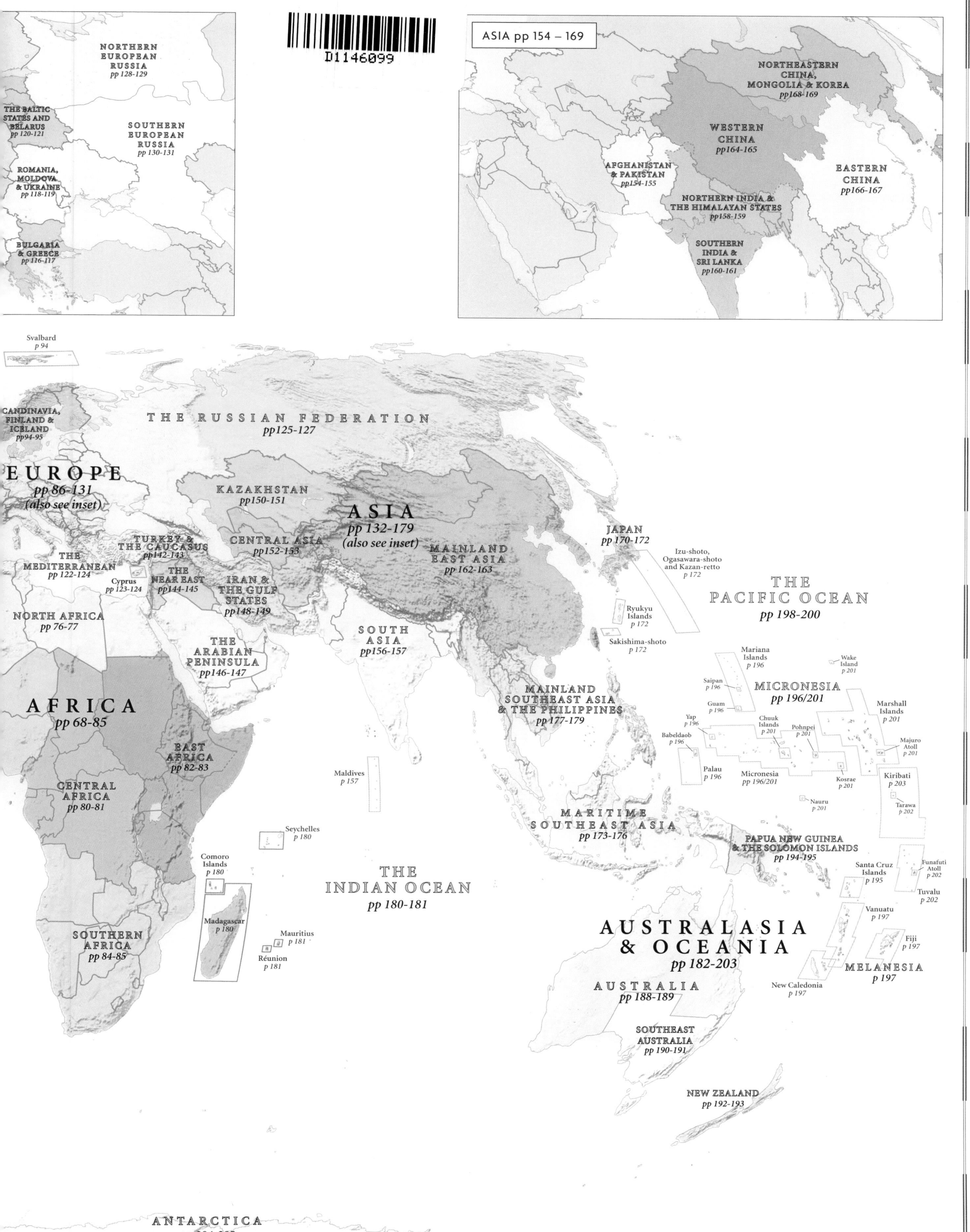

D1146099

NORTHERN EUROPEAN RUSSIA
pp 128-129
THE BALTIC STATES AND BELARUS
pp 120-121
SOUTHERN EUROPEAN RUSSIA
pp 130-131
ROMANIA, MOLDOVA & UKRAINE
pp 118-119
BULGARIA & GREECE
pp 116-117
ASIA pp 154 – 169
NORTHEASTERN CHINA, MONGOLIA & KOREA
pp168-169
WESTERN CHINA
pp164-165
AFGHANISTAN & PAKISTAN
pp154-155
EASTERN CHINA
pp166-167
NORTHERN INDIA & THE HIMALAYAN STATES
pp158-159
SOUTHERN INDIA & SRI LANKA
pp160-161
Svalbard
p 94
CANDINAVIA, FINLAND & ICELAND
pp94-95
THE RUSSIAN FEDERATION
pp125-127
EUROPE
pp 86-131
(also see inset)
KAZAKHSTAN
pp150-151
ASIA
pp 132-179
(also see inset)
TURKEY & THE CAUCASUS
pp142-143
CENTRAL ASIA
pp152-153
MAINLAND EAST ASIA
pp 162-163
JAPAN
pp 170-172
Izu-shoto, Ogasawara-shoto and Kazan-retto
p 172
THE MEDITERRANEAN
pp 122-124
Cyprus
pp 123-124
THE NEAR EAST
pp144-145
IRAN & THE GULF STATES
pp148-149
THE PACIFIC OCEAN
pp 198-200
Ryukyu Islands
p 172
NORTH AFRICA
pp 76-77
SOUTH ASIA
pp156-157
Sakishima-shoto
p 172
THE ARABIAN PENINSULA
pp146-147
Mariana Islands
p 196
Wake Island
p 201
MAINLAND SOUTHEAST ASIA & THE PHILIPPINES
pp 177-179
Saipan
p 196
MICRONESIA
pp 196/201
AFRICA
pp 68-85
Guam
p 196
Marshall Islands
p 201
Yap
p 196
Chuuk Islands
p 201
Pohnpei
p 201
EAST AFRICA
pp 82-83
Babeldaob
p 196
Majuro Atoll
p 201
Maldives
p 157
Palau
p 196
Micronesia
pp 196/201
Kosrae
p 201
Kiribati
p 203
CENTRAL AFRICA
pp 80-81
Nauru
p 201
Tarawa
p 202
MARITIME SOUTHEAST ASIA
pp 173-176
Seychelles
p 180
PAPUA NEW GUINEA & THE SOLOMON ISLANDS
pp 194-195
Comoro Islands
p 180
THE INDIAN OCEAN
pp 180-181
Funafuti Atoll
p 202
Santa Cruz Islands
p 195
Tuvalu
p 202
Vanuatu
p 197
Madagascar
p 180
Mauritius
p 181
AUSTRALASIA & OCEANIA
pp 182-203
Fiji
p 197
SOUTHERN AFRICA
pp 84-85
Réunion
p 181
MELANESIA
p 197
New Caledonia
p 197
AUSTRALIA
pp 188-189
SOUTHEAST AUSTRALIA
pp 190-191
NEW ZEALAND
pp 192-193
ANTARCTICA
pp 204-205

REFERENCE
ATLAS
OF THE WORLD

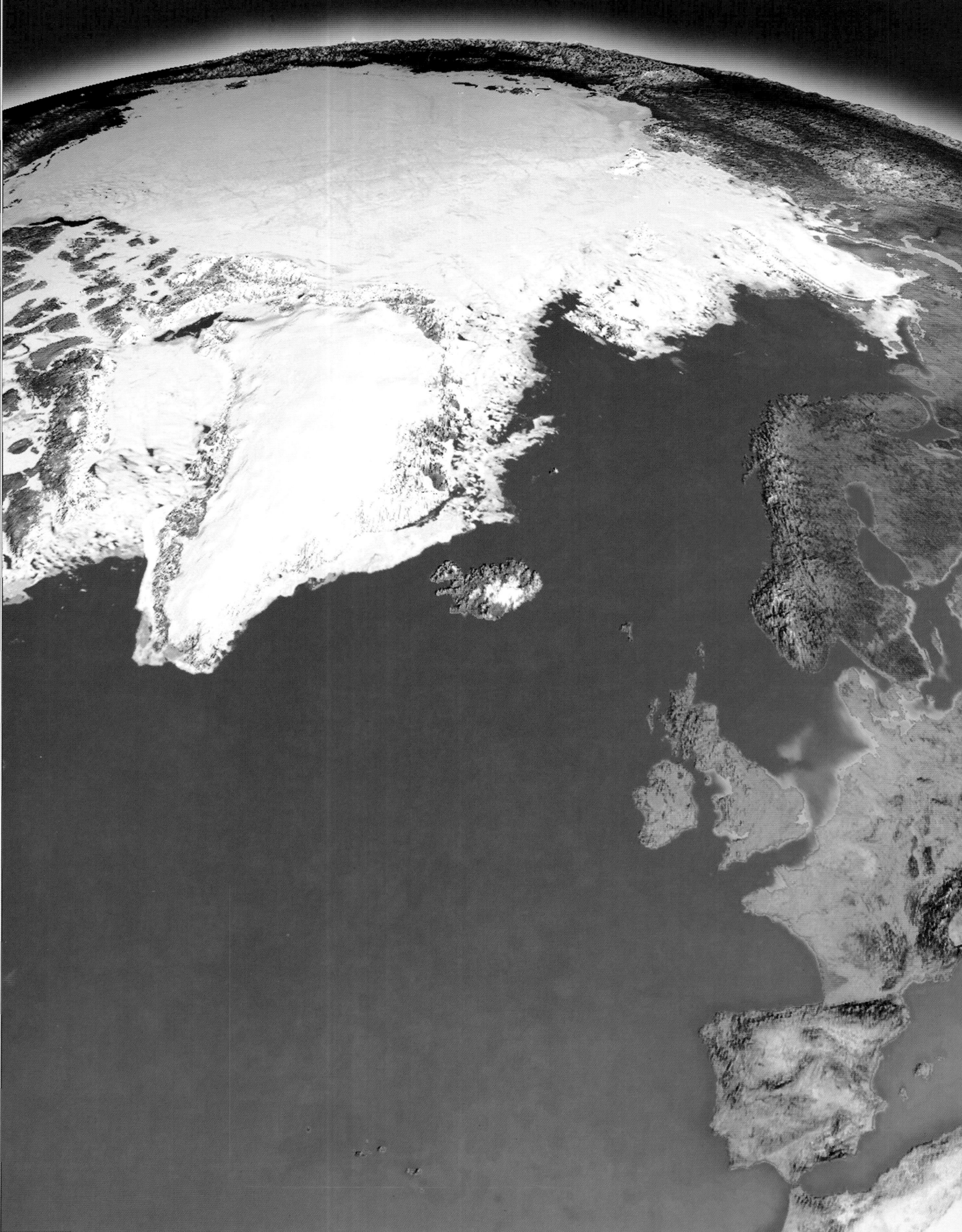

REFERENCE ATLAS
OF THE WORLD

London • New York • Munich • Melbourne • Delhi

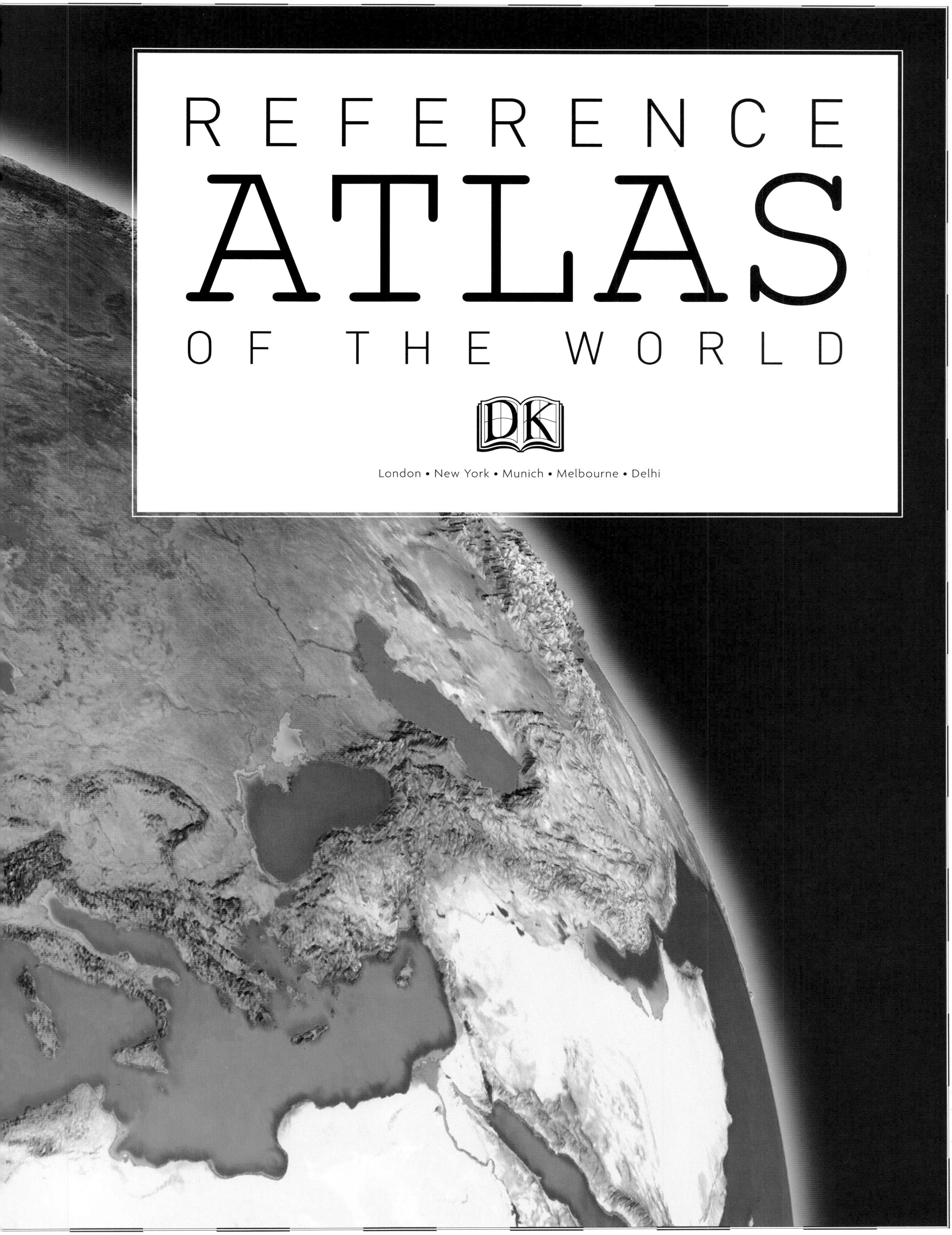

LONDON, NEW YORK, MELBOURNE, MUNICH, DELHI

FOR THE SEVENTH EDITION

Publishing Director Jonathan Metcalf **Managing Cartographers** David Roberts • Simon Mumford **Art Director** Bryn Walls
Managing Editor Debra Wolter **Designers** Nimbus Design, Langworth, UK • Giraffe, London, UK • Yak El-Droubie
Cartographers Roger Bullen • DEMAP, Strathdale, Australia • Paul Eames • Encompass Graphics Ltd, Brighton, UK • Ed Merritt • Rob Stokes • Iorwerth Watkins
Jacket Designers Lee Ellwood • Duncan Turner **Systems Co-ordinator** Philip Rowles

General Geographical Consultants

Physical Geography Denys Brunsden, Emeritus Professor, Department of Geography, King's College, London
Human Geography Professor J Malcolm Wagstaff, Department of Geography, University of Southampton
Place Names Caroline Burgess, Permanent Committee on Geographical Names, London
Boundaries International Boundaries Research Unit, Mountjoy Research Centre, University of Durham

Digital Mapping Consultants

DK Cartopia developed by George Galfalvi and XMap Ltd, London
Professor Jan-Peter Muller, Department of Photogrammetry and Surveying, University College, London
Cover globes, planets and information on the Solar System provided by Philip Eales and Kevin Tildsley, Planetary Visions Ltd, London

Regional Consultants

North America Dr David Green, Department of Geography, King's College, London • Jim Walsh, Head of Reference, Wessell Library, Tufts University, Medford, Massachussetts
South America Dr David Preston, School of Geography, University of Leeds **Europe** Dr Edward M Yates, formerly of the Department of Geography, King's College, London
Africa Dr Philip Amis, Development Administration Group, University of Birmingham • Dr Ieuan Ll Griffiths, Department of Geography, University of Sussex
Dr Tony Binns, Department of Geography, University of Sussex
Central Asia Dr David Turnock, Department of Geography, University of Leicester **South and East Asia** Dr Jonathan Rigg, Department of Geography, University of Durham
Australasia and Oceania Dr Robert Allison, Department of Geography, University of Durham

Acknowledgements

Digital terrain data created by Eros Data Center, Sioux Falls, South Dakota, USA. Processed by GVS Images Inc, California, USA and Planetary Visions Ltd, London, UK
• Cambridge International Reference on Current Affairs (CIRCA), Cambridge, UK • Digitization by Robertson Research International, Swanley, UK • Peter Clark
British Isles maps generated from a dataset supplied by Map Marketing Ltd/European Map Graphics Ltd in combination with DK Cartopia copyright data

DORLING KINDERSLEY CARTOGRAPHY

Editor-in-Chief Andrew Heritage **Managing Cartographer** David Roberts **Senior Cartographic Editor** Roger Bullen
Editorial Direction Louise Cavanagh **Database Manager** Simon Lewis **Art Direction** Chez Picthall

Cartographers

Pamela Alford • James Anderson • Caroline Bowie • Dale Buckton • Tony Chambers • Jan Clark • Bob Croser • Martin Darlison • Damien Demaj • Claire Ellam • Sally Gable
Jeremy Hepworth • Geraldine Horner • Chris Jackson • Christine Johnston • Julia Lunn • Michael Martin • Ed Merritt • James Mills-Hicks • Simon Mumford • John Plumer
John Scott • Ann Stephenson • Gail Townsley • Julie Turner • Sarah Vaughan • Jane Voss • Scott Wallace • Iorwerth Watkins • Bryony Webb • Alan Whitaker • Peter Winfield

Digital Maps Created in DK Cartopia by
Tom Coulson • Thomas Robertshaw
Philip Rowles • Rob Stokes
Managing Editor
Lisa Thomas
Editors
Thomas Heath • Wim Jenkins • Jane Oliver
Siobhan Ryan • Elizabeth Wyse
Editorial Research
Helen Dangerfield • Andrew Rebeiro-Hargrave
Additional Editorial Assistance
Debra Clapson • Robert Damon • Ailsa Heritage
Constance Novis • Jayne Parsons • Chris Whitwell

Placenames Database Team
Natalie Clarkson • Ruth Duxbury • Caroline Falce • John Featherstone • Dan Gardiner
Ciárán Hynes • Margaret Hynes • Helen Rudkin • Margaret Stevenson • Annie Wilson
Senior Managing Art Editor
Philip Lord
Designers
Scott David • Carol Ann Davis • David Douglas • Rhonda Fisher
Karen Gregory • Nicola Liddiard • Paul Williams
Illustrations
Ciárán Hughes • Advanced Illustration, Congleton, UK
Picture Research
Melissa Albany • James Clarke • Anna Lord
Christine Rista • Sarah Moule • Louise Thomas

Production
Rita Sinha

First published in Great Britain in 1997 as the DK World Atlas by Dorling Kindersley Limited, 80 Strand, London WC2R 0RL.

A Penguin Company

Reprinted with revisions 1998, 1999. Second Edition (revised) 2001. Third Edition (revised) 2003. Reprinted with revisions 2004. Sixth Edition 2005. Seventh Edition 2007.
Copyright © 1997, 1998, 1999, 2001, 2003, 2004, 2005, 2007 Dorling Kindersley Limited, London

A CIP catalogue record for this book is available from the British Library

ISBN: 978-1-4053-1776-4

Reprographics by MDP Ltd, Wiltshire, UK
Printed and bound by Star Standard, Singapore.

See our complete catalogue at www.dk.com

Introduction

For many, the outstanding legacy of the twentieth century was the way in which the Earth shrank. As we enter the third millennium, it is increasingly important for us to have a clear vision of the World in which we live. The human population has increased fourfold since 1900. The last scraps of *terra incognita* – the polar regions and ocean depths – have been penetrated and mapped. New regions have been colonized, and previously hostile realms claimed for habitation. The advent of aviation technology and mass tourism allows many of us to travel further, faster and more frequently than ever before. In doing so we are given a bird's-eye view of the Earth's surface denied to our forebears.

At the same time, the amount of information about our world has grown enormously. Telecommunications can span the greatest distances in fractions of a second: our multi-media environment hurls uninterrupted streams of data at us, on the printed page, through the airwaves and across our television and computer screens; events from all corners of the globe reach us instantaneously, and are witnessed as they unfold. Our sense of stability and certainty has been eroded; instead, we are aware that the World is in a constant state of flux and change. Natural disasters, man-made cataclysms and conflicts between nations remind us daily of the enormity and fragility of our domain. The events of September 11, 2001, threw into a very stark relief the levels of ignorance and inaccessibility that exist when trying to 'know' or 'understand' our planet and its many cultures.

The current crisis in our 'global' culture has made the need greater than ever before for everyone to possess an atlas. The *DK Reference Atlas of the World* has been conceived to meet this need. At its core, like all atlases, it seeks to define where places are, to describe their main characteristics, and to locate them in relation to other places. Every attempt has been made to make the information on the maps as clear and accessible as possible. In addition, each page of the atlas provides a wealth of further information, bringing the maps to life. Using photographs, diagrams, 'at-a-glance' maps, introductory texts and captions, the atlas builds up a detailed portait of those features – cultural, political, economic and geomorphological – which make each region unique, and which are also the main agents of change.

This Seventh Edition of the *DK Reference Atlas of the World* incorporates thousands of revisions and updates affecting every map and every page, and reflects many of the geo-political developments which continue to alter the shape of our world. Since its first publication in 1997 the book has proved extremely popular – going into 22 editions around the world –and has been translated into 13 languages, including Greek and Russian.

CONTENTS

THE WORLD

THE BRITISH ISLES

Atlas of the world
North America

South America

Africa

Europe

Asia

Australasia & Oceania

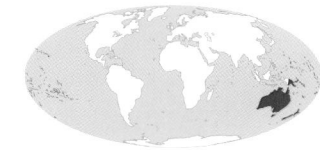

INDEX–GAZETTEER

Key to maps

Regional

Physical features

elevation

6000m / 19,686ft
4000m / 13,124ft
3000m / 9843ft
2000m / 6562ft
1000m / 3281ft
500m / 1640ft
250m / 820ft
100m / 328ft
sea level
below sea level

▲ elevation above sea level (mountain height)
▲ volcano
✕ pass
▼ elevation below sea level (depression depth)

sand desert
lava flow
coastline
reef
atoll

sea depth

sea level
-250m / -820ft
-500m / -1640ft
-1000m / -3281ft
-2000m / -6562ft
-3000m / -9843ft

▲ seamount / guyot symbol
▼ undersea spot depth

Drainage features

main river
secondary river
tertiary river
minor river
main seasonal river
secondary seasonal river
canal
waterfall
rapids
dam
perennial lake
seasonal lake
perennial salt lake
seasonal salt lake
reservoir
salt flat / salt pan
marsh / salt marsh
mangrove
wadi
spring / well / waterhole / oasis

Ice features

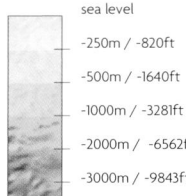

ice cap / sheet
ice shelf
glacier / snowfield
summer pack ice limit
winter pack ice limit

Communications

motorway / highway
motorway / highway (under construction)
major road
minor road
tunnel (road)
main line
minor line
tunnel (rail)
✈ international airport

Borders

full international border
undefined international border
disputed de facto border
disputed territorial claim border
indication of country extent (Pacific only)
indication of dependent territory extent (Pacific only)
demarcation/ cease fire line
autonomous / federal region border
2nd order internal administrative border
3rd order internal administrative border

Settlements

built up area

settlement population symbols

▪ more than 5 million
▣ 1 million to 5 million
◉ 500,000 to 1 million
◎ 100,000 to 500,000
⊕ 50,000 to 100,000
○ 10,000 to 50,000
○ fewer than 10,000

▪●● country/dependent territory capital city
▪●● autonomous / federal region / 2nd order internal administrative centre
▪●● 3rd order internal administrative centre

Miscellaneous features

ancient wall
◇ site of interest
⊕ scientific station

Graticule features

lines of latitude and longitude / Equator
Tropics / Polar circles
45° degrees of longitude / latitude

Typographic key

Physical features

landscape features ... *Namib Desert*
Massif Central
ANDES

headland .... *Nordkapp*

elevation / volcano / pass .... Mount Meru 4556 m

drainage features .... *Lake Geneva*

rivers / canals spring / well / waterhole / oasis / waterfall / rapids / dam .... *Mekong*

ice features .... *Vatnajökull*

sea features .... *Golfe de Lion*
Andaman Sea
INDIAN OCEAN

undersea features ... *Barracuda Fracture Zone*

Regions

country .... **ARMENIA**

dependent territory with parent state ..... **NIUE (to NZ)**

region outside feature area .... ANGOLA

autonomous / federal region .... MINAS GERAIS

2nd order internal administrative region .... **MINSKAYA VOBLASTS'**

3rd order internal administrative region .... Vaucluse

cultural region .... New England

Settlements

capital city .... **BEIJING**

dependent territory capital city .... FORT-DE-FRANCE

other settlements ... **Chicago**
Adana
Tizi Ozou
Yonezawa
Farnham

Miscellaneous

sites of interest / miscellaneous .... *Valley of the Kings*

Tropics / Polar circles .... *Antarctic Circle*

How to use this Atlas

The atlas is organized by continent, moving eastwards from the International Date Line. The opening section describes the world's structure, systems and its main features. The Atlas of the World which follows, is a continent-by-continent guide to today's world, starting with a comprehensive insight into the physical, political and economic structure of each continent, followed by integrated mapping and descriptions of each region or country.

The world

The introductory section of the Atlas deals with every aspect of the planet, from physical structure to human geography, providing an overall picture of the world we live in. Complex topics such as the landscape of the Earth, climate, oceans, population and economic patterns are clearly explained with the aid of maps, diagrams drawn from the latest information.

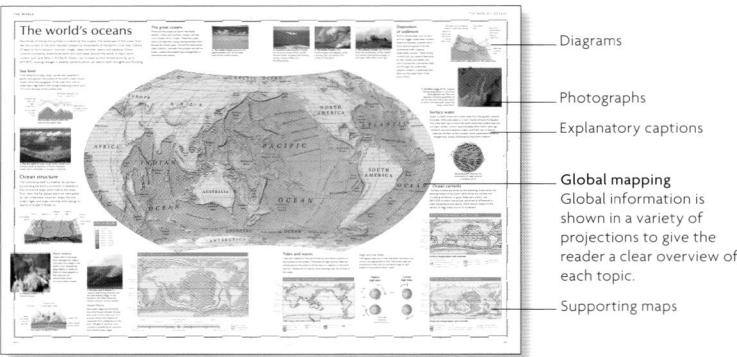

Diagrams
Photographs
Explanatory captions
Global mapping
Global information is shown in a variety of projections to give the reader a clear overview of each topic.
Supporting maps

The political continent

The political portrait of the continent is a vital reference point for every continental section, showing the position of countries relative to one another, and the relationship between human settlement and geographic location. The complex mosaic of languages spoken in each continent is mapped, as is the effect of communications networks on the pattern of settlement.

Locator map
Introductory text
Communications map
Population map
Political map
All the countries in each continent are shown, with their political capitals and most populous cities.
Communications map

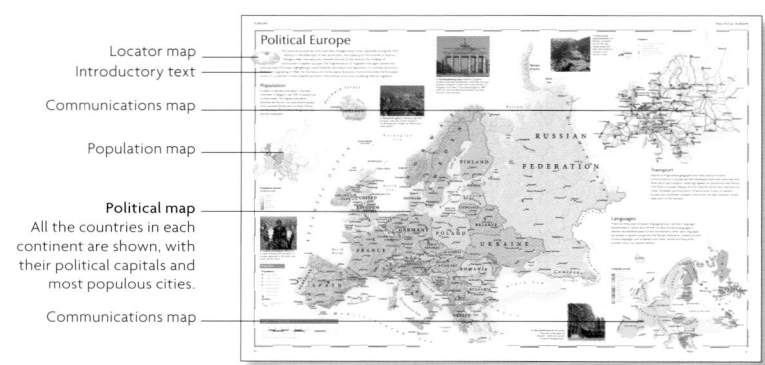

Continental resources

The Earth's rich natural resources, including oil, gas, minerals and fertile land, have played a key role in the development of society. These pages show the location of minerals and agricultural resources on each continent, and how they have been instrumental in dictating industrial growth and the varieties of economic activity across the continent.

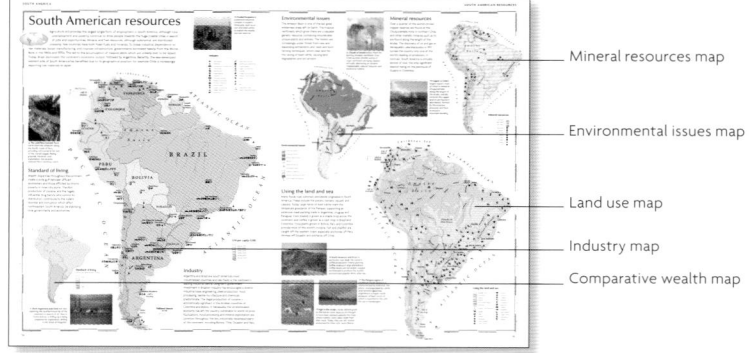

Mineral resources map
Environmental issues map
Land use map
Industry map
Comparative wealth map

The physical continent

The astonishing variety of landforms, and the dramatic forces that created and continue to shape the landscape, are explained in the continental physical spread. Cross-sections, illustrations and terrain maps highlight the different parts of the continent, showing how nature's forces have produced the landscapes we see today.

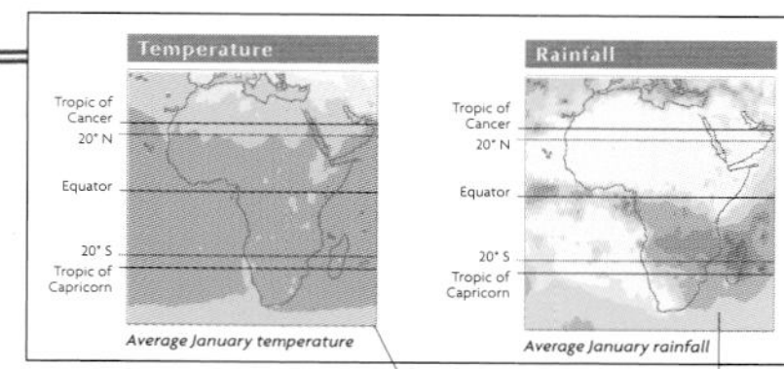

Climate charts
Rainfall and temperature charts clearly show the continental patterns of rainfall and temperature.

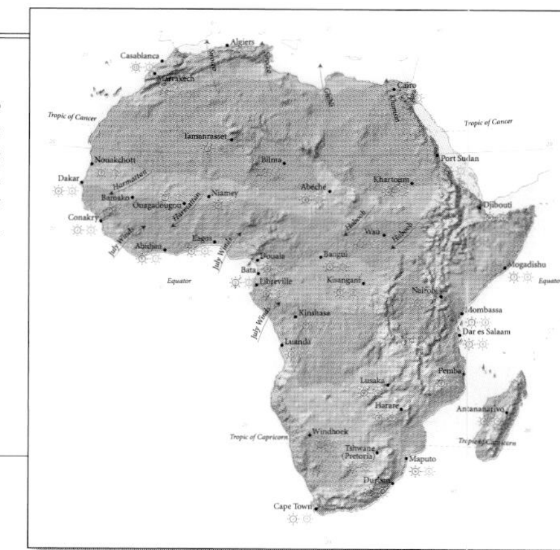

Climate map
Climatic regions vary across each continent. The map displays the differing climatic regions, as well as daily hours of sunshine at selected weather stations.

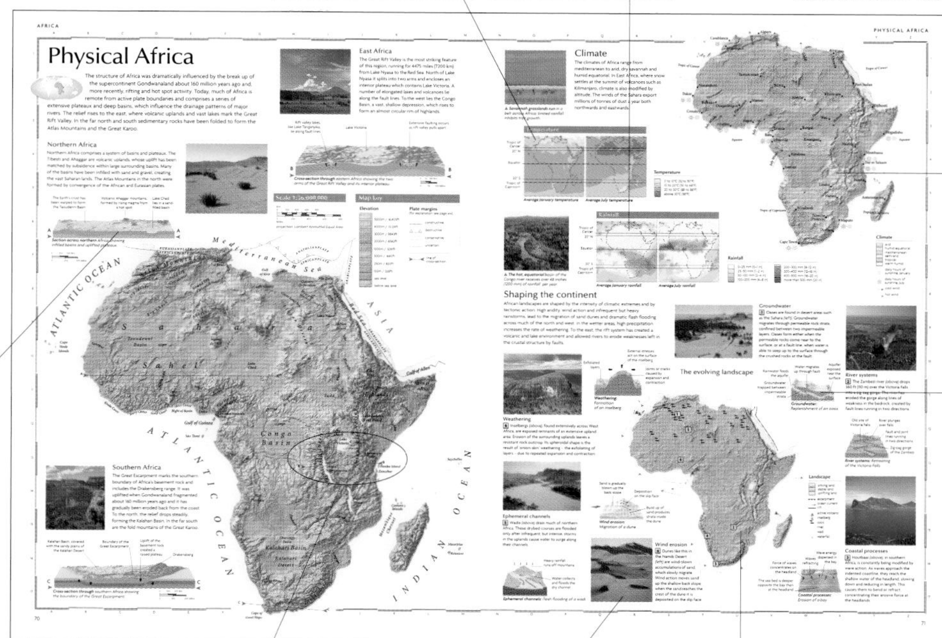

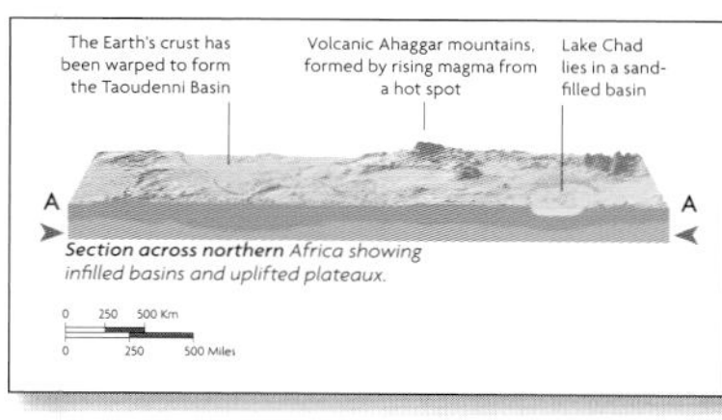

Cross-sections
Detailed cross-sections through selected parts of the continent show the underlying geomorphic structure.

The Earth's crust has been warped to form the Taoudenni Basin

Volcanic Ahaggar mountains, formed by rising magma from a hot spot

Lake Chad lies in a sand-filled basin

Section across northern Africa showing infilled basins and uplifted plateaux.

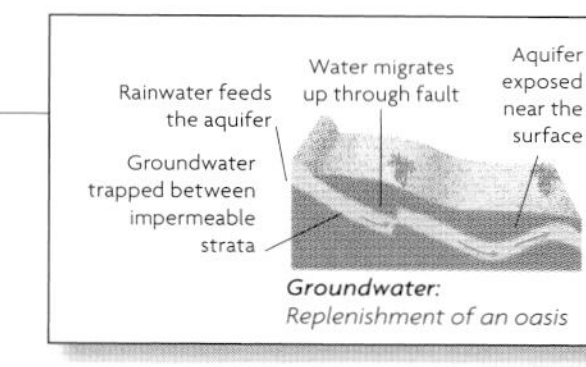

Landform diagrams
The complex formation of many typical landforms is summarized in these easy-to-understand illustrations.

Rainwater feeds the aquifer

Water migrates up through fault

Aquifer exposed near the surface

Groundwater trapped between impermeable strata

Groundwater: Replenishment of an oasis

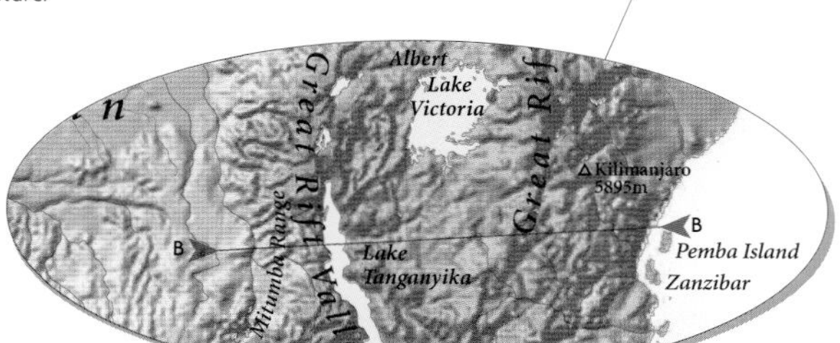

Main physical map
Detailed satellite data has been used to create an accurate and visually striking picture of the surface of the continent.

Photographs
A wide range of beautiful photographs bring the world's regions to life.

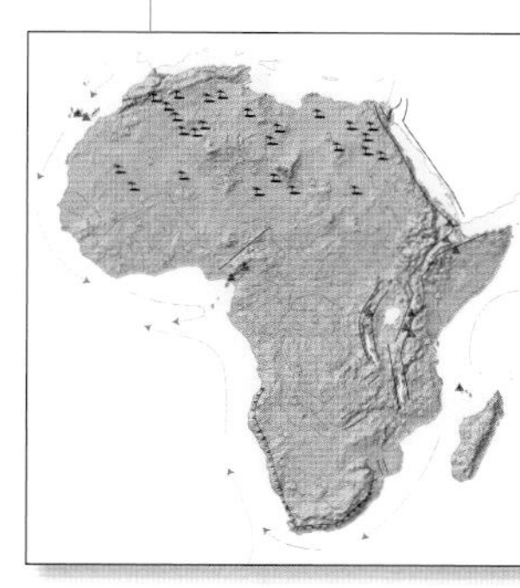

Landscape evolution map
The physical shape of each continent is affected by a variety of forces which continually sculpt and modify the landscape. This map shows the major processes which affect different parts of the continent.

Regional mapping

The main body of the Atlas is a unique regional map set, with detailed information on the terrain, the human geography of the region and its infrastructure. Around the edge of the map, additional 'at-a-glance' maps, give an instant picture of regional industry, land use and agriculture. The detailed terrain map (shown in perspective), focuses on the main physical features of the region, and is enhanced by annotated illustrations, and photographs of the physical structure.

The transport network

340,090 miles (544,144 km)		4813 miles (7700 km)
12,872 miles (20,592 km)		2108 miles (3389 km)

New York's commercial success is tied historically to its transport connections. The Erie Canal, completed in 1825, opened up the Great Lakes and the interior to New York's markets and carried a stream of immigrants into the Midwest.

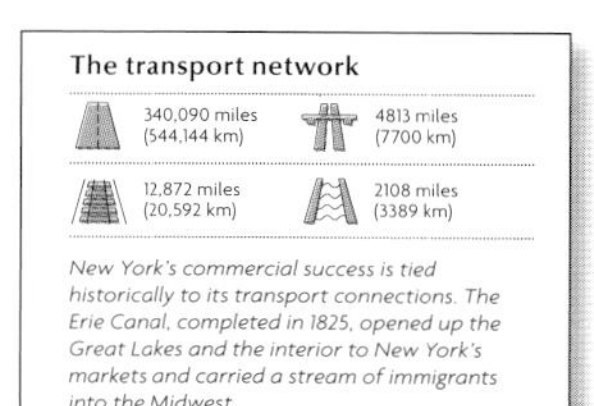

Transport network
The differing extent of the transport network for each region is shown here, along with key facts about the transport system.

Regional Locator
This small map shows the location of each country in relation to its continent.

Key to main map
A key to the population symbols and land heights accompanies the main map.

World locator
This locates the continent in which the region is found on a small world map.

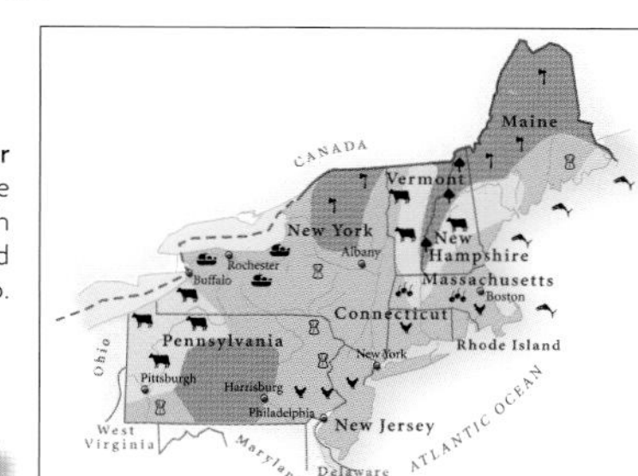

Land use map
This shows the different types of land use which characterize the region, as well as indicating the principal agricultural activities.

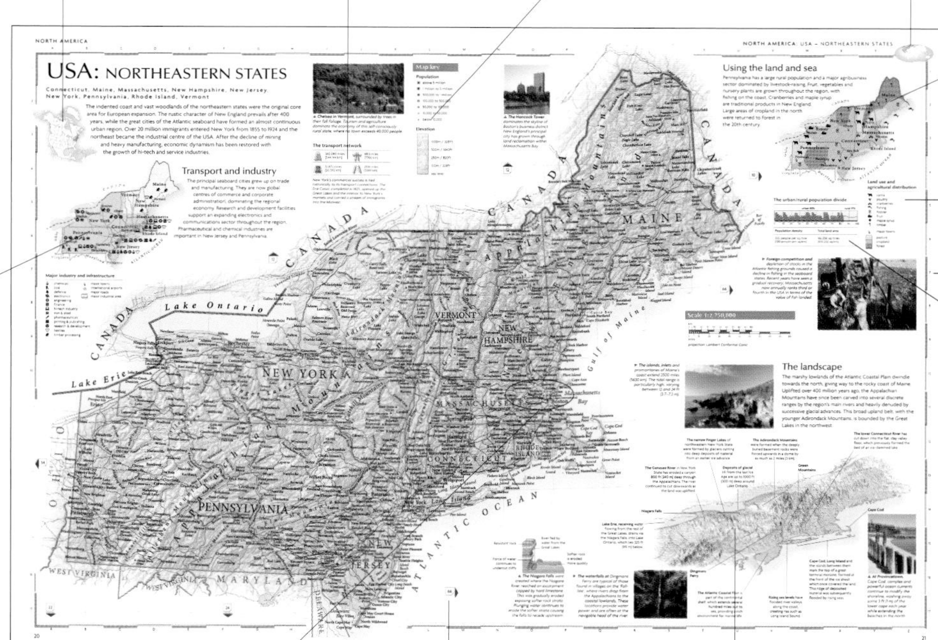

Map keys
Each supporting map has its own key.

Grid reference
The framing grid provides a location reference for each place listed in the Index.

The urban/rural population divide

urban 83%   rural 17%

| 0 | 10 | 20 | 30 | 40 | 50 | 60 | 70 | 80 | 90 | 100 |

Population density	Total land area
335 people per sq mile (120 people per sq km)	162,258 sq miles (420,232 sq km)

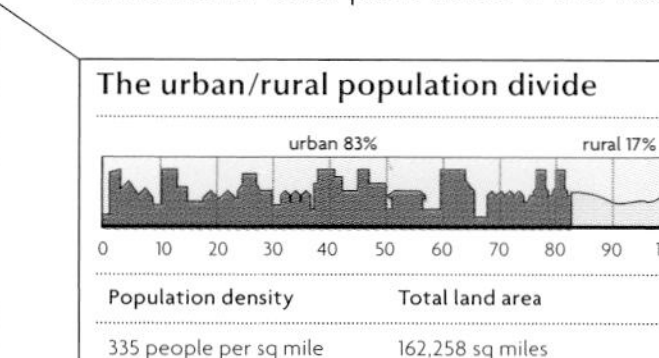

Urban/rural population divide
The proportion of people in the region who live in urban and rural areas, as well as the overall population density and land area are clearly shown in these simple graphics.

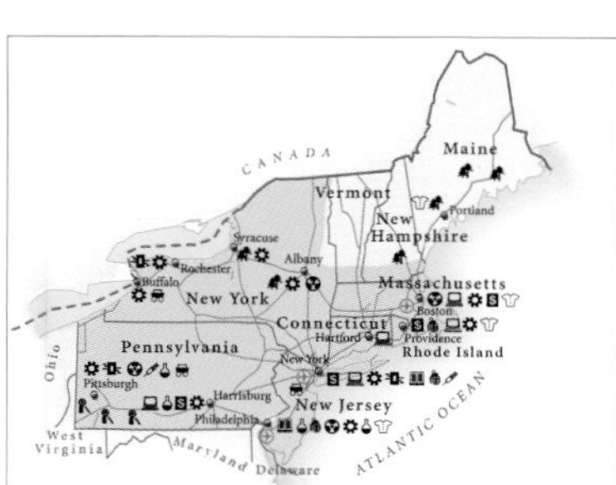

Transport and industry map
The main industrial areas are mapped, and the most important industrial and economic activities of the region are shown.

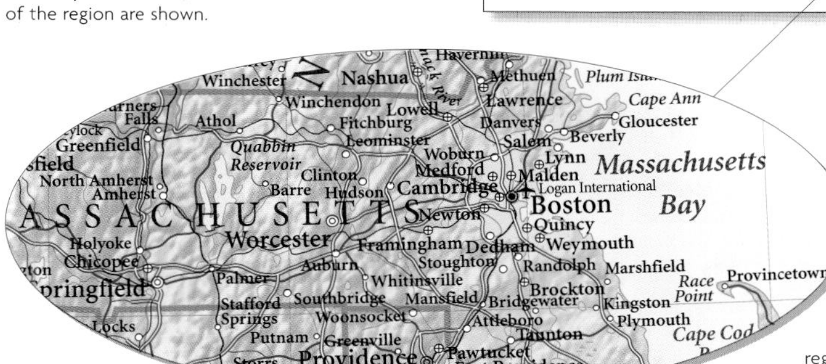

Continuation symbols
These symbols indicate where adjacent maps can be found.

Main regional map
A wealth of information is displayed on the main map, building up a rich portrait of the interaction between the physical landscape and the human and political geography of each region. The key to the regional maps can be found on page viii.

Landscape map
The computer-generated terrain model accurately portrays an oblique view of the landscape. Annotations highlight the most important geographic features of the region.

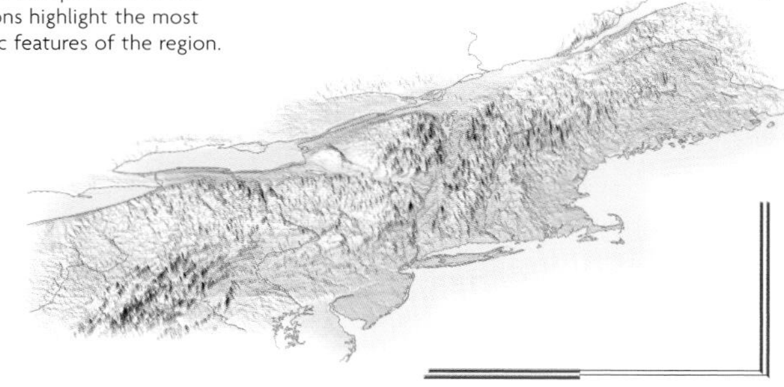

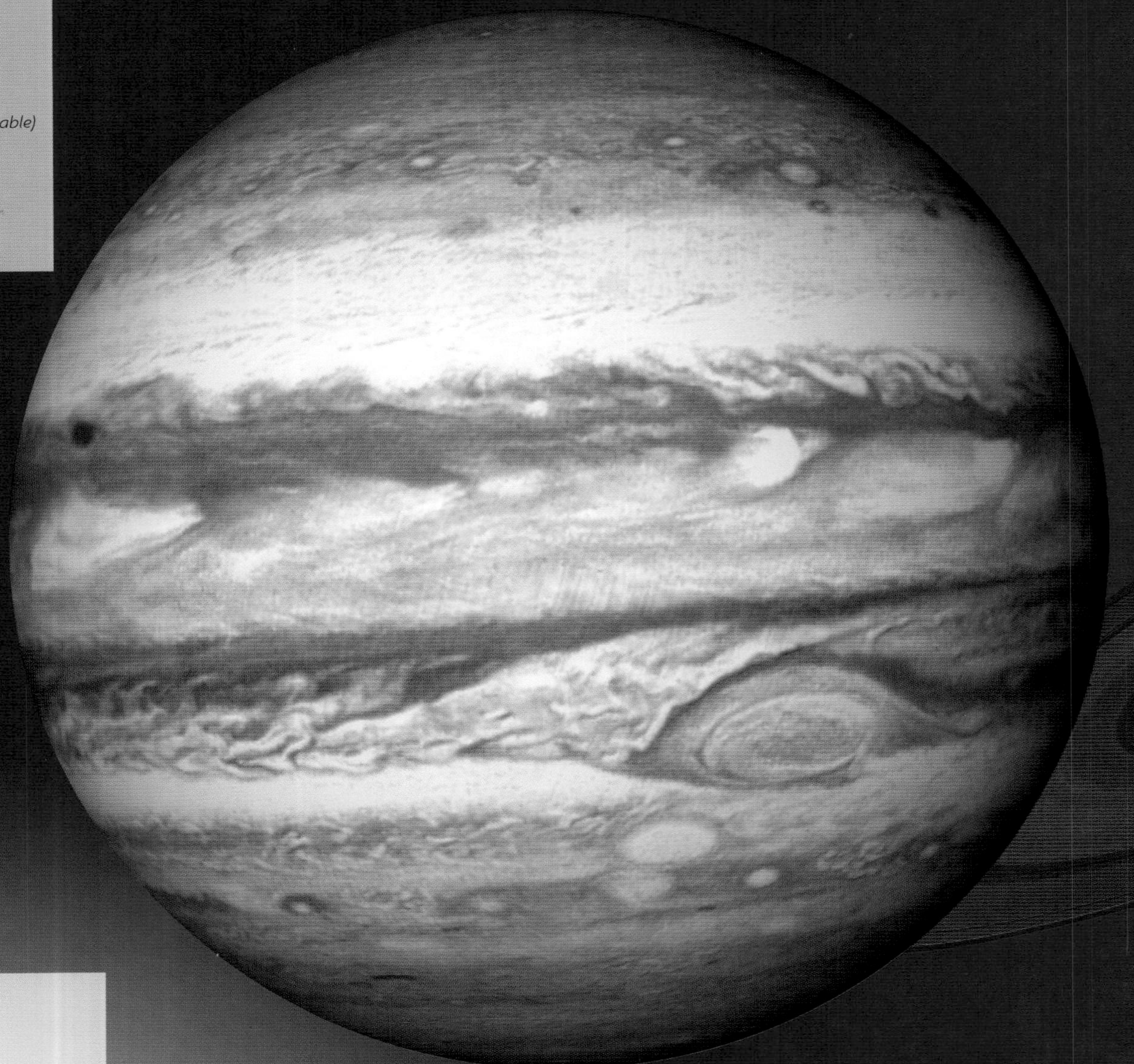

Jupiter

- ⊖ **Diameter:** 88,846 miles (142,984 km)
- ⬤ **Mass:** 1,900,000 million million million tons
- ○ **Temperature:** -153°C (extremes not available)
- ▯ **Distance from Sun:** 483 million miles (778 million km)
- ◑ **Length of day:** 9.84 hours
- ◑ **Length of year:** 11.86 earth years
- ⊖ **Surface gravity:** 1 kg = 2.53 kg

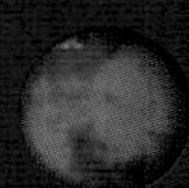

Mars

- ⊖ **Diameter:** 4217 miles (6786 km)
- ⬤ **Mass:** 642 million million million tons
- ○ **Temperature:** -137 to 37°C
- ▯ **Distance from Sun:** 142 million miles (228 million km)
- ◑ **Length of day:** 24.623 hours
- ◑ **Length of year:** 1.88 earth years
- ⊖ **Surface gravity:** 1 kg = 0.38 kg

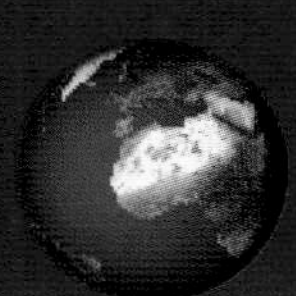

Earth

- ⊖ **Diameter:** 7926 miles (12,756 km)
- ⬤ **Mass:** 5976 million million million tons
- ○ **Temperature:** -70 to 55°C
- ▯ **Distance from Sun:** 93 million miles (150 million km)
- ◑ **Length of day:** 23.92 hours
- ◑ **Length of year:** 365.25 earth days
- ⊖ **Surface gravity:** 1 kg = 1 kg

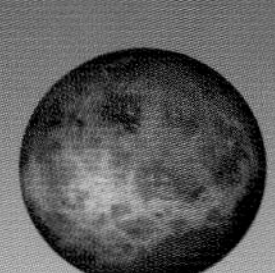

Venus

- ⊖ **Diameter:** 7520 miles (12,102 km)
- ⬤ **Mass:** 4870 million million million tons
- ○ **Temperature:** 457°C (extremes not available)
- ▯ **Distance from Sun:** 67 million miles (108 million km)
- ◑ **Length of day:** 243.01 earth days
- ◑ **Length of year:** 224.7 earth days
- ⊖ **Surface gravity:** 1 kg = 0.88 kg

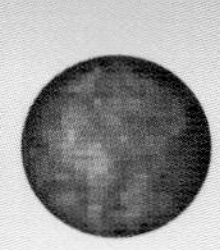

Mercury

- ⊖ **Diameter:** 3031 miles (4878 km)
- ⬤ **Mass:** 330 million million million tons
- ○ **Temperature:** -173 to 427°C
- ▯ **Distance from Sun:** 36 million miles (58 million km)
- ◑ **Length of day:** 58.65 earth days
- ◑ **Length of year:** 87.97 earth days
- ⊖ **Surface gravity:** 1 kg = 0.38 kg

The Solar System

Nine major planets, their satellites and countless minor planets (asteroids) orbit the Sun to form the Solar System. The Sun, our nearest star, creates energy from nuclear reactions deep within its interior, providing all the light and heat which make life on Earth possible. The Earth is unique in the Solar System in that it supports life: its size, gravitational pull and distance from the Sun have all created the optimum conditions for the evolution of life. The planetary images seen here are composites derived from actual spacecraft images (not shown to scale).

The Sun

- ⊖ **Diameter:** 864,948 miles (1,392,000 km)
- ⬤ **Mass:** 1990 million million million tons

The Sun was formed when a swirling cloud of dust and gas contracted, pulling matter into its centre. When the temperature at the centre rose to 1,000,000°C, nuclear fusion – the fusing of hydrogen into helium, creating energy – occurred, releasing a constant stream of heat and light.

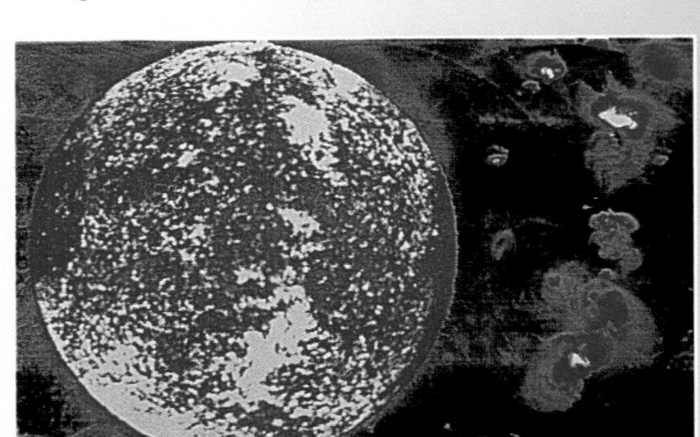

▲ **Solar flares are** sudden bursts of energy from the Sun's surface. They can be 125,000 miles (200,000 km) long.

The formation of the Solar System

The cloud of dust and gas thrown out by the Sun during its formation cooled to form the Solar System. The smaller planets nearest the Sun are formed of minerals and metals. The outer planets were formed at lower temperatures, and consist of swirling clouds of gases.

The Milankovitch cycle

The amount of radiation from the Sun which reaches the Earth is affected by variations in the Earth's orbit and the tilt of the Earth's axis, as well as by 'wobbles' in the axis. These variations cause three separate cycles, corresponding with the durations of recent ice ages.

Stretch
100,000 year cycle

Earth's orbit varies from circular to eliptical

Sun

Tilt
41,000 year cycle

Sun

Angle of tilt varies by 2.4°

Wobble
21,000 year cycle

Sun

The Earth wobbles like a spinning top as it rotates

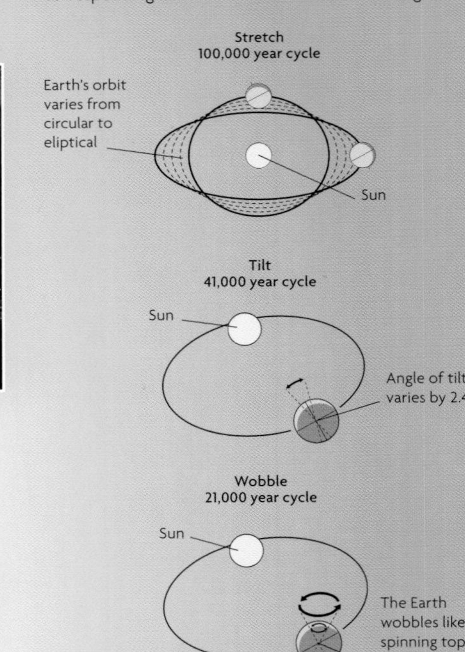

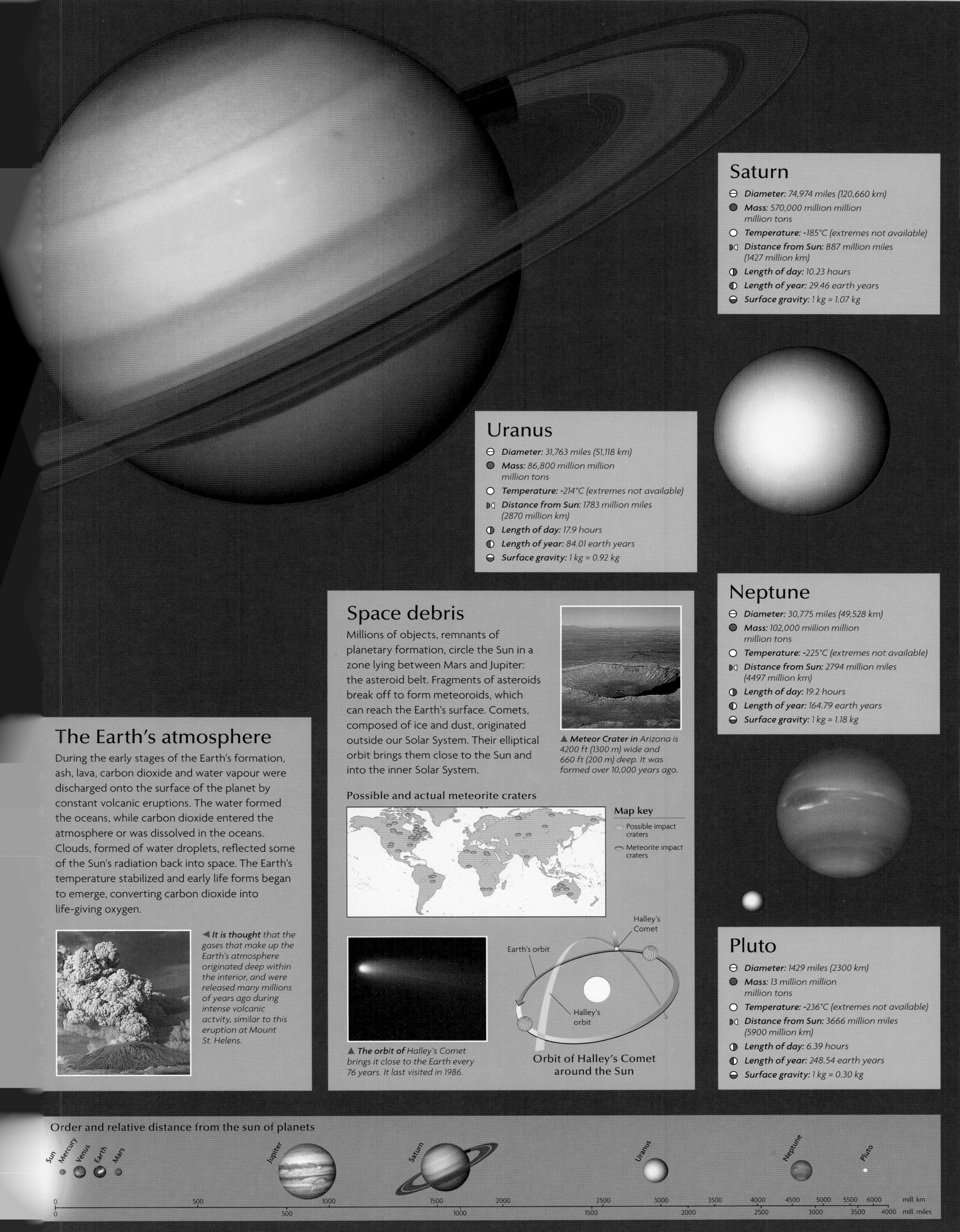

Saturn

- **Diameter:** 74,974 miles (120,660 km)
- **Mass:** 570,000 million million million tons
- **Temperature:** -185°C (extremes not available)
- **Distance from Sun:** 887 million miles (1427 million km)
- **Length of day:** 10.23 hours
- **Length of year:** 29.46 earth years
- **Surface gravity:** 1 kg = 1.07 kg

Uranus

- **Diameter:** 31,763 miles (51,118 km)
- **Mass:** 86,800 million million million tons
- **Temperature:** -214°C (extremes not available)
- **Distance from Sun:** 1783 million miles (2870 million km)
- **Length of day:** 17.9 hours
- **Length of year:** 84.01 earth years
- **Surface gravity:** 1 kg = 0.92 kg

Neptune

- **Diameter:** 30,775 miles (49,528 km)
- **Mass:** 102,000 million million million tons
- **Temperature:** -225°C (extremes not available)
- **Distance from Sun:** 2794 million miles (4497 million km)
- **Length of day:** 19.2 hours
- **Length of year:** 164.79 earth years
- **Surface gravity:** 1 kg = 1.18 kg

Pluto

- **Diameter:** 1429 miles (2300 km)
- **Mass:** 13 million million million tons
- **Temperature:** -236°C (extremes not available)
- **Distance from Sun:** 3666 million miles (5900 million km)
- **Length of day:** 6.39 hours
- **Length of year:** 248.54 earth years
- **Surface gravity:** 1 kg = 0.30 kg

Space debris

Millions of objects, remnants of planetary formation, circle the Sun in a zone lying between Mars and Jupiter: the asteroid belt. Fragments of asteroids break off to form meteoroids, which can reach the Earth's surface. Comets, composed of ice and dust, originated outside our Solar System. Their elliptical orbit brings them close to the Sun and into the inner Solar System.

▲ **Meteor Crater in** Arizona is 4200 ft (1300 m) wide and 660 ft (200 m) deep. It was formed over 10,000 years ago.

Possible and actual meteorite craters

Map key
- Possible impact craters
- Meteorite impact craters

▲ **The orbit of** Halley's Comet brings it close to the Earth every 76 years. It last visited in 1986.

Halley's Comet

Earth's orbit

Halley's orbit

Orbit of Halley's Comet around the Sun

The Earth's atmosphere

During the early stages of the Earth's formation, ash, lava, carbon dioxide and water vapour were discharged onto the surface of the planet by constant volcanic eruptions. The water formed the oceans, while carbon dioxide entered the atmosphere or was dissolved in the oceans. Clouds, formed of water droplets, reflected some of the Sun's radiation back into space. The Earth's temperature stabilized and early life forms began to emerge, converting carbon dioxide into life-giving oxygen.

◄ **It is thought** that the gases that make up the Earth's atmosphere originated deep within the interior, and were released many millions of years ago during intense volcanic actvity, similar to this eruption at Mount St. Helens.

Order and relative distance from the sun of planets

Sun | Mercury | Venus | Earth | Mars | Jupiter | Saturn | Uranus | Neptune | Pluto

0 500 1000 1500 2000 2500 3000 3500 4000 4500 5000 5500 6000 mill. km

0 500 1000 1500 2000 2500 3000 3500 4000 mill. miles

The physical world

The Earth's surface is constantly being transformed: it is uplifted, folded and faulted by tectonic forces; weathered and eroded by wind, water and ice. Sometimes change is dramatic, the spectacular results of earthquakes or floods. More often it is a slow process lasting millions of years. A physical map of the world represents a snapshot of the ever-evolving architecture of the Earth. This terrain map shows the whole surface of the Earth, both above and below the sea.

The world in section

These cross-sections around the Earth, one in the northern hemisphere; one straddling the Equator, reveal the limited areas of land above sea level in comparison with the extent of the sea floor. The greater erosive effects of weathering by wind and water limit the upward elevation of land above sea level, while the deep oceans retain their dramatic mountain and trench profiles.

Aleutian Trench   Pacific Ocean   Rocky Mountains

60°N

180°   150°W   120°W

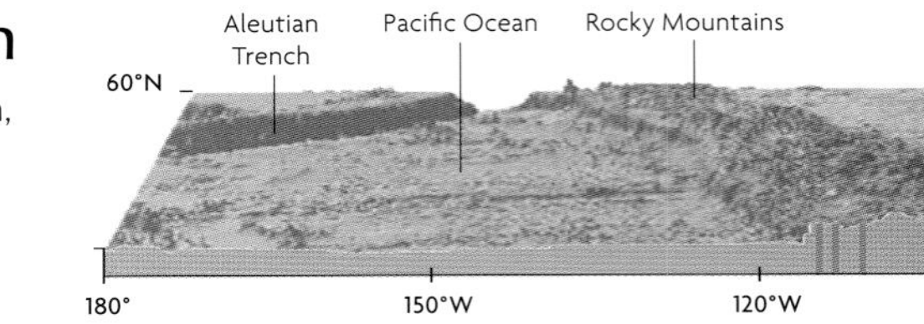

Cross-section: Northern hemisphere

Hawaiian Islands

20°N

10°S

180°   150°W   120°W

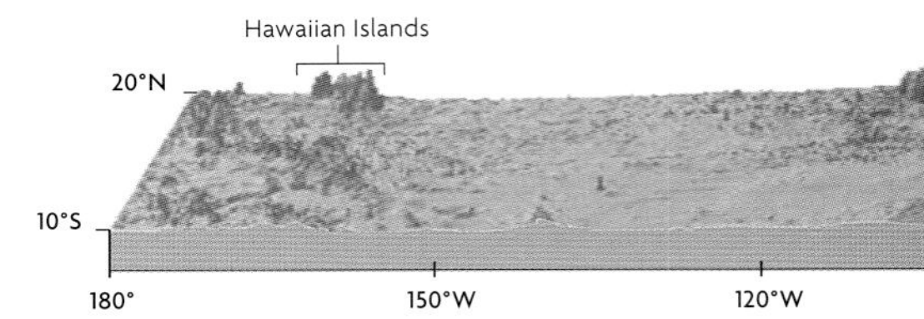

Cross-section: Southern hemisphere

Map key

Geographical regions

- ice
- tundra
- needleleaf forest
- broadleaf forest
- cultivated land
- hot desert
- cold desert
- tropical grassland
- tropical rainforest
- mountain
- submarine regions

Scale 1:66,000,000

Km
0 250 500 1000 1500 2000

Miles
0 250 500 1000 1500 2000

projection: Wagner VII

Northern hemisphere

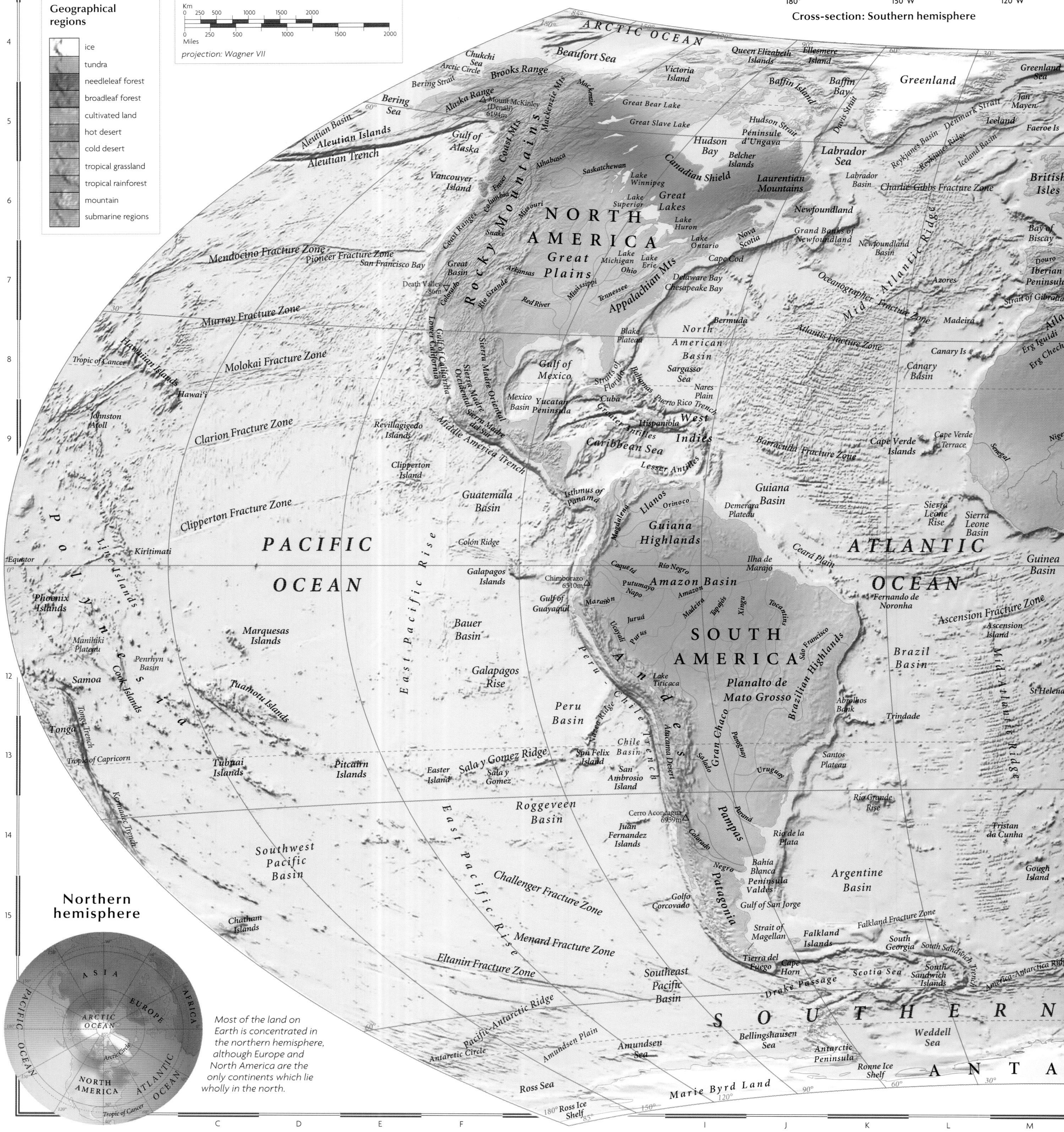

Most of the land on Earth is concentrated in the northern hemisphere, although Europe and North America are the only continents which lie wholly in the north.

ASIA
EUROPE
AFRICA
PACIFIC OCEAN
ARCTIC OCEAN
Arctic Circle
ATLANTIC OCEAN
NORTH AMERICA
Tropic of Cancer

ARCTIC OCEAN

Beaufort Sea
Chukchi Sea
Bering Strait
Arctic Circle
Bering Sea
Brooks Range
Aleutian Islands
Aleutian Trench
Alaska Range
Mount McKinley (Denali) 6194m
Gulf of Alaska
Vancouver Island
Coast Ranges
Mendocino Fracture Zone
Pioneer Fracture Zone
San Francisco Bay
Murray Fracture Zone
Tropic of Cancer
Hawaiian Islands
Johnston Atoll
Hawai'i
Molokai Fracture Zone
Clarion Fracture Zone
Clipperton Island
Revillagigedo Islands
Clipperton Fracture Zone

Queen Elizabeth Islands
Victoria Island
Great Bear Lake
Great Slave Lake
Mackenzie Mts
Canadian Shield
Baffin Island
Baffin Bay
Ellesmere Island
Greenland
Greenland Sea
Jan Mayen
Iceland
Faeroe Is
Denmark Strait
Davis Strait
Hudson Strait
Péninsule d'Ungava
Hudson Bay
Belcher Islands
Laurentian Mountains
Labrador Sea
Labrador Basin
Charlie Gibbs Fracture Zone
Reykjanes Basin
Reykjanes Ridge
British Isles

NORTH AMERICA
Great Plains
Rocky Mountains
Athabasca
Saskatchewan
Lake Winnipeg
Great Lakes
Lake Superior
Lake Michigan
Lake Huron
Lake Ontario
Lake Erie
Missouri
Snake
Columbia
Arkansas
Great Basin
Death Valley -86m
Colorado
Rio Grande
Red River
Tennessee
Mississippi
Ohio
Newfoundland
Nova Scotia
Cape Cod
Appalachian Mts
Delaware Bay
Chesapeake Bay
Grand Banks of Newfoundland
Newfoundland Basin
Bay of Biscay
Douro
Iberian Peninsula
Strait of Gibraltar
Madeira

Sierra Madre Occidental
Sierra Madre Oriental
Sierra Madre del Sur
Gulf of California
Mexico Basin
Yucatan Peninsula
Gulf of Mexico
Cuba
Straits of Florida
Blake Plateau
Bahamas
Hispaniola
Greater Antilles
West Indies
Caribbean Sea
Lesser Antilles
North American Basin
Sargasso Sea
Bermuda
Nares Plain
Puerto Rico Trench
Azores
Oceanographer Fracture Zone
Atlantis Fracture Zone
Mid Atlantic Ridge
Canary Is
Canary Basin
Atlas
Erg Iguidi
Erg Chech
Cape Verde Islands
Cape Verde Terrace
Niger

Middle America Trench
Guatemala Basin
Isthmus of Panama
Colón Ridge
Galapagos Islands
Galapagos Rise
Bauer Basin

PACIFIC OCEAN
Polynesia
Line Islands
Kiritimati
Equator 0°
Phoenix Islands
Manihiki Plateau
Penrhyn Basin
Cook Islands
Samoa
Tonga
Tonga Trench
Kermadec Trench
Tropic of Capricorn
Marquesas Islands
Tuamotu Islands
Tubuai Islands
Pitcairn Islands
Easter Island
Sala y Gomez Ridge
Sala y Gomez
East Pacific Rise
East Pacific Rise
Peru Basin
Roggeveen Basin
Southwest Pacific Basin
Chatham Islands
Challenger Fracture Zone
Menard Fracture Zone
Eltanin Fracture Zone
Pacific Antarctic Ridge
Antarctic Circle
Southeast Pacific Basin

Llanos
Orinoco
Guiana Highlands
Magdalena
Demerara Plateau
Guiana Basin
Ceará Plain
Sierra Leone Rise
Sierra Leone Basin
ATLANTIC OCEAN
Guinea Basin

Cauca
Chimborazo 6310m
Putumayo
Napo
Río Negro
Amazon
Amazon Basin
Madeira
Gulf of Guayaquil
Marañón
Jurua
Ucayali
Purus
Tapajós
Xingu
Tocantins
São Francisco
Ilha de Marajó
Fernando de Noronha
Ascension Fracture Zone
Ascension Island
Mid-Atlantic Ridge

SOUTH AMERICA
Andes
Peru-Chile Trench
Lake Titicaca
Nazca Ridge
San Felix Island
San Ambrosio Island
Atacama Desert
Chile Basin
Gran Chaco
Paraguay
Salado
Planalto de Mato Grosso
Brazilian Highlands
Paraná
Brazil Basin
Abrolhos Bank
Trindade
St Helena
Santos Plateau
Rio Grande Rise

Cerro Aconcagua 6959m
Juan Fernandez Islands
Colorado
Negro
Pampas
Bahía Blanca
Peninsula Valdés
Rio de la Plata
Uruguay
Gulf of San Jorge
Golfo Corcovado
Patagonia
Strait of Magellan
Tierra del Fuego
Cape Horn
Drake Passage
Scotia Sea
Falkland Islands
Falkland Fracture Zone
South Georgia
South Sandwich Islands
South Sandwich Trench
Argentine Basin
Tristan da Cunha
Gough Island

SOUTHERN

Ross Sea
Marie Byrd Land
Ross Ice Shelf
Amundsen Plain
Amundsen Sea
Bellingshausen Sea
Antarctic Peninsula
Ronne Ice Shelf
Weddell Sea
ANTA

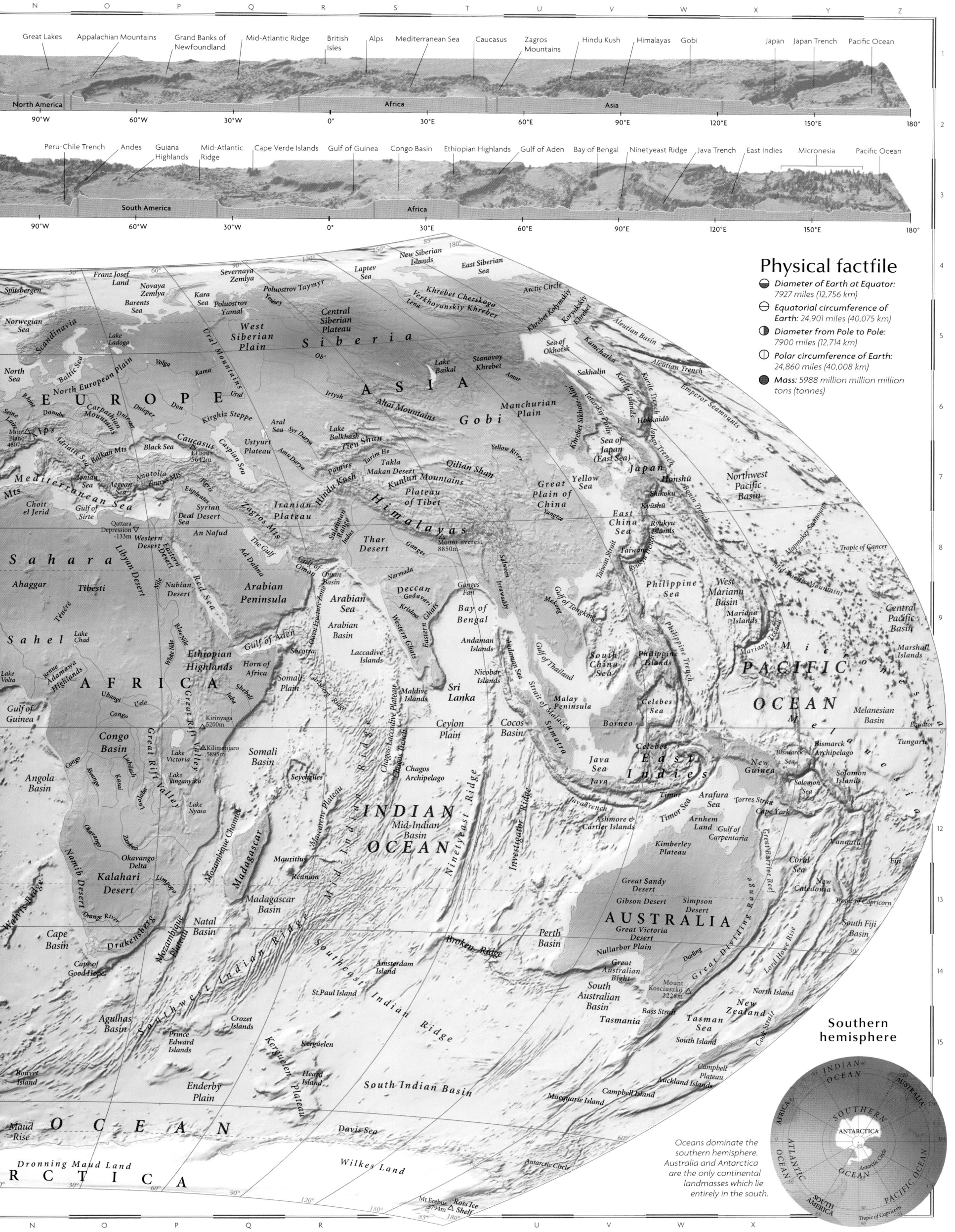

Physical factfile

- *Diameter of Earth at Equator:* 7927 miles (12,756 km)
- *Equatorial circumference of Earth:* 24,901 miles (40,075 km)
- *Diameter from Pole to Pole:* 7900 miles (12,714 km)
- *Polar circumference of Earth:* 24,860 miles (40,008 km)
- *Mass:* 5988 million million million tons (tonnes)

Southern hemisphere

Oceans dominate the southern hemisphere. Australia and Antarctica are the only continental landmasses which lie entirely in the south.

Structure of the Earth

The Earth as it is today is just the latest phase in a constant process of evolution which has occurred over the past 4.5 billion years. The Earth's continents are neither fixed nor stable; over the course of the Earth's history, propelled by currents rising from the intense heat at its centre, the great plates on which they lie have moved, collided, joined together, and separated. These processes continue to mould and transform the surface of the Earth, causing earthquakes and volcanic eruptions and creating oceans, mountain ranges, deep ocean trenches and island chains.

Inside the Earth

The Earth's hot inner core is made up of solid iron, while the outer core is composed of liquid iron and nickel. The mantle nearest the core is viscous, whereas the rocky upper mantle is fairly rigid. The crust is the rocky outer shell of the Earth. Together, the upper mantle and the crust form the lithosphere.

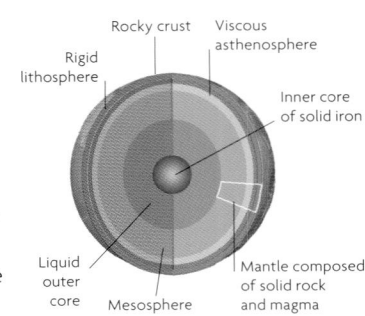

Rigid lithosphere
Rocky crust
Viscous asthenosphere
Inner core of solid iron
Liquid outer core
Mesosphere
Mantle composed of solid rock and magma

The dynamic Earth

The Earth's crust is made up of eight major (and several minor) rigid continental and oceanic tectonic plates, which fit closely together. The positions of the plates are not static. They are constantly moving relative to one another. The type of movement between plates affects the way in which they alter the structure of the Earth. The oldest parts of the plates, known as shields, are the most stable parts of the Earth and little tectonic activity occurs here.

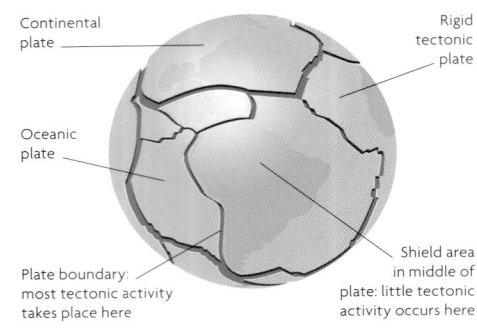

Continental plate
Rigid tectonic plate
Oceanic plate
Plate boundary: most tectonic activity takes place here
Shield area in middle of plate: little tectonic activity occurs here

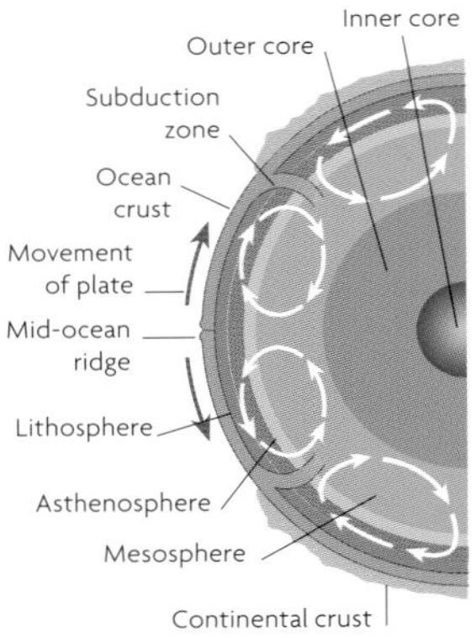

Convection currents

Deep within the Earth, at its inner core, temperatures may exceed 8100°F (4500°C). This heat warms rocks in the mesosphere which rise through the partially molten mantle, displacing cooler rocks just below the solid crust, which sink, and are warmed again by the heat of the mantle. This process is continually repeated, creating convection currents which form the moving force beneath the Earth's crust.

Inner core
Outer core
Subduction zone
Ocean crust
Movement of plate
Mid-ocean ridge
Lithosphere
Asthenosphere
Mesosphere
Continental crust

Plate boundaries

The boundaries between the plates are the areas where most tectonic activity takes place. Three types of movement occur at plate boundaries: the plates can either move towards each other, move apart, or slide past each other. The effect this has on the Earth's structure depends on whether the margin is between two continental plates, two oceanic plates or an oceanic and continental plate.

Mid-ocean ridges

Mid-ocean ridges are formed when two adjacent oceanic plates pull apart, allowing magma to force its way up to the surface, which then cools to form solid rock. Vast amounts of volcanic material are discharged at these mid-ocean ridges which can reach heights of 10,000 ft (3000 m).

▲ *The Mid-Atlantic Ridge rises above sea level in Iceland, producing geysers and volcanoes.*

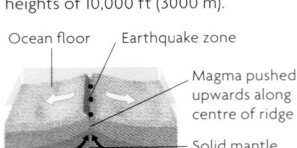

Ocean floor
Earthquake zone
Magma pushed upwards along centre of ridge
Solid mantle

Formation of a mid-ocean ridge

Ocean plates meeting

△△ Oceanic crust is denser and thinner than continental crust; on average it is 3 miles (5 km) thick, while continental crust averages 18–24 miles (30–40 km). When oceanic plates of similar density meet, the crust is contorted as one plate overrides the other, forming deep sea trenches and volcanic island arcs above sea level.

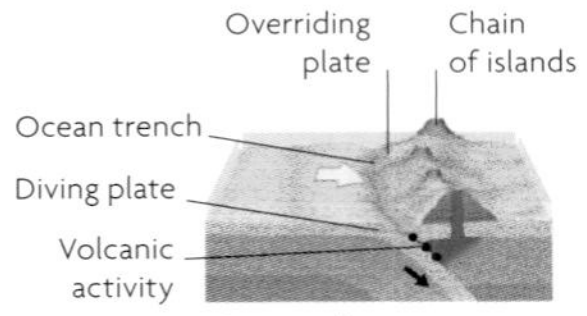

▲ *Mount Pinatubo is an active volcano, lying on the Pacific 'Ring of Fire'.*

Overriding plate
Chain of islands
Ocean trench
Diving plate
Volcanic activity

Ocean plates meeting to form an island arc

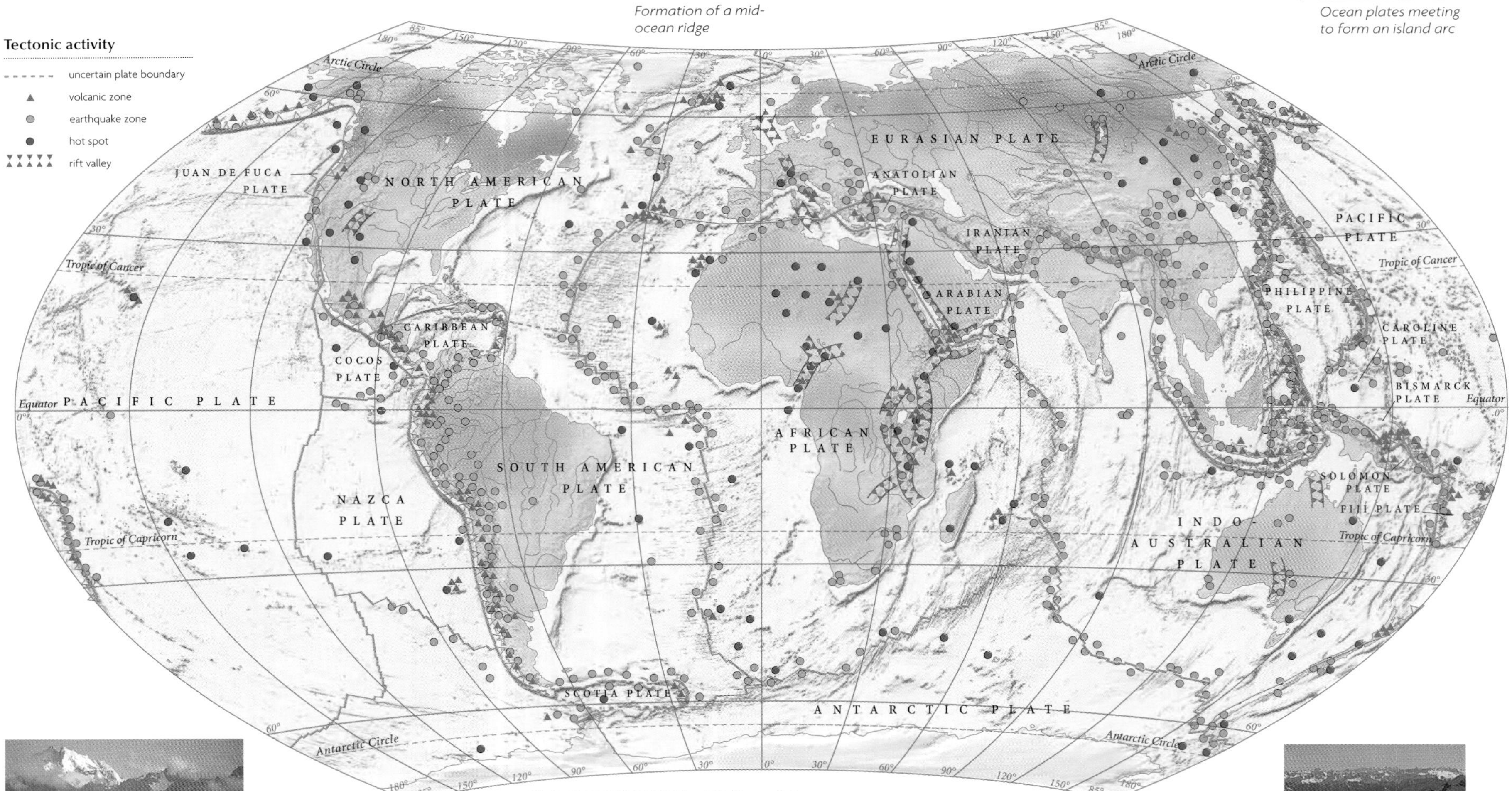

Tectonic activity

- – – – – uncertain plate boundary
- ▲ volcanic zone
- ● earthquake zone
- ● hot spot
- ▼▼▼▼▼ rift valley

JUAN DE FUCA PLATE
NORTH AMERICAN PLATE
EURASIAN PLATE
ANATOLIAN PLATE
IRANIAN PLATE
ARABIAN PLATE
PACIFIC PLATE
PHILIPPINE PLATE
CAROLINE PLATE
BISMARCK PLATE
CARIBBEAN PLATE
COCOS PLATE
PACIFIC PLATE
AFRICAN PLATE
SOUTH AMERICAN PLATE
NAZCA PLATE
SOLOMON PLATE
FIJI PLATE
INDO-AUSTRALIAN PLATE
SCOTIA PLATE
ANTARCTIC PLATE

Arctic Circle
Tropic of Cancer
Equator
Tropic of Capricorn
Antarctic Circle

Diving plates

△△ When an oceanic and a continental plate meet, the denser oceanic plate is driven underneath the continental plate, which is crumpled by the collision to form mountain ranges. As the ocean plate plunges downward, it heats up, and molten rock (magma) is forced up to the surface.

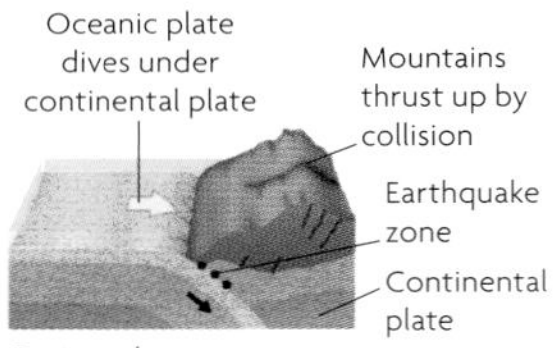

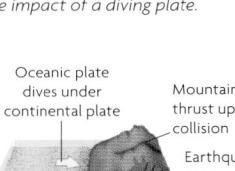

◄ *The Andean mountain chain is the typical result of the impact of a diving plate.*

Oceanic plate dives under continental plate
Mountains thrust up by collision
Earthquake zone
Continental plate

Diving plate

Sliding plates

When two plates slide past each other, friction is caused along the fault line which divides them. The plates do not move smoothly, and the uneven movement causes earthquakes.

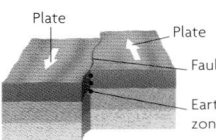

▲ *The deep fracture caused by the sliding plates of the San Andreas Fault can be clearly seen in parts of California.*

Plate
Plate
Fault line
Earthquake zone

Sliding plates

Colliding plates

▲▲▲ When two continental plates collide, great mountain chains are thrust upwards as the crust buckles and folds under the force of the impact.

► *The Alps were formed when the African Plate collided with the Eurasian Plate, about 65 million years ago.*

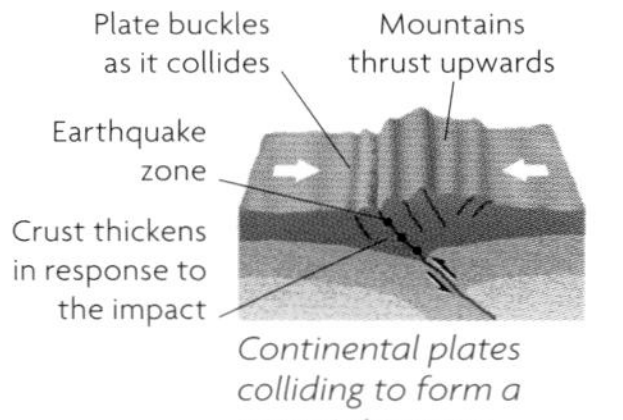

Plate buckles as it collides
Mountains thrust upwards
Earthquake zone
Crust thickens in response to the impact

Continental plates colliding to form a mountain range

Continental drift

Although the plates which make up the Earth's crust move only a few centimetres in a year, over the millions of years of the Earth's history, its continents have moved many thousands of kilometres, to create new continents, oceans and mountain chains.

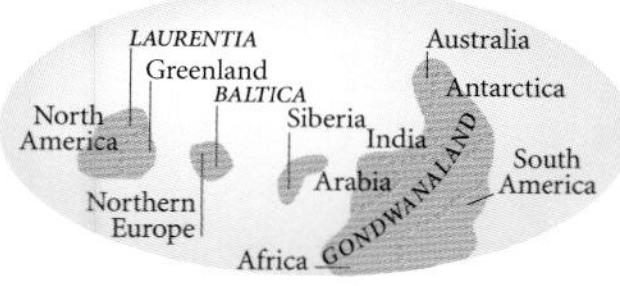

1: Cambrian period
570–510 million years ago. Most continents are in tropical latitudes. The supercontinent of Gondwanaland reaches the South Pole.

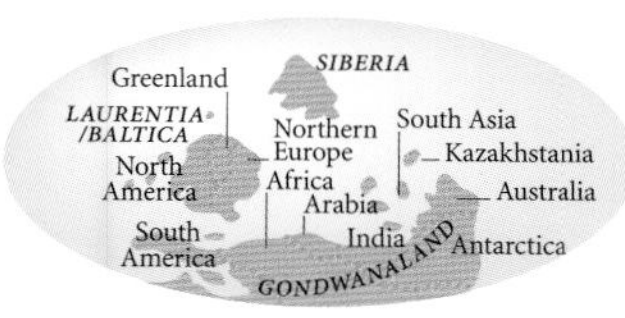

2: Devonian period
408–362 million years ago. The continents of Gondwanaland and Laurentia are drifting northwards.

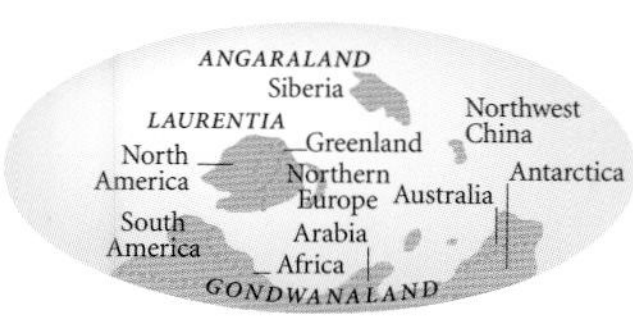

3: Carboniferous period
362–290 million years ago. The Earth is dominated by three continents; Laurentia, Angaraland and Gondwanaland.

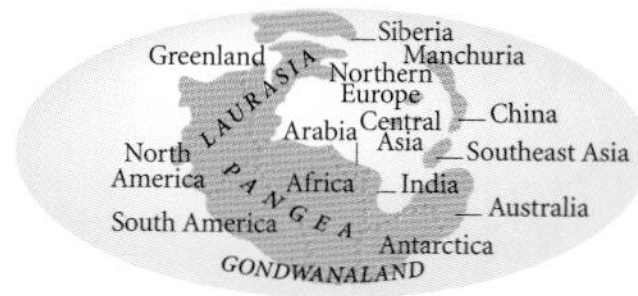

4: Triassic period
245–208 million years ago. All three major continents have joined to form the super-continent of Pangea.

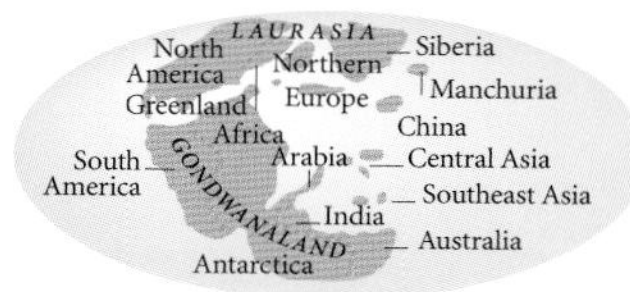

5: Jurassic period
208–145 million years ago. The super-continent of Pangea begins to break up, causing an overall rise in sea levels.

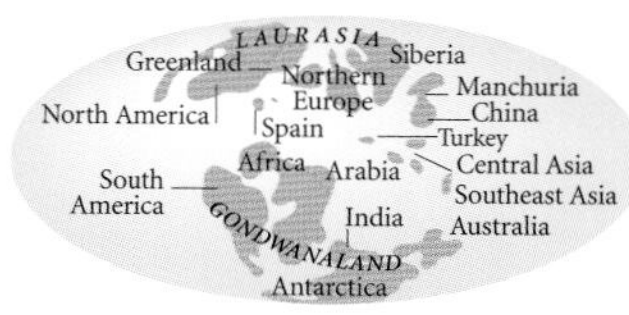

6: Cretaceous period
145–65 million years ago. Warm shallow seas cover much of the land: sea levels are about 80 ft (25 m) above present levels.

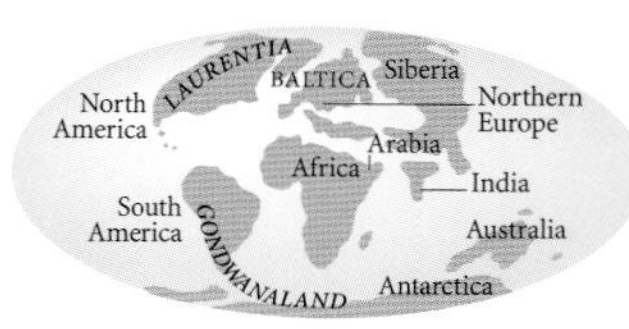

7: Tertiary period
65–2 million years ago. Although the world's geography is becoming more recognizable, major events such as the creation of the Himalayan mountain chain, are still to occur during this period.

Continental shields

The centres of the Earth's continents, known as shields, were established between 2500 and 500 million years ago; some contain rocks over three billion years old. They were formed by a series of turbulent events: plate movements, earthquakes and volcanic eruptions. Since the Pre-Cambrian period, over 570 million years ago, they have experienced little tectonic activity, and today, these flat, low-lying slabs of solidified molten rock form the stable centres of the continents. They are bounded or covered by successive belts of younger sedimentary rock.

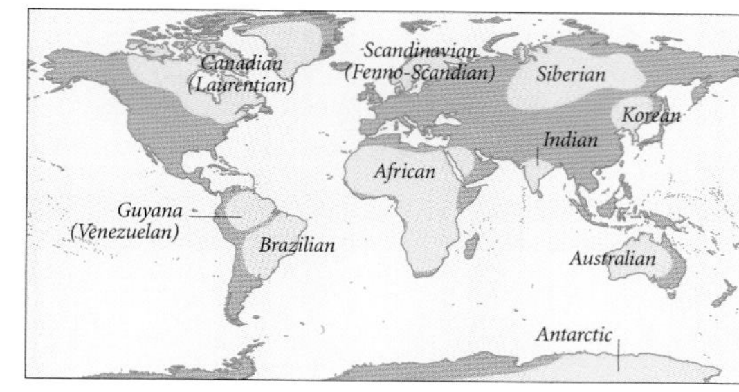

The Hawaiian island chain

A hot spot lying deep beneath the Pacific Ocean pushes a plume of magma from the Earth's mantle up through the Pacific Plate to form volcanic islands. While the hot spot remains stationary, the plate on which the islands sit is moving slowly. A long chain of islands has been created as the plate passes over the hot spot.

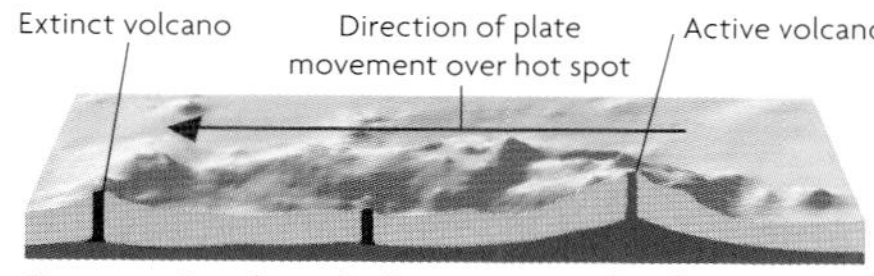

Cross-section through the Hawaiian Islands

Evolution of the Hawaiian Islands

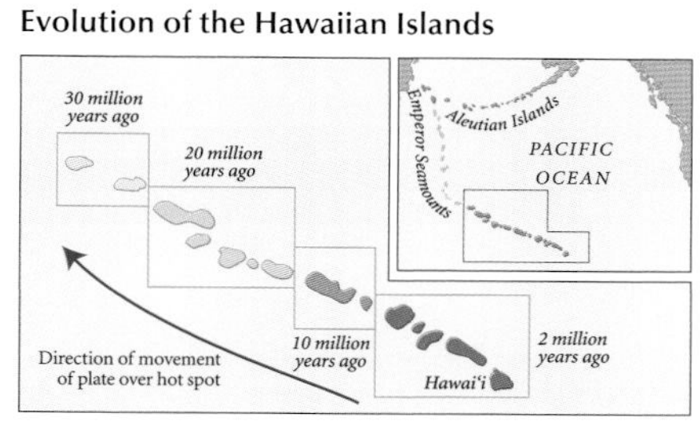

Creation of the Himalayas

Between 10 and 20 million years ago, the Indian subcontinent, part of the ancient continent of Gondwanaland, collided with the continent of Asia. The Indo-Australian Plate continued to move northwards, displacing continental crust and uplifting the Himalayas, the world's highest mountain chain.

Movements of India

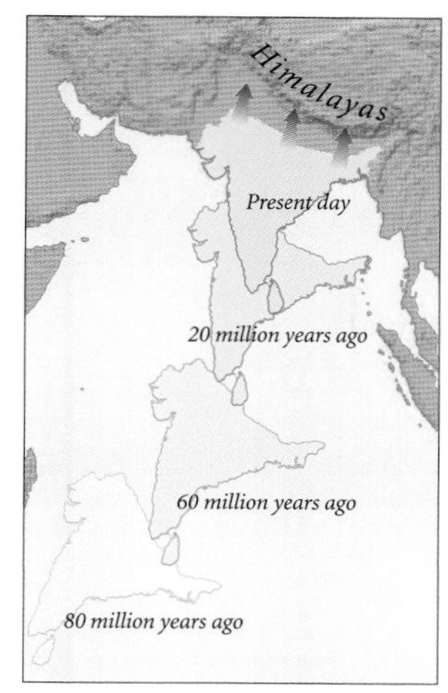

Cross-section through the Himalayas

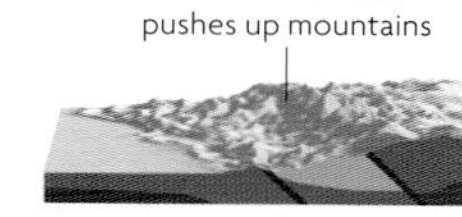

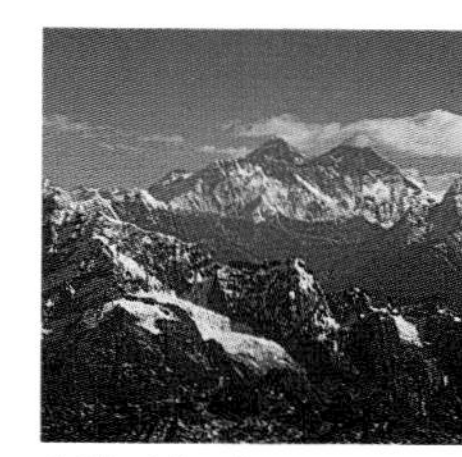

▲ *The Himalayas were uplifted when the Indian subcontinent collided with Asia.*

The Earth's geology

The Earth's rocks are created in a continual cycle. Exposed rocks are weathered and eroded by wind, water and chemicals and deposited as sediments. If they pass into the Earth's crust they will be transformed by high temperatures and pressures into metamorphic rocks or they will melt and solidify as igneous rocks.

Sandstone

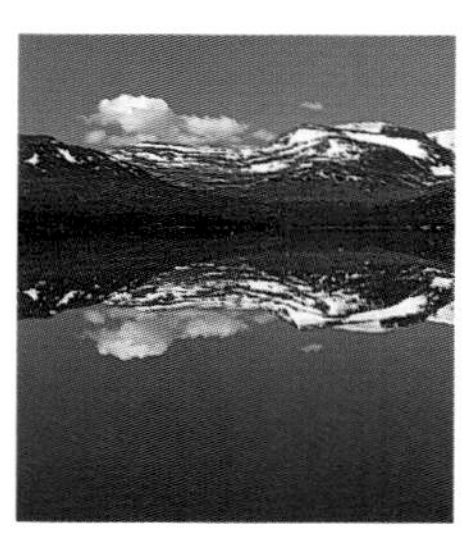

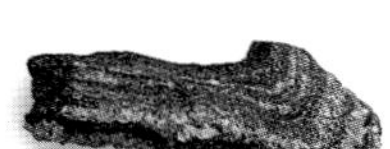

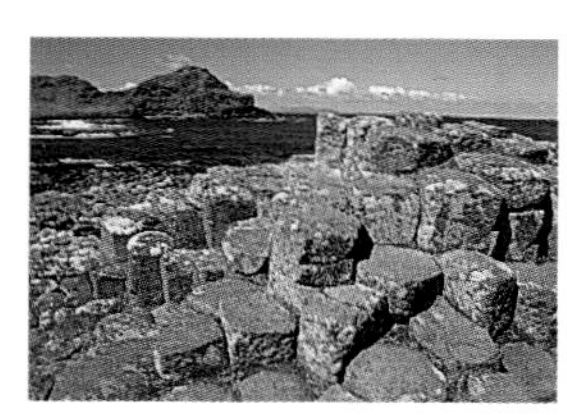

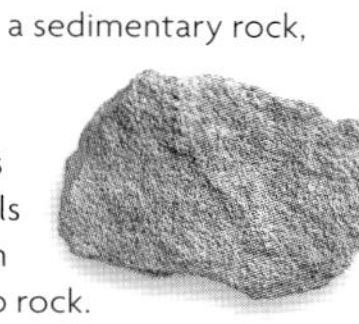

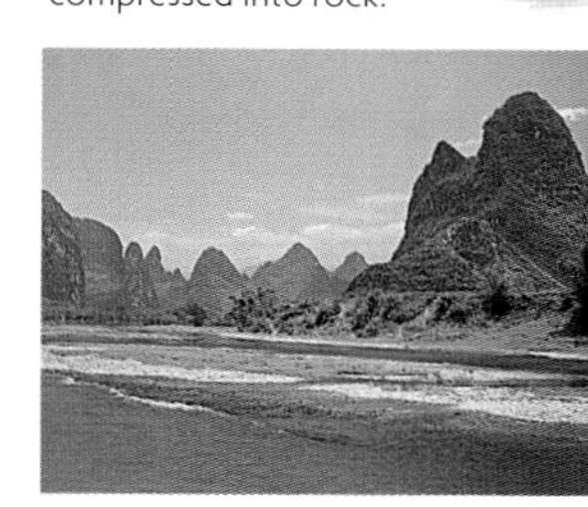

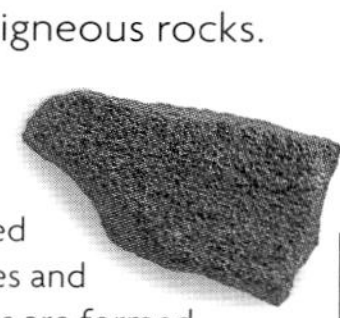

8 Sandstones are sedimentary rocks formed mainly in deserts, beaches and deltas. Desert sandstones are formed of grains of quartz which have been well rounded by wind erosion.

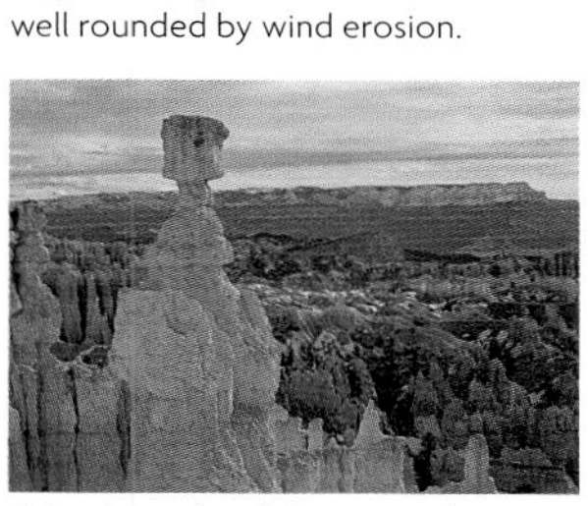

▲ *Rock stacks of desert sandstone, at Bryce Canyon National Park, Utah, USA.*

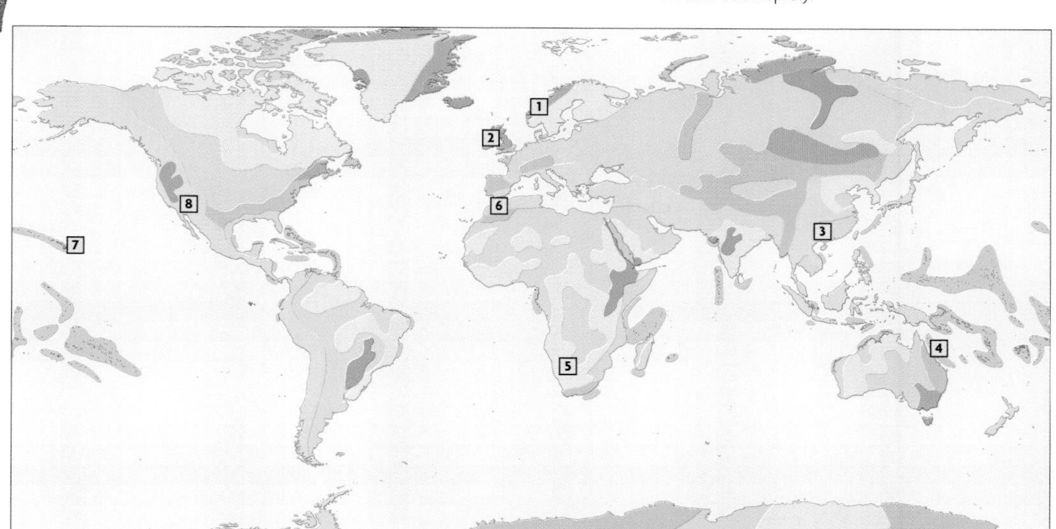

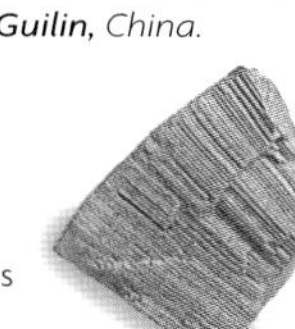

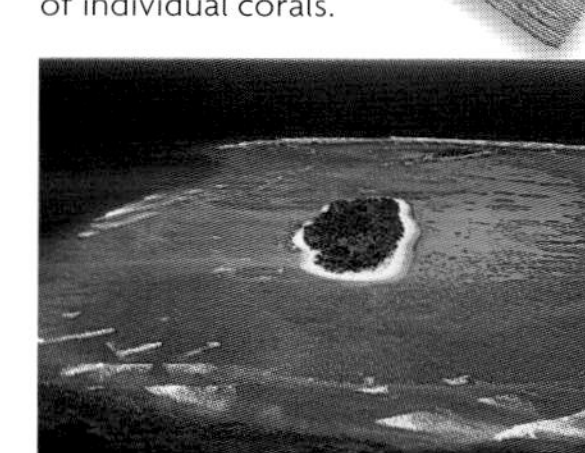

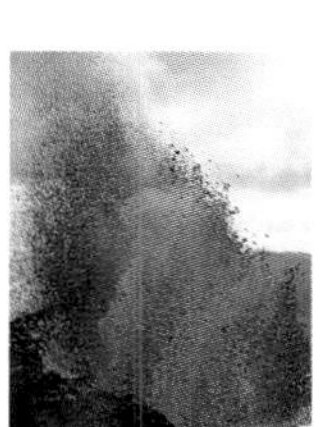

◄ *Extrusive igneous rocks are formed during volcanic eruptions, as here in Hawai'i.*

Andesite

7 Andesite is an extrusive igneous rock formed from magma which has solidified on the Earth's crust after a volcanic eruption.

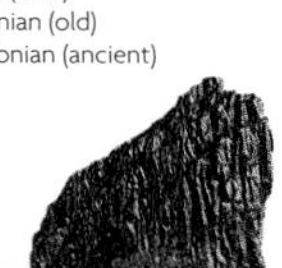

Gneiss

1 Gneiss is a metamorphic rock made at great depth during the formation of mountain chains, when intense heat and pressure transform sedimentary or igneous rocks.

▲ *Gneiss formations in Norway's Jotunheimen Mountains.*

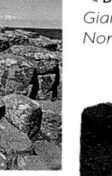

◄ *Basalt columns at Giant's Causeway, Northern Ireland, UK.*

Basalt

2 Basalt is an igneous rock, formed when small quantities of magma lying close to the Earth's surface cool rapidly.

Limestone

3 Limestone is a sedimentary rock, which is formed mainly from the calcite skeletons of marine animals which have been compressed into rock.

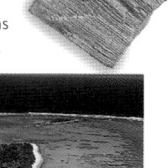

▲ *Limestone hills, Guilin, China.*

Coral

4 Coral reefs are formed from the skeletons of millions of individual corals.

▲ *Great Barrier Reef, Australia.*

Geological regions

- continental shield
- sedimentary cover
- coral formation
- igneous rock types

Mountain ranges

- Alpine (new)
- Hercynian (old)
- Caledonian (ancient)

Schist

6 Gchist is a metamorphic rock formed during mountain building, when temperature and pressure are comparatively high. Both mudstones and shales reform into schist under these conditions.

► *Schist formations in the Atlas Mountains, northwestern Africa.*

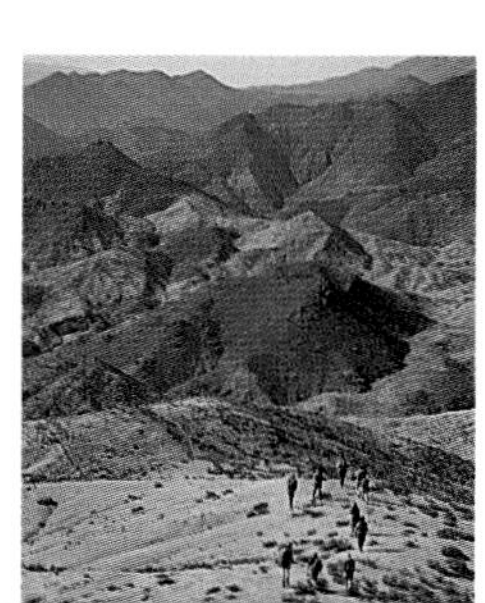

Granite

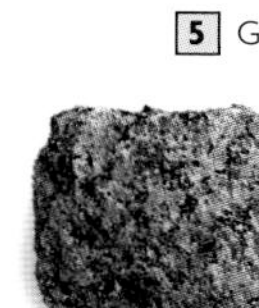

5 Granite is an intrusive igneous rock formed from magma which has solidified deep within the Earth's crust. The magma cools slowly, producing a coarse-grained rock.

► *Namibia's Namaqualand Plateau is formed of granite.*

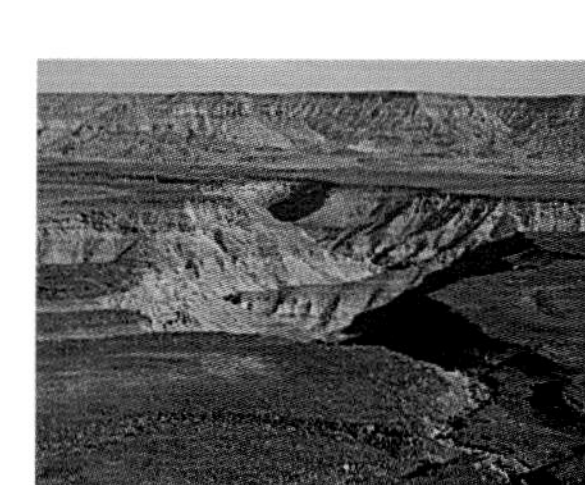

Shaping the landscape

The basic material of the Earth's surface is solid rock: valleys, deserts, soil and sand are all evidence of the powerful agents of weathering, erosion and deposition which constantly shape and transform the Earth's landscapes. Water, either flowing continually in rivers or seas, or frozen and compacted into solid sheets of ice, has the most clearly visible impact on the Earth's surface. But wind can transport fragments of rock over huge distances and strip away protective layers of vegetation, exposing rock surfaces to the impact of extreme heat and cold.

Coastal water

The world's coastlines are constantly changing; every day, tides deposit, sift and sort sand and gravel on the shoreline. Over longer periods, powerful wave action erodes cliffs and headlands and carves out bays.

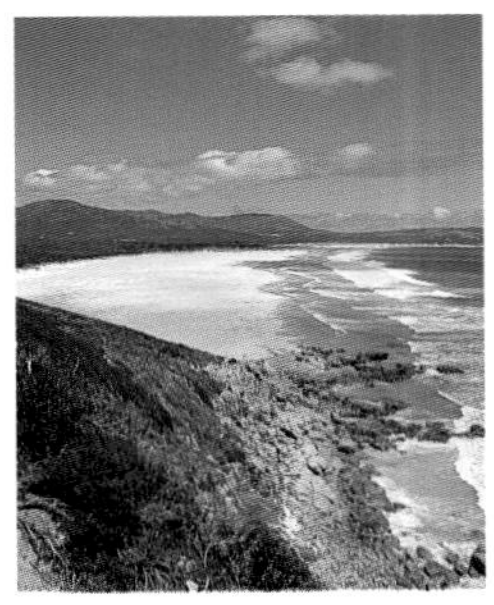

▶ *A low, wide* sandy beach on South Africa's Cape Peninsula is continually re-shaped by the action of the Atlantic waves.

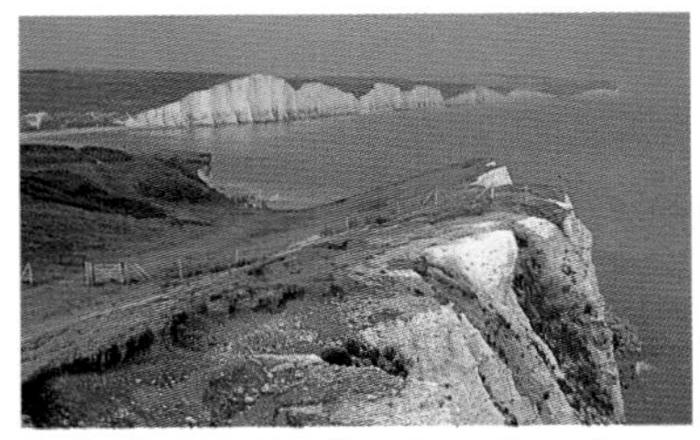

▲ *The sheer chalk* cliffs at Seven Sisters in southern England are constantly under attack from waves.

Water

Less than 2% of the world's water is on the land, but it is the most powerful agent of landscape change. Water, as rainfall, groundwater and rivers, can transform landscapes through both erosion and deposition. Eroded material carried by rivers forms the world's most fertile soils.

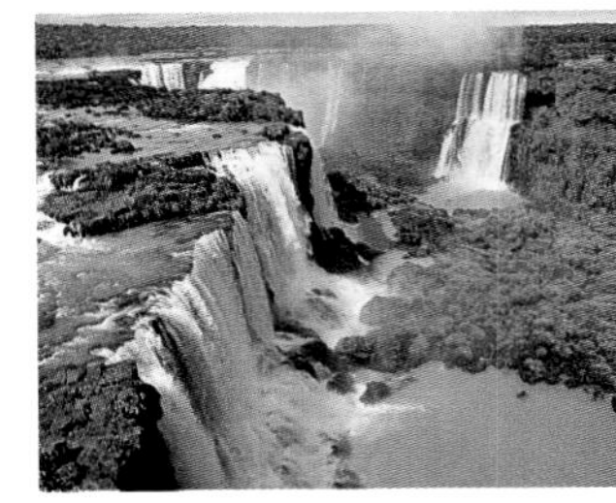

▲ *Waterfalls such as* the Iguaçu Falls on the border between Argentina and southern Brazil, erode the underlying rock, causing the falls to retreat.

Groundwater

In regions where there are porous rocks such as chalk, water is stored underground in large quantities; these reservoirs of water are known as aquifers. Rain percolates through topsoil into the underlying bedrock, creating an underground store of water. The limit of the saturated zone is called the water table.

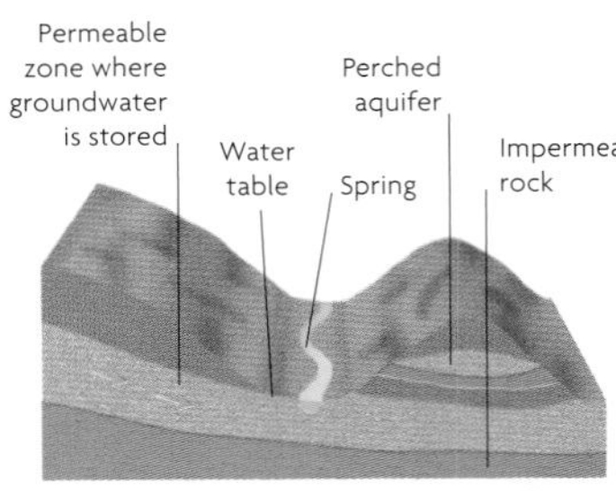

Storage of groundwater in an aquifer

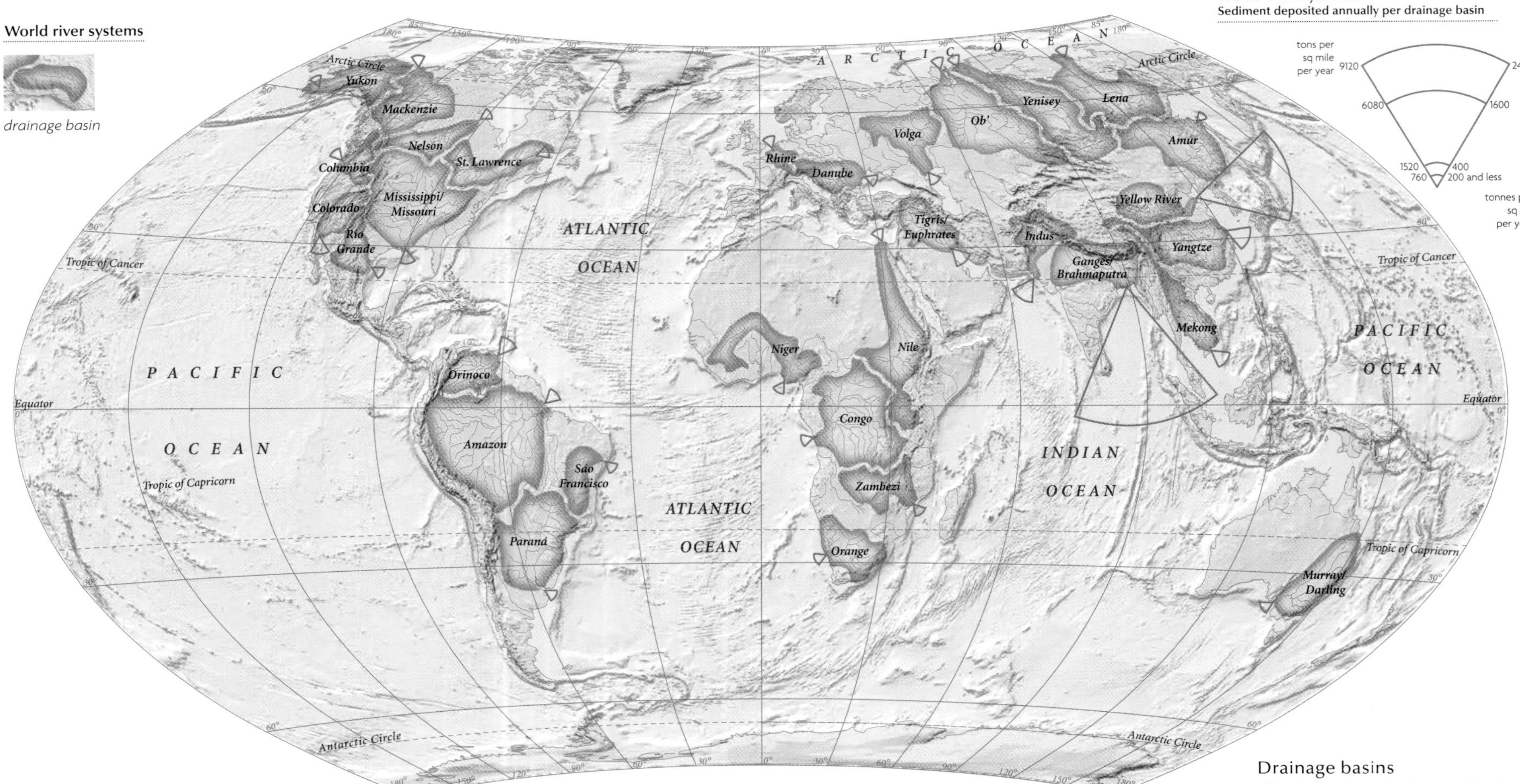

World river systems

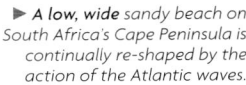

drainage basin

World river systems:
Sediment deposited annually per drainage basin

tons per sq mile per year 9120 · 6080 · 1520 · 760 · 400 · 200 and less · 2400 · 1600

tonnes per sq km per year

Rivers

Rivers erode the land by grinding and dissolving rocks and stones. Most erosion occurs in the river's upper course as it flows through highland areas. Rock fragments are moved along the river bed by fast-flowing water and deposited in areas where the river slows down, such as flat plains, or where the river enters seas or lakes.

River valleys

Over long periods of time rivers erode uplands to form characteristic V-shaped valleys with smooth sides.

Resistant rock · River · Chemical erosion cuts valley in softer rock

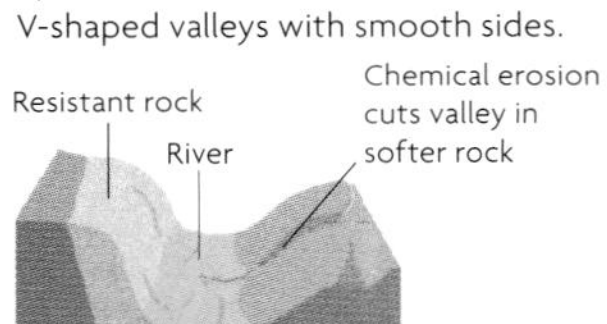

River valley erosion

Deltas

When a river deposits its load of silt and sediment (alluvium) on entering the sea, it may form a delta. As this material accumulates, it chokes the mouth of the river, forcing it to create new channels to reach the sea.

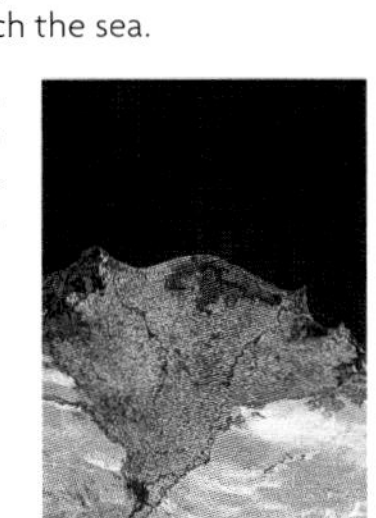

▶ *The Nile forms* a broad delta as it flows into the Mediterranean.

Drainage basins

The drainage basin is the area of land drained by a major trunk river and its smaller branch rivers or tributaries. Drainage basins are separated from one another by natural boundaries known as watersheds.

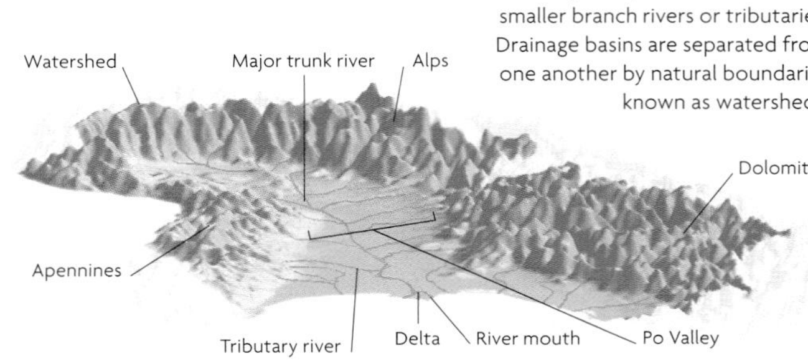

Watershed · Major trunk river · Alps · Dolomites · Apennines · Tributary river · Delta · River mouth · Po Valley

The drainage basin of the Po river, northern Italy.

Meanders

In their lower courses, rivers flow slowly. As they flow across the lowlands, they form looping bends called meanders.

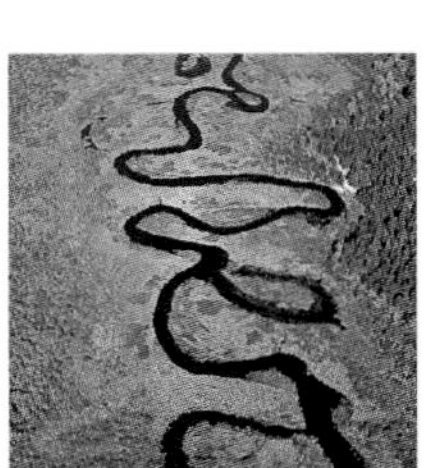

▲ *The Mississippi River* forms meanders as it flows across the southern USA.

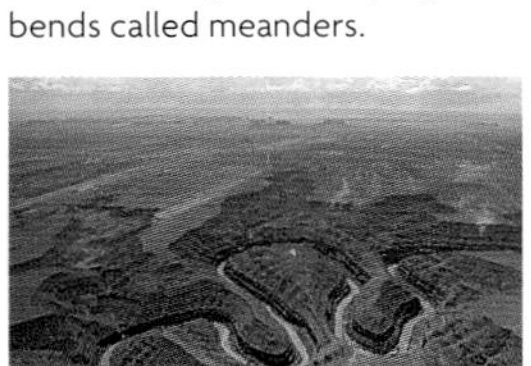

▲ *The meanders of* Utah's San Juan River have become deeply incised.

Deposition

When rivers have deposited large quantities of fertile alluvium, they are forced to find new channels through the alluvium deposits, creating braided river systems.

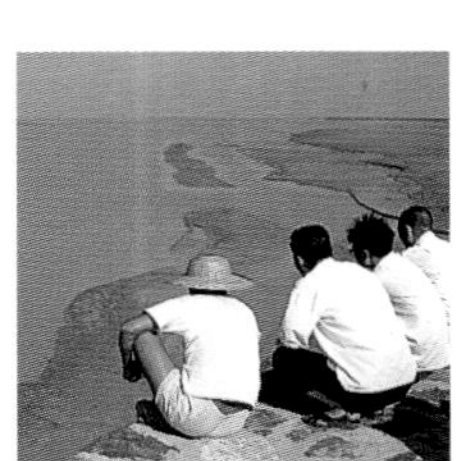

◀ *Mud is deposited* by China's Yellow River in its lower course.

Landslides

Heavy rain and associated flooding on slopes can loosen underlying rocks, which crumble, causing the top layers of rock and soil to slip.

▶ *A huge landslide* in the Swiss Alps has left massive piles of rocks and pebbles called scree.

Gullies

In areas where soil is thin, rainwater is not effectively absorbed, and may flow overland. The water courses downhill in channels, or gullies, and may lead to rapid erosion of soil.

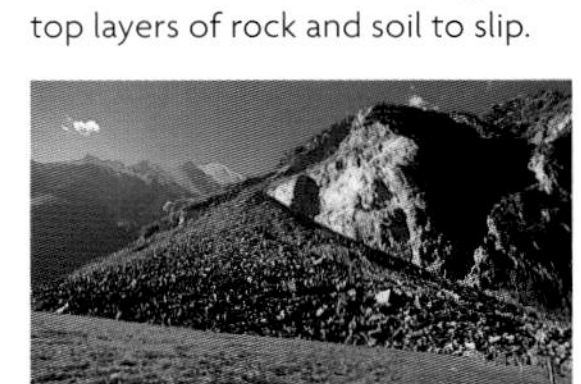

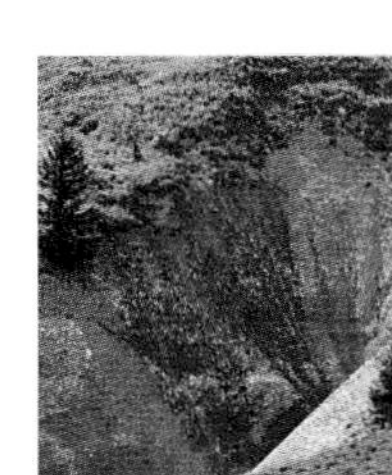

▲ *A deep gully* in the French Alps caused by the scouring of upper layers of turf.

Ice

During its long history, the Earth has experienced a number of glacial episodes when temperatures were considerably lower than today. During the last Ice Age, 18,000 years ago, ice covered an area three times larger than it does today. Over these periods, the ice has left a remarkable legacy of transformed landscapes.

Glaciers

Glaciers are formed by the compaction of snow into 'rivers' of ice. As they move over the landscape, glaciers pick up and carry a load of rocks and boulders which erode the landscape they pass over, and are eventually deposited at the end of the glacier.

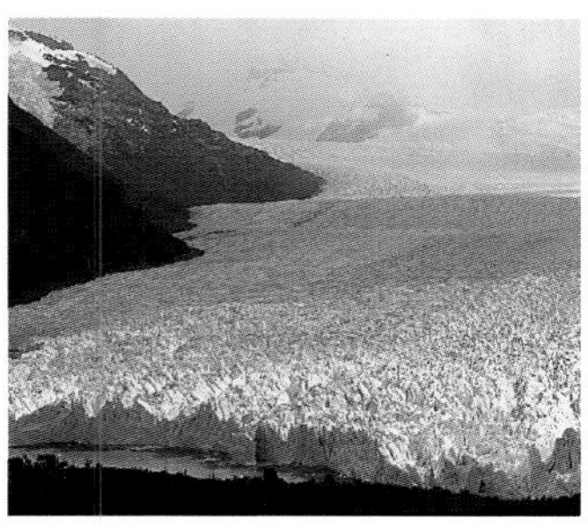

▲ **A massive glacier** advancing down a valley in southern Argentina.

Post-glacial features

When a glacial episode ends, the retreating ice leaves many features. These include depositional ridges called moraines, which may be eroded into low hills known as drumlins; sinuous ridges called eskers; kames which are rounded hummocks; depressions known as kettle holes; and windblown loess deposits.

Glacial valleys

Glaciers can erode much more powerfully than rivers. They form steep-sided, flat-bottomed valleys with a typical U-shaped profile. Valleys created by tributary glaciers, whose floors have not been eroded to the same depth as the main glacial valley floor, are called hanging valleys.

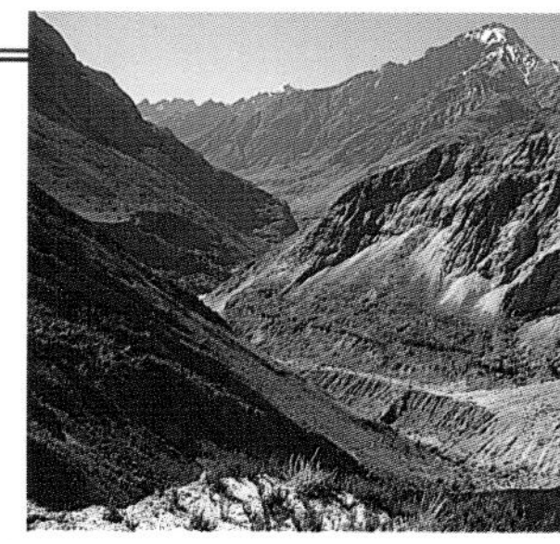

▲ **The U-shaped profile** and piles of morainic debris are characteristic of a valley once filled by a glacier.

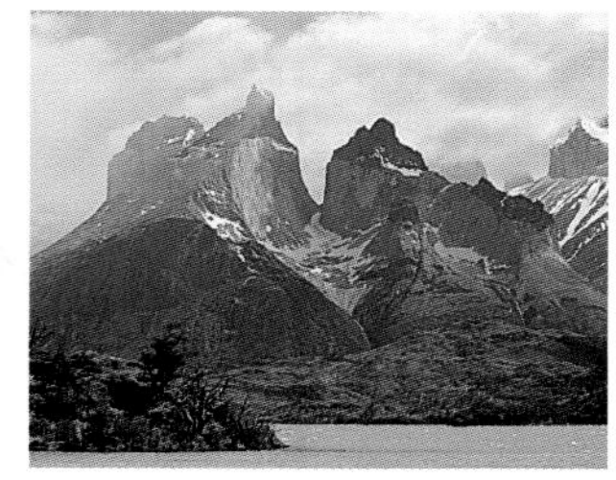

▲ **A series of** hanging valleys high up in the Chilean Andes.

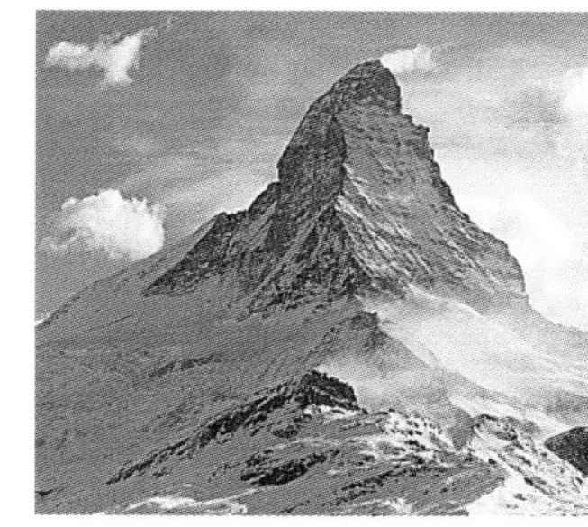

▲ **The profile of** the Matterhorn has been formed by three cirques lying 'back-to-back'.

Cirques

Cirques are basin-shaped hollows which mark the head of a glaciated valley. Where neighbouring cirques meet, they are divided by sharp rock ridges called arêtes. It is these arêtes which give the Matterhorn its characteristic profile.

Fjords

Fjords are ancient glacial valleys flooded by the sea following the end of a period of glaciation. Beneath the water, the valley floor can be 4000 ft (1300 m) deep.

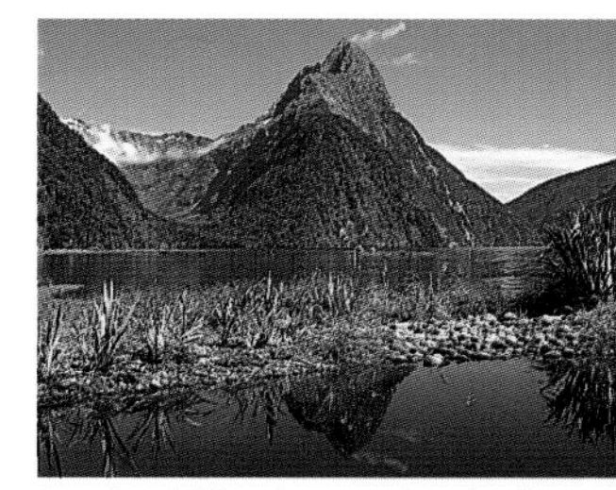

▲ **A fjord fills** a former glacial valley in southern New Zealand.

Periglaciation

Periglacial areas occur near to the edge of ice sheets. A layer of frozen ground lying just beneath the surface of the land is known as permafrost. When the surface melts in the summer, the water is unable to drain into the frozen ground, and so 'creeps' downhill, a process known as solifluction.

Past and present world ice-cover and glacial features

Past and present world ice cover and glacial features

- extent of last Ice Age
- loess deposits
- post-glacial feature
- glacial feature
- present day ice cover
- glacial field

Kame terrace
Retreating glacier
Kettle hole
Esker
Drumlin
Braided river
Terminal moraine
Windblown loess
Glacial till
Bedrock

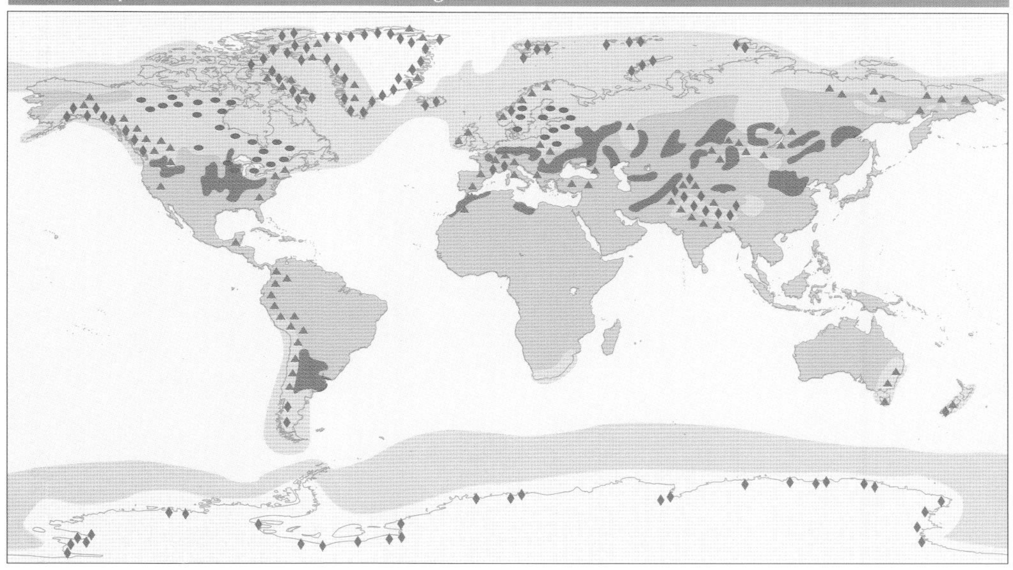

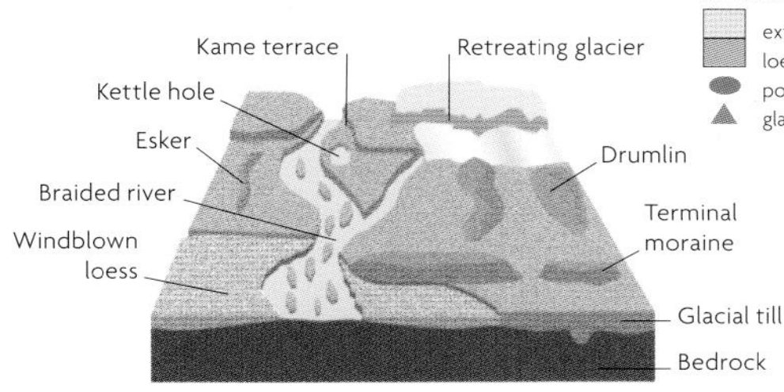

Post-glacial landscape features

Ice shattering

Water drips into fissures in rocks and freezes, expanding as it does so. The pressure weakens the rock, causing it to crack, and eventually to shatter into polygonal patterns.

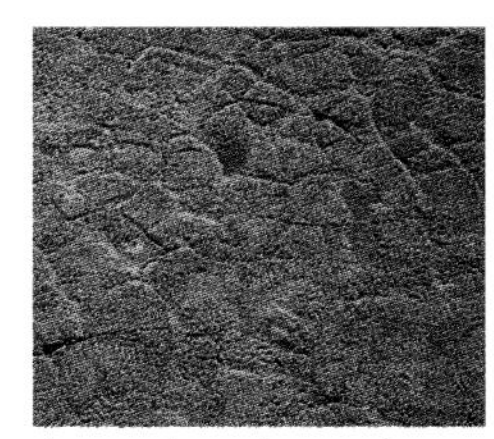

▲ **Irregular polygons show** through the sedge-grass tundra in the Yukon, Canada.

Wind

Strong winds can transport rock fragments great distances, especially where there is little vegetation to protect the rock. In desert areas, wind picks up loose, unprotected sand particles, carrying them over great distances. This powerfully abrasive debris is blasted at the surface by the wind, eroding the landscape into dramatic shapes.

Deposition

The rocky, stony floors of the world's deserts are swept and scoured by strong winds. The smaller, finer particles of sand are shaped into surface ripples, dunes, or sand mountains, which rise to a height of 650 ft (200 m). Dunes usually form single lines, running perpendicular to the direction of the prevailing wind. These long, straight ridges can extend for over 100 miles (160 km).

Dunes

Dunes are shaped by wind direction and sand supply. Where sand supply is limited, crescent-shaped barchan dunes are formed.

Prevailing winds and dust trajectories

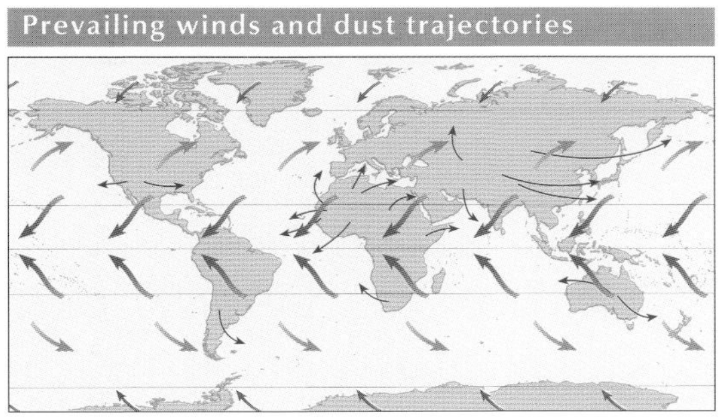

Prevailing winds
- northeast trade
- southeast trade
- westerly
- westerly
- polar easterly
- polar easterly

Dust trajectories
- trajectory of aeolian dust

Hot and cold deserts

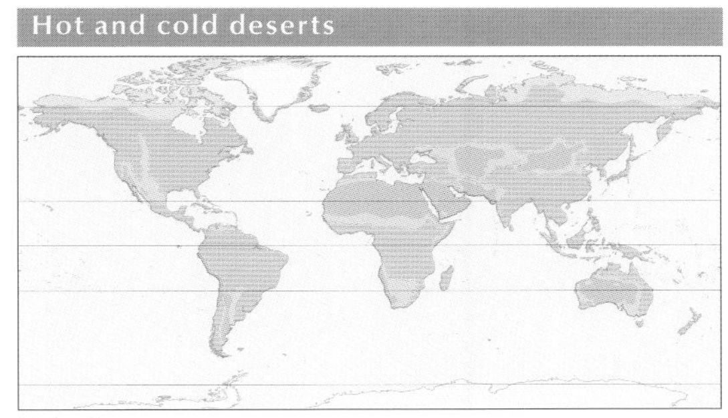

Main desert types
- hot arid
- semi-arid
- cold polar

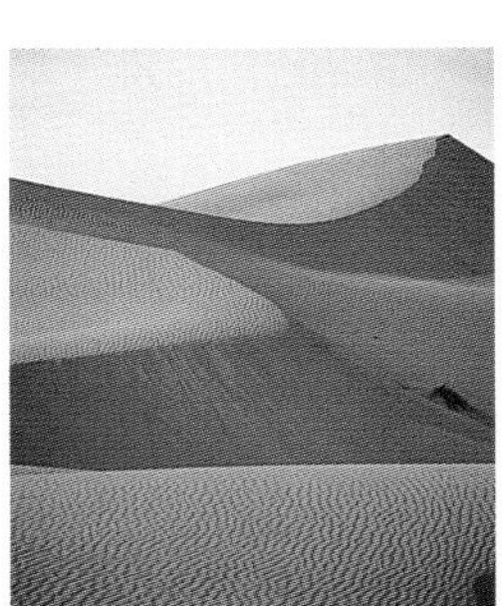

▲ **Barchan dunes in** the Arabian Desert.

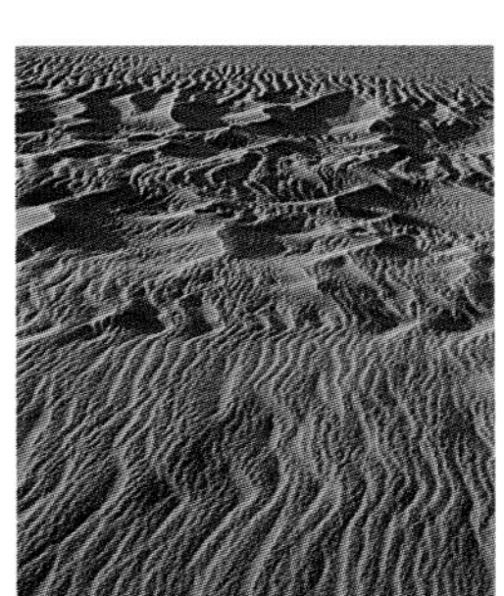

▲ **Complex dune system in** the Sahara.

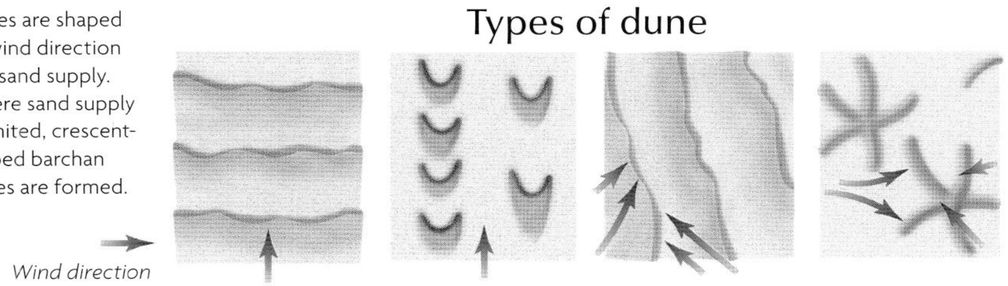

Heat

Fierce sun can heat the surface of rock, causing it to expand more rapidly than the cooler, underlying layers. This creates tensions which force the rock to crack or break up. In arid regions, the evaporation of water from rock surfaces dissolves certain minerals within the water, causing salt crystals to form in small openings in the rock. The hard crystals force the openings to widen into cracks and fissures.

Temperature

Most of the world's deserts are in the tropics. The cold deserts which occur elsewhere are arid because they are a long way from the rain-giving sea. Rock in deserts is exposed because of lack of vegetation and is susceptible to changes in temperature; extremes of heat and cold can cause both cracks and fissures to appear in the rock.

Desert abrasion

Abrasion creates a wide range of desert landforms from faceted pebbles and wind ripples in the sand, to large-scale features such as yardangs (low, streamlined ridges), and scoured desert pavements.

Wind abrasion
Faceted rock
Wind direction
Desert pavement
Gravel
Sand desert
Wind rippling
Thermal fracturing

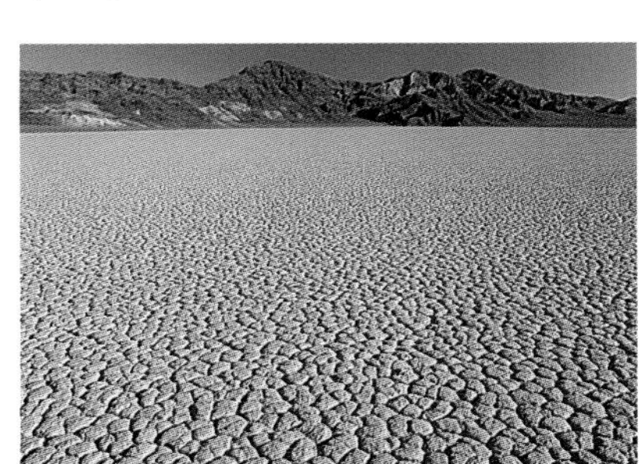

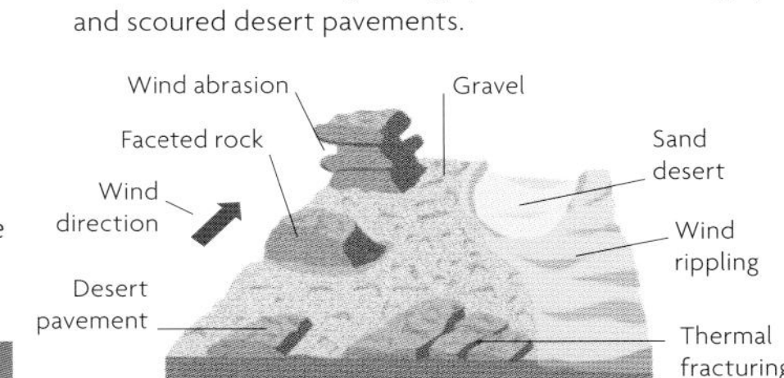

Features of a desert surface

Types of dune

Wind direction

Transverse dune

Barchan dune

Linear dune

Star dune

▲ **The cracked and** parched floor of Death Valley, California. This is one of the hottest deserts on Earth.

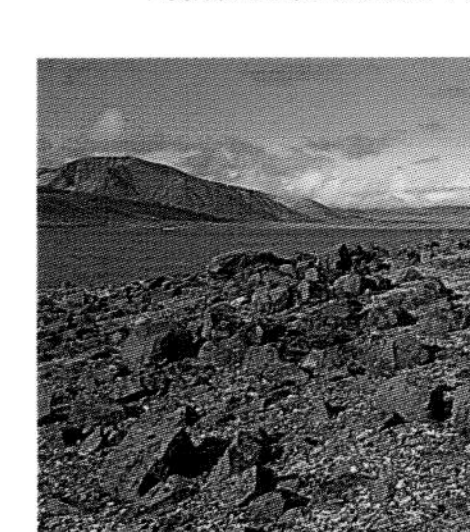

◄ **This dry valley** at Ellesmere Island in the Canadian Arctic is an example of a cold desert. The cracked floor and scoured slopes are features also found in hot deserts.

A B C D E F G H I J K L M

The world's oceans

Two-thirds of the Earth's surface is covered by the oceans. The landscape of the ocean floor, like the surface of the land, has been shaped by movements of the Earth's crust over millions of years to form volcanic mountain ranges, deep trenches, basins and plateaux. Ocean currents constantly redistribute warm and cold water around the world. A major warm current, such as El Niño in the Pacific Ocean, can increase surface temperature by up to 46°F (8°C), causing changes in weather patterns which can lead to both droughts and flooding.

The great oceans

There are five oceans on Earth: the Pacific, Atlantic, Indian and Southern oceans, and the much smaller Arctic Ocean. These five ocean basins are relatively young, having evolved within the last 80 million years. One of the most recent plate collisions, between the Eurasian and African plates, created the present-day arrangement of continents and oceans.

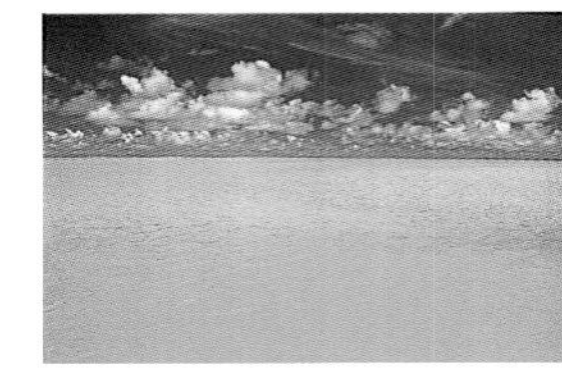

▲ **The Indian Ocean** accounts for approximately 20% of the total area of the world's oceans.

Sea level

If the influence of tides, winds, currents and variations in gravity were ignored, the surface of the Earth's oceans would closely follow the topography of the ocean floor, with an underwater ridge 3000 ft (915 m) high producing a rise of up to 3 ft (1 m) in the level of the surface water.

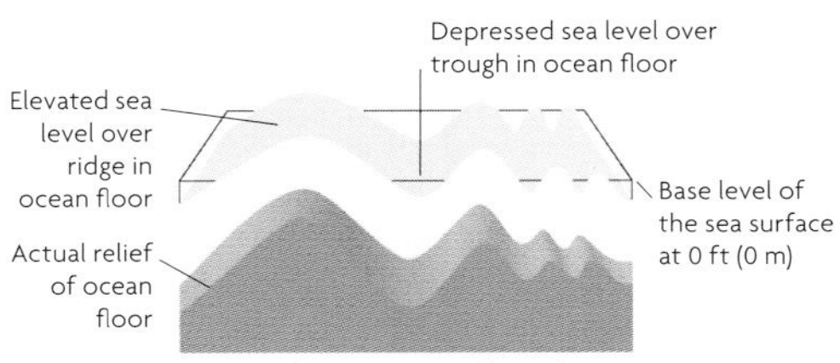

How surface waters reflect the relief of the ocean floor

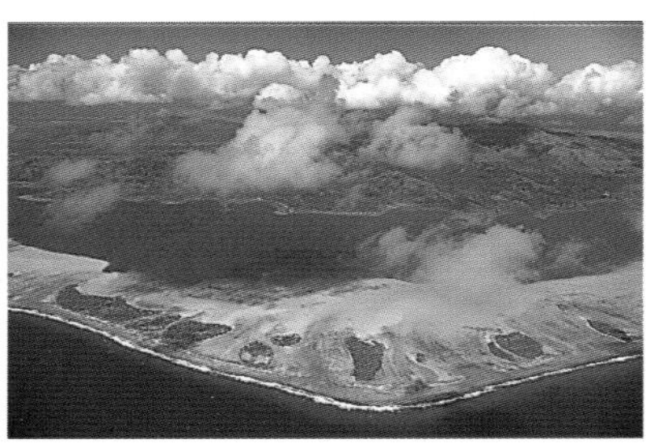

▲ **The low relief** of many small Pacific islands such as these atolls at Huahine in French Polynesia makes them vulnerable to changes in sea level.

Ocean structure

The continental shelf is a shallow, flat sea-bed surrounding the Earth's continents. It extends to the continental slope, which falls to the ocean floor. Here, the flat abyssal plains are interrupted by vast, underwater mountain ranges, the mid-ocean ridges, and ocean trenches which plunge to depths of 35,828 ft (10,920 m).

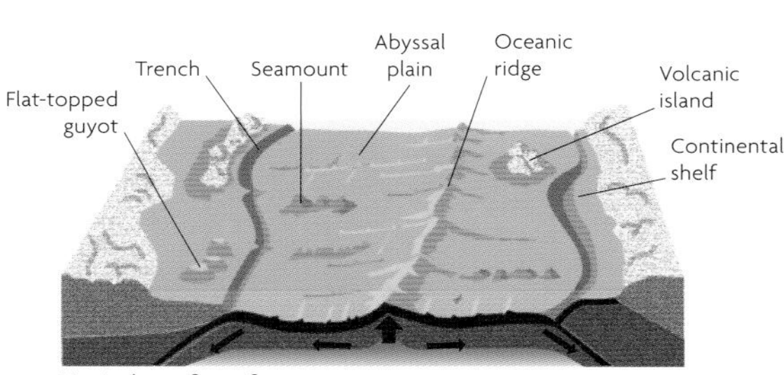

Typical sea-floor features

Ocean depth

| Sea level |
| 200m / 656ft |
| 1000m / 3281ft |
| 2000m / 6562ft |
| 3000m / 9843ft |
| 4000m / 13,124ft |
| 5000m / 16,400ft |
| 6000m / 19,686ft |

Black smokers

These vents in the ocean floor disgorge hot, sulphur-rich water from deep in the Earth's crust. Despite the great depths, a variety of lifeforms have adapted to the chemical-rich environment which surrounds black smokers.

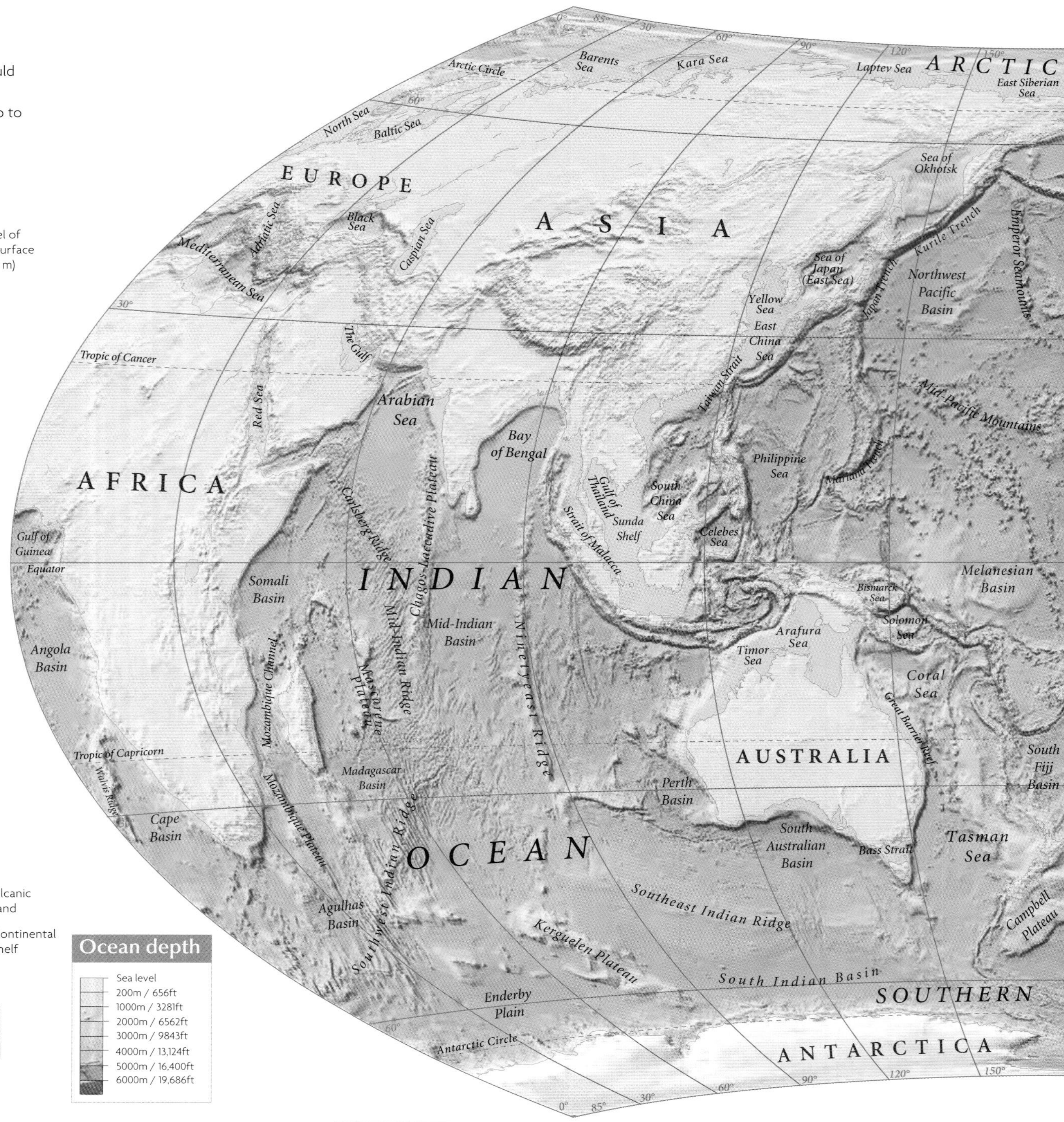

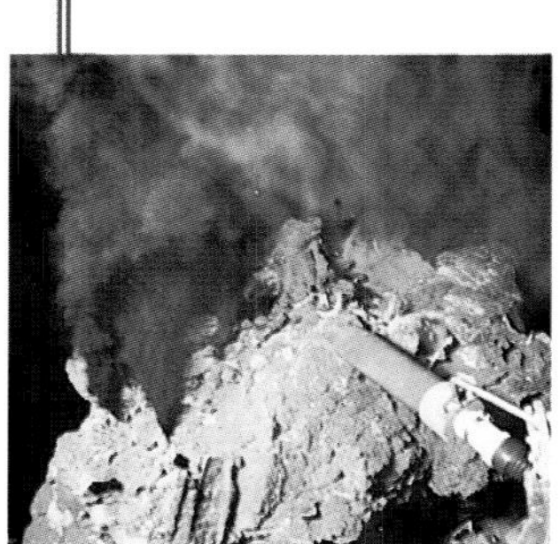

▲ **A black smoker** in the Atlantic Ocean.

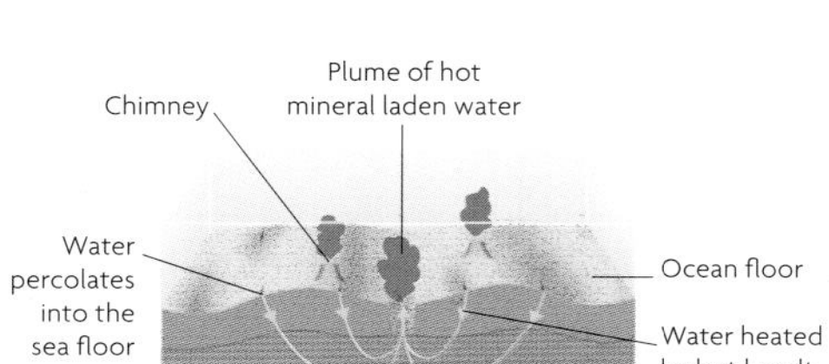

Formation of black smokers

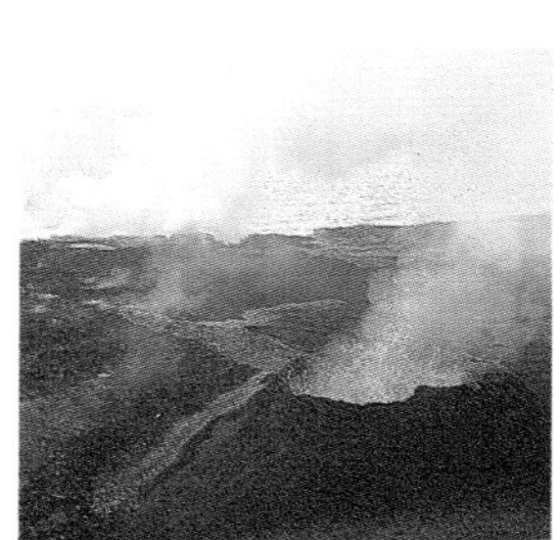

▲ **Surtsey, near Iceland,** is a volcanic island lying directly over the Mid-Atlantic Ridge. It was formed in the 1960s following intense volcanic activity nearby.

Ocean floors

Mid-ocean ridges are formed by lava which erupts beneath the sea and cools to form solid rock. This process mirrors the creation of volcanoes from cooled lava on the land. The ages of sea floor rocks increase in parallel bands outwards from central ocean ridges.

Ages of the ocean floor

Arctic Circle
Tropic of Cancer
Equator
Tropic of Capricorn
Antarctic Circle

Jurassic | Cretaceous | Tertiary (Paleogene) | Quaternary | Cretaceous | Jurassic

208 million years old — 145 — 65 — 23 — 0 — 23 — 65 — 145 — 208 million years old
Tertiary (Neogene)

Age uncertain
Continental shelf and island arcs

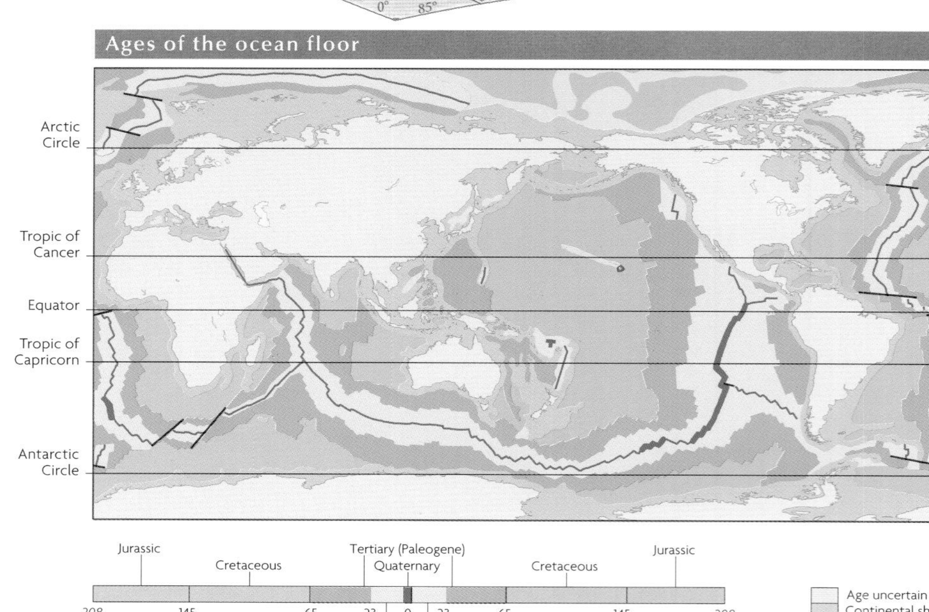

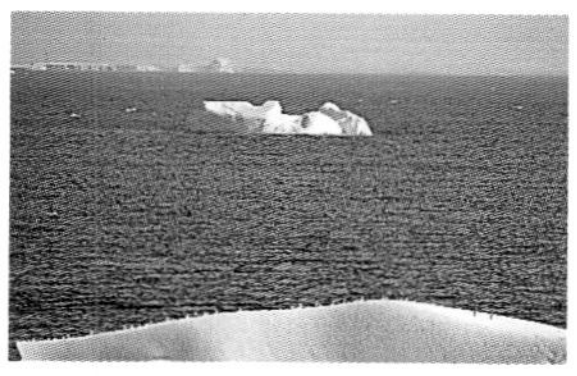

▲ **Currents in the** *Southern Ocean are driven by some of the world's fiercest winds, including the Roaring Forties, Furious Fifties and Shrieking Sixties.*

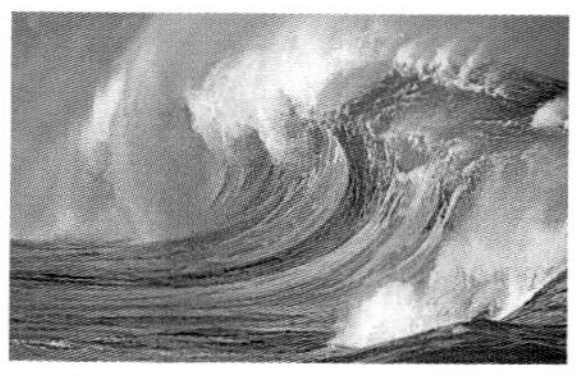

▲ **The Pacific Ocean** *is the world's largest and deepest ocean, covering over one-third of the surface of the Earth.*

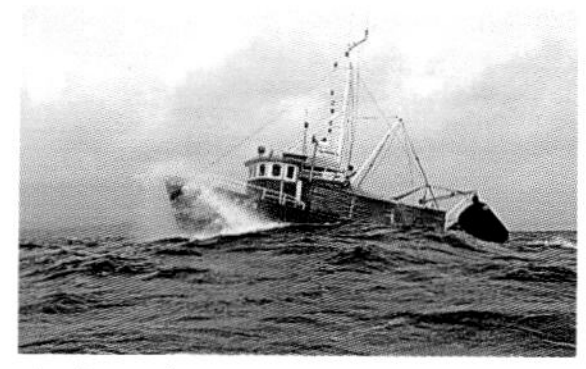

▲ **The Atlantic Ocean** *was formed when the landmasses of the eastern and western hemispheres began to drift apart 180 million years ago.*

Deposition of sediment

Storms, earthquakes, and volcanic activity trigger underwater currents known as turbidity currents which scour sand and gravel from the continental shelf, creating underwater canyons. These strong currents pick up material deposited at river mouths and deltas, and carry it across the continental shelf and through the underwater canyons, where it is eventually laid down on the ocean floor in the form of fans.

Sediment accumulates at head of underwater canyon *Continental shelf* *Rocks and Other debris, flow from shelf to ocean floor* *Recently-deposited sediments overlay older rocks* *Deep sea turbidity flow*

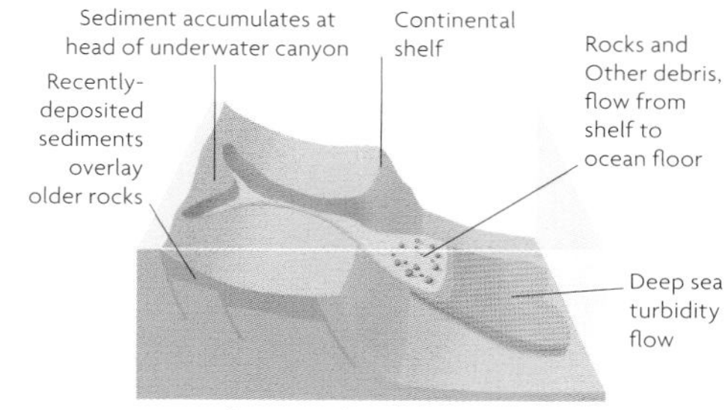

How sediment is deposited on the ocean floor

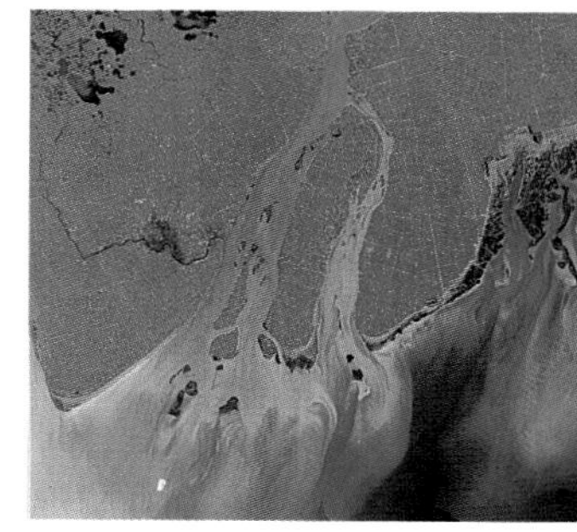

▶ *Satellite image of the Yangtze (Chang Jiang) Delta, in which the land appears red. The river deposits immense quantities of silt into the East China Sea, much of which will eventually reach the deep ocean floor.*

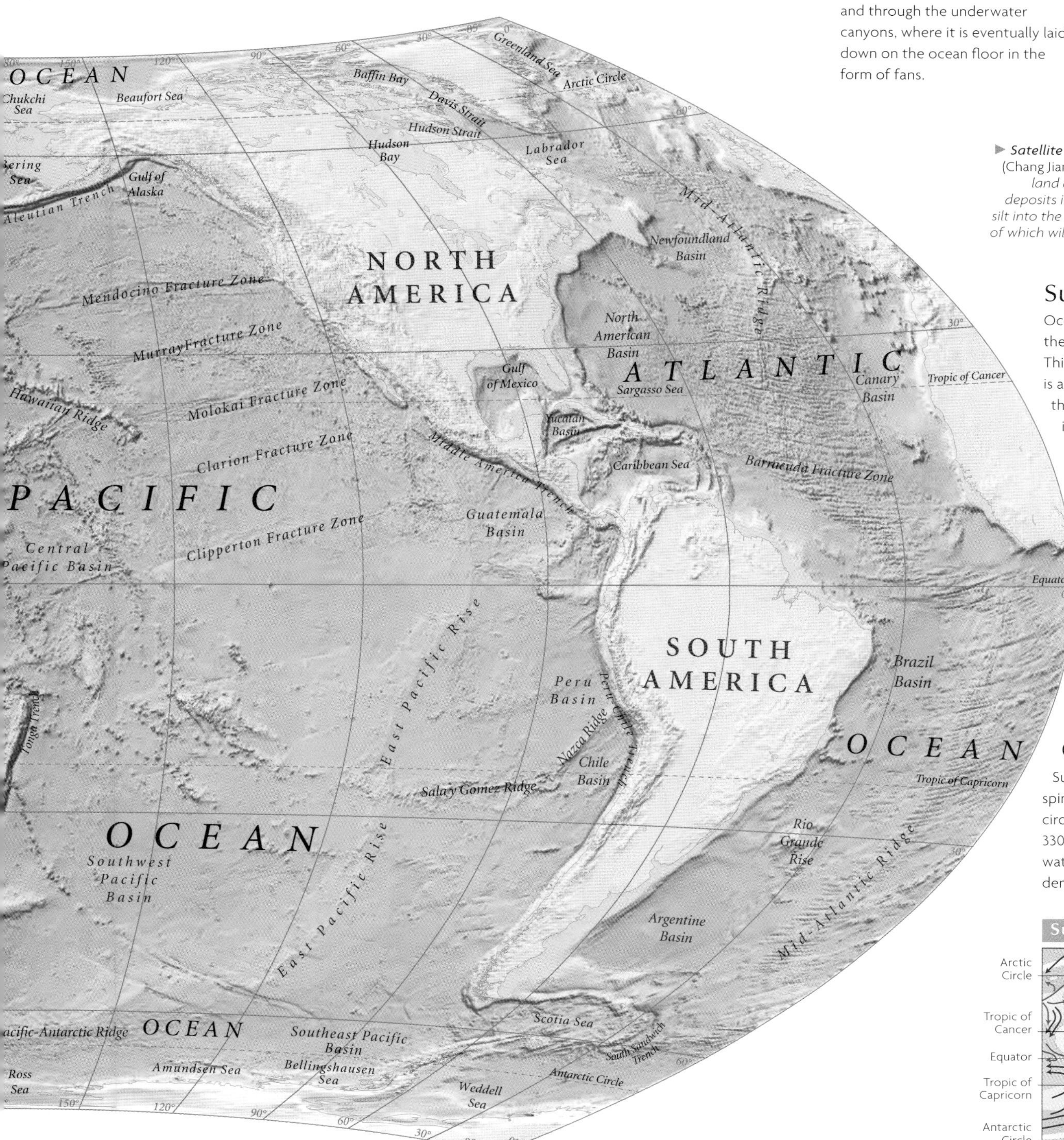

Surface water

Ocean currents move warm water away from the Equator towards the poles, while cold water is, in turn, moved towards the Equator. This is the main way in which the Earth distributes surface heat and is a major climatic control. Approximately 4000 million years ago, the Earth was dominated by oceans and there was no land to interrupt the flow of the currents, which would have flowed as straight lines, simply influenced by the Earth's rotation.

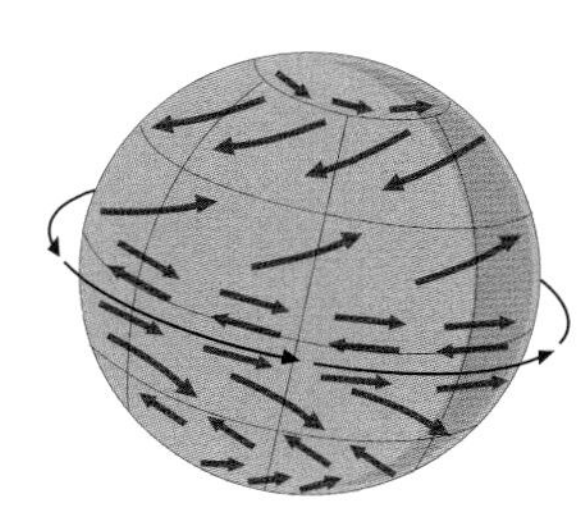

Idealized globe showing the movement of water around a landless Earth.

Ocean currents

Surface currents are driven by the prevailing winds and by the spinning motion of the Earth, which drives the currents into circulating whirlpools, or gyres. Deep sea currents, over 330 ft (100 m) below the surface, are driven by differences in water temperature and salinity, which have an impact on the density of deep water and on its movement.

Surface temperature and currents

Arctic Circle
Tropic of Cancer
Equator
Tropic of Capricorn
Antarctic Circle

Surface temperature and currents

- - - - - Ice-shelf (below 0°C / 32°F)
Sea-ice* (average) below -2°C / 28°F
Sea-water -2–0°C / 28–32°F
* Sea-water freezes at -19°C / 28.4°F

0–10°C / 32–50°F
10–20°C / 50–68°F
20–30°C / 68–86°F

→ warm current
→ cold current

Map labels

OCEAN, Chukchi Sea, Bering Sea, Beaufort Sea, Gulf of Alaska, Aleutian Trench, Baffin Bay, Davis Strait, Hudson Strait, Hudson Bay, Greenland Sea, Arctic Circle, Labrador Sea, NORTH AMERICA, Newfoundland Basin, Mid-Atlantic Ridge, North American Basin, ATLANTIC, Mendocino Fracture Zone, Murray Fracture Zone, Hawaiian Ridge, Molokai Fracture Zone, Gulf of Mexico, Sargasso Sea, Canary Basin, Tropic of Cancer, Clarion Fracture Zone, Mid-Atlantic Ridge, Yucatan Basin, Caribbean Sea, Bermuda Fracture Zone, PACIFIC, Clipperton Fracture Zone, Guatemala Basin, Central Pacific Basin, Peru Basin, SOUTH AMERICA, Brazil Basin, East Pacific Rise, Peru-Chile Trench, Nazca Ridge, Chile Basin, OCEAN, Equator, Sala y Gomez Ridge, Tropic of Capricorn, Rio Grande Rise, OCEAN, Southwest Pacific Basin, East Pacific Rise, Argentine Basin, Mid-Atlantic Ridge, Pacific-Antarctic Ridge, OCEAN, Southeast Pacific Basin, Scotia Sea, Ross Sea, Amundsen Sea, Bellingshausen Sea, Weddell Sea, South Sandwich Trench, Antarctic Circle, Tonga Trench

Tides and waves

Tides are created by the pull of the Sun and Moon's gravity on the surface of the oceans. The levels of high and low tides are influenced by the position of the Moon in relation to the Earth and Sun. Waves are formed by wind blowing over the surface of the water.

High and low tides

The highest tides occur when the Earth, the Moon and the Sun are aligned *(below left)*. The lowest tides are experienced when the Sun and Moon align at right angles to one another *(below right)*.

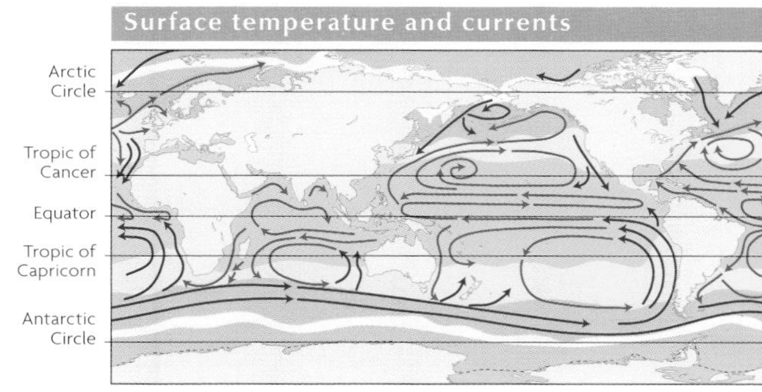

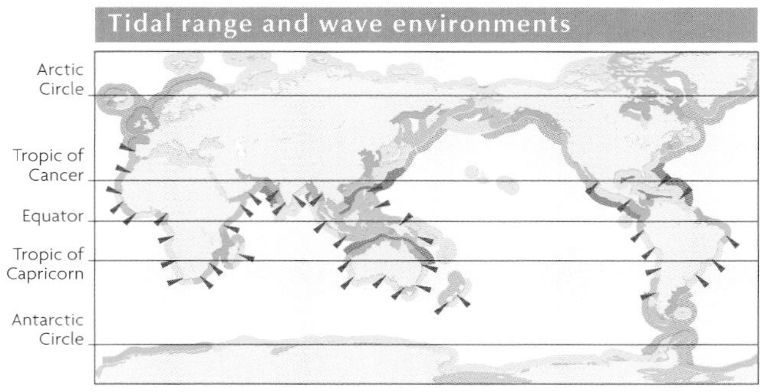

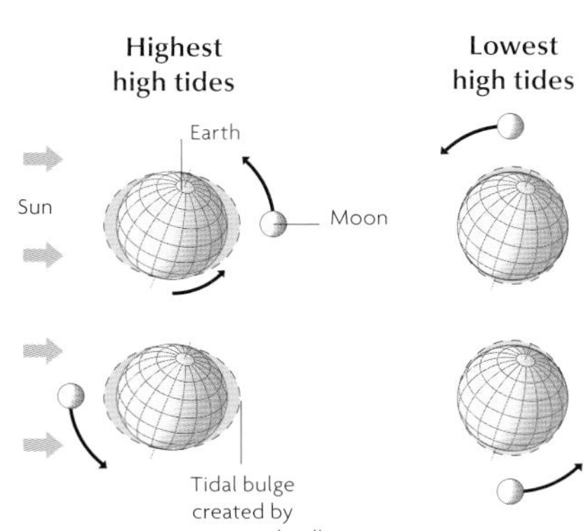

Tidal range and wave environments

Arctic Circle
Tropic of Cancer
Equator
Tropic of Capricorn
Antarctic Circle

Tidal range and wave environments

less than 2m / 7ft
2–4m / 7–13ft
greater than 4m / 13ft
east coast swell
west coast swell
tropical cyclone
storm wave
ice-shelf

Highest high tides

Earth
Sun
Moon
Tidal bulge created by gravitational pull

Lowest high tides

Deep sea temperature and currents

Arctic Circle
Tropic of Cancer
Equator
Tropic of Capricorn
Antarctic Circle

Deep sea temperature and currents

Ice-shelf (below 0°C / 32°F)
Sea-water -2–0°C / 28–32°F (below 5000m / 16,400ft)
Sea-water 0–5°C / 32–41°F (below 4000m / 13,120ft)

→ Primary currents
→ Secondary currents

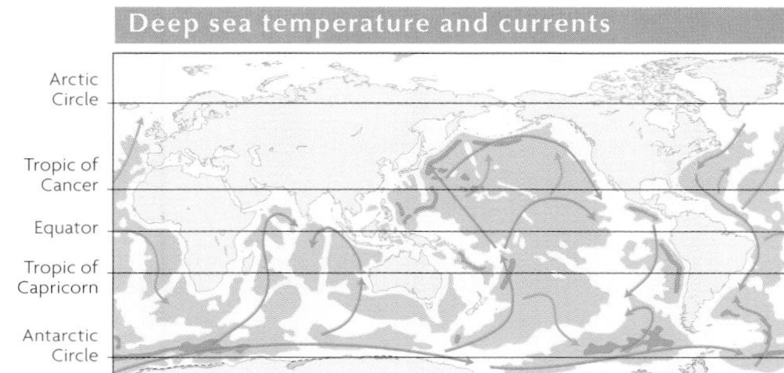

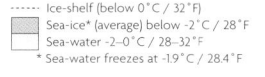

The global climate

The Earth's climatic types consist of stable patterns of weather conditions averaged out over a long period of time. Different climates are categorized according to particular combinations of temperature and humidity. By contrast, weather consists of short-term fluctuations in wind, temperature and humidity conditions. Different climates are determined by latitude, altitude, the prevailing wind and circulation of ocean currents. Longer-term changes in climate, such as global warming or the onset of ice ages, are punctuated by shorter-term events which comprise the day-to-day weather of a region, such as frontal depressions, hurricanes and blizzards.

The atmosphere, wind and weather

The Earth's atmosphere has been compared to a giant ocean of air which surrounds the planet. Its circulation patterns are influenced by three factors; the currents in the oceans and are influenced by three factors; the Earth's orbit around the Sun and rotation about its axis, and variations in the amount of heat radiation received from the Sun. If both heat and moisture were not redistributed between the Equator and the poles, large areas of the Earth would be uninhabitable.

◀ *Heavy fogs, as* here in southern England, form as moisture-laden air passes over cold ground.

Temperature

The world can be divided into three major climatic zones, stretching like large belts across the latitudes: the tropics which are warm; the cold polar regions and the temperate zones which lie between them. Temperatures across the Earth range from above 30°C (86°F) in the deserts to as low as -55°C (-70°F) at the poles. Temperature is also controlled by altitude; because air becomes cooler and less dense the higher it gets, mountainous regions are typically colder than those areas which are at, or close to, sea level.

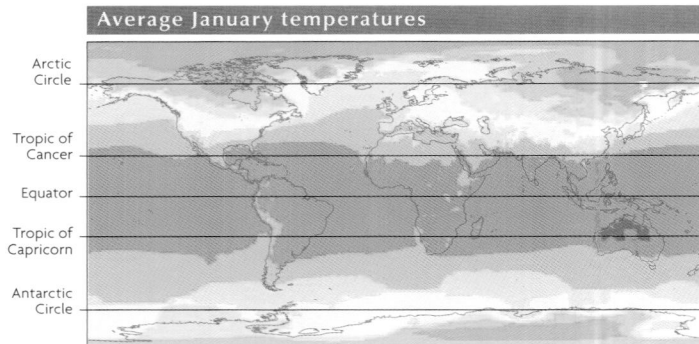

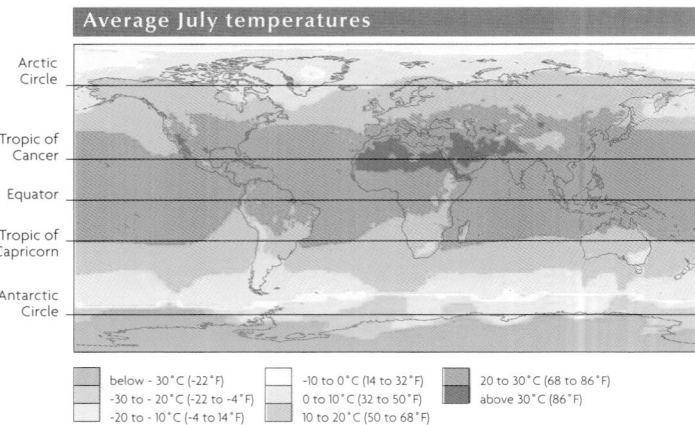

Global air circulation

Air does not simply flow from the Equator to the poles, it circulates in giant cells known as Hadley and Ferrel cells. As air warms it expands, becoming less dense and rising; this creates areas of low pressure. As the air rises it cools and condenses, causing heavy rainfall over the tropics and slight snowfall over the poles. This cool air then sinks, forming high pressure belts. At surface level in the tropics these sinking currents are deflected polewards as the westerlies and towards the equator as the trade winds. At the poles they become the polar easterlies.

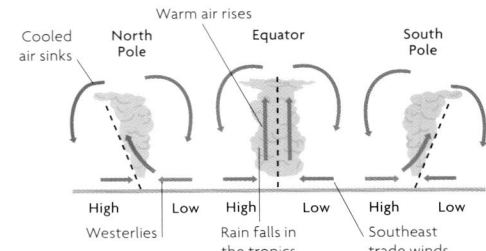

▲ *The Antarctic pack ice* expands its area by almost seven times during the winter as temperatures drop and surrounding seas freeze.

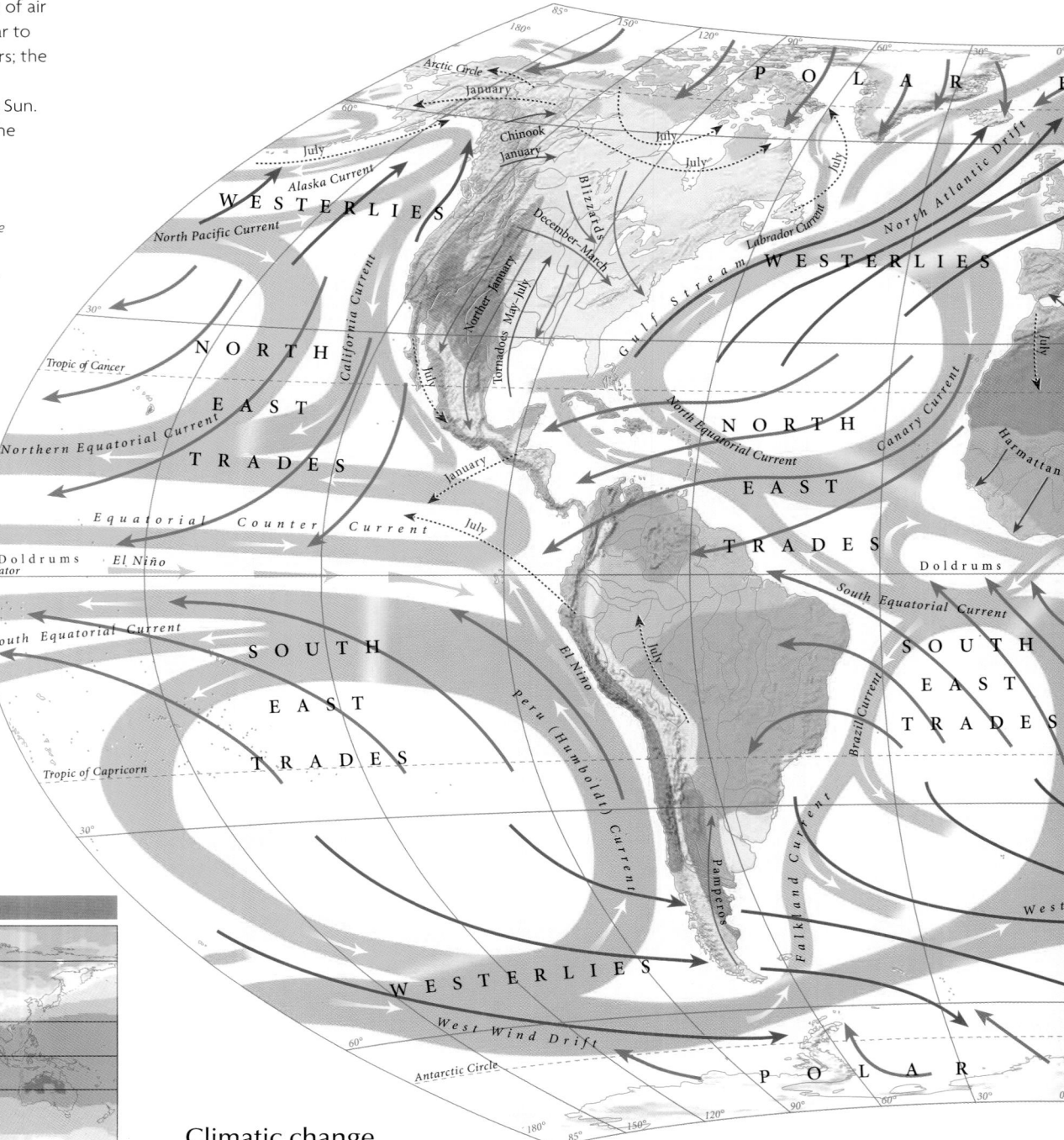

Climatic change

The Earth is currently in a warm phase between ice ages. Warmer temperatures result in higher sea levels as more of the polar ice caps melt. Most of the world's population lives near coasts, so any changes which might cause sea levels to rise, could have a potentially disastrous impact.

▲ *This ice fair,* painted by Pieter Brueghel the Younger in the 17th century, shows the Little Ice Age which peaked around 300 years ago.

The greenhouse effect

Gases such as carbon dioxide are known as 'greenhouse gases' because they allow shortwave solar radiation to enter the Earth's atmosphere, but help to stop longwave radiation from escaping. This traps heat, raising the Earth's temperature. An excess of these gases, such as that which results from the burning of fossil fuels, helps trap more heat and can lead to global warming.

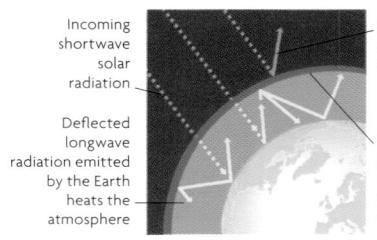

Incoming shortwave solar radiation

Deflected shortwave solar radiation

Deflected longwave radiation emitted by the Earth heats the atmosphere

Greenhouse gases prevent the escape of longwave radiation

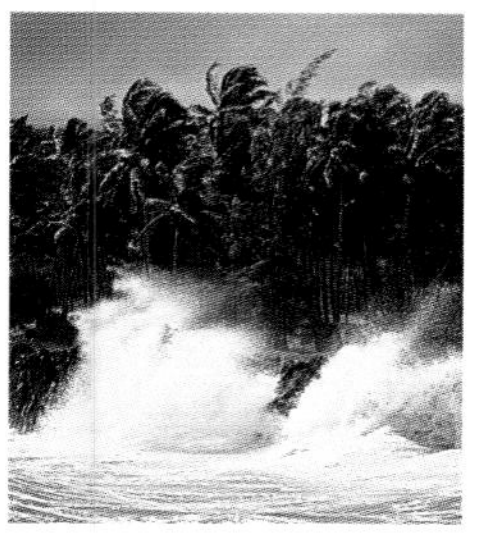

◄ *The islands of the Caribbean, Mexico's Gulf coast and the southeastern USA are often hit by hurricanes formed far out in the Atlantic.*

Oceanic water circulation

In general, ocean currents parallel the movement of winds across the Earth's surface. Incoming solar energy is greatest at the Equator and least at the poles. So, water in the oceans heats up most at the Equator and flows polewards, cooling as it moves north or south towards the Arctic or Antarctic. The flow is eventually reversed and cold water currents move back towards the Equator. These ocean currents act as a vast system for moving heat from the Equator towards the poles and are a major influence on the distribution of the Earth's climates.

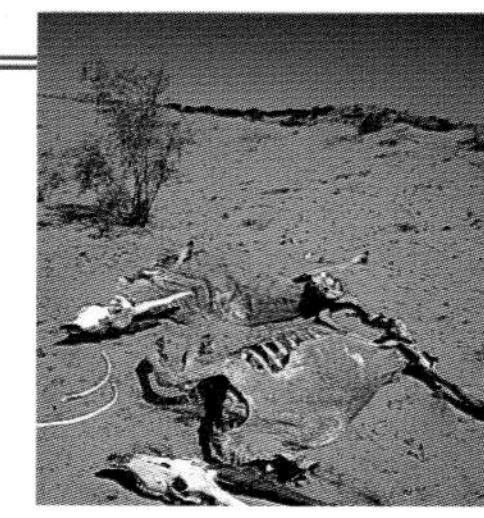

▲ *In marginal climatic zones years of drought can completely dry out the land and transform grassland to desert.*

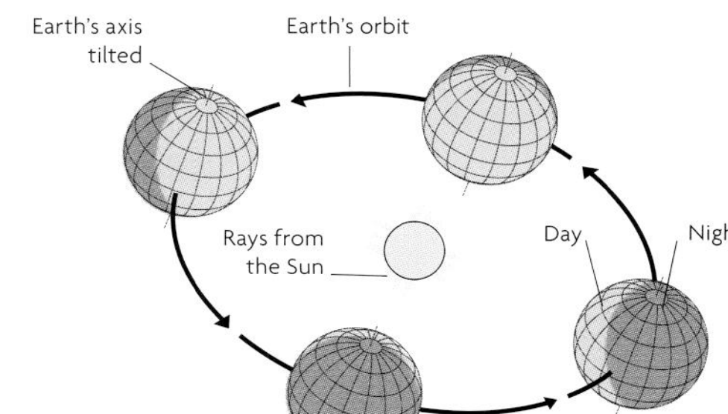

Map key

Climate zones

- ice cap
- subarctic
- tundra
- continental
- temperate
- warm temperate
- mediterranean
- semi-arid
- arid
- hot humid
- humid equatorial
- tropical

Ocean currents
- warm
- cold

Prevailing winds
- → warm
- → cold

Local winds
- → warm
- → cold
- June → seasonal*
- * (seasonal winds which can either be warm or cold)

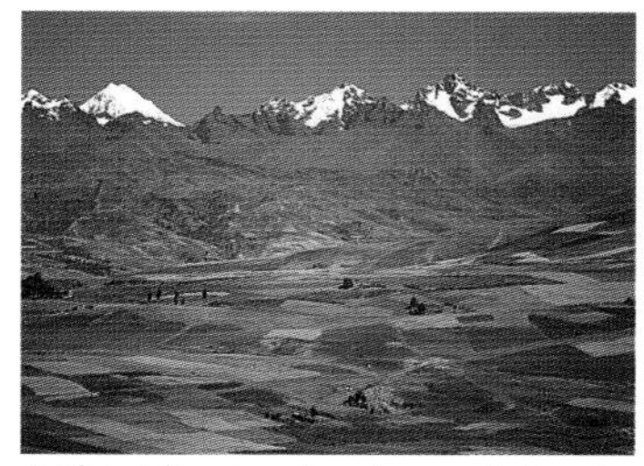

▲ *The wide range of environments found in the Andes is strongly related to their altitude, which modifies climatic influences. While the peaks are snow-capped, many protected interior valleys are semi-tropical.*

Tilt and rotation

The tilt and rotation of the Earth during its annual orbit largely control the distribution of heat and moisture across its surface, which correspondingly controls its large-scale weather patterns. As the Earth annually rotates around the Sun, half its surface is receiving maximum radiation, creating summer and winter seasons. The angle of the Earth means that on average the tropics receive two and a half times as much heat from the Sun each day as the poles.

Earth's axis tilted — Earth's orbit
Rays from the Sun — Day — Night

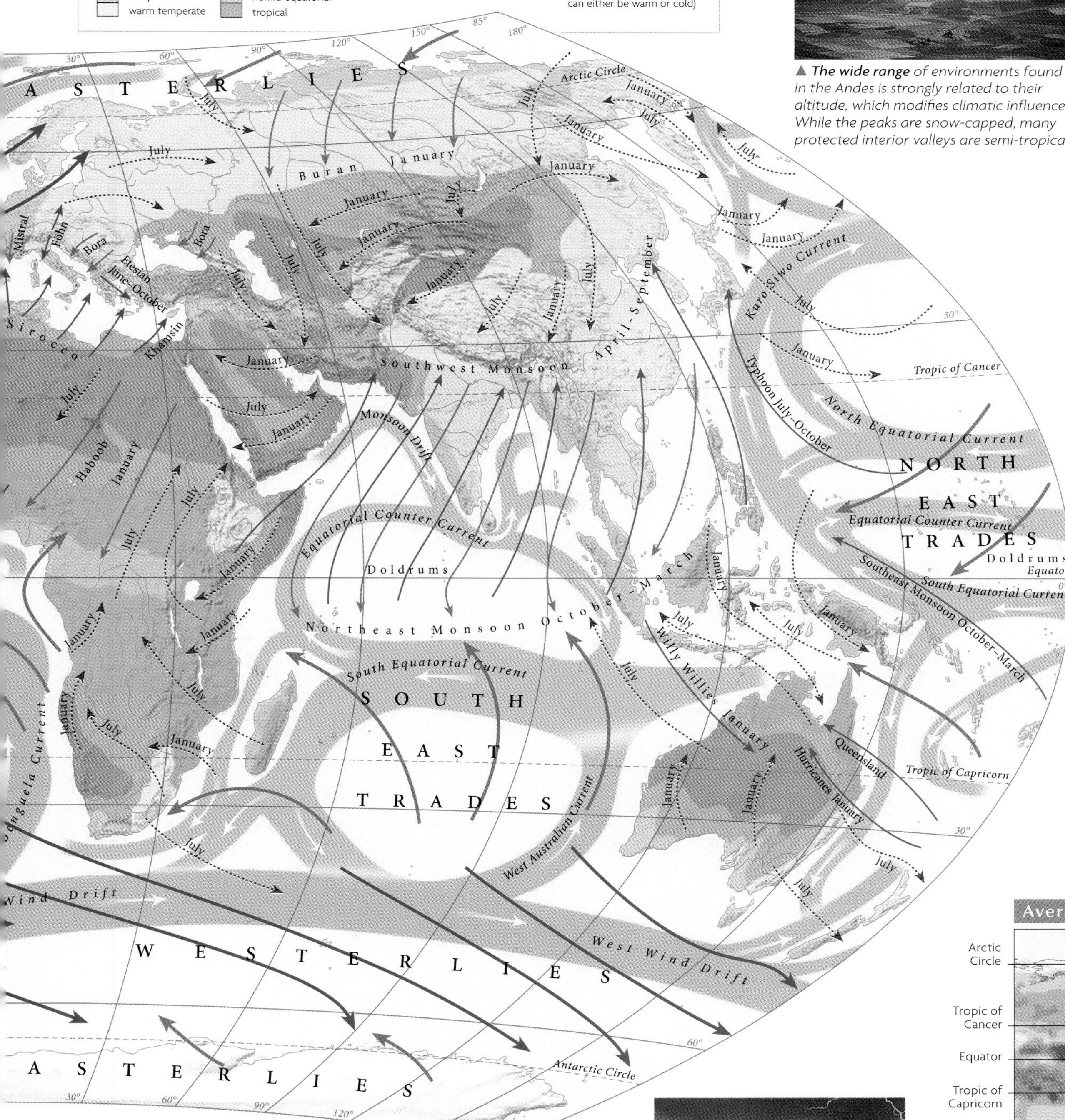

The Coriolis effect

The rotation of the Earth influences atmospheric circulation by deflecting winds and ocean currents. Winds blowing in the northern hemisphere are deflected to the right and those in the southern hemisphere are deflected to the left, creating large-scale patterns of wind circulation, such as the northeast and southeast trade winds and the westerlies. This effect is greatest at the poles and least at the Equator.

Maximum deflection at North pole
Deflection to right in northern hemisphere, creates northeast trade winds — Westerlies
No deflection at Equator
Polar easterlies — Deflection to left in southern hemisphere, creates southeast trade winds
Maximum deflection at South Pole

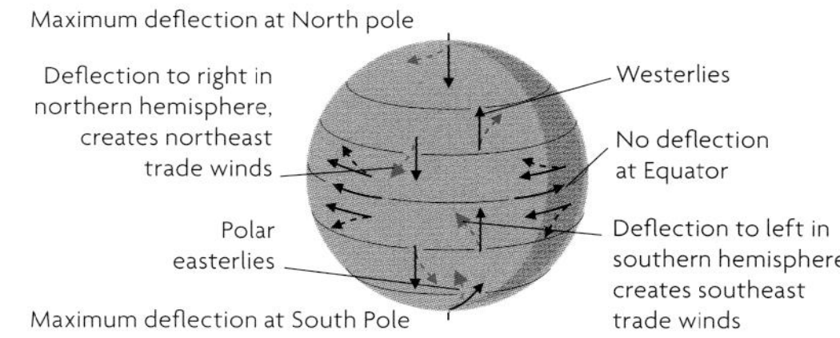

Precipitation

When warm air expands, it rises and cools, and the water vapour it carries condenses to form clouds. Heavy, regular rainfall is characteristic of the equatorial region, while the poles are cold and receive only slight snowfall. Tropical regions have marked dry and rainy seasons, while in the temperate regions rainfall is relatively unpredictable.

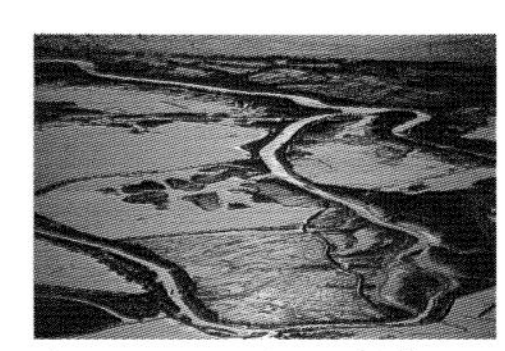

▲ *Monsoon rains, which affect southern Asia from May to September, are caused by sea winds blowing across the warm land.*

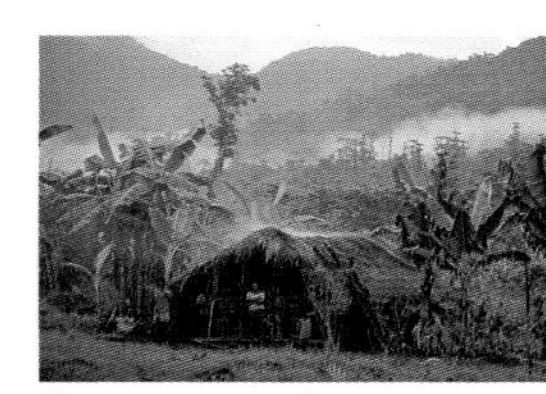

▲ *Heavy tropical rainstorms occur frequently in Papua New Guinea, often causing soil erosion and landslides in cultivated areas.*

Average January rainfall

Arctic Circle
Tropic of Cancer
Equator
Tropic of Capricorn
Antarctic Circle

Average July rainfall

Arctic Circle
Tropic of Cancer
Equator
Tropic of Capricorn
Antarctic Circle

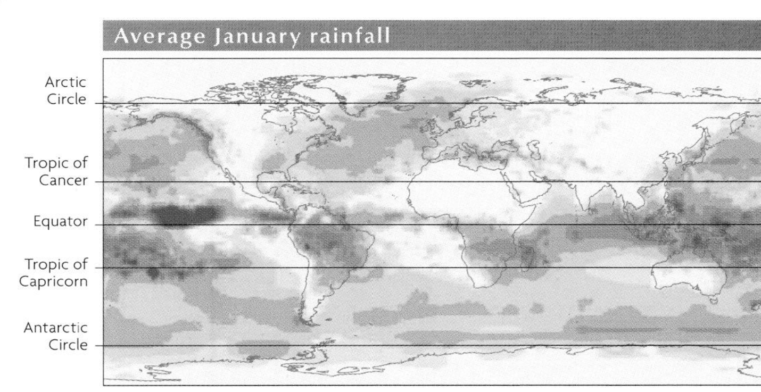

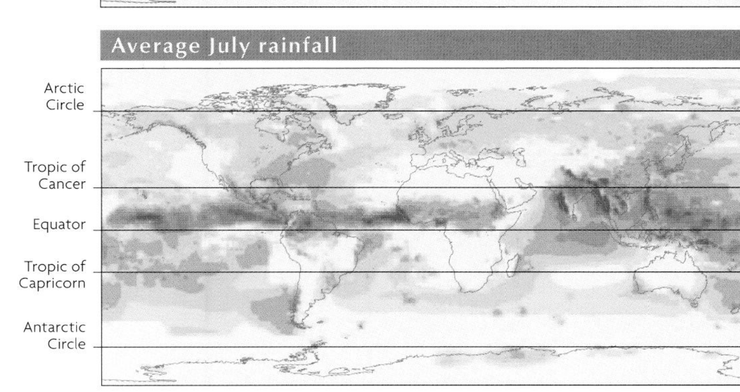

- 0–25 mm (0–1 in)
- 25–50 mm (1–2 in)
- 50–100 mm (2–4 in)
- 100–200 mm (4–8 in)
- 200–300 mm (8–12 in)
- 300–400 mm (12–16 in)
- 400–500 mm (16–20 in)
- above 500 mm (20 in)

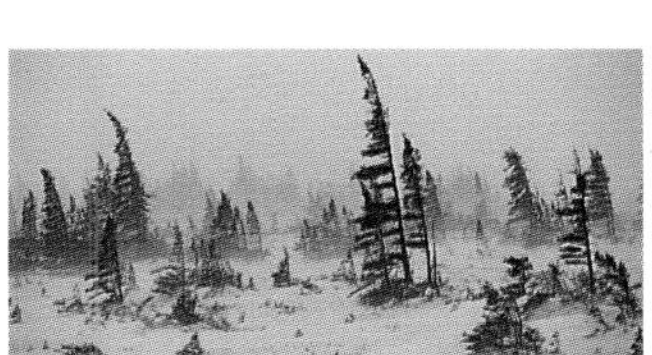

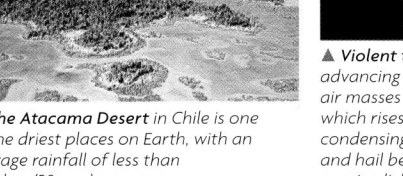

▲ *The intensity of some blizzards in Canada and the northern USA can give rise to snowdrifts as high as 10 ft (3 m).*

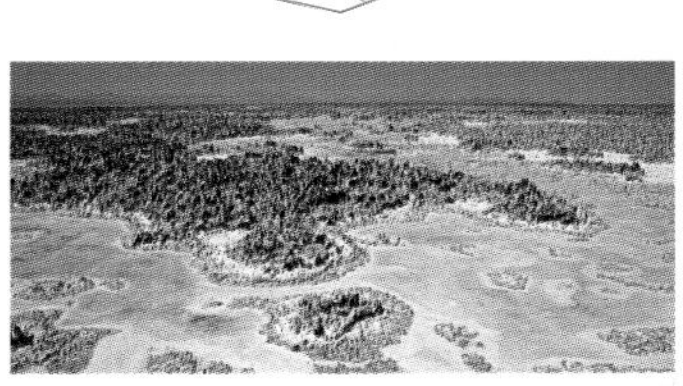

▲ *The Atacama Desert in Chile is one of the driest places on Earth, with an average rainfall of less than 2 inches (50 mm) per year.*

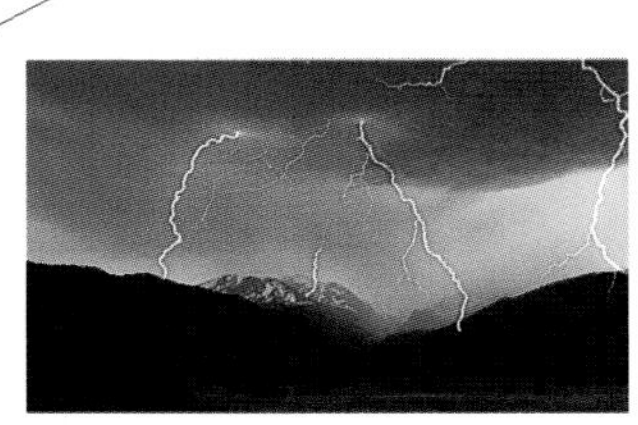

▲ *Violent thunderstorms occur along advancing cold fronts, when cold, dry air masses meet warm, moist air, which rises rapidly, its moisture condensing into thunderclouds. Rain and hail become electrically charged, causing lightning.*

The rainshadow effect

When moist air is forced to rise by mountains, it cools and the water vapour falls as precipitation, either as rain or snow. Only the dry, cold air continues over the mountains, leaving inland areas with little or no rain. This is called the rainshadow effect and is one reason for the existence of the Mojave Desert in California, which lies east of the Coast Ranges.

Moist air travels inland from the sea
As air rises it cools and condenses leading to cloud
Dry air in 'shadow' of mountain

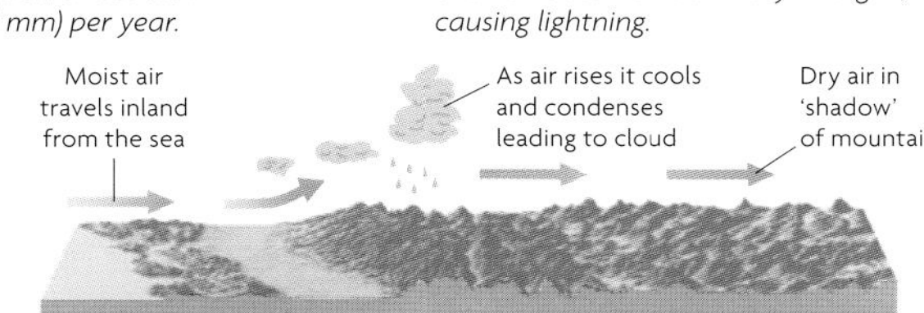

The rainshadow effect

Life on Earth

A unique combination of an oxygen-rich atmosphere and plentiful water is the key to life on Earth. Apart from the polar ice caps, there are few areas which have not been colonized by animals or plants over the course of the Earth's history. Plants process sunlight to provide them with their energy, and ultimately all the Earth's animals rely on plants for survival. Because of this reliance, plants are known as primary producers, and the availability of nutrients and temperature of an area is defined as its primary productivity, which affects the quantity and type of animals which are able to live there. This index is affected by climatic factors – cold and aridity restrict the quantity of life, whereas warmth and regular rainfall allow a greater diversity of species.

Biogeographical regions

The Earth can be divided into a series of biogeographical regions, or biomes, ecological communities where certain species of plant and animal co-exist within particular climatic conditions. Within these broad classifications, other factors including soil richness, altitude and human activities such as urbanization, intensive agriculture and deforestation, affect the local distribution of living species within each biome.

Polar regions
☐ A layer of permanent ice at the Earth's poles covers both seas and land. Very little plant and animal life can exist in these harsh regions.

Tundra
☐ A desolate region, with long, dark freezing winters and short, cold summers. With virtually no soil and large areas of permanently frozen ground known as permafrost, the tundra is largely treeless, though it is briefly clothed by small flowering plants in the summer months.

Needleleaf forests
☐ With milder summers than the tundra and less wind, these areas are able to support large forests of coniferous trees.

Broadleaf forests
☐ Much of the northern hemisphere was once covered by deciduous forests, which occurred in areas with marked seasonal variations. Most deciduous forests have been cleared for human settlement.

Temperate rainforests
☐ In warmer wetter areas, such as southern China, temperate deciduous forests are replaced by evergreen forest.

Deserts
☑ Deserts are areas with negligible rainfall. Most hot deserts lie within the tropics; cold deserts are dry because of their distance from the moisture-providing sea.

Mediterranean
☐ Hot, dry summers and short winters typify these areas, which were once covered by evergreen shrubs and woodland, but have now been cleared by humans for agriculture.

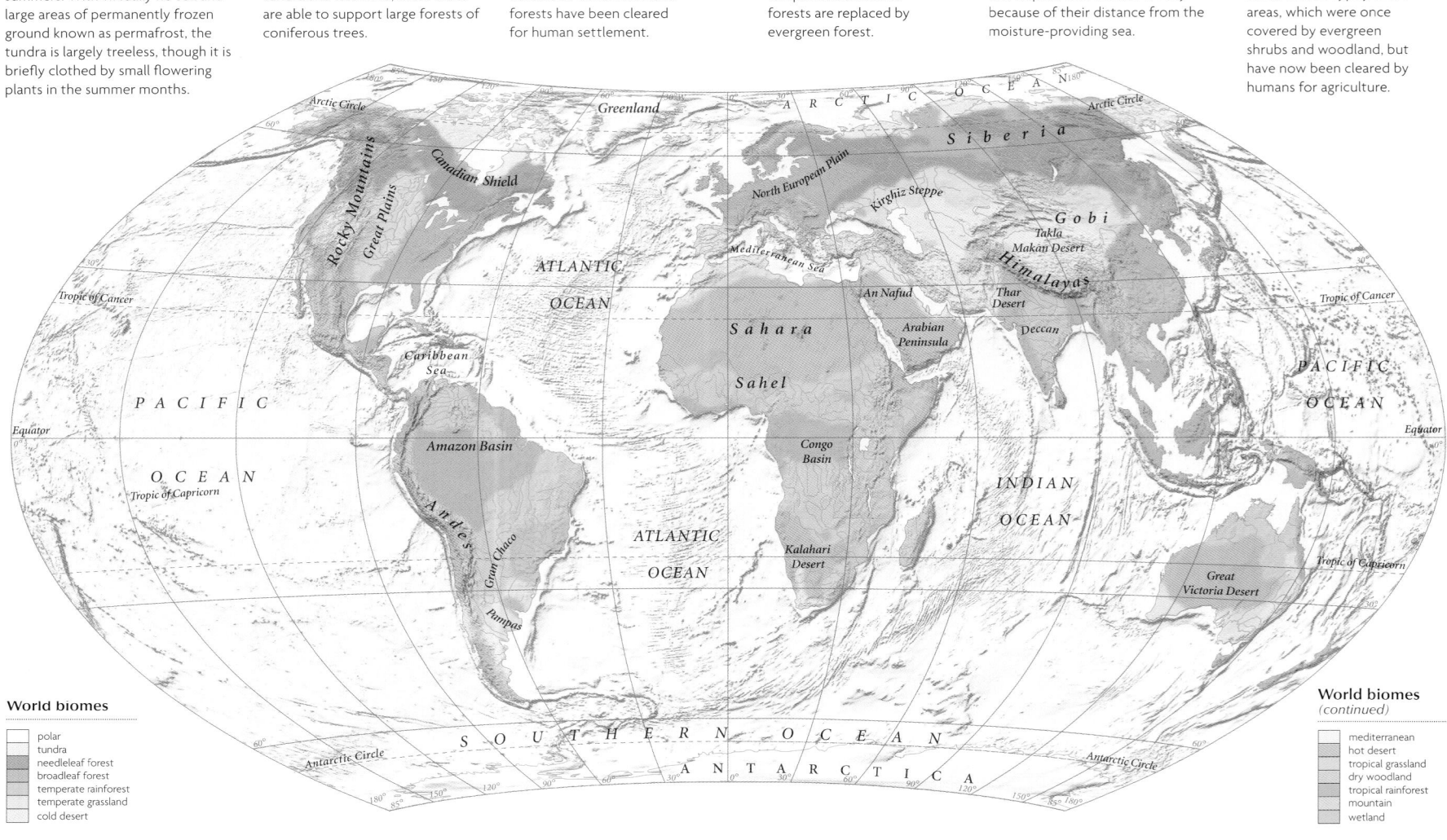

World biomes

☐ polar
☐ tundra
☐ needleleaf forest
☐ broadleaf forest
☐ temperate rainforest
☐ temperate grassland
☐ cold desert

World biomes
(continued)

☐ mediterranean
☐ hot desert
☐ tropical grassland
☐ dry woodland
☐ tropical rainforest
☐ mountain
☐ wetland

Tropical and temperate grasslands
☑ The major grassland areas are found in the centres of the larger continental landmasses. In Africa's tropical savannah regions, seasonal rainfall alternates with drought. Temperate grasslands, also known as steppes and prairies are found in the northern hemisphere, and in South America, where they are known as the pampas.

Dry woodlands
☐ Trees and shrubs, adapted to dry conditions, grow widely spaced from one another, interspersed by savannah grasslands.

Tropical rainforests
☐ Characterized by year-round warmth and high rainfall, tropical rainforests contain the highest diversity of plant and animal species on Earth.

Mountains
☐ Though the lower slopes of mountains may be thickly forested, only ground-hugging shrubs and other vegetation will grow above the tree line which varies according to both altitude and latitude.

Wetlands
☐ Rarely lying above sea level, wetlands are marshes, swamps and tidal flats. Some, with their moist, fertile soils, are rich feeding grounds for fish and breeding grounds for birds. Others have little soil structure and are too acidic to support much plant and animal life.

Biodiversity

The number of plant and animal species, and the range of genetic diversity within the populations of each species, make up the Earth's biodiversity. The plants and animals which are endemic to a region – that is, those which are found nowhere else in the world – are also important in determining levels of biodiversity. Human settlement and intervention have encroached on many areas of the world once rich in endemic plant and animal species. Increasing international efforts are being made to monitor and conserve the biodiversity of the Earth's remaining wild places.

Animal adaptation

The degree of an animal's adaptability to different climates and conditions is extremely important in ensuring its success as a species. Many animals, particularly the largest mammals, are becoming restricted to ever-smaller regions as human development and modern agricultural practices reduce their natural habitats. In contrast, humans have been responsible – both deliberately and accidentally – for the spread of some of the world's most successful species. Many of these introduced species are now more numerous than the indigenous animal populations.

Polar animals

The frozen wastes of the polar regions are able to support only a small range of species which derive their nutritional requirements from the sea. Animals such as the walrus *(left)* have developed insulating fat, stocky limbs and double-layered coats to enable them to survive in the freezing conditions.

Desert animals

Many animals which live in the extreme heat and aridity of the deserts are able to survive for days and even months with very little food or water. Their bodies are adapted to lose heat quickly and to store fat and water. The Gila monster *(above)* stores fat in its tail.

Amazon rainforest

The vast Amazon Basin is home to the world's greatest variety of animal species. Animals are adapted to live at many different levels from the treetops to the tangled undergrowth which lies beneath the canopy. The sloth *(below)* hangs upside down in the branches. Its fur grows from its stomach to its back to enable water to run off quickly.

Diversity of animal species

Number of animal species per country

- more than 2000
- 1000–1999
- 700–999
- 400–699
- 200–399
- 100–199
- 0–99
- data not available

High altitudes

Few animals exist in the rarefied atmosphere of the highest mountains. However, birds of prey such as eagles and vultures *(above)*, with their superb eyesight can soar as high as 23,000 ft (7000 m) to scan for prey below.

Urban animals

The growth of cities has reduced the amount of habitat available to many species. A number of animals are now moving closer into urban areas to scavenge from the detritus of the modern city *(left)*. Rodents, particularly rats and mice, have existed in cities for thousands of years, and many insects, especially moths, quickly develop new colouring to provide them with camouflage.

Marine biodiversity

The oceans support a huge variety of different species, from the world's largest mammals like whales and dolphins down to the tiniest plankton. The greatest diversities occur in the warmer seas of continental shelves, where plants are easily able to photosynthesize, and around coral reefs, where complex ecosystems are found. On the ocean floor, nematodes can exist at a depth of more than 10,000 ft (3000 m) below sea level.

Endemic species

Isolated areas such as Australia and the island of Madagascar, have the greatest range of endemic species. In Australia, these include marsupials such as the kangaroo *(below)*, which carry their young in pouches on their bodies. Destruction of habitat, pollution, hunting, and predators introduced by humans, are threatening this unique biodiversity.

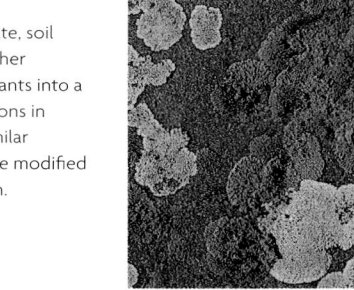

Plant adaptation

Environmental conditions, particularly climate, soil type and the extent of competition with other organisms, influence the development of plants into a number of distinctive forms. Similar conditions in quite different parts of the world create similar adaptations in the plants, which may then be modified by other, local, factors specific to the region.

Cold conditions

In areas where temperatures rarely rise above freezing, plants such as lichens *(left)* and mosses grow densely, close to the ground.

Rainforests

Most of the world's largest and oldest plants are found in rainforests; warmth and heavy rainfall provide ideal conditions for vast plants like the world's largest flower, the rafflesia *(left)*.

Hot, dry conditions

Arid conditions lead to the development of plants whose surface area has been reduced to a minimum to reduce water loss. In cacti *(above)*, which can survive without water for months, leaves are minimal or not present at all.

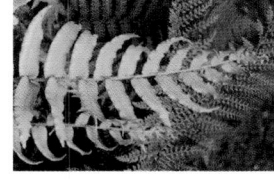

Ancient plants

Some of the world's most primitive plants still exist today, including algae, cycads and many ferns *(above)*, reflecting the success with which they have adapted to changing conditions.

Resisting predators

A great variety of plants have developed devices including spines *(above)*, poisons, stinging hairs and an unpleasant taste or smell to deter animal predators.

Diversity of plant species

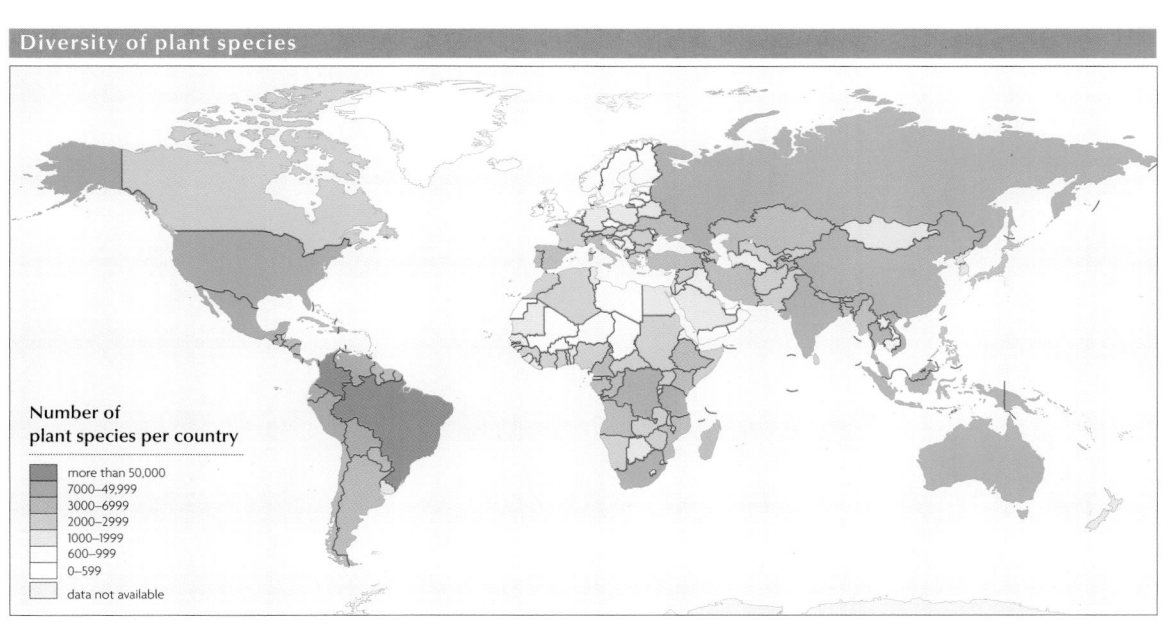

Number of plant species per country

- more than 50,000
- 7000–49,999
- 3000–6999
- 2000–2999
- 1000–1999
- 600–999
- 0–599
- data not available

Weeds

Weeds such as bindweed *(above)* are fast-growing, easily dispersed, and tolerant of a number of different environments, enabling them to quickly colonize suitable habitats. They are among the most adaptable of all plants.

Population and settlement

The Earth's population is projected to rise from its current level of about 6.5 billion to reach some 10 billion by 2025. The global distribution of this rapidly growing population is very uneven, and is dictated by climate, terrain and natural and economic resources. The great majority of the Earth's people live in coastal zones, and along river valleys. Deserts cover over 20% of the Earth's surface, but support less than 5% of the world's population. It is estimated that over half of the world's population live in cities – most of them in Asia – as a result of mass migration from rural areas in search of jobs. Many of these people live in the so-called 'megacities', some with populations as great as 40 million.

Patterns of settlement

The past 200 years have seen the most radical shift in world population patterns in recorded history.

Nomadic life

All the world's peoples were hunter-gatherers 10,000 years ago. Today nomads, who live by following available food resources, account for less than 0.0001% of the world's population. They are mainly pastoral herders, moving their livestock from place to place in search of grazing land.

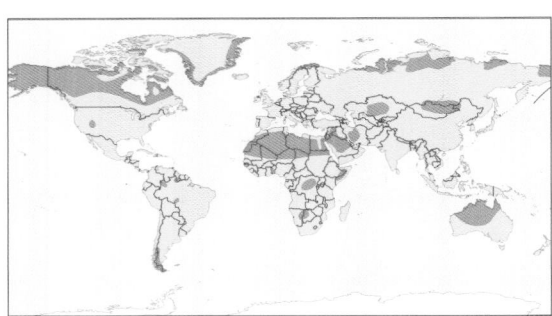

Nomadic population

▨ Nomadic population area

The growth of cities

In 1900 there were only 14 cities in the world with populations of more than a million, mostly in the northern hemisphere. Today, as more and more people in the developing world migrate to towns and cities, there are 29 cities whose population exceeds 5 million, and around 440 million-cities.

Million-cities in 1900

Million-cities in 1900

• Cities over 1 million population

Million-cities in 2005

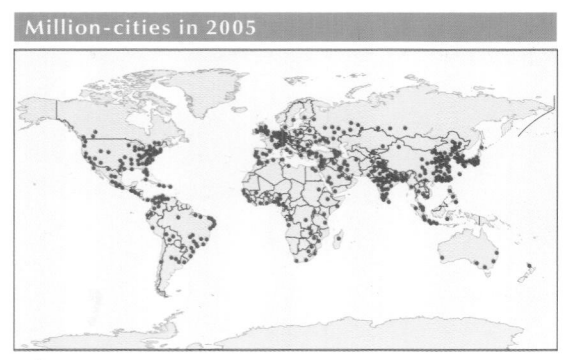

Million-cities in 2005

• Cities over 1 million population

North America

The eastern and western seaboards of the USA, with huge expanses of interconnected cities, towns and suburbs, are vast, densely-populated megalopolises. Central America and the Caribbean also have high population densities. Yet, away from the coasts and in the wildernesses of northern Canada the land is very sparsely settled.

▲ *Vancouver on Canada's west coast, grew up as a port city. In recent years it has attracted many Asian immigrants, particularly from the Pacific Rim.*

▲ *North America's central plains, the continent's agricultural heartland, are thinly populated and highly productive.*

Population density
(inhabitants per sq km)

More than 200
101–200
51–100
21–50
11–20
6–10
1–5
Less than 1

South America

Most settlement in South America is clustered in a narrow belt in coastal zones and in the northern Andes. During the 20th century, cities such as São Paulo and Buenos Aires grew enormously, acting as powerful economic magnets to the rural population. Shanty towns have grown up on the outskirts of many major cities to house these immigrants, often lacking basic amenities.

▲ *Many people in western South America live at high altitudes in the Andes, both in cities and in villages such as this one in Bolivia.*

▲ *Venezuela is one of the most highly urbanized countries in South America, with nearly 90% of the population living in cities such as Caracas.*

Africa

▲ *Cities such as Nairobi (above), Cairo and Johannesburg have grown rapidly in recent years, although only Cairo has a significant population on a global scale.*

The arid climate of much of Africa means that settlement of the continent is sparse, focusing in coastal areas and fertile regions such as the Nile Valley. Africa still has a high proportion of nomadic agriculturalists, although many are now becoming settled, and the population is predominantly rural.

▲ *Traditional lifestyles and homes persist across much of Africa, which has a higher proportion of rural or village-based population than any other continent.*

Europe

With its temperate climate, and rich mineral and natural resources, Europe is generally very densely settled. The continent acts as a magnet for economic migrants from the developing world, and immigration is now widely restricted. Birth rates in Europe are generally low, and in some countries, such as Germany, the populations have stabilized at zero growth, with a fast-growing elderly population.

▲ *Many European cities, like Siena, once reflected the 'ideal' size for human settlements. Modern technological advances have enabled them to grow far beyond the original walls.*

▲ *Within the densely-populated Netherlands the reclamation of coastal wetlands is vital to provide much-needed land for agriculture and settlement.*

Asia

Most Asian settlement originally centred around the great river valleys such as the Indus, the Ganges and the Yangtze. Today, almost 60% of the world's population lives in Asia, many in burgeoning cities – particularly in the economically-buoyant Pacific Rim countries. Even rural population densities are high in many countries; practices such as terracing in Southeast Asia making the most of the available land.

▲ *Many of China's cities are now vast urban areas with populations of more than 5 million people.*

▲ *This stilt village in Bangladesh is built to resist the regular flooding. Pressure on land, even in rural areas, forces many people to live in marginal areas.*

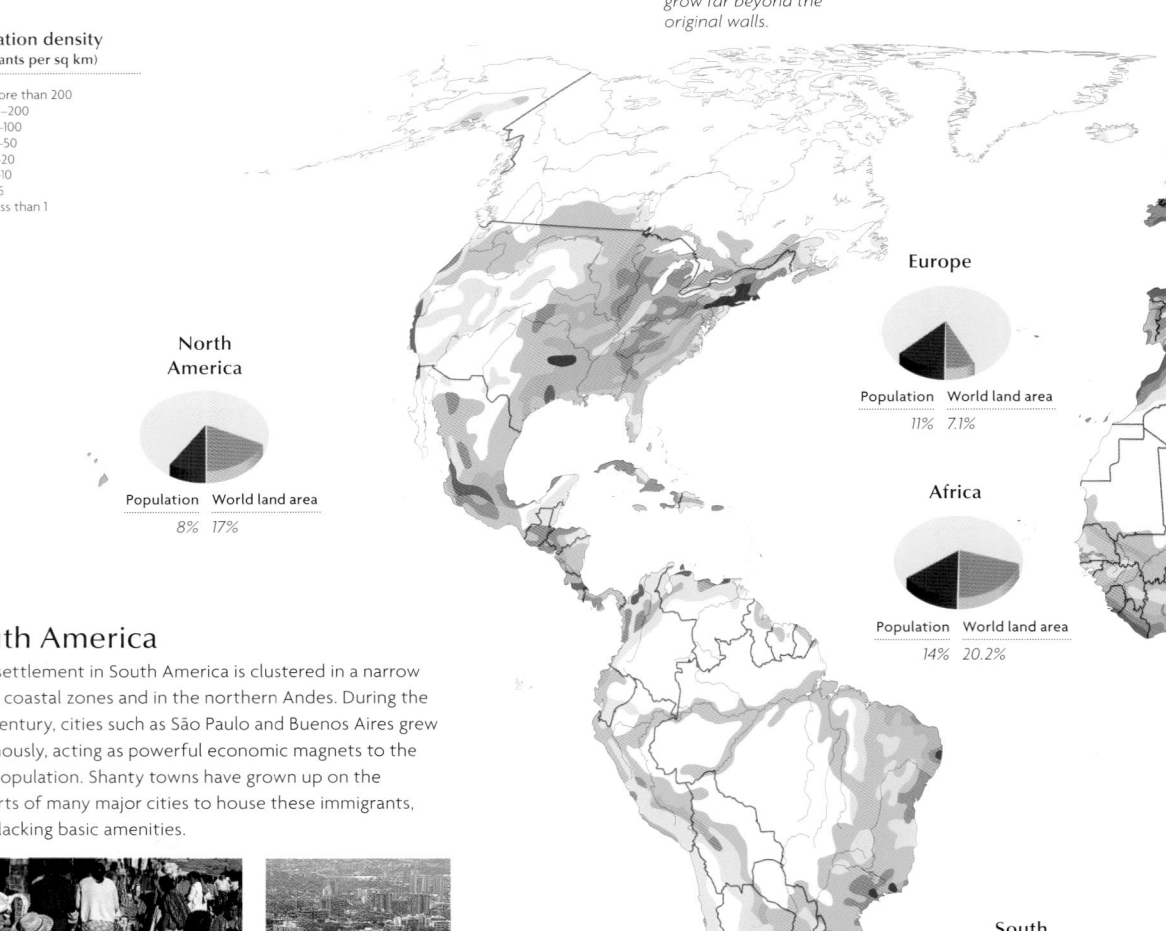

North America

Population 8% World land area 17%

Europe

Population 11% World land area 7.1%

Africa

Population 14% World land area 20.2%

South America

Population 6% World land area 11.8%

Population structures

Population pyramids are an effective means of showing the age structures of different countries, and highlighting changing trends in population growth and decline. The typical pyramid for a country with a growing, youthful population, is broad-based *(left)*, reflecting a high birth rate and a far larger number of young rather than elderly people. In contrast, countries with populations whose numbers are stabilizing have a more balanced distribution of people in each age band, and may even have lower numbers of people in the youngest age ranges, indicating both a high life expectancy, and that the population is now barely replacing itself *(right)*. The Russian Federation *(centre)* still bears the scars of the Second World War, reflected in the dramatically lower numbers of men than women in the 60–80+ age range.

Youthful population
(India)

Males | 80+ | Females
70–79
60–69
50–59
40–49
30–39
20–29
10–19
0–9

100 80 60 40 20 0 20 40 60 80 100
Population in millions

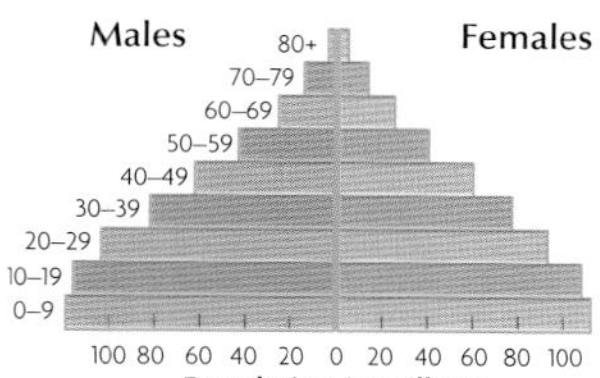

Distorted population
(Russian Federation)

Males | 80+ | Females
70–79
60–69
50–59
40–49
30–39
20–29
10–19
0–9

12 10 8 6 4 2 0 2 4 6 8 10 12
Population in millions

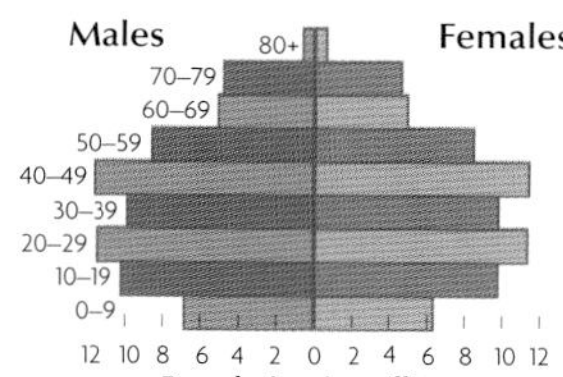

Ageing population
(United States of America)

Males | 80+ | Females
70–79
60–69
50–59
40–49
30–39
20–29
10–19
0–9

20 16 12 8 4 0 4 8 12 16 20
Population in millions

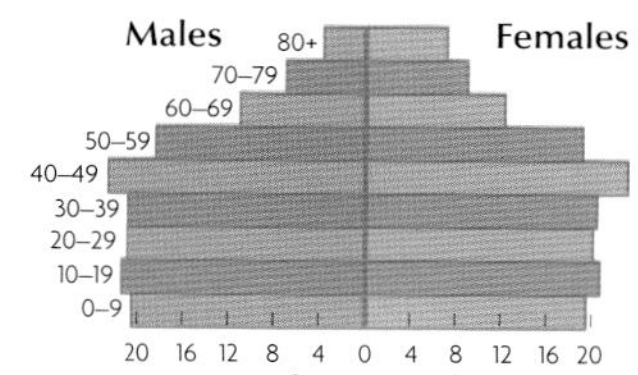

Population growth

Improvements in food supply and advances in medicine have both played a major role in the remarkable growth in global population, which has increased five-fold over the last 150 years. Food supplies have risen with the mechanization of agriculture and improvements in crop yields. Better nutrition, together with higher standards of public health and sanitation, have led to increased longevity and higher birth rates.

World population growth
1500 to present day

1500 1600 1700 1800 1900 2000

Asia

Population World land area
60% 29.1%

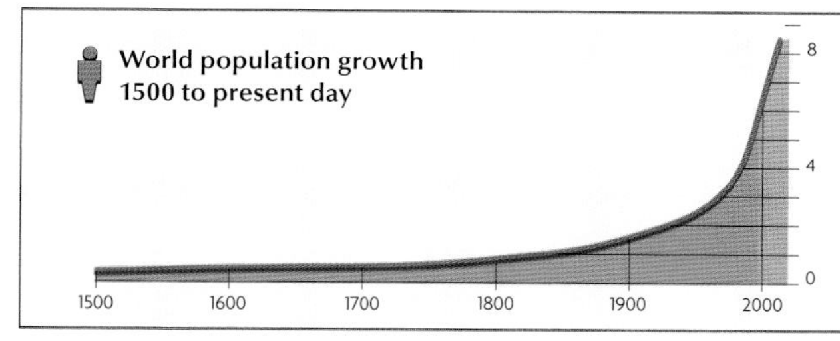

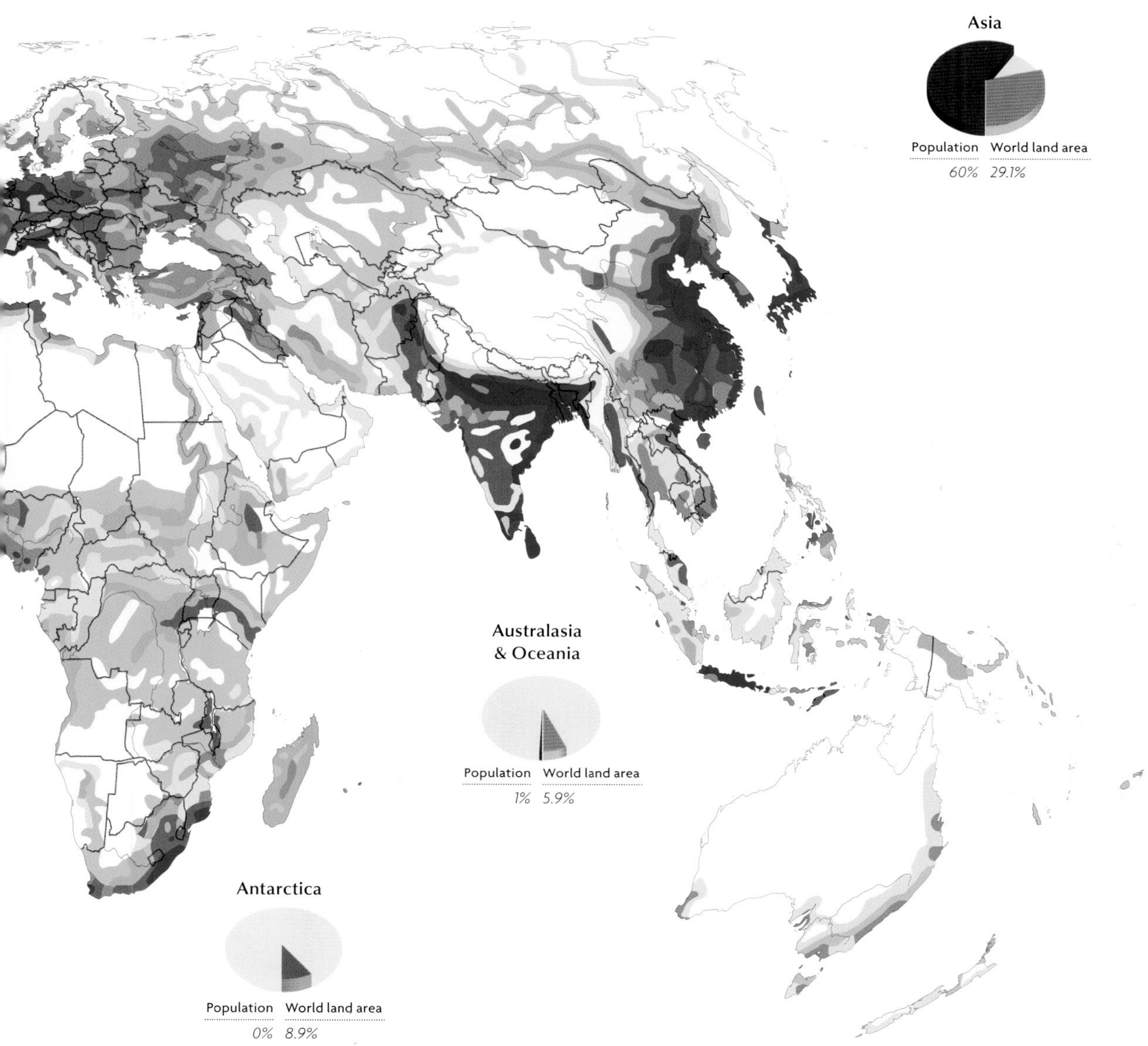

World nutrition

Two-thirds of the world's food supply is consumed by the industrialized nations, many of which have a daily calorific intake far higher than is necessary for their populations to maintain a healthy body weight. In contrast, in the developing world, about 800 million people do not have enough food to meet their basic nutritional needs.

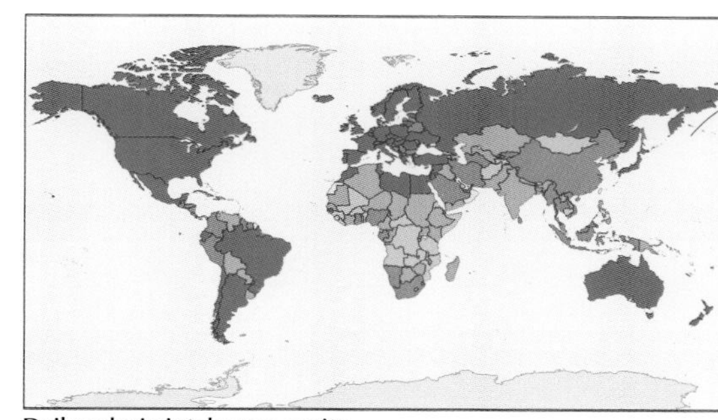

Daily calorie intake per capita

- above 3000
- 2500–2999
- 2000–2499
- below 2000
- data not available

World life expectancy

Improved public health and living standards have greatly increased life expectancy in the developed world, where people can now expect to live twice as long as they did 100 years ago. In many of the world's poorest nations, inadequate nutrition and disease, means that the average life expectancy still does not exceed 45 years.

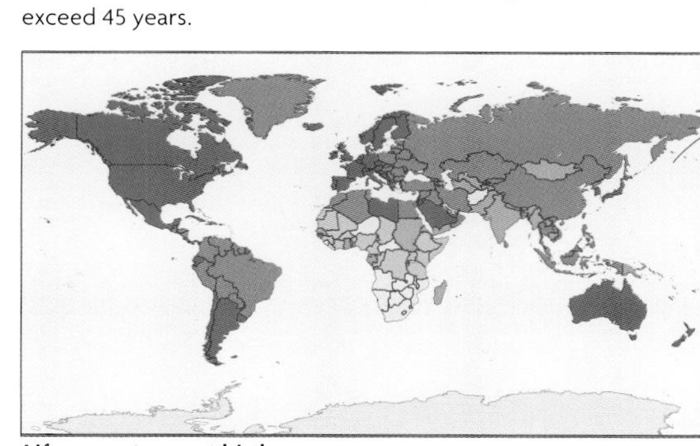

Life expectancy at birth

- above 75 years
- 65–74 years
- 55–64 years
- 45–54 years
- below 44 years
- data not available

Australasia & Oceania

Population World land area
1% 5.9%

Antarctica

Population World land area
0% 8.9%

Australasia and Oceania

This is the world's most sparsely settled region. The peoples of Australia and New Zealand live mainly in the coastal cities, with only scattered settlements in the arid interior. The Pacific islands can only support limited populations because of their remoteness and lack of resources.

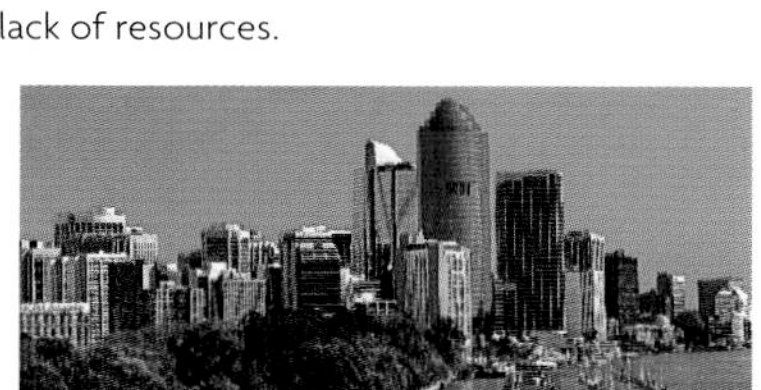

▶ *Brisbane, on Australia's Gold Coast is the most rapidly expanding city in the country. The great majority of Australia's population lives in cities near the coasts.*

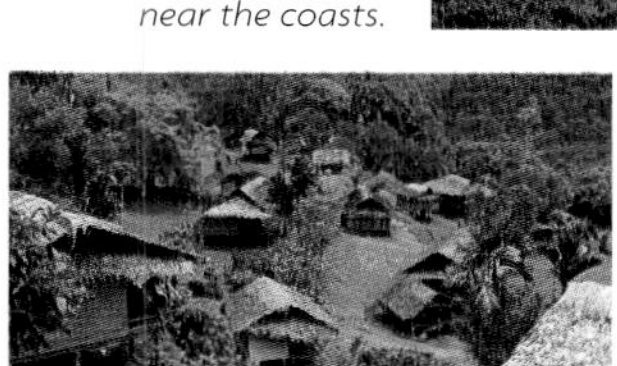

◀ *The remote highlands of Papua New Guinea are home to a wide variety of peoples, many of whom still subsist by traditional hunting and gathering.*

Average world birth rates

Birth rates are much higher in Africa, Asia and South America than in Europe and North America. Increased affluence and easy access to contraception are both factors which can lead to a significant decline in a country's birth rate.

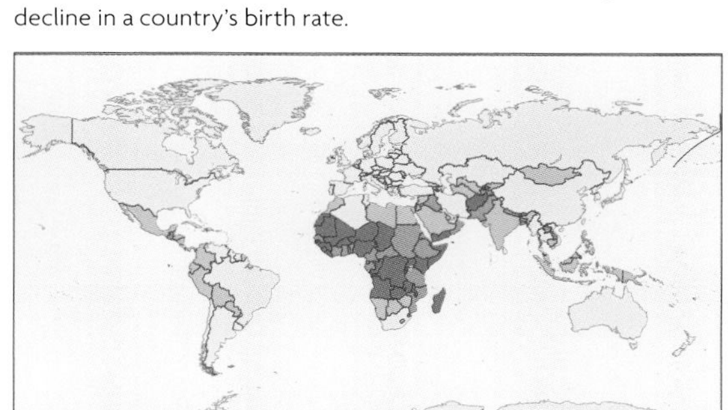

Number of births (per 1000 people)

- above 40
- 30–39
- 20–29
- below 20
- data not available

World infant mortality

In parts of the developing world infant mortality rates are still high; access to medical services such as immunization, adequate nutrition and the promotion of breast-feeding have been important in combating infant mortality.

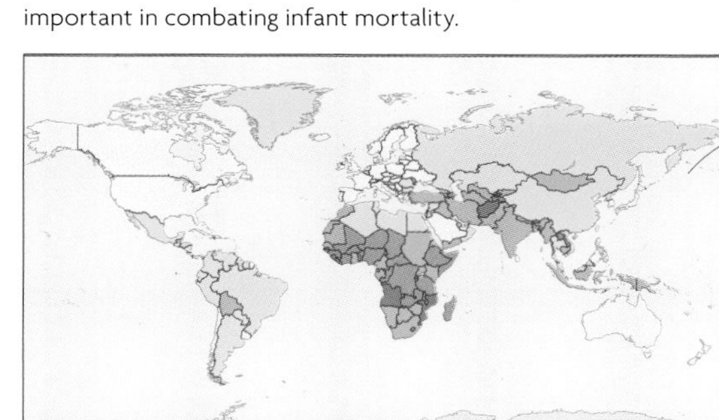

World infant mortality rates (deaths per 1000 live births)

- above 125
- 75–124
- 35–74
- 15–34
- below 15
- data not available

The economic system

The wealthy countries of the developed world, with their aggressive, market-led economies and their access to productive new technologies and international markets, dominate the world economic system. At the other extreme, many of the countries of the developing world are locked in a cycle of national debt, rising populations and unemployment. The state-managed economies of the former communist bloc began to be dismantled during the 1990s, and China is emerging as a major economic power following decades of isolation.

Trade blocs

Trade blocs

- EU
- CACM
- NAFTA
- SADC
- ASEAN
- ECOWAS
- LAIA
- CEEAC

International trade blocs are formed when groups of countries, often already enjoying close military and political ties, join together to offer mutually preferential terms of trade for both imports and exports. Increasingly, global trade is dominated by three main blocs: the EU, NAFTA, and ASEAN. They are supplanting older trade blocs such as the Commonwealth, a legacy of colonialism.

International trade flows

World trade acts as a stimulus to national economies, encouraging growth. Over the last three decades, as heavy industries have declined, services – banking, insurance, tourism, airlines and shipping – have taken an increasingly large share of world trade. Manufactured articles now account for nearly two-thirds of world trade; raw materials and food make up less than a quarter of the total.

Shipping
Ships carry 80% of international cargo, and extensive container ports, where cargo is stored, are vital links in the international transport network.

Multinationals
Multinational companies are increasingly penetrating inaccessible markets. The reach of many American commodities is now global.

Primary products
Many countries, particularly in the Caribbean and Africa, are still reliant on primary products such as rubber and coffee, which makes them vulnerable to fluctuating prices.

Service industries
Service industries such as banking, tourism and insurance were the fastest-growing industrial sector in the last half of the 20th century. Lloyds of London is the centre of the world insurance market.

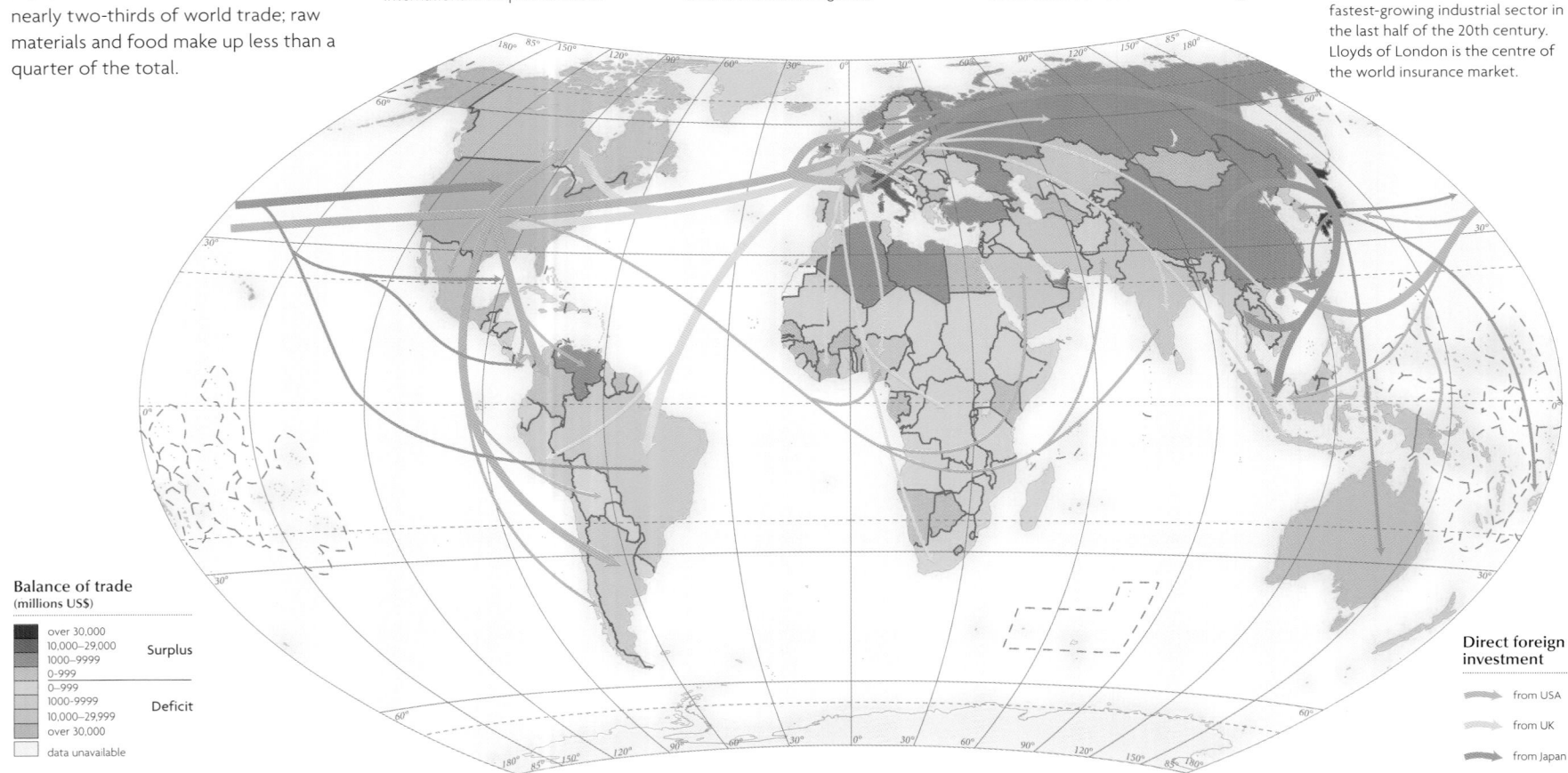

Balance of trade
(millions US$)

Surplus
- over 30,000
- 10,000–29,000
- 1000–9999
- 0–999

Deficit
- 0–999
- 1000–9999
- 10,000–29,999
- over 30,000

- data unavailable

Direct foreign investment
- from USA
- from UK
- from Japan

World money markets

The financial world has traditionally been dominated by three major centres – Tokyo, New York and London, which house the headquarters of stock exchanges, multinational corporations and international banks. Their geographic location means that, at any one time in a 24-hour day, one major market is open for trading in shares, currencies and commodities. Since the late 1980s, technological advances have enabled transactions between financial centres to occur at ever-greater speed, and new markets have sprung up throughout the world.

New stock markets

New stock markets are now opening in many parts of the world, where economies have recently emerged from state controls. In Moscow and Beijing, and several countries in eastern Europe, newly-opened stock exchanges reflect the transition to market-driven economies.

The developing world

International trade in capital and currency is dominated by the rich nations of the northern hemisphere. In parts of Africa and Asia, where exports of any sort are extremely limited, home-produced commodities are simply sold in local markets.

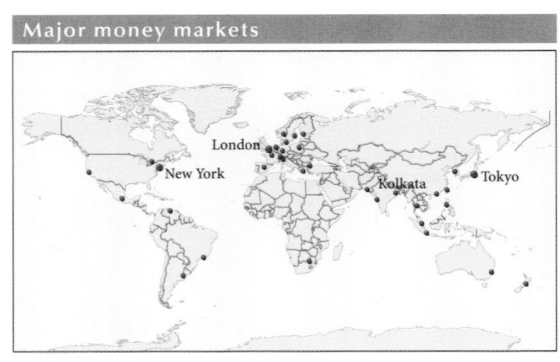

Major money markets

London
New York
Kolkata
Tokyo

Location of major stock markets
- Major stock markets

▲ *The Tokyo Stock Market crashed in 1990, leading to slow-down in the growth of the world's most powerful economy, and a refocusing on economic policy away from export-led growth and towards the domestic market.*

▲ *Dealers at the Kolkata Stock Market. The Indian economy has been opened up to foreign investment and many multinationals now have bases there.*

▲ *Markets have thrived in communist Vietnam since the introduction of a liberal economic policy.*

World wealth disparity

A global assessment of Gross Domestic Product (GDP) by nation reveals great disparities. The developed world, with only a quarter of the world's population, has 80% of the world's manufacturing income. Civil war, conflict and political instability further undermine the economic self-sufficiency of many of the world's poorest nations.

Urban sprawl

Cities are expanding all over the developing world, attracting economic migrants in search of work and opportunities. In cities such as Rio de Janeiro, housing has not kept pace with the population explosion, and squalid shanty towns *(favelas)* rub shoulders with middle-class housing.

▲ *The* **favelas of** *Rio de Janeiro sprawl over the hills surrounding the city.*

Agricultural economies

In parts of the developing world, people survive by subsistence farming – only growing enough food for themselves and their families. With no surplus product, they are unable to exchange goods for currency, the only means of escaping the poverty trap. In other countries, farmers have been encouraged to concentrate on growing a single crop for the export market. This reliance on cash crops leaves farmers vulnerable to crop failure and to changes in the market price of the crop.

Urban decay

Although the USA still dominates the global economy, it faces deficits in both the federal budget and the balance of trade. Vast discrepancies in personal wealth, high levels of unemployment, and the dismantling of welfare provisions throughout the 1980s have led to severe deprivation in several of the inner cities of North America's industrial heartland.

▲ *Cities such as* Detroit *have been badly hit by the decline in heavy industry.*

Booming cities

Since the 1980s the Chinese government has set up special industrial zones, such as Shanghai, where foreign investment is encouraged through tax incentives. Migrants from rural China pour into these regions in search of work, creating 'boomtown' economies.

◀ *Foreign investment has* encouraged new infrastructure development in cities like Shanghai.

Economic 'tigers'

The economic 'tigers' of the Pacific Rim – China, Singapore, and South Korea – have grown faster than Europe and the USA over the last decade. Their export- and service-led economies have benefited from stable government, low labour costs, and foreign investment.

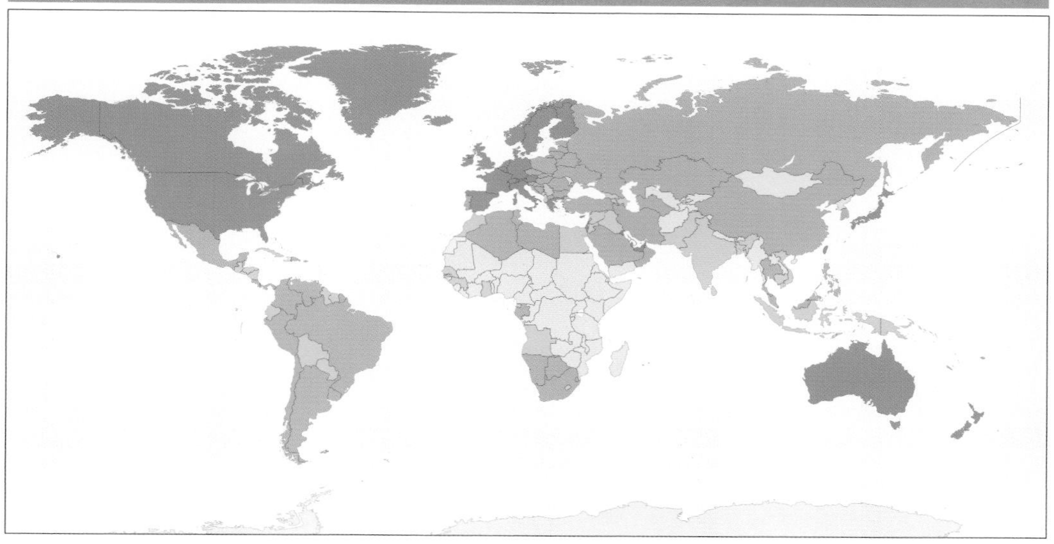

▲ *Hong Kong, with* its fine natural harbour, is one of the most important ports in Asia.

Comparative world wealth

World economies - average GDP per capita (US$)
- above 20,000
- 5000–20,000
- 2000–5000
- below 2000
- data unavailable

▲ *The* **Ugandan uplands** *are fertile, but poor infrastructure hampers the export of cash crops.*

▲ *A* **shopping arcade** *in Paris displays a great profusion of luxury goods.*

The affluent West

The capital cities of many countries in the developed world are showcases for consumer goods, reflecting the increasing importance of the service sector, and particularly the retail sector, in the world economy. The idea of shopping as a leisure activity is unique to the western world. Luxury goods and services attract visitors, who in turn generate tourist revenue.

Tourism

In 2004, there were over 700 million tourists worldwide. Tourism is now the world's biggest single industry, employing 130 million people, though frequently in low-paid unskilled jobs. While tourists are increasingly exploring inaccessible and less-developed regions of the world, the benefits of the industry are not always felt at a local level. There are also worries about the environmental impact of tourism, as the world's last wildernesses increasingly become tourist attractions.

▲ *Botswana's* **Okavango Delta** *is an area rich in wildlife. Tourists make safaris to the region, but the impact of tourism is controlled.*

Money flows

Foreign investment in the developing world during the 1970s led to a global financial crisis in the 1980s, when many countries were unable to meet their debt repayments. The International Monetary Fund (IMF) was forced to reschedule the debts and, in some cases, write them off completely. Within the developing world, austerity programmes have been initiated to cope with the debt, leading in turn to high unemployment and galloping inflation. In many parts of Africa, stricken economies are now dependent on international aid.

◀ *In rural* **Southeast Asia,** *babies are given medical checks by* UNICEF *as part of a global aid programme sponsored by the* UN.

Tourist arrivals

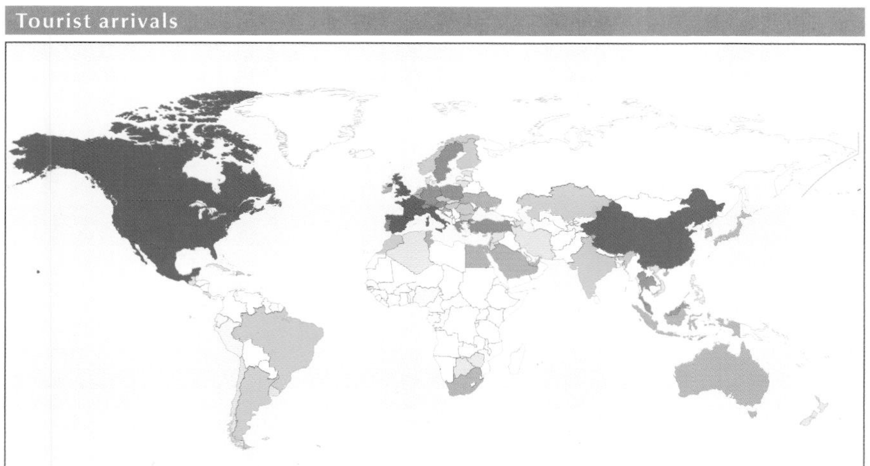

Tourist arrivals
- over 20 million
- 10–20 million
- 5–10 million
- 2.5–5 million
- 1–2.5 million
- 700,000–999,000
- under 700,000
- data unavailable

International debt

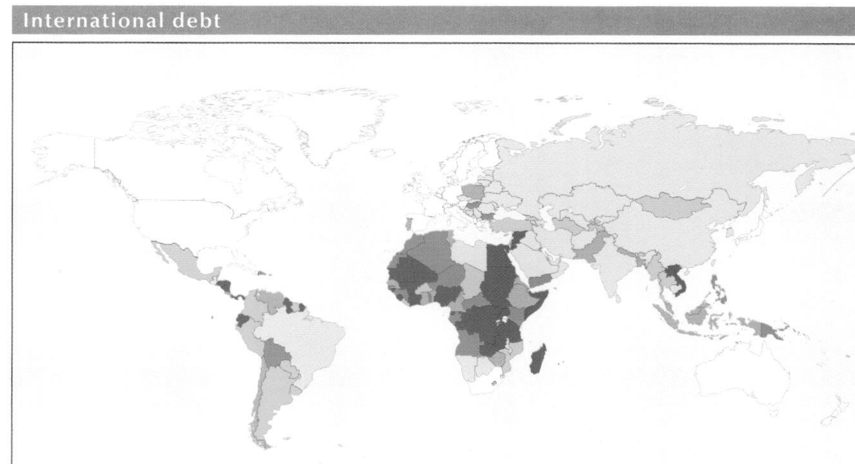

International debt (as percentage of GNI)
- over 100%
- 70–99%
- 50–69%
- 30–49%
- 10–29%
- below 10%
- data unavailable

The political world

There are 194 independent countries in the world today. With the exception of Antarctica, where territorial claims have been deferred by international treaty, every land area of the Earth's surface either belongs to, or is claimed by, one country or another. The largest country in the world is the Russian Federation, the smallest is Vatican City. Some 60 overseas dependent territories remain, administered variously by France, Australia, Denmark, New Zealand, Norway, Portugal, the UK, the US and the Netherlands.

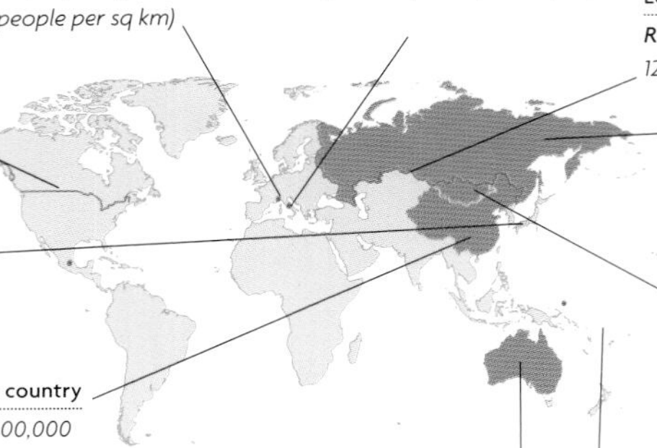

International borders

The map shows three main types of boundary between states. Full borders represent internationally agreed and recognized territorial boundaries. Undefined borders exist where no fixed boundary between states has been demarcated; the boundaries indicated in this way show approximate areas of sovereignty. A disputed border is indicated where a *de facto* territorial boundary exists, which is not agreed or is subject to arbitration.

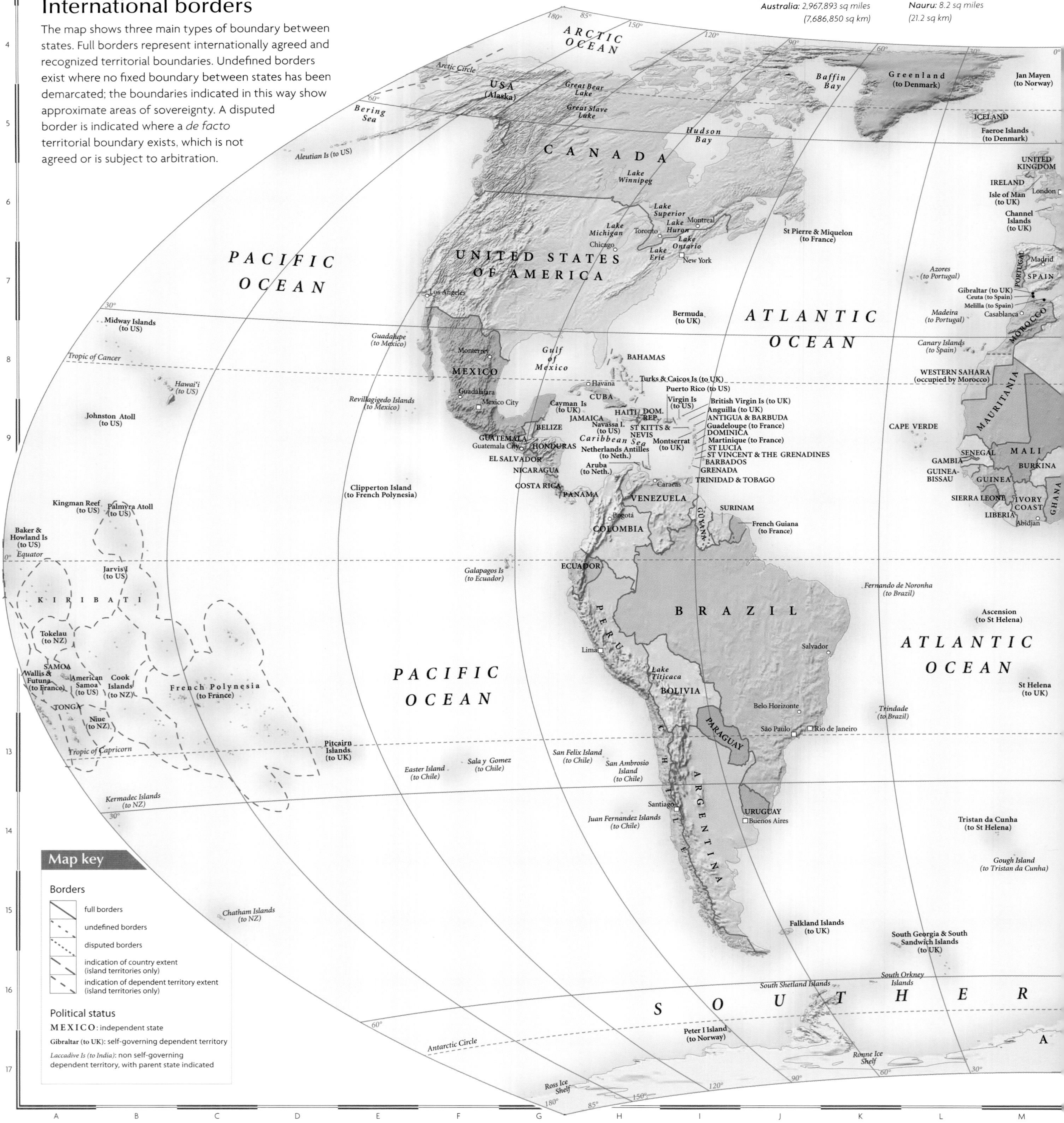

Most densely populated country
Monaco: 16,620 people per sq mile
(43,213 people per sq km)

Smallest country
Vatican City: 0.17 sq miles (0.44 sq km)

Longest land borders
Russian Federation:
12,427 miles (20,000 km)

Longest single land border
Canada/USA: 5526 miles
(8893 km)

Largest country
Russian Federation:
6,592,735 sq miles
(17,075,200 sq km)

Most populous City
Tokyo: 34,200,000
people

Most sparsely populated country
Mongolia:
4 people per sq mile
(2 people per sq km)

Most populous country
China: 1,315,800,000
people (estimated)

Largest island country
Australia: 2,967,893 sq miles
(7,686,850 sq km)

Smallest island country
Nauru: 8.2 sq miles
(21.2 sq km)

Map key

Borders

full borders
undefined borders
disputed borders
indication of country extent
(island territories only)
indication of dependent territory extent
(island territories only)

Political status

MEXICO : independent state
Gibraltar (to UK): self-governing dependent territory
Laccadive Is (to India): non self-governing
dependent territory, with parent state indicated

The world in 1914

The early years of the 20th century saw the mainly European colonial empires reaching their greatest extents by 1914. Two world wars inaugurated their disintegration, but even in 1950 there were only 82 independent countries. Since then, over 100 have gained their independence, culminating in the breakup of the Soviet Union and former Yugoslavia in the early 1990s.

Percentage of Earth's land surface controlled by colonial empires in 1914

- Independent: 29.8%
- Chinese: 6%
- Ottoman: 1.5%
- Russian: 15%
- Portuguese: 1%
- Spanish: 1%
- British: 21.5%
- French: 7.7%
- Belgian: 1.6%
- Italian: 1.8%
- German: 1.6%
- Japanese: 0.4%
- United States: 7.6%
- Dutch: 1.4%
- Danish: 1.5%

Colonial empires in 1914

Colonial Empires in 1914

- Belgian
- British
- Chinese
- Danish
- Dutch
- French
- German
- Italian
- Japanese
- Ottoman
- Portuguese
- Russian
- Spanish
- United States
- Independent
- Disputed

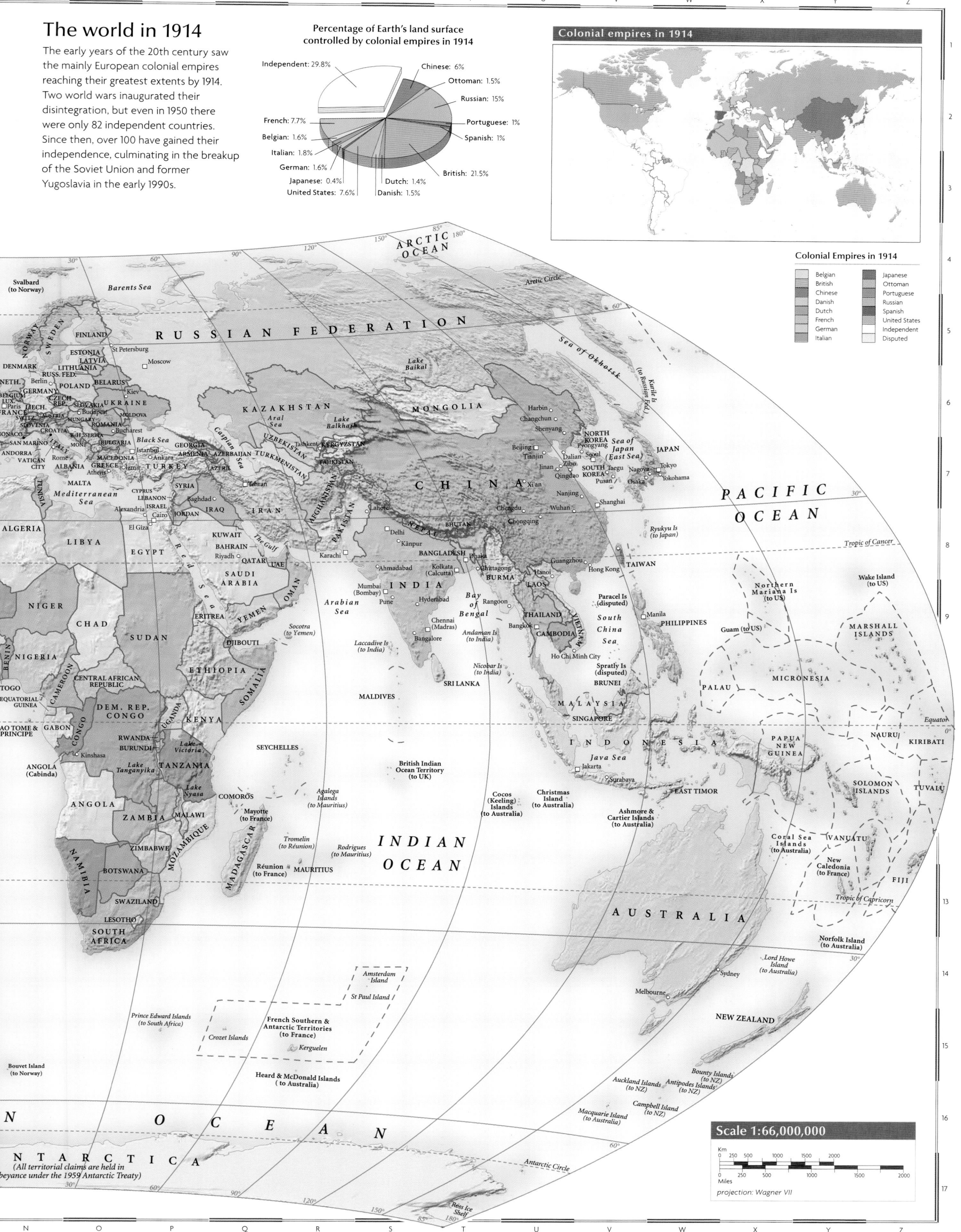

States and boundaries

There are over 190 sovereign states in the world today; in 1950 there were only 82. Over the last half-century national self-determination has been a driving force for many states with a history of colonialism and oppression. As more borders have been added to the world map, the number of international border disputes has increased.

In many cases, where the impetus towards independence has been religious or ethnic, disputes with minority groups have also caused violent internal conflict. While many newly-formed states have moved peacefully towards independence, successfully establishing government by multiparty democracy, dictatorship by military regime or individual despot is often the result of the internal power-struggles which characterize the early stages in the lives of new nations.

The nature of politics

Democracy is a broad term: it can range from the ideal of multiparty elections and fair representation to, in countries such as Singapore, a thin disguise for single-party rule. In despotic regimes, on the other hand, a single, often personal authority has total power; institutions such as parliament and the military are mere instruments of the dictator.

◀ The stars and stripes of the US flag are a potent symbol of the country's status as a federal democracy.

The changing world map

Decolonization

In 1950, large areas of the world remained under the control of a handful of European countries (page xxviii). The process of decolonization had begun in Asia, where, following the Second World War, much of south and southeast Asia sought and achieved self-determination. In the 1960s, a host of African states achieved independence, so that by 1965, most of the larger tracts of the European overseas empires had been substantially eroded. The final major stage in decolonization came with the break-up of the Soviet Union and the Eastern bloc after 1990. The process continues today as the last toeholds of European colonialism, often tiny island nations, press increasingly for independence.

▲ Icons of communism, including statues of former leaders such as Lenin and Stalin, were destroyed when the Soviet bloc was dismantled in 1989, creating several new nations.

▲ Iran has been one of the modern world's few true theocracies; Islam has an impact on every aspect of political life.

◀ Saddam Hussein, former autocratic leader of Iraq, promoted an extreme personality cult for over 20 years. He was ousted by a US-led coalition in 2003.

New nations 1945–1965

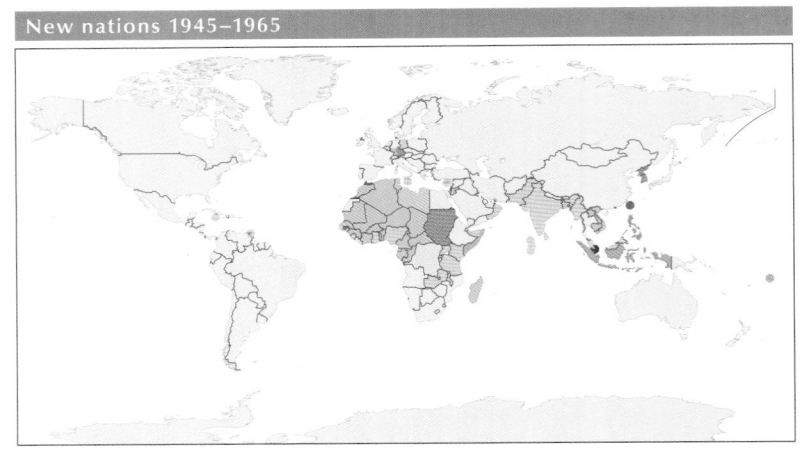

New nations 1965–present

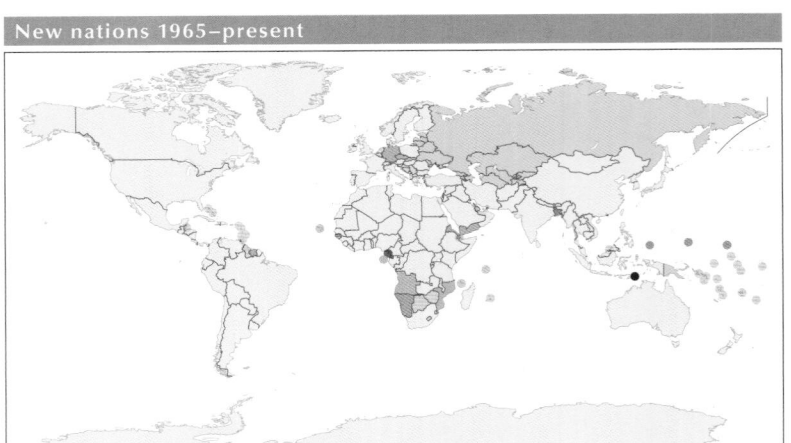

▲ North Korea is an independent communist republic. Power is concentrated in the hands of Kim Jong Il.

◀ South Africa became a democracy in 1994, when elections ended over a century of white minority rule.

Administration at the time of independence

Australia	Malaysia
Aust/NZ/UK	Netherlands
Belgium	New Zealand
China	Pakistan
Czechoslovakia	Portugal
Egypt/UK	South Africa
Ethiopia	Spain
France	UK
France/UK	Unified country
Indonesia	USA
Italy	USSR
Japan	Yugoslavia

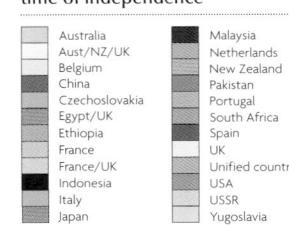

▲ In Brunei the Sultan has ruled by decree since 1962; power is closely tied to the royal family. The Sultan's brothers are responsible for finance and foreign affairs.

Types of government

- Multiparty democracy for more than 10 yrs
- Multiparty/transitional democracy within last 10 yrs
- Single-party government
- Military regime
- Theocracy
- Absolute monarchy
- ♠ Current civil unrest

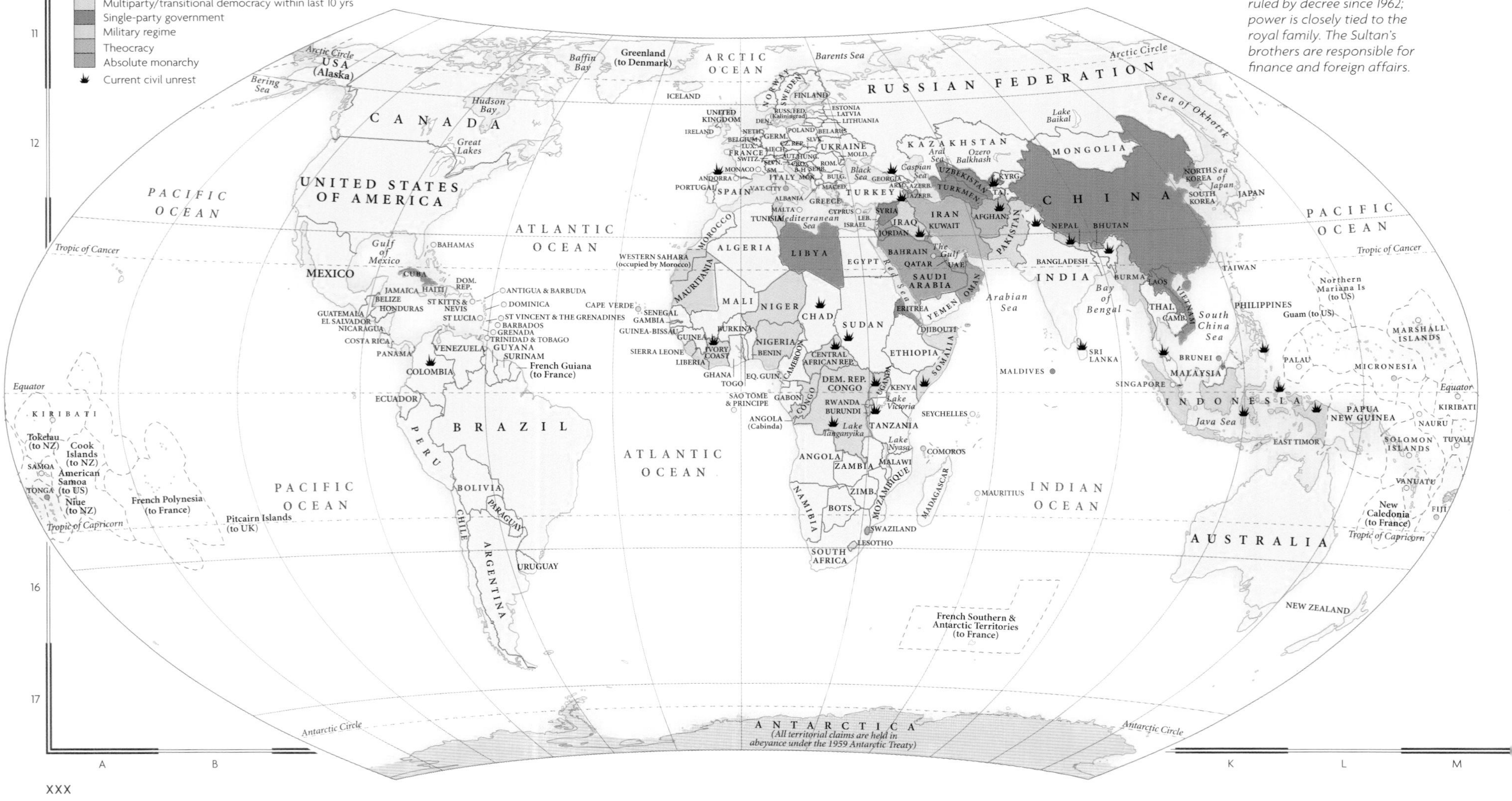

[World map with country labels including: CANADA, UNITED STATES OF AMERICA, MEXICO, BRAZIL, ARGENTINA, RUSSIAN FEDERATION, CHINA, INDIA, AUSTRALIA, and many others]

ANTARCTICA
(All territorial claims are held in abeyance under the 1959 Antarctic Treaty)

Lines on the map

The determination of international boundaries can use a variety of criteria. Many of the borders between older states follow physical boundaries; some mirror religious and ethnic differences; others are the legacy of complex histories of conflict and colonialism, while others have been imposed by international agreements or arbitration.

Post-colonial borders

When the European colonial empires in Africa were dismantled during the second half of the 20th century, the outlines of the new African states mirrored colonial boundaries. These boundaries had been drawn up by colonial administrators, often based on inadequate geographical knowledge. Such arbitrary boundaries were imposed on people of different languages, racial groups, religions and customs. This confused legacy often led to civil and international war.

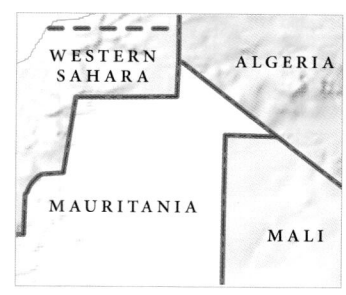

Physical borders

Many of the world's countries are divided by physical borders: lakes, rivers, mountains. The demarcation of such boundaries can, however, lead to disputes. Control of waterways, water supplies and fisheries are frequent causes of international friction.

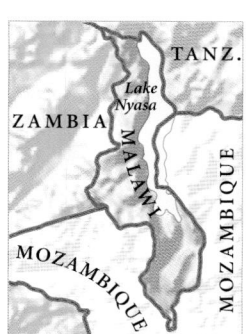

▲ The conflict that has plagued many African countries since independence has caused millions of people to become refugees.

Enclaves

The shifting political map over the course of history has frequently led to anomalous situations. Parts of national territories may become isolated by territorial agreement, forming an enclave. The West German part of the city of Berlin, which until 1989 lay a hundred miles (160 km) within East German territory, was a famous example.

Antarctica

When Antarctic exploration began a century ago, seven nations, Australia, Argentina, Britain, Chile, France, New Zealand and Norway, laid claim to the new territory. In 1961 the Antarctic Treaty, now signed by 45 nations, agreed to hold all territorial claims in abeyance.

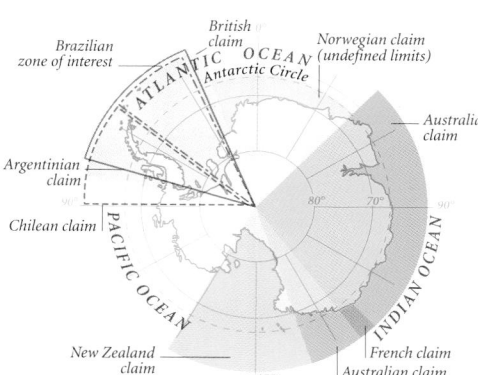

▲ Since the independence of Lithuania and Belarus, the peoples of the Russian enclave of Kaliningrad have become physically isolated.

Geometric borders

Straight lines and lines of longitude and latitude have occasionally been used to determine international boundaries; and indeed the world's second longest continuous international boundary, between Canada and the USA, follows the 49th Parallel for over one-third of its course. Many Canadian, American and Australian internal administrative boundaries are similarly determined using a geometric solution.

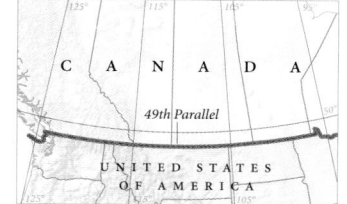

▲ Different farming techniques in Canada and the USA clearly mark the course of the international boundary in this satellite map.

World boundaries

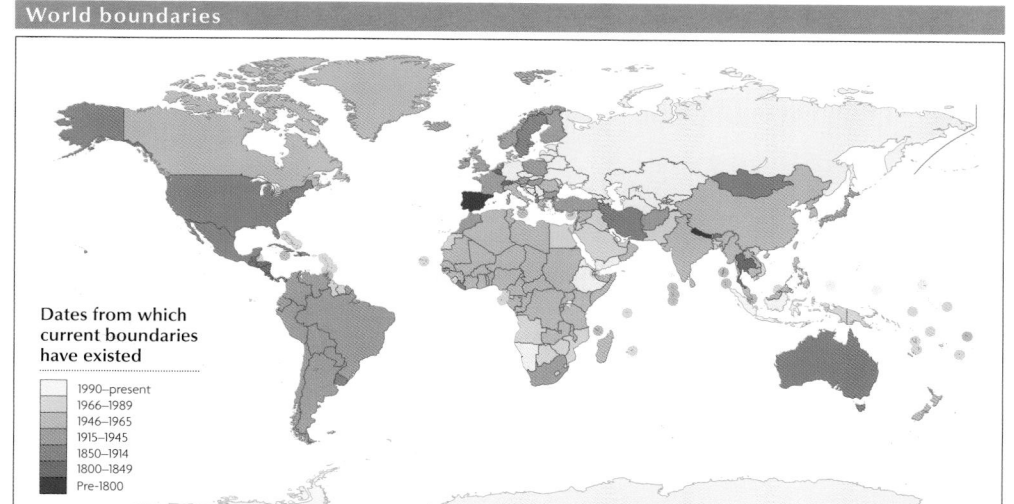

Dates from which current boundaries have existed

- 1990–present
- 1966–1989
- 1946–1965
- 1915–1945
- 1850–1914
- 1800–1849
- Pre-1800

Lake borders

Countries which lie next to lakes usually fix their borders in the middle of the lake. Unusually the Lake Nyasa border between Malawi and Tanzania runs along Tanzania's shore.

▲ Complicated agreements between colonial powers led to the awkward division of Lake Nyasa.

River borders

Rivers alone account for one-sixth of the world's borders. Many great rivers form boundaries between a number of countries. Changes in a river's course and interruptions of its natural flow can lead to disputes, particularly in areas where water is scarce. The centre of the river's course is the nominal boundary line.

▲ The Danube forms all or part of the border between nine European nations.

Mountain borders

Mountain ranges form natural barriers and are the basis for many major borders, particularly in Europe and Asia. The watershed is the conventional boundary demarcation line, but its accurate determination is often problematic.

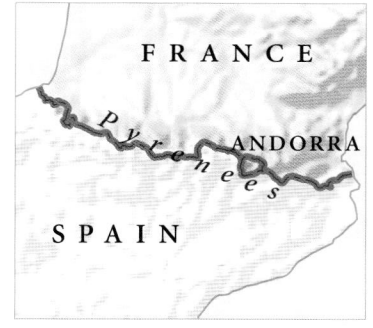

▲ The Pyrenees form a natural mountain border between France and Spain.

Shifting boundaries – Poland

Borders between countries can change dramatically over time. The nations of eastern Europe have been particularly affected by changing boundaries. Poland is an example of a country whose boundaries have changed so significantly that it has literally moved around Europe. At the start of the 16th century, Poland was the largest nation in Europe. Between 1772 and 1795, it was absorbed into Prussia, Austria and Russia, and it effectively ceased to exist. After the First World War, Poland became an independent country once more, but its borders changed again after the Second World War following invasions by both Soviet Russia and Nazi Germany.

▲ In 1634, Poland was the largest nation in Europe, its eastern boundary reaching towards Moscow.

▲ From 1772–1795, Poland was gradually partitioned between Austria, Russia and Prussia. Its eastern boundary receded by over 100 miles (160 km).

▲ Following the First World War, Poland was reinstated as an independent state, but it was less than half the size it had been in 1634.

▲ After the Second World War the Baltic Sea border was extended westwards, but much of the eastern territory was annexed by Russia.

International disputes

There are more than 60 disputed borders or territories in the world today. Although many of these disputes can be settled by peaceful negotiation, some areas have become a focus for international conflict. Ethnic tensions have been a major source of territorial disagreement throughout history, as has the ownership of, and access to, valuable natural resources. The turmoil of the post-colonial era in many parts of Africa is partly a result of the 19th century 'carve-up' of the continent, which created potential for conflict by drawing often arbitrary lines through linguistic and cultural areas.

Jammu and Kashmir

Disputes over Jammu and Kashmir have caused three serious wars between India and Pakistan since 1947. Pakistan wishes to annex the largely Muslim territory, while India refuses to cede any territory or to hold a referendum, and also lays claim to the entire territory. Most international maps show the 'line of control' agreed in 1972 as the *de facto* border. In addition India has territorial disputes with neighbouring China. The situation is further complicated by a Kashmiri independence movement, active since the late 1980s.

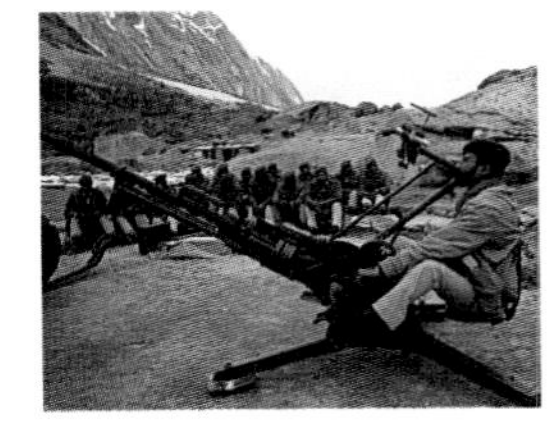

▲ **Indian army troops** maintain their positions in the mountainous terrain of northern Kashmir.

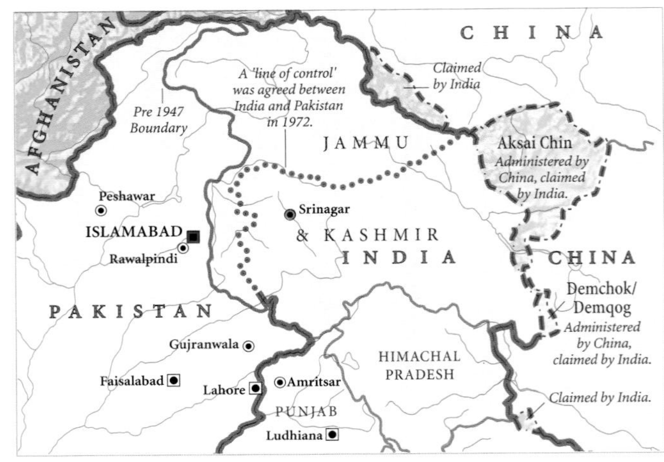

North and South Korea

Since 1953, the *de facto* border between North and South Korea has been a ceasefire line which straddles the 38th Parallel and is designated as a demilitarized zone. Both countries have heavy fortifications and troop concentrations behind this zone.

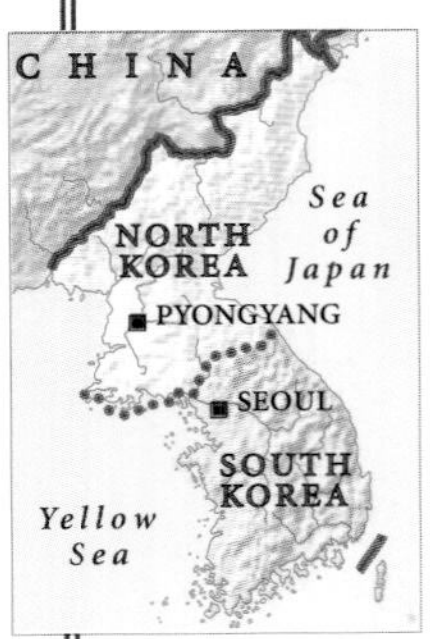

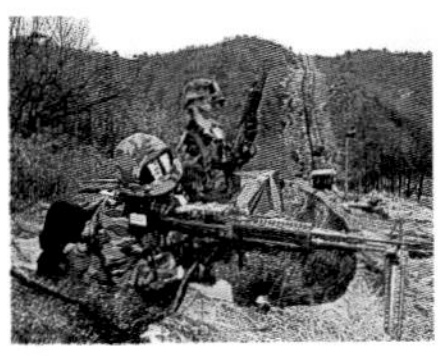

▲ **Heavy fortifications** on the border between North and South Korea.

Cyprus

Cyprus was partitioned in 1974, following an invasion by Turkish troops. The south is now the Greek Cypriot Republic of Cyprus, while the self-proclaimed Turkish Republic of Northern Cyprus is recognized only by Turkey.

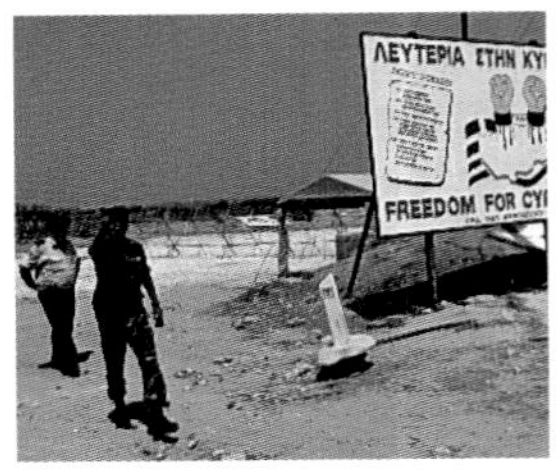

▲ **The so-called 'green line'** divides Cyprus into Greek and Turkish sectors.

The Falkland Islands

The British dependent territory of the Falkland Islands was invaded by Argentina in 1982, sparking a full-scale war with the UK. In 1995, the UK and Argentina reached an agreement on the exploitation of oil reserves around the islands.

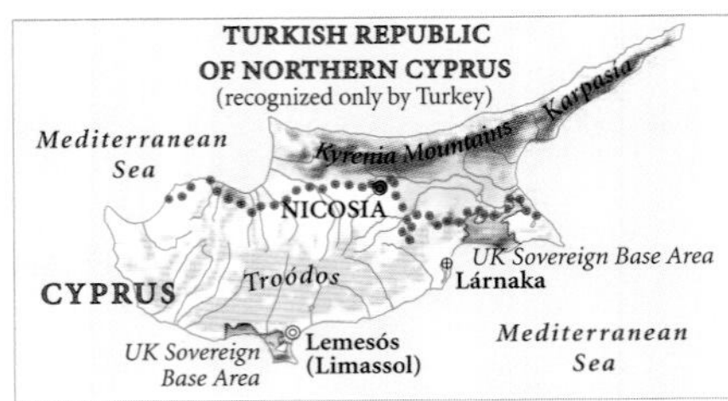

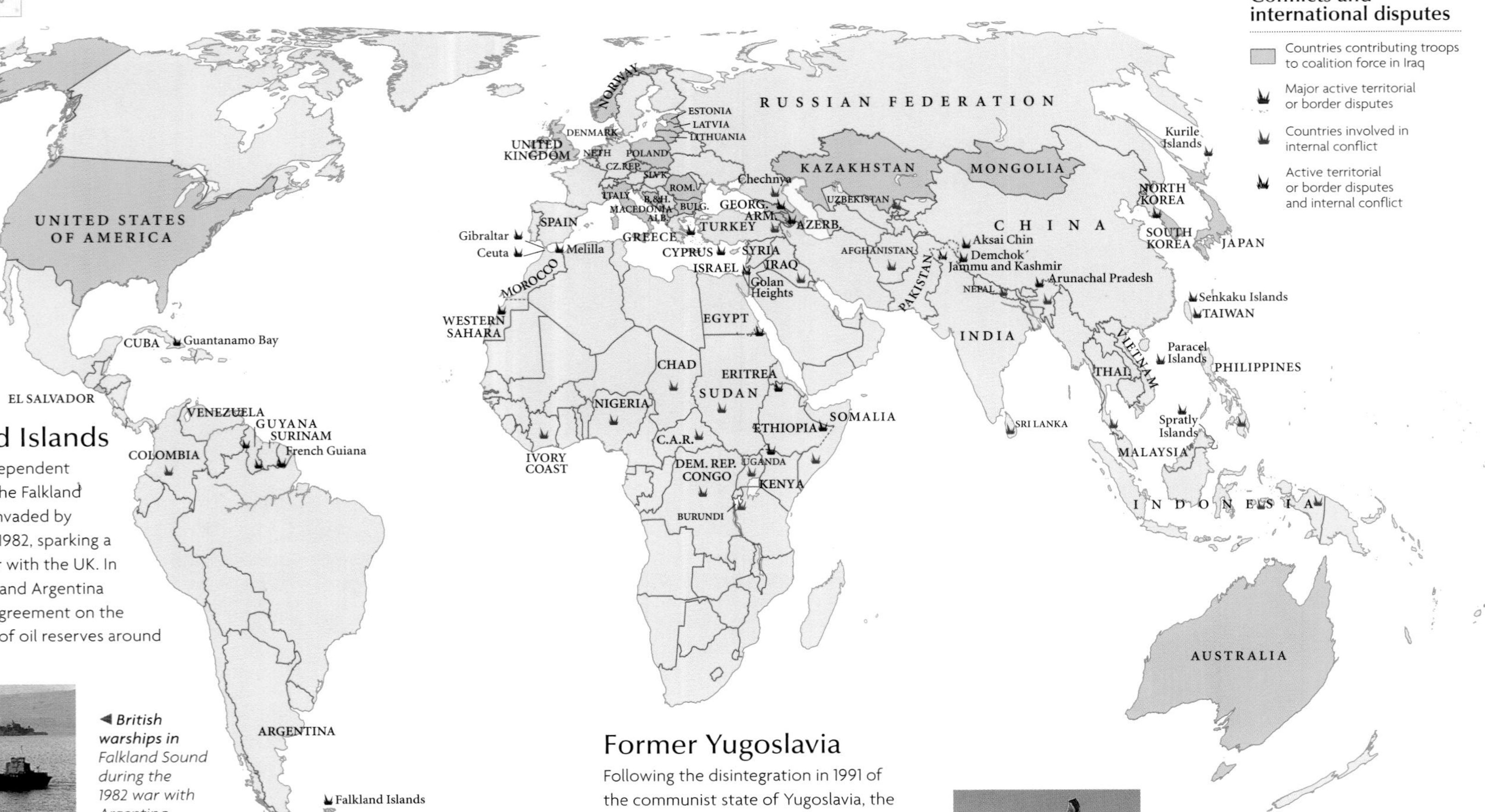

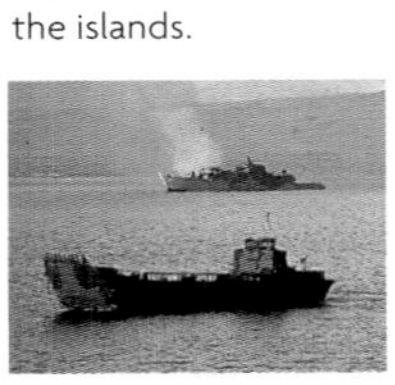

◀ **British warships** in Falkland Sound during the 1982 war with Argentina.

Israel

Israel was created in 1948 following the 1947 UN Resolution (147) on Palestine. Until 1979 Israel had no borders, only ceasefire lines from a series of wars in 1948, 1967 and 1973. Treaties with Egypt in 1979 and Jordan in 1994 led to these borders being defined and agreed. Negotiations over Israeli settlements and Palestinian self-government have seen little effective progress since 2000.

Former Yugoslavia

Following the disintegration in 1991 of the communist state of Yugoslavia, the breakaway states of Croatia and Bosnia and Herzegovina came into conflict with the 'parent' state (consisting of Serbia and Montenegro). Warfare focused on ethnic and territorial ambitions in Bosnia. The tenuous Dayton Accord of 1995 sought to recognize the post-1990 borders, whilst providing for ethnic partition and required international peace-keeping troops to maintain the terms of the peace.

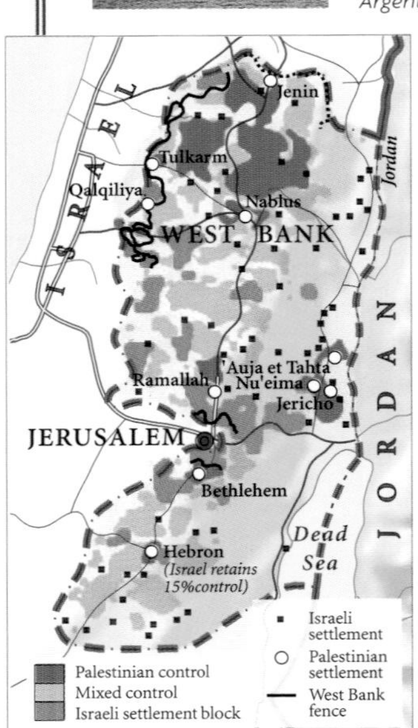

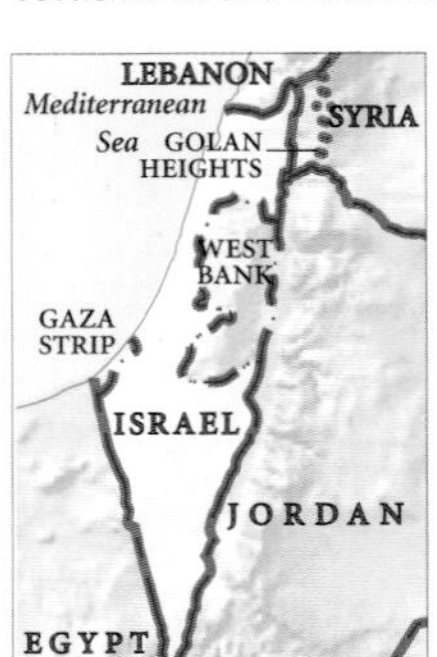

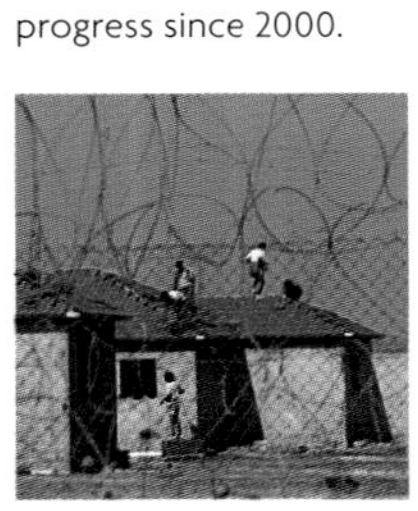

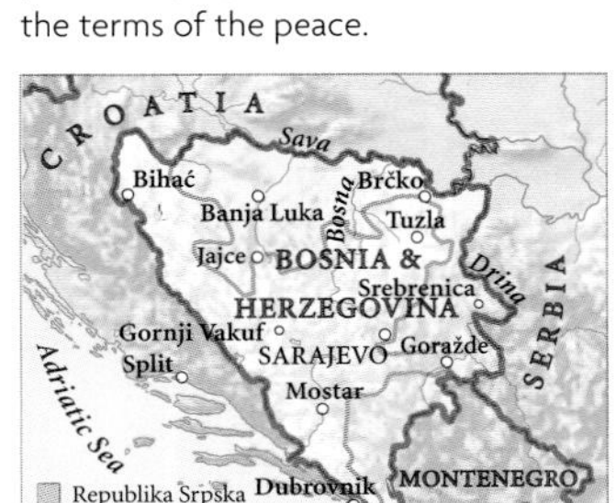

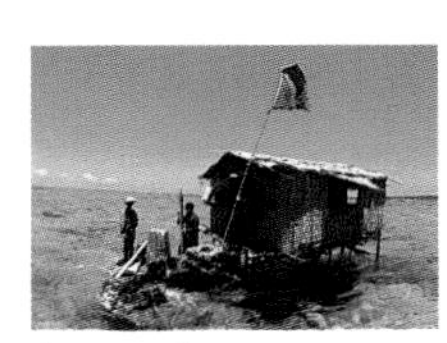

▲ **Most claimant states** have small military garrisons on the Spratly Islands.

The Spratly Islands

The site of potential oil and natural gas reserves, the Spratly Islands in the South China Sea have been claimed by China, Vietnam, Taiwan, Malaysia and the Philippines since the Japanese gave up a wartime claim in 1951.

Palestinian control
Mixed control
Israeli settlement block
Israeli settlement
Palestinian settlement
West Bank fence

▲ **Barbed-wire fences** surround a settlement in the Golan Heights.

Republika Srpska
Federacija Bosna i Hercegovina

Occupied by Taiwan
Occupied by Philippines
Occupied by Malaysia
Occupied by China
Occupied by Vietnam

Conflicts and international disputes

Countries contributing troops to coalition force in Iraq

Major active territorial or border disputes

Countries involved in internal conflict

Active territorial or border disputes and internal conflict

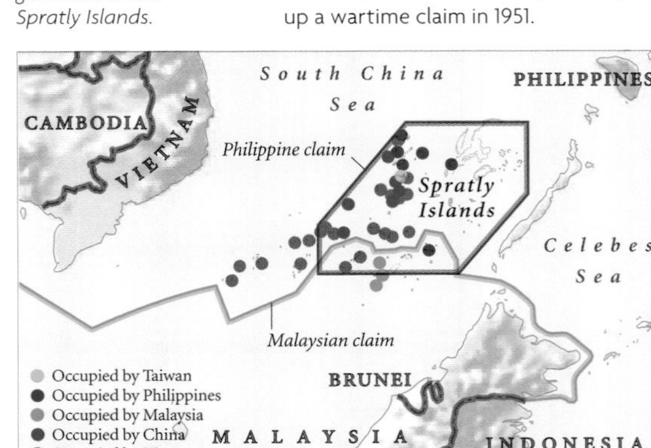

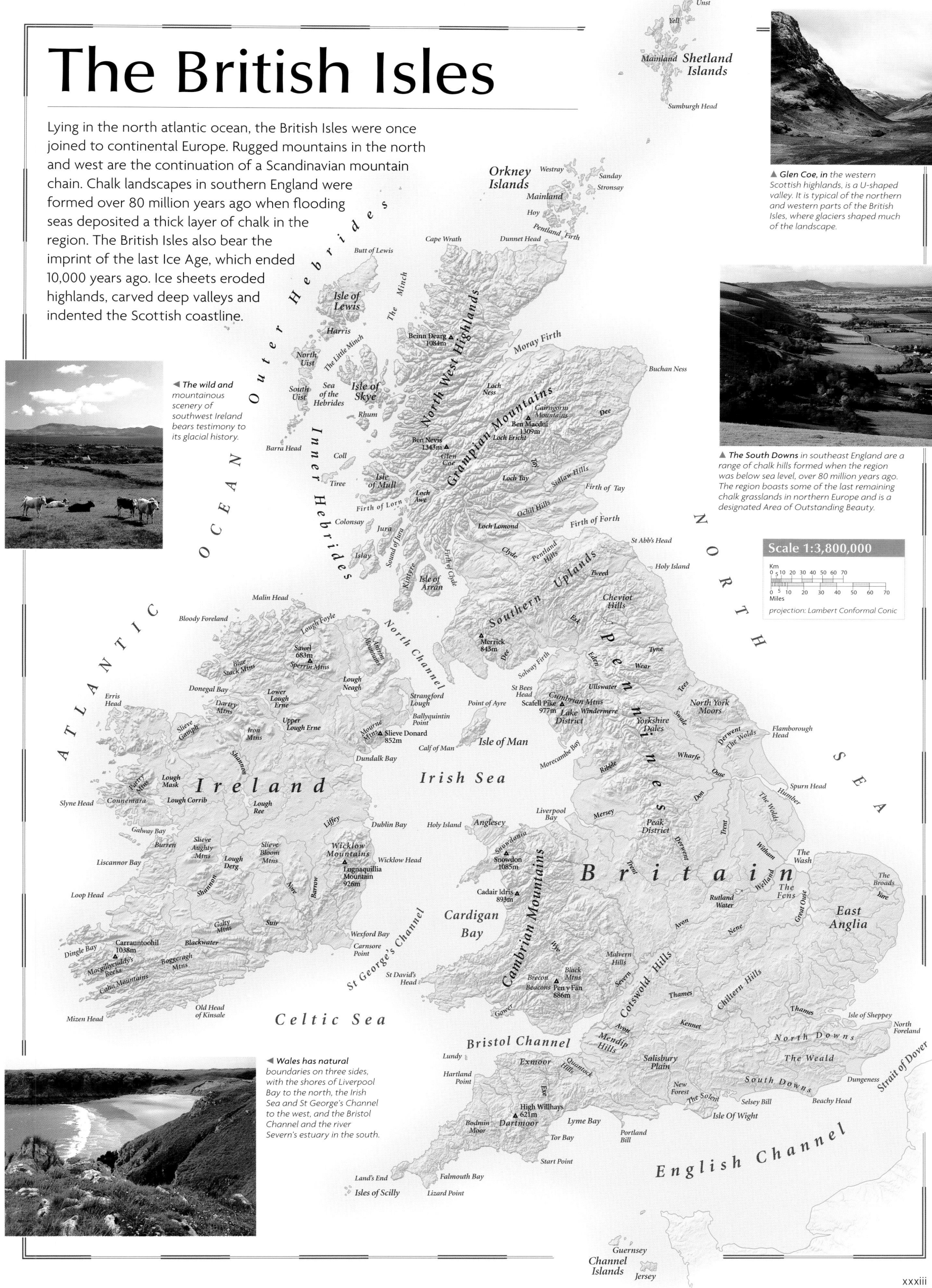

The British Isles

Lying in the north atlantic ocean, the British Isles were once joined to continental Europe. Rugged mountains in the north and west are the continuation of a Scandinavian mountain chain. Chalk landscapes in southern England were formed over 80 million years ago when flooding seas deposited a thick layer of chalk in the region. The British Isles also bear the imprint of the last Ice Age, which ended 10,000 years ago. Ice sheets eroded highlands, carved deep valleys and indented the Scottish coastline.

▲ **Glen Coe, in** the western Scottish highlands, is a U-shaped valley. It is typical of the northern and western parts of the British Isles, where glaciers shaped much of the landscape.

▲ **The South Downs** in southeast England are a range of chalk hills formed when the region was below sea level, over 80 million years ago. The region boasts some of the last remaining chalk grasslands in northern Europe and is a designated Area of Outstanding Beauty.

◀ **The wild and** mountainous scenery of southwest Ireland bears testimony to its glacial history.

◀ **Wales has natural** boundaries on three sides, with the shores of Liverpool Bay to the north, the Irish Sea and St George's Channel to the west, and the Bristol Channel and the river Severn's estuary in the south.

Scale 1:3,800,000

Km
0 5 10 20 30 40 50 60 70

Miles
0 5 10 20 30 40 50 60 70

projection: Lambert Conformal Conic

Political British Isles

The United Kingdom's system of government has evolved over a long period, uninterrupted by any successful foreign invasion since 1066. Democracy takes the form of a constitutional monarchy, in which the monarch is a passive figurehead. The identity of the UK is being challenged by the prospect of a federal Europe, by the establishment of national assemblies in Scotland and Wales and by the introduction of an assembly in Northern Ireland which represents Unionist and Republican views. Ireland grew out of the Irish Free State, established in 1921, and has become an independent democracy with membership of the UN and the EU. The Anglo-Irish Accord of 1985 established a permanent cabinet-level channel for dialogue between Britain and Ireland.

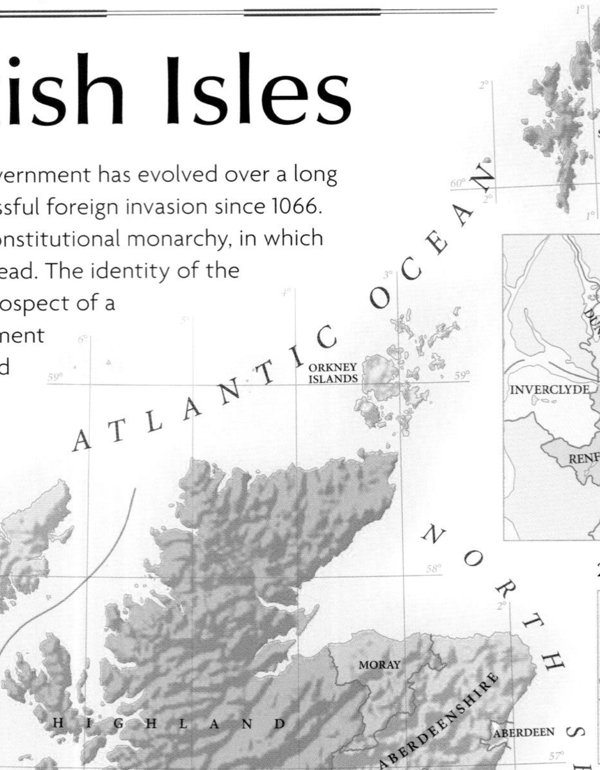

1: Central Scotland

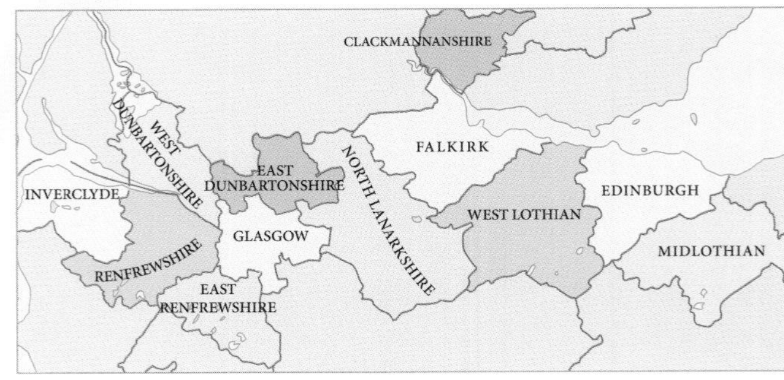

CLACKMANNANSHIRE
WEST DUNBARTONSHIRE
EAST DUNBARTONSHIRE
NORTH LANARKSHIRE
FALKIRK
INVERCLYDE
RENFREWSHIRE
GLASGOW
WEST LOTHIAN
EDINBURGH
EAST RENFREWSHIRE
MIDLOTHIAN

2: The Northeast

NORTH TYNESIDE
NEWCASTLE UPON TYNE
SOUTH TYNESIDE
GATESHEAD
SUNDERLAND

3: Teeside

HARTLEPOOL
STOCKTON-ON-TEES
DARLINGTON
MIDDLESBROUGH
REDCAR AND CLEVELAND

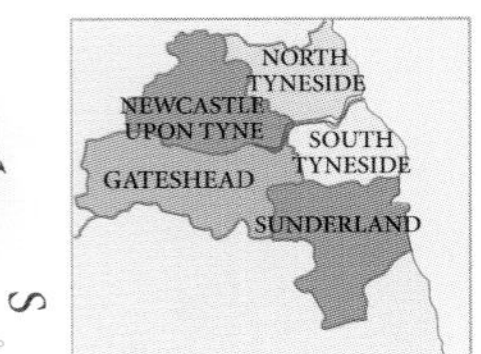

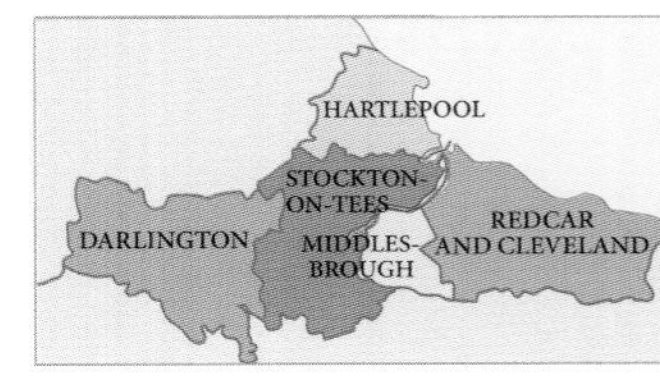

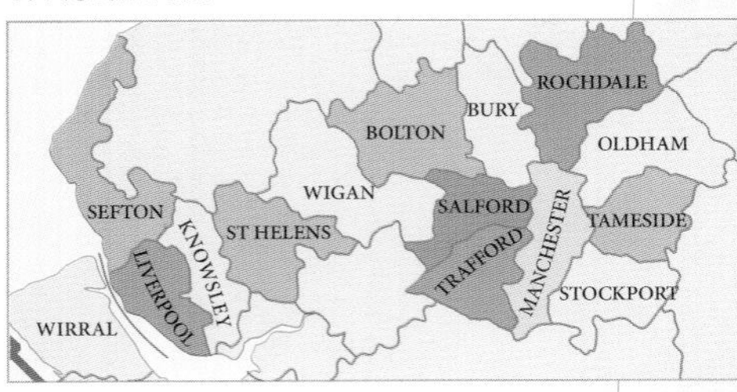

UK Administrative Regions

The UK radically reformed its administrative structure in the mid-1990s. A single-tier system of unitary authorities for local government was introduced for Scotland and Wales and the most densely-populated parts of England. The traditional two-tier system of counties subdivided into districts remains in the more rural parts of England. Northern Ireland has had a system of unitary authorities since 1972, although the county names are still commonly used.

Scale 1:4,200,000

Km
0 5 10 20 30 40 50 60 70 80
Miles
0 5 10 20 30 40 50 60 70 80

projection: Lambert Conformal Conic

4: Northwest

ROCHDALE
BURY
BOLTON
OLDHAM
WIGAN
ST HELENS
SALFORD
TAMESIDE
SEFTON
KNOWSLEY
TRAFFORD
MANCHESTER
STOCKPORT
WIRRAL
LIVERPOOL

Republic of Ireland Administrative Regions

The Republic of Ireland has been divided into 26 counties since independence in 1921. When the six counties of Northern Ireland were included, the island could be divided into the four historic provinces of Ulster, Connaught, Leinster and Munster (see map of Ireland on page xliv), although these have little or no administrative function today.

5: South Wales

BLAENAU GWENT
MERTHYR TYDFIL
TORFAEN
NEATH PORT TALBOT
RHONDDA CYNON TAFF
CAERPHILLY
SWANSEA
NEWPORT
BRIDGEND
CARDIFF
THE VALE OF GLAMORGAN

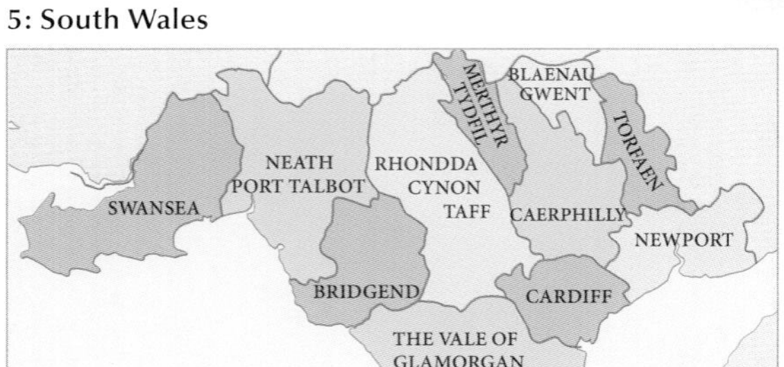

6: The West Midlands

WOLVERHAMPTON
WALSALL
DUDLEY
SANDWELL
BIRMINGHAM
SOLIHULL
COVENTRY

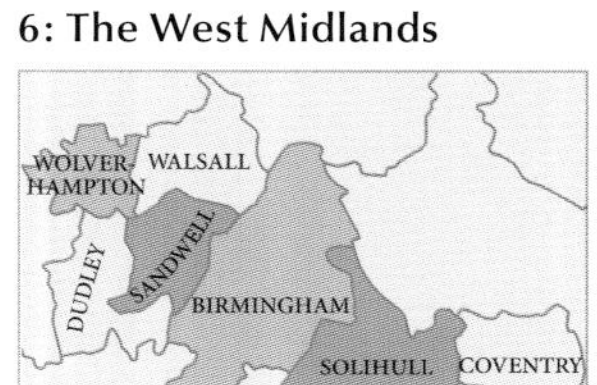

Greater London Administrative Regions

London is divided into 32 boroughs (plus the Corporation of the City of London), which effectively have the same status as other unitary authorities in the UK. Until the Mayor of London elections in 2000, London had not had a directly elected council since the abolition of the Greater London Council (GLC) in 1986.

7: Greater London

ENFIELD
BARNET
HARINGEY
WALTHAM FOREST
REDBRIDGE
HAVERING
HARROW
BRENT
CAMDEN
ISLINGTON
HACKNEY
NEWHAM
BARKING & DAGENHAM
HILLINGDON
EALING
BEXLEY
HOUNSLOW
RICHMOND
MERTON
KINGSTON
SUTTON
CROYDON
BROMLEY
GREENWICH

1. HAMMERSMITH & FULHAM
2. KENSINGTON & CHELSEA
3. WESTMINSTER
4. ISLINGTON
5. HACKNEY
6. CITY OF LONDON
7. TOWER HAMLETS
8. SOUTHWARK
9. WANDSWORTH

Map labels: ATLANTIC OCEAN · NORTH SEA · Irish Sea · Celtic Sea · English Channel · SHETLAND ISLANDS · ORKNEY ISLANDS · WESTERN ISLES · HIGHLAND · SCOTLAND · MORAY · ABERDEENSHIRE · ABERDEEN · PERTH AND KINROSS · ANGUS · DUNDEE · FIFE · STIRLING · ARGYLL AND BUTE · NORTH AYRSHIRE · SOUTH LANARKSHIRE · EAST AYRSHIRE · SCOTTISH BORDERS · SOUTH AYRSHIRE · DUMFRIES AND GALLOWAY · NORTHUMBERLAND · UNITED KINGDOM · CUMBRIA · DURHAM · NORTH YORKSHIRE · ISLE OF MAN (British Crown dependency) · NORTHERN IRELAND · LANCASHIRE · BRADFORD · LEEDS · YORK · EAST RIDING OF YORKSHIRE · KINGSTON UPON HULL · BLACKPOOL · BLACKBURN WITH DARWEN · CALDERDALE · WAKEFIELD · NORTH LINCOLNSHIRE · NORTH EAST LINCOLNSHIRE · KIRKLEES · BARNSLEY · DONCASTER · ROTHERHAM · WARRINGTON · HALTON · SHEFFIELD · CHESHIRE · DERBYSHIRE · ISLE OF ANGLESEY · CONWY · FLINTSHIRE · DENBIGHSHIRE · WREXHAM · STOKE-ON-TRENT · NOTTINGHAM · DERBY · NOTTINGHAMSHIRE · LINCOLNSHIRE · GWYNEDD · TELFORD AND WREKIN · STAFFORDSHIRE · LEICESTERSHIRE · LEICESTER · RUTLAND · NORFOLK · WALES · SHROPSHIRE · ENGLAND · POWYS · WORCESTERSHIRE · WARWICKSHIRE · NORTHAMPTONSHIRE · BEDFORDSHIRE · MILTON KEYNES · PETERBOROUGH · CAMBRIDGESHIRE · SUFFOLK · CEREDIGION · HEREFORDSHIRE · MONMOUTHSHIRE · GLOUCESTERSHIRE · OXFORDSHIRE · BUCKINGHAMSHIRE · LUTON · HERTFORDSHIRE · ESSEX · PEMBROKESHIRE · CARMARTHENSHIRE · SOUTH GLOUCESTERSHIRE · SWINDON · WINDSOR AND MAIDENHEAD · READING · WEST BERKSHIRE · WOKINGHAM · BRACKNELL FOREST · SLOUGH · THURROCK · SOUTHEND-ON-SEA · MEDWAY · BRISTOL · NORTH SOMERSET · BATH AND NORTH EAST SOMERSET · WILTSHIRE · HAMPSHIRE · SURREY · KENT · SOMERSET · SOUTHAMPTON · PORTSMOUTH · WEST SUSSEX · EAST SUSSEX · BRIGHTON AND HOVE · DEVON · DORSET · POOLE · BOURNEMOUTH · ISLE OF WIGHT · CORNWALL · PLYMOUTH · TORBAY · ISLES OF SCILLY · GUERNSEY (British Crown dependency) · JERSEY (British Crown dependency)

Ireland labels: IRELAND · DONEGAL · LONDONDERRY · MOYLE · BALLYMONEY · COLERAINE · LIMAVADY · LARNE · STRABANE · MAGHERAFELT · ANTRIM · CARRICKFERGUS · NEWTOWNABBEY · NORTH DOWN · OMAGH · COOKSTOWN · BELFAST · CASTLEREAGH · ARDS · DUNGANNON · CRAIGAVON · LISBURN · FERMANAGH · ARMAGH · BANBRIDGE · DOWN · MONAGHAN · NEWRY AND MOURNE · SLIGO · LEITRIM · CAVAN · LOUTH · MAYO · ROSCOMMON · LONGFORD · WESTMEATH · MEATH · GALWAY · OFFALY · KILDARE · DUBLIN · CLARE · LAOIS · WICKLOW · CARLOW · LIMERICK · TIPPERARY · KILKENNY · WEXFORD · KERRY · WATERFORD · CORK

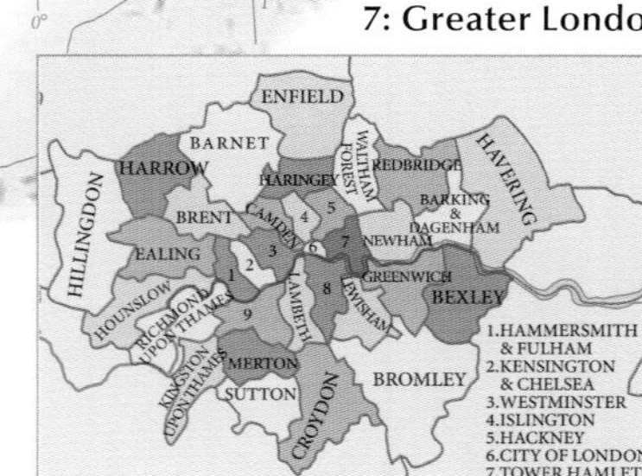

Wales

The ancient Cambrian mountains form the backbone of this green, mountainous country, which has been a stronghold of Celtic culture for about 3000 years. Wales had been incorporated with England from 1535 until a pro-devolution majority vote in a referendum in 1997. Over one-fifth of the people speak Welsh, a Celtic language with a rich poetic tradition. About 60 per cent of the country's 2.8 million population live in the south or extreme northeast. The old coal-based industries that transformed these areas last century have since given way to a service-led economy.

Transport and Industry

The mining industries, particularly slate and coal, have declined greatly this century. Factories in South Wales are served by deepwater ports such as Milford Haven, which has a large oil refinery and steel works. Electronics and light manufacturing industries, supported by government incentives, have grown rapidly in the south and also in central rural areas.

◀ *Snowdonia National Park* contains Snowdon, the highest mountain in England and Wales. The park is renowned for its jagged peaks and deep valleys, eroded by glaciers during the last Ice Age.

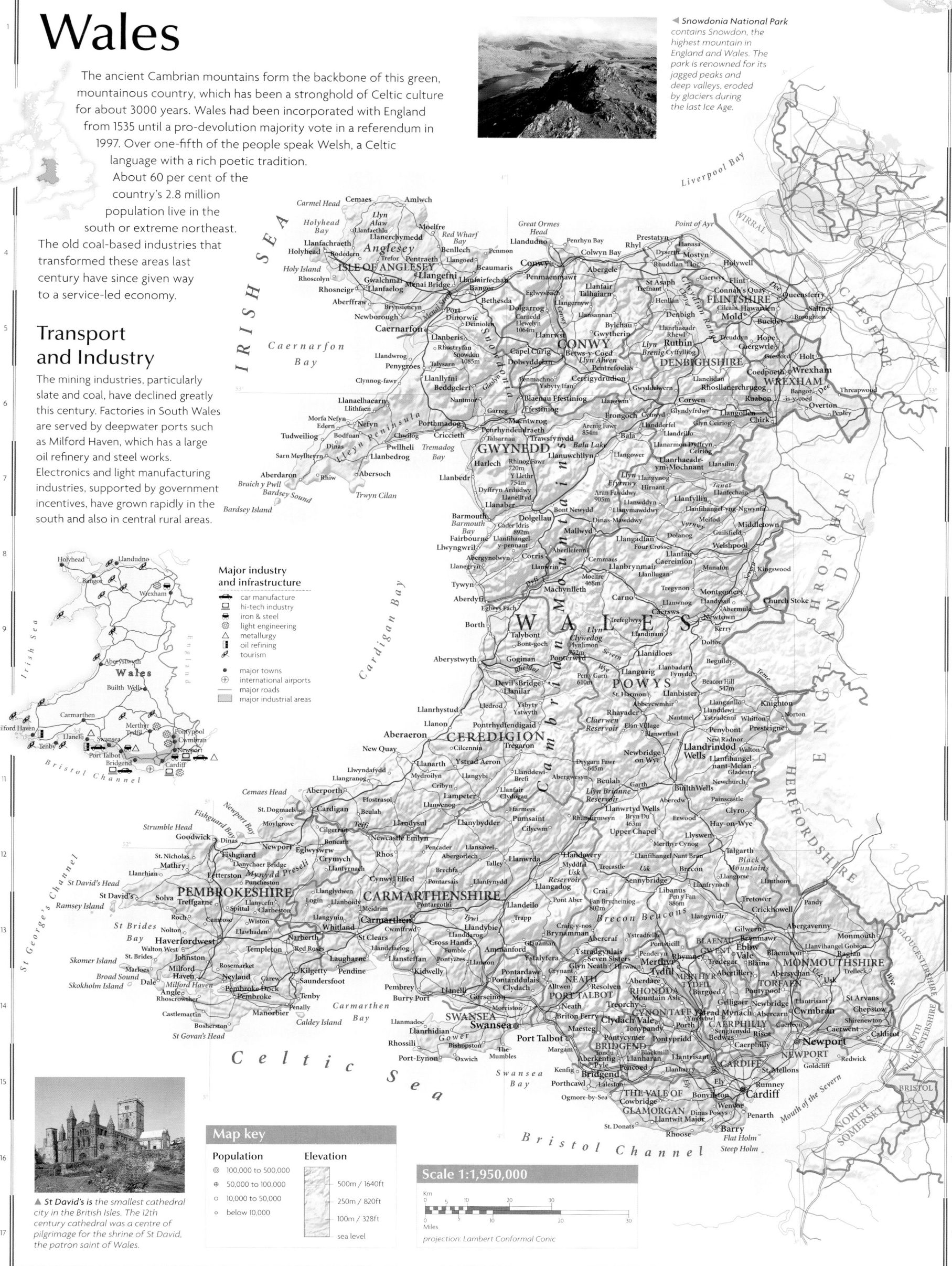

Major industry and infrastructure
- car manufacture
- hi-tech industry
- iron & steel
- light engineering
- metallurgy
- oil refining
- tourism
- • major towns
- ⊕ international airports
- major roads
- major industrial areas

▲ *St David's is* the smallest cathedral city in the British Isles. The 12th century cathedral was a centre of pilgrimage for the shrine of St David, the patron saint of Wales.

Map key

Population
- ◎ 100,000 to 500,000
- ⊕ 50,000 to 100,000
- ○ 10,000 to 50,000
- ○ below 10,000

Elevation
- 500m / 1640ft
- 250m / 820ft
- 100m / 328ft
- sea level

Scale 1:1,950,000

projection: Lambert Conformal Conic

A B C D E F G H I J K L M

Southern England

Southern England is the most affluent part of the British Isles, benefiting from close proximity to Europe, fertile agricultural land, and the capital, London, as a focus of wealth, political power and population. The physical landscape varies dramatically from the bleak uplands of the southwestern Cornish peninsula through the rolling Cotswold Hills to the flat, often marshy, expanses of Essex. The southeast of England is the most densely populated region of the UK, and the growth of industries such as communications and financial services since the 1980s, has put considerable strain on transport and housing provision, with the building of new infrastructure becoming an issue of political controversy in the 1990s.

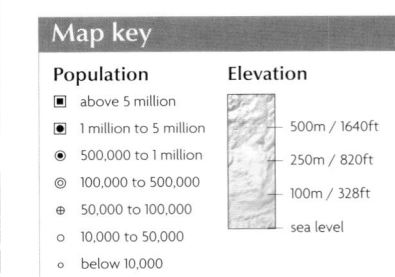

◀ *The city of* Bath is built on the site of the Roman spa, Aquae Sulis. It is one of the most architecturally distinguished of British cities, noted for its elegant Georgian crescents built from the distinctive honey-coloured local stone.

Map key

Population

- ■ above 5 million
- ◩ 1 million to 5 million
- ◉ 500,000 to 1 million
- ◎ 100,000 to 500,000
- ⊕ 50,000 to 100,000
- ⊕ 10,000 to 50,000
- ○ below 10,000

Elevation

- 500m / 1640ft
- 250m / 820ft
- 100m / 328ft
- sea level

▲ *Clifton Suspension Bridge,* which spans the Avon Gorge, was designed by the great Victorian engineer, Isambard Kingdom Brunel and completed in 1864. It served as an important transport link for Bristol's then growing import and export trade in meat, tobacco and fruit.

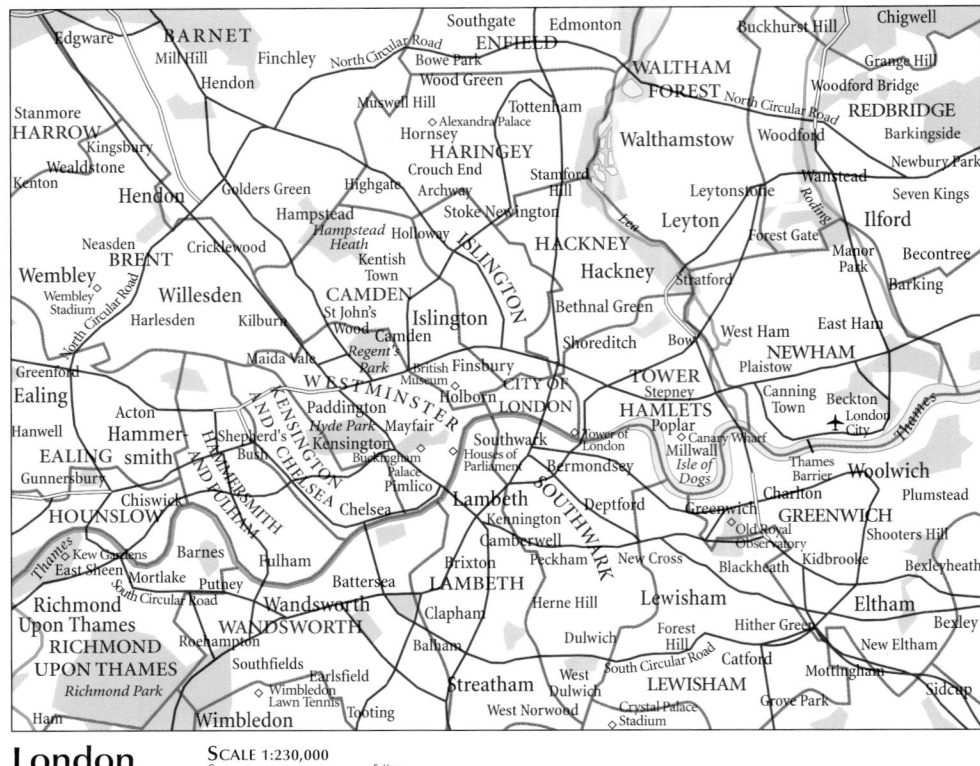

London

SCALE 1:230,000

0   5 Km
0   5 Miles

▲ *The cliffs of* north Devon bear the full force of the Atlantic Ocean. The entire British land mass is gradually tilting, with uplift continuing on the west coast, while the east faces the increasing threat of flooding by the sea.

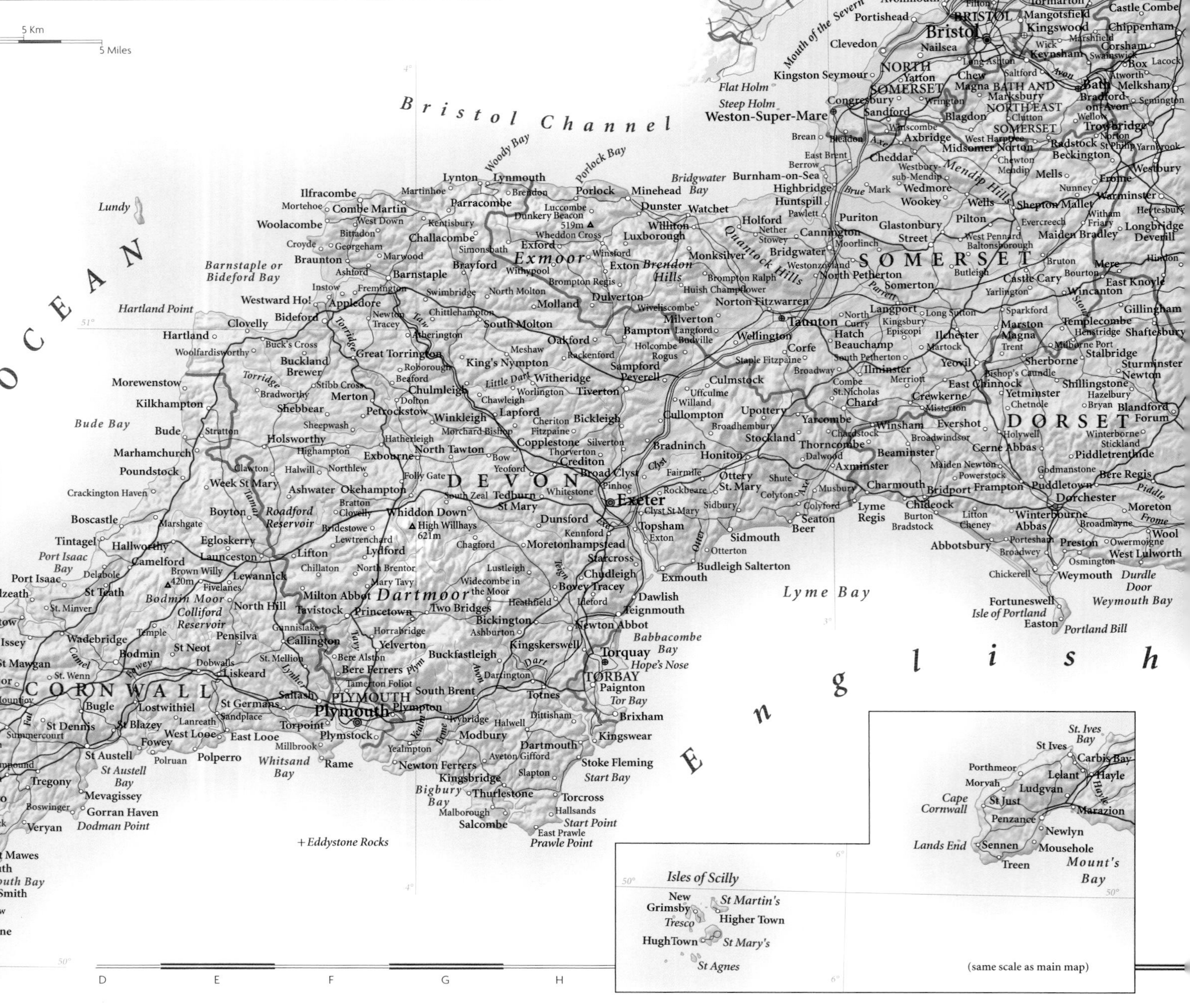

(same scale as main map)

Transport and industry

Throughout the southeast, service industries are growing, most notably in the areas of tourism, business support and retailing. At the heart of the capital, the City of London is one of the world's leading financial centres. In contrast to the flourishing service sector, engineering industries such as aerospace and car manufacture have faced long-term decline. Lightweight manufacturing industries such as pharmaceuticals and electronics are expanding around cities and along major transport corridors such as the M4. The southwest remains far less industrialized.

▲ *The luxury homes* and offices at Canary Wharf are part of the Docklands development project, an attempt to revitalize east London following the decline of the dockyards and provide space for the expansion of the City of London.

Major industry and infrastructure

- ✈ aerospace
- 🚗 car manufacture
- ⚗ chemicals
- ⚙ engineering
- Ⓢ finance
- 🏭 food processing
- 🖥 hi-tech industry
- ⚙ light engineering
- 🖨 printing & publishing
- ✎ tourism
- ■ capital cities
- • major towns
- ✈ international airports
- — major roads
- ▨ major industrial areas

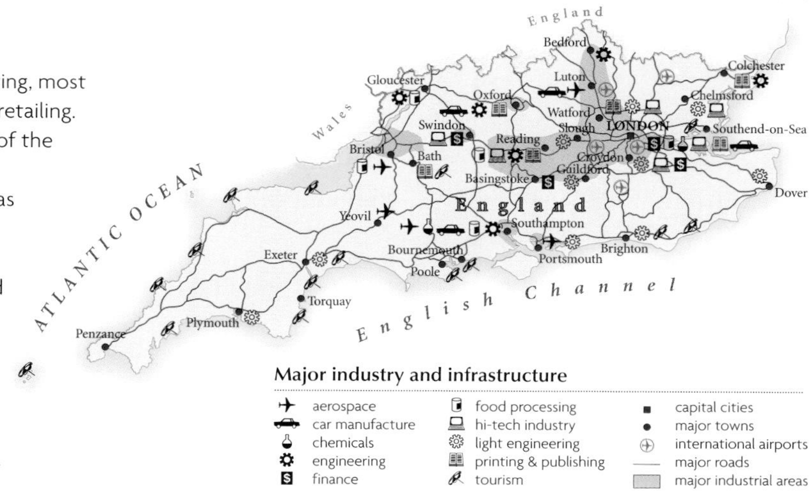

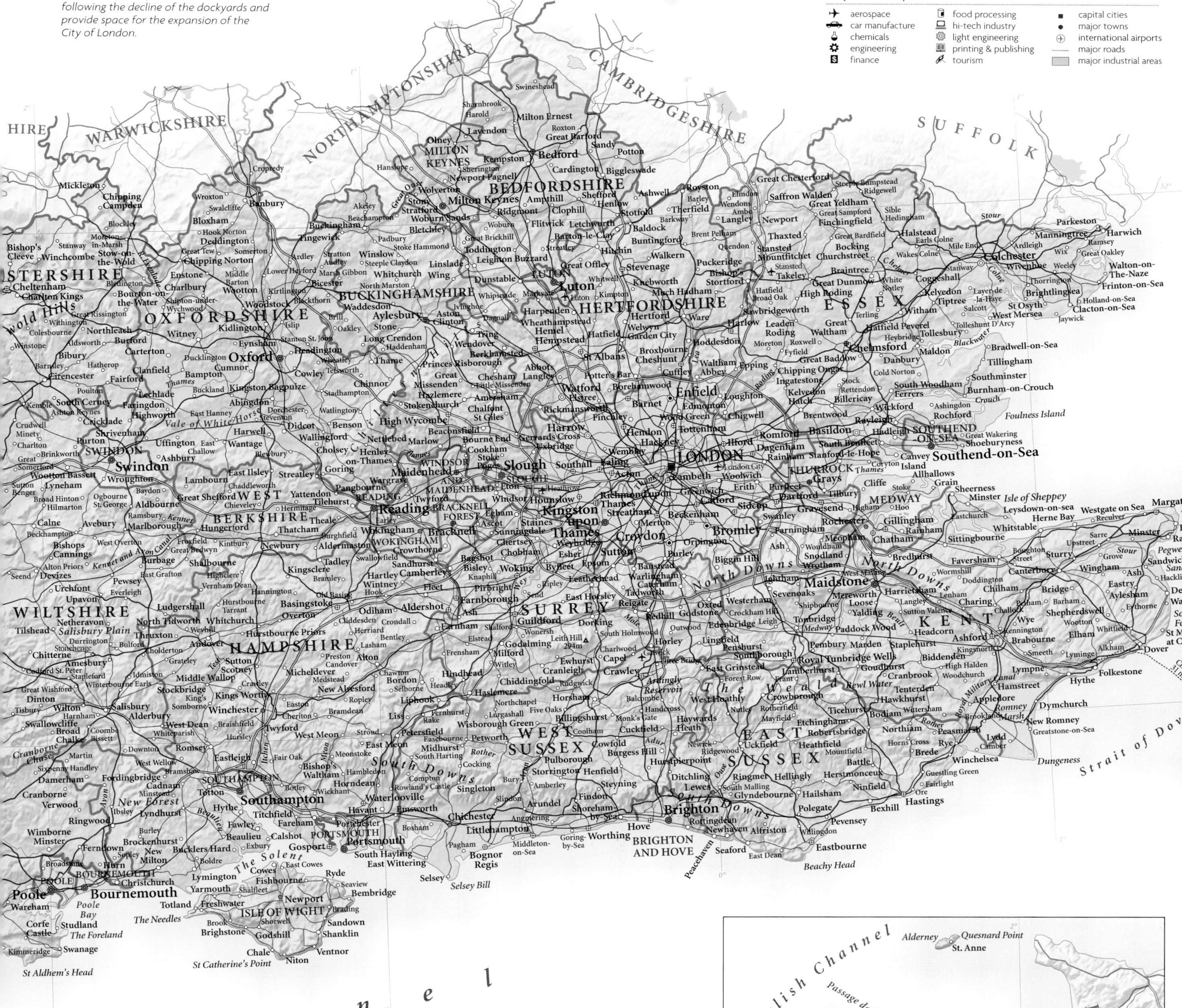

▲ *Leeds Castle, near* Maidstone, is one of a number of important castles in the southeast. First started in the 12th century, the castle has been inhabited continuously, and has been extended and rebuilt countless times.

Scale 1:1,000,000

projection: Lambert Conformal Conic

CHANNEL ISLANDS (to UK)

(same scale as main map)

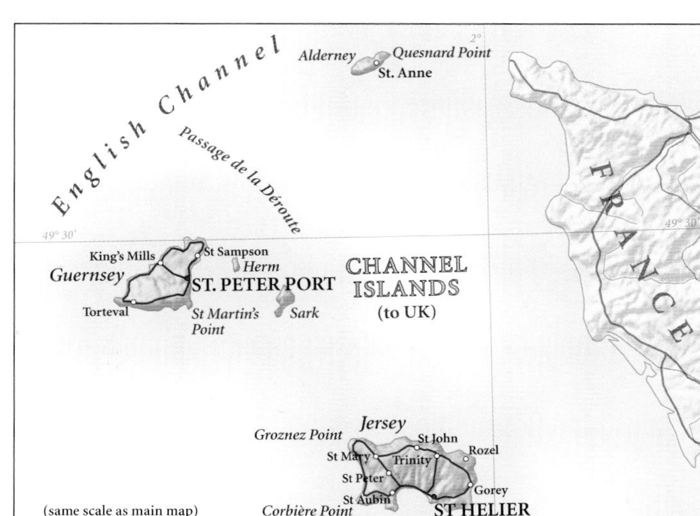

Central England

The industrial regions around Birmingham, Coventry and the Potteries of Stoke-on-Trent, the dramatic hills of the Derbyshire's Peak District, and the windy fenlands of Lincolnshire and Norfolk, all illustrate the great diversity of England's central counties. Many of the most important developments of the Industrial Revolution occurred in this area, including the construction of the canal system. The traditional industrial heartland remains the most populous part of this region with far lower densities in East Anglia, although counties such as Cambridgeshire have recently seen large influxes of people from the crowded southeast.

Transport and Industry

The mass production of iron and steel, ceramics and textiles was important in this region from the end of the 18th century onwards. This great industrial base provided an ideal location for automotive manufacturing throughout much of the 20th century, particularly around Coventry and Birmingham. In recent years, the growth of hi-tech and service industries, particularly in and around Cambridge, has attracted new investment, while agriculture remains important in both Hereford and the East Anglian counties.

Major industry and infrastructure

✈ aerospace	🏭 food processing	● major towns
🍺 brewing	🖥 hi-tech industry	🛫 international airports
🚗 car manufacture	△ metallurgy	— major roads
⚙ ceramics	🖨 printing & publishing	▨ major industrial areas
⚗ chemicals	▦ textiles	
⚙ engineering		
🐟 fish processing		

The West Midlands

SCALE 1:560,000

Scale 1:9,000,000

projection: Lambert Conformal Conic

One of the most important developments of the Industrial Revolution took place at Ironbridge. In 1709, Abraham Darby I discovered how to smelt iron ore using local coke, rather than charcoal, of which there was a shortage. This paved the way for the mass production of iron, used for bridges, ships and buildings.

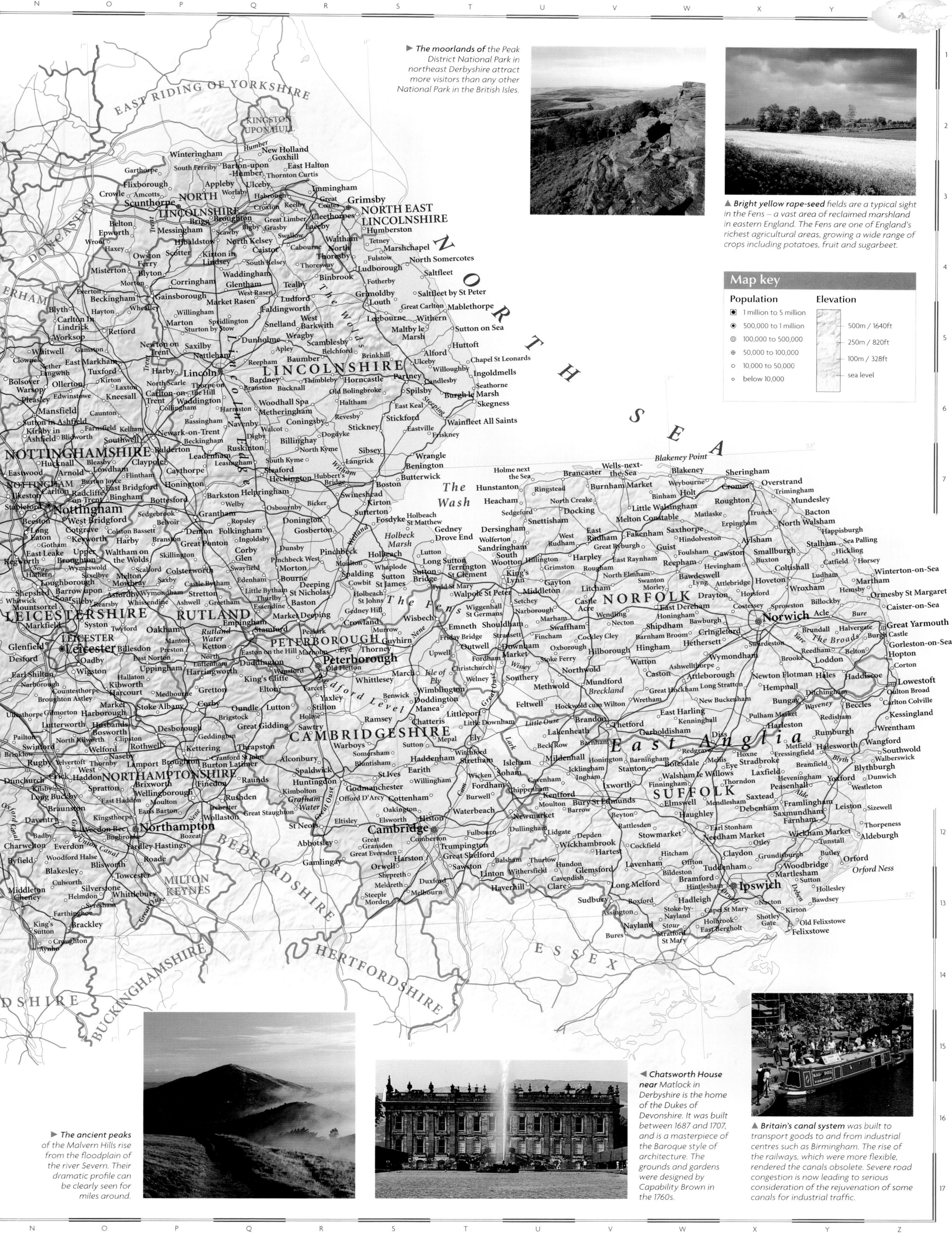

▶ The moorlands of the Peak District National Park in northeast Derbyshire attract more visitors than any other National Park in the British Isles.

▲ Bright yellow rape-seed fields are a typical sight in the Fens – a vast area of reclaimed marshland in eastern England. The Fens are one of England's richest agricultural areas, growing a wide range of crops including potatoes, fruit and sugarbeet.

Map key

Population

- ◉ 1 million to 5 million
- ◉ 500,000 to 1 million
- ◉ 100,000 to 500,000
- ⊕ 50,000 to 100,000
- ○ 10,000 to 50,000
- ○ below 10,000

Elevation

- 500m / 1640ft
- 250m / 820ft
- 100m / 328ft
- sea level

▶ The ancient peaks of the Malvern Hills rise from the floodplain of the river Severn. Their dramatic profile can be clearly seen for miles around.

◀ Chatsworth House near Matlock in Derbyshire is the home of the Dukes of Devonshire. It was built between 1687 and 1707, and is a masterpiece of the Baroque style of architecture. The grounds and gardens were designed by Capability Brown in the 1760s.

▲ Britain's canal system was built to transport goods to and from industrial centres such as Birmingham. The rise of the railways, which were more flexible, rendered the canals obsolete. Severe road congestion is now leading to serious consideration of the rejuvenation of some canals for industrial traffic.

Northern England

The dramatic Pennine range provides a central upland spine for northern England's fine and varied landscape, flanked to the west by the famous Lake District. The modern world's first industrial cities, including Manchester, Sheffield and Bradford, rose to greatness across this region from the mid 18th century, fuelled by local coal fields, with each specializing in particular trades including textiles, metal products and shipbuilding. The decline of manufacturing – particularly in the heavy industries – in the 20th century hit northern England hard, leading to prolonged economic depression. However, following major economic restructuring in the late 1980s, the north has been highly successful in attracting foreign investment. The great industrial cities such as Manchester, Liverpool, Leeds and Newcastle have maintained their position at the centre of northern England's cultural and economic life.

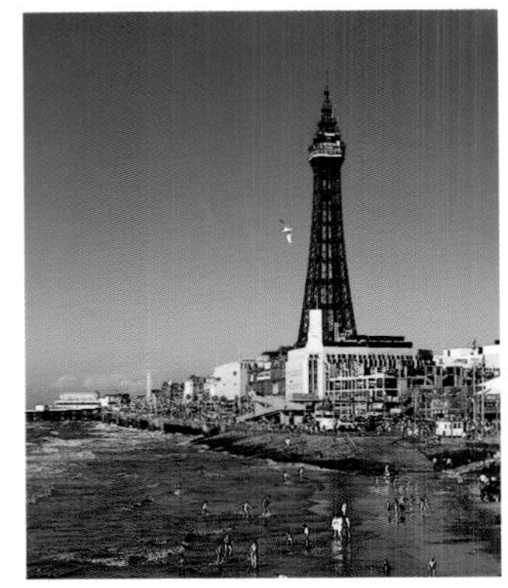

◀ *Blackpool's famous tower,* built in 1895, stands as a testament to the rise of the tourist industry in late 19th century Britain, as workers from the nearby Lancashire cotton mills and Yorkshire woollen mills flocked to the town on their annual holidays. Blackpool remains a popular tourist resort today.

Transport and Industry

Once the centre of heavy manufacturing, service industries now dominate the northern economy, following a difficult period of transition. Massive inward investment by multinational companies has helped northern England retain a majority share of current manufacturing activity in the UK. New light engineering and car production plants have developed in and around the region's cities, alongside more traditional industries such as iron and steel, and textiles.

Scale 1:9,000,000

Km
0   5   10   20   30

Miles
0   10   20   30

projection: Lambert Conformal Conic

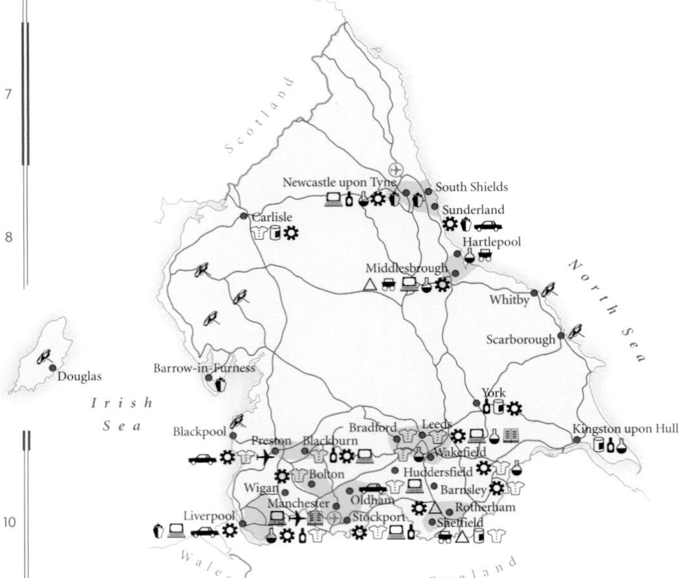

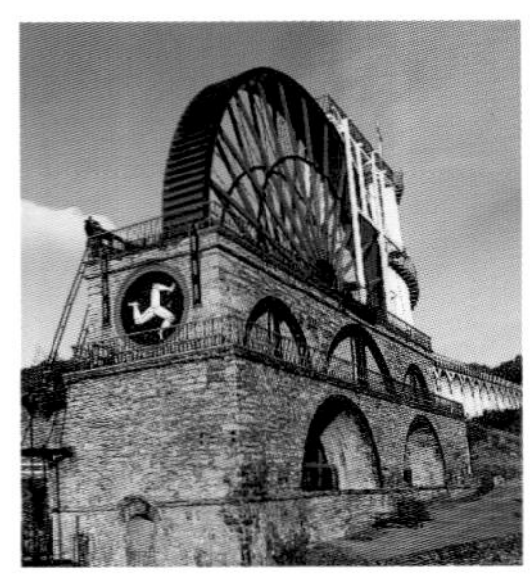

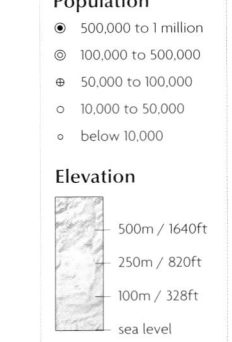

▲ *The Laxey Wheel* on the Isle of Man – 72 ft (22 m) high is the largest waterwheel in the world. During the 19th century it was used to pump water from the nearby iron ore mines. The 'Three Legs of Man' on the front of the wheel is an ancient symbol, first thought to have been used by the Vikings.

Map key

Population
- ◉ 500,000 to 1 million
- ◎ 100,000 to 500,000
- ⊕ 50,000 to 100,000
- ○ 10,000 to 50,000
- ○ below 10,000

Elevation
- 500m / 1640ft
- 250m / 820ft
- 100m / 328ft
- sea level

Major industry and infrastructure

✈ aerospace	⚒ iron & steel	● major towns
🍺 brewing	⚙ metallurgy	⊕ international airports
🚗 car manufacture	🖨 printing & publishing	— major roads
⚗ chemicals	⚓ shipbuilding	major industrial areas
⚙ engineering	⚞ textiles	
🍴 food processing	✎ tourism	
💻 hi-tech industry		

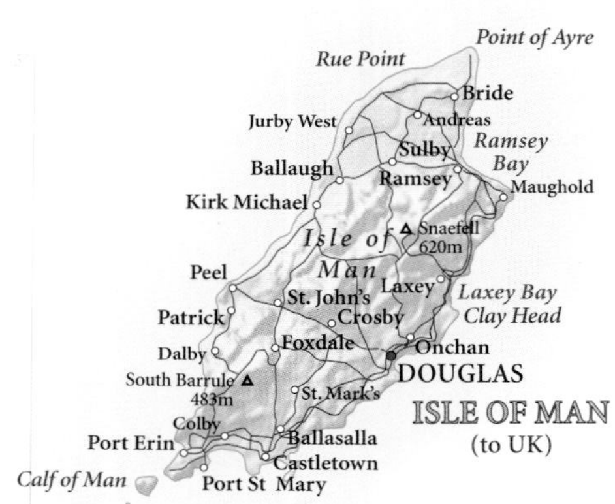

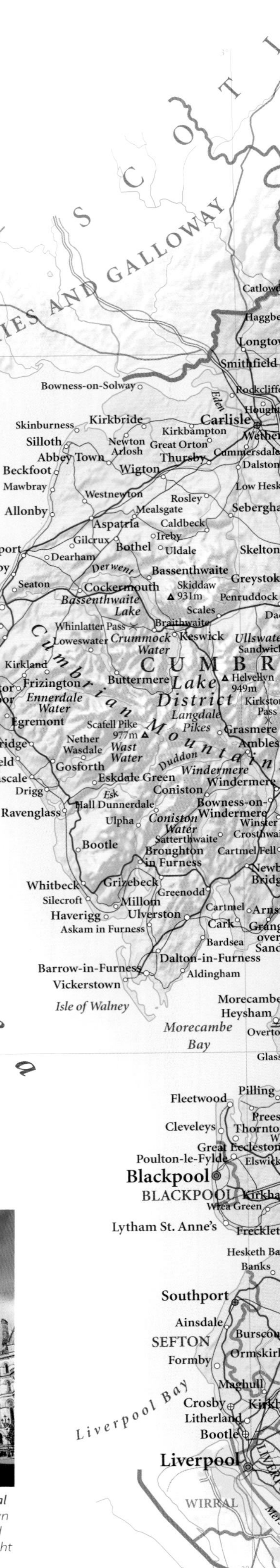

The Northwest

SCALE 1:560,000

0   5   10 Km
0   5   10 Miles

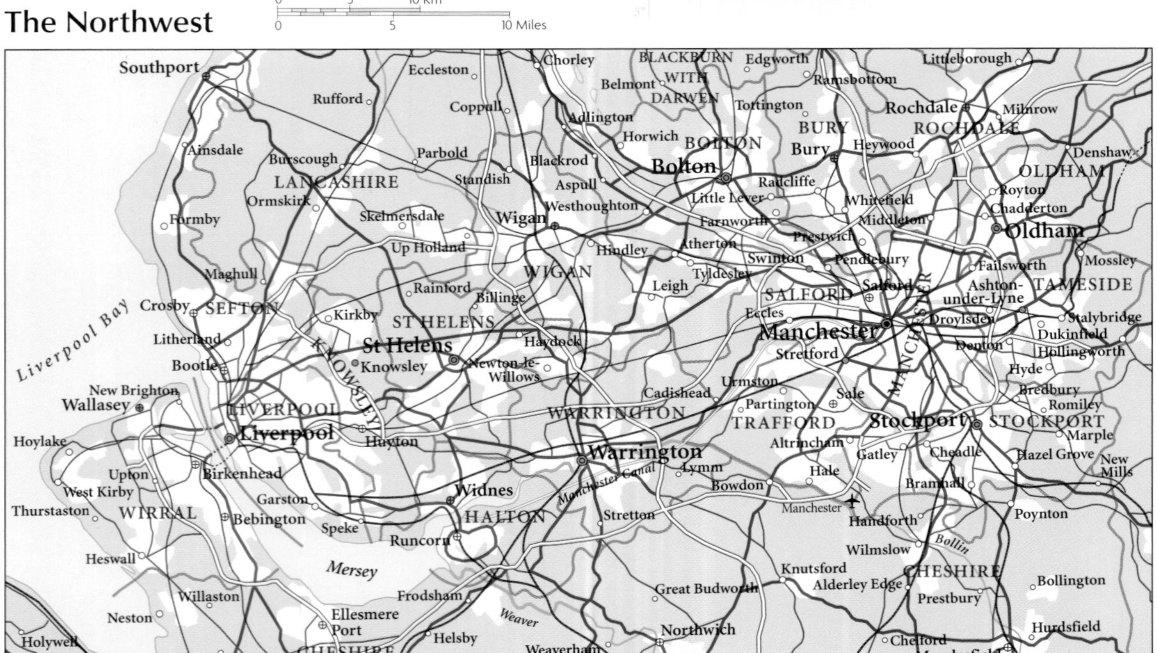

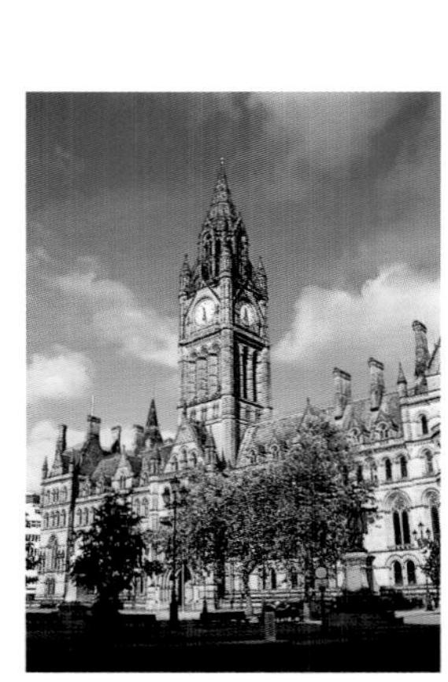

▲ *The spectacular gothic-revival architecture of Manchester Town Hall recalls the great wealth and civic pride of the city at the height of the Industrial Revolution.*

The Northeast

SCALE 1:560,000

0   5   10 Km
0   5   10 Miles

NORTH SEA

SCOTTISH BORDERS

NORTHUMBERLAND

Berwick-upon-Tweed
Tweedmouth
Norham
Ancroft
Duddo
Lowick
Beal
Crookham
Ford
Fenwick
Milfield
Belford
Bamburgh
Holy Island
Seahouses
North Sunderland
Beadnell
Embleton
Dunstan
Howick
Longhoughton
Alnmouth
Shilbottle
Amble
Broomhill
Acklington
Widdrington
The Scars
Druridge Bay
Newbiggin-by-the-Sea

△ The Cheviot 816m

Cheviot Hills

Kielder Forest
Kielder Water

Alnwick
Rothbury
Longframlington
Felton

P e n n i n e s

DURHAM
Durham

Newcastle upon Tyne
NEWCASTLE UPON TYNE
Gateshead
GATESHEAD
Sunderland
SUNDERLAND
NORTH TYNESIDE
SOUTH TYNESIDE
South Shields
Tynemouth
Whitley Bay

Hadrian's Wall
Hexham
Corbridge
Consett
Chester-le-Street
Hetton-le-Hole
Peterlee
Seaham

Hartlepool
HARTLEPOOL
Hartlepool Bay
Seaton Carew
Tees Bay

REDCAR AND CLEVELAND
Redcar
Middlesbrough
MIDDLESBROUGH
Saltburn-by-the-Sea
Whitby
Robin Hood's Bay
Ravenscar
Scarborough

DARLINGTON
Darlington
STOCKTON-ON-TEES
Stockton-on-Tees
Billingham
Northallerton

North York Moors
Cleveland Hills

NORTH YORKSHIRE
York
YORK

Yorkshire Dales

Richmond
Catterick
Leyburn
Ripon
Harrogate
Knaresborough
Skipton

LANCASHIRE
Preston
Blackburn
BLACKBURN WITH DARWEN

BRADFORD
Bradford
LEEDS
Leeds
Halifax
CALDERDALE
Huddersfield
KIRKLEES
Wakefield
WAKEFIELD
ROCHDALE
OLDHAM
Oldham
BOLTON
Bolton
BURY
Bury
MANCHESTER
Manchester
Stockport
STOCKPORT
TAMESIDE
TRAFFORD
SALFORD
St Helens
ST HELENS
WIGAN
Wigan

Sheffield
SHEFFIELD
ROTHERHAM
Rotherham
Barnsley
BARNSLEY
DONCASTER
Doncaster

EAST RIDING OF YORKSHIRE
Beverley
Kingston upon Hull
KINGSTON UPON HULL
Bridlington
Flamborough Head
Filey
Filey Bay
Bridlington Bay
Driffield
Spurn Head

NORTH LINCOLNSHIRE
NOTTINGHAMSHIRE
DERBYSHIRE
CHESHIRE
WARRINGTON
HALTON

The Northeast (inset)
Belsay
Milbourne
Ponteland
Cramlington
Seaton Delaval
Whitley Bay
NORTHUMBERLAND
Blyth
NORTH TYNESIDE
Tynemouth
North Shields
Newcastle upon Tyne
NEWCASTLE UPON TYNE
Gosforth
Wallsend
Jarrow
South Shields
SOUTH TYNESIDE
Gateshead
GATESHEAD
Whitburn
Boldon
SUNDERLAND
Sunderland
Washington
Chester-le-Street
Houghton-le-Spring
Murton
Seaham
Ryhope
Consett
Durham
Stanley
Sacriston
Sherburn
Easington
Easington Colliery
Horden
Peterlee
Wheatley Hill
Wingate
Bishop Auckland
Spennymoor
Ferryhill
Sedgefield
Trimdon
Trimdon Colliery
Hart
Hartlepool
HARTLEPOOL
Hartlepool Bay
Seaton Carew
Tees Bay
Wolviston
STOCKTON-ON-TEES
Billingham
Stockton-on-Tees
Thornaby on Tees
DARLINGTON
Darlington
Piercebridge
Newton Aycliffe
Shildon
REDCAR AND CLEVELAND
Redcar
Marske-by-the-Sea
South Bank
Ormesby
MIDDLESBROUGH
Middlesbrough
Eston
Guisborough

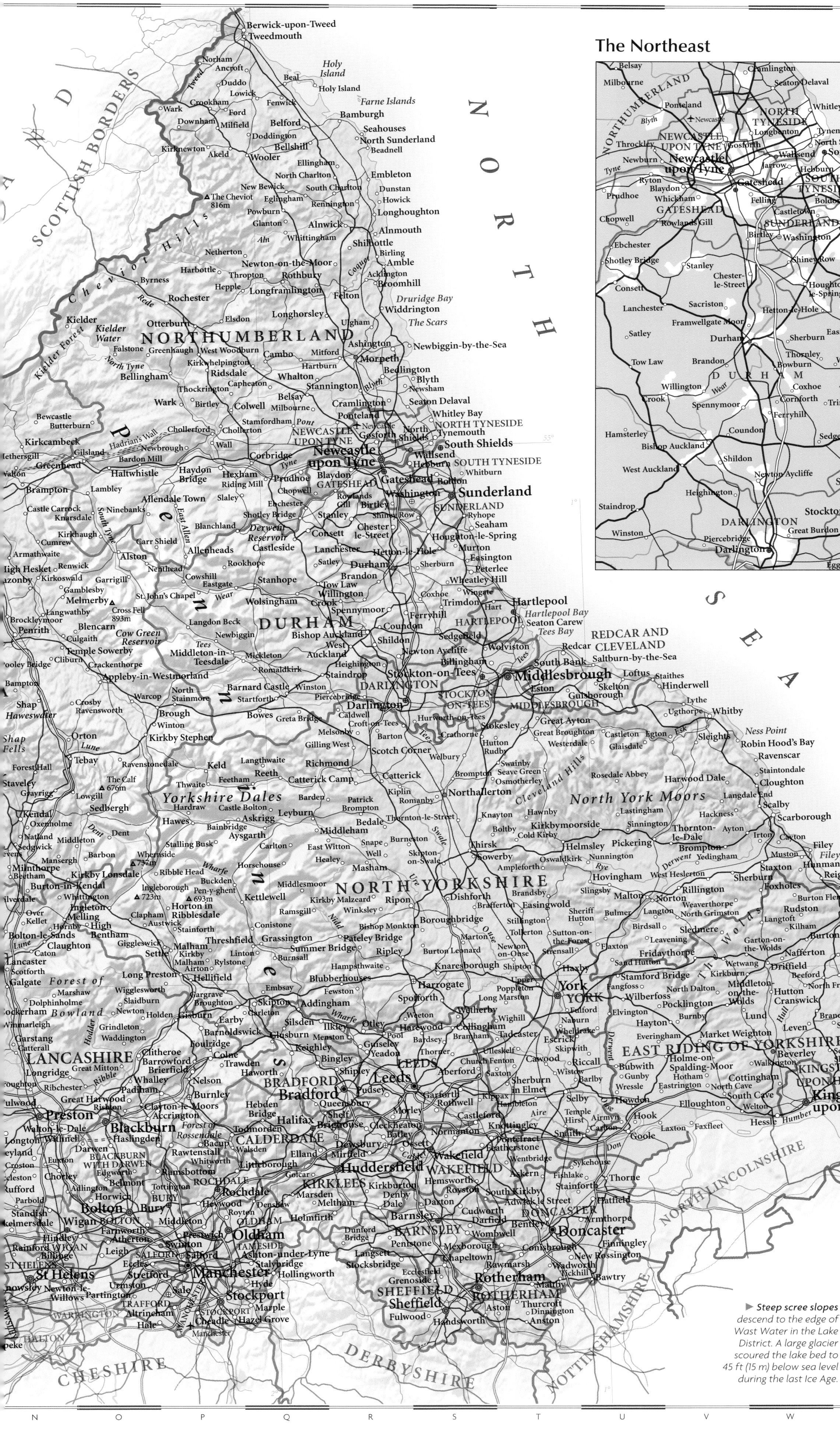

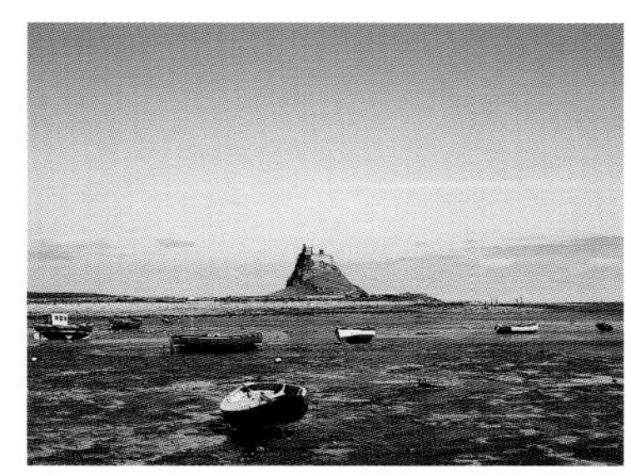

▲ *At low tide*, Holy Island – or Lindisfarne – becomes linked to Northumberland by a rocky causeway. Lindisfarne is famous for its monastery, which was founded in ad 635, and also the beautifully illustrated Lindisfarne Gospels, which were written there.

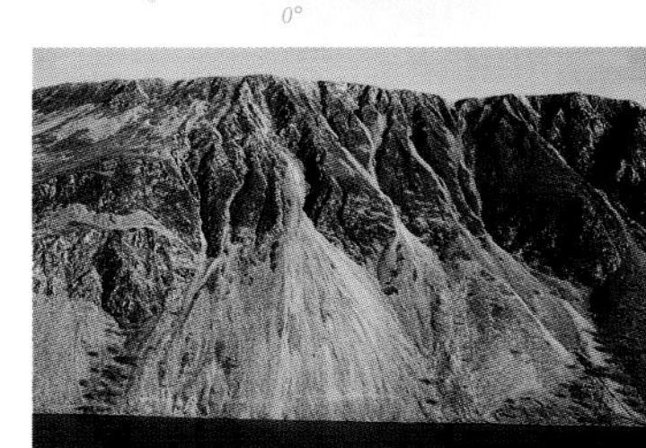

▶ *Steep scree slopes* descend to the edge of Wast Water in the Lake District. A large glacier scoured the lake bed to 45 ft (15 m) below sea level during the last Ice Age.

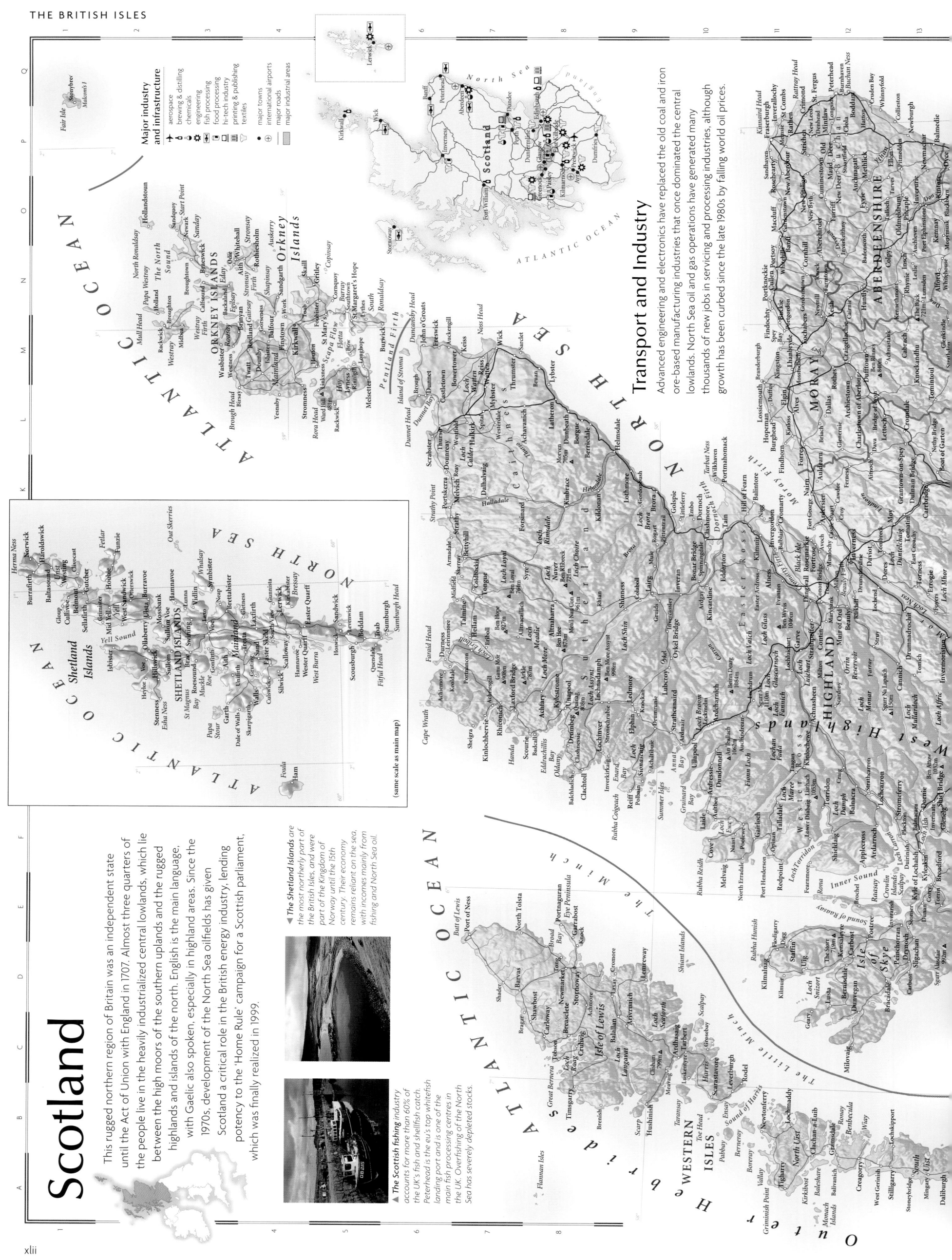

Scotland

This rugged northern region of Britain was an independent state until the Act of Union with England in 1707. Almost three quarters of the people live in the heavily industrialized central lowlands, which lie between the high moors of the southern uplands and the rugged highlands and islands of the north. English is the main language, with Gaelic also spoken, especially in highland areas. Since the 1970s, development of the North Sea oilfields has given Scotland a critical role in the British energy industry, lending potency to the 'Home Rule' campaign for a Scottish parliament, which was finally realized in 1999.

▼ *The Shetland Islands* are the most northerly part of the British Isles, and were part of the Kingdom of Norway until the 15th century. Their economy remains reliant on the sea, with incomes mainly from fishing and North Sea oil.

▲ *The Scottish fishing* industry accounts for more than 60% of the UK's fish and shellfish catch. Peterhead is the eu's top whitefish landing port and is one of the main fish processing centres in the U.K. Overfishing of the North Sea has severely depleted stocks.

Transport and Industry

Advanced engineering and electronics have replaced the old coal and iron ore-based manufacturing industries that once dominated the central lowlands. North Sea oil and gas operations have generated many thousands of new jobs in servicing and processing industries, although growth has been curbed since the late 1980s by falling world oil prices.

Major industry and infrastructure
- aerospace
- brewing & distilling
- chemicals
- engineering
- fish processing
- food processing
- hi-tech industry
- printing & publishing
- textiles
- major towns
- international airports
- major roads
- major industrial areas

(same scale as main map)

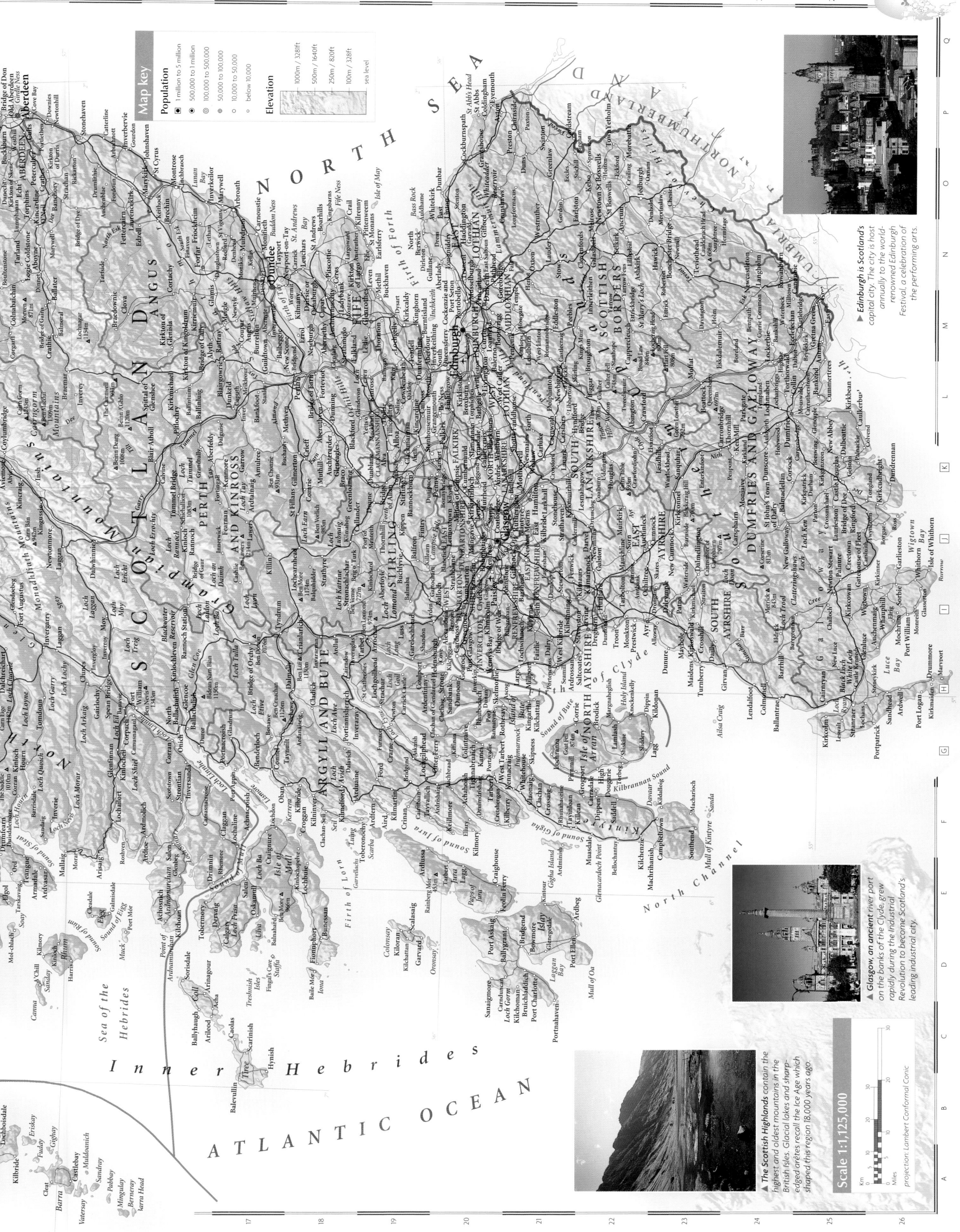

▲ Edinburgh is Scotland's capital city. The city is host annually to the world-renowned Edinburgh Festival, a celebration of the performing arts.

▲ Glasgow, an ancient river port on the banks of the Clyde, grew rapidly during the Industrial Revolution to become Scotland's leading industrial city.

▲ The Scottish Highlands contain the highest and oldest mountains in the British Isles. Glacial lakes and sharp-edged arêtes recall the Ice Age which shaped this region 18,000 years ago.

Scale 1:1,125,000

projection: Lambert Conformal Conic

Ireland

The unspoilt scenery and folk culture of Ireland reflect its remote position on the western fringe of Europe, and contrast with the so-called 'troubles' which have long hindered its development. Ireland emerged from British rule as a free state in 1921 and is separated from Northern Ireland by the UK's only land border. Coastal hill ranges encircle a central undulating plain, strewn with many lakes and bogs. Ireland has benefited from EU grants since the 1980s, which have contributed to the growth of industry and infrastructure.

Map key

Population

- ◉ 100,000 to 500,000
- ⊕ 50,000 to 100,000
- ○ 10,000 to 50,000
- ○ below 10,000

Elevation

- 500m / 1640ft
- 250m / 820ft
- 100m / 328ft
- sea level

▲ The Campanile in Trinity College, Dublin, was built by Sir Charles Lanyon, architect of Queen's College, Belfast. It is 98 ft (30 m) high.

▶ The Burren is a massive limestone plateau in the northwest of County Clare. A wide range of Mediterranean and Alpine plants flourish in the pastures, near shallow lakes and in the cracks in the limestone pavement.

Transport and Industry

Northern Ireland's industries are concentrated in Belfast, once a great textiles and shipbuilding centre which has faced chronic recession since the 1970s. Industrialization in Ireland began properly in the 1950s. A broad range of goods are now produced for export near Dublin, and in many other larger towns.

Scale 1:1,600,000

Km
0 5 10   20   30   40   50

Miles
0 5 10   20   30   40   50

projection: Lambert Conformal Conic

Major industry and infrastructure

- ✈ aerospace
- brewing
- chemicals
- engineering
- food processing
- hi-tech industry
- textiles
- tourism
- ■ capital cities
- • major towns
- ✈ international airports
- — major roads
- ▨ major industrial areas

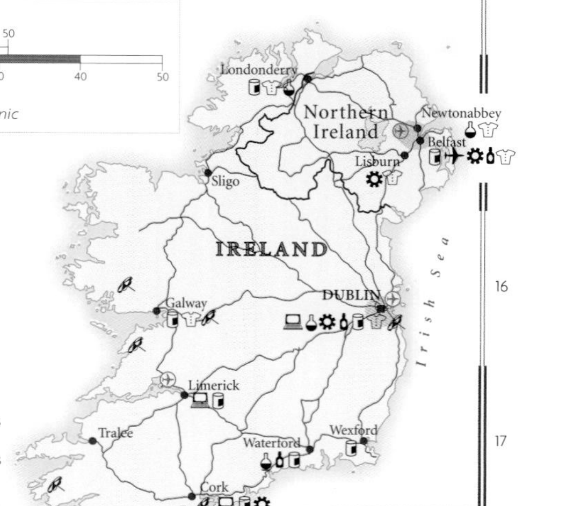

Index: British Isles & Ireland

The place names of the British Isles reflect the languages of both the present and the past. The distribution of these settlement names on maps indicates where these languages are now, and where they were once spoken. The early inhabitants of the British Isles were Celts. Their names now survive in the west; the region to which they were driven by successive invasions of Romans, Anglo-Saxons and Norwegian Vikings. The most immediately recognisable of these names are Welsh names. These are found both in north Wales, where the language is still the mother tongue of more than half a million people, and in the south, where the language generally spoken is now English. The familiar initial elements Llan– (church) and Aber– (river mouth, confluence) are found throughout Wales and many anglicised names on maps and signposts are now accompanied by their original Welsh forms: Cardiff (Caerdydd), Swansea (Abertawe), Carmarthen (Caerfyrddin).

Less than 100,000 people in Scotland still speak Gaelic. They are found principally in the Hebrides and the northwest highlands. Surviving Gaelic names are more widely dispersed throughout western Scotland as a whole. Some physical feature names are preserved in their Gaelic spelling, for example, Sgurr a 'Choire Ghlais – but most settlement names, and the names of prominent features such as Oban and Ben Nevis, have long been anglicised. However as in Wales, there is now increasing recognition of Gaelic spellings: Benbecula (Beinn na Faoghla) and North Uist (Uibhist a'Tuath).

Most of the Irish Gaelic names in Ireland were systematically anglicised during the years of British rule and the language itself all but disappeared; barely 60,000 people in the western extremities of the country still speak Irish as their mother tongue. Since independence in 1922, the Irish government has tried to remedy this situation by decreeing Irish the official national language and making it a compulsory subject in schools. As a result, over half a million people in the island of Ireland now claim to be able to speak some Irish. A commission has also been set up by the Irish government to determine the true Irish form of every place name in the country and many of these are now being given recognition on maps, for example, Dublin (Baile Átha Cliath), Cork (Corcaigh) and Limerick (Luimneach). Very few names exist in Irish only. Examples are Dun Laoghaire (formerly Kingstown) and Cobh (formerly Queenstown). Typical anglicised Irish elements in place names are Bally- (Town) and Inish- (island).

Two lesser Celtic languages, both now dead, survive in a few place names: Cornish, with names beginning with Tre- (Village), and Manx with names prefaced by Balla-.

Little place name evidence remains of the Roman occupation of Britain. Though the Romans latinized the mainly Celtic names they found throughout the country, these soon disappeared as later Anglo-Saxon and Norwegian newcomers imposed their own names. Old Sarum is a rare example of a surviving Latin name. The Language continued to be used occasionally; Magna (big), Parva (little) and Super-Mare (on the sea) were added to place names to differentiate villages of the same name.

Anglo-Saxons began their invasion of southern Britain only thirty years after the Romans left in ad 410. Norwegian Viking invasions of Scotland and northern Britain followed in the late eighth and early ninth centuries. Thus it came about that Norwegian and Anglo-Saxon place names spread across the country from Shetland in the north, to Hampshire in the south and westwards to the Celtic fringe. These are the names that survive today, though their spellings are very different from the Old English forms recorded in the Domesday Book of 1086. The dividing line between the two linguistic strands is geographically complex but as a general rule it can be stated that names ending in –by and –thorpe are Norwegian in origin, while those with –ham and –ton are Anglo-Saxon.

The Norman Invasion of 1066 brought the French language with it. French, therefore, contributed in a minor way to the formation of place names in southern England; names with Beau- and Bel- (beautiful) being the most conspicuous. Norman French prepositions survive in such names as Ashby de la Zouch and Chapel en le Frith.

◆ Country   ◇ Dependent Territory   ▲ Administrative Region   ▲ Mountain   ◎ Lake   ⌁ River
● Country Capital   ◈ Dependent Territory Capital   ✕ International Airport   ▲ Mountain Range   ⊡ Reservoir

Legend:
♦ Country ◇ Dependent Territory ▲ Administrative Region ▲ Mountain
● Country Capital ◉ Dependent Territory Capital ✕ International Airport ▲ Mountain Range ◎ Lake ≈ River ▨ Reservoir

BRINYAN – CLYST ST MARY

xlii M3 **Brinyan** Orkney Islands, N Scotland, UK
xxxvi L10 **Bristol** ***anc.*** Bricgstow. City of Bristol, SW England, UK
xxxv H16 **Bristol Channel** *inlet* England/ Wales, UK
xxxvi K9 **Bristol, City of** ◐ *unitary authority* SW England, UK
xxxv H14 **Briton Ferry** Neath Port Talbot, S Wales, UK
xxxvi H16 **Brixham** Devon, SW England, UK
xxxvi D8 **Brixton** Lambeth, SE England, UK
xxxix O12 **Brixworth** Northamptonshire, C England, UK
xlii D8 **Broad Bay** *bay* NW Scotland, UK
xxxvii N12 **Broad Chalke** Wiltshire, S England, UK
xxxvi I14 **Broad Clyst** Devon, SW England, UK
xliv E12 **Broadford** Limerick, SW Ireland
xlii E13 **Broadford** Highland, N Scotland, UK
xliv C5 **Broad Haven** *inlet* NW Ireland
xxxvi I13 **Broadhembury** Devon, SW England, UK
xxxvii N9 **Broad Hinton** Wiltshire, S England, UK
xliii L22 **Broad Law** ▲ S Scotland, UK
xxxvi L14 **Broadmayne** Dorset, S England, UK
xxxv B14 **Broad Sound** *sound* SW Wales, UK
xxxvii Z10 **Broadstairs** Kent, SE England, UK
xxxix Y9 **Broads, The** *wetland* E England, UK
xxxvii N13 **Broadstone** Poole, S England, UK
xxxvi J13 **Broadway** Somerset, SW England, UK
xxxviii L14 **Broadway** Worcestershire, W England, UK
xxxvi L14 **Broadwey** Dorset, S England, UK
xxxvi K13 **Broadwindsor** Dorset, S England, UK
xlii E12 **Brochel** Highland, NW Scotland, UK
xxxvii O13 **Brockenhurst** Hampshire, S England, UK
xli N8 **Brockleymoor** Cumbria, NW England, UK
xliii G21 **Brodick** North Ayrshire, W Scotland, UK
xxxviii H11 **Bromfield** Shropshire, W England, UK
xxxvii U9 **Bromley** Bromley, SE England, UK
xxxiv L17 **Bromley** ◐ *London borough* SE England, UK
xli V11 **Brompton** North Yorkshire, N England, UK
xli S11 **Brompton** North Yorkshire, N England, UK
xxxvi I12 **Brompton Ralph** Somerset, SW England, UK
xxxvi H12 **Brompton Regis** Somerset, SW England, UK
xxxviii B16 **Bromsgrove** Worcestershire, W England, UK
xxxviii I12 **Bromyard** Herefordshire, W England, UK
xxxvii P14 **Brook** Isle of Wight, S England, UK
xxxix X10 **Brooke** Norfolk, E England, UK
xxxvii X12 **Brookland** Kent, SE England, UK
xli R4 **Broomhill** Northumberland, N England, UK
xlii G10 **Broom, Loch** *inlet* NW Scotland, UK
xlii K9 **Brora** Highland, N Scotland, UK
xlii J9 **Brora** ≈ N Scotland, UK
xlii K9 **Brora, Loch** ◎ N Scotland, UK
xxxviii I10 **Broseley** Shropshire, W England, UK
xliv D12 **Brosna** Kerry, SW Ireland
xliv I9 **Brosna** ≈ Westmeath, C Ireland
xli O9 **Brough** Cumbria, NW England, UK
xlii L6 **Brough** Highland, N Scotland, UK
xlii L3 **Brough Head** *island* N Scotland, UK
xliv L3 **Broughshane** Ballymena, NE Northern Ireland, UK
xli N14 **Broughton** Lancashire, NW England, UK
xxxix P11 **Broughton** Northamptonshire, C England, UK
xxxix P3 **Broughton** North Lincolnshire, N England, UK
xli P13 **Broughton** North Yorkshire, N England, UK
xlii M2 **Broughton** Orkney Islands, N Scotland, UK
xliii L21 **Broughton** The Borders, S Scotland, UK
xxxv K5 **Broughton** Flintshire, N Wales, UK
xxxix N10 **Broughton Astley** Leicestershire, C England, UK
xl L11 **Broughton in Furness** Cumbria, NW England, UK
xlii N3 **Broughtown** Orkney Islands, N Scotland, UK
xxxviii C13 **Brownhills** Walsall, C England, UK
xxxvi D14 **Brown Willy** *hill* SW England, UK
xxxvii T8 **Broxbourne** Hertfordshire, E England, UK
xliii L20 **Broxburn** City of Edinburgh, E Scotland, UK
xxxviii H7 **Broxton** Cheshire, W England, UK
xlii M7 **Bruan** Highland, N Scotland, UK
xxxvi J11 **Brue** ≈ SW England, UK
xliv F12 **Bruff** Limerick, SW Ireland
xliii D20 **Bruichladdich** Argyll and Bute, W Scotland, UK
xxxix Y9 **Brundall** Norfolk, E England, UK
xliv F12 **Bruree** Limerick, SW Ireland
xxxvi L12 **Bruton** Somerset, SW England, UK
xliii M24 **Brydekirk** Dumfries and Galloway, SW Scotland, UK
xxxv H13 **Brynamman** Carmarthenshire, S Wales, UK
xxxv I12 **Bryn Du** *hill* E Wales, UK
xxxv J13 **Brynmawr** Blaenau Gwent, SE Wales, UK
xxxv F5 **Brynsiencyn** Isle of Anglesey, NW Wales, UK
xli U14 **Bubwith** East Riding of Yorkshire, N England, UK
xlii Q12 **Buchan Ness** *headland* NE Scotland, UK
xliii K17 **Buchanty** Perth and Kinross, C Scotland, UK
xliii J19 **Buchlyvie** Stirling, C Scotland, UK
xli P11 **Buckden** North Yorkshire, N England, UK
xxxvi G15 **Buckfastleigh** Devon, SW England, UK
xliii M18 **Buckhaven** Fife, E Scotland, UK
xxxvi F5 **Buckhurst Hill** Redbridge, SE England, UK
xlii M11 **Buckie** Moray, NE Scotland, UK
xxxvii Q6 **Buckingham** Buckinghamshire, C England, UK
xxxvii Q7 **Buckinghamshire** ◐ *county* SE England, UK
xxxvii O8 **Buckland** Oxfordshire, C England, UK
xxxvi F12 **Buckland Brewer** Devon, SW England, UK
xxxvii P13 **Bucklers Hard** Hampshire, S England, UK
xxxv K5 **Buckley** Flintshire, N Wales, UK
xxxix R6 **Bucknall** Lincolnshire, E England, UK
xxxviii G12 **Bucknell** Shropshire, W England, UK
xlii P13 **Bucksburn** City of Aberdeen, NE Scotland, UK
xxxvi E12 **Buck's Cross** Devon, SW England, UK
xlii M13 **Buck, The** ▲ N Scotland, UK
xliii N17 **Buddon Ness** *headland* E Scotland, UK
xxxvi E13 **Bude** Cornwall, SW England, UK
xxxvi D13 **Bude Bay** *bay* SW England, UK
xxxvi I14 **Budleigh Salterton** Devon, SW England, UK
xxxix O12 **Bugbrooke** Northamptonshire, C England, UK
xxxvi D16 **Bugle** Cornwall, SW England, UK
xxxv J11 **Builth Wells** Powys, E Wales, UK
xxxvii O11 **Bulford** Wiltshire, S England, UK
xliv A15 **Bull, The** *island* S Ireland
xli U12 **Bulmer** North Yorkshire, N England, UK
xliv G2 **Bunbeg** Donegal, N Ireland
xxxviii H7 **Bunbury** Cheshire, W England, UK
xliv K11 **Bunclody** Wexford, SE Ireland
xliv I2 **Buncrana** ***Ir.*** Bun Cranncha. Donegal, NW Ireland
xliv G5 **Bundoran** ***Ir.*** Bun Dobhráin. Donegal, NW Ireland
xliii D18 **Bunessan** Argyll and Bute, W Scotland, UK
xxxix Y10 **Bungay** Suffolk, E England, UK
xliv I13 **Bunmahon** Waterford, S Ireland
xliv F10 **Bunnaglass** Galway, W Ireland
xliv F11 **Bunratty** Clare, W Ireland
xxxvii U6 **Buntingford** Hertfordshire, SE England, UK
xxxviii K6 **Burbage** Derbyshire, C England, UK
xxxvii O10 **Burbage** Wiltshire, S England, UK
xxxix Y9 **Bure** ≈ E England, UK
xxxix V14 **Bures** Essex, E England, UK
xxxviii I7 **Burfard** Cheshire, C England, UK
xxxvii O7 **Burford** Oxfordshire, C England, UK
xxxvii T12 **Burgess Hill** West Sussex, SE England, UK
xxxix Y9 **Burgh Castle** Norfolk, E England, UK
xlii L11 **Burghead** Moray, N Scotland, UK
xxxvii Q10 **Burghfield** West Berkshire, S England, UK
xxxix T6 **Burgh le Marsh** Lincolnshire, E England, UK
xxxvii O13 **Burley** Hampshire, S England, UK
xxxviii H8 **Burlton** Shropshire, W England, UK
xli V13 **Burnby** East Riding of Yorkshire, N England, UK
xli R11 **Burneston** North Yorkshire, N England, UK
xxxix V7 **Burnham** Market Norfolk, E England, UK
xxxvii X8 **Burnham-on-Crouch** Essex, SE England, UK
xxxvi J11 **Burnham-on-Sea** Somerset, SW England, UK
xlii Q12 **Burnhaven** Aberdeenshire, NE Scotland, UK
xli P14 **Burnley** Lancashire, NW England, UK
xli Q12 **Burnsall** North Yorkshire, N England, UK
xliii J23 **Burnside** East Ayrshire, W Scotland, UK
xliii M19 **Burntisland** Fife, E Scotland, UK
xxxviii C13 **Burntwood** Staffordshire, C England, UK
xlii J1 **Burrafirth** Shetland Islands, NE Scotland, UK
xlii I2 **Burravoe** Shetland Islands, NE Scotland, UK
xlii N5 **Burray** *island* NE Scotland, UK
xliii M17 **Burrelton** Perth and Kinross, C Scotland, UK
xliv E9 **Burren** Clare, W Ireland
xliv E10 **Burren** *physical region* W Ireland
xliii I26 **Burrow Head** *headland* SW Scotland, UK
xxxv F14 **Burry Port** Carmarthenshire, S Wales, UK
xl M15 **Burscough** Lancashire, NW England, UK
xl B17 **Burton** Cheshire, W England, UK
xli W12 **Burton Agnes** East Riding of Yorkshire, N England, UK
xxxvi K14 **Burton Bradstock** Dorset, S England, UK
xli W11 **Burton Fleming** East Riding of Yorkshire, N England, UK
xli N11 **Burton-in-Kendal** Cumbria, NW England, UK
xxxix O7 **Burton Joyce** Nottinghamshire, C England, UK
xxxix P11 **Burton Latimer** Northamptonshire, C England, UK
xli S12 **Burton Leonard** North Yorkshire, N England, UK
xli X14 **Burton Pidsea** East Riding of Yorkshire, N England, UK
xliv G3 **Burtonport** Donegal, N Ireland
xxxviii L9 **Burton upon Trent** ***var.*** Burton on Trent, Burton-upon-Trent. Staffordshire, C England, UK
xxxviii H7 **Burwardsley** Cheshire, W England, UK
xxxix T12 **Burwell** Cambridgeshire, E England, UK
xlii M5 **Burwick** Orkney Islands, N Scotland, UK
xl G14 **Bury** Bury, NW England, UK
xxxvii S13 **Bury** West Sussex, SE England, UK
xl F14 **Bury** ◐ *unitary authority* NW England, UK
xxxix U12 **Bury St Edmunds** ***hist.*** Beodericsworth. Suffolk, E England, UK
xliv K2 **Bushmills** Moyle, N Northern Ireland, UK
xliii G20 **Bute, Island of** *island* SW Scotland, UK
xliii G21 **Bute, Sound of** *sound* W Scotland, UK
xxxvi K12 **Butleigh** Somerset, SW England, UK
xxxix Y13 **Butley** Suffolk, SW England, UK
xli O6 **Butterburn** Cumbria, NW England, UK
xl L9 **Buttermere** Cumbria, NW England, UK
xxxix S7 **Butterwick** Lincolnshire, E England, UK
xliv F13 **Buttevant** Cork, S Ireland
xxxviii K6 **Buxton** Derbyshire, C England, UK
xxxix X8 **Buxton** Norfolk, E England, UK
xxxix N13 **Byfield** Northamptonshire, C England, UK
xxxvii S10 **Byfleet** Surrey, SE England, UK
xxxv I5 **Bylchau** Conwy, N Wales, UK
xli O4 **Byrness** Northumberland, N England, UK

C

xxxix Q4 **Cabourne** Lincolnshire, E England, UK
xlii M13 **Cabrach** Moray, N Scotland, UK
xxxv H8 **Cader Idris** ▲ NW Wales, UK
xl F15 **Cadishead** Salford, NW England, UK
xxxvii O13 **Cadnam** Hampshire, S England, UK
xxxv K5 **Caergwrle** Flintshire, N Wales, UK
xxxv K14 **Caerleon** Newport, SE Wales, UK
xxxv F5 **Caernarfon** ***var.*** Caernarvon, Carnarvon. Gwynedd, NW Wales, UK
xxxv D5 **Caernarfon Bay** *bay* NW Wales, UK
xxxv J15 **Caerphilly** Caerphilly, S Wales, UK
xxxv J14 **Caerphilly** ◐ *unitary authority* S Wales, UK
xxxv I9 **Caersws** Powys, C Wales, UK
xxxv L14 **Caerwent** Monmouthshire, SE Wales, UK
xxxv J4 **Caerwys** Flintshire, N Wales, UK
xliv C14 **Caha Mountains** ***Ir.*** An Cheacha. ▲▲ SW Ireland
xliv H12 **Caher** ***Ir.*** An Cathair. Tipperary, S Ireland
xliv B13 **Caherciveen** ***Ir.*** Cathair Saidhbhín. Kerry, SW Ireland
xliv B14 **Caherdaniel** Kerry, SW Ireland
xliv L12 **Cahore Point** ***Ir.*** Rinn Chathóir. *headland* SE Ireland
xliii F19 **Cairnbaan** Argyll and Bute, W Scotland, UK
xliii H18 **Cairndow** Argyll and Bute, W Scotland, UK
xliii L14 **Cairn Gorm** ▲ C Scotland, UK
xliii L14 **Cairngorm Mountains** ▲▲ C Scotland, UK
xlii N12 **Cairnie** Aberdeenshire, NE Scotland, UK
xliii H24 **Cairnryan** Dumfries and Galloway, SW Scotland, UK
xliii J23 **Cairnsmore of Carsphairn** ▲ SW Scotland, UK
xliii K22 **Cairn Table** ▲ C Scotland, UK
xliii L15 **Cairnwell, The** ▲ C Scotland, UK
xxxix Z9 **Caister-on-Sea** Norfolk, E England, UK
xxxix Q4 **Caistor** Lincolnshire, E England, UK
xl M8 **Caldbeck** Cumbria, NW England, UK
xli R15 **Calder** ≈ N England, UK
xl K10 **Calder Bridge** Cumbria, NW England, UK
xliii K20 **Caldercruix** North Lanarkshire, C Scotland, UK
xli P15 **Calderdale** ◐ *unitary authority* N England, UK
xlii K6 **Calder, Loch** ◎ N Scotland, UK
xliii J21 **Caldermill** South Lanarkshire, C Scotland, UK
xxxv D14 **Caldey Island** *island* SW Wales, UK
xxxv L14 **Caldicot** Monmouthshire, SE Wales, UK
xli R9 **Caldwell** North Yorkshire, N England, UK
xl F12 **Calf of Man** *island* SW Isle of Man
xlii N3 **Calfsound** Orkney Islands, N Scotland, UK
xli O10 **Calf, The** ▲ NW England, UK
xliii D16 **Calgary** Argyll and Bute, W Scotland, UK
xliv I12 **Callan** ***Ir.*** Callain. Kilkenny, S Ireland
xliii J18 **Callander** Stirling, C Scotland, UK
xxxvi E15 **Callington** Cornwall, SW England, UK
xxxvii N9 **Calne** Wiltshire, S England, UK
xxxvii P13 **Calshot** Hampshire, S England, UK
xliv G8 **Caltra** Galway, W Ireland
xliii K15 **Calvine** Perth and Kinross, C Scotland, UK
xxxix T12 **Cam** ≈ E England, UK
xliii F16 **Camasnacroise** Highland, NW Scotland, UK
xxxvii X12 **Camber** East Sussex, SE England, UK
xxxvii R10 **Camberley** Surrey, SE England, UK
xxxvi D8 **Camberwell** Southwark, SE England, UK
xli Q5 **Cambo** Northumberland, N England, UK
xxxvi B17 **Camborne** Cornwall, SW England, UK
xxxv H11 **Cambrian Mountains** ▲▲ C Wales, UK
xxxix S12 **Cambridge** ***Lat.*** Cantabrigia. Cambridgeshire, E England, UK
xxxix Q11 **Cambridgeshire** ◐ *county* E England, UK
xxxiv K16 **Camden** ◐ *London borough* SE England, UK
xxxvi C7 **Camden** Camden, SE England, UK
xxxvi D15 **Camel** ≈ SW England, UK
xxxvi D14 **Camelford** Cornwall, SW England, UK
xliii P14 **Cammachmore** Aberdeenshire, NE Scotland, UK
xliv C12 **Camp** Kerry, SW Ireland
xliii F22 **Campbeltown** Argyll and Bute, W Scotland, UK
xliii J19 **Campsie Fells** ▲▲ Stirling, C Scotland, UK
xxxv C13 **Camrose** Pembrokeshire, SW Wales, UK
xliii G15 **Camusnagaul** Highland, NW Scotland, UK
xxxix S6 **Candlesby** Lincolnshire, E England, UK
xliii C14 **Canna** *island* NW Scotland, UK
xlii H12 **Cannich** Highland, NW Scotland, UK
xxxvi J11 **Cannington** Somerset, SW England, UK
xxxvi F7 **Canning Town** Newham, SE England, UK
xxxviii B13 **Cannock** Staffordshire, C England, UK
xxxviii K9 **Cannock Chase** *forest* C England, UK
xliii N24 **Canonbie** Dumfries and Galloway, SW Scotland, UK
xxxvii X10 **Canterbury** ***hist.*** Cantwaraburh, ***anc.*** Durovernum, ***Lat.*** Cantuaria. Kent, SE England, UK
xxxvii W9 **Canvey Island** Essex, SE England, UK
xliii C16 **Caolas** Argyll and Bute, W Scotland, UK
xxxvii T11 **Capel** Surrey, SE England, UK
xxxv H5 **Capel Curig** Conwy, N Wales, UK
xxxix W13 **Capel St Mary** Suffolk, E England, UK
xli Q5 **Capheaton** Northumberland, N England, UK
xliii M22 **Cappercleuch** The Borders, S Scotland, UK
xliv H13 **Cappoquin** Waterford, S Ireland
xliii L17 **Caputh** Perth and Kinross, C Scotland, UK
xxxvi L16 **Carbis Bay** Cornwall, SW England, UK
xlii D13 **Carbost** Highland, NW Scotland, UK
xlii D12 **Carbost** Highland, NW Scotland, UK
xliv J9 **Carbury** Kildare, E Ireland
xxxv J15 **Cardiff** ◐ *unitary authority* S Wales, UK
xxxv K15 **Cardiff** ***Wel.*** Caerdydd. *national region capital* Cardiff, S Wales, UK
xxxv E11 **Cardigan** ***Wel.*** Aberteifi. Ceredigion, SW Wales, UK
xxxv E10 **Cardigan Bay** *bay* W Wales, UK
xxxviii H10 **Cardington** Shropshire, W England, UK
xxxvii T6 **Cardington** Bedfordshire, C England, UK
xliii I19 **Cardross** Argyll and Bute, W Scotland, UK
xxxv D14 **Carew** Pembrokeshire, SW Wales, UK
xliii L24 **Cargenbridge** Dumfries and Galloway, SW Scotland, UK
xl M11 **Cark** Cumbria, NW England, UK
xliv H3 **Cark Mountain** *hill* N Ireland
xli P13 **Carleton** North Yorkshire, N England, UK
xliv L6 **Carlingford** Louth, NE Ireland
xliv L6 **Carlingford Lough** *inlet* Ireland/ Northern Ireland, UK
xl M7 **Carlisle** ***anc.*** Caer Luel, Luguvallium, Luguvallum. Cumbria, NW England, UK
xliii L20 **Carlops** The Borders, S Scotland, UK
xliv J11 **Carlow** ***Ir.*** Ceatharlach. Carlow, SE Ireland
xliv J11 **Carlow** ***Ir.*** Cheatharlach. ◐ *county* SE Ireland
xlii C8 **Carloway** Western Isles, NW Scotland, UK
xli U14 **Carlton** North Yorkshire, N England, UK
xli Q11 **Carlton** North Yorkshire, N England, UK
xxxix N7 **Carlton** Nottinghamshire, C England, UK
xxxix Z10 **Carlton Colville** Suffolk, E England, UK
xxxix N5 **Carlton in Lindrick** Nottinghamshire, C England, UK
xxxix P6 **Carlton-on-Trent** Nottinghamshire, C England, UK
xliii K21 **Carluke** South Lanarkshire, C Scotland, UK
xxxv F13 **Carmarthen** Carmarthenshire, SW Wales, UK
xxxv E14 **Carmarthen Bay** *bay* S Wales, UK
xxxv E13 **Carmarthenshire** ◐ *unitary authority* S Wales, UK
xxxv E3 **Carmel Head** *headland* NW Wales, UK
xliv C9 **Carna** Galway, W Ireland
xliii J14 **Carn Bàn** ▲ NW Scotland, UK
xliv I2 **Carndonagh** ***Ir.*** Carn Domhnach. Donegal, NW Ireland
xliii D20 **Carnduncan** Argyll and Bute, W Scotland, UK
xxxv G5 **Carnedd Llywelyn** ▲ NW Wales, UK
xlii H13 **Carn Eige** ▲ N Scotland, UK
xliv K11 **Carnew** Wicklow, E Ireland
xliv F5 **Carney** Sligo, N Ireland
xliv L3 **Carnlough** Larne, E Northern Ireland, UK
xxxv I9 **Carno** Powys, C Wales, UK
xliii N17 **Carnoustie** Angus, E Scotland, UK
xliv K13 **Carnsore Point** ***Ir.*** Ceann an Chairn. headland SE Ireland
xliii L21 **Carnwath** South Lanarkshire, C Scotland, UK
xliii F21 **Carradale** Argyll and Bute, W Scotland, UK
xliv E7 **Carra, Lough** ◎ NW Ireland
xliv D9 **Carraroe** Galway, W Ireland
xliv C13 **Carrauntoohil** ***Ir.*** Carrantual, Carrauntohil, Corrán Tuathail. ▲ SW Ireland
xlii K13 **Carrbridge** Highland, NW Scotland, UK
xliii N17 **Carrick** Fife, E Scotland, UK
xliv F4 **Carrick** Donegal, N Ireland
xliv H2 **Carrickart** ***var.*** Carrigart, ***Ir.*** Carraig *Airt*. Donegal, N Ireland
xliii H19 **Carrick Castle** Argyll and Bute, W Scotland, UK
xliv M4 **Carrickfergus** ◐ *district* E Northern Ireland, UK
xliv M4 **Carrickfergus** ***Ir.*** Carraig Fhearghais. Carrickfergus, NE Northern Ireland, UK
xliv J6 **Carrickmacross** ***Ir.*** Carraig Mhachaire Rois. Monaghan, N Ireland
xliv J4 **Carrickmore** Omagh, W Northern Ireland, UK
xliv G7 **Carrick-on-Shannon** ***Ir.*** Cora Droma Rúisc. Leitrim/Roscommon, NW Ireland
xliv I12 **Carrick-on-Suir** ***Ir.*** Carraig na Siúire. Tipperary, S Ireland
xliv E14 **Carrigadrohid Reservoir** ▣ S Ireland
xliv C11 **Carrigaholt** Clare, W Ireland
xliv G10 **Carrigahorig** Tipperary, S Ireland
xliv F14 **Carrigaline** Cork, S Ireland
xliv H7 **Carrigallen** Leitrim, N Ireland
xliv I3 **Carrigans** Donegal, N Ireland
xlii H10 **Carron** ≈ NW Scotland, UK
xliii K23 **Carronbridge** Dumfries and Galloway, SW Scotland, UK
xlii F12 **Carron, Loch** *inlet* NW Scotland, UK
xliv J2 **Carrowkeel** ***var.*** Kerrykeel. Donegal, N Ireland
xliv D5 **Carrowmore Lake** ◎ NW Ireland
xli O7 **Carr Shield** Northumberland, N England, UK
xliii L24 **Carrutherstown** Dumfries and Galloway, SW Scotland, UK
xliv L5 **Carryduff** Castlereagh, E Northern Ireland, UK
xliii J25 **Carsluith** Dumfries and Galloway, SW Scotland, UK
xliii J23 **Carsphairn** Dumfries and Galloway, SW Scotland, UK
xliii K21 **Carstairs** South Lanarkshire, C Scotland, UK
xxxvii O8 **Carterton** Oxfordshire, C England, UK
xl M11 **Cartmel** Cumbria, NW England, UK
xl M11 **Cartmel Fell** Cumbria, NW England, UK
xliv C9 **Cashel** Galway, W Ireland
xliv H12 **Cashel** ***Ir.*** Caiseal. Tipperary, S Ireland
xliv D12 **Cashen** ≈ SW Ireland
xliii I17 **Cashlie** Perth and Kinross, C Scotland, UK
xxxix V9 **Castle Acre** Norfolk, E England, UK
xliv E7 **Castlebar** ***Ir.*** Caisleán an Bharraigh. Mayo, W Ireland
xliii A14 **Castlebay** Western Isles, NW Scotland, UK
xliv K7 **Castlebellingham** Louth, NE Ireland
xliv K6 **Castleblayney** ***Ir.*** Baile na Lorgan. Monaghan, N Ireland
xli Q10 **Castle Bolton** North Yorkshire, N England, UK
xliv K12 **Castlebridge** Wexford, SE Ireland
xxxviii D15 **Castle Bromwich** Birmingham, C England, UK
xxxix Q9 **Castle Bytham** Lincolnshire, E England, UK
xli N7 **Castle Carrock** Cumbria, NW England, UK
xxxvi L12 **Castle Cary** Somerset, SW England, UK
xxxvi M9 **Castle Combe** Wiltshire, S England, UK
xliv I11 **Castlecomer** Kilkenny, SE Ireland
xliv B14 **Castlecove** Kerry, SW Ireland
xliii L21 **Castlecraig** The Borders, S Scotland, UK
xliv K3 **Castledawson** Magherafelt, C Northern Ireland, UK
xliv I4 **Castlederg** Strabane, W Northern Ireland, UK
xliv J10 **Castledermot** Kildare, E Ireland
xliii K25 **Castle Douglas** Dumfries and Galloway, S Scotland, UK
xliv K12 **Castleellis** Wexford, SE Ireland
xliv I3 **Castlefinn** ***Ir.*** Caisleán na Finne. Donegal, NW Ireland
xli S14 **Castleford** Wakefield, N England, UK
xliv C12 **Castlegregory** Kerry, SW Ireland
xliv D12 **Castleisland** ***Ir.*** Oileán Ciarral. Kerry, SW Ireland
xliii H25 **Castle Kennedy** Dumfries and Galloway, SW Scotland, UK
xliv C13 **Castlemaine** Kerry, SW Ireland
xxxv C14 **Castlemartin** Pembrokeshire, SW Wales, UK
xliv G14 **Castlemartyr** Cork, S Ireland
xliv I8 **Castlepollard** Westmeath, C Ireland
xliv F7 **Castlerea** ***Ir.*** An Caisleán Riabhach. Roscommon, W Ireland
xliv L4 **Castlereagh** ***Ir.*** An Caisleán Riabhach. Castlereagh, N Northern Ireland, UK
xliv L4 **Castlereagh** ◐ *district* E Northern Ireland, UK
xliv J2 **Castlerock** Coleraine, N Northern Ireland, UK
xli Q7 **Castleside** Durham, N England, UK
xlii J12 **Castle Stuart** Highland, NW Scotland, UK
xli U9 **Castleton** North Yorkshire, N England, UK
xl F12 **Castletown** SE Isle of Man
xli W3 **Castletown** Sunderland, NE England, UK
xlii L6 **Castletown** Highland, N Scotland, UK
xliv C14 **Castletown Bere** Cork, S Ireland
xliv F13 **Castletownroche** Cork, S Ireland
xliv D15 **Castletownshend** Cork, S Ireland
xliv L6 **Castlewellan** Down, E Northern Ireland, UK
xxxix V10 **Caston** Norfolk, E England, UK
xxxvii U10 **Caterham** Surrey, SE England, UK
xxxix Y8 **Catfield** Norfolk, E England, UK
xxxvi F9 **Catford** Lewisham, SE England, UK
xl M5 **Catlowdy** Cumbria, NW England, UK
xli N12 **Caton** Lancashire, NW England, UK
xliii J22 **Catrine** East Ayrshire, SW Scotland, UK
xxxviii B16 **Catshill** Worcestershire, W England, UK
xli N13 **Catterall** Lancashire, NW England, UK
xli R10 **Catterick** North Yorkshire, N England, UK
xli R10 **Catterick Camp** North Yorkshire, N England, UK
xliii N23 **Cauldcleuch Head** ▲ S Scotland, UK
xliii L25 **Caulkerbush** Dumfries and Galloway, SW Scotland, UK
xxxix O6 **Caunton** Nottinghamshire, C England, UK
xliv I7 **Cavan** ***Ir.*** Cabhán. Cavan, N Ireland
xliv I6 **Cavan** ***Ir.*** An Cabhán. ◐ *county* N Ireland
xxxix U13 **Cavendish** Suffolk, E England, UK
xxxix U11 **Cavenham** Suffolk, E England, UK
xli T14 **Cawood** North Yorkshire, N England, UK
xxxix W8 **Cawston** Norfolk, E England, UK
xxxix P7 **Caythorpe** Lincolnshire, E England, UK
xli W11 **Cayton** North Yorkshire, N England, UK
xliv K9 **Celbridge** Kildare, E Ireland
xxxviii K7 **Cellarhead** Staffordshire, C England, UK
xxxv E3 **Cemaes** Isle of Anglesey, NW Wales, UK
xxxv D11 **Cemaes Head** *headland* SW Wales, UK
xxxv H8 **Cemmaes** Powys, C Wales, UK
xxxv F10 **Ceredigion** ◐ *unitary authority* W Wales, UK
xliii M18 **Ceres** Fife, E Scotland, UK
xxxvi L13 **Cerne Abbas** Dorset, S England, UK
xxxv I6 **Cerrigydrudion** Conwy, N Wales, UK
xl H14 **Chadderton** Oldham, NW England, UK
xxxviii B16 **Chaddesley Corbett** Worcestershire, W England, UK
xxxvii P9 **Chaddleworth** West Berkshire, S England, UK
xxxvi G14 **Chagford** Devon, SW England, UK
xxxvii P14 **Chale** Isle of Wight, S England, UK
xxxvii S8 **Chalfont St Giles** Buckinghamshire, C England, UK
xxxvi G11 **Challacombe** Devon, SW England, UK
xliii I24 **Challoch** Dumfries and Galloway, SW Scotland, UK
xxxvii X10 **Challock** Kent, SE England, UK
xxxvii X15 **Channel Islands** ***Fr.*** Îles Normandes. *island group* S English Channel
xxxvii Z11 **Channel Tunnel** *tunnel* France/UK
xxxviii K5 **Chapel-en-le-Frith** Derbyshire, C England, UK
xxxix T5 **Chapel St Leonards** Lincolnshire, E England, UK
xli S16 **Chapeltown** Sheffield, N England, UK
xxxvi K13 **Chard** Somerset, SW England, UK
xxxvi J13 **Chardstock** Devon, SW England, UK
xxxvii X11 **Charing** Kent, SE England, UK
xxxvii P7 **Charlbury** Oxfordshire, C England, UK
xlii M12 **Charlestown of Aberlour** Moray, N Scotland, UK
xliv F6 **Charlestown** Mayo, NW Ireland
xxxvi F8 **Charlton** Greenwich, SE England, UK
xxxvii N9 **Charlton** Wiltshire, S England, UK
xxxvii N7 **Charlton Kings** Gloucestershire, C England, UK
xxxvii T11 **Charlwood** Surrey, SE England, UK
xxxvi K14 **Charmouth** Dorset, S England, UK
xxxix N12 **Charwelton** Northamptonshire, C England, UK
xxxvii W10 **Chatham** Kent, SE England, UK
xxxix S11 **Chatteris** Cambridgeshire, E England, UK
xxxvi G13 **Chawleigh** Devon, SW England, UK
xxxvii Q11 **Chawton** Hampshire, S England, UK
xxxviii K7 **Cheadle** Staffordshire, C England, UK
xli P17 **Cheadle** Stockport, NW England, UK
xxxvi K11 **Cheddar** Somerset, SW England, UK
xxxviii K7 **Cheddleton** Staffordshire, C England, UK
xl G17 **Chelford** Cheshire, W England, UK
xxxviii M8 **Chellaston** City of Derby, C England, UK
xxxvii W7 **Chelmer** ≈ E England, UK
xxxvii W8 **Chelmsford** Essex, E England, UK
xxxvi C8 **Chelsea** Kensington and Chelsea, SE England, UK
xxxvi M7 **Cheltenham** Gloucestershire, C England, UK
xxxv M14 **Chepstow** Monmouthshire, SE Wales, UK
xxxvii Q12 **Cheriton** Hampshire, S England, UK
xxxvi H13 **Cheriton Fitzpaine** Devon, SW England, UK
xxxvii S10 **Chertsey** Surrey, SE England, UK
xxxvii S8 **Chesham** Buckinghamshire, C England, UK
xl H17 **Cheshire** ◐ *county* C England, UK
xxxvii U8 **Cheshunt** Hertfordshire, SE England, UK
xxxviii B13 **Cheslyn Hay** Staffordshire, C England, UK
xxxviii G6 **Chester** ***Wel.*** Caerleon; ***hist.*** Legaceaster, ***Lat.*** Deva, Devana Castra. Cheshire, C England, UK
xxxviii M6 **Chesterfield** Derbyshire, C England, UK
xli R7 **Chester-le-Street** Durham, N England, UK
xliii O22 **Chesters** The Borders, S Scotland, UK
xxxviii I8 **Cheswardine** Shropshire, W England, UK
xxxvi L13 **Chetnole** Dorset, S England, UK
xliii O23 **Cheviot Hills** *hill range* England/ Scotland, UK
xli P3 **Cheviot, The** ▲ NE England, UK
xxxvi L10 **Chew Magna** Bath and North East Somerset, SW England, UK
xxxvi L11 **Chewton Mendip** Somerset, SW England, UK
xxxvii R13 **Chichester** West Sussex, SE England, UK
xxxvi L14 **Chickerell** Dorset, S England, UK
xxxvii S11 **Chiddingfold** Surrey, SE England, UK
xxxvi K14 **Chideock** Dorset, S England, UK
xxxvii P9 **Chieveley** West Berkshire, S England, UK
xxxvi G5 **Chigwell** Essex, SE England, UK
xxxviii I8 **Child's Ercall** Shropshire, W England, UK
xxxvii Y10 **Chilham** Kent, SE England, UK
xxxvi F14 **Chillaton** Devon, SW England, UK
xxxvii R8 **Chiltern Hills** *hill range* S England, UK
xxxvii R8 **Chinnor** Oxfordshire, C England, UK
xxxix U12 **Chippenham** Cambridgeshire, E England, UK
xxxvi M9 **Chippenham** Wiltshire, S England, UK
xxxvii N6 **Chipping Campden** Gloucestershire, C England, UK
xxxvii O7 **Chipping Norton** Oxfordshire, C England, UK
xxxvii V8 **Chipping Ongar** Essex, SE England, UK
xxxvi M9 **Chipping Sodbury** South Gloucestershire, SW England, UK
xxxviii G10 **Chirbury** Shropshire, W England, UK
xxxv K6 **Chirk** Wrexham, NE Wales, UK
xliii P20 **Chirnside** The Borders, S Scotland, UK
xxxvi B8 **Chiswick** Hounslow, SE England, UK
xxxvii N11 **Chitterne** Wiltshire, S England, UK
xxxvi G12 **Chittlehampton** Devon, SW England, UK
xxxvii S10 **Chobham** Surrey, SE England, UK
xlii J8 **Choire, Loch** ◎ NW Scotland, UK
xxxvii O11 **Cholderton** Wiltshire, S England, UK
xli P6 **Chollerford** Northumberland, N England, UK
xli P6 **Chollerton** Northumberland, N England, UK
xxxvii Q9 **Cholsey** Oxfordshire, C England, UK
xli Q7 **Chopwell** Gateshead, NE England, UK
xli N15 **Chorley** Lancashire, NW England, UK
xxxix T10 **Christchurch** Cambridgeshire, E England, UK
xxxvii O14 **Christchurch** Dorset, S England, UK
xxxvi H14 **Chudleigh** Devon, SW England, UK
xxxvi G13 **Chulmleigh** Devon, SW England, UK
xxxvi M7 **Churchdown** Gloucestershire, C England, UK
xxxviii J9 **Church Eaton** Staffordshire, C England, UK
xli T14 **Church Fenton** North Yorkshire, N England, UK
xxxviii H6 **Church Minshull** Cheshire, W England, UK
xxxv K9 **Church Stoke** Powys, C Wales, UK
xxxviii H10 **Church Stretton** Shropshire, W England, UK
xliv K13 **Churchtown** Wexford, SE Ireland
xliv J13 **Churchtown** Wexford, SE Ireland
xxxv F6 **Chwilog** Gwynedd, NW Wales, UK
xxxv J5 **Cilcain** Flintshire, N Wales, UK
xxxv G11 **Cilcennin** Ceredigion, W Wales, UK
xxxv E12 **Cilgerran** Pembrokeshire, SW Wales, UK
xxxv H12 **Cilycwm** Carmarthenshire, S Wales, UK
xxxvi L7 **Cinderford** Gloucestershire, C England, UK
xxxvii N8 **Cirencester** ***anc.*** Corinium, Corinium Dobunorum. Gloucestershire, C England, UK
xliii H19 **Clachaig** Argyll and Bute, W Scotland, UK
xliii F21 **Clachan** Argyll and Bute, W Scotland, UK
xlii A11 **Clachan-a-Luib** Western Isles, NW Scotland, UK
xliii G19 **Clachan of Glendaruel** Argyll and Bute, W Scotland, UK
xliii F18 **Clachan-Seil** Argyll and Bute, W Scotland, UK
xlii G8 **Clachtoll** Highland, NW Scotland, UK
xliii K19 **Clackmannan** Clackmannan, C Scotland, UK
xliii K18 **Clackmannan** ◐ *unitary authority* C Scotland, UK
xxxvii Y7 **Clacton-on-Sea** ***var.*** Clacton. Essex, E England, UK
xliii H18 **Cladich** Argyll and Bute, W Scotland, UK
xxxv H10 **Claerwen Reservoir** ▣ E Wales, UK
xliii F16 **Claggan** Highland, NW Scotland, UK
xliv K9 **Clane** Kildare, E Ireland
xxxvii O8 **Clanfield** Oxfordshire, C England, UK
xliii G20 **Claonaig** Argyll and Bute, W Scotland, UK
xxxvi D9 **Clapham** Lambeth, SE England, UK
xli O12 **Clapham** North Yorkshire, N England, UK
xxxv D13 **Clarbeston** Pembrokeshire, SW Wales, UK
xxxix V13 **Clare** Suffolk, E England, UK
xliv E10 **Clare** ***Ir.*** An Clár. ◐ *county* W Ireland
xliv F8 **Clare** ≈ W Ireland
xliv E10 **Clarecastle** Clare, W Ireland
xliv H10 **Clareen** Offaly, C Ireland
xliv E9 **Claregalway** Galway, W Ireland
xliv C7 **Clare Island** ***Ir.*** Cliara. *island* W Ireland
xliv E7 **Claremorris** ***Ir.*** Clár Chlainne Mhuiris. Mayo, W Ireland
xliv F9 **Clarinbridge** Galway, W Ireland
xlii J10 **Clashmore** Highland, NW Scotland, UK
xlii G8 **Clashnessie** Highland, NW Scotland, UK
xliii J24 **Clatteringshaws Loch** ◎ SW Scotland, UK
xliv J3 **Claudy** Londonderry, NW Northern Ireland, UK
xli N12 **Claughton** Lancashire, NW England, UK
xxxviii D17 **Claverdon** Warwickshire, C England, UK
xxxvi E13 **Clawton** Devon, SW England, UK
xxxviii M6 **Clay Cross** Derbyshire, C England, UK
xxxix W13 **Claydon** Suffolk, E England, UK
xl G11 *headland* C Isle of Man
xxxix P7 **Claypole** Lincolnshire, E England, UK
xli O14 **Clayton-le-Moors** Lancashire, NW England, UK
xliii E15 **Cleadale** Highland, NW Scotland, UK
xliv C15 **Clear, Cape** ***var.*** The Bill of Cape Clear, ***Ir.*** Ceann Cléire. *headland* SW Ireland
xliv D15 **Clear Island** *island* S Ireland
xliii A14 **Cleat** Western Isles, NW Scotland, UK
xl K9 **Cleator Moor** Cumbria, NW England, UK
xli R14 **Cleckheaton** Kirklees, N England, UK
xxxviii H11 **Clee St Margaret** Shropshire, W England, UK
xxxix R3 **Cleethorpes** North East Lincolnshire, E England, UK
xxxviii I11 **Cleobury Mortimer** Shropshire, W England, UK
xxxvi K10 **Clevedon** North West Somerset, SW England, UK
xli T10 **Cleveland Hills** *hill range* N England, UK
xl M13 **Cleveleys** Lancashire, NW England, UK
xliv C7 **Clew Bay** ***Ir.*** Cuan Mó. *inlet* W Ireland
xli N9 **Cliburn** Cumbria, NW England, UK
xxxvii Q11 **Cliddesden** Hampshire, S England, UK
xliv C8 **Clifden** ***Ir.*** An Clochán. Galway, W Ireland
xxxvii W9 **Cliffe** Kent, SE England, UK
xxxviii G13 **Clifford** Herefordshire, W England, UK
xxxviii I12 **Clifton upon Teme** Worcestershire, W England, UK
xxxix O11 **Clipston** Northamptonshire, C England, UK
xlii C9 **Clisham** ▲ NW Scotland, UK
xli O13 **Clitheroe** Lancashire, NW England, UK
xxxviii H9 **Clive** Shropshire, W England, UK
xlii J1 **Clivocast** Shetland Islands, NE Scotland, UK
xliv H3 **Cloghan** Donegal, N Ireland
xliv H9 **Cloghan** Offaly, C Ireland
xliv G12 **Clogheen** Tipperary, S Ireland
xliv I5 **Clogher** Dungannon, C Northern Ireland, UK
xliv L7 **Clogher Head** *headland* E Ireland
xliv L7 **Clogherhead** Louth, NE Ireland
xliv M5 **Cloghy Ards**, E Northern Ireland, UK
xliv L3 **Clog Mills** Ballymena, NE Northern Ireland, UK
xlii P12 **Clola** Aberdeenshire, NE Scotland, UK
xliv E15 **Clonakilty** ***Ir.*** Cloich na Coillte. Cork, SW Ireland
xliv E15 **Clonakilty Bay** *bay* S Ireland
xliv I9 **Clonaslee** Laois, C Ireland
xliv F8 **Clonbern** Galway, W Ireland
xliv D8 **Clonbur** Galway, W Ireland
xliv K9 **Clondalkin** ***Ir.*** Cluain Dolcáin. Dublin, E Ireland
xliv I13 **Clonea Bay** *bay* S Ireland
xliv I5 **Clones** ***Ir.*** Cluain Eois. Monaghan, N Ireland
xliv G9 **Clonfert** Galway, W Ireland
xliv H9 **Clonmacnoise** Offaly, C Ireland
xliv H12 **Clonmel** ***Ir.*** Cluain Meala. Tipperary, S Ireland
xliv K12 **Clonroche** Wexford, SE Ireland
xliv J6 **Clontibret** Monaghan, NE Ireland
xliv E8 **Cloonboo** Galway, W Ireland
xliv F11 **Cloonlara** Clare, W Ireland
xliv G10 **Cloonoon** Galway, W Ireland
xliv F9 **Cloonymorris** Galway, W Ireland
xxxvii S6 **Clophill** Bedfordshire, C England, UK
xli W10 **Cloughton** North Yorkshire, N England, UK
xliii M15 **Clova** Angus, E Scotland, UK
xxxvi E12 **Clovelly** Devon, SW England, UK
xliii N21 **Clovenfords** The Borders, S Scotland, UK
xxxix N5 **Clowne** Derbyshire, C England, UK
xxxviii J11 **Clows Top** Worcestershire, W England, UK
xlii G13 **Cluanie, Loch** ◎ NW Scotland, UK
xxxviii G11 **Clun** Shropshire, W England, UK
xliii H14 **Clunes** Highland, NW Scotland, UK
xxxviii G11 **Clungunford** Shropshire, W England, UK
xxxvi L10 **Clutton** Bath and North East Somerset, SW England, UK
xxxv J4 **Clwyd** ≈ N Wales, UK
xxxv J4 **Clwydian Range** ▲▲ N Wales, UK
xxxv H14 **Clydach** Swansea, S Wales, UK
xxxv I14 **Clydach Vale** Rhondda Cynon Taff, S Wales, UK
xliii K22 **Clyde** ≈ W Scotland, UK
xliii I20 **Clydebank** West Dunbartonshire, W Scotland, UK
xliii H20 **Clyde, Firth of** *inlet* S Scotland, UK
xxxv F6 **Clynnog-fawr** Gwynedd, NW Wales, UK
xxxv K11 **Clyro** Powys, C Wales, UK
xxxvi I13 **Clyst** ≈ SW England, UK
xxxvi I14 **Clyst St Mary** Devon, SW England, UK

◆ Country ◇ Dependent Territory ◐ Administrative Region ▲ Mountain ◎ Lake ≈ River
● Country Capital ○ Dependent Territory Capital ✈ International Airport ▲▲ Mountain Range ▣ Reservoir

◆ Country   ◇ Dependent Territory   ◄ Administrative Region   ▲ Mountain   ☉ Lake   ≈ River
● Country Capital   ○ Dependent Territory Capital   ✕ International Airport   ▲ Mountain Range   ☐ Reservoir

F

G

Legend:
◆ Country | ◇ Dependent Territory | ◉ Administrative Region | ▲ Mountain | ◎ Lake | ✦ River
◆ Country Capital | ◉ Dependent Territory Capital | ✕ International Airport | ▲ Mountain Range | ▣ Reservoir

GRANGEMOUTH – JURA, PAPS OF

xliii *K19* **Grangemouth** Falkirk, C Scotland, UK
xl *M11* **Grange-over-Sands** Cumbria, NW England, UK
xli *Y6* **Grangetown** Redcar and Cleveland, N England, UK
xxxix *P8* **Grantham** Lincolnshire, E England, UK
xlii *L13* **Grantown-on-Spey** Highland, N Scotland, UK
xliii *O20* **Grantshouse** The Borders, S Scotland, UK
xxxix *Q4* **Grasby** Lincolnshire, E England, UK
xl *M10* **Grasmere** Cumbria, NW England, UK
xli *Q12* **Grassington** North Yorkshire, N England, UK
xxxvii *O11* **Grateley** Hampshire, S England, UK
xxxviii *G10* **Gravels** Shropshire, W England, UK
xxxvii *V9* **Gravesend** Kent, SE England, UK
xli *N10* **Grayrigg** Cumbria, NW England, UK
xxxvii *V9* **Grays** Essex, SE England, UK
xli *T9* **Great Ayton** North Yorkshire, N England, UK
xxxvii *W8* **Great Baddow** Essex, SE England, UK
xxxvii *V6* **Great Bardfield** Essex, SE England, UK
xxxvii *S5* **Great Barford** Bedfordshire, C England, UK
xxxvii *O10* **Great Bedwyn** Wiltshire, S England, UK
xlii *B8* **Great Bernera** *island* NW Scotland, UK
xliv *A13* **Great Blasket Island** ***Ir.*** An Blascaod Mór. *island* SW Ireland
xxxvii *R6* **Great Brickhill** Buckinghamshire, C England, UK
xli *T10* **Great Broughton** North Yorkshire, N England, UK
xl *E17* **Great Budworth** Cheshire, W England, UK
xli *W7* **Great Burdon** Darlington, N England, UK
xxxix *S5* **Great Carlton** Lincolnshire, E England, UK
xxxvii *V6* **Great Chesterford** Essex, SE England, UK
xxxix *R3* **Great Coates** North East Lincolnshire, E England, UK
xxxvii *V7* **Great Dunmow** Essex, SE England, UK
xl *M14* **Great Eccleston** Lancashire, NW England, UK
xxxix *S12* **Great Eversden** Cambridgeshire, E England, UK
xxxix *Q11* **Great Gidding** Cambridgeshire, E England, UK
xxxix *S12* **Great Gransden** Cambridgeshire, E England, UK
xli *O14* **Great Harwood** Lancashire, NW England, UK
xxxix *V10* **Great Hockham** Norfolk, E England, UK
xxxix *Q3* **Great Limber** Lincolnshire, E England, UK
xxxviii *J13* **Great Malvern** Worcestershire, W England, UK
xxxvii *R8* **Great Missenden** Buckinghamshire, C England, UK
xli *O14* **Great Mitton** Lancashire, NW England, UK
xxxvii *Y6* **Great Oakley** Essex, SE England, UK
xxxvii *T7* **Great Offley** Hertfordshire, SE England, UK
xxxv *H4* **Great Ormes Head** *headland* N Wales, UK
xl *M7* **Great Orton** Cumbria, NW England, UK
xxxix *T10* **Great Ouse** ***var.*** Ouse. ≈ E England, UK
xxxix *P8* **Great Ponton** Lincolnshire, E England, UK
xxxvii *O7* **Great Rissington** Gloucestershire, C England, UK
xxxix *V8* **Great Ryburgh** Norfolk, E England, UK
xxxvii *V6* **Great Sampford** Essex, SE England, UK
xxxvii *P9* **Great Shefford** West Berkshire, S England, UK
xxxix *T13* **Great Shelford** Cambridgeshire, E England, UK
xxxvii *N9* **Great Somerford** Wiltshire, S England, UK
xxxix *R12* **Great Staughton** Cambridgeshire, E England, UK
xxxvii *Y12* **Greatstone-on-Sea** Kent, SE England, UK
xxxvii *P7* **Great Tew** Oxfordshire, C England, UK
xxxvi *F12* **Great Torrington** Devon, SW England, UK
xxxvii *X9* **Great Wakering** Essex, SE England, UK
xxxvii *W7* **Great Waltham** Essex, SE England, UK
xxxvii *N11* **Great Wishford** Wiltshire, S England, UK
xxxviii *I12* **Great Witley** Worcestershire, W England, UK
xxxix *Z9* **Great Yarmouth** ***var.*** Yarmouth. Norfolk, E England, UK
xxxvii *V6* **Great Yeldham** Essex, SE England, UK
xliv *J2* **Greencastle** Donegal, N Ireland
xliv *L6* **Greencastle** Newry and Mourne, S Northern Ireland, UK
xxxvi *A7* **Greenford** Ealing, SE England, UK
xli *O5* **Greenhaugh** Northumberland, N England, UK
xli *N6* **Greenhead** Northumberland, N England, UK
xliii *O21* **Greenlaw** The Borders, S Scotland, UK
xliii *K18* **Greenloaning** Perth and Kinross, C Scotland, UK
xliii *K22* **Green Lowther** ▲ C Scotland, UK
xliii *H19* **Greenock** Inverclyde, W Scotland, UK
xl *M11* **Greenodd** Cumbria, NW England, UK
xliv *L13* **Greenore Point** *headland* SE Ireland
xxxiv *L16* **Greenwich** ◐ *London borough* SE England, UK
xxxvii *U9* **Greenwich** ***hist.*** Grenawic. Greenwich, SE England, UK
xxxix *P9* **Greetham** Rutland, C England, UK
xli *S16* **Grenoside** Sheffield, N England, UK
xxxv *K5* **Gresford** Wrexham, NE Wales, UK
xli *Q9* **Greta Bridge** Durham, N England, UK
xliii *M24* **Gretna** Dumfries and Galloway, SW Scotland, UK
xliii *M24* **Gretna Green** Dumfries and Galloway, SW Scotland, UK
xxxix *P10* **Gretton** Northamptonshire, C England, UK
xliv *M5* **Greyabbey** Ards, E Northern Ireland, UK
xl *M8* **Greystoke** Cumbria, NW England, UK
xliv *L10* **Greystones** ***Ir.*** Na Clocha Liatha. Wicklow, E Ireland
xlii *A11* **Griminish Point** *headland* NW Scotland, UK
xlii *I2* **Grimister** Shetland Islands, NE Scotland, UK
xxxix *S5* **Grimoldby** Lincolnshire, E England, UK
xxxix *R3* **Grimsby** ***prev.*** Great Grimsby. North East Lincolnshire, E England, UK
xxxix *U8* **Grimston** Norfolk, E England, UK
xli *O13* **Grindleton** Lancashire, NW England, UK
xlii *N4* **Gritley** Orkney Islands, N Scotland, UK
xl *L11* **Grizebeck** Cumbria, NW England, UK
xliii *F21* **Grogport** Argyll and Bute, W Scotland, UK
xlii *C10* **Grosebay** Western Isles, NW Scotland, UK
xxxvii *Y10* **Grove** Kent, SE England, UK
xxxvi *F9* **Grove Park** Lewisham, SE England, UK
xxxvii *W16* **Groznez Point** *headland* Jersey, Channel Islands
xlii *I9* **Gruids** Highland, NW Scotland, UK
xlii *F10* **Gruinard Bay** *bay* NW Scotland, UK
xxxix *X13* **Grundisburgh** Suffolk, E England, UK
xlii *H4* **Gruting** Shetland Islands, NE Scotland, UK
xxxiv *H16* **Guernsey** ***off.*** Bailiwick of Guernsey. ◇ *UK crown dependency* NW Europe
xxxvii *V15* **Guernsey** *island* Channel Islands, NW Europe
xxxvii *W12* **Guestling Green** East Sussex, SE England, UK
xxxvii *S11* **Guildford** Surrey, SE England, UK
xliii *L17* **Guildtown** Perth and Kinross, C Scotland, UK
xxxv *K8* **Guilsfield** Powys, C Wales, UK
xli *T9* **Guisborough** Redcar and Cleveland, N England, UK
xli *R13* **Guiseley** Leeds, N England, UK
xxxix *W8* **Guist** Norfolk, E England, UK
xliii *N19* **Gullane** East Lothian, SE Scotland, UK
xli *U14* **Gunby** East Riding of Yorkshire, N England, UK
xxxvi *A8* **Gunnersbury** Hounslow, SE England, UK
xxxvi *F15* **Gunnislake** Cornwall, SW England, UK
xlii *I4* **Gunnista** Shetland Islands, NE Scotland, UK
xxxvi *B17* **Gunwalloe** Cornwall, SW England, UK
xlii *I1* **Gutcher** Shetland Islands, NE Scotland, UK
xxxix *S9* **Guyhirn** Cambridgeshire, E England, UK
xxxv *F4* **Gwalchmai** Isle of Anglesey, NW Wales, UK
xliv *F3* **Gweebarra Bay** ***Ir.*** Béal an Bheara. *inlet* W Ireland
xliv *G2* **Gweedore** ***Ir.*** Gaoth Dobhair. Donegal, NW Ireland
xxxv *J6* **Gwyddelwern** Denbighshire, N Wales, UK
xxxv *G7* **Gwynedd** ◐ *unitary authority* NW Wales, UK
xxxv *H5* **Gwytherin** Conwy, N Wales, UK

H

xxxix *Q3* **Habrough** North East Lincolnshire, E England, UK
xxxvii *Z10* **Hacklinge** Kent, SE England, UK
xli *V10* **Hackness** North Yorkshire, N England, UK
xxxvi *E6* **Hackney** Hackney, SE England, UK
xxxiv *L16* **Hackney** ◐ *London borough* SE England, UK
xxxvii *R8* **Haddenham** Buckinghamshire, C England, UK
xxxix *T11* **Haddenham** Cambridgeshire, E England, UK
xliii *N19* **Haddington** East Lothian, SE Scotland, UK
xxxix *Y10* **Haddiscoe** Norfolk, E England, UK
xxxvii *W9* **Hadleigh** Essex, SE England, UK
xxxix *W13* **Hadleigh** Suffolk, E England, UK
xxxviii *I9* **Hadley** Shropshire, W England, UK
xxxviii *H9* **Hadnall** Shropshire, W England, UK
xli *O6* **Hadrian's Wall** *ancient wall* N England, UK
xxxviii *B17* **Hadzor** Worcestershire, W England, UK
xl *M6* **Haggbeck** Cumbria, NW England, UK
xxxviii *B15* **Hagley** Worcestershire, W England, UK
xliv *D10* **Hag's Head** ***Ir.*** Ceann Caillí. *headland* W Ireland
xxxvii *V13* **Hailsham** East Sussex, SE England, UK
xli *O17* **Hale** Trafford, NW England, UK
xxxix *Y10* **Hales** Norfolk, E England, UK
xxxviii *B15* **Halesowen** Dudley, C England, UK
xxxix *Y11* **Halesworth** Suffolk, E England, UK
xxxviii *M13* **Halford** Warwickshire, C England, UK
xli *Q14* **Halifax** Calderdale, N England, UK
xlii *L6* **Halkirk** Highland, N Scotland, UK
xlii *K7* **Halladale** ≈ N Scotland, UK
xxxix *P10* **Hallaton** Leicestershire, C England, UK
xl *L10* **Hall Dunnerdale** Cumbria, NW England, UK
xxxviii *J13* **Hallow** Worcestershire, W England, UK
xxxvi *H17* **Hallsands** Devon, SW England, UK
xxxvi *D14* **Hallworthy** Cornwall, SW England, UK
xli *X14* **Halsham** East Riding of Yorkshire, N England, UK
xxxvii *W6* **Halstead** Essex, SE England, UK
xxxix *R6* **Haltham** Lincolnshire, E England, UK
xl *D16* **Halton** ◐ *unitary authority* NW England, UK
xli *O6* **Haltwhistle** Northumberland, N England, UK
xxxix *Y9* **Halvergate** Norfolk, E England, UK
xxxvi *H16* **Halwell** Devon, SW England, UK
xxxvi *F13* **Halwill** Devon, SW England, UK
xxxvi *A9* **Ham** Richmond upon Thames, SE England, UK
xlii *G4* **Ham** Shetland Islands, NE Scotland, UK
xxxvii *Q12* **Hambledon** Hampshire, S England, UK
xli *T14* **Hambleton** North Yorkshire, N England, UK
xliii *J20* **Hamilton** South Lanarkshire, S Scotland, UK
xxxvi *A7* **Hammersmith** *London borough capital* Hammersmith and Fulham, SE England, UK
xxxiv *K16* **Hammersmith and Fulham** ◐ *London borough* SE England, UK
xlii *I3* **Hamnavoe** Shetland Islands, NE Scotland, UK
xlii *I4* **Hamnavoe** Shetland Islands, NE Scotland, UK
xxxvii *P11* **Hampshire** ◐ *county* S England, UK
xxxvi *C6* **Hampstead** Camden, SE England, UK
xli *R12* **Hampsthwaite** North Yorkshire, N England, UK
xli *U5* **Hamsterley** Durham, N England, UK
xxxvii *X11* **Hamstreet** Kent, SE England, UK
xlii *G7* **Handa Island** *island* NW Scotland, UK
xxxvii *T12* **Handcross** West Sussex, SE England, UK
xl *G16* **Handforth** Cheshire, W England, UK
xli *S17* **Handsworth** Rotherham, N England, UK
xxxviii *J7* **Hanley** City of Stoke-on-Trent, C England, UK
xxxvii *Q10* **Hannington** Hampshire, S England, UK
xxxvii *R6* **Hanslope** Milton Keynes, C England, UK
xxxvi *A7* **Hanwell** Ealing, SE England, UK
xxxix *Y8* **Happisburgh** Norfolk, E England, UK
xli *P4* **Harbottle** Northumberland, N England, UK
xxxviii *M12* **Harbury** Warwickshire, C England, UK
xxxix *O8* **Harby** Leicestershire, C England, UK
xxxix *P6* **Harby** Nottinghamshire, C England, UK
xli *P10* **Hardrow** North Yorkshire, N England, UK
xli *S13* **Harewood** Leeds, N England, UK
xxxiv *K16* **Haringey** ◐ *London borough* SE England, UK
xxxv *G7* **Harlech** Gwynedd, NW Wales, UK
xxxvi *B7* **Harlesden** Brent, SE England, UK
xxxix *X11* **Harleston** Norfolk, E England, UK
xxxvii *U7* **Harlow** Essex, E England, UK
xxxix *P6* **Harmston** Lincolnshire, E England, UK
xxxvii *N12* **Harnham** Wiltshire, S England, UK
xxxvii *S5* **Harold** Bedfordshire, C England, UK
xlii *J1* **Haroldswick** Shetland Islands, NE Scotland, UK
xxxvii *S7* **Harpenden** Hertfordshire, E England, UK
xxxix *U8* **Harpley** Norfolk, E England, UK
xxxvii *W10* **Harrietsham** Kent, SE England, UK
xxxix *P10* **Harringworth** Northamptonshire, C England, UK
xliii *D14* **Harris** Highland, NW Scotland, UK
xlii *C10* **Harris** *physical region* NW Scotland, UK
xlii *B10* **Harris, Sound of** *strait* NW Scotland, UK
xli *S12* **Harrogate** North Yorkshire, N England, UK
xxxvii *T8* **Harrow** Harrow, SE England, UK
xxxiv *K16* **Harrow** ◐ *London borough* SE England, UK
xxxix *S13* **Harston** Cambridgeshire, E England, UK
xli *S8* **Hart** Hartlepool, N England, UK
xli *Q5* **Hartburn** Northumberland, N England, UK
xxxix *V12* **Hartest** Suffolk, E England, UK
xliii *L22* **Hart Fell** ▲ SW Scotland, UK
xl *E17* **Hartford** Cheshire, C England, UK
xxxviii *L6* **Hartington** Derbyshire, C England, UK
xxxvi *E12* **Hartland** Devon, SW England, UK
xxxvi *D12* **Hartland Point** *headland* SW England, UK
xxxviii *A16* **Hartlebury** Worcestershire, W England, UK
xli *Y5* **Hartlepool** Hartlepool, N England, UK
xli *X5* **Hartlepool** ◐ *unitary authority* NE England, UK
xli *T8* **Hartlepool Bay** *bay* N England, UK
xxxvii *R10* **Hartley Wintney** Hampshire, S England, UK
xxxvi *M7* **Hartpury** Gloucestershire, C England, UK
xxxviii *K13* **Harvington** Worcestershire, W England, UK
xxxvii *P9* **Harwell** Oxfordshire, C England, UK
xxxvii *Y6* **Harwich** Essex, E England, UK
xli *V10* **Harwood Dale** North Yorkshire, N England, UK
xxxvii *S12* **Haslemere** Surrey, SE England, UK
xli *O15* **Haslingden** Lancashire, NW England, UK
xxxvii *W13* **Hastings** East Sussex, SE England, UK
xxxvi *J12* **Hatch Beauchamp** Somerset, SW England, UK
xli *U15* **Hatfield** Doncaster, N England, UK
xxxviii *I12* **Hatfield** Herefordshire, W England, UK
xxxvii *T7* **Hatfield** Hertfordshire, E England, UK
xxxvii *V7* **Hatfield Broad Oak** Essex, SE England, UK
xxxvii *W7* **Hatfield Peverel** Essex, SE England, UK
xxxvi *F13* **Hatherleigh** Devon, SW England, UK
xxxix *N9* **Hathern** Leicestershire, C England, UK
xxxvii *N8* **Hatherop** Gloucestershire, C England, UK
xxxviii *L5* **Hathersage** Derbyshire, C England, UK
xxxviii *L8* **Hatton** Derbyshire, C England, UK
xlii *P12* **Hatton** Aberdeenshire, NE Scotland, UK
xxxix *W12* **Haughley** Suffolk, E England, UK
xxxviii *J9* **Haughton** Staffordshire, C England, UK
xxxvii *R13* **Havant** Hampshire, S England, UK
xxxv *C13* **Haverfordwest** Pembrokeshire, SW Wales, UK
xxxix *U13* **Haverhill** Suffolk, E England, UK
xl *K11* **Haverigg** Cumbria, NW England, UK
xxxiv *M16* **Havering** ◐ *London borough* SE England, UK
xxxv *K5* **Hawarden** Flintshire, N Wales, UK
xli *P11* **Hawes** North Yorkshire, N England, UK
xli *N9* **Haweswater** ◎ NW England, UK
xliii *N22* **Hawick** The Borders, SE Scotland, UK
xxxvii *W12* **Hawkhurst** Kent, SE England, UK
xli *T11* **Hawnby** North Yorkshire, N England, UK
xli *Q14* **Haworth** Bradford, N England, UK
xli *T12* **Haxby** York, N England, UK
xxxix *O4* **Haxey** North Lincolnshire, N England, UK
xl *D15* **Haydock** St Helens, NW England, UK
xli *P6* **Haydon Bridge** Northumberland, N England, UK
xxxviii *K5* **Hayfield** Derbyshire, C England, UK
xxxvi *M16* **Hayle** Cornwall, SW England, UK
xxxvi *M16* **Hayle** ≈ SW England, UK
xxxv *K12* **Hay-on-Wye** Powys, E Wales, UK
xli *V13* **Hayton** East Riding of Yorkshire, N England, UK
xxxix *O5* **Hayton** Nottinghamshire, C England, UK
xxxvii *U12* **Haywards Heath** West Sussex, SE England, UK
xxxvi *L13* **Hazelbury Bryan** Dorset, S England, UK
xli *P17* **Hazel Grove** Stockport, NW England, UK
xxxvii *R8* **Hazlemere** Buckinghamshire, SE England, UK
xxxix *U7* **Heacham** Norfolk, E England, UK
xxxvii *W11* **Headcorn** Kent, SE England, UK
xliv *E8* **Headford** Galway, W Ireland
xxxvii *Q8* **Headington** Oxfordshire, S England, UK
xxxvii *R11* **Headley** Hampshire, S England, UK
xli *R11* **Healey** North Yorkshire, N England, UK
xxxviii *M7* **Heanor** Derbyshire, C England, UK
xxxvi *H15* **Heathfield** Devon, SW England, UK
xxxvii *V12* **Heathfield** East Sussex, SE England, UK
xxxviii *C13* **Heath Hayes** Staffordshire, C England, UK
xxxvii *S9* **Heathrow** ✕ (London)SE England, UK
xli *R6* **Hebburn** South Tyneside, NE England, UK
xli *Q14* **Hebden Bridge** Calderdale, N England, UK
xliii *C15* **Hebrides, Sea of the** *sea* NW Scotland, UK
xxxix *Q7* **Heckington** Lincolnshire, E England, UK
xxxviii *C13* **Hednesford** Staffordshire, C England, UK
xli *R9* **Heighington** Darlington, N England, UK
xlii *I7* **Heilam** Highland, NW Scotland, UK
xliii *O21* **Heiton** The Borders, S Scotland, UK
xliii *H19* **Helensburgh** Argyll and Bute, W Scotland, UK
xli *P13* **Hellifield** North Yorkshire, N England, UK
xxxvii *V13* **Hellingly** East Sussex, SE England, UK
xxxix *N13* **Helmdon** Northamptonshire, C England, UK
xlii *L9* **Helmsdale** Highland, N Scotland, UK
xlii *K8* **Helmsdale** ≈ N Scotland, UK
xli *T11* **Helmsley** North Yorkshire, N England, UK
xxxix *Q7* **Helpringham** Lincolnshire, E England, UK
xl *D17* **Helsby** Cheshire, W England, UK
xxxvi *B17* **Helston** Cornwall, SW England, UK
xl *M9* **Helvellyn** ▲ NW England, UK
xliv *H13* **Helvick Head** *headland* S Ireland
xxxvii *S8* **Hemel Hempstead** Hertfordshire, E England, UK
xxxix *X10* **Hempnall** Norfolk, E England, UK
xxxix *Y9* **Hemsby** Norfolk, E England, UK
xli *S15* **Hemsworth** Wakefield, N England, UK
xxxvi *B6* **Hendon** Barnet, SE England, UK
xxxvii *T12* **Henfield** West Sussex, SE England, UK
xxxviii *G8* **Hengoed** Shropshire, W England, UK
xxxviii *D17* **Henley-in-Arden** Warwickshire, C England, UK
xxxvii *Q9* **Henley-on-Thames** Oxfordshire, C England, UK
xxxv *I5* **Henllan** Conwy, N Wales, UK
xxxvii *T6* **Henlow** Bedfordshire, C England, UK
xxxvi *L12* **Henstridge** Somerset, SW England, UK
xli *P4* **Hepple** Northumberland, N England, UK
xxxviii *H13* **Hereford** Herefordshire, W England, UK
xxxvi *K6* **Herefordshire** ◐ *unitary authority* W England, UK
xliii *N20* **Heriot** The Borders, S Scotland, UK
xxxvii *W15* **Herm** *island* Channel Islands
xlii *J1* **Herma Ness** *headland* NE Scotland, UK
xxxvii *P9* **Hermitage** West Berkshire, S England, UK
xliii *N23* **Hermitage** The Borders, S Scotland, UK
xxxvii *Y10* **Herne** Bay Kent, SE England, UK
xxxvi *D9* **Herne** Hill Southwark, SE England, UK
xxxvii *Q11* **Herriard** Hampshire, S England, UK
xxxvii *V12* **Herstmonceux** East Sussex, SE England, UK
xxxvii *T7* **Hertfordshire** ◐ *county* E England, UK
xl *M15* **Hesketh Bank** Lancashire, NW England, UK
xli *W14* **Hessle** East Riding of Yorkshire, N England, UK
xl *B16* **Heswall** Wirral, NW England, UK
xxxix *X9* **Hethersett** Norfolk, E England, UK
xl *M6* **Hethersgill** Cumbria, NW England, UK
xli *W4* **Hetton-le-Hole** Sunderland, NE England, UK
xxxix *Y11* **Heveningham** Suffolk, E England, UK
xxxix *X8* **Hevingham** Norfolk, E England, UK
xli *Q6* **Hexham** Northumberland, N England, UK
xxxvii *W8* **Heybridge** Essex, SE England, UK
xlii *H2* **Heylor** Shetland Islands, NE Scotland, UK
xl *M12* **Heysham** Lancashire, NW England, UK
xxxvi *M11* **Heytesbury** Wiltshire, S England, UK
xli *P15* **Heywood** Rochdale, NW England, UK
xxxix *P4* **Hibaldstow** North Lincolnshire, N England, UK
xxxix *Y8* **Hickling** Norfolk, E England, UK
xxxviii *M6* **Higham** Derbyshire, C England, UK
xxxvii *W9* **Higham** Kent, SE England, UK
xxxvi *F13* **Highampton** Devon, SW England, UK
xli *O12* **High Bentham** North Yorkshire, N England, UK
xxxvi *J11* **Highbridge** Somerset, SW England, UK
xxxvii *P10* **Highclere** Hampshire, S England, UK
xxxviii *I9* **High Ercall** Shropshire, W England, UK
xxxvi *I17* **Higher Town** Isles of Scilly, SW England, UK
xxxvi *C6* **Highgate** Haringey, SE England, UK
xxxvii *X11* **High Halden** Kent, SE England, UK
xl *K8* **High Harrington** Cumbria, NW England, UK
xl *M7* **High Hesket** Cumbria, NW England, UK
xlii *H12* **Highland** ◐ *unitary authority* NW Scotland, UK
xxxviii *I11* **Highley** Shropshire, W England, UK
xxxvii *V7* **High Roding** Essex, SE England, UK
xliii *L24* **Hightae** Dumfries and Galloway, SW Scotland, UK
xxxvi *G14* **High Willhays** ▲ SW England, UK
xxxvii *O8* **Highworth** Swindon, S England, UK
xxxvii *R8* **High Wycombe** ***prev.*** Chepping Wycombe, Chipping Wycombe. Buckinghamshire, SE England, UK
xxxix *V10* **Hilborough** Norfolk, E England, UK
xxxviii *J8* **Hilderstone** Staffordshire, C England, UK
xli *X12* **Hilderthorpe** East Riding of Yorkshire, N England, UK
xxxiv *K16* **Hillingdon** ◐ *London borough* SE England, UK
xxxix *U8* **Hillington** Norfolk, E England, UK
xlii *K10* **Hill of Fearn** Highland, N Scotland, UK
xliv *L5* **Hillsborough** Lisburn, E Northern Ireland, UK
xlii *H2* **Hillswick** Shetland Islands, NE Scotland, UK
xliv *L6* **Hilltown** Newry and Mourne, S Northern Ireland, UK
xxxvii *N9* **Hilmarton** Wiltshire, S England, UK
xxxviii *M10* **Hinckley** Leicestershire, C England, UK
xli *U9* **Hinderwell** North Yorkshire, N England, UK
xxxvii *R11* **Hindhead** Surrey, SE England, UK
xli *N16* **Hindley** Wigan, NW England, UK
xxxix *W8* **Hindolveston** Norfolk, E England, UK
xxxvi *M12* **Hindon** Wiltshire, S England, UK
xxxix *W10* **Hingham** Norfolk, E England, UK
xxxix *W13* **Hintlesham** Suffolk, E England, UK
xxxv *I7* **Hirnant** Powys, C Wales, UK
xxxv *I14* **Hirwaun** Rhondda Cynon Taff, S Wales, UK
xxxix *S12* **Histon** Cambridgeshire, E England, UK
xxxix *W13* **Hitcham** Suffolk, E England, UK
xxxvii *T6* **Hitchin** Hertfordshire, E England, UK
xxxvi *F9* **Hither Green** Lewisham, SE England, UK
xxxix *U10* **Hockwold cum Wilton** Norfolk, E England, UK
xli *O13* **Hodder** ≈ NW England, UK
xxxvii *U8* **Hoddesdon** Hertfordshire, SE England, UK
xxxviii *I8* **Hodnet** Shropshire, W England, UK
xxxix *S8* **Holbeach** Lincolnshire, E England, UK
xxxix *S9* **Holbeach St Johns** Lincolnshire, E England, UK
xxxix *S8* **Holbeach St Matthew** Lincolnshire, E England, UK
xxxix *S8* **Holbeck Marsh** *physical region* E England, UK
xxxvi *D7* **Holborn** Camden, SE England, UK
xxxix *X13* **Holbrook** Suffolk, E England, UK
xxxvi *I12* **Holcombe Rogus** Devon, SW England, UK
xli *O13* **Holden** Lancashire, NW England, UK
xxxvi *I11* **Holford** Somerset, SW England, UK
xlii *M2* **Holland** Orkney Islands, N Scotland, UK
xxxvii *Y7* **Holland-on-Sea** Essex, SE England, UK
xlii *O2* **Hollandstoun** Orkney Islands, N Scotland, UK
xxxix *Y13* **Hollesley** Suffolk, E England, UK
xl *I15* **Hollingworth** Tameside, NW England, UK
xxxvi *C6* **Holloway** Islington, SE England, UK
xli *Y14* **Hollym** East Riding of Yorkshire, N England, UK
xliv *E7* **Hollymount** Mayo, NW Ireland
xliv *K10* **Hollywood** Wicklow, E Ireland
xliii *M23* **Holm** Dumfries and Galloway, SW Scotland, UK
xxxix *R10* **Holme** Cambridgeshire, E England, UK
xxxix *U7* **Holme next the Sea** Norfolk, E England, UK
xli *U13* **Holme on Spalding Moor** East Riding of Yorkshire, N England, UK
xxxviii *I6* **Holmes Chapel** Cheshire, W England, UK
xli *R15* **Holmfirth** Kirklees, N England, UK
xxxvi *E13* **Holsworthy** Devon, SW England, UK
xxxix *W7* **Holt** Norfolk, E England, UK
xxxv *L5* **Holt** Wrexham, NE Wales, UK
xliv *H11* **Holycross** Tipperary, S Ireland
xxxv *E4* **Holyhead** ***Wel.*** Caer Gybi. Isle of Anglesey, NW Wales, UK
xxxv *E4* **Holyhead Bay** *bay* NW Wales, UK
xli *Q1* **Holy Island** Northumberland, N England, UK
xli *Q1* **Holy Island** *island* NE England, UK
xliii *H22* **Holy Island** *island* W Scotland, UK
xxxv *D4* **Holy Island** *island* NW Wales, UK
xxxvi *L13* **Holywell** Dorset, S England, UK
xl *A17* **Holywell** Flintshire, N Wales, UK
xliii *L24* **Holywood** Dumfries and Galloway, SW Scotland, UK
xxxix *W9* **Honingham** Norfolk, E England, UK
xxxix *P7* **Honington** Lincolnshire, E England, UK
xxxix *V11* **Honington** Suffolk, E England, UK
xxxvi *J13* **Honiton** Devon, SW England, UK
xxxvii *W9* **Hoo** Kent, SE England, UK
xli *U14* **Hook** East Riding of Yorkshire, N England, UK
xxxvii *R10* **Hook** Hampshire, S England, UK
xliv *J13* **Hook Head** ***Ir.*** Rinn Duáin. *headland* SE Ireland
xxxvii *P6* **Hook Norton** Oxfordshire, C England, UK
xxxviii *L5* **Hope** Derbyshire, C England, UK
xxxv *K5* **Hope** Flintshire, N Wales, UK
xxxviii *H10* **Hope Bowdler** Shropshire, W England, UK
xlii *L11* **Hopeman** Moray, N Scotland, UK
xxxvi *H15* **Hope's Nose** *headland* SW England, UK
xxxviii *H13* **Hope under Dinmore** Herefordshire, W England, UK
xxxix *Z10* **Hopton** Norfolk, E England, UK
xli *X4* **Horden** Durham, N England, UK
xxxvii *U11* **Horley** Surrey, SE England, UK
xli *N12* **Hornby** Lancashire, NW England, UK
xxxix *R6* **Horncastle** Lincolnshire, E England, UK
xxxvii *Q13* **Horndean** Hampshire, S England, UK
xliv *H2* **Horn Head** *headland* N Ireland
xxxvii *W12* **Horns Cross** East Sussex, SE England, UK
xli *X13* **Hornsea** East Riding of Yorkshire, E England, UK
xxxvi *C5* **Hornsey** Haringey, SE England, UK
xxxvi *F15* **Horrabridge** Devon, SW England, UK
xli *Q11* **Horsehouse** North Yorkshire, N England, UK
xliv *H9* **Horseleap** Westmeath, C Ireland
xxxix *Y8* **Horsey** Norfolk, E England, UK
xxxix *X9* **Horsford** Norfolk, E England, UK
xxxvii *T12* **Horsham** West Sussex, SE England, UK
xxxvi *M8* **Horsley** Gloucestershire, C England, UK
xli *P12* **Horton in Ribblesdale** North Yorkshire, N England, UK
xli *O15* **Horwich** Bolton, NW England, UK
xlii *I5* **Hoswick** Shetland Islands, NE Scotland, UK
xli *V14* **Hotham** East Riding of Yorkshire, N England, UK
xlii *J2* **Houbie** Shetland Islands, NE Scotland, UK
xl *M7* **Houghton** Cumbria, NW England, UK
xli *S7* **Houghton-le-Spring** Sunderland, NE England, UK
xxxvii *S9* **Hounslow** Hounslow, SE England, UK
xxxiv *K16* **Hounslow** ◐ *London borough* SE England, UK
xliii *F14* **Hourn, Loch** *inlet* NW Scotland, UK
xlii *M4* **Houton** Orkney Islands, N Scotland, UK
xxxvii *T13* **Hove** Brighton and Hove, SE England, UK
xxxix *X9* **Hoveton** Norfolk, E England, UK
xli *U11* **Hovingham** North Yorkshire, N England, UK
xli *U14* **Howden** East Riding of Yorkshire, N England, UK
xliii *M20* **Howgate** Midlothian, SE Scotland, UK
xli *R3* **Howick** Northumberland, N England, UK
xliv *L9* **Howth** Dublin, E Ireland
xxxix *X11* **Hoxne** Suffolk, E England, UK
xlii *L5* **Hoy** *island* N Scotland, UK
xl *A16* **Hoylake** Wirral, NW England, UK
xxxix *R7* **Hubbert's Bridge** Lincolnshire, E England, UK
xxxix *N7* **Hucknall** Nottinghamshire, C England, UK
xli *R15* **Huddersfield** Kirklees, N England, UK
xxxvi *I17* **Hugh Town** Isles of Scilly, SW England, UK
xxxvi *I12* **Huish Champflower** Somerset, SW England, UK
xli *W13* **Hull** ≈ N England, UK
xxxvi *M9* **Hullavington** Wiltshire, S England, UK
xli *W14* **Humber** *estuary* E England, UK
xxxix *R4* **Humberston** North East Lincolnshire, E England, UK
xxxix *U13* **Hundon** Suffolk, E England, UK
xxxvii *P10* **Hungerford** West Berkshire, S England, UK
xliv *C14* **Hungry Hill** ▲ SW Ireland
xlii *D11* **Hunish, Rubha** *headland* NW Scotland, UK
xli *W11* **Hunmanby** North Yorkshire, N England, UK
xxxix *U7* **Hunstanton** Norfolk, E England, UK
xxxix *R12* **Huntingdon** Cambridgeshire, E England, UK
xxxvi *L7* **Huntley** Gloucestershire, C England, UK
xlii *N12* **Huntly** Aberdeenshire, NE Scotland, UK
xxxvi *J11* **Huntspill** Somerset, SW England, UK
xl *H17* **Hurdsfield** Cheshire, C England, UK
xliii *I21* **Hurlford** East Ayrshire, W Scotland, UK
xxxvii *N13* **Hurn** Dorset, S England, UK
xxxvii *P12* **Hursley** Hampshire, S England, UK
xxxvii *P11* **Hurstbourne Priors** Hampshire, S England, UK
xxxvii *P11* **Hurstbourne Tarrant** Hampshire, S England, UK
xxxvii *U12* **Hurstpierpoint** West Sussex, SE England, UK
xli *R9* **Hurworth-on-Tees** Darlington, N England, UK
xxxix *O11* **Husbands Bosworth** Leicestershire, C England, UK
xlii *B9* **Hushinish** Western Isles, NW Scotland, UK
xxxix *T5* **Huttoft** Lincolnshire, E England, UK
xli *W13* **Hutton Cranswick** East Riding of Yorkshire, N England, UK
xli *S10* **Hutton Rudby** North Yorkshire, N England, UK
xl *C16* **Huyton Knowsley**, NW England, UK
xli *P16* **Hyde** Tameside, NW England, UK
xliii *K21* **Hyndford Bridge** South Lanarkshire, C Scotland, UK
xliii *B17* **Hynish** Argyll and Bute, W Scotland, UK
xxxvii *P13* **Hythe** Hampshire, S England, UK
xxxvii *Y11* **Hythe** Kent, SE England, UK

I

xxxvii *O13* **Ibsley** Hampshire, S England, UK
xxxviii *M9* **Ibstock** Leicestershire, C England, UK
xxxix *U11* **Icklingham** Suffolk, E England, UK
xxxvi *H15* **Ideford** Devon, SW England, UK
xxxvii *O11* **Idmiston** Wiltshire, S England, UK
xxxviii *H8* **Ightfield** Shropshire, W England, UK
xxxvii *V10* **Ightham** Kent, SE England, UK
xxxvi *K12* **Ilchester** Somerset, SW England, UK
xxxvi *G6* **Ilford** Redbridge, SE England, UK
xxxvi *F11* **Ilfracombe** Devon, SW England, UK
xxxix *N7* **Ilkeston** Derbyshire, C England, UK
xli *R13* **Ilkley** Bradford, N England, UK
xxxviii *L13* **Ilmington** Warwickshire, C England, UK
xxxvi *K13* **Ilminster** Somerset, SW England, UK
xxxix *R3* **Immingham** North East Lincolnshire, E England, UK
xliv *E10* **Inagh** Clare, W Ireland
xliv *C13* **Inch** Kerry, SW Ireland
xliii *O16* **Inchbraoch** Angus, E Scotland, UK
xliv *E14* **Inchigeelagh** Cork, S Ireland
xliii *M19* **Inchkeith** *island* C Scotland, UK
xliii *G20* **Inchmarnock** *island* W Scotland, UK
xlii *H8* **Inchnadamph** Highland, NW Scotland, UK
xxxvii *V8* **Ingatestone** Essex, SE England, UK
xxxix *V11* **Ingham** Suffolk, E England, UK
xli *O11* **Ingleborough** ▲ N England, UK
xli *O12* **Ingleton** North Yorkshire, N England, UK
xxxix *T6* **Ingoldmells** Lincolnshire, E England, UK
xxxix *Q8* **Ingoldsby** Lincolnshire, E England, UK
xliv *F14* **Inishannon** Cork, S Ireland
xliv *B8* **Inishark** *island* W Ireland
xliv *B7* **Inishbofin** ***Ir.*** Inis Bó Finne. *island* W Ireland
xliv *D10* **Inisheer** ***var.*** Inishere, ***Ir.*** Inis Oírr. *island* W Ireland
xliv *B6* **Inishkea North** *island* NW Ireland
xliv *B6* **Inishkea South** *island* NW Ireland
xliv *C9* **Inishmaan** ***Ir.*** Inis Meáin. *island* W Ireland
xliv *D9* **Inishmore** ***Ir.*** Árainn. *island* W Ireland
xliv *F5* **Inishmurray** *island* N Ireland
xliv *J2* **Inishowen Head** *headland* N Ireland
xliv *J1* **Inishtrahull** ***Ir.*** Inis Trá Tholl. *island* NW Ireland
xliv *I1* **Inishtrahull Sound** *sound* N Ireland
xliv *B8* **Inishturk** ***Ir.*** Inis Toirc. *island* W Ireland
xliv *J12* **Inistioge** Kilkenny, SE Ireland
xxxviii *K12* **Inkberrow** Worcestershire, W England, UK
xliii *B17* **Inner Hebrides** *island group* W Scotland, UK
xliii *M21* **Innerleithen** The Borders, S Scotland, UK
xlii *E12* **Inner Sound** *strait* NW Scotland, UK
xliii *J16* **Innerwick** Perth and Kinross, C Scotland, UK
xliv *E5* **Inniscrone** Sligo, N Ireland
xliv *B14* **Inny** ≈ SW Ireland
xlii *N12* **Insch** Aberdeenshire, NE Scotland, UK
xliii *K14* **Insh** Highland, NW Scotland, UK
xxxvi *F12* **Instow** Devon, SW England, UK
xliii *I18* **Invararnan** Stirling, C Scotland, UK
xliv *G4* **Inver** Donegal, N Ireland
xliii *L17* **Inver** Perth and Kinross, C Scotland, UK
xlii *P11* **Inverallochy** Aberdeenshire, NE Scotland, UK
xliv *D9* **Inveran** Galway, W Ireland
xlii *I9* **Inveran** Highland, NW Scotland, UK
xliii *H18* **Inveraray** Argyll and Bute, W Scotland, UK
xlii *E12* **Inverarish** Highland, NW Scotland, UK
xliii *O15* **Inverbervie** Aberdeenshire, NE Scotland, UK
xlii *I9* **Invercassley** Highland, NW Scotland, UK
xliii *H20* **Inverclyde** ◐ *unitary authority* C Scotland, UK
xliii *L14* **Inverey** Aberdeenshire, NE Scotland, UK
xliii *H14* **Invergarry** Highland, NW Scotland, UK
xliii *H15* **Invergloy** Highland, NW Scotland, UK
xlii *J11* **Invergordon** Highland, N Scotland, UK
xliii *M17* **Invergowrie** City of Dundee, E Scotland, UK
xliii *F14* **Inverie** Highland, NW Scotland, UK
xlii *G13* **Inverinate** Highland, NW Scotland, UK
xliii *O16* **Inverkeilor** Angus, E Scotland, UK
xliii *L19* **Inverkeithing** Fife, E Scotland, UK
xlii *N12* **Inverkeithny** Aberdeenshire, NE Scotland, UK
xliii *H20* **Inverkip** Inverclyde, W Scotland, UK
xlii *G8* **Inverkirkaig** Highland, NW Scotland, UK
xlii *I13* **Invermoriston** Highland, NW Scotland, UK
xlii *J12* **Inverness** Highland, N Scotland, UK
xliii *H15* **Inverroy** Highland, NW Scotland, UK
xliii *G16* **Inversanda** Highland, NW Scotland, UK
xliii *I18* **Inveruglas** Argyll and Bute, W Scotland, UK
xlii *O13* **Inverurie** Aberdeenshire, NE Scotland, UK
xliii *D18* **Iona** *island* W Scotland, UK
xxxviii *K7* **Ipstones** Staffordshire, C England, UK
xxxix *X13* **Ipswich** ***hist.*** Gipeswic. Suffolk, E England, UK
xxxix *P12* **Irchester** Northamptonshire, C England, UK
xl *L8* **Ireby** Cumbria, NW England, UK
xliv *F8* **Ireland** ***off.*** Ireland, ***prev.*** Ireland, Republic of, ***Ir.*** Éire. ◆ *republic* NW Europe
xxxvi *L9* **Iron Acton** South Gloucestershire, SW England, UK
xxxviii *I10* **Ironbridge** The Wrekin, W England, UK
xliv *I8* **Iron, Lough** ◎ C Ireland
xliv *H6* **Iron Mountains** ▲▲ N Ireland
xli *W11* **Irton** North Yorkshire, N England, UK
xliii *I21* **Irvine** North Ayrshire, W Scotland, UK
xliv *I5* **Irvinestown** Fermanagh, W Northern Ireland, UK
xlii *M4* **Isbister** Orkney Islands, N Scotland, UK
xlii *I2* **Isbister** Shetland Islands, NE Scotland, UK
xliii *L17* **Isla** ≈ C Scotland, UK
xliii *D21* **Islay** *island* SW Scotland, UK
xxxix *U11* **Isleham** Cambridgeshire, E England, UK
xxxv *E4* **Isle of Anglesey** ◐ *unitary authority* NW Wales, UK
xl *G12* **Isle of Man** ◇ *UK crown dependency* NW Europe
xliii *I26* **Isle of Whithorn** Dumfries and Galloway, SW Scotland, UK
xxxvii *P14* **Isle of Wight** ◐ *unitary authority* S England, UK
xxxiv *L16* **Islington** ◐ *London borough* SE England, UK
xxxvi *D7* **Islington** *London borough capital* Islington, SE England, UK
xxxvii *P7* **Islip** Oxfordshire, C England, UK
xxxvii *P12* **Itchen** ≈ S England, UK
xxxvii *S7* **Ivinghoe** Buckinghamshire, C England, UK
xxxvi *G16* **Ivybridge** Devon, SW England, UK
xxxix *V11* **Ixworth** Suffolk, E England, UK

J

xli *W2* **Jarrow** South Tyneside, NE England, UK
xxxvii *Y7* **Jaywick** Essex, SE England, UK
xliii *O22* **Jedburgh** The Borders, SE Scotland, UK
xxxiv *I16* **Jersey** ◇ *UK crown dependency* NW Europe
xxxvii *X16* **Jersey** *island* NW Europe
xlii *M6* **John o'Groats** Highland, N Scotland, UK
xliii *O15* **Johnshaven** Aberdeenshire, NE Scotland, UK
xxxv *C13* **Johnston** Pembrokeshire, SW Wales, UK
xliii *I20* **Johnstone** Renfrewshire, W Scotland, UK
xliv *H11* **Johnstown** Kilkenny, SE Ireland
xliii *E19* **Jura** *island* SW Scotland, UK
xliii *E20* **Jura, Paps of** ▲▲ W Scotland, UK

◆ Country ● Country Capital ◇ Dependent Territory ○ Dependent Territory Capital ◐ Administrative Region ✕ International Airport ▲ Mountain ▲▲ Mountain Range ◎ Lake ⊡ Reservoir ≈ River

LLANTWIT MAJOR – NEW ABBEY

xxxv *I16* **Llantwit Major** The Vale of Glamorgan, S Wales, UK
xxxv *I7* **Llanuwchllyn** Gwynedd, NW Wales, UK
xxxv *K13* **Llanvihangel Gobion** Monmouthshire, SE Wales, UK
xxxv *I7* **Llanwddyn** Powys, C Wales, UK
xxxv *F11* **Llanwenog** Ceredigion, W Wales, UK
xxxv *I9* **Llanwnog** Powys, C Wales, UK
xxxv *H12* **Llanwrda** Carmarthenshire, S Wales, UK
xxxv *H8* **Llanwrin** Powys, C Wales, UK
xxxv *I10* **Llanwrthwl** Powys, C Wales, UK
xxxv *I11* **Llanwrtyd Wells** Powys, C Wales, UK
xxxv *G12* **Llanybydder** Carmarthenshire, S Wales, UK
xxxv *D13* **Llanycefn** Pembrokeshire, SW Wales, UK
xxxv *D12* **Llanychaer Bridge** Pembrokeshire, SW Wales, UK
xxxv *I7* **Llanymawddwy** Gwynedd, NW Wales, UK
xxxv *D13* **Llawhaden** Pembrokeshire, SW Wales, UK
xxxv *G10* **Lledrod** Ceredigion, W Wales, UK
xxxv *E7* **Lleyn Peninsula** *peninsula* NW Wales, UK
xxxv *F6* **Llithfaen** Gwynedd, NW Wales, UK
xxxv *J4* **Lloc** Flintshire, N Wales, UK
xxxv *F11* **Llwyndafydd** Ceredigion, W Wales, UK
xxxv *G8* **Llwyngwril** Gwynedd, NW Wales, UK
xxxv *J12* **Llyswen** Powys, C Wales, UK
xliii *M20* **Loanhead** Midlothian, SE Scotland, UK
xliii *F15* **Lochailort** Highland, NW Scotland, UK
xliii *F16* **Lochaline** Highland, NW Scotland, UK
xliii *H25* **Lochans** Dumfries and Galloway, SW Scotland, UK
xliii *L24* **Locharbriggs** Dumfries and Galloway, SW Scotland, UK
xliii *H17* **Lochawe** Argyll and Bute, W Scotland, UK
xlii *A13* **Lochboisdale** Western Isles, NW Scotland, UK
xliii *E17* **Lochbuie** Argyll and Bute, W Scotland, UK
xlii *F12* **Lochcarron** Highland, NW Scotland, UK
xliii *M22* **Lochcraig Head** ▲ S Scotland, UK
xliii *F17* **Lochdon** Argyll and Bute, W Scotland, UK
xlii *H10* **Lochdrum** Highland, NW Scotland, UK
xliii *J17* **Lochearnhead** Stirling, C Scotland, UK
xlii *J12* **Lochend** Highland, NW Scotland, UK
xliii *M19* **Lochgelly** Fife, E Scotland, UK
xliii *G19* **Lochgilphead** Argyll and Bute, W Scotland, UK
xliii *H18* **Lochgoilhead** Argyll and Bute, W Scotland, UK
xlii *G8* **Lochinver** Highland, N Scotland, UK
xlii *H11* **Lochluichart** Highland, NW Scotland, UK
xliii *L24* **Lochmaben** Dumfries and Galloway, SW Scotland, UK
xlii *B11* **Lochmaddy** Western Isles, NW Scotland, UK
xliii *M14* **Lochnagar** ▲ C Scotland, UK
xliii *G21* **Lochranza** North Ayrshire, W Scotland, UK
xliii *I21* **Lochwinnoch** Renfrewshire, W Scotland, UK
xliii *H14* **Lochy, Loch** ◎ N Scotland, UK
xliii *L24* **Lockerbie** Dumfries and Galloway, S Scotland, UK
xxxix *Y10* **Loddon** Norfolk, E England, UK
xli *U9* **Loftus** Redcar and Cleveland, N England, UK
xliii *N14* **Logie Coldstone** Aberdeenshire, NE Scotland, UK
xxxv *E13* **Login** Carmarthenshire, S Wales, UK
xliii *I19* **Lomond, Loch** ◎ C Scotland, UK
xxxvii *U9* **London** *anc.* Augusta, ***Lat.*** Londinium. ● (UK) SE England, UK
xxxvi *G7* **London City** ✈ City of London, SE England, UK
xxxiv *L16* **London, City of** ◈ *London borough* SE England, UK
xliv *I3* **Londonderry** ***var.*** Derry, ***Ir.*** Doire. Londonderry, NW Northern Ireland, UK
xliv *I3* **Londonderry** ◈ *district* NW Northern Ireland, UK
xxxvi *K10* **Long Ashton** North West Somerset, SW England, UK
xli *V2* **Longbenton** North Tyneside, NE England, UK
xxxviii *C16* **Longbridge** Birmingham, C England, UK
xxxvi *M11* **Longbridge Deverill** Wiltshire, S England, UK
xxxix *O12* **Long Buckby** Northamptonshire, C England, UK
xxxvii *Q8* **Long Crendon** Buckinghamshire, C England, UK
xxxix *N8* **Long Eaton** Derbyshire, C England, UK
xliv *H7* **Longford** ***Ir.*** An Longfort. Longford, C Ireland
xxxviii *M11* **Longford** Coventry, C England, UK
xxxviii *L8* **Longford** Derbyshire, C England, UK
xliv *H7* **Longford** ***Ir.*** An Longfort. ◈ *county* C Ireland
xliii *O20* **Longformacus** The Borders, S Scotland, UK
xli *Q4* **Longframlington** Northumberland, N England, UK
xlii *M5* **Longhope** Orkney Islands, N Scotland, UK
xli *Q4* **Longhorsley** Northumberland, N England, UK
xli *R3* **Longhoughton** Northumberland, N England, UK
xliii *H19* **Long, Loch** *inlet* W Scotland, UK
xli *T13* **Long Marston** North Yorkshire, N England, UK
xxxviii *L13* **Long Marston** Warwickshire, C England, UK
xxxix *V13* **Long Melford** Suffolk, E England, UK
xxxviii *H10* **Long Mynd, The** *hill range* W England, UK
xxxvi *L7* **Longney** Gloucestershire, C England, UK
xliii *N19* **Longniddry** East Lothian, SE Scotland, UK
xxxviii *K6* **Longnor** Staffordshire, C England, UK
xli *P12* **Long Preston** North Yorkshire, N England, UK
xli *N14* **Longridge** Lancashire, NW England, UK
xlii *P12* **Longside** Aberdeenshire, NE Scotland, UK
xxxix *X10* **Long Stratton** Norfolk, E England, UK
xxxix *S8* **Long Sutton** Lincolnshire, E England, UK
xxxvi *K12* **Long Sutton** Somerset, SW England, UK
xli *N14* **Longton** Lancashire, NW England, UK
xl *M6* **Longtown** Cumbria, NW England, UK
xxxviii *G14* **Longtown** Herefordshire, W England, UK
xliv *C11* **Loop Head** ***Ir.*** Ceann Léime. *headland* W Ireland
xxxvii *W10* **Loose** Kent, SE England, UK
xliii *E18* **Lorn, Firth of** *inlet* W Scotland, UK
xlii *L11* **Lossiemouth** Moray, NE Scotland, UK
xxxvi *D16* **Lostwithiel** Cornwall, SW England, UK
xlii *K9* **Lothmore** Highland, N Scotland, UK
xxxix *N9* **Loughborough** Leicestershire, C England, UK
xliv *L5* **Loughbrickland** Banbridge, SE Northern Ireland, UK
xliv *F9* **Loughrea** ***Ir.*** Baile Locha Riach. Galway, W Ireland
xliv *C7* **Louisburgh** Mayo, NW Ireland
xliv *K7* **Louth** Louth, NE Ireland
xxxix *S5* **Louth** Lincolnshire, E England, UK
xliv *K7* **Louth** ***Ir.*** Lú. ◈ *county* NE Ireland
xliv *K5* **Louthgall** Armagh, S Northern Ireland, UK
xxxix *O7* **Lowdham** Nottinghamshire, C England, UK
xlii *F11* **Lower Diabaig** Highland, NW Scotland, UK
xxxvii *P7* **Lower Heyford** Oxfordshire, C England, UK
xliv *I5* **Lower Lough Erne** ◎ SW Northern Ireland, UK
xxxix *Z10* **Lowestoft** Suffolk, E England, UK
xl *K9* **Loweswater** Cumbria, NW England, UK
xli *N10* **Lowgill** Cumbria, NW England, UK
xl *M7* **Low Hesket** Cumbria, NW England, UK
xli *Q2* **Lowick** Northumberland, N England, UK
xlii *I7* **Loyal, Loch** ◎ N Scotland, UK
xliii *G14* **Loyne, Loch** ◎ NW Scotland, UK
xlii *H9* **Lubcroy** Highland, NW Scotland, UK
xliii *J18* **Lubnaig, Loch** ◎ C Scotland, UK
xliv *K9* **Lucan** ***Ir.*** Leamhcán. Dublin, E Ireland
xxxvi *H11* **Luccombe** Somerset, SW England, UK
xliii *H26* **Luce Bay** *inlet* SW Scotland, UK
xxxix *R4* **Ludborough** Lincolnshire, E England, UK
xxxix *R4* **Ludford** Lincolnshire, E England, UK
xxxvii *O11* **Ludgershall** Wiltshire, S England, UK
xxxvi *A17* **Ludgvan** Cornwall, SW England, UK
xxxix *Y9* **Ludham** Norfolk, E England, UK
xxxviii *H11* **Ludlow** Shropshire, W England, UK
xliv *K10* **Lugnaquillia Mountain** ***Ir.*** Log na Coille. ▲ E Ireland
xlii *H11* **Luichart, Loch** ◎ NW Scotland, UK
xliii *F18* **Luing** *island* W Scotland, UK
xliv *I12* **Lukeswell** Kilkenny, SE Ireland
xliv *J9* **Lullymore** Kildare, E Ireland
xliii *N14* **Lumphanan** Aberdeenshire, NE Scotland, UK
xlii *N13* **Lumsden** Aberdeenshire, NE Scotland, UK
xliii *O16* **Lunan Bay** *bay* E Scotland, UK
xli *V13* **Lund** East Riding of Yorkshire, N England, UK
xxxvi *D11* **Lundy** *island* SW England, UK
xli *N10* **Lune** ≈ NW England, UK
xlii *I3* **Lunna** Shetland Islands, NE Scotland, UK
xliv *L5* **Lurgan** ***Ir.*** An Lorgain. Craigavon, S Northern Ireland, UK
xxxvii *S12* **Lurgashall** West Sussex, SE England, UK
xliv *L8* **Lusk** Dublin, E Ireland
xlii *C10* **Luskentyre** Western Isles, NW Scotland, UK
xliii *I19* **Luss** Argyll and Bute, W Scotland, UK
xlii *D12* **Lusta** Highland, NW Scotland, UK
xxxvi *H14* **Lustleigh** Devon, SW England, UK
xxxvii *T7* **Luton** Luton, E England, UK
xxxvii *S7* **Luton** ◈ *unitary authority* C England, UK
xxxvii *T7* **Luton** ✈ (London) Luton, SE England, UK
xxxix *N11* **Lutterworth** Leicestershire, C England, UK
xxxix *S8* **Lutton** Lincolnshire, E England, UK
xxxix *R10* **Lutton** Northamptonshire, C England, UK
xxxvi *H11* **Luxborough** Somerset, SW England, UK
xlii *L8* **Lybster** Highland, N Scotland, UK
xxxvii *X12* **Lydd** Kent, SE England, UK
xxxvi *F14* **Lydford** Devon, SW England, UK
xxxviii *G11* **Lydham** Shropshire, W England, UK
xxxvi *L8* **Lydney** Gloucestershire, C England, UK
xxxvi *J15* **Lyme Bay** *bay* S England, UK
xxxvi *K14* **Lyme Regis** Dorset, S England, UK
xxxvii *Y11* **Lyminge** Kent, SE England, UK
xxxvii *P14* **Lymington** Hampshire, S England, UK
xl *E16* **Lymm** Cheshire, W England, UK
xxxvii *Y11* **Lympne** Kent, SE England, UK
xxxvii *O13* **Lyndhurst** Hampshire, S England, UK
xxxvii *N9* **Lyneham** Wiltshire, S England, UK
xlii *M5* **Lyness** Orkney Islands, N Scotland, UK
xxxix *W9* **Lyng** Norfolk, E England, UK
xxxvi *E15* **Lynher** ≈ SW England, UK
xxxvi *G11* **Lynmouth** Devon, SW England, UK
xxxvi *G11* **Lynton** Devon, SW England, UK
xliii *I17* **Lyon, Loch** ◎ C Scotland, UK
xl *M14* **Lytham St Anne's** Lancashire, NW England, UK
xli *V9* **Lythe** North Yorkshire, N England, UK
xlii *M5* **Lythes** Orkney Islands, N Scotland, UK

M

xliv *D8* **Maam Cross** Galway, W Ireland
xliv *D8* **Maamturk Mountains** ▲▲ W Ireland
xliv *G3* **Maas** Donegal, N Ireland
xxxix *T5* **Mablethorpe** Lincolnshire, E England, UK
xl *H17* **Macclesfield** Cheshire, C England, UK
xlii *O11* **Macduff** Aberdeenshire, NE Scotland, UK
xliv *C13* **Macgillycuddy's Reeks** ***var.*** Macgillicuddy's Reeks Mountains, ***Ir.*** Na Cruacha Dubha. ▲▲ SW Ireland
xliii *F23* **Macharioch** Argyll and Bute, W Scotland, UK
xliii *F22* **Machrihanish** Argyll and Bute, W Scotland, UK
xxxv *H8* **Machynlleth** Powys, C Wales, UK
xliv *E14* **Macroom** ***Ir.*** Maigh Chromtha. Cork, SW Ireland
xxxviii *I7* **Madeley** Staffordshire, C England, UK
xxxv *G6* **Maentwrog** Gwynedd, NW Wales, UK
xxxv *I14* **Maesteg** Bridgend, S Wales, UK
xliv *M4* **Magee, Island** *island* E Northern Ireland, UK
xliv *K3* **Maghera** ***Ir.*** Machaire Rátha. Magherafelt, C Northern Ireland, UK
xliv *F10* **Maghera** *hill* W Ireland
xliv *K3* **Magherafelt** ***Ir.*** Machaire Fíolta. Magherafelt, C Northern Ireland, UK
xliv *K4* **Magherafelt** ◈ *district* C Northern Ireland, UK
xliv *L5* **Magheralin** Craigavon, C Northern Ireland, UK
xl *M16* **Maghull** Sefton, NW England, UK
xliv *I6* **Maguiresbridge** Fermanagh, W Northern Ireland, UK
xxxvi *B7* **Maida Vale** Westminster, SE England, UK
xxxvi *L11* **Maiden Bradley** Wiltshire, S England, UK
xxxvii *R9* **Maidenhead** Windsor and Maidenhead, S England, UK
xxxvi *L13* **Maiden Newton** Dorset, S England, UK
xliii *H23* **Maidens** South Ayrshire, W Scotland, UK
xliv *M3* **Maidens, The** *island group* E Northern Ireland, UK
xxxvii *W10* **Maidstone** Kent, SE England, UK
xliv *F11* **Maigue** ≈ W Ireland
xlii *L4* **Mainland** *island* Orkney, N Scotland, UK
xlii *I3* **Mainland** *island* Shetland, NE Scotland, UK
xliv *L8* **Malahide** ***Ir.*** Mullach Íde. Dublin, E Ireland
xxxvi *G17* **Malborough** Devon, SW England, UK
xlii *P1* **Malcom's Head** *headland* NE Scotland, UK
xxxvii *W8* **Maldon** Essex, E England, UK
xli *P12* **Malham** North Yorkshire, N England, UK
xliv *I2* **Malin** ***Ir.*** Málainn. Donegal, NW Ireland
xliv *I1* **Malin Head** ***Ir.*** Cionn Mhálanna. *headland* NW Ireland
xliv *F4* **Malin More** Donegal, N Ireland
xliii *F14* **Mallaig** Highland, N Scotland, UK
xliv *F13* **Mallow** ***Ir.*** Mala. Cork, SW Ireland
xxxv *I8* **Mallwyd** Gwynedd, NW Wales, UK
xxxvi *M9* **Malmesbury** Wiltshire, S England, UK
xxxviii *H7* **Malpas** Cheshire, W England, UK
xli *T16* **Maltby** Rotherham, N England, UK
xxxix *S5* **Maltby le Marsh** Lincolnshire, E England, UK
xli *U11* **Malton** North Yorkshire, N England, UK
xxxviii *I13* **Malvern Hills** *hill range* W England, UK
xxxviii *J13* **Malvern Link** Worcestershire, W England, UK
xxxv *J8* **Manafon** Powys, C Wales, UK
xl *G15* **Manchester** ***Lat.*** Mancunium. Manchester, NW England, UK
xli *P16* **Manchester** ◈ *unitary authority* NW England, UK
xl *E16* **Manchester Canal** *canal* NW England, UK
xxxix *S10* **Manea** Cambridgeshire, E England, UK
xliv *D13* **Mangerton Mountain** ▲ SW Ireland
xxxvi *L9* **Mangotsfield** South Gloucestershire, SW England, UK
xl *G11* **Man, Isle of** *island* British Isles
xxxvii *Y6* **Manningtree** Essex, SE England, UK
xxxv *D14* **Manorbier** Pembrokeshire, SW Wales, UK
xliv *G5* **Manorhamilton** ***Ir.*** Cluainín. Leitrim, NW Ireland
xxxvi *F6* **Manor Park** Newham, SE England, UK
xli *N11* **Mansergh** Cumbria, NW England, UK
xxxix *N6* **Mansfield** Nottinghamshire, C England, UK
xxxix *P9* **Manton** Rutland, C England, UK
xxxvi *L16* **Marazion** Cornwall, SW England, UK
xxxix *S10* **March** Cambridgeshire, E England, UK
xxxvii *W11* **Marden** Kent, SE England, UK
xlii *F11* **Maree, Loch** ◎ N Scotland, UK
xxxv *H15* **Margam** Neath Port Talbot, S Wales, UK
xxxvii *Z9* **Margate** ***prev.*** Mergate. Kent, SE England, UK
xliii *G22* **Margnaheglish** North Ayrshire, W Scotland, UK
xxxix *U9* **Marham** Norfolk, E England, UK
xxxvi *E13* **Marhamchurch** Cornwall, SW England, UK
xxxix *R10* **Marholm** Cambridgeshire, E England, UK
xxxvi *K11* **Mark** Somerset, SW England, UK
xxxviii *M10* **Market Bosworth** Leicestershire, C England, UK
xxxix *R9* **Market Deeping** Lincolnshire, E England, UK
xxxviii *I8* **Market Drayton** Shropshire, W England, UK
xxxix *O10* **Market Harborough** Leicestershire, C England, UK
xliv *K5* **Markethill** Armagh, S Northern Ireland, UK
xxxix *Q5* **Market Rasen** Lincolnshire, E England, UK
xli *V13* **Market Weighton** East Riding of Yorkshire, N England, UK
xxxix *N9* **Markfield** Leicestershire, C England, UK
xxxvi *L10* **Marksbury** Bath and North East Somerset, SW England, UK
xxxvii *S7* **Markyate** Hertfordshire, E England, UK
xxxvii *O10* **Marlborough** Wiltshire, S England, UK
xxxv *C14* **Marloes** Pembrokeshire, SW Wales, UK
xxxvii *R9* **Marlow** Buckinghamshire, C England, UK
xli *Q17* **Marple** Stockport, NW England, UK
xli *Q15* **Marsden** Kirklees, N England, UK
xli *N13* **Marshaw** Lancashire, NW England, UK
xxxix *S4* **Marshchapel** Lincolnshire, E England, UK
xxxvi *M9* **Marshfield** South Gloucestershire, SW England, UK
xxxvi *D14* **Marshgate** Cornwall, SW England, UK
xxxvii *Q7* **Marsh Gibbon** Buckinghamshire, C England, UK
xli *Z6* **Marske-by-the-Sea** Redcar and Cleveland, N England, UK
xxxvi *L12* **Marston Magna** Somerset, SW England, UK
xxxix *Y9* **Martham** Norfolk, E England, UK
xxxvii *N12* **Martin** Hampshire, S England, UK
xxxvi *G11* **Martinhoe** Devon, SW England, UK
xxxix *X13* **Martlesham** Suffolk, E England, UK
xxxviii *I12* **Martley** Worcestershire, W England, UK
xxxvi *K12* **Martock** Somerset, SW England, UK
xxxix *P5* **Marton** Lincolnshire, E England, UK
xli *S12* **Marton** North Yorkshire, N England, UK
xxxvi *F12* **Marwood** Devon, SW England, UK
xlii *I11* **Marybank** Highland, NW Scotland, UK
xliii *O15* **Marykirk** Aberdeenshire, NE Scotland, UK
xl *K8* **Maryport** Cumbria, NW England, UK
xliii *H26* **Maryport** Dumfries and Galloway, SW Scotland, UK
xxxvi *F14* **Mary Tavy** Devon, SW England, UK
xliii *N14* **Marywell** Aberdeenshire, NE Scotland, UK
xliii *O16* **Marywell** Angus, E Scotland, UK
xli *R11* **Masham** North Yorkshire, N England, UK
xliv *D8* **Mask, Lough** ***Ir.*** Loch Measca. ◎ W Ireland
xxxv *C12* **Mathry** Pembrokeshire, SW Wales, UK
xxxix *X8* **Matlaske** Norfolk, E England, UK
xxxviii *M6* **Matlock** Derbyshire, C England, UK
xxxviii *L6* **Matlock Bath** Derbyshire, C England, UK
xliii *I22* **Mauchline** East Ayrshire, W Scotland, UK
xlii *P12* **Maud** Aberdeenshire, NE Scotland, UK
xl *H11* **Maughold** E Isle of Man
xliv *D8* **Maum** Galway, W Ireland
xl *K7* **Mawbray** Cumbria, NW England, UK
xxxvi *C17* **Mawgan** Cornwall, SW England, UK
xxxvi *C17* **Mawnan Smith** Cornwall, SW England, UK
xliii *I23* **Maybole** South Ayrshire, W Scotland, UK
xxxvi *C7* **Mayfair** Westminster, SE England, UK
xxxvii *V12* **Mayfield** East Sussex, SE England, UK
xxxviii *L7* **Mayfield** Staffordshire, C England, UK
xliii *O18* **May, Isle of** *island* E Scotland, UK
xliv *K9* **Maynooth** Kildare, E Ireland
xliv *E7* **Mayo** ***Ir.*** Maigh Eo. ◈ *county* W Ireland
xlii *I7* **Meadie, Loch** ◎ NW Scotland, UK
xlii *I8* **Meall Nom Con** ▲ NW Scotland, UK
xl *L8* **Mealsgate** Cumbria, NW England, UK
xxxviii *F13* **Measham** Leicestershire, C England, UK
xliv *J8* **Meath** ***Ir.*** An Mhí. ◈ *county* E Ireland
xlii *C9* **Meavaig** Western Isles, NW Scotland, UK
xxxix *P10* **Medbourne** Leicestershire, C England, UK
xxxvii *Q11* **Medstead** Hampshire, S England, UK
xxxvii *V11* **Medway** ≈ SE England, UK
xxxv *E13* **Meidrim** Carmarthenshire, S Wales, UK
xxxv *J8* **Meifod** Powys, C Wales, UK
xliii *M16* **Meigle** Perth and Kinross, C Scotland, UK
xliii *L17* **Meikleour** Perth and Kinross, C Scotland, UK
xxxviii *M8* **Melbourne** Derbyshire, C England, UK
xxxix *S13* **Meldreth** Cambridgeshire, E England, UK
xxxvi *M10* **Melksham** Wiltshire, S England, UK
xliv *H13* **Melleray, Mount** ▲ S Ireland
xli *N12* **Melling** Lancashire, NW England, UK
xxxix *W11* **Mellis** Suffolk, E England, UK
xxxvi *L11* **Mells** Somerset, SW England, UK
xli *N8* **Melmerby** Cumbria, NW England, UK
xliii *N21* **Melrose** The Borders, S Scotland, UK
xlii *M5* **Melsetter** Orkney Islands, N Scotland, UK
xli *R9* **Melsonby** North Yorkshire, N England, UK
xli *Q15* **Meltham** Kirklees, N England, UK
xxxix *W8* **Melton Constable** Norfolk, E England, UK
xxxix *P9* **Melton Mowbray** Leicestershire, C England, UK
xlii *F10* **Melvaig** Highland, NW Scotland, UK
xlii *K6* **Melvich** Highland, N Scotland, UK
xliv *G5* **Melvin, Lough** ***Ir.*** Loch Meilbhe. ◎ S Northern Ireland, UK/Ireland
xlii *P11* **Memsie** Aberdeenshire, NE Scotland, UK
xxxv *G4* **Menai Bridge** Isle of Anglesey, NW Wales, UK
xxxv *F5* **Menai Strait** *strait* NW Wales, UK
xxxvi *K11* **Mendip Hills** ***var.*** Mendips. *hill range* S England, UK
xxxix *W12* **Mendlesham** Suffolk, E England, UK
xli *Q13* **Menston** Leeds, N England, UK
xxxvii *Q12* **Meon** ≈ S England, UK
xxxvii *Q12* **Meonstoke** Hampshire, S England, UK
xxxvii *W10* **Meopham** Kent, SE England, UK
xxxix *T11* **Mepal** Cambridgeshire, E England, UK
xxxvi *M12* **Mere** Wiltshire, S England, UK
xxxvii *V10* **Mereworth** Kent, SE England, UK
xxxviii *E15* **Meriden** Solihull, C England, UK
xliii *I24* **Merrick** ▲ S Scotland, UK
xxxvi *K13* **Merriott** Somerset, SW England, UK
xl *M17* **Mersey** ≈ NW England, UK
xxxv *I12* **Merthyr** Cynog Powys, C Wales, UK
xxxv *J13* **Merthyr Tydfil** Merthyr Tydfil, S Wales, UK
xxxv *J14* **Merthyr Tydfil** ◈ *unitary authority* S Wales, UK
xxxvi *F13* **Merton** Devon, SW England, UK
xxxvii *T9* **Merton** Merton, SE England, UK
xxxiv *K17* **Merton** ◈ *London borough* SE England, UK
xliii *O22* **Mervinslaw** The Borders, S Scotland, UK
xxxvi *G12* **Meshaw** Devon, SW England, UK
xxxix *P4* **Messingham** North Lincolnshire, N England, UK
xxxix *X11* **Metfield** Suffolk, E England, UK
xxxix *Q6* **Metheringham** Lincolnshire, E England, UK
xliii *M18* **Methil** Fife, E Scotland, UK
xlii *O12* **Methlick** Aberdeenshire, NE Scotland, UK
xliii *L17* **Methven** Perth and Kinross, C Scotland, UK
xxxix *U10* **Methwold** Norfolk, E England, UK
xxxvi *D16* **Mevagissey** Cornwall, SW England, UK
xliv *M4* **Mew Island** *island* E Northern Ireland, UK
xli *S16* **Mexborough** Doncaster, N England, UK
xlii *I13* **Mhor, Loch** ◎ NW Scotland, UK
xxxviii *G14* **Michaelchurch Escley** Herefordshire, W England, UK
xxxvii *P11* **Micheldever** Hampshire, S England, UK
xli *P9* **Mickleton** Durham, N England, UK
xxxvii *N6* **Mickleton** Gloucestershire, C England, UK
xlii *M3* **Midbea** Orkney Islands, N Scotland, UK
xxxvii *P7* **Middle Barton** Oxfordshire, C England, UK
xli *Q11* **Middleham** North Yorkshire, N England, UK
xli *Y6* **Middlesbrough** Middlesborough, N England, UK
xli *Y7* **Middlesbrough** ◈ *unitary authority* N England, UK
xli *Q11* **Middlesmoor** North Yorkshire, N England, UK
xli *N11* **Middleton** Cumbria, NW England, UK
xxxix *U9* **Middleton** Norfolk, E England, UK
xl *G14* **Middleton** Rochdale, NW England, UK
xxxix *N13* **Middleton Cheney** Northamptonshire, C England, UK
xli *P8* **Middleton in Teesdale** Durham, N England, UK
xxxvii *S13* **Middleton-on-Sea** West Sussex, SE England, UK
xli *V13* **Middleton-on-the-Wolds** East Riding of Yorkshire, N England, UK
xliv *J5* **Middletown** Armagh, S Northern Ireland, UK
xxxv *K8* **Middletown** Powys, C Wales, UK
xxxviii *M13* **Middle Tysoe** Warwickshire, C England, UK
xxxvii *O11* **Middle Wallop** Hampshire, S England, UK
xxxviii *I6* **Middlewich** Cheshire, W England, UK
xlii *I6* **Midfield** Highland, N Scotland, UK
xxxvii *R12* **Midhurst** West Sussex, SE England, UK
xliv *G14* **Midleton** ***Ir.*** Mainistir na Corann. Cork, SW Ireland
xliii *M20* **Midlothian** ◈ *unitary authority* S Scotland, UK
xxxvi *L10* **Midsomer Norton** Bath and North East Somerset, SW England, UK
xlii *I2* **Mid Yell** Shetland Islands, NE Scotland, UK
xxxvi *L12* **Milborne Port** Somerset, SW England, UK
xli *Q5* **Milbourne** Northumberland, N England, UK
xxxix *U11* **Mildenhall** Suffolk, E England, UK
xxxvii *X6* **Mile End** Essex, SE England, UK
xliv *G11* **Milestone** Tipperary, S Ireland
xli *P2* **Milfield** Northumberland, N England, UK
xxxvii *S11* **Milford** Surrey, SE England, UK
xxxv *C14* **Milford Haven** ***prev.*** Milford. Pembrokeshire, SW Wales, UK
xxxv *C14* **Milford Haven** *inlet* SW Wales, UK
xxxvi *F16* **Millbrook** Cornwall, SW England, UK
xliv *I2* **Millford** ***Ir.*** Baile na nGallóglach. Donegal, NW Ireland
xxxvi *B5* **Mill Hill** Barnet, SE England, UK
xliii *P15* **Mill of Uras** Aberdeenshire, NE Scotland, UK
xl *L11* **Millom** Cumbria, NW England, UK
xliii *H21* **Millport** North Ayrshire, W Scotland, UK
xliv *E13* **Millstreet** Cork, S Ireland
xliii *M24* **Milltown** Dumfries and Galloway, SW Scotland, UK
xliv *D10* **Milltown Malbay** ***Ir.*** Sráid na Cathrach. Clare, W Ireland
xxxvi *E8* **Millwall** Tower Hamlets, SE England, UK
xliii *J20* **Milngavie** East Dunbartonshire, C Scotland, UK
xl *H13* **Milnow** Rochdale, NW England, UK
xli *N11* **Milnthorpe** Cumbria, NW England, UK
xlii *C12* **Milovaig** Highland, NW Scotland, UK
xlii *H11* **Milton** Highland, NW Scotland, UK
xlii *J12* **Milton** Highland, NW Scotland, UK
xxxvi *F15* **Milton Abbot** Devon, SW England, UK
xxxvii *S5* **Milton Ernest** Bedfordshire, C England, UK
xxxvii *R6* **Milton Keynes** Milton Keynes, SE England, UK
xxxvii *R5* **Milton Keynes** ◈ *unitary authority* C England, UK
xliii *J19* **Milton of Campsie** East Dunbartonshire, C Scotland, UK
xxxvi *I12* **Milverton** Somerset, SW England, UK
xlii *E9* **Minch, The** ***var.*** North Minch. *strait* NW Scotland, UK
xliv *H14* **Mine Head** ***Ir.*** Mionn Ard. *headland* S Ireland
xxxvi *I11* **Minehead** Somerset, SW England, UK
xxxvii *N9* **Minety** Wiltshire, S England, UK
xlii *A13* **Mingary** Western Isles, NW Scotland, UK
xliii *A15* **Mingulay** *island* NW Scotland, UK
xxxvii *O13* **Minstead** Hampshire, S England, UK
xxxvii *X9* **Minster** Kent, SE England, UK
xxxvii *Z10* **Minster** Kent, SE England, UK
xxxviii *G10* **Minsterley** Shropshire, W England, UK
xlii *P11* **Mintlaw** Aberdeenshire, NE Scotland, UK
xli *R15* **Mirfield** Kirklees, N England, UK
xxxix *O4* **Misterton** Nottinghamshire, C England, UK
xxxvi *K13* **Misterton** Somerset, SW England, UK
xliv *G12* **Mitchelstown** ***Ir.*** Baile Mhistéala. Cork, SW Ireland
xli *R5* **Mitford** Northumberland, N England, UK
xliv *C15* **Mizen Head** ***Ir.*** Carn Uí Néid. *headland* SW Ireland
xliv *H9* **Moate** Westmeath, C Ireland
xliii *I25* **Mochrum** Dumfries and Galloway, SW Scotland, UK
xxxvi *G16* **Modbury** Devon, SW England, UK
xxxv *F4* **Moelfre** Isle of Anglesey, NW Wales, UK
xxxv *H8* **Moelfre** *hill* E Wales, UK
xliii *L23* **Moffat** Dumfries and Galloway, S Scotland, UK
xliv *D10* **Moher, Cliffs of** *cliff* W Ireland
xliv *H7* **Mohill** Leitrim, N Ireland
xliv *L5* **Moira** Craigavon, C Northern Ireland, UK
xlii *D13* **Mol-chlach** Highland, NW Scotland, UK
xxxv *J5* **Mold** Flintshire, NE Wales, UK
xxxvii *T11* **Mole** ≈ SE England, UK
xxxvi *H12* **Molland** Devon, SW England, UK
xlii *A11* **Monach Islands** *island group* NW Scotland, UK
xliii *J14* **Monadhliath Mountains** ▲▲ N Scotland, UK
xliv *J5* **Monaghan** ***Ir.*** Muineachán. Monaghan, N Ireland
xliv *J6* **Monaghan** ***Ir.*** Muineachán. ◈ *county* N Ireland
xlii *H12* **Monar, Loch** ◎ NW Scotland, UK
xliv *J9* **Monasterevin** Kildare, E Ireland
xliv *H10* **Moneygall** Offaly, C Ireland
xliv *K4* **Moneymore** Cookstown, C Northern Ireland, UK
xliii *K23* **Moniaive** Dumfries and Galloway, SW Scotland, UK
xliii *N17* **Monifieth** Angus, E Scotland, UK
xliii *N17* **Monikie** Angus, E Scotland, UK
xxxviii *H13* **Monkland** Herefordshire, W England, UK
xxxvii *T12* **Monk's Gate** West Sussex, SE England, UK
xxxvi *I11* **Monksilver** Somerset, SW England, UK
xliii *I22* **Monkton** South Ayrshire, W Scotland, UK
xxxv *L13* **Monmouth** ***Wel.*** Trefynwy. Monmouthshire, SE Wales, UK
xxxv *K13* **Monmouthshire** ◈ *unitary authority* SE Wales, UK
xliii *I26* **Monreith** Dumfries and Galloway, SW Scotland, UK
xxxv *K9* **Montgomery** Powys, E Wales, UK
xliii *M18* **Montrave** Fife, E Scotland, UK
xliii *O16* **Montrose** Angus, E Scotland, UK
xlii *O13* **Monymusk** Aberdeenshire, NE Scotland, UK
xxxvi *K11* **Moorlinch** Somerset, SW England, UK
xliii *F14* **Morar** Highland, NW Scotland, UK
xliii *F14* **Morar, Loch** ◎ N Scotland, UK
xlii *L11* **Moray** ◈ *unitary authority* N Scotland, UK
xlii *K11* **Moray Firth** *inlet* N Scotland, UK
xxxvi *G13* **Morchard Bishop** Devon, SW England, UK
xxxviii *H14* **Mordiford** Herefordshire, W England, UK
xliii *O22* **Morebattle** The Borders, S Scotland, UK
xl *M12* **Morecambe** Lancashire, NW England, UK
xl *M12* **Morecambe Bay** *inlet* NW England, UK
xlii *H8* **More, Loch** ◎ NW Scotland, UK
xxxvi *M14* **Moreton** Dorset, S England, UK
xxxvii *V8* **Moreton** Essex, SE England, UK
xxxvi *H14* **Moretonhampstead** Devon, SW England, UK
xxxvii *O6* **Moreton-in-Marsh** Gloucestershire, C England, UK
xxxvi *E13* **Morewenstow** Cornwall, SW England, UK
xxxv *E6* **Morfa Nefyn** Gwynedd, NW Wales, UK
xlii *I13* **Mor, Glen** ***var.*** Glen Albyn, Great Glen. *valley* N Scotland, UK
xli *R14* **Morley** Leeds, N England, UK
xli *R5* **Morpeth** Northumberland, N England, UK
xxxv *H14* **Morriston** Swansea, S Wales, UK
xxxvi *F11* **Mortehoe** Devon, SW England, UK
xxxviii *H12* **Mortimer's Cross** Herefordshire, W England, UK
xxxvi *B8* **Mortlake** Richmond upon Thames, SE England, UK
xxxix *Q8* **Morton** Lincolnshire, E England, UK
xxxix *O4* **Morton** Lincolnshire, E England, UK
xxxvi *L16* **Morvah** Cornwall, SW England, UK
xliii *M14* **Morven** ▲ NE Scotland, UK
xlii *K8* **Morven** ▲ N Scotland, UK
xxxviii *I10* **Morville** Shropshire, W England, UK
xlii *I2* **Mossbank** Shetland Islands, NE Scotland, UK
xliv *L4* **Mossley** Newtownabbey, E Northern Ireland, UK
xl *H14* **Mossley** Tameside, NW England, UK
xlii *M11* **Mosstodloch** Moray, N Scotland, UK
xxxv *J4* **Mostyn** Flintshire, N Wales, UK
xliii *K20* **Motherwell** North Lanarkshire, C Scotland, UK
xxxvi *F9* **Mottingham** Bromley, SE England, UK
xxxix *R8* **Moulton** Lincolnshire, E England, UK
xxxix *P12* **Moulton** Northamptonshire, C England, UK
xxxix *U12* **Moulton** Suffolk, E England, UK
xxxv *J14* **Mountain Ash** Rhondda Cynon Taff, S Wales, UK
xliv *F8* **Mount Bellew** Galway, W Ireland
xxxvii *W12* **Mountfield** East Sussex, SE England, UK
xliv *J4* **Mount Hamilton** Strabane, W Northern Ireland, UK
xxxvi *C16* **Mountjoy** Cornwall, SW England, UK
xliv *I10* **Mountmellick** ***Ir.*** Móinteach Mílic. Laois, C Ireland
xliv *I10* **Mountrath** Laois, C Ireland
xxxvi *M17* **Mount's Bay** *inlet* SW England, UK
xliv *F10* **Mountshannon** Clare, W Ireland
xxxix *N9* **Mountsorrel** Leicestershire, C England, UK
xliv *G8* **Mount Talbot** Roscommon, C Ireland
xliv *I4* **Mourne** ≈ W Northern Ireland, UK
xliv *L6* **Mourne Mountains** ***Ir.*** Beanna Boirche. ▲▲ SE Northern Ireland, UK
xxxvi *M16* **Mousehole** Cornwall, SW England, UK
xliii *L24* **Mouswald** Dumfries and Galloway, SW Scotland, UK
xliv *J2* **Moville** Donegal, N Ireland
xxxviii *J7* **Mow Cop** Staffordshire, C England, UK
xliv *K5* **Moy** Dungannon, C Northern Ireland, UK
xlii *J12* **Moy** Highland, NW Scotland, UK
xliii *I15* **Moy** Highland, NW Scotland, UK
xliv *E6* **Moy** ≈ NW Ireland
xliv *C8* **Moyard** Galway, W Ireland
xliv *E9* **Moycullen** Galway, W Ireland
xliv *K5* **Moygashel** Dungannon, C Northern Ireland, UK
xliv *L2* **Moyle** ◈ *district* N Northern Ireland, UK
xxxv *D12* **Moylgrove** Pembrokeshire, SW Wales, UK
xliii *I15* **Moy, Loch** ◎ NW Scotland, UK
xliv *F8* **Moylough** Galway, W Ireland
xliii *F21* **Muasdale** Argyll and Bute, W Scotland, UK
xxxvii *U7* **Much Hadham** Hertfordshire, SE England, UK
xxxviii *I14* **Much Marcle** Herefordshire, W England, UK
xxxviii *I10* **Much Wenlock** Shropshire, W England, UK
xliii *D15* **Muck** *island* W Scotland, UK
xlii *H3* **Muckle Roe** *island* NE Scotland, UK
xliv *J6* **Muckno Lough** ◎ NE Ireland
xliv *D13* **Muckross** Kerry, SW Ireland
xlii *J9* **Muie** Highland, NW Scotland, UK
xliv *J11* **Muine Bheag** ***Eng.*** Bagenalstown. Carlow, SE Ireland
xliii *N17* **Muirdrum** Angus, E Scotland, UK
xliii *J20* **Muirhead** Angus, E Scotland, UK
xliii *M17* **Muirhead** North Lanarkshire, C Scotland, UK
xliii *J22* **Muirkirk** East Ayrshire, W Scotland, UK
xlii *I12* **Muir of Ord** Highland, NW Scotland, UK
xliii *A14* **Muldoanich** *island* NW Scotland, UK
xliv *F11* **Mulkear** ≈ W Ireland
xliv *E12* **Mullaghareirk Mountains** *hill range* W Ireland
xliv *K10* **Mullaghcleevaun** ▲ E Ireland
xliv *G5* **Mullaghmore** Sligo, N Ireland
xliv *H6* **Mullan** Fermanagh, W Northern Ireland, UK
xlii *H13* **Mullardoch, Loch** ◎ NW Scotland, UK
xlii *M2* **Mull Head** *headland* N Scotland, UK
xliv *I12* **Mullinavat** Kilkenny, SE Ireland
xliv *I8* **Mullingar** ***Ir.*** An Muileann gCearr. Westmeath, C Ireland
xxxvi *B17* **Mullion** Cornwall, SW England, UK
xliii *E17* **Mull, Isle of** *island* W Scotland, UK
xliii *E16* **Mull, Sound of** *strait* NW Scotland, UK
xliv *D7* **Mulrany** Mayo, NW Ireland
xxxix *X7* **Mundesley** Norfolk, E England, UK
xxxix *V10* **Mundford** Norfolk, E England, UK
xliv *F11* **Mungret** Limerick, SW Ireland
xlii *J11* **Munlochy** Highland, NW Scotland, UK
xliv *D13* **Munster** ***Ir.*** Cúige Mumhan. *province* S Ireland
xliv *E9* **Murroogh** Clare, W Ireland
xxxix *S9* **Murrow** Cambridgeshire, E England, UK
xli *S7* **Murton** Durham, N England, UK
xxxvi *J14* **Musbury** Devon, SW England, UK
xliv *E13* **Musheramore** ▲ S Ireland
xliii *M20* **Musselburgh** East Lothian, SE Scotland, UK
xli *W11* **Muston** North Yorkshire, N England, UK
xxxvi *C5* **Muswell Hill** Haringey, SE England, UK
xliii *K18* **Muthill** Perth and Kinross, C Scotland, UK
xliv *D10* **Mutton Island** *island* W Ireland.
xliv *C7* **Mweelrea** ***Ir.*** Caoc Maol Réidh. ▲ W Ireland
xlii *L7* **Mybster** Highland, N Scotland, UK
xxxv *H12* **Myddfai** Carmarthenshire, S Wales, UK
xxxviii *H9* **Myddle** Shropshire, W England, UK
xxxv *F11* **Mydroilyn** Ceredigion, W Wales, UK

N

xliv *K9* **Naas** ***Ir.*** An Nás, Nás na Ríogh. Kildare, C Ireland
xlii *F10* **Naast** Highland, NW Scotland, UK
xli *T13* **Naburn** York, N England, UK
xxxix *X13* **Nacton** Suffolk, E England, UK
xliv *E13* **Nad** Cork, S Ireland
xli *W12* **Nafferton** East Riding of Yorkshire, N England, UK
xliv *F13* **Nagles Mountains** ▲▲ S Ireland
xxxvi *K10* **Nailsea** North West Somerset, SW England, UK
xxxvi *M8* **Nailsworth** Gloucestershire, C England, UK
xlii *K11* **Nairn** Highland, N Scotland, UK
xxxv *J10* **Nantmel** Powys, C Wales, UK
xxxv *G6* **Nantmor** Gwynedd, NW Wales, UK
xxxviii *H7* **Nantwich** Cheshire, W England, UK
xxxv *D13* **Narberth** Pembrokeshire, SW Wales, UK
xxxix *N10* **Narborough** Leicestershire, C England, UK
xxxix *U9* **Narborough** Norfolk, E England, UK
xliv *G3* **Narin** Donegal, N Ireland
xxxix *O11* **Naseby** Northamptonshire, C England, UK
xli *N11* **Natland** Cumbria, NW England, UK
xliv *K8* **Navan** ***Ir.*** An Uaimh. Meath, E Ireland
xxxix *Q6* **Navenby** Lincolnshire, E England, UK
xlii *J8* **Naver, Loch** ◎ NW Scotland, UK
xxxix *W14* **Nayland** Suffolk, E England, UK
xliv *K5* **Neagh, Lough** ◎ E Northern Ireland, UK
xliv *E8* **Neale** Mayo, NW Ireland
xlii *I3* **Neap** Shetland Islands, NE Scotland, UK
xxxvi *A6* **Neasden** Brent, SE England, UK
xxxv *H14* **Neath** Neath Port Talbot, S Wales, UK
xxxv *H14* **Neath Port Talbot** ◈ *unitary authority* S Wales, UK
xxxix *V9* **Necton** Norfolk, E England, UK
xxxix *W12* **Needham Market** Suffolk, E England, UK
xxxvii *O14* **Needles, The** *rocks* Isle of Wight, S England, UK
xxxv *E6* **Nefyn** Gwynedd, NW Wales, UK
xli *P14* **Nelson** Lancashire, NW England, UK
xliv *G10* **Nenagh** ***Ir.*** An tAonach. Tipperary, C Ireland
xxxix *S9* **Nene** ≈ E England, UK
xli *O7* **Nenthead** Cumbria, NW England, UK
xliv *D6* **Nephin** ***Ir.*** Néifinn. ▲ W Ireland
xxxviii *G9* **Nesscliffe** Shropshire, W England, UK
xlii *I13* **Ness, Loch** ◎ N Scotland, UK
xli *V9* **Ness Point** *headland* N England, UK
xl *B17* **Neston** Cheshire, W England, UK
xxxvii *O11* **Netheravon** Wiltshire, S England, UK
xxxix *N6* **Nether Langwith** Nottinghamshire, C England, UK
xxxvi *J11* **Nether Stowey** Somerset, SW England, UK
xli *P4* **Netherton** Northumberland, N England, UK
xl *K10* **Nether Wasdale** Cumbria, NW England, UK
xlii *K13* **Nethy Bridge** Highland, NW Scotland, UK
xxxvii *Q9* **Nettlebed** Oxfordshire, C England, UK
xxxix *Q5* **Nettleham** Lincolnshire, E England, UK
xliii *F14* **Nevis, Loch** *inlet* NW Scotland, UK
xliii *L24* **New Abbey** Dumfries and Galloway, SW Scotland, UK

◆ Country
● Country Capital
◇ Dependent Territory
○ Dependent Territory Capital
◈ Administrative Region
✈ International Airport
▲ Mountain
▲▲ Mountain Range
◎ Lake
▣ Reservoir
≈ River

◆ Country ◇ Dependent Territory ● Administrative Region ▲ Mountain ≈ River
● Country Capital ○ Dependent Territory Capital × International Airport ▲▲ Mountain Range ⊚ Lake ⊚ Reservoir

S

◆ Country   ◇ Dependent Territory   ✦ Administrative Region   ▲ Mountain   ⊙ Lake   ⌁ River
● Country Capital   ◎ Dependent Territory Capital   ✈ International Airport   ▲ Mountain Range   ▣ Reservoir

SORBIE – ULDALE

xliii I25 **Sorbie** Dumfries and Galloway, SW Scotland, UK
xliii D16 **Sorisdale** Argyll and Bute, W Scotland, UK
xliii J22 **Sorn** East Ayrshire, W Scotland, UK
xxxvii T9 **Southall** Ealing, SE England, UK
xxxviii M12 **Southam** Warwickshire, C England, UK
xxxvii P13 **Southampton** ***hist.*** Hamwih, ***Lat.*** Clausentum. City of Southampton, S England, UK
xxxvii P12 **Southampton, City of** ◐ *unitary authority* S England, UK
xliii H23 **South** Ayrshire ◐ *unitary authority* W Scotland, UK
xli U9 **South Bank** Redcar and Cleveland, N England, UK
xl F12 **South Barrule** *hill* S Isle of Man
xxxvii W9 **South Benfleet** Essex, SE England, UK
xxxvii V11 **Southborough** Kent, SE England, UK
xxxvi G16 **South Brent** Devon, SW England, UK
xli V14 **South Cave** East Riding of Yorkshire, N England, UK
xxxvii N8 **South Cerney** Gloucestershire, C England, UK
xli R3 **South Charlton** Northumberland, N England, UK
xxxvii R12 **South Downs** *hill range* SE England, UK
xliii F23 **Southend** Argyll and Bute, W Scotland, UK
xxxvii X9 **Southend-on-Sea** Essex, E England, UK
xxxvii W9 **Southend-on-Sea** ◐ *unitary authority* SE England, UK
xliii K23 **Southern Uplands** ▲▲ S Scotland, UK
xxxix T10 **Southery** Norfolk, E England, UK
xliii N16 **South Esk** ≈ E Scotland, UK
xxxix P3 **South Ferriby** North Lincolnshire, N England, UK
xxxvi B9 **Southfields** Wandsworth, SE England, UK
xxxvii Z11 **South Foreland** *headland* SE England, UK
xxxvi D5 **Southgate** Enfield, SE England, UK
xxxvi L8 **South Gloucestershire** ◐ *unitary authority* W England, UK
xxxvii R12 **South Harting** West Sussex, SE England, UK
xxxvii Q13 **South Hayling** Hampshire, S England, UK
xxxvii T11 **South Holmwood** Surrey, SE England, UK
xxxix Q4 **South Kelsey** Lincolnshire, E England, UK
xli S15 **South Kirkby** Wakefield, N England, UK
xxxix R7 **South Kyme** Lincolnshire, E England, UK
xliii J21 **South Lanarkshire** ◐ *unitary authority* C Scotland, UK
xxxviii K13 **South Littleton** Worcestershire, C England, UK
xxxvii U13 **South Malling** East Sussex, SE England, UK
xxxvii X8 **Southminster** Essex, SE England, UK
xxxvi G12 **South Molton** Devon, SW England, UK
xxxvi K12 **South Petherton** Somerset, SW England, UK
xl B13 **Southport** Sefton, NW England, UK
xliii L19 **South Queensferry** City of Edinburgh, SE Scotland, UK
xlii N5 **South Ronaldsay** *island* NE Scotland, UK
xli W2 **South Shields** South Tyneside, NE England, UK
xli W13 **South Skirlaugh** East Riding of Yorkshire, N England, UK
xliv D10 **South Sound** *sound* W Ireland
xlii N5 **Southtown** Orkney Islands, N Scotland, UK
xli O7 **South Tyne** ≈ N England, UK
xli S6 **South Tyneside** ◐ *unitary authority* NE England, UK
xlii A13 **South Uist** *island* NW Scotland, UK
xlii I4 **South View** Shetland Islands, NE Scotland, UK
xxxiv L16 **Southwark** ◐ *London borough* SE England, UK
xxxvi D8 **Southwark** *London borough capital* Southwark, SE England, UK
xxxix O7 **Southwell** Nottinghamshire, C England, UK
xxxix Z11 **Southwold** Suffolk, E England, UK
xxxvii W8 **South Woodham Ferrers** Essex, E England, UK
xxxix T8 **South Wootton** Norfolk, E England, UK
xxxvi G14 **South Zeal** Devon, SW England, UK
xli S11 **Sowerby** North Yorkshire, N England, UK
xxxix R8 **Spalding** Lincolnshire, E England, UK
xxxix R11 **Spaldwick** Cambridgeshire, E England, UK
xliv D10 **Spanish Point** *headland* W Ireland
xxxvi L12 **Sparkford** Somerset, SW England, UK
xliii H15 **Spean Bridge** Highland, NW Scotland, UK
xl M17 **Speke** Liverpool, NW England, UK
xli R8 **Spennymoor** Durham, N England, UK
xliv J3 **Sperrin Mountains** ▲▲ N Northern Ireland, UK
xxxviii J13 **Spetchley** Worcestershire, W England, UK
xlii M11 **Spey** ≈ NE Scotland, UK
xlii M11 **Spey Bay** Moray, N Scotland, UK
xliv E9 **Spiddle** Galway, W Ireland
xxxix S6 **Spilsby** Lincolnshire, E England, UK
xlii J10 **Spinningdale** Highland, NW Scotland, UK
xlii L7 **Spital** Highland, N Scotland, UK
xxxv D13 **Spittal** Pembrokeshire, SW Wales, UK
xliii L15 **Spittal of Glenshee** Perth and Kinross, C Scotland, UK
xli R13 **Spofforth** North Yorkshire, N England, UK
xxxix O12 **Spratton** Northamptonshire, C England, UK
xxxix Q5 **Spridlington** Lincolnshire, E England, UK
xliii O21 **Sprouston** The Borders, S Scotland, UK
xxxix X9 **Sprowston** Norfolk, E England, UK
xli Y15 **Spurn Head** *headland* E England, UK
xliv L10 **Sraghmore** Wicklow, E Ireland
xlii J4 **Stack Skerry** *island* N Scotland, UK
xxxvii Q8 **Stadhampton** Oxfordshire, C England, UK
xliii D17 **Staffa** *island* W Scotland, UK
xlii E11 **Staffin** Highland, NW Scotland, UK
xxxviii J9 **Stafford** Staffordshire, C England, UK
xxxviii C13 **Staffordshire** ◐ *county* C England, UK
xli Q9 **Staindrop** Durham, N England, UK
xxxvii S9 **Staines** Surrey, SE England, UK
xli T15 **Stainforth** Doncaster, N England, UK
xli P12 **Stainforth** North Yorkshire, N England, UK
xli W10 **Staintondale** North Yorkshire, N England, UK
xli U9 **Staithes** Redcar and Cleveland, N England, UK
xxxvi L12 **Stalbridge** Dorset, S England, UK
xxxix Y8 **Stalham** Norfolk, E England, UK
xli P11 **Stalling Busk** North Yorkshire, N England, UK
xli Q16 **Stalybridge** Tameside, NW England, UK
xxxix Q9 **Stamford** Lincolnshire, E England, UK
xli U12 **Stamford Bridge** East Riding of Yorkshire, N England, UK
xli Q6 **Stamfordham** Northumberland, N England, UK
xxxvi D6 **Stamford Hill** Hackney, SE England, UK
xli N15 **Standish** Wigan, NW England, UK
xxxviii J8 **Standon** Staffordshire, C England, UK
xxxvii W9 **Stanford-le-Hope** Essex, SE England, UK
xli Q8 **Stanhope** Durham, N England, UK
xliii L22 **Stanhope** The Borders, S Scotland, UK
xli Q7 **Stanley** Durham, N England, UK
xliii L17 **Stanley** Perth and Kinross, C Scotland, UK
xxxvi A5 **Stanmore** Harrow, SE England, UK
xli R5 **Stannington** Northumberland, N England, UK
xxxvii V7 **Stansted** ✕ (London) Essex, E England, UK
xxxvii V7 **Stansted** Mountfitchet Hertfordshire, E England, UK
xxxix V11 **Stanton** Suffolk, E England, UK
xxxvii Q8 **Stanton St John** Oxfordshire, C England, UK
xxxvii X7 **Stanway** Essex, SE England, UK
xxxvii N6 **Stanway** Gloucestershire, C England, UK
xxxvi J12 **Staple Fitzpaine** Somerset, SW England, UK
xxxix N8 **Stapleford** Nottinghamshire, C England, UK
xxxvii N11 **Stapleford** Wiltshire, S England, UK
xxxvii W11 **Staplehurst** Kent, SE England, UK
xxxvi I14 **Starcross** Devon, SW England, UK
xxxvi H16 **Start Bay** *bay* SW England, UK
xli Q9 **Startforth** Durham, N England, UK
xxxvi H17 **Start Point** *headland* SW England, UK
xlii O3 **Start Point** *headland* N Scotland, UK
xxxvi M7 **Staunton** Gloucestershire, C England, UK
xxxvi K7 **Staunton** Gloucestershire, C England, UK
xxxviii G13 **Staunton on Wye** Herefordshire, W England, UK
xli N10 **Staveley** Cumbria, NW England, UK
xxxviii M5 **Staveley** Derbyshire, C England, UK
xxxvi M7 **Staverton** Gloucestershire, C England, UK
xli W11 **Staxton** North Yorkshire, N England, UK
xxxvi I10 **Steep Holm** *island* S England, UK
xxxix S6 **Steeping** ≈ E England, UK
xxxvii W6 **Steeple Bumpstead** Essex, SE England, UK
xxxvii R7 **Steeple Claydon** Buckinghamshire, C England, UK
xxxix R13 **Steeple Morden** Cambridgeshire, E England, UK
xliii K19 **Stenhousemuir** Falkirk, C Scotland, UK
xlii H2 **Stenness** Shetland Islands, NE Scotland, UK
xliii O19 **Stenton** East Lothian, SE Scotland, UK
xxxvi E7 **Stepney** Tower Hamlets, SE England, UK
xliii J20 **Stepps** North Lanarkshire, C Scotland, UK
xxxvii T7 **Stevenage** Hertfordshire, E England, UK
xliii I21 **Stevenston** North Ayrshire, W Scotland, UK
xxxvii P8 **Steventon** Oxfordshire, C England, UK
xliii I21 **Stewarton** East Ayrshire, W Scotland, UK
xxxvii T13 **Steyning** West Sussex, SE England, UK
xxxvi F13 **Stibb Cross** Devon, SW England, UK
xliii O21 **Stichill** The Borders, S Scotland, UK
xxxix S6 **Stickford** Lincolnshire, E England, UK
xxxix S6 **Stickney** Lincolnshire, E England, UK
xlii A12 **Stilligarry** Western Isles, NW Scotland, UK
xli T12 **Stillington** North Yorkshire, N England, UK
xxxix R10 **Stilton** Cambridgeshire, E England, UK
xliii H23 **Stinchar** ≈ W Scotland, UK
xliii K19 **Stirling** Stirling, C Scotland, UK
xliii I19 **Stirling** ◐ *unitary authority* C Scotland, UK
xxxvi B17 **Stithians** Cornwall, SW England, UK
xxxvii W8 **Stock** Essex, SE England, UK
xxxvii P11 **Stockbridge** Hampshire, S England, UK
xxxvi J13 **Stockland** Devon, SW England, UK
xl H16 **Stockport** Stockport, NW England, UK
xli P16 **Stockport** ◐ *unitary authority* NW England, UK
xli R16 **Stocksbridge** Sheffield, N England, UK
xli X6 **Stockton-on-Tees** ***var.*** Stockton on Tees. Stockton-on-Tees, N England, UK
xli S9 **Stockton-on-Tees** ◐ *unitary authority* NE England, UK
xxxvii W9 **Stoke** Kent, SE England, UK
xxxix P10 **Stoke Albany** Northamptonshire, C England, UK
xxxix W13 **Stoke-by-Nayland** Suffolk, E England, UK
xxxix U10 **Stoke Ferry** Norfolk, E England, UK
xxxvi H16 **Stoke Fleming** Devon, SW England, UK
xxxviii M10 **Stoke Golding** Leicestershire, C England, UK
xxxvii R7 **Stoke Hammond** Buckinghamshire, C England, UK
xxxvii R8 **Stokenchurch** Buckinghamshire, C England, UK
xxxvi D6 **Stoke Newington** Hackney, SE England, UK
xxxviii J7 **Stoke-on-Trent** ***var.*** Stoke. City of Stoke-on-Trent, C England, UK
xxxviii J7 **Stoke-on-Trent, City of** ◐ *unitary authority* C England, UK
xxxvii S9 **Stoke Poges** Buckinghamshire, C England, UK
xxxviii B17 **Stoke Prior** Worcestershire, W England, UK
xli T9 **Stokesley** North Yorkshire, N England, UK
xxxvii R7 **Stone** Buckinghamshire, C England, UK
xxxvi L8 **Stone** Gloucestershire, C England, UK
xxxviii J8 **Stone** Staffordshire, C England, UK
xliii P14 **Stonehaven** Aberdeenshire, NE Scotland, UK
xxxvii N11 **Stonehenge** *ancient monument* Wiltshire, S England, UK
xliii J21 **Stonehouse** South Lanarkshire, C Scotland, UK
xlii A13 **Stoneybridge** Western Isles, NW Scotland, UK
xliii H25 **Stoneykirk** Dumfries and Galloway, SW Scotland, UK
xlii Q1 **Stonybreck** Shetland Islands, NE Scotland, UK
xxxvii R6 **Stony Stratford** Milton Keynes, C England, UK
xlii D8 **Stornoway** Western Isles, NW Scotland, UK
xxxvii S12 **Storrington** West Sussex, S England, UK
xlii E12 **Storr, The** ▲ NW Scotland, UK
xxxvii T6 **Stotfold** Bedfordshire, E England, UK
xxxix W13 **Stour** ≈ E England, UK
xxxvi L12 **Stour** ≈ S England, UK
xxxvii Z10 **Stour** ≈ SE England, UK
xxxviii B15 **Stourbridge** Dudley, C England, UK
xxxviii A16 **Stourport-on-Severn** Worcestershire, W England, UK
xliii N21 **Stow** The Borders, S Scotland, UK
xxxix W12 **Stowmarket** Suffolk, E England, UK
xxxvii N7 **Stow-on-the-Wold** Gloucestershire, C England, UK
xliv I3 **Strabane** ***Ir.*** An Srath Bán. Strabane, W Northern Ireland, UK
xliv I3 **Strabane** ◐ *district* W Northern Ireland, UK
xliii O14 **Strachan** Aberdeenshire, NE Scotland, UK
xliii H18 **Strachur** Argyll and Bute, W Scotland, UK
xliv J10 **Stradbally** Laois, C Ireland
xxxix X11 **Stradbroke** Suffolk, E England, UK
xliv I6 **Stradone** Cavan, N Ireland
xxxix U9 **Stradsett** Norfolk, E England, UK
xliii I23 **Straiton** South Ayrshire, W Scotland, UK
xliv F5 **Strandhill** Sligo, N Ireland
xliv M5 **Strangford** Down, E Northern Ireland, UK
xliv M5 **Strangford Lough** ***Ir.*** Loch Cuan. *inlet* E Northern Ireland, UK
xliv H3 **Stranorlar** ***Ir.*** Srath an Urláir. Donegal, NW Ireland
xliii H25 **Stranraer** Dumfries and Galloway, S Scotland, UK
xxxvi E6 **Stratford** Newham, SE England, UK
xxxix W14 **Stratford St Mary** Suffolk, E England, UK
xxxviii K13 **Stratford-upon-Avon** ***var.*** Stratford. Warwickshire, C England, UK
xxxviii D17 **Stratford upon Avon Canal** *canal* C England, UK
xliii J21 **Strathaven** South Lanarkshire, C Scotland, UK
xliii J19 **Strathblane** Stirling, C Scotland, UK
xlii H9 **Strathcanaird** Highland, NW Scotland, UK
xlii G12 **Strathcarron** Highland, NW Scotland, UK
xlii M13 **Strathdon** Aberdeenshire, NE Scotland, UK
xliii M18 **Strathmiglo** Fife, E Scotland, UK
xlii I11 **Strathpeffer** Highland, NW Scotland, UK
xlii K6 **Strathy** Highland, N Scotland, UK
xlii J6 **Strathy Point** *headland* N Scotland, UK
xliii J18 **Strathyre** Stirling, C Scotland, UK
xxxvi E13 **Stratton** Cornwall, SW England, UK
xxxvii Q7 **Stratton Audley** Oxfordshire, C England, UK
xxxvi D9 **Streatham** Lambeth, SE England, UK
xxxvii S6 **Streatley** Bedfordshire, C England, UK
xxxvii Q9 **Streatley** West Berkshire, S England, UK
xxxvi K11 **Street** Somerset, SW England, UK
xli T12 **Strensall** York, N England, UK
xli P16 **Stretford** Trafford, NW England, UK
xxxix T11 **Stretham** Cambridgeshire, E England, UK
xl E16 **Stretton** Cheshire, W England, UK
xxxix Q9 **Stretton** Rutland, C England, UK
xlii P11 **Strichen** Aberdeenshire, NE Scotland, UK
xliv G7 **Strokestown** Roscommon, C Ireland
xlii L6 **Stroma, Island of** *island* N Scotland, UK
xlii F12 **Stromeferry** Highland, N Scotland, UK
xlii L4 **Stromness** Orkney Islands, N Scotland, UK
xliii I18 **Stronachlachar** Stirling, C Scotland, UK
xliii H19 **Strone** Argyll and Bute, W Scotland, UK
xlii H8 **Stronechrubie** Highland, NW Scotland, UK
xlii N3 **Stronsay** *island* NE Scotland, UK
xlii N3 **Stronsay Firth** *inlet* N Scotland, UK
xliii F16 **Strontian** Highland, NW Scotland, UK
xxxvi M8 **Stroud** Gloucestershire, C England, UK
xxxvii R12 **Stroud** Hampshire, S England, UK
xxxv C12 **Strumble Head** *headland* SW Wales, UK
xlii I12 **Struy** Highland, NW Scotland, UK
xlii P12 **Stuartfield** Aberdeenshire, NE Scotland, UK
xxxvii N14 **Studland** Dorset, S England, UK
xxxviii C17 **Studley** Warwickshire, C England, UK
xxxvi M13 **Sturminster Newton** Dorset, S England, UK
xxxvii Y10 **Sturry** Kent, SE England, UK
xxxix P5 **Sturton by Stow** Lincolnshire, E England, UK
xliv G8 **Suck** ≈ C Ireland
xxxviii L8 **Sudbury** Derbyshire, C England, UK
xxxix V13 **Sudbury** Suffolk, E England, UK
xxxix W12 **Suffolk** ◐ *county* E England, UK
xliv H12 **Suir** ***Ir.*** An tSiúir. ≈ S Ireland
xl G11 **Sulby** N Isle of Man
xlii J4 **Sule Skerry** *island* N Scotland, UK
xlii I2 **Sullom** Shetland Islands, NE Scotland, UK
xlii I5 **Sumburgh** Shetland Islands, NE Scotland, UK
xlii I6 **Sumburgh Head** *headland* NE Scotland, UK
xli R12 **Summer Bridge** North Yorkshire, N England, UK
xxxvi C16 **Summercourt** Cornwall, SW England, UK
xlii F9 **Summer Isles** *island group* NW Scotland, UK
xliii F16 **Sunart, Loch** *inlet* NW Scotland, UK
xli X3 **Sunderland** ***var.*** Wearmouth. Sunderland, NE England, UK
xli W3 **Sunderland** ◐ *unitary authority* NE England, UK
xli X15 **Sunk Island** East Riding of Yorkshire, N England, UK
xxxvii S10 **Sunningdale** Surrey, SE England, UK
xxxvii S11 **Surrey** ◐ *county* SE England, UK
xxxix R8 **Sutterton** Lincolnshire, E England, UK
xxxix S11 **Sutton** Cambridgeshire, E England, UK
xxxix Y13 **Sutton** Suffolk, E England, UK
xxxvii T10 **Sutton** Sutton, SE England, UK
xxxiv K17 **Sutton** ◐ *London borough* SE England, UK
xxxvi M9 **Sutton Benger** Wiltshire, S England, UK
xxxix T8 **Sutton Bridge** Lincolnshire, E England, UK
xxxviii D14 **Sutton Coldfield** Birmingham, C England, UK
xxxix N6 **Sutton in Ashfield** Nottinghamshire, C England, UK
xxxix T5 **Sutton on Sea** Lincolnshire, E England, UK
xli T12 **Sutton-on-the-Forest** North Yorkshire, N England, UK
xxxix S9 **Sutton St James** Lincolnshire, E England, UK
xxxvii P11 **Sutton Scotney** Hampshire, S England, UK
xxxvii W11 **Sutton Valence** Kent, SE England, UK
xxxviii L9 **Swadlincote** Derbyshire, C England, UK
xxxix V9 **Swaffham** Norfolk, E England, UK
xli S10 **Swainby** North Yorkshire, N England, UK
xxxvi M10 **Swainswick** Bath and North East Somerset, SW England, UK
xxxvii P6 **Swalcliffe** Oxfordshire, C England, UK
xli S11 **Swale** ≈ N England, UK
xliv H6 **Swalinbar** Cavan, N Ireland
xxxix Q4 **Swallow** Lincolnshire, E England, UK
xxxvii N12 **Swallowcliffe** Wiltshire, S England, UK
xxxvii R10 **Swallowfield** Wokingham, S England, UK
xxxvii N14 **Swanage** Dorset, S England, UK
xxxvii V9 **Swanley** Kent, SE England, UK
xxxv G14 **Swansea** ***Wel.*** Abertawe. Swansea, S Wales, UK
xxxv G14 **Swansea** ◐ *unitary authority* S Wales, UK
xxxv G15 **Swansea Bay** *bay* S Wales, UK
xxxix W9 **Swanton Morley** Norfolk, E England, UK
xxxix X10 **Swardeston** Norfolk, E England, UK
xxxix Q8 **Swayfield** Lincolnshire, E England, UK
xliv H3 **Swilly** ≈ N Ireland
xliv I2 **Swilly, Lough** ***Ir.*** Loch Súilí. *inlet* N Ireland
xxxvi G12 **Swimbridge** Devon, SW England, UK
xxxvii O9 **Swindon** Thamesdown, S England, UK
xxxvii N9 **Swindon** ◐ *unitary authority* C England, UK
xxxvii S5 **Swineshead** Bedfordshire, C England, UK
xxxix R7 **Swineshead** Lincolnshire, E England, UK
xliv E6 **Swinford** Mayo, NW Ireland
xxxix N11 **Swinford** Leicestershire, C England, UK
xlii I3 **Swining** Shetland Islands, NE Scotland, UK
xli O16 **Swinton** Salford, NW England, UK
xliii P21 **Swinton** The Borders, S Scotland, UK
xliv L8 **Swords** ***Ir.*** Sord, Sórd Choluim Chille. Dublin, E Ireland
xli T15 **Sykehouse** Doncaster, N England, UK
xlii I3 **Symbister** Shetland Islands, NE Scotland, UK
xxxviii H15 **Symonds Yat** Herefordshire, W England, UK
xlii J7 **Syre** Highland, N Scotland, UK
xxxix O13 **Syresham** Northamptonshire, C England, UK
xxxix O9 **Syston** Leicestershire, C England, UK

T

xli S13 **Tadcaster** North Yorkshire, N England, UK
xxxvii Q10 **Tadley** Hampshire, S England, UK
xxxvii T11 **Tadworth** Surrey, SE England, UK
xxxv J15 **Taff** ≈ SE Wales, UK
xliv K12 **Taghmon** Wexford, SE Ireland
xlii J10 **Tain** Highland, N Scotland, UK
xxxvii V7 **Takeley** Essex, SE England, UK
xxxv J12 **Talgarth** Powys, C Wales, UK
xlii F11 **Talladale** Highland, NW Scotland, UK
xliv L9 **Tallaght** Dublin, E Ireland
xxxv G12 **Talley** Carmarthenshire, S Wales, UK
xliv G13 **Tallow** Waterford, S Ireland
xlii I6 **Talmine** Highland, N Scotland, UK
xxxv G6 **Talsarnau** Gwynedd, NW Wales, UK
xxxv G9 **Talybont** Ceredigion, W Wales, UK
xxxv F6 **Talysarn** Gwynedd, NW Wales, UK
xxxviii D14 **Tam** ≈ C England, UK
xxxvi E14 **Tamar** ≈ SW England, UK
xxxvi F15 **Tamerton Foliot** Devon, SW England, UK
xli P16 **Tameside** ◐ *unitary authority* NW England, UK
xxxviii D13 **Tamworth** Staffordshire, C England, UK
xxxv J7 **Tanat** ≈ E Wales, UK
xliv K5 **Tandragee** Armagh, S Northern Ireland, UK
xlii B9 **Taransay** *island* NW Scotland, UK
xlii K10 **Tarbat Ness** *headland* N Scotland, UK
xliv D11 **Tarbert** Kerry, SW Ireland
xliii G20 **Tarbert** Argyll and Bute, W Scotland, UK
xliii E19 **Tarbert** Argyll and Bute, W Scotland, UK
xlii C10 **Tarbert** Western Isles, NW Scotland, UK
xliii I18 **Tarbet** Argyll and Bute, W Scotland, UK
xliii I22 **Tarbolton** South Ayrshire, W Scotland, UK
xliii N15 **Tarfside** Angus, E Scotland, UK
xliii N14 **Tarland** Aberdeenshire, NE Scotland, UK
xxxviii I6 **Tarporley** Cheshire, W England, UK
xliii E14 **Tarskavaig** Highland, NW Scotland, UK
xxxviii H6 **Tarvin** Cheshire, W England, UK
xxxviii H6 **Tattenhall** Cheshire, W England, UK
xxxvi J12 **Taunton** Somerset, SW England, UK
xxxvi F15 **Tavistock** Devon, SW England, UK
xxxvi F15 **Tavy** ≈ SW England, UK
xxxvi G12 **Taw** ≈ SW England, UK
xliv F7 **Tawnyinah** Mayo, NW Ireland
xliii L17 **Tay** ≈ C Scotland, UK
xliii M17 **Tay, Firth of** *inlet* E Scotland, UK
xliii F21 **Tayinloan** Argyll and Bute, W Scotland, UK
xliii J17 **Tay, Loch** ◎ C Scotland, UK
xliii G17 **Taynuilt** Argyll and Bute, W Scotland, UK
xliii N17 **Tayport** Fife, E Scotland, UK
xliii F19 **Tayvallich** Argyll and Bute, W Scotland, UK
xxxix R4 **Tealby** Lincolnshire, E England, UK
xliii E14 **Teangue** Highland, NW Scotland, UK
xli N10 **Tebay** Cumbria, NW England, UK
xxxvi G14 **Tedburn St Mary** Devon, SW England, UK
xli R9 **Tees** ≈ N England, UK
xli T8 **Tees Bay** *bay* N England, UK
xxxv E12 **Teifi** ***var.*** River Teif. ≈ SW Wales, UK
xxxvi H14 **Teign** ≈ SW England, UK
xxxvi H15 **Teignmouth** Devon, SW England, UK
xxxviii I9 **Telford** Shropshire, W England, UK
xxxviii J13 **Teme** ≈ England/Wales, UK
xliv H11 **Tempelmore** Tipperary, S Ireland
xliii L24 **Templand** Dumfries and Galloway, SW Scotland, UK
xxxvi D15 **Temple** Cornwall, SW England, UK
xliii M20 **Temple** Midlothian, SE Scotland, UK
xxxvi L12 **Templecombe** Somerset, SW England, UK
xli T14 **Temple Hirst** North Yorkshire, N England, UK
xliv L4 **Templepatrick** Antrim, NE Northern Ireland, UK
xli N8 **Temple Sowerby** Cumbria, NW England, UK
xxxv D13 **Templeton** Pembrokeshire, SW Wales, UK
xxxviii I12 **Tenbury Wells** Worcestershire, W England, UK
xxxv E14 **Tenby** Pembrokeshire, SW Wales, UK
xxxvii X11 **Tenterden** Kent, SE England, UK
xxxvii W7 **Terling** Essex, SE England, UK
xliv H2 **Termon** Donegal, N Ireland
xxxix T8 **Terrington St Clement** Norfolk, E England, UK
xxxvii P11 **Test** ≈ S England, UK
xxxvi M8 **Tetbury** Gloucestershire, C England, UK
xxxix S4 **Tetney** Lincolnshire, E England, UK
xxxvii Q8 **Tetsworth** Oxfordshire, C England, UK
xxxviii A14 **Tettenhall** Wolverhampton, C England, UK
xliii M23 **Teviot** ≈ SE Scotland, UK
xliii N23 **Teviothead** The Borders, S Scotland, UK
xxxvi M6 **Tewkesbury** Gloucestershire, C England, UK
xxxvii Q8 **Thame** Oxfordshire, C England, UK
xxxvii T9 **Thames** ≈ S England, UK
xxxvii P10 **Thatcham** West Berkshire, S England, UK
xxxvii V6 **Thaxted** Essex, SE England, UK
xxxvii Q10 **Theale** West Berkshire, S England, UK
xliii M22 **The Borders** ◐ *unitary authority* S Scotland, UK
xxxvii V9 **The Medway Towns** ◐ *unitary authority* SE England, UK
xxxv G15 **The Mumbles** Swansea, S Wales, UK
xxxvii U6 **Therfield** Hertfordshire, SE England, UK
xxxix V11 **Thetford** Norfolk, E England, UK
xxxv I15 **The Vale of Glamorgan** ◐ *unitary authority* S Wales, UK
xxxviii H9 **The Wrekin** ◐ *unitary authority* C England, UK
xxxix R6 **Thimbleby** Lincolnshire, E England, UK
xli S11 **Thirsk** North Yorkshire, N England, UK
xli P5 **Thockrington** Northumberland, N England, UK
xliv G8 **Thomas Street** Roscommon, C Ireland
xliv I12 **Thomastown** Kilkenny, SE Ireland
xxxix R4 **Thoresway** Lincolnshire, E England, UK
xli X7 **Thornaby on Tees** Middlesborough, NE England, UK
xxxvi L9 **Thornbury** South Gloucestershire, SW England, UK
xxxix O11 **Thornby** Northamptonshire, C England, UK
xxxvi K13 **Thorncombe** Dorset, S England, UK
xxxix W12 **Thorndon** Suffolk, E England, UK
xli U15 **Thorne** Doncaster, N England, UK
xli S13 **Thorner** Leeds, N England, UK
xxxix R9 **Thorney** Cambridgeshire, E England, UK
xliii K23 **Thornhill** Dumfries and Galloway, S Scotland, UK
xliii J18 **Thornhill** Stirling, C Scotland, UK
xli W5 **Thornley** Durham, N England, UK
xl M13 **Thornton** Lancashire, NW England, UK
xliii M18 **Thornton** Fife, E Scotland, UK
xxxix Q3 **Thornton Curtis** North Lincolnshire, N England, UK
xli V11 **Thornton Dale** North Yorkshire, N England, UK
xli S11 **Thornton-le-Street** North Yorkshire, N England, UK
xxxix Y12 **Thorpeness** Suffolk, E England, UK
xxxix P6 **Thorpe on the Hill** Lincolnshire, E England, UK
xxxvii Y7 **Thorrington** Essex, SE England, UK
xxxvi H13 **Thorverton** Devon, SW England, UK
xxxix Q11 **Thrapston** Northamptonshire, C England, UK
xxxvii U11 **Three Bridges** West Sussex, S England, UK
xli P12 **Threshfield** North Yorkshire, N England, UK
xli U2 **Throckley** Newcastle upon Tyne, NE England, UK
xli Q4 **Thropton** Northumberland, N England, UK
xlii M7 **Thrumster** Highland, N Scotland, UK
xxxvii O11 **Thruxton** Hampshire, S England, UK
xli T16 **Thurcroft** Rotherham, N England, UK
xxxix Q9 **Thurlby** Lincolnshire, E England, UK
xliv H11 **Thurles** ***Ir.*** Durlas. Tipperary, S Ireland
xxxvi G16 **Thurlestone** Devon, SW England, UK
xxxix U13 **Thurlow** Suffolk, E England, UK
xxxvii V9 **Thurrock** ◐ *unitary authority* SE England, UK
xl M7 **Thursby** Cumbria, NW England, UK
xlii L6 **Thurso** Highland, N Scotland, UK
xlii K7 **Thurso** ≈ NW Scotland, UK
xl B16 **Thurstaston** Wirral, NW England, UK
xli P10 **Thwaite** North Yorkshire, N England, UK
xxxvi L7 **Tibberton** Gloucestershire, C England, UK
xxxvii W12 **Ticehurst** East Sussex, SE England, UK
xli T16 **Tickhill** Doncaster, N England, UK
xxxvi K8 **Tidenham** Gloucestershire, C England, UK
xxxviii L5 **Tideswell** Derbyshire, C England, UK
xlii A11 **Tigharry** Western Isles, NW Scotland, UK
xliii G20 **Tighnabruaich** Argyll and Bute, W Scotland, UK
xxxvii V9 **Tilbury** Essex, SE England, UK
xxxvii Q9 **Tilehurst** Reading, S England, UK
xliii K19 **Tillicoultry** Clackmannan, C Scotland, UK
xxxvii X8 **Tillingham** Essex, SE England, UK
xxxvii N11 **Tilshead** Wiltshire, S England, UK
xxxviii H8 **Tilstock** Shropshire, W England, UK
xxxviii H7 **Tilston** Cheshire, W England, UK
xliii K15 **Tilt** ≈ C Scotland, UK
xliv E15 **Timoleague** Cork, S Ireland
xlii B8 **Timsgarry** Western Isles, NW Scotland, UK
xliv K11 **Tinahely** Wicklow, E Ireland
xxxvii Q6 **Tingewick** Buckinghamshire, C England, UK
xxxvi D14 **Tintagel** Cornwall, SW England, UK
xliii L21 **Tinto** ▲ C Scotland, UK
xliii K22 **Tinto Hills** ▲▲ South Lanarkshire, C Scotland, UK
xliv G12 **Tipperary** ***Ir.*** Tiobraid Árann. Tipperary, S Ireland
xliv G11 **Tipperary** ***Ir.*** Tiobraid Árann. ◐ *county* S Ireland
xxxviii B14 **Tipton** Sandwell, C England, UK
xxxvii X7 **Tiptree** Essex, SE England, UK
xliii B17 **Tiree** *island* W Scotland, UK
xxxvii N12 **Tisbury** Wiltshire, S England, UK
xxxviii L7 **Tissington** Derbyshire, C England, UK
xxxvii Q13 **Titchfield** Hampshire, S England, UK
xxxvi I13 **Tiverton** Devon, SW England, UK
xlii N4 **Toab** Orkney Islands, N Scotland, UK
xlii I5 **Toab** Shetland Islands, NE Scotland, UK
xliv F6 **Tobercurry** Sligo, N Ireland
xliii E16 **Tobermory** Argyll and Bute, W Scotland, UK
xliii F18 **Toberonochy** Argyll and Bute, W Scotland, UK
xlii C8 **Tobson** Western Isles, NW Scotland, UK
xxxvii S6 **Toddington** Bedfordshire, C England, UK
xli P14 **Todmorden** Calderdale, N England, UK
xliv D15 **Toe Head** *headland* SW Ireland
xlii B10 **Toe Head** *headland* NW Scotland, UK
xli T12 **Tollerton** North Yorkshire, N England, UK
xxxvii X7 **Tollesbury** Essex, SE England, UK
xxxvii X7 **Tolleshunt d'Arcy** Essex, SE England, UK
xlii K13 **Tomatin** Highland, NW Scotland, UK
xlii J12 **Tombreck** Highland, NW Scotland, UK
xliii H14 **Tomdoun** Highland, NW Scotland, UK
xliv F10 **Tomgraney** Clare, W Ireland
xlii H13 **Tomich** Highland, NW Scotland, UK
xlii L13 **Tomintoul** Moray, N Scotland, UK
xxxvii V11 **Tonbridge** Kent, SE England, UK
xxxv I15 **Tondu** Bridgend, S Wales, UK
xlii D8 **Tong** Western Isles, NW Scotland, UK
xliii J25 **Tongland** Dumfries and Galloway, SW Scotland, UK
xlii I7 **Tongue** Highland, N Scotland, UK
xxxv I14 **Tonypandy** Rhondda Cynon Taff, S Wales, UK
xliv C8 **Toombeola** Galway, W Ireland
xliv K4 **Toome Bridge** Antrim, NE Northern Ireland, UK
xliv G10 **Toomyvara** Tipperary, S Ireland
xliv C15 **Toormore** Cork, S Ireland
xxxvi C9 **Tooting** Wandsworth, SE England, UK
xxxvi I14 **Topsham** Devon, SW England, UK
xxxvi H16 **Tor Bay** *bay* SW England, UK
xxxvi H15 **Torbay** ◐ *unitary authority* SW England, UK
xliii G22 **Torbeg** North Ayrshire, W Scotland, UK
xxxvi H16 **Torcross** Devon, SW England, UK
xlii J11 **Tore** Highland, NW Scotland, UK
xxxv K14 **Torfaen** ◐ *unitary authority* SE Wales, UK
xxxvi M9 **Tormarton** South Gloucestershire, SW England, UK
xlii J13 **Torness** Highland, NW Scotland, UK
xliii L20 **Torphichen** West Lothian, SE Scotland, UK
xliii N14 **Torphins** Aberdeenshire, NE Scotland, UK
xxxvi F16 **Torpoint** Cornwall, SW England, UK
xxxvi H15 **Torquay** Devon, SW England, UK
xxxvi F12 **Torridge** ≈ SW England, UK
xlii F11 **Torridon** Highland, NW Scotland, UK
xlii F11 **Torridon, Loch** *inlet* NW Scotland, UK
xlii E13 **Torrin** Highland, NW Scotland, UK
xxxvii V16 **Torteval** Guernsey, Channel Islands
xliii L24 **Torthorwald** Dumfries and Galloway, SW Scotland, UK
xliv G2 **Tory Island** ***Ir.*** Toraigh. island NW Ireland
xliv G2 **Tory Sound** *sound* N Ireland
xxxvii P14 **Totland** Isle of Wight, S England, UK
xxxvi H15 **Totnes** Devon, SW England, UK
xxxvi D5 **Tottenham** Haringey, SE England, UK
xli O15 **Tottington** Bury, NW England, UK
xxxvii P13 **Totton** Hampshire, S England, UK
xxxix O13 **Towcester** Northamptonshire, C England, UK
xxxiv L16 **Tower Hamlets** ◐ *London borough* SE England, UK
xli Q8 **Tow Law** Durham, N England, UK
xliii O22 **Town Yetholm** The Borders, S Scotland, UK
xli O17 **Trafford** ◐ *unitary authority* NW England, UK
xliv C12 **Tralee** ***Ir.*** Trá Lí. Kerry, SW Ireland
xliv C12 **Tralee Bay** ***Ir.*** Bá Thrá Lí. *bay* SW Ireland
xliv I13 **Tramore** ***Ir.*** Tráigh Mhór, Trá Mhór. Waterford, S Ireland
xliii N20 **Tranent** East Lothian, SE Scotland, UK
xxxv G13 **Trapp** Carmarthenshire, S Wales, UK
xli P14 **Trawden** Lancashire, NW England, UK
xxxv H6 **Trawsfynydd** Gwynedd, NW Wales, UK
xxxv I12 **Trecastle** Powys, C Wales, UK
xxxv J13 **Tredegar** Blaenau Gwent, SE Wales, UK
xxxvi L17 **Treen** Cornwall, SW England, UK
xxxv I9 **Trefeglwys** Powys, C Wales, UK
xxxv C13 **Treffgarne** Pembrokeshire, SW Wales, UK
xxxv I4 **Trefnant** Denbighshire, N Wales, UK
xxxviii G8 **Trefonen** Shropshire, W England, UK
xxxv F4 **Trefor** Isle of Anglesey, NW Wales, UK
xxxv H11 **Tregaron** Ceredigion, W Wales, UK
xxxvi C16 **Tregony** Cornwall, SW England, UK
xxxv J8 **Tregynon** Powys, C Wales, UK
xliii H15 **Treig, Loch** ◎ NW Scotland, UK
xxxv L14 **Trelleck** Monmouthshire, SE Wales, UK
xxxv F7 **Tremadog Bay** *bay* NW Wales, UK
xxxvi L12 **Trent** Somerset, SW England, UK
xxxviii M8 **Trent** ≈ C England, UK
xxxv I14 **Treorchy** Rhondda Cynon Taff, S Wales, UK
xxxvi I17 **Tresco** *island* SW England, UK
xliii D17 **Treshnish Isles** *island group* W Scotland, UK
xxxvi C16 **Tresillian** Cornwall, SW England, UK
xlii I4 **Tresta** Shetland Islands, NE Scotland, UK
xxxv J13 **Tretower** Powys, C Wales, UK
xxxv K5 **Treuddyn** Flintshire, N Wales, UK
xxxvi B15 **Trevose Head** *headland* SW England, UK
xliv J8 **Trim** ***Ir.*** Baile Átha Troim. Meath, E Ireland
xli S8 **Trimdon** Durham, N England, UK
xli X5 **Trimdon Colliery** Durham, N England, UK
xxxix X7 **Trimingham** Norfolk, E England, UK
xxxvii S7 **Tring** Hertfordshire, SE England, UK
xxxvii X17 **Trinity** Jersey, Channel Islands
xliii I24 **Trool, Loch** ◎ Dumfries and Galloway, SW Scotland, UK
xliii H22 **Troon** South Ayrshire, W Scotland, UK
xxxvi M10 **Trowbridge** Wiltshire, S England, UK
xxxix T12 **Trumpington** Cambridgeshire, E England, UK
xxxix X8 **Trunch** Norfolk, E England, UK
xxxvi C16 **Truro** Cornwall, SW England, UK
xliv G5 **Truskmore** ▲ N Ireland
xxxv E7 **Trwyn Cilan** *headland* NW Wales, UK
xliv F8 **Tuam** ***Ir.*** Tuaim. Galway, W Ireland
xxxix X13 **Tuddenham** Suffolk, E England, UK
xxxv E6 **Tudweiliog** Gwynedd, NW Wales, UK
xliv F10 **Tulla** Clare, W Ireland
xliii H16 **Tulla, Loch** ◎ W Scotland, UK
xliv I9 **Tullamore** ***Ir.*** Tulach Mhór. Offaly, C Ireland
xliii K19 **Tullibody** Clackmannan, C Scotland, UK
xlii O12 **Tulloch** Aberdeenshire, NE Scotland, UK
xliv J11 **Tullow** ***Ir.*** An Tullach. Carlow, SE Ireland
xliv H5 **Tully** Fermanagh, SW Northern Ireland, UK
xliv G7 **Tulsk** Roscommon, C Ireland
xxxv G13 **Tumble** Carmarthenshire, S Wales, UK
xliii K16 **Tummel** ≈ C Scotland, UK
xliii K16 **Tummel Bridge** Perth and Kinross, C Scotland, UK
xliii K16 **Tummel, Loch** ◎ C Scotland, UK
xxxviii J7 **Tunstall** City of Stoke-on-Trent, C England, UK
xli X14 **Tunstall** East Riding of Yorkshire, N England, UK
xxxix Y12 **Tunstall** Suffolk, E England, UK
xliii H23 **Turnberry** South Ayrshire, W Scotland, UK
xlii O11 **Turriff** Aberdeenshire, NE Scotland, UK
xxxviii L8 **Tutbury** Staffordshire, C England, UK
xxxix O6 **Tuxford** Nottinghamshire, C England, UK
xlii M4 **Twatt** Orkney Islands, N Scotland, UK
xliii P21 **Tweed** ≈ England/Scotland, UK
xli P1 **Tweedmouth** Northumberland, N England, UK
xliii L22 **Tweedsmuir** The Borders, S Scotland, UK
xliv C8 **Twelve Pins, The** ▲▲ W Ireland
xxxvi A9 **Twickenham** Richmond upon Thames, SE England, UK
xxxvi G15 **Two Bridges** Devon, SW England, UK
xxxviii E13 **Twycross** Leicestershire, C England, UK
xxxvii P12 **Twyford** Hampshire, S England, UK
xxxix O9 **Twyford** Leicestershire, C England, UK
xxxvii R9 **Twyford** Wokingham, S England, UK
xliii J25 **Twynholm** Dumfries and Galloway, SW Scotland, UK
xxxix S9 **Tydd St Mary** Lincolnshire, E England, UK
xliv J5 **Tyholland** Monaghan, NE Ireland
xl E14 **Tyldesley** Wigan, NW England, UK
xliii I17 **Tyndrum** Stirling, C Scotland, UK
xli Q6 **Tyne** ≈ N England, UK
xli S6 **Tynemouth** North Tyneside, NE England, UK
xxxv G13 **Tywi** ≈ S Wales, UK
xxxv G8 **Tywyn** Gwynedd, W Wales, UK

U

xxxvii U12 **Uckfield** East Sussex, SE England, UK
xliii K21 **Uddington** South Lanarkshire, C Scotland, UK
xxxvi I13 **Uffculme** Devon, SW England, UK
xxxvii O9 **Uffington** Oxfordshire, C England, UK
xli U9 **Ugthorpe** North Yorkshire, N England, UK
xlii D11 **Uig** Highland, N Scotland, UK
xxxix S5 **Ulceby** Lincolnshire, E England, UK
xxxix Q3 **Ulceby** North Lincolnshire, N England, UK
xl L8 **Uldale** Cumbria, NW England, UK

◆ Country ◇ Dependent Territory ◐ Administrative Region ▲ Mountain ◎ Lake ≈ River
● Country Capital ○ Dependent Territory Capital ✕ International Airport ▲▲ Mountain Range ▣ Reservoir

◆ Country   ◇ Dependent Territory   ▲ Administrative Region   ▲ Mountain   ◎ Lake   ∿ River
● Country Capital   ○ Dependent Territory Capital   ✕ International Airport   ⌃ Mountain Range   ▣ Reservoir

ATLAS
OF THE WORLD

THE MAPS IN THIS ATLAS ARE ARRANGED CONTINENT BY CONTINENT, STARTING
FROM THE INTERNATIONAL DATE LINE, AND MOVING EASTWARD. THE MAPS PROVIDE
A UNIQUE VIEW OF TODAY'S WORLD, COMBINING TRADITIONAL CARTOGRAPHIC
TECHNIQUES WITH THE LATEST REMOTE-SENSED AND DIGITAL TECHNOLOGY.

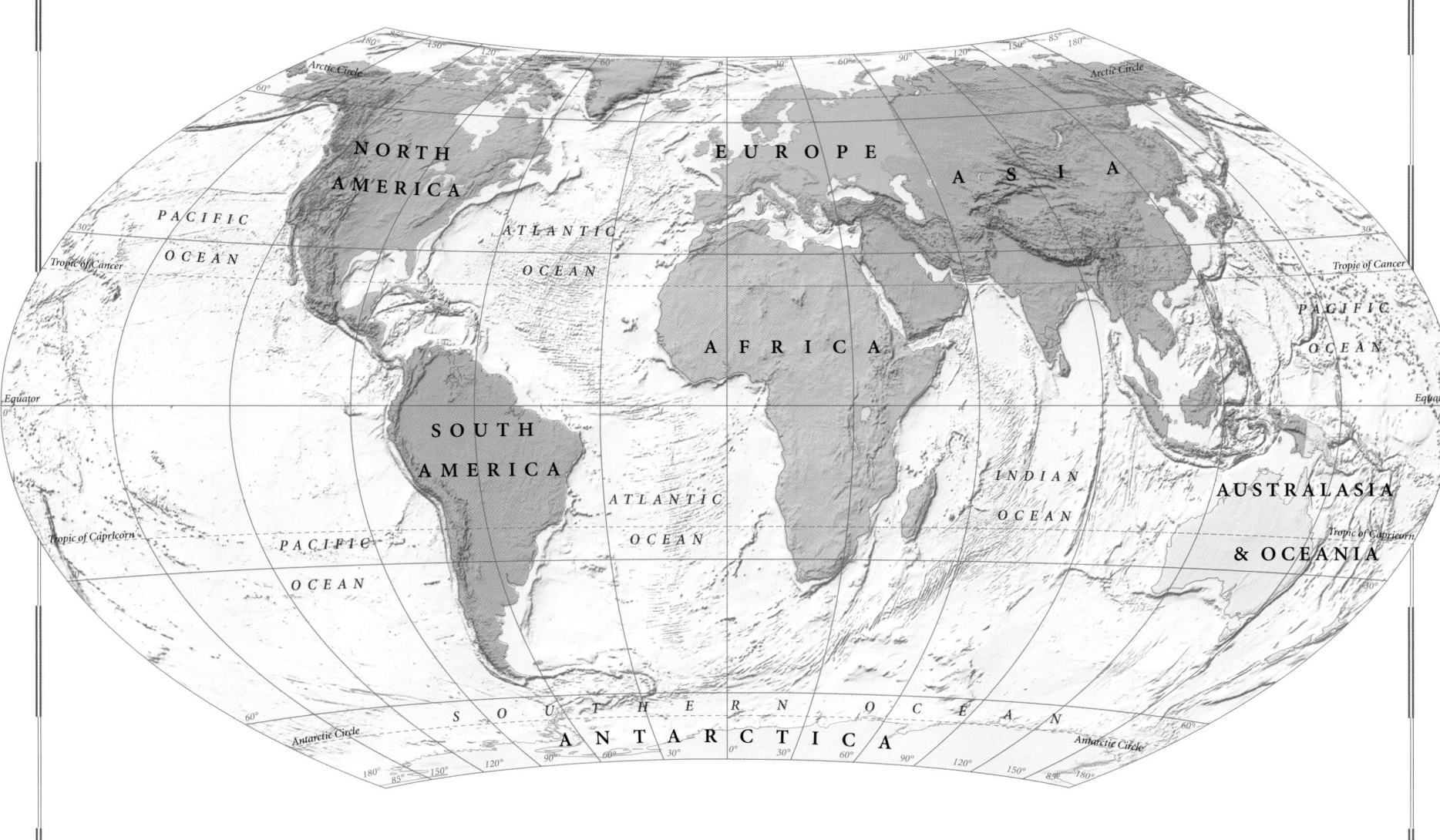

North America

North America is the world's third largest continent with a total area of 9,358,340 sq miles

(24,238,000 sq km) including Greenland and the Caribbean islands.

It lies wholly within the Northern Hemisphere.

- ⬤ **Greatest extent, North–South:** *4600 miles / 7400 km*
- ⬛ **Greatest extent, East–West:** *3500 miles / 5700 km*

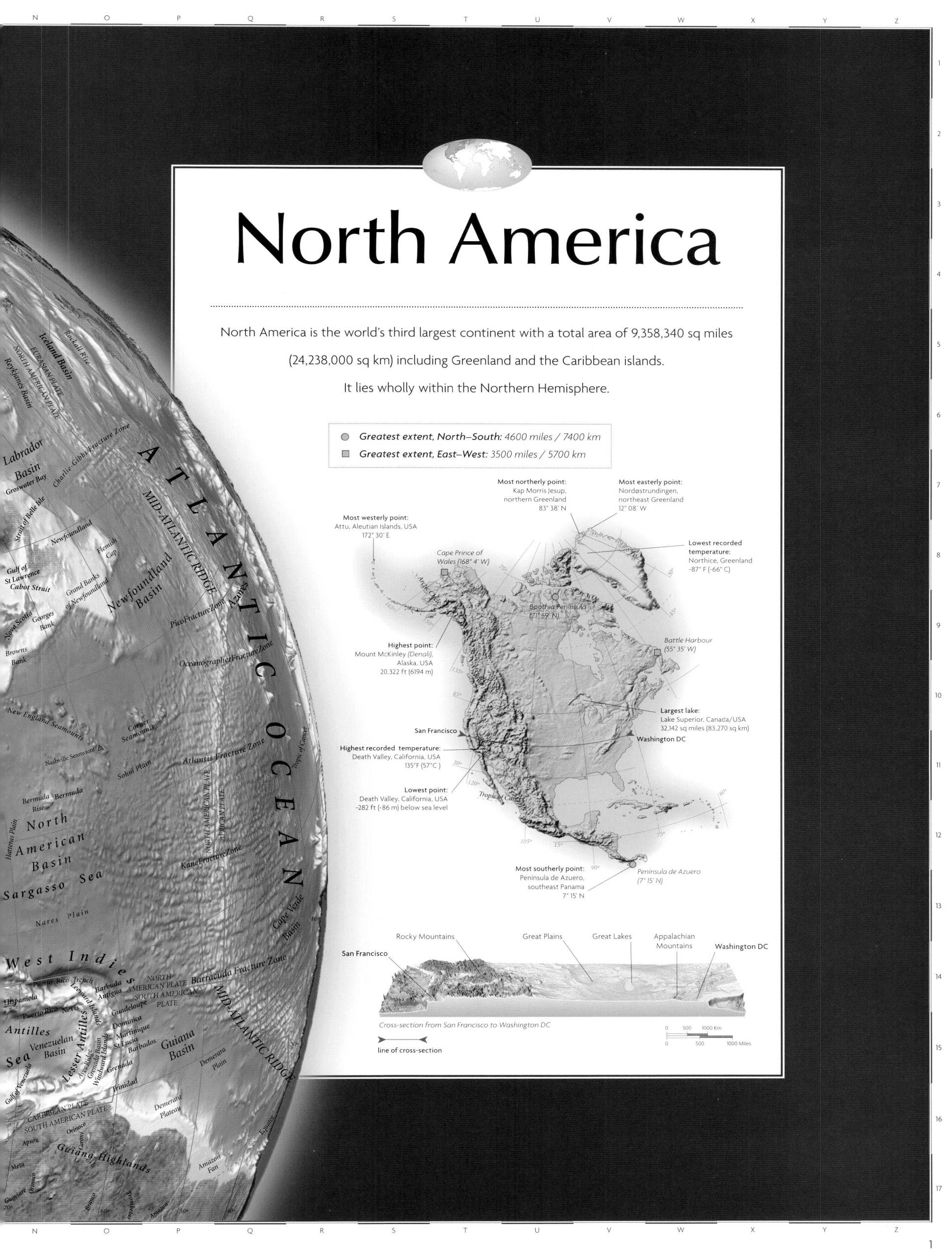

Most northerly point:
Kap Morris Jesup,
northern Greenland
83° 38′ N

Most easterly point:
Nordøstrundingen,
northeast Greenland
12° 08′ W

Most westerly point:
Attu, Aleutian Islands, USA
172° 30′ E

*Cape Prince of
Wales (168° 4′ W)*

**Lowest recorded
temperature:**
Northice, Greenland
-87° F (-66° C)

*Boothia Peninsula
(71° 59′ N)*

Highest point:
Mount McKinley *(Denali),*
Alaska, USA
20,322 ft (6194 m)

*Battle Harbour
(55° 35′ W)*

Largest lake:
Lake Superior, Canada/USA
32,142 sq miles (83,270 sq km)

San Francisco

Washington DC

Highest recorded temperature:
Death Valley, California, USA
135°F (57°C)

Tropic of Cancer

Lowest point:
Death Valley, California, USA
-282 ft (-86 m) below sea level

Most southerly point:
Peninsula de Azuero,
southeast Panama
7° 15′ N

*Peninsula de Azuero
(7° 15′ N)*

San Francisco — Rocky Mountains — Great Plains — Great Lakes — Appalachian Mountains — Washington DC

Cross-section from San Francisco to Washington DC

line of cross-section

| 0 | 500 | 1000 Km |
| 0 | 500 | 1000 Miles |

Ocean floor labels

ATLANTIC OCEAN
MID-ATLANTIC RIDGE

Iceland Basin
Rockall Rise
EURASIAN PLATE
NORTH AMERICAN PLATE
Reykjanes Basin
Labrador Basin
Groswater Bay
Charlie-Gibbs Fracture Zone
Strait of Belle Isle
Newfoundland
Flemish Cap
Gulf of St Lawrence
Cabot Strait
Grand Banks of Newfoundland
Newfoundland Basin
Azores
Nova Scotia
Georges Bank
Pico Fracture Zone
Browns Bank
Oceanographer Fracture Zone
New England Seamounts
Corner Seamounts
Nashville Seamount
Atlantis Fracture Zone
Sohm Plain
Bermuda
Bermuda Rise
NORTH AMERICAN PLATE
Hatteras Plain
North American Basin
Kane Fracture Zone
Sargasso Sea
Nares Plain
Cape Verde Basin
West Indies
MID-ATLANTIC RIDGE
Puerto Rico Trench
Barbuda
NORTH AMERICAN PLATE
Barracuda Fracture Zone
Hispaniola
Leeward Islands
Antigua
SOUTH AMERICAN PLATE
Puerto Rico
Nevis
Guadeloupe
Antilles
Dominica
Venezuelan Basin
Martinique
Lesser Antilles
St Lucia
Grenada Basin
Barbados
Caribbean Sea
Windward Islands
Grenada
Guiana Basin
Gulf of Venezuela
Trinidad
Demerara Plain
CARIBBEAN PLATE
SOUTH AMERICAN PLATE
Demerara Plateau
Apure
Orinoco
Meta
Guiana Highlands
Amazon Fan
Guaviare
Amazon

Physical North America

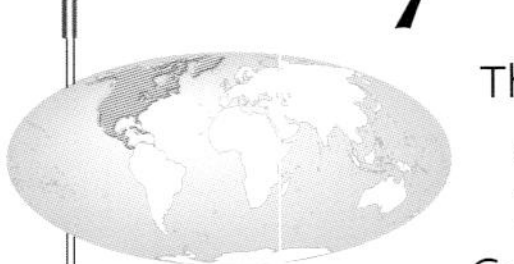

The North American continent can be divided into a number of major structural areas: the Western Cordillera, the Canadian Shield, the Great Plains and Central Lowlands, and the Appalachians. Other smaller regions include the Gulf Atlantic Coastal Plain which borders the southern coast of North America from the southern Appalachians to the Great Plains. This area includes the expanding Mississippi Delta. A chain of volcanic islands, running in an arc around the margin of the Caribbean Plate, lie to the east of the Gulf of Mexico.

The Canadian Shield

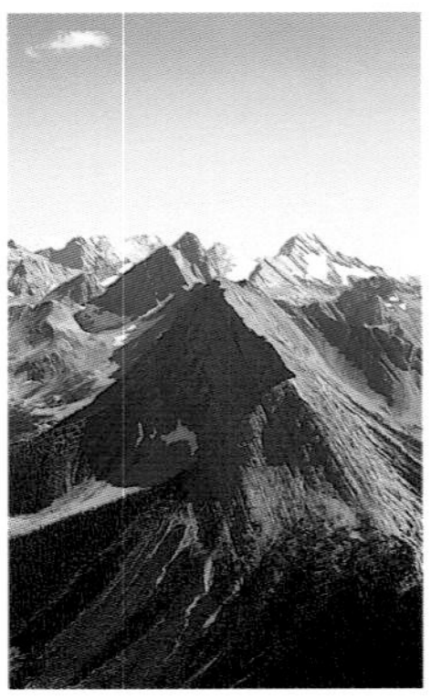

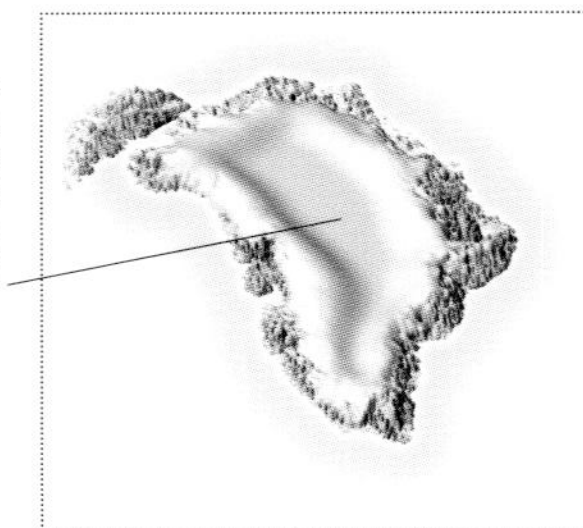

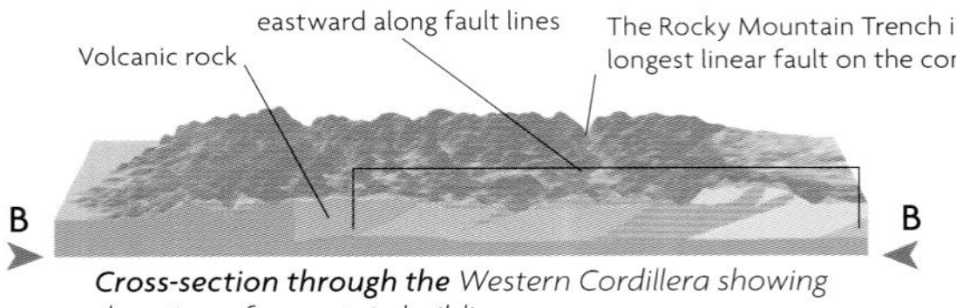

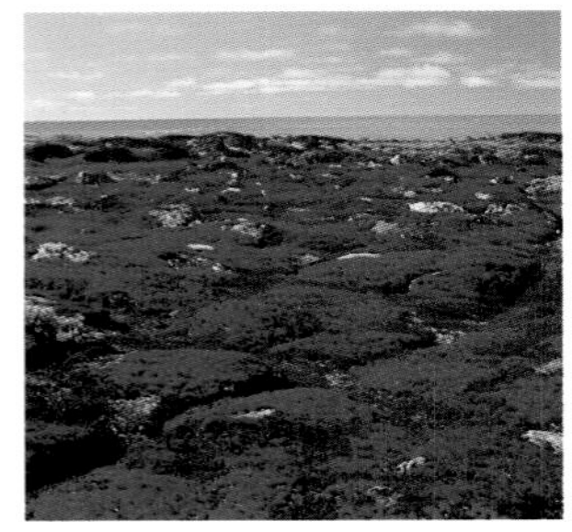

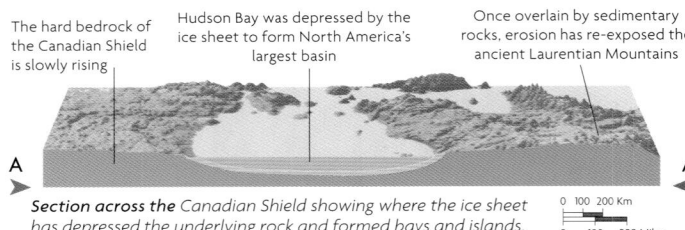

Spanning northern Canada and Greenland, this geologically stable plain forms the heart of the continent, containing rocks over two billion years old. A long history of weathering and repeated glaciation has scoured the region, leaving flat plains, gentle hummocks, numerous small basins and lakes, and the bays and islands of the Arctic.

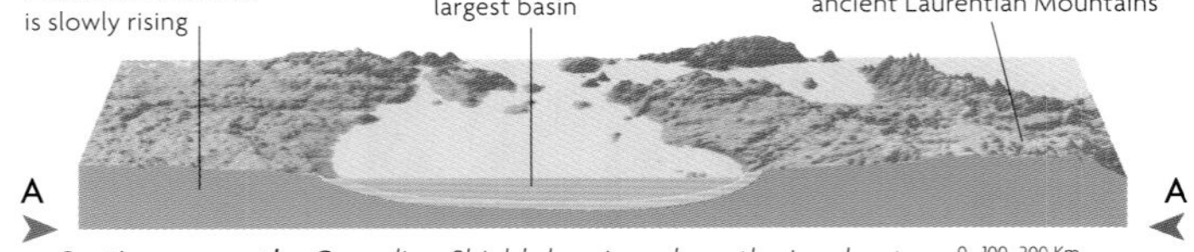

The Western Cordillera

About 80 million years ago the Pacific and North American plates collided, uplifting the Western Cordillera. This consists of the Aleutian, Coast, Cascade and Sierra Nevada mountains, and the inland Rocky Mountains. These run parallel from the Arctic to Mexico.

The weight of the ice sheet, 1.8 miles (3 km) thick, has depressed the land to 0.6 miles (1 km) below sea level

▲ This computer-generated view shows the ice-covered island of Greenland without its ice cap.

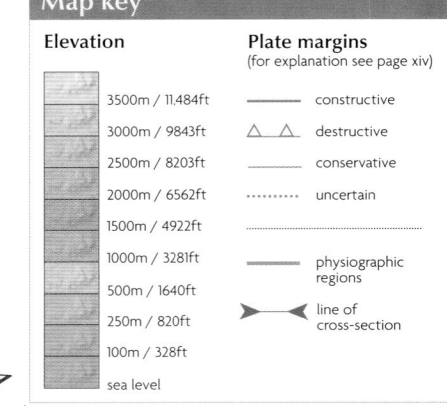

The hard bedrock of the Canadian Shield is slowly rising

Hudson Bay was depressed by the ice sheet to form North America's largest basin

Once overlain by sedimentary rocks, erosion has re-exposed the ancient Laurentian Mountains

Section across the Canadian Shield showing where the ice sheet has depressed the underlying rock and formed bays and islands.

0   100 200 Km
0   100   200 Miles

Strata have been thrust eastward along fault lines

Volcanic rock

The Rocky Mountain Trench is the longest linear fault on the continent

Cross-section through the Western Cordillera showing direction of mountain building.

0   50   100 Km
0   50   100 Miles

Map key

Elevation

	3500m / 11,484ft
	3000m / 9843ft
	2500m / 8203ft
	2000m / 6562ft
	1500m / 4922ft
	1000m / 3281ft
	500m / 1640ft
	250m / 820ft
	100m / 328ft
	sea level

Plate margins
(for explanation see page xiv)

——	constructive
△ △	destructive
——	conservative
······	uncertain
——	physiographic regions
►◄	line of cross-section

Scale 1:38,000,000

Km
0 200 400 600 800 1000
0 200 400 600 800 1000
Miles

projection: Lambert Azimuthal Equal Area

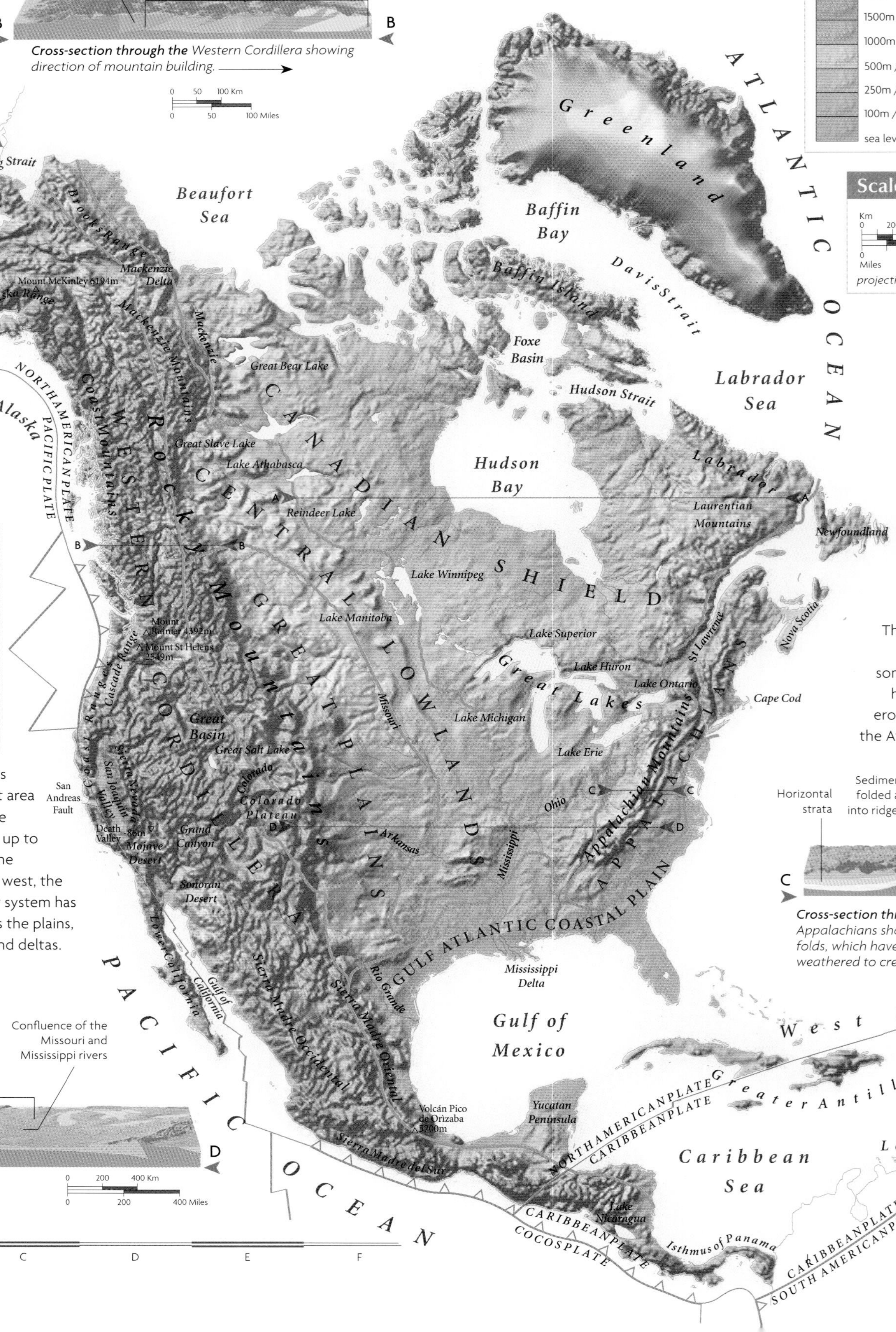

The Great Plains and Central Lowlands

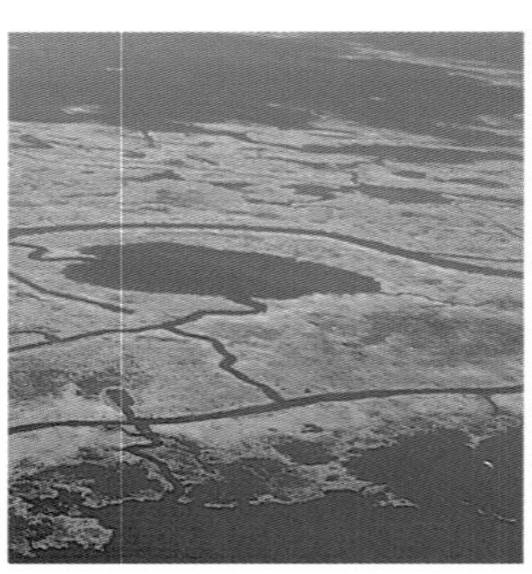

Deposits left by retreating glaciers and rivers have made this vast flat area very fertile. In the north this is the result of glaciation, with deposits up to one mile (1.7 km) thick, covering the basement rock. To the south and west, the massive Missouri/Mississippi river system has for centuries deposited silt across the plains, creating broad, flat flood plains and deltas.

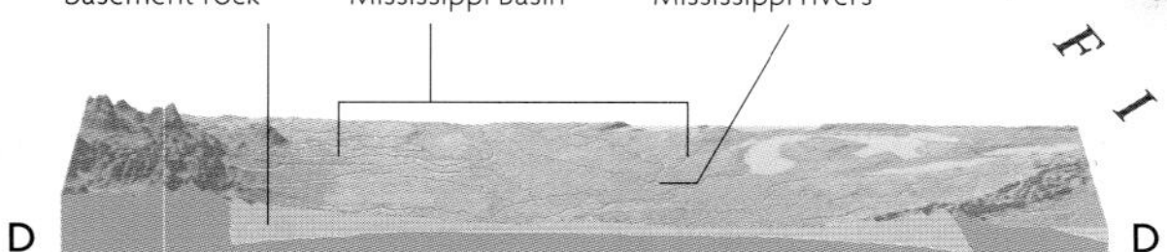

The Appalachians

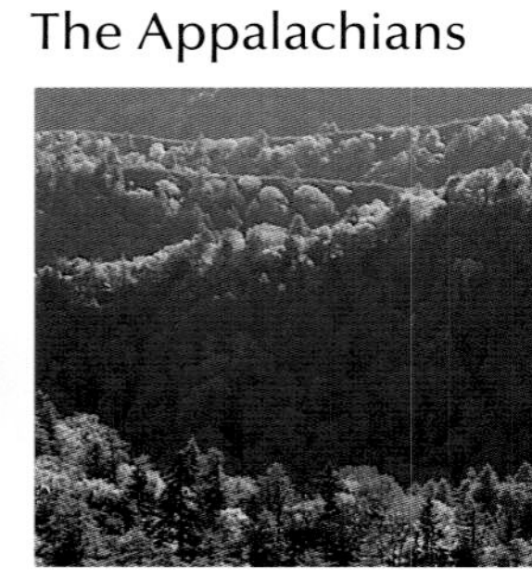

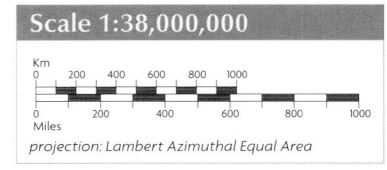

The Appalachian Mountains, uplifted about 400 million years ago, are some of the oldest in the world. They have been lowered and rounded by erosion and now slope gently towards the Atlantic across a broad coastal plain.

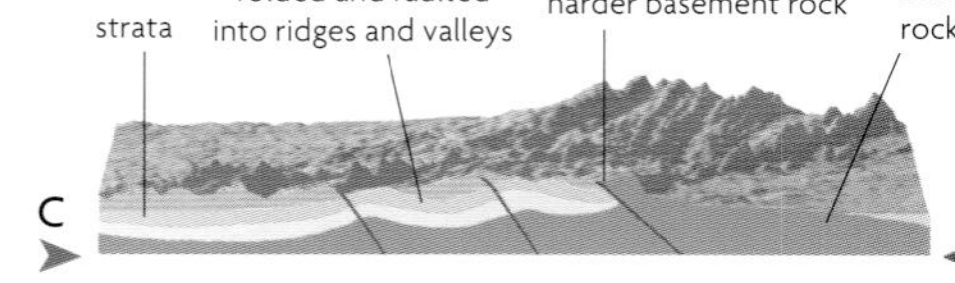

Horizontal strata

Sedimentary strata folded and faulted into ridges and valleys

Softer strata has been crumpled against the harder basement rock

Hard basement rock

Cross-section through the Appalachians showing the numerous folds, which have subsequently been weathered to create a rounded relief.

0   25   50 Km
0   25   50 Miles

Sedimentary layers overlay domed basement rock

Upland rivers drain south towards the Mississippi Basin

Confluence of the Missouri and Mississippi rivers

Section across the Great Plains and Central Lowlands showing river systems and structure.

0   200 400 Km
0   200 400 Miles

Map labels

ASIA

Bering Strait

Beaufort Sea

Bering Sea

Aleutian Islands

Aleutian Range

Brooks Range

Alaska Range

Mount McKinley 6194m

Mackenzie Delta

Gulf of Alaska

NORTH AMERICAN PACIFIC PLATE

Mackenzie Mountains

Mackenzie

Great Bear Lake

Coast Mountains

Great Slave Lake

Lake Athabasca

WESTERN CORDILLERA

ROCKY MOUNTAINS

CANADIAN SHIELD

Reindeer Lake

CENTRAL LOWLANDS

Greenland

ATLANTIC OCEAN

Baffin Bay

Baffin Island

Davis Strait

Foxe Basin

Hudson Strait

Labrador Sea

Hudson Bay

Labrador

Laurentian Mountains

Newfoundland

Lake Winnipeg

Lake Manitoba

GREAT PLAINS

Nova Scotia

Missouri

Lake Superior

Lake Huron

St Lawrence

Lake Ontario

Cape Cod

Lake Michigan

Great Lakes

Lake Erie

APPALACHIAN MOUNTAINS

APPALACHIANS

Ohio

Cascade Range

Mount Rainier 4392m

Mount St Helens 2549m

Sierra Nevada

Great Basin

Great Salt Lake

Colorado Plateau

Arkansas

San Joaquin

San Andreas Fault

Death Valley

Sierra Nevada

Mojave Desert

Grand Canyon

Sonoran Desert

Mississippi

GULF ATLANTIC COASTAL PLAIN

PACIFIC OCEAN

Lower California

Sierra Madre Occidental

Gulf of California

Sierra Madre Oriental

Rio Grande

Mississippi Delta

Gulf of Mexico

West Indies

Greater Antilles

Lesser Antilles

Volcán Pico de Orizaba 5700m

Yucatan Peninsula

NORTH AMERICAN PLATE

CARIBBEAN PLATE

Caribbean Sea

Sierra Madre del Sur

COCOS PLATE

CARIBBEAN PLATE

Lake Nicaragua

Isthmus of Panama

SOUTH AMERICAN PLATE

SOUTH AMERICA

Climate

North America's climate includes extremes ranging from freezing Arctic conditions in Alaska and Greenland, to desert in the southwest, and tropical conditions in southeastern Florida, the Caribbean and Central America. Central and southern regions are prone to severe storms including tornadoes and hurricanes.

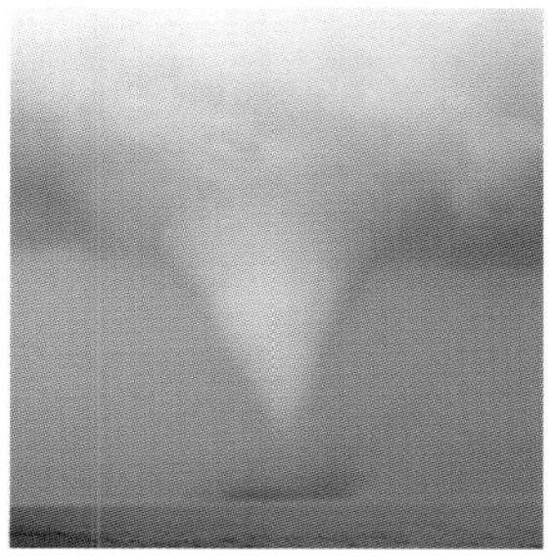

▲ *'Tornado alley' in the Mississippi Valley suffers frequent tornadoes.*

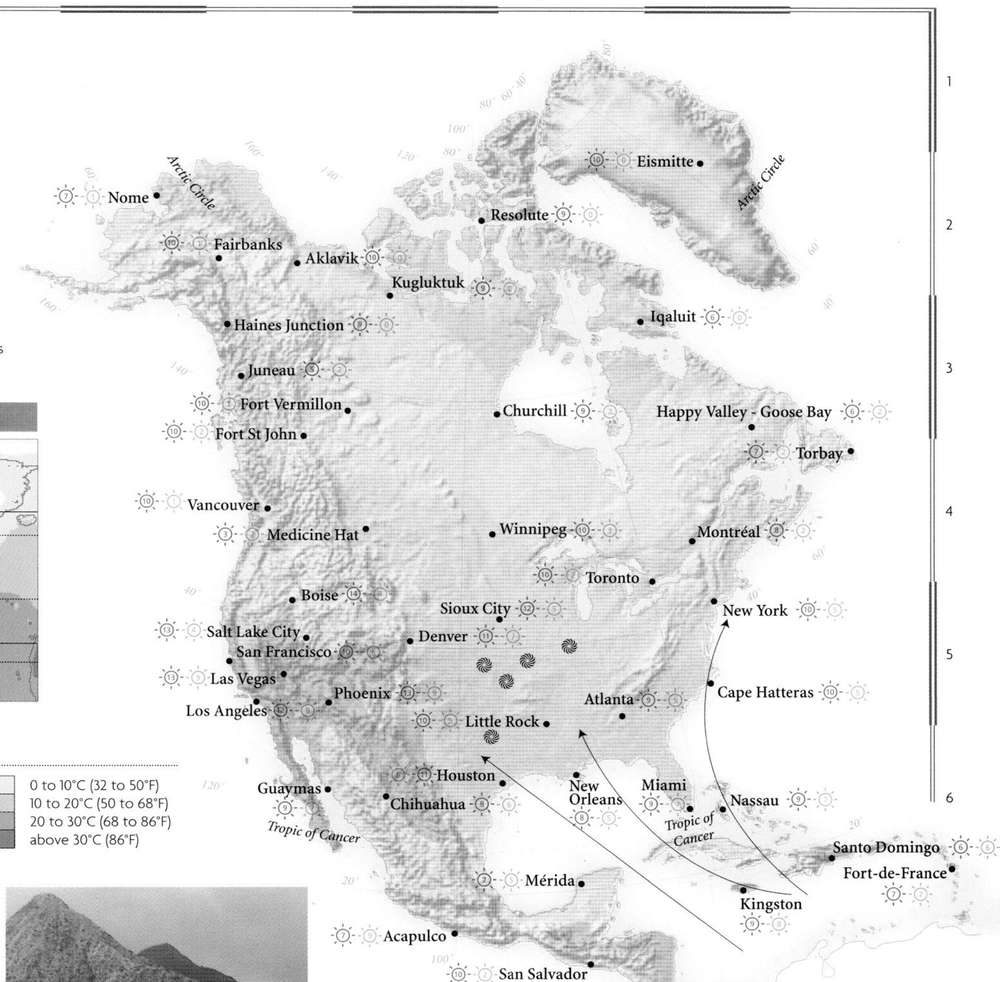

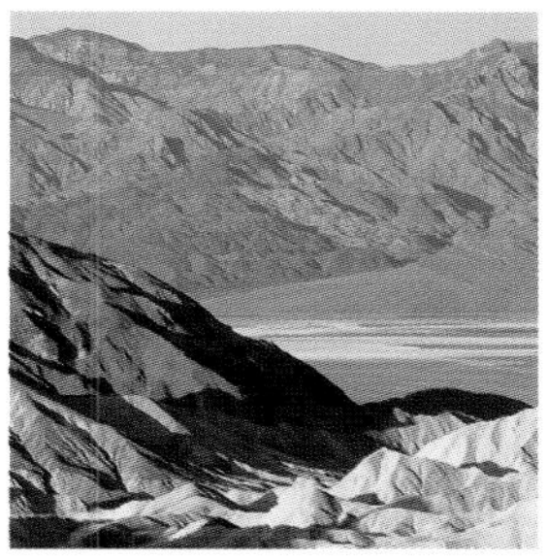

▲ *Much of the* southwest is semi-desert; receiving less than 12 inches (300 mm) of rainfall a year.

Climate

	ice cap
	tundra
	subarctic
	cool continental
	warm humid
	semi-arid
	arid
	humid equatorial
	tropical
☼	daily hours of sunshine, January
☀	daily hours of sunshine, July
→	direction of hurricanes
⊛	tornado zones

Temperature

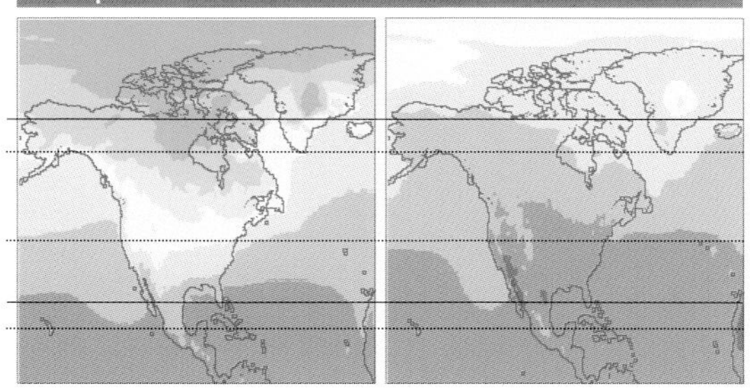

Average January temperature

Average July temperature

Temperature

	below -30°C (-22°F)
	-30 to -20°C (-22 to -4°F)
	-20 to -10°C (-4 to 14°F)
	-10 to 0°C (14 to 32°F)
	0 to 10°C (32 to 50°F)
	10 to 20°C (50 to 68°F)
	20 to 30°C (68 to 86°F)
	above 30°C (86°F)

Rainfall

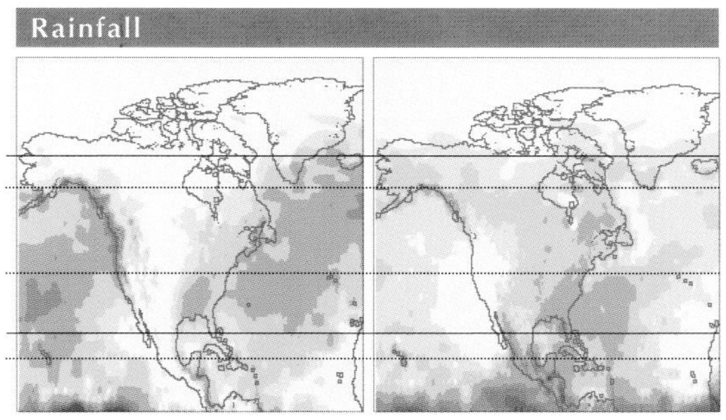

Average January rainfall

Average July rainfall

Rainfall

	0–25 mm (0–1 in)
	25–50 mm (1–2 in)
	50–100 mm (2–4 in)
	100–200 mm (4–8 in)
	200–300 mm (8–12 in)
	300–400 mm (12–16 in)
	400–500 mm (16–20 in)
	more than 500 mm (20 in)

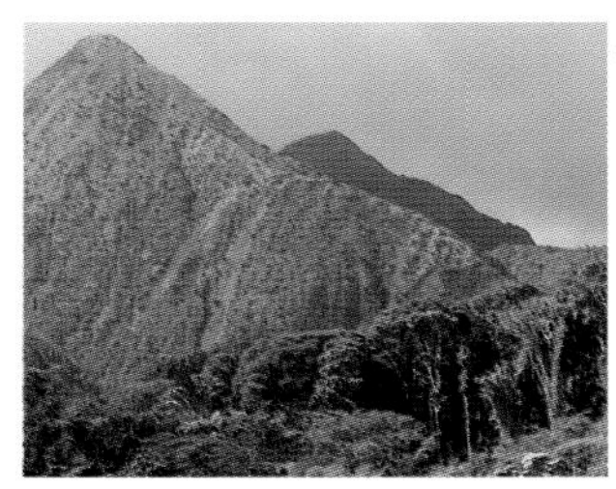

◄ *The lush, green mountains of the Lesser Antilles receive annual rainfalls of up to 360 inches (9000 mm).*

Map labels: Nome, Fairbanks, Aklavik, Kugluktuk, Resolute, Eismitte, Haines Junction, Iqaluit, Juneau, Churchill, Happy Valley - Goose Bay, Fort Vermillon, Torbay, Fort St John, Vancouver, Winnipeg, Montréal, Medicine Hat, Toronto, Boise, Sioux City, New York, Salt Lake City, Denver, San Francisco, Atlanta, Cape Hatteras, Las Vegas, Los Angeles, Phoenix, Little Rock, Houston, Miami, Nassau, Guaymas, Chihuahua, New Orleans, Santo Domingo, Fort-de-France, Mérida, Kingston, Acapulco, San Salvador, San José

Arctic Circle, Tropic of Cancer

Shaping the continent

Glacial processes affect much of northern Canada, Greenland and the Western Cordillera. Along the western coast of North America, Central America and the Caribbean, underlying plates moving together lead to earthquakes and volcanic eruptions. The vast river systems, fed by mountain streams, constantly erode and deposit material along their paths.

Volcanic activity

1 Mount St Helens volcano *(right)* in the Cascade Range erupted violently in May 1980, killing 57 people and levelling large areas of forest. The lateral blast filled a valley for 15 miles (25 km) with debris.

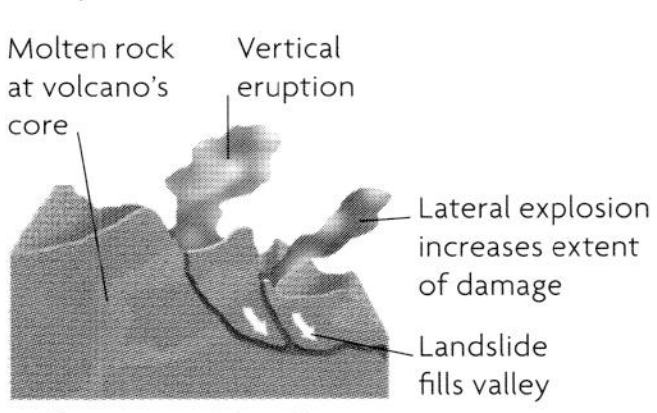

Molten rock at volcano's core
Vertical eruption
Lateral explosion increases extent of damage
Landslide fills valley

Volcanic activity: Eruption of Mount St Helens

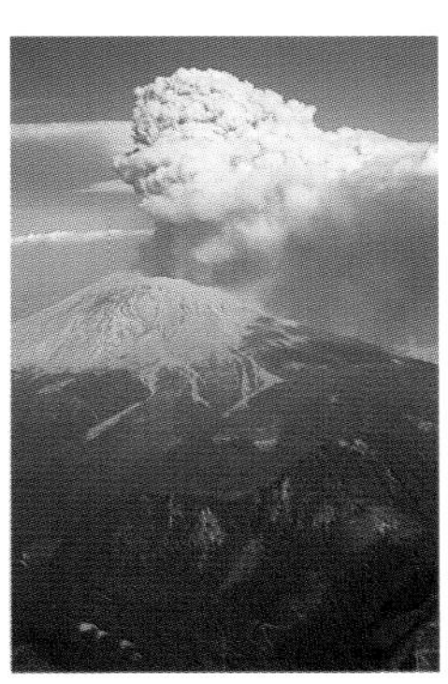

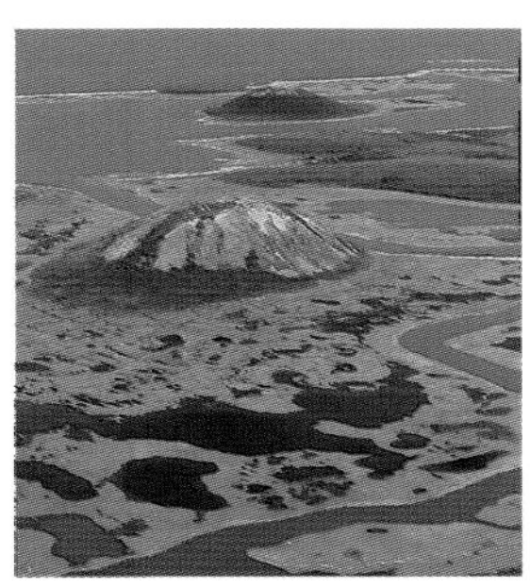

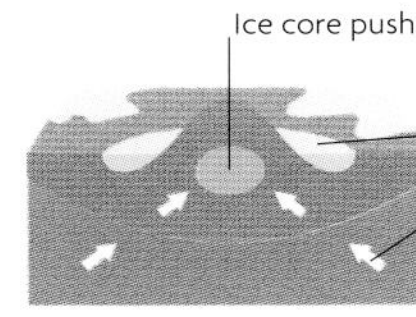

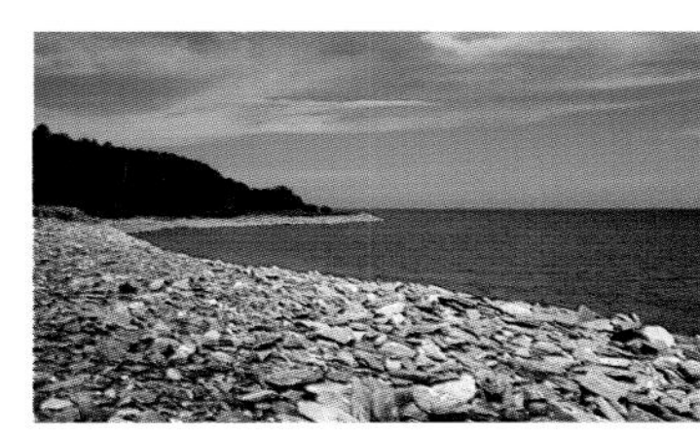

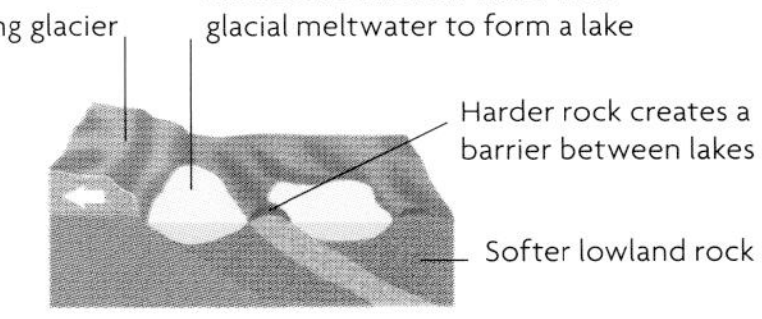

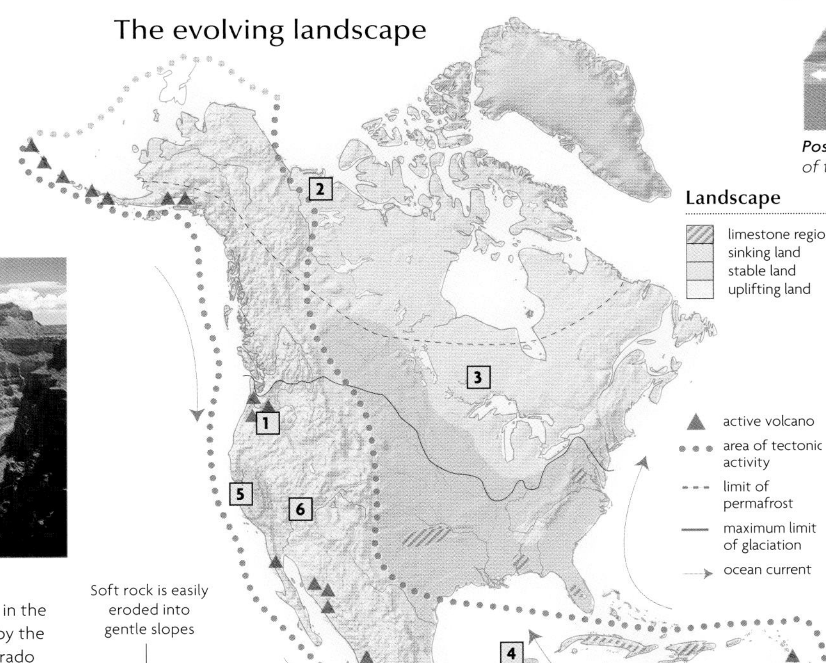

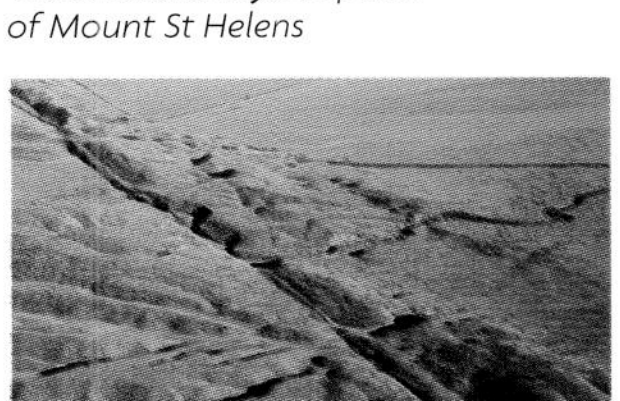

Seismic activity

5 The San Andreas Fault *(above)* places much of the North America's west coast under constant threat from earthquakes. It is caused by the Pacific Plate grinding past the North American Plate at a faster rate, though in the same direction.

Pacific Plate
San Andreas Fault
Fault is caused by faster movement of Pacific Plate
North American Plate

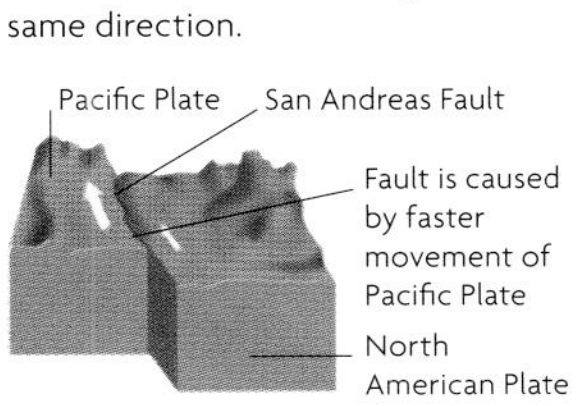

Seismic activity: Action of the San Andreas Fault

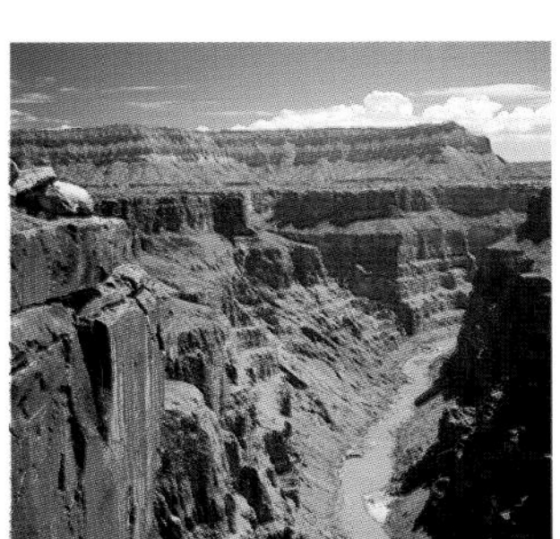

River erosion

6 The Grand Canyon *(above)* in the Colorado Plateau was created by the downward erosion of the Colorado River, combined with the gradual uplift of the plateau, over the past 30 million years. The contours of the canyon formed as the softer rock layers eroded into gentle slopes, and the hard rock layers into cliffs. The depth varies from 3855–6560 ft (1175–2000 m).

Soft rock is easily eroded into gentle slopes
Hard rock resists erosion
Colorado River cuts down through rock

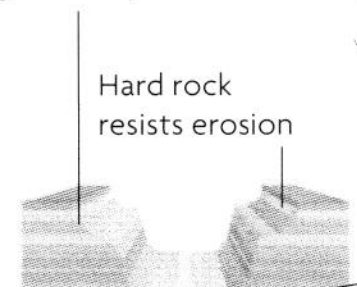

River Erosion: Formation of the Grand Canyon

Periglaciation

2 The ground in the far north is nearly always frozen: the surface thaws only in summer. This freeze-thaw process produces features such as pingos *(left)* formed by the freezing of groundwater. With each successive winter ice accumulates producing a mound with a core of ice.

Ice core pushes up ground to form pingo
Unfrozen lake
Groundwater attracted to ice core

Periglaciation: Formation of a pingo in the Mackenzie Delta

The evolving landscape

Landscape

	limestone region
	sinking land
	stable land
	uplifting land

▲ active volcano
⋯ area of tectonic activity
--- limit of permafrost
— maximum limit of glaciation
→ ocean current

Post-glacial lakes

3 A chain of lakes from Great Bear Lake to the Great Lakes *(above)* was created as the ice retreated northwards. Glaciers scoured hollows in the softer lowland rock. Glacial deposits at the lip of the hollows, and ridges of harder rock, trapped water to form lakes.

Retreating glacier
Ice-scoured hollow filled with glacial meltwater to form a lake
Harder rock creates a barrier between lakes
Softer lowland rock

Post-glacial lakes: Formation of the Great Lakes

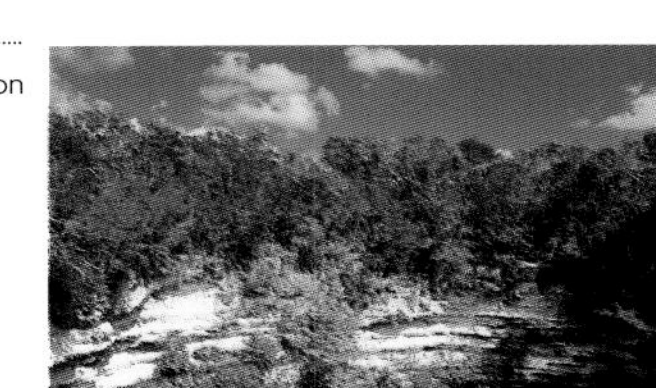

Weathering

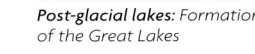

4 The Yucatan Peninsula is a vast, flat limestone plateau in southern Mexico. Weathering action from both rainwater and underground streams has enlarged fractures in the rock to form caves and hollows, called sinkholes *(above)*.

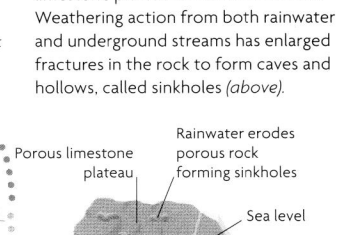

Porous limestone plateau
Rainwater erodes porous rock forming sinkholes
Sea level
Underground stream further erodes rock

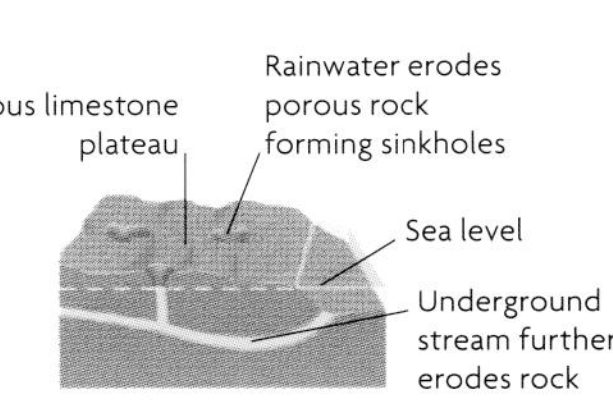

Weathering: Water erosion on the Yucatan Peninsula

Political North America

Democracy is well established in some parts of the continent but is a recent phenomenon in others. The economically dominant nations of Canada and the USA have a long democratic tradition but elsewhere, notably in the countries of Central America, political turmoil has been more common. In Nicaragua and Haiti, harsh dictatorships have only recently been superseded by democratically-elected governments. North America's largest countries, Canada, Mexico and the USA have federal state systems, sharing political power between national and state governments. The USA has intervened militarily on several occasions in Central America and the Caribbean to protect its strategic interests.

Transport

In the 19th century, railways were used to open up the North American continent. Air transport is now more common for long distance passenger travel, although railways are still extensively used for bulk freight transport. Waterways, like the Mississippi River, are important for the transport of bulk materials, and the Panama Canal is a vital link between the Pacific Ocean and the Caribbean. In the 20th century, road transport increased massively in North America, with the introduction of cheap, mass-produced motor cars and extensive highway construction.

◀ *This busy suburban* interchange in Los Angeles is part of the USA's Interstate freeway system. Construction of the 55,000 mile (88,500 km) freeway network began in the 1950s, and it now connects most major cities, and carries one-fifth of the USA's road traffic.

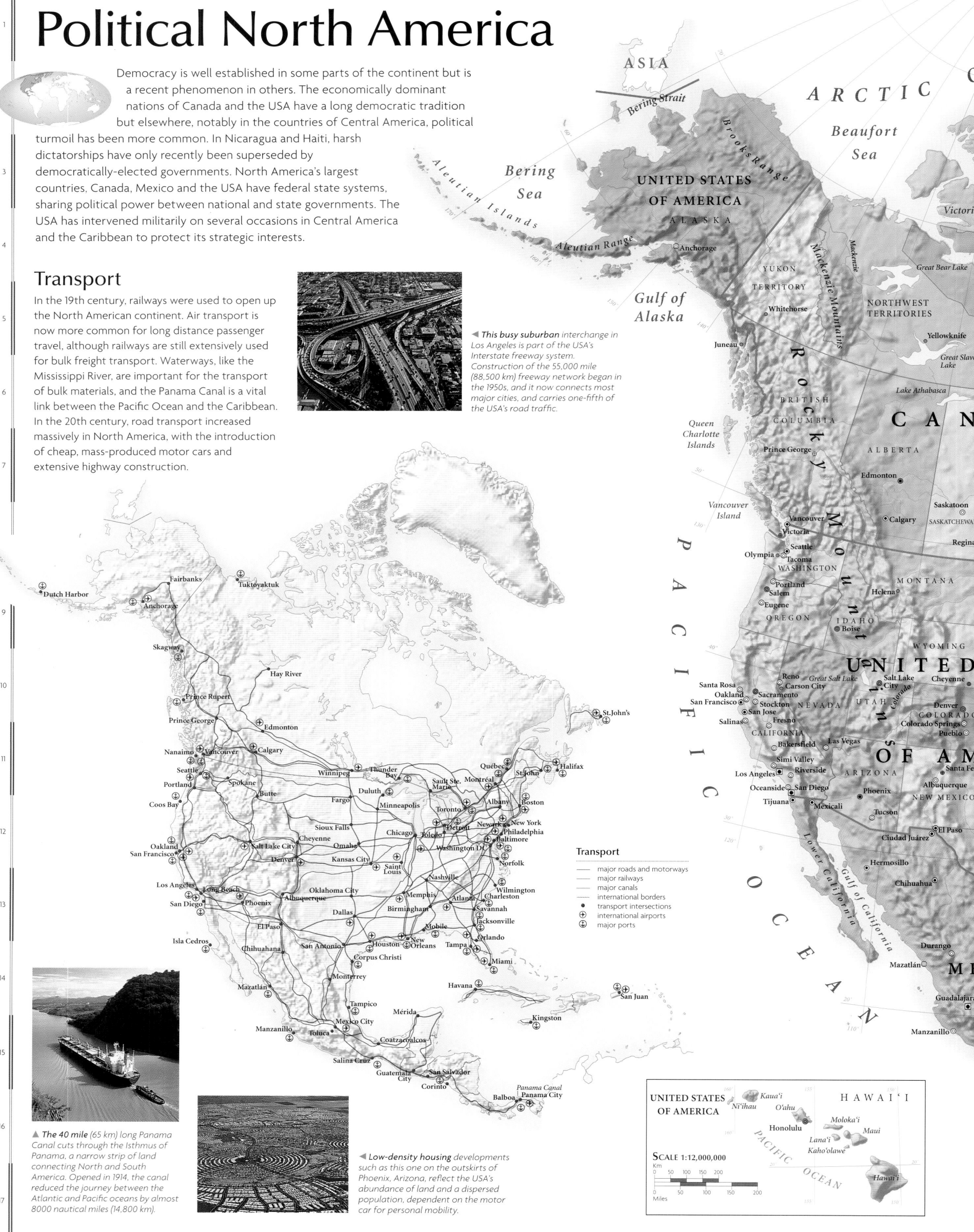

Transport
— major roads and motorways
— major railways
— major canals
— international borders
● transport intersections
✈ international airports
⊕ major ports

▲ *The 40 mile* (65 km) long Panama Canal cuts through the Isthmus of Panama, a narrow strip of land connecting North and South America. Opened in 1914, the canal reduced the journey between the Atlantic and Pacific oceans by almost 8000 nautical miles (14,800 km).

◀ *Low-density housing* developments such as this one on the outskirts of Phoenix, Arizona, reflect the USA's abundance of land and a dispersed population, dependent on the motor car for personal mobility.

UNITED STATES OF AMERICA

SCALE 1:12,000,000

HAWAI'I

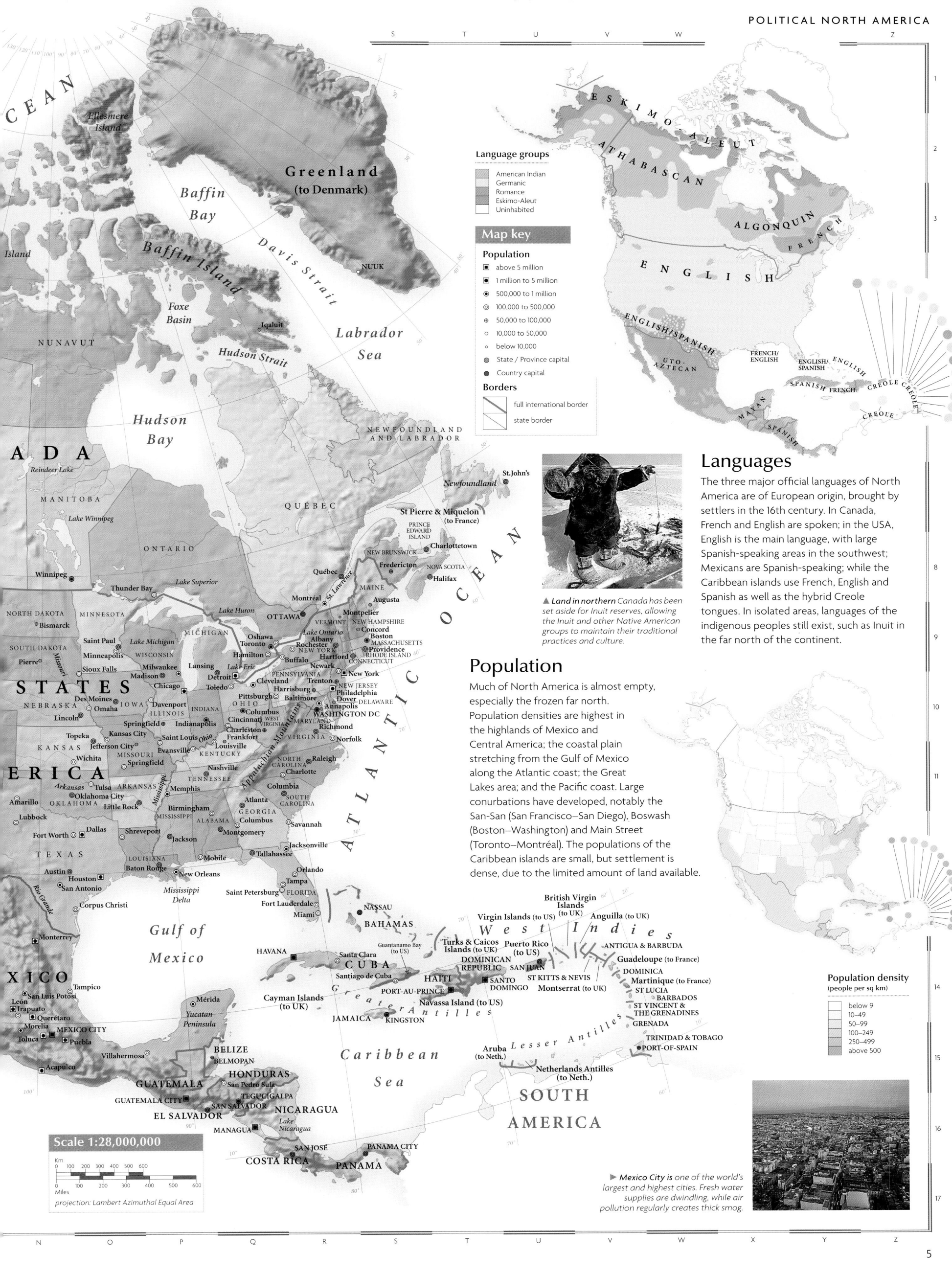

Language groups

- American Indian
- Germanic
- Romance
- Eskimo-Aleut
- Uninhabited

Map key

Population

- ■ above 5 million
- ▣ 1 million to 5 million
- ◉ 500,000 to 1 million
- ◎ 100,000 to 500,000
- ⊕ 50,000 to 100,000
- ○ 10,000 to 50,000
- ∘ below 10,000
- ◻ State / Province capital
- ● Country capital

Borders

- full international border
- state border

Languages

The three major official languages of North America are of European origin, brought by settlers in the 16th century. In Canada, French and English are spoken; in the USA, English is the main language, with large Spanish-speaking areas in the southwest; Mexicans are Spanish-speaking; while the Caribbean islands use French, English and Spanish as well as the hybrid Creole tongues. In isolated areas, languages of the indigenous peoples still exist, such as Inuit in the far north of the continent.

▲ Land in northern Canada has been set aside for Inuit reserves, allowing the Inuit and other Native American groups to maintain their traditional practices and culture.

Population

Much of North America is almost empty, especially the frozen far north. Population densities are highest in the highlands of Mexico and Central America; the coastal plain stretching from the Gulf of Mexico along the Atlantic coast; the Great Lakes area; and the Pacific coast. Large conurbations have developed, notably the San-San (San Francisco–San Diego), Boswash (Boston–Washington) and Main Street (Toronto–Montréal). The populations of the Caribbean islands are small, but settlement is dense, due to the limited amount of land available.

Population density
(people per sq km)

- below 9
- 10–49
- 50–99
- 100–249
- 250–499
- above 500

► Mexico City is one of the world's largest and highest cities. Fresh water supplies are dwindling, while air pollution regularly creates thick smog.

Scale 1:28,000,000

projection: Lambert Azimuthal Equal Area

5

North American resources

The two northern countries of Canada and the USA are richly endowed with natural resources which have helped to fuel economic development. The USA is the world's largest economy, although today it is facing stiff competition from the Far East. Mexico has relied on oil revenues but there are hopes that the North American Free Trade Agreement (NAFTA), will encourage trade growth with Canada and the USA. The poorer countries of Central America and the Caribbean depend largely on cash crops and tourism.

Industry

The modern, industrialized economies of the USA and Canada contrast sharply with those of Mexico, Central America and the Caribbean. Manufacturing is especially important in the USA; vehicle production is concentrated around the Great Lakes, while electronic and hi-tech industries are increasingly found in the western and southern states. Mexico depends on oil exports and assembly work, taking advantage of cheap labour. Many Central American and Caribbean countries rely heavily on agricultural exports.

◀ After its purchase from Russia in 1867, Alaska's frozen lands were largely ignored by the USA. Oil reserves similar in magnitude to those in eastern Texas were discovered in Prudhoe Bay, Alaska in 1968. Freezing temperatures and a fragile environment hamper oil extraction.

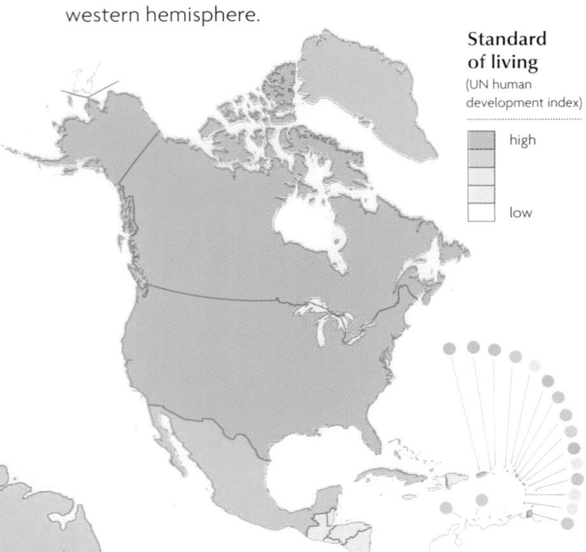

▲ South of San Francisco, 'Silicon Valley' is both a national and international centre for hi-tech industries, electronic industries and research institutions.

▲ Multinational companies rely on cheap labour and tax benefits to assemble vehicles in Mexican factories.

Standard of living

The USA and Canada have one of the highest overall standards of living in the world. However, many people still live in poverty, especially in inner city ghettos and some rural areas. Central America and the Caribbean are markedly poorer than their wealthier northern neighbours. Haiti is the poorest country in the western hemisphere.

Standard of living
(UN human development index)
high
low

▲ Fish such as cod, flounder and plaice are caught in the Grand Banks, off the Newfoundland coast, and processed in many North Atlantic coastal settlements.

▲ The health of the Wall Street stock market in New York is the standard measure of the state of the world's economy.

Industry

- aerospace
- brewing
- car/vehicle manufacture
- chemicals
- defence
- electronics
- engineering
- film industry
- finance
- food processing
- hi-tech industry
- iron & steel
- pharmaceuticals
- printing & publishing
- research & development
- shipbuilding
- sugar processing
- textiles
- timber processing
- tobacco processing
- coal
- oil
- gas
- industrial cities
- major industrial areas

GNI per capita (US$)

- below 1999
- 2000–4999
- 5000–9999
- 10,000–19,999
- 20,000–24,999
- above 25,000

Map labels

ARCTIC OCEAN
Beaufort Sea
Bering Strait
RUSS. FED.
Bering Sea
Prudhoe Bay
USA
Gulf of Alaska
PACIFIC OCEAN
Baffin Bay
Greenland (to Denmark)
Labrador Sea
Hudson Strait
Hudson Bay
CANADA
Vancouver
Calgary
Seattle
Winnipeg
Portland
Montréal
Minneapolis
Milwaukee
Toronto
Boston
Albany
Detroit
Buffalo
New York
UNITED STATES OF AMERICA
Chicago
Cleveland
Pittsburgh
Philadelphia
Baltimore
San Francisco
Denver
Kansas City
Saint Louis
Cincinnati
Dayton
Wichita
Nashville
Greensboro
Los Angeles
Tulsa
Charlotte
San Diego
Phoenix
Dallas
Birmingham
Atlanta
Tijuana
Ciudad Juárez
El Paso
Houston
New Orleans
Jacksonville
Orlando
Tampa
Monterrey
Gulf of Mexico
Miami
ATLANTIC OCEAN
Guadalajara
Mexico City
MEXICO
West Indies
BAHAMAS
Havana
CUBA
Turks & Caicos Islands (to UK)
Virgin Islands (to US)
British Virgin Islands (to UK)
Anguilla (to UK)
ST KITTS & NEVIS
ANTIGUA & BARBUDA
Montserrat (to UK)
Puerto Rico (to US)
San Juan
Guadeloupe (to France)
DOMINICA
Martinique (to France)
ST LUCIA
BARBADOS
ST VINCENT & THE GRENADINES
GRENADA
TRINIDAD & TOBAGO
Port-of-Spain
Cayman Islands (to UK)
JAMAICA
HAITI
Port-au-Prince
DOMINICAN REPUBLIC
Santo Domingo
Greater Antilles
Navassa Island (to US)
Aruba (to Neth.)
Lesser Antilles
Caribbean Sea
Netherlands Antilles (to Neth.)
VENEZUELA
BELIZE
GUATEMALA
Guatemala City
HONDURAS
Tegucigalpa
EL SALVADOR
San Salvador
NICARAGUA
Managua
San José
COSTA RICA
Panama City
PANAMA
COLOMBIA

Environmental issues

Many fragile environments are under threat throughout the region. In Haiti, all the primary rainforest has been destroyed, while air pollution from factories and cars in Mexico City is amongst the worst in the world. Elsewhere, industry and mining pose threats, particularly in the delicate arctic environment of Alaska where oil spills have polluted coastlines and decimated fish stocks.

Mineral resources

Fossil fuels are exploited in considerable quantities throughout the continent. Coal mining in the Appalachians is declining but vast open pits exist further west in Wyoming. Oil and natural gas are found in Alaska, Texas, the Gulf of Mexico, and the Canadian West. Canada has large quantities of nickel, while Jamaica has considerable deposits of bauxite, and Mexico has large reserves of silver.

Mineral resources

- oil field
- gas field
- coal field
- bauxite
- copper
- gold
- iron
- lead
- nickel
- phosphates
- silver
- uranium

Environmental issues

- national parks
- acid rain
- tropical forest
- forest destroyed
- desert
- desertification
- polluted rivers
- radioactive contamination
- marine pollution
- heavy marine pollution
- poor urban air quality

▲ **In addition to** fossil fuels, North America is also rich in exploitable metallic ores. This vast, mile-deep (1.6 km) pit is a copper mine in New Mexico.

▲ **Wild bison** graze in Yellowstone National Park, the world's first national park. Designated in 1872, geothermal springs and boiling mud are among its natural spectacles, making it a major tourist attraction.

▲ **In agriculturally marginal** areas where the soil is either too poor, or the climate too dry for crops, cattle ranching proliferates – especially in Mexico and the western reaches of the Great Plains.

Using the land and sea

Abundant land and fertile soils stretch from the Canadian prairies to Texas creating North America's agricultural heartland. Cereals and cattle ranching form the basis of the farming economy, with corn and soya beans also important. Fruit and vegetables are grown in California using irrigation, while Florida is a leading producer of citrus fruits. Caribbean and Central American countries depend on cash crops such as bananas, coffee and sugar cane, often grown on large plantations. This reliance on a single crop can leave these countries vulnerable to fluctuating world crop prices.

Using the land and sea

- cropland
- forest
- ice cap
- mountain region
- pasture
- tundra
- wetland
- desert
- major conurbations
- cattle
- goats
- pigs
- poultry
- reindeer
- sheep
- bananas
- citrus fruits
- coffee
- corn (maize)
- cotton
- fishing
- fruit
- maple syrup
- peanuts
- rice
- shellfish
- soya beans
- sugar cane
- timber
- tobacco
- vineyards
- wheat

◀ **Sugar cane is** Cuba's main agricultural crop, and is grown and processed throughout the Caribbean. Fermented sugar is used to make rum.

◀ **The Great Plains** support large-scale arable farming throughout central North America. Corn is grown in a belt south and west of the Great Lakes, while further west where the climate is drier, wheat is grown.

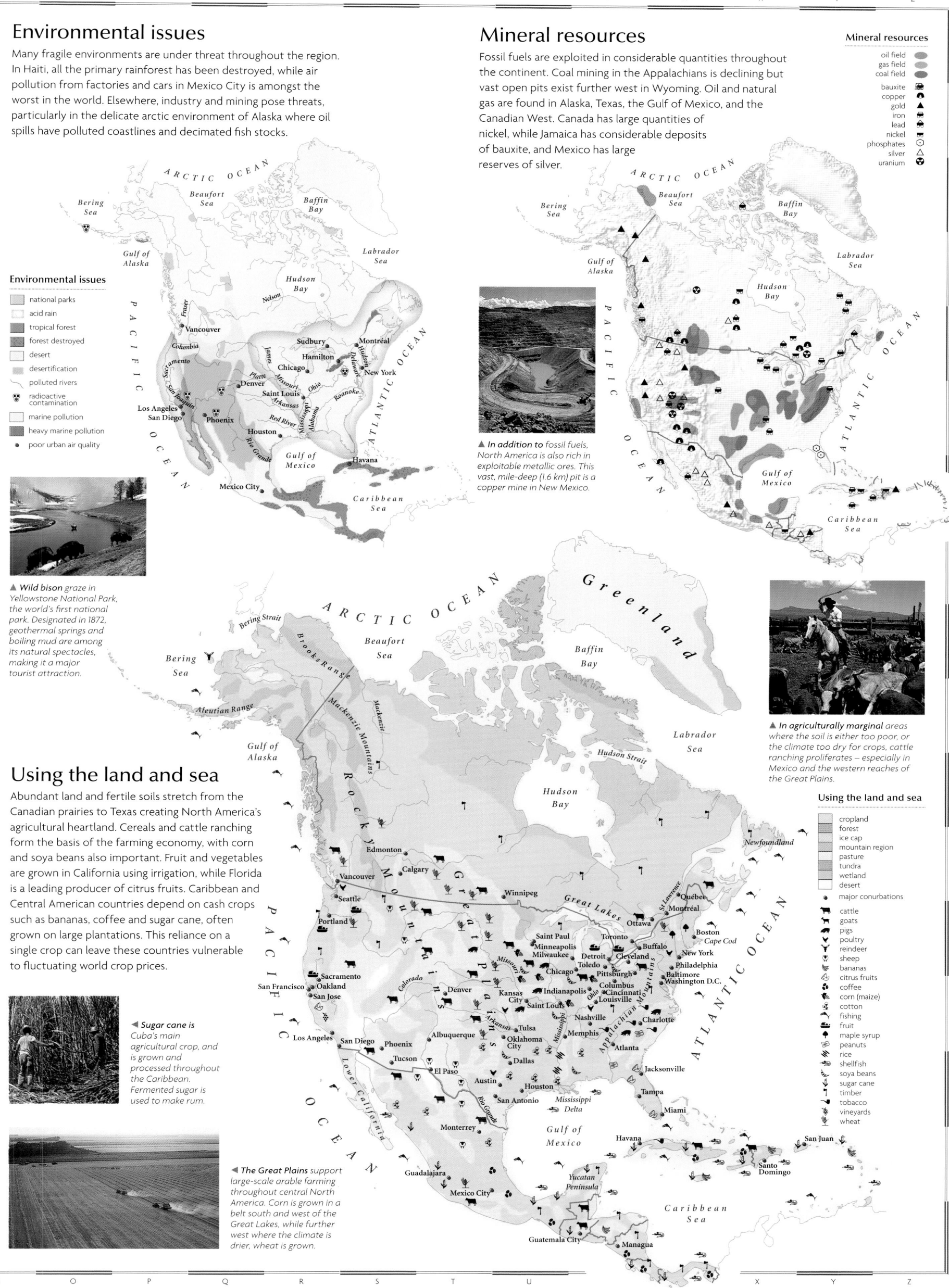

A   B   C   D   E   F   G   K   L   M

Canada:
WESTERN PROVINCES

Alberta, British Columbia, Manitoba,
Saskatchewan, Yukon Territory

The mountains of the west coast, incorporating British Columbia and
the Yukon Territory, descend into the vast, flat prairies of Alberta,
Saskatchewan and Manitoba. The empty lands and fertile soils of
the prairie provinces attracted migrants, and the descendants of
early European immigrants still make up a large proportion of
the population. The mechanization of agriculture has
reduced the need for labour, and rural population
densities remain low. The majority of the people live
within 100 miles (160 km) of the southern Canada—USA
border, and in British Columbia, one of the leading Canadian provinces in
terms of economic wealth. The Yukon Territory, in the far north, remains a
relatively unspoilt wilderness, containing large, untapped mineral reserves.
This province has a significant population of Native Americans,
many of whom maintain a traditional lifestyle.

Using the land and sea

Wheat farming is the economic mainstay of Alberta, Manitoba and
Saskatchewan, which contain 82% of farmland in Canada. Cattle
are also raised on the prairies. Forestry and fishing are the most
prominent resource-based industries in British Columbia. Despite
the mountainous terrain, fruit and specialized grains can be grown
in the Okanagan and Fraser valleys.

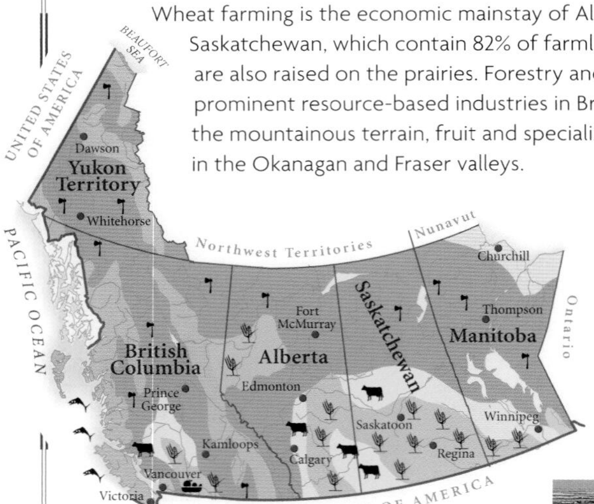

Land use and agricultural distribution

- cattle
- cereals
- fishing
- fruit
- timber
- major towns
- pasture
- cropland
- forest
- wetland
- barren
- tundra

The urban/rural population divide

urban 83%   rural 17%

0 10 20 30 40 50 60 70 80 90 100

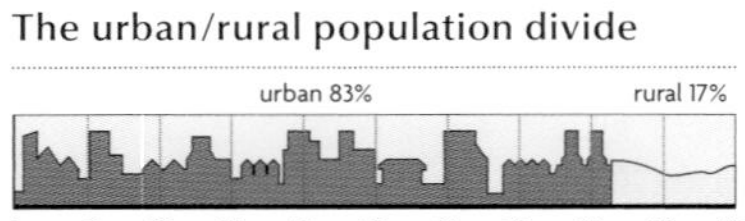

Population density	Total land area
8 people per sq mile (3 people per sq km)	1,230,547 sq miles (3,187,120 sq km)

Transport and industry

The western provinces contain a wealth of mineral resources.
Alberta holds the bulk of Canada's fossil fuels; the other
provinces contain reserves of metallic ores, such as zinc, lead
and silver. Isolation from markets has slowed the development
of manufacturing, restricting it to the large cities like Vancouver,
Winnipeg and Calgary. Hydro-electric power is widely
exploited, although there is increasing concern about potential
ecological damage.

Major industry and infrastructure

- aerospace
- chemicals
- coal
- engineering
- food processing
- hydro-electric power
- mining
- oil & gas
- timber processing
- major towns
- international airports
- major roads
- major industrial areas

The transport network

82,438 miles (135,145 km)	
6459 miles (10,401 km)	
24,041 miles (38,694 km)	
None	

The transport network of the
western provinces is dominated
by east–west routes that weave
through mountain passes and
spread across the plains. Access
to some northern areas is
restricted to air travel.

▲ The Fraser River valley is a major
area of settlement in British
Columbia. Railways cross the
Rocky Mountains via this valley.

▲ Established in 1907,
Jasper National Park lies
in the heart of the Rocky
Mountains. It is noted for
its spectacular alpine
scenery and contains
part of the large
Columbia Icefield.

▲ Large, highly-mechanized and
often very specialized farms,
requiring huge investment but little
labour, characterize modern
farming in the prairies.

◄ Much of the Yukon Territory
is uninhabited tundra. Industry
is based on the extraction of
mineral resources, and to a
lesser extent, on the scattered
forests of the south.

17
198

The landscape

The massive Rocky Mountains form a continental divide between rivers flowing eastward and westward. East of the mountains, stretching from the Arctic Circle south into the USA, lie the interior plains. Covered with glacial deposits from the last Ice Age, these are interspersed with hilly regions and long, steep escarpments.

Map key

Population

- ◉ 500,000 to 1 million
- ◎ 100,000 to 500,000
- ⊙ 50,000 to 100,000
- ○ 10,000 to 50,000
- ○ below 10,000

Elevation

- 6000m / 19,686ft
- 4000m / 13,124ft
- 3000m / 9843ft
- 2000m / 6562ft
- 1000m / 3281ft
- 500m / 1640ft
- 250m / 820ft
- 100m / 328ft
- sea level

Scale 1:7,500,000

Km
0 25 50 100 150 200 250

Miles
0 25 50 100 150 200 250

projection: Lambert Conformal Conic

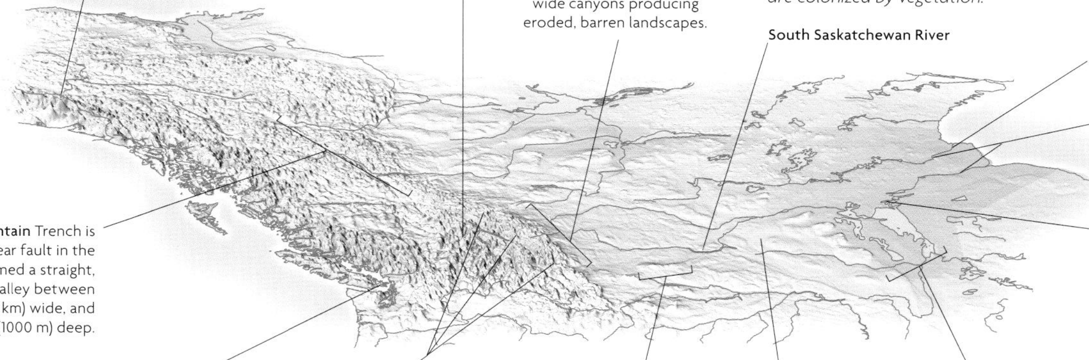

Mount Logan rises 19,551 ft (5959 m). It is the highest peak in Canada.

The Columbia Icefield in the Rocky Mountains is the source of two major rivers, the Athabasca and the North Saskatchewan.

The badlands of Alberta were created when east-flowing rivers, swollen by meltwater at the end of the last Ice Age, cut deep, wide canyons producing eroded, barren landscapes.

South Saskatchewan River

Vegetated island · Bar
River flow is diverted by deposited sediments · Sand flat

▲ **Braided rivers are** shallow and fast-flowing. The interlaced branches are formed when excess sediments, which can no longer be transported, are deposited. The sediments collect in the river channel forming bars and sand flats. Islands form when the bars are colonized by vegetation.

▲ **Across the tundra** of northern Manitoba, widespread permafrost inhibits water from permeating the soil. This causes rivers like the Churchill to flow in many channels, which can be frozen for up to six months during the winter.

The Nelson and Churchill rivers drain northward across the Canadian Shield to Hudson Bay. The shield covers three-fifths of Saskatchewan.

Setting Lake

The Rocky Mountain Trench is the longest linear fault in the world. It has formed a straight, flat-bottomed valley between 2–9 miles (4–15 km) wide, and up to 3280 ft (1000 m) deep.

Hundreds of islands dot the fjord-indented coast of British Columbia; the largest is Vancouver Island.

Three major passes cut through the Rocky Mountains: Yellowhead, Kicking Horse and Crowsnest. They are all used as transport routes through the mountains.

The Cypress Hills rise to 4806 ft (1465 m) above the surrounding plain. Having escaped the last glaciation they contain unique plant and animal life. The silvery lupine, bunchberry and lodgepole pine all grow in the cool, moist climate of the hills.

The Alberta and Saskatchewan plains bear strong testament to past glaciations. The Assiniboine, Saskatchewan and Qu'Appelle rivers occupy flat-bottomed, steep-sided valleys eroded during the last Ice Age by glacial meltwater.

▲ **Ancient granite outcrops,** part of the Canadian Shield, rise above the surface of Setting Lake, which was initially formed by meltwater from the last Ice Age.

The lowlands of Manitoba are a basin that once held the vast post-glacial Lake Agassiz, remnants of which include Lake Winnipeg, Lake Winnipegosis and Lake Manitoba.

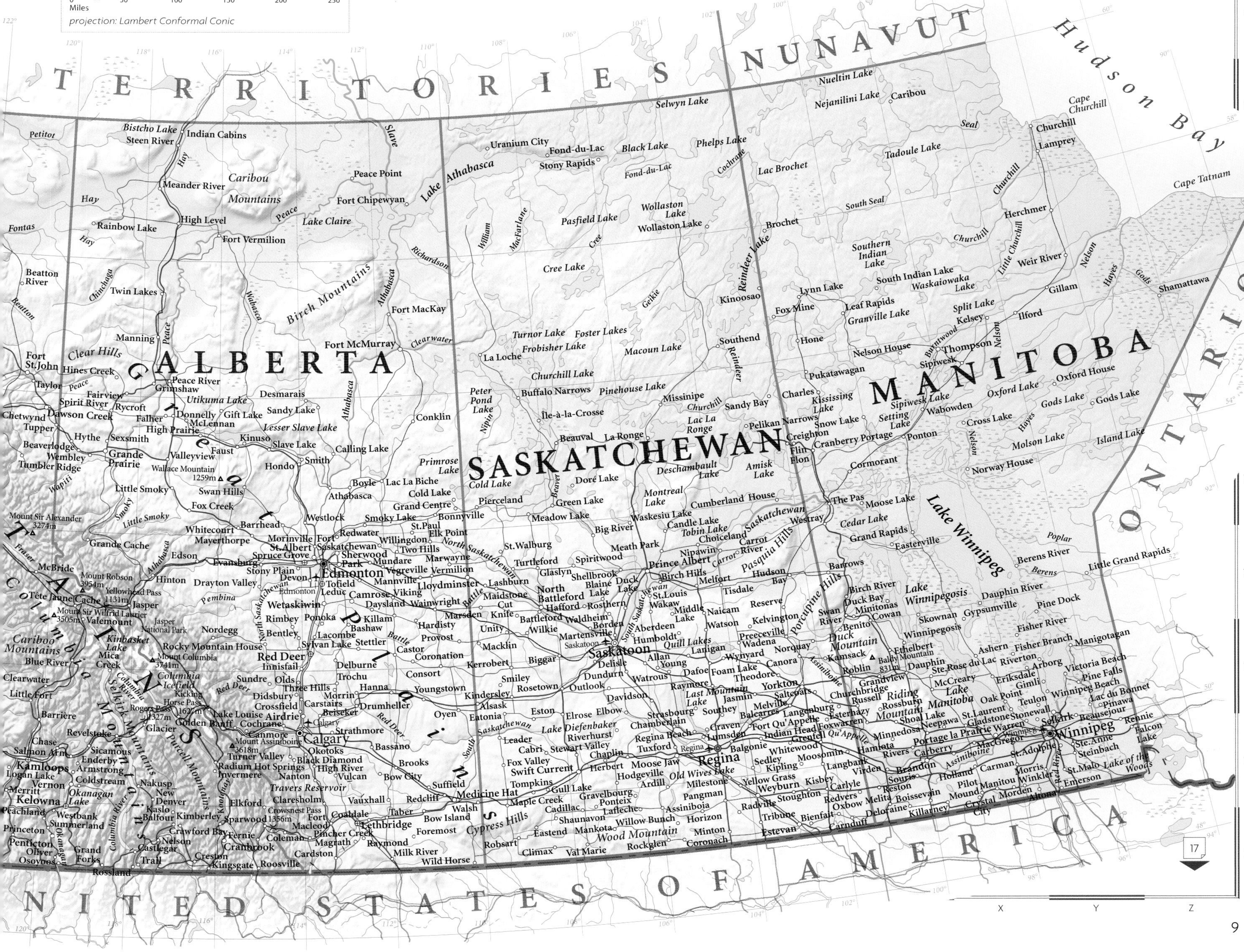

Canada: EASTERN PROVINCES

New Brunswick, Newfoundland & Labrador, Nova Scotia, Ontario,
Prince Edward Island, Québec, *St Pierre & Miquelon (to France)*

Colonized by both the English and the French during the 16th century, Canada's eastern provinces are still marked by their dual influences. They contain the last fragment of once-sizeable French territories, the islands of St Pierre and Miquelon. French remains Canada's second official language and Québec's first language. The population of the eastern provinces is highly concentrated in the south, especially along the border with the USA. A recent decline in fishing in the Atlantic provinces has encouraged a steady flow of westerly migration to more prosperous regions. The north, around Hudson Bay, remains snow-covered for most of the year and the indigenous Inuit people make up the bulk of its sparse population.

◀ *Rocher Percé, is 290 ft (88 m) high. Lying off the southeastern coast of Québec, it is a sanctuary for sea birds.*

Scale 1:7,000,000

Km
0 25 50 100 150 200

Miles
0 25 50 100 150 200

projection: Lambert Conformal Conic

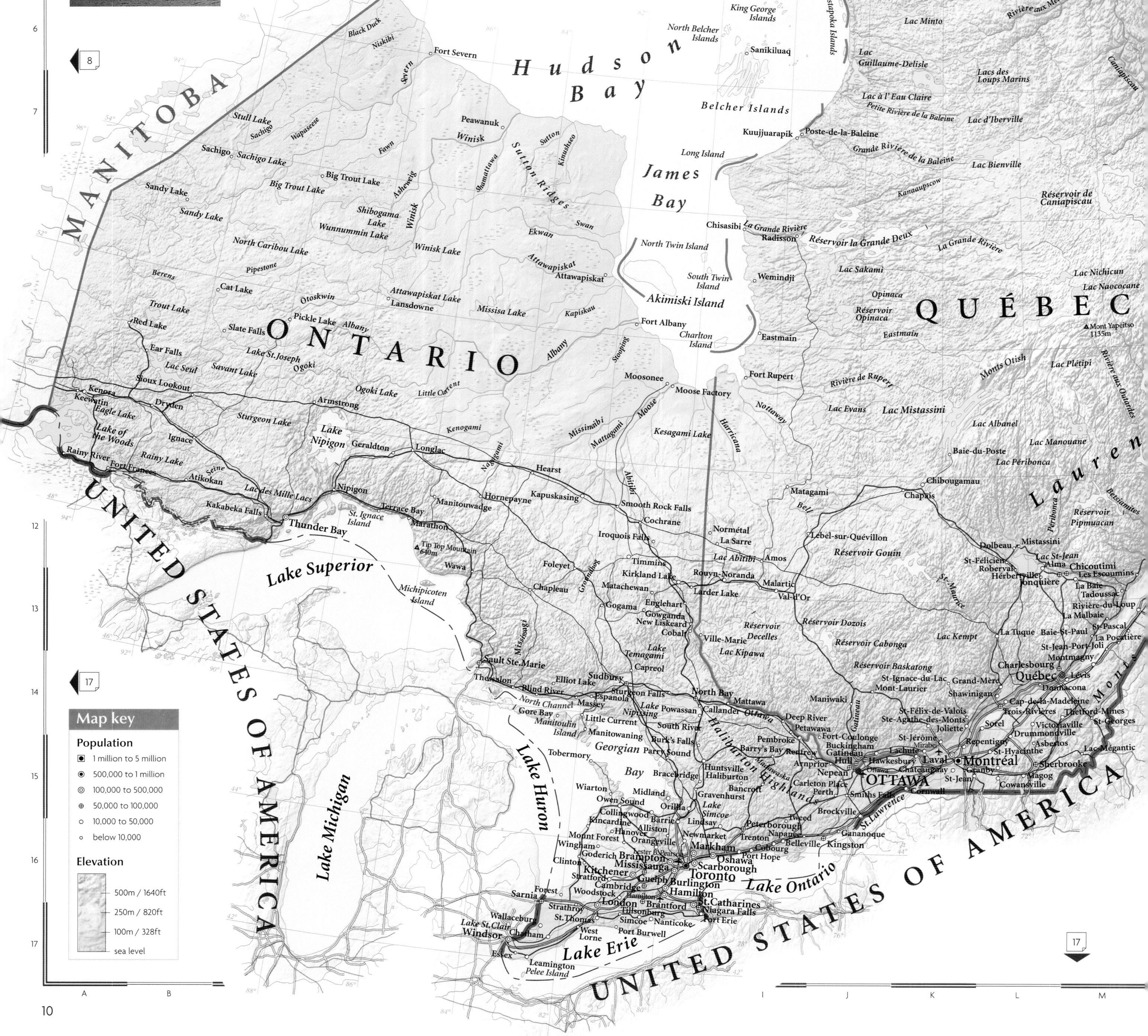

Map key

Population
- ▣ 1 million to 5 million
- ◉ 500,000 to 1 million
- ◎ 100,000 to 500,000
- ⊕ 50,000 to 100,000
- ○ 10,000 to 50,000
- ○ below 10,000

Elevation

500m / 1640ft
250m / 820ft
100m / 328ft
sea level

The landscape

Much of eastern Canada is part of the Canadian Shield. Glaciers have scoured the land leaving deposits that have dammed and diverted streams, to create a rocky landscape strewn with lakes and swamps. Much of the ground is subject to permafrost, which further impedes drainage. The uplands in the far east are the most northerly extension of the Appalachian mountain chain.

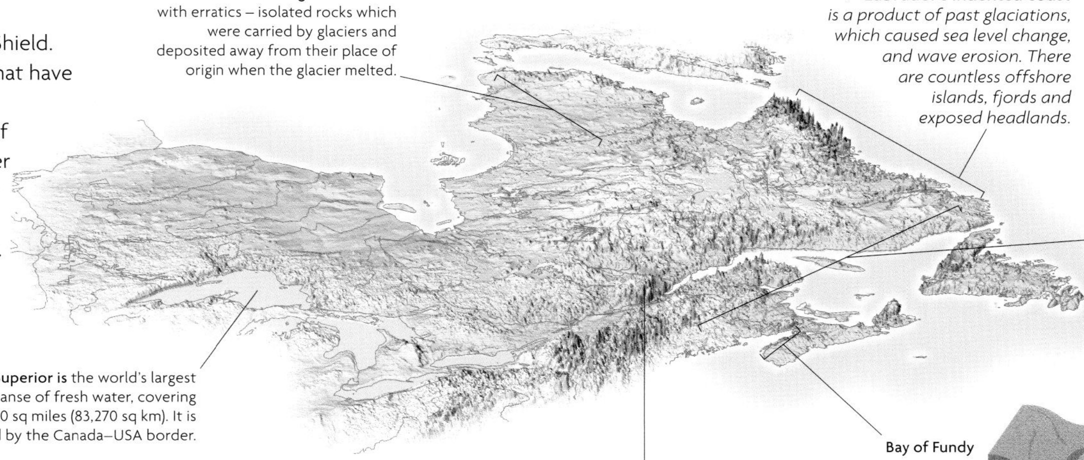

The Péninsule d'Ungava is littered with erratics – isolated rocks which were carried by glaciers and deposited away from their place of origin when the glacier melted.

▶ **Labrador's indented coast** is a product of past glaciations, which caused sea level change, and wave erosion. There are countless offshore islands, fjords and exposed headlands.

The eroded highlands of New Brunswick, Nova Scotia and Newfoundland are part of the Appalachian mountain chain, formed over 400 million years ago.

Lake Superior is the world's largest expanse of fresh water, covering 32,150 sq miles (83,270 sq km). It is crossed by the Canada–USA border.

Laurentides Park

Steep cliffs bound the bay

Bay of Fundy
Tidal waters are channelled down the bay

The bay is 94 miles (151 km) long

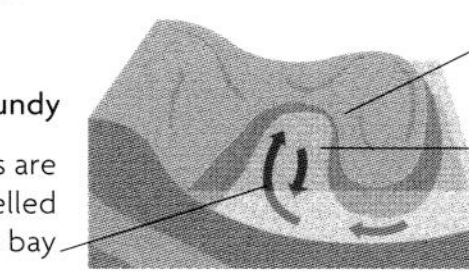

▶ **The forested Laurentides Park** incorporates part of the Laurentian Mountains. Within its boundaries are over 1600 lakes.

▲ **At the Bay of Fundy**, incoming waves are funnelled down the long, narrow, steep-sided bay. These topographical features cause fast-flowing tides which can rise 70 ft (21 m).

▲ **The tides at** the Bay of Fundy are among the highest in the world. At low tide the tree-topped rocks have been likened to flowerpots.

Transport and industry

Both Québec and Ontario have a diversified manufacturing sector located in the south. Across the rest of the region, industry is largely based around local resources, which accounts for the large number of fish and timber processing plants and mines. Many of the fast-flowing rivers are also gradually being harnessed for hydro-electric power.

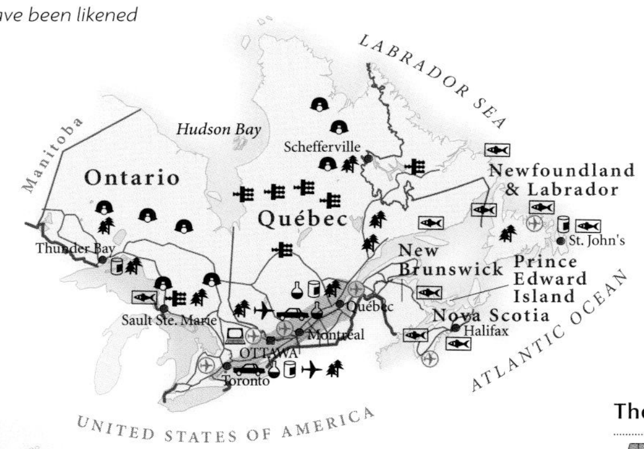

Major industry and infrastructure

- ✈ aerospace
- 🚗 vehicle manufacture
- chemicals
- fish processing
- food processing
- hi-tech industry
- hydro-electric power
- mining
- timber processing
- ■ capital cities
- ● major towns
- ✈ international airports
- — major roads
- major industrial areas

The transport network

🛣	84,522 miles (136,325 km)
🛤	1858 miles (2998 km)
	20,602 miles (33,159 km)
	376 miles (606 km)

The majority of Canada's large ports lie in the east. Since the 1960s the region's rail network has been steadily reduced; Newfoundland recently lost its last remaining line, the Long-Cross Island line.

▲ **Fish processing is** a major industry in the Atlantic provinces. Fogo Island, off Newfoundland, has barely a thousand inhabitants but it is able to sustain a number of cod canneries.

Using the land and sea

With thin soils restricting farming to the south, the forests which grow in vast unbroken tracts across eastern Canada provide an important source of revenue. Coastal communities rely heavily on the rich fishing grounds of the Atlantic Ocean, although foreign competition and overfishing have resulted in strict policies to conserve stocks.

The urban/rural population divide

urban 84% | rural 16%

0 10 20 30 40 50 60 70 80 90 100

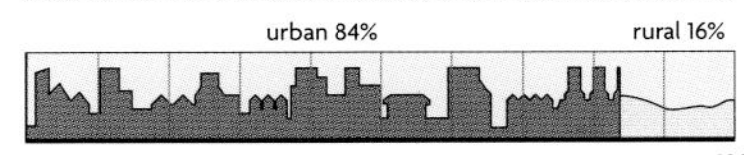

Population density	Total land area
21 people per sq mile (8 people per sq km)	1,076,227 sq miles (2,787,431 sq km)

Land use and agricultural distribution

- cattle
- cereals
- fishing
- fruit
- timber
- ■ capital cities
- ● major towns
- pasture
- cropland
- forest
- tundra

▶ **Prince Edward Island is** the only Atlantic province with notable agricultural land. The island is Canada's leading producer of potatoes.

Southeastern Canada

Southern Ontario, Southern Québec

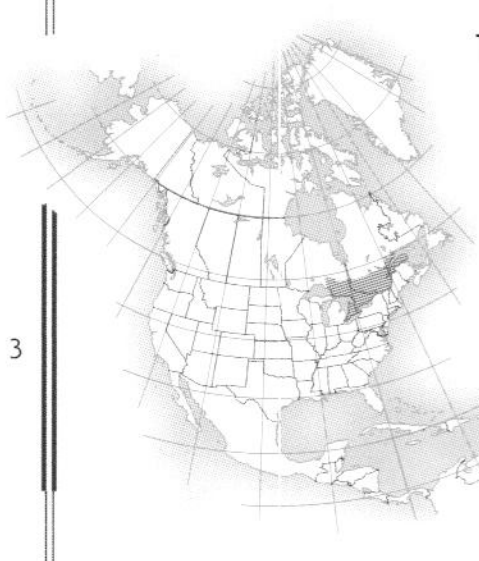

The southern parts of Québec and Ontario form the economic heart of Canada. The two provinces are divided by their language and culture; in Québec, French is the main language, whereas English is spoken in Ontario. Separatist sentiment in Québec has led to a provincial referendum on the question of a sovereignty association with Canada. The region contains Canada's capital, Ottawa and its two largest cities: Toronto, the centre of commerce and Montréal, the cultural and administrative heart of French Canada.

▶ **Niagara Falls lies** on the border between Canada and the USA. It comprises a system of two falls: American Falls, in New York, is separated from Horseshoe Falls, in Ontario, by Goat Island. Horseshoe Falls, seen here, plunges 184 ft (56 m) and is 2500 ft (762 m) wide.

▲ **The port at** Montréal is situated on the St. Lawrence Seaway. A network of 16 locks allows sea-going vessels access to routes once plied by fur-trappers and early settlers.

Transport and industry

The cities of southern Québec and Ontario, and their hinterlands, form the heart of Canadian manufacturing industry. Toronto is Canada's leading financial centre, and Ontario's motor and aerospace industries have developed around the city. A major centre for nickel mining lies to the north of Toronto. Most of Québec's industry is located in Montréal, the oldest port in North America. Chemicals, paper manufacture and the construction of transport equipment are leading industrial activities.

Major industry and infrastructure

- car manufacture
- chemicals
- engineering
- finance
- food processing
- hi-tech industry
- mining
- iron & steel
- textiles
- paper industry
- timber processing
- capital cities
- major towns
- international airports
- major roads
- major industrial areas

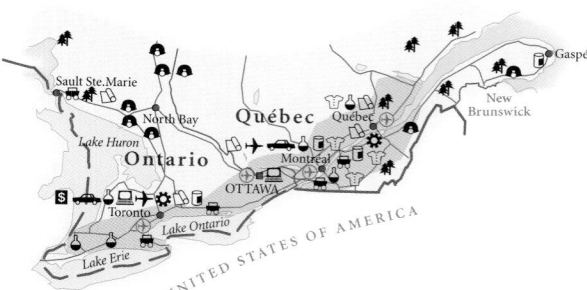

The transport network

The opening of the St. Lawrence Seaway in 1959 finally allowed ocean-going ships (up to 24,000 tons (tonnes)) access to the interior of Canada, creating a vital trading route.

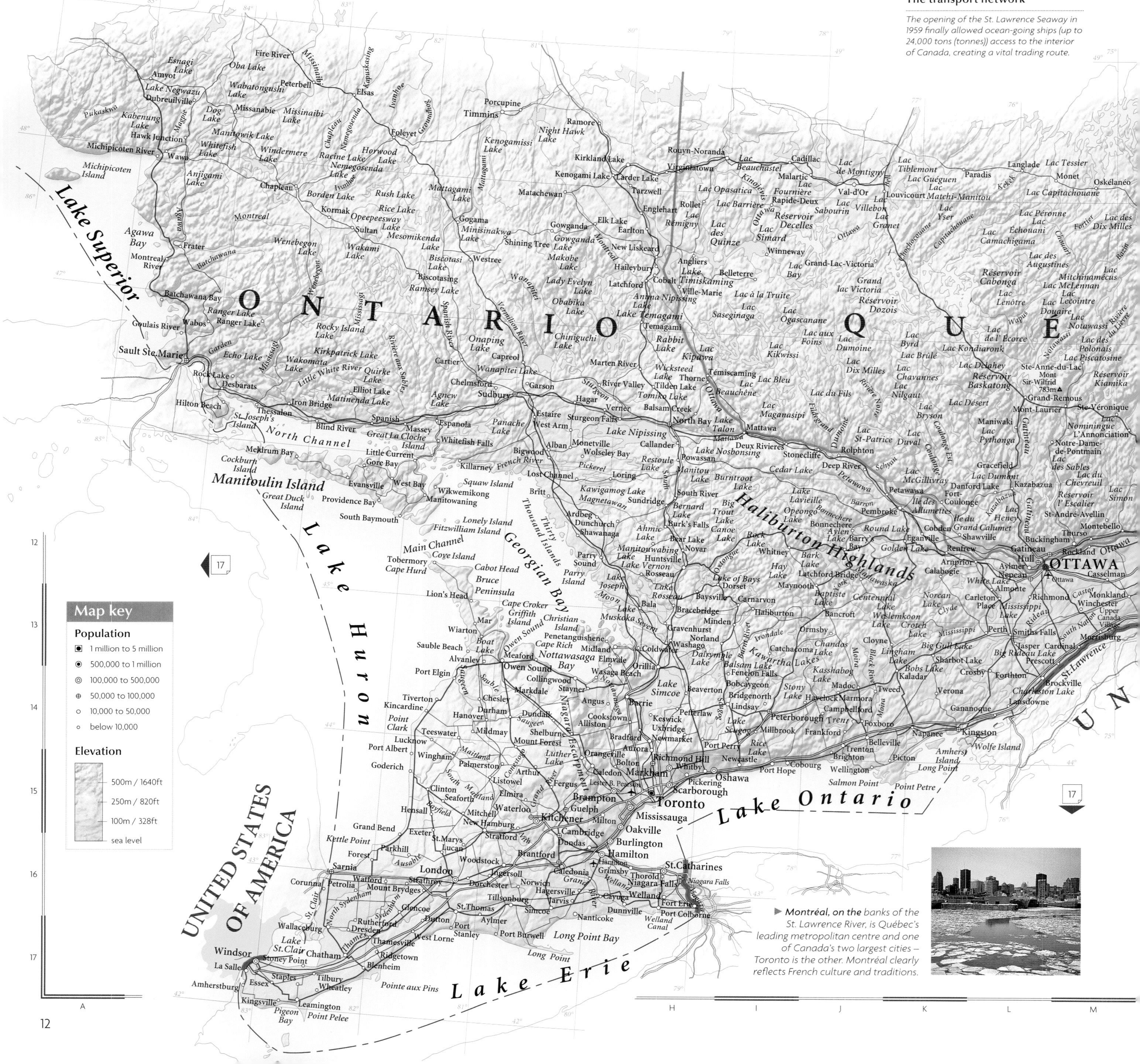

Map key

Population
- 1 million to 5 million
- 500,000 to 1 million
- 100,000 to 500,000
- 50,000 to 100,000
- 10,000 to 50,000
- below 10,000

Elevation
- 500m / 1640ft
- 250m / 820ft
- 100m / 328ft
- sea level

▶ **Montréal, on the** banks of the St. Lawrence River, is Québec's leading metropolitan centre and one of Canada's two largest cities — Toronto is the other. Montréal clearly reflects French culture and traditions.

Using the land and sea

The productive Niagara 'fruit belt' on the shores of Lake Erie and Lake Ontario is a major farming region, although available farmland is being challenged by urban expansion. Québec is Canada's leading producer of maple syrup and dairy products. In the north, farmland gives way to extensive areas of forest, partly used for commercial logging. Fishing occurs in Atlantic waters and in the Great Lakes.

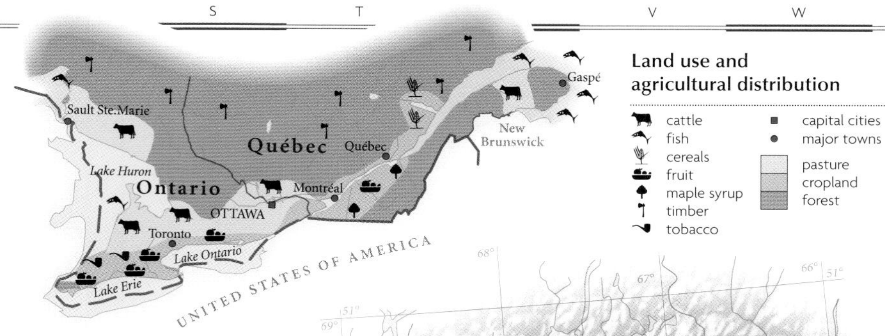

The urban/rural population divide

urban 87%   rural 13%

0 10 20 30 40 50 60 70 80 90 100

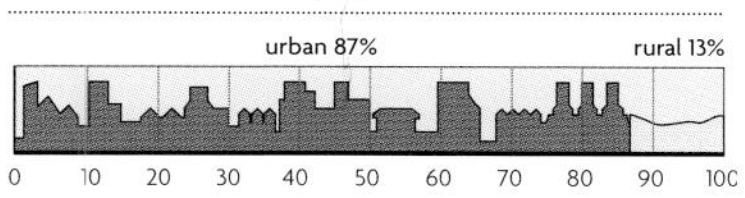

Population density	Total land area
64 people per sq mile (25 people per sq km)	214,230 sq miles (555,000 sq km)

Land use and agricultural distribution

- cattle
- fish
- cereals
- fruit
- maple syrup
- timber
- tobacco
- capital cities
- major towns
- pasture
- cropland
- forest

▲ Pumpkins are just one of the crops grown in the Niagara 'fruit belt'. The mild climate, moderated by the lakes, allows the cultivation of a wide range of fruit and vegetables, including cherries, apples, peaches, grapes and asparagus. Fruit and vegetable growing is confined to southern Canada, due to the colder climate and short growing season of the northern regions.

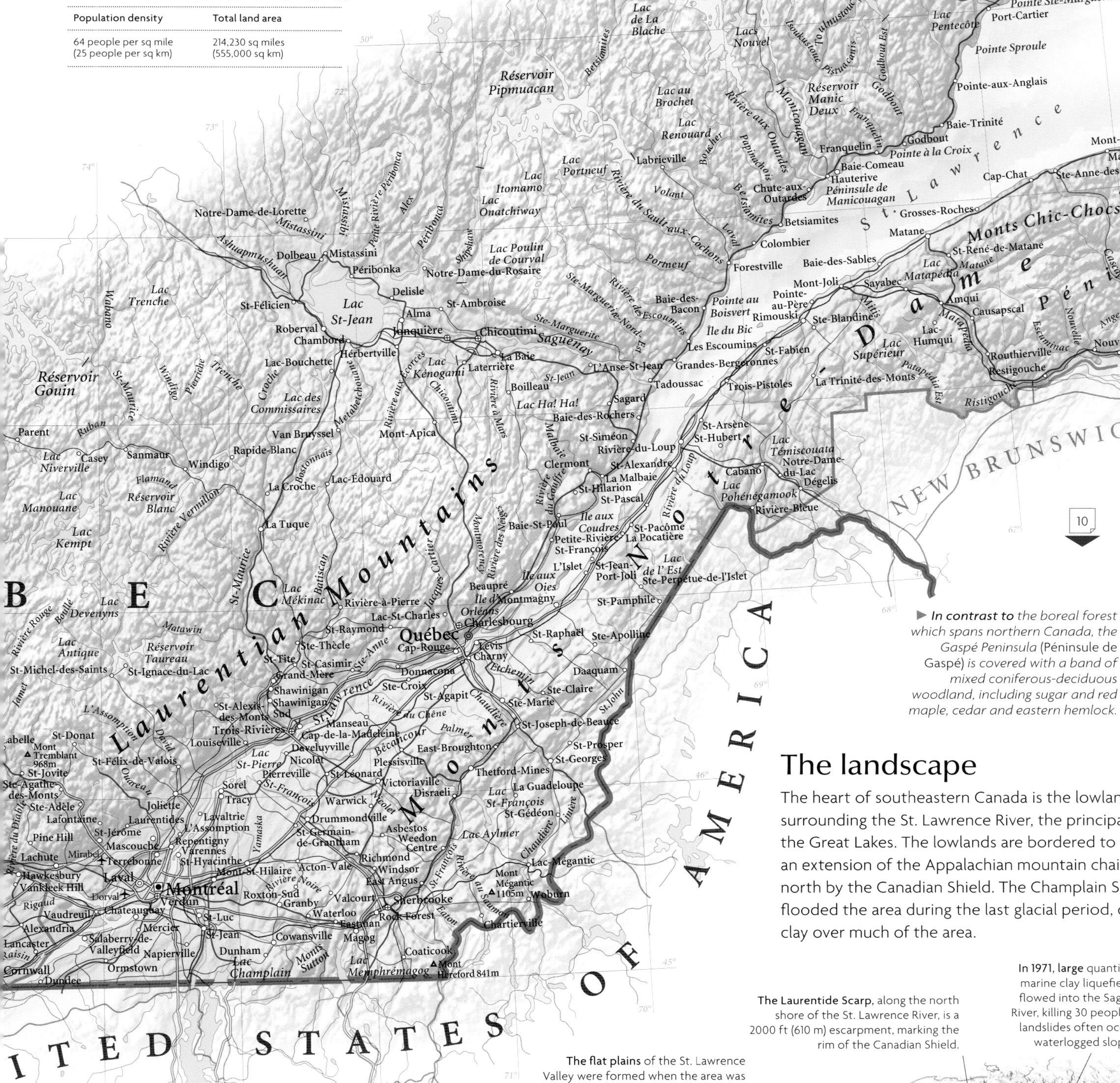

▶ In contrast to the boreal forest which spans northern Canada, the Gaspé Peninsula (Péninsule de Gaspé) is covered with a band of mixed coniferous-deciduous woodland, including sugar and red maple, cedar and eastern hemlock.

The landscape

The heart of southeastern Canada is the lowland area surrounding the St. Lawrence River, the principal outlet for the Great Lakes. The lowlands are bordered to the east by an extension of the Appalachian mountain chain and to the north by the Canadian Shield. The Champlain Sea, which flooded the area during the last glacial period, deposited clay over much of the area.

▲ The wooded Gaspé Peninsula (Péninsule de Gaspé) includes the Notre Dame and Shickshock Mountains (Monts Chic-Chocs). These are a northerly outcrop of the Appalachian mountain chain.

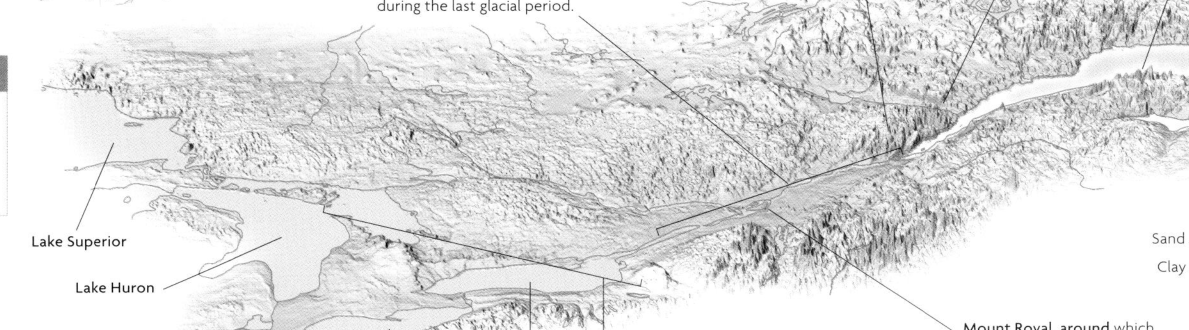

The Laurentide Scarp, along the north shore of the St. Lawrence River, is a 2000 ft (610 m) escarpment, marking the rim of the Canadian Shield.

In 1971, large quantities of marine clay liquefied and flowed into the Saguenay River, killing 30 people. Large landslides often occur on waterlogged slopes.

The flat plains of the St. Lawrence Valley were formed when the area was inundated by the Champlain Sea during the last glacial period.

Scale 1:3,000,000

Km
0 5 10 20 30 40 50 60 70

Miles
0 5 10 20 30 40 50 60 70

projection: Lambert Conformal Conic

◀ Point Pelee is a world-famous site for bird migration. Over 250 species of bird have been sighted on the sandspit which forms the southern tip of the Canadian mainland.

Lake Superior

Lake Huron

Lake Erie   Lake Ontario

The Great Lakes moderate the climate of the area surrounding the St. Lawrence River. Their water, which cools more slowly than the land, acts as a reservoir for warmth, extending the growing season into the early autumn.

Mount Royal, around which the city of Montréal has developed, is the result of an igneous intrusion which occurred between 135 and 65 million years ago.

River bank or bluff
Earthflow
Sand
Clay
River

▲ In the lowlands around the St. Lawrence, earthflows have developed along gentle river banks where sand overlies clay, making the surface layers very unstable. When the slope's natural equilibrium is disturbed, an earthflow can occur.

Canada

Canada is the second largest country in the world, and with only about one-tenth of its land area inhabited, it is one of the most sparsely populated. Canada became a confederation in 1867, though Newfoundland did not join until 1949. As a founding member of the UN and of the Commonwealth, Canada has played an important role in international affairs. A constitutional crisis, focusing on the French-speaking Québécois, and Inuit and Native American land rights, dominated politics in the 1990s. In 1999, part of the Northwest Territories, Nunavut, became a self-governing homeland for the Inuit.

▲ *The Selwyn Mountains* in northwestern Canada form part of the Rocky Mountains. The highest point, Keele Peak, rises to 9750 ft (2972 m).

Transport and industry

Abundant energy in the form of coal, oil, natural gas and hydro-electric power underpins Canadian industry. Over 75% of manufacturing is concentrated in the Great Lakes–St. Lawrence region, including prospering aerospace, transport and hi-tech industries. Across Canada as a whole, manufacturing has developed around a diversified, high-quality resource base and a wide range of metallic and non-metallic minerals.

41

198

The transport network

309,019 miles (497,375 km)	10,500 miles (16,900 km)
8049 miles (12,995 km)	1864 miles (3000 km)

In recent years the road network has been expanded, especially links to remote areas. Meanwhile, for long-distance travel, air transport now supersedes the declining rail network, which focuses mainly on east–west routes.

Major industry and infrastructure

- ✈ aerospace
- 🚗 car manufacture
- ⚗ chemicals
- ⚙ engineering
- 🍴 food processing
- 🖥 hi-tech industry
- ⊞ hydro-electric power
- ♦ oil & gas
- ⚒ mining
- 🏭 timber processing
- ● capital cities
- ● major towns
- ✈ international airports
- — major roads
- ▨ major industrial areas

◄ *Canada has one* of the world's highest rates of energy consumption per person. It is endowed with vast hydro-electric potential from which more than 60% of its electricity requirements are generated.

The landscape

Glaciers on islands in the Arctic Ocean are the last remnants of the ice sheet that once covered and shaped Canada. Hudson Bay is the centre of the Canadian Shield, a huge, eroded plateau marked at its southern extremity by a string of lakes running southeastwards from Great Bear Lake to the Great Lakes. In contrast to the rolling relief of the Shield and the central lowland region, the Rocky Mountains rise to peaks of over 13,000 ft (4000 m), stretching 500 miles (800 km) along the west coast.

▲ *Along the northeastern* coast of Baffin Island the mountains rise to 8000 ft (2440 m). Glaciers move down through the valleys to the sea, eroding wide U-shaped valleys.

Top layer thaws in the summer

Marginal areas of permafrost thaw in summer

Permanently frozen ground

Unfrozen ground where temperature is more moderate

▲ *Permanently frozen ground* known as permafrost is common in Canada's northern tundra. It thickens further north, becoming hundreds of metres deep in parts of the Arctic.

The Mackenzie river, flowing north over the permafrost, forms a wide river channel with many tributaries. Together with the Peel river it has created a long, narrow delta at its mouth. The entire river freezes during the winter.

Exposure to three phases of mountain-building and subsequent erosion over millions of years has moulded the ancient Canadian Shield into a series of basins and ridges.

Great Bear Lake

The Rocky Mountains were formed some 80 million years ago, when the Pacific plate was driven under the North American plate, forcing up the land.

◄ *Isolated pillars, known* as hoodoos near Red Deer river in the badlands of Alberta are a product of wind and water erosion, especially flash floods. The badlands lie in the rain shadow of the Rocky Mountains, which creates a semi-arid climate.

Fertile prairies stretch from the southern rim of the Canadian Shield, south into the USA.

The Great Lakes lie on the Canada–USA border. The basins they now occupy were fashioned by repeated ice advance. At one time, Lakes Superior, Huron and Michigan formed a single large lake, Lake Nipissing.

The St. Lawrence River is 2350 miles (3782 km) long. It flows from the western shore of Lake Superior through the Great Lakes and on to the Atlantic Ocean. From December to April, the St. Lawrence Seaway freezes between Lake Ontario and Montréal.

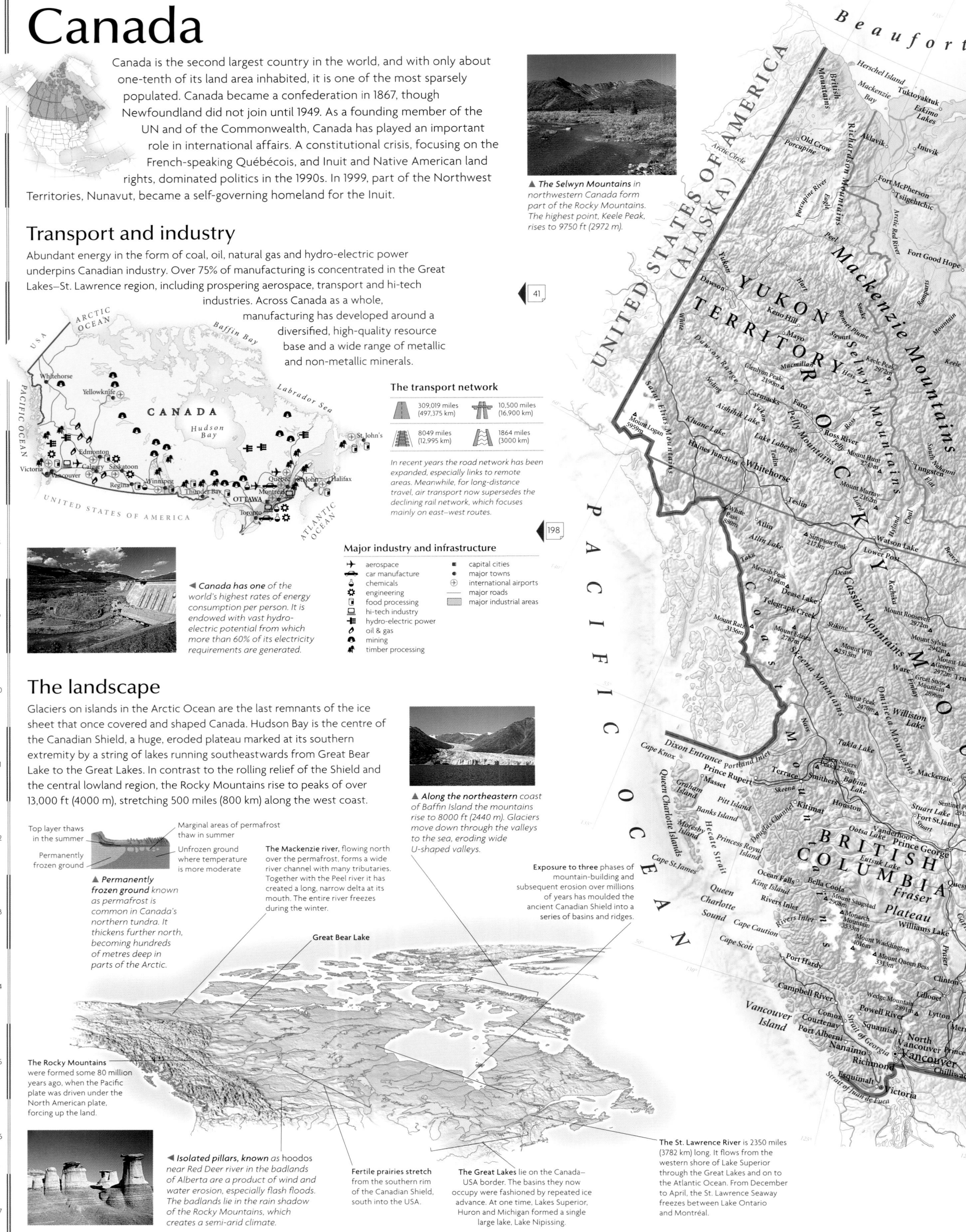

Gg

Banks Island
Cape Kellett
Sachs Harbour
Cape Lambton
Cape Wollaston
Holman
Prince Albert Peninsula
Cape Bathurst
Cape Parry
Cape Lyon
Amundsen Gulf
Paulatuk
Franklin Bay
Horton
Anderson
Prince Albert Sound
Dolphin & Union Strait
Wollaston Peninsula
Victoria Island

Sea
130°
125°
120°
115°
110°
105°
100°

Passage Point
Peel Point
Viscount Melville Sound
Stefansson Island
Hadley Bay
Prince of Wales Strait
Zeta Lake
Gateshead Island
Larsen Sound
Kent Peninsula
Coronation Gulf
Cambridge Bay
Jenny Lind Island
Queen Maud Gulf
Bathurst Inlet
Ellice
Bowes Point
Adelaide Peninsula
Chantrey Inlet

Cape Krusenstern
Rae
Kugluktuk
Takijuq Lake

Somerset Island
Peel Sound
Prince of Wales Island
Franklin Strait
Boothia Peninsula
King William Island
Gjoa Haven
Rae Strait

Admiralty Inlet
Brodeur Peninsula
Prince Regent Inlet
Gulf of Boothia
Cape Englefield
Cape Chapman
Taloyoak
Pelly Bay
Simpson Peninsula
Committee Bay
Wales Island

Borden Peninsula
Gifford
Igloolik
Hall Beach
Melville Peninsula

Cape Henry Kater
Baffin
Rowley Island
Baird Peninsula
Prince Charles Island
Air Force Island
Nettilling
Koukdjuak

Foxe Basin
Bowman Bay
Cape Dorchester
Foxe Peninsula
Cape Dorset
Salisbury Island
Foxe Channel
Nottingham Island
Mansel Island

C
A
H
Z

NORTHWEST TERRITORIES

Norman Wells
Déline
Great Bear Lake
Echo Bay
Tulita
Hottah Lake
Wrigley
Lac La Martre
Wha Ti
Willowlake
Horn
Edzo
Fort Simpson
Yellowknife
Reliance
Lutselk'e
Snowdrift
Nonacho Lake
Fort Providence
Great Slave Lake
Fort Resolution
Hay River
Pine Point
Trout
Fort Liard
Fort Smith

Aylmer Lake
Clinton-Colden Lake
Hanbury
Thelon
Dubawnt
Talston
Thoa
Wholdaia Lake

Aberdeen Lake
Back
Garry Lake
Dubawnt Lake
Yathkyed Lake
Kazan
Kasba Lake
Nueltin Lake
Tha-Anne
Thlewiaza

Baker Lake
Baker Lake
Whale Cove
Eskimo Point
Arviat

NUNAVUT
Back
Wager Bay
Repulse Bay
Hayes

Chesterfield Inlet
Chesterfield Inlet
Rankin Inlet

Hudson Bay

Cape Kendall
Cape Low
Southampton Island
Coral Harbour
Roes Welcome Sound
Evans Strait

Fisher Strait
Coats Island

Ottawa Islands

ALBERTA
Fort Nelson
Fort Nelson
Petitot
Fontas
Bistcho Lake
Steen River
High Level
Fort Vermilion
Caribou Mountains
Clear Hills
Fort St.John
Grimshaw
Fairview
Manning
Peace River
Dawson Creek
Chetwynd
Grande Prairie
Wapiti
Valleyview
High Prairie
Swan Hills
Grande Cache
Whitecourt
Edson
Barrhead
Westlock
Hinton
Morinville
St.Albert
Spruce Grove
Stony Plain
Edmonton
Drayton Valley
Devon
Leduc
Rocky Mountain House
Wetaskiwin
Ponoka
Lacombe
Sylvan Lake
Stettler
Red Deer
Innisfail
Didsbury
Olds
Drumheller
Airdrie
Calgary
Okotoks
Strathmore
High River
Canmore
Invermere
Claresholm
Travers Reservoir
Nanton
Fort Macleod
Coaldale
Lethbridge
Taber
Pincher Creek
Raymond
Cardston
Milk River

Fort Chipewyan
Lake Athabasca
Uranium City
Lake Claire
Birch Mountains
Athabasca
Fort McMurray
William
Lake Athabasca
Black Lake
Pasfield Lake
MacFarlane
Cree Lake
Cree
Clearwater
La Loche
Turnor Lake
Frobisher Lake
Foster Lakes
Macoun Lake
Primrose Lake
Cold Lake
Peter Pond Lake
Buffalo Narrows
Churchill Lake
Pinehouse Lake
Missinipe
SASKATCHEWAN
Beaver
La Ronge
Lac La Ronge
Deschambault Lake
Cold Lake
Grand Centre
Meadow Lake
Montreal Lake
Amisk Lake
Creighton
Flin Flon
Tobin Lake
Wabowden
St.Walburg
Nipawin
Hudson Bay
Pasquia Hills
The Pas
Cedar Lake
Grand Rapids
Melfort
Tisdale
Porcupine Hills
Swan River
Prince Albert
North Battleford
Battleford
Unity
Martensville
Saskatoon
Lanigan
Watrous
Humboldt
Quill Lakes
Wynyard
Biggar
Rosetown
Kindersley
Outlook
Lake Diefenbaker
Last Mountain Lake
Fort Qu'Appelle
Lumsden
Regina
Moose Jaw
Swift Current
Old Wives Lake
Assiniboia
Val Marie
Wood Mountain
Rockglen
Weyburn
Estevan
Medicine Hat
Redcliff
Maple Creek
Cypress Hills

Phelps Lake
Wollaston Lake
Wollaston Lake
Reindeer Lake
South Seal
Southern Indian Lake
Lynn Lake
Leaf Rapids
Granville Lake
Split Lake
Thompson
Burntwood
Nelson
Sipiwesk Lake
Kississing Lake
Oxford Lake
Gods Lake
Island Lake
MANITOBA
Lake Winnipegosis
Lake Winnipeg
Dauphin
Duck Mountain
Baldy Mountain
Riding Mountain
Neepawa
Minnedosa
Brandon
Virden
Portage la Prairie
Winnipeg
Steinbach
Stonewall
Selkirk
Beausejour
Pinawa
Carman
Morris
Morden
Winkler
Altona
Lake of the Woods

Lac Brochet
Tadoule Lake
Seal
Churchill
Churchill
Cape Churchill
Nejanilini Lake

Cape Tatnam
Fort Severn
Severn
Winisk
Winisk Lake
Attawapiskat
Attawapiskat Lake
ONTARIO
Sandy Lake
North Caribou Lake
Big Trout Lake
Sachigo
Sachigo Lake
Pipestone
Red Lake
Ear Falls
Sioux Lookout
Lac Seul
Lake St.Joseph
Pickle Lake
Armstrong
Lake Nipigon
Lake Nipigon
Nipigon
Kenora
Dryden
Fort Frances
Rainy Lake
Rainy River
Atikokan
Thunder Bay
Lac des Milles Lacs
Eagle Lake

UNITED STATES OF AMERICA

Scale 1:9,250,000

Km
0 25 50 100 150 200 250 300 350

Miles
0 25 50 100 150 200 250 300 350

projection: Lambert Azimuthal Equal Area

Gg   H   Hh   I   Ii   J   Jj   K   Kk   L   Ll   M   Mm

Map key
Population
- above 5 million
- 1 million to 5 million
- 500,000 to 1 million
- 100,000 to 500,000
- 50,000 to 100,000
- 10,000 to 50,000
- below 10,000
Elevation
- 4000m / 13,124ft
- 3000m / 9843ft
- 2000m / 6562ft
- 1000m / 3281ft
- 500m / 1640ft
- 250m / 820ft
- 100m / 328ft
- sea level
▲ *The Sonoran Desert in southwestern Arizona stretches into Mexico and merges to the northwest with California's Mojave Desert. Much of the southwest is very arid, especially the 'rain-starved' areas between the Coast Ranges and the Rocky Mountains.*

A　Aa　B　Bb　C　Cc　D　Dd　E　Ee　F

The United States of America

COTERMINOUS USA (FOR ALASKA AND HAWAI'I SEE PAGES 40-41)

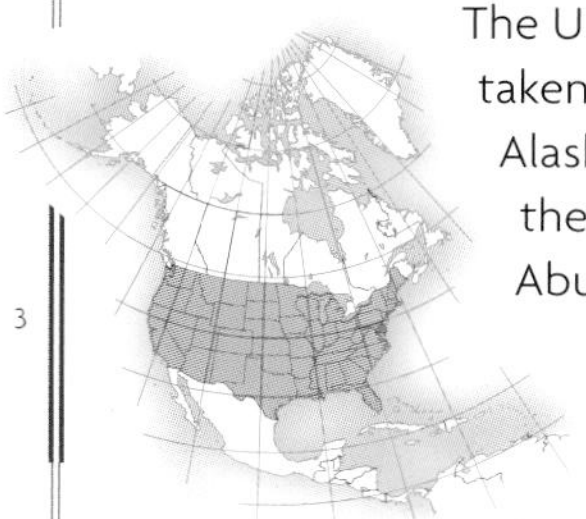

The USA's progression from frontier territory to economic and political superpower has taken less than 200 years. The 48 coterminous states, along with the outlying states of Alaska and Hawaii, are part of a federal union, held together by the guiding principles of the US Constitution, which enshrines the ideals of democracy and liberty for all. Abundant fertile land and a rich resource-base fuelled and sustained the USA's economic development. With the spread of agriculture and the growth of trade and industry came the need for a larger workforce, which was supplied by millions of immigrants, many seeking an escape from poverty and political or religious persecution. Immigration continues today, particularly from Central America and Asia.

▲ *Mount Rainier is a dormant volcano in the Cascade Range, Washington. This 14,090 ft (4392 m) peak is flanked by the most extensive glacier outside Alaska.*

Transport and industry

The USA has been the industrial powerhouse of the world since the Second World War, pioneering mass-production and the consumer lifestyle. Initially, heavy engineering and manufacturing in the northeast led the economy. Today, heavy industry has declined and the USA's economy is driven by service and financial industries, with the most important being defence, hi-tech and electronics.

◀ *Washington DC was established as the site for the nation's capital in 1790. It is home to the seat of national government, on Capitol Hill, as well as the President's official residence, the White House.*

Major industry and infrastructure

- ✈ aerospace
- 🚗 car manufacture
- chemicals
- coal
- electronics
- engineering
- food processing
- hi-tech industry
- oil & gas
- ✇ research & development
- textiles
- tourism
- ■ capital cities
- ⊕ major towns
- ✈ international airports
- major roads
- major industrial areas

The transport network

3,875,040 miles (6,240,000 km)		52,388 miles (84,361 km)	
148,308 miles (235,238 km)		25,467 miles (41,009 km)	

Transport in the USA is dominated by the car which, with the extensive Interstate Highway system, allows great personal mobility. Today, internal air flights between major cities provide the most rapid cross-country travel.

The landscape

The high, rugged mountain ranges of the west are about 80 million years old, geologically young compared to the old, eroded, Appalachian mountain chain, which dates from when North America and Europe were joined together as part of the supercontinent Pangaea, 400 million years ago. In contrast, the Great Plains and Mississippi Basin have a low relief and fertile soils.

▲ *Devils Tower, in Wyoming is a 1280 ft (390 m) intrusion of basalt rock, which cooled to form octagonal pillars. In 1906 it became the first US National Monument.*

Missouri River
Ohio River
Mississippi River
Mississippi Delta

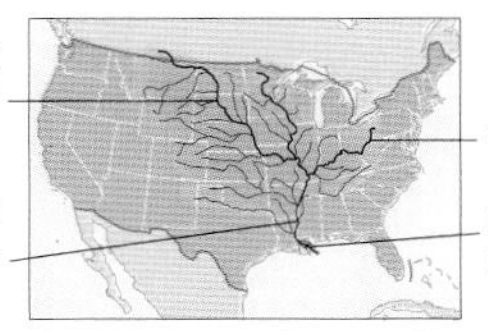

▲ *The massive drainage basin of the Mississippi covers 1,250,000 sq miles (3,200,000 sq km). It includes all areas drained by the Mississippi and its chief tributaries, the Missouri and Ohio rivers, and drains the entire region from the Appalachians to the Rockies.*

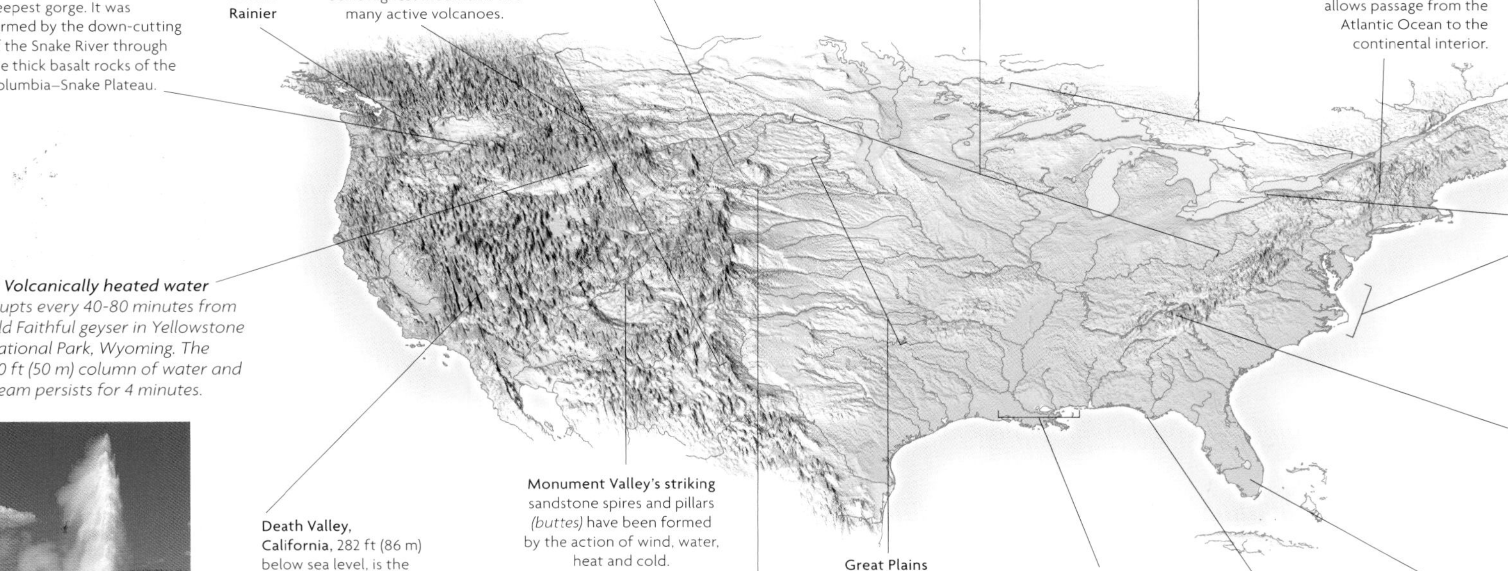

Hells Canyon running through part of Idaho and Oregon, is North America's deepest gorge. It was formed by the down-cutting of the Snake River through the thick basalt rocks of the Columbia–Snake Plateau.

Mount Rainier

The Rocky Mountains form the backbone of the USA, running from Alaska to New Mexico. They contain the USA's highest mountains and many active volcanoes.

The Hudson-Mohawk Gap, lying at the point where the two rivers join, allows passage from the Atlantic Ocean to the continental interior.

The Great Lakes

Niagara Falls

Barrier beaches, bars and spits are typical of the Atlantic coast. These sand formations around Cape Hatteras stretch along the coast for 200 miles (320 km).

▼ *Volcanically heated water erupts every 40-80 minutes from Old Faithful geyser in Yellowstone National Park, Wyoming. The 170 ft (50 m) column of water and steam persists for 4 minutes.*

The Great Smoky Mountains, part of the ancient Appalachian mountain chain, formed a natural barrier to early settlers attempting to penetrate the country's interior.

Death Valley, California, 282 ft (86 m) below sea level, is the lowest point in the western hemisphere, and one of the hottest places on Earth. Temperatures of 190° F (88° C) have been recorded here.

Monument Valley's striking sandstone spires and pillars *(buttes)* have been formed by the action of wind, water, heat and cold.

Great Plains

The deep gullies of South Dakota's badlands are created by periodic, torrential rainfall, which erodes the soft soils and rocks. Their form has been greatly affected by changes in land use.

Most of the USA is drained by the great Mississippi River system. At its mouth, where levées are breached, floodwaters are carried to the swamps through a series of channels. This region is known as the bayou.

The USA's Gulf Coast is seriously affected by hurricane erosion which reshapes its beaches and sandbanks.

The Everglades are a vast area of saw-grass swamp covering 4000 sq miles (10,300 sq km) of southern Florida.

Map labels

Cape Flattery
Port Angeles
Mount Olympus 428m
Bremerton
Seattle
Aberdeen
Olympia
Astoria
Portland
Vance
McMinnville
Salem
Albany
Corvallis
Eugene
Springfield
Coos Bay
Roseburg
Cape Blanco
Grants Pass
Crescent City
Medford
Ashland
Upper Klamath Lake
Klamath Falls
Yreka
Eureka
Mount Shasta 4316m
Cape Mendocino
Redding
Honey Lake
Susanville
Point Arena
Chico
Pyramid Lake
Santa Rosa
Yuba City
Reno
Vallejo
Berkeley
Sacramento
Oakland
San Francisco
Stockton
Modesto
San Jose
Merced
Santa Cruz
Monterey
Salinas
Fresno
Visalia
San Luis Obispo
Santa Maria
Santa Barbara
Bakersfie
Los Angeles
Long Beach
Channel Islands
Oceanside
San Diego

PACIFIC OCEAN

Coast Ranges
Central Valley
Sierra Nevada
California
San Joaquin River
Sacramento River

CANADA
Seattle
Portland
Minneapolis
Milwaukee
Detroit
Buffalo
Boston
Chicago
Cleveland
New York
San Francisco
Denver
Pittsburgh
Philadelphia
Cincinnati
WASHINGTON DC
Kansas City
Saint Louis
Greensboro
Los Angeles
Phoenix
Nashville
Raleigh
San Diego
Atlanta
Birmingham
Dallas
Jacksonville
Houston
Orlando
New Orleans
Tampa
Miami
Gulf of Mexico
MEXICO
PACIFIC OCEAN
ATLANTIC OCEAN

198

A　Aa　B　Bb　C　Cc　D　Dd　E　Ee　F　Ff

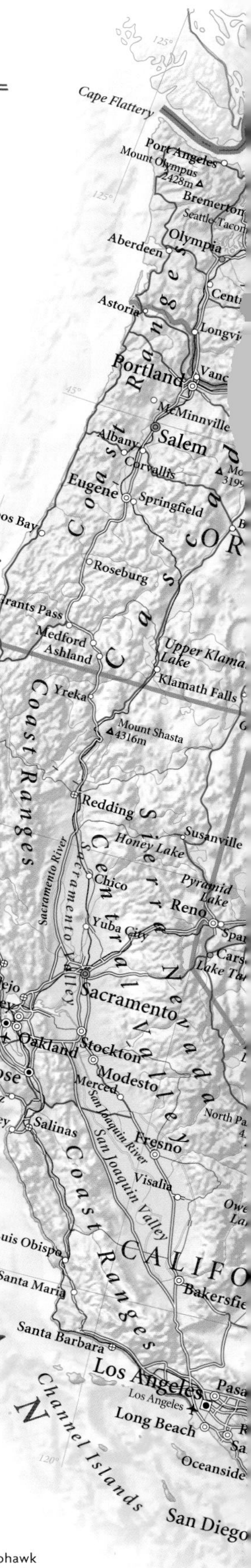

Using the land and sea

The majority of Canada's agricultural land is found in the prairies, which cover 140 million acres (57 million ha) and support wheat and grain-fed cattle. More specialized crops, such as fruit and vegetables, are grown in pockets of agricultural land in the east and west. Of Canada's many islands, only Prince Edward Island has notable farmland. Further north, boreal forests, exploited for timber, run in an almost unbroken arc, giving way to uncultivable tundra and ice sheets in the far north.

The urban/rural population divide

urban 77%   rural 23%

Population density	Total land area
9 people per sq mile (3 people per sq km)	3,559,294 sq miles (9,220,970 sq km)

Land use and agricultural distribution

- cattle
- cereals
- fishing
- fruit
- timber

- ◼ capital cities
- ● major towns

- pasture
- cropland
- forest
- wetland
- mountain region
- barren
- tundra

▲ *The climate and topography of the prairies makes them ideally suited to farming. Long summer days, moderate temperatures, limited rainfall and flat plains provide excellent conditions for wheat farming.*

▶ *Ottawa was selected by Queen Victoria as the Canadian capital in 1858. Prior to this date it was a notorious work camp centred around the lumber industry. Today, the city is known as 'Silicon Valley North', due to its concentration of hi-tech industries.*

Map key

Population

- ◉ 1 million to 5 million
- ◉ 500,000 to 1 million
- ◎ 100,000 to 500,000
- ⊕ 50,000 to 100,000
- ○ 10,000 to 50,000
- ∘ below 10,000

Elevation

- 6000m / 19,686ft
- 4000m / 13,124ft
- 3000m / 9843ft
- 2000m / 6562ft
- 1000m / 3281ft
- 500m / 1640ft
- 250m / 820ft
- 100m / 328ft
- sea level

▲ *The Great Lakes are drained by the St. Lawrence River which flows down through a wide tectonic depression. It forms a broad estuary for much of its course, the width varying from 1.2 miles (1.9 km) in the upper reaches to 90 miles (145 km) at its mouth.*

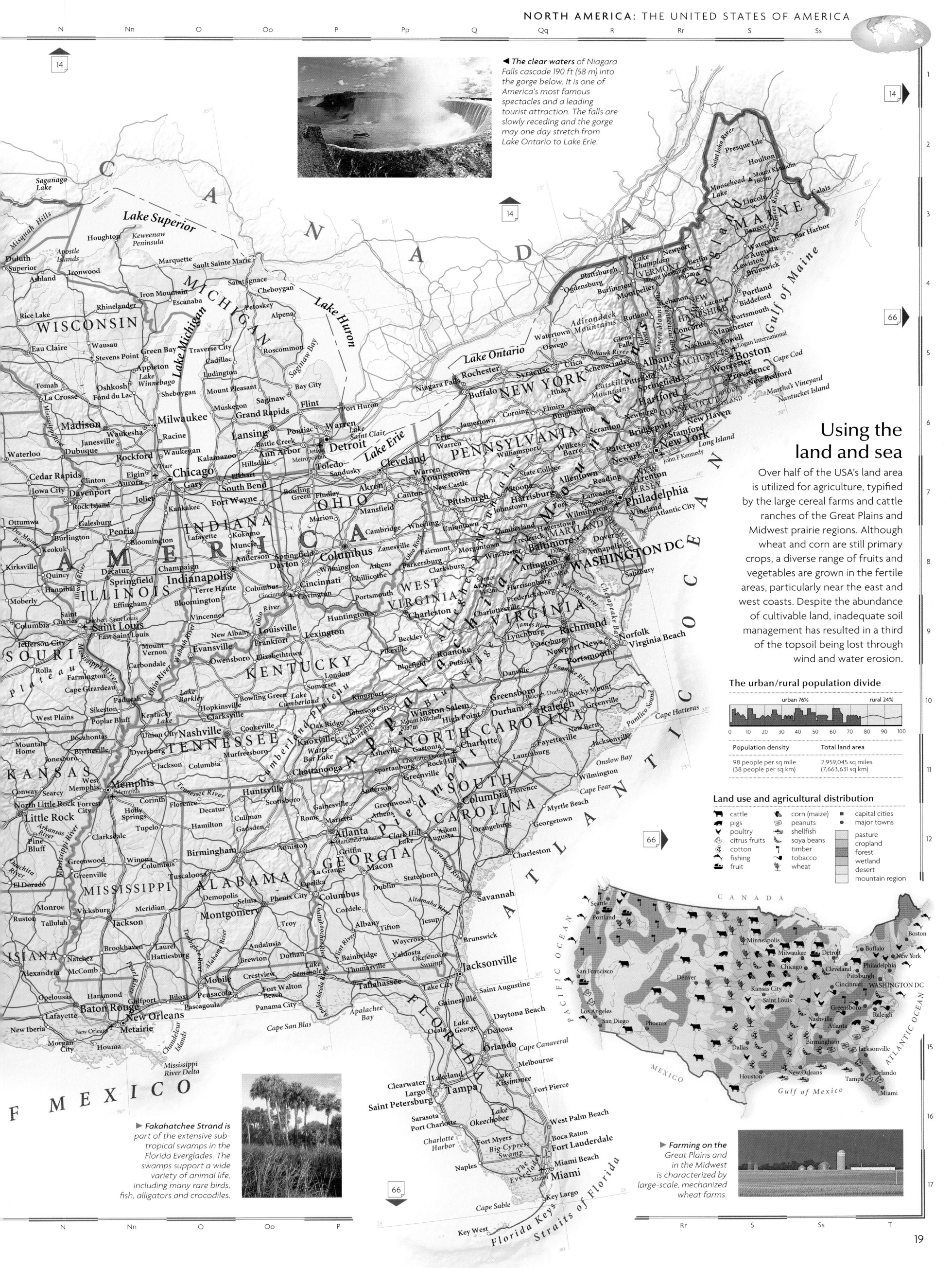

◀ *The clear waters* of Niagara Falls cascade 190 ft (58 m) into the gorge below. It is one of America's most famous spectacles and a leading tourist attraction. The falls are slowly receding and the gorge may one day stretch from Lake Ontario to Lake Erie.

Using the land and sea

Over half of the USA's land area is utilized for agriculture, typified by the large cereal farms and cattle ranches of the Great Plains and Midwest prairie regions. Although wheat and corn are still primary crops, a diverse range of fruits and vegetables are grown in the fertile areas, particularly near the east and west coasts. Despite the abundance of cultivable land, inadequate soil management has resulted in a third of the topsoil being lost through wind and water erosion.

The urban/rural population divide

urban 76%   rural 24%

0 10 20 30 40 50 60 70 80 90 100

Population density	Total land area
98 people per sq mile (38 people per sq km)	2,959,045 sq miles (7,663,631 sq km)

Land use and agricultural distribution

- cattle
- pigs
- poultry
- citrus fruits
- cotton
- fishing
- fruit
- corn (maize)
- peanuts
- shellfish
- soya beans
- timber
- tobacco
- wheat
- capital cities
- major towns
- pasture
- cropland
- forest
- wetland
- desert
- mountain region

▶ *Fakahatchee Strand is* part of the extensive sub-tropical swamps in the Florida Everglades. The swamps support a wide variety of animal life, including many rare birds, fish, alligators and crocodiles.

▶ *Farming on the* Great Plains and in the Midwest is characterized by large-scale, mechanized wheat farms.

USA: NORTHEASTERN STATES

Connecticut, Maine, Massachusetts, New Hampshire, New Jersey,
New York, Pennsylvania, Rhode Island, Vermont

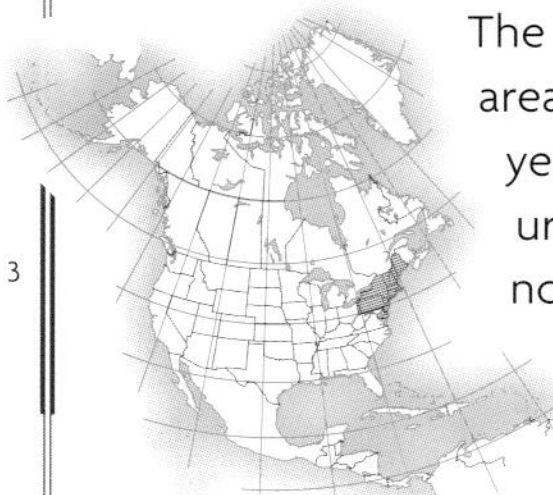

The indented coast and vast woodlands of the northeastern states were the original core area for European expansion. The rustic character of New England prevails after 400 years, while the great cities of the Atlantic seaboard have formed an almost continuous urban region. Over 20 million immigrants entered New York from 1855 to 1924 and the northeast became the industrial centre of the USA. After the decline of mining and heavy manufacturing, economic dynamism has been restored with the growth of hi-tech and service industries.

▲ Chelsea in Vermont, surrounded by trees in their fall foliage. Tourism and agriculture dominate the economy of this self-consciously rural state, where no town exceeds 40,000 people.

Map key

Population
- ◼ above 5 million
- ◼ 1 million to 5 million
- ◉ 500,000 to 1 million
- ◎ 100,000 to 500,000
- ⊙ 50,000 to 100,000
- ○ 10,000 to 50,000
- ○ below 10,000

Elevation
- 1000m / 3281ft
- 500m / 1640ft
- 250m / 820ft
- 100m / 328ft
- sea level

Transport and industry

The principal seaboard cities grew up on trade and manufacturing. They are now global centres of commerce and corporate administration, dominating the regional economy. Research and development facilities support an expanding electronics and communications sector throughout the region. Pharmaceutical and chemical industries are important in New Jersey and Pennsylvania.

The transport network

340,090 miles (544,144 km)	4813 miles (7700 km)
12,872 miles (20,592 km)	2108 miles (3389 km)

New York's commercial success is tied historically to its transport connections. The Erie Canal, completed in 1825, opened up the Great Lakes and the interior to New York's markets and carried a stream of immigrants into the Midwest.

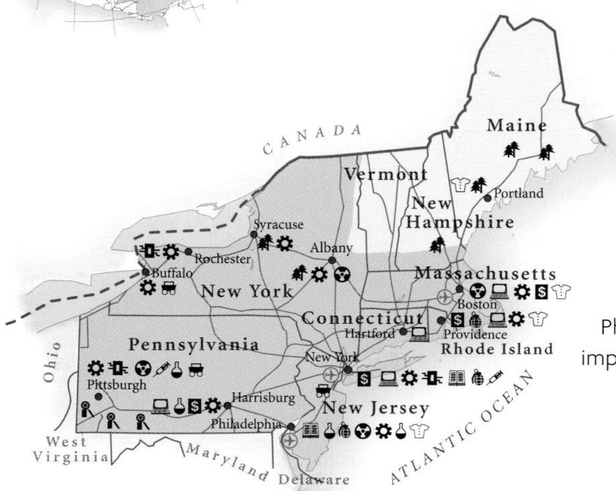

Major industry and infrastructure
- ♠ chemicals
- coal
- defence
- ✿ electronics
- ✿ engineering
- finance
- hi-tech industry
- iron & steel
- pharmaceuticals
- printing & publishing
- research & development
- ▼ textiles
- timber processing
- ⊕ major towns
- ✈ international airports
- — major roads
- major industrial area

Inset map labels: CANADA, Maine, Vermont, New Hampshire, Portland, Syracuse, Albany, New York, Rochester, Buffalo, Massachusetts, Boston, Connecticut, Hartford, Providence, Rhode Island, New York, Pennsylvania, Ohio, Pittsburgh, Harrisburg, Philadelphia, New Jersey, West Virginia, Maryland, Delaware, ATLANTIC OCEAN

Main map labels (selected): CANADA, Lake Ontario, Lake Erie, OHIO, WEST VIRGINIA, MARYLAND, DELAWARE, NEW YORK, PENNSYLVANIA, NEW JERSEY, VERMONT, MASSAC, CONNECT, ATLANTIC, Adirondack Mountains, Catskill Mountains, Allegheny Plateau, Appalachian Mountains, Lake Champlain, Saint Lawrence River, Finger Lakes, Thousand Islands

Buffalo, Niagara Falls, Rochester, Syracuse, Utica, Albany, Schenectady, Troy, Binghamton, Elmira, Ithaca, Watertown, Oswego, Ogdensburg, Plattsburgh, Burlington, Montpelier, Rutland, Bennington, Pittsfield, Springfield, Hartford, New Haven, Bridgeport, Stamford, Yonkers, New York, Jersey City, Newark, Paterson, Trenton, Philadelphia, Camden, Atlantic City, Cape May, Scranton, Wilkes Barre, Williamsport, Harrisburg, Lancaster, York, Reading, Allentown, Bethlehem, Easton, Altoona, Johnstown, Pittsburgh, Erie

14
12
34
22
24
66

20

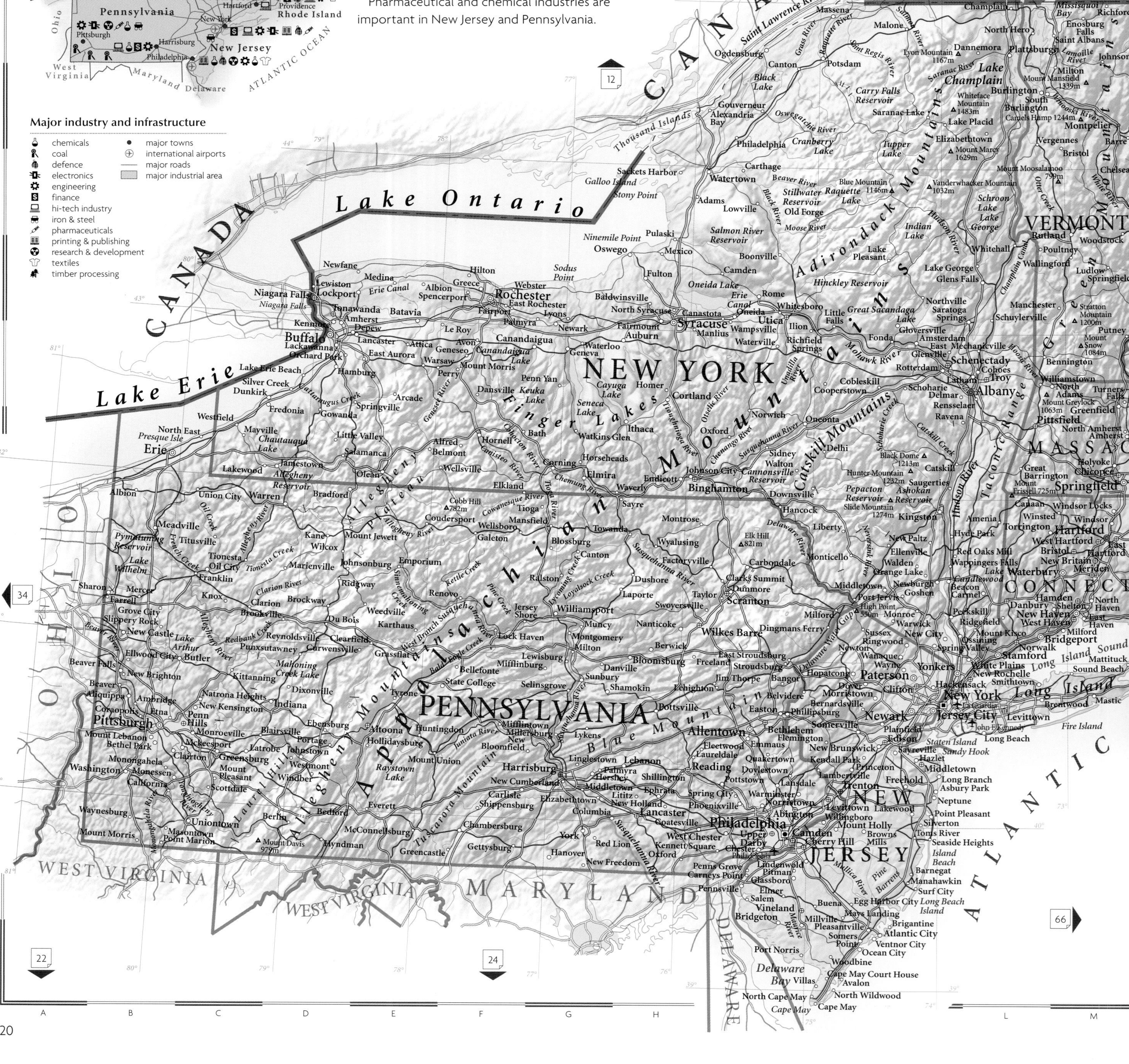

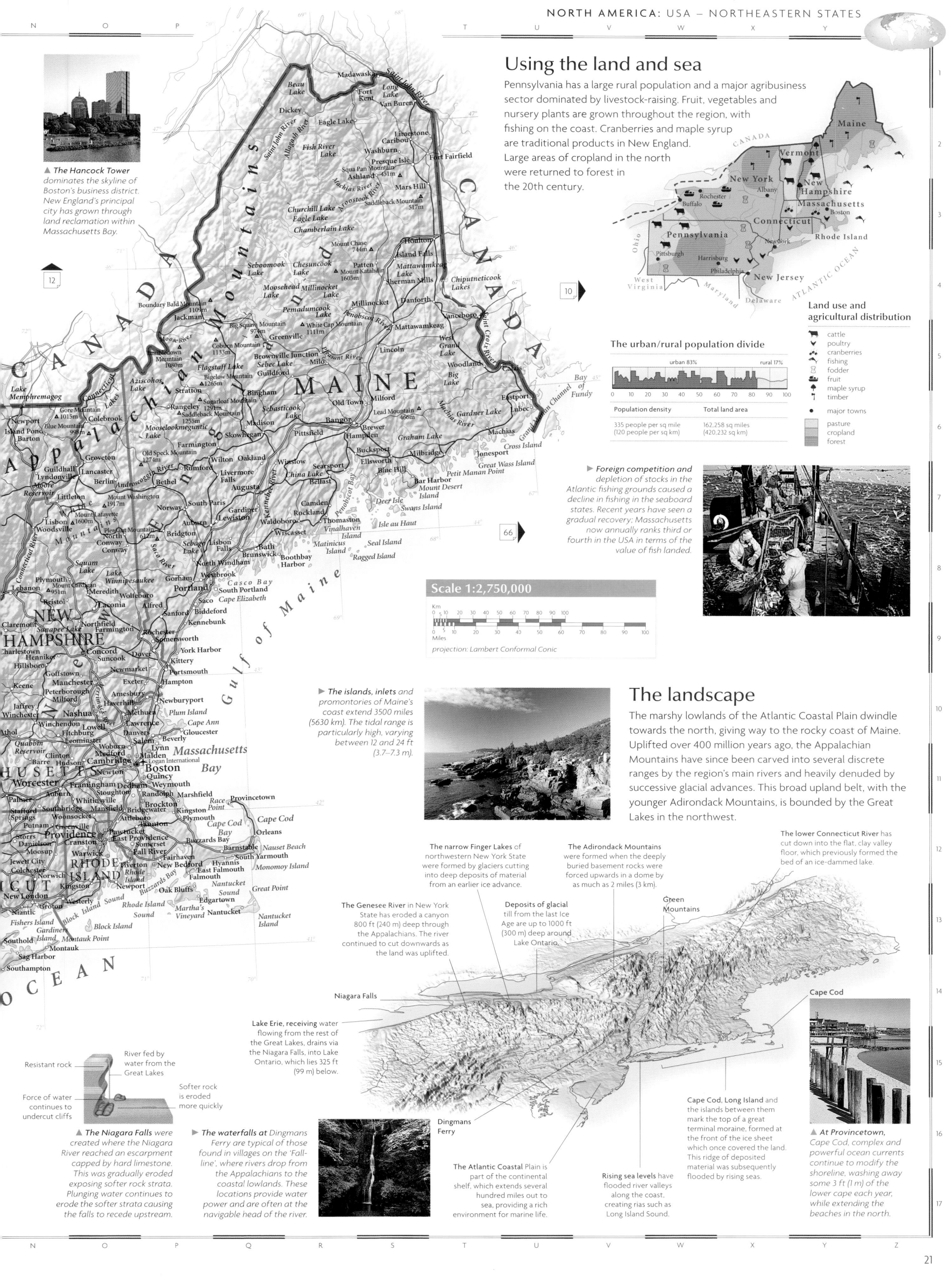

▲ *The Hancock Tower dominates the skyline of Boston's business district. New England's principal city has grown through land reclamation within Massachusetts Bay.*

Using the land and sea

Pennsylvania has a large rural population and a major agribusiness sector dominated by livestock-raising. Fruit, vegetables and nursery plants are grown throughout the region, with fishing on the coast. Cranberries and maple syrup are traditional products in New England. Large areas of cropland in the north were returned to forest in the 20th century.

Land use and agricultural distribution

- cattle
- poultry
- cranberries
- fishing
- fodder
- fruit
- maple syrup
- timber
- major towns

pasture
cropland
forest

The urban/rural population divide

urban 83%   rural 17%

0 10 20 30 40 50 60 70 80 90 100

Population density	Total land area
335 people per sq mile (120 people per sq km)	162,258 sq miles (420,232 sq km)

▶ *Foreign competition and depletion of stocks in the Atlantic fishing grounds caused a decline in fishing in the seaboard states. Recent years have seen a gradual recovery; Massachusetts now annually ranks third or fourth in the USA in terms of the value of fish landed.*

▶ *The islands, inlets and promontories of Maine's coast extend 3500 miles (5630 km). The tidal range is particularly high, varying between 12 and 24 ft (3.7–7.3 m).*

Scale 1:2,750,000

Km
0 5 10 20 30 40 50 60 70 80 90 100

0 5 10 20 30 40 50 60 70 80 90 100
Miles

projection: Lambert Conformal Conic

The landscape

The marshy lowlands of the Atlantic Coastal Plain dwindle towards the north, giving way to the rocky coast of Maine. Uplifted over 400 million years ago, the Appalachian Mountains have since been carved into several discrete ranges by the region's main rivers and heavily denuded by successive glacial advances. This broad upland belt, with the younger Adirondack Mountains, is bounded by the Great Lakes in the northwest.

The narrow Finger Lakes of northwestern New York State were formed by glaciers cutting into deep deposits of material from an earlier ice advance.

The Adirondack Mountains were formed when the deeply buried basement rocks were forced upwards in a dome by as much as 2 miles (3 km).

The lower Connecticut River has cut down into the flat, clay valley floor, which previously formed the bed of an ice-dammed lake.

The Genesee River in New York State has eroded a canyon 800 ft (240 m) deep through the Appalachians. The river continued to cut downwards as the land was uplifted.

Deposits of glacial till from the last Ice Age are up to 1000 ft (300 m) deep around Lake Ontario.

Green Mountains

Niagara Falls

Cape Cod

▲ *The Niagara Falls were created where the Niagara River reached an escarpment capped by hard limestone. This was gradually eroded exposing softer rock strata. Plunging water continues to erode the softer strata causing the falls to recede upstream.*

Resistant rock

River fed by water from the Great Lakes

Force of water continues to undercut cliffs

Softer rock is eroded more quickly

▲ *The waterfalls at Dingmans Ferry are typical of those found in villages on the 'Fall-line', where rivers drop from the Appalachians to the coastal lowlands. These locations provide water power and are often at the navigable head of the river.*

Dingmans Ferry

Lake Erie, receiving water flowing from the rest of the Great Lakes, drains via the Niagara Falls, into Lake Ontario, which lies 325 ft (99 m) below.

The Atlantic Coastal Plain is part of the continental shelf, which extends several hundred miles out to sea, providing a rich environment for marine life.

Rising sea levels have flooded river valleys along the coast, creating rias such as Long Island Sound.

Cape Cod, Long Island and the islands between them mark the top of a great terminal moraine, formed at the front of the ice sheet which once covered the land. This ridge of deposited material was subsequently flooded by rising seas.

▲ *At Provincetown, Cape Cod, complex and powerful ocean currents continue to modify the shoreline, washing away some 3 ft (1 m) of the lower cape each year, while extending the beaches in the north.*

21

USA: MID-EASTERN STATES

Delaware, District of Columbia, Kentucky, Maryland, North Carolina, South Carolina, Tennessee, Virginia, West Virginia

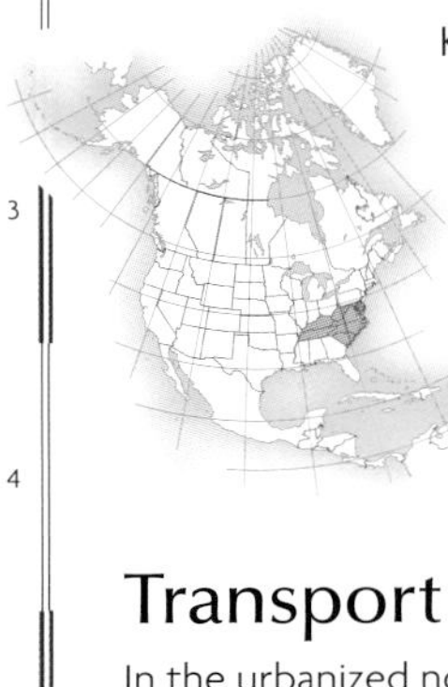

Key events in the history of the USA took place in this diverse region, which became the front line in the Civil War of 1861–65 between North and South. Strong regional contrasts exist between the fertile coastal plains, the isolated upcountry of the Appalachian Mountains and the cotton-growing areas of the Mississippi lowlands to the west. Whilst coal mining, a traditional industry in the Appalachians, has declined in recent years leaving much rural poverty, service industries elsewhere have increased, especially in the US federal capital, Washington DC.

Map key

Population
- ◉ 500,000 to 1 million
- ◎ 100,000 to 500,000
- ⊕ 50,000 to 100,000
- ○ 10,000 to 50,000
- · below 10,000

Elevation
- 6000m / 19,686ft
- 4000m / 13,124ft
- 3000m / 9843ft
- 2000m / 6562ft
- 1000m / 3281ft
- 500m / 1640ft
- 250m / 820ft
- 100m / 328ft
- sea level

Scale 1:3,000,000

Km
0 5 10 20 30 40 50 60 70 80

Miles
0 5 10 20 30 40 50 60 70 80

projection: Lambert Conformal Conic

▲ *The Bluegrass region* of Kentucky centres on the town of Lexington. This exceptionally fertile rolling plain is well known for its thoroughbred horse-breeding ranches.

Transport and industry

In the urbanized northeast, manufacturing remains important, alongside a burgeoning service sector. North Carolina is a major centre for industrial research and development. Traditional industries include Tennessee whiskey, and textiles in South Carolina. The decline of open-cast coal mining in the Appalachians has been hastened by environmental controls, although adventure-tourism is a flourishing new industry.

Major industry and infrastructure

- adventure-tourism
- car manufacture
- coal
- electronics
- engineering
- finance
- food processing
- hi-tech industry
- mining
- research & development
- textiles
- ■ capital cities
- ■ major towns
- ✈ international airports
- — major roads
- major industrial areas

The transport network

452,218 miles (723,548 km)		5737 miles (8267 km)	
18,336 miles (29,503 km)		4404 miles (7081 km)	

Tennessee's rivers are part of an important inland bulk-transport network. Memphis is connected with New Orleans in the south, and with cities as distant as Minneapolis, Sioux City, Chicago and Pittsburgh, via the Mississippi and its tributaries.

The landscape

The eastern tributaries of the Mississippi drain the interior lowlands. The Cumberland Plateau and the parallel ranges of the Appalachians have been successively uplifted and eroded over time, with the eastern side reduced to a series of foothills known as the Piedmont. The broad coastal plain gradually falls away into salt marshes, lagoons and offshore bars, broken by flooded estuaries along the shores of the Atlantic.

Natural Bridge in eastern Kentucky is an arch 78 ft (26 m) long and 65 ft (20 m) high. It has been shaped from resistant sandstone by gradual weathering processes, which removed the softer rock lying underneath.

The Allegheny Mountains form the northwestern edge of the Appalachian mountain chain. Continuous folding has formed rich seams of bituminous coal.

◄ *Farmland on the* eastern shores of Chesapeake Bay is sustained by artificial drainage. The area also provides refuge for a variety of waterfowl.

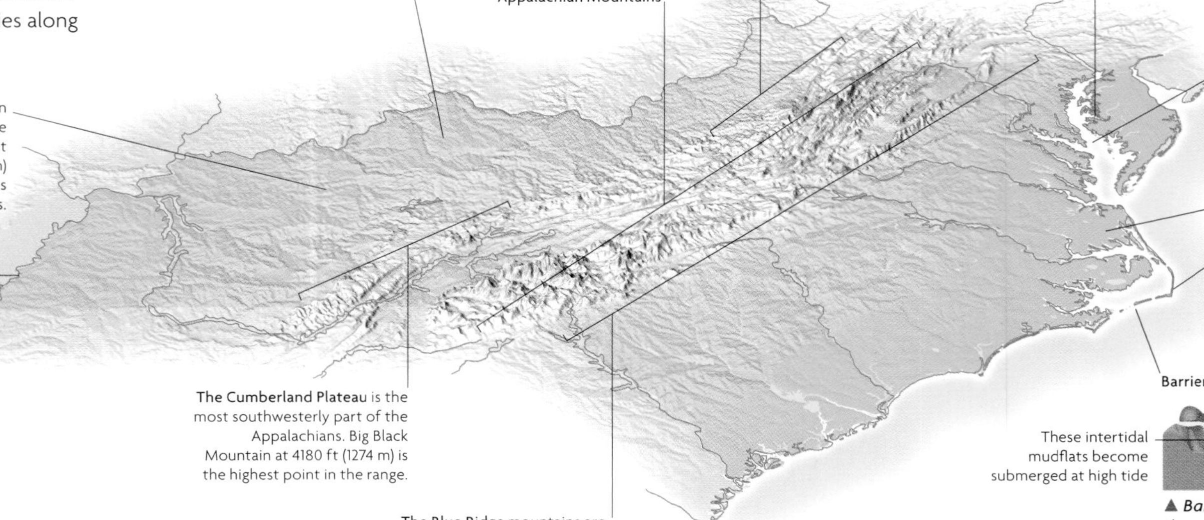

Appalachian Mountains

The many inlets of Chesapeake Bay are the flooded tributaries of the main river valley, which have been inundated by rising sea levels.

Salt marshes such as Great Dismal Swamp, develop where the coast is sheltered. Vast areas of such marshland have been reclaimed for farmland and settlement.

Cape Hatteras is the easternmost point of an offshore barrier island; a wave-deposited sand-bar which has become permanent, establishing its own vegetation.

Barrier islands

The Mammoth Cave is part of an extensive cave system in the limestone region of southwestern Kentucky. It stretches for over 300 miles (485 km) on five different levels and contains three rivers and three lakes.

The Mississippi River and its tributary the Ohio River form the western border of the region.

These intertidal mudflats become submerged at high tide

Tidal inlet

Barrier island

The Cumberland Plateau is the most southwesterly part of the Appalachians. Big Black Mountain at 4180 ft (1274 m) is the highest point in the range.

◄ *The Great Smoky Mountains* form the western escarpment of the Appalachians. The region is heavily forested, with over 130 species of tree.

The Blue Ridge mountains are a steep ridge, culminating in Mount Mitchell, the highest point in the Appalachians, at 6684 ft (2037 m).

▲ *Barrier islands are* common along the coasts of North and South Carolina. As sea levels rise, wave action builds up ridges of sand and pebbles parallel to the coast, separated by lagoons or intertidal mudflats, which are flooded at high tide.

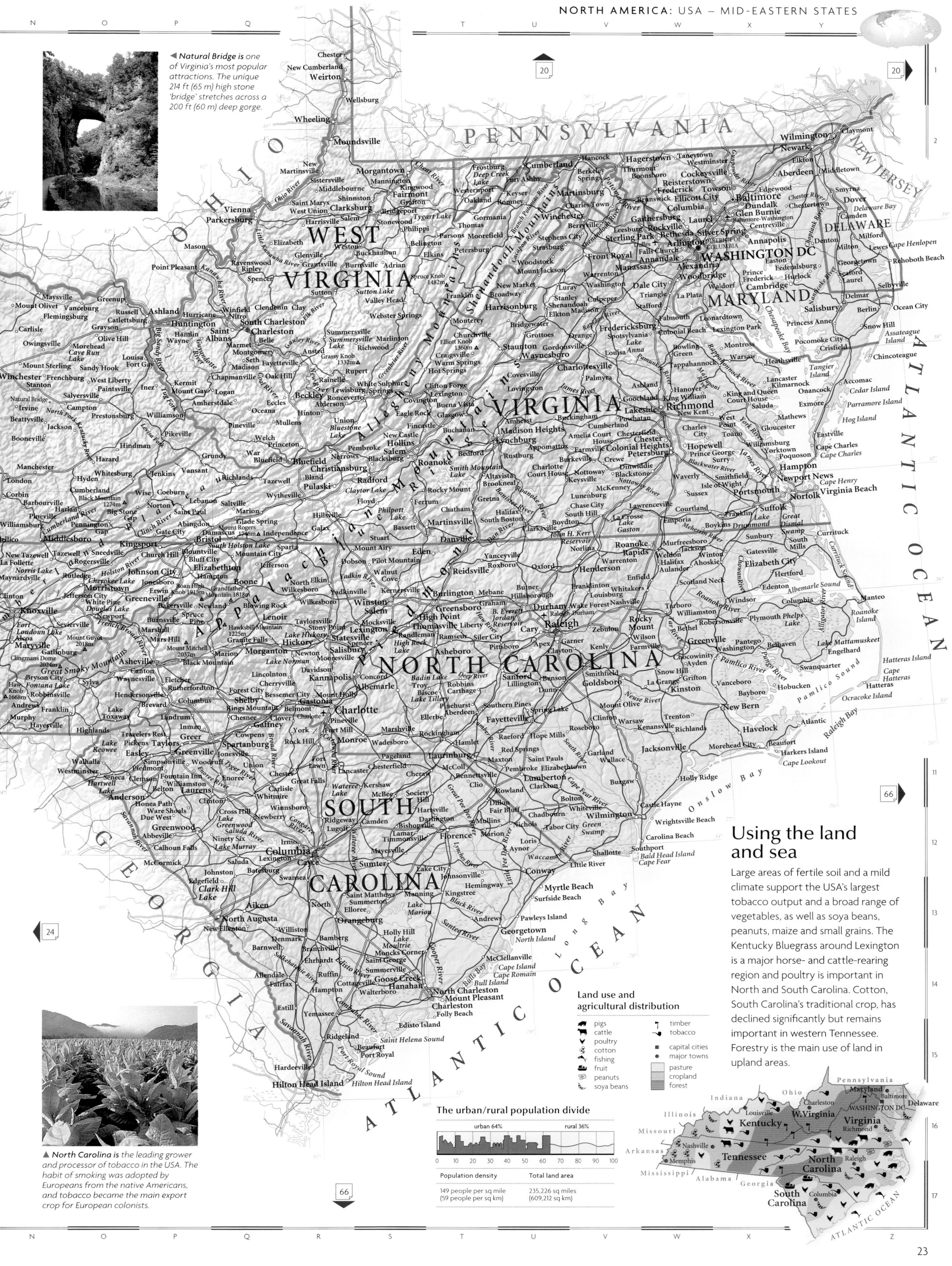

◀ *Natural Bridge is* one of Virginia's most popular attractions. The unique 214 ft (65 m) high stone 'bridge' stretches across a 200 ft (60 m) deep gorge.

Using the land and sea

Large areas of fertile soil and a mild climate support the USA's largest tobacco output and a broad range of vegetables, as well as soya beans, peanuts, maize and small grains. The Kentucky Bluegrass around Lexington is a major horse- and cattle-rearing region and poultry is important in North and South Carolina. Cotton, South Carolina's traditional crop, has declined significantly but remains important in western Tennessee. Forestry is the main use of land in upland areas.

Land use and agricultural distribution

- pigs
- cattle
- poultry
- cotton
- fishing
- fruit
- peanuts
- soya beans
- timber
- tobacco
- ■ capital cities
- ● major towns
- pasture
- cropland
- forest

The urban/rural population divide

urban 64%   rural 36%

0 10 20 30 40 50 60 70 80 90 100

Population density	Total land area
149 people per sq mile (59 people per sq km)	235,226 sq miles (609,212 sq km)

▲ *North Carolina is* the leading grower and processor of tobacco in the USA. The habit of smoking was adopted by Europeans from the native Americans, and tobacco became the main export crop for European colonists.

USA: SOUTHERN STATES

Alabama, Florida, Georgia, Louisiana, Mississippi

The South has maintained a separate identity and outlook throughout the history of the USA. Defeat in the American Civil War (1861–65) brought chronic poverty to the Confederate states, while the subsequent liberation of four million black slaves began a struggle not resolved until the 1960s, when the Civil Rights movement achieved an end to legal racial segregation. Since then many parts of the region have experienced rapid change: tourism and retirement communities, together with agriculture, have fuelled growth in Florida whilst defence-related industries have boosted the growth of cities such as Miami and Atlanta. Despite these changes, many people retain a strong attachment to their history: in Louisiana, French is still spoken in Cajun communities near the coast.

Transport and industry

Florida's tourist trade is only part of a flourishing service sector, which has swelled the principal cities of the south. Petroleum and mineral extraction has made the Gulf coast a major industrial region. Traditional textile production remains important in Georgia, while advanced new industries have grown from the Space Program.

The transport network

441,625 miles (706,600 km)	
5116 miles (8186 km)	
16,597 miles (26,555 km)	
6179 miles (9942 km)	

Atlanta's Hartsfield International airport is one of the busiest in the world. A dramatic rise in the use of regional air transport has helped to integrate the major cities of the southern states.

◀ *The French Quarter is the traditional cultural centre of New Orleans. The city, extensively damaged by Hurricane Katrina in 2005, once thrived on the cotton trade but now relies mainly on tourism and on oil from the Gulf of Mexico.*

Major industry and infrastructure

- ✈ aerospace
- 🚗 car manufacture
- chemicals
- coal
- defence
- electronics
- engineering
- food processing
- oil
- textiles
- tourism
- • major towns
- ⊕ international airports
- — major roads
- major industrial areas

The landscape

The Blue Ridge mountains in the north are skirted by the gentle hills of the Piedmont, whose rivers drain south on to the great flat expanse of the coastal plain. Sandy barrier beaches and islands dominate the sea shore, tracing round the swampy limestone arm of Florida. In the west, the Mississippi meanders towards its delta, crossing the thickly mantled alluvial plain of the interior lowlands.

▲ *The cypress swamps of the Mississippi Delta form in the backswamps behind the levées of the river and in the multitude of subsiding delta basins.*

The Mississippi is the world's third longest river and moves over 1000 million tonnes of sediment a year, creating deep alluvial plains. Flooding is a constant threat in lowland areas.

The Yazoo River flows parallel to the Mississippi through a common flood plain. The confluence of the rivers is deferred downstream because flood deposition has built the Mississippi channel up above the level of the Yazoo.

Cathedral Caverns near Huntsville in Alabama is a system of vast limestone caves, with a main opening 1000 ft (300 m) high and 150 ft (50 m) wide.

At De Soto Falls, Alabama, the Little River descends into the deepest canyon east of the Mississippi, with sheer cliff walls up to 700 ft (230 m) high.

Brasstown Bald in the Blue Ridge mountains of Georgia is the region's highest point, at 4784 ft (1458 m).

▲ *In Providence Canyon, Georgia, the Chattahoochee River has cut straight down through the sandy bedrock, to leave sheer rock faces and pinnacles, which have been smoothed by subsequent weathering.*

Sand bars, deposited by waves breaking offshore, form barrier beaches along much of the coastline, creating sheltered lagoons and salt marshes behind them.

Across Florida the coastal plain is mostly less than 75 ft (25 m) above sea level. The land is underlain by limestone, pitted with hollows which have been filled by over 10,000 lakes.

Mississippi Delta

Delta lobe

The delta of the Mississippi over 5000 years ago

Present-day delta

Lake Okeechobee is actually a shallow, slow-moving river, 150 miles (240 km) long and 50 miles (80 km) wide.

▲ *Over the last 5000 years the lower course of the Mississippi has moved back and forth over great distances. These changes, caused by varying sediment loads and human modification, have resulted in a 'bird's foot' delta with several lobes, each reflecting the river's different historic position.*

The Everglades lie in a limestone hollow formed over two million years ago, which has gradually become in-filled with swamp deposits.

Atchafalaya Bay

Piedmont

Florida Keys

Scale 1:3,500,000

projection: Lambert Conformal Conic

Map key

Population
- 500,000 to 1 million
- 100,000 to 500,000
- 50,000 to 100,000
- 10,000 to 50,000
- below 10,000

Elevation
- 4000m / 13,124ft
- 3000m / 9843ft
- 2000m / 6562ft
- 1000m / 3281ft
- 500m / 1640ft
- 250m / 820ft
- 100m / 328ft
- sea level

▲ Mangrove swamps and islets merge across Whitewater Bay, in the Everglades National Park. Alligators, crocodiles, endangered aquatic mammals such as manatees, and a great variety of birds inhabit the subtropical sanctuary.

◄ New Orleans was devastated by Hurricane Katrina in August 2005. Around 1200 lives were lost across the region. Florida and the Gulf coast are prone to hurricanes every autumn.

Using the land and sea

In recent years a wide variety of cash crops has been grown in lands once dominated by cotton. The semi-tropical Florida climate has made it a world leader in the growing of citrus fruit. Georgia has a similar reputation for peanuts; elsewhere soya beans, sugar cane, poultry and cattle are important. Fishing takes place in Atlantic and Gulf waters, with shellfishing in the shallow Louisiana 'bayou'.

The urban/rural population divide

urban 72%   rural 28%

0 10 20 30 40 50 60 70 80 90 100

Population density	Total land area
149 people per sq mile (57 people per sq km)	253,046 sq miles (655,364 sq km)

▲ Cotton production, once the economic mainstay of the 'deep south', has fallen by more than 50% since 1900. Soil erosion, pests and new farming techniques have shifted the cotton belt west towards Texas and California.

Land use and agricultural distribution

- cattle
- pigs
- poultry
- citrus
- cotton
- fishing
- peanuts
- shellfish
- soya beans
- sugar cane
- timber
- major towns
- pasture
- cropland
- forest
- wetland

► Duck Key is one of the chain of limestone and coral islands which form the Florida Keys. The Overseas Highway, completed in 1938, extends 100 miles (160 km) from the mainland to Key West along a series of causeways and bridges.

25

USA: Texas

First explored by Spaniards moving north from Mexico in search of gold, Texas was controlled by Spain and then Mexico, before becoming an independent republic in 1836, and joining the Union of States in 1845. During the 19th century, many of the migrants who came to Texas raised cattle on the abundant land; in the 20th century, they were joined by prospectors attracted by the promise of oil riches. Today, although natural resources, especially oil, still form the basis of its wealth, the diversified Texan economy includes thriving hi-tech and finance industries. The major urban centres, home to 80% of the population, lie in the south and east, and include Houston, the 'oil-city', and Dallas–Fort Worth. Hispanic influences remain strong, especially in the south and west.

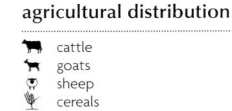

▲ **Dallas was founded** in 1841 as a prairie trading post and its development was stimulated by the arrival of railroads. Cotton and then oil funded the town's early growth. Today, the modern, high-rise skyline of Dallas reflects the city's position as a leading centre of banking, insurance and the petroleum industry in the southwest.

38

Using the land

Cotton production and livestock-raising, particularly cattle, dominate farming, although crop failures and the demands of local markets have led to some diversification. Following the introduction of modern farming techniques, cotton production spread out from the east to the plains of western Texas. Cattle ranches are widespread, while sheep and goats are raised on the dry Edwards Plateau.

Land use and agricultural distribution

- cattle
- goats
- sheep
- cereals
- cotton
- major towns

pasture
cropland
forest
barren

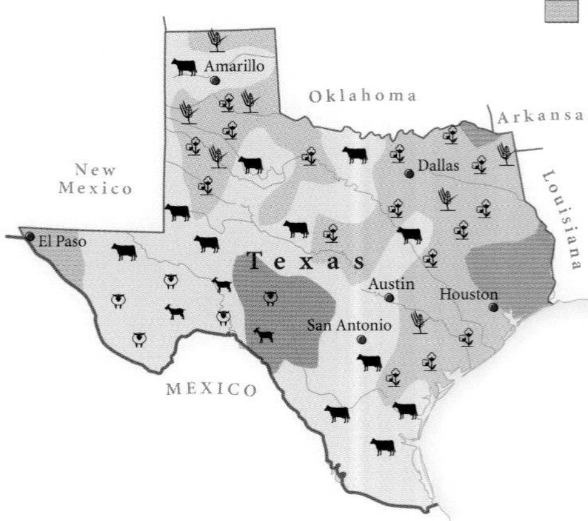

The urban/rural population divide

urban 80% rural 20%

0 10 20 30 40 50 60 70 80 90 100

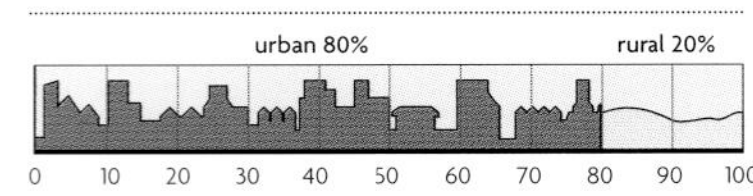

Population density	Total land area
84 people per sq mile (33 people per sq km)	261,797 sq miles (678,028 sq km)

▲ **The huge cattle** ranches of Texas developed during the 19th century when land was plentiful and could be acquired cheaply. Today, more cattle and sheep are raised in Texas than in any other state.

The landscape

Texas is made up of a series of massive steps descending from the mountains and high plains of the west and northwest to the coastal lowlands in the southeast. Many of the state's borders are delineated by water. The Rio Grande flows from the Rocky Mountains to the Gulf of Mexico, marking the border with Mexico.

▲ **Cap Rock Escarpment** juts out from the plains, running 200 miles (320 km) from north to south. Its height varies from 300 ft (90 m) rising to sheer cliffs up to 1000 ft (300 m).

42

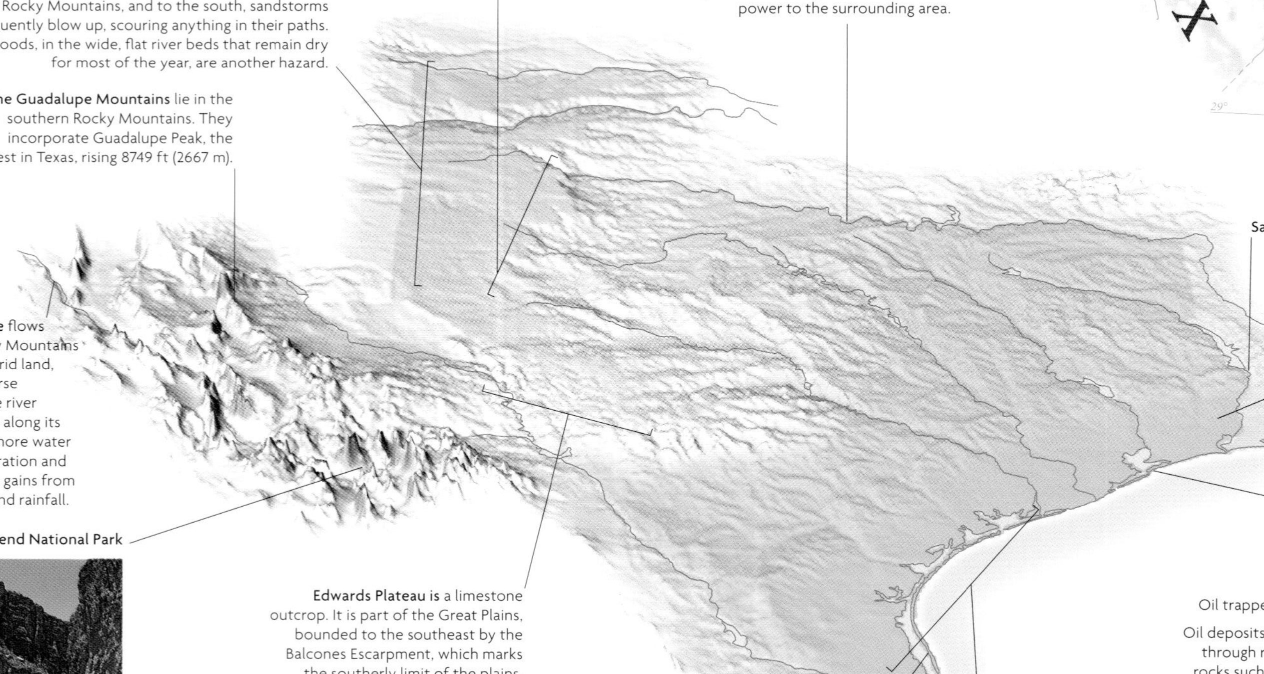

The Llano Estacado or Staked Plain in northern Texas is known for its harsh environment. In the north, freezing winds carrying ice and snow sweep down from the Rocky Mountains, and to the south, sandstorms frequently blow up, scouring anything in their paths. Flash floods, in the wide, flat river beds that remain dry for most of the year, are another hazard.

The Guadalupe Mountains lie in the southern Rocky Mountains. They incorporate Guadalupe Peak, the highest in Texas, rising 8749 ft (2667 m).

The Rio Grande flows from the Rocky Mountains through semi-arid land, supporting sparse vegetation. The river actually shrinks along its course, losing more water through evaporation and seepage than it gains from its tributaries and rainfall.

Big Bend National Park

The Red River flows for 1300 miles (2090 km), marking most of the northern border of Texas. A dam and reservoir along its course provide vital irrigation and hydro-electric power to the surrounding area.

Sabine River

Extensive forests of pine and cypress grow in the eastern corner of the coastal lowlands where the average rainfall is 45 inches (1145 mm) a year. This is higher than the rest of the state and over twice the average in the west.

In the coastal lowlands of southeastern Texas the Earth's crust is warping, causing the land to subside and allowing the sea to invade. Around Galveston, the rate of downward tilting is 6 inches (15 cm) per year. Erosion of the coast is also exacerbated by hurricanes.

Edwards Plateau is a limestone outcrop. It is part of the Great Plains, bounded to the southeast by the Balcones Escarpment, which marks the southerly limit of the plains.

◀ **Flowing through** 1500 ft (450 m) high gorges, the shallow, muddy Rio Grande makes a 90° bend, which marks the southern border of Big Bend National Park, giving it its name. The area is a mixture of forested mountains, deserts and canyons.

Laguna Madre in southern Texas has been almost completely cut off from the sea by Padre Island. This sand bank was created by wave action, carrying and depositing material along the coast. The process is known as longshore drift.

Padre Island

Oil deposits

Oil trapped by fault

Oil deposits migrate through reservoir rocks such as shale

Oil accumulates beneath impermeable cap rock

Impermeable rock strata

Salt dome

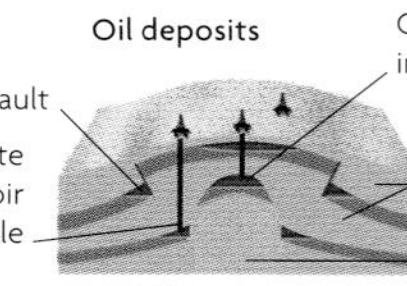

▲ **Oil deposits are** found beneath much of Texas. They collect as oil migrates upwards through porous layers of rock until it is trapped, either by a cap of rock above a salt dome, or by a fault line which exposes impermeable rock through which the oil cannot rise.

Map labels

NEW MEXICO

Texline Kerrick
Dalhart
Hartley
Channing
Canadian River
High
Adrian Vega
Wildorado
Dawn
Hereford
Friona Dimmitt
Bovina
Farwell Running Water Draw
Springlake
Muleshoe Earth
Sudan Olton Amherst
Enochs Littlefield Anton
Morton Whiteface Levelland
Ropesville
Meadow Brownfield
Plains Tokio Sulphur Springs Draw
Denver City Wellman Welch
Seagraves Cedar Lake
Seminole
Goldsmith
Mustang Draw Andrews Midland
Kermit
Wink Penwell Odessa
Mentone Wickett
Pecos Monahans Royalty Crane
Barstow Grandfalls Imperial
Toyah Salt Draw Girvin McCamey
Saragosa Balmorhea Bakersfield
Fort Stockton
Davis Stockton Plateau
Mountains Big Canyon
Mount Livermore 2554m
Fort Davis Marathon Sanderson
Marfa Alpine Glass Mountains
Candelaria Cathedral Mountain 2093m
Dryden
Shafter Casa Piedra
Presidio Redford
Terlingua Emory Peak 2385m Big Bend National Park

Amarillo
Oklahoma Arkansas
New Mexico Dallas Louisiana
El Paso Texas Austin
San Antonio Houston
MEXICO

Cornudo El Paso
San Elizario Clint
Fabens Tornillo
Fort Hancock McNary
Esperanza Sierra Blanca 2100m
Dell City Guadalupe Mountains Red Bluff Reservoir
Salt Basin Guadalupe Peak 2667m Orla
Salt Flat Pecos River
Hueco Mountains Delaware Mountains
Sierra Diablo Apache Mountains
Van Horn Kent
Rio Grande
Sierra Vieja
Ruidosa Chinati Mountains
Santiago Mountains
Alamito Creek
Terlingua Creek

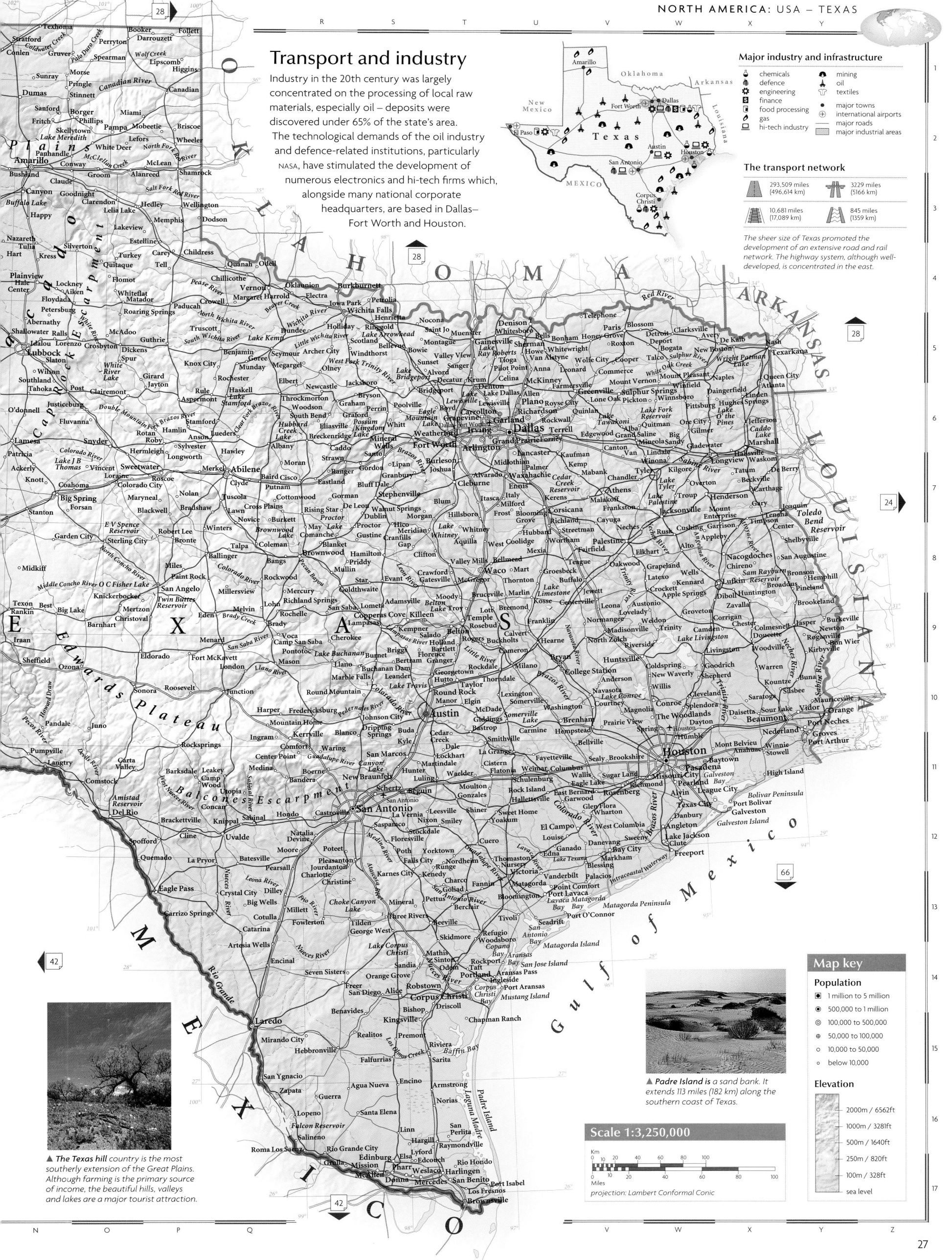

Transport and industry

Industry in the 20th century was largely concentrated on the processing of local raw materials, especially oil – deposits were discovered under 65% of the state's area. The technological demands of the oil industry and defence-related institutions, particularly NASA, have stimulated the development of numerous electronics and hi-tech firms which, alongside many national corporate headquarters, are based in Dallas–Fort Worth and Houston.

Major industry and infrastructure

- chemicals
- defence
- engineering
- finance
- food processing
- gas
- hi-tech industry
- mining
- oil
- textiles
- major towns
- international airports
- major roads
- major industrial areas

The transport network

293,509 miles (496,614 km)	3229 miles (5166 km)
10,681 miles (17,089 km)	845 miles (1359 km)

The sheer size of Texas promoted the development of an extensive road and rail network. The highway system, although well-developed, is concentrated in the east.

▲ The Texas hill country is the most southerly extension of the Great Plains. Although farming is the primary source of income, the beautiful hills, valleys and lakes are a major tourist attraction.

▲ Padre Island is a sand bank. It extends 113 miles (182 km) along the southern coast of Texas.

Map key

Population

- ▣ 1 million to 5 million
- ◉ 500,000 to 1 million
- ◉ 100,000 to 500,000
- ◉ 50,000 to 100,000
- ⊕ 10,000 to 50,000
- ○ below 10,000

Elevation

- 2000m / 6562ft
- 1000m / 3281ft
- 500m / 1640ft
- 250m / 820ft
- 100m / 328ft
- sea level

Scale 1:3,250,000

projection: Lambert Conformal Conic

USA: SOUTH MIDWESTERN STATES

Arkansas, Kansas, Missouri, Oklahoma

The expansion of the USA focused on this region in the mid-19th century. Settlers spread from the confluence of the Missouri and Mississippi rivers up onto the Great Plains. This treeless expanse, which early explorers had called the 'Great American Desert', was turned into one of the world's richest agricultural regions; but periodic droughts, coupled with over-intensive farming, led to the 'Dustbowl' soil erosion crisis of the 1930s, the abandonment of many farms, and a mass exodus to the west coast. The land has since recovered, although the mechanization of agriculture has led to a decline in the rural population. In recent years, suburban residential development has spread rapidly across the wooded Ozark Plateau in the east of the region.

Transport and industry

The processing of agricultural products, such as brewing and meat packing, has been traditionally important in these states. In Kansas and Oklahoma, diversified manufacturing now supplements income from fossil fuels; Wichita has become a world centre for aeronautical engineering, an industry which also employs many people in neighbouring Missouri.

Major industry and infrastructure

- ✈ aerospace
- ✿ engineering
- S finance
- food processing
- gas
- mining
- oil
- vehicle manufacture
- major towns
- ✈ international airports
- — major roads
- major industrial areas

The transport network

380,307 miles (608,491 km)	4068 miles (6508 km)
16,185 miles (25,896 km)	1994 miles (3208 km)

The Arkansas River and its tributaries allow access to over half of the USA's navigable inland waterways. A system of locks and dams along the river provides Tulsa in Oklahoma with a navigable water route to the Gulf of Mexico.

► *Agricultural produce from the plains is moved by barges along the Mississippi. The river now carries a far greater tonnage of freight than any other waterway system in the USA.*

The landscape

Most of the region consists of high, treeless plains, which gradually descend east from the Rocky Mountains. Drainage follows this slope, with rivers flowing towards the alluvial lowlands of the Mississippi in the southeast. Between the plains and the lowlands lie various ranges of wooded hills, including the deeply incised Ozark Plateau.

▲ *The Mississippi, North America's longest river, is joined by the Missouri, its main tributary, on a flood plain which spreads south to the Gulf of Mexico.*

Collapsed limestone caverns led to the formation of Big Basin in Kansas; a depression 100 ft (33 m) deep and 1 mile (1.6 km) wide.

The Great Salt Plains of northern Oklahoma cover 45 sq mile (116 sq km). The arid, white flats were left by the gradual evaporation of an ancient salt lake.

Underground water reserves

Flint Hills is the region's easternmost major escarpment. Steep, grassy uplands are interspersed with rocky, wooded ravines and outcrops of limestone and chert.

Missouri River

The Ozark Plateau is a wooded, hilly region of rivers and narrow, winding lakes. The Lake of the Ozarks was created by the damming of the Osage River in 1930.

Crowleys Ridge is a long, sandy ridge, rising from the Mississippi flood plain. It was formed over thousands of years by the deposition of sand blown eastwards from the Great Plains.

▼ *Lake Ouachita, in Arkansas is one of a number of irregularly-shaped lakes found among the ridges of the Ouachita Mountains.*

▲ *The Ogallala Aquifer, beneath the Great Plains, is the largest known source of underground water in the world. There is concern about the rapid depletion of this finite water supply by irrigation schemes.*

Devil's Den is a dry badland area. The rugged landscape, strewn with large boulders, is the eroded remnant of a spur extending from the Arbuckle mountains to the west.

Ouachita Mountains

Mississippi River

Red River

▲ *The landscape of northeast Kansas is interlaced by rivers which have cut broad wooded valleys through the gentle hills. All the rivers in Kansas form part of the massive Missouri/Mississippi drainage basin.*

Map key

Population
- ◉ 100,000 to 500,000
- ⊕ 50,000 to 100,000
- ○ 10,000 to 50,000
- ○ below 10,000

Elevation
- 1000m / 3281ft
- 500m / 1640ft
- 250m / 820ft
- 100m / 328ft
- sea level

Scale 1:3,000,000

projection: Lambert Conformal Conic

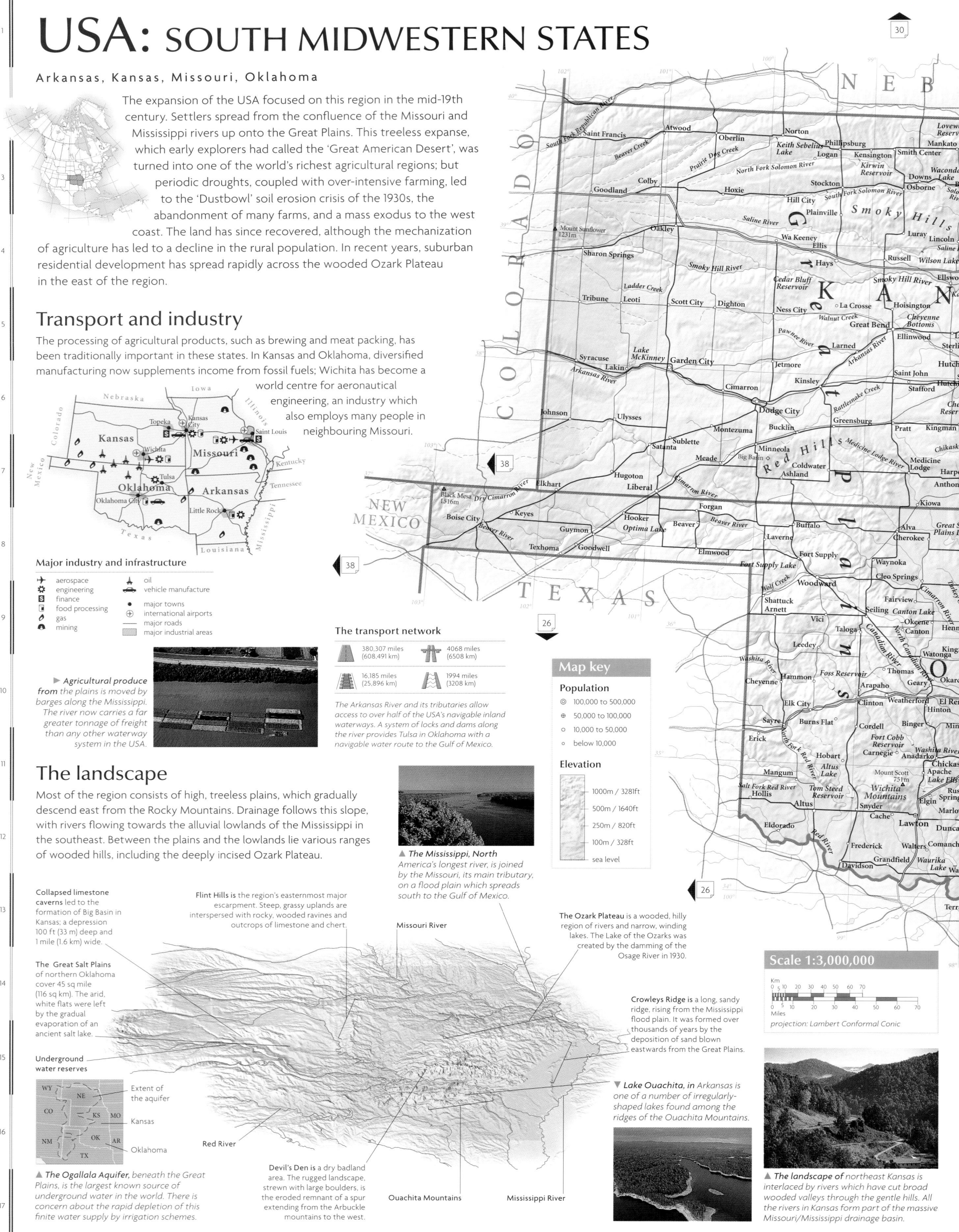

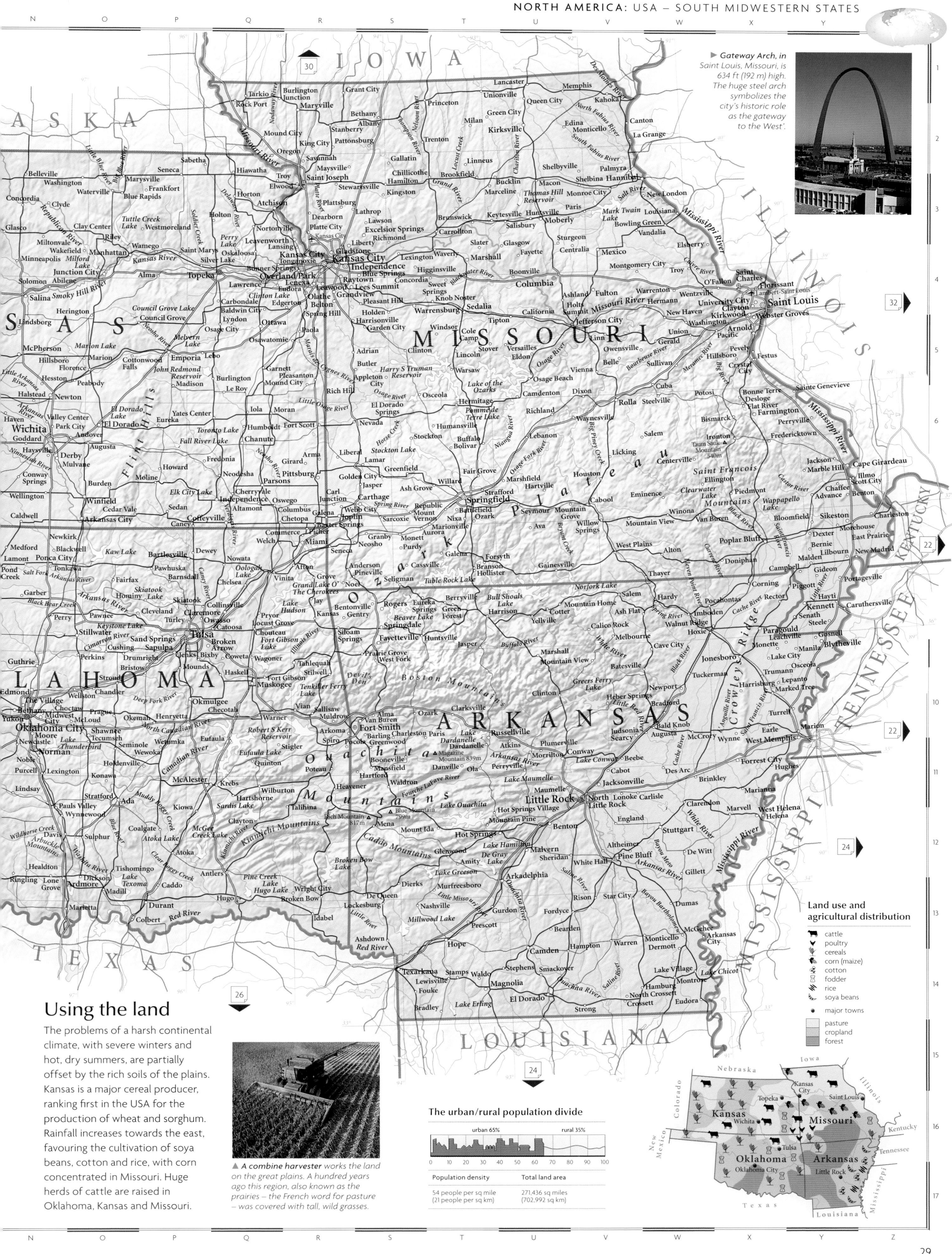

▶ *Gateway Arch, in Saint Louis, Missouri, is 634 ft (192 m) high. The huge steel arch symbolizes the city's historic role as the gateway to the West'.*

Using the land

The problems of a harsh continental climate, with severe winters and hot, dry summers, are partially offset by the rich soils of the plains. Kansas is a major cereal producer, ranking first in the USA for the production of wheat and sorghum. Rainfall increases towards the east, favouring the cultivation of soya beans, cotton and rice, with corn concentrated in Missouri. Huge herds of cattle are raised in Oklahoma, Kansas and Missouri.

▲ *A combine harvester* works the land on the great plains. A hundred years ago this region, also known as the prairies – the French word for pasture – was covered with tall, wild grasses.

The urban/rural population divide

urban 65%   rural 35%

0   10   20   30   40   50   60   70   80   90   100

Population density
54 people per sq mile
(21 people per sq km)

Total land area
271,436 sq miles
(702,992 sq km)

Land use and agricultural distribution

- cattle
- poultry
- cereals
- corn (maize)
- cotton
- fodder
- rice
- soya beans
- major towns

pasture
cropland
forest

USA: NORTH MIDWESTERN STATES

Iowa, Minnesota, Nebraska, North Dakota, South Dakota

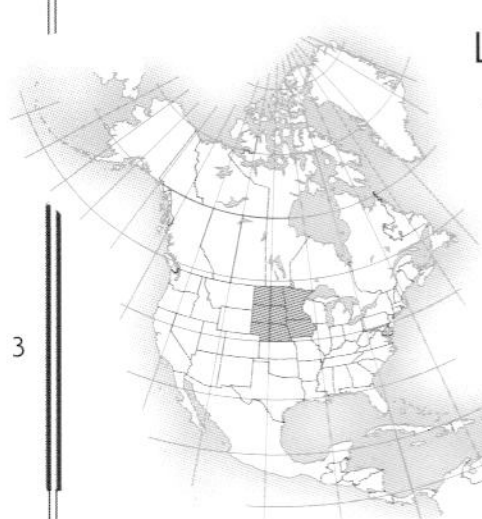

Lying at the very heart of the North American continent, much of this region was acquired from France as part of the Louisiana Purchase in 1803. The area was largely by-passed by the early waves of westward migrants. When Europeans did settle, during the 19th century, they displaced the Native Americans who lived on the plains. The settlers planted arable crops and raised cattle on the immensely fertile prairie land, founding an agrarian tradition which flourishes today. Most of this region remains rural; of the five states, only in Minnesota has there been significant diversification away from agriculture and resource-based industries into the hi-tech and service sectors.

Using the land

The popular image of these states as agricultural is entirely justified; prairies stretch uninterrupted across most of the area. Croplands fall into two regions: the wheat belt of the plains, and the corn belt of the central USA. Cash crops, such as soya beans, are grown to supplement incomes. Livestock, particularly pigs and cattle, are raised throughout this region.

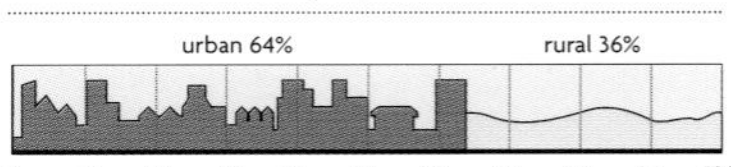

▶ *Dark, fertile prairie* soils in the southeast provide Minnesota's most productive farmland. Hot, humid summers create a long growing season for corn cultivation.

The urban/rural population divide

urban 64% rural 36%

0 10 20 30 40 50 60 70 80 90 100

Population density	Total land area
31 people per sq mile (12 people per sq km)	357,212 sq miles (925,143 sq km)

Land use and agricultural distribution

- cattle
- pigs
- corn (maize)
- soya beans
- wheat
- ● major towns
- pasture
- cropland
- forest
- wetland

Transport and industry

Food processing and the production of farm machinery are supported by the large agricultural sector. Mineral exploitation is also an important activity: gold is mined in the ore-rich Black Hills of South Dakota, and both North Dakota and Nebraska are emerging as major petroleum producers.

▶ *Water erosion along* the Little Missouri River has carried away sedimentary deposits, creating rugged landscapes known as badlands.

The transport network

504,522 miles (807,235 km)	3422 miles (5475 km)
16,940 miles (27,104 km)	683 miles (1098 km)

Nebraska's central location has made it an important transport artery for east–west traffic. Minnesota's road network radiates out from the hub of the twin cities, Minneapolis–Saint Paul.

Major industry and infrastructure

- coal
- engineering
- electronics
- finance
- food processing
- oil & gas
- mining
- ● major towns
- ⊕ international airports
- — major roads
- major industrial areas

The landscape

These states straddle the Great Plains and the lowlands of the central USA, with Minnesota lying in a transition zone between the eastern forests and the prairies. The region was shaped by repeated ice advances and retreats, leaving a flat relief, broken only by the numerous lakes and broad river networks which drain the prairies.

Escarpment Ridge

In permeable strata hollows are formed by small mudslides

Water flowing into gullies erodes back the escarpment

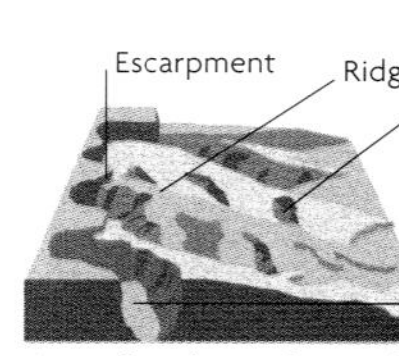

▲ *Badlands are formed* by stormwater run-off which flows down the impermeable strata of the escarpment and saturates the permeable strata leading to mudslides and the formation of gullies.

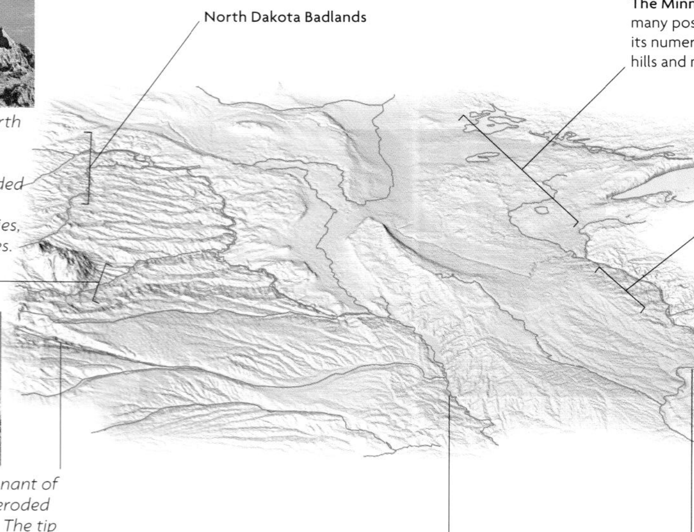

The Minnesota landscape contains many post-glacial features, including its numerous lakes, boulder-strewn hills and mineral-rich deposits.

North Dakota Badlands

▲ *In the badlands* of North and South Dakota, horizontal layers of sandstone have been eroded by rivers, leaving a landscape of narrow gullies, sharp crests and pinnacles.

South Dakota Badlands

Although it escaped the last glaciation, the limestone bedrock of southeastern Minnesota has been eroded by surface and subterranean streams, leaving a network of underground caverns and steepsided valleys.

▲ *Chimney Rock is* a remnant of an ancient land surface, eroded by the North Platte River. The tip of its spire stands 500 ft (150 m) above the plain.

Missouri River

Mississippi River

◀ *In northeastern Iowa,* the Mississippi and its tributaries have deeply incised the underlying bedrock creating a hilly terrain, with bluffs standing 300 ft (90 m) above the valley.

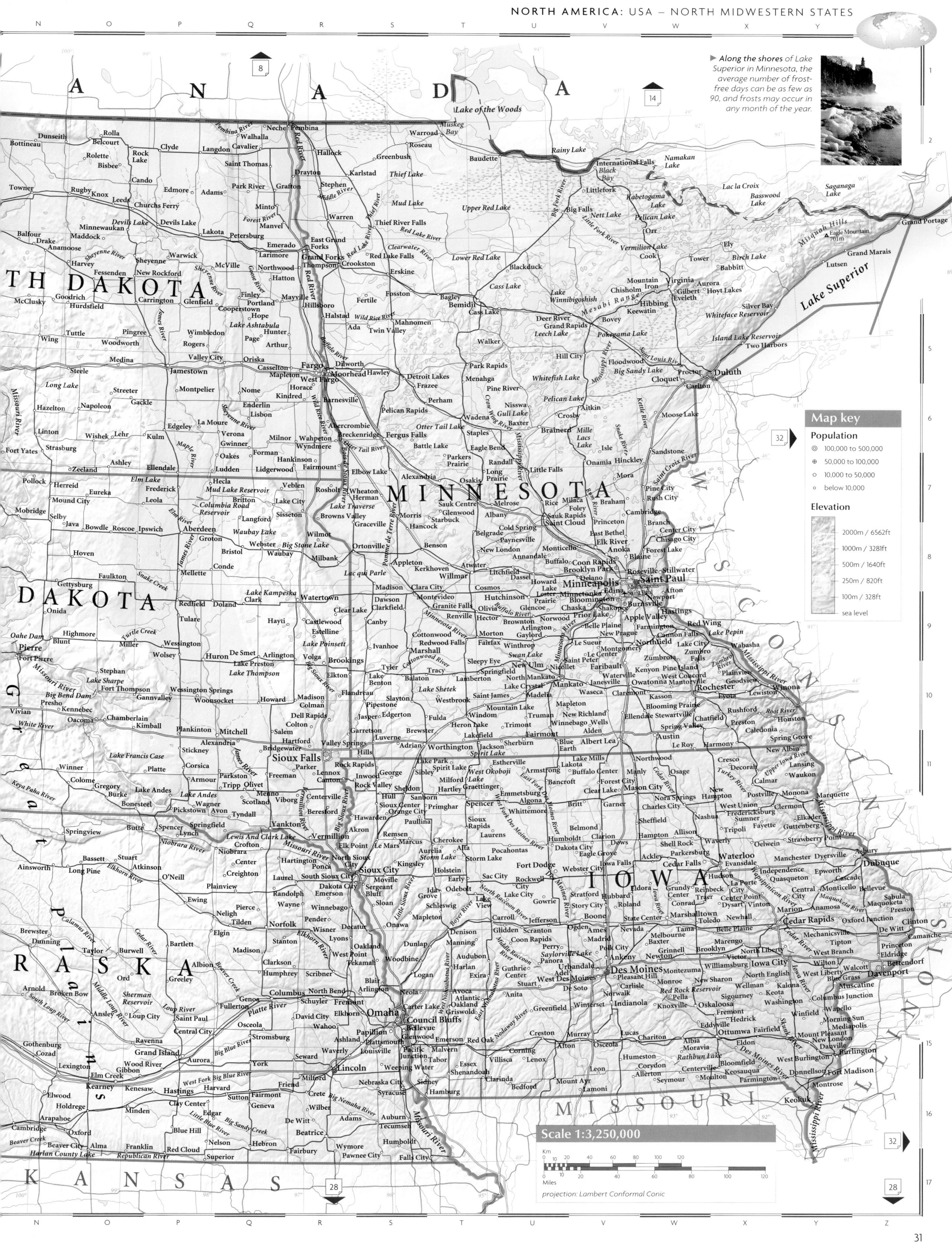

▶ Along the shores of Lake Superior in Minnesota, the average number of frost-free days can be as few as 90, and frosts may occur in any month of the year.

Map key

Population
⊚ 100,000 to 500,000
⊕ 50,000 to 100,000
⊙ 10,000 to 50,000
○ below 10,000

Elevation
2000m / 6562ft
1000m / 3281ft
500m / 1640ft
250m / 820ft
100m / 328ft
sea level

Scale 1:3,250,000

projection: Lambert Conformal Conic

USA: GREAT LAKES STATES

Illinois, Indiana, Michigan, Ohio, Wisconsin

The states bordering the Great Lakes developed rapidly in the second half of the 19th century as a result of improvements in communications: rail to the west and waterways to the south and east. Fertile land and good links with growing eastern seaboard cities encouraged the development of agriculture and food processing. Migrants from Europe and other parts of the USA flooded into the region and for much of the 20th century the region's economy boomed. However, in recent years heavy industry has declined, earning the region the unwanted label the 'Rustbelt'.

Transport and industry

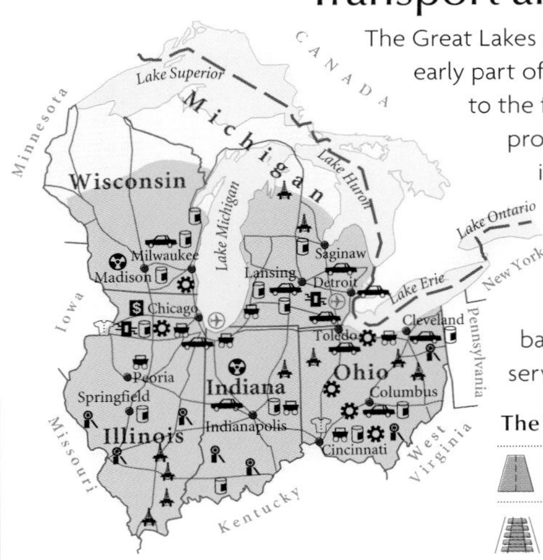

The Great Lakes region is the centre of the USA's car industry. Since the early part of the 20th century, its prosperity has been closely linked to the fortunes of automobile manufacturing. Iron and steel production has expanded to meet demand from this industry. In the 1970s, nationwide recession, cheaper foreign competition in the automobile sector, pollution in and around the Great Lakes and the collapse of the meat-packing industry, centred on Chicago, forced these states to diversify their industrial base. New industries have emerged, notably electronics, service and finance industries.

The transport network

540,682 miles (865,091 km)		6550 miles (10,480 km)	
24,928 miles (39,884 km)		2330 miles (3748 km)	

Few areas of the USA have a comparable transport system. Chicago is a principal transport terminus with a dense network of roads, railways and Interstate freeways radiating from the city.

▶ *Ever since Ransom Olds and Henry Ford started mass-producing automobiles in Detroit early in the 20th century, the city's name has become synonymous with the American automotive industry.*

Major industry and infrastructure

- car manufacture
- coal
- electronics
- engineering
- finance
- food processing
- iron & steel
- oil
- research & development
- textiles
- major towns
- international airports
- major roads
- major industrial areas

The landscape

Much of this region shows the impact of glaciation which lasted until about 10,000 years ago, and extended as far south as Illinois and Ohio. Although the relief of the region slopes towards the Great Lakes, because the ice sheets blocked northerly drainage, most of the rivers today flow southwards, forming part of the massive Mississippi/Missouri drainage basin.

◀ *The dunes near Sleeping Bear Point rise 400 ft (120 m) from the banks of Lake Michigan. They are constantly being resculpted by wind action.*

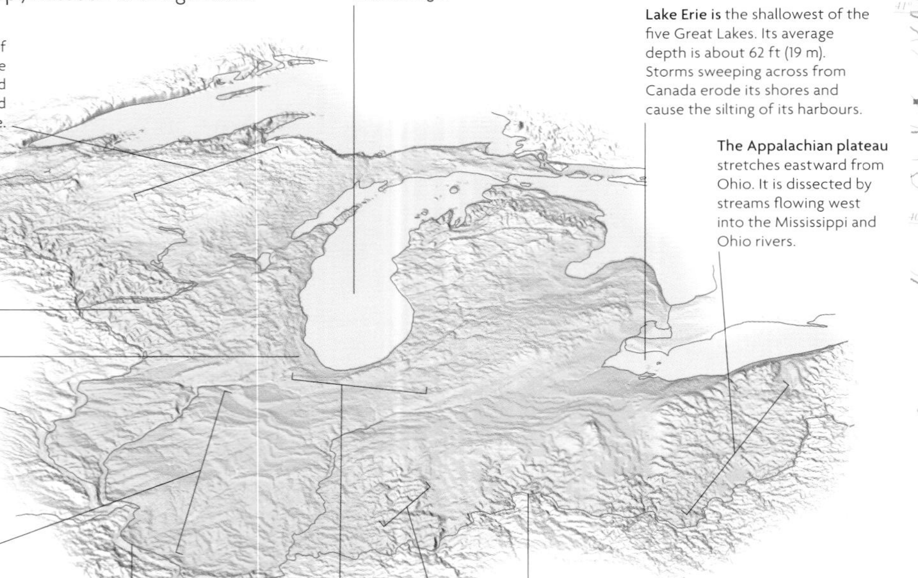

Lake Michigan

The many lakes and marshes of Wisconsin and Michigan are the result of glacial erosion and deposition which occurred during the last Ice Age.

Southwestern Wisconsin is known as a 'driftless' area. Unlike most of the region, low hills protected it from erosion by the advancing ice sheet.

Most of the water used in northern Illinois is pumped from underground reservoirs. Due to increased demand, many areas now face a water shortage. Around Joliet, the water table was lowered by more than 700 ft (210 m) over the last century.

Lake Erie is the shallowest of the five Great Lakes. Its average depth is about 62 ft (19 m). Storms sweeping across from Canada erode its shores and cause the silting of its harbours.

The Appalachian plateau stretches eastward from Ohio. It is dissected by streams flowing west into the Mississippi and Ohio rivers.

Illinois plains

▲ *The plains of Illinois are characteristic of drift landscapes, scoured and flattened by glacial erosion and covered with fertile glacial deposits.*

Mississippi River

Ohio River

Relic landforms from the last glaciation, such as shallow basins and ridges, cover all but the south of this region. Ridges, known as moraines, up to 300 ft (100 m) high, lie to the south of Lake Michigan.

Unlike the level prairie to the north, southern Indiana is relatively rugged. Limestone in the hills has been dissolved by water, producing features such as sinkholes and underground caves.

Glacial till

Present-day river or stream

Channels caused by outwash from melting glacier

Most recent till deposits

Older till sheet

Bedrock

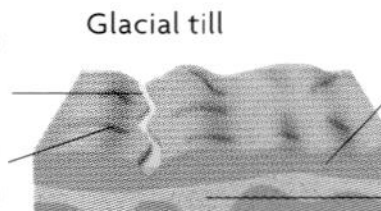

▲ *As a result of successive glacial depositions, the total depth of till along the former southern margin of the Laurentide ice sheet can exceed 1300 ft (400 m).*

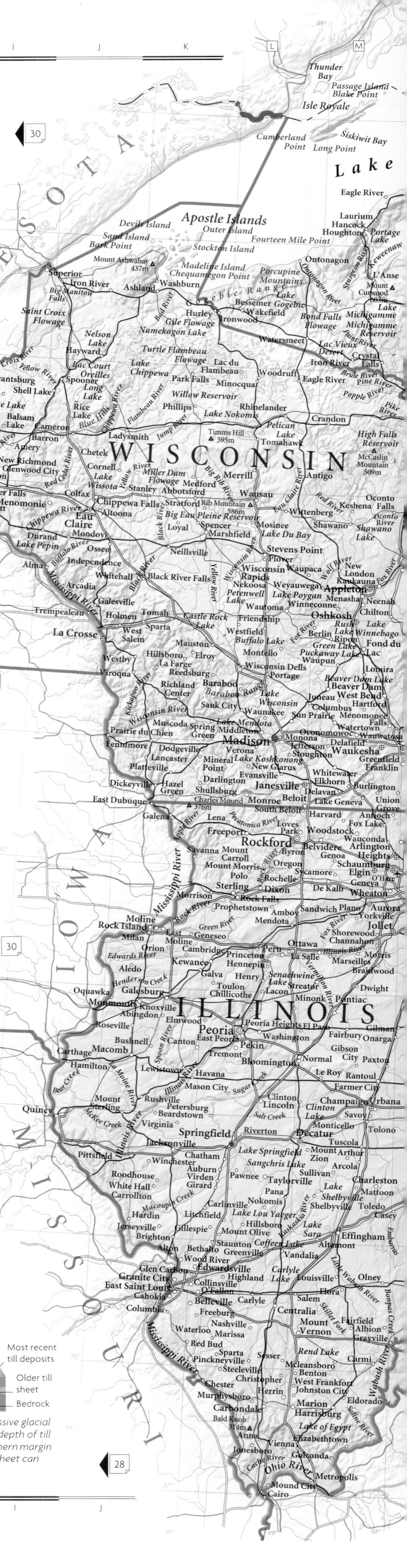

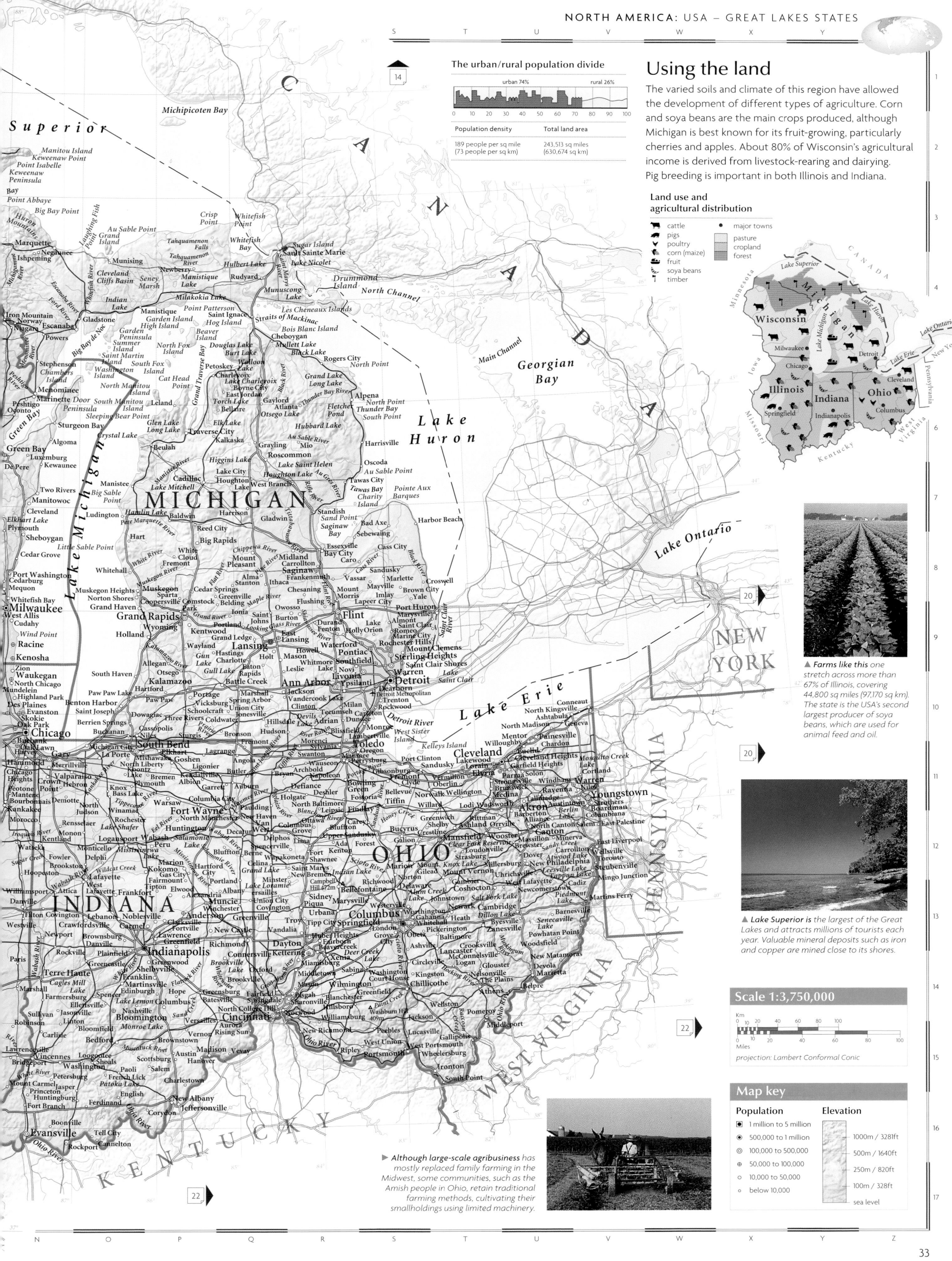

Using the land

The varied soils and climate of this region have allowed the development of different types of agriculture. Corn and soya beans are the main crops produced, although Michigan is best known for its fruit-growing, particularly cherries and apples. About 80% of Wisconsin's agricultural income is derived from livestock-rearing and dairying. Pig breeding is important in both Illinois and Indiana.

The urban/rural population divide

urban 74%   rural 26%

0 10 20 30 40 50 60 70 80 90 100

Population density	Total land area
189 people per sq mile (73 people per sq km)	243,513 sq miles (630,674 sq km)

Land use and agricultural distribution

- cattle
- pigs
- poultry
- corn (maize)
- fruit
- soya beans
- timber
- major towns
- pasture
- cropland
- forest

▲ Farms like this one stretch across more than 67% of Illinois, covering 44,800 sq miles (97,170 sq km). The state is the USA's second largest producer of soya beans, which are used for animal feed and oil.

▲ Lake Superior is the largest of the Great Lakes and attracts millions of tourists each year. Valuable mineral deposits such as iron and copper are mined close to its shores.

Scale 1:3,750,000

Km
0 20 40 60 80 100

Miles
0 20 40 60 80 100

projection: Lambert Conformal Conic

Map key

Population
- 1 million to 5 million
- 500,000 to 1 million
- 100,000 to 500,000
- 50,000 to 100,000
- 10,000 to 50,000
- below 10,000

Elevation
- 1000m / 3281ft
- 500m / 1640ft
- 250m / 820ft
- 100m / 328ft
- sea level

▶ Although large-scale agribusiness has mostly replaced family farming in the Midwest, some communities, such as the Amish people in Ohio, retain traditional farming methods, cultivating their smallholdings using limited machinery.

USA: NORTH MOUNTAIN STATES

Idaho, Montana, Oregon, Washington, Wyoming

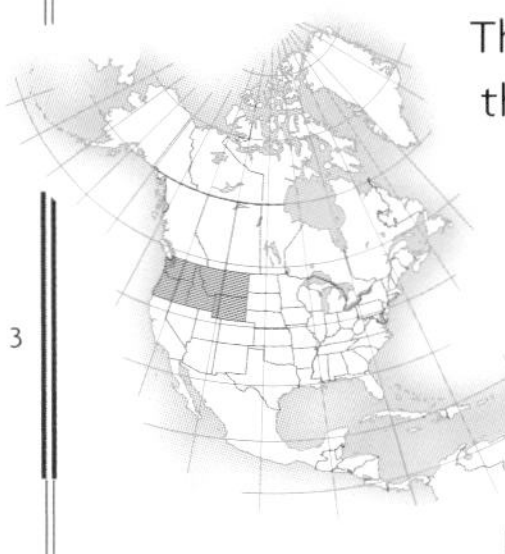

The remoteness of the northwestern states, coupled with the rugged landscape, ensured that this was one of the last areas settled by Europeans in the 19th century. Fur-trappers and gold-prospectors followed the Snake River westwards as it wound its way through the Rocky Mountains. The states of the northwest have pioneered many conservationist policies, with the USA's first national park opened at Yellowstone in 1872. More recently, the Cascades and Rocky Mountains have become havens for adventure tourism. The mountains still serve to isolate the western seaboard from the rest of the continent. This isolation has encouraged west coast cities to expand their trade links with countries of the Pacific Rim.

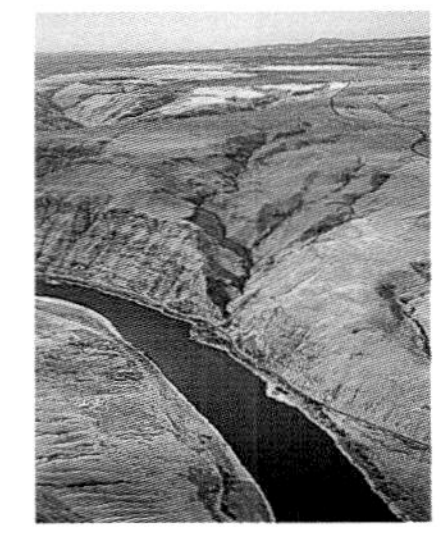

▲ **The Snake River** has cut down into the basalt of the Columbia Basin to form Hells Canyon, the deepest in the USA, with cliffs up to 7900 ft (2408 m) high.

Map key

Population
- ◉ 500,000 to 1 million
- ◎ 100,000 to 500,000
- ⊕ 50,000 to 100,000
- ○ 10,000 to 50,000
- ○ below 10,000

Elevation
- 4000m / 13,124ft
- 3000m / 9843ft
- 2000m / 6562ft
- 1000m / 3281ft
- 500m / 1640ft
- 250m / 820ft
- 100m / 328ft
- sea level

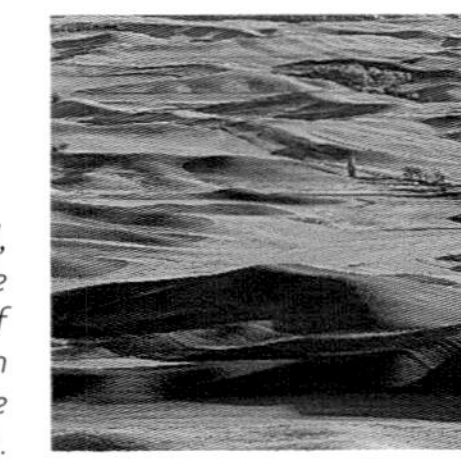

▶ **Fine-textured, volcanic soils** in the hilly Palouse region of eastern Washington are susceptible to erosion.

Using the land

Wheat farming in the east gives way to cattle ranching as rainfall decreases. Irrigated farming in the Snake River valley produces large yields of potatoes and other vegetables. Dairying and fruit-growing take place in the wet western lowlands between the mountain ranges.

The urban/rural population divide

urban 74%   rural 26%

0 10 20 30 40 50 60 70 80 90 100

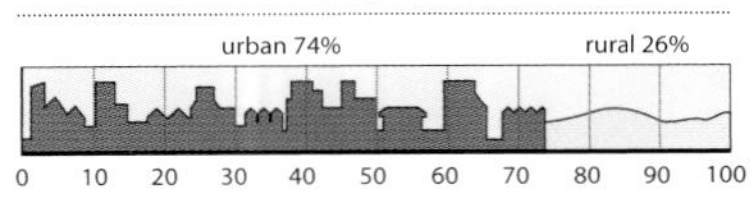

Population density	Total land area
26 people per sq mile (10 people per sq km)	487,970 sq miles (1,263,716 sq km)

Scale 1:3,750,000

Km
0 20 40 60 80 100
Miles
0 10 20 40 60 80 100

projection: Lambert Conformal Conic

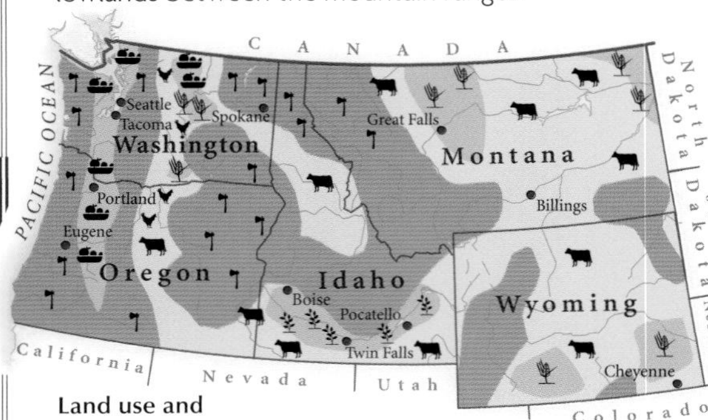

Land use and agricultural distribution

- cattle
- poultry
- cereals
- fruit
- potatoes
- timber
- major towns
- pasture
- cropland
- forest

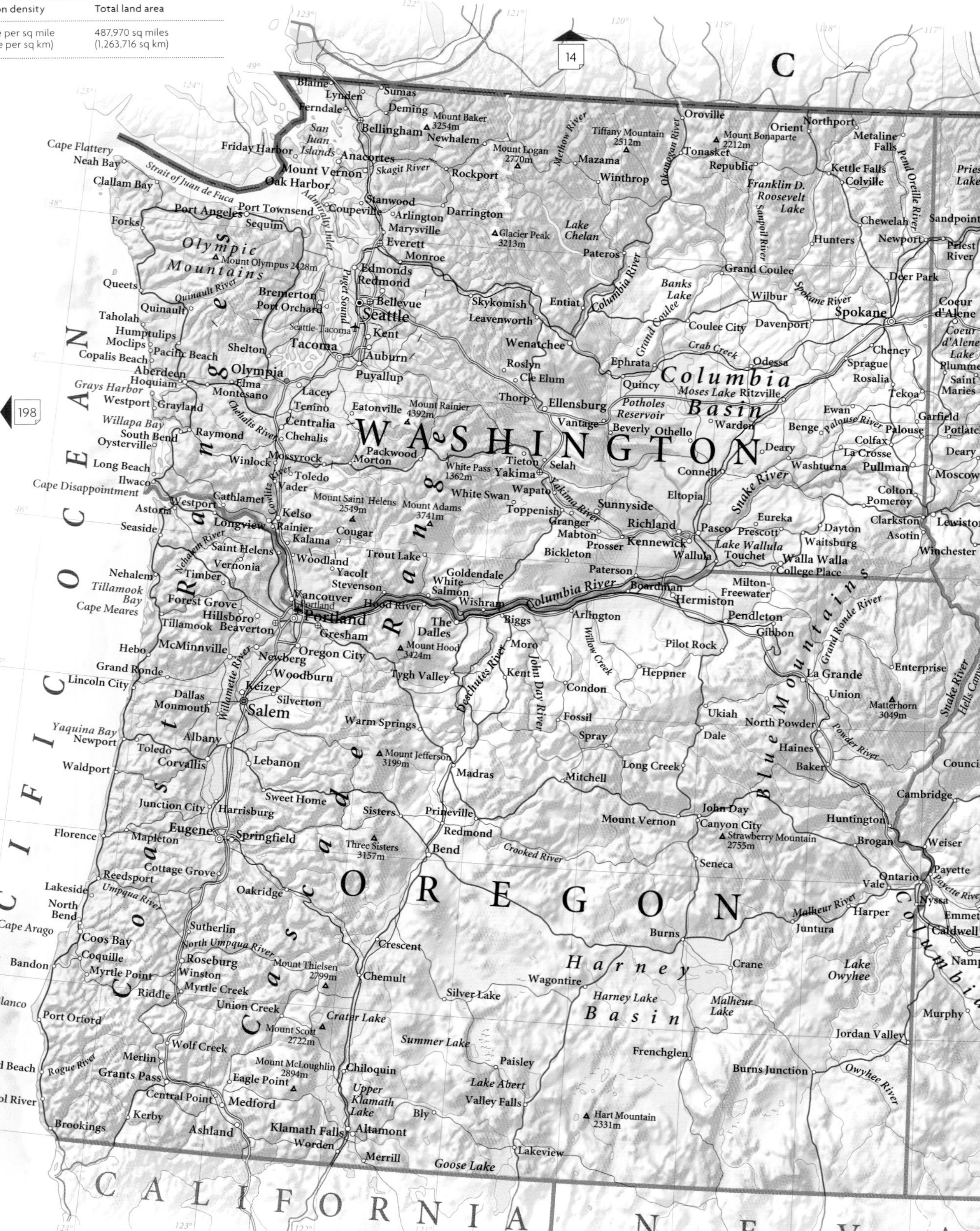

Transport and industry

Minerals and timber are extremely important in this region. Uranium, precious metals, copper and coal are all mined, the latter in vast open-cast pits in Wyoming; oil and natural gas are extracted further north. Manufacturing, notably related to the aerospace and electronics industries, is important in western cities.

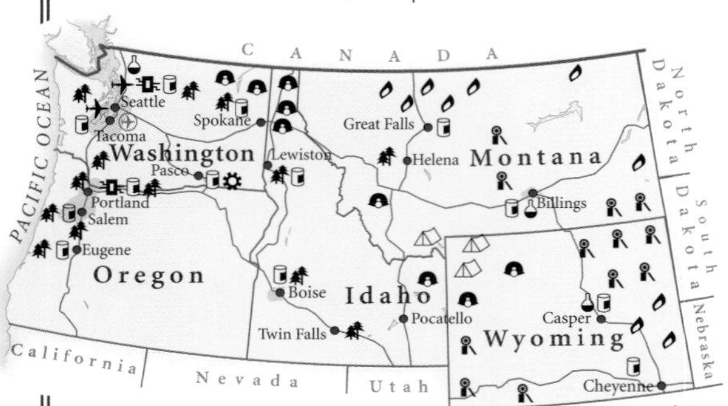

The transport network

- 347,857 miles (556,571 km)
- 4200 miles (6720 km)
- 12,354 miles (19,766 km)
- 1108 miles (1782 km)

Major industry and infrastructure

- adventure tourism
- aerospace
- coal
- chemicals
- electronics
- food processing
- mining
- oil & gas
- timber processing
- major towns
- international airports
- major roads
- major industrial areas

The Union Pacific Railroad has been in service across Wyoming since 1867. The route through the Rocky Mountains is now shared with the Interstate 80, a major east–west highway.

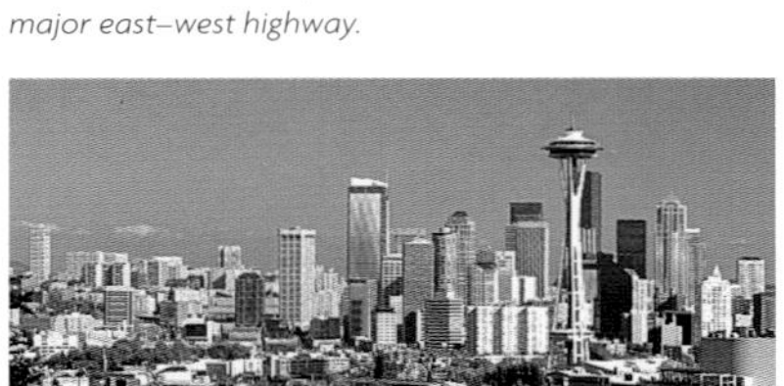

◀ **Seattle lies in** one of Puget Sound's many inlets. The city receives oil and other resources from Alaska, and benefits from expanding trade across the Pacific.

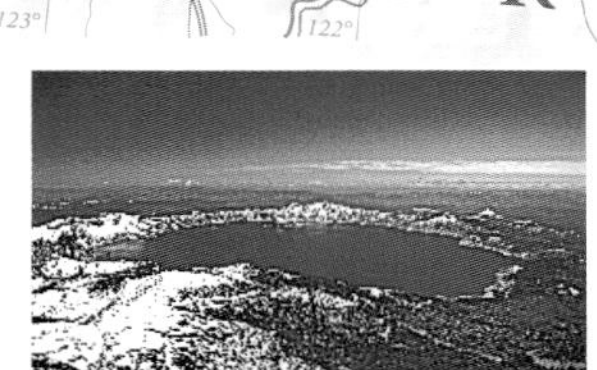

◀ **Crater Lake, Oregon,** is 6 miles (10 km) wide and 1800 ft (600 m) deep. It marks the site of a volcanic cone, which collapsed after an eruption within the last 7000 years.

The landscape

The Rocky Mountains are flanked by lower parallel ranges, which spread onto the Great Plains in the east and surmount the broad lava plateau which extends westwards. The Cascade Range divides the Columbia Basin from the coastlands, where the low areas skirting Puget Sound are broken by the steep, volcanic Olympic Mountains and the wooded hills of the Coast Ranges.

Molten rock cools, forming parallel columns

Surrounding strata eroded away

Molten rock wells up from the Earth's core

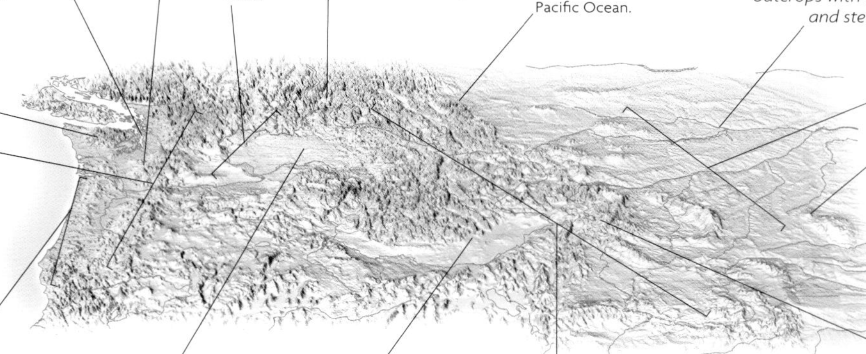

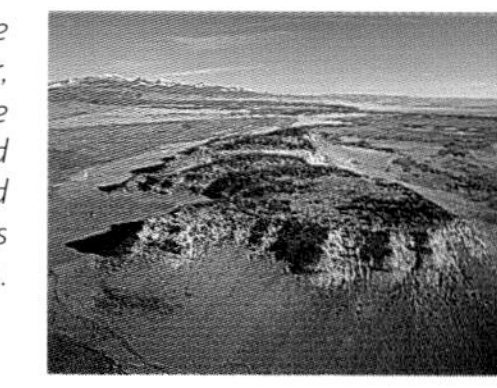

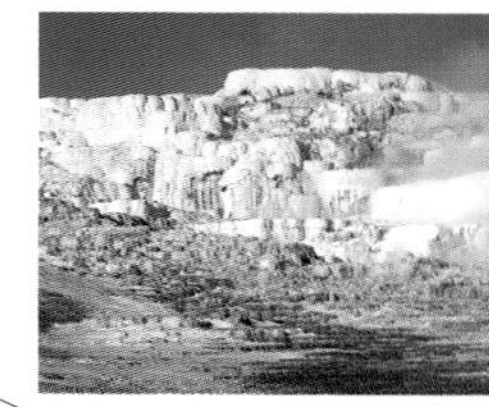

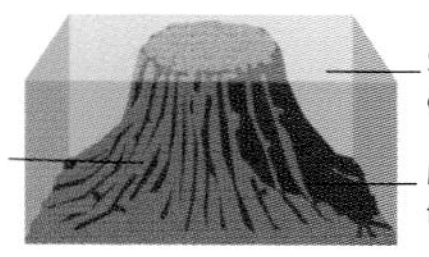

▲ *Devil's Tower in Wyoming* is an igneous intrusion, formed below the Earth's surface. Molten rock intruded through cracks in the overlying strata and cooled. Over time, the softer rock layers have been eroded away, leaving only the tower standing.

Puget Sound

Mount St Helens erupted in 1980, killing 57 people and devastating a huge area.

Columbia Basin

Grand Coulee and the lesser *coulées* (ravines) were cut by cataclysmic floods, from the release of an ice-dammed lake, at the end of the last Ice Age.

The Continental Divide, or watershed, crosses the Lewis Range. From here, rivers flow east to Hudson Bay, south to the Gulf of Mexico and west to the Pacific Ocean.

▶ *Piney Buttes are* the remnants of an older, higher land surface gradually weathered and eroded into isolated outcrops with flat tops and steep sides.

Glacial valleys on the seaward side of the Olympic Mountains receive about 142 inches (3600 mm) of rain per year, supporting the only true rainforest of the northern hemisphere.

The Cascades are glacially scoured volcanic mountains, the highest of which is Mount Rainier, a dormant volcano at 14,409 ft (4392 m).

Coast Ranges

Great Plains

Devil's Tower

Rocky Mountains

The plateaux of the Columbia and Snake rivers represent one of the world's largest accumulations of lava. Over 5 million years ago, successive flows of molten basalt buried the existing land surface by up to 450 ft (150 m).

The contorted rock shapes at 'Craters of the Moon' National Monument in Idaho were left 2000 years ago by the sporadic upwelling of viscous lava from fissures in the basalt plateau.

▲ *Water from the* hot springs in Yellowstone National Park deposits minerals as it cools in rock pools. Long periods of deposition have created these rock terraces.

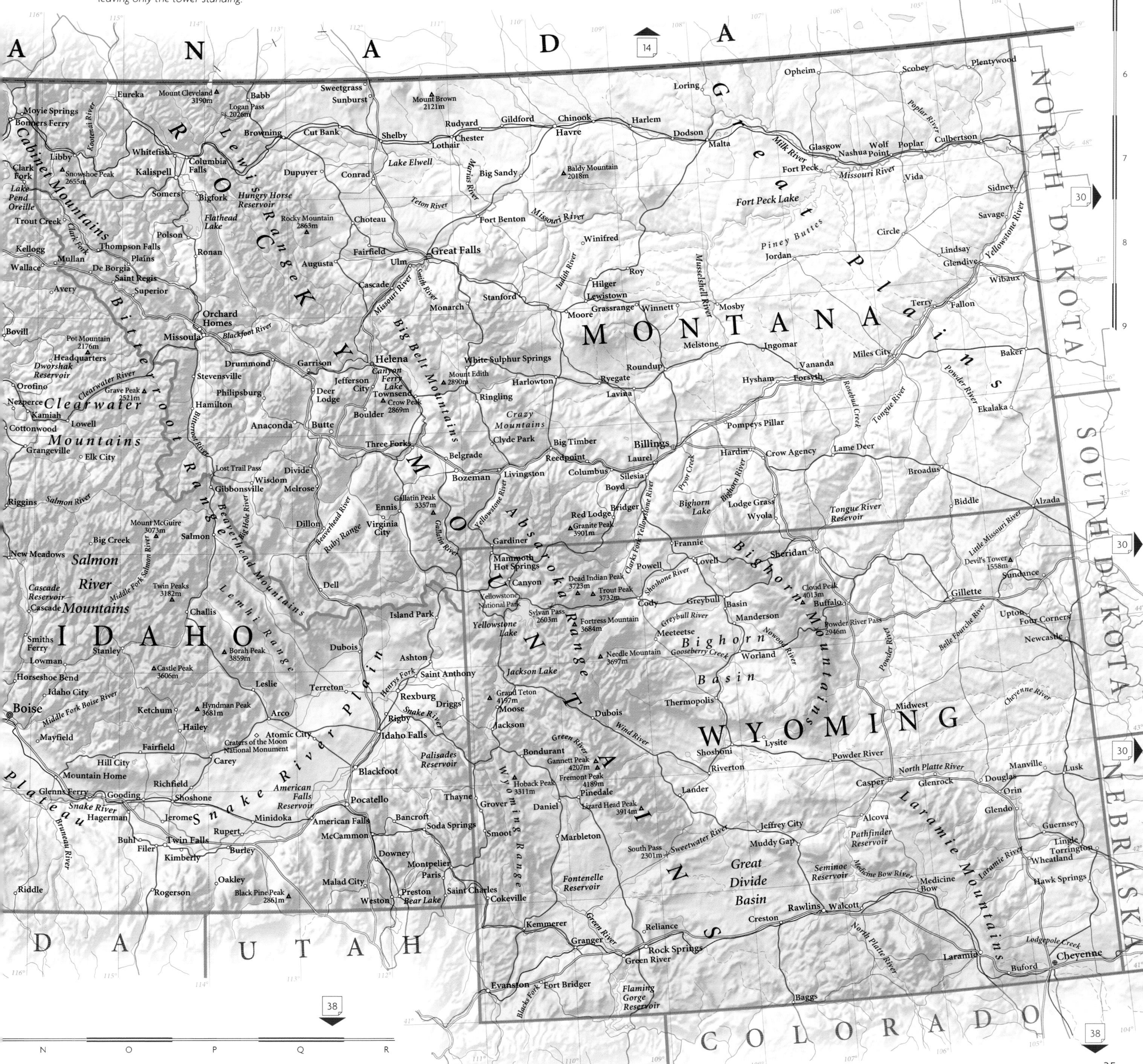

A B C D E F G H I J

USA: CALIFORNIA & NEVADA

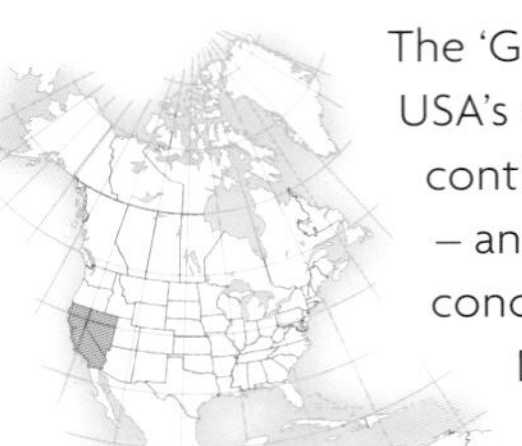

The 'Gold Rush' of 1849 attracted the first major wave of European settlers to the USA's west coast. The pleasant climate, beautiful scenery and dynamic economy continue to attract immigrants – despite the ever-present danger of earthquakes – and California has become the USA's most populous state. The population is concentrated in the vast conurbations of Los Angeles, San Francisco and San Diego; new immigrants include people from South Korea, the Philippines, Vietnam and Mexico. Nevada's arid lands were initially exploited for minerals; in recent years, revenue from mining has been superseded by income from the tourist and gambling centres of Las Vegas and Reno.

Map key

Population

- ◉ 1 million to 5 million
- ◉ 500,000 to 1 million
- ◉ 100,000 to 500,000
- ⊕ 50,000 to 100,000
- ○ 10,000 to 50,000
- ○ below 10,000

Elevation

- 4000m / 13,124ft
- 3000m / 9843ft
- 2000m / 6562ft
- 1000m / 3281ft
- 500m / 1640ft
- 250m / 820ft
- 100m / 328ft
- sea level

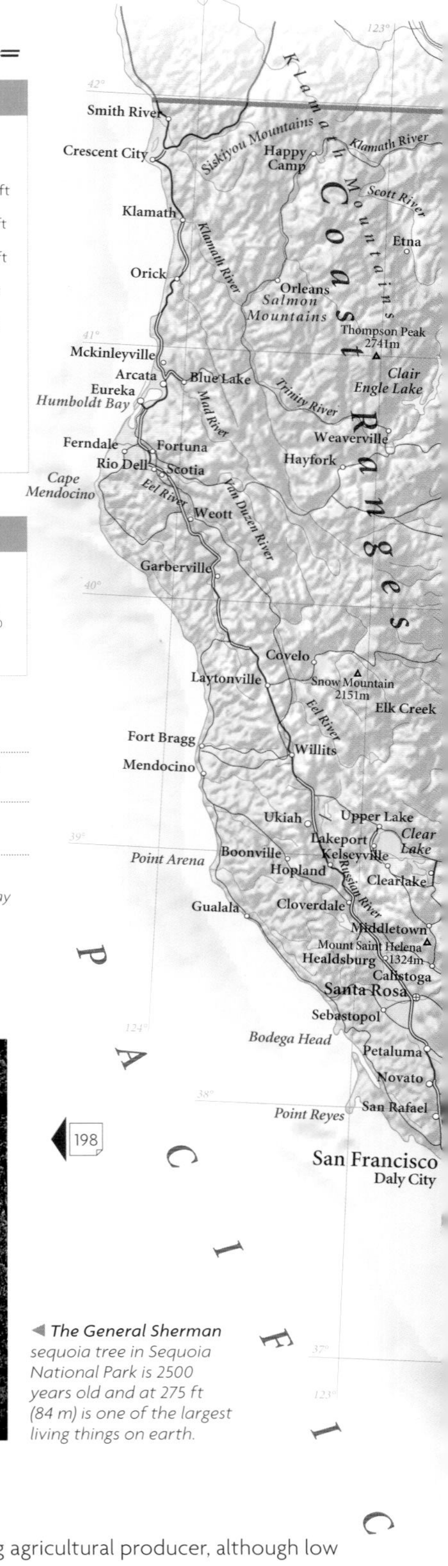

Transport and industry

Nevada's rich mineral reserves ushered in a period of mining wealth which has now been replaced by revenue generated from gambling. California supports a broad set of activities including defence-related industries and research and development facilities. 'Silicon Valley', near San Francisco, is a world leading centre for micro-electronics, while tourism and the Los Angeles film industry also generate large incomes.

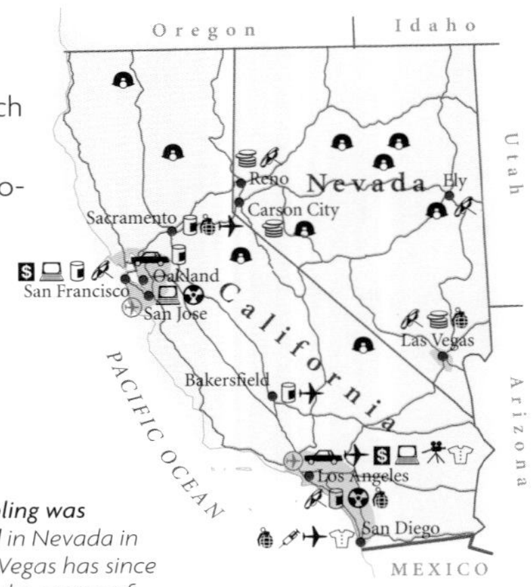

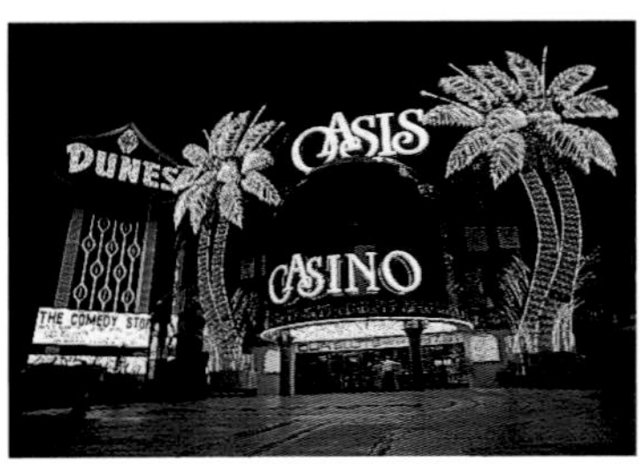

◀ *Gambling was legalized in Nevada in 1931. Las Vegas has since become the centre of this multi-million dollar industry.*

Major industry and infrastructure

- ✈ aerospace
- 🚗 car manufacture
- 🛡 defence
- Ⓢ film industry
- $ finance
- 🍴 food processing
- 🎲 gambling
- 💻 hi-tech industry
- ⛏ mining
- ☢ pharmaceuticals
- ☢ research & development
- ⊤ textiles
- 🏖 tourism
- • major towns
- ⊕ international airports
- ▬ major roads
- ▨ major industrial areas

Scale 1:3,000,000

Km
0 5 10 20 30 40 50 60 70 80

Miles
0 5 10 20 30 40 50 60 70 80

projection: Lambert Conformal Conic

The transport network

🛣 211,459 miles (338,334 km)		🛣 2944 miles (4710 km)
🚆 7822 miles (12,595 km)		🚆 190 miles (360 km)

In California, the motor vehicle is a vital part of daily life, and an extensive freeway system runs throughout the state, cementing its position as the most important mode of transport

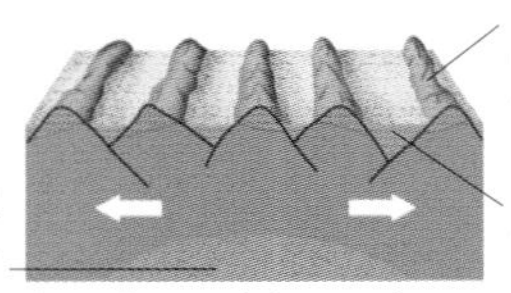

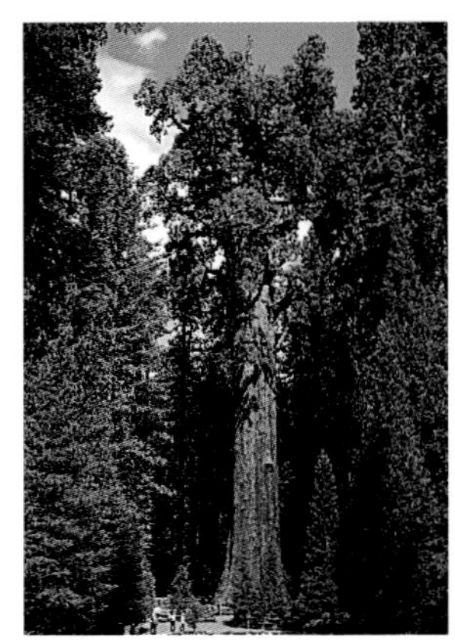

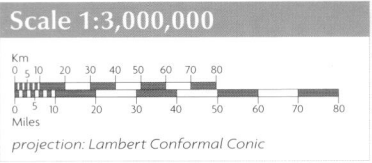

◀ *The General Sherman sequoia tree in Sequoia National Park is 2500 years old and at 275 ft (84 m) is one of the largest living things on earth.*

The landscape

The broad Central Valley divides California's coastal mountains from the Sierra Nevada. The San Andreas Fault, running beneath much of the state, is the site of frequent earth tremors and sometimes more serious earthquakes. East of the Sierra Nevada, the landscape is characterized by the basin and range topography with stony deserts and many salt lakes.

Rising molten rock causes stretching of the Earth's crust

Extensive cracking (faulting) uplifted a series of ridges

As ridges are eroded they fill intervening valleys with sediments

▲ *Molten rock (magma) welling up to form a dome in the Earth's interior, causes the brittle surface rocks to stretch and crack. Some areas were uplifted to form mountains (ranges), while others sunk to form flat valleys (basins).*

Most of California's agriculture is confined to the fertile and extensively irrigated Central Valley, running between the Coast Ranges and the Sierra Nevada. It incorporates the San Joaquin and Sacramento valleys.

The dramatic granitic rock formations of Half Dome and El Capitan, and the verdant coniferous forests, attract millions of visitors annually to Yosemite National Park in the Sierra Nevada.

Sierra Nevada

The Great Basin dominates most of Nevada's topography containing large open basins, punctuated by eroded features such as *buttes* and *mesas*. River flow tends to be seasonal, dependent upon spring showers and winter snow melt.

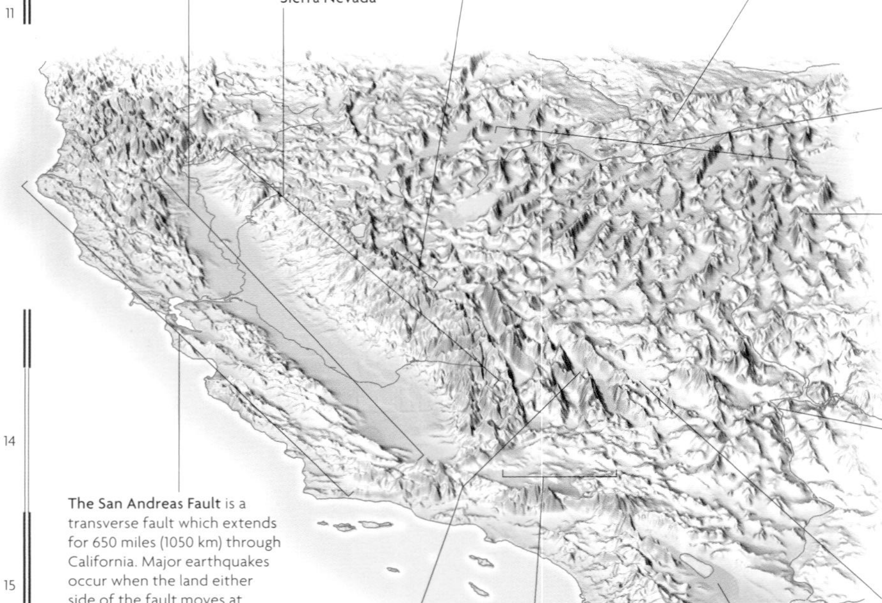

Wheeler Peak is home to some of the world's oldest trees, bristlecone pines, which live for up to 5000 years.

Using the land

California is the USA's leading agricultural producer, although low rainfall makes irrigation essential. The long growing season and abundant sunshine allow many crops to be grown in the fertile Central Valley including grapes, citrus fruits, vegetables and cotton. Almost 17 million acres (6.8 million hectares) of California's forests are used commercially. Nevada's arid climate and poor soil are largely unsuitable for agriculture; 85% of its land is state owned and large areas are used for underground testing of nuclear weapons.

Land use and agricultural distribution

- 🐄 cattle
- 🍊 citrus fruits
- 🍎 fruit
- 🌾 irrigation
- 🌲 timber
- 🍇 vineyards
- • major towns
- pasture
- cropland
- forest
- desert

When the Hoover Dam across the Colorado River was completed in 1936, it created Lake Mead, one of the largest artificial lakes in the world, extending for 115 miles (285 km) upstream.

The San Andreas Fault is a transverse fault which extends for 650 miles (1050 km) through California. Major earthquakes occur when the land either side of the fault moves at different rates. San Francisco was devastated by an earthquake in 1906.

Death Valley

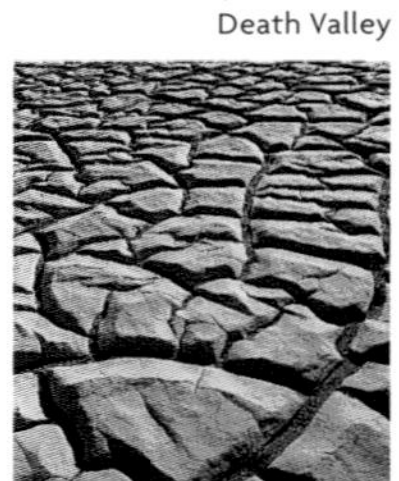

▶ *Named by migrating settlers in 1849, Death Valley is the driest, hottest place in North America, as well as being the lowest point on land in the western hemisphere, at 282 ft (86 m) below sea level.*

The sparsely populated Mojave Desert receives less than 8 inches (200 mm) of rainfall a year. It is used extensively for weapons-testing and military purposes.

The Salton Sea was created accidentally between 1905 and 1907 when an irrigation channel from the Colorado River broke out of its banks and formed this salty 300 sq mile (777 sq km), land-locked lake.

Amargosa Desert

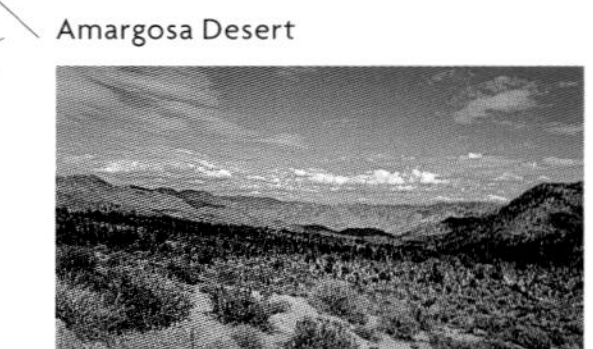

▲ *The Sierra Nevada create a 'rainshadow', preventing rain from reaching much of Nevada. Pacific air masses, passing over the mountains, are stripped of their moisture.*

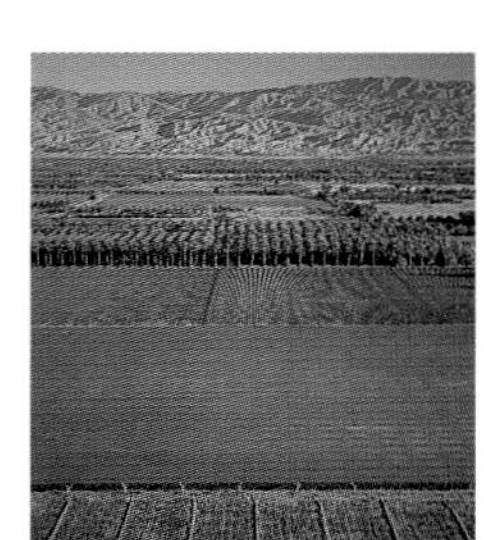

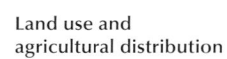

▲ *Without considerable irrigation, this fertile valley at Palm Springs would still be part of the Sonoran Desert. California's farmers account for about 80% of the state's total water usage.*

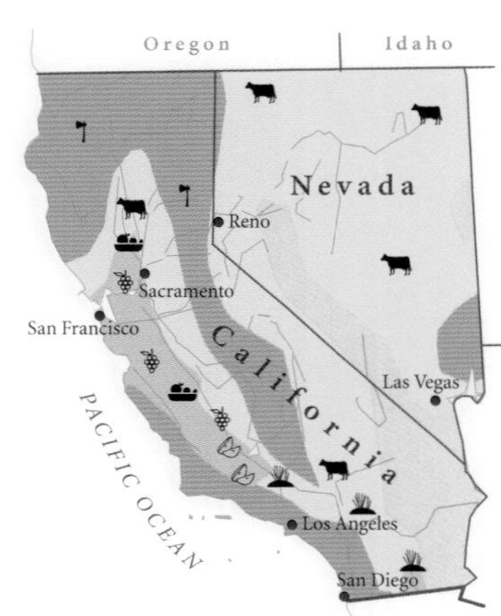

The urban/rural population divide

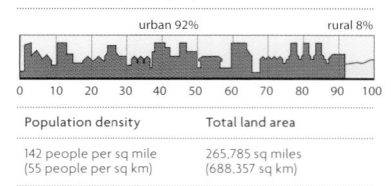

urban 92%   rural 8%

0 10 20 30 40 50 60 70 80 90 100

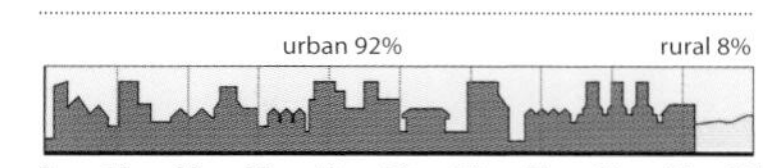

Population density	Total land area
142 people per sq mile (55 people per sq km)	265,785 sq miles (688,357 sq km)

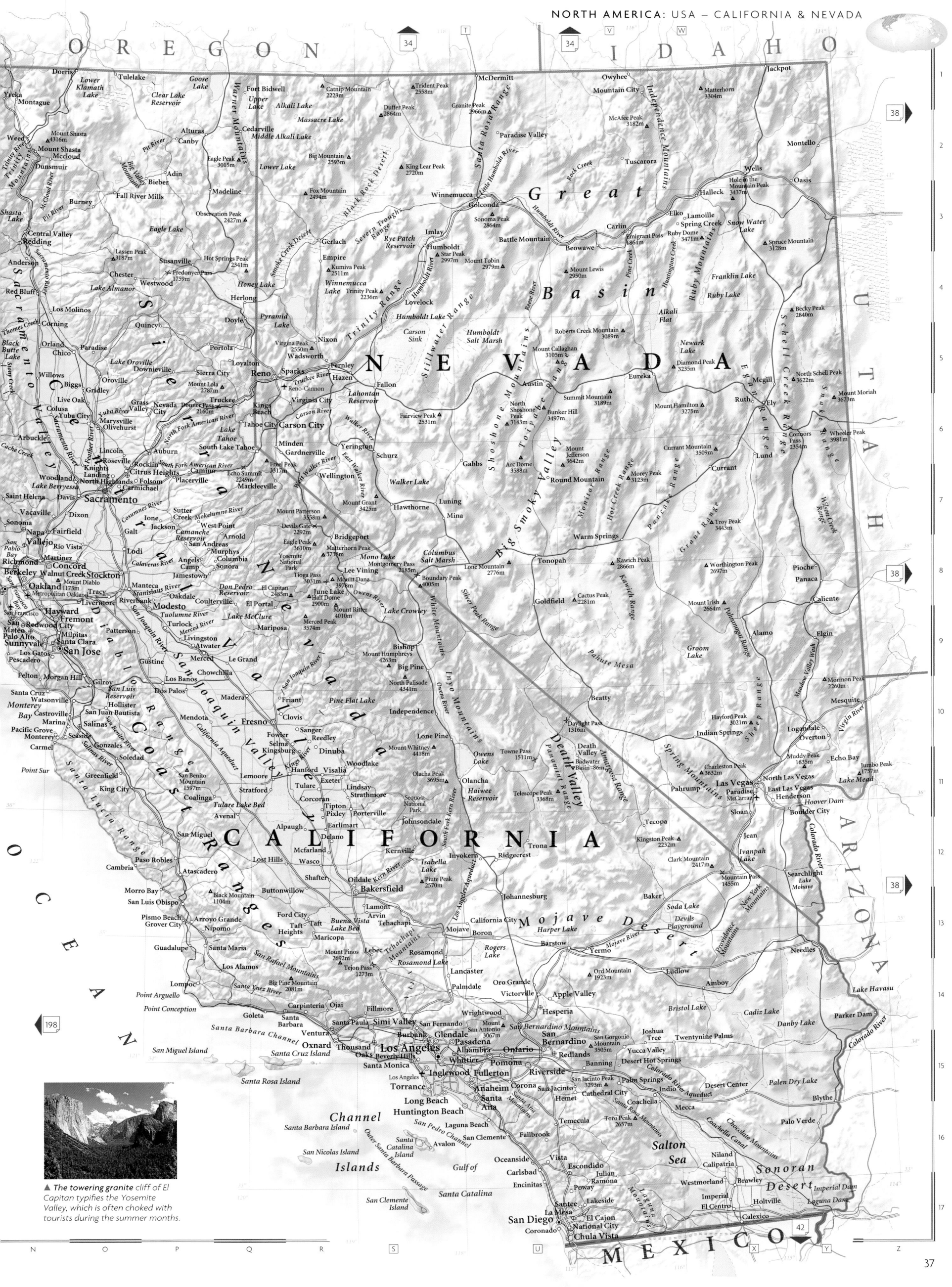

▲ **The towering granite** cliff of El Capitan typifies the Yosemite Valley, which is often choked with tourists during the summer months.

USA: SOUTH MOUNTAIN STATES

Arizona, Colorado, New Mexico, Utah

This arid region, characterized by expansive plateaux and spectacular canyons is home to several distinct peoples. The ruins of cliff dwellings built a thousand years ago by the Anasazi people still exist today, and native Americans own one-third of the land in Arizona. Spanish and Mexican conquest and settlement left a hispanic presence which is strongest in New Mexico. The Mormons, who came to the Great Salt Lake seeking religious freedom in 1847, were among the earliest Anglo-American settlers and now make up over 70% of Utah's population. The region's mineral wealth drove rapid development in the 20th century, yet the constraints of a fragile environment, including widespread water shortages, may limit prospects for growth.

The landscape

The arid, rocky expanse of the Colorado Plateau is dissected by immense canyons of the Colorado River. Desert lies to the north and south and branches of the Rocky Mountains run to the east and west. The Great Salt Lake and Desert lie within the Great Basin, a barren region of parallel mountain ranges which extends into Arizona.

When water evaporates it leaves a salt pan

Mudflats

Lake is fed by seasonal snow melt

Water level of lake varies according to quantity of run-off received from snow melt

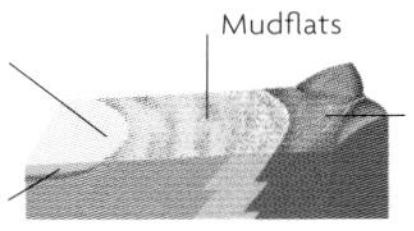

▲ *The Great Salt Lake is an ephemeral lake; it can remain dry for extended periods, leaving a pan of evaporated mineral salts in its centre.*

Over 13 million years of weathering has created thousands of spires and pinnacles from the alternating rock strata of Bryce Canyon.

The parallel basins and ridges, which run north-south along the Great Basin, reflect a major series of block-faults in the underlying bedrock.

Parts of the Grand Canyon, which cuts through the Colorado Plateau, are 16 miles (25 km) wide. The Colorado River has cut down 6262 ft (2000 m), exposing rock strata more than 2 billion years old.

Lake Powell

The Rio Grande has its source in several meltwater streams, which have cut deep valleys into the platform of the San Juan Mountains.

Sand dunes, 600 ft (180 m) high, have been deposited in San Luis Valley, by winds funnelled through the San Juan and Sangre de Cristo mountains in the Rockies.

Rainbow Bridge is the world's largest natural arch. The 309 ft (94 m) span probably began to grow when the sandstone spur of a meandering creek was breached during a flash flood.

The striking colour effects seen in the Painted Desert come from minerals such as gypsum and haematite, combined with ambient heat and dust.

Shifting gypsum sands produce a constantly changing land surface, overwhelming plants and any other obstacles in Tularosa Valley.

Petrified Forest

Carlsbad Caverns

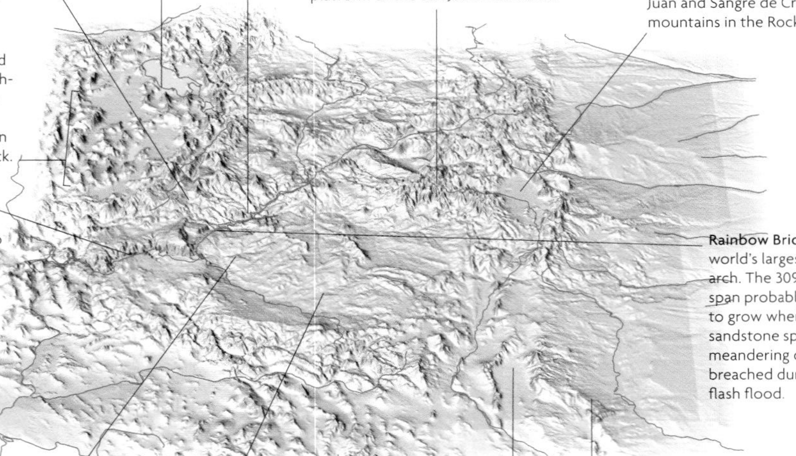

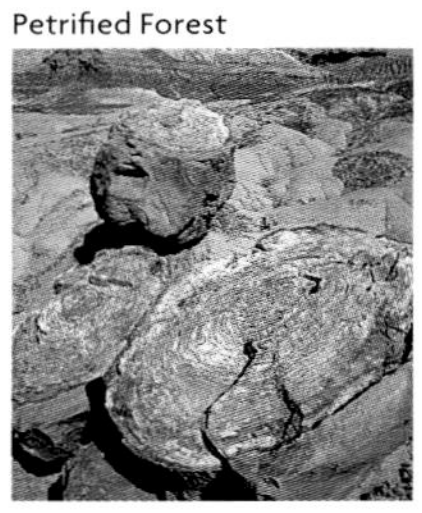

▶ *In the arid landscape of Petrified Forest National Park in Arizona, the grain of prehistoric trees has been preserved as a fossil imprint in the rocks. The bog-preserved trees were gradually turned to stone by seeping mineral-rich water.*

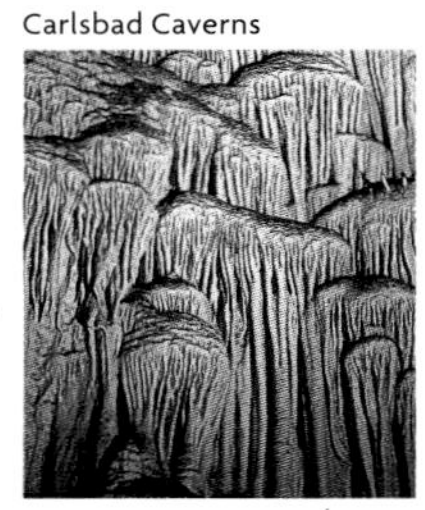

▶ *The intricate stalactites of Carlsbad Caverns have grown with the seepage of calcium-rich water, over the last 100,000 years. The huge caves are home to around 100,000 Mexican freetail bats.*

Transport and industry

New industries have helped reduce the region's dependence on the extraction of minerals and fossil fuels. Precision manufacture has grown rapidly, particularly in Arizona and Colorado. Salt Lake City and Denver are well-established financial centres and New Mexico, the USA's main producer of uranium, is a prominent region for nuclear research. Colorado is the USA's most important centre for winter sports.

The transport network

232,434 miles (373,986 km)		4059 miles (6515 km)
8627 miles (13,881 km)		none

The Colorado Rockies are crossed by 32 mountain passes, some as high as 12,183 ft (3713 m). The Eisenhower Tunnel west of Denver carries Interstate Highway 70 straight through the Continental Divide.

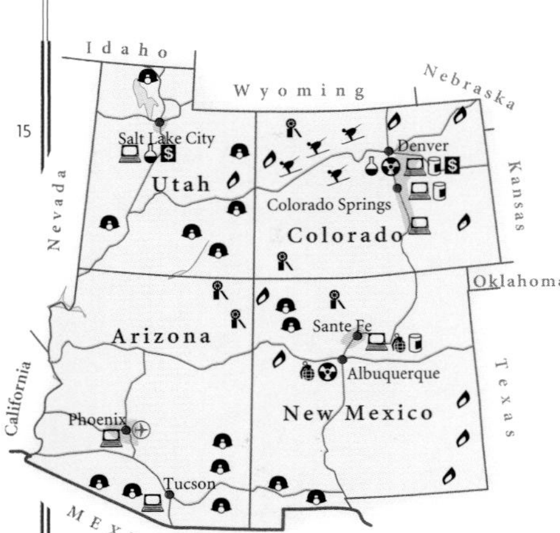

Major industry and infrastructure

- chemicals
- coal
- defence
- finance
- food processing
- hi-tech industry
- oil & gas
- mining
- research & development
- winter sports
- ⊙ major towns
- ⊕ international airports
- major roads
- ▨ major industrial areas

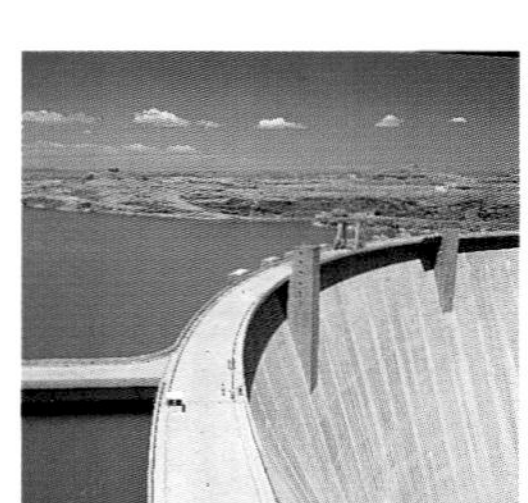

▲ *Glen Canyon Dam on the Colorado river was completed in 1964. It provides hydro-electric power and irrigation water as part of a long-term federal project to harness the river.*

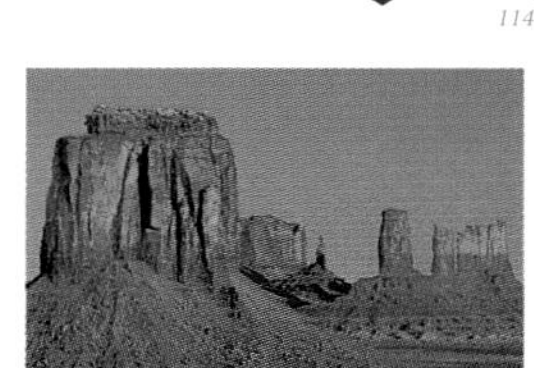

◀ *The flat tablelands (mesas), and the isolated pinnacles (buttes) which rise from the floor of Monument Valley are the resistant remnants of an earlier land surface, gradually cut back by erosion under arid conditions.*

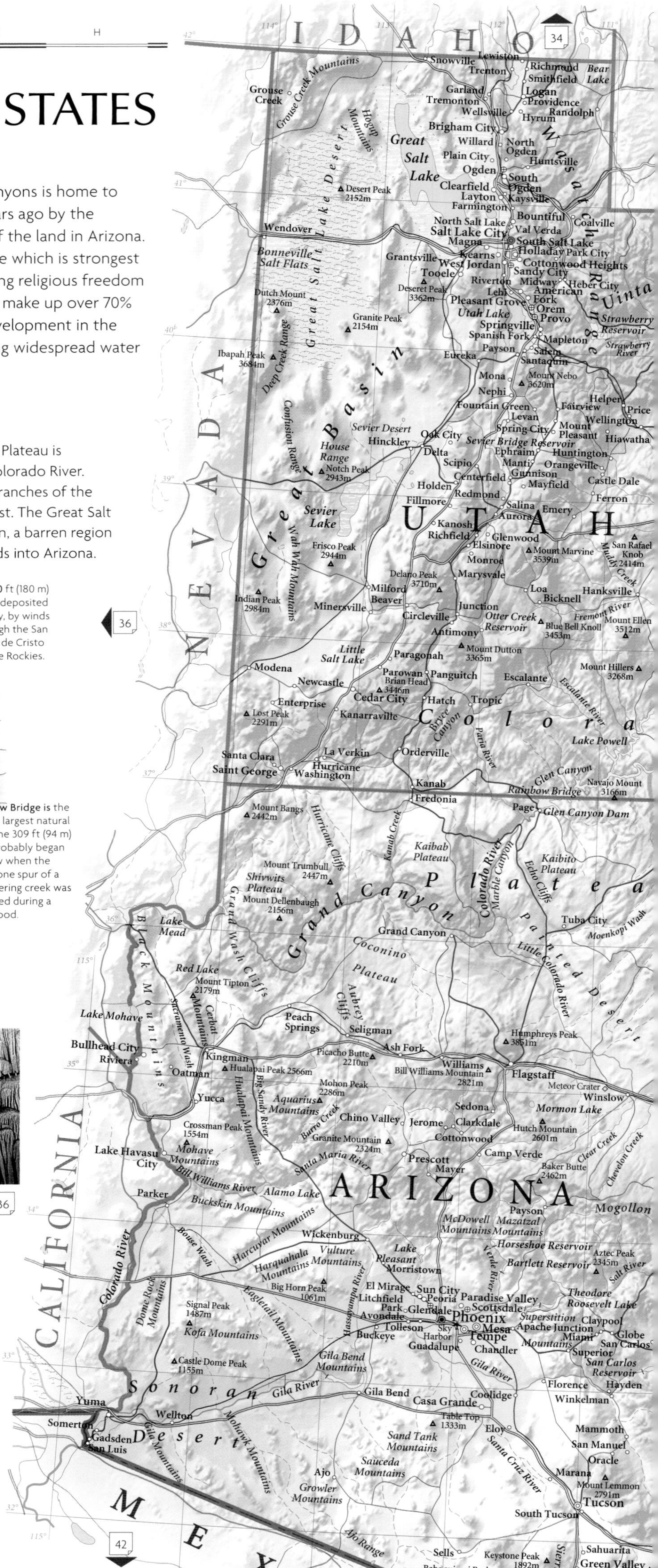

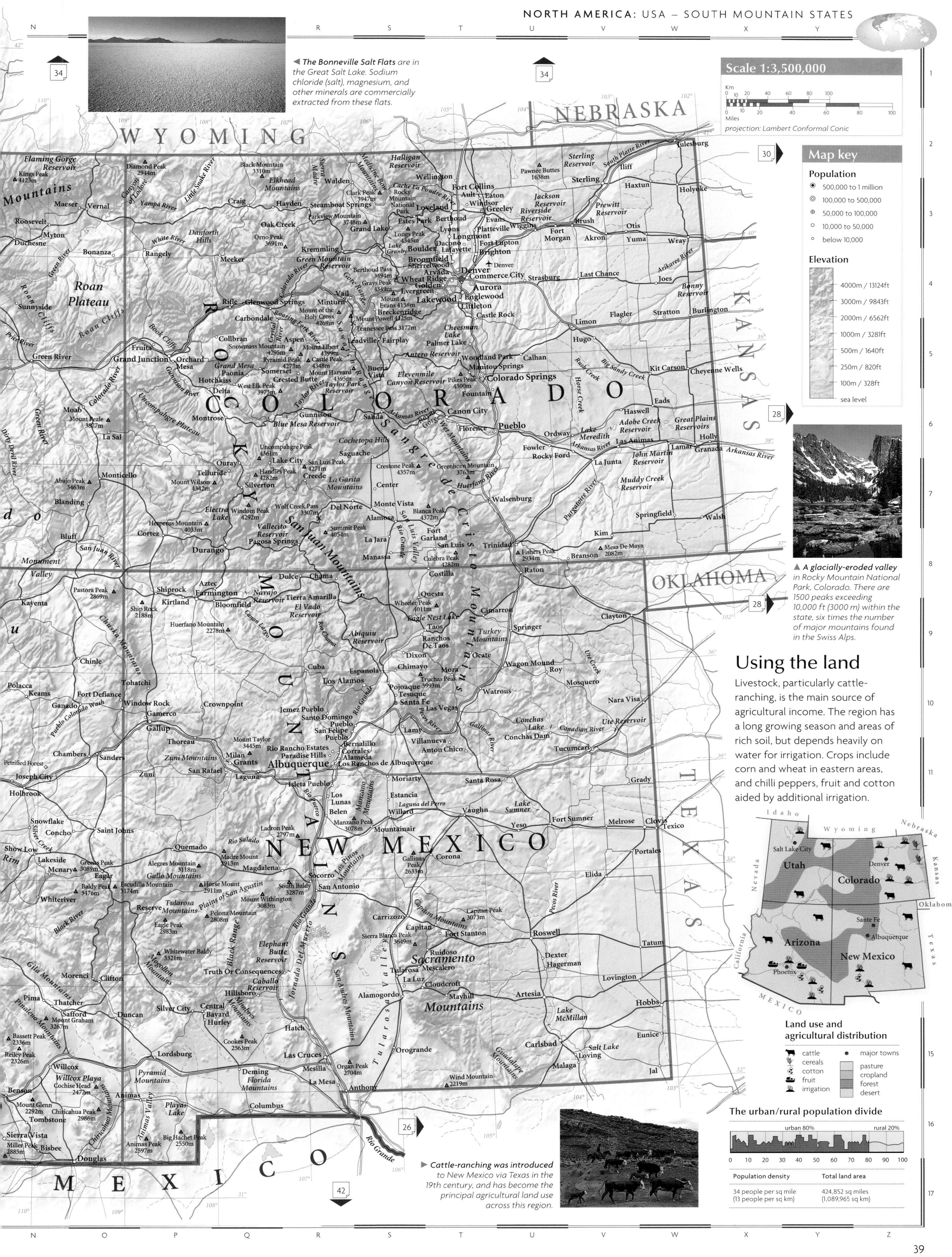

The Bonneville Salt Flats are in the Great Salt Lake. Sodium chloride (salt), magnesium, and other minerals are commercially extracted from these flats.

Scale 1:3,500,000

projection: Lambert Conformal Conic

Map key

Population

- ◉ 500,000 to 1 million
- ◎ 100,000 to 500,000
- ⊕ 50,000 to 100,000
- ○ 10,000 to 50,000
- ○ below 10,000

Elevation

- 4000m / 13124ft
- 3000m / 9843ft
- 2000m / 6562ft
- 1000m / 3281ft
- 500m / 1640ft
- 250m / 820ft
- 100m / 328ft
- sea level

▲ *A glacially-eroded valley* in Rocky Mountain National Park, Colorado. There are 1500 peaks exceeding 10,000 ft (3000 m) within the state, six times the number of major mountains found in the Swiss Alps.

Using the land

Livestock, particularly cattle-ranching, is the main source of agricultural income. The region has a long growing season and areas of rich soil, but depends heavily on water for irrigation. Crops include corn and wheat in eastern areas, and chilli peppers, fruit and cotton aided by additional irrigation.

Land use and agricultural distribution

- cattle
- cereals
- cotton
- fruit
- irrigation
- ● major towns
- pasture
- cropland
- forest
- desert

The urban/rural population divide

urban 80%   rural 20%

0 10 20 30 40 50 60 70 80 90 100

Population density	Total land area
34 people per sq mile (13 people per sq km)	424,852 sq miles (1,089,965 sq km)

▶ *Cattle-ranching* was introduced to New Mexico via Texas in the 19th century, and has become the principal agricultural land use across this region.

USA: HAWAI‘I

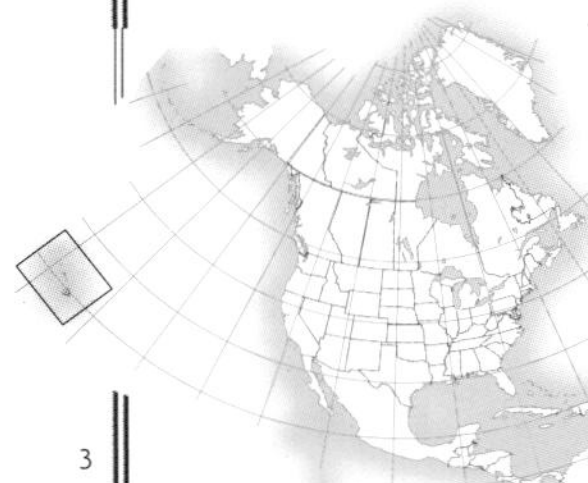

The 122 islands of the Hawaiian archipelago – which are part of Polynesia – are the peaks of the world's largest volcanoes. They rise approximately 6 miles (9.7 km) from the floor of the Pacific Ocean. The largest, the island of Hawai‘i, remains highly active. Hawai‘i became the USA's 50th state in 1959. A tradition of receiving immigrant workers is reflected in the islands' ethnic diversity, with peoples drawn from around the rim of the Pacific. Only 9% of the current population are native Polynesians.

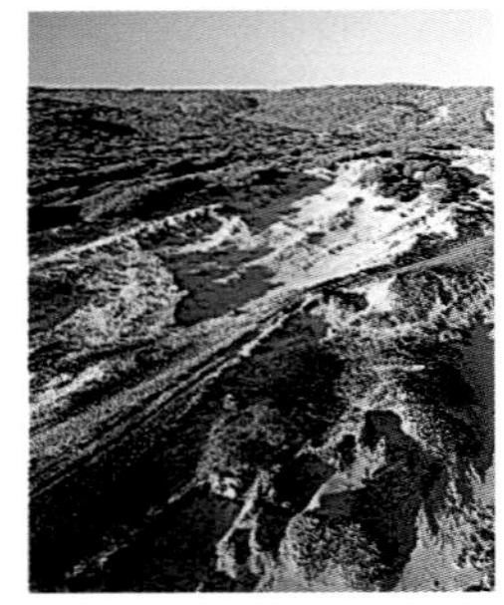

▲ The island of Moloka‘i is formed from volcanic rock. Mature sand dunes cover the rocks in coastal areas.

Transport and industry

Tourism dominates the economy, with over 90% of the population employed in services. The naval base at Pearl Harbor is also a major source of employment. Industry is concentrated on the island of O‘ahu and relies mostly on imported materials, while agricultural produce is processed locally.

The transport network

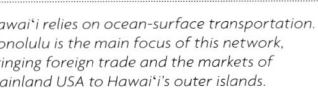

4102 miles (6600 km)	43 miles (69 km)
none	none

Hawai‘i relies on ocean-surface transportation. Honolulu is the main focus of this network, bringing foreign trade and the markets of mainland USA to Hawai‘i's outer islands.

Major industry and infrastructure

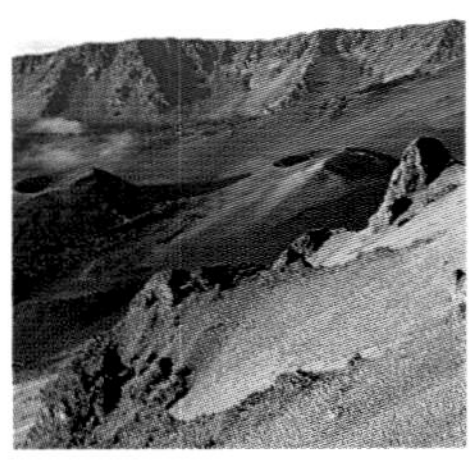

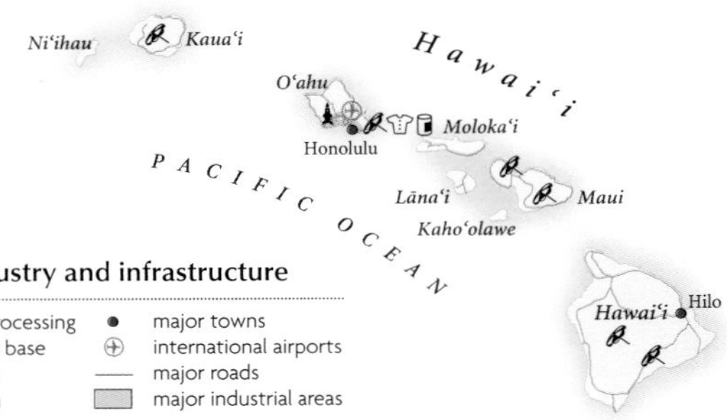

- food processing
- military base
- textiles
- tourism
- major towns
- international airports
- major roads
- major industrial areas

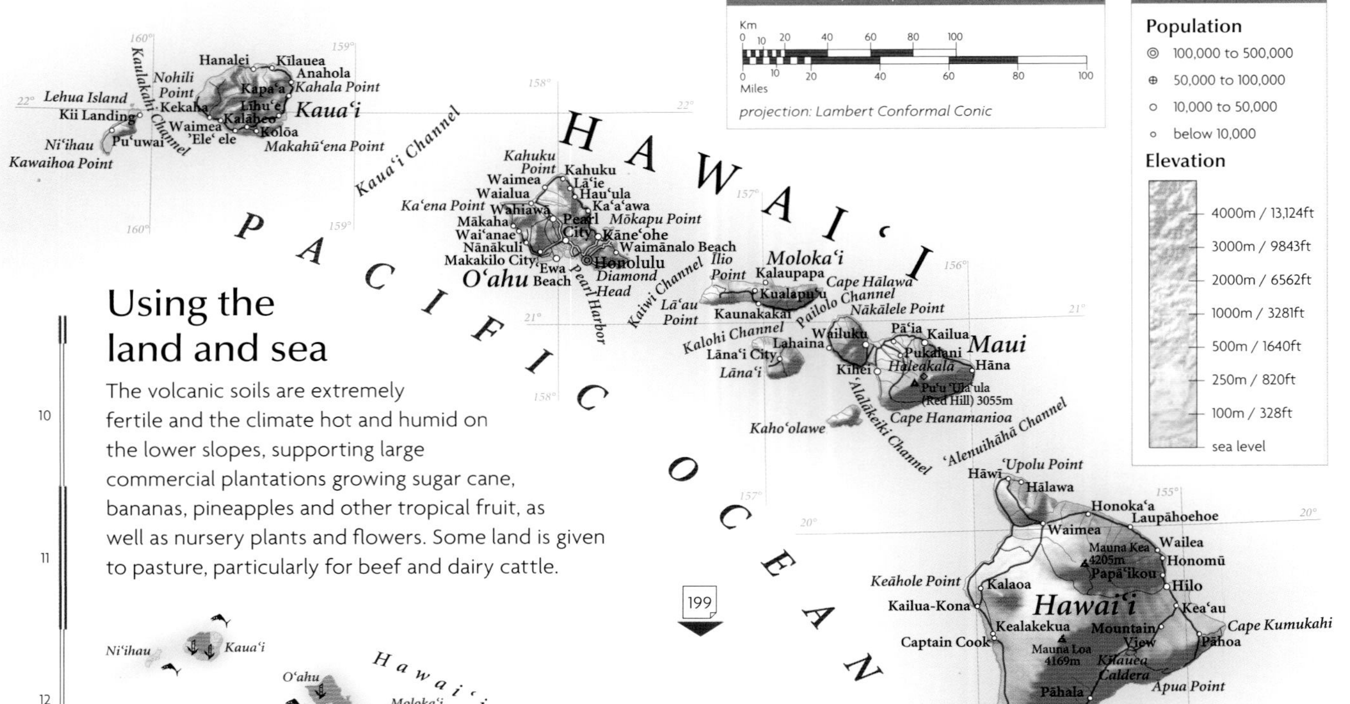

◄ Haleakala's extinct volcanic crater is the world's largest. The giant caldera, containing many secondary cones, is 2000 ft (600 m) deep and 20 miles (32 km) in circumference.

Using the land and sea

The ice-free coastline of Alaska provides access to salmon fisheries and more than 129 million acres (52.2 million ha) of forest. Most of Alaska is uncultivable, and around 90% of food is imported. Barley, hay and hothouse products are grown around Anchorage, where dairy farming is also concentrated.

The urban/rural population divide

urban 68%   rural 32%

0 10 20 30 40 50 60 70 80 90 100

Population density	Total land area
1 person per sq mile (0.4 people per sq km)	571,951 sq miles (1,481,296 sq km)

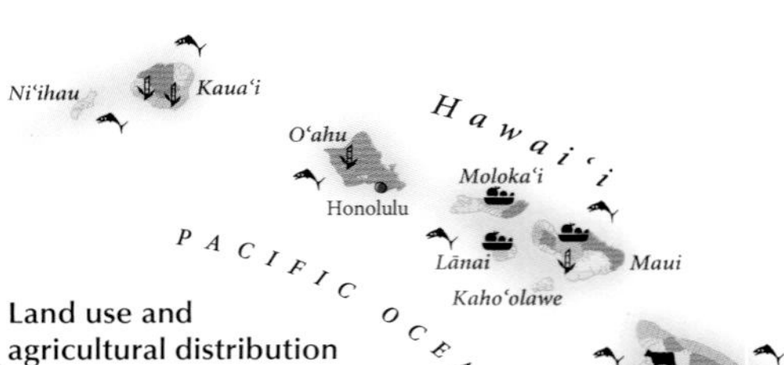

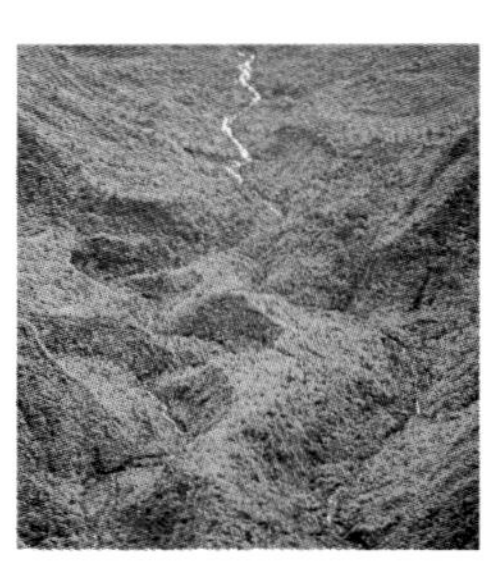

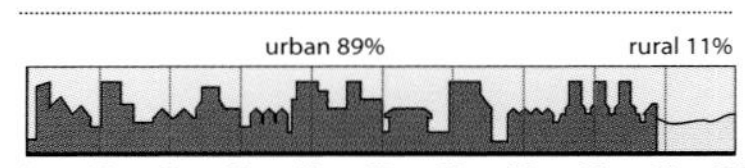

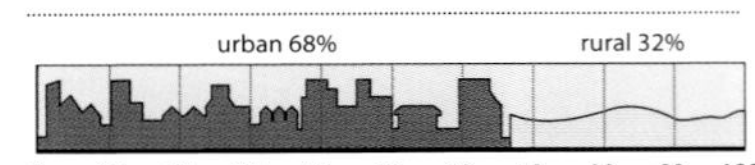

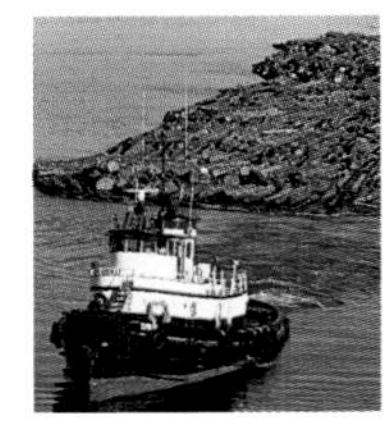

◄ A raft of timber from the Tongass forest is hauled by a tug, bound for the pulp mills of the Alaskan coast between Juneau and Ketchikan.

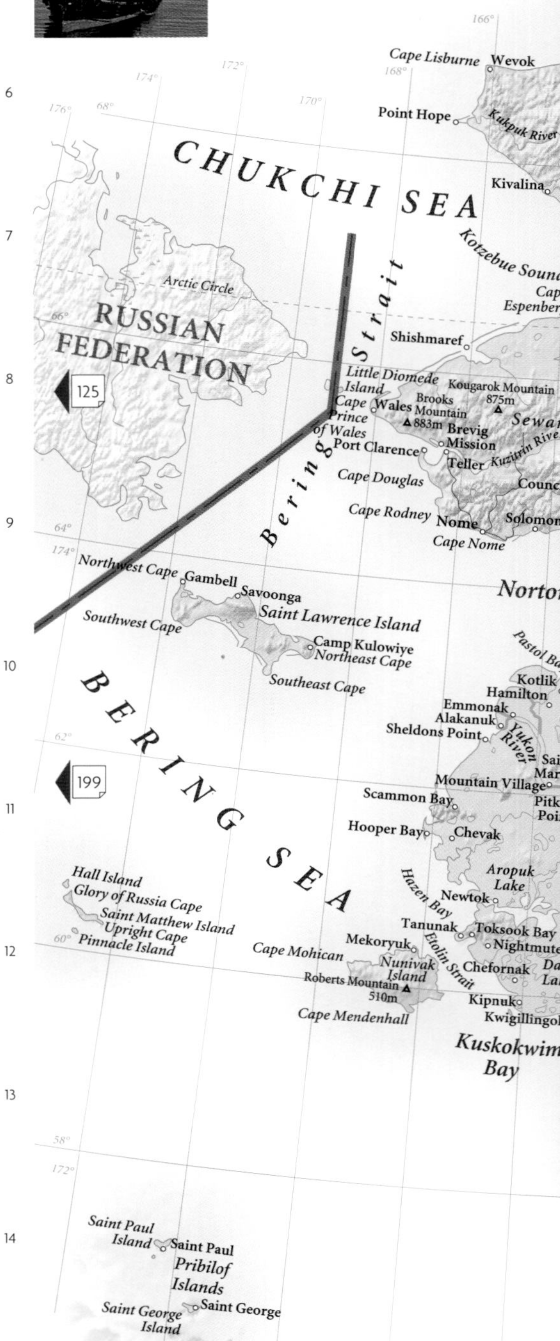

Scale 1:3,500,000

Km
0 10 20   40   60   80   100

Miles
0 10 20   40   60   80   100

projection: Lambert Conformal Conic

Map key

Population
- ◎ 100,000 to 500,000
- ⊕ 50,000 to 100,000
- ○ 10,000 to 50,000
- ○ below 10,000

Elevation
- 4000m / 13,124ft
- 3000m / 9843ft
- 2000m / 6562ft
- 1000m / 3281ft
- 500m / 1640ft
- 250m / 820ft
- 100m / 328ft
- sea level

Using the land and sea

The volcanic soils are extremely fertile and the climate hot and humid on the lower slopes, supporting large commercial plantations growing sugar cane, bananas, pineapples and other tropical fruit, as well as nursery plants and flowers. Some land is given to pasture, particularly for beef and dairy cattle.

Land use and agricultural distribution

- cattle
- fishing
- fruit
- sugar cane
- major towns
- pasture
- cropland
- forest
- mountain region

▶ The island of Kaua‘i is one of the wettest places in the world, receiving some 450 inches (11,500 mm) of rain a year.

The urban/rural population divide

urban 89%   rural 11%

0 10 20 30 40 50 60 70 80 90 100

Population density	Total land area
189 people per sq mile (73 people per sq km)	6,423 sq miles (16,636 sq km)

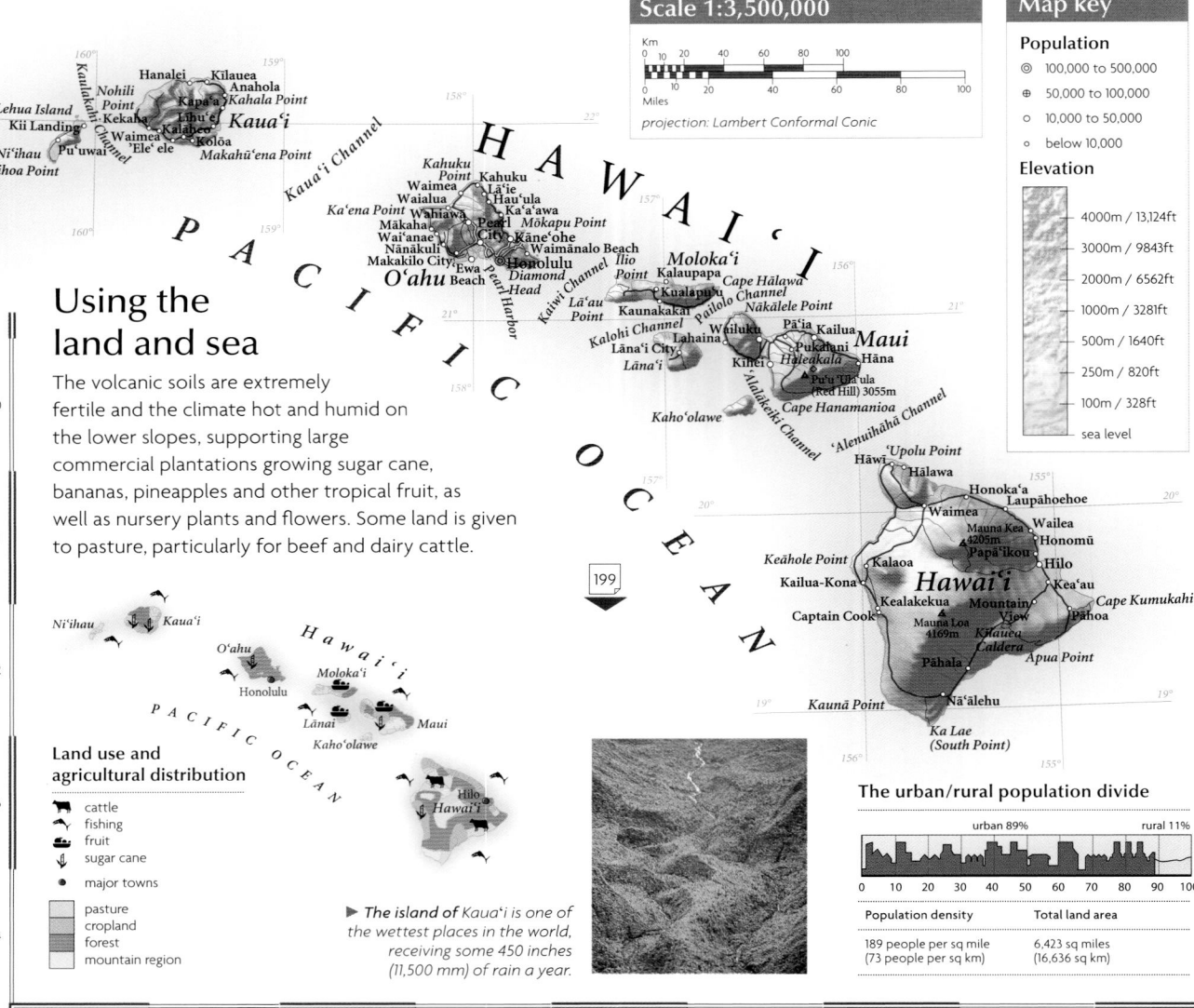

Map key

Population
- ◎ 100,000 to 500,000
- ⊕ 50,000 to 100,000
- ○ 10,000 to 50,000
- ○ below 10,000

Elevation
- 4000m / 13,124ft
- 3000m / 9843ft
- 2000m / 6562ft
- 1000m / 3281ft
- 500m / 1640ft
- 250m / 820ft
- 100m / 328ft
- sea level

Scale 1:8,000,000

Km
0 25 50   100   150   200   250

Miles
0 25 50   100   150   200   250

projection: Lambert Conformal Conic

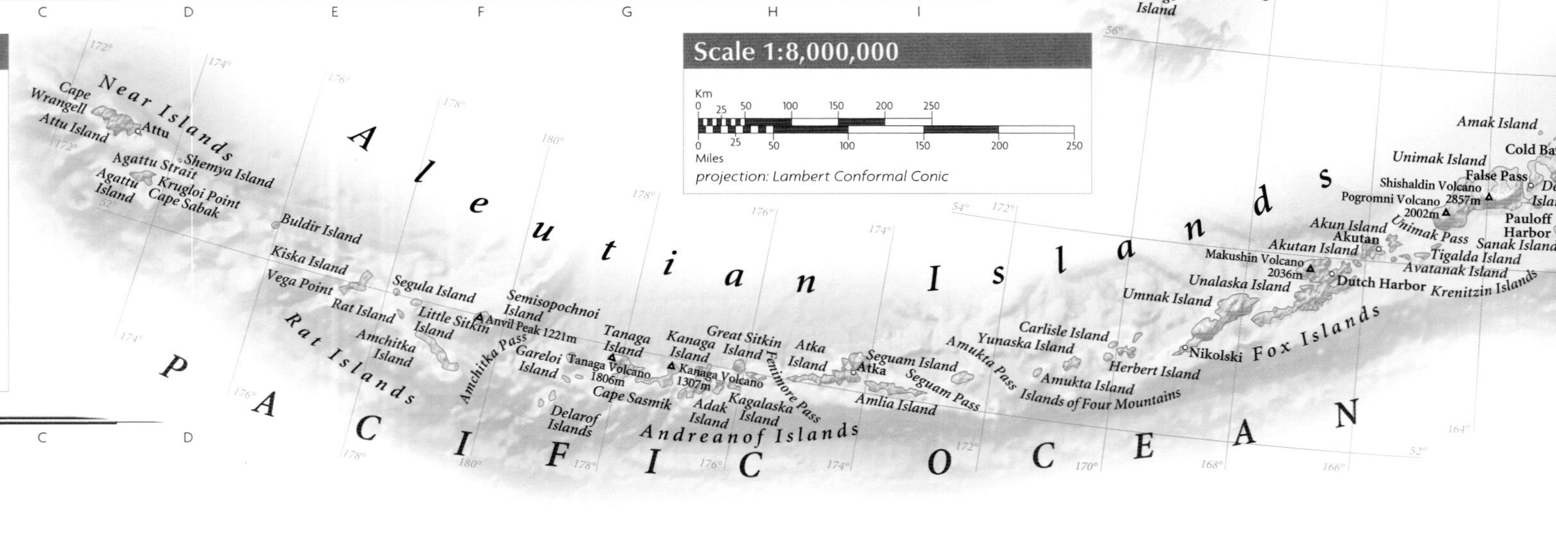

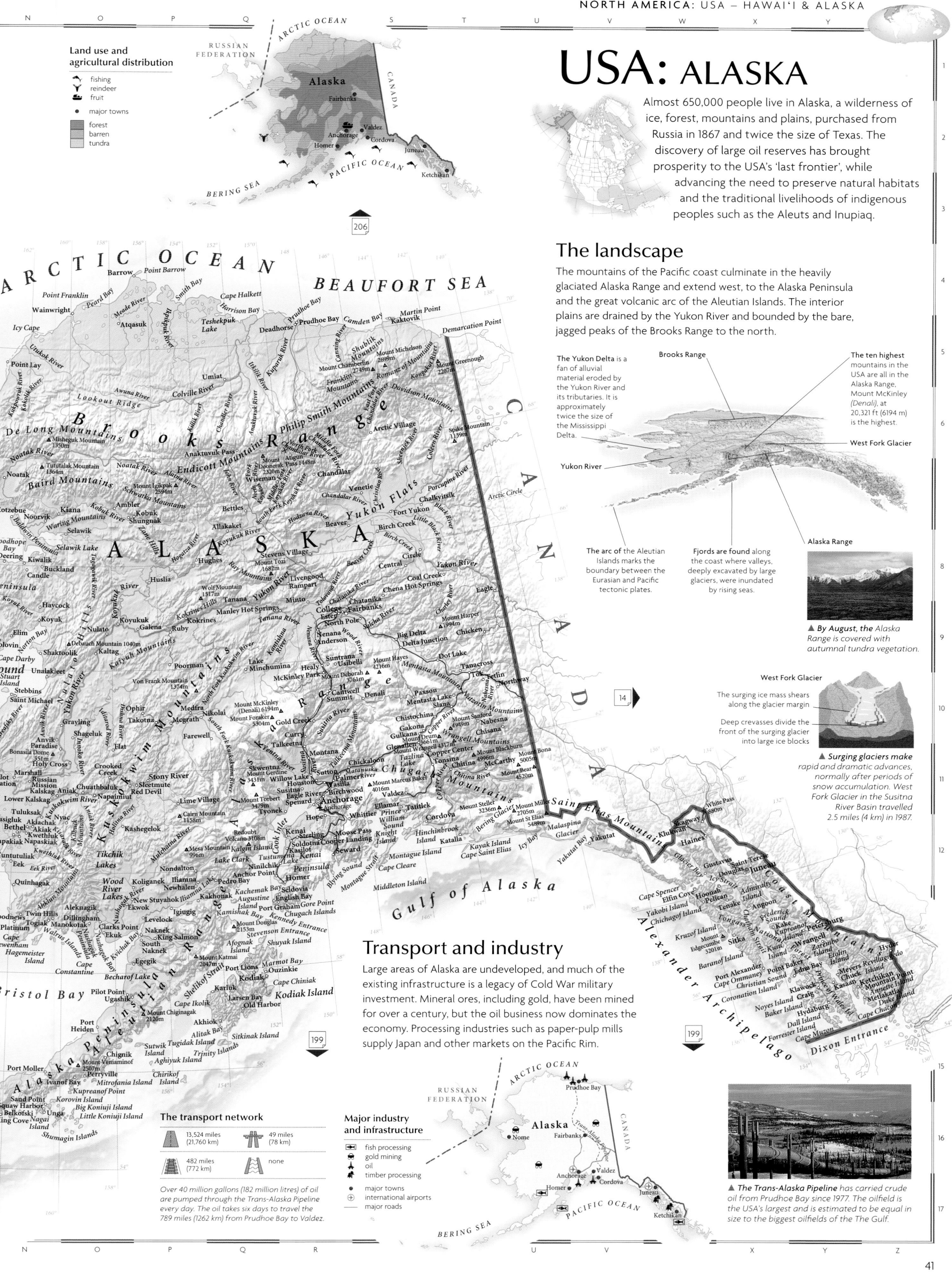

USA: ALASKA

Almost 650,000 people live in Alaska, a wilderness of ice, forest, mountains and plains, purchased from Russia in 1867 and twice the size of Texas. The discovery of large oil reserves has brought prosperity to the USA's 'last frontier', while advancing the need to preserve natural habitats and the traditional livelihoods of indigenous peoples such as the Aleuts and Inupiaq.

The landscape

The mountains of the Pacific coast culminate in the heavily glaciated Alaska Range and extend west, to the Alaska Peninsula and the great volcanic arc of the Aleutian Islands. The interior plains are drained by the Yukon River and bounded by the bare, jagged peaks of the Brooks Range to the north.

The Yukon Delta is a fan of alluvial material eroded by the Yukon River and its tributaries. It is approximately twice the size of the Mississippi Delta.

Brooks Range

The ten highest mountains in the USA are all in the Alaska Range, Mount McKinley (Denali), at 20,321 ft (6194 m) is the highest.

West Fork Glacier

Yukon River

The arc of the Aleutian Islands marks the boundary between the Eurasian and Pacific tectonic plates.

Fjords are found along the coast where valleys, deeply excavated by large glaciers, were inundated by rising seas.

Alaska Range

▲ By August, the Alaska Range is covered with autumnal tundra vegetation.

West Fork Glacier

The surging ice mass shears along the glacier margin

Deep crevasses divide the front of the surging glacier into large ice blocks

▲ Surging glaciers make rapid and dramatic advances, normally after periods of snow accumulation. West Fork Glacier in the Susitna River Basin travelled 2.5 miles (4 km) in 1987.

Transport and industry

Large areas of Alaska are undeveloped, and much of the existing infrastructure is a legacy of Cold War military investment. Mineral ores, including gold, have been mined for over a century, but the oil business now dominates the economy. Processing industries such as paper-pulp mills supply Japan and other markets on the Pacific Rim.

▲ The Trans-Alaska Pipeline has carried crude oil from Prudhoe Bay since 1977. The oilfield is the USA's largest and is estimated to be equal in size to the biggest oilfields of the The Gulf.

Land use and agricultural distribution

- ⌁ fishing
- reindeer
- fruit
- • major towns

  forest
  barren
  tundra

The transport network

13,524 miles (21,760 km)		49 miles (78 km)	
482 miles (772 km)		none	

Over 40 million gallons (182 million litres) of oil are pumped through the Trans-Alaska Pipeline every day. The oil takes six days to travel the 789 miles (1262 km) from Prudhoe Bay to Valdez.

Major industry and infrastructure

- fish processing
- gold mining
- oil
- timber processing
- • major towns
- ⊕ international airports
- — major roads

41

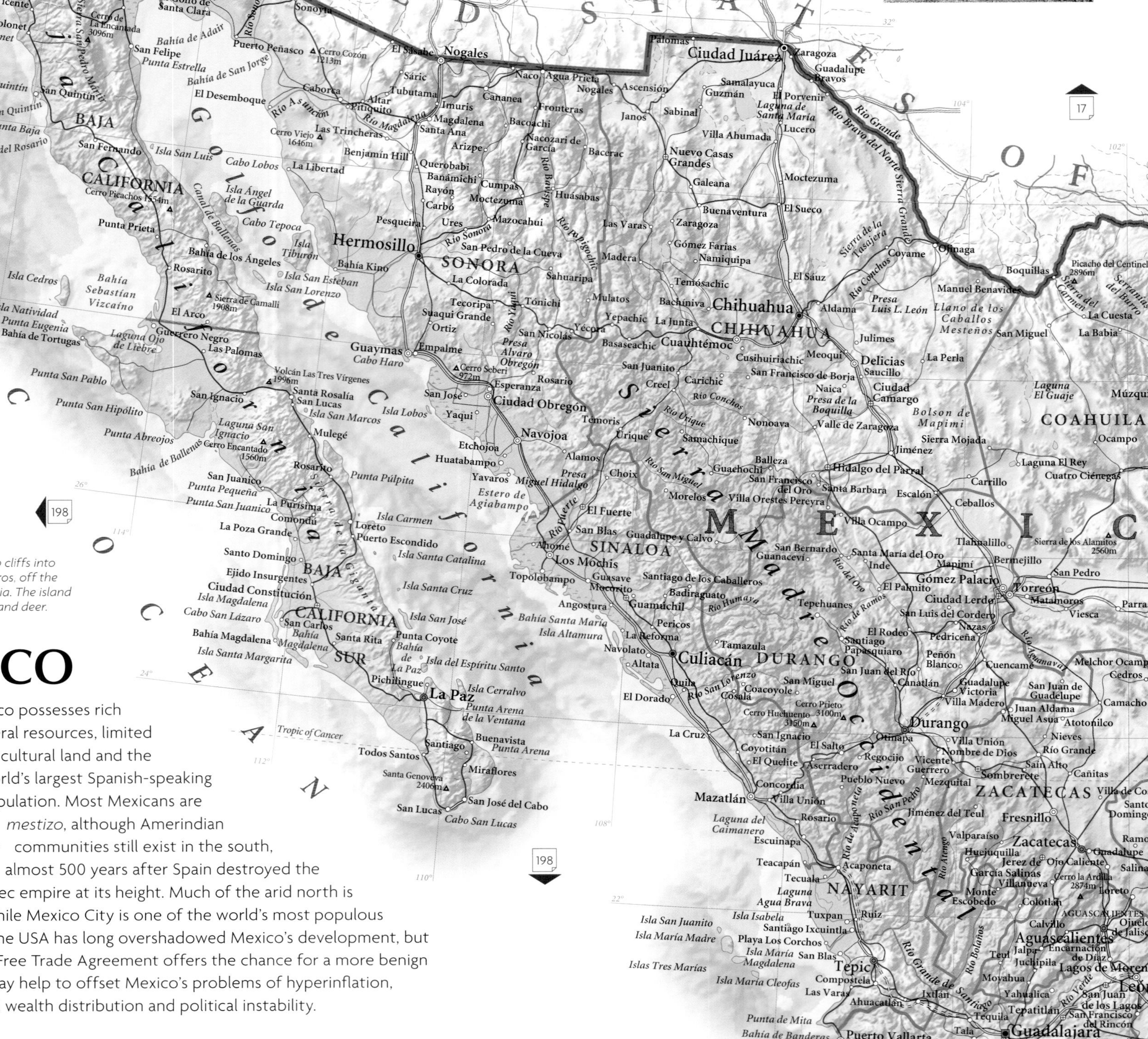

A B C D E F G H I J K L M

▶ **The rugged, desert** landscape of the Sierra Madre del Sur is a product of complex tectonic processes, where the fold mountains in western North America, running north–south, meet the Caribbean mountain arc which runs east–west.

Scale 1:6,250,000

Km 0 75 150 200
Miles 0 25 50 100 150 200

projection: Lambert Conformal Conic

▲ **Wave action has** cut steep cliffs into the igneous rocks of Isla Cedros, off the Pacific coast of Baja California. The island is home to sea lions, reptiles and deer.

Mexico

Mexico possesses rich mineral resources, limited agricultural land and the world's largest Spanish-speaking population. Most Mexicans are *mestizo*, although Amerindian communities still exist in the south, almost 500 years after Spain destroyed the Aztec empire at its height. Much of the arid north is sparsely inhabited, while Mexico City is one of the world's most populous cities. Conflict with the USA has long overshadowed Mexico's development, but the North American Free Trade Agreement offers the chance for a more benign relationship, which may help to offset Mexico's problems of hyperinflation, foreign debt, unequal wealth distribution and political instability.

Using the land and sea

Corn occupies much of the cultivated area. Commercial plantations of coffee, sugar, vanilla and cotton are found along the Gulf coastal plain and in irrigated parts of the arid north, which is otherwise used for extensive ranching. Fishing is important, particularly shellfish for export. A soaring population has created the need for grain imports since 1980.

The urban/rural population divide

urban 74%   rural 26%

0 10 20 30 40 50 60 70 80 90 100

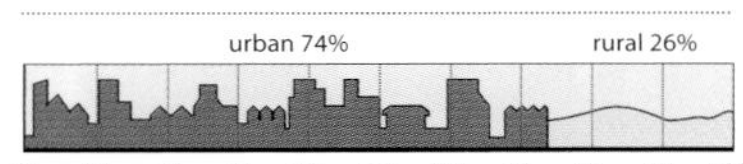

Population density	Total land area
140 people per sq mile (54 people per sq km)	755,865 sq miles (1,958,200 sq km)

Land use and agricultural distribution

- cattle
- coffee
- corn (maize)
- cotton
- fishing
- shellfish
- sugar cane
- timber
- vanilla
- capital cities
- major towns
- pasture
- cropland
- forest
- desert

▶ **Coffee beans spread** out to dry in the sun. Coffee, grown mainly on the Gulf coastal plain, is Mexico's most valuable export crop.

Map key

Mexico: Administrative regions

① Distrito Federal

Population
- ■ above 5 million
- ◨ 1 million to 5 million
- ◉ 500,000 to 1 million
- ◎ 100,000 to 500,000
- ⊕ 50,000 to 100,000
- ○ 10,000 to 50,000
- ○ below 10,000

Elevation
- 4000m / 13,124ft
- 3000m / 9843ft
- 2000m / 6562ft
- 1000m / 3281ft
- 500m / 1640ft
- 250m / 820ft
- 100m / 328ft
- sea level

The landscape

The great central plateau rises gently southwards from the Rio Grande, isolated from the coastal plains by the Sierra Madre Oriental and Occidental. The two ranges converge from east and west respectively, culminating in high volcanic peaks around Mexico City. Further ranges of the Sierra Madre rise to the south of the Balsas basin, skirted by the low-lying Isthmus of Tehuantepec (*Istmo de Tehuantepec*) and Yucatan Peninsula.

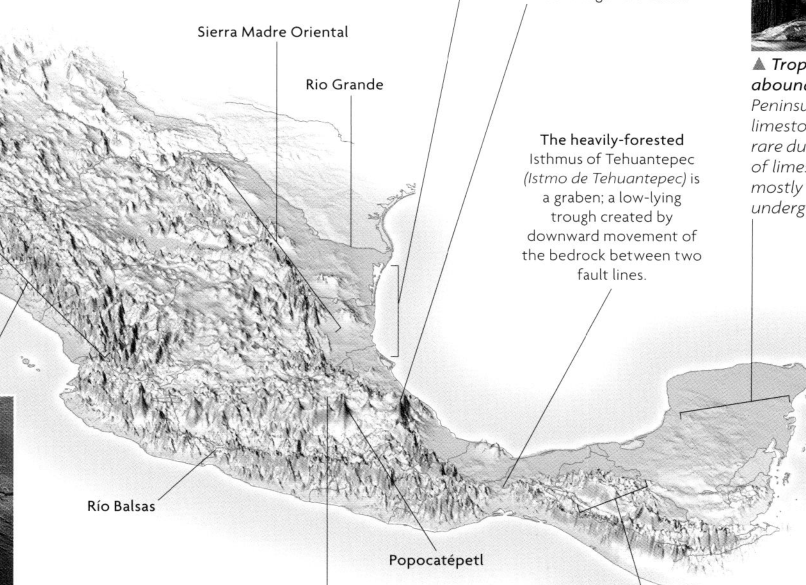

The long, narrow, extremely arid peninsula of Baja (lower) California is an elongated granite block, separated from the mainland by the flooded rift valley of the Gulf of California (*Golfo de California*).

Wave action has constructed sand bars which shelter lagoons along the shore of the Gulf coastal plain.

The dormant cone of Volcán Pico de Orizaba is, at 18,700 ft (5700 m), the highest peak in Mexico. In North America, only Mount McKinley and Mount Logan are taller.

Sierra Madre Oriental

Rio Grande

The heavily-forested Isthmus of Tehuantepec (*Istmo de Tehuantepec*) is a graben; a low-lying trough created by downward movement of the bedrock between two fault lines.

▲ *Tropical rainforest abounds* in the Yucatan Peninsula, a broad, low limestone shelf. Rivers are rare due to the porous nature of limestone, so the forest is mostly fed by streams and underground water.

Formation of the Gulf of California

Direction of plate movement
Baja California
Transform fault
Gulf of California
Edge of continental crust
Spreading oceanic ridge

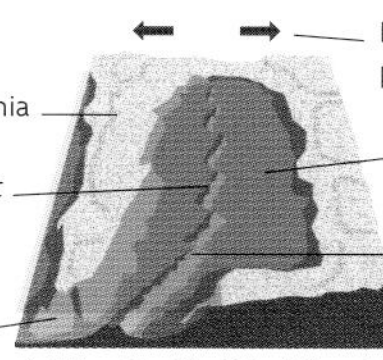

▲ *The Gulf of California* (Golfo de California) began to open out about 4 million years ago as a result of rifting and plate displacement along transform faults.

Sierra Madre Occidental

▲ *Popocatépetl is a* dormant volcano, part of the Pacific 'Ring of Fire'. The crater is over half a mile (1 km) wide.

Río Balsas

Popocatépetl

The unstable, earthquake-prone, upland basin around Mexico City was once a region of shallow lakes. Flood control measures and domestic consumption over the last four centuries have caused the virtual disappearance of this surface water.

The highlands of Chiapas are a series of *horsts*, blocks of land thrust upwards between two fault lines. Volcanic cones have developed where lava has flowed out from the faults.

Transport and industry

Oil and gas on the Gulf coast are Mexico's main sources of export income. Metal mining has declined but the country remains a leading global producer of silver. Manufacturing is heavily concentrated around the Mexico City metropolitan area, while the duty-free movement of goods in the USA border region, under the *Maquiladora* (twin plant) scheme, has created new hi-tech and service growth centres.

Major industry and infrastructure

brewing	oil & gas
car manufacture	textiles
chemicals	
electronics	capital cities
fish processing	major towns
maquiladoras	international airports
mining	major roads
	major industrial areas

The transport network

67,564 miles (108,746 km)

3994 miles (6429 km)

16,561 miles (26,656 km)

1801 miles (2900 km)

Fast, modern highways or autopistas now link Mexico City with Toluca, Puebla and other satellite cities, yet distant centres like Chihuahua are still served by narrow roads and an outdated rail network.

▲ *A stone figure* reclines by the Temple of Warriors, within the Mayan city of Chichén-Itzá. The Maya civilization flourished across the Yucatan Peninsula between 200 and 900 AD.

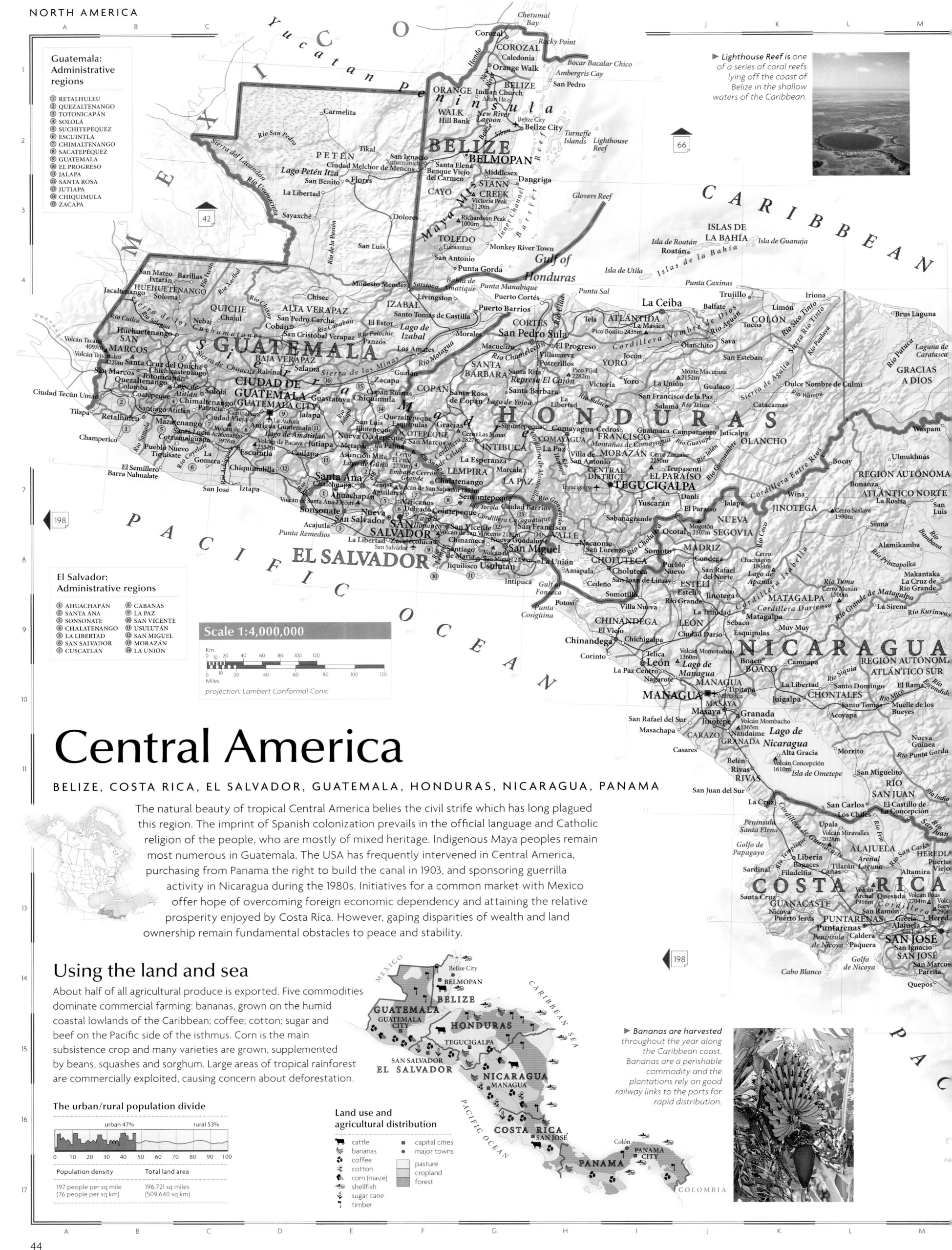

A B C D E F G H I J K L M

Guatemala: Administrative regions

① RETALHULEU
② QUEZALTENANGO
③ TOTONICAPÁN
④ SOLOLÁ
⑤ SUCHITEPÉQUEZ
⑥ ESCUINTLA
⑦ CHIMALTENANGO
⑧ SACATEPÉQUEZ
⑨ GUATEMALA
⑩ EL PROGRESO
⑪ JALAPA
⑫ SANTA ROSA
⑬ JUTIAPA
⑭ CHIQUIMULA
⑮ ZACAPA

► *Lighthouse Reef is* one of a series of coral reefs lying off the coast of Belize in the shallow waters of the Caribbean.

El Salvador: Administrative regions

① AHUACHAPÁN
② SANTA ANA
③ SONSONATE
④ CHALATENANGO
⑤ LA LIBERTAD
⑥ SAN SALVADOR
⑦ CUSCATLÁN
⑧ CABAÑAS
⑨ LA PAZ
⑩ SAN VICENTE
⑪ USULUTÁN
⑫ SAN MIGUEL
⑬ MORAZÁN
⑭ LA UNIÓN

Scale 1:4,000,000

Km 0 10 20 40 60 80 100 120
Miles 0 20 40 60 80 100 120

projection: Lambert Conformal Conic

Central America

BELIZE, COSTA RICA, EL SALVADOR, GUATEMALA, HONDURAS, NICARAGUA, PANAMA

The natural beauty of tropical Central America belies the civil strife which has long plagued this region. The imprint of Spanish colonization prevails in the official language and Catholic religion of the people, who are mostly of mixed heritage. Indigenous Maya peoples remain most numerous in Guatemala. The USA has frequently intervened in Central America, purchasing from Panama the right to build the canal in 1903, and sponsoring guerrilla activity in Nicaragua during the 1980s. Initiatives for a common market with Mexico offer hope of overcoming foreign economic dependency and attaining the relative prosperity enjoyed by Costa Rica. However, gaping disparities of wealth and land ownership remain fundamental obstacles to peace and stability.

Using the land and sea

About half of all agricultural produce is exported. Five commodities dominate commercial farming: bananas, grown on the humid coastal lowlands of the Caribbean; coffee; cotton; sugar and beef on the Pacific side of the isthmus. Corn is the main subsistence crop and many varieties are grown, supplemented by beans, squashes and sorghum. Large areas of tropical rainforest are commercially exploited, causing concern about deforestation.

The urban/rural population divide

urban 47%   rural 53%

Population density	Total land area
197 people per sq mile (76 people per sq km)	196,721 sq miles (509,640 sq km)

Land use and agricultural distribution

- cattle
- bananas
- coffee
- cotton
- corn (maize)
- shellfish
- sugar cane
- timber
- ■ capital cities
- ● major towns
- pasture
- cropland
- forest

► *Bananas are harvested* throughout the year along the Caribbean coast. Bananas are a perishable commodity and the plantations rely on good railway links to the ports for rapid distribution.

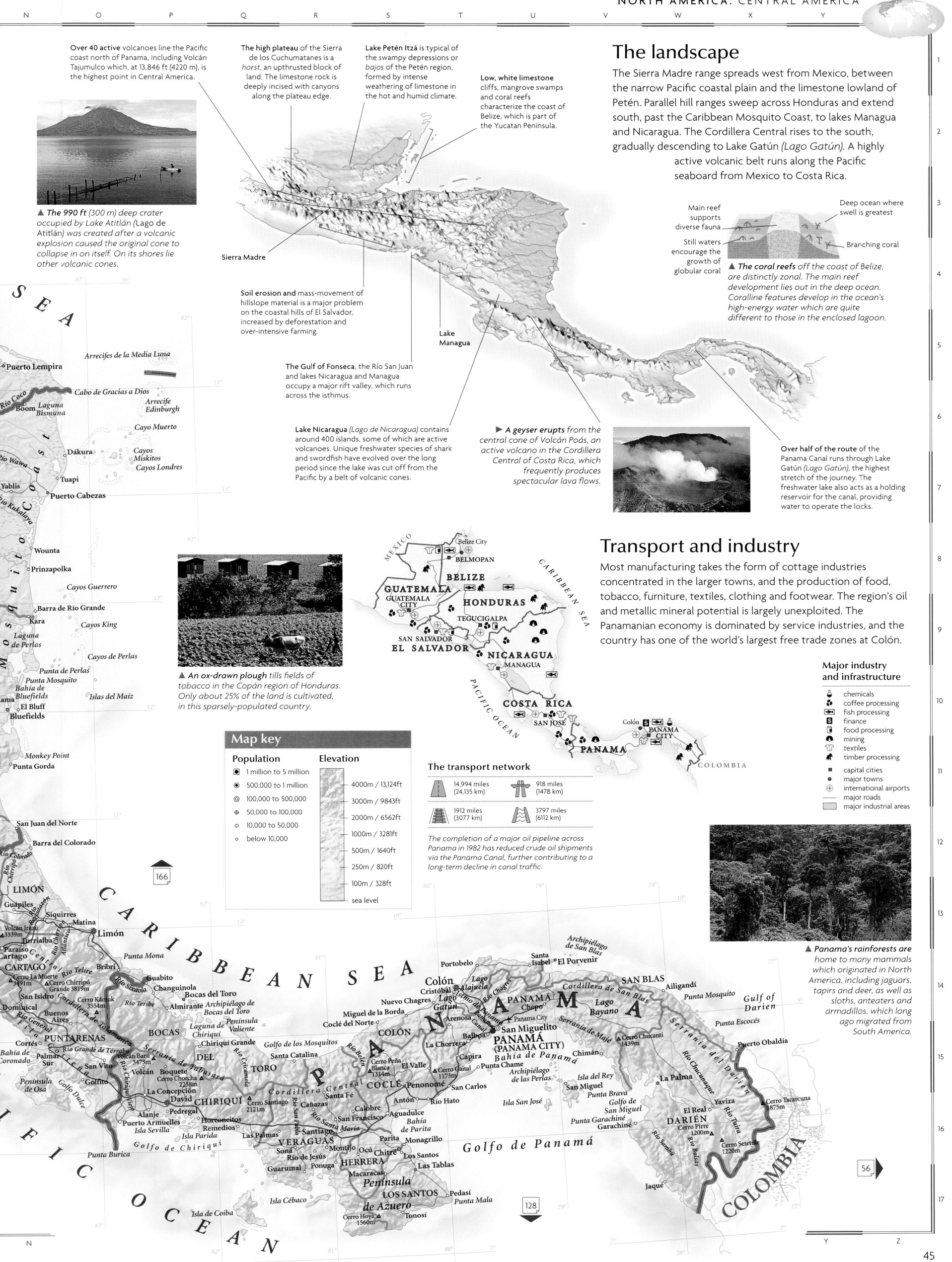

Over 40 active volcanoes line the Pacific coast north of Panama, including Volcán Tajumulco which, at 13,846 ft (4220 m), is the highest point in Central America.

The high plateau of the Sierra de los Cuchumatanes is a *horst*, an upthrusted block of land. The limestone rock is deeply incised with canyons along the plateau edge.

Lake Petén Itzá is typical of the swampy depressions or *bajos* of the Petén region, formed by intense weathering of limestone in the hot and humid climate.

Low, white limestone cliffs, mangrove swamps and coral reefs characterize the coast of Belize, which is part of the Yucatan Peninsula.

▲ *The 990 ft (300 m) deep crater occupied by Lake Atitlán (Lago de Atitlán) was created after a volcanic explosion caused the original cone to collapse in on itself. On its shores lie other volcanic cones.*

Sierra Madre

Soil erosion and mass-movement of hillslope material is a major problem on the coastal hills of El Salvador, increased by deforestation and over-intensive farming.

Lake Managua

The Gulf of Fonseca, the Río San Juan and lakes Nicaragua and Managua occupy a major rift valley, which runs across the isthmus.

Lake Nicaragua (*Lago de Nicaragua*) contains around 400 islands, some of which are active volcanoes. Unique freshwater species of shark and swordfish have evolved over the long period since the lake was cut off from the Pacific by a belt of volcanic cones.

▲ *A geyser erupts from the central cone of Volcán Poás, an active volcano in the Cordillera Central of Costa Rica, which frequently produces spectacular lava flows.*

The landscape

The Sierra Madre range spreads west from Mexico, between the narrow Pacific coastal plain and the limestone lowland of Petén. Parallel hill ranges sweep across Honduras and extend south, past the Caribbean Mosquito Coast, to lakes Managua and Nicaragua. The Cordillera Central rises to the south, gradually descending to Lake Gatún (*Lago Gatún*). A highly active volcanic belt runs along the Pacific seaboard from Mexico to Costa Rica.

Main reef supports diverse fauna

Deep ocean where swell is greatest

Still waters encourage the growth of globular coral

Branching coral

▲ *The coral reefs off the coast of Belize, are distinctly zonal. The main reef development lies out in the deep ocean. Coralline features develop in the ocean's high-energy water which are quite different to those in the enclosed lagoon.*

Over half of the route of the Panama Canal runs through Lake Gatún (*Lago Gatún*), the highest stretch of the journey. The freshwater lake also acts as a holding reservoir for the canal, providing water to operate the locks.

Transport and industry

Most manufacturing takes the form of cottage industries concentrated in the larger towns, and the production of food, tobacco, furniture, textiles, clothing and footwear. The region's oil and metallic mineral potential is largely unexploited. The Panamanian economy is dominated by service industries, and the country has one of the world's largest free trade zones at Colón.

▲ *An ox-drawn plough tills fields of tobacco in the Copán region of Honduras. Only about 25% of the land is cultivated, in this sparsely-populated country.*

Major industry and infrastructure

- chemicals
- coffee processing
- fish processing
- finance
- food processing
- mining
- textiles
- timber processing
- capital cities
- major towns
- international airports
- major roads
- major industrial areas

Map key

Population
- 1 million to 5 million
- 500,000 to 1 million
- 100,000 to 500,000
- 50,000 to 100,000
- 10,000 to 50,000
- below 10,000

Elevation
- 4000m / 13,124ft
- 3000m / 9843ft
- 2000m / 6562ft
- 1000m / 3281ft
- 500m / 1640ft
- 250m / 820ft
- 100m / 328ft
- sea level

The transport network

14,994 miles (24,135 km)	918 miles (1478 km)
1912 miles (3077 km)	3797 miles (6112 km)

The completion of a major oil pipeline across Panama in 1982 has reduced crude oil shipments via the Panama Canal, further contributing to a long-term decline in canal traffic.

▲ *Panama's rainforests are home to many mammals which originated in North America, including jaguars, tapirs and deer, as well as sloths, anteaters and armadillos, which long ago migrated from South America.*

◀ **The Caribbean's virgin** rainforest, seen here in Jamaica, is increasingly at risk from agricultural, industrial and tourist development. On some islands, the rainforest has virtually disappeared.

▲ **The large bar** which lies submerged in front of Marina Cay in the British Virgin Islands, has been built up by waves, depositing a bank of sand which partially encloses the islet.

Scale 1:5,500,000

Km
0 10 20 40 60 80 100 120 140 160

Miles
0 20 40 60 80 100 120 140 160

projection: Lambert Conformal Conic

The Caribbean

BAHAMAS, GREATER ANTILLES, LESSER ANTILLES

The islands known as the West Indies form a great arc which trails eastwards from the Gulf of Mexico almost to Venezuela, enclosing the Caribbean Sea. During the period of European colonization, which began in the 16th century, Britain, France, Spain and the Netherlands struggled for control of the area. Some countries remained politically tied to their colonial rulers until late in the 20th century, and most islands' economies still bear the legacy of the plantation system. A diverse mix of peoples, with roots drawn from Africa, East Asia and Europe replaced the original Amerindian population, creating a unique and remarkably homogeneous culture, reflected in the various Creole languages and musical forms such as reggae and calypso.

Using the land and sea

Agriculture has long been the basis of most Caribbean economies. Much agricultural land is set aside for cash crops such as sugar, spices, citrus fruits, bananas and cocoa, which are grown for export. Diversification is being encouraged to reduce the islands' reliance on imported grain and vulnerability to price fluctuations.

▶ **Market traders in** St George's, the capital of Grenada, sell a wide variety of fresh fruit and vegetables. The island is known particularly for its spices and is the world's second-largest producer of nutmeg after Indonesia.

The urban/rural population divide

urban 65%　　　　rural 35%

0 10 20 30 40 50 60 70 80 90 100

Population density

435 people per sq mile
(168 people per sq km)

Total land area

88,396 sq miles
(229,005 sq km)

Land use and agricultural distribution

- cattle
- bananas
- coffee
- fishing
- shellfish
- sugar cane
- tobacco

● major towns

pasture
cropland
forest

Map key

Population

- ◙ 1 million to 5 million
- ◉ 500,000 to 1 million
- ◎ 100,000 to 500,000
- ⊕ 50,000 to 100,000
- ⊙ 10,000 to 50,000
- ○ below 10,000

Elevation

3000m / 9843ft
2000m / 6562ft
1000m / 3281ft
500m / 1640ft
250m / 820ft
100m / 328ft
sea level

SCALE 1:2,500,000

0　5　10　20 Km
0　5　10　20 Miles

Transport and industry

Caribbean industry remains, with few exceptions, agricultural and export-led, or service-based, supporting the flourishing tourist industry. However, several countries including Jamaica, Barbados, Trinidad and Tobago and Puerto Rico have developed important mineral industries, and Cuba is attempting to diversify its economy by importing capital goods to start up new manufacturing businesses.

▶ **Cruise ships,** such as this one moored at Castries in St Lucia, have become a popular way for tourists to travel round the Caribbean islands, stopping off at several islands for sightseeing and shopping.

The transport network

53,439 miles (86,012 km)		661 miles (1064 km)	
3376 miles (5434 km)		211 miles (340 km)	

Air links are well-developed between most of the Caribbean islands. The importance of the tourist trade has recently encouraged many countries to upgrade their paved roads.

Major industry and infrastructure

- fish processing
- finance
- mining
- oil refining
- sugar refining
- tourism
- major towns
- international airports
- major roads
- major industrial areas

▶ **This rock stack** on the coast of St-Martin in the Leeward Islands has been created by wave action which undercut the cliffs, forming an arch. Continued wave action weakened the arch, which eventually collapsed leaving a single tower of rock.

▶ **The Pitons** in St Lucia are two volcanic domes; the tallest is 2620 ft (798 m) high. Their steep slopes are covered in thick forest.

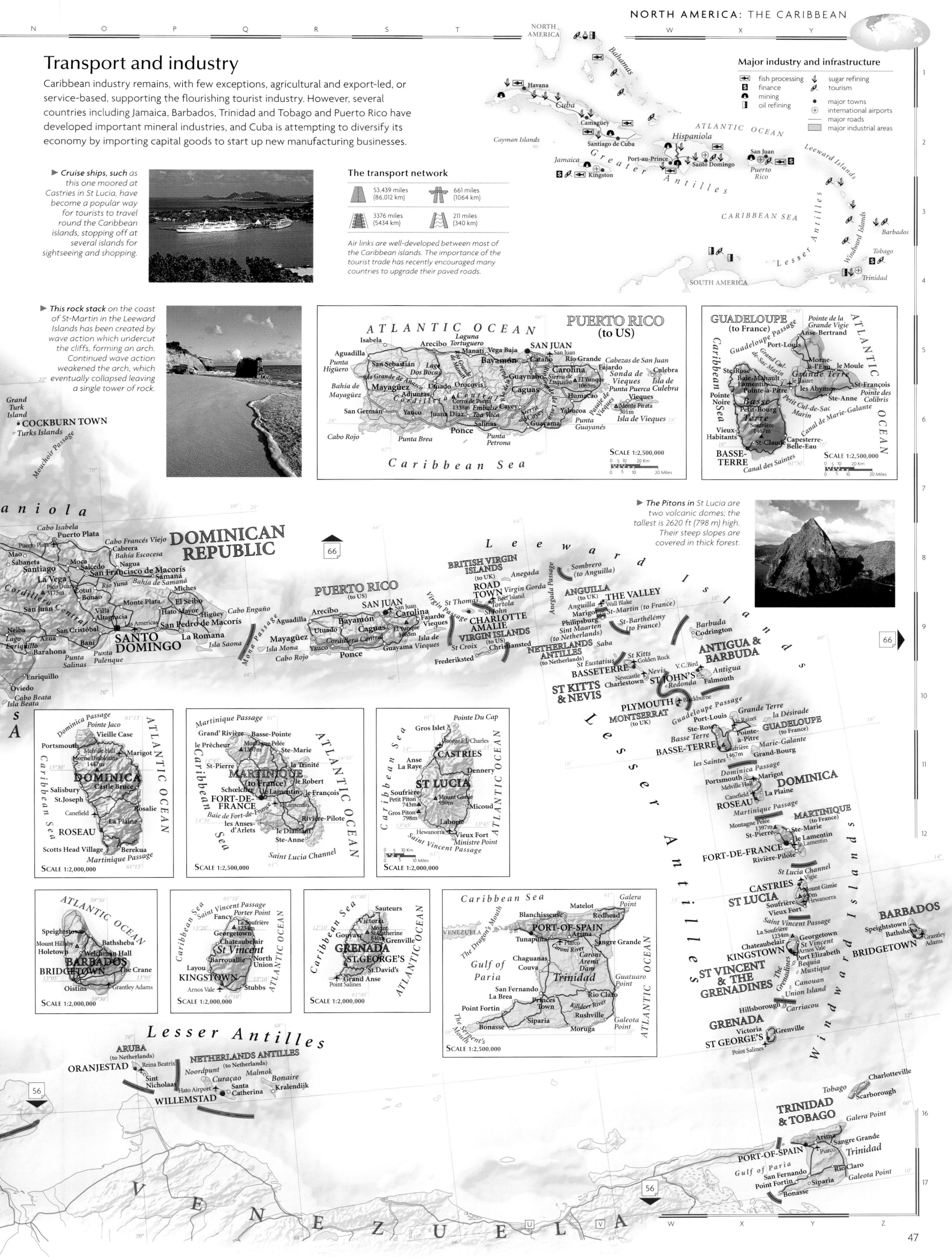

South America

Reaching from the humid tropics down into the cold south Atlantic, South America has an area of 6,886,000 sq miles (17,835,000 sq km). There are 12 separate countries, with the largest, Brazil, covering almost half the continent.

- ● *Greatest extent, North–South: 4750 miles / 7640 km*
- ■ *Greatest extent, East–West: 3100 miles / 4990 km*

Most northerly point:
Punta Gallinas, Colombia
12° 28' N

Punta Gallinas,
Colombia 12° 28' N

Most westerly point:
Galapagos Islands,
Ecuador 92° W

Equator

Punta Pariñas, Peru
81° 20' W

Cabo Branco /
Ponta do Seixas,
Brazil 34° 50' W

Largest lake: Lake Titicaca,
Bolivia/Peru 3220 sq miles
(8340 sq km)

Highest recorded temperature:
Rivadavia, Argentina
120°F (49°C)

Tropic of Capricorn

Antofagasta

São Paulo

Most easterly point:
Ilhas Martin Vaz, Brazil
28° 51' W

Highest point:
Cerro Aconcagua, Argentina
22,833 ft (6959 m)

Lowest point:
Peninsula Valdés, Argentina
-131 ft (-40 m) below sea level

Lowest recorded temperature:
Sarmiento, Argentina
-27°F (-33°C)

Froward Cape, Chile
53° 54' S

Most southerly point:
Cape Horn, Chile
55° 59' S

Antofagasta,
Chile

Atacama Desert

Andes

Paraguay river

Planalto de Mato Grosso

São Paulo, Brazil

Cross-section from Antofagasta, Chile to São Paulo, Brazil

line of cross-section

| 0 | 250 | 500 | 750 | 1000 Km |
| 0 | 250 | 500 | 750 | 1000 Miles |

NORTH

Cedros Trench

Rio Grande

Sierra Madre Oriental

Mexico
Basin

San Lucas
Cape

Lago de Chapala

Popocatépetl
5452m

East Pacific Rise

South Pacific

PACIFIC

Union Reefs

Clipperton Seamounts

Clipperton
Island

COCOS PLATE
NAZCA PLATE

NAZCA PLATE
PACIFIC PLATE

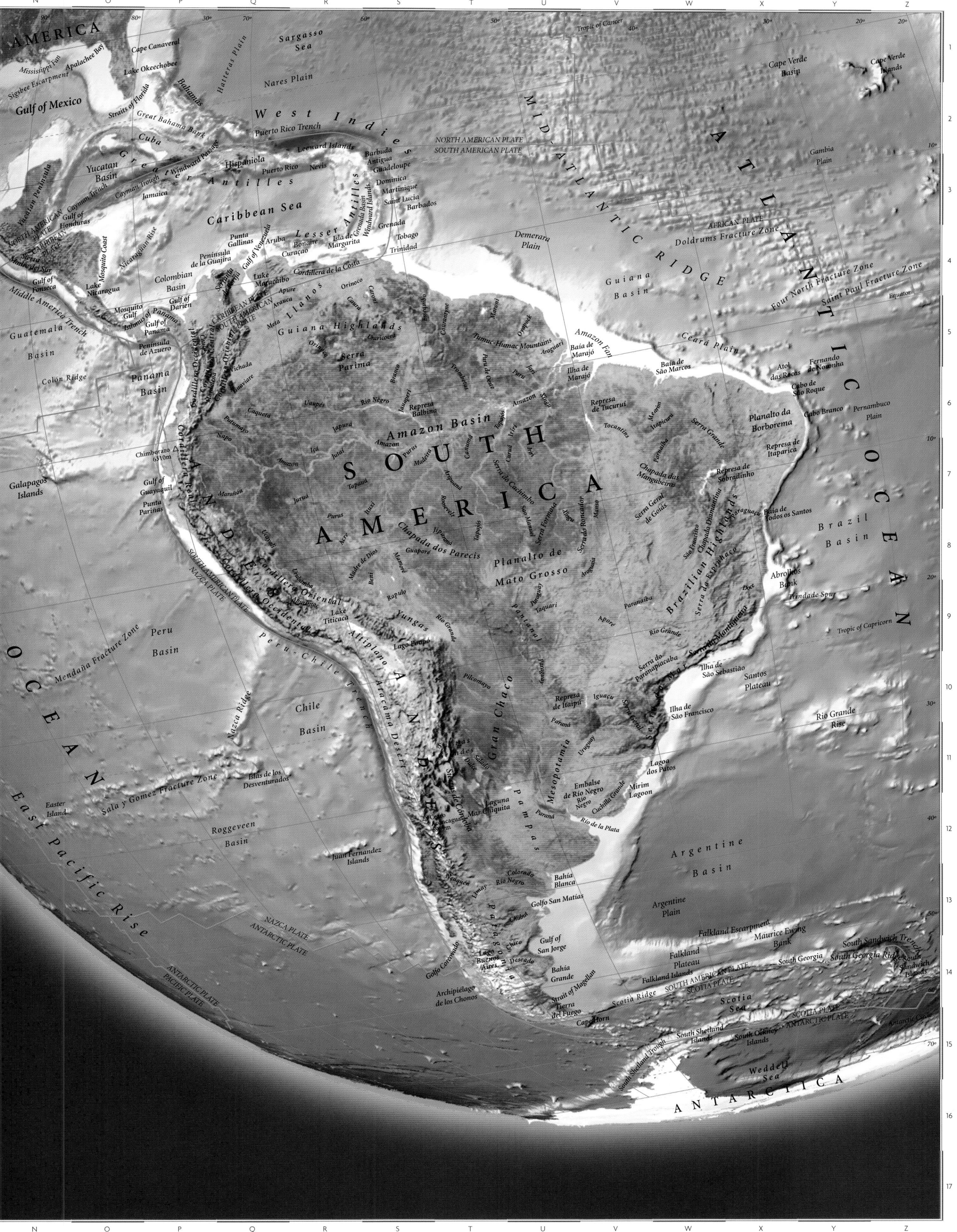

N O P Q R S T U V W X Y Z

AMERICA

Mississippi Fan
Apalachee Bay
Cape Canaveral
Lake Okeechobee
Sigsbee Escarpment
Gulf of Mexico
Straits of Florida
Great Bahama Bank
Bahamas
Hatteras Plain
Sargasso Sea
Nares Plain
Cape Verde Basin
Cape Verde Islands

Yucatan Peninsula
Cuba
Yucatan Basin
Windward Passage
Puerto Rico Trench
Gambia Plain

Cayman Trench
Jamaica
Hispaniola
Puerto Rico
Nevis
Leeward Islands
Barbuda
Antigua
Guadeloupe
NORTH AMERICAN PLATE
SOUTH AMERICAN PLATE
AFRICAN PLATE

Gulf of Honduras
NORTH AMERICAN PLATE
CARIBBEAN PLATE
Caribbean Sea
Lesser Antilles
Dominica
Martinique
Saint Lucia
Barbados
Doldrums Fracture Zone

Banks del Sur
Nicaraguan Rise
Punta Gallinas
Aruba
Bonaire
Curaçao
Isla de Margarita
Grenada
Tobago
Trinidad
Demerara Plain

Middle America Trench
Lake Nicaragua
Mosquito Coast
Peninsula de la Guajira
Gulf of Venezuela
Lake Maracaibo
Guiana Basin
Four North Fracture Zone
Saint Paul Fracture Zone
Equator

Guatemala Basin
Gulf of Fonseca
Colombian Basin
Apure
Arauca
Orinoco
Caroni
Guaviare
Amazon Fan
Ceará Plain

Colón Ridge
Isthmus of Panama
Gulf of Darien
SOUTH AMERICAN PLATE
CARIBBEAN PLATE
Meta
Llanos
Guiana Highlands
Charicora
Baía de Marajó
Baía de São Marcos
Fernando de Noronha
Atol das Rocas
Cabo de São Roque

Panama Basin
Peninsula de Azuero
Gulf of Panama
Orituco
Serra Parima
Branco
Uaupés
Rio Negro
Caquetá
Japurá
Içá
Napo
Amazon
Ilha de Marajó
Xingu
Cabo Branco
Pernambuco Plain

Galapagos Islands
Chimborazo 6310m
Putumayo
Amazon
Purus
Maú
Tapajós
SOUTH
Trombetas
Tapajós
Xingu
Tocantins
Serra do Cachimbo
Planalto da Borborema
Represa de Itaparica

Gulf of Guayaquil
Punta Parinas
Marañón
Jurua
Purus
AMERICA
Araguaia
São Manuel
Serra Formosa
Chapada das Mangabeiras
Represa de Sobradinho

Mendaña Fracture Zone
Peru Basin
Napo
Amazon Basin
Juruá
Madre de Dios
Guaporé
Chapada dos Parecis
Paraguai
Araguaia
São Francisco
Chapada Diamantina
Baía de Todos os Santos
Brazil Basin

Cordillera Occidental
Cordillera Oriental
Beni
Mamoré
Guaporé
Planalto de Mato Grosso
Paraguay
Doce
Abrolhos Bank
Trindade Spur

Nazca Ridge
Lake Titicaca
Yungas
ANDES
Rio Grande
Pantanal
Taquari
Apore
Paranaíba
Brazilian Highlands
Serra de Espinhaço
Tropic of Capricorn

Altiplano
Lago Poopó
Pilcomayo
Paraná
Paranapanema
Serra do Paranapiacaba
Serra da Mantiqueira
Ilha de São Sebastião
Santos Plateau

Sala y Gomez Fracture Zone
Chile Basin
Gran Chaco
Represa de Itaipu
Iguaçu
Paraná
Uruguay
Ilha de São Francisco

Easter Island
Islas de los Desventurados
Atacama Desert
Salado
Salta
Mesopotamia
Lagoa dos Patos
Rio Grande Rise

Roggeveen Basin
Juan Fernandez Islands
Andes
Mar Chiquita
Embalse de Río Negro
Rio Negro
Mirim Lagoon

Colorado
Rio Negro
Bahía Blanca
Argentine Basin

Pampas
Río de la Plata

East Pacific Rise
NAZCA PLATE
ANTARCTIC PLATE
Limay
Chubut
Golfo San Matías
Argentine Plain
Falkland Escarpment
Maurice Ewing Bank
South Sandwich Trench

Golfo Corcovado
Chico
Gulf of San Jorge
Falkland Plateau
South Georgia
South Georgia Ridge
South Sandwich Islands

ANTARCTIC PLATE
PACIFIC PLATE
NAZCA PLATE
ANTARCTIC PLATE
Lago Buenos Aires
Deseado
Bahía Grande
Falkland Islands
Scotia Ridge
SOUTH AMERICAN PLATE
SCOTIA PLATE

Archipiélago de los Chonos
Strait of Magellan
Tierra del Fuego
Cape Horn
Scotia Sea
SCOTIA PLATE
ANTARCTIC PLATE
Antarctic Circle

South Shetland Islands
South Orkney Islands

South Shetland Trough
Weddell Sea

ANTARCTICA

AMERICA

West Indies

Greater Antilles

MID-ATLANTIC RIDGE

A T L A N T I C   O C E A N

P A C I F I C   O C E A N

Physical South America

Three major physiographic regions characterize South America. The oldest, the ancient Brazilian Shield and the smaller Guyana and Patagonian shields, form the stable core of the continent. Stretching along the entire west coast are the younger Andean fold mountains with many summits rising to 20,000 ft (6100 m). These two diverse regions are separated by a number of sedimentary basins carrying South America's large river systems to the sea. These include the massive Amazon Basin and the basin of the Gran Chaco.

The Amazon Basin and Guyana Shield

The Amazon river occupies a large depression in the Earth's crust, formed by the uplift of the Andes. It is covered by thick volcanic deposits and layers of alluvium – these have been laid down by the Amazon's many tributaries. To the north is the smaller Guyana Shield.

Headwaters of the Amazon rise in the Andes
Thick alluvium deposits
Mouths of the Amazon

A — A

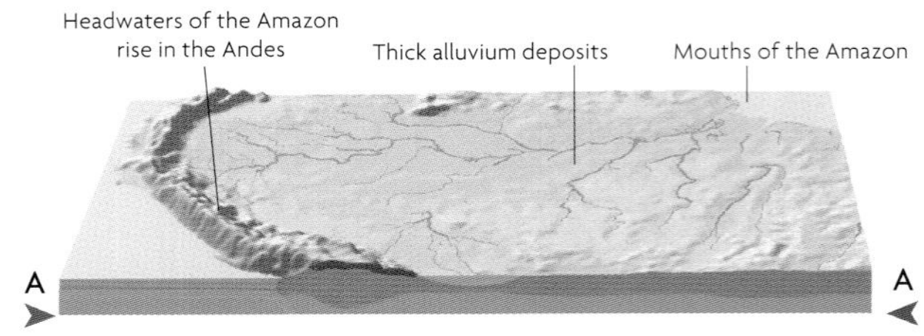

Section across northern South America showing Amazon Basin and its drainage pattern.

0   500   1000 Km
0   500   1000 Miles

Scale 1:27,500,000

Km
0   200   400   600   800

Miles
0   200   400   600   800

projection: Lambert Azimuthal Equal Area

The Andean Uplands

The Andean Uplands run along the west coast of South America. They are being uplifted as the Nazca Plate is subducted beneath the South American Plate. They contain some of the world's largest volcanoes, such as Cotopaxi, and Lake Titicaca which occupies a dormant site. The far south has many large ice-sheets and a fragmented coastline.

Nazca Plate
South American Plate
Volcanic intrusions

B — B

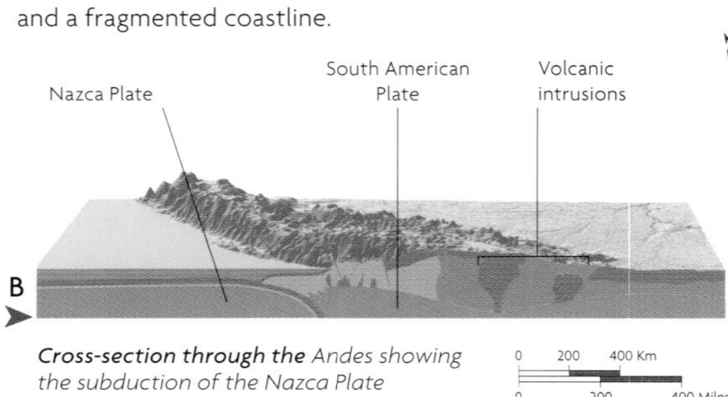

Cross-section through the Andes showing the subduction of the Nazca Plate beneath the South American Plate.

0   200   400 Km
0   200   400 Miles

The Brazilian Shield and Gran Chaco

The immense Brazilian Shield underlies more than one-third of South America. It is pitted with numerous volcanic intrusions, and a large basaltic plateau exists between the Paraná river and the Atlantic Ocean. The flat Gran Chaco lies to the west of the shield, covered by sedimentary deposits eroded from the Andes, and transported by South America's mighty rivers.

Young, folded Andes mountains
Volcanic intrusions
Major rivers drain to the south through the Gran Chaco
Ancient resistant shield

C — C

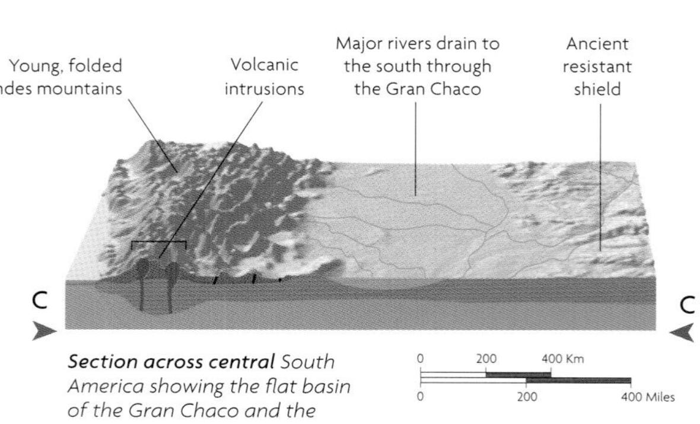

Section across central South America showing the flat basin of the Gran Chaco and the ancient Brazilian Shield.

0   200   400 Km
0   200   400 Miles

Map key

Elevation

6000m / 19,686ft
4000m / 13,124ft
3000m / 9843ft
2000m / 6562ft
1500m / 4922ft
1000m / 3281ft
500m / 1640ft
250m / 820ft
100m / 328ft
sea level

Plate margins
(for explanation see page xiv)

constructive
destructive
conservative
uncertain

physiographic regions
line of cross-section

Map labels

Punta Gallinas
Gulf of Venezuela
Lake Maracaibo
Gulf of Darien
Gulf of Panama
COCOS PLATE
NAZCA PLATE
Cauca
Magdalena
Llanos
Orinoco
Pakaraima Mountains
GUYANA SHIELD
Guiana Highlands
Tumuc-Humac Mountains
Río Negro
Japurá
Branco
Cordillera Occidental
Cordillera Central
Cordillera Oriental
Cordillera Real
Cotopaxi 5897m
Chimborazo 6310m
Gulf of Guayaquil
Putumayo
Amazon
Represa Balbina
Amazon
Ilha de Marajó
Marañón
Amazon
Juruá
Purús
Madeira
Tapajós
Xingú
Tocantins
Serra dos Carajás
Punta Negra
Nevado Huascarán 6768m
Ucayali
Serra do Cachimbo
Araguaia
Tocantins
Cabo de São Roque
Planalto da Borborema
Madre de Dios
Chapada dos Parecis
Guaporé
Serra Formosa
BRAZILIAN
Serra do Roncador
Serra Dourada
Represa de Sobradinho
São Francisco
Lake Titicaca
Planalto de Mato Grosso
SHIELD
Brazilian Highlands
Lago Poopó
Pantanal
Serra do Caiapó
Serra Geral
Serra do Espinhaço
Altiplano
Atacama Desert
Pilcomayo
Gran Chaco
Paraná
Serra do Mar
Serra da Mantiqueira
Cerro Ojos del Salado 6880m
Paraguay
Serra da Mantiqueira
Paraguay
Mesopotamia
Uruguay
Cerro Aconcagua 6959m
PATAGONIAN SHIELD
Pampas
Paraná
Lagoa dos Patos
Mirim Lagoon
Salado
Río de la Plata
Colorado
Río Negro
Península Valdés
Isla de Chiloé
Lago Colhué Huapí
Chico
Gulf of San Jorge
Deseado
Golfo de Penas
Bahía Grande
Strait of Magellan
Falkland Islands
Tierra del Fuego
Cape Horn
NAZCA PLATE
SOUTH AMERICAN PLATE
PACIFIC OCEAN
ATLANTIC OCEAN
ANDEAN SYSTEM
SUB-ANDEAN SYSTEM
Amazon Basin
Patagonia
ANTARCTIC PLATE
SOUTH AMERICAN PLATE
SCOTIA PLATE

Climate

The climate of South America is influenced by three principal factors: the seasonal shift of high pressure air masses over the tropics, cold ocean currents along the western coast, affecting temperature and precipitation, and the mountain barrier produced by the Andes, which creates a rain shadow over much of the south.

▲ *Mild winters and cool summers typify the extensive Pampas grasslands of Argentina.*

▲ *Chile's hyper-arid Atacama Desert is renowned as one of the driest places on Earth.*

Climate
- tundra
- cool continental
- warm humid
- semi-arid
- arid
- humid equatorial
- tropical
- ☼ daily hours of sunshine, January
- ☼ daily hours of sunshine, July
- → cold wind

Temperature

Average January temperature *Average July temperature*

Temperature
- below -30°C (-22°F)
- -30 to -20°C (-22 to -4°F)
- -20 to -10°C (-4 to 14°F)
- -10 to 0°C (14 to 32°F)
- 0 to 10°C (32 to 50°F)
- 10 to 20°C (50°F)
- 20 to 30°C (68 to 86°F)
- above 30°C (86°F)

Rainfall

Average January rainfall *Average July rainfall*

Rainfall
- 0–25 mm (0–1 in)
- 25–50 mm (1–2 in)
- 50–100 mm (2–4 in)
- 100–200 mm (4–8 in)
- 200–300 mm (8–12 in)
- 300–400 mm (12–16 in)
- 400–500 mm (16–20 in)
- more than 500 mm (20 in)

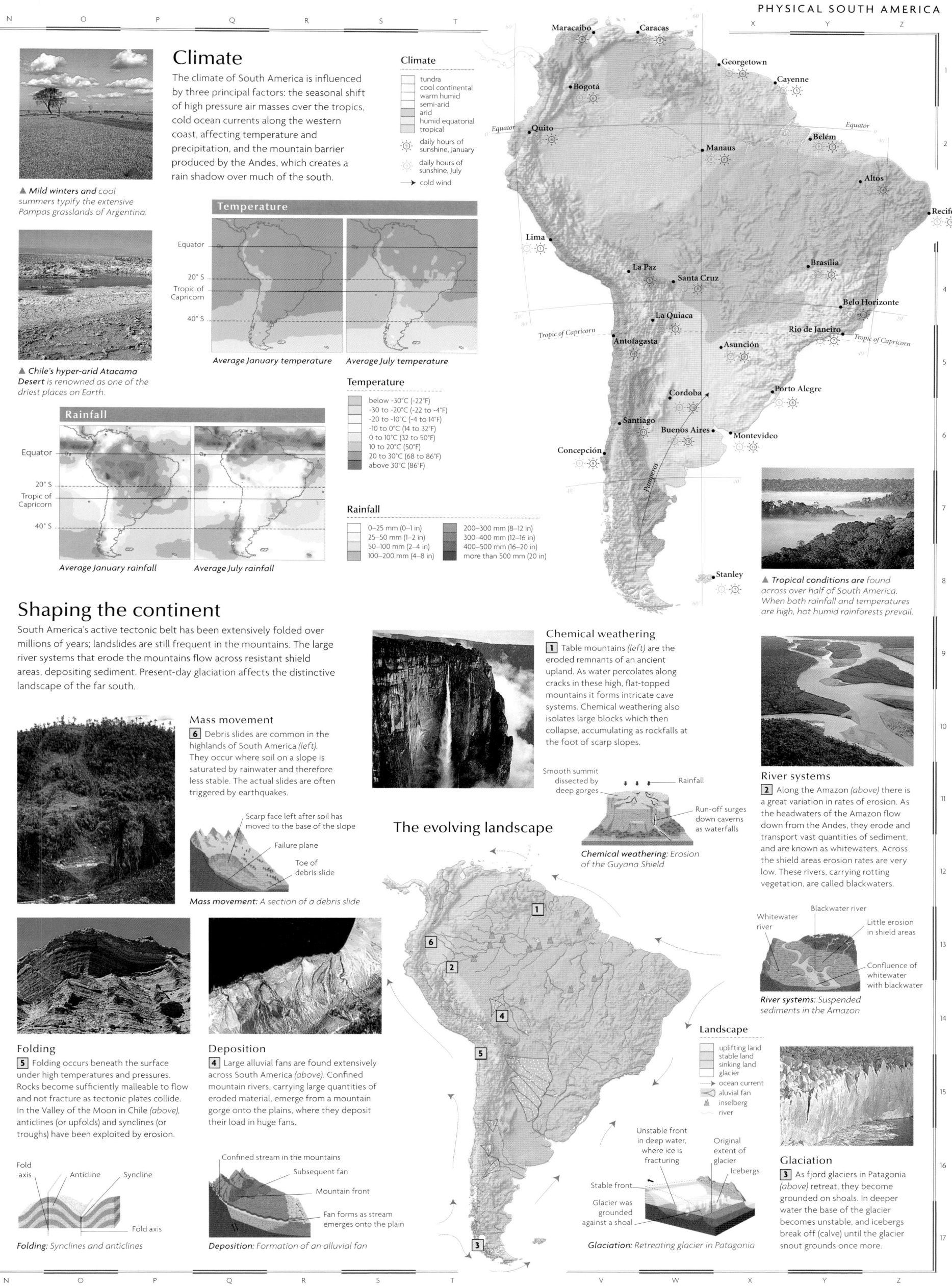

▲ *Tropical conditions are found across over half of South America. When both rainfall and temperatures are high, hot humid rainforests prevail.*

Shaping the continent

South America's active tectonic belt has been extensively folded over millions of years; landslides are still frequent in the mountains. The large river systems that erode the mountains flow across resistant shield areas, depositing sediment. Present-day glaciation affects the distinctive landscape of the far south.

Mass movement

6 Debris slides are common in the highlands of South America *(left)*. They occur where soil on a slope is saturated by rainwater and therefore less stable. The actual slides are often triggered by earthquakes.

Scarp face left after soil has moved to the base of the slope
Failure plane
Toe of debris slide

Mass movement: *A section of a debris slide*

Chemical weathering

1 Table mountains *(left)* are the eroded remnants of an ancient upland. As water percolates along cracks in these high, flat-topped mountains it forms intricate cave systems. Chemical weathering also isolates large blocks which then collapse, accumulating as rockfalls at the foot of scarp slopes.

Smooth summit dissected by deep gorges
Rainfall
Run-off surges down caverns as waterfalls

Chemical weathering: *Erosion of the Guyana Shield*

The evolving landscape

River systems

2 Along the Amazon *(above)* there is a great variation in rates of erosion. As the headwaters of the Amazon flow down from the Andes, they erode and transport vast quantities of sediment, and are known as whitewaters. Across the shield areas erosion rates are very low. These rivers, carrying rotting vegetation, are called blackwaters.

Whitewater river
Blackwater river
Little erosion in shield areas
Confluence of whitewater with blackwater

River systems: *Suspended sediments in the Amazon*

Landscape
- uplifting land
- stable land
- sinking land
- glacier
- → ocean current
- alluvial fan
- ▲ inselberg
- river

Folding

5 Folding occurs beneath the surface under high temperatures and pressures. Rocks become sufficiently malleable to flow and not fracture as tectonic plates collide. In the Valley of the Moon in Chile *(above)*, anticlines (or upfolds) and synclines (or troughs) have been exploited by erosion.

Fold axis
Anticline Syncline
Fold axis

Folding: *Synclines and anticlines*

Deposition

4 Large alluvial fans are found extensively across South America *(above)*. Confined mountain rivers, carrying large quantities of eroded material, emerge from a mountain gorge onto the plains, where they deposit their load in huge fans.

Confined stream in the mountains
Subsequent fan
Mountain front
Fan forms as stream emerges onto the plain

Deposition: *Formation of an alluvial fan*

Glaciation

3 As fjord glaciers in Patagonia *(above)* retreat, they become grounded on shoals. In deeper water the base of the glacier becomes unstable, and icebergs break off (calve) until the glacier snout grounds once more.

Unstable front in deep water, where ice is fracturing
Original extent of glacier
Icebergs
Stable front
Glacier was grounded against a shoal

Glaciation: *Retreating glacier in Patagonia*

Political South America

Modern South America's political boundaries have their origins in the territorial endeavours of explorers during the 16th century, who claimed almost the entire continent for Portugal and Spain. The Portuguese land in the east later evolved into the federal states of Brazil, while the Spanish vice-royalties eventually emerged as separate independent nation-states in the early 19th century. South America's growing population has become increasingly urbanized, with the expansion of coastal cities into large conurbations like Rio de Janeiro and Buenos Aires. In Brazil, Argentina, Chile and Uruguay, a succession of military dictatorships has given way to fragile, but strengthening, democracies.

◄ *Europe retains a* small foothold in South America. Kourou in French Guiana was the site chosen by the European Space Agency to launch the Ariane rocket. As a result of its status as a French overseas department, French Guiana is actually part of the European Union.

Scale 1:21,500,000

projection: Lambert Azimuthal Equal Area

Transport

Most major road and rail routes are confined to the coastal regions by the forbidding natural barriers of the Andes mountains and the Amazon Basin. Few major cross-continental routes exist, although Buenos Aires serves as a transport centre for the main rail links to La Paz and Valparaíso, while the construction of the Trans-Amazon and Pan-American Highways have made direct road travel possible from Recife to Lima and from Puerto Montt up the coast into central America. A new waterway project is proposed to transform the Paraguay river into a major shipping route, although it involves considerable wetland destruction.

▶ *South America's most* extensive rail network is centred on the Argentinian capital, Buenos Aires. The construction of new rail lines from this important port, allowed the colonization of the Pampas lands for agriculture.

Languages

Prior to European exploration in the 16th century, a diverse range of indigenous languages were spoken across the continent. With the arrival of Iberian settlers, Spanish became the dominant language, with Portuguese spoken in Brazil, and Native American languages such as Quechua and Guaraní, becoming concentrated in the continental interior. Today this pattern persists, although successive European colonization has led to Dutch being spoken in Surinam, English in Guyana, and French in French Guiana, while in large urban areas, Japanese and Chinese are increasingly common.

Transport

— major roads and motorways
— major railways
— international borders
• transport intersections
⊕ international airports
⊕ major ports

Language groups

American Indian
Germanic
Romance

▶ *Chile's main port,* Valparaíso, is a vital national shipping centre, in addition to playing a key role in the growing trade with Pacific nations. The country's awkward, elongated shape means that sea transport is frequently used for internal travel and communications in Chile.

▲ *Indigenous South American* lifestyles have not been totally submerged by European cultures and languages. The continental interior, and particularly the Amazon Basin, is still home to many different ethnic peoples.

▶ *Lima's magnificent* cathedral reflects South America's colonial past with its unmistakably Spanish style. In July 1821, Peru became the last Spanish colony on the mainland to declare independence.

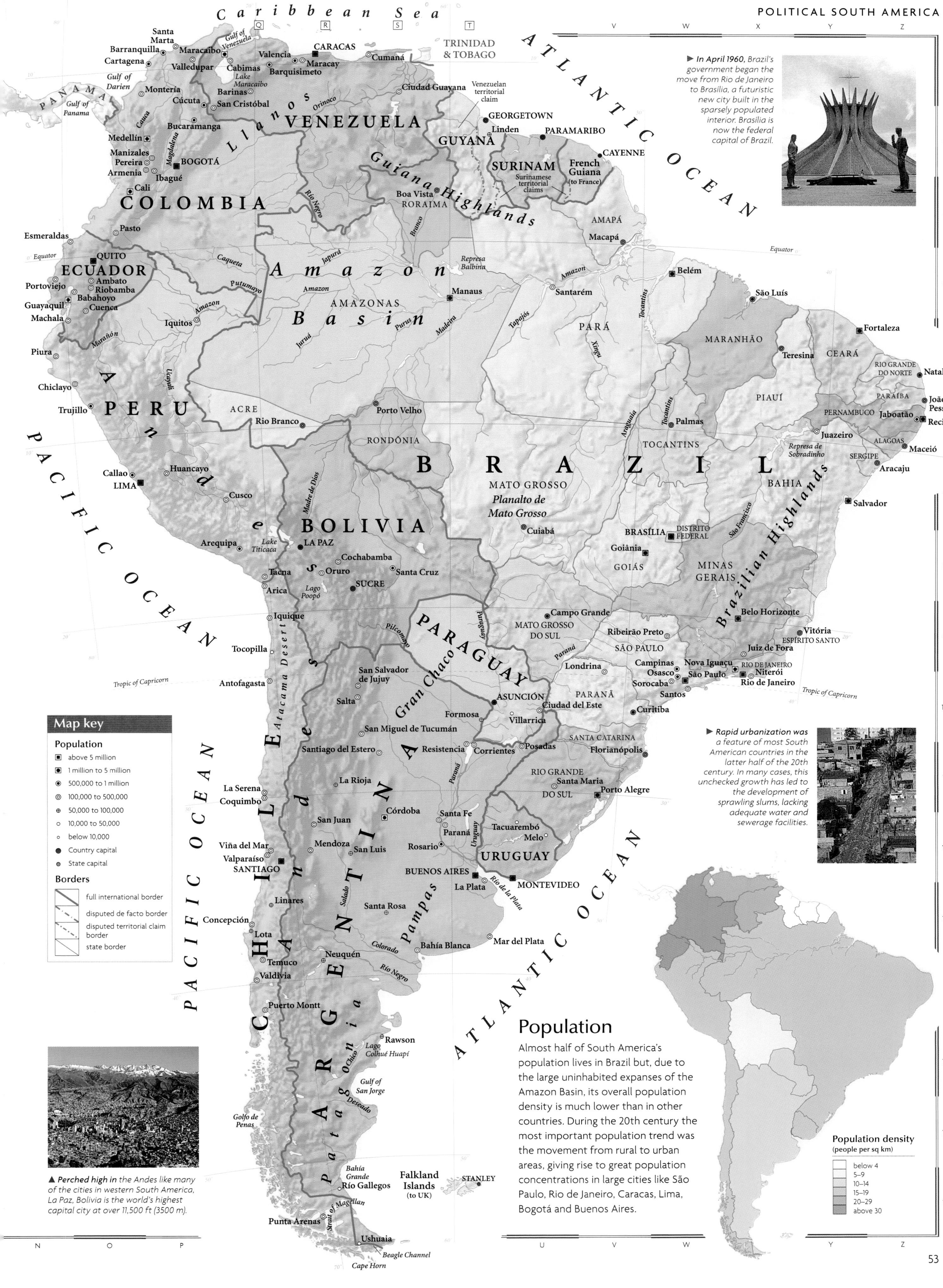

Caribbean Sea

TRINIDAD & TOBAGO

ATLANTIC OCEAN

▶ *In April 1960, Brazil's government began the move from Rio de Janeiro to Brasília, a futuristic new city built in the sparsely populated interior. Brasília is now the federal capital of Brazil.*

VENEZUELA

Santa Marta
Barranquilla
Cartagena
Maracaibo
Gulf of Venezuela
Valledupar
Cabimas
Valencia
Maracay
CARACAS
Cumaná
Gulf of Darien
Montería
Barinas
Cúcuta
San Cristóbal
Ciudad Guayana
Venezuelan territorial claim
PANAMA
Gulf of Panama
Bucaramanga
Lake Maracaibo
Barquisimeto
Medellín
Manizales
Pereira
BOGOTÁ
GEORGETOWN
Linden
PARAMARIBO
CAYENNE
Armenia
Ibagué
Llanos
GUYANA
SURINAM
French Guiana (to France)
Cali
Orinoco
Río Negro
Guiana Highlands
Surinamese territorial claims

COLOMBIA

Boa Vista
RORAIMA
AMAPÁ
Macapá
Esmeraldas
Equator
QUITO
ECUADOR
Ambato
Riobamba
Babahoyo
Cuenca
Caqueta
Japurá
Amazon
Manaus
Amazon
Belém
São Luís
Equator
Portoviejo
Putumayo
AMAZONAS
Santarém
Guayaquil
Machala
Iquitos
Amazon
A m a z o n   B a s i n
PARÁ
MARANHÃO
Fortaleza
Piura
Marañón
Jurua
Purus
Madeira
Tapajós
Tocantins
Teresina
CEARÁ
RIO GRANDE DO NORTE
Chiclayo
Ucayali
Xingu
Araguaia
Tocantins
PIAUÍ
Natal
Trujillo
ACRE
Porto Velho
Tocantins
Palmas
PARAÍBA
João Pessoa
Jaboatão
P E R U
Rio Branco
RONDÔNIA
PERNAMBUCO
Recife
Juazeiro
Callao
LIMA
Huancayo
B R A Z I L
TOCANTINS
Represa de Sobradinho
ALAGOAS
Maceió
SERGIPE
Aracaju
Cusco
MATO GROSSO
Planalto de Mato Grosso
São Francisco
BAHIA
Brazilian Highlands
Madre de Dios
BOLIVIA
Cuiabá
BRASÍLIA
DISTRITO FEDERAL
Salvador
Arequipa
Lake Titicaca
LA PAZ
Cochabamba
Goiânia
MINAS GERAIS
Tacna
Oruro
Santa Cruz
GOIÁS
Arica
SUCRE
Lago Poopó
Campo Grande
Belo Horizonte
Iquique
Pilcomayo
Paraguay
MATO GROSSO DO SUL
Ribeirão Preto
Vitória
ESPÍRITO SANTO
Atacama Desert
PARAGUAY
Paraná
SÃO PAULO
Juiz de Fora
Tocopilla
Gran Chaco
Campinas
Nova Iguaçu
RIO DE JANEIRO
Antofagasta
San Salvador de Jujuy
Londrina
Osasco
São Paulo
Niterói
Sorocaba
Rio de Janeiro
Tropic of Capricorn
Salta
Formosa
ASUNCIÓN
Ciudad del Este
PARANÁ
Santos
Villarrica
Curitiba
San Miguel de Tucumán
Posadas
SANTA CATARINA
Santiago del Estero
Resistencia
Corrientes
Florianópolis
La Rioja
Paraná
RIO GRANDE DO SUL
Santa Maria
Porto Alegre
A R G E N T I N A
La Serena
Coquimbo
Córdoba
Santa Fe
Tacuarembó
Melo
San Juan
Paraná
Uruguay
Viña del Mar
Valparaíso
SANTIAGO
Mendoza
San Luis
Rosario
URUGUAY
Salado
Pampas
BUENOS AIRES
MONTEVIDEO
Linares
Santa Rosa
La Plata
Río de la Plata
Concepción
Colorado
Bahía Blanca
Mar del Plata
Lota
Temuco
Neuquén
Río Negro
C H I L E
Valdivia
Puerto Montt
Patagonia
Chubut
Lago Colhué Huapí
Rawson
Deseado
Golfo de Penas
Gulf of San Jorge
Bahía Grande
Río Gallegos
Falkland Islands (to UK)
STANLEY
Strait of Magellan
Punta Arenas
Ushuaia
Beagle Channel
Cape Horn

Andes

Andes

PACIFIC OCEAN

ATLANTIC OCEAN

Map key

Population

- ■ above 5 million
- ◾ 1 million to 5 million
- ◉ 500,000 to 1 million
- ◎ 100,000 to 500,000
- ⊕ 50,000 to 100,000
- ○ 10,000 to 50,000
- • below 10,000
- ● Country capital
- ◉ State capital

Borders

- full international border
- disputed de facto border
- disputed territorial claim border
- state border

▲ *Perched high in the Andes like many of the cities in western South America, La Paz, Bolivia is the world's highest capital city at over 11,500 ft (3500 m).*

▶ *Rapid urbanization was a feature of most South American countries in the latter half of the 20th century. In many cases, this unchecked growth has led to the development of sprawling slums, lacking adequate water and sewerage facilities.*

Population

Almost half of South America's population lives in Brazil but, due to the large uninhabited expanses of the Amazon Basin, its overall population density is much lower than in other countries. During the 20th century the most important population trend was the movement from rural to urban areas, giving rise to great population concentrations in large cities like São Paulo, Rio de Janeiro, Caracas, Lima, Bogotá and Buenos Aires.

Population density
(people per sq km)

- below 4
- 5–9
- 10–14
- 15–19
- 20–29
- above 30

South American resources

Agriculture still provides the largest single form of employment in South America, although rural unemployment and poverty continue to drive people towards the huge coastal cities in search of jobs and opportunities. Mineral and fuel resources, although substantial, are distributed unevenly; few countries have both fossil fuels and minerals. To break industrial dependence on raw materials, boost manufacturing, and improve infrastructure, governments borrowed heavily from the World Bank in the 1960s and 1970s. This led to the accumulation of massive debts which are unlikely ever to be repaid. Today, Brazil dominates the continent's economic output, followed by Argentina. Recently, the less-developed western side of South America has benefited due to its geographical position; for example Chile is increasingly exporting raw materials to Japan.

◀ *Ciudad Guayana is a planned industrial complex in eastern Venezuela, built as an iron and steel centre to exploit the nearby iron ore reserves.*

Industry

aerospace	pharmaceuticals
brewing	printing & publishing
car/vehicle manufacture	shipbuilding
chemicals	sugar processing
electronics	textiles
engineering	timber processing
finance	tobacco processing
fish processing	wine
food processing	oil
hi-tech industry	gas
iron & steel	
meat processing	industrial cities
metal refining	major industrial areas
narcotics	

Caribbean Sea

Gulf of Panama

PANAMA

Barranquilla
Cartagena
Maracaibo
Barquisimeto
Caracas
Valencia
VENEZUELA
Ciudad Guayana
Georgetown
GUYANA
Paramaribo
SURINAM
French Guiana (to France)
Medellín
Bogotá
Cali
COLOMBIA
Quito
ECUADOR
Guayaquil
Iquitos
Belém

Amazon Basin

Manaus
Fortaleza
Natal

BRAZIL

Chiclayo
Chimbote
PERU
Lima
Cusco
Recife
Maceió
Salvador
Arequipa
La Paz
BOLIVIA
Santa Cruz
Sucre
Brasília
Arica
Iquique
Belo Horizonte
Chuquicamata
Antofagasta
PARAGUAY
São Paulo
Rio de Janeiro
Asunción
Ciudad del Este
Curitiba
San Miguel de Tucumán
Corrientes
Porto Alegre
Córdoba
Santa Fe
Rosario
URUGUAY
Rio Grande
Valparaíso
Mendoza
Buenos Aires
Montevideo
Santiago
Talca
Concepción
ARGENTINA
Bahía Blanca
Neuquén
Valdivia
Comodoro Rivadavia
Gulf of San Jorge

Falkland Islands (to UK)

Bahía Grande

Punta Arenas
Strait of Magellan
Cape Horn

ATLANTIC OCEAN

PACIFIC OCEAN

CHILE

▲ *The cold Peru Current flows north from the Antarctic along the Pacific coast of Peru, providing rich nutrients for one of the world's largest fishing grounds. However, over-exploitation has severely reduced Peru's anchovy catch.*

Standard of living

Wealth disparities throughout the continent create a wide gulf between affluent landowners and those afflicted by chronic poverty in inner-city slums. The illicit production of cocaine, and the hugely influential drug barons who control its distribution, contribute to the violent disorder and corruption which affect northwestern South America, de-stabilizing local governments and economies.

Standard of living
(UN human development index)
low
high

▶ *Both Argentina and Chile are now exploring the southernmost tip of the continent in search of oil. Here in Punta Arenas, a drilling rig is being prepared for exploratory drilling in the Strait of Magellan.*

GNI per capita (US$)
below 999
1000–1999
2000–2999
3000–3999
4000–4999
above 5000

Industry

Argentina and Brazil are South America's most industrialized countries and São Paulo is the continent's leading industrial centre. Long-term government investment in Brazilian industry has encouraged a diverse industrial base; engineering, steel production, food processing, textile manufacture and chemicals predominate. The illegal production of cocaine is economically significant in the Andean countries of Colombia and Bolivia. In Venezuela, the oil-dominated economy has left the country vulnerable to world oil price fluctuations. Food processing and mineral exploitation are common throughout the less industrially developed parts of the continent, including Bolivia, Chile, Ecuador and Peru.

Environmental issues

The Amazon Basin is one of the last great wilderness areas left on Earth. The tropical rainforests which grow there are a valuable genetic resource, containing innumerable unique plants and animals. The forests are increasingly under threat from new and expanding settlements and 'slash and burn' farming techniques, which clear land for the raising of beef cattle, causing land degradation and soil erosion.

◀ **Clouds of smoke** billow from the burning Amazon rainforest. Over 11,500 sq miles (30,000 sq km) of virgin rainforest are being cleared annually, destroying an ancient, irreplaceable, natural resource and biodiverse habitat.

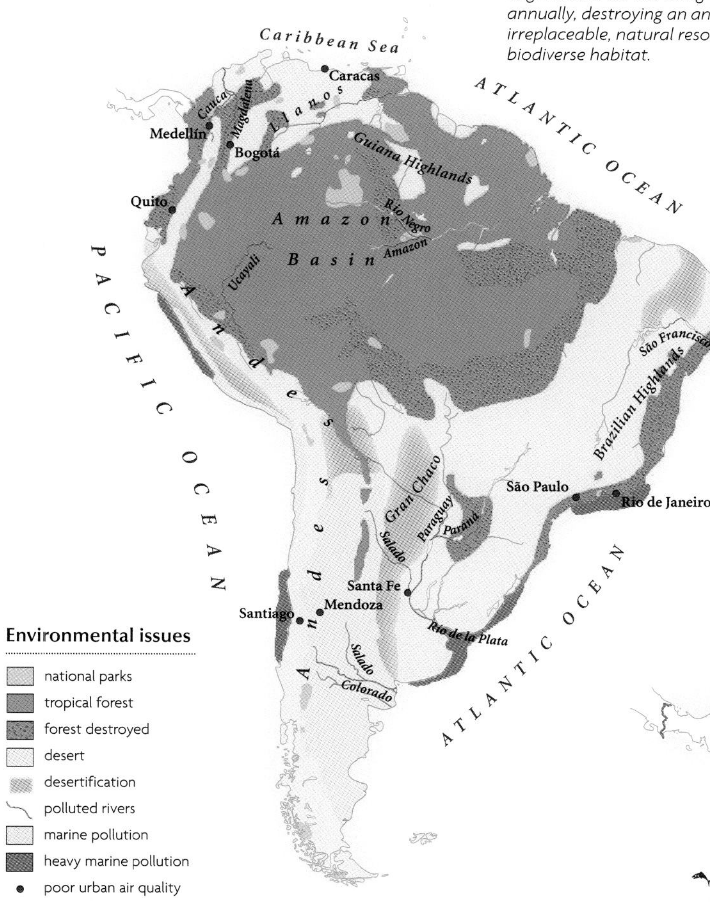

Environmental issues
- national parks
- tropical forest
- forest destroyed
- desert
- desertification
- polluted rivers
- marine pollution
- heavy marine pollution
- poor urban air quality

Using the land and sea

Many foods now common worldwide originated in South America. These include the potato, tomato, squash, and cassava. Today, large herds of beef cattle roam the temperate grasslands of the Pampas, supporting an extensive meat-packing trade in Argentina, Uruguay and Paraguay. Corn (maize) is grown as a staple crop across the continent and coffee is grown as a cash crop in Brazil and Colombia. Coca plants grown in Bolivia, Peru and Colombia provide most of the world's cocaine. Fish and shellfish are caught off the western coast, especially anchovies off Peru, shrimps off Ecuador and pilchards off Chile.

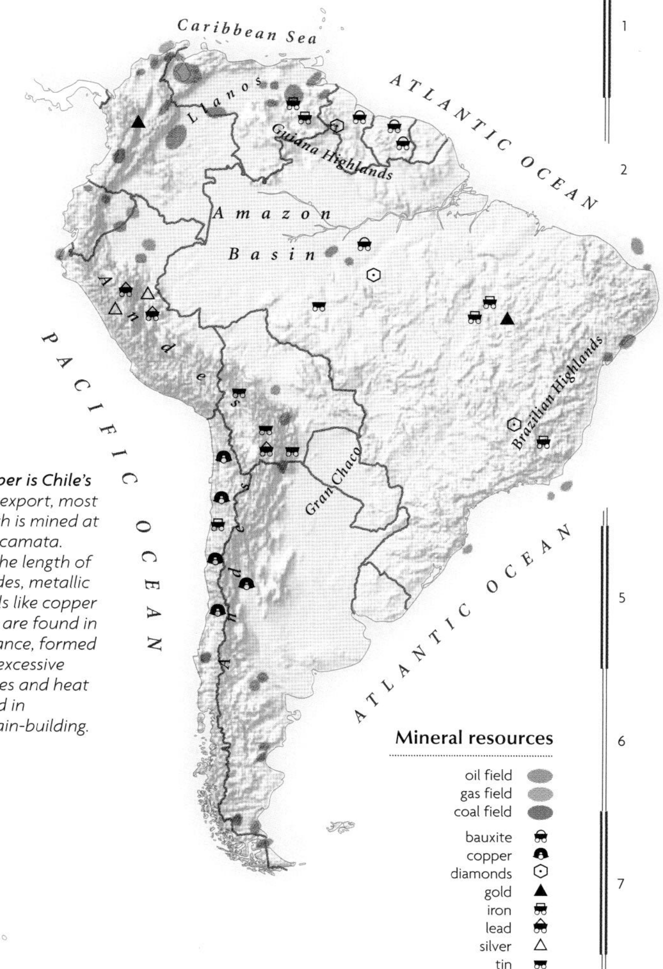

◀ **South America, and** Brazil in particular, now leads the world in coffee production, mainly growing Coffea Arabica in large plantations. Coffee beans are harvested, roasted and brewed to produce the world's second most popular drink, after tea.

◀ **The Pampas region** of southeast South America is characterized by extensive, flat plains, and populated by cattle and ranchers (gauchos). Argentina is a major world producer of beef, much of which is exported to the USA for use in hamburgers.

◀ **High in the Andes**, hardy alpacas graze on the barren land. Alpacas are thought to have been domesticated by the Incas, whose nobility wore robes made from their wool. Today, they are still reared and prized for their soft, warm fleeces.

Mineral resources

Over a quarter of the world's known copper reserves are found at the Chuquicamata mine in northern Chile, and other metallic minerals such as tin are found along the length of the Andes. The discovery of oil and gas at Venezuela's Lake Maracaibo in 1917 turned the country into one of the world's leading oil producers. In contrast, South America is virtually devoid of coal, the only significant deposit being on the peninsula of Guajira in Colombia.

◀ **Copper is Chile's** largest export, most of which is mined at Chuquicamata. Along the length of the Andes, metallic minerals like copper and tin are found in abundance, formed by the excessive pressures and heat involved in mountain-building.

Mineral resources
- oil field
- gas field
- coal field
- bauxite
- copper
- diamonds
- gold
- iron
- lead
- silver
- tin

Using the land and sea
- barren land
- cropland
- desert
- forest
- mountain region
- pasture
- major conurbations
- cattle
- pigs
- sheep
- bananas
- corn (maize)
- citrus fruits
- cocoa
- cotton
- coffee
- fishing
- oil palms
- peanuts
- rubber
- shellfish
- soya beans
- sugar cane
- vineyards
- wheat

55

Northern South America

COLOMBIA, GUYANA, SURINAM, VENEZUELA, French Guiana (to France)

Fringed by the Pacific and Atlantic oceans and the Caribbean Sea, South America's northern region has a rich range of natural resources, some exploited for centuries by colonial powers including the Spanish, French, Dutch and British, others still to be fully explored. The prospects for further economic development in Colombia, Guyana and Surinam are blighted by drug-related violence and political instability. Venezuela, despite huge incomes from its oil reserves, remains less developed in other industrial sectors. French Guiana is an overseas *département* of France, now seeking greater autonomy. Most of the major population centres, such as Bogotá, have grown up in the temperate conditions of the high Andes or, like Caracas, at strategic points along the Caribbean coast.

► Flowers grown in Colombia are exported all over the world, and include fine carnations and roses. Here, workers are cutting roses which have been grown in plastic greenhouses.

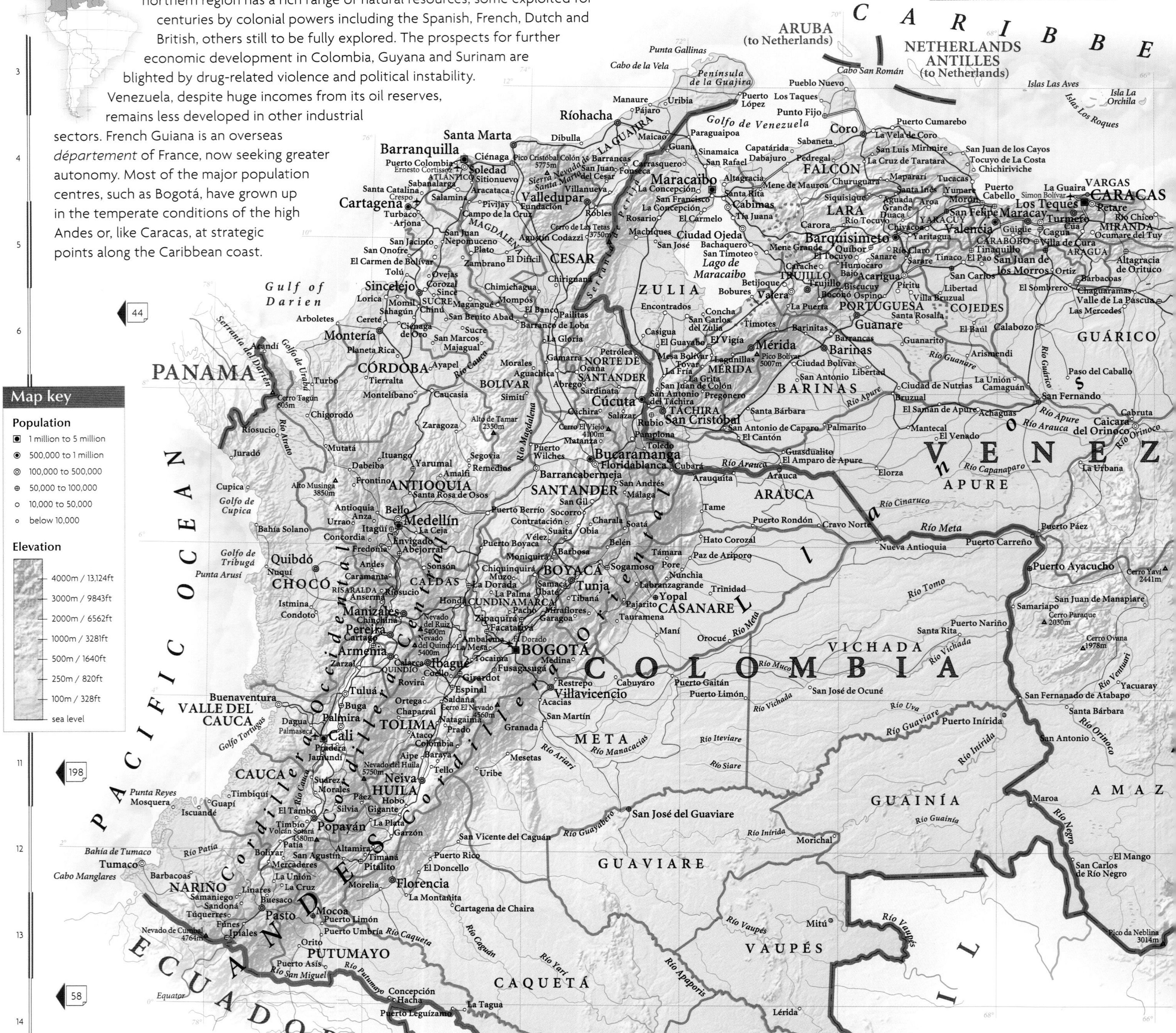

Map key

Population
- ▣ 1 million to 5 million
- ◉ 500,000 to 1 million
- ◎ 100,000 to 500,000
- ⊕ 50,000 to 100,000
- ⊙ 10,000 to 50,000
- ○ below 10,000

Elevation
- 4000m / 13,124ft
- 3000m / 9843ft
- 2000m / 6562ft
- 1000m / 3281ft
- 500m / 1640ft
- 250m / 820ft
- 100m / 328ft
- sea level

▲ Large open squares like the Plaza de Bolívar in Bogotá are characteristic of many cities founded by the Spanish.

◄ Scattered farms and villages have grown up on the gentle slopes of this Colombian river valley, utilizing the fertile soils for farming.

Scale 1:6,500,000

Km
0 25 50   100   150   200

Miles
0 25 50   100   150   200

projection: Lambert Azimuthal Equal Area

▲ The Orinoco river flows from its source in the southern Guiana Highlands to form a broad delta on Venezuela's Atlantic coast. One of its distributary channels opens into a wide bay called the Serpent's Mouth.

Transport and industry

Many mineral resources are mined in Colombia, including fuels, gold and precious and semi-precious stones. Revenues from coffee and exports of illegal narcotics are crucial to the economy. Venezuela's major economic activity is the oil industry around Lake Maracaibo (*Lago de Maracaibo*). Sugar and bauxite are exported from Guyana and Surinam.

The transport network

31,720 miles (51,054 km)	
3411 miles (5490 km)	
2448 miles (3940 km)	
22,429 miles (36,100 km)	

Rivers are an important means of transport in Colombia; many are extensively navigable. The Pan-American Highway runs through Colombia. In Venezuela, much infrastructure investment is linked to the oil industry.

Major industry and infrastructure

- chemicals
- finance
- food processing
- iron & steel
- narcotics
- mining
- oil
- oil refining
- pharmaceuticals
- textiles
- timber processing
- ● capital cities
- ■ major towns
- ⊕ international airports
- — major roads
- major industrial areas

▲ *Vast oil reserves around Lake Maracaibo (Lago de Maracaibo) form the focus of Venezuelan industry. Incomes from oil are used to invest in other industries and in the development of infrastructure.*

Using the land

The Andean basins support cereals and potatoes. Livestock graze at higher altitudes and on the drier tropical grasslands known as the *llanos*; hardy goats are reared in scrubland areas. Grown at higher elevations, coffee is an important cash crop, as is cotton, sugar cane, bananas, citrus fruits, cocoa and rice, farmed on the Caribbean lowlands. Coca is the most widely-grown narcotic plant, with heroin poppies grown in Colombia and marijuana in lowland areas throughout the region.

The urban/rural population divide

urban 80%   rural 20%

0 10 20 30 40 50 60 70 80 90 100

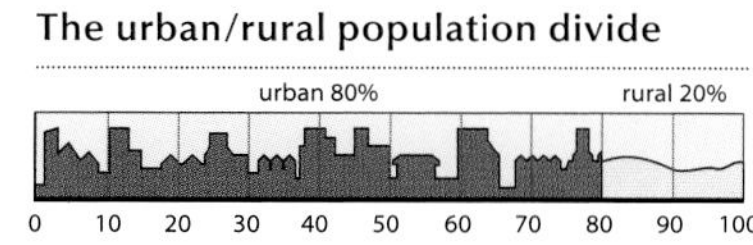

Population density	Total land area
78 people per sq mile (30 people per sq km)	1,111,317 sq miles (2,879,060 sq km)

Land use and agricultural distribution

- cattle
- goats
- bananas
- cereals
- coffee
- cotton
- sugar cane
- ■ capital cities
- ● major towns
- pasture
- cropland
- forest
- wetlands
- mountain region

The landscape

At its northernmost reaches, in western Colombia and Venezuela, the great Andean mountain chain splits into three distinct ranges: the Cordillera Oriental, Cordillera Central and Cordillera Occidental, intercut by a complex series of lesser ranges and basins. The relief becomes lower toward the coast and the interior plains of the northern Amazon Basin, rising again into the tropical hills of the Guiana Highlands.

▲ *The Sierra Nevada de Santa Marta is a granite massif which rises sharply from the Caribbean lowlands to snow-covered peaks, the tallest of which is 18,947 ft (5775 m) high.*

Lake Maracaibo (*Lago de Maracaibo*) is not a true lake but a shallow inlet of the Caribbean Sea. It is the main source of Venezuela's oil.

The drainage basin of the Magdalena River and the Cauca, its main tributary, covers over 20% of Colombia's total surface area.

Colombia's eastern lowlands are known locally as *llanos*, meaning grasslands.

In the Guiana Highlands, Venezuela's most remote region, the ancient crystalline rocks contain deposits of iron ore, gold and diamonds.

Angel Falls (*Salto Ángel*), at 3212 ft (979 m), is the world's highest waterfall.

Igneous intrusions into the crystalline plateau which forms most of central Guyana have led to the formation of the many rapids which characterize Guyana's rivers.

Guyana Shield
- Alluvial plains
- Inselbergs
- Table mountains

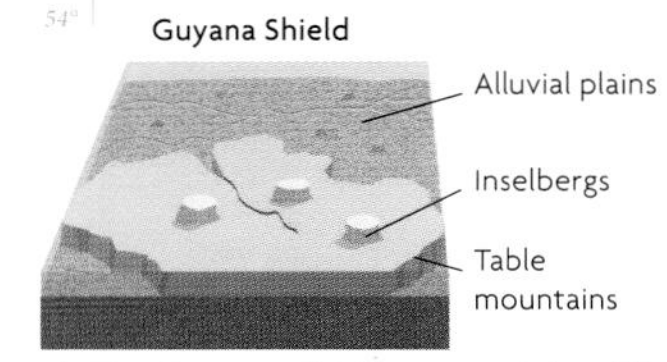

▲ *The Guyana Shield is one of the oldest land surfaces in the world – probably formed more than 4 billion years ago. Chemical weathering over millions of years has created flat-topped table mountains and large numbers of inselbergs.*

Over 80% of Surinam is covered by tropical rainforest.

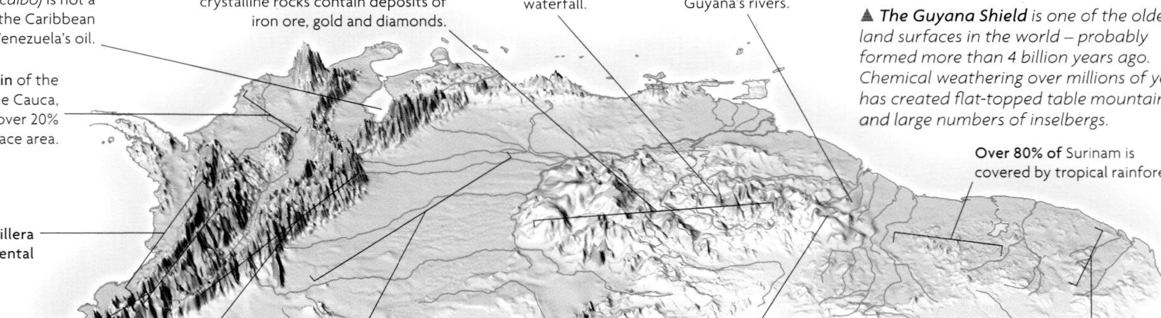

▶ *The Potaru river descends 741 ft (226 m) over a sandstone ledge at the Kaieteur Falls in Guyana.*

Most of the land in French Guiana is low-lying; here, the rocks of the Guiana Highlands have been eroded by rivers flowing towards the sea.

Cordillera Occidental
Cordillera Central
Cordillera Oriental
Potaru river

Western South America

BOLIVIA, ECUADOR, PERU

The three states of Western South America share a similar geography and recent history. Dominated by the Inca empire until Spanish conquest in the 16th century, they achieved independence from Spain in the early 19th century. The precipitous terrain of the Andes presents severe difficulties for overland transport and continues to be a barrier to national unity and stability. Although Ecuador is now a relatively stable democracy, the military is highly influential in Peru and Bolivia, while the drug trade and associated corruption discourages external aid and economic progress. Wealth and power are still largely concentrated in the hands of a small elite of families, who attained their position during the Spanish colonial period. Energy resources and political recognition for the indigenous peoples are becoming increasingly important issues, particularly in Bolivia.

The landscape

Bolivia, Peru and Ecuador each possess a high Andean mountain region and an eastern region consisting of tropical lowlands and the Andean slope leading down to them. Towards the south of the region, the mountains widen to form the high plateau of the Altiplano. Peru and Ecuador also have fertile, lowland coastal plains. A wide variety of environments include selva (tropical rainforest), montaña (mountain forest) and grassland.

▲ **There are many** large and active volcanoes in the Andes. Magma generated in the heart of the volcano erupts in a huge cloud of ash. Ash-fall deposits are common throughout the Andes and the rock produced is known as andesite. This is rapidly soaked by heavy rain, causing massive debris flows.

Cotopaxi is the world's highest active volcano, with a peak 19,347 ft (5897 m) high. A massive eruption in 1877 caused a mudflow which destroyed everything in its path for 150 miles (240 km).

Fast-flowing tributaries of the Amazon, which rise in the Andes, run eastwards through the front ranges to reach the tropical lowlands. They cut valleys so deep that tropical environments can be found extending well into mountainous areas.

Much of eastern Ecuador is covered by the tropical rainforest of the Amazon Basin.

Rolling hills and level plains typify the montaña and selva region, which makes up more than 65% of Peru.

The Bolivian oriente covers more than two-thirds of the country. It includes llanos – low alluvial plains, massive swamps, flooded bottomlands, savannah grassland and tropical forests.

The Altiplano is a flat, high plateau lying between the Cordillera Oriental and the Cordillera Occidental at a height of up to 12,500 ft (3800 m). At its margins lie many spurs and alluvial fans.

The steepness of the Andean slopes means that avalanches and debris flows are an ever-present danger. A landslide starting from Nevado Huascarán in Peru in 1970 killed 20,000 people in 2.5 minutes when it engulfed an inhabited valley.

The Peruvian Andes are relatively young mountains which are continually being uplifted, making the area very unstable, with frequent earthquakes. The transport difficulties that they present continue to form a barrier to national unity.

▲ **Lake Titicaca, which** forms part of the border between Peru and Bolivia, is the largest lake in South America and the highest significant body of water in the world at an altitude of 12,507 ft (3812 m).

Lake Titicaca

Bolivian Andes

▲ **Nevado de Illampu** and Nevado de Ancohuma, at 21,275 ft (6485 m) and 21,490 ft (6550 m) respectively, form Illampu, the highest mountain in the Bolivian Andes.

▲ **Ecuador's capital city,** Quito, lies high in the Andes, nestling between snow-capped peaks. At 9350 ft (2850 m), Quito is the second highest capital in the world – La Paz in Bolivia is the highest.

Scale 1:7,750,000

projection: Lambert Azimuthal Equal Area

Map key

Population
- ■ above 5 million
- ◉ 1 million to 5 million
- ◎ 500,000 to 1 million
- ⊕ 100,000 to 500,000
- ○ 50,000 to 100,000
- ○ 10,000 to 50,000
- ○ below 10,000

Elevation
- 6000m / 19,686ft
- 4000m / 13,124ft
- 3000m / 9843ft
- 2000m / 6562ft
- 1000m / 3281ft
- 500m / 1640ft
- 250m / 820ft
- 100m / 328ft
- sea level

Ecuador: Administrative regions
① CARCHI
② TUNGURAHUA
③ BOLIVAR
④ CHIMBORAZO
⑤ ZAMORA CHINCHIPE

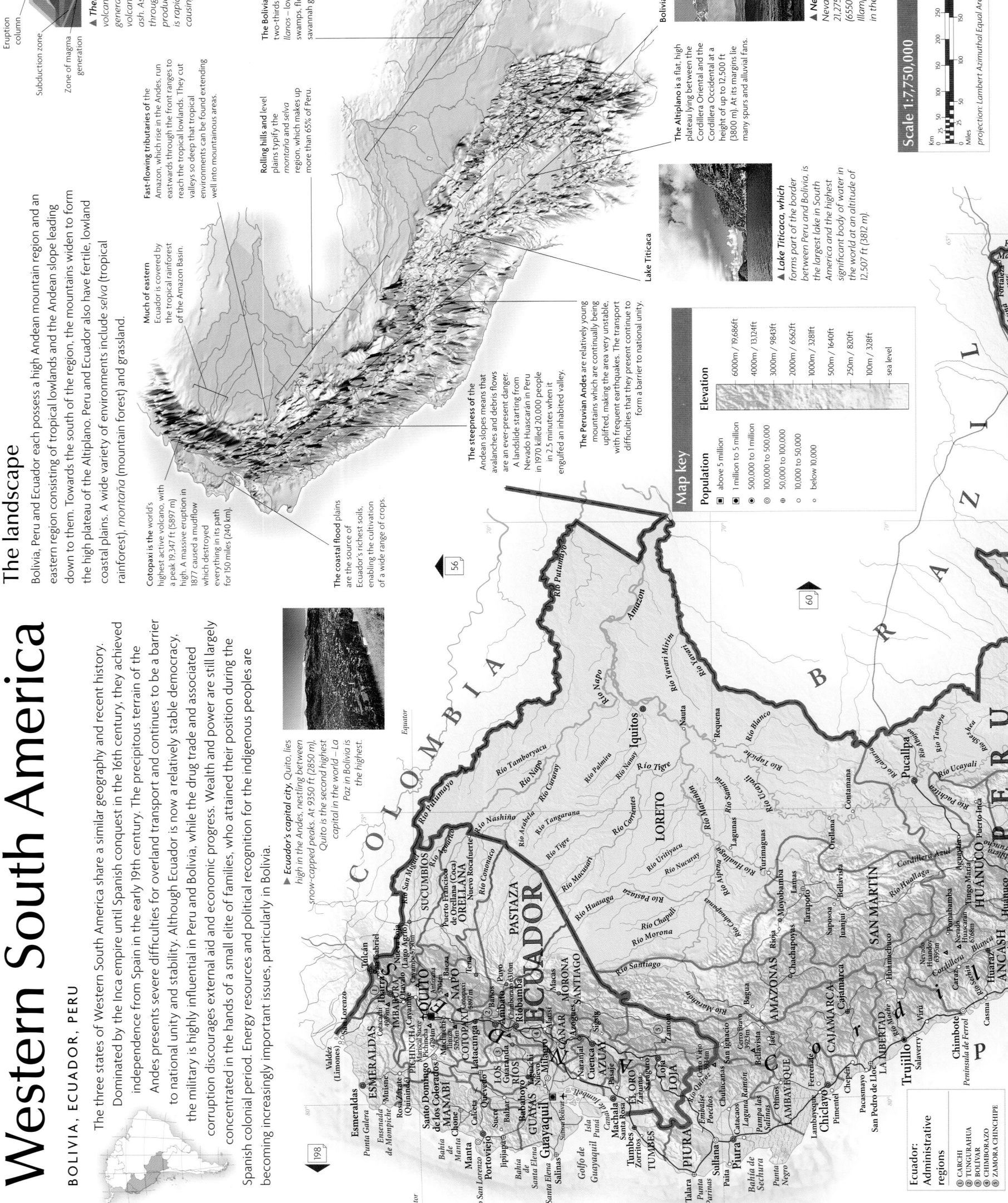

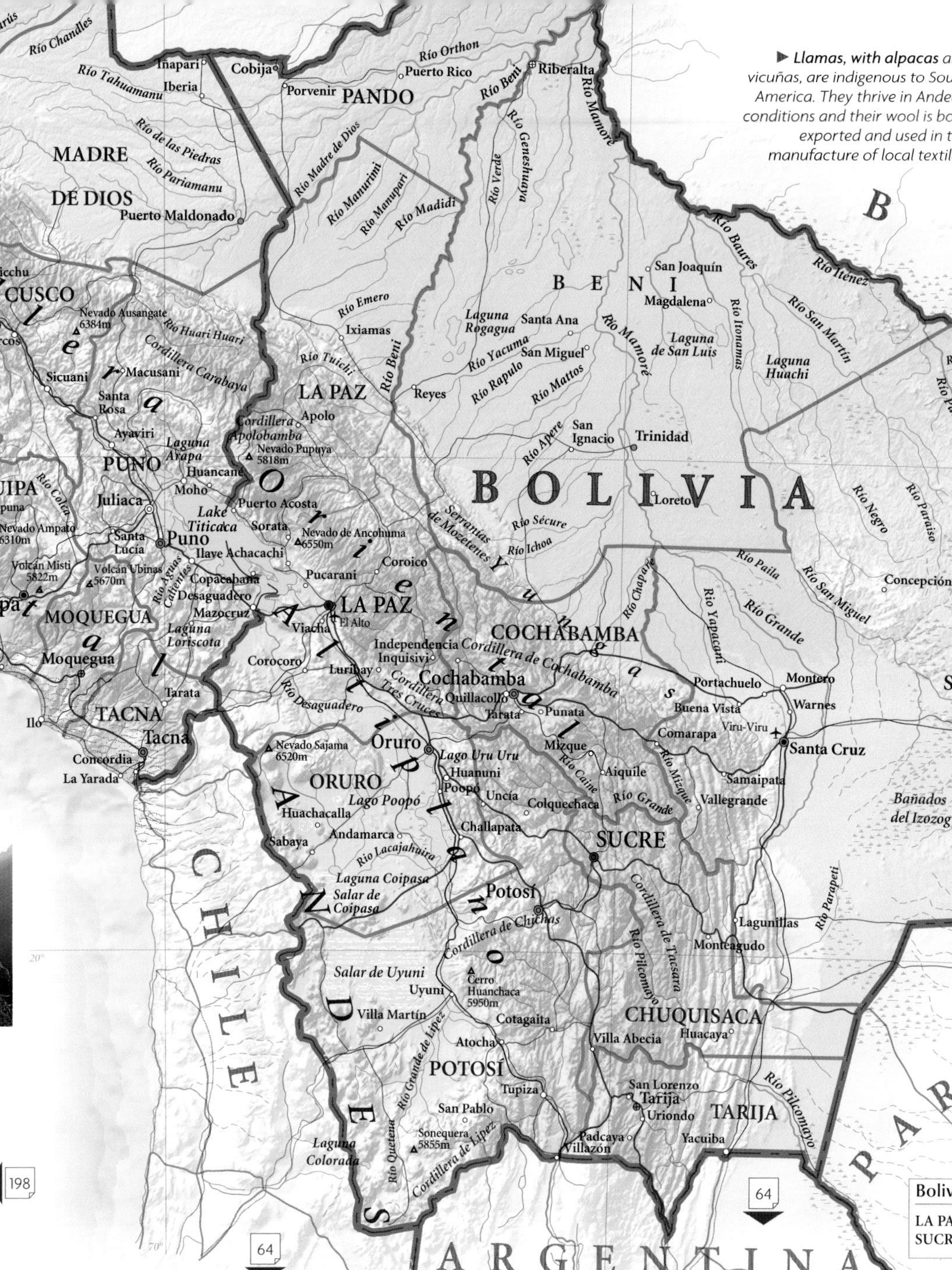

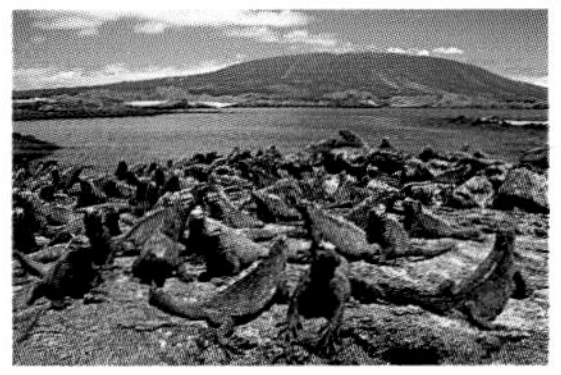

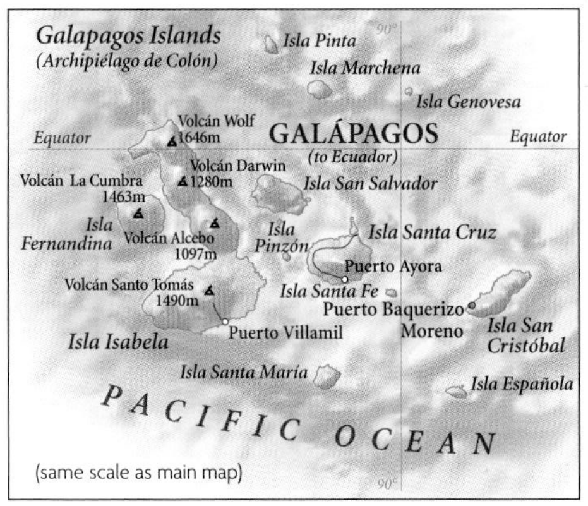

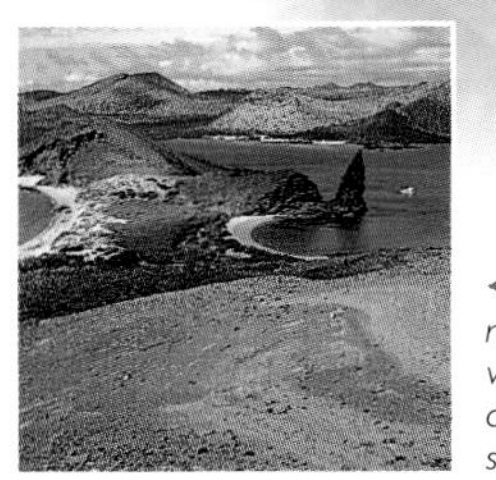

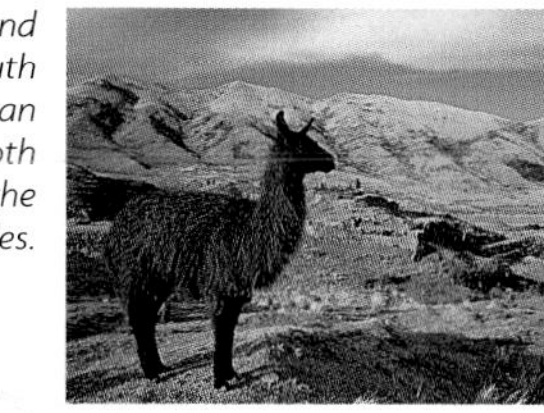

▲ *Llamas, with alpacas and vicuñas, are indigenous to South America. They thrive in Andean conditions and their wool is both exported and used in the manufacture of local textiles.*

Bolivia: Capital cities
LA PAZ – legislative and administrative capital
SUCRE – legal capital

The urban/rural population divide

urban 69%   rural 31%

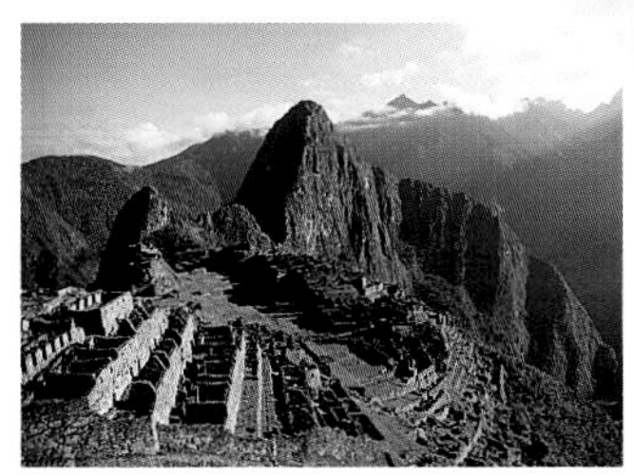

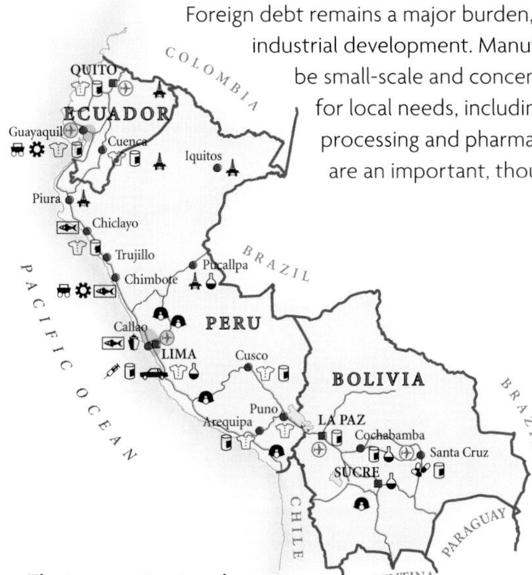

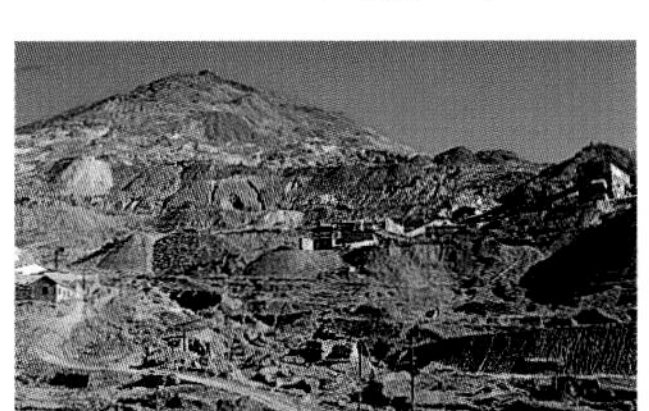

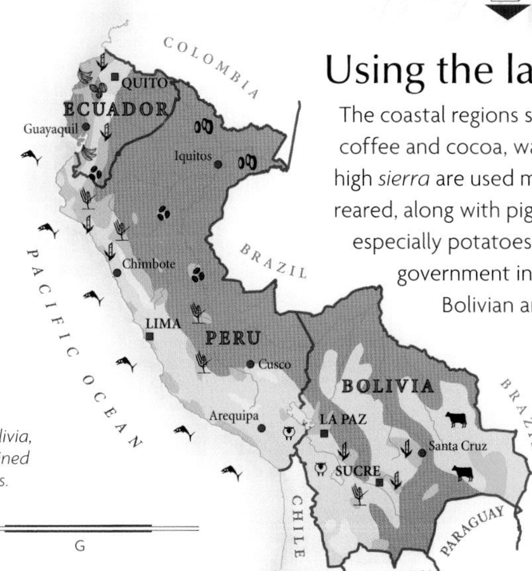

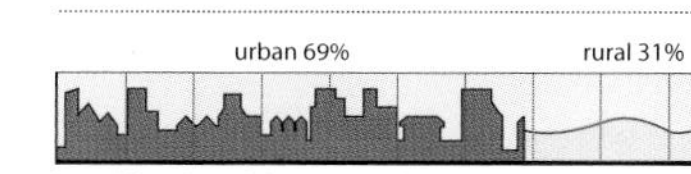

Population density   Total land area
48 people per sq mile   1,019,515 sq miles
(19 people per sq km)   (2,641,230 sq km)

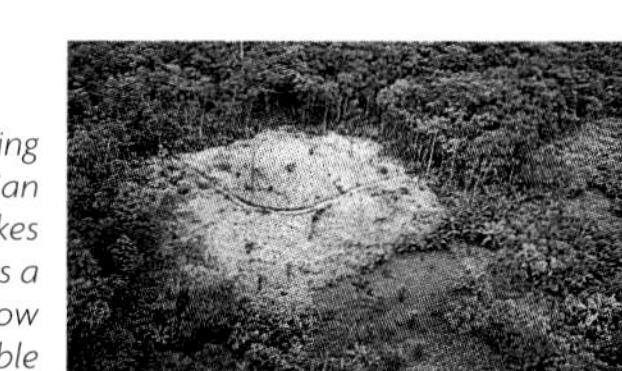

▲ *Clearance of the forest in coca-growing regions is encouraged by the Bolivian government. The inaccessible terrain makes policing the growers very difficult. Coca is a popular crop because it is simple to grow and to transport, and is very profitable when illegally processed as cocaine.*

Using the land and sea

The coastal regions support a variety of cash crops including rice, sugar cane, bananas, coffee and cocoa, watered by rainfall or by irrigation schemes. The grasslands of the high *sierra* are used mainly for grazing a wide range of livestock; cattle and sheep are reared, along with pigs, and the indigenous llama and alpaca. Subsistence crops, especially potatoes and cereals, are grown lower down the mountain flanks. Despite government incentives to grow alternative crops, coca, used for cocaine, is the Bolivian and Peruvian *oriente's* most profitable commercial crop.

Land use and agricultural distribution

cattle
sheep
bananas
cereals
cocoa
coffee
fishing
rubber
sugar cane

● capital cities
▪ major towns

pasture
cropland
forest
mountain region
desert
wetlands

▲ *A colony of marine iguanas basks on the rocks of Isla Fernandina in the Galapagos Islands. Charles Darwin's theory of evolution was inspired by the differences he found between the animal species on neighbouring islands in the Galapagos.*

Galapagos Islands
(Archipiélago de Colón)

(same scale as main map)

▼ *The Galapagos Islands are mainly composed of lava, with very little vegetation near to the coasts, although the wetter inland slopes are mantled with forest.*

▲ *The ancient city of Machupicchu, in the Peruvian Andes was built prior to the Inca period. Its impressive ruins reflect a culture which had developed a high degree of sophistication.*

Transport and industry

The mountain regions are rich in minerals including lead, copper, silver, gold, zinc and tungsten, though high production and transport costs have meant that they are expensive to extract and vulnerable to price collapses. Foreign debt remains a major burden, hampering industrial development. Manufacturing tends to be small-scale and concentrates on products for local needs, including textiles, food processing and pharmaceuticals. Narcotics are an important, though illegal, export.

Major industry and infrastructure

car manufacture
chemicals
engineering
fish processing
food processing
iron & steel
mining
narcotics
oil
pharmaceuticals
shipbuilding

● capital cities
▪ major towns
✈ international airports
— major roads
major industrial areas

▼ *At Potosi in Bolivia, silver has been mined for over 400 years.*

The transport network

13,326 miles (21,449 km)
4217 miles (6787 km)
1993 miles (3208 km)
22,429 miles (36,100 km)

A trans-continental highway is under construction to link Ilo, on Peru's Pacific coast, to Porto Esperanza in Brazil, via Puerto Suárez in Bolivia. Establishing port facilities on the Pacific coast is crucial to landlocked Bolivia's further development.

Brazil

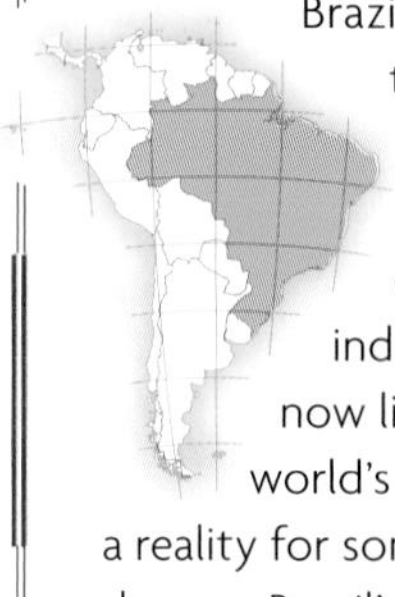

Brazil is the largest country in South America, with a population of 179 million – greater than the combined total for the whole of the rest of the continent. The 26 states which make up the federal republic of Brazil are administered from the purpose-built capital, Brasília. Tropical rainforest, covering more than one-third of the country, contains rich natural resources, but great tracts are sacrificed to agriculture, industry and urban expansion on a daily basis. Most of Brazil's multi-ethnic population now live in cities, some of which are vast areas of urban sprawl; São Paulo is one of the world's biggest conurbations, with more than 19 million inhabitants. Although prosperity is a reality for some, many people still live in great poverty, and mounting foreign debts continue to damage Brazil's prospects of economic advancement.

Using the land

Brazil has immense natural resources, including minerals and hardwoods, many of which are found in the fragile rainforest. Brazil is the world's leading coffee grower and a major producer of livestock, sugar and orange juice concentrate. Soya beans for animal feed, particularly for poultry feed, have become the country's most significant crop.

Land use and agricultural distribution

- cattle
- pigs
- sheep
- citrus fruits
- coffee
- cotton
- soya beans
- sugar cane
- timber
- capital cities
- major towns

pasture
cropland
forest

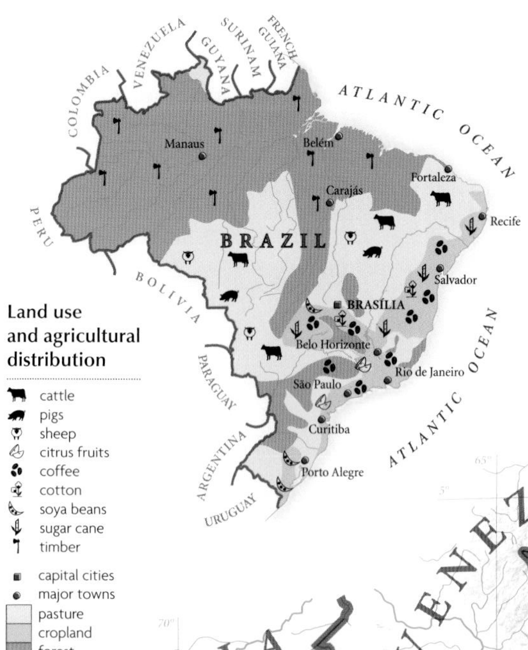

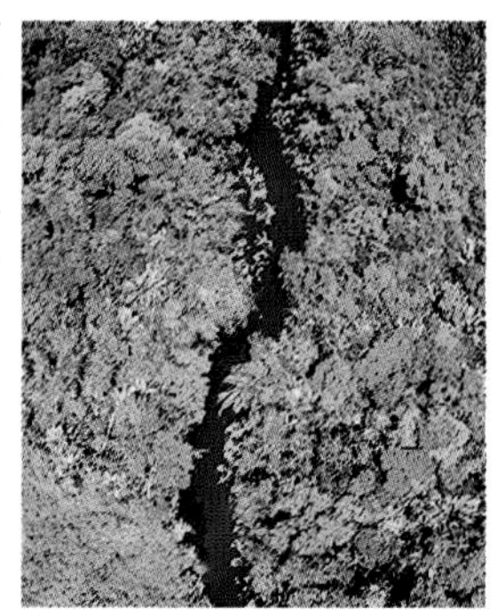

▲ *The fecundity of parts of Brazil's rainforest results from exceptionally high levels of rainfall and the quantities of silt deposited by the Amazon river system.*

The urban/rural population divide

urban 78%   rural 22%

Population density	Total land area
55 people per sq mile (21 people per sq km)	3,286,472 sq miles (8,511,970 sq km)

The landscape

The Amazon Basin, containing the largest area of tropical rainforest on Earth, covers nearly half of Brazil. It is bordered by two shield areas: in the south by the Brazilian Highlands, and in the north by the Guiana Highlands. The east coast is dominated by a great escarpment which runs for 1600 miles (2565 km).

The ancient Brazilian Highlands have a varied topography. Their plateaux, hills and deep valleys are bordered by highly-eroded mountains containing important mineral deposits. They are drained by three great river systems, the Amazon, the Paraguay–Paraná and the São Francisco.

The São Francisco Basin has a climate unique in Brazil. Known as the drought polygon, it has almost no rain during the dry season, leading to regular disastrous droughts.

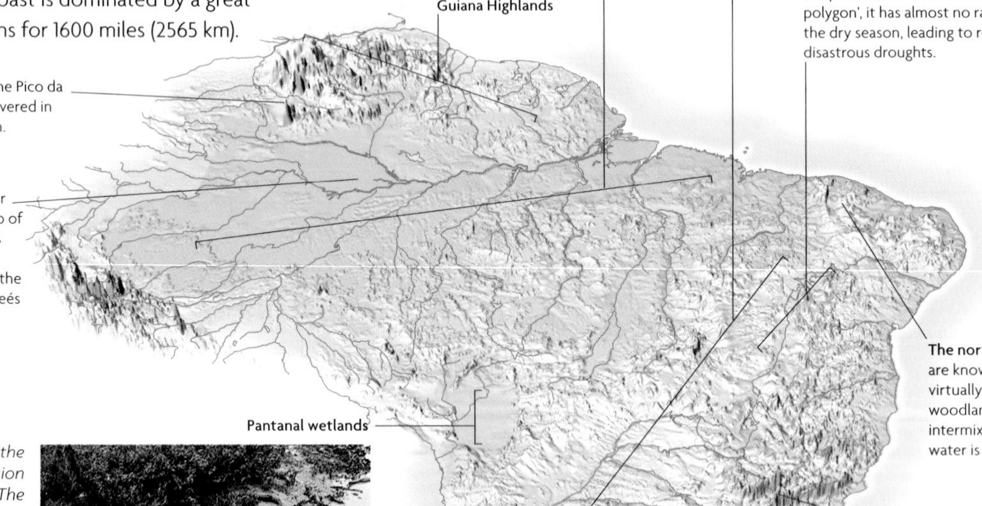

The Amazon Basin is the largest river basin in the world. The Amazon river and over a thousand tributaries drain an area of 2,375,000 sq miles (6,150,000 sq km) and carry one-fifth of the world's fresh water out to sea.

Guiana Highlands

Brazil's highest mountain is the Pico da Neblina which was only discovered in 1962. It is 9888 ft (3014 m) high.

The flood plains which border the Amazon river are made up of a variety of different features including shallow lakes and swamps, mangrove forests in the tidal delta area and fertile levees on river banks and point bars.

Pantanal wetlands

The northeastern scrublands are known as the *caatinga*, a virtually impenetrable thorny woodland, sometimes intermixed with cacti where water is scarce.

The famous Sugar Loaf Mountain (*Pão de Açúcar*) which overlooks Rio de Janeiro is a fine example of a volcanic plug; a domed core of solidified lava left after the slopes of the original volcano have eroded away.

Deep natural harbours such as Baía de Guanabara were created where the steep slopes of the Serra da Mantiqueira plunge directly into the ocean.

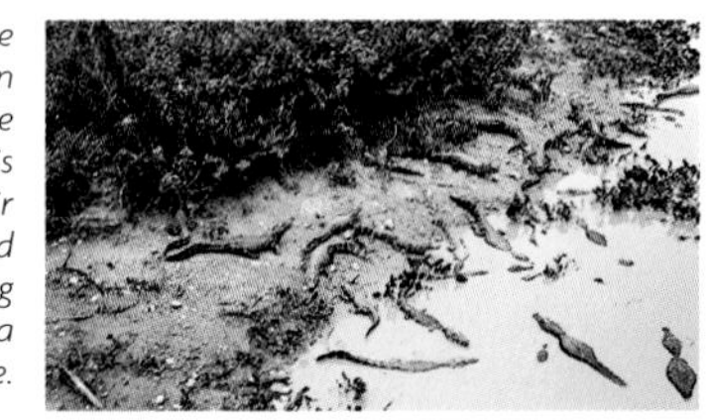

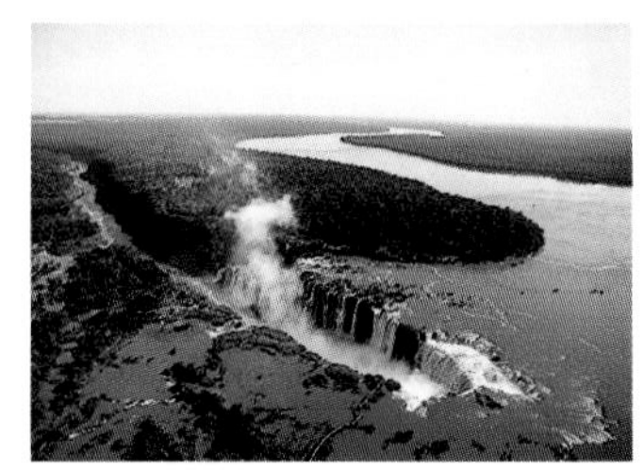

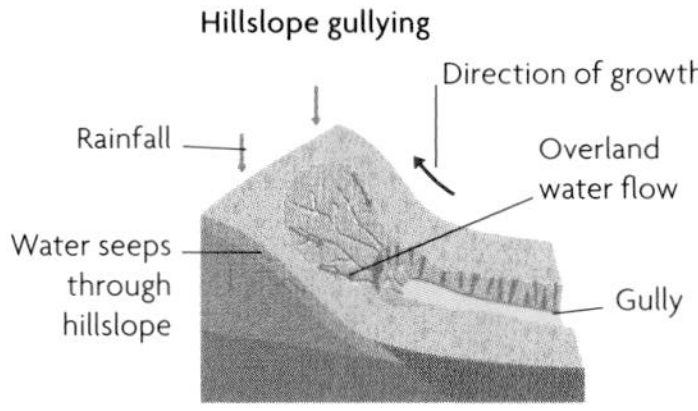

▼ *Large-scale gullies are common in Brazil, particularly on hillslopes from which vegetation has been removed. Gullies grow headwards (up the slope), aided by a combination of erosion through water seepage and rainwater runoff.*

Direction of growth
Overland water flow
Gully

Hillslope gullying
Rainfall
Water seeps through hillslope

▲ *The Pantanal region in the south of Brazil is an extension of the Gran Chaco plain. The swamps and marshes of this area are renowned for their beauty, and abundant and unique wildlife, including wildfowl and these caimans, a type of crocodile.*

▼ *The Iguaçu river surges over the spectacular Iguaçu Falls (Saltos do Iguaçu) towards the Paraná river. Falls like these are increasingly under pressure from large-scale hydro-electric projects such as that at Itaipú.*

Map key

Population
- above 5 million
- 1 million to 5 million
- 500,000 to 1 million
- 100,000 to 500,000
- 50,000 to 100,000
- 10,000 to 50,000
- below 10,000

Elevation
- 3000m / 9843ft
- 2000m / 6562ft
- 1000m / 3281ft
- 500m / 1640ft
- 250m / 820ft
- 100m / 328ft
- sea level

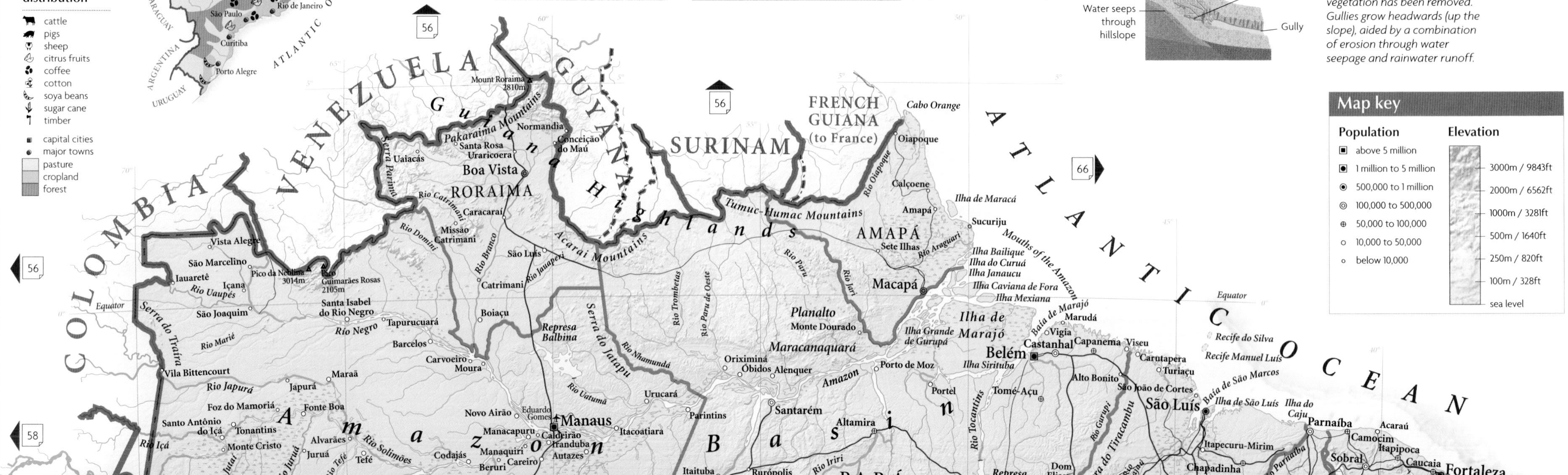

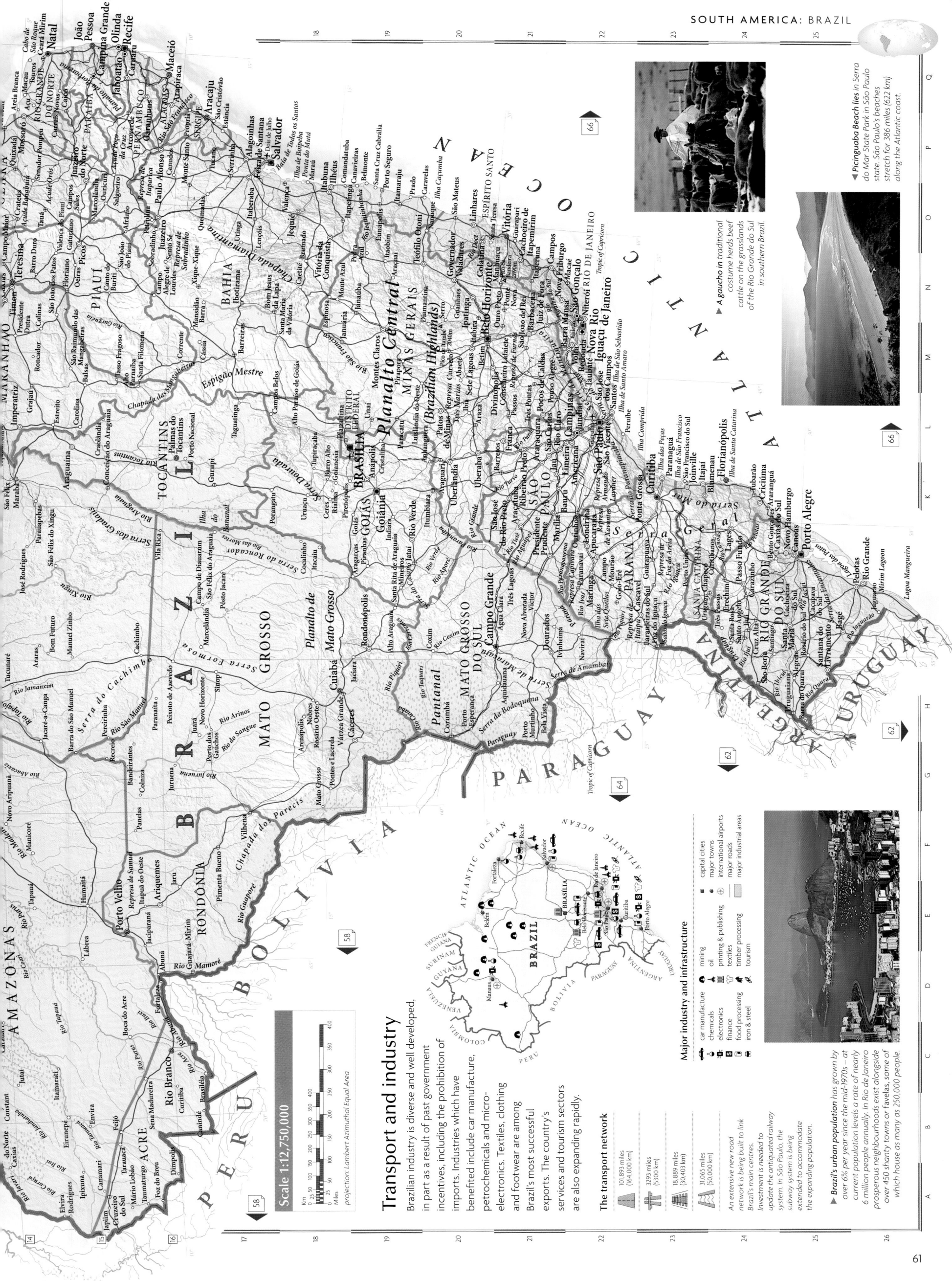

▶ *Picinguaba Beach lies in Serra do Mar State Park in São Paulo state. São Paulo's beaches stretch for 386 miles (612 km) along the Atlantic coast.*

▶ *A gaucho in traditional costume herds beef cattle on the grasslands of the Rio Grande do Sul in southern Brazil.*

Transport and industry

Brazilian industry is diverse and well developed, in part as a result of past government incentives, including the prohibition of imports. Industries which have benefited include car manufacture, and microelectronics and micro-petrochemicals and microelectronics. Textiles, clothing and footwear are among Brazil's most successful exports. The country's services and tourism sectors are also expanding rapidly.

Scale 1:12,750,000

projection: Lambert Azimuthal Equal Area

The transport network

- 101,893 miles (164,000 km)
- 3293 miles (5300 km)
- 18,889 miles (30,403 km)
- 31,065 miles (50,000 km)

An extensive new road network is being built to link Brazil's main centres. Investment is needed to update the antiquated railway system. In São Paulo, the subway system is being extended to accommodate the expanding population.

Major industry and infrastructure

- car manufacture
- chemicals
- electronics
- finance
- food processing
- iron & steel
- mining
- oil
- printing & publishing
- textiles
- timber processing
- tourism
- capital cities
- major towns
- international airports
- major roads
- major industrial areas

▶ *Brazil's urban population has grown by over 6% per year since the mid-1970s – at current population levels a rate of nearly 6 million people annually. In Rio de Janeiro prosperous neighbourhoods exist alongside over 450 shanty towns or favelas, some of which house as many as 250,000 people.*

Eastern South America

URUGUAY, NORTHEAST ARGENTINA, SOUTHEAST BRAZIL

The vast conurbations of Rio de Janeiro, São Paulo and Buenos Aires form the core of South America's highly-urbanized eastern region. São Paulo state, with over 40 million inhabitants, is among the world's 20 most powerful economies, and São Paulo is the fastest growing city on the continent. Rio de Janeiro and Buenos Aires, transformed in the last hundred years from port cities to great metropolitan areas each with more than 10 million inhabitants, typify the unstructured growth and wealth disparities of South America's great cities. In Uruguay, two fifths of the population lives in the capital.

Montevideo, which faces Buenos Aires across the River Plate (Rio de la Plata). Immigration from the countryside has created severe pressure on the urban infrastructure, particularly on available housing, leading to a profusion of crowded shanty settlements (favelas or barrios).

Using the land

Most of Uruguay and the Pampas of northern Argentina are devoted to the rearing of livestock, especially cattle and sheep, which are central to both countries' economies. Soya beans, first produced in Brazil's Rio Grande do Sul, are now more widely grown for large-scale export, as are cereals, sugar cane and grapes. Subsistence crops, including potatoes, corn and sugar beet, are grown on the remaining arable land.

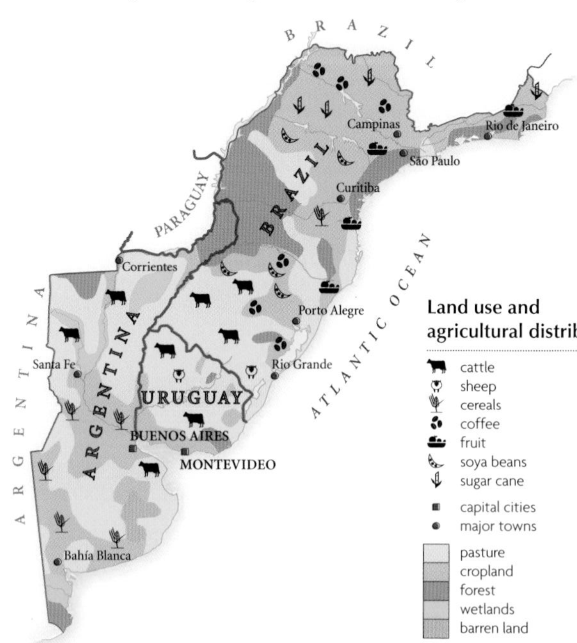

▼ The rolling grasslands of Uruguay are ideally suited to the rearing of cattle, which are concentrated in great herds throughout the region.

Land use and agricultural distribution

- ⚘ cattle
- ⚘ sheep
- ⚘ cereals
- ⚘ coffee
- ⚘ fruit
- ⚘ soya beans
- ⚘ sugar cane
- ⚘ major cities

- pasture
- cropland
- forest
- wetlands
- barren land

Transport and industry

Southeast Brazil is home to much of the important motor and capital goods industry, largely based around São Paulo; iron and steel production is also concentrated in this region. Uruguay's economy continues to be based mainly on the export of livestock products including meat and leather goods. Buenos Aires is Argentina's chief port, and the region has a varied and sophisticated economic base including service-based industries such as finance and publishing, as well as primary processing.

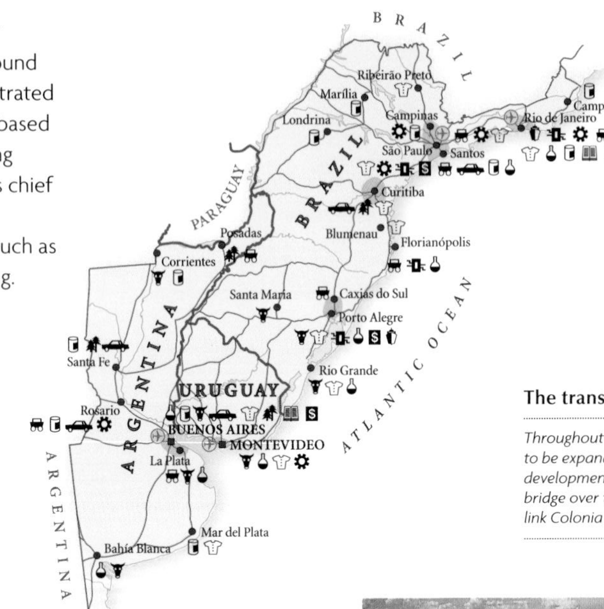

Major industry and infrastructure

- 🚗 car manufacture
- chemicals
- engineering
- finance
- food processing
- iron & steel
- meat processing
- printing & publishing
- shipbuilding
- textiles
- timber processing
- capital cities
- major towns
- international airports
- major roads
- major industrial areas

The transport network

Throughout the region, road networks need to be expanded to cope with urban development. Plans are underway to build a bridge over the River Plate (Rio de la Plata) to link Colonia and Buenos Aires.

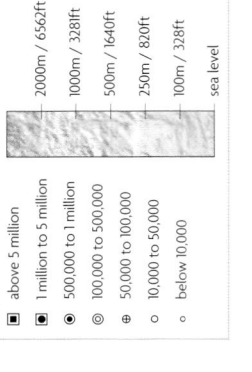

▲ Soya beans are harvested, pressed, and processed into soya cake, which is used as animal feed. The cake is fed mainly to chickens on large-scale factory farms, and the growth in soya production has been an important factor in the expansion of the Brazilian poultry trade.

Map key

Population
- ■ above 5 million
- ■ 1 million to 5 million
- ◉ 500,000 to 1 million
- ⊕ 100,000 to 500,000
- ⊙ 50,000 to 100,000
- ○ 10,000 to 50,000
- ∘ below 10,000

Elevation
- 2000m / 6562ft
- 1000m / 3281ft
- 500m / 1640ft
- 250m / 820ft
- 100m / 328ft
- sea level

Scale 1:6,250,000

Km 0 25 50 75 100 150 200
Miles 0 25 50 75 100 150 200

projection: Lambert Azimuthal Equal Area

▲ The Itaipú dam on the Paraná river is one of the largest hydro-electric projects in the world, jointly financed by Brazil and Paraguay.

▲ Rio de Janeiro's annual carnival, Mardi Gras, which ushers in the start of Lent, is an extravagant five-day parade through the city, characterized by fantastically decorated floats, exuberant dancing and samba music.

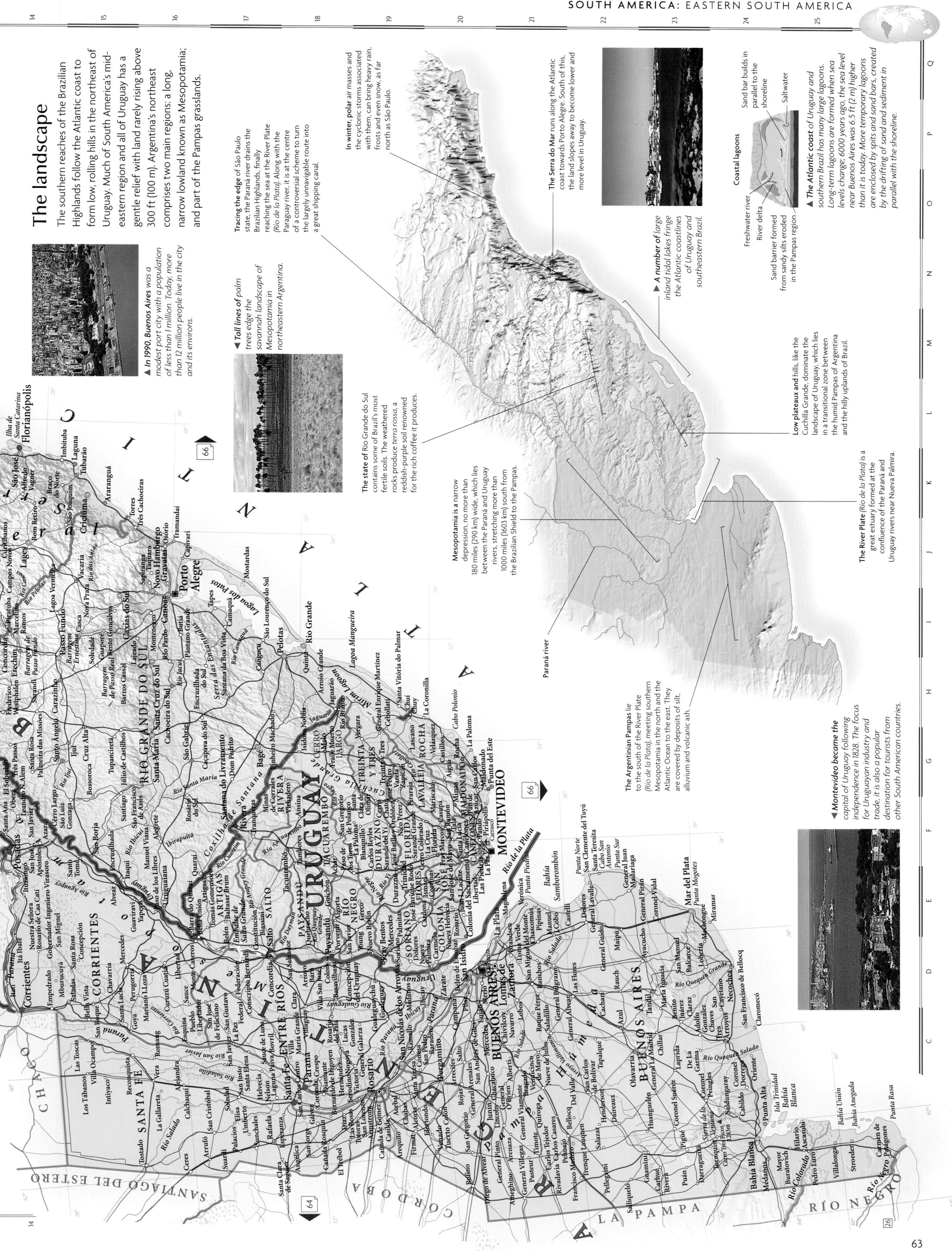

The landscape

The southern reaches of the Brazilian Highlands follow the Atlantic coast to form low, rolling hills in the northeast of Uruguay. Much of South America's mid-eastern region and all of Uruguay has a gentle relief with land rarely rising above 300 ft (100 m). Argentina's northeast comprises two main regions: a long, narrow lowland known as Mesopotamia; and part of the Pampas grasslands.

Tracing the edge of São Paulo state, the Paraná river drains the Brazilian Highlands, finally reaching the sea at the River Plate (Rio de la Plata). Along with the Paraguay river, it is at the centre of a controversial scheme to turn the largely unnavigable route into a great shipping canal.

▲ *In 1990, Buenos Aires was a modest port city with a population of less than 1 million. Today, more than 12 million people live in the city and its environs.*

▼ *Tall lines of palm trees edge the savannah landscape of Mesopotamia in northeastern Argentina.*

The state of Rio Grande do Sul contains some of Brazil's most fertile soils. The weathered rocks produce terra rossa, a reddish-purple soil renowned for the rich coffee it produces.

In winter, polar air masses and the cyclonic storms associated with them, can bring heavy rain, frosts and even snow, as far north as São Paulo.

The Serra do Mar runs along the Atlantic coast towards Porto Alegre. South of this, the land slopes away to become lower and more level in Uruguay.

▲ *A number of large inland tidal lakes fringe the Atlantic coastlines of Uruguay and southeastern Brazil.*

Coastal lagoons

Sand bar builds in parallel to the shoreline

Freshwater river

River delta

Sand barrier formed from sandy silts eroded

Saltwater

▲ *The Atlantic coast of Uruguay and southern Brazil has many large lagoons. Long-term lagoons are formed when sea levels change; 6000 years ago, the sea level near Buenos Aires was 6.5 ft (2 m) higher than it is today. More temporary lagoons are enclosed by spits and sand bars, created by the drifting of sand and sediment in parallel with the shoreline.*

Low plateaux and hills, like the Cuchilla Grande, dominate the landscape of Uruguay, which lies in a transitional zone between the humid Pampas of Argentina and the hilly uplands of Brazil.

Mesopotamia is a narrow depression, no more than 180 miles (290 km) wide, which lies between the Paraná and Uruguay rivers, stretching more than 1000 miles (1603 km) south from the Brazilian Shield to the Pampas.

The River Plate (Rio de la Plata) is a great estuary formed at the confluence of the Paraná and Uruguay rivers near Nueva Palmira.

Paraná river

The Argentinian Pampas lie to the south of the River Plate (Rio de la Plata), meeting southern Mesopotamia in the north and the Atlantic Ocean to the east. They are covered by deposits of silt, alluvium and volcanic ash.

▼ *Montevideo became the capital of Uruguay following independence in 1828. The focus for Uruguayan industry and trade, it is also a popular destination for tourists from other South American countries.*

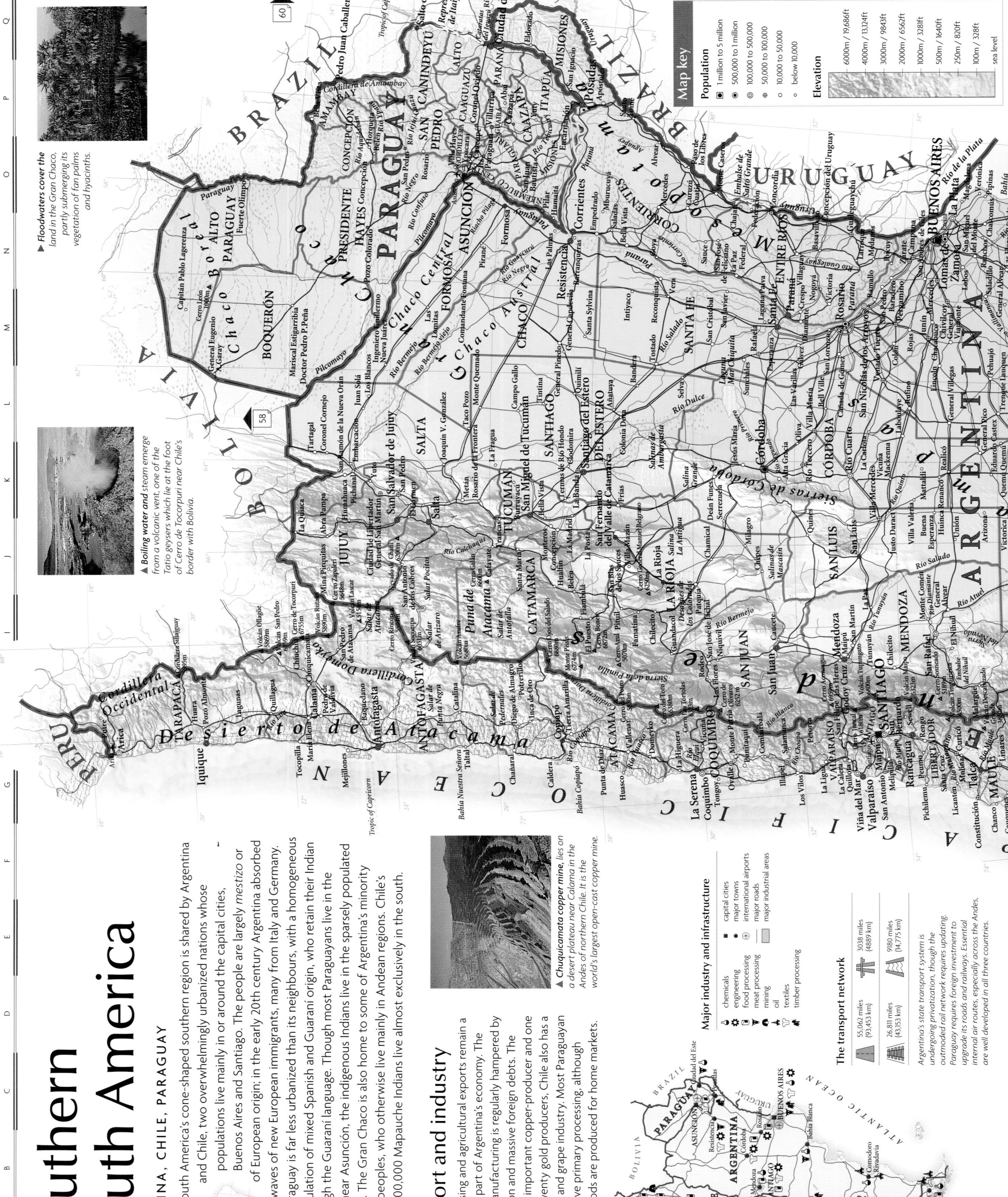

Southern South America

ARGENTINA, CHILE, PARAGUAY

South America's cone-shaped southern region is shared by Argentina and Chile, two overwhelmingly urbanized nations whose populations live mainly in or around the capital cities, Buenos Aires and Santiago. The people are largely *mestizo* or of European origin; in the early 20th century Argentina absorbed waves of new European immigrants, many from Italy and Germany. Paraguay is far less urbanized than its neighbours, with a homogeneous population of mixed Spanish and Guaraní origin, who retain their Indian roots through the Guaraní language. Though most Paraguayans live in the southeast, near Asunción, the indigenous Indians live in the sparsely populated Gran Chaco. The Gran Chaco is also home to some of Argentina's minority indigenous peoples, who otherwise live mainly in Andean regions. Chile's estimated 800,000 Mapuche Indians live almost exclusively in the south.

Transport and industry

Food processing and agricultural exports remain a fundamental part of Argentina's economy. The growth of manufacturing is regularly hampered by hyper-inflation and massive foreign debts. The world's most important copper-producer and one of the top twenty gold producers, Chile also has a thriving wine and grape industry. Most Paraguayan exports involve primary processing, although domestic goods are produced for home markets.

▲ *Floodwaters cover the land in the Gran Chaco, partly submerging its vegetation of fan palms and hyacinths.*

▲ *Boiling water and steam emerge from a volcanic vent, one of the Tatio geysers which lie at the foot of Cerro de Tocorpuri near Chile's border with Bolivia.*

▲ *Chuquicamata copper mine, lies on a desert plateau near Calama in the Andes of northern Chile. It is the world's largest open-cast copper mine.*

Map key

Population
- ◉ 1 million to 5 million
- ◉ 500,000 to 1 million
- ⊕ 100,000 to 500,000
- ⊕ 50,000 to 100,000
- ○ 10,000 to 50,000
- ○ below 10,000

Elevation
- 6000m / 19,686ft
- 4000m / 13,124ft
- 3000m / 9843ft
- 2000m / 6562ft
- 1000m / 3281ft
- 500m / 1640ft
- 250m / 820ft
- 100m / 328ft
- sea level

Major industry and infrastructure

- chemicals
- engineering
- food processing
- meat processing
- mining
- oil
- textiles
- timber processing

- ■ capital cities
- • major cities
- • major towns
- ✈ international airports
- — major roads
- ▭ major industrial areas

The transport network

55,062 miles (93,453 km)	3038 miles (4889 km)
26,811 miles (43,153 km)	9180 miles (14,775 km)

Argentina's state transport system is undergoing privatization, though the outmoded rail network requires updating. Paraguay requires foreign investment to upgrade its roads and railways. Essential internal air routes, especially across the Andes, are well developed in all three countries.

The landscape

The Andes run from north to south, forming a precipitous natural border between Chile and Argentina. East of the Andes are the scrublands of the Gran Chaco and the plains of the Pampas, which extend northward towards Paraguay. In the far southwest, Chile's indented Pacific coastline has many features typical of areas which have been affected by glaciation.

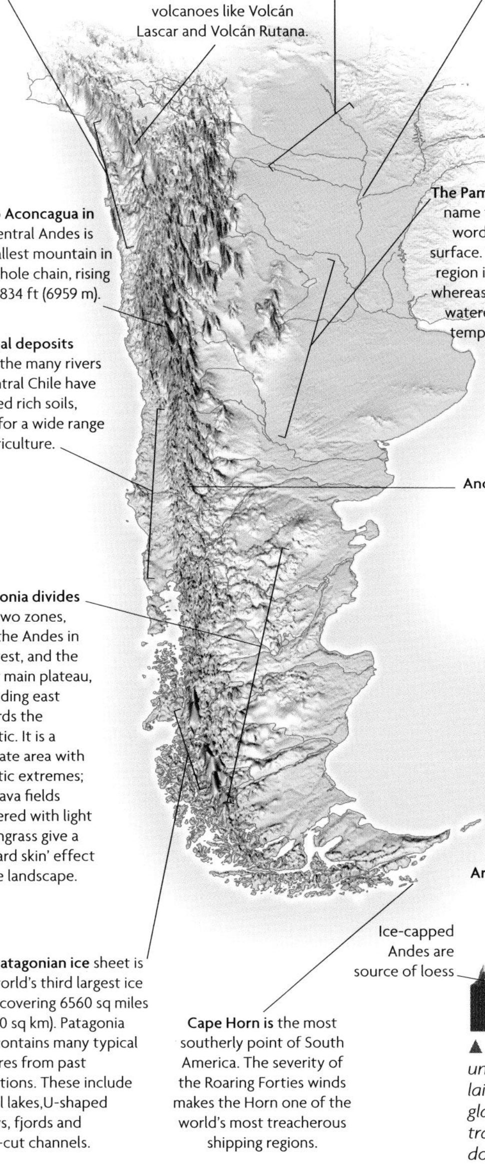

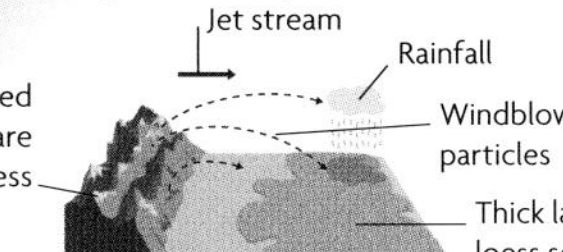

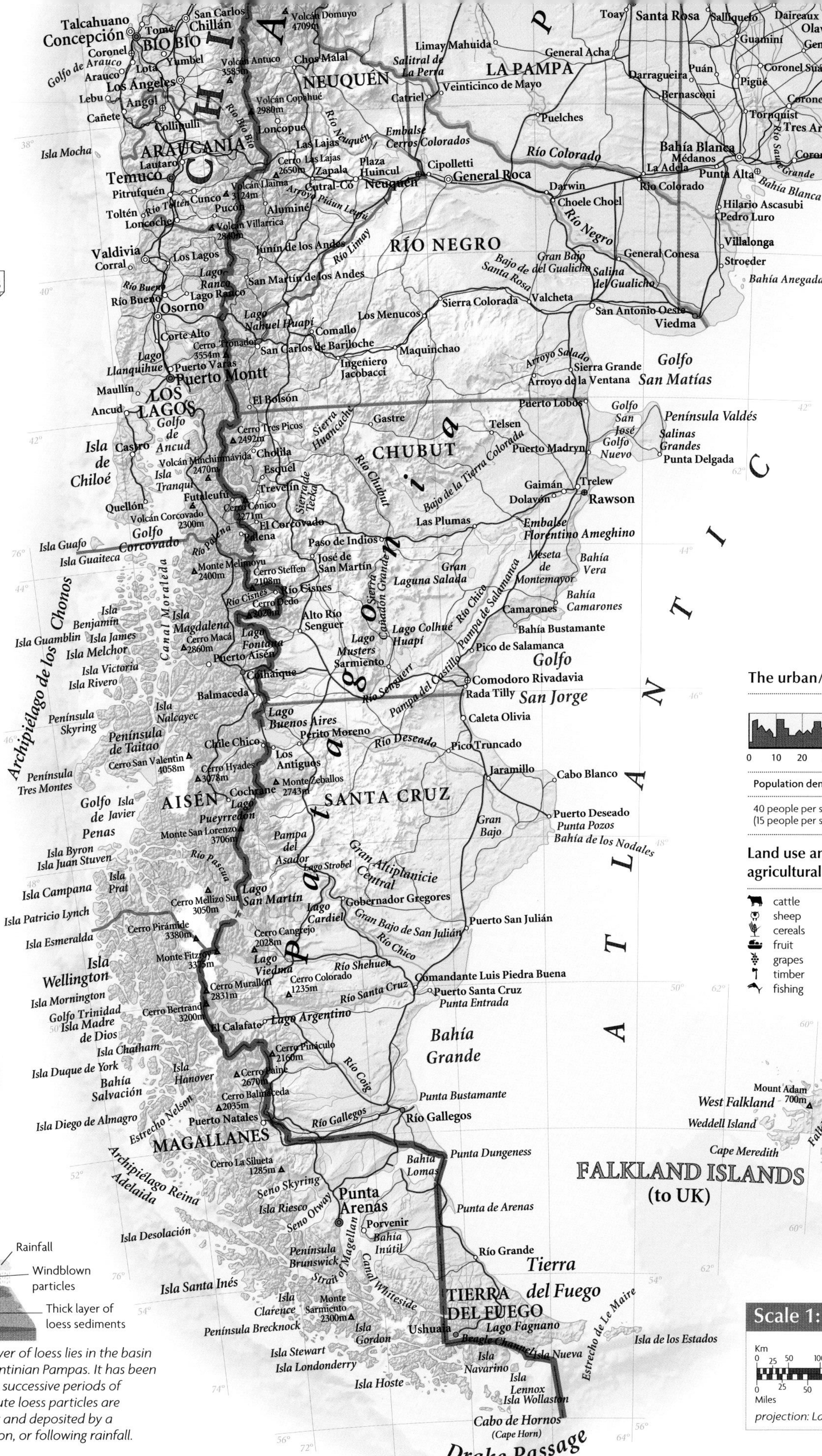

▲ *Great blocks of ice break away from the jagged blue peaks of these ice mountains to form icebergs off the coast of Patagonia, Argentina's most southerly region.*

▲ *The Atacama Desert (Desierto de Atacama) in Chile is one of the driest places on Earth where some areas have never recorded any rain. It contains a number of salt lakes.*

The Gran Chaco combines poor drainage, extremely hot temperatures and thorn-infested scrub to make it one of South America's most inhospitable regions.

Landlocked Paraguay relies on its river system for access to the sea and to produce hydro-electric power. The most important river system is the Paraguay–Paraná which provides links into neighbouring countries including Brazil, Uruguay and Argentina.

Cerro Aconcagua in the Andes is the tallest mountain in the whole chain, rising to 22,834 ft (6959 m).

Alluvial deposits from the many rivers in central Chile have created rich soils, ideal for a wide range of agriculture.

Most of the highest mountains in Chile's northern Andes are volcanoes like Volcán Lascar and Volcán Rutana.

The Pampas derive their name from an Indian word meaning flat surface. The severity of the dry western region is largely desert, whereas the east is well-watered, supporting temperate grasses.

Patagonia divides into two zones, with the Andes in the west, and the lower main plateau, extending east towards the Atlantic. It is a desolate area with climatic extremes; dark lava fields scattered with light bunchgrass give a 'leopard skin' effect to the landscape.

The Patagonian ice sheet is the world's third largest ice field, covering 6560 sq miles (17,000 sq km). Patagonia also contains many typical features from past glaciations. These include glacial lakes, U-shaped valleys, fjords and deep-cut channels.

Cape Horn is the most southerly point of South America. The severity of the Roaring Forties winds makes the Horn one of the world's most treacherous shipping regions.

Ice-capped Andes are source of loess

Andes

Argentinian Pampas

Rainfall
Windblown particles
jet stream
Thick layer of loess sediments

▲ *A thick, fertile layer of loess lies in the basin underlying the Argentinian Pampas. It has been laid down following successive periods of glaciation. The minute loess particles are transported as dust and deposited by a downward air motion, or following rainfall.*

Using the land and sea

The rich plains of the Pampas support massive herds of cattle, producing meat, milk and hides essential to the domestic and export markets of both Argentina and Paraguay. Wheat and fruit are Argentina's other major agricultural products. A wide range of soft fruits, citrus fruits and more specialized crops such as walnuts, and grapes for wine and the table, are grown in Chile's fertile Central Valley, while the landscape to the south is dominated by forestry, mainly growing commercial radiata pine. Paraguay is self-sufficient in wheat and other staples. Cotton, coffee, tobacco and oilseeds such as soya, are the major export crops.

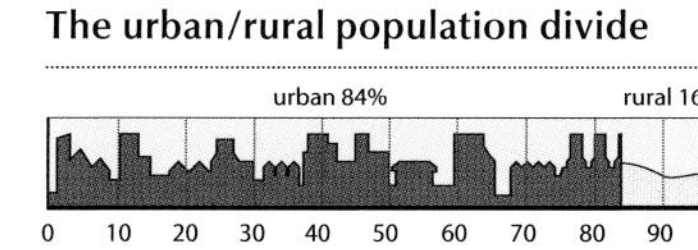

▲ *Charred tree stumps surround a cattle enclosure on the island of Tierra del Fuego in southern Argentina. Forest clearance to provide grazing land for cattle is of major environmental concern.*

The urban/rural population divide
urban 84%   rural 16%

Population density
40 people per sq mile
(5 people per sq km)

Total land area
1,498,757 sq miles
(3,882,790 sq km)

Land use and agricultural distribution
- capital cities
- major towns
- pasture
- cropland
- forest
- barren land
- mountain region
- desert

cattle, sheep, cereals, fruit, grapes, timber, fishing

Scale 1:8,750,000
projection: Lambert Azimuthal Equal Area

The Atlantic Ocean

The Atlantic is the youngest of the world's oceans, formed about 180 million years ago when the landmasses of the eastern and western hemispheres separated. Its underwater topography is dominated by the Mid-Atlantic Ridge, a huge mountain system running north to south along the centre of the ocean. Although most of the ridge's peaks lie below the sea, some emerge as volcanic islands, like Iceland and the Azores.

The Atlantic contains a wealth of resources, including substantial oil and gas reserves and rich fishing grounds. Until the 1950s, the north Atlantic was the world's busiest shipping route; cheaper air transport and alternative routes have shifted patterns of world trade.

Resources

Development of the oil and gas reserves in the Atlantic began in the 1940s around the Gulf of Mexico. Since then other areas have been exploited, including the North Sea, the west coast of Africa and the area east of Newfoundland and Nova Scotia. There is also extensive mining of sand, gravel and shell deposits by the USA and UK. For centuries, the north Atlantic's fishing grounds have been utilized more heavily than other oceans, leading to a serious decline in many fish stocks.

▲ Surtsey near Iceland, lies on the Mid-Atlantic Ridge. The island was formed in 1963 following a volcanic eruption caused by sea-floor spreading.

▲ On 5 January 1993, the oil tanker Braer ran aground in the Shetland Islands, spilling 83,660 tons (85,000 tonnes) of light crude oil into the ocean, devastating the local marine ecosystem.

▲ Fishing in the seas around northwestern Europe dates back over 1500 years. The high nutrient content of the seas makes them ideal breeding grounds for many species of fish.

Resources (including wildlife)
- fish
- whales
- aggregates
- oil & gas
- major towns
- major ports

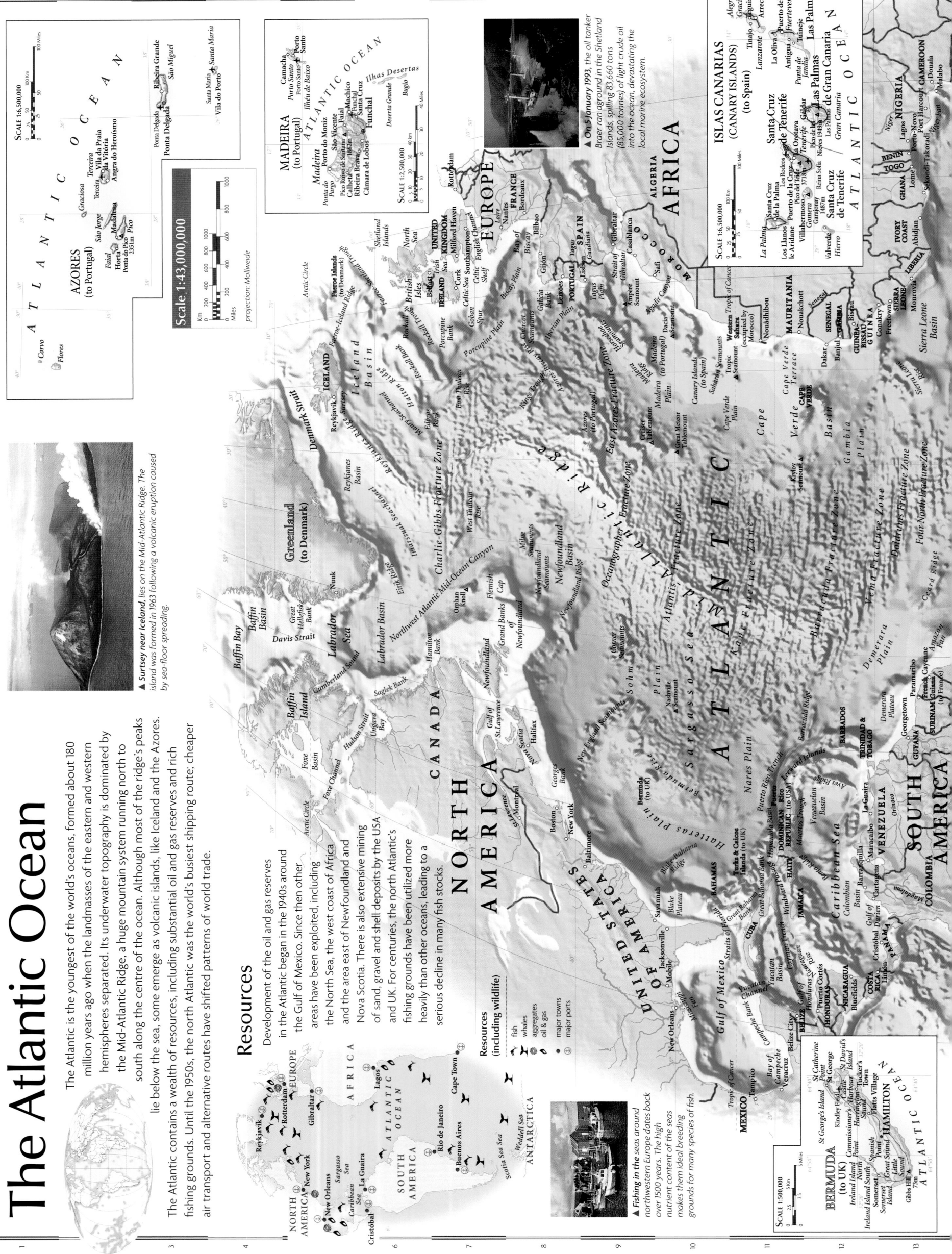

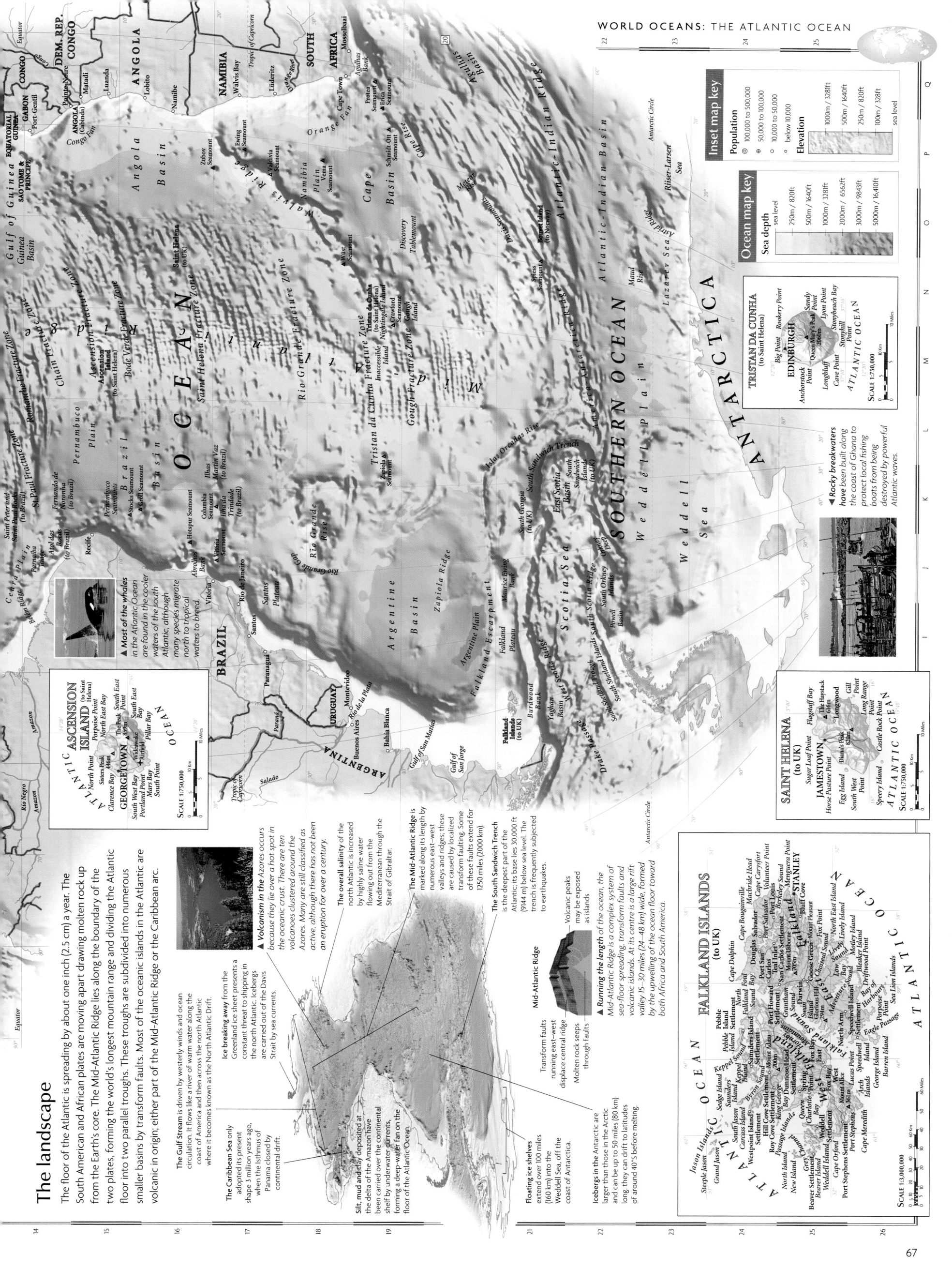

The landscape

The floor of the Atlantic is spreading by about one inch (2.5 cm) a year. The South American and African plates are moving apart drawing molten rock up from the Earth's core. The Mid-Atlantic Ridge lies along the boundary of the two plates, forming the world's longest mountain range and dividing the Atlantic floor into two parallel troughs. These troughs are subdivided into numerous smaller basins by transform faults. Most of the oceanic islands in the Atlantic are volcanic in origin; either part of the Mid-Atlantic Ridge or the Caribbean arc.

▲ Most of the whales in the Atlantic Ocean are found in the cooler waters of the south Atlantic, although many species migrate north to tropical waters to breed.

The Gulf Stream is driven by westerly winds and ocean circulation. It flows like a river of warm water along the coast of America and then across the north Atlantic where it becomes known as the North Atlantic Drift.

Ice breaking away from the Greenland ice sheet presents a constant threat to shipping in the north Atlantic. Icebergs are carried out of the Davis Strait by sea currents.

Silt, mud and clay deposited at the delta of the Amazon have shape 3 million years ago, when the Isthmus of Panama closed by continental drift.

Floating ice shelves extend over 100 miles (160 km) into the Weddell Sea, off the coast of Antarctica.

Icebergs in the Antarctic are larger than those in the Arctic and can be up to 50 miles (80 km) long, they can drift to latitudes of around 40°S before melting.

▲ **Volcanism in the Azores** occurs because they lie over a hot spot in the oceanic crust. There are ten volcanoes clustered around the Azores. Many are still classified as active, although there has not been an eruption for over a century.

The overall salinity of the north Atlantic is increased by highly saline water flowing out from the Mediterranean through the Strait of Gibraltar.

The Mid-Atlantic Ridge is marked along its length by numerous east–west valleys and ridges; these are caused by localized transform faulting. Some of these faults extend for 1250 miles (2000 km).

The South Sandwich Trench is the deepest part of the Atlantic; its base lies 30,000 ft (9144 m) below sea level. The trench is frequently subjected to earthquakes.

Volcanic peaks may be exposed as islands

Transform faults running east–west displace central ridge

Molten rock seeps through faults

Mid-Atlantic Ridge

▲ **Running the length** of the ocean, the Mid-Atlantic Ridge is a complex system of sea-floor spreading, transform faults and volcanic islands. At its centre is a large rift valley 15–30 miles (24–48 km) wide, formed by the upwelling of the ocean floor toward both Africa and South America.

▲ **Rocky breakwaters have been built along** the coast of Ghana to protect local fishing boats from being destroyed by powerful Atlantic waves.

Inset map key

Population
◉ 100,000 to 500,000
⊕ 50,000 to 100,000
○ 10,000 to 50,000
○ below 10,000

Elevation
1000m / 3281ft
500m / 1640ft
250m / 820ft
100m / 328ft
sea level

Ocean map key

Sea depth
sea level
250m / 820ft
500m / 1640ft
1000m / 3281ft
2000m / 6562ft
3000m / 9843ft
5000m / 16,404ft

TRISTAN DA CUNHA (to Saint Helena)
EDINBURGH
ATLANTIC OCEAN
SCALE 1:750,000

SAINT HELENA (to UK)
JAMESTOWN
ATLANTIC OCEAN
SCALE 1:750,000

ASCENSION ISLAND (to Saint Helena)
GEORGETOWN
ATLANTIC OCEAN
SCALE 1:750,000

FALKLAND ISLANDS (to UK)
STANLEY
ATLANTIC OCEAN
SCALE 1:3,000,000

Africa

The world's second largest continent, Africa covers an area of 11,712,434 sq miles (30,335,000 sq km). It has 53 separate countries, including Madagascar in the Indian Ocean – the highest number of any continent.

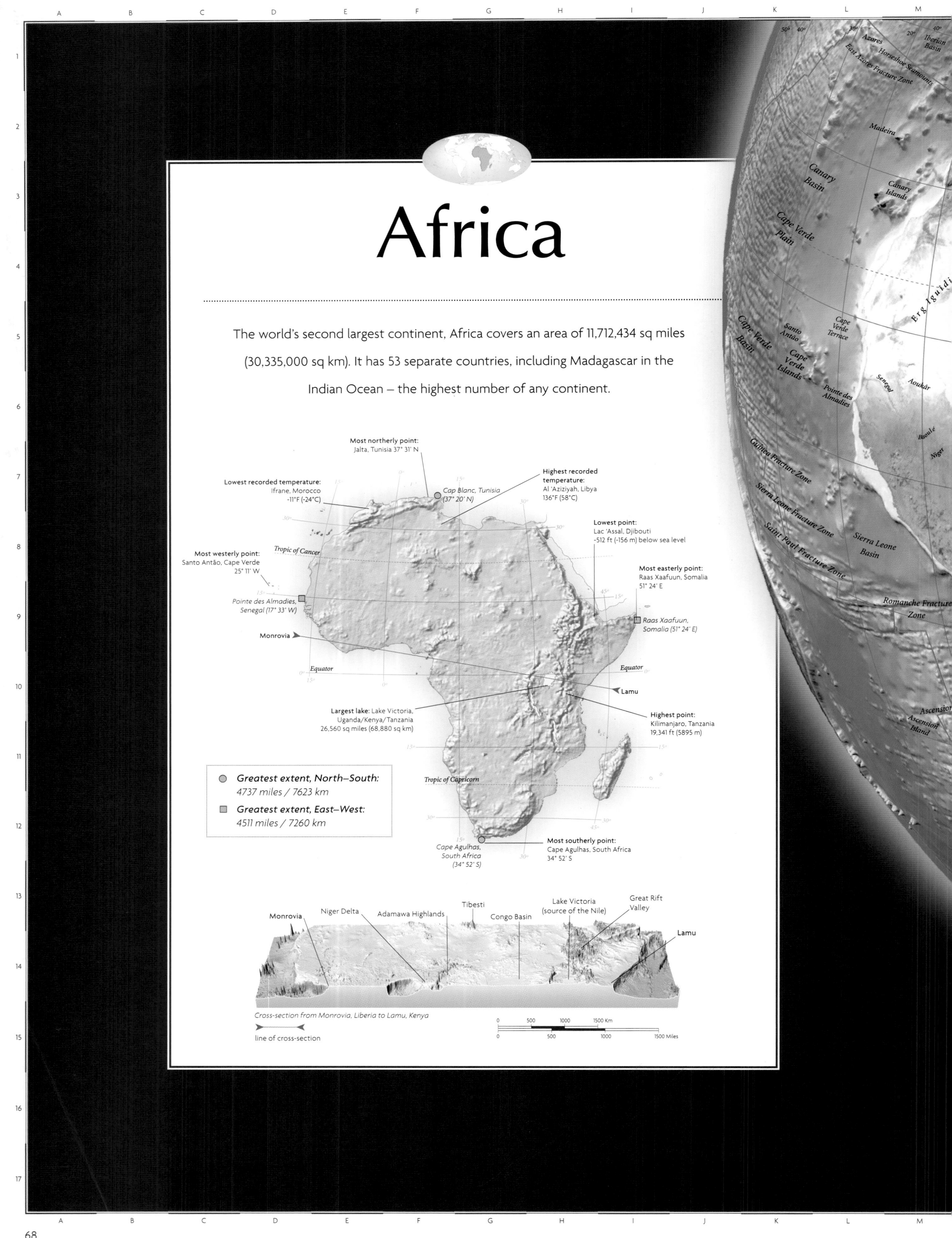

Most northerly point:
Jalta, Tunisia 37° 31' N

Lowest recorded temperature:
Ifrane, Morocco
-11°F (-24°C)

Cap Blanc, Tunisia
(37° 20' N)

Highest recorded
temperature:
Al 'Aziziyah, Libya
136°F (58°C)

Lowest point:
Lac 'Assal, Djibouti
-512 ft (-156 m) below sea level

Most westerly point:
Santo Antão, Cape Verde
25° 11' W

Tropic of Cancer

Most easterly point:
Raas Xaafuun, Somalia
51° 24' E

Pointe des Almadies,
Senegal (17° 33' W)

Raas Xaafuun,
Somalia (51° 24' E)

Monrovia

Equator

Equator

Lamu

Largest lake: Lake Victoria,
Uganda/Kenya/Tanzania
26,560 sq miles (68,880 sq km)

Highest point:
Kilimanjaro, Tanzania
19,341 ft (5895 m)

⬤ **Greatest extent, North–South:**
4737 miles / 7623 km

◼ **Greatest extent, East–West:**
4511 miles / 7260 km

Tropic of Capricorn

Cape Agulhas,
South Africa
(34° 52' S)

Most southerly point:
Cape Agulhas, South Africa
34° 52' S

Monrovia | Niger Delta | Adamawa Highlands | Tibesti | Congo Basin | Lake Victoria (source of the Nile) | Great Rift Valley | Lamu

Cross-section from Monrovia, Liberia to Lamu, Kenya

line of cross-section

| 0 | 500 | 1000 | 1500 Km |
| 0 | 500 | 1000 | 1500 Miles |

Iberian
Basin

Azores

Horseshoe Seamounts

East Azore Fracture Zone

Madeira

Canary
Basin

Canary
Islands

Cape Verde
Plain

Erg Iguîdî

Cape Verde
Basin

Santo
Antão

Cape
Verde
Terrace

Cape
Verde
Islands

Pointe des
Almadies

Senegal

Aoukâr

Guinea Fracture Zone

Bîoû I.

Niger

Sierra Leone Fracture Zone

Sierra Leone
Basin

Saint Paul Fracture Zone

Romanche Fracture
Zone

Ascension

Ascension
Island

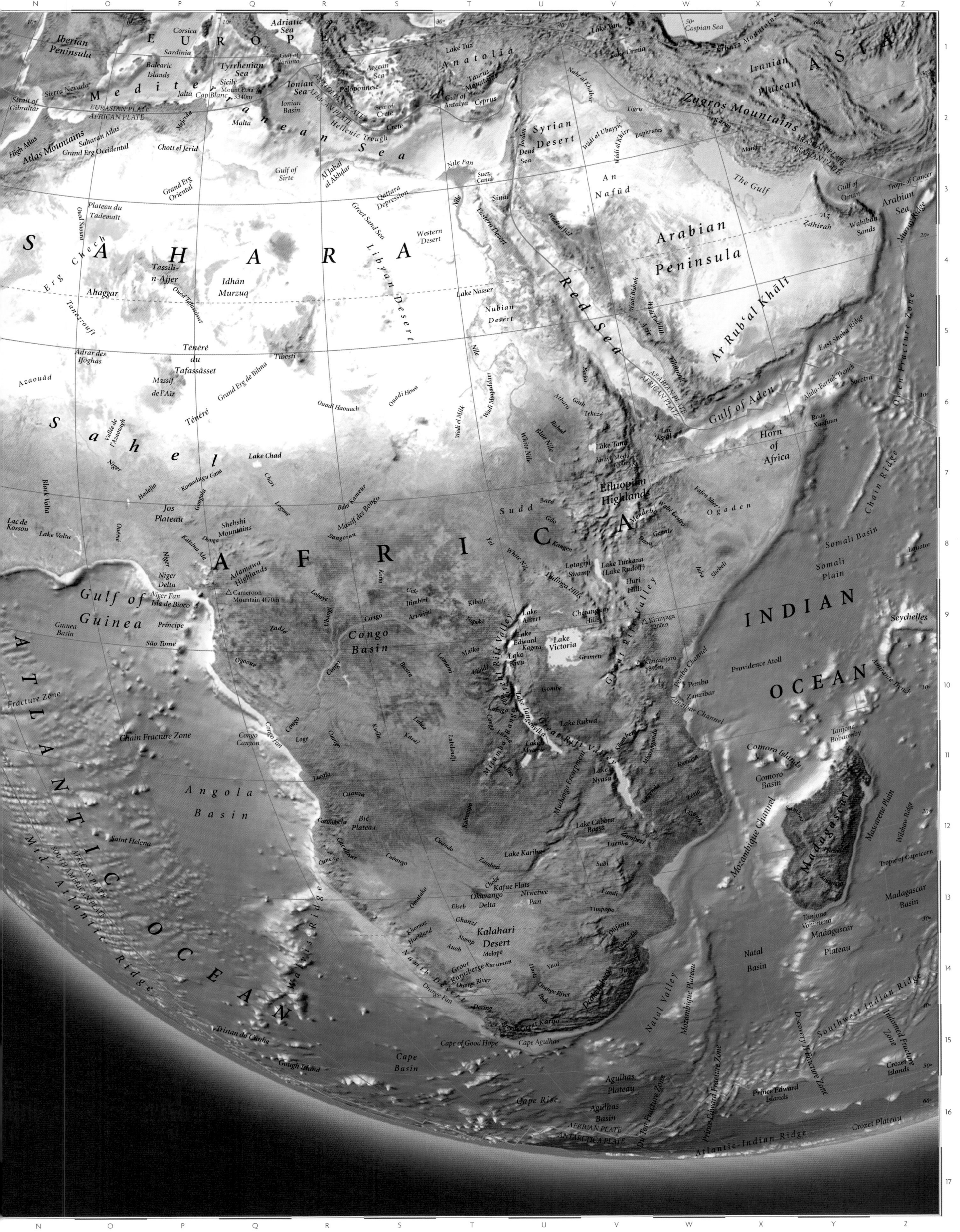

N O P Q R S T U V W X Y Z
1 2 3 4 5 6 7 8 9 10 11 12 13 14 15 16 17
E U R O P E
Iberian Peninsula
Corsica
Sardinia
Adriatic Sea
Balearic Islands
Tyrrhenian Sea
Gulf of Taranto
Sicily
Mount Etna 3340m
Ionian Sea
Ionian Basin
Aegean Sea
Peloponnese
Sea of Crete
Crete
Hellenic Trough
ANATOLIAN PLATE
AFRICAN PLATE
Lake Tuz
A n a t o l i a
Taurus Mountains
Gulf of Antalya
Cyprus
Lake Van
Lake Urmia
Caspian Sea
Elburz Mountains
Iranian Plateau
A S I A
Zagros Mountains
Strait of Gibraltar
Sierra Nevada
M e d i t e r r a n e a n S e a
Jalta
Cap Blanc
EURASIAN PLATE
AFRICAN PLATE
Malta
Mejerda
High Atlas
Atlas Mountains
Saharan Atlas
Grand Erg Occidental
Chott el Jerid
Gulf of Sirte
Al Jabal al Akhdar
Grand Erg Oriental
Nile Fan
Suez Canal
Sinai
Nile
Qattara Depression
Jordan
Dead Sea
Syrian Desert
Nahr al Khabur
Tigris
Wadi al Ubayyid
Wadi al Khirr
Euphrates
Kārūn
Mand
IRANIAN PLATE
ARABIAN PLATE
An Nafūd
The Gulf
Gulf of Oman
Tropic of Cancer
Arabian Sea
Az Zāhirah
Wahibah Sands
Murray Ridge
Plateau du Tademaït
Oued Saoura
Great Sand Sea
Western Desert
Eastern Desert
Wadi al Hamd
S A H A R A
Erg Chech
Tassili-n-Ajjer
Idhān Murzuq
Ahaggar
Oued Tafassâsset
Libyan Desert
Lake Nasser
Nubian Desert
Red Sea
Arabian Peninsula
Wadi Bishah
Wadi Tathlith
Asir
Ar Rub' al Khālī
Tanezrouft
Adrar des Ifôghas
Ténéré du Tafassâsset
Tibesti
Grand Erg de Bilma
Massif de l'Aïr
Azaouâd
Ténéré
Ouadi Haouach
Ouadi Howa
Wadi al Milk
Wadi Muqaddam
Barka
Atbara
Gash
Tekezē
Rahad
Blue Nile
White Nile
East Sheba Ridge
Alula-Fartak Trench
Socotra
Owen Fracture Zone
ARABIAN PLATE
AFRICAN PLATE
Gulf of Aden
Lac Assal
Raas Xaafuun
Horn of Africa
Lake Tana
Ras Dashen 4533m
Ethiopian Highlands
S a h e l
Vallée de l'Azaouagh
Niger
Lake Chad
Chari
Komadugu Gana
Hadejia
Gongola
Black Volta
Lac de Kossou
Lake Volta
Oueme
Jos Plateau
Shebshi Mountains
Donga
Katsina Ala
Logone
Bahr Kameur
Massif des Bongo
Bangoran
Sudd
Baro
Gilo
Mendebo
Wabe Gestro
Genale
Dawa
Fafen Shet'
Ogaden
Chain Ridge
Somali Basin
Somali Plain
Equator
A F R I C A
Niger
Adamawa Highlands
Niger Delta
Niger Fan
Isla de Bioco
Cameroon Mountain 4070m
Gulf of Guinea
Principe
Guinea Basin
São Tomé
Kotto
Lobaye
Uele
Itimbiri
Aruwimi
Kibali
Ubangi
Congo
Zadié
Congo Basin
Ogooué
Yei
White Nile
Kangen
Lotagipi Swamp
Lake Turkana (Lake Rudolf)
Jubba
Shebeli
Dufinga Hills
Huri Hills
Cherangany Hills
Great Rift Valley
Kirinyaga 5200m
Lake Albert
Lake Edward
Kagera
Lake Kivu
Lake Victoria
Grumeti
Ngoko
Maiko
Lomami
Lualaba
Busira
Rift Valley
INDIAN OCEAN
Seychelles
Providence Atoll
Amirante Trench
Kilimanjaro 5895m
Pemba Channel
Pemba
Zanzibar
Zanzibar Channel
Gombe
Lake Tanganyika
Lake Rukwa
Kilombero
Lake Mweru
Luvua
Luapula
Mitumba Range
Chain Fracture Zone
Fracture Zone
Congo Canyon
Congo Fan
Congo
Loge
Cuango
Kwilu
Lulua
Kasai
Lubilandji
Lukuga
Muchinga Escarpment
Lake Nyasa
Ruvuma
Mbemkuru
Tanjona Bobaomby
Comoro Islands
Comoro Basin
Lugenda
Lurio
Ligonha
Lucala
Cuanza
Angola Basin
Bié Plateau
Catumbela
Cunene
Cubango
Cuando
Kabompo
Zambezi
Lake Cabora Bassa
Luenha
Lake Kariba
Sambao
Madagascar
Mozambique Channel
Mascarene Plain
Wildham Ridge
Tropic of Capricorn
Saint Helena
SOUTH AMERICAN PLATE
AFRICAN PLATE
Mid-Atlantic Ridge
ATLANTIC OCEAN
Kafue Flats
Ntwetwe Pan
Okavango Delta
Sabi
Lundi
Limpopo
Omatako
Eiseb
Ghanzi
Khomas Hochland
Nosop
Auob
Kalahari Desert
Molopo
Kuruman
Olifants
Groot Karasberge
Orange River
Namib Desert
Orange Fan
Walvis Ridge
Vaal
Harts
Orange River
Drakensberg
Great Karoo
Cape of Good Hope
Cape Agulhas
Tanjona Vohimena
Madagascar Plateau
Madagascar Basin
Natal Basin
Natal Valley
Mozambique Plateau
Discovery II Fracture Zone
Southwest Indian Ridge
Indomed Fracture Zone
Tristan da Cunha
Gough Island
Cape Basin
Agulhas Plateau
Cape Rise
Agulhas Basin
AFRICAN PLATE
ANTARCTICA PLATE
Du Toit Fracture Zone
Prince Edward Fracture Zone
Prince Edward Islands
Atlantic-Indian Ridge
Crozet Islands
Crozet Plateau
10° 30° 50° 20° 40° 60°

Physical Africa

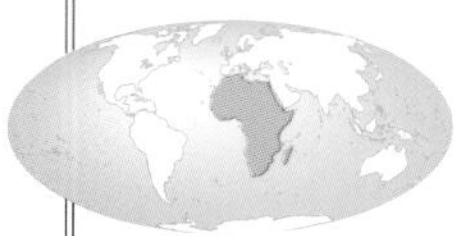

The structure of Africa was dramatically influenced by the break up of the supercontinent Gondwanaland about 160 million years ago and, more recently, rifting and hot spot activity. Today, much of Africa is remote from active plate boundaries and comprises a series of extensive plateaux and deep basins, which influence the drainage patterns of major rivers. The relief rises to the east, where volcanic uplands and vast lakes mark the Great Rift Valley. In the far north and south sedimentary rocks have been folded to form the Atlas Mountains and the Great Karoo.

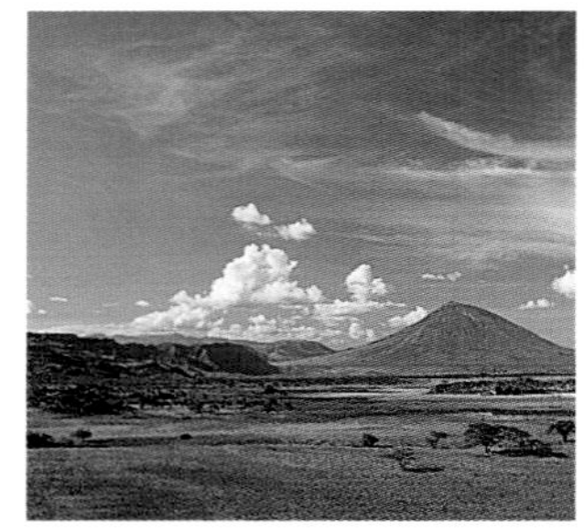

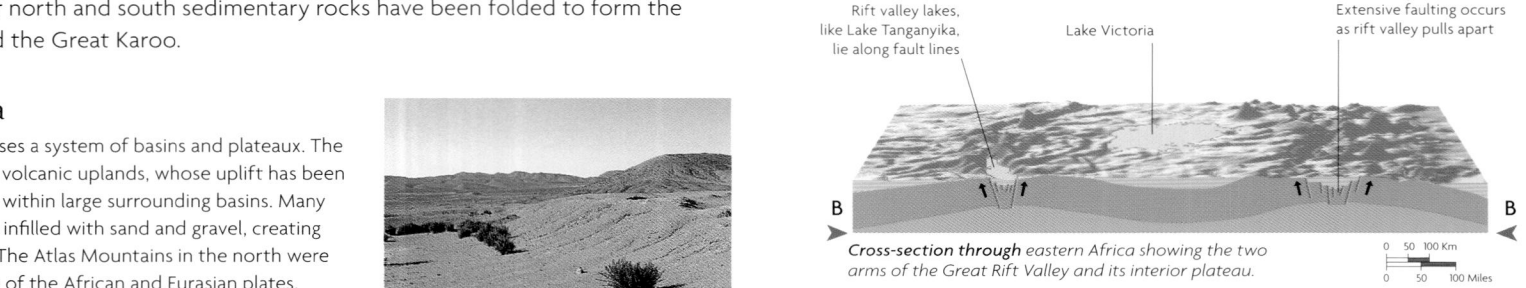

East Africa

The Great Rift Valley is the most striking feature of this region, running for 4475 miles (7200 km) from Lake Nyasa to the Red Sea. North of Lake Nyasa it splits into two arms and encloses an interior plateau which contains Lake Victoria. A number of elongated lakes and volcanoes lie along the fault lines. To the west lies the Congo Basin, a vast, shallow depression, which rises to form an almost circular rim of highlands.

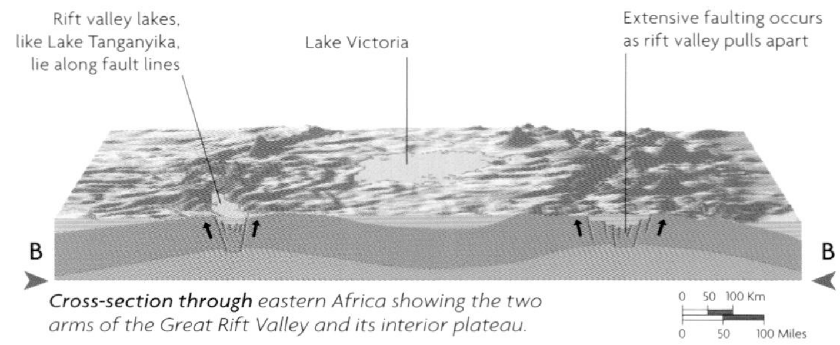

Rift valley lakes, like Lake Tanganyika, lie along fault lines

Lake Victoria

Extensive faulting occurs as rift valley pulls apart

Cross-section through eastern Africa showing the two arms of the Great Rift Valley and its interior plateau.

0   50   100 Km
0   50   100 Miles

Northern Africa

Northern Africa comprises a system of basins and plateaux. The Tibesti and Ahaggar are volcanic uplands, whose uplift has been matched by subsidence within large surrounding basins. Many of the basins have been infilled with sand and gravel, creating the vast Saharan lands. The Atlas Mountains in the north were formed by convergence of the African and Eurasian plates.

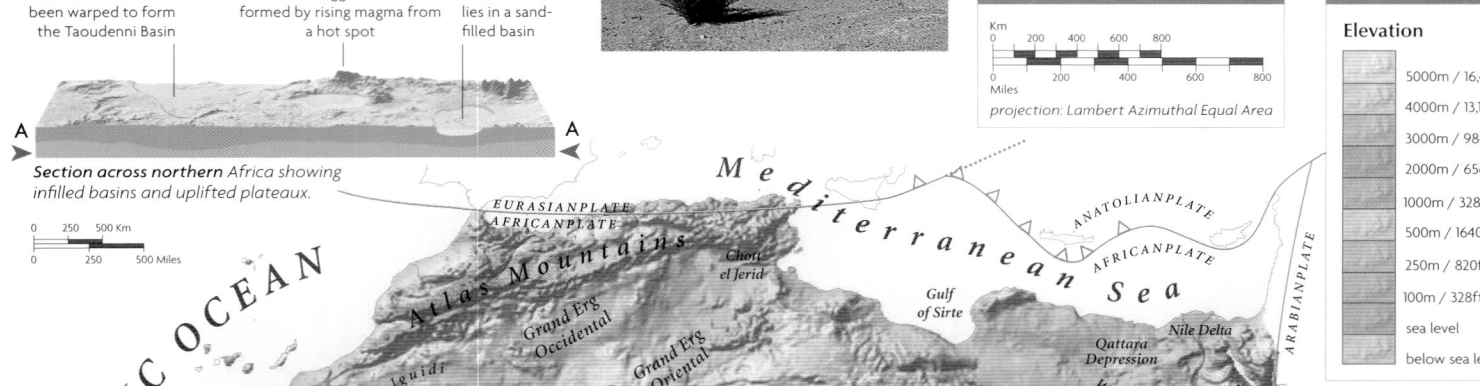

The Earth's crust has been warped to form the Taoudenni Basin

Volcanic Ahaggar mountains, formed by rising magma from a hot spot

Lake Chad lies in a sand-filled basin

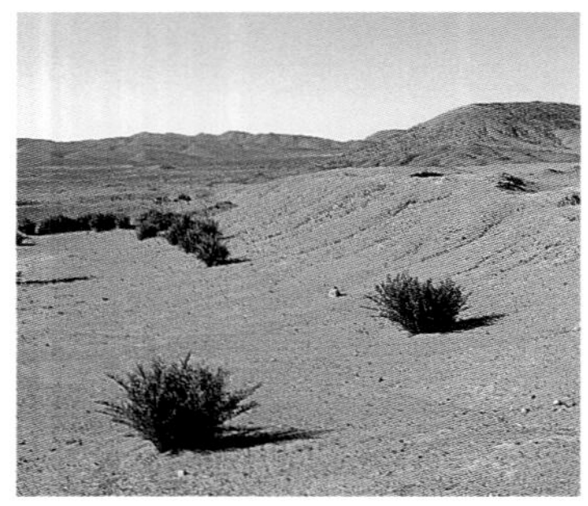

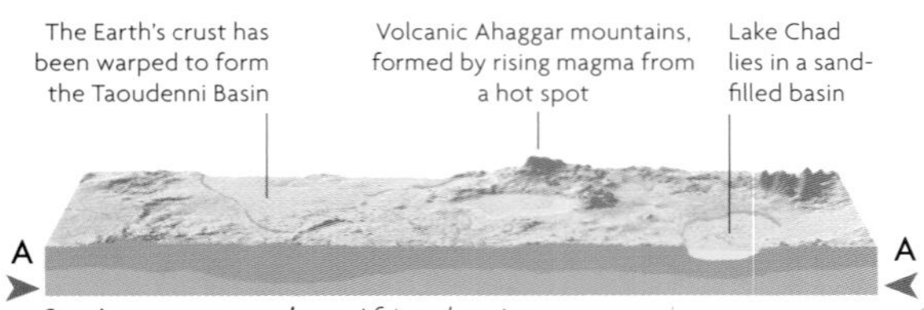

Section across northern Africa showing infilled basins and uplifted plateaux.

0   250   500 Km
0   250   500 Miles

Scale 1:36,000,000

Km
0   200   400   600   800

Miles
0   200   400   600   800

projection: Lambert Azimuthal Equal Area

Map key

Elevation

5000m / 16,405ft
4000m / 13,124ft
3000m / 9843ft
2000m / 6562ft
1000m / 3281ft
500m / 1640ft
250m / 820ft
100m / 328ft
sea level
below sea level

Plate margins
(for explanation see page xiv)

———— constructive
△ △ destructive
———— conservative
·········· uncertain
◄—► line of cross-section

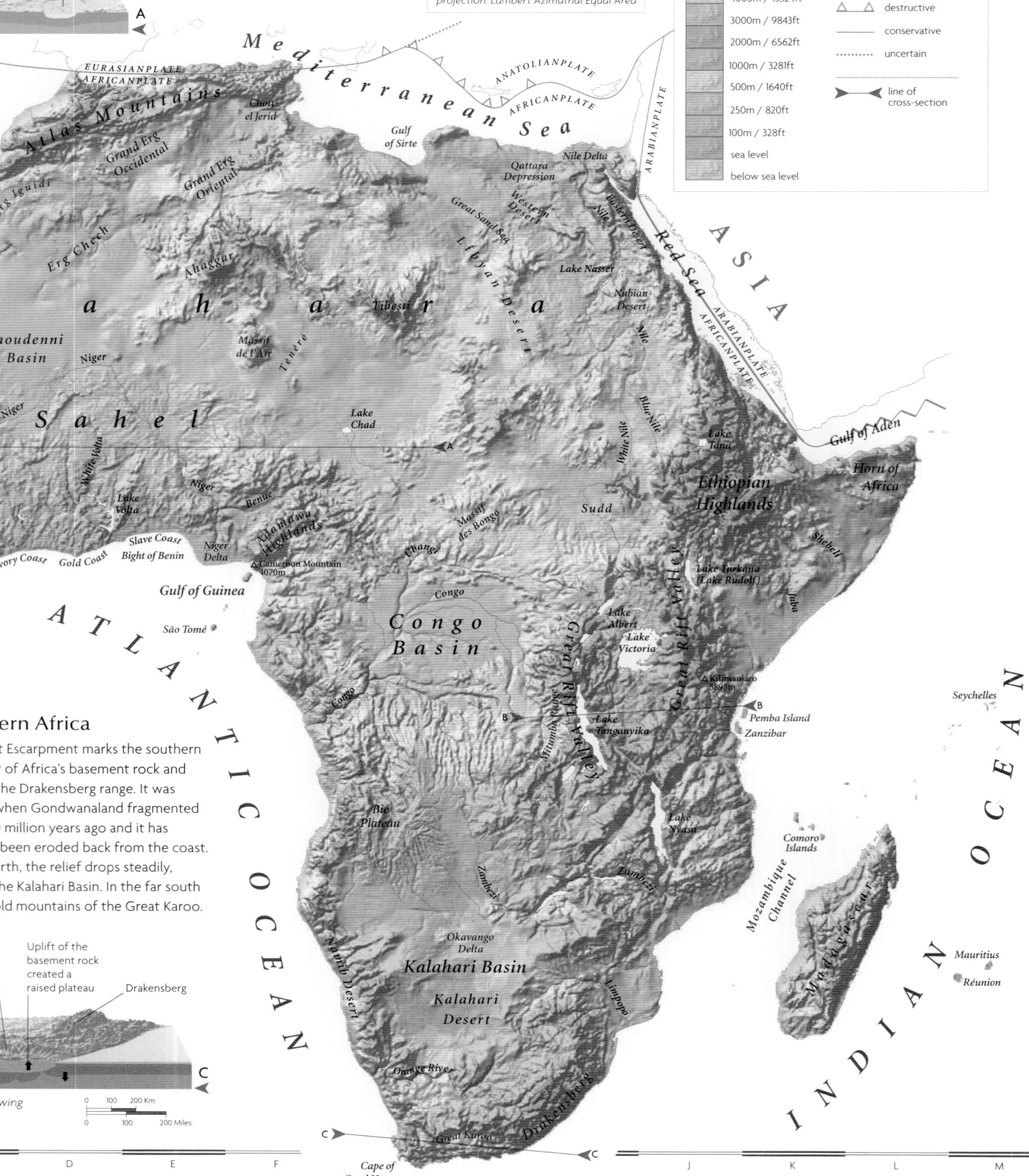

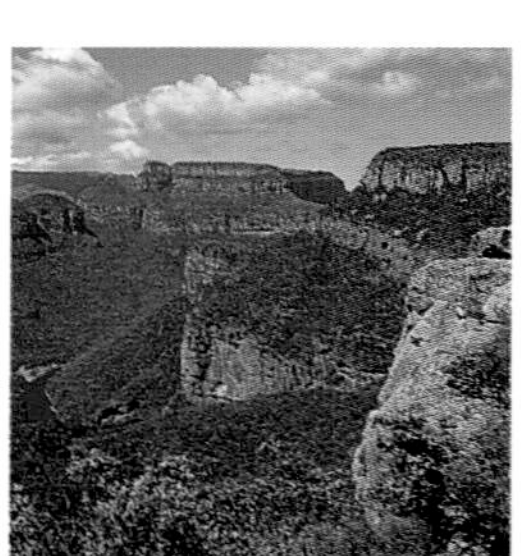

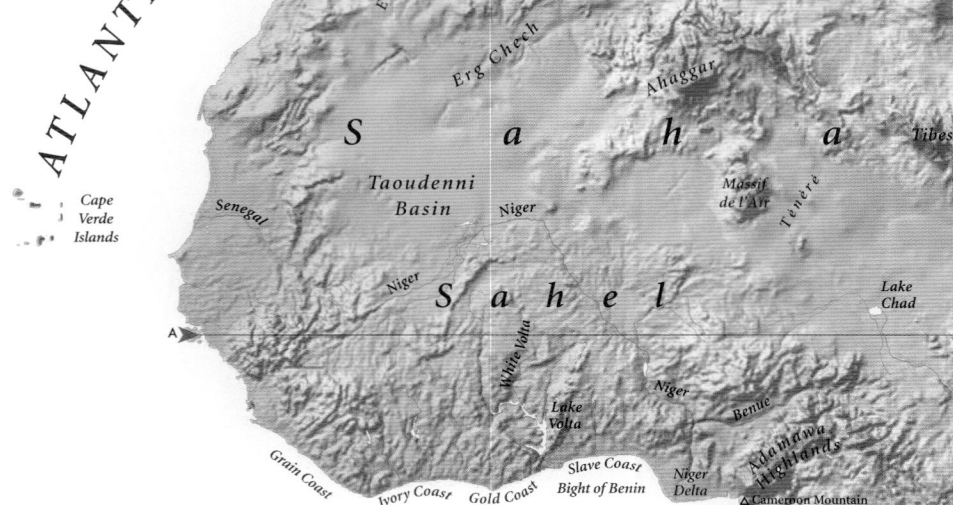

Southern Africa

The Great Escarpment marks the southern boundary of Africa's basement rock and includes the Drakensberg range. It was uplifted when Gondwanaland fragmented about 160 million years ago and it has gradually been eroded back from the coast. To the north, the relief drops steadily, forming the Kalahari Basin. In the far south are the fold mountains of the Great Karoo.

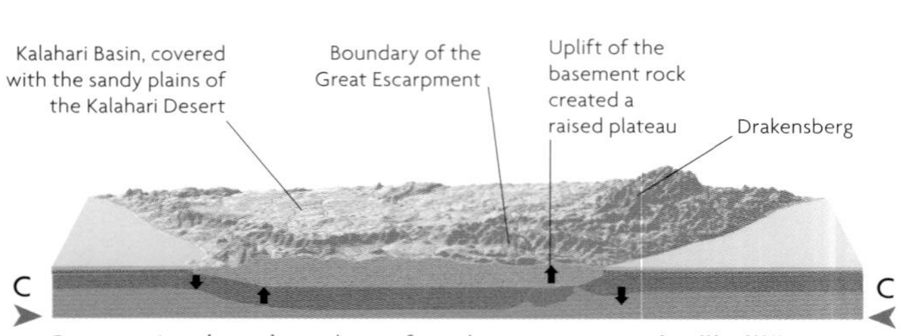

Kalahari Basin, covered with the sandy plains of the Kalahari Desert

Boundary of the Great Escarpment

Uplift of the basement rock created a raised plateau

Drakensberg

Cross-section through southern Africa showing the boundary of the Great Escarpment.

0   100   200 Km
0   100   200 Miles

Map labels

ATLANTIC OCEAN

Mediterranean Sea

EURASIAN PLATE
AFRICAN PLATE
ANATOLIAN PLATE
AFRICAN PLATE
ARABIAN PLATE

Atlas Mountains
Chott el Jerid
Gulf of Sirte
Qattara Depression
Nile Delta
Grand Erg Occidental
Grand Erg Oriental
Great Sand Sea
Western Desert
Libyan Desert
Lake Nasser
Nubian Desert
ARABIAN PLATE
Red Sea
ASIA
ARABIAN PLATE
AFRICAN PLATE

Erg Iguidi
Erg Chech
Ahaggar
Ténéré
Tibesti
Nile

Cape Verde Islands
Senegal

S a h a r a

Taoudenni Basin
Niger
Massif de l'Aïr

Gulf of Aden

Lake Tana
Blue Nile
White Nile
Ethiopian Highlands
Horn of Africa

Niger
S a h e l
Lake Chad

Grain Coast
Ivory Coast   Gold Coast
White Volta
Lake Volta
Niger
Benue
Slave Coast   Bight of Benin   Niger Delta
Adamawa Highlands
△ Cameroon Mountain 4070m

Gulf of Guinea

São Tomé

A T L A N T I C   O C E A N

Ubangi
Congo
Massif des Bongo
Sudd

Congo
Congo
B a s i n

Lake Turkana (Lake Rudolf)
Shebeli
Juba

Great Rift Valley
Lake Albert
Lake Victoria
△ Kilimanjaro 5895m

Mbomu
Lomami
Great Rift Valley
Lake Tanganyika

Pemba Island
Zanzibar

Seychelles

Bié Plateau

Lake Nyasa

Comoro Islands

Zambezi

Mozambique Channel

Madagascar

Namib Desert

Okavango Delta
Kalahari Basin
Kalahari Desert
Limpopo

Mauritius
Réunion

Orange River
Drakensberg
Great Karoo

I N D I A N   O C E A N

Cape of Good Hope

Climate

The climates of Africa range from mediterranean to arid, dry savannah and humid equatorial. In East Africa, where snow settles at the summit of volcanoes such as Kilimanjaro, climate is also modified by altitude. The winds of the Sahara export millions of tonnes of dust a year both northwards and eastwards.

▲ *Savannah grasslands run in a belt across Africa; limited rainfall inhibits tree growth.*

Temperature

Tropic of Cancer
20° N
Equator
20° S
Tropic of Capricorn

Average January temperature   *Average July temperature*

Temperature
- 0 to 10°C (32 to 50°F)
- 10 to 20°C (50 to 68°F)
- 20 to 30°C (68 to 86°F)
- above 30°C (86°F)

Rainfall

Tropic of Cancer
20° N
Equator
20° S
Tropic of Capricorn

Average January rainfall   *Average July rainfall*

Rainfall
- 0–25 mm (0–1 in)
- 25–50 mm (1–2 in)
- 50–100 mm (2–4 in)
- 100–200 mm (4–8 in)
- 200–300 mm (8–12 in)
- 300–400 mm (12–16 in)
- 400–500 mm (16–20 in)
- more than 500 mm (20 in)

▲ *The hot, equatorial basin of the Congo river receives over 48 inches (1200 mm) of rainfall per year.*

Climate
- arid
- humid equatorial
- mediterranean
- semi-arid
- tropical
- warm humid
- ☼ daily hours of sunshine, January
- ☼ daily hours of sunshine, July
- → cold wind
- → hot wind

Shaping the continent

African landscapes are shaped by the intensity of climatic extremes and by tectonic action. High aridity, wind action and infrequent but heavy rainstorms, lead to the migration of sand dunes and dramatic flash flooding across much of the north and west. In the wetter areas, high precipitation increases the rate of weathering. To the east, the rift system has created a volcanic and lake environment and allowed rivers to erode weaknesses left in the crustal structure by faults.

The evolving landscape

Groundwater

1 Oases are found in desert areas such as the Sahara *(left)*. Groundwater migrates through permeable rock strata, confined between two impermeable layers. Oases form either when the permeable rocks come near to the surface, or at a fault line, when water is able to seep up to the surface through the crushed rocks at the fault.

Rainwater feeds the aquifer
Water migrates up through fault
Aquifer exposed near the surface
Groundwater trapped between impermeable strata

Groundwater: Replenishment of an oasis

River systems

2 The Zambezi river *(above)* drops 360 ft (110 m) over the Victoria Falls into a zig-zag gorge. The river has eroded the gorge along lines of weakness in the bedrock, created by fault lines running in two directions.

Old site of Victoria Falls
River plunges over falls
Fault and joint lines running in two directions
Zig-zag gorge of the Zambezi

River systems: Retreating of the Victoria Falls

Weathering

External stresses act on the surface of the inselberg
Exfoliated layers
Joints or cracks caused by expansion and contraction

Weathering: Formation of an inselberg

6 Inselbergs *(above)*, found extensively across West Africa, are exposed remnants of an extensive upland area. Erosion of the surrounding uplands leaves a resistant rock outcrop. Its spheroidal shape is the result of 'onion-skin' weathering – the exfoliating of layers – due to repeated expansion and contraction.

Landscape
- sinking land
- stable land
- uplifting land
- ⌄⌄⌄ escarpment
- → ocean current
- ⊢ rift
- ▲ active volcano
- ⬛ inselberg
- oasis
- river
- wadi
- waterfall

Ephemeral channels

5 Wadis *(above)* drain much of northern Africa. These drybed courses are flooded only after infrequent, but intense, storms in the uplands cause water to surge along their channels.

Heavy rainfall runs off mountains
Water collects and floods the dry channel

Ephemeral channels: Flash flooding of a wadi

Wind erosion

Sand is gradually blown up the back slope
Deposition on the slip face
Build up of sand produces strata inside the dune

Wind erosion: Migration of a dune

4 Dunes like this in the Namib Desert *(left)* are wind-blown accumulations of sand, which slowly migrate. Wind action moves sand up the shallow back slope; when the sand reaches the crest of the dune it is deposited on the slip face.

Coastal processes

Wave energy dispersed in the bay
Waves refracting
Force of waves concentrates on the headland
The sea bed is deeper opposite the bay than at the headland

Coastal processes: Erosion of a bay

3 Houtbaai *(above)*, in southern Africa, is constantly being modified by wave action. As waves approach the indented coastline, they reach the shallow water of the headland, slowing down and reducing in length. This causes them to bend or refract, concentrating their erosive force at the headlands.

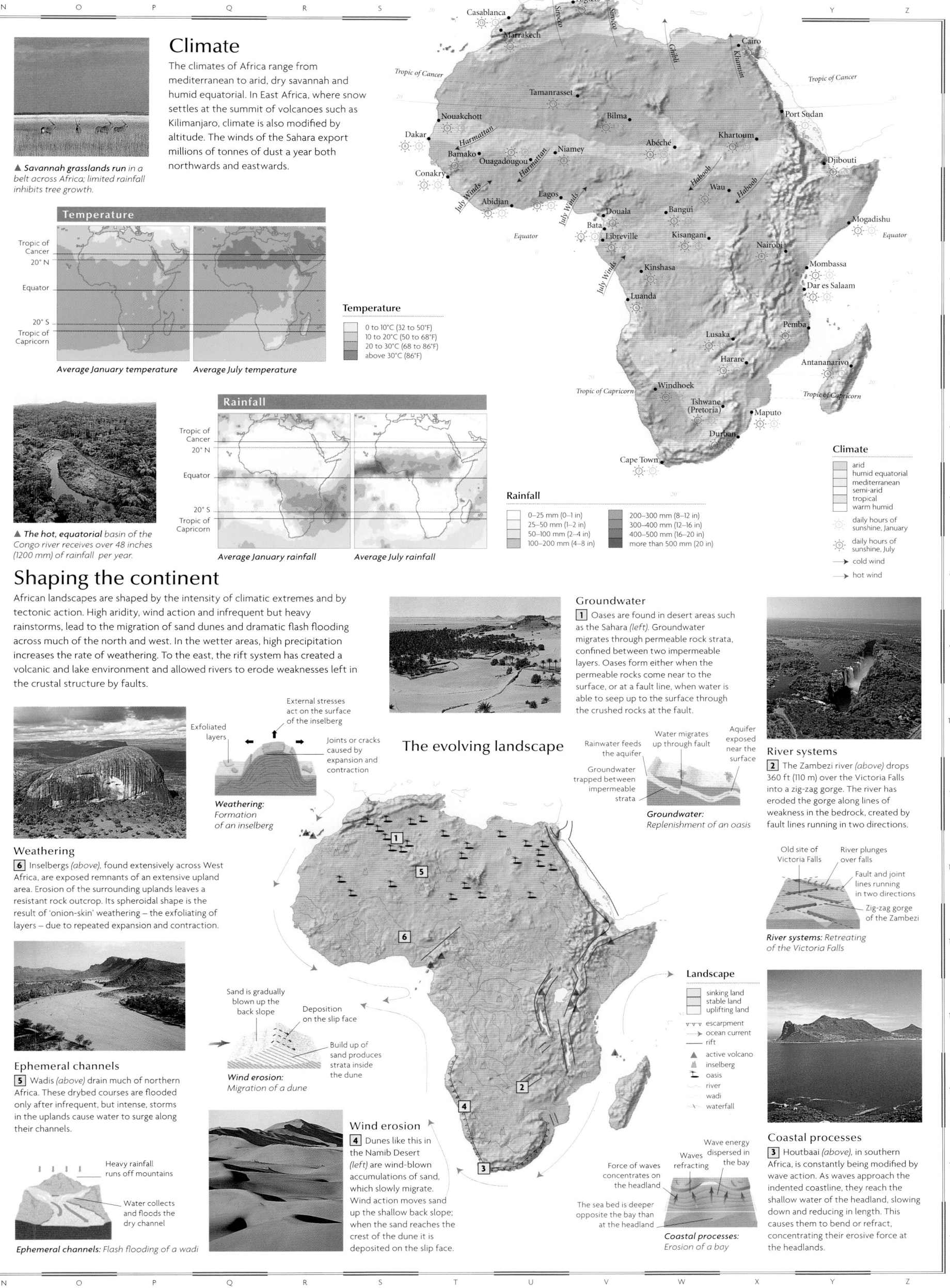

Political Africa

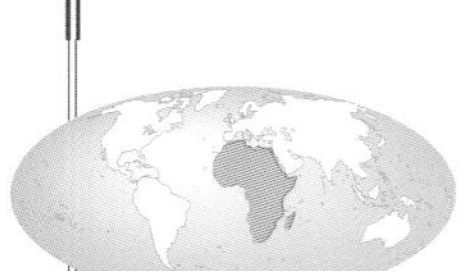

The political map of modern Africa only emerged following the end of the Second World War. Over the next half-century, all of the countries formerly controlled by European powers gained independence from their colonial rulers – only Liberia and Ethiopia were never colonized. The post-colonial era has not been an easy period for many countries, but there have been moves towards multi-party democracy across much of the continent. In South Africa, democratic elections replaced the internationally-condemned apartheid system only in 1994. Other countries have still to find political stability; corruption in government and ethnic tensions are serious problems. National infrastructures, based on the colonial transport systems built to exploit Africa's resources, are often inappropriate for independent economic development.

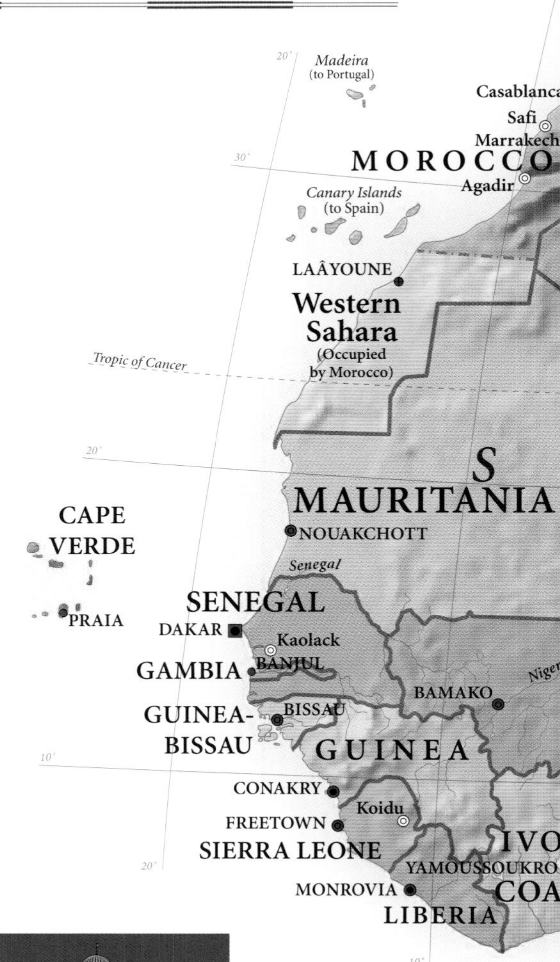

Languages

Three major world languages act as *lingua francas* across the African continent: Arabic in North Africa; English in southern and eastern Africa and Nigeria; and French in Central and West Africa, and in Madagascar. A huge number of African languages are spoken as well – over 2000 have been recorded, with more than 400 in Nigeria alone – reflecting the continuing importance of traditional cultures and values. In the north of the continent, the extensive use of Arabic reflects Middle Eastern influences while Bantu is widely-spoken across much of southern Africa.

Language groups

- Afro-Asiatic (Hamito-Semitic)
- Niger-Congo
- Nilo-Saharan
- Khoisan
- Indo-European
- Austronesian

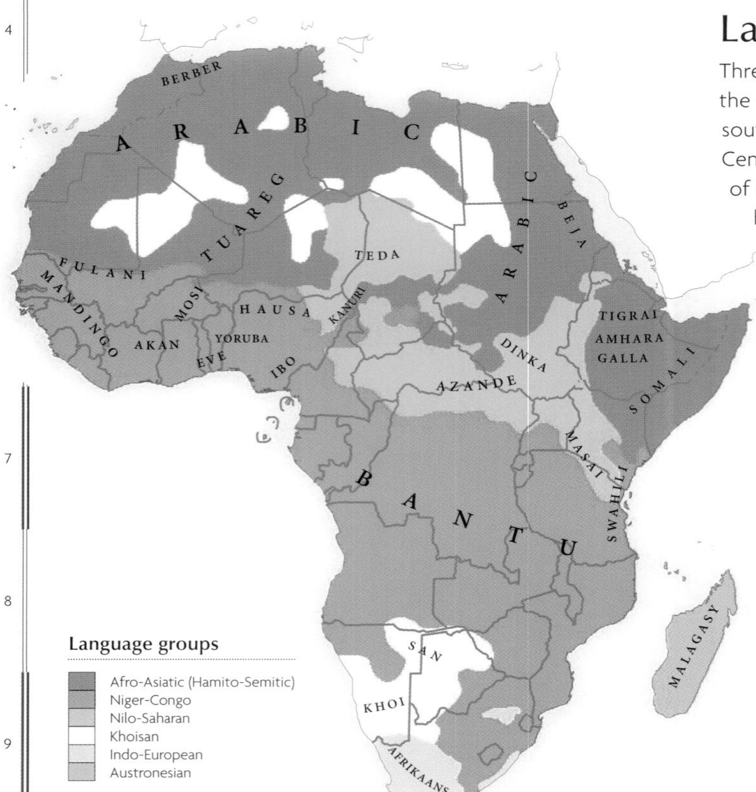

Official African languages

- French
- English
- Arabic
- Portuguese
- Swahili
- Amharic
- Spanish
- French/English
- French/Arabic
- French/Malagasy
- English/Swahili
- Arabic/Somali

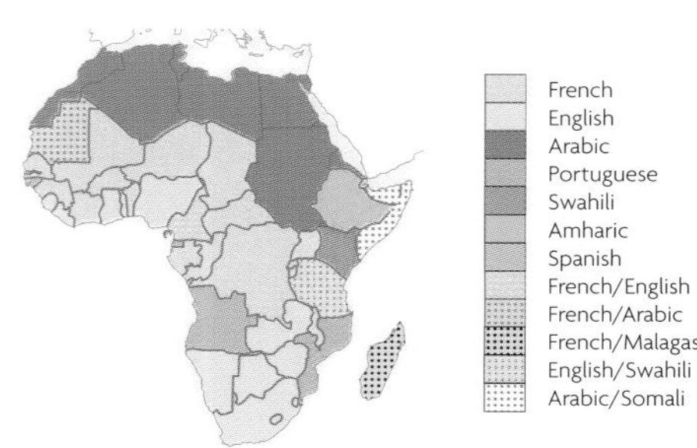

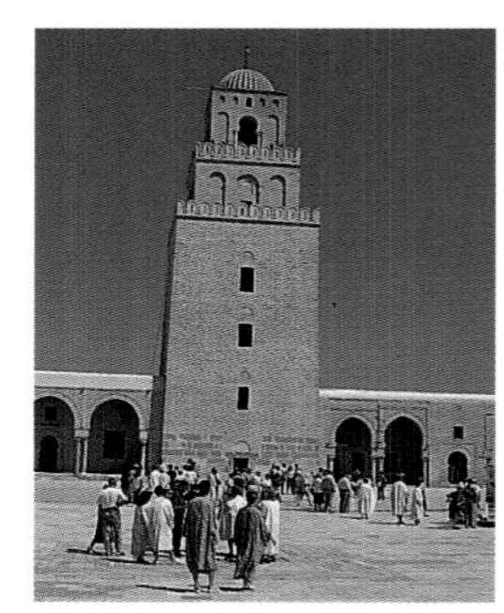

▲ *Islamic influences are evident throughout North Africa. The Great Mosque at Kairouan, Tunisia, is Africa's holiest Islamic place.*

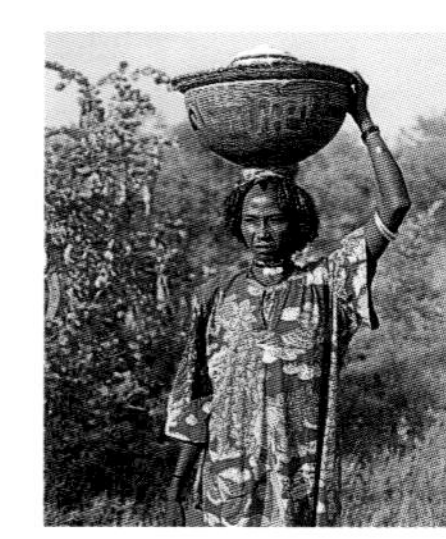

▲ *In northeastern Nigeria, people speak Kanuri – a dialect of the Nilo-Saharan language group.*

Transport

African railways were built to aid the exploitation of natural resources, and most offer passage only from the interior to the coastal cities, leaving large parts of the continent untouched – five land-locked countries have no railways at all. The Congo, Nile and Niger river networks offer limited access to land within the continental interior, but have a number of waterfalls and cataracts which prevent navigation from the sea. Many roads were developed in the 1960s and 1970s, but economic difficulties are making the maintenance and expansion of the networks difficult.

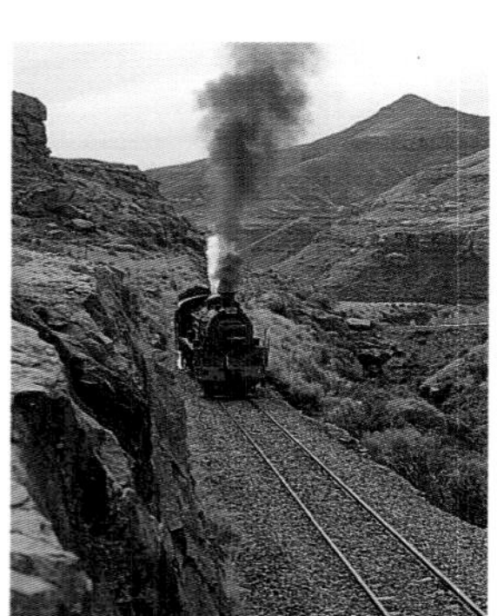

▶ *South Africa has the largest concentration of railways in Africa. Over 20,000 miles (32,000 km) of routes have been built since 1870.*

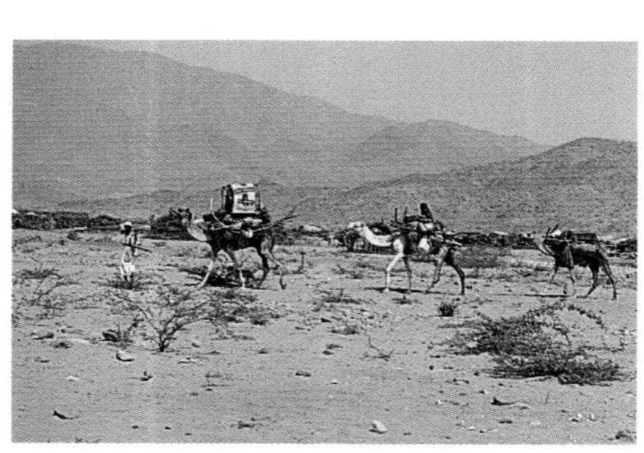

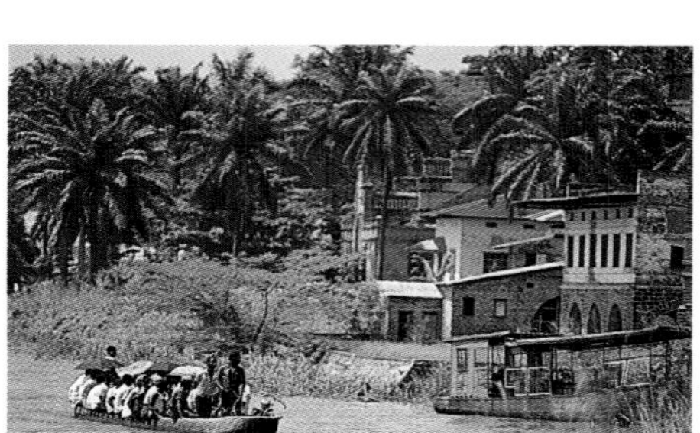

◀ *The Congo river, though not suitable for river transport along its entire length, forms a vital link for people and goods in its navigable inland reaches.*

▲ *Traditional means of transport, such as the camel, are still widely used across the less accessible parts of Africa.*

Transport

- — major roads and motorways
- — major railways
- — major canal
- — international borders
- ⊕ transport intersections
- ⊕ international airports
- ⊕ major ports

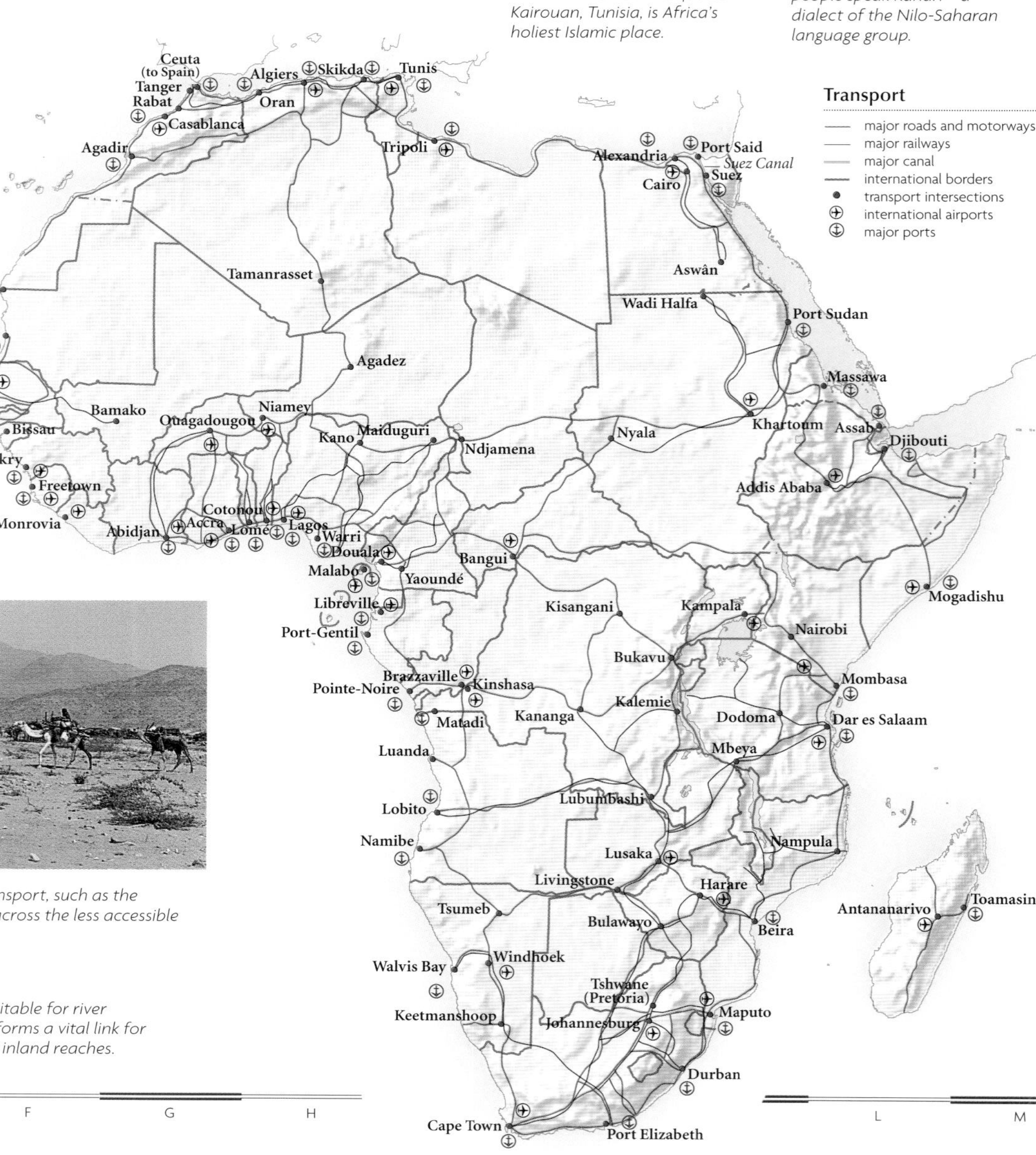

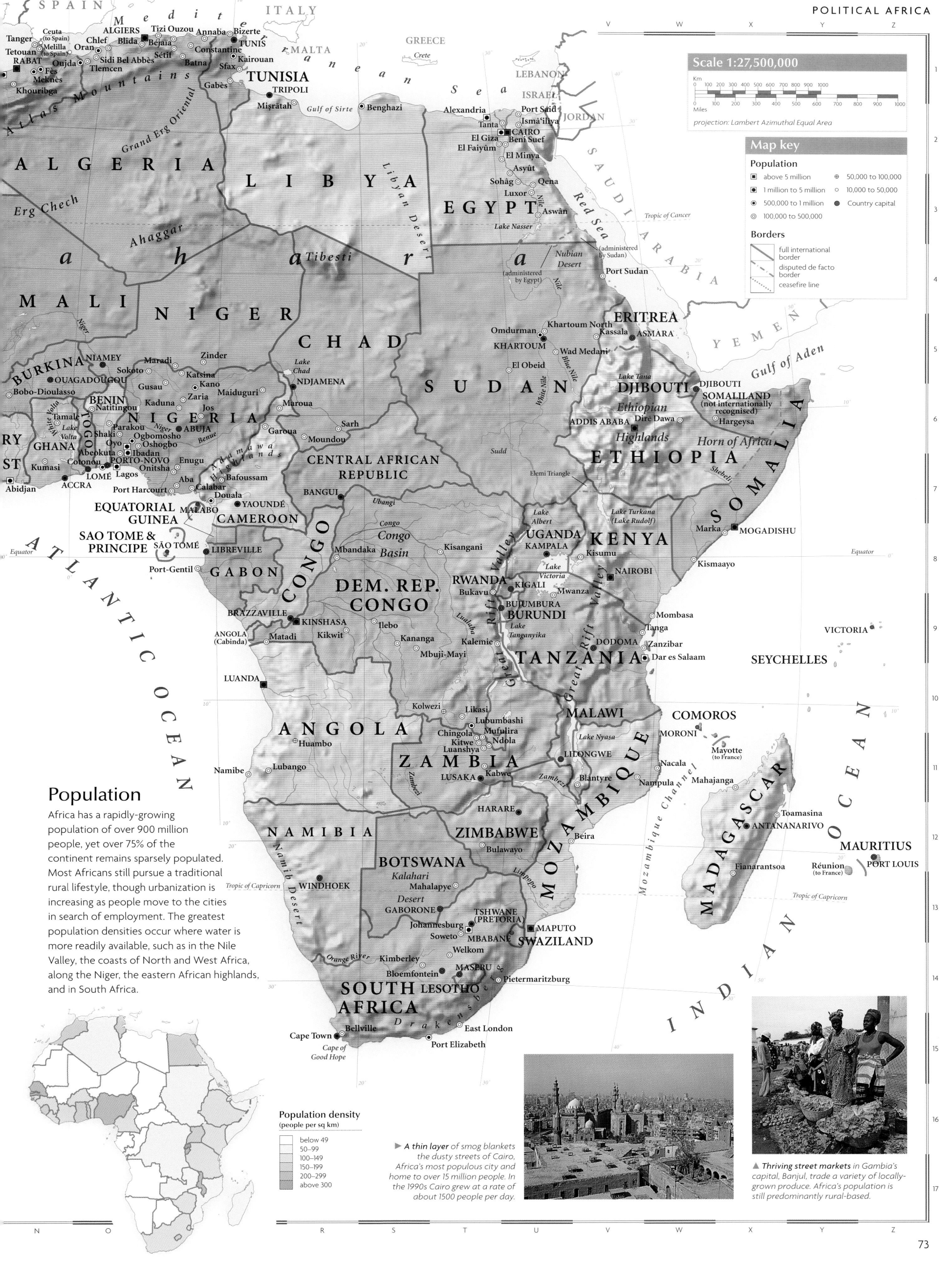

SPAIN · ITALY · GREECE

Tanger · Ceuta (to Spain) · Melilla (to Spain) · ALGIERS · Tizi Ouzou · Annaba · Bizerte · MALTA · LEBANON
Tetouan · Oran · Chlef · Blida · Bejaïa · Constantine · TUNIS · ISRAEL · JORDAN
RABAT · Oujda · Sidi Bel Abbès · Sétif · Batna · Kairouan · TUNISIA
Fès · Meknès · Tlemcen · Sfax · Gabès
Khouribga
Mişrātah · TRIPOLI · Alexandria · Port Said · Ismâ'îliya

ALGERIA · LIBYA · EGYPT

Tanta · CAIRO · Beni Suef
El Giza · El Minya
El Faiyûm · Asyût
Sohâg · Qena
Luxor
Aswân

Benghazi · Gulf of Sirte

Erg Chech · Ahaggar · Tibesti · Libyan Desert · Lake Nasser

SAUDI ARABIA

Nubian Desert (administered by Sudan)
(administered by Egypt)
Port Sudan

MALI · NIGER · CHAD · SUDAN

Omdurman · Khartoum North · Kassala · ERITREA
KHARTOUM · Wad Medani · ASMARA
El Obeid

YEMEN

Gulf of Aden

DJIBOUTI · DJIBOUTI · SOMALILAND (not internationally recognised)
Dire Dawa · Hargeysa
ADDIS ABABA

BURKINA · NIAMEY · Maradi · Zinder · Lake Chad
Sokoto · Katsina · Kano
Bobo-Dioulasso · OUAGADOUGOU · Gusau · Zaria · NDJAMENA · Maiduguri
BENIN · Natitingou · Kaduna · Jos · Maroua
Tamale · Parakou · Oyo · Oshogbo · ABUJA · Garoua · Moundou · Sarh
GHANA · Shaki · Ibadan · Enugu · Benue
Kumasi · Abeokuta · Onitsha · Bafoussam
Abidjan · LOMÉ · ACCRA · Lagos · Aba · Calabar · Douala
Port Harcourt · YAOUNDÉ

TOGO · NIGERIA · CENTRAL AFRICAN REPUBLIC

Ethiopian Highlands · Horn of Africa
ETHIOPIA · Shebeli

Elemi Triangle · SOMALIA

EQUATORIAL GUINEA · MALABO
SAO TOME & PRINCIPE · SÃO TOMÉ · LIBREVILLE
Port-Gentil · GABON

CAMEROON · BANGUI · Ubangi · Congo

Mbandaka · Congo Basin · Kisangani

Lake Albert · Lake Turkana (Lake Rudolf)
UGANDA · KENYA
KAMPALA · Kisumu · Marka · MOGADISHU
Lake Victoria · NAIROBI · Kismaayo
Equator

CONGO · BRAZZAVILLE · KINSHASA · Ilebo
DEM. REP. CONGO · Kikwit
ANGOLA (Cabinda) · Matadi · Kananga · Mbuji-Mayi

RWANDA · Bukavu · KIGALI
BUJUMBURA · BURUNDI
Lake Tanganyika · Kalemie
Great Rift Valley · DODOMA
TANZANIA · Dar es Salaam · Zanzibar · Tanga · Mombasa · Mwanza

VICTORIA
SEYCHELLES

LUANDA

ANGOLA · Huambo · Kolwezi · Likasi · Lubumbashi · Chingola · Mufulira · Ndola
Kitwe · Luanshya · MALAWI · COMOROS · MORONI
ZAMBIA · LILONGWE · Mayotte (to France)
Namibe · Lubango · LUSAKA · Kabwe · Lake Nyasa · Nacala · Nampula · Mahajanga
Blantyre

HARARE · Beira · MADAGASCAR · ANTANANARIVO · Toamasina

NAMIBIA · ZIMBABWE · MOZAMBIQUE · Mozambique Channel
Bulawayo

MAURITIUS
Fianarantsoa · Réunion (to France) · PORT LOUIS

BOTSWANA · Kalahari Desert · Mahalapye · Zambezi · Limpopo
WINDHOEK · GABORONE
Namib Desert · TSHWANE (PRETORIA)
Johannesburg · Soweto · MBABANE · MAPUTO
Welkom · SWAZILAND
SOUTH AFRICA · Kimberley · Orange River · MASERU
Bloemfontein · LESOTHO · Pietermaritzburg
Cape Town · Bellville · East London
Cape of Good Hope · Port Elizabeth · Drakensberg
Tropic of Capricorn

ATLANTIC OCEAN · INDIAN OCEAN

Population

Africa has a rapidly-growing population of over 900 million people, yet over 75% of the continent remains sparsely populated. Most Africans still pursue a traditional rural lifestyle, though urbanization is increasing as people move to the cities in search of employment. The greatest population densities occur where water is more readily available, such as in the Nile Valley, the coasts of North and West Africa, along the Niger, the eastern African highlands, and in South Africa.

Population density
(people per sq km)
below 49
50–99
100–149
150–199
200–299
above 300

▶ A thin layer of smog blankets the dusty streets of Cairo, Africa's most populous city and home to over 15 million people. In the 1990s Cairo grew at a rate of about 1500 people per day.

▲ Thriving street markets in Gambia's capital, Banjul, trade a variety of locally-grown produce. Africa's population is still predominantly rural-based.

African resources

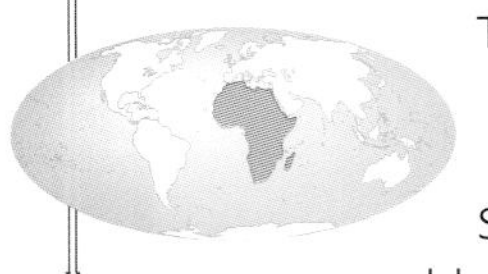

The economies of most African countries are dominated by subsistence and cash crop agriculture, with limited industrialization. Manufacturing industry is largely confined to South Africa. Many countries depend on a single resource, such as copper or gold, or a cash crop, such as coffee, for export income, which can leave them vulnerable to fluctuations in world commodity prices. In order to diversify their economies and develop a wider industrial base, investment from overseas is being actively sought by many African governments.

Industry

Many African industries concentrate on the extraction and processing of raw materials. These include the oil industry, food processing, mining and textile production. South Africa accounts for over half of the continent's industrial output with much of the remainder coming from the countries along the northern coast. Over 60% of Africa's workforce is employed in agriculture.

◀ *The unspoilt natural* splendour of wildlife reserves, like the Serengeti National Park in Tanzania, attract tourists to Africa from around the globe. The tourist industry in Kenya and Tanzania is particularly well developed, where it accounts for almost 10% of GNI.

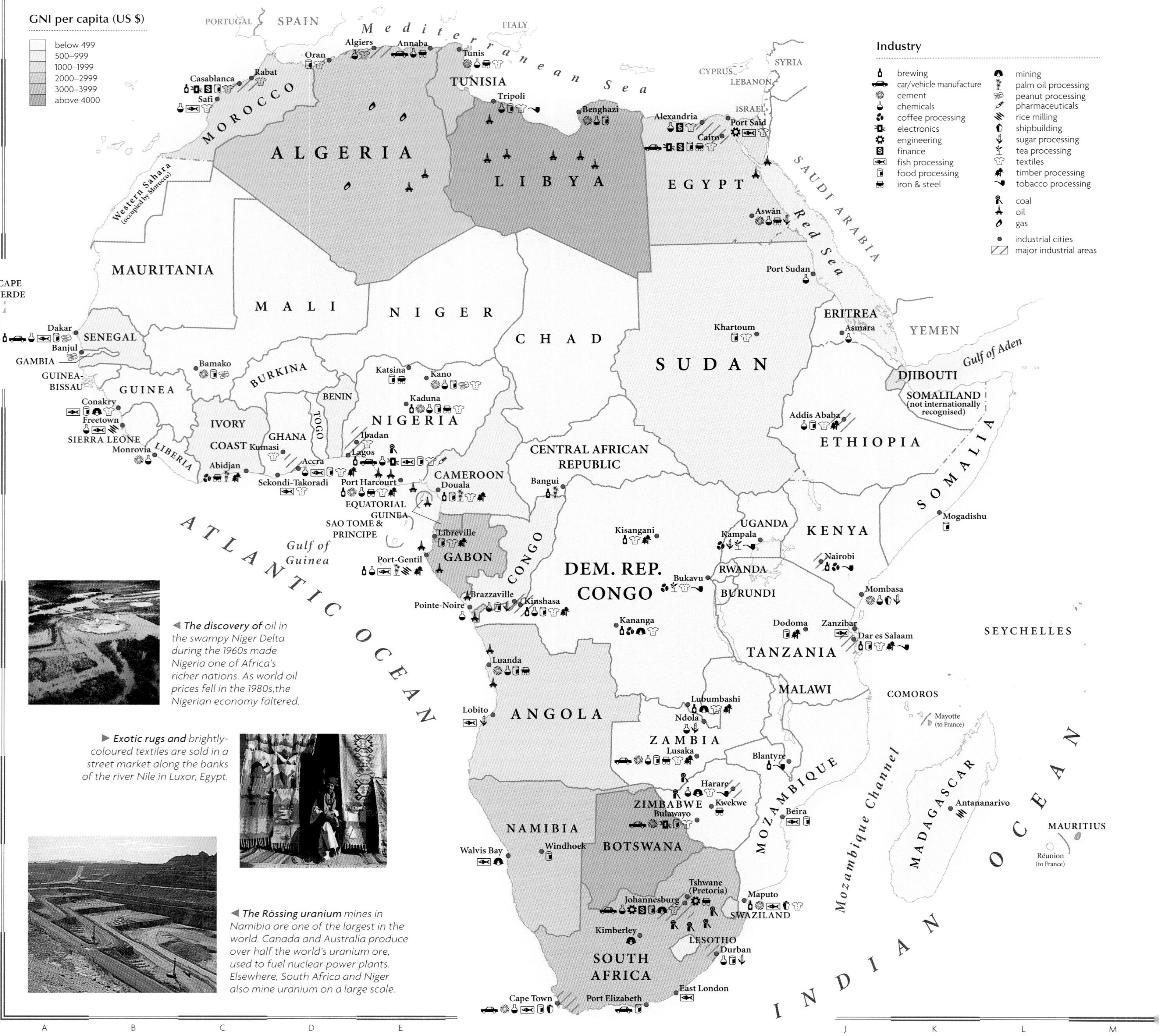

Standard of living

Since the 1960s most countries in Africa have seen significant improvements in life expectancy, healthcare and education. However, 28 of the 30 most deprived countries in the world are African, and the continent as a whole lies well behind the rest of the world in terms of meeting many basic human needs.

Standard of living
(UN human development index)

high

low

GNI per capita (US $)

below 499
500–999
1000–1999
2000–2999
3000–3999
above 4000

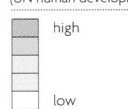

◀ *The discovery of* oil in the swampy Niger Delta during the 1960s made Nigeria one of Africa's richer nations. As world oil prices fell in the 1980s, the Nigerian economy faltered.

▶ *Exotic rugs and* brightly-coloured textiles are sold in a street market along the banks of the river Nile in Luxor, Egypt.

◀ *The Rössing uranium* mines in Namibia are one of the largest in the world. Canada and Australia produce over half the world's uranium ore, used to fuel nuclear power plants. Elsewhere, South Africa and Niger also mine uranium on a large scale.

Industry

brewing	mining
car/vehicle manufacture	palm oil processing
cement	peanut processing
chemicals	pharmaceuticals
coffee processing	rice milling
electronics	shipbuilding
engineering	sugar processing
finance	tea processing
fish processing	textiles
food processing	timber processing
iron & steel	tobacco processing

coal
oil
gas

• industrial cities
major industrial areas

(Map of Africa showing countries and industrial cities)

PORTUGAL SPAIN
ITALY
CYPRUS SYRIA
LEBANON
ISRAEL
Mediterranean Sea
Algiers Annaba
Oran Tunis
Casablanca Rabat
Safi
MOROCCO
Tripoli
TUNISIA
Benghazi
Alexandria
Port Said
Cairo
ALGERIA
LIBYA
EGYPT
Aswân
Western Sahara (occupied by Morocco)
MAURITANIA
MALI
NIGER
CHAD
SUDAN
ERITREA
Asmara
Khartoum
Port Sudan
YEMEN
DJIBOUTI
SOMALILAND (not internationally recognised)
CAPE VERDE
Dakar
SENEGAL
Banjul
GAMBIA
GUINEA-BISSAU
GUINEA
Bamako
BURKINA
BENIN
Katsina Kano
Kaduna
NIGERIA
Conakry
Freetown
SIERRA LEONE
Monrovia
LIBERIA
IVORY COAST
GHANA
TOGO
Kumasi
Ibadan
Lagos
Accra
Abidjan
Sekondi-Takoradi
Port Harcourt
CAMEROON
Douala
CENTRAL AFRICAN REPUBLIC
Bangui
Addis Ababa
ETHIOPIA
SOMALIA
Mogadishu
EQUATORIAL GUINEA
SAO TOME & PRINCIPE
Libreville
GABON
Port-Gentil
CONGO
Kisangani
UGANDA
Kampala
KENYA
Nairobi
DEM. REP. CONGO
Bukavu
RWANDA
BURUNDI
Mombasa
Brazzaville
Kinshasa
Pointe-Noire
Kananga
Dodoma
Zanzibar
Dar es Salaam
SEYCHELLES
TANZANIA
Luanda
MALAWI
COMOROS
Lubumbashi
Ndola
ZAMBIA
Lusaka
Blantyre
Mayotte (to France)
Lobito
ANGOLA
ATLANTIC OCEAN
Gulf of Guinea
Harare
Kwekwe
Beira
ZIMBABWE
Bulawayo
MOZAMBIQUE
MADAGASCAR
Antananarivo
MAURITIUS
Réunion (to France)
Mozambique Channel
NAMIBIA
Walvis Bay
Windhoek
BOTSWANA
Tshwane (Pretoria)
Johannesburg
Maputo
SWAZILAND
Kimberley
LESOTHO
Durban
SOUTH AFRICA
East London
Cape Town
Port Elizabeth
INDIAN OCEAN
Red Sea
SAUDI ARABIA
Gulf of Aden

74

Environmental issues

One of Africa's most serious environmental problems occurs in marginal areas such as the Sahel where scrub and forest clearance, often for cooking fuel, combined with overgrazing, are causing desertification. Game reserves in southern and eastern Africa have helped to preserve many endangered animals, although the needs of growing populations have led to conflict over land use, and poaching is a serious problem.

Environmental issues
- national parks
- tropical forest
- forest destroyed
- desert
- desertification
- polluted rivers
- radioactive contamination
- marine pollution
- heavy marine pollution
- poor urban air quality

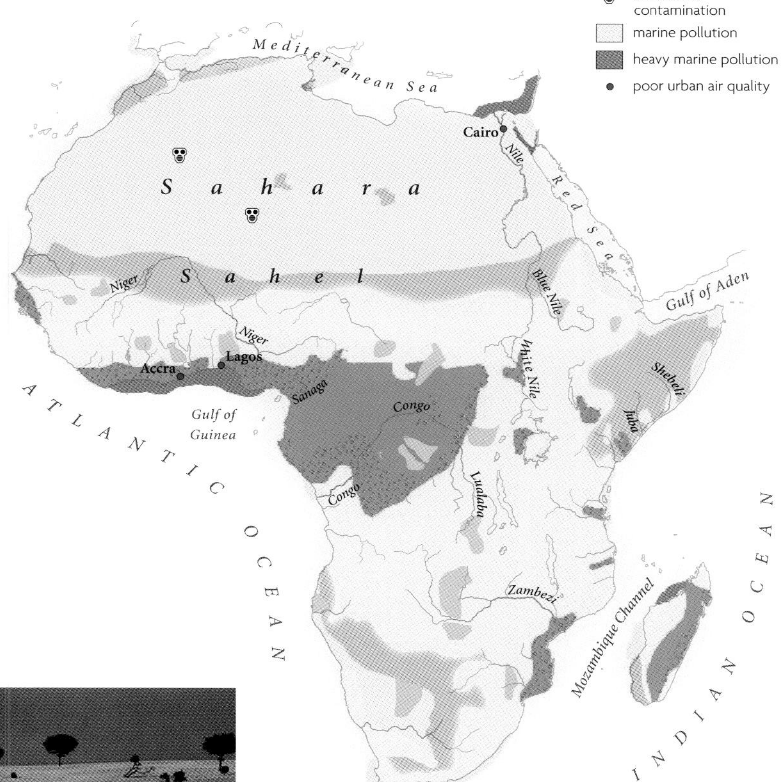

▲ The Sahel's delicate natural equilibrium is easily destroyed by the clearing of vegetation, drought and overgrazing. This causes the Sahara to advance south, engulfing the savannah grasslands.

Mineral resources

Africa's ancient plateaux contain some of the world's most substantial reserves of precious stones and metals. About 15% of the world's gold is mined in South Africa; Zambia has great copper deposits; and diamonds are mined in Botswana, Dem. Rep. Congo and South Africa. Oil has brought great economic benefits to Algeria, Libya and Nigeria.

Mineral resources
- oil field
- gas field
- coal field
- bauxite
- copper
- diamonds
- gold
- iron
- phosphates
- tin
- uranium

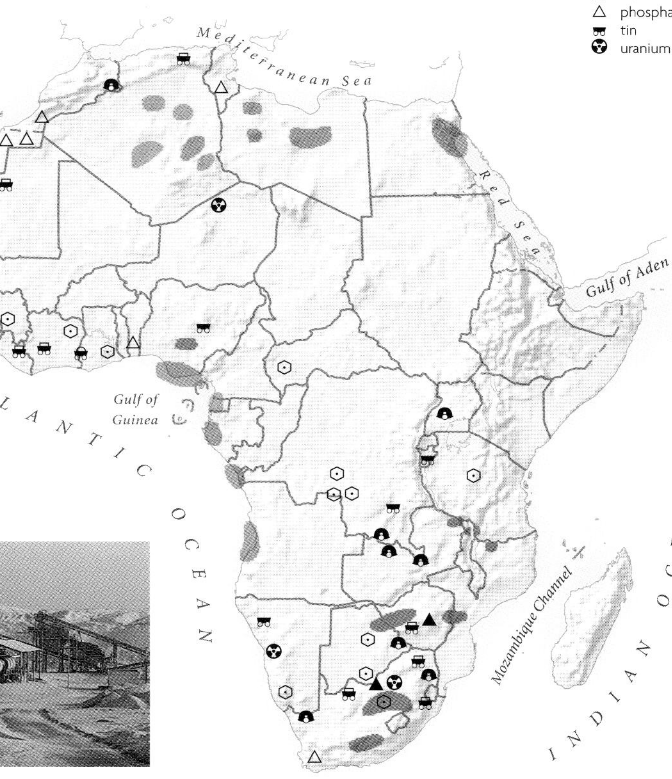

▲ North and West Africa have large deposits of white phosphate minerals, which are used in making fertilizers. Morocco, Senegal, and Tunisia are among the continent's leading producers.

▲ Workers on a tea plantation gather one of Africa's most important cash crops, providing a valuable source of income. Coffee, rubber, bananas, cotton and cocoa are also widely grown as cash crops.

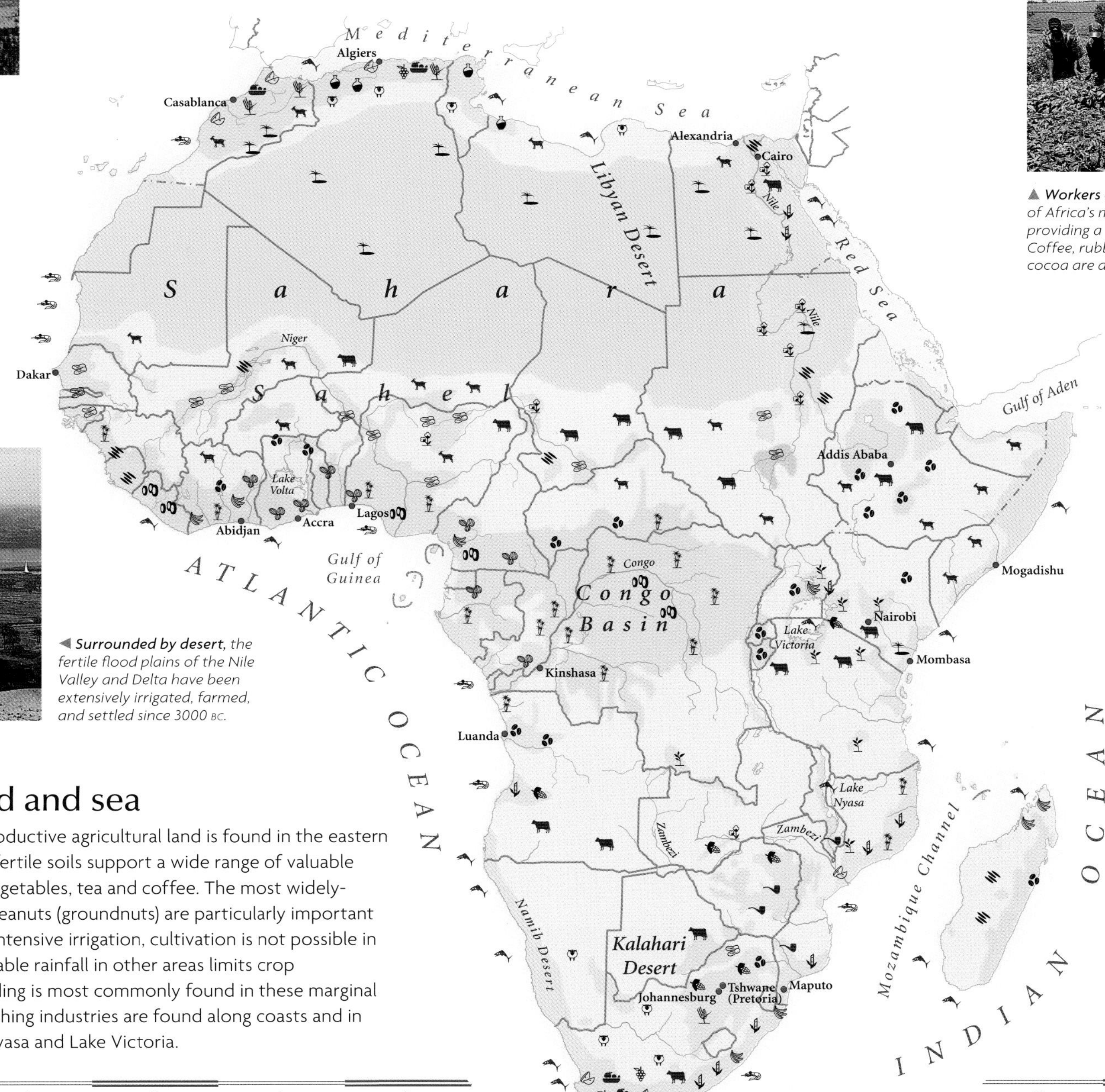

◄ Surrounded by desert, the fertile flood plains of the Nile Valley and Delta have been extensively irrigated, farmed, and settled since 3000 BC.

Using the land and sea

Some of Africa's most productive agricultural land is found in the eastern volcanic uplands, where fertile soils support a wide range of valuable export crops including vegetables, tea and coffee. The most widely-grown grain is corn and peanuts (groundnuts) are particularly important in West Africa. Without intensive irrigation, cultivation is not possible in desert regions and unreliable rainfall in other areas limits crop production. Pastoral herding is most commonly found in these marginal lands. Substantial local fishing industries are found along coasts and in vast lakes such as Lake Nyasa and Lake Victoria.

Using the land and sea
- cropland
- desert
- forest
- pasture
- wetland
- major conurbations
- cattle
- goats
- cereals
- sheep
- bananas
- corn (maize)
- citrus fruits
- cocoa
- cotton
- coffee
- dates
- fishing
- fruit
- oil palms
- olives
- peanuts
- rice
- rubber
- shellfish
- sugar cane
- tea
- tobacco
- vineyards
- wheat

North Africa

ALGERIA, EGYPT, LIBYA, MOROCCO, TUNISIA, WESTERN SAHARA

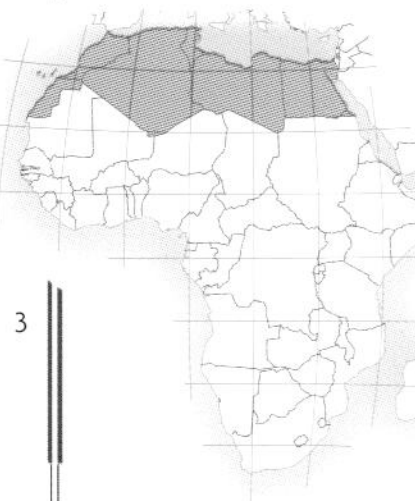

Fringed by the Mediterranean along the northern coast and by the arid Sahara in the south, North Africa reflects the influence of many invaders, both European and, most importantly, Arab, giving the region an almost universal Islamic flavour and a common Arabic language. The countries lying to the west of Egypt are often referred to as the Maghreb, an Arabic term for 'west'. Today, Morocco and Tunisia exploit their culture and landscape for tourism, while rich oil and gas deposits aid development in Libya and Algeria, despite political turmoil. Egypt, with its fertile, Nile-watered agricultural land and varied industrial base, is the most populous nation.

The landscape

The Atlas Mountains, which extend across much of Morocco, northern Algeria and Tunisia, are part of the fold mountain system which also runs through much of southern Europe. They recede to the south and east, becoming a steppe landscape before meeting the Sahara desert which covers more than 90% of the region. The sediments of the Sahara overlie an ancient plateau of crystalline rock, some of which is more than four billion years old.

▲ *These rock piles* in Algeria's Ahaggar mountains are the result of weathering caused by extremes of temperature. Great cracks or joints appear in the rocks, which are then worn and smoothed by the wind.

Map key

Population
- ■ above 5 million
- ■ 1 million to 5 million
- ◉ 500,000 to 1 million
- ◎ 100,000 to 500,000
- ⊕ 50,000 to 100,000
- ○ 10,000 to 50,000
- ○ below 10,000

Elevation
- 4000m / 13,124ft
- 3000m / 9843ft
- 2000m / 6562ft
- 1000m / 3281ft
- 500m / 1640ft
- 250m / 820ft
- 100m / 328ft
- sea level

Scale 1:11,000,000

projection: Lambert Azimuthal Equal Area

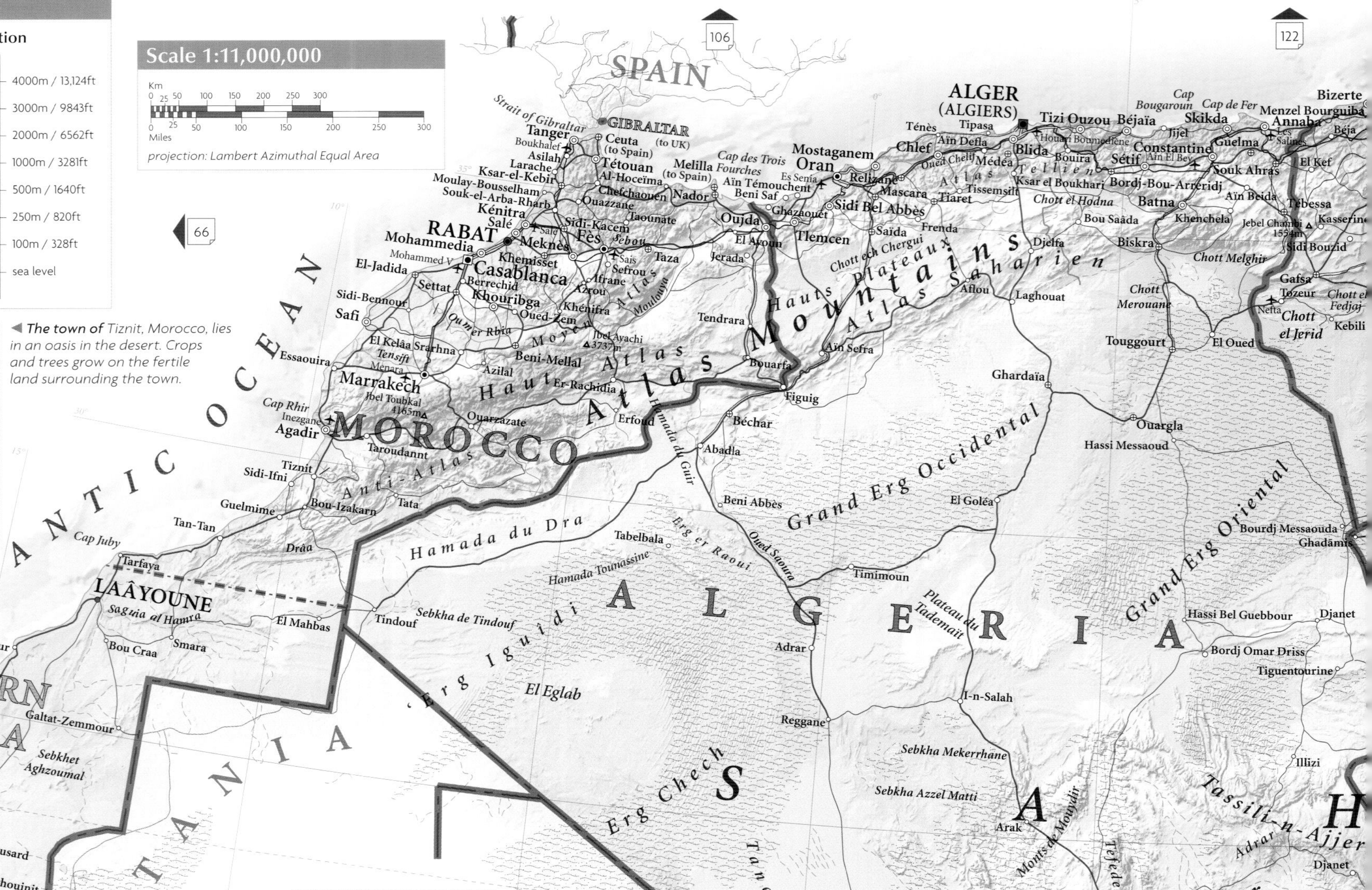

◀ *The town of* Tiznit, Morocco, lies in an oasis in the desert. Crops and trees grow on the fertile land surrounding the town.

▶ *The Grand Erg Occidental* is one of Algeria's great Saharan sand seas. Wind force and direction determines the nature of landforms such as the linear or seif dunes in the foreground.

Using the land and sea

Sheltered valleys in the Atlas Mountains, the Nile Valley and Delta, and the Mediterranean coast are the main sources of good farming land. A wide variety of valuable crops including cereals, rice and cotton, and woods such as cedar and cork, are grown. Typical Mediterranean crops such as olives, figs, dates and citrus fruits also thrive in these areas. The Nile Valley is particularly fertile, and most of Egypt's population lives close to the river. Elsewhere, irrigation is essential to improve crop yields on the desert margins.

The urban/rural population divide

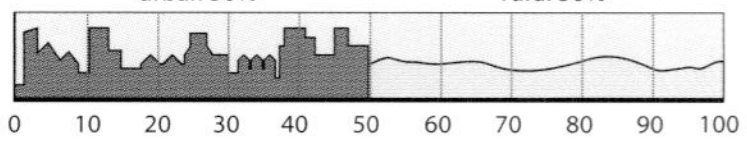

urban 50%	rural 50%

0 10 20 30 40 50 60 70 80 90 100

Population density

65 people per sq mile
(25 people per sq km)

Total land area

2,215,020 sq miles
(5,738,394 sq km)

Land use and agricultural distribution
- goats
- sheep
- cereals
- citrus fruits
- cork
- cotton
- dates
- fishing
- olives
- vineyards
- ■ capital cities
- • major towns
- pasture
- cropland
- forest
- desert

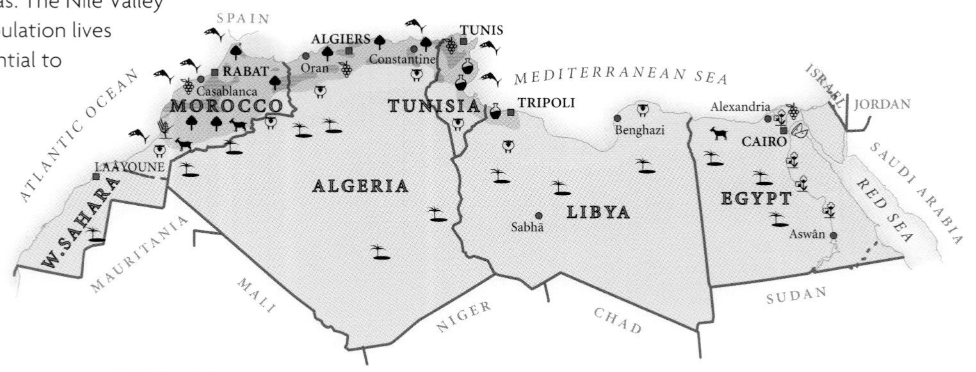

▲ *Many North African* nomads, such as the Bedouin, maintain a traditional pastoral lifestyle on the desert fringes, moving their herds of sheep, goats and camels from place to place – crossing country borders in order to find sufficient grazing land.

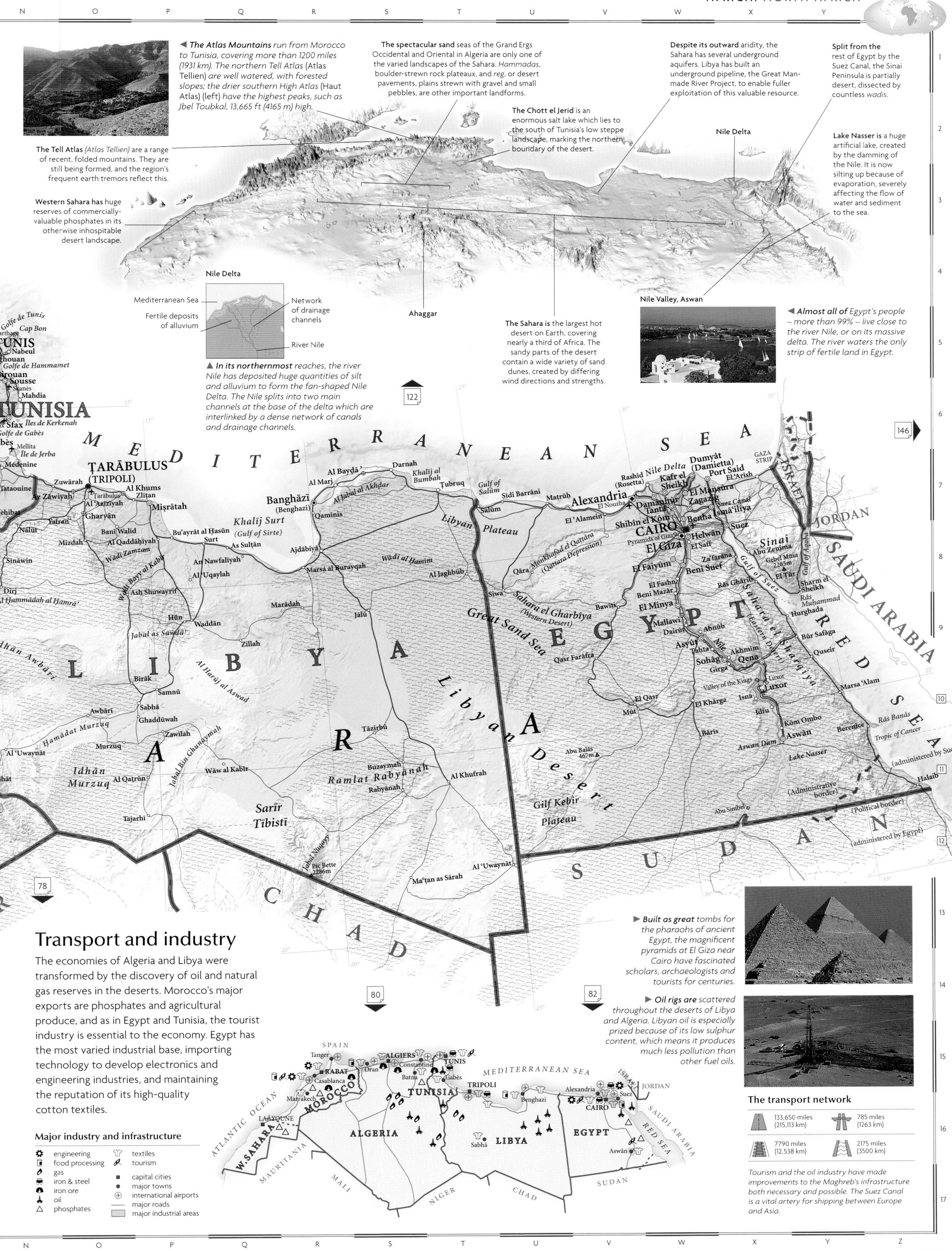

The Atlas Mountains run from Morocco to Tunisia, covering more than 1200 miles (1931 km). The northern Tell Atlas (Atlas Tellien) are well watered, with forested slopes; the drier southern High Atlas (Haut Atlas) (left) have the highest peaks, such as Jbel Toubkal, 13,665 ft (4165 m) high.

The spectacular sand seas of the Grand Ergs Occidental and Oriental in Algeria are only one of the varied landscapes of the Sahara. *Hammadas*, boulder-strewn rock plateaux, and *reg*, or desert pavements, plains strewn with gravel and small pebbles, are other important landforms.

Despite its outward aridity, the Sahara has several underground aquifers. Libya has built an underground pipeline, the Great Man-made River Project, to enable fuller exploitation of this valuable resource.

Split from the rest of Egypt by the Suez Canal, the Sinai Peninsula is partially desert, dissected by countless *wadis*.

The Tell Atlas (Atlas Tellien) are a range of recent, folded mountains. They are still being formed, and the region's frequent earth tremors reflect this.

The Chott el Jerid is an enormous salt lake which lies to the south of Tunisia's low steppe landscape, marking the northern boundary of the desert.

Lake Nasser is a huge artificial lake, created by the damming of the Nile. It is now silting up because of evaporation, severely affecting the flow of water and sediment to the sea.

Nile Delta

Western Sahara has huge reserves of commercially-valuable phosphates in its otherwise inhospitable desert landscape.

Nile Delta

Mediterranean Sea
Fertile deposits of alluvium
Network of drainage channels
River Nile

Ahaggar

The Sahara is the largest hot desert on Earth, covering nearly a third of Africa. The sandy parts of the desert contain a wide variety of sand dunes, created by differing wind directions and strengths.

Nile Valley, Aswan

Almost all of Egypt's people – more than 99% – live close to the river Nile, or on its massive delta. The river waters the only strip of fertile land in Egypt.

In its northernmost reaches, the river Nile has deposited huge quantities of silt and alluvium to form the fan-shaped Nile Delta. The Nile splits into two main channels at the base of the delta which are interlinked by a dense network of canals and drainage channels.

Transport and industry

The economies of Algeria and Libya were transformed by the discovery of oil and natural gas reserves in the deserts. Morocco's major exports are phosphates and agricultural produce, and as in Egypt and Tunisia, the tourist industry is essential to the economy. Egypt has the most varied industrial base, importing technology to develop electronics and engineering industries, and maintaining the reputation of its high-quality cotton textiles.

Built as great tombs for the pharaohs of ancient Egypt, the magnificent pyramids at El Giza near Cairo have fascinated scholars, archaeologists and tourists for centuries.

Oil rigs are scattered throughout the deserts of Libya and Algeria. Libyan oil is especially prized because of its low sulphur content, which means it produces much less pollution than other fuel oils.

Major industry and infrastructure

engineering	textiles
food processing	tourism
gas	capital cities
iron & steel	major towns
iron ore	international airports
oil	major roads
phosphates	major industrial areas

The transport network

133,650 miles (215,113 km)	785 miles (1263 km)
7790 miles (12,538 km)	2175 miles (3500 km)

Tourism and the oil industry have made improvements to the Maghreb's infrastructure both necessary and possible. The Suez Canal is a vital artery for shipping between Europe and Asia.

West Africa

BENIN, BURKINA, CAPE VERDE, GAMBIA, GHANA, GUINEA, GUINEA-BISSAU, IVORY COAST, LIBERIA, MALI, MAURITANIA, NIGER, NIGERIA, SENEGAL, SIERRA LEONE, TOGO

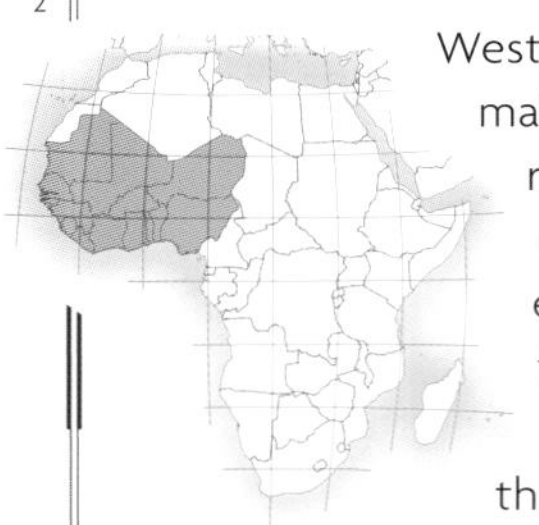

West Africa is an immensely diverse region, encompassing the desert landscapes and mainly Muslim populations of the southern Saharan countries, and the tropical rainforests of the more humid south, with a great variety of local languages and cultures. The rich natural resources and accessibility of the area were quickly exploited by Europeans; most of the Africans taken by slave traders came from this region, causing serious depopulation. The very different influences of West Africa's leading colonial powers, Britain and France, remain today, reflected in the languages and institutions of the countries they once governed.

► *The dry scrub* of the Sahel is only suitable for grazing herd animals like these cattle in Mali.

Scale 1:9,000,000

projection: Lambert Azimuthal Equal Area

Transport and industry

Abundant natural resources including oil and metallic minerals are found in much of West Africa, although investment is required for their further exploitation. Nigeria experienced an oil boom during the 1970s but subsequent growth has been sporadic. Most industry in other countries has a primary basis, including mining, logging and food processing.

The transport network

62,154 miles (100,038 km)	1037 miles (1669 km)
6752 miles (10,867 km)	10,192 miles (16,405 km)

The road and rail systems are most developed near the coasts. Some of the land-locked countries remain disadvantaged by the difficulty of access to ports, and their poor road networks.

Major industry and infrastructure

- chemicals
- cotton spinning
- food processing
- mining
- oil
- palm oil processing
- peanut processing
- textiles
- vehicle manufacture
- ● capital cities
- · major towns
- ✈ international airports
- — major roads
- ▓ major industrial areas

Map key

Population
- ■ 1 million to 5 million
- ⊙ 500,000 to 1 million
- ⊙ 100,000 to 500,000
- ⊕ 50,000 to 100,000
- ○ 10,000 to 50,000
- ○ below 10,000

Elevation
- 2000m / 6562ft
- 1000m / 3281ft
- 500m / 1640ft
- 250m / 820ft
- 100m / 328ft
- sea level

CAPE VERDE

Santo Antão, Pombas, Ilhas de Barlavento, Pedra Lume, Mindelo, São Vicente, Ribeira Brava, Amilcar Cabral, Sal, São Nicolau, Boa Vista, João Barrosa

ATLANTIC OCEAN

Tarrafal, Maio, Fogo, São Filipe, Santiago, Maio, PRAIA, Ilhas de Sotavento

(same scale as main map)

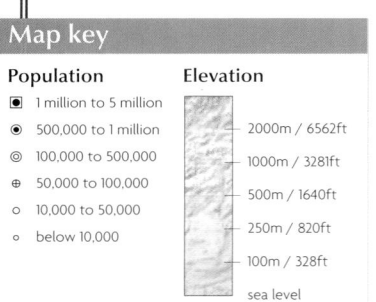

◄ *The southern regions* of West Africa still contain great swathes of tropical rainforest, including some of the world's most prized hardwood trees, such as mahogany and iroko.

Using the land and sea

The humid southern regions are most suitable for cultivation; in these areas, cash crops such as coffee, cotton, cocoa and rubber are grown in large quantities. Peanuts (groundnuts) are grown throughout West Africa. In the north, advancing desertification has made the Sahel increasingly unviable for cultivation, and pastoral farming is more common. Great herds of sheep, cattle and goats are grazed on the savannah grasses, and fishing is important in coastal and delta areas.

▲ *The Gambia, mainland* Africa's smallest country, produces great quantities of peanuts (groundnuts). Winnowing is used to separate the nuts from their stalks.

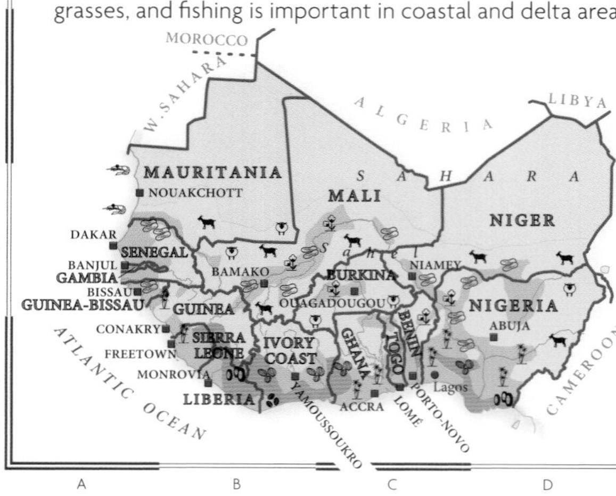

Land use and agricultural distribution

- goats
- sheep
- cocoa
- coffee
- cotton
- oil palms
- peanuts
- rubber
- shellfish
- ■ capital cities
- · major towns
- pasture
- cropland
- forest
- desert

The urban/rural population divide

urban 36%   rural 64%

0 10 20 30 40 50 60 70 80 90 100

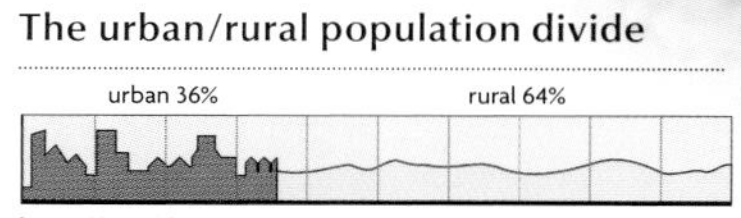

Population density	Total land area
104 people per sq mile (40 people per sq km)	2,337,137 sq miles (6,054,760 sq km)

Main map labels

WESTERN SAHARA (occupied by Morocco)

'Aïn Ben Tili, Yetti, Bir Mogreïn, 'Ayoûn 'Abd el Mâlek

TIRIS ZEMMOUR, Kâghet, El Hank, El Mreiti, El Mrâyer

Tropic of Cancer, Zouérat, El Hammâmi, Fdérik, Touâjil, Tourine, Char, Choûm, Ouadâne, Maqteïr, Ouarâne, Erg

Ras Nouâdhibou, Nouâdhibou, Bou Lanouar, Azefâl, Akchâr, Ouâne

DAKHLET NOUÂDHIBOU, Dakhlet Nouâdhibou, Et Tidra, Ras Timiris, Nouâmghâr, ADRAR, El Mrâyer

INCHIRI, Atâr, Chinguetti

Akjoujt, Bennichâb, Bou Rjeimât, MAURITANIA, El Mreyyé, S

NOUAKCHOTT, Sebkhet Te-n-Dghâmcha, Beila, Nouakchott, Idini, Rachid, TAGANT, Tichit, HODH

TRARZA, Tidjikja, Moudjéria, Aoukâr, ECH CHARGUI

ATLANTIC OCEAN

Boutilimit, Magta' Lahjar, Boûmdeïd, Tâmchekket, Oualâta

Mederdra, Rkiz, BRAKNA, Aleg, Guérou, Kiffa, HODH EL GHARBI, Néma

Rosso, Richard Toll, Dagana, Podor, Bogué, Bababé, Môguel, Kaédi, Sîntiou, 'Ayoûn el 'Atroûs, Timbedgha, Amourj, Bassikounou

Saint Louis, Lac de Guier, Vallée du Ferlo, Mbout, ASSABA, Kankossa, Kobenni, Adel Bagrou

DAKAR, Louga, Mékhé, Kébémer, Dara, Linguère, Ranérou, Maghama, GORGOL, GUIDIMAKA, Sélibabi, Ould Yenjé, Yélimané, Nioro, Ballé, Nara

Tivaouane, Thiès, Touba, Mbaké, Vélingara, Kayes, Ambidédi, Maréna, Diéma, Mourdiah, Sokolo, Niono

Rufisque, Bambey, Diourbel, KAYES, Kidira, Diamou, Bafoulabé, Kita, Kolokani, Banamba, SÉGOU

Mbour, Fatick, Kaolack, Sebikhotane, Kaffrine, Koungheul, Goudiri, Sadiola, Toukoto, Sébékoro, KOULIKORO, Didiéni, Markala

Joal-Fadiout, Sokone, Nioro du Rip, Maka, Tambacounda, Dialakoto, Kokofata, Kati, Koulikoro, Fana, SÉGOU

SENEGAL, BANJUL, Bignona, Kolda, Vélingara, Médina Gounas, Saraya, Kédougou, Niagassola, BAMAKO, Bla

GAMBIA, Brikama, Mansa Konko, Georgetown, Basse Santa Su, Koundara, Mali, Tinguage, Dioïla

Diouloulou, Ziguinchor, Séédhiou, Farim, Bissorã, Gabú, Gaoual, Maléa, Doko, Kangaba, Ouéléssébougou, Niéna

GUINEA-BISSAU, Cacheu, Mansôa, BISSAU, Fulacunda, Bolama, Buba, Catió, Boké, Fouta, Labé, Tougué, Dinguiraye, Tikinso, Siguiri, Yanfolila, Bougouni, SIKASSO, Sikasso

Quinhámel, Bafatá, Fulacunda, Arquipélago dos Bijagós, Kamsar, Télimélé, Djallon, Dabola, Kouroussa, Mandiana, Garalo, Kolondiéba

Kindia, Fria, Boffa, Konkouré, Mamou, GUINEA, Kankan, Samatigula, Kadiolo, Tengréla, Niellé

CONAKRY, Dubréka, Coyah, Forécariah, Moriba, Kabala, Faranah, Tokounou, Kérouané, Madinani, Odienné, Boundiali, Korhogo

Port Loko, Kambia, Pendembu, Kissidougou, Macenta, IVORY, Touba, Kani, Séguéla, Kounahiri, Réoumi

FREETOWN, Lungi, Makeni, Magburaka, Koidu, Guéckédou, Beyla, Sifié, Vavoua

SIERRA LEONE, Lunsar, Bo, Kenema, Mano, Zorzor, Nzérékoré, Lola, Sanniquellie, Man, Zuénoula, Vavoua, Lac de Kossou

Moyamba, Shenge, Sewa, Koïahun, Voinjama, Bonthe, Sherbro Island, Sulima, Tubmanburg, Ganta, Danané, Daloa, Zoukougbeu

MONROVIA, Monrovia, Marshall, Robertsport, Gbanga, Harbel, LIBERIA, Tapeta, Guiglo, Issia, Gagnoa

Buchanan, Cestos, River Cess, Zwedru, Duékoué, Lac de Buyo, Soubré

Greenville, Sassandra

ATLANTIC OCEAN, Grand Cess, Plibo, Grabo, San-Pédro, Grand-Béréby, Cape Palmas, Harper, Tabou

Inset maps (Transport and Using the land)

MOROCCO, W. SAHARA, ALGERIA, LIBYA, SAHARA, MAURITANIA, NOUAKCHOTT, MALI, NIGER, CHAD, DAKAR, SENEGAL, BANJUL, GAMBIA, GUINEA-BISSAU, BAMAKO, BURKINA, NIAMEY, OUAGADOUGOU, CONAKRY, GUINEA, SIERRA LEONE, FREETOWN, IVORY COAST, GHANA, BENIN, TOGO, NIGERIA, ABUJA, Kano, MONROVIA, LIBERIA, ACCRA, LOMÉ, PORTO-NOVO, Lagos, Ibadan, Port Harcourt, YAMOUSSOUKRO, CAMEROON, ATLANTIC OCEAN

▲ *Inselbergs, found across* the Sahel, are isolated hills, or outcrops, formed where the surrounding plain has eroded away, leaving only the more resistant remnants of the original plateau.

The dry grasslands of the Sahel border the southern reaches of the Sahara. Overgrazing, drought and the cutting down of trees for firewood, means that much of the Sahel is turning irrevocably to desert.

► *The Niger river flows for 2600 miles (4181 km) from Fouta Djallon, on the plateau of Guinea, via southern Mali, where it supports rich fish stocks, on through the desert, and finally through Nigeria to the Gulf of Guinea.*

The landscape

There are two major topographical areas in West Africa: the northern deserts are part of the Saharan region which stretches across the whole continent; the grasslands of the Sahel and the southern Guinea coast are part of Africa's central plateau. The landscape is generally low, rarely rising above 1500 ft (457 m) and consists mainly of plains, broken by an occasional high plateau or mountain range.

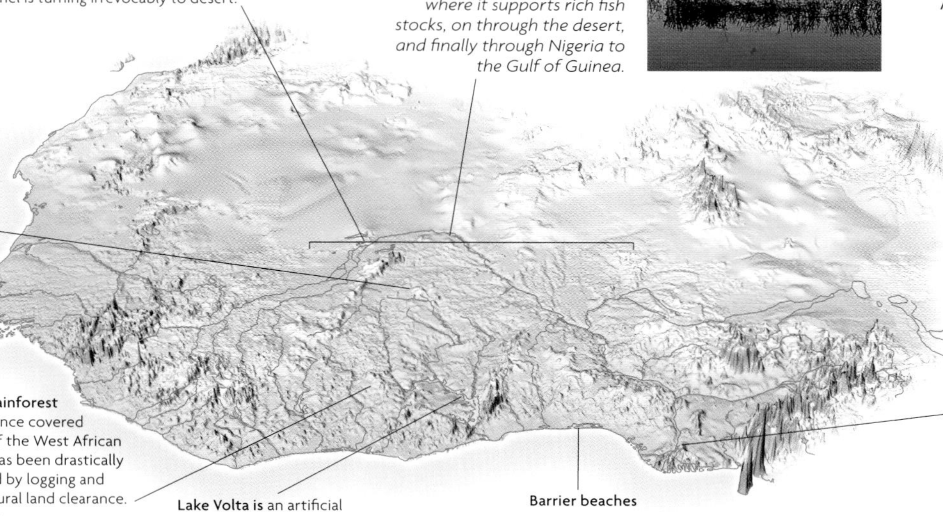

Two types of coastline characterize West Africa. Swampy, muddy coasts colonized by mangroves occur on river deltas and where ocean currents are weak, like the coast of Senegal. Sandy beaches, with barrier ridges and lagoons, form where currents are stronger.

As it nears the Gulf of Guinea, the Niger forks into many strands. When the river floods, alluvium is deposited over a wide area. This creates fertile soils, able to support both crops and livestock.

Virgin rainforest which once covered much of the West African coast, has been drastically reduced by logging and agricultural land clearance.

Lake Volta is an artificial lake, created by the damming of the Volta river. It links the drier northern areas with the coast and is intended to provide fresh water for drinking, fisheries and irrigation.

Barrier beaches

Fluvial deposits — Lagoon
River dammed by — Barrier beach
barrier beach — Estuarine deposits

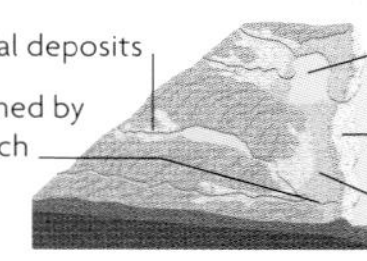

▲ *Along much of* the West African coast, barrier beaches have built up and dammed river mouths, forming fluvial and estuarine plains.

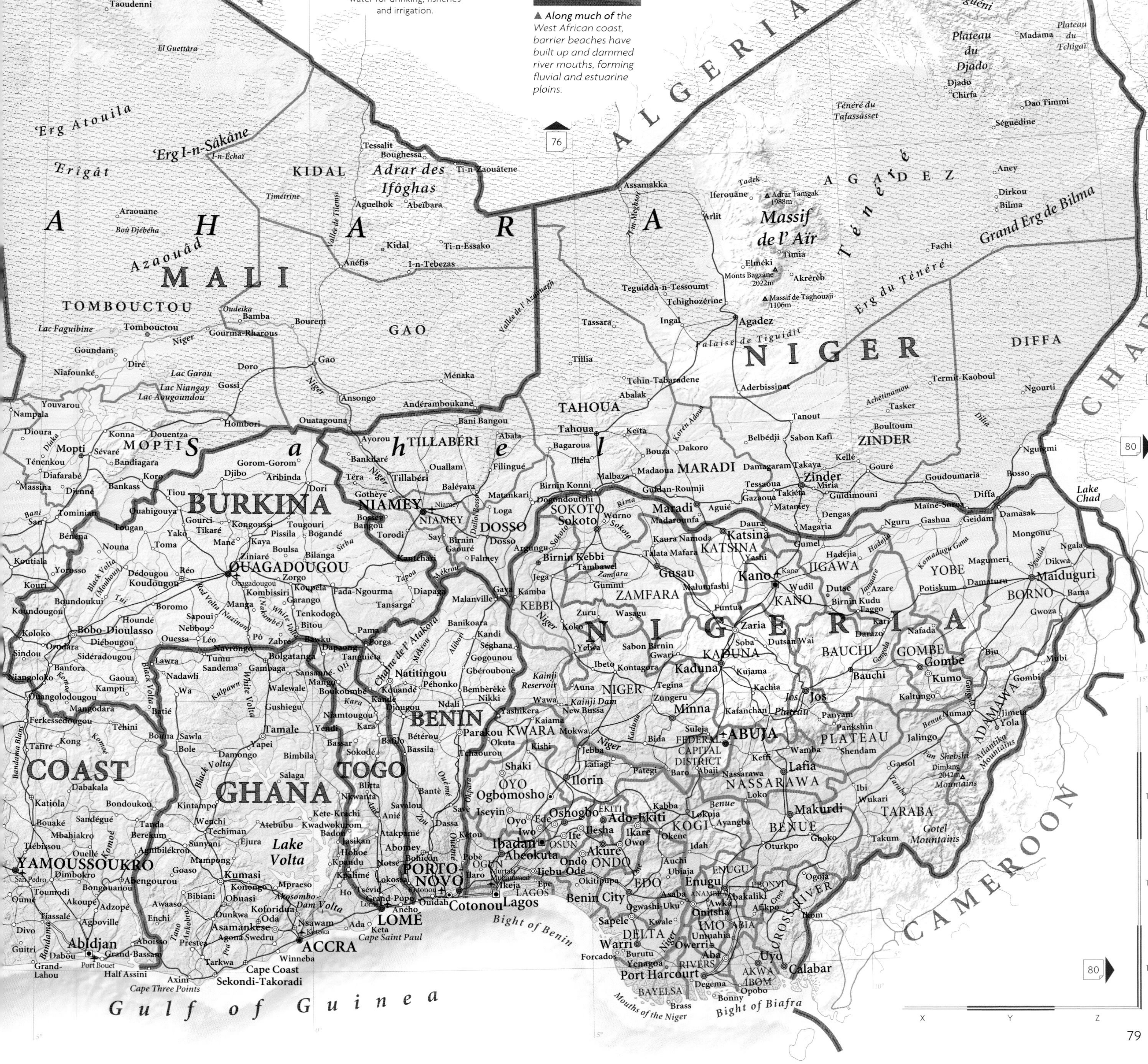

Central Africa

CAMEROON, CENTRAL AFRICAN REPUBLIC, CHAD, CONGO, DEM. REP. CONGO, EQUATORIAL GUINEA, GABON, SAO TOME & PRINCIPE

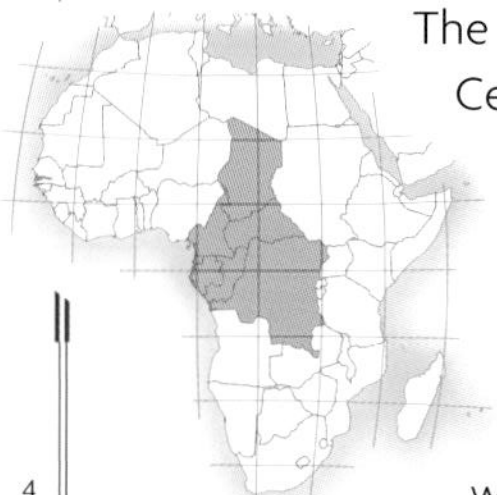

The great rainforest basin of the Congo river embraces most of remote Central Africa. The interior was largely unknown to Europeans until late in the 19th century, when its tribal kingdoms were split – principally between France and Belgium – with Sao Tome and Principe the lone Portuguese territory, and Equatorial Guinea controlled by Spain. Open democracy and regional economic integration are important goals for these nations – several of which have only recently emerged from restrictive regimes – and investment is needed to improve transport infrastructures. Many of the small, but fast-growing and increasingly urban population, speak French, the regional *lingua franca*, along with several hundred Pygmy, Bantu and Sudanic dialects.

The landscape

Lake Chad lies in a desert basin bounded by the volcanic Tibesti mountains in the north, plateaux in the east and, in the south, the broad watershed of the Congo basin. The vast circular depression of the Congo is isolated from the coastal plain by the granite Massif du Chaillu. To the northwest, the volcanoes and fold mountains of the Cameroon Ridge (*Dorsale Camerounaise*) extend as islands into the Gulf of Guinea. The high fold mountains fringing the east of the Congo Basin fall steeply to the lakes of the Great Rift Valley.

Transport and industry

Large reserves of valuable minerals are found in Central Africa: copper, cobalt and diamonds are mined in Dem. Rep. Congo and manganese in Gabon, Congo, Cameroon, Gabon and Equatorial Guinea have oil deposits and oil has also been recently discovered in Chad. Goods such as palm oil and rubber are processed for export.

The transport network

102,747 miles (165,774 km)
37 miles (60 km)
3985 miles (6414 km)
1410 miles (2270 km)

The Trans-Gabon railway, which began operating in 1987, has opened up new sources of timber and manganese. Elsewhere, much investment is needed to update and improve road, rail and water transport.

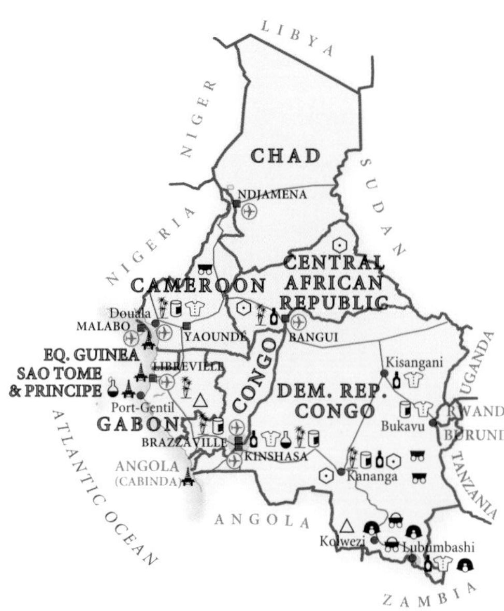

Major industry and infrastructure

- brewing
- chemicals
- cobalt
- copper
- diamonds
- food processing
- manganese
- oil
- palm oil processing
- textiles
- tin
- capital cities
- major towns
- international airports
- major roads
- major industrial areas

The ancient rocks of Dem. Rep. Congo hold immense and varied mineral reserves. This open pit copper mine is at Kolwezi in the far south.

The Tibesti mountains are the highest in the Sahara. They were pushed up by the movement of the African Plate over a hot spot, which first formed the northern Ahaggar mountains and is now thought to lie under the Great Rift Valley.

The Congo river is second only to the Amazon in the volume of water it carries, and in the size of its drainage basin.

Lake Tanganyika, the world's second deepest lake, is the largest of a series of linear 'ribbon' lakes occupying a trench within the Great Rift Valley.

Rich mineral deposits in the 'Copper Belt' of Dem. Rep. Congo were formed under intense heat and pressure when the ancient African Shield was uplifted to form the region's mountains.

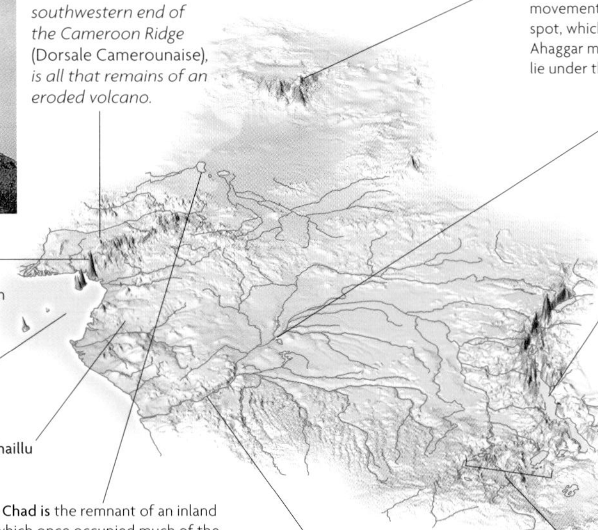

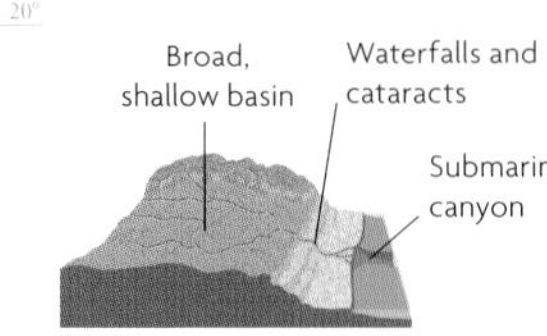

▲ *Virgin tropical rainforest covers the Ruwenzori range on the borders of Dem. Rep. Congo and Uganda.*

The lake-like expansion of the Congo river at Stanley Pool is the lowest point of the interior basin, although the river still descends more than 1000 ft (300 m) to reach the sea.

▲ *The Congo river flows sluggishly through the rainforest of the interior basin. Towards the coast, the river drops steeply in a series of waterfalls and cataracts. At this point, the erosional power of the river becomes so great that it has formed a deep submarine canyon offshore.*

Waterfalls and cataracts
Submarine canyon
Broad, shallow basin

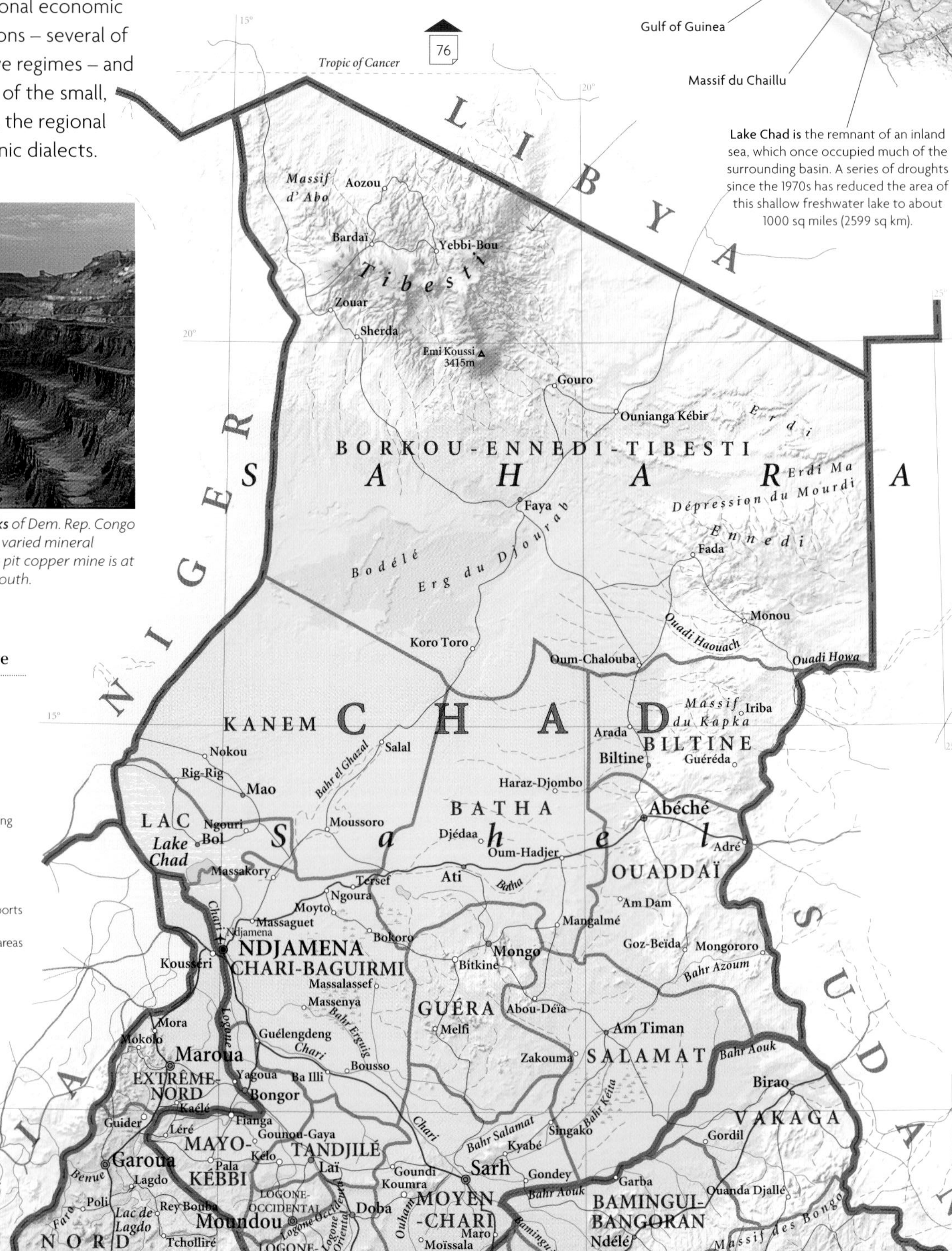

▲ *The vast sand flats surrounding Lake Chad were once covered by water. Changing climatic patterns caused the lake to shrink, and desert now covers much of its previous area.*

▲ *A plug of resistant lava, at the southwestern end of the Cameroon Ridge (Dorsale Camerounaise), is all that remains of an eroded volcano.*

The volcanic massif of Cameroon Mountain occupies an area which remains volcanically active.

Lake Chad is the remnant of an inland sea, which once occupied much of the surrounding basin. A series of droughts since the 1970s has reduced the area of this shallow freshwater lake to about 1000 sq miles (2599 sq km).

Map key

Population
- 1 million to 5 million
- 500,000 to 1 million
- 100,000 to 500,000
- 50,000 to 100,000
- 10,000 to 50,000
- below 10,000

Elevation
- 4000m / 13,124ft
- 3000m / 9843ft
- 2000m / 6562ft
- 1000m / 3281ft
- 500m / 1640ft
- 250m / 820ft
- 100m / 328ft
- sea level

Scale 1:9,500,000

projection: Lambert Azimuthal Equal Area

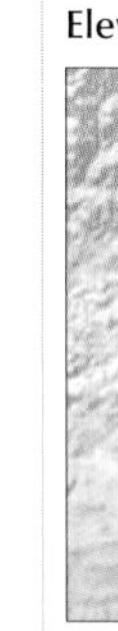

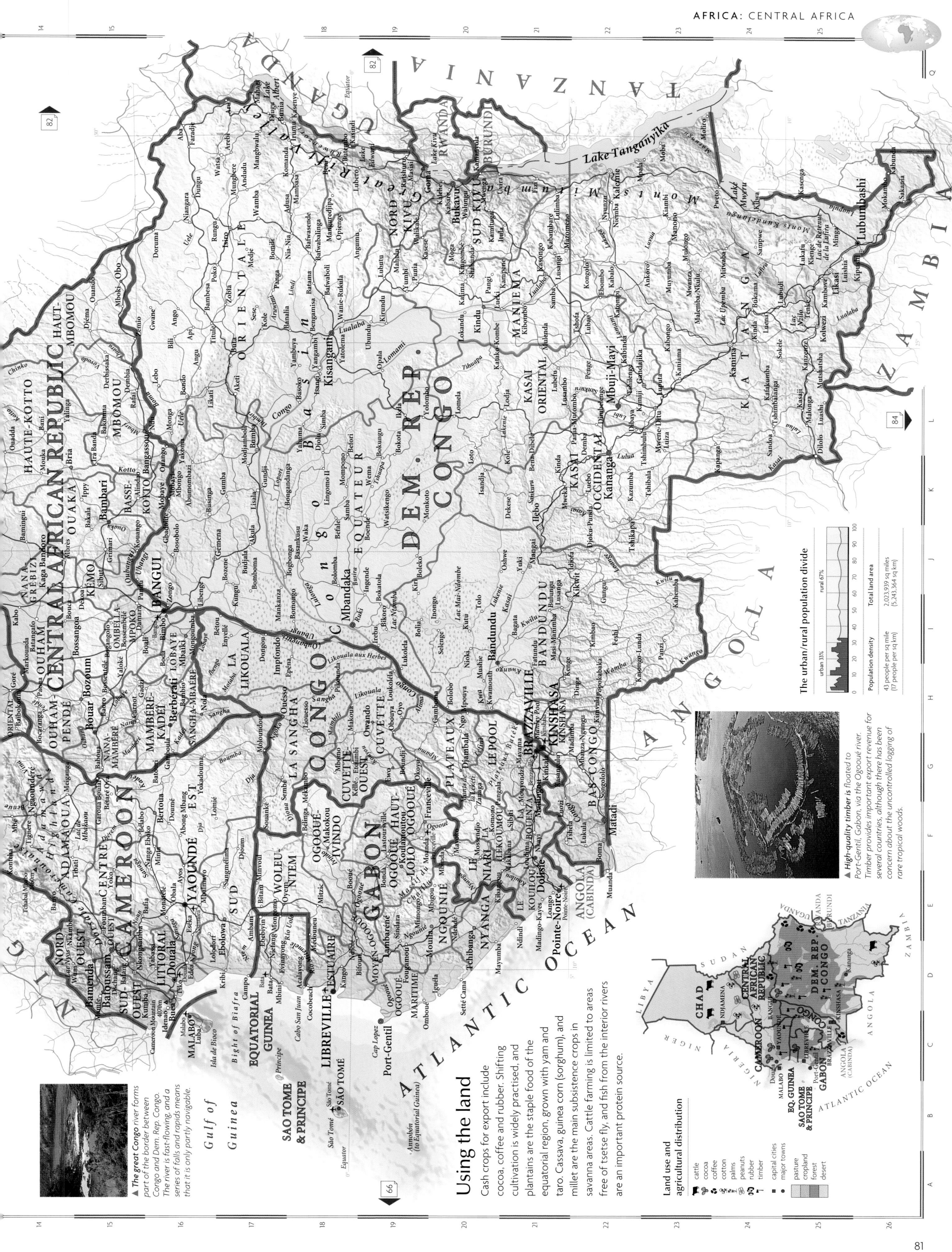

Using the land

Cash crops for export include cocoa, coffee and rubber. Shifting cultivation is widely practised, and plantains are the staple food of the equatorial region, grown with yam and taro. Cassava, guinea corn (sorghum), and millet are the main subsistence crops in savanna areas. Cattle farming is limited to areas free of tsetse fly, and fish from the interior rivers are an important protein source.

Land use and agricultural distribution

- cattle
- cocoa
- coffee
- cotton
- palms
- peanuts
- rubber
- timber
- capital cities
- major towns
- pasture
- cropland
- forest
- desert

▲ The great Congo river forms part of the border between Congo and Dem. Rep. Congo. The river is fast-flowing, and a series of falls and rapids means that it is only partly navigable.

▲ High-quality timber is floated to Port-Gentil, Gabon, via the Ogooué river. Timber provides important export revenue for several countries, although there has been concern about the uncontrolled logging of rare tropical woods.

The urban/rural population divide

urban 33%   rural 67%

Total land area
2,023,939 sq miles
(5,243,364 sq km)

Population density
43 people per sq mile
(17 people per sq km)

East Africa

BURUNDI, DJIBOUTI, ERITREA, ETHIOPIA, KENYA, RWANDA, SOMALIA, SUDAN, TANZANIA, UGANDA

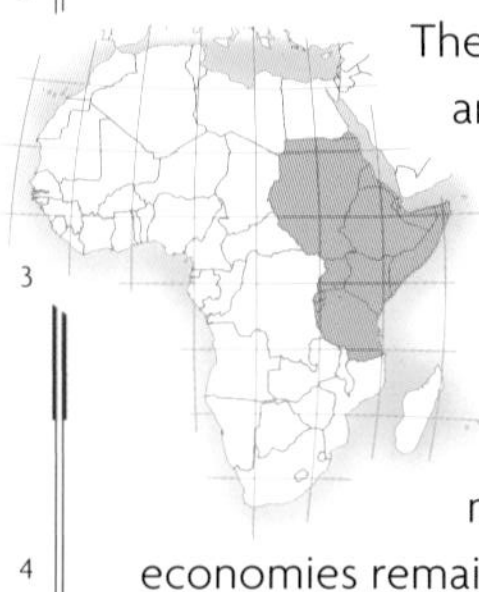

The countries of East Africa divide into two distinct cultural regions. Sudan and the 'Horn' nations have been influenced by the Middle East; Ethiopia was the home of one of the earliest Christian civilizations, and Sudan reflects both Muslim and Christian influences, while the southern countries share a closer cultural affinity with other sub-Saharan nations. Some of Africa's most densely populated countries lie in this region, and the needs of a growing number of people have put pressure on marginal lands and fragile environments. Although most East African economies remain strongly agricultural, Kenya has developed a varied industrial base.

The landscape

East Africa's most significant landscape feature is the Great Rift Valley, which formed during the most recent phase of continental movement when the rigid basement rocks cracked and buckled. Great blocks of land were raised and lowered, creating huge flat-bottomed valleys and steep escarpments, sometimes covered by volcanic extrusions in highland areas.

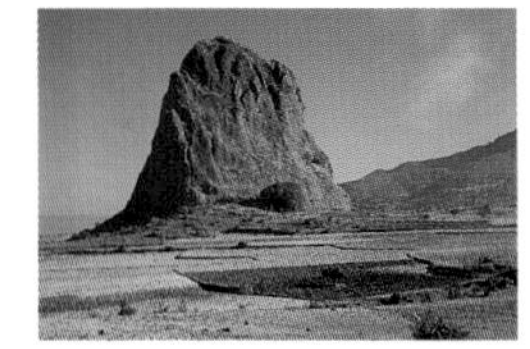

▼ This dome at Gonder, in Ethiopia, is a volcanic intrusion, formed when molten rock pushed up the surface of the Earth and then solidified, leaving an outcrop of igneous rock.

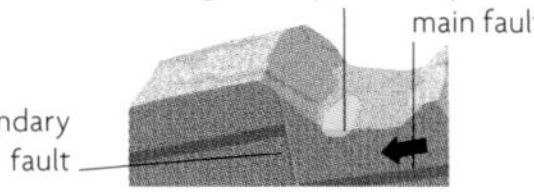

▲ The eastern arm of the Great Rift Valley is gradually being pulled apart; however the forces on one side are greater than the other causing the land to slope. This affects regional drainage which migrates down the slope.

Ephemeral lake forms at far edge of slope

Central block slopes towards main fault

Boundary fault

Lava flows on uplifted areas either side of the eastern branch of the Great Rift Valley gave the Ethiopian Highlands – a series of high, wide plateaux – their distinctive rounded appearance and fertile soils.

Kilimanjaro

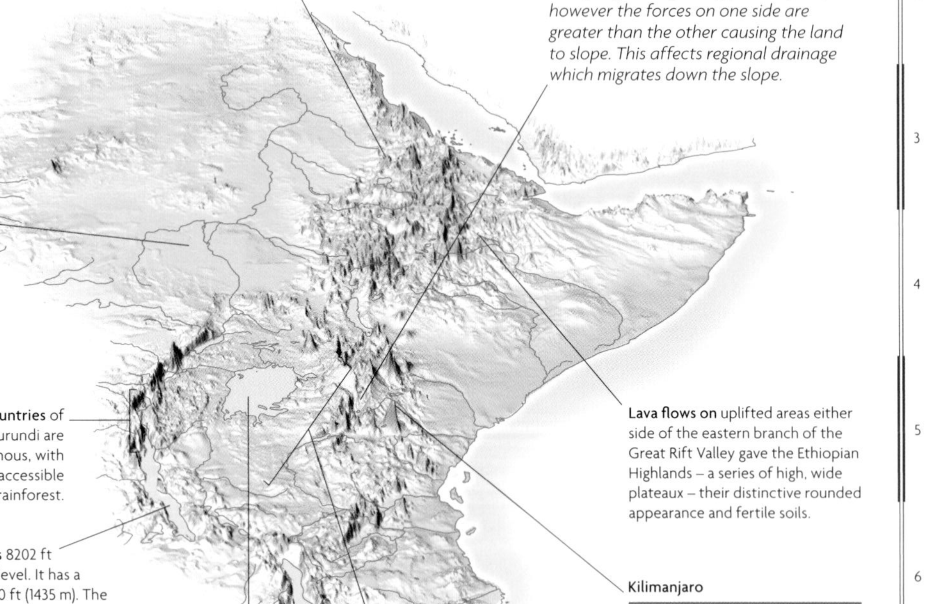

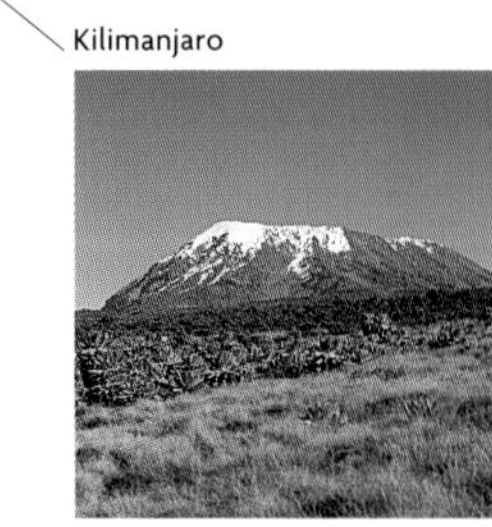

▲ An extinct volcano, Kilimanjaro is Africa's highest mountain, rising 19,340 ft (5895 m). Once famed for its snow-capped peak, this has almost completely melted due to changing climatic conditions.

A vast plateau lies between the eastern and western rift valleys in Kenya, Uganda and western Tanzania. It has been levelled by long periods of erosion to form a peneplain, but is dotted with inselbergs – outcrops of more resistant rocks.

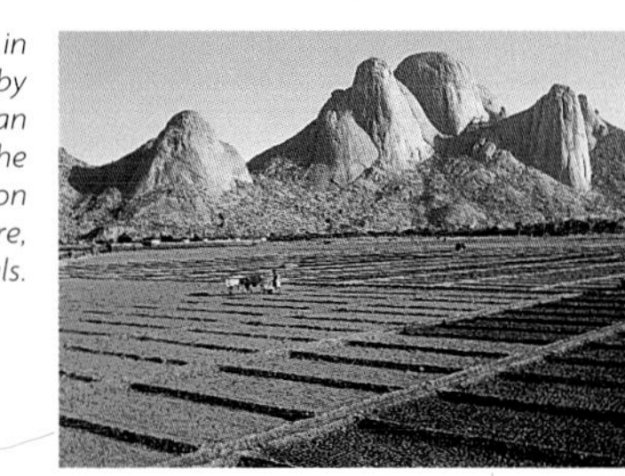

▼ The Kassala region in eastern Sudan is watered by the Atbara river, an important tributary of the Nile. Most of the population is engaged in agriculture, growing cotton and cereals.

Lake Victoria occupies a vast basin between the two arms of the Great Rift Valley. It is the world's second largest lake in terms of surface area, extending 26,560 sq miles (68,880 sq km). The lake contains numerous islands and coral reefs.

The tiny countries of Rwanda and Burundi are mainly mountainous, with large areas of inaccessible tropical rainforest.

Lake Tanganyika lies 8202 ft (2500 m) above sea level. It has a depth of nearly 4700 ft (1435 m). The lake traces the valley floor for some 400 miles (644 km) of the western arm of the Great Rift Valley.

Much of northern Sudan is covered by desert. However, in the tropical wetlands of the southern Sudd region, annual rainfall can sometimes exceed 40 inches (1000 mm).

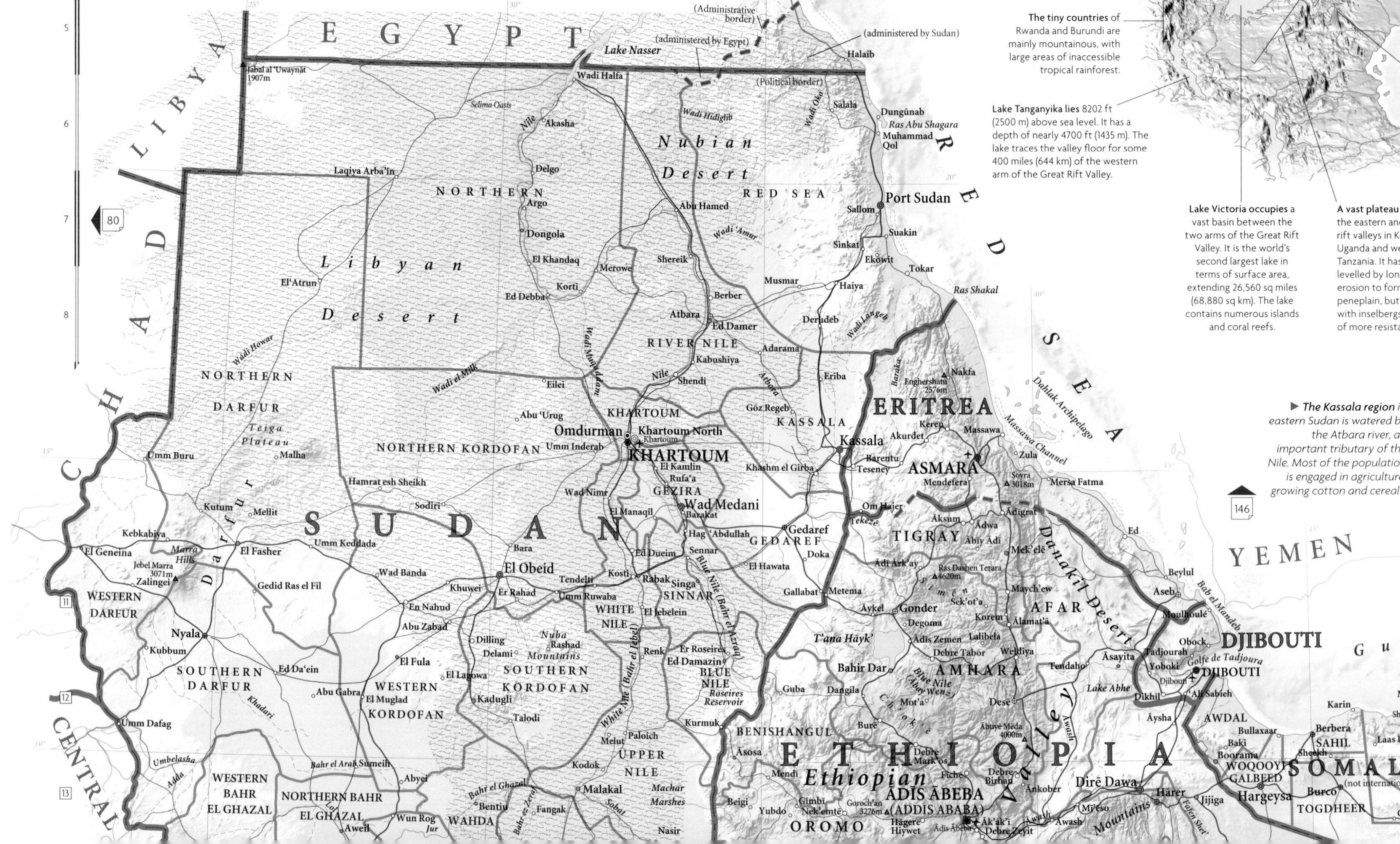

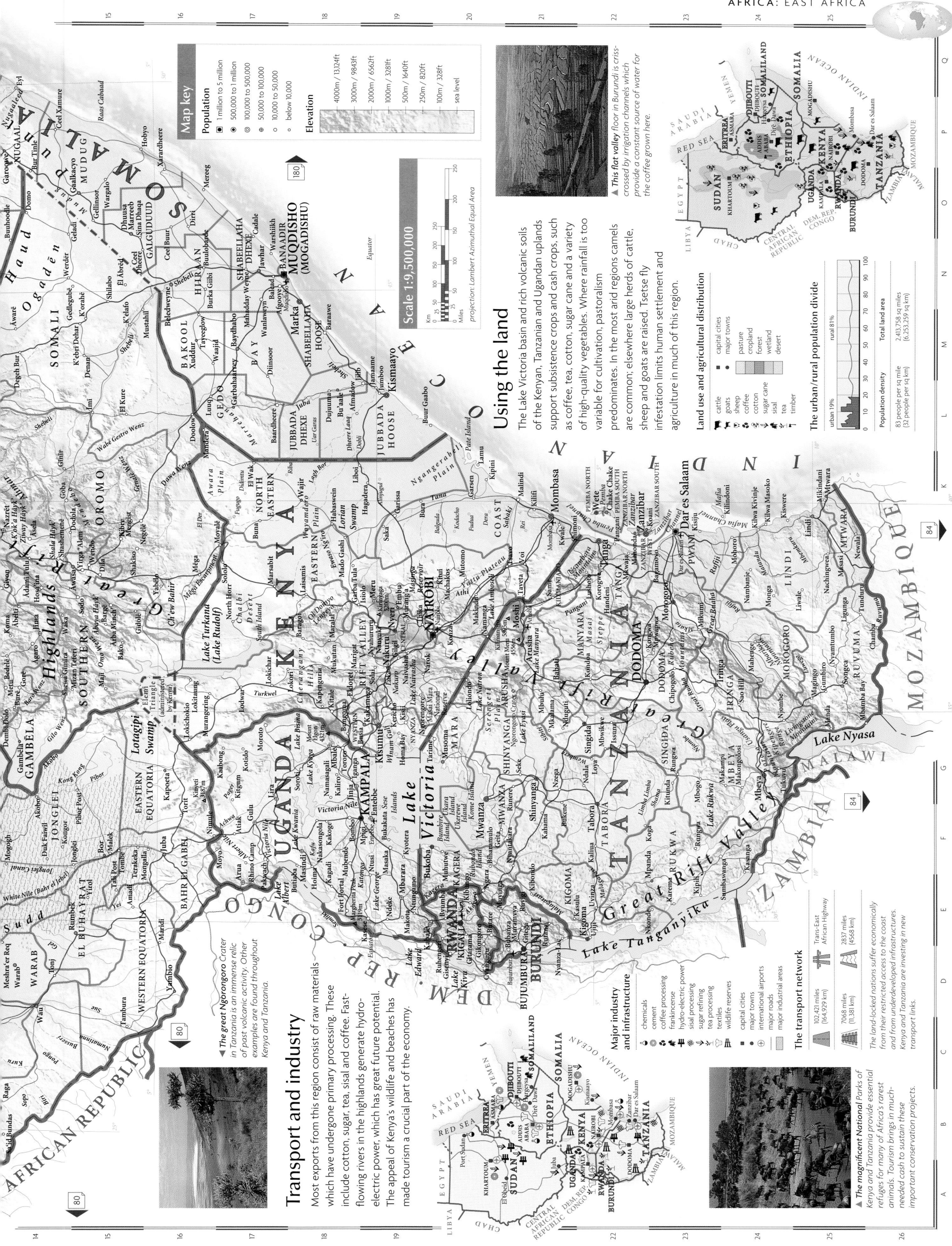

Map key

Population

- ◉ 1 million to 5 million
- ◎ 500,000 to 1 million
- ⊕ 100,000 to 500,000
- ○ 50,000 to 100,000
- ○ 10,000 to 50,000
- ○ below 10,000

Elevation

- 4000m / 13,124ft
- 3000m / 9843ft
- 2000m / 6562ft
- 1000m / 3281ft
- 500m / 1640ft
- 250m / 820ft
- 100m / 328ft
- sea level

Scale 1:9,500,000

projection: Lambert Azimuthal Equal Area

▲ *This flat valley floor in Burundi is criss-crossed by irrigation channels which provide a constant source of water for the coffee grown here.*

Using the land

The Lake Victoria basin and rich volcanic soils of the Kenyan, Tanzanian and Ugandan uplands support subsistence crops and cash crops, such as coffee, tea, cotton, sugar cane and a variety of high-quality vegetables. Where rainfall is too variable for cultivation, pastoralism predominates. In the most arid regions camels are common; elsewhere large herds of cattle, sheep and goats are raised. Tsetse fly infestation limits human settlement and agriculture in much of this region.

Land use and agricultural distribution

- ● capital cities
- • major cities
- pasture
- cropland
- forest
- wetland
- desert
- cattle
- goats
- sheep
- coffee
- cotton
- sugar cane
- sisal
- tea
- timber

The urban/rural population divide

- urban 19%
- rural 81%

Population density
83 people per sq mile
(32 people per sq km)

Total land area
2,413,758 sq miles
(6,253,259 sq km)

Transport and industry

Most exports from this region consist of raw materials which have undergone primary processing. These include cotton, sugar, tea, sisal and coffee. Fast-flowing rivers in the highlands generate hydro-electric power, which has great future potential. The appeal of Kenya's wildlife and beaches has made tourism a crucial part of the economy.

▲ *The great Ngorongoro Crater in Tanzania is an immense relic of past volcanic activity. Other examples are found throughout Kenya and Tanzania.*

Major industry and infrastructure

- chemicals
- cement
- coffee processing
- frankincense
- sisal processing
- hydro-electric power
- sugar refining
- tea processing
- textiles
- wildlife reserves
- ● capital cities
- • major towns
- international airports
- major roads
- major industrial areas

The transport network

- Trans-East African Highway
- 2837 miles (4568 km)
- 102,421 miles (164,929 km)
- 7068 miles (11,381 km)

The land-locked nations suffer economically from their restricted access to the coast and from underdeveloped infrastructures. Kenya and Tanzania are investing in new transport links.

▲ *The magnificent National Parks of Kenya and Tanzania provide essential refuges for many of Africa's rarest animals. Tourism brings in much-needed cash to sustain these important conservation projects.*

Southern Africa

ANGOLA, BOTSWANA, LESOTHO, MALAWI, MOZAMBIQUE,
NAMIBIA, SOUTH AFRICA, SWAZILAND, ZAMBIA, ZIMBABWE

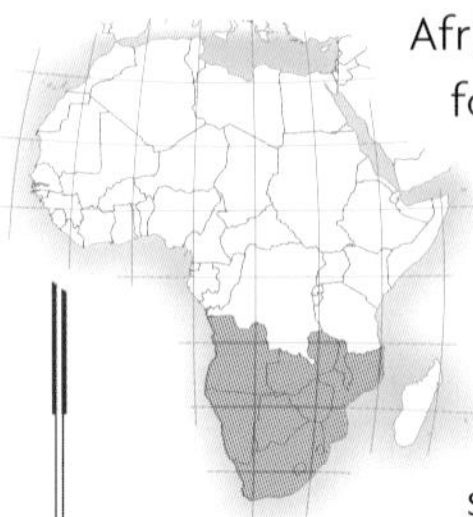

Africa's vast southern plateau has been a contested homeland for disparate peoples for many centuries. The European incursion began with the slave trade and quickened in the 19th century, when the discovery of enormous mineral wealth secured South Africa's regional economic dominance. The struggle against white minority rule led to strife in Namibia, Zimbabwe, and the former Portuguese territories of Angola and Mozambique. South Africa's notorious apartheid laws, which denied basic human rights to more than 75% of the people, led to the state being internationally ostracized until 1994, when the first fully democratic elections inaugurated a new era of racial justice.

The landscape

Most of southern Africa rests on a concave plateau comprising the Kalahari basin and a mountainous fringe, skirted by a coastal plain which widens out in Mozambique. The plateau extends north, towards the Planalto de Bié in Angola, the Congo Basin and the lake-filled troughs of the Great Rift Valley. The eastern region is drained by the Zambezi and Limpopo rivers, and the Orange is the major western river.

Transport and industry

South Africa, the world's largest exporter of gold, has a varied economy which generates about 75% of the region's income and draws migrant labour from neighbouring states. Angola exports petroleum; Botswana and Namibia rely on diamond mining; and Zambia is seeking to diversify its economy to compensate for declining copper reserves.

▼ *Almost all new mining ventures in Zimbabwe are now subject to government control. This mine at Bindura in northeastern Zimbabwe produces nickel, one of the country's top three minerals in terms of economic value.*

Major industry and infrastructure

- ⚙ car manufacture
- ◆ coal
- ⬤ copper
- ◇ diamonds
- ⊙ food processing
- ▲ gold
- ⊕ oil
- ⊤ textiles
- ⚑ uranium
- ▲ wildlife reserves

- ◼ capital cities
- ■ major towns
- ⊕ international airports
- major roads
- major industrial areas

At Victoria Falls
At Victoria Falls, the Zambezi river has cut a spectacular gorge taking advantage of large joints in the basalt, which were first formed as the lava cooled and contracted.

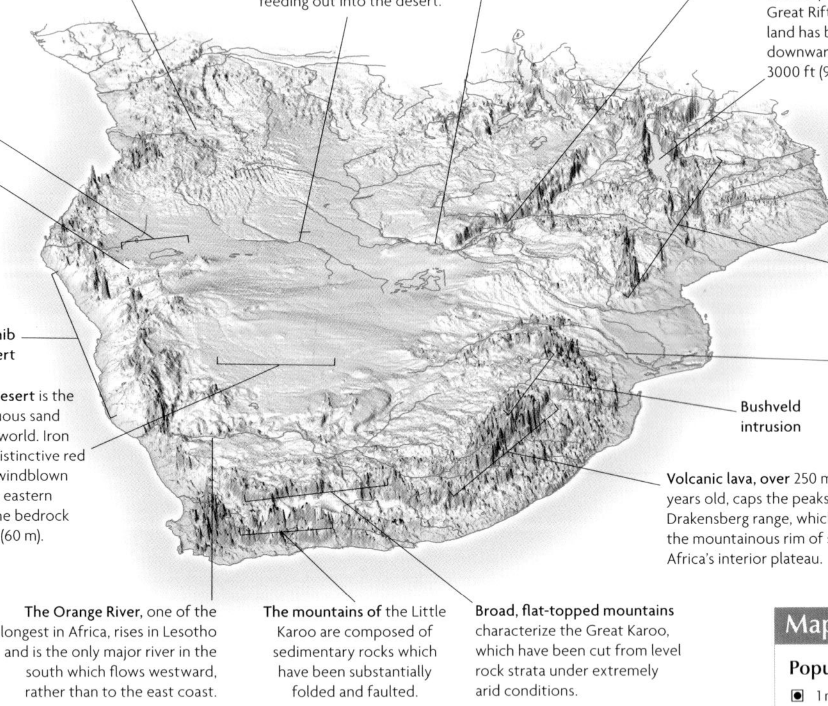

▼ *The fast-flowing Zambezi river cuts a deep, wide channel as it flows along the Zimbabwe/Zambia border.*

Lake Nyasa
Lake Nyasa occupies one of the deep troughs of the Great Rift Valley, where the land has been displaced downwards by as much as 3000 ft (920 m).

Great Rift Valley

Limpopo river

Bushveld intrusion

Volcanic lava
Volcanic lava, over 250 million years old, caps the peaks of the Drakensberg range, which lie on the mountainous rim of southern Africa's interior plateau.

Broad, flat-topped mountains
Broad, flat-topped mountains characterize the Great Karoo, which have been cut from level rock strata under extremely arid conditions.

The Okavango/Cubango river flows from the Planalto de Bié to the swamplands of the Okavango Delta, one of the world's largest inland deltas, where it divides into countless distributary channels, feeding out into the desert.

Planalto de Bié

Thousands of years of evaporating water have produced the Etosha Pan, one of the largest salt flats in the world. Lake and river sediments in the area indicate that the region was once less arid.

Khorixas, Namibia

▲ *Finger Rock, near Khorixas, Namibia is a remnant of a former land surface, which has been denuded by erosion over the last 5 million years. These occasional stacks of partially weathered rocks interrupt the plains of the dry southern interior.*

Namib Desert

The Kalahari Desert is the largest continuous sand surface in the world. Iron oxide gives a distinctive red colour to the windblown sand, which, in eastern areas covers the bedrock by over 200 ft (60 m).

The Orange River, one of the longest in Africa, rises in Lesotho and is the only major river in the south which flows westward, rather than to the east coast.

The mountains of the Little Karoo are composed of sedimentary rocks which have been substantially folded and faulted.

The transport network

✈ 84,213 miles (135,609 km)	🚂 746 miles (1202 km)	
🛣 23,208 miles (37,372 km)	🚂 3815 miles (6144 km)	

Southern Africa's Cape-gauge rail network is by far the largest in the continent. About two-thirds of the 20,000 miles (32,000 km) system lies within South Africa. Lines such as the Harare–Bulawayo route have become corridors for industrial growth.

▲ *Following a series of droughts, this baobab tree in Zimbabwe now stands alone in a field once filled by sugar cane. The thick trunk and small leaves of the baobab help it to conserve water, enabling it to survive even in drought conditions.*

Map key

Population
- ◉ 1 million to 5 million
- ⊙ 500,000 to 1 million
- ⊛ 100,000 to 500,000
- ⊕ 50,000 to 100,000
- ⊕ 10,000 to 50,000
- ○ below 10,000

Elevation
- 3000m / 9843ft
- 2000m / 6562ft
- 1000m / 3281ft
- 500m / 1640ft
- 250m / 820ft
- 100m / 328ft
- sea level

Bushveld intrusion
- Granite
- Chromite
- Gabbro and peridotite
- Magnetite
- Platinum minerals

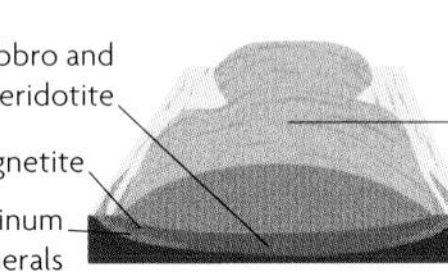

▲ *The Bushveld intrusion lies on South Africa's high 'veld'. Molten magma intruded into the Earth's crust creating a saucer-shaped feature, more than 180 miles (300 km) across, containing regular layers of precious minerals, overlain by a dome of granite.*

South Africa: Capital cities
TSHWANE (PRETORIA) – administrative capital
CAPE TOWN – legislative capital
BLOEMFONTEIN – judicial capital

Scale 1:9,500,000
Km 0 25 50 100 150 200 250 300
Miles 0 25 50 100 150 200
projection: Lambert Azimuthal Equal Area

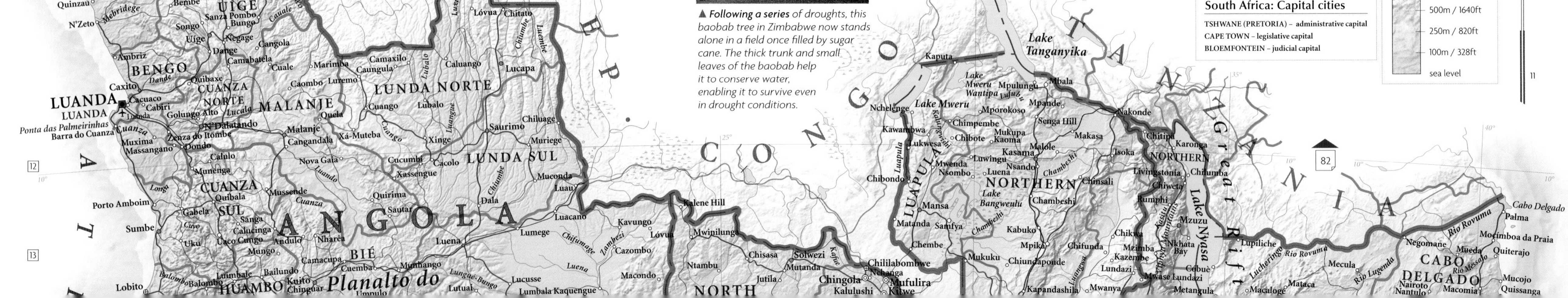

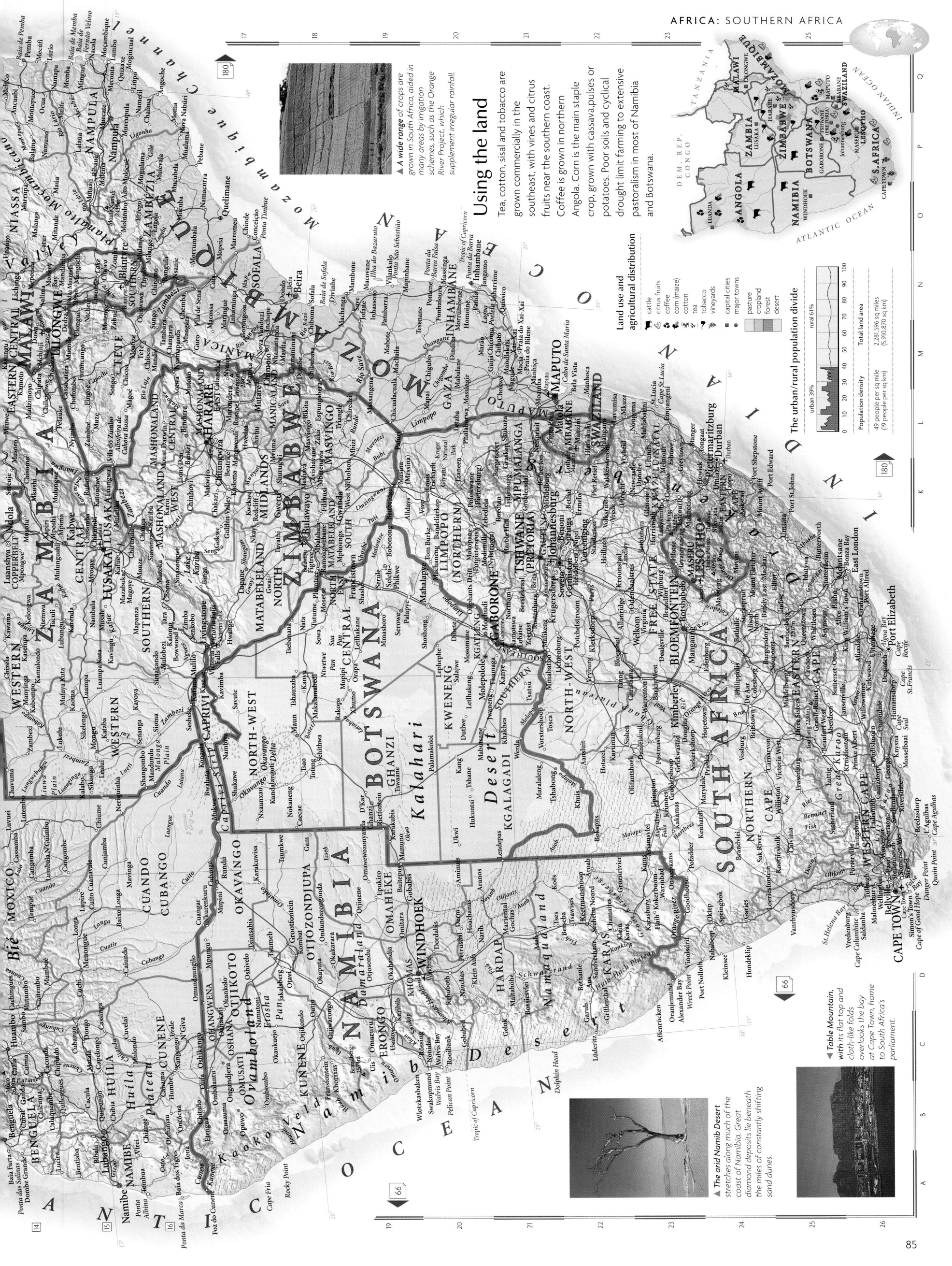

▲ A wide range of crops are grown in South Africa, aided in many areas by irrigation schemes, such as the Orange River Project, which supplement irregular rainfall.

Using the land

Tea, cotton, sisal and tobacco are grown commercially in the southeast, with vines and citrus fruits near the southern coast. Coffee is grown in northern Angola. Corn is the main staple crop, grown with cassava, pulses or potatoes. Poor soils and cyclical drought limit farming to extensive pastoralism in most of Namibia and Botswana.

Land use and agricultural distribution

- cattle
- citrus fruits
- coffee
- corn (maize)
- cotton
- tea
- tobacco
- vineyards
- capital cities
- major towns

pasture | cropland | forest | desert

The urban/rural population divide

urban 39% | rural 61%

Population density
49 people per sq mile
(19 people per sq km)

Total land area
2,281,596 sq miles
(5,910,870 sq km)

▼ Table Mountain, with its flat top and cloth-like folds overlooks the bay at Cape Town, home to South Africa's parliament.

▲ The arid Namib Desert stretches along much of the coast of Namibia. Great diamond deposits lie beneath the miles of constantly shifting sand dunes.

ARCTIC OCEAN
North Pole
Laptev Sea

Ellesmere Island

Greenland

King Frederik
VIII Land

King Christian X Land

Severnaya
Zemlya
Ostrov
Rudol'fa
Franz Josef Land

Kara Sea
Poluostrov Taymyr
Mys
Flissingskiy

Poluostrov Yamal
Baydaratskaya Guba
Gulf of Ob

Yenisey

Greenland
Sea

Spitsbergen
NORTH AMERICAN PLATE
EURASIAN PLATE

Bjørnøya

Barents
Sea

Novaya Zemlya

Kara Strait
Ostrov
Kolguyev
Poluostrov
Kanin

West Siberian Plain

ASIA

Ural Mountains

Jan Mayen Fracture Zone
Jan Mayen
Barents
Trough
North Cape
Nordkinn

Murmansk Rise
Pechora
Timanskiy Kryazh

Denmark Strait

Arctic Circle

Bjargtangar

Iceland
Plateau

Kolbeinsey Ridge
Jan Mayen Ridge

Reykjanes Ridge

Iceland
Basin

Iceland
Vatnajökull

Faeroe-Iceland Ridge

Tromsøflaket
Fugløya Bank

Vesterålen

Lofoten

Norwegian Sea

Vøring Plateau

Norwegian Basin

Kola Peninsula
Inari
Imandra

White Sea

Kvitøya
Kandalaksha
Mezen'
Severnaya Dvina

Onega Bay
Lake
Onega

Inarijärvi
Torneälven
Tuloma

Kemijoki
Oulujoki

Ozero
Vygozero

Lake
Ladoga

Onega
Ozero
Beloye

Mologa
Sukhona
Yug

Vychegda

Vychegda

Galdhøpiggen
2469m

Kølen

Kebnekaise
2117m

Ljusnan

Gulf of Bothnia

Åland

Vänern

Lake
Ladoga

Sukhona
Yug

Sot'

Rybinsk
Reservoir

Kostroma

Kazan'

Hatton Ridge

Rockall
Rise

Feni Ridge

Faeroe Islands

Bill Baileys
Bank

Faeroe-Shetland Trough

Rockall Trough

Shetland
Islands

Orkney Islands

Viking Bank

Norwegian Trench

Jutland
Bank

Åland
Gotland

Gulf of Finland
Lake
Peipus
Lake Pskov

Gulf of
Riga

Lake Ilmen
Lake Ilmen

Msta

Volga

Moskva

Oka

Volga Upland

Volga

Outer Hebrides

Ben Nevis
1343m

Grampian
Mountains

North Channel

Ireland
Irish Sea

Shannon

British
Isles

Snowdon
1085m

Pennines

Trent
Severn

North
Sea

Great
Fisher
Bank

Skagerrak

Kattegat

Jylland

Sjælland

Fyn

Baltic Sea

North European Plain

Western Dvina

Neman

Pripet
Marshes

Desna

Central Russian Upland

Don

Kirghiz Steppe

Celtic Sea
Celtic
Shelf

St. George's
Channel
Bristol Channel

Land's End

The
Fens

Thames

Frisian Islands

Elbe

Oder

Vistula

Warta

Bug

EUROPE

Seym

Dnieper Lowlands

Seym

Tsimlyansk
Reservoir

Caspian

Porcupine
Plain

English Channel

Channel Islands

Strait of Dover

Seine

Marne

Ardennes
Rhine
Meuse

Moselle

Harz

Danube

Lake Constance

Vistula

Carpathian
Mountains

Dniester

Podil's'ka Vysochina
Pivdennyy Buh

Kiev
Reservoir
Kremenchuk
Reservoir

Dnieper

Black Sea Lowland

Sea of
Azov
Crimea

Kuban'

Manych

Yergeni

Azores-Biscay Rise

Charcot Seamounts

Theta Gap

Galicia
Bank

Bay of
Biscay

Biscay
Plain

Loire

Vienne
Cher

Garonne

Massif
Central

Lake Geneva
Mont
Blanc

Lake Garda

Dordogne

Lot

Cévennes

Saône

Po

Bakony
Drava

Lake Balaton

Great
Hungarian
Plain

Dinaric Alps

Sava

Tisza

Danube

Balkan Mountains

Transylvanian Alps

Danube

Black Sea

Iberian
Plain

Miño

Duero

Douro

Cordillera Cantábrica

Aragón

Ebro

Iberian
Peninsula

Sistema Central

Tagus

Sistema Ibérica

Gulf of Lion

Ligurian
Sea

Adriatic Sea

Corno Grande
2912m

Adriatic
Basin

Balkan Mountains

Sea of
Marmara

EURASIAN PLATE
ANATOLIAN PLATE

Black Sea

Cabo
da Roca

Tagus Plain

Gorringe
Ridge

Horseshoe Seamounts

Ampère Seamount

Cape
Saint Vincent

Punta de
Tarifa

Guadiana

Sierra Morena

Guadalquivir

Júcar

Gulf of
Valencia

Segura

Sistemas Béticos

Balearic Islands

Algerian Basin

Sardinia

Corsica

Strait of Bonifacio

Tyrrhenian
Sea

Tyrrhenian
Basin

Mount Etna
3340m

Gulf of
Taranto

Strait of Otranto

Lake
Ohrid

Lake
Prespa

Aegean
Sea

Sea of Crete

Ionian Sea

Mediterranean
Sea

Peloponnese

Mirtoan
Sea

Karpathos
Strait

Anatolia

Taurus Mountains

Gulf of
Antalya

Rhodes

Cyprus

Seine Plain

Seine Seamount

Madeira

Dacia Seamount

Agadir Canyon

Strait of
Gibraltar

Sebou

Alboran Sea

Oued Chelif

EURASIAN PLATE
AFRICAN PLATE

Mediterranean Ridge

Levantine Basin

Gávdos

Mediterranean Sea

Cyprus
Basin

Nile Fan

Dead
Sea

Canary Islands

Rif

Oum er Rbia

Middle Atlas

High Atlas

Atlas Mountains

Tell Atlas

Saharan Atlas

Chott el Jerid

Gulf of
Sirte

Suez Canal
Sinai

Gulf of Suez

'Erg Iguidi

Erg Chech

SAHARA

Grand Erg Occidental

Grand Erg Oriental

AFRICA

Qattara Depression
-133m

Western Desert

Libyan Desert

86

Europe

Europe is the world's second smallest continent, covering 4,053,309 sq miles (10,498,000 sq km). It comprises 45 separate countries, including Turkey and the Russian Federation, although the greater parts of these nations lie in Asia.

● **Greatest extent, North–South:** 2700 miles / 4300 km

■ **Greatest extent, East–West:** 3500 miles / 5600 km

Most northerly point: Ostrov Rudol'fa, Russian Federation 81° 47′ N

Most easterly point: Mys Flissingskiy, Novaya Zemlya, Russian Federation 69° 03′ E

N Ural Mountains, Russian Federation (66° 12′ E)

Most westerly point: Bjargtangar, Iceland 24° 33′ W

Norkinn, Norway (71° 08′ N)

Lowest recorded temperature: Ust 'Shchugor, Russian Federation -67°F (-55°C)

Largest lake: Lake Ladoga, Russian Federation 7100 sq miles (18,390 sq km)

Ural Mountains

Cabo da Roca, Portugal (9° 32′ W)

Cape Saint Vincent

Punta de Tarifa, Spain (36° 01′ N)

Lowest point: Caspian Depression, Russian Federation -92 ft (-28 m) below sea level

Highest recorded temperature: Seville, Spain 122°F (50°C)

Highest point: El'brus, Russian Federation 18,510 ft (5642 m)

Most southerly point: Gávdos, Greece 34° 51′ N

British Isles Massif Central Scandinavia Carpathian Mountains North European Plain Ural Mountains

Iberian Peninsula Pyrenees Alps Baltic Sea

Cape Saint Vincent

Cross-section from Cape Saint Vincent, Portugal to the Ural Mountains, Russian Federation

line of cross-section

0   200   400 Km
0   200   400 Miles

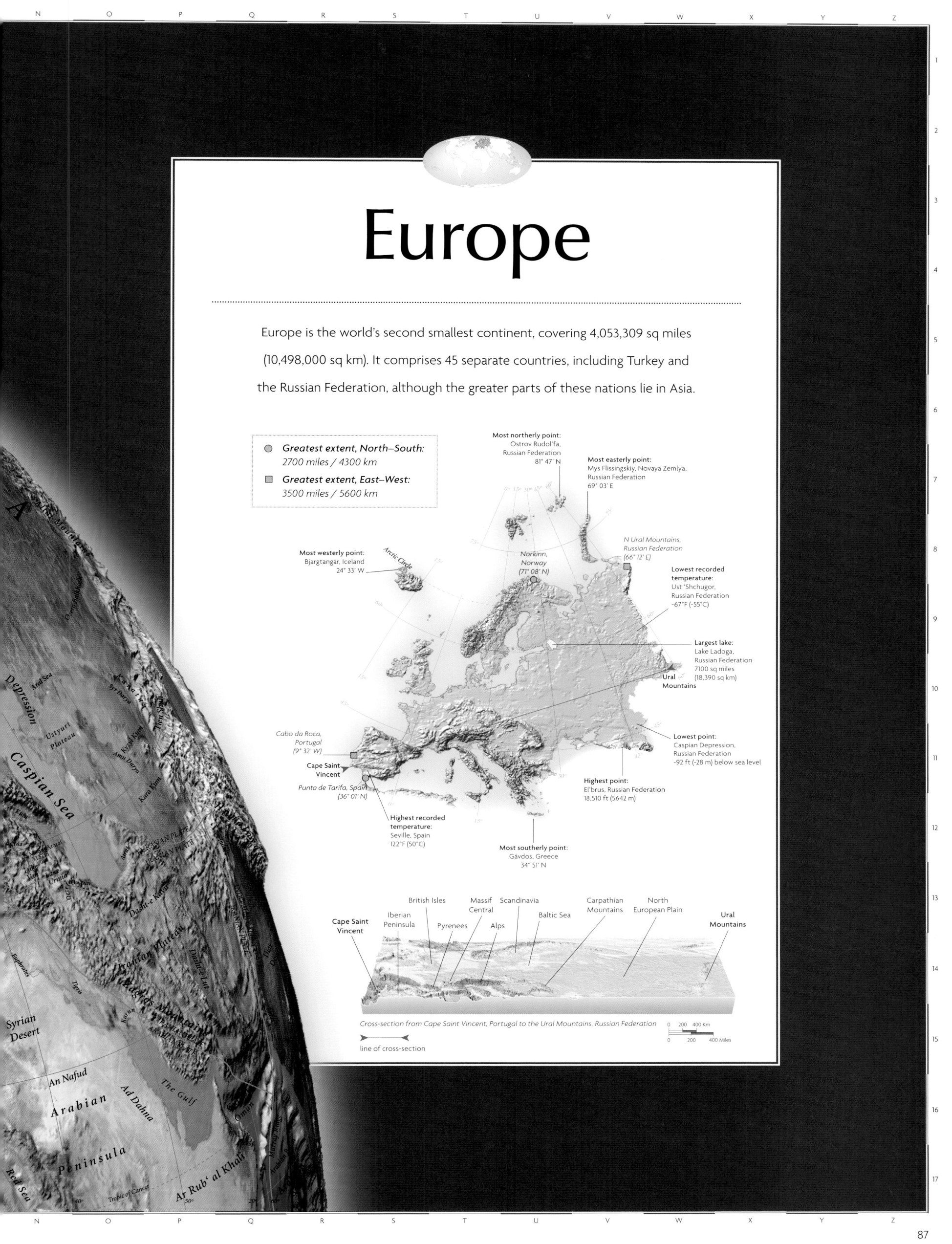

A B C D E F G H I J K L M

Physical Europe

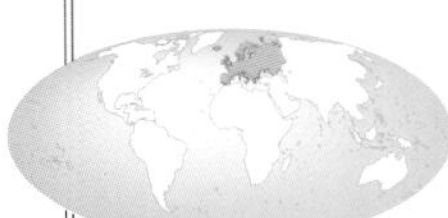

The physical diversity of Europe belies its relatively small size. To the northwest and south it is enclosed by mountains. The older, rounded Atlantic Highlands of Scandinavia and the British Isles lie to the north and the younger, rugged peaks of the Alpine Uplands to the south. In between lies the North European Plain, stretching 2485 miles (4000 km) from The Fens in England to the Ural Mountains in Russia. South of the plain lies a series of gently folded sedimentary rocks separated by ancient plateaux, known as massifs.

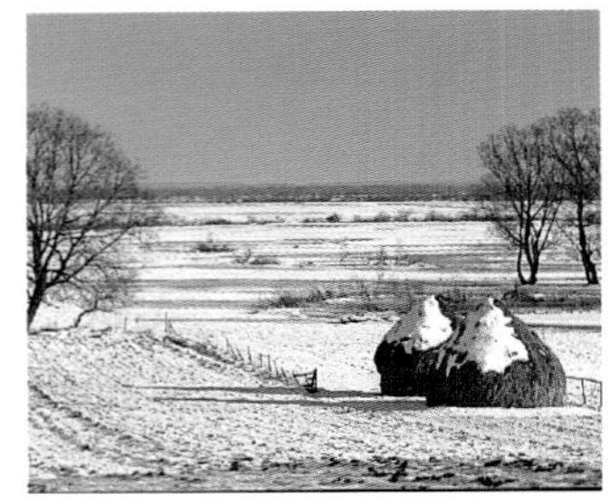

The North European Plain

Rising less than 1000 ft (300 m) above sea level, the North European Plain strongly reflects past glaciation. Ridges of both coarse moraine and finer, windblown deposits have accumulated over much of the region. The ice sheet also diverted a number of river channels from their original courses.

The Atlantic Highlands

The Atlantic Highlands were formed by compression against the Scandinavian Shield during the Caledonian mountain-building period over 500 million years ago. The highlands were once part of a continuous mountain chain, now divided by the North Sea and a submerged rift valley.

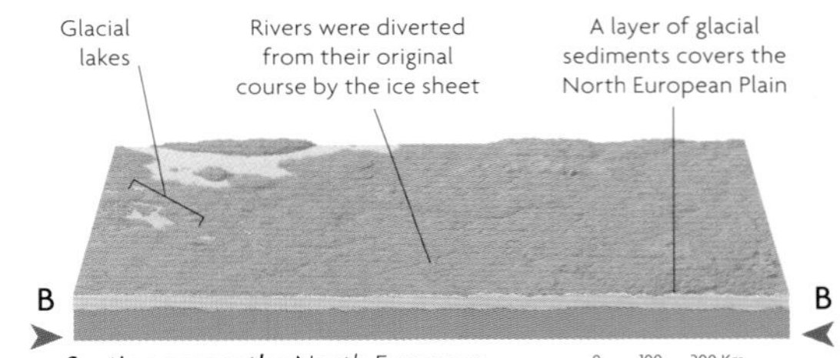

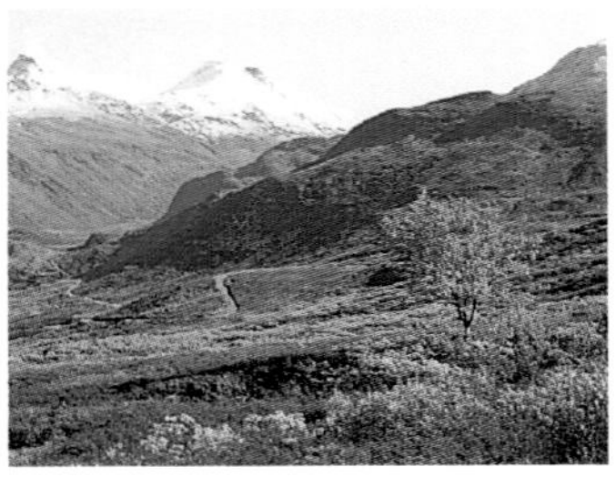

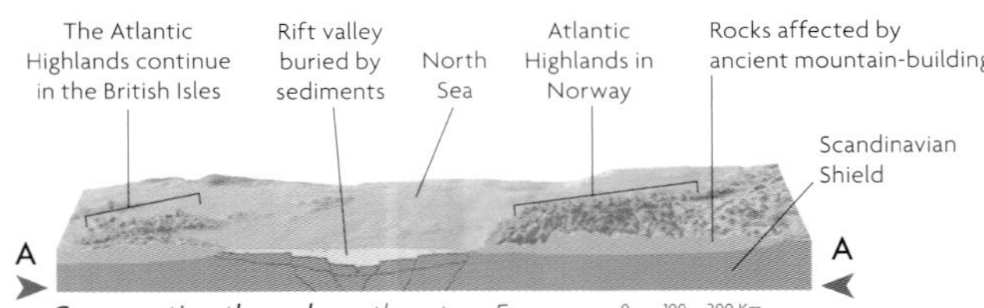

The Atlantic Highlands continue in the British Isles | Rift valley buried by sediments | North Sea | Atlantic Highlands in Norway | Rocks affected by ancient mountain-building | Scandinavian Shield

A — A

Cross-section through *northeastern Europe showing the continuous mountain chain and rift valley system.*

0   100   200 Km
0   100   200 Miles

Glacial lakes | Rivers were diverted from their original course by the ice sheet | A layer of glacial sediments covers the North European Plain

B — B

Section across the *North European Plain showing its low relief and drainage.*

0   100   200 Km
0   100   200 Miles

Scale 1:23,000,000

Km
0 100 200 300 400 500 600

Miles
0   100   200   300   400   600

projection: Lambert Azimuthal Equal Area

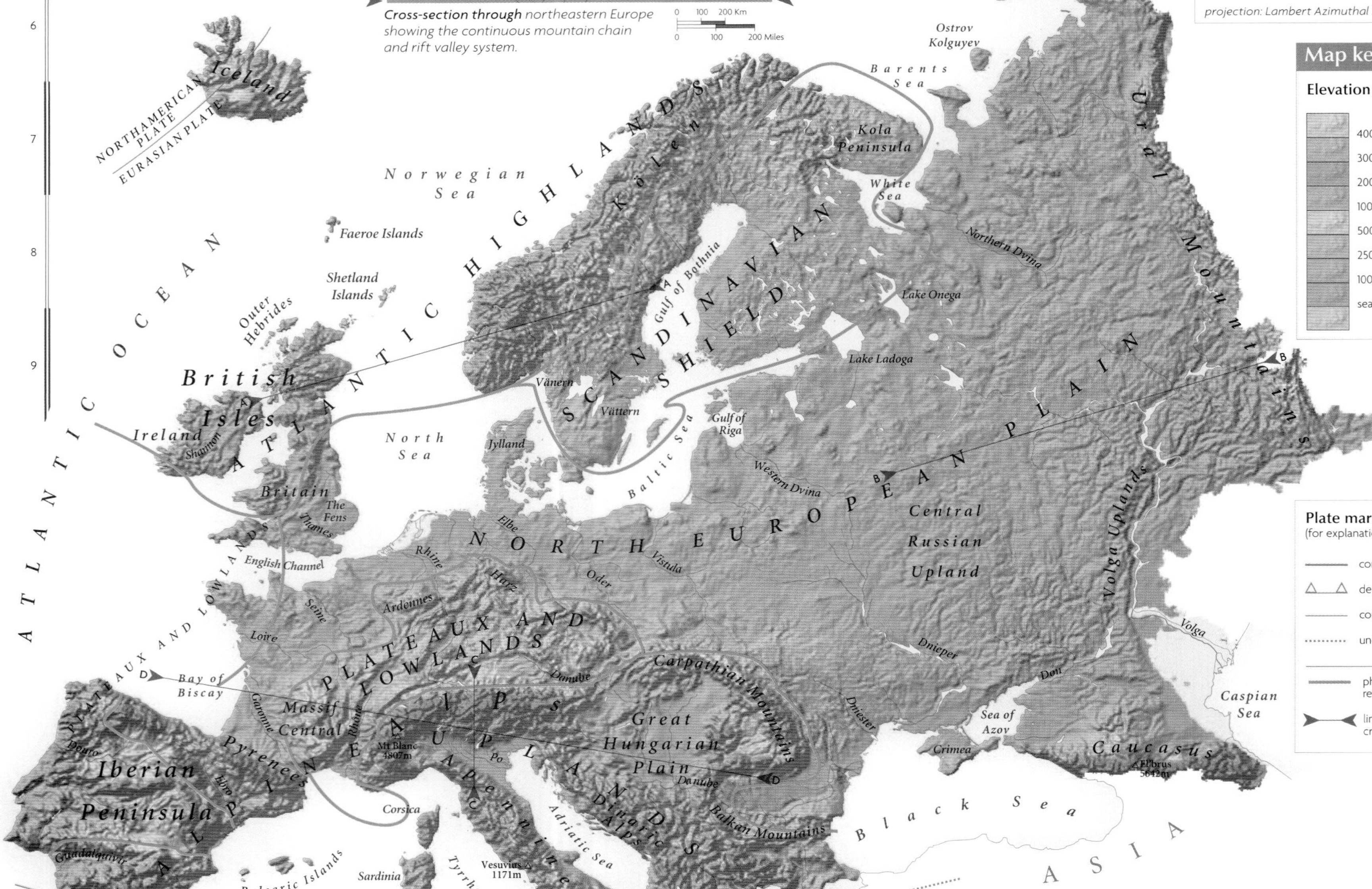

Map key

Elevation

4000m / 13,124ft
3000m / 9843ft
2000m / 6562ft
1000m / 3281ft
500m / 1640ft
250m / 820ft
100m / 328ft
sea level

Plate margins
(for explanation see page xiv)

——— constructive
△   △ destructive
——— conservative
·········· uncertain

——— physiographic regions
▶◀ line of cross-section

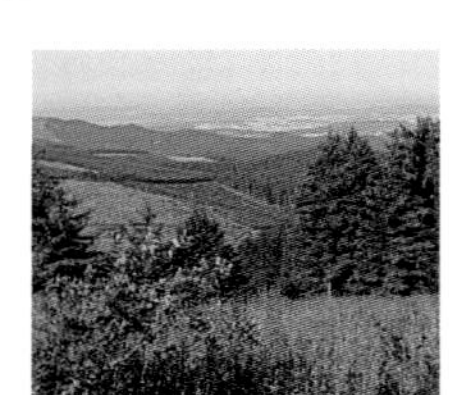

The plateaux and lowlands

The uplifted plateaux or massifs of southern central Europe are the result of long-term erosion, later followed by uplift. They are the source areas of many of the rivers which drain Europe's lowlands. In some of the higher reaches, fractures have enabled igneous rocks from deep in the Earth to reach the surface.

Igneous rocks have intruded into the Massif Central | Older, eroded massifs lie behind the arc of the Alps | Po Valley | Tectonically formed basins | Great Hungarian Plain

D — D

Cross-section through *the plateaux and lowlands showing the lower elevation of the ancient massifs.*

0   100   100 Km
0   100   100 Miles

The Alpine Uplands

The collision of the African and European continents, which began about 65 million years ago, folded and then uplifted a series of mountain ranges running across southern Europe and into Asia. Two major lines of folding can be traced: one includes the Pyrenees, the Alps and the Carpathian Mountains; the other incorporates the Apennines and the Dinaric Alps.

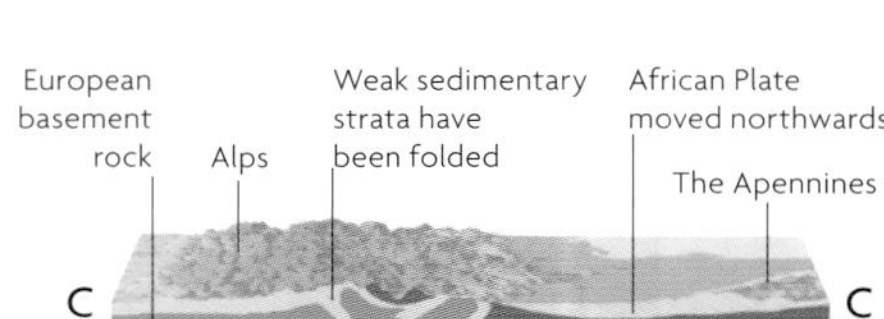

European basement rock | Alps | Weak sedimentary strata have been folded | African Plate moved northwards | The Apennines

C — C

Cross-section through *the Alps showing folding and faulting caused by plate tectonics.*

0   50   100 Km
0   50   100 Miles

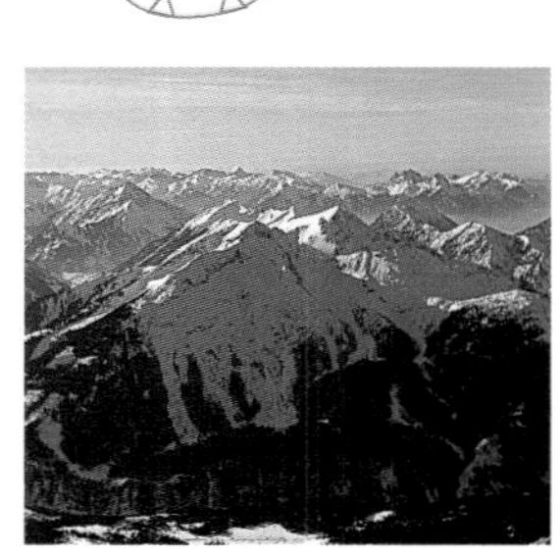

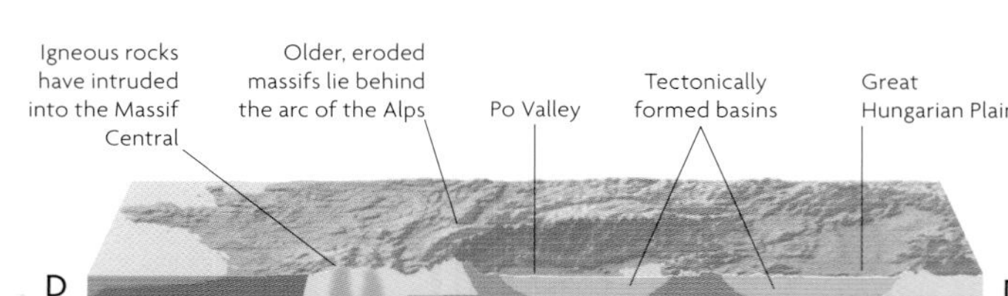

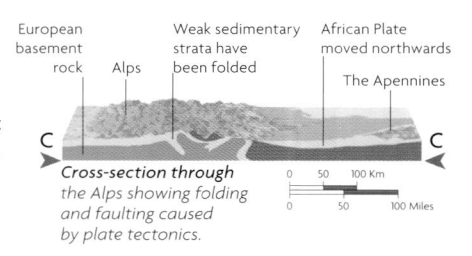

Map labels

NORTH AMERICAN PLATE
EURASIAN PLATE
Iceland
ATLANTIC OCEAN
Norwegian Sea
Faeroe Islands
Shetland Islands
Outer Hebrides
British Isles
Ireland
Britain
The Fens
Thames
English Channel
North Sea
ATLANTIC HIGHLANDS
Kjølen
SCANDINAVIAN SHIELD
Gulf of Bothnia
Baltic Sea
Gulf of Riga
Jylland
Väneren
Vättern
Elbe
Rhine
Maas
Oder
Vistula
Seine
Loire
Ardennes
PLATEAUX AND LOWLANDS
Bay of Biscay
Massif Central
Garonne
Pyrenees
Mt Blanc 4807m
ALPINE UPLANDS
Iberian Peninsula
Tagus
Guadiana
Ebro
Guadalquivir
Balearic Islands
Sardinia
Corsica
Po
Apennines
Adriatic Sea
Tyrrhenian Sea
Vesuvius 1171m
Sicily
Etna 3283m
Malta
Ionian Sea
EURASIAN PLATE
AFRICAN PLATE
Mediterranean Sea
Danube
ALPS
Carpathian Mountains
Great Hungarian Plain
Danube
Dinaric Alps
Balkan Mountains
Peloponnese
Aegean Sea
ANATOLIAN PLATE
AFRICAN PLATE
Crete
Black Sea
Dnieper
Dniester
Dnieper
Don
Sea of Azov
Crimea
Caucasus
Elbrus 5642m
Caspian Sea
Volga
Volga Uplands
Central Russian Upland
Western Dvina
Lake Ladoga
Lake Onega
Northern Dvina
White Sea
Kola Peninsula
Barents Sea
Ostrov Kolguyev
Novaya Zemlya
Kara Sea
Ural Mountains
NORTH EUROPEAN PLAIN
ASIA

Climate

Europe experiences few extremes in either rainfall or temperature, with the exception of the far north and south. Along the west coast, the warm currents of the North Atlantic Drift moderate temperatures. Although east–west air movement is relatively unimpeded by relief, the Alpine Uplands halt the progress of north–south air masses, protecting most of the Mediterranean from cold, north winds.

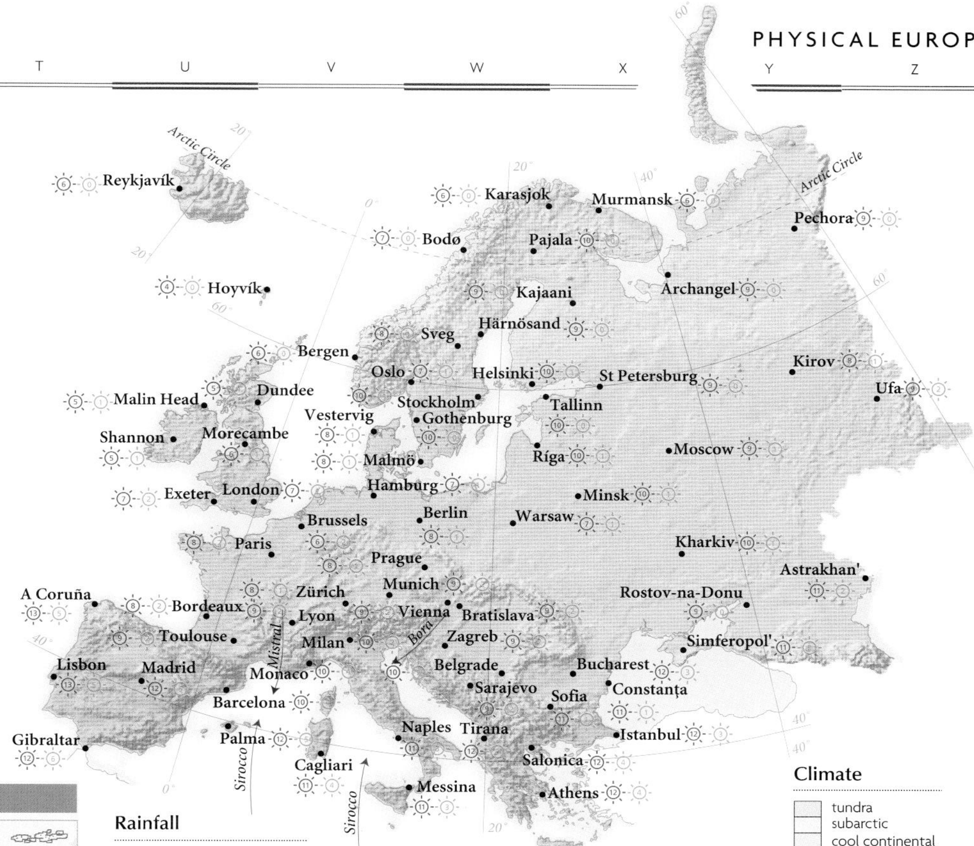

▲ *Frost grips northern and eastern Europe during the long cold winters. Lakes and rivers frequently freeze.*

Temperature

Temperature

- below -30°C (-22°F)
- -30 to -20°C (-22 to -4°F)
- -20 to -10°C (-4 to 14°F)
- -10 to 0°C (14 to 32°F)
- 0 to 10°C (32 to 50°F)
- 10 to 20°C (50 to 60°F)
- 20 to 30°C (68 to 86°F)
- above 30°C (86°F)

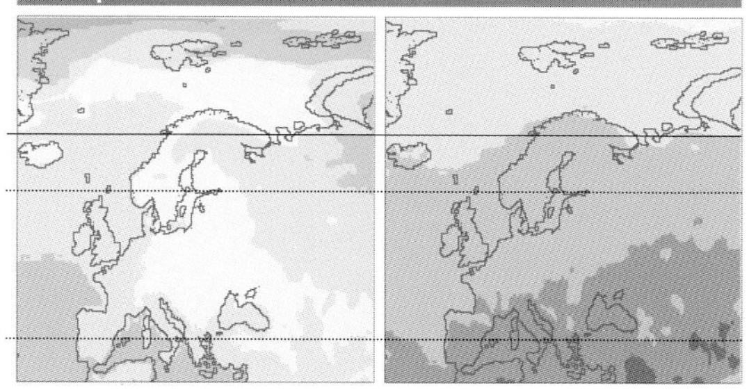

Average January temperature

Average July temperature

▲ *Mild temperatures and frequent rainfall contribute to the fertile farming land found over much of northwestern Europe.*

Rainfall

Rainfall

- 0–25 mm (0–1 in)
- 25–50 mm (1–2 in)
- 50–100 mm (2–4 in)
- 100–200 mm (4–8 in)
- 200–300 mm (8–12 in)
- 300–400 mm (12–16 in)
- 400–500 mm (16–20 in)
- more than 500 mm (20 in)

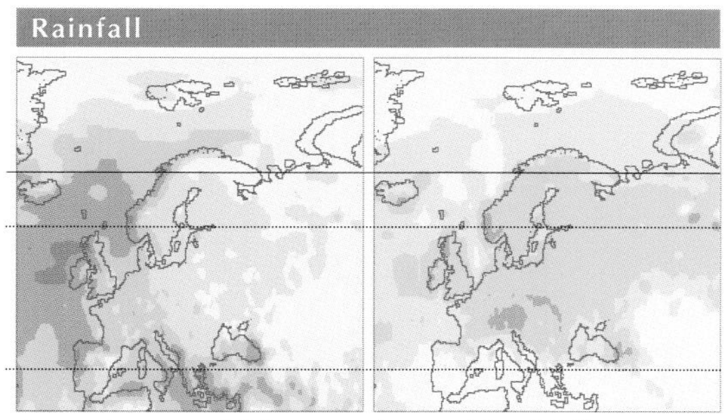

Average January rainfall

Average July rainfall

▶ *Dusty Sirocco winds from Africa help create the semi-arid scrubland common across the Mediterranean coastlands of southern Europe.*

Climate

- tundra
- subarctic
- cool continental
- warm humid
- mediterranean
- semi-arid

☼ daily hours of sunshine, January

☼ daily hours of sunshine, July

→ cold wind

→ hot wind

Shaping the continent

Successive Ice Ages have left many relict landforms across Europe. Present glaciers continue to carve peaks and valleys in the northern Atlantic Highlands and Alpine Uplands. Tectonic activity, both past and present, has shaped southern Europe and Iceland. Active volcanoes and earthquakes still occur in Italy and Greece. Europe's extensive coastline, particularly in the northwest, is constantly modified by wave action and fluvial deposits.

Glaciation

1 Valley glaciers, such as this one *(left)* in Iceland, form in hollows at the top of valleys and flow downwards, drawn by gravity. Their growth is dynamic; new snowfall constantly accumulates at the head of the glacier, while the snout melts, depositing material eroded and carried by the glacier.

Snow accumulates at the head of glacier

Glacier movement erodes valley

Glacier snout melts depositing eroded debris

Glaciation: Development of a glacier

Landscape

- uplifting land
- stable land
- sinking land
- limestone region
- glacier

▲ active volcano

→ ocean current

⋯ area of tectonic activity

— maximum limit of glaciation

River systems

2 Rivers are continuously transporting eroded material towards the sea. Slow-moving, low-gradient rivers, like this one in western Russia *(above)*, deposit their alluvium load, infilling valleys creating a flood plain. Subsequent climatic and tectonic fluctuations may erode the flood plain to form terraces.

Terrace created by erosion

Flood plain

Deposited alluvium

River channel

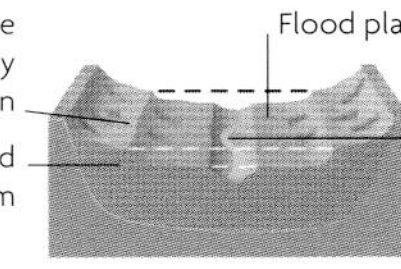

River systems: Formation of a flood plain and terraces

Coastal processes

5 Spits are narrow bands of sand or shingle, formed by longshore drift; a process whereby waves carry material along the beach. They usually form where the coastline changes direction, and their growth is then halted by an opposing river current, as at Spurn Head, in the British Isles *(left)*. Coastal features such as these are constantly being created and destroyed.

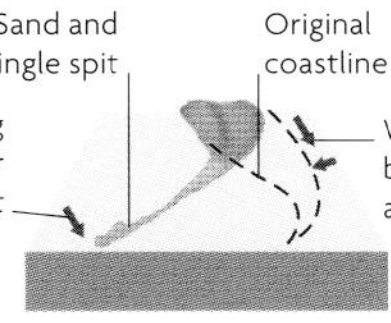

Sand and shingle spit

Original coastline

Opposing river current

Waves breaking at an angle

Coastal processes: Formation of a spit

The evolving landscape

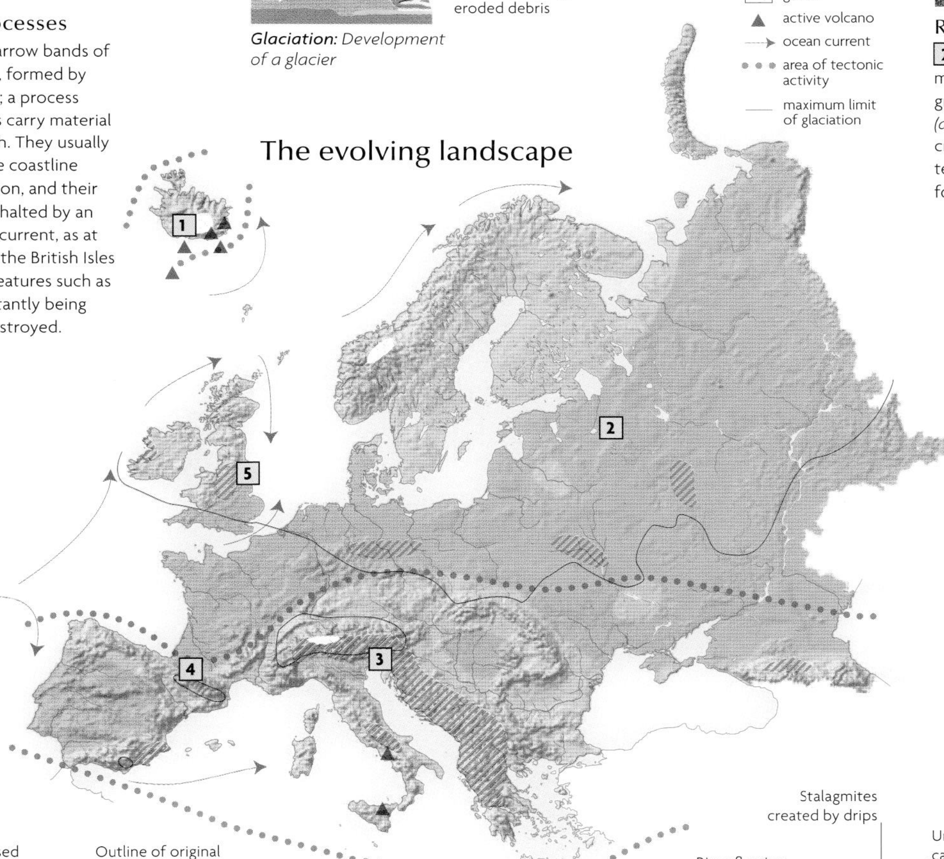

Erosion and weathering

4 Much of Europe was once subjected to folding and faulting, exposing hard and soft rock layers. Subsequent erosion and weathering has worn away the softer strata, leaving up-ended layers of hard rock as in the French Pyrenees *(above)*.

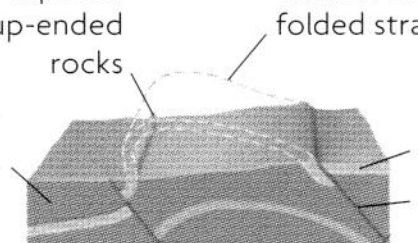

Exposed up-ended rocks

Outline of original folded strata

Soft rock

Hard rock

Fault line

Folded rock strata

Erosion and weathering: Modification of a fold

Stalagmites created by drips

Underground cavern

River flowing underground dissolves rocks and creates caves

Stalactites formed by seeping water

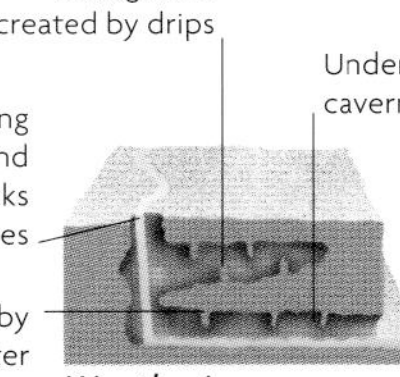

Weathering: Formation of a cave

Weathering

3 As surface water filters through permeable limestone, the rock dissolves to form underground caves, like Postojna in the Karst region of Slovenia *(above)*. Stalactites grow downwards as lime-enriched water seeps from roof fractures; stalagmites grow upwards where drips splash down.

Political Europe

The political boundaries of Europe have changed many times, especially during the 20th century in the aftermath of two world wars, the break-up of the empires of Austria-Hungary, Nazi Germany and, towards the end of the century, the collapse of communism in eastern Europe. The fragmentation of Yugoslavia has again altered the political map of Europe, highlighting a trend towards nationalism and devolution. In contrast, economic federalism is growing. In 1958, the formation of the European Economic Community (now the European Union or EU) started a move towards economic and political union and increasing internal migration.

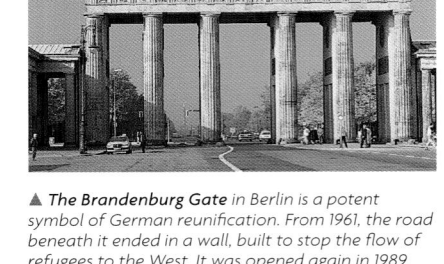

▲ *The Brandenburg Gate* in Berlin is a potent symbol of German reunification. From 1961, the road beneath it ended in a wall, built to stop the flow of refugees to the West. It was opened again in 1989 when the wall was destroyed and East and West Germany were reunited.

Population

Europe is a densely populated, urbanized continent; in Belgium over 90% of people live in urban areas. The highest population densities are found in an area stretching east from southern Britain and northern France, into Germany. The northern fringes are only sparsely populated.

▲ *Demand for space* in densely populated European cities like London has led to the development of high-rise offices and urban sprawl.

Population density
(people per sq km)

- below 49
- 50–99
- 100–149
- 150–199
- 200–299
- above 300

▲ *Traditional lifestyles still* persist in many remote and rural parts of Europe, especially in the south, east, and in the far north.

Map key

Population

- ▣ above 5 million
- ▪ 1 million to 5 million
- ◉ 500,000 to 1 million
- ◉ 100,000 to 500,000
- ⊕ 50,000 to 100,000
- ○ 10,000 to 50,000
- ● Country capital

Borders

⬠ full international border

Scale 1:15,500,000

Km
0 100 200 300 400 500 600 700

Miles
0 100 200 300 400 500 600 700

projection: Lambert Azimuthal Equal Area

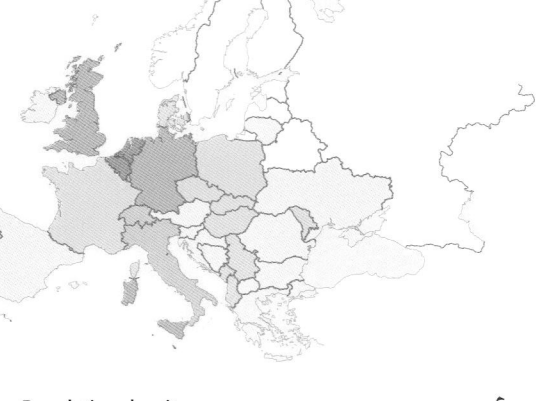

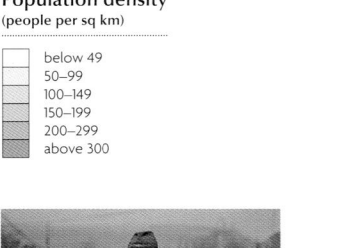

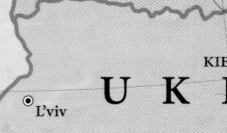

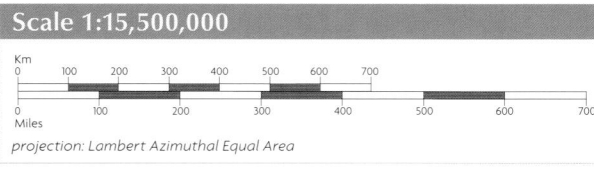

Denmark Strait

ICELAND
REYKJAVÍK

Arctic Circle

Norwegian Sea

Faeroe Islands
(to Denmark)

ATLANTIC OCEAN

Shetland Islands

Outer Hebrides
Orkney Islands

NORWAY
Trondheim
Bergen
OSLO
Stavanger
Kristiansand

SWEDEN
Uppsala
Örebro
STOCKHOLM
Vänern
Gothenburg
Jönköping
Vättern

Gulf of Bothnia

FINLAND
Tampere
Åland
Turku
HELSINKI
Lake Ladoga

Murmansk
St Petersburg

Baltic Sea
Gotland
Ventspils

ESTONIA
TALLINN

LATVIA
RĪGA
Liepāja
Western Dvina

LITHUANIA
Kaunas
VILNIUS
Vitsyebsk

MINSK

BELARUS
Babruysk
Homyel'
Brest

SCOTLAND
Aberdeen
Glasgow Dundee
Edinburgh
NORTHERN IRELAND
Belfast

North Sea

DENMARK
Helsingborg
COPENHAGEN Malmö
Odense
Ålborg

Helsinki

IRELAND
DUBLIN
Isle of Man (to UK)
UNITED KINGDOM
Liverpool
Manchester Sheffield
Leeds
WALES
Birmingham
ENGLAND
Cardiff
LONDON
Southampton
Newcastle upon Tyne
Thames

Groningen
AMSTERDAM NETH.
THE HAGUE
Rotterdam
Antwerp
BELGIUM
BRUSSELS
Liège
Bonn
le Havre
Seine

Hamburg
Bremen
Hannover
Elbe
BERLIN
GERMANY
Düsseldorf
Leipzig
Dresden
Frankfurt am Main
Rhine
Nuremberg
Stuttgart
Munich

Oder
Gdańsk
Bydgoszcz
Poznań
Łódź
WARSAW
POLAND
Wrocław
Kraków

Vistula

KIEV
UKR
L'viv
Chernivtsi

Dniester
MOLDOVA
CHIŞINĂU

Channel Islands (to UK)
English Channel

FRANCE
Rennes
PARIS
Orléans
St-Nazaire
Nantes
Loire
Limoges
Bordeaux
Lyon
Geneva

LUXEMBOURG
LUXEMBOURG

Strasbourg

PRAGUE
CZECH REPUBLIC

Salzburg
SLOVAKIA
BRATISLAVA
VIENNA
Győr
AUSTRIA
LIECHTENSTEIN
Innsbruck
HUNGARY
BUDAPEST

Miskolc

Cluj-Napoca

ROMANIA
Braşov

Bay of Biscay

A Coruña
Porto
Duero
Valladolid
Ebro
Zaragoza

PORTUGAL
LISBON
Tagus
Setúbal
MADRID
SPAIN
Seville
Córdoba
Cádiz
Málaga
Gibraltar (to UK)
Ceuta (to Spain)
Melilla (to Spain)

Pyrenees
ANDORRA
ANDORRA LA VELLA
Toulouse
Marseille
Nice

Zürich
BERN
SWITZERLAND
ALPS
Milan
Turin
Verona
Po
Genoa
Bologna
LJUBLJANA
SLOVENIA
Venice Trieste
ZAGREB
CROATIA
Florence
Pisa
SAN MARINO
ITALY
Corsica

MONACO

Valencia
Barcelona
Murcia
Ibiza
Palma
Mallorca
Menorca
Balearic Islands

Sardinia

VATICAN CITY
ROME
Naples
Bari
Cagliari

BOS. & HERZ.
SARAJEVO
Mostar
MONTENEGRO
PODGORICA
SERBIA
BELGRADE
Danube
BUCHAREST
Constanţa
Ruse
Varna
BULGARIA
SOFIA
Stara Zagora
Burgas
SKOPJE
MACEDONIA
TIRANA
ALBANIA
Salonica

TUR

Adriatic Sea
Tyrrhenian Sea
Palermo
Sicily
Catania
Messina
Cosenza

Ionian Sea

MALTA
VALLETTA

Mediterranean Sea

GREECE
Lárisa
Aegean Sea
Piraeus ATHENS
Irákleio
Crete

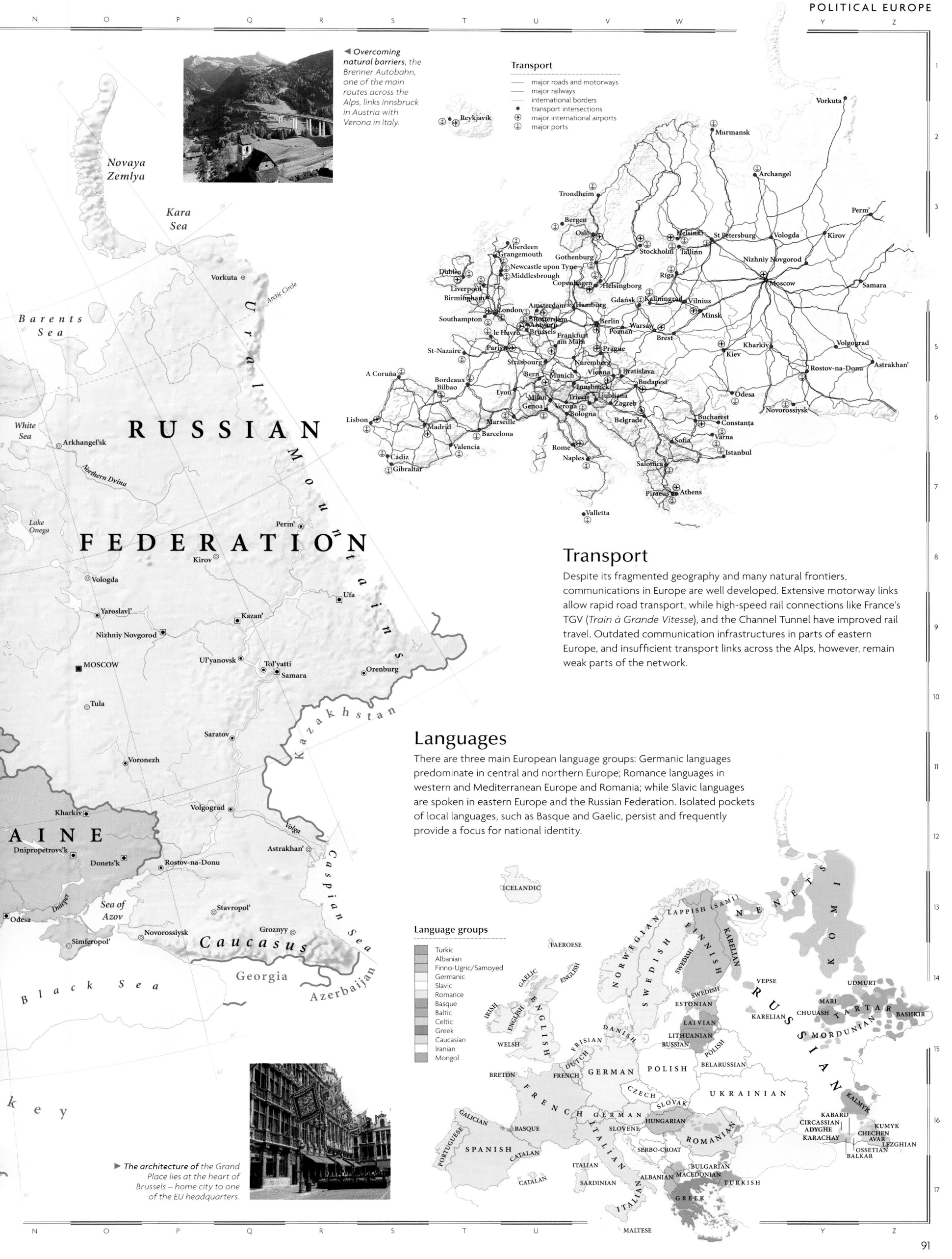

◀ *Overcoming natural barriers,* the Brenner Autobahn, one of the main routes across the Alps, links Innsbruck in Austria with Verona in Italy.

Transport

- major roads and motorways
- major railways
- international borders
- • transport intersections
- ⊕ major international airports
- ⊕ major ports

Transport

Despite its fragmented geography and many natural frontiers, communications in Europe are well developed. Extensive motorway links allow rapid road transport, while high-speed rail connections like France's TGV (*Train à Grande Vitesse*), and the Channel Tunnel have improved rail travel. Outdated communication infrastructures in parts of eastern Europe, and insufficient transport links across the Alps, however, remain weak parts of the network.

Languages

There are three main European language groups: Germanic languages predominate in central and northern Europe; Romance languages in western and Mediterranean Europe and Romania; while Slavic languages are spoken in eastern Europe and the Russian Federation. Isolated pockets of local languages, such as Basque and Gaelic, persist and frequently provide a focus for national identity.

Language groups

- Turkic
- Albanian
- Finno-Ugric/Samoyed
- Germanic
- Slavic
- Romance
- Basque
- Baltic
- Celtic
- Greek
- Caucasian
- Iranian
- Mongol

▶ *The architecture of* the Grand Place lies at the heart of Brussels – home city to one of the EU headquarters.

European resources

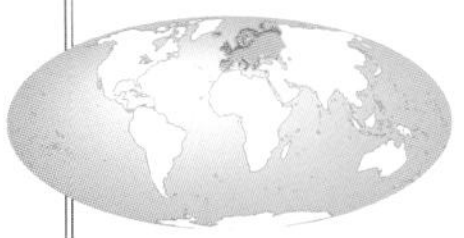

Europe's large tracts of fertile, accessible land, combined with its generally temperate climate, have allowed a greater percentage of land to be used for agricultural purposes than in any other continent. Extensive coal and iron ore deposits were used to create steel and manufacturing industries during the 19th and 20th centuries. Today, although natural resources have been widely exploited, and heavy industry is of declining importance, the growth of hi-tech and service industries has enabled Europe to maintain its wealth.

Industry

Europe's wealth was generated by the rise of industry and colonial exploitation during the 19th century. The mining of abundant natural resources made Europe the industrial centre of the world. Adaptation has been essential in the changing world economy, and a move to service-based industries has been widespread except in eastern Europe, where heavy industry still dominates.

▲ *Countries like Hungary* are still struggling to modernize inefficient factories left over from extensive, centrally-planned industrialization during the communist era.

◀ *Frankfurt am Main* is an example of a modern service-based city. The skyline is dominated by headquarters from the worlds of banking and commerce.

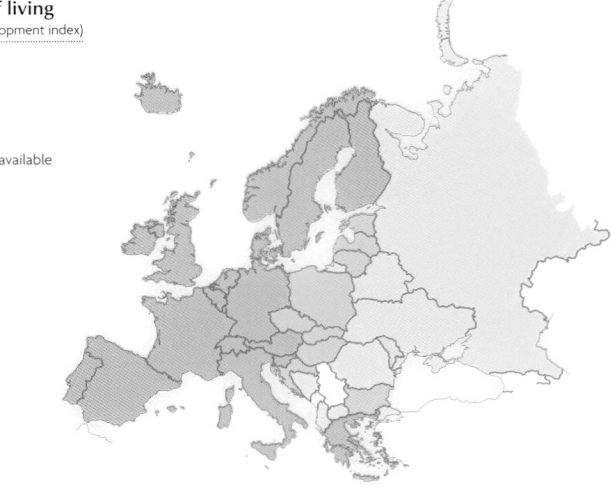

▲ *Other power sources* are becoming more attractive as fossil fuels run out; 16% of Europe's electricity is now provided by hydro-electric power.

Standard of living

Living standards in western Europe are among the highest in the world, although there is a growing sector of homeless, jobless people. Eastern Europeans have lower overall standards of living – a legacy of stagnated economies.

Standard of living
(UN human development index)

	low
	high
	data not available

▶ *Skiing brings millions* of tourists to the slopes each year, which means that even unproductive, marginal land is used to create wealth in the French, Swiss, Italian and Austrian Alps.

GNI per capita (US $)

	below 1999
	2000–4999
	5000–9999
	10,000–19,999
	20,000–24,999
	above 25,000

Industry

✈ aerospace	▣ food processing	⚥ wine
⚗ brewing	▭ hi-tech industry	⚒ coal
⛟ car/vehicle manufacture	⚙ iron & steel	▲ oil
⚗ chemicals	⚚ pharmaceuticals	▲ gas
⚔ defence	⚐ printing & publishing	
⚡ electronics	⚓ shipbuilding	• industrial cities
⚙ engineering	⬗ textiles	▨ major industrial areas
▤ finance	⚘ timber processing	

Map labels:

ICELAND — Reykjavík

Novaya Zemlya

Ostrov Kolguyev

Barents Sea

Murmansk · Archangel

NORWAY — Trondheim, Bergen, Oslo
SWEDEN — Stockholm, Gothenburg
FINLAND — Turku, Helsinki
Norwegian Sea
Gulf of Bothnia
Faeroe Islands (to Denmark)

RUSSIAN FEDERATION — Perm', Cherepovets, Yaroslavl', Ivanovo, Nizhniy Novgorod, Kazan', Ufa, Moscow, Tol'yatti, Samara, Ryazan', Tula, Saratov, Voronezh, Kursk, Volgograd, Rostov-na-Donu, St Petersburg

IRELAND — Dublin
UNITED KINGDOM — Glasgow, Belfast, Newcastle upon Tyne, Isle of Man (to UK), Manchester, Liverpool, Cardiff, Birmingham, London
North Sea
DENMARK — Copenhagen
ESTONIA — Tallinn
LATVIA — Riga
LITHUANIA — Vilnius
RUSS. FED. (Kaliningrad)
Baltic Sea
Malmö, Hamburg, Gdańsk

POLAND — Poznań, Łódź, Warsaw
BELARUS — Minsk
UKRAINE — Kiev, Kharkiv, Dnipropetrovs'k, Donets'k, Kryvyy Rih
MOLDOVA
Channel Islands (to UK)
NETH. — Amsterdam, Rotterdam, Antwerp
BELG. — Brussels, Liège
Rouen, Lille, Ghent, Essen, Cologne, Berlin, Leipzig, Dresden
GERMANY — Frankfurt am Main, Prague, Katowice, Kraków
CZECH REP.
LUX.
Metz, Strasbourg, Stuttgart, Munich, Nuremberg
Paris, Nantes
FRANCE
SLOVAKIA — Bratislava
Zürich, LIECH., Vienna, Linz
SWITZ. — AUSTRIA
SLVN. — Zagreb
HUNGARY — Budapest
Bordeaux, Lyon, Turin, Milan, Genoa, Venice, Bologna
Bay of Biscay
A Coruña, Porto, Bilbao, Toulouse, Marseille
PORTUGAL — Lisbon
SPAIN — Madrid, Barcelona, Seville
ANDORRA
Corsica
MONACO
ITALY — Rome, Naples, Taranto, Palermo
VATICAN CITY
SAN MARINO
CROATIA
BOSNIA & HERZ.
MONT.
SERBIA — Belgrade
ROMANIA — Ploesti, Bucharest, Constanța
BULGARIA — Sofia, Varna
MACED.
ALBANIA
GREECE — Salonica, Athens, Piraeus
TURKEY — Istanbul
Gibraltar (to UK), Ceuta (to Spain), Melilla (to Spain)
MOROCCO
Sardinia, Sicily, MALTA, Crete
Balearic Islands
Tyrrhenian Sea, Ionian Sea, Aegean Sea, Adriatic Sea
Mediterranean Sea
Black Sea, Odesa
Caspian Sea
GEORGIA, AZERBAIJAN
KAZAKHSTAN
Atlantic Ocean

Mineral resources

Fossil fuels are Europe's main mineral resource, although fuel demand far outstrips production. Sizeable coal reserves remain in the Donbass in Ukraine, Germany's Ruhr Valley and Poland. Oil and gas reserves are found mainly in the North Sea, the Volga Basin, and the Caucasus.

▶ **The valuable oil** and gas reserves in the North Sea were first discovered in the early 1960s, and are exploited by the UK, Denmark, Germany and Norway.

Mineral resources
- oil field
- gas field
- coal field
- bauxite
- iron
- lead
- mercury
- potassium
- uranium
- zinc

Environmental issues
- national parks
- acid rain
- polluted rivers
- radioactive contamination
- marine pollution
- heavy marine pollution
- poor urban air quality

Environmental issues

The partially enclosed waters of the Baltic and Mediterranean seas have become heavily polluted, while the Barents Sea is contaminated with spent nuclear fuel from Russia's navy. Acid rain, caused by emissions from factories and power stations, is actively destroying northern forests. As a result, pressure is growing to safeguard Europe's natural environment and prevent further deterioration.

▲ **Coniferous forest covers** vast swathes of northern Scandinavia and the Russian Federation. Pollutants from other parts of Europe mixing with rainfall are causing defoliation and serious damage to many forests.

▶ **The Camargue in** the Rhône Delta, southern France, is a protected wetland area, famous for its native population of white horses, and unique bird and plant life.

Using the land and sea

Europe's swelling urban population and the outward expansion of many cities has created acute competition for land. Despite this, European resourcefulness has maximized land potential, and over half of Europe's land is still used for a wide variety of agricultural purposes. Land in northern Europe is used for cattle-rearing, pasture, and arable crops. Towards the Mediterranean, the mild climate allows the growing of grapes for wine; olives, sunflowers, tobacco and citrus fruits. EU subsidies, however, have resulted in massive overproduction and a land 'set-aside' policy has been introduced.

Using the land and sea
- cropland
- forest
- ice cap
- mountain region
- pasture
- tundra
- wetland
- major conurbations
- cattle
- goats
- pigs
- poultry
- reindeer
- sheep
- cereals
- citrus fruits
- cotton
- fishing
- fodder
- fruit
- olive oil
- potatoes
- rice
- root crops
- roses
- shellfish
- sunflowers
- timber
- tobacco
- vineyards

▲ **Bulgarian roses are** one of the many diverse crops grown in Europe. Rose oil, extracted from the petals, is used in perfume making.

▲ **Lowland pastures are** used for dairy farming. Good transport links and refrigeration allow fresh milk to be distributed throughout Europe.

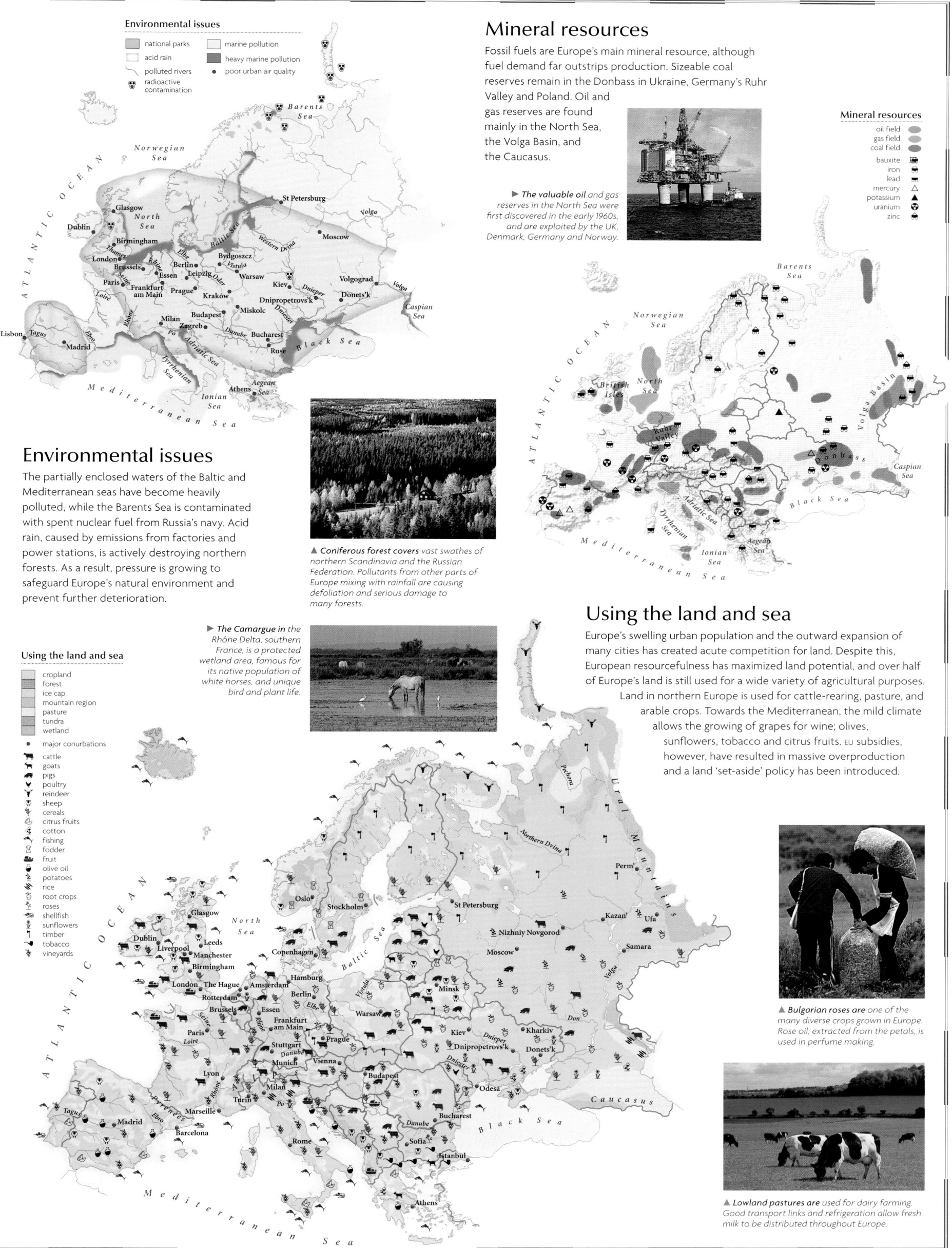

Scandinavia, Finland & Iceland

DENMARK, NORWAY, SWEDEN, FINLAND, ICELAND

Jutting into the Arctic Circle, this northern swathe of Europe has some of the continent's harshest environments, but benefits from great reserves of oil, gas and natural evergreen forests. While most early settlers came from the south, migrants to Finland came from the east, giving it a distinct language and culture. Since the late 19th century, the Scandinavian states have developed strong egalitarian traditions. Today, their welfare benefits systems are among the most extensive in the world, and standards of living are high. The Lapps, or Sami, maintain their traditional lifestyle in the northern regions of Norway, Sweden and Finland.

The landscape

Glaciers up to 10,000 ft (3000 m) deep covered most of Scandinavia and Finland during the last Ice Age. The effects of glaciation mark the entire landscape, from the mountains to the lowlands, across the tundra landscape of Lapland, and the lake districts of Sweden and Finland.

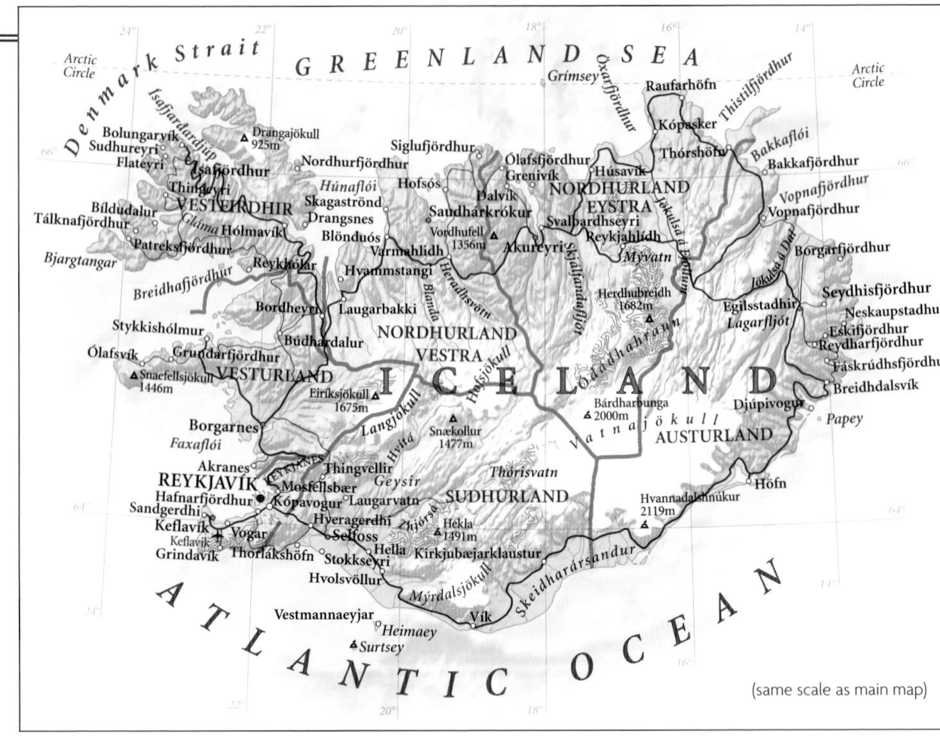

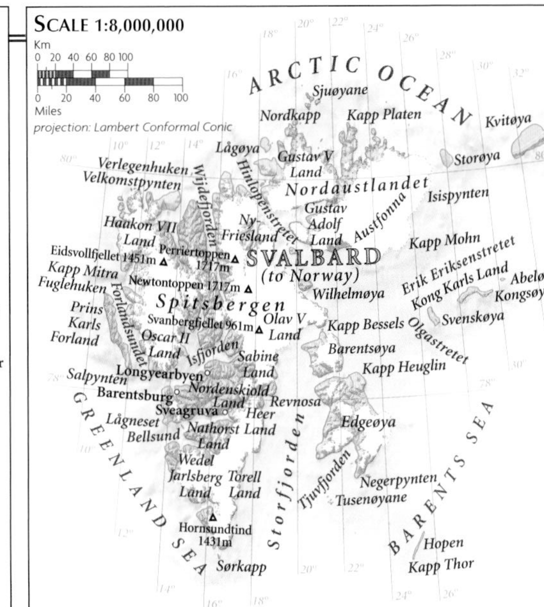

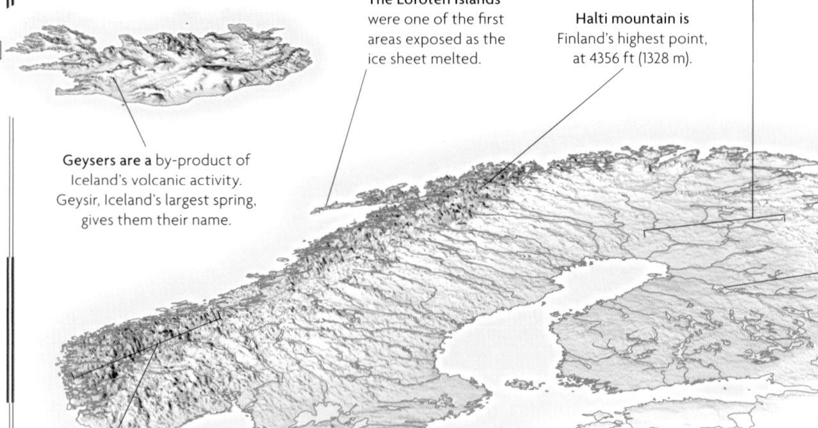

Geysers are a by-product of Iceland's volcanic activity. Geysir, Iceland's largest spring, gives them their name.

The Lofoten Islands were one of the first areas exposed as the ice sheet melted.

Halti mountain is Finland's highest point, at 4356 ft (1328 m).

Lapland, north of the Arctic Circle, is an area of undulating fells and plains known as tundra. The subsoil is permanently frozen and therefore impermeable. There are many peat bogs. Pools reappear in the summer when the surface thaws.

▼ **Finland's landscape was** fashioned by ice action. Glaciers gouged out its distinctive shallow lake basins, such as Oulujärvi, and left debris called moraines in their wake.

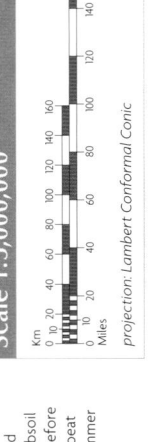

Fjords

▲ **The fjords on the western** coast of Norway were once gentle river valleys. Their deep floors and steep sides were carved out by glaciers during the last Ice Age, and they were later flooded by the sea.

▲ **On the coast of** Sjælland, these cliffs have been eroded by the sea, exposing layers of chalk and limestone.

Sjælland coast

Area of maximum yearly uplift 0.3 in/yr (9 mm/yr)

Slower rates of uplift 0.1 in/yr (3 mm/yr)

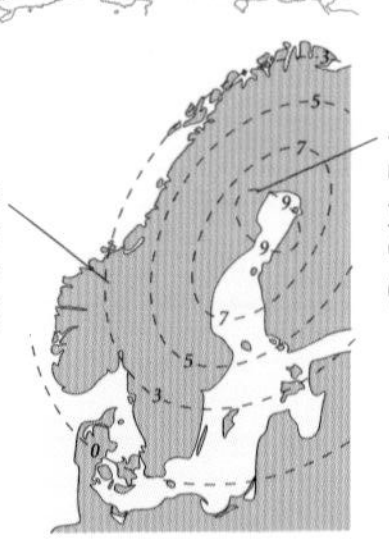

▲ **Scandinavia is still** recovering from the last Ice Age, when ice depressed the land by 2000 ft (600 m). This gradual uplift is known as isostatic rebound.

Using the land and sea

The cold climate, short growing season, poorly developed soil, steep slopes, and exposure to high winds across northern regions means that most agriculture is concentrated, with the population, in the south. Most of Finland and much of Norway and Sweden are covered by dense forests of pine, spruce and birch, which supply the timber industries.

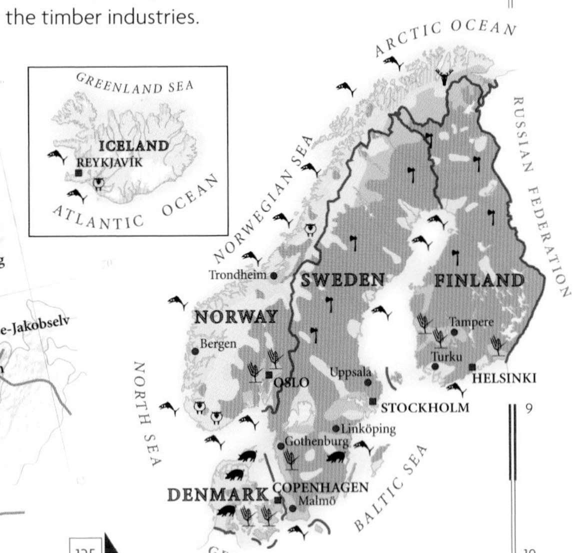

Land use and agricultural distribution

- capital cities
- major towns
- pasture
- cropland
- forest
- mountain region
- tundra

- fishing
- pigs
- reindeer
- sheep
- cereals
- timber

The urban/rural population divide

urban 77%   rural 23%

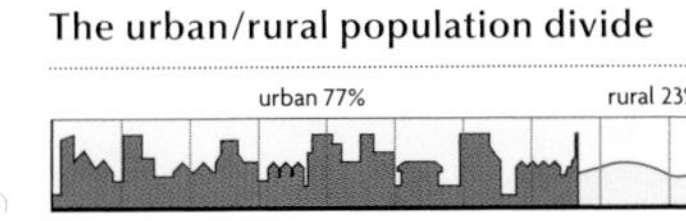

Population density

Total land area

51 people per sq mile
(20 people per sq km)

473,970 sq miles
(1,227,610 sq km)

SCALE 1:8,000,000

Km 0 20 40 60 80 100
Miles 0 20 40 60 80 100

projection: Lambert Conformal Conic

Scale 1:5,000,000

Km 0 20 40 60 80 100 120 140 160
Miles 0 20 40 60 80 100 120 140 160

projection: Lambert Conformal Conic

(same scale as main map)

▲ **Sweden is one of the** world's largest producers of wood and wood-based products. The traditional movement of logs by floating them down rivers has now been largely replaced by the use of trucks.

Map key

Population
- ⊚ 500,000 to 1 million
- ◉ 100,000 to 500,000
- ◎ 50,000 to 100,000
- ○ 10,000 to 50,000
- ○ below 10,000

Elevation
- 2000m / 6562ft
- 1000m / 3281ft
- 500m / 1640ft
- 250m / 820ft
- 100m / 328ft
- sea level

Transport and industry

Norway derives its premier industry, the production of oil and gas, from the North Sea, while Denmark exploits its own oil and gas reserves. Hydro-electric power is a major industry, particularly in Sweden and Iceland. Timber processing remains significant in Finland and Sweden, but metal and engineering industries are increasingly important. In Iceland, fish products are the main source of export earnings.

The transport network

- 226,735 miles (364,936 km)
- 2042 miles (3386 km)
- 13,704 miles (22,057 km)
- 6,661 miles (10,721km)

Although roads now reach most areas, the railways are markedly less developed. Much of the north is not served by rail and may rely on air and sea services for long distance travel and freight transportation.

Major industry and infrastructure

- ✿ car manufacture
- ⚙ engineering
- ⛏ fish processing
- ⚡ hydro-electric power
- ⚛ nuclear power
- ⛽ oil & gas
- 🌲 timber processing
- ■ capital cities
- ● major cities
- • major towns
- ⊕ international airports
- — major roads
- ▨ major industrial areas

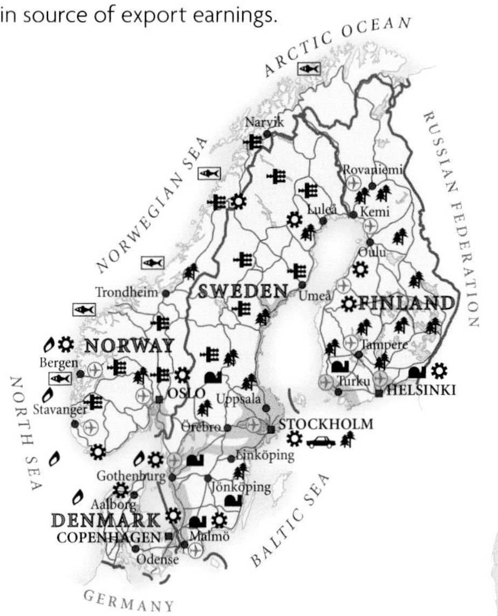

▲ **The use of geothermal power in** Iceland began half a century ago. Today geothermal power stations supply 89% of the country's domestic heating requirements.

▲ **Many Lappish people**, in addition to traditional reindeer herding, now also make their living from fishing and farming, or working in cities. Tourism provides some with an extra source of income.

NORWEGIAN SEA

NORTH SEA

BALTIC SEA

Gulf of Finland

Gulf of Bothnia

Skagerrak

Kattegat

Southern Scandinavia

SOUTHERN NORWAY, SOUTHERN SWEDEN, DENMARK

Scandinavia's economic and political hub is the more habitable and accessible southern region. Many of the area's major cities are on the southern coasts, including Oslo and Stockholm, the capital of Norway and Sweden. In Denmark, most of the population and the capital, Copenhagen, are located on its many islands. A cultural unity links the three Scandinavian countries. Their main languages, Danish, Swedish and Norwegian, are mutually intelligible, and they all retain their monarchies, although the parliaments have legislative control.

Using the land

Agriculture in southern Scandinavia is highly mechanized although farms are small. Denmark is the most intensively farmed country and its western pastureland is used mainly for pig farming. Cereal crops including wheat, barley and oats, predominate in eastern Denmark and in the far south of Sweden. Southern Norway and Sweden have large tracts of forest which are exploited for logging.

Land use and agricultural distribution

cattle
pigs
sheep
cereals
fodder
root crops
timber

capital cities
major towns

pasture
cropland
forest
mountain region

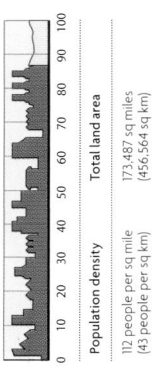

NORWAY
Trondheim
SWEDEN
Uppsala
Örebro
STOCKHOLM
Linköping
Oslo
DENMARK
Göteborg
Aalborg
COPENHAGEN
Odense
Malmö

NORWEGIAN SEA
NORTH SEA
BALTIC SEA
KATTEGAT
GERMANY

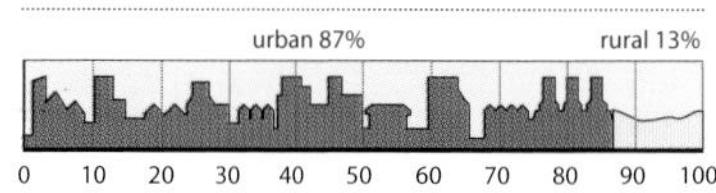

▲ In Norway winters are longer and colder inland than in coastal areas, where the warm current of the North Atlantic Drift moderates the climate.

The landscape

Southern Scandinavia, with the exception of Norway, has a flatter terrain than the rest of the region. Denmark and southern Sweden are both extensions of the North European Plain. In this area, because of glacial deposition rather than erosion, the soils are deeper and more fertile.

Acid rain, caused by industrial pollution carried north from elsewhere in Europe, harms plant and animal life in Scandinavian forests and lakes. The region's surface rocks lack lime to neutralize the acid, so making the problem more serious.

The urban/rural population divide

urban 87%   rural 13%

Population density	Total land area
112 people per sq mile (43 people per sq km)	173,487 sq miles (456,564 sq km)

▲ In the past, glaciers such as this one in Olden, Norway, were much larger. Today, many are retreating to yield the spectacular glacial scenery.

The peak of Glittertind in the Jotunheimen mountains is 8110 ft (2472 m) high.

Olden

▲ Limestone pillars eroded by the sea dot the coast of Gotland and surrounding islands.

Distinctive low ridges, called eskers, are found across southern Sweden. They are formed from sand and gravel deposits left by retreating glaciers.

The lakes of southern Sweden remain from a period when the land was completely flooded. As the ice which covered the area melted, the land rose, leaving lakes in shallow, ice-scoured depressions. Sweden has over 90,000 lakes.

Vänern in Sweden is the largest lake in Scandinavia. It covers an area of 2080 sq miles (5390 sq km).

Denmark's flat and fertile soils are formed on glacial deposits between 100–160 ft (30–50 m) deep.

When the ice retreated the valley was flooded by the sea

Old valley floor

Sognefjorden

Erosion by glaciers deepened existing river valleys

Sea level

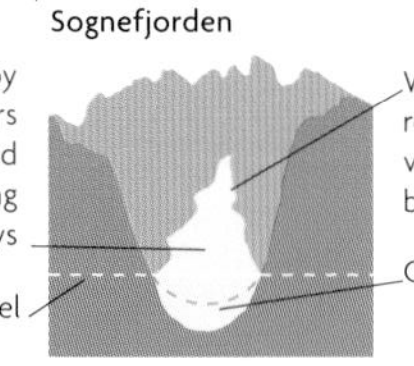

▲ Sognefjorden is the deepest of Norway's many fjords. It drops to 4291 ft (1308 m) below sea level.

Map key

Population
◉ 500,000 to 1 million
◎ 100,000 to 500,000
⊕ 50,000 to 100,000
○ 10,000 to 50,000
∘ below 10,000

Elevation
2000m / 6562ft
1000m / 3281ft
500m / 1640ft
250m / 820ft
100m / 328ft
sea level

Scale 1:2,900,000

projection: Lambert Conformal Conic

Gulf of Bothnia

VÄSTERNORRLAND
GÄVLEBORG
JÄMTLAND
DALARNA
HEDMARK
OPPLAND
SØR-TRØNDELAG
NORD-TRØNDELAG
MØRE OG ROMSDAL
SOGN OG FJORDANE

NORWEGIAN SEA

Trondheim
Oslo

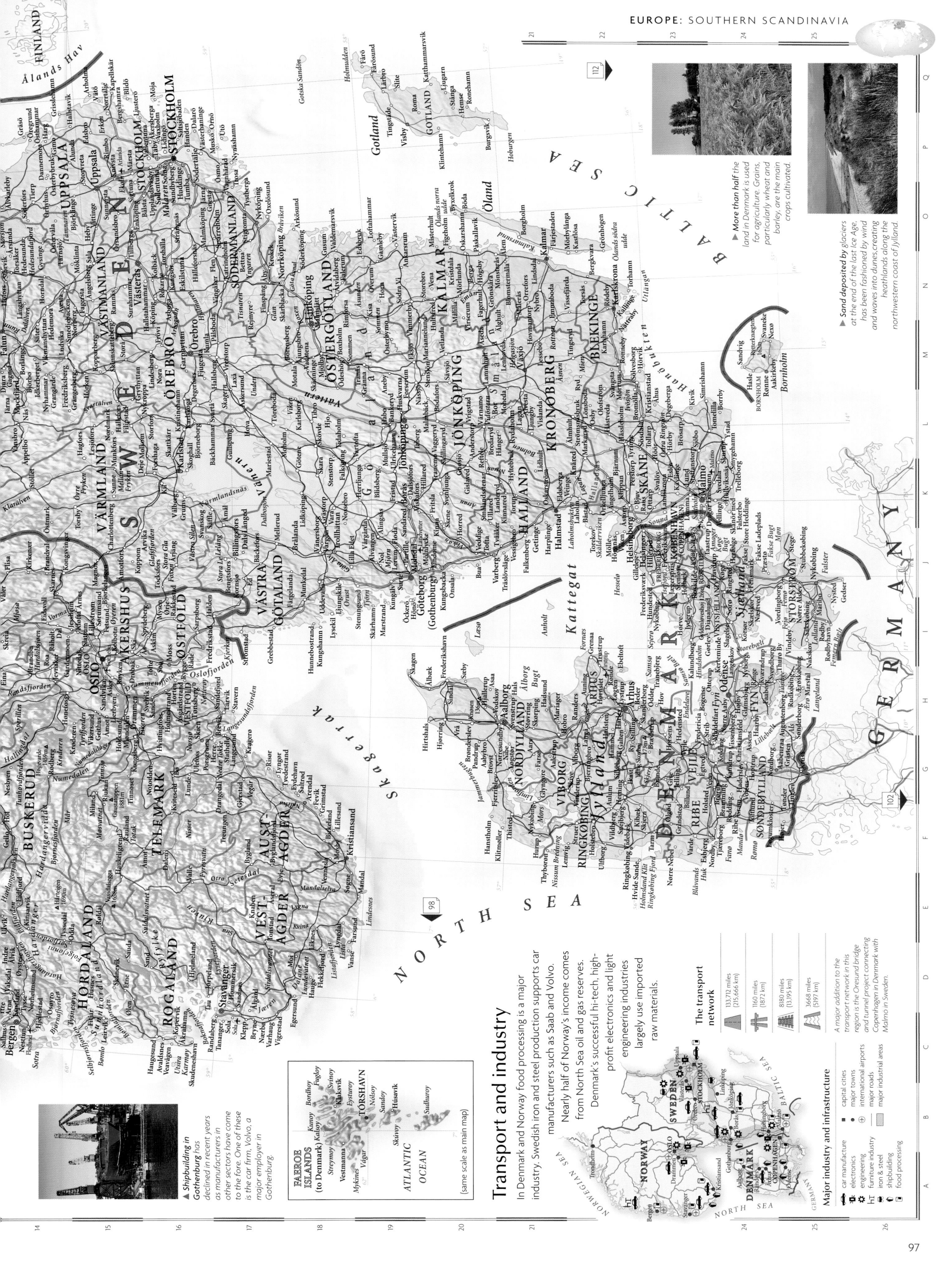

▲ *More than half the land in Denmark is used for agriculture. Grains, particularly wheat and barley, are the main crops cultivated.*

▲ *Sand deposited by glaciers at the end of the last Ice Age, has been fashioned by wind and waves into dunes, creating heathlands along the northwestern coast of Jylland.*

Transport and industry

In Denmark and Norway food processing is a major industry. Swedish iron and steel production supports car manufacturers such as Saab and Volvo. Nearly half of Norway's income comes from North Sea oil and gas reserves. Denmark's successful hi-tech, high-profit electronics and light engineering industries largely use imported raw materials.

The transport network

🛣	133,712 miles (215,666 km)
🚆	1160 miles (1872 km)
✈	8180 miles (13,195 km)
⛴	3668 miles (5197 km)

A major addition to the transport network in this region is the Oresund bridge and tunnel project connecting Copenhagen in Denmark with Malmö in Sweden.

Major industry and infrastructure

- ● capital cities
- • major towns
- ⊕ international airports
- — major roads
- ▨ major industrial areas

Major industry
- car manufacture
- electronics
- engineering
- furniture industry
- iron & steel
- shipbuilding
- food processing

▲ *Shipbuilding in Gothenburg has declined in recent years as manufacturers in other sectors have come to the fore. One of these is the car firm, Volvo, a major employer in Gothenburg.*

FÆRØE ISLANDS (to Denmark)
(same scale as main map)

ATLANTIC OCEAN

The British Isles

UNITED KINGDOM, IRELAND

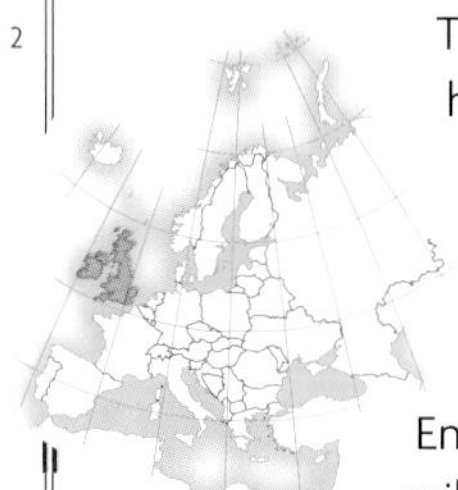

The British Isles have for centuries played a central role in European and world history. England, Wales, Scotland and Northern Ireland together form the United Kingdom (UK), while the southern portion of Ireland is an independent country, self-governing since 1921. Although England has tended to be the politically and economically dominant partner in the UK, the Scots, Welsh and Irish maintain independent cultures, distinct national identities and languages. Southeastern England is the most densely populated part of this crowded region, with over eight million people living in and around the London area.

Transport and industry

The British Isles' industrial base was founded primarily on coal, iron and textiles, based largely in the north. Today, the most productive sectors include hi-tech industries clustered mainly in southeastern England, chemicals, finance and the service sector, particularly tourism.

Major industry and infrastructure

- car manufacture
- chemicals
- engineering
- hi-tech industry
- iron & steel
- tourism
- capital cities
- major towns
- international airports
- major roads
- major industrial areas

The transport network

285,947 miles (460,240 km)	2023 miles (3578 km)
11,825 miles (19,032km)	3976 miles (6400 km)

The UK's congested roads have become a major focus of environmental concern in recent years. No longer an island, the UK was finally linked to continental Europe by the Channel Tunnel in 1994.

▼ Clew Bay in western Ireland, is characteristic of the heavily indented west coast, where deep wide-mouthed bays separate the mountains of Mayo, Donegal and Kerry as they thrust out into the Atlantic Ocean.

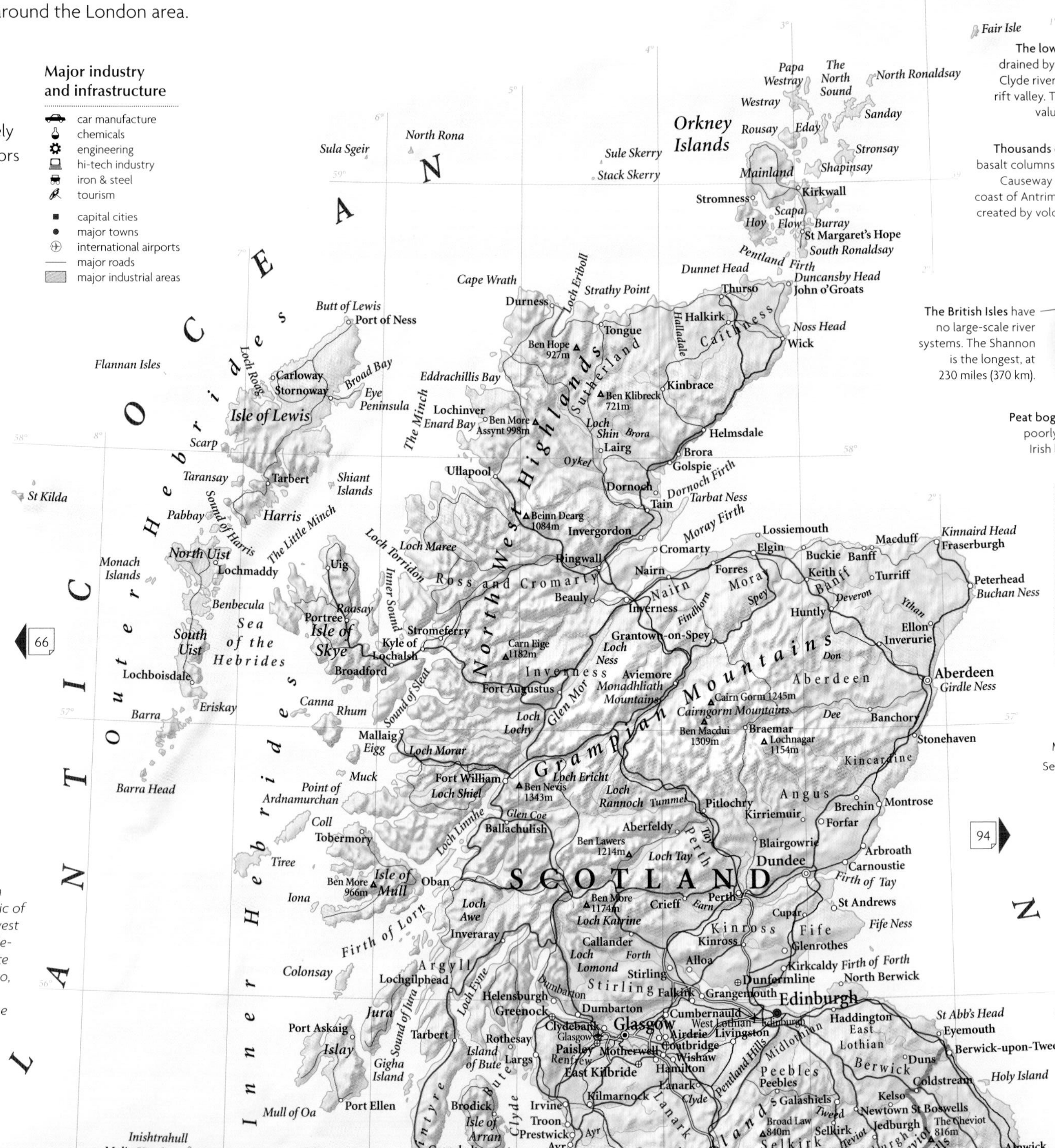

The landscape

Rugged uplands dominate the landscape of Scotland, Wales and northern England. All the peaks in the British Isles over 4000 ft (1219 m) lie in highland Scotland. Lowland England rises into several ranges of rolling hills, including the older Mendips, and the Cotswolds and the Chilterns, which were formed at the same time as the Alps in southern Europe.

▲ The valley of Glen Coe in the Scottish Highlands is a U-shaped valley, typical of the north and west of the British Isles, where glaciers shaped much of the landscape.

Over 600 islands, mostly uninhabited, lie west and north of the Scottish mainland.

The lowlands of Scotland, drained by the Tay, Forth and Clyde rivers, are centred on a rift valley. The region contains valuable coal reserves.

Thousands of hexagonal basalt columns form Giant's Causeway on the north coast of Antrim. These were created by volcanic activity.

The British Isles have no large-scale river systems. The Shannon is the longest, at 230 miles (370 km).

Peat bogs dot the poorly-drained Irish lowlands.

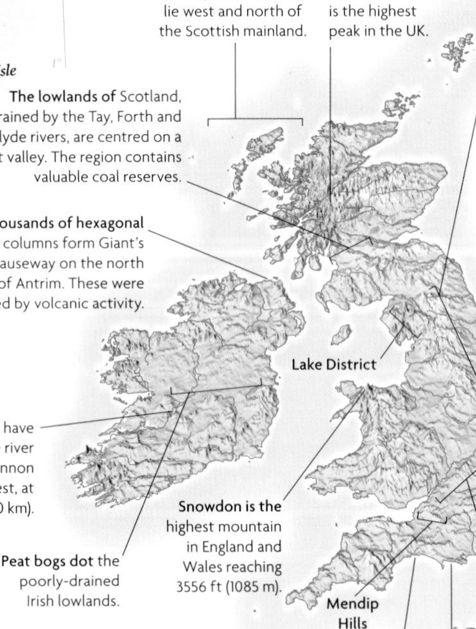

▲ Ullswater in the Lake District fills a deep valley formed by glacial erosion.

The Fens are a low-lying area reclaimed from the sea.

The Pennines, sometimes called the backbone of England, are formed of limestones and grits.

Chiltern Hills

The Cotswold Hills are characterized by a series of limestone ridges overlooking clay vales.

Ben Nevis at 4409 ft (1343 m) is the highest peak in the UK.

Snowdon is the highest mountain in England and Wales reaching 3556 ft (1085 m).

Mendip Hills

Lake District

▼ Dartmoor, studded with tors, is an exposed part of a vast granite dome, formed when molten rock intruded into the Earth's crust.

Black Ven, Lyme Regis

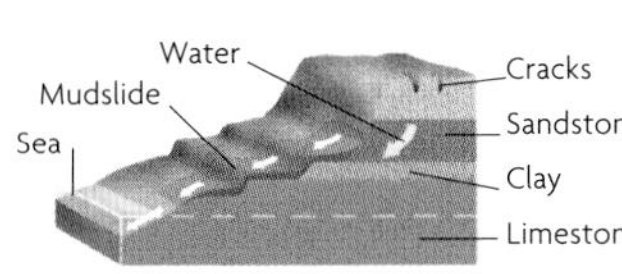

▲ Much of the south coast is subject to landslides. Following rain, water seeps into the underlying, less permeable clays which then crumble and slide into the sea.

- Water
- Mudslide
- Sea
- Cracks
- Sandstone
- Clay
- Limestone

▲ Coastal erosion around the British Isles forms striking features such as this limestone arch, Durdle Door in Dorset.

Durdle Door

Map key

Population
- ■ above 5 million
- ◉ 1 million to 5 million
- ◎ 500,000 to 1 million
- ⊙ 100,000 to 500,000
- ⊕ 50,000 to 100,000
- ○ 10,000 to 50,000
- ○ below 10,000

Elevation
- 1000m / 3281ft
- 500m / 1640ft
- 250m / 820ft
- 100m / 328ft
- sea level

Shetland Islands

Unst, Fetlar, Herma Ness, Out Skerries, Whalsay, Hillswick, Sullom Voe, Yell, Yell Sound, St Magnus Bay, Mainland, Leirwick, Bressay, Papa Stour, Scalloway, West Burra, Foula, Fitful Head, Sumburgh Head

Fair Isle

Orkney Islands

North Ronaldsay, Sanday, Westray, Papa Westray, Stronsay, Rousay, Eday, Shapinsay, The North Sound, Mainland, Kirkwall, Stromness, Scapa, Hoy, Flotta, Burray, South Ronaldsay, St Margaret's Hope, Duncansby Head, John o'Groats

Sula Sgeir, North Rona

SCOTLAND

Cape Wrath, Durness, Ben Hope, Loch Eriboll, Tongue, Strathy Point, Bettyhill, Halladale, Dunnet Head, Thurso, Halkirk, Wick, Helmsdale, Brora, Golspie, Dornoch, Tain, Dornoch Firth, Noss Head, Duncansby Head

Butt of Lewis, Port of Ness, Eye Peninsula, Broad Bay, Stornoway, Carloway, Loch Roag, Isle of Lewis, Tarbert, Harris, Sound of Harris, North Uist, Benbecula, Lochboisdale, South Uist, Eriskay, Barra, Barra Head, Monach Islands

St Kilda

Flannan Isles, Scarp, Taransay, Pabbay, Shiant Islands

Ben More Assynt 998m, Lochinver, Eddrachillis Bay, Enard Bay, Ben More, Ullapool, Loch Broom, Inner Sound, Loch Torridon, Loch Maree, Kyle of Lochalsh, Broadford, Portree, Isle of Skye, Raasay, Uig, Rhum, Eigg, Muck, Canna, Coll, Tiree, Point of Ardnamurchan, Tobermory, Iona, Isle of Mull, Colonsay, Oban, Firth of Lorn, Port Askaig, Islay, Jura, Sound of Jura, Gigha Island, Mull of Oa, Port Ellen, Campbeltown, Mull of Kintyre

Beinn Dearg 1084m, Cromarty, Dingwall, Beauly, Inverness, Loch Ness, Fort Augustus, Fort William, Ben Nevis 1343m, Glen Coe, Loch Shiel, Loch Linnhe, Mallaig, Glenfinnan, Ben More 966m, Inveraray, Loch Fyne, Lochgilphead, Loch Awe, Crinan, Brodick, Isle of Arran, Isle of Bute, Rothesay, Largs, Ardrossan, Irvine, Troon, Prestwick, Ayr

Bonar Bridge, Lairg, Loch Shin, Carn Eige 1183m, Invergordon, Alness, Nairn, Forres, Elgin, Lossiemouth, Buckie, Keith, Huntly, Banff, Macduff, Turriff, Fraserburgh, Peterhead, Buchan Ness, Girdle Ness, Aberdeen, Kinnaird Head, Stonehaven, Montrose, Arbroath, Brechin, Forfar, Kirriemuir, Blairgowrie, Braemar 1154m, Cairn Gorm 1245m, Cairngorm Mountains, Grantown-on-Spey, Aviemore, Kingussie, Ben Macdui 1309m, Pitlochry, Aberfeldy, Loch Tay, Ben Lawers, Loch Rannoch, Loch Earn, Crieff, Callander, Ben More 1174m, Dunkeld, Perth, Dundee, St Andrews, Fife Ness, Firth of Tay, Carnoustie, Kirkcaldy, Firth of Forth, North Berwick, Dunbar, St Abb's Head, Eyemouth, Berwick-upon-Tweed, Holy Island, Alnwick

Kinross, Loch Leven, Stirling, Falkirk, Alloa, Dunfermline, Grangemouth, Cumbernauld, Dumbarton, Dunoon, Greenock, Paisley, Glasgow, Clyde, Motherwell, Hamilton, East Kilbride, Kilmarnock, Lanark, Cumnock, Dumfries

Edinburgh, Haddington, Peebles, Galashiels, Selkirk, Melrose, Lauder, Jedburgh, Hawick, Newtown St Boswells, Kelso, Coldstream, Duns, Roxburgh, Cheviot Hills, The Cheviot, Wooler

NORTH SEA

NORTH ATLANTIC OCEAN

England & Wales (transport map)

Aberdeen, Dundee, Glasgow, Edinburgh, Newcastle upon Tyne, UNITED KINGDOM, Leeds, Liverpool, Manchester, Sheffield, Nottingham, Birmingham, Norwich, Leicester, Cardiff, Bristol, LONDON, DUBLIN, IRELAND, Belfast, Cork, English Channel, NORTH SEA, ATLANTIC OCEAN

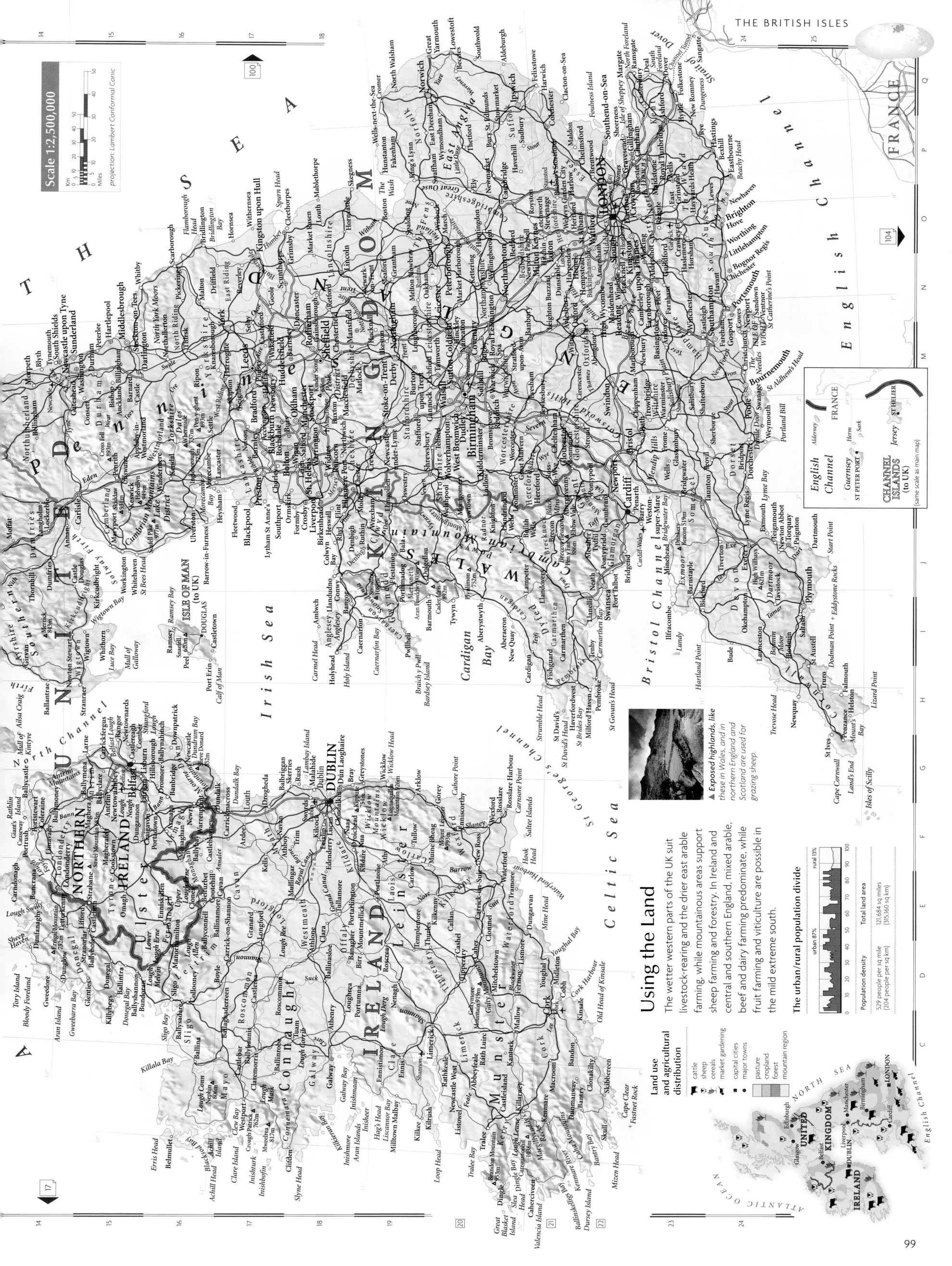

Scale 1:2,500,000

projection: Lambert Conformal Conic

Using the Land

The wetter western parts of the UK suit livestock-rearing and the drier east arable farming, while mountainous areas support sheep farming and forestry. In Ireland and central and southern England, mixed arable, beef and dairy farming predominate, while fruit farming and viticulture are possible in the mild extreme south.

▲ Exposed highlands, like these in Wales, and in northern England and Scotland are used for grazing sheep.

Land use and agricultural distribution

cattle
sheep
cereals
market gardening
capital cities
major towns

pasture
cropland
forest
mountain region

The urban/rural population divide

	urban 87%	rural 13%

Population density
529 people per sq mile
(204 people per sq km)

Total land area
121,684 sq miles
(315,160 sq km)

CHANNEL ISLANDS (to UK)
(same scale as main map)

English Channel

FRANCE

The Low Countries

BELGIUM, LUXEMBOURG, NETHERLANDS

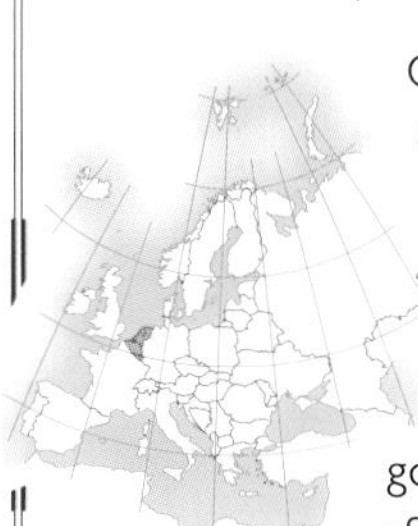

One of northwestern Europe's strategic crossroads, the Low Countries are united by a common history in which they have often been a battleground in European wars. For over a thousand years they were ruled by foreign powers. Even after they achieved independence, the three countries maintained close links, later forming the world's first totally free labour and goods market, the Benelux Economic Union, which became the core of the European Community (now the European Union or EU). These states have remained at the forefront of wider European co-operation; Brussels, The Hague and Luxembourg are hosts to major institutions of the EU.

The landscape

The main geographical regions of the Netherlands are the northern glacial heathlands, the low-lying lands of the Rhine and Maas/Meuse, the reclaimed polders, and the dune coast and islands. Belgium includes part of the Ardennes, together with the coalfields on its northern flanks, and the fertile Flanders plain.

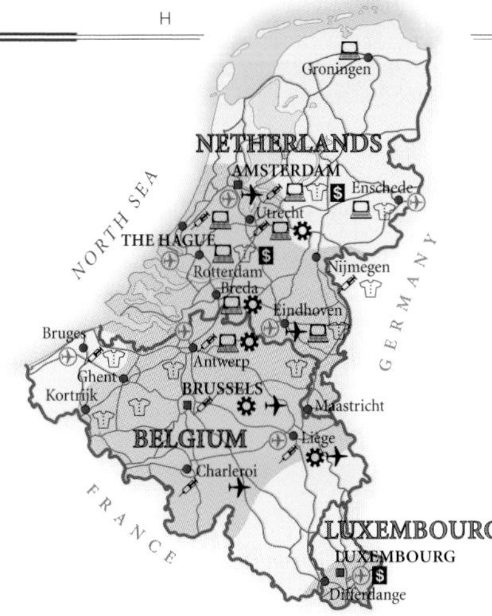

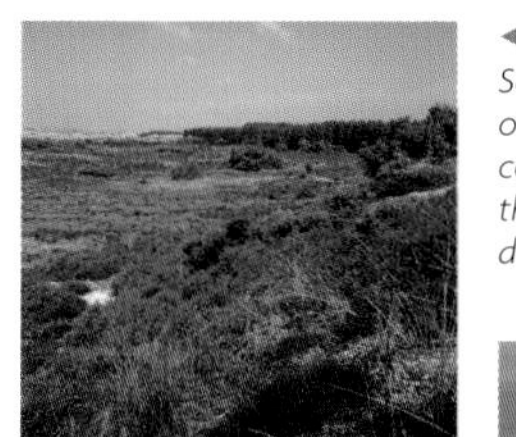

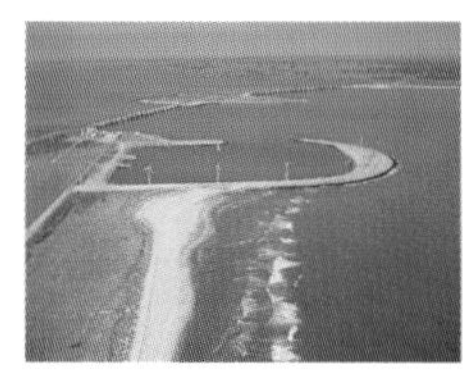

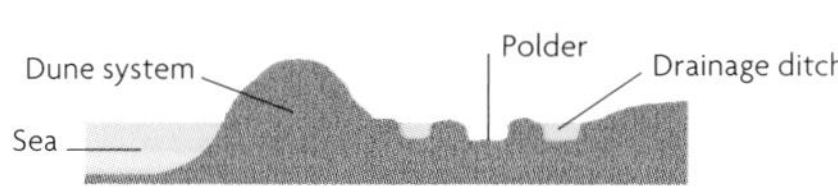

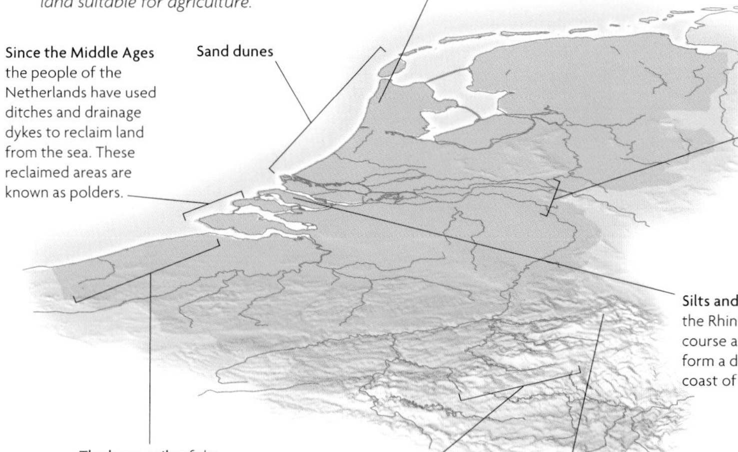

Since the Middle Ages the people of the Netherlands have used ditches and drainage dykes to reclaim land from the sea. These reclaimed areas are known as polders.

▲ **Extensive sand dune** systems along the coast have prevented flooding of the land. Behind the dunes, marshy land is drained to form polders, usable land suitable for agriculture.

Dune system
Sea
Polder — Drainage ditch
Sand dunes
Schoorl

▶ **Heathlands, like these** at Schoorl, are found along the coast of the Netherlands. Much of the coast was breached by the sea in the 5th century, creating its distinctive inlets and islands.

▲ **One-third of the** Netherlands lies below sea level and flooding is a constant threat. Barrages have been built across the mouths of many rivers to contain floodwaters.

The parallel valleys of the Maas/Meuse and Rhine rivers were created when the Rhine was deflected from its previous course by the ice sheet which formed during the last Ice Age.

Silts and sands eroded by the Rhine throughout its course are deposited to form a delta on the west coast of the Netherlands.

Hautes Fagnes is the highest part of Belgium. The bogs and streams in this upland region result from high rainfall and low temperatures.

The loess soils of the Flanders Plain in western Belgium provide excellent conditions for arable farming.

Ardennes

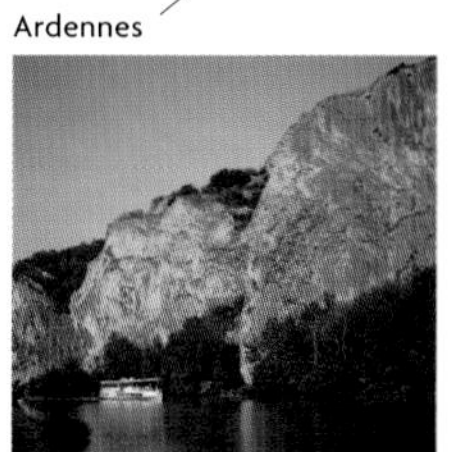

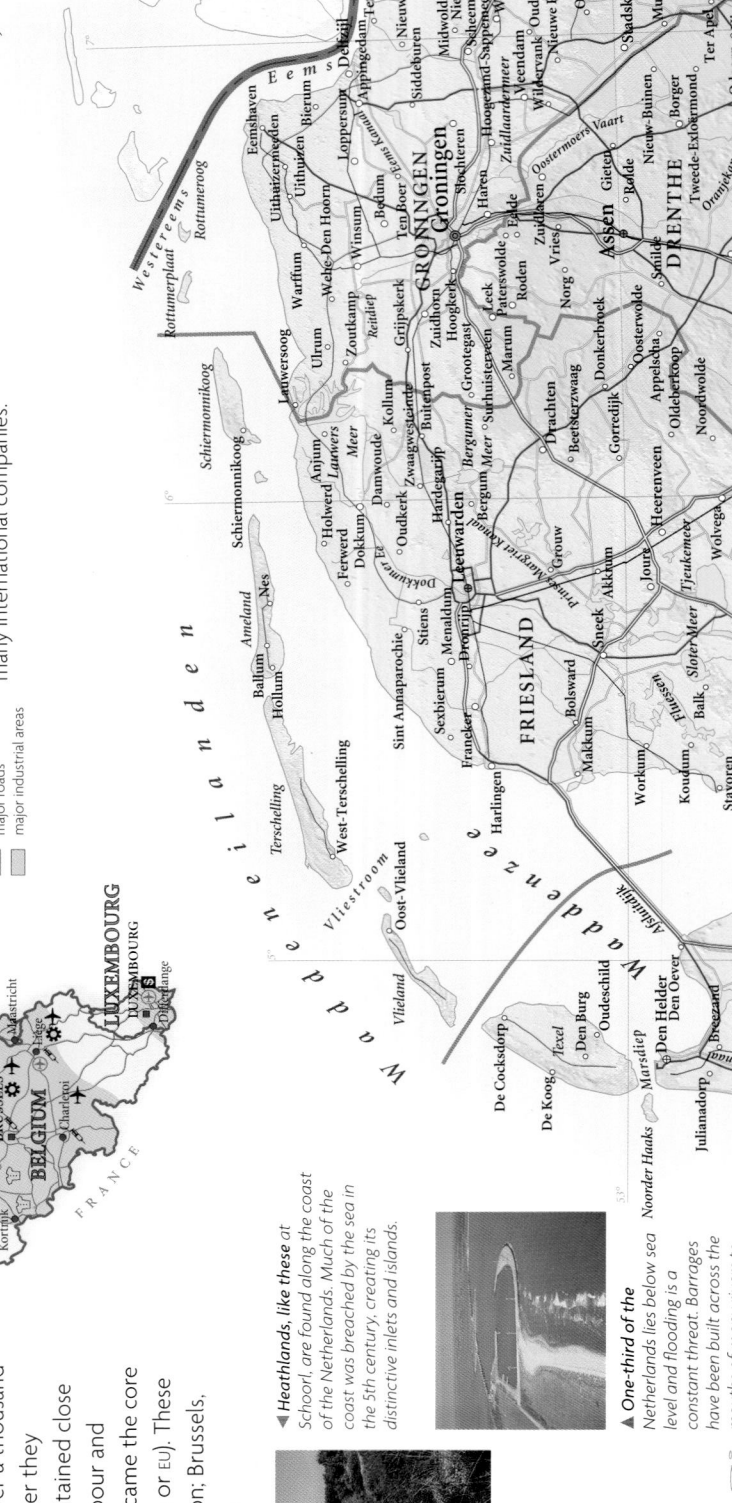

▶ **Uplifted and folded** 220 million years ago, the Ardennes have since been reduced to relatively level plateaux, then sharply incised by rivers such as the Maas/Meuse.

Transport and industry

In the western Netherlands, a massive, sprawling industrialized zone encompasses many new hi-tech and service industries. Belgium's central region has emerged as the country's light manufacturing and services centre. Luxembourg city is home to more than 160 banks and the European headquarters of many international companies.

Major industry and infrastructure

➤ aerospace
✿ finance
⚙ engineering
💻 hi-tech industry
⚗ pharmaceuticals
▣ textiles
● capital cities
● major cities
● major towns
✈ international airports
— major roads
▨ major industrial areas

The Low Countries hold a key position on the North Sea, containing Europe's two largest ports, Rotterdam and Antwerp, which are connected to a comprehensive system of inland waterways.

The transport network		
140,588 miles (226,281 km)	2565 miles (4129 km)	4134 miles (6653 km)
4099 miles (6598 km)		

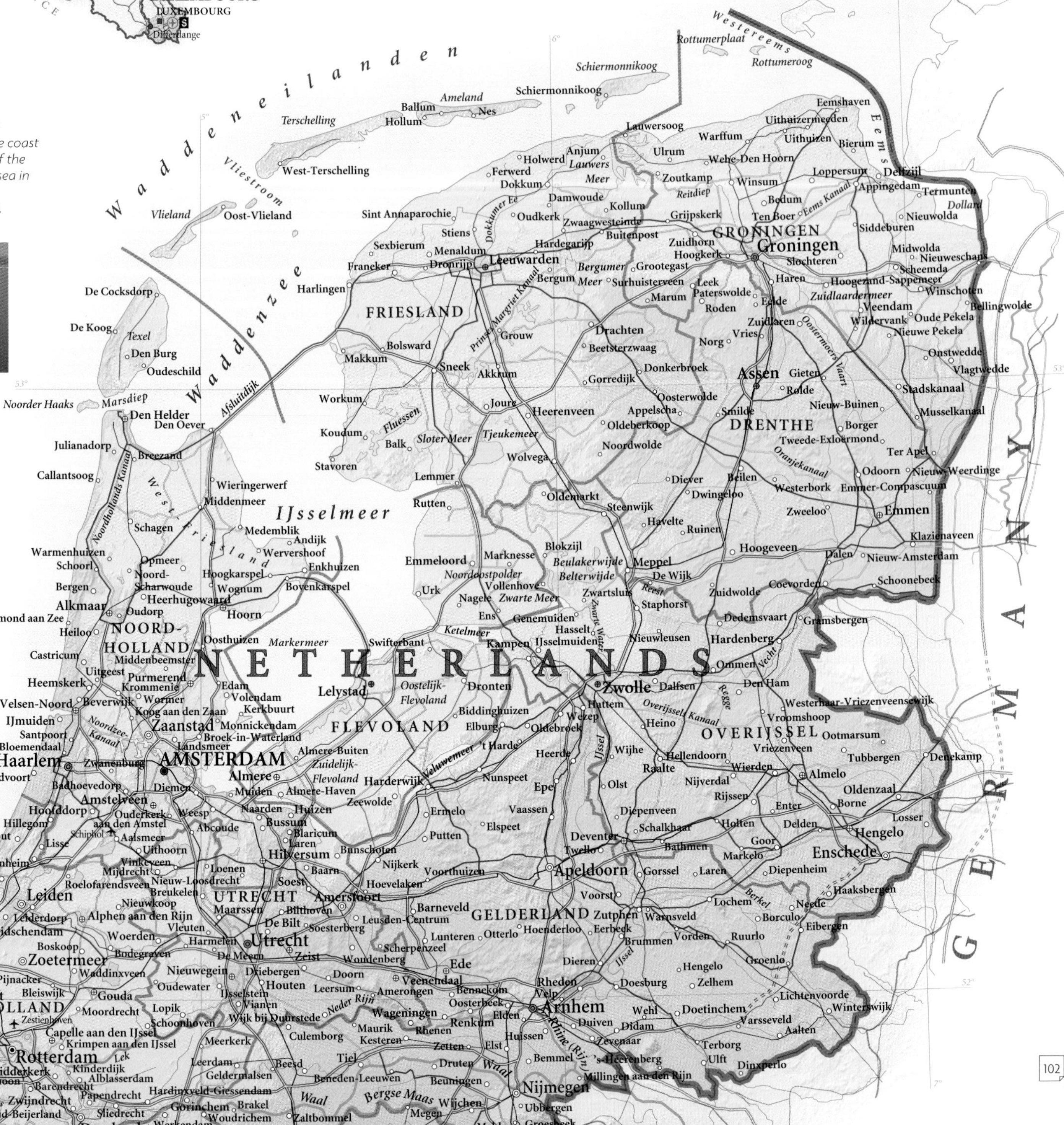

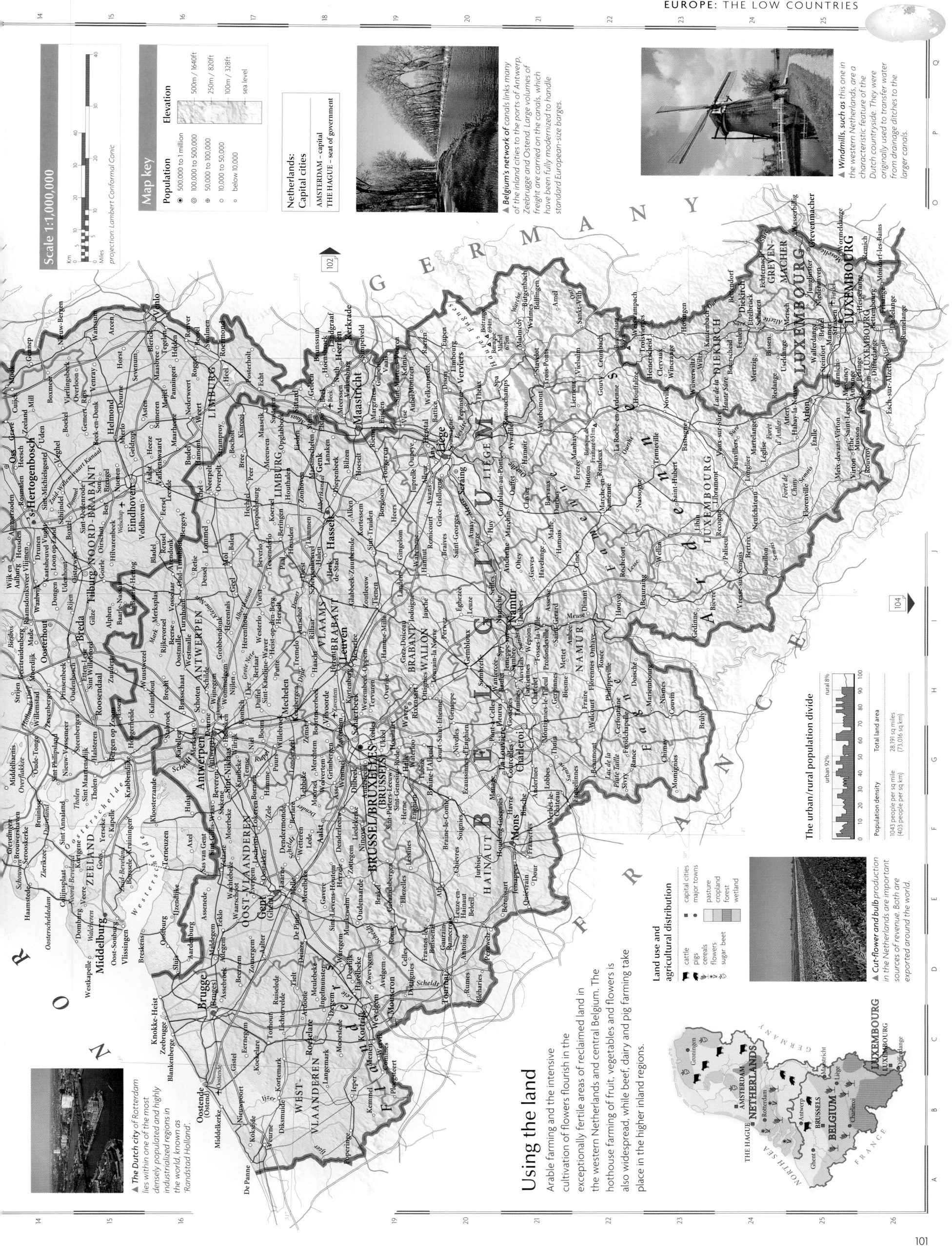

Scale 1:1,000,000

projection: Lambert Conformal Conic

Map key

Elevation

500m / 1640ft
250m / 820ft
100m / 328ft
sea level

Population
- ◉ 500,000 to 1 million
- ◎ 100,000 to 500,000
- ⊕ 50,000 to 100,000
- ○ 10,000 to 50,000
- ○ below 10,000

Netherlands:
Capital cities
AMSTERDAM – capital
THE HAGUE – seat of government

▲ *Belgium's network of canals links many of the inland cities to the ports of Antwerp, Zeebrugge and Ostend. Large volumes of freight are carried on the canals, which have been fully modernized to handle standard European-size barges.*

▲ *Windmills, such as this one in the western Netherlands, are a characteristic feature of the Dutch countryside. They were originally used to transfer water from drainage ditches to the larger canals.*

▲ *The Dutch city of Rotterdam lies within one of the most densely populated and highly industrialized regions in the world, known as 'Randstad Holland'.*

Using the land

Arable farming and the intensive cultivation of flowers flourish in the exceptionally fertile areas of reclaimed land in the western Netherlands and central Belgium. The hothouse farming of fruit, vegetables and flowers is also widespread, while beef, dairy and pig farming take place in the higher inland regions.

Land use and agricultural distribution

- cattle
- pigs
- cereals
- flowers
- sugar beet

- capital cities
- major towns
- pasture
- cropland
- forest
- wetland

▲ *Cut-flower and bulb production in the Netherlands are important sources of revenue. Both are exported around the world.*

The urban/rural population divide

urban 92%
rural 8%

Population density	Total land area
104 people per sq mile (403 people per sq km)	28,191 sq miles (73,016 sq km)

Germany

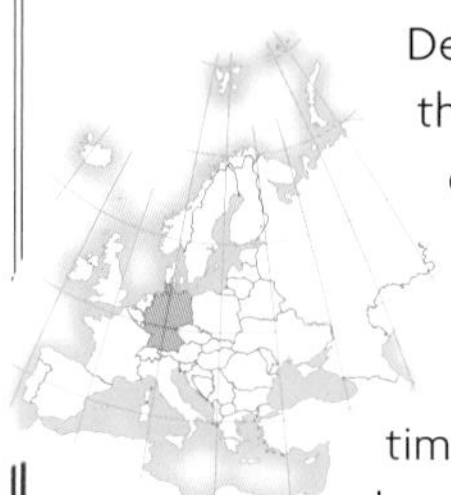

Despite the devastation of its industry and infrastructure during the Second World War and its separation from eastern Germany during the Cold War, West Germany made a rapid recovery in the following generation to become Europe's most formidable economic power. When the Berlin Wall was dismantled in 1989, the two halves of Germany were politically united for the first time in 40 years. Complete social and economic unity remain a longer term goal, as East German industry and society adapt to a free market. Germany has been a key player in the creation of the European Union (EU) and in moves toward a single European currency.

Using the land

Germany has a large, efficient agricultural sector, and produces more than three-quarters of its own food. The major crops grown are cereals and sugar beet on the more fertile soils, and root crops, rye, oats and fodder on the poorer soils of the northern plains and central uplands. Southern Germany is also a principal producer of high quality wines. Vineyards cover the slopes surrounding the Rhine and its tributaries.

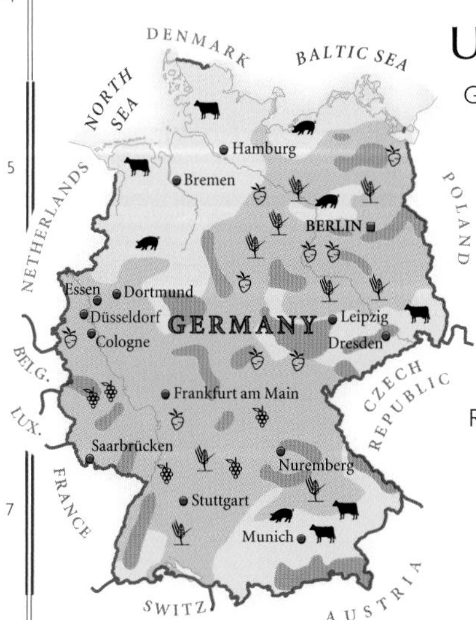

Land use and agricultural distribution

- cattle
- pigs
- cereals
- sugar beet
- vineyards
- capital cities
- major towns
- pasture
- cropland
- forest

The urban/rural population divide

| urban 87% | rural 13% |

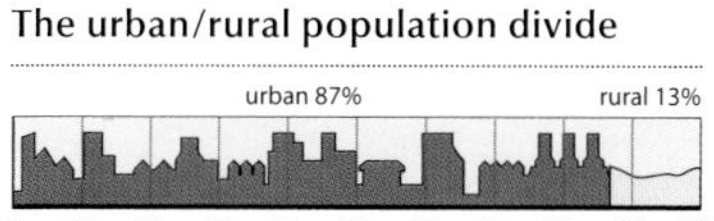

Population density
612 people per sq mile
(236 people per sq km)

Total land area
137,804 sq miles
(356,910 sq km)

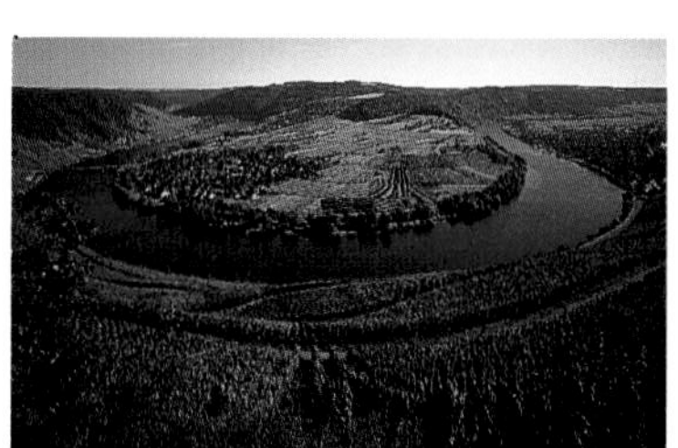

▲ The Moselle river flows through the Rhine State Uplands (Rheinisches Schiefergebirge). During a period of uplift, pre-existing river meanders were deeply incised, to form its present dramatic contours.

The landscape

The plains of northern Germany, the volcanic plateaux and mountains of the central uplands, and the Bavarian Alps are the three principal geographic regions in Germany. North to south the land rises steadily from barely 300 ft (90 m) in the plains to 6500 ft (2000 m) in the Bavarian Alps, which are a small but distinct region in the far south.

The Harz Mountains were formed 300 million years ago. They are block-faulted mountains, formed when a section of the Earth's crust was thrust up between two faults.

Elbe river

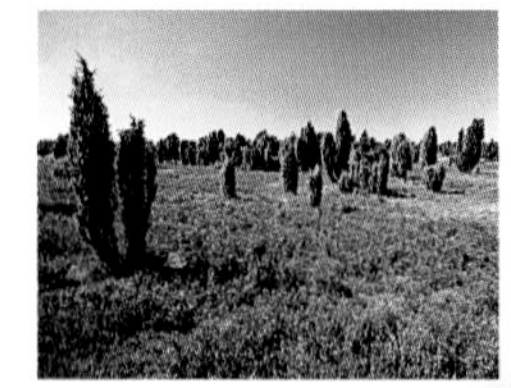

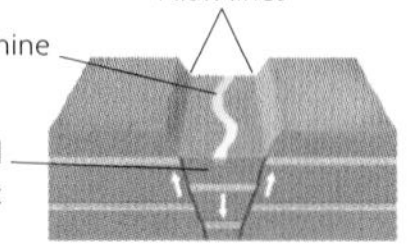

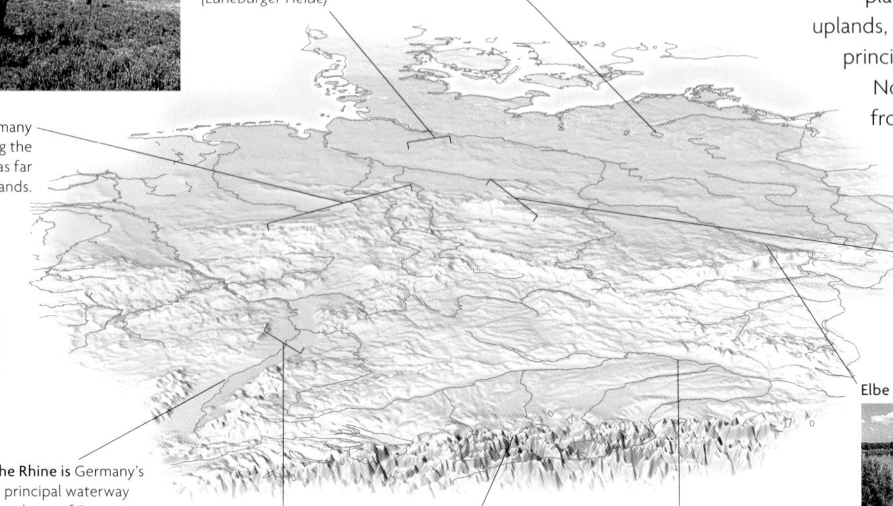

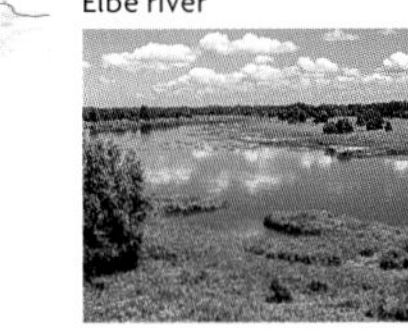

▼ The Elbe flows in wide meanders across the north German plain to the North Sea. At its mouth it is 10 miles (16 km) wide

Scale 1:2,250,000

projection: Lambert Conformal Conic

Müritz lake covers 45 sq miles (117 sq km), but is only 108 ft (33 m) deep. It lies in a shallow valley formed by meltwater flowing out from a retreating ice sheet. These valleys are known as Urstromtaler.

Zugspitze, the highest peak in Germany at 9719 ft (2962 m), was formed during the Alpine mountain-building period, 30 million years ago.

The Danube rises in the Black Forest (Schwarzwald) and flows east, across a wide valley, on its course to the Black Sea.

Rhine Rift Valley

The Rhine is Germany's principal waterway and one of Europe's longest rivers, flowing 820 miles (1320 km).

▲ The heathlands of northern Germany are covered by glacial deposits of sandy outwash soil which makes them largely infertile. They support only sheep and solitary trees.

Lüneburg Heath (Lüneburger Heide)

Much of the landscape of northern Germany has been shaped by glaciation. During the last Ice Age, the ice sheet advanced as far as the northern slopes of the central uplands.

Fault lines

Rhine

Downfaulted block

▲ Part of the floor of the Rhine Rift Valley was let down between two parallel faults in the Earth's crust.

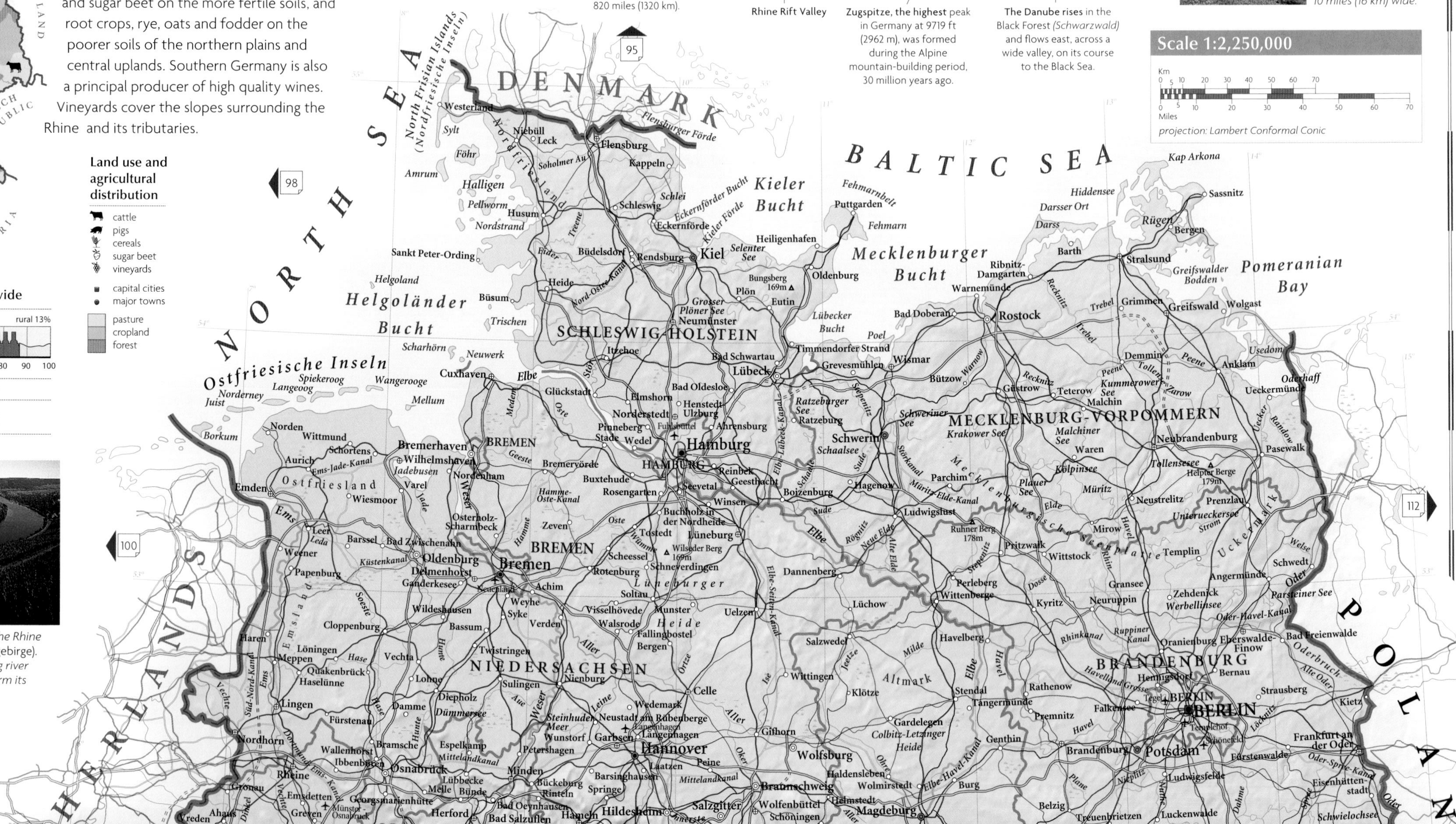

D

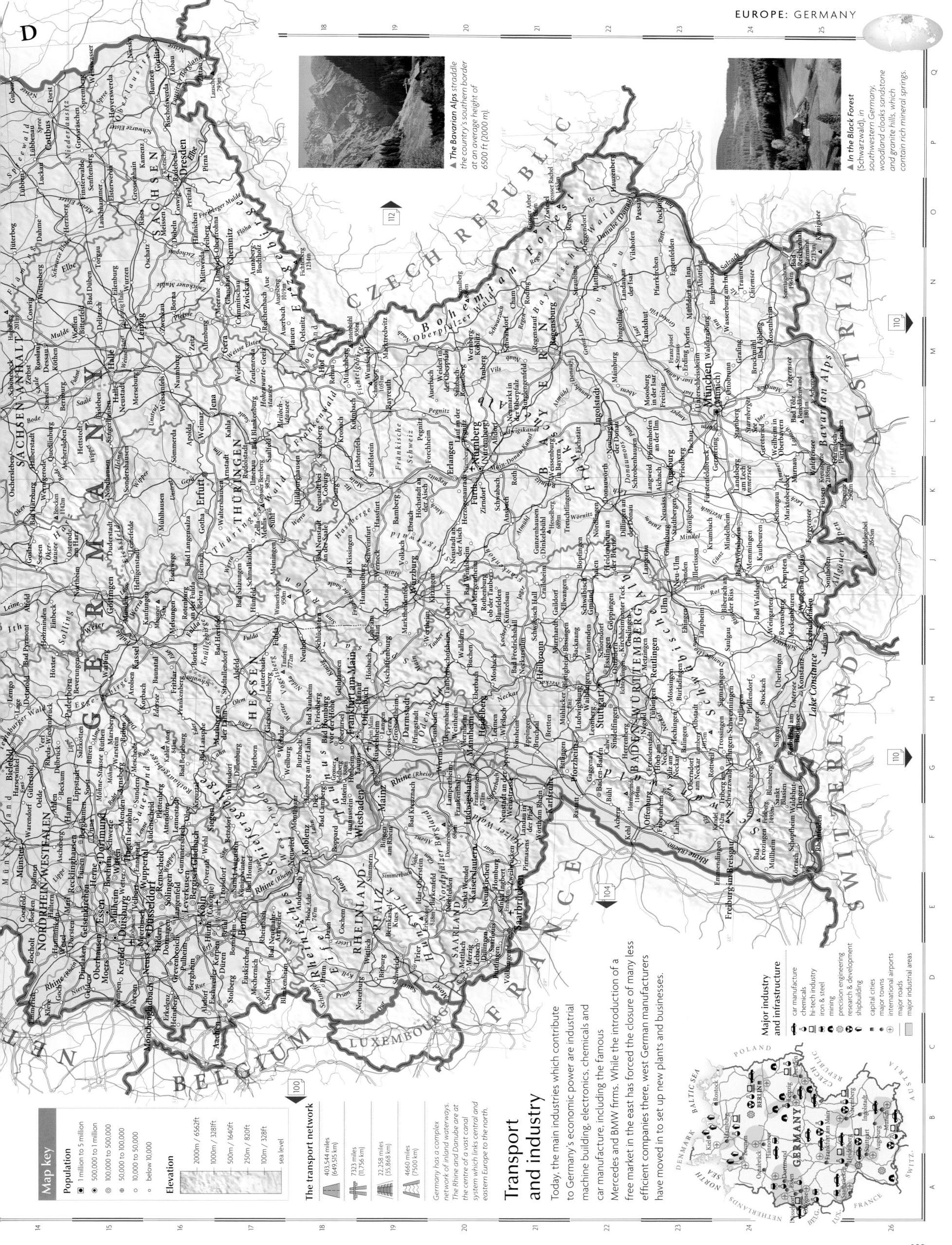

▲ *The Bavarian Alps* straddle the country's southern border at an average height of 6500 ft (2000 m).

▲ *In the Black Forest* (Schwarzwald), in southwestern Germany, woodland clocks sandstone and granite hills, which contain rich mineral springs.

Transport and industry

Today, the main industries which contribute to Germany's economic power are industrial machine building, electronics, chemicals and car manufacture, including the famous Mercedes and BMW firms. While the introduction of a free market in the east has forced the closure of many less efficient companies there, west German manufacturers have moved in to set up new plants and businesses.

Germany has a complex network of inland waterways. The Rhine and Danube are at the centre of a vast canal system which links central and eastern Europe to the north.

The transport network

403,544 miles (649,515 km)	
7323 miles (11,756 km)	
22,258 miles (35,868 km)	
4660 miles (7500 km)	

Major industry and infrastructure

- car manufacture
- chemicals
- hi-tech industry
- iron & steel
- mining
- precision engineering
- research & development
- shipbuilding
- capital cities
- major towns
- international airports
- major roads
- major industrial areas

Map key

Population
- 1 million to 5 million
- 500,000 to 1 million
- 100,000 to 500,000
- 50,000 to 100,000
- 10,000 to 50,000
- below 10,000

Elevation
- 2000m / 6562ft
- 1000m / 3281ft
- 500m / 1640ft
- 250m / 820ft
- 100m / 328ft
- sea level

France

FRANCE, MONACO

A major centre of culture and fashion, and a leading producer of both industrial and agricultural goods, France is a key player in the push towards European unity. The founder of modern Republican government in the 18th century, France has been closely involved in European events for many centuries. The Paris Basin is the most highly populated area; Île de France is home to over 11 million people. Large parts of rural France remain thinly populated, particularly the mountainous Massif Central, Pyrenees and southern Alps.

◄ *The chalk cliffs* of Normandy (Normandie) and southeastern England form part of a single geological region, now divided in two by the English Channel.

The landscape

France's landscape was fashioned by two phases of mountain-building. The northwestern peninsula, the Massif Central and the Vosges date from 220 million years ago. The complex folds of the Alps and Pyrenees, the gently-folded Jura, and the low-lying sedimentary areas of the Paris, Garonne and Rhône basins started to form 65 million years ago.

The coast of Brittany (Bretagne) is highly indented where deep valleys in the northwestern peninsula were drowned by the sea.

The Normandy (Normandie) coastline is characterized by high chalk cliffs.

The coastline of France is 2141 miles (3427 km) long.

▲ *The Paris Basin* consists of a layered sequence of sedimentary rocks. Fertile soils over much of the area make good agricultural land.

The gently rounded summits of the Vosges are over 200 million years old.

The Biscay coast, like the Mediterranean, is characterized by flat sandy beaches, interspersed with lagoons.

Garonne Basin

The Dordogne region contains spectacular examples of limestone scenery including caves and gorges.

The Pyrenees form a natural border between France and Spain.

The ancient Massif Central, disturbed by the formation of the Alps, was subject to volcanism that only ceased during the last 10,000 years.

The folded Jura form low ridges and long narrow valleys.

The Alps were forced up during several phases of mountain-building beginning 65 million years ago.

Rhône Basin

Corsica's northeastern peninsula has dramatic cliffs of folded limestone.

Rhône Delta

Rhône

Delta plain

The marshes of the Camargue

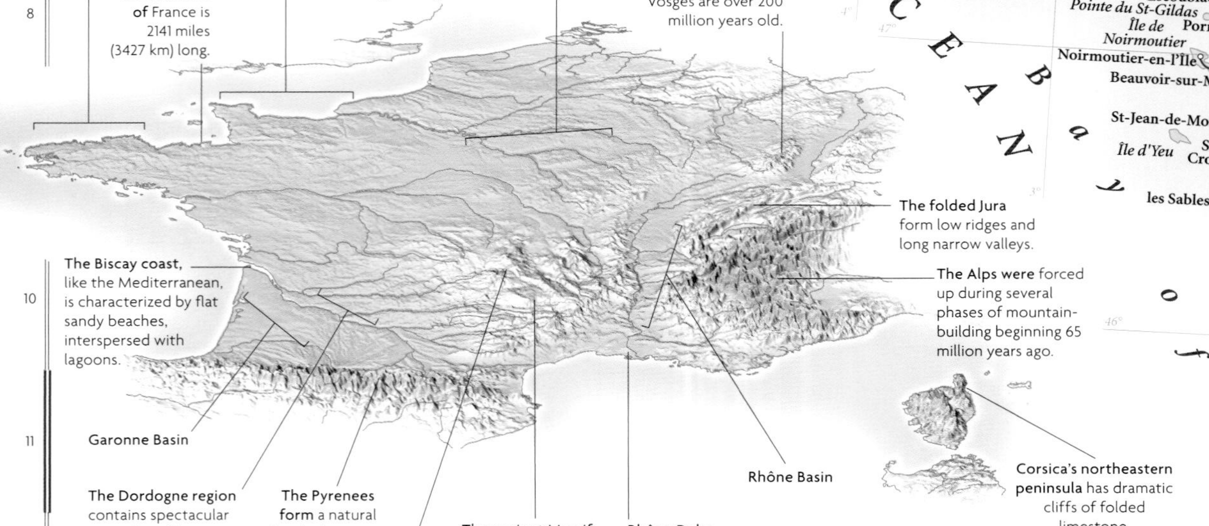

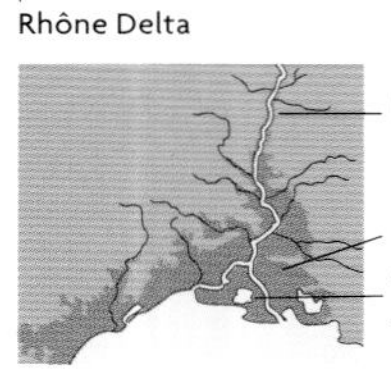

◄ *The volcanic landscape* of the Auvergne where the cones of its extinct volcanoes have worn away to leave 'plugs' of lava.

▲ *Deposition in the Rhône* Delta is wave-dominated. Sea currents carry river sediments extending the delta plain westwards.

Transport and industry

Today the main French growth industries are hi-tech, including micro-electronics, telecommunications and aerospace. Other important sectors are the nuclear industry, only rivalled in scale by that of the USA, car manufacture, dominated by the giants Renault and Peugeot, and a highly diversified tourist industry.

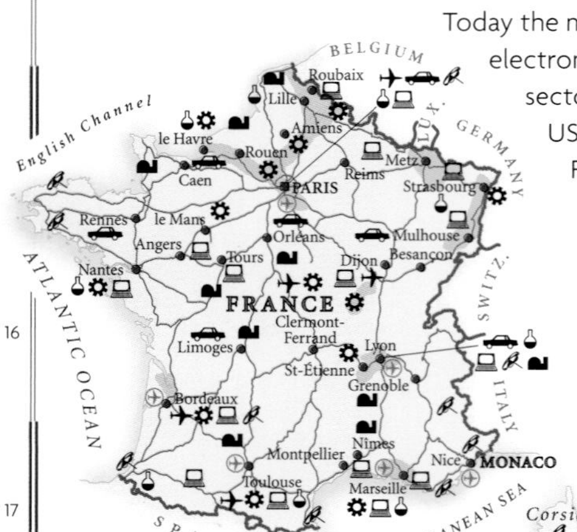

Major industry and infrastructure

- ✈ aerospace industry
- 🚗 car manufacture
- ⚗ chemicals
- ⚙ engineering
- 💻 hi-tech industry
- 🔋 nuclear power
- 🏖 tourism

- ■ capital cities
- • major towns
- ✈ international airports
- — major roads
- ▨ major industrial areas

The transport network

🛣	555,473 miles (894,050 km)	🛣	7305 miles (11,758 km)
🚆	10,399 miles (16,737 km)	🚇	1159 miles (1863 km)

The French TGV (Train à Grande Vitesse) leads the world in high-speed train technology, and provides a service which can be faster, door-to-door, than air travel.

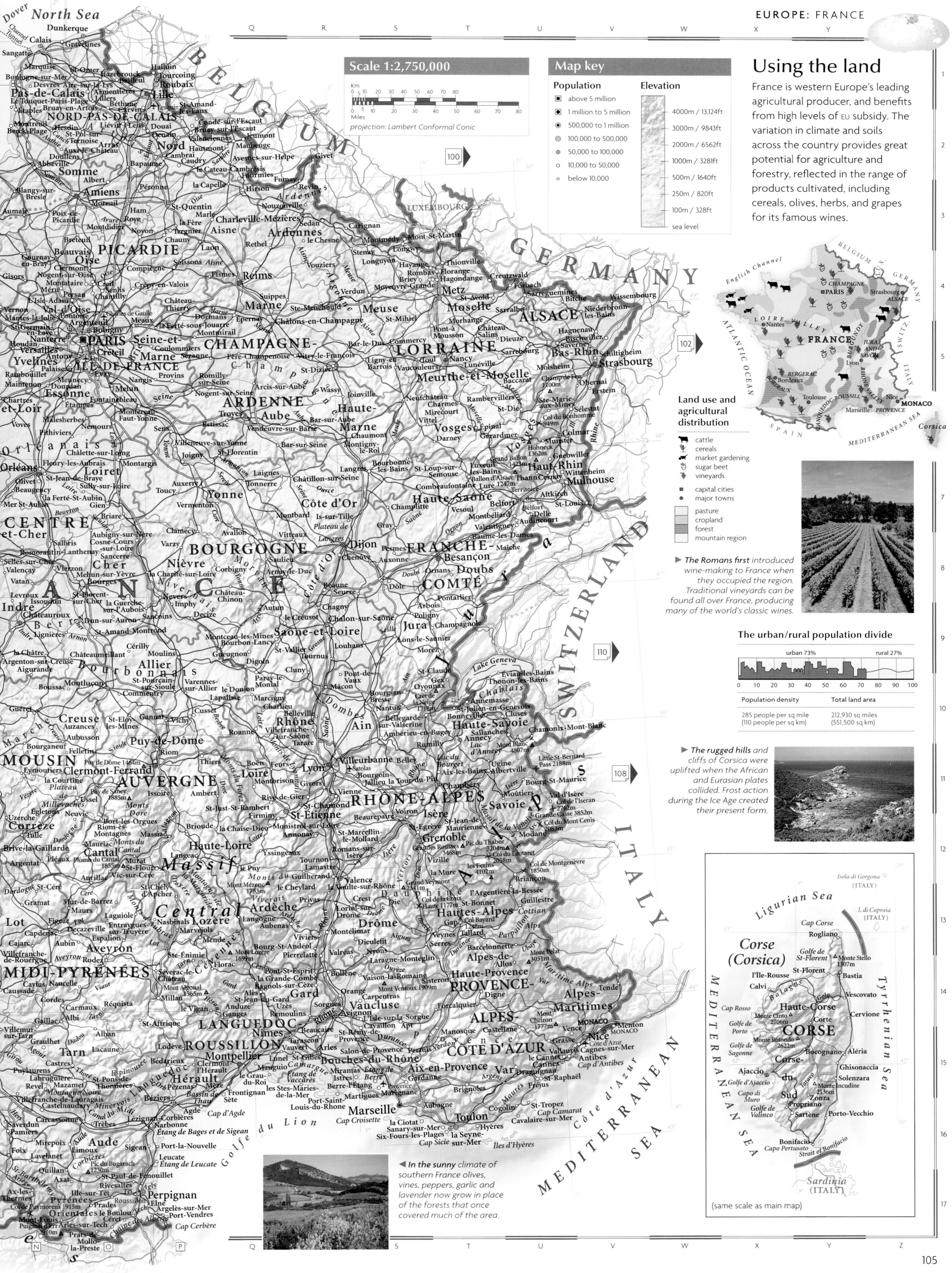

Using the land

France is western Europe's leading agricultural producer, and benefits from high levels of EU subsidy. The variation in climate and soils across the country provides great potential for agriculture and forestry, reflected in the range of products cultivated, including cereals, olives, herbs, and grapes for its famous wines.

Scale 1:2,750,000

projection: Lambert Conformal Conic

Map key

Population
- above 5 million
- 1 million to 5 million
- 500,000 to 1 million
- 100,000 to 500,000
- 50,000 to 100,000
- 10,000 to 50,000
- below 10,000

Elevation
- 4000m / 13,124ft
- 3000m / 9843ft
- 2000m / 6562ft
- 1000m / 3281ft
- 500m / 1640ft
- 250m / 820ft
- 100m / 328ft
- sea level

Land use and agricultural distribution

- cattle
- cereals
- market gardening
- sugar beet
- vineyards
- capital cities
- major towns
- pasture
- cropland
- forest
- mountain region

▶ **The Romans first** introduced wine-making to France when they occupied the region. Traditional vineyards can be found all over France, producing many of the world's classic wines.

The urban/rural population divide

urban 73%   rural 27%

0 10 20 30 40 50 60 70 80 90 100

Population density	Total land area
285 people per sq mile (110 people per sq km)	212,930 sq miles (551,500 sq km)

▶ **The rugged hills** and cliffs of Corsica were uplifted when the African and Eurasian plates collided. Frost action during the Ice Age created their present form.

◀ **In the sunny** climate of southern France olives, vines, peppers, garlic and lavender now grow in place of the forests that once covered much of the area.

Corse (Corsica)

(same scale as main map)

The Iberian peninsula

ANDORRA, GIBRALTAR, PORTUGAL,
SPAIN (Azores, Canary Islands, Madeira on p.66)

The Iberian peninsula is separated from the rest of
Europe by the Pyrenees, and at its most southerly
point is only 5 miles (8 km) from North Africa.
The location of Iberia has been central to its
diverse history. The Greeks, Carthaginians, Romans,
Visigoths and most recently the Moors, invaded
Iberia at various times. For much of the 20th century,
both Spain and Portugal were governed by right-wing
dictators. Since the establishment of democratic governments in the
mid-1970s, modernization has been rapid and both countries are now
among the most popular of European holiday destinations.

Using the land

The principal crops grown in Iberia are
cereals, especially wheat and barley. Both
countries are major wine producers, most
notably of Rioja, sherry and port. Sheep
are kept throughout the region, and citrus
fruits thrive on the Mediterranean coast.
The successful forest industry in Iberia
produces 84% of the world's cork.

▲ The steep, terraced slopes of the
Douro Valley in northern Portugal,
are used to cultivate vines. The
grapes harvested produce Portugal's
famous port wine.

The urban/rural population divide

urban 68%   rural 32%

0 10 20 30 40 50 60 70 80 90 100

Population density	Total land area
215 people per sq mile (83 people per sq km)	230,569 sq miles (597,170 sq km)

Land use and agricultural distribution

- sheep
- cereals
- citrus fruit
- olives
- vineyards
- cork
- capital cities
- major towns
- pasture
- cropland
- forest
- mountain region

Transport and industry

Since the 1970s, the economies of Spain and Portugal
have expanded and diversified. In both countries,
tourism has outstripped agriculture in economic
importance. Spain's resource base is varied, including
coal, iron and the world's largest reserves of mercury.
Portugal is a leading producer of tungsten ore.

Major industry and infrastructure

- car manufacture
- chemicals
- engineering
- fish processing
- mining
- textiles
- tourism
- capital cities
- major towns
- international airports
- major roads
- major industrial areas

The transport network

241,720 miles (388,990 km)	1552 miles (2529 km)
11,793 miles (18,979 km)	1159 miles (1865 km)

Radiating from Madrid, the road network in
Spain dates from the 18th century, but now
includes many motorways. Portugal's road
system has been completely modernized in
recent years.

◄ The eroded cliffs of the
Algarve in southern Portugal
were carved by Atlantic waves.
The numerous rocky bays and
beaches, and the region's
pleasant climate, have made it
a popular tourist destination.

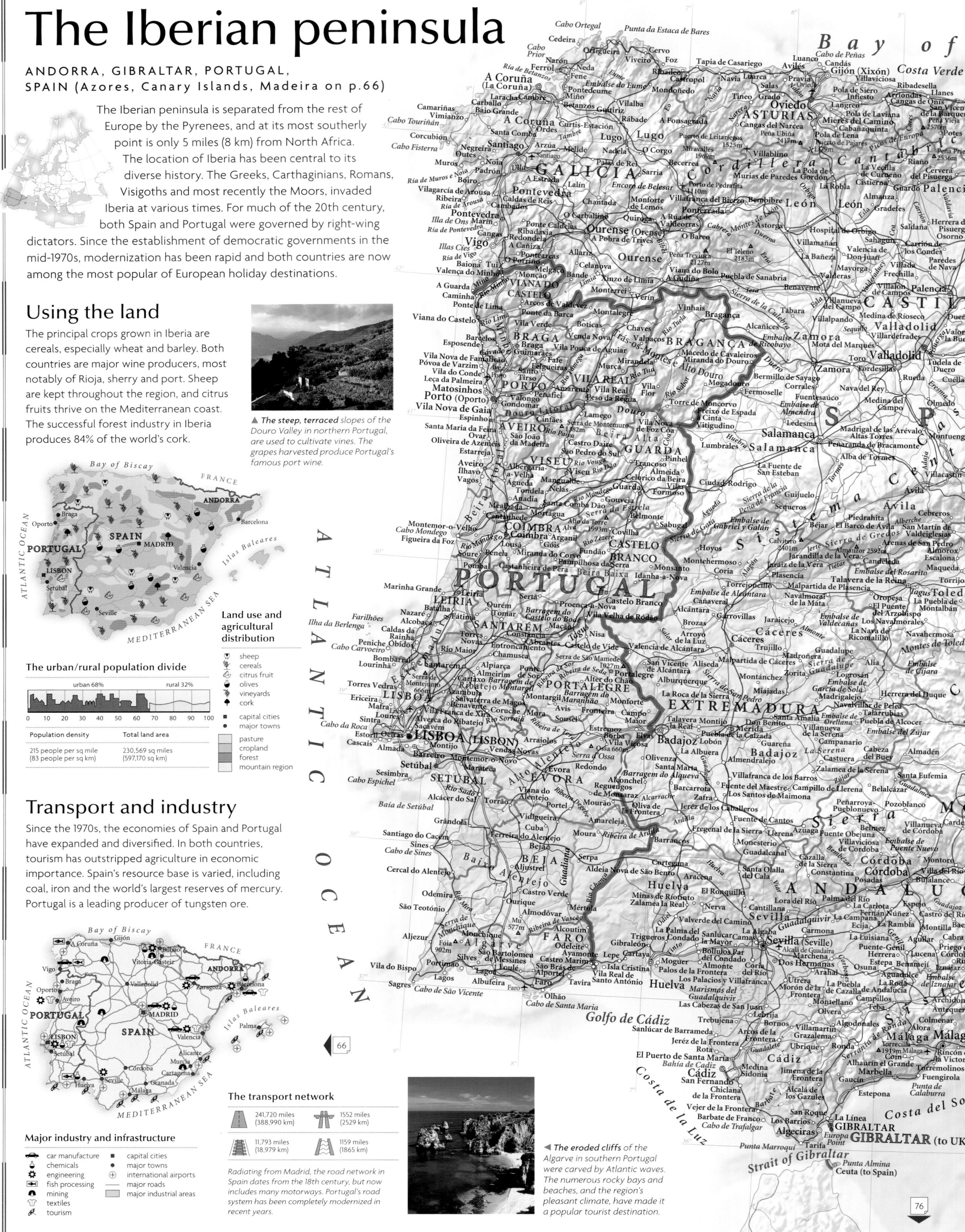

▶ The climate in northwestern Spain is milder in both summer and winter than in the rest of the country, creating a verdant environment, more commonly associated with northwestern Europe.

Map key

Population

- ◉ 1 million to 5 million
- ◉ 500,000 to 1 million
- ◉ 100,000 to 500,000
- ⊕ 50,000 to 100,000
- ⊙ 10,000 to 50,000
- ○ below 10,000

Elevation

- 3000m / 9843ft
- 2000m / 6562ft
- 1000m / 3281ft
- 500m / 1640ft
- 250m / 820ft
- 100m / 328ft
- sea level

Scale 1:2,750,000

Km
0 5 10 20 30 40 50 60 70 80

Miles
0 5 10 20 30 40 50 60 70 80

projection: Lambert Conformal Conic

The landscape

A vast plateau, the Meseta dominates the centre of the peninsula, enclosed by the Cordillera Cantábrica to the north and the Sierra Morena to the south. It is drained by three major rivers, the Douro/Duero, the Tagus, and the Guadalquivir. The peninsula experiences great variations in climate and rainfall, both regionally and locally.

▲ The Pyrenees form Iberia's northeastern boundary, running for 270 miles (440 km), dividing the peninsula from the rest of Europe.

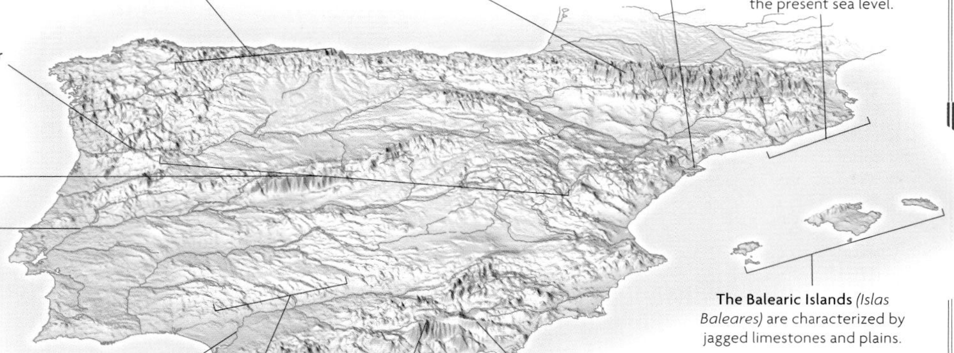

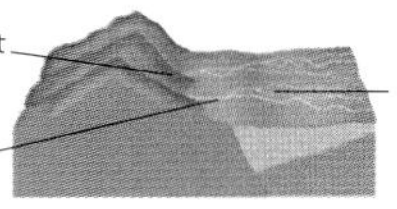

The Ebro river has formed the peninsula's largest delta. Recently, sediment flows have been seriously disturbed by nearby reservoirs.

On the northeastern coast sea level changes are evident from wave-cut beaches which rise up to 200 ft (60 m) above the present sea level.

Cordillera Cantábrica

Douro/Duero river

The Meseta plateau averages 1970 ft (600 m) in height and is now largely dry and treeless.

Tagus River

The Balearic Islands (Islas Baleares) are characterized by jagged limestones and plains.

Mountain front
Weathered material
Pediment

▲ Pediments are characteristic of semi-arid lands across Iberia. A pediment is a flat, low-lying, eroded platform, cut into the bedrock. Weathered material is transported by streams and deposited in broad fan shapes on the pediment.

The Guadalquivir river brings vital irrigation water to the plains, and like many of Iberia's rivers, is prone to flooding.

Sierra Morena

The Sierra Nevada in southern Spain contain Iberia's highest peak, Mulhacén, which rises 11,418 ft (3481 m).

▶ In the Sierra de los Filabres deforestation and overgrazing, which cause soil erosion, have created semi-desert badlands.

The Italian peninsula

ITALY, SAN MARINO, VATICAN CITY

The Italian peninsula is a land of great contrasts. Until unification in 1861, Italy was a collection of independent states, whose competitiveness during the Renaissance resulted in the architectural and artistic magnificence of cities such as Rome, Florence and Venice. The majority of Italy's population and economic activity is concentrated in the north, centred on the sophisticated industrial city of Milan. Southern Italy, the *Mezzogiorno*, has a harsh and difficult terrain, and remains far less developed than the north. Attempts to attract industry and investment in the south are frequently deterred by the entrenched network of organized crime and corruption.

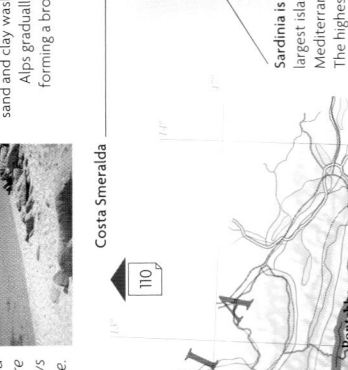

The landscape

The mainly mountainous and hilly Italian peninsula took its present form following a collision between the African and Eurasian tectonic plates. The Alps in the northwest rise to a high point of 15,772 ft (4807 m) at Mont Blanc (*Monte Bianco*) on the French border, while the Apennines (*Appennino*) form a rugged backbone, running along the entire length of the country.

▲ *The island of Sardinia is an ancient land mass; an uplifted section of very old igneous rocks. Its rugged mountainous regions provide pasture for sheep and goats, while its valleys support some agriculture.*

Mont Blanc
(*Monte Bianco*)

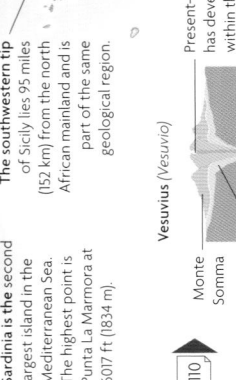

▲ *The Dolomites* (Alpi Dolomitiche) are formed of thick limestones, overlying weaker marine strata. They have distinctive serrated peaks and many massive landslides occur.

The distinctive square shape of the Gulf of Taranto (*Golfo di Taranto*) was defined by numerous block faults. Earthquakes are common in this region.

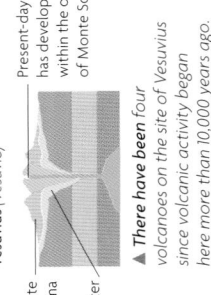

The Apennines (*Appennino*) are the source of most of Italy's rivers. They run 823 miles (1324 km) down the length of the peninsula.

The Po Valley once formed part of the Adriatic Sea. Sediments of gravel, sand and clay washed down from the Alps gradually filling the bay and forming a broad, cultivable plain.

Vesuvius (*Vesuvio*)

The Pontine Marshes (*Agro Pontino*) are bounded by low sand hills which prevent natural drainage.

Costa Smeralda

The Strait of Messina (*Stretto di Messina*) is between 2 and 12 miles (3–19 km) wide, and is a rich fishing ground.

Sicily is the largest island in the Mediterranean at 9926 sq miles (25,708 sq km).

The southwestern tip of Sicily lies 95 miles (152 km) from the north African mainland and is part of the same geological region.

Sardinia is the second largest island in the Mediterranean Sea. The highest point is Punta La Marmora at 6017 ft (1834 m).

Present-day crater has developed within the old crater of Monte Somma.

▲ *There have been four volcanoes on the site of Vesuvius since volcanic activity began here more than 10,000 years ago.*

Vesuvius (*Vesuvio*)

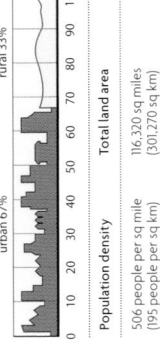
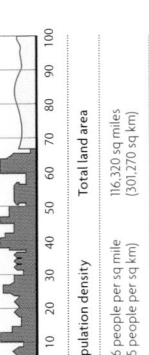

Monte Somma

Old crater

Using the land

Italy produces 95% of its own food. The best farming land is in the Po Valley in northern Italy, where soft wheat and rice are grown. Irrigation is essential to agriculture in much of the south. Italy is a major producer and exporter of citrus fruits, olives, tomatoes and wine.

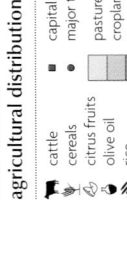

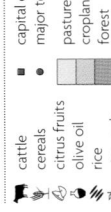
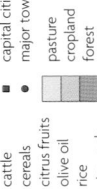

SLOVENIA
CROATIA
AUSTRIA
SWITZERLAND
SAN MARINO
ROME
ITALY
FRANCE
Milan
Bologna
Florence
Turin
Naples
Palermo
Sicily
Catania
Bari
Sardinia
Sassari
Cagliari
Adriatic Sea
Ionian Sea
Tyrrhenian Sea
MEDITERRANEAN SEA

Land use and agricultural distribution

- cattle
- cereals
- citrus fruits
- olive oil
- rice
- vineyards
- capital cities
- major towns
- pasture
- cropland
- forest
- mountain region

The urban/rural population divide

urban 67%   rural 33%

Population density	Total land area
506 people per sq mile (195 people per sq km)	116,320 sq miles (301,270 sq km)

Scale 1:2,500,000

projection Lambert Conformal Conic

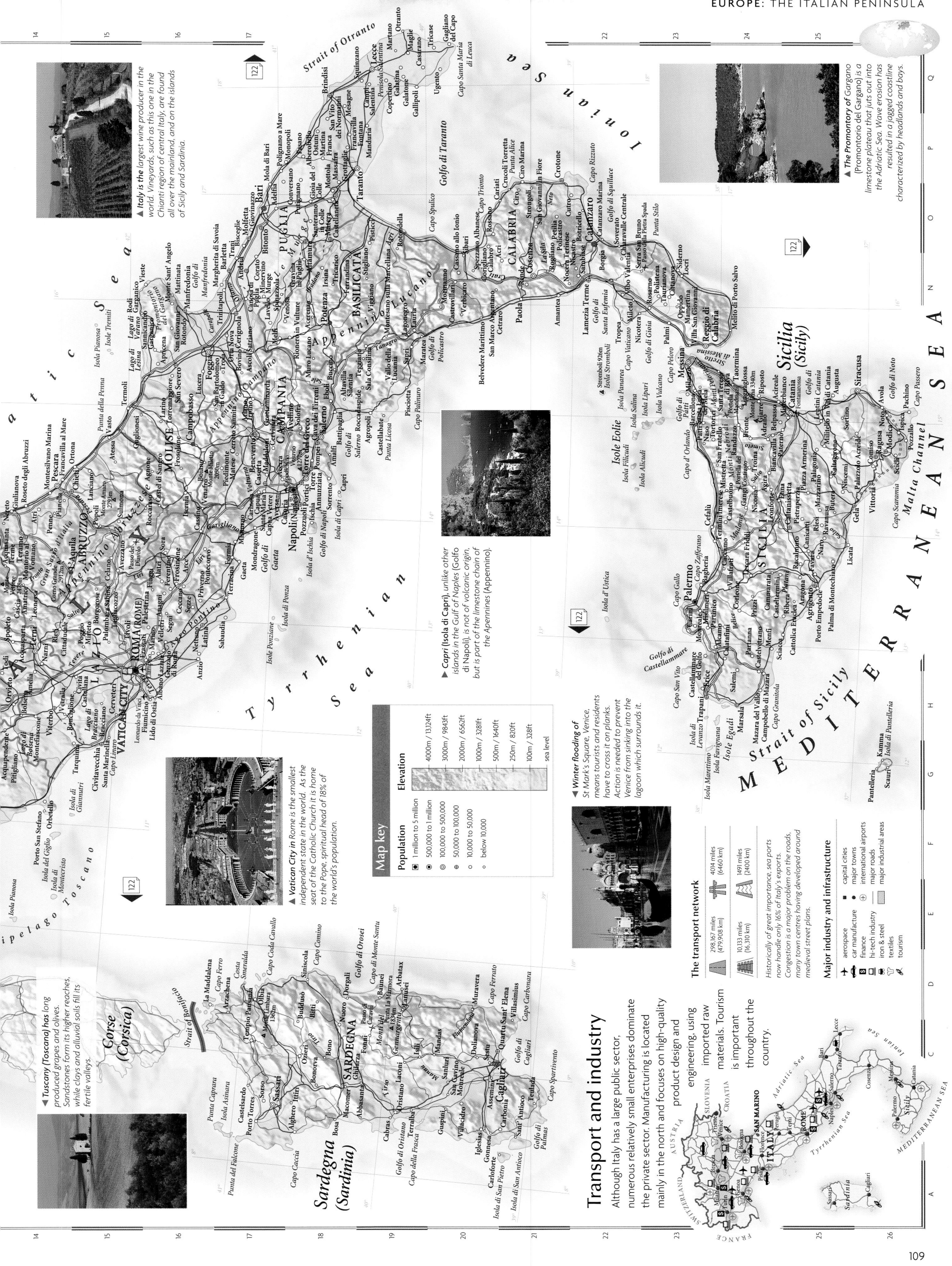

▲ **Italy is the** largest wine producer in the world. Vineyards, such as this one in the Chianti region of central Italy, are found all over the mainland, and on the islands of Sicily and Sardinia.

▲ **The Promontory of Gargano** (Promontorio del Gargano) is a limestone plateau that juts out into the Adriatic Sea. Wave erosion has resulted in a jagged coastline characterized by headlands and bays.

▲ **Capri** (Isola di Capri), unlike other islands in the Gulf of Naples (Golfo di Napoli), is not of volcanic origin, but is part of the limestone chain of the Apennines (Appennino).

▼ **Winter flooding of** St Mark's Square, Venice, means tourists and residents have to cross it on planks. Action is needed to prevent Venice from sinking into the lagoon which surrounds it.

▲ **Vatican City in Rome** is the smallest independent state in the world. As the home to the Pope, spiritual head of 18% of the world's population, it is the seat of the Catholic Church.

▼ **Tuscany** (Toscana) has long produced grapes and olives. Sandstones form its higher reaches, while clays and alluvial soils fill its fertile valleys.

Map key

Population
- ◉ 1 million to 5 million
- ◎ 500,000 to 1 million
- ⊙ 100,000 to 500,000
- ⊚ 50,000 to 100,000
- ○ 10,000 to 50,000
- ○ below 10,000

Elevation
- 4000m / 13,124ft
- 3000m / 9843ft
- 2000m / 6562ft
- 1000m / 3281ft
- 500m / 1640ft
- 250m / 820ft
- 100m / 328ft
- sea level

The transport network

- 298,167 miles (479,908 km)
- 4014 miles (6460 km)
- 10,133 miles (16,310 km)
- 1491 miles (2400 km)

Historically of great importance, sea ports now handle only 16% of Italy's exports. Congestion is a major problem on the roads, many town centres having developed around medieval street plans.

Major industry and infrastructure

- ✈ aerospace
- 🚗 car manufacture
- Ⓢ finance
- hi-tech industry
- iron & steel
- textiles
- tourism
- ● capital cities
- ○ major towns
- ✈ international airports
- — major roads
- ▨ major industrial areas

Transport and industry

Although Italy has a large public sector, numerous relatively small enterprises dominate the private sector. Manufacturing is located mainly in the north and focuses on high-quality product design and engineering, using imported raw materials. Tourism is important throughout the country.

The Alpine states

AUSTRIA, LIECHTENSTEIN, SLOVENIA, SWITZERLAND

The Alpine countries of Austria, Switzerland, Liechtenstein and Slovenia form a narrow strip across western Europe's geographical core, lying on the main north–south trading routes across the Alps. Switzerland, politically neutral since 1815, is an important international meeting place and houses one of the headquarters of the United Nations, although it only became a member in 2002. Austria, once at the heart of the great Habsburg Empire has been a fully independent nation since 1955, and maintains a deserved reputation as an international centre of culture. Slovenia declared independence from the former Yugoslavia in 1991 and despite initial economic hardship, is now starting to achieve the prosperity enjoyed by its Alpine neighbours.

Using the land

The Alpine region's mountainous terrain discourages cultivation over much of the land area. The primary agricultural activity is the raising of dairy and beef cattle on the pasture land of the lower mountain slopes. Austria is self-supporting in grains, and crops such as wheat, barley and grapes are grown on the east Austrian lowlands. Woodlands are more prevalent in the eastern Alps; both Austria and Slovenia have large tracts of forest.

Land use and agricultural distribution

- cattle
- pigs
- cereals
- vineyards
- capital cities
- major towns
- pasture
- cropland
- forest
- mountain region

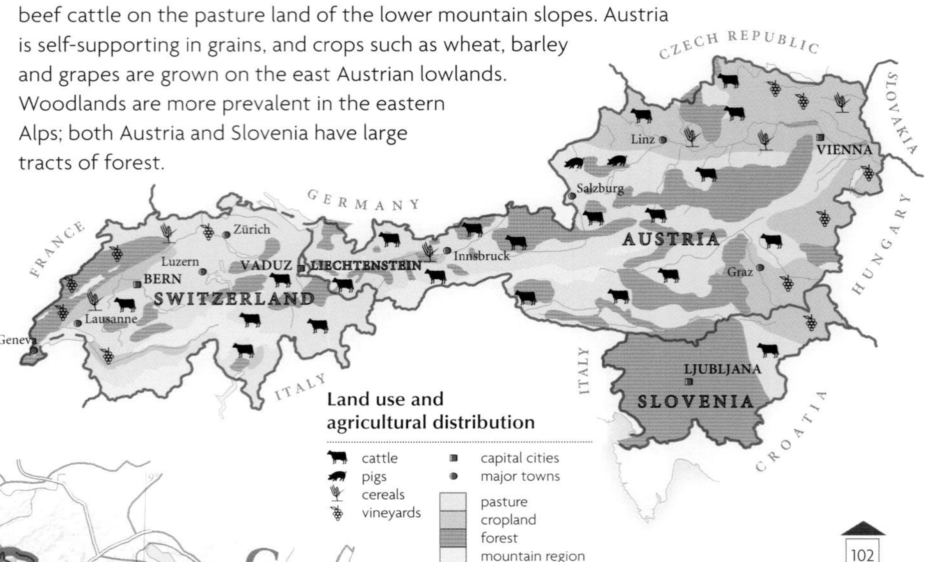

◀ *The Matterhorn, on* the Swiss-Italian border, is one of the highest mountains in the Alps, at 14,692 ft (4478 m). The term 'horn' refers to its distinctive peak, formed by three glaciers eroding hollows, known as cirques, in each of its sides.

The landscape

The Alps occupy three-fifths of Switzerland, most of southern Austria and the northwest of Slovenia. They were formed by the collision of the African and Eurasian tectonic plates, which began 65 million years ago. Their complex geology is reflected in the differing heights and rock types of the various ranges. The Rhine flows along Liechtenstein's border with Switzerland, creating a broad flood plain in the north and west of Liechtenstein. In the far northeast and east are a number of lowland regions, including the Vienna Basin, Burgenland and the plain of the Danube. Slovenia's major rivers flow across the lower eastern regions; in the west, the rivers flow largely underground through the limestone Karst region.

Original height after uplift and folding
Folded strata are overturned creating a *nappe*
Eurasian Plate
Present-day height of Alps
African Plate

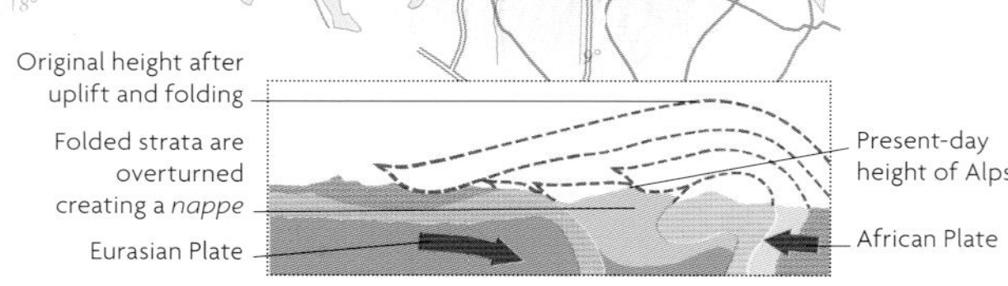

▲ *The convergence of* the African and Eurasian plates compressed and folded huge masses of rock strata. As the plates continued to move together, the folded strata were overturned, creating complex nappes. Much of the rock strata has since been eroded, resulting in the current topography of the Alps.

▲ *Constricted as it* cuts through ridges in the Alps, the Danube meanders across the lowlands, where uplift combined with river erosion has deepened meanders.

The Vienna Basin lies mainly below 390 ft (120 m). It gradually subsided and filled with sediment as the Alps were uplifted.

Neusiedler See straddles the border of Austria and Hungary; the area around it provides some of the best wine-growing land in Austria.

The Austrian Alps comprise three distinct mountain ranges, separated by deep trenches. The northern and southern ranges are rugged limestones, while the Tauern range is formed of crystalline rocks.

The mountains of the Jura form a natural border between Switzerland and France. Their marine limestones date from over 200 million years ago. When the Alps were formed the Jura were folded into a series of parallel ridges and troughs.

Tectonic activity has resulted in dramatic changes in land height over very short distances. Lake Geneva, lying at 1221 ft (372 m) is only 43 miles (70 km) away from the 15,772 ft (4807 m) peak of Mont Blanc, on the France–Italy border.

The Bernese Alps (*Berner Alpen*) contain the Aletsch, which at 15 miles (24 km) is the longest Alpine glacier.

The Rhine, like other major Alpine rivers, follows a broad, flat trough between the mountains. Along part of its course, the Rhine forms the boundary between Switzerland and Liechtenstein.

The first road through the Brenner Pass was built in 1772, although it has been used as a mountain route since Roman times. It is the lowest of the main Alpine passes at 4298 ft (1374 m).

▶ *The deep, blue lakes of* the Karst region are part of a drainage network which runs largely underground through this limestone area.

Karst region

The limestone cave system at Postojna extends for more than 10 miles (16 km) and includes caverns reaching 125 ft (40 m) in height and width.

The Tauern range in the central Austrian Alps contains the highest mountain in Austria, the towering Grossglockner, rising 12,461 ft (3798 m).

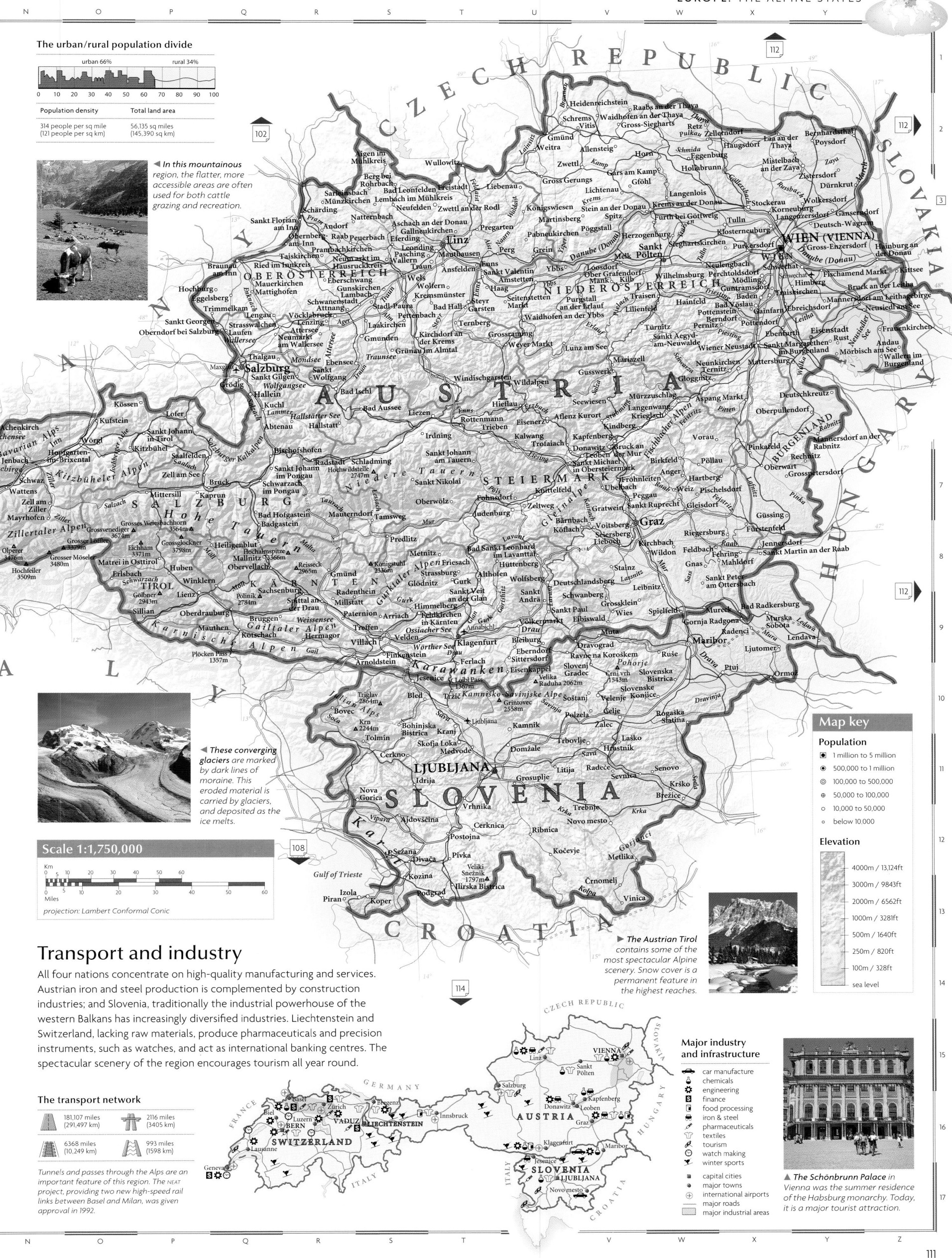

The urban/rural population divide

urban 66%   rural 34%

0 10 20 30 40 50 60 70 80 90 100

Population density	Total land area
314 people per sq mile (121 people per sq km)	56,135 sq miles (145,390 sq km)

◀ *In this mountainous region, the flatter, more accessible areas are often used for both cattle grazing and recreation.*

◀ *These converging glaciers are marked by dark lines of moraine. This eroded material is carried by glaciers, and deposited as the ice melts.*

Scale 1:1,750,000

Km
0 10 20 30 40 50 60

Miles
0 10 20 30 40 50 60

projection: Lambert Conformal Conic

Transport and industry

All four nations concentrate on high-quality manufacturing and services. Austrian iron and steel production is complemented by construction industries; and Slovenia, traditionally the industrial powerhouse of the western Balkans has increasingly diversified industries. Liechtenstein and Switzerland, lacking raw materials, produce pharmaceuticals and precision instruments, such as watches, and act as international banking centres. The spectacular scenery of the region encourages tourism all year round.

The transport network

181,107 miles (291,497 km)		2116 miles (3405 km)	
6368 miles (10,249 km)		993 miles (1598 km)	

Tunnels and passes through the Alps are an important feature of this region. The NEAT project, providing two new high-speed rail links between Basel and Milan, was given approval in 1992.

▶ *The Austrian Tirol contains some of the most spectacular Alpine scenery. Snow cover is a permanent feature in the highest reaches.*

Map key

Population
- 1 million to 5 million
- 500,000 to 1 million
- 100,000 to 500,000
- 50,000 to 100,000
- 10,000 to 50,000
- below 10,000

Elevation
- 4000m / 13,124ft
- 3000m / 9843ft
- 2000m / 6562ft
- 1000m / 3281ft
- 500m / 1640ft
- 250m / 820ft
- 100m / 328ft
- sea level

Major industry and infrastructure

- car manufacture
- chemicals
- engineering
- finance
- food processing
- iron & steel
- pharmaceuticals
- textiles
- tourism
- watch making
- winter sports
- capital cities
- major towns
- international airports
- major roads
- major industrial areas

▲ *The Schönbrunn Palace in Vienna was the summer residence of the Habsburg monarchy. Today, it is a major tourist attraction.*

Central Europe

CZECH REPUBLIC, HUNGARY, POLAND, SLOVAKIA

When Slovakia and the Czech Republic became separate countries in 1993, they joined Hungary and Poland in a new role as independent nation states, following centuries of shifting boundaries and imperial strife. This turbulent history bequeathed the region a rich cultural heritage, shared through the works of its many great writers and composers, and celebrated in the vibrant historic capitals of Prague, Budapest and Warsaw. Having shaken off years of Soviet domination in 1989, these states are confronting the challenge of winning commercial investment to modernize outmoded industries as they integrate their economies with those of the European Union.

The landscape

The forested Carpathian Mountains, uplifted with the Alps, lie southeast of the older Bohemian Massif, which contains the Sudeten and Krusné Hory (Erzgebirge) ranges. They divide the fertile plains of the Danube to the south and the Vistula (Wisła), which flows north across vast expanses of glacial deposits into the Baltic Sea.

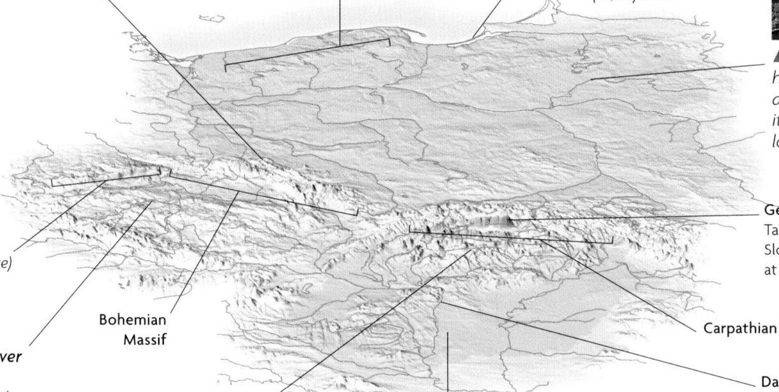

Transport and industry

Heavy industry has dominated post-war life in Central Europe. Poland has large coal reserves, having inherited the Silesian coalfield from Germany after the Second World War, allowing the export of large quantities of coal, along with other minerals. Hungary specializes in consumer goods and services, while Slovakia's industrial base is still relatively small. The Czech Republic's traditional glassworks and breweries bring some stability to its precarious Soviet-built manufacturing sector.

Hot mineral springs occur where geothermally heated water wells up through faults and fractures in the rocks of the Sudeten Mountains.

Pomerania is a sandy coastal region of glacially-formed lakes stretching west from the Vistula (Wisła).

Longshore currents moving east along the Baltic coast have built a 40 mile (65 km) spit composed of material from the Vistula (Wisła) river.

▲ **The Biebrza river** has left meanders and oxbow lakes as it flows across low-lying ground.

Gerlachovsky stit, in the Tatra Mountains, is Slovakia's highest mountain, at 8711ft (2655 m).

Carpathian Mountains

Danube river

Slip-off slope

Bluff

Direction of flow

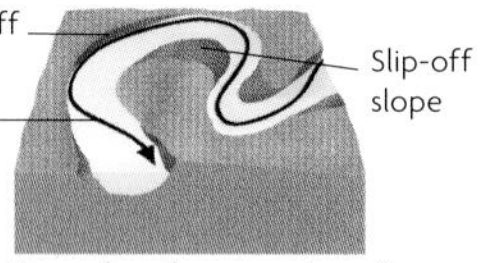

▲ **Meanders form as rivers flow** across plains at a low gradient. A steep cliff or bluff, forms on the outside curve and a gentler slip-off slope on the inside bend.

The Great Hungarian Plain formed by the flood plain of the Danube is a mixture of steppe and cultivated land, covering nearly half of Hungary's total area.

The Slovak Ore Mountains (Slovenské Rudohorie) are noted for their mineral resources, including high-grade iron ore.

Bohemian Massif

Krusné Hory (Erzgebirge)

▲ **The Berounka river** cuts through the precipitous wooded landscape of the Bohemian Massif, banked by a broad flood plain.

Major industry and infrastructure

- car manufacture
- chemicals
- engineering
- food processing
- mining
- shipbuilding
- tourism
- capital cities
- major towns
- international airports
- major roads
- major industrial areas

The transport network

| 213,997 miles (344,600 km) | 817 miles (315 km) |
| 27,479 miles (44,249 km) | 3784 miles (6094 km) |

The huge growth of tourism and business has prompted major investment in the transport infrastructure, with new road-building schemes within and between the main cities of the region.

▲ **Budapest, the capital** of Hungary, straddles the Danube. It comprises the historic towns of Buda, on the west bank, and Pest, which contains the Parliament Building, seen here on the far bank.

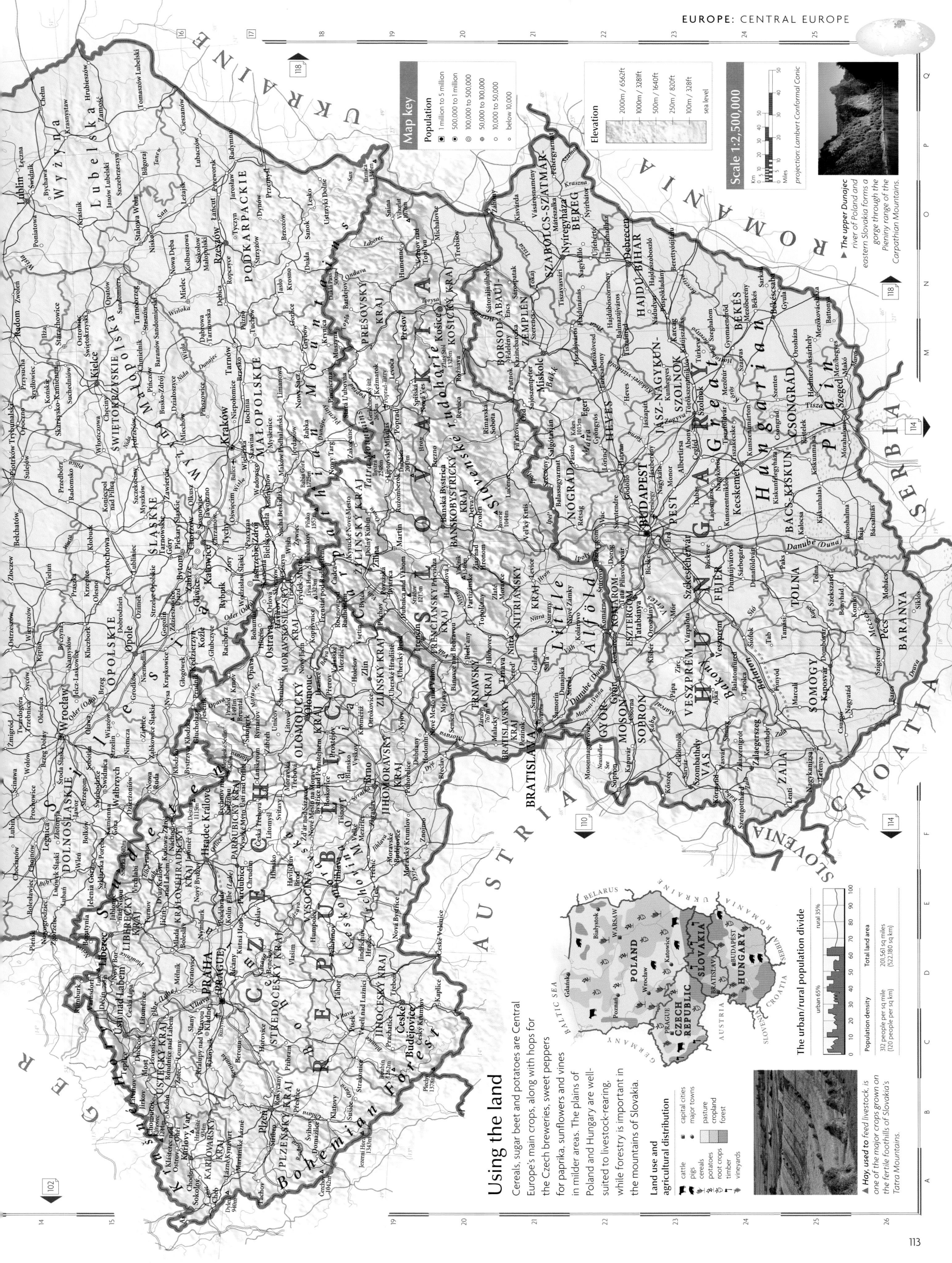

Map key

Population

- ◉ 1 million to 5 million
- ◉ 500,000 to 1 million
- ⊕ 100,000 to 500,000
- ⊕ 50,000 to 100,000
- ○ 10,000 to 50,000
- ○ below 10,000

Elevation

- 2000m / 6562ft
- 1000m / 3281ft
- 500m / 1640ft
- 250m / 820ft
- 100m / 328ft
- sea level

Scale 1:2,500,000

projection: Lambert Conformal Conic

▲ The upper Dunajec river of Poland and eastern Slovakia forms a gorge range through the Pieniny range of the Carpathian Mountains.

▲ The upper Dunajec river of Poland and eastern Slovakia forms a gorge range through the Pieniny range of the Carpathian Mountains.

Using the land

Cereals, sugar beet and potatoes are Central Europe's main crops, along with hops for the Czech breweries, sweet peppers for paprika, sunflowers and vines in milder areas. The plains of Poland and Hungary are well-suited to livestock-rearing, while forestry is important in the mountains of Slovakia.

Land use and agricultural distribution

- ■ capital cities
- • major towns
- pasture
- cropland
- forest

cattle
pigs
cereals
potatoes
root crops
timber
vineyards

The urban/rural population divide

urban 65%   rural 35%

Population density
312 people per sq mile
(120 people per sq km)

Total land area
201,561 sq miles
(522,180 sq km)

▲ Hay, used to feed livestock, is one of the major crops grown on the fertile foothills of Slovakia's Tatra Mountains.

Southeast Europe

ALBANIA, BOSNIA & HERZEGOVINA, CROATIA, MACEDONIA, MONTENEGRO, SERBIA

For 46 years the federation of Yugoslavia held together the most diverse ethnic region in Europe, along the picturesque mountain hinterland of the Dalmatian coast. Economic collapse resulted in internal tensions. In the early 1990s, civil war broke out in both Croatia and Bosnia as the ethnic populations struggled to establish their own exclusive territories. Peace was only restored by the UN after NATO launched air strikes in 1995. Montenegro voted to split from Serbia in 2006 while the future of the province of Kosovo, whose attempts to gain autonomy in 1998 were crushed by the Serbian government, is still unresolved. Neighbouring Albania is slowly improving its fragile economy but remains one of Europe's poorest nations.

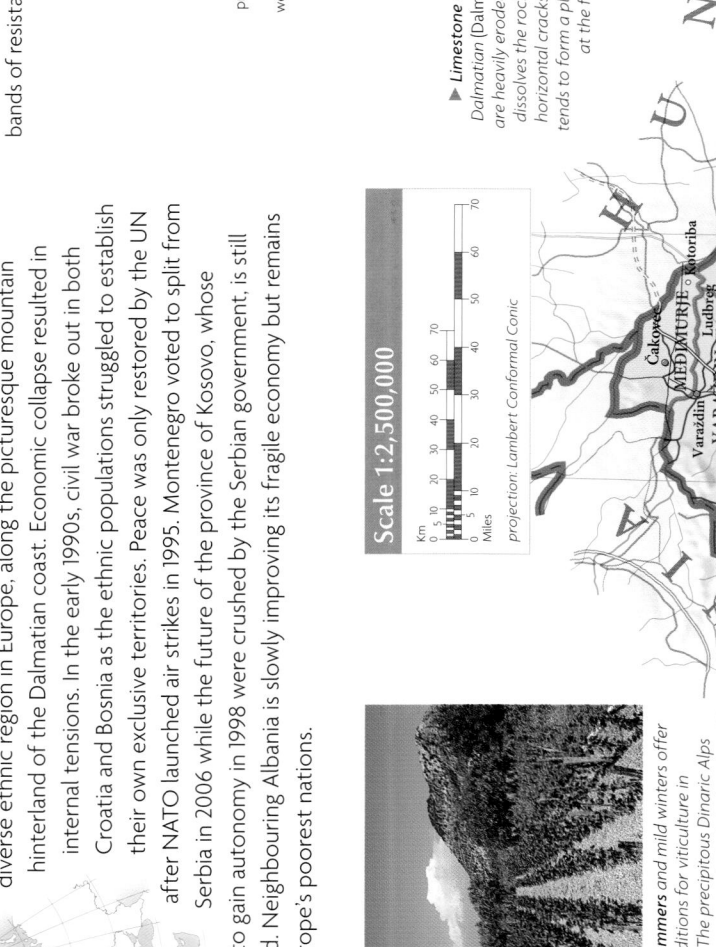

▲ *Hot, dry summers and mild winters offer excellent conditions for viticulture in Montenegro. The precipitous Dinaric Alps have kept this region relatively isolated for centuries.*

The landscape

The Tisza, Sava and Drava rivers drain the broad northern lowland, meeting the Danube after it crosses the Hungarian border. In the west, the Dinaric Alps divide the Adriatic Sea from the interior. Mainland valleys and elongated islands run parallel to the steep Dalmatian (*Dalmacija*) coastline, following alternating bands of resistant limestone.

Poljes in the Kosovo region

Sheer limestone walls enclose all sides

Flat *polje* floor

Underground drainage along joints in the rock

Spring at foot of cliff

Rain and underground water dissolve limestone along massive vertical joints (cracks). This creates poljes: depressions several miles across with steep walls and broad, flat floors.

At Iron Gate (*Derdap*), on the border with Romania, the Danube narrows and cuts through foothills of the Balkan and Carpathian mountains, forming the deepest gorge in Europe.

A major earthquake at Skopje, Macedonia, in 1963 killed 1000 people. The whole region lies on an active crustal plate margin.

At least 70% of the fresh water in the western Balkans drains eastwards into the Black Sea, mostly via the Danube (*Dunov*).

The river flood plains of the Pannonian Basin are flanked by terraces of gravel and wind-blown glacial deposits known as loess.

Tisza river

Drava river

Sava river

A series of river valleys breaking through the Dinaric Alps from the lowlands of western Albania, give access to the interior.

The elongated islands, promontories and straits of the Dalmatian (*Dalmacija*) coast were formed as the Adriatic Sea rose to flood valleys running parallel to the shore.

Lake Ohrid

▲ *Lake Ohrid borders Albania and Macedonia. Ohrid is the deepest lake in the western Balkans, reaching depths of 938 ft (286 m).*

Dalmatian (*Dalmacijo*) coast

▲ *Limestone cliffs along the Dalmatian (*Dalmacija*) shoreline are heavily eroded, as salt water dissolves the rock along existing horizontal cracks, or joints. This tends to form a platform of rock at the foot of the cliff.*

Scale 1:2,500,000

projection: Lambert Conformal Conic

Map key

Population

- ⊙ 1 million to 5 million
- ◉ 500,000 to 1 million
- ⊚ 100,000 to 500,000
- ⊙ 50,000 to 100,000
- ○ 10,000 to 50,000
- ○ below 10,000

Elevation

2000m / 6562ft
1000m / 3281ft
500m / 1640ft
250m / 820ft
100m / 328ft
sea level

▲ *The Tara river is one of Montenegro's major rivers. It flows into the Danube via the Drina and Sava rivers. Along its course the Tara has eroded spectacular gorges up to 3280 ft (1000 m) deep.*

▲ *The ancient Croatian port of Dubrovnik was one of the former Yugoslavia's most popular tourist resorts and an important point of access to the sea along the Dalmatian (Dalmacija) coast. Shelling of the old city by Serb forces in 1991 provoked international condemnation.*

The transport network

🚗	46,996 miles (75,642 km)
🚂	5413 miles (8713 km)
✈	685 miles (1103 km)
🚢	879 miles (1415 km)

The war resulted in the destruction or disintegration of infrastructure for transport, communications and power supply, though this is now in the process of recovery.

▲ *Industrial processing plants were established throughout Albania by the Hoxha regime, which collapsed in 1992. They remain incongruous among the villages of one of Europe's most conservative rural societies.*

Land use and agricultural distribution

- 🐖 pigs
- 🐑 sheep
- 🌾 cereals
- 🍎 fruit
- 🫒 olives
- sugar beet
- timber
- tobacco
- vineyards

- ● capital cities
- ● major towns
- pasture
- cropland
- forest
- mountain region

The urban/rural population divide

urban 51%   rural 49%

Population density
240 people per sq mile
(93 people per sq km)

Total land area
95,038 sq miles
(246,278 sq km)

▼ *Sweet red peppers are dried in the sun, ready to make paprika. Macedonia's economy is mainly agricultural and its fertile soils support a broad range of crops.*

Major industry and infrastructure

- △ aluminium refining
- car manufacture
- chemicals
- engineering
- food processing
- hydro-electric power
- mining
- shipbuilding
- textiles
- timber processing
- ● capital cities
- ● major towns
- ✈ international airports
- major roads

Transport and industry

Processing industries based on the region's wealth of mineral reserves predominate in Albania and Macedonia. In other regions, industrial plants have been commandeered, if not destroyed in the war and mineral extraction has severely declined. The fast-flowing rivers found throughout the Dinaric Alps are exploited to generate hydro-electric power.

▲ *The historic centre of Mostar in southern Bosnia, with its famous 16th-century Turkish bridge, was destroyed by shelling during 1993. The town was formerly the capital of Herzegovina.*

Using the land

Crops of wheat, maize, sugar beet, vegetables and fruit are widely grown. The hilly terrain is suited to forestry and livestock farming. The mild, mediterranean climate of the coastal regions provides ideal conditions for growing vines and olives. Albania's largely agricultural economy has been adversely affected by the recent dismantling of state farms.

115

Bulgaria & Greece

Including EUROPEAN TURKEY

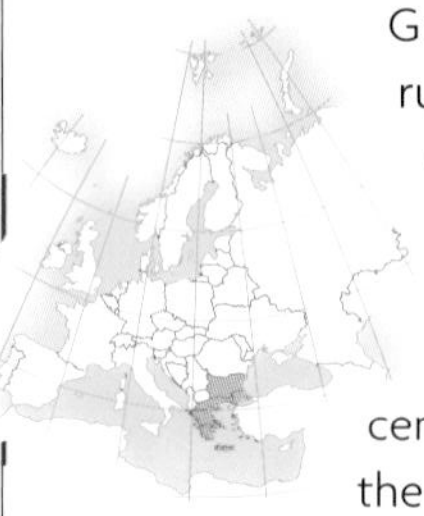

Greece is renowned as the original hearth of western civilization. The rugged terrain and numerous islands have profoundly affected its development, creating a strong agricultural and maritime tradition. In the past 50 years, this formerly rural society has rapidly urbanized, with one third of the population now living in the capital, Athens, and in the northern city of Salonica. Bulgaria, dominated for centuries by the Ottoman Turks, became part of the eastern bloc after the Second World War, only slowly emerging from Soviet influence in 1989. Moves towards democracy led to some instability in Bulgaria and Greece, now outweighed by the challenge of integration with the European Union.

The landscape

Bulgaria's Balkan mountains divide the Danubian Plain (*Dunavska Ravnina*) and Maritsa Basin, meeting the Black Sea in the east along sandy beaches. The steep Rhodope Mountains form a natural barrier with Greece, while the younger Pindus form a rugged central spine which descends into the Aegean Sea to give a vast archipelago of over 2000 islands, the largest of which is Crete.

Balkan Mountains

Maritsa Basin

Pindus Mountains

Rhodope Mountains

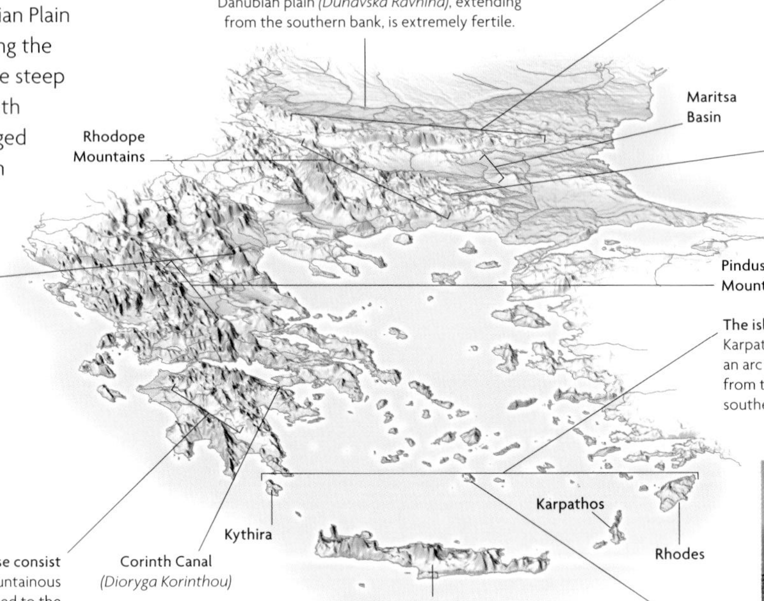

The Danube, Europe's second longest river, forms most of Bulgaria's northern border. The Danubian plain (*Dunavska Ravnina*), extending from the southern bank, is extremely fertile.

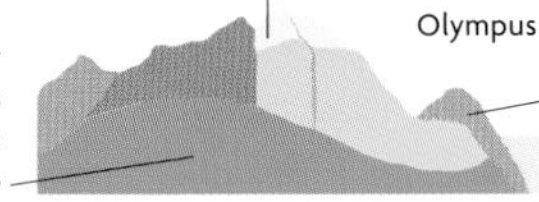

▲ *The Arda river cuts through the Rhodope Mountains in rugged, rocky gorges.*

The islands of Crete, Kythira, Karpathos and Rhodes are part of an arc which bends southeastwards from the Peloponnese, forming the southern boundary of the Aegean.

Rhodes

Karpathos

Crete

Kythira

▲ *Layers of black volcanic ash still cover the island of Santorini. This volcano last erupted 3500 years ago, but still shows signs of volcanic activity.*

Mount Olympus is the mythical home of the Greek Gods and, at 9570 ft (2917 m), is the highest mountain in Greece.

Corinth Canal (*Dioryga Korinthou*)

The Peloponnese consist of several mountainous peninsulas, linked to the mainland by the isthmus of Corinth. The Corinth Canal (*Dioryga Korinthou*), built in 1893, cuts through the isthmus, linking the Aegean and Ionian seas.

Ancient metamorphic rock, formed miles below the surface

Mount Olympus

Limestone rocks exposed by erosion of metamorphic rocks

Younger limestones created in shallow seas

▲ *Mount Olympus is a composite of rocks formed by two major tectonic events. First the older metamorphic rocks were thrust over the limestones, then two million years ago regional warping and subsequent erosion, re-exposed the limestone.*

Transport and industry

Soviet investment introduced heavy industry into Bulgaria, and the processing of agricultural produce, such as tobacco, is important throughout the country. Both countries have substantial shipyards and Greece has one of the world's largest merchant fleets. Many small craft workshops, producing textiles and processed foods, are clustered around Greek cities. The service and construction sectors have profited from the successful tourist industry.

Major industry and infrastructure

- chemicals
- engineering
- food processing
- shipbuilding
- textiles
- tourism

- capital cities
- major towns
- international airports
- major roads
- major industrial areas

The transport network

103,930 miles (167,630 km)	
345 miles (557 km)	
4346 miles (6995 km)	
294 miles (474 km)	

Bulgaria's railways require investment to revive an outdated infrastructure. In Greece, despite a developing road network, ferry-boats remain the most effective form of transport in many areas.

▲ *A towering pinnacle at Meteora in central Greece is home to the monastery of Roussanou. The 24 rock towers which dominate the plain of Thessaly (Thessalia) are remnants of an old plateau. Long-term weathering along fissures in the rock has worn away the rest of the plateau.*

Scale 1:2,500,000

projection: Lambert Conformal Conic

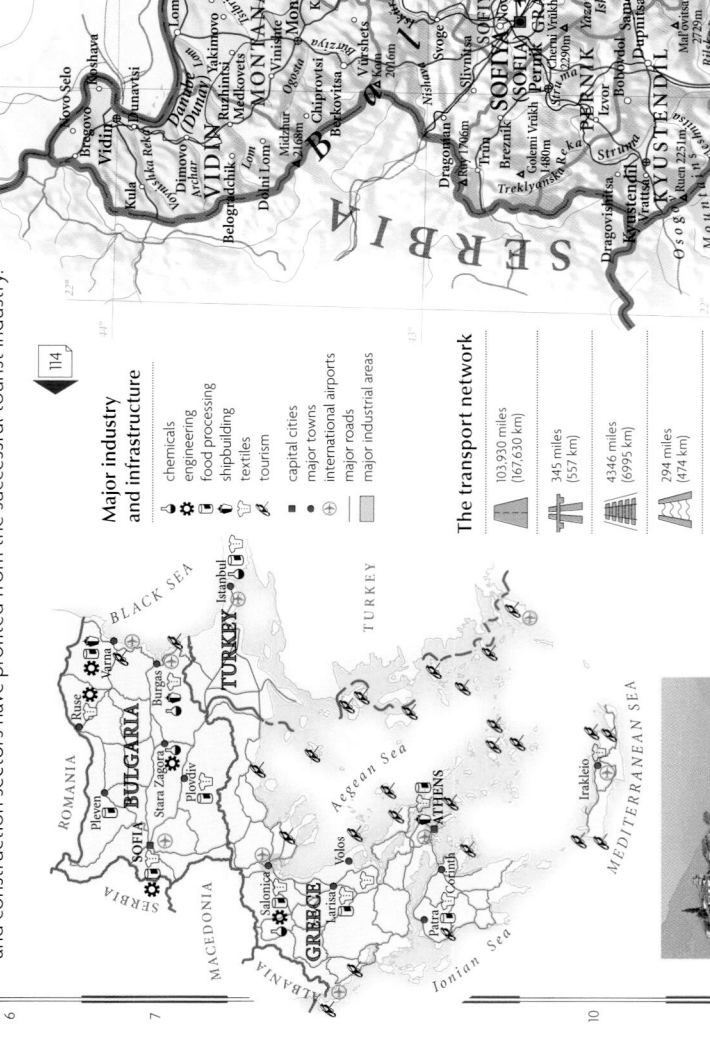

BLACK SEA

TURKEY

BULGARIA

ROMANIA

SERBIA

MACEDONIA

ALBANIA

GREECE

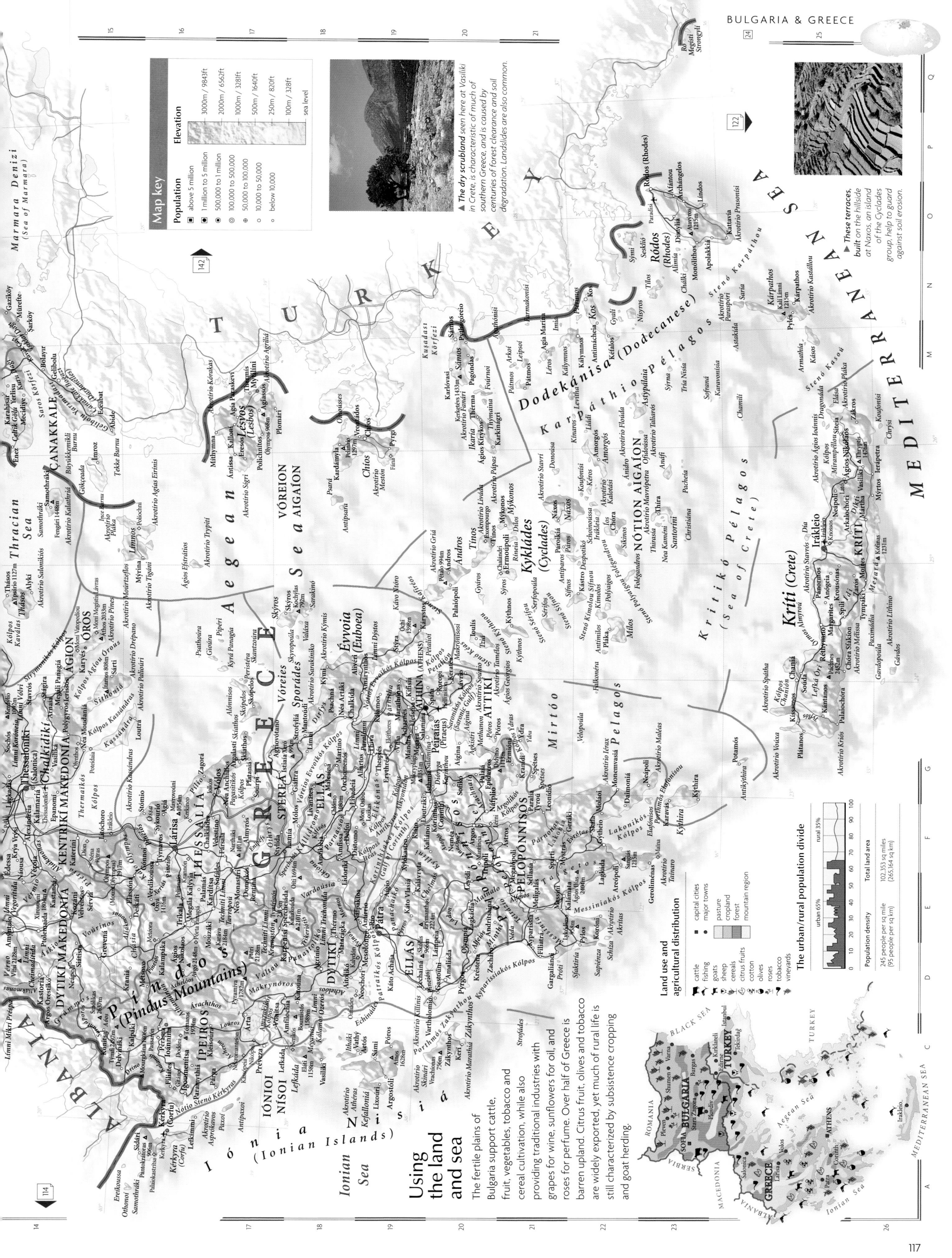

Map key

Population

- ▪ above 5 million
- ▪ 1 million to 5 million
- ◉ 500,000 to 1 million
- ⊛ 100,000 to 500,000
- ⊕ 50,000 to 100,000
- ⊙ 10,000 to 50,000
- ○ below 10,000

Elevation

- 3000m / 9843ft
- 2000m / 6562ft
- 1000m / 3281ft
- 500m / 1640ft
- 250m / 820ft
- 100m / 328ft
- sea level

▲ *The dry scrubland seen here at Vasiliki in Crete, is characteristic of much of southern Greece, and is caused by centuries of forest clearance and soil degradation. Landslides are also common.*

▲ *These terraces, built on the hillside at Naxos, an island of the Cyclades group, help to guard against soil erosion.*

Using the land and sea

The fertile plains of Bulgaria support cattle, fruit, vegetables, tobacco and cereal cultivation, while also providing traditional industries with grapes for wine, sunflowers for oil, and roses for perfume. Over half of Greece is barren upland. Citrus fruit, olives and tobacco are widely exported, yet much of rural life is still characterized by subsistence cropping and goat herding.

Land use and agricultural distribution

- cattle
- fishing
- goats
- sheep
- cereals
- citrus fruits
- cotton
- olives
- roses
- tobacco
- vineyards

- ▪ capital cities
- • major towns
- pasture
- cropland
- forest
- mountain region

The urban/rural population divide

urban 65%   rural 35%

Population density: 245 people per sq mile (95 people per sq km)

Total land area: 102,353 sq miles (265,164 sq km)

Romania, Moldova & Ukraine

The industrial, social and cultural make-up of Romania and the former Soviet states of Moldova and Ukraine still bear the imprint of their communist past. As part of the USSR, Ukraine was a leading agricultural, industrial and energy producer. These industries, like those in Moldova and Romania, are now being reoriented more firmly towards western markets. As a result of shifting borders, and Soviet policy actively encouraging Russian immigration into other Soviet states like Ukraine and Moldova, all three countries now contain large numbers of foreign nationals. Moldovans and Romanians are still close in terms of language and culture, although Moldova is striving to remain an independent nation.

Using the land

The fertile black soils of Ukraine, often called 'the breadbasket of Europe', have enabled the cultivation of a variety of cereals and vegetables, which are widely exported. Romania and Moldova also grow cereals, sunflowers and vegetables, and are noted for the quality of their wines.

◀ *The fertile lands and tolerant climate of Moldova are ideally suited to growing grapes for wine.*

Land use and agricultural distribution

- cattle
- pigs
- poultry
- sheep
- cereals
- cotton
- sugar beet
- sunflowers
- vineyards
- ● capital cities
- ● major towns

pasture
cropland
forest
wetland

The urban/rural population divide

urban 65%   rural 35%

0 10 20 30 40 50 60 70 80 90 100

Population density	Total land area
222 people per sq mile (86 people per sq km)	334,947 sq miles (867,740 sq km)

◀ *Glacial lakes are found throughout the Transylvanian Alps (Carpatii Meridionali), although the mountains no longer have any permanent snow cover.*

Transport and industry

Heavy industry using local raw materials characterizes much of this region. The industrial heartland of Ukraine, specializing in metal and machine-building industries, is based around its vast mineral reserves in the Donbass region. In Moldova, food processing draws on produce from its agricultural sector. Romanian industry relies both on local raw materials and imported iron, steel and oil.

Major industry and infrastructure

- car manufacture
- chemicals
- coal
- engineering
- food processing
- mining
- oil & gas
- textiles
- tourism
- ● capital cities
- ● major towns
- ✈ international airports
- major roads
- major industrial areas

The transport network

170,707 miles (274,757 km)		1170 miles (1883 km)	
21,474 miles (34,563 km)		4130 miles (6647 km)	

Increased industrialization has necessitated the upgrading of road and rail networks in all three countries. Modernization has tended to focus only on major cities and industrial areas.

▶ *During the 1960s and 1970s, many industries, like this carbon factory, developed using the mineral resources on the flanks of the Transylvanian Alps (Carpatii Meridionali).*

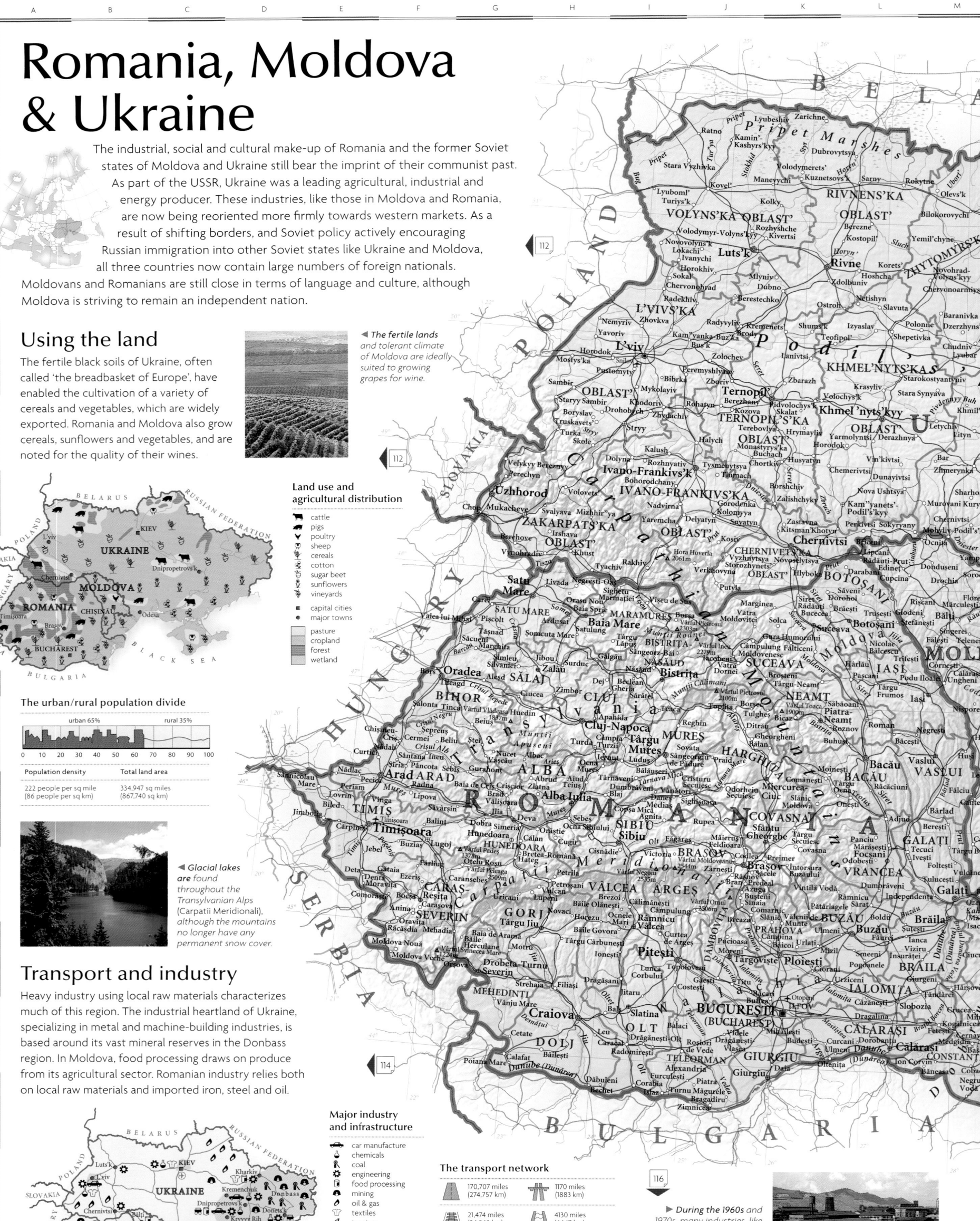

Scale 1:3,250,000

Km
0 10 20 30 40 50 60 70 80 90 100

Miles
0 10 20 30 40 50 60 70 80 90 100

projection: Lambert Conformal Conic

Map key

Population

- ◉ 1 million to 5 million
- ◎ 500,000 to 1 million
- ⊙ 100,000 to 500,000
- ⊕ 50,000 to 100,000
- ○ 10,000 to 50,000
- ∘ below 10,000

Elevation

- 2000m / 6562ft
- 1000m / 3281ft
- 500m / 1640ft
- 250m / 820ft
- 100m / 328ft
- sea level

RUSSIAN FEDERATION

RUSSIA

UKRAINE

MOLDOVA

CHERNIHIVS'KA OBLAST'

KYYIVS'KA OBLAST'

SUMS'KA OBLAST'

POLTAVS'KA OBLAST'

KHARKIVS'KA OBLAST'

LUHANS'KA OBLAST'

CHERKAS'KA OBLAST'

VINNYTS'KA OBLAST'

KIROVOHRADS'KA OBLAST'

DNIPROPETROVS'KA OBLAST'

DONETS'KA OBLAST'

ODES'KA OBLAST'

MYKOLAYIVS'KA OBLAST'

KHERSONS'KA OBLAST'

ZAPORIZ'KA OBLAST'

TRANSNISTRIA

RESPUBLIKA KRYM

KYYIV (KIEV)
Zhytomyr
Vinnytsya
Chernihiv
Sumy
Kharkiv
Poltava
Cherkasy
Kirovohrad
Dnipropetrovs'k
Zaporizhzhya
Luhans'k
Donets'k
Mariupol'
Berdyans'k
Melitopol'
Mykolayiv
Kherson
Odesa
Illichivs'k
Simferopol'
Sevastopol'
Yalta
Kerch
Yevpatoriya
CHIŞINĂU
Tiraspol
Constanța
Tulcea

Black Sea

Sea of Azov

Gulf of Taganrog

Dnieper Lowland

Kerch Strait

Black Sea Lowland

Roman-Kash 1545m

▲ The Swallow's Nest castle at Yalta is one of many tourist resorts on the Crimean (Krym) coast, dubbed the 'Russian Riviera'.

Old glaciated valley — Water has eroded a new post-glacial valley

▲ Balkas are common throughout Ukraine. They are large U-shaped valleys, formed during the last Ice Age, which contain narrower, deep valleys. These were incised by a sudden flow of water, following an ice melt.

Anti-clockwise currents have created the sandspits which fringe the Sea of Azov.

The landscape

Vast flat lowlands and gently rolling hills cover most of southeastern Europe. In the southwest, the Carpathian Mountains form a gentle arc. To the south of the Carpathian Mountains lies the Danube Plain, across which the Danube river flows to the Black Sea. To the north and east, the hills of Moldova level out into low plains, running east to the steppes of Ukraine.

▶ Divided into crystalline massifs, the southern arm of the Carpathian Mountains, the Transylvanian Alps (Carpatii Meridionali), extend 170 miles (274 km) across southwestern Romania.

Steppe landscape covers two-thirds of Ukraine. These flat, treeless grasslands extend from central Europe to central Asia.

The Codrii Hills dominate the landscape of central Moldova; they are intersected by deep, flat valleys and ravines.

Most of the major rivers in southeastern Europe, like the Danube, the Dniester and Dnieper flow south and east to the Black Sea.

Uplifted and folded at the same time as the Alps, some 250 miles (400 km) of the eastern Carpathian Mountains contain ancient volcanic cones and craters.

The Apuseni Mountains (Muntii Apuseni) are rich in mineral deposits, including gold and iron ore.

Transylvanian Alps (Carpatii Meridionali)

The Danube forms a natural border between Romania and Bulgaria.

The three branches of the Danube Delta (Delta Dunării) form a triangle of wetlands covering some 1950 sq miles (5050 sq km).

At Kryms'ki Hory, three flat-topped, parallel limestone ridges run 80 miles (128 km) along the southern coast of the Crimean (Krym) Peninsula.

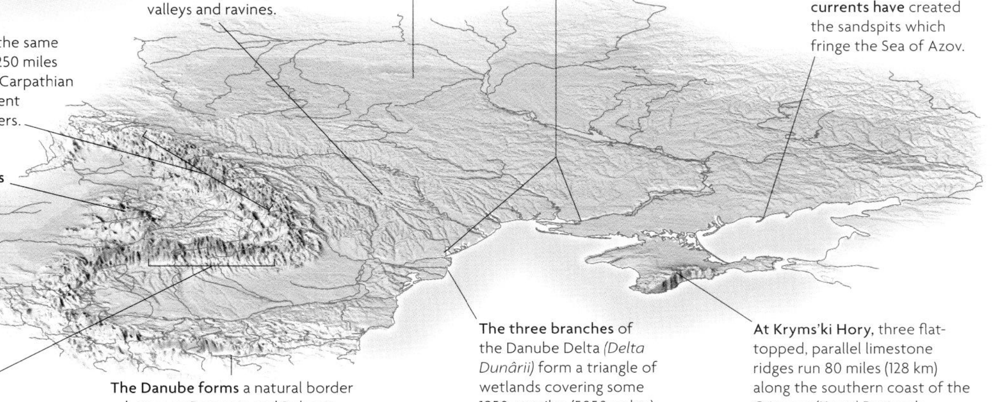

The Baltic states & Belarus

BELARUS, ESTONIA, LATVIA, LITHUANIA, Kaliningrad

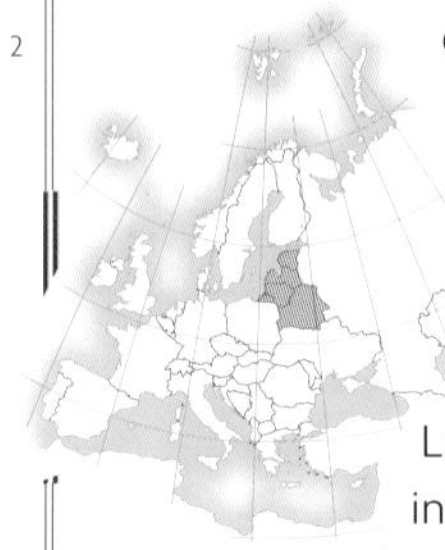

Occupying Europe's main corridor to Russia, the four distinct cultures of Estonia, Latvia, Lithuania and Belarus share a history of struggle for nationhood against the interests of more powerful neighbours. As the first republics to declare their independence from the Soviet Union in 1990–91, the Baltic states of Estonia, Latvia and Lithuania sought an economic role in the EU, while reaffirming their European cultural roots through the church and a strong musical tradition. Meanwhile, Belarus has shown economic and political allegiance to Russia by joining the Commonwealth of Independent States.

▲ *The seaport of Riga is Latvia's capital and the centre of economic and cultural life. With a 32% Russian minority in Latvia, language and the right to national citizenship are key issues.*

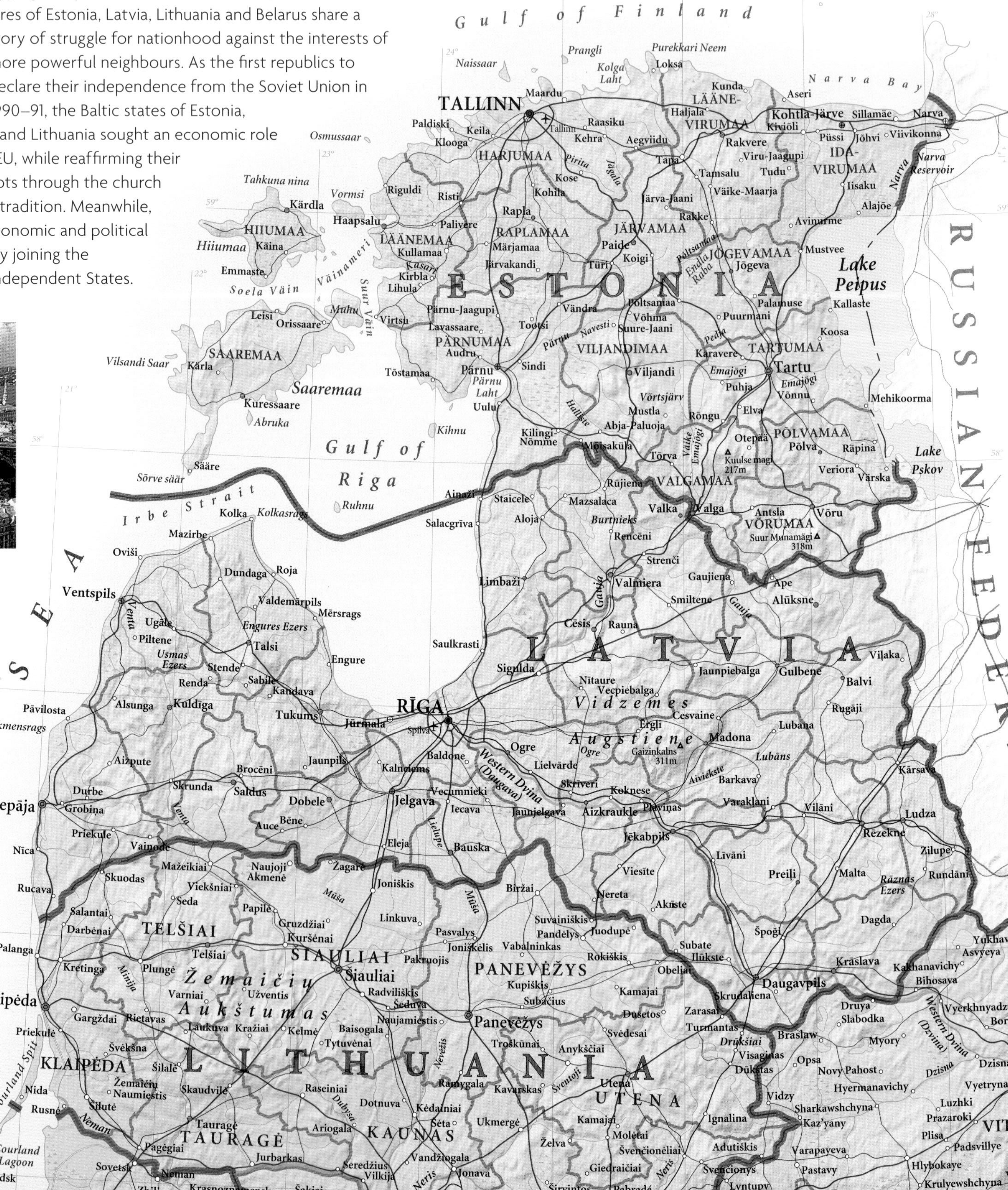

Using the land

Across the four nations cattle and pig farming are widespread, together with diverse arable crops, including flax for making linen, potatoes used to produce vodka, cereals and other vegetables. Almost a third of the land is forested; demand for timber has increased the importance of forest management.

Land use and agricultural distribution

- cattle
- pigs
- cereals
- flax
- potatoes
- timber
- capital cities
- major towns
- pasture
- cropland
- forest
- wetland

The urban/rural population divide

urban 69% rural 31%

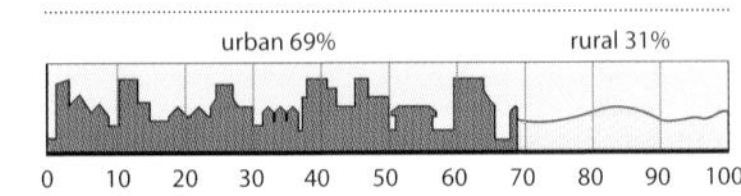

Population density	Total land area
122 people per sq mile (47 people per sq km)	145,006 sq miles (375,656 sq km)

0 10 20 30 40 50 60 70 80 90 100

▲ *A pine forest in northern Belarus. Conifers in the north give way to hardwood forest further south. Timber mills are supplied with logs floated along the country's many navigable waterways.*

▲ *The Western Dvina river provides hydro-electric power and, during the summer months, access to the Baltic Sea. The lower course of the river freezes from December to April.*

Map key

Population
- ● 1 million to 5 million
- ◉ 500,000 to 1 million
- ⊕ 100,000 to 500,000
- ⊙ 50,000 to 100,000
- ○ 10,000 to 50,000
- ○ below 10,000

Elevation
- 250m / 820ft
- 100m / 328ft
- sea level

RUSSIAN FEDERATION

BELARUS

ESTONIA

LATVIA

LITHUANIA

RUSS. FED.

POLAND

Kaliningrad

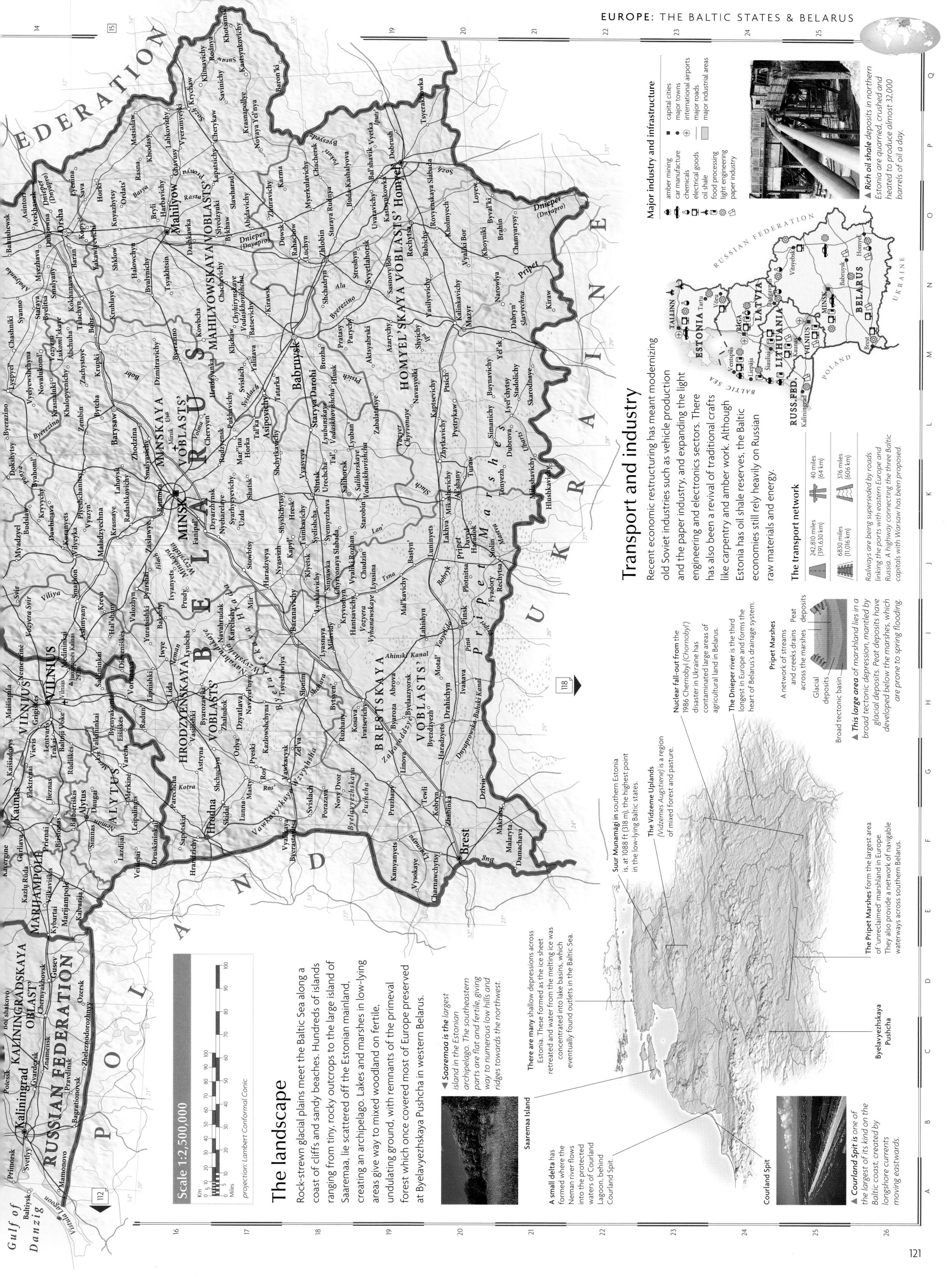

Major industry and infrastructure

- amber mining
- car manufacture
- chemicals
- electrical goods
- oil shale
- food processing
- light engineering
- paper industry

- capital cities
- major towns
- international airports
- major roads
- major industrial areas

▲ *Rich oil shale deposits in northern Estonia are quarried, crushed and heated to produce almost 32,000 barrels of oil a day.*

Transport and industry

Recent economic restructuring has meant modernizing old Soviet industries such as vehicle production and the paper industry, and expanding the light engineering and electronics sectors. There has also been a revival of traditional crafts like carpentry and amber work. Although Estonia has oil shale reserves, the Baltic economies still rely heavily on Russian raw materials and energy.

The transport network

242,810 miles (390,630 km)	40 miles (64 km)
6830 miles (11,016 km)	376 miles (606 km)

Railways are being superseded by roads linking the ports with eastern Europe and Russia. A highway connecting the three Baltic capitals with Warsaw has been proposed.

Nuclear fall-out from the 1986 Chernobyl (*Chornobyl*) disaster in Ukraine has contaminated large areas of agricultural land in Belarus.

The Dnieper river is the third longest in Europe and forms the heart of Belarus's drainage system.

Pripet Marshes
A network of streams and creeks drains across the marshes

- Peat deposits
- Glacial deposits
- Broad tectonic basin

▲ *This large area of marshland lies in a broad tectonic depression, mantled by glacial deposits. Peat deposits have developed below the marshes, which are prone to spring flooding.*

The landscape

Rock-strewn glacial plains meet the Baltic Sea along a coast of cliffs and sandy beaches. Hundreds of islands ranging from tiny, rocky outcrops to the large island of Saaremaa, lie scattered off the Estonian mainland, creating an archipelago. Lakes and marshes in low-lying areas give way to mixed woodland on fertile, undulating ground, with remnants of the primeval forest which once covered most of Europe preserved at Byelavyezhskaya Pushcha in western Belarus.

▲ *Saaremaa is the largest island in the Estonian archipelago. The southeastern parts are flat and fertile, giving way to numerous low hills and ridges towards the northwest.*

There are many shallow depressions across Estonia. These formed as the ice sheet retreated and water from the melting ice was concentrated into lake basins, which eventually found outlets in the Baltic Sea.

Suur Munamägi in southern Estonia is, at 1088 ft (318 m), the highest point in the low-lying Baltic states.

The Vidzeme Uplands (*Vidzemes Augstiene*) is a region of mixed forest and pasture.

The Pripet Marshes form the largest area of 'unreclaimed' marshland in Europe. They also provide a network of navigable waterways across southern Belarus.

A small delta has formed where the Neman river flows into the protected waters of Courland Lagoon, behind Courland Spit.

Saaremaa Island

Courland Spit

Byelavyezhskaya Pushcha

▲ *Courland Spit is one of the largest of its kind on the Baltic coast, created by longshore currents moving eastwards.*

Scale 1:2,500,000

projection: Lambert Conformal Conic

121

The Mediterranean

The Mediterranean Sea stretches over 2500 miles (4000 km) east to west, separating Europe from Africa. At its most westerly point it is connected to the Atlantic Ocean through the Strait of Gibraltar. In the east, the Suez canal, opened in 1869, gives passage to the Indian Ocean. In the northeast, linked by the Sea of Marmara, lies the Black Sea. The Mediterranean is bordered by almost 30 states and territories, and more than 100 million people live on its shores and islands. Throughout history, the Mediterranean has been a focal area for many great empires and civilizations, reflected in the variety of cultures found on its shores. Since the 1960s, development along the southern coast of Europe has expanded rapidly to accommodate increasing numbers of tourists and to enable the exploitation of oil and gas reserves. This has resulted in rising levels of pollution, threatening the future of the sea.

Using the land and sea

A quarter of the fish species found in the Mediterranean are economically important. Sardines are the main catch in northern and western regions and aquaculture, including oyster farming, is becoming increasingly important in the eastern Mediterranean. Olives, citrus fruit, cork trees and vines thrive in the mediterranean climate, enjoying hot, dry summers and mild, wet winters. Italy and Spain are world leaders in commercial olive production.

Transport and industry

The opening of the Suez Canal in 1869 made the Mediterranean a key shipping route to Asia. Oil and gas reserves, although comparatively small on a world scale, are being explored and exploited off the coasts of Libya, Greece, Italy, Spain and Tunisia. The Mediterranean's greatest natural resources are its miles of beaches and warm sea. Over half the world's income from tourism is generated in the Mediterranean.

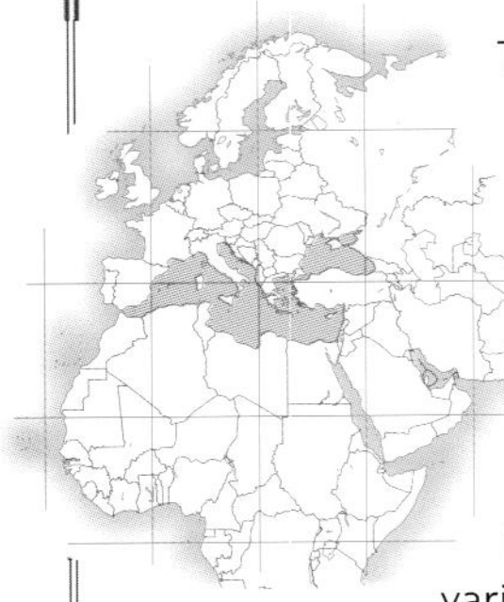

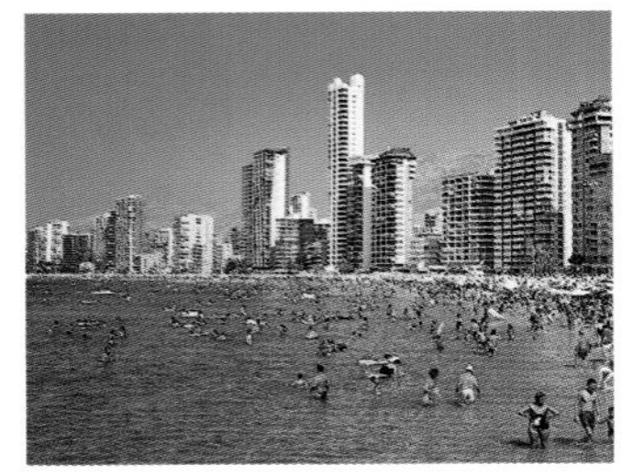

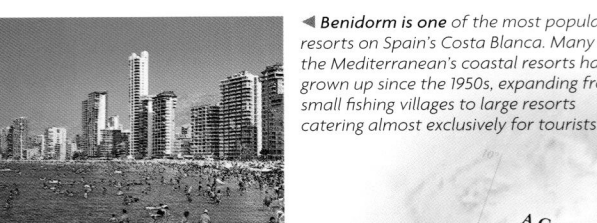

◄ *Benidorm is one* of the most popular resorts on Spain's Costa Blanca. Many of the Mediterranean's coastal resorts have grown up since the 1950s, expanding from small fishing villages to large resorts catering almost exclusively for tourists.

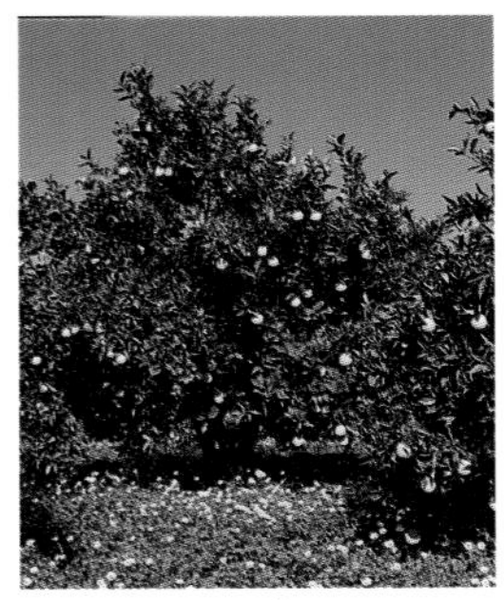

◄ *The growing of* citrus fruit such as lemons, limes, oranges and grapefruit is common along the coasts surrounding the Mediterranean.

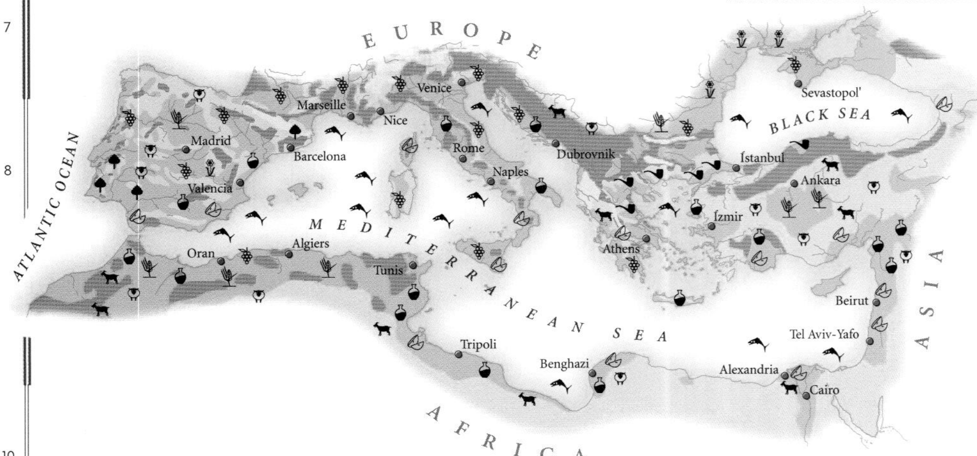

Land use and agricultural distribution

- 🐐 goats
- 🐑 sheep
- 🌾 cereals
- 🍊 citrus fruits
- 🌳 cork
- 🎣 fishing
- 🫒 olives
- 🌻 sunflowers
- 🌿 tobacco
- 🍇 vineyards
- ● major towns

	pasture
	cropland
	forest
	mountain region
	wetland
	desert

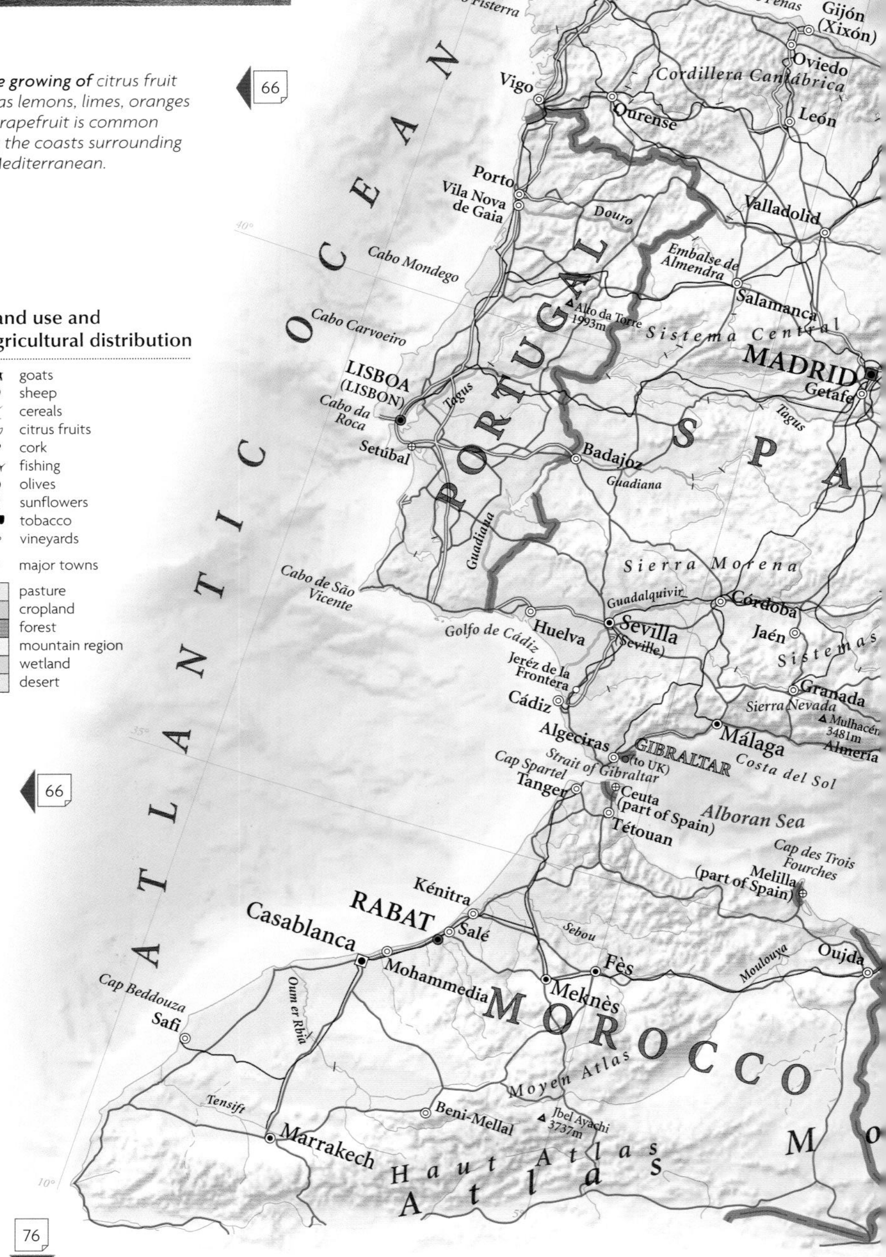

The landscape

The Mediterranean Sea is almost totally landlocked, joined to the Atlantic Ocean through the Strait of Gibraltar, which is only 8 miles (13 km) wide. Lying on an active plate margin, sea floor movements have formed a variety of basins, troughs and ridges. A submarine ridge running from Tunisia to the island of Sicily divides the Mediterranean into two distinct basins. The western basin is characterized by broad, smooth abyssal (or ocean) plains. In contrast, the eastern basin is dominated by a large ridge system, running east to west.

The narrow Strait of Gibraltar inhibits water exchange between the Mediterranean Sea and the Atlantic Ocean, producing a high degree of salinity and a low tidal range within the Mediterranean. The lack of tides has encouraged the build-up of pollutants in many semi-enclosed bays.

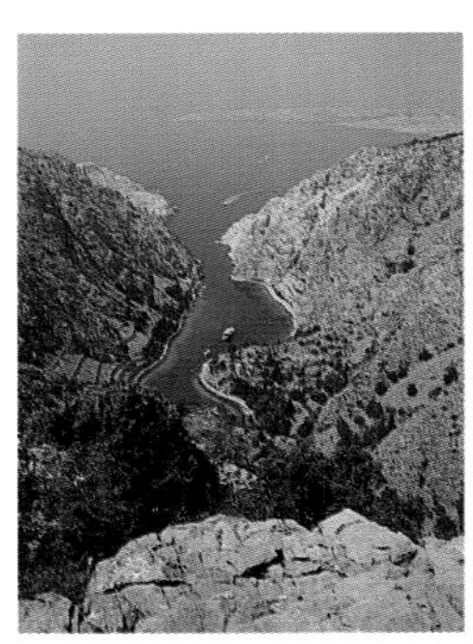

▲ *The Dalmatian* (Dalmacija) coast has many long, elongated islands running parallel to the mainland. These resulted when rising sea levels drowned valleys running parallel with the coast.

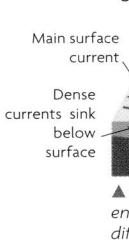

Main surface current

Denser, more saline currents flow back to Atlantic

Dense currents sink below surface

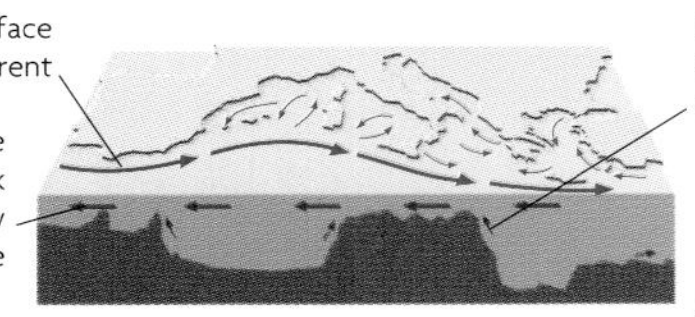

▲ *Because the Mediterranean* is almost enclosed by land, its circulation is quite different to the oceans. There is one major current which flows in from the Atlantic and moves east. Currents flowing back to the Atlantic are denser and flow below the main current.

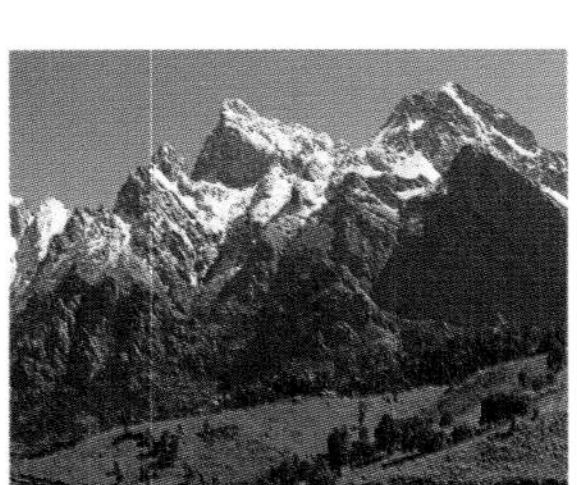

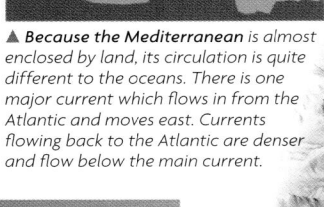

◄ *The Atlas Mountains* are a range of fold mountains which lie in Morocco and Algeria. They run parallel to the Mediterranean, forming a topographical and climatic divide between the Mediterranean coast and the western Sahara.

The edge of the Eurasian Plate is edged by a continental shelf. In the Mediterranean Sea this is widest at the Ebro Fan where it extends 60 miles (96 km).

Beneath the Strait of Sicily lies a submarine ridge which rises to 1200 ft (360 m) below sea level. It divides the eastern and western basins of the Mediterranean.

An arc of active submarine, island and mainland volcanoes, including Etna and Vesuvius, lie in and around southern Italy. The area is also susceptible to earthquakes and landslides.

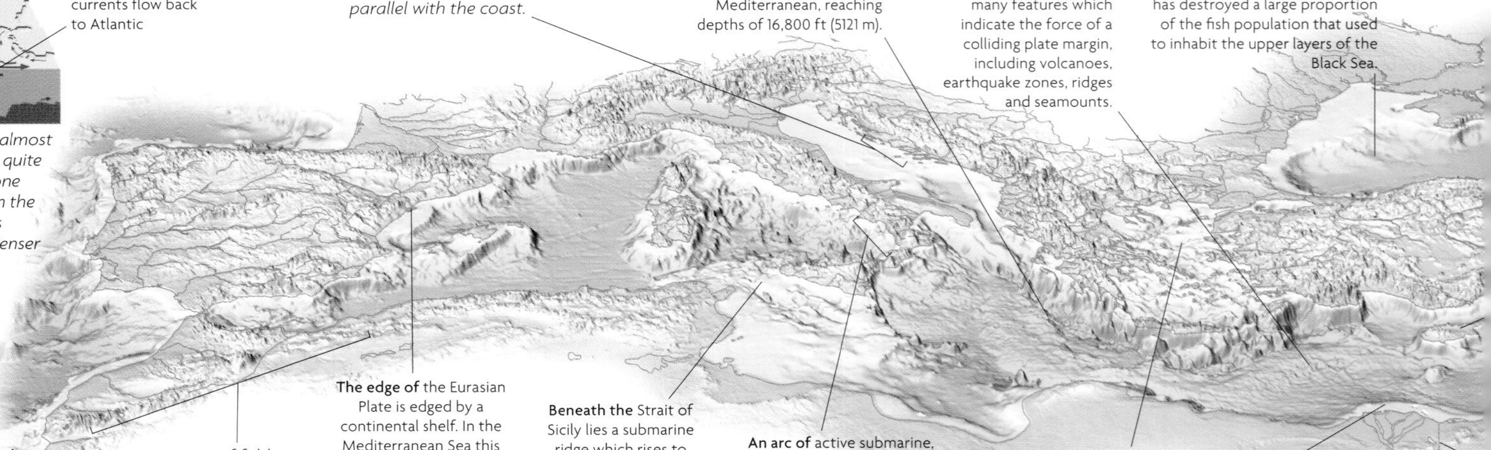

The Ionian Basin is the deepest in the Mediterranean, reaching depths of 16,800 ft (5121 m).

The eastern basin of the Mediterranean contains many features which indicate the force of a colliding plate margin, including volcanoes, earthquake zones, ridges and seamounts.

The shallow basin of the Aegean contains numerous small islands, many of volcanic origin.

Industrial pollution flowing from the Dnieper and Danube rivers has destroyed a large proportion of the fish population that used to inhabit the upper layers of the Black Sea.

Nutrient flows into the eastern Mediterranean, and sediment flows to the Nile Delta have been severely lowered by the building of the Aswan Dam across the Nile in Egypt. This is causing the delta to shrink.

(Map of Iberia and North Africa with labels:)

Cabo Ortegal, A Coruña, Cabo Fisterra, Cabo de Peñas, Gijón (Xixón), Oviedo, Cordillera Cantábrica, León, Vigo, Ourense, Vila Nova de Gaia, Porto, Douro, Valladolid, Embalse de Almendra, Salamanca, Alto da Torre 1993m, Sistema Central, MADRID, LISBOA (LISBON), Cabo da Roca, Setúbal, Tejo, Badajoz, Guadiana, Sierra Morena, Cabo de São Vicente, Golfo de Cádiz, Huelva, Guadalquivir, Sevilla (Seville), Córdoba, Jaén, Jerez de la Frontera, Cádiz, Granada, Sierra Nevada, Mulhacén 3481m, Málaga, Costa del Sol, Almería, Algeciras (no UK), Strait of Gibraltar, GIBRALTAR, Cap Spartel, Tánger, Ceuta (part of Spain), Alborán Sea, Cap des Trois Fourches, Melilla (part of Spain), Tétouan, Kénitra, Casablanca, RABAT, Salé, Mohammedia, Sebou, Fès, Moulouya, Oujda, Cap Beddouza, Safi, Meknès, Oum er Rbia, MOROCCO, Beni-Mellal, Moyen Atlas, Tensift, Marrakech, Jbel Ayachi 3757m, Haut Atlas

ATLANTIC OCEAN

(Map labels on land-use map:) EUROPE, Marseille, Venice, Nice, Rome, Madrid, Barcelona, Naples, Dubrovnik, BLACK SEA, Sevastopol', Istanbul, Valencia, Ankara, İzmir, Athens, ASIA, Algiers, Oran, Tunis, MEDITERRANEAN SEA, Beirut, Tel Aviv-Yafo, Tripoli, Benghazi, Alexandria, Cairo, AFRICA

The Russian Federation

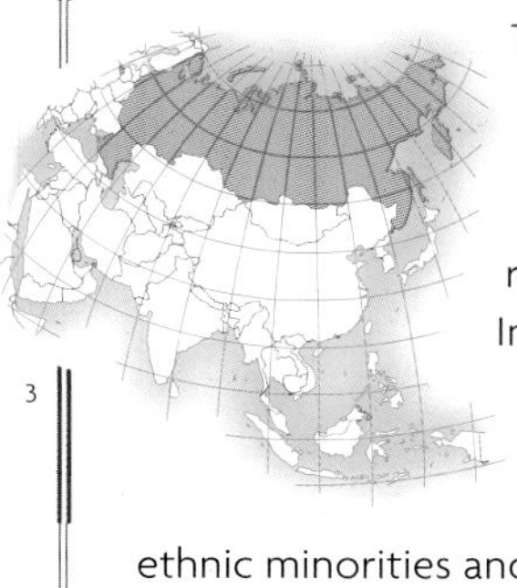

The Cold War era of global relations was concluded in 1991 with the formal dissolution of the Soviet Union. The Russian Federation declared its separate sovereignty from the foundering communist empire following independence declarations from a number of former Soviet republics. As the leading member of the Commonwealth of Independent States, the Russian Federation has a central role in the development of post-Soviet Eurasia. Crossing 11 time zones, the Russian Federation is almost twice the size of the USA, and with more than 150 ethnic minorities and 21 autonomous republics, regionalist dissent within its own territory remains a danger.

▶ *Summer beds of moss and lichen scatter a 90% surface cover of ice across the islands of Franz Josef Land (Zemlya Frantsa-Iosifa), the northernmost land in the eastern hemisphere.*

Map key

Population
- ▪ above 5 million
- ◾ 1 million to 5 million
- ◉ 500,000 to 1 million
- ◎ 100,000 to 500,000
- ⊕ 50,000 to 100,000
- ○ 10,000 to 50,000
- ○ below 10,000

Elevation
- 4000m / 13,124ft
- 3000m / 9843ft
- 2000m / 6562ft
- 1000m / 3281ft
- 500m / 1640ft
- 250m / 820ft
- 100m / 328ft
- sea level

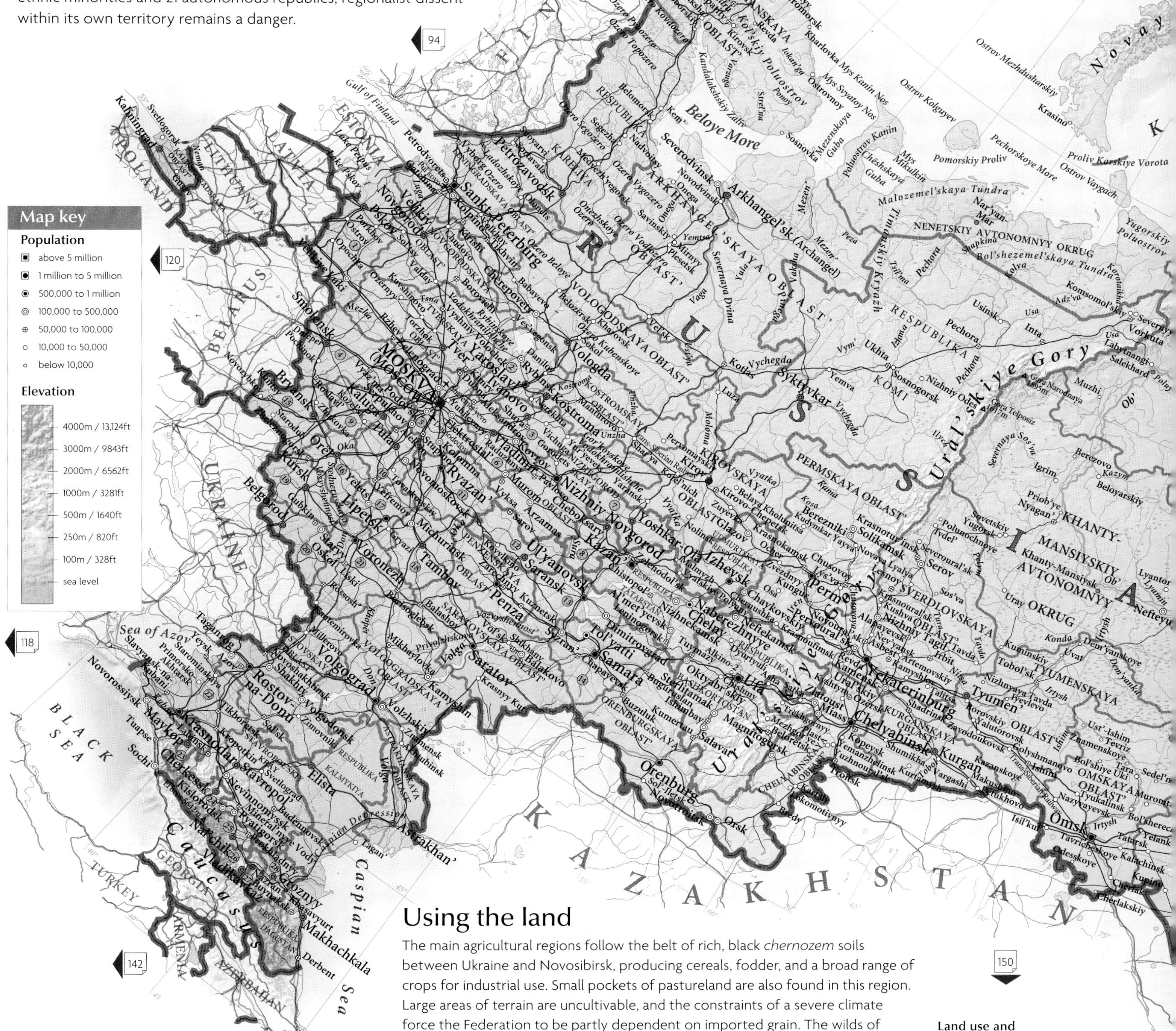

Using the land

The main agricultural regions follow the belt of rich, black *chernozem* soils between Ukraine and Novosibirsk, producing cereals, fodder, and a broad range of crops for industrial use. Small pockets of pastureland are also found in this region. Large areas of terrain are uncultivable, and the constraints of a severe climate force the Federation to be partly dependent on imported grain. The wilds of Siberia are given over to hunting and reindeer herding, and contain the world's largest timber reserves.

Map key

The Russian Federation: Administrative regions
1. PSKOVSKAYA OBLAST'
2. YAROSLAVSKAYA OBLAST'
3. IVANOVSKAYA OBLAST'
4. SMOLENSKAYA OBLAST'
5. MOSKOVSKAYA OBLAST'
6. VLADIMIRSKAYA OBLAST'
7. RESPUBLIKA MARIY EL
8. CHAVASH RESPUBLIKI
9. KALUZHSKAYA OBLAST'
10. TUL'SKAYA OBLAST'
11. RYAZANSKAYA OBLAST'
12. RESPUBLIKA MORDOVIYA
13. UL'YANOVSKAYA OBLAST'
14. SAMARSKAYA OBLAST'
15. BRYANSKAYA OBLAST'
16. ORLOVSKAYA OBLAST'
17. LIPETSKAYA OBLAST'
18. TAMBOVSKAYA OBLAST'
19. KURSKAYA OBLAST'
20. BELGORODSKAYA OBLAST'
21. VORONEZHSKAYA OBLAST'
22. KRASNODARSKIY KRAY
23. RESPUBLIKA ADYGEYA
24. KARACHAYEVO-CHERKESSKAYA RESPUBLIKA
25. KABARDINO-BALKARSKAYA RESPUBLIKA
26. RESPUBLIKA SEVERNAYA OSETIYA - ALANIYA
27. INGUSHSKAYA RESPUBLIKA
28. CHECHENSKAYA RESPUBLIKA
29. YEVREYSKAYA AVTONOMNAYA OBLAST'

Land use and agricultural distribution
- cattle
- cereals
- root crops
- timber
- capital cities
- major towns
- pasture
- cropland
- forest
- desert
- mountain region
- barren

The urban/rural population divide
urban 76% — rural 24%

0 10 20 30 40 50 60 70 80 90 100

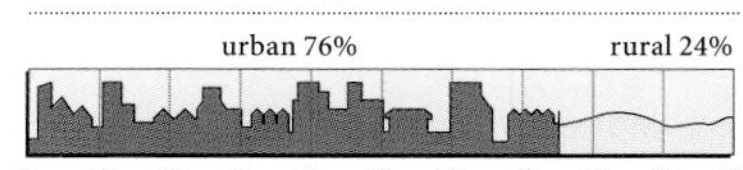

Population density	Total land area
22 people per sq mile (9 people per sq km)	65,592,800 sq miles (17,075,400 sq km)

RUSSIAN FEDERATION

Siberia

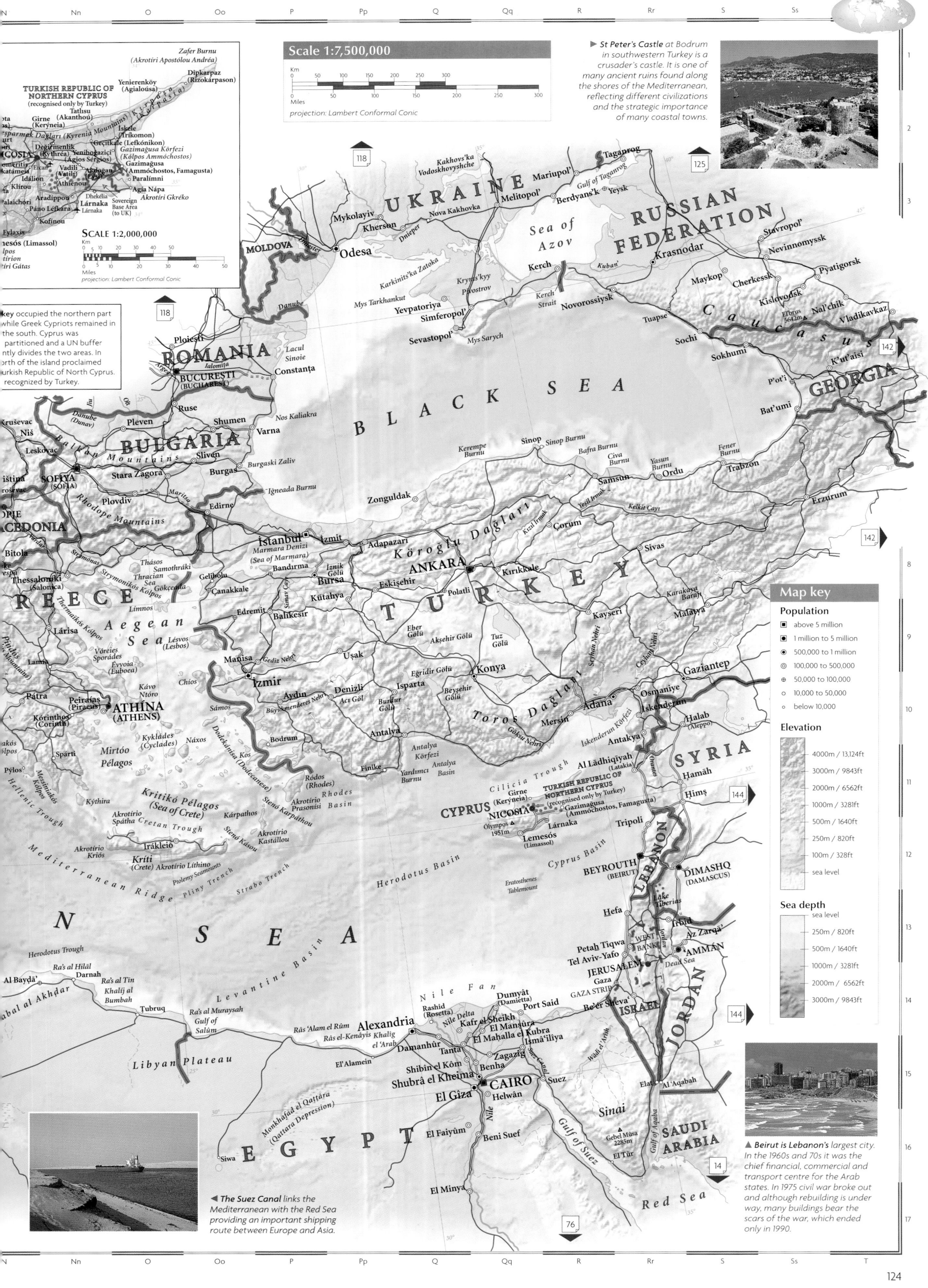

St Peter's Castle at Bodrum in southwestern Turkey is a crusader's castle. It is one of many ancient ruins found along the shores of the Mediterranean, reflecting different civilizations and the strategic importance of many coastal towns.

The Suez Canal links the Mediterranean with the Red Sea providing an important shipping route between Europe and Asia.

Beirut is Lebanon's largest city. In the 1960s and 70s it was the chief financial, commercial and transport centre for the Arab states. In 1975 civil war broke out and although rebuilding is under way, many buildings bear the scars of the war, which ended only in 1990.

Major industry and infrastructure

- fishing port
- oil & gas
- tourism
- major towns
- international airports
- major roads
- major industrial areas

ATLANTIC OCEAN

MEDITERRANEAN SEA

BLACK SEA

EUROPE

ASIA

AFRICA

Madrid · Marseille · Nice · Livorno · Venice · Rome · Napoli · Dubrovnik · Novorossiysk · Sevastopol' · Constanța · Burgas · İstanbul · Sofia · Ankara · Trabzon · Barcelona · Valencia · Malaga · Oran · Algiers · Tunis · Sfax · Tripoli · Benghazi · Athens · İzmir · Antalya · Beirut · Tel Aviv-Yafo · Alexandria · Cairo · Port Said · Suez

▶ **Monaco is just** one of the luxurious resorts scattered along the Riviera, which stretches along the coast from Cannes in France to La Spezia in Italy. The region's mild winters and hot summers have attracted wealthy tourists since the early 19th century.

CYPRUS

Koruçam Burnu (Akrotiri Kormakiti) · Güzelyurt Körfezi (Kólpos Mórfou) · Kólpos Chrysochoú · Akrotíri Arnaoúti · Páno Panajia · Pégeia · Páfos · Pólis · Ársos · Olympos 1951m · Kouklia · Sovereign Base Area (to UK) · Akrotírion

In 1974 T... of Cyprus ... control o... effective... zone cur... 1983 the... itself the... It was or...

104

110

110

114

Bay of Biscay

Bordeaux · Santander · Donostia-San Sebastián · San Vicente de Barakaldo · Bilbao · Vitoria-Gasteiz · Burgos · Pamplona (Iruña) · Logroño · Zaragoza · Lleida · Terrassa · Sabadell · Mataró · Barcelona · Tarragona · Castellón de la Plana · Valencia · Albacete · Alicante · Elche · Murcia · Cartagena · Cabo de Palos · Cabo de Gata

FRANCE · Lyon · Villeurbanne · St-Étienne · Grenoble · Toulouse · Montpellier · Nîmes · Aix-en-Provence · Marseille · Toulon · Cannes · MONACO · Nice

SWITZERLAND · AUSTRIA · SLOVENIA · LJUBLJANA · ZAGREB · Maribor · CROATIA

Lake Geneva · Mont Blanc 4807m · Matterhorn 4478m · Lago Maggiore · Lago di Como · Bolzano · Trento · Alpi Dolomitiche · Udine · Trieste · Venezia (Venice) · Torino (Turin) · Novara · Monza · Bergamo · Brescia · Vicenza · Padova · Milano (Milan) · Alessandria · Piacenza · Parma · Verona · Chioggia · Pula · Rijeka · Genova (Genoa) · Reggio nell'Emilia · Modena · Bologna · Ferrara · Ravenna · Forlì · Rimini · La Spezia · Prato · Firenze (Florence) · Pisa · Livorno · Ancona · Pescara · Perugia

Pyrenees · Vignemale 3298m · ANDORRA

ITALY · APPENNINO

San Marino · Zadar · Šibenik · Split · Brač · Hvar · Korčula · Pelješac · Mljet · BOSNIA & HERZEGOVINA · Banja Luka · Zenica · SARAJEVO · Mostar · Dubrovnik · MONTENEGRO · PODGORICA · Kosovska Mitrovica · Peć · Prizren · SERBIA · Kragujevac · Kraljevo · Lake Scutari · Kepi i Rodonit · TIRANË (TIRANA) · Durrës · ALBANIA · Lake Ohri

Ligurian Sea · Corse (Corsica) (to France) · Isola d'Elba · Golfo di Genova

Adriatic Sea · Adriatic Basin · Gulf of Venice · Dugi Otok · Krk · Cres · Pag

Sistema Ibérico · Duero · Ebro · Golfo de San Jordi · Cap Tortosa · Ebro Fan

Mallorca (Majorca) · Menorca (Minorca) · Palma · Ibiza · Formentera · Islas Baleares (Balearic Islands)

Golfo de Valencia · Cabo de La Nao · Benidorm · Costa Blanca

Béticos · Júcar

MEDITERRANEAN · Algerian Basin

Isola Asinara · Sardegna (Sardinia) (to Italy) · Sassari · Macomer · Ajaccio · Strait of Bonifacio · Sardinia-Corsica Trough · VATICAN CITY · ROMA (ROME) · Capo Circeo · Golfo di Gaeta · Napoli (Naples) · Vesuvio 1277m · Torre del Greco · Salerno · Golfo di Salerno

Civitavecchia · Termi · Vasto · Termoli · Foggia · Bari · Brindisi · Lecce · Golfo di Manfredonia · Taranto · Golfo di Taranto · Otranto · Capo Santa Maria di Leuca · Kérkyra (Corfu) · Strait of Otranto · Lumi i Vjosës

Tyrrhenian Sea · Tyrrhenian Basin · Golfo di Oristano · Tirso · Isola di San Pietro · Golfo di Palmas · Cagliari · Capo Carbonara · Capo Spartivento · Golfo di Cagliari

Cosenza · Crotone · Capo Rizzuto · Catanzaro · Iónia Nisiá (Ionian Islands) · Lefkáda · Ionian Sea · Kefalloniá · Zákynthos · Kyparis...

ALGER (ALGIERS) · Cap de Bordj El Bahri · Chlef · Tizi Ouzou · Blida · Béjaïa · Skikda · Annaba · Bizerte · Golfe de Tunis · Cap Blanc · Cap Bon · Oran · Cap Ferrat · Mostaganem · Sidi Bel Abbès · Constantine · Sétif · Batna · TUNIS · Tlemcen

Atlas Tellien · ALGERIA · Chott El Hodna · Zahrez Chergui · Massif de l'Aurès

Chott ech Chergui · Hauts Plateaux · Atlas Saharien · Montains

TUNISIA · Golfe de Hammamet · Sousse · Capo Granitola · Agrigento · Capo Scaramia · Capo Passero · Siracusa · Catania · Monte Etna 3340m · Reggio di Calabria · Messina · Stretto di Messina · Palermo · Sicilia (Sicily) · Capo · Simeto · Salso · Isola di Pantelleria (to Italy) · Medina Bank

Ionian Basin

Gozo · VALLETTA · Malta · MALTA · Malta Channel

Golfe de Gabès · Sfax · Îles de Kerkenah · Sebkhet de Sidi el Hani · Rass Kaboudia · Isole Pelagie (to Italy) · Sebkhet en Noual · Gabès · Île de Jerba · Médenine

ṬARĀBULUS (TRIPOLI) · Zuwārah · Al 'Azīzīyah · Gharyān · Miṣrātah · Al Khums · Rās Miṣrātah · Tūkrah · Banghāzī (Benghazi)

Khalīj Surt (Gulf of Sirte) · Surt · As Sultān · An Nawfalīyah · Ajdābiyā · Sabkhat Ghuzayyil · Wādī al Fārigh

LIBYA

SCALE 1:900,000

MALTA · Ras San Dimitri · Gozo · Ras il-Wardija · Victoria · Nadur · Mġarr · Comino (Kemmuna) · Mellieha · San Pawl il-Bahar · Malta · Mosta · St Julian's · Sliema · Hamrun · Paola · Rabat · Luqa · VALLETTA · Birżebbuġa · Il-Kullana · Marsaxlokk Bay · Mediterranean Sea · projection: Lambert Conformal Conic

Oxygen in the Black Sea is dissolved only in its upper layers; at depths below 230–300 ft (70–100 m) the sea is 'dead' and can support no lifeforms other than specially-adapted bacteria.

▲ **The city of** Venice is built on an archipelago of islands and mud-flats in the middle of a lagoon at the head of the Adriatic Sea. The city's numerous canals follow water routes between the original 118 islands.

▲ **Cyprus is the** third largest Mediterranean island after Sardinia and Sicily. The island is mountainous; containing two main ranges, the Troodos and the Kyrenia mountains .

Both the Dead Sea in Jordan and the Gulf of Aqaba are extensions of the Great Rift Valley which runs through eastern Africa.

The Suez Canal, opened in 1869, extends 100 miles (160 km) from Port Said to the Gulf of Suez.

◀ **Commercial fisheries are** found throughout the Mediterranean. Operations have traditionally been small-scale. As elsewhere, high demand has caused a decline in fish stocks.

76 · 76 · 76

◄ A *fishing trawler* lies at anchor in the icy waters of Karaginskiy Zaliv, at the northern end of the Kamchatka Peninsula (Poluostrov Kamchatka) in eastern Siberia. The Russian Federation's fishing fleet is the largest in the world and operates worldwide.

◄ The *shores of* Lake Baikal (Ozero Baykal) are a mixture of forest and the grassy steppe seen here. The lake freezes to a depth of 33 ft (10 m) in winter.

Scale 1:13,800,000

projection: Lambert Conformal Conic

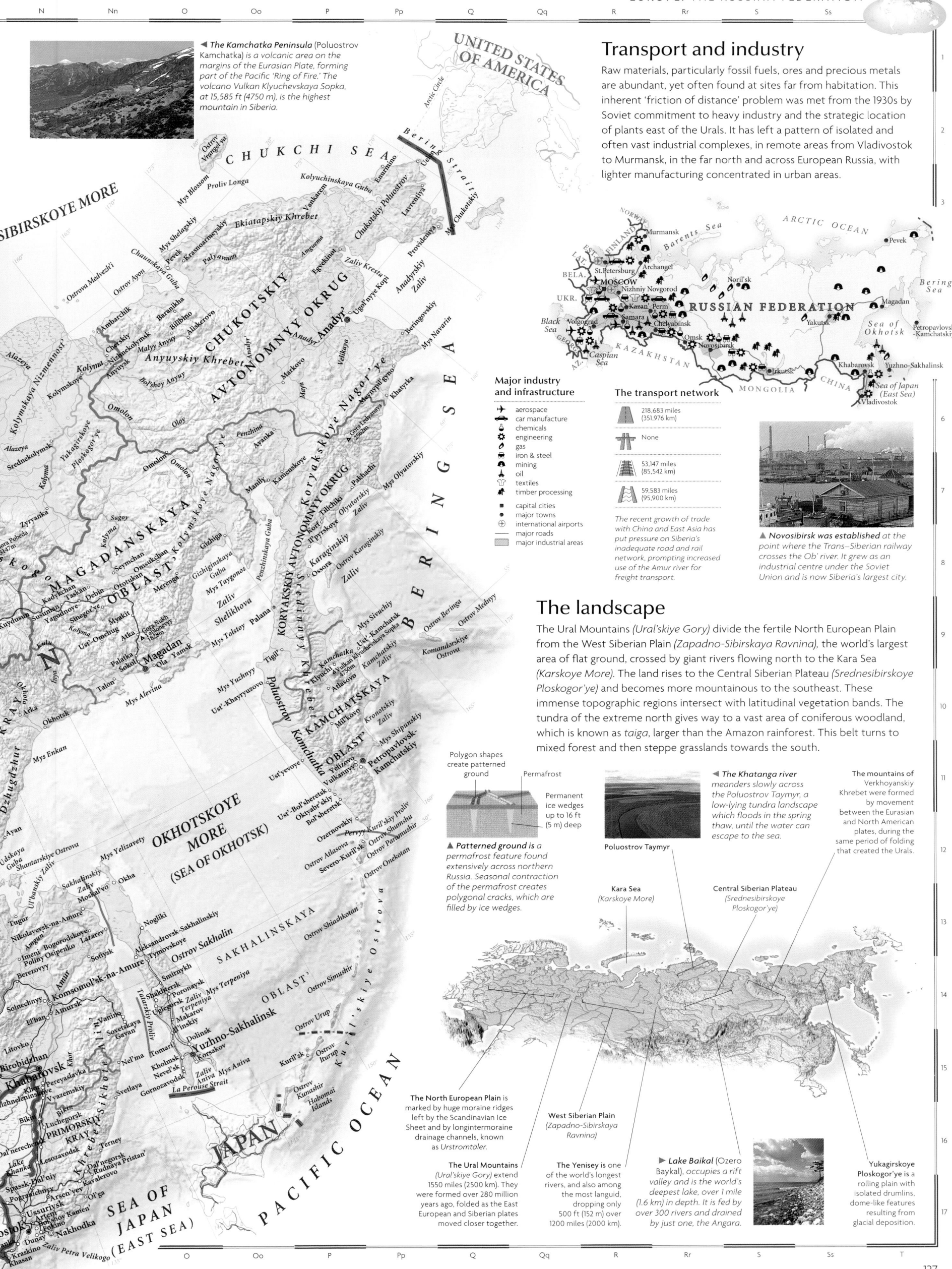

◀ *The Kamchatka Peninsula* (Poluostrov Kamchatka) *is a volcanic area on the margins of the Eurasian Plate, forming part of the Pacific 'Ring of Fire.' The volcano Vulkan Klyuchevskaya Sopka, at 15,585 ft (4750 m), is the highest mountain in Siberia.*

Transport and industry

Raw materials, particularly fossil fuels, ores and precious metals are abundant, yet often found at sites far from habitation. This inherent 'friction of distance' problem was met from the 1930s by Soviet commitment to heavy industry and the strategic location of plants east of the Urals. It has left a pattern of isolated and often vast industrial complexes, in remote areas from Vladivostok to Murmansk, in the far north and across European Russia, with lighter manufacturing concentrated in urban areas.

Major industry and infrastructure

- ✈ aerospace
- 🚗 car manufacture
- ⚗ chemicals
- ⚙ engineering
- 🔥 gas
- iron & steel
- ⛏ mining
- oil
- 👕 textiles
- timber processing
- ■ capital cities
- • major towns
- ⊕ international airports
- — major roads
- ▨ major industrial areas

The transport network

218,683 miles (351,976 km)	
None	
53,147 miles (85,542 km)	
59,583 miles (95,900 km)	

The recent growth of trade with China and East Asia has put pressure on Siberia's inadequate road and rail network, prompting increased use of the Amur river for freight transport.

▲ *Novosibirsk was established at the point where the Trans–Siberian railway crosses the Ob' river. It grew as an industrial centre under the Soviet Union and is now Siberia's largest city.*

The landscape

The Ural Mountains (Ural'skiye Gory) divide the fertile North European Plain from the West Siberian Plain (Zapadno-Sibirskaya Ravnina), the world's largest area of flat ground, crossed by giant rivers flowing north to the Kara Sea (Karskoye More). The land rises to the Central Siberian Plateau (Srednesibirskoye Ploskogor'ye) and becomes more mountainous to the southeast. These immense topographic regions intersect with latitudinal vegetation bands. The tundra of the extreme north gives way to a vast area of coniferous woodland, which is known as *taiga*, larger than the Amazon rainforest. This belt turns to mixed forest and then steppe grasslands towards the south.

Polygon shapes create patterned ground
Permafrost
Permanent ice wedges up to 16 ft (5 m) deep

▲ *Patterned ground is a permafrost feature found extensively across northern Russia. Seasonal contraction of the permafrost creates polygonal cracks, which are filled by ice wedges.*

▶ *The Khatanga river meanders slowly across the Poluostrov Taymyr, a low-lying tundra landscape which floods in the spring thaw, until the water can escape to the sea.*

Poluostrov Taymyr

The mountains of Verkhoyanskiy Khrebet were formed by movement between the Eurasian and North American plates, during the same period of folding that created the Urals.

Kara Sea (Karskoye More)

Central Siberian Plateau (Srednesibirskoye Ploskogor'ye)

The North European Plain is marked by huge moraine ridges left by the Scandinavian Ice Sheet and by long intermoraine drainage channels, known as *Urstromtäler.*

The Ural Mountains (Ural'skiye Gory) extend 1550 miles (2500 km). They were formed over 280 million years ago, folded as the East European and Siberian plates moved closer together.

West Siberian Plain (Zapadno-Sibirskaya Ravnina)

The Yenisey is one of the world's longest rivers, and also among the most languid, dropping only 500 ft (152 m) over 1200 miles (2000 km).

▶ *Lake Baikal* (Ozero Baykal), *occupies a rift valley and is the world's deepest lake, over 1 mile (1.6 km) in depth. It is fed by over 300 rivers and drained by just one, the Angara.*

Yukagirskoye Ploskogor'ye is a rolling plain with isolated drumlins, dome-like features resulting from glacial deposition.

Northern European Russia

Reaching into the Arctic Circle, this region of lakeland, forest and tundra is historically bound to Europe by St Petersburg, the old imperial capital of Tsarist Russia and home to a third of the region's population. Communist rule from Moscow left the north politically marginalized, contributing to the present problems of outmoded industry, poor infrastructure and serious environmental neglect. However, with borders embracing Finland, Norway, the Baltic and the northern sea route to the Atlantic, the region's success in foreign trade is now of prime importance to the Russian economy.

The landscape

The ancient bedrock of the Scandinavian Shield lies exposed across the glacially scoured Khibiny Mountains of the Kola Peninsula (*Kol'skiy Poluostrov*), becoming mantled with till towards the North European Plain. The Valdai Hills (*Valdayskaya Vozvyshennost'*) form an important watershed for the plain's rivers, while thick forest veils a complicated topography of moraines, lakes and ground disturbed by frost action. The Ural Mountains (*Ural'skiye Gory*) form a border with Asia in the east.

◀ *The Kola Peninsula* (Kol'skiy Poluostrov) is part of the Scandinavian Shield, an area of ancient bedrock underlying Scandinavia. Rocks in excess of 2500 million years old are exposed across the peninsula.

▲ *The Khibiny mountains* were formed by volcanic intrusions into the Scandinavian Shield, over 570 million years ago.

Kola Peninsula (*Kol'skiy Poluostrov*)

Karst features, including sinkholes, lakes and caverns, are found in limestone outcrops across the plain of the Severnaya Dvina and Mezen' rivers.

The low-lying plains of the Pechora, Mezen' and Severnaya Dvina rivers were flooded by the sea while the land was still isostatically depressed following the last Ice Age, a process which has hidden the landforms created by glacial deposition.

Retreating glacier — Meltwater channels
Terminal moraine

▲ *Terminal moraines are* crescent-shaped ridges of glacial deposits, widely found in central Russia. Detritus is carried by the glacier and deposited at its terminus (snout) as it melts, marking the limit of the ice advance.

Ural Mountains (*Ural'skiye Gory*)

Two of Europe's biggest rivers, the Volga and Western Dvina, rise in the swampy uplands of the Valdai Hills (*Valdayskaya Vozvyshennost'*).

▶ *Lake Onega* (Onezhskoye Ozero) is the remnant of a body of water which, 12,000 years ago, connected the White Sea (Beloye More) with the Gulf of Finland and the Baltic Sea.

Using the land and sea

The cold climate confines agriculture mainly to southern and western provinces, where dairy farming predominates and arable land is given over to fodder crops as well as flax, potatoes, oats and rye. Areas beyond the northern margins of cultivation are used for forestry, hunting, herding and fishing, with some vegetables grown in hothouses around urban areas.

Land use and agricultural distribution

- cattle
- fishing
- reindeer
- timber
- fodder
- • major towns

- pasture
- cropland
- forest
- mountain region
- wetland
- tundra
- barren
- ice

The urban/rural population divide

urban 80% rural 20%

0 10 20 30 40 50 60 70 80 90 100

Population density	Total land area
26 people per sq mile (10 people per sq km)	829,398 sq miles (2,148,700 sq km)

◀ *Many rapids are found along the 175 mile (280 km) course of the Suna river.*

▶ *St Peter and Paul Fortress* is the oldest building in St Petersburg, founded by Peter the Great in 1703 as a modern, European capital for Russia.

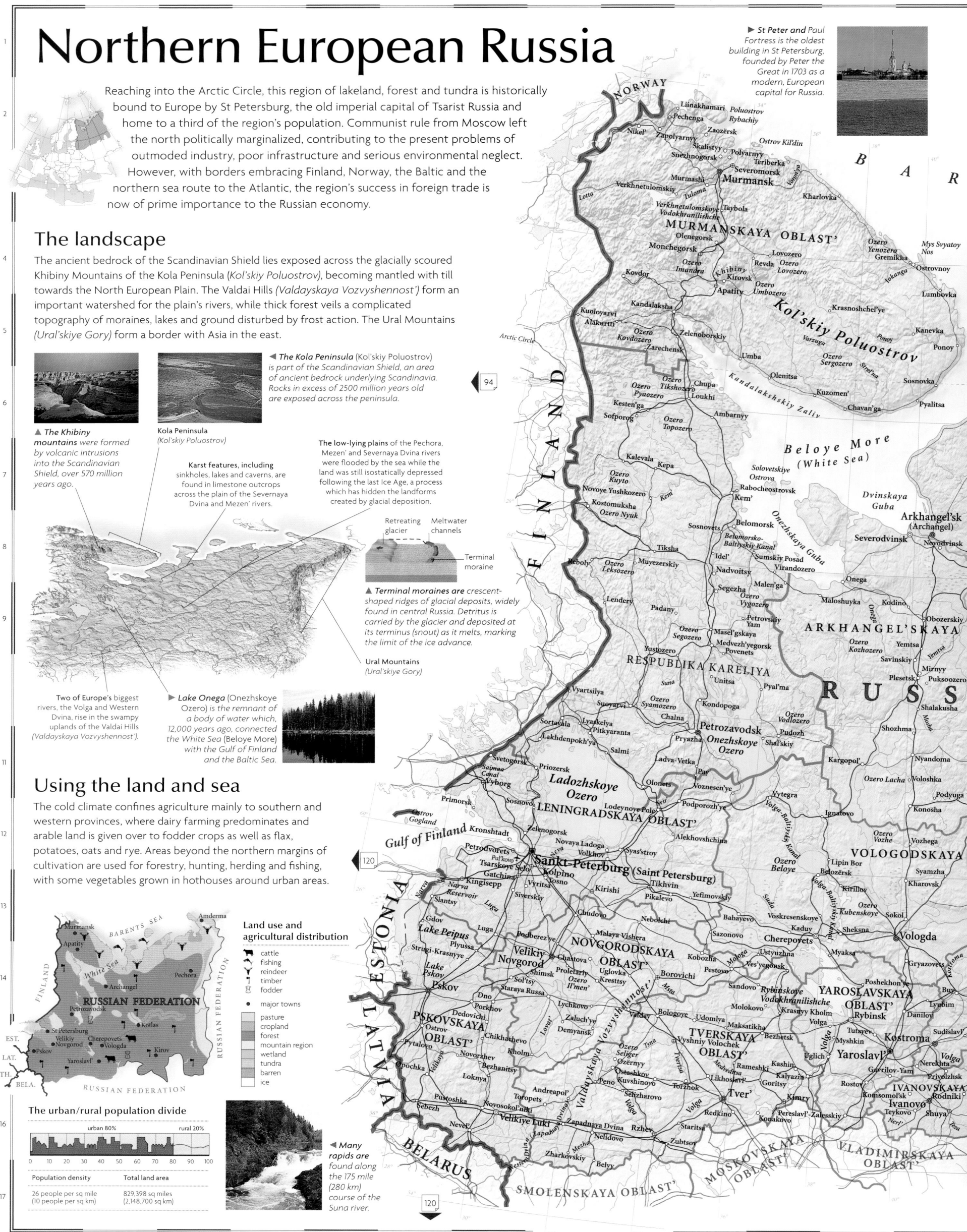

◄ *The Ural Mountains* (Ural'skiye Gory) form the traditional boundary between Europe and Asia. Elevations rarely exceed 6000 ft (1830 m). The region is extremely barren in the far northern latitudes.

Scale 1:5,500,000

projection: Lambert Conformal Conic

Map key

Population
- 1 million to 5 million
- 500,000 to 1 million
- 100,000 to 500,000
- 50,000 to 100,000
- 10,000 to 50,000
- below 10,000

Elevation
- 1000m / 3281ft
- 500m / 1640ft
- 250m / 820ft
- 100m / 328ft
- sea level

Transport and industry

The ports of St Petersburg, Murmansk and Archangel serve a regional economy led by large-scale resource extraction. Nickel, iron ore and apatite are mined in the Kola Peninsula (Kol'skiy Poluostrov), and fossil fuels in the Pechora Basin. Paper production is central to Archangel's vast timber industry, while St Petersburg, drawing on ample labour, has become a major manufacturing centre.

Major industry and infrastructure
- chemicals
- coal
- defence
- engineering
- food processing
- hydro-electric power
- mining
- oil & gas
- textiles
- timber processing
- major towns
- international airports
- major roads
- major industrial areas

The transport network
- 53,700 miles (85,920 km)
- None
- 10,300 miles (16,572 km)
- 12,500 miles (20,000 km)

Railways linking remote industrial centres with the region's ports are the principal means of supply, although the impressive system of canals, linking natural waterways, is used for freight haulage during the summer.

► *Ice forces the* port at St Petersburg to close in winter, yet Murmansk, on the Barents Sea, remains open, its waters prevented from freezing by warmer ocean currents extending from the North Atlantic Drift.

▶ *Kaliningrad has been a Russian enclave since 1945. The port is an important centre for the Russian Federation's Baltic fishing fleet.*

◀ *St Basil's Cathedral, completed in 1561, stands in Moscow's Red Square next to the Kremlin; the original fortified stronghold of the city.*

Southern European Russia

This region, divided from Asia by desert, seas and mountains, has exerted a powerful influence both east and west since the 13th century. Over 70 years of Communist rule produced a highly urbanized, industrial society dominated by Moscow, which was the capital of the Soviet Union until 1991. Almost two-thirds of the Russian Federation's population live in this core area, with a relatively high *per capita* share of its wealth. However, the rapid growth of a market economy has caused great social upheaval, with rising crime and political instability.

The landscape

Ancient folds in the deep sedimentary strata of the North European Plain have created a sequence of high and low regions. The Central Russian Upland (*Srednerusskaya Vozvyshennost'*) in the west is deeply incised by rivers draining into the lowland of the Oka and Don rivers. In the east the Volga, Europe's longest river, flows south to the Caspian Sea, dividing the Volga Uplands (*Privolzhskaya Vozvyshennost'*) from the foothills of the Ural Mountains (*Ural'skiye Gory*). The Caucasus mountains and the Black Sea form a natural border to the southwest.

▲ *A plantation of Scots pine helps consolidate the loose sandy soils of the Meshchera Lowland (Meshcherskaya Nizina), which lies on the bed of an old glacial lake.*

The **Smolensk-Moscow Upland** (*Smolensko-Moskovskaya Vozvyshennost'*) is a series of terminal moraine ridges marking the southern extent of the last glaciation.

Glacial till covers the bedrock to the north of the North European Plain, giving a gentle surface relief.

The **lowland of** the Oka and Don rivers lies over a broad trough, between the upfolds of the Volga Uplands (*Privolzhskaya Vozvyshennost'*) to the east, and the Central Russian Upland (*Srednerusskaya Vozvyshennost'*) to the west.

The **southern Ural Mountains** (*Ural'skiye Gory*) consist of several parallel ranges of ancient fold mountains running from north to south.

Central Russian Upland (*Srednerusskaya Vozvyshennost'*).

The **flood plain** of the Volga forms a long oasis of verdant vegetation, contrasting with the aridity of the surrounding Caspian hinterland.

The **marshlands** of the Volga Delta are visited by over 260 species of bird each year, migrating between South Africa and Arctic Siberia.

The **Caspian Depression** is a large downfold (or syncline) which became flooded, forming the Caspian Sea. The shoreline is 98 ft (30 m) below sea level.

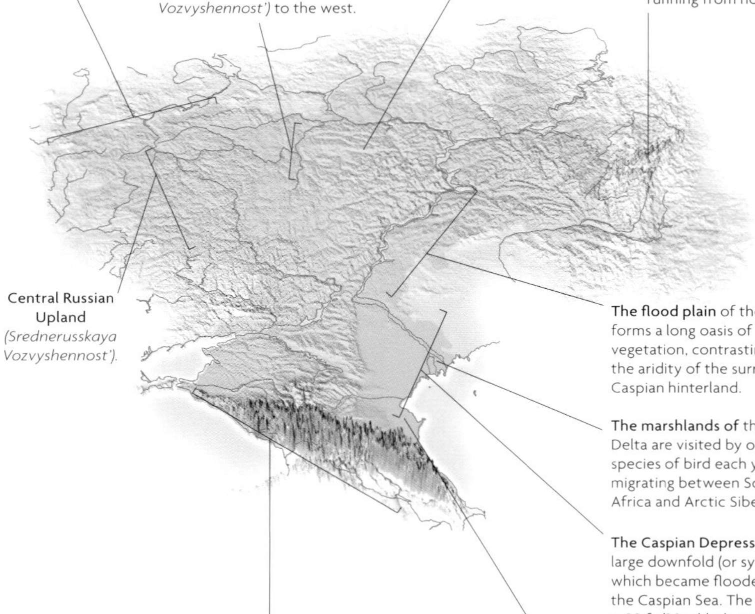

◀ *The Caucasus mountains run from the Black Sea to the Caspian Sea. They include El' brus which, at 18,511 ft (5642 m), is the highest point in Europe. It is still uplifting at a rate of 0.4 inches (10 mm) per year.*

Drifting sand occupies large areas of the south, forming dunes up to 50 ft (15 m) high.

Salt dome

Salt dome is forced up and through the rock strata

Sedimentary strata

Salts are forced upwards by denser overlying strata

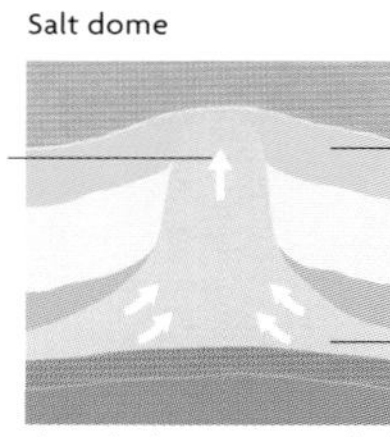

▲ *Salt domes, rounded hills up to 500 ft (150 m) high, are produced as less dense rock salts are displaced under the extreme pressure of denser, overlying strata and forced up towards the surface creating domes. They are widespread in the Caspian Depression.*

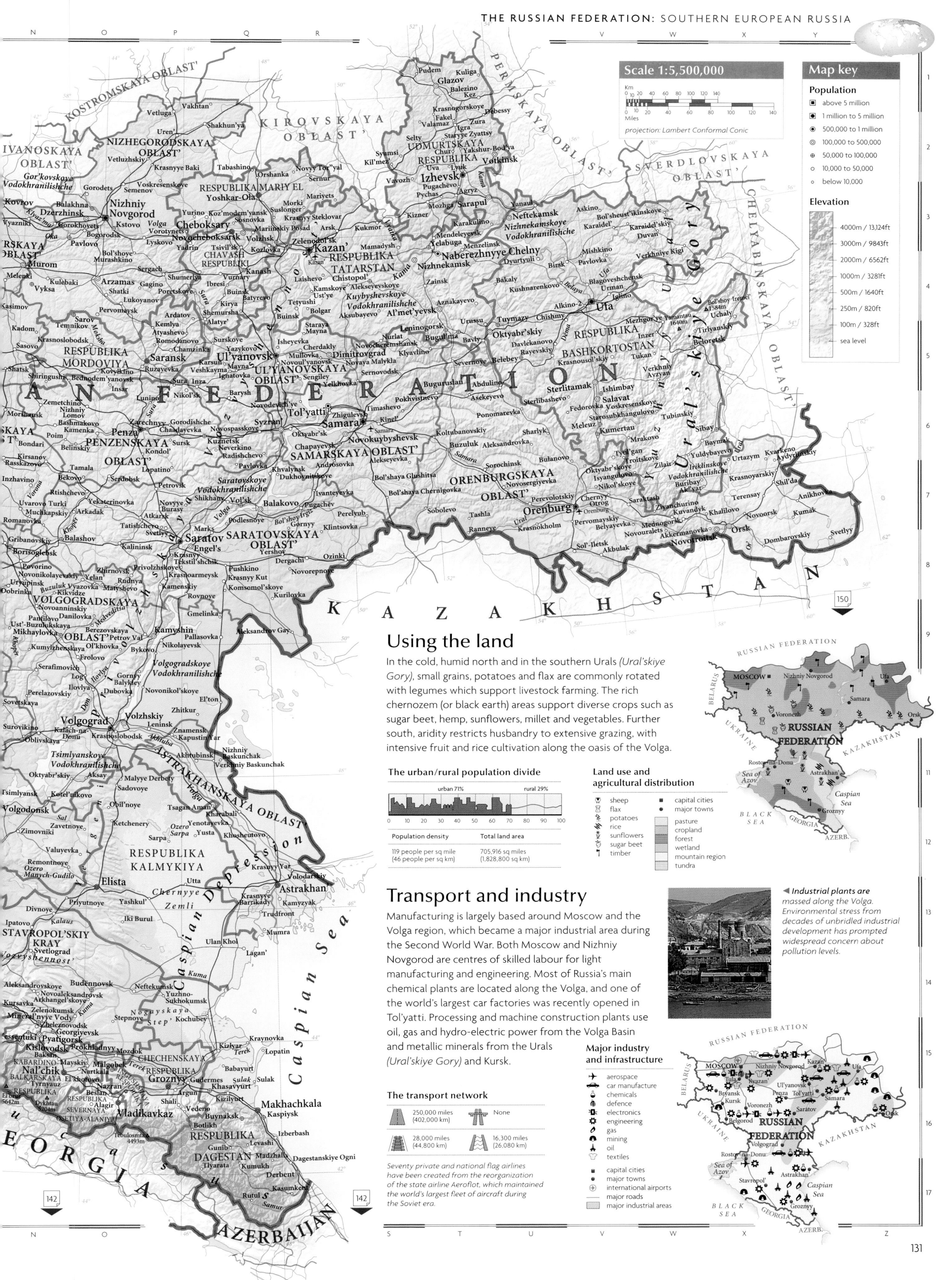

Scale 1:5,500,000

projection: Lambert Conformal Conic

Map key

Population
- ■ above 5 million
- ▣ 1 million to 5 million
- ◉ 500,000 to 1 million
- ◎ 100,000 to 500,000
- ⊕ 50,000 to 100,000
- ○ 10,000 to 50,000
- ○ below 10,000

Elevation
- 4000m / 13,124ft
- 3000m / 9843ft
- 2000m / 6562ft
- 1000m / 3281ft
- 500m / 1640ft
- 250m / 820ft
- 100m / 328ft
- sea level

Using the land

In the cold, humid north and in the southern Urals *(Ural'skiye Gory)*, small grains, potatoes and flax are commonly rotated with legumes which support livestock farming. The rich chernozem (or black earth) areas support diverse crops such as sugar beet, hemp, sunflowers, millet and vegetables. Further south, aridity restricts husbandry to extensive grazing, with intensive fruit and rice cultivation along the oasis of the Volga.

The urban/rural population divide

urban 71%   rural 29%

0 10 20 30 40 50 60 70 80 90 100

Population density
119 people per sq mile
(46 people per sq km)

Total land area
705,916 sq miles
(1,828,800 sq km)

Land use and agricultural distribution

- sheep
- flax
- potatoes
- rice
- sunflowers
- sugar beet
- timber
- ■ capital cities
- • major towns

- pasture
- cropland
- forest
- wetland
- mountain region
- tundra

Transport and industry

Manufacturing is largely based around Moscow and the Volga region, which became a major industrial area during the Second World War. Both Moscow and Nizhniy Novgorod are centres of skilled labour for light manufacturing and engineering. Most of Russia's main chemical plants are located along the Volga, and one of the world's largest car factories was recently opened in Tol'yatti. Processing and machine construction plants use oil, gas and hydro-electric power from the Volga Basin and metallic minerals from the Urals *(Ural'skiye Gory)* and Kursk.

◄ *Industrial plants are massed along the Volga. Environmental stress from decades of unbridled industrial development has prompted widespread concern about pollution levels.*

Major industry and infrastructure

- aerospace
- car manufacture
- chemicals
- defence
- electronics
- engineering
- gas
- mining
- oil
- textiles
- ■ capital cities
- • major towns
- ⊕ international airports
- major roads
- major industrial areas

The transport network

- 250,000 miles (402,000 km)
- None
- 28,000 miles (44,800 km)
- 16,300 miles (26,080 km)

Seventy private and national flag airlines have been created from the reorganization of the state airline Aeroflot, which maintained the world's largest fleet of aircraft during the Soviet era.

Asia

Asia, the world's largest continent, covers 16,838,365 sq miles (43,608,000 sq km).
It comprises 49 separate countries, including 97% of Turkey and 72% of the
Russian Federation. Almost 60% of the world's population lives in Asia.

- ● **Greatest extent, North–South:**
  4000 miles / 6440 km
- ■ **Greatest extent, East–West:**
  6000 miles / 9650 km

Most northerly point:
Mys Articesku,
Russian Federation
81° 12' N

Mys Dezhneva,
Russian Federation
169° 40' W

Largest lake:
Caspian Sea
143,205 sq miles
(371,000 sq km)

Mys Chelyuskin,
Russian Federation
77° 44' N

Most easterly point:
Mys Dezhneva,
Russian Federation
169° 40' W

Most westerly point:
Bozca Adası, Turkey
26° 2' E

Baba Bur-nu,
Turkey
26° 4' E

Lowest recorded temperature:
Verkhoyansk,
Russian Federation
-90°F (-68°C)

Lowest point:
Dead Sea,
Israel/Jordan
-1286 ft (-392 m)
below sea level

Kagoshima

Highest point:
Mount Everest,
China/Nepal
29,035 ft (8850 m)

Hodeida

Highest recorded temperature:
Tirat Tsvi, Israel
129°F (54°C)

Equator

Tanjong Piai,
Malaysia
1° 16' N

Most southerly point:
Pulau Pamana,
Indonesia 11° S

| Hodeida, Yemen | The Gulf | Zagros Mountains | Plateau of Tibet | Gobi | Manchurian Plain | Kagoshima, Japan |

Cross-section from Hodeida, Yemen to Kagoshima, Japan

line of cross-section

| 0 | 500 | 1000 | 1500 Km |
| 0 | 500 | 1000 | 1500 Miles |

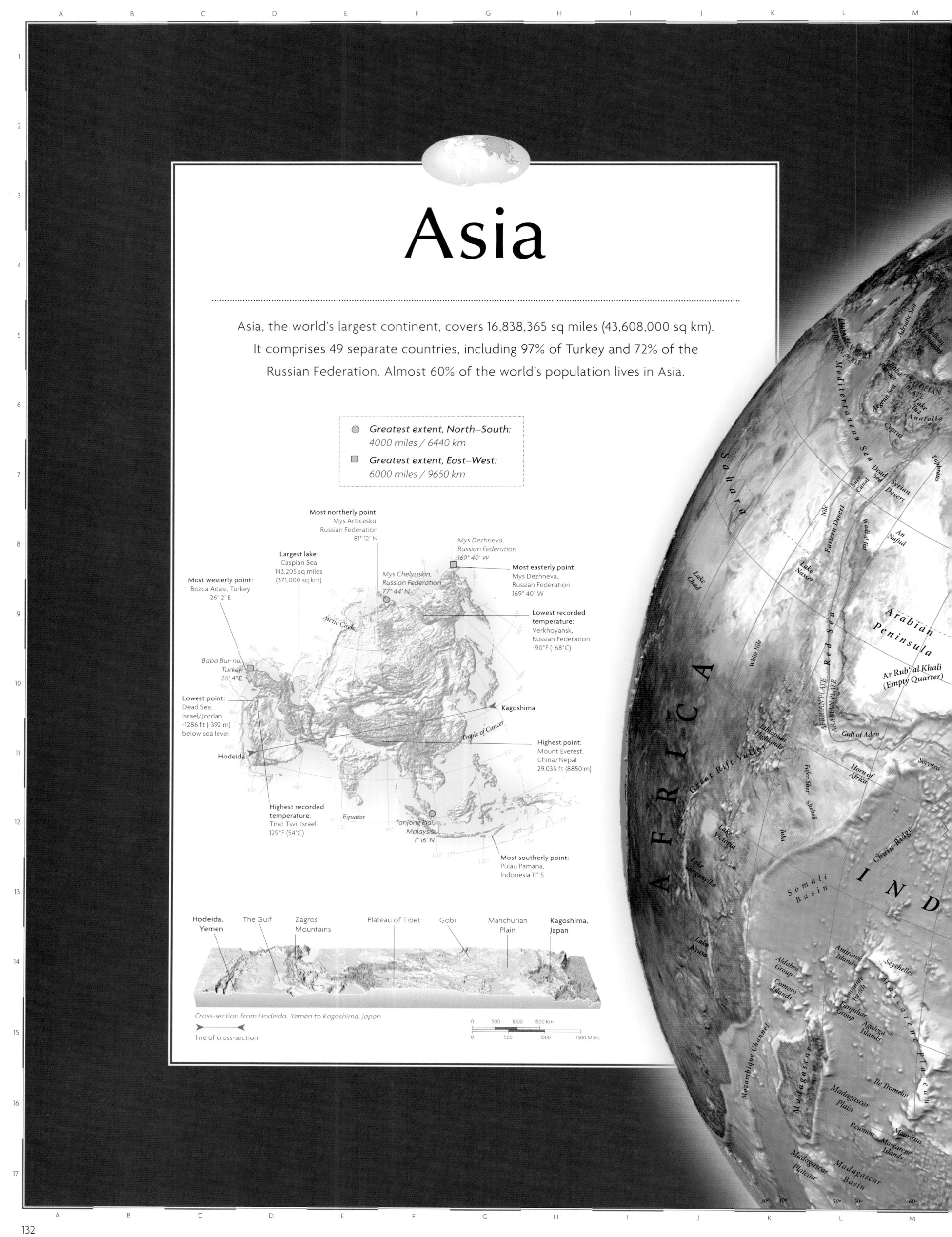

ARCTIC OCEAN
North Pole
NORTH AMERICAN PLATE
EURASIAN PLATE

EUROPE

ASIA

Norwegian Sea
Scandinavia
North Sea
Gulf of Bothnia
Baltic Sea
Gulf of Finland
North Cape
Barents Sea
Kola Peninsula
White Sea
Novaya Zemlya
Kara Sea
Severnaya Zemlya
Mys Chelyuskin
Poluostrov Taymyr
Laptev Sea
New Siberian Islands
East Siberian Sea
Long Strait
Bering Strait
Bering Sea

North European Plain
Central Russian Upland
Ural Mountains
West Siberian Plain
North Siberian Lowland
Central Siberian Plateau
Siberia
Khrebet Cherskogo
Verkhoyanskiy Khrebet
Kolyma Range
Koryak Range

Black Sea
Caucasus
Caspian Depression
Aral Sea
Kirghiz Steppe
Lake Chany
Altai Mountains
Plateau of Mongolia
Stanovoy Khrebet
Zeya Reservoir
Manchurian Plain
Kamchatka
Sea of Okhotsk
Kuril Islands

Caspian Sea
Ustyurt Plateau
Turan Lowland
Kara Kum
Syr Darya
Lake Balkhash
Tien Shan
Dzungaria
Gobi
Yellow River
Sea of Japan (East Sea)
Japan
Hokkaido

Iranian Plateau
Zagros Mountains
Hindu Kush
Karakoram Range
Takla Makan Desert
Kunlun Mountains
Plateau of Tibet
Altun Shan
Nan Shan
Qilian Shan
Ordos Desert
Wutai Shan
Bo Hai
Korea Bay
Yellow Sea
Cheju-do
Korea Strait
Shikoku
Kyushu

The Gulf
Strait of Hormuz
Thar Desert
Himalayas
Annapurna 8091m
Mount Everest 8850m
Great Plain of China
East China Sea
Ryukyu Islands

Arabian Sea
Deccan
Western Ghats
Eastern Ghats
Bay of Bengal
Mouths of the Ganges
Taiwan
Philippine Sea

Arabian Basin
Laccadive Islands
Malabar Coast
Coromandel Coast
Sri Lanka
Andaman Islands
Gulf of Martaban
South China Sea
Luzon
Philippine Basin

INDIAN OCEAN
Maldives
Ceylon Plain
Andaman Sea
Nicobar Islands
Gulf of Thailand
Mouths of the Mekong
South China Basin
Palawan
Mindoro
Panay
Negros
Samar
Mindanao
Celebes Sea

Carlsberg Ridge
Chagos-Laccadive Plateau
Ninetyeast Ridge
Sumatra
Malay Peninsula
Sunda Shelf
Borneo
Greater Sunda Islands
Sulu Sea
Celebes Sea
Moluccas
Halmahera
New Guinea Trench

Mid-Indian Ridge
Chagos Bank
Chagos Trench
Mid-Indian Basin
Cocos Basin
Cocos Islands
Christmas Island
Java Trench
Java
Java Sea
East Indies
Lesser Sunda Islands
Bali
Flores Sea
Sumba Islands
Timor
Banda Sea
Arafura Sea
Torres Strait

AUSTRALIA

PACIFIC OCEAN

Tropic of Cancer
Equator
Tropic of Capricorn

Asian resources

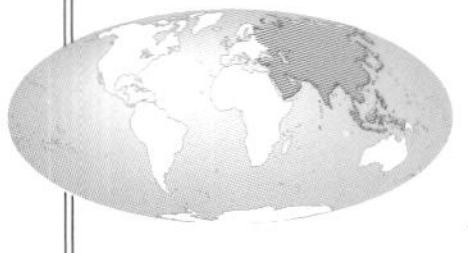

Although agriculture remains the economic mainstay of most Asian countries, the number of people employed in agriculture has steadily declined, as new industries have been developed during the past 30 years. China, Indonesia, Malaysia, Thailand and Turkey have all experienced far-reaching structural change in their economies, while the breakup of the Soviet Union has created a new economic challenge in the Central Asian republics. The countries of The Gulf illustrate the rapid transformation from rural nomadism to modern, urban society which oil wealth has brought to parts of the continent. Asia's most economically dynamic countries, Japan, Singapore, South Korea, and Taiwan, fringe the Pacific Ocean and are known as the Pacific Rim. In contrast, other Southeast Asian countries like Laos and Cambodia remain both economically and industrially underdeveloped.

Industry

East Asian industry leads the continent in both productivity and efficiency; electronics, hi-tech industries, car manufacture and shipbuilding are important. The so-called economic 'tigers' of the Pacific Rim are Japan, South Korea and Taiwan and in recent years China has rediscovered its potential as an economic superpower. Heavy industries such as engineering, chemicals, and steel typify the industrial complexes along the corridor created by the Trans-Siberian Railway, the Fergana Valley in Central Asia, and also much of the huge industrial plain of east China. The discovery of oil in The Gulf has brought immense wealth to countries that previously relied on subsistence agriculture on marginal desert land.

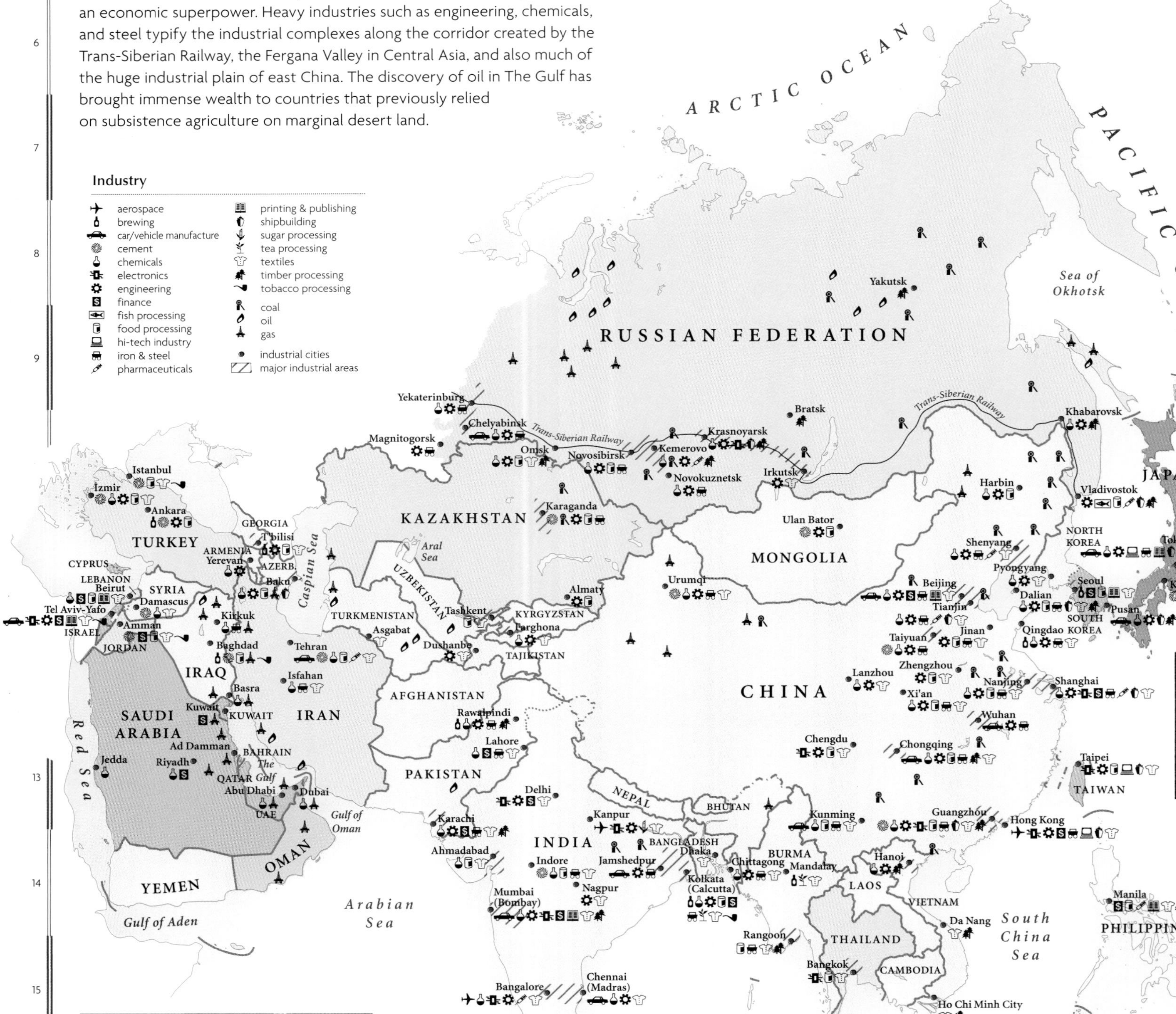

Standard of living

Despite Japan's high standards of living, and Southwest Asia's oil-derived wealth, immense disparities exist across the continent. Afghanistan remains one of the world's most underdeveloped nations, as do the mountain states of Nepal and Bhutan. Further rapid population growth is exacerbating poverty and overcrowding in many parts of India and Bangladesh.

Standard of living
(UN human development index)
- low
- high

▲ *On a small island* at the southern tip of the Malay Peninsula lies Singapore, one of the Pacific Rim's most vibrant economic centres. Multinational banking and finance form the core of the city's wealth.

GNI per capita (US$)
- below 1999
- 2000–4999
- 5000–9999
- 10,000–19,999
- 20,000–24,999
- above 25,000

Industry
- ✈ aerospace
- brewing
- car/vehicle manufacture
- cement
- chemicals
- electronics
- engineering
- finance
- fish processing
- food processing
- hi-tech industry
- iron & steel
- pharmaceuticals
- printing & publishing
- shipbuilding
- sugar processing
- tea processing
- textiles
- timber processing
- tobacco processing
- coal
- oil
- gas
- ■ industrial cities
- ▨ major industrial areas

▲ *Iron and steel*, engineering and shipbuilding typify the heavy industry found in eastern China's industrial cities, especially the nation's leading manufacturing centre, Shanghai.

◀ *Traditional industries are* still crucial to many rural economies across Asia. Here, on the Vietnamese coast, salt has been extracted from seawater by evaporation and is being loaded into a van to take to market.

ARCTIC OCEAN

PACIFIC OCEAN

RUSSIAN FEDERATION

Sea of Okhotsk

Yakutsk

Trans-Siberian Railway

Yekaterinburg
Chelyabinsk
Magnitogorsk
Omsk
Novosibirsk
Kemerovo
Krasnoyarsk
Novokuznetsk
Irkutsk
Bratsk
Khabarovsk
Vladivostok

Istanbul
Izmir
Ankara
TURKEY
CYPRUS
LEBANON
Beirut
Tel Aviv-Yafo
ISRAEL
SYRIA
Damascus
Amman
JORDAN
GEORGIA
Tbilisi
ARMENIA
Yerevan
AZERB.
Baku
Caspian Sea
Aral Sea
KAZAKHSTAN
Karaganda

Kirkuk
Baghdad
IRAQ
Basra
Kuwait
KUWAIT
SAUDI ARABIA
Ad Damman
BAHRAIN
The Gulf
QATAR
Abu Dhabi
Dubai
UAE
Gulf of Oman
Jedda
Riyadh
Red Sea
YEMEN
Gulf of Aden
OMAN

Tehran
Isfahan
IRAN
UZBEKISTAN
TURKMENISTAN
Asgabat
Tashkent
Farghona
KYRGYZSTAN
Dushanbe
TAJIKISTAN
AFGHANISTAN
Rawalpindi
Lahore
PAKISTAN
Karachi
Ahmadabad
Indore
Mumbai (Bombay)
Nagpur
Arabian Sea
INDIA
Delhi
Kanpur
Jamshedpur
BANGLADESH
Dhaka
Chittagong
Kolkata (Calcutta)
Bangalore
Chennai (Madras)
SRI LANKA
INDIAN OCEAN

Almaty
Urumqi
MONGOLIA
Ulan Bator
CHINA
Lanzhou
Xi'an
Chengdu
Chongqing
Kunming
NEPAL
BHUTAN
BURMA
Mandalay
Rangoon
THAILAND
Bangkok
CAMBODIA
LAOS
VIETNAM
Hanoi
Da Nang
Ho Chi Minh City
South China Sea

Harbin
Shenyang
NORTH KOREA
Pyongyang
Beijing
Tianjin
Dalian
Jinan
Taiyuan
Qingdao
SOUTH KOREA
Seoul
Pusan
Zhengzhou
Nanjing
Shanghai
Wuhan
Guangzhou
Hong Kong
Taipei
TAIWAN
JAPAN
Tokyo
Nagoya
Kobe
Vladivostok

Manila
PHILIPPINES

Kuala Lumpur
MALAYSIA
BRUNEI
Singapore
SINGAPORE
INDONESIA
Jakarta
Surabaya
EAST TIMOR

Environmental issues

The transformation of Uzbekistan by the former Soviet Union into the world's fifth largest producer of cotton led to the diversion of several major rivers for irrigation. Starved of this water, the Aral Sea diminished in volume by over 75% since 1960, irreversibly altering the ecology of the area. Heavy industries in eastern China have polluted coastal waters, rivers and urban air, while in Burma, Malaysia and Indonesia, ancient hardwood rainforests are felled faster than they can regenerate.

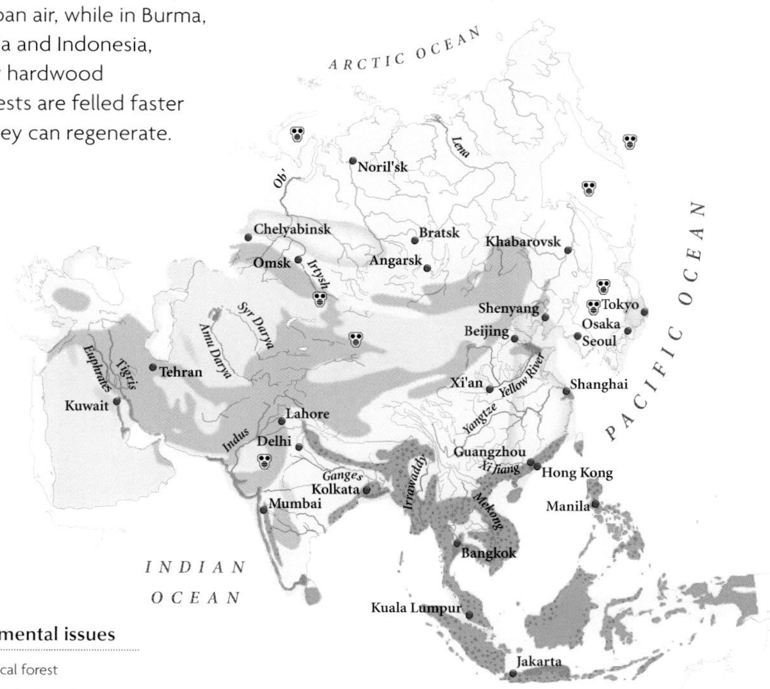

▲ *Although Siberia remains* a quintessentially frozen, inhospitable wasteland, vast untapped mineral reserves – especially the oil and gas of the West Siberian Plain – have lured industrial development to the area since the 1950s and 1960s.

Mineral resources

At least 60% of the world's known oil and gas deposits are found in Asia; notably the vast oil fields of The Gulf, and the less-exploited oil and gas fields of the Ob' basin in west Siberia. Immense coal reserves in Siberia and China have been utilized to support large steel industries. Southeast Asia has some of the world's largest deposits of tin, found in a belt running down the Malay Peninsula to Indonesia.

Mineral resources

- oil field
- gas field
- coal field
- chromite
- copper
- gold
- iron
- lead
- nickel
- platinum
- tin
- wolfram

Environmental issues

- tropical forest
- forest destroyed
- desert
- desertification
- acid rain
- polluted rivers
- marine pollution
- heavy marine pollution
- radioactive contamination
- poor urban air quality

◀ *The long-term environmental* impact of the Gulf War (1991) is still uncertain. As Iraqi troops left Kuwait, equipment was abandoned to rust and thousands of oil wells were set alight, pouring crude oil into The Gulf.

Using the land and sea

Vast areas of Asia remain uncultivated as a result of unsuitable climatic and soil conditions. In favourable areas such as river deltas, farming is intensive. Rice is the staple crop of most Asian countries, grown in paddy fields on waterlogged alluvial plains and terraced hillsides, and often irrigated for higher yields. Across the black earth region of the Eurasian steppe in southern Siberia and Kazakhstan, wheat farming is the dominant activity. Cash crops, like tea in Sri Lanka and dates in the Arabian Peninsula, are grown for export, and provide valuable income. The sovereignty of the rich fishing grounds in the South China Sea is disputed by China, Malaysia, Taiwan, the Philippines and Vietnam, because of potential oil reserves.

Using the land and sea

- cropland
- desert
- forest
- mountain region
- pasture
- tundra
- wetland
- major conurbations
- cattle
- pigs
- goats
- sheep
- coconuts
- corn (maize)
- cotton
- dates
- fishing
- fruit
- jute
- peanuts
- rice
- rubber
- shellfish
- soya beans
- sugar beet
- sugar cane
- tea
- timber
- wheat

▲ *Date palms have* been cultivated in oases throughout the Arabian Peninsula since antiquity. In addition to the fruit, palms are used for timber, fuel, rope, and for making vinegar, syrup and a liquor known as arrack.

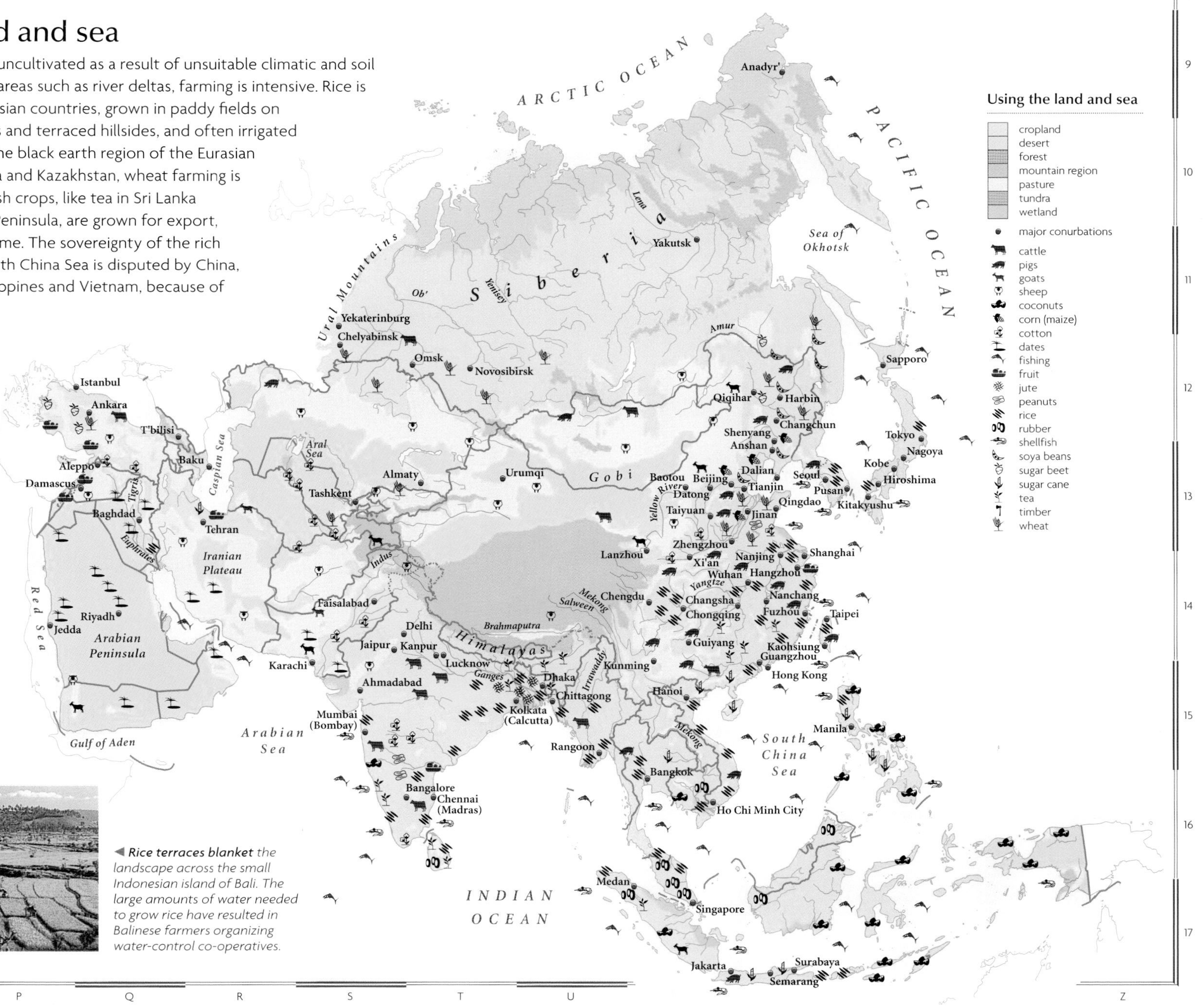

◀ *Rice terraces blanket* the landscape across the small Indonesian island of Bali. The large amounts of water needed to grow rice have resulted in Balinese farmers organizing water-control co-operatives.

Siberian Plateau and Plain

The West Siberian Plain is one of the largest in the world, and contains a vast system of marshes. The whole area is covered by glacial deposits, underlain by the Angara Shield, a remnant of the ancient continent of Laurasia. The flat relief of the region and thick surface deposits result in poor drainage; this, combined with the freezing and thawing of the extensive permafrost layer leads to the formation of the vast swamps which cover the area. Many of the north-flowing rivers are also frozen for up to half the year.

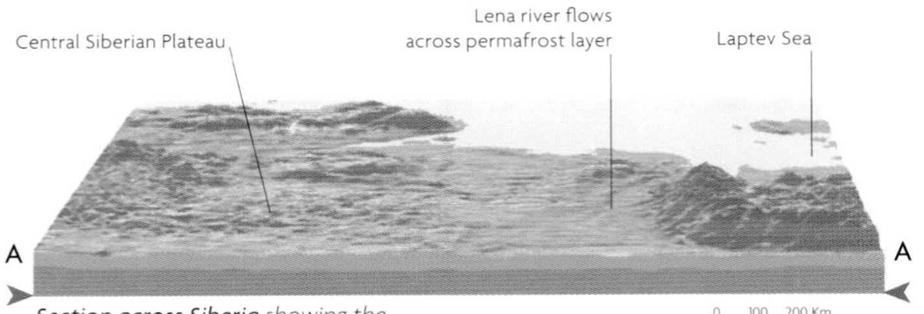

Section across Siberia showing the
Central Siberian Plateau and its drainage.

Central Siberian Plateau

Lena river flows across permafrost layer

Laptev Sea

0   100   200 Km
0   100   200 Miles

The Arabian Shield and Iranian Plateau

Approximately five million years ago, rifting of the continental crust split the Arabian Plate from the African Plate and flooded the Red Sea. As this rift spread, the Arabian Plate collided with the Eurasian Plate, transforming part of the Tethys seabed into the Zagros Mountains which run northwest-southeast across western Iran.

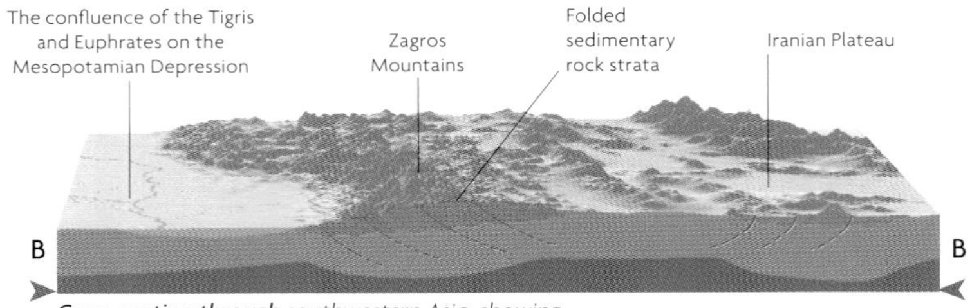

The confluence of the Tigris and Euphrates on the Mesopotamian Depression

Zagros Mountains

Folded sedimentary rock strata

Iranian Plateau

Cross-section through southwestern Asia, showing
*the Mesopotamian Depression, the folded Zagros
Mountains and the Iranian Plateau.*

0   50   100 Km
0   50   100 Miles

The Turan Basin and Kazakh Uplands

The Turan Basin and Kazakh Uplands are a complex mixture of mountain foothills, an arid limestone plateau and deserts including the Kyzl Kum and Kara Kum. In the centre of the Turan Lowland – an area of inland drainage – is the desiccated Aral Sea, reduced to a fraction of its former size because of the diversion of its flow into irrigation channels. The only rivers with sufficient water to cross this arid region are the Syr Dayra and Amu Dayra.

The Indian Shield and Himalayan System

The large shield area beneath the Indian subcontinent is between 2.5 and 3.5 billion years old. As the floor of the southern Indian Ocean spread, it pushed the Indian Shield north. This was eventually driven beneath the Plateau of Tibet. This process closed up the ancient Tethys Sea and uplifted the world's highest mountain chain, the Himalayas. Much of the uplifted rock strata was from the seabed of the Tethys Sea, partly accounting for the weakness of the rocks and the high levels of erosion found in the Himalayas.

Indo-Gangetic Depression

Crushed sediment from seabed of the Tethys Sea

Himalayas

Thrust zone

Plateau of Tibet

Cross-section through the Himalayas showing
thrust faulting of the rock strata.

0   50   100 Km
0   50   100 Miles

Central Asian Plateaux and Basins

The Plateau of Tibet lies north of the Himalayas and covers 965,250 sq miles (2,500,000 sq km); its average elevation is 16,500 ft (5000 m). The region is noted for its extreme aridity. In the south, the Himalayan mountain belt blocks moisture-bearing winds. The pressure from the Indo-Australian Plate against the plateau is causing both uplift and, when combined with the downward force caused by weight of the plateau, extension east and west of the of the more malleable underlying crust. The brittle upper rock layers are extensively faulted.

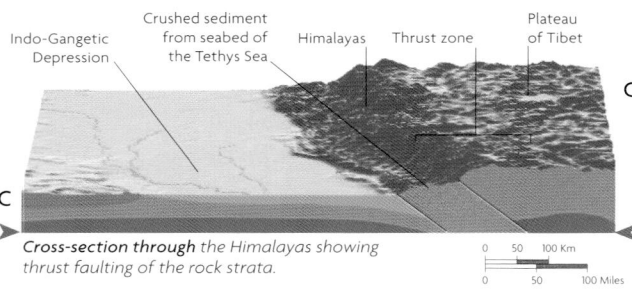

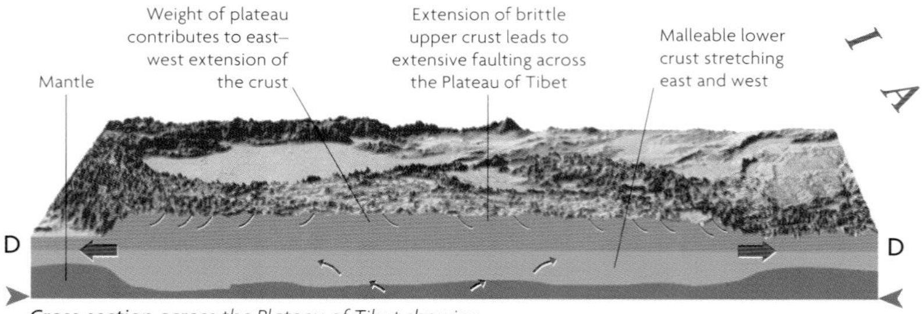

Weight of plateau contributes to east–west extension of the crust

Extension of brittle upper crust leads to extensive faulting across the Plateau of Tibet

Malleable lower crust stretching east and west

Mantle

Cross-section across the Plateau of Tibet showing
*uplift and crustal extension caused by the collision
of the Indo-Australian and Eurasian plates.*

0   200   400 Km
0   200   400 Miles

ARC

Franz Josef Land

Kara Sea

EUROPE

SIBERIAN

West Siberian Plain

Ural Mountains

Ob

Nadym

Gulf of Ob

Poluostrov Yamal

Tobol

Ishim

Irtysh

Black Sea

Sea of Azov

EURASIAN PLATE

ANATOLIAN PLATE

Anatolia

Taurus Mountains

Gulf of Antalya

Kizil Irmak

Caucasus

Kura

Caspian Sea

Kirghiz Steppe

Kulunda Steppe

Elburz Mountains

Ustyurt Plateau

Aral Sea

TURAN BASIN & KAZAKH UPLANDS

Turan Lowland

Kazakh Uplands

Lake Balkhash

Ili

Ozero Zaysan

AFRICAN PLATE

Mediterranean Sea

Syrian Desert

Euphrates

Tigris

ARABIAN PLATE

ARABIAN SHIELD & IRANIAN PLATEAU

Great Salt Desert

Iranian Plateau

Zagros Mountains

Kyzyl Kum

Amu Darya

Kara Kum

Syr Darya

Chatkal Range

Kirghiz Range

Turkestan Range

Issyk-Kul'

Ozero Issyk-Kul'

Tien Shan

Tarim He

Tarim

Takla Makan

AFRICA

An Nafūd

As Summān

Ad Dahnā'

Al Biyāḍ

'Asīr

Red Sea

ARABIAN PLATE

AFRICAN PLATE

Arabian Peninsula

Ar Rub' al Khālī (Empty Quarter)

Hadhramaut

The Gulf

Strait of Hormuz

Gulf of Oman

IRANIAN PLATE

Hindu Kush

Kabul

Khyber Pass 1080m

Solaimānrange

Indus

K2 861 1m

Karakoram Range

Karakoram Pass 5568m

Kunlun

Thar Desert

Sutlej

INDIAN SHIELD & HIMALAYAN SYSTEM

Himal

Mouths of the Indus

Rann of Kachchh

Vindhya Range

Narmada

Satpura Range

Gulf of Kachchh

Gulf of Khambhat

Arabian Sea

INDO-AUSTRALIAN PLATE

Gulf of Aden

ARABIAN PLATE

AFRICAN PLATE

Socotra

Godavari

Krishna

Deccan

Western Ghats

Eastern Ghats

INDIAN OCEAN

Sri Lanka

Gulf of Mannar

Physical Asia

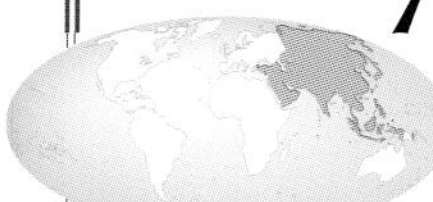

The structure of Asia can be divided into two distinct regions. The landscape of northern Asia consists of old mountain chains, shields, plateaux and basins, like the Ural Mountains in the west and the Central Siberian Plateau to the east. To the south of this region, are a series of plateaux and basins, including the vast Plateau of Tibet and the Tarim Basin. In contrast, the landscapes of southern Asia are much younger, formed by tectonic activity beginning about 65 million years ago, leading to an almost continuous mountain chain running from Europe, across much of Asia, and culminating in the mighty Himalayan mountain belt, formed when the Indo-Australian Plate collided with the Eurasian Plate. They are still being uplifted today. North of the mountains lies a belt of deserts, including the Gobi and the Takla Makan. In the far south, tectonic activity has formed narrow island arcs, extending over 4000 miles (7000 km). To the west lies the Arabian Shield, once part of the African Plate. As it was rifted apart from Africa, the Arabian Plate collided with the Eurasian Plate, uplifting the Zagros Mountains.

Shaping the landscape

In the north, melting of extensive permafrost leads to typical periglacial features such as thermokarst. In the arid areas wind action transports sand creating extensive dune systems. An active tectonic margin in the south causes continued uplift, and volcanic and seismic activity, but also high rates of weathering and erosion. Across the continent, huge rivers erode and transport vast quantities of sediment depositing it on the plains or forming large deltas.

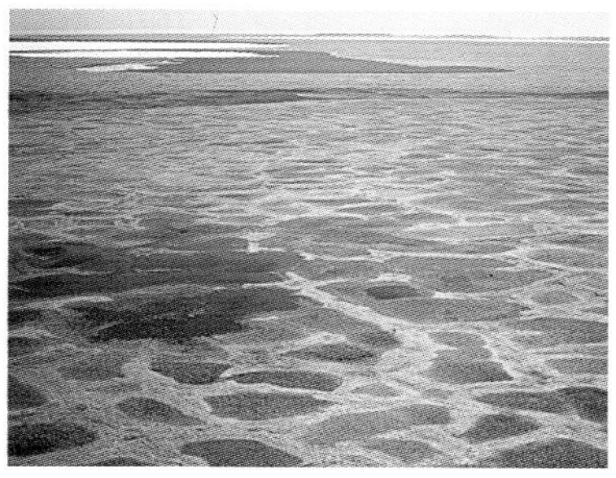

Periglaciation

1 Permafrost is widespread across northern Siberia. When ground ice, which makes up a large proportion of the soil layer, melts, it contracts and extensive ground subsidence occurs. Over time this process leads to depressions in the landscape and the gradual movement of soil down slopes. Eventually the accumulation of water in the depressions leads to thermokarstic lakes *(left)*.

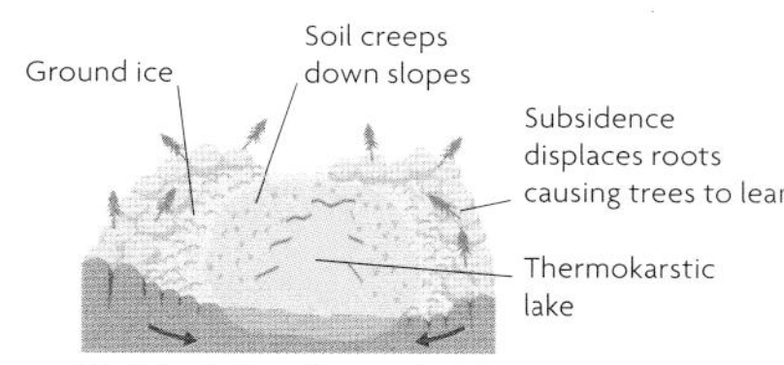

Periglaciation: formation of thermokarst

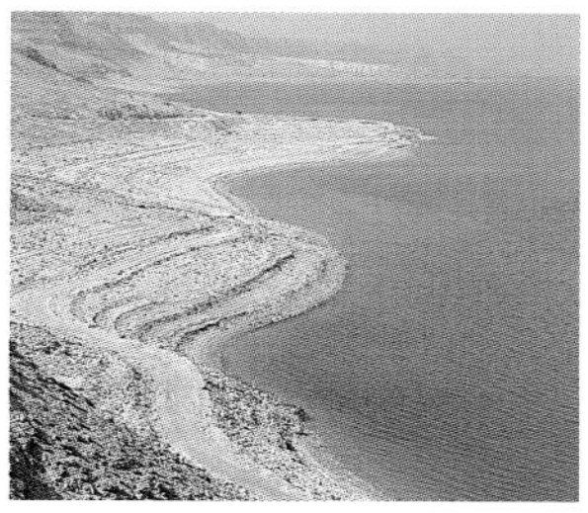

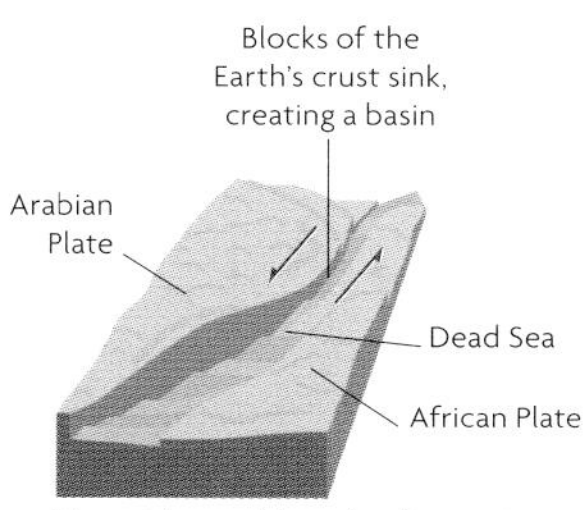

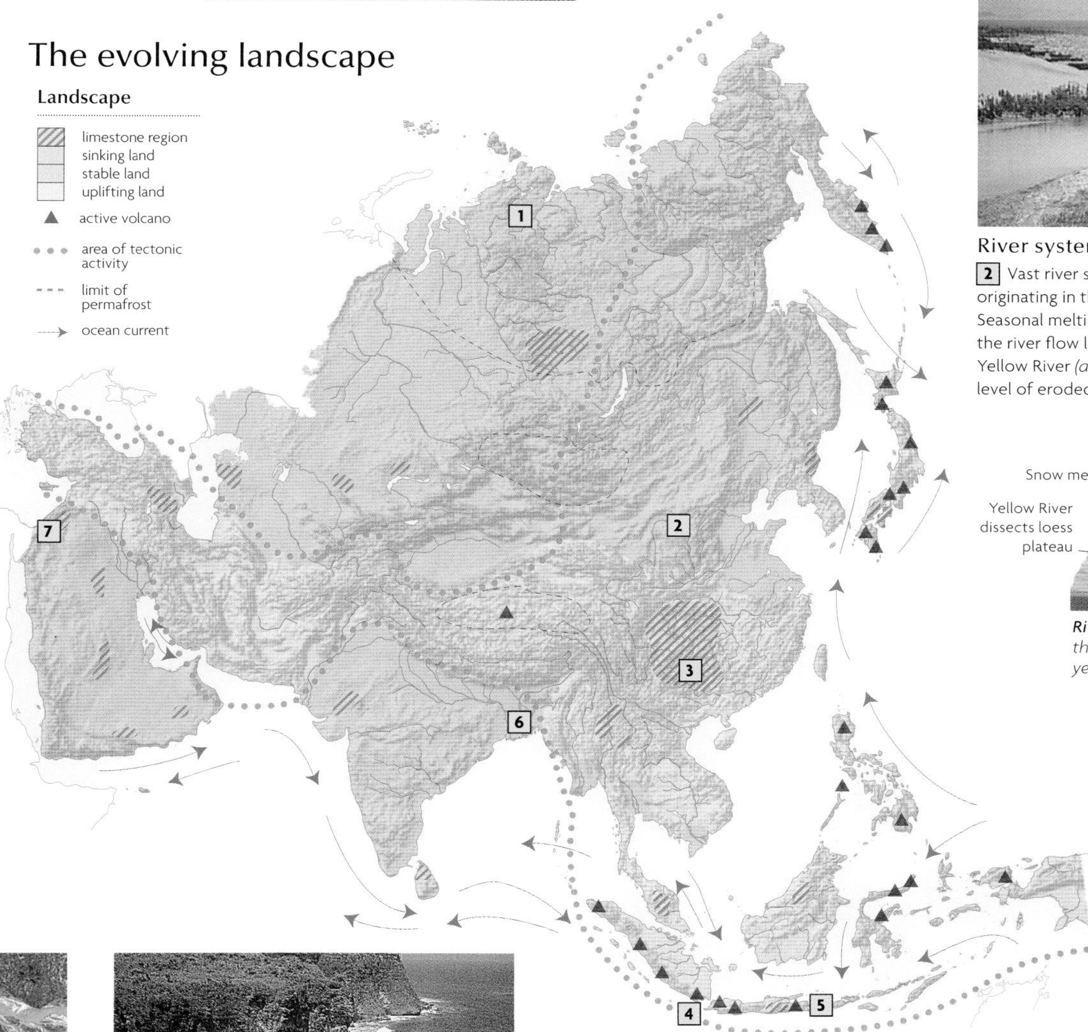

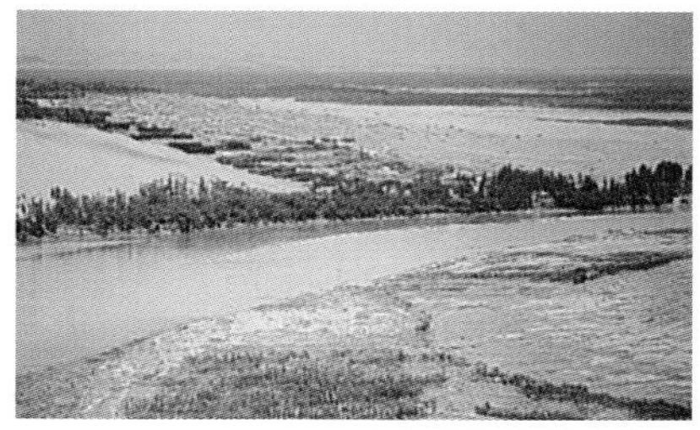

River systems

2 Vast river systems flow across Asia, many originating in the Himalayas and the Plateau of Tibet. Seasonal melting of snow and monsoon rains swell the river flow leading to flooding and erosion. The Yellow River *(above)* gets its colour from the high level of eroded material from the loess plateau.

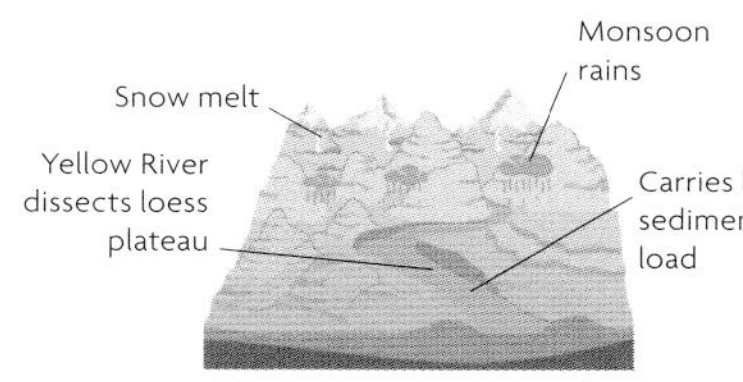

River systems: erosion of the loess plateau by the yellow river

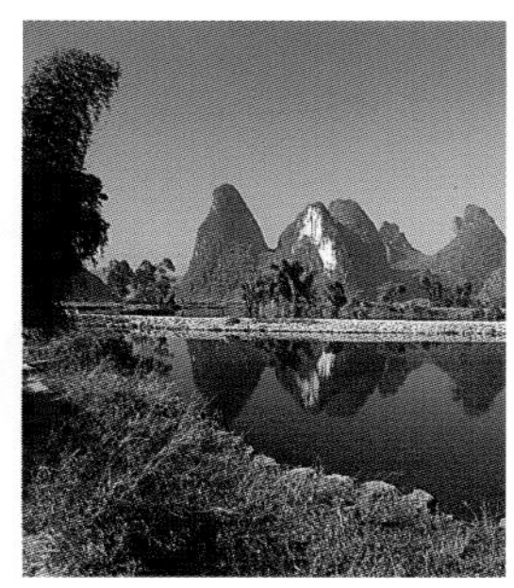

The evolving landscape

Landscape

- limestone region
- sinking land
- stable land
- uplifting land
- ▲ active volcano
- ● ● ● area of tectonic activity
- – – – limit of permafrost
- → ocean current

Tectonic activity

7 The Dead Sea *(above)* lies in a pull-apart basin. The sliding of the African Plate against the Arabian Plate, at unequal rates, led to the sinking of blocks of crust. This depression has been filled by the waters of the Dead Sea and Lake Tiberias *(Sea of Galilee)*. The plates continue to move causing intermittent earthquakes.

Tectonic activity: the formation of a pull-apart basin

Chemical weathering

3 Tower karsts are widespread across south China *(above)* and Vietnam. It is thought the karstic towers were formed under a soil cover, where small depressions in the limestone bedrock began to be weathered by soil water acids, eventually creating larger hollows. This process continued over millions of years, deepening the hollows and leaving steep-sided limestone hills.

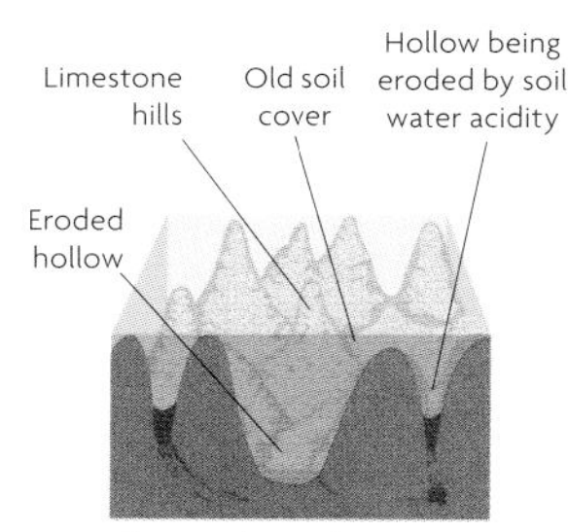

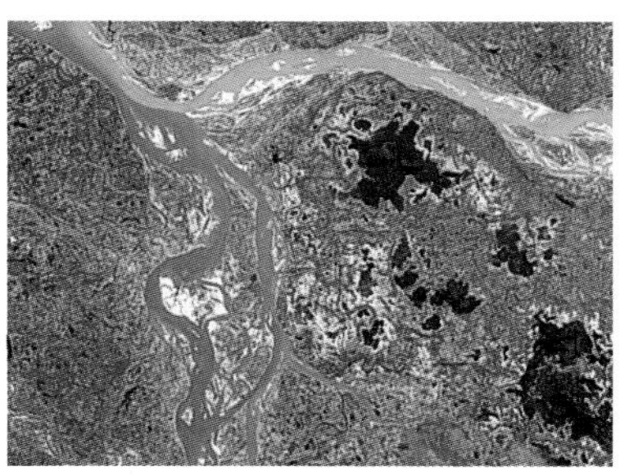

Sedimentation

6 The Ganges/Brahmaputra is a tide-dominated delta *(above)*. The two rivers transport huge quantities of mountain sediment, which is deposited on the delta plain. This debris is then redistributed by tidal currents, to form extensions to the bars, beach ridges and deltaic deposits.

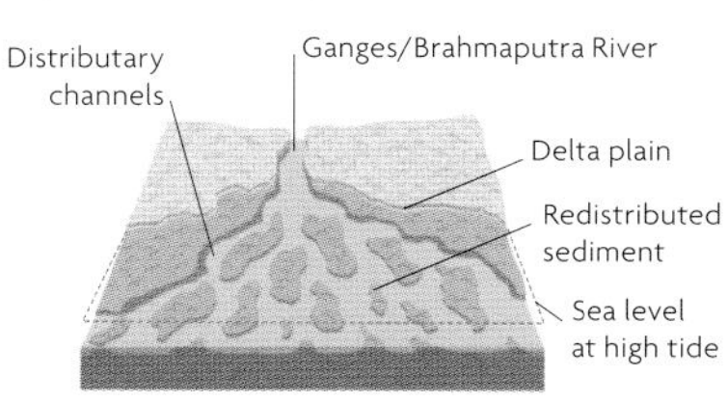

Sedimentation: the destruction of a delta

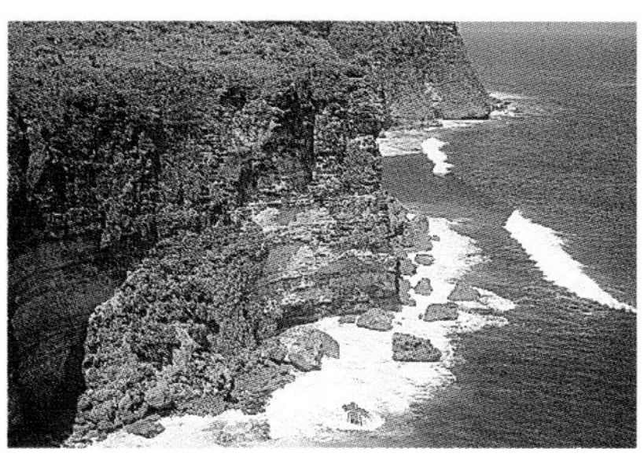

Coastal erosion

5 The erosion of cliffs along the coast of Indonesia *(above)* and Thailand occurs when waves and currents undermine the base leading to collapse of material. The surf then gradually erodes this material away, exposing the cliff to further undercutting. This process eventually creates shore platforms.

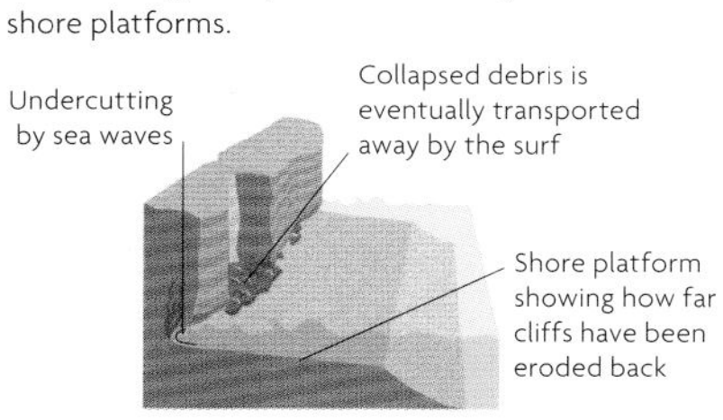

Coastal erosion: the undercutting of a cliff

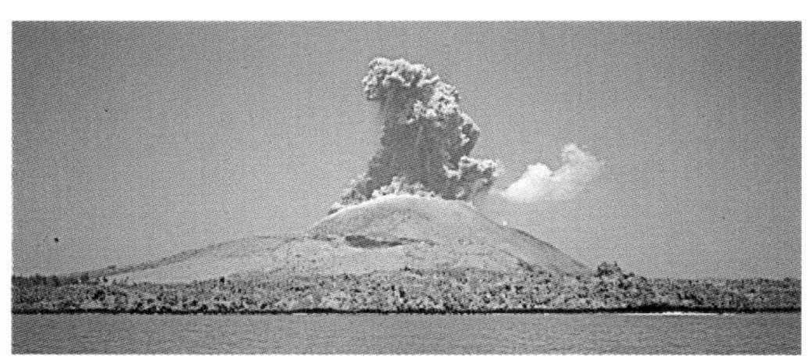

Volcanic activity

4 Volcanic eruptions occur frequently across Southeast Asia's island arcs *(above)*. Low-level eruptions occur when groundwater, superheated by underlying magma, becomes pressurized, forcing hot fluid and rocks up through cracks in the volcanic cone. This is known as a phreatic eruption.

Volcanic activity: a phreatic eruption

Chemical weathering: formation of tower karst

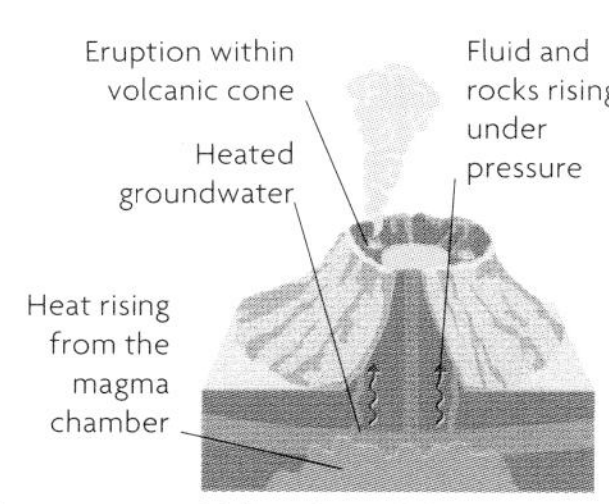

Political Asia

Asia is the world's largest continent, encompassing many different and discrete realms, from the desert Arab lands of the southwest to the subtropical archipelago of Indonesia; from the vast barren wastes of Siberia to the fertile river valleys of China and South Asia, seats of some of the world's most ancient civilizations. The collapse of the Soviet Union has fragmented the north of the continent into the Siberian portion of the Russian Federation, and the new republics of Central Asia. Strong religious traditions heavily influence the politics of South and Southwest Asia. Hindu and Muslim rivalries threaten to upset the political equilibrium in South Asia where India – in terms of population – remains the world's largest democracy. Communist China, another population giant, is reasserting its position as a world political and economic power, while on its doorstep, the dynamic Pacific Rim countries, led by Japan, continue to assert their worldwide economic force.

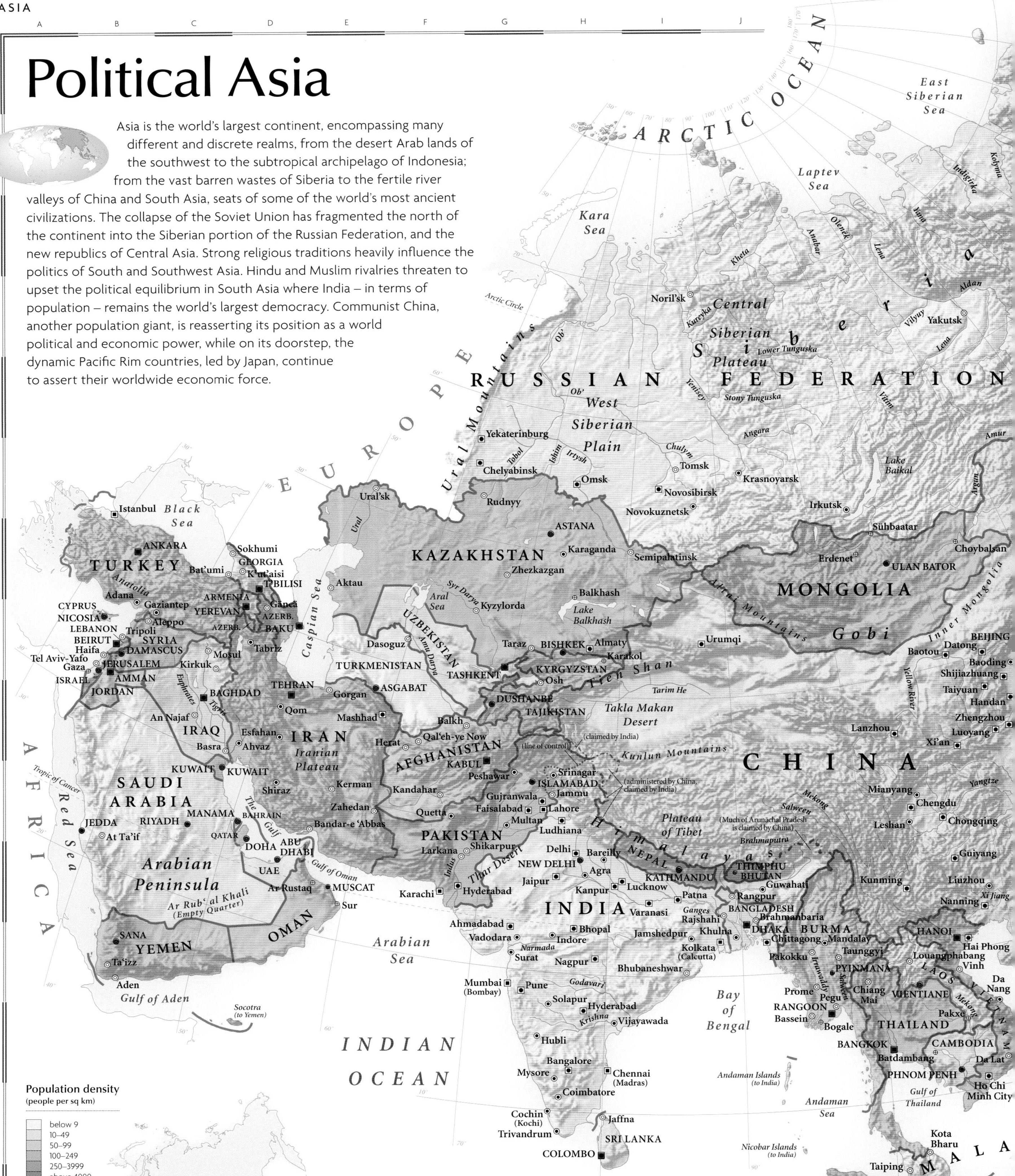

Population density
(people per sq km)

- below 9
- 10–49
- 50–99
- 100–249
- 250–3999
- above 4000

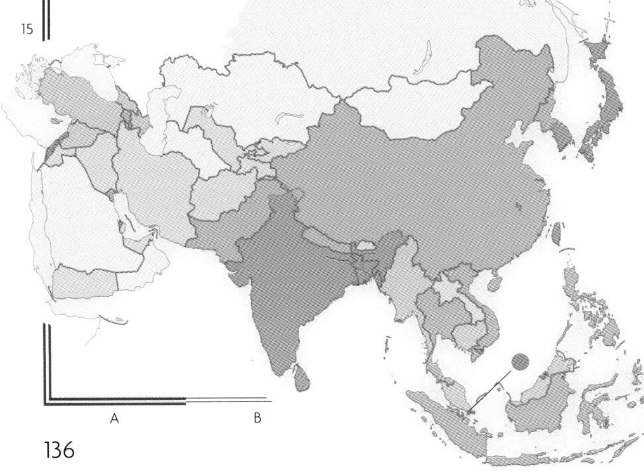

Population

Some of the world's most populous and least populous regions are in Asia. The plains of eastern China, the Ganges river plains in India, Japan and the Indonesian island of Java, all have very high population densities; by contrast parts of Siberia and the Plateau of Tibet are virtually uninhabited. China has the world's greatest population – 20% of the globe's total – while India, with the second largest, is likely to overtake China within 30 years.

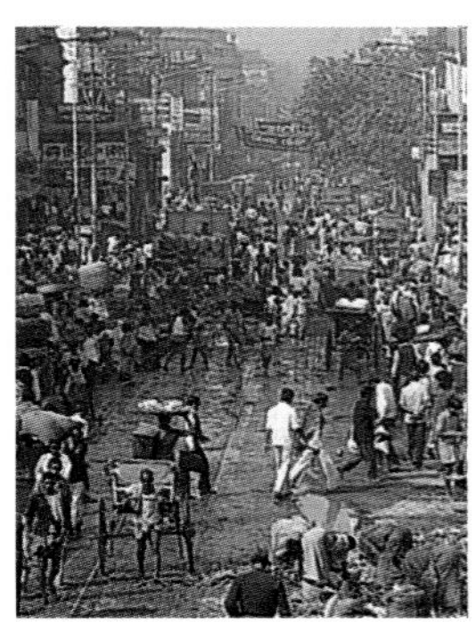

◀ *Kolkata's 13 million inhabitants bustle through a maze of crowded, narrow streets. Population densities in India's largest city reach almost 85,000 per sq mile (33,000 per sq km).*

Map labels

ARCTIC OCEAN
East Siberian Sea
Laptev Sea
Kara Sea
Arctic Circle
RUSSIAN FEDERATION
Siberia
Central Siberian Plateau
Lower Tunguska
Stony Tunguska
West Siberian Plain
Noril'sk
Yekaterinburg
Chelyabinsk
Ural'sk
Rudnyy
Omsk
Tomsk
Novosibirsk
Novokuznetsk
Krasnoyarsk
Irkutsk
Lake Baikal
Yakutsk
Vilyuy
Sühbaatar
Erdenet
Choybalsan
ULAN BATOR
MONGOLIA
Gobi
Inner Mongolia
Altai Mountains
EUROPE
Ural Mountains
ASTANA
Karaganda
KAZAKHSTAN
Zhezkazgan
Semipalatinsk
Balkhash
Lake Balkhash
Kyzylorda
Aral Sea
Aktau
Syr Darya
Istanbul
Black Sea
ANKARA
TURKEY
Anatolia
Adana
Sokhumi
Bat'umi
GEORGIA
K'ut'aisi
T'BILISI
ARMENIA
YEREVAN
AZERB.
Ganca
BAKU
Tabriz
Caspian Sea
CYPRUS
NICOSIA
Gaziantep
Aleppo
LEBANON
Tripoli
BEIRUT
SYRIA
DAMASCUS
Haifa
Tel Aviv-Yafo
JERUSALEM
Gaza
ISRAEL
AMMAN
JORDAN
Kirkuk
Mosul
Euphrates
Tigris
BAGHDAD
An Najaf
IRAQ
Basra
Ahvaz
Esfahan
Herat
Qom
TEHRAN
Gorgan
Mashhad
Dasoguz
Amu Darya
TURKMENISTAN
ASGABAT
UZBEKISTAN
TASHKENT
Taraz
BISHKEK
KYRGYZSTAN
Osh
DUSHANBE
TAJIKISTAN
Balkh
Qal'eh-ye Now
Tien Shan
Urumqi
Karakol
Almaty
Tarim He
Takla Makan Desert
Kunlun Mountains
CHINA
Lanzhou
Xi'an
Zhengzhou
Luoyang
Handan
Taiyuan
Shijiazhuang
Baoding
BEIJING
Datong
Baotou
Yellow River
IRAN
Iranian Plateau
Kerman
Shiraz
Zahedan
Bandar-e 'Abbas
Kandahar
AFGHANISTAN
KABUL
Quetta
Peshawar
Srinagar
ISLAMABAD
Jammu
(line of control)
(claimed by India)
(administered by China, claimed by India)
Gujranwala
Faisalabad
Lahore
Multan
Ludhiana
Larkana
Shikarpur
PAKISTAN
Karachi
Hyderabad
Thar Desert
Indus
Delhi
NEW DELHI
Jaipur
Bareilly
Agra
Kanpur
Lucknow
Varanasi
Patna
Ganges
Plateau of Tibet
Brahmaputra
(Much of Arunachal Pradesh is claimed by China)
Himalayas
NEPAL
KATHMANDU
THIMPHU
BHUTAN
Guwahati
Rangpur
BANGLADESH
DHAKA
Brahmanbaria
Rajshahi
Khulna
Kolkata (Calcutta)
Jamshedpur
Chittagong
Pakokku
BURMA
Mandalay
Taunggyi
PYINMANA
Irrawaddy
Prome
Pegu
RANGOON
Bassein
Bogale
Salween
Mekong
Mianyang
Chengdu
Leshan
Chongqing
Guiyang
Kunming
Liuzhou
Nanning
Xi Jiang
Yangtze
HANOI
Hai Phong
Louangphabang
Vinh
Da Nang
LAOS
VIETNAM
Chiang Mai
VIENTIANE
Pakxe
THAILAND
BANGKOK
Batdambang
CAMBODIA
Da Lat
PHNOM PENH
Ho Chi Minh City
Gulf of Thailand
Kota Bharu
MALA
Taiping
KUALA LUMPUR
PUTRAJAYA
SINGAPORE
Medan
Sumatra
Jambi
Padang
Palembang
JAKARTA
Equator
INDIA
Ahmadabad
Vadodara
Bhopal
Indore
Surat
Nagpur
Bhubaneshwar
Narmada
Mumbai (Bombay)
Pune
Solapur
Hyderabad
Godavari
Krishna
Vijayawada
Hubli
Bangalore
Mysore
Coimbatore
Chennai (Madras)
Cochin (Kochi)
Trivandrum
Jaffna
SRI LANKA
COLOMBO
Bay of Bengal
Andaman Islands (to India)
Andaman Sea
Nicobar Islands (to India)
Arabian Sea
INDIAN OCEAN
SAUDI ARABIA
JEDDA
RIYADH
At Ta'if
MANAMA
BAHRAIN
QATAR
DOHA
ABU DHABI
UAE
MUSCAT
OMAN
Sur
Ar Rustaq
Gulf of Oman
The Gulf
KUWAIT
Arabian Peninsula
Ar Rub' al Khali (Empty Quarter)
SANA
YEMEN
Ta'izz
Aden
Gulf of Aden
Socotra (to Yemen)
Red Sea
Tropic of Cancer
AFRICA

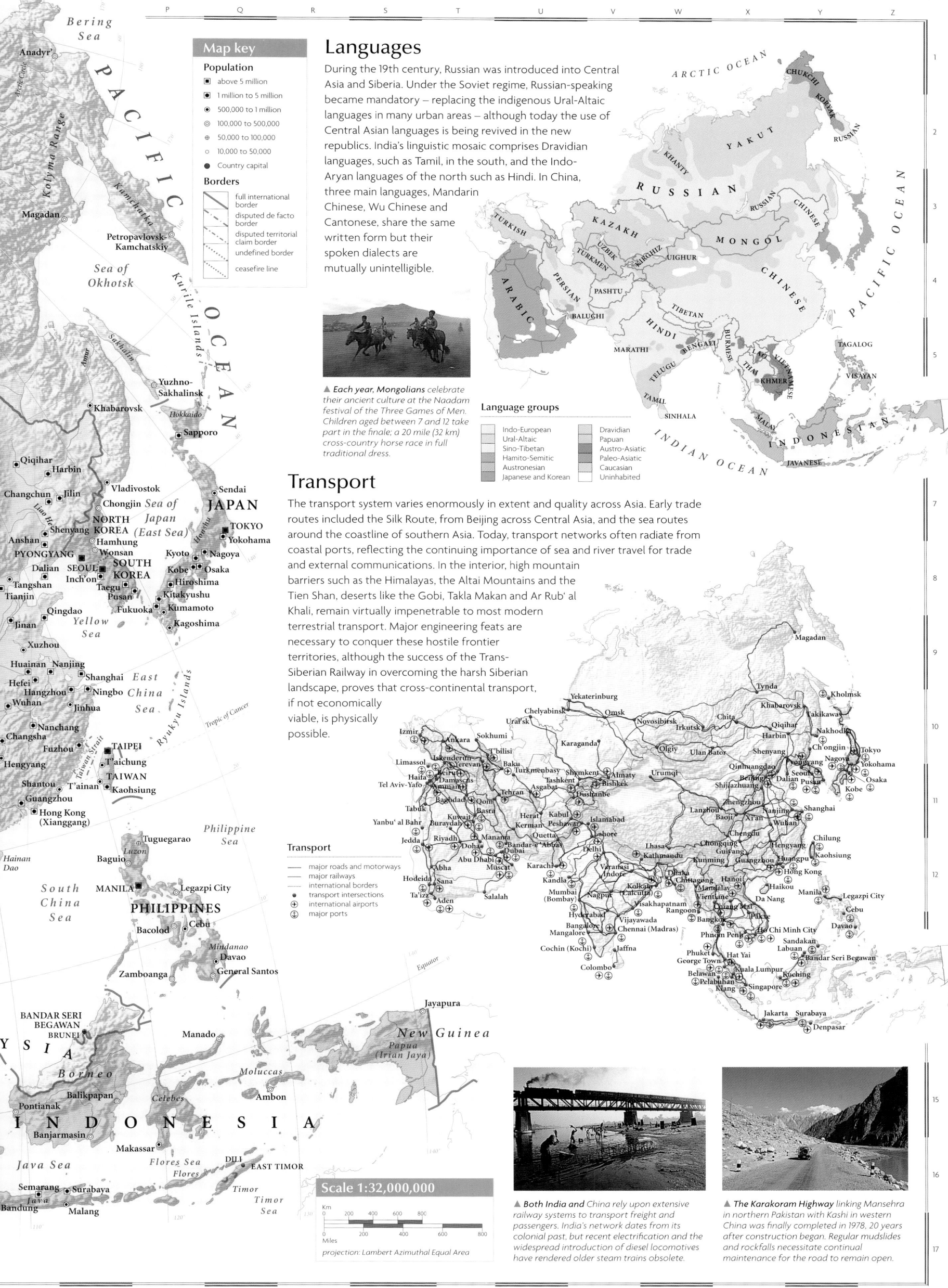

Languages

During the 19th century, Russian was introduced into Central Asia and Siberia. Under the Soviet regime, Russian-speaking became mandatory – replacing the indigenous Ural-Altaic languages in many urban areas – although today the use of Central Asian languages is being revived in the new republics. India's linguistic mosaic comprises Dravidian languages, such as Tamil, in the south, and the Indo-Aryan languages of the north such as Hindi. In China, three main languages, Mandarin Chinese, Wu Chinese and Cantonese, share the same written form but their spoken dialects are mutually unintelligible.

▲ *Each year, Mongolians* celebrate *their ancient culture at the Naadam festival of the Three Games of Men. Children aged between 7 and 12 take part in the finale; a 20 mile (32 km) cross-country horse race in full traditional dress.*

Map key

Population
- ◼ above 5 million
- ◾ 1 million to 5 million
- ◉ 500,000 to 1 million
- ◎ 100,000 to 500,000
- ⊕ 50,000 to 100,000
- ○ 10,000 to 50,000
- ● Country capital

Borders
- full international border
- disputed de facto border
- disputed territorial claim border
- undefined border
- ceasefire line

Language groups
- Indo-European
- Ural-Altaic
- Sino-Tibetan
- Hamito-Semitic
- Austronesian
- Japanese and Korean
- Dravidian
- Papuan
- Austro-Asiatic
- Paleo-Asiatic
- Caucasian
- Uninhabited

Transport

The transport system varies enormously in extent and quality across Asia. Early trade routes included the Silk Route, from Beijing across Central Asia, and the sea routes around the coastline of southern Asia. Today, transport networks often radiate from coastal ports, reflecting the continuing importance of sea and river travel for trade and external communications. In the interior, high mountain barriers such as the Himalayas, the Altai Mountains and the Tien Shan, deserts like the Gobi, Takla Makan and Ar Rub' al Khali, remain virtually impenetrable to most modern terrestrial transport. Major engineering feats are necessary to conquer these hostile frontier territories, although the success of the Trans-Siberian Railway in overcoming the harsh Siberian landscape, proves that cross-continental transport, if not economically viable, is physically possible.

Transport
- —— major roads and motorways
- —— major railways
- —— international borders
- ● transport intersections
- ⊕ international airports
- ⊕ major ports

Scale 1:32,000,000

Km 0 200 400 600 800

Miles 0 200 400 600 800

projection: Lambert Azimuthal Equal Area

▲ *Both India and* China rely upon extensive *railway systems to transport freight and passengers. India's network dates from its colonial past, but recent electrification and the widespread introduction of diesel locomotives have rendered older steam trains obsolete.*

▲ *The Karakoram Highway linking Mansehra in northern Pakistan with Kashi in western China was finally completed in 1978, 20 years after construction began. Regular mudslides and rockfalls necessitate continual maintenance for the road to remain open.*

Climate

The climate of Asia exhibits marked differences from region to region, with freezing polar conditions in the north, hot and cold deserts in central regions and subtropical conditions throughout the south. Much of this variation can be attributed to enormous mountain barriers and internal depressions found across the continent. Monsoon winds, which reverse semi-annually, cause alternate wet and dry seasons across southern Asia. These air masses moving north from the ocean are stripped of their moisture over the Himalayas causing arid conditions across the Plateau of Tibet. Both the south and east are susceptible to tropical cyclones or typhoons.

◄ *Treeless, frozen plains,* with permanently frozen soil layers characterize much of Siberia. Even during the summer only the top 2–3 ft (1 m) of soil thaws.

▲ *Tundra-like marshes* are found alongside vast sand dunes in the Takla Makan Desert in China. In the spring, windstorms of hurricane-force can send dust as high as 13,000 ft (4000 m) in the air.

▲ *The Gobi Desert* experiences major extremes in climate, with winter temperatures sometimes falling below -40°C (-40°F) and summer temperatures exceeding 45°C (113°F).

Climate

	tundra
	subarctic
	cool continental
	warm humid
	mediterranean
	semi-arid
	arid
	humid equatorial
	tropical

☀ daily hours of sunshine, January
☀ daily hours of sunshine, July
→ cyclone
→ typhoon
→ cold/dry monsoon
→ warm/wet monsoon
→ cold wind

Map labels

Mys Chelyuskin, Anadyr', Salekhard, Okhotsk, Petropavlovsk-Kamchatskiy, Yakutsk, Stony Tunguska, Yekaterinburg, Omsk, Novosibirsk, Irkutsk, Khabarovsk, Sapporo, Buran, Karaganda, Buran, Harbin, Vladivostok, Ankara, T'bilisi, Fort-Shevchenko, Urumqi, Beijing, Seoul, Tokyo, Osaka, Jerusalem, Baghdad, Tehran, Asgabat, Tashkent, Taiyuan, Nagasaki, Kuwait, Kabul, Lanzhou, Shanghai, Bandar-e 'Abbas, Lahore, Chengdu, Wuhan, Muscat, Karachi, New Delhi, Kathmandu, Kunming, Hong Kong (Xianggang), Taipei, Dhaka, Hanoi, Kolkata (Calcutta), Chiang Mai, Vientiane, Mumbai (Bombay), Rangoon, Bangkok, Chennai (Madras), Cyclone, Phnom Penh, Ho Chi Minh City, Port Blair, Phuket, Bandar Seri Begawan, Manokwari, Colombo, Ambon, Singapore, Padang, Jakarta, Kupang, Typhoon

Tropic of Cancer, Arctic Circle, Equator

Temperature

	below -30°C (-22°F)
	-30 to -20°C (-22 to -4°F)
	-20 to -10°C (-4 to 14°F)
	-10 to 0°C (14 to 32°F)
	0 to 10°C (32 to 50°F)
	10 to 20°C (50°F)
	20 to 30°C (68 to 86°F)
	above 30°C (86°F)

Arctic Circle, 60° N, 40° N, Tropic of Cancer, 20° N, Equator, 20° S, Tropic of Capricorn, 40° S

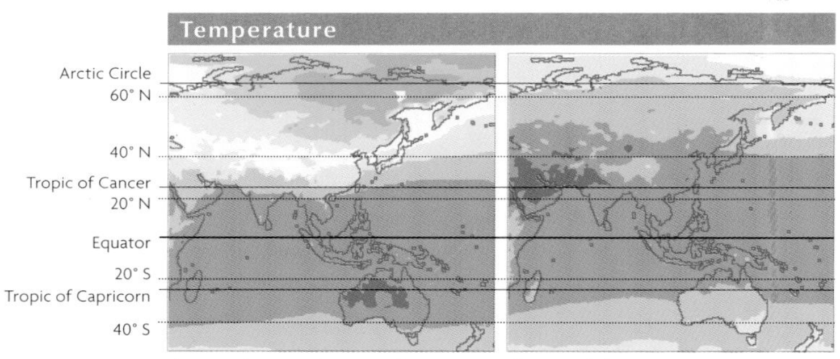

Average January temperature   *Average July temperature*

Rainfall

	0 –25 mm (0–1 in)
	25–50 mm (1–2 in)
	50–100 mm (2–4 in)
	100–200 mm (4–8 in)
	200–300 mm (8–12 in)
	300–400 mm (12–16 in)
	400–500 mm (16–20 in)
	more than 500 mm (20 in)

Arctic Circle, 60° N, 40° N, Tropic of Cancer, 20° N, Equator, 20° S, Tropic of Capricorn, 40° S

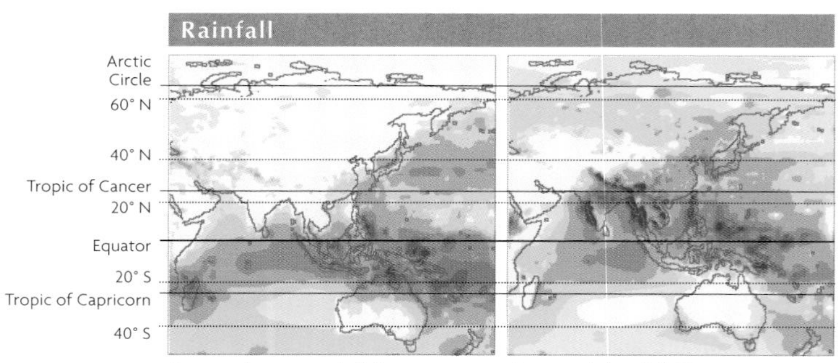

Average January rainfall   *Average July rainfall*

▲ *Tropical cyclones occur* principally during late summer and early autumn. The intense winds and heavy rainfall can devastate entire villages.

▲ *Through India, the* southwest monsoon, which brings heavy rainfall from May to September, accounts for 80% of annual precipitation.

East Siberian Mountains

The fold mountains along the coast of northeast Asia are formed from folded sedimentary strata from an ancient sea shelf. The peninsula of Kamchatka, in the far northeast, extends 600 miles (1000 km) into the Pacific Ocean. The mountain range continues as the Kurile Island arc. Kamchatka lies at the boundary of the Eurasian and Pacific plates, and contains 74 volcanoes, of which only 13 are still active.

Scale 1:30,000,000

Km
0 200 400 600 800

Miles
0 200 400 600 800

projection: Lambert Azimuthal Equal Area

Map key

Elevation

- 6000m / 19,686ft
- 4000m / 13,124ft
- 3000m / 9843ft
- 2000m / 6562ft
- 1000m / 3281ft
- 500m / 1640ft
- 250m / 820ft
- 100m / 328ft
- sea level

Plate margins
(for explanation see page xiv)

- ——— constructive
- △ △ destructive
- ——— conservative
- ·········· uncertain
- ─────── physiographic regions
- ►——◄ line of cross-section

East Asian Plains and Uplands

Several, small, isolated shield areas, such as the Shandong Peninsula, are found in east Asia. Between these stable shield areas, large river systems like the Yangtze and the Yellow River have deposited thick layers of sediment, forming extensive alluvial plains. The largest of these is the Great Plain of China, the relief of which does not rise above 300 ft (100 m).

Coastal Lowlands and Island Arcs

The coastal plains that fringe Southeast Asia contain many large delta systems, caused by high levels of rainfall and erosion of the Himalayas, the Plateau of Tibet and relict loess deposits. To the south is an extensive island archipelago, lying on the drowned Sunda Shelf. Most of these islands are volcanic in origin, caused by the subduction of the Indo-Australian Plate beneath the Eurasian Plate.

Cross-section through Southeast Asia showing the subduction zone between the Indo-Australian and Eurasian plates and the island arc.

A B C D E F G H I J K L M

Turkey & the Caucasus

ARMENIA, AZERBAIJAN, GEORGIA, TURKEY

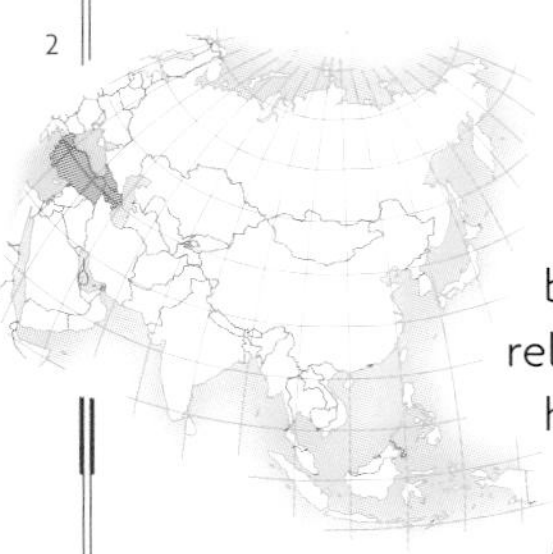

This region occupies the fragmented junction between Europe, Asia and the Russian Federation. Sunni Islam provides a common identity for the secular state of Turkey, which the revered leader Kemal Atatürk established from the remnants of the Ottoman Empire after the First World War. Turkey has a broad resource base and expanding trade links with Europe, but the east is relatively undeveloped and strife between the state and a large Kurdish minority has yet to be resolved. Georgia is similarly challenged by ethnic separatism, while the Christian state of Armenia and the mainly Muslim and oil-rich Azerbaijan are locked in conflict over the territory of Nagorno-Karabakh.

Transport and industry

Turkey leads the region's well-diversified economy. Petrochemicals, textiles, engineering and food processing are the main industries. Azerbaijan is able to export oil, while the other states rely heavily on hydro-electric power and imported fuel. Georgia produces precision machinery. War and earthquake damage have devastated Armenia's infrastructure.

Using the land and sea

Turkey is largely self-sufficient in food. The irrigated Black Sea coastlands have the world's highest yields of hazelnuts. Tobacco, cotton, sultanas, tea and figs are the region's main cash crops and a great range of fruit and vegetables are grown. Wine grapes are among the labour-intensive crops which allow full use of limited agricultural land in the Caucasus. Sturgeon fishing is particularly important in Azerbaijan.

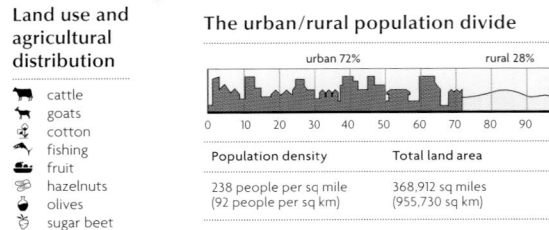

▲ Azerbaijan has substantial oil reserves, located in and around the Caspian Sea. They were some of the earliest oilfields in the world to be exploited.

Major industry and infrastructure

- carpet weaving
- cement
- chemicals
- coal
- engineering
- food processing
- oil
- textiles
- tourism
- vehicle manufacture
- ■ capital cities
- ● major towns
- ⊕ international airports
- major roads
- major industrial areas

The transport network

114,867 miles (184,882 km)

5778 miles (9300 km)

8120 miles (13,069 km)

745 miles (1200 km)

Physical and political barriers have severely limited communications between Armenia, Georgia and Azerbaijan. Turkey has a relatively well-developed transport network.

Land use and agricultural distribution

- cattle
- goats
- cotton
- fishing
- fruit
- hazelnuts
- olives
- sugar beet
- tobacco
- vineyards
- ■ capital cities
- major towns
- pasture
- cropland
- forest

The urban/rural population divide

urban 72%   rural 28%

0 10 20 30 40 50 60 70 80 90 100

Population density	Total land area
238 people per sq mile (92 people per sq km)	368,912 sq miles (955,730 sq km)

▲ For many centuries, Istanbul has held tremendous strategic importance as a crucial gateway between Europe and Asia. Founded by the Greeks as Byzantium, the city became the centre of the East Roman Empire and was known as Constantinople to the Romans. From the 15th century onwards the city became the centre of the great Ottoman Empire.

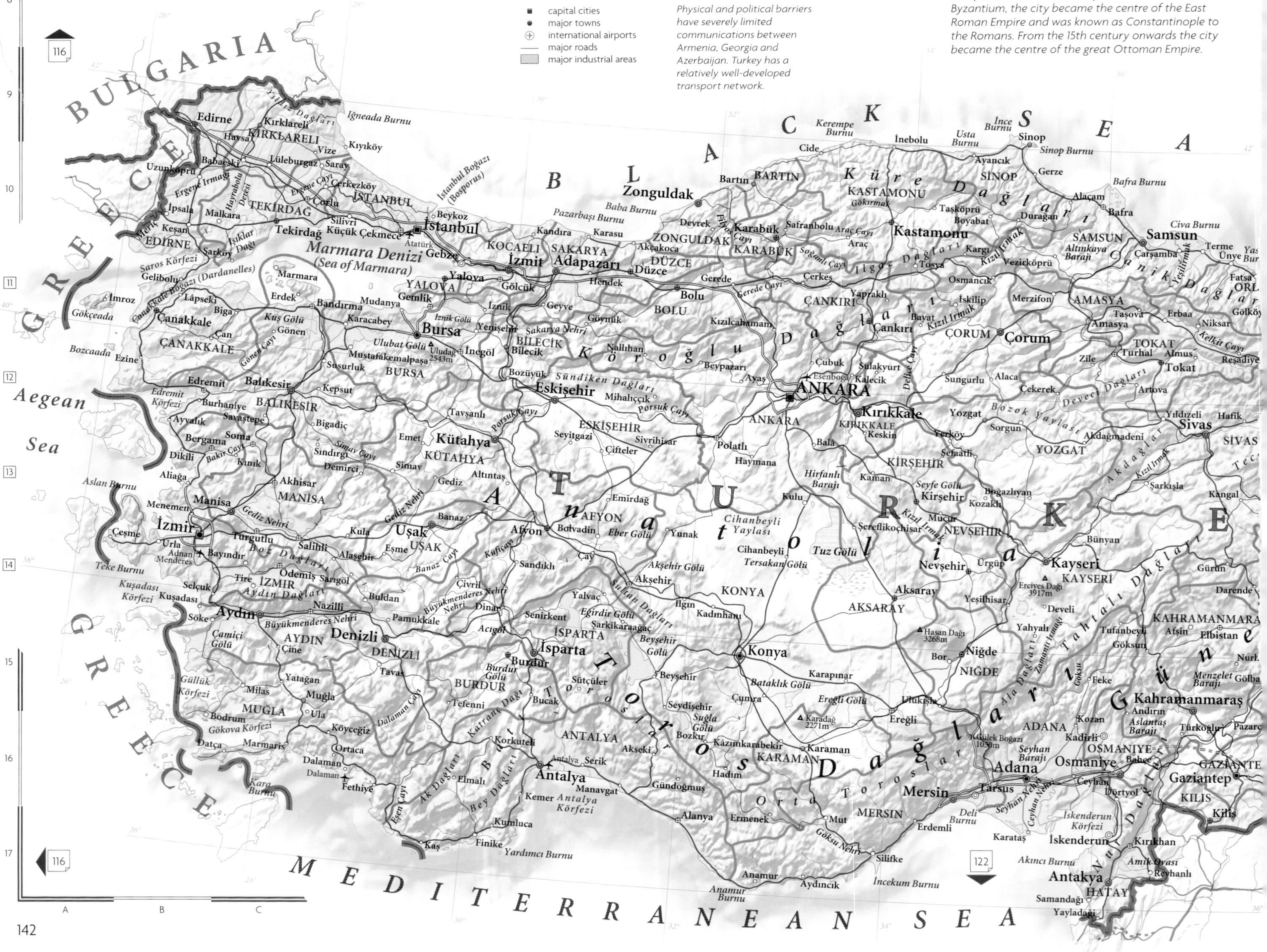

The landscape

The deeply-eroded hills and salty basins of the Anatolian Plateau are bordered by several mountain ranges along the Black Sea coast, and the limestone Taurus Mountains (Toros Daglari) in the south. A lowland trough divides the Caucasus and the Lesser Caucasus, which form a formidable barrier of peaks in the north.

Limestone weathering in the Anatolian Plateau

Eroded gully — High plateau

Layers of tephra — Remnant landforms

▲ **In central Turkey**, rainwater has chemically weathered away numerous layers of limestone, leaving isolated outcrops and pinnacles and deep eroded gullies.

▶ **The Caucasus are** fold mountains, which formed around the same time as the Taurus Mountains (Toros Daglari) around 65 million years ago and have since been modified by volcanic erruptions.

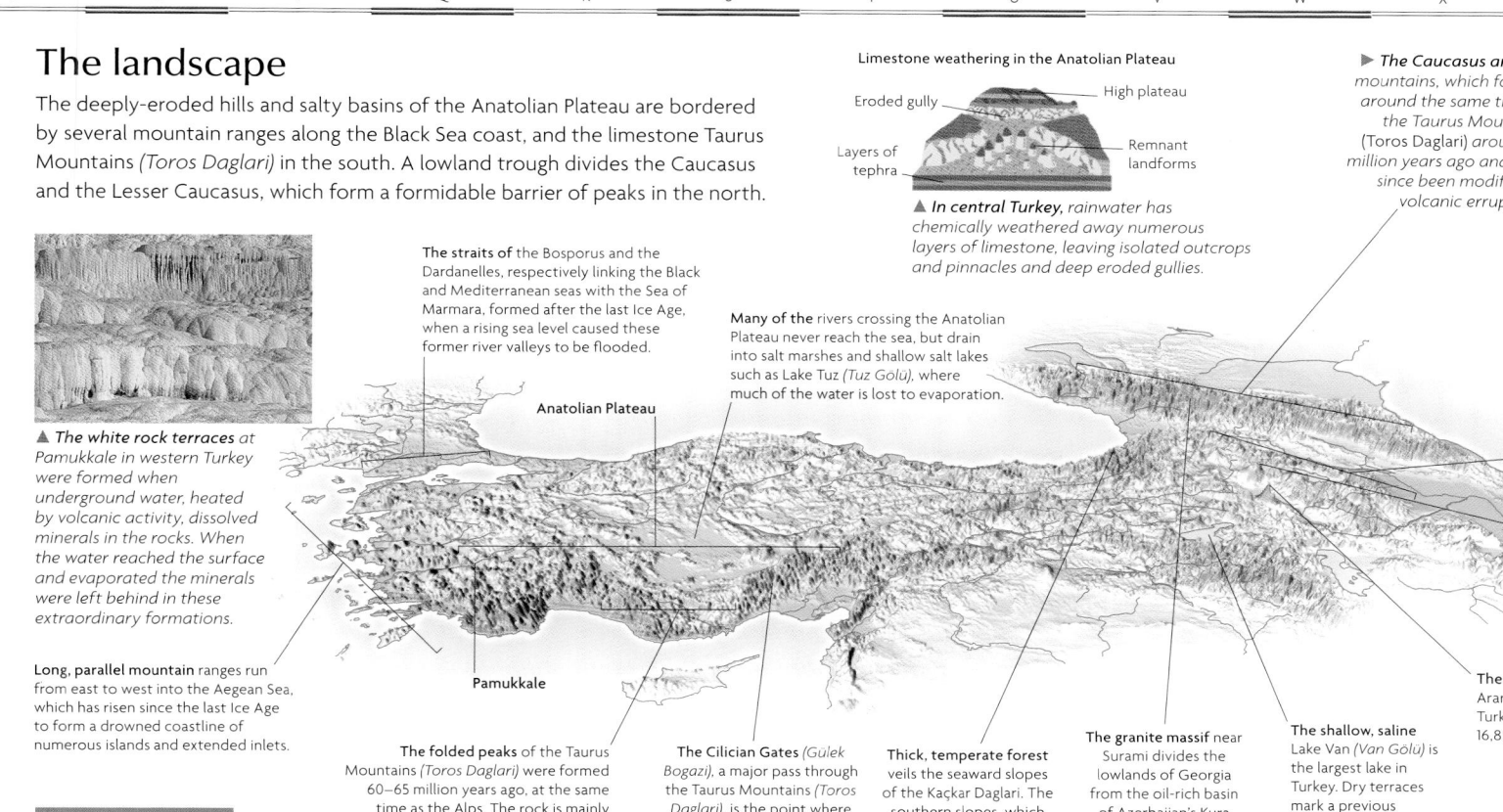

The straits of the Bosporus and the Dardanelles, respectively linking the Black and Mediterranean seas with the Sea of Marmara, formed after the last Ice Age, when a rising sea level caused these former river valleys to be flooded.

Many of the rivers crossing the Anatolian Plateau never reach the sea, but drain into salt marshes and shallow salt lakes such as Lake Tuz (Tuz Gölü), where much of the water is lost to evaporation.

Anatolian Plateau

Lava has flowed over large areas of the Lesser Caucasus within the last five million years, producing extensive basalt plateaux.

▲ **The white rock terraces** at Pamukkale in western Turkey were formed when underground water, heated by volcanic activity, dissolved minerals in the rocks. When the water reached the surface and evaporated the minerals were left behind in these extraordinary formations.

Pamukkale

The earthquake that struck Armenia in 1988 killed over 55,000 people and devastated the country's infrastructure.

Long, parallel mountain ranges run from east to west into the Aegean Sea, which has risen since the last Ice Age to form a drowned coastline of numerous islands and extended inlets.

The volcanic cone of Mount Ararat is the highest peak in Turkey, with an altitude of 16,853 ft (5137 m).

The folded peaks of the Taurus Mountains (Toros Daglari) were formed 60–65 million years ago, at the same time as the Alps. The rock is mainly limestone, with deep caves, gorges and underground rivers.

The Cilician Gates (Gülek Bogazi), a major pass through the Taurus Mountains (Toros Daglari), is the point where streams flow from the interior plateau onto the lowland of Adana.

Thick, temperate forest veils the seaward slopes of the Kaçkar Daglari. The southern slopes, which lie in a rainshadow, are dry and barren.

The granite massif near Surami divides the lowlands of Georgia from the oil-rich basin of Azerbaijan's Kura river, which has built a large delta into the Caspian Sea.

The shallow, saline Lake Van (Van Gölü) is the largest lake in Turkey. Dry terraces mark a previous shoreline 181 ft (55 m) above the present water level.

Map key

Population

- ▣ above 5 million
- ▣ 1 million to 5 million
- ◉ 500,000 to 1 million
- ◎ 100,000 to 500,000
- ⊕ 50,000 to 100,000
- ○ 10,000 to 50,000
- ○ below 10,000

Elevation

	4000m / 13,124ft
	3000m / 9843ft
	2000m / 6562ft
	1000m / 3281ft
	500m / 1640ft
	250m / 820ft
	100m / 328ft
	sea level

▶ **Since the 6th century** BC, the pinnacles and caves of east-central Anatolia have been utilized as dwellings. Many are still inhabited today.

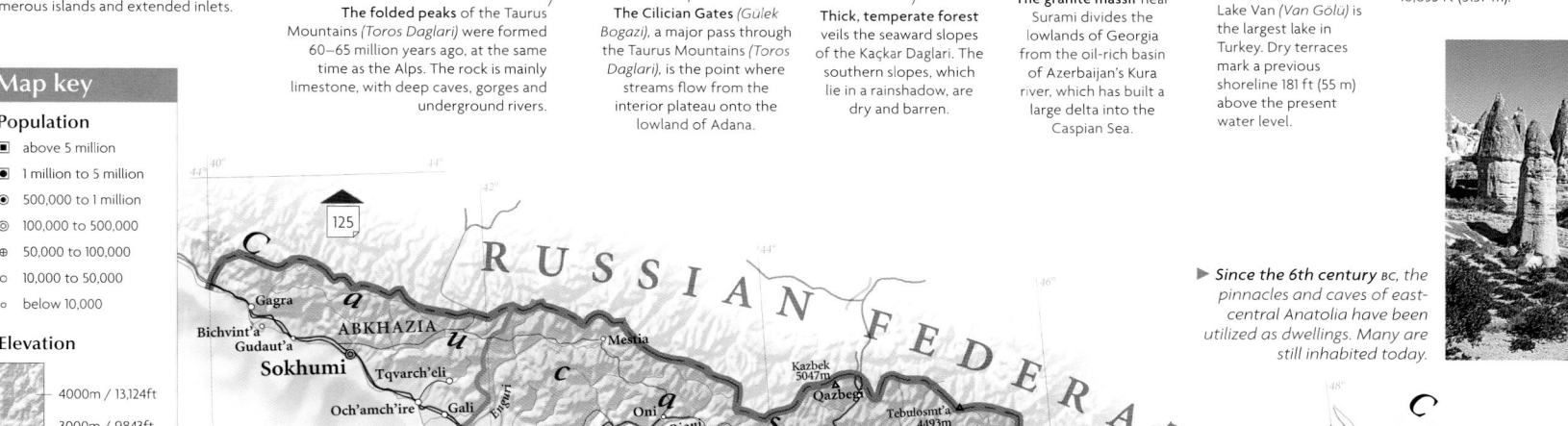

Scale 1:4,000,000

Km
0 20 40 60 80 100 120
Miles
0 10 20 40 60 80 120

projection: Lambert Conformal Conic

▲ **The fisheries of** Azerbaijan are noted for their hauls of sturgeon, and the Caspian Sea accounts for 80% of the world's total catch. However, stocks are now under serious threat due to overfishing.

▲ **Traditional steam baths** are found throughout the region, and are used for socializing as well as for bathing.

The Near East

IRAQ, ISRAEL, JORDAN, LEBANON, SYRIA

Some of the world's oldest civilizations developed in this region – the Fertile Crescent – which is venerated by Jews, Muslims and Christians, but torn by competing religious, ethnic and national claims to the land. Turkish Ottoman rule ended with the First World War and the region was divided into areas administered by Britain and France. The UN endorsed calls for a Jewish homeland in what was then Palestine and in 1948 the state of Israel was declared. Hostility towards the Jewish state led to a series of wars with its Arab neighbours. After 2000, attempts to broker peaceful resolutions with both the Palestinian population and with adjacent Arab states were hampered by a revival of Islamic militarism and conflicting international interests in the oil-rich region. This led to an Israeli retrenchment and culminated in a US-led invasion of Iraq in 2003, which toppled the Ba'athist regime of Saddam Hussein in the name of a 'war on terror'.

Using the land and sea

Water scarcity limits cropland to the north and to areas watered principally by the Tigris, Euphrates and Jordan rivers. In Israel, new irrigation techniques are allowing cultivation in the arid Negev. Wheat is the chief grain and large areas of scrub support livestock herding. Commercial produce includes dates, tobacco, citrus fruits, olives, grapes and cotton, which is Syria's main export crop. Fishing is still important in the Mediterranean.

The urban/rural population divide

urban 70%   rural 30%

Population density	Total land area
217 people per sq mile (84 people per sq km)	325,460 sq miles (843,160 sq km)

Land use and agricultural distribution

- sheep
- cereals
- citrus fruits
- cotton
- dates
- fishing
- rice
- tobacco
- capital cities
- major towns
- pasture
- cropland
- wetland
- desert

Transport and industry

The petrochemical industry is well established, and central to the economies of Syria and Iraq, which was the world's second largest oil exporter before the war with Iran which began in 1980. Lebanon has traditionally been a centre for commerce, while Israel has a well-diversified economy with an expanding tourist industry, despite few natural resources.

The transport network

- 49,859 miles (80,249 km)
- 1365 miles (2197 km)
- 3826 miles (6158 km)
- 1171 miles (1885 km)

Jordan's sea port of Al 'Aqabah is connected to Damascus in Syria by road and rail. This route to the Red Sea provides for large exports of phosphate and trade with states in The Gulf.

Major industry and infrastructure

- car manufacture
- cement
- chemicals
- electronics
- finance
- food processing
- iron & steel
- oil
- oil refining
- textiles
- capital cities
- major towns
- international airports
- major roads
- major industrial areas

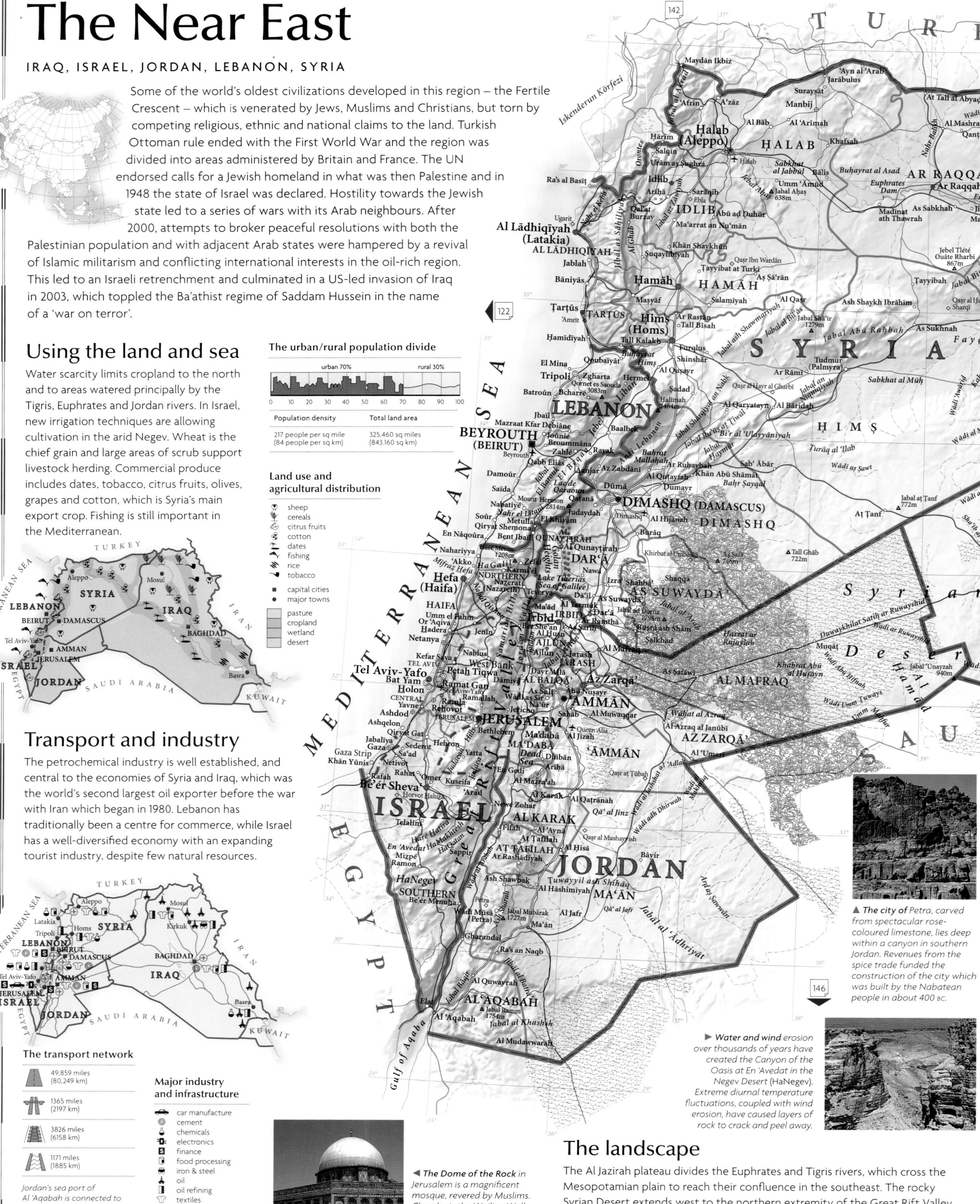

▲ *The city of Petra, carved from spectacular rose-coloured limestone, lies deep within a canyon in southern Jordan. Revenues from the spice trade funded the construction of the city which was built by the Nabatean people in about 400 BC.*

▶ *Water and wind erosion over thousands of years have created the Canyon of the Oasis at En 'Avedat in the Negev Desert (HaNegev). Extreme diurnal temperature fluctuations, coupled with wind erosion, have caused layers of rock to crack and peel away.*

◀ *The Dome of the Rock in Jerusalem is a magnificent mosque, revered by Muslims. Close by is the Wailing Wall, the city's most sacred Jewish landmark and the Church of the Holy Sepulchre, a famous Christian place of worship.*

The landscape

The Al Jazirah plateau divides the Euphrates and Tigris rivers, which cross the Mesopotamian plain to reach their confluence in the southeast. The rocky Syrian Desert extends west to the northern extremity of the Great Rift Valley, which runs from the mountains of Lebanon to the Gulf of Aqaba. The Jordan river flows south along this trough into the Dead Sea, divided from the Mediterranean coastal plain by a steep-sided plateau.

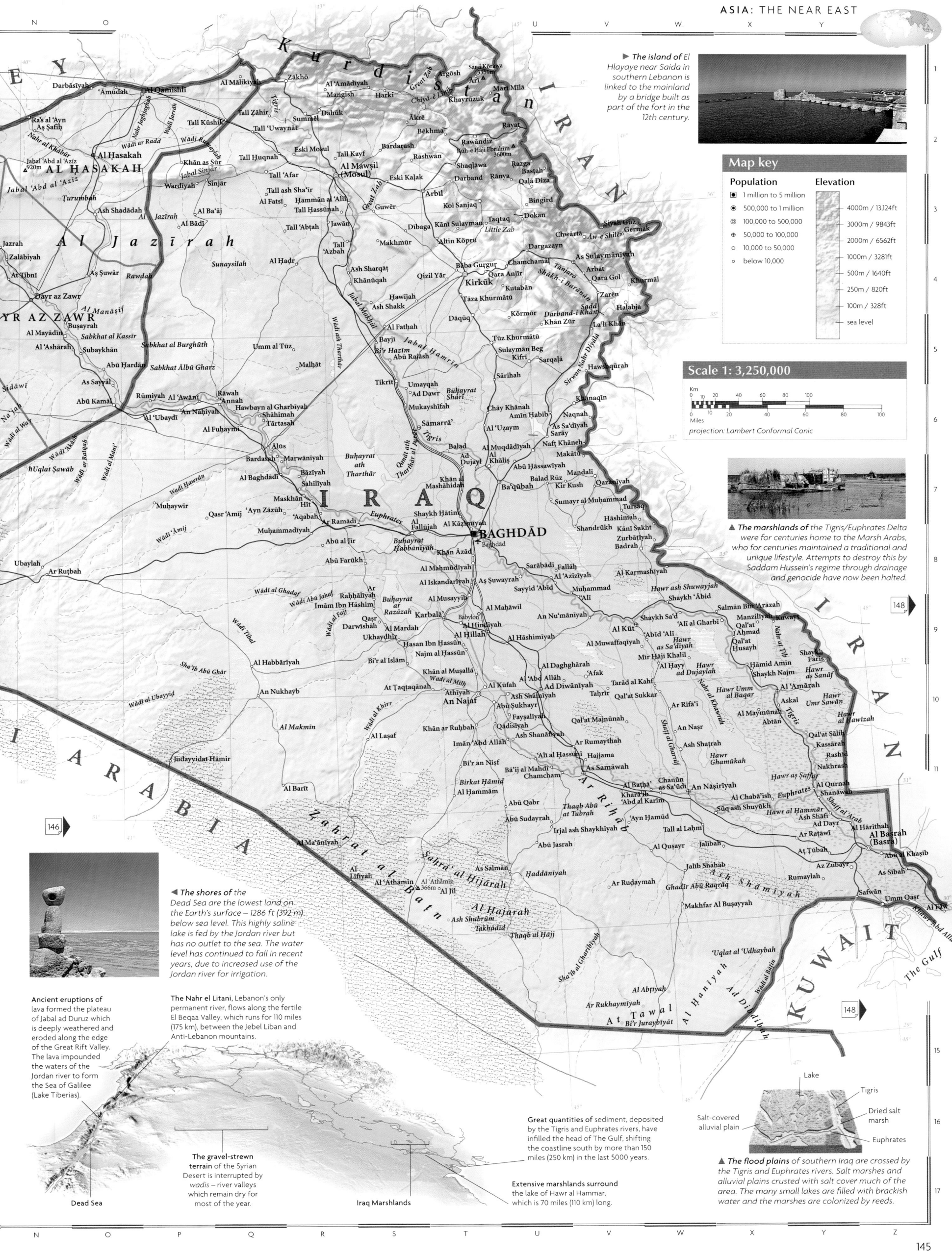

▶ The island of *El Hlayaye* near Saida in southern Lebanon is linked to the mainland by a bridge built as part of the fort in the 12th century.

Map key

Population

- ◉ 1 million to 5 million
- ◉ 500,000 to 1 million
- ◉ 100,000 to 500,000
- ◉ 50,000 to 100,000
- ○ 10,000 to 50,000
- ○ below 10,000

Elevation

- 4000m / 13,124ft
- 3000m / 9843ft
- 2000m / 6562ft
- 1000m / 3281ft
- 500m / 1640ft
- 250m / 820ft
- 100m / 328ft
- sea level

Scale 1: 3,250,000

Km 0 10 20 40 60 80 100
Miles 0 20 40 60 80 100

projection: Lambert Conformal Conic

▲ The marshlands of the Tigris/Euphrates Delta were for centuries home to the Marsh Arabs, who for centuries maintained a traditional and unique lifestyle. Attempts to destroy this by Saddam Hussein's regime through drainage and genocide have now been halted.

◀ The shores of the Dead Sea are the lowest land on the Earth's surface – 1286 ft (392 m) below sea level. This highly saline lake is fed by the Jordan river but has no outlet to the sea. The water level has continued to fall in recent years, due to increased use of the Jordan river for irrigation.

Dead Sea

Ancient eruptions of lava formed the plateau of Jabal ad Duruz which is deeply weathered and eroded along the edge of the Great Rift Valley. The lava impounded the waters of the Jordan river to form the Sea of Galilee (Lake Tiberias).

The Nahr el Litani, Lebanon's only permanent river, flows along the fertile El Beqaa Valley, which runs for 110 miles (175 km), between the Jebel Liban and Anti-Lebanon mountains.

The gravel-strewn terrain of the Syrian Desert is interrupted by wadis – river valleys which remain dry for most of the year.

Iraq Marshlands

Great quantities of sediment, deposited by the Tigris and Euphrates rivers, have infilled the head of The Gulf, shifting the coastline south by more than 150 miles (250 km) in the last 5000 years.

Extensive marshlands surround the lake of Hawr al Hammar, which is 70 miles (110 km) long.

Lake
Tigris
Dried salt marsh
Euphrates
Salt-covered alluvial plain

▲ The flood plains of southern Iraq are crossed by the Tigris and Euphrates rivers. Salt marshes and alluvial plains crusted with salt cover much of the area. The many small lakes are filled with brackish water and the marshes are colonized by reeds.

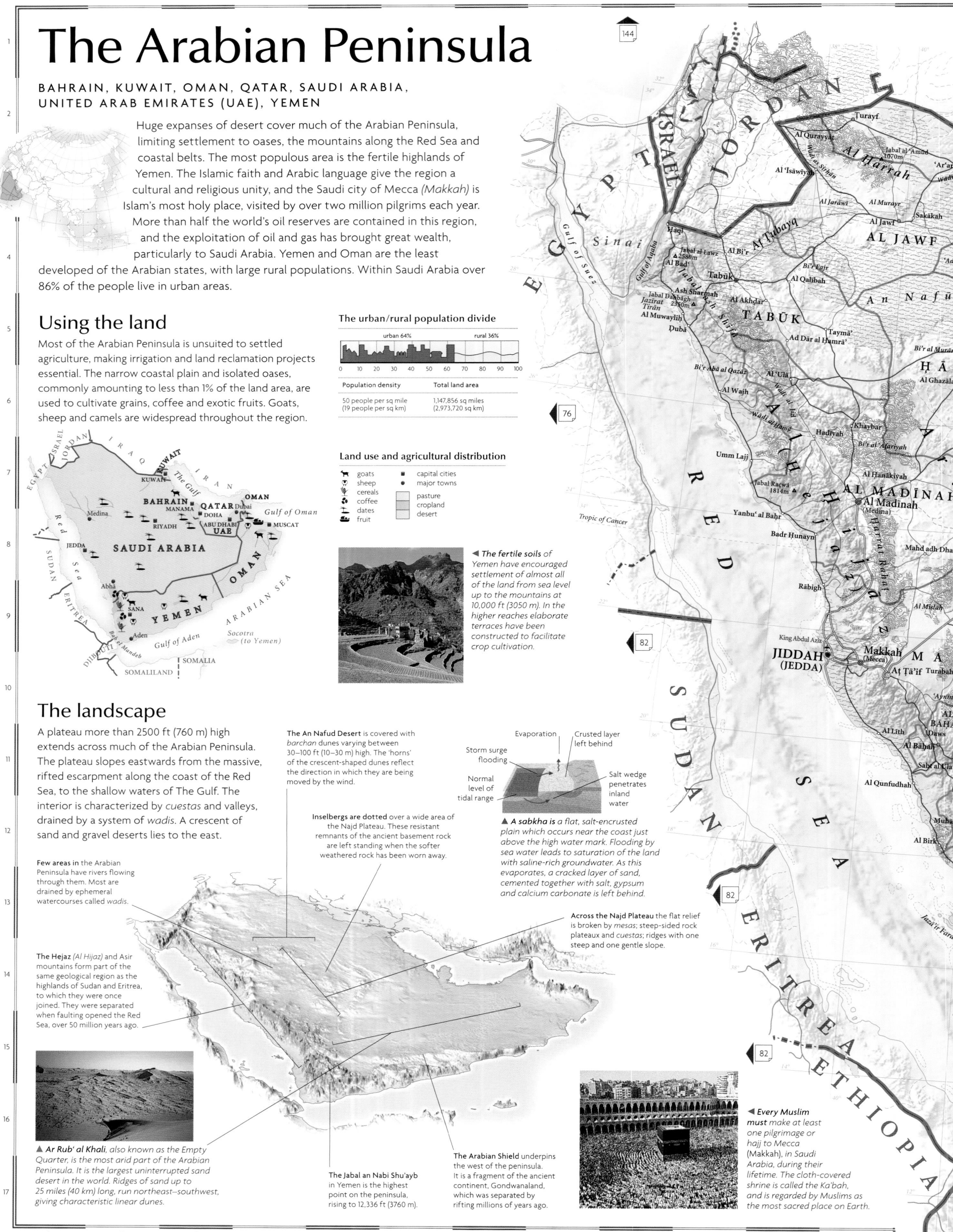

The Arabian Peninsula

BAHRAIN, KUWAIT, OMAN, QATAR, SAUDI ARABIA,
UNITED ARAB EMIRATES (UAE), YEMEN

Huge expanses of desert cover much of the Arabian Peninsula,
limiting settlement to oases, the mountains along the Red Sea and
coastal belts. The most populous area is the fertile highlands of
Yemen. The Islamic faith and Arabic language give the region a
cultural and religious unity, and the Saudi city of Mecca (Makkah) is
Islam's most holy place, visited by over two million pilgrims each year.
More than half the world's oil reserves are contained in this region,
and the exploitation of oil and gas has brought great wealth,
particularly to Saudi Arabia. Yemen and Oman are the least
developed of the Arabian states, with large rural populations. Within Saudi Arabia over
86% of the people live in urban areas.

Using the land

Most of the Arabian Peninsula is unsuited to settled
agriculture, making irrigation and land reclamation projects
essential. The narrow coastal plain and isolated oases,
commonly amounting to less than 1% of the land area, are
used to cultivate grains, coffee and exotic fruits. Goats,
sheep and camels are widespread throughout the region.

The urban/rural population divide

urban 64%   rural 36%

0 10 20 30 40 50 60 70 80 90 100

Population density	Total land area
50 people per sq mile (19 people per sq km)	1,147,856 sq miles (2,973,720 sq km)

Land use and agricultural distribution

- goats
- sheep
- cereals
- coffee
- dates
- fruit
- capital cities
- major towns
- pasture
- cropland
- desert

◄ *The fertile soils* of
Yemen have encouraged
settlement of almost all
of the land from sea level
up to the mountains at
10,000 ft (3050 m). In the
higher reaches elaborate
terraces have been
constructed to facilitate
crop cultivation.

The landscape

A plateau more than 2500 ft (760 m) high
extends across much of the Arabian Peninsula.
The plateau slopes eastwards from the massive,
rifted escarpment along the coast of the Red
Sea, to the shallow waters of The Gulf. The
interior is characterized by *cuestas* and valleys,
drained by a system of *wadis*. A crescent of
sand and gravel deserts lies to the east.

The An Nafud Desert is covered with
barchan dunes varying between
30–100 ft (10–30 m) high. The 'horns'
of the crescent-shaped dunes reflect
the direction in which they are being
moved by the wind.

Inselbergs are dotted over a wide area of
the Najd Plateau. These resistant
remnants of the ancient basement rock
are left standing when the softer
weathered rock has been worn away.

Evaporation

Crusted layer
left behind

Storm surge
flooding

Normal
level of
tidal range

Salt wedge
penetrates
inland
water

▲ *A sabkha is* a flat, salt-encrusted
plain which occurs near the coast just
above the high water mark. Flooding by
sea water leads to saturation of the land
with saline-rich groundwater. As this
evaporates, a cracked layer of sand,
cemented together with salt, gypsum
and calcium carbonate is left behind.

Few areas in the Arabian
Peninsula have rivers flowing
through them. Most are
drained by ephemeral
watercourses called *wadis*.

The Hejaz (Al Hijaz) and Asir
mountains form part of the
same geological region as the
highlands of Sudan and Eritrea,
to which they were once
joined. They were separated
when faulting opened the Red
Sea, over 50 million years ago.

Across the Najd Plateau the flat relief
is broken by *mesas*; steep-sided rock
plateaux and *cuestas*; ridges with one
steep and one gentle slope.

▲ *Ar Rub' al Khali*, also known as the Empty
Quarter, is the most arid part of the Arabian
Peninsula. It is the largest uninterrupted sand
desert in the world. Ridges of sand up to
25 miles (40 km) long, run northeast–southwest,
giving characteristic linear dunes.

The Jabal an Nabi Shu'ayb
in Yemen is the highest
point on the peninsula,
rising to 12,336 ft (3760 m).

The Arabian Shield underpins
the west of the peninsula.
It is a fragment of the ancient
continent, Gondwanaland,
which was separated by
rifting millions of years ago.

◄ *Every Muslim
must* make at least
one pilgrimage or
hajj to Mecca
(Makkah), in Saudi
Arabia, during their
lifetime. The cloth-covered
shrine is called the Ka'bah,
and is regarded by Muslims as
the most sacred place on Earth.

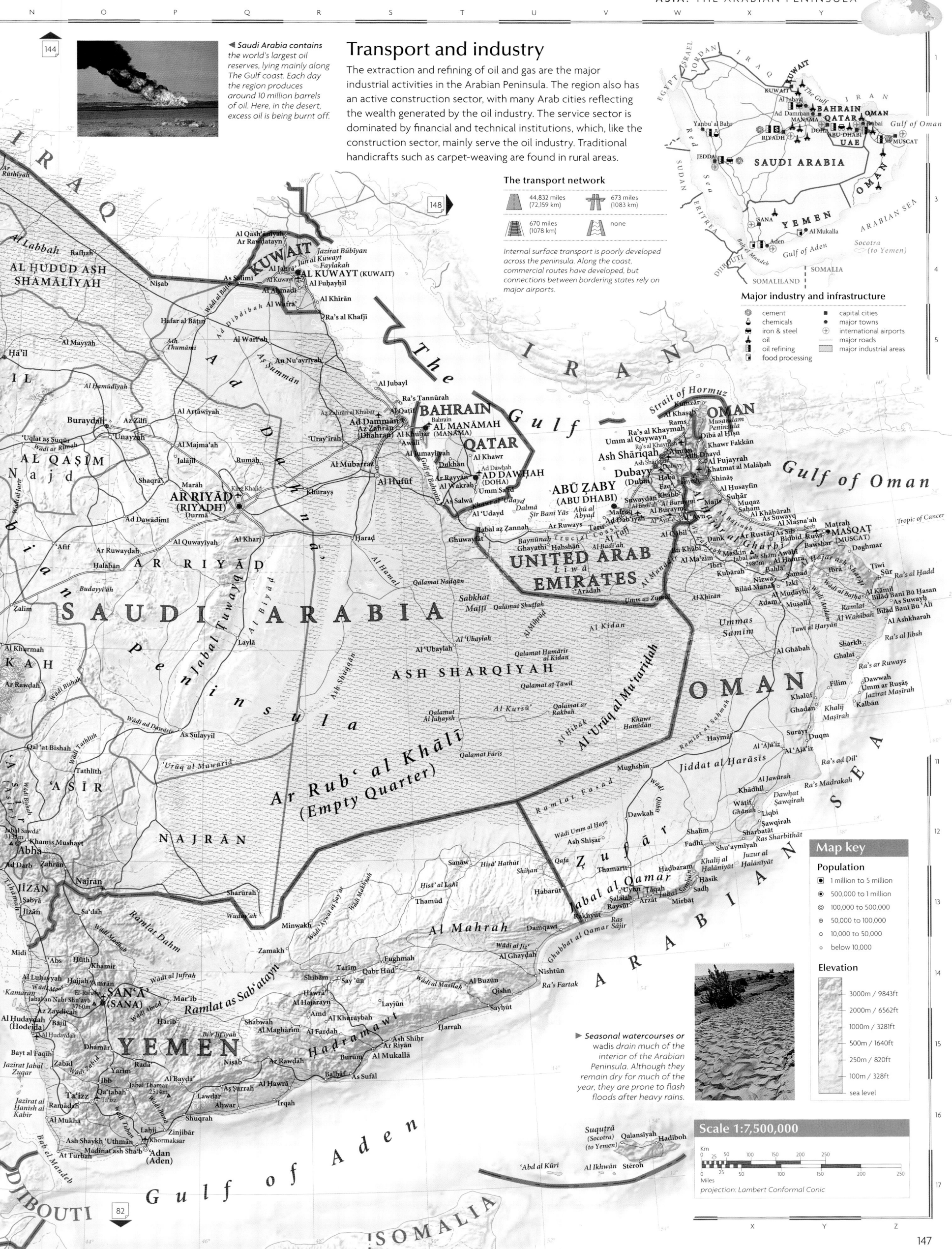

Saudi Arabia contains the world's largest oil reserves, lying mainly along The Gulf coast. Each day the region produces around 10 million barrels of oil. Here, in the desert, excess oil is being burnt off.

Transport and industry

The extraction and refining of oil and gas are the major industrial activities in the Arabian Peninsula. The region also has an active construction sector, with many Arab cities reflecting the wealth generated by the oil industry. The service sector is dominated by financial and technical institutions, which, like the construction sector, mainly serve the oil industry. Traditional handicrafts such as carpet-weaving are found in rural areas.

The transport network

44,832 miles (72,159 km)		673 miles (1083 km)
670 miles (1078 km)		none

Internal surface transport is poorly developed across the peninsula. Along the coast, commercial routes have developed, but connections between bordering states rely on major airports.

Major industry and infrastructure

- cement
- chemicals
- iron & steel
- oil
- oil refining
- food processing
- capital cities
- major towns
- international airports
- major roads
- major industrial areas

Seasonal watercourses or wadis drain much of the interior of the Arabian Peninsula. Although they remain dry for much of the year, they are prone to flash floods after heavy rains.

Map key

Population

- 1 million to 5 million
- 500,000 to 1 million
- 100,000 to 500,000
- 50,000 to 100,000
- 10,000 to 50,000
- below 10,000

Elevation

- 3000m / 9843ft
- 2000m / 6562ft
- 1000m / 3281ft
- 500m / 1640ft
- 250m / 820ft
- 100m / 328ft
- sea level

Scale 1:7,500,000

projection: Lambert Conformal Conic

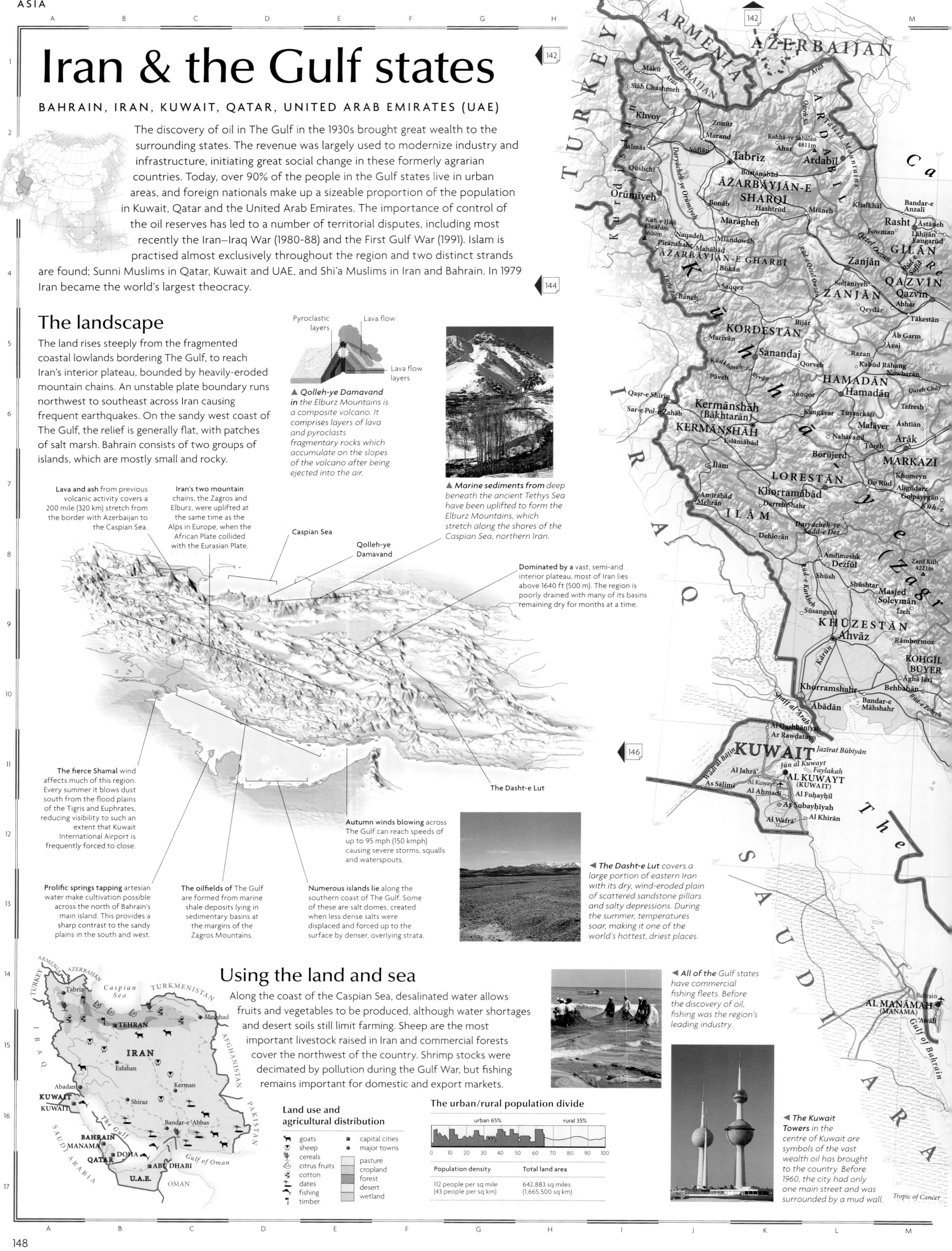

Iran & the Gulf states

BAHRAIN, IRAN, KUWAIT, QATAR, UNITED ARAB EMIRATES (UAE)

The discovery of oil in The Gulf in the 1930s brought great wealth to the surrounding states. The revenue was largely used to modernize industry and infrastructure, initiating great social change in these formerly agrarian countries. Today, over 90% of the people in the Gulf states live in urban areas, and foreign nationals make up a sizeable proportion of the population in Kuwait, Qatar and the United Arab Emirates. The importance of control of the oil reserves has led to a number of territorial disputes, including most recently the Iran–Iraq War (1980-88) and the First Gulf War (1991). Islam is practised almost exclusively throughout the region and two distinct strands are found; Sunni Muslims in Qatar, Kuwait and UAE, and Shi'a Muslims in Iran and Bahrain. In 1979 Iran became the world's largest theocracy.

The landscape

The land rises steeply from the fragmented coastal lowlands bordering The Gulf, to reach Iran's interior plateau, bounded by heavily-eroded mountain chains. An unstable plate boundary runs northwest to southeast across Iran causing frequent earthquakes. On the sandy west coast of The Gulf, the relief is generally flat, with patches of salt marsh. Bahrain consists of two groups of islands, which are mostly small and rocky.

Pyroclastic layers / Lava flow / Lava flow layers

▲ Qolleh-ye Damavand in the Elburz Mountains is a composite volcano. It comprises layers of lava and pyroclasts fragmentary rocks which accumulate on the slopes of the volcano after being ejected into the air.

▲ Marine sediments from deep beneath the ancient Tethys Sea have been uplifted to form the Elburz Mountains, which stretch along the shores of the Caspian Sea, northern Iran.

Lava and ash from previous volcanic activity covers a 200 mile (320 km) stretch from the border with Azerbaijan to the Caspian Sea.

Iran's two mountain chains, the Zagros and Elburz, were uplifted at the same time as the Alps in Europe, when the African Plate collided with the Eurasian Plate.

Caspian Sea

Qolleh-ye Damavand

Dominated by a vast, semi-arid interior plateau, most of Iran lies above 1640 ft (500 m). The region is poorly drained with many of its basins remaining dry for months at a time.

The fierce Shamal wind affects much of this region. Every summer it blows dust south from the flood plains of the Tigris and Euphrates, reducing visibility to such an extent that Kuwait International Airport is frequently forced to close.

The Dasht-e Lut

Autumn winds blowing across The Gulf can reach speeds of up to 95 mph (150 kmph) causing severe storms, squalls and waterspouts.

Prolific springs tapping artesian water make cultivation possible across the north of Bahrain's main island. This provides a sharp contrast to the sandy plains in the south and west.

The oilfields of The Gulf are formed from marine shale deposits lying in sedimentary basins at the margins of the Zagros Mountains.

Numerous islands lie along the southern coast of The Gulf. Some of these are salt domes, created when less dense salts were displaced and forced up to the surface by denser, overlying strata.

◀ The Dasht-e Lut covers a large portion of eastern Iran with its dry, wind-eroded plain of scattered sandstone pillars and salty depressions. During the summer, temperatures soar, making it one of the world's hottest, driest places.

Using the land and sea

Along the coast of the Caspian Sea, desalinated water allows fruits and vegetables to be produced, although water shortages and desert soils still limit farming. Sheep are the most important livestock raised in Iran and commercial forests cover the northwest of the country. Shrimp stocks were decimated by pollution during the Gulf War, but fishing remains important for domestic and export markets.

◀ All of the Gulf states have commercial fishing fleets. Before the discovery of oil, fishing was the region's leading industry.

◀ The Kuwait Towers in the centre of Kuwait are symbols of the vast wealth oil has brought to the country. Before 1960, the city had only one main street and was surrounded by a mud wall.

Land use and agricultural distribution

- goats
- sheep
- cereals
- citrus fruits
- cotton
- dates
- fishing
- timber
- ● capital cities
- • major towns
- pasture
- cropland
- forest
- desert
- wetland

The urban/rural population divide

urban 65% | rural 35%

0 10 20 30 40 50 60 70 80 90 100

Population density: 112 people per sq mile (43 people per sq km)

Total land area: 642,883 sq miles (1,665,500 sq km)

Tropic of Cancer

◄ Many volcanoes lie in Iran's 1200 mile (1930 km) volcanic belt, including the country's highest peak, the now-extinct Qolleh-ye Damavand at 18,600 ft (5671 m).

▶ Extensive oil and gas exploitation in the Gulf region has allowed the economic transformation of the Gulf states. Consequently, many of these states have a hugely improved per capita income compared to the 1960's.

Transport and industry

Both onshore and offshore oil reserves are exploited throughout the region. Kuwait not only extracts but also refines 80% of its oil. Bahrain has diversified its economy to become the main commercial and financial centre in The Gulf. Iran produces a wide range of products: textile mills are widespread and carpet-weaving is an important export industry.

Major industry and infrastructure

- carpet manufacture
- chemicals
- ⑤ finance
- food processing
- oil
- oil refining
- ⊤ textiles
- ■ capital city
- ● major towns
- ✈ international airports
- — major roads
- major industrial areas

The transport network

63,543 miles (102,274 km)		884 miles (1423 km)	
3822 miles (6151 km)		562 miles (904 km)	

Major towns and neighbouring countries are linked by adequate road networks, although rural areas are less well served. Bahrain is linked to the mainland by a 15 mile (25 km) long causeway.

Map key

Population
- ■ above 5 million
- ⊡ 1 million to 5 million
- ⊙ 500,000 to 1 million
- ⊚ 100,000 to 500,000
- ⊕ 50,000 to 100,000
- ○ 10,000 to 50,000
- ○ below 10,000

Elevation
- 4000m / 13,124ft
- 3000m / 9843ft
- 2000m / 6562ft
- 1000m / 3281ft
- 500m / 1640ft
- 250m / 820ft
- 100m / 328ft
- sea level

Scale 1:5,500,000

projection: Lambert Conformal Conic

149

Kazakhstan

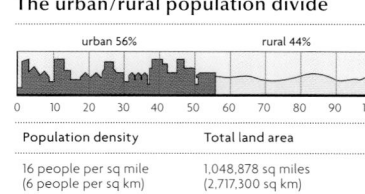

Abundant natural resources lie in the immense steppe grasslands, deserts and central plateau of the former Soviet republic of Kazakhstan. An intensive programme of industrial and agricultural development to exploit these resources during the Soviet era resulted in catastrophic industrial pollution, including fallout from nuclear testing and the shrinkage of the Aral Sea. Since independence, the government has encouraged foreign investment and liberalized the economy to promote growth. The adoption of Kazakh as the national language is intended to encourage a new sense of national identity in a state where living conditions for the majority remain harsh, both in cramped urban centres and impoverished rural areas.

Transport and industry

The single most important industry in Kazakhstan is mining, based around extensive oil deposits near the Caspian Sea, the world's largest chromium mine, and vast reserves of iron ore. Recent foreign investment has helped to develop industries including food processing and steel manufacture, and to expand the exploitation of mineral resources. The Russian space programme is still based at Baykonyr, near Kyzylorda in central Kazakhstan.

Major industry and infrastructure

⚗ chemicals	■ capital cities
⚙ engineering	● major towns
🐟 fish processing	✈ international airports
🍴 food processing	— major roads
△ iron & steel	major industrial areas
⛏ metallurgy	
⛰ mining	
🛢 oil	

The transport network

48,263 miles
(77,680 km)

8483 miles
(13,660 km)

3900 miles
(2423 km)

Industrial areas in the north and east are well-connected to Russia. Air and rail links with Germany and China have been established through foreign investment. Better access to Baltic ports is being sought.

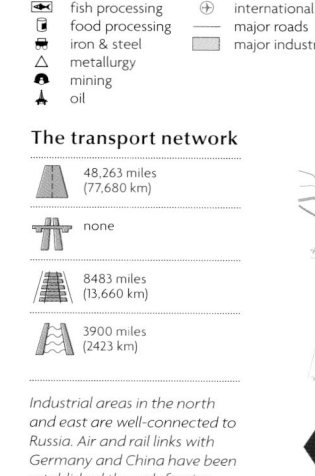

◄ An open-cast coal mine in Kazakhstan. Foreign investment is being actively sought by the Kazakh government in order to fully exploit the potential of the country's rich mineral reserves.

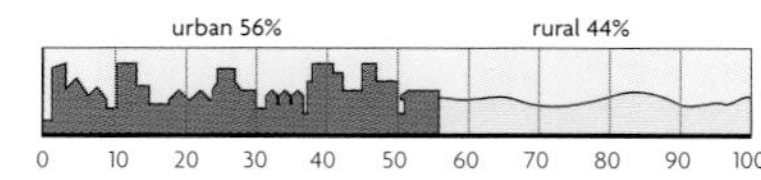

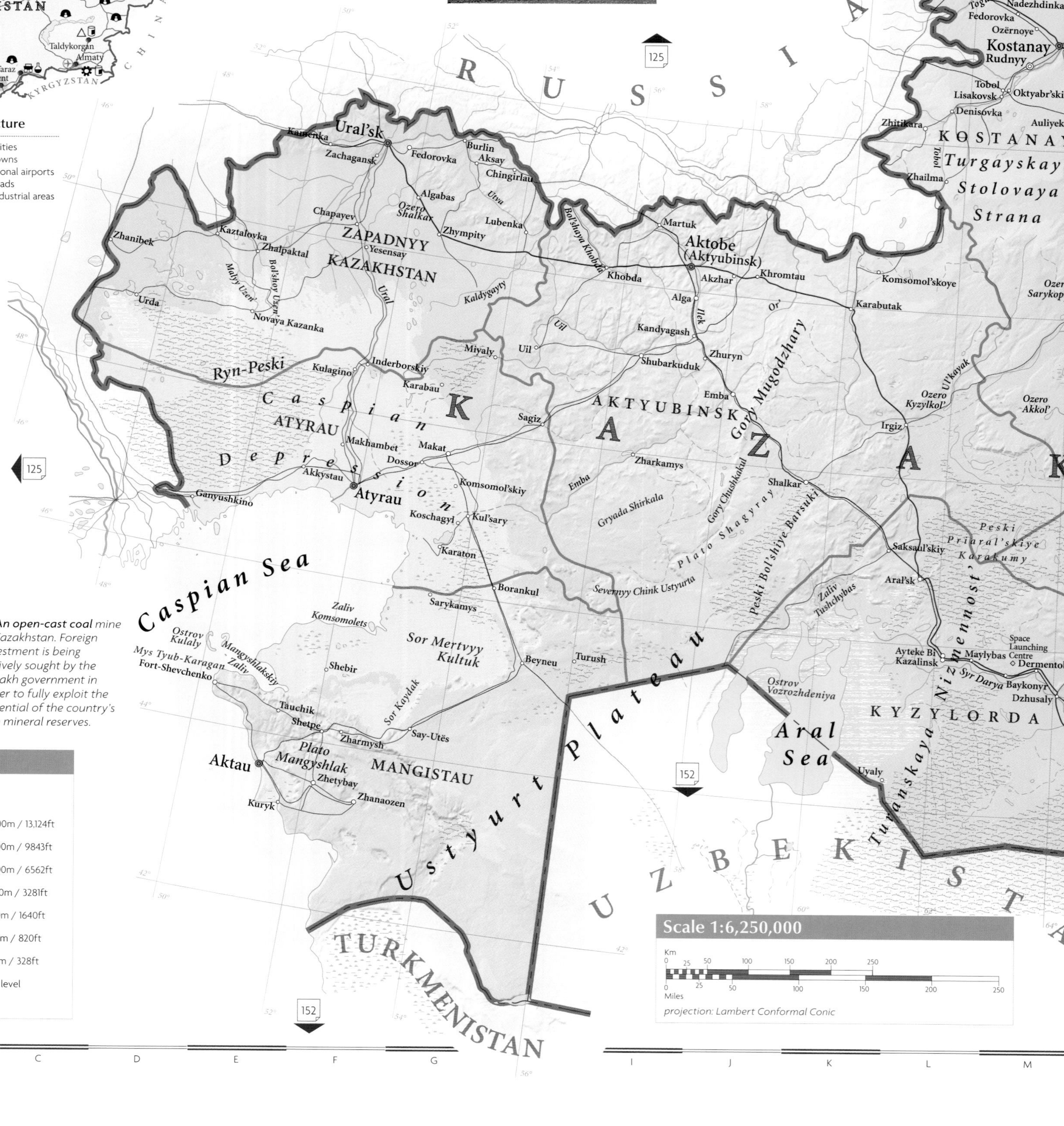

Map key

Population

- ▣ 1 million to 5 million
- ◉ 500,000 to 1 million
- ◍ 100,000 to 500,000
- ⊕ 50,000 to 100,000
- ○ 10,000 to 50,000
- ○ below 10,000

Elevation

- 4000m / 13,124ft
- 3000m / 9843ft
- 2000m / 6562ft
- 1000m / 3281ft
- 500m / 1640ft
- 250m / 820ft
- 100m / 328ft
- sea level

Using the land and sea

The rearing of large herds of sheep and goats on the steppe grasslands forms the core of Kazakh agriculture. Arable cultivation and cotton-growing in pasture and desert areas was encouraged during the Soviet era, but relative yields are low. The heavy use of fertilizers and the diversion of natural water sources for irrigation has degraded much of the land.

The urban/rural population divide

urban 56% rural 44%

0 10 20 30 40 50 60 70 80 90 100

Population density	Total land area
16 people per sq mile (6 people per sq km)	1,048,878 sq miles (2,717,300 sq km)

Land use and agricultural distribution

- 🐂 cattle
- 🐐 goats
- 🐑 sheep
- ❋ cotton
- 🐟 fishing
- 🌾 wheat
- ■ capital cities
- ● major towns
- pasture
- cropland
- forest
- mountain region
- desert

◄ The nomadic peoples who moved their herds around the steppe grasslands are now largely settled, although echoes of their traditional lifestyle, in particular their superb riding skills, remain.

Scale 1:6,250,000

projection: Lambert Conformal Conic

The landscape

Stretching more than 1250 miles (2000 km) from the Caspian Sea in the west to China in the east, more than 40% of Kazakhstan is covered by steppe grasslands which give way to barren desert in the south. The land rises eastwards towards the mineral-rich central plateau, to form the Altai Mountains.

1960 **1996** **2010**

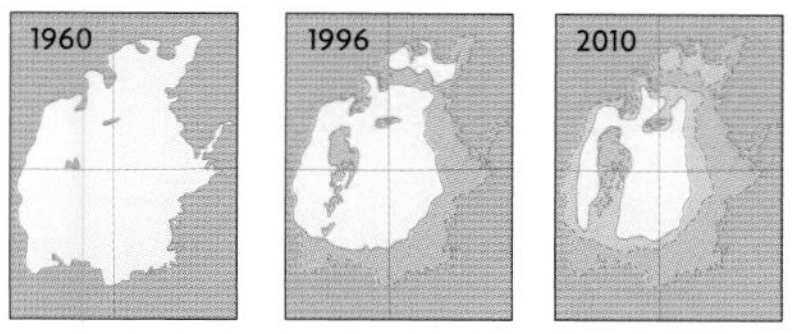

▲ **Since 1960, the** Aral Sea has shrunk by 75%, become extremely saline, and lost all but five of its once-abundant fish species. Factors in this ecological disaster include the excessive use of fertilizers, defoliants and the diversion of its main source rivers for the irrigation of desert lands.

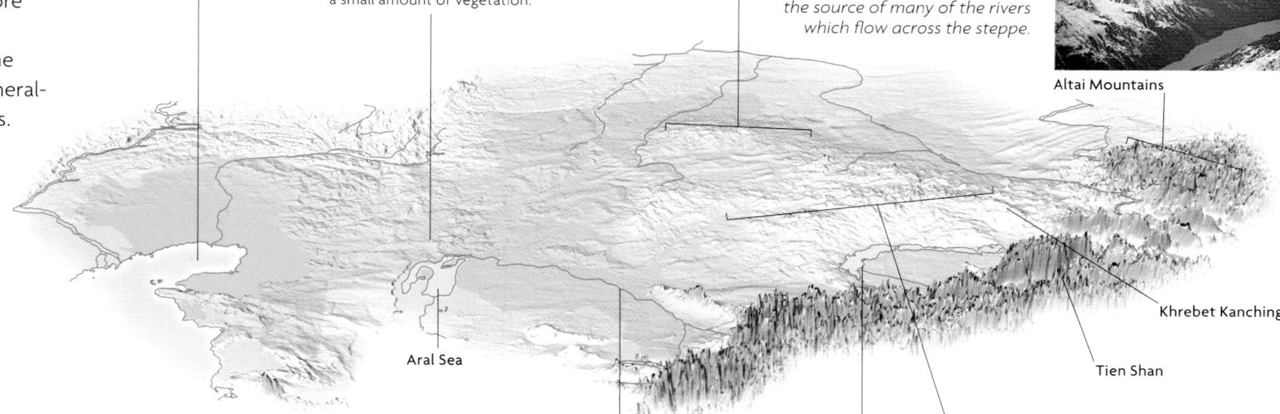

The Caspian Sea is the largest body of inland water in the world.

The desert of Peski Bol'shiye Barsuki is mainly sandy, displaying a number of classic dune formations. Groundwater supports a small amount of vegetation.

A large number of salt lakes fill depressions in the rolling uplands of central Kazakhstan.

▶ **The Altai Mountains** lie on Kazakhstan's eastern borders with China and the Russian Federation. Cold and largely barren, they are the source of many of the rivers which flow across the steppe.

Altai Mountains

Aral Sea

Khrebet Kanchingiz

Tien Shan

Its waters taken for industry and irrigation, the Syr Darya, one of Kazakhstan's major rivers, now barely reaches the Aral Sea which it used to fill. Like many Kazakh rivers it has been heavily polluted with chemicals and its flow has been restricted by up to 60%.

The waters of Lake Balkhash (Ozero Balkhash), unlike those of the Aral Sea, are still able to support a fishing industry.

The central Kazakh Uplands (Kazakhskiy Melkosopochnik) contain much of the country's mineral riches. The landscape is largely flat with occasional rocky outcrops and hillocks.

▶ **Immense stretches of** steppe grasslands characterize much of the Kazakh landscape. These lowland areas have been used for arable cultivation in recent years, although problems with irrigation have meant that much of the land is being allowed to revert to its natural vegetation and pastoral usage.

▲ **Rows of pine** trees edge this valley near Almaty. The snow-covered slopes in the background are used for skiing.

[Map of Kazakhstan showing cities, regions, and physical features including: Petropavlovsk, Mamlyutka, Bulayevo, Kokshetau, Astana, Karaganda, Zhezkazgan, Kyzylorda, Taraz, Shymkent, Almaty (Alma-Ata), Semipalatinsk, Ust'-Kamenogorsk, Pavlodar, Ekibastuz, Temirtau, Taldykorgan; regions: SEVERNYY KAZAKHSTAN, AKMOLA, PAVLODAR, KARAGANDA, VOSTOCHNYY KAZAKHSTAN, ALMATY, ZHAMBYL, YUZHNYY KAZAKHSTAN; physical features: Ozero Balkhash, Betpak-Dala, Peski Moyynkum, Peski Saryyesik-Atyrau, Melkosopochnik, Altai Mountains, Tien Shan, Khrebet Tarbagatay, Kirghiz Range, Ozero Zaysan; bordering countries: FEDERATION (RUSSIAN), KYRGYZSTAN, CHINA]

151

Central Asia

KYRGYZSTAN, TAJIKISTAN, TURKMENISTAN, UZBEKISTAN

The four republics that declared independence in 1991 were created in the early years of the Soviet Union, promoting ethnic divisions in a region whose common focus, since the 8th century, has been Islam. Traditional rural and nomadic ways of life have survived the Soviet era, while the benefits of modern industry and grand irrigation schemes have resulted in severe pollution in the delicate, arid environment of the steppe, particularly in Uzbekistan. Many ethnic minority groups are scattered among the four republics, with isolated communities in the mountains of Kyrgyzstan. The current Islamic revival has brought hope of greater regional unity, in spite of religious factionalism which, in 1992, plunged Tajikistan into civil war.

◄ *The desert of* the Kara Kum (Garagum) occupies over 70% of Turkmenistan; its wind-scoured surface of dune ridges and depressions severely limits human settlement.

Map key

Population
- ◉ 1 million to 5 million
- ◉ 500,000 to 1 million
- ◉ 100,000 to 500,000
- ⊕ 50,000 to 100,000
- ○ 10,000 to 50,000
- ○ below 10,000

Elevation
- 6000m / 19,686ft
- 4000m / 13,124ft
- 3000m / 9843ft
- 2000m / 6562ft
- 1000m / 3281ft
- 500m / 1640ft
- 250m / 820ft
- 100m / 328ft
- sea level

▲ *The southern shoreline* of the Aral Sea has retreated over 30 miles (48 km) since 1960. A major cause is the diversion of water from the Amu Darya river for irrigation via the Kara Kum Canal (Garagum Kanaly).

Transport and industry

Fossil fuels are extracted and processed in all four states, with scope for further exploitation. Agriculture provides raw materials for many industries, including food and textiles processing, and the manufacture of leather goods, clothing and carpets. Farm machinery is also produced.

The transport network

73,658 miles (118,555 km)		87 miles (140 km)	
4773 miles (7683 km)		1180 miles (1900 km)	

The Kara Kum Canal (Garagumskiy Kanal) runs for 870 miles (1400 km) from the Amu Darya river to the Caspian Sea. The canal is principally used for irrigation but is navigable for 280 miles (450 km).

Major industry and infrastructure

- carpet weaving
- chemicals
- engineering
- food processing
- oil & gas
- textiles
- ■ capital cities
- ■ major towns
- ✈ international airports
- — major roads
- ▨ major industrial areas

The landscape

The great Tien Shan and Pamir ranges meet in a succession of high mountain chains. These mountains encircle the fertile Fergana Valley and reach west into the desert of the Kyzyl Kum, dividing the Syr Darya and Amu Darya rivers. Sandy steppeland extends to the shores of the Caspian Sea, with the desert of the Kara Kum (Garagum) in the south. The Amu Darya drains into the Aral Sea in the north.

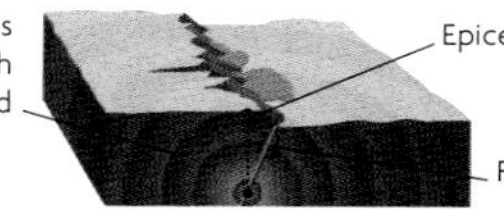

Salt marshes fill many of the depressions in the Ustyurt Plateau, a barren, rocky tableland about 650 ft (200 m) above sea level.

Some of the world's largest deposits of marine salts are found in Garabogaz Aylagy. This shallow, saline gulf has an average depth of only 33 ft (10 m), and a very high evaporation rate, producing the salty deposits.

The Kara Kum (Garagum) is one of the world's largest expanses of sand. Wind action has created a terrain of shifting, crescent-shaped sand dunes known as barchans.

A series of major rock faults has created the Fergana Valley, a deep depression surrounded by high mountains. Water from the Syr Darya river and from underground sources supports intensive agriculture, despite minimal rainfall.

The Amu Darya is the only river in Central Asia with a sufficient volume of water to cross the desert of the Kara Kum (Garagum) from the Pamirs to the Aral Sea, where it forms a delta largely vegetated by scrub grasses.

Kyzyl Kum

Syr Darya

Earthquake zone

▲ In the heavily-fractured and faulted mountain region, earthquakes are common, caused by the sudden release of tension along active fault lines.

Naryn river

Mount Communism (Qullai Kommunizm), in the northern Pamirs, was so named for being the highest point in the former Soviet Union, rising to 24,590 ft (7495 m).

Shock waves travel through ground

Epicentre

Fault

Qarokul

◀ Bare mountains provide a stark background to the croplands along the Naryn river in Kyrgyzstan. Irrigation is essential for cultivation in this dry region.

Ozero Issyk-Kul' lies at an altitude of 5193 ft (1584 m). The lake remains ice-free throughout the year, due to the slight salinity of the water.

Tien Shan

▲ The Tien Shan extend from China in the east, reaching heights over 24,420 ft (7443 m) and branching into many parallel ranges in the west.

◀ Nestling high in the Pamir range, and fed by glacial meltwater, Qarokul is the largest of the lakes in this region.

Scale 1:4,250,000

projection: Lambert Conformal Conic

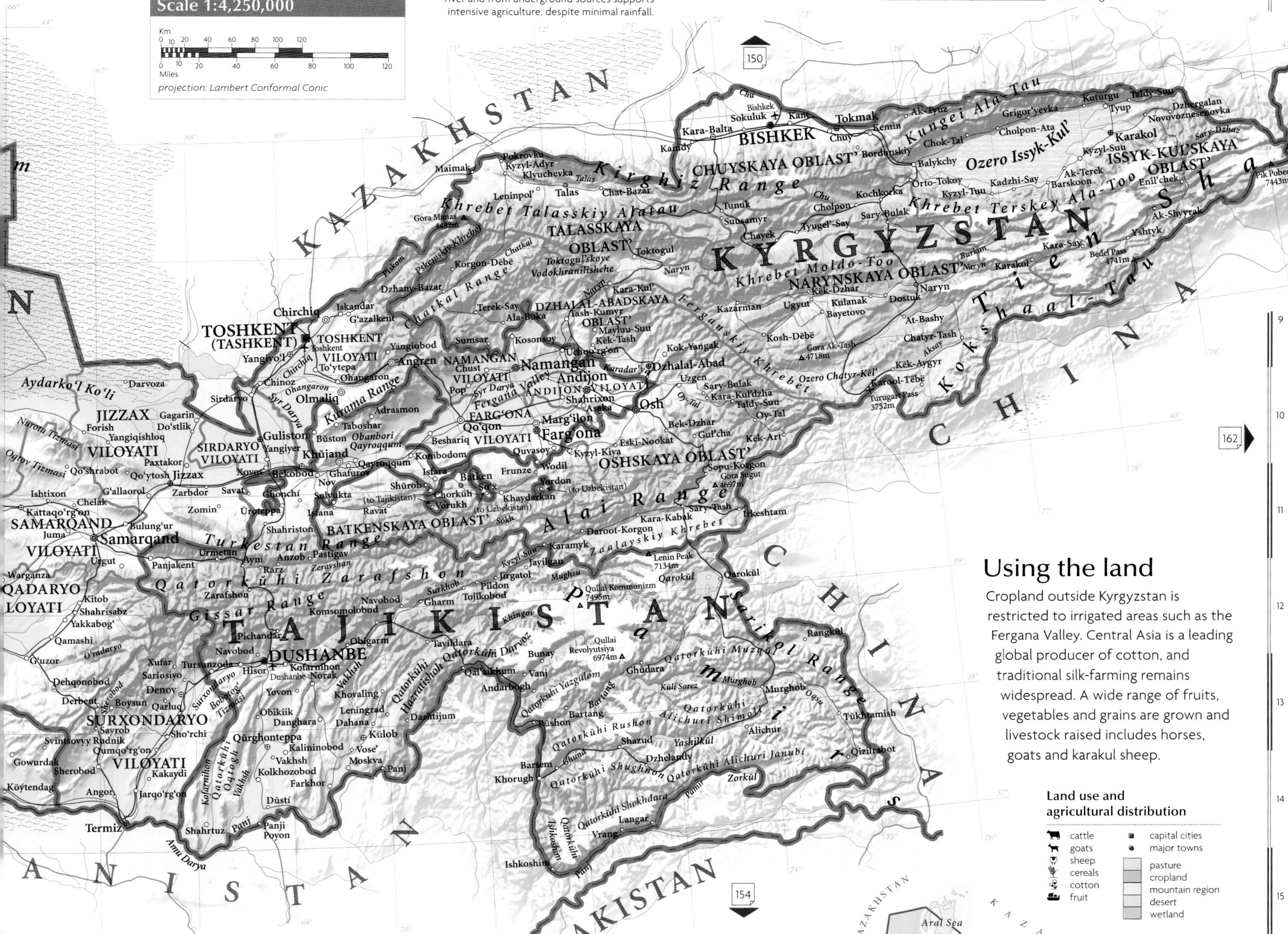

Using the land

Cropland outside Kyrgyzstan is restricted to irrigated areas such as the Fergana Valley. Central Asia is a leading global producer of cotton, and traditional silk-farming remains widespread. A wide range of fruits, vegetables and grains are grown and livestock raised includes horses, goats and karakul sheep.

Land use and agricultural distribution

- cattle
- goats
- sheep
- cereals
- cotton
- fruit
- capital cities
- major towns
- pasture
- cropland
- mountain region
- desert
- wetland

▶ Plentiful sunshine, rich soils and massive irrigation schemes have made Uzbekistan the world's fifth largest cotton producer, although water shortages now prevent any further expansion of irrigated land.

The urban/rural population divide

urban 36%   rural 64%

0 10 20 30 40 50 60 70 80 90 100

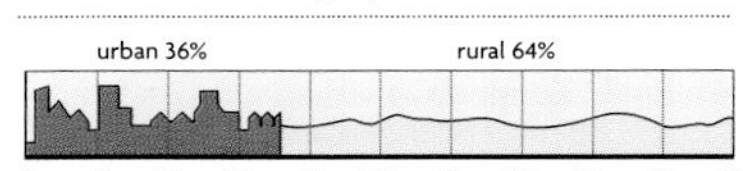

Population density	Total land area
88 people per sq mile (34 people per sq km)	492,961 sq miles (1,277,100 sq km)

Afghanistan & Pakistan

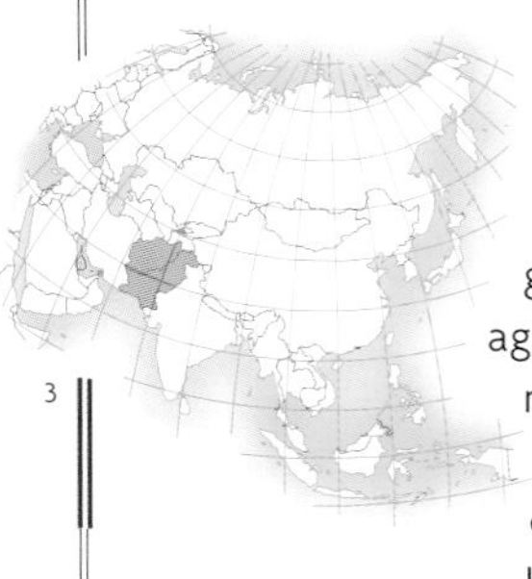

Pakistan was created by the partition of British India in 1947, becoming the western arm of a new Islamic state for Indian Muslims; the eastern sector, in Bengal, seceded to become the separate country of Bangladesh in 1971. Over half of Pakistan's 158 million people live in the Punjab, at the fertile head of the great Indus Basin. The river sustains a national economy based on irrigated agriculture, including cotton for the vital textiles industry. Afghanistan, a mountainous, landlocked country, with an ancient and independent culture, has been wracked by war since 1979. Factional strife escalated into an international conflict in late 2001, as US-led troops ousted the militant and fundamentally Islamist *taliban* regime as part of their 'war on terror'.

◄ *The town of* Bamian lies high in the Hindu Kush west of Kabul. Between the 2nd and 5th centuries two huge statues of Buddha were carved into the nearby rock, the largest of which stood 125 ft (38 m) high. The statues were destroyed by the taliban regime in March 2001.

Transport and industry

Pakistan is highly dependent on the cotton textiles industry, although diversified manufacture is expanding around cities such as Karachi and Lahore. Afghanistan's limited industry is based mainly on the processing of agricultural raw materials and includes traditional crafts such as carpet-making.

Major industry and infrastructure

- carpet weaving
- chemicals
- engineering
- finance
- food processing
- iron & steel
- oil & gas
- textiles
- capital cities
- major towns
- international airports
- major roads
- major industrial areas

The transport network

96,154 miles (154,763 km)	
211 miles (340 km)	
4852 miles (7814 km)	
745 miles (1200 km)	

▶ *The Karakoram Highway* is one of the highest major roads in the world. It took over 24,000 workers almost 20 years to complete.

The Karakoram Highway was completed after 20 years of construction in 1978. It breaches the Himalayan mountain barrier providing a commercial motor route linking lowland Pakistan and China.

The landscape

Afghanistan's topography is dominated by the mountains of the Hindu Kush, which spread south and west into numerous mountain spurs. The dry plateau of southwestern Afghanistan extends into Pakistan and the hills which overlook the great Indus Basin. In northern Pakistan the Hindu Kush, Himalayan and Karakoram ranges meet to form one of the world's highest mountain regions.

◄ *The Hunza river* rises in the northern Karakoram Range, running for 120 miles (193 km) before joining the Gilgit river.

Hunza river

▶ *The arid Hindu Kush* makes much of Afghanistan uninhabitable, with over 50% of the land lying above 6500 ft (2000 m).

The plains and foothills which extend from the northern slopes of the Hindu Kush are part of the great grassy steppe lands of Central Asia.

Hindu Kush

K2 (Mount Godwin Austen), in the Karakoram Range, is the second highest mountain in the world, at an altitude of 28,251 ft (8611 m).

Frequent earthquakes mean that mountain-building processes are continuing in this region, as the Indo-Australian Plate drifts northwards, colliding with the Eurasian Plate.

Some of the largest glaciers outside the polar regions are found in the Karakoram Range, including Siachen Glacier (Siachen Muztagh), which is 40 miles (72 km) long.

Himalayas

Mountain chains running southwest from the Hindu Kush into Pakistan form a barrier to the humid winds which blow from the Indian Ocean, creating arid conditions across southern Afghanistan.

The soils of the Punjab plain are nourished by enormous quantities of sediment, carried from the Himalayas by the five tributaries of the Indus river.

The Indus Basin is part of the Indus-Ganges lowland, a vast depression which has been filled with layers of sediment over the last 50 million years. These deposits are estimated to be over 16,400 ft (5000 m) deep.

The Indus Delta is prone to heavy flooding and high levels of salinity. It remains a largely uncultivated wilderness area.

Glacis covered by coarse-grained sediment

Sediments washed down from mountains accumulate on glacis slopes

Bedrock

Fine sediments deposited on salt flats are removed by wind erosion.

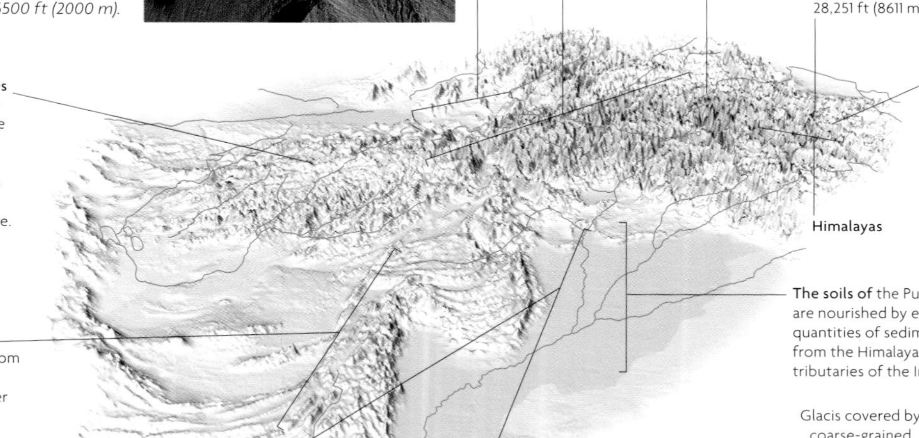

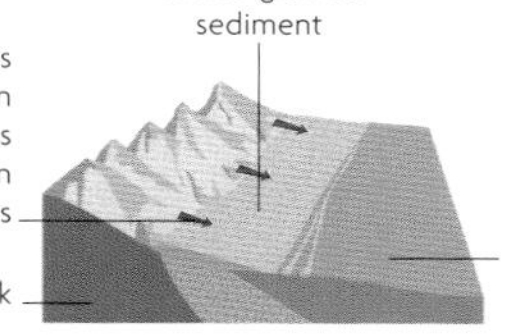

▲ *Glacis are gentle*, debris-covered slopes which lead into salt flats or deserts. They typically occur at the base of mountains in arid regions such as

Map labels

TURKMEN
BA
Balā Morghāb
Selseleh-ye Band-e
BĀDGHIS
Kāriz-e Elyās
Towraghoudī
Qarah Bāgh
Kūshk
Qal'eh-ye Now
Qādes
Darya-ye Morghāb
Eslām Qal'eh
Kūhestān Dasht-e Hamdam Āb
Zendeh Jān
Ghūriān
Herāt
Selseleh-ye Sefīd Kūh
HERĀT
Shahrak
GHOWR
A F G H A
Shindand
Farāh Rūd
Kūh-e Chehel Abdālān
Dak
Dasht-e Bābūs
Anār Darreh
FARĀH
Hāmūn-e Şāberī
Farāh Rūd
Farāh
Delārām
Now Zād
Sangīn
Dasht-e Khāsh
Hāmūn-e Pūzak
NĪMRŪZ
Gereshk
Lashkar Gāh
Chakhānsūr
Shelleh-ye Pūdeh Tal
Darvīshān
Zaranj
Dasht-e Mārgow
Kūchnay Darweyshān
HELMAND
Daryā-ye Helmand
Deh Shū
Dasht-e Gowd-e Zereh
Chāgai Hills
Hāmūn-i Lora
BAL
Nok Kundi
Yakmach
Dasht-i Tāhlāb
Dālbandin
Tāhlāb
Hāmūn-i Māshkel
Kamarod
Sīāhān Range
Tagas
Panjgūr
IRAN
Central Makrān
Ispikān
Nīhing
Nasīrābād Kech Hoshāb
Kolwa
Mand
Turbat
Dasht
Suntsar
Khor Kalmat
Jīwanī
Gwādar West Bay
Gwādar
Gwādar East Bay
Pasni
Astola Island
Ormāra

Inset map

UZBEKISTAN
TAJIKISTAN
CHINA
TURKMENISTAN
Mazar-e Sharīf
Herat
KABUL
Peshawar
AFGHANISTAN
ISLAMABAD
Rawalpindi
Kandahar
Lahore
Quetta
Faisalabad
Multan
Bahawalpur
PAKISTAN
Sukkur
INDIA
IRAN
Karachi
Hyderabad
A R A B I A N   S E A

Scale

Scale 1:4,500,000

Km
0 10 20   40   60   80   100   120   140   160
Miles
0   10   20   40   60   80   100   120   140 160

projection: Lambert Conformal Conic

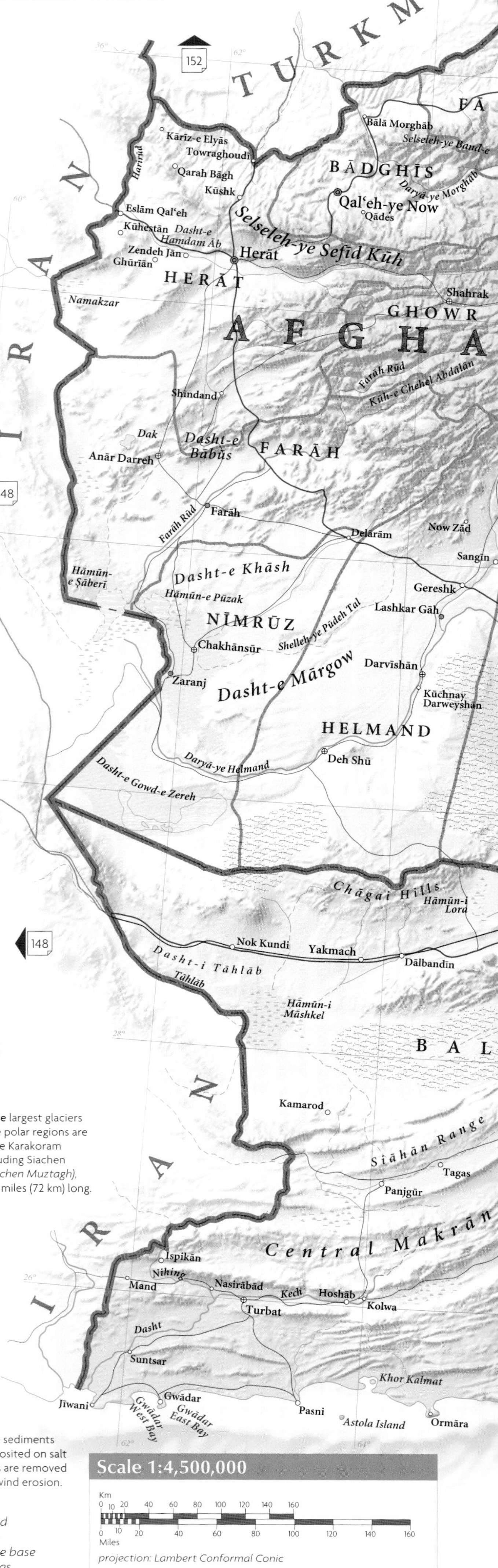

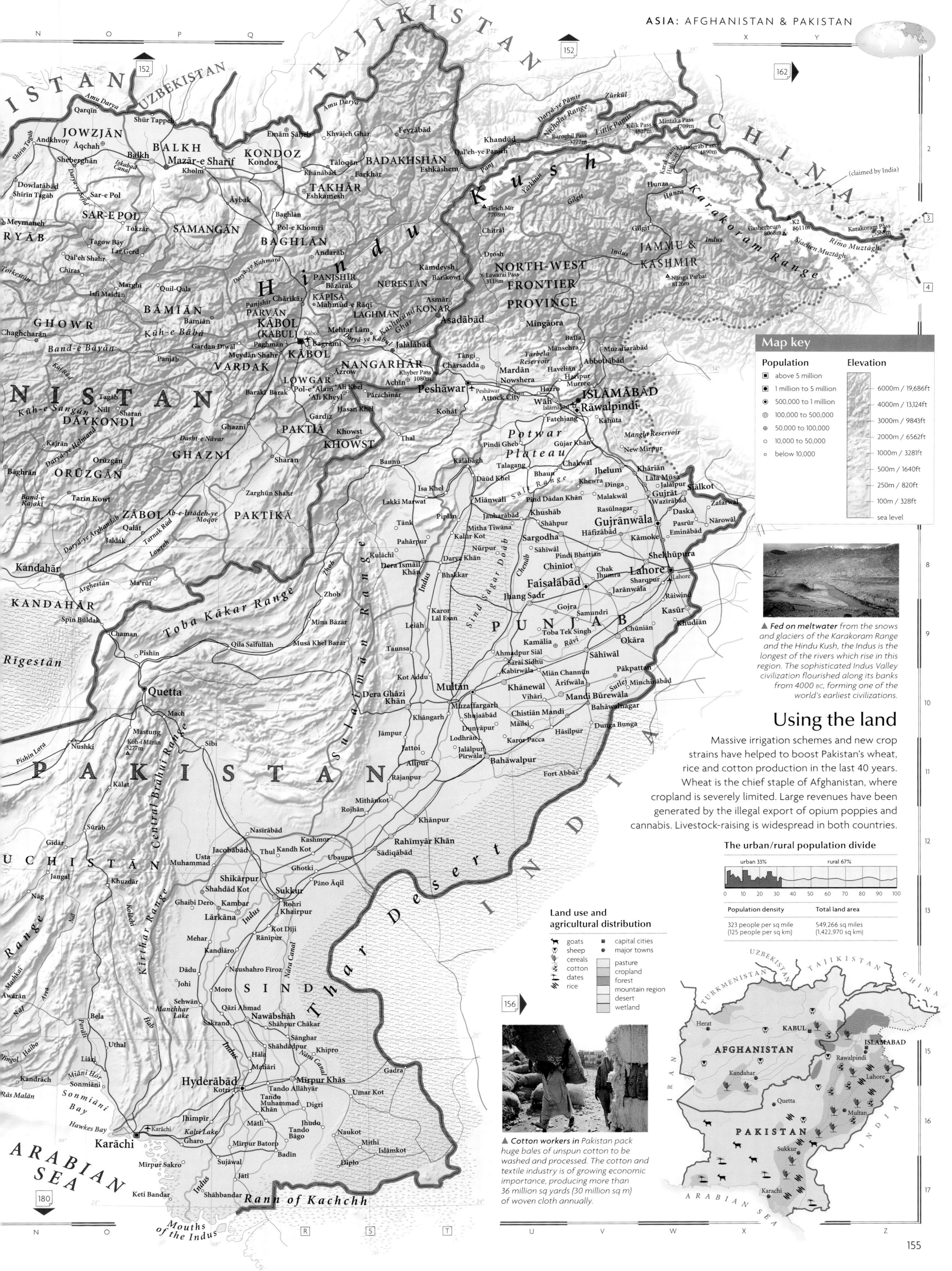

Map key

Population
- ■ above 5 million
- ◼ 1 million to 5 million
- ⬤ 500,000 to 1 million
- ◉ 100,000 to 500,000
- ⊕ 50,000 to 100,000
- ○ 10,000 to 50,000
- ∘ below 10,000

Elevation
- 6000m / 19,686ft
- 4000m / 13,124ft
- 3000m / 9843ft
- 2000m / 6562ft
- 1000m / 3281ft
- 500m / 1640ft
- 250m / 820ft
- 100m / 328ft
- sea level

▲ *Fed on meltwater* from the snows and glaciers of the Karakoram Range and the Hindu Kush, the Indus is the longest of the rivers which rise in this region. The sophisticated Indus Valley civilization flourished along its banks from 4000 BC, forming one of the world's earliest civilizations.

Using the land

Massive irrigation schemes and new crop strains have helped to boost Pakistan's wheat, rice and cotton production in the last 40 years. Wheat is the chief staple of Afghanistan, where cropland is severely limited. Large revenues have been generated by the illegal export of opium poppies and cannabis. Livestock-raising is widespread in both countries.

The urban/rural population divide

urban 33% | rural 67%

0 10 20 30 40 50 60 70 80 90 100

Population density	Total land area
323 people per sq mile (125 people per sq km)	549,266 sq miles (1,422,970 sq km)

Land use and agricultural distribution
- goats
- sheep
- cereals
- cotton
- dates
- rice
- ■ capital cities
- • major towns
- pasture
- cropland
- forest
- mountain region
- desert
- wetland

▲ *Cotton workers in* Pakistan pack huge bales of unspun cotton to be washed and processed. The cotton and textile industry is of growing economic importance, producing more than 36 million sq yards (30 million sq m) of woven cloth annually.

South Asia

BANGLADESH, BHUTAN, INDIA, MALDIVES, NEPAL, PAKISTAN, SRI LANKA

More than one-fifth of the world's population lives in the south Asian subcontinent. Great cultural diversity has come from a long succession of foreign invaders, including Hindu Aryans, Islamic Moguls and the British, whose empire incorporated the princely states of the Maharajas and extended to the borders of Nepal and Bhutan in the Himalayas. Independent since 1947, India is the world's largest democracy, and at the current rate of growth, may overtake China as the world's most populous country during the 21st century. There are points of tension in the region over claims for independence by the Sikhs in the Indian Punjab and the Tamil separatists in Sri Lanka, and the long-standing dispute with Pakistan over Jammu and Kashmir in the north.

The landscape

South Asia is effectively isolated from the rest of Asia by desert along the western flank of Pakistan, and a continuous wall of mountains, dominated by the Himalayas, to the north and east. The great basins of the Indus and Ganges separate this mountain fringe from the rolling plateau of the Indian peninsula, which is bordered by a line of coastal hills, the Eastern and Western Ghats.

The Himalayas are the highest and most extensive mountain system in the world. They were formed when the Indo-Australian Plate collided with the Eurasian Plate about 40 million years ago, thrusting up huge masses of land and creating a 'ripple' effect, which formed lesser mountain ranges in Tibet and Southeast Asia. Mount Everest is the world's tallest mountain at 29,035 ft (8850 m).

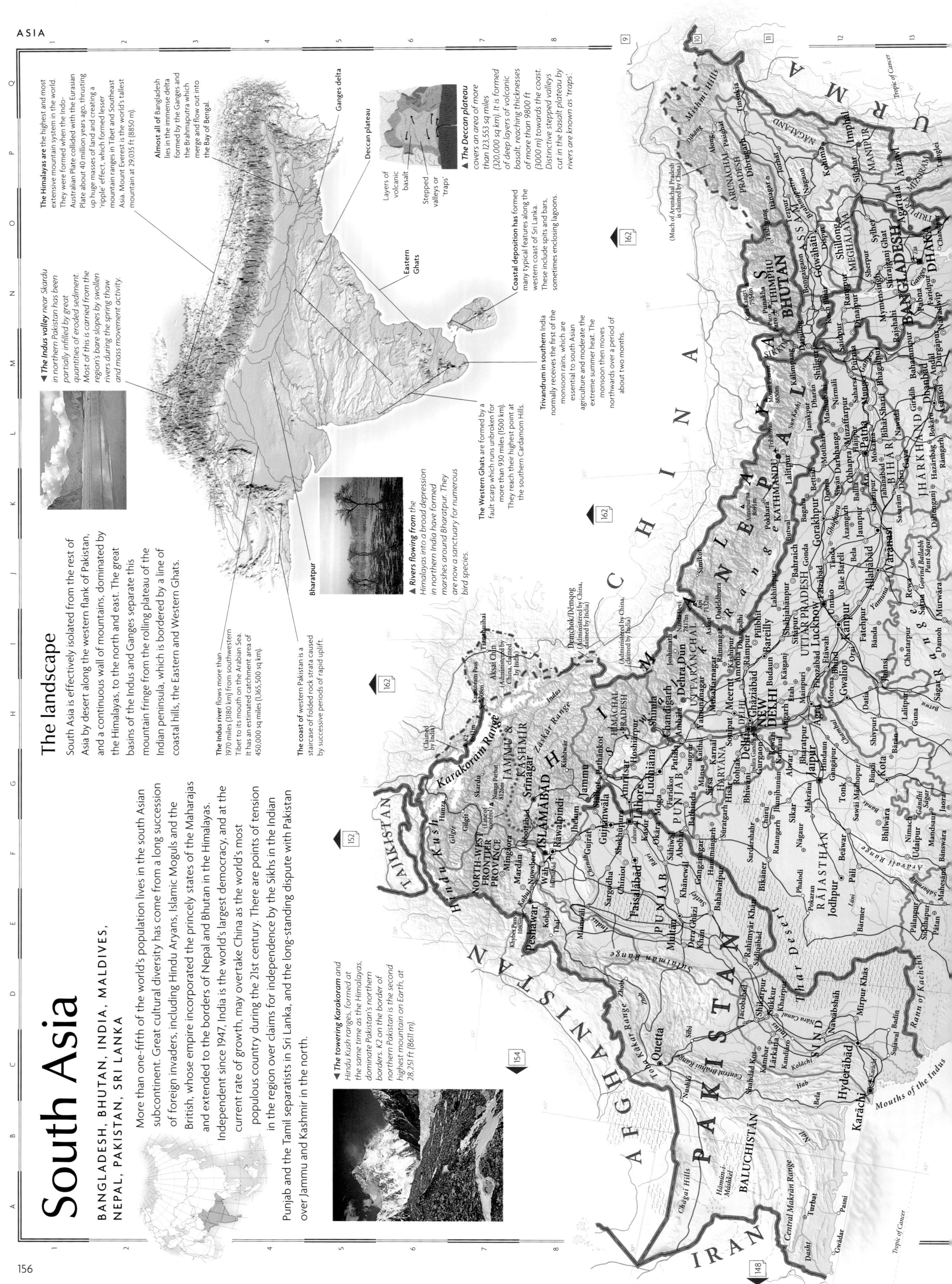

▼ *The Indus valley near Skardu in northern Pakistan has been partially infilled by great quantities of eroded sediment. Most of this is carried from the region's bare slopes by swollen rivers during the spring thaw and mass movement activity.*

▼ *The towering Karakoram and Hindu Kush ranges, formed at the same time as the Himalayas, dominate Pakistan's northern borders. K2 on the border of northern Pakistan is the second highest mountain on Earth, at 28,251 ft (8611 m).*

Almost all of Bangladesh lies in the immense delta formed by the Ganges and the Brahmaputra which merge and flow out into the Bay of Bengal.

The Deccan plateau covers an area of more than 123,553 sq miles (320,000 sq km). It is formed of deep layers of volcanic basalt, reaching thicknesses of more than 9800 ft (3000 m) towards the coast. Distinctive stepped valleys cut in the basalt plateau by rivers are known as 'traps'.

Layers of volcanic basalt

Stepped valleys or 'traps'

Deccan plateau

Ganges delta

Eastern Ghats

Coastal deposition has formed many typical features along the western coast of India. These include spits and bars, sometimes enclosing lagoons.

Trivandrum in southern India normally receives the first of the monsoon rains, which are essential to south Asian agriculture and moderate the extreme summer heat. The monsoon then moves northwards over a period of about two months.

The Western Ghats are formed by a fault scarp which runs unbroken for more than 930 miles (1500 km). They reach their highest point at the southern Cardamom Hills.

▼ *Rivers flowing from the Himalayas into a broad depression in northern India have formed marshes around Bharatpur. They are now a sanctuary for numerous bird species.*

Bharatpur

The Indus river flows more than 1970 miles (3180 km) from southwestern Tibet to its mouth on the Arabian Sea. It has an estimated catchment area of 450,000 sq miles (1,165,500 sq km).

The coast of western Pakistan is a staircase of folded rock strata caused by successive periods of rapid uplift.

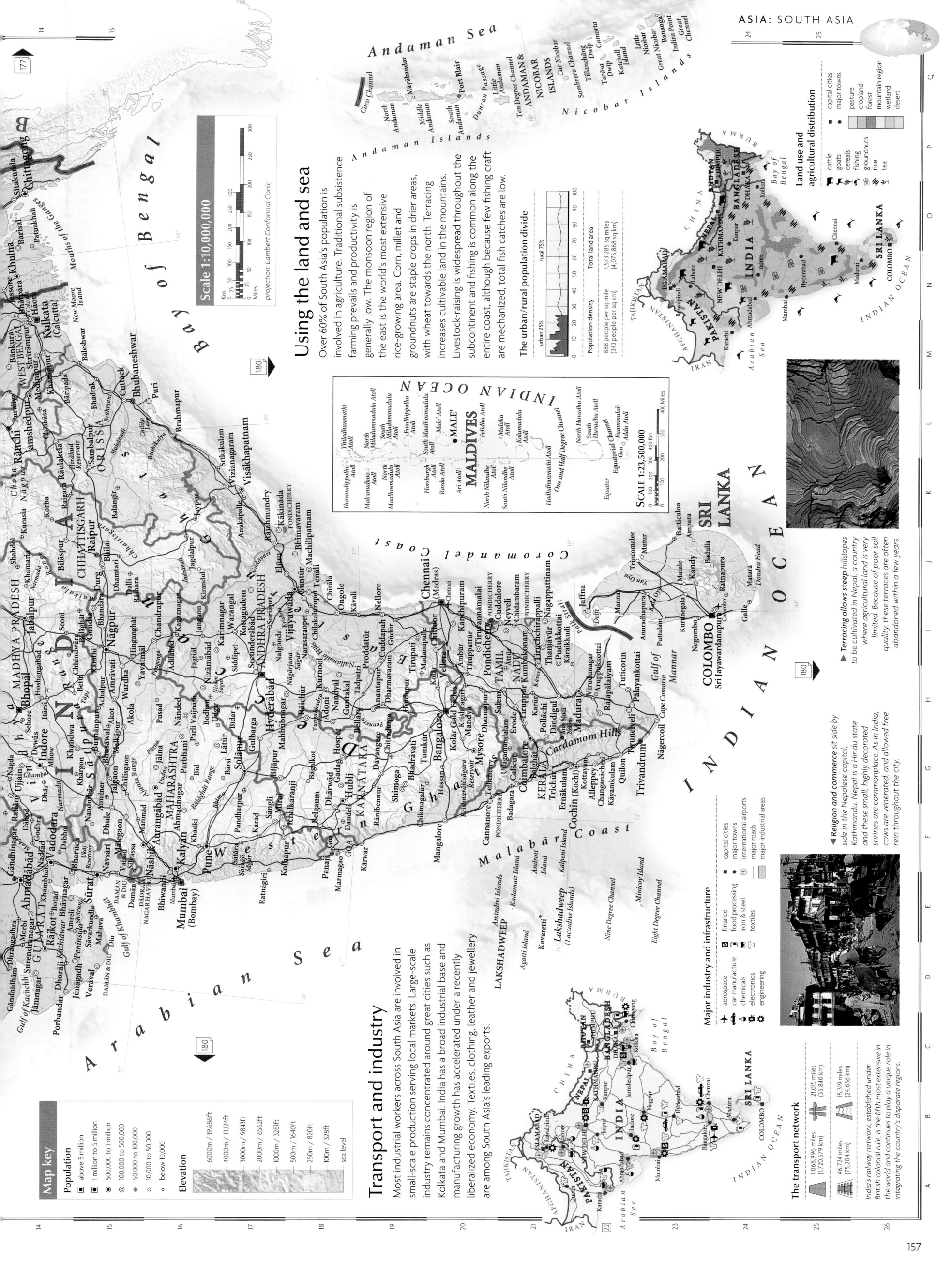

Using the land and sea

Over 60% of South Asia's population is involved in agriculture. Traditional subsistence farming prevails and productivity is generally low. The monsoon region of the east is the world's most extensive rice-growing area. Corn, millet and groundnuts are staple crops in drier areas, with wheat towards the north. Terracing increases cultivable land in the mountains. Livestock-raising is widespread throughout the subcontinent and fishing is common along the entire coast, although because few fishing craft are mechanized, total fish catches are low.

Transport and industry

Most industrial workers across South Asia are involved in small-scale production serving local markets. Large-scale industry remains concentrated around great cities such as Kolkata and Mumbai. India has a broad industrial base and manufacturing growth has accelerated under a recently liberalized economy. Textiles, clothing, leather and jewellery are among South Asia's leading exports.

Terracing allows steep hillslopes to be cultivated in Nepal, a country where agricultural land is very limited. Because of poor soil quality, these terraces are often abandoned within a few years.

Religion and commerce sit side by side in the Nepalese capital, Kathmandu. Nepal is a Hindu state and these small, highly decorated shrines are commonplace. As in India, cows are venerated, and allowed free rein throughout the city.

India's railway network, established under British colonial rule, is the fifth most extensive in the world and continues to play a unique role in integrating the country's disparate regions.

Scale 1:10,000,000
projection: Lambert Conformal Conic

SCALE 1:23,500,000

Northern India & the Himalayan states

BANGLADESH, BHUTAN, NEPAL, Arunachal Pradesh, Assam, Bihar, Chandigarh, Delhi, Haryana, Himachal Pradesh, Jammu & Kashmir, Jharkhand, Manipur, Meghalaya, Mizoram, Nagaland, Punjab, Rajasthan, Sikkim, Tripura, Uttaranchal, Uttar Pradesh, West Bengal

The Ganges and Brahmaputra river basins and the massive mountain barrier of the Himalayas define this region's landscape and have served to reinforce potent cultural and religious differences among its people. Hinduism pervades most aspects of national life and is a growing political force within India, a secular country which also encompasses the centre of Sikhism at Amritsar and the world's largest Muslim minority. Nepal is a crowded mountain state, which faces severe ecological problems from deforestation, while the tiny Himalayan Buddhist kingdom of Bhutan is emerging from long-term isolation, to welcome selected visitors. The Muslim state of Bangladesh, formerly East Pakistan, is one of the world's most densely populated countries and one of the poorest, with more than 145 million people living largely on the massive Ganges/Brahmaputra delta. Many Bangladeshis live under threat of repeated, catastrophic floods.

◄ *The Golden Temple in Amritsar, the most sacred shrine of the Sikh religion, was the scene of violent clashes between Sikh separatists and government forces in 1984.*

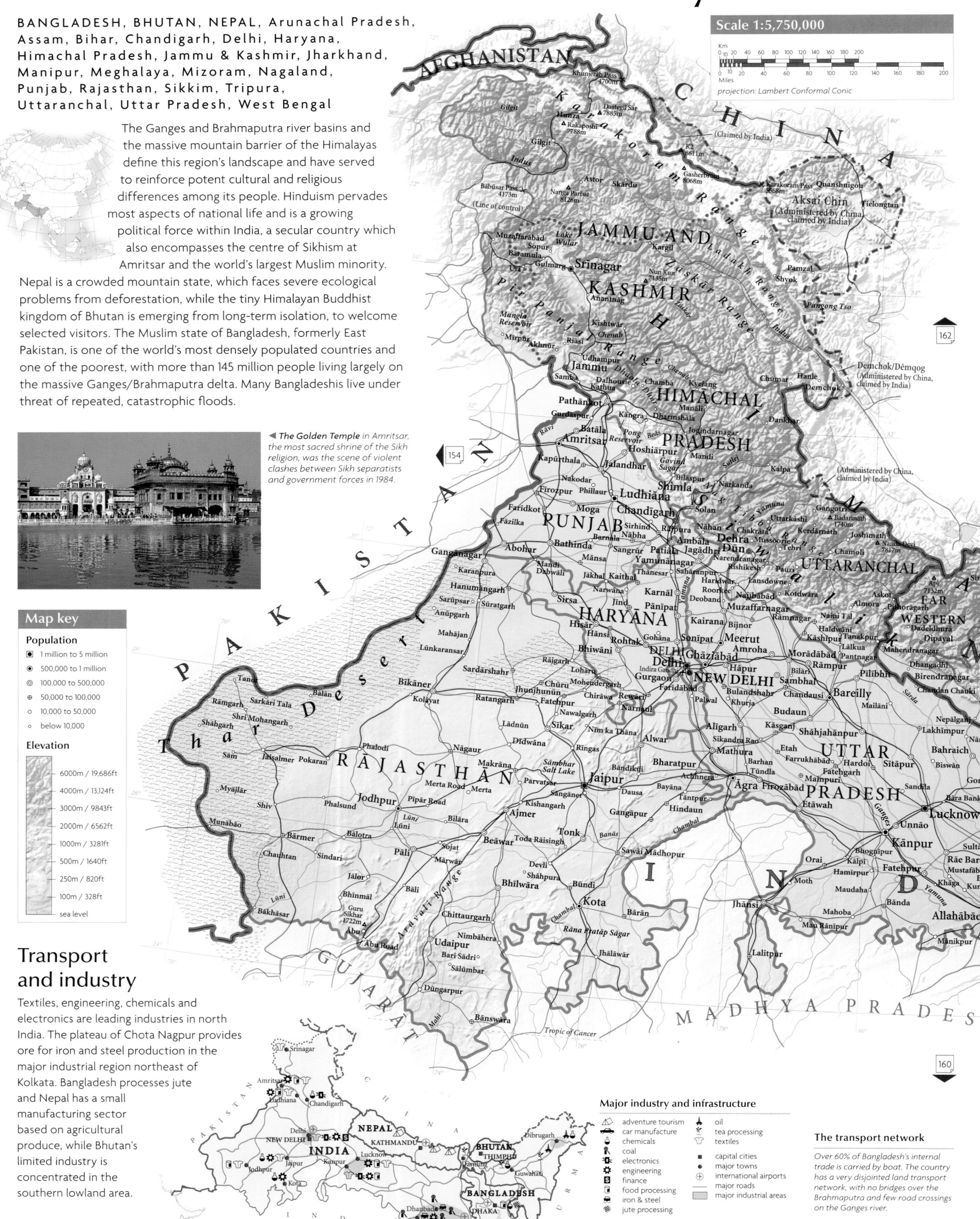

Map key

Population
⊡ 1 million to 5 million
⊚ 500,000 to 1 million
⊙ 100,000 to 500,000
⊕ 50,000 to 100,000
○ 10,000 to 50,000
○ below 10,000

Elevation
6000m / 19,686ft
4000m / 13,124ft
3000m / 9843ft
2000m / 6562ft
1000m / 3281ft
500m / 1640ft
250m / 820ft
100m / 328ft
sea level

Transport and industry

Textiles, engineering, chemicals and electronics are leading industries in north India. The plateau of Chota Nagpur provides ore for iron and steel production in the major industrial region northeast of Kolkata. Bangladesh processes jute and Nepal has a small manufacturing sector based on agricultural produce, while Bhutan's limited industry is concentrated in the southern lowland area.

Major industry and infrastructure
🚠 adventure tourism
🚗 car manufacture
⚗ chemicals
⬛ coal
⚙ electronics
⚙ engineering
$ finance
🍴 food processing
🚂 iron & steel
❋ jute processing
🛢 oil
🍵 tea processing
�️ textiles
■ capital cities
● major towns
✈ international airports
— major roads
▨ major industrial areas

The transport network
Over 60% of Bangladesh's internal trade is carried by boat. The country has a very disjointed land transport network, with no bridges over the Brahmaputra and few road crossings on the Ganges river.

Scale 1:5,750,000
projection: Lambert Conformal Conic

The landscape

Most of the region is drained by the Ganges river, which meets the Brahmaputra in Bangladesh to form an immense delta before flowing into the Bay of Bengal. The Himalayas extend eastwards over 1500 miles (2400 km), from the parallel ranges running through Jammu and Kashmir. The Thar Desert occupies the southwest.

▶ *The Pir Panjal* range *in southwestern Kashmir rises to elevations of 12,500 ft (3810 m). Despite the freezing conditions, settlements and extensive pastures are found above the tree line.*

The northern ranges of the Himalayas contain the highest mountains in the world, with average heights of more than 23,000 ft (7000 m) and many peaks higher than 26,000 ft (8000 m).

In the last 40 million years, the course of the Brahmaputra has been diverted hundreds of miles to the east by the rising landmass of the Himalayas.

The Khasi Hills are an example of a *horst*, a fractured block of bedrock which has been thrust upwards.

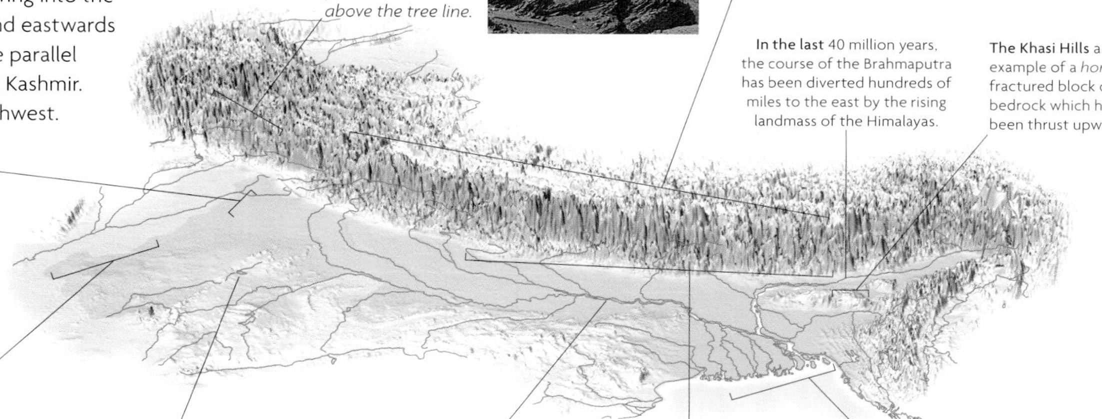

▲ *The summit of* Machhapuchhre *rises to 22,942 ft (6993 m). It is also known as the 'Fish's Tail' because of its distinctive peak.*

The Indian Punjab lies mainly to the west of the Ganges watershed and its rivers flow into the Indus. Control of this water resource has been a source of great friction with neighbouring Pakistan.

The border between India and Pakistan runs through the Thar Desert, an area of sandy *seif* dunes 50–100 ft (15–30 m) in height. Fossils found in the desert indicate that the dunes, stabilized by vegetation, have been in their current position for about 3000 years.

Sambhar Salt Lake in Rajasthan is India's largest lake. Unlike most of the Himalayan lakes which are glacial in origin – formed in ice-scoured basins or as the result of depositional damming – it is an ephemeral salt lake filled periodically by flash flooding.

The Ganges river, sacred to the Hindu people, drains a vast lowland area at the base of the Himalayas. The northern plains are covered by sandy deposits, broken by mud-banks formed when the river floods.

The rapid deforestation of Himalayan valleys has led to acute soil erosion and increased rates of rainwater run-off, both cited as possible causes of the worsening floods downstream in the Ganges/Brahmaputra delta, although natural rates are high and may be the real cause.

Over half of the great Ganges/Brahmaputra delta floods each year during the monsoon as rivers, swollen by meltwater from the Himalayas and by excess rainwater, break their banks and fertilize the land with nutrient-rich sediment.

Debris slides in the middle Himalayas

Debris fans at base of slope

Soil blocks

Slide plain

Slide plain

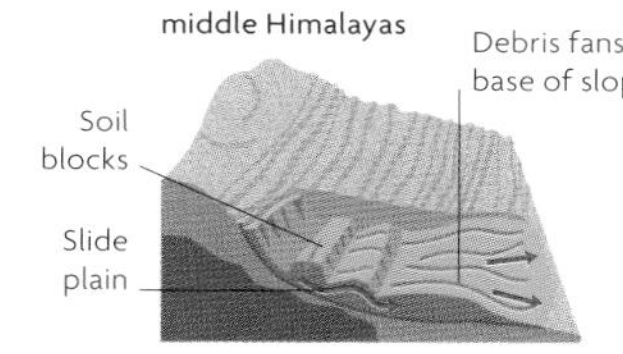

▲ *Soil loss in the middle Himalayas has largely been attributed to debris slides, where large blocks of soil are mobilized by saturation along a slide plane. Once mobile, the soil slides down the slope, gaining speed and thinning to form a fan at the base of the slope.*

Using the land

Grain production dominates land use. Rice is most widely grown in the east. Irrigation and new crop strains have dramatically increased yields in the Punjab, a major wheat-producing area. River flood plains are intensively farmed and livestock-herding is widespread, particularly in Bhutan. Regional crops include jute in Bangladesh, tea in Assam, cardamom in Sikkim and saffron in Kashmir.

The urban/rural population divide

urban 23%   rural 77%

0 10 20 30 40 50 60 70 80 90 100

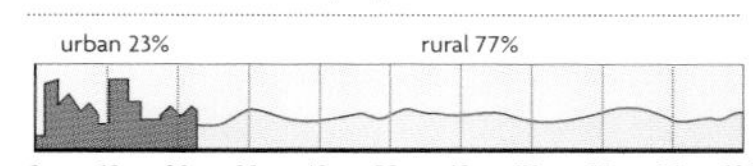

Population density	Total land area
993 people per sq mile (384 people per sq km)	665,104 sq miles (1,723,068 sq km)

▲ *An adverse climate, steep slopes and poor soils limit crop cultivation in Bhutan, which is a largely agrarian economy. Rice, corn and wheat are the main staples, although orchards are being established as the soil and climate suit this type of farming.*

Land use and agricultural distribution

- cattle
- goats
- sheep
- cereals
- jute
- rice
- tea
- capital cities
- major towns

- pasture
- cropland
- forest
- mountain region
- wetland
- desert

▲ *Flooded streets in Dhaka, Bangladesh are a testament to the region's vulnerability to flooding. In 1988 alone, 75% of the country was flooded, leaving thousands of people dead and over 25 million homeless.*

Southern India & Sri Lanka

SRI LANKA, Andhra Pradesh, Chhattisgarh, Dadra & Nagar Haveli, Daman & Diu, Goa, Gujarat, Karnataka, Kerala, Lakshadweep, Madhya Pradesh, Maharashtra, Orissa, Pondicherry, Tamil Nadu

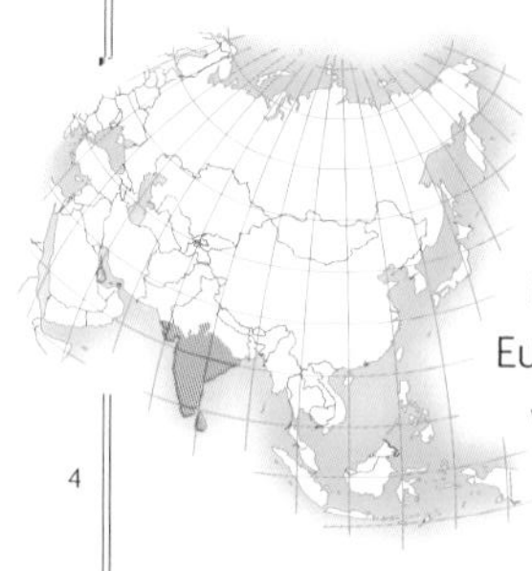

The unique and highly independent southern states reflect the diverse and decentralized nature of India, which has fourteen official languages. The southern half of the peninsula lay beyond the reach of early invaders from the north and retained the distinct and ancient culture of Dravidian peoples such as the Tamils, whose language is spoken in preference to Hindi throughout southern India. The interior plateau of southern India is less densely populated than the coastal lowlands, where the European colonial imprint is strongest. Urban and industrial growth is accelerating, but southern India's vast population remains predominantly rural. The island of Sri Lanka has two distinct cultural groups; the mainly Buddhist Sinhalese majority, and the Tamil minority whose struggle for a homeland in the northeast has led to prolonged civil war.

Using the land and sea

Rice is the main staple in the east; in Sri Lanka and along the humid Malabar Coast. Groundnuts are grown on the Deccan plateau, with wheat, corn and chickpeas, towards the north. Sri Lanka is a leading exporter of tea, coconuts and rubber. Cotton plantations supply local mills around Nagpur and Mumbai. Fishing supports many communities in Kerala and the Laccadive Islands.

Land use and agricultural distribution

- cattle
- goats
- cereals
- cotton
- fishing
- groundnuts
- rice
- rubber
- tea
- capital cities
- major towns

pasture
cropland
forest
wetland

The urban/rural population divide

urban 33%   rural 67%

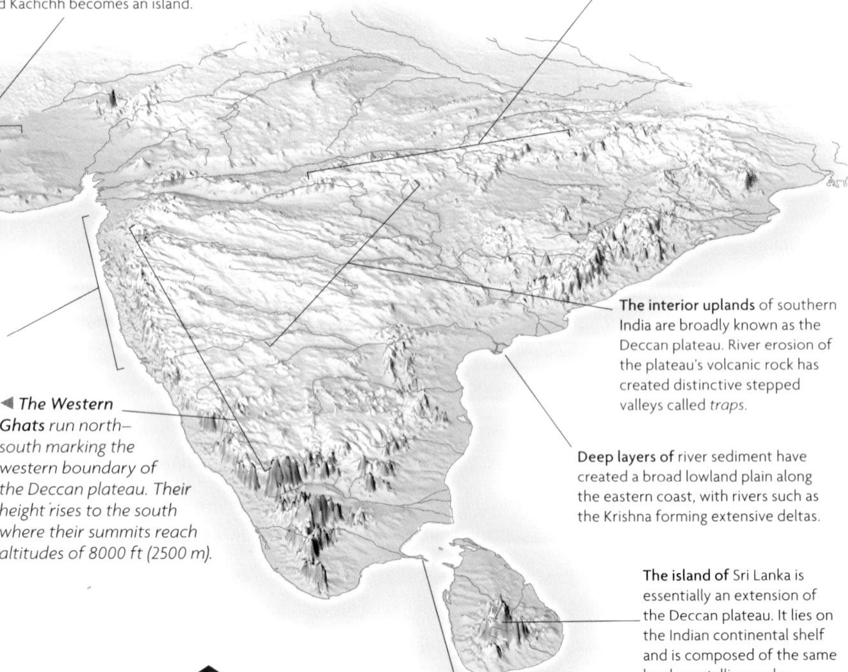

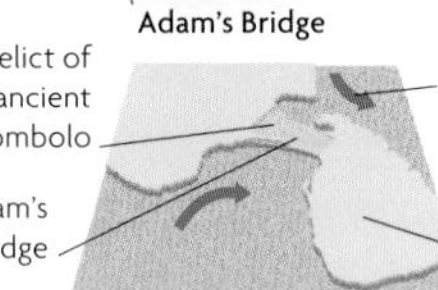

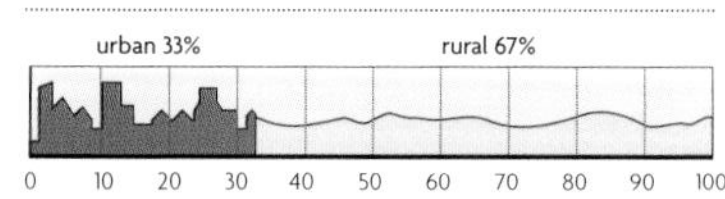

Population density	730 people per sq mile (282 people per sq km)
Total land area	698,295 sq miles (1,809,054 sq km)

The landscape

The undulating Deccan plateau underlies most of southern India: it slopes gently down towards the east and is largely enclosed by the Ghats coastal hill ranges. The Western Ghats run continuously along the Arabian Sea coast, while the Eastern Ghats are interrupted by rivers which follow the slope of the plateau and flow across broad lowlands into the Bay of Bengal. The plateaux and basins of Sri Lanka's central highlands are surrounded by a broad plain.

Along the northern boundary of the Deccan plateau, old basement rocks are interspersed with younger sedimentary strata. This creates spectacular scarplands, cut by numerous waterfalls along the softer sedimentary strata.

The Rann of Kachchh tidal marshes encircle the low-lying Kachchh peninsula. For several months during the rainy season the water level of the marshes rises and Kachchh becomes an island.

The interior uplands of southern India are broadly known as the Deccan plateau. River erosion of the plateau's volcanic rock has created distinctive stepped valleys called traps.

Deep layers of river sediment have created a broad lowland plain along the eastern coast, with rivers such as the Krishna forming extensive deltas.

The island of Sri Lanka is essentially an extension of the Indian continental shelf and is composed of the same hard, crystalline rocks.

The Western Ghats run north–south marking the western boundary of the Deccan plateau. Their height rises to the south where their summits reach altitudes of 8000 ft (2500 m).

The Konkan coast, which runs between Daman and Goa, is characterized by rocky headlands, and bays with crescent-shaped beaches. Flooded river valleys known as rias extend inland.

Ocean currents cause sediment build up

Adam's Bridge

Relict of ancient tombolo

Adam's Bridge

▲ Adam's Bridge (Rama's Bridge) is a chain of sandy shoals lying about 4 ft (1.2 m) under the sea between India and Sri Lanka. They once formed the world's longest tombolo, or land bridge, before the sea level began to rise several thousand years ago.

Sri Lanka

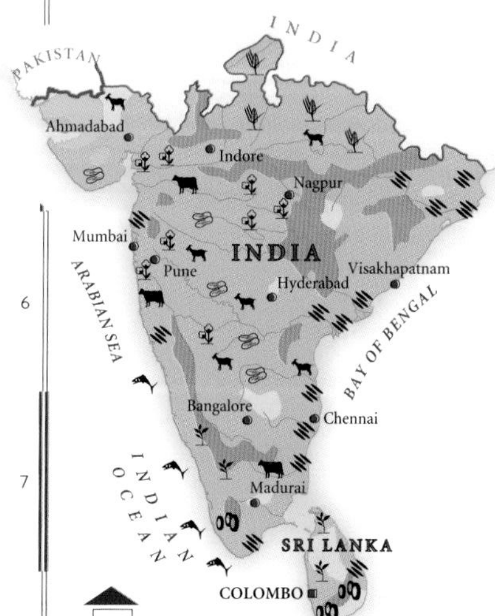

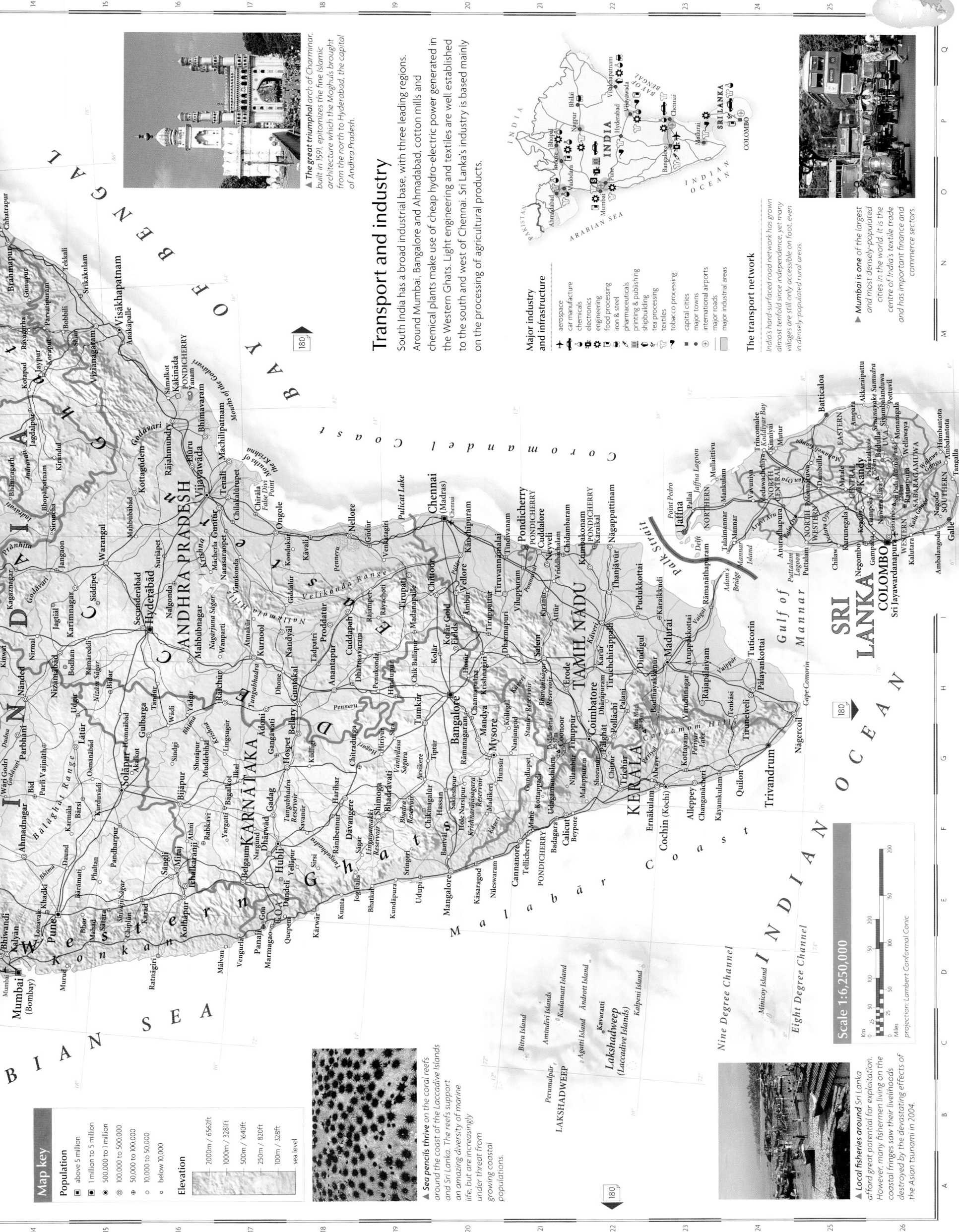

▲ *The great triumphal arch of Charminar,
built in 1591, epitomizes the fine Islamic
architecture which the Moghuls brought
from the north to Hyderabad, the capital
of Andhra Pradesh.*

Transport and industry

South India has a broad industrial base, with three leading regions.
Around Mumbai, Bangalore and Ahmadabad, cotton mills and
chemical plants make use of cheap hydro-electric power generated in
the Western Ghats. Light engineering and textiles are well established
to the south and west of Chennai. Sri Lanka's industry is based mainly
on the processing of agricultural products.

Major industry
and infrastructure

- ✈ aerospace
- 🚗 car manufacture
- ⚗ chemicals
- ⚡ electronics
- ⚙ engineering
- 🍴 food processing
- ⛏ iron & steel
- 💊 pharmaceuticals
- 🖨 printing & publishing
- 🚢 shipbuilding
- 🧵 textiles
- 🍃 tea processing
- 🌿 tobacco processing
- ■ capital cities
- ● major towns
- ⊕ international airports
- major roads
- major industrial areas

The transport network

India's hard-surfaced road network has grown
almost tenfold since independence, yet many
villages are still only accessible on foot, even
in densely-populated rural areas.

▲ *Mumbai is one of the largest
and most densely-populated
cities in the world. It is the
centre of India's textile trade
and has important finance and
commerce sectors.*

▲ *Sea pencils thrive on the coral reefs
around the coast of the Laccadive Islands
and Sri Lanka. The reefs support
an amazing diversity of marine
life, but are increasingly
under threat from
growing coastal
populations.*

▲ *Local fisheries around Sri Lanka
afford great potential for exploitation.
However, many fishermen living on the
coastal fringes saw their livelihoods
destroyed by the devastating effects of
the Asian tsunami in 2004.*

Scale 1:6,250,000

projection Lambert Conformal Conic

Map key

Population
- ■ above 5 million
- ■ 1 million to 5 million
- ◉ 500,000 to 1 million
- ◉ 100,000 to 500,000
- ⊕ 50,000 to 100,000
- ⊙ 10,000 to 50,000
- ∘ below 10,000

Elevation
- 2000m / 6562ft
- 1000m / 3281ft
- 500m / 1640ft
- 250m / 820ft
- 100m / 328ft
- sea level

Mainland East Asia

CHINA, MONGOLIA, NORTH KOREA, SOUTH KOREA, TAIWAN

China, the world's most populous nation, has an unbroken cultural history, longer than that of any other country, and is rapidly emerging as a leading world power. When Mao Zedong established Communist rule in 1949, China had become a backward feudal empire, stricken by civil war and over a century of European and Japanese incursions. The closed regime withstood the traumas of rapid industrialization, communalized farming and the brutal purges of the Cultural Revolution but, since the 1980s has introduced economic reforms, led by expanded foreign trade. China's population is heavily concentrated in the east and, despite accelerating urban growth, remains predominantly rural. One cultural group, the Han, make up over 90% of the people, while five 'Autonomous Regions' have been established in the south and west for the main ethnic minorities.

Transport and industry

Large-scale industrial growth has always been a priority of the Communist government. Metals and machine production, chemicals and engineering are among the leading industries, concentrated in the major cities of the east coast. Textiles and clothing manufacture, the main consumer goods sector, is relatively well dispersed, with a few significant centres such as Shanghai, Beijing and Hong Kong.

Major industry and infrastructure

- car manufacture
- chemicals
- electronics
- engineering
- finance
- food processing
- iron & steel
- shipbuilding
- textiles
- capital cities
- major towns
- international airports
- major roads
- major industrial areas

The transport network

829,790 miles (1,335,571 km)		12,740 miles (20,506 km)	
43,976 miles (70,780 km)		70,991 miles (114,262 km)	

Ever-increasing demand for rail transportation has led to major improvement and expansion of the network, notably the 690 mile (1100 km) link between Golmud and Lhasa opened in 2006.

◀ *Coal is China's most abundant mineral resource. This mine at Fuxin in Liaoning province is used to provide coal for a nearby power station.*

The landscape

The East Asian landmass is arranged in three distinct levels, the highest of which is the Plateau of Tibet in the southwest. The arid uplands of northwestern China form a barren middle step. The main rivers flow eastward from these two platforms to the East China and South China sea coasts, across a broad region of alluvial lowlands and low hills.

◀ *Gansu province, through which the ancient Silk Route passes on its way to the west, is characterized by extensive loess deposits which are terraced and used for crop cultivation.*

◀ *Paektu-san, at 9023 ft (2750 m), is North Korea's highest peak; an extinct volcanic cone now filled by a crater lake.*

The loess plateau of northern China is the world's greatest expanse of loess, a loose soil made up of wind-blown material. The plateau has been heavily eroded by tributaries of the Yellow River.

Shifting sand dunes are found in the arid west of the northeast China Plain, while the eastern part of this great expanse is wet and swampy.

River-eroded fine soils

Thick blanket of loess

▲ *Because of its very small grain-size, loess has been easily transported and deposited by winds which scour the plains, and in northern China, deposits of loess can be up to 3000 ft (1000 m) thick. Loess-based soils are very fertile, but clearing land for agriculture quickly destabilizes the soil and allows it to be eroded.*

The Gobi Desert extends across the Nei Mongol Gaoyuan; a vast saucer-shaped upland surrounded by a rim of higher mountains.

Tarim Basin (Tarim Pendi)

Plateau of Tibet

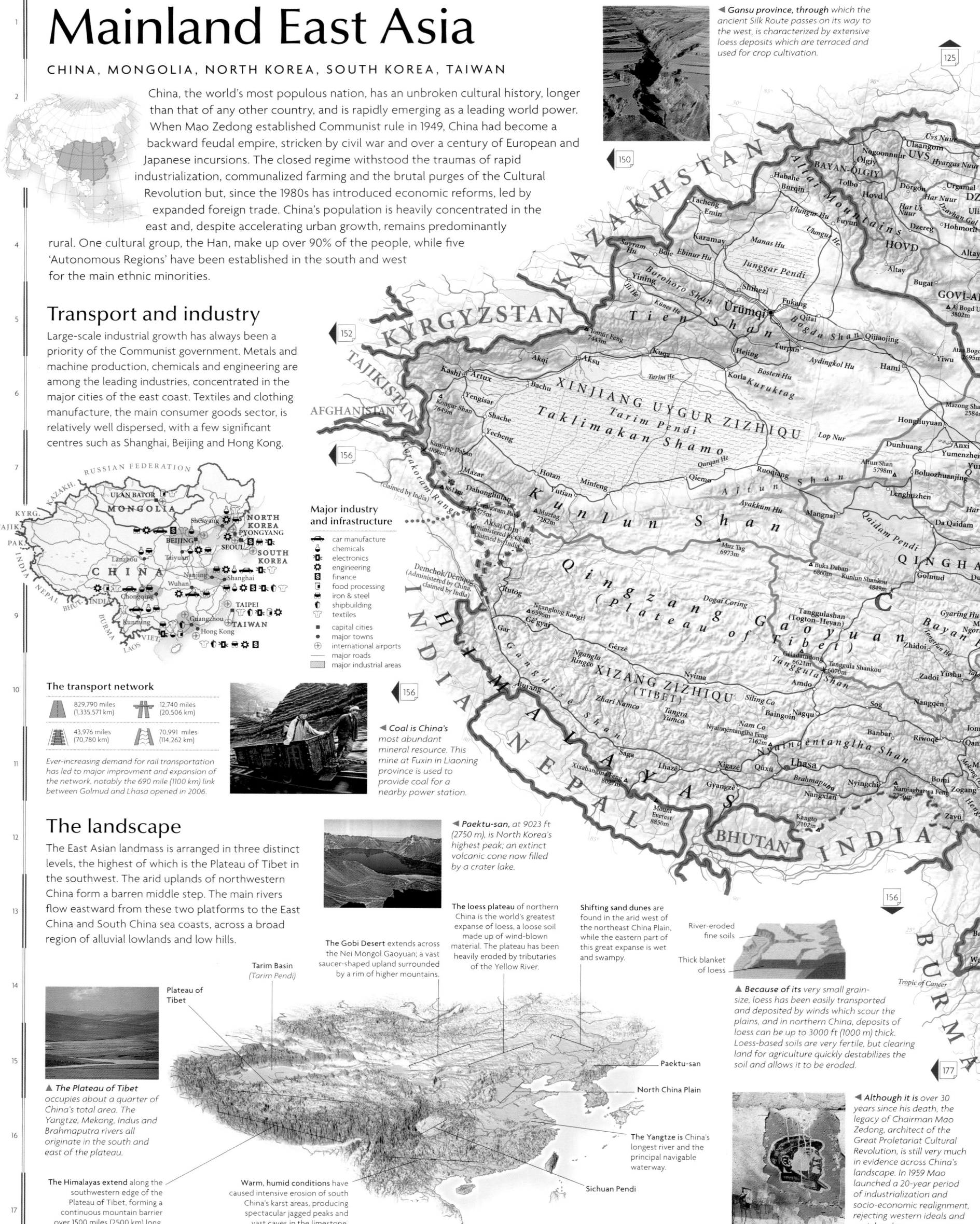

Paektu-san

North China Plain

The Yangtze is China's longest river and the principal navigable waterway.

Sichuan Pendi

▲ *The Plateau of Tibet occupies about a quarter of China's total area. The Yangtze, Mekong, Indus and Brahmaputra rivers all originate in the south and east of the plateau.*

The Himalayas extend along the southwestern edge of the Plateau of Tibet, forming a continuous mountain barrier over 1500 miles (2500 km) long.

Warm, humid conditions have caused intensive erosion of south China's karst areas, producing spectacular jagged peaks and vast caves in the limestone.

◀ *Although it is over 30 years since his death, the legacy of Chairman Mao Zedong, architect of the Great Proletariat Cultural Revolution, is still very much in evidence across China's landscape. In 1959 Mao launched a 20-year period of industrialization and socio-economic realignment, rejecting western ideals and social codes.*

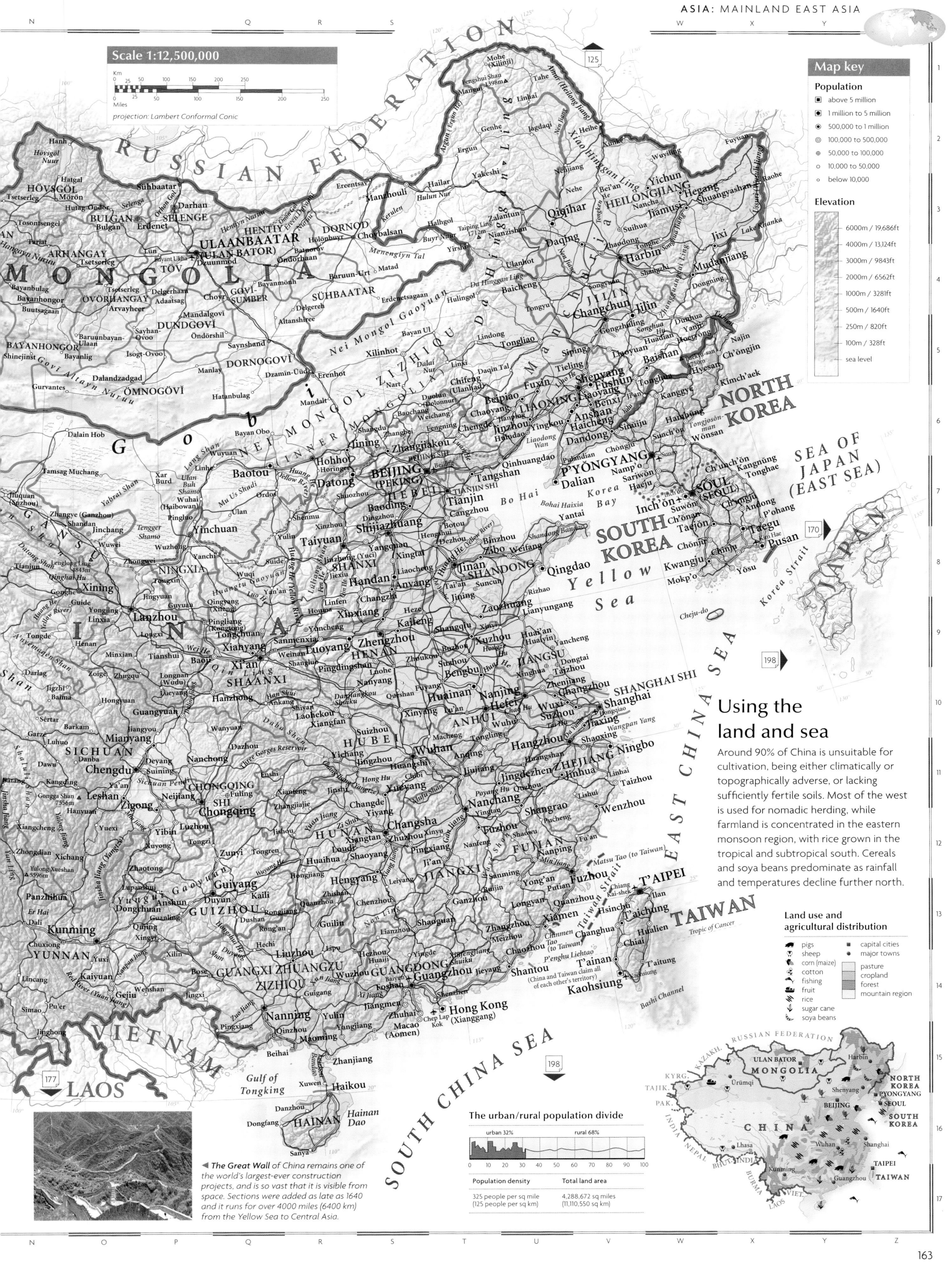

Scale 1:12,500,000

Km
0 25 50   100   150   200   250
Miles
0 25 50   100   150   200   250

projection: Lambert Conformal Conic

Map key

Population

- ▣ above 5 million
- ▣ 1 million to 5 million
- ◉ 500,000 to 1 million
- ◎ 100,000 to 500,000
- ⊙ 50,000 to 100,000
- ○ 10,000 to 50,000
- ○ below 10,000

Elevation

- 6000m / 19,686ft
- 4000m / 13,124ft
- 3000m / 9843ft
- 2000m / 6562ft
- 1000m / 3281ft
- 500m / 1640ft
- 250m / 820ft
- 100m / 328ft
- sea level

Using the land and sea

Around 90% of China is unsuitable for cultivation, being either climatically or topographically adverse, or lacking sufficiently fertile soils. Most of the west is used for nomadic herding, while farmland is concentrated in the eastern monsoon region, with rice grown in the tropical and subtropical south. Cereals and soya beans predominate as rainfall and temperatures decline further north.

Land use and agricultural distribution

- pigs
- sheep
- corn (maize)
- cotton
- fishing
- fruit
- rice
- sugar cane
- soya beans
- ■ capital cities
- ● major towns
- pasture
- cropland
- forest
- mountain region

◀ **The Great Wall** of China remains one of the world's largest-ever construction projects, and is so vast that it is visible from space. Sections were added as late as 1640 and it runs for over 4000 miles (6400 km) from the Yellow Sea to Central Asia.

The urban/rural population divide

urban 32%   rural 68%

0 10 20 30 40 50 60 70 80 90 100

Population density	Total land area
325 people per sq mile (125 people per sq km)	4,288,672 sq miles (11,110,550 sq km)

Western China

Gansu, Ningxia, Qinghai, Tibet, Xinjiang

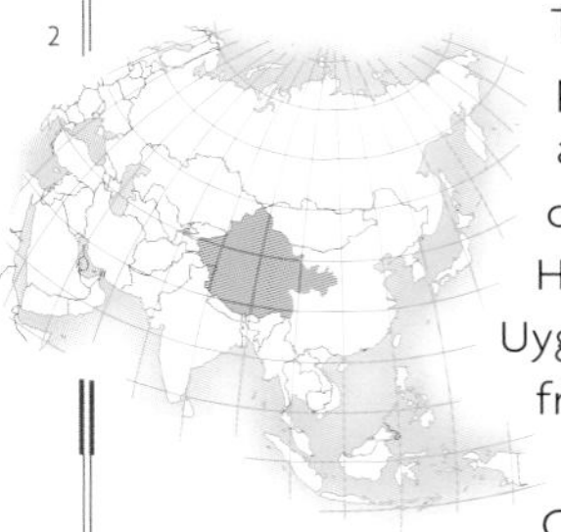

The plateaux and basins of China's dry, desolate western domain are sparsely populated and largely undeveloped, although they have rich mineral reserves; they also form a critical buffer zone for China, in a geographically important and culturally sensitive part of the Asian continent. Across most of the west, the Han Chinese are outnumbered by a range of cultural groups, including the Uygur, the largest group of the various semi-nomadic Muslim peoples from Central Asia. The remote, inhospitable Plateau of Tibet is the world's coldest and highest plateau. It has been occupied by the Chinese since 1950. Tibet is one of western China's five 'Autonomous Regions', but its reclusive Buddhist culture has been systematically undermined by the Chinese government.

Map key

Population

- ▣ 1 million to 5 million
- ◉ 500,000 to 1 million
- ◎ 100,000 to 500,000
- ⊕ 50,000 to 100,000
- ⊙ 10,000 to 50,000
- ○ below 10,000

Elevation

	6000m / 19,686ft
	4000m / 13,124ft
	3000m / 9843ft
	2000m / 6562ft
	1000m / 3281ft
	500m / 1640ft
	250m / 820ft
	100m / 328ft
	sea level

Scale 1:7,000,000

Km 0 25 50 100 150 200
Miles 0 25 50 100 150 200

projection: Lambert Conformal Conic

▲ *The Lhasa He is one of the many rivers which drain the vast Plateau of Tibet. From its source in the Nyainqêntanglha Shan range and fed by the spring meltwater, it eventually joins the upper Brahmaputra 40 miles (65 km) southwest of Lhasa.*

Using the land

Agriculture is constrained by the cold, dry climate and lack of fertile soils in the region, although irrigation and glasshouse farming are increasing agricultural potential. Large quantities of fruit, like melons and grapes, are grown at the oases of Hami and Turpan in Xinjiang, and new irrigation schemes have greatly increased cotton and wheat production in the Tarim Basin (Tarim Pendi). Most of the great area of Tibet and Qinghai is devoted to pastoralism. Sheep are the principal livestock.

Land use and agricultural distribution

- goats
- sheep
- cereals
- cotton
- grapes
- melons
- oases
- • major towns
- pasture
- cropland
- forest
- mountain region
- desert

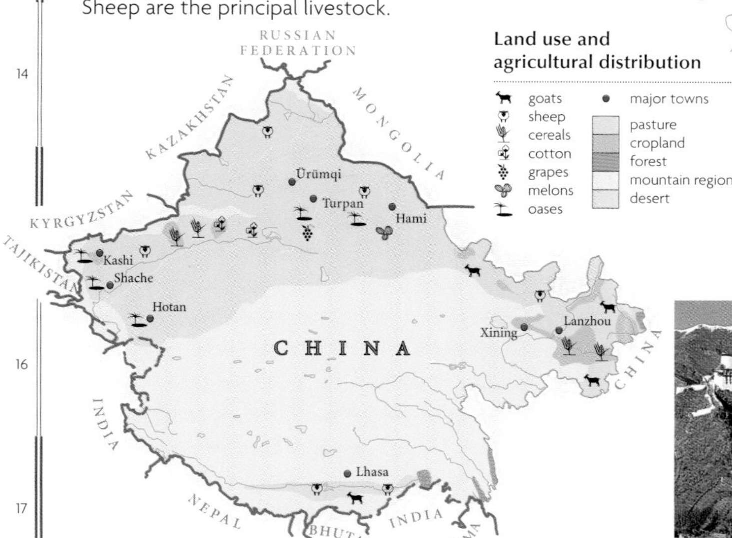

◀ *The Potala Palace, in Tibet's capital, Lhasa, was the former residence of the Dalai Lama, Tibetan Buddhism's spiritual leader. Tibet remains only sparsely populated; forming over 20% of China's landmass, it supports fewer than 1% of its population.*

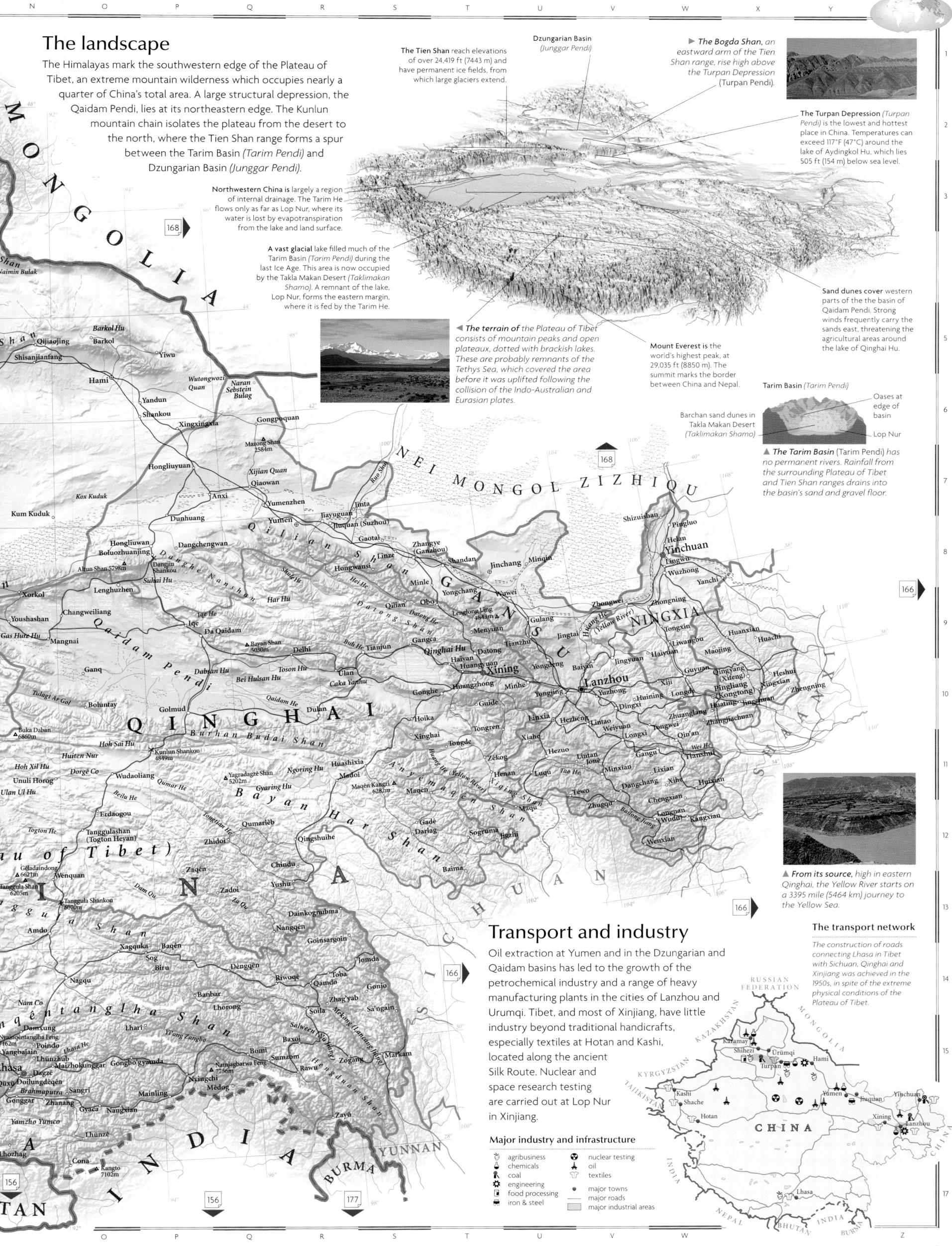

The landscape

The Himalayas mark the southwestern edge of the Plateau of Tibet, an extreme mountain wilderness which occupies nearly a quarter of China's total area. A large structural depression, the Qaidam Pendi, lies at its northeastern edge. The Kunlun mountain chain isolates the plateau from the desert to the north, where the Tien Shan range forms a spur between the Tarim Basin (Tarim Pendi) and Dzungarian Basin (Junggar Pendi).

Northwestern China is largely a region of internal drainage. The Tarim He flows only as far as Lop Nur, where its water is lost by evapotranspiration from the lake and land surface.

A vast glacial lake filled much of the Tarim Basin (Tarim Pendi) during the last Ice Age. This area is now occupied by the Takla Makan Desert (Taklimakan Shamo). A remnant of the lake, Lop Nur, forms the eastern margin, where it is fed by the Tarim He.

◀ **The terrain of** the Plateau of Tibet consists of mountain peaks and open plateaux, dotted with brackish lakes. These are probably remnants of the Tethys Sea, which covered the area before it was uplifted following the collision of the Indo-Australian and Eurasian plates.

The Tien Shan reach elevations of over 24,419 ft (7443 m) and have permanent ice fields, from which large glaciers extend.

Dzungarian Basin (Junggar Pendi)

▶ **The Bogda Shan,** an eastward arm of the Tien Shan range, rise high above the Turpan Depression (Turpan Pendi).

The Turpan Depression (Turpan Pendi) is the lowest and hottest place in China. Temperatures can exceed 117°F (47°C) around the lake of Aydingkol Hu, which lies 505 ft (154 m) below sea level.

Mount Everest is the world's highest peak, at 29,035 ft (8850 m). The summit marks the border between China and Nepal.

Sand dunes cover western parts of the the basin of Qaidam Pendi. Strong winds frequently carry the sands east, threatening the agricultural areas around the lake of Qinghai Hu.

Tarim Basin (Tarim Pendi)

Oases at edge of basin

Barchan sand dunes in Takla Makan Desert (Taklimakan Shamo)

Lop Nur

▲ **The Tarim Basin** (Tarim Pendi) has no permanent rivers. Rainfall from the surrounding Plateau of Tibet and Tien Shan ranges drains into the basin's sand and gravel floor.

▲ **From its source,** high in eastern Qinghai, the Yellow River starts on a 3395 mile (5464 km) journey to the Yellow Sea.

Transport and industry

Oil extraction at Yumen and in the Dzungarian and Qaidam basins has led to the growth of the petrochemical industry and a range of heavy manufacturing plants in the cities of Lanzhou and Urumqi. Tibet, and most of Xinjiang, have little industry beyond traditional handicrafts, especially textiles at Hotan and Kashi, located along the ancient Silk Route. Nuclear and space research testing are carried out at Lop Nur in Xinjiang.

The transport network

The construction of roads connecting Lhasa in Tibet with Sichuan, Qinghai and Xinjiang was achieved in the 1950s, in spite of the extreme physical conditions of the Plateau of Tibet.

Major industry and infrastructure

- agribusiness
- chemicals
- coal
- engineering
- food processing
- iron & steel
- nuclear testing
- oil
- textiles
- major towns
- major roads
- major industrial areas

Eastern China

TAIWAN, Anhui, Beijing, Chongqing, Fujian, Guangdong, Guangxi, Guizhou, Hainan, Hebei, Henan, Hubei, Hunan, Jiangsu, Jiangxi, Shaanxi, Shandong, Shanghai, Shanxi, Sichuan, Tianjin, Yunnan, Zhejiang

The east is China's heartland. Massive industrial development since 1949 has transformed much of the densely populated rural landscape, in a region still prone to flooding and drought. Over 30 cities have populations of over a million, including the giant metropolis of Shanghai and the capital Beijing, which has been China's cultural and political centre since the 13th century. The ethnically diverse southwest and the oil-rich interior provinces of Sichuan and Shaanxi have largely missed out on the remarkable economic growth occurring in designated free-trade areas along the coasts of the South and East China seas. The republic of Taiwan was established in 1949 by Chinese nationalists ousted from the mainland by the victorious Communist forces. Taiwan now has one of the strongest economies in the world but its sovereignty is not recognized by China. Hong Kong provides a major international trade link for China; a 99-year 'lease' period of British control was concluded in 1997.

▲ North of the Qin Ling range in Shaanxi province, is an agriculturally fertile region covered with fine, wind-blown deposits and known as the loess plateau. The loose sediments are vulnerable to water erosion.

Using the land and sea

This is a region of intensive cultivation. Wheat, millet, sorghum and cotton are the main crops of the Yellow River basin. South from Sichuan, rice becomes the principal crop, grown with wheat, corn and cotton along the Yangtze river. Tea is produced in the hills and sugar cane along the coast of the southeast, where flat land is limited. Pigs and poultry are raised in great numbers.

Land use and agricultural distribution

- cattle
- pigs
- cereals
- corn (maize)
- cotton
- fishing
- peanuts
- rice
- sugar cane
- tea
- capital cities
- major towns
- pasture
- cropland
- forest
- mountain region

▲ On the hills above the North China Plain, slopes are terraced to utilize the rich loess soils of the Taihang Shan range.

Map key

Population
- ■ above 5 million
- ▣ 1 million to 5 million
- ◉ 500,000 to 1 million
- ◎ 100,000 to 500,000
- ⊕ 50,000 to 100,000
- ○ 10,000 to 50,000
- ○ below 10,000

Elevation
- 6000m / 19,686ft
- 4000m / 13,124ft
- 3000m / 9843ft
- 2000m / 6562ft
- 1000m / 3281ft
- 500m / 1640ft
- 250m / 820ft
- 100m / 328ft
- sea level

Scale 1:7,750,000

Km
0 25 50 100 150 200 250 300

Miles
0 25 50 100 150 200 250 300

projection: Lambert Conformal Conic

◄ The former Portuguese territory of Macao, with its colonial architecture, bars and casinos, reverted to Chinese rule in 1999.

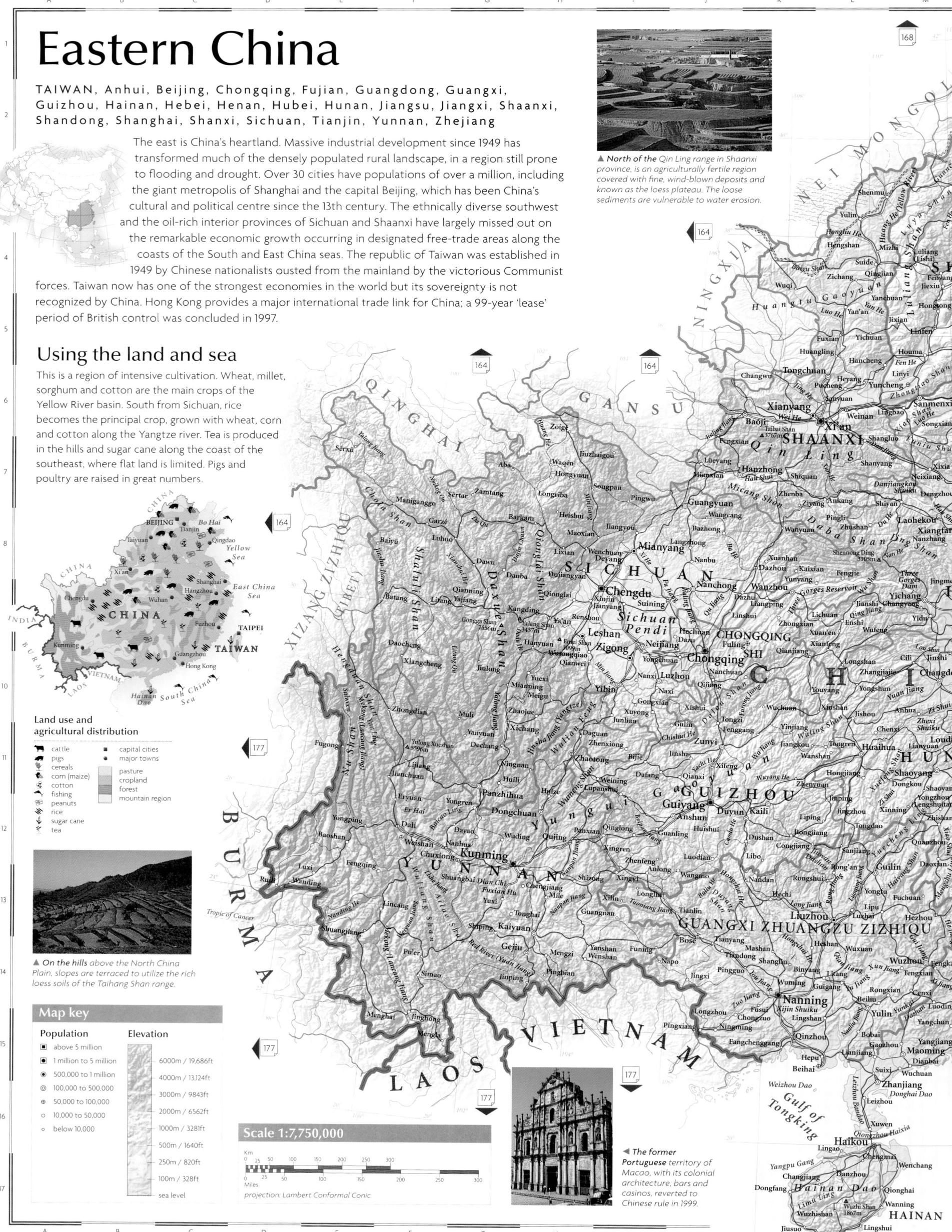

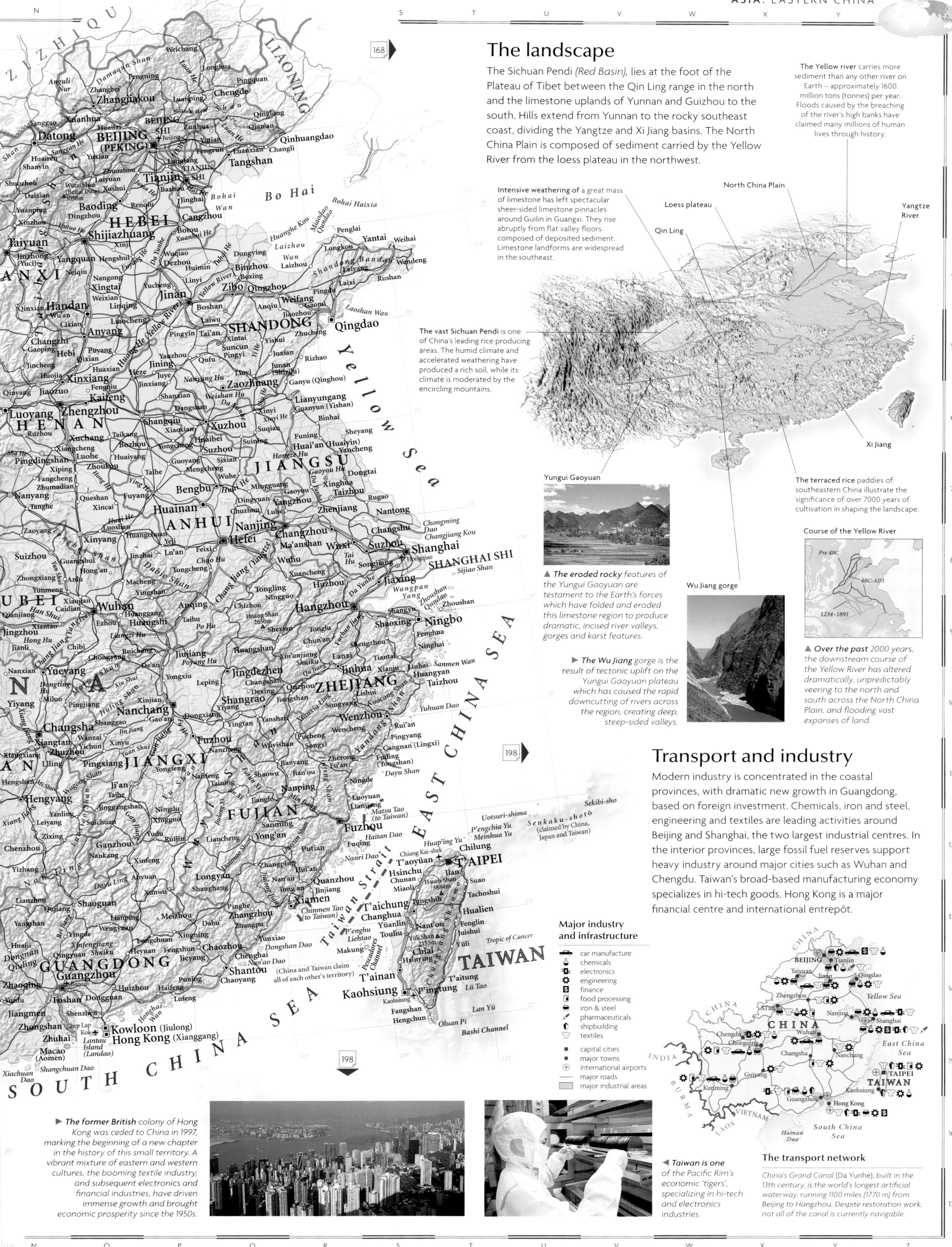

The landscape

The Sichuan Pendi (*Red Basin*), lies at the foot of the Plateau of Tibet between the Qin Ling range in the north and the limestone uplands of Yunnan and Guizhou to the south. Hills extend from Yunnan to the rocky southeast coast, dividing the Yangtze and Xi Jiang basins. The North China Plain is composed of sediment carried by the Yellow River from the loess plateau in the northwest.

The Yellow river carries more sediment than any other river on Earth – approximately 1600 million tons (tonnes) per year. Floods caused by the breaching of the river's high banks have claimed many millions of human lives through history.

Intensive weathering of a great mass of limestone has left spectacular sheer-sided limestone pinnacles around Guilin in Guangxi. They rise abruptly from flat valley floors composed of deposited sediment. Limestone landforms are widespread in the southeast.

The vast Sichuan Pendi is one of China's leading rice producing areas. The humid climate and accelerated weathering have produced a rich soil, while its climate is moderated by the encircling mountains.

Yungui Gaoyuan

▲ The eroded rocky features of the Yungui Gaoyuan are testament to the Earth's forces which have folded and eroded this limestone region to produce dramatic, incised river valleys, gorges and karst features.

Wu Jiang gorge

▶ The Wu Jiang gorge is the result of tectonic uplift on the Yungui Gaoyuan plateau which has caused the rapid downcutting of rivers across the region, creating deep, steep-sided valleys.

The terraced rice paddies of southeastern China illustrate the significance of over 7000 years of cultivation in shaping the landscape.

Course of the Yellow River

Pre 4BC
4BC–AD1
1234–1891

▲ Over the past 2000 years, the downstream course of the Yellow River has altered dramatically, unpredictably veering to the north and south across the North China Plain, and flooding vast expanses of land.

Transport and industry

Modern industry is concentrated in the coastal provinces, with dramatic new growth in Guangdong, based on foreign investment. Chemicals, iron and steel, engineering and textiles are leading activities around Beijing and Shanghai, the two largest industrial centres. In the interior provinces, large fossil fuel reserves support heavy industry around major cities such as Wuhan and Chengdu. Taiwan's broad-based manufacturing economy specializes in hi-tech goods. Hong Kong is a major financial centre and international entrepôt.

Major industry and infrastructure

- car manufacture
- chemicals
- electronics
- engineering
- finance
- food processing
- iron & steel
- pharmaceuticals
- shipbuilding
- textiles

- capital cities
- major towns
- international airports
- major roads
- major industrial areas

▶ The former British colony of Hong Kong was ceded to China in 1997, marking the beginning of a new chapter in the history of this small territory. A vibrant mixture of eastern and western cultures, the booming textile industry, and subsequent electronics and financial industries, have driven immense growth and brought economic prosperity since the 1950s.

◀ Taiwan is one of the Pacific Rim's economic 'tigers', specializing in hi-tech and electronics industries.

The transport network

China's Grand Canal (Da Yunhe), built in the 13th century, is the world's longest artificial waterway, running 1100 miles (1770 m) from Beijing to Hangzhou. Despite restoration work, not all of the canal is currently navigable.

Northeastern China, Mongolia & Korea

MONGOLIA, NORTH KOREA, SOUTH KOREA, Heilongjiang, Inner Mongolia, Jilin, Liaoning

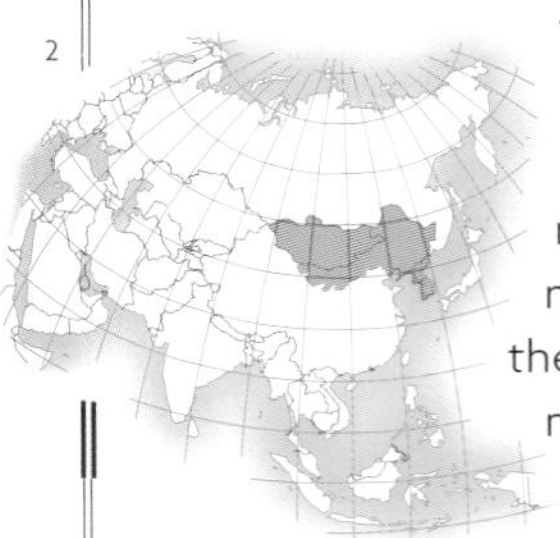

This northerly region has for centuries been a domain of shifting borders and competing colonial powers. Mongolia was the heartland of Chinghiz Khan's vast Mongol empire in the 13th century, while northeastern China was home to the Manchus, China's last ruling dynasty (1644–1911). The mineral and forest wealth of the northeast helped make this China's principal region of heavy industry, although the outdated state factories now face decline. South Korea's state-led market economy has grown dramatically and Seoul is now one of the world's largest cities. The austere communist regime of North Korea has isolated itself from the expanding markets of the Pacific Rim and faces continuing economic stagnation.

▲ *The Eurasian steppe* stretches from the mouth of the Danube in Europe, to Mongolia. In Mongolia, nomadic people have lived in felt huts called yurts or gers, for thousands of years.

Map key

Population
- ▣ above 5 million
- ▢ 1 million to 5 million
- ◉ 500,000 to 1 million
- ◎ 100,000 to 500,000
- ⊕ 50,000 to 100,000
- ○ 10,000 to 50,000
- ○ below 10,000

Elevation
- 4000m / 13,124ft
- 3000m / 9843ft
- 2000m / 6562ft
- 1000m / 3281ft
- 500m / 1640ft
- 250m / 820ft
- 100m / 328ft
- sea level

Scale 1:7,000,000

Km 0 25 50 100 150 200
Miles 0 25 50 100 150 200

projection: Lambert Conformal Conic

The landscape

The great North China Plain is largely enclosed by mountain ranges including the Great and Lesser Khingan Ranges (*Da Hinggan Ling* and *Xiao Hinggan Ling*) in the north, and the Changbai Shan, which extend south into the rugged peninsula of Korea. The broad steppeland plateau of Nei Mongol Gaoyuan borders the southeastern edge of the great cold desert of the Gobi which extends west across the southern reaches of Mongolia. In northwest Mongolia the Altai Mountains and various lesser ranges are interspersed with lakeland basins.

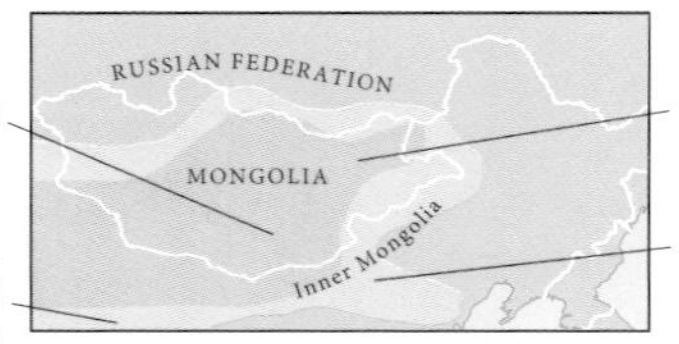

Gobi

Semi-arid zone

Desert zone

Ordos Desert (*Mu Us Shadi*)

RUSSIAN FEDERATION

MONGOLIA

Inner Mongolia

▲ *Much of Mongolia* and Inner Mongolia is a vast desert area. To the south and east, a semi-arid region extends into China proper.

▲ *The Gobi desert* stretches from Central Asia, through Mongolia and into China. Bare rock surfaces, rather than sand dunes, typify the cold desert landscape of the Gobi.

Tributaries of the Amur river follow U-shaped valleys through the Great Khingan Range (*Da Hinggan Ling*). These were cut by ice-age glaciers between 3 and 10 million years ago.

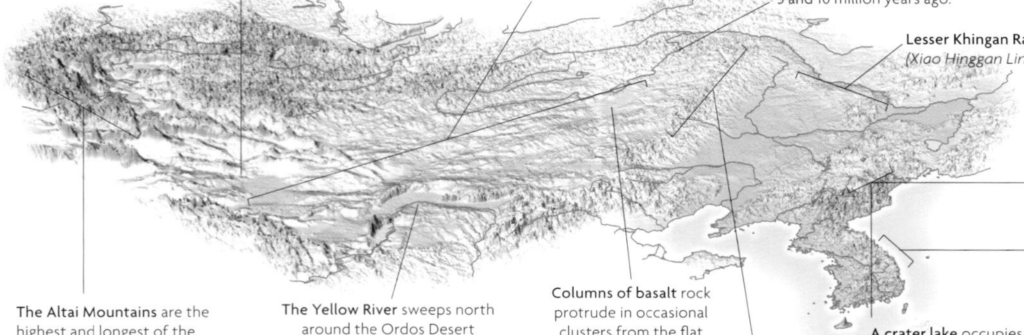

Lesser Khingan Range (*Xiao Hinggan Ling*)

Changbai Shan

T'aebaek-sanmaek

The Altai Mountains are the highest and longest of the mountain ranges which extend into Mongolia from the northwest. These mountains provide one of the last refuges for the endangered snow leopard.

The Yellow River sweeps north around the Ordos Desert (*Mu Us Shadi*), bringing water to an otherwise barren region.

Columns of basalt rock protrude in occasional clusters from the flat surface of the eastern Gobi. Their regular, six-sided form was produced when the rock cooled and contracted from its molten state.

Great Khingan Range (*Da Hinggan Ling*)

A crater lake occupies the 9023 ft (2750 m) snowy summit of the extinct volcano Paektu-san, the highest peak in the mountains of the Changbai Shan.

◄ *The wooded mountain* range of T'aebaek-sanmaek forms the backbone of the Korean peninsula, running north–south along the eastern coastline.

Transport and industry

North Korea's centrally-planned economy is strongly oriented towards heavy industry, while South Korea has a broad manufacturing base which includes textiles, steel, electronics, and one of the world's largest shipbuilding industries. Mongolia and Inner Mongolia's great mineral resource potential is largely undeveloped. The heavy industrial region around Shenyang produces iron, steel, chemicals and cement on a massive scale.

Major industry and infrastructure

- car manufacture
- chemicals
- coal
- electronics
- engineering
- finance
- food processing
- iron & steel
- pharmaceuticals
- shipbuilding
- textiles
- capital cities
- major towns
- international airports
- major roads
- major industrial areas

The transport network

Liaoning has China's most comprehensive railway network, the legacy of the Japanese occupation of Manchuria in the 20th century. The railways are used primarily for freight transport.

▲ *Ulan Bator, the Mongolian capital bears many of the hallmarks of Soviet-style central planning, the result of economic and industrial assistance from the Soviet Union following Mongolian independence in 1921.*

▶ *While North Korea has remained politically and economically isolated from the rest of the world, South Korea has enjoyed immense economic growth. It has benefited considerably from US economic aid in the aftermath of the Korean war of 1950–1953.*

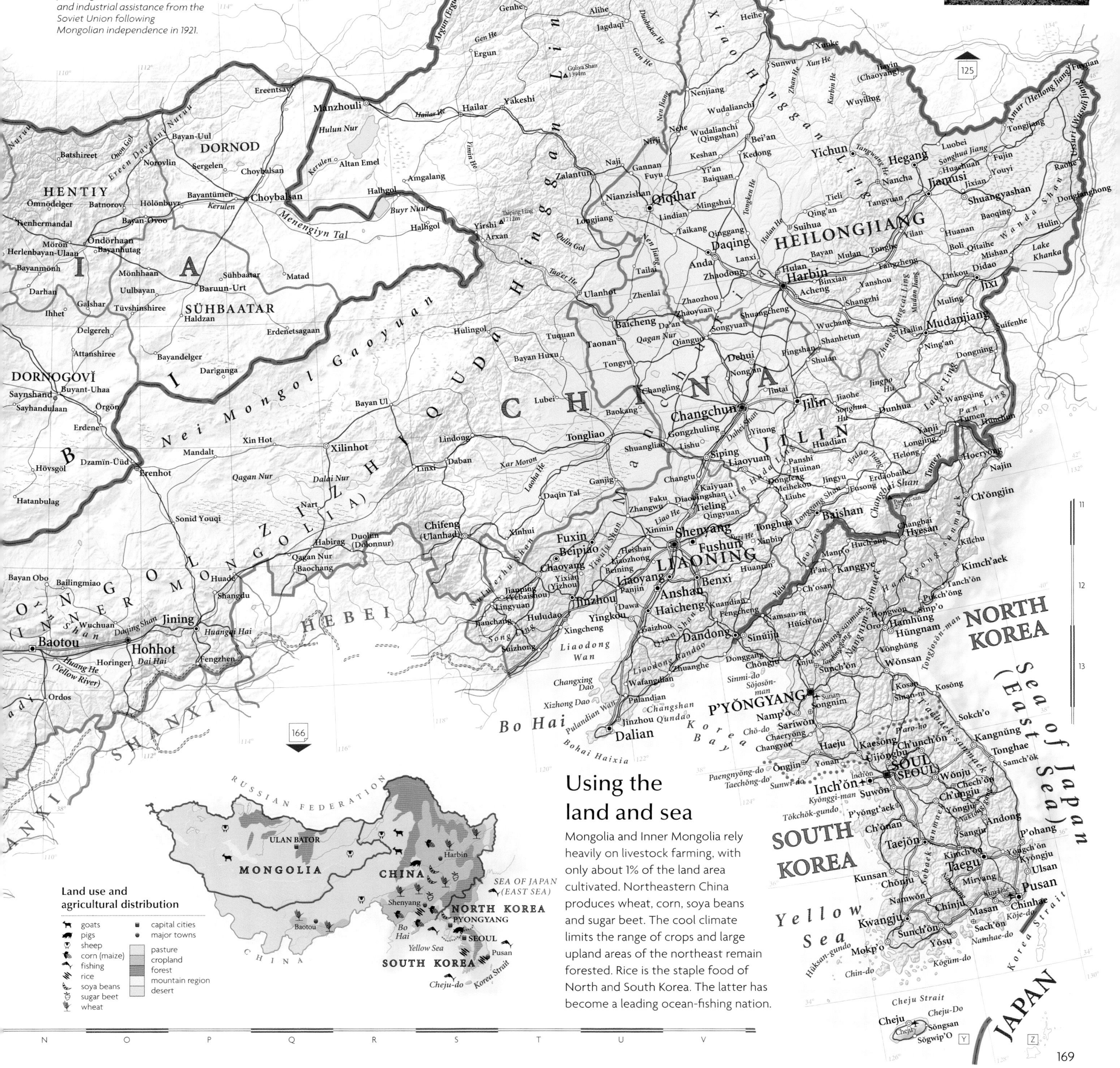

Using the land and sea

Mongolia and Inner Mongolia rely heavily on livestock farming, with only about 1% of the land area cultivated. Northeastern China produces wheat, corn, soya beans and sugar beet. The cool climate limits the range of crops and large upland areas of the northeast remain forested. Rice is the staple food of North and South Korea. The latter has become a leading ocean-fishing nation.

Land use and agricultural distribution

- goats
- pigs
- sheep
- corn (maize)
- fishing
- rice
- soya beans
- sugar beet
- wheat
- capital cities
- major towns
- pasture
- cropland
- forest
- mountain region
- desert

Japan

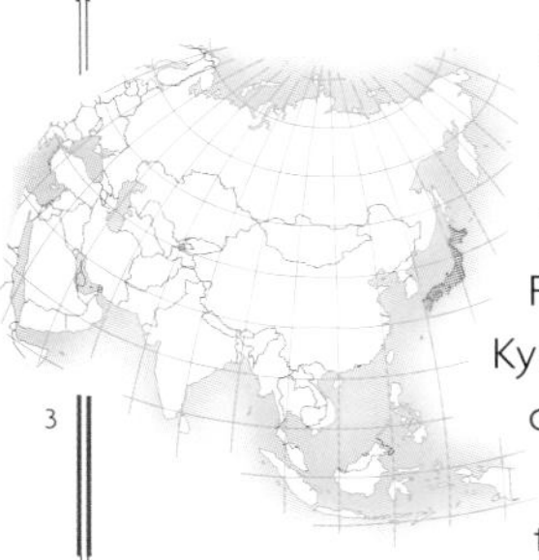

In the years since the end of the Second World War, Japan has become the world's most dynamic industrial nation. The country comprises a string of over 4000 islands which lie in a great northeast to southwest arc in the northwest Pacific. Four major islands: Hokkaido, Honshu, Shikoku and Kyushu are home to the great majority of Japan's population of 128 million people, although the mountainous terrain of the central region means that most cities are situated on the coast. A densely populated industrial belt stretches along much of Honshu's southern coast, including Japan's crowded capital, Tokyo. Alongside its spectacular economic growth and the increasing westernization of its cities, Japan still maintains a most singular culture, reflected in its traditional food, formal behavioural codes, unique Shinto religion and a deep reverence for the emperor.

Transport and industry

Japan is the world's second largest market economy, outranked only by the USA. Technological development, particularly of computers, electronic goods, cars and motorcycles is second to none. Japanese industry invests in its workforce, and in long-term research and development to maintain the high standard of its products, and a reputation for innovation. Japanese businesses are now global both in their manufacturing bases and in the distribution of goods.

The transport network

557,978 miles (898,082 km)		4257 miles (6851 km)	
12,486 miles (20,096 km)		1099 miles (1770 km)	

Japanese road construction traditionally lagged behind that of its extensive and technologically advanced railway network. The road network's relative lack of development has led to severe urban congestion, although expressways have now been built in some cities.

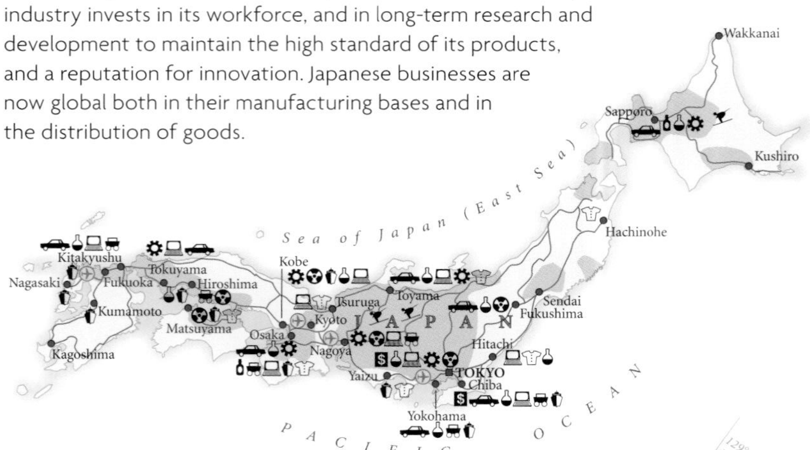

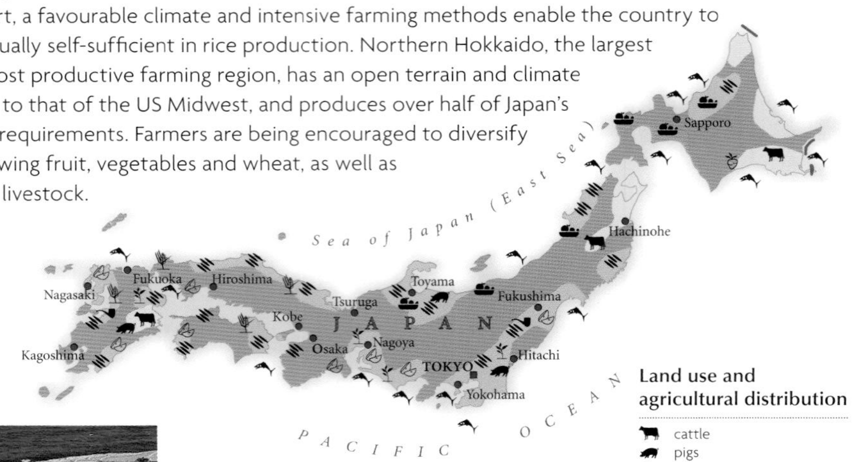

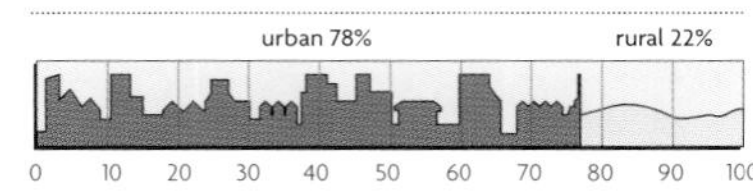

▲ *Known in the* west as the 'bullet train', the Shinkansen is the second-fastest train in the world. It speeds past the snow-capped peak of Mount Fuji between the cities of Tokyo and Osaka.

Using the land and sea

Although only about 11% of Japan is suitable for cultivation, substantial government support, a favourable climate and intensive farming methods enable the country to be virtually self-sufficient in rice production. Northern Hokkaido, the largest and most productive farming region, has an open terrain and climate similar to that of the US Midwest, and produces over half of Japan's cereal requirements. Farmers are being encouraged to diversify by growing fruit, vegetables and wheat, as well as raising livestock.

▲ *Cutting terraces maximizes* the limited agricultural land, enabling Japan to produce large quantities of rice.

The urban/rural population divide

urban 78%	rural 22%
0 10 20 30 40 50 60 70 80 90 100	

Population density	Total land area
885 people per sq mile (342 people per sq km)	145,869 sq miles (377,800 sq km)

Land use and agricultural distribution

- cattle
- pigs
- fishing
- cereals
- citrus fruits
- fruit
- herbs
- rice
- root crops
- tobacco
- ■ capital cities
- ● major towns
- pasture
- cropland
- forest

Major industry and infrastructure

- brewing
- car manufacture
- chemicals
- hi-tech industry
- engineering
- finance
- iron & steel
- research & development
- shipbuilding
- textiles
- winter sports
- ■ capital cities
- major towns
- ⊕ international airports
- —— major roads
- major industrial areas

▶ *The Kobe earthquake* in January 1995 highlighted Japan's vulnerability to earthquakes, despite technological advances. It shattered much of the infrastructure of this important port. More than 5000 people died as buildings and overhead highways collapsed and fires broke out.

◀ *A number of* new volcanoes emerged in Japan during the 20th century. They exist alongside older cones like this one in Aso-Kuju National Park on Kyushu, now dormant and grass-covered.

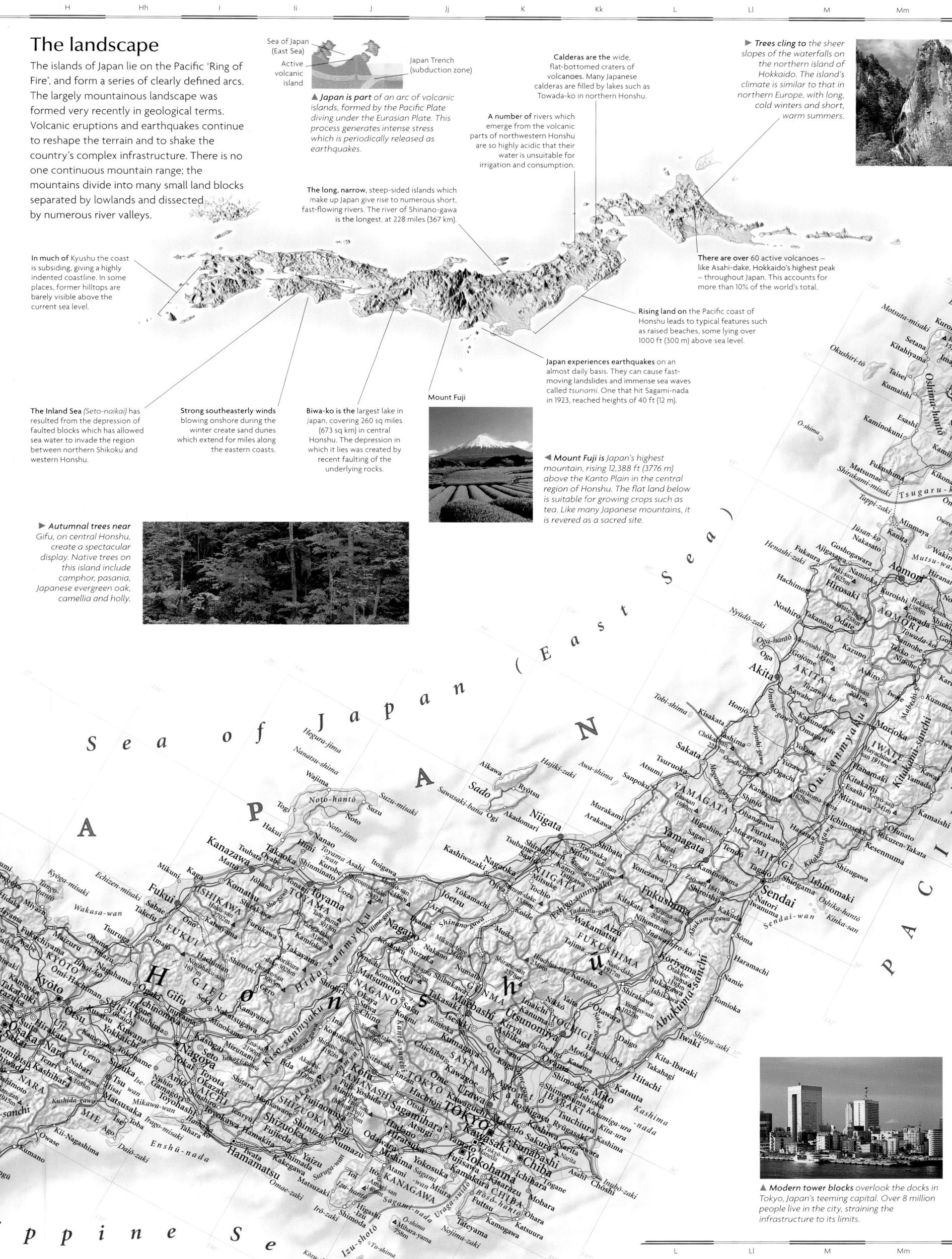

The landscape

The islands of Japan lie on the Pacific 'Ring of Fire', and form a series of clearly defined arcs. The largely mountainous landscape was formed very recently in geological terms. Volcanic eruptions and earthquakes continue to reshape the terrain and to shake the country's complex infrastructure. There is no one continuous mountain range; the mountains divide into many small land blocks separated by lowlands and dissected by numerous river valleys.

Sea of Japan (East Sea)
Active volcanic island
Japan Trench (subduction zone)

▲ **Japan is part** of an arc of volcanic islands, formed by the Pacific Plate diving under the Eurasian Plate. This process generates intense stress which is periodically released as earthquakes.

Calderas are the wide, flat-bottomed craters of volcanoes. Many Japanese calderas are filled by lakes such as Towada-ko in northern Honshu.

A number of rivers which emerge from the volcanic parts of northwestern Honshu are so highly acidic that their water is unsuitable for irrigation and consumption.

▶ **Trees cling to** the sheer slopes of the waterfalls on the northern island of Hokkaido. The island's climate is similar to that in northern Europe, with long, cold winters and short, warm summers.

The long, narrow, steep-sided islands which make up Japan give rise to numerous short, fast-flowing rivers. The river of Shinano-gawa is the longest, at 228 miles (367 km).

In much of Kyushu the coast is subsiding, giving a highly indented coastline. In some places, former hilltops are barely visible above the current sea level.

There are over 60 active volcanoes – like Asahi-dake, Hokkaido's highest peak – throughout Japan. This accounts for more than 10% of the world's total.

Rising land on the Pacific coast of Honshu leads to typical features such as raised beaches, some lying over 1000 ft (300 m) above sea level.

Japan experiences earthquakes on an almost daily basis. They can cause fast-moving landslides and immense sea waves called *tsunami*. One that hit Sagami-nada in 1923, reached heights of 40 ft (12 m).

The Inland Sea (*Seto-naikai*) has resulted from the depression of faulted blocks which has allowed sea water to invade the region between northern Shikoku and western Honshu.

Strong southeasterly winds blowing onshore during the winter create sand dunes which extend for miles along the eastern coasts.

Biwa-ko is the largest lake in Japan, covering 260 sq miles (673 sq km) in central Honshu. The depression in which it lies was created by recent faulting of the underlying rocks.

Mount Fuji

◀ **Mount Fuji is** Japan's highest mountain, rising 12,388 ft (3776 m) above the Kanto Plain in the central region of Honshu. The flat land below is suitable for growing crops such as tea. Like many Japanese mountains, it is revered as a sacred site.

▶ **Autumnal trees near** Gifu, on central Honshu, create a spectacular display. Native trees on this island include camphor, pasania, Japanese evergreen oak, camellia and holly.

▲ **Modern tower blocks** overlook the docks in Tokyo, Japan's teeming capital. Over 8 million people live in the city, straining the infrastructure to its limits.

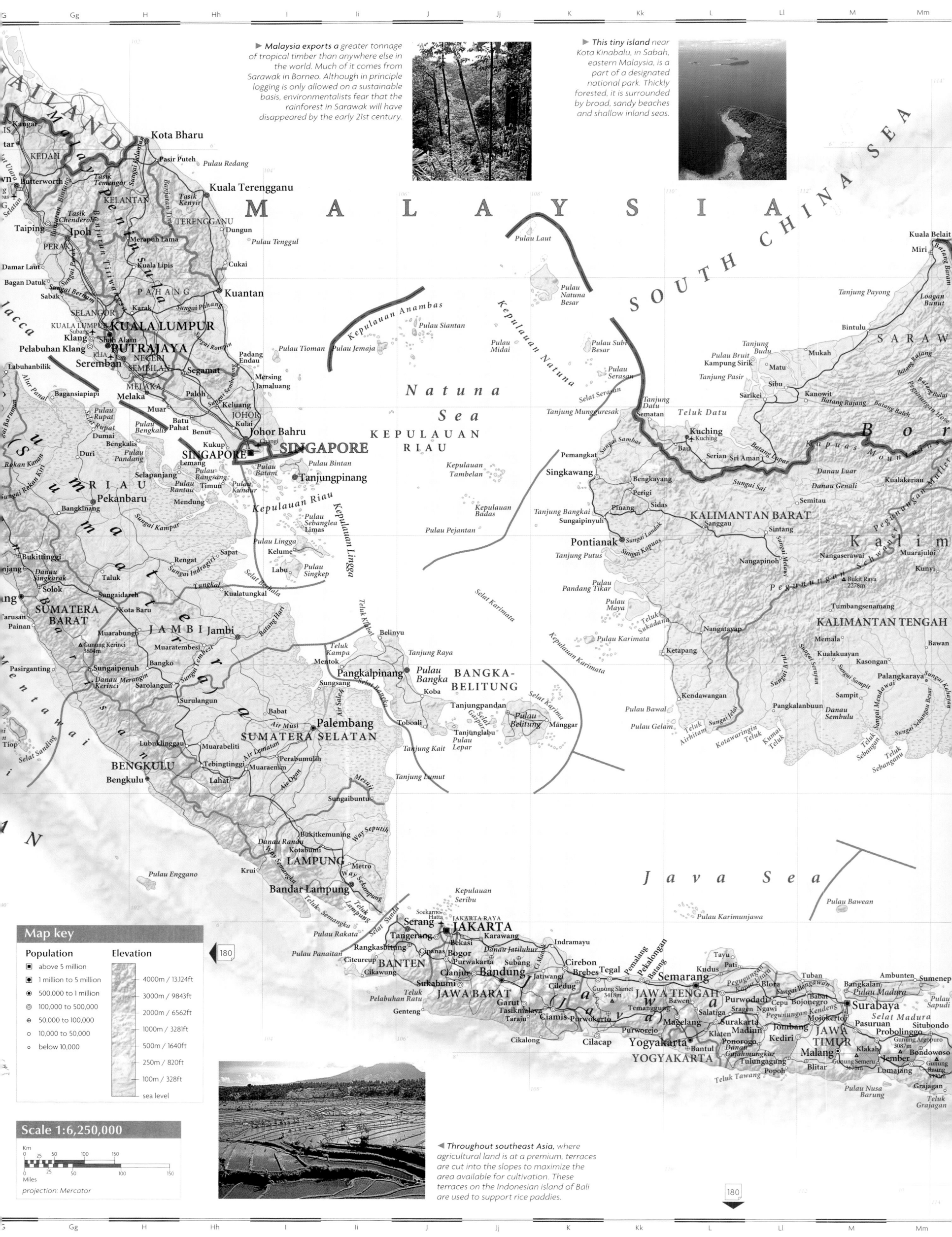

► Malaysia exports a greater tonnage of tropical timber than anywhere else in the world. Much of it comes from Sarawak in Borneo. Although in principle logging is only allowed on a sustainable basis, environmentalists fear that the rainforest in Sarawak will have disappeared by the early 21st century.

► This tiny island near Kota Kinabalu, in Sabah, eastern Malaysia, is a part of a designated national park. Thickly forested, it is surrounded by broad, sandy beaches and shallow inland seas.

◄ Throughout southeast Asia, where agricultural land is at a premium, terraces are cut into the slopes to maximize the area available for cultivation. These terraces on the Indonesian island of Bali are used to support rice paddies.

Map key

Population
- ■ above 5 million
- ▣ 1 million to 5 million
- ◉ 500,000 to 1 million
- ⊕ 100,000 to 500,000
- ⊕ 50,000 to 100,000
- ○ 10,000 to 50,000
- ∘ below 10,000

Elevation
- 4000m / 13,124ft
- 3000m / 9843ft
- 2000m / 6562ft
- 1000m / 3281ft
- 500m / 1640ft
- 250m / 820ft
- 100m / 328ft
- sea level

Scale 1:6,250,000

Km 0 25 50 100 150
Miles 0 25 50 100 150

projection: Mercator

Maritime Southeast Asia

BRUNEI, EAST TIMOR, INDONESIA, MALAYSIA, SINGAPORE

The intricate arc of islands which runs from peninsular Malaysia east to Papua in western New Guinea sustains a huge variety of peoples, languages and cultures. Indonesia is by far the largest country in the region, and 59% of its huge, predominantly Muslim, population is crowded onto Java, the most habitable of Indonesia's 13,677 islands. Malaysia, split between the mainland and the east Malaysian states of Sabah and Sarawak on Borneo, has a diverse population, as well as a fast-growing economy that is increasingly challenging that of its prosperous southern neighbour, Singapore. This small island nation is the financial and commercial capital of Southeast Asia, and an Asian 'tiger' economy. The Sultanate of Brunei in northern Borneo, one of the world's last princely states, also has an extremely high standard of living, based on its oil revenues.

Using the land and sea

Rice is the most important arable crop in Indonesia and Malaysia, and both countries manage to meet almost all of their domestic demand. Malaysian rubber accounts for 25% of world production and is the main cash crop, grown on plantations and small farms, along with oil palms and copra. Timber is exported from both Malaysia and Indonesia. Modern agricultural techniques enable Singapore to produce fruit and vegetables despite a shortage of suitable land.

◀ *Spiral cuts in* the bark of this rubber palm show where it has been tapped. Sophisticated 'cloning' techniques mean that trees which produce consistently high quantities of rubber can be easily reproduced.

The urban/rural population divide

urban 44%   rural 56%

0 10 20 30 40 50 60 70 80 90 100

Population density	Total land area
297 people per sq mile (115 people per sq km)	828,356 sq miles (2,146,000 sq km)

Land use and agricultural distribution

- coconuts
- fishing
- oil palms
- rice
- rubber
- shellfish
- sugar cane
- timber
- capital cities
- major towns
- pasture
- cropland
- forest
- wetland

The landscape

From Sumatra in the west, the volcanic islands of Indonesia run for nearly 3100 miles (5000 km). The Sunda Shelf, an extension of the Eurasian Plate, lies between Java, Bali, Sumatra, Lombok and Borneo. Their volcanic mountains rise from a base below the sea and they were once joined together by dry land, which has since been submerged by rising sea levels.

▶ *The river of* Sungai Mahakam cuts through the central highlands of Borneo, the third largest island in the world, with a total area of 290,000 sq miles (757,050 sq km). Although mountainous, Borneo is one of the most stable of the Indonesian islands, with little volcanic activity.

▲ *The Sunda Shelf* underlies this whole region. It is one of the largest submarine shelves in the world, covering an area of 714,285 sq miles (1,850,000 sq km). During the early Quaternary period, when sea levels were lower, the shelf was exposed.

Borneo — Broad, shallow valleys on sea floor
Malay Peninsula — Present sea level
Sumatra — Quaternary sea level, 460 ft (140 m) below present sea level
Drowned rivers

Malay Peninsula has a rugged east coast, but the west coast, fronting the Strait of Malacca, has many sheltered beaches and bays. The two coasts are divided by the Banjaran Titiwangsa, which run the length of the peninsula.

Gunung Kinabalu is the highest peak in Malaysia, rising 13,455 ft (4101 m).

The four-pronged island of Celebes is the product of complex tectonic activity which ruptured and then reattached small fragments of the Earth's crust to form the island's many peninsulas.

Papua (Irian Jaya) contains some of the most dense and least explored tropical rainforests in the world, inhabited by many rare species of plants and animals.

The island of Krakatau *(Pulau Rakata),* lying between Sumatra and Java, was all but destroyed in 1883, when the volcano erupted. The release of gas and dust into the atmosphere disrupted cloud cover and global weather patterns for several years.

Gunung Semeru

▶ *The volcano of* Gunung Semeru *in eastern Java lies on the Pacific 'Ring of Fire'. It is part of the ancient Tennegger volcano and remains highly active.*

Indonesia has more than 220 volcanoes, most of which are still active. They are strung out along the island arc from Sumatra through the Lesser Sunda Islands, into the Moluccas and Celebes.

Coral islands such as Timor in eastern Indonesia show evidence of very recent and dramatic movements of the Earth's plates. Reefs in Timor have risen by as much as 4000 ft (1300 m) in the last million years.

The Pegunungan Jayawijaya range in central Papua (Irian Jaya) contains the world's highest range of limestone mountains, some with peaks more than 16,400 ft (5000 m) high. Heavy rainfall and high temperatures, which promote rapid weathering, have led to the creation of large underground caves and river systems such as the river of Sungai Baliem.

Malaysia: capital cities

KUALA LUMPUR – capital
PUTRAJAYA – administrative capital

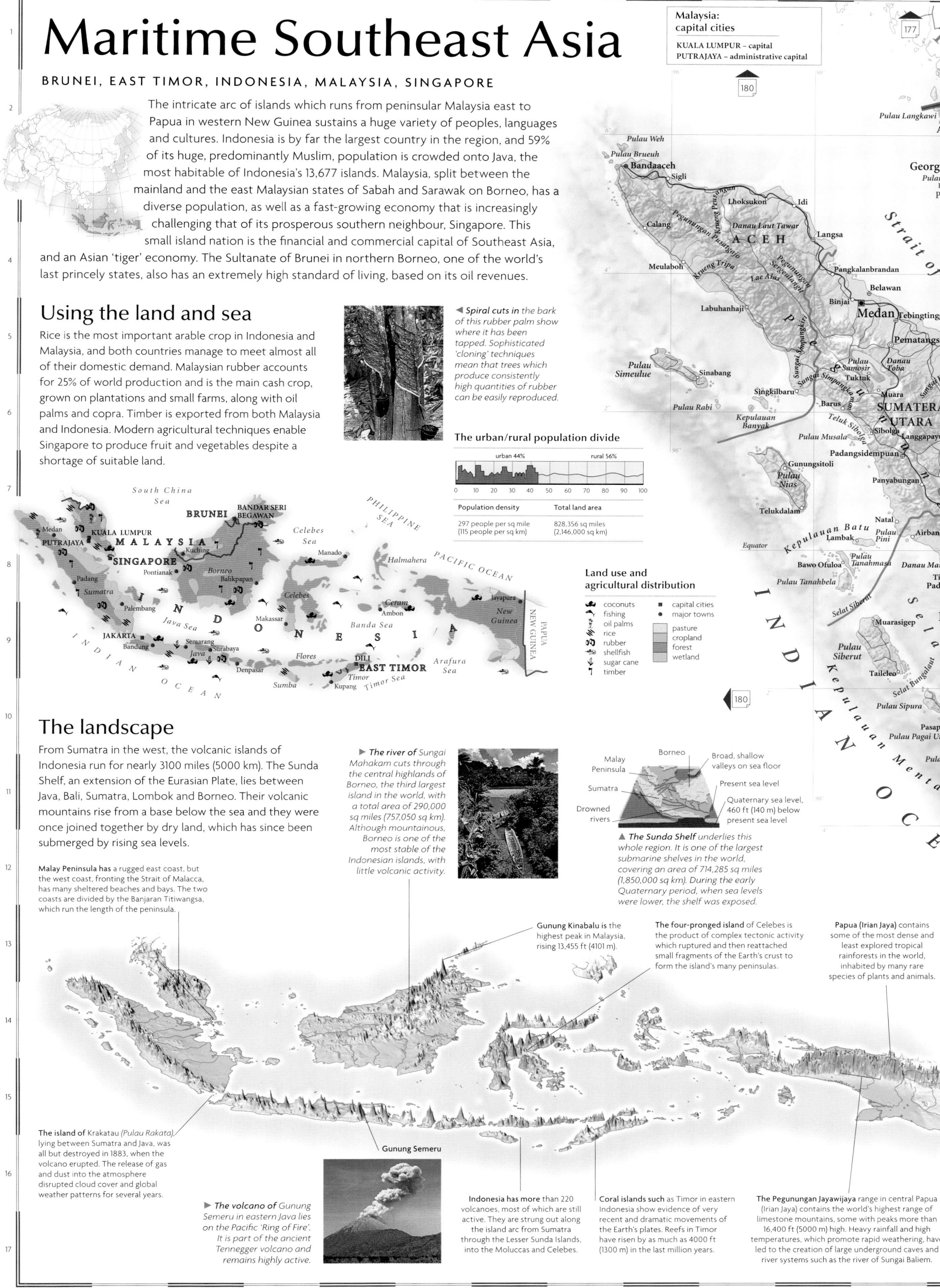

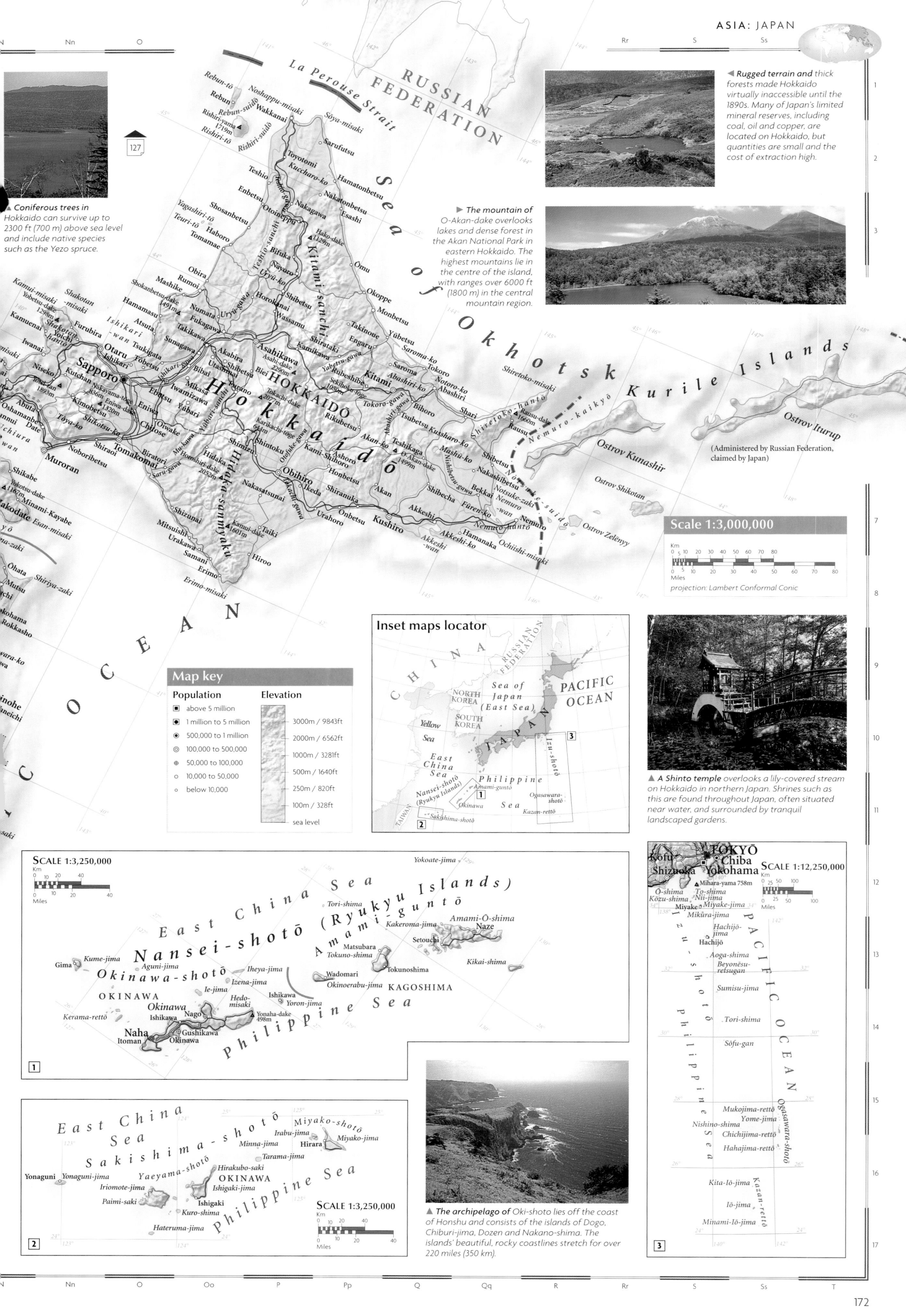

◀ *Rugged terrain and* thick forests made Hokkaido virtually inaccessible until the 1890s. Many of Japan's limited mineral reserves, including coal, oil and copper, are located on Hokkaido, but quantities are small and the cost of extraction high.

▶ *The mountain of* O-Akan-dake overlooks lakes and dense forest in the Akan National Park in eastern Hokkaido. The highest mountains lie in the centre of the island, with ranges over 6000 ft (1800 m) in the central mountain region.

▲ *Coniferous trees in* Hokkaido can survive up to 2300 ft (700 m) above sea level and include native species such as the Yezo spruce.

(Administered by Russian Federation, claimed by Japan)

Scale 1:3,000,000

Km
0 5 10 20 30 40 50 60 70 80

Miles
0 5 10 20 30 40 50 60 70 80

projection: Lambert Conformal Conic

Map key

Population

■ above 5 million
◉ 1 million to 5 million
◉ 500,000 to 1 million
◉ 100,000 to 500,000
⊕ 50,000 to 100,000
○ 10,000 to 50,000
○ below 10,000

Elevation

3000m / 9843ft
2000m / 6562ft
1000m / 3281ft
500m / 1640ft
250m / 820ft
100m / 328ft
sea level

Inset maps locator

▲ *A Shinto temple* overlooks a lily-covered stream on Hokkaido in northern Japan. Shrines such as this are found throughout Japan, often situated near water, and surrounded by tranquil landscaped gardens.

SCALE 1:3,250,000

Km
0 10 20 40

Miles
0 10 20 40

SCALE 1:12,250,000

Km
0 25 50 100

Miles
0 50 100

SCALE 1:3,250,000

Km
0 10 20 40

Miles
0 10 20 40

▲ *The archipelago of* Oki-shoto lies off the coast of Honshu and consists of the islands of Dogo, Chiburi-jima, Dozen and Nakano-shima. The islands' beautiful, rocky coastlines stretch for over 220 miles (350 km).

Mainland Southeast Asia & the Philippines

BURMA, CAMBODIA, LAOS, PHILIPPINES, THAILAND, VIETNAM

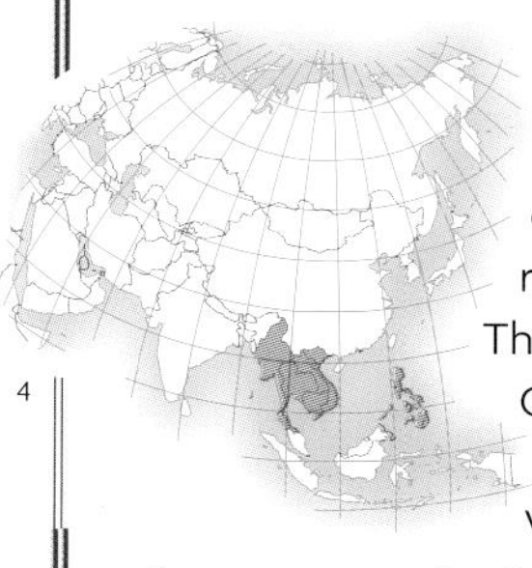

Thickly forested mountains, intercut by the broad valleys of five great rivers characterize the landscape of Southeast Asia's mainland countries. Agriculture remains the main activity for much of the population, which is concentrated in the river flood plains and deltas. Linked ethnic and cultural roots give the region a distinct identity. Most people on the mainland are Theravada Buddhists, and the Philippines is the only predominantly Christian country in Southeast Asia. Foreign intervention began in the 16th century with the opening of the spice trade; Cambodia, Laos and Vietnam were French colonies until the end of the Second World War, Burma was under British control; and the Philippines was controlled by Spain and the USA in the 20th century. Only Thailand was never colonized. Today, Thailand and the Philippines are poised to play a leading role in the economic development of the Pacific Rim, and Laos and Vietnam have begun to mend the devastation of the Vietnam War, and to develop their economies. With continuing political instability and a shattered infrastructure, Cambodia faces an uncertain future, while Burma is seeking investment and the ending of its long isolation from the world community.

The landscape

A series of mountain ranges runs north–south through the mainland, formed as the result of the collision between the Eurasian Plate and the Indian subcontinent, which created the Himalayas. They are interspersed by the valleys of a number of great rivers. On their passage to the sea these rivers have deposited sediment, forming huge, fertile flood plains and deltas. The Philippines' 7000 islands are mountainous and volcanic, with narrow coastal plains.

▲ *The Irrawaddy river* is Burma's vital central artery, watering the ricefields and providing a rich source of fish, as well as an important transport link, particularly for local traffic.

▲ *Commercial logging* – still widespread in Burma – has now been stopped in Thailand because of over-exploitation of the tropical rainforest.

▲ *Lake Taal on* the Philippine island of Luzon lies within the crater of an immense volcano which erupted twice in the 20th century, first in 1911 and again in 1965, causing the deaths of more than 3200 people.

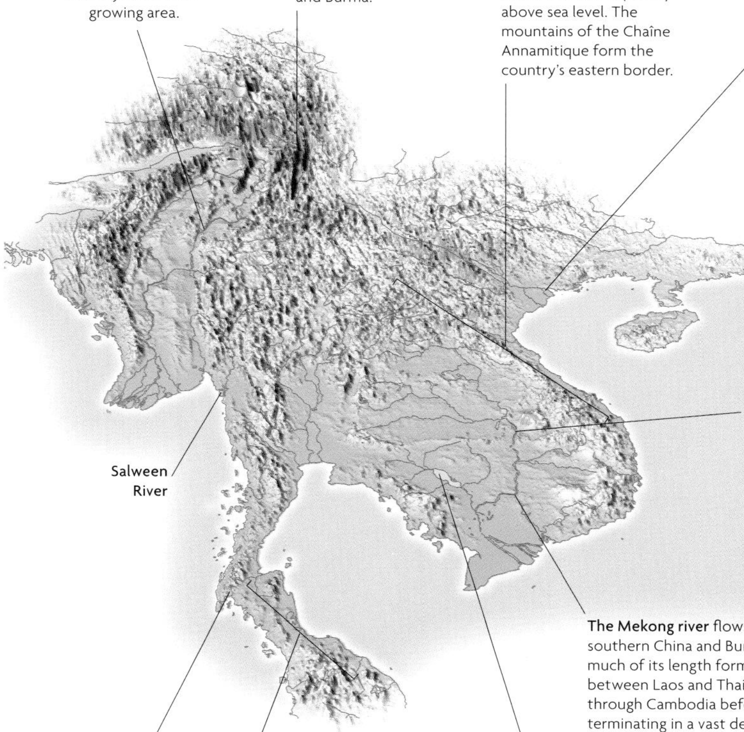

The Irrawaddy river runs virtually north–south, draining the plains of northern Burma. The Irrawaddy delta is the country's main rice-growing area.

Hkakabo Razi is the highest point in mainland Southeast Asia. It rises 19,300 ft (5885 m) at the border between China and Burma.

Mountains dominate the Laotian landscape with more than 90% of the land lying more than 600 ft (180 m) above sea level. The mountains of the Chaîne Annamitique form the country's eastern border.

The Red River delta in northern Vietnam is fringed to the north by steep-sided, round-topped limestone hills, typical of karst scenery.

▲ *The fast-flowing waters of* the Mekong river cascade over this waterfall in Champasak province in Laos. The force of the water erodes rocks at the base of the fall.

Salween River

Malay Peninsula

Tonle Sap, a freshwater lake, drains into the Mekong delta via the Mekong river. It is the largest lake in Southeast Asia.

The Mekong river flows through southern China and Burma, then for much of its length forms the border between Laos and Thailand, flowing through Cambodia before terminating in a vast delta on the southern Vietnamese coast.

Mindanao has five mountain ranges, many of which have large numbers of active volcanoes. Lying just west of the Philippine Trench, which forms the boundary between the colliding Philippine and Eurasian plates, the entire island chain is subject to earthquakes and volcanic activity.

Bohol

◀ *Bohol in the* southern Philippines is famous for its so-called 'chocolate hills'. There are more than 1000 of these regular mounds on the island. The hills are limestone in origin, the smoothed remains of an earlier cycle of erosion. Their brown appearance in the dry season gives the hills their name.

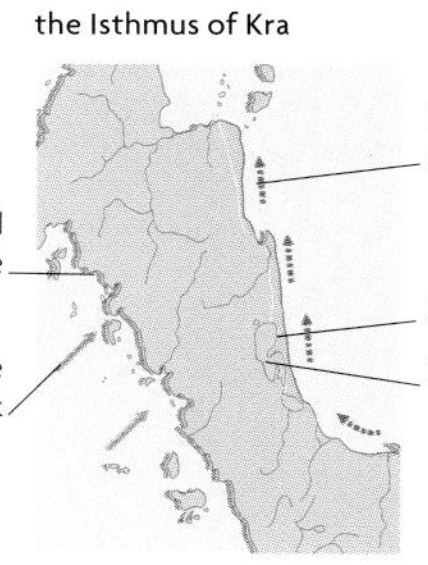

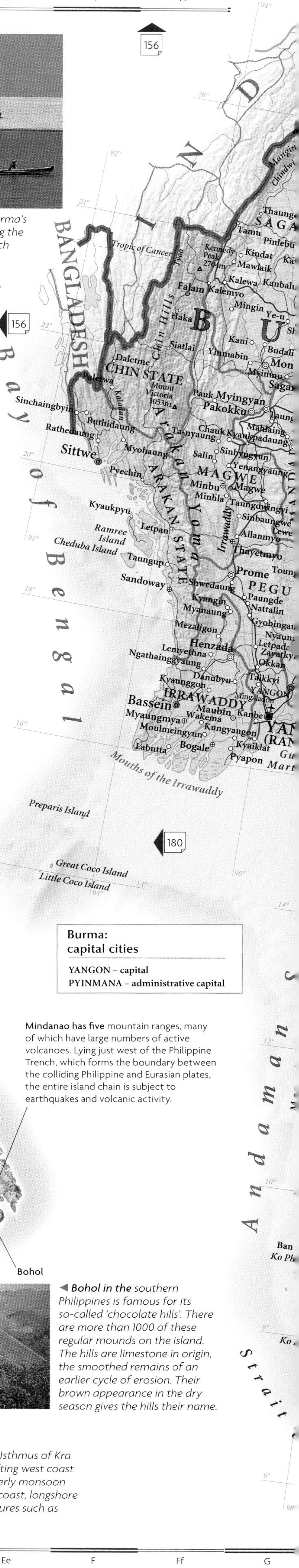

Burma: capital cities

YANGON – capital
PYINMANA – administrative capital

Thailand

◀ *The coast of* the Isthmus of Kra, in southeast Thailand has many small, precipitous islands like these, formed by chemical erosion on limestone, which is weathered along vertical cracks. The humidity of the climate in Southeast Asia increases the rate of weathering.

The coastline of the Isthmus of Kra

Longshore drift

Eroded coastline

Spit

Wave attack

Lagoon

◀ *The east and* west coasts of the Isthmus of Kra differ greatly. The tectonically uplifting west coast is exposed to the harsh south-westerly monsoon and is heavily eroded. On the east coast, longshore currents produce depositional features such as spits and lagoons.

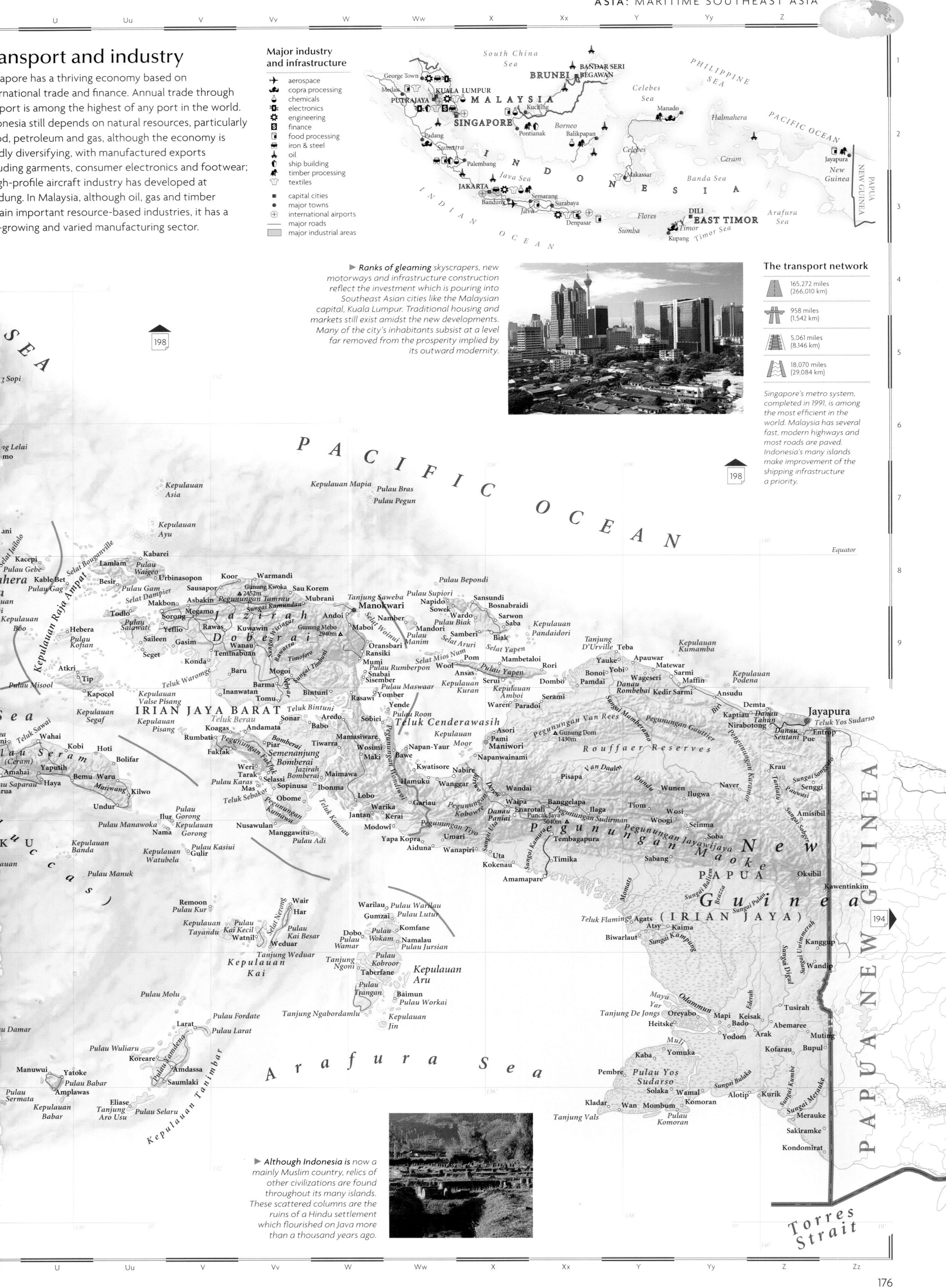

...ansport and industry

...apore has a thriving economy based on ...rnational trade and finance. Annual trade through ...port is among the highest of any port in the world. ...onesia still depends on natural resources, particularly ...od, petroleum and gas, although the economy is ...dly diversifying, with manufactured exports ...uding garments, consumer electronics and footwear; ...gh-profile aircraft industry has developed at ...dung. In Malaysia, although oil, gas and timber ...ain important resource-based industries, it has a ...-growing and varied manufacturing sector.

Major industry and infrastructure

- ✈ aerospace
- copra processing
- ♨ chemicals
- electronics
- ✿ engineering
- finance
- food processing
- iron & steel
- oil
- ship building
- timber processing
- textiles

- ■ capital cities
- major towns
- ⊕ international airports
- major roads
- major industrial areas

▶ *Ranks of gleaming* skyscrapers, new motorways and infrastructure construction reflect the investment which is pouring into Southeast Asian cities like the Malaysian capital, Kuala Lumpur. Traditional housing and markets still exist amidst the new developments. Many of the city's inhabitants subsist at a level far removed from the prosperity implied by its outward modernity.

The transport network

165,272 miles (266,010 km)

958 miles (1,542 km)

5,061 miles (8,146 km)

18,070 miles (29,084 km)

Singapore's metro system, completed in 1991, is among the most efficient in the world. Malaysia has several fast, modern highways and most roads are paved. Indonesia's many islands make improvement of the shipping infrastructure a priority.

▶ *Although Indonesia is* now a mainly Muslim country, relics of other civilizations are found throughout its many islands. These scattered columns are the ruins of a Hindu settlement which flourished on Java more than a thousand years ago.

Tr

Sin
inte
the
Ind
wo
rap
inc
a h
Bar
ren
fas

PHILIPPINES

PHILIPPINE

Sulu Sea

Pulau Balambangan
Balabac Strait
Pulau Banggi
Kudat
Tiga Tarok
Teluk Paitan
Kanibongan
Tuaran
Gunung Kinabalu
410tm
Kota Kinabalu
Ranau
Sandakan
Kota Kinabalu
Teluk Labuk
Kuala Penyu
Sungai Sugut
Teluk Kimanis
LABUAN
Pulau Labuan
Tambunan
SABAH
Sungai Labuk
Labuan
Keningau
Sungai Kinabatangan
Sungai Segama
Bandar Seri Begawan
Brunei Bay
Tenom
Lahad Datu
BANDAR
SERI
BEGAWAN
Banjaran Brassey
Teluk
Lahad Datu
BRUNEI
Pulau Timbun Mata
Pulau Bum Bun
Tawau
Pulau Sebatik

Celebes

Sea

Kepulauan
Nanusa

Kepulauan
Kawio

Pulau
Karakelong
Melanguane
Pulau Salibabu
Kepulauan
Talaud
Damau
Pulau Kaburuang

Sungai Sembakung
Sungai Sesayap
Pulau Mandul
Bunyu
Pulau Bunyu
Tarakan
Pulau Tarakan
Pulau Mapat

Kepulauan
Sangir
Ulu
Pulau Siau
Sopi Tanju
Pulau
Morotai
Sabatini

Sungai Kayan
Tanjungbatu
Pulau Maratua
Teluk
Pantai
Pulau
Sangihe
Tahuna
Kepulauan
Loloda Utara
Tanjung Bisoa
Galela
Tobelo

Sungai Berau
Tanjungredeb
Teluk
Sangkulirang
Serai
Selat Bangka
Pulau Bangka
Pediwang
Iga
Tan
Ak

neo

KALIMANTAN TIMUR
Gunung Antu
750m
Salumpaga
Oan
Teluk Kuandang
Manado
Tomohon
Airmadidi
Tondano
Bitung
Danau Tondano
SULAWESI
UTARA
Pulau Mayu
Bobopayo
Dodaga

Gunung Menyapa
2000m
Tolitoli
Leok
Teluk Bilang
Lanu
Ternate
Pulau Ternate
Kusu
Teluk
Kau
Buli
Muarawahau
Tompo
Teluk
Dondo
Gunung Malino
2499m
Kuandang
Gorontalo
Amurang
Kotamobagu
Soasiu
Pulau Tidore
Pulau
Halmahera

Sangkulirang
Sepasu
Pegunungan Paleleh
GORONTALO
Danau
Limboto
Gorontalo
Pegunungan Kotai
MALUKU
UTARA
Bicoli

Longiram
Danau
Semayang
Molosipat
Lemito
Bubaa
Gunung
Bulowa
1970m
Molibagu
Pulau Makian
Teluk
Weda
Metulang
Danau Melintang
Teluk Gorontalo
Mafa

Tenggarong
Tanjung Ayu
Danau Jempang
Samarinda
Towera
Kepulauan
Togian
Pulau
Batudaka
Molucca
Sea
Pulau
Kasiruta
Pulau Bacan
Halm
Se

Danau
Sangasanga
Tanjung Bayur
Tate
Donggala
Lambogo
Dondo
Selat Walea
Maliku
Teku
Kepulauan
Bacan
Pulau
Mandioli
Gani
Kepul

Palu
Pegunungan Tokalekaju
Tambarana
Toima
Teluk Poh
Luwuk
Teku
Selat Obi
Balikpapan
Pakuli
Danau
Lindu
Bolang
Pegunungan Balingara
Balo
Pulau Bisa

Waru
Poso
Tobamawu
Pulau Peleng
SULAWESI
Kembani
Penu
Pulau Mangole
Sesepe
Pulau Obi

Muarakaman
Teluk Balikpapan
Gimpo
Pandiri
Pelei
TENGAH
Kepulauan
Treko
Pulau
Banggai
Tano
Capalulu
Pulau Gomumu

Dayu
Tanjung
Tentena
Pegunungan
Pompangeo
Baturebe
Kepulauan Banggai
Selat Salue Timpaus
Kepulauan
Sula
Ceram
Tanjung Nan
Lasahata
Pa

Amuntai
Karossa
Taripa
Danau Poso
Teluk Towori
Teluk
Tolo
Pulau Taliabu
Sanana
Pulau
Sanana
Pulau Boano
Piru
Pu

Negara
Rantau
Babana
SULAWESI
BARAT
Sulawesi
(Celebes)
Saroako
Danau Matana
Mahalona
Pulau Luha
Danau Towuti
Kepulauan
Salabangka
Gunung Kaubalatmada
2729m
Danau
Rana
Namlea
Pulau
Kelang

KALIMANTAN
SELATAN
Banjarmasin
Mamuju
Masamba
Wotu
Usu
Pulau Buru
Luhu
Pulau
Manipa
Watawa
Halong
Latu
Sap
Ha

Martapura
Malunda
Rantepao
Wiau
Asera
Pulau Manui
Waflia
Tifu
Ambon
Pulau Ambon
Haruku

Pelaihari
Pulau Sebuku
Majene
SULAWESI
SELATAN
Polewali
Enrekang
Pegunungan
Mekongka
Elara
Pulau
Ambelau
Kepulauan Leas
M

Kotabaru
Teluk
Mandar
Sungai
Jadiwa
SULAWESI
Kendari
Pulau Wowoni
MALU

Pulau
Laut
Parepare
Danau Sidenreng
Anabanua
Kolaka
Teluk Staring
Teluk Wowoni
Kepu
Peny

Karambu
Danau Tempe
Singkang
TENGGARA
Pulau
Padamarang
Pulau Muna
Pulau Buton
Kepulauan
Lucipara

Watampone
Singkang
Bugingkalo
Tampo
Bonelipu
Teluk
Kolonawatobo

Kepulauan
Laut Kecil
Maros
Bulukumba
Lasihao
Raha
Kamaru

Pulau Karamain
Makassar
Takalar
Pising
Pulau
Muna
Baubau
Kepulauan
Langkesi

Pulau
Masalembo-besar
Jeneponto
Selat Kabaena
Selat Mana
Pulau
Kaledupa
Kepulauan
Tukangbesi

Selat Selayar
Pulau Kabaena
Pulau Binongko

Benteng
Kepulauan
Macan
Pulau
Batuata
Banda Sea

Pulau
Kangean
Kepulauan
Kangean
Kepulauan
Bonerate

Kepulauan
Sabalana
Pulau
Tanahjampea
Pulau Kalao

Bali Sea
Flores
Sea
Pulau Bonerate
Pulau Kalaotoa

Bali
Singaraja
Tejakula
Danau Butur
Bayan
Pulau Moyo
Gunung Api
1949m
Pulau
Komodo
Teluk
Maumere
Kepulauan Damar
Pulau Romang
Kepulauan
Leti

Banyuwangi
Negara
BALI
Karangasem
NUSA TENGGARA BARAT
Gunung Tambora
2821m
Sumbawabesar
Dompu
Raba
Teluk
Saleh
Larantuka
Pulau Wetar
Selat Romang
Pulau Moa

Denpasar
Mataram
Taliwang
Lunyuk
Gunung Takan
1400m
Gerampi
Komodo
Ruteng
Bajawa
Endeh
Teluk Geliting
Kepulauan
Solor
Kabir
Kalabahi
DILI
Manatuto
Tutuala

Ngurah Rai
Nusa
Penida
Kuta
Sumbawa
Selat Sumba
Flores
Sunda Islands
Maumere
Kepulauan Alor
Pulau Alor
Pulau Pantar
EAST TIMOR
Lospalos

NUSA TENGGARA TIMUR
Bondokodi
Waikabubak
Waingapu
Sumba
Savu Sea
Kefamenanu
Soe
Nikiniki
Maliana
Suai

Gunung Kekneno
2070m
Sulamu
Kupang
Toineke
Timor Sea

Baing
Kepulauan
Sawu
Pulau Sawu
Selat Roti
Baa

Makassar Strait

Gulf of Tomini

Teluk Bone

Maluku

INDONESIA

Nusa Tenggara (Lesser Sunda Islands)

Timor Sea

Using the land and sea

The fertile flood plains of rivers such as the Mekong and Salween, and the humid climate, enable the production of rice throughout the region. Cambodia, Burma and Laos still have substantial forests, producing hardwoods such as teak and rosewood. Cash crops include tropical fruits such as coconuts, bananas and pineapples, rubber, oil palm, sugar cane and the jute substitute, kenaf. Pigs and cattle are the main livestock raised. Large quantities of marine and freshwater fish are caught throughout the region.

Land use and agricultural distribution

- cattle
- pigs
- bananas
- coconuts
- fishing
- oil palms
- rice
- rubber
- sugar cane
- timber
- capital cities
- major towns
- pasture
- cropland
- forest
- wetland

The urban/rural population divide

urban 30%   rural 70%

Population density	Total land area
345 people per sq mile (133 people per sq km)	733,828 sq miles (1,901,110 sq km)

The Paracel Islands and the Spratly Islands are two strategically sensitive island groups, disputed by several surrounding countries. The Paracels are claimed by China, Taiwan and Vietnam, though only China has actually occupied them. The Spratlys are claimed by China, Taiwan, Vietnam, Malaysia and the Philippines and are particularly important as they lie on oil and gas deposits.

▶ *The city of* Hue in central Vietnam was the country's capital under the 13 emperors of the Nguyen dynasty from 1802 to 1945. It is the site of a number of religious monuments, including the Thien-Mu Pagoda.

N Nn O Oo P Pp Q Qq R Rr S Ss

Transport and industry

Industrial manufacturing has become increasingly important in Thailand, Vietnam and the Philippines in recent years. The assembling of component-based electrical and electronic goods is becoming more common throughout this region, with foreign companies benefiting from low labour costs and the upgrading of technology. The economies of Burma and Cambodia are still based on agricultural produce and the processing of raw materials. Tin is the region's most important metal, and nickel, copper and chromite are also mined, although the quantities produced are not significant on a global scale. Thailand's successful tourist industry is the country's highest earner of foreign exchange.

The transport network

	82,958 miles (133,524 km)		267 miles (430 km)
	7500 miles (12,071 km)		28,585 miles (46,008 km)

Transport development has concentrated on the building of road networks. Water and sea transport remain important, although air links have improved, particularly in Thailand and the Philippines.

Major industry and infrastructure

chemicals	oil & gas	■	capital cities
electronics	mining	●	major towns
engineering	shipbuilding	⊕	international airports
finance	textiles	—	major roads
food processing	timber processing		major industrial areas
iron & steel			

Map inset labels

BANGLADESH INDIA CHINA
Mandalay PYINMANA HANOI Hai Phong
BURMA Chiang Mai VIENTIANE Gulf of Tongking
Bay of Bengal LAOS
RANGOON Moulmein THAILAND VIETNAM Hue Da Nang
Andaman Sea BANGKOK CAMBODIA South China Sea
Gulf of Thailand PHNOM PENH Ho Chi Minh City
Hat Yai BRUNEI MALAYSIA

Luzon Strait Luzon Philippine Sea
MANILA PHILIPPINES Cebu
Sulu Sea Mindanao Davao
Zamboanga Celebes Sea
MALAYSIA

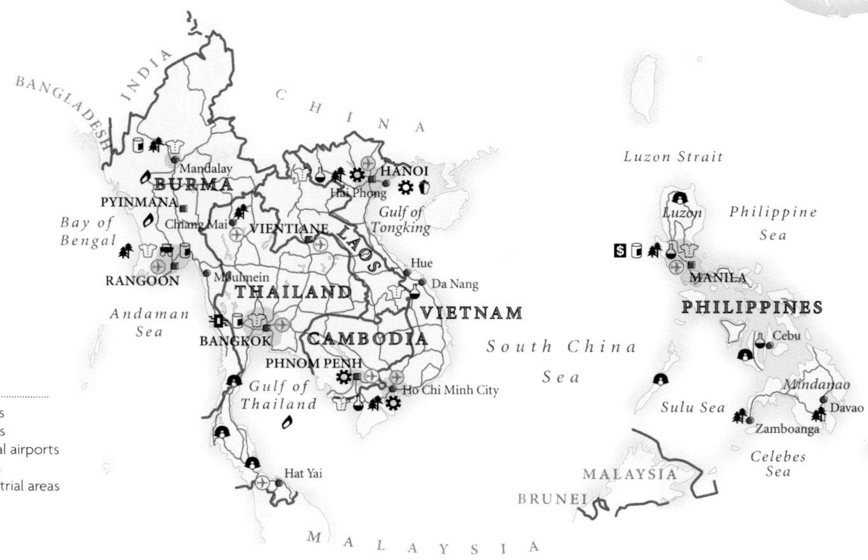

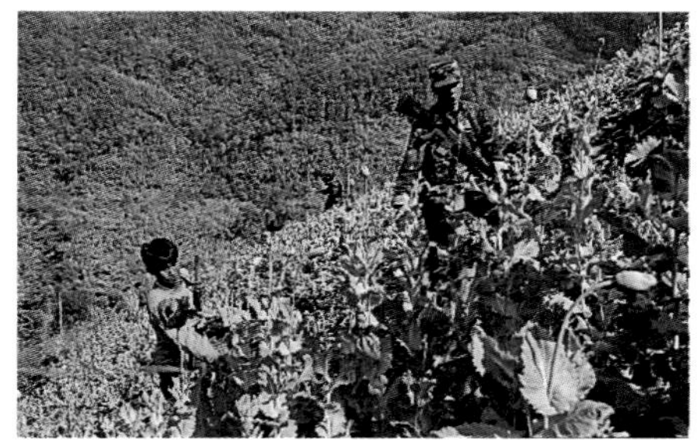

◀ Opium poppies are destroyed under army supervision in Thailand. This action is part of a government-sponsored initiative to reduce the trade in drugs such as heroin, which is derived from these plants. Drug trafficking is a major problem throughout the region; the area is known as the 'Golden Triangle', and Laos is the third-largest producer of opium poppies in the world.

▶ The terracing of land to restrict soil erosion and create flat surfaces for agriculture is a common practice throughout Southeast Asia, particularly where land is scarce. These terraces are on Luzon in the Philippines.

Main map labels

Bashi Channel
Batan Islands
Luzon Strait Balintang Channel Babuyan Island
Babuyan Channel Escarpada Point
Mayraira Point Claveria Aparri
Laoag Mount Cagua 1133m
Cabugao Dingras Tuao Tuguegarao
Vigan Bangued Tabuk Ilagan
Candon Bontoc Lagawe Cauayan
San Fernando Bangar Echague
Bauang Ta Bayombong Bayombong
Baguio Trinidad San Ildefonso Peninsula
Bolinao Dagupan Luzon
Lingayen Gulf San Jose City Baler
San Carlos Tarlac Palayan City
Camiling Cabanatuan
Masinloc Iba High Peak 2037m San Fernando
Mount Pinatubo 1485m Angeles Polillo Islands
Olongapo Malolos Caloocan Quezon City
Balanga Pasig Labo
MANILA Ninoy Aquino Daet
Corregidor Island Imus Laguna de Bay Caramoan
Tagaytay San Pablo Naga Catanduanes Island
Nasugbu Lipa Calauag Virac
Lake Taal Lucena Pili Tabaco City
Batangas Catanauan Mayon Volcano 2422m
Lubang Island Boac San Francisco Legazpi City
Cape Calavite Calapan Ligao Donsol Sorsogon
Mamburao Marinduque Burias Island Bulan Laoang Samar
Sablayan Mindoro Pinamalayan Tablas Sibuyan Masbate Catarman Dolores
Mount Baco 2488m Roxas Sibuyan Sea Cajidiocan Catbalogan
Busuanga Island San Jose Odiongan Masbate Borongan
Coron Balud Biliran Island Calbiga
Culion Island Calamian Group Jintotolo Channel Placer Naval Borongan
Roxas City Ibajay Kalibo Visayan Sea Carigara Tacloban Guiuan
Linapacan Island Culasi Bogo Ormoc Leyte Gulf
El Nido Panay Island Passi Cadiz Sagay Baybay Leyte
West York Island Taytay Iloilo Silay Cebu Danao Sogod Dinagat Island
Flat Island Nanshan Island San Jose de Buenavista Miagao San Carlos City Toledo Lapu-Lapu Maasin Dinagat
SPRATLY ISLANDS (disputed) Bago Camotes Sea Ubay Siargao Island
La Carlota Bais Cebu Argao Surigao
Himamaylan Bacolod Bohol Jagna
Puerto Princesa Negros Sipalay Dumaguete Camiguin Island Cabadbaran Tandag
Palawan Cagayan Islands Siquijor Island Butuan Prosperidad
Quezon Bayawan Siaton Point Siaton Gingoog Lianga
Brooke's Point Siocon Dapitan Iligan Bay Cagayan de Oro Tagoloan Hinatuan
Dipolog Oroquieta Ozamiz Iligan Bislig
Sulu Sea Mount Malindang 2425m Tubod Malaybalay Monkayo
Sindangan Labason Kapatagan Marawi Nabunturan
Liloy Pagadian Sultan Kudarat Lake Lanao Maramag Baganga
Balabac Island Kabasalan Malabang Mindanao Tagum Pantukan
Balabac Strait Tungawan Midsayap Davao Manay
Cagayan de Tawi Tawi Siocon Cotabato Kidapawan Mount Apo 2954m Mati Lupon
Dumagasa Point Zamboanga Lebak Mount Busa 2085m Digos Governor Generoso
Isabela Lamitan Istalan Koronadal Davao Gulf Cape San Agustin
Pangutaran Group Basilan Palimbang Surallah Malita Tacurong
Samales Group Kiamba Parker Volcano 1842m General Santos Jose Abad Santos
Jolo Jolo Celebes Sea Tinaca Point Sarangani Islands
Tapul Group
Tawitawi Balimbing Sulu Archipelago
Sibutu Passage Sibutu
MALAYSIA

West York Island
Flat Island
Nanshan Island
PHILIPPINE SEA

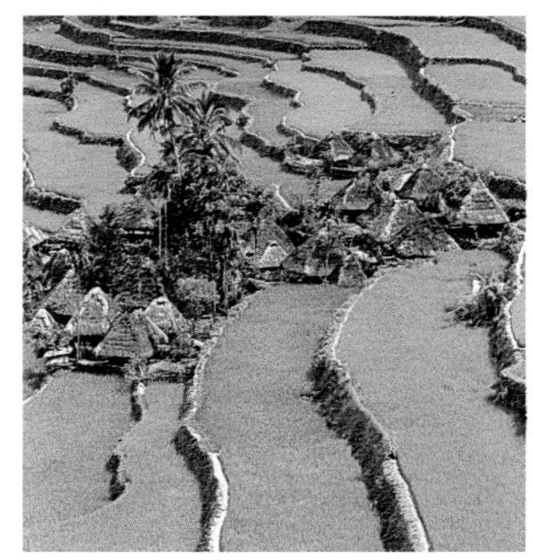

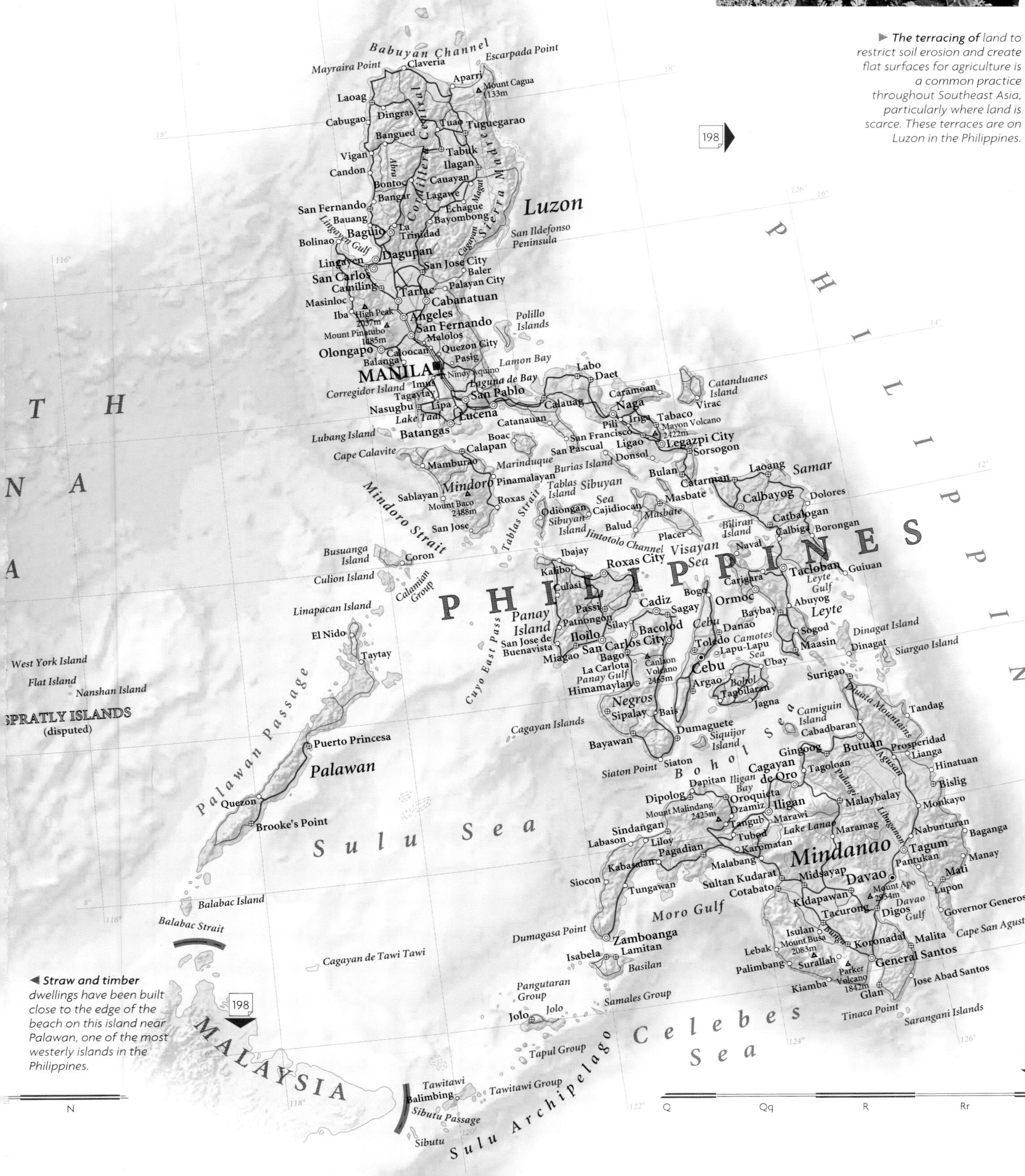

◀ Straw and timber dwellings have been built close to the edge of the beach on this island near Palawan, one of the most westerly islands in the Philippines.

Scale box

Scale 1:7,750,000

Km 0 25 50 100 150 200
Miles 0 25 50 100 150 200

projection: Lambert Conformal Conic

Map key

Population
- ■ above 5 million
- ◪ 1 million to 5 million
- ◉ 500,000 to 1 million
- ◎ 100,000 to 500,000
- ⊕ 50,000 to 100,000
- ○ 10,000 to 50,000
- ○ below 10,000

Elevation
- 4000m / 13,124ft
- 3000m / 9843ft
- 2000m / 6562ft
- 1000m / 3281ft
- 500m / 1640ft
- 250m / 820ft
- 100m / 328ft
- sea level

The Indian Ocean

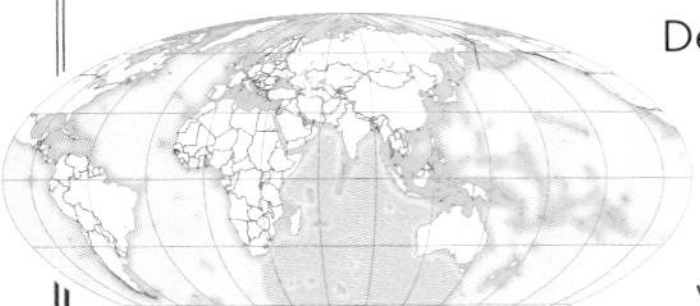

Despite being the smallest of the three major oceans, the evolution of the Indian Ocean was the most complex. The ocean basin was formed during the break up of the supercontinent Gondwanaland, when the Indian subcontinent moved northeast, Africa moved west and Australia separated from Antarctica. Like the Pacific Ocean, the warm waters of the Indian Ocean are punctuated by coral atolls and islands. About one-fifth of the world's population – over 1000 million people – live on its shores. Those people living along the northern coasts are constantly threatened by flooding and typhoons caused by the monsoon winds.

The landscape

The Indian Ocean began forming about 150 million years ago, but in its present form it is relatively young, only about 36 million years old. Along the three subterranean mountain chains of its mid-ocean ridge the seafloor is still spreading. The Indian Ocean has fewer trenches than other oceans and only a narrow continental shelf around most of its surrounding land.

Sediments come from Ganges/Brahmaputra river system

Submarine canyons transport sediment to fan – some of these are more than 1500 miles (2500 km) long

Sri Lanka

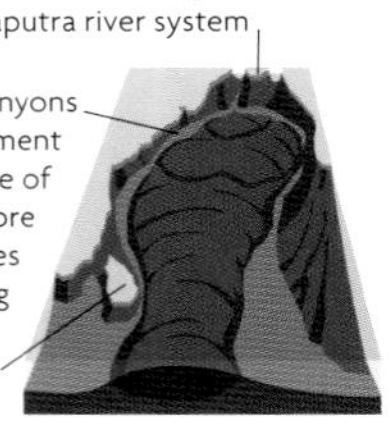

▲ **The Ganges Fan** is one of the world's largest submarine accumulations of sediment, extending far beyond Sri Lanka. It is fed by the Ganges/Brahmaputra river system, whose sediment is carried through a network of underwater canyons at the edge of the continental shelf.

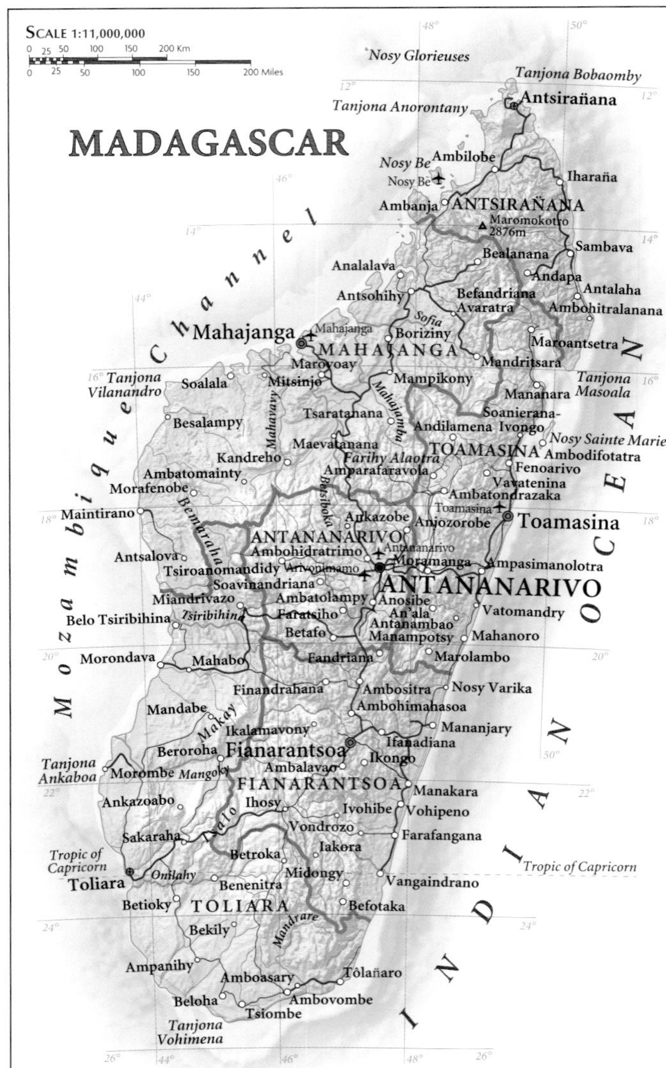

The mid-oceanic ridge runs from the Arabian Sea. It diverges east of Madagascar, one arm runs southwest to join the Mid-Atlantic Ridge, the other branches southeast, joining the Pacific-Antarctic Ridge, southeast of Tasmania.

The Ninetyeast Ridge takes its name from the line of longitude it follows. It is the world's longest and straightest under-sea ridge.

Two of the world's largest rivers flow into the Indian Ocean; the Indus and the Ganges/Brahmaputra. Both have deposited enormous fans of sediment.

Indus River

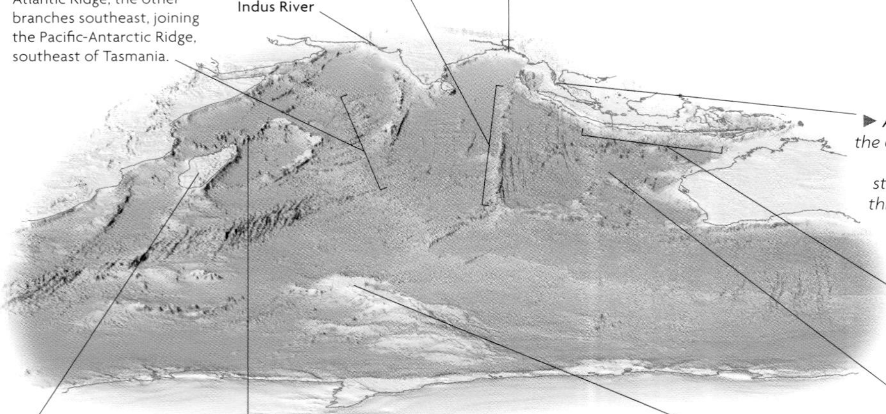

▶ **A large proportion** of the coast of Thailand, on the Isthmus of Kra, is stabilized by mangrove thickets. They act as an important breeding ground for wildlife.

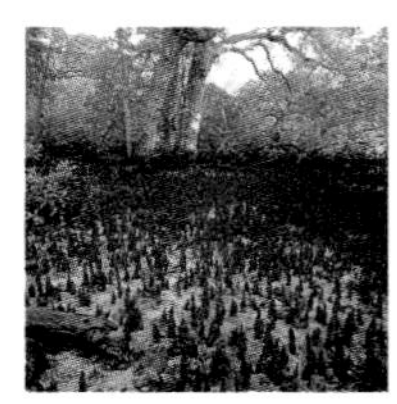

The Java Trench is the world's longest, it runs 1600 miles (2570 km) from the southwest of Java, but is only 50 miles (80 km) wide.

The relief of Madagascar rises from a low-lying coastal strip in the east, to the central plateau. The plateau is also a major watershed separating Madagascar's three main river basins.

▶ **The central group** of the Seychelles are mountainous, granite islands. They have a narrow coastal belt and lush, tropical vegetation cloaks the highlands.

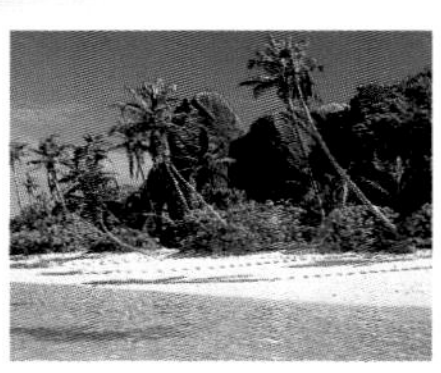

The Kerguelen Islands in the Southern Ocean were created by a hot spot in the Earth's crust. The islands were formed in succession as the Antarctic Plate moved slowly over the hot spot.

The circulation in the northern Indian Ocean is controlled by the monsoon winds. Biannually these winds reverse their pattern, causing a reversal in the surface currents and alternative high and low pressure conditions over Asia and Australia.

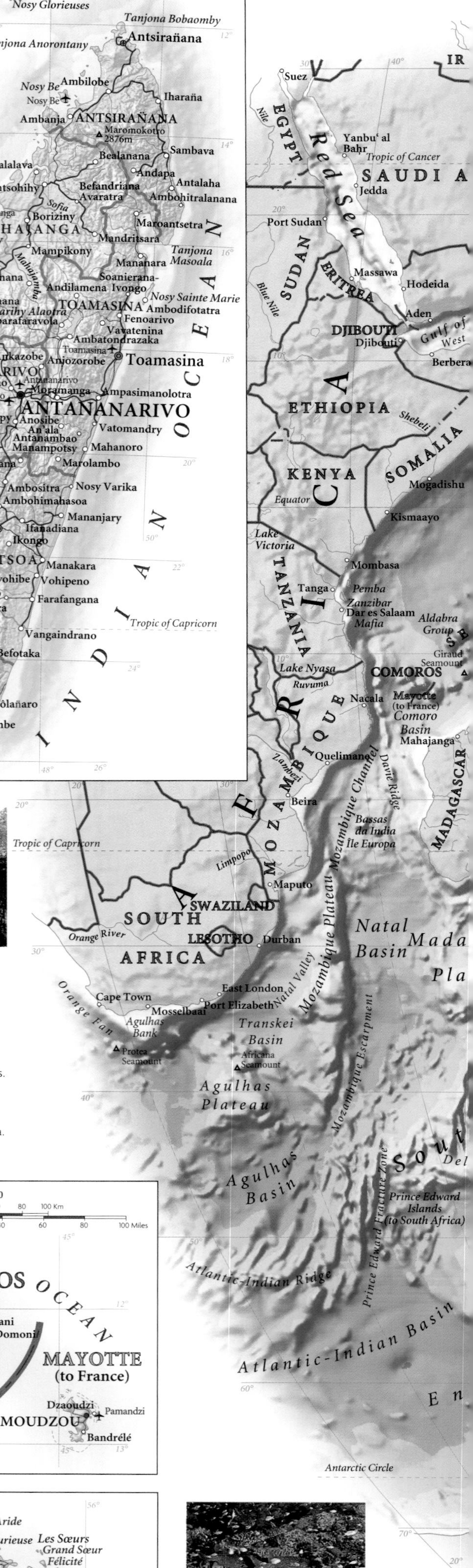

Resources

Many of the small islands in the Indian Ocean rely exclusively on tuna-fishing and tourism to maintain their economies. Most fisheries are artisanal, although large-scale tuna-fishing does take place in the Seychelles, Mauritius and the western Indian Ocean. Other resources include oil in The Gulf, pearls in the Red Sea and tin from deposits off the shores of Burma, Thailand and Indonesia.

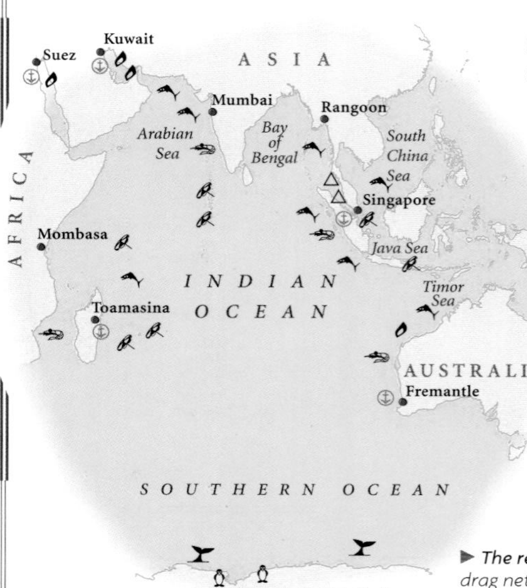

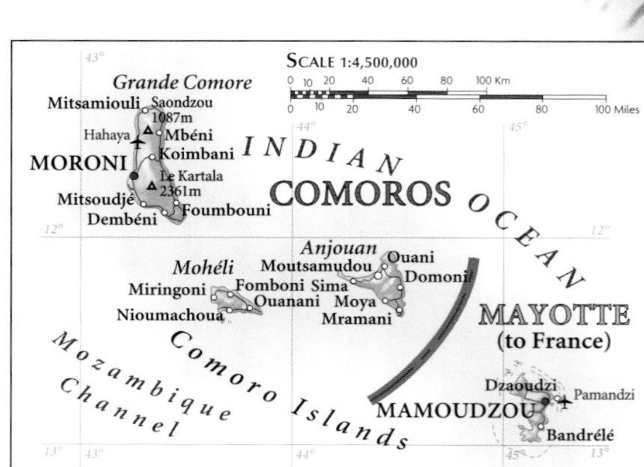

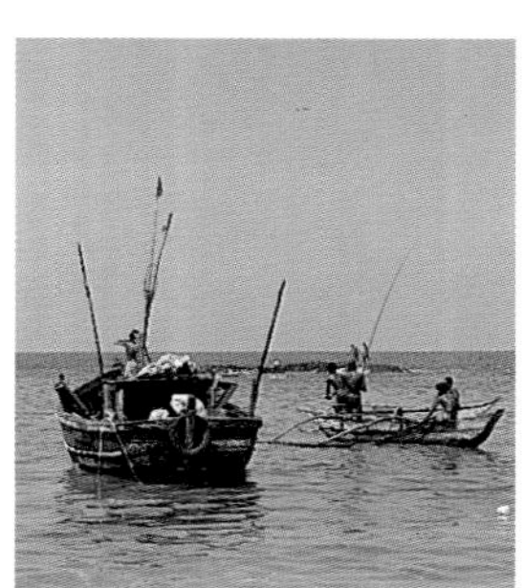

▶ **The recent use** of large drag nets for tuna-fishing has not only threatened the livelihoods of many small-scale fisheries, but also caused widespread environmental concern about the potential impact on other marine species.

Resources (including wildlife)

- 🐟 fish
- 🐧 penguins
- 🦪 shellfish
- 🐋 whales
- ⛽ oil & gas
- △ tin deposits
- ● tourism
- ● major towns
- ⊕ major ports

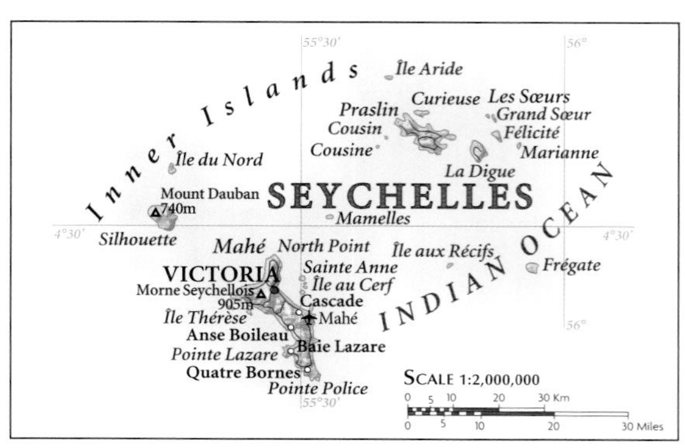

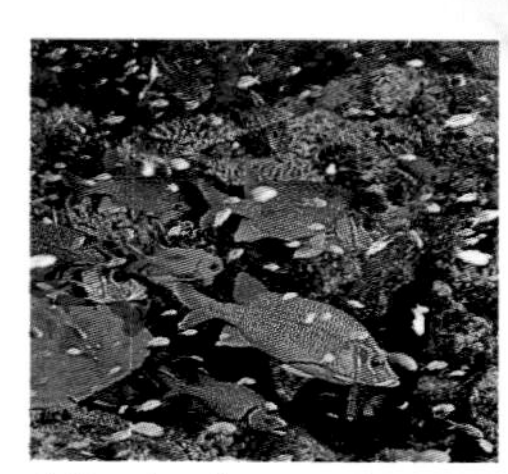

▲ **Coral reefs support** an enormous diversity of animal and plant life. Many species of tropical fish, like these squirrel fish, live and feed around the profusion of reefs and atolls in the Indian Ocean.

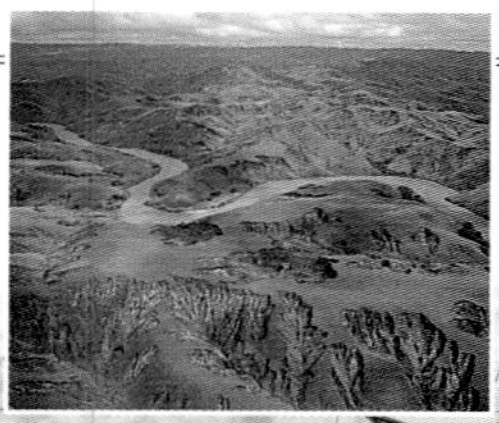

◄ **The steeper eastern** side of Madagascar is drained by numerous short, fast-flowing rivers. In contrast, larger, more languid rivers flow across the west. Both erode huge quantities of Madagascar's reddish soil.

► **There are over** 1300 small coral islands in the Maldives, but only about 200 are inhabited. They are based around an ancient submerged volcanic mountain range and all the islands are low-lying, none rising more than 6 ft (1.8 m) above sea level.

Scale 1:42,000,000

Km
0   200   400   600   800   1000
Miles
0   200   400   600   800   1000

projection: Mollweide

Map labels

AQ
KUWAIT
Kuwait
Ad Dammām, BAHRAIN
QATAR Doha
Abu Dhabi UAE
Dubai
Mīnā' Qābūs
RABIA

IRAN
Bandar-e 'Abbās
OMAN
PAKISTAN
Gwādar
Karachi
Indus

A S I A

Ganges
Brahmaputra
BANGLADESH
Dhaka
Kolkata (Calcutta)
Chittagong
CHINA

Narmada
INDIA
Bhāvnagar
Mumbai (Bombay)
Godavari
Visākhapatnam
Krishna
Ganges Fan
BURMA
Rangoon
Salween
Mekong
LAOS
VIETNAM
TAIWAN
Ryukyu Islands
Tropic of Cancer
East China Sea

YEMEN
OMAN
Salalah
Aden
Socotra (to Yemen)
Arabian Sea
Arabian Basin
Mangalore
Chennai (Madras)
Cochin
Tuticorin
Laccadive Islands (to India)
Trincomalee
Sri Lanka
SRI LANKA
Colombo
Bay of Bengal
Andaman Islands (to India)
Andaman Basin
Andaman Sea
THAILAND
Gulf of Thailand
CAMBODIA
Gulf of Tongking
South China Sea
PHILIPPINES
Philippine Sea

Andrew Tablemount
Carlsberg Ridge
Chain Ridge
Somali Basin
Amirante Islands
Amirante Basin
Seychelles Bank
Mahé
SEYCHELLES
Farquhar Group
Coco-de-Mer Seamounts
Madingley Rise
Saya de Malha Bank
Nazareth Bank
Cargados Carajos Bank
Mid-Indian Ocean Basin
Chagos Archipelago
Diego Garcia
British Indian Ocean Territory (to UK)
Mid-Indian Basin
Chagos-Laccadive Plateau
Ninetyeast Ridge
Ceylon Plain
Cocos Basin
Nicobar Islands (to India)
Kepulauan
Bedawan
Strait of Malacca
Klang
Singapore
MALAYSIA
Sumatra
INDONESIA
Borneo
Celebes Sea
Sulu Sea
Celebes
Makassar Strait
Molucca Sea
Ceram Sea
Banda Sea
New Guinea
Equator

Mascarene Plateau
Mascarene Basin
Agalega Islands (to Mauritius)
Rodrigues (to Mauritius)
Mascarene Islands
MAURITIUS
Réunion (to France)
Toamasina
Mascarene Plain
Madagascar Basin
Walters Shoal
Mauritius Trench
INDIAN
OCEAN
Egeria Fracture Zone
Argo Fracture Zone
Osborn Plateau
Broken Ridge
Ob' Trench
Cocos Islands (to Australia)
Christmas Island (to Australia)
Java Trench
Java Ridge
Java
Bali
Sumbawa
Lombok Basin
Savu
Timor
EAST TIMOR
Ashmore & Cartier Islands (to Australia)
Timor Sea
Timor Trough
Arafura Sea
Joseph Bonaparte Gulf
Darwin
Gulf of Carpentaria
Wyndham

Wharton Basin
Wallaby Plateau
Batavia Seamount
East Indiaman Ridge
Gulden Draak Seamount
Cuvier Plateau
Cuvier Basin
Shark Bay
North Australian Basin
Gascoyne Plain
Sahul Shelf
King Sound
Rowley Shoals
Broome
Exmouth Plateau
Port Hedland
Tropic of Capricorn
AUSTRALIA

Perth Basin
Naturaliste Plateau
Geraldton
Fremantle
Bunbury
Albany
Great Australian Bight
Port Augusta
Darling
Murray
Adelaide
Spencer Gulf
Kangaroo Island
Melbourne
King Island
Bass Strait
Tasmania

INDIAN OCEAN

Crozet Basin
Crozet Plateau
Crozet Islands
Cano Rise
Ob' Tablemount
Lena Tablemount
Amsterdam Fracture Zone
Amsterdam Island
St. Paul Island
French Southern & Antarctic Territories (to France)
Kerguelen
Kerguelen Plateau
Heard & McDonald Islands (to Australia)
Southeast Indian Ridge
South Australian Plain
South Australian Basin
King Island
Tasman Plateau
Tasmania

Southwest Indian Ridge
derby Plain
Banzare Seamounts
SOUTHERN OCEAN
South Indian Basin

Prydz Bay
ANTARCTICA
Antarctic Circle

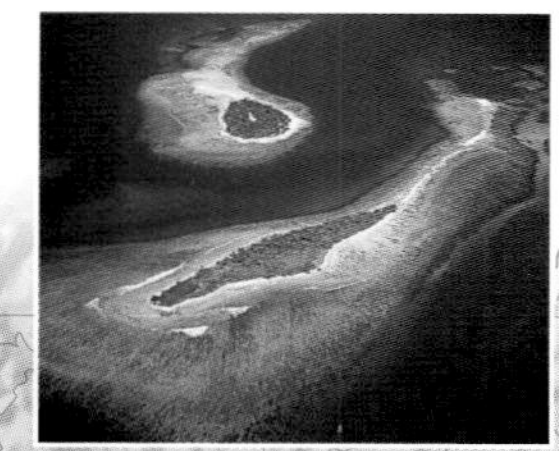

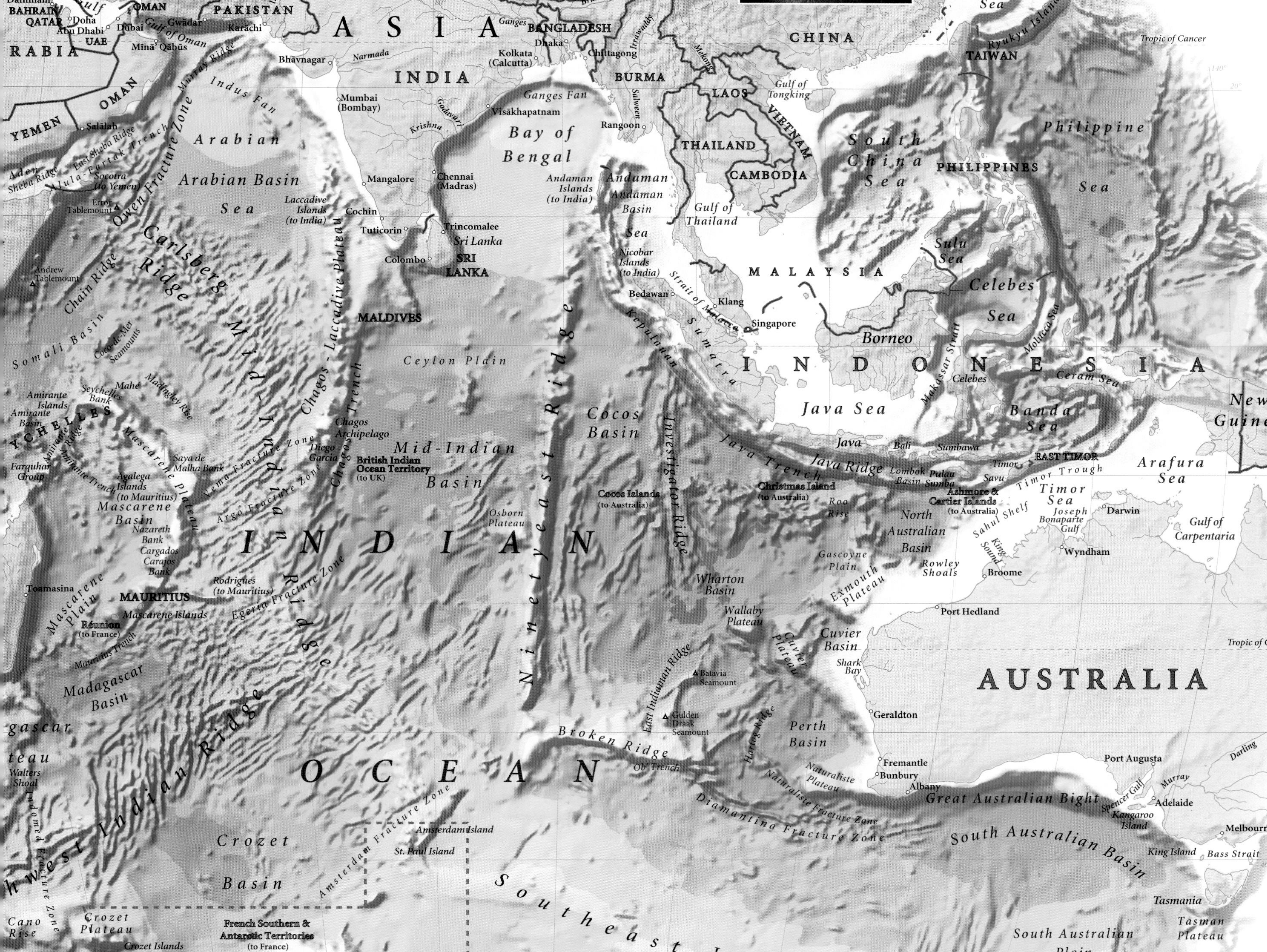

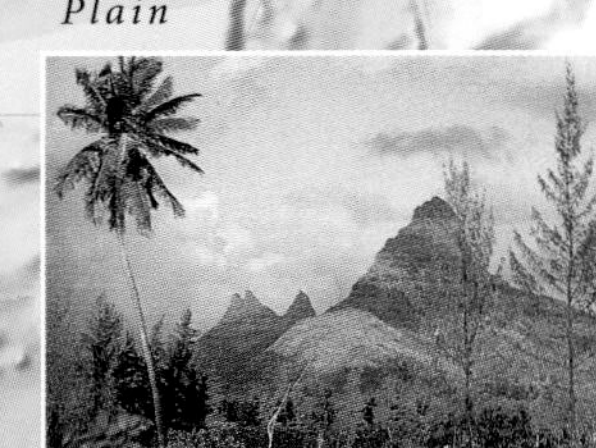

▲ **The island of** Mauritius is volcanic in origin. Its central plateau is bounded by mountains which may once have formed the rim of a volcanic crater.

RÉUNION (to France)

SCALE 1:2,000,000
0   5   10   20   30 Km
0   5   10   20 Miles

ST-DENIS
Le Port
St-Paul
Pointe des Aigrettes
Trois-Bassins
St-Leu
Pointe au Sel
Ste-Marie
Gillot
St-Gilles-les-Bains
Salazie
Piton des Neiges 3070m
Cilaos
La Plaine-des-Palmistes
Ste-Suzanne
Ste-André
St-Benoit
Ste-Rose
Piton de la Fournaise 2632m
Le Tampon
St-Louis
Point de la Rivière St-Etienne
St-Pierre
St-Joseph
Pointe de la Table
St-Philippe
INDIAN OCEAN

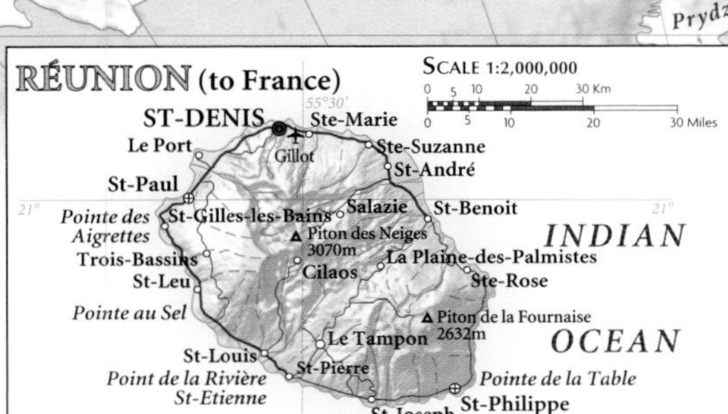

Ocean map key

Sea Depth

sea level
250m / 820ft
500m / 1640ft
1000m / 3281ft
2000m / 6562ft
3000m / 9843ft

Inset map key

Population

◉ 500,000 to 1 million
◎ 100,000 to 500,000
⊕ 50,000 to 100,000
○ 10,000 to 50,000
○ below 10,000

Elevation

3000m / 9843ft
2000m / 6562ft
1000m / 3281ft
500m / 1640ft
250m / 820ft
100m / 328ft
sea level

MAURITIUS

Round Island
Flat Island
Gunner's Quoin
Ile D'Ambre
Canonniers Point
Triolet
Pamplemousses
Goodlands
Rivière du Rempart
PORT LOUIS
Beau Bassin
Mont du Rempart 545m
Quatre Bornes
Rose Hill
Centre de Flacq
Bel Air
Tamarin
Vacoas
Curepipe
Piton de la Petite
Rivière Noire 828m
Rose Belle
Mahebourg
Chemin Grenier
Sir Seewoosagur Ramgoolam
Souillac
Pointe Sud Ouest

INDIAN OCEAN

SCALE 1:2,000,000
0   5   10   20   30 Km
0   5   10   20   30 Miles

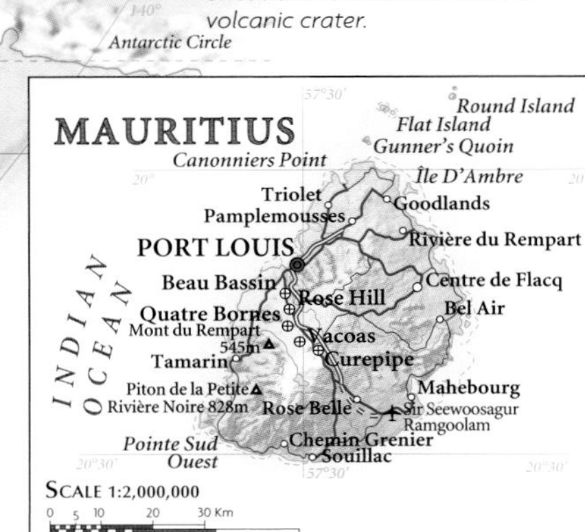

Australasia & Oceania

Australasia and Oceania, covering a land area of 3,285,048 sq miles (8,508,238 sq km), takes in 14 countries including the continent of Australia, New Zealand, Papua New Guinea and many island groups scattered across the Pacific Ocean.

● **Greatest extent, North–South:** 2000 miles / 3200 km

■ **Greatest extent, East–West:** 2500 miles /4000 km

Most northerly point: Eastern Island, Midway Islands 28° 15' N

Highest point: Mount Wilhelm, Papua New Guinea 14,794 ft (4509 m)

Most easterly point: Clipperton Island, 109° 12' W

Largest lake: Lake Eyre, Australia 3430 sq miles (8884 sq km)

Highest recorded temperature: Bourke, Australia 128°F (53°C)

Lowest point: Lake Eyre, Australia -53 ft (-16 m) below sea level

Most westerly point: Cape Inscription, Australia 112° 57' E

Equator

Cape York, Australia 10° 41'S

Ducie Island

Cape Byron, Australia 153° 37' E

Lowest recorded temperature: Canberra, Australia -8°F (-22°C)

Steep Point, Australia 113° 9' E

Dirk Hartog Island

South East Point, Australia, 39° 10' S

Most southerly point: Macquarie Island, New Zealand 54° 30' S

Dirk Hartog Island, Australia

Great Dividing Range

New Caledonia

New Zealand

Tonga

Tuamoto Islands

Ducie Island, Pitcairn Islands

Cross-section from Dirk Hartog Island, Australia to Ducie Island, Pitcairn Islands

▶ line of cross-section

0   500   1000 1500 Km
0   500   1000 1500 Miles

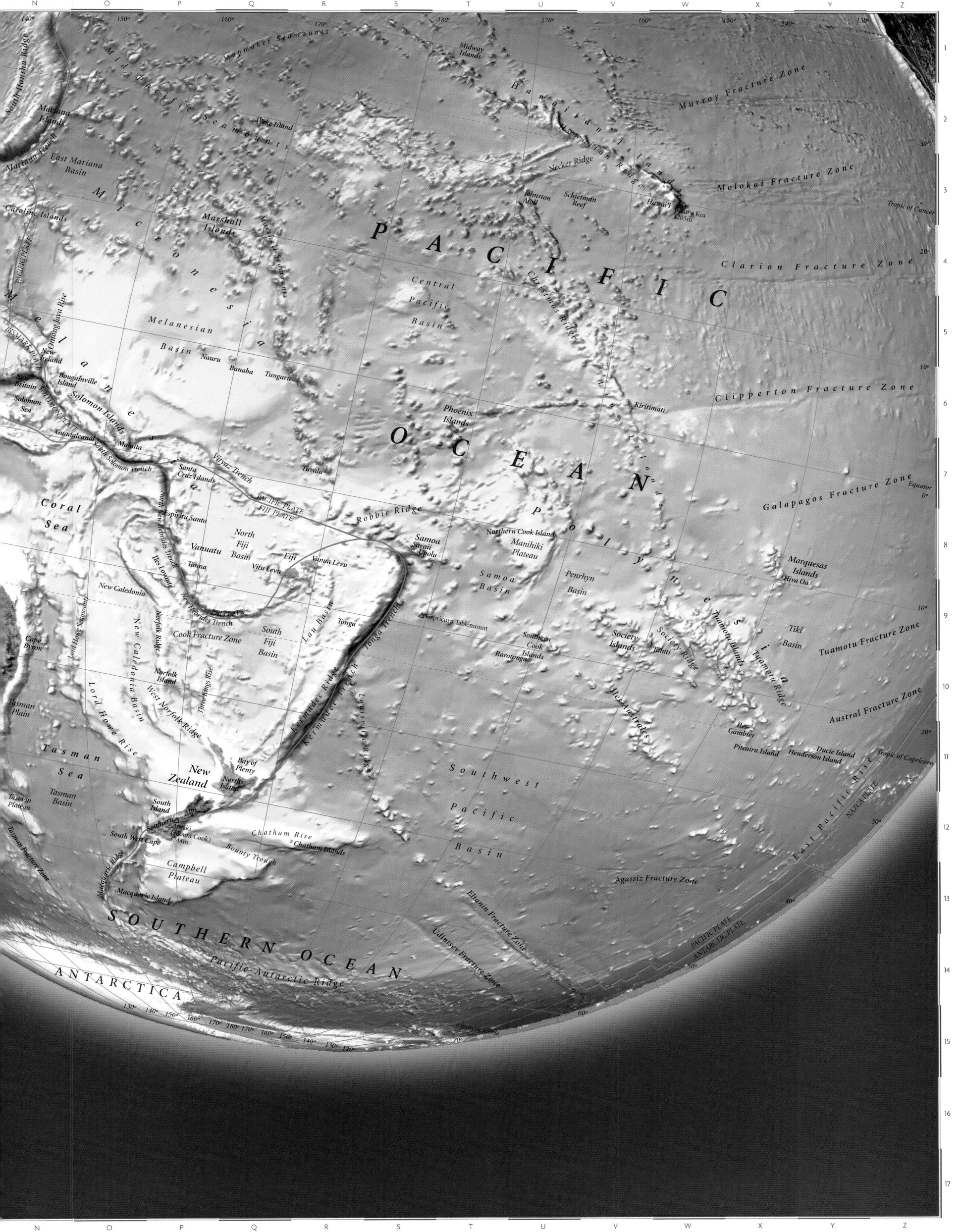

PACIFIC OCEAN
SOUTHERN OCEAN
ANTARCTICA
Midway Islands
Mapmaker Seamounts
Mid-Pacific Seamounts
Hawaiian Islands
Hawaiian Ridge
Murray Fracture Zone
Molokai Fracture Zone
Clarion Fracture Zone
Clipperton Fracture Zone
Galapagos Fracture Zone
Tuamotu Fracture Zone
Austral Fracture Zone
Agassiz Fracture Zone
Eltanin Fracture Zone
Udintsev Fracture Zone
Tropic of Cancer
Equator
Tropic of Capricorn
Antarctic Circle
Necker Ridge
Johnston Atoll
Schjetman Reef
Hawai'i
Mauna Kea 4205m
Wake Island
South Honshu Ridge
Mariana Islands
Mariana Trench
East Mariana Basin
Caroline Islands
Micronesia
Marshall Islands
Marshall Seamounts
Central Pacific Basin
Christmas Ridge
Line Islands
Kiritimati
Melanesian Basin
Melanesia
Ontong Java Rise
New Ireland
New Britain
Bougainville Island
Solomon Sea
Solomon Islands
Guadalcanal
Malaita
South Solomon Trench
Nauru
Banaba
Tungaru
Phoenix Islands
Tuvalu
Santa Cruz Islands
Vityaz Trench
PACIFIC PLATE
FIJI PLATE
BISMARCK PLATE
SOLOMON PLATE
Robbie Ridge
Coral Sea
Espiritu Santo
North New Hebrides Trench
Vanuatu
North Fiji Basin
Fiji
Vitu Levu
Vanua Levu
Samoa
Savai'i
Upolu
Northern Cook Islands
Manihiki Plateau
Samoa Basin
Penrhyn Basin
Polynesia
Marquesas Islands
Hiva Oa
Tiki Basin
Tuamotu Islands
Tuamotu Ridge
Society Islands
Society Ridge
Tahiti
Southern Cook Islands
Rarotonga
Capricorn Tablemount
Tonga
Tonga Trench
Lau Basin
South Fiji Basin
Cook Fracture Zone
New Caledonia
Iles Loyauté
Tanna
New Hebrides Trench
Lord Howe Seamounts
Norfolk Ridge
New Caledonia Basin
Norfolk Island
West Norfolk Ridge
Three Kings Rise
Kermadec Ridge
Kermadec Trench
Louisville Ridge
Iles Australes
Iles Gambier
Pitcairn Island
Henderson Island
Ducie Island
East Pacific Rise
NAZCA PLATE
Cape Byron
Tasman Plain
Lord Howe Rise
Tasman Sea
Tasman Plateau
Tasman Basin
Tasman Fracture Zone
New Zealand
North Island
South Island
Bay of Plenty
Southern Alps
Aoraki (Mount Cook) 3754m
South West Cape
Chatham Rise
Chatham Islands
Bounty Trough
Campbell Plateau
Macquarie Ridge
Macquarie Island
Southwest Pacific Basin
Pacific-Antarctic Ridge
PACIFIC PLATE
ANTARCTIC PLATE

Political Australasia & Oceania

Vast expanses of ocean separate this geographically fragmented realm, characterized more by each country's isolation than by any political unity. Australia's and New Zealand's traditional ties with the United Kingdom, as members of the Commonwealth, are now being called into question as Australasian and Oceanian nations are increasingly looking to forge new relationships with neighbouring Asian countries like Japan. External influences have featured strongly in the politics of the Pacific Islands; the various territories of Micronesia were largely under US control until the late 1980s, and France, New Zealand, the USA and the UK still have territories under colonial rule in Polynesia. Nuclear weapons-testing by Western superpowers was widespread during the Cold War period, but has now been discontinued.

◄ *Western Australia's mineral* wealth has transformed its state capital, Perth, into one of Australia's major cities. Perth is one of the world's most isolated cities – over 2500 miles (4000 km) from the population centres of the eastern seaboard.

Scale 1:32,000,000

projection: Lambert Azimuthal Equal Area

Population

Density of settlement in the region is generally low. Australia is one of the least densely populated countries on Earth with over 80% of its population living within 25 miles (40 km) of the coast – mostly in the southeast of the country. New Zealand, and the island groups of Melanesia, Micronesia and Polynesia, are much more densely populated, although many of the smaller islands remain uninhabited.

Population density
(people per sq km)

| below 4 |
| 5-24 |
| 25-49 |
| 50-99 |
| 100-199 |
| 200-299 |
| above 300 |

▲ *The myriad of* small coral islands which are scattered across the Pacific Ocean are often uninhabited, as they offer little shelter from the weather, often no fresh water, and only limited food supplies.

◄ *The planes of* the Australian Royal Flying Doctor Service are able to cover large expanses of barren land quickly, bringing medical treatment to the most inaccessible and far-flung places.

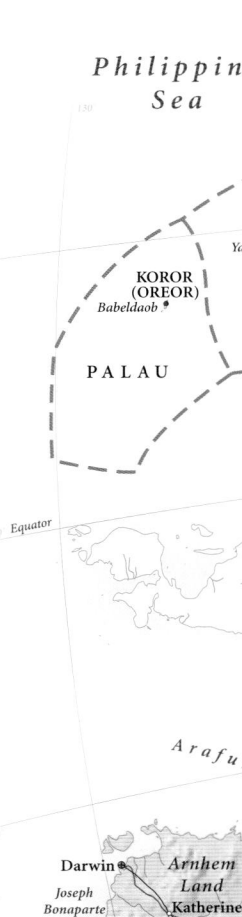

Languages

English is spoken throughout Australia and New Zealand. In Australia, English has been superimposed on a mosaic of Aboriginal languages. In New Zealand, the indigenous language, Maori, is the official language besides English. In Papua New Guinea, Melanesian Pidgin has become a *lingua franca* alongside several hundred indigenous languages. Across the region, the indigenous languages can be grouped into (1) the Aboriginal languages of Australia, (2) the Papuan languages spoken mostly inland in Papua New Guinea, and (3) the widely dispersed Austronesian, which includes coastal languages of Papua New Guinea, New Zealand Maori and languages of Oceania.

Language groups

- Australian
- Papuan
- Indo-European
- Austronesian

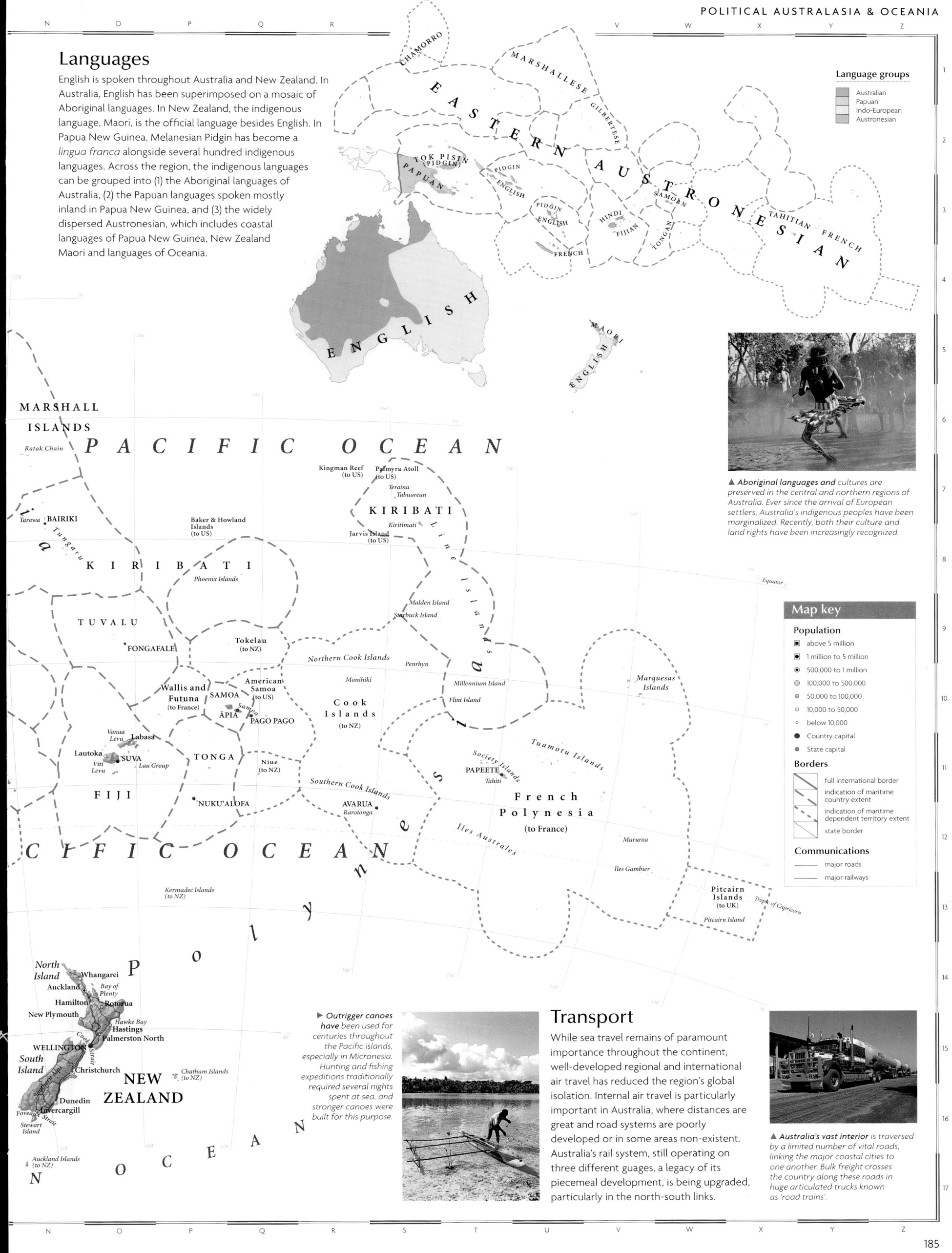

▲ *Aboriginal languages and* cultures are preserved in the central and northern regions of Australia. Ever since the arrival of European settlers, Australia's indigenous peoples have been marginalized. Recently, both their culture and land rights have been increasingly recognized.

Map key

Population

- ▪ above 5 million
- ◪ 1 million to 5 million
- ◉ 500,000 to 1 million
- ◎ 100,000 to 500,000
- ⊕ 50,000 to 100,000
- ○ 10,000 to 50,000
- ∘ below 10,000
- ● Country capital
- ◦ State capital

Borders

- full international border
- indication of maritime country extent
- indication of maritime dependent territory extent
- state border

Communications

- major roads
- major railways

▶ *Outrigger canoes have* been used for centuries throughout the Pacific islands, especially in Micronesia. Hunting and fishing expeditions traditionally required several nights spent at sea, and stronger canoes were built for this purpose.

Transport

While sea travel remains of paramount importance throughout the continent, well-developed regional and international air travel has reduced the region's global isolation. Internal air travel is particularly important in Australia, where distances are great and road systems are poorly developed or in some areas non-existent. Australia's rail system, still operating on three different guages, a legacy of its piecemeal development, is being upgraded, particularly in the north-south links.

▲ *Australia's vast interior is traversed* by a limited number of vital roads, linking the major coastal cities to one another. Bulk freight crosses the country along these roads in huge articulated trucks known as 'road trains'.

Australasian & Oceanian resources

Natural resources are of major economic importance throughout Australasia and Oceania. Australia in particular is a major world exporter of raw materials such as coal, iron ore and bauxite, while New Zealand's agricultural economy is dominated by sheep-raising. Trade with western Europe has declined significantly in the last 20 years, and the Pacific Rim countries of Southeast Asia are now the main trading partners, as well as a source of new settlers to the region. Australasia and Oceania's greatest resources are its climate and environment; tourism increasingly provides a vital source of income for the whole continent.

▲ *The largely unpolluted* waters of the Pacific Ocean support rich and varied marine life, much of which is farmed commercially. Here, oysters are gathered for market off the coast of New Zealand's South Island.

▶ *Huge flocks of* sheep are a common sight in New Zealand, where they outnumber people by 12 to 1. New Zealand is one of the world's largest exporters of wool and frozen lamb.

Standard of living

In marked contrast to its neighbour, Australia, with one of the world's highest life expectancies and standards of living, Papua New Guinea is one of the world's least developed countries. In addition, high population growth and urbanization rates throughout the Pacific islands contribute to overcrowding. The Aboriginal and Maori people of Australia and New Zealand have been isolated for many years. Recently, their traditional land ownership rights have begun to be legally recognized in an effort to ease their social and economic isolation, and to improve living standards.

Standard of living
(UN human development index)
- low
- high
- figures unavailable

Environmental issues

The prospect of rising sea levels poses a threat to many low-lying islands in the Pacific. Nuclear weapons-testing, once common throughout the region, was finally discontinued in 1996. Australia's ecological balance has been irreversibly altered by the introduction of alien species. Although it has the world's largest underground water reserve, the Great Artesian Basin, the availability of fresh water in Australia remains critical. Periodic droughts combined with over-grazing lead to desertification and increase the risk of devastating bush fires, and occasional flash floods.

Environmental issues
- national parks
- tropical forest
- forest destroyed
- desert
- desertification
- polluted rivers
- radioactive contamination
- marine pollution
- heavy marine pollution
- poor urban air quality

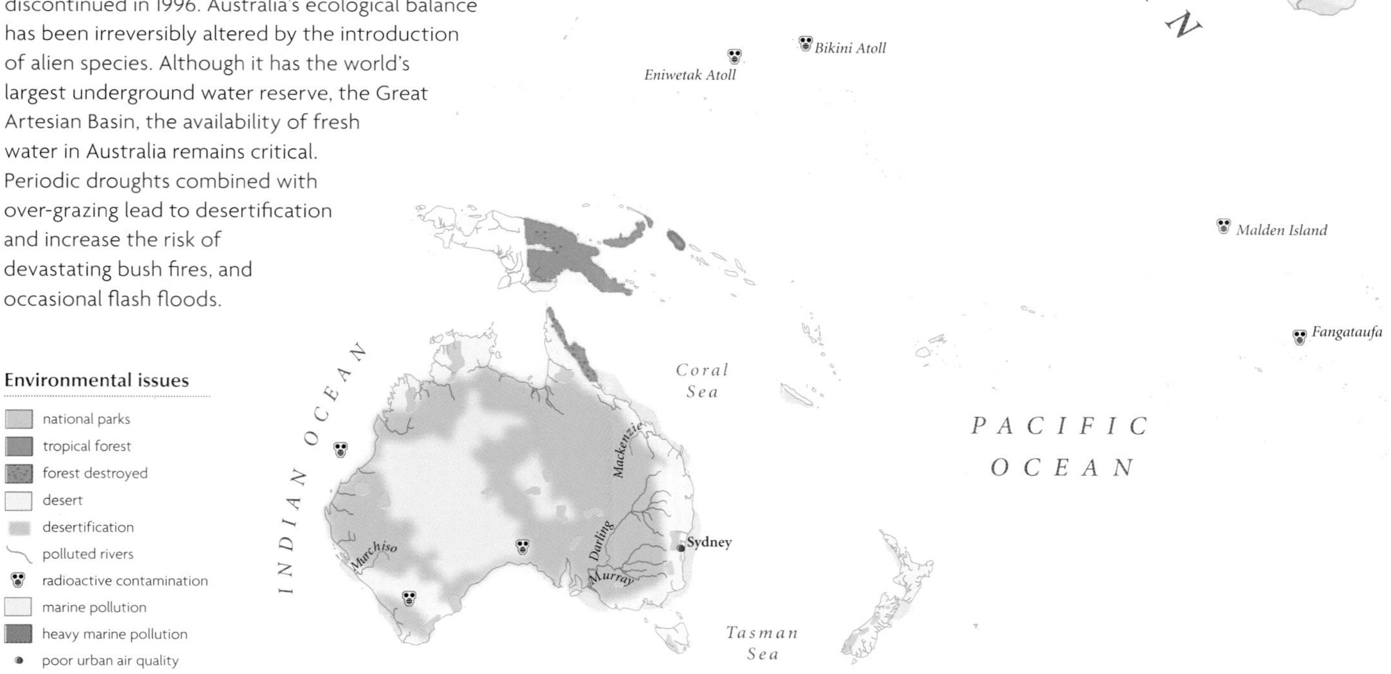

▲ *In 1946 Bikini Atoll,* in the Marshall Islands, was chosen as the site for Operation Crossroads – investigating the effects of atomic bombs upon naval vessels. Further nuclear tests continued until the early 1990s. The long-term environmental effects are unknown.

Agriculture, industry and minerals

Much of the region's industry is resource-based: sheep farming for wool and meat in Australia and New Zealand; mining in Australia and Papua New Guinea and fishing throughout the Pacific islands. Manufacturing is mainly limited to the large coastal cities in Australia and New Zealand, like Sydney, Adelaide, Melbourne, Brisbane, Perth and Auckland, although small-scale enterprises operate in the Pacific islands, concentrating on processing of fish and foods. Tourism continues to provide revenue to the area – in Fiji it accounts for 15% of GNP.

▲ *The massive Ok Tedi* copper mine was opened in 1988. It is situated in the midst of remote tropical jungle in Papua New Guinea.

▲ *Plumes of steam* rise from the electricity turbines on New Zealand's North Island. New Zealand is one of the few countries in the world where geothermal energy makes a significant contribution to national energy production.

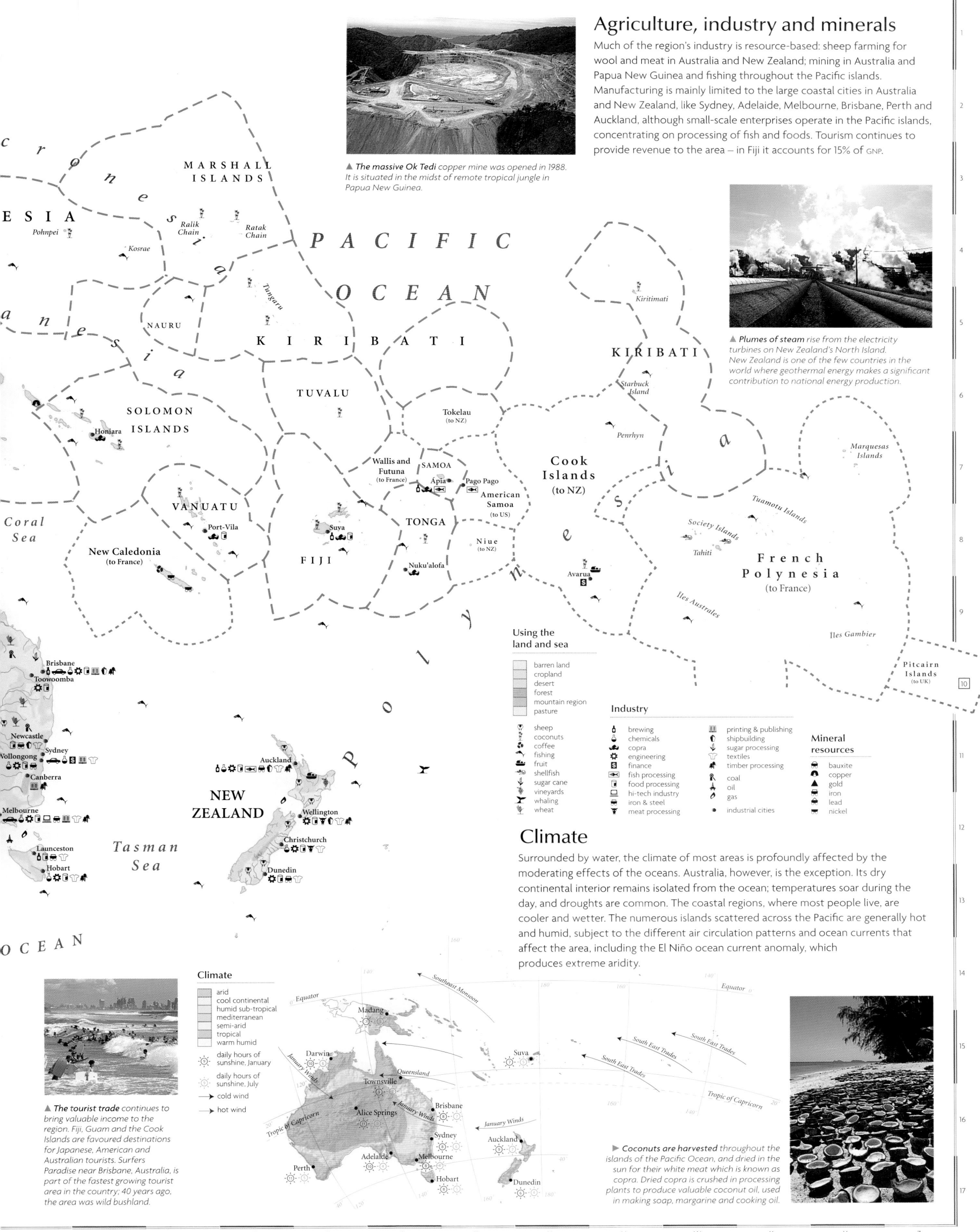

Using the land and sea

- barren land
- cropland
- desert
- forest
- mountain region
- pasture

Industry

sheep	brewing	printing & publishing
coconuts	chemicals	shipbuilding
coffee	copra	sugar processing
fishing	engineering	textiles
fruit	finance	timber processing
shellfish	fish processing	coal
sugar cane	food processing	oil
vineyards	hi-tech industry	gas
whaling	iron & steel	industrial cities
wheat	meat processing	

Mineral resources

- bauxite
- copper
- gold
- iron
- lead
- nickel

Climate

Surrounded by water, the climate of most areas is profoundly affected by the moderating effects of the oceans. Australia, however, is the exception. Its dry continental interior remains isolated from the ocean; temperatures soar during the day, and droughts are common. The coastal regions, where most people live, are cooler and wetter. The numerous islands scattered across the Pacific are generally hot and humid, subject to the different air circulation patterns and ocean currents that affect the area, including the El Niño ocean current anomaly, which produces extreme aridity.

Climate

- arid
- cool continental
- humid sub-tropical
- mediterranean
- semi-arid
- tropical
- warm humid
- daily hours of sunshine, January
- daily hours of sunshine, July
- cold wind
- hot wind

▲ *The tourist trade* continues to bring valuable income to the region. Fiji, Guam and the Cook Islands are favoured destinations for Japanese, American and Australian tourists. Surfers Paradise near Brisbane, Australia, is part of the fastest growing tourist area in the country; 40 years ago, the area was wild bushland.

▶ *Coconuts are harvested* throughout the islands of the Pacific Ocean, and dried in the sun for their white meat which is known as copra. Dried copra is crushed in processing plants to produce valuable coconut oil, used in making soap, margarine and cooking oil.

Australia

Australia is the world's smallest continent, a stable landmass lying between the Indian and Pacific oceans. Previously home to its aboriginal peoples only, since the end of the 18th century immigration has transformed the face of the country. Initially settlers came mainly from western Europe, particularly the UK, and for years Australia remained wedded to its British colonial past. More recent immigrants have come from eastern Europe, and from Asian countries such as Japan, South Korea and Indonesia. Australia is now forging strong trading links with these 'Pacific Rim' countries and its economic future seems to lie with Asia and the Americas, rather than Europe, its traditional partner.

Using the land

Over 104 million sheep are dispersed in vast herds around the country, contributing to a major export industry. Cattle-ranching is important, particularly in the west. Wheat, and grapes for Australia's wine industry, are grown mainly in the south. Much of the country is desert, unsuitable for agriculture unless irrigation is used.

The urban/rural population divide

urban 85%   rural 15%

Population density	Total land area
6 people per sq mile (2 people per sq km)	2,967,893 sq miles (7,686,850 sq km)

Land use and agricultural distribution

- cattle
- sheep
- cereals
- sugar cane
- timber
- vineyards
- ■ capital cities
- ● major towns
- pasture
- cropland
- forest
- desert
- mountain region

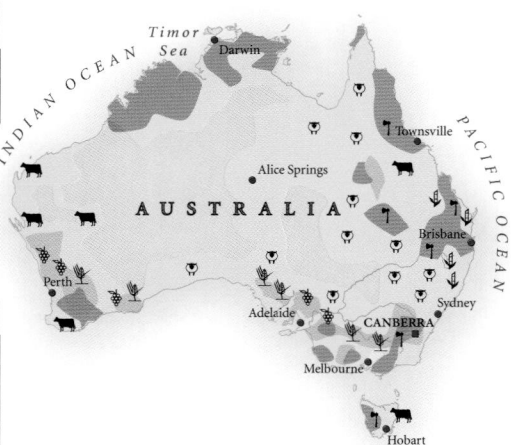

▲ *Lines of ripening* vines stretch for miles in Barossa Valley, a major wine-growing region near Adelaide.

The landscape

Australia consists of many eroded plateaux, lying firmly in the middle of the Indo-Australian Plate. It is the world's flattest continent, and the driest, after Antarctica. The coasts tend to be more hilly and fertile, especially in the east. The mountains of the Great Dividing Range form a natural barrier between the eastern coastal areas and the flat, dry plains and desert regions of the Australian 'outback.'

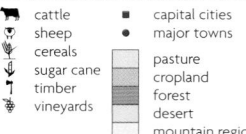

▲ *The Great Barrier Reef* is the world's largest area of coral islands and reefs. It runs for about 1240 miles (2000 km) along the Queensland coast.

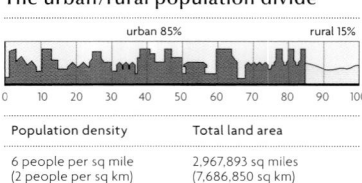

The ancient Kimberley Plateau is the source of some of Australia's richest mineral deposits, including diamonds.

The tropical rain forest of the Cape York Peninsula contains more than 600 different varieties of tree.

Uluru (Ayers Rock)

Arnhem Land

Great Artesian Basin

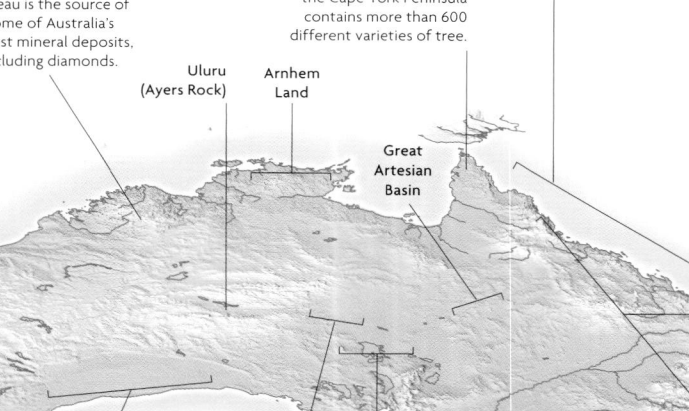

▲ *The Pinnacles are* a series of rugged sandstone pillars. Their strange shapes have been formed by water and wind erosion.

More than half of Australia rests on a uniform shield over 600 million years old. It is one of the Earth's original geological plates.

The Nullarbor Plain is a low-lying limestone plateau which is so flat that the Trans-Australian Railway runs through it in a straight line for more than 300 miles (483 km).

The Simpson Desert has a number of large salt pans, created by the evaporation of past rivers and now sourced by seasonal rains. Some are crusted with gypsum, but most are covered by common salt crystals.

The Lake Eyre basin, lying 51 ft (16 m) below sea level, is one of the largest inland drainage systems in the world, covering an area of more than 500,000 sq miles (1,300,000 sq km).

Tasmania has the same geological structure as the Australian Alps. During the last period of glaciation, 18,000 years ago, sea levels were some 300 ft (100 m) lower and it was joined to the mainland.

Australian Alps

The Great Dividing Range forms a watershed between east- and west-flowing rivers. Erosion has created deep valleys, gorges and waterfalls where rivers tumble over escarpments on their way to the sea.

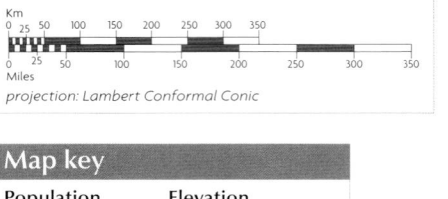

◄ *Uluru (Ayers Rock),* the world's largest free-standing rock, is a massive outcrop of red sandstone in Australia's desert centre. Wind and sandstorms have ground the rock into the smooth curves seen here. Uluru is revered as a sacred site by many aboriginal peoples.

Scale 1:10,500,000

Km
0 25 50   100   150   200   250   300 350

Miles
0 25 50   100   150   200   250   300 350

projection: Lambert Conformal Conic

Map key

Population	
▣	1 million to 5 million
◉	500,000 to 1 million
◎	100,000 to 500,000
⊕	50,000 to 100,000
○	10,000 to 50,000
∘	below 10,000

Elevation

- 2000m / 6562ft
- 1000m / 3281ft
- 500m / 1640ft
- 250m / 820ft
- 100m / 328ft
- sea level

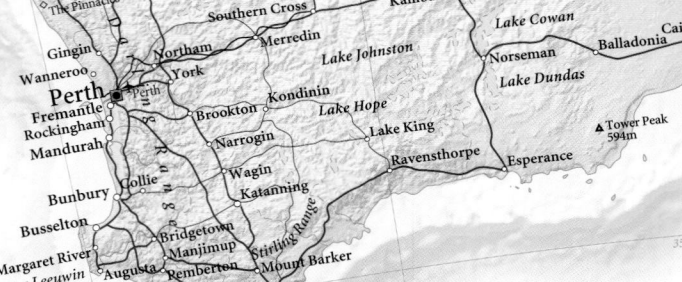

Great Artesian Basin

Rainwater replenishes aquifer

Aquifers from which artesian water is obtained

Lake Eyre

Underground water movements

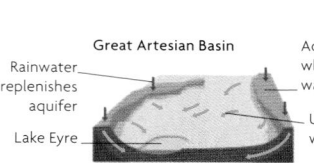

▲ *The Great Artesian Basin* underlies nearly 20% of the total area of Australia, providing a valuable store of underground water, essential to Australian agriculture. The ephemeral rivers which drain the northern part of the basin have highly braided courses and, in consequence, the area is known as 'channel country.'

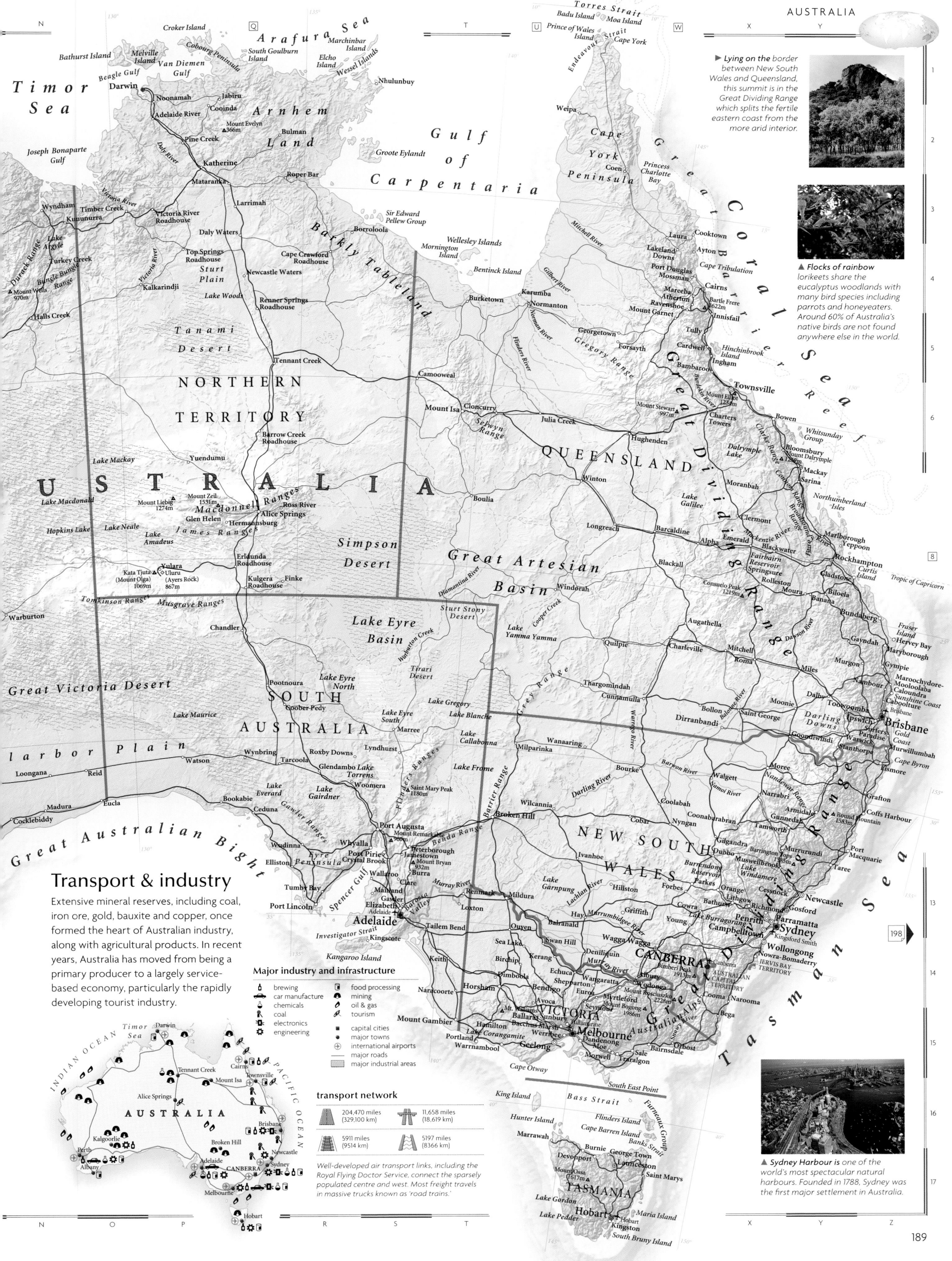

► Lying on the border between New South Wales and Queensland, this summit is in the Great Dividing Range which splits the fertile eastern coast from the more arid interior.

▲ Flocks of rainbow lorikeets share the eucalyptus woodlands with many bird species including parrots and honeyeaters. Around 60% of Australia's native birds are not found anywhere else in the world.

Transport & industry

Extensive mineral reserves, including coal, iron ore, gold, bauxite and copper, once formed the heart of Australian industry, along with agricultural products. In recent years, Australia has moved from being a primary producer to a largely service-based economy, particularly the rapidly developing tourist industry.

Major industry and infrastructure

- ♨ brewing
- 🚗 car manufacture
- ⚗ chemicals
- ⬟ coal
- electronics
- ✦ engineering
- 🏭 food processing
- ⚒ mining
- ◭ oil & gas
- ☂ tourism

- ■ capital cities
- ● major towns
- ✈ international airports
- — major roads
- ▨ major industrial areas

transport network

204,470 miles (329,100 km)		11,658 miles (18,619 km)	
5911 miles (9514 km)		5197 miles (8366 km)	

Well-developed air transport links, including the Royal Flying Doctor Service, connect the sparsely populated centre and west. Most freight travels in massive trucks known as 'road trains.'

▲ Sydney Harbour is one of the world's most spectacular natural harbours. Founded in 1788, Sydney was the first major settlement in Australia.

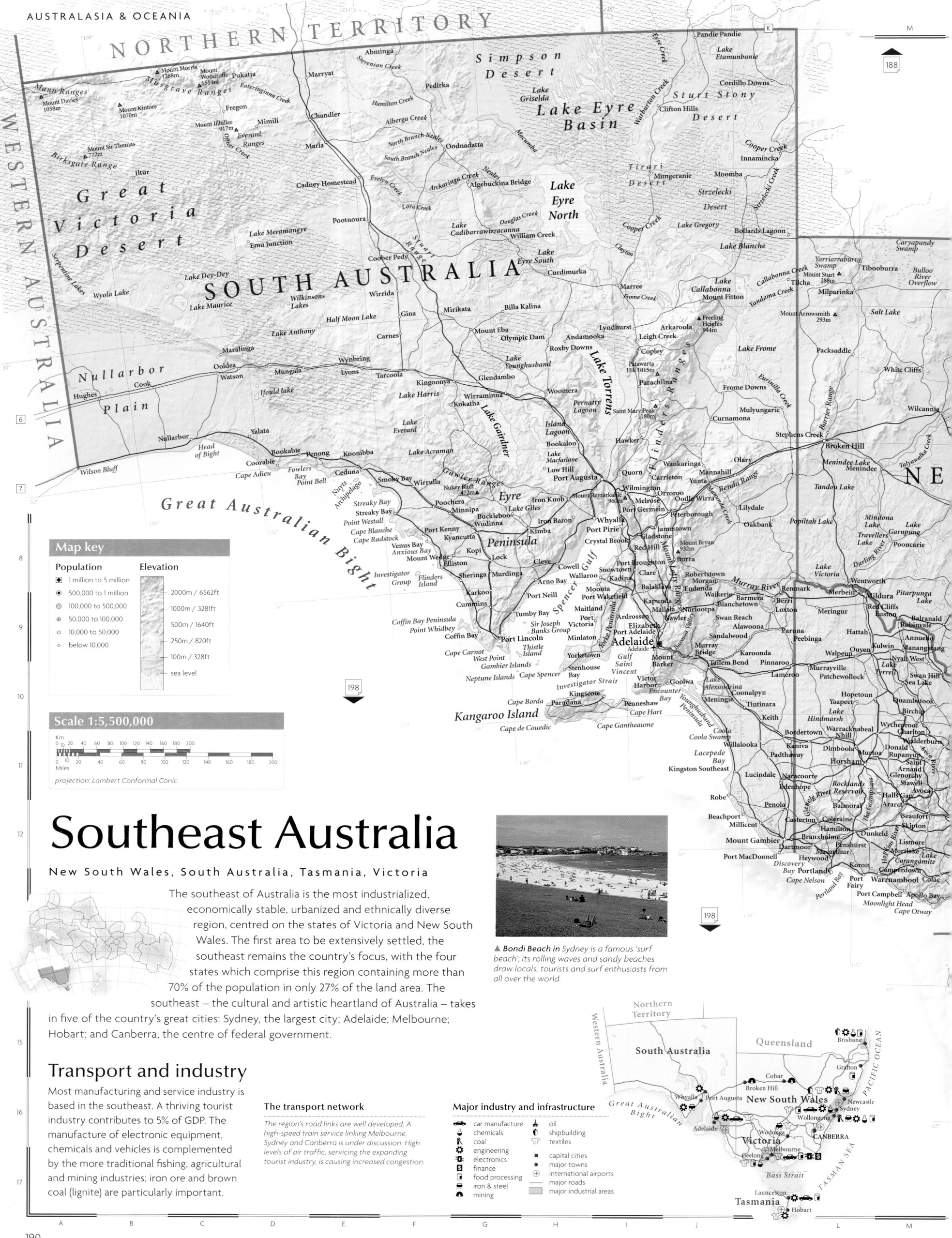

Southeast Australia

New South Wales, South Australia, Tasmania, Victoria

The southeast of Australia is the most industrialized, economically stable, urbanized and ethnically diverse region, centred on the states of Victoria and New South Wales. The first area to be extensively settled, the southeast remains the country's focus, with the four states which comprise this region containing more than 70% of the population in only 27% of the land area. The southeast – the cultural and artistic heartland of Australia – takes in five of the country's great cities: Sydney, the largest city; Adelaide; Melbourne; Hobart; and Canberra, the centre of federal government.

Transport and industry

Most manufacturing and service industry is based in the southeast. A thriving tourist industry contributes to 5% of GDP. The manufacture of electronic equipment, chemicals and vehicles is complemented by the more traditional fishing, agricultural and mining industries; iron ore and brown coal (lignite) are particularly important.

The transport network

The region's road links are well developed. A high-speed train service linking Melbourne, Sydney and Canberra is under discussion. High levels of air traffic, servicing the expanding tourist industry, is causing increased congestion.

Major industry and infrastructure

- car manufacture
- chemicals
- coal
- engineering
- electronics
- finance
- food processing
- iron & steel
- mining
- oil
- shipbuilding
- textiles
- capital cities
- major towns
- international airports
- major roads
- major industrial areas

▲ *Bondi Beach in Sydney is a famous 'surf beach'; its rolling waves and sandy beaches draw locals, tourists and surf enthusiasts from all over the world.*

Map key

Population
- 1 million to 5 million
- 500,000 to 1 million
- 100,000 to 500,000
- 50,000 to 100,000
- 10,000 to 50,000
- below 10,000

Elevation
- 2000m / 6562ft
- 1000m / 3281ft
- 500m / 1640ft
- 250m / 820ft
- 100m / 328ft
- sea level

Scale 1:5,500,000

projection: Lambert Conformal Conic

Using the land and sea

The western flanks of the Great Dividing Range and the northern deserts of South Australia support massive herds of sheep and cattle, while more intensive stock-rearing occurs near the cities. Sugar cane is the most important industrial crop, and cereals including wheat, maize, barley and sorghum are also grown. Grapes, citrus and orchard fruits are among the wide range of fruit and vegetables cultivated in this region. Tasmania's forestry and fishing contributes to over one-third of the state's exports.

▲ *The fertile Darling Downs, known as the 'breadbasket of Australia', support a wide range of crops including cereals, sugar cane and fruit.*

▶ *The Murray River has its source in the eastern uplands of the Great Dividing Range. Fed by melting snow, it runs for 1609 miles (2589 km), and has sufficient volume to reach the ocean southeast of Adelaide despite a minimal gradient for most of its lower reaches.*

The urban/rural population divide

urban 85%   rural 15%

0 10 20 30 40 50 60 70 80 90 100

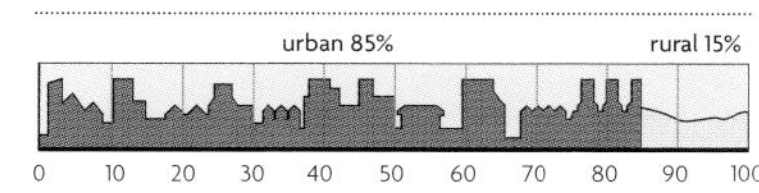

Population density	Total land area
18 people per sq mile (7 people per sq km)	778,022 sq miles (2,015,600 sq km)

Land use and agricultural distribution

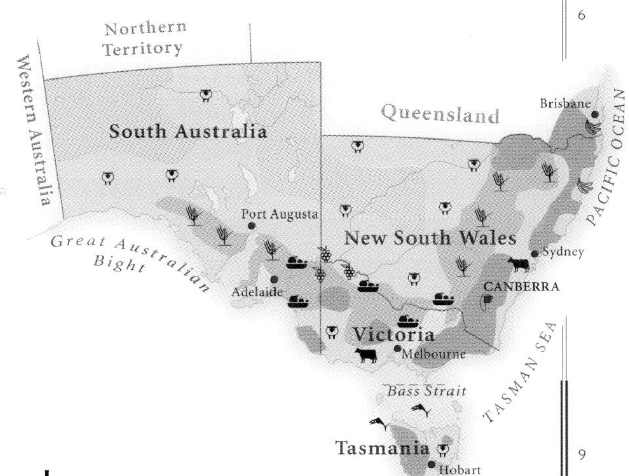

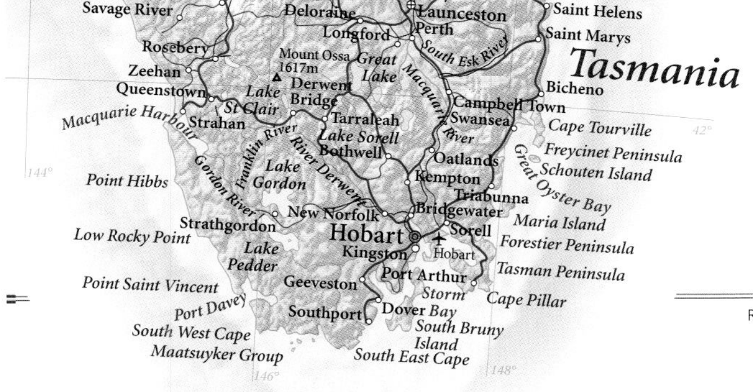

- cattle
- sheep
- bananas
- fishing
- fruit
- vineyards
- wheat

- ▪ capital cities
- • major towns

- pasture
- cropland
- forest
- desert
- mountain region

The landscape

The southern half of the Great Dividing Range runs parallel to the eastern coast of Victoria and New South Wales as far as Tasmania, which, though divided from the mainland is part of the same mountain chain. South Australia comprises the Australian shield and half of the dry, flat Nullarbor Plain. The Murray/Darling river basin is the only major river system.

◀ *The heavily folded Flinders Ranges is part of an arc of sedimentary rocks reaching northward from Kangaroo Island.*

Shallow continental shelf
Past land link
Bass Strait
Tasmania

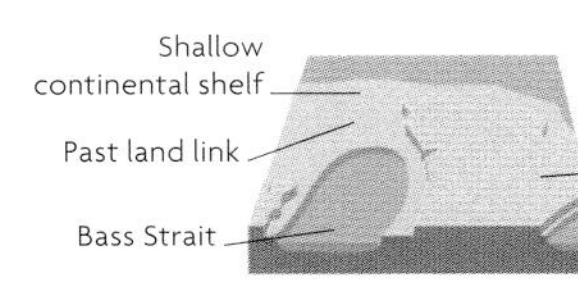

▲ *Tasmania is part of Australia's eastern highlands, separated from the mainland by 155 miles (250 km) of the Bass Strait. In the recent geological past, dry land links between Tasmania and Victoria would have been possible during periods of world-wide glaciation, when the sea level was more than 180 ft (55 m) below that of present sea levels.*

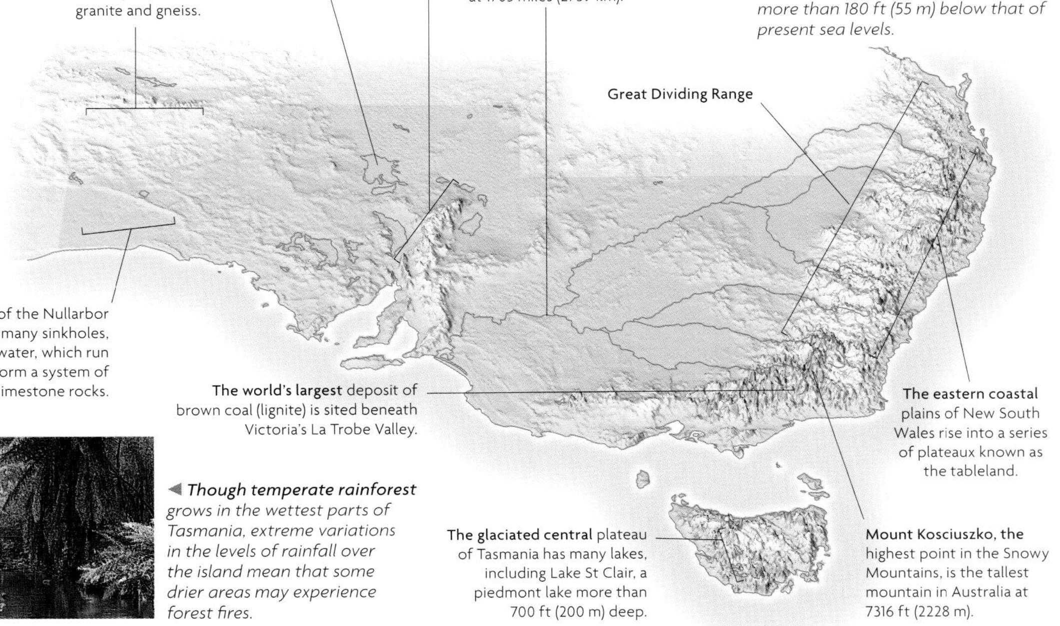

Lake Eyre is the largest of southern Australia's dry lakes. Lying -51 ft (-16 m) below sea level, it has flooded only three times in the last century.

The Musgrave and Everard ranges form bare, rounded hills made up of ancient granite and gneiss.

The Murray/Darling is Australia's longest river at 1703 miles (2739 km).

Great Dividing Range

The eastern part of the Nullarbor Plain has many sinkholes, eroded by rainwater, which run underground to form a system of long caves in the limestone rocks.

The world's largest deposit of brown coal (lignite) is sited beneath Victoria's La Trobe Valley.

The eastern coastal plains of New South Wales rise into a series of plateaux known as the tableland.

◀ *Though temperate rainforest grows in the wettest parts of Tasmania, extreme variations in the levels of rainfall over the island mean that some drier areas may experience forest fires.*

The glaciated central plateau of Tasmania has many lakes, including Lake St Clair, a piedmont lake more than 700 ft (200 m) deep.

Mount Kosciuszko, the highest point in the Snowy Mountains, is the tallest mountain in Australia at 7316 ft (2228 m).

New Zealand

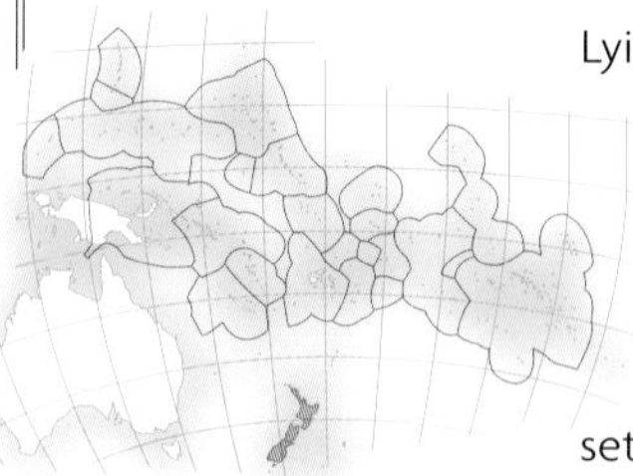

Lying 1500 miles east-southeast of Australia, New Zealand was originally settled by the Maori, a people with Polynesian roots. It was one of the last major landmasses to be visited by Europeans. The islands' rugged topography means that most settlement has concentrated in coastal areas. People of European origin make up about 70% of the population of 4 million, following immigration from the 1920s onwards. Many recent settlers have come from Asia, including India and China, and a number of the Pacific Islands. Although the Maori now make up a minority of less than half a million, their ancient claims to at least half of national territory are gaining increasing legal credence.

The landscape

New Zealand comprises two large islands and many scattered smaller islands. On South Island the Alpine Fault marks the boundary between the Pacific and Indo-Australian plates. Tectonic activity has strongly influenced the formation of the Southern Alps, snow-capped mountains with several peaks over 9800 ft (3000 m). North Island has a lower and less extensive mountain region, containing forested hills, a central volcanic plateau and downlands.

Mountain-building in the Southern Alps

North Island
Alpine Fault
Pacific Plate
South Island
Southern Alps
Indo-Australian Plate

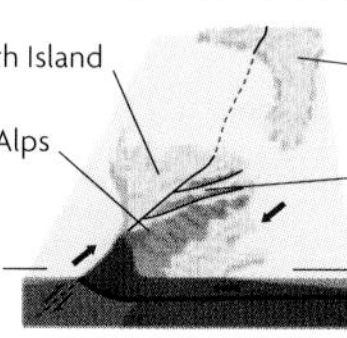

▲ **The Southern Alps** have been formed by 'slip' faulting. The Indo-Australian and Pacific plates run in opposite directions along the Alpine Fault. Although they slide past each other, they are also being thrust over one another, causing the continental crust of the Pacific Plate to be uplifted to form the Alps.

The Southern Alps run for more than 300 miles, (483 km) forming the backbone of South Island. They were uplifted following the collision of the Pacific and Indo-Australian plates.

Fiordland in the far south west, contains a large number of flooded glacial valleys.

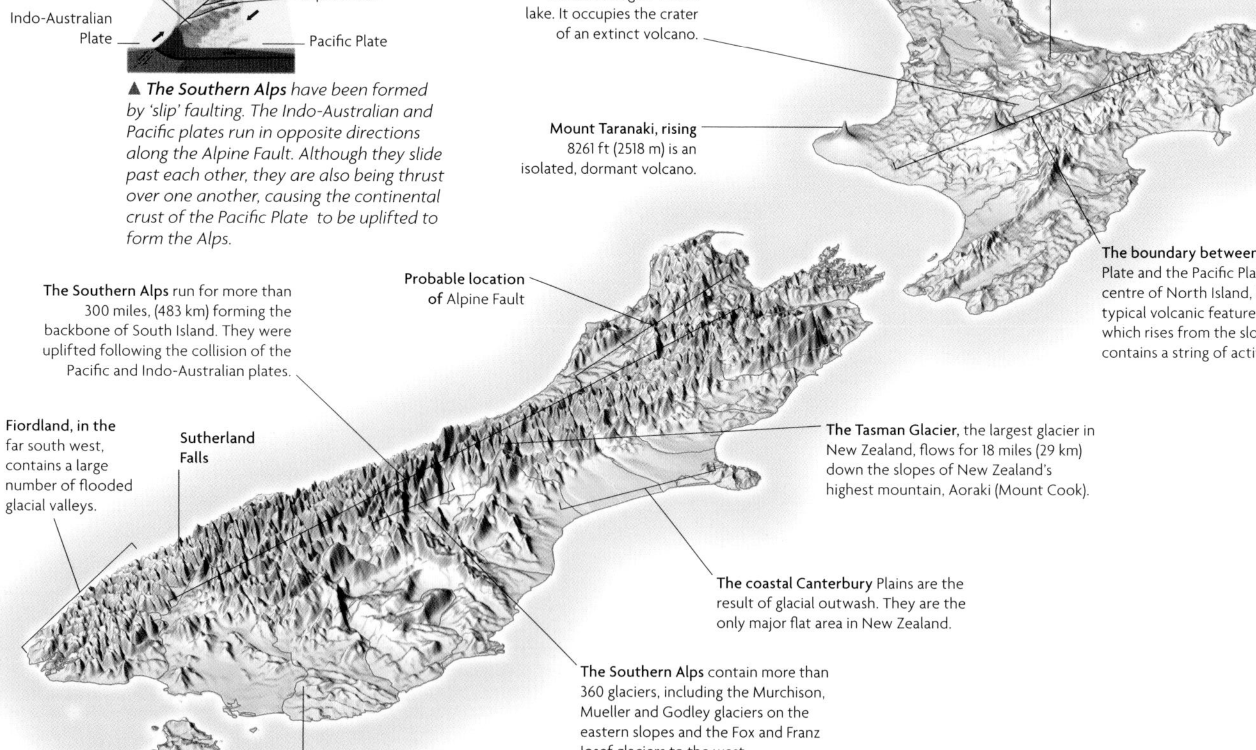

▲ **Clouds of steam** rise from White Island, an active, offshore volcano lying in the Bay of Plenty, off the northern coast of North Island.

Scale 1:2,750,000
projection: Lambert Conformal Conic

▼ **The Northland region** is characterized by many coastal inlets. These are lined by mangrove swamps, signalling the change to a subtropical climate in the far north of the island.

Northland

▼ **The Rotorua and** Taupo valleys have some of the largest and most spectacular thermal springs in New Zealand. These occur when superheated groundwater rises to the surface through joints in the rocks.

Rotorua

The boundary between the Indo-Australian Plate and the Pacific Plate runs through the centre of North Island, leading to many typical volcanic features. The plateau which rises from the slopes of Lake Taupo contains a string of active volcanoes.

Lake Taupo is New Zealand's largest inland lake. It occupies the crater of an extinct volcano.

Mount Taranaki, rising 8261 ft (2518 m) is an isolated, dormant volcano.

Probable location of Alpine Fault

Sutherland Falls

High levels of rainfall and a steep topography has made New Zealand's rivers swift-running. In the southern reaches of both islands, the rivers such as the Mokoreta form broad, braided streams.

The Southern Alps contain more than 360 glaciers, including the Murchison, Mueller and Godley glaciers on the eastern slopes and the Fox and Franz Josef glaciers to the west.

The coastal Canterbury Plains are the result of glacial outwash. They are the only major flat area in New Zealand.

The Tasman Glacier, the largest glacier in New Zealand, flows for 18 miles (29 km) down the slopes of New Zealand's highest mountain, Aoraki (Mount Cook).

PACIFIC OCEAN

TASMAN SEA

North Island

South Island

NEW ZEALAND

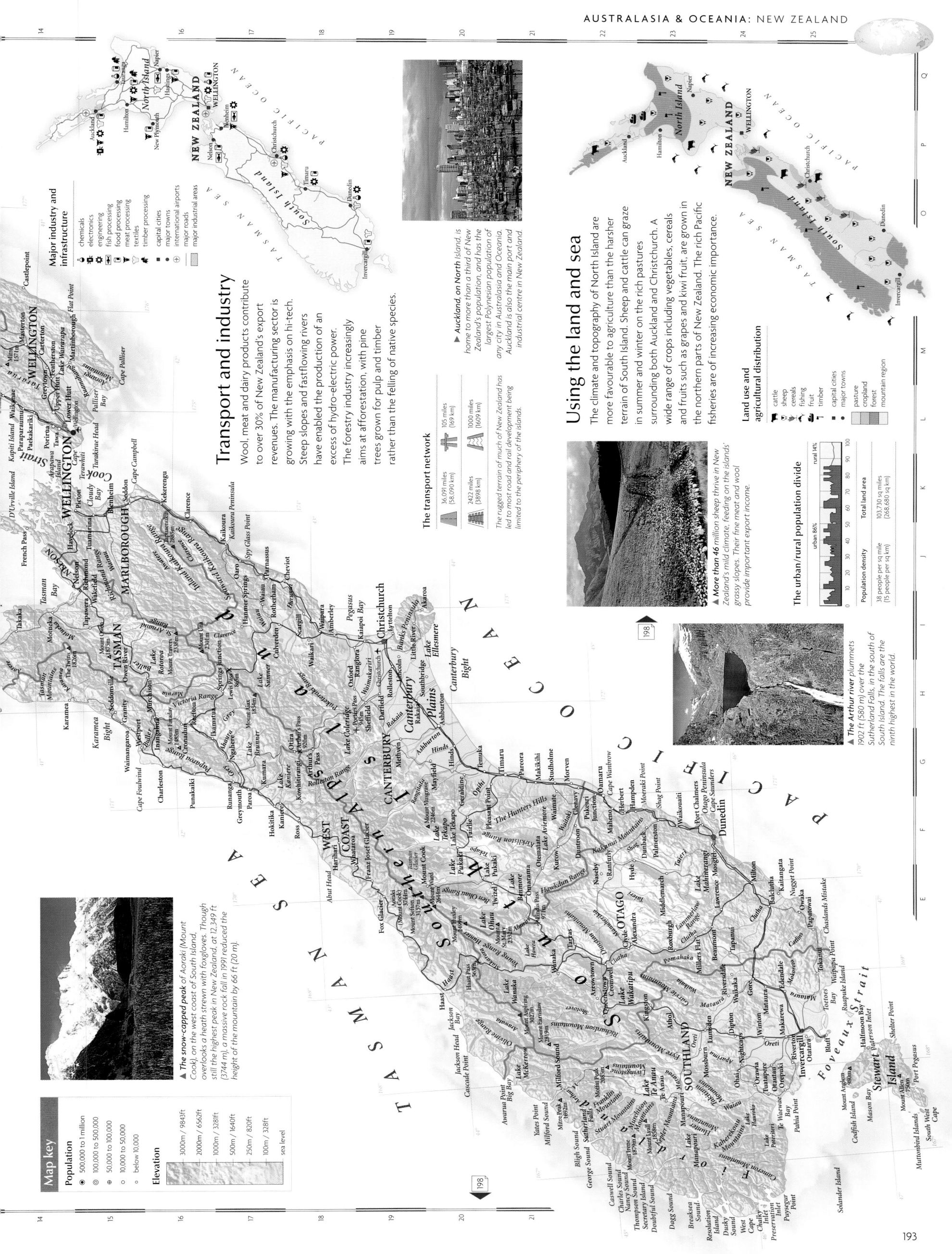

Transport and industry

Wool, meat and dairy products contribute to over 30% of New Zealand's export revenues. The manufacturing sector is growing with the emphasis on hi-tech. Steep slopes and fastflowing rivers have enabled the production of an excess of hydro-electric power. The forestry industry increasingly aims at afforestation, with pine trees grown for pulp and timber rather than the felling of native species.

The transport network

36,091 miles (58,090 km)	105 miles (169 km)
2442 miles (3898 km)	1000 miles (1609 km)

The rugged terrain of much of New Zealand has led to most road and rail development being limited to the periphery of the islands.

Major industry and infrastructure

- chemicals
- electronics
- engineering
- fish processing
- food processing
- meat processing
- textiles
- timber processing
- capital cities
- major towns
- international airports
- major roads
- major industrial areas

▲ *Auckland, on North Island, is home to more than a third of New Zealand's population, and has the largest Polynesian population of any city in Australasia and Oceania. Auckland is also the main port and industrial centre in New Zealand.*

Using the land and sea

The climate and topography of North Island are more favourable to agriculture than the harsher terrain of South Island. Sheep and cattle can graze in summer and winter on the rich pastures surrounding both Auckland and Christchurch. A wide range of crops including vegetables, cereals and fruits such as grapes and kiwi fruit, are grown in the northern parts of New Zealand. The rich Pacific fisheries are of increasing economic importance.

▲ *More than 46 million sheep thrive in New Zealand's mild climate, feeding on the islands' grassy slopes. Their fine meat and wool provide important export income.*

▲ *The Arthur river plummets 1902 ft (580 m) over the Sutherland Falls, in the south of South Island. The falls are the ninth highest in the world.*

Land use and agricultural distribution

- cattle
- sheep
- cereals
- fruit
- timber
- capital cities
- major towns
- pasture
- cropland
- forest
- mountain region

The urban/rural population divide

Population density	Total land area
38 people per sq mile (15 people per sq km)	103,730 sq miles (268,680 sq km)

urban 86% · rural 14%

Map key

Population

- 500,000 to 1 million
- 100,000 to 500,000
- 50,000 to 100,000
- 10,000 to 50,000
- below 10,000

Elevation

- 3000m / 9843ft
- 2000m / 6562ft
- 1000m / 3281ft
- 500m / 1640ft
- 250m / 820ft
- 100m / 328ft
- sea level

▲ *The snow-capped peak of Aoraki (Mount Cook), on the west coast of South Island, overlooks a heath strewn with foxgloves. Though still the highest peak in New Zealand, at 12,349 ft (3744 m), a massive rock fall in 1991 reduced the height of the mountain by 66 ft (20 m).*

Papua New Guinea & the Solomon Islands

Cut off by inaccessible, largely mountainous terrain, the peoples of Papua New Guinea have maintained a remarkable diversity of language and culture. There are over 750 separate languages, and yet more distinct tribes. Much of the country remains isolated, with many of the indigenous inhabitants of the interior living as hunter-gatherers. To the east of Papua New Guinea, the Solomons form an archipelago of several hundred islands, scattered over an area of 252,897 sq miles (655,000 sq km). The Solomon Islanders, a mainly Melanesian people, live on the six largest islands.

Using the land and sea

Most agriculture in Papua New Guinea is at a subsistence level, with more than two-thirds of the land used for rough grazing, particularly for pigs. The tropical rainforest is a rich timber resource. The Solomon Islanders rely heavily on coconuts for export revenue and fishing, mainly for tuna, is a staple industry.

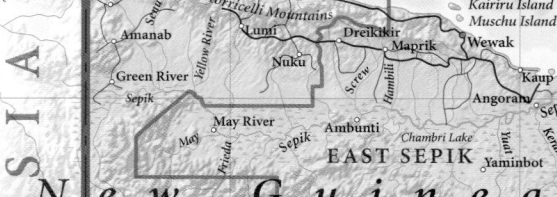

Land use and agricultural distribution

- bananas
- cocoa
- coconuts
- fishing
- oil palms
- rubber
- timber
- capital cities
- major towns
- cropland
- forest
- wetland

◄ Over 70% of Papua New Guinea is covered by dense, tropical rainforest, sustained by high levels of rainfall. Uncontrolled logging in the formerly inaccessible rainforest has led to species loss and soil erosion on steep slopes.

The urban/rural population divide

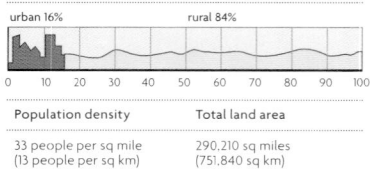

urban 16%   rural 84%

0 10 20 30 40 50 60 70 80 90 100

Population density	Total land area
33 people per sq mile (13 people per sq km)	290,210 sq miles (751,840 sq km)

Map key

Population
- ⊚ 100,000 to 500,000
- ⊕ 50,000 to 100,000
- ○ 10,000 to 50,000
- ○ below 10,000

Elevation
- 4000m / 13,124ft
- 3000m / 9843ft
- 2000m / 6562ft
- 1000m / 3281ft
- 500m / 1640ft
- 250m / 820ft
- 100m / 328ft
- sea level

◄ Huli tribesmen from Southern Highlands Province in Papua New Guinea parade in ceremonial dress, their powdered wigs decorated with exotic plumage and their faces and bodies painted with coloured pigments.

Transport and industry

Papua New Guinea has substantial mineral resources including the world's largest copper reserves at Panguna on Bougainville Island; gold, and potential oil and natural gas. Political instability on Bougainville and an undeveloped infrastructure deters the investment necessary for exploition of these reserves. The Solomon Islanders rely mainly on copra and timber with some production of palm oil and cocoa. Traditional crafts are made for the tourist market and for export.

The transport network

🛣	513 miles (825 km)
	None
	None
	6794 miles (10,940 km)

Much of Papua New Guinea and the Solomons is inaccessible by road. A network of airstrips serves even remote villages on the islands. The Solomons' airport has been extended to take jumbo jets to improve connections for tourism.

► The slopes of this extinct volcano near Talasea on the island of New Britain have been almost entirely colonized by rainforest vegetation.

Major industry and infrastructure

- beverages
- coffee processing
- copra processing
- food processing
- mining
- textiles
- timber processing
- ■ capital cities
- ● major towns
- ⊕ international airports
- — major roads

Scale 1:5,500,000

Km
0 10 20 40 60 80 100 120 140 160 180 200

Miles
0 10 20 40 60 80 100 120 140 160 180 200

projection: Mercator

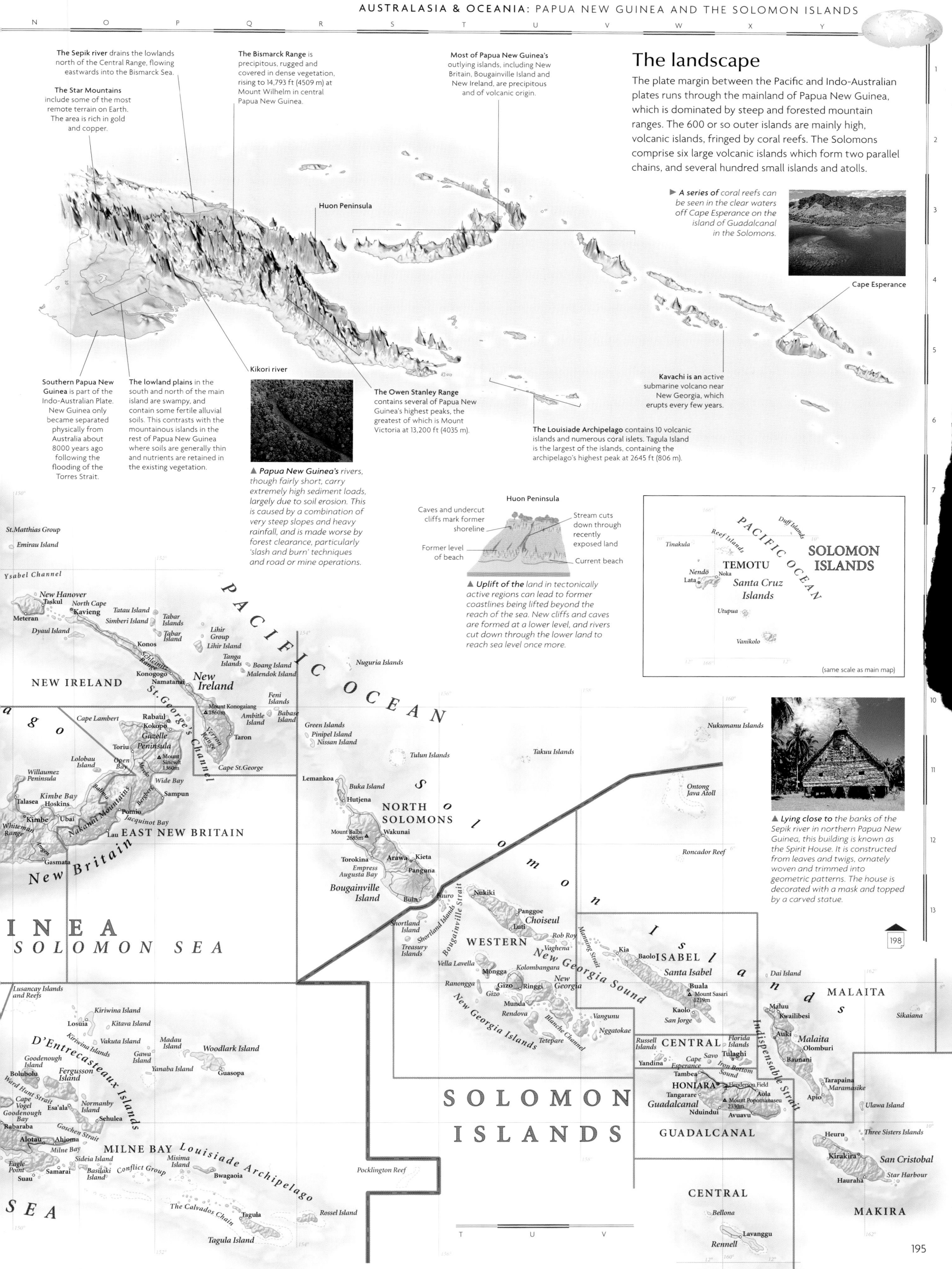

N O P Q R S T U V W X Y

The Sepik river drains the lowlands north of the Central Range, flowing eastwards into the Bismarck Sea.

The Star Mountains include some of the most remote terrain on Earth. The area is rich in gold and copper.

The Bismarck Range is precipitous, rugged and covered in dense vegetation, rising to 14,793 ft (4509 m) at Mount Wilhelm in central Papua New Guinea.

Most of Papua New Guinea's outlying islands, including New Britain, Bougainville Island and New Ireland, are precipitous and of volcanic origin.

Huon Peninsula

The landscape

The plate margin between the Pacific and Indo-Australian plates runs through the mainland of Papua New Guinea, which is dominated by steep and forested mountain ranges. The 600 or so outer islands are mainly high, volcanic islands, fringed by coral reefs. The Solomons comprise six large volcanic islands which form two parallel chains, and several hundred small islands and atolls.

▶ *A series of coral reefs can be seen in the clear waters off Cape Esperance on the island of Guadalcanal in the Solomons.*

Cape Esperance

Southern Papua New Guinea is part of the Indo-Australian Plate. New Guinea only became separated physically from Australia about 8000 years ago following the flooding of the Torres Strait.

The lowland plains in the south and north of the main island are swampy, and contain some fertile alluvial soils. This contrasts with the mountainous islands in the rest of Papua New Guinea where soils are generally thin and nutrients are retained in the existing vegetation.

Kikori river

The Owen Stanley Range contains several of Papua New Guinea's highest peaks, the greatest of which is Mount Victoria at 13,200 ft (4035 m).

Kavachi is an active submarine volcano near New Georgia, which erupts every few years.

The Louisiade Archipelago contains 10 volcanic islands and numerous coral islets. Tagula Island is the largest of the islands, containing the archipelago's highest peak at 2645 ft (806 m).

▲ *Papua New Guinea's rivers, though fairly short, carry extremely high sediment loads, largely due to soil erosion. This is caused by a combination of very steep slopes and heavy rainfall, and is made worse by forest clearance, particularly 'slash and burn' techniques and road or mine operations.*

Huon Peninsula

Caves and undercut cliffs mark former shoreline

Former level of beach

Stream cuts down through recently exposed land

Current beach

▲ *Uplift of the land in tectonically active regions can lead to former coastlines being lifted beyond the reach of the sea. New cliffs and caves are formed at a lower level, and rivers cut down through the lower land to reach sea level once more.*

SOLOMON ISLANDS

PACIFIC OCEAN

Duff Islands

Reef Islands

Tinakula

TEMOTU

Nendö
Lata
Noka

Santa Cruz Islands

Utupua

Vanikolo

(same scale as main map)

▲ *Lying close to the banks of the Sepik river in northern Papua New Guinea, this building is known as the Spirit House. It is constructed from leaves and twigs, ornately woven and trimmed into geometric patterns. The house is decorated with a mask and topped by a carved statue.*

198

St.Matthias Group
Emirau Island

Ysabel Channel

New Hanover
Taskul
North Cape
Kavieng
Meteran
Dyaul Island

Tatau Island
Simberi Island
Tabar Islands
Tabar Island

Lihir Group
Lihir Island

Konos
Schleinitz Range
Konogogo
Namatanai

Tanga Islands
Boang Island
Malendok Island

Nuguria Islands

St.George's Channel

NEW IRELAND
New Ireland

Feni Islands
Mount Konogaiang
1860m
Ambitle Island
Babase Island

PACIFIC OCEAN

Cape Lambert
Rabaul
Kokopo
Gazelle Peninsula
Toriu
Open Bay
Mount Sinewit
1360m

Taron

Varron Range
Cape St.George

Green Islands
Pinipel Island
Nissan Island

Tulun Islands

Takuu Islands

Nukumanu Islands

Lolobau Island
Willaumez Peninsula
Talasea
Kimbe Bay
Hoskins
Kimbe
Ubai
Whiteman Range
Gasmata

Nakanai Mountains
Baining
Wide Bay
Sampun
Jacquinot Bay
Pomio
Lau EAST NEW BRITAIN

Lemankoa
Buka Island
Hutjena

S o l o m o n

Ontong Java Atoll

New Britain

INEA
SOLOMON SEA

NORTH SOLOMONS
Wakunai
Mount Balbi
2685m
Torokina
Arawa
Kieta
Panguna
Empress Augusta Bay
Bougainville Island
Buin
Kauro

Nukiki

Panggoe
Luti
Choiseul

Roncador Reef

I s l a n d s

Lusancay Islands and Reefs

Shortland Island
Shortland Islands
Treasury Islands

Bougainville Strait

Rob Roy
Kia

WESTERN
Vaghena
New Georgia Sound

Baolo
ISABEL
Santa Isabel
Buala
Mount Sasari
1219m

Dai Island

MALAITA

Kiriwina Island
Kitava Island
Losuia
Vakuta Island
D'Entrecasteaux Islands
Kiriwina Islands
Gawa Island
Madau Island
Yanaba Island
Woodlark Island
Guasopa

Vella Lavella
Mongga
Kolombangara
Ranongga
Gizo
Gizo
Ringgi
New Georgia
Munda
Rendova

Manning Strait

Kaolo
San Jorge

Maluu
Kwailibesi
Auki
Malaita
Olomburi

Sikaiana

Goodenough Island
Bolubolu
Fergusson Island
Ward Hunt Strait
Cape Vogel
Goodenough Bay
Rabaraba
Esa'ala
Normanby Island
Sehulea

Gawa Island

Blanche Channel
Vangunu
Nggatokae
Tetepare

Russell Islands
Yandina

CENTRAL
Florida Islands
Savo
Tulaghi
Cape Esperance
Tambea
Iron Bottom Sound

Tarapaina
Maramasike
Apio

Ulawa Island

Goschen Strait
Alotau
Ahioma
Milne Bay
MILNE BAY
Samarai
Basilaki Island

Misima Island

SOLOMON ISLANDS

HONIARA
Tangarare
Guadalcanal
Nduindui
Avuavu

Henderson Field
Aola
Mount Popomanaseu
2330m

Heruru
Three Sisters Islands
Kirakira
Hauraha
San Cristobal
Star Harbour

Eagle Point
Suau

Conflict Group

Louisiade Archipelago
Bwagaoia
Tagula

Pocklington Reef

GUADALCANAL

CENTRAL

MAKIRA

SEA

The Calvados Chain
Tagula
Tagula Island

Rossel Island

Bellona
Rennell

Lavanggu

The Pacific Ocean

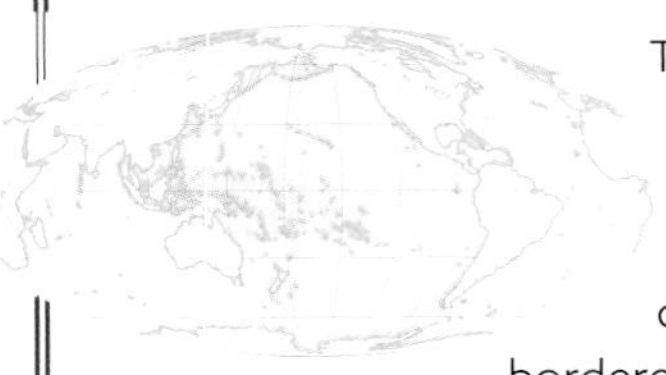

The Pacific is the world's largest and deepest ocean. It is nearly twice the area of the Atlantic and contains almost three times as much water. The ocean is dotted with islands and surrounded by some of the world's most populous states; over half the world's population lives on its shores. The Pacific is bordered by active plate margins known as the 'Ring of Fire', causing earthquakes and tsunamis, and creating volcanic islands and subterranean mountain chains. The largest underwater mountains break the surface as island arcs. The fisheries of the Pacific are some of the most productive in the world and provide a vital resource for many of the Pacific islands. Since the Second World War there has been a shift in trading patterns, with a considerable growth in trade between the United States and the countries of the Pacific Rim.

Map key

Population
○ below 10,000

Elevation
- 1000m / 3281ft
- 500m / 1640ft
- 250m / 820ft
- 100m / 328ft
- sea level

Sea Depth
- sea level
- 250m / 820ft
- 500m / 1640ft
- 1000m / 3281ft
- 2000m / 6562ft
- 3000m / 9843ft
- 5000m / 16,410ft

Scale 1:50,000,000
Km 0 200 400 600 800 1000
Miles 0 200 400 600 800 1000
projection: Mollweide

American Samoa and Samoa

American Samoa and Samoa are part of the island archipelago of Polynesia. The two most populous islands are Tutuila in American Samoa and Upolu in Samoa. Although the economies of both these states remain predominantly resource-based, both are expanding their light manufacturing sectors, and the US administration is the primary employer in American Samoa. Tuna fishing is particularly important: 25% of all tuna consumed in the USA is processed and canned in Pago Pago.

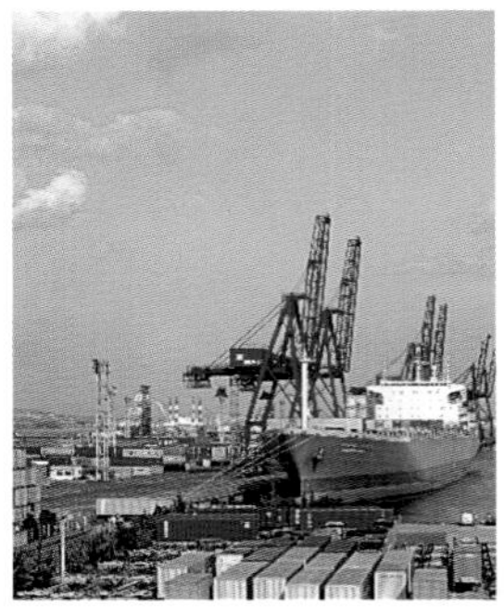

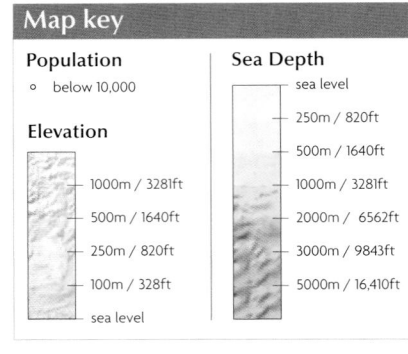

► *Japan is one of the major trading nations within the Pacific, importing iron and steel from Australia, and grain from the USA. The major exports from the 'Pacific Rim' are electronics, precision equipment and motor cars.*

SCALE 1:3,000,000
0 10 20 40 Km
0 10 20 40 Miles

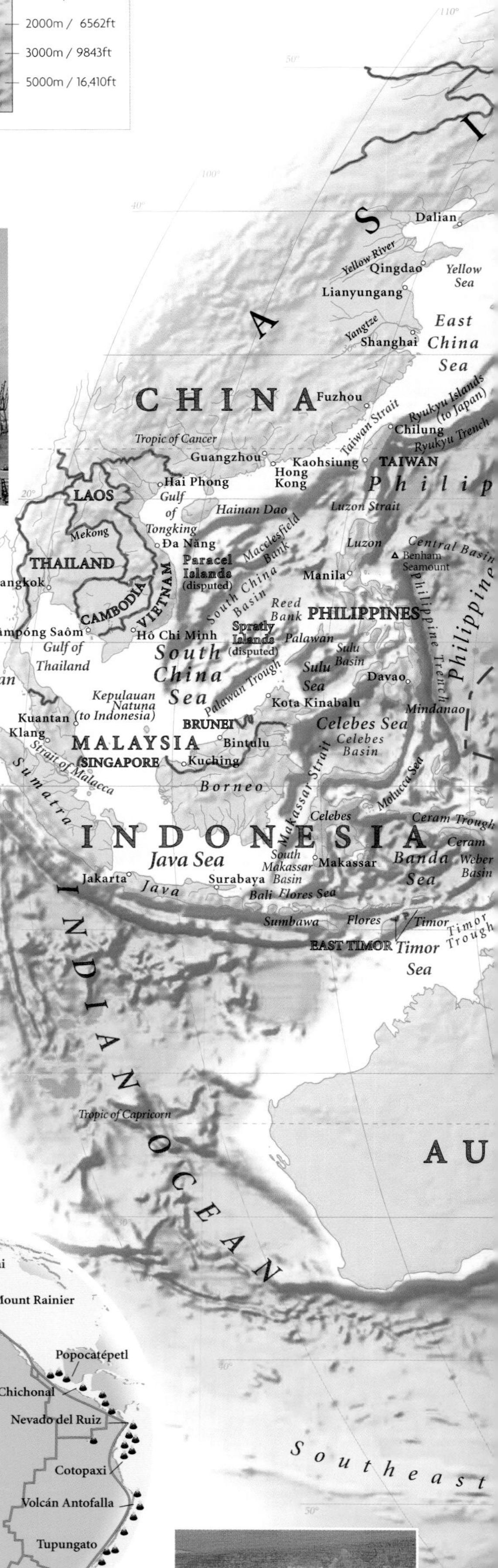

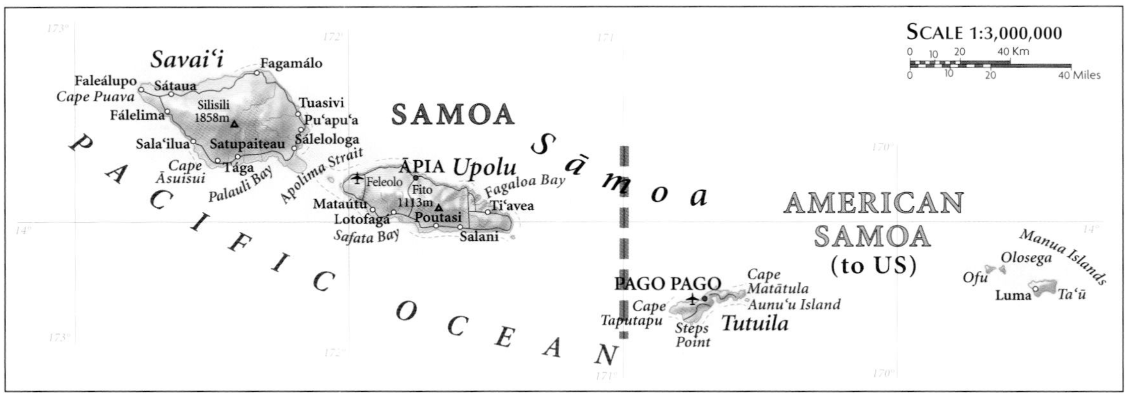

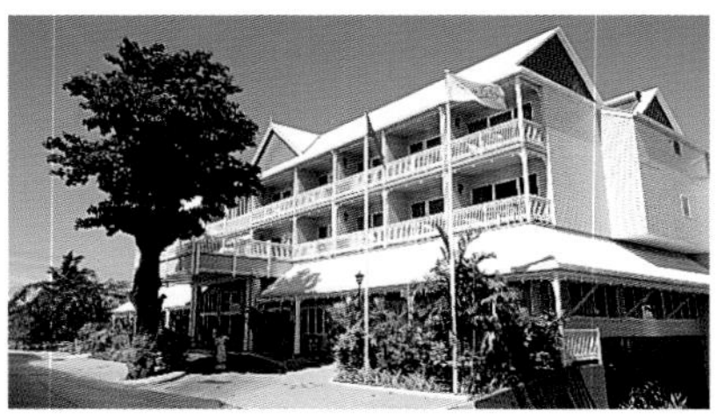

◄ *Many of the buildings in Samoa reflect the country's colonial past. Once a colony of New Zealand, Samoa is now an independent state; American Samoa remains an unincorporated territory of the United States.*

The Ring of Fire

The active plate margins surrounding the Pacific have created numerous land and island volcanoes along its border. The actual basin of the Pacific is made up of a number of separate tectonic plates which move away from each other, colliding with other plates. When they collide, the oceanic plates, being thinner, are forced beneath the thicker continental plates, forming deep ocean trenches and high ridges. These collision zones are known as subduction zones and are characterized by intense seismic and volcanic activity.

Resources

Many of the small islands in the Pacific rely heavily on marine resources to provide valuable export incomes. These fisheries tend to be small-scale and are forced to compete with the large commercial fleets from Japan and the Russian Federation. Although many metallic mineral deposits have been discovered in the Pacific, few are exploited. The major areas of oil and gas extraction are off the coast of Vietnam, along the Kamchatka Peninsula and off the coast of Alaska.

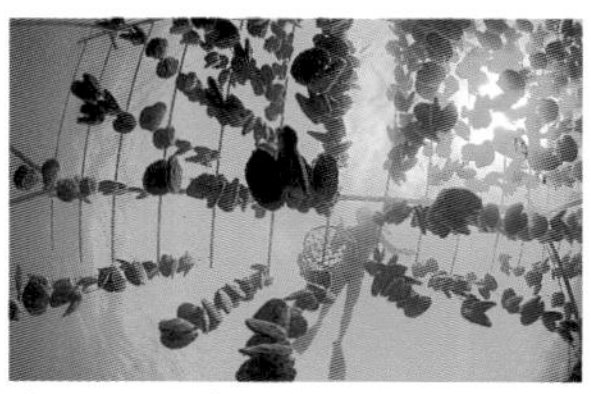

▲ *Farms such as this black pearl oyster farm in Tahiti are widespread throughout the Pacific. The culturing or farming of marine organisms, such as molluscs and crustaceans, has been practised for hundreds of years.*

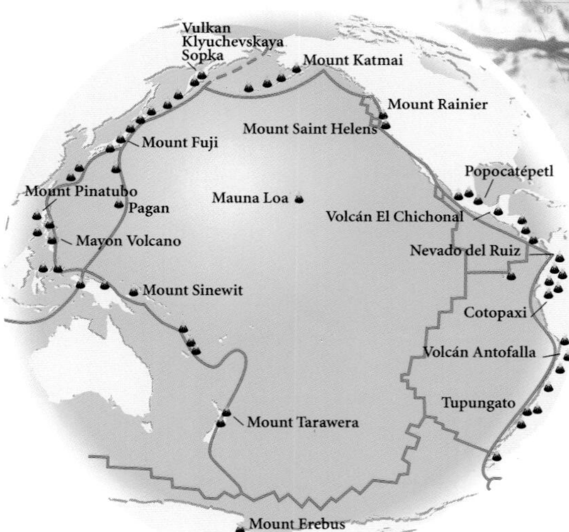

Ring of Fire
— plate boundaries
● major volcanoes

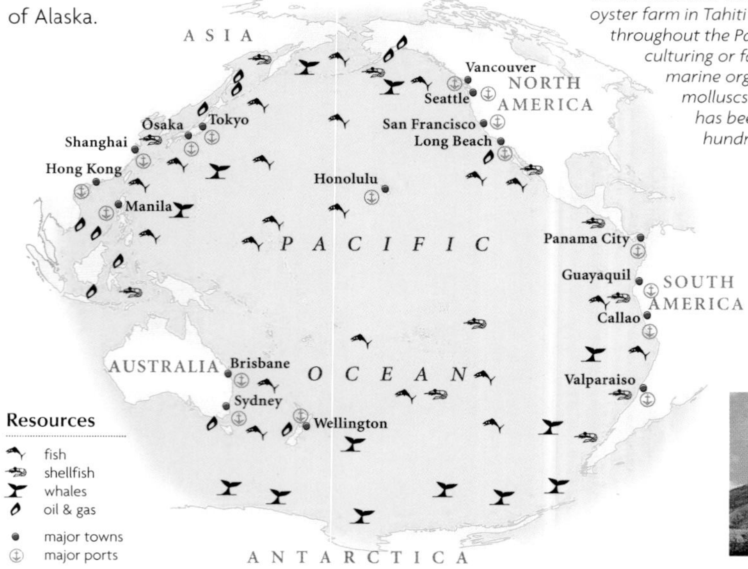

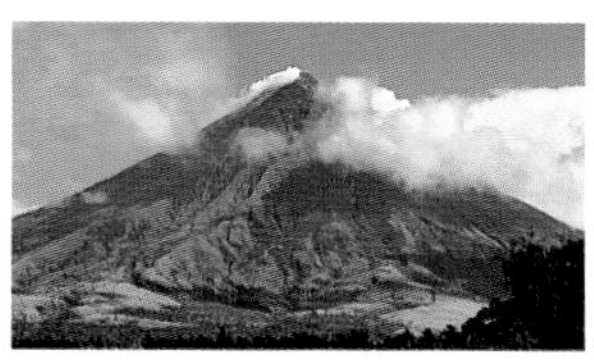

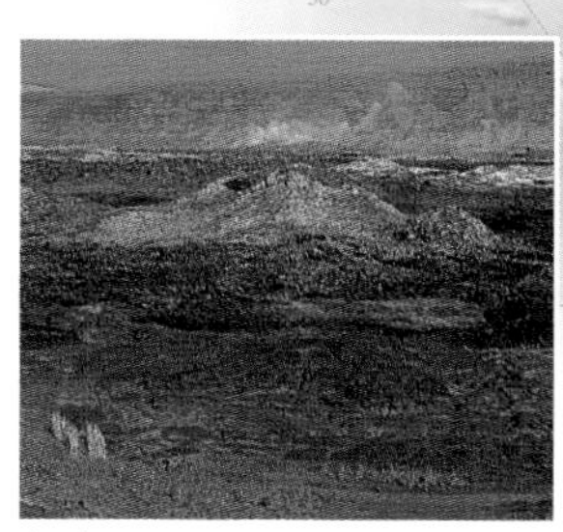

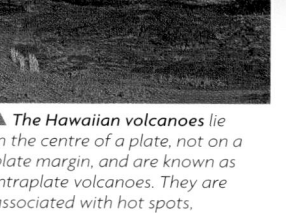

▲ *The Hawaiian volcanoes lie in the centre of a plate, not on a plate margin, and are known as intraplate volcanoes. They are associated with hot spots, whereby a plume of hot molten rock rises to the surface as the plate moves over it.*

◄ *Mayon Volcano in the Philippines is one of many active volcanoes on the Pacific 'Ring of Fire'. It is noted for its perfect conical shape; the base of the cone is 80 miles (130 km) in circumference.*

Resources
- fish
- shellfish
- whales
- oil & gas
- ● major towns
- ⊕ major ports

Melanesia

FIJI, VANUATU, New Caledonia *(to France)*

Three main island groups make up the area of southern Melanesia in the southwestern Pacific: the independent countries of Fiji and Vanuatu and the French overseas territory of New Caledonia. The major Melanesian island group, the Solomon Islands, lies to the east of Papua New Guinea (pages 336–337). Most of the larger islands are volcanic in origin; the smaller ones are mainly coral atolls and are largely uninhabited. The economy in all three island groups is increasingly driven by tourism, not necessarily to the benefit of other economic activities.

Vanuatu

A string of mountainous volcanic islands covering more than 4706 sq miles (12,190 sq km) of the south Pacific, Vanuatu achieved independence from France and the UK in 1980. The majority of the population relies on subsistence fishing and agriculture. Once-important copra and cocoa exports are declining as a result of cost-effective substitutes from elsewhere, and alternatives are being explored. There is further resource potential in the forests and fishing grounds, and beef and arable farming are of growing importance. Tourism, accounting for 40% of GDP, is the fastest-growing sector of the economy, and further expansion is planned.

SCALE 1:6,000,000

projection: Lambert Conformal Conic

CORAL SEA

New Caledonia *(to France)*

New Caledonia, a French overseas territory known as Kanaky by its indigenous peoples, comprises a large main island, 260 miles (418 km) long, and many smaller islands and atolls. Socio-economic inequality, unemployment and the issue of independence have caused tension between the Kanaks and the French-speaking expatriate population. This resulted in a long history of political violence, although the Nouméa accord, signed in 1998, allowed for greater autonomy. New Caledonia produces 20% of the world's nickel, and improved incomes from tourism and agriculture have benefited the economy.

▲ On New Caledonia's main island, relatively high interior plateaux descend to coastal plains. Nickel is the most important mineral resource, but the hills also harbour metallic deposits including chrome, cobalt, iron, gold, silver and copper.

Map key

Population
⊕ 50,000 to 100,000
○ 10,000 to 50,000
○ below 10,000

Elevation
1000m / 3281ft
500m / 1640ft
250m / 820ft
100m / 328ft
sea level

Fiji

Fiji is a volcanic archipelago in the southwestern Pacific consisting of two large islands and 880 smaller islets, and covering a total area of 7054 sq miles (18,270 sq km). The majority of the population lives on the two largest islands. The people are split fairly evenly between Indo-Fijians, who arrived when Fiji was still a British colony, and the indigenous Fijians who have, since 1987, controlled the government. Sugar and copra are the most important crops in a diversified agricultural base and forestry is becoming increasingly important. A relatively varied economy has potential for mineral and hydro-electric exploitation, while Fiji's climate and location on the main Pacific air routes are an impetus to tourism.

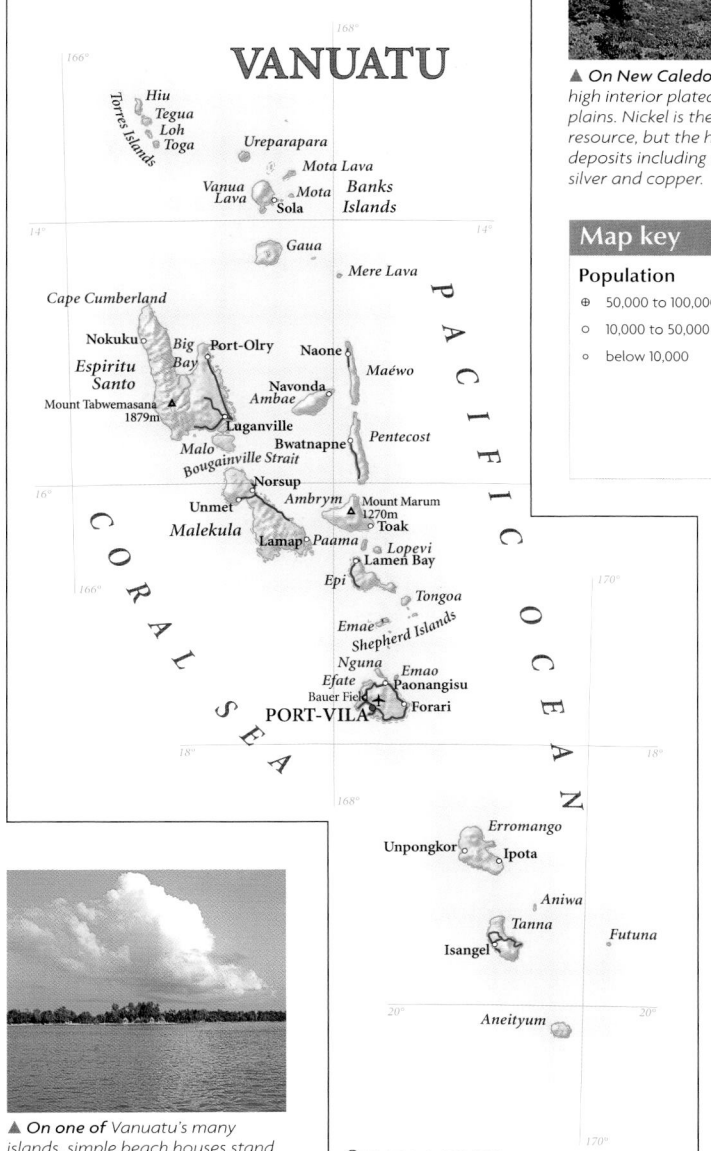

SCALE 1:6,000,000

projection: Mercator

▲ On one of Vanuatu's many islands, simple beach houses stand at the water's edge, surrounded by coconut palms and other tropical vegetation. The unspoilt beaches and tranquillity of its islands are drawing ever-larger numbers of tourists to Vanuatu.

SCALE 1:6,000,000

projection: Lambert Conformal Conic

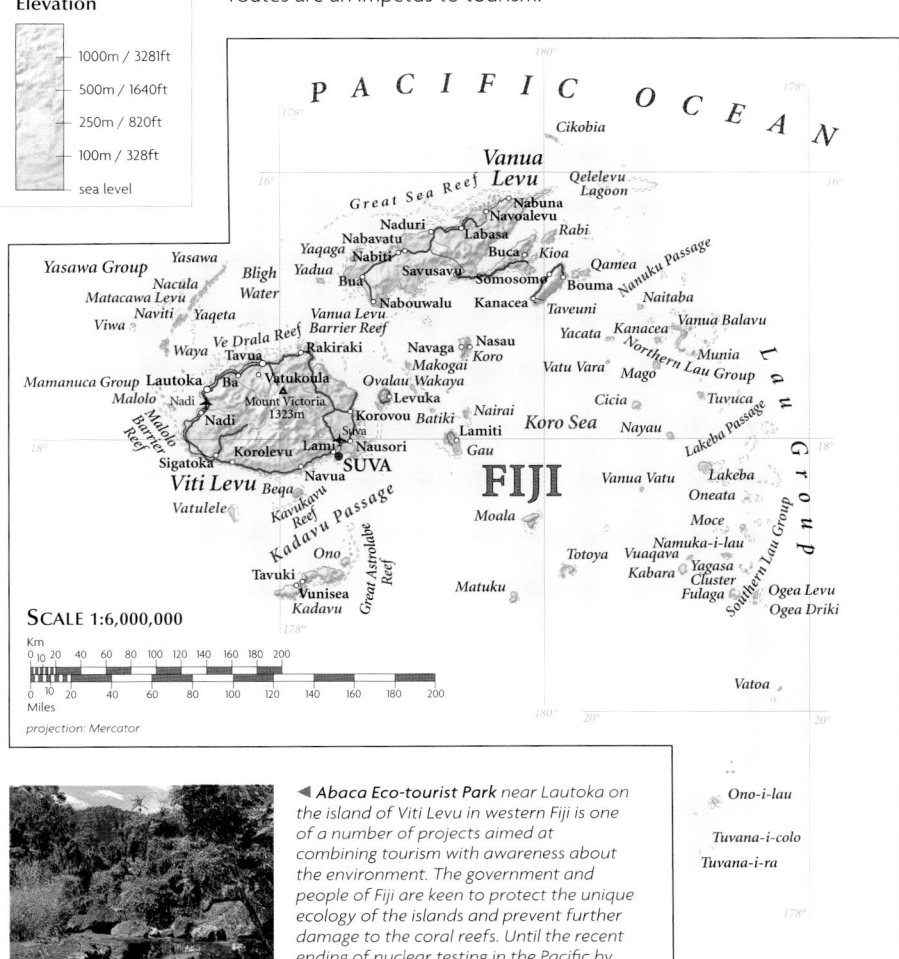

◀ Abaca Eco-tourist Park near Lautoka on the island of Viti Levu in western Fiji is one of a number of projects aimed at combining tourism with awareness about the environment. The government and people of Fiji are keen to protect the unique ecology of the islands and prevent further damage to the coral reefs. Until the recent ending of nuclear testing in the Pacific by Western nations, Fiji lay downwind of some of the main testing sites.

Micronesia

MARSHALL ISLANDS, MICRONESIA, NAURU, PALAU,
Guam, Northern Mariana Islands, Wake Island

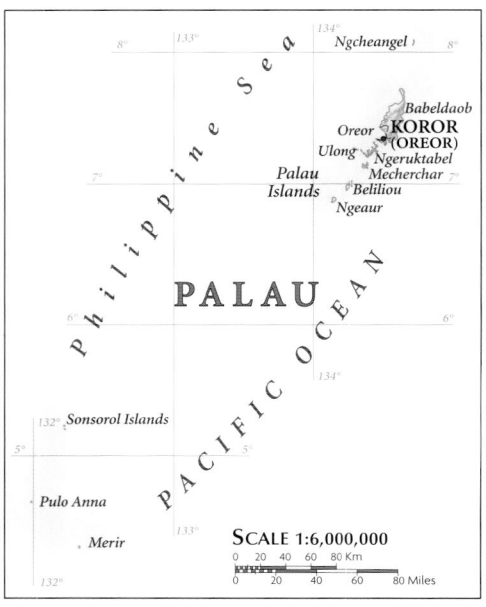

The Micronesian islands lie in the western reaches of the Pacific Ocean and are all part of the same volcanic zone. The Federated States of Micronesia is the largest group, with more than 600 atolls and forested volcanic islands in an area of more than 1120 sq miles (2900 sq km). Micronesia is a mixture of former colonies, overseas territories and dependencies. Most of the region still relies on aid and subsidies to sustain economies limited by resources, isolation, and an emigrating population, drawn to New Zealand and Australia by the attractions of a western lifestyle.

Palau

Palau is an archipelago of over 200 islands, only eight of which are inhabited. It was the last remaining UN trust territory in the Pacific, controlled by the USA until 1994, when it became independent. The economy operates on a subsistence level, with coconuts and cassava the principal crops. Fishing licences and tourism provide foreign currency.

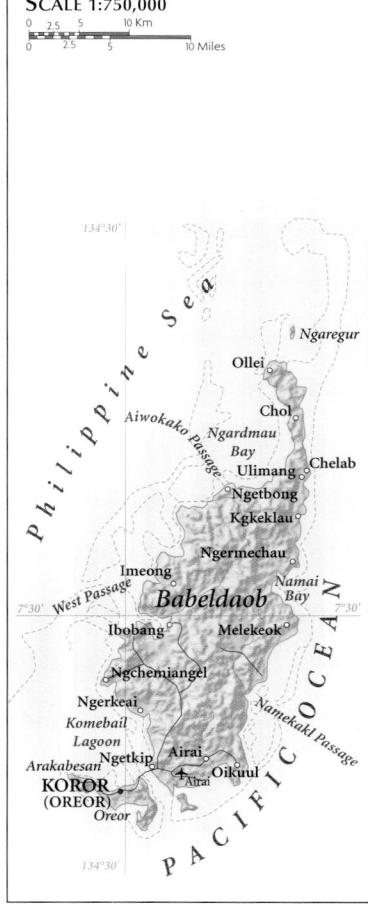

SCALE 1:750,000

SCALE 1:6,000,000

Guam (to US)

Lying at the southern end of the Mariana Islands, Guam is an important US military base and tourist destination. Social and political life is dominated by the indigenous Chamorro, who make up just under half the population, although the increasing prevalence of western culture threatens Guam's traditional social stability.

◀ The tranquillity of these coastal lagoons, at Inarajan in southern Guam, belies the fact that the island lies in a region where typhoons are common.

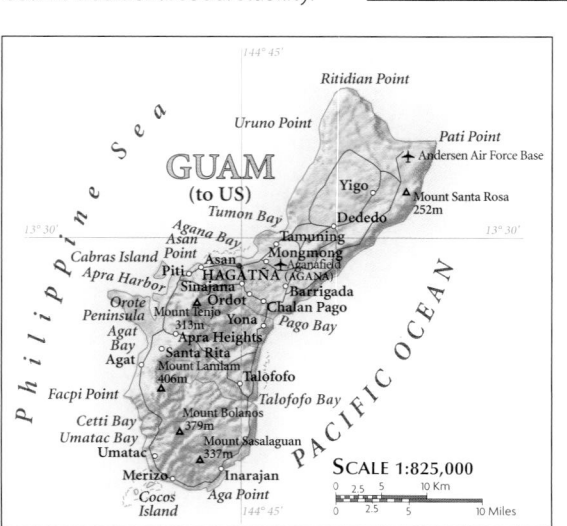

SCALE 1:825,000

Northern Mariana Islands (to US)

A US Commonwealth territory, the Northern Marianas comprise the whole of the Mariana archipelago except for Guam. The islands retain their close links with the United States and continue to receive US aid. Tourism, though bringing in much-needed revenue, has speeded the decline of the traditional subsistence economy. Most of the population lives on Saipan.

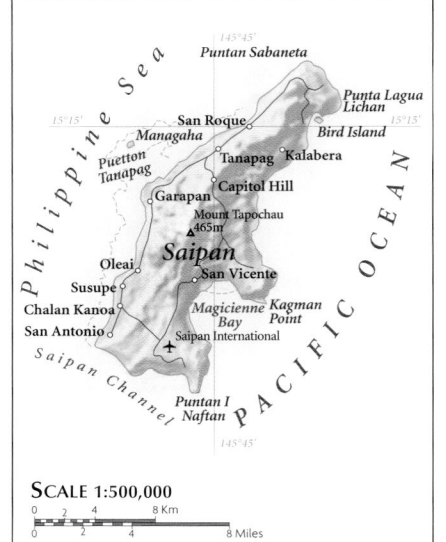

SCALE 1:500,000

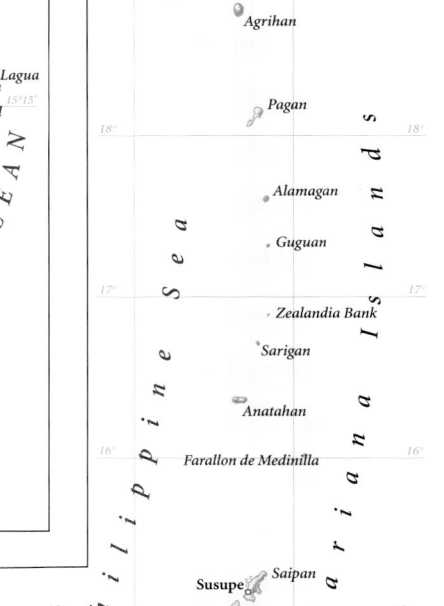

NORTHERN MARIANA ISLANDS (to US)

SCALE 1:5,000,000

▲ The Palau Islands have numerous hidden lakes and lagoons. These sustain their own ecosystems which have developed in isolation. This has produced adaptations in the animals and plants which are often unique to each lake.

Micronesia

A mixture of high volcanic islands and low-lying coral atolls, the Federated States of Micronesia include all the Caroline Islands except Palau. Pohnpei, Kosrae, Chuuk and Yap are the four main island cluster states, each of which has its own language, with English remaining the official language. Nearly half the population is concentrated on Pohnpei, the largest island. Independent since 1986, the islands continue to receive considerable aid from the USA which supplements an economy based primarily on fishing and copra processing.

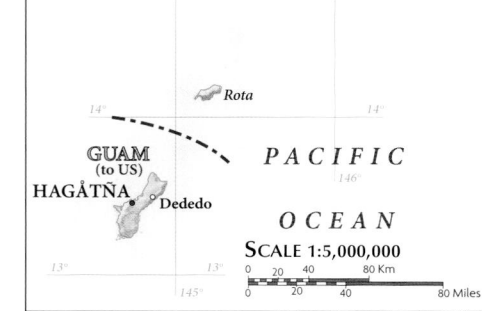

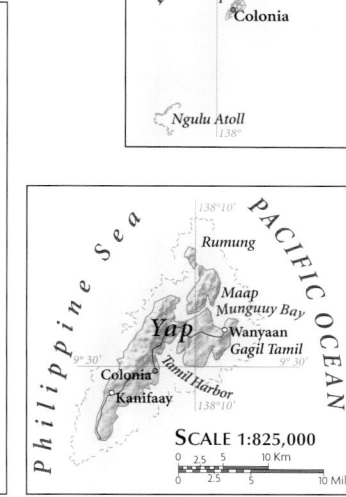

SCALE 1:825,000

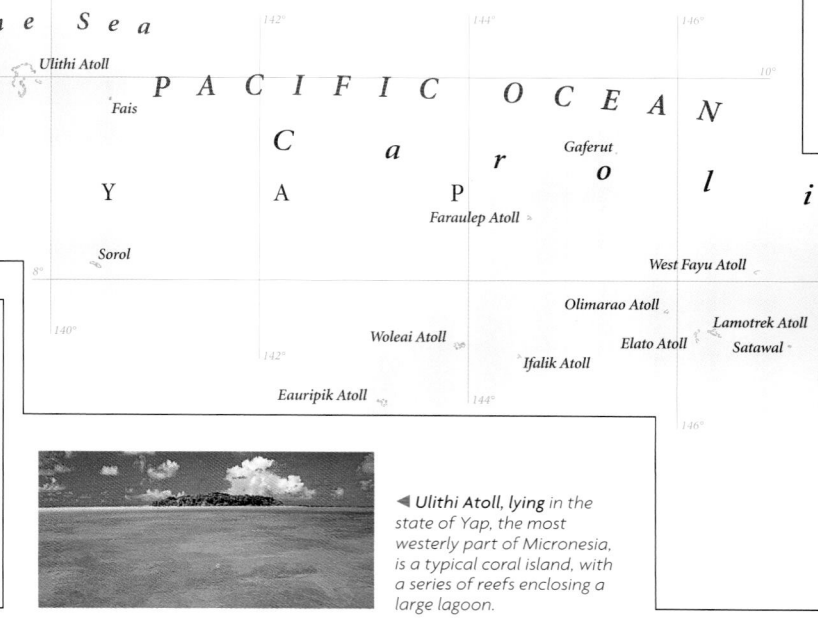

◀ Ulithi Atoll, lying in the state of Yap, the most westerly part of Micronesia, is a typical coral island, with a series of reefs enclosing a large lagoon.

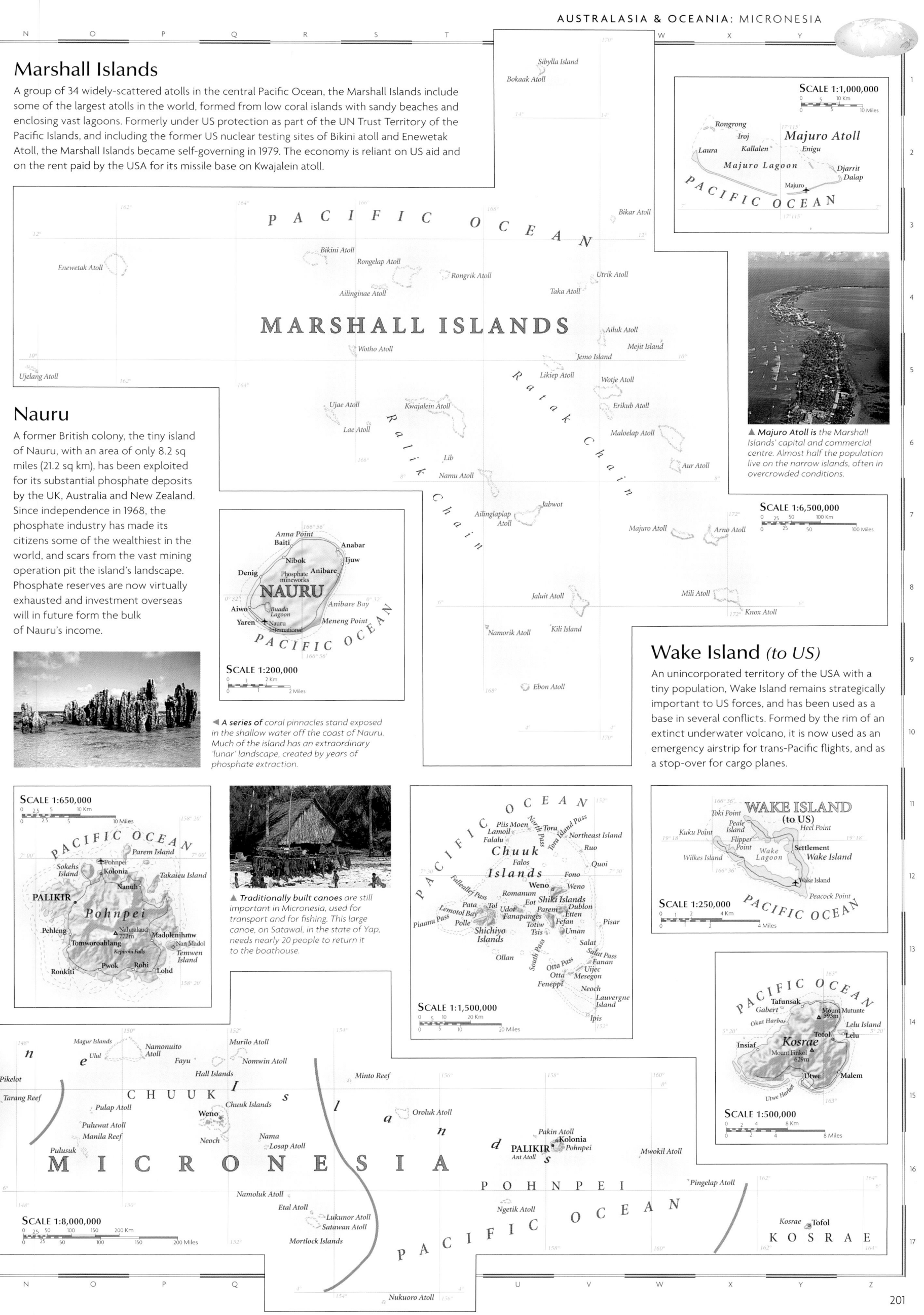

Marshall Islands

A group of 34 widely-scattered atolls in the central Pacific Ocean, the Marshall Islands include some of the largest atolls in the world, formed from low coral islands with sandy beaches and enclosing vast lagoons. Formerly under US protection as part of the UN Trust Territory of the Pacific Islands, and including the former US nuclear testing sites of Bikini atoll and Enewetak Atoll, the Marshall Islands became self-governing in 1979. The economy is reliant on US aid and on the rent paid by the USA for its missile base on Kwajalein atoll.

▲ *Majuro Atoll is* the Marshall Islands' capital and commercial centre. Almost half the population live on the narrow islands, often in overcrowded conditions.

Nauru

A former British colony, the tiny island of Nauru, with an area of only 8.2 sq miles (21.2 sq km), has been exploited for its substantial phosphate deposits by the UK, Australia and New Zealand. Since independence in 1968, the phosphate industry has made its citizens some of the wealthiest in the world, and scars from the vast mining operation pit the island's landscape. Phosphate reserves are now virtually exhausted and investment overseas will in future form the bulk of Nauru's income.

◀ *A series of* coral pinnacles stand exposed in the shallow water off the coast of Nauru. Much of the island has an extraordinary 'lunar' landscape, created by years of phosphate extraction.

Wake Island *(to US)*

An unincorporated territory of the USA with a tiny population, Wake Island remains strategically important to US forces, and has been used as a base in several conflicts. Formed by the rim of an extinct underwater volcano, it is now used as an emergency airstrip for trans-Pacific flights, and as a stop-over for cargo planes.

▲ *Traditionally built canoes* are still important in Micronesia, used for transport and for fishing. This large canoe, on Satawal, in the state of Yap, needs nearly 20 people to return it to the boathouse.

The Landscape

Although it is still the largest ocean, the basin of the Pacific has been gradually decreasing in size due to the movement of the Indo-Australian Plate. The oldest parts are about 135 million years old. The eastern border of the Pacific is characterized by a continuous mountain chain running the length of the North and South American continents. The eastern basin has a low, uninterrupted relief, at depths averaging 15,000 ft (4570 m). In contrast, the western Pacific is scattered with island arcs and bounded by a series of deep ocean trenches. An almost continuous chain of volcanoes surrounds the ocean and an active mid-ocean ridge runs northeast–southwest.

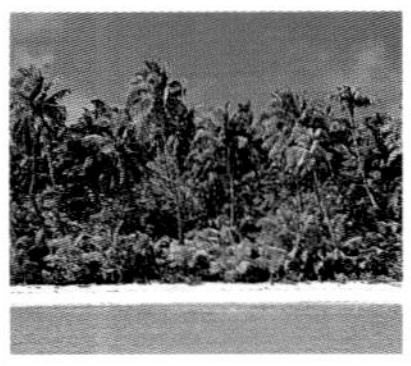

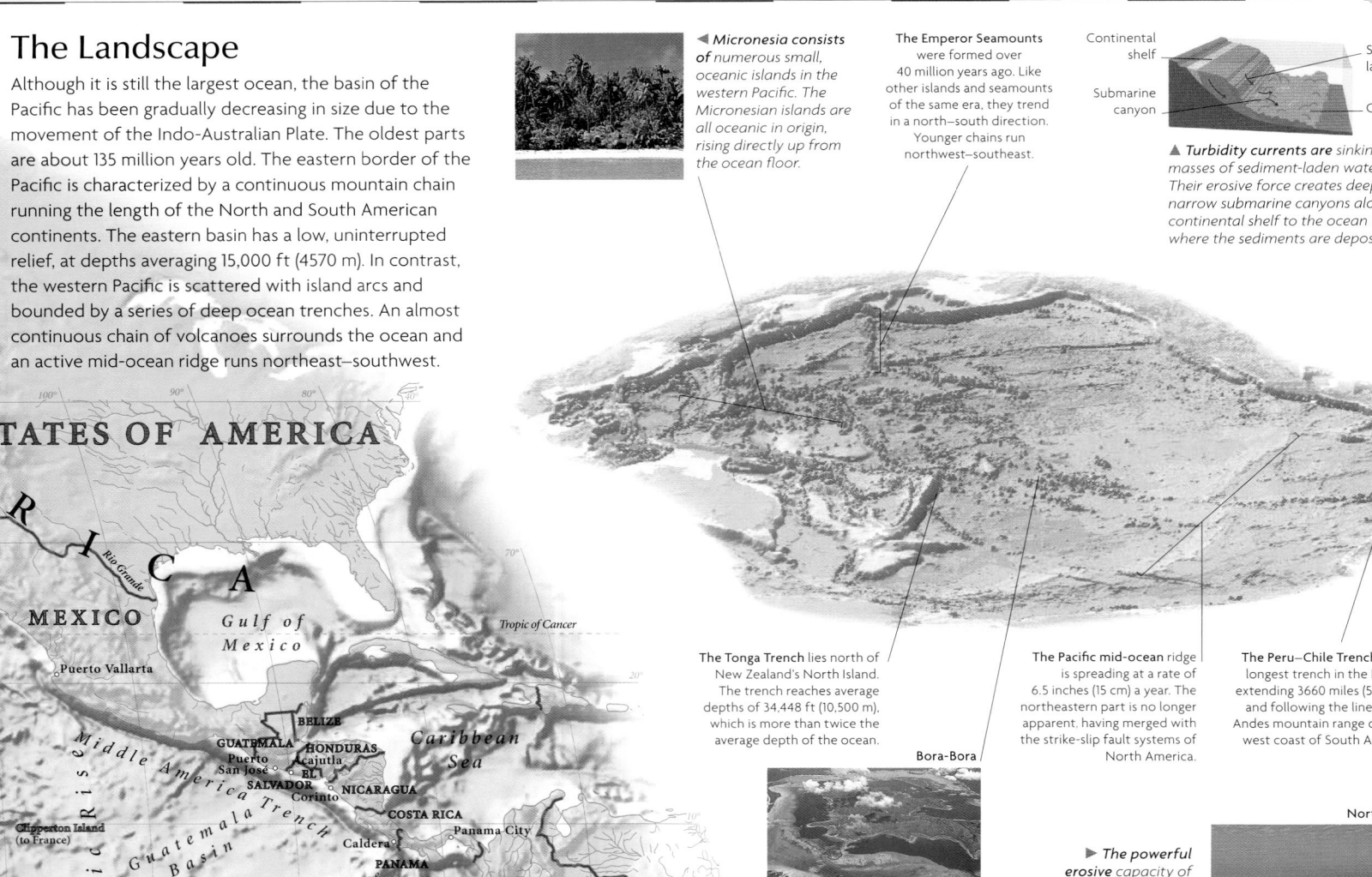

◄ *Micronesia consists of* numerous small, oceanic islands in the western Pacific. The Micronesian islands are all oceanic in origin, rising directly up from the ocean floor.

The Emperor Seamounts were formed over 40 million years ago. Like other islands and seamounts of the same era, they trend in a north–south direction. Younger chains run northwest–southeast.

Continental shelf
Submarine canyon
Sediment-laden current
Ocean floor

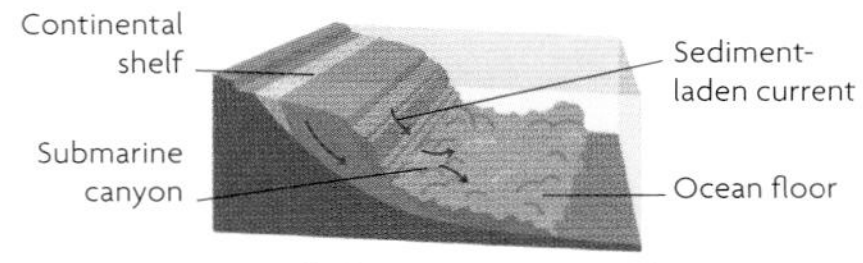

▲ *Turbidity currents are* sinking masses of sediment-laden water. Their erosive force creates deep, narrow submarine canyons along the continental shelf to the ocean floor, where the sediments are deposited.

STATES OF AMERICA

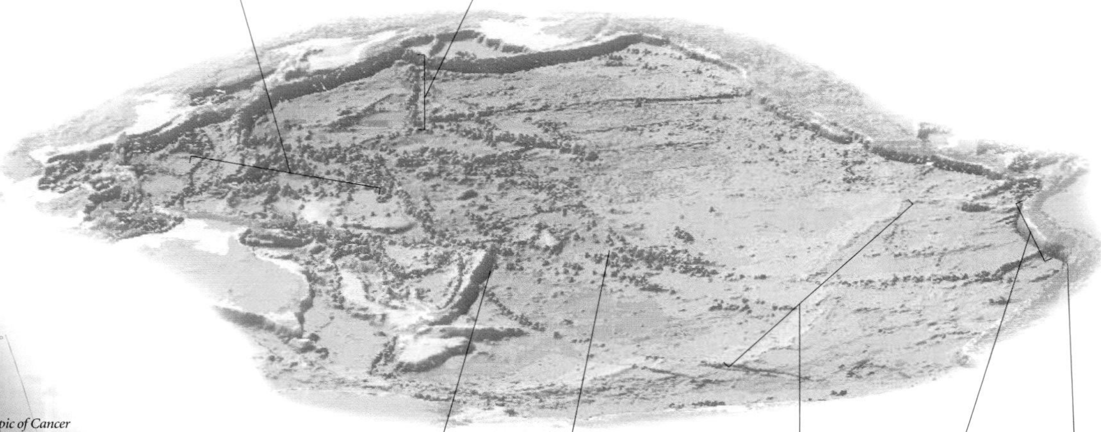

The Tonga Trench lies north of New Zealand's North Island. The trench reaches average depths of 34,448 ft (10,500 m), which is more than twice the average depth of the ocean.

The Pacific mid-ocean ridge is spreading at a rate of 6.5 inches (15 cm) a year. The northeastern part is no longer apparent, having merged with the strike-slip fault systems of North America.

The Peru–Chile Trench is the longest trench in the Pacific, extending 3660 miles (5900 km), and following the line of the Andes mountain range down the west coast of South America.

Bora-Bora

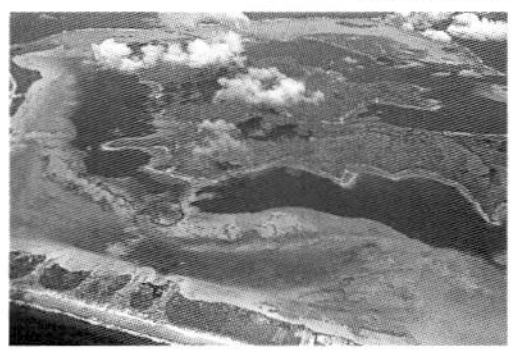

▲ *Bora-Bora's twin mountain* peaks are the remnants of an ancient volcano, now surrounded by a large lagoon, fringed with coral.

Northern Chile

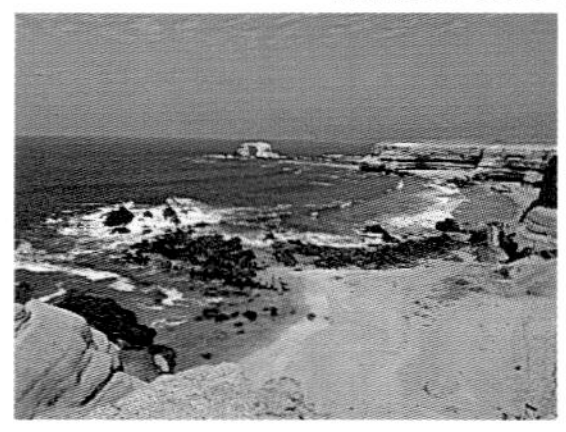

► *The powerful erosive* capacity of Pacific waves can be seen along this stretch of coastline in northern Chile. Wave erosion has cut back the bedrock, exposing numerous rock layers.

Tonga

The Kingdom of Tonga lies in the southwest Pacific, about 2000 miles (3000 km) off the east coast of Australia. It comprises 169 islands of which only 36 are permanently inhabited. The majority of the population live on the largest island, Tongatapu. There are only three sizeable towns and the main commercial centre is the capital Nuku'alofa. Tonga's economy is based mainly on agriculture; coconuts, bananas and vanilla are grown as cash crops for export. Although there is some light manufacturing, growing land shortages have forced increased migration to New Zealand and Australia.

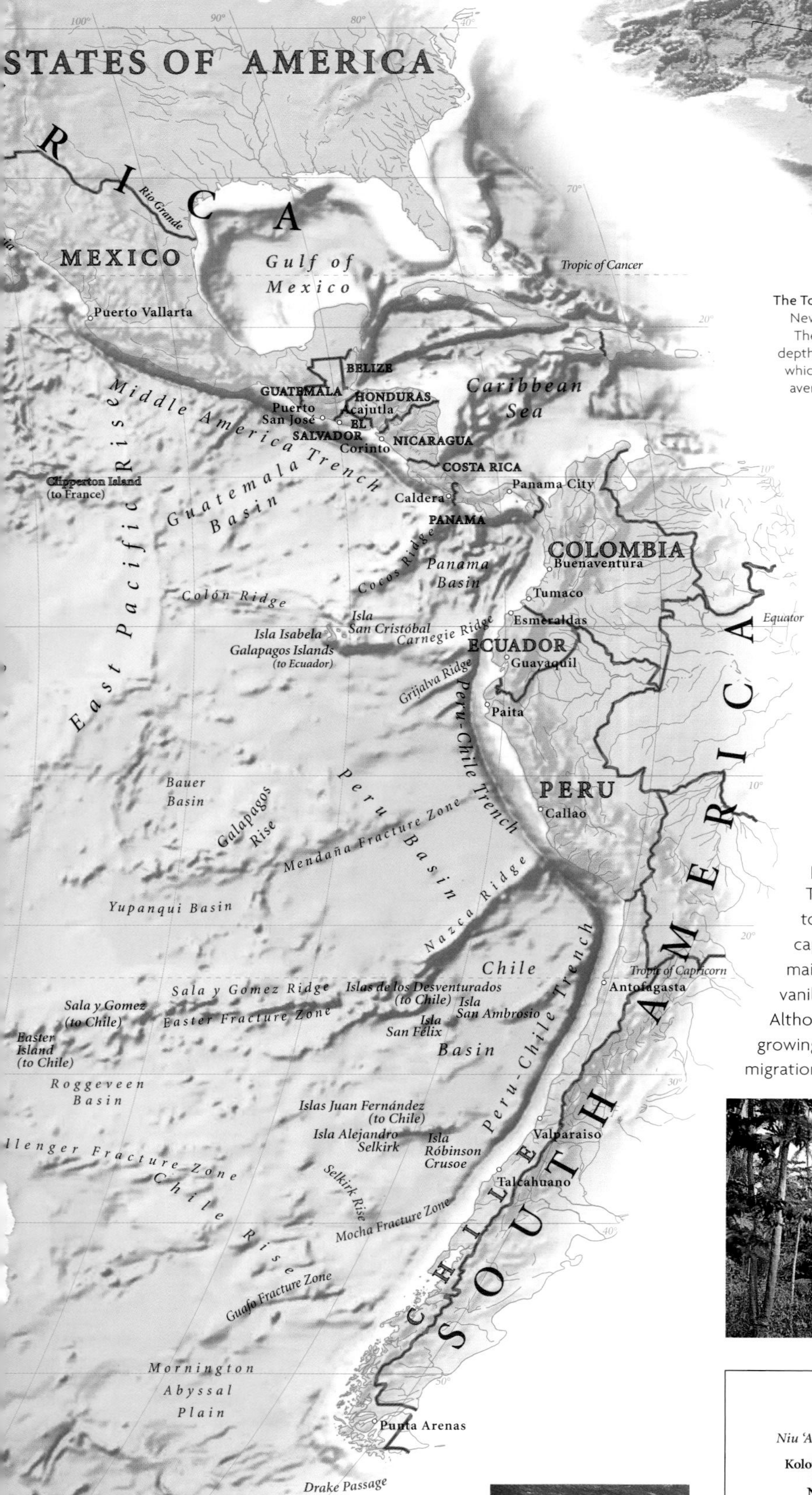

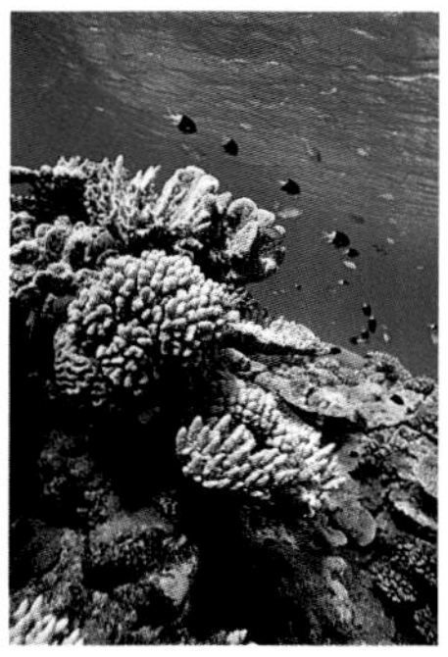

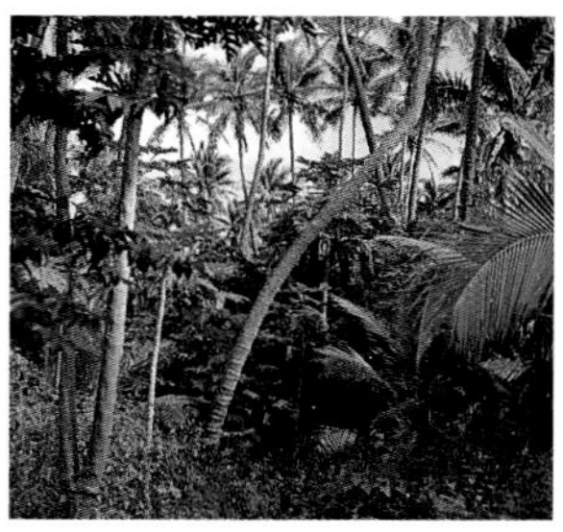

◄ *The islands of* Tonga fall into two belts; those in the east are low, coral islands, while those in the west are high and volcanic. Four of the islands still contain active volcanoes. The mountainous, western islands are covered with verdant tropical vegetation.

► *Coral reefs and* atolls are found throughout the warm waters of the south Pacific. Reefs build up from the skeletons of millions of coral polyps – tiny sea creatures that cling to the reef and secrete calcium carbonate around their bodies, forming a hard protective skeleton.

SCALE 1:1,000,000

SCALE 1:6,000,000

TONGA

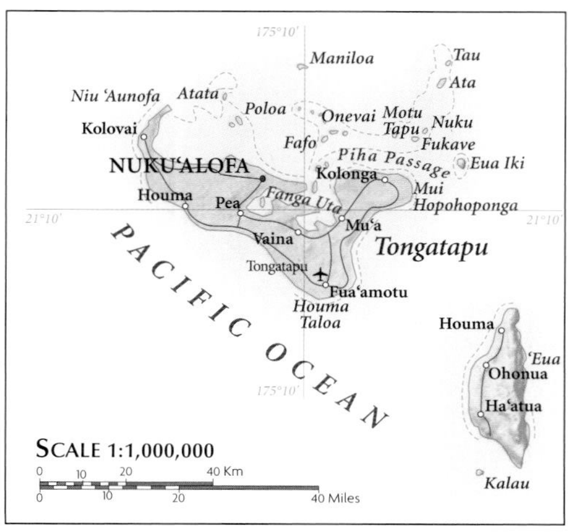

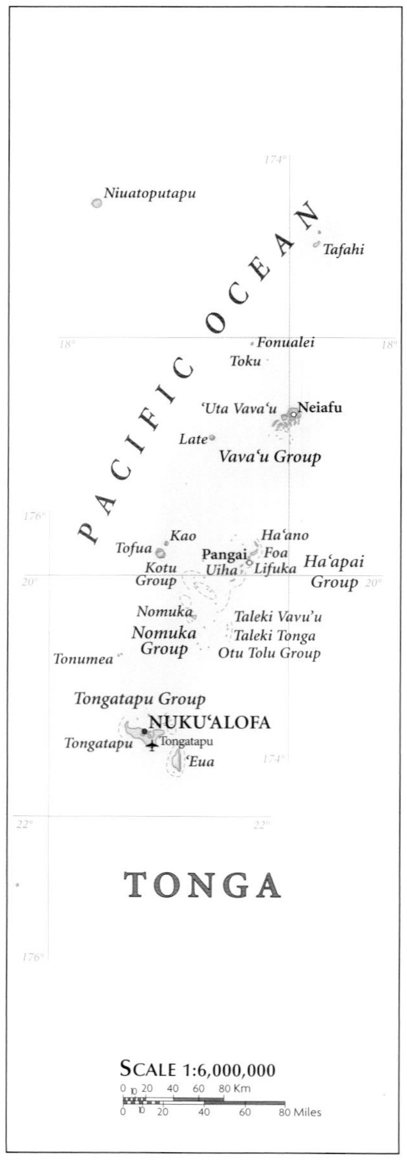

Wave action has eroded this shoreline near Port Campbell in southeastern Australia leaving isolated pinnacles of rock cut off from the main coastline. They are known as the 'Twelve Apostles'.

Polynesia

KIRIBATI, TUVALU, Cook Islands, Easter Island, French Polynesia, Niue, Pitcairn Islands, Tokelau, Wallis & Futuna

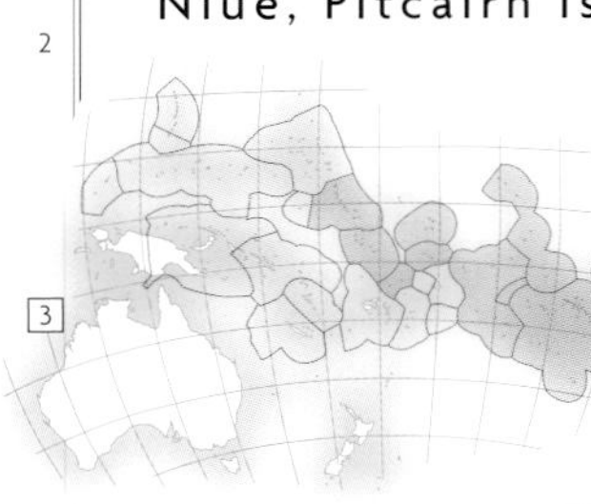

The numerous island groups of Polynesia lie to the east of Australia, scattered over a vast area in the south Pacific. The islands are a mixture of low-lying coral atolls, some of which enclose lagoons, and the tips of great underwater volcanoes. The populations on the islands are small, and most people are of Polynesian origin, as are the Maori of New Zealand. Local economies remain simple, relying mainly on subsistence crops, mineral deposits – many now exhausted – fishing and tourism.

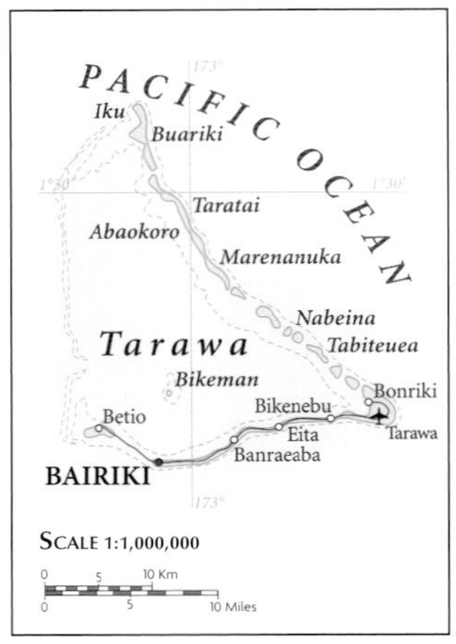

Kiribati

A former British colony, Kiribati became independent in 1979. Banaba's phosphate deposits ran out in 1980, following decades of exploitation by the British. Economic development remains slow and most agriculture is at a subsistence level, though coconuts provide export income, and underwater agriculture is being developed.

SCALE 1:1,000,000

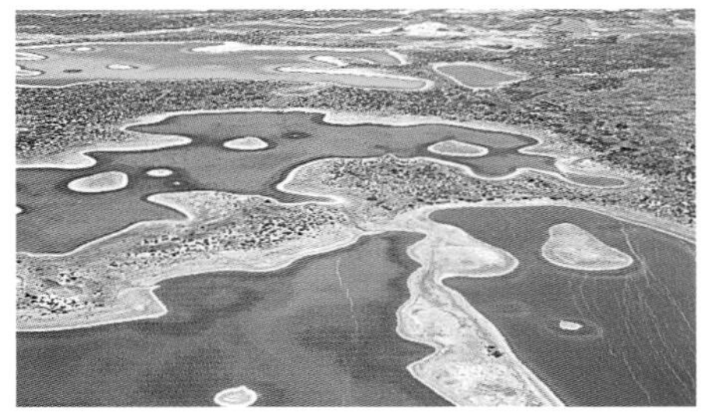

▶ *With the exception* of Banaba all the islands in Kiribati's three groups are low-lying, coral atolls. This aerial view shows the sparsely vegetated islands, intercut by many small lagoons.

Tuvalu

A chain of nine coral atolls, 360 miles (579 km) long with a land area of just over 9 sq miles (23 sq km), Tuvalu is one of the world's smallest and most isolated states. As the Ellice Islands, Tuvalu was linked to the Gilbert Islands (now part of Kiribati) as a British colony until independence in 1978. Politically and socially conservative, Tuvaluans live by fishing and subsistence farming.

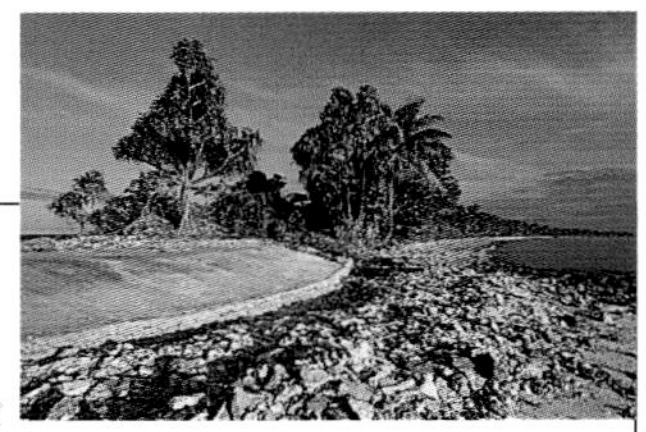

▲ *Funafuti Atoll contains* more than 40% of Tuvalu's people, giving it an extremely high population density.

SCALE 1:500,000

SCALE 1:6,000,000

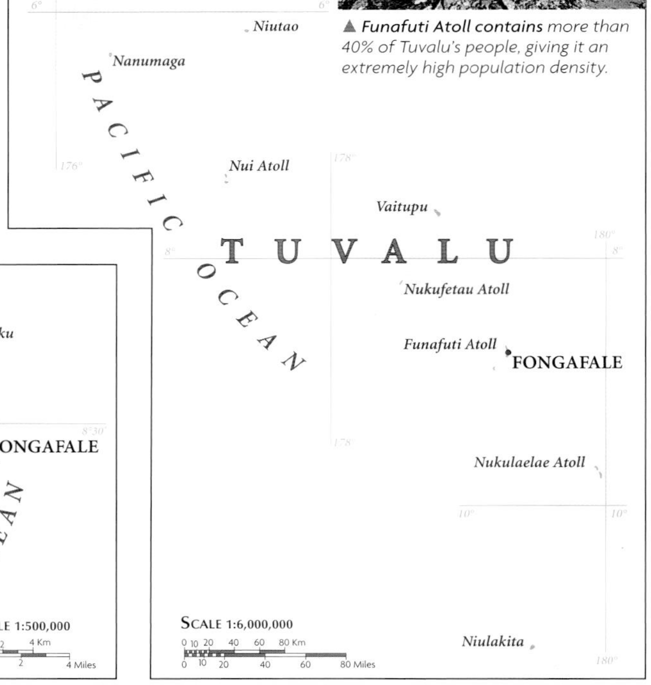

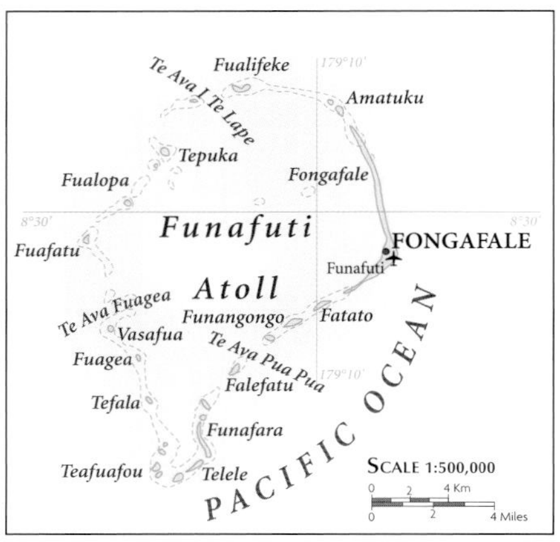

Tokelau *(to New Zealand)*

A low-lying coral atoll, Tokelau is a dependent territory of New Zealand with few natural resources. Although a 1990 cyclone destroyed crops and infrastructure, a tuna cannery and the sale of fishing licences have raised revenue and a catamaran link between the islands has increased their tourism potential. Tokelau's small size and economic weakness makes independence from New Zealand unlikely.

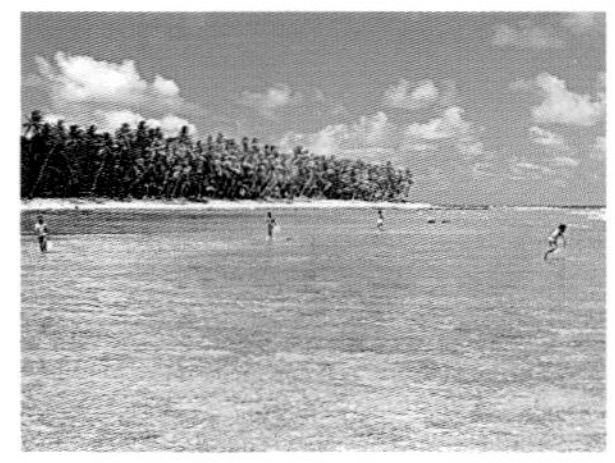

▲ *Fishermen cast their* nets to catch small fish in the shallow waters off Atafu Atoll, the most westerly island in Tokelau.

SCALE 1:2,000,000

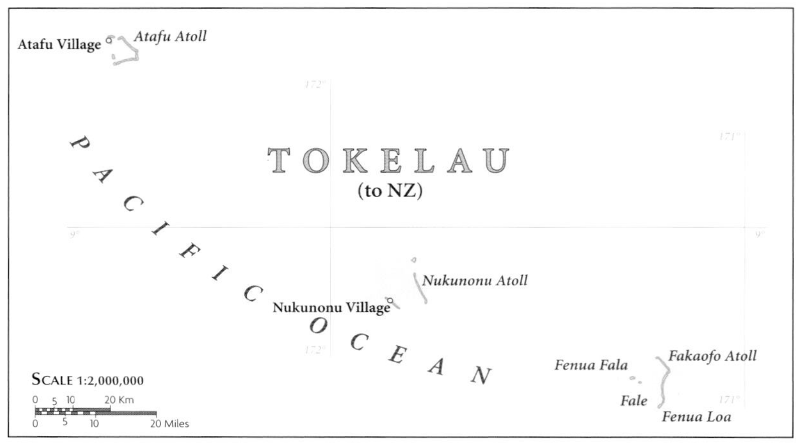

Wallis & Futuna *(to France)*

In contrast to other French overseas territories in the south Pacific, the inhabitants of Wallis and Futuna have shown little desire for greater autonomy. A subsistence economy produces a variety of tropical crops, while foreign currency remittances come from expatriates and from the sale of licences to Japanese and Korean fishing fleets.

SCALE 1:1,000,000

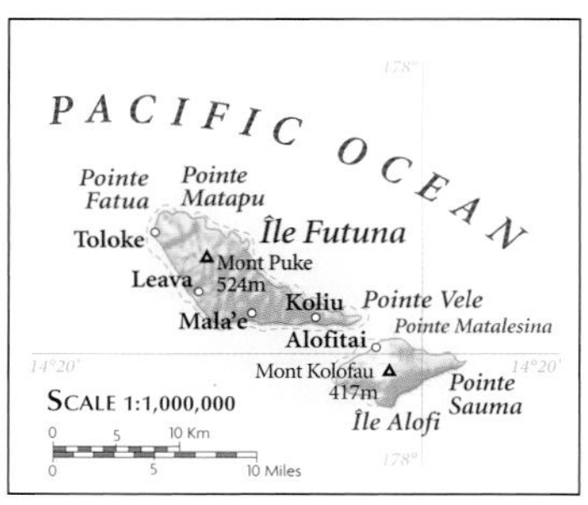

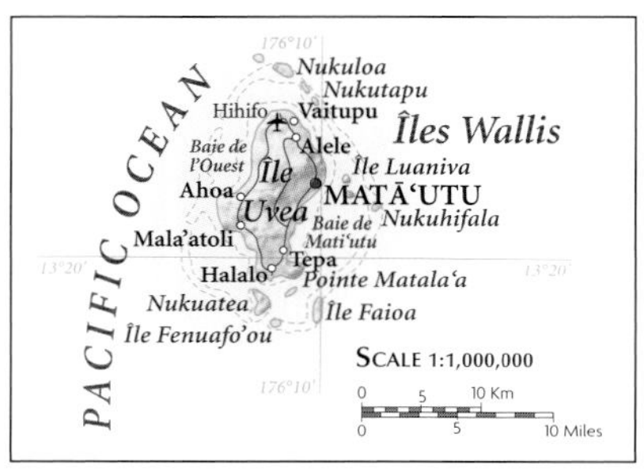

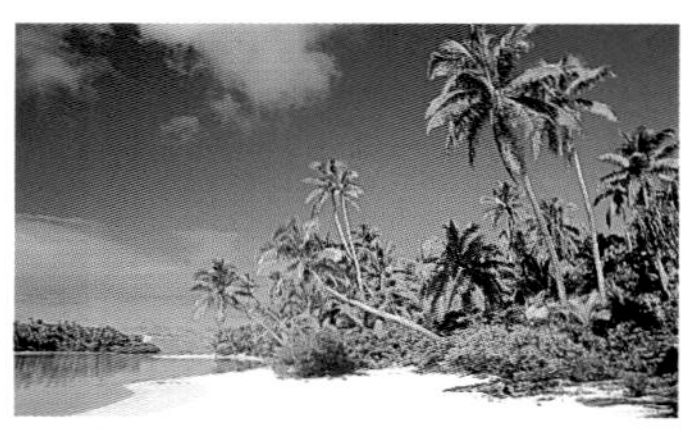

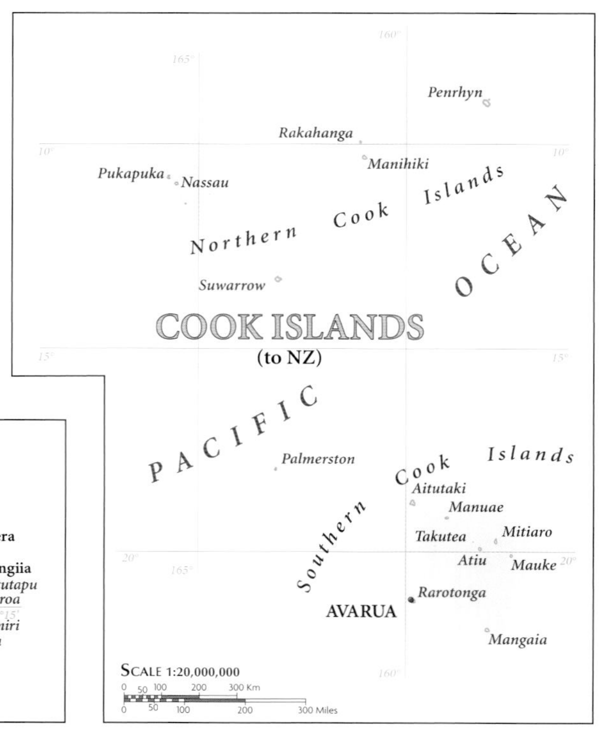

Niue *(to New Zealand)*

Niue, the world's largest coral island, is self-governing but exists in free association with New Zealand. Tropical fruits are grown for local consumption; tourism and the sale of postage stamps provide foreign currency. The lack of local job prospects has led more than 10,000 Niueans to emigrate to New Zealand, which has now invested heavily in Niue's economy in the hope of reversing this trend.

SCALE 1:1,000,000

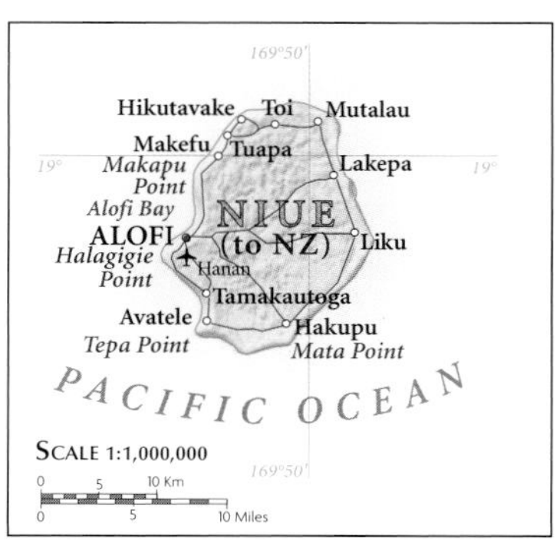

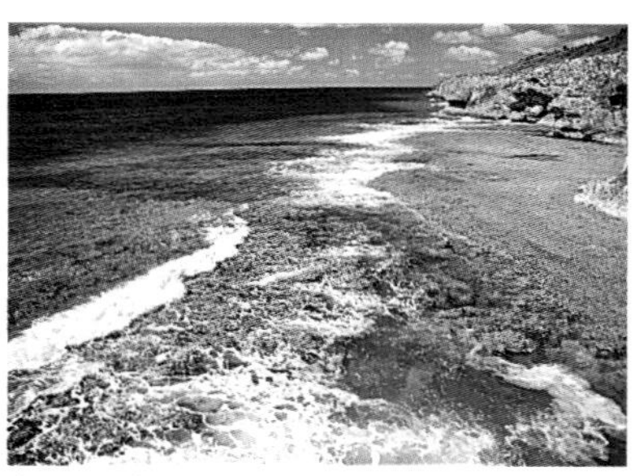

▲ *Waves have cut* back the original coastline, exposing a sandy beach, near Mutalau in the northeast corner of Niue.

Cook Islands *(to New Zealand)*

A mixture of coral atolls and volcanic peaks, the Cook Islands achieved self-government in 1965 but exist in free association with New Zealand. A diverse economy includes pearl and giant clam farming, and an ostrich farm, plus tourism and banking. A 1991 friendship treaty with France provides for French surveillance of territorial waters.

▲ *Palm trees fringe* the white sands of a beach on Aitutaki in the Southern Cook Islands, where tourism is of increasing economic importance.

SCALE 1:325,000

SCALE 1:20,000,000

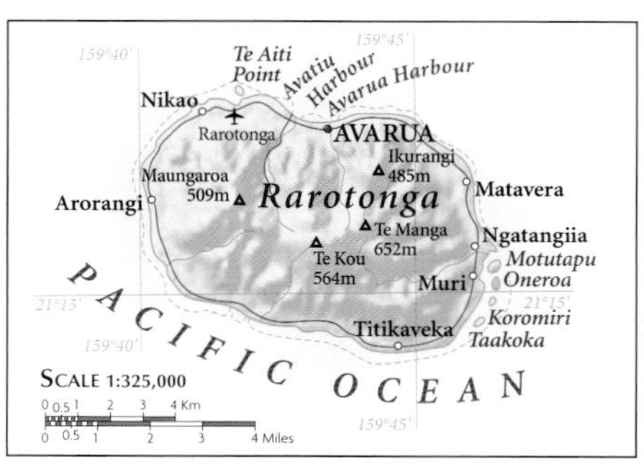

Tungaru (Gilbert Islands)

Makin
Butaritari
Abaiang   Marakei
BAIRIKI   Tarawa
Maiana
Kuria   Abemama
Aranuka
Banaba   Nonouti
Tabiteuea   Beru   Nikunau
Onotoa   Arorae
Tamana

Equator

Teraina
Tabuaeran
Kiritimati
(Christmas Island)

L i n e   I s l a n d s

Equator

K I R I B A T I

P h o e n i x   I s l a n d s

Kanton
McKean Island   Birnie Island   Enderbury Island
Rawaki
Nikumaroro   Manra
Orona

Malden Island

Starbuck Island

P A C I F I C   O C E A N

Millennium Island
Vostok Island
Flint Island

SCALE 1:20,000,000
0 50 100 200 300 400 Km
0 50 100 200 300 400 Miles

PACIFIC OCEAN

Northwest Point   Cape Manning   Northeast Point
Cook Island   **London**   **Banana**   Kiritimati
Saint   Manulu Lagoon
Paris   Stanislas
Bay
Poland   Vaskess   Bay of
South   Bay   Isles Lagoon   Wrecks
West   Joe's Hill
Point   12m   Aeon
Azur Lagoon   Point
Pelican
Lagoon
South East Point

Kiritimati
(Christmas Island)

SCALE 1:1,175,000
0   10 Miles

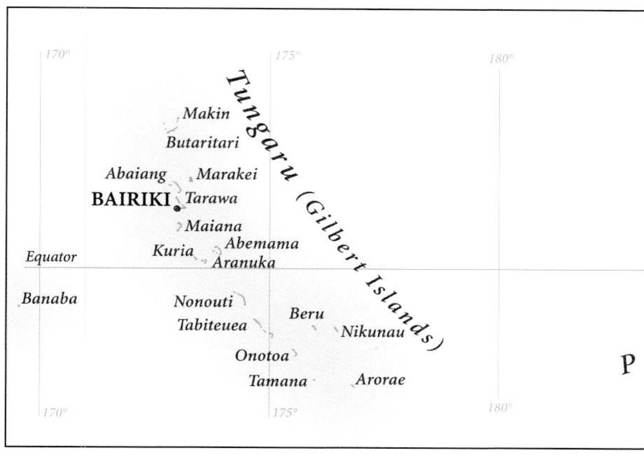

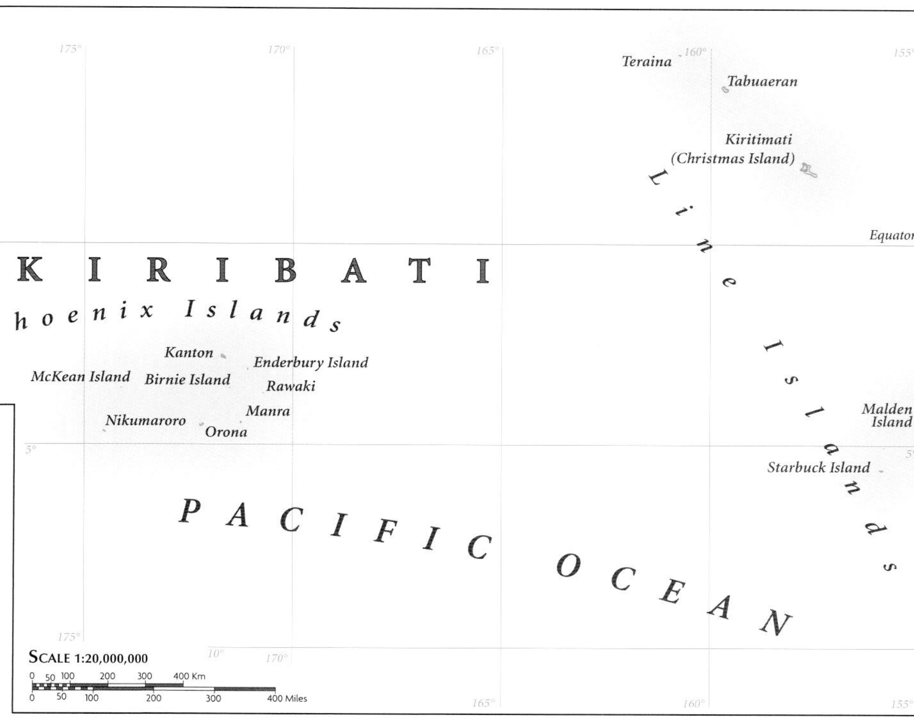

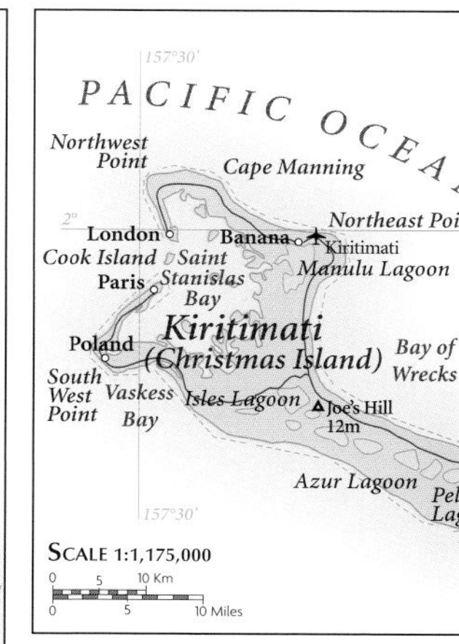

French Polynesia *(to France)*

The 130 islands of French Polynesia cover 4 million sq miles (10.5 million sq km). Nearly 75% of the people live on Tahiti. The use of Mururoa as a nuclear testing site by the French military transformed the economy, creating many jobs. The end of testing led to calls from the Polynesian majority for greater autonomy from France, the rebuilding of indigenous trade, and a reduction in tourism to stop the erosion of the islands' traditional culture.

Baie d'Opunohu
Baie de Cook
Papetoai   Pointe Aroa   *Î l e s   d u   V e n t*
Matotea   Paopao   Baie de Mataval   Pointe Vénus
714m   Mahina   Papenoo
Moorea   Afareaitu   **PAPEETE**   Pirea   Tiarei
Haapiti   Mont Tohiea   Faaa
1207m   Faa   Mont Aorai   Hitiaa
Pointe Nuupere   2066m
Punaauia   Mont Orohena   *Tahiti*
Pointe Nuuroa   2241m   Passe Tamotoe
Mont Tetufera   Baie de
1799m   Faaone   Taravao
Paea   Taravao
Maraa   Isthme de Taravao
Pointe Maraa   Papara   Afaahiti   Tautira
Mataiea   Teohatu   Presqu'île
Récif Tepeae   Vairao   de Taiarapu
Mont Ronui
Teahupoo   1332m

P A C I F I C   O C E A N

SCALE 1:1,000,000
0   5   10 Km
0   5   10 Miles

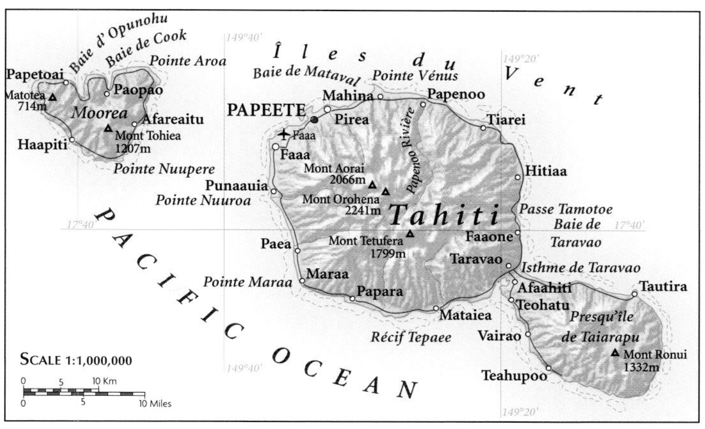

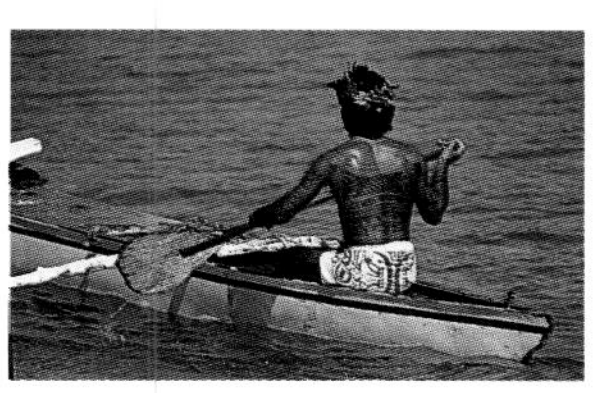

◄ *The traditional Tahitian* welcome for visitors, who are greeted by parties of canoes, has become a major tourist attraction.

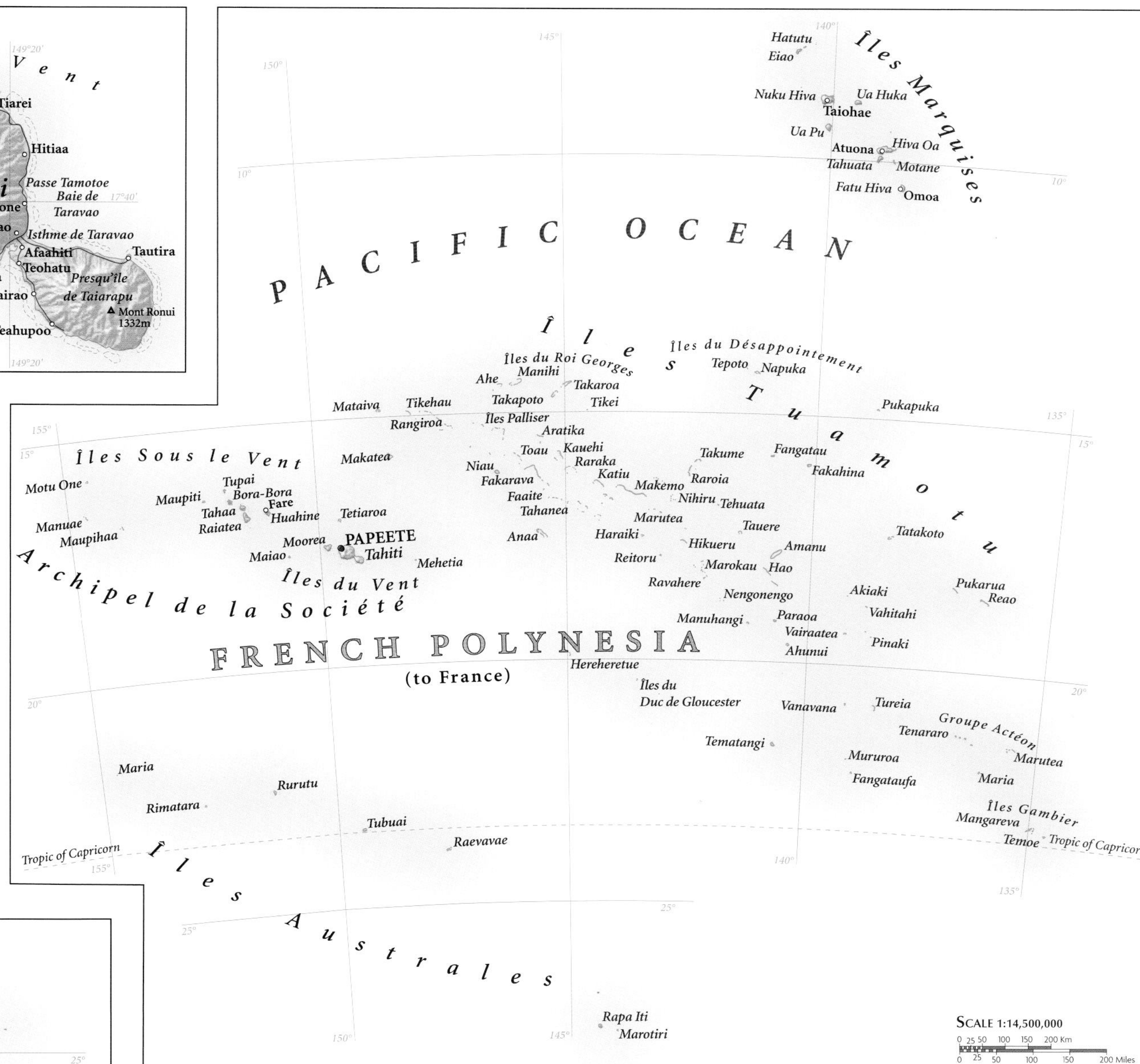

Î l e s   M a r q u i s e s

Hatutu
Eiao
Nuku Hiva   Ua Huka
Taiohae
Ua Pu   Hiva Oa
Atuona   Motane
Tahuata
Fatu Hiva   Omoa

P A C I F I C   O C E A N

Î l e s   T u a m o t u

Îles du Roi Georges   Îles du Désappointement
Manihi   Tepoto   Napuka
Ahe   Takaroa   Pukapuka
Mataiva   Tikehau   Takapoto   Tikei
Rangiroa   Îles Palliser
Aratika   Takume   Fangatau
Makatea   Toau   Kauehi   Fakahina
Niau   Raraka   Raroia
Î l e s   S o u s   l e   V e n t   Fakarava   Katiu   Nihiru   Tehuata
Motu One   Tupai   Faaite   Makemo
Maupiti   Bora-Bora   Tahanea   Marutea   Tauere   Tatakoto
Manuae   Tahaa   Fare   Huahine   Haraiki   Hikueru   Amanu
Maupihaa   Raiatea   Tetiaroa   Reitoru   Marokau   Pukarua
Moorea   **PAPEETE**   Anaa   Ravahere   Akiaki   Reao
Maiao   Tahiti   Nengonengo   Pukarua
Mehetia   Manuhangi   Paraoa   Vahitahi
Î l e s   d u   V e n t   Vairaatea   Pinaki
A r c h i p e l   d e   l a   S o c i é t é   Ahunui

Hereheretue
F R E N C H   P O L Y N E S I A   Îles du
(to France)   Duc de Gloucester   Vanavana   Tureia
Tenararo   *Groupe Actéon*
Tematangi   Mururoa   Marutea
Maria   Fangataufa   Maria
Rurutu   *Îles Gambier*
Rimatara   Mangareva
Tubuai   Temoe   *Tropic of Capricorn*
Tropic of Capricorn   Raevavae
Î l e s   A u s t r a l e s

Rapa Iti
Marotiri

SCALE 1:14,500,000
0 25 50   100   150   200 Km
0 25 50   100   150   200 Miles

Pitcairn Islands *(to UK)*

Britain's most isolated dependency, Pitcairn Island was first populated by mutineers from the HMS *Bounty* in 1790. Emigration is further depleting the already limited gene pool of the island's inhabitants, with associated social and health problems. Barter, fishing and subsistence farming form the basis of the economy although postage stamp sales provide foreign currency earnings, and offshore mineral exploitation may boost the economy in future.

PITCAIRN ISLANDS
(to UK)

Oeno Island
Henderson Island
Ducie Island
Pitcairn Island

P A C I F I C   O C E A N

SCALE 1:10,000,000
0   25 50   100 Km
0   25   50   100 Miles

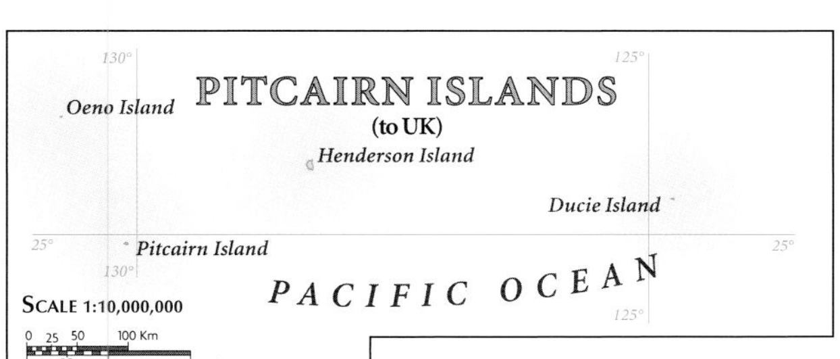

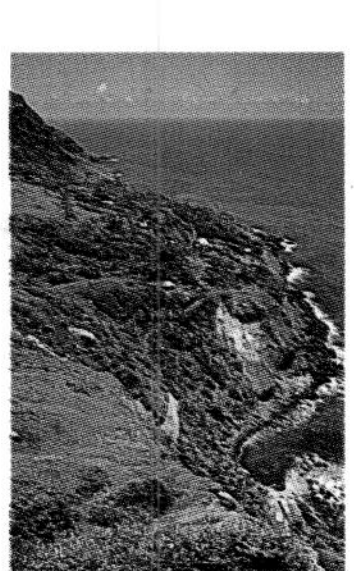

◄ *The Pitcairn Islanders* rely on regular airdrops from New Zealand and periodic visits by supply vessels to provide them with basic commodities.

Young's Rock   Bounty Bay
Adam's Rock
ADAMSTOWN   *Pitcairn Island*
Point Christian   St Paul's Point

P A C I F I C   O C E A N

SCALE 1:125,000
0   0.5   1   2 Km
0   0.5   1 Miles

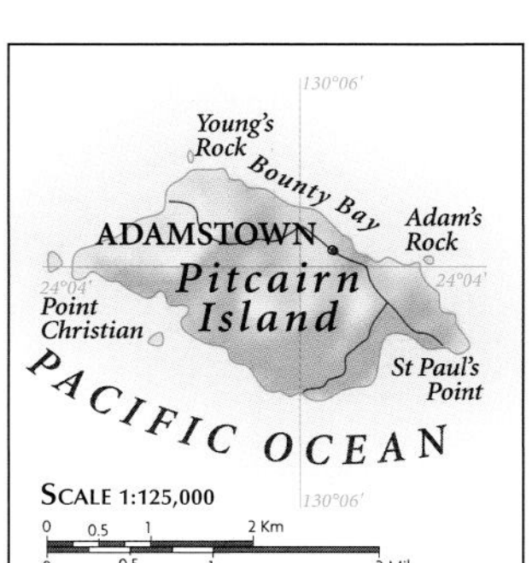

Easter Island *(to Chile)*

One of the most easterly islands in Polynesia, Easter Island *(Isla de Pascua)* – also known as Rapa Nui, is part of Chile. The mainly Polynesian inhabitants support themselves by farming, which is mainly of a subsistence nature, and includes cattle rearing and crops such as sugar cane, bananas, corn, gourds and potatoes. In recent years, tourism has become the most important source of income and the island sustains a small commercial airport.

Easter Island
(Isla de Pascua)
(to Chile)

Cabo   Punta   Playa de Anakena
San Juan
Punta   Punta
Norte   Rosalia
Maunga Terevaka   Bahía de La
506m   Naunau   Pérouse
Ahu Akivi   Cabo
Ahu   Maunga Pukatikei   O'Higgins
Motu   Tautara   370m
Tautara   Rano Raraku
Hanga Roa   Maunga Tangaroa   Cabo
270m   Roggewein
Mataveri   Vaihu   Punta
Ahu Vinapu   Punta   Cuidado
Rano Kau   Akahanga
Orongo   Punta Baja   *P A C I F I C*
Motu Nui   *O C E A N*
Cabo Sur

SCALE 1:500,000
0   2   4   6 Km
0   2   4   6   8 Miles

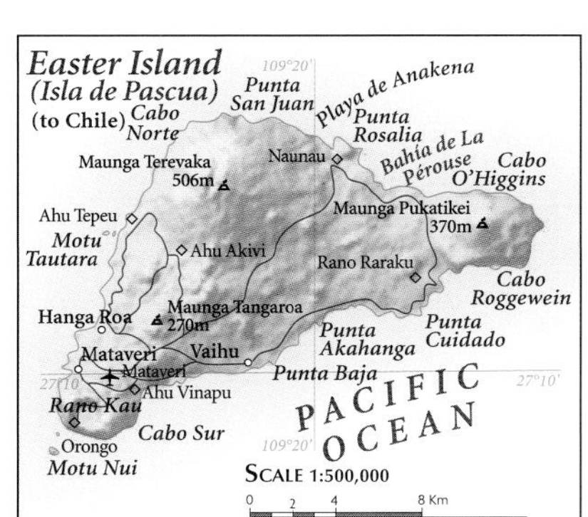

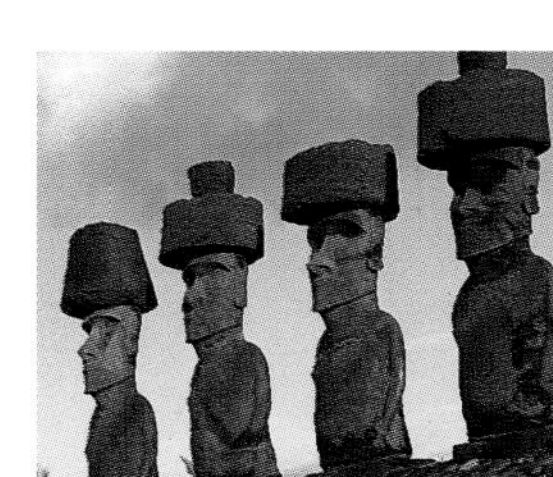

▲ *The Naunau,* a series of huge stone statues overlook Playa de Anakena, on Easter Island. Carved from a soft volcanic rock, they were erected between 400 and 900 years ago.

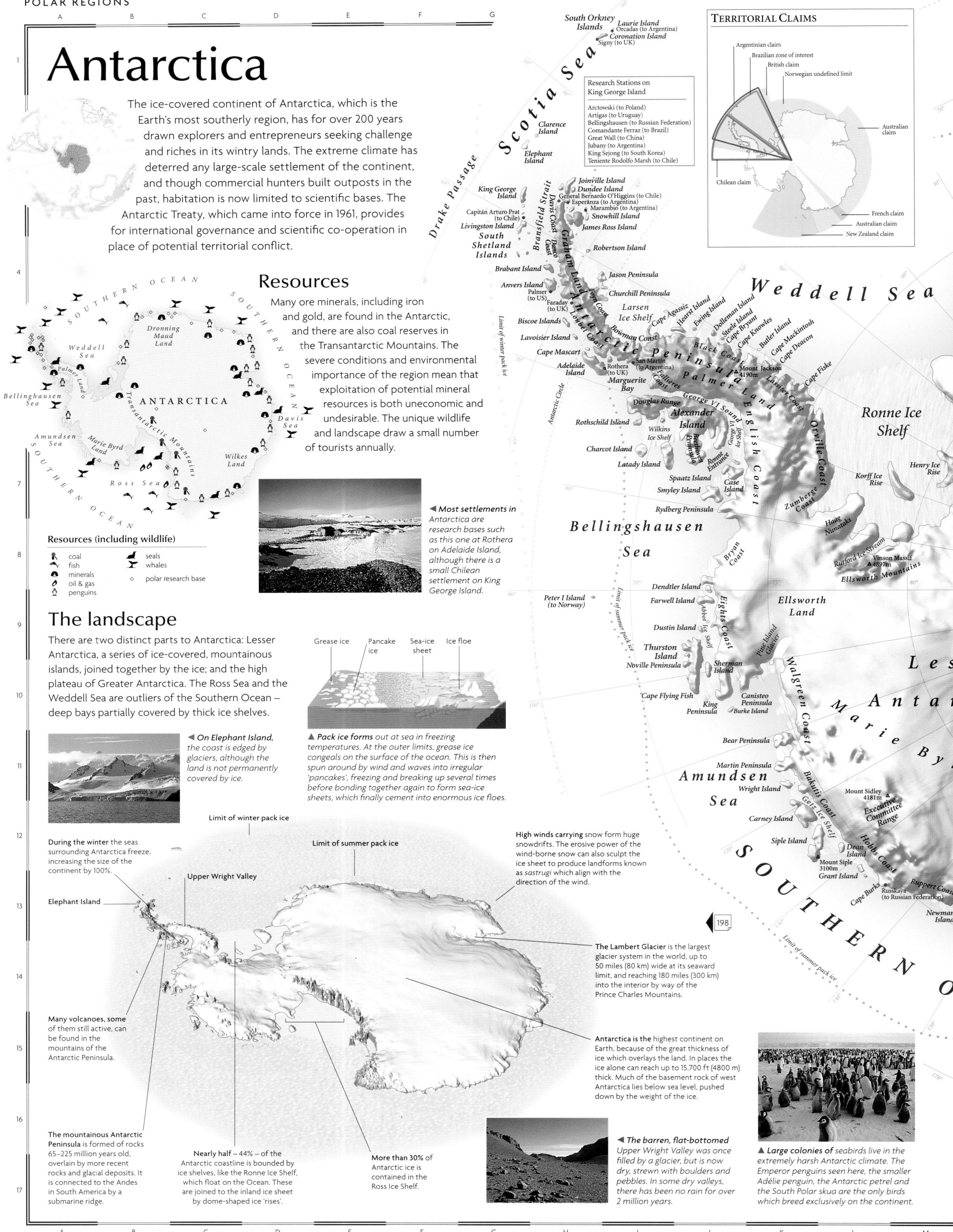

Antarctica

The ice-covered continent of Antarctica, which is the Earth's most southerly region, has for over 200 years drawn explorers and entrepreneurs seeking challenge and riches in its wintry lands. The extreme climate has deterred any large-scale settlement of the continent, and though commercial hunters built outposts in the past, habitation is now limited to scientific bases. The Antarctic Treaty, which came into force in 1961, provides for international governance and scientific co-operation in place of potential territorial conflict.

Resources

Many ore minerals, including iron and gold, are found in the Antarctic, and there are also coal reserves in the Transantarctic Mountains. The severe conditions and environmental importance of the region mean that exploitation of potential mineral resources is both uneconomic and undesirable. The unique wildlife and landscape draw a small number of tourists annually.

Resources (including wildlife)

- coal
- fish
- minerals
- oil & gas
- penguins
- seals
- whales
- polar research base

◀ *Most settlements in Antarctica are research bases such as this one at Rothera on Adelaide Island, although there is a small Chilean settlement on King George Island.*

The landscape

There are two distinct parts to Antarctica: Lesser Antarctica, a series of ice-covered, mountainous islands, joined together by the ice; and the high plateau of Greater Antarctica. The Ross Sea and the Weddell Sea are outliers of the Southern Ocean – deep bays partially covered by thick ice shelves.

Grease ice   Pancake ice   Sea-ice sheet   Ice floe

◀ *On Elephant Island, the coast is edged by glaciers, although the land is not permanently covered by ice.*

▲ *Pack ice forms out at sea in freezing temperatures. At the outer limits, grease ice congeals on the surface of the ocean. This is then spun around by wind and waves into irregular 'pancakes', freezing and breaking up several times before bonding together again to form sea-ice sheets, which finally cement into enormous ice floes.*

Limit of winter pack ice

Upper Wright Valley

Elephant Island

During the winter the seas surrounding Antarctica freeze, increasing the size of the continent by 100%.

Limit of summer pack ice

High winds carrying snow form huge snowdrifts. The erosive power of the wind-borne snow can also sculpt the ice sheet to produce landforms known as *sastrugi* which align with the direction of the wind.

Many volcanoes, some of them still active, can be found in the mountains of the Antarctic Peninsula.

The Lambert Glacier is the largest glacier system in the world, up to 50 miles (80 km) wide at its seaward limit, and reaching 180 miles (300 km) into the interior by way of the Prince Charles Mountains.

Antarctica is the highest continent on Earth, because of the great thickness of ice which overlays the land. In places the ice alone can reach up to 15,700 ft (4800 m) thick. Much of the basement rock of west Antarctica lies below sea level, pushed down by the weight of the ice.

The mountainous Antarctic Peninsula is formed of rocks 65–225 million years old, overlain by more recent rocks and glacial deposits. It is connected to the Andes in South America by a submarine ridge.

Nearly half – 44% – of the Antarctic coastline is bounded by ice shelves, like the Ronne Ice Shelf, which float on the Ocean. These are joined to the inland ice sheet by dome-shaped ice 'rises'.

More than 30% of Antarctic ice is contained in the Ross Ice Shelf.

◀ *The barren, flat-bottomed Upper Wright Valley was once filled by a glacier, but is now dry, strewn with boulders and pebbles. In some dry valleys, there has been no rain for over 2 million years.*

▲ *Large colonies of seabirds live in the extremely harsh Antarctic climate. The Emperor penguins seen here, the smaller Adélie penguin, the Antarctic petrel and the South Polar skua are the only birds which breed exclusively on the continent.*

TERRITORIAL CLAIMS

- Argentinian claim
- Brazilian zone of interest
- British claim
- Norwegian undefined limit
- Australian claim
- Chilean claim
- French claim
- Australian claim
- New Zealand claim

Research Stations on King George Island

- Arctowski (to Poland)
- Artigas (to Uruguay)
- Bellingshausen (to Russian Federation)
- Comandante Ferraz (to Brazil)
- Great Wall (to China)
- Jubany (to Argentina)
- King Sejong (to South Korea)
- Teniente Rodolfo Marsh (to Chile)

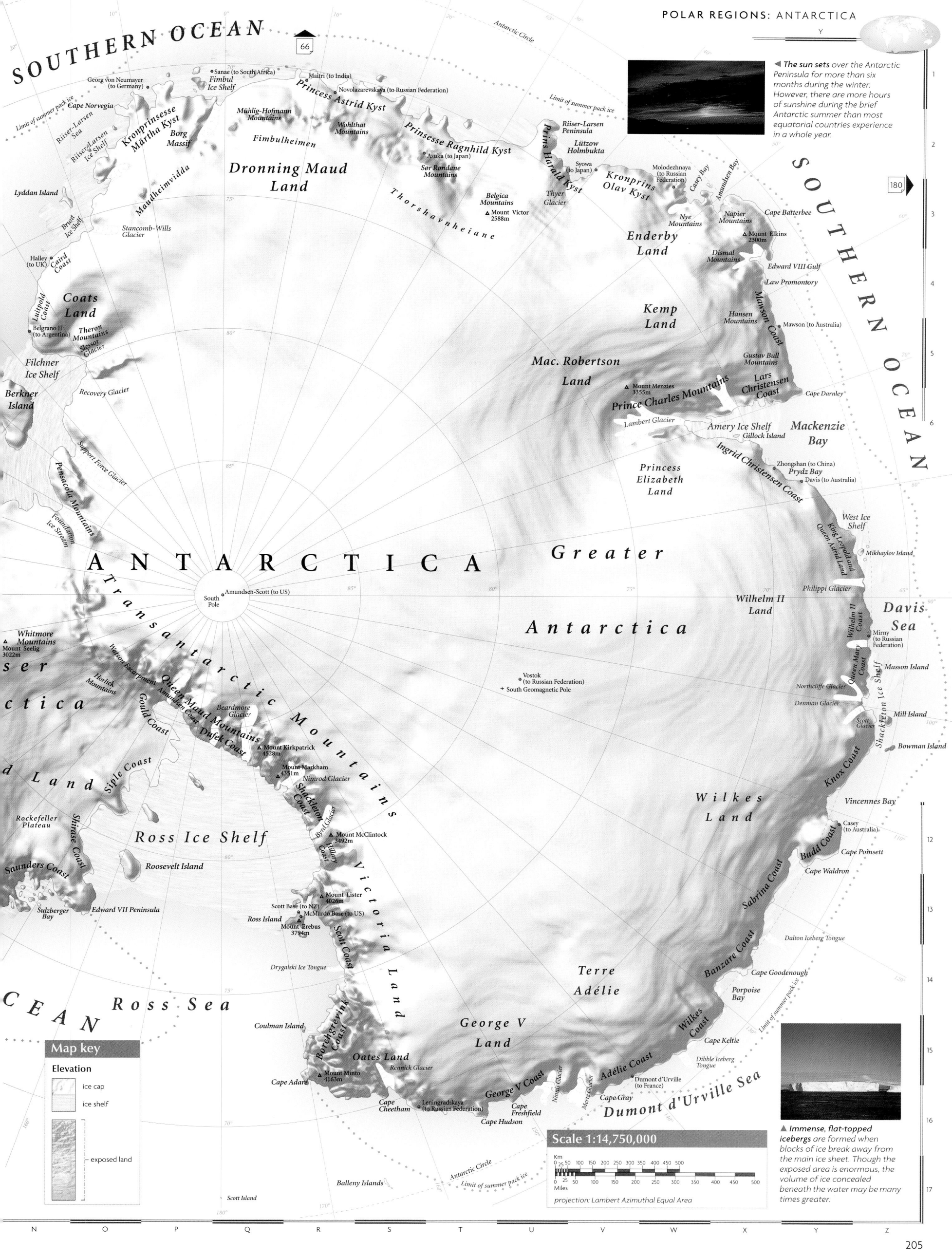

The sun sets over the Antarctic Peninsula for more than six months during the winter. However, there are more hours of sunshine during the brief Antarctic summer than most equatorial countries experience in a whole year.

▲ *Immense, flat-topped icebergs* are formed when blocks of ice break away from the main ice sheet. Though the exposed area is enormous, the volume of ice concealed beneath the water may be many times greater.

Map key

Elevation

- ice cap
- ice shelf
- exposed land

Scale 1:14,750,000

Km
0 25 50 100 150 200 250 300 350 400 450 500

Miles
0 25 50 100 150 200 250 300 350 400 450 500

projection: Lambert Azimuthal Equal Area

The Arctic

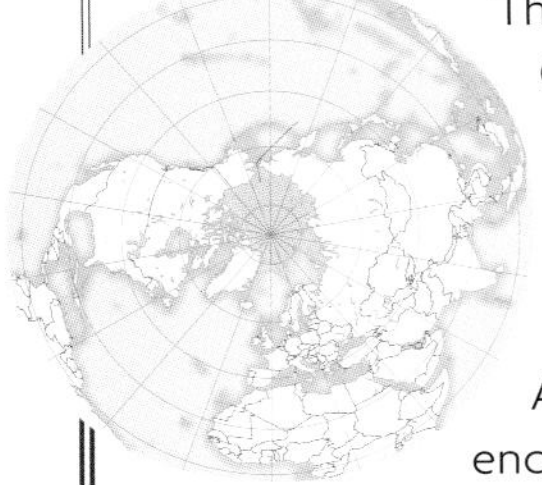

Three continents, Asia, North America and Europe, reach into the Arctic Circle at their northernmost limits, almost entirely encircling the Arctic Ocean. Despite the region's extraordinarily harsh climate, it has been inhabited for thousands of years by peoples such as the European Lapps, the Russian Nenet, and the North American Inuit, who draw a living from fishing, herding and hunting. More recently, particularly in the Russian Arctic, opportunities to exploit oil and other mineral reserves have encouraged immigration. Pollution of the Arctic's unique ecology and damage to the traditional lifestyles of many native peoples have been the unfortunate results of this activity, and international co-operation is needed to safeguard the future of the region.

Map key

Population

- ■ above 5 million
- ▣ 1 million to 5 million
- ◉ 500,000 to 1 million
- ⊚ 100,000 to 500,000
- ⊕ 50,000 to 100,000
- ○ 10,000 to 50,000
- ○ below 10,000

Sea Depth

sea level
- 250m / 820ft
- 500m / 1640ft
- 1000m / 3281ft
- 2000m / 6562ft
- 3000m / 9843ft

Scale 1:21,000,000

Km 0 100 200 300 400 500 600
Miles 0 100 200 300 400 500 600

projection: Lambert Azimuthal Equal Area

▲ *Wind-blown snow etches* deep patterns in the ice sheet known as sastrugi. They align with the direction of the wind.

Resources

Large quantities of coal, oil and natural gas are to be found in the basins of the Arctic Ocean, and in northern Canada, Alaska and the Russian Federation. The cost and difficulty of extraction and, more recently, awareness of damage to the environment, have limited exploitation to coastal regions. The unfrozen waters have stocks of fish including cod, plaice and haddock. Quotas have now been put in place to restrict the number of fish caught annually. Reindeer are herded in large numbers by many of the native Arctic peoples. Most grain and vegetables are imported from elsewhere.

Bering Sea

NORTH AMERICA   *ASIA*

ARCTIC OCEAN

Inuvik
Tiksi
Noril'sk
Qaanaaq
Murmansk
Reykjavík

ATLANTIC OCEAN   *EUROPE*

▲ *Icebreakers, ships with* specially strengthened hulls, designed to break a path through the ice, are used to keep important routes open during the winter, when falling temperatures cause much of the Arctic Ocean to freeze over.

Resources

- coal
- fish
- mining
- oil & gas
- radioactive contamination
- major towns
- major ports

The landscape

The Arctic Ocean comprises two large ocean basins divided by three submarine ridges, the greatest of which, the Lomonosov Ridge, is a huge underwater mountain range which has an average height of more than 10,000 ft (3000 m). The lands which encircle the Arctic Ocean are underlain by great shield areas of ancient rocks, which were heavily glaciated during the last Ice Age.

◀ *Icebergs are constantly* broken up and re-shaped by wind and the oceans. This flat-topped iceberg has been undercut, leaving a craggy ice cliff.

The Canadian Shield underlies almost all of the Canadian Arctic. It is a very stable plateau of ancient rock, now covered by glacial lakes and sediment, which supports tundra vegetation.

The Arctic Ocean is the world's smallest ocean with a total area of 5,440,000 sq miles (15,100,000 sq km).

At a latitude of more than 75° N, the Arctic Ocean is almost permanently covered by pack-ice, though high winds and the movement of the seas may cause the ice to crack and break up.

In the more southerly reaches of the Arctic, like Siberia, much of the land is covered by permafrost. In the summer, higher temperatures warm the frozen ground, causing a number of typical phenomena. These include solifluction, the fast downhill movement of top soil layers; freeze/thaw activity, which patterns the ground into regular polygonal shapes, and the formation of large domes with a frozen ice core, known as pingos.

Lomonosov Ridge

Arctic ice shelf

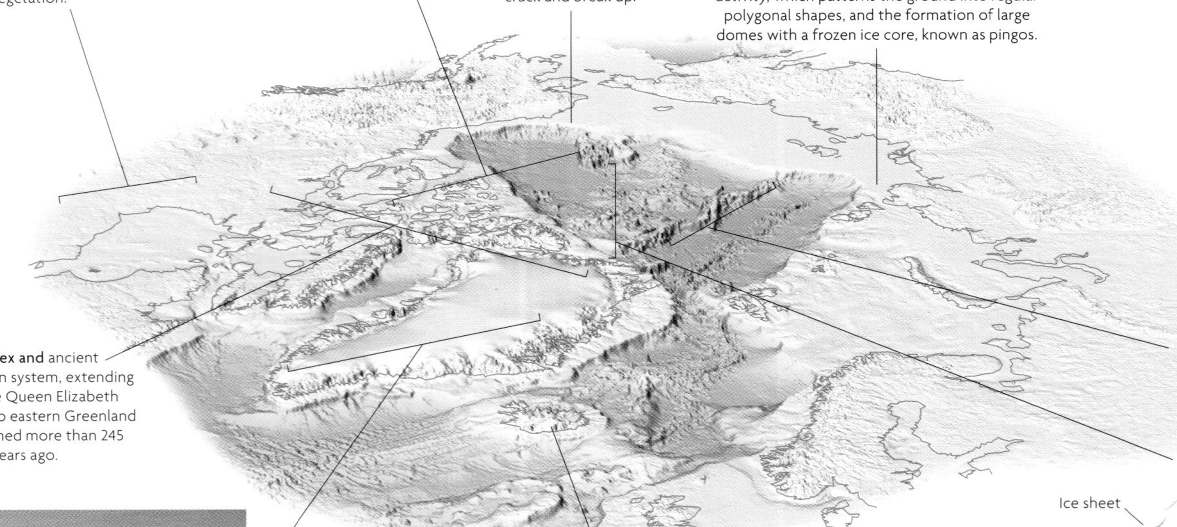

A complex and ancient mountain system, extending from the Queen Elizabeth Islands to eastern Greenland was formed more than 245 million years ago.

◀ *Much of Greenland is* covered by a massive ice sheet more than 650,000 sq miles (1,683,400 sq km) in extent. The weight of the ice has depressed the central land area to form a basin lying more than 1000 ft (300 m) below sea level. Only at the edges of the island is bare rock visible.

Iceland has five major glaciers, sustained by heavy snowfall. Parts of the ice cap cover active volcanoes, such as Bárdharbunga, which periodically erupt causing the melted ice to form a great lake at the glacier margins.

Ice sheet
Iceberg

Crevasses occur at the edge of the ice sheet

Sea water melts the edge of the ice sheet

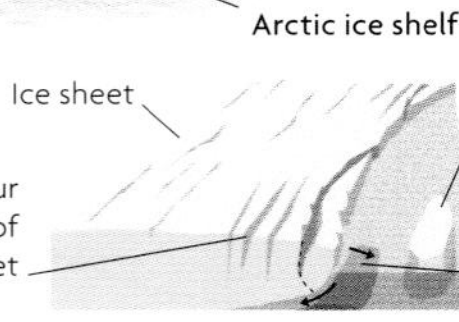

▲ *At the boundary* of the Arctic ice shelves, sea water flows under the ice causing melting and forming crevasses on the surface. This eventually weakens blocks of ice which break away as icebergs. This process is known as calving.

Map labels (main map, right)

CANADA

NORTH AMERICA

Mackenzie

Great Bear Lake

Great Slave Lake

Kugluktuk

Bathurst Inlet

Cambridge Bay

Queen Maud Gulf

King William Island

Boothia Peninsula

Nelson

Churchill

Back

Gulf

Southampton Island

Repulse Bay

Melville Peninsula

Hudson Bay

Coats Island

Mansel Island

Foxe Basin

Prince Charles Island

Ivujivik

Inukjuak

Baffin Island

Hudson Strait

Lake Harbour

Frobisher Bay

Cumberland Sound

Home Bay

Ungava Bay

Cape Chidley

Davis Strait

Maniitsoq

NUUK

Nain

Labrador Sea

Paamiut

Ivittuut

Qaqortoq

Nanortalik

Narsarsuaq

Labrador Basin

Nunap Isua (Kap Farvel) Eirik Ridge

ATLANTIC

198
14
14
66

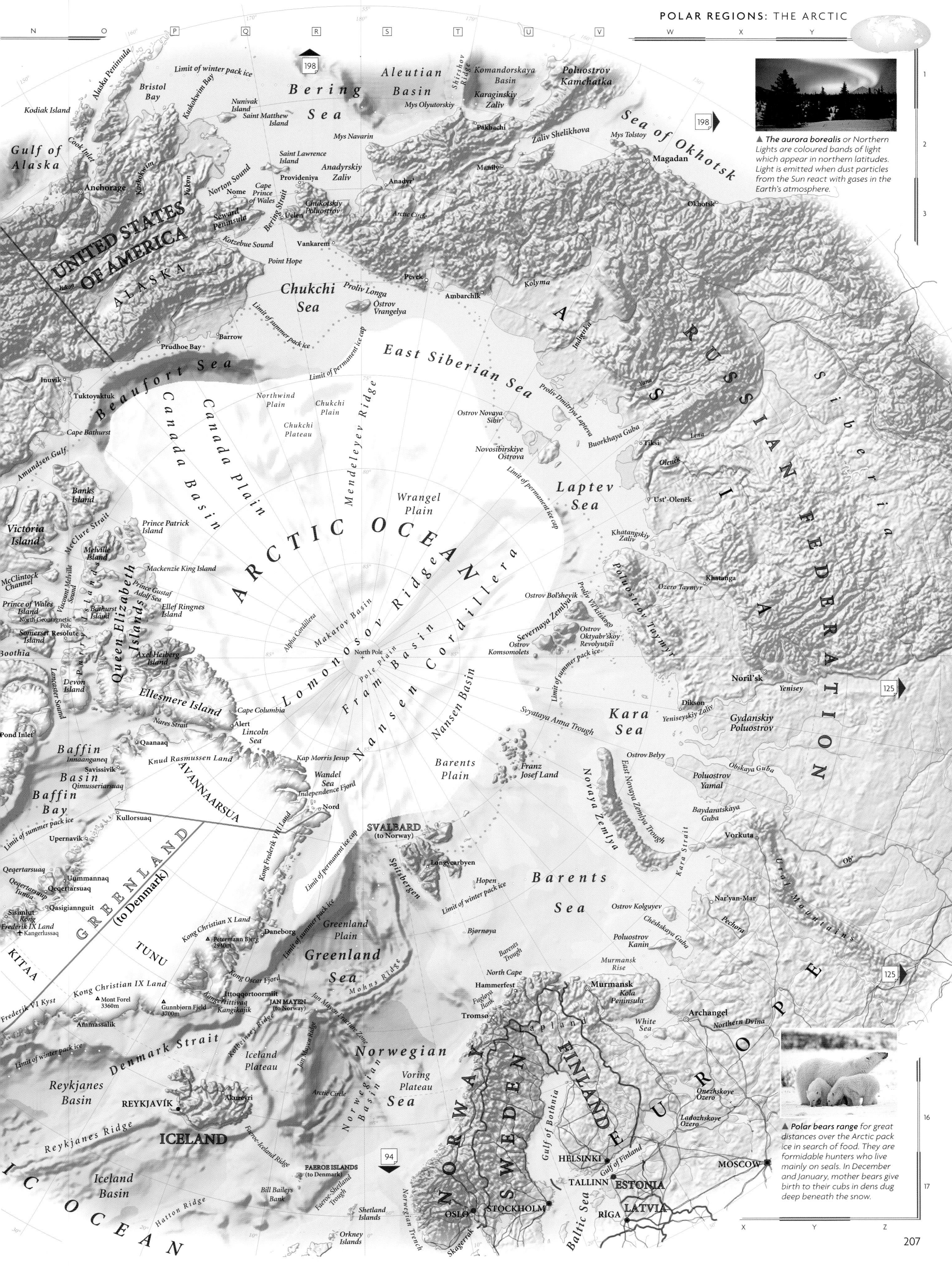

▲ The aurora borealis or Northern Lights are coloured bands of light which appear in northern latitudes. Light is emitted when dust particles from the Sun react with gases in the Earth's atmosphere.

▲ Polar bears range for great distances over the Arctic pack ice in search of food. They are formidable hunters who live mainly on seals. In December and January, mother bears give birth to their cubs in dens dug deep beneath the snow.

Geographical comparisons

Largest countries

Russian Federation	6,592,735 sq miles	(17,075,200 sq km)
Canada	3,851,788 sq miles	(9,976,140 sq km)
USA	3,717,792 sq miles	(9,629,091 sq km)
China	3,705,386 sq miles	(9,596,960 sq km)
Brazil	3,286,470 sq miles	(8,511,965 sq km)
Australia	2,967,893 sq miles	(7,686,850 sq km)
India	1,269,339 sq miles	(3,287,590 sq km)
Argentina	1,068,296 sq miles	(2,766,890 sq km)
Kazakhstan	1,049,150 sq miles	(2,717,300 sq km)
Sudan	967,493 sq miles	(2,505,815 sq km)

Smallest countries

Vatican City	0.17 sq miles	(0.44 sq km)
Monaco	0.75 sq miles	(1.95 sq km)
Nauru	8.2 sq miles	(21.2 sq km)
Tuvalu	10 sq miles	(26 sq km)
San Marino	24 sq miles	(61 sq km)
Liechtenstein	62 sq miles	(160 sq km)
Marshall Islands	70 sq miles	(181 sq km)
St. Kitts & Nevis	101 sq miles	(261 sq km)
Maldives	116 sq miles	(300 sq km)
Malta	124 sq miles	(320 sq km)

Largest islands

	To the nearest 1000 – or 100,000 for the largest	
Greenland	849,400 sq miles	(2,200,000 sq km)
New Guinea	312,000 sq miles	(808,000 sq km)
Borneo	292,222 sq miles	(757,050 sq km)
Madagascar	229,300 sq miles	(594,000 sq km)
Sumatra	202,300 sq miles	(524,000 sq km)
Baffin Island	183,800 sq miles	(476,000 sq km)
Honshu	88,800 sq miles	(230,000 sq km)
Britain	88,700 sq miles	(229,800 sq km)
Victoria Island	81,900 sq miles	(212,000 sq km)
Ellesmere Island	75,700 sq miles	(196,000 sq km)

Richest countries

	GNI per capita, in US$
Luxembourg	56,230
Norway	52,030
Liechtenstein	50,000
Switzerland	48,230
USA	41,400
Denmark	40,650
Iceland	38,620
Japan	37,810
Sweden	35,770
Ireland	34,280

Poorest countries

	GNI per capita, in US$
Burundi	90
Ethiopia	110
Liberia	110
Congo, Dem. Rep.	120
Somalia	120
Guinea-Bissau	160
Malawi	170
Eritrea	180
Sierra Leone	200
Rwanda	220
Afghanistan	222
Niger	230

Most populous countries

China	1,315,800,000
India	1,103,400,000
USA	298,200,000
Indonesia	222,800,000
Brazil	186,400,000
Cameroon	163,000,000
Pakistan	157,900,000
Russian Federation	143,200,000
Bangladesh	141,800,000
Nigeria	131,500,000

Least populous countries

Vatican City	921
Tuvalu	11,636
Nauru	13,048
Palau	20,303
San Marino	28,880
Monaco	32,409
Liechtenstein	33,717
St Kitts & Nevis	38,958
Marshall Islands	59,071
Antigua & Barbuda	68,722
Dominica	69,029
Andorra	70,549

Most densely populated countries

Monaco	43,212 people per sq mile	(16,620 per sq km)
Singapore	18,220 people per sq mile	(7049 per sq km)
Vatican City	5418 people per sq mile	(2093 per sq km)
Malta	3242 people per sq mile	(1256 per sq km)
Maldives	2836 people per sq mile	(1097 per sq km)
Bangledesh	2743 people per sq mile	(1059 per sq km)
Bahrain	2663 people per sq mile	(1030 per sq km)
China	1838 people per sq mile	(710 per sq km)
Mauritius	1671 people per sq mile	(645 per sq km)
Barbados	1627 people per sq mile	(628 per sq km)

Most sparsely populated countries

Mongolia	4 people per sq mile	(2 per sq km)
Namibia	6 people per sq mile	(2 per sq km)
Australia	7 people per sq mile	(3 per sq km)
Mauritania	8 people per sq mile	(3 per sq km)
Surinam	8 people per sq mile	(3 per sq km)
Botswana	8 people per sq mile	(3 per sq km)
Iceland	8 people per sq mile	(3 per sq km)
Canada	9 people per sq mile	(4 per sq km)
Libya	9 people per sq mile	(4 per sq km)
Guyana	10 people per sq mile	(4 per sq km)

Most widely spoken languages

1. Chinese (Mandarin)	6. Arabic
2. English	7. Bengali
3. Hindi	8. Portuguese
4. Spanish	9. Malay-Indonesian
5. Russian	10. French

Largest conurbations

	Population
Tokyo	34,200,000
Mexico City	22,800,000
Seoul	22,300,000
New York	21,900,000
São Paulo	20,200,000
Mumbai	19,850,000
Delhi	19,700,000
Shanghai	18,150,000
Los Angeles	18,000,000
Osaka	16,800,000
Jakarta	16,550,000
Kolkata	15,650,000
Cairo	15,600,000
Manila	14,950,000
Karachi	14,300,000
Moscow	13,750,000
Buenos Aires	13,450,000
Dacca	13,250,000
Rio de Janeiro	12,150,000
Beijing	12,100,000
London	12,000,000
Tehran	11,850,000
Istanbul	11,500,000
Lagos	11,100,000
Shenzhen	10,700,000

Countries with the most land borders

14: China		(Afghanistan, Bhutan, Burma, India, Kazakhstan, Kyrgyzstan, Laos, Mongolia, Nepal, North Korea, Pakistan, Russian Federation, Tajikistan, Vietnam)
14: Russian Federation		(Azerbaijan, Belarus, China, Estonia, Finland, Georgia, Kazakhstan, Latvia, Lithuania, Mongolia, North Korea, Norway, Poland, Ukraine)
10: Brazil		(Argentina, Bolivia, Colombia, French Guiana, Guyana, Paraguay, Peru, Surinam, Uruguay, Venezuela)
9: Congo, Dem. Rep.		(Angola, Burundi, Central African Republic, Congo, Rwanda, Sudan, Tanzania, Uganda, Zambia)
9: Germany		(Austria, Belgium, Czech Republic, Denmark, France, Luxembourg, Netherlands, Poland, Switzerland)
9: Sudan		(Central African Republic, Chad, Dem. Rep.Congo, Egypt, Eritrea, Ethiopia, Kenya, Libya, Uganda)
8: Austria		(Czech Republic, Germany, Hungary, Italy, Liechtenstein, Slovakia, Slovenia, Switzerland)
8: France		(Andorra, Belgium, Germany, Italy, Luxembourg, Monaco, Spain, Switzerland)
8: Tanzania		(Burundi, Dem. Rep.Congo, Kenya, Malawi, Mozambique, Rwanda, Uganda, Zambia)
8: Turkey		(Armenia, Azerbaijan, Bulgaria, Georgia, Greece, Iran, Iraq, Syria)
8: Zambia		(Angola, Botswana, Dem. Rep.Congo, Malawi, Mozambique, Namibia, Tanzania, Zimbabwe)

Longest rivers

Nile (NE Africa)	4160 miles	(6695 km)
Amazon (South America)	4049 miles	(6516 km)
Yangtze (China)	3915 miles	(6299 km)
Mississippi/Missouri (USA)	3710 miles	(5969 km)
Ob'-Irtysh (Russian Federation)	3461 miles	(5570 km)
Yellow River (China)	3395 miles	(5464 km)
Congo (Central Africa)	2900 miles	(4667 km)
Mekong (Southeast Asia)	2749 miles	(4425 km)
Lena (Russian Federation)	2734 miles	(4400 km)
Mackenzie (Canada)	2640 miles	(4250 km)
Yenisey (Russian Federation)	2541 miles	(4090km)

Highest mountains

		Height above sea level
Everest	29,035 ft	(8850 m)
K2	28,253 ft	(8611 m)
Kanchenjunga I	28,210 ft	(8598 m)
Makalu I	27,767 ft	(8463 m)
Cho Oyu	26,907 ft	(8201 m)
Dhaulagiri I	26,796 ft	(8167 m)
Manaslu I	26,783 ft	(8163 m)
Nanga Parbat I	26,661 ft	(8126 m)
Annapurna I	26,547 ft	(8091 m)
Gasherbrum I	26,471 ft	(8068 m)

Largest bodies of inland water

		With area and depth
Caspian Sea	143,243 sq miles (371,000 sq km)	3215 ft (980 m)
Lake Superior	31,151 sq miles (83,270 sq km)	1289 ft (393 m)
Lake Victoria	26,828 sq miles (69,484 sq km)	328 ft (100 m)
Lake Huron	23,436 sq miles (60,700 sq km)	751 ft (229 m)
Lake Michigan	22,402 sq miles (58,020 sq km)	922 ft (281 m)
Lake Tanganyika	12,703 sq miles (32,900 sq km)	4700 ft (1435 m)
Great Bear Lake	12,274 sq miles (31,790 sq km)	1047 ft (319 m)
Lake Baikal	11,776 sq miles (30,500 sq km)	5712 ft (1741 m)
Great Slave Lake	10,981 sq miles (28,440 sq km)	459 ft (140 m)
Lake Erie	9,915 sq miles (25,680 sq km)	197 ft (60 m)

Deepest ocean features

Challenger Deep, Mariana Trench (Pacific)	36,201 ft	(11,034 m)
Vityaz III Depth, Tonga Trench (Pacific)	35,704 ft	(10,882 m)
Vityaz Depth, Kurile-Kamchatka Trench (Pacific)	34,588 ft	(10,542 m)
Cape Johnson Deep, Philippine Trench (Pacific)	34,441 ft	(10,497 m)
Kermadec Trench (Pacific)	32,964 ft	(10,047 m)
Ramapo Deep, Japan Trench (Pacific)	32,758 ft	(9984 m)
Milwaukee Deep, Puerto Rico Trench (Atlantic)	30,185 ft	(9200 m)
Argo Deep, Torres Trench (Pacific)	30,070 ft	(9165 m)
Meteor Depth, South Sandwich Trench (Atlantic)	30,000 ft	(9144 m)
Planet Deep, New Britain Trench (Pacific)	29,988 ft	(9140 m)

Greatest waterfalls

		Mean flow of water
Boyoma (Congo (Zaire))	600,400 cu. ft/sec	(17,000 cu.m/sec)
Khône (Laos/Cambodia)	410,000 cu. ft/sec	(11,600 cu.m/sec)
Niagara (USA/Canada)	195,000 cu. ft/sec	(5500 cu.m/sec)
Grande (Uruguay)	160,000 cu. ft/sec	(4500 cu.m/sec)
Paulo Afonso (Brazil)	100,000 cu. ft/sec	(2800 cu.m/sec)
Urubupunga (Brazil)	97,000 cu. ft/sec	(2750 cu.m/sec)
Iguaçu (Argentina/Brazil)	62,000 cu. ft/sec	(1700 cu.m/sec)
Maribondo (Brazil)	53,000 cu. ft/sec	(1500 cu.m/sec)
Victoria (Zimbabwe)	39,000 cu. ft/sec	(1100 cu.m/sec)
Kabalega (Uganda)	42,000 cu. ft/sec	(1200 cu.m/sec)
Churchill (Canada)	35,000 cu. ft/sec	(1000 cu.m/sec)
Cauvery (India)	33,000 cu. ft/sec	(900 cu.m/sec)

Highest waterfalls

	* Indicates that the total height is a single leap	
Angel (Venezuela)	3212 ft	(979 m)
Tugela (South Africa)	3110 ft	(948 m)
Utigard (Norway)	2625 ft	(800 m)
Mongefossen (Norway)	2539 ft	(774 m)
Mtarazi (Zimbabwe)	2500 ft	(762 m)
Yosemite (USA)	2425 ft	(739 m)
Ostre Mardola Foss (Norway)	2156 ft	(657 m)
Tyssestrengane (Norway)	2119 ft	(646 m)
*Cuquenan (Venezuela)	2001 ft	(610 m)
Sutherland (New Zealand)	1903 ft	(580 m)
*Kjellfossen (Norway)	1841 ft	(561 m)

Largest deserts

	NB -- Most of Antarctica is a polar desert, with only 50mm of precipitation annually	
Sahara	3,450,000 sq miles	(9,065,000 sq km)
Gobi	500,000 sq miles	(1,295,000 sq km)
Ar Rub al Khali	289,600 sq miles	(750,000 sq km)
Great Victorian	249,800 sq miles	(647,000 sq km)
Sonoran	120,000 sq miles	(311,000 sq km)
Kalahari	120,000 sq miles	(310,800 sq km)
Kara Kum	115,800 sq miles	(300,000 sq km)
Takla Makan	100,400 sq miles	(260,000 sq km)
Namib	52,100 sq miles	(135,000 sq km)
Thar	33,670 sq miles	(130,000 sq km)

Hottest inhabited places

Djibouti (Djibouti)	86° F	(30 °C)
Timbouctou (Mali)	84.7° F	(29.3 °C)
Tirunelveli (India)		
Tuticorin (India)		
Nellore (India)	84.5° F	(29.2 °C)
Santa Marta (Colombia)		
Aden (Yemen)	84° F	(28.9 °C)
Madurai (India)		
Niamey (Niger)		
Hodeida (Yemen)	83.8° F	(28.8 °C)
Ouagadougou (Burkina)		
Thanjavur (India)		
Tiruchchirappalli (India)		

Driest inhabited places

Aswân (Egypt)	0.02 in	(0.5 mm)
Luxor (Egypt)	0.03 in	(0.7 mm)
Arica (Chile)	0.04 in	(1.1 mm)
Ica (Peru)	0.1 in	(2.3 mm)
Antofagasta (Chile)	0.2 in	(4.9 mm)
El Minya (Egypt)	0.2 in	(5.1 mm)
Asyût (Egypt)	0.2 in	(5.2 mm)
Callao (Peru)	0.5 in	(12.0 mm)
Trujillo (Peru)	0.55 in	(14.0 mm)
El Faiyûm (Egypt)	0.8 in	(19.0 mm)

Wettest inhabited places

Buenaventura (Colombia)	265 in	(6743 mm)
Monrovia (Liberia)	202 in	(5131 mm)
Pago Pago (American Samoa)	196 in	(4990 mm)
Moulmein (Burma)	191 in	(4852 mm)
Lae (Papua New Guinea)	183 in	(4645 mm)
Baguio (Luzon Island, Philippines)	180 in	(4573 mm)
Sylhet (Bangladesh)	176 in	(4457 mm)
Padang (Sumatra, Indonesia)	166 in	(4225 mm)
Bogor (Java, Indonesia)	166 in	(4225 mm)
Conakry (Guinea)	171 in	(4341 mm)

The time zones

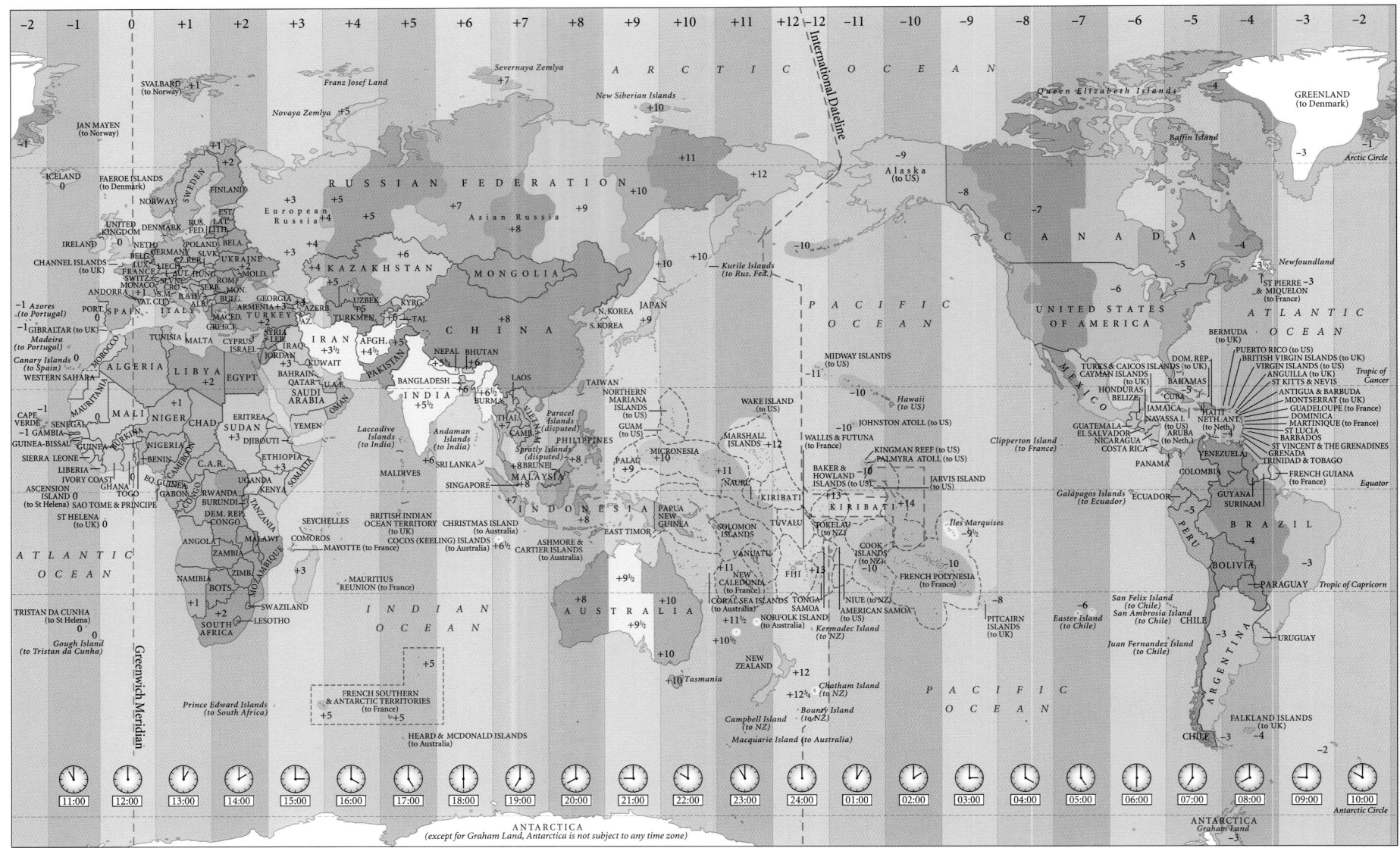

The numbers at the top of the map indicate the number of hours each time zone is ahead or behind Greenwich Mean Time (GMT). The clocks and 24-hour times given at the bottom of the map show the time in each time zone when it is 12:00 hours noon GMT.

Time zones

The present system of international timekeeping divides the world into 24 time zones by means of 24 standard meridians of longitude, each 15° apart. Time is measured in each zone as so many hours ahead or behind the time at the Greenwich Meridian (GMT). Countries, or parts of countries, falling in the vicinity of each zone, adopt its time as shown on the map above. Therefore, using the map, when it is 12:00 noon GMT, it will be 2:00 pm in Zambia; similarly, when it is 4:30 pm GMT, it will be 11:30 am in Peru.

Greenwich Mean Time (GMT)

Greenwich Mean Time (or Universal Time, as it is more correctly called) has been the internationally accepted basis for calculating solar time – measured in relation to the Earth's rotation around the Sun – since 1884. Greenwich Mean Time is specifically the solar time at the site of the former Royal Observatory in the London Borough of Greenwich, United Kingdom. The Greenwich Meridian is an imaginary line around the world that runs through the North and South poles. It corresponds to 0° of longitude, which lies on this site at Greenwich. Time is measured around the world in relation to the official time along the Meridian.

Standard time

Standard time is the official time, designated by law, in any specific country or region. Standard time was

initiated in 1884, after it became apparent that the practice of keeping various systems of local time was causing confusion – particularly in the USA and Canada, where several railroad routes passed through scores of areas which calculated local time by different rules. The standard time of a particular region is calculated in reference to the longitudinal time zone in which it falls. In practice, these zones do not always match their longitudinal position; in some places the area of the zone has been altered in shape for the convenience of inhabitants, as can be seen in the map. For example, while China occupies five time zones, time is standardized across the whole country at +8 hours GMT. So as the sun rises in Beijing, there are still four more hours of darkness in western China despite it being the in the same standard time zone.

The International Dateline

The International Dateline is an imaginary line that extends from pole to pole, and roughly corresponds to a line of 180° longitude for much of its length. This line is the arbitrary marker between calendar days. By moving from east to west across the line, a traveller will need to set their calendar back one day, while those travelling in the opposite direction will need to add a day. This is to compensate for the use of standard time around the world, which is based on the time at noon along the Greenwich Meridian, approximately halfway around the world. Wide deviations from 180° longitude

occur through the Bering Strait – to avoid dividing Siberia into two separate calendar days – and in the Pacific Ocean – to allow certain Pacific islands the same calendar day as New Zealand. Changes were made to the International Dateline in 1995 that made Millennium Island (formerly Caroline Island) in Kiribati the first land area to witness the beginning of the year 2000.

Daylight saving time

Also known as summer time, daylight saving is a system of advancing clocks in order to extend the waking day during periods of later daylight hours. This normally means advancing clocks by one hour in early spring, and reverting back to standard time in early autumn. The system of daylight saving is used throughout much of Europe, the USA, Australia, and many other countries worldwide, although there are no standardized dates for the changeover to summer time due to the differences in hours of daylight at different latitudes. Daylight saving was first introduced in certain countries during the First World War, to decrease the need for artificial light and heat – the system stayed in place after the war, as it proved practical. During the Second World War, some countries went so far as to keep their clocks an hour ahead of standard time continuously, and the UK temporarily introduced 'double summer time', which advanced clocks two hours ahead of standard time during the summer months.

Countries of the World

There are currently 194 independent countries in the world – more than at any previous time – and 59 dependencies. Antarctica is the only land area on Earth that is not officially part of, and does not belong to, any single country.

In 1950, the world comprised 82 countries. In the decades following, many more states came into being as they achieved independence from their former colonial rulers. Most recent additions were caused by the breakup of the former Soviet Union in 1991, and the former Yugoslavia in 1992, which swelled the ranks of independent states. In May 2006 Montenegro voted to split from Serbia, making it the latest country to gain independence.

Country factfile key

Formation Date of independence / date current borders were established

Population Total population / population density – based on total *land* area / percentage of urban-based population

Languages An asterisk (*) denotes the official language(s)

Calorie consumption Average number of calories consumed daily per person

AFGHANISTAN
Central Asia

Official name Islamic State of Afghanistan
Formation 1919 / 1919
Capital Kabul
Population 29.9 million / 119 people per sq mile (46 people per sq km) / 22%
Total area 250,000 sq miles (647,500 sq km)
Languages Pashtu*, Tajik, Dari, Farsi, Uzbek, Turkmen
Religions Sunni Muslim 84%, Shi'a Muslim 15%, Other 1%
Ethnic mix Pashtun 38%, Tajik 25%, Hazara 19%, Uzbek and Turkmen 15%, Other 3%
Government Transitional regime
Currency New afghani = 100 puls
Literacy rate 36%
Calorie consumption 1539 calories

ALBANIA
Southeast Europe

Official name Republic of Albania
Formation 1912 / 1921
Capital Tirana
Population 3.1 million / 293 people per sq mile (113 people per sq km) / 42%
Total area 11,100 sq miles (28,748 sq km)
Languages Albanian*, Greek
Religions Sunni Muslim 70%, Orthodox Christian 20%, Roman Catholic 10%
Ethnic mix Albanian 93%, Greek 5%, Other 2%
Government Parliamentary system
Currency Lek = 100 qindarka (qintars)
Literacy rate 99%
Calorie consumption 2848 calories

ALGERIA
North Africa

Official name People's Democratic Republic of Algeria
Formation 1962 / 1962
Capital Algiers
Population 32.9 million / 36 people per sq mile (14 people per sq km) / 60%
Total area 919,590 sq miles (2,381,740 sq km)
Languages Arabic, Tamazight (Kabyle, Shawia, Tamashek), French
Religions Sunni Muslim 99%, Christian and Jewish 1%
Ethnic mix Arab 75%, Berber 24%, European and Jewish 1%
Government Presidential system
Currency Algerian dinar = 100 centimes
Literacy rate 70%
Calorie consumption 3022 calories

ANDORRA
Southwest Europe

Official name Principality of Andorra
Formation 1278 / 1278
Capital Andorra la Vella
Population 70,549 / 392 people per sq mile (152 people per sq km) / 63%
Total area 181 sq miles (468 sq km)
Languages Spanish, Catalan, French, Portuguese
Religions Roman Catholic 94%, Other 6%
Ethnic mix Spanish 46%, Andorran 28%, Other 18%, French 8%
Government Parliamentary system
Currency Euro = 100 cents
Literacy rate 99%
Calorie consumption Not available

ANGOLA
Southern Africa

Official name Republic of Angola
Formation 1975 / 1975
Capital Luanda
Population 15.9 million / 33 people per sq mile (13 people per sq km) / 34%
Total area 481,351 sq miles (1,246,700 sq km)
Languages Portuguese*, Umbundu, Kimbundu, Kikongo
Religions Roman Catholic 50%, Other 30%, Protestant 20%
Ethnic mix Ovimbundu 37%, Other 25%, Kimbundu 25%, Bakongo 13%
Government Presidential system
Currency Readjusted kwanza = 100 lwei
Literacy rate 67%
Calorie consumption 2083 calories

ANTIGUA & BARBUDA
West Indies

Official name Antigua and Barbuda
Formation 1981 / 1981
Capital St. John's
Population 68,722 / 404 people per sq mile (156 people per sq km) / 37%
Total area 170 sq miles (442 sq km)
Languages English, English patois
Religions Anglican 45%, Other Protestant 42%, Roman Catholic 10%, Other 2%, Rastafarian 1%
Ethnic mix Black African 95%, Other 5%
Government Parliamentary system
Currency Eastern Caribbean dollar = 100 cents
Literacy rate 86%
Calorie consumption 2349 calories

ARGENTINA
South America

Official name Republic of Argentina
Formation 1816 / 1816
Capital Buenos Aires
Population 38.7 million / 37 people per sq mile (14 people per sq km) / 90%
Total area 1,068,296 sq miles (2,766,890 sq km)
Languages Spanish*, Italian, Amerindian languages
Religions Roman Catholic 90%, Other 6%, Protestant 2%, Jewish 2%
Ethnic mix Indo-European 83%, Mestizo 14%, Jewish 2%, Amerindian 1%
Government Presidential system
Currency new Argentine peso = 100 centavos
Literacy rate 97%
Calorie consumption 2992 calories

ARMENIA
Southwest Asia

Official name Republic of Armenia
Formation 1991 / 1991
Capital Yerevan
Population 3 million / 261 people per sq mile (101 people per sq km) / 70%
Total area 11,506 sq miles (29,800 sq km)
Languages Armenian*, Azeri, Russian
Religions Armenian Apostolic Church (Orthodox) 94%, Other 6%
Ethnic mix Armenian 93%, Azeri 3%, Other 2%, Russian 2%
Government Presidential system
Currency Dram = 100 luma
Literacy rate 99%
Calorie consumption 2268 calories

AUSTRALIA
Australasia & Oceania

Official name Commonwealth of Australia
Formation 1901 / 1901
Capital Canberra
Population 20.2 million / 7 people per sq mile (3 people per sq km) / 85%
Total area 2,967,893 sq miles (7,686,850 sq km)
Languages English*, Italian, Cantonese, Greek, Arabic, Vietnamese, Aboriginal languages
Religions Roman Catholic 26%, Anglican 24%, Other 23%, Nonreligious 13%, United Church 8%, Other Protestant 6%
Ethnic mix European 92%, Asian 5%, Aboriginal and other 3%
Government Parliamentary system
Currency Australian dollar = 100 cents
Literacy rate 99%
Calorie consumption 3054 calories

AUSTRIA
Central Europe

Official name Republic of Austria
Formation 1918 / 1919
Capital Vienna
Population 8.2 million / 257 people per sq mile (99 people per sq km) / 65%
Total area 32,378 sq miles (83,858 sq km)
Languages German*, Croatian, Slovenian, Hungarian (Magyar)
Religions Roman Catholic 78%, Nonreligious 9%, Other (including Jewish and Muslim) 8%, Protestant 5%
Ethnic mix Austrian 93%, Croat, Slovene, and Hungarian 6%, Other 1%
Government Parliamentary system
Currency Euro = 100 cents
Literacy rate 99%
Calorie consumption 3673 calories

AZERBAIJAN
Southwest Asia

Official name Republic of Azerbaijan
Formation 1991 / 1991
Capital Baku
Population 8.4 million / 251 people per sq mile (97 people per sq km) / 57%
Total area 33,436 sq miles (86,600 sq km)
Languages Azeri, Russian
Religions Shi'a Muslim 68%, Sunni Muslim 26%, Russian Orthodox 3%, Armenian Apostolic Church (Orthodox) 2%, Other 1%
Ethnic mix Azeri 90%, Dagestani 3%, Russian 3%, Other 2%, Armenian 2%
Government Presidential system
Currency Manat = 100 gopik
Literacy rate 99%
Calorie consumption 2575 calories

BAHAMAS
West Indies

Official name Commonwealth of the Bahamas
Formation 1973 / 1973
Capital Nassau
Population 323,000 / 84 people per sq mile (32 people per sq km) / 89%
Total area 5382 sq miles (13,940 sq km)
Languages English*, English Creole, French Creole
Religions Baptist 32%, Anglican 20%, Roman Catholic 19%, Other 17%, Methodist 6%, Church of God 6%
Ethnic mix Black African 85%, Other 15%
Government Parliamentary system
Currency Bahamian dollar = 100 cents
Literacy rate 96%
Calorie consumption 2755 calories

BAHRAIN
Southwest Asia

Official name Kingdom of Bahrain
Formation 1971 / 1971
Capital Manama
Population 727,000 / 2663 people per sq mile (1030 people per sq km) / 97%
Total area 239 sq miles (620 sq km)
Languages Arabic*
Religions Muslim (mainly Shi'a) 99%, Other 1%
Ethnic mix Bahraini 70%, Iranian, Indian, and Pakistani 24%, Other Arab 4%, European 2%
Government Monarchy
Currency Bahraini dinar = 1000 fils
Literacy rate 88%
Calorie consumption Not available

BANGLADESH
South Asia

Official name People's Republic of Bangladesh
Formation 1971 / 1971
Capital Dhaka
Population 142 million / 2743 people per sq mile (1059 people per sq km) / 25%
Total area 55,598 sq miles (144,000 sq km)
Languages Bengali*, Urdu, Chakma, Marma (Magh), Garo, Khasi, Santhali, Tripuri, Mro
Religions Muslim (mainly Sunni) 87%, Hindu 12%, Other 1%
Ethnic mix Bengali 98%, Other 2%
Government Parliamentary system
Currency Taka = 100 poisha
Literacy rate 41%
Calorie consumption 2205 calories

BARBADOS
West Indies

Official name Barbados
Formation 1966 / 1966
Capital Bridgetown
Population 270,000 / 1627 people per sq mile (628 people per sq km) / 50%
Total area 166 sq miles (430 sq km)
Languages English*, Bajan (Barbadian English)
Religions Anglican 40%, Other 24%, Nonreligious 17%, Pentecostal 8%, Methodist 7%, Roman Catholic 4%
Ethnic mix Black African 90%, Other 10%
Government Parliamentary system
Currency Barbados dollar = 100 cents
Literacy rate 99%
Calorie consumption 3091 calories

BELARUS
Eastern Europe

Official name Republic of Belarus
Formation 1991 / 1991
Capital Minsk
Population 9.8 million / 122 people per sq mile (47 people per sq km) / 71%
Total area 80,154 sq miles (207,600 sq km)
Languages Belarussian*, Russian
Religions Orthodox Christian 60%, Other 32%, Roman Catholic 8%
Ethnic mix Belarussian 78%, Russian 13%, Polish 4%, Ukrainian 3%, Other 2%
Government Presidential system
Currency Belarussian rouble = 100 kopeks
Literacy rate 99%
Calorie consumption 3000 calories

BELGIUM
Northwest Europe

Official name Kingdom of Belgium
Formation 1830 / 1919
Capital Brussels
Population 10.4 million / 821 people per sq mile (317 people per sq km) / 97%
Total area 11,780 sq miles (30,510 sq km)
Languages Dutch*, French*, German
Religions Roman Catholic 88%, Other 10%, Muslim 2%
Ethnic mix Fleming 58%, Walloon 33%, Other 6%, Italian 2%, Moroccan 1%
Government Parliamentary system
Currency Euro = 100 cents
Literacy rate 99%
Calorie consumption 3584 calories

BELIZE
Central America

Official name Belize
Formation 1981 / 1981
Capital Belmopan
Population 270,000 / 31 people per sq mile (12 people per sq km) / 54%
Total area 8867 sq miles (22,966 sq km)
Languages English*, English Creole, Spanish, Mayan, Garifuna (Carib)
Religions Roman Catholic 62%, Other 13%, Anglican 12%, Methodist 6%, Mennonite 4%, Seventh-day Adventist 3%
Ethnic mix Mestizo 44%, Creole 30%, Maya 11%, Garifuna 7%, Other 4%, Asian Indian 4%
Government Parliamentary system
Currency Belizean dollar = 100 cents
Literacy rate 77%
Calorie consumption 2869 calories

BENIN
West Africa

Official name Republic of Benin
Formation 1960 / 1960
Capital Porto-Novo
Population 8.4 million / 197 people per sq mile (76 people per sq km) / 42%
Total area 43,483 sq miles (112,620 sq km)
Languages French*, Fon, Bariba, Yoruba, Adja, Houeda, Somba
Religions Voodoo 50%, Muslim 30%, Christian 20%
Ethnic mix Fon 47%, Other 31%, Adja 12%, Bariba 10%
Government Presidential system
Currency CFA franc = 100 centimes
Literacy rate 34%
Calorie consumption 2548 calories

BHUTAN
South Asia

Official name Kingdom of Bhutan
Formation 1656 / 1865
Capital Thimphu
Population 2.2 million / 121 people per sq mile (47 people per sq km) / 7%
Total area 18,147 sq miles (47,000 sq km)
Languages Dzongkha*, Nepali, Assamese
Religions Mahayana Buddhist 70%, Hindu 24%, Other 6%
Ethnic mix Bhute 50%, Other 25%, Nepalese 25%
Government Monarchy
Currency Ngultrum = 100 chetrum
Literacy rate 47%
Calorie consumption Not available

BOLIVIA
South America

Official name Republic of Bolivia
Formation 1825 /1938
Capital La Paz (administrative); Sucre (judicial)
Population 9.2 million / 22 people per sq mile (8 people per sq km) / 63%
Total area 424,162 sq miles (1,098,580 sq km)
Languages Aymara*, Quechua*, Spanish*
Religions Roman Catholic 93%, Other 7%
Ethnic mix Quechua 37%, Aymara 32%, Mixed race 13%, European 10%, Other 8%
Government Presidential system
Currency Boliviano = 100 centavos
Literacy rate 87%
Calorie consumption 2235 calories

BOSNIA & HERZEGOVINA
Southeast Europe

Official name Bosnia and Herzegovina
Formation 1992 / 1992
Capital Sarajevo
Population 3.9 million / 198 people per sq mile (76 people per sq km) / 43%
Total area 19,741 sq miles (51,129 sq km)
Languages Serbo-Croat*
Religions Muslim (mainly Sunni) 40%, Orthodox Christian 31%, Roman Catholic 15%, Other 10%, Protestant 4%
Ethnic mix Bosniak 48%, Serb 38%, Croat 14%
Government Parliamentary system
Currency Marka = 100 pfeninga
Literacy rate 95%
Calorie consumption 2894 calories

BOTSWANA
Southern Africa

Official name Republic of Botswana
Formation 1966 / 1966
Capital Gaborone
Population 1.8 million / 8 people per sq mile (3 people per sq km) / 50%
Total area 231,803 sq miles (600,370 sq km)
Languages English*, Setswana, Shona, San, Khoikhoi, isiNdebele
Religions Traditional beliefs 50%, Christian (mainly Protestant) 30%, Other (including Muslim) 20%
Ethnic mix Tswana 98%, Other 2%
Government Presidential system
Currency Pula = 100 thebe
Literacy rate 79%
Calorie consumption 2151 calories

BRAZIL
South America

Official name Federative Republic of Brazil
Formation 1822 / 1828
Capital Brasilia
Population 186 million / 57 people per sq mile (22 people per sq km) / 81%
Total area 3,286,470 sq miles (8,511,965 sq km)
Languages Portuguese*, German, Italian, Spanish, Polish, Japanese, Amerindian languages
Religions Roman Catholic 74%, Protestant 15%, Atheist 7%, Other 4%
Ethnic mix Black 53%, Mixed race 40%, White 6%, Other 1%
Government Presidential system
Currency Real = 100 centavos
Literacy rate 88%
Calorie consumption 3049 calories

BRUNEI
Southeast Asia

Official name Sultanate of Brunei
Formation 1984 / 1984
Capital Bandar Seri Begawan
Population 374,000 / 184 people per sq mile (71 people per sq km) / 72%
Total area 2228 sq miles (5770 sq km)
Languages Malay*, English, Chinese
Religions Muslim (mainly Sunni) 66%, Buddhist 14%, Other 10%, Christian 10%
Ethnic mix Malay 67%, Chinese 16%, Other 11%, Indigenous 6%
Government Monarchy
Currency Brunei dollar = 100 cents
Literacy rate 93%
Calorie consumption 2855 calories

BULGARIA
Southeast Europe

Official name Republic of Bulgaria
Formation 1908 / 1947
Capital Sofia
Population 7.7 million / 180 people per sq mile (70 people per sq km) / 70%
Total area 42,822 sq miles (110,910 sq km)
Languages Bulgarian*, Turkish, Romani
Religions Orthodox Christian 83%, Muslim 12%, Other 4%, Roman Catholic 1%
Ethnic mix Bulgarian 84%, Turkish 9%, Roma 5%, Other 2%
Government Parliamentary system
Currency Lev = 100 stotinki
Literacy rate 98%
Calorie consumption 2848 calories

BURKINA
West Africa

Official name Burkina Faso
Formation 1960 / 1960
Capital Ouagadougou
Population 13.2 million / 125 people per sq mile (48 people per sq km) / 19%
Total area 105,869 sq miles (274,200 sq km)
Languages French*, Mossi, Fulani, Tuareg, Dyula, Songhai
Religions Muslim 55%, Traditional beliefs 35%, Roman Catholic 9%, Other Christian 1%
Ethnic mix Other 50%, Mossi 50%
Government Presidential system
Currency CFA franc = 100 centimes
Literacy rate 13%
Calorie consumption 2462 calories

BURMA (MYANMAR)
Southeast Asia

Official name Union of Myanmar
Formation 1948 / 1948
Capital Rangoon (Yangon), Pyinmana
Population 50.5 million / 199 people per sq mile (77 people per sq km) / 28%
Total area 261,969 sq miles (678,500 sq km)
Languages Burmese*, Shan, Karen, Rakhine, Chin, Yangbye, Kachin, Mon
Religions Buddhist 87%, Christian 6%, Muslim 4%, Other 2%, Hindu 1%
Ethnic mix Burman (Bamah) 68%, Other 13%, Shan 9%, Karen 6%, Rakhine 4%
Government Military-based regime
Currency Kyat = 100 pyas
Literacy rate 90%
Calorie consumption 2937 calories

BURUNDI
Central Africa

Official name Republic of Burundi
Formation 1962 / 1962
Capital Bujumbura
Population 7.5 million / 757 people per sq mile (292 people per sq km) / 9%
Total area 10,745 sq miles (27,830 sq km)
Languages Kirundi*, French*, Kiswahili
Religions Christian 60%, Traditional beliefs 39%, Muslim 1%
Ethnic mix Hutu 85%, Tutsi 14%, Twa 1%
Government Presidential system
Currency Burundi franc = 100 centimes
Literacy rate 59%
Calorie consumption 1649 calories

CAMBODIA
Southeast Asia

Official name Kingdom of Cambodia
Formation 1953 / 1953
Capital Phnom Penh
Population 14.1 million / 207 people per sq mile (80 people per sq km) / 16%
Total area 69,900 sq miles (181,040 sq km)
Languages Khmer*, French, Chinese, Vietnamese, Cham
Religions Buddhist 93%, Muslim 6%, Christian 1%
Ethnic mix Khmer 90%, Other 5%, Vietnamese 4%, Chinese 1%
Government Parliamentary system
Currency Riel = 100 sen
Literacy rate 74%
Calorie consumption 2046 calories

CAMEROON
Central Africa

Official name Republic of Cameroon
Formation 1960 / 1961
Capital Yaoundé
Population 163 million / 907 people per sq mile (350 people per sq km) / 49%
Total area 183,567 sq miles (475,400 sq km)
Languages English*, French*, Bamileke, Fang, Fulani
Religions Roman Catholic 35%, Traditional beliefs 25%, Muslim 22%, Protestant 18%
Ethnic mix Cameroon highlanders 31%, Other 21%, Equatorial Bantu 19%, Kirdi 11%, Fulani 10%, Northwestern Bantu 8%
Government Presidential system
Currency CFA franc = 100 centimes
Literacy rate 68%
Calorie consumption 2273 calories

CANADA
North America

Official name Canada
Formation 1867 / 1949
Capital Ottawa
Population 32.3 million / 9 people per sq mile (4 people per sq km) / 77%
Total area 3,717,792 sq miles (9,984,670 sq km)
Languages English*, French*, Chinese, Italian, German, Ukrainian, Inuktitut, Cree
Religions Roman Catholic 44%, Protestant 29%, Other and nonreligious 27%
Ethnic mix British origin 44%, French origin 25%, Other European 20%, Other 11%
Government Parliamentary system
Currency Canadian dollar = 100 cents
Literacy rate 99%
Calorie consumption 3589 calories

CAPE VERDE
Atlantic Ocean

Official name Republic of Cape Verde
Formation 1975
Capital Praia
Population 507,000 / 326 people per sq mile (126 people per sq km) / 62%
Total area 1557 sq miles (4033 sq km)
Languages Portuguese*, Portuguese Creole
Religions Roman Catholic 97%, Other 2%, Protestant (Church of the Nazarene) 1%
Ethnic mix Mestiço 60%, African 30%, Other 10%
Government Mixed presidential–parliamentary system
Currency Cape Verde escudo = 100 centavos
Literacy rate 76%
Calorie consumption 3243 calories

CENTRAL AFRICAN REPUBLIC
Central Africa

Official name Central African Republic
Formation 1960 / 1960
Capital Bangui
Population 4 million / 17 people per sq mile (6 people per sq km) / 41%
Total area 240,534 sq miles (622,984 sq km)
Languages Sango, Banda, Gbaya, French
Religions Traditional beliefs 60%, Christian (mainly Roman Catholic) 35%, Muslim 5%
Ethnic mix Baya 34%, Banda 27%, Mandjia 21%, Sara 10%, Other 8%
Government Presidential system
Currency CFA franc = 100 centimes
Literacy rate 49%
Calorie consumption 1980 calories

CHAD
Central Africa

Official name Republic of Chad
Formation 1960 / 1960
Capital N'Djamena
Population 9.7 million / 20 people per sq mile (8 people per sq km) / 24%
Total area 495,752 sq miles (1,284,000 sq km)
Languages French, Sara, Arabic, Maba
Religions Muslim 55%, Traditional beliefs 35%, Christian 10%
Ethnic mix Nomads (Tuareg and Toubou) 38%, Sara 30%, Other 17%, Arab 15%
Government Presidential system
Currency CFA franc = 100 centimes
Literacy rate 26%
Calorie consumption 2114 calories

CHILE
South America

Official name Republic of Chile
Formation 1818 / 1883
Capital Santiago
Population 16.3 million / 56 people per sq mile (22 people per sq km) / 86%
Total area 292,258 sq miles (756,950 sq km)
Languages Spanish*, Amerindian languages
Religions Roman Catholic 80%, Other and nonreligious 20%
Ethnic mix Mixed race and European 90%, Amerindian 10%
Government Presidential system
Currency Chilean peso = 100 centavos
Literacy rate 96%
Calorie consumption 2863 calories

CHINA
East Asia

Official name People's Republic of China
Formation 960 / 1999
Capital Beijing
Population 1.32 billion / 365 people per sq mile (141 people per sq km) / 32%
Total area 3,705,386 sq miles (9,596,960 sq km)
Languages Mandarin*, Wu, Cantonese, Hsiang, Min, Hakka, Kan
Religions Nonreligious 59%, Traditional beliefs 20%, Other 13%, Buddhist 6%, Muslim 2%
Ethnic mix Han 92%, Other 6%, Hui 1%, Zhuang 1%
Government One-party state
Currency Renminbi (known as yuan) = 10 jiao
Literacy rate 91%
Calorie consumption 2951 calories

COLOMBIA
South America

Official name Republic of Colombia
Formation 1819 / 1903
Capital Bogotá
Population 45.6 million / 114 people per sq mile (44 people per sq km) / 74%
Total area 439,733 sq miles (1,138,910 sq km)
Languages Spanish*, Wayuu, Páez, and other Amerindian languages
Religions Roman Catholic 95%, Other 5%
Ethnic mix Mestizo 58%, White 20%, European–African 14%, African 4%, African–Amerindian 3%, Amerindian 1%
Government Presidential system
Currency Colombian peso = 100 centavos
Literacy rate 94%
Calorie consumption 2585 calories

COMOROS
Indian Ocean

Official name Union of the Comoros
Formation 1975 / 1975
Capital Moroni
Population 798,000 / 927 people per sq mile (358 people per sq km) / 33%
Total area 838 sq miles (2170 sq km)
Languages Arabic*, Comoran, French
Religions Muslim (mainly Sunni) 98%, Other 1%, Roman Catholic 1%
Ethnic mix Comoran 97%, Other 3%
Government Presidential system
Currency Comoros franc = 100 centimes
Literacy rate 56%
Calorie consumption 1754 calories

CONGO
Central Africa

Official name Republic of the Congo
Formation 1960 / 1960
Capital Brazzaville
Population 4 million / 30 people per sq mile (12 people per sq km) / 63%
Total area 132,046 sq miles (342,000 sq km)
Languages French*, Kongo, Teke, Lingala
Religions Traditional beliefs 50%, Roman Catholic 25%, Protestant 23%, Muslim 2%
Ethnic mix Bakongo 48%, Sangha 20%, Teke 17%, Mbochi 12%, Other 3%
Government Presidential system
Currency CFA franc = 100 centimes
Literacy rate 83%
Calorie consumption 2162 calories

CONGO, DEM. REP.
Central Africa

Official name Democratic Republic of the Congo
Formation 1960 / 1960
Capital Kinshasa
Population 57.5 million / 66 people per sq mile (25 people per sq km) / 30%
Total area 905,563 sq miles (2,345,410 sq km)
Languages French*, Kiswahili, Tshiluba, Kikongo, Lingala
Religions Roman Catholic 50%, Protestant 20%, Traditional beliefs and other 10%, Muslim 10%, Kimbanguist 10%
Ethnic mix Other 55%, Bantu and Hamitic 45%
Government Transitional regime
Currency Congolese franc = 100 centimes
Literacy rate 65%
Calorie consumption 1599 calories

COSTA RICA
Central America

Official name Republic of Costa Rica
Formation 1838 / 1838
Capital San José
Population 4.3 million / 218 people per sq mile (84 people per sq km) / 52%
Total area 19,730 sq miles (51,100 sq km)
Languages Spanish*, English Creole, Bribri, Cabecar
Religions Roman Catholic 76%, Other (including Protestant) 24%
Ethnic mix Mestizo and European 96%, Black 2%, Chinese 1%, Amerindian 1%
Government Presidential system
Currency Costa Rican colón = 100 centimos
Literacy rate 96%
Calorie consumption 2876 calories

CROATIA
Southeast Europe

Official name Republic of Croatia
Formation 1991 / 1991
Capital Zagreb
Population 4.6 million / 211 people per sq mile (81 people per sq km) / 58%
Total area 21,831 sq miles (56,542 sq km)
Languages Croatian*
Religions Roman Catholic 88%, Other 7%, Orthodox Christian 4%, Muslim 1%
Ethnic mix Croat 90%, Other 5%, Serb 4%, Bosniak 1%
Government Parliamentary system
Currency Kuna = 100 lipas
Literacy rate 98%
Calorie consumption 2799 calories

CUBA
West Indies

Official name Republic of Cuba
Formation 1902 / 1902
Capital Havana
Population 11.3 million / 264 people per sq mile (102 people per sq km) / 75%
Total area 42,803 sq miles (110,860 sq km)
Languages Spanish*
Religions Nonreligious 49%, Roman Catholic 40%, Atheist 6%, Other 4%, Protestant 1%
Ethnic mix White 66%, European–African 22%, Black 12%
Government One-party state
Currency Cuban peso = 100 centavos
Literacy rate 97%
Calorie consumption 3152 calories

CYPRUS
Southeast Europe

Official name Republic of Cyprus
Formation 1960 / 1960
Capital Nicosia
Population 835,000 / 234 people per sq mile (90 people per sq km) / 57%
Total area 3571 sq miles (9250 sq km)
Languages Greek, Turkish
Religions Orthodox Christian 78%, Muslim 18%, Other 4%
Ethnic mix Greek 85%, Turkish 12%, Other 3%
Government Presidential system
Currency Cyprus pound (Turkish lira in TRNC) = 100 cents (Cyprus pound); 100 kurus (Turkish lira)
Literacy rate 97%
Calorie consumption 3255 calories

CZECH REPUBLIC
Central Europe

Official name Czech Republic
Formation 1993 / 1993
Capital Prague
Population 10.2 million / 335 people per sq mile (129 people per sq km) / 75%
Total area 30,450 sq miles (78,866 sq km)
Languages Czech*, Slovak, Hungarian (Magyar)
Religions Roman Catholic 39%, Atheist 38%, Other 18%, Protestant 3%, Hussite 2%
Ethnic mix Czech 81%, Moravian 13%, Slovak 6%
Government Parliamentary system
Currency Czech koruna = 100 haleru
Literacy rate 99%
Calorie consumption 3171 calories

DENMARK
Northern Europe

Official name Kingdom of Denmark
Formation AD 950 / 1945
Capital Copenhagen
Population 5.4 million / 330 people per sq mile (127 people per sq km) / 85%
Total area 16,639 sq miles (43,094 sq km)
Languages Danish*
Religions Evangelical Lutheran 89%, Other 10%, Roman Catholic 1%
Ethnic mix Danish 96%, Other (including Scandinavian and Turkish) 3%, Faeroese and Inuit 1%
Government Parliamentary system
Currency Danish krone = 100 øre
Literacy rate 99%
Calorie consumption 3439 calories

DJIBOUTI
East Africa

Official name Republic of Djibouti
Formation 1977 / 1977
Capital Djibouti
Population 793,000 / 89 people per sq mile (34 people per sq km) / 83%
Total area 8494 sq miles (22,000 sq km)
Languages French*, Arabic*, Somali, Afar
Religions Muslim (mainly Sunni) 94%, Christian 6%
Ethnic mix Issa 60%, Afar 35%, Other 5%
Government Presidential system
Currency Djibouti franc = 100 centimes
Literacy rate 66%
Calorie consumption 2220 calories

DOMINICA
West Indies

Official name Commonwealth of Dominica
Formation 1978 / 1978
Capital Roseau
Population 69,029 / 238 people per sq mile (92 people per sq km) / 71%
Total area 291 sq miles (754 sq km)
Languages English*, French Creole
Religions Roman Catholic 77%, Protestant 15%, Other 8%
Ethnic mix Black 91%, Mixed race 6%, Carib 2%, Other 1%
Government Parliamentary system
Currency Eastern Caribbean dollar = 100 cents
Literacy rate 88%
Calorie consumption 2763 calories

DOMINICAN REPUBLIC
West Indies

Official name Dominican Republic
Formation 1865 / 1865
Capital Santo Domingo
Population 8.9 million / 476 people per sq mile (184 people per sq km) / 65%
Total area 18,679 sq miles (48,380 sq km)
Languages Spanish*, French Creole
Religions Roman Catholic 92%, Other and nonreligious 8%
Ethnic mix Mixed race 75%, White 15%, Black 10%
Government Presidential system
Currency Dominican Republic peso = 100 centavos
Literacy rate 88%
Calorie consumption 2347 calories

EAST TIMOR
Southeast Asia

Official name Democratic Republic of Timor-Leste
Formation 2002 / 2002
Capital Dili
Population 947,000 / 168 people per sq mile (65 people per sq km) / 8%
Total area 5756 sq miles (14,874 sq km)
Languages Tetum (Portuguese/Austronesian), Bahasa Indonesia, and Portuguese
Religions Roman Catholic 95%, Other (including Muslim and Protestant) 5%
Ethnic mix Papuan groups approx 85%, Indonesian approx 13%, Chinese 2%
Government Parliamentary system
Currency US dollar = 100 cents
Literacy rate 59%
Calorie consumption 2806 calories

ECUADOR
South America

Official name Republic of Ecuador
Formation 1830 / 1941
Capital Quito
Population 13.2 million / 123 people per sq mile (48 people per sq km) / 65%
Total area 109,483 sq miles (283,560 sq km)
Languages Spanish*, Quechua*, other Amerindian languages
Religions Roman Catholic 93%, Protestant, Jewish, and other 7%
Ethnic mix Mestizo 55%, Amerindian 25%, White 10%, Black 10%
Government Presidential system
Currency US dollar = 100 cents
Literacy rate 91%
Calorie consumption 2754 calories

EGYPT
North Africa

Official name Arab Republic of Egypt
Formation 1936 / 1982
Capital Cairo
Population 74 million / 193 people per sq mile (74 people per sq km) / 45%
Total area 386,660 sq miles (1,001,450 sq km)
Languages Arabic*, French, English, Berber
Religions Muslim (mainly Sunni) 94%, Coptic Christian and other 6%
Ethnic mix Eastern Hamitic 90%, Nubian, Armenian, and Greek 10%
Government Presidential system
Currency Egyptian pound = 100 piastres
Literacy rate 56%
Calorie consumption 3338 calories

EL SALVADOR
Central America

Official name Republic of El Salvador
Formation 1841 / 1841
Capital San Salvador
Population 6.9 million / 862 people per sq mile (333 people per sq km) / 47%
Total area 8124 sq miles (21,040 sq km)
Languages Spanish*
Religions Roman Catholic 80%, Evangelical 18%, Other 2%
Ethnic mix Mestizo 94%, Amerindian 5%, White 1%
Government Presidential system
Currency Salvadorean colón & US dollar = 100 centavos (colón); 100 cents (US dollar)
Literacy rate 80%
Calorie consumption 2584 calories

EQUATORIAL GUINEA
Central Africa

Official name Republic of Equatorial Guinea
Formation 1968 / 1968
Capital Malabo
Population 504,000 / 47 people per sq mile (18 people per sq km) / 48%
Total area 10,830 sq miles (28,051 sq km)
Languages Spanish*, Fang, Bubi
Religions Roman Catholic 90%, Other 10%
Ethnic mix Fang 85%, Other 11%, Bubi 4%
Government Presidential system
Currency CFA franc = 100 centimes
Literacy rate 84%
Calorie consumption Not available

ERITREA
East Africa

Official name State of Eritrea
Formation 1993 / 2002
Capital Asmara
Population 4.4 million / 97 people per sq mile (37 people per sq km) / 19%
Total area 46,842 sq miles (121,320 sq km)
Languages Arabic*, Tigrinya*, English, Tigre, Afar, Bilen, Kunama, Nara, Saho, Hadareb
Religions Christian 45%, Muslim 45%, Other 10%
Ethnic mix Tigray 50%, Tigray and Kunama 40%, Afar 4%, Other 3%, Saho 3%
Government Transitional regime
Currency Nakfa = 100 cents
Literacy rate 57%
Calorie consumption 1513 calories

ESTONIA
Northeast Europe

Official name Republic of Estonia
Formation 1991 / 1991
Capital Tallinn
Population 1.3 million / 75 people per sq mile (29 people per sq km) / 69%
Total area 17,462 sq miles (45,226 sq km)
Languages Estonian*, Russian
Religions Evangelical Lutheran 56%, Orthodox Christian 25%, Other 19%
Ethnic mix Estonian 62%, Russian 30%, Other 8%
Government Parliamentary system
Currency Kroon = 100 senti
Literacy rate 99%
Calorie consumption 3002 calories

ETHIOPIA
East Africa

Official name Federal Democratic Republic of Ethiopia
Formation 1896 / 2002
Capital Addis Ababa
Population 77.4 million / 181 people per sq mile (70 people per sq km) / 18%
Total area 435,184 sq miles (1,127,127 sq km)
Languages Amharic*, Tigrinya, Galla, Sidamo, Somali, English, Arabic
Religions Orthodox Christian 40%, Muslim 40%, Traditional beliefs 15%, Other 5%
Ethnic mix Oromo 40%, Amhara 25%, Other 14%, Sidamo 9%, Berta 6%, Somali 6%
Government Parliamentary system
Currency Ethiopian birr = 100 cents
Literacy rate 42%
Calorie consumption 1857 calories

FIJI
Australasia & Oceania

Official name Republic of the Fiji Islands
Formation 1970 / 1970
Capital Suva
Population 848,000 / 120 people per sq mile (46 people per sq km) / 49%
Total area 7054 sq miles (18,270 sq km)
Languages English*, Fijian*, Hindi, Urdu, Tamil, Telugu
Religions Hindu 38%, Methodist 37%, Roman Catholic 9%, Other 8%, Muslim 8%
Ethnic mix Melanesian 48%, Indian 46%, Other 6%
Government Parliamentary system
Currency Fiji dollar = 100 cents
Literacy rate 93%
Calorie consumption 2894 calories

FINLAND
Northern Europe

Official name Republic of Finland
Formation 1917 / 1947
Capital Helsinki
Population 5.2 million / 44 people per sq mile (17 people per sq km) / 67%
Total area 130,127 sq miles (337,030 sq km)
Languages Finnish*, Swedish*, Sámi
Religions Evangelical Lutheran 89%, Orthodox Christian 1%, Roman Catholic 1%, Other 9%
Ethnic mix Finnish 93%, Other (including Sámi) 7%
Government Parliamentary system
Currency Euro = 100 cents
Literacy rate 99%
Calorie consumption 3100 calories

FRANCE
Western Europe

Official name French Republic
Formation 987 / 1919
Capital Paris
Population 60.5 million / 285 people per sq mile (110 people per sq km) / 76%
Total area 211,208 sq miles (547,030 sq km)
Languages French*, Provençal, German, Breton, Catalan, Basque
Religions Roman Catholic 88%, Muslim 8%, Protestant 2%, Buddhist 1%, Jewish 1%
Ethnic mix French 90%, North African (mainly Algerian) 6%, German (Alsace) 2%, Breton 1%, Other (including Corsicans) 1%
Government Mixed presidential–parliamentary system
Currency Euro = 100 cents
Literacy rate 99%
Calorie consumption 3654 calories

GABON
Central Africa

Official name Gabonese Republic
Formation 1960 / 1960
Capital Libreville
Population 1.4 million / 14 people per sq mile (5 people per sq km) / 81%
Total area 103,346 sq miles (267,667 sq km)
Languages French*,Fang, Punu, Sira, Nzebi, Mpongwe
Religions Christian (mainly Roman Catholic) 55%, Traditional beliefs 40%, Other 4%, Muslim 1%
Ethnic mix Fang 35%, Other Bantu 29%, Eshira 25%, European and other African 11%
Government Presidential system
Currency CFA franc = 100 centimes
Literacy rate 71%
Calorie consumption 2637 calories

GAMBIA
West Africa

Official name Republic of the Gambia
Formation 1965 / 1965
Capital Banjul
Population 1.5 million / 389 people per sq mile (150 people per sq km) / 33%
Total area 4363 sq miles (11,300 sq km)
Languages English*, Mandinka, Fulani, Wolof, Jola, Soninke
Religions Sunni Muslim 90%, Christian 9%, Traditional beliefs 1%
Ethnic mix Mandinka 42%, Fulani 18%, Wolof 16%, Jola 10%, Serahuli 9%, Other 5%
Government Presidential system
Currency Dalasi = 100 butut
Literacy rate 38%
Calorie consumption 2273 calories

GEORGIA
Southwest Asia

Official name Georgia
Formation 1991 / 1991
Capital Tbilisi
Population 4.5 million / 167 people per sq mile (65 people per sq km) / 61%
Total area 26,911 sq miles (69,700 sq km)
Languages Georgian*, Russian, Azeri, Armenian, Mingrelian, Ossetian, Abkhazian
Religions Georgian Orthodox 65%, Muslim 11%, Russian Orthodox 10%, Armenian Orthodox 8%, Other 6%
Ethnic mix Georgian 70%, Armenian 8%, Russian 6%, Azeri 6%, Ossetian 3%, Other 7%
Government Presidential system
Currency Lari = 100 tetri
Literacy rate 99%
Calorie consumption 2354 calories

GERMANY
Northern Europe

Official name Federal Republic of Germany
Formation 1871 / 1990
Capital Berlin
Population 82.7 million / 613 people per sq mile (237 people per sq km) / 88%
Total area 137,846 sq miles (357,021 sq km)
Languages German*, Turkish
Religions Protestant 34%, Roman Catholic 33%, Other 30%, Muslim 3%
Ethnic mix German 92%, Other 3%, Other European 3%, Turkish 2%
Government Parliamentary system
Currency Euro = 100 cents
Literacy rate 99%
Calorie consumption 3496 calories

GHANA
West Africa

Official name Republic of Ghana
Formation 1957 / 1957
Capital Accra
Population 22.1 million / 249 people per sq mile (96 people per sq km) / 38%
Total area 92,100 sq miles (238,540 sq km)
Languages Twi, Fanti, Ewe, Ga, Adangbe, Gurma, Dagomba (Dagbani)
Religions Christian 69%, Muslim 16%, Traditional beliefs 9%, Other 6%
Ethnic mix Ashanti and Fanti 52%, Moshi-Dagomba 16%, Ewe 12%, Other 11%, Ga and Ga-adanbe 8%, Yoruba 1%
Government Presidential system
Currency Cedi = 100 psewas
Literacy rate 54%
Calorie consumption 2667 calories

GREECE
Southeast Europe

Official name Hellenic Republic
Formation 1829 / 1947
Capital Athens
Population 11.1 million / 220 people per sq mile (85 people per sq km) / 60%
Total area 50,942 sq miles (131,940 sq km)
Languages Greek*, Turkish, Macedonian, Albanian
Religions Orthodox Christian 98%, Other 1%, Muslim 1%
Ethnic mix Greek 98%, Other 2%
Government Parliamentary system
Currency Euro = 100 cents
Literacy rate 91%
Calorie consumption 3721 calories

GRENADA
West Indies

Official name Grenada
Formation 1974 / 1974
Capital St. George's
Population 89,502 / 683 people per sq mile (263 people per sq km) / 38%
Total area 131 sq miles (340 sq km)
Languages English*, English Creole
Religions Roman Catholic 68%, Anglican 17%, Other 15%
Ethnic mix Black African 82%, Mulatto (mixed race) 13%, East Indian 3%, Other 2%
Government Parliamentary system
Currency Eastern Caribbean dollar = 100 cents
Literacy rate 96%
Calorie consumption 2932 calories

GUATEMALA
Central America

Official name Republic of Guatemala
Formation 1838 / 1838
Capital Guatemala City
Population 12.6 million / 301 people per sq mile (116 people per sq km) / 40%
Total area 42,042 sq miles (108,890 sq km)
Languages Spanish*, Quiché, Mam, Cakchiquel, Kekchí
Religions Roman Catholic 65%, Protestant 33%, Other and nonreligious 2%
Ethnic mix Amerindian 60%, Mestizo 30%, Other 10%
Government Presidential system
Currency Quetzal = 100 centavos
Literacy rate 69%
Calorie consumption 2219 calories

GUINEA
West Africa

Official name Republic of Guinea
Formation 1958 / 1958
Capital Conakry
Population 9.4 million / 99 people per sq mile (38 people per sq km) / 33%
Total area 94,925 sq miles (245,857 sq km)
Languages French*, Fulani, Malinke, Soussou
Religions Muslim 65%, Traditional beliefs 33%, Christian 2%
Ethnic mix Fulani 30%, Malinke 30%, Soussou 15%, Kissi 10%, Other tribes 10%, Other 5%
Government Presidential system
Currency Guinea franc = 100 centimes
Literacy rate 41%
Calorie consumption 2409 calories

GUINEA-BISSAU
West Africa

Official name Republic of Guinea-Bissau
Formation 1974 / 1974
Capital Bissau
Population 1.6 million / 147 people per sq mile (57 people per sq km) / 24%
Total area 13,946 sq miles (36,120 sq km)
Languages Portuguese*, Balante, Fulani, Malinke, Portuguese Creole
Religions Traditional beliefs 52%, Muslim 40%, Christian 8%
Ethnic mix Other tribes 31%, Balante 25%, Fula 20%, Mandinka 12%, Mandyako 11%, Other 1%
Government Presidential system
Currency CFA franc = 100 centimes
Literacy rate 40%
Calorie consumption 2024 calories

GUYANA
South America

Official name Cooperative Republic of Guyana
Formation 1966 / 1966
Capital Georgetown
Population 751,000 / 10 people per sq mile (4 people per sq km) / 38%
Total area 83,000 sq miles (214,970 sq km)
Languages English*, Hindi, Tamil, Amerindian languages, English Creole
Religions Christian 57%, Hindu 33%, Muslim 9%, Other 1%
Ethnic mix East Indian 52%, Black African 38%, Other 4%, Amerindian 4%, European and Chinese 2%
Government Presidential system
Currency Guyanese dollar = 100 cents
Literacy rate 97%
Calorie consumption 2692 calories

HAITI
West Indies

Official name Republic of Haiti
Formation 1804 / 1844
Capital Port-au-Prince
Population 8.5 million / 799 people per sq mile (308 people per sq km) / 36%
Total area 10,714 sq miles (27,750 sq km)
Languages French Creole*, French*
Religions Roman Catholic 80%, Protestant 16%, Other (including Voodoo) 3%, Nonreligious 1%
Ethnic mix Black African 95%, Mulatto (mixed race) and European 5%
Government Transitional regime
Currency Gourde = 100 centimes
Literacy rate 52%
Calorie consumption 2086 calories

HONDURAS
Central America

Official name Republic of Honduras
Formation 1838 / 1838
Capital Tegucigalpa
Population 7.2 million / 167 people per sq mile (64 people per sq km) / 53%
Total area 43,278 sq miles (112,090 sq km)
Languages Spanish*, Garífuna (Carib), English Creole
Religions Roman Catholic 97%, Protestant 3%
Ethnic mix Mestizo 90%, Black African 5%, Amerindian 4%, White 1%
Government Presidential system
Currency Lempira = 100 centavos
Literacy rate 80%
Calorie consumption 2356 calories

HUNGARY
Central Europe

Official name Republic of Hungary
Formation 1918 / 1947
Capital Budapest
Population 10.1 million / 283 people per sq mile (109 people per sq km) / 64%
Total area 35,919 sq miles (93,030 sq km)
Languages Hungarian (Magyar)*
Religions Roman Catholic 52%, Calvinist 16%, Other 15%, Nonreligious 14%, Lutheran 3%
Ethnic mix Magyar 90%, Other 7%, Roma 2%, German 1%
Government Parliamentary system
Currency Forint = 100 fillér
Literacy rate 99%
Calorie consumption 3483 calories

ICELAND
Northwest Europe

Official name Republic of Iceland
Formation 1944 / 1944
Capital Reykjavík
Population 295,000 / 8 people per sq mile (3 people per sq km) / 93%
Total area 39,768 sq miles (103,000 sq km)
Languages Icelandic*
Religions Evangelical Lutheran 93%, Nonreligious 6%, Other (mostly Christian) 1%
Ethnic mix Icelandic 94%, Other 5%, Danish 1%
Government Parliamentary system
Currency Icelandic króna = 100 aurar
Literacy rate 99%
Calorie consumption 3249 calories

INDIA
South Asia

Official name Republic of India
Formation 1947 / 1947
Capital New Delhi
Population 1.1 billion / 961 people per sq mile (371 people per sq km) / 28%
Total area 1,269,338 sq miles (3,287,590 sq km)
Languages Hindi*, English*, Bengali, Marathi, Telugu, Tamil, Bihari, Gujarati, Kanarese, Urdu
Religions Hindu 83%, Muslim 11%, Christian 2%, Sikh 2%, Other 1%, Buddhist 1%
Ethnic mix Indo-Aryan 72%, Dravidian 25%, Mongoloid and other 3%
Government Parliamentary system
Currency Indian rupee = 100 paise
Literacy rate 61%
Calorie consumption 2459 calories

INDONESIA
Southeast Asia

Official name Republic of Indonesia
Formation 1949 / 1999
Capital Jakarta
Population 223 million / 321 people per sq mile (124 people per sq km) / 41%
Total area 741,096 sq miles (1,919,440 sq km)
Languages Bahasa Indonesia*, Javanese, Sundanese, Madurese, Dutch
Religions Sunni Muslim 87%, Protestant 6%, Roman Catholic 3%, Hindu 2%, Other 1%, Buddhist 1%
Ethnic mix Javanese 45%, Sundanese 14%, Coastal Malays 8%, Madurese 8%, Other 25%
Government Presidential system
Currency Rupiah = 100 sen
Literacy rate 88%
Calorie consumption 2904 calories

IRAN
Southwest Asia

Official name Islamic Republic of Iran
Formation 1502 / 1990
Capital Tehran
Population 69.5 million / 110 people per sq mile (42 people per sq km) / 62%
Total area 636,293 sq miles (1,648,000 sq km)
Languages Farsi*, Azeri, Luri, Gilaki, Mazanderani, Kurdish, Turkmen, Arabic, Baluchi
Religions Shi'a Muslim 93%, Sunni Muslim 6%, Other 1%
Ethnic mix Persian 50%, Azari 24%, Other 10%, Kurdish 8%, Lur and Bakhtiari 8%
Government Islamic theocracy
Currency Iranian rial = 100 dinars
Literacy rate 77%
Calorie consumption 3085 calories

IRAQ
Southwest Asia

Official name Republic of Iraq
Formation 1932 / 1990
Capital Baghdad
Population 28.8 million / 171 people per sq mile (66 people per sq km) / 77%
Total area 168,753 sq miles (437,072 sq km)
Languages Arabic*, Kurdish, Turkic languages, Armenian, Assyrian
Religions Shi'a Muslim 60%, Sunni Muslim 35%, Other (including Christian) 5%
Ethnic mix Arab 80%, Kurdish 15%, Turkmen 3%, Other 2%
Government Transitional regime
Currency New Iraqi dinar = 1000 fils
Literacy rate 40%
Calorie consumption 2197 calories

IRELAND
Northwest Europe

Official name Ireland
Formation 1922 / 1922
Capital Dublin
Population 4.1 million / 154 people per sq mile (60 people per sq km) / 59%
Total area 27,135 sq miles (70,280 sq km)
Languages English*, Irish Gaelic*
Religions Roman Catholic 88%, Other and nonreligious 9%, Anglican 3%
Ethnic mix Irish 93%, Other 4%, British 3%
Government Parliamentary system
Currency Euro = 100 cents
Literacy rate 99%
Calorie consumption 3656 calories

ISRAEL
Southwest Asia

Official name State of Israel
Formation 1948 / 1994
Capital Jerusalem (not internationally recognized)
Population 6.7 million / 854 people per sq mile (330 people per sq km) / 91%
Total area 8019 sq miles (20,770 sq km)
Languages Hebrew*, Arabic, Yiddish, German, Russian, Polish, Romanian, Persian
Religions Jewish 80%, Muslim (mainly Sunni) 16%, Druze and other 2%, Christian 2%
Ethnic mix Jewish 80%, Other (mostly Arab) 20%
Government Parliamentary system
Currency Shekel = 100 agorot
Literacy rate 97%
Calorie consumption 3666 calories

ITALY
Southern Europe

Official name Italian Republic
Formation 1861 / 1947
Capital Rome
Population 58.1 million / 512 people per sq mile (198 people per sq km) / 67%
Total area 116,305 sq miles (301,230 sq km)
Languages Italian*, German, French, Rhaeto-Romanic, Sardinian
Religions Roman Catholic 85%, Other and nonreligious 13%, Muslim 2%
Ethnic mix Italian 94%, Other 4%, Sardinian 2%
Government Parliamentary system
Currency Euro = 100 cents
Literacy rate 99%
Calorie consumption 3671 calories

IVORY COAST
West Africa

Official name Republic of Côte d'Ivoire
Formation 1960 / 1960
Capital Yamoussoukro
Population 18.2 million / 148 people per sq mile (57 people per sq km) / 46%
Total area 124,502 sq miles (322,460 sq km)
Languages French*, Akan, Kru, Voltaic
Religions Muslim 38%, Traditional beliefs 25%, Roman Catholic 25%, Protestant 6%, Other 6%
Ethnic mix Baoulé 23%, Other 19%, Bété 18%, Senufo 15%, Agni-Ashanti 14%, Mandinka 11%
Government Presidential system
Currency CFA franc = 100 centimes
Literacy rate 48%
Calorie consumption 2631 calories

JAMAICA
West Indies

Official name Jamaica
Formation 1962 / 1962
Capital Kingston
Population 2.7 million / 646 people per sq mile (249 people per sq km) / 56%
Total area 4243 sq miles (10,990 sq km)
Languages English*, English Creole
Religions Other and nonreligious 45%, Other Protestant 20%, Church of God 18%, Baptist 10%, Anglican 7%
Ethnic mix Black African 75%, Mulatto (mixed race) 13%, European and Chinese 11%, East Indian 1%
Government Parliamentary system
Currency Jamaican dollar = 100 cents
Literacy rate 88%
Calorie consumption 2685 calories

JAPAN
East Asia

Official name Japan
Formation 1590 / 1972
Capital Tokyo
Population 128 million / 881 people per sq mile (340 people per sq km) / 79%
Total area 145,882 sq miles (377,835 sq km)
Languages Japanese, Korean, Chinese
Religions Shinto and Buddhist 76%, Buddhist 16%, Other (including Christian) 8%
Ethnic mix Japanese 99%, Other (mainly Korean) 1%
Government Parliamentary system
Currency Yen = 100 sen
Literacy rate 99%
Calorie consumption 2761 calories

JORDAN
Southwest Asia

Official name Hashemite Kingdom of Jordan
Formation 1946 / 1967
Capital Amman
Population 5.6 million / 163 people per sq mile (63 people per sq km) / 74%
Total area 35,637 sq miles (92,300 sq km)
Languages Arabic*
Religions Muslim (mainly Sunni) 92%, Other (mostly Christian) 8%
Ethnic mix Arab 98%, Circassian 1%, Armenian 1%
Government Monarchy
Currency Jordanian dinar = 1000 fils
Literacy rate 90%
Calorie consumption 2673 calories

KAZAKHSTAN
Central Asia

Official name Republic of Kazakhstan
Formation 1991 / 1991
Capital Astana
Population 14.8 million / 14 people per sq mile (5 people per sq km) / 56%
Total area 1,049,150 sq miles (2,717,300 sq km)
Languages Kazakh*, Russian*, Ukrainian, Tatar, German, Uzbek, Uighur
Religions Muslim (mainly Sunni) 47%, Orthodox Christian 44%, Other 9%
Ethnic mix Kazakh 53%, Russian 30%, Other 9%, Ukrainian 4%, Tatar 2%, German 2%
Government Presidential system
Currency Tenge = 100 tiyn
Literacy rate 99%
Calorie consumption 2677 calories

KENYA
East Africa

Official name Republic of Kenya
Formation 1963 / 1963
Capital Nairobi
Population 34.3 million / 157 people per sq mile (60 people per sq km) / 33%
Total area 224,961 sq miles (582,650 sq km)
Languages Kiswahili*, English*, Kikuyu, Luo, Kalenjin, Kamba
Religions Christian 60%, Traditional beliefs 25%, Other 9%, Muslim 6%
Ethnic mix Other 30%, Kikuyu 21%, Luhya 14%, Luo 13%, Kalenjin 11%, Kamba 11%
Government Presidential system
Currency Kenya shilling = 100 cents
Literacy rate 74%
Calorie consumption 2090 calories

KIRIBATI
Australasia & Oceania

Official name Republic of Kiribati
Formation 1979 / 1979
Capital Bairiki (Tarawa Atoll)
Population 103,092 / 376 people per sq mile (145 people per sq km) / 36%
Total area 277 sq miles (717 sq km)
Languages English*, Kiribati
Religions Roman Catholic 53%, Kiribati Protestant Church 39%, Other 8%
Ethnic mix Micronesian 96%, Other 4%
Government Nonparty system
Currency Australian dollar = 100 cents
Literacy rate 99%
Calorie consumption 2859 calories

KUWAIT
Southwest Asia

Official name State of Kuwait
Formation 1961 / 1961
Capital Kuwait City
Population 2.7 million / 392 people per sq mile (152 people per sq km) / 98%
Total area 6880 sq miles (17,820 sq km)
Languages Arabic*, English
Religions Sunni Muslim 45%, Shi'a Muslim 40%, Christian, Hindu, and other 15%
Ethnic mix Kuwaiti 45%, Other Arab 35%, South Asian 9%, Other 7%, Iranian 4%
Government Monarchy
Currency Kuwaiti dinar = 1000 fils
Literacy rate 83%
Calorie consumption 3010 calories

KYRGYZSTAN
Central Asia

Official name Kyrgyz Republic
Formation 1991 / 1991
Capital Bishkek
Population 5.3 million / 69 people per sq mile (27 people per sq km) / 33%
Total area 76,641 sq miles (198,500 sq km)
Languages Kyrgyz*, Russian*, Uzbek, Tatar, Ukrainian
Religions Muslim (mainly Sunni) 70%, Orthodox Christian 30%
Ethnic mix Kyrgyz 57%, Russian 19%, Uzbek 13%, Other 7%, Tatar 2%, Ukrainian 2%
Government Presidential system
Currency Som = 100 tyyn
Literacy rate 99%
Calorie consumption 2999 calories

LAOS
Southeast Asia

Official name Lao People's Democratic Republic
Formation 1953 / 1953
Capital Vientiane
Population 5.9 million / 66 people per sq mile (26 people per sq km) / 24%
Total area 91,428 sq miles (236,800 sq km)
Languages Lao*, Mon-Khmer, Yao, Vietnamese, Chinese, French
Religions Buddhist 85%, Other (including animist) 15%
Ethnic mix Lao Loum 66%, Lao Theung 30%, Other 2%, Lao Soung 2%
Government One-party state
Currency New kip = 100 at
Literacy rate 69%
Calorie consumption 2312 calories

LATVIA
Northeast Europe

Official name Republic of Latvia
Formation 1991 / 1991
Capital Riga
Population 2.3 million / 92 people per sq mile (36 people per sq km) / 69%
Total area 24,938 sq miles (64,589 sq km)
Languages Latvian*, Russian
Religions Lutheran 55%, Roman Catholic 24%, Other 12%, Orthodox Christian 9%
Ethnic mix Latvian 57%, Russian 32%, Belarussian 4%, Ukrainian 3%, Polish 2%, Other 2%
Government Parliamentary system
Currency Lats = 100 santims
Literacy rate 99%
Calorie consumption 2938 calories

LEBANON
Southwest Asia

Official name Republic of Lebanon
Formation 1941 / 1941
Capital Beirut
Population 3.6 million / 911 people per sq mile (352 people per sq km) / 90%
Total area 4015 sq miles (10,400 sq km)
Languages Arabic*, French, Armenian, Assyrian
Religions Muslim 70%, Christian 30%
Ethnic mix Arab 94%, Armenian 4%, Other 2%
Government Parliamentary system
Currency Lebanese pound = 100 piastres
Literacy rate 87%
Calorie consumption 3196 calories

LESOTHO
Southern Africa

Official name Kingdom of Lesotho
Formation 1966 / 1966
Capital Maseru
Population 1.8 million / 154 people per sq mile (59 people per sq km) / 28%
Total area 11,720 sq miles (30,355 sq km)
Languages English*, Sesotho*, isiZulu
Religions Christian 90%, Traditional beliefs 10%
Ethnic mix Sotho 97%, European and Asian 3%
Government Parliamentary system
Currency Loti = 100 lisente
Literacy rate 81%
Calorie consumption 2638 calories

LIBERIA
West Africa

Official name Republic of Liberia
Formation 1847 / 1847
Capital Monrovia
Population 3.3 million / 89 people per sq mile (34 people per sq km) / 45%
Total area 43,000 sq miles (111,370 sq km)
Languages English*, Kpelle, Vai, Bassa, Kru, Grebo, Kissi, Gola, Loma
Religions Christian 68%, Traditional beliefs 18%, Muslim 14%
Ethnic mix Indigenous tribes (16 main groups) 95%, Americo-Liberians 5%
Government Transitional regime
Currency Liberian dollar = 100 cents
Literacy rate 58%
Calorie consumption 1900 calories

LIBYA
North Africa

Official name Great Socialist People's Libyan Arab Jamahariyah
Formation 1951 / 1951
Capital Tripoli
Population 5.9 million / 9 people per sq mile (3 people per sq km) / 88%
Total area 679,358 sq miles (1,759,540 sq km)
Languages Arabic*, Tuareg
Religions Muslim (mainly Sunni) 97%, Other 3%
Ethnic mix Arab and Berber 95%, Other 5%
Government One-party state
Currency Libyan dinar = 1000 dirhams
Literacy rate 82%
Calorie consumption 3320 calories

LIECHTENSTEIN
Central Europe

Official name Principality of Liechtenstein
Formation 1719 / 1719
Capital Vaduz
Population 33,717 / 544 people per sq mile (211 people per sq km) / 21%
Total area 62 sq miles (160 sq km)
Languages German*, Alemannish dialect, Italian
Religions Roman Catholic 81%, Other 12%, Protestant 7%
Ethnic mix Liechtensteiner 62%, Foreign residents 38%
Government Parliamentary system
Currency Swiss franc = 100 rappen/centimes
Literacy rate 99%
Calorie consumption Not available

LITHUANIA
Northeast Europe

Official name Republic of Lithuania
Formation 1991 / 1991
Capital Vilnius
Population 3.4 million / 135 people per sq mile (52 people per sq km) / 68%
Total area 25,174 sq miles (65,200 sq km)
Languages Lithuanian*, Russian
Religions Roman Catholic 83%, Other 12%, Protestant 5%
Ethnic mix Lithuanian 80%, Russian 9%, Polish 7%, Other 2%, Belarussian 2%
Government Parliamentary system
Currency Litas (euro is also legal tender) = 100 centu
Literacy rate 99%
Calorie consumption 3324 calories

LUXEMBOURG
Northwest Europe

Official name Grand Duchy of Luxembourg
Formation 1867 / 1867
Capital Luxembourg-Ville
Population 465,000 / 466 people per sq mile (180 people per sq km) / 92%
Total area 998 sq miles (2586 sq km)
Languages Luxembourgish*, German*, French*
Religions Roman Catholic 97%, Protestant, Orthodox Christian, and Jewish 3%
Ethnic mix Luxembourger 73%, Foreign residents 27%
Government Parliamentary system
Currency Euro = 100 cents
Literacy rate 99%
Calorie consumption 3701 calories

MACEDONIA
Southeast Europe

Official name Republic of Macedonia
Formation 1991 / 1991
Capital Skopje
Population 2 million / 201 people per sq mile (78 people per sq km) / 62%
Total area 9781 sq miles (25,333 sq km)
Languages Macedonian, Albanian, Serbo-Croat
Religions Orthodox Christian 59%, Muslim 26%, Other 10%, Roman Catholic 4%, Protestant 1%
Ethnic mix Macedonian 64%, Albanian 25%, Turkish 4%, Roma 3%, Other 2%, Serb 2%
Government Mixed presidential–parliamentary system
Currency Macedonian denar = 100 deni
Literacy rate 96%
Calorie consumption 2655 calories

MADAGASCAR
Indian Ocean

Official name Republic of Madagascar
Formation 1960 / 1960
Capital Antananarivo
Population 18.6 million / 83 people per sq mile (32 people per sq km) / 30%
Total area 226,656 sq miles (587,040 sq km)
Languages Malagasy*, French*
Religions Traditional beliefs 52%, Christian (mainly Roman Catholic) 41%, Muslim 7%
Ethnic mix Other Malay 46%, Merina 26%, Betsimisaraka 15%, Betsileo 12%, Other 1%
Government Presidential system
Currency Ariary = 5 iraimbilanja
Literacy rate 71%
Calorie consumption 2005 calories

MALAWI
Southern Africa

Official name Republic of Malawi
Formation 1964 / 1964
Capital Lilongwe
Population 12.9 million / 355 people per sq mile (137 people per sq km) / 25%
Total area 45,745 sq miles (118,480 sq km)
Languages English*, Chewa*, Lomwe, Yao, Ngoni
Religions Protestant 55%, Roman Catholic 20%, Muslim 20%, Traditional beliefs 5%
Ethnic mix Bantu 99%, Other 1%
Government Presidential system
Currency Malawi kwacha = 100 tambala
Literacy rate 64%
Calorie consumption 2155 calories

MALAYSIA
Southeast Asia

Official name Federation of Malaysia
Formation 1963 / 1965
Capital Kuala Lumpur; Putrajaya (administrative)
Population 25.3 million / 199 people per sq mile (77 people per sq km) / 57%
Total area 127,316 sq miles (329,750 sq km)
Languages Malay*, Chinese*, Bahasa Malaysia, Tamil, English
Religions Muslim (mainly Sunni) 53%, Buddhist 19%, Chinese faiths 12%, Other 7%, Christian 7%, Traditional beliefs 2%
Ethnic mix Malay 48%, Chinese 29%, Indigenous tribes 12%, Indian 6%, Other 5%
Government Parliamentary system
Currency Ringgit = 100 sen
Literacy rate 89%
Calorie consumption 2881 calories

MALDIVES
Indian Ocean

Official name Republic of Maldives
Formation 1965 / 1965
Capital Male'
Population 329,000 / 2836 people per sq mile (1097 people per sq km) / 30%
Total area 116 sq miles (300 sq km)
Languages Dhivehi (Maldivian)*, Sinhala, Tamil, Arabic
Religions Sunni Muslim 100%
Ethnic mix Arab–Sinhalese–Malay 100%
Government Nonparty system
Currency Rufiyaa = 100 lari
Literacy rate 97%
Calorie consumption 2548 calories

MALI
West Africa

Official name Republic of Mali
Formation 1960 / 1960
Capital Bamako
Population 13.5 million / 29 people per sq mile (11 people per sq km) / 30%
Total area 478,764 sq miles (1,240,000 sq km)
Languages French*, Bambara, Fulani, Senufo, Soninke
Religions Muslim (mainly Sunni) 80%, Traditional beliefs 18%, Christian 1%, Other 1%
Ethnic mix Bambara 32%, Other 26%, Fulani 14%, Senufu 12%, Soninka 9%, Tuareg 7%
Government Presidential system
Currency CFA franc = 100 centimes
Literacy rate 19%
Calorie consumption 2174 calories

MALTA
Southern Europe

Official name Republic of Malta
Formation 1964 / 1964
Capital Valletta
Population 402,000 / 3242 people per sq mile (1256 people per sq km) / 91%
Total area 122 sq miles (316 sq km)
Languages Maltese*, English
Religions Roman Catholic 98%, Other and nonreligious 2%
Ethnic mix Maltese 96%, Other 4%
Government Parliamentary system
Currency Maltese lira = 100 cents
Literacy rate 88%
Calorie consumption 3587 calories

MARSHALL ISLANDS
Australasia & Oceania

Official name Republic of the Marshall Islands
Formation 1986 / 1986
Capital Majuro
Population 59,071 / 844 people per sq mile (326 people per sq km) / 69%
Total area 70 sq miles (181 sq km)
Languages Marshallese*, English*, Japanese, German
Religions Protestant 90%, Roman Catholic 8%, Other 2%
Ethnic mix Micronesian 97%, Other 3%
Government Presidential system
Currency US dollar = 100 cents
Literacy rate 91%
Calorie consumption Not available

MAURITANIA
West Africa

Official name Islamic Republic of Mauritania
Formation 1960 / 1960
Capital Nouakchott
Population 3.1 million / 8 people per sq mile (3 people per sq km) / 58%
Total area 397,953 sq miles (1,030,700 sq km)
Languages French*, Hassaniyah Arabic, Wolof
Religions Sunni Muslim 100%
Ethnic mix Maure 81%, Wolof 7%, Tukolor 5%, Other 4%, Soninka 3%
Government Transitional regime
Currency Ouguiya = 5 khoums
Literacy rate 51%
Calorie consumption 2772 calories

MAURITIUS
Indian Ocean

Official name Republic of Mauritius
Formation 1968 / 1968
Capital Port Louis
Population 1.2 million / 1671 people per sq mile (645 people per sq km) / 41%
Total area 718 sq miles (1860 sq km)
Languages English*, French Creole, Hindi, Urdu, Tamil, Chinese, French
Religions Hindu 52%, Roman Catholic 26%, Muslim 17%, Other 3%, Protestant 2%
Ethnic mix Indo-Mauritian 68%, Creole 27%, Sino-Mauritian 3%, Franco-Mauritian 2%
Government Parliamentary system
Currency Mauritian rupee = 100 cents
Literacy rate 84%
Calorie consumption 2955 calories

MEXICO
North America

Official name United Mexican States
Formation 1836 / 1848
Capital Mexico City
Population 107 million / 145 people per sq mile (56 people per sq km) / 74%
Total area 761,602 sq miles (1,972,550 sq km)
Languages Spanish*, Nahuatl, Mayan, Zapotec, Mixtec, Otomi, Totonac, Tzotzil, Tzeltal
Religions Roman Catholic 88%, Other 7%, Protestant 5%
Ethnic mix Mestizo 60%, Amerindian 30%, European 9%, Other 1%
Government Presidential system
Currency Mexican peso = 100 centavos
Literacy rate 90%
Calorie consumption 3145 calories

MICRONESIA
Australasia & Oceania

Official name Federated States of Micronesia
Formation 1986 / 1986
Capital Palikir (Pohnpei Island)
Population 108,105 / 399 people per sq mile (154 people per sq km) / 28%
Total area 271 sq miles (702 sq km)
Languages Trukese, Pohnpeian, Mortlockese, Kosraean, English
Religions Roman Catholic 50%, Protestant 48%, Other 2%
Ethnic mix Micronesian 100%
Government Nonparty system
Currency US dollar = 100 cents
Literacy rate 81%
Calorie consumption Not available

MOLDOVA
Southeast Europe

Official name Republic of Moldova
Formation 1991 / 1991
Capital Chisinau
Population 4.2 million / 323 people per sq mile (125 people per sq km) / 46%
Total area 13,067 sq miles (33,843 sq km)
Languages Moldovan*, Ukrainian, Russian
Religions Orthodox Christian 98%, Jewish 2%
Ethnic mix Moldovan 65%, Ukrainian 14%, Russian 13%, Other 4%, Gagauz 4%
Government Parliamentary system
Currency Moldovan leu = 100 bani
Literacy rate 96%
Calorie consumption 2806 calories

MONACO
Southern Europe

Official name Principality of Monaco
Formation 1861 / 1861
Capital Monaco-Ville
Population 32,409 / 43212 people per sq mile (16620 people per sq km) / 100%
Total area 0.75 sq miles (1.95 sq km)
Languages French*, Italian, Monégasque, English
Religions Roman Catholic 89%, Protestant 6%, Other 5%
Ethnic mix French 47%, Other 20%, Monégasque 17%, Italian 16%
Government Monarchy
Currency Euro = 100 cents
Literacy rate 99%
Calorie consumption Not available

MONGOLIA
East Asia

Official name Mongolia
Formation 1924 / 1924
Capital Ulan Bator
Population 2.6 million / 4 people per sq mile (2 people per sq km) / 64%
Total area 604,247 sq miles (1,565,000 sq km)
Languages Khalkha Mongolian*, Kazakh, Chinese, Russian
Religions Tibetan Buddhist 96%, Muslim 4%
Ethnic mix Mongol 90%, Kazakh 4%, Other 2%, Chinese 2%, Russian 2%
Government Mixed presidential–parliamentary system
Currency Tugrik (tögrög) = 100 möngö
Literacy rate 98%
Calorie consumption 2249 calories

MONTENEGRO
Europe

Official name Republic of Montenegro
Formation 2006 / 2006
Capital Podgorica
Population 620,145 / 116 people per sq mile (45 people per sq km) / 62%
Total area 5,332 sq miles (13,812 sq km)
Languages Montenegrin, Serbian, Albanian
Religions Orthodox Christian 74%, Muslim 18%, Roman Catholic 4%, Other 4%
Ethnic mix Montenegrin 43%, Serb 32%, Bosniak 8%, Albanian 5%, Other 12%
Government Parliamentary system
Currency Euro = 100 cents
Literacy rate 98%
Calorie consumption Not available

MOROCCO
North Africa

Official name Kingdom of Morocco
Formation 1956 / 1956
Capital Rabat
Population 31.5 million / 183 people per sq mile (71 people per sq km) / 56%
Total area 172,316 sq miles (446,300 sq km)
Languages Arabic*, Tamazight (Berber), French, Spanish
Religions Muslim (mainly Sunni) 99%, Other (mostly Christian) 1%
Ethnic mix Arab 70%, Berber 29%, European 1%
Government Monarchy
Currency Moroccan dirham = 100 centimes
Literacy rate 51%
Calorie consumption 3052 calories

MOZAMBIQUE
Southern Africa

Official name Republic of Mozambique
Formation 1975 / 1975
Capital Maputo
Population 19.8 million / 65 people per sq mile (25 people per sq km) / 40%
Total area 309,494 sq miles (801,590 sq km)
Languages Portuguese*, Makua, Xitsonga, Sena, Lomwe
Religions Traditional beliefs 56%, Christian 30%, Muslim 14%
Ethnic mix Makua Lomwe 47%, Tsonga 23%, Malawi 12%, Shona 11%, Yao 4%, Other 3%
Government Presidential system
Currency Metical = 100 centavos
Literacy rate 47%
Calorie consumption 2079 calories

NAMIBIA
Southern Africa

Official name Republic of Namibia
Formation 1990 / 1994
Capital Windhoek
Population 2 million / 6 people per sq mile (2 people per sq km) / 31%
Total area 318,694 sq miles (825,418 sq km)
Languages English*, Ovambo, Kavango, Bergdama, German, Afrikaans
Religions Christian 90%, Traditional beliefs 10%
Ethnic mix Ovambo 50%, Other tribes 16%, Kavango 9%, Other 9%, Damara 8%, Herero 8%
Government Presidential system
Currency Namibian dollar = 100 cents
Literacy rate 85%
Calorie consumption 2278 calories

NAURU
Australasia & Oceania

Official name Republic of Nauru
Formation 1968 / 1968
Capital None
Population 13,048 / 1611 people per sq mile (621 people per sq km) / 100%
Total area 8.1 sq miles (21 sq km)
Languages Nauruan*, Kiribati, Chinese, Tuvaluan, English
Religions Nauruan Congregational Church 60%, Roman Catholic 35%, Other 5%
Ethnic mix Nauruan 62%, Other Pacific islanders 25%, Chinese and Vietnamese 8%, European 5%
Government Parliamentary system
Currency Australian dollar = 100 cents
Literacy rate 95%
Calorie consumption Not available

NEPAL
South Asia

Official name Kingdom of Nepal
Formation 1769 / 1769
Capital Kathmandu
Population 27.1 million / 513 people per sq mile (198 people per sq km) / 12%
Total area 54,363 sq miles (140,800 sq km)
Languages Nepali*, Maithili, Bhojpuri
Religions Hindu 90%, Buddhist 5%, Muslim 3%, Other (including Christian) 2%
Ethnic mix Nepalese 52%, Other 19%, Maithili 11%, Tibeto-Burmese 10%, Bhojpuri 8%
Government Monarchy
Currency Nepalese rupee = 100 paise
Literacy rate 49%
Calorie consumption 2453 calories

NETHERLANDS
Northwest Europe

Official name Kingdom of the Netherlands
Formation 1648 / 1839
Capital Amsterdam; The Hague (administrative)
Population 16.3 million / 1245 people per sq mile (481 people per sq km) / 89%
Total area 16,033 sq miles (41,526 sq km)
Languages Dutch*, Frisian
Religions Roman Catholic 36%, Other 34%, Protestant 27%, Muslim 3%
Ethnic mix Dutch 82%, Other 12%, Surinamese 2%, Turkish 2%, Moroccan 2%
Government Parliamentary system
Currency Euro = 100 cents
Literacy rate 99%
Calorie consumption 3362 calories

NEW ZEALAND
Australasia & Oceania

Official name New Zealand
Formation 1947 / 1947
Capital Wellington
Population 4 million / 39 people per sq mile (15 people per sq km) / 86%
Total area 103,737 sq miles (268,680 sq km)
Languages English*, Maori
Religions Anglican 24%, Other 22%, Presbyterian 18%, Nonreligious 16%, Roman Catholic 15%, Methodist 5%
Ethnic mix European 77%, Maori 12%, Other immigrant 6%, Pacific islanders 5%
Government Parliamentary system
Currency New Zealand dollar = 100 cents
Literacy rate 99%
Calorie consumption 3219 calories

NICARAGUA
Central America

Official name Republic of Nicaragua
Formation 1838 / 1838
Capital Managua
Population 5.5 million / 120 people per sq mile (46 people per sq km) / 65%
Total area 49,998 sq miles (129,494 sq km)
Languages Spanish*, English Creole, Miskito
Religions Roman Catholic 80%, Protestant Evangelical 17%, Other 3%
Ethnic mix Mestizo 69%, White 14%, Black 8%, Amerindian 5%, Zambo 4%
Government Presidential system
Currency Córdoba oro = 100 centavos
Literacy rate 77%
Calorie consumption 2298 calories

NIGER
West Africa

Official name Republic of Niger
Formation 1960 / 1960
Capital Niamey
Population 14 million / 29 people per sq mile (11 people per sq km) / 21%
Total area 489,188 sq miles (1,267,000 sq km)
Languages French*, Hausa, Djerma, Fulani, Tuareg, Teda
Religions Muslim 85%, Traditional beliefs 14%, Other (including Christian) 1%
Ethnic mix Hausa 54%, Djerma and Songhai 21%, Fulani 10%, Tuareg 9%, Other 6%
Government Presidential system
Currency CFA franc = 100 centimes
Literacy rate 14%
Calorie consumption 2130 calories

NIGERIA
West Africa

Official name Federal Republic of Nigeria
Formation 1960 / 1961
Capital Abuja
Population 132 million / 374 people per sq mile (144 people per sq km) / 44%
Total area 356,667 sq miles (923,768 sq km)
Languages English*, Hausa, Yoruba, Ibo
Religions Muslim 50%, Christian 40%, Traditional beliefs 10%
Ethnic mix Other 29%, Hausa 21%, Yoruba 21%, Ibo 18%, Fulani 11%
Government Presidential system
Currency Naira = 100 kobo
Literacy rate 67%
Calorie consumption 2726 calories

NORTH KOREA
East Asia

Official name Democratic People's Republic of Korea
Formation 1948 / 1953
Capital Pyongyang
Population 22.5 million / 484 people per sq mile (187 people per sq km) / 60%
Total area 46,540 sq miles (120,540 sq km)
Languages Korean*
Religions Atheist 100%
Ethnic mix Korean 100%
Government One-party state
Currency North Korean won = 100 chon
Literacy rate 99%
Calorie consumption 2142 calories

NORWAY
Northern Europe

Official name Kingdom of Norway
Formation 1905 / 1905
Capital Oslo
Population 4.6 million / 39 people per sq mile (15 people per sq km) / 76%
Total area 125,181 sq miles (324,220 sq km)
Languages Norwegian* (Bokmål "book language" and Nynorsk "new Norsk"), Sámi
Religions Evangelical Lutheran 89%, Other and nonreligious 10%, Roman Catholic 1%
Ethnic mix Norwegian 93%, Other 6%, Sámi 1%
Government Parliamentary system
Currency Norwegian krone = 100 øre
Literacy rate 99%
Calorie consumption 3484 calories

OMAN
Southwest Asia

Official name Sultanate of Oman
Formation 1951 / 1951
Capital Muscat
Population 2.6 million / 32 people per sq mile (12 people per sq km) / 84%
Total area 82,031 sq miles (212,460 sq km)
Languages Arabic*, Baluchi, Farsi, Hindi, Punjabi
Religions Ibadi Muslim 75%, Other Muslim and Hindu 25%
Ethnic mix Arab 88%, Baluchi 4%, Persian 3%, Indian and Pakistani 3%, African 2%
Government Monarchy
Currency Omani rial = 1000 baizas
Literacy rate 74%
Calorie consumption Not available

PAKISTAN
South Asia

Official name Islamic Republic of Pakistan
Formation 1947 / 1971
Capital Islamabad
Population 158 million / 531 people per sq mile (205 people per sq km) / 37%
Total area 310,401 sq miles (803,940 sq km)
Languages Urdu*, Baluchi, Brahui, Pashtu, Punjabi, Sindhi
Religions Sunni Muslim 77%, Shi'a Muslim 20%, Hindu 2%, Christian 1%
Ethnic mix Punjabi 56%, Pathan (Pashtun) 15%, Sindhi 14%, Mohajir 7%, Other 4%, Baluchi 4%
Government Presidential system
Currency Pakistani rupee = 100 paisa
Literacy rate 49%
Calorie consumption 2419 calories

PALAU
Australasia & Oceania

Official name Republic of Palau
Formation 1994 / 1994
Capital Koror
Population 20,303 / 104 people per sq mile (40 people per sq km) / 70%
Total area 177 sq miles (458 sq km)
Languages Palauan, English, Japanese, Angaur, Tobi, Sonsorolese
Religions Christian 66%, Modekngei 34%
Ethnic mix Micronesian 87%, Filipino 8%, Chinese and other Asian 5%
Government Nonparty system
Currency US dollar = 100 cents
Literacy rate 98%
Calorie consumption Not available

PANAMA
Central America

Official name Republic of Panama
Formation 1903 / 1903
Capital Panama City
Population 3.2 million / 109 people per sq mile (42 people per sq km) / 56%
Total area 30,193 sq miles (78,200 sq km)
Languages Spanish*, English Creole, Amerindian languages, Chibchan languages
Religions Roman Catholic 86%, Other 8%, Protestant 6%
Ethnic mix Mestizo 60%, White 14%, Black 12%, Amerindian 8%, Asian 4%, Other 2%
Government Presidential system
Currency Balboa = 100 centesimos
Literacy rate 92%
Calorie consumption 2272 calories

PAPUA NEW GUINEA
Australasia & Oceania

Official name Independent State of Papua New Guinea
Formation 1975 / 1975
Capital Port Moresby
Population 5.9 million / 34 people per sq mile (13 people per sq km) / 17%
Total area 178,703 sq miles (462,840 sq km)
Languages Pidgin English*, Papuan*, English, Motu, 750 (est.) native languages
Religions Protestant 60%, Roman Catholic 37%, Other 3%
Ethnic mix Melanesian and mixed race 100%
Government Parliamentary system
Currency Kina = 100 toeas
Literacy rate 57%
Calorie consumption 2193 calories

PARAGUAY
South America

Official name Republic of Paraguay
Formation 1811 / 1938
Capital Asunción
Population 6.2 million / 40 people per sq mile (16 people per sq km) / 56%
Total area 157,046 sq miles (406,750 sq km)
Languages Guarani*, Spanish*, German
Religions Roman Catholic 96%, Protestant (including Mennonite) 4%
Ethnic mix Mestizo 90%, Other 8%, Amerindian 2%
Government Presidential system
Currency Guaraní = 100 centimos
Literacy rate 92%
Calorie consumption 2565 calories

PERU
South America

Official name Republic of Peru
Formation 1824 / 1941
Capital Lima
Population 28 million / 57 people per sq mile (22 people per sq km) / 73%
Total area 496,223 sq miles (1,285,200 sq km)
Languages Spanish*, Quechua*, Aymara*
Religions Roman Catholic 95%, Other 5%
Ethnic mix Amerindian 50%, Mestizo 40%, White 7%, Other 3%
Government Presidential system
Currency New sol = 100 centimos
Literacy rate 88%
Calorie consumption 2571 calories

PHILIPPINES
Southwest Asia

Official name Republic of the Philippines
Formation 1946 / 1946
Capital Manila
Population 83.1 million / 722 people per sq mile (279 people per sq km) / 59%
Total area 115,830 sq miles (300,000 sq km)
Languages Filipino*, English*, Tagalog, Cebuano, Ilocano, Hiligaynon, many other local languages
Religions Roman Catholic 83%, Protestant 9%, Muslim 5%, Other (including Buddhist) 3%
Ethnic mix Malay 95%, Other 3%, Chinese 2%
Government Presidential system
Currency Philippine peso = 100 centavos
Literacy rate 93%
Calorie consumption 2379 calories

POLAND
Northern Europe

Official name Republic of Poland
Formation 1918 / 1945
Capital Warsaw
Population 38.5 million / 328 people per sq mile (126 people per sq km) / 66%
Total area 120,728 sq miles (312,685 sq km)
Languages Polish*
Religions Roman Catholic 93%, Other and nonreligious 5%, Orthodox Christian 2%
Ethnic mix Polish 97%, Other 2%, Silesian 1%
Government Parliamentary system
Currency Zloty = 100 groszy
Literacy rate 99%
Calorie consumption 3374 calories

PORTUGAL
Southwest Europe

Official name Republic of Portugal
Formation 1139 / 1640
Capital Lisbon
Population 10.5 million / 296 people per sq mile (114 people per sq km) / 64%
Total area 35,672 sq miles (92,391 sq km)
Languages Portuguese
Religions Roman Catholic 97%, Other 2%, Protestant 1%
Ethnic mix Portuguese 98%, African and other 2%
Government Parliamentary system
Currency Euro = 100 cents
Literacy rate 93%
Calorie consumption 3741 calories

QATAR
Southwest Asia

Official name State of Qatar
Formation 1971 / 1971
Capital Doha
Population 813,000 / 191 people per sq mile (74 people per sq km) / 93%
Total area 4416 sq miles (11,437 sq km)
Languages Arabic*
Religions Muslim (mainly Sunni) 95%, Other 5%
Ethnic mix Arab 40%, Indian 18%, Pakistani 18%, Other 14%, Iranian 10%
Government Monarchy
Currency Qatar riyal = 100 dirhams
Literacy rate 89%
Calorie consumption Not available

ROMANIA
Southest Europe

Official name Romania
Formation 1878 / 1947
Capital Bucharest
Population 21.7 million / 244 people per sq mile (94 people per sq km) / 56%
Total area 91,699 sq miles (237,500 sq km)
Languages Romanian*, Hungarian (Magyar), Romani, German
Religions Romanian Orthodox 87%, Roman Catholic 5%, Protestant 4%, Other 2%, Greek Orthodox 1%, Greek Catholic (Uniate) 1%
Ethnic mix Romanian 89%, Magyar 7%, Roma 3%, Other 1%
Government Presidential system
Currency Romanian leu = 100 bani
Literacy rate 97%
Calorie consumption 3455 calories

RUSSIAN FEDERATION
Europe / Asia

Official name Russian Federation
Formation 1480 / 1991
Capital Moscow
Population 143 million / 22 people per sq mile (8 people per sq km) / 78%
Total area 6,592,735 sq miles (17,075,200 sq km)
Languages Russian*, Tatar, Ukrainian, Chavash, various other national languages
Religions Orthodox Christian 75%, Other 15%, Muslim 10%
Ethnic mix Russian 82%, Other 10%, Tatar 4%, Ukrainian 3%, Chavash 1%
Government Presidential system
Currency Russian rouble = 100 kopeks
Literacy rate 99%
Calorie consumption 3072 calories

RWANDA
Central Africa

Official name Republic of Rwanda
Formation 1962 / 1962
Capital Kigali
Population 9 million / 934 people per sq mile (361 people per sq km) / 6%
Total area 10,169 sq miles (26,338 sq km)
Languages Kinyarwanda*, French*, Kiswahili, English
Religions Roman Catholic 56%, Traditional beliefs 25%, Muslim 10%, Protestant 9%
Ethnic mix Hutu 90%, Tutsi 9%, Other (including Twa) 1%
Government Presidential system
Currency Rwanda franc = 100 centimes
Literacy rate 64%
Calorie consumption 2084 calories

SAINT KITTS & NEVIS
West Indies

Official name Federation of Saint Christopher and Nevis
Formation 1983 / 1983
Capital Basseterre
Population 38,958 / 280 people per sq mile (108 people per sq km) / 34%
Total area 101 sq miles (261 sq km)
Languages English*, English Creole
Religions Anglican 33%, Methodist 29%, Other 22%, Moravian 9%, Roman Catholic 7%
Ethnic mix Black 94%, Mixed race 3%, Other and Amerindian 2%, White 1%
Government Parliamentary system
Currency Eastern Caribbean dollar = 100 cents
Literacy rate 98%
Calorie consumption 2609 calories

SAINT LUCIA
West Indies

Official name Saint Lucia
Formation 1979 / 1979
Capital Castries
Population 166,312 / 705 people per sq mile (273 people per sq km) / 38%
Total area 239 sq miles (620 sq km)
Languages English*, French Creole
Religions Roman Catholic 90%, Other 10%
Ethnic mix Black 90%, Mulatto (mixed race) 6%, Asian 3%, White 1%
Government Parliamentary system
Currency Eastern Caribbean dollar = 100 cents
Literacy rate 90%
Calorie consumption 2988 calories

SAINT VINCENT & THE GRENADINES
West Indies

Official name Saint Vincent and the Grenadines
Formation 1979 / 1979
Capital Kingstown
Population 117,534 / 897 people per sq mile (346 people per sq km) / 55%
Total area 150 sq miles (389 sq km)
Languages English*, English Creole
Religions Anglican 47%, Methodist 28%, Roman Catholic 13%, Other 12%
Ethnic mix Black 66%, Mulatto (mixed race) 19%, Asian 6%, Other 5%, White 4%
Government Parliamentary system
Currency Eastern Caribbean dollar = 100 cents
Literacy rate 88%
Calorie consumption 2599 calories

SAMOA
Australasia & Oceania

Official name Independent State of Samoa
Formation 1962 / 1962
Capital Apia
Population 185,000 / 169 people per sq mile (65 people per sq km) / 22%
Total area 1104 sq miles (2860 sq km)
Languages Samoan*, English*
Religions Christian 99%, Other 1%
Ethnic mix Polynesian 90%, Euronesian 9%, Other 1%
Government Parliamentary system
Currency Tala = 100 sene
Literacy rate 99%
Calorie consumption 2945 calories

SAN MARINO
Southern Europe

Official name Republic of San Marino
Formation 1631 / 1631
Capital San Marino
Population 28,880 / 1203 people per sq mile (473 people per sq km) / 94%
Total area 23.6 sq miles (61 sq km)
Languages Italian*
Religions Roman Catholic 93%, Other and nonreligious 7%
Ethnic mix Sammarinese 80%, Italian 19%, Other 1%
Government Parliamentary system
Currency Euro = 100 cents
Literacy rate 99%
Calorie consumption Not available

SÃO TOMÉ & PRÍNCIPE
West Africa

Official name Democratic Republic of São Tomé and Príncipe
Formation 1975 / 1975
Capital São Tomé
Population 187,410 / 505 people per sq mile (195 people per sq km) / 47%
Total area 386 sq miles (1001 sq km)
Languages Portuguese*, Portuguese Creole
Religions Roman Catholic 84%, Other 16%
Ethnic mix Black 90%, Portuguese and Creole 10%
Government Presidential system
Currency Dobra = 100 centimos
Literacy rate 83%
Calorie consumption 2460 calories

SAUDI ARABIA
Souhwest Asia

Official name Kingdom of Saudi Arabia
Formation 1932 / 1932
Capital Riyadh; Jiddah (administrative)
Population 24.6 million / 30 people per sq mile (12 people per sq km) / 86%
Total area 756,981 sq miles (1,960,582 sq km)
Languages Arabic*
Religions Sunni Muslim 85%, Shi'a Muslim 15%
Ethnic mix Arab 90%, Afro-Asian 10%
Government Monarchy
Currency Saudi riyal = 100 halalat
Literacy rate 79%
Calorie consumption 2844 calories

SENEGAL
West Africa

Official name Republic of Senegal
Formation 1960 / 1960
Capital Dakar
Population 11.7 million / 157 people per sq mile (61 people per sq km) / 47%
Total area 75,749 sq miles (196,190 sq km)
Languages French*, Diola, Mandinka, Malinke, Pulaar, Serer, Soninke, Wolof
Religions Sunni Muslim 90%, Christian (mainly Roman Catholic) 5%, Traditional beliefs 5%
Ethnic mix Wolof 43%, Toucouleur 24%, Serer 15%, Other 11%, Diola 4%, Malinke 3%
Government Presidential system
Currency CFA franc = 100 centimes
Literacy rate 39%
Calorie consumption 2279 calories

SERBIA
Europe

Official name Republic of Serbia
Formation 2006 /2006
Capital Belgrade
Population 9.7 million / 290 people per sq mile (112 people per sq km) / 52%
Total area 34,116 sq miles (88,361 sq km)
Languages Serbo-Croat*, Albanian, Hungarian
Religions Orthodox Christian 85%, Muslim 6%, Other 6%, Roman Catholic 3%
Ethnic mix Serb 66%, Albanian 19%, Hungarian 4%, Bosniak 2%, Other 9%
Government Parliamentary system
Currency Dinar (Serbia) = 100 para
Literacy rate 98%
Calorie consumption Not available

SEYCHELLES
Indian Ocean

Official name Republic of Seychelles
Formation 1976 / 1976
Capital Victoria
Population 81,188 / 781 people per sq mile (301 people per sq km) / 64%
Total area 176 sq miles (455 sq km)
Languages French Creole*, English, French
Religions Roman Catholic 90%, Anglican 8%, Other (including Muslim) 2%
Ethnic mix Creole 89%, Indian 5%, Other 4%, Chinese 2%
Government Presidential system
Currency Seychelles rupee = 100 cents
Literacy rate 92%
Calorie consumption 2465 calories

SIERRA LEONE
West Africa

Official name Republic of Sierra Leone
Formation 1961 / 1961
Capital Freetown
Population 5.5 million / 199 people per sq mile (77 people per sq km) / 37%
Total area 27,698 sq miles (71,740 sq km)
Languages English*, Mende, Temne, Krio
Religions Muslim 30%, Traditional beliefs 30%, Other 30%, Christian 10%
Ethnic mix Mende 35%, Temne 32%, Other 21%, Limba 8%, Kuranko 4%
Government Presidential system
Currency Leone = 100 cents
Literacy rate 30%
Calorie consumption 1936 calories

SINGAPORE
Southeast Asia

Official name Republic of Singapore
Formation 1965 / 1965
Capital Singapore
Population 4.3 million / 18220 people per sq mile (7049 people per sq km) / 100%
Total area 250 sq miles (648 sq km)
Languages English*, Malay*, Mandarin*, Tamil*
Religions Buddhist 55%, Taoist 22%, Muslim 16%, Hindu, Christian, and Sikh 7%
Ethnic mix Chinese 77%, Malay 14%, Indian 8%, Other 1%
Government Parliamentary system
Currency Singapore dollar = 100 cents
Literacy rate 93%
Calorie consumption Not available

SLOVAKIA
Central Europe

Official name Slovak Republic
Formation 1993 / 1993
Capital Bratislava
Population 5.4 million / 285 people per sq mile (110 people per sq km) / 57%
Total area 18,859 sq miles (48,845 sq km)
Languages Slovak*, Hungarian (Magyar), Czech
Religions Roman Catholic 60%, Other 18%, Atheist 10%, Protestant 8%, Orthodox Christian 4%
Ethnic mix Slovak 85%, Magyar 11%, Other 2%, Roma 1%, Czech 1%
Government Parliamentary system
Currency Slovak koruna = 100 halierov
Literacy rate 99%
Calorie consumption 2889 calories

SLOVENIA
Central Europe

Official name Republic of Slovenia
Formation 1991 / 1991
Capital Ljubljana
Population 2 million / 256 people per sq mile (99 people per sq km) / 50%
Total area 7820 sq miles (20,253 sq km)
Languages Slovene*, Serbo-Croat
Religions Roman Catholic 96%, Other 3%, Muslim 1%
Ethnic mix Slovene 83%, Other 12%, Serb 2%, Croat 2%, Bosniak 1%
Government Parliamentary system
Currency Tolar = 100 stotinov
Literacy rate 99%
Calorie consumption 3001 calories

SOLOMON ISLANDS
Australasia & Oceania

Official name Solomon Islands
Formation 1978 / 1978
Capital Honiara
Population 478,000 / 44 people per sq mile (17 people per sq km) / 20%
Total area 10,985 sq miles (28,450 sq km)
Languages English*, Melanesian Pidgin, Pidgin English
Religions Anglican 34%, Roman Catholic 19%, Methodist 11%, Seventh-day Adventist 10%, South Seas Evangelical Church 17%, Other 9%
Ethnic mix Melanesian 94%, Polynesian 4%, Other 2%
Government Parliamentary system
Currency Solomon Islands dollar = 100 cents
Literacy rate 77%
Calorie consumption 2265 calories

SOMALIA
East Africa

Official name Somalia
Formation 1960 / 1960
Capital Mogadishu
Population 8.2 million / 34 people per sq mile (13 people per sq km) / 28%
Total area 246,199 sq miles (637,657 sq km)
Languages Somali*, Arabic*, English, Italian
Religions Sunni Muslim 98%, Christian 2%
Ethnic mix Somali 85%, Other 15%
Government Transitional regime
Currency Somali shilling = 100 centesimi
Literacy rate 24%
Calorie consumption 1628 calories

SOUTH AFRICA
Southern Africa

Official name Republic of South Africa
Formation 1934 / 1994
Capital Pretoria; Cape Town; Bloemfontein
Population 47.4 million / 101 people per sq mile (39 people per sq km) / 55%
Total area 471,008 sq miles (1,219,912 sq km)
Languages English, isiZulu, isiXhosa, Afrikaans, Sepedi, Setswana, Sesotho, Xitsonga, siSwati, Tshivenda, isiNdebele
Religions Christian 68%, Traditional beliefs and animist 29%, Muslim 2%, Hindu 1%
Ethnic mix Black 79%, White 10%, Colored 9%, Asian 2%
Government Presidential system
Currency Rand = 100 cents
Literacy rate 82%
Calorie consumption 2956 calories

SOUTH KOREA
East Asia

Official name Republic of Korea
Formation 1948 / 1953
Capital Seoul
Population 47.8 million / 1254 people per sq mile (484 people per sq km) / 82%
Total area 38,023 sq miles (98,480 sq km)
Languages Korean*
Religions Mahayana Buddhist 47%, Protestant 38%, Roman Catholic 11%, Confucianist 3%, Other 1%
Ethnic mix Korean 100%
Government Presidential system
Currency South Korean won = 100 chon
Literacy rate 98%
Calorie consumption 3058 calories

SPAIN
Southeast Europe

Official name Kingdom of Spain
Formation 1492 / 1713
Capital Madrid
Population 43.1 million / 224 people per sq mile (86 people per sq km) / 78%
Total area 194,896 sq miles (504,782 sq km)
Languages Spanish*, Catalan*, Galician*, Basque*
Religions Roman Catholic 96%, Other 4%
Ethnic mix Castilian Spanish 72%, Catalan 17%, Galician 6%, Basque 2%, Other 2%, Roma 1%
Government Parliamentary system
Currency Euro = 100 cents
Literacy rate 98%
Calorie consumption 3371 calories

SRI LANKA
South Asia

Official name Democratic Socialist Republic of Sri Lanka
Formation 1948 / 1948
Capital Colombo
Population 20.7 million / 828 people per sq mile (320 people per sq km) / 24%
Total area 25,332 sq miles (65,610 sq km)
Languages Sinhala, Tamil, Sinhala-Tamil, English
Religions Buddhist 69%, Hindu 15%, Muslim 8%, Christian 8%
Ethnic mix Sinhalese 74%, Tamil 18%, Moor 7%, Burgher, Malay, and Veddha 1%
Government Mixed presidential–parliamentary system
Currency Sri Lanka rupee = 100 cents
Literacy rate 90%
Calorie consumption 2385 calories

SUDAN
East Africa

Official name Republic of the Sudan
Formation 1956 / 1956
Capital Khartoum
Population 36.2 million / 37 people per sq mile (14 people per sq km) / 36%
Total area 967,493 sq miles (2,505,810 sq km)
Languages Arabic*, Dinka, Nuer, Nubian, Beja, Zande, Bari, Fur, Shilluk, Lotuko
Religions Muslim (mainly Sunni) 70%, Traditional beliefs 20%, Christian 9%, Other 1%
Ethnic mix Other Black 52%, Arab 40%, Dinka and Beja 7%, Other 1%
Government Presidential system
Currency Sudanese pound or dinar = 100 piastres
Literacy rate 59%
Calorie consumption 2228 calories

SURINAM
South America

Official name Republic of Suriname
Formation 1975 / 1975
Capital Paramaribo
Population 499,000 / 8 people per sq mile (3 people per sq km) / 74%
Total area 63,039 sq miles (163,270 sq km)
Languages Dutch*, Sranan (Creole), Javanese, Sarnami Hindi, Saramaccan, Chinese, Carib
Religions Hindu 27%, Protestant 25%, Roman Catholic 23%, Muslim 20%, Traditional beliefs 5%
Ethnic mix Creole 34%, South Asian 34%, Javanese 18%, Black 9%, Other 5%
Government Parliamentary system
Currency Suriname dollar (guilder until 2004) = 100 cents
Literacy rate 88%
Calorie consumption 2652 calories

SWAZILAND
Southern Africa

Official name Kingdom of Swaziland
Formation 1968 / 1968
Capital Mbabane
Population 1 million / 151 people per sq mile (58 people per sq km) / 26%
Total area 6704 sq miles (17,363 sq km)
Languages English*, siSwati*, isiZulu, Xitsonga
Religions Christian 60%, Traditional beliefs 40%
Ethnic mix Swazi 97%, Other 3%
Government Monarchy
Currency Lilangeni = 100 cents
Literacy rate 79%
Calorie consumption 2322 calories

SWEDEN
Northern Europe

Official name Kingdom of Sweden
Formation 1523 / 1905
Capital Stockholm
Population 9 million / 57 people per sq mile (22 people per sq km) / 83%
Total area 173,731 sq miles (449,964 sq km)
Languages Swedish*, Finnish, Sámi
Religions Evangelical Lutheran 82%, Other 13%, Roman Catholic 2%, Muslim 2%, Orthodox Christian 1%
Ethnic mix Swedish 88%, Foreign-born or first-generation immigrant 10%, Finnish and Sámi 2%
Government Parliamentary system
Currency Swedish krona = 100 öre
Literacy rate 99%
Calorie consumption 3185 calories

SWITZERLAND
Central Europe

Official name Swiss Confederation
Formation 1291 / 1857
Capital Bern
Population 7.3 million / 475 people per sq mile (184 people per sq km) / 68%
Total area 15,942 sq miles (41,290 sq km)
Languages German*, French*, Italian*, Romansch*, Swiss-German
Religions Roman Catholic 46%, Protestant 40%, Other and nonreligious 12%, Muslim 2%
Ethnic mix German 65%, French 18%, Italian 10%, Other 6%, Romansch 1%
Government Parliamentary system
Currency Swiss franc = 100 rappen/centimes
Literacy rate 99%
Calorie consumption 3526 calories

SYRIA
Southwest Asia

Official name Syrian Arab Republic
Formation 1941 / 1967
Capital Damascus
Population 19 million / 267 people per sq mile (103 people per sq km) / 55%
Total area 71,498 sq miles (184,180 sq km)
Languages Arabic*, French, Kurdish, Armenian, Circassian, Turkic languages, Assyrian, Aramaic
Religions Sunni Muslim 74%, Other Muslim 16%, Christian 10%
Ethnic mix Arab 89%, Kurdish 6%, Other 3%, Armenian, Turkmen, and Circassian 2%
Government One-party state
Currency Syrian pound = 100 piasters
Literacy rate 83%
Calorie consumption 3038 calories

TAIWAN
East Asia

Official name Republic of China (ROC)
Formation 1949 / 1949
Capital Taipei
Population 22.9 million / 1838 people per sq mile (710 people per sq km) / 69%
Total area 13,892 sq miles (35,980 sq km)
Languages Amoy Chinese, Mandarin Chinese, Hakka Chinese
Religions Buddhist, Confucianist, and Taoist 93%, Christian 5%, Other 2%
Ethnic mix Han (pre-20th-century migration) 84%, Han (20th-century migration) 14%, Aboriginal 2%
Government Presidential system
Currency Taiwan dollar = 100 cents
Literacy rate 97%
Calorie consumption Not available

TAJIKISTAN
Central Asia

Official name Republic of Tajikistan
Formation 1991 / 1991
Capital Dushanbe
Population 6.5 million / 118 people per sq mile (45 people per sq km) / 28%
Total area 55,251 sq miles (143,100 sq km)
Languages Tajik*, Uzbek, Russian
Religions Sunni Muslim 80%, Other 15%, Shi'a Muslim 5%
Ethnic mix Tajik 62%, Uzbek 24%, Russian 8%, Other 4%, Tatar 1%, Kyrgyz 1%
Government Presidential system
Currency Somoni = 100 diram
Literacy rate 99%
Calorie consumption 1828 calories

TANZANIA
East Africa

Official name United Republic of Tanzania
Formation 1964 / 1964
Capital Dodoma
Population 38.3 million / 112 people per sq mile (43 people per sq km) / 33%
Total area 364,898 sq miles (945,087 sq km)
Languages English*, Kiswahili*, Sukuma, Chagga, Nyamwezi, Hehe, Makonde, Yao, Sandawe
Religions Muslim 33%, Christian 33%, Traditional beliefs 30%, Other 4%
Ethnic mix Native African (over 120 tribes) 99%, European and Asian 1%
Government Presidential system
Currency Tanzanian shilling = 100 cents
Literacy rate 69%
Calorie consumption 1975 calories

THAILAND
Southeastern Asia

Official name Kingdom of Thailand
Formation 1238 / 1907
Capital Bangkok
Population 64.2 million / 325 people per sq mile (126 people per sq km) / 22%
Total area 198,455 sq miles (514,000 sq km)
Languages Thai*, Chinese, Malay, Khmer, Mon, Karen, Miao
Religions Buddhist 95%, Muslim 4%, Other (including Christian) 1%
Ethnic mix Thai 83%, Chinese 12%, Malay 3%, Khmer and Other 2%
Government Parliamentary system
Currency Baht = 100 stang
Literacy rate 93%
Calorie consumption 2467 calories

TOGO
Western Africa

Official name Republic of Togo
Formation 1960 / 1960
Capital Lomé
Population 6.1 million / 290 people per sq mile (112 people per sq km) / 33%
Total area 21,924 sq miles (56,785 sq km)
Languages French*, Ewe, Kabye, Gurma
Religions Traditional beliefs 50%, Christian 35%, Muslim 15%
Ethnic mix Ewe 46%, Kabye 27%, Other African 26%, European 1%
Government Presidential system
Currency CFA franc = 100 centimes
Literacy rate 53%
Calorie consumption 2345 calories

TONGA
Australasia & Oceania

Official name Kingdom of Tonga
Formation 1970 / 1970
Capital Nuku'alofa
Population 112,422 / 404 people per sq mile (156 people per sq km) / 43%
Total area 289 sq miles (748 sq km)
Languages Tongan*, English
Religions Free Wesleyan 41%, Roman Catholic 16%, Church of Jesus Christ of Latter-day Saints 14%, Free Church of Tonga 12%, Other 17%
Ethnic mix Polynesian 99%, Other 1%
Government Monarchy
Currency Pa'anga (Tongan dollar) = 100 seniti
Literacy rate 99%
Calorie consumption Not available

TRINIDAD & TOBAGO
West Indies

Official name Republic of Trinidad and Tobago
Formation 1962 / 1962
Capital Port-of-Spain
Population 1.3 million / 656 people per sq mile (253 people per sq km) / 74%
Total area 1980 sq miles (5128 sq km)
Languages English*, English Creole, Hindi, French, Spanish
Religions Christian 60%, Hindu 24%, Other and nonreligious 9%, Muslim 7%
Ethnic mix East Indian 40%, Black 40%, Mixed race 19%, White and Chinese 1%
Government Parliamentary system
Currency Trinidad and Tobago dollar = 100 cents
Literacy rate 99%
Calorie consumption 2732 calories

TUNISIA
North Africa

Official name Republic of Tunisia
Formation 1956 / 1956
Capital Tunis
Population 10.1 million / 168 people per sq mile (65 people per sq km) / 68%
Total area 63,169 sq miles (163,610 sq km)
Languages Arabic*, French
Religions Muslim (mainly Sunni) 98%, Christian 1%, Jewish 1%
Ethnic mix Arab and Berber 98%, Jewish 1%, European 1%
Government Presidential system
Currency Tunisian dinar = 1000 millimes
Literacy rate 74%
Calorie consumption 3238 calories

TURKEY
Asia / Europe

Official name Republic of Turkey
Formation 1923 / 1939
Capital Ankara
Population 73.2 million / 246 people per sq mile (95 people per sq km) / 75%
Total area 301,382 sq miles (780,580 sq km)
Languages Turkish*, Kurdish, Arabic, Circassian, Armenian, Greek, Georgian, Ladino
Religions Muslim (mainly Sunni) 99%, Other 1%
Ethnic mix Turkish 70%, Kurdish 20%, Other 8%, Arab 2%
Government Parliamentary system
Currency new Turkish lira = 100 kurus
Literacy rate 88%
Calorie consumption 3357 calories

TURKMENISTAN
Central Asia

Official name Turkmenistan
Formation 1991 / 1991
Capital Ashgabat
Population 4.8 million / 25 people per sq mile (10 people per sq km) / 45%
Total area 188,455 sq miles (488,100 sq km)
Languages Turkmen*, Uzbek, Russian, Kazakh, Tatar
Religions Sunni Muslim 87%, Orthodox Christian 11%, Other 2%
Ethnic mix Turkmen 77%, Uzbek 9%, Russian 7%, Other 4%, Kazakh 2%, Tatar 1%
Government One-party state
Currency Manat = 100 tenga
Literacy rate 99%
Calorie consumption 2742 calories

TUVALU
Australasia & Oceania

Official name Tuvalu
Formation 1978 / 1978
Capital Fongafale, on Funafuti Atoll
Population 11,636 / 1164 people per sq mile (448 people per sq km) / 45%
Total area 10 sq miles (26 sq km)
Languages Tuvaluan, Kiribati, English
Religions Church of Tuvalu 97%, Other 1%, Baha'i 1%, Seventh-day Adventist 1%
Ethnic mix Polynesian 96%, Other 4%
Government Nonparty system
Currency Australian dollar and Tuvaluan dollar = 100 cents
Literacy rate 98%
Calorie consumption Not available

UGANDA
East Africa

Official name Republic of Uganda
Formation 1962 / 1962
Capital Kampala
Population 28.8 million / 374 people per sq mile (144 people per sq km) / 14%
Total area 91,135 sq miles (236,040 sq km)
Languages English*, Luganda, Nkole, Chiga, Lango, Acholi, Teso, Lugbara
Religions Roman Catholic 38%, Protestant 33%, Traditional beliefs 13%, Muslim (mainly Sunni) 8%, Other 8%
Ethnic mix Bantu tribes 50%, Other 45%, Sudanese 5%
Government Nonparty system
Currency New Uganda shilling = 100 cents
Literacy rate 69%
Calorie consumption 2410 calories

UKRAINE
Eastern Europe

Official name Ukraine
Formation 1991 / 1991
Capital Kiev
Population 46.5 million / 199 people per sq mile (77 people per sq km) / 68%
Total area 223,089 sq miles (603,700 sq km)
Languages Ukrainian*, Russian, Tatar
Religions Christian (mainly Orthodox) 95%, Other 4%, Jewish 1%
Ethnic mix Ukrainian 73%, Russian 22%, Other 4%, Jewish 1%
Government Presidential system
Currency Hryvna = 100 kopiykas
Literacy rate 99%
Calorie consumption 3054 calories

UNITED ARAB EMIRATES
Southwest Asia

Official name United Arab Emirates
Formation 1971 / 1972
Capital Abu Dhabi
Population 4.5 million / 139 people per sq mile (54 people per sq km) / 86%
Total area 32,000 sq miles (82,880 sq km)
Languages Arabic*, Farsi, Indian and Pakistani languages, English
Religions Muslim (mainly Sunni) 96%, Christian, Hindu, and other 4%
Ethnic mix Asian 60%, Emirian 25%, Other Arab 12%, European 3%
Government Monarchy
Currency UAE dirham = 100 fils
Literacy rate 77%
Calorie consumption 3225 calories

UNITED KINGDOM
Northwest Europe

Official name United Kingdom of Great Britain and Northern Ireland
Formation 1707 / 1922
Capital London
Population 59.7 million / 640 people per sq mile (247 people per sq km) / 90%
Total area 94,525 sq miles (244,820 sq km)
Languages English*, Welsh, Scottish Gaelic
Religions Anglican 45%, Roman Catholic 9%, Presbyterian 4%, Other 42%
Ethnic mix English 80%, Scottish 9%, West Indian, Asian, and other 5%, Northern Irish 3%, Welsh 3%
Government Parliamentary system
Currency Pound sterling = 100 pence
Literacy rate 99%
Calorie consumption 3412 calories

UNITED STATES
North America

Official name United States of America
Formation 1776 / 1959
Capital Washington D.C.
Population 298 million / 84 people per sq mile (33 people per sq km) / 77%
Total area 3,717,792 sq miles (9,626,091 sq km)
Languages English*, Spanish, Chinese, French, German, Tagalog, Vietnamese, Italian, Korean, Russian, Polish
Religions Protestant 52%, Roman Catholic 25%, Muslim 2%, Jewish 2%, Other 19%
Ethnic mix White 69%, Hispanic 13%, Black American/African 13%, Asian 4%, Native American 1%
Government Presidential system
Currency US dollar = 100 cents
Literacy rate 99%
Calorie consumption 3774 calories

URUGUAY
South America

Official name Eastern Republic of Uruguay
Formation 1828 / 1828
Capital Montevideo
Population 3.5 million / 52 people per sq mile (20 people per sq km) / 91%
Total area 68,039 sq miles (176,220 sq km)
Languages Spanish*
Religions Roman Catholic 66%, Other and nonreligious 30%, Jewish 2%, Protestant 2%
Ethnic mix White 90%, Mestizo 6%, Black 4%
Government Presidential system
Currency Uruguayan peso = 100 centésimos
Literacy rate 98%
Calorie consumption 2828 calories

UZBEKISTAN
Central Asia

Official name Republic of Uzbekistan
Formation 1991 / 1991
Capital Tashkent
Population 26.6 million / 154 people per sq mile (59 people per sq km) / 37%
Total area 172,741 sq miles (447,400 sq km)
Languages Uzbek*, Russian, Tajik, Kazakh
Religions Sunni Muslim 88%, Orthodox Christian 9%, Other 3%
Ethnic mix Uzbek 71%, Other 12%, Russian 8%, Tajik 5%, Kazakh 4%
Government Presidential system
Currency Som = 100 tiyin
Literacy rate 99%
Calorie consumption 2241 calories

VANUATU
Australasia & Oceania

Official name Republic of Vanuatu
Formation 1980 / 1980
Capital Port Vila
Population 211,000 / 45 people per sq mile (17 people per sq km) / 20%
Total area 4710 sq miles (12,200 sq km)
Languages Bislama* (Melanesian pidgin), English*, French*, other indigenous languages
Religions Presbyterian 37%, Other 19%, Anglican 15%, Roman Catholic 15%, Traditional beliefs 8%, Seventh-day Adventist 6%
Ethnic mix Melanesian 94%, Other 3%, Polynesian 3%
Government Parliamentary system
Currency Vatu = 100 centimes
Literacy rate 74%
Calorie consumption 2587 calories

VATICAN CITY
Southern Europe

Official name State of the Vatican City
Formation 1929 / 1929
Capital Vatican City
Population 921 / 5418 people per sq mile (2093 people per sq km) / 100%
Total area 0.17 sq miles (0.44 sq km)
Languages Italian*, Latin*
Religions Roman Catholic 100%
Ethnic mix The current pope is German. Cardinals are from many nationalities, but Italians form the largest group. Most of the resident lay persons are Italian.
Government Papal state
Currency Euro = 100 cents
Literacy rate 99%
Calorie consumption Not available

VENEZUELA
South America

Official name Bolivarian Republic of Venezuela
Formation 1830 / 1830
Capital Caracas
Population 26.7 million / 78 people per sq mile (30 people per sq km) / 87%
Total area 352,143 sq miles (912,050 sq km)
Languages Spanish*, Amerindian languages
Religions Roman Catholic 89%, Protestant and other 11%
Ethnic mix Mestizo 69%, White 20%, Black 9%, Amerindian 2%
Government Presidential system
Currency Bolívar = 100 centimos
Literacy rate 93%
Calorie consumption 2336 calories

VIETNAM
Southeast Asia

Official name Socialist Republic of Vietnam
Formation 1976 / 1976
Capital Hanoi
Population 84.2 million / 670 people per sq mile (259 people per sq km) / 20%
Total area 127,243 sq miles (329,560 sq km)
Languages Vietnamese*, Chinese, Thai, Khmer, Muong, Nung, Miao, Yao, Jarai
Religions Buddhist 55%, Other and nonreligious 38%, Christian (mainly Roman Catholic) 7%
Ethnic mix Vietnamese 88%, Other 6%, Chinese 4%, Thai 2%
Government One-party state
Currency Dông = 10 hao = 100 xu
Literacy rate 90%
Calorie consumption 2566 calories

YEMEN
Southwest Asia

Official name Republic of Yemen
Formation 1990 / 1990
Capital Sana
Population 21 million / 97 people per sq mile (37 people per sq km) / 25%
Total area 203,849 sq miles (527,970 sq km)
Languages Arabic*
Religions Sunni Muslim 55%, Shi'a Muslim 42%, Christian, Hindu, and Jewish 3%
Ethnic mix Arab 95%, Afro-Arab 3%, Indian, Somali, and European 2%
Government Presidential system
Currency Yemeni rial = 100 sene
Literacy rate 49%
Calorie consumption 2038 calories

ZAMBIA
Southern Africa

Official name Republic of Zambia
Formation 1964 / 1964
Capital Lusaka
Population 11.7 million / 41 people per sq mile (16 people per sq km) / 45%
Total area 290,584 sq miles (752,614 sq km)
Languages English*, Bemba, Tonga, Nyanja, Lozi, Lala-Bisa, Nsenga
Religions Christian 63%, Traditional beliefs 36%, Muslim and Hindu 1%
Ethnic mix Bemba 34%, Other African 26%, Tonga 16%, Nyanja 14%, Lozi 9%, European 1%
Government Presidential system
Currency Zambian kwacha = 100 ngwee
Literacy rate 68%
Calorie consumption 1927 calories

ZIMBABWE
Southern Africa

Official name Republic of Zimbabwe
Formation 1980 / 1980
Capital Harare
Population 13 million / 87 people per sq mile (34 people per sq km) / 35%
Total area 150,803 sq miles (390,580 sq km)
Languages English*, Shona, isiNdebele
Religions Syncretic (Christian/traditional beliefs) 50%, Christian 25%, Traditional beliefs 24%, Other (including Muslim) 1%
Ethnic mix Shona 71%, Ndebele 16%, Other African 11%, White 1%, Asian 1%
Government Presidential system
Currency Zimbabwe dollar = 100 cents
Literacy rate 90%
Calorie consumption 1943 calories

Geographical names

The following glossary lists all geographical terms occurring on the maps and in main-entry names in the Index-Gazetteer. These terms may precede, follow or be run together with the proper element of the name; where they precede it the term is reversed for indexing purposes - thus Poluostrov Yamal is indexed as Yamal, Poluostrov.

Key

Geographical term
Language, Term

A

Å *Danish, Norwegian*, River
Āb *Persian*, River
Adrar *Berber*, Mountains
Agía, Ágios *Greek*, Saint
Air *Indonesian*, River
Ákra *Greek*, Cape, point
Alpen *German*, Alps
Alt- *German*, Old
Altiplanicie *Spanish*, Plateau
Älve(en) *Swedish*, River
-ån *Swedish*, River
Anse *French*, Bay
'Aqabat *Arabic*, Pass
Archipiélago *Spanish*, Archipelago
Arcipelago *Italian*, Archipelago
Arquipélago *Portuguese*, Archipelago
Arrecife(s) *Spanish*, Reef(s)
Aru *Tamil*, River
Augstiene *Latvian*, Upland
Aukštuma *Lithuanian*, Upland
Aust- *Norwegian*, Eastern
Avtonomnyy Okrug *Russian*, Autonomous district
Āw *Kurdish*, River
'Ayn *Arabic*, Spring, well
'Ayoûn *Arabic*, Wells

B

Baelt *Danish*, Strait
Bahía *Spanish*, Bay
Baḩr *Arabic*, River
Baía *Portuguese*, Bay
Baie *French*, Bay
Bañado *Spanish*, Marshy land
Bandao *Chinese*, Peninsula
Banjaran *Malay*, Mountain range
Barajı *Turkish*, Dam
Barragem *Portuguese*, Reservoir
Bassin *French*, Basin
Batang *Malay*, Stream
Beinn, Ben *Gaelic*, Mountain
-berg *Afrikaans, Norwegian*, Mountain
Besar *Indonesian, Malay*, Big
Birkat, Birket *Arabic*, Lake, well,
Boğazi *Turkish*, Lake
Boka *Serbo-Croatian*, Bay
Bol'sh-aya, -iye, -oy, -oye *Russian*, Big
Botigh(i) *Uzbek*, Depression basin
-bre(en) *Norwegian*, Glacier
Bredning *Danish*, Bay
Bucht *German*, Bay
Bugt(en) *Danish*, Bay
Buḩayrat *Arabic*, Lake, reservoir
Buḩeirat *Arabic*, Lake
Bukit *Malay*, Mountain
-bukta *Norwegian*, Bay
bukten *Swedish*, Bay
Bulag *Mongolian*, Spring
Bulak *Uighur*, Spring
Burnu *Turkish*, Cape, point
Buuraha *Somali*, Mountains

C

Cabo *Portuguese*, Cape
Caka *Tibetan*, Salt lake
Canal *Spanish*, Channel
Cap *French*, Cape
Capo *Italian*, Cape, headland
Cascada *Portuguese*, Waterfall
Cayo(s) *Spanish*, Islet(s), rock(s)
Cerro *Spanish*, Mountain
Chaîne *French*, Mountain range
Chapada *Portuguese*, Hills, upland
Chau *Cantonese*, Island
Chāy *Turkish*, River
Chhâk *Cambodian*, Bay
Chhu *Tibetan*, River
-chŏsuji *Korean*, Reservoir
Chott *Arabic*, Depression, salt lake
Chŭli *Uzbek*, Grassland, steppe
Ch'ün-tao *Chinese*, Island group
Chuŏr Phnum *Cambodian*, Mountains
Ciudad *Spanish*, City, town
Co *Tibetan*, Lake
Colline(s) *French*, Hill(s)
Cordillera *Spanish*, Mountain range
Costa *Spanish*, Coast
Côte *French*, Coast
Coxilha *Portuguese*, Mountains
Cuchilla *Spanish*, Mountains

D

Daban *Mongolian, Uighur*, Pass
Daği *Azerbaijani, Turkish*, Mountain
Dağlari *Azerbaijani, Turkish*, Mountains
-dake *Japanese*, Peak
-dal(en) *Norwegian*, Valley
Danau *Indonesian*, Lake
Dao *Chinese*, Island
Đao *Vietnamese*, Island
Daryā *Persian*, River
Daryācheh *Persian*, Lake
Dasht *Persian*, Desert, plain
Dawḩat *Arabic*, Bay
Denizi *Turkish*, Sea
Dere *Turkish*, Stream
Desierto *Spanish*, Desert
Dili *Azerbaijani*, Spit
-do *Korean*, Island
Dooxo *Somali*, Valley
Düzü *Azerbaijani*, Steppe
-dwīp *Bengali*, Island

E

-eilanden *Dutch*, Islands
Embalse *Spanish*, Reservoir
Ensenada *Spanish*, Bay
Erg *Arabic*, Dunes
Estany *Catalan*, Lake
Estero *Spanish*, Inlet
Estrecho *Spanish*, Strait
Étang *French*, Lagoon, lake
-ey *Icelandic*, Island
Ezero *Bulgarian, Macedonian*, Lake
Ezers *Latvian*, Lake

F

Feng *Chinese*, Peak
Fjord *Danish*, Fjord
-fjord(en) *Danish, Norwegian, Swedish*, fjord
-fjørdhur *Faeroese*, Fjord
Fleuve *French*, River
Fliegu *Maltese*, Channel
-fljör *Icelandic*, River
-flói *Icelandic*, Bay
Forêt *French*, Forest

G

-gan *Japanese*, Rock
-gang *Korean*, River
Ganga *Hindi, Nepali, Sinhala*, River
Gaoyuan *Chinese*, Plateau
Garagumy *Turkmen*, Sands
-gawa *Japanese*, River
Gebel *Arabic*, Mountain
-gebirge *German*, Mountain range
Ghadīr *Arabic*, Well
Ghubbat *Arabic*, Bay
Gjiri *Albanian*, Bay
Gol *Mongolian*, River
Golfe *French*, Gulf
Golfo *Italian, Spanish*, Gulf
Göl(ü) *Turkish*, Lake
Golyam, -a *Bulgarian*, Big
Gora *Russian, Serbo-Croatian*, Mountain
Góra *Polish*, mountain
Gory *Russian*, Mountain
Gryada *Russian*, ridge
Guba *Russian*, Bay
-gundo *Korean*, island group
Gunung *Malay*, Mountain

H

Ḩadd *Arabic*, Spit
-haehyŏp *Korean*, Strait
Haff *German*, Lagoon
Hai *Chinese*, Bay, lake, sea
Haixia *Chinese*, Strait
Hamada *Arabic*, Plateau
Ḩammādat *Arabic*, Plateau
Hāmūn *Persian*, Lake
-hantō *Japanese*, Peninsula
Har, Haré *Hebrew*, Mountain
Ḩarrat *Arabic*, Lava-field
Hav(et) *Danish, Swedish*, Sea
Hawr *Arabic*, Lake
Hāyk' *Amharic*, Lake
He *Chinese*, River
-hegység *Hungarian*, Mountain range
Heide *German*, Heath, moorland
Helodrano *Malagasy*, Bay
Higashi- *Japanese*, East(ern)
Ḩiṣā' *Arabic*, Well
Hka *Burmese*, River
-ho *Korean*, Lake
Hô *Korean*, Reservoir
Holot *Hebrew*, Dunes
Hora *Belarussian, Czech*, Mountain
Hrada *Belarussian*, Mountain, ridge
Hsi *Chinese*, River
Hu *Chinese*, Lake
Huk *Danish*, Point

I

Île(s) *French*, Island(s)
Ilha(s) *Portuguese*, Island(s)
Ilhéu(s) *Portuguese*, Islet(s)
Imeni *Russian*, In the name of
Inish- *Gaelic*, Island
Insel(n) *German*, Island(s)
Irmağı, Irmak *Turkish*, River
Isla(s) *Spanish*, Island(s)
Isola (Isole) *Italian*, Island(s)

J

Jabal *Arabic*, Mountain
Jāl *Arabic*, Ridge
-järv *Estonian*, Lake
-järvi *Finnish*, Lake
Jazā'ir *Arabic*, Islands
Jazīrat *Arabic*, Island
Jazīreh *Persian*, Island
Jebel *Arabic*, Mountain
Jezero *Serbo-Croatian*, Lake
Jezioro *Polish*, Lake
Jiang *Chinese*, River
-jima *Japanese*, Island
Jižní *Czech*, Southern
-jõgi *Estonian*, River
-joki *Finnish*, River
-jökull *Icelandic*, Glacier
Jūn *Arabic*, Bay
Juzur *Arabic*, Islands

K

Kaikyō *Japanese*, Strait
-kaise *Lappish*, Mountain
Kali *Nepali*, River
Kalnas *Lithuanian*, Mountain
Kalns *Latvian*, Mountain
Kang *Chinese*, Harbour
Kangri *Tibetan*, Mountain(s)
Kaôh *Cambodian*, Island
Kapp *Norwegian*, Cape
Káto *Greek*, Lower
Kavīr *Persian*, Desert
K'edi *Georgian*, Mountain range
Kediet *Arabic*, Mountain
Kepi *Albanian*, Cape, point
Kepulauan *Indonesian, Malay*, Island group
Khalīg, Khalīj *Arabic*, Gulf
Khawr *Arabic*, Inlet
Khola *Nepali*, River
Khrebet *Russian*, Mountain range
Ko *Thai*, Island
-ko *Japanese*, Inlet, lake
Kólpos *Greek*, Bay
-kopf *German*, Peak
Körfäzi *Azerbaijani*, Bay
Körfezi *Turkish*, Bay
Kõrgustik *Estonian*, Upland
Kosa *Russian, Ukrainian*, Spit
Koshi *Nepali*, River
Kou *Chinese*, River-mouth
Kowtal *Persian*, Pass
Kray *Russian*, Region, territory
Kryazh *Russian*, Ridge
Kuduk *Uighur*, Well
Kūh(hā) *Persian*, Mountain(s)
-kul' *Russian*, Lake
Kŭl(i) *Tajik, Uzbek*, Lake
-kundo *Korean*, Island group
-kysten *Norwegian*, Coast
Kyun *Burmese*, Island

L

Laaq *Somali*, Watercourse
Lac *French*, Lake
Lacul *Romanian*, Lake
Lagh *Somali*, Stream
Lago *Italian, Portuguese, Spanish*, Lake
Lagoa *Portuguese*, Lagoon
Laguna *Italian, Spanish*, Lagoon, lake
Laht *Estonian*, Bay
Laut *Indonesian*, Bay
Lembalemba *Malagasy*, Plateau
Lerr *Armenian*, Mountain
Lerrnashght'a *Armenian*, Mountain range
Les *Czech*, Forest
Lich *Armenian*, Lake
Liehtao *Chinese*, Island group
Liqeni *Albanian*, Lake
Límni *Greek*, Lake
Ling *Chinese*, Mountain range
Llano *Spanish*, Plain, prairie
Lumi *Albanian*, River
Lyman *Ukrainian*, Estuary

M

Madīnat *Arabic*, City, town
Mae Nam *Thai*, River
-mägi *Estonian*, Hill
Maja *Albanian*, Mountain
Mal *Albanian*, Mountains
Mal-aya, -oye, -yy, *Russian*, Small
-man *Korean*, Bay
Mar *Spanish*, Lake
Marios *Lithuanian*, Lake
Massif *French*, Mountains
Meer *German*, Lake
-meer *Dutch*, Lake
Melkosopochnik *Russian*, Plain
-meri *Estonian*, Sea
Mifraz *Hebrew*, Bay
Minami- *Japanese*, South(ern)
-misaki *Japanese*, Cape, point
Monkhafad *Arabic*, Depression
Montagne(s) *French*, Mountain(s)
Montañas *Spanish*, Mountains
Mont(s) *French*, Mountain(s)
Monte *Italian, Portuguese*, Mountain
More *Russian*, Sea
Mörön *Mongolian*, River
Mys *Russian*, Cape, point

N

-nada *Japanese*, Open stretch of water
Nagor'ye *Russian*, Upland
Naḩal *Hebrew*, River
Nahr *Arabic*, River
Nam *Laotian*, River
Namakzār *Persian*, Salt desert
Né-a, -on, -os *Greek*, New
Nedre- *Norwegian*, Lower
-neem *Estonian*, Cape, point
Nehri *Turkish*, River
-nes *Norwegian*, Cape, point
Nevado *Spanish*, Mountain (snow-capped)
Nieder- *German*, Lower
Nishi- *Japanese*, West(ern)
-nísi *Greek*, Island
Nisoi *Greek*, Islands
Nizhn-eye, -iy, -iye, -yaya *Russian*, Lower
Nizmennost' *Russian*, Lowland, plain
Nord *Danish, French, German*, North
Norte *Portuguese, Spanish*, North
Nos *Bulgarian*, Point, spit
Nosy *Malagasy*, Island
Nov-a, -i, *Bulgarian, Serbo-Croatian*, New
Nov-aya, -o, -oye, -yy, -yye *Russian*, New
Now-a, -e, -y *Polish*, New
Nur *Mongolian*, Lake
Nuruu *Mongolian*, Mountains
Nuur *Mongolian*, Lake
Nyzovyna *Ukrainian*, Lowland, plain

O

-ø *Danish*, Island
Ober- *German*, Upper
Oblast' *Russian*, Province
Órmos *Greek*, Bay
Orol(i) *Uzbek*, Island
Øster- *Norwegian*, Eastern
Ostrov(a) *Russian*, Island(s)
Otok *Serbo-Croatian*, Island
Oued *Arabic*, Watercourse
-oy *Faeroese*, Island
-øy(a) *Norwegian*, Island
Oya *Sinhala*, River
Ozero *Russian, Ukrainian*, Lake

P

Passo *Italian*, Pass
Pegunungan *Indonesian, Malay*, Mountain range
Pélagos *Greek*, Sea
Pendi *Chinese*, Basin
Penisola *Italian*, Peninsula
Pertuis *French*, Strait
Peski *Russian*, Sands
Phanom *Thai*, Mountain
Phou *Laotian*, Mountain
Pi *Chinese*, Point
Pic *Catalan, French*, Peak
Pico *Portuguese, Spanish*, Peak
-piggen *Danish*, Peak
Pik *Russian*, Peak
Pivostriv *Ukrainian*, Peninsula
Planalto *Portuguese*, Plateau
Planina, Planini *Bulgarian, Macedonian, Serbo-Croatian*, Mountain range
Plato *Russian*, Plateau
Ploskogor'ye *Russian*, Upland
Poluostrov *Russian*, Peninsula
Ponta *Portuguese*, Point
Porthmós *Greek*, Strait
Pótamos *Greek*, River
Presa *Spanish*, Dam
Prokhod *Bulgarian*, Pass
Proliv *Russian*, Strait
Pulau *Indonesian, Malay*, Island
Pulu *Malay*, Island
Punta *Spanish*, Point
Pushcha *Belorussian*, Forest
Puszcza *Polish*, Forest

Q

Qā' *Arabic*, Depression
Qalamat *Arabic*, Well
Qatorkŭh(i) *Tajik*, Mountain
Qiuling *Chinese*, Hills
Qolleh *Persian*, Mountain
Qu *Tibetan*, Stream
Quan *Chinese*, Well
Qulla(i) *Tajik*, Peak
Qundao *Chinese*, Island group

R

Raas *Somali*, Cape
-rags *Latvian*, Cape
Ramlat *Arabic*, Sands
Ra's *Arabic*, Cape, headland, point
Ravnina *Bulgarian, Russian*, Plain
Récif *French*, Reef
Recife *Portuguese*, Reef
Reka *Bulgarian*, River
Represa (Rep.) *Portuguese, Spanish*, Reservoir
Reshteh *Persian*, Mountain range
Respublika *Russian*, Republic, first-order administrative division
Respublika(si) *Uzbek*, Republic, first-order administrative division
-retsugan *Japanese*, Chain of rocks
-rettō *Japanese*, Island chain
Riacho *Spanish*, Stream
Riban' *Malagasy*, Mountains
Rio *Portuguese*, River
Río *Spanish*, River
Riu *Catalan*, River
Rivier *Dutch*, River
Rivière *French*, River
Rowd *Pashtu*, River
Rt *Serbo-Croatian*, Point
Rūd *Persian*, River
Rūdkhāneh *Persian*, River
Rudohorie *Slovak*, Mountains
Ruisseau *French*, Stream

S

-saar *Estonian*, Island
-saari *Finnish*, Island
Sabkhat *Arabic*, Salt marsh
Sāgar(a) *Hindi*, Lake, reservoir
Şaḩrā' *Arabic*, Desert
Saint, Sainte *French*, Saint
Salar *Spanish*, Salt-pan
Salto *Portuguese, Spanish*, Waterfall
Samudra *Sinhala*, Reservoir
-san *Japanese, Korean*, Mountain
-sanchi *Japanese*, Mountains
-sandur *Icelandic*, Beach
Sankt *German, Swedish*, Saint
-sanmaek *Korean*, Mountain range
-sanmyaku *Japanese*, Mountain range
San, Santa, Santo *Italian, Portuguese, Spanish*, Saint
São *Portuguese*, Saint
Sarīr *Arabic*, Desert
Sebkha, Sebkhet *Arabic*, Depression, salt marsh
Sedlo *Czech*, Pass
See *German*, Lake
Selat *Indonesian*, Strait
Selatan *Indonesian*, Southern
-selkä *Finnish*, Lake, ridge
Selseleh *Persian*, Mountain range
Serra *Portuguese*, Mountain
Serranía *Spanish*, Mountain
-seto *Japanese*, Channel, strait
Sever-naya, -noye, -nyy, -o *Russian*, Northern
Sha'īb *Arabic*, Watercourse
Shākh *Kurdish*, Mountain
Shamo *Chinese*, Desert
Shan *Chinese*, Mountain(s)
Shankou *Chinese*, Pass
Shanmo *Chinese*, Mountain range
Shaţţ *Arabic*, Distributary
Shet' *Amharic*, River
Shi *Chinese*, Municipality
-shima *Japanese*, Island
Shiqqat *Arabic*, Depression
-shotō *Japanese*, Group of islands
Shuiku *Chinese*, Reservoir
Shūrkhog(i) *Uzbek*, Salt marsh
Sierra *Spanish*, Mountains
Sint *Dutch*, Saint
-sjø(en) *Norwegian*, Lake
-sjön *Swedish*, Lake
Solonchak *Russian*, Salt lake
Solonchakovyye Vpadiny *Russian*, Salt basin, wetlands
Son *Vietnamese*, Mountain
Sông *Vietnamese*, River
Sør- *Norwegian*, Southern
-spitze *German*, Peak
Star-á, -é *Czech*, Old
Star-aya, -oye, -yy, -yye *Russian*, Old
Stenó *Greek*, Strait
Step' *Russian*, Steppe
Štít *Slovak*, Peak
Stœng *Cambodian*, River
Stolovaya Strana *Russian*, Plateau
Stredné *Slovak*, Middle
Střední *Czech*, Middle
Stretto *Italian*, Strait
Su Anbari *Azerbaijani*, Reservoir
-suidō *Japanese*, Channel, strait
Sund *Swedish*, Sound, strait
Sungai *Indonesian, Malay*, River
Suu *Turkish*, River

T

Tal *Mongolian*, Plain
Tandavan' *Malagasy*, Mountain range
Tangorombohitr' *Malagasy*, Mountain massif
Tanjung *Indonesian, Malay*, Cape, point
Tao *Chinese*, Island
Ţaraq *Arabic*, Hills
Tassili *Berber*, Mountain, plateau
Tau *Russian*, Mountain(s)
Taungdan *Burmese*, Mountain range
Techníti Límni *Greek*, Reservoir
Tekojärvi *Finnish*, Reservoir
Teluk *Indonesian, Malay*, Bay
Tengah *Indonesian*, Middle
Terara *Amharic*, Mountain
Timur *Indonesian*, Eastern
-tind(an) *Norwegian*, Peak
Tizma(si) *Uzbek*, Mountain range, ridge
-tō *Japanese*, island
Tog *Somali*, Valley
-tōge *Japanese*, pass
Togh(i) *Uzbek*, mountain
Tônlé *Cambodian*, Lake
Top *Dutch*, Peak
-tunturi *Finnish*, Mountain
Ţurāq *Arabic*, hills
Tur'at *Arabic*, Channel

U

Udde(n) *Swedish*, Cape, point
'Uqlat *Arabic*, Well
Utara *Indonesian*, Northern
Uul *Mongolian*, Mountains

V

Väin *Estonian*, Strait
Vallée *French*, Valley
-vatn *Icelandic*, Lake
-vatnet *Norwegian*, Lake
Velayat *Turkmen*, Province
-vesi *Finnish*, Lake
Vestre- *Norwegian*, Western
-vidda *Norwegian*, Plateau
-vík *Icelandic*, Bay
-viken *Swedish*, Bay, inlet
Vinh *Vietnamese*, Bay
Víztárloló *Hungarian*, Reservoir
Vodaskhovishcha *Belarussian*, Reservoir
Vodokhranilishche (Vdkhr.) *Russian*, Reservoir
Vodoskhovyshche (Vdskh.) *Ukrainian*, Reservoir
Volcán *Spanish*, Volcano
Vostochn-o, yy *Russian*, Eastern
Vozvyshennost' *Russian*, Upland, plateau
Vozyera *Belarussian*, Lake
Vpadina *Russian*, Depression
Vrchovina *Czech*, Mountains
Vrha *Macedonian*, Peak
Vychodné *Slovak*, Eastern
Vysochyna *Ukrainian*, Upland
Vysočina *Czech*, Upland

W

Waadi *Somali*, Watercourse
Wādī *Arabic* Watercourse
Wāḩat, Wâhat *Arabic*, Oasis
Wald *German*, Forest
Wan *Chinese*, Bay
Way *Indonesian*, River
Webi *Somali*, River
Wenz *Amharic*, River
Wiloyat(i) *Uzbek*, Province
Wyżyna *Polish*, Upland
Wzgórza *Polish*, Upland
Wzvyshsha *Belarussian*, Upland

X

Xé *Laotian*, River
Xi *Chinese*, Stream

Y

-yama *Japanese*, Mountain
Yanchi *Chinese*, Salt lake
Yang *Chinese*, Bay
Yanhu *Chinese*, Salt lake
Yarımadası *Azerbaijani, Turkish*, Peninsula
Yaylası *Turkish*, Plateau
Yazovir *Bulgarian*, Reservoir
Yoma *Burmese*, Mountains
Ytre- *Norwegian*, Outer
Yü *Chinese*, Island
Yunhe *Chinese*, Canal
Yuzhn-o, -yy *Russian*, Southern

Z

-zaki *Japanese*, Cape, point
Zaliv *Bulgarian, Russian*, Bay
-zan *Japanese*, Mountain
Zangbo *Tibetan*, River
Zapadn-aya, -o, -yy *Russian*, Western
Západné *Slovak*, Western
Západní *Czech*, Western
Zatoka *Polish, Ukrainian*, Bay
-zee *Dutch*, Sea
Zemlya *Russian*, Earth, land
Zizhiqu *Chinese*, Autonomous region

25 de Mayo – Abu Simbel

Index

Glossary of Abbreviations

This glossary provides a comprehensive guide to the abbreviations used in this Atlas, and in the Index.

A
abbrev. abbreviated
AD Anno Domini
Afr. Afrikaans
Alb. Albanian
Amh. Amharic
anc. ancient
approx. approximately
Ar. Arabic
Arm. Armenian
ASEAN Association of South East Asian Nations
ASSR Autonomous Soviet Socialist Republic
Aust. Australian
Az. Azerbaijani
Azerb. Azerbaijan

B
Basq. Basque
BC before Christ
Bel. Belorussian
Ben. Bengali
Ber. Berber
B-H Bosnia-Herzegovina
bn billion (one thousand million)
BP British Petroleum
Bret. Breton
Brit. British
Bul. Bulgarian
Bur. Burmese

C
C central
C. Cape
°C degrees Centigrade
CACM Central America Common Market
Cam. Cambodian
Cant. Cantonese
CAR Central African Republic
Cast. Castilian
Cat. Catalan
CEEAC Central America Common Market
Chin. Chinese
CIS Commonwealth of Independent States
cm centimetre(s)
Cro. Croat
Cz. Czech
Czech Rep. Czech Republic

D
Dan. Danish
Div. Divehi
Dom. Rep. Dominican Republic
Dut. Dutch

E
E east
EC *see* EU
EEC *see* EU
ECOWAS Economic Community of West African States
ECU European Currency Unit
EMS European Monetary System
Eng. English
est estimated
Est. Estonian
EU European Union (previously European Community [EC], European Economic Community [EEC])

F
°F degrees Fahrenheit
Faer. Faeroese
Fij. Fijian
Fin. Finnish
Fr. French
Fris. Frisian
ft foot/feet
FYROM Former Yugoslav Republic of Macedonia

G
g gram(s)
Gael. Gaelic
Gal. Galician
GDP Gross Domestic Product (the total value of goods and services produced by a country excluding income from foreign countries)
Geor. Georgian
Ger. German
Gk Greek
GNP Gross National Product (the total value of goods and services produced by a country)

H
Heb. Hebrew
HEP hydro-electric power
Hind. Hindi
hist. historical
Hung. Hungarian

I
I. Island
Icel. Icelandic
in inch(es)
In. Inuit (Eskimo)
Ind. Indonesian
Intl International
Ir. Irish
Is Islands
It. Italian

J
Jap. Japanese

K
Kaz. Kazakh
kg kilogram(s)
Kir. Kirghiz
km kilometre(s)
km² square kilometre (singular)
Kor. Korean
Kurd. Kurdish

L
L. Lake
LAIA Latin American Integration Association
Lao. Laotian
Lapp. Lappish
Lat. Latin
Latv. Latvian
Liech. Liechtenstein
Lith. Lithuanian
Lus. Lusatian
Lux. Luxembourg

M
m million/metre(s)
Mac. Macedonian
Maced. Macedonia
Mal. Malay
Malg. Malagasy
Malt. Maltese
mi. mile(s)
Mong. Mongolian
Mt. Mountain
Mts Mountains

N
N north
NAFTA North American Free Trade Agreement
Nep. Nepali
Neth. Netherlands
Nic. Nicaraguan
Nor. Norwegian
NZ New Zealand

P
Pash. Pashtu
PNG Papua New Guinea
Pol. Polish
Poly. Polynesian
Port. Portuguese
prev. previously

R
Rep. Republic
Res. Reservoir
Rmsch Romansch
Rom. Romanian
Rus. Russian
Russ. Fed. Russian Federation

S
S south
SADC Southern Africa Development Community
SCr. Serbian, Croatian
Sinh. Sinhala
Slvk Slovak
Slvn. Slovene
Som. Somali
Sp. Spanish
St., St Saint
Strs Straits
Swa. Swahili
Swe. Swedish
Switz. Switzerland

T
Taj. Tajik
Th. Thai
Thai. Thailand
Tib. Tibetan
Turk. Turkish
Turkm. Turkmenistan

U
UAE United Arab Emirates
Uigh. Uighur
UK United Kingdom
Ukr. Ukrainian
UN United Nations
Urd. Urdu
US/USA United States of America
USSR Union of Soviet Socialist Republics
Uzb. Uzbek

V
var. variant
Vdkhr. Vodokhranilishche (Russian for reservoir)
Vdskh. Vodoskhovyshche (Ukrainian for reservoir)
Vtn. Vietnamese

W
W west
Wel. Welsh

This index lists all the placenames and features shown on the regional and continental maps in this Atlas. Placenames are referenced to the largest scale map on which they appear. The policy followed throughout the Atlas is to use the local spelling or local name at regional level; commonly-used English language names may occasionally be added (in parentheses) where this is an aid to identification e.g. Firenze (Florence). English names, where they exist, have been used for all international features e.g. oceans and country names; they are also used on the continental maps and in the introductory World Today section; these are then fully cross-referenced to the local names found on the regional maps. The index also contains commonly-found alternative names and variant spellings, which are also fully cross-referenced.

All main entry names are those of settlements unless otherwise indicated by the use of italicized definitions or representative symbols, which are keyed at the foot of each page.

1

25 de Mayo *see* Veinticinco de Mayo
143 *Y13* **26 Bakı Komissarı** ***Rus.*** Imeni 26 Bakinskikh Komissarov. SE Azerbaijan *39.18N 49.13E*
26 Baku Komissarlary Adyndaky *see* Uzboý
8 *M16* **100 Mile House** ***var.*** Hundred Mile House. British Columbia, SW Canada *51.39N 121.19W*

A

Aa *see* Gauja
97 *G24* **Aabenraa** ***var.*** Åbenrå, ***Ger.*** Apenrade. Sønderjylland, SW Denmark *55.03N 9.25E*
97 *G20* **Aabybro** ***var.*** Åbybro. Nordjylland, N Denmark *57.09N 9.45E*
103 *C16* **Aachen** ***Dut.*** Aken, ***Fr.*** Aix-la-Chapelle; ***anc.*** Aquae Grani, Aquisgranum. Nordrhein-Westfalen, W Germany *50.47N 6.06E*
Aaiún *see* Laâyoune
97 *M24* **Aakirkeby** ***var.*** Åkirkeby. Bornholm, E Denmark *55.04N 14.55E*
Ãak Nông *see* Gia Nghia
97 *G20* **Aalborg** ***var.*** Ålborg, Ålborg-Nørresundby; ***anc.*** Alburgum. Nordjylland, N Denmark *57.03N 9.55E*
Aalborg Bugt *see* Ålborg Bugt
103 *J21* **Aalen** Baden-Württemberg, S Germany *48.49N 10.06E*
97 *G21* **Aalestrup** ***var.*** Ålestrup. Viborg, NW Denmark *56.42N 9.31E*
100 *I11* **Aalsmeer** Noord-Holland, C Netherlands *52.16N 4.43E*
101 *F18* **Aalst** ***Fr.*** Alost. Oost-Vlaanderen, C Belgium *50.57N 4.03E*
101 *K18* **Aalst** Noord-Brabant, S Netherlands *51.46N 5.07E*
100 *O12* **Aalten** Gelderland, E Netherlands *51.55N 6.34E*
101 *D17* **Aalter** Oost-Vlaanderen, NW Belgium *51.04N 3.28E*
Aanaar *see* Inari
Aanaarjävri *see* Inarijärvi
95 *M17* **Äänekoski** Länsi-Suomi, W Finland *62.33N 25.44E*
144 *H7* **Aanjar** ***var.*** 'Anjar. C Lebanon *33.45N 35.56E*
85 *G21* **Aansluit** Northern Cape, N South Africa *26.41S 22.24E*
Aar *see* Aare
110 *F7* **Aarau** Aargau, N Switzerland *47.22N 8.00E*
110 *D8* **Aarberg** Bern, W Switzerland *47.02N 7.15E*
101 *D16* **Aardenburg** Zeeland, SW Netherlands *51.16N 3.27E*
110 *D8* **Aare** ***var.*** Aar. ≈ W Switzerland
110 *F7* **Aargau** ***Fr.*** Argovie. ◈ *canton* N Switzerland
Aarhus *see* Århus
Aarlen *see* Arlon
97 *G21* **Aars** ***var.*** Års. Nordjylland, N Denmark *56.49N 9.31E*
101 *I17* **Aarschot** Vlaams Brabant, C Belgium *50.58N 4.49E*
Aassi, Nahr el *see* Orontes
Aat *see* Ath
166 *G7* **Aba** ***prev.*** Ngawa. Sichuan, C China *32.51N 101.46E*
79 *V17* **Aba** Abia, S Nigeria *5.06N 7.22E*
81 *P16* **Aba** Orientale, NE Dem. Rep. Congo *3.52N 30.13E*
146 *J6* **Abā al Qazāz, Bi'r** *well* NW Saudi Arabia *26.37N 36.50E*
Abā as Su'ūd *see* Najrān
61 *G14* **Abacaxis, Rio** ≈ NW Brazil
Abaco Island *see* Great Abaco/Little Abaco
Abaco Island *see* Great Abaco, N Bahamas
148 *K10* **Ābādān** Khūzestān, SW Iran *30.24N 48.18E*
152 *F13* **Abadan** ***prev.*** Bezmein, Büzmeýin, ***Rus.*** Byuzmeyin. Ahal Welaýaty, C Turkmenistan *38.07N 57.52E*
149 *O10* **Ābādeh** Fārs, C Iran *31.10N 52.39E*
76 *H8* **Abadla** W Algeria *31.04N 2.39W*
61 *M20* **Abaeté** Minas Gerais, SE Brazil *19.10S 45.24W*
Abag Qi *see* Xin Hot
64 *P7* **Abaí** Caazapá, S Paraguay *25.58S 55.54W*
203 *O2* **Abaiang** ***var.*** Apia; ***prev.*** Charlotte Island. *atoll* Tungaru, W Kiribati
Abaj *see* Abay
79 *U15* **Abaji** Federal Capital District, C Nigeria *8.35N 6.54E*
39 *O7* **Abajo Peak** ▲ Utah, W USA *37.51N 109.28W*
79 *V16* **Abakaliki** Ebonyi, SE Nigeria *6.18N 8.07E*
126 *Hh15* **Abakan** Respublika Khakasiya, S Russian Federation *53.43N 91.25E*
126 *Hh15* **Abakan** ≈ S Russian Federation
79 *S11* **Abala** Tillabéri, SW Niger *14.55N 3.27E*
79 *U11* **Abalak** Tahoua, C Niger *15.28N 6.18E*
121 *N14* **Abalyanka** ***Rus.*** Obolyanka. ≈ N Belarus
126 *Ii14* **Aban** Krasnoyarskiy Kray, S Russian Federation *56.41N 96.04E*
149 *P9* **Āb Anbār-e Kān Sorkh** Yazd, C Iran *31.22N 53.37E*
59 *G16* **Abancay** Apurímac, SE Peru *13.37S 72.52W*
202 *H2* **Abaokoro** *atoll* Tungaru, W Kiribati
Abariringa *see* Kanton
149 *P10* **Abarkū** Yazd, C Iran
172 *Qq5* **Abashiri** ***var.*** Abasiri. Hokkaidō, NE Japan *44.00N 144.15E*
172 *Q6* **Abashiri-gawa** ≈ Hokkaidō, NE Japan
172 *Q5* **Abashiri-ko** ◎ Hokkaidō, NE Japan
Abasiri *see* Abashiri
43 *P10* **Abasolo** Tamaulipas, C Mexico *24.02N 98.18W*
194 *L16* **Abau** Central, S PNG *10.09S 148.40E*
151 *R10* **Abay** ***var.*** Abaj. Karaganda, C Kazakhstan *49.34N 72.54E*
83 *I15* **Ābaya Hāyk'** ***Eng.*** Lake Margherita, ***It.*** Abbaia. ◎ SW Ethiopia
Ābay Wenz *see* Blue Nile
126 *Hh15* **Abaza** Respublika Khakasiya, S Russian Federation *52.40N 89.58E*
Abbaia *see* Ābaya Hāyk'
149 *Q13* **Āb Bārīk** Fārs, S Iran
109 *C18* **Abbasanta** Sardegna, Italy, C Mediterranean Sea *40.08N 8.49E*
Abbatis Villa *see* Abbeville
32 *M3* **Abbaye, Point** *headland* Michigan, N USA *46.58N 88.08W*
Abbazia *see* Opatija
Abbé, Lake *see* Abhe, Lake
105 *N2* **Abbeville** ***anc.*** Abbatis Villa. Somme, N France *50.06N 1.50E*
25 *R7* **Abbeville** Alabama, S USA *31.34N 85.16W*
25 *U6* **Abbeville** Georgia, SE USA *31.58N 83.18W*
24 *I9* **Abbeville** Louisiana, S USA *29.58N 92.08W*
23 *P12* **Abbeville** South Carolina, SE USA *34.10N 82.22W*
99 *B20* **Abbeyfeale** ***Ir.*** Mainistir na Féile. SW Ireland *52.24N 9.21W*
108 *D8* **Abbiategrasso** Lombardia, NW Italy *45.24N 9.04E*
95 *I14* **Abborrträsk** Norrbotten, N Sweden *65.24N 19.33E*
204 *J9* **Abbot Ice Shelf** *ice shelf* Antarctica
8 *M17* **Abbotsford** British Columbia, SW Canada *49.01N 122.18W*
32 *K6* **Abbotsford** Wisconsin, N USA *44.57N 90.19W*
155 *U5* **Abbottābād** North-West Frontier Province, NW Pakistan *34.08N 73.10E*
121 *M14* **Abchuha** ***Rus.*** Obchuga. Minskaya Voblasts', NW Belarus *54.30N 29.23E*
100 *I10* **Abcoude** Utrecht, C Netherlands *52.16N 4.58E*
145 *N2* **'Abd al 'Azīz, Jabal** ▲▲ NE Syria
147 *U17* **'Abd al Kūrī** *island* SE Yemen
145 *Z13* **'Abd Allāh, Khawr** *bay* Iraq/Kuwait
131 *U6* **Abdulino** Orenburgskaya Oblast', W Russian Federation *53.37N 53.39E*
80 *J10* **Abéché** ***var.*** Abécher, Abeshr. Ouaddaï, SE Chad *13.49N 20.49E*
Abécher *see* Abéché
149 *S8* **Āb-e Garm va Sard** Yazd, E Iran
79 *R8* **Abeïbara** Kidal, NE Mali *19.07N 1.52E*
107 *P5* **Abejar** Castilla-León, N Spain *41.48N 2.46W*
56 *E9* **Abejorral** Antioquia, W Colombia *5.52N 75.34W*
Abela *see* Ávila
Abellinum *see* Avellino
94 *Q2* **Abeløya** *island* Kong Karls Land, E Svalbard
82 *I13* **Ābeltī** Oromo, C Ethiopia *8.09N 37.31E*
203 *O2* **Abemama** ***var.*** Apamama; ***prev.*** Roger Simpson Island. *atoll* Tungaru, W Kiribati
176 *Yy14* **Abemaree** ***var.*** Abemarre. Papua, E Indonesia *7.03S 140.10E*
79 *O16* **Abengourou** E Ivory Coast *6.42N 3.27W*
Åbenrå *see* Aabenraa
103 *L22* **Abens** ≈ SE Germany
79 *S16* **Abeokuta** Ogun, SW Nigeria *7.07N 3.21E*
99 *I20* **Aberaeron** SW Wales, UK *52.15N 4.15W*
Aberbrothock *see* Arbroath
Abercorn *see* Mbala
31 *R6* **Abercrombie** North Dakota, N USA *46.25N 96.42W*
191 *T7* **Aberdeen** New South Wales, SE Australia *32.09S 150.55E*
9 *T15* **Aberdeen** Saskatchewan, S Canada *52.15N 106.19W*
85 *H25* **Aberdeen** Eastern Cape, S South Africa *32.30S 24.00E*
98 *L9* **Aberdeen** ***anc.*** Devana. NE Scotland, UK *57.10N 2.04W*
23 *X2* **Aberdeen** Maryland, NE USA *39.28N 76.09W*
25 *N3* **Aberdeen** Mississippi, S USA *33.49N 88.32W*
23 *T10* **Aberdeen** North Carolina, SE USA *35.07N 79.25W*
31 *P8* **Aberdeen** South Dakota, N USA *45.27N 98.29W*
34 *F8* **Aberdeen** Washington, NW USA *46.57N 123.48W*
98 *K9* **Aberdeen** *cultural region* NE Scotland, UK
15 *K6* **Aberdeen Lake** ◎ Nunavut, NE Canada
98 *J10* **Aberfeldy** C Scotland, UK *56.38N 3.48W*
99 *K21* **Abergavenny** ***anc.*** Gobannium. SE Wales, UK *51.50N 3.00W*
Abergwaun *see* Fishguard
Abermarre *see* Abemaree
27 *N5* **Abernathy** Texas, SW USA *33.49N 101.50W*
Abersee *see* Wolfgangsee
Abertawe *see* Swansea
Aberteifi *see* Cardigan
34 *I15* **Abert, Lake** ◎ Oregon, NW USA
99 *I20* **Aberystwyth** W Wales, UK *52.25N 4.04W*
Abeshr *see* Abéché
Ábeskovvu *see* Abisko
108 *F10* **Abetone** Toscana, C Italy *44.09N 10.42E*
129 *V5* **Abez'** Respublika Komi, NW Russian Federation *66.32N 61.41E*
148 *M5* **Āb Garm** Qazvin, N Iran
147 *N12* **Abhā** 'Asīr, SW Saudi Arabia *18.16N 42.31E*
148 *M5* **Abhar** Zanjān, NW Iran *36.07N 49.19E*
Abhé Bad/Ābhē Bid Hāyk' *see* Abhe, Lake
82 *K12* **Abhe, Lake** ***var.*** Lake Abbé, ***Amh.*** Ābhē Bid Hāyk', ***Som.*** Abhé Bad. ◎ Djibouti/Ethiopia
79 *V17* **Abia** ◈ *state* SE Nigeria
145 *V9* **'Abīd 'Alī** E Iraq *32.20N 45.58E*
121 *O17* **Abidavichy** ***Rus.*** Obidovichi. Mahilyowskaya Voblasts', E Belarus *53.21N 30.24E*
117 *L15* **Abide** Çanakkale, NW Turkey *40.04N 26.13E*
79 *N17* **Abidjan** S Ivory Coast *5.19N 4.01W*
Āb-i-Istāda *see* Īstādeh-ye Moqor, Āb-e-
29 *N4* **Abilene** Kansas, C USA *38.55N 97.12W*
27 *Q7* **Abilene** Texas, SW USA *32.27N 99.43W*
Abindonia *see* Abingdon
99 *M21* **Abingdon** ***anc.*** Abindonia. S England, UK *51.40N 1.16W*
32 *K12* **Abingdon** Illinois, N USA *40.48N 90.24W*
23 *P8* **Abingdon** Virginia, NE USA *36.42N 81.58W*
Abingdon *see* Pinta, Isla
20 *J15* **Abington** Pennsylvania, NE USA *40.06N 75.05W*
130 *K14* **Abinsk** Krasnodarskiy Kray, SW Russian Federation *44.51N 38.12E*
39 *R9* **Abiquiu Reservoir** ▣ New Mexico, SW USA
94 *I10* **Abisko** ***Lapp.*** Ábeskovvu. Norrbotten, N Sweden *68.21N 18.49E*
10 *G12* **Abitibi** ≈ Ontario, S Canada
10 *H12* **Abitibi, Lac** ◎ Ontario/Québec, S Canada
82 *J10* **Ābīy Ādī** Tigray, N Ethiopia *13.40N 38.57E*
120 *H6* **Abja-Paluoja** Viljandimaa, S Estonia *58.07N 25.19E*
143 *Q8* **Abkhazia** ◈ *autonomous republic* NW Georgia
190 *F1* **Abminga** South Australia *26.07S 134.49E*
77 *W9* **Abnûb** C Egypt *27.18N 31.09E*
Åbo *see* Turku
158 *G9* **Abohar** Punjab, N India *30.10N 74.12E*
79 *O17* **Aboisso** SE Ivory Coast *5.27N 3.06W*
80 *H5* **Abo, Massif d'** ▲▲ NW Chad
79 *R16* **Abomey** S Benin *7.14N 2.00E*
81 *F16* **Abong Mbang** Est, SE Cameroon *3.58N 13.10E*
113 *L23* **Abony** Pest, C Hungary *47.10N 20.00E*
80 *J11* **Abou-Déïa** Salamat, SE Chad *11.30N 19.18E*
Aboudouhour *see* Abū aḍ Ḍuhūr
Abou Kémal *see* Abū Kamāl
Abou Simbel *see* Abu Simbel
143 *T12* **Abovyan** C Armenia *40.16N 44.33E*
179 *P8* **Abra** ≈ Luzon, N Philippines
147 *P15* **Abrād, Wādī** *seasonal river* W Yemen
Abraham Bay *see* The Carlton
106 *G10* **Abrantes** ***var.*** Abrántes. Santarém, C Portugal *39.28N 8.12W*
64 *J4* **Abra Pampa** Jujuy, N Argentina *22.46S 65.40W*
Abrashlare *see* Brezovo
56 *G7* **Abrego** Norte de Santander, N Colombia *8.07N 73.15W*
Abrene *see* Pytalovo
42 *C7* **Abreojos, Punta** *headland* W Mexico *26.43N 113.36W*
67 *J16* **Abrolhos Bank** *undersea feature* W Atlantic Ocean
121 *H19* **Abrova** ***Rus.*** Obrovo. Brestskaya Voblasts', SW Belarus *52.30N 25.31E*
118 *G11* **Abrud** ***Ger.*** Gross-Schlatten, ***Hung.*** Abrudbánya. Alba, SW Romania *46.15N 23.07E*
Abrudbánya *see* Abrud
120 *E6* **Abruka** *island* SW Estonia
109 *J15* **Abruzzese, Appennino** ▲▲ C Italy
109 *J14* **Abruzzo** ◈ *region* C Italy
147 *N14* **'Abs** ***var.*** Sūq 'Abs. W Yemen *16.42N 42.55E*
35 *T12* **Absaroka Range** ▲▲ Montana/Wyoming, NW USA
143 *Z11* **Abşeron Yarımadası** ***Rus.*** Apsheronskiy Poluostrov. *peninsula* E Azerbaijan
149 *N6* **Āb Shīrīn** Eşfahān, C Iran
145 *X10* **Abtān** SE Iraq *31.37N 47.06E*
111 *R6* **Abtenau** Salzburg, NW Austria *47.33N 13.21E*
170 *Dd12* **Abu** Yamaguchi, Honshū, SW Japan *34.30N 131.26E*
158 *E14* **Ābu** Rājasthān, N India *24.40N 72.49E*
144 *I4* **Abū aḍ Ḍuhūr** ***Fr.*** Aboudouhour. Idlib, NW Syria *35.30N 37.00E*
149 *P17* **Abū al Abyaḍ** *island* C UAE
144 *K10* **Abū al Ḥuşayn, Khabrat** ◎ N Jordan
145 *R8* **Abū al Jīr** C Iraq *33.16N 42.55E*
145 *Y12* **Abū al Khaşīb** ***var.*** Abul Khasib. SE Iraq *30.26N 48.00E*
145 *U12* **Abū at Tubrah, Thaqb** *well* S Iraq *30.54N 45.02E*
77 *V11* **Abu Balâs** ▲ SW Egypt *24.28N 27.36E*
Abu Dhabi *see* Abū Ẓaby
145 *R8* **Abū Farūkh** C Iraq *33.06N 43.18E*
82 *C12* **Abu Gabra** Southern Darfur, W Sudan *11.01N 26.49E*
145 *P10* **Abū Ghār, Sha'īb** *dry watercourse* S Iraq
82 *G7* **Abu Hamed** River Nile, N Sudan *19.31N 33.19E*
145 *O5* **Abū Ḥardān** ***var.*** Hajîne. Dayr az Zawr, E Syria *34.45N 40.49E*
145 *T7* **Abū Ḥāssawīyah** E Iraq *33.52N 44.47E*
144 *K10* **Abū Ḥifnah, Wādī** *dry watercourse* N Jordan
79 *V15* **Abuja** ● (Nigeria) Federal Capital District, C Nigeria *9.04N 7.28E*
145 *R9* **Abū Jahaf, Wādī** *dry watercourse* C Iraq
58 *F12* **Abujao, Río** ≈ E Peru
145 *U12* **Abū Jasrah** S Iraq *30.43N 44.50E*
145 *O6* **Abū Kamāl** ***Fr.*** Abou Kémal. Dayr az Zawr, E Syria *34.28N 40.55E*
175 *Q11* **Abuki, Pegunungan** ▲▲ Sulawesi, C Indonesia
171 *Ll14* **Abukuma-gawa** ≈ Honshū, C Japan
171 *Ll15* **Abukuma-sanchi** ▲▲ Honshū, C Japan
Abula *see* Ávila
Abul Khasib *see* Abū al Khaşīb
81 *K16* **Abumombazi** ***var.*** Abumonbazi. Equateur, N Dem. Rep. Congo *3.43N 22.06E*
Abumonbazi *see* Abumombazi
61 *D15* **Abunã** Rondônia, W Brazil *9.40S 65.19W*
58 *K13* **Abunã, Rio** ***var.*** Río Abuná. ≈ Bolivia/Brazil
144 *G10* **Abū Nuşayr** ***var.*** Abu Nuseir. 'Ammān, W Jordan *32.03N 35.58E*
Abu Nuseir *see* Abū Nuşayr
145 *T12* **Abū Qabr** S Iraq *31.03N 44.34E*
144 *K5* **Abū Raḩbah, Jabal** ▲▲ C Syria
145 *S5* **Abū Rajāsh** N Iraq *34.47N 43.36E*
145 *W13* **Abū Raqrāq, Ghadīr** *well* S Iraq *30.15N 45.57E*
158 *E14* **Ābu Road** Rājasthān, N India *24.28N 72.46E*
82 *I6* **Abu Shagara, Ras** *headland* NE Sudan *18.04N 38.31E*
77 *W12* **Abu Simbel** ***var.*** Abou Simbel, Abū Sunbul. *ancient monument* S Egypt *22.25N 31.37E*

◆ Country
● Country Capital
◇ Dependent Territory
○ Dependent Territory Capital
◈ Administrative Region
✈ International Airport
▲ Mountain
▲▲ Mountain Range
Ѫ Volcano
≈ River
◎ Lake
▣ Reservoir

ABŪ SUDAYRAH – AÍNOS

145 U12 **Abū Sudayrah** S Iraq 30.55N 44.58E
145 T10 **Abū Şukhayr** S Iraq 31.54N 44.27E
Abū Sunbul see Abu Simbel
172 Nn6 **Abuta** Hokkaidō, NE Japan 42.34N 140.44E
193 E18 **Abut Head** headland South Island, NZ 43.06S 170.16E
82 E9 **Abu 'Urug** Northern Kordofan, C Sudan 15.52N 30.25E
82 K12 **Ābuyē Mēda** ▲ C Ethiopia 10.23N 39.46E
179 R13 **Abuyog** Leyte, C Philippines 10.45N 124.58E
82 D11 **Abu Zabad** Western Kordofan, C Sudan 12.21N 29.16E
Abū Ẓabī see Abū Ẓaby
149 P16 **Abū Ẓaby** var. Abū Ẓabī, Eng. Abu Dhabi. ● (UAE) Abū Ẓaby, C UAE 24.30N 54.20E
77 X8 **Abu Zenîma** E Egypt 29.01N 33.08E
97 N17 **Åby** Östergötland, S Sweden 58.40N 16.19E
Abyaḍ, Al Baḥr al see White Nile
Åbybro see Aabybro
82 D13 **Abyei** Western Kordofan, S Sudan 9.34N 28.28E
Abyla see Ávila
Abymes see les Abymes
Abyssinia see Ethiopia
Açâba see Assaba
56 F11 **Acacias** Meta, C Colombia 3.58N 73.46W
60 L13 **Açailandia** Maranhão, E Brazil 4.51S 47.25W
Acaill see Achill Island
44 E8 **Acajutla** Sonsonate, W El Salvador 13.35N 89.48W
81 D17 **Acalayong** SW Equatorial Guinea 1.05N 9.34E
43 N13 **Acámbaro** Guanajuato, C Mexico 20.01N 100.45W
56 C6 **Acandí** Chocó, NW Colombia 8.28N 77.18W
106 H4 **A Cañiza** var. La Cañiza. Galicia, NW Spain 42.13N 8.16W
42 J11 **Acaponeta** Nayarit, C Mexico 22.30N 105.21W
42 J11 **Acaponeta, Río de** ≈ C Mexico
43 O16 **Acapulco** var. Acapulco de Juárez. Guerrero, S Mexico 16.51N 99.53W
Acapulco de Juárez see Acapulco
57 T13 **Acarai Mountains** Sp. Serra Acaraí. ⛰ Brazil/Guyana
Acaraí, Serra see Acarai Mountains
60 O13 **Acaraú** Ceará, NE Brazil 4.35S 37.37W
56 J6 **Acarigua** Portuguesa, N Venezuela 9.34N 69.12W
44 C6 **Acatenango, Volcán de** 🌋 S Guatemala 14.30N 90.52W
43 Q15 **Acatlán** var. Acatlán de Osorio. Puebla, S Mexico 18.12N 98.01W
Acatlán de Osorio see Acatlán
43 S15 **Acayucan** var. Acayucán. Veracruz-Llave, E Mexico 17.58N 94.58W
Accho see 'Akko
23 Y5 **Accomac** Virginia, NE USA 37.43N 75.39W
79 Q17 **Accra** ● (Ghana) SE Ghana 5.33N 0.15W
99 L17 **Accrington** NW England, UK 53.46N 2.21W
63 B19 **Acebal** Santa Fe, C Argentina 33.13S 60.49W
173 Ee4 **Aceh** off. Daerah Istimewa Aceh, var. Acheen, Achin, Atchin, Atjeh. ⬖ autonomous district NW Indonesia
109 M18 **Acerenza** Basilicata, S Italy 40.46N 15.51E
109 K17 **Acerra** anc. Acerrae. Campania, S Italy 40.55N 14.22E
Acerrae see Acerra
Ach'asar Lerr see Achkasar
59 J17 **Achacachi** La Paz, W Bolivia 16.04S 68.39W
56 K7 **Achaguas** Apure, C Venezuela 7.46N 68.13W
160 H12 **Achalpur** prev. Elichpur, Ellichpur. Mahārāshtra, C India 21.19N 77.30E
63 F18 **Achar** Tacuarembó, C Uruguay 32.26S 56.10W
117 H19 **Acharnés** var. Aharnes; prev. Akharnaí. Attikí, C Greece 38.09N 23.58E
Acheen see Aceh
101 K16 **Achel** Limburg, NE Belgium 51.15N 5.31E
117 D16 **Achelóos** var. Akhelóös, Aspropótamos; anc. Achelous. ≈ W Greece
Achelous see Achelóos
169 W8 **Acheng** Heilongjiang, NE China 45.31N 126.55E
111 N6 **Achenkirch** Tirol, W Austria 47.31N 11.42E
103 L24 **Achenpass** pass Austria/Germany 47.35N 11.39E
111 N7 **Achensee** ◎ W Austria
103 F22 **Achern** Baden-Württemberg, SW Germany 48.37N 8.04E
117 C16 **Acherón** ≈ W Greece
79 W11 **Achétinamou** ≈ S Niger
158 J12 **Achhnera** Uttar Pradesh, N India 27.10N 77.45E
44 C7 **Achiguate, Río** ≈ S Guatemala
99 A16 **Achill Head** Ir. Ceann Acla. headland W Ireland 53.58N 10.14W
99 A16 **Achill Island** Ir. Acaill. island W Ireland
102 H11 **Achim** Niedersachsen, NW Germany 53.01N 9.01E
155 S5 **Achīn** Nangarhār, E Afghanistan 34.04N 70.40E
Achin see Aceh
126 Hh14 **Achinsk** Krasnoyarskiy Kray, S Russian Federation 56.21N 90.25E
168 E5 **Achit Nuur** ◎ NW Mongolia
143 T11 **Achkasar** Arm. Ach'asar Lerr. ▲ Armenia/Georgia 41.09N 43.55E
130 K13 **Achuyevo** Krasnodarskiy Kray, SW Russian Federation 46.00N 38.01E
83 F16 **Achwa** var. Aswa. ≈ N Uganda
142 E15 **Acıgöl** salt lake SW Turkey
109 L24 **Acireale** Sicilia, Italy, C Mediterranean Sea 37.36N 15.10E
Aciris see Agri
27 N7 **Ackerly** Texas, SW USA 32.31N 101.43W
24 M4 **Ackerman** Mississippi, S USA 33.18N 89.10W
31 W13 **Ackley** Iowa, C USA 42.33N 93.03W
46 J5 **Acklins Island** island SE Bahamas
Acla, Ceann see Achill Head
64 H11 **Aconcagua, Cerro** ▲ W Argentina 32.36S 69.53W
Açores/Açores, Arquipélago dos/Açores, Ilhas dos see Azores
106 G2 **A Coruña** Cast. La Coruña ⬖ province Galicia, NW Spain
106 H2 **A Coruña** Cast. La Coruña, Eng. Corunna; anc. Caronium. Galicia, NW Spain 43.22N 8.24W
44 L10 **Acoyapa** Chontales, S Nicaragua 12.01N 85.08W
108 H13 **Acquapendente** Lazio, C Italy 42.44N 11.52E
108 J13 **Acquasanta Terme** Marche, C Italy 42.46N 13.24E
108 I13 **Acquasparta** Lazio, C Italy 42.41N 12.31E
108 C9 **Acqui Terme** Piemonte, NW Italy 44.40N 8.28E
Acrae see Palazzolo Acreide
190 F7 **Acraman, Lake** salt lake South Australia
61 A15 **Acre** off. Estado do Acre. ⬖ state W Brazil
Acre see 'Akko
61 C16 **Acre, Rio** ≈ W Brazil
109 N20 **Acri** Calabria, SW Italy 39.30N 16.22E
Acte see Ágion Óros
203 Y12 **Actéon, Groupe** island group Îles Tuamotu, SE French Polynesia
13 P12 **Acton-Vale** Québec, SE Canada 45.39N 72.31W
43 P13 **Actopan** var. Actopán. Hidalgo, C Mexico 20.16N 98.57W
61 P14 **Açu** var. Assu. Rio Grande do Norte, E Brazil 5.33S 36.55W
Acunum Acusio see Montélimar
79 Q17 **Ada** SE Ghana 5.46N 0.37E
31 R5 **Ada** Minnesota, N USA 47.18N 96.31W
33 R12 **Ada** Ohio, N USA 40.46N 83.49W
29 O12 **Ada** Oklahoma, C USA 34.48N 96.38W
114 L8 **Ada** Serbia, N Serbia 45.48N 20.08E
168 L8 **Adaatsag** var. Tavin. Dundgovĭ, C Mongolia 46.27N 105.43E
Ada Bazar see Adapazarı
42 D3 **Adair, Bahía de** bay NW Mexico
106 M7 **Adaja** ≈ N Spain
40 H17 **Adak Island** island Aleutian Islands, Alaska, USA
Adalia see Antalya
Adalia, Gulf of see Antalya Körfezi
147 X9 **Adam** N Oman 22.22N 57.30E
Adama see Nazrēt
62 I8 **Adamantina** São Paulo, S Brazil 21.40S 51.04W
81 E14 **Adamaoua** Eng. Adamawa. ⬖ province N Cameroon
70 F11 **Adamaoua, Massif d'** Eng. Adamawa Highlands. plateau NW Cameroon
79 Y14 **Adamawa** ⬖ state E Nigeria
Adamawa see Adamaoua
Adamawa Highlands see Adamaoua, Massif d'
108 F6 **Adamello** ▲ N Italy 46.09N 10.33E
83 J14 **Ādamī Tulu** Oromo, C Ethiopia 7.52N 38.39E
65 M23 **Adam, Mount** var. Monte Independencia. ▲ West Falkland, Falkland Islands 51.36S 60.00W
31 R16 **Adams** Nebraska, C USA 40.25N 96.30W
20 H8 **Adams** New York, NE USA 43.48N 75.57W
31 Q3 **Adams** North Dakota, N USA 48.23N 98.01W
161 I23 **Adam's Bridge** chain of shoals NW Sri Lanka
34 H10 **Adams, Mount** ▲ Washington, NW USA 46.12N 121.29W
Adam's Peak see Sri Pada
203 R16 **Adam's Rock** island Pitcairn Island, Pitcairn Islands
203 P16 **Adamstown** ○ (Pitcairn Islands) Pitcairn Island, Pitcairn Islands 25.04S 130.04W
22 G10 **Adamsville** Tennessee, S USA 35.14N 88.23W
27 S9 **Adamsville** Texas, SW USA 31.15N 98.09W
147 O17 **'Adan** Eng. Aden. SW Yemen 12.51N 45.04E
142 K16 **Adana** var. Seyhan. Adana, S Turkey 37.00N 35.19E
142 K16 **Adana** var. Seyhan. ⬖ province S Turkey
Adâncata see Horlivka
175 Nn10 **Adang, Teluk** bay Borneo, C Indonesia
142 F11 **Adapazarı** prev. Ada Bazar. Sakarya, NW Turkey 40.48N 30.24E
82 H8 **Adarama** River Nile, NE Sudan 17.04N 34.57E
205 Q16 **Adare, Cape** headland Antarctica 71.24S 170.27E
108 E6 **Adda** anc. Addua. ≈ N Italy
82 A13 **Adda** ≈ W Sudan
149 Q17 **Aḍ Ḍab'īyah** Abū Ẓaby, C UAE 24.16N 54.07E
149 O18 **Aḍ Ḍafrah** desert S UAE
147 Q6 **Ad Dahnā'** desert E Saudi Arabia
76 A11 **Ad Dakhla** var. Dakhla. SW Western Sahara 23.46N 15.56W
Ad Dalanj see Dilling
Ad Damar see Ed Damer
Ad Damazīn see Ed Damazin
Ad Dāmir see Ed Damer
181 N2 **Ad Dammām** desert NE Saudi Arabia
147 R6 **Ad Dammān** var. Dammām. Ash Sharqīyah, NE Saudi Arabia 26.23N 50.04E
Ad Dāmūr see Damoûr
146 K5 **Ad Dār al Ḥamrā'** Tabūk, NW Saudi Arabia 27.21N 37.45E
146 M13 **Ad Darb** Jīzān, SW Saudi Arabia 17.45N 42.15E
147 O8 **Ad Dawādimī** Ar Riyāḍ, C Saudi Arabia 24.31N 44.21E
149 N16 **Ad Dawḥah** Eng. Doha. ● (Qatar) C Qatar 25.15N 51.36E
149 N16 **Ad Dawḥah** Eng. Doha. ✈ C Qatar 25.11N 51.37E
145 S6 **Ad Dawr** N Iraq 34.30N 43.49E
145 Y12 **Ad Dayr** var. Dayr, Shahbān. E Iraq 30.45N 47.36E
Addi Arkay see Ādī Ārk'ay
145 X15 **Ad Dibdibah** physical region Iraq/Kuwait
Aḍ Ḍiffah see Libyan Plateau
Addis Ababa see Ādīs Ābeba
Addison see Webster Springs
145 U10 **Ad Dīwānīyah** var. Diwaniyah. C Iraq 32.00N 44.57E
Addua see Adda
157 K22 **Addu Atoll** atoll S Maldives
Ad Dujail see Ad Dujayl
145 T7 **Ad Dujayl** var. Ad Dujail. N Iraq 33.49N 44.16E
Ad Duwaym/Ad Duwēm see Ed Dueim
101 D16 **Adegem** Oost-Vlaanderen, NW Belgium 51.12N 3.31E
25 U7 **Adel** Georgia, SE USA 31.08N 83.25W
31 U14 **Adel** Iowa, C USA 41.36N 94.01W
190 I9 **Adelaide** state capital South Australia 34.55S 138.36E
46 H2 **Adelaide** New Providence, N Bahamas 24.59N 77.30W
190 I9 **Adelaide** ✈ South Australia 34.55S 138.31E
204 H6 **Adelaide Island** island Antarctica
15 K4 **Adelaide Peninsula** peninsula Nunavut, N Canada
189 P2 **Adelaide River** Northern Territory, N Australia 13.12S 131.06E
78 M10 **'Adel Bagrou** Hodh ech Chargui, SE Mauritania 15.33N 7.04W
194 I11 **Adelbert Range** ⛰ N PNG
188 K3 **Adele Island** island Western Australia
109 O17 **Adelfia** Puglia, SE Italy 41.01N 16.52E
205 V16 **Adélie Coast** physical region Antarctica
205 V14 **Adélie, Terre** physical region Antarctica
Adelnau see Odolanów
Adelsberg see Postojna
Aden see 'Adan
147 Q17 **Aden, Gulf of** gulf SW Arabian Sea
79 V10 **Aderbissinat** Agadez, C Niger 15.30N 7.57E
Adhaim see Al 'Uẓaym
149 R16 **Adh Dhayd** var. Al Dhaid. Ash Shāriqah, NE UAE 25.19N 55.51E
146 M4 **'Adhfā'** spring/well NW Saudi Arabia 29.15N 41.24E
144 I13 **'Ādhriyāt, Jabāl al** ⛰ S Jordan
194 L12 **Adi** ≈ New Britain, C PNG
82 I10 **Ādī Ārk'ay** var. Addi Arkay. Amhara, N Ethiopia 13.18N 37.56E
190 C7 **Adieu, Cape** headland South Australia 32.01S 132.12E
108 H8 **Adige** Ger. Etsch. ≈ N Italy
82 J10 **Ādīgrat** Tigray, N Ethiopia 14.17N 39.27E
160 I13 **Ādilabād** var. Ādilābād. Andhra Pradesh, C India 19.40N 78.31E
37 P2 **Adin** California, W USA 41.10N 120.57W
176 Vv12 **Adi, Pulau** island E Indonesia
20 K8 **Adirondack Mountains** ⛰ New York, NE USA
82 J13 **Ādīs Ābeba** Eng. Addis Ababa. ● (Ethiopia) Ādīs Ābeba, C Ethiopia 8.59N 38.43E
82 J13 **Ādīs Ābeba** ✈ Ādīs Ābeba, C Ethiopia 8.58N 38.53E
82 I11 **Ādīs Zemen** Amhara, N Ethiopia 12.00N 37.43E
Adi Ugri see Mendefera
143 N15 **Adıyaman** Adıyaman, SE Turkey 37.46N 38.15E
143 N15 **Adıyaman** ⬖ province S Turkey
118 L11 **Adjud** Vrancea, E Romania 46.06N 27.11E
47 T6 **Adjuntas** C Puerto Rico 18.10N 66.44W
Adjuntas, Presa de las see Vicente Guerrero, Presa
Ādkup see Erikub Atoll
130 L15 **Adler** Krasnodarskiy Kray, SW Russian Federation 43.25N 39.58E
Adler see Orlice
110 G7 **Adliswil** Zürich, NW Switzerland 47.20N 8.30E
15 L1 **Admiralty Inlet** fjord Baffin Island, Nunavut, NE Canada
34 G7 **Admiralty Inlet** inlet Washington, NW USA
41 X13 **Admiralty Island** island Alexander Archipelago, Alaska, USA
194 K8 **Admiralty Islands** island group N PNG
142 B14 **Adnan Menderes** ✈ (İzmir) İzmir, W Turkey 38.16N 27.09E
39 V6 **Adobe Creek Reservoir** ⊞ Colorado, C USA
79 T16 **Ado-Ekiti** Ekiti, SW Nigeria 7.42N 5.13E
Adola see Kibre Mengist
63 C23 **Adolfo González Chaues** Buenos Aires, E Argentina
161 H17 **Ādoni** Andhra Pradesh, C India 15.37N 77.16E
104 K15 **Adour** anc. Aturus. ≈ SW France
Adowa see Ādwa
107 O15 **Adra** Andalucía, S Spain 36.45N 3.01W
109 L24 **Adrano** Sicilia, Italy, C Mediterranean Sea 37.39N 14.49E
76 I9 **Adrar** C Algeria 27.55N 0.12W
78 K7 **Adrar** ⬖ region C Mauritania
76 L11 **Adrar** ⛰ SE Algeria
76 A12 **Adrar Souttouf** ⛰ SW Western Sahara
Adrasman see Adrasmon
153 Q10 **Adrasmon** Rus. Adrasman. NW Tajikistan 40.38N 69.56E
80 K10 **Adré** Ouaddaï, E Chad 13.39N 22.09E
108 H9 **Adria** anc. Atria, Hadria, Hatria. Veneto, NE Italy 45.03N 12.04E
33 R10 **Adrian** Michigan, N USA 41.54N 84.02W
31 S11 **Adrian** Minnesota, N USA 43.38N 95.55W
29 R5 **Adrian** Missouri, C USA 38.24N 94.21W
26 M2 **Adrian** Texas, SW USA 35.16N 102.39W
23 S4 **Adrian** West Virginia, NE USA 38.53N 80.14W
Adrianople/Adrianopolis see Edirne
123 Mm8 **Adriatic Basin** undersea feature Adriatic Sea, N Mediterranean Sea
Adriatico, Mare see Adriatic Sea
108 L13 **Adriatic Sea** Alb. Deti Adriatik, It. Mare Adriatico, SCr. Jadransko More, Slvn. Jadransko Morje. sea N Mediterranean Sea
Adriatik, Deti see Adriatic Sea
Adua see Ādwa
Aduana del Sásabe see El Sásabe
81 O17 **Adusa** Orientale, NE Dem. Rep. Congo 1.25N 28.04E
120 J13 **Adutiškis** Vilnius, E Lithuania 55.09N 26.34E
29 Y7 **Advance** Missouri, C USA 37.06N 89.54W
67 D25 **Adventure Sound** bay East Falkland, Falkland Islands
82 J10 **Ādwa** var. Adowa, It. Adua. Tigray, N Ethiopia 14.08N 38.51E
126 M8 **Adycha** ≈ NE Russian Federation
130 L14 **Adygeya, Respublika** ⬖ autonomous republic SW Russian Federation
Adzhikui see Ajyguýy
79 N17 **Adzopé** SE Ivory Coast 6.07N 3.54W
129 U4 **Adz'va** ≈ NW Russian Federation
129 U5 **Adz'vavom** Respublika Komi, NW Russian Federation 66.35N 59.13E
Ædua see Autun
117 K19 **Aegean Islands** island group Greece/Turkey
Aegean North see Vóreion Aigaíon
117 I17 **Aegean Sea** Gk. Aigaíon Pélagos, Aigaío Pélagos, Turk. Ege Denizi. sea NE Mediterranean Sea
Aegean South see Nótion Aigaíon
120 H3 **Aegviidu** Ger. Charlottenhof. Harjumaa, NW Estonia 59.16N 25.37E
Aegyptus see Egypt
Aelana see Al 'Aqabah
Aelok see Ailuk Atoll
Aelōninae see Ailinginae Atoll
Aeḷōnḷapḷap see Ailinglaplap Atoll
Æmilia see Emilia-Romagna
Æmilianum see Millau
Aemona see Ljubljana
Aenaria see Ischia
Aeolian Islands see Eolie, Isole
203 Z3 **Aeon Point** headland Kiritimati, NE Kiribati 1.46N 157.10W
97 G24 **Ærø** Ger. Arrö. island C Denmark
97 H24 **Ærøskøbing** Fyn, C Denmark 54.52N 10.24E
Æsernia see Isernia
106 G3 **A Estrada** Galicia, NW Spain 42.40N 8.28W
117 C18 **Aetós** Itháki, Iónia Nisiá, Greece, C Mediterranean Sea 38.21N 20.40E
203 Q8 **Afaahiti** Tahiti, W French Polynesia 17.43S 149.18W
145 U10 **'Afak** C Iraq 32.04N 45.16E
Afanasjevo see Afanas'yevo
129 T14 **Afanas'yevo** var. Afanasjevo. Kirovskaya Oblast', NW Russian Federation 58.55N 53.13E
Afándou see Afántou
117 O23 **Afántou** var. Afándou. Ródos, Dodekánisa, Greece, Aegean Sea 36.16N 28.10E
Afar Depression see Danakil Desert
82 K11 **Afar** ⬖ region NE Ethiopia
203 O7 **Afareaitu** Moorea, W French Polynesia 17.33S 149.46W
146 L7 **'Afariyah, Bi'r al** well NW Saudi Arabia 25.28N 39.21E
Afars et des Issas, Territoire Français des see Djibouti
85 D22 **Affenrücken** Karas, SW Namibia 28.05S 15.49E
Afghānestān, Dowlat-e Eslāmī-ye see Afghanistan
154 M6 **Afghanistan** off. Islamic State of Afghanistan, Per. Dowlat-e Eslāmī-ye Afghānestān; prev. Republic of Afghanistan. ◆ Islamic state C Asia
Afgoi see Afgooye
83 N17 **Afgooye** It. Afgoi. Shabeellaha Hoose, S Somalia 2.09N 45.07E
147 N8 **'Afīf** Ar Riyāḍ, C Saudi Arabia 23.57N 42.57E
79 V17 **Afikpo** Ebonyi, SE Nigeria 5.52N 7.58E
Afiun Karahissar see Afyon
Åfjord see Åi Åfjord
111 V6 **Aflenz Kurort** Steiermark, E Austria 47.33N 15.14E
76 J6 **Aflou** N Algeria 34.09N 2.06E
83 L18 **Afmadow** Jubbada Hoose, S Somalia 0.24N 42.03E
41 Q14 **Afognak Island** island Alaska, USA
106 J2 **A Fonsagrada** Galicia, NW Spain 43.09N 7.03W
194 L15 **Afore** Northern, S PNG 9.01S 148.22E
61 O15 **Afrânio** Pernambuco, E Brazil 8.31S 40.54W
68-69 **Africa** continent
70 L11 **Africa, Horn of** physical region Ethiopia/Somalia
180 K11 **Africana Seamount** undersea feature SW Indian Ocean 37.10S 29.10E
88 A14 **African Plate** tectonic feature
144 I2 **'Afrīn** Ḥalab, N Syria 36.31N 36.51E
142 M15 **Afşin** Kahramanmaraş, C Turkey 38.13N 36.54E
100 J7 **Afsluitdijk** dam N Netherlands 53.00N 5.10E
31 U15 **Afton** Iowa, C USA 41.01N 94.12W
31 W9 **Afton** Minnesota, N USA 44.54N 92.46W
29 R8 **Afton** Oklahoma, C USA 36.41N 94.57W
142 F14 **Afyon** prev. Afyonkarahisar. Afyon, W Turkey 38.46N 30.31E
142 F14 **Afyon** var. Afiun Karahissar, Afyonkarahisar. ⬖ province W Turkey
Afyonkarahisar see Afyon
Agadès see Agadez
79 V10 **Agadez** prev. Agadès. Agadez, C Niger 16.57N 7.55E
79 W8 **Agadez** ⬖ department N Niger
76 E8 **Agadir** SW Morocco 30.30N 9.36W
66 M9 **Agadir Canyon** undersea feature SE Atlantic Ocean
151 R12 **Agadyr'** Karaganda, C Kazakhstan 48.15N 72.54E
181 O7 **Agalega Islands** island group N Mauritius
44 K6 **Agalta, Sierra de** ⛰ E Honduras
126 Gg10 **Agan** ≈ C Russian Federation
Agana/Agaña see Hagåtña
196 B15 **Agana Bay** bay NW Guam
196 C16 **Agana Field** ✈ (Agana) C Guam 13.28N 144.48E
171 Kk13 **Agano-gawa** ≈ Honshū, C Japan
196 B17 **Aga Point** headland S Guam
160 G9 **Agar** Madhya Pradesh, C India 23.43N 76.01E
83 I14 **Āgaro** Oromo, C Ethiopia 7.52N 36.36E
159 V15 **Agartala** Tripura, NE India 23.49N 91.15E
204 I5 **Agassiz, Cape** headland Antarctica 68.28S 62.58W
183 V13 **Agassiz Fracture Zone** tectonic feature S Pacific Ocean
196 B16 **Agat** W Guam 13.20N 144.38E
196 B16 **Agat Bay** bay W Guam
151 P13 **Agat, Gory** hill C Kazakhstan 46.55N 69.13E
Agatha see Agde
117 M20 **Agathónisi** island Dodekánisa, Greece, Aegean Sea
176 Y13 **Agats** Papua, E Indonesia 5.33S 138.07E
161 C21 **Agatti Island** island Lakshadweep, India, N Indian Ocean
40 D16 **Agattu Island** island Aleutian Islands, Alaska, USA
40 D16 **Agattu Strait** strait Aleutian Islands, Alaska, USA
12 B8 **Agawa** ≈ Ontario, S Canada
12 B8 **Agawa Bay** lake bay Ontario, S Canada
79 N17 **Agboville** SE Ivory Coast 5.56N 4.13W
143 V12 **Ağdam** Rus. Agdam. SW Azerbaijan 40.04N 46.00E
105 P16 **Agde** anc. Agatha. Hérault, S France 43.19N 3.28E
105 P16 **Agde, Cap d'** headland S France 43.17N 3.30E
Agedabia see Ajdābiyā
104 L14 **Agen** anc. Aginnum. Lot-et-Garonne, SW France 44.12N 0.37E
Agendicum see Sens
171 K16 **Ageo** Saitama, Honshū, S Japan 35.58N 139.36E
111 R5 **Ager** ≈ N Austria
Agere Hiywet see Hāgere Hiywet
110 G8 **Ägerisee** ◎ W Switzerland
148 M10 **Āghā Jārī** Khūzestān, SW Iran 30.48N 49.45E
41 P15 **Aghiyuk Island** island Alaska, USA
76 B12 **Aghouinit** SE Western Sahara 22.14N 13.10W
Aghri Dagh see Büyükağrı Dağı
76 B10 **Aghzoumal, Sebkhet** var. Sebjet Agsumal. salt lake E Western Sahara
117 F15 **Agiá** var. Ayiá. Thessalía, C Greece 39.43N 22.45E
42 G7 **Agiabampo, Estero de** estuary NW Mexico
124 Nn4 **Agía Fýlaxis** var. Ayia Phyla. S Cyprus 34.43N 33.02E
Agialoúsa see Yenierenköy
117 M21 **Agía Marína** Léros, Dodekánisa, Greece, Aegean Sea 37.09N 26.51E
124 Oo3 **Agía Nápa** var. Ayia Napa. E Cyprus 34.59N 34.00E
117 L16 **Agía Paraskeví** Lésvos, E Greece 39.13N 26.19E
117 J15 **Agías Eirínis, Akrotírio** headland Límnos, E Greece 39.47N 25.21E
Agiasós see Agiassós
117 L17 **Agiassós** var. Agiasós, Ayiásos, Ayiássos. Lésvos, E Greece 39.04N 26.22E
Aginnum see Agen
126 K16 **Aginskiy Buryatskiy Avtonomnyy Okrug** ⬖ autonomous district S Russian Federation
126 Kk16 **Aginskoye** Aginskiy Buryatskiy Avtonomnyy Okrug, S Russian Federation 51.10N 114.31E
117 I14 **Ágion Óros** Eng. Mount Athos. ⬖ monastic republic NE Greece
117 H14 **Ágion Óros** var. Akte, Aktí; anc. Acte. peninsula NE Greece
116 D13 **Ágios Achílleios** religious building Dytikí Makedonía, N Greece 40.46N 21.04E
117 J16 **Ágios Efstrátios** var. Áyios Evstrátios, Hagios Evstrátios. island E Greece
117 H20 **Ágios Geórgios** island Kykládes, Greece, Aegean Sea
Ágios Geórgios see Ro
117 E21 **Ágios Ilías** ▲ S Greece 36.57N 22.19E
117 K25 **Ágios Ioánnis, Akrotírio** headland Kríti, Greece, E Mediterranean Sea 35.19N 25.46E
117 L20 **Ágios Kírykos** var. Áyios Kírikos. Ikaría, Dodekánisa, Greece, Aegean Sea 37.04N 26.16E
117 D16 **Ágios Nikolaos** Thessalía, C Greece 39.33N 21.21E
117 K25 **Ágios Nikólaos** var. Áyios Nikólaos. Kríti, Greece, E Mediterranean Sea 35.12N 25.43E
Ágios Sérgios see Yeniboğaziçi
117 H14 **Agíou Órous, Kólpos** gulf N Greece
109 K24 **Agira** anc. Agyrium. Sicilia, Italy, C Mediterranean Sea 37.39N 14.31E
117 G20 **Agkístri** island S Greece
116 G12 **Ágkistro** var. Angistro. ▲ NE Greece 41.21N 23.29E
105 O17 **Agly** ≈ S France
Agnetheln see Agnita
12 E10 **Agnew Lake** ◎ Ontario, S Canada
79 O16 **Agnibilékrou** E Ivory Coast 7.10N 3.10W
118 I11 **Agnita** Ger. Agnetheln, Hung. Szentágota. Sibiu, SW Romania 45.59N 24.39E
109 K15 **Agnone** Molise, C Italy 41.49N 14.21E
171 Hh17 **Ago** Mie, Honshū, SW Japan 34.18N 136.50E
108 C8 **Agogna** ≈ N Italy
Agoitz see Agoiz
107 R3 **Agoiz** var. Agoitz, Aoiz. Navarra, N Spain 42.47N 1.23W
79 P17 **Agona Swedru** var. Swedru. SE Ghana 5.31N 0.42W
Agordat see Akurdet
Agosta see Augusta
105 N15 **Agout** ≈ S France
158 J12 **Āgra** Uttar Pradesh, N India 27.09N 78.00E
Agra and Oudh, United Provinces of see Uttar Pradesh
Agram see Zagreb
107 U5 **Agramunt** Cataluña, NE Spain 41.48N 1.07E
107 Q5 **Agreda** Castilla-León, N Spain 41.51N 1.55W
143 S13 **Ağrı** var. Karaköse; prev. Karakılısse. Ağrı, NE Turkey 39.43N 43.04E
143 S13 **Ağrı** ⬖ province NE Turkey
109 N19 **Agri** anc. Aciris. ≈ S Italy
Agri Dagi see Büyükağrı Dağı
109 J24 **Agrigento** Gk. Akragas; prev. Girgenti. Sicilia, Italy, C Mediterranean Sea 37.19N 13.33E
196 K4 **Agrihan** island N Northern Mariana Islands
117 L17 **Agriliá, Akrotírio** prev. Ákra Maléas. headland Lésvos, E Greece 39.01N 26.36E
117 D18 **Agrínio** prev. Agrinion. Dytikí Ellás, W Greece 38.37N 21.25E
Agrinion see Agrínio
117 G17 **Agriovótano** Évvoia, C Greece 39.00N 23.18E
109 L18 **Agropoli** Campania, S Italy 40.21N 14.58E
131 T3 **Agryz** Udmurtskaya Respublika, NW Russian Federation 56.27N 52.58E
143 U11 **Ağstafa** Rus. Akstafa. NW Azerbaijan 41.06N 45.28E
143 X11 **Ağsu** Rus. Akhsu. C Azerbaijan 40.34N 48.24E
Agsumal, Sebjet see Aghzoumal, Sebkhet
42 J11 **Agua Brava, Laguna** lagoon W Mexico
56 F7 **Aguachica** Cesar, N Colombia 8.16N 73.35W
61 J20 **Água Clara** Mato Grosso do Sul, SW Brazil 20.21S 52.58W
46 D5 **Aguada de Pasajeros** Cienfuegos, C Cuba 22.22N 80.50W
56 J5 **Aguada Grande** Lara, N Venezuela 10.34N 69.30W
47 S5 **Aguadilla** W Puerto Rico 18.24N 67.09W
45 S16 **Aguadulce** Coclé, S Panama 8.16N 80.31W
106 L14 **Aguadulce** Andalucía, S Spain 37.15N 4.58W
43 O8 **Agualeguas** Nuevo León, NE Mexico 26.17N 99.30W
42 L9 **Aguanaval, Río** ≈ C Mexico
44 J5 **Aguán, Río** ≈ N Honduras
27 R16 **Agua Nueva** Texas, SW USA 26.57N 98.34W
62 J8 **Aguapeí, Rio** ≈ S Brazil
63 E14 **Aguapey, Río** ≈ NE Argentina
42 G3 **Agua Prieta** Sonora, NW Mexico 31.16N 109.33W
106 G5 **A Guarda** var. A Guardia, Laguardia, La Guardia. Galicia, NW Spain 41.54N 8.52W
A Guardia see A Guarda
58 E6 **Aguarico, Río** ≈ Ecuador/Peru
57 O6 **Aguasay** Monagas, NE Venezuela 9.25N 63.43W
42 M12 **Aguascalientes** Aguascalientes, C Mexico 21.53N 102.17W
42 L12 **Aguascalientes** ⬖ state C Mexico
59 I18 **Aguas Calientes, Río** ≈ S Peru
107 R7 **Aguasvivas** ≈ NE Spain
62 J7 **Água Vermelha, Represa de** ⊞ S Brazil
58 E12 **Aguaytía** Ucayali, C Peru 9.04S 75.32W
106 I5 **A Gudiña** var. La Gudiña. Galicia, NW Spain 42.04N 7.07W
106 G7 **Águeda** Aveiro, N Portugal 40.34N 8.28W
106 J8 **Águeda** ≈ Portugal/Spain
79 Q8 **Aguelhok** Kidal, NE Mali 19.18N 0.50E
79 V12 **Aguié** Maradi, S Niger 13.28N 7.43E
196 K8 **Aguijan** island S Northern Mariana Islands
106 M14 **Aguilar** var. Aguilar de la Frontera. Andalucía, S Spain 37.31N 4.40W
106 M3 **Aguilar de Campóo** Castilla-León, N Spain 42.46N 4.15W
Aguilar de la Frontera see Aguilar
44 F7 **Aguilares** San Salvador, C El Salvador 13.56N 89.09W
107 Q14 **Aguilas** Murcia, SE Spain 37.24N 1.36W
42 L15 **Aguililla** Michoacán de Ocampo, SW Mexico 18.43N 102.45W
Agulhas see L'Agulhas
180 J11 **Agulhas Bank** undersea feature SW Indian Ocean
180 K11 **Agulhas Basin** undersea feature SW Indian Ocean
85 F26 **Agulhas, Cape** Afr. Kaap Agulhas. headland SW South Africa 34.51S 19.59E
Agulhas, Kaap see Agulhas, Cape
62 O9 **Agulhas Negras, Pico das** ▲ SE Brazil 22.21S 44.39W
180 K11 **Agulhas Plateau** undersea feature SW Indian Ocean
172 Oo14 **Aguni-jima** island Nansei-shotō, SW Japan
Agurain see Salvatierra
179 Rr15 **Agusan** ≈ Mindanao, S Philippines
56 G5 **Agustín Codazzi** var. Codazzi. Cesar, N Colombia 10.01N 73.15W
Agyrium see Agira
76 L12 **Ahaggar** high plateau region SE Algeria
152 E12 **Ahal Welaýaty** Rus. Akhalskiy Velayat. ⬖ province C Turkmenistan
148 K2 **Ahar** Āẕarbāyjān-e Sharqī, NW Iran 38.25N 47.07E
Aharnes see Acharnés
144 J3 **Aḥaṣ, Jabal** ▲ NW Syria
144 J3 **Aḥaṣ, Jebal** ⛰ W Syria
193 G16 **Ahaura** ≈ South Island, NZ
102 E13 **Ahaus** Nordrhein-Westfalen, NW Germany 52.04N 7.01E
203 U9 **Ahe** atoll Îles Tuamotu, C French Polynesia
192 N10 **Ahimanawa Range** ⛰ North Island, NZ
121 I19 **Ahinski Kanal** Rus. Oginskiy Kanal. canal SW Belarus
195 N16 **Ahioma** SE PNG 10.18S 150.33E
192 I2 **Ahipara** Northland, North Island, NZ 35.11S 173.07E
192 I2 **Ahipara Bay** bay SE Tasman Sea
Áhkká see Akka
41 N13 **Ahklun Mountains** ⛰ Alaska, USA
143 R14 **Ahlat** Bitlis, E Turkey 38.45N 42.30E
103 F14 **Ahlen** Nordrhein-Westfalen, W Germany 51.46N 7.52E
160 D10 **Ahmadābād** var. Ahmedabad. Gujarāt, W India 23.03N 72.40E
149 R10 **Ahmadābād** Kermān, C Iran 35.51N 59.36E
Ahmadi see Al Aḥmadī
Ahmad Khel see Ḥasan Khēl
161 F14 **Ahmadnagar** var. Ahmednagar. Mahārāshtra, W India 19.07N 74.48E
155 T9 **Ahmadpur Siāl** Punjab, E Pakistan 30.40N 71.47E
79 N5 **Aḥmar, 'Erg el** desert N Mali
82 K13 **Ahmar Mountains** ⛰ C Ethiopia
Ahmedabad see Ahmadābād
Ahmednagar see Ahmadnagar
116 N12 **Ahmetbey** Kırklareli, NW Turkey 41.26N 27.35E
12 H12 **Ahmic Lake** ◎ Ontario, S Canada
202 G12 **Ahoa** Île Uvea, E Wallis and Futuna 13.16S 176.12W
42 G8 **Ahomé** Sinaloa, C Mexico 25.55N 109.10W
23 X8 **Ahoskie** North Carolina, SE USA 36.17N 76.59W
103 D17 **Ahr** ≈ W Germany
149 N12 **Ahram** var. Ahrom. Būshehr, S Iran 28.52N 51.18E
102 J9 **Ahrensburg** Schleswig-Holstein, N Germany 53.40N 10.13E
Ahrom see Ahram
95 L17 **Ähtäri** Länsi-Suomi, W Finland 62.31N 24.11E
42 K12 **Ahuacatlán** Nayarit, C Mexico 21.04N 104.32W
44 E7 **Ahuachapán** Ahuachapán, W El Salvador 13.55N 89.49W
44 A9 **Ahuachapán** ⬖ department W El Salvador
203 V16 **Ahu Akivi** var. Siete Moai. ancient monument Easter Island, Chile, E Pacific Ocean
203 W11 **Ahunui** atoll Îles Tuamotu, C French Polynesia
193 E20 **Ahuriri** ≈ South Island, NZ
97 L22 **Åhus** Skåne, S Sweden 55.55N 14.18E
Ahu Tahira see Ahu Vinapu
203 V16 **Ahu Tepeu** ancient monument Easter Island, Chile, E Pacific Ocean
203 V17 **Ahu Vinapu** var. Ahu Tahira. ancient monument Easter Island, Chile, E Pacific Ocean
148 L9 **Ahvāz** var. Ahwāz; prev. Nāsiri. Khūzestān, SW Iran 31.19N 48.37E
Ahvenanmaa see Åland
147 Q16 **Aḥwar** SW Yemen 13.34N 46.41E
Ahwāz see Ahvāz
96 H7 **Åi Åfjord** var. Åfjord, Årnes. Sør-Trondelag, C Norway 63.57N 10.12E
Aibak see Āybak
103 K22 **Aichach** Bayern, SE Germany 48.26N 11.06E
171 I16 **Aichi** off. Aichi-ken, var. Aiti. ⬖ prefecture Honshū, SW Japan
Aïdin see Aydın
176 Ww12 **Aiduna** Papua, E Indonesia 4.20S 135.15E
Aidussina see Ajdovščina
194 F13 **Aiema** ≈ W PNG
Aifir, Clochán an see Giant's Causeway
Aigaíon Pélagos/Aigaío Pélagos see Aegean Sea
111 S3 **Aigen im Mülkreis** Oberösterreich, N Austria 48.39N 13.57E
117 G20 **Aígina** var. Aíyina, Egina. Aígina, C Greece 37.45N 23.25E
117 G20 **Aígina** island S Greece
117 E18 **Aígio** var. Egio; prev. Aíyion. Dytikí Ellás, S Greece 38.15N 22.04E
110 C10 **Aigle** Vaud, SW Switzerland 46.19N 6.58E
105 P14 **Aigoual, Mont** ▲ S France 44.09N 3.34E
181 O16 **Aigrettes, Pointe des** headland W Réunion 21.01S 55.13E
63 G19 **Aiguá** var. Aigua. Maldonado, S Uruguay 34.13S 54.46W
105 S13 **Aigues** ≈ SE France
105 N10 **Aigurande** Indre, C France 46.26N 1.49E
Ai-hun see Heihe
171 K11 **Aikawa** Niigata, Sado, C Japan 38.04N 138.15E
23 Q13 **Aiken** South Carolina, SE USA 33.33N 81.43W
27 N4 **Aiken** Texas, SW USA 34.06N 101.31W
166 F13 **Ailao Shan** ⛰ SW China
45 W14 **Ailigandí** San Blas, NE Panama 9.13N 78.04W
201 R4 **Ailinginae Atoll** var. Aelōninae. atoll Ralik Chain, SW Marshall Islands
201 T7 **Ailinglaplap Atoll** var. Aelōnlaplap. atoll Ralik Chain, S Marshall Islands
Aillionn, Loch see Allen, Lough
98 H13 **Ailsa Craig** island SW Scotland, UK
201 V5 **Ailuk Atoll** var. Aelok. atoll Ratak Chain, NE Marshall Islands
126 Mm12 **Aim** Khabarovskiy Kray, E Russian Federation 58.45N 134.08E
105 R11 **Ain** ⬖ department E France
105 S10 **Ain** ≈ E France
120 G7 **Ainaži** Est. Heinaste, Ger. Hainasch. Limbaži, N Latvia 57.51N 24.24E
76 L6 **Aïn Beida** NE Algeria 35.52N 7.25E
78 K4 **'Aïn Ben Tili** Tiris Zemmour, N Mauritania 25.58N 9.30W
76 J5 **Aïn Defla** var. Aïn Eddefla. N Algeria 36.16N 1.58E
Aïn Eddefla see Aïn Defla
76 L5 **Ain El Bey** ✈ (Constantine) NE Algeria 36.15N 6.36E
117 C19 **Aínos** ▲ Kefalloniá, Iónia Nisiá, Greece, C Mediterranean Sea 38.08N 20.39E

◆ Country
● Country Capital
◇ Dependent Territory
○ Dependent Territory Capital
⬖ Administrative Region
✈ International Airport
▲ Mountain
⛰ Mountain Range
🌋 Volcano
≈ River
◎ Lake
⊞ Reservoir

AINSA – ALCOY

107 T4 **Ainsa** Aragón, NE Spain 42.25N 0.07E
76 I7 **Aïn Sefra** NW Algeria 32.45N 0.32W
31 N13 **Ainsworth** Nebraska, C USA 42.33N 99.51W
Aintab see Gaziantep
76 H5 **Aïn Témouchent** N Algeria 35.18N 1.09W
194 H11 **Aiome** Madang, N PNG 5.04S 144.43E
Aïoun el Atrous/ Aïoun el Atroûss see 'Ayoûn el 'Atroûs
56 E11 **Aipe** Huila, C Colombia 3.15N 75.16W
58 D9 **Aipena, Río** ≈ N Peru
59 L19 **Aiquile** Cochabamba, C Bolivia 18.10S 65.10W
Aïr see Aïr, Massif de l'
196 E10 **Airai** Babeldaob, C Palau
196 E10 **Airai** ✕ (Oreor) Babeldaob, N Palau 7.22N 134.34E
173 Ff8 **Airbangis** Sumatera, NW Indonesia 0.12N 99.22E
9 Q16 **Airdrie** Alberta, SW Canada 51.20N 114.00W
98 I12 **Airdrie** S Scotland, UK 55.52N 3.58W
Air du Azbine see Aïr, Massif de l'
99 M17 **Aire** ≈ N England, UK
104 K15 **Aire-sur-l'Adour** Landes, SW France 43.43N 0.16W
105 O1 **Aire-sur-la-Lys** Pas-de-Calais, N France 50.39N 2.24E
16 N2 **Air Force Island** *island* Baffin Island, Nunavut, NE Canada
174 L11 **Airhitam, Teluk** *bay* Borneo, C Indonesia
175 Rr7 **Airmadidi** Sulawesi, N Indonesia 1.25N 124.58E
79 V8 **Aïr, Massif de l'** *var.* Aïr, Air du Azbine, Asben. ⛰ NC Niger
110 G10 **Airolo** Ticino, S Switzerland 46.32N 8.38E
104 K9 **Airvault** Deux-Sèvres, W France 46.51N 0.07W
103 K19 **Aisch** ≈ S Germany
65 G20 **Aisén** *off.* Región Aisén del General Carlos Ibañez del Campo, *var.* Aysen. ◈ *region* S Chile
8 H7 **Aishihik Lake** ◎ Yukon Territory, W Canada
105 P3 **Aisne** ◈ *department* N France
105 R4 **Aisne** ≈ NE France
111 T4 **Aist** ≈ N Austria
116 K13 **Aisými** Anatolikí Makedonía kai Thráki, NE Greece 41.00N 25.55E
107 S11 **Aitana** ▲ E Spain 38.39N 0.15W
194 F9 **Aitape** *var.* Eitape. Sandaun, NW PNG 3.07S 142.22E
Aiti see Aichi
31 V6 **Aitkin** Minnesota, N USA 46.31N 93.42W
117 D18 **Aitolikó** *var.* Etoliko; *prev.* Aitolikón. Dytikí Ellás, C Greece 38.25N 21.21E
Aitolikón see Aitolikó
202 L15 **Aitutaki** *island* S Cook Islands
118 H11 **Aiud** *Ger.* Strassburg, *Hung.* Nagyenyed; *prev.* Engeten. Alba, SW Romania 46.16N 23.42E
120 I9 **Aiviekste** ≈ C Latvia
201 Q8 **Aiwo** SW Nauru 0.32S 166.54E
196 E8 **Aiwokako Passage** *passage* Babeldaob, N Palau
Aix see Aix-en-Provence
105 S15 **Aix-en-Provence** *var.* Aix; *anc.* Aquae Sextiae. Bouches-du-Rhône, SE France 43.31N 5.27E
Aix-la-Chapelle see Aachen
105 T11 **Aix-les-Bains** Savoie, E France 45.40N 5.55E
194 E11 **Aiyang, Mount** ▲ NW PNG 5.03S 141.15E
Aíyina see Aígina
Aíyion see Aígio
159 W15 **Āīzawl** Mizoram, NE India 23.40N 92.45E
120 H9 **Aizkraukle** Aizkraukle, S Latvia 56.36N 25.06E
120 C9 **Aizpute** Liepāja, W Latvia 56.43N 21.32E
171 L14 **Aizu-Wakamatsu** *var.* Aizuwakamatu. Fukushima, Honshū, C Japan 37.27N 139.55E
Aizuwakamatu see Aizu-Wakamatsu
105 X15 **Ajaccio** Corse, France, C Mediterranean Sea 41.54N 8.43E
105 X15 **Ajaccio, Golfe d'** *gulf* Corse, France, C Mediterranean Sea
43 Q15 **Ajalpán** Puebla, S Mexico 18.25N 97.19W
160 F13 **Ajanta Range** ⛰ C India
143 R10 **Ajaria** ◈ *autonomous republic* SW Georgia
Ajastan see Armenia
95 G14 **Ajaureforsen** Västerbotten, N Sweden 65.31N 15.43E
193 H17 **Ajax, Mount** ▲ South Island, NZ 42.34S 172.06E
168 F9 **Aj Bogd Uul** ▲ SW Mongolia 44.49N 95.01E
77 R8 **Ajdābiyā** *var.* Agedabia, Ajdābiyah. NE Libya 30.46N 20.13E
Ajdābiyah see Ajdābiyā
111 S12 **Ajdovščina** *Ger.* Haidenschaft, *It.* Aidussina. W Slovenia 45.52N 13.55E
171 Mm8 **Ajigasawa** Aomori, Honshū, C Japan 40.45N 140.11E
Ajjinena see El Geneina
113 H23 **Ajka** Veszprém, W Hungary 47.07N 17.31E
144 G9 **'Ajlūn** Irbid, N Jordan 32.19N 35.45E
144 H9 **'Ajlūn, Jabal** ⛰ W Jordan
Ájluokta see Drag
149 R15 **'Ajmān** *var.* Ajman, 'Ujmān. 'Ajmān, NE UAE 25.36N 55.42E
158 G12 **Ajmer** *var.* Ajmere. Rājasthān, N India 26.28N 74.40E
38 J15 **Ajo** Arizona, SW USA 32.22N 112.51W
107 N2 **Ajo, Cabo de** *headland* N Spain 43.31N 3.36W
38 J16 **Ajo Range** ⛰ Arizona, SW USA
152 C14 **Ajyguýy** *Rus.* Adzhikui. Balkan Welaýaty, W Turkmenistan 39.46N 53.57E
Akaba see Al 'Aqabah
172 P5 **Akabira** Hokkaidō, NE Japan 43.31N 142.03E
171 K12 **Akadomari** Niigata, Sado, C Japan 37.54N 138.24E
83 E20 **Akagera** *var.* Kagera. ≈ Rwanda/Tanzania *see also* Kagera
203 W16 **Akahanga, Punta** *headland* Easter Island, Chile, E Pacific Ocean
171 Ii16 **Akaishi-dake** ▲ Honshū, S Japan 35.26N 138.09E
171 J16 **Akaishi-sanmyaku** ⛰ Honshū, S Japan
82 J13 **Āk'ak'i** Oromo, C Ethiopia 8.50N 38.51E
161 G15 **Akalkot** Mahārāshtra, W India 17.36N 76.10E
Akamagaseki see Shimonoseki
172 Q7 **Akan** Hokkaidō, NE Japan 43.09N 144.08E
172 Q6 **Akan-ko** ◎ Hokkaidō, NE Japan
Akanthoú see Tatlısu
193 I19 **Akaroa** Canterbury, South Island, NZ 43.48S 172.58E
82 E6 **Akasha** Northern, N Sudan 21.03N 30.45E
170 G14 **Akashi** *var.* Akasi. Hyōgo, Honshū, SW Japan 34.37N 134.59E
145 N7 **'Akāsh, Wādī** *var.* Wādī 'Ukash. *dry watercourse* W Iraq
Akasi see Akashi
94 K11 **Äkäsjokisuu** Lappi, N Finland 67.28N 23.44E
143 S11 **Akbaba Dağı** ▲ Armenia/Turkey 41.04N 43.28E
Akbük Limanı see Güllük Körfezi
131 V8 **Akbulak** Orenburgskaya Oblast', W Russian Federation 51.01N 55.35E
143 O11 **Akçaabat** Trabzon, NE Turkey 41.00N 39.36E
143 N15 **Akçadağ** Malatya, C Turkey 38.21N 37.58E
142 G11 **Akçakoca** Düzce, NW Turkey 41.04N 31.07E
Akchakaya, Vpadina see Akdzhakaya, Vpadina
78 H7 **Akchâr** *desert* W Mauritania
151 S12 **Akchatau** *Kaz.* Aqshataū. Karaganda, C Kazakhstan 47.58N 74.01E
142 L13 **Akdağlar** ⛰ C Turkey
142 E17 **Ak Dağları** ⛰ SW Turkey
142 K13 **Akdağmadeni** Yozgat, C Turkey 39.39N 35.48E
152 G8 **Akdepe** *prev.* Ak-Tepe, Leninsk, *Turkm.* Lenin. Daşoguz Welaýaty, N Turkmenistan 42.10N 59.17E
Ak-Dere see Byala
124 O3 **Akdoğan** *Gk.* Lýsi. C Cyprus 35.06N 33.42E
126 Hh16 **Ak-Dovurak** Respublika Tyva, S Russian Federation 51.09N 90.36E
152 F9 **Akdzhakaya, Vpadina** *var.* Vpadina Akchakaya. *depression* N Turkmenistan
175 Tt7 **Akelamo** Pulau Halmahera, E Indonesia 1.27N 128.39E
Aken see Aachen
Akermanceaster see Bath
97 P15 **Åkersberga** Stockholm, C Sweden 59.28N 18.19E
97 H15 **Akershus** ◈ *county* S Norway
81 L16 **Aketi** Orientale, N Dem. Rep. Congo 2.46N 23.42E
152 C10 **Akgyr Erezi** *Rus.* Gryada Akkyr. *hill range* NW Turkmenistan
Akhalskiy Velayat see Ahal Welaýaty
143 S10 **Akhalts'ikhe** SW Georgia 41.38N 43.03E
Akhangaran see Ohangaron
Akharnaí see Acharnés
77 R7 **Akhḑar, Al Jabal al** *hill range* NE Libya
Akhelóös see Achelóos
41 Q15 **Akhiok** Kodiak Island, Alaska, USA 56.57N 154.12W
142 C13 **Akhisar** Manisa, W Turkey 38.54N 27.49E
77 X10 **Akhmîm** *anc.* Panopolis. C Egypt 26.24N 31.50E
158 H6 **Akhnūr** Jammu and Kashmir, NW India 32.57N 74.43E
Akhsu see Ağsu
131 P11 **Akhtuba** ≈ SW Russian Federation
131 P11 **Akhtubinsk** Astrakhanskaya Oblast', SW Russian Federation 48.16N 46.13E
Akhtyrka see Okhtyrka
170 F15 **Aki** Kōchi, Shikoku, SW Japan 33.30N 133.54E
41 N12 **Akiachak** Alaska, USA 60.54N 161.25W
41 N12 **Akiak** Alaska, USA 60.54N 161.12W
203 X11 **Akiaki** *atoll* Îles Tuamotu, E French Polynesia
10 H9 **Akimiski Island** *island* Nunavut, C Canada
142 K17 **Akıncı Burnu** *headland* S Turkey 36.21N 35.47E
Akıncılar see Selçuk
119 U10 **Akinovka** Zaporiz'ka Oblast', S Ukraine
Åkirkeby see Aakirkeby
171 M10 **Akita** Akita, Honshū, C Japan 39.44N 140.06E
171 M10 **Akita** *off.* Akita-ken. ◈ *prefecture* Honshū, C Japan
78 H8 **Akjoujt** *prev.* Fort-Repoux. Inchiri, W Mauritania 19.42N 14.28W
94 H11 **Akka** *Lapp.* Áhkká. ⛰ N Sweden
94 H11 **Akkajaure** ◎ N Sweden
Akkala see Oqqal'a
161 L25 **Akkaraipattu** Eastern Province, E Sri Lanka 7.13N 81.51E
151 P13 **Akkense** Karaganda, C Kazakhstan 46.39N 68.06E
Akkerman see Bilhorod-Dnistrovs'kyy
131 W8 **Akkermanovka** Orenburgskaya Oblast', W Russian Federation 51.11N 58.03E
172 Qq7 **Akkeshi** Hokkaidō, NE Japan 43.03N 144.48E
172 Qq7 **Akkeshi-ko** ◎ Hokkaidō, NE Japan
172 Qq8 **Akkeshi-wan** *bay* NW Pacific Ocean
144 F8 **'Akko** *Eng.* Acre, *Fr.* Saint-Jean-d'Acre; *Bibl.* Accho, Ptolemaïs. Northern, N Israel 32.55N 35.04E
151 Q8 **Akkol'** *Kaz.* Aqköl; *prev.* Alekseyevka, *Kaz.* Alekseevka. Akmola, C Kazakhstan 51.58N 70.58E
151 T14 **Akkol'** *Kaz.* Aqköl. Almaty, SE Kazakhstan 45.01N 75.38E
151 Q16 **Akkol'** *Kaz.* Aqköl. Zhambyl, S Kazakhstan 43.25N 70.46E
150 M11 **Akkol', Ozero** *prev.* Ozero Zhaman-Akkol'. ◎ C Kazakhstan
100 L6 **Akkrum** Friesland, N Netherlands 53.01N 5.52E
151 U8 **Akku** *prev.* Lebyazh'ye. Pavlodar, NE Kazakhstan 51.29N 77.48E
150 F12 **Akkystau** *Kaz.* Aqqystaū. Atyrau, SW Kazakhstan 47.13N 51.01E
14 Ff3 **Aklavik** Northwest Territories, NW Canada 68.15N 135.01W
Akmeņrags see Akmensrags
120 B9 **Akmensrags** *prev.* Akmeņrags. *headland* W Latvia 56.49N 21.03E
164 E9 **Akmeqit** Xinjiang Uygur Zizhiqu, NW China 37.10N 76.59E
152 J14 **Akmeydan** Mary Welaýaty, C Turkmenistan 37.50N 62.08E
Akmola see Astana
151 P9 **Akmola** *off.* Akmolinskaya Oblast', *Kaz.* Aqmola Oblysy; *prev.* Tselinogradskaya Oblast. ◈ *province* C Kazakhstan
Akmolinsk see Astana
Akmolinskaya Oblast' see Akmola
Aknavásár see Târgu Ocna
120 I11 **Aknīste** Jēkabpils, S Latvia 56.09N 25.43E
170 G14 **Akō** Hyōgo, Honshū, SW Japan 34.44N 134.22E
83 G14 **Akobo** Jonglei, SE Sudan 7.49N 33.04E
83 G14 **Akobo** *var.* Ākobowenz. ≈ Ethiopia/Sudan
Ākobowenz see Akobo
160 H12 **Akola** Mahārāshtra, C India 20.44N 77.00E
Akordat see Akurdet
79 Q16 **Akosombo Dam** *dam* SE Ghana 6.23N 0.06E
160 H12 **Akot** Mahārāshtra, C India 20.45N 77.00E
79 N16 **Akoupé** SE Ivory Coast 6.19N 3.54W
10 M3 **Akpatok Island** *island* Nunavut, E Canada
164 G7 **Akqi** Xinjiang Uygur Zizhiqu, NW China 40.51N 78.20E
144 I2 **Akrād, Jabal al** ⛰ N Syria
Akragas see Agrigento
94 H3 **Akranes** Vesturland, W Iceland 64.19N 22.01W
145 S2 **Ākrē** *Ar.* 'Aqrah. N Iraq 36.46N 43.52E
97 C16 **Åkrahamn** Rogaland, S Norway 59.15N 5.12E
79 V9 **Akrérèb** Agadez, C Niger 17.45N 9.01E
117 D22 **Akrítas, Akrotírio** *headland* S Greece 36.43N 21.52E
39 V3 **Akron** Colorado, C USA 40.09N 103.12W
31 R12 **Akron** Iowa, C USA 42.49N 96.33W
33 U12 **Akron** Ohio, N USA 41.04N 81.31W
Akrotiri see Akrotírion
Akrotiri Bay see Akrotírion, Kólpos
124 N4 **Akrotírion** *var.* Akrotiri. *UK air base* S Cyprus 34.36N 32.57E
124 Nn4 **Akrotírion, Kólpos** *var.* Akrotiri Bay. *bay* S Cyprus
123 Mm4 **Akrotiri Sovereign Base Area** *UK military installation* S Cyprus 34.34N 32.58E
164 F11 **Aksai Chin** *Chin.* Aksayqin. *disputed region* China/India
Aksaj see Aksay
142 I15 **Aksaray** Aksaray, C Turkey 38.23N 33.50E
142 I15 **Aksaray** ◈ *province* C Turkey
150 G8 **Aksay** *var.* Aksaj, *Kaz.* Aqsay. Zapadnyy Kazakhstan, NW Kazakhstan 51.10N 53.03E
131 O11 **Aksay** Volgogradskaya Oblast', SW Russian Federation 47.59N 43.54E
153 W10 **Aksay** *var.* Toxkan He. ≈ China/Kyrgyzstan
Aksay/Aksay Kazaksu Zizhixian see Boluozhuanjing/Hongliuwan
Aksayqin see Aksai Chin
164 G11 **Aksayqin Hu** ◎ NW China
142 G14 **Akşehir** Konya, W Turkey 38.22N 31.24E
142 G14 **Akşehir Gölü** ◎ C Turkey
142 G16 **Akseki** Antalya, SW Turkey 37.03N 31.46E
126 L15 **Aksenovo-Zilovskoye** Chitinskaya Oblast', S Russian Federation 53.01N 117.26E
126 Kk16 **Aksha** Chitinskaya Oblast', S Russian Federation 50.16N 113.22E
151 V11 **Akshatau, Khrebet** ⛰ E Kazakhstan
153 Y8 **Ak-Shyyrak** Issyk-Kul'skaya Oblast', E Kyrgyzstan 41.46N 78.34E
Akstafa see Ağstafa
164 H7 **Aksu** Xinjiang Uygur Zizhiqu, NW China 41.16N 80.15E
151 R8 **Aksu** *Kaz.* Aqsū. Akmola, N Kazakhstan 52.31N 72.00E
151 T8 **Aksu** *var.* Jermak, *Kaz.* Ermak; *prev.* Yermak. Pavlodar, NE Kazakhstan 52.03N 76.55E
151 W13 **Aksu** *Kaz.* Aqsū. Almaty, SE Kazakhstan 45.31N 79.28E
151 V13 **Aksu** *Kaz.* Aqsū. ≈ SE Kazakhstan
151 X11 **Aksuat** *Kaz.* Aqsūat. Vostochnyy Kazakhstan, E Kazakhstan 47.46N 82.49E
151 Y11 **Aksuat** *Kaz.* Aqsūat. Vostochnyy Kazakhstan, SE Kazakhstan 48.16N 83.39E
131 S4 **Aksubayevo** Respublika Tatarstan, W Russian Federation 54.52N 50.50E
164 H7 **Aksu He** *Rus.* Sary-Dzhaz. ≈ China/Kyrgyzstan *see also* Sary-Dzhaz
82 J10 **Āksum** Tigray, N Ethiopia 14.06N 38.42E
151 O12 **Aktas** *Kaz.* Aqtas. Karaganda, C Kazakhstan 48.03N 66.21E
Aktash see Oqtosh
153 V9 **Ak-Tash, Gora** ▲ C Kyrgyzstan 40.53N 74.39E
151 R10 **Aktau** *Kaz.* Aqtaū. Karaganda, C Kazakhstan 50.13N 73.06E
150 E11 **Aktau** *Kaz.* Aqtaū; *prev.* Shevchenko. Mangistau, W Kazakhstan 43.37N 51.13E
Aktau, Khrebet see Oqtogh, SW Tajikistan
Aktau, Khrebet see Oqtov Tizmasi, C Uzbekistan
Akte see Ágion Óros
Ak-Tepe see Akdepe
153 X7 **Ak-Terek** Issyk-Kul'skaya Oblast', E Kyrgyzstan 42.14N 77.46E
Aktí see Ágion Óros
164 E8 **Akto** Xinjiang Uygur Zizhiqu, NW China 39.07N 75.43E
150 I10 **Aktobe** *Kaz.* Aqtöbe, *prev.* Aktyubinsk. Aktyubinsk, NW Kazakhstan 50.18N 57.09E
151 V12 **Aktogay** *Kaz.* Aqtoghay. Vostochnyy Kazakhstan, E Kazakhstan 46.56N 79.40E
121 M18 **Aktsyabrski** *Rus.* Oktyabr'skiy; *prev.* Karpilovka. Homyel'skaya Voblasts', SE Belarus 52.37N 28.52E
Aktyubinsk see Aktobe
150 H11 **Aktyubinsk** *off.* Aktyubinskaya Oblast', *Kaz.* Aqtöbe Oblysy. ◈ *province* W Kazakhstan
Aktyubinsk see Aktobe
153 W7 **Ak-Tyuz** *var.* Aktyuz. Chuyskaya Oblast', N Kyrgyzstan 42.50N 76.05E
81 J17 **Akula** Equateur, NW Dem. Rep. Congo 2.21N 20.13E
170 Bb15 **Akune** Kagoshima, Kyūshū, SW Japan 31.59N 130.11E
40 L16 **Akun Island** *island* Aleutian Islands, Alaska, USA
82 J9 **Akurdet** *var.* Agordat, Akordat. C Eritrea 15.33N 38.01E
79 T16 **Akure** Ondo, SW Nigeria 7.18N 5.12E
94 J2 **Akureyri** Nordhurland Eystra, N Iceland 65.40N 18.06W
40 L17 **Akutan** Akutan Island, Alaska, USA 54.08N 165.47W
40 K17 **Akutan Island** *island* Aleutian Islands, Alaska, USA
79 V17 **Akwa Ibom** ◈ *state* SE Nigeria
Akyab see Sittwe
131 W7 **Ak"yar** Respublika Bashkortostan, W Russian Federation 51.51N 58.13E
150 J10 **Akzhar** *prev.* Novorossiyskiy, Novorossiyskoye. Aktyubinsk, NW Kazakhstan 50.13N 57.57E
151 Y11 **Akzhar** *Kaz.* Aqzhar. Vostochnyy Kazakhstan, E Kazakhstan 47.36N 83.37E
96 F13 **Ål** Buskerud, S Norway 60.37N 8.33E
121 N18 **Ala** *Rus.* Ola. ≈ SE Belarus
22 H11 **Alabama** *off.* State of Alabama; also known as Camellia State, Heart of Dixie, The Cotton State, Yellowhammer State. ◈ *state* S USA
25 P6 **Alabama River** ≈ Alabama, S USA
25 P4 **Alabaster** Alabama, S USA 33.14N 86.49W
145 U10 **Al 'Abd Allāh** *var.* Al Abdullah. S Iraq 32.06N 45.08E
Al Abdullah see Al 'Abd Allāh
145 W14 **Al Abṭīyah** *well* S Iraq 29.27N 45.56E
153 S9 **Ala-Buka** Dzhalal-Abadskaya Oblast', W Kyrgyzstan 41.22N 71.27E
194 K15 **Alabule** ≈ C PNG
142 J12 **Alaca** Çorum, N Turkey 40.10N 34.52E
142 K10 **Alaçam** Samsun, N Turkey 41.35N 35.37E
Alacant see Alicante
25 V9 **Alachua** Florida, SE USA 29.48N 82.29W
143 S13 **Aladağlar** ⛰ W Turkey
142 K15 **Ala Dağları** ⛰ C Turkey
168 I5 **Alag-Erdene** *var.* Manhan. Hövsgöl, N Mongolia 50.05N 100.01E
131 O16 **Alagir** Respublika Severnaya Osetiya, SW Russian Federation 43.02N 44.10E
108 B6 **Alagna Valsesia** Valle d'Aosta, NW Italy 45.51N 7.50E
105 P12 **Alagnon** ≈ C France
61 P16 **Alagoas** *off.* Estado de Alagoas. ◈ *state* E Brazil
61 P17 **Alagoinhas** Bahia, E Brazil 12.09S 38.21W
107 R5 **Alagón** Aragón, NE Spain 41.46N 1.07W
106 J9 **Alagón** ≈ W Spain
95 K16 **Alahärmä** Länsi-Suomi, W Finland 63.15N 22.49E
al Ahdar see Al Akhḑar
Álaheaieatnu see Altaelva
148 K12 **Al Aḩmadī** *var.* Ahmadi. E Kuwait 29.02N 48.01E
Al Ain see Al 'Ayn
107 Z8 **Alaior** *prev.* Alayor. Menorca, Spain, W Mediterranean Sea 39.55N 4.07E
153 T11 **Alai Range** *Rus.* Alayskiy Khrebet. ⛰ Kyrgyzstan/Tajikistan
Alais see Alès
147 X11 **Al 'Ajā'iz** E Oman 19.33N 57.12E
147 X11 **Al 'Ajā'iz** *oasis* SE Oman 19.40N 57.13E
95 L16 **Alajärvi** Länsi-Suomi, W Finland 63.00N 23.50E
120 K4 **Alajõe** Ida-Virumaa, NE Estonia 59.00N 27.26E
44 M13 **Alajuela** Alajuela, C Costa Rica 10.00N 84.12W
44 L12 **Alajuela** *off.* Provincia de Alajuela. ◈ *province* N Costa Rica
45 T14 **Alajuela, Lago** ◎ C Panama
40 M11 **Alakanuk** Alaska, USA 62.41N 164.37W
146 K5 **Al Akhḑar** *var.* al Ahdar. Tabūk, NW Saudi Arabia 28.04N 37.13E
Alaköl see Alakol', Ozero
151 X13 **Alakol', Ozero** *Kaz.* Alaköl. ◎ SE Kazakhstan
128 I5 **Alakurtti** Murmanskaya Oblast', NW Russian Federation 66.57N 30.27E
40 F10 **'Alalākeiki Channel** *var.* Alalakeiki Channel *channel* Hawai'i, USA, C Pacific Ocean
Al 'Alamayn see El 'Alamein
145 R1 **Al 'Amādīyah** N Iraq 37.09N 43.27E
196 K5 **Alamagan** *island* C Northern Mariana Islands
145 X10 **Al 'Amārah** *var.* Amara. E Iraq 31.51N 47.10E
82 J11 **Ālamat'ā** Tigray, N Ethiopia 12.22N 39.32E
39 R11 **Alameda** New Mexico, SW USA 35.09N 106.37W
124 Pp15 **'Alam el Rûm, Râs** *headland* N Egypt 31.21N 27.23E
Alamícamba see Alamikamba
44 M8 **Alamikamba** *var.* Alamícamba. Región Autónoma Atlántico Norte, NE Nicaragua 13.29N 84.17W
26 K11 **Alamito Creek** ≈ Texas, SW USA
42 M8 **Alamitos, Sierra de los** ▲ NE Mexico 26.15N 102.14W
37 X9 **Alamo** Nevada, W USA 37.21N 115.07W
22 F9 **Alamo** Tennessee, S USA 35.46N 89.07W
43 Q12 **Álamo** Veracruz-Llave, C Mexico 20.55N 97.40W
39 S14 **Alamogordo** New Mexico, SW USA 32.52N 105.57W
38 J12 **Alamo Lake** ▣ Arizona, SW USA
42 H7 **Alamos** Sonora, NW Mexico 26.59N 108.53W
39 S7 **Alamosa** Colorado, C USA 37.25N 105.51W
95 J20 **Åland** *var.* Aland Islands, *Fin.* Ahvenanmaa. ◈ *province* SW Finland
95 J19 **Åland** *Fin.* Ahvenanmaa. *island* SW Finland
90 K9 **Åland** *var.* Aland Islands, *Fin.* Ahvenanmaa. *island group* SW Finland
Aland Islands see Åland
Aland Sea see Ålands Hav
97 Q14 **Ålands Hav** *var.* Aland Sea. *strait* Baltic Sea/Gulf of Bothnia
45 P16 **Alanje** Chiriquí, SW Panama 8.22N 82.36W
27 O2 **Alanreed** Texas, SW USA 35.12N 100.45W
142 G17 **Alanya** Antalya, S Turkey 36.31N 32.01E
25 U7 **Alapaha River** ≈ Florida/Georgia, SE USA
125 Ee11 **Alapayevsk** Sverdlovskaya Oblast', C Russian Federation 57.48N 61.50E
Alappuzha see Alleppey
144 F14 **Al 'Aqabah** *var.* Akaba, Aqaba, 'Aqaba; *anc.* Aelana, Elath. Al 'Aqabah, SW Jordan 29.32N 35.00E
144 G14 **Al 'Aqabah** *off.* Muḩāfaẓat Al 'Aqabah. ◈ *governorate* SW Jordan
Al 'Arabīyah as Su'ūdīyah see Saudi Arabia
al Araïch see Larache
107 Q10 **Alarcón** Castilla-La Mancha, C Spain 39.33N 2.04W
107 Q9 **Alarcón, Embalse de** ▣ C Spain
144 J2 **Al 'Arīmah** *Fr.* Arime. Ḩalab, N Syria 36.27N 37.41E
Al 'Arīsh see El 'Arîsh
147 P6 **Al Arṭāwīyah** Ar Riyāḑ, N Saudi Arabia 26.33N 45.19E
175 O16 **Alas** Sumbawa, S Indonesia 8.27S 117.04E
Alasca, Golfo de see Alaska, Gulf of
142 D14 **Alaşehir** Manisa, W Turkey 38.19N 28.30E
145 N5 **Al 'Ashārah** *var.* Ashara. Dayr az Zawr, E Syria 34.51N 40.36E
Al 'Āṣimah see 'Ammān
Al Ashkhara see Al Ashkharah
147 Z9 **Al Ashkharah** *var.* Al Ashkhara. NE Oman 21.46N 59.30E
41 P8 **Alaska** *off.* State of Alaska; also known as Land of the Midnight Sun, The Last Frontier, Seward's Folly; *prev.* Russian America. ◈ *state* NW USA
41 T13 **Alaska, Gulf of** *var.* Golfo de Alasca. *gulf* Canada/USA
41 O15 **Alaska Peninsula** *peninsula* Alaska, USA
41 Q11 **Alaska Range** ⛰ Alaska, USA
173 Ee4 **Alas, Lae** ≈ Sumatera, NW Indonesia
Al-Asnam see Chlef
175 O16 **Alas, Selat** *strait* Nusa Tenggara, C Indonesia
108 B10 **Alassio** Liguria, NW Italy 44.01N 8.12E
Alat see Olot
143 Y12 **Älät** *Rus.* Alyat; *prev.* Alyaty-Pristan'. SE Azerbaijan 39.57N 49.24E
145 S13 **Al 'Athāmīn** S Iraq 30.27N 43.40E
41 P7 **Alatna River** ≈ Alaska, USA
109 J15 **Alatri** Lazio, C Italy 41.43N 13.21E
Alattio see Alta
131 P5 **Alatyr'** Chavash Respubliki, W Russian Federation 54.50N 46.28E
58 C7 **Alausí** Chimborazo, C Ecuador 2.07S 78.44W
107 O3 **Álava** *Basq.* Araba. ◈ *province* País Vasco, N Spain
143 T11 **Alaverdi** N Armeni 41.06N 44.37E
Alavo see Alavus
95 N14 **Ala-Vuokki** Oulu, E Finland 64.46N 29.29E
95 K17 **Alavus** *Swe.* Alavo. Länsi-Suomi, W Finland 62.33N 23.37E
Al 'Awābī see Awābī
145 P6 **Al 'Awānī** W Iraq 34.28N 41.43E
Al Awaynāt see Al 'Uwaynāt
190 K9 **Alawoona** South Australia 34.45S 140.28E
Alaykel'/Alay-Kuu see Këk-Art
149 R17 **Al 'Ayn** *var.* Al Ain. Abū Ẓaby, E UAE 24.13N 55.44E
149 R17 **Al 'Ayn** *var.* Al Ain. ✕ Abū Ẓaby, E UAE 24.16N 55.31E
144 G12 **Al 'Aynā** Al Karak, W Jordan 30.59N 35.43E
Alayor see Alaior
Alayskiy Khrebet see Alai Range
127 N7 **Alazeya** ≈ NE Russian Federation
145 U8 **Al 'Azīzīyah** *var.* Aziziya. E Iraq 32.54N 45.05E
123 L14 **Al 'Azīzīyah** NW Libya 32.31N 13.01E
144 I10 **Al Azraq al Janūbī** Az Zarqā', N Jordan 31.49N 36.48E
108 B9 **Alba** *anc.* Alba Pompeia. Piemonte, NW Italy 44.40N 8.01E
27 V6 **Alba** Texas, SW USA 32.47N 95.37W
118 G11 **Alba** ◈ *county* W Romania
145 P3 **Al Ba'āj** N Iraq 36.02N 41.43E
144 J2 **Al Bāb** Ḩalab, N Syria 36.24N 37.31E
118 G10 **Albac** *Hung.* Fehérvölgy; *prev.* Álbák. Alba, SW Romania 46.25N 22.58E
107 Q11 **Albacete** Castilla-La Mancha, C Spain 39.00N 1.52W
107 P11 **Albacete** ◈ *province* Castilla-La Mancha, C Spain
146 I4 **Al Bad'** Tabūk, NW Saudi Arabia 28.28N 35.00E
106 L7 **Alba de Tormes** Castilla-León, N Spain 40.49N 5.30W
145 P3 **Al Bādī** N Iraq 35.57N 41.37E
147 V8 **Al Badī'ah** ✕ (Abū Ẓaby) Abū Ẓaby, C UAE 24.27N 54.39E
149 P17 **Al Badī'ah** *var.* Al Bedei'ah. *spring/well* C UAE 23.44N 53.50E
145 Q7 **Al Baghdādī** *var.* Khān al Baghdādī. SW Iraq 33.19N 44.22E
Al Bāha see Al Bāḩah
146 M11 **Al Bāḩah** *var.* Al Bāha. Al Bāḩah, SW Saudi Arabia 20.00N 41.29E
146 M11 **Al Bāḩah** *off.* Minṭaqat al Bāḩah. ◈ *province* W Saudi Arabia
Al Baḩrayn see Bahrain
107 S11 **Albaida** País Valenciano, E Spain 38.51N 0.31W
118 H11 **Alba Iulia** *Ger.* Weissenburg, *Hung.* Gyulafehérvár; *prev.* Bălgrad, Karlsburg, Károly-Fehérvár. Alba, W Romania 46.06N 23.33E
Álbák see Albac
144 G10 **Al Balqā'** *off.* Muḩāfaẓat al Balqā', *var.* Balqā'. ◈ *governorate* NW Jordan
12 F11 **Alban** Ontario, S Canada 46.07N 80.37W
105 O15 **Alban** Tarn, S France 43.52N 2.30E
10 K11 **Albanel, Lac** ◎ Québec, SE Canada
115 L20 **Albania** *off.* Republic of Albania, *Alb.* Republika e Shqipërisë, Shqipëria; *prev.* People's Socialist Republic of Albania. ◆ *republic* SE Europe
Albania see Aubagne
109 H15 **Albano Laziale** Lazio, C Italy 41.43N 12.40E
188 J14 **Albany** Western Australia 35.03S 117.54E
25 S7 **Albany** Georgia, SE USA 31.34N 84.09W
33 P13 **Albany** Indiana, N USA 40.18N 85.14W
22 L8 **Albany** Kentucky, S USA 36.41N 85.07W
31 U7 **Albany** Minnesota, N USA 45.39N 94.33W
29 R2 **Albany** Missouri, C USA 40.15N 94.15W
20 L10 **Albany** *state capital* New York, NE USA 42.39N 73.45W
34 G12 **Albany** Oregon, NW USA 44.38N 123.06W
27 Q6 **Albany** Texas, SW USA 32.43N 99.18W
10 F10 **Albany** ≈ Ontario, S Canada
Alba Pompeia see Alba
Alba Regia see Székesfehérvár
144 J6 **Al Bāridah** *var.* Bāridah. Ḩimş, C Syria 34.15N 37.39E
145 Q11 **Al Barīt** S Iraq 31.16N 42.28E
107 R8 **Albarracín** Aragón, NE Spain 40.24N 1.25W
145 Y12 **Al Baṣrah** *Eng.* Basra; *hist.* Busra, Bussora. SE Iraq 30.30N 47.49E
145 V11 **Al Baṭḩā'** SE Iraq 31.06N 45.49E
147 X8 **Al Bāṭinah** *var.* Batinah. *coastal region* N Oman
(0) H16 **Albatross Plateau** *undersea feature* E Pacific Ocean
Al Batrūn see Batroûn
124 Nn14 **Al Bayḑā'** *var.* Beida. NE Libya 32.46N 21.43E
147 P16 **Al Bayḑā'** *var.* Al Beida. SW Yemen 13.58N 45.38E
Al Bedei'ah see Al Badī'ah
Al Beida see Al Bayḑā'
23 S10 **Albemarle** *var.* Albermarle. North Carolina, SE USA 35.21N 80.12W
Albemarle Island see Isabela, Isla
23 N8 **Albemarle Sound** *inlet* W Atlantic Ocean
108 B10 **Albenga** Liguria, NW Italy 44.04N 8.13E
106 L8 **Alberche** ≈ C Spain
105 O17 **Albères, Chaîne des** *var.* les Albères, Montes Albères. ⛰ France/Spain
Albères, Montes see Albères, Chaîne des
190 F2 **Alberga Creek** *seasonal river* South Australia
106 G7 **Albergaria-a-Velha** Aveiro, N Portugal 40.42N 8.28W
107 S10 **Alberic** País Valenciano, E Spain 39.07N 0.31W
Albermarle see Albemarle
109 P18 **Alberobello** Puglia, SE Italy 40.47N 17.14E
110 J7 **Alberschwende** Vorarlberg, W Austria 47.28N 9.49E
105 O3 **Albert** Somme, N France 50.00N 2.37E
9 O12 **Alberta** ◈ *province* SW Canada
194 K14 **Albert Edward, Mount** ▲ S PNG 8.23S 147.23E
Albert Edward Nyanza see Edward, Lake
63 C20 **Alberti** Buenos Aires, E Argentina 35.03S 60.15W
113 K23 **Albertirsa** Pest, C Hungary 47.15N 19.36E
101 I16 **Albertkanaal** *canal* N Belgium
81 P17 **Albert, Lake** *var.* Albert Nyanza, Lac Mobutu Sese Seko. ◎ Uganda/Dem. Rep. Congo
31 V11 **Albert Lea** Minnesota, N USA 43.39N 93.22W
83 F16 **Albert Nile** ≈ NW Uganda
Albert Nyanza see Albert, Lake
105 T11 **Albertville** Savoie, E France 45.41N 6.24E
25 Q2 **Albertville** Alabama, S USA 34.16N 86.12W
Albertville see Kalemie
105 N15 **Albi** *anc.* Albiga. Tarn, S France 43.55N 2.09E
31 W15 **Albia** Iowa, C USA 41.01N 92.48W
Albiga see Albi
57 X9 **Albina** Marowijne, NE Surinam 5.31N 54.04W
85 A15 **Albina, Ponta** *headland* SW Angola 15.52S 11.45E
32 M16 **Albion** Illinois, N USA 38.22N 88.03W
33 P11 **Albion** Indiana, N USA 41.22N 85.23W
31 P14 **Albion** Nebraska, C USA 41.41N 98.00W
20 E9 **Albion** New York, NE USA 43.13N 78.09W
20 B12 **Albion** Pennsylvania, NE USA 41.52N 80.18W
Al Biqā' see El Beqaa
146 J4 **Al Bi'r** *var.* Bi'r Ibn Hirmās. Tabūk, NW Saudi Arabia 28.52N 36.16E
146 M12 **Al Birk** Makkah, SW Saudi Arabia 18.12N 41.36E
147 Q9 **Al Biyāḑ** *desert* C Saudi Arabia
100 H13 **Alblasserdam** Zuid-Holland, SW Netherlands 51.52N 4.40E
Albocácer see Albocàsser
107 T8 **Albocàsser** *Cast.* Albocácer. País Valenciano, E Spain 40.21N 0.01E
97 H19 **Ålbæk** Nordjylland, N Denmark 57.33N 10.24E
Albona see Labin
107 O17 **Alborán, Isla de** *island* S Spain
Alborán, Mar de see Alboran Sea
107 N17 **Alboran Sea** *Sp.* Mar de Alborán. *sea* SW Mediterranean Sea
Ålborg see Aalborg
97 H21 **Ålborg Bugt** *var.* Aalborg Bugt. *bay* N Denmark
Ålborg-Nørresundby see Aalborg
149 O5 **Alborz, Reshteh-ye Kūhhā-ye** *Eng.* Elburz Mountains. ⛰ N Iran
107 Q14 **Albox** Andalucía, S Spain 37.22N 2.08W
103 H23 **Albstadt** Baden-Württemberg, SW Germany 48.13N 9.01E
106 G14 **Albufeira** Beja, S Portugal 37.04N 8.15W
145 P5 **Ālbū Gharz, Sabkhat** ◎ W Iraq
107 O15 **Albuñol** Andalucía, S Spain 36.48N 3.10W
39 Q11 **Albuquerque** New Mexico, SW USA 35.04N 106.37W
147 W8 **Al Buraymī** *var.* Buraimi. N Oman 24.16N 55.48E
149 R17 **Al Buraymī** *var.* Buraimi. *spring/well* Oman/UAE 24.27N 55.33E
Al Burayqah see Marsá al Burayqah
Alburgum see Aalborg
106 I10 **Alburquerque** Extremadura, W Spain 39.12N 7.00W
189 V14 **Albury** New South Wales, SE Australia 36.03S 146.52E
147 T14 **Al Buzūn** SE Yemen 15.40N 50.53E
95 G17 **Alby** Västernorrland, C Sweden 62.30N 15.25E
Albyn, Glen see Mor, Glen
106 G12 **Alcácer do Sal** Setúbal, W Portugal 38.21N 8.29W
Alcalá de Chisvert/Alcalá de Chivert see Alcalà de Xivert
106 K14 **Alcalá de Guadaira** Andalucía, S Spain 37.19N 5.49W
107 O8 **Alcalá de Henares** *Ar.* Alkal'a; *anc.* Complutum. Madrid, C Spain 40.28N 3.22W
106 K16 **Alcalá de los Gazules** Andalucía, S Spain 36.28N 5.43W
107 T8 **Alcalà de Xivert** *var.* Alcalá de Chisvert, *Cast.* Alcalá de Chivert. País Valenciano, E Spain 40.19N 0.13E
107 N14 **Alcalá La Real** Andalucía, S Spain 37.28N 3.55W
109 I23 **Alcamo** Sicilia, Italy, C Mediterranean Sea 37.58N 12.58E
107 T4 **Alcanadre** ≈ NE Spain
107 T8 **Alcanar** Cataluña, NE Spain 40.33N 0.28E
106 J5 **Alcañices** Castilla-León, N Spain 41.40N 6.21W
107 T7 **Alcañiz** Aragón, NE Spain 41.03N 0.09W
106 I9 **Alcántara** Extremadura, W Spain 39.42N 6.54W
106 J9 **Alcántara, Embalse de** ▣ W Spain
107 R13 **Alcantarilla** Murcia, SE Spain 37.58N 1.12W
107 P11 **Alcaraz** Castilla-La Mancha, C Spain 38.40N 2.28W
107 P12 **Alcaraz, Sierra de** ⛰ C Spain
106 I12 **Alcarrache** ≈ SW Spain
107 T6 **Alcarràs** Cataluña, NE Spain 41.34N 0.31E
107 N14 **Alcaudete** Andalucía, S Spain 37.34N 4.04W
Alcázar see Ksar-el-Kebir
107 O10 **Alcázar de San Juan** *anc.* Alce. Castilla-La Mancha, C Spain 39.24N 3.12W
Alcazarquivir see Ksar-el-Kebir
Alce see Alcázar de San Juan
59 B17 **Alcebo, Volcán** △ Galapagos Islands, Ecuador, E Pacific Ocean 0.25S 91.06W
145 X12 **Al Chabā'ish** *var.* Al Kaba'ish. SE Iraq 30.58N 47.01E
119 Y7 **Alchevs'k** *prev.* Kommunarsk, Voroshilovsk. Luhans'ka Oblast', E Ukraine 48.29N 38.52E
Alcira see Alzira
23 N9 **Alcoa** Tennessee, S USA 35.47N 83.58W
106 F9 **Alcobaça** Leiria, C Portugal 39.31N 8.58W
107 N8 **Alcobendas** Madrid, C Spain 40.31N 3.37W
Alcoi see Alcoy
107 P7 **Alcolea del Pinar** Castilla-La Mancha, C Spain 41.01N 2.28W
106 I11 **Alconchel** Extremadura, W Spain 38.31N 7.04W
Alcora see L'Alcora
107 N8 **Alcorcón** Madrid, C Spain 40.20N 3.52W
107 S7 **Alcorisa** Aragón, NE Spain 40.52N 0.22W
63 B19 **Alcorta** Santa Fe, C Argentina 33.31S 61.07W
106 H14 **Alcoutim** Faro, S Portugal 37.28N 7.28W
35 W15 **Alcova** Wyoming, C USA 42.33N 106.40W
107 S11 **Alcoy** *Cat.* Alcoi. País Valenciano, E Spain 38.42N 0.28W

◆ Country ● Country Capital ◇ Dependent Territory ○ Dependent Territory Capital ◈ Administrative Region ✕ International Airport ▲ Mountain ⛰ Mountain Range △ Volcano ≈ River ◎ Lake ▣ Reservoir
221

Alcúdia – Alpha

107 Y9 **Alcúdia** Mallorca, Spain, W Mediterranean Sea 39.52N 3.07E
107 Y9 **Alcúdia, Badia d'** bay Mallorca, Spain, W Mediterranean Sea
180 M7 **Aldabra Group** island group SW Seychelles
145 U10 **Al Daghghārah** C Iraq 32.10N 44.57E
42 J5 **Aldama** Chihuahua, N Mexico 28.49N 105.52W
43 P11 **Aldama** Tamaulipas, C Mexico 22.55N 98.03W
126 Ll12 **Aldan** Respublika Sakha (Yakutiya), NE Russian Federation 58.31N 125.15E
126 Mm12 **Aldan** ≈ NE Russian Federation
Aldar see Aldarhaan
al Dar al Baida see Rabat
168 G7 **Aldarhaan** var. Aldar. Dzavhan, W Mongolia 47.43N 96.36E
99 Q20 **Aldeburgh** E England, UK 52.12N 1.35E
107 P5 **Aldehuela de Calatañazor** Castilla-León, N Spain 41.42N 2.46W
Aldeia Nova see Aldeia Nova de São Bento
106 H13 **Aldeia Nova de São Bento** var. Aldeia Nova. Beja, S Portugal 37.55N 7.24W
31 V11 **Alden** Minnesota, N USA 43.40N 93.34W
192 N6 **Aldermen Islands, The** island group N NZ
99 L25 **Alderney** island Channel Islands
99 N22 **Aldershot** S England, UK 51.15N 0.46W
23 R6 **Alderson** West Virginia, NE USA 37.43N 80.38W
Al Dhaid see Adh Dhayd
32 J11 **Aledo** Illinois, N USA 41.12N 90.45W
78 H9 **Aleg** Brakna, SW Mauritania 17.03N 13.52W
66 Q10 **Alegranza** island Islas Canarias, Spain, NE Atlantic Ocean
39 P12 **Alegres Mountain** ▲ New Mexico, SW USA 34.09N 108.11W
63 F15 **Alegrete** Rio Grande do Sul, S Brazil 29.46S 55.46W
63 C16 **Alejandra** Santa Fe, C Argentina 29.54S 59.49W
200 Oo12 **Alejandro Selkirk, Isla** island Islas Juan Fernández, Chile, E Pacific Ocean
128 I12 **Alekhovshchina** Leningradskaya Oblast', NW Russian Federation 60.22N 33.57E
41 O13 **Aleknagik** Alaska, USA 59.16N 158.37W
Aleksandriya see Oleksandriya
Aleksandropol' see Gyumri
130 L3 **Aleksandrov** Vladimirskaya Oblast', W Russian Federation 56.24N 38.42E
115 N14 **Aleksandrovac** Serbia, C Serbia 43.28N 21.05E
131 R9 **Aleksandrov Gay** Saratovskaya Oblast', W Russian Federation 50.08N 48.34E
131 U6 **Aleksandrovka** Orenburgskaya Oblast', W Russian Federation 52.47N 54.14E
Aleksandrovka see Oleksandrivka
116 J8 **Aleksandrovo** Lovech, N Bulgaria 43.16N 24.53E
129 V13 **Aleksandrovsk** Permskaya Oblast', NW Russian Federation 59.12N 57.27E
Aleksandrovsk see Zaporizhzhya
131 N14 **Aleksandrovskoye** Stavropol'skiy Kray, SW Russian Federation 44.43N 42.56E
127 O14 **Aleksandrovsk-Sakhalinskiy** Ostrov Sakhalin, Sakhalinskaya Oblast', SE Russian Federation 50.55N 142.12E
112 J10 **Aleksandrów Kujawski** Kujawskio-pomorskie, C Poland 52.51N 18.42E
112 K12 **Aleksandrów Łódzki** Łódzkie, C Poland 51.48N 19.18E
Alekseevka see Terekty
130 L9 **Alekseyevka** Belgorodskaya Oblast', W Russian Federation 50.35N 38.41E
151 P7 **Alekseyevka** Kaz. Alekseevka. Akmola, N Kazakhstan 53.31N 69.30E
131 S7 **Alekseyevka** Samarskaya Oblast', W Russian Federation 52.37N 51.20E
Alekseyevka see Akkol', Akmola, Kazakhstan
Alekseyevka see Terekty, Vostochnyy Kazakhstan, Kazakhstan
126 Jj13 **Alekseyevsk** Irkutskaya Oblast', C Russian Federation 57.46N 108.07E
131 R4 **Alekseyevskoye** Respublika Tatarstan, W Russian Federation 55.18N 50.11E
130 K5 **Aleksin** Tul'skaya Oblast', W Russian Federation 54.30N 37.07E
115 O14 **Aleksinac** Serbia, SE Serbia 43.33N 21.43E
202 G11 **Alele** Île Uvea, E Wallis and Futuna 13.13S 176.09W
97 N20 **Ålem** Kalmar, S Sweden 56.57N 16.25E
104 L6 **Alençon** Orne, N France 48.25N 0.04E
60 I12 **Alenquer** Pará, NE Brazil 1.58S 54.45W
40 G10 **'Alenuihāhā Channel** var. Alenuihaha Channel channel Hawai'i, USA, C Pacific Ocean
Alep/Aleppo see Ḩalab
105 Y15 **Aléria** Corse, France, C Mediterranean Sea 42.06N 9.29E
207 Q11 **Alert** Ellesmere Island, Nunavut, N Canada 82.28N 62.13W
105 Q14 **Alès** prev. Alais. Gard, S France 44.07N 4.04E
118 G9 **Aleşd** Hung. Élesd. Bihor, SW Romania 47.03N 22.22E
108 C9 **Alessandria** Fr. Alexandrie. Piemonte, N Italy 44.54N 8.37E
Ålestrup see Aalestrup
96 D9 **Ålesund** Møre og Romsdal, S Norway 62.28N 6.10E
110 E10 **Aletschhorn** ▲ SW Switzerland 46.33N 8.01E
207 S1 **Aleutian Basin** undersea feature Bering Sea
40 H17 **Aleutian Islands** island group Alaska, USA
41 P14 **Aleutian Range** ⛰ Alaska, USA
(0) B5 **Aleutian Trench** undersea feature S Bering Sea
127 O10 **Alevina, Mys** headland E Russian Federation 58.52N 151.21E
13 Q6 **Alex** ≈ Québec, SE Canada
30 J3 **Alexander** North Dakota, N USA 47.48N 103.38W
41 W14 **Alexander Archipelago** island group Alaska, USA
Alexanderbaai see Alexander Bay
85 D23 **Alexander Bay** Afr. Alexanderbaai. Northern Cape, W South Africa 28.35S 16.30E
25 Q5 **Alexander City** Alabama, S USA 32.56N 85.57W
204 J6 **Alexander Island** island Antarctica
Alexander Range see Kirghiz Range
191 O12 **Alexandra** Victoria, SE Australia 37.12S 145.43E
193 D22 **Alexandra** Otago, South Island, NZ 45.15S 169.24E
117 F14 **Alexándreia** var. Alexándria. Kentrikí Makedonía, N Greece 40.38N 22.27E
Alexandretta see İskenderun
Alexandretta, Gulf of see İskenderun Körfezi
13 N13 **Alexandria** Ontario, SE Canada 45.19N 74.37W
124 Q15 **Alexandria** Ar. Al Iskandarīyah. N Egypt 31.07N 29.51E
46 J12 **Alexandria** C Jamaica 18.18N 77.21W
118 J15 **Alexandria** Teleorman, S Romania 43.58N 25.18E
33 P13 **Alexandria** Indiana, N USA 40.15N 85.40W
22 M4 **Alexandria** Kentucky, S USA 38.56N 84.21W
24 H7 **Alexandria** Louisiana, S USA 31.18N 92.27W
31 T7 **Alexandria** Minnesota, N USA 45.54N 95.22W
31 Q11 **Alexandria** South Dakota, N USA 43.39N 97.46W
23 W4 **Alexandria** Virginia, NE USA 38.48N 77.03W
Alexándria see Alexándreia
20 I7 **Alexandria Bay** New York, NE USA 44.20N 75.54W
Alexandrie see Alessandria
190 J10 **Alexandrina, Lake** ◎ South Australia
116 K13 **Alexandroúpoli** var. Alexandroúpolis, Turk. Dedeagaç, Dedeagach. Anatolikí Makedonía kai Thráki, NE Greece 40.51N 25.52E
Alexandroúpolis see Alexandroúpoli
8 L15 **Alexis Creek** British Columbia, SW Canada 52.06N 123.25W
126 Gg15 **Aleysk** Altayskiy Kray, S Russian Federation 52.32N 82.46E
8 L15 **Alexis Creek** British Columbia, SW Canada 52.06N 123.25W
126 Gg15 **Aleysk** Altayskiy Kray, S Russian Federation 52.32N 82.46E
145 S8 **Al Fallūjah** var. Falluja. C Iraq 33.21N 43.46E
107 R8 **Alfambra** ≈ E Spain
Al Faqa see Faq'
147 R15 **Al Farḑah** C Yemen 14.51N 48.33E
107 Q4 **Alfaro** La Rioja, N Spain 42.09N 1.46W
107 U5 **Alfarràs** Cataluña, NE Spain 41.49N 0.34E
Al Fāshir see El Fasher
Al Fashn see El Fashn
116 M7 **Alfatar** Silistra, NE Bulgaria 43.56N 27.17E
145 S5 **Al Fatḩah** C Iraq 35.06N 43.34E
145 Q3 **Al Fatsī** N Iraq 36.04N 42.39E
145 Z13 **Al Fāw** var. Fao. SE Iraq 29.55N 48.25E
Al Fayyūm see El Faiyûm
117 D20 **Alfeiós** prev. Alfiós, anc. Alpheius, Alpheus. ≈ S Greece
102 I13 **Alfeld** Niedersachsen, C Germany 51.58N 9.49E
Alfiós see Alfeiós
Alföld see Great Hungarian Plain
96 C11 **Ålfotbreen** glacier S Norway
21 P9 **Alfred** Maine, NE USA 43.28N 70.43W
20 F11 **Alfred** New York, NE USA 42.15N 77.47W
63 K14 **Alfredo Vagner** Santa Catarina, S Brazil 27.40S 49.22W
96 M12 **Alfta** Gävleborg, C Sweden 61.19N 16.04E
146 K12 **Al Fuḩayḩīl** var. Fahaheel. SE Kuwait 29.01N 48.04E
145 Q6 **Al Fuḩaymī** C Iraq 34.17N 42.09E
149 S16 **Al Fujayrah** Eng. Fujairah. Al Fujayrah, NE UAE 25.09N 56.18E
149 S16 **Al Fujayrah** Eng. Fujairah. ✕ Al Fujayrah, NE UAE 25.04N 56.12E
Al Furāt see Euphrates
150 I10 **Alga** Kaz. Algha. Aktyubinsk, NW Kazakhstan 49.55N 57.19E
150 G9 **Algabas** Zapadnyy Kazakhstan, NW Kazakhstan 50.45N 52.07E
97 C17 **Ålgård** Rogaland, S Norway 58.45N 5.52E
106 G14 **Algarve** cultural region S Portugal
190 G3 **Algebuckina Bridge** South Australia 28.03S 135.48E
106 K16 **Algeciras** Andalucía, SW Spain 36.07N 5.27W
107 S10 **Algemesí** País Valenciano, E Spain 39.10N 0.27W
Al-Genain see El Geneina
123 I11 **Alger** var. Algiers, El Djazaïr, Al Jazair. ● (Algeria) N Algeria 36.47N 2.58E
76 H9 **Algeria** off. Democratic and Popular Republic of Algeria. ◆ republic N Africa
123 J9 **Algerian Basin** var. Balearic Plain undersea feature W Mediterranean Sea
Algha see Alga
144 I4 **Al Ghāb** ◎ NW Syria
147 X10 **Al Ghābah** var. Ghaba. C Oman 21.21N 57.13E
147 U14 **Al Ghayḑah** E Yemen 16.15N 52.13E
146 M6 **Al Ghazālah** Ḩā'il, NW Saudi Arabia 26.55N 41.23E
109 B17 **Alghero** Sardegna, Italy, C Mediterranean Sea 40.34N 8.19E
97 M20 **Älghult** Kronoberg, S Sweden 57.00N 15.34E
Al Ghurdaqah see Hurghada
Algiers see Alger
107 S10 **Alginet** País Valenciano, E Spain 39.13N 0.28W
85 I26 **Algoa Bay** bay S South Africa
106 L15 **Algodonales** Andalucía, S Spain 36.54N 5.24W
107 N9 **Algodor** ≈ C Spain
Al Golea see El Goléa
33 N6 **Algoma** Wisconsin, N USA 44.41N 87.24W
31 U12 **Algona** Iowa, C USA 43.04N 94.13W
22 L8 **Algood** Tennessee, S USA 36.12N 85.27W
107 O2 **Algorta** País Vasco, N Spain 43.20N 3.00W
63 E18 **Algorta** Río Negro, W Uruguay 32.21S 57.12W
Al Haba see Haba
145 Q10 **Al Habbārīyah** S Iraq 32.16N 42.12E
Al Hadhar see Al Ḩaḑr
145 Q4 **Al Ḩaḑr** var. Al Hadhar; anc. Hatra. NW Iraq 35.33N 42.43E
145 T13 **Al Ḩajarah** desert S Iraq
147 W8 **Al Ḩajār al Gharbī** ⛰ N Oman
147 Y8 **Al Ḩajar ash Sharqī** ⛰ NE Oman
147 R15 **Al Hajarayn** C Yemen 15.29N 48.24E
144 L10 **Al Ḩamād** desert Jordan/Saudi Arabia
Al Hamad see Syrian Desert
77 N9 **Al Ḩamādah al Ḩamrā'** var. Al Ḩamrā'. desert NW Libya
107 N15 **Alhama de Granada** Andalucía, S Spain 37.00N 3.58W
107 R13 **Alhama de Murcia** Murcia, SE Spain 37.51N 1.25W
37 T15 **Alhambra** California, W USA 34.07N 118.06W
145 T12 **Al Ḩammām** S Iraq 31.09N 44.04E
147 X8 **Al Ḩamrā'** NE Oman 23.07N 57.22E
Al Ḩamrā' see Al Ḩamādah al Ḩamrā'
147 O6 **Al Ḩamūdīyah** spring/well N Saudi Arabia 27.05N 44.24E
146 M7 **Al Ḩanākīyah** Al Madīnah, W Saudi Arabia 24.54N 40.31E
145 W14 **Al Ḩanīyah** escarpment Iraq/Saudi Arabia
145 Y12 **Al Hārithah** SE Iraq 30.43N 47.43E
146 L3 **Al Ḩarrah** desert NW Saudi Arabia
77 Q10 **Al Harūj al Aswad** desert C Libya
Al Hasaifin see Al Ḩusayfīn
145 N2 **Al Ḩasakah** var. Al Hasijah, El Haseke, Fr. Hassetché. Al Ḩasakah, NE Syria 36.22N 40.43E
145 O2 **Al Ḩasakah** off. Muḩāfaẓat al Ḩasakah, var. Al Hasakah, Āl Hasakah, Hasakah, Hassakeh. ◈ governorate NE Syria
145 T9 **Al Hāshimīyah** C Iraq 32.24N 44.39E
144 G13 **Al Hāshimīyah** Ma'ān, S Jordan 30.31N 35.46E
Al Hasijah see Al Ḩasakah
106 M15 **Alhaurín el Grande** Andalucía, S Spain 36.39N 4.40W
147 Q16 **Al Ḩawrā** S Yemen 13.54N 47.36E
145 V10 **Al Ḩayy** var. Kut al Hai, Kūt al Ḩayy. E Iraq 32.10N 46.03E
147 U11 **Al Ḩibāk** desert E Saudi Arabia
144 H8 **Al Hījānah** var. Hejanah, Hijanah. Dimashq, W Syria 33.23N 36.34E
146 K7 **Al Ḩijāz** Eng. Hejaz. physical region NW Saudi Arabia
Al Hilbeh see 'Ulayyānīyah, Bi'r al
145 T9 **Al Ḩillah** var. Hilla. C Iraq 32.28N 44.28E
145 T9 **Al Hindīyah** var. Hindiya. C Iraq 32.31N 44.13E
144 G12 **Al Ḩisā** Aţ Ţafilah, W Jordan 30.49N 35.58E
76 G5 **Al-Hoceïma** var. al Hoceima, Al-Hoceima, Alhucemas; prev. Villa Sanjurjo. N Morocco 35.13N 3.55W
Alhucemas see Al-Hoceïma
107 N17 **Alhucemas, Peñon de** island group S Spain
147 N15 **Al Ḩudaydah** Eng. Hodeida. W Yemen 15.00N 42.50E
147 N15 **Al Ḩudaydah** Eng. Hodeida. ✕ W Yemen 14.45N 43.01E
146 M4 **Al Ḩudūd ash Shamālīyah** var. Minţaqat al Ḩudūd ash Shamālīyah, Eng. Northern Border Region. ◈ province N Saudi Arabia
147 S7 **Al Hufūf** var. Hofuf. Ash Sharqīyah, NE Saudi Arabia 25.21N 49.33E
al-Hurma see Al Khurmah
147 X7 **Al Ḩusayfīn** var. Al Hasaifin. N Oman 24.33N 56.33E
144 G9 **Al Ḩuşn** var. Husn. Irbid, N Jordan 32.28N 35.52E
145 U9 **'Alī** E Iraq 32.43N 45.21E
106 L10 **Alia** Extremadura, W Spain 39.25N 5.12W
149 P9 **'Alīābād** Yazd, C Iran 36.55N 54.33E
'Alīābad see Qā'emshahr
107 S7 **Aliaga** Aragón, NE Spain 40.40N 0.42W
142 B13 **Aliağa** İzmir, W Turkey 38.49N 26.58E
Aliákmon see Aliákmonas
117 F14 **Aliákmonas** prev. Aliákmon, anc. Haliacmon. ≈ N Greece
145 W9 **'Alī al Gharbī** E Iraq 32.28N 46.42E
145 U11 **'Alī al Ḩassūnī** S Iraq 31.25N 44.50E
117 G18 **Alíartos** Stereá Ellás, C Greece 38.22N 23.06E
143 Y12 **Äli-Bayramlı** Rus. Ali-Bayramly. SE Azerbaijan 39.57N 48.54E
Ali-Bayramly see Äli-Bayramlı
116 P12 **Alibey Barajı** ⊠ NW Turkey
79 S13 **Alibori** ≈ N Benin
114 M10 **Alibunar** Serbia, NE Serbia 45.06N 20.59E
107 S12 **Alicante** Cat. Alacant; Lat. Lucentum. País Valenciano, SE Spain 38.21N 0.28W
107 S12 **Alicante** ◈ province País Valenciano, SE Spain
107 S12 **Alicante** ✕ Murcia, E Spain 38.21N 0.28W
85 I25 **Alice** Eastern Cape, S South Africa 32.49S 26.49E
27 S14 **Alice** Texas, SW USA 27.45N 98.04W
85 I25 **Alicedale** Eastern Cape, S South Africa 33.19S 26.04E
67 B25 **Alice, Mount** hill West Falkland, Falkland Islands
109 P20 **Alice, Punta** headland S Italy 39.24N 17.09E
189 Q7 **Alice Springs** Northern Territory, C Australia 23.42S 133.52E
25 N4 **Aliceville** Alabama, S USA 33.07N 88.09W
153 U13 **Alichur** SE Tajikistan 37.49N 73.45E
153 U14 **Alichuri Janubí, Qatorkŭhi** Rus. Yuzhno-Alichurskiy Khrebet. ⛰ SE Tajikistan
153 U13 **Alichuri Shimolí, Qatorkŭhi** Rus. Severo-Alichurskiy Khrebet. ⛰ SE Tajikistan
109 K22 **Alicudi, Isola** island Isole Eolie, S Italy
158 J11 **Alīgarh** Uttar Pradesh, N India 27.54N 78.04E
148 M7 **Alīgūdarz** Lorestān, W Iran 33.27N 49.33E
169 U5 **Alihe** var. Oroqen Zizhiqi. Nei Mongol Zizhiqu, N China 50.34N 123.40E
(0) F12 **Alijos, Islas** island group California, SW USA
155 R6 **'Alī Kbel** Pash. 'Alī Khēl. Paktīkā, E Afghanistan 33.55N 69.49E
Ali Khel see 'Alī Kheyl, Paktīā, Afghanistan
'Alī Khēl see 'Alī Kbel, Paktīkā, Afghanistan
155 R6 **'Alī Kheyl** var. Ali Khel, Jajı. Paktīā, SE Afghanistan 33.55N 69.46E
147 V17 **Al Ikhwān** island group SE Yemen
Aliki see Alykí
81 H19 **Alima** ≈ C Congo
Al Imārāt al 'Arabīyah al Muttaḩidah see United Arab Emirates
194 M12 **Alimbit** ≈ New Britain, C PNG
117 N23 **Alimía** island Dodekánisa, Greece, Aegean Sea
57 V12 **Alimimuni Piek** ▲ S Surinam 2.25N 55.46W
81 K15 **Alindao** Basse-Kotto, S Central African Republic 4.58N 21.16E
97 J18 **Alingsås** Västra Götaland, S Sweden 57.55N 12.30E
83 K18 **Alinjugul** spring/well E Kenya 0.03S 40.31E
155 S11 **Alīpur** Punjab, E Pakistan 29.22N 70.58E
159 T12 **Alīpur Duār** West Bengal, NE India 26.28N 89.25E
20 B14 **Aliquippa** Pennsylvania, NE USA 40.36N 80.15W
82 L12 **'Ali Sabieh** var. 'Alī Sabīḩ. S Djibouti 11.07N 42.44E
'Alī Sabīḩ see 'Ali Sabieh
146 K3 **Al 'Īsāwīyah** Al Jawf, NW Saudi Arabia 30.41N 37.58E
106 J10 **Aliseda** Extremadura, W Spain 39.25N 6.42W
145 T8 **Al Iskandarīyah** C Iraq 32.52N 44.22E
Al Iskandarīyah see Alexandria
127 Oo5 **Aliskerovo** Chukotskiy Avtonomnyy Okrug, NE Russian Federation 67.40N 167.37E
116 H13 **Alistráti** Kentrikí Makedonía, NE Greece 41.03N 23.58E
41 P15 **Alitak Bay** bay Kodiak Island, Alaska, USA
Al Ittiḩād see Madīnat ash Sha'b
117 H18 **Alivéri** var. Alivérion. Évvoia, C Greece 38.25N 24.02E
Alivérion see Alivéri
Aliwal-Noord see Aliwal North
85 I24 **Aliwal North** Afr. Aliwal-Noord. Eastern Cape, SE South Africa 30.39S 26.43E
124 Nn15 **Al Jabal al Akhḑar** ⛰ NE Libya
144 H13 **Al Jafr** Ma'ān, S Jordan 30.18N 36.13E
77 T8 **Al Jaghbūb** NE Libya 29.45N 24.31E
148 K11 **Al Jahrā'** var. Al Jahrah, Jahra. C Kuwait 29.17N 47.36E
Al Jahrah see Al Jahrā'
Al Jamāhīrīyah al 'Arabīyah al Lībīyah ash Sha'bīyah al Ishtirāk see Libya
146 K3 **Al Jarāwī** spring/well NW Saudi Arabia 30.12N 38.48E
147 X11 **Al Jawārah** oasis SE Oman 18.59N 57.16E
146 L3 **Al Jawf** var. Jauf. Al Jawf, NW Saudi Arabia 29.51N 39.49E
146 L4 **Al Jawf** off. Minţaqat al Jawf. ◈ province N Saudi Arabia
Al Jawlān see Golan Heights
Al Jazair see Alger
145 N4 **Al Jazīrah** physical region Iraq/Syria
106 F14 **Aljezur** Faro, S Portugal 37.18N 8.49W
145 S13 **Al Jīl** S Iraq 30.28N 43.57E
144 G11 **Al Jīzah** var. Jiza. 'Ammān, N Jordan 31.42N 35.57E
Al Jīzah see El Gîza
Al Jubail see Al Jubayl
147 S6 **Al Jubayl** var. Al Jubail. Ash Sharqīyah, NE Saudi Arabia 27.00N 49.36E
147 T10 **Āl Juḩaysh, Qalamat** well SE Saudi Arabia 20.35N 51.00E
149 N15 **Al Jumaylīyah** N Qatar 25.37N 51.04E
Al Junaynah see El Geneina
106 G13 **Aljustrel** Beja, S Portugal 37.52N 8.10W
Al Kaba'ish see Al Chabā'ish
Al-Kadhimain see Al Kāẓimīyah
Al Kāf see El Kef
Alkal'a see Alcalá de Henares
37 W4 **Alkali Flat** salt flat Nevada, W USA
37 Q1 **Alkali Lake** ◎ Nevada, W USA
147 Z9 **Al Kāmil** NE Oman 22.15N 59.12E
144 G11 **Al Karak** var. El Kerak, Karak, Kerak; anc. Kir Moab, Kir of Moab. Al Karak, W Jordan 31.10N 35.42E
144 G12 **Al Karak** off. Muḩāfaẓat al Karak. ◈ governorate W Jordan
145 W8 **Al Karmashīyah** E Iraq 32.57N 46.10E
Al-Kashaniya see Al Qash'ānīyah
Al-Kasr al-Kebir see Ksar-el-Kebir
145 T8 **Al Kāẓimīyah** var. Al-Kadhimain, Kadhimain. C Iraq 33.22N 44.19E
101 J18 **Alken** Limburg, NE Belgium 50.52N 5.19E
147 X8 **Al Khābūrah** var. Khabura. N Oman 23.56N 57.06E
Al Khalīl see Hebron
145 T7 **Al Khāliş** C Iraq 33.51N 44.33E
Al Khaluf see Khalūf
Al Khārijah see El Khârga
147 Q8 **Al Kharj** Ar Riyāḑ, C Saudi Arabia 24.12N 47.12E
147 W6 **Al Khaşab** var. Khasab. N Oman 26.10N 56.18E
Al Khaur see Al Khawr
149 N15 **Al Khawr** var. Al Khaur, Al Khor. N Qatar 25.40N 51.33E
148 K12 **Al Khīrān** var. Al Khiran. SE Kuwait 28.34N 48.21E
147 W9 **Al Khīrān** spring/well NW Oman 22.31N 55.42E
Al Khiyām see El Khiyam
Al-Khobar see Al Khubar
Al Khor see Al Khawr
147 S6 **Al Khubar** var. Al-Khobar. Ash Sharqīyah, NE Saudi Arabia 26.15N 50.10E
77 T11 **Al Khufrah** SE Libya 24.10N 23.19E
123 L14 **Al Khums** var. Homs, Khoms, Khums. NW Libya 32.39N 14.16E
147 R15 **Al Khuraybah** C Yemen 15.05N 48.16E
146 M9 **Al Khurmah** var. al-Hurma. Makkah, W Saudi Arabia 21.58N 42.00E
147 V9 **Al Kidan** desert NE Saudi Arabia
131 V4 **Alkino-2** Respublika Bashkortostan, W Russian Federation 54.30N 55.40E
100 H9 **Alkmaar** Noord-Holland, NW Netherlands 52.37N 4.45E
145 T10 **Al Kūfah** var. Kufa. S Iraq 32.01N 44.25E
147 T10 **Al Kursū'** desert E Saudi Arabia
145 V9 **Al Kūt** var. Kūt al 'Amārah, Kut al Imara. E Iraq 32.30N 45.51E
Al-Kuwait see Al Kuwayt
Al Kuwayr see Guwēr
148 K11 **Al Kuwayt** var. Al-Kuwait, Eng. Kuwait, Kuwait City; prev. Qurein. ● (Kuwait) E Kuwait 29.23N 48.00E
148 K11 **Al Kuwayt** ✕ C Kuwait 29.13N 47.57E
117 G19 **Alkyonidón, Kólpos** gulf C Greece
147 N4 **Al Labbah** physical region N Saudi Arabia
144 G4 **Al Lādhiqīyah** Eng. Latakia, Fr. Lattaquié; anc. Laodicea, Laodicea ad Mare. Al Lādhiqīyah, W Syria 35.31N 35.46E
144 H4 **Al Lādhiqīyah** off. Muḩāfaẓat al Ļādhiqīyah, var. Al Lathqiyah, Latakia, Lattakia. ◈ governorate W Syria
21 R2 **Allagash River** ≈ Maine, NE USA
158 M13 **Allahābād** Uttar Pradesh, N India 25.27N 81.49E
149 S3 **Allāh Dāgh, Reshteh-ye** ⛰ NE Iran
41 Q8 **Allakaket** Alaska, USA 66.34N 152.39W
126 Mm11 **Allakh-Yun'** ≈ NE Russian Federation
9 T15 **Allan** Saskatchewan, S Canada 51.50N 105.59W
177 Ff6 **Allanmyo** Magwe, C Burma 19.25N 95.13E
85 I22 **Allanridge** Free State, C South Africa 27.43S 26.43E
106 H4 **Allariz** Galicia, NW Spain 42.10N 7.48W
145 R11 **Al Laşaf** var. Al Lussuf. S Iraq 31.38N 43.16E
Al Lathqiyah see Al Lādhiqīyah
25 S2 **Allatoona Lake** ⊠ Georgia, SE USA
85 J19 **Alldays** :Limpopo NE South Africa 22.39S 29.04E
Alle see Łyna
33 P10 **Allegan** Michigan, N USA 42.31N 85.51W
19 Qq8 **Allegheny Mountains** ⛰ NE USA
20 E12 **Allegheny Plateau** ⛰ New York/Pennsylvania, NE USA
20 D11 **Allegheny Reservoir** ⊠ New York/Pennsylvania, NE USA
20 E12 **Allegheny River** ≈ New York/Pennsylvania, NE USA
24 K9 **Allemands, Lac des** ◎ Louisiana, S USA
27 U6 **Allen** Texas, SW USA 33.06N 96.40W
23 R14 **Allendale** South Carolina, SE USA 33.01N 81.19W
43 N6 **Allende** Coahuila de Zaragoza, NE Mexico 28.22N 100.47W
43 O9 **Allende** Nuevo León, NE Mexico 25.19N 100.01W
99 D16 **Allen, Lough** Ir. Loch Aillionn. ◎ NW Ireland
193 B26 **Allen, Mount** ▲ Stewart Island, Southland, SW NZ 47.05S 167.49E
111 V2 **Allensteig** Niederösterreich, N Austria 48.40N 15.24E
Allenstein see Olsztyn
20 I14 **Allentown** Pennsylvania, NE USA 40.37N 75.30W
161 G23 **Alleppey** var. Alappuzha; prev. Alleppi. Kerala, SW India 9.30N 76.22E
Alleppi see Alleppey
102 J12 **Aller** ≈ NW Germany
31 V16 **Allerton** Iowa, C USA 40.42N 93.22W
101 K19 **Alleur** Liège, E Belgium 50.40N 5.33E
103 J25 **Allgäuer Alpen** ⛰ Austria/Germany
30 J13 **Alliance** Nebraska, C USA 42.05N 102.52W
33 U12 **Alliance** Ohio, N USA 40.55N 81.06W
105 O10 **Allier** ◈ department N France
145 R13 **Al Līfīyah** S Iraq 30.25N 43.03E
46 J13 **Alligator Pond** C Jamaica 17.52N 77.34W
23 Y9 **Alligator River** ≈ North Carolina, SE USA
31 W12 **Allison** Iowa, C USA 42.45N 92.48W
12 G14 **Alliston** Ontario, S Canada 44.09N 79.51W
146 L11 **Al Līth** Makkah, SW Saudi Arabia 21.00N 41.00E
Al Liwā' see Līwā
98 J12 **Alloa** C Scotland, UK 56.07N 3.49W
105 U14 **Allos** Alpes-de-Haute-Provence, SE France 44.16N 6.37E
110 D6 **Allschwil** Basel-Land, NW Switzerland 47.34N 7.32E
Al Lubnān see Lebanon
147 N14 **Al Luḩayyah** W Yemen 15.43N 42.45E
12 K12 **Allumettes, Île des** island Québec, SE Canada
Al Lussuf see Al Laşaf
111 S5 **Alm** ≈ N Austria
13 Q7 **Alma** Québec, SE Canada 48.33N 71.43W
29 S10 **Alma** Arkansas, C USA 35.28N 94.13W
25 V7 **Alma** Georgia, SE USA 31.32N 82.27W
29 P4 **Alma** Kansas, C USA 39.01N 96.17W
33 Q8 **Alma** Michigan, N USA 43.22N 84.39W
31 O17 **Alma** Nebraska, C USA 40.06N 99.21W
32 I7 **Alma** Wisconsin, N USA 44.21N 91.54W
145 R12 **Al Ma'ānīyah** S Iraq 30.45N 42.57E
Alma-Ata see Almaty
Alma-Atinskaya Oblast' see Almaty
Almacellas see Almacelles
107 T5 **Almacelles** var. Almacellas. Cataluña, NE Spain 41.43N 0.25E
106 F11 **Almada** Setúbal, W Portugal 38.40N 9.09W
106 L11 **Almadén** Castilla-La Mancha, C Spain 38.46N 4.49W
68 L6 **Almadies, Pointe des** headland W Senegal 14.43N 17.31W
146 L7 **Al Madīnah** Eng. Medina. Al Madīnah, W Saudi Arabia 24.25N 39.29E
146 L7 **Al Madīnah** off. Minţaqat al Madīnah. ◈ province W Saudi Arabia
144 H9 **Al Mafraq** var. Mafraq. Al Mafraq, N Jordan 32.19N 36.12E
144 J10 **Al Mafraq** off. Muḩāfaẓat al Mafraq. ◈ governorate NW Jordan
147 R15 **Al Maghārīm** C Yemen 15.00N 47.49E
107 N11 **Almagro** Castilla-La Mancha, C Spain 38.54N 3.43W
Al Maḩallah al Kubrá see El Maḩalla el Kubra
145 T9 **Al Maḩāwīl** var. Khān al Maḩāwīl. C Iraq 32.39N 44.28E
Al Mahdīyah see Mahdia
145 T8 **Al Maḩmūdīyah** var. Mahmudiya. C Iraq 33.04N 44.22E
147 T14 **Al Mahrah** ⛰ E Yemen
147 P7 **Al Majma'ah** Ar Riyāḑ, C Saudi Arabia 25.55N 45.18E
145 Q11 **Al Makmīn** well S Iraq 31.38N 42.10E
145 Q1 **Al Mālikīyah** var. Malkiye. Al Ḩasakah, N Syria 37.12N 42.13E
Almalyk see Olmaliq
Al Mamlakah al Urdunīyah al Hāshimīyah see Jordan
Al Mamlakah see Morocco
149 Q18 **Al Manādir** var. Al Manadir. desert Oman/UAE
148 L15 **Al Manāmah** Eng. Manama. ● (Bahrain) N Bahrain 26.13N 50.33E
145 O5 **Al Manāşif** ⛰ E Syria
37 O4 **Almanor, Lake** ⊠ California, W USA
107 R11 **Almansa** Castilla-La Mancha, C Spain 38.52N 1.06W
Al Manşūrah see El Manşûra
106 L3 **Almanza** Castilla-León, N Spain 42.40N 5.01W
106 L8 **Almanzor** ▲ W Spain 40.13N 5.18W
107 P14 **Almanzora** ≈ SE Spain
145 S9 **Al Mardah** C Iraq 32.35N 43.30E
Al-Mariyya see Almería
77 R7 **Al Marj** var. Barka, It. Barce. NE Libya 32.30N 20.54E
144 L2 **Al Mashrafah** Ar Raqqah, N Syria 36.25N 39.07E
147 X8 **Al Maşna'ah** var. Al Muşana'a. NE Oman 23.45N 57.37E
Almassora see Almazora
Almatinskaya Oblast' see Almaty
151 U15 **Almaty** var. Alma-Ata. Almaty, SE Kazakhstan 43.19N 76.55E
151 S14 **Almaty** off. Almatinskaya Oblast', Kaz. Almaty Oblysy; prev. Alma-Atinskaya Oblast'. ◈ province SE Kazakhstan
151 U15 **Almaty** ✕ Almaty, SE Kazakhstan 43.15N 76.57E
Almaty Oblysy see Almaty
al-Mawailih see Al Muwayliḩ
145 R3 **Al Mawşil** Eng. Mosul. N Iraq 36.21N 43.07E
145 N5 **Al Mayādīn** var. Mayadin, Fr. Meyadine. Dayr az Zawr, E Syria 35.00N 40.31E
145 X10 **Al Maymūnah** var. Maimuna. SE Iraq 31.43N 46.55E
147 N5 **Al Mayyāh** Ḩā'il, N Saudi Arabia 27.56N 42.53E
Al Ma'zam see Al Ma'zim
107 P6 **Almazán** Castilla-León, N Spain 41.28N 2.31W
147 W8 **Al Ma'zim** var. Al Ma'zam. NW Oman 23.22N 56.16E
126 Kk11 **Almaznyy** Respublika Sakha (Yakutiya), NE Russian Federation 62.19N 114.14E
107 T9 **Almazora** Cat. Almassora. País Valenciano, E Spain 39.55N 0.02W
Al Mazra' see Al Mazra'ah
144 G11 **Al Mazra'ah** var. Al Mazra', Mazra'a. Al Karak, W Jordan 31.17N 35.31E
103 G15 **Alme** ≈ W Germany
106 I7 **Almeida** Guarda, N Portugal 40.43N 6.52W
106 G10 **Almeirim** Santarém, C Portugal 39.12N 8.37W
100 O10 **Almelo** Overijssel, E Netherlands 52.22N 6.42E
107 S9 **Almenara** País Valenciano, E Spain 39.46N 0.13W
107 P12 **Almenaras** ▲ S Spain 38.31N 2.27W
107 P5 **Almenar de Soria** Castilla-León, N Spain 41.40N 2.12W
106 J6 **Almendra, Embalse de** ⊠ Castilla-León, NW Spain
106 J11 **Almendralejo** Extremadura, W Spain 38.40N 6.25W
100 J10 **Almere** var. Almere-stad. Flevoland, C Netherlands 52.22N 5.12E
100 J10 **Almere-Buiten** Flevoland, C Netherlands 52.24N 5.15E
100 J10 **Almere-Haven** Flevoland, C Netherlands 52.19N 5.13E
Almere-stad see Almere
107 P15 **Almería** Ar. Al-Mariyya; anc. Unci, Lat. Portus Magnus. Andalucía, S Spain 36.49N 2.25W
107 P14 **Almería** ◈ province Andalucía, S Spain
107 P15 **Almería, Golfo de** gulf S Spain
131 S5 **Al'met'yevsk** Respublika Tatarstan, W Russian Federation 54.52N 52.19E
97 L21 **Älmhult** Kronoberg, S Sweden 56.31N 14.10E
147 U9 **Al Miḩrāḑ** desert NE Saudi Arabia
Al Mīnā' see El Mina
106 L17 **Almina, Punta** headland Ceuta, Spain, N Africa 35.54N 5.16W
Al Minyā see El Minya
Al Miqdādīyah see Al Muqdādīyah
45 P14 **Almirante** Bocas del Toro, NW Panama 9.16N 82.24W
Almirós see Almyrós
146 M9 **Al Mislaḩ** spring/well W Saudi Arabia 22.46N 40.47E
Almissa see Omiš
106 G13 **Almodôvar** var. Almodóvar. Beja, S Portugal 37.31N 8.03W
106 M11 **Almodóvar del Campo** Castilla-La Mancha, C Spain 38.43N 4.10W
107 Q9 **Almodóvar del Pinar** Castilla-La Mancha, C Spain 39.43N 1.55W
33 S9 **Almont** Michigan, N USA 42.53N 83.02W
12 L13 **Almonte** Ontario, SE Canada 45.13N 76.12W
106 J14 **Almonte** Andalucía, S Spain 37.16N 6.31W
106 K9 **Almonte** ≈ W Spain
158 K9 **Almora** Uttaranchal, N India 29.36N 79.40E
106 M8 **Almorox** Castilla-La Mancha, C Spain 40.13N 4.22W
147 S7 **Al Mubarraz** Ash Sharqīyah, E Saudi Arabia 25.28N 49.34E
Al Muḑaibī see Al Muḑaybī
144 G15 **Al Mudawwarah** Ma'ān, SW Jordan 29.20N 36.00E
147 Y9 **Al Muḑaybī** var. Al Muḑaibī. NE Oman 22.34N 58.07E
Almudébar see Almudévar
107 S5 **Almudévar** var. Almudébar. Aragón, NE Spain 42.03N 0.34W
147 S15 **Al Mukallā** var. Mukalla. SE Yemen 14.36N 49.07E
147 N16 **Al Mukhā** Eng. Mocha. SW Yemen 13.18N 43.16E
107 N15 **Almuñécar** Andalucía, S Spain 36.43N 3.40W
145 U7 **Al Muqdādīyah** var. Al Miqdādīyah. C Iraq 33.58N 44.58E
146 L3 **Al Murayr** spring/well NW Saudi Arabia 30.06N 39.54E
142 M12 **Almus** Tokat, N Turkey 40.22N 36.54E
Al Muşana'a see Al Maşna'ah
145 T9 **Al Musayyib** var. Musaiyib. C Iraq 32.46N 44.19E
145 V9 **Al Muwaffaqīyah** S Iraq 32.19N 45.22E
144 H10 **Al Muwaqqar** var. El Muwaqqar. 'Ammān, W Jordan 31.49N 36.06E
146 J5 **Al Muwayliḩ** var. al-Mawailih. Tabūk, NW Saudi Arabia 27.39N 35.33E
117 F17 **Almyrós** var. Almirós. Thessalía, C Greece 39.10N 22.45E
117 I24 **Almyroú, Órmos** bay Krití, Greece, E Mediterranean Sea
Al Nūwfalīyah see An Nawfalīyah
98 L13 **Alnwick** N England, UK 55.26N 1.44W
Al Obayyid see El Obeid
Al Odaid see Al 'Udayd
202 B16 **Alofi** ○ (Niue) W Niue 19.01S 169.55E
202 A16 **Alofi Bay** bay W Niue, C Pacific Ocean
202 E13 **Alofi, Île** island S Wallis and Futuna
202 E13 **Alofitai** Île Alofi, W Wallis and Futuna 14.21S 178.03W
Aloha State see Hawaii
120 G7 **Aloja** Limbaži, N Latvia 57.47N 24.53E
159 X10 **Along** Arunāchel Pradesh, NE India 28.15N 94.56E
117 H16 **Alónnisos** island Vóreies Sporádes, Greece, Aegean Sea
106 M15 **Álora** Andalucía, S Spain 36.49N 4.43W
175 Rr15 **Alor, Kepulauan** island group E Indonesia
175 Rr16 **Alor, Pulau** prev. Ombai. island Kepulauan Alor, E Indonesia
175 R16 **Alor, Selat** strait Flores Sea/Savu Sea
173 G2 **Alor Setar** var. Alor Star, Alur Setar. Kedah, Peninsular Malaysia 6.06N 100.22E
Alost see Aalst
160 F9 **Ālot** Madhya Pradesh, C India 23.58N 75.40E
195 N16 **Alotau** Milne Bay, SE PNG 10.18S 150.39E
176 Yy15 **Alotip** Papua, E Indonesia 8.07S 140.06E
Al Oued see El Oued
37 R12 **Alpaugh** California, W USA 35.52N 119.29W
Alpen see Alps
33 R6 **Alpena** Michigan, N USA 45.04N 83.27W
Alpes see Alps
105 S14 **Alpes-de-Haute-Provence** ◈ department SE France
105 U14 **Alpes-Maritimes** ◈ department SE France
189 W8 **Alpha** Queensland, E Australia 23.40S 146.38E

◆ Country
● Country Capital
◇ Dependent Territory
○ Dependent Territory Capital
◈ Administrative Region
✕ International Airport
▲ Mountain
⛰ Mountain Range
Volcano
≈ River
◎ Lake
⊠ Reservoir

Alpha Cordillera – Anakāpalle

207 R9 **Alpha Cordillera** *var.* Alpha Ridge. *undersea feature* Arctic Ocean
Alpha Ridge *see* Alpha Cordillera
Alpheius *see* Alfeiós
101 I15 **Alphen** Noord-Brabant, S Netherlands *51.29N 4.57E*
100 H11 **Alphen aan den Rijn** *var.* Alphen. Zuid-Holland, C Netherlands *52.07N 4.40E*
Alpheus *see* Alfeiós
Alpi *see* Alps
106 G10 **Alpiarça** Santarém, C Portugal *39.15N 8.34W*
26 K10 **Alpine** Texas, SW USA *30.22N 103.40W*
110 F8 **Alpnach** Unterwalden, W Switzerland *46.56N 8.17E*
110 D11 **Alps** *Fr.* Alpes, *Ger.* Alpen, *It.* Alpi. ▲ C Europe
147 W8 **Al Qābil** *var.* Qabil. N Oman *23.55N 55.49E*
Al Qaḍārif *see* Gedaref
77 P8 **Al Qaddāḥīyah** N Libya *31.21N 15.16E*
Al Qāhirah *see* Cairo
146 K4 **Al Qalībah** Tabūk, NW Saudi Arabia *28.28N 37.40E*
145 O1 **Al Qāmishlī** *var.* Kamishli, Qamishly. Al Ḥasakah, NE Syria *37.00N 41.00E*
144 I6 **Al Qaryatayn** *var.* Qaryatayn, *Fr.* Qariateïne. Ḥimṣ, C Syria *34.13N 37.13E*
148 K11 **Al Qash'ānīyah** *var.* Al-Kashaniya. NE Kuwait *29.59N 47.42E*
147 N7 **Al Qaşim** *off.* Mintaqat Qaşim, Qassim. ◆ *province* C Saudi Arabia
144 J5 **Al Qaşr** Ḥimṣ, C Syria *35.06N 37.39E*
Al Qaşr *see* El Qasr
Al Qaşrayn *see* Kasserine
147 S6 **Al Qaţīf** Ash Sharqīyah, NE Saudi Arabia *26.27N 50.01E*
144 G11 **Al Qaṭrānah** *var.* El Qatrani, Qatrana. Al Karak, W Jordan *31.13N 36.03E*
77 P11 **Al Qaṭrūn** SW Libya *24.57N 14.40E*
Al Qayrawān *see* Kairouan
Al-Qsar al-Kbir *see* Ksar-el-Kebir
Al Qubayyāt *see* Qoubaïyât
Al Quds/Al Quds ash Sharīf *see* Jerusalem
106 H12 **Alqueva, Barragem do** ⊠ Portugal/Spain
144 G8 **Al Qunayţirah** *var.* El Kuneitra, El Quneitra, Kuneitra, Qunaytra. Al Qunayţirah, SW Syria *33.07N 35.49E*
144 G8 **Al Qunayţirah** *off.* Muḥāfaẓat al Qunayţirah, *var.* El Q'unaytirah, Qunaytirah, *Fr.* Kuneitra. ◆ *governorate* SW Syria
146 M11 **Al Qunfudhah** Makkah, SW Saudi Arabia *19.19N 41.02E*
146 K2 **Al Qurayyāt** Al Jawf, NW Saudi Arabia *31.24N 37.25E*
145 Y11 **Al Qurnah** *var.* Kurna. SE Iraq *31.01N 47.27E*
145 V12 **Al Quşayr** S Iraq *30.36N 45.52E*
144 I6 **Al Quşayr** *var.* El Quseir, Quşayr, *Fr.* Kousseir. Ḥimṣ, W Syria *34.36N 36.36E*
Al Quşayr *see* Quseir
144 H7 **Al Quţayfah** *var.* Quţayfah, Qutayfe, Quteife, *Fr.* Kouteifé. Dimashq, W Syria *33.44N 36.33E*
147 P8 **Al Quwayīyah** Ar Riyāḍ, C Saudi Arabia *24.06N 45.18E*
Al Quwayr *see* Guwēr
144 F14 **Al Quwayrah** *var.* El Quweira. Al 'Aqabah, SW Jordan *29.49N 35.19E*
Al Rayyan *see* Ar Rayyān
Al Ruweis *see* Ar Ruways
97 G24 **Als** *Ger.* Alsen. *island* SW Denmark
105 U5 **Alsace** *Ger.* Elsass; *anc.* Alsatia. ◆ *region* NE France
9 R16 **Alsask** Saskatchewan, S Canada *51.24N 109.55W*
Alsasua *see* Altsasu
Alsatia *see* Alsace
103 C16 **Alsdorf** Nordrhein-Westfalen, W Germany *50.52N 6.09E*
8 G8 **Alsek** ∾ Canada/USA
Alsen *see* Als
103 F19 **Alsenz** ∾ W Germany
103 H17 **Alsfeld** Hessen, C Germany *50.45N 9.14E*
121 K20 **Al'shany** *Rus.* Ol'shany. Brestskaya Voblasts', SW Belarus *52.04N 27.19E*
Alsókubin *see* Dolný Kubín
120 C9 **Alsunga** Kuldīga, W Latvia *56.59N 21.31E*
Alt *see* Olt
94 K9 **Alta** *Fin.* Alattio. Finnmark, N Norway *69.58N 23.16E*
31 T12 **Alta** Iowa, C USA *42.40N 95.17W*
110 I7 **Altach** Vorarlberg, W Austria *47.22N 9.39E*
94 K9 **Altaelva** *Lapp.* Álaheaieatnu. ∾ N Norway
94 J8 **Altafjorden** *fjord* NE Norwegian Sea
64 K10 **Alta Gracia** Córdoba, C Argentina *31.42S 64.25W*
44 K11 **Alta Gracia** Rivas, SW Nicaragua *11.33N 85.35W*
56 H4 **Altagracia** Zulia, NW Venezuela *10.43N 71.30W*
56 M5 **Altagracia de Orituco** Guárico, N Venezuela *9.49N 66.22W*
Altai *see* Altai Mountains
133 T7 **Altai Mountains** *var.* Altai, *Chin.* Altay Shan, *Rus.* Altay. ▲ Asia/Europe
25 V6 **Altamaha River** ∾ Georgia, SE USA
60 J13 **Altamira** Pará, NE Brazil *3.13S 52.15W*
56 D12 **Altamira** Huila, S Colombia *2.02N 75.51W*
44 M13 **Altamira** Alajuela, N Costa Rica *10.25N 84.21W*
43 Q11 **Altamira** Tamaulipas, C Mexico *22.24N 97.57W*
32 L15 **Altamont** Illinois, N USA *39.03N 88.45W*
29 Q7 **Altamont** Kansas, C USA *37.11N 95.18W*
34 H16 **Altamont** Oregon, NW USA *42.12N 121.44W*
22 K10 **Altamont** Tennessee, S USA *35.25N 85.42W*
25 X11 **Altamonte Springs** Florida, SE USA *28.39N 81.22W*
109 O17 **Altamura** *anc.* Lupatia. Puglia, SE Italy *40.50N 16.33E*
42 H9 **Altamura, Isla** *island* C Mexico
Altan *see* Erdenehayrhan
Altanbulag *see* Bayanhayrhan
169 Q7 **Altan Emel** *var.* Xin Barag Youqi. Nei Mongol Zizhiqu, N China *48.37N 116.40E*
Altan-Ovoo *see* Tsenher
169 N9 **Altanshiree** *var.* Chandmanī. Dornogovĭ, SE Mongolia *45.36N 110.30E*
Altanteel *see* Dzereg
168 D5 **Altantsögts** *var.* Tsagaantüngi. Bayan-Ölgiy, NW Mongolia *49.06N 90.26E*
42 F3 **Altar** Sonora, NW Mexico *30.44N 111.49W*
42 D2 **Altar, Desierto de** *var.* Sonoran Desert. *desert* Mexico/USA *see also* Sonoran Desert
107 Q8 **Alta, Sierra** ▲ N Spain *40.29N 1.36W*
42 H9 **Altata** Sinaloa, C Mexico *24.39N 107.55W*
44 D4 **Alta Verapaz** *off.* Departamento de Alta Verapaz. ◆ *department* C Guatemala
109 L18 **Altavilla Silentia** Campania, S Italy *40.32N 15.06E*
23 T7 **Altavista** Virginia, NE USA *37.06N 79.17W*
164 L2 **Altay** Xinjiang Uygur Zizhiqu, NW China *47.51N 88.06E*
168 D6 **Altay** *var.* Chihertey. Bayan-Ölgiy, W Mongolia *48.10N 89.35E*
168 F9 **Altay** *var.* Bayan-Ovoo. Govĭ-Altay, SW Mongolia *44.39N 94.45E*
168 G8 **Altay** *prev.* Yösönbulag. Govĭ-Altay, W Mongolia *46.23N 96.16E*
168 E8 **Altay** *var.* Bor-Üdzüür. Hovd, W Mongolia *45.46N 92.13E*
Altay *see* Altai Mountains, Asia/Europe
Altay *see* Bayantes, Mongolia
126 H16 **Altay, Respublika** *var.* Gornyy Altay; *prev.* Gorno-Altayskaya Respublika. ◆ *autonomous republic* S Russian Federation
Altay Shan *see* Altai Mountains
125 G15 **Altayskiy Kray** ◆ *territory* S Russian Federation
Altbetsche *see* Bečej
103 L20 **Altdorf** Bayern, SE Germany *49.23N 11.22E*
110 G8 **Altdorf** *var.* Altorf. Uri, C Switzerland *46.52N 8.37E*
107 T11 **Altea** País Valenciano, E Spain *38.37N 0.03W*
102 L10 **Alte Elde** ∾ N Germany
103 M16 **Altenburg** Thüringen, E Germany *50.58N 12.27E*
Altenburg *see* Bucureşti, Romania
Altenburg *see* Baia de Criş, Romania
102 P12 **Alte Oder** ∾ NE Germany
106 H10 **Alter do Chão** Portalegre, C Portugal *39.12N 7.40W*
94 I10 **Altevatnet** *Lapp.* Álttesjávri. ◎ N Norway
29 V12 **Altheimer** Arkansas, C USA *34.19N 91.51W*
111 T9 **Althofen** Kärnten, S Austria *46.52N 14.27E*
116 H7 **Altimir** Vratsa, NW Bulgaria *43.33N 23.48E*
142 K11 **Altınkaya Barajı** ⊠ N Turkey
145 S3 **Altin Köprü** *var.* Altun Kupri. N Iraq *35.45N 44.08E*
142 E13 **Altıntaş** Kütahya, W Turkey *39.04N 30.07E*
59 K18 **Altiplano** *physical region* W South America
Altkanischa *see* Kanjiža
105 U7 **Altkirch** Haut-Rhin, NE France *47.37N 7.14E*
Altlublau *see* Stará Ľubovňa
102 L12 **Altmark** *cultural region* N Germany
Altmoldowa *see* Moldova Veche
27 W8 **Alto** Texas, SW USA *31.39N 95.04W*
106 H11 **Alto Alentejo** *physical region* S Portugal
61 I19 **Alto Araguaia** Mato Grosso, C Brazil *17.19S 53.10W*
60 L12 **Alto Bonito** Pará, NE Brazil *1.48S 46.18W*
85 O15 **Alto Molócuè** Zambézia, NE Mozambique *15.41S 37.42E*
32 K15 **Alton** Illinois, N USA *38.53N 90.10W*
29 W8 **Alton** Missouri, C USA *36.41N 91.24W*
9 X17 **Altona** Manitoba, S Canada *49.12N 97.38W*
20 E14 **Altoona** Pennsylvania, NE USA *40.31N 78.22W*
32 J6 **Altoona** Wisconsin, N USA *44.49N 91.22W*
64 N3 **Alto Paraguay** *off.* Departamento del Alto Paraguay. ◆ *department* N Paraguay
61 L17 **Alto Paraíso de Goiás** Goiás, S Brazil *14.04S 47.15W*
64 P6 **Alto Paraná** *off.* Departamento del Alto Paraná. ◆ *department* E Paraguay
Alto Paraná *see* Paraná
61 L15 **Alto Parnaíba** Maranhão, E Brazil *9.07S 45.55W*
58 H13 **Alto Purús, Río** ∾ E Peru
Altorf *see* Altdorf
65 H19 **Alto Río Senguer** *var.* Alto Río Senguerr. Chubut, S Argentina *45.03S 70.48W*
43 Q13 **Altotonga** Veracruz-Llave, E Mexico *19.43N 97.12W*
103 N23 **Altötting** Bayern, SE Germany *48.12N 12.37E*
Altpasua *see* Stara Pazova
Altraga *see* Bayandzürh
Alt-Schwanenburg *see* Gulbene
107 P3 **Altsasu** *Cast.* Alsasua. Navarra, N Spain *42.54N 2.10W*
Altsohl *see* Zvolen
110 I7 **Altstätten** Sankt Gallen, NE Switzerland *47.22N 9.33E*
Áltteesjávri *see* Altevatnet
44 G1 **Altun Ha** *ruins* Belize, N Belize *17.46N 88.20W*
Altun Kupri *see* Altin Köprü
164 D8 **Altun Shan** ▲ C China *39.19N 93.37E*
164 L9 **Altun Shan** *var.* Altyn Tagh. ▲ NW China
37 P2 **Alturas** California, W USA *41.28N 120.32W*
28 K12 **Altus** Oklahoma, C USA *34.38N 99.19W*
28 K11 **Altus Lake** ⊠ Oklahoma C USA
Altvater *see* Praděd
Altyn Tagh *see* Altun Shan
Alu *see* Shortland Island
al-'Ubaila *see* Al 'Ubaylah
145 O6 **Al 'Ubaydī** W Iraq *34.22N 41.15E*
147 T9 **Al 'Ubaylah** *var.* al-'Ubaila. Ash Sharqīyah, E Saudi Arabia *22.01N 50.57E*
147 T9 **Al 'Ubaylah** *spring/well* E Saudi Arabia *22.02N 50.56E*
Al Ubayyiḍ *see* El Obeid
147 T7 **Al 'Udayd** *var.* Al Odaid. Abū Ẓaby, W UAE *24.34N 51.27E*
120 J8 **Alūksne** *Ger.* Marienburg. Alūksne, NE Latvia *57.26N 27.02E*
146 K6 **Al 'Ulā** Al Madīnah, NW Saudi Arabia *26.39N 37.55E*
181 N4 **Alula-Fartak Trench** *var.* Illaue Fartak Trench. *undersea feature* W Indian Ocean
144 I11 **Al 'Umarī** 'Ammān, E Jordan *37.30N 31.30E*
33 S13 **Alum Creek Lake** ⊠ Ohio, N USA
65 H15 **Aluminé** Neuquén, C Argentina *39.15S 71.00W*
97 O14 **Alunda** Uppsala, C Sweden *60.04N 18.04E*
119 T14 **Alupka** Respublika Krym, S Ukraine *44.24N 34.01E*
77 P8 **Al 'Uqaylah** N Libya *30.13N 16.10E*
Al Uqşur *see* Luxor
Al Urdunn *see* Jordan
173 G6 **Alur Panal** *bay* Sumatera, W Indonesia
147 V10 **Al 'Urūq al Mu'tariḍah** *salt lake* SE Saudi Arabia
145 Q7 **Ālūs** C Iraq *34.04N 42.27E*
119 T13 **Alushta** Respublika Krym, S Ukraine *44.40N 34.24E*
77 U12 **Al 'Uwaynāt** SE Libya *21.46N 24.51E*
77 N11 **Al 'Uwaynāt** *var.* Al Awaynāt. SW Libya *25.47N 10.34E*
145 T6 **Al 'Uzaym** *var.* Adhaim. E Iraq *34.12N 44.31E*
28 L8 **Alva** Oklahoma, C USA *36.48N 98.40W*
106 H8 **Alva** ∾ N Portugal
97 J18 **Älvängen** Västra Götaland, S Sweden *57.55N 12.09E*
12 F14 **Alvanley** Ontario, S Canada *44.33N 81.05W*
43 S14 **Alvarado** Veracruz-Llave, E Mexico *18.46N 95.45W*
27 T7 **Alvarado** Texas, SW USA *32.24N 97.12W*
60 D13 **Alvarães** Amazonas, NW Brazil *3.13S 64.53W*
42 G6 **Álvaro Obregón, Presa** ⊠ W Mexico
96 H10 **Alvdal** Hedmark, S Norway *62.07N 10.39E*
96 K12 **Älvdalen** Dalarna, C Sweden *61.13N 14.04E*
63 E15 **Alvear** Corrientes, NE Argentina *29.03S 56.30W*
106 F10 **Alverca do Ribatejo** Lisboa, C Portugal *38.55N 9.01W*
97 L20 **Alvesta** Kronoberg, S Sweden *56.52N 14.34E*
27 W12 **Alvin** Texas, SW USA *29.25N 95.14W*
96 O13 **Älvkarleby** Uppsala, C Sweden *60.34N 17.30E*
27 S5 **Alvord** Texas, SW USA *33.22N 97.39W*
95 G18 **Älvros** Jämtland, C Sweden *62.04N 14.30E*
94 J13 **Älvsbyn** Norrbotten, N Sweden *65.41N 21.00E*
148 K12 **Al Wafrā'** SE Kuwait *28.37N 47.56E*
146 J6 **Al Wajh** Tabūk, NW Saudi Arabia *26.15N 36.29E*
147 N16 **Al Wakrah** *var.* Wakra. C Qatar *25.09N 51.36E*
144 M8 **al Walaj, Sha'īb** *dry watercourse* W Iraq
158 I11 **Alwar** Rājasthān, N India *27.31N 76.34E*
147 Q5 **Al Wari'ah** Ash Sharqīyah, N Saudi Arabia *27.54N 47.22E*
161 G22 **Alwaye** Kerala, SW India *10.06N 76.22E*
Alxa Zuoqi *see* Bayan Hot
Alx Youqi *see* Ehen Hudag
Al Yaman *see* Yemen
144 G9 **Al Yarmūk** Irbid, N Jordan *32.41N 35.55E*
Alyat/Alyaty-Pristan' *see* Älät
117 I14 **Alykí** *var.* Aliki. Thásos, N Greece *40.36N 24.45E*
121 F14 **Alytus** *Pol.* Olita. Alytus, S Lithuania *54.24N 24.02E*
121 F15 **Alytus** ◆ *province* S Lithuania
103 N23 **Alz** ∾ SE Germany
35 Y11 **Alzada** Montana, NW USA *45.00N 104.24W*
126 Ii14 **Alzamay** Irkutskaya Oblast', S Russian Federation *55.33N 98.36E*
101 M25 **Alzette** ∾ S Luxembourg
107 S10 **Alzira** *var.* Alcira; *anc.* Saetabicula, Suero. País Valenciano, E Spain *39.10N 0.27W*
Al Zubair *see* Az Zubayr
189 O8 **Amadeus, Lake** *seasonal lake* Northern Territory, C Australia
83 E15 **Amadi** Western Equatoria, SW Sudan *5.31N 30.19E*
16 Nn3 **Amadjuak Lake** ◎ Baffin Island, Nunavut, N Canada
97 J23 **Amager** *island* E Denmark
170 Cc13 **Amagi** Fukuoka, Kyūshū, SW Japan *33.24N 130.37E*
171 J17 **Amagi-san** ▲ Honshū, S Japan *34.51N 138.57E*
175 Tt11 **Amahai** *var.* Masohi. Pulau Seram, E Indonesia *3.19S 128.55E*
40 M16 **Amak Island** *island* Alaska, USA
170 Bb14 **Amakusa-nada** *gulf* Kyūshū, SW Japan
97 J16 **Åmål** Västra Götaland, S Sweden *59.04N 12.40E*
56 E8 **Amalfi** Antioquia, N Colombia *6.54N 75.04W*
109 L18 **Amalfi** Campania, S Italy *40.37N 14.35E*
117 D19 **Amaliáda** *var.* Amaliás. Dytikí Ellás, S Greece *37.48N 21.21E*
Amaliás *see* Amaliáda
160 F12 **Amalner** Mahārāshtra, C India *21.03N 75.04E*
176 X12 **Amamapare** Papua, E Indonesia *4.51S 136.43E*
61 H21 **Amambaí, Serra de** *var.* Cordillera de Amambay, Serra de Amambay. ▲ Brazil/Paraguay *see also* Amambay, Cordillera de
64 P4 **Amambay** *off.* Departamento del Amambay. ◆ *department* E Paraguay
64 P5 **Amambay, Cordillera de** *var.* Serra de Amambaí, Serra de Amambay. ▲ Brazil/Paraguay *see also* Amambaí, Serra de
Amambay, Serra de *see* Amambaí, Serra de/Amambay, Cordillera de
172 Q13 **Amami-guntō** *island group* SW Japan
172 Qq13 **Amami-Ō-shima** *island* S Japan
194 E10 **Amanab** Sandaun, NW PNG *3.34S 141.10E*
108 J13 **Amandola** Marche, C Italy *42.58N 13.22E*
109 N21 **Amantea** Calabria, SW Italy *39.06N 16.05E*
203 W10 **Amanu** *island* Îles Tuamotu, C French Polynesia
60 J10 **Amapá** Amapá, NE Brazil *02.00N 50.50W*
60 J11 **Amapá** *off.* Estado de Amapá; *prev.* Território de Amapá. ◆ *state* NE Brazil
44 H8 **Amapala** Valle, S Honduras *13.18N 87.37W*
Amara *see* Al 'Amārah
106 H6 **Amarante** Porto, N Portugal *41.16N 8.04W*
177 G5 **Amarapura** Mandalay, C Burma *21.54N 96.01E*
Amardalay *see* Delgertsogt
106 I12 **Amareleja** Beja, S Portugal *38.12N 7.13W*
37 V11 **Amargosa Range** ▲ California, W USA
27 N2 **Amarillo** Texas, SW USA *35.13N 101.49W*
Amarinthos *see* Amárynthos
109 K15 **Amaro, Monte** ▲ C Italy *42.03N 14.06E*
117 H18 **Amárynthos** *var.* Amarinthos. Évvoia, C Greece *38.24N 23.53E*
Amasia *see* Amasya
142 K12 **Amasya** *anc.* Amasia. Amasya, N Turkey *40.40N 35.49E*
142 K11 **Amasya** ◆ *province* N Turkey
44 F4 **Amatique, Bahía de** *bay* Gulf of Honduras, W Caribbean Sea
44 D6 **Amatitlán, Lago de** ◎ S Guatemala
109 J14 **Amatrice** Lazio, C Italy *42.38N 13.19E*
202 C8 **Amatuku** *atoll* C Tuvalu
101 J20 **Amay** Liège, E Belgium *50.33N 5.19E*
50 F7 **Amazon** *Sp.* Amazonas. ∾ Brazil/Peru
61 C14 **Amazonas** *off.* Estado do Amazonas. ◆ *state* N Brazil
56 G15 **Amazonas** *off.* Comisaria del Amazonas. ◆ *province* SE Colombia
58 C10 **Amazonas** *off.* Departamento de Amazonas. ◆ *department* N Peru
56 M12 **Amazonas** *off.* Territorio Amazonas. ◆ *federal territory* S Venezuela
Amazonas *see* Amazon
50 F7 **Amazon Basin** *basin* N South America
49 V5 **Amazon Fan** *undersea feature* W Atlantic Ocean
60 K11 **Amazon, Mouths of the** *delta* NE Brazil
197 C12 **Ambae** *var.* Aoba, Omba. *island* C Vanuatu
158 I9 **Ambāla** Haryāna, NW India *30.22N 76.49E*
161 J26 **Ambalangoda** Southern Province, SW Sri Lanka *6.13N 80.03E*
161 K26 **Ambalantota** Southern Province, S Sri Lanka *6.07N 81.01E*
180 I6 **Ambalavao** Fianarantsoa, C Madagascar *21.49S 46.55E*
56 E10 **Ambalema** Tolima, C Colombia *4.49N 74.48W*
81 E17 **Ambam** Sud, S Cameroon *2.22N 11.16E*
180 J2 **Ambanja** Antsirañana, N Madagascar *13.40S 48.27E*
127 O5 **Ambarchik** Respublika Sakha (Yakutiya), NE Russian Federation *69.33N 162.08E*
64 K9 **Ambargasta, Salinas de** *salt lake* C Argentina
128 J6 **Ambarnyy** Respublika Kareliya, NW Russian Federation *65.53N 33.44E*
58 C7 **Ambato** Tungurahua, C Ecuador *1.18S 78.39W*
180 I5 **Ambatolampy** Antananarivo, C Madagascar *19.21S 47.27E*
180 H4 **Ambatomainty** Mahajanga, W Madagascar *17.40S 45.39E*
180 J4 **Ambatondrazaka** Toamasina, C Madagascar *17.49S 48.28E*
175 Ss12 **Ambelau, Pulau** *see* Ambelau, Pulau
103 L20 **Amberg** *var.* Amberg in der Oberpfalz. Bayern, SE Germany *49.27N 11.51E*
Amberg in der Oberpfalz *see* Amberg
44 H1 **Ambergris Cay** *island* NE Belize
105 S11 **Ambérieu-en-Bugey** Ain, E France *45.57N 5.21E*
193 I18 **Amberley** Canterbury, South Island, NZ *43.09S 172.43E*
105 P11 **Ambert** Puy-de-Dôme, C France *45.34N 3.42E*
Ambianum *see* Amiens
78 J11 **Ambidédi** Kayes, SW Mali *14.37N 11.49W*
160 M10 **Ambikāpur** Chhattīsgarh, C India *23.09N 83.12E*
180 J2 **Ambilobe** Antsirañana, N Madagascar *13.10S 49.03E*
195 Q10 **Ambitle Island** *island* Feni Islands, NE PNG
41 O7 **Ambler** Alaska, USA *67.05N 157.51W*
Amblève *see* Amel
Ambo *see* Hāgere Hiywet
180 I8 **Amboasary** Toliara, S Madagascar *25.01S 46.22E*
180 J4 **Ambodifotatra** *var.* Ambodifototra. Toamasina, E Madagascar *16.58S 49.51E*
Amboenten *see* Ambunten
180 I5 **Ambohidratrimo** Antananarivo, C Madagascar *18.48S 47.25E*
180 I6 **Ambohimahasoa** Fianarantsoa, SE Madagascar *21.07S 47.13E*
180 K3 **Ambohitralanana** Antsirañana, NE Madagascar *15.13S 50.28E*
176 X10 **Amboi, Kepulauan** *island group* E Indonesia
Amboina *see* Ambon
104 M8 **Amboise** Indre-et-Loire, C France *47.25N 1.00E*
175 T11 **Ambon** *prev.* Amboina, Amboyna. Pulau Ambon, E Indonesia *3.40S 128.10E*
175 T12 **Ambon, Pulau** *island* E Indonesia
83 I20 **Amboseli, Lake** ◎ Kenya/Tanzania
180 I6 **Ambositra** Fianarantsoa, SE Madagascar *20.31S 47.15E*
180 I8 **Ambovombe** Toliara, S Madagascar *25.10S 46.06E*
37 W14 **Amboy** California, W USA *34.33N 115.44W*
32 L11 **Amboy** Illinois, N USA *41.42N 89.19W*
Amboyna *see* Ambon
Ambracia *see* Árta
20 B14 **Ambridge** Pennsylvania, NE USA *40.33N 80.11W*
Ambrim *see* Ambrym
84 A11 **Ambriz** Bengo, NW Angola *7.55S 13.11E*
Ambrizete *see* N'Zeto
197 C13 **Ambrym** *var.* Ambrim. *island* C Vanuatu
174 Mm14 **Ambunten** *prev.* Amboenten. Pulau Madura, E Indonesia *6.55S 113.45E*
194 G10 **Ambunti** East Sepik, NW PNG *4.06S 142.49E*
161 I20 **Āmbūr** Tamil Nādu, SE India *12.48N 78.43E*
40 E17 **Amchitka Island** *island* Aleutian Islands, Alaska, USA
40 F17 **Amchitka Pass** *strait* Aleutian Islands, Alaska, USA
147 R15 **'Amd** C Yemen *15.09N 47.58E*
80 J10 **Am Dam** Ouaddaï, E Chad *12.46N 20.28E*
176 Uu15 **Amdassa** Pulau Yamdena, E Indonesia *7.40S 131.24E*
129 U1 **Amderma** Nenetskiy Avtonomnyy Okrug, NW Russian Federation *69.45N 61.36E*
165 N14 **Amdo** Xizang Zizhiqu, W China *32.15N 91.43E*
42 K13 **Ameca** Jalisco, SW Mexico *20.31N 104.02W*
43 P14 **Amecameca** *var.* Amecameca de Juárez. México, C Mexico *19.07N 98.45W*
Amecameca de Juárez *see* Amecameca
63 A20 **Ameghino** Buenos Aires, E Argentina *34.51S 62.28W*
101 M21 **Amel** *Fr.* Amblève. Liège, E Belgium *50.20N 6.13E*
100 K4 **Ameland** *Fris.* It Amelân. *island* Waddeneilanden, N Netherlands
Amelân, It *see* Ameland
109 H14 **Amelia** Umbria, C Italy *42.33N 12.26E*
23 V6 **Amelia Court House** Virginia, NE USA *37.19N 77.57W*
25 W8 **Amelia Island** *island* Florida, SE USA
20 L12 **Amenia** New York, NE USA *41.51N 73.31W*
America *see* United States of America
67 M21 **America-Antarctica Ridge** *undersea feature* S Atlantic Ocean
America in Miniature *see* Maryland
62 L9 **Americana** São Paulo, S Brazil *22.43S 47.19W*
35 Q15 **American Falls** Idaho, NW USA *42.47N 112.51W*
35 Q15 **American Falls Reservoir** ⊠ Idaho, NW USA
38 L3 **American Fork** Utah, W USA *40.24N 111.47W*
198 D8 **American Samoa** ◇ US *unincorporated territory* W Polynesia
25 S6 **Americus** Georgia, SE USA *32.04N 84.13W*
100 K12 **Amerongen** Utrecht, C Netherlands *52.00N 5.30E*
100 K11 **Amersfoort** Utrecht, C Netherlands *52.09N 5.22E*
99 N21 **Amersham** SE England, UK *51.39N 0.37W*
32 I5 **Amery** Wisconsin, N USA *45.18N 92.20W*
205 W6 **Amery Ice Shelf** *ice shelf* Antarctica
31 V13 **Ames** Iowa, C USA *42.01N 93.37W*
21 P10 **Amesbury** Massachusetts, NE USA *42.51N 70.55W*
Amestratus *see* Mistretta
117 F18 **Amfíkleia** *var.* Amfíklia. Stereá Ellás, C Greece *38.37N 22.34E*
Amfíklia *see* Amfíkleia
117 D17 **Amfilochía** *var.* Amfilokhía. Dytikí Ellás, C Greece *38.52N 21.09E*
Amfilokhía *see* Amfilochía
116 H13 **Amfípoli** *anc.* Amphipolis. *site of ancient city* Kentrikí Makedonía, NE Greece *40.49N 23.51E*
117 F18 **Ámfissa** Stereá Ellás, C Greece *38.31N 22.22E*
126 M11 **Amga** Respublika Sakha (Yakutiya), NE Russian Federation *60.55N 131.45E*
126 M11 **Amga** ∾ NE Russian Federation
169 R7 **Amgalang** *var.* Xin Barag Zuoqi. Nei Mongol Zizhiqu, N China *48.12N 118.15E*
195 N12 **Amgen** ∾ New Britain, C PNG
127 P4 **Amguema** ∾ NE Russian Federation
127 Nn14 **Amgun'** ∾ SE Russian Federation
82 J12 **Amhara** ◆ *region* N Ethiopia
11 P15 **Amherst** Nova Scotia, SE Canada *45.49N 64.13W*
20 M11 **Amherst** Massachusetts, NE USA *42.22N 72.31W*
20 D10 **Amherst** New York, NE USA *42.57N 78.47W*
26 M4 **Amherst** Texas, SW USA *33.59N 102.24W*
23 U6 **Amherst** Virginia, NE USA *37.35N 79.03W*
Amherst *see* Kyaikkami
12 C18 **Amherstburg** Ontario, S Canada *42.05N 83.06W*
23 Q6 **Amherstdale** West Virginia, NE USA *37.46N 81.46W*
12 K15 **Amherst Island** *island* Ontario, SE Canada
Amida *see* Diyarbakır
30 J6 **Amidon** North Dakota, N USA *46.26N 103.18W*
105 O3 **Amiens** *anc.* Ambianum, Samarobriva. Somme, N France *49.54N 2.18E*
145 P8 **'Amīj, Wādī** *var.* Wadi 'Amīq. *dry watercourse* W Iraq
142 L17 **Amik Ovası** ◎ S Turkey
78 E9 **Amilcar Cabral** ✕ Sal, NE Cape Verde *16.45N 22.56E*
Amilhayt, Wādī *see* Umm al Ḥayt, Wādī
Amíndaion/Amindeo *see* Amýntaio
161 C21 **Amīndīvi Islands** *island group* Lakshadweep, India, N Indian Ocean
145 U6 **Amīn Ḥabīb** E Iraq *34.17N 45.10E*
85 E20 **Aminuis** Omaheke, E Namibia *23.37S 19.21E*
'Amīq, Wadi *see* 'Amīj, Wādī
148 J7 **Amīrābād** Īlām, NW Iran *33.19N 46.16E*
Amirante Bank *see* Amirante Ridge
181 N6 **Amirante Basin** *undersea feature* W Indian Ocean
181 N6 **Amirante Islands** *var.* Amirantes Group. *island group* C Seychelles
181 N7 **Amirante Ridge** *var.* Amirante Bank. *undersea feature* W Indian Ocean
Amirantes Group *see* Amirante Islands
181 N7 **Amirante Trench** *undersea feature* W Indian Ocean
176 Z12 **Amisibil** Papua, E Indonesia *3.59S 140.35E*
9 U13 **Amisk Lake** ◎ Saskatchewan, C Canada
Amistad, Presa de la *see* Amistad Reservoir
27 O12 **Amistad Reservoir** *var.* Presa de la Amistad. ⊠ Mexico/USA
Amisus *see* Samsun
24 K8 **Amite** *var.* Amite City. Louisiana, S USA *30.40N 90.30W*
Amite City *see* Amite
29 T12 **Amity** Arkansas, C USA *34.15N 93.27W*
160 H11 **Amla** *prev.* Amulla. Madhya Pradesh, C India *21.57N 78.06E*
40 I17 **Amlia Island** *island* Aleutian Islands, Alaska, USA
99 I18 **Amlwch** NW Wales, UK *53.25N 4.22W*
Ammaia *see* Portalegre
144 H10 **'Ammān** *var.* Amman; *anc.* Philadelphia, *Bibl.* Rabbah Ammon, Rabbath Ammon. ● (Jordan) 'Ammān, NW Jordan *31.57N 35.55E*
144 H10 **'Ammān** *off.* Muḥāfaẓat 'Ammān, *prev.* Al 'Āşimah. ◆ *governorate* NW Jordan
95 N14 **Ämmänsaari** Oulu, E Finland *64.51N 28.58E*
94 H13 **Ammarnäs** Västerbotten, N Sweden *65.58N 16.10E*
207 O15 **Ammassalik** *var.* Angmagssalik. Tunu, S Greenland *65.51N 37.30W*
103 K24 **Ammer** ∾ SE Germany
103 K24 **Ammersee** ◎ SE Germany
100 J13 **Ammerzoden** Gelderland, C Netherlands *51.46N 5.07E*
Ammóchostos *see* Gazimağusa
Ammóchostos, Kólpos *see* Gazimağusa Körfezi
Amnok-kang *see* Yalu
Amoea *see* Portalegre
Amoentai *see* Amuntai
Amoerang *see* Amurang
149 O4 **Āmol** *var.* Amul. Māzandarān, N Iran *36.30N 52.24E*
117 K21 **Amorgós** Amorgós, Kykládes, Greece, Aegean Sea *36.49N 25.54E*
117 K22 **Amorgós** *island* Kykládes, Greece, Aegean Sea
25 N3 **Amory** Mississippi, S USA *33.58N 88.29W*
10 I13 **Amos** Québec, SE Canada *48.34N 78.07W*
97 G15 **Åmot** Buskerud, S Norway *59.52N 9.55E*
97 E15 **Åmot** Telemark, S Norway *59.34N 7.59E*
97 J15 **Åmotfors** Värmland, C Sweden *59.46N 12.24E*
78 L10 **Amourj** Hodh ech Chargui, SE Mauritania *16.04N 7.12W*
Amoy *see* Xiamen
180 H7 **Ampanihy** Toliara, SW Madagascar *24.40S 44.45E*
161 L25 **Ampara** *var.* Amparai. Eastern Province, E Sri Lanka *7.16N 81.40E*
180 J4 **Amparafaravola** Toamasina, E Madagascar *17.33S 48.13E*
Amparai *see* Ampara
62 M9 **Amparo** São Paulo, S Brazil *22.40S 46.49W*
180 J5 **Ampasimanolotra** Toamasina, E Madagascar *18.49S 49.04E*
59 H17 **Ampato, Nevado** ▲ S Peru *15.52S 71.51W*
103 L23 **Amper** ∾ SE Germany
66 M9 **Ampère Seamount** *undersea feature* E Atlantic Ocean *35.05N 13.00W*
Amphipolis *see* Amfípoli
178 M10 **Amphitrite Group** *island group* N Paracel Islands
176 U15 **Amplawas** *var.* Emplawas. Pulau Babar, E Indonesia *8.01S 129.42E*
107 U7 **Amposta** Cataluña, NE Spain *40.43N 0.34E*
13 V7 **Amqui** Québec, SE Canada *48.28N 67.27W*
147 O14 **'Amrān** W Yemen *15.39N 43.59E*
Amraoti *see* Amrāvati
160 H12 **Amrāvati** *prev.* Amraoti. Mahārāshtra, C India *20.55N 77.45E*
160 C11 **Amreli** Gujarāt, W India *21.36N 71.19E*
110 H6 **Amriswil** Thurgau, NE Switzerland *47.33N 9.18E*
144 H5 **'Amrīt** *ruins* Ṭarţūs, W Syria *34.48N 35.54E*
158 H7 **Amritsar** Punjab, N India *31.38N 74.54E*
158 J10 **Amroha** Uttar Pradesh, N India *28.54N 78.28E*
102 G7 **Amrum** *island* NW Germany
95 I15 **Åmsele** Västerbotten, N Sweden *64.31N 19.24E*
100 I10 **Amstelveen** Noord-Holland, C Netherlands *52.18N 4.49E*
100 I10 **Amsterdam** ● (Netherlands) Noord-Holland, C Netherlands *52.22N 4.54E*
20 K10 **Amsterdam** New York, NE USA *42.56N 74.11W*
181 Q11 **Amsterdam Fracture Zone** *tectonic feature* S Indian Ocean
181 R11 **Amsterdam Island** *island* NE French Southern and Antarctic Territories
111 U4 **Amstetten** Niederösterreich, N Austria *48.07N 14.52E*
80 J11 **Am Timan** Salamat, SE Chad *11.01N 20.16E*
152 L12 **Amu-Buxoro Kanali** *var.* Aral-Bukhorskiy Kanal. *canal* C Uzbekistan
145 O1 **'Āmūdah** *var.* Amude. Al Ḥasakah, N Syria *37.06N 40.56E*
153 O15 **Amu Darya** *Rus.* Amudar'ya, *Taj.* Dar"yoi Amu, *Turkm.* Amyderya, *Uzb.* Amudaryo; *anc.* Oxus. ∾ C Asia
Amu-Dar'ya *see* Amyderya
Amudar'ya/Amudaryo/Amu, Dar"yoi *see* Amu Darya
Amude *see* 'Āmūdah
146 L3 **'Amūd, Jabal al** ▲ NW Saudi Arabia *30.59N 39.17E*
40 J17 **Amukta Island** *island* Aleutian Islands, Alaska, USA
40 I17 **Amukta Pass** *strait* Aleutian Islands, Alaska, USA
Amul *see* Āmol
Amulla *see* Amla
Amundsen Basin *see* Fram Basin
205 X3 **Amundsen Bay** *bay* Antarctica
205 P10 **Amundsen Coast** *physical region* Antarctica
15 H2 **Amundsen Gulf** *gulf* Northwest Territories, N Canada
199 Ll16 **Amundsen Plain** *undersea feature* S Pacific Ocean
205 Q9 **Amundsen-Scott** *US research station* Antarctica *89.59S 10.00E*
204 J11 **Amundsen Sea** *sea* S Pacific Ocean
96 M12 **Amungen** ◎ C Sweden
175 N10 **Amuntai** *prev.* Amoentai. Borneo, C Indonesia *2.24S 115.13E*
133 W6 **Amur** *Chin.* Heilong Jiang. ∾ China/Russian Federation
175 Rr7 **Amurang** *prev.* Amoerang. Sulawesi, C Indonesia *1.12N 124.37E*
175 Rr7 **Amurang, Teluk** *bay* Sulawesi, C Indonesia
107 O3 **Amurrio** País Vasco, N Spain *43.03N 3.00W*
127 Nn15 **Amursk** Khabarovskiy Kray, SE Russian Federation *50.13N 136.34E*
126 M14 **Amurskaya Oblast'** ◆ *province* SE Russian Federation
82 G7 **'Amur, Wadi** ∾ NE Sudan
117 C17 **Amvrakikós Kólpos** *gulf* W Greece
Amvrosiyevka *see* Amvrosiyivka
119 X8 **Amvrosiyivka** *Rus.* Amvrosiyevka. Donets'ka Oblast', SE Ukraine *47.46N 38.31E*
152 M14 **Amyderya** *Rus.* Amu-Dar'ya. Lebap Welaýaty, NE Turkmenistan *37.58N 65.14E*
Amyderya *see* Amu Darya
116 E13 **Amýntaio** *var.* Amindeo; *prev.* Amíndaion. Dytikí Makedonía, N Greece *40.42N 21.42E*
12 B6 **Amyot** Ontario, S Canada *48.28N 84.58W*
203 U10 **Anaa** *atoll* Îles Tuamotu, C French Polynesia
Anabanoea *see* Anabanua
175 Pp12 **Anabanua** *prev.* Anabanoea. Sulawesi, C Indonesia *3.58S 120.07E*
201 R8 **Anabar** NE Nauru *0.30S 166.56E*
126 K7 **Anabar** ∾ NE Russian Federation
An Abhainn Mhór *see* Blackwater
57 O6 **Anaco** Anzoátegui, NE Venezuela *9.30N 64.28W*
35 Q10 **Anaconda** Montana, NW USA *46.09N 112.55W*
34 H7 **Anacortes** Washington, NW USA *48.30N 122.36W*
28 M11 **Anadarko** Oklahoma, C USA *35.04N 98.14W*
116 N12 **Ana Dere** ∾ NW Turkey
106 G8 **Anadia** Aveiro, N Portugal *40.25N 8.27W*
Anadolu Dağları *see* Doğu Karadeniz Dağları
127 Pp5 **Anadyr'** Chukotskiy Avtonomnyy Okrug, NE Russian Federation *64.40N 177.22E*
127 P5 **Anadyr'** ∾ NE Russian Federation
Anadyr, Gulf of *see* Anadyrskiy Zaliv
133 X4 **Anadyrskiy Khrebet** *var.* Chukot Range. ▲ NE Russian Federation
127 Q4 **Anadyrskiy Zaliv** *Eng.* Gulf of Anadyr. *gulf* NE Russian Federation
117 K22 **Anáfi** *anc.* Anaphe. *island* Kykládes, Greece, Aegean Sea
109 J15 **Anagni** Lazio, C Italy *41.43N 13.12E*
'Ānah *see* 'Annah
37 T15 **Anaheim** California, W USA *33.50N 117.54W*
8 L15 **Anahim Lake** British Columbia, SW Canada *52.26N 125.13W*
40 B8 **Anahola** Kaua'i, Hawai'i, USA, C Pacific Ocean *22.09N 159.19W*
27 X11 **Anahuac** Texas, SW USA *29.46N 94.40W*
43 O7 **Anáhuac** Nuevo León, NE Mexico *27.13N 100.09W*
161 G22 **Anai Mudi** ▲ S India *10.16N 77.08E*
Anaiza *see* 'Unayzah
161 M15 **Anakāpalle** Andhra Pradesh, E India *17.42N 83.06E*

◆ Country ● Country Capital ◇ Dependent Territory ○ Dependent Territory Capital ◆ Administrative Region ✕ International Airport ▲ Mountain ▲ Mountain Range ⋏ Volcano ∾ River ◎ Lake ⊠ Reservoir
223

ANAKENA, PLAYA DE – APARIMA

203 W15 **Anakena, Playa de** beach Easter Island, Chile, E Pacific Ocean
41 Q7 **Anaktuvuk Pass** Alaska, USA 68.08N 151.44W
41 Q6 **Anaktuvuk River** ≈ Alaska, USA
180 J3 **Analalava** Mahajanga, NW Madagascar 14.37S 47.46E
46 F6 **Ana Maria, Golfo de** gulf C Cuba
Anambas Islands see Anambas, Kepulauan
174 Ii5 **Anambas, Kepulauan** var. Anambas Islands island group W Indonesia
79 U17 **Anambra** ◈ state SE Nigeria
31 N4 **Anamoose** North Dakota, N USA 47.50N 100.14W
31 Y13 **Anamosa** Iowa, C USA 42.06N 91.17W
142 H17 **Anamur** Mersin, S Turkey 36.06N 32.49E
142 H17 **Anamur Burnu** headland S Turkey 36.03N 32.49E
170 Ff16 **Anan** Tokushima, Shikoku, SW Japan 33.54N 134.40E
160 O12 **Ānandadur** Orissa, E India 21.13N 86.08E
161 H18 **Anantapur** Andhra Pradesh, S India 14.40N 77.36E
158 H5 **Anantnāg** var. Islamabad. Jammu and Kashmir, NW India 33.43N 75.10E
Ananyev see Anan'yiv
119 O9 **Anan'yiv** Rus. Ananyev. Odes'ka Oblast', SW Ukraine 47.43N 29.51E
130 J14 **Anapa** Krasnodarskiy Kray, SW Russian Federation 44.55N 37.20E
Anaphe see Anáfi
61 K18 **Anápolis** Goiás, C Brazil 16.19S 48.58W
149 R10 **Anār** Kermān, C Iran 30.48N 55.17E
Anár see Inari
149 P7 **Anārak** Eşfahān, C Iran 33.21N 53.43E
Anar Dara see Anār Darreh
154 J7 **Anār Darreh** var. Anar Dara. Farāh, W Afghanistan 32.45N 61.37E
Anárjohka see Inarijoki
25 X9 **Anastasia Island** island Florida, SE USA
196 K7 **Anatahan** island C Northern Mariana Islands
132 M6 **Anatolia** plateau C Turkey
88 F14 **Anatolian Plate** tectonic feature Asia/Europe
116 H13 **Anatolikí Makedonía kai Thráki** Eng. Macedonia East and Thrace. ◈ region NE Greece
Anatom see Aneityum
64 L8 **Añatuya** Santiago del Estero, N Argentina 28.27S 62.52W
An Baile Meánach see Ballymena
An Bhearú see Barrow
An Bhóinn see Boyne
An Blascaod Mór see Great Blasket Island
An Cabhán see Cavan
An Caisleán Nua see Newcastle
An Caisleán Riabhach see Castlereagh, Northern Ireland, UK
An Caisleán Riabhach see Castlerea, Ireland
58 C13 **Ancash** off. Departamento de Ancash. ◈ department W Peru
An Cathair see Caher
104 J8 **Ancenis** Loire-Atlantique, NW France 47.22N 1.10W
An Chanáil Ríoga see Royal Canal
An Cheacha see Caha Mountains
41 R11 **Anchorage** Alaska, USA 61.12N 149.52W
41 R12 **Anchorage** ✕ Alaska, USA 61.08N 150.00W
41 Q13 **Anchor Point** Alaska, USA 59.46N 151.49W
An Chorr Chríochach see Cookstown
67 M24 **Anchorstack Point** headland W Tristan da Cunha 37.07S 12.21W
An Clár see Clare
An Clochán see Clifden
An Clochán Liath see Dunglow
25 U12 **Anclote Keys** island group Florida, SE USA
An Cóbh see Cobh
59 J17 **Ancohuma, Nevado de** ▲ W Bolivia 15.51S 68.33W
An Comar see Comber
59 D14 **Ancón** Lima, W Peru 11.47S 77.09W
108 J12 **Ancona** Marche, C Italy 43.37N 13.30E
Ancuabe see Ancuabi
84 Q13 **Ancuabi** var. Ancuabe. Cabo Delgado, NE Mozambique 12.57S 39.54E
65 F17 **Ancud** prev. San Carlos de Ancud. Los Lagos, S Chile 41.52S 73.49W
65 G17 **Ancud, Golfo de** gulf S Chile
Ancyra see Ankara
169 V8 **Anda** Heilongjiang, NE China 46.22N 125.15E
59 G16 **Andahuaylas** Apurímac, S Peru 13.38S 73.20W
An Daingean see Dingle
159 R15 **Andāl** West Bengal, NE India 23.34N 87.13E
96 E9 **Åndalsnes** Møre og Romsdal, S Norway 62.33N 7.42E
106 K13 **Andalucía** Eng. Andalusia. ◈ autonomous community S Spain
25 P7 **Andalusia** Alabama, S USA 31.18N 86.29W
Andalusia see Andalucía
157 Q21 **Andaman and Nicobar Islands** var. Andamans and Nicobars. ◈ union territory India, NE Indian Ocean
181 T4 **Andaman Basin** undersea feature NE Indian Ocean
157 P19 **Andaman Islands** island group India, NE Indian Ocean
181 T4 **Andaman Sea** sea NE Indian Ocean
59 K19 **Andamarca** Oruro, C Bolivia 18.50S 67.24W
176 V10 **Andamata** Papua, E Indonesia 2.40S 132.30E
190 H5 **Andamooka** South Australia 30.26S 137.12E
147 Y9 **'Andām, Wādī** seasonal river NE Oman
180 J3 **Andapa** Antsirañana, NE Madagascar 14.39S 49.40E
155 R4 **Andarāb** var. Banow. Baghlān, NE Afghanistan 35.36N 69.18E
Andarbag see Andarbogh
153 S13 **Andarbogh** Rus. Andarbag, Anderbak. S Tajikistan 37.51N 71.45E
111 Z5 **Andau** Burgenland, E Austria 47.46N 17.03E
110 I10 **Andeer** Graubünden, S Switzerland 46.36N 9.24E
94 H9 **Andenes** Nordland, C Norway 69.18N 16.06E
101 J20 **Andenne** Namur, SE Belgium 50.28N 5.06E
79 S11 **Andéramboukane** Gao, E Mali 15.24N 3.03E
Anderbak see Andarbogh
101 G18 **Anderlecht** Brussels, C Belgium 50.50N 4.18E
101 G21 **Anderlues** Hainaut, S Belgium 50.24N 4.16E
110 G9 **Andermatt** Uri, C Switzerland 46.39N 8.36E
103 E17 **Andernach** anc. Antunnacum. Rheinland-Pfalz, SW Germany 50.25N 7.25E
196 D15 **Andersen Air Force Base** air base NE Guam 13.34N 144.55E
41 R9 **Anderson** Alaska, USA 64.20N 149.11W
37 N4 **Anderson** California, W USA 40.26N 122.21W
33 P13 **Anderson** Indiana, N USA 40.06N 85.40W
29 R8 **Anderson** Missouri, C USA 36.39N 94.26W
23 P11 **Anderson** South Carolina, SE USA 34.30N 82.39W
27 V10 **Anderson** Texas, SW USA 30.29N 96.00W
15 Gg3 **Anderson** ≈ Northwest Territories, NW Canada
97 K20 **Anderstorp** Jönköping, S Sweden 57.16N 13.46E
56 D9 **Andes** Antioquia, W Colombia 5.40N 75.55W
49 P7 **Andes** ▲▲ W South America
31 P12 **Andes, Lake** ◎ South Dakota, N USA
94 H9 **Andfjorden** fjord E Norwegian Sea
161 H16 **Andhra Pradesh** ◈ state E India
100 J8 **Andijk** Noord-Holland, NW Netherlands 52.38N 5.00E
153 S10 **Andijon** Rus. Andizhan. Andijon Viloyati, E Uzbekistan 40.46N 72.19E
153 S10 **Andijon Viloyati** Rus. Andizhanskaya Oblast'. ◈ province E Uzbekistan
Andikíthira see Antikýthira
180 J4 **Andilamena** Toamasina, C Madagascar 17.00S 48.35E
148 L8 **Andīmeshk** var. Andimishk; prev. Salehābād. Khūzestān, SW Iran 32.28N 48.21E
Andimishk see Andīmeshk
Andipáros see Antíparos
Andipaxi see Antípaxoi
Andípsara see Antípsara
142 L16 **Andırın** Kahramanmaraş, S Turkey 37.33N 36.18E
164 J8 **Andirlangar** Xinjiang Uygur Zizhiqu, NW China 37.38N 83.40E
Andírrion see Antírrio
Ándissa see Ántissa
Andizhan see Andijon
Andizhanskaya Oblast' see Andijon Viloyati
155 N2 **Andkhvoy** Fāryāb, N Afghanistan 36.55N 65.07E
107 Q2 **Andoain** País Vasco, N Spain 43.13N 2.01W
176 W9 **Andoi** Papua, E Indonesia 0.53S 133.59E
169 Y15 **Andong** Jap. Antō. E South Korea 36.34N 128.43E
111 R4 **Andorf** Oberösterreich, N Austria 48.22N 13.33E
107 S7 **Andorra** Aragón, NE Spain 40.58N 0.27W
107 V4 **Andorra** off. Principality of Andorra, Cat. Valls d'Andorra, Fr. Vallée d'Andorre. ◆ monarchy SW Europe
Andorra see Andorra la Vella
107 V4 **Andorra la Vella** var. Andorra, Fr. Andorre la Vielle, Sp. Andorra la Vieja. ● (Andorra) C Andorra 42.30N 1.30E
Andorra la Vieja see Andorra la Vella
Andorra, Valls d'/Andorre, Vallée d' see Andorra
Andorre la Vielle see Andorra la Vella
99 M22 **Andover** S England, UK 51.13N 1.28W
29 N6 **Andover** Kansas, C USA 37.42N 97.08W
94 G10 **Andøya** island C Norway
62 I8 **Andradina** São Paulo, S Brazil 20.54S 51.25W
107 X9 **Andratx** Mallorca, Spain, W Mediterranean Sea 39.35N 2.25E
41 N10 **Andreafsky River** ≈ Alaska, USA
40 H17 **Andreanof Islands** island group Aleutian Islands, Alaska, USA
128 H16 **Andreapol'** Tverskaya Oblast', W Russian Federation 56.38N 32.17E
Andreas, Cape see Zafer Burnu
Andreevka see Kabanbay
23 N10 **Andrews** North Carolina, SE USA 35.19N 84.01W
23 T13 **Andrews** South Carolina, SE USA 33.27N 79.33W
26 M7 **Andrews** Texas, SW USA 32.19N 102.33W
181 N5 **Andrew Tablemount** var. Gora Andryu. undersea feature W Indian Ocean 6.45N 50.30E
Andreyevka see Kabanbay
109 N17 **Andria** Puglia, SE Italy 41.13N 16.16E
115 K16 **Andrijevica** E-Montenegro 42.45N 19.45E
117 E20 **Andrítsaina** Pelopónnisos, S Greece 37.29N 21.52E
An Droichead Nua see Newbridge
Andropov see Rybinsk
117 J19 **Ándros** Ándros, Kykládes, Greece, Aegean Sea 37.49N 24.55E
117 J20 **Ándros** island Kykládes, Greece, Aegean Sea
21 O7 **Androscoggin River** ≈ Maine/New Hampshire, NE USA
46 F3 **Andros Island** island NW Bahamas
131 R7 **Androsovka** Samarskaya Oblast', W Russian Federation 52.41N 49.34E
46 G3 **Andros Town** Andros Island, NW Bahamas 24.40N 77.47W
161 D21 **Āndrott Island** island Lakshadweep, India, N Indian Ocean
119 N5 **Andrushivka** Zhytomyrs'ka Oblast', N Ukraine 50.01N 29.02E
113 K17 **Andrychów** Małopolskie, S Poland 49.51N 19.23E
Andryu, Gora see Andrew Tablemount
94 I10 **Andselv** Troms, N Norway 69.05N 18.30E
81 O17 **Andudu** Orientale, NE Dem. Rep. Congo 2.25N 28.39E
107 N13 **Andújar** anc. Illiturgis. Andalucía, SW Spain 38.01N 4.03W
84 C12 **Andulo** Bié, W Angola 11.28S 16.43E
105 Q14 **Anduze** Gard, S France 44.03N 3.59E
An Earagail see Errigal Mountain
97 L19 **Aneby** Jönköping, S Sweden 57.49N 14.45E
Anécho see Aného
79 Q9 **Anéfis** Kidal, NE Mali 18.05N 0.38E
47 U8 **Anegada** island NE British Virgin Islands
63 B25 **Anegada, Bahía** bay E Argentina
47 U9 **Anegada Passage** passage Anguilla/British Virgin Islands
79 R17 **Aného** var. Anécho; prev. Petit-Popo. S Togo 6.13N 1.36E
197 D17 **Aneityum** var. Anatom; prev. Kéamu. island S Vanuatu
119 N10 **Anenii Noi** Rus. Novyye Aneny. C Moldova 46.52N 29.10E
194 L12 **Anepmete** New Britain, E PNG 5.47S 148.37E
107 U4 **Aneto** ▲ NE Spain 42.36N 0.37E
152 F13 **Ānew** Rus. Annau. Ahal Welaýaty, C Turkmenistan 37.51N 58.22E
Ānewetak see Enewetak Atoll
79 Y8 **Aney** Agadez, NE Niger 19.22N 13.00E
An Fheoir see Nore
126 Ii13 **Angara** ≈ C Russian Federation
126 J15 **Angarsk** Irkutskaya Oblast', S Russian Federation 52.31N 103.55E
95 G17 **Ånge** Västernorrland, C Sweden 62.31N 15.40E
Angel see Úhlava
42 D4 **Ángel de la Guarda, Isla** island NW Mexico
179 P10 **Angeles** off. Angeles City. Luzon, N Philippines 15.16N 120.37E
Angeles City see Angeles
Angel Falls see Ángel, Salto
97 J22 **Ängelholm** Skåne, S Sweden 56.14N 12.52E
63 A17 **Angélica** Santa Fe, C Argentina 31.33S 61.33W
27 W8 **Angelina River** ≈ Texas, SW USA
57 Q9 **Ángel, Salto** Eng. Angel Falls. waterfall E Venezuela 5.52N 62.19W
97 M15 **Ängelsberg** Västmanland, C Sweden 59.57N 16.01E
37 P8 **Angels Camp** California, W USA 38.03N 120.31W
111 W7 **Anger** Steiermark, SE Austria 47.16N 15.41E
Angerapp see Ozersk
Angerburg see Węgorzewo
95 H15 **Ångermanälven** ≈ N Sweden
102 P11 **Angermünde** Brandenburg, NE Germany 53.01N 13.59E
104 K7 **Angers** anc. Juliomagus. Maine-et-Loire, NW France 47.30N 0.33W
13 W7 **Angers** ≈ Québec, SE Canada
95 J16 **Ängesön** island N Sweden
Angistro see Ágkistro
116 H13 **Angítis** ≈ NE Greece
178 J14 **Ângk Tasaôm** prev. Angtassom. Takêv, S Cambodia 10.59N 104.39E
193 C25 **Anglem, Mount** ▲ Stewart Island, Southland, SW NZ 46.44S 167.56E
99 I18 **Anglesey** cultural region NW Wales, UK
99 I18 **Anglesey** island NW Wales, UK
104 I15 **Anglet** Pyrénées-Atlantiques, SW France 43.28N 1.30W
27 W12 **Angleton** Texas, SW USA 29.10N 95.25W
Anglia see England
12 H9 **Angliers** Québec, SE Canada 47.33N 79.17W
Anglo-Egyptian Sudan see Sudan
Angmagssalik see Ammassalik
178 Ii8 **Ang Nam Ngum** ◎ C Laos
81 N16 **Ango** Orientale, N Dem. Rep. Congo 4.02N 25.49E
85 Q15 **Angoche** Nampula, E Mozambique 16.12S 39.55E
65 G14 **Angol** Araucanía, C Chile 37.48S 72.40W
33 Q11 **Angola** Indiana, N USA 41.37N 85.00W
84 A9 **Angola** off. Republic of Angola; prev. People's Republic of Angola, Portuguese West Africa. ◆ republic SW Africa
67 P15 **Angola Basin** undersea feature E Atlantic Ocean
41 X13 **Angoon** Admiralty Island, Alaska, USA 57.33N 134.30W
153 O14 **Angor** Surkhondaryo Viloyati, S Uzbekistan 37.30N 67.06E
Angora see Ankara
194 H10 **Angoram** East Sepik, NW PNG 4.01S 144.03E
42 H8 **Angostura** Sinaloa, C Mexico 25.18N 108.10W
Angostura see Ciudad Bolívar
43 U17 **Angostura, Presa de la** ⊠ SE Mexico
30 J11 **Angostura Reservoir** ⊠ South Dakota, N USA
104 L11 **Angoulême** anc. Iculisma. Charente, W France 45.39N 0.10E
104 K11 **Angoumois** cultural region W France
66 O2 **Angra do Heroísmo** Terceira, Azores, Portugal, NE Atlantic Ocean 38.40N 27.13W
62 O10 **Angra dos Reis** Rio de Janeiro, SE Brazil 22.58S 44.16W
Angra Pequena see Lüderitz
153 Q10 **Angren** Toshkent Viloyati, E Uzbekistan 41.04N 70.17E
Angtassom see Ângk Tasaôm
178 Hh11 **Ang Thong** var. Angthong. Ang Thong, C Thailand 14.34N 100.25E
81 M16 **Angu** Orientale, N Dem. Rep. Congo 3.38N 24.14E
107 S5 **Angües** Aragón, NE Spain 42.07N 0.10W
47 U9 **Anguilla** ◇ UK dependent territory E West Indies
47 V9 **Anguilla** island E West Indies
46 F4 **Anguilla Cays** islets SW Bahamas
Angul see Anugul
167 N1 **Anguli Nur** ◎ E China
81 O18 **Angumu** Orientale, E Dem. Rep. Congo 0.10S 27.42E
12 G14 **Angus** Ontario, S Canada 44.19N 79.52W
98 J10 **Angus** cultural region E Scotland, UK
61 K19 **Anhangüera** Goiás, S Brazil 18.12S 48.19W
101 I21 **Anhée** Namur, S Belgium 50.18N 4.52E
97 I21 **Anholt** island C Denmark
166 M11 **Anhua** var. Dongping. Hunan, S China 28.25N 111.10E
167 P8 **Anhui** var. Anhui Sheng, Anhwei, Wan. ◈ province E China
Anhui Sheng/Anhwei see Anhui
41 O11 **Aniak** Alaska, USA 61.34N 159.31W
41 O12 **Aniak River** ≈ Alaska, USA
An Iarmhí see Westmeath
201 R8 **Anibare** E Nauru 0.31S 166.56E
201 R8 **Anibare Bay** bay E Nauru, W Pacific Ocean
Anicium see le Puy
117 K22 **Ánidro** island Kykládes, Greece, Aegean Sea
79 R15 **Anié** C Togo 7.48N 1.12E
79 Q15 **Anié** ≈ C Togo
104 J16 **Anie, Pic d'** ▲ SW France 42.56N 0.44W
131 Y7 **Anikhovka** Orenburgskaya Oblast', W Russian Federation 51.27N 60.17E
12 G9 **Anima Nipissing Lake** ◎ Ontario, S Canada
39 O16 **Animas** New Mexico, SW USA 31.55N 108.49W
39 P16 **Animas Peak** ▲ New Mexico, SW USA 31.34N 108.46W
39 P16 **Animas Valley** valley New Mexico, SW USA
118 F13 **Anina** Ger. Steierdorf, Hung. Stájerlakanina; prev. Ştaierdorf-Anina, Steierdorf-Anina, Steyerlak-Anina. Caraş-Severin, SW Romania 45.04N 21.51E
31 U14 **Anita** Iowa, C USA 41.27N 94.45W
127 Oo16 **Aniva, Mys** headland Ostrov Sakhalin, SE Russian Federation 46.02N 143.25E
127 Oo16 **Aniva, Zaliv** bay SE Russian Federation
197 E16 **Aniwa** island S Vanuatu
95 M19 **Anjalankoski** Etelä-Suomi, S Finland 60.39N 26.54E
'Anjar see Aanjar
Anjiangying see Luanping
12 B8 **Anjigami Lake** ◎ Ontario, S Canada
171 Hh16 **Anjō** var. Anzyô. Aichi, Honshū, SW Japan 34.58N 137.07E
104 J8 **Anjou** cultural region NW France
180 I13 **Anjouan** var. Nzwani, Johanna Island. island SE Comoros
180 J4 **Anjozorobe** Antananarivo, C Madagascar 18.22S 47.52E
169 W13 **Anju** W North Korea 39.36N 125.44E
100 M5 **Anjum** Fris. Eanjum. Friesland, N Netherlands 53.22N 6.09E
180 G6 **Ankaboa, Tanjona** headland W Madagascar 21.57S 43.16E
166 L7 **Ankang** prev. Xing'an. Shaanxi, C China 32.45N 109.00E
142 I12 **Ankara** prev. Angora, anc. Ancyra. ● (Turkey) Ankara, C Turkey 39.55N 32.49E
142 H12 **Ankara** ◈ province C Turkey
97 N19 **Ankarsrum** Kalmar, S Sweden 57.40N 16.19E
180 H6 **Ankazoabo** Toliara, SW Madagascar 22.18S 44.30E
180 I4 **Ankazobe** Antananarivo, C Madagascar 18.19S 47.07E
31 V14 **Ankeny** Iowa, C USA 41.43N 93.37W
178 Kk11 **An Khê** Gia Lai, C Vietnam 13.57N 108.39E
102 O9 **Anklam** Mecklenburg-Vorpommern, NE Germany 53.51N 13.42E
82 K13 **Ānkober** Amhara, N Ethiopia 9.36N 39.44E
79 O17 **Ankobra** ≈ S Ghana
81 N22 **Ankoro** Katanga, SE Dem. Rep. Congo 6.45S 26.58E
101 L24 **Anlier, Forêt d'** forest SE Belgium
166 I13 **Anlong** Guizhou, S China 25.05N 105.29E
An Longfort see Longford
178 Ii11 **Ânlong Vêng** Siĕmréab, NW Cambodia 14.16N 104.07E
An Lorgain see Lurgan
167 N8 **Anlu** Hubei, C China 31.15N 113.41E
An Mhí see Meath
An Mhuir Cheilteach see Celtic Sea
An Muileann gCearr see Mullingar
95 F16 **Ånn** Jämtland, C Sweden 63.19N 12.34E
130 M8 **Anna** Voronezhskaya Oblast', W Russian Federation 51.31N 40.23E
32 L17 **Anna** Illinois, N USA 37.27N 89.15W
27 U5 **Anna** Texas, SW USA 33.21N 96.33W
76 L5 **Annaba** prev. Bône. NE Algeria 36.55N 7.46E
An Nabatīyah at Taḥtā see Nabatîyé
103 N17 **Annaberg-Buchholz** Sachsen, E Germany 50.34N 13.01E
111 T9 **Annabichl** ✕ (Klagenfurt) Kärnten, S Austria 46.39N 14.21E
146 M5 **An Nafūd** desert NW Saudi Arabia
145 P6 **'Annah** var. 'Ānah. NW Iraq 33.27N 43.19E
145 P6 **An Nāḥiyah** W Iraq 34.24N 41.33E
145 T10 **An Najaf** var. Najaf. S Iraq 31.58N 44.19E
23 V5 **Anna, Lake** ⊠ Virginia, NE USA
99 F16 **Annalee** ≈ N Ireland
178 Jj9 **Annamitique, Chaîne** ▲▲ C Laos
99 J14 **Annan** S Scotland, UK 55.00N 3.19W
31 U8 **Annandale** Minnesota, N USA 45.15N 94.07W
23 W4 **Annandale** Virginia, NE USA 38.48N 77.10W
201 Q7 **Anna Point** headland N Nauru 0.30S 166.55E
23 X3 **Annapolis** state capital Maryland, NE USA 38.58N 76.29W
196 A10 **Anna, Pulo** island S Palau
159 O10 **Annapurṇa** ▲ C Nepal 28.30N 83.49E
An Nāqūrah see En Nâqoûra
33 R10 **Ann Arbor** Michigan, N USA 42.16N 83.45W
An Nás see Naas
145 W12 **An Nāṣirīyah** var. Nasiriya. SE Iraq 31.04N 46.16E
145 W11 **An Naṣr** E Iraq 31.34N 46.08E
Annau see Ānew
123 Mm16 **An Nawfalīyah** var. Al Nūwfalīyah. N Libya 30.46N 17.48E
21 P10 **Ann, Cape** headland Massachusetts, NE USA 42.39N 70.35W
188 I10 **Annean, Lake** ◎ Western Australia
Anneciacum see Annecy
105 T11 **Annecy** anc. Anneciacum. Haute-Savoie, E France 45.53N 6.09E
105 T11 **Annecy, Lac d'** ◎ E France
105 T10 **Annemasse** Haute-Savoie, E France 46.10N 6.13E
41 Z14 **Annette Island** island Alexander Archipelago, Alaska, USA
An Nhơn see Binh Đinh
An Nīl al Abyaḍ see White Nile
An Nīl al Azraq see Blue Nile
25 Q3 **Anniston** Alabama, S USA 33.39N 85.49W
81 A19 **Annobón** island W Equatorial Guinea
105 R12 **Annonay** Ardèche, E France 45.15N 4.40E
46 K12 **Annotto Bay** C Jamaica 18.16N 76.45W
147 R5 **An Nu'ayrīyah** var. Narıya. Ash Sharqīyah, NE Saudi Arabia 27.30N 48.30E
190 M9 **Annuello** Victoria, SE Australia 34.54S 142.50E
145 Q10 **An Nukhayb** S Iraq 32.01N 42.15E
145 U9 **An Nu'mānīyah** E Iraq 32.34N 45.22E
Áno Arkhánai see Archánes
117 J25 **Anógeia** var. Anogia, Anóyia. Kríti, Greece, E Mediterranean Sea 35.17N 24.55E
Anogia see Anógeia
31 V8 **Anoka** Minnesota, N USA 45.15N 93.26W
An Ómaigh see Omagh
180 I1 **Anorontany, Tanjona** headland N Madagascar
180 J5 **Anosibe An'Ala** Toamasina, E Madagascar 19.24S 48.10E
Anóyia see Anógeia
An Pointe see Warrenpoint
167 P9 **Anqing** Anhui, E China 30.31N 116.58E
167 Q5 **Anqiu** Shandong, E China 36.25N 119.10E
An Ráth see Ráth Luirc
An Ribhéar see Kenmare River
An Ros see Rush
101 K19 **Ans** Liège, E Belgium 50.39N 5.31E
Anṣāb see Niṣāb
176 Ww10 **Ansas** Papua, E Indonesia 1.44S 135.52E
103 J20 **Ansbach** Bayern, SE Germany 49.15N 10.34E
An Sciobairín see Skibbereen
An Scoil see Skull
An Seancheann see Old Head of Kinsale
47 Y5 **Anse-Bertrand** Grande Terre, N Guadeloupe 16.28N 61.30W
180 H17 **Anse Boileau** Mahé, NE Seychelles 4.43S 55.28E
47 S11 **Anse La Raye** NW Saint Lucia 13.57N 61.01W
56 D9 **Anserma** Caldas, W Colombia 5.15N 75.46W
111 T4 **Ansfelden** Oberösterreich, N Austria 48.12N 14.17E
169 U12 **Anshan** Liaoning, NE China 41.06N 122.55E
166 J12 **Anshun** Guizhou, S China 26.15N 105.58E
63 F17 **Ansina** Tacuarembó, C Uruguay 31.58S 55.28W
31 O15 **Ansley** Nebraska, C USA 41.16N 99.22W
27 P6 **Anson** Texas, SW USA 32.45N 99.54W
79 Q10 **Ansongo** Gao, E Mali 15.39N 0.33E
An Srath Bán see Strabane
23 R5 **Ansted** West Virginia, NE USA 38.08N 81.06W
176 Yy10 **Ansudu** Papua, E Indonesia 2.09S 139.19E
59 G15 **Anta** Cusco, S Peru 13.31S 72.12W
59 G16 **Antabamba** Apurímac, C Peru 14.26S 72.51W
Antafalva see Kovačica
142 L17 **Antakya** anc. Antioch, Antiochia. Hatay, S Turkey 36.12N 36.10E
180 K3 **Antalaha** Antsirañana, NE Madagascar 14.52S 50.16E
142 F17 **Antalya** prev. Adalia, anc. Attaleia, Bibl. Attalia. Antalya, SW Turkey 36.52N 30.42E
142 F17 **Antalya** ◈ province SW Turkey
142 F16 **Antalya** ✕ Antalya, SW Turkey 36.53N 30.45E
124 Qq11 **Antalya Basin** undersea feature E Mediterranean Sea
Antalya, Gulf of see Antalya Körfezi
142 F16 **Antalya Körfezi** var. Gulf of Adalia, Eng. Gulf of Antalya. gulf SW Turkey
180 J5 **Antanambao Manampotsy** Toamasina, E Madagascar 19.30S 48.36E
180 I5 **Antananarivo** prev. Tananarive. ● (Madagascar) Antananarivo, C Madagascar 18.52S 47.30E
180 I4 **Antananarivo** ◈ province C Madagascar
180 J5 **Antananarivo** ✕ Antananarivo, C Madagascar 18.52S 47.30E
An tAonach see Nenagh
204-205 **Antarctica** continent
204 I5 **Antarctic Peninsula** peninsula Antarctica
63 J15 **Antas, Rio das** ≈ S Brazil
201 U16 **Ant Atoll** atoll Caroline Islands, E Micronesia
An Teampall Mór see Templemore
Antep see Gaziantep
106 M15 **Antequera** anc. Anticaria, Antiquaria. Andalucía, S Spain 37.01N 4.34W
Antequera see Oaxaca
39 S5 **Antero Reservoir** ⊠ Colorado, C USA
28 M7 **Anthony** Kansas, C USA 37.09N 98.01W
39 R16 **Anthony** New Mexico, SW USA 32.00N 106.36W
190 D5 **Anthony, Lake** salt lake South Australia
76 E8 **Anti-Atlas** ▲▲ SW Morocco
105 U15 **Antibes** anc. Antipolis. Alpes-Maritimes, SE France 43.34N 7.07E
105 U15 **Antibes, Cap d'** headland SE France 43.33N 7.08E
Anticaria see Antequera
11 Q11 **Anticosti, Île d'** Eng. Anticosti Island. island Québec, E Canada
Anticosti Island see Anticosti, Île d'
104 K3 **Antifer, Cap d'** headland N France 49.43N 0.10E
32 L6 **Antigo** Wisconsin, N USA 45.10N 89.10W
11 Q15 **Antigonish** Nova Scotia, SE Canada 45.39N 62.00W
66 P11 **Antigua** Fuerteventura, Islas Canarias, NE Atlantic Ocean
47 X10 **Antigua** island S Antigua and Barbuda, Leeward Islands
Antigua see Antigua Guatemala
47 W9 **Antigua and Barbuda** ◆ commonwealth republic E West Indies
44 C6 **Antigua Guatemala** var. Antigua. Sacatepéquez, SW Guatemala 14.33N 90.39W
43 P11 **Antiguo Morelos** var. Antiguo-Morelos. Tamaulipas, C Mexico 22.34N 99.06W
117 F19 **Antíkyras, Kólpos** gulf C Greece
117 G24 **Antikýthira** var. Andikíthira. island S Greece
144 I7 **Anti-Lebanon** var. Jebel esh Sharqi, Ar. Al Jabal ash Sharqī, Fr. Anti-Liban. ▲▲ Lebanon/Syria
Anti-Liban see Anti-Lebanon
117 M22 **Antimácheia** Kos, Dodekánisa, Greece, Aegean Sea 36.48N 27.05E
117 I22 **Antímilos** island Kykládes, Greece, Aegean Sea
38 L6 **Antimony** Utah, W USA 38.07N 112.00W
An tInbhear Mór see Arklow
32 M10 **Antioch** Illinois, N USA 42.28N 88.06W
Antioch see Antakya
104 I10 **Antioche, Pertuis d'** inlet W France
Antiochia see Antakya
56 D8 **Antioquia** Antioquia, C Colombia 6.24N 75.52W
56 E8 **Antioquia** off. Departamento de Antioquia. ◈ province C Colombia
117 J21 **Antíparos** var. Andipáros. island Kykládes, Greece, Aegean Sea
117 B17 **Antípaxoi** var. Andipaxi. island Iónia Nisiá, Greece, C Mediterranean Sea
126 H7 **Antipayuta** Yamalo-Nenetskiy Avtonomnyy Okrug, N Russian Federation 69.08N 76.43E
199 J14 **Antipodes Islands** island group S NZ
Antipolis see Antibes
117 J18 **Antípsara** var. Andípsara. island E Greece
Antiquaria see Antequera
13 N10 **Antique, Lac** ◎ Québec, SE Canada
117 E18 **Antírrio** var. Andírrion. Dytikí Ellás, C Greece 38.20N 21.46E
117 K16 **Ántissa** var. Ándissa. Lésvos, E Greece 39.15N 25.59E
An tIúr see Newry
Antivari see Bar
58 C6 **Antizana** ▲ N Ecuador 0.29S 78.08W
29 Q13 **Antlers** Oklahoma, C USA 34.13N 95.37W
95 J14 **Antnäs** Norrbotten, N Sweden 65.32N 21.53E
Antō see Andong
64 G5 **Antofagasta** Antofagasta, N Chile 23.40S 70.22W
64 G6 **Antofagasta** off. Región de Antofagasta. ◈ region N Chile
64 I7 **Antofalla, Salar de** salt lake NW Argentina
101 D20 **Antoing** Hainaut, SW Belgium 50.34N 3.26E
26 M5 **Anton** Texas, SW USA 33.48N 102.09W
45 S16 **Antón** Coclé, C Panama 8.22N 80.15W
39 T11 **Anton Chico** New Mexico, SW USA 35.12N 105.09W
62 K12 **Antonina** Paraná, S Brazil 25.28S 48.43W
105 O5 **Antony** Hauts-de-Seine, N France 48.45N 2.16E
Antratsit see Antratsyt
119 Y8 **Antratsyt** Rus. Antratsit. Luhans'ka Oblast', E Ukraine 48.07N 39.04E
99 G15 **Antrim** Ir. Aontroim. NE Northern Ireland, UK 54.43N 6.13W
99 G14 **Antrim** Ir. Aontroim. cultural region NE Northern Ireland, UK
99 G14 **Antrim Mountains** ▲▲ NE Northern Ireland, UK
180 H5 **Antsalova** Mahajanga, W Madagascar 18.40S 44.37E
Antserana see Antsirañana
An tSionainn see Shannon
180 J2 **Antsirañana** var. Antserana; prev. Antsirane, Diégo-Suarez. Antsirañana, N Madagascar 12.19S 49.16E
180 J2 **Antsirañana** ◈ province N Madagascar
Antsirane see Antsirañana
An tSiúir see Suir
120 I7 **Antsla** Ger. Anzen. Võrumaa, SE Estonia 57.49N 26.34E
An tSláine see Slaney
180 J3 **Antsohihy** Mahajanga, NW Madagascar 14.49S 47.58E
65 G14 **Antuco, Volcán** ▲ C Chile 37.29S 71.25W
175 P7 **Antu, Gunung** ▲ Borneo, N Indonesia 0.57N 118.51E
An Tullach see Tullow
An-tung see Dandong
Antunnacum see Andernach
Antwerp see Antwerpen
101 G16 **Antwerpen** Eng. Antwerp, Fr. Anvers. Antwerpen, N Belgium 51.13N 4.25E
101 H16 **Antwerpen** Eng. Antwerp. ◈ province N Belgium
An Uaimh see Navan
160 N12 **Anugul** var. Angul. Orissa, E India 20.51N 84.59E
158 F9 **Anūpgarh** Rājasthān, NW India 29.10N 73.13E
160 K10 **Anūppur** Madhya Pradesh, C India 23.06N 81.45E
161 K24 **Anuradhapura** North Central Province, C Sri Lanka 8.19N 80.25E
Anvers see Antwerpen
204 G4 **Anvers Island** island Antarctica
41 N11 **Anvik** Alaska, USA 62.39N 160.12W
41 N10 **Anvik River** ≈ Alaska, USA
40 F17 **Anvil Peak** ▲ Semisopochnoi Island, Alaska, USA 51.59N 179.36E
165 P7 **Anxi** var. Yuanquan. Gansu, N China 40.31N 95.45E
190 F8 **Anxious Bay** bay South Australia
167 O5 **Anyang** Henan, C China 36.10N 114.18E
165 S11 **A'nyêmaqên Shan** ▲▲ C China
120 H12 **Anykščiai** Utena, E Lithuania 55.30N 25.34E
167 P13 **Anyuan** var. Xinshan. Jiangxi, S China 25.10N 115.25E
127 O6 **Anyuysk** Chukotskiy Avtonomnyy Okrug, NE Russian Federation 68.22N 161.33E
127 Oo5 **Anyuyskiy Khrebet** ▲▲ NE Russian Federation
56 D8 **Anza** Antioquia, C Colombia 6.18N 75.54W
Anzen see Antsla
126 H13 **Anzhero-Sudzhensk** Kemerovskaya Oblast', S Russian Federation 56.00N 85.42E
109 I16 **Anzio** Lazio, C Italy 41.27N 12.37E
57 O6 **Anzoátegui** off. Estado Anzoátegui. ◈ state NE Venezuela
153 P12 **Anzob** W Tajikistan 39.24N 68.55E
Anzyô see Anjō
Aoba see Ambae
172 Ss13 **Aoga-shima** island Izu-shotō, SE Japan
Aohan Qi see Xinhui
Aoiz see Agoiz
195 X16 **Aola** var. Tenaghau. Guadalcanal, C Solomon Islands 9.32S 160.28E
178 Gg15 **Ao Luk Nua** Krabi, SW Thailand 8.21N 98.43E
Aomen see Macao
172 N8 **Aomori** Aomori, Honshū, C Japan 40.49N 140.43E
171 Mm9 **Aomori** off. Aomori-ken. ◈ prefecture Honshū, C Japan
Aontroim see Antrim
117 C15 **Aóos** var. Vijosa, Vijosë, Alb. Lumi i Vjosës,. ≈ Albania/Greece see also Vjosës, Lumi i
203 Q7 **Aorai, Mont** ⩘ Tahiti, W French Polynesia 17.36S 149.28W
193 E19 **Aoraki** prev. Aorangi, Mount Cook. ▲ South Island, NZ 43.38S 170.05E
178 Ii13 **Aôral, Phnum** prev. Phnom Aural. ▲ W Cambodia 12.01N 104.10E
Aorangi see Aoraki
193 L15 **Aorangi Mountains** ▲▲ North Island, NZ
192 H13 **Aorere** ≈ South Island, NZ
108 A7 **Aosta** anc. Augusta Praetoria. Valle d'Aosta, NW Italy 45.43N 7.19E
79 O11 **Aougoundou, Lac** ◎ S Mali
78 K9 **Aoukâr** var. Aouker. plateau C Mauritania
80 J13 **Aouk, Bahr** ≈ Central African Republic/Chad
Aouker see Aoukâr
76 B11 **Aousard** SE Western Sahara 22.42N 14.22W
170 G12 **Aoya** Tottori, Honshū, SW Japan 35.31N 134.01E
Aoyang see Shanggao
80 H5 **Aozou** Borkou-Ennedi-Tibesti, N Chad 22.00N 17.11E
28 M11 **Apache** Oklahoma, C USA 34.57N 98.21W
38 L14 **Apache Junction** Arizona, SW USA 33.25N 111.33W
26 J9 **Apache Mountains** ▲▲ Texas, SW USA
38 M16 **Apache Peak** ▲ Arizona, SW USA 31.50N 110.25W
118 H10 **Apahida** Cluj, NW Romania 46.49N 23.45E
25 T9 **Apalachee Bay** bay Florida, SE USA
25 T3 **Apalachee River** ≈ Georgia, SE USA
25 S10 **Apalachicola** Florida, SE USA 29.43N 84.58W
25 S10 **Apalachicola Bay** bay Florida, SE USA
25 R9 **Apalachicola River** ≈ Florida, SE USA
Apam see Apan
Apamama see Abemama
43 P14 **Apan** var. Apam. Hidalgo, C Mexico 19.41N 98.24W
44 J8 **Apanás, Lago de** ◎ NW Nicaragua
56 H14 **Apaporis, Río** ≈ Brazil/Colombia
193 C23 **Aparima** ≈ South Island, NZ

◆ Country
● Country Capital
◇ Dependent Territory
○ Dependent Territory Capital
◈ Administrative Region
✕ International Airport
▲ Mountain
▲▲ Mountain Range
⩘ Volcano
≈ River
◎ Lake
⊠ Reservoir

APARRI – ARNAOÚTI, AKROTÍRI

179 P7 Aparri Luzon, N Philippines 18.16N 121.42E
114 J9 Apatin Serbia, NW Serbia 45.40N 19.01E
128 J4 Apatity Murmanskaya Oblast', NW Russian Federation 67.33N 33.26E
57 X9 Apatou NW French Guiana 5.07N 54.20W
42 M14 Apatzingán var. Apatzingán de la Constitución. Michoacán de Ocampo, SW Mexico 19.04N 102.19W
176 Y9 Apauwar Papua, E Indonesia 1.36S 138.10E
Apaxtla see Apaxtla de Castrejón
43 O15 Apaxtla de Castrejón var. Apaxtla. Guerrero, S Mexico 18.06N 99.55W
120 J7 Ape Alūksne, NE Latvia 57.32N 26.42E
100 L11 Apeldoorn Gelderland, E Netherlands 52.13N 5.57E
Apennines see Appennino
Apenrade see Aabenraa
59 L17 Apere, Río ≈ C Bolivia
57 W11 Apetina Sipaliwini, SE Surinam 3.30N 55.03W
23 U9 Apex North Carolina, SE USA 35.43N 78.51W
81 M16 Api Orientale, N Dem. Rep. Congo 3.42N 25.22E
158 M9 Api ▲ NW Nepal 30.07N 80.57E
Apia see Abaiang
198 Bb8 Āpia ● (Samoa) Upolu, SE Samoa 13.49S 171.46W
62 K11 Apiaí São Paulo, S Brazil 24.28S 48.51W
175 P16 Api, Gunung ▲ Pulau Sangeang, S Indonesia 8.09S 119.03E
195 Y16 Apio Maramasike Island, N Solomon Islands 9.36S 161.25E
43 O15 Apipilulco Guerrero, S Mexico 18.10N 99.40W
43 P14 Apizaco Tlaxcala, S Mexico 19.24N 98.10W
106 I4 A Pobla de Trives Cast. Puebla de Trives. Galicia, NW Spain 42.21N 7.16W
57 U9 Apoera Sipaliwini, NW Surinam 5.10N 57.08W
117 O23 Apolakkiá Ródos, Dodekánisa, Greece, Aegean Sea 36.02N 27.48E
103 L16 Apolda Thüringen, C Germany 51.01N 11.31E
198 B8 Apolima Strait strait C Pacific Ocean
190 M13 Apollo Bay Victoria, SE Australia 38.40S 143.44E
Apollonia see Sozopol
59 J16 Apolo La Paz, W Bolivia 14.40S 68.33W
59 J16 Apolobamba, Cordillera ▲▲ Bolivia/Peru
179 Rr16 Apo, Mount ⛰ Mindanao, S Philippines 6.54N 125.16E
25 W11 Apopka Florida, SE USA 28.40N 81.30W
25 W11 Apopka, Lake ◎ Florida, SE USA
61 J19 Aporé, Rio ≈ SW Brazil
32 K2 Apostle Islands island group Wisconsin, N USA
Apostolas Andreas, Cape see Zafer Burnu
63 F14 Apóstoles Misiones, NE Argentina 27.54S 55.45W
Apostólou Andréa, Akrotíri see Zafer Burnu
119 S9 Apostolove Rus. Apostolovo. Dnipropetrovs'ka Oblast', E Ukraine 47.40N 33.45E
Apostolovo see Apostolove
19 Qq9 Appalachian Mountains ▲▲ E USA
97 K14 Äppelbo Dalarna, C Sweden 60.30N 14.00E
100 N7 Appelscha Fris. Appelskea. Friesland, N Netherlands 52.57N 6.19E
Appelskea see Appelscha
108 G11 Appennino Eng. Apennines. ▲▲ Italy/San Marino
109 L17 Appennino Campano ▲▲ C Italy
110 I7 Appenzell Appenzell, NW Switzerland 47.19N 9.25E
110 H7 Appenzell ◈ canton NE Switzerland
57 V12 Appikalo Sipaliwini, S Surinam 2.07N 56.16W
100 O5 Appingedam Groningen, NE Netherlands 53.18N 6.52E
27 X8 Appleby Texas, SW USA 31.43N 94.36W
99 L15 Appleby-in-Westmorland NW England, UK 54.34N 2.26W
32 K10 Apple River ≈ Illinois, N USA
32 I5 Apple River ≈ Wisconsin, N USA
27 W9 Apple Springs Texas, SW USA 31.13N 94.57W
31 S8 Appleton Minnesota, N USA 45.12N 96.01W
32 M7 Appleton Wisconsin, N USA 44.16N 88.24W
29 S5 Appleton City Missouri, C USA 38.11N 94.01W
37 U14 Apple Valley California, W USA 34.30N 117.11W
31 V9 Apple Valley Minnesota, N USA 44.43N 93.13W
23 U6 Appomattox Virginia, NE USA 37.21N 78.49W
196 B16 Apra Harbour harbor W Guam
196 B16 Apra Heights W Guam
108 F6 Aprica, Passo dell' pass N Italy 46.10N 10.08E
109 M15 Apricena anc. Hadria Picena. Puglia, SE Italy 41.46N 15.27E
130 L14 Apsheronsk Krasnodarskiy Kray, SW Russian Federation 44.27N 39.45E
Apsheronskiy Poluostrov see Abşeron Yarımadası
105 S15 Apt anc. Apta Julia. Vaucluse, SE France 43.54N 5.24E
Apta Julia see Apt
40 H12 'Āpua Point var. Apua Point headland Hawai'i, USA, C Pacific Ocean 19.15N 155.13W
62 I10 Apucarana Paraná, S Brazil 23.34S 51.28W
Apulia see Puglia
56 K8 Apure off. Estado Apure. ◈ state C Venezuela
56 J7 Apure, Río ≈ W Venezuela
59 F16 Apurímac off. Departamento de Apurímac. ◈ department C Peru
59 F15 Apurímac, Río ≈ S Peru
118 G10 Apuseni, Munţii ▲▲ W Romania
Aqaba/'Aqaba see Al 'Aqabah
144 F15 Aqaba, Gulf of var. Gulf of Elat, Ar. Khalīj al 'Aqabah; anc. Sinus Aelaniticus. gulf NE Red Sea
145 R7 'Aqabah C Iraq 33.33N 42.55E
'Aqabah, Khalīj al see Aqaba, Gulf of
155 O2 Āqchah var. Āqcheh. Jowzjān, N Afghanistan 36.59N 66.07E
Āqcheh see Āqchah
Aqköl see Akkol'
Aqmola see Astana
Aqmola Oblysy see Akmola
164 L10 Aqqikkol Hu ◎ NW China
Aqqystaū see Akkystau
'Aqrah see Ākrē
Aqsay see Aksay
Aqshataū see Akchatau
Aqsū see Aksu
Aqsūat see Aksuat
Aqtas see Aktas
Aqtaū see Aktau
Aqtöbe/Aqtöbe Oblysy see Aktobe
Aqtoghay see Aktogay
Aquae Augustae see Dax
Aquae Calidae see Bath
Aquae Flaviae see Chaves
Aquae Grani see Aachen
Aquae Panoniae see Baden
Aquae Sextiae see Aix-en-Provence
Aquae Solis see Bath
Aquae Tarbelicae see Dax
38 J11 Aquarius Mountains ▲▲ Arizona, SW USA
64 O5 Aquidabán, Río ≈ E Paraguay
61 H20 Aquidauana Mato Grosso do Sul, S Brazil 20.27S 55.45W
42 L15 Aquila Michoacán de Ocampo, S Mexico 18.36N 103.32W
Aquila/Aquila degli Abruzzi see L'Aquila
27 T8 Aquilla Texas, SW USA 31.51N 97.13W
46 L9 Aquin S Haiti 18.16N 73.24W
Aquisgranum see Aachen
104 J13 Aquitaine ◈ region SW France
Aqzhar see Akzhar
159 P13 Āra prev. Arrah. Bihār, N India 25.34N 84.40E
107 S4 Ara ≈ NE Spain
25 P2 Arab Alabama, S USA 34.19N 86.30W
Araba see Álava
144 G12 'Arabah, Wādī al Heb. Ha'Arava. dry watercourse Israel/Jordan
119 U12 Arabats'ka Strilka, Kosa spit S Ukraine
119 U12 Arabats'ka Zatoka gulf S Ukraine
'Arab, Baḩr al see Arab, Bahr el
82 C12 Arab, Bahr el var. Baḩr al 'Arab. ≈ S Sudan
58 E7 Arabela, Río ≈ N Peru
181 O4 Arabian Basin undersea feature N Arabian Sea
Arabian Desert see Sahara el Sharqîya
147 N9 Arabian Peninsula peninsula SW Asia
87 P15 Arabian Plate tectonic feature Africa/Asia/Europe
147 W14 Arabian Sea sea NW Indian Ocean
Arabicus, Sinus see Red Sea
'Arabī, Khalīj al see Gulf, The
Arabistan see Khūzestān
'Arabīyah as Su'ūdīyah, Al Mamlakah al see Saudi Arabia
'Arabīyah Jumhūrīyah, Mişr al see Egypt
144 I9 'Arab, Jabal al ▲▲ S Syria
124 Pp14 'Arab, Khalîg el Eng. Arabs Gulf. gulf N Egypt
Arab Republic of Egypt see Egypt
Arabs Gulf see 'Arab, Khalîg el
145 Y12 'Arab, Shaţţ al Eng. Shatt al Arab, Per. Arvand Rūd. ≈ Iran/Iraq
142 I11 Araç Kastamonu, N Turkey 41.13N 33.19E
61 P16 Aracaju state capital Sergipe, E Brazil 10.45S 37.07W
56 F5 Aracataca Magdalena, N Colombia 10.36N 74.13W
60 P13 Aracati Ceará, E Brazil 4.31S 37.45W
62 J8 Araçatuba São Paulo, S Brazil 21.12S 50.24W
106 J13 Aracena Andalucía, S Spain 37.54N 6.33W
117 F20 Arachnaío ▲▲ S Greece
117 D16 Árachthos var. Arta; prev. Árakhthos, anc. Arachthus. ≈ W Greece
Arachthus see Árachthos
61 N19 Araçuai Minas Gerais, SE Brazil 16.52S 42.03W
142 I11 Araç Çayı ≈ N Turkey
144 F11 'Arad Southern, S Israel 31.16N 35.09E
118 F11 Arad Arad, W Romania 46.12N 21.20E
118 F11 Arad ◈ county W Romania
80 J9 Arada Biltine, NE Chad 15.00N 20.38E
149 P18 'Arādah Abū Z̧aby, S UAE 22.57N 53.24E
Aradhippou see Aradíppou
124 O3 Aradíppou var. Aradhippou. SE Cyprus 34.57N 33.37E
182 K6 Arafura Sea Ind. Laut Arafuru. sea W Pacific Ocean
182 L6 Arafura Shelf undersea feature C Arafura Sea
Arafuru, Laut see Arafura Sea
61 J18 Aragarças Goiás, C Brazil 15.55S 52.12W
Aragats, Gora see Aragats Lerr
143 T12 Aragats Lerr Rus. Gora Aragats. ▲ W Armenia 40.31N 44.06E
34 E14 Arago, Cape headland Oregon, NW USA 43.17N 124.25W
107 R6 Aragón ◈ autonomous community E Spain
107 Q4 Aragón ≈ NE Spain
109 I24 Aragona Sicilia, Italy, C Mediterranean Sea 37.25N 13.37E
107 Q7 Aragoncillo ▲ C Spain 40.59N 2.01W
56 L5 Aragua off. Estado Aragua. ◈ state N Venezuela
57 N6 Aragua de Barcelona Anzoátegui, NE Venezuela 9.30N 64.45W
57 O5 Aragua de Maturín Monagas, NE Venezuela 9.58N 63.30W
61 K15 Araguaia, Río var. Araguaya. ≈ C Brazil
61 K19 Araguari Minas Gerais, SE Brazil 18.37S 48.13W
60 J11 Araguari, Rio ≈ SW Brazil
Araguaya see Araguaia, Río
106 K14 Arahal Andalucía, S Spain 37.15N 5.33W
171 Jj13 Arai Niigata, Honshū, C Japan 36.58N 138.14E
Árainn see Inishmore
Árainn Mhór see Aran Island
Ara Jovis see Aranjuez
76 J11 Arak C Algeria 25.17N 3.45E
176 Yy15 Arak Papua, E Indonesia 7.14S 139.40E
148 M7 Arāk prev. Sultānābād. Markazī, W Iran 34.07N 49.39E
196 D10 Arakabesan island Palau Islands, N Palau
57 S7 Arakaka NW Guyana 7.37N 59.58W
177 Ff6 Arakan State var. Rakhine State. ◈ state W Burma
177 Ff5 Arakan Yoma ▲▲ W Burma
171 Kk12 Arakawa Niigata, Honshū, C Japan 38.06N 139.25E
Árakhthos see Árachthos
Araks/Arak's see Aras
164 H7 Aral Xinjiang Uygur Zizhiqu, NW China 40.40N 81.19E
Aral see Aral'sk, Kazakhstan
Aral see Vose', Tajikistan
Aral-Bukhorskiy Kanal see Amu-Buxoro Kanali
143 T12 Aralik Iğdır, E Turkey 39.54N 44.28E
152 H5 Aral Sea Kaz. Aral Tengizi, Rus. Aral'skoye More, Uzb. Orol Dengizi. inland sea Kazakhstan/Uzbekistan
150 L13 Aral'sk Kaz. Aral. Kzylorda, SW Kazakhstan 46.48N 61.40E
Aral'skoye More/Aral Tengizi see Aral Sea
43 O10 Aramberri Nuevo León, NE Mexico 24.05N 99.52W
194 F14 Aramia ≈ SW PNG
149 N6 Ārān var. Golārā. Eşfahān, C Iran 34.03N 51.30E
107 N5 Aranda de Duero Castilla-León, N Spain 41.40N 3.40W
114 M12 Aranđelovac prev. Arandjelovac. Serbia, C Serbia 44.18N 20.32E
Arandjelovac see Aranđelovac
99 J19 Aran Fawddwy ▲ NW Wales, UK 52.48N 3.42W
99 C14 Aran Island Ir. Árainn Mhór. island NW Ireland
99 A18 Aran Islands island group W Ireland
107 N9 Aranjuez anc. Ara Jovis. Madrid, C Spain 40.01N 3.37W
85 E20 Aranos Hardap, SE Namibia 24.11S 19.07E
27 U14 Aransas Bay inlet Texas, SW USA
27 T14 Aransas Pass Texas, SW USA 27.54N 97.09W
203 O3 Aranuka prev. Nanouki. atoll Tungaru, W Kiribati
178 I11 Aranyaprathet Prachin Buri, S Thailand 13.42N 102.32E
Aranyosasztal see Zlatý Stôl
Aranyosgyéres see Câmpia Turzii
Aranyosmarót see Zlaté Moravce
170 Cc14 Arao Kumamoto, Kyūshū, SW Japan 33.16N 130.25E
79 O8 Araouane Tombouctou, N Mali 18.58N 3.39W
28 L10 Arapaho Oklahoma, C USA 35.34N 98.57W
31 N16 Arapahoe Nebraska, C USA 40.18N 99.54W
59 I16 Arapa, Laguna ◎ SE Peru
193 K14 Arapawa Island island C NZ
63 E17 Arapey Grande, Río ≈ N Uruguay
61 P16 Arapiraca Alagoas, E Brazil 9.45S 36.40W
146 M3 'Ar'ar Al Ḩudūd ash Shamālīyah, NW Saudi Arabia 31.00N 41.00E
56 G15 Araracuara Caquetá, S Colombia 0.36S 72.24W
63 K15 Araranguá Santa Catarina, S Brazil 28.55S 49.30W
62 L8 Araraquara São Paulo, S Brazil 21.46S 48.07W
61 O13 Araras Ceará, E Brazil 4.08S 40.30W
60 I14 Araras Pará, N Brazil 6.03S 54.34W
62 L9 Araras São Paulo, S Brazil 22.21S 47.21W
62 H11 Araras, Serra das ▲▲ S Brazil
143 U12 Ararat S Armenia 39.49N 44.45E
190 M12 Ararat Victoria, SE Australia 37.18S 142.57E
Ararat, Mount see Büyükağrı Dağı
146 M3 'Ar'ar, Wādī dry watercourse Iraq/Saudi Arabia
133 N7 Aras Arm. Arak's, Az. Araz Nehri, Per. Rūd-e Aras, Rus. Araks; prev. Araxes. ≈ SW Asia
107 R9 Aras de Alpuente País Valenciano, E Spain 39.55N 1.09W
143 S13 Aras Güneyi Dağları ▲▲ NE Turkey
Aras, Rūd-e see Aras
203 U9 Aratika atoll Îles Tuamotu, C French Polynesia
Aratürük see Yiwu
56 I8 Arauca Arauca, NE Colombia 7.03N 70.46W
56 I8 Arauca off. Intendencia de Arauca. ◈ province NE Colombia
65 G15 Araucanía off. Región de la Araucanía. ◈ region C Chile
56 L7 Arauca, Río ≈ Colombia/Venezuela
65 F14 Arauco Bío Bío, C Chile 37.16S 73.15W
65 F14 Arauco, Golfo de gulf S Chile
56 H8 Arauquita Arauca, C Colombia 7.01N 71.20W
Arausio see Orange
158 F13 Arāvali Range ▲▲ N India
195 S12 Arawa Bougainville Island, NE PNG 6.13S 155.37E
193 C20 Arawata ≈ South Island, NZ
194 L12 Arawe Islands island group E PNG
61 L20 Araxá Minas Gerais, SE Brazil 19.37S 46.49W
Araxes see Aras
57 O5 Araya Sucre, N Venezuela 10.34N 64.15W
107 R4 Arba ≈ N Spain
83 I15 Ārba Minch' Southern, S Ethiopia 6.02N 37.34E
145 U4 Arbat NE Iraq 35.26N 45.34E
109 D19 Arbatax Sardegna, Italy, C Mediterranean Sea 39.57N 9.42E
Arbe see Rab
Arbela see Arbīl
145 S3 Arbīl var. Erbil, Irbīl, Kurd. Hawlēr; anc. Arbela. N Iraq 36.12N 44.01E
97 M16 Arboga Västmanland, C Sweden 59.24N 15.49E
97 M16 Arbogaån ≈ C Sweden
105 S9 Arbois Jura, E France 46.54N 5.45E
56 D6 Arboletes Antioquia, NW Colombia 8.52N 76.25W
9 X15 Arborg Manitoba, S Canada 50.52N 97.20W
96 N12 Arbrå Gävleborg, C Sweden 61.27N 16.21E
98 K10 Arbroath anc. Aberbrothock. E Scotland, UK 56.34N 2.34W
37 N6 Arbuckle California, W USA 39.00N 122.05W
29 N12 Arbuckle Mountains ▲▲ Oklahoma, C USA
168 I5 Arbulag var. Mandal. Hövsgöl, N Mongolia 49.55N 99.21E
Arbuzinka see Arbyzynka
119 Q8 Arbyzynka Rus. Arbuzinka. Mykolayivs'ka Oblast', S Ukraine 47.54N 31.19E
105 U12 Arc ≈ E France
104 J13 Arcachon Gironde, SW France 44.40N 1.10W
104 J13 Arcachon, Bassin d' inlet SW France
20 E10 Arcade New York, NE USA 42.32N 78.19W
25 W14 Arcadia Florida, SE USA 27.13N 81.51W
24 H5 Arcadia Louisiana, S USA 32.33N 92.55W
32 J7 Arcadia Wisconsin, N USA 44.15N 91.30W
Arcae Remorum see Châlons-en-Champagne
46 L9 Arcahaie C Haiti 18.46N 72.32W
36 K3 Arcata California, W USA 40.51N 124.06W
37 U6 Arc Dome ▲ Nevada, W USA 38.52N 117.20W
109 J16 Arce Lazio, C Italy 41.35N 13.34E
43 O15 Arcelia Guerrero, S Mexico 18.19N 100.16W
101 M15 Arcen Limburg, SE Netherlands 51.28N 6.10E
117 J25 Archánes var. Áno Arkhánai, Epáno Archánes; prev. Epáno Arkhánai.
Archangel see Arkhangel'sk
Archangel Bay see Chëshskaya Guba
117 O23 Archángelos var. Arhangelos, Arkhángelos. Ródos, Dodekánisa, Greece, Aegean Sea 36.13N 28.07E
116 F7 Archar ≈ NW Bulgaria
33 R11 Archbold Ohio, N USA 41.31N 84.18W
107 R12 Archena Murcia, SE Spain 38.07N 1.16W
27 R5 Archer City Texas, SW USA 33.36N 98.37W
106 M14 Archidona Andalucía, S Spain 37.06N 4.22W
67 B25 Arch Islands island group SW Falkland Islands
108 G13 Arcidosso Toscana, C Italy 42.52N 11.30E
105 Q5 Arcis-sur-Aube Aube, N France 48.32N 4.09E
190 F3 Arckaringa Creek seasonal river South Australia
108 G7 Arco Trentino-Alto Adige, N Italy 45.53N 10.51E
35 Q14 Arco Idaho, NW USA 43.38N 113.18W
32 M14 Arcola Illinois, N USA 39.39N 88.19W
107 P6 Arcos de Jalón Castilla-León, N Spain 41.12N 2.13W
106 K15 Arcos de la Frontera Andalucía, S Spain 36.45N 5.49W
106 G5 Arcos de Valdevez Viana do Castelo, N Portugal 41.51N 8.25W
61 P15 Arcoverde Pernambuco, E Brazil 08.23S 37.00W
104 H5 Arcovest, Pointe de l' headland NW France 48.49N 2.58W
Arctic-Mid Oceanic Ridge see Nansen Cordillera
207 R8 Arctic Ocean ocean
14 G4 Arctic Red River ≈ Northwest Territories/Yukon Territory, NW Canada
Arctic Red River see Tsiigehtchic
41 S6 Arctic Village Alaska, USA 68.07N 145.32W
204 H1 Arctowski Polish research station South Shetland Islands, Antarctica 61.57S 58.23W
116 I12 Arda var. Ardhas, Gk. Ardas. ≈ Bulgaria/Greece see also Ardas
148 L2 Ardabīl var. Ardebil. Ardabīl, NW Iran 38.15N 48.18E
148 L2 Ardabīl off. Ostān-e Ardabīl. ◈ province NW Iran
143 R11 Ardahan Ardahan, NE Turkey 41.07N 42.40E
143 S11 Ardahan ◈ province NE Turkey
149 P8 Ardakān Yazd, C Iran 32.20N 54.02E
96 E12 Årdalstangen Sogn og Fjordane, S Norway 61.13N 7.43E
143 R11 Ardanuç Artvin, NE Turkey 41.07N 42.04E
116 L12 Ardas var. Ardhas, Bul. Arda. ≈ Bulgaria/Greece see also Arda
144 I13 Arḑ aş Şawwān var. Ardh es Suwwān. plain S Jordan
131 P5 Ardatov Respublika Mordoviya, W Russian Federation 54.49N 46.13E
12 G12 Ardbeg Ontario, S Canada 45.38N 80.05W
Ardeal see Transylvania
Ardebil see Ardabīl
105 Q13 Ardèche ≈ C France
105 Q13 Ardèche ◈ department E France
99 F17 Ardee Ir. Baile Átha Fhirdhia. NE Ireland 53.52N 6.33W
105 Q3 Ardennes ◈ department NE France
101 J23 Ardennes physical region Belgium/France
143 Q11 Ardeşen Rize, NE Turkey 41.12N 41.02E
149 O7 Ardestān var. Ardistan. Eşfahān, C Iran 33.29N 52.16E
110 J9 Ardez Graubünden, SE Switzerland 46.47N 10.09E
Ardhas see Arda/Ardas
Ardh es Suwwān see Arḑ aş Şawwān
106 I12 Ardila, Ribeira de Sp. Ardilla. ≈ Portugal/Spain see also Ardilla
9 T17 Ardill Saskatchewan, S Canada 49.56N 105.49W
106 I12 Ardilla Port. Ribeira de Ardila. ≈ Portugal/Spain see also Ardila, Ribeira de
42 M11 Ardilla, Cerro la ▲ C Mexico 22.15N 102.33W
116 J12 Ardino Kŭrdzhali, S Bulgaria 41.38N 25.22E
Ardistan see Ardestān
191 P9 Ardlethan New South Wales, SE Australia 34.24S 146.52E
Ard Mhacha see Armagh
25 P1 Ardmore Alabama, S USA 34.59N 86.51W
29 N13 Ardmore Oklahoma, C USA 34.10N 97.08W
22 J10 Ardmore Tennessee, S USA 35.00N 86.48W
98 G10 Ardnamurchan, Point of headland N Scotland, UK 56.42N 6.15W
Árdni see Arnøya
101 C17 Ardooie West-Vlaanderen, W Belgium 50.59N 3.10E
190 I9 Ardrossan South Australia 34.27S 137.54E
118 H9 Ardusat Hung. Erdőszáda. Maramureş, N Romania 47.36N 23.25E
95 F16 Åre Jämtland, C Sweden 63.25N 13.04E
81 P16 Arebi Orientale, NE Dem. Rep. Congo 2.46N 29.34E
47 T5 Arecibo C Puerto Rico 18.28N 66.43W
176 W10 Aredo Papua, E Indonesia 2.27S 133.59E
61 P14 Areia Branca Rio Grande do Norte, E Brazil 4.53S 37.03W
121 O14 Arekhawsk Rus. Orekhovsk. Vitsyebskaya Voblasts', N Belarus 54.42N 30.30E
Arel see Arlon
Arelas/Arelate see Arles
Arenal, Embalse de see Arenal Laguna
44 L12 Arenal Laguna var. Embalse de Arenal. ◎ NW Costa Rica
44 L13 Arenal, Volcán ⛰ NW Costa Rica 10.21N 84.42W
36 K6 Arena, Point headland California, W USA 38.57N 123.44W
61 H17 Arenápolis Mato Grosso, W Brazil 14.25S 56.52W
42 G10 Arena, Punta headland W Mexico 23.28N 109.24W
106 L8 Arenas de San Pedro Castilla-León, N Spain 40.12N 5.04W
65 I24 Arenas, Punta de headland S Argentina 53.10S 68.15W
63 B20 Arenaza Buenos Aires, E Argentina 34.55S 61.45W
97 F17 Arendal Aust-Agder, S Norway 58.27N 8.45E
101 J16 Arendonk Antwerpen, N Belgium 51.18N 5.06E
45 T15 Arenosa Panamá, N Panama 9.02N 79.57W
Arensburg see Kuressaare
107 W5 Arenys de Mar Cataluña, NE Spain 41.34N 2.33E
108 C9 Arenzano Liguria, NW Italy 44.25N 8.43E
117 F22 Areópoli prev. Areópolis. Pelopónnisos, S Greece 36.39N 22.24E
Areópolis see Areópoli
59 H18 Arequipa Arequipa, SE Peru 16.24S 71.33W
59 G17 Arequipa off. Departamento de Arequipa. ◈ department SW Peru
63 B19 Arequito Santa Fe, C Argentina 33.09S 61.28W
106 M7 Arévalo Castilla-León, N Spain 41.04N 4.43W
108 H12 Arezzo anc. Arretium. Toscana, C Italy 43.28N 11.49E
107 Q4 Arga ≈ N Spain
Argaeus see Erciyes Dağı
117 G17 Argalastí Thessalía, C Greece 39.13N 23.14E
107 O10 Argamasilla de Alba Castilla-La Mancha, C Spain 39.07N 3.04W
164 L8 Argan Xinjiang Uygur Zizhiqu, NW China 40.09N 88.16E
107 O8 Arganda Madrid, C Spain 40.19N 3.25W
106 H8 Arganil Coimbra, N Portugal 40.13N 8.03W
179 Qq14 Argao Cebu, C Philippines 9.52N 123.33E
159 V15 Argartala Tripura, NE India
126 K9 Arga-Sala ≈ NE Russian Federation
105 P17 Argelès-sur-Mer Pyrénées-Orientales, S France 42.33N 3.01E
105 T15 Argens ≈ SE France
108 H9 Argenta Emilia-Romagna, N Italy 44.37N 11.49E
104 K5 Argentan Orne, N France 48.45N 0.01W
105 N12 Argentat Corrèze, C France 45.06N 1.57E
108 A9 Argentera Piemonte, NE Italy 44.25N 6.57E
105 N5 Argenteuil Val-d'Oise, N France 48.57N 2.13E
64 K13 Argentina off. Republic of Argentina. ◆ republic S South America
Argentina Basin see Argentine Basin
Argentine Abyssal Plain see Argentine Plain
67 I19 Argentine Basin var. Argentina Basin. undersea feature SW Atlantic Ocean
67 I20 Argentine Plain var. Argentine Abyssal Plain. undersea feature SW Atlantic Ocean
Argentine Rise see Falkland Plateau
65 H22 Argentino, Lago ◎ S Argentina
104 K8 Argenton-Château Deux-Sèvres, W France 46.59N 0.22W
104 M9 Argenton-sur-Creuse Indre, C France 46.34N 1.32E
Argentoratum see Strasbourg
118 I12 Argeş ◈ county S Romania
118 K14 Argeş ≈ S Romania
155 O8 Arghandāb, Daryā-ye ≈ SE Afghanistan
Arghastān see Arghestān
155 O8 Arghestān Pash. Arghastān. ≈ SE Afghanistan
Argirocastro see Gjirokastër
82 E7 Argo Northern, N Sudan 19.31N 30.25E
181 P7 Argo Fracture Zone tectonic feature C Indian Ocean
117 F20 Argolikós Kólpos gulf S Greece
105 R4 Argonne physical region NE France
174 Mm15 Argopuro, Gunung ▲ Jawa, S Indonesia 7.57S 113.32E
117 F20 Árgos Pelopónnisos, S Greece 37.38N 22.42E
145 S1 Argōsh N Iraq 37.07N 44.13E
117 D14 Árgos Orestikó Dytikí Makedonía, N Greece 40.27N 21.15E
117 B19 Argostóli var. Argostólion. Kefalloniá, Iónia Nisiá, Greece, C Mediterranean Sea 38.10N 20.29E
Argostólion see Argostóli
Argovie see Aargau
37 O14 Arguello, Point headland California, W USA 34.34N 120.39W
131 P16 Argun Chechenskaya Respublika, SW Russian Federation 43.16N 45.53E
163 T2 Argun Chin. Ergun He, Rus. Argun'. ≈ China/Russian Federation
79 T12 Argungu Kebbi, NW Nigeria 12.45N 4.24E
Arguut see Guchin-Us
189 N3 Argyle, Lake salt lake Western Australia
98 G12 Argyll cultural region W Scotland, UK
Argyrokastron see Gjirokastër
168 I7 Arhangay ◈ province C Mongolia
Arhangelos see Archángelos
97 P14 Arholma Stockholm, C Sweden 59.51N 19.01E
97 G22 Århus var. Aarhus. Århus, C Denmark 56.09N 10.10E
97 G22 Århus ◈ county C Denmark
145 T1 Ārī E Iraq 37.07N 44.34E
194 M12 Aria ≈ New Britain, E PNG
Aria see Herāt
170 C13 Ariake-kai bay NE East China Sea
85 F22 Ariamsvlei Karas, SE Namibia 28.07S 19.49E
109 L17 Ariano Irpino Campania, S Italy 41.08N 15.00E
56 F11 Ariari, Río ≈ C Colombia
157 K19 Ari Atoll atoll C Maldives
79 P11 Aribinda N Burkina 14.12N 0.50W
64 G2 Arica hist. San Marcos de Arica. Tarapacá, N Chile 18.30S 70.18W
56 H16 Arica Amazonas, S Colombia 2.09S 71.48W
64 G2 Arica ✈ Tarapacá, N Chile 18.30S 70.19W
170 G16 Arida Wakayama, Honshū, SW Japan 34.05N 135.07E
116 E13 Aridaía var. Aridea, Aridhaía. Dytikí Makedonía, N Greece 40.58N 22.04E
Aridea see Aridaía
180 I15 Aride, Île island Inner Islands, NE Seychelles
Aridhaía see Aridaía
105 N17 Ariège ◈ department S France
104 M16 Ariège var. la Riege. ≈ Andorra/France
118 H11 Arieş ≈ W Romania
155 U10 Ārifwāla Punjab, E Pakistan 30.14N 73.04E
Ariguaní see El Difícil
144 G11 Arīhā Al Karak, W Jordan 31.25N 35.46E
144 I3 Arīḩā var. Arīhā. Idlib, W Syria 35.49N 36.36E
Arīḩā see Jericho
39 W4 Arikaree River ≈ Colorado/Nebraska, C USA
170 Bb12 Arikawa Nagasaki, Nakadōri-jima, SW Japan 32.58N 129.06E
114 L13 Arilje Serbia, W Serbia 43.45N 20.06E
47 U14 Arima Trinidad, Trinidad and Tobago 10.38N 61.16W
Arime see Al 'Arīmah
Ariminum see Rimini
61 H16 Arinos, Rio ≈ W Brazil
42 M14 Ario de Rosales var. Ario de Rosáles. Michoacán de Ocampo, SW Mexico 19.12N 101.43W
120 F12 Ariogala Kaunas, C Lithuania 55.16N 23.30E
49 T7 Aripuanã ≈ W Brazil
61 E15 Ariquemes Rondônia, W Brazil 9.55S 63.06W
124 Rr15 'Arîsh, Wâdi el ≈ NE Egypt
56 K6 Arismendi Barinas, C Venezuela 8.28N 68.22W
8 J14 Aristazabal Island island SW Canada
62 F13 Aristóbulo del Valle Misiones, NE Argentina 27.09S 54.54W
180 I5 Arivonimamo ✈ (Antananarivo) Antananarivo, C Madagascar 19.00S 47.11E
Arixang see Wenquan
107 Q6 Ariza Aragón, NE Spain 41.19N 2.03W
64 I6 Arizaro, Salar de salt lake NW Argentina
107 O2 Arizgoiti var. Basauri. País Vasco, N Spain 43.13N 2.54W
64 K13 Arizona San Luis, C Argentina 35.43S 65.16W
38 J12 Arizona off. State of Arizona; also known as Copper State, Grand Canyon State. ◈ state SW USA
42 G4 Arizpe Sonora, NW Mexico 30.19N 110.11W
97 J16 Årjäng Värmland, C Sweden 59.24N 12.09E
149 P8 Arjenān Yazd, C Iran 32.19N 53.48E
94 I13 Arjeplog Norrbotten, N Sweden 66.04N 18.00E
56 E5 Arjona Bolívar, N Colombia 10.13N 75.22W
107 N13 Arjona Andalucía, S Spain 37.55N 4.04W
127 N11 Arka Khabarovskiy Kray, E Russian Federation 60.04N 142.17E
24 L2 Arkabutla Lake ⊡ Mississippi, S USA
131 O7 Arkadak Saratovskaya Oblast', W Russian Federation 51.55N 43.29E
29 T13 Arkadelphia Arkansas, C USA 34.07N 93.03W
117 J25 Arkalochóri prev. Arkalohori, Arkalokhórion. Kríti, Greece, E Mediterranean Sea 35.09N 25.15E
Arkalohori/Arkalokhórion see Arkalochóri
151 O10 Arkalyk Kaz. Arqalyq. Kostanay, N Kazakhstan 50.15N 66.52E
29 U10 Arkansas off. State of Arkansas; also known as The Land of Opportunity. ◈ state S USA
29 W14 Arkansas City Arkansas, C USA 33.36N 91.12W
29 O7 Arkansas City Kansas, C USA 37.03N 97.02W
18 Kk10 Arkansas River ≈ C USA
190 J5 Arkaroola South Australia 30.21S 139.20E
Arkhángelos see Archángelos
128 L8 Arkhangel'sk Eng. Archangel. Arkhangel'skaya Oblast', NW Russian Federation 64.31N 40.40E
128 L9 Arkhangel'skaya Oblast' ◈ province NW Russian Federation
131 O14 Arkhangel'skoye Stavropol'skiy Kray, SW Russian Federation 44.37N 44.03E
127 N16 Arkhara Amurskaya Oblast', S Russian Federation 49.20N 130.04E
99 G19 Arklow Ir. An tInbhear Mór. SE Ireland 52.48N 6.09W
117 M20 Arkoí island Dodekánisa, Greece, Aegean Sea
29 R11 Arkoma Oklahoma, C USA 35.19N 94.27W
102 O7 Arkona, Kap headland NE Germany 54.40N 13.24E
97 N17 Arkösund Östergötland, S Sweden 58.28N 16.55E
126 H4 Arkticheskogo Instituta, Ostrova island N Russian Federation
97 O15 Arlanda ✈ (Stockholm) Stockholm, C Sweden 59.40N 17.58E
152 C11 Arlandag Rus. Gora Arlan. ▲ W Turkmenistan 39.39N 54.28E
Arlan, Gora see Arlandag
107 O5 Arlanza ≈ N Spain
107 N5 Arlanzón ≈ N Spain
105 R15 Arles var. Arles-sur-Rhône; anc. Arelas, Arelate. Bouches-du-Rhône, SE France 43.40N 4.37E
Arles-sur-Rhône see Arles
105 O17 Arles-sur-Tech Pyrénées-Orientales, S France 42.27N 2.37E
31 U9 Arlington Minnesota, N USA 44.36N 94.04W
31 R15 Arlington Nebraska, C USA 41.27N 96.21W
34 J11 Arlington Oregon, NW USA 45.43N 120.10W
31 R10 Arlington South Dakota, N USA 44.21N 97.07W
22 E10 Arlington Tennessee, S USA 35.17N 89.40W
27 T6 Arlington Texas, SW USA 32.43N 97.04W
23 W4 Arlington Virginia, NE USA 38.54N 77.09W
34 H7 Arlington Washington, NW USA 48.12N 122.07W
32 M10 Arlington Heights Illinois, N USA 42.08N 88.03W
79 U8 Arlit Agadez, C Niger 18.54N 7.25E
101 L24 Arlon Dut. Aarlen, Ger. Arel; Lat. Orolaunum. Luxembourg, SE Belgium 49.40N 5.49E
29 R7 Arma Kansas, C USA 37.32N 94.42W
99 F16 Armagh Ir. Ard Mhacha. S Northern Ireland, UK 54.15N 6.33W
99 F16 Armagh cultural region S Northern Ireland, UK
104 K15 Armagnac cultural region S France
105 Q7 Armançon ≈ C France
62 K10 Armando Laydner, Represa ⊡ S Brazil
117 M24 Armathía island SE Greece
130 M14 Armavir Krasnodarskiy Kray, SW Russian Federation 44.59N 41.07E
143 T12 Armavir prev. Hoktemberyan, Rus. Oktemberyan. SW Armenia 40.09N 43.58E
56 E10 Armenia Quindío, W Colombia 4.31N 75.40W
143 T12 Armenia off. Republic of Armenia, var. Ajastan, Arm. Hayastani Hanrapetut'yun; prev. Armenian Soviet Socialist Republic. ◆ republic SW Asia
Armenierstadt see Gherla
105 O1 Armentières Nord, N France 50.40N 2.52E
42 K14 Armería Colima, SW Mexico 18.55N 103.55W
191 T5 Armidale New South Wales, SE Australia 30.31S 151.40E
31 P11 Armour South Dakota, N USA 43.19N 98.21W
63 B18 Armstrong Santa Fe, C Argentina 32.46S 61.39W
9 N16 Armstrong British Columbia, SW Canada 50.27N 119.13W
10 D11 Armstrong Ontario, S Canada 50.19N 89.01W
31 U11 Armstrong Iowa, C USA 43.24N 94.28W
27 S16 Armstrong Texas, SW USA 26.55N 97.47W
119 S11 Armyans'k Rus. Armyansk. Respublika Krym, S Ukraine 46.05N 33.43E
117 H14 Arnaía var. Arnea. Kentrikí Makedonía, N Greece 40.30N 23.36E
123 Mm3 Arnaoúti, Akrotíri var. Arnaoútis, Cape Arnaouti. headland W Cyprus 35.06N 32.16E

◆ Country ● Country Capital ◇ Dependent Territory ○ Dependent Territory Capital ◈ Administrative Region ✈ International Airport ▲ Mountain ▲▲ Mountain Range ⛰ Volcano ≈ River ◎ Lake ⊡ Reservoir

Arnaouti, Cape/Arnaoútis – Athens

Arnaouti, Cape/Arnaoútis see Arnaoúti, Akrotíri
10 L4 Arnaud ≈ Québec, E Canada
105 Q8 Arnay-le-Duc Côte d'Or, C France 47.08N 4.27E
Arnea see Arnaía
107 Q4 Arnedo La Rioja, N Spain 42.13N 2.04W
97 I14 Årnes Akershus, S Norway 60.07N 11.28E
Årnes see Åi Åfjord
28 K9 Arnett Oklahoma, C USA 36.07N 99.46W
100 L12 Arnhem Gelderland, SE Netherlands 51.58N 5.54E
189 Q2 Arnhem Land physical region Northern Territory, N Australia
108 F11 Arno ≈ C Italy
Arno see Arno Atoll
201 W7 Arno Atoll var. Arṇo. atoll Ratak Chain, NE Marshall Islands
190 H8 Arno Bay South Australia 33.55S 136.31E
37 Q8 Arnold California, W USA 38.15N 120.19W
29 X5 Arnold Missouri, C USA 38.25N 90.22W
31 N15 Arnold Nebraska, C USA 41.25N 100.11W
111 R10 Arnoldstein Slvn. Pod Klošter. Kärnten, S Austria 46.34N 13.43E
105 N9 Arnon ≈ C France
47 P14 Arnos Vale ✕ (Kingstown) Saint Vincent, SE Saint Vincent and the Grenadines 13.08N 61.13W
94 I8 Arnøya Lapp. Árdni. island N Norway
12 L12 Arnprior Ontario, SE Canada 45.31N 76.11W
103 G15 Arnsberg Nordrhein-Westfalen, W Germany 51.24N 8.04E
103 K16 Arnstadt Thüringen, C Germany 50.49N 10.57E
Arnswalde see Choszczno
56 K5 Aroa Yaracuy, N Venezuela 10.25N 68.54W
85 E21 Aroab Karas, SE Namibia 26.47S 19.37E
Ároania see Chelmós
203 O6 Aroa, Pointe headland Moorea, W French Polynesia 17.27S 149.45W
Aroe Islands see Aru, Kepulauan
103 H15 Arolsen Niedersachsen, C Germany 51.23N 9.00E
108 C7 Arona Piemonte, NE Italy 45.45N 8.33E
21 R3 Aroostook River ≈ Canada/USA
Arop Island see Long Island
40 M12 Aropuk Lake ◎ Alaska, USA
203 P4 Arorae atoll Tungaru, W Kiribati
202 G16 Arorangi Rarotonga, S Cook Islands 21.13S 159.49W
110 I9 Arosa Graubünden, S Switzerland 46.48N 9.42E
106 F4 Arousa, Ría de estuary E Atlantic Ocean
176 Uu16 Aro Usu, Tanjung headland Pulau Selaru, SE Indonesia 8.19S 130.45E
192 P8 Arowhana ▲ North Island, NZ 38.07S 177.52E
143 V12 Arp'a Az. Arpaçay. ≈ Armenia/Azerbaijan
143 S11 Arpaçay Kars, NE Turkey 40.51N 43.19E
Arpaçay see Arp'a
Arqalyq see Arkalyk
155 N14 Arra ≈ SW Pakistan
Arrabona see Győr
Arrah see Āra
Ar Rahad see Er Rahad
145 R9 Ar Raḥḥālīyah C Iraq 32.53N 43.21E
62 Q10 Arraial do Cabo Rio de Janeiro, SE Brazil 22.57S 42.00W
106 H11 Arraiolos Évora, S Portugal 38.43N 7.58W
145 R8 Ar Ramādī var. Ramadi, Rumadiya. SW Iraq 33.27N 43.19E
146 J6 Ar Rāmī Ḥimṣ, C Syria 34.32N 37.54E
Ar Rams see Rams
144 H9 Ar Ramthā var. Ramtha. Irbid, N Jordan 32.34N 36.00E
98 H13 Arran, Isle of island SW Scotland, UK
144 L3 Ar Raqqah var. Rakka; anc. Nicephorium. Ar Raqqah, N Syria 35.57N 39.03E
144 L3 Ar Raqqah off. Muḥāfaẓat al Raqqah, var. Raqqah, Fr. Rakka. ⬖ governorate N Syria
105 O2 Arras anc. Nemetocenna. Pas-de-Calais, N France 50.16N 2.46E
107 P3 Arrasate Cast. Mondragón. País Vasco, N Spain 43.04N 2.30W
144 G12 Ar Rashādiyah Aṭ Ṭafilah, W Jordan 30.42N 35.37E
144 I5 Ar Rastān var. Rastâne. Ḥimṣ, W Syria 34.57N 36.43E
145 X12 Ar Raṭāwī E Iraq 30.37N 47.12E
104 L15 Arrats ≈ S France
147 N10 Ar Rawḍah Makkah, S Saudi Arabia 21.19N 42.48E
147 Q15 Ar Rawḍah S Yemen 14.26N 47.13E
148 K11 Ar Rawḍatayn var. Raudhatain. N Kuwait 29.52N 47.42E
149 N16 Ar Rayyān var. Al Rayyan. C Qatar 25.18N 51.24E
104 L17 Arreau Hautes-Pyrénées, S France 42.55N 0.21E
66 Q11 Arrecife var. Arrecife de Lanzarote, Puerto Arrecife. Lanzarote, Islas Canarias, NE Atlantic Ocean 28.57N 13.33W
Arrecife de Lanzarote see Arrecife
45 P6 Arrecife Edinburgh reef NE Nicaragua
63 C19 Arrecifes Buenos Aires, E Argentina 34.06S 60.09W
104 F6 Arrée, Monts d' ▲▲ NW France
Ar Refā'ī see Ar Rifā'ī
Arretium see Arezzo
Arriaca see Guadalajara
111 S9 Arriach Kärnten, S Austria 46.43N 13.52E
43 T16 Arriaga Chiapas, SE Mexico 16.13N 93.54W
43 N12 Arriaga San Luis Potosí, C Mexico 21.55N 101.22W
145 W10 Ar Rifā'ī var. Ar Refā'ī. SE Iraq 31.46N 46.07E
145 V12 Ar Riḥāb salt flat S Iraq
106 L2 Arriondas Asturias, N Spain 43.22N 5.10W
147 Q7 Ar Riyāḍ Eng. Riyadh. ● (Saudi Arabia) Ar Riyāḍ, C Saudi Arabia 24.49N 46.49E
147 O8 Ar Riyāḍ off. Minṭaqat ar Riyāḍ. ⬖ province C Saudi Arabia
147 S15 Ar Riyān S Yemen 14.43N 49.18E
Arrō see Ærø
63 H18 Arroio Grande Rio Grande do Sul, S Brazil 32.15S 53.02W
104 K15 Arros ≈ S France
105 Q9 Arroux ≈ C France
27 R5 Arrowhead, Lake ▣ Texas, SW USA
190 L5 Arrowsmith, Mount hill New South Wales, SE Australia 30.07S 141.37E
193 D21 Arrowtown Otago, South Island, NZ 44.57S 168.51E
63 D17 Arroyo Barú Entre Ríos, E Argentina 31.52S 58.25W
106 J10 Arroyo de la Luz Extremadura, W Spain 39.28N 6.36W
65 J16 Arroyo de la Ventana Río Negro, SE Argentina 41.41S 66.03W
37 P13 Arroyo Grande California, W USA 35.07N 120.35W
Ar Ru'ays see Ar Ruways
147 R11 Ar Rub' al Khālī Eng. Empty Quarter, Great Sandy Desert. desert SW Asia
145 V13 Ar Ruḍaymah S Iraq 30.19N 45.25E
63 A16 Arrufó Santa Fe, C Argentina 30.15S 61.45W
144 I7 Ar Ruḥaybah var. Ruhaybeh, Fr. Rouhaïbé. Dimashq, W Syria 33.45N 36.40E
145 V15 Ar Rukhaymīyah well S Iraq 29.22N 45.43E
145 U11 Ar Rumaythah var. Rumaitha. S Iraq 31.31N 45.15E
147 X8 Ar Rustāq var. Rostak, Rustaq. N Oman 23.34N 57.25E
145 N8 Ar Ruṭbah var. Rutba. SW Iraq 33.03N 40.16E
146 M3 Ar Rūthīyah spring/well NW Saudi Arabia 31.18N 41.23E
ar-Ruwaida see Ar Ruwayḍah
147 O8 Ar Ruwayḍah var. ar-Ruwaida. Jīzān, C Saudi Arabia 23.48N 44.44E
149 N15 Ar Ruways var. Al Ruweis, Ar Ru'ays, Ruwais. N Qatar 26.07N 51.13E
149 O17 Ar Ruways var. Ar Ru'ays, Ruwaisv. Abū Ẓaby, W UAE 24.09N 52.57E
Ārs see Aars
Arsanias see Murat Nehri
127 Nn18 Arsen'yev Primorskiy Kray, SE Russian Federation 44.09N 133.28E
161 G19 Arsikere Karnātaka, W India 13.18N 76.15E
131 R3 Arsk Respublika Tatarstan, W Russian Federation 56.07N 49.54E
96 N10 Årskogen Gävleborg, C Sweden 62.07N 17.19E
124 N3 Ársos C Cyprus 34.51N 32.46E
96 N13 Årsunda Gävleborg, C Sweden 60.31N 16.45E
117 C17 Árta anc. Ambracia. Ípeiros, W Greece 39.07N 20.59E
107 Y9 Artà Mallorca, Spain, W Mediterranean Sea 39.42N 3.20E
Arta see Árachthos
143 T12 Artashat S Armenia 39.57N 44.34E
42 M15 Arteaga Michoacán de Ocampo, SW Mexico 18.20N 102.18W
127 Nn18 Artem Primorskiy Kray, SE Russian Federation 43.24N 132.20E
46 C4 Artemisa La Habana, W Cuba 22.49N 82.46W
119 W7 Artemivs'k Donets'ka Oblast', E Ukraine 48.35N 37.58E
126 I14 Artemovsk Krasnoyarskiy Kray, S Russian Federation 54.22N 93.24E
126 Kk13 Artemovskiy Irkutskaya Oblast', C Russian Federation 58.15N 114.51E
125 Ee13 Artemovskiy Sverdlovskaya Oblast', C Russian Federation 57.22N 61.55E
107 U5 Artesa de Segre Cataluña, NE Spain 41.54N 1.03E
39 U14 Artesia New Mexico, SW USA 32.50N 104.24W
27 Q14 Artesia Wells Texas, SW USA 28.13N 99.18W
110 G8 Arth Schwyz, C Switzerland 47.05N 8.39E
12 F15 Arthur Ontario, S Canada 43.49N 80.31W
32 M14 Arthur Illinois, N USA 39.42N 88.28W
30 L14 Arthur Nebraska, C USA 41.32N 101.42W
31 Q5 Arthur North Dakota, N USA 47.03N 97.12W
193 B21 Arthur ≈ South Island, NZ
20 B13 Arthur, Lake ▣ Pennsylvania, NE USA
191 N15 Arthur River ≈ Tasmania, SE Australia
193 G18 Arthur's Pass Canterbury, South Island, NZ 42.59S 171.33E
193 G17 Arthur's Pass pass South Island, NZ 42.57S 171.33E
46 I3 Arthur's Town Cat Island, C Bahamas 24.34N 75.39W
46 M9 Artibonite, Rivière de l' ≈ C Haiti
63 E16 Artigas prev. San Eugenio, San Eugenio del Cuareim. Artigas, N Uruguay 30.25S 56.28W
63 E16 Artigas ⬖ department N Uruguay
204 H1 Artigas Uruguayan research station Antarctica 61.57S 58.23W
143 T11 Art'ik W Armenia 40.38N 43.57E
197 G4 Art, Île island Îles Belep, W New Caledonia
105 O2 Artois cultural region N France
142 L12 Artova Tokat, N Turkey 40.06N 36.18E
107 Y9 Artrutx, Cap d' var. Cabo Dartuch. headland Menorca, Spain, W Mediterranean Sea 39.55N 3.49E
Artsiz see Artsyz
119 N11 Artsyz Rus. Artsiz. Odes'ka Oblast', SW Ukraine 45.58N 29.25E
164 E7 Artux Xinjiang Uygur Zizhiqu, NW China 39.45N 76.09E
143 R11 Artvin Artvin, NE Turkey 41.12N 41.48E
143 R11 Artvin ⬖ province NE Turkey
152 G14 Artyk Ahal Welaýaty, C Turkmenistan 37.32N 59.16E
81 Q16 Aru Orientale, NE Dem. Rep. Congo 2.52N 30.49E
83 E17 Arua NW Uganda 3.01N 30.55E
106 I4 A Rúa de Valdeorras var. La Rúa. Galicia, NW Spain 42.22N 7.12W
Aruângua see Luangwa
47 O15 Aruba var. Oruba. ◇ Dutch autonomous region S West Indies
49 Q4 Aruba island Aruba, Lesser Antilles
Aru Islands see Aru, Kepulauan
176 Ww14 Aru, Kepulauan Eng. Aru Islands; prev. Aroe Islands. island group E Indonesia
159 W10 Arunāchal Pradesh prev. North East Frontier Agency, North East Frontier Agency of Assam. ⬖ state NE India
Arun Qi see Naji
161 H23 Aruppukkottai Tamil Nādu, SE India 9.31N 78.03E
176 Ww9 Aruri, Selat strait Papua, E Indonesia
83 I20 Arusha Arusha, N Tanzania 3.22S 36.40E
83 I20 Arusha ⬖ region E Tanzania
83 I21 Arusha ✕ Arusha, N Tanzania 3.26S 37.07E
56 C9 Arusí, Punta headland NW Colombia 5.36N 77.30W
174 Ll10 Arut, Sungai ≈ Borneo, C Indonesia
161 J23 Aruvi Aru ≈ NW Sri Lanka
81 M17 Aruwimi var. Ituri (upper course). ≈ NE Dem. Rep. Congo
Árva see Orava
39 T4 Arvada Colorado, C USA 39.48N 105.06W
Arvand Rūd see 'Arab, Shaṭṭ al
168 J8 Arvayheer Övörhangay, C Mongolia 46.13N 102.47E
15 L8 Arviat prev. Eskimo Point. Nunavut, C Canada 61.10N 94.15W
95 I14 Arvidsjaur Norrbotten, N Sweden 65.34N 19.12E
97 J15 Arvika Värmland, C Sweden 59.40N 12.37E
94 J8 Årviksand Troms, N Norway 70.10N 20.30E
37 S13 Arvin California, W USA 35.12N 118.52W
169 S8 Arxan Nei Mongol Zizhiqu, N China 47.11N 119.58E
151 P7 Arykbalyk Kaz. Aryqbalyq. Severnyy Kazakhstan, N Kazakhstan 53.00N 68.11E
Aryqbalyq see Arykbalyk
151 P17 Arys' Kaz. Arys. Yuzhnyy Kazakhstan, S Kazakhstan 42.25N 68.49E
Arys see Orzysz
Arys Köli see Arys, Ozero
151 O14 Arys, Ozero Kaz. Arys Köli. ◎ C Kazakhstan
109 D16 Arzachena Sardegna, Italy, C Mediterranean Sea 41.05N 9.21E
131 O4 Arzamas Nizhegorodskaya Oblast', W Russian Federation 55.25N 43.51E
147 V13 Arzāt S Oman 17.03N 54.19E
106 H3 Arzúa Galicia, NW Spain 42.55N 8.10W
113 A16 Aš Ger. Asch. Karlovarský Kraj, W Czech Republic 50.12N 12.12E
97 H15 Ås Akershus, S Norway 59.39N 10.48E
Aså see Asaa
97 H20 Asaa var. Aså. Nordjylland, N Denmark 57.07N 10.24E
85 E21 Asab Karas, S Namibia 25.28S 17.58E
79 U16 Asaba Delta, S Nigeria 6.10N 6.44E
155 S4 Asadābād var. Asadābād; prev. Chaghasarāy. Konar, E Afghanistan 34.52N 71.09E
144 K3 Asad, Buḥayrat al ◎ N Syria
65 H20 Asador, Pampa del plain S Argentina
171 Kk17 Asahi Chiba, Honshū, S Japan 36.08N 140.37E
171 J13 Asahi Toyama, Honshū, SW Japan 36.56N 137.34E
172 Pp5 Asahi-dake ▲ Hokkaidō, N Japan 43.42N 142.50E
170 Ff13 Asahi-gawa ≈ Honshū, SW Japan
172 P5 Asahikawa Hokkaidō, N Japan 43.46N 142.22E
153 S10 Asaka Rus. Assake; prev. Leninsk. Andijon Viloyati, E Uzbekistan 40.39N 72.16E
79 P17 Asamankese SE Ghana 5.46N 0.41W
171 Jj15 Asama-yama ▲ Honshū, S Japan 36.25N 138.34E
196 B15 Asan W Guam 13.28N 144.43E
196 B15 Asan Point headland W Guam
159 R15 Āsānsol West Bengal, NE India 23.40N 86.58E
82 K12 Āsayita Āfar, NE Ethiopia 11.35N 41.23E
176 V9 Asbakin Papua, E Indonesia 0.45S 131.40E
Asben see Aïr, Massif de l'
125 Ee11 Asbest Sverdlovskaya Oblast', C Russian Federation 57.12N 61.18E
13 Q12 Asbestos Québec, SE Canada 45.46N 71.55W
31 Y13 Asbury Iowa, C USA 42.30N 90.45W
20 K15 Asbury Park New Jersey, NE USA 40.13N 74.00W
43 Z12 Ascención, Bahiá de la bay NW Caribbean Sea
42 I3 Ascensión Chihuahua, N Mexico 31.07N 107.58W
67 M14 Ascension Fracture Zone tectonic feature C Atlantic Ocean
67 G14 Ascension Island ◇ dependency of St. Helena C Atlantic Ocean
67 N16 Ascension Island island C Atlantic Ocean
Asch see Aš
111 S3 Aschach an der Donau Oberösterreich, N Austria 48.22N 14.00E
103 H18 Aschaffenburg Bayern, SW Germany 49.58N 9.09E
103 F14 Ascheberg Nordrhein-Westfalen, W Germany 51.46N 7.36E
103 L14 Aschersleben Sachsen-Anhalt, C Germany 51.46N 11.28E
108 G12 Asciano Toscana, C Italy 43.15N 11.32E
108 J13 Ascoli Piceno anc. Asculum Picenum. Marche, C Italy 42.51N 13.34E
109 M17 Ascoli Satriano anc. Asculub, Ausculum Apulum. Puglia, SE Italy 41.13N 15.31E
110 G11 Ascona Ticino, S Switzerland 46.10N 8.45E
Asculub see Ascoli Satriano
Asculum Picenum see Ascoli Piceno
82 L11 Āseb var. Assab, Amh. Āseb. SE Eritrea 13.03N 42.36E
97 M20 Åseda Kronoberg, S Sweden 57.10N 15.19E
131 T6 Asekeyevo Orenburgskaya Oblast', W Russian Federation 53.36N 52.53E
194 J13 Aseki Morobe, C PNG 7.18S 146.16E
83 J14 Āsela var. Asella, Aselle, Asselle. Oromo, C Ethiopia 7.55N 39.08E
95 H15 Åsele Västerbotten, N Sweden 64.10N 17.19E
Asella/Aselle see Āsela
96 K12 Åsen Dalarna, C Sweden 61.18N 13.49E
116 J11 Asenovgrad prev. Stanimaka. Plovdiv, C Bulgaria 42.01N 24.54E
175 Q11 Asera Sulawesi, C Indonesia 3.24S 121.42E
97 E17 Åseral Vest-Agder, S Norway 58.37N 7.27E
120 J3 Aseri var. Asserien, Ger. Asserin. Ida-Virumaa, NE Estonia 59.28N 26.50E
42 J10 Aserradero Durango, W Mexico
152 F13 Aşgabat prev. Ashgabat, Ashkhabad, Poltoratsk. ● (Turkmenistan) Ahal Welaýaty, C Turkmenistan 37.58N 58.22E
152 F13 Aşgabat ✕ Ahal Welaýaty, C Turkmenistan 38.06N 58.10E
97 H16 Åsgårdstrand Vestfold, S Norway 59.19N 10.28E
125 E11 Asha Chelyabinskaya Oblast', C Russian Federation 55.01N 57.11E
Ashara see Al 'Ashārah
25 T6 Ashburn Georgia, SE USA 31.42N 83.39W
193 G19 Ashburton Canterbury, South Island, NZ 43.55S 171.46E
193 G19 Ashburton ≈ South Island, NZ
188 H8 Ashburton River ≈ Western Australia
151 V10 Ashchysu ≈ E Kazakhstan
8 M16 Ashcroft British Columbia, SW Canada 50.40N 121.16W
144 E10 Ashdod anc. Azotos, Lat. Azotus. Central, W Israel 31.48N 34.37E
29 S14 Ashdown Arkansas, C USA 33.40N 94.07W
23 T9 Asheboro North Carolina, SE USA 35.42N 79.48W
9 X15 Ashern Manitoba, S Canada 51.10N 98.22W
23 P10 Asheville North Carolina, SE USA 35.36N 82.33W
10 E8 Asheweig ≈ Ontario, C Canada
29 V9 Ash Flat Arkansas, C USA 36.13N 91.36W
191 T4 Ashford New South Wales, SE Australia 29.18S 151.09E
99 P22 Ashford SE England, UK 51.09N 0.52E
38 K11 Ash Fork Arizona, SW USA 35.12N 112.31W
Ashgabat see Aşgabat
29 T7 Ash Grove Missouri, C USA 37.19N 93.35W
171 K15 Ashikaga var. Asikaga. Tochigi, Honshū, S Japan 36.19N 139.26E
171 Mm10 Ashiro Iwate, Honshū, C Japan 40.04N 141.00E
170 E16 Ashizuri-misaki headland Shikoku, SW Japan 32.43N 132.59E
Ashkelon see Ashqelon
Ashkhabad see Aşgabat
25 Q4 Ashland Alabama, S USA 33.16N 85.50W
28 K7 Ashland Kansas, C USA 37.11N 99.46W
23 P5 Ashland Kentucky, S USA 38.28N 82.39W
21 S2 Ashland Maine, NE USA 46.36N 68.24W
24 M1 Ashland Mississippi, S USA 34.51N 89.10W
29 U4 Ashland Missouri, C USA 38.46N 92.15W
31 S15 Ashland Nebraska, C USA 41.01N 96.21W
33 T12 Ashland Ohio, N USA 40.52N 82.19W
34 G15 Ashland Oregon, NW USA 42.11N 122.42W
23 W6 Ashland Virginia, NE USA 37.45N 77.28W
32 K3 Ashland Wisconsin, N USA 46.34N 90.54W
22 I8 Ashland City Tennessee, S USA 36.16N 87.03W
191 S4 Ashley New South Wales, SE Australia 29.21S 149.49E
31 O7 Ashley North Dakota, N USA 46.00N 99.22W
181 W7 Ashmore and Cartier Islands ◇ Australian external territory E Indian Ocean
121 I14 Ashmyany Rus. Oshmyany. Hrodzyenskaya Voblasts', W Belarus 54.24N 25.57E
20 K12 Ashokan Reservoir ▣ New York, NE USA
172 Pp6 Ashoro Hokkaidō, NE Japan 43.16N 143.33E
144 E10 Ashqelon var. Ashkelon. Southern, C Israel 31.40N 34.34E
Ashraf see Behshahr
145 O3 Ash Shadādah var. Ash Shaddādah, Jisr ash Shadadi, Shaddādī, Shedadi, Tell Shedadi. Al Ḥasakah, NE Syria 36.00N 40.42E
Ash Shaddādah see Ash Shadādah
145 Y12 Ash Shāfī E Iraq 30.49N 47.30E
145 R4 Ash Shakk var. Shaykh. C Iraq 35.15N 43.27E
Ash Sham/Ash Shām see Dimashq
145 T10 Ash Shāmīyah var. Shamiya. C Iraq 31.55N 44.37E
145 Y13 Ash Shāmīyah var. Al Bādiyah al Janūbīyah. desert S Iraq
145 T11 Ash Shanāfīyah var. Ash Shināfiyah. S Iraq 31.34N 44.38E
144 G13 Ash Sharāh var. Esh Sharā. ▲▲ W Jordan
149 R16 Ash Shāriqah Eng. Sharjah. Ash Shāriqah, NE UAE 25.22N 55.28E
149 R16 Ash Shāriqah var. Sharjah. ✕ Ash Shāriqah, NE UAE 25.19N 55.37E
146 I4 Ash Sharmah var. Šarma. Tabūk, NW Saudi Arabia 28.01N 35.16E
145 R4 Ash Sharqāṭ NW Iraq 35.30N 43.15E
147 S10 Ash Sharqīyah off. Al Minṭaqah ash Sharqīyah, Eng. Eastern Region. ⬖ province E Saudi Arabia
145 W11 Ash Shaṭrah var. Shatra. SE Iraq 31.25N 46.10E
144 G13 Ash Shawbak Ma'ān, W Jordan 30.31N 35.34E
144 L5 Ash Shaykh Ibrāhīm Ḥimṣ, C Syria 35.03N 38.50E
147 O17 Ash Shaykh 'Uthmān SW Yemen 12.53N 45.00E
147 S15 Ash Shiḥr SE Yemen 14.45N 49.24E
Ash Shināfiyah see Ash Shanāfīyah
147 V12 Ash Shiṣar var. Shisur. SW Oman 18.13N 53.34E
145 S13 Ash Shubrūm well S Iraq 30.09N 43.59E
147 R10 Ash Shuqqān desert E Saudi Arabia
77 O9 Ash Shuwayrif var. Ash Shwayrif. N Libya 29.54N 14.16E
Ash Shwayrif see Ash Shuwayrif
33 U10 Ashtabula Ohio, N USA 41.54N 80.46W
31 Q5 Ashtabula, Lake ▣ North Dakota, N USA
143 T12 Ashtarak W Armenia 40.18N 44.22E
148 M6 Āshtiān var. Āshtiyān. Markazī, W Iran 34.24N 49.55E
Āshtiyān see Āshtiān
35 R13 Ashton Idaho, NW USA 44.04N 111.27W
11 O10 Ashuanipi Lake ◎ Newfoundland and Labrador, E Canada
13 P6 Ashuapmushuan ≈ Québec, SE Canada
25 Q3 Ashville Alabama, S USA 33.50N 86.15W
33 S14 Ashville Ohio, N USA 39.43N 82.57W
32 K3 Ashwabay, Mount hill Wisconsin, N USA 46.49N 90.57W
176 Uu7 Asia, Kepulauan island group E Indonesia
160 N13 Āsika Orissa, E India 19.37N 84.40E
Asikaga see Ashikaga
95 M18 Asikkala var. Vääksy. Etelä-Suomi, S Finland 61.09N 25.36E
76 G5 Asilah N Morocco 35.18N 6.04W
'Aṣī, Nahr al see Orontes
109 B16 Asinara, Isola island W Italy
126 H13 Asino Tomskaya Oblast', C Russian Federation 56.56N 86.02E
121 O14 Asintorf Rus. Osintorf. Vitsyebskaya Voblasts', N Belarus 54.43N 30.35E
121 L17 Asipovichy Rus. Osipovichi. Mahilyowskaya Voblasts', C Belarus 53.18N 28.40E
147 N12 'Asīr off. Minṭaqat 'Asīr. ⬖ province SW Saudi Arabia
146 M11 'Asīr Eng. Asir. ▲▲ SW Saudi Arabia
145 X10 Askal E Iraq 31.45N 47.07E
143 P13 Aşkale Erzurum, NE Turkey 39.56N 40.39E
119 T11 Askaniya-Nova Khersons'ka Oblast', S Ukraine 46.27N 33.54E
97 H15 Asker Akershus, S Norway 59.49N 10.29E
97 L17 Askersund Örebro, C Sweden 58.55N 14.55E
Aski Kalak see Eski Kaļak
97 I15 Askim Østfold, S Norway 59.34N 11.10E
131 V3 Askino Respublika Bashkortostan, W Russian Federation 56.07N 56.39E
117 D14 Áskio ▲▲ N Greece
158 L9 Askot Uttaranchal, N India 29.43N 80.19E
96 C12 Askvoll Sogn og Fjordane, S Norway 61.21N 5.04E
142 A13 Aslan Burnu headland W Turkey 38.44N 26.43E
142 L16 Aslantaş Barajı ▣ S Turkey
155 S4 Asmār var. Bar Kunar. Konar, E Afghanistan 34.58N 71.28E
82 I9 Asmara Amh. Āsmera. ● (Eritrea) C Eritrea 15.15N 38.57E
Āsmera see Asmara
97 L21 Åsnen ◎ S Sweden
117 F19 Asopós ≈ S Greece
176 X10 Asori Papua, E Indonesia 2.37S 136.06E
82 G12 Āsosa Benishangul, W Ethiopia 10.06N 34.27E
34 M10 Asotin Washington, NW USA 46.18N 117.03W
Aspadana see Eşfahān
Aspang see Aspang Markt
111 X6 Aspang Markt var. Aspang. Niederösterreich, E Austria 47.34N 16.07E
107 S12 Aspe País Valenciano, E Spain 38.21N 0.43W
39 R5 Aspen Colorado, C USA 39.12N 106.49W
27 P6 Aspermont Texas, SW USA 33.07N 100.13W
Asphaltites, Lacus see Dead Sea
Aspinwall see Colón
193 C20 Aspiring, Mount ▲ South Island, NZ 44.21S 168.47E
117 B16 Asprókavos, Akrotírio headland Kérkyra, Iónia Nisiá, Greece, C Mediterranean Sea 39.22N 20.07E
Aspropótamos see Achelóos
Assab see Aseb
78 J10 Assaba var. Açâba. ⬖ region S Mauritania
144 I4 As Sabkhah var. Sabkha. Ar Raqqah, NE Syria 35.30N 35.54E
145 U6 As Sa'dīyah E Iraq 34.11N 45.09E
Assad, Lake see Asad, Buḥayrat al
144 I8 Aş Şafā ▲ S Syria 33.03N 37.07E
144 I10 Aş Şafāwī Al Mafraq, N Jordan 37.12N 32.30E
Aş Şaff see El Şaff
145 N2 Aş Şafīḥ Al Ḥasakah, N Syria 36.42N 40.12E
Aş Şaḥrā' al Gharbīyah see Sahara el Gharbîya
Aş Şaḥrā' ash Sharqīyah see Sahara el Sharqîya
Assake see Asaka
As Salamīyah see Salamīyah
147 Q4 As Sālimī var. Salemy. SW Kuwait 29.07N 46.41E
69 W7 'Assal, Lac ◎ C Djibouti
As Sallūm see Salûm
145 T13 As Salmān S Iraq 30.28N 44.34E
144 G10 As Salṭ var. Salt. Al Balqā', NW Jordan 32.03N 35.43E
148 M16 As Salwā var. Salwa, Salwah. S Qatar 24.43N 50.52E
159 V12 Assam ⬖ state NE India
Assamaka see Assamakka
79 T8 Assamakka var. Assamaka. Agadez, NW Niger 19.24N 5.52E
145 U11 As Samāwah var. Samawa. S Iraq 31.17N 45.05E
As Saqia al Hamra see Saguia al Hamra
144 J4 Aş Şā'rān Ḥamāh, C Syria 35.15N 37.28E
144 G9 Aş Şarīḥ Irbid, N Jordan 32.31N 35.54E
23 Z5 Assateague Island island Maryland, NE USA
145 O6 As Sayyāl var. Sayyāl. Dayr az Zawr, E Syria 34.37N 40.52E
101 G18 Asse Vlaams Brabant, C Belgium 50.55N 4.12E
101 D16 Assebroek West-Vlaanderen, NW Belgium 51.12N 3.16E
Asselle see Āsela
109 C20 Assemini Sardegna, Italy, C Mediterranean Sea 39.16N 8.58E
100 N7 Assen Drenthe, NE Netherlands 53.00N 6.34E
101 E16 Assenede Oost-Vlaanderen, NW Belgium 51.15N 3.43E
97 G24 Assens Fyn, C Denmark 55.16N 9.54E
Asserien/Asserin see Aseri
101 I21 Assesse Namur, SE Belgium 50.22N 5.01E
147 Y8 As Sīb var. Seeb. NE Oman 23.40N 58.03E
145 Z13 As Sībah var. Sibah. SE Iraq 30.13N 47.24E
9 T17 Assiniboia Saskatchewan, S Canada 49.39N 105.58W
9 V15 Assiniboine ≈ Manitoba, S Canada
9 P16 Assiniboine, Mount ▲ Alberta/British Columbia, SW Canada 50.54N 115.43W
Assiout see Asyût
62 J9 Assis São Paulo, S Brazil 22.37S 50.25W
108 I13 Assisi Umbria, C Italy 43.04N 12.36E
Assiut see Asyût
Assling see Jesenice
Assouan see Aswân
Assu see Açu
Assuan see Aswân
148 K12 Aş Şubayḥīyah var. Subiyah. S Kuwait 28.55N 47.57E
147 R16 As Sufāl S Yemen 14.06N 48.42E
144 L5 As Sukhnah var. Sukhne, Fr. Soukhné. Ḥimṣ, C Syria 34.55N 38.52E
145 U4 As Sulaymānīyah var. Sulaimaniya, Kurd. Slēmānī. NE Iraq 35.31N 45.27E
147 P11 As Sulayyil Ar Riyāḍ, S Saudi Arabia 20.28N 45.33E
123 M16 As Sulţān N Libya 31.01N 17.21E
147 Q5 Aş Şummān desert N Saudi Arabia
147 Q16 Aş Şurrah SW Yemen 13.56N 46.23E
145 N4 Aş Şuwār var. Şuwār. Dayr az Zawr, E Syria 35.31N 40.37E
144 H9 As Suwaydā' var. El Suweida, Es Suweida, Suweida, Fr. Soueida. As Suwaydā', SW Syria 32.43N 36.33E
144 H9 As Suwaydā' off. Muḥāfaẓat as Suwaydā', var. As Suwaydā, Suwaydá, Suweida, Fr. Soueida. ⬖ governorate S Syria
147 Z9 As Suwayḥ NE Oman 22.07N 59.42E
147 X8 As Suwayq var. Suwaik. N Oman 23.51N 57.20E
145 T8 Aş Şuwayrah var. Suwaira. E Iraq 32.57N 44.46E
As Suways see Suez
Asta Colonia see Asti
Astacus see İzmit
117 M23 Astakída island SE Greece
151 Q9 Astana prev. Akmola, Akmolinsk, Tselinograd, Aqmola. ● (Kazakhstan) Akmola, N Kazakhstan 51.12N 71.25E
148 M3 Āstāneh Gīlān, NW Iran 37.16N 49.58E
Asta Pompeia see Asti
143 Y14 Astara S Azerbaijan 38.28N 48.51E
Astarabad see Gorgān
101 L15 Asten Noord-Brabant, SE Netherlands 51.24N 5.45E
Asterābād see Gorgān
108 C8 Asti anc. Asta Colonia, Asta Pompeia, Hasta Colonia, Hasta Pompeia. Piemonte, NW Italy 44.54N 8.10E
Astigi see Ecija
Astipálaia see Astypálaia
154 L16 Astola Island island SW Pakistan
158 H4 Astor Jammu and Kashmir, NW India 35.21N 74.52E
106 K4 Astorga anc. Asturica Augusta. Castilla-León, N Spain 42.27N 6.04W
34 F10 Astoria Oregon, NW USA 46.12N 123.49W
(0) F8 Astoria Fan undersea feature E Pacific Ocean
97 J22 Åstorp Skåne, S Sweden 56.09N 12.57E
Astrabad see Gorgān
131 Q13 Astrakhan' Astrakhanskaya Oblast', SW Russian Federation 46.20N 48.00E
Astrakhan-Bazar see Călilabad
131 Q11 Astrakhanskaya Oblast' ⬖ province SW Russian Federation
95 J15 Åsträsk Västerbotten, N Sweden 64.38N 20.00E
Astrida see Butare
67 O22 Astrid Ridge undersea feature S Atlantic Ocean
194 J11 Astrolabe Bay inlet N PNG
197 I4 Astrolabe, Récifs de l' reef C New Caledonia
124 Nn3 Astromerítis N Cyprus 35.09N 33.02E
117 F20 Ástros Pelopónnisos, S Greece 37.24N 22.43E
121 G16 Astryna Rus. Ostryna. Hrodzyenskaya Voblasts', W Belarus 53.44N 24.33E
106 J2 Asturias ⬖ autonomous community NW Spain
Asturias see Oviedo
Asturica Augusta see Astorga
117 L22 Astypálaia var. Astipálaia, It. Stampalia. island Kykládes, Greece, Aegean Sea
198 Aa8 Āsuisui, Cape headland Savai'i, W Samoa 13.43S 172.28W
205 S2 Asuka Japanese research station Antarctica 71.49S 23.52E
64 O6 Asunción ● (Paraguay) Central, S Paraguay 25.16S 57.36W
64 O6 Asunción ✕ Central, S Paraguay 25.15S 57.40W
196 K3 Asuncion Island island N Northern Mariana Islands
44 E6 Asunción Mita Jutiapa, SE Guatemala 14.19N 89.42W
Asunción Nochixtlán see Nochixtlán
42 E3 Asunción, Río ≈ NW Mexico
97 M18 Åsunden ◎ S Sweden
120 K11 Asvyeya Rus. Osveya. Vitsyebskaya Voblasts', N Belarus 56.00N 28.05E
Aswa see Achwa
77 X11 Aswân var. Assouan, Assuan; anc. Syene. SE Egypt 24.03N 32.58E
77 X11 Aswân High Dam dam SE Egypt 23.54N 32.51E
77 W9 Asyût var. Assiout, Assiut, Siut; anc. Lycopolis. C Egypt 27.05N 31.10E
200 R15 Ata island Tongatapu Group, SW Tonga
64 G8 Atacama off. Región de Atacama. ⬖ region C Chile
Atacama Desert see Atacama, Desierto de
64 H4 Atacama, Desierto de Eng. Atacama Desert. desert N Chile
64 I6 Atacama, Puna de ▲▲ NW Argentina
64 I5 Atacama, Salar de salt lake N Chile
56 E11 Ataco Tolima, C Colombia 3.33N 75.25W
202 H8 Atafu Atoll island NW Tokelau
202 H8 Atafu Village Atafu Atoll, NW Tokelau 8.40S 172.40W
76 K12 Atakor ▲▲ SE Algeria
79 R14 Atakora, Chaîne de l' var. Atakora Mountains. ▲▲ N Benin
Atakora Mountains see Atakora, Chaîne de l'
79 R16 Atakpamé C Togo 7.31N 1.07E
152 F11 Atakui Ahal Welaýaty, C Turkmenistan 40.04N 58.03E
60 B13 Atalaia do Norte Amazonas, N Brazil 4.22S 70.10W
171 J17 Atami Shizuoka, Honshū, S Japan 35.04N 139.03E
152 M14 Atamyrat prev. Kerki. Lebap Welaýaty, E Turkmenistan 37.51N 65.06E
78 I7 Aţâr Adrar, W Mauritania 20.30N 13.03W
168 G10 Atas Bogd ▲ SW Mongolia 43.17N 96.47E
37 P12 Atascadero California, W USA 35.28N 120.40W
27 S13 Atascosa River ≈ Texas, SW USA
151 R11 Atasu Karaganda, C Kazakhstan 48.42N 71.37E
151 R12 Atasu ≈ C Kazakhstan
200 Qq15 Atata island Tongatapu Group, S Tonga
142 H10 Atatürk ✕ (İstanbul) İstanbul, NW Turkey 40.58N 28.50E
143 N16 Atatürk Barajı ▣ S Turkey
117 O23 Atavýros prev. Attávyros. ▲ Ródos, Dodekánisa, Greece, Aegean Sea 36.10N 27.50E
Atax see Aude
82 G8 Atbara var. 'Aṭbārah. River Nile, NE Sudan 17.42N 34.00E
82 H8 Atbara var. Nahr 'Aṭbarah. ≈ Eritrea/Sudan
'Aṭbārah/'Aṭbarah, Nahr see Atbara
151 P9 Atbasar Akmola, N Kazakhstan 51.49N 68.18E
At-Bashi see At-Bashy
153 W9 At-Bashy var. At-Bashi. Narynskaya Oblast', C Kyrgyzstan 41.07N 75.48E
24 I10 Atchafalaya Bay bay Louisiana, S USA
24 I8 Atchafalaya River ≈ Louisiana, S USA
Atchin see Aceh
29 Q3 Atchison Kansas, C USA 39.31N 95.07W
79 P16 Atebubu C Ghana 7.47N 1.00W
107 Q6 Ateca Aragón, NE Spain 41.19N 1.49W
42 K11 Atengo, Río ≈ C Mexico
Aternum see Pescara
109 K15 Atessa Abruzzo, C Italy 42.03N 14.25E
Ateste see Este
101 E19 Ath var. Aat. Hainaut, SW Belgium 50.37N 3.46E
9 Q13 Athabasca Alberta, SW Canada 54.43N 113.15W
9 Q12 Athabasca var. Athabaska. ≈ Alberta, SW Canada
9 R10 Athabasca, Lake ◎ Alberta/Saskatchewan, SW Canada
Athabaska see Athabasca
117 C16 Athamánon ▲▲ C Greece
99 F17 Athboy Ir. Baile Átha Buí. E Ireland 53.37N 6.54W
Athenae see Athína
99 C18 Athenry Ir. Baile Átha an Rí. W Ireland 53.19N 8.49W
25 P2 Athens Alabama, S USA 34.48N 86.58W

◆ Country ● Country Capital ◇ Dependent Territory ○ Dependent Territory Capital ⬖ Administrative Region ✕ International Airport ▲ Mountain ▲▲ Mountain Range Volcano ≈ River ◎ Lake ▣ Reservoir

ATHENS – AZUL

25 T3 **Athens** Georgia, SE USA *33.57N 83.24W*
33 T14 **Athens** Ohio, N USA *39.19N 82.06W*
22 M10 **Athens** Tennessee, SE USA *35.26N 84.35W*
27 V7 **Athens** Texas, SW USA *32.12N 95.51W*
Athens *see* Athína
117 B18 **Athéras, Akrotírio** *headland* Kefalloniá, Iónia Nisiá, Greece, C Mediterranean Sea *38.20N 20.24E*
189 W4 **Atherton** Queensland, NE Australia *17.18S 145.29E*
83 I19 **Athi** ≈ S Kenya
124 O3 **Athiénou** SE Cyprus *35.01N 33.31E*
117 H19 **Athína** *Eng.* Athens; *prev.* Athínai, *anc.* Athenae. ● (Greece) Attikí, C Greece *37.58N 23.44E*
Athínai *see* Athína
145 S10 **Athīyah** C Iraq *32.01N 44.04E*
99 D18 **Athlone** *Ir.* Baile Átha Luain. C Ireland *53.25N 7.55W*
161 F16 **Athni** Karnātaka, W India *16.43N 75.04E*
193 C23 **Athol** Southland, South Island, NZ *45.30S 168.35E*
21 N11 **Athol** Massachusetts, NE USA *42.35N 72.11W*
117 I15 **Áthos** ▲ NE Greece *40.10N 24.21E*
Athos, Mount *see* Ágion Óros
Ath Thawrah *see* Madīnat ath Thawrah
147 P5 **Ath Thumāmī** *spring/well* N Saudi Arabia *27.56N 45.06E*
101 L25 **Athus** Luxembourg, SE Belgium *49.34N 5.49E*
99 E19 **Athy** *Ir.* Baile Átha Í. C Ireland *52.58N 6.59W*
80 I10 **Ati** Batha, C Chad *13.10N 18.19E*
83 F16 **Atiak** NW Uganda *3.13N 32.04E*
59 G17 **Atico** Arequipa, SW Peru *16.13S 73.13W*
107 O6 **Atienza** Castilla-La Mancha, C Spain *41.12N 2.52W*
41 Q6 **Atigun Pass** *pass* Alaska, USA *68.01N 149.36W*
10 B12 **Atikokan** Ontario, S Canada *48.45N 91.37W*
11 O9 **Atikonak Lac** ◎ Newfoundland and Labrador, E Canada
44 C6 **Atitlán, Lago de** ◎ W Guatemala
202 L16 **Atiu** *island* S Cook Islands
Atjeh *see* Aceh
127 O9 **Atka** Magadanskaya Oblast', E Russian Federation *60.45N 151.34E*
40 H17 **Atka** Atka Island, Alaska, USA *52.12N 174.13W*
40 H17 **Atka Island** *island* Aleutian Islands, Alaska, USA
131 O7 **Atkarsk** Saratovskaya Oblast', W Russian Federation *52.15N 43.48E*
29 U11 **Atkins** Arkansas, C USA *35.15N 92.56W*
31 O13 **Atkinson** Nebraska, C USA *42.31N 98.57W*
176 U10 **Atkri** Papua, E Indonesia *1.45S 130.04E*
43 O13 **Atlacomulco** *var.* Atlacomulco de Fabela. México, C Mexico *19.48N 99.52W*
Atlacomulco de Fabela *see* Atlacomulco
25 S3 **Atlanta** *state capital* Georgia, SE USA *33.45N 84.22W*
33 R6 **Atlanta** Michigan, N USA *45.01N 84.07W*
27 X6 **Atlanta** Texas, SW USA *33.06N 94.09W*
31 T15 **Atlantic** Iowa, C USA *41.24N 95.00W*
23 Y10 **Atlantic** North Carolina, SE USA *34.52N 76.20W*
25 W8 **Atlantic Beach** Florida, SE USA *30.19N 81.24W*
20 J17 **Atlantic City** New Jersey, NE USA *39.22N 74.27W*
180 L14 **Atlantic-Indian Basin** *undersea feature* SW Indian Ocean
180 K13 **Atlantic-Indian Ridge** *undersea feature* SW Indian Ocean
56 E4 **Atlántico** *off.* Departamento del Atlántico. ◈ *province* NW Colombia
66-67 **Atlantic Ocean** *ocean*
44 K7 **Atlántico Norte, Región Autónoma** *prev.* Zelaya Norte. ◈ *autonomous region* NE Nicaragua
44 L10 **Atlántico Sur, Región Autónoma** *prev.* Zelaya Sur. ◈ *autonomous region* SE Nicaragua
44 I5 **Atlántida** ◈ *department* N Honduras
79 Y15 **Atlantika Mountains** ▲▲ E Nigeria
66 J10 **Atlantis Fracture Zone** *tectonic feature* NW Atlantic Ocean
76 H7 **Atlas Mountains** ▲▲ NW Africa
127 Pp13 **Atlasova, Ostrov** *island* SE Russian Federation
127 Pp10 **Atlasovo** Kamchatskaya Oblast', E Russian Federation *55.42N 159.34E*
123 H13 **Atlas Saharien** *var.* Saharan Atlas. ▲▲ Algeria/Morocco
Atlas, Tell *see* Atlas Tellien
123 Gg10 **Atlas Tellien** *Eng.* Tell Atlas. ▲▲ N Algeria
8 I9 **Atlin** British Columbia, W Canada *59.31N 133.40W*
8 I9 **Atlin Lake** ◎ British Columbia, W Canada
43 P14 **Atlixco** Puebla, S Mexico *18.55N 98.25W*
96 B11 **Atløyna** *island* S Norway
161 I17 **Ātmakūr** Andhra Pradesh, C India *15.52N 78.42E*
25 O8 **Atmore** Alabama, S USA *31.01N 87.29W*
103 J20 **Atmühl** ≈ S Germany
96 H11 **Atna** ≈ S Norway
170 E12 **Atō** Yamaguchi, Honshū, SW Japan *34.24N 131.42E*
59 L21 **Atocha** Potosí, S Bolivia *20.55S 66.13W*
29 P12 **Atoka** Oklahoma, C USA *34.23N 96.07W*
29 O12 **Atoka Lake** *var.* Atoka Reservoir. ⊡ Oklahoma, C USA
Atoka Reservoir *see* Atoka Lake
35 Q14 **Atomic City** Idaho, NW USA *43.26N 112.48W*
42 L10 **Atotonilco** Zacatecas, C Mexico *24.12N 102.46W*
42 M13 **Atotonilco el Alto** *var.* Atotonilco. Jalisco, SW Mexico *20.32N 102.27W*
79 N7 **Atouila, 'Erg** *desert* N Mali
43 N16 **Atoyac** *var.* Atoyac de Alvarez. Guerrero, S Mexico *17.10N 100.27W*
Atoyac de Alvarez *see* Atoyac
43 P15 **Atoyac, Río** ≈ S Mexico
41 O5 **Atqasuk** Alaska, USA *70.28N 157.24W*
Atrak/Atrak, Rūd-e *see* Etrek
97 J20 **Ätran** ≈ S Sweden
56 C7 **Atrato, Río** ≈ NW Colombia
Atrek *see* Etrek
109 K14 **Atri** Abruzzo, C Italy *42.34N 13.58E*
Atria *see* Adria
171 Jj16 **Atsugi** *var.* Atugi. Kanagawa, Honshū, S Japan *35.27N 139.21E*
171 L12 **Atsumi** Yamagata, Honshū, C Japan *38.38N 139.36E*
172 Oo4 **Atsuta** Hokkaidō, NE Japan *43.28N 141.24E*
176 Y13 **Atsy** Papua, E Indonesia *5.40S 138.19E*
149 Q17 **Aṭ Ṭaff** *desert* C UAE
144 G12 **Aṭ Ṭafilah** *var.* Et Tafila, Tafila. Aṭ Ṭafilah, W Jordan *30.52N 35.36E*
144 G12 **Aṭ Ṭafilah** *off.* Muḥāfaẓat aṭ Ṭafilah. ◈ *governorate* W Jordan
146 L10 **Aṭ Ṭā'if** Makkah, W Saudi Arabia *21.49N 40.49E*
Attaleia/Attalia *see* Antalya
25 Q3 **Attalla** Alabama, S USA *34.01N 86.05W*
144 L2 **At Tall al Abyaḍ** *var.* Tall al Abyaḍ, Tell Abyad, *Fr.* Tell Abiad. Ar Raqqah, N Syria *36.36N 34.00E*
144 L7 **At Tanf** Ḥimṣ, S Syria *33.29N 38.39E*
Attapu *see* Samakhixai
145 S10 **At Taqṭaqānah** C Iraq *32.03N 43.54E*
Attávyros *see* Atavýros
145 V15 **At Tawal** *desert* Iraq/Saudi Arabia
10 G9 **Attawapiskat** Ontario, C Canada *52.55N 82.25W*
10 F9 **Attawapiskat** ≈ Ontario, S Canada
10 D9 **Attawapiskat Lake** ◎ Ontario, C Canada
At Taybé *see* Ṭayyibah
103 F16 **Attendorn** Nordrhein-Westfalen, W Germany *51.07N 7.54E*
111 R5 **Attersee** Salzburg, NW Austria *47.55N 13.31E*
111 R5 **Attersee** ◎ N Austria
101 L24 **Attert** Luxembourg, SE Belgium *49.45N 5.47E*
144 M4 **At Tibnī** *var.* Tibnī. Dayr az Zawr, NE Syria *35.30N 39.48E*
33 N13 **Attica** Indiana, N USA *40.17N 87.15W*
20 E10 **Attica** New York, NE USA *42.51N 78.13W*
Attica *see* Attikí
11 N7 **Attikamagen Lake** ◎ Newfoundland and Labrador, E Canada
117 H20 **Attikí** *Eng.* Attica. ◈ *region* C Greece
21 O12 **Attleboro** Massachusetts, NE USA *41.55N 71.15W*
111 R5 **Attnang** Oberösterreich, N Austria *48.01N 13.43E*
155 U6 **Attock City** Punjab, E Pakistan *33.52N 72.19E*
Attopeu *see* Samakhixai
27 X8 **Attoyac River** ≈ Texas, SW USA
40 D16 **Attu** Attu Island, Alaska, USA *52.53N 173.18E*
145 Y12 **Aṭ Ṭūbah** E Iraq *30.29N 47.28E*
146 K4 **Aṭ Ṭubayq** *plain* Jordan/Saudi Arabia
40 C16 **Attu Island** *island* Aleutian Islands, Alaska, USA
Aṭ Ṭūr *see* El Ṭûr
161 I21 **Āttūr** Tamil Nādu, SE India *11.34N 78.39E*
147 N17 **At Turbah** SW Yemen *12.42N 43.31E*
64 I12 **Atuel, Río** ≈ C Argentina
Atugi *see* Atsugi
203 X7 **Atuona** Hiva Oa, NE French Polynesia *9.46S 139.03W*
Aturus *see* Adour
97 M18 **Åtvidaberg** Östergötland, S Sweden *58.12N 16.00E*
37 P9 **Atwater** California, W USA *37.19N 120.33W*
31 T8 **Atwater** Minnesota, N USA *45.08N 94.48W*
28 I2 **Atwood** Kansas, C USA *39.48N 101.02W*
33 U12 **Atwood Lake** ⊡ Ohio, N USA
131 P5 **Atyashevo** Respublika Mordoviya, W Russian Federation *54.36N 46.04E*
150 F12 **Atyrau** *prev.* Gur'yev. Atyrau, W Kazakhstan *47.07N 51.55E*
150 E11 **Atyrau** *off.* Atyrauskaya Oblast', *var. Kaz.* Atyraū Oblysy; *prev.* Gur'yevskaya Oblast'. ◈ *province* W Kazakhstan
Atyraū Oblysy/Atyrauskaya Oblast' *see* Atyrau
110 J7 **Au** Vorarlberg, NW Austria *47.19N 10.01E*
194 G8 **Aua Island** *island* NW PNG
105 S16 **Aubagne** *anc.* Albania. Bouches-du-Rhône, SE France *43.16N 5.34E*
101 L25 **Aubange** Luxembourg, SE Belgium *49.34N 5.48E*
105 Q6 **Aube** ◈ *department* N France
105 R6 **Aube** ≈ N France
101 L19 **Aubel** Liège, E Belgium *50.45N 5.49E*
105 Q13 **Aubenas** Ardèche, E France *44.37N 4.24E*
105 O8 **Aubigny-sur-Nère** Cher, C France *47.30N 2.27E*
105 O13 **Aubin** Aveyron, S France *44.30N 2.18E*
105 O13 **Aubrac, Monts d'** ▲▲ S France
38 J10 **Aubrey Cliffs** *cliff* Arizona, SW USA
25 R5 **Auburn** Alabama, S USA *32.37N 85.30W*
37 P6 **Auburn** California, W USA *38.53N 121.03W*
32 K14 **Auburn** Illinois, N USA *39.35N 89.45W*
33 Q11 **Auburn** Indiana, N USA *41.22N 85.03W*
22 J7 **Auburn** Kentucky, S USA *36.52N 86.42W*
21 P8 **Auburn** Maine, NE USA *44.05N 70.15W*
21 N11 **Auburn** Massachusetts, NE USA *42.11N 71.47W*
31 S16 **Auburn** Nebraska, C USA *40.23N 95.50W*
20 H10 **Auburn** New York, NE USA *42.55N 76.31W*
34 H8 **Auburn** Washington, NW USA *47.18N 122.13W*
105 N11 **Aubusson** Creuse, C France *45.58N 2.10E*
120 E10 **Auce** *Ger.* Autz. Dobele, SW Latvia *56.28N 22.54E*
104 L15 **Auch** *Lat.* Augusta Auscorum, Elimberrum. Gers, S France *43.39N 0.37E*
79 U16 **Auchi** Edo, S Nigeria *7.01N 6.17E*
25 T9 **Aucilla River** ≈ Florida/Georgia, SE USA
192 L6 **Auckland** Auckland, North Island, NZ *36.53S 174.46E*
192 K5 **Auckland** *off.* Auckland Region. ◈ *region* North Island, NZ
192 L6 **Auckland** ✕ Auckland, North Island, NZ *37.01S 174.49E*
199 Ii15 **Auckland Islands** *island group* S NZ
105 O16 **Aude** ◈ *department* S France
105 N16 **Aude** *anc.* Atax. ≈ S France
Audenarde *see* Oudenaarde
Audern *see* Audru
104 E6 **Audierne** Finistère, NW France *48.01N 4.30W*
104 E6 **Audierne, Baie d'** *bay* NW France
105 U7 **Audincourt** Doubs, E France *47.28N 6.49E*
120 G5 **Audru** *Ger.* Audern. Pärnumaa, SW Estonia *58.25N 24.21E*
31 T14 **Audubon** Iowa, C USA *41.44N 94.56W*
103 N17 **Aue** Sachsen, E Germany *50.34N 12.42E*
102 H12 **Aue** ≈ NW Germany
102 L9 **Auerbach** Bayern, SE Germany *49.41N 11.41E*
103 M17 **Auerbach** Sachsen, E Germany *50.30N 12.24E*
110 I10 **Auererrhein** ≈ SW Switzerland
103 N17 **Auersberg** ▲ E Germany *50.30N 12.42E*
189 W9 **Augathella** Queensland, E Australia *25.54S 146.38E*
33 Q12 **Auglaize River** ≈ Ohio, N USA
85 F22 **Augrabies Falls** *waterfall* W South Africa *28.37S 20.24E*
33 R7 **Au Gres River** ≈ Michigan, N USA
Augsbourg *see* Augsburg
103 K22 **Augsburg** *Fr.* Augsbourg; *anc.* Augusta Vindelicorum. Bayern, S Germany *48.22N 10.54E*
188 I14 **Augusta** Western Australia *34.18S 115.10E*
109 L25 **Augusta** *It.* Agosta. Sicilia, Italy, C Mediterranean Sea *37.19N 15.13E*
29 W11 **Augusta** Arkansas, C USA *35.16N 91.22W*
25 V3 **Augusta** Georgia, SE USA *33.29N 81.58W*
29 O6 **Augusta** Kansas, C USA *37.40N 96.59W*
21 Q7 **Augusta** *state capital* Maine, NE USA *44.19N 69.44W*
35 Q8 **Augusta** Montana, NW USA *47.28N 112.23W*
Augusta *see* London
Augusta Auscorum *see* Auch
Augusta Emerita *see* Mérida
Augusta Praetoria *see* Aosta
Augusta Suessionum *see* Soissons
Augusta Trajana *see* Stara Zagora
Augusta Treverorum *see* Trier
Augusta Vangionum *see* Worms
Augusta Vindelicorum *see* Augsburg
97 G24 **Augustenborg** *Ger.* Augustenburg. Sønderjylland, SW Denmark *54.57N 9.52E*
Augustenburg *see* Augustenborg
41 Q13 **Augustine Island** *island* Alaska, USA
12 L9 **Augustines, Lac des** ◎ Québec, SE Canada
Augustobona Tricassium *see* Troyes
Augustodunum *see* Autun
Augustodurum *see* Bayeux
Augustoritum Lemovicensium *see* Limoges
112 O8 **Augustów** *Rus.* Avgustov. Podlaskie, NE Poland *53.51N 22.58E*
Augustow Canal *see* Augustowski, Kanał
112 O8 **Augustowski, Kanał** *Eng.* Augustow Canal, *Rus.* Avgustovskiy Kanal. *canal* NE Poland
188 I9 **Augustus, Mount** ▲ Western Australia *24.42S 117.42E*
195 X15 **Auki** Malaita, N Solomon Islands *8.48S 160.45E*
23 W8 **Aulander** North Carolina, SE USA *36.15N 77.16W*
188 L7 **Auld, Lake** *salt lake* Western Australia
Aulie Ata/Auliye-Ata *see* Taraz
150 M8 **Auliyekol'** *prev.* Semiozernoye. Kostanay, N Kazakhstan *52.22N 64.06E*
108 E10 **Aulla** Toscana, C Italy *44.15N 10.00E*
104 F6 **Aulne** ≈ NW France
Aulong *see* Ulong
39 T3 **Ault** Colorado, C USA *40.34N 104.43W*
97 F22 **Aulum** *var.* Avlum. Ringkøbing, C Denmark *56.16N 8.48E*
105 N3 **Aumale** Seine-Maritime, N France *49.45N 1.43E*
Auminzatau, Gory *see* Ovminzatovo Tog'lari
79 T14 **Auna** Niger, W Nigeria *10.13N 4.43E*
97 H21 **Auning** Århus, C Denmark *56.25N 10.22E*
198 Cc9 **Aunu'u Island** *island* W American Samoa
85 E20 **Auob** *var.* Oup. ≈ Namibia/South Africa
95 K19 **Aura** Länsi-Suomi, W Finland *60.37N 22.34E*
111 R5 **Aurach** ≈ N Austria
Aural, Phnom *see* Aôral, Phnum
159 O14 **Aurangābād** Bihār, N India *24.48N 84.22E*
160 F13 **Aurangābād** Mahārāshtra, C India *19.52N 75.22E*
201 V7 **Aur Atoll** *atoll* E Marshall Islands
104 G7 **Auray** Morbihan, NW France *47.40N 2.58W*
96 G13 **Aurdal** Oppland, S Norway *60.51N 9.25E*
96 F8 **Aure** Møre og Romsdal, S Norway *63.16N 8.31E*
31 T12 **Aurelia** Iowa, C USA *42.42N 95.26W*
Aurelia Aquensis *see* Baden-Baden
Aurelianum *see* Orléans
123 J12 **Aurès, Massif de l'** ▲▲ NE Algeria
102 F10 **Aurich** Niedersachsen, NW Germany *53.28N 7.28E*
105 O13 **Aurillac** Cantal, C France *44.55N 2.25E*
Aurine, Alpi *see* Zillertaler Alpen
Aurium *see* Ourense
12 H15 **Aurora** Ontario, S Canada *44.00N 79.26W*
57 S8 **Aurora** NW Guyana *6.46N 59.45W*
39 T4 **Aurora** Colorado, C USA *39.42N 104.51W*
32 M11 **Aurora** Illinois, N USA *41.45N 88.19W*
33 Q15 **Aurora** Indiana, N USA *39.01N 84.55W*
31 W4 **Aurora** Minnesota, N USA *47.31N 92.14W*
29 S8 **Aurora** Missouri, C USA *36.58N 93.43W*
31 P16 **Aurora** Nebraska, C USA *40.52N 98.00W*
38 J5 **Aurora** Utah, W USA *38.55N 111.55W*
Aurora *see* Maéwo, Vanuatu
Aurora *see* San Francisco, Philippines
96 F10 **Aursjøen** ◎ S Norway
96 I8 **Aursunden** ◎ S Norway
85 D21 **Aus** Karas, SW Namibia *26.37S 16.18E*
Ausa *see* Vic
12 E16 **Ausable** ≈ Ontario, S Canada
33 O3 **Au Sable Point** *headland* Michigan, N USA *46.40N 86.08W*
33 S7 **Au Sable Point** *headland* Michigan, N USA *44.19N 83.20W*
33 R6 **Au Sable River** ≈ Michigan, N USA
59 H16 **Ausangate, Nevado** ▲ C Peru *13.46S 71.13W*
Auschwitz *see* Oświęcim
Ausculum Apulum *see* Ascoli Satriano
107 Q4 **Ausejo** La Rioja, N Spain *42.21N 2.10W*
Aussig *see* Ústí nad Labem
97 F17 **Aust-Agder** ◈ *county* S Norway
207 Q7 **Austfonna** *glacier* NE Svalbard
33 P15 **Austin** Indiana, N USA *38.45N 85.48W*
31 W11 **Austin** Minnesota, N USA *43.40N 92.58W*
37 U5 **Austin** Nevada, W USA *39.28N 117.04W*
27 S10 **Austin** *state capital* Texas, S USA *30.16N 97.44W*
188 J10 **Austin, Lake** *salt lake* Western Australia
33 V11 **Austintown** Ohio, N USA *41.06N 80.45W*
27 V9 **Austonio** Texas, SW USA *31.09N 95.39W*
Australes, Archipel des *see* Australes, Îles
Australes et Antarctiques Françaises, Terres *see* French Southern and Antarctic Territories
203 T14 **Australes, Îles** *var.* Archipel des Australes, Îles Tubuai, Tubuai Islands, *Eng.* Austral Islands. *island group* SW French Polynesia
183 Y11 **Austral Fracture Zone** *tectonic feature* S Pacific Ocean
189 O7 **Australia** *off.* Commonwealth of Australia. ◆ *commonwealth republic*
182 M8 **Australia** *continent*
191 Q12 **Australian Alps** ▲▲ SE Australia
191 R11 **Australian Capital Territory** *prev.* Federal Capital Territory. ◈ *territory* SE Australia
Australie, Bassin Nord de l' *see* North Australian Basin
Austral Islands *see* Australes, Îles
Austrava *see* Ostrov
111 T6 **Austria** *off.* Republic of Austria, *Ger.* Österreich. ◆ *republic* C Europe
94 K3 **Austurland** ◈ *region* SE Iceland
96 G10 **Austvågøya** *island* C Norway
60 G13 **Autazes** Amazonas, N Brazil *3.37S 59.07W*
104 M16 **Auterive** Haute-Garonne, S France *43.22N 1.28E*
Autesiodorum *see* Auxerre
105 N2 **Authie** ≈ N France
Autissiodorum *see* Auxerre
42 K14 **Autlán** *var.* Autlán de Navarro. Jalisco, SW Mexico *19.46N 104.22W*
Autlán de Navarro *see* Autlán
Autricum *see* Chartres
105 Q9 **Autun** *anc.* Ædua, Augustodunum. Saône-et-Loire, C France *46.57N 4.18E*
Autz *see* Auce
101 H20 **Auvelais** Namur, S Belgium *50.27N 4.37E*
105 P11 **Auvergne** ◈ *region* C France
104 M12 **Auvézère** ≈ W France
105 P7 **Auxerre** *anc.* Autesiodorum, Autissiodorum. Yonne, C France *47.48N 3.34E*
105 N2 **Auxi-le-Château** Pas-de-Calais, N France *50.14N 2.06E*
105 S8 **Auxonne** Côte d'Or, C France *47.12N 5.22E*
57 P9 **Auyan Tebuy** ▲ SE Venezuela *5.48N 62.27W*
105 O10 **Auzances** Creuse, C France *46.01N 2.29E*
29 U8 **Ava** Missouri, C USA *36.57N 92.39W*
148 M5 **Āvaj** Qazvīn, N Iran *35.36N 49.15E*
97 C15 **Avaldsnes** Rogaland, S Norway *59.21N 5.16E*
105 Q8 **Avallon** Yonne, C France *47.30N 3.54E*
104 K6 **Avaloirs, Mont des** ▲ NW France *48.27N 0.11W*
37 S16 **Avalon** Santa Catalina Island, California, W USA *33.20N 118.19W*
20 J17 **Avalon** New Jersey, NE USA *39.04N 74.42W*
11 V13 **Avalon Peninsula** *peninsula* Newfoundland and Labrador, E Canada
207 Q11 **Avannaarsua** ◈ *province* N Greenland
62 K10 **Avaré** São Paulo, S Brazil *23.06S 48.57W*
Avaricum *see* Bourges
202 H16 **Avarua** ○ (Cook Islands) Rarotonga, S Cook Islands *21.12S 159.46E*
202 H16 **Avarua Harbour** *harbor* Rarotonga, S Cook Islands
Avasfelsőfalu *see* Negreşti-Oaş
40 L17 **Avatanak Island** *island* Aleutian Islands, Alaska, USA
202 B16 **Avatele** S Niue *19.06S 169.55E*
202 H16 **Avatiu** Rarotonga, S Cook Islands *21.12S 159.46W*
202 H15 **Avatiu Harbour** *harbor* Rarotonga, S Cook Islands
Avdeyevka *see* Avdiyivka
116 J13 **Ávdira** Anatolikí Makedonía kai Thráki, NE Greece *40.58N 24.58E*
119 X8 **Avdiyivka** *Rus.* Avdeyevka. Donets'ka Oblast', SE Ukraine *48.05N 37.45E*
Avdzaga *see* Gurvanbulag
106 G6 **Ave** ≈ N Portugal
106 G7 **Aveiro** *anc.* Talabriga. Aveiro, W Portugal *40.37N 8.40W*
106 G7 **Aveiro** ◈ *district* N Portugal
Avela *see* Ávila
101 D18 **Avelgem** West-Vlaanderen, W Belgium *50.46N 3.25E*
63 D20 **Avellaneda** Buenos Aires, E Argentina *34.43S 58.23W*
109 L17 **Avellino** *anc.* Abellinum. Campania, S Italy *40.54N 14.46E*
37 Q12 **Avenal** California, W USA *36.00N 120.07W*
Avenio *see* Avignon
96 E8 **Averøya** *island* S Norway
109 K17 **Aversa** Campania, S Italy *40.58N 14.12E*
35 N9 **Avery** Idaho, NW USA *47.14N 115.48W*
27 W5 **Avery** Texas, SW USA *33.33N 94.46W*
Aves, Islas de *see* Las Aves, Islas
Avesnes *see* Avesnes-sur-Helpe
105 Q2 **Avesnes-sur-Helpe** *var.* Avesnes. Nord, N France *50.07N 3.57E*
66 G12 **Aves Ridge** *undersea feature* SE Caribbean Sea
97 M14 **Avesta** Dalarna, C Sweden *60.09N 16.10E*
105 O14 **Aveyron** ◈ *department* S France
105 N14 **Aveyron** ≈ S France
109 J15 **Avezzano** Abruzzo, C Italy *42.01N 13.25E*
117 D16 **Avgó** ▲ C Greece *39.31N 21.24E*
Avgustov *see* Augustów
Avgustovskiy Kanal *see* Augustowski, Kanał
98 J9 **Aviemore** N Scotland, UK *57.06N 4.01W*
193 F21 **Aviemore, Lake** ◎ South Island, NZ
105 R15 **Avignon** *anc.* Avenio. Vaucluse, SE France *43.57N 4.49E*
106 M7 **Ávila** *var.* Avila; *anc.* Abela, Abula, Abyla, Avela. Castilla-León, C Spain *40.39N 4.42W*
106 L8 **Ávila** ◈ *province* Castilla-León, C Spain
106 K2 **Avilés** Asturias, NW Spain *43.33N 5.55W*
120 J4 **Avinurme** *Ger.* Awwinorm. Ida-Virumaa, NE Estonia *58.58N 26.52E*
106 H10 **Avis** Portalegre, C Portugal *39.03N 7.52W*
Avlum *see* Aulum
190 M11 **Avoca** Victoria, SE Australia *37.09S 143.34E*
31 T14 **Avoca** Iowa, C USA *41.27N 95.20W*
190 M11 **Avoca River** ≈ Victoria, SE Australia
109 L25 **Avola** Sicilia, Italy, C Mediterranean Sea *36.54N 15.07E*
20 F10 **Avon** New York, NE USA *42.53N 77.41W*
31 P12 **Avon** South Dakota, N USA *43.00N 98.03W*
99 M23 **Avon** ≈ S England, UK
99 L20 **Avon** ≈ C England, UK
38 K13 **Avondale** Arizona, SW USA *33.25N 112.20W*
25 X13 **Avon Park** Florida, SE USA *27.36N 81.30W*
104 J5 **Avranches** Manche, N France *48.42N 1.21W*
105 O3 **Avre** ≈ N France
195 X16 **Avuavu** *var.* Kolotambu. Guadalcanal, C Solomon Islands *9.52S 160.25E*
Avveel *see* Ivalo, Finland
Avveel *see* Ivalojoki, Finland
Avvil *see* Ivalo
79 O17 **Awaaso** *var.* Awaso. SW Ghana *6.10N 2.18W*
147 X8 **Awābī** *var.* Al'Awābī. NE Oman *23.19N 57.34E*
170 G15 **Awaji-shima** *island* SW Japan
192 L9 **Awakino** Waikato, North Island, NZ *38.40S 174.37E*
148 M15 **'Awālī** C Bahrain *26.06N 50.33E*
101 K19 **Awans** Liège, E Belgium *50.39N 5.30E*
192 I2 **Awanui** Northland, North Island, NZ *35.01S 173.16E*
154 M14 **Awārān** Baluchistān, SW Pakistan *26.31N 65.10E*
83 K16 **Awara Plain** *plain* NE Kenya
82 M13 **Āwarē** Somali, E Ethiopia *8.12N 44.09E*
144 M6 **'Awāriḍ, Wādī** *dry watercourse* E Syria
193 B20 **Awarua Point** *headland* South Island, NZ *44.15S 168.03E*
83 J14 **Āwasa** Southern, S Ethiopia *6.54N 38.26E*
82 K13 **Āwash** Afar, NE Ethiopia *8.59N 40.15E*
82 K12 **Āwash** *var.* Hawash. ≈ C Ethiopia
171 Kk11 **Awa-shima** *island* C Japan
Awaso *see* Awaaso
164 H7 **Awat** Xinjiang Uygur Zizhiqu, NW China *40.36N 80.22E*
193 J15 **Awatere** ≈ South Island, NZ
77 O10 **Awbārī** SW Libya *26.34N 12.46E*
77 N9 **Awbārī, Idhān** *var.* Edeyen d'Oubari. *desert* Algeria/Libya
82 M12 **Awdal** *off.* Gobolka Awdal. ◈ *region* N Somalia
82 C13 **Aweil** Northern Bahr el Ghazal, SW Sudan *8.44N 27.25E*
98 H11 **Awe, Loch** ◎ W Scotland, UK
79 U16 **Awka** Anambra, SW Nigeria *6.12N 7.04E*
41 O6 **Awuna River** ≈ Alaska, USA
Awwinorm *see* Avinurme
Ax *see* Dax
Axarfjördhur *see* Öxarfjördhur
105 N17 **Axat** Aude, S France *42.46N 2.13E*
101 F16 **Axel** Zeeland, SW Netherlands *51.16N 3.55E*
207 P9 **Axel Heiberg Island** *var.* Axel Heiburg. *island* Nunavut, N Canada
Axel Heiburg *see* Axel Heiberg Island
79 O17 **Axim** S Ghana *4.52N 2.13W*
116 F13 **Axiós** *var.* Vardar. ≈ Greece/FYR Macedonia *see also* Vardar
105 N17 **Ax-les-Thermes** Ariège, S France *42.43N 1.49E*
171 Gg14 **Ayabe** Kyōto, Honshū, SW Japan *35.16N 135.15E*
122 F13 **Ayachi, Jbel** ▲ C Morocco *32.30N 5.00W*
63 D22 **Ayacucho** Buenos Aires, E Argentina *37.09S 58.30W*
59 F15 **Ayacucho** Ayacucho, S Peru *13.10S 74.15W*
59 E16 **Ayacucho** *off.* Departamento de Ayacucho. ◈ *department* SW Peru
151 W11 **Ayagoz** *var.* Ayaguz, *Kaz.* Ayaköz; *prev.* Sergiopol. Vostochnyy Kazakhstan, E Kazakhstan *47.54N 80.25E*
151 V12 **Ayagoz** *var.* Ayaguz, *Kaz.* Ayaköz. ≈ E Kazakhstan
Ayaguz *see* Ayagoz
Ayakagytma *see* Oyoqog'itma
Ayakkuduk *see* Oyoqquduq
164 L10 **Ayakkum Hu** ◎ NW China
Ayaköz *see* Ayagoz
106 H14 **Ayamonte** Andalucía, S Spain *37.13N 7.24W*
127 N12 **Ayan** Khabarovskiy Kray, E Russian Federation *56.27N 138.09E*
142 J10 **Ayancık** Sinop, N Turkey *41.55N 34.34E*
57 S9 **Ayanganna Mountain** ▲ C Guyana *5.21N 59.54W*
79 U16 **Ayangba** Kogi, C Nigeria *7.36N 7.10E*
127 P6 **Ayanka** Koryakskiy Avtonomnyy Okrug, E Russian Federation *63.42N 167.31E*
56 E7 **Ayapel** Córdoba, NW Colombia *8.16N 75.10W*
142 H12 **Ayaş** Ankara, N Turkey *40.01N 32.21E*
59 I16 **Ayaviri** Puno, S Peru *14.52S 70.34W*
155 P3 **Āybak** *var.* Aibak, Haibak; *prev.* Samangān. Samangān, NE Afghanistan *36.16N 68.04E*
153 N10 **Aydarko'l Ko'li** *Rus.* Ozero Aydarkul'. ◎ C Uzbekistan
Aydarkul', Ozero *see* Aydarko'l Ko'li
23 W10 **Ayden** North Carolina, SE USA *35.28N 77.25W*
142 C15 **Aydın** *var.* Aidin; *anc.* Tralles. Aydın, SW Turkey *37.51N 27.51E*
142 C15 **Aydın** *var.* Aidin. ◈ *province* SW Turkey
142 I17 **Aydıncık** Mersin, S Turkey *36.10N 33.16E*
142 C15 **Aydın Dağları** ▲▲ W Turkey
164 L6 **Aydingkol Hu** ◎ NW China
131 X7 **Aydyrlinskiy** Orenburgskaya Oblast', W Russian Federation *52.03N 59.54E*
107 S4 **Ayerbe** Aragón, NE Spain *42.16N 0.40W*
Ayers Rock *see* Uluru
Ayeyarwady *see* Irrawaddy
Ayia Napa *see* Agía Nápa
Ayia Phyla *see* Agía Fýlaxis
Ayiásos/Ayiássos *see* Agiassós
Áyios Evstrátios *see* Ágios Efstrátios
Áyios Kírikos *see* Ágios Kírykos
Áyios Nikólaos *see* Ágios Nikólaos
Ayios Seryios *see* Yeniboğaziçi
82 I11 **Āykel** Amhara, N Ethiopia *12.33N 37.01E*
126 K10 **Aykhal** Respublika Sakha (Yakutiya), NE Russian Federation *66.07N 110.25E*
12 J12 **Aylen Lake** ◎ Ontario, SE Canada
99 N21 **Aylesbury** SE England, UK *51.49N 0.49W*
107 O6 **Ayllón** Castilla-León, N Spain *41.25N 3.22W*
12 F17 **Aylmer** Ontario, S Canada *42.46N 80.57W*
12 L12 **Aylmer** Québec, SE Canada *45.22N 75.51W*
13 R12 **Aylmer, Lac** ◎ Québec, SE Canada
15 J6 **Aylmer Lake** ◎ Northwest Territories, NW Canada
151 V14 **Aynabulak** Almaty, SE Kazakhstan *44.37N 77.58E*
144 K2 **'Ayn al 'Arab** Ḥalab, N Syria *36.55N 38.21E*
Aynayn *see* 'Aynīn
145 V12 **'Ayn Ḥamūd** S Iraq *30.51N 45.37E*
153 P12 **Ayni** *prev. Rus.* Varzimanor Ayni. W Tajikistan *39.24N 68.30E*
146 M10 **'Aynīn** *var.* Aynayn. *spring/well* SW Saudi Arabia *20.52N 41.41E*
23 U12 **Aynor** South Carolina, SE USA *33.59N 79.11W*
145 Q7 **'Ayn Zāzūh** C Iraq *33.29N 42.34E*
159 N12 **Ayodhya** Uttar Pradesh, N India *26.46N 82.12E*
127 O5 **Ayon, Ostrov** *island* NE Russian Federation
107 R11 **Ayora** País Valenciano, E Spain *39.04N 1.04W*
79 Q11 **Ayorou** Tillabéri, W Niger *14.44N 0.54E*
81 E16 **Ayos** Centre, S Cameroon *3.52N 12.31E*
78 L5 **'Ayoûn 'Abd el Mâlek** *well* N Mauritania *24.51N 7.38W*
78 K10 **'Ayoûn el 'Atroûs** *var.* Aïoun el Atrous, Aïoun el Atroûss. Hodh el Gharbi, SE Mauritania *16.37N 9.36W*
98 I13 **Ayr** W Scotland, UK *55.28N 4.37W*
98 I13 **Ayr** ≈ W Scotland, UK
98 I13 **Ayrshire** *cultural region* SW Scotland, UK
Aysen *see* Aisén
82 L12 **Āysha** Somali, E Ethiopia *10.36N 42.31E*
150 L14 **Ayteke Bi** *Kaz.* Zhangaqazaly *prev.* Novokazalinsk. Kyzylorda, SW Kazakhstan *45.52N 62.09E*
152 K8 **Aytim** Navoiy Viloyati, N Uzbekistan *42.15N 63.25E*
189 W4 **Ayton** Queensland, NE Australia *15.54S 145.19E*
116 M9 **Aytos** Burgas, E Bulgaria *42.43N 27.13E*
176 Uu7 **Ayu, Kepulauan** *island group* E Indonesia
A Yun Pa *see* Cheo Reo
175 O8 **Ayu, Tanjung** *headland* Borneo, N Indonesia *0.25N 117.34E*
42 K13 **Ayutla** Jalisco, C Mexico *20.07N 104.18W*
43 P16 **Ayutlá** *var.* Ayutla de los Libres. Guerrero, S Mexico *16.56N 99.22W*
Ayutla de los Libres *see* Ayutlá
178 H11 **Ayutthaya** *var.* Phra Nakhon Si Ayutthaya. Phra Nakhon Si Ayutthaya, C Thailand *14.19N 100.34E*
142 B13 **Ayvalık** Balıkesir, W Turkey *39.18N 26.42E*
101 L20 **Aywaille** Liège, E Belgium *50.28N 5.40E*
147 R13 **'Aywat aş Şay'ar, Wādī** *seasonal river* N Yemen
Azaffal *see* Azeffâl
107 T9 **Azahar, Costa del** *coastal region* E Spain
107 S6 **Azaila** Aragón, NE Spain *41.16N 0.30W*
106 F10 **Azambuja** Lisboa, C Portugal *39.04N 8.52W*
159 N13 **Āzamgarh** Uttar Pradesh, N India *26.03N 83.10E*
79 O9 **Azaouâd** *desert* C Mali
79 S10 **Azaouagh, Vallée de l'** *var.* Azaouak. ≈ W Niger
Azaouak *see* Azaouagh, Vallée de l'
63 F14 **Azara** Misiones, NE Argentina *28.03S 55.42W*
Āzarān *see* Hashtrūd
Azärbaycan/Azärbaycan Respublikası *see* Azerbaijan
Āzarbāyjān-e Bākhtarī *see* Āzarbāyjān-e Gharbī
148 I4 **Āzarbāyjān-e Gharbī** *off.* Ostān-e Āzarbāyjān-e Gharbī *Eng.* West Azerbaijan *prev.* Āzarbāyjān-e Bākhtarī . ◈ *province* NW Iran
Āzarbāyjān-e Khāvarī *see* Āzarbāyjān-e Sharqī
148 J3 **Āzarbāyjān-e Sharqī** *off.* Ostān-e Āzarbāyjān-e Sharqī, *Eng.* East Azerbaijan; *prev.* Āzarbāyjān-e Khāvarī. ◈ *province* NW Iran
79 W13 **Azare** Bauchi, N Nigeria *11.41N 10.09E*
121 M19 **Azarychy** *Rus.* Ozarichi. Homyel'skaya Voblasts', SE Belarus *52.31N 29.19E*
104 L8 **Azay-le-Rideau** Indre-et-Loire, C France *47.16N 0.25E*
144 I2 **A'zāz** Ḥalab, NW Syria *36.34N 37.03E*
78 H7 **Azeffâl** *var.* Azaffal. *desert* Mauritania/Western Sahara
143 V12 **Azerbaijan** *off.* Azerbaijani Republic, *Az.* Azärbaycan, Azärbaycan Respublikası; *prev.* Azerbaijan SSR. ◆ *republic* SW Asia
151 T7 **Azhbulat, Ozero** ◎ NE Kazakhstan
76 F7 **Azilal** C Morocco *31.58N 6.53W*
Azimabad *see* Patna
21 O6 **Aziscohos Lake** ⊡ Maine, NE USA
Azizbekov *see* Vayk'
Azizie *see* Telish
Aziziya *see* Al 'Azīzīyah
131 T4 **Aznakayevo** Respublika Tatarstan, W Russian Federation *54.55N 53.15E*
58 C8 **Azogues** Cañar, S Ecuador *2.41S 78.54W*
66 N2 **Azores** *var.* Açores, Ilhas dos Açores, *Port.* Arquipélago dos Açores. *island group* Portugal, NE Atlantic Ocean
66 L8 **Azores-Biscay Rise** *undersea feature* E Atlantic Ocean
Azotos/Azotus *see* Ashdod
80 K11 **Azoum, Bahr** *seasonal river* SE Chad
130 L12 **Azov** Rostovskaya Oblast', SW Russian Federation *47.06N 39.26E*
130 J13 **Azov, Sea of** *Rus.* Azovskoye More, *Ukr.* Azovs'ke More. *sea* NE Black Sea
Azovs'ke More/Azovskoye More *see* Azov, Sea of
144 I10 **Azraq, Wāḥat al** *oasis* N Jordan *31.51N 36.51E*
Āzro *see* Āzrow
76 G6 **Azrou** C Morocco *33.30N 5.12W*
155 R5 **Āzrow** *var.* Āzro. Lowgar, E Afghanistan *34.10N 69.39E*
39 P8 **Aztec** New Mexico, SW USA *36.49N 107.59W*
38 M13 **Aztec Peak** ▲ Arizona, SW USA *33.48N 110.54W*
47 N9 **Azua** *var.* Azua de Compostela. S Dominican Republic *18.25N 70.44W*
Azua de Compostela *see* Azua
106 K12 **Azuaga** Extremadura, W Spain *38.16N 5.40W*
58 B8 **Azuay** ◈ *province* W Ecuador
170 Bb11 **Azuchi-Ō-shima** *island* SW Japan
107 O11 **Azuer** ≈ C Spain
45 S17 **Azuero, Península de** *peninsula* S Panama
64 I6 **Azufre, Volcán** *var.* Volcán Lastarria. ▲ N Chile *25.16S 68.35W*
118 J12 **Azuga** Prahova, SE Romania *45.27N 25.34E*
63 C22 **Azul** Buenos Aires, E Argentina *36.46S 59.49W*

◆ Country ● Country Capital ◇ Dependent Territory ○ Dependent Territory Capital ◈ Administrative Region ✕ International Airport ▲ Mountain ▲▲ Mountain Range Volcano ≈ River ◎ Lake ⊡ Reservoir
227

AZUL, CERRO – BALATON, LAKE

64 I8 **Azul, Cerro** ▲ NW Argentina 28.28S 68.43W
58 E12 **Azul, Cordillera** ▲▲ C Peru
171 Ll14 **Azuma-san** ▲ Honshū, C Japan 37.44N 140.05E
105 V15 **Azur, Côte d'** coastal region SE France
203 Z3 **Azur Lagoon** ◎ Kiritimati, E Kiribati
'Azza see Gaza
Az Zāb al Kabīr see Great Zab
144 H7 **Az Zabdānī** var. Zabadani. Dimashq, W Syria 33.45N 36.07E
147 W8 **Aẓ Ẓāhirah** desert NW Oman
147 S6 **Aẓ Ẓahrān** Eng. Dhahran. Ash Sharqīyah, NE Saudi Arabia 26.18N 50.01E
147 R6 **Aẓ Ẓahrān al Khubar** var. Dhahran Al Khobar. ✕ Ash Sharqīyah, NE Saudi Arabia 26.28N 49.42E
Az Zaqāzīq see Zagazig
144 H10 **Az Zarqā'** var. Zarqa. Az Zarqā', NW Jordan 32.04N 36.06E
144 I11 **Az Zarqā'** off. Muḥāfaẓat az Zarqā', var. Zarqa. ◐ governorate N Jordan
77 O7 **Az Zāwiyah** var. Zawia. NW Libya 32.45N 12.43E
147 N15 **Az Zaydīyah** W Yemen 15.19N 43.03E
76 I11 **Azzel Matti, Sebkha** var. Sebkra Azz el Matti. salt flat C Algeria
147 P6 **Az Zilfī** Ar Riyāḍ, N Saudi Arabia 26.16N 44.48E
145 Y13 **Az Zubayr** var. Al Zubair. SE Iraq 30.24N 47.45E
Az Zuqur see Jabal Zuuqar, Jazīrat

B

197 H14 **Ba** prev. Mba. Viti Levu, W Fiji 17.34S 177.40E
Ba see Đa Răng
175 R18 **Baa** Pulau Rote, C Indonesia 10.43S 123.06E
197 G5 **Baaba, Île** island Îles Belep, W New Caledonia
144 H7 **Baalbek** var. Ba'labakk; anc. Heliopolis. E Lebanon 34.00N 36.15E
110 G8 **Baar** Zug, N Switzerland 47.12N 8.31E
83 L17 **Baardheere** var. Bardere, It. Bardera. Gedo, SW Somalia 2.13N 42.19E
82 Q12 **Baargaal** Bari, NE Somalia 11.12N 51.04E
101 I15 **Baarle-Hertog** Antwerpen, N Belgium 51.26N 4.56E
101 I15 **Baarle-Nassau** Noord-Brabant, S Netherlands 51.27N 4.56E
100 J11 **Baarn** Utrecht, C Netherlands 52.13N 5.16E
168 H9 **Baatsagaan** var. Bayansayr. Bayanhongor, C Mongolia 45.36N 99.27E
116 D13 **Baba** var. Buševa, Gk. Varnoús. ▲▲ FYR Macedonia/Greece
78 H10 **Bababé** Brakna, W Mauritania 16.22N 13.57W
142 G10 **Baba Burnu** headland NW Turkey 41.18N 31.24E
119 N13 **Babadag** Tulcea, SE Romania 44.53N 28.46E
143 X10 **Babadağ Dağı** ▲ NE Azerbaijan 41.02N 48.04E
152 H14 **Babadaýhan** Rus. Babadaykhan; prev. Kirovsk. Ahal Welaýaty, C Turkmenistan 37.39N 60.17E
Babadaykhan see Babadaýhan
152 G14 **Babadurmaz** Ahal Welaýaty, C Turkmenistan 37.39N 59.03E
116 M12 **Babaeski** Kırklareli, NW Turkey 41.26N 27.06E
145 T4 **Bāba Gurgur** N Iraq 35.34N 44.18E
58 B7 **Babahoyo** prev. Bodegas. Los Ríos, C Ecuador 1.49S 79.33W
155 P5 **Bābā, Kūh-e** ▲▲ C Afghanistan
175 P10 **Babana** Sulawesi, C Indonesia 2.03S 119.13E
Babao see Qilian
176 U16 **Babar, Kepulauan** island group E Indonesia
176 U15 **Babar, Pulau** island Kepulauan Babar, E Indonesia
158 G4 **Bābāsar Pass** pass India/Pakistan
195 Q10 **Babase Island** island Feni Islands, NE PNG
Babashy, Gory see Babaşy
152 C9 **Babaşy** Rus. Gory Babashy. ▲▲ W Turkmenistan
174 Ll15 **Babat** Jawa, S Indonesia 7.07S 112.07E
174 I10 **Babat** Sumatera, W Indonesia 2.45S 104.01E
Babatag, Khrebet see Botogot', Tizmasi
83 H21 **Babati** Manyara, NE Tanzania 4.12S 35.45E
128 J13 **Babayevo** Vologodskaya Oblast', NW Russian Federation 59.22N 35.51E
131 Q15 **Babayurt** Respublika Dagestan, SW Russian Federation 43.38N 46.49E
35 P6 **Babb** Montana, NW USA 48.51N 113.26W
31 X4 **Babbitt** Minnesota, N USA 47.42N 91.56W
196 E9 **Babeldaob** var. Babeldaop, Babelthuap. island N Palau
Babeldaop see Babeldaob
147 N17 **Bab el Mandeb** strait Gulf of Aden/Red Sea
Babelthuap see Babeldaob
113 K17 **Babia Góra** var. Babia Hora. ▲ Poland/Slovakia 49.33N 19.32E
Babia Hora see Babia Góra
Babian Jiang see Black River
Babichi see Babichy
121 N19 **Babichy** Rus. Babichi. Homyel'skaya Voblasts', SE Belarus 52.17N 30.00E
114 I10 **Babina Greda** Vukovar-Srijem, E Croatia 45.09N 18.33E
8 K13 **Babine Lake** ◎ British Columbia, SW Canada
176 Vv10 **Babo** Papua, E Indonesia 2.29S 133.30E
149 O4 **Bābol** var. Babul, Balfrush, Barfrush; prev. Barfurush. Māzandarān, N Iran 36.34N 52.39E
149 O4 **Bābolsar** var. Babulsar; prev. Meshed-i-Sar. Māzandarān, N Iran 36.42N 52.37E
38 L16 **Baboquivari Peak** ▲ Arizona, SW USA 31.46N 111.36W
81 G15 **Baboua** Nana-Mambéré, W Central African Republic 5.46N 14.47E
121 M17 **Babruysk** Rus. Bobruysk. Mahilyowskaya Voblasts', E Belarus 53.07N 29.13E
Babu see Hezhou
Babul see Bābol
Babulsar see Bābolsar
115 O19 **Babuna** ≈ C FYR Macedonia
115 O19 **Babuna** ▲▲ C FYR Macedonia
154 K7 **Bābūs, Dasht-e** Pash. Bebas, Dasht-i. ▲▲ W Afghanistan
126 Jj16 **Babushkin** Respublika Buryatiya, S Russian Federation 51.35N 105.49E
179 P7 **Babuyan Channel** channel N Philippines
179 Pp7 **Babuyan Island** island N Philippines
145 T9 **Babylon** site of ancient city C Iraq 32.33N 44.25E
114 J9 **Bač** Ger. Batsch. Serbia, NW Serbia 45.24N 19.17E
60 M13 **Bacabal** Maranhão, E Brazil 4.15S 44.45W
43 Y14 **Bacalar** Quintana Roo, SE Mexico 18.38N 88.17W
43 Y14 **Bacalar Chico, Boca** strait SE Mexico
175 Ss8 **Bacan, Kepulauan** island group E Indonesia
175 T8 **Bacan, Pulau** prev. Batjan. island Maluku, E Indonesia
118 L10 **Bacău** Hung. Bákó. Bacău, NE Romania 46.36N 26.55E
118 K11 **Bacău** ◐ county E Romania
Băc Bô, Vinh see Tongking, Gulf of
178 Jj5 **Băc Can** var. Bach Thông. Băc Thai, N Vietnam 22.07N 105.50E
105 T5 **Baccarat** Meurthe-et-Moselle, NE France 48.27N 6.46E
191 N12 **Bacchus Marsh** Victoria, SE Australia 37.46S 144.27E
42 H4 **Bacerac** Sonora, NW Mexico 30.27N 108.55W
118 L10 **Băceşti** Vaslui, E Romania 46.49N 27.13E
178 Jj6 **Băc Giang** Ha Băc, N Vietnam 21.17N 106.12E
56 I5 **Bachaquero** Zulia, NW Venezuela 9.57N 71.09W
Bacher see Pohorje
120 M13 **Bacheykava** Rus. Bocheykovo. Vitsyebskaya Voblasts', N Belarus 55.01N 29.09E
42 I5 **Bachíniva** Chihuahua, N Mexico 28.41N 107.13W
Bach Thông see Băc Can
164 G8 **Bachu** Xinjiang Uygur Zizhiqu, NW China 39.46N 78.30E
15 J6 **Back** ≈ Nunavut, N Canada
114 K10 **Bačka Palanka** prev. Palanka. Serbia, NW Serbia 44.22N 20.57E
114 K8 **Bačka Topola** Hung. Topolya; prev. Hung. Bácstopolya. Serbia, N Serbia 45.48N 19.39E
97 J17 **Bäckefors** Västra Götaland, S Sweden 58.49N 12.07E
Bäckermühle Schulzenmühle see Żywiec
97 L16 **Bäckhammar** Värmland, C Sweden 59.09N 14.13E
114 K9 **Bački Petrovac** Hung. Petrőcz; prev. Petrovac, Petrovácz. Serbia, NW Serbia 45.22N 19.34E
103 I21 **Backnang** Baden-Württemberg, SW Germany 48.46N 9.25E
178 J15 **Bac Liêu** var. Vinh Loi. Minh Hai, S Vietnam 9.19N 105.42E
178 Jj6 **Băc Ninh** Ha Băc, N Vietnam 21.10N 106.04E
42 G4 **Bacoachi** Sonora, NW Mexico 30.37N 109.57W
179 Q13 **Bacolod** off. Bacolod City. Negros, C Philippines 10.43N 122.58E
179 P12 **Baco, Mount** ▲ Mindoro, N Philippines 12.50N 121.08E
113 K25 **Bácsalmás** Bács-Kiskun, S Hungary 46.09N 19.17E
Bácsjózseffalva see Žednik
113 J24 **Bács-Kiskun** off. Bács-Kiskun Megye. ◐ county S Hungary
Bácsszenttamás see Srbobran
Bácstopolya see Bačka Topola
Bactra see Balkh
Bada see Xilin
161 F21 **Badagara** Kerala, SW India 11.24N 75.45E
103 M24 **Bad Aibling** Bayern, SE Germany 47.52N 12.00E
168 I13 **Badain Jaran Shamo** desert N China
106 I11 **Badajoz** anc. Pax Augusta. Extremadura, W Spain 38.52N 6.58W
106 J11 **Badajoz** ◐ province Extremadura, W Spain
155 S2 **Badakhshān** ◐ province NE Afghanistan
107 W6 **Badalona** anc. Baetulo. Cataluña, E Spain 41.27N 2.15E
160 O11 **Bādāmapāhārh** Orissa, E India 22.04N 86.06E
158 K8 **Badarīnāth** ▲ N India 30.43N 79.28E
174 Jj8 **Badas, Kepulauan** island group W Indonesia
111 S6 **Bad Aussee** Salzburg, E Austria 47.35N 13.44E
33 S8 **Bad Axe** Michigan, N USA 43.48N 83.00W
103 G16 **Bad Berleburg** Nordrhein-Westfalen, W Germany 51.03N 8.24E
103 L17 **Bad Blankenburg** Thüringen, C Germany 50.43N 11.19E
Bad Borseck see Borsec
103 G18 **Bad Camberg** Hessen, W Germany 50.18N 8.15E
102 L8 **Bad Doberan** Mecklenburg-Vorpommern, N Germany 54.06N 11.55E
103 N14 **Bad Düben** Sachsen, E Germany 51.35N 12.34E
111 X4 **Baden** var. Baden bei Wien; anc. Aquae Panoniae, Thermae Pannonicae. Niederösterreich, NE Austria 48.01N 16.13E
110 F9 **Baden** Aargau, N Switzerland 47.28N 8.19E
103 G21 **Baden-Baden** anc. Aurelia Aquensis. Baden-Württemberg, SW Germany 48.46N 8.13E
Baden bei Wien see Baden
103 G22 **Baden-Württemberg** Fr. Bade-Wurtemberg. ◐ state SW Germany
114 A10 **Baderna** Istra, NW Croatia 45.12N 13.45E
Bade-Wurtemberg see Baden-Württemberg
103 H20 **Bad Fredrichshall** Baden-Württemberg, S Germany 49.13N 9.15E
102 P11 **Bad Freienwalde** Brandenburg, NE Germany 52.46N 14.03E
111 Q8 **Badgastein** var. Gastein. Salzburg, NW Austria 47.07N 13.09E
Badger State see Wisconsin
154 L4 **Bādghīs** ◐ province NW Afghanistan
111 T5 **Bad Hall** Oberösterreich, N Austria 48.03N 14.13E
103 J14 **Bad Harzburg** Niedersachsen, C Germany 51.52N 10.34E
103 I16 **Bad Hersfeld** Hessen, C Germany 50.52N 9.41E
100 I10 **Badhoevedorp** Noord-Holland, C Netherlands 52.21N 4.46E
111 Q8 **Bad Hofgastein** Salzburg, NW Austria 47.10N 13.07E
Bad Homburg see Bad Homburg vor der Höhe
103 G18 **Bad Homburg vor der Höhe** var. Bad Homburg. Hessen, W Germany 50.13N 8.37E
103 E17 **Bad Honnef** Nordrhein-Westfalen, W Germany 50.39N 7.13E
155 Q17 **Badīn** Sind, SE Pakistan 24.40N 68.49E
23 S10 **Badin Lake** ▣ North Carolina, SE USA
42 I8 **Badiraguato** Sinaloa, C Mexico 25.26N 107.33W
111 R6 **Bad Ischl** Oberösterreich, N Austria 47.43N 13.35E
Badjawa see Bajawa
Badje-Sohppar see Övre Soppero
103 J18 **Bad Kissingen** Bayern, SE Germany 50.12N 10.04E
Bad Königswart see Lázně Kynžvart
103 F19 **Bad Kreuznach** Rheinland-Pfalz, SW Germany 49.49N 7.52E
103 F24 **Bad Krozingen** Baden-Württemberg, SW Germany 47.55N 7.43E
103 G16 **Bad Laasphe** Nordrhein-Westfalen, W Germany 50.57N 8.24E
30 J6 **Badlands** physical region North Dakota, N USA
103 K16 **Bad Langensalza** Thüringen, C Germany 51.05N 10.40E
111 T3 **Bad Leonfelden** Oberösterreich, N Austria 48.31N 14.17E
103 I20 **Bad Mergentheim** Baden-Württemberg, SW Germany 49.30N 9.46E
103 H17 **Bad Nauheim** Hessen, W Germany 50.22N 8.45E
103 E17 **Bad Neuenahr-Arhweiler** Rheinland-Pfalz, W Germany 50.33N 7.07E
Bad Neustadt see Bad Neustadt an der Saale
103 J18 **Bad Neustadt an der Saale** var. Bad Neustadt. Berlin, C Germany 50.21N 10.13E
Badnur see Betūl
176 Yy15 **Bado** Papua, E Indonesia 7.06S 139.33E
102 H13 **Bad Oeynhausen** Nordrhein-Westfalen, NW Germany 52.12N 8.48E
102 J9 **Bad Oldesloe** Schleswig-Holstein, N Germany 53.49N 10.22E
79 Q16 **Badou** C Togo 7.37N 0.37E
Bad Polzin see Połczyn-Zdrój
102 H13 **Bad Pyrmont** Niedersachsen, C Germany 51.58N 9.16E
111 X9 **Bad Radkersburg** Steiermark, SE Austria 46.40N 16.02E
145 V8 **Badrah** E Iraq 33.06N 45.58E
Badrah see Tarialan
103 N24 **Bad Reichenhall** Bayern, SE Germany 47.43N 12.52E
146 K8 **Badr Ḥunayn** Al Madīnah, W Saudi Arabia 23.46N 38.45E
30 M10 **Bad River** ≈ South Dakota, N USA
32 K4 **Bad River** ≈ Wisconsin, N USA
102 H13 **Bad Salzuflen** Nordrhein-Westfalen, NW Germany 52.04N 8.45E
103 J16 **Bad Salzungen** Thüringen, C Germany 50.48N 10.15E
111 V8 **Bad Sankt Leonhard im Lavanttal** Kärnten, S Austria 46.55N 14.51E
102 K9 **Bad Schwartau** Schleswig-Holstein, N Germany 53.55N 10.42E
103 L24 **Bad Tölz** Bayern, SE Germany 47.44N 11.34E
189 U1 **Badu Island** island Queensland, NE Australia
161 K25 **Badulla** Uva Province, C Sri Lanka 6.58N 81.03E
111 X5 **Bad Vöslau** Niederösterreich, NE Austria 47.58N 16.12E
103 I24 **Bad Waldsee** Baden-Württemberg, S Germany 47.54N 9.44E
37 U11 **Badwater Basin** depression California, W USA
103 J20 **Bad Windsheim** Bayern, C Germany 49.30N 10.25E
103 J23 **Bad Wörishofen** Bayern, S Germany 48.00N 10.36E
102 G10 **Bad Zwischenahn** Niedersachsen, NW Germany 53.10N 8.01E
106 M13 **Baena** Andalucía, S Spain 37.37N 4.22W
Baeterrae/Baeterrae Septimanorum see Béziers
Baetic Cordillera/Baetic Mountains see Béticos, Sistemas
Baetulo see Badalona
59 K18 **Baeza** Napo, NE Ecuador 0.30S 77.52W
107 N13 **Baeza** Andalucía, S Spain 38.00N 3.28W
81 D15 **Bafang** Ouest, W Cameroon 5.10N 10.10E
78 H12 **Bafatá** C Guinea-Bissau 12.09N 14.37W
155 U5 **Baffa** North-West Frontier Province, NW Pakistan 34.28N 73.14E
207 O11 **Baffin Basin** undersea feature N Labrador Sea
207 N12 **Baffin Bay** bay Canada/Greenland
27 T15 **Baffin Bay** inlet Texas, SW USA
206 M12 **Baffin Island** island Nunavut, NE Canada
81 E15 **Bafia** Centre, C Cameroon 4.49N 11.13E
79 R14 **Bafilo** NE Togo 9.22N 1.19E
78 J12 **Bafing** ≈ W Africa
78 J12 **Bafoulabé** Kayes, W Mali 13.43N 10.49W
81 D15 **Bafoussam** Ouest, W Cameroon 5.31N 10.25E
149 R9 **Bāfq** Yazd, C Iran 31.34N 55.21E
142 L10 **Bafra** Samsun, N Turkey 41.34N 35.55E
142 L10 **Bafra Burnu** headland N Turkey 41.42N 36.02E
149 S12 **Bāft** Kermān, S Iran 29.12N 56.36E
81 N18 **Bafwabalinga** Orientale, NE Dem. Rep. Congo 0.52N 26.55E
81 N18 **Bafwaboli** Orientale, NE Dem. Rep. Congo 0.42N 26.06E
81 N17 **Bafwasende** Orientale, NE Dem. Rep. Congo 1.00N 27.09E
194 J11 **Bagabag Island** island N PNG
44 K13 **Bagaces** Guanacaste, NW Costa Rica 10.29N 85.13W
159 O12 **Bagaha** Bihār, N India 27.07N 84.04E
161 F16 **Bāgalkot** Karnātaka, W India 16.10N 75.42E
83 J22 **Bagamoyo** Pwani, E Tanzania 6.25S 38.55E
174 Gg4 **Bagan Datuk** var. Bagan Datok. Perak, Peninsular Malaysia 3.58N 100.46E
179 Rr15 **Baganga** Mindanao, S Philippines 7.31N 126.34E
174 Gg6 **Bagansiapiapi** var. Pasirpangarayan. Sumatera, W Indonesia 2.09N 100.50E
168 M8 **Baganuur** var. Nüürst. Töv, C Mongolia 47.44N 108.22E
Bagaria see Bagheria
79 T11 **Bagaroua** Tahoua, W Niger 14.34N 4.24E
81 I20 **Bagata** Bandundu, W Dem. Rep. Congo 3.46S 17.57E
Bagdad see Baghdād
126 Kk15 **Bagdarin** Respublika Buryatiya, S Russian Federation 54.27N 113.34E
63 G17 **Bagé** Rio Grande do Sul, S Brazil 31.22S 54.06W
Bagenalstown see Muine Bheag
Bagerhat see Bagherhat
105 P16 **Bages et de Sigean, Étang de** ◎ S France
35 W17 **Baggs** Wyoming, C USA 41.02N 107.39W
160 F11 **Bāgh** Madhya Pradesh, C India 22.22N 74.49E
145 T8 **Baghdād** var. Bagdad, Eng. Baghdad. ● (Iraq) C Iraq 33.19N 44.25E
145 T8 **Baghdād** ✕ C Iraq 33.19N 44.25E
159 T16 **Bagherhat** var. Bagerhat. Khulna, S Bangladesh 22.40N 89.48E
109 J23 **Bagheria** var. Bagaria. Sicilia, Italy, C Mediterranean Sea 38.04N 13.31E
149 S10 **Bāghīn** Kermān, C Iran 30.50N 57.00E
155 Q3 **Baghlān** Baghlān, NE Afghanistan 36.10N 68.43E
155 Q3 **Baghlān** var. Bāghlān. ◐ province NE Afghanistan
154 M7 **Bāghrān** Helmand, S Afghanistan 32.55N 64.57E
31 T4 **Bagley** Minnesota, N USA 47.31N 95.24W
108 H10 **Bagnacavallo** Emilia-Romagna, C Italy 44.00N 12.59E
104 K16 **Bagnères-de-Bigorre** Hautes-Pyrénées, S France 43.04N 0.09E
104 L17 **Bagnères-de-Luchon** Hautes-Pyrénées, S France 42.46N 0.34E
108 F11 **Bagni di Lucca** Toscana, C Italy 44.01N 10.38E
108 H11 **Bagno di Romagna** Emilia-Romagna, C Italy 43.51N 11.57E
105 R14 **Bagnols-sur-Cèze** Gard, S France 44.10N 4.37E
168 M14 **Bag Nur** ◎ N China
179 Q13 **Bago** off. Bago City. Negros, C Philippines 10.30N 122.49E
Bago see Pegu
78 M13 **Bagoé** ≈ Ivory Coast/Mali
Bagrāmē see Bagrāmī
155 R5 **Bagrāmī** var. Bagrāmē. Kābōl, E Afghanistan 34.28N 69.16E
121 B14 **Bagrationovsk** Ger. Preussisch Eylau. Kaliningradskaya Oblast', W Russian Federation 54.24N 20.39E
Bagrax see Bohu
Bagrax Hu see Bosten Hu
58 C10 **Bagua** Amazonas, NE Peru 5.34S 78.24W
179 P9 **Baguio** off. Baguio City. Luzon, N Philippines 16.25N 120.36E
79 V9 **Bagzane, Monts** ▲ N Niger 17.48N 8.43E
Bāḥah, Minṭaqat al see Al Bāḥah
Bahama Islands see Bahamas
46 H3 **Bahamas** off. Commonwealth of the Bahamas. ◆ commonwealth republic N West Indies
(0) L13 **Bahamas** var. Bahama Islands. island group N West Indies
159 S15 **Baharampur** prev. Berhampore. West Bengal, NE India 24.03N 88.16E
152 E12 **Baharly** var. Bäherden, Rus. Bakharden; prev. Bakherden. Ahal Welaýaty, C Turkmenistan 38.30N 57.18E
175 Nn6 **Bahau, Sungai** ≈ Borneo, N Indonesia
155 U10 **Bahāwalnagar** Punjab, E Pakistan 30.00N 73.03E
155 T11 **Bahāwalpur** Punjab, E Pakistan 29.24N 71.39E
142 L16 **Bahçe** Osmaniye, S Turkey 37.11N 36.32E
166 J8 **Ba He** ≈ C China
Bäherden see Baharly
61 N16 **Bahia** off. Estado da Bahia. ◐ state E Brazil
63 B24 **Bahía Blanca** Buenos Aires, E Argentina 38.43S 62.19W
42 L15 **Bahía Bufadero** Michoacán de Ocampo, SW Mexico
65 J19 **Bahía Bustamante** Chubut, SE Argentina 45.06S 66.30W
42 D5 **Bahía de los Ángeles** Baja California, NW Mexico
42 C6 **Bahía de Tortugas** Baja California Sur, W Mexico 27.42N 114.54W
44 J4 **Bahía, Islas de la** Eng. Bay Islands. island group N Honduras
42 E5 **Bahía Kino** Sonora, NW Mexico 28.48N 111.55W
42 E9 **Bahía Magdalena** var. Puerto Magdalena. Baja California Sur, W Mexico 24.34N 112.07W
56 C8 **Bahía Solano** var. Ciudad Mutis, Solano. Chocó, W Colombia 6.13N 77.27W
82 I11 **Bahir Dar** var. Bahr Dar, Bahrdar Giyorgis. Amhara, N Ethiopia 11.33N 37.22E
147 X8 **Bahlā'** var. Bahlah, Bahlat. NW Oman 22.55N 57.16E
Bāhla see Bālān
Bahlah/Bahlat see Bahlā'
158 M11 **Bahraich** Uttar Pradesh, N India 27.34N 81.36E
149 M14 **Bahrain** off. State of Bahrain, Dawlat al Bahrayn, Ar. Al Baḥrayn; prev. Bahrein, anc. Tylos or Tyros. ◆ monarchy SW Asia
148 M14 **Bahrain** ✕ C Bahrain 26.15N 50.39E
148 M15 **Bahrain, Gulf of** gulf Persian Gulf, NW Arabian Sea
144 I7 **Baḥrat Mallāḥah** ◎ W Syria
Bahrayn, Dawlat al see Bahrain
Bahr Dar/Bahrdar Giyorgis see Bahir Dar
Bahrein see Bahrain
83 E16 **Bahr el Gabel** ◐ state S Sudan
82 E13 **Bahr ez Zaref** ≈ C Sudan
69 R8 **Bahr Kameur** ≈ N Central African Republic
Bahr Tabariya, Sea of see Tiberias, Lake
149 W15 **Bāhū Kalāt** Sīstān va Balūchestān, SE Iran 25.42N 61.28E
120 N13 **Bahushewsk** Rus. Bogushëvsk. Vitsyebskaya Voblasts', NE Belarus 54.51N 30.13E
Bai see Tagow Bāy
118 G13 **Baia de Aramă** Mehedinţi, SW Romania 45.00N 22.43E
118 G11 **Baia de Criş** Ger. Altenburg, Hung. Körösbánya. Hunedoara, SW Romania 46.10N 22.40E
85 A16 **Baia dos Tigres** Namibe, SW Angola 16.36S 11.44E
84 A13 **Baia Farta** Benguela, W Angola 12.38S 13.12E
118 H9 **Baia Mare** Ger. Frauenbach, Hung. Nagybánya; prev. Neustadt. Maramureş, NW Romania 47.39N 23.35E
118 H8 **Baia Sprie** Ger. Mittelstadt, Hung. Felsőbánya. Maramureş, NW Romania 47.40N 23.42E
80 G13 **Baïbokoum** Logone-Oriental, SW Chad 7.46N 15.43E
166 F12 **Baicao Ling** ▲▲ SW China
169 U9 **Baicheng** var. Pai-ch'eng; prev. T'aon-an. Jilin, NE China 45.31N 122.50E
164 I6 **Baicheng** var. Bay. Xinjiang Uygur Zizhiqu, NW China 41.49N 81.45E
118 J13 **Băicoi** Prahova, SE Romania 45.01N 25.52E
Baidoa see Baydhabo
13 U6 **Baie-Comeau** Québec, SE Canada 49.12N 68.10W
13 T7 **Baie-des-Bacon** Québec, SE Canada 48.31N 69.17W
13 S8 **Baie-des-Rochers** Québec, SE Canada 47.57N 69.50W
13 U6 **Baie-des-Sables** Québec, SE Canada 48.41N 67.55W
10 K11 **Baie-du-Poste** Québec, SE Canada 50.19N 73.49W
180 H17 **Baie Lazare** Mahé, NE Seychelles 4.45S 55.28E
47 Y5 **Baie-Mahault** Basse Terre, C Guadeloupe 16.17N 61.34W
13 R9 **Baie-St-Paul** Québec, SE Canada 47.27N 70.30W
13 V5 **Baie-Trinité** Québec, SE Canada 49.25N 67.19W
11 T11 **Baie Verte** Newfoundland and Labrador, SE Canada 49.58N 56.06W
Baihe see Erdaobaihe
Baiguan see Shangyu
145 U11 **Bā'ij al Mahdī** S Iraq 31.21N 44.57E
Baiji see Bayjī
Baikal, Lake see Baykal, Ozero
Bailādila see Kirandul
Baile an Chaistil see Ballycastle
Baile an Róba see Ballinrobe
Baile an tSratha see Ballintra
Baile Átha an Rí see Athenry
Baile Átha Buí see Athboy
Baile Átha Cliath see Dublin
Baile Átha Fhirdhia see Ardee
Baile Átha Í see Athy
Baile Átha Luain see Athlone
Baile Átha Troim see Trim
Baile Brigín see Balbriggan
Baile Easa Dara see Ballysadare
118 I13 **Băile Govora** Vâlcea, SW Romania 45.00N 24.08E
118 F13 **Băile Herculane** Ger. Herkulesbad, Hung. Herkulesfürdő. Caraş-Severin, SW Romania 44.50N 22.23E
Baile Locha Riach see Loughrea
Baile Mhistéala see Mitchelstown
Baile Monaidh see Ballymoney
107 N12 **Bailén** Andalucía, S Spain 38.06N 3.46W
Baile na hInse see Ballynahinch
Baile na Lorgan see Castleblayney
Baile na Mainistreach see Newtownabbey
Baile Nua na hArda see Newtownards
118 I12 **Băile Olăneşti** Vâlcea, SW Romania 45.16N 24.13E
118 H14 **Băileşti** Dolj, SW Romania 44.01N 23.20E
169 N12 **Bailingmiao** var. Darhan Muminggan Lianheqi. Nei Mongol Zizhiqu, N China 41.41N 110.25E
60 K11 **Bailique, Ilha** island NE Brazil
105 O1 **Bailleul** Nord, N France 50.43N 2.43E
80 H12 **Ba Illi** Chari-Baguirmi, SW Chad 10.31N 16.28E
165 V12 **Bailong Jiang** ≈ C China
84 C13 **Bailundo** Port. Vila Teixeira da Silva. Huambo, C Angola 12.12S 15.52E
165 T13 **Baima** var. Sêraitang. Qinghai, C China 32.55N 100.44E
Baima see Baxoi
176 W14 **Baimun** Pulau Workai, E Indonesia 6.41S 134.40E
194 H14 **Baimuru** Gulf, S PNG 7.31S 144.44E
164 M16 **Bainang** Xizang Zizhiqu, W China 28.57N 89.31E
25 S8 **Bainbridge** Georgia, SE USA 30.54N 84.33W
175 Pp17 **Baing** Pulau Sumba, SE Indonesia 10.09S 120.34E
164 M14 **Baingoin** Xizang Zizhiqu, W China 31.25N 90.01E
106 G2 **Baio Grande** Galicia, NW Spain 43.08N 8.58W
106 G4 **Baiona** Galicia, NW Spain 42.06N 8.49W
169 V7 **Baiquan** Heilongjiang, NE China 47.37N 126.04E
Bā'ir see Bāyir
164 I11 **Bairab Co** ◎ W China
27 Q7 **Baird** Texas, SW USA 32.23N 99.23W
41 N7 **Baird Mountains** ▲▲ Alaska, USA
15 Mm2 **Baird Peninsula** peninsula Baffin Island, Nunavut, NE Canada
Baireuth see Bayreuth
202 H3 **Bairiki** ● (Kiribati) Tarawa, NW Kiribati 1.19N 173.01E
Bairin Youqi see Daban
Bairin Zuoqi see Lindong
151 P17 **Bairkum** Kaz. Bayyrqum. Yuzhnyy Kazakhstan, S Kazakhstan 41.57N 68.05E
191 P12 **Bairnsdale** Victoria, SE Australia 37.51S 147.37E
179 Q14 **Bais** Negros, S Philippines 9.36N 123.07E
104 L15 **Baïse** var. Baise. ≈ S France
169 W11 **Baishan** prev. Hunjiang. Jilin, NE China 41.57N 126.31E
Baishan see Mashan
120 F12 **Baisogala** Šiauliai, C Lithuania 55.38N 23.44E
201 Q7 **Baiti** N Nauru 0.30S 166.55E
106 G13 **Baixo Alentejo** physical region S Portugal
66 P5 **Baixo, Ilhéu de** island Madeira, Portugal, NE Atlantic Ocean
85 E15 **Baixo Longa** Cuando Cubango, SE Angola 15.39S 18.39E
165 V10 **Baiyin** Gansu, C China 36.33N 104.11E
166 E8 **Baiyü** var. Jianshe. Sichuan, C China 30.37N 97.15E
167 N14 **Baiyun** ✕ (Guangzhou) Guangdong, S China 23.12N 113.19E
166 K4 **Baiyu Shan** ▲▲ C China
113 J25 **Baja** Bács-Kiskun, S Hungary 46.12N 18.56E
42 C4 **Baja California** ◐ state NW Mexico
42 C4 **Baja California** Eng. Lower California. peninsula NW Mexico
42 E9 **Baja California Sur** ◐ state W Mexico
Bājah see Béja
Bajan see Bayan
203 V16 **Baja, Punta** headland Easter Island, Chile, E Pacific Ocean 27.10S 109.21W
42 B4 **Baja, Punta** headland NW Mexico 29.57N 115.48W
57 R5 **Baja, Punta** headland NE Venezuela
44 D5 **Baja Verapaz** off. Departamento de Baja Verapaz. ◐ department C Guatemala
175 Q16 **Bajawa** prev. Badjawa. Flores, S Indonesia 8.46S 120.58E
159 S16 **Baj Baj** prev. Budge-Budge. West Bengal, E India 22.28N 88.10E
147 N15 **Bājil** W Yemen 15.05N 43.16E
191 U4 **Bajimba, Mount** ▲ New South Wales, SE Australia 29.19S 152.04E
114 K13 **Bajina Bašta** Serbia, W Serbia 43.58N 19.33E
159 U14 **Bajitpur** Dhaka, E Bangladesh 24.12N 90.57E
114 K8 **Bajmok** Serbia, NW Serbia 45.59N 19.25E
Bajo Boquete see Boquete
115 L17 **Bajram Curri** Kukës, N Albania 42.22N 20.06E
81 J14 **Bakala** Ouaka, C Central African Republic 6.03N 20.31E
131 T4 **Bakaly** Respublika Bashkortostan, W Russian Federation 55.10N 53.46E
Bakan see Shimonoseki
151 U14 **Bakanas** Kaz. Baqanas. Almaty, SE Kazakhstan 44.50N 76.13E
151 V12 **Bakanas** Kaz. Baqanas. ≈ E Kazakhstan
155 R4 **Bākārak** Panjshīr, NE Afghanistan 35.16N 69.28E
151 U14 **Bakbakty** Kaz. Baqbaqty. Almaty, SE Kazakhstan 44.36N 76.41E
126 Gg13 **Bakchar** Tomskaya Oblast', C Russian Federation 56.58N 81.59E
78 I11 **Bakel** E Senegal 13.43N 13.40W
37 W13 **Baker** California, W USA 35.15N 116.04W
24 J8 **Baker** Louisiana, S USA 30.35N 91.10W
35 Y9 **Baker** Montana, NW USA 46.22N 104.16W
34 L12 **Baker** Oregon, NW USA 44.46N 117.49W
199 Jj8 **Baker and Howland Islands** ◇ US unincorporated territory W Polynesia
38 L12 **Baker Butte** ▲ Arizona, SW USA 34.24N 111.22W
41 X15 **Baker Island** island Alexander Archipelago, Alaska, USA
15 Kk6 **Baker Lake** Nunavut, N Canada 64.19N 96.10W
15 Kk6 **Baker Lake** ◎ Nunavut, N Canada
34 H6 **Baker, Mount** ▲ Washington, NW USA 48.46N 121.48W
37 R13 **Bakersfield** California, W USA 35.22N 119.01W
26 M9 **Bakersfield** Texas, SW USA 30.54N 102.21W
23 P9 **Bakersville** North Carolina, SE USA 36.03N 82.10W
Bakhābī see Bū Khābī
Bakharden see Baharly
Bakhardok see Bokurdak
149 U5 **Bākharz, Kuhhā-ye** ▲▲ NE Iran
158 D13 **Bākhāsar** Rājasthān, NW India 24.43N 71.09E
Bakhchisaray see Bakhchysaray
119 T13 **Bakhchysaray** Rus. Bakhchisaray. Respublika Krym, S Ukraine 44.43N 33.53E
Bakherden see Baharly
119 R3 **Bakhmach** Chernihivs'ka Oblast', N Ukraine 51.10N 32.48E
126 Hh11 **Bakhta** Krasnoyarskiy Kray, C Russian Federation 62.25N 88.56E
Bākhtarān see Kermānshāh
149 Q11 **Bakhtegān, Daryācheh-ye** ◎ C Iran
151 X12 **Bakhty** Vostochnyy Kazakhstan, E Kazakhstan 46.41N 82.45E
143 Z11 **Bakı** Eng. Baku. ● (Azerbaijan) E Azerbaijan 40.23N 49.51E
82 M12 **Baki** Awdal, N Somalia 10.10N 43.45E
143 Z11 **Bakı** ✕ E Azerbaijan 40.26N 49.55E
142 C13 **Bakır Çayı** ≈ W Turkey
94 L1 **Bakkafjördhur** Austurland, NE Iceland 66.01N 14.49W
94 L1 **Bakkaflói** sea area W Norwegian Sea
83 I15 **Bako** Southern, S Ethiopia 5.45N 36.39E
78 L15 **Bako** NW Ivory Coast 9.06N 7.34W
Bákó see Bacău
113 H23 **Bakony** Eng. Bakony Mountains, Ger. Bakonywald. ▲▲ W Hungary
Bakony Mountains/Bakonywald see Bakony
83 M16 **Bakool** off. Gobolka Bakool. ◐ region W Somalia
81 L15 **Bakouma** Mbomou, SE Central African Republic 5.42N 22.43E
131 N15 **Baksan** Kabardino-Balkarskaya Respublika, SW Russian Federation 43.43N 43.31E
121 I16 **Bakshty** Hrodzyenskaya Voblasts', W Belarus 53.56N 26.13E
Baku see Bakı
204 K12 **Bakutis Coast** physical region Antarctica
Bakwanga see Mbuji-Mayi
151 O15 **Bakyrly** Yuzhnyy Kazakhstan, S Kazakhstan 44.30N 67.41E
12 H13 **Bala** Ontario, S Canada 45.01N 79.37W
99 J19 **Bala** NW Wales, UK 52.54N 3.31W
142 I13 **Balâ** Ankara, C Turkey 39.34N 33.07E
179 O16 **Balabac Island** island W Philippines
Balabac, Selat see Balabac Strait
175 O1 **Balabac Strait** var. Selat Balabac. strait Malaysia/Philippines
Ba'labakk see Baalbek
175 O10 **Balabalangan, Kepulauan** island group N Indonesia
197 H4 **Balabio, Île** island Province Nord, W New Caledonia
118 I14 **Balaci** Teleorman, S Romania 44.21N 24.55E
145 S7 **Balad** N Iraq 34.00N 44.07E
127 N14 **Baladek** Khabarovskiy Kray, SE Russian Federation 53.45N 133.22E
145 U7 **Balad Rūz** E Iraq 33.42N 45.04E
126 J15 **Balagansk** Irkutskaya Oblast', S Russian Federation 54.02N 102.48E
160 J11 **Bālāghāt** Madhya Pradesh, C India 21.48N 80.10E
161 F14 **Bālāghāt Range** ▲▲ W India
105 X14 **Balagne** physical region Corse, France, C Mediterranean Sea
107 U5 **Balaguer** Cataluña, NE Spain 41.48N 0.48E
107 S3 **Balaïtous** var. Pic de Balaitous, Pic de Balaïtous. ▲ France/Spain 42.51N 0.17W
Balaitous, Pic de see Balaïtous
Bálák see Ballangen
131 O3 **Balakhna** Nizhegorodskaya Oblast', W Russian Federation 56.26N 43.43E
126 I14 **Balakhta** Krasnoyarskiy Kray, S Russian Federation 55.22N 91.24E
190 I9 **Balaklava** South Australia 34.10S 138.22E
Balakleya see Balakliya
119 V6 **Balakliya** Rus. Balakleya. Kharkivs'ka Oblast', E Ukraine 49.26N 36.51E
131 Q7 **Balakovo** Saratovskaya Oblast', W Russian Federation 52.03N 47.47E
85 P14 **Balama** Cabo Delgado, N Mozambique 13.18S 38.39E
175 Nn1 **Balambangan, Pulau** island East Malaysia
154 L3 **Bālā Morghāb** Laghmān, NW Afghanistan 35.37N 63.21E
158 E11 **Bālān** prev. Bāhla. Rājasthān, NW India 27.45N 71.31E
118 J10 **Bălan** Hung. Balánbánya. Harghita, C Romania 46.39N 25.45E
Balánbánya see Bălan
179 P10 **Balanga** Luzon, N Philippines 14.40N 120.32E
160 M12 **Balāngīr** prev. Bolangir. Orissa, E India 20.46N 83.31E
131 N8 **Balashov** Saratovskaya Oblast', W Russian Federation 51.31N 43.14E
Balasore see Bāleshwar
113 K21 **Balassagyarmat** Nógrád, N Hungary 48.04N 19.16E
31 S10 **Balaton** Minnesota, N USA 44.13N 95.52W
113 H24 **Balaton** var. Lake Balaton, Ger. Plattensee. ◎ W Hungary
113 I23 **Balatonfüred** var. Füred. Veszprém, W Hungary 46.56N 17.51E
Balaton, Lake see Balaton

228

◆ Country ● Country Capital ◇ Dependent Territory ○ Dependent Territory Capital ◐ Administrative Region ✕ International Airport ▲ Mountain ▲▲ Mountain Range Volcano ≈ River ◎ Lake ▣ Reservoir

BĂLĂUŞERI – BARATARIA BAY

118 I11 **Bălăuşeri** Ger. Bladenmarkt, Hung. Balavásár. Mureş, C Romania 46.24N 24.41E
Balavásár see Bălăuşeri
107 Q11 **Balazote** Castilla-La Mancha, C Spain 38.54N 2.09W
Balázsfalva see Blaj
121 F14 **Balbieriškis** Kaunas, S Lithuania 54.29N 23.52E
195 S12 **Balbi, Mount** ▲ Bougainville Island, NE PNG 5.51S 154.58E
60 F11 **Balbina, Represa** ⊠ NW Brazil
45 T15 **Balboa** Panamá, C Panama 8.55N 79.36W
99 G17 **Balbriggan** Ir. Baile Brigín. E Ireland 53.37N 6.10W
Balbunar see Kubrat
83 N17 **Balcad** Shabeellaha Dhexe, C Somalia 2.19N 45.19E
63 D23 **Balcarce** Buenos Aires, E Argentina 37.51S 58.16W
9 U16 **Balcarres** Saskatchewan, S Canada 50.49N 103.31W
116 O8 **Balchik** Dobrich, NE Bulgaria 43.25N 28.11E
193 E24 **Balclutha** Otago, South Island, NZ 46.15S 169.44E
27 Q12 **Balcones Escarpment** escarpment Texas, SW USA
20 F14 **Bald Eagle Creek** ≈ Pennsylvania, NE USA
Baldenburg see Biały Bór
23 V12 **Bald Head Island** island North Carolina, SE USA
29 W10 **Bald Knob** Arkansas, C USA 35.18N 91.34W
32 K17 **Bald Knob** hill Illinois, N USA 37.33N 89.21W
Baldohn see Baldone
120 G9 **Baldone** Ger. Baldohn. Rīga, W Latvia 56.46N 24.18E
24 I9 **Baldwin** Louisiana, S USA 29.50N 91.32W
33 P7 **Baldwin** Michigan, N USA 43.54N 85.49W
29 Q4 **Baldwin City** Kansas, C USA 38.43N 95.12W
41 N8 **Baldwin Peninsula** headland Alaska, USA 66.45N 162.19W
20 H9 **Baldwinsville** New York, NE USA 43.09N 76.19W
25 N2 **Baldwyn** Mississippi, S USA 34.30N 88.38W
9 W15 **Baldy Mountain** ▲ Manitoba, S Canada 51.29N 100.46W
35 T7 **Baldy Mountain** ▲ Montana, NW USA 48.09N 109.39W
39 O13 **Baldy Peak** ▲ Arizona, SW USA 33.56N 109.37W
Bâle see Basel
Baleares see Illes Balears
107 X11 **Baleares, Islas** Eng. Balearic Islands. island group Spain, W Mediterranean Sea
Baleares Major see Mallorca
Balearic Islands see Baleares, Islas
Balearic Plain see Algerian Basin
Balearis Minor see Menorca
174 M6 **Baleh, Batang** ≈ East Malaysia
10 J8 **Baleine, Grande Rivière de la** ≈ Québec, E Canada
10 K7 **Baleine, Petite Rivière de la** ≈ Québec, SE Canada
11 N6 **Baleine, Rivière à la** ≈ Québec, E Canada
101 J16 **Balen** Antwerpen, N Belgium 51.11N 5.12E
179 P9 **Baler** Luzon, N Philippines 15.47N 121.30E
160 P11 **Bāleshwar** prev. Balasore. Orissa, E India 21.31N 86.58E
126 L16 **Baley** Chitinskaya Oblast', S Russian Federation 51.30N 116.16E
79 S12 **Baléyara** Tillabéri, W Niger 13.48N 2.57E
131 T1 **Balezino** Udmurtskaya Respublika, NW Russian Federation 57.57N 53.03E
44 J4 **Balfate** Colón, N Honduras 15.47N 86.24W
9 O17 **Balfour** British Columbia, SW Canada 49.39N 116.57W
31 N3 **Balfour** North Dakota, N USA 47.55N 100.34W
Balfrush see Bābol
126 I16 **Balgazyn** Respublika Tyva, S Russian Federation 50.53N 95.12E
9 U16 **Balgonie** Saskatchewan, S Canada 50.30N 104.12W
Bălgrad see Alba Iulia
83 J19 **Balguda** spring/well S Kenya 1.28S 39.50E
164 K6 **Balguntay** Xinjiang Uygur Zizhiqu, NW China 42.51N 86.19E
147 R16 **Balḥāf** S Yemen 14.02N 48.15E
158 F13 **Bāli** Rājasthān, N India 25.17N 73.16E
175 N15 **Bali** ◈ province S Indonesia
175 N16 **Bali** island C Indonesia
113 K16 **Balice** ✈ (Kraków) Małopolskie, S Poland 49.57N 19.49E
176 Yy13 **Baliem, Sungai** ≈ Papua, E Indonesia
142 C12 **Balıkesir** Balıkesir, W Turkey 39.38N 27.52E
142 C12 **Balıkesir** ◈ province NW Turkey
144 L3 **Balīkh, Nahr** ≈ N Syria
175 O9 **Balikpapan** Borneo, C Indonesia 1.15S 116.49E
175 O9 **Balikpapan, Teluk** bay Borneo, C Indonesia
Bali, Laut see Bali Sea
195 O11 **Balima** ≈ New Britain, C PNG
179 P17 **Balimbing** Tawitawi, SW Philippines 5.10N 120.00E
194 G14 **Balimo** Western, SW PNG 8.01S 142.52E
Bálinc see Balinţ
175 Qq9 **Balingara, Pegunungan** ▲ Sulawesi, N Indonesia
103 H23 **Balingen** Baden-Württemberg, SW Germany 48.16N 8.51E
118 F11 **Balinţ** Hung. Bálinc. Timiş, W Romania 45.52N 21.54E
179 Pp6 **Balintang Channel** channel N Philippines
144 K3 **Bālis** Ḥalab, N Syria 36.01N 38.03E
175 N15 **Bali Sea** Ind. Laut Bali. sea C Indonesia
175 N16 **Bali, Selat** strait C Indonesia
100 K7 **Balk** Friesland, N Netherlands 52.54N 5.34E
152 B11 **Balkanabat** Rus. Nebitdag. Balkan Welaýaty, W Turkmenistan 39.33N 54.19E
124 O7 **Balkan Mountains** Bul./SCr. Stara Planina. ▲ Bulgaria/Serbia
Balkanskiy Velayat see Balkan Welaýaty
152 B9 **Balkan Welaýaty** Rus. Balkanskiy Velayat. ◈ province W Turkmenistan
151 P8 **Balkashino** Akmola, N Kazakhstan 52.32N 68.43E
155 O2 **Balkh** anc. Bactra. Balkh, N Afghanistan 36.46N 66.54E
155 P2 **Balkh** ◈ province N Afghanistan
151 T13 **Balkhash** Kaz. Balqash. Karaganda, SE Kazakhstan 46.52N 74.54E
Balkhash, Lake see Balkhash, Ozero
151 T13 **Balkhash, Ozero** Eng. Lake Balkhash, Kaz. Balqash. ⊛ SE Kazakhstan
Balla Balla see Mbalabala
98 H10 **Ballachulish** N Scotland, UK 56.40N 5.10W
188 M12 **Balladonia** Western Australia 32.21S 123.31E
99 C16 **Ballaghaderreen** Ir. Bealach an Doirín. C Ireland 53.51N 8.29W
94 H10 **Ballangen** Lapp. Bálák. Nordland, NW Norway 68.18N 16.48E
99 H14 **Ballantrae** W Scotland, UK 55.04N 5.00W
191 N12 **Ballarat** Victoria, SE Australia 37.36S 143.51E
188 K11 **Ballard, Lake** salt lake Western Australia
Ballari see Bellary
78 L11 **Ballé** Koulikoro, W Mali 15.18N 8.31W
42 D7 **Ballenas, Bahía de** bay W Mexico
42 D5 **Ballenas, Canal de** channel NW Mexico
205 R17 **Balleny Islands** island group Antarctica
42 J7 **Balleza** var. San Pablo Balleza. Chihuahua, N Mexico 26.55N 106.21W
116 M13 **Ballı** Tekirdağ, NW Turkey 40.48N 27.03E
159 O13 **Ballia** Uttar Pradesh, N India 25.45N 84.09E
191 V4 **Ballina** New South Wales, SE Australia 28.49S 153.33E
99 C16 **Ballina** Ir. Béal an Átha. W Ireland 54.07N 9.09W
99 D16 **Ballinamore** Ir. Béal an Átha Móir. NW Ireland 54.03N 7.46W
99 D18 **Ballinasloe** Ir. Béal Átha na Sluaighe. W Ireland 53.19N 8.13W
27 P8 **Ballinger** Texas, SW USA 31.44N 99.57W
99 C17 **Ballinrobe** Ir. Baile an Róba. W Ireland 53.37N 9.14W
99 A21 **Ballinskelligs Bay** Ir. Bá na Scealg. inlet SW Ireland
99 D15 **Ballintra** Ir. Baile an tSratha. NW Ireland 54.34N 8.07W
105 T7 **Ballon d'Alsace** ▲ NE France 47.50N 6.54E
Ballon de Guebwiller see Grand Ballon
115 K21 **Ballsh** var. Ballshi. Fier, SW Albania 40.35N 19.45E
Ballshi see Ballsh
100 K4 **Ballum** Friesland, N Netherlands 53.27N 5.40E
99 F16 **Ballybay** Ir. Béal Átha Beithe. N Ireland 54.07N 6.54W
99 E14 **Ballybofey** Ir. Bealach Féich. NW Ireland 54.48N 7.46W
99 G14 **Ballycastle** Ir. Baile an Chaistil. N Northern Ireland, UK 55.12N 6.13W
99 G15 **Ballyclare** Ir. Bealach Cláir. E Northern Ireland, UK 54.45N 6.00W
99 E16 **Ballyconnell** Ir. Béal Átha Conaill. N Ireland 54.07N 7.34W
99 C17 **Ballyhaunis** Ir. Beál Átha hAmhnais. W Ireland 53.45N 8.45W
99 G14 **Ballymena** Ir. An Baile Meánach. NE Northern Ireland, UK 54.52N 6.16W
99 F14 **Ballymoney** Ir. Baile Monaidh. NE Northern Ireland, UK 55.10N 6.30W
99 G15 **Ballynahinch** Ir. Baile na hInse. SE Northern Ireland, UK 54.24N 5.54W
99 D16 **Ballysadare** Ir. Baile Easa Dara. NW Ireland 54.13N 8.30W
99 D15 **Ballyshannon** Ir. Béal Átha Seanaidh. NW Ireland 54.30N 8.10W
65 H19 **Balmaceda** Aisén, S Chile 45.54S 71.47W
65 G23 **Balmaceda, Cerro** ▲ S Chile 51.27S 73.26W
113 N22 **Balmazújváros** Hajdú-Bihar, E Hungary 47.36N 21.18E
110 E10 **Balmhorn** ▲ SW Switzerland 46.27N 7.41E
190 L12 **Balmoral** Victoria, SE Australia 37.16S 141.38E
26 K9 **Balmorhea** Texas, SW USA 30.58N 103.44W
Balneario Claromecó see Claromecó
175 R9 **Balo** Sulawesi, N Indonesia 0.58S 123.19E
Balochistān see Baluchistān
84 B13 **Balombo** Port. Norton de Matos, Vila Norton de Matos. Benguela, W Angola 12.21S 14.46E
84 B13 **Balombo** ≈ W Angola
189 X10 **Balonne River** ≈ Queensland, E Australia
158 E13 **Bālotra** Rājasthān, N India 25.51N 72.18E
151 V14 **Balpyk Bi** prev. Kirovskiy Kaz. Kīrov. Almaty, SE Kazakhstan 44.52N 78.10E
Balqā'/Balqā', Muḥāfaẓat al see Al Balqā'
Balqash see Balkhash/Balkhash, Ozero
158 M12 **Balrāmpur** Uttar Pradesh, N India 27.25N 82.10E
190 M9 **Balranald** New South Wales, SE Australia 34.39S 143.33E
118 H14 **Balş** Olt, S Romania 44.19N 24.06E
12 H11 **Balsam Creek** Ontario, S Canada 46.26N 79.10W
32 I5 **Balsam Lake** Wisconsin, N USA 45.27N 92.28W
12 I14 **Balsam Lake** ⊛ Ontario, SE Canada
61 M14 **Balsas** Maranhão, E Brazil 07.30S 46.00W
42 M15 **Balsas, Río** var. Río Mexcala. ≈ S Mexico
45 W16 **Balsas, Río** ≈ SE Panama
121 O18 **Bal'shavik** Rus. Bol'shevik. Homyel'skaya Voblasts', SE Belarus 52.34N 30.49E
97 O15 **Bålsta** Uppsala, C Sweden 59.33N 17.35E
110 E7 **Balsthal** Solothurn, NW Switzerland 47.20N 7.50E
119 O8 **Balta** Odes'ka Oblast', SW Ukraine 47.58N 29.39E
107 N5 **Baltanás** Castilla-León, N Spain 41.56N 4.12W
63 E16 **Baltasar Brum** Artigas, N Uruguay 30.43S 57.19W
118 M9 **Bălţi** Rus. Bel'tsy. N Moldova 47.45N 27.57E
Baltic Port see Paldiski
120 B10 **Baltic Sea** Ger. Ostee, Rus. Baltiskoye More. sea N Europe
23 X3 **Baltimore** Maryland, NE USA 39.17N 76.36W
33 T13 **Baltimore** Ohio, N USA 39.48N 82.33W
23 X3 **Baltimore-Washington** ✈ Maryland, E USA 39.10N 76.40W
Baltischport/Baltiski see Paldiski
Baltiskoye More see Baltic Sea
121 A14 **Baltiysk** Ger. Pillau. Kaliningradskaya Oblast', W Russian Federation 54.39N 19.54E
Baltkrievija see Belarus
121 H14 **Baltoji Vokė** Vilnius, SE Lithuania 54.35N 25.13E
194 K9 **Baluan Island** island N PNG
Balūchestān va Sīstān see Sīstān va Balūchestān
154 M12 **Baluchistān** var. Balochistān, Beluchistan. ◈ province SW Pakistan
179 Q12 **Balud** Masbate, N Philippines 12.03N 123.12E
174 Mm6 **Balui, Batang** ≈ East Malaysia
159 S13 **Bālurghat** West Bengal, NE India 25.14N 88.43E
120 J8 **Balvi** Balvi, NE Latvia 57.07N 27.14E
194 H12 **Balyer River** Western Highlands, C PNG
153 W7 **Balykchy** Kir. Ysyk-Köl; prev. Issyk-Kul', Rybach'ye. Issyk-Kul'skaya Oblast', NE Kyrgyzstan 42.28N 76.08E
58 B7 **Balzar** Guayas, W Ecuador 1.25S 79.54W
110 I8 **Balzers** S Liechtenstein 47.04N 9.31E
149 T12 **Bam** Kermān, SE Iran 29.08N 58.27E
79 Y13 **Bama** Borno, NE Nigeria 11.28N 13.46E
78 L12 **Bamako** ● (Mali) Capital District, SW Mali 12.39N 8.01W
79 P10 **Bamba** Gao, C Mali 17.03N 1.19W
44 M8 **Bambana, Río** ≈ NE Nicaragua
81 J15 **Bambari** Ouaka, C Central African Republic 5.45N 20.37E
189 W5 **Bambaroo** Queensland, NE Australia 19.00S 146.16E
103 K19 **Bamberg** Bayern, SE Germany 49.54N 10.52E
23 R14 **Bamberg** South Carolina, SE USA 33.18N 81.02W
81 M16 **Bambesa** Orientale, N Dem. Rep. Congo 3.25N 25.43E
78 G11 **Bambey** W Senegal 14.43N 16.26W
81 H16 **Bambio** Sangha-Mbaéré, SW Central African Republic 3.57N 16.54E
85 I24 **Bamboesberge** ▲ S South Africa 31.24S 26.10E
81 D14 **Bamenda** Nord-Ouest, W Cameroon 5.55N 10.09E
8 K17 **Bamfield** Vancouver Island, British Columbia, SW Canada 48.48N 125.05W
Bami see Bamy
155 P4 **Bāmīān** var. Bāmiān. Bāmīān, NE Afghanistan 34.50N 67.51E
155 O4 **Bāmīān** ◈ province C Afghanistan
81 J14 **Bamingui** Bamingui-Bangoran, C Central African Republic 7.38N 20.06E
80 J13 **Bamingui** ≈ N Central African Republic
80 J13 **Bamingui-Bangoran** ◈ prefecture N Central African Republic
149 V13 **Bampūr** Sīstān va Balūchestān, SE Iran 27.13N 60.28E
194 G14 **Bamu** ≈ SW PNG
152 E12 **Bamy** Rus. Bami. Ahal Welaýaty, C Turkmenistan 38.42N 56.47E
Bán see Bánovce nad Bebravou
83 N17 **Banaadir** off. Gobolka Banaadir. ◈ region S Somalia
203 N3 **Banaba** var. Ocean Island. island Tungaru, W Kiribati
61 O14 **Banabuiú, Açude** ⊠ NE Brazil
59 O19 **Bañados del Izozog** salt lake SE Bolivia
99 D18 **Banagher** Ir. Beannchar. C Ireland 53.12N 7.56W
81 M17 **Banalia** Orientale, N Dem. Rep. Congo 1.39N 25.19E
78 L12 **Banamba** Koulikoro, W Mali 13.33N 7.25W
42 G4 **Banámichi** Sonora, NW Mexico 30.01N 110.13W
189 Y9 **Banana** Queensland, E Australia 24.33S 150.07E
203 Z2 **Banana** prev. Main Camp. Kiritimati, E Kiribati 02.00N 157.25W
61 K16 **Bananal, Ilha do** island C Brazil
25 Y12 **Banana River** lagoon Florida, SE USA
157 Q22 **Bananga** Andaman and Nicobar Islands, India, NE Indian Ocean 6.57N 93.54E
Banaras see Vārānasi
116 N13 **Banarlı** Tekirdağ, NW Turkey 41.04N 27.21E
158 H12 **Banās** ≈ N India
77 Z11 **Banâs, Râs** headland E Egypt 23.55N 35.47E
114 N10 **Banatski Karlovac** Serbia, NE Serbia 45.03N 21.02E
147 P16 **Banā, Wādī** dry watercourse SW Yemen
142 E14 **Banaz** Uşak, W Turkey 38.46N 29.46E
142 E14 **Banaz Çayı** ≈ W Turkey
165 P14 **Banbar** var. Coka. Xizang Zizhiqu, W China 31.01N 94.43E
99 G15 **Banbridge** Ir. Droichead na Banna. SE Northern Ireland, UK 54.21N 6.16W
Ban Bua Yai see Bua Yai
99 M21 **Banbury** S England, UK 52.04N 1.19W
178 H7 **Ban Chiang Dao** Chiang Mai, NW Thailand 19.22N 98.59E
98 K9 **Banchory** NE Scotland, UK 58.04N 0.35W
12 J13 **Bancroft** Ontario, SE Canada 45.04N 77.49W
35 R15 **Bancroft** Idaho, NW USA 42.43N 111.54W
31 U11 **Bancroft** Iowa, C USA 43.17N 94.13W
160 I9 **Banda** Madhya Pradesh, C India 24.04N 78.57E
158 L13 **Bānda** Uttar Pradesh, N India 25.28N 80.19E
173 E3 **Bandaaceh** var. Banda Atjeh; prev. Koetaradja, Kutaradja, Kutaraja. Sumatera, W Indonesia 5.30N 95.19E
Banda Atjeh see Bandaaceh
176 U12 **Banda, Kepulauan** island group E Indonesia
Banda, Laut see Banda Sea
79 N17 **Bandama** var. Bandama Fleuve. ≈ S Ivory Coast
79 N15 **Bandama Blanc** ≈ C Ivory Coast
Bandama Fleuve see Bandama
Bandar 'Abbās see Bandar-e 'Abbās
159 W16 **Bandarban** Chittagong, SE Bangladesh 22.13N 92.13E
82 Q13 **Bandarbeyla** var. Bender Beila, Bender Beyla. Bari, NE Somalia 9.28N 50.48E
149 R14 **Bandar-e 'Abbās** var. Bandar 'Abbās; prev. Gombroon. Hormozgān, S Iran 27.10N 56.10E
148 M3 **Bandar-e Anzalī** Gīlān, NW Iran 37.25N 49.28E
149 N12 **Bandar-e Būshehr** var. Būshehr, Eng. Bushire. Būshehr, S Iran 28.58N 50.49E
148 M11 **Bandar-e Genāveh** var. Ganāveh; prev. Gonāveh. Būshehr, SW Iran 29.33N 50.39E
149 T15 **Bandar-e Jāsk** var. Jāsk. Hormozgān, SE Iran 25.35N 58.06E
149 O13 **Bandar-e Kangān** var. Kangān. Būshehr, S Iran 25.50N 57.30E
149 R14 **Bandar-e Khamīr** Hormozgān, S Iran 26.59N 55.30E
149 Q14 **Bandar-e Langeh** var. Bandar-e Lengeh, Lingeh. Hormozgān, S Iran 26.34N 54.52E
Bandar-e Lengeh see Bandar-e Langeh
148 L10 **Bandar-e Māhshahr** var. Māh-Shahr; prev. Bandar-e Ma'shūr. Khūzestān, SW Iran 30.33N 49.10E
Bandar-e Ma'shūr see Bandar-e Māhshahr
149 O14 **Bandar-e Nakhīlū** Hormozgān, S Iran
Bandar-e Shāh see Bandar-e Torkaman
149 P4 **Bandar-e Torkaman** var. Bandar-e Torkeman, Bandar-e Torkman; prev. Bandar-e Shāh. Golestān, N Iran 36.55N 54.04E
Bandar-e Torkeman/Bandar-e Torkman see Bandar-e Torkaman
Bandar Kassim see Boosaaso
174 Ii13 **Bandar Lampung** var. Bandarlampung, Tanjungkarang-Telukbetung; prev. Tandjoengkarang, Tanjungkarang, Teloekbetoeng, Telukbetung. Sumatera, W Indonesia 5.28N 105.16E
Bandar Maharani see Muar
Bandar Masulipatnam see Machilīpatnam
Bandar Penggaram see Batu Pahat
175 N3 **Bandar Seri Begawan** prev. Brunei Town. ● (Brunei) N Brunei 4.55N 114.58E
174 Mm3 **Bandar Seri Begawan** ✈ N Brunei 4.55N 114.58E
175 Ss13 **Banda Sea** var. Laut Banda. sea E Indonesia
106 H5 **Bande** Galicia, NW Spain 42.01N 7.58W
61 G15 **Bandeirantes** Mato Grosso, W Brazil 9.04S 57.53W
61 N20 **Bandeira, Pico da** ▲ SE Brazil 20.25S 41.45W
85 K19 **Bandelierkop** Limpopo, NE South Africa 23.21S 29.46E
64 L8 **Bandera** Santiago del Estero, N Argentina 28.52S 62.15W
27 Q11 **Bandera** Texas, SW USA 29.43N 99.07W
42 J13 **Banderas, Bahía de** bay W Mexico
79 O11 **Bandiagara** Mopti, C Mali 14.22N 3.42W
158 I12 **Bāndīkūi** Rājasthān, N India 27.07N 76.34E
142 C11 **Bandırma** var. Penderma. Balıkesir, NW Turkey 40.21N 27.58E
Bandjarmasin see Banjarmasin
Bandoeng see Bandung
99 C21 **Bandon** Ir. Droicheadna Bandan. SW Ireland 51.43N 8.43W
34 E14 **Bandon** Oregon, NW USA 43.07N 124.24W
178 J8 **Ban Dong Bang** Nong Khai, E Thailand 18.00N 104.08E
178 I6 **Ban Donkon** Oudômxai, N Laos 20.20N 101.37E
180 J14 **Bandrélé** SE Mayotte
81 H20 **Bandundu** prev. Banningville. Bandundu, W Dem. Rep. Congo 3.18S 17.24E
81 I21 **Bandundu** off. Région de Bandundu. ◈ region W Dem. Rep. Congo
174 Jj14 **Bandung** prev. Bandoeng. Jawa, C Indonesia 6.47S 107.28E
118 L15 **Băneasa** Constanţa, SW Romania 44.03N 27.42E
148 J4 **Bāneh** Kordestān, N Iran 35.58N 45.54E
46 I7 **Banes** Holguín, E Cuba 20.58N 75.43W
9 P16 **Banff** Alberta, SW Canada 51.10N 115.34W
98 K8 **Banff** NE Scotland, UK 57.39N 2.33W
98 K8 **Banff** cultural region NE Scotland, UK
Bánffyhunyad see Huedin
79 N14 **Banfora** SW Burkina 10.36N 4.45W
161 H19 **Bangalore** Karnātaka, S India 12.58N 77.34E
159 S16 **Bangaon** West Bengal, NE India 23.01N 88.49E
179 P9 **Bangar** Luzon, N Philippines 16.51N 120.25E
81 L15 **Bangassou** Mbomou, SE Central African Republic 4.51N 22.55E
194 K12 **Bangeta, Mount** ▲ C PNG 6.11S 147.02E
175 Qq10 **Banggai, Kepulauan** island group C Indonesia
175 R9 **Banggai, Pulau** island Kepulauan Banggai, N Indonesia
176 X11 **Banggelapa** Papua, E Indonesia 3.47S 136.53E
Banggi see Banggi, Pulau
175 O1 **Banggi, Pulau** var. Banggi. island East Malaysia
124 N15 **Banghāzī** Eng. Bengazi, Benghazi, It. Bengasi. NE Libya 32.07N 20.04E
Bang Hieng see Xé Banghiang
174 J10 **Bangka-Belitung** off. Propinsi Bangka-Belitung. ◈ province W Indonesia
174 K8 **Bangkai, Tanjung** var. Bankai. headland Borneo, N Indonesia 0.21N 108.53E
174 M14 **Bangkalan** Pulau Madura, C Indonesia 7.04S 112.43E
175 S6 **Bangka, Pulau** island N Indonesia
174 J10 **Bangka, Pulau** island W Indonesia
174 Ii10 **Bangka, Selat** strait Sumatera, W Indonesia
175 Rr6 **Bangka, Selat** var. Selat Likupang. strait Sulawesi, N Indonesia
174 Gg8 **Bangkinang** Sumatera, W Indonesia 0.21N 100.56E
174 H10 **Bangko** Sumatera, W Indonesia 2.03S 102.15E
Bangkok see Krung Thep
Bangkok, Bight of see Krung Thep, Ao
159 T14 **Bangladesh** off. People's Republic of Bangladesh; prev. East Pakistan. ◆ republic S Asia
178 Kk13 **Ba Ngoi** Khanh Hoa, S Vietnam 11.55N 109.07E
158 K5 **Bangong Co** var. Pangong Tso. ⊛ China/India
see also Pangong Tso
99 G15 **Bangor** Ir. Beannchar. E Northern Ireland, UK 54.40N 5.40W
99 I18 **Bangor** NW Wales, UK 53.13N 4.07W
21 R6 **Bangor** Maine, NE USA 44.48N 68.46W
20 I14 **Bangor** Pennsylvania, NE USA 40.52N 75.12W
69 R8 **Bangoran** ≈ S Central African Republic
Bang Phra see Trat
Bang Pla Soi see Chon Buri
27 Q8 **Bangs** Texas, SW USA 31.43N 99.07W
178 H13 **Bang Saphan** var. Bang Saphan Yai. Prachuap Khiri Khan, SW Thailand 11.10N 99.27E
Bang Saphan Yai see Bang Saphan
38 I8 **Bangs, Mount** ▲ Arizona, SW USA 36.47N 113.51W
95 E15 **Bangsund** Nord-Trøndelag, C Norway 64.22N 11.22E
179 P8 **Bangued** Luzon, N Philippines 17.36N 120.40E
81 I15 **Bangui** ● (Central African Republic) Ombella-Mpoko, SW Central African Republic 4.21N 18.31E
81 I15 **Bangui** ✈ Ombella-Mpoko, SW Central African Republic 4.19N 18.34E
85 N16 **Bangula** Southern, S Malawi 16.38S 35.04E
Bangwaketse see Southern
84 K12 **Bangweulu, Lake** var. Lake Bengweulu. ⊛ N Zambia
Banhā see Benha
Ban Hat Yai see Hat Yai
178 I8 **Ban Hin Heup** Viangchan, C Laos 18.37N 102.19E
Ban Houayxay/Ban Houei Sai see Houayxay
178 H12 **Ban Hua Hin** var. Hua Hin. Prachuap Khiri Khan, SW Thailand 12.29N 99.55E
81 L14 **Bani** Haute-Kotto, E Central African Republic 7.06N 22.51E
79 N12 **Bani** ≈ S Mali
47 O9 **Baní** S Dominican Republic 18.14N 70.18W
Banias see Bāniyās
79 S11 **Bani Bangou** Tillabéri, SW Niger 15.04N 2.40E
78 M12 **Banifing** var. Ngorolaka. ≈ Burkina/Mali
79 R13 **Banikoara** N Benin 11.18N 2.25E
Banī Mazār see Beni Mazâr
116 K8 **Baniski Lom** ≈ N Bulgaria
23 U7 **Banister River** ≈ Virginia, NE USA
Banī Suwayf see Beni Suef
77 O8 **Banī Walīd** NW Libya 31.46N 13.58E
144 H5 **Bāniyās** var. Banias, Baniyas, Paneas. Ṭarṭūs, W Syria 35.12N 35.57E
115 K14 **Banja** Serbia, W Serbia 43.33N 19.35E
Banjak, Kepulauan see Banyak, Kepulauan
114 J12 **Banja Koviljača** Serbia, W Serbia 44.31N 19.11E
114 G11 **Banja Luka** Republika Srpska, NW Bosnia and Herzegovina 44.46N 17.10E
175 N11 **Banjarmasin** prev. Bandjarmasin. Borneo, C Indonesia 3.22S 114.33E
Banjoewangi see Banyuwangi
78 F11 **Banjul** prev. Bathurst. ● (Gambia) W Gambia 13.25N 16.43W
78 F11 **Banjul** ✈ W Gambia 13.18N 16.39W
Banjuwangi see Banyuwangi
Bank see Bankä
143 Y13 **Bankä** Rus. Bank. SE Azerbaijan 39.25N 49.13E
178 Jj11 **Ban Kadian** var. Ban Kadiene. Champasak, S Laos 14.25N 105.42E
Ban Kadiene see Ban Kadian
Bankai see Bangkai, Tanjung
178 Gg15 **Ban Kam Phuam** Phangnga, SW Thailand 9.16N 98.24E
Ban Kantang see Kantang
79 O11 **Bankass** Mopti, S Mali 14.05N 3.30W
97 L19 **Bankeryd** Jönköping, S Sweden 57.51N 14.07E
85 K16 **Banket** Mashonaland West, N Zimbabwe 17.25S 30.25E
178 Jj11 **Ban Khamphô** Attapu, S Laos 14.35N 106.18E
25 O4 **Bankhead Lake** ⊠ Alabama, S USA
79 Q11 **Bankilaré** Tillabéri, SW Niger 14.34N 0.41E
Banks, Îles see Banks Islands
8 I14 **Banks Island** island British Columbia, SW Canada
15 Hh1 **Banks Island** island Banks Island, Northwest Territories, NW Canada
197 C10 **Banks Islands** Fr. Îles Banks. island group N Vanuatu
25 U8 **Banks Lake** ⊛ Georgia, SE USA
34 K8 **Banks Lake** ⊠ Washington, NW USA
193 I19 **Banks Peninsula** peninsula South Island, NZ
191 Q15 **Banks Strait** strait SW Tasman Sea
Ban Kui Nua see Kui Buri
159 R16 **Bānkura** West Bengal, NE India 23.13N 87.04E
178 J8 **Ban Lakxao** var. Lak Sao. Bolikhamxai, C Laos 18.10N 104.58E
178 H17 **Ban Lam Phai** Songkhla, SW Thailand 6.43N 100.57E
Ban Mae Sot see Mae Sot
Ban Mae Suai see Mae Suai
Ban Mak Khaeng see Udon Thani
177 G3 **Banmauk** Sagaing, N Burma 24.25N 95.54E
Banmo see Bhamo
178 Jj10 **Ban Mun-Houamuang** S Laos 15.11N 106.44E
99 F14 **Bann** var. Lower Bann, Upper Bann. ≈ N Northern Ireland, UK
178 Jj10 **Ban Nadou** Salavan, S Laos 15.51N 105.37E
178 J10 **Ban Nakala** Savannakhét, S Laos 16.14N 105.09E
178 I8 **Ban Nakha** Viangchan, C Laos 18.13N 102.29E
178 Jj9 **Ban Nakham** Khammouan, S Laos 17.10N 105.25E
178 I8 **Ban Namoun** Xaignabouli, N Laos 18.40N 101.34E
178 Hh17 **Ban Nang Sata** Yala, SW Thailand 6.15N 101.13E
178 Gg15 **Ban Na San** Surat Thani, SW Thailand 8.52N 99.21E
178 Ii7 **Ban Nasi** Xiangkhoang, N Laos 19.37N 103.33E
46 I3 **Bannerman Town** Eleuthera Island, C Bahamas 24.38N 76.09W
37 V15 **Banning** California, W USA 33.55N 116.52W
Banningville see Bandundu
178 Jj11 **Ban Nongsim** Champasak, S Laos 14.45N 106.00E
155 S7 **Bannu** prev. Edwardesabad. North-West Frontier Province, NW Pakistan 32.00N 70.36E
Bañolas see Banyoles
58 C7 **Baños** Tungurahua, C Ecuador 1.20S 78.24W
Bánovce see Bánovce nad Bebravou
113 I19 **Bánovce nad Bebravou** var. Bánovce, Hung. Bán. Trenčiansky Kraj, W Slovakia 48.43N 18.15E
114 I12 **Banovići** Federacija Bosna I Hercegovina, E Bosnia and Herzegovina 44.25N 18.31E
Banow see Andarāb
Ban Pak Phanang see Pak Phanang
178 Hh7 **Ban Pan Nua** Lampang, NW Thailand 18.51N 99.57E
178 I10 **Ban Phai** Khon Kaen, E Thailand 16.00N 102.42E
178 Jj9 **Ban Phou A Douk** Khammouan, C Laos 17.12N 106.07E
178 I8 **Ban Phu** Uthai Thani, W Thailand
178 H11 **Ban Pong** Ratchaburi, W Thailand 13.49N 99.52E
202 I3 **Banraeaba** Tarawa, W Kiribati 1.19N 173.01E
178 Gg11 **Ban Sai Yok** Kanchanaburi, W Thailand 14.24N 98.54E
Ban Sattahip/Ban Sattahipp see Sattahip
Ban Sichon see Sichon
Ban Si Racha see Siracha
113 J19 **Banská Bystrica** Ger. Neusohl, Hung. Besztercebánya. Banskobystrický Kraj, C Slovakia 48.45N 19.08E
113 K20 **Banskobystrický Kraj** ◈ region C Slovakia
178 J8 **Ban Sôppheung** Bolikhamxai, C Laos 18.33N 104.18E
Ban Sop Prap see Sop Prap
158 G15 **Bānswāra** Rājasthān, N India 23.31N 74.28E
178 Gg15 **Ban Ta Khun** Surat Thani, SW Thailand 8.53N 98.52E
Ban Takua Pa see Takua Pa
178 Jj9 **Ban Talak** Khammouan, C Laos 17.33N 105.40E
79 R15 **Bantè** W Benin 8.21N 1.55E
174 Ii14 **Banten** off. Propinsi Banten. ◈ province W Indonesia
178 Ii8 **Ban Thabôk** Bolikhamxai, C Laos 18.21N 103.12E
178 Jj10 **Ban Tôp** Savannakhét, S Laos 16.07N 106.07E
99 B21 **Bantry** Ir. Beanntraí. SW Ireland 51.40N 9.27W
99 A21 **Bantry Bay** Ir. Bá Bheanntraí. bay SW Ireland
174 L15 **Bantul** prev. Bantoel. Jawa, C Indonesia 7.55S 110.21E
161 F19 **Bantvāl** var. Bantwāl. Karnātaka, E India 12.57N 75.04E
Bantwāl see Bantvāl
116 N9 **Banya** Burgas, E Bulgaria 42.46N 27.49E
173 Ee6 **Banyak, Kepulauan** prev. Kepulauan Banjak. island group NW Indonesia
107 U8 **Banya, La** headland E Spain 40.34N 0.37E
81 E14 **Banyo** Adamaoua, NW Cameroon 6.46N 11.49E
107 X4 **Banyoles** var. Bañolas. Cataluña, NE Spain 42.07N 2.46E
178 H16 **Ban Yong Sata** Trang, SW Thailand 7.09N 99.42E
174 Mm16 **Banyuwangi** var. Banjuwangi; prev. Banjoewangi. Jawa, S Indonesia 8.12S 114.22E
205 X14 **Banzare Coast** physical region Antarctica
181 Q14 **Banzare Seamounts** undersea feature S Indian Ocean
Banzart see Bizerte
169 Q12 **Baochang** var. Taibus Qi. Nei Mongol Zizhiqu, N China 41.55N 115.22E
167 O3 **Baoding** var. Pao-ting; prev. Tsingyuan. Hebei, E China 38.52N 115.28E
Baoebaoe see Baubau
Baoi, Oileán see Dursey Island
166 J6 **Baoji** var. Pao-chi, Paoki. Shaanxi, C China 34.22N 107.16E
169 U9 **Baokang** var. Hoqin Zuoyi Zhongji. Nei Mongol Zizhiqu, N China 44.08N 123.18E
195 V14 **Baolo** Santa Isabel, N Solomon Islands 7.41S 158.47E
178 K13 **Bao Lôc** Lâm Đông, S Vietnam 11.33N 107.48E
169 Z7 **Baoqing** Heilongjiang, NE China 46.15N 132.12E
Baoqing see Shaoyang
81 H15 **Baoro** Nana-Mambéré, W Central African Republic 5.40N 16.00E
166 E12 **Baoshan** var. Pao-shan. Yunnan, SW China 25.04N 99.07E
169 N13 **Baotou** var. Pao-t'ou, Paotow. Nei Mongol Zizhiqu, N China 40.37N 109.58E
78 L14 **Baoulé** ≈ S Mali
78 K12 **Baoulé** ≈ W Mali
Bao Yên see Phơ Rang
105 O2 **Bapaume** Pas-de-Calais, N France 50.06N 2.50E
12 J13 **Baptiste Lake** ⊛ Ontario, SE Canada
Bapu see Meigu
Baqanas see Bakanas
Baqbaqty see Bakbakty
165 P14 **Baqên** var. Dartang. Xizang Zizhiqu, W China 31.50N 94.08E
144 F14 **Bāqir, Jabal** ▲ S Jordan
145 T7 **Ba'qūbah** var. Qubba. C Iraq 33.45N 44.40E
64 H5 **Baquedano** Antofagasta, N Chile 23.19S 69.49W
118 M6 **Bar** Vinnyts'ka Oblast', C Ukraine 49.04N 27.39E
115 J18 **Bar** It. Antivari, S-Montenegro 42.02N 19.09E
82 E10 **Bara** Northern Kordofan, C Sudan 13.42N 30.21E
83 M18 **Baraawe** It. Brava. Shabeellaha Hoose, S Somalia 1.09N 43.59E
158 M12 **Bāra Banki** Uttar Pradesh, N India 26.55N 81.10E
125 G13 **Barabinsk** Novosibirskaya Oblast', C Russian Federation 55.19N 78.01E
32 L8 **Baraboo** Wisconsin, N USA 43.27N 89.45W
32 K8 **Baraboo Range** hill range Wisconsin, N USA
Baracaldo see San Vicente de Barakaldo
13 Y6 **Barachois** Québec, SE Canada 48.37N 64.14W
46 J7 **Baracoa** Guantánamo, E Cuba 20.19N 74.31W
63 C19 **Baradero** Buenos Aires, E Argentina 33.47S 59.29W
191 R6 **Baradine** New South Wales, SE Australia 30.55S 149.03E
Baraf Daja Islands see Damar, Kepulauan
160 M12 **Baragarh** Orissa, E India 21.20N 83.36E
83 I17 **Baragoi** Rift Valley, W Kenya 1.39N 36.46E
47 N9 **Barahona** SW Dominican Republic 18.13N 71.07W
159 W13 **Barail Range** ▲ NE India
82 I9 **Baraka** var. Barka, Ar. Khawr Barakah. seasonal river Eritrea/Sudan
82 G10 **Barakat** Gezira, C Sudan 14.18N 33.31E
Barakī see Barakī Barak
155 Q6 **Barakī Barak** var. Barakī, Baraki Rajan. Lowgar, E Afghanistan 33.58N 68.58E
Baraki Rajan see Barakī Barak
160 N11 **Bārākot** Orissa, E India 21.35N 85.00E
Baram see Baram, Batang
57 S7 **Barama River** ≈ N Guyana
161 E14 **Bārāmati** Mahārāshtra, W India 18.12N 74.39E
174 Mm4 **Baram, Batang** var. Baram, Barram. ≈ East Malaysia
158 H5 **Bārāmūla** Jammu and Kashmir, NW India 34.15N 74.24E
121 N14 **Baran'** Vitsyebskaya Voblasts', NE Belarus 54.28N 30.18E
158 I14 **Bārān** Rājasthān, N India 25.07N 76.31E
145 U4 **Barānān, Shākh-i** ▲ E Iraq
121 I17 **Baranavichy** Pol. Baranowicze, Rus. Baranovichi. Brestskaya Voblasts', SW Belarus 53.07N 26.01E
127 Oo5 **Baranikha** Chukotskiy Avtonomnyy Okrug, NE Russian Federation 68.29N 168.13E
118 M4 **Baranivka** Zhytomyrs'ka Oblast', N Ukraine 50.16N 27.40E
41 W14 **Baranof Island** island Alexander Archipelago, Alaska, USA
Baranovichi/Baranowicze see Baranavichy
113 N15 **Baranów Sandomierski** Podkarpackie, SE Poland 50.28N 21.31E
113 I26 **Baranya** off. Baranya Megye. ◈ county S Hungary
159 R13 **Barāri** Bihār, NE India 25.31N 87.22E
24 L10 **Barataria Bay** bay Louisiana, S USA

◆ Country
● Country Capital
◇ Dependent Territory
○ Dependent Territory Capital
◈ Administrative Region
✈ International Airport
▲ Mountain
▲ Mountain Range
Volcano
≈ River
⊛ Lake
⊠ Reservoir

Barat Daya, Kepulauan see Damar, Kepulauan
120 L12 **Baravukha** Rus. Borovukha. Vitsyebskaya Voblasts', N Belarus 55.36N 28.33E
56 E11 **Baraya** Huila, C Colombia 3.10N 75.04W
61 M21 **Barbacena** Minas Gerais, SE Brazil 21.13S 43.46W
56 B13 **Barbacoas** Nariño, SW Colombia 1.37N 78.07W
56 L6 **Barbacoas** Aragua, N Venezuela 9.28N 66.58W
47 Z13 **Barbados** ◆ commonwealth republic SE West Indies
49 S3 **Barbados** island Barbados
107 U11 **Barbaria, Cap de** var. Cabo de Berbería. headland Formentera, E Spain 38.39N 1.24E
116 N13 **Barbaros** Tekirdağ, NW Turkey 40.55N 27.28E
76 A11 **Barbas, Cap** headland S Western Sahara 22.14N 16.45W
107 T5 **Barbastro** Aragón, NE Spain 42.01N 0.07E
106 K16 **Barbate** ♣ SW Spain
106 K16 **Barbate de Franco** Andalucía, S Spain 36.11N 5.55W
85 K21 **Barberton** Mpumalanga, NE South Africa 25.45S 31.01E
33 U12 **Barberton** Ohio, N USA 41.02N 81.37W
104 K12 **Barbezieux-St-Hilaire** Charente, W France 45.28N 0.09W
56 G9 **Barbosa** Boyacá, C Colombia 5.57N 73.37W
23 N7 **Barbourville** Kentucky, S USA 36.52N 83.53W
47 W9 **Barbuda** island N Antigua and Barbuda
189 W8 **Barcaldine** Queensland, E Australia 23.33S 145.20E
Barcarozsnyó see Râşnov
106 I11 **Barcarrota** Extremadura, W Spain 38.31N 6.51W
Barcău see Berettyó
Barce see Al Marj
109 L23 **Barcellona** var. Barcellona Pozzo di Gotto. Sicilia, Italy, C Mediterranean Sea 38.09N 15.15E
Barcellona Pozzo di Gotto see Barcellona
107 W6 **Barcelona** anc. Barcino. Barcinona. Cataluña, E Spain 41.25N 2.10E
57 N5 **Barcelona** Anzoátegui, NE Venezuela 10.07N 64.43W
107 S5 **Barcelona** ◆ province Cataluña, NE Spain
107 W6 **Barcelona** ✕ Cataluña, E Spain 41.25N 2.10E
105 U14 **Barcelonnette** Alpes-de-Haute-Provence, SE France 44.24N 6.37E
60 E12 **Barcelos** Amazonas, N Brazil 0.58S 62.58W
106 G5 **Barcelos** Braga, N Portugal 41.31N 8.37W
112 I10 **Barcin** Ger. Bartschin. Kujawski-pomorskie, C Poland 52.51N 17.55E
Barcino/Barcinona see Barcelona
Barcoo see Cooper Creek
113 H26 **Barcs** Somogy, SW Hungary 45.57N 17.26E
143 W11 **Bärdä** Rus. Barda. C Azerbaijan 40.25N 47.07E
80 H5 **Bardaï** Borkou-Ennedi-Tibesti, N Chad 21.21N 16.55E
145 R2 **Bardaṛash** N Iraq 36.32N 43.36E
145 Q7 **Bardasah** SW Iraq 34.02N 42.28E
159 S16 **Barddhaman** West Bengal, NE India 23.10N 88.03E
113 N18 **Bardejov** Ger. Bartfeld, Hung. Bártfa. Prešovský Kraj, E Slovakia 49.17N 21.18E
107 R4 **Bárdenas Reales** physical region N Spain
Bardera/Bardere see Baardheere
Bardesir see Bardsir
94 K3 **Bárdharbunga** ▲ C Iceland 64.39N 17.30W
Bardhē, Drini i see Beli Drim
108 E9 **Bardi** Emilia-Romagna, C Italy 44.09N 9.44E
108 A8 **Bardonecchia** Piemonte, W Italy 45.04N 6.40E
99 H19 **Bardsey Island** island NW Wales, UK
149 S11 **Bardsir** var. Bardesir, Mashiz. Kermān, C Iran 29.57N 56.29E
22 L6 **Bardstown** Kentucky, S USA 37.48N 85.28W
Barduli see Barletta
22 G7 **Bardwell** Kentucky, S USA 36.52N 89.01W
158 K11 **Bareilly** var. Bareli. Uttar Pradesh, N India 28.19N 79.24E
Bareli see Bareilly
98 H13 **Barendrecht** Zuid-Holland, SW Netherlands 51.52N 4.31E
104 M3 **Barentin** Seine-Maritime, N France 49.33N 0.57E
94 N3 **Barentsburg** Spitsbergen, W Svalbard 78.01N 14.19E
Barentsevo More/Barents Havet see Barents Sea
94 O3 **Barentsøya** island E Svalbard
207 T11 **Barents Plain** undersea feature N Barents Sea
129 P3 **Barents Sea** Nor. Barents Havet, Rus. Barentsovo More. sea Arctic Ocean
207 U14 **Barents Trough** undersea feature SW Barents Sea
82 I9 **Barentu** W Eritrea 15.08N 37.35E
104 J3 **Barfleur** Manche, N France 49.41N 1.18W
104 J3 **Barfleur, Pointe de** headland N France 49.46N 1.09W
Barfrush/Barfurush see Bābol
164 H14 **Barga** Xizang Zizhiqu, W China 30.51N 81.19E
107 N9 **Bargas** Castilla-La Mancha, C Spain 39.54N 4.00W
83 I15 **Bargë** Southern, S Ethiopia 6.11N 37.04E
108 A9 **Barge** Piemonte, NE Italy 44.49N 7.21E
159 U16 **Barguna** Barisal, S Bangladesh 22.09N 90.07E
126 K15 **Barguzin** Respublika Buryatiya, S Russian Federation 53.37N 109.47E
159 O13 **Barhaj** Uttar Pradesh, N India 26.16N 83.43E

191 N10 **Barham** New South Wales, SE Australia 35.39S 144.09E
158 J12 **Barhan** Uttar Pradesh, N India 27.21N 78.10E
21 S7 **Bar Harbor** Mount Desert Island, Maine, NE USA 44.23N 68.14W
159 R14 **Barharwa** Jhārkhand, NE India
159 P15 **Barhi** Jhārkhand, N India 24.19N 85.25E
109 O17 **Bari** var. Bari delle Puglie; anc. Barium. Puglia, SE Italy 41.06N 16.52E
82 P12 **Bari** off. Gobolka Bari. ◆ region NE Somalia
178 K14 **Ba Ria** var. Châu Thanh. Ba Ria-Vung Tau, S Vietnam 10.30N 107.10E
Bāridah see Al Bāridah
Bari delle Puglie see Bari
155 T4 **Barikot** see Barīkowṭ
Barīkowṭ var. Barikot. Konar, NE Afghanistan 35.18N 71.36E
44 C4 **Barillas** var. Santa Cruz Barillas. Huehuetenango, NW Guatemala 15.49N 91.19W
56 J6 **Barinas** Barinas, W Venezuela 8.36N 70.15W
56 J7 **Barinas** off. Estado Barinas; prev. Zamora. ◆ state W Venezuela
56 J6 **Barinitas** Barinas, NW Venezuela 8.45N 70.25W
160 P11 **Bāripada** Orissa, E India 21.58N 86.45E
62 K9 **Baririri** São Paulo, S Brazil 22.05S 48.45W
77 W11 **Bāris** E Egypt 24.28N 30.39E
158 G14 **Bari Sādri** Rājasthān, N India 24.25N 74.28E
159 U16 **Barisal** Barisal, S Bangladesh 22.40N 90.19E
159 U16 **Barisal** ◆ division S Bangladesh
173 G7 **Barisan, Pegunungan** ▲ Sumatera, W Indonesia
175 N10 **Barito, Sungai** ♣ Borneo, C Indonesia
Barium see Bari
Bārjās see Porjus
Barka see Baraka
Barka see Al Marj
166 H8 **Barkam** Sichuan, C China 31.56N 102.22E
120 J9 **Barkava** Madona, C Latvia 56.43N 26.34E
8 M15 **Barkerville** British Columbia, SW Canada 53.06N 121.34W
12 I12 **Bark Lake** ◎ Ontario, SE Canada
22 H7 **Barkley, Lake** ☐ Kentucky/Tennessee, S USA
8 K17 **Barkley Sound** inlet British Columbia, W Canada
85 J24 **Barkly East** Afr. Barkly-Oos. Eastern Cape, SE South Africa 30.58S 27.34E
Barkly-Oos see Barkly East
189 S4 **Barkly Tableland** plateau Northern Territory/Queensland, N Australia
Barkly-Wes see Barkly West
85 H22 **Barkly West** Afr. Barkly-Wes. Northern Cape, N South Africa 28.31S 24.31E
165 O5 **Barkol** var. Barkol Kazak Zizhixian. Xinjiang Uygur Zizhiqu, NW China 43.37N 93.01E
165 O5 **Barkol Hu** ◎ NW China
Barkol Kazak Zizhixian see Barkol
109 P11 **Bark Point** headland Wisconsin, N USA 46.53N 91.11W
27 P11 **Barksdale** Texas, SW USA 29.43N 100.03W
Bar Kunar see Asmār
118 L10 **Bârlad** prev. Bîrlad. Vaslui, E Romania 46.12N 27.39E
118 M11 **Bârlad** prev. Bîrlad. ♣ E Romania
78 D9 **Barlavento, Ilhas de** var. Windward Islands. island group N Cape Verde
165 R5 **Bar-le-Duc** var. Bar-sur-Ornain. Meuse, NE France 48.46N 5.10E
188 K11 **Barlee, Lake** ◎ Western Australia
188 H8 **Barlee Range** ▲ Western Australia
109 N16 **Barletta** anc. Barduli. Puglia, SE Italy 41.19N 16.18E
112 E10 **Barlinek** Ger. Berlinchen. Zachodnio-pomorskie, NW Poland 53.00N 15.11E
29 S11 **Barling** Arkansas, C USA 35.19N 94.18W
176 Vv10 **Barma** Papua, E Indonesia 1.55S 132.57E
191 Q9 **Barmedman** New South Wales, SE Australia 34.09S 147.21E
158 D12 **Bärmer** Rājasthān, NW India 25.46N 71.24E
190 K9 **Barmera** South Australia 34.14S 140.26E
99 I21 **Barmouth** NW Wales, UK 52.44N 4.03W
158 F10 **Barnagar** Madhya Pradesh, C India 23.01N 75.28E
158 H9 **Barnala** Punjab, NW India 30.19N 75.33E
99 L15 **Barnard Castle** N England, UK 54.34N 1.55W
191 O6 **Barnato** New South Wales, SE Australia 31.39S 145.01E
126 H14 **Barnaul** Altayskiy Kray, C Russian Federation 53.21N 83.45E
111 V8 **Bärnbach** Steiermark, SE Austria 47.05N 15.07E
20 K16 **Barnegat** New Jersey, NE USA 39.43N 74.12W
25 S4 **Barnesville** Georgia, SE USA 33.03N 84.09W
31 R6 **Barnesville** Minnesota, N USA 46.39N 96.25W
33 U13 **Barnesville** Ohio, N USA 39.59N 81.10W
98 M7 **Barneveld** var. Barnveld. Gelderland, C Netherlands 52.09N 5.35E
27 O9 **Barnhart** Texas, SW USA 31.07N 101.09W
29 P8 **Barnsdall** Oklahoma, C USA 36.33N 96.09W
99 M17 **Barnsley** N England, UK 53.34N 1.28W
21 Q12 **Barnstable** Massachusetts, NE USA 41.42N 70.16W
99 I23 **Barnstaple** SW England, UK 51.04N 4.04W

Barnveld see Barneveld
23 Q14 **Barnwell** South Carolina, SE USA 33.14N 81.21W
69 U8 **Baro** var. Baro Wenz. ♣ Ethiopia/Sudan
79 U15 **Baro** Niger, C Nigeria 8.35N 6.28E
Baro see Baro Wenz
Baroda see Vadodara
121 Q17 **Baron'ki** Rus. Boron'ki. Mahilyowskaya Voblasts', E Belarus 53.07N 32.09E
190 J9 **Barossa Valley** valley South Australia
Baroui see Salisbury
83 H14 **Baro Wenz** var. Baro, Nahr Bārū. ♣ Ethiopia/Sudan
159 U12 **Barpeta** Assam, NE India 26.19N 91.05E
23 S7 **Barques, Pointe Aux** headland Michigan, N USA 44.04N 82.57W
56 I5 **Barquisimeto** Lara, NW Venezuela 10.03N 69.18W
61 N16 **Barra** Bahia, E Brazil 11.06S 43.15W
191 T5 **Barraba** New South Wales, SE Australia 30.24S 150.37E
62 L9 **Barra Bonita** São Paulo, S Brazil 22.30S 48.34W
66 J12 **Barracuda Fracture Zone** var. Fifteen Twenty Fracture Zone. tectonic feature SW Atlantic Ocean
66 G11 **Barracuda Ridge** undersea feature N Atlantic Ocean
45 N12 **Barra del Colorado** Limón, NE Costa Rica 10.44N 83.35W
45 N9 **Barra de Río Grande** Región Autónoma Atlántico Sur, E Nicaragua 12.56N 83.30W
58 A11 **Barra do Cuanza** Luanda, NW Angola 9.12S 13.08E
62 O9 **Barra do Piraí** Rio de Janeiro, SE Brazil 22.30S 43.47W
63 D16 **Barra do Quaraí** Rio Grande do Sul, SE Brazil 31.03S 58.10W
61 G14 **Barra do São Manuel** Pará, N Brazil 7.12S 58.03W
85 N19 **Barra Falsa, Ponta da** headland S Mozambique 22.57S 35.36E
98 E10 **Barra Head** headland NW Scotland, UK 56.46N 7.37W
62 O9 **Barra Mansa** Rio de Janeiro, SE Brazil 22.34S 44.03W
59 D14 **Barranca** Lima, W Peru 10.46S 77.46W
56 F8 **Barrancabermeja** Santander, N Colombia 7.00N 73.51W
56 H4 **Barrancas** La Guajira, N Colombia 10.58N 72.46W
56 J6 **Barrancas** Barinas, NW Venezuela 8.46N 70.07W
57 Q6 **Barrancas** Monagas, NE Venezuela 8.55N 62.12W
56 F6 **Barranco de Loba** Bolívar, N Colombia 8.55N 74.07W
106 I12 **Barrancos** Beja, S Portugal 38.07N 6.58W
64 N7 **Barranqueras** Chaco, E Argentina 27.31S 58.53W
56 E4 **Barranquilla** Atlántico, N Colombia 10.58N 74.48W
85 N20 **Barra, Ponta da** headland S Mozambique 23.46S 35.33E
107 P11 **Barrax** Castilla-La Mancha, C Spain 39.04N 2.12W
21 N11 **Barre** Massachusetts, NE USA 42.24N 72.06W
20 M7 **Barre** Vermont, NE USA 44.09N 72.25W
61 M17 **Barreiras** Bahia, E Brazil 12.09S 44.58W
106 F11 **Barreiro** Setúbal, W Portugal 38.40N 9.04W
67 C26 **Barren Island** island S Falkland Islands
22 K7 **Barren River Lake** ☐ Kentucky, S USA
62 L7 **Barretos** São Paulo, S Brazil 20.33S 48.33W
11 P14 **Barrhead** Alberta, SW Canada 54.08N 114.28W
12 I12 **Barrie** Ontario, S Canada 44.24N 79.39W
11 N16 **Barrière** British Columbia, SW Canada 51.10N 120.06W
12 H8 **Barrière, Lac** ◎ Québec, SE Canada
190 L6 **Barrier Range** hill range New South Wales, SE Australia
44 G3 **Barrier Reef** reef E Belize
196 C16 **Barrigada** ○ Guam 13.27N 144.48E
Barrington Island see Santa Fe, Isla
191 T7 **Barrington Tops** ▲ New South Wales, SE Australia 32.06S 151.18E
191 O4 **Barringun** New South Wales, SE Australia 29.02S 145.45E
61 K18 **Barro Alto** Goiás, S Brazil 15.07S 48.56W
61 H14 **Barro Duro** Piauí, NE Brazil 5.49S 42.30W
32 I5 **Barron** Wisconsin, N USA 45.24N 91.49W
12 I12 **Barron** ♣ Ontario, SE Canada
63 H15 **Barros Cassal** Rio Grande do Sul, S Brazil 29.12S 52.33W
47 P14 **Barrouallie** Saint Vincent, W Saint Vincent and the Grenadines 13.13N 61.16W
10 O4 **Barrow** Alaska, USA 71.17N 156.47W
97 E18 **Barrow** Ir. An Bhearú. ♣ SE Ireland
189 O6 **Barrow Creek Roadhouse** Northern Territory, N Australia 21.30S 133.52E
96 J16 **Barrow-in-Furness** NW England, UK 54.07N 3.13W
188 G7 **Barrow Island** island Western Australia
41 O4 **Barrow, Point** headland Alaska, USA 71.23N 156.28W
9 V13 **Barrows** Manitoba, C Canada 52.49N 101.36W
190 J22 **Barry's** S Wales, UK 51.24N 3.18W
12 J12 **Barry's Bay** Ontario, SE Canada
150 K14 **Barsakel'mes, Ostrov** island SW Kazakhstan

151 V11 **Barshatas** Vostochnyy Kazakhstan, E Kazakhstan 48.04N 78.38E
161 F14 **Bārsi** Mahārāshtra, W India 18.13N 75.42E
153 X8 **Barskoon** Issyk-Kul'skaya Oblast', E Kyrgyzstan 42.07N 77.34E
102 F10 **Barssel** Niedersachsen, NW Germany 53.10N 7.46E
37 U14 **Barstow** California, W USA 34.52N 117.00W
26 L8 **Barstow** Texas, SW USA 31.27N 103.23W
105 R6 **Bar-sur-Aube** Aube, NE France 48.13N 4.43E
105 Q6 **Bar-sur-Seine** Aube, N France 48.06N 4.22E
Bar-sur-Ornain see Bar-le-Duc
180 L9 **Bartang** Tajikistan 38.06N 71.48E
151 T13 **Bartang** ♣ SE Tajikistan
Bartenstein see Bartoszyce
Bártfa/Bártfeld see Bardejov
177 N7 **Barth** Mecklenburg-Vorpommern, NE Germany 54.21N 12.43E
29 W13 **Bartholomew, Bayou** ♣ Arkansas/Louisiana, S USA
57 T8 **Bartica** N Guyana 6.24N 58.36W
142 H10 **Bartın** Bartın, NW Turkey 41.37N 32.19E
142 H10 **Bartın** ◆ province NW Turkey
189 W4 **Bartle Frere** ▲ Queensland, E Australia 17.15S 145.43E
29 P8 **Bartlesville** Oklahoma, C USA 36.45N 95.58W
31 P14 **Bartlett** Nebraska, C USA 41.51N 98.32W
20 E10 **Bartlett** Tennessee, S USA 35.12N 89.52W
27 T9 **Bartlett** Texas, SW USA 30.47N 97.25W
38 L13 **Bartlett Reservoir** ☐ Arizona, SW USA
21 N6 **Barton** Vermont, NE USA 44.44N 72.09W
112 L7 **Bartoszyce** Ger. Bartenstein. Warmińsko-Mazurskie, NE Poland 54.16N 20.49E
25 W12 **Bartow** Florida, SE USA 27.54N 81.50W
Bartschin see Barcin
176 V10 **Baru** Papua, E Indonesia 1.44S 132.16E
173 G6 **Barumun, Sungai** ♣ Sumatera, W Indonesia
Barū, Nahr see Baro Wenz
173 M16 **Barung, Nusa** island S Indonesia
31 X3 **Barwood Lake** ◎ Canada/USA
173 Ff6 **Barus** Sumatera, NW Indonesia 2.08N 98.15E
168 I9 **Baruunbayan-Ulaan** var. Höövör. Övörhangay, C Mongolia 45.10N 101.19E
Baruunsuu see Tsogttsetsiy
169 P8 **Baruun-Urt** Sühbaatar, E Mongolia 46.39N 113.19E
45 P15 **Barú, Volcán** var. Volcán de Chiriquí. ▲ W Panama 8.49N 82.32W
101 K21 **Barvaux** Luxembourg, SE Belgium 50.21N 5.30E
44 M13 **Barva, Volcán** ▲ NW Costa Rica 10.07N 84.08W
119 W6 **Barvinkove** Kharkiv's'ka Oblast', E Ukraine 48.54N 37.03E
160 G11 **Barwāh** Madhya Pradesh, C India 22.17N 76.01E
Bärwalde Neumark see Mieszkowice
160 F11 **Barwāni** Madhya Pradesh, C India 22.01N 74.55E
191 P5 **Barwon River** ♣ New South Wales, SE Australia
121 L15 **Barysaw** Rus. Borisov. Minskaya Voblasts', NE Belarus 54.14N 28.30E
131 Q6 **Barysh** Ul'yanovskaya Oblast', W Russian Federation 53.32N 47.06E
119 Q4 **Baryshivka** Kyyivs'ka Oblast', N Ukraine 50.21N 31.21E
81 J17 **Basankusu** Equateur, NW Dem. Rep. Congo 1.12N 19.50E
119 N11 **Basarabeasca** Rus. Bessarabka. SE Moldova 46.22N 28.58E
118 M14 **Basarabi** Constanţa, SW Romania 44.07N 28.27E
42 H9 **Basaseachic** Chihuahua, N Mexico 28.18N 108.13W
Basauri see Arizgoiti
63 D18 **Basavilbaso** Entre Ríos, E Argentina 32.23S 58.48W
81 F21 **Bas-Congo** off. Région du Bas-Congo; prev. Bas-Zaïre. ◆ region SW Dem. Rep. Congo
110 E6 **Basel** Eng. Basle, Fr. Bâle. Basel-Stadt, NW Switzerland 47.33N 7.36E
110 E7 **Basel** Eng. Basle, Fr. Bâle. ◆ canton NW Switzerland
149 T14 **Bashākerd, Kūhhā-ye** ▲ SE Iran
9 Q15 **Bashaw** Alberta, SW Canada 52.40N 112.53W
52 K16 **Bashbedeng** Mary Welaýaty, S Turkmenistan 35.44N 63.07E
167 T15 **Bashi Channel** Chin. Pa-shih Hai-hsia. channel Philippines/Taiwan
Bashkiria see Bashkortostan, Respublika
125 Dd12 **Bashkortostan, Respublika** prev. Bashkiria. ◆ autonomous republic W Russian Federation
131 N6 **Bashmakovo** Penzenskaya Oblast', W Russian Federation 53.13N 43.00E
181 T9 **Bashsakarba** Lebap Welaýaty, NE Turkmenistan 40.25N 62.16E
119 R9 **Bashtanka** Mykolayivs'ka Oblast', S Ukraine 47.24N 32.27E
195 O13 **Basilaki Island** island SE PNG
24 H1 **Basile** Louisiana, S USA 30.29N 92.36W
190 M18 **Basilicata** ◆ region S Italy
35 V13 **Basin** Wyoming, C USA 44.22N 108.02W
99 N22 **Basingstoke** S England, UK 51.16N 1.08W
149 U8 **Başiran** Khorāsān-e Janūbī, E Iran 31.57N 59.07E
114 B10 **Baška** It. Bescanuova. Primorje-Gorski Kotar, NW Croatia 44.58N 14.43E
23 Q13 **Başkale** Van, SE Turkey 38.03N 44.01E
30 M7 **Basland** South Dakota, N USA 45.05N 100.40W
143 O14 **Baskil** Elazığ, E Turkey 38.35N 38.52E

Basle see Basel
160 H9 **Bāsoda** Madhya Pradesh, C India 23.54N 77.58E
81 L17 **Basoko** Orientale, N Dem. Rep. Congo 1.13N 23.25E
Basque Country, The see País Vasco
Basra see Al Başrah
105 U5 **Bas-Rhin** ◆ department NE France
Bassam see Grand-Bassam
9 Q16 **Bassano** Alberta, SW Canada 50.48N 112.28W
108 H7 **Bassano del Grappa** Veneto, NE Italy 45.45N 11.45E
79 S16 **Bassar** var. Bassari. NW Togo 9.15N 0.46E
Bassari see Bassar
180 L9 **Bassas da India** island group W Madagascar
158 H9 **Bassecourt** Jura, W Switzerland 47.20N 7.16E
100 M11 **Bassein** var. Pathein. Irrawaddy, SW Burma 16.46N 94.45E
81 J15 **Basse-Kotto** ◆ prefecture S Central African Republic
107 V5 **Bassella** Cataluña, NE Spain 42.01N 1.16E
47 Q11 **Basse-Normandie** Eng. Lower Normandy. ◆ region N France
47 X6 **Basse-Pointe** N Martinique 14.52N 61.07W
78 H12 **Basse Santa Su** E Gambia 13.18N 14.10W
Basse-Saxe see Niedersachsen
47 X6 **Basse-Terre** ○ (Guadeloupe) Basse Terre, SW Guadeloupe 16.07N 61.40W
47 X6 **Basse Terre** island W Guadeloupe
47 V10 **Basseterre** ● (Saint Kitts and Nevis) Saint Kitts, Saint Kitts and Nevis 17.15S 62.41W
31 O13 **Bassett** Nebraska, C USA 42.34N 99.32W
23 S7 **Bassett** Virginia, NE USA 36.45N 79.59W
39 N15 **Bassett Peak** ▲ Arizona, SW USA 32.30N 110.16W
78 M10 **Bassikounou** Hodh ech Chargui, SE Mauritania 15.55N 5.58W
79 R15 **Bassila** S Benin 9.01N 1.46E
Bass, Îlots de see Marotiri
33 S13 **Bass Lake** Indiana, N USA 41.12N 86.35W
191 O14 **Bass Strait** strait SE Australia
102 H11 **Bassum** Niedersachsen, NW Germany 52.51N 8.43E
32 M7 **Basswood Lake** ◎ Canada/USA
3 S7 **Båstad** Skåne, S Sweden 56.26N 12.51E
145 U2 **Başʿan** E Iraq 36.20N 45.14E
159 N12 **Basti** Uttar Pradesh, N India 26.48N 82.43E
101 L23 **Bastogne** Luxembourg, SE Belgium 50.00N 5.43E
24 I5 **Bastrop** Louisiana, S USA 32.46N 91.54W
27 T11 **Bastrop** Texas, SW USA 30.06N 97.19W
95 J15 **Bastuträsk** Västerbotten, N Sweden 64.46N 20.05E
121 J19 **Bastyn'** Rus. Bostyn'. Brestskaya Voblasts', SW Belarus 52.23N 26.46E
Basuo see Dongfang
Basutoland see Lesotho
81 G15 **Batouri** Est, E Cameroon 4.26N 14.24E

24 L2 **Batesville** Mississippi, S USA 34.18N 89.56W
27 Q13 **Batesville** Texas, SW USA 28.56N 99.38W
46 L13 **Bath** E Jamaica 17.56N 76.20W
99 L22 **Bath** anc. Aquae Calidae, Aquae Solis. SW England, UK 51.22N 2.22W
21 Q8 **Bath** Maine, NE USA 43.54N 69.49W
20 F11 **Bath** New York, NE USA 42.20N 77.16W
Bath see Berkeley Springs
80 I10 **Batha** ◆ prefecture C Chad
147 Y8 **Batha** seasonal river C Chad
147 Y8 **Baṭhāʾ, Wādī al** dry watercourse NE Oman
158 H9 **Bathinda** Punjab, NW India 30.13N 74.54E
100 M11 **Bathmen** Overijssel, E Netherlands 52.15N 6.16E
47 Z14 **Bathsheba** E Barbados 13.12N 59.31W
191 R8 **Bathurst** New South Wales, SE Australia 33.32S 149.34E
11 O13 **Bathurst** New Brunswick, SE Canada 47.37N 65.40W
Bathurst see Banjul
15 Gg2 **Bathurst, Cape** headland Northwest Territories, NW Canada 70.33N 128.00W
206 L8 **Bathurst Inlet** Nunavut, N Canada 66.23N 107.00W
15 J4 **Bathurst Inlet** inlet Nunavut, N Canada
189 N1 **Bathurst Island** island Northern Territory, N Australia
207 O9 **Bathurst Island** island Parry Islands, Nunavut, N Canada
79 O14 **Batié** SW Burkina 9.53N 2.57W
197 O14 **Batiki** prev. Mbatiki. island C Fiji
Batīnah see Al Bāṭinah
147 Y9 **Bāṭin, Wādī al** dry watercourse SW Asia
13 R9 **Batiscan** ♣ Québec, SE Canada
142 F16 **Batı Toroslar** ▲ SW Turkey
Batjan see Bacan, Pulau
153 R11 **Batken** Batkenskaya Oblast', SW Kyrgyzstan 40.03N 70.50E
153 Q11 **Batkenskaya Oblast'** Kir. Batken Oblasty. ◆ province SW Kyrgyzstan
Batken Oblasty see Batkenskaya Oblast'
143 O13 **Batman** SE Turkey 37.52N 41.06E
143 Q15 **Batman** ◆ province SE Turkey
76 L6 **Batna** NE Algeria 35.34N 6.11E
24 J8 **Baton Rouge** state capital Louisiana, S USA 30.28N 91.09W
144 G14 **Bāt, Jibāl al** ▲ S Jordan
144 G6 **Batroûn** var. Al Batrūn. N Lebanon 34.15N 35.42E
Batsch see Bač
121 M17 **Batsevichy** Rus. Batsevichi. Mahilyowskaya Voblasts', E Belarus 53.24N 29.13E
94 M7 **Båtsfjord** Finnmark, N Norway 70.37N 29.42E
169 N7 **Batshireet** var. Eg. Hentiy, N Mongolia 48.22N 110.07E
168 L7 **Batsümber** var. Mandal. Töv, C Mongolia 48.24N 106.47E
168 M8 **Battambang** see Bátdâmbâng
205 X3 **Batterbee, Cape** headland Antarctica
101 L17 **Battice** Liège, E Belgium 50.39N 5.50E
109 L19 **Battipaglia** Campania, S Italy 40.36N 14.58E
9 R15 **Battle** ♣ Alberta/Saskatchewan, SW Canada
Battle Born State see Nevada
32 H9 **Battle Creek** Michigan, N USA 42.19N 85.10W
31 S15 **Battlefield** Missouri, C USA 37.07N 93.22W
9 T14 **Battleford** Saskatchewan, SW Canada 52.45N 108.19W
31 S6 **Battle Lake** Minnesota, N USA 46.16N 95.42W
37 T7 **Battle Mountain** Nevada, W USA 40.37N 116.55W
113 M25 **Battonya** Békés, SE Hungary 46.16N 21.00E
179 Pp6 **Batu Islands** island group N Philippines
20 L8 **Batu** São Paulo, S Brazil 20.54S 47.37W
Batu, Île de see Pulau
175 Qq14 **Batuata, Pulau** island C Indonesia
175 Q13 **Batudaka, Pulau** island N Indonesia
173 T9 **Batu, Kepulauan** prev. Batoe. island group W Indonesia
143 O14 **Bat'umi** W Georgia 41.39N 41.37E
174 H6 **Batu Pahat** prev. Bandar Penggaram. Johor, Peninsular Malaysia 1.51N 102.55E
175 Rr8 **Baturaja** Sumatera, S Indonesia 4.10N 104.10E
126 H13 **Baturino** Tomskaya Oblast', C Russian Federation 57.46N 85.08E
119 U3 **Baturyn** Chernihivs'ka Oblast', N Ukraine 51.20N 32.52E
191 S11 **Batemans Bay** New South Wales, SE Australia 35.45S 150.09E
144 P9 **Bat Yam** Tel Aviv, C Israel 32.01N 34.45E
104 F5 **Batz, Île de** ♣ NW France
174 T11 **Bau** Sarawak, East Malaysia 1.25N 110.10E

179 P9 **Bauang** Luzon, N Philippines 16.33N 120.20E
175 Qq13 **Baubau** var. Baoebaoe. Pulau Buton, C Indonesia 5.30S 122.37E
79 W14 **Bauchi** Bauchi, NE Nigeria 10.18N 9.46E
79 W14 **Bauchi** ◆ state C Nigeria
104 H7 **Baud** Morbihan, NW France 47.52N 2.59W
31 T2 **Baudette** Minnesota, N USA 48.42N 94.36W
200 Nn10 **Bauer Basin** undersea feature E Pacific Ocean
197 C14 **Bauer Field** var. Port Vila. ✕ (Port-Vila) Éfaté, C Vanuatu 17.42S 168.21E
11 T8 **Bauld, Cape** headland Newfoundland and Labrador, E Canada 51.35N 55.22W
105 T8 **Baume-les-Dames** Doubs, E France 47.22N 6.20E
195 X15 **Baumann** N Solomon Islands 9.06S 160.52E
103 I15 **Baunatal** Hessen, C Germany 51.15N 9.25E
109 D18 **Baunei** Sardegna, Italy, C Mediterranean Sea 40.04N 9.36E
59 M15 **Baures, Río** ♣ N Bolivia
62 K9 **Baurú** São Paulo, S Brazil 22.19S 49.07W
120 G10 **Bauska** Ger. Bauske. Bauska, S Latvia 56.24N 24.11E
Bauske see Bauska
103 Q15 **Bautzen** Lus. Budyšin. Sachsen, E Germany 51.10N 14.26E
151 Q16 **Baūyrzhan Momyshuly** Kaz. Baūyrzhan Momyshuly; prev. Burnoye. Zhambyl, S Kazakhstan 42.36N 70.46E
Bauzanum see Bolzano
Bavaria see Bayern
Bavière see Bayern
111 N7 **Bavarian Alps** Ger. Bayerische Alpen. ▲ Austria/Germany
42 H4 **Bavispe, Río** ♣ NW Mexico
131 T5 **Bavly** Respublika Tatarstan, W Russian Federation 54.20N 53.21E
191 O12 **Baw Baw, Mount** ▲ Victoria, SE Australia 37.49S 146.16E
176 W11 **Bawe** Papua, E Indonesia 2.56S 134.39E
174 L15 **Bawean, Pulau** island S Indonesia
174 L15 **Bawen** Jawa, S Indonesia 7.13S 110.25E
77 W14 **Bawiti** N Egypt 28.18N 28.52E
178 Gg7 **Bawlakè** Kayah State, C Burma 19.10N 97.19E
173 T9 **Bawo Ofuloa** Pulau Tanahmasa, W Indonesia 0.10S 98.24E
147 X8 **Bawshar** var. Baushar. NE Oman 23.26N 58.19E
Ba Xian see Bazhou
164 M8 **Baxkorgan** Xinjiang Uygur Zizhiqu, W China 39.05N 90.00E
25 V6 **Baxley** Georgia, SE USA 31.46N 82.21W
165 R15 **Baxoi** var. Baima. Xizang Zizhiqu, W China 30.01N 96.53E
31 W14 **Baxter** Iowa, C USA 41.49N 93.09W
31 U6 **Baxter** Minnesota, N USA 46.21N 94.18W
29 R8 **Baxter Springs** Kansas, C USA 37.01N 94.45W
83 M17 **Bay** off. Gobolka Bay. ◆ region SW Somalia
Bay see Baicheng
46 H8 **Bayamo** Granma, E Cuba 20.21N 76.38W
47 S9 **Bayamón** E Puerto Rico 18.24N 66.09W
169 R7 **Bayan** Heilongjiang, NE China 46.04N 127.24E
175 Nn16 **Bayan** prev. Bajan. Pulau Lombok, C Indonesia 8.16S 116.28E
168 M8 **Bayan** var. Maaniït. Töv, C Mongolia 47.21N 107.32E
168 M8 **Bayan** Bayanhutag, Hentiy, Mongolia
Bayan var. Bayan-Uul, Govĭ-Altay, Mongolia
Bayan var. Bürentogtoh, Hövsgöl, Mongolia
Bayan see Hölönbuyr, Dornod, Mongolia
Bayan see Ihhet, Dornogovĭ, Mongolia
158 I12 **Bayāna** Rājasthān, N India 26.55N 77.18E
155 N5 **Bāyān, Band-e** ▲ C Afghanistan
168 H8 **Bayanbulag** Bayanhongor, C Mongolia 46.46N 98.07E
Bayanbulag see Ölziyt
164 I5 **Bayanbulak** Xinjiang Uygur Zizhiqu, W China 43.04N 84.09E
168 L7 **Bayanchandmanĭ** var. Ihsüüj. Töv, C Mongolia 48.12N 106.23E
168 J11 **Bayandalay** var. Dalay. Ömnögovĭ, S Mongolia 43.27N 103.30E
126 Jj15 **Bayandelger** var. Shireet. Sühbaatar, SE Mongolia 45.33N 112.19E
168 I9 **Bayandelger** var. Altraga. Hövsgöl, N Mongolia 50.08N 98.54E
Bayangol see Bugat, Mongolia
168 I9 **Bayangovĭ** var. Örgön. Bayanhongor, C Mongolia 44.43N 100.23E
165 R12 **Bayan Har Shan** var. Bayan Khar. ▲ C China
168 G6 **Bayanhayrhan** var. Altanbulag. Dzavhan, W Mongolia 49.16N 96.22E
119 R3 **Bayanhongor** Bayanhongor, C Mongolia 46.07N 100.42E
168 I8 **Bayanhongor** ◆ province C Mongolia
168 K14 **Bayan Hot** var. Alxa Zuoqi. Nei Mongol Zizhiqu, N China 38.49N 105.40E
169 O8 **Bayan Huxu** var. Horqin Zuoyi Zhongji. Nei Mongol Zizhiqu, N China 45.02N 121.33E

◆ COUNTRY ◇ DEPENDENT TERRITORY ◆ ADMINISTRATIVE REGION ▲ MOUNTAIN ▼ VOLCANO ◎ LAKE
● COUNTRY CAPITAL ○ DEPENDENT TERRITORY CAPITAL ✕ INTERNATIONAL AIRPORT ▲ MOUNTAIN RANGE ♣ RIVER ☐ RESERVOIR

◆ COUNTRY   ◇ DEPENDENT TERRITORY   ■ ADMINISTRATIVE REGION   ▲ MOUNTAIN   ☼ VOLCANO   ◙ LAKE
● COUNTRY CAPITAL   ○ DEPENDENT TERRITORY CAPITAL   ✈ INTERNATIONAL AIRPORT   ▲ MOUNTAIN RANGE   ◈ RIVER   ▭ RESERVOIR

231

BELORUSSIA/BELORUSSIAN SSR – BHATNI JUNCTION

Belorussia/Belorussian SSR see Belarus
Belorusskaya Gryada see Byelaruskaya Hrada
Belorusskaya SSR see Belarus
Beloshchel'ye see Nar'yan-Mar
116 N8 **Beloslav** Varna, E Bulgaria 43.13N 27.42E
Belostok see Białystok
180 H5 **Belo Tsiribihina** var. Belo-sur-Tsiribihina. Toliara, W Madagascar 19.40S 44.30E
Belovár see Bjelovar
Belovezhskaya Pushcha see Białowieska, Puszcza/Byelavyezhskaya Pushcha
116 H10 **Belovo** Pazardzhik, C Bulgaria 42.12N 24.02E
126 H14 **Belovo** Kemerovskaya Oblast', S Russian Federation 54.25N 86.13E
Belovodsk see Bilovods'k
125 Ff9 **Beloyarskiy** Khanty-Mansiyskiy Avtonomnyy Okrug, N Russian Federation 63.40N 66.31E
128 K7 **Beloye More** Eng. White Sea. sea NW Russian Federation
128 K13 **Beloye, Ozero** ◎ NW Russian Federation
116 J10 **Belozem** Plovdiv, C Bulgaria 42.11N 25.00E
128 K13 **Belozërsk** Vologodskaya Oblast', NW Russian Federation 59.58N 37.49E
101 E20 **Belœil** Hainaut, SW Belgium 50.33N 3.45E
110 D8 **Belp** Bern, W Switzerland 46.54N 7.31E
110 D8 **Belp** ✈ (Bern) Bern, C Switzerland 46.55N 7.29E
109 L24 **Belpasso** Sicilia, Italy, C Mediterranean Sea 37.34N 14.58E
33 U14 **Belpre** Ohio, N USA 39.14N 81.34W
100 M8 **Belterwijde** ◎ N Netherlands
29 R4 **Belton** Missouri, C USA 38.48N 94.31W
23 P11 **Belton** South Carolina, SE USA 34.31N 82.29W
27 T9 **Belton** Texas, SW USA 31.03N 97.27W
27 S9 **Belton Lake** ⊠ Texas, SW USA
Bel'tsy see Bălţi
99 E16 **Belturbet** Ir. Béal Tairbirt. N Ireland 54.06N 7.25W
Beluchistan see Baluchistān
151 Z9 **Belukha, Gora** ▲ Kazakhstan/Russian Federation 49.42N 86.33E
109 M20 **Belvedere Marittimo** Calabria, SW Italy 39.37N 15.52E
32 L10 **Belvidere** Illinois, N USA 42.15N 88.50W
20 J14 **Belvidere** New Jersey, NE USA 40.49N 75.03W
Bely see Belyy
131 V8 **Belyayevka** Orenburgskaya Oblast', W Russian Federation 51.25N 56.26E
Belynichi see Byalynichy
128 H17 **Belyy** var. Bely, Beyj. Tverskaya Oblast', W Russian Federation 55.51N 32.57E
130 I6 **Belyye Berega** Bryanskaya Oblast', W Russian Federation 53.11N 34.42E
126 H5 **Belyy, Ostrov** island N Russian Federation
126 H12 **Belyy Yar** Tomskaya Oblast', C Russian Federation 58.26N 84.57E
102 N13 **Belzig** Brandenburg, NE Germany 52.09N 12.37E
24 K4 **Belzoni** Mississippi, S USA 33.10N 90.29W
180 H4 **Bemaraha** var. Plateau du Bemaraha. ▲▲ W Madagascar
84 B10 **Bembe** Uíge, NW Angola 7.01S 14.18E
79 S14 **Bembèrèkè** var. Bimbéréké. N Benin 10.10N 2.40E
106 K12 **Bembézar** ~ SW Spain
106 J3 **Bembibre** Castilla-León, N Spain 42.37N 6.25W
31 T4 **Bemidji** Minnesota, N USA 47.27N 94.53W
100 L12 **Bemmel** Gelderland, SE Netherlands 51.52N 5.54E
176 U11 **Bemu** Pulau Seram, E Indonesia 3.21S 129.58E
Benāb see Bonāb
107 T5 **Benabarre** var. Benavarn. Aragón, NE Spain 42.06N 0.28E
Benaco see Garda, Lago di
81 L20 **Bena-Dibele** Kasai Oriental, C Dem. Rep. Congo 4.01S 22.50E
107 R9 **Benageber, Embalse de** ⊠ E Spain
191 O11 **Benalla** Victoria, SE Australia 36.33S 146.00E
106 M14 **Benamejí** Andalucía, S Spain 37.16N 4.33W
Benares see Vārānasi
Benavarn see Benabarre
106 F10 **Benavente** Santarém, C Portugal 38.58N 8.49W
106 K5 **Benavente** Castilla-León, N Spain 42.00N 5.40W
27 S15 **Benavides** Texas, SW USA 27.36N 98.24W
98 F8 **Benbecula** island NW Scotland, UK
Bencovazzo see Benkovac
34 H13 **Bend** Oregon, NW USA 44.03N 121.18W
190 K7 **Benda Range** ▲▲ South Australia
191 T6 **Bendemeer** New South Wales, SE Australia 30.54S 151.12E
Bender see Tighina
Bender Beila/Bender Beyla see Bandarbeyla
Bender Cassim/Bender Qaasim see Boosaaso
Bendery see Tighina
191 N11 **Bendigo** Victoria, SE Australia 36.46S 144.18E
120 E10 **Bēne** Dobele, SW Latvia 56.30N 23.04E
100 K13 **Beneden-Leeuwen** Gelderland, C Netherlands 51.52N 5.32E
103 L24 **Benediktenwand** ▲ S Germany 47.39N 11.28E
Benemérita de San Cristóbal see San Cristóbal
79 N12 **Bénéna** Ségou, S Mali 13.04N 4.20W
180 I7 **Benenitra** Toliara, S Madagascar 23.25S 45.06E
Beneschau see Benešov
Beneški Zaliv see Venice, Gulf of
113 D17 **Benešov** Ger. Beneschau. Středočeský Kraj, W Czech Republic 49.48N 14.40E
126 Ll3 **Benetta, Ostrov** island Novosibirskiye Ostrova, NE Russian Federation
109 L17 **Benevento** anc. Beneventum, Malventum. Campania, S Italy 41.07N 14.45E
Beneventum see Benevento
181 S3 **Bengal, Bay of** bay N Indian Ocean
81 M17 **Bengamisa** Orientale, N Dem. Rep. Congo 0.58N 25.10E
Bengasi see Banghāzī
174 Ll15 **Bengawan, Sungai** ~ Jawa, S Indonesia
Bengazi see Banghāzī
167 P7 **Bengbu** var. Peng-pu. Anhui, E China 32.57N 117.17E
34 L9 **Benge** Washington, NW USA 46.55N 118.01W
Benghazi see Banghāzī
174 H7 **Bengkalis** Pulau Bengkalis, W Indonesia 1.29N 102.07E
174 H6 **Bengkalis, Pulau** island W Indonesia
174 Kk7 **Bengkayang** Borneo, C Indonesia 0.45N 109.28E
Bengkoelen/Bengkoeloe see Bengkulu
174 H12 **Bengkulu** prev. Bengkoeloe, Benkoelen, Benkulen. Sumatera, W Indonesia 3.46S 102.16E
174 H11 **Bengkulu** off. Propinsi Bengkulu; prev. Bengkoelen, Benkoelen, Benkulen. ⬖ province W Indonesia
84 A11 **Bengo** ⬖ province W Angola
97 J16 **Bengtsfors** Västra Götaland, S Sweden 59.03N 12.13E
84 B13 **Benguela** var. Benguella. Benguela, W Angola 12.34S 13.30E
85 A14 **Benguela** ⬖ province W Angola
Benguella see Benguela
Bengweulu, Lake see Bangweulu, Lake
124 Qq15 **Benha** var. Banhā. N Egypt 30.22N 31.16E
198 G6 **Benham Seamount** undersea feature W Philippine Sea 15.48N 124.15E
98 H6 **Ben Hope** ▲ N Scotland, UK 58.25N 4.36W
81 P18 **Beni** Nord Kivu, NE Dem. Rep. Congo 0.31N 29.29E
59 L15 **Beni** var. El Beni. ⬖ department N Bolivia
76 H8 **Beni Abbès** W Algeria 30.07N 2.09W
107 T8 **Benicarló** País Valenciano, E Spain 40.25N 0.25E
107 T9 **Benicasim** Cat. Benicàssim. País Valenciano, E Spain 40.03N 0.03E
Benicàssim see Benicasim
107 T12 **Benidorm** País Valenciano, SE Spain 38.33N 0.09W
77 W9 **Beni Mazâr** var. Banī Mazār. C Egypt 28.24N 30.38E
122 F12 **Beni-Mellal** C Morocco 32.20N 6.21W
79 R14 **Benin** off. Republic of Benin; prev. Dahomey. ◆ republic W Africa
79 S17 **Benin, Bight of** gulf W Africa
79 U16 **Benin City** Edo, SW Nigeria 6.22N 5.39E
59 K16 **Beni, Río** ~ N Bolivia
123 Gg11 **Beni Saf** var. Beni-Saf. NW Algeria 35.16N 1.33W
82 H12 **Benishangul** ⬖ region W Ethiopia
107 T11 **Benissa** País Valenciano, E Spain 38.43N 0.03E
124 Qq17 **Beni Suef** var. Banī Suwayf. N Egypt 29.09N 31.03E
9 V15 **Benito** Manitoba, S Canada 51.57N 101.24W
Benito see Uolo, Río
63 C23 **Benito Juárez** Buenos Aires, E Argentina 37.43S 59.48W
43 P14 **Benito Juaréz Internacional** ✈ (México) México, S Mexico 19.24N 99.02W
27 P5 **Benjamin** Texas, SW USA 33.34N 99.47W
60 B13 **Benjamin Constant** Amazonas, N Brazil 4.22S 70.01W
42 F4 **Benjamín Hill** Sonora, NW Mexico 30.13N 111.07W
65 F19 **Benjamín, Isla** island Archipiélago de los Chonos, S Chile
172 N5 **Benkei-misaki** headland Hokkaidō, NE Japan 42.49N 140.10E
30 L17 **Benkelman** Nebraska, C USA 40.04N 101.30W
98 I7 **Ben Klibreck** ▲ N Scotland, UK 58.15N 4.23W
Benkoelen see Bengkulu
114 D13 **Benkovac** It. Bencovazzo. Zadar, SW Croatia 44.02N 15.36E
Benkulen see Bengkulu
98 I11 **Ben Lawers** ▲ C Scotland, UK 56.33N 4.13W
98 J9 **Ben Macdui** var. Beinn MacDuibh. ▲ C Scotland, UK 57.02N 3.42W
98 G11 **Ben More** ▲ W Scotland, UK 56.26N 6.00W
98 I11 **Ben More** ▲ C Scotland, UK 56.22N 4.31W
98 H7 **Ben More Assynt** ▲ N Scotland, UK 58.09N 4.51W
193 E20 **Benmore, Lake** ◎ South Island, NZ
100 L12 **Bennekom** Gelderland, SE Netherlands 52.00N 5.40E
23 T11 **Bennettsville** South Carolina, SE USA 34.37N 79.41W
98 H10 **Ben Nevis** ▲ N Scotland, UK 56.46N 5.01W
192 M9 **Benneydale** Waikato, North Island, NZ 38.31S 175.22E
Bennichab see Bennichchâb
78 H8 **Bennichchâb** var. Bennichab. Inchiri, W Mauritania 19.25N 15.21W
20 L10 **Bennington** Vermont, NE USA 42.51N 73.09W
193 E20 **Ben Ohau Range** ▲▲ South Island, NZ
85 J21 **Benoni** Gauteng, NE South Africa 26.04S 28.18E
180 J2 **Be, Nosy** var. Nossi-Bé. island NW Madagascar
Bénoué see Benue
44 F2 **Benque Viejo del Carmen** Cayo, W Belize 17.04N 89.08W
103 G19 **Bensheim** Hessen, W Germany 49.40N 8.37E
39 N16 **Benson** Arizona, SW USA 31.55N 110.16W
31 S8 **Benson** Minnesota, N USA 45.19N 95.36W
23 U10 **Benson** North Carolina, SE USA 35.22N 78.33W
175 Pp14 **Benteng** Pulau Selayar, C Indonesia 6.07S 120.28E
85 A14 **Bentiaba** Namibe, SW Angola 14.18S 12.27E
189 T4 **Bentinck Island** island Wellesley Islands, Queensland, N Australia
82 E13 **Bentiu** Wahda, S Sudan 9.13N 29.49E
144 G8 **Bent Jbaïl** var. Bint Jubayl. S Lebanon 33.07N 35.25E
9 Q15 **Bentley** Alberta, SW Canada 52.27N 114.02W
63 I15 **Bento Gonçalves** Rio Grande do Sul, S Brazil 29.06S 51.29W
29 U12 **Benton** Arkansas, C USA 34.33N 92.35W
32 L16 **Benton** Illinois, N USA 38.00N 88.55W
22 H7 **Benton** Kentucky, S USA 36.51N 88.21W
24 G5 **Benton** Louisiana, S USA 32.41N 93.44W
29 Y7 **Benton** Missouri, C USA 37.05N 89.34W
22 M10 **Benton** Tennessee, S USA 35.10N 84.39W
33 O10 **Benton Harbor** Michigan, N USA 42.07N 86.27W
29 S9 **Bentonville** Arkansas, C USA 36.22N 94.12W
79 V16 **Benue** ⬖ state SE Nigeria
80 F13 **Benue** Fr. Bénoué. ~ Cameroon/Nigeria
174 Hh6 **Benut** Johor, Peninsular Malaysia 1.37N 103.15E
169 V12 **Benxi** prev. Pen-ch'i, Penhsihu, Penki. Liaoning, NE China 41.11N 123.46E
Benyakoni see Byenyakoni
114 K10 **Beočin** Serbia, N Serbia 45.13N 19.43E
Beodericsworth see Bury St Edmunds
114 M11 **Beograd** Eng. Belgrade, Ger. Belgrad; anc. Singidunum. ● (Serbia) Serbia, N Serbia 44.48N 20.27E
114 L11 **Beograd** Eng. Belgrade. ✈ Serbia, N Serbia 44.45N 20.21E
78 M16 **Béoumi** C Ivory Coast 7.40N 5.34W
37 V3 **Beowawe** Nevada, W USA 40.33N 116.31W
176 Ww8 **Bepondi, Pulau** see Bepondi, Pulau
170 D13 **Beppu** Ōita, Kyūshū, SW Japan 33.16N 131.28E
170 Dd14 **Beppu-wan** bay SW Japan
197 H15 **Beqa** prev. Mbengga. island W Fiji
Beqa Barrier Reef see Kavukavu Reef
47 Y14 **Bequia** island C Saint Vincent and the Grenadines
115 L16 **Berane** prev. Ivangrad, E-Montenegro 42.51N 19.51E
115 L21 **Berat** var. Berati, SCr. Beligrad. Berat, C Albania 40.42N 19.57E
115 L21 **Berat** ⬖ district C Albania
Berătău see Berettyó
Berati see Berat
Beraun see Berounka, Czech Republic
Beraun see Beroun, Czech Republic
175 O6 **Berau, Sungai** ~ Borneo, N Indonesia
176 V10 **Berau, Teluk** var. MacCluer Gulf. bay Papua, E Indonesia
82 G8 **Berber** River Nile, NE Sudan 18.01N 34.00E
82 N12 **Berbera** Sahil, NW Somalia 10.24N 45.01E
81 H16 **Berbérati** Mambéré-Kadéï, SW Central African Republic 4.13N 15.49E
Berberia, Cabo de see Barbaria, Cap de
57 T9 **Berbice River** ~ NE Guyana
Berchid see Berrechid
105 N2 **Berck-Plage** Pas-de-Calais, N France 50.24N 1.34E
27 T13 **Berclair** Texas, SW USA 28.33N 97.32W
119 W10 **Berda** ~ SE Ukraine
Berdichev see Berdychiv
126 Ll11 **Berdigestyakh** Respublika Sakha (Yakutiya), NE Russian Federation 62.02N 127.03E
126 H14 **Berdsk** Novosibirskaya Oblast', C Russian Federation 54.42N 82.56E
119 W10 **Berdyans'k** Rus. Berdyansk; prev. Osipenko. Zaporiz'ka Oblast', SE Ukraine 46.46N 36.48E
119 W10 **Berdyans'ka Kosa** spit SE Ukraine
119 V10 **Berdyans'ka Zatoka** gulf S Ukraine
119 N5 **Berdychiv** Rus. Berdichev. Zhytomyrs'ka Oblast', N Ukraine 49.52N 28.39E
22 M6 **Berea** Kentucky, S USA 37.34N 84.18W
Beregovo/Beregszász see Berehove
118 G8 **Berehove** Cz. Berehovo, Hung. Beregszász, Rus. Beregovo. Zakarpats'ka Oblast', W Ukraine 48.13N 22.39E
Berehovo see Berehove
194 J15 **Bereina** Central, S PNG 8.33S 146.25E
152 C11 **Bereket** prev. Rus. Gazandzhyk, Kazandzhik, Turkm. Gazanjyk. Balkan Welaýaty, W Turkmenistan 39.16N 55.27E
47 O12 **Berekua** S Dominica 15.14N 61.19W
79 O16 **Berekum** W Ghana 7.27N 2.34W
77 Y11 **Berenice** var. Mînâ Baranîs. SE Egypt 23.58N 35.29E
15 L14 **Berens** ~ Manitoba/Ontario, C Canada
9 X14 **Berens River** Manitoba, C Canada 52.22N 97.00W
31 R12 **Beresford** South Dakota, N USA 43.02N 96.45W
118 J4 **Berestechko** Volyns'ka Oblast', NW Ukraine 50.21N 25.06E
118 M11 **Bereşti** Galaţi, E Romania 46.04N 27.54E
119 U6 **Berestova** ~ E Ukraine
Beretău see Berettyó
113 N23 **Berettyó** Rom. Barcău; prev. Berătău, Beretău. ~ Hungary/Romania
113 N23 **Berettyóújfalu** Hajdú-Bihar, E Hungary 47.15N 21.33E
Berëza/Bereza Kartuska see Byaroza
119 Q4 **Berezan'** Kyyivs'ka Oblast', N Ukraine 50.18N 31.30E
119 Q10 **Berezanka** Mykolayivs'ka Oblast', S Ukraine 46.51N 31.24E
118 J6 **Berezhany** Pol. Brzeżany. Ternopil's'ka Oblast', W Ukraine 49.29N 25.00E
Berezina see Byerezino
Berezino see Byerazino
119 P10 **Berezivka** Rus. Berezovka. Odes'ka Oblast', SW Ukraine 47.12N 30.55E
119 Q2 **Berezna** Chernihivs'ka Oblast', NE Ukraine 51.35N 31.50E
118 L3 **Berezne** Rivnens'ka Oblast', NW Ukraine 51.00N 26.46E
119 R9 **Bereznehuvate** Mykolayivs'ka Oblast', S Ukraine 47.18N 32.52E
129 N10 **Bereznik** Arkhangel'skaya Oblast', NW Russian Federation 62.50N 42.40E
129 U13 **Berezniki** Permskaya Oblast', NW Russian Federation 59.25N 56.49E
Berezovka see Berezivka, Ukraine
Berezovka see Byarozawka, Belarus
125 Ff9 **Berezovo** Khanty-Mansiyskiy Avtonomnyy Okrug, N Russian Federation 63.48N 64.38E
131 O9 **Berezovskaya** Volgogradskaya Oblast', SW Russian Federation 50.17N 43.58E
126 H14 **Berezovskiy** Kemerovskaya Oblast', S Russian Federation 55.40N 86.06E
127 N14 **Berezovyy** Khabarovskiy Kray, E Russian Federation 51.42N 135.39E
85 E25 **Berg** ~ W South Africa
Berg see Berg bei Rohrbach
107 V4 **Berga** Cataluña, NE Spain 42.06N 1.40E
97 N20 **Berga** Kalmar, S Sweden 57.13N 16.03E
142 B13 **Bergama** İzmir, W Turkey 39.07N 27.10E
108 E7 **Bergamo** anc. Bergomum. Lombardia, N Italy 45.42N 9.40E
107 P3 **Bergara** País Vasco, N Spain 43.05N 2.25W
111 S3 **Berg bei Rohrbach** var. Berg. Oberösterreich, N Austria 48.34N 14.02E
195 O11 **Bergberg** ~ New Britain, C Papau New Guinea
102 O6 **Bergen** Mecklenburg-Vorpommern, NE Germany 54.25N 13.24E
103 I11 **Bergen** Niedersachsen, NW Germany 52.49N 9.57E
100 H8 **Bergen** Noord-Holland, NW Netherlands 52.40N 4.42E
96 C13 **Bergen** Hordaland, S Norway 60.24N 5.19E
Bergen see Mons
57 W9 **Berg en Dal** Brokopondo, C Surinam 5.15N 55.20W
101 G15 **Bergen op Zoom** Noord-Brabant, S Netherlands 51.30N 4.18E
104 L13 **Bergerac** Dordogne, SW France 44.51N 0.30E
101 J16 **Bergeyk** Noord-Brabant, S Netherlands 51.19N 5.21E
103 D16 **Bergheim** Nordrhein-Westfalen, W Germany 50.57N 6.39E
57 X10 **Bergi** Sipaliwini, E Surinam 4.36N 54.24W
103 E16 **Bergisch Gladbach** Nordrhein-Westfalen, W Germany 50.59N 7.07E
103 F14 **Bergkamen** Nordrhein-Westfalen, W Germany 51.36N 7.39E
97 N21 **Bergkvara** Kalmar, S Sweden 56.22N 16.04E
Bergomum see Bergamo
100 K13 **Bergse Maas** ~ S Netherlands
97 P15 **Bergshamra** Stockholm, C Sweden 59.37N 18.40E
96 N10 **Bergsjö** Gävleborg, C Sweden 62.00N 17.10E
95 J14 **Bergsviken** Norrbotten, N Sweden 65.16N 21.24E
100 L6 **Bergum** Fris. Burgum. Friesland, N Netherlands 53.12N 5.58E
100 M6 **Bergumer Meer** ◎ N Netherlands
96 N12 **Bergviken** ◎ C Sweden
174 I9 **Berhala, Selat** strait Sumatera, W Indonesia
Berhampore see Baharampur
127 Q9 **Beringa, Ostrov** island E Russian Federation
101 J17 **Beringen** Limburg, NE Belgium 51.04N 5.13E
41 T12 **Bering Glacier** glacier Alaska, USA
Beringov Proliv see Bering Strait
127 Q5 **Beringovskiy** Chukotskiy Avtonomnyy Okrug, NE Russian Federation 63.04N 179.09E
199 K2 **Bering Sea** sea N Pacific Ocean
40 L9 **Bering Strait** Rus. Beringov Proliv. strait Bering Sea/Chukchi Sea
Berislav see Beryslav
107 O15 **Berja** Andalucía, S Spain 36.51N 2.55W
96 H9 **Berkåk** Sør-Trøndelag, S Norway 62.50N 10.01E
100 N11 **Berkel** ~ Germany/Netherlands
37 N8 **Berkeley** California, W USA 37.52N 122.16W
67 E24 **Berkeley Sound** sound NE Falkland Islands
23 V2 **Berkeley Springs** var. Bath. West Virginia, NE USA 39.36N 78.12W
205 N6 **Berkner Island** island Antarctica
116 G8 **Berkovitsa** Montana, NW Bulgaria 43.16N 23.07E
99 M22 **Berkshire** cultural region S England, UK
101 H17 **Berlaar** Antwerpen, N Belgium 51.08N 4.39E
Berlanga see Berlanga de Duero
107 P6 **Berlanga de Duero** var. Berlanga. Castilla-León, N Spain 41.28N 2.51W
(0) I16 **Berlanga Rise** undersea feature E Pacific Ocean
101 F17 **Berlare** Oost-Vlaanderen, NW Belgium 51.01N 4.01E
106 E9 **Berlenga, Ilha da** island C Portugal
94 M7 **Berlevåg** Lapp. Bearalváhki. Finnmark, N Norway 70.51N 29.04E
102 O12 **Berlin** ● (Germany) Berlin, NE Germany 52.31N 13.26E
23 Z4 **Berlin** Maryland, NE USA 38.19N 75.13W
21 O7 **Berlin** New Hampshire, NE USA 44.27N 71.13W
20 D16 **Berlin** Pennsylvania, NE USA 39.54N 78.57W
32 L7 **Berlin** Wisconsin, N USA 43.57N 88.59W
102 O12 **Berlin** ⬖ state NE Germany
Berlinchen see Barlinek
33 U12 **Berlin Lake** ⊠ Ohio, N USA
191 R11 **Bermagui** New South Wales, SE Australia 36.26S 150.01E
42 L8 **Bermejillo** Durango, C Mexico 25.55N 103.39W
64 M6 **Bermejo (viejo), Río** ~ N Argentina
64 L5 **Bermejo, Río** ~ N Argentina
64 I10 **Bermejo, Río** ~ W Argentina
107 P2 **Bermeo** País Vasco, N Spain 43.25N 2.43W
106 K6 **Bermillo de Sayago** Castilla-León, N Spain 41.22N 6.07W
108 E6 **Bermina, Pizzo** Rmsch. Piz Bernina. ▲ Italy/Switzerland see also Bernina, Piz 46.22N 9.52E
66 A12 **Bermuda** var. Bermuda Islands, Bermudas; prev. Somers Islands. ◇ UK crown colony NW Atlantic Ocean
1 N11 **Bermuda** var. Great Bermuda, Long Island, Main Island. island Bermuda
Bermuda Islands see Bermuda
Bermuda-New England Seamount Arc see New England Seamounts
1 N11 **Bermuda Rise** undersea feature C Sargasso Sea
Bermudas see Bermuda
110 D8 **Bern** Fr. Berne. ● (Switzerland) Bern, W Switzerland 46.57N 7.25E
110 D9 **Bern** Fr. Berne. ⬖ canton W Switzerland
39 R11 **Bernalillo** New Mexico, SW USA 35.18N 106.33W
12 H12 **Bernard Lake** ◎ Ontario, S Canada
63 B18 **Bernardo de Irigoyen** Santa Fe, NE Argentina 32.09S 61.06W
20 J14 **Bernardsville** New Jersey, NE USA 40.43N 74.34W
65 K14 **Bernasconi** La Pampa, C Argentina 37.55S 63.43W
102 O12 **Bernau** Brandenburg, NE Germany 52.40N 13.36E
104 L4 **Bernay** Eure, N France 49.04N 0.36E
103 L14 **Bernburg** Sachsen-Anhalt, C Germany 51.46N 11.45E
111 X5 **Berndorf** Niederösterreich, NE Austria 47.55N 16.10E
33 Q12 **Berne** Indiana, N USA 40.39N 84.57W
Berne see Bern
110 D10 **Berner Alpen** var. Berner Oberland, Eng. Bernese Oberland. ▲▲ SW Switzerland
Berner Oberland/Bernese Oberland see Berner Alpen
111 Y2 **Bernhardsthal** Niederösterreich, N Austria 48.40N 16.51E
24 H4 **Bernice** Louisiana, S USA 32.49N 92.39W
29 Y8 **Bernie** Missouri, C USA 36.40N 89.58W
188 G9 **Bernier Island** island Western Australia
Bernina Pass see Bernina, Passo del
110 J10 **Bernina, Passo del** Eng. Bernina Pass. pass SE Switzerland 46.23N 10.00E
110 J10 **Bernina, Piz** It. Pizzo Bermina. ▲ Italy/Switzerland see also Bermina, Pizzo 46.22N 9.55E
101 E20 **Bérnissart** Hainaut, SW Belgium 50.29N 3.37E
103 E18 **Bernkastel-Kues** Rheinland-Pfalz, W Germany 49.55N 7.04E
Beroea see Ḥalab
180 H6 **Beroroha** Toliara, SW Madagascar 21.40S 45.10E
Béroubouay see Gbéroubouè
113 C17 **Beroun** Ger. Beraun. Středočeský Kraj, W Czech Republic 49.58N 14.04E
113 C16 **Berounka** Ger. Beraun. ~ W Czech Republic
115 Q18 **Berovo** E FYR Macedonia 41.45N 22.50E
76 F6 **Berrechid** var. Berchid. W Morocco 33.16N 7.32W
105 R15 **Berre, Étang de** ◎ SE France
105 S15 **Berre-l'Étang** Bouches-du-Rhône, SE France 43.28N 5.10E
190 K9 **Berri** South Australia 34.16S 140.35E
33 O10 **Berrien Springs** Michigan, N USA 41.57N 86.20W
191 O10 **Berrigan** New South Wales, SE Australia 35.41S 145.50E
105 N9 **Berry** cultural region C France
37 N7 **Berryessa, Lake** ◎ California, W USA
46 G2 **Berry Islands** island group N Bahamas
29 T9 **Berryville** Arkansas, C USA 36.21N 93.30W
23 V3 **Berryville** Virginia, NE USA 39.09N 77.58W
85 D21 **Berseba** Karas, S Namibia 26.00S 17.46E
119 O8 **Bershad'** Vinnyts'ka Oblast', C Ukraine 48.19N 29.28E
30 L3 **Berthold** North Dakota, N USA 48.16N 101.48W
39 T3 **Berthoud** Colorado, C USA 40.18N 105.04W
39 S4 **Berthoud Pass** pass Colorado, C USA 39.48N 105.46W
81 F15 **Bertoua** Est, E Cameroon 4.34N 13.42E
27 S10 **Bertram** Texas, SW USA 30.44N 98.03W
65 G22 **Bertrand, Cerro** ▲ S Argentina 50.00S 73.27W
101 J23 **Bertrix** Luxembourg, SE Belgium 49.52N 5.15E
203 P3 **Beru** var. Peru. atoll Tungaru, W Kiribati
Beruni see Beruniy
152 I9 **Beruniy** var. Biruni, Rus. Beruni. Qoraqalpog'iston Respublikasi, W Uzbekistan 41.48N 60.39E
60 F13 **Beruri** Amazonas, NW Brazil 3.44S 61.13W
20 H14 **Berwick** Pennsylvania, NE USA 41.03N 76.13W
98 K12 **Berwick** cultural region SE Scotland, UK
98 L12 **Berwick-upon-Tweed** N England, UK 55.46N 2.00W
119 S10 **Beryslav** Rus. Berislav. Khersons'ka Oblast', S Ukraine 46.51N 33.27E
Berytus see Beyrouth
180 H4 **Besalampy** Mahajanga, W Madagascar 16.43S 44.28E
105 T8 **Besançon** anc. Besontium, Vesontio. Doubs, E France 47.13N 6.01E
105 P10 **Besbre** ~ C France
Bescanuova see Baška
Besdan see Bezdan
Besed' see Byesyedz'
153 R10 **Beshariq** Rus. Besharyk; prev. Kirovo. Farg'ona Viloyati, E Uzbekistan 40.26N 70.33E
Besharyk see Beshariq
152 L9 **Beshbuloq** Rus. Beshulak. Navoiy Viloyati, N Uzbekistan 41.55N 64.13E
Beshenkovichi see Byeshankovichy
152 M13 **Beshkent** Qashqadaryo Viloyati, S Uzbekistan 38.47N 65.42E
Beshulak see Beshbuloq
176 Uu8 **Besir** Papua, E Indonesia 0.25S 130.38E
114 L10 **Beška** Serbia, N Serbia 45.09N 20.04E
Beskra see Biskra
131 O16 **Beslan** Respublika Severnaya Osetiya, SW Russian Federation 43.12N 44.33E
115 P16 **Besna Kobila** ▲ SE Serbia 42.30N 22.16E
143 N16 **Besni** Adıyaman, S Turkey 37.42N 37.52E
Besontium see Besançon
124 Nn2 **Beşparmak Dağları** Eng. Kyrenia Mountains. ▲▲ N Cyprus
Bessarabka see Basarabeasca
94 O2 **Bessels, Kapp** headland C Svalbard 78.36N 21.43E
25 P4 **Bessemer** Alabama, S USA 33.24N 86.57W
32 K3 **Bessemer** Michigan, N USA 46.28N 90.03W
23 Q10 **Bessemer City** North Carolina, SE USA 35.16N 81.16W
104 M10 **Bessines-sur-Gartempe** Haute-Vienne, C France 46.06N 1.22E
101 K15 **Best** Noord-Brabant, S Netherlands 51.31N 5.24E
27 N9 **Best** Texas, SW USA 31.13N 101.34W
129 O11 **Bestuzhevo** Arkhangel'skaya Oblast', NW Russian Federation 61.36N 43.54E
126 M11 **Bestyakh** Respublika Sakha (Yakutiya), NE Russian Federation 61.25N 129.05E
Beszterce see Bistriţa
Besztercebánya see Banská Bystrica
180 I5 **Betafo** Antananarivo, C Madagascar 19.49S 46.49E
106 H2 **Betanzos** Galicia, NW Spain 43.16N 8.16W
106 G2 **Betanzos, Ría de** estuary NW Spain
81 G15 **Bétaré Oya** Est, E Cameroon 5.34N 14.09E
107 S9 **Bétera** País Valenciano, E Spain 39.34N 0.28W
79 R15 **Bétérou** C Benin 9.13N 2.18E
85 K21 **Bethal** Mpumalanga, NE South Africa 26.27S 29.28E
32 K15 **Bethalto** Illinois, N USA 38.54N 90.02W
85 D21 **Bethanie** var. Bethanien, Bethany. Karas, S Namibia 26.26S 17.06E
Bethanien see Bethanie
29 S2 **Bethany** Missouri, C USA 40.15N 94.03W
29 N10 **Bethany** Oklahoma, C USA 35.31N 97.37W
Bethany see Bethanie
41 N12 **Bethel** Alaska, USA 60.47N 161.45W
21 P7 **Bethel** Maine, NE USA 44.24N 70.47W
23 W9 **Bethel** North Carolina, SE USA 35.46N 77.21W
20 B15 **Bethel Park** Pennsylvania, NE USA 40.21N 80.03W
23 W3 **Bethesda** Maryland, NE USA 38.58N 77.06W
85 J22 **Bethlehem** Free State, C South Africa 28.11S 28.16E
20 I14 **Bethlehem** Pennsylvania, NE USA 40.36N 75.22W
144 F10 **Bethlehem** Ar. Bayt Laḥm, Heb. Bet Leḥem. C West Bank 31.43N 35.12E
Bethlen see Beclean
85 I24 **Bethulie** Free State, C South Africa 30.29S 25.54E
105 O1 **Béthune** Pas-de-Calais, N France 50.31N 2.37E
104 M3 **Béthune** ~ N France
106 M14 **Béticos, Sistemas** var. Sistema Penibético, Eng. Baetic Cordillera, Baetic Mountains. ▲▲ S Spain
56 I6 **Betijoque** Trujillo, NW Venezuela 9.27N 70.47W
61 M20 **Betim** Minas Gerais, SE Brazil 19.55S 44.10W
202 H3 **Betio** Tarawa, W Kiribati 1.21N 172.55E
180 H7 **Betioky** Toliara, S Madagascar 23.42S 44.22E
Bet Leḥem see Bethlehem
Betlen see Beclean
178 H17 **Betong** Yala, SW Thailand 5.47N 101.04E
81 I16 **Bétou** La Likouala, N Congo 3.07N 18.30E
151 P14 **Betpak-Dala** Kaz. Betpaqdala. plateau S Kazakhstan
Betpaqdala see Betpak-Dala
180 H7 **Betroka** Toliara, S Madagascar 23.15S 46.07E
Betschau see Bečva
144 G9 **Bet She'an** Ar. Baysān, Beisān; anc. Scythopolis. Northern, N Israel 32.29N 35.25E
13 T6 **Betsiamites** Québec, SE Canada 48.55N 68.40W
13 T6 **Betsiamites** ~ Québec, SE Canada
180 I4 **Betsiboka** ~ N Madagascar
101 M25 **Bettembourg** Luxembourg, S Luxembourg 49.31N 6.06E
101 M23 **Bettendorf** Diekirch, NE Luxembourg 49.52N 6.13E
31 Z14 **Bettendorf** Iowa, C USA 41.31N 90.31W
77 R13 **Bette, Pic** var. Bīkkū Bīttī, It. Picco Bette. ▲ S Libya 22.02N 19.07E
Bette, Picco see Bette, Pic
159 P12 **Bettiah** Bihār, N India 26.49N 84.30E
41 Q7 **Bettles** Alaska, USA 66.54N 151.40W
97 N17 **Bettna** Södermanland, C Sweden 58.52N 16.40E
160 H11 **Betūl** prev. Badnur. Madhya Pradesh, C India 21.55N 77.54E
160 H9 **Betwa** ~ C India
103 F16 **Betzdorf** Rheinland-Pfalz, W Germany 50.47N 7.50E
84 C9 **Béu** Uíge, NW Angola 6.16S 15.28E
33 P6 **Beulah** Michigan, N USA 44.37N 86.04W
30 L5 **Beulah** North Dakota, N USA 47.16N 101.48W
100 M8 **Beulakerwijde** ◎ N Netherlands
100 L13 **Beuningen** Gelderland, SE Netherlands 51.52N 5.47E
Beuthen see Bytom
105 N7 **Beuvron** ~ C France
101 F16 **Beveren** Oost-Vlaanderen, N Belgium 51.13N 4.15E
23 T9 **B.Everett Jordan Reservoir** var. Jordan Lake. ⊠ North Carolina, SE USA
99 N17 **Beverley** E England, UK 53.51N 0.25W
Beverley see Beverly
101 J17 **Beverlo** Limburg, NE Belgium 51.06N 5.14E
21 P11 **Beverly** Massachusetts, NE USA 42.33N 70.49W
34 J9 **Beverly** var. Beverley. Washington, NW USA 46.50N 119.57W
37 S15 **Beverly Hills** California, W USA 34.02N 118.25W
103 I14 **Beverungen** Nordrhein-Westfalen, C Germany 51.39N 9.22E
100 H9 **Beverwijk** Noord-Holland, W Netherlands 52.28N 4.37E
110 C10 **Bex** Vaud, W Switzerland 46.15N 7.00E
99 P23 **Bexhill** var. Bexhill-on-Sea. SE England, UK 50.49N 0.28E
Bexhill-on-Sea see Bexhill
142 E17 **Bey Dağları** ▲▲ SW Turkey
Beyj see Belyy
142 E10 **Beykoz** İstanbul, NW Turkey 41.09N 29.06E
78 K15 **Beyla** SE Guinea 8.43N 8.41W
143 X12 **Beyläqan** prev. Zhdanov. SW Azerbaijan 39.43N 47.38E
82 L10 **Beylul** var. Beilul. SE Eritrea 13.10N 42.27E
150 H14 **Beyneu** Kaz. Beyneū. Mangistau, SW Kazakhstan 45.19N 55.11E
Beyneū see Beyneu
172 Ss14 **Beyonēsu-retsugan** Eng. Bayonnaise Rocks. island group SE Japan
142 G12 **Beypazarı** Ankara, NW Turkey 40.10N 31.55E
161 F21 **Beypore** Kerala, SW India 11.10N 75.49E
144 G7 **Beyrouth** var. Bayrūt, Eng. Beirut; anc. Berytus. ● (Lebanon) W Lebanon 33.54N 35.31E
144 G7 **Beyrouth** ✈ W Lebanon 33.52N 35.30E
142 G15 **Beyşehir** Konya, SW Turkey 37.39N 31.42E
142 G15 **Beyşehir Gölü** ◎ C Turkey
110 J7 **Bezau** Vorarlberg, NW Austria 47.24N 9.55E
114 J8 **Bezdan** Ger. Besdan, Hung. Bezdán. Serbia, NW Serbia 45.51N 19.00E
Bezdezh see Byezdzyezh
128 G15 **Bezhanitsy** Pskovskaya Oblast', W Russian Federation 56.57N 29.53E
128 K15 **Bezhetsk** Tverskaya Oblast', W Russian Federation 57.47N 36.42E
105 P16 **Béziers** anc. Baeterrae, Baeterrae Septimanorum, Julia Beterrae. Hérault, S France 43.21N 3.13E
Bezmein see Abadan
Bezwada see Vijayawāda
160 P12 **Bhadrak** var. Bhadrakh. Orissa, E India 21.06N 86.31E
Bhadrakh see Bhadrak
161 F19 **Bhadra Reservoir** ⊠ SW India
161 F18 **Bhadrāvati** Karnātaka, SW India 13.52N 75.43E
159 R14 **Bhāgalpur** Bihār, NE India 25.13N 86.58E
Bhairab see Bhairab Bazar
159 U14 **Bhairab Bazar** var. Bhairab. Dhaka, C Bangladesh 24.04N 91.00E
159 O11 **Bhairahawā** Western, S Nepal 27.31N 83.27E
155 S8 **Bhakkar** Punjab, E Pakistan 31.41N 71.04E
159 P11 **Bhaktapur** Central, C Nepal 27.47N 85.21E
178 Gg3 **Bhamo** var. Banmo. Kachin State, N Burma 24.15N 97.15E
Bhāmragad see Bhāmragarh
160 K13 **Bhāmragarh** var. Bhāmragad. Mahārāshtra, C India 19.28N 80.39E
160 J12 **Bhandāra** Mahārāshtra, C India 21.10N 79.40E
Bhārat see India
158 J12 **Bharatpur** prev. Bhurtpore. Rājasthān, N India 27.13N 77.28E
160 D11 **Bharūch** Gujarāt, W India 21.48N 72.54E
161 E18 **Bhatkal** Karnātaka, W India 13.59N 74.34E
159 O13 **Bhatni** var. Bhatni Junction. Uttar Pradesh, N India 26.22N 83.55E
Bhatni Junction see Bhatni

◆ Country
● Country Capital
◇ Dependent Territory
○ Dependent Territory Capital
⬖ Administrative Region
✈ International Airport
▲ Mountain
▲▲ Mountain Range
Volcano
~ River
◎ Lake
⊠ Reservoir

BHĀTPĀRA – BLACKPOOL

159 S16 **Bhātpāra** West Bengal, NE India 22.55N 88.30E
155 U7 **Bhaun** Punjab, E Pakistan 32.53N 72.45E
Bhaunagar see Bhāvnagar
160 M13 **Bhavānīpātna** Orissa, E India 19.56N 83.09E
161 H21 **Bhavānīsāgar Reservoir** ▣ S India
160 D11 **Bhāvnagar** prev. Bhaunagar. Gujarāt, W India 21.46N 72.13E
Bheanntraí, Bá see Bantry Bay
Bheara, Béal an see Gweebarra Bay
160 K12 **Bhilai** Chhattīsgarh, C India 21.13N 81.26E
158 G13 **Bhīlwāra** Rājasthān, N India 25.22N 74.39E
161 E14 **Bhīma** ≈ S India
161 K16 **Bhīmavaram** Andhra Pradesh, E India 16.34N 81.34E
160 I7 **Bhind** Madhya Pradesh, C India 26.33N 78.46E
158 E13 **Bhīnmāl** Rājasthān, N India 25.01N 72.22E
Bhir see Bīd
160 D13 **Bhiwandi** Mahārāshtra, W India 19.21N 73.07E
158 H10 **Bhiwāni** Haryāna, N India 28.49N 76.07E
158 L13 **Bhognīpur** Uttar Pradesh, N India 26.12N 79.48E
159 U16 **Bhola** Barisal, S Bangladesh 22.42N 90.43E
160 H10 **Bhopāl** Madhya Pradesh, C India 23.16N 77.24E
161 J14 **Bhopālpatnam** Chhattīsgarh, C India 18.51N 80.22E
161 E14 **Bhor** Mahārāshtra, W India 18.10N 73.55E
160 O12 **Bhubaneshwar** prev. Bhubaneswar, Bhuvaneshwar. Orissa, E India 20.16N 85.51E
Bhubaneswar see Bhubaneshwar
160 B9 **Bhuj** Gujarāt, W India 23.16N 69.40E
Bhuket see Phuket
Bhurtpore see Bharatpur
Bhusaval see Bhusāwal
160 G12 **Bhusāwal** prev. Bhusaval. Mahārāshtra, C India 21.01N 75.49E
159 T12 **Bhutan** off. Kingdom of Bhutan, var. Druk-yul. ◆ monarchy S Asia
Bhuvaneshwar see Bhubaneshwar
149 T15 **Bīābān, Kūh-e** ▲▲ S Iran
79 V18 **Biafra, Bight of** var. Bight of Bonny. bay W Africa
176 X9 **Biak** Papua, E Indonesia 1.10S 136.04E
176 Ww9 **Biak, Pulau** island E Indonesia
112 P12 **Biała Podlaska** Lubelskie, E Poland 52.03N 23.08E
112 F7 **Białogard** Ger. Belgard. Zachodnio-pomorskie, NW Poland 54.00N 15.58E
112 P10 **Białowieska, Puszcza** Bel. Byelavyezhskaya Pushcha, Rus. Belovezhskaya Pushcha. physical region Belarus/Poland see also Byelavyezhskaya Pushcha
112 G8 **Biały Bór** Ger. Baldenburg. Zachodnio-pomorskie, NW Poland 53.53N 16.49E
112 P9 **Białystok** Rus. Belostok, Bielostok. Podlaskie, NE Poland 53.08N 23.09E
109 L24 **Biancavilla** prev. Inessa. Sicilia, Italy, C Mediterranean Sea 37.37N 14.52E
Bianco, Monte see Blanc, Mont
Bianjing see Xunke
78 L15 **Biankouma** W Ivory Coast 7.43N 7.37W
178 Ii7 **Bia, Phou** var. Pou Bia. ▲ C Laos 18.59N 103.09E
Bia, Pou see Bia, Phou
149 R5 **Biārjmand** Semnān, N Iran 36.04N 55.49E
107 P4 **Biarra** ≈ NE Spain
104 I15 **Biarritz** Pyrénées-Atlantiques, SW France 43.24N 1.39W
110 H10 **Biasca** Ticino, S Switzerland 46.22N 8.59E
63 E17 **Biassini** Salto, N Uruguay 31.18S 57.05W
Biasteri see Laguardia
172 Oo5 **Bibai** Hokkaidō, NE Japan 43.22N 141.52E
85 B15 **Bibala** Port. Vila Arriaga. Namibe, SW Angola 14.45S 13.18E
106 I4 **Bibéi** ≈ NW Spain
Biberach see Biberach an der Riss
103 I23 **Biberach an der Riss** var. Biberach, Ger. Biberach an der Riß. Baden-Württemberg, S Germany 48.06N 9.46E
110 E7 **Biberist** Solothurn, NW Switzerland 47.10N 7.34E
79 O16 **Bibiani** SW Ghana 6.28N 2.19W
114 C13 **Bibinje** Zadar, SW Croatia 44.04N 15.17E
Biblical Gebal see Jbaïl
118 I5 **Bibrka** Pol. Bóbrka, Rus. Bobrka. L'vivs'ka Oblast', NW Ukraine 49.39N 24.16E
119 N10 **Bîc** ≈ S Moldova
115 M18 **Bicaj** Kukës, NE Albania 42.00N 20.24E
118 K10 **Bicaz** Hung. Békás. Neamţ, NE Romania 46.53N 26.04E
191 Q16 **Bicheno** Tasmania, SE Australia 41.56S 148.15E
Bichiş see Békés
Bichiş-Ciaba see Békéscsaba
Bichitra see Phichit
143 P8 **Bichvint'a** Rus. Pitsunda. NW Georgia 43.12N 40.21E
13 T7 **Bic, Île du** island Québec, SE Canada
34 J10 **Bickleton** Washington, NW USA 46.00N 120.16W
38 L6 **Bicknell** Utah, W USA 38.20N 111.32W
175 Tt7 **Bicoli** Pulau Halmahera, E Indonesia 0.34N 128.33E
113 J22 **Bicske** Fejér, C Hungary 47.28N 18.38E
161 F14 **Bīd** prev. Bhir. Mahārāshtra, W India 19.17N 75.22E
79 U15 **Bida** Niger, C Nigeria 9.06N 6.02E
161 H15 **Bīdar** Karnātaka, C India 17.55N 77.34E
147 Y8 **Bidbid** NE Oman 23.25N 58.07E
21 P9 **Biddeford** Maine, NE USA 43.28N 70.27W
100 L9 **Biddinghuizen** Flevoland, C Netherlands 52.28N 5.41E
35 X11 **Biddle** Montana, NW USA 45.04N 105.21W
99 J23 **Bideford** SW England, UK 51.01N 4.12W
84 D13 **Bié** ◈ province C Angola
37 O2 **Bieber** California, W USA 41.07N 121.09W
112 O9 **Biebrza** ≈ NE Poland
172 P5 **Biei** Hokkaidō, NE Japan 43.33N 142.28E
110 D8 **Biel** Fr. Bienne. Bern, W Switzerland 47.09N 7.16E
102 G13 **Bielefeld** Nordrhein-Westfalen, NW Germany 52.01N 8.31E
110 D8 **Bieler See** Fr. Lac de Bienne. ◎ W Switzerland
Bielitz/Bielitz-Biala see Bielsko-Biała
108 C7 **Biella** Piemonte, N Italy 45.33N 8.03E
Bielostok see Białystok
113 J17 **Bielsko-Biała** Ger. Bielitz, Bielitz-Biala. Śląskie, S Poland 49.48N 19.01E
112 P10 **Bielsk Podlaski** Białystok, E Poland 52.45N 23.11E
Bien Bien see Điện Biên
Biên Đông see South China Sea
9 V17 **Bienfait** Saskatchewan, S Canada 49.06N 102.47W
178 Jj14 **Biên Hoa** Đông Nai, S Vietnam 10.58N 106.49E
Bienne see Biel
Bienne, Lac de see Bieler See
10 K8 **Bienville, Lac** ◎ Québec, C Canada
84 D13 **Bié, Planalto do** var. Bié Plateau. plateau C Angola
Bié Plateau see Bié, Planalto do
110 B9 **Bière** Vaud, W Switzerland 46.32N 6.19E
100 O4 **Bierum** Groningen, NE Netherlands 53.25N 6.51E
100 I13 **Biesbos** var. Biesbosch. wetland S Netherlands
Biesbosch see Biesbos
101 H21 **Biesme** Namur, S Belgium 50.19N 4.43E
103 H21 **Bietigheim-Bissingen** Baden-Württemberg, SW Germany 48.57N 9.07E
101 I23 **Bièvre** Namur, SE Belgium 49.56N 5.01E
81 D18 **Bifoun** Moyen-Ogooué, NW Gabon 0.15S 10.24E
172 Pp3 **Bifuka** Hokkaidō, NE Japan 44.28N 142.20E
142 C11 **Biga** Çanakkale, NW Turkey 40.13N 27.13E
142 C13 **Bigadiç** Balıkesir, W Turkey 39.24N 28.07E
28 J7 **Big Basin** basin Kansas, C USA
193 B20 **Big Bay** bay South Island, NZ
197 B12 **Big Bay** bay C Vanuatu
33 O5 **Big Bay de Noc** ◎ Michigan, N USA
33 N3 **Big Bay Point** headland Michigan, N USA 46.51N 87.40W
35 R10 **Big Belt Mountains** ▲▲ Montana, NW USA
31 N10 **Big Bend Dam** dam South Dakota, N USA 44.03N 99.27W
26 K12 **Big Bend National Park** national park Texas, S USA
24 K5 **Big Black River** ≈ Mississippi, S USA
29 O3 **Big Blue River** ≈ Kansas/Nebraska, C USA
26 M10 **Big Canyon** ≈ Texas, SW USA
35 N12 **Big Creek** Idaho, NW USA 45.05N 115.20W
25 N8 **Big Creek Lake** ▣ Alabama, S USA
25 X15 **Big Cypress Swamp** wetland Florida, SE USA
41 S9 **Big Delta** Alaska, USA 64.09N 145.50W
32 K6 **Big Eau Pleine Reservoir** ▣ Wisconsin, N USA
21 P5 **Bigelow Mountain** ▲ Maine, NE USA 45.09N 70.17W
168 G9 **Biger** var. Jargalant. Govĭ-Altay, W Mongolia 45.39N 97.10E
31 U3 **Big Falls** Minnesota, N USA 48.13N 93.48W
35 P8 **Bigfork** Montana, NW USA 48.03N 114.04W
31 U3 **Big Fork River** ≈ Minnesota, N USA
9 S15 **Biggar** Saskatchewan, S Canada 52.03N 107.58W
188 L3 **Bigge Island** island Western Australia
37 O5 **Biggs** California, W USA 39.24N 121.44W
34 I11 **Biggs** Oregon, NW USA 45.39N 120.49W
12 K13 **Big Gull Lake** ◎ Ontario, SE Canada
39 P16 **Big Hachet Peak** ▲ New Mexico, SW USA 31.38N 108.24W
35 P11 **Big Hole River** ≈ Montana, NW USA
35 V13 **Bighorn Basin** basin Wyoming, C USA
35 U11 **Bighorn Lake** ◎ Montana/Wyoming, N USA
35 W13 **Bighorn Mountains** ▲▲ Wyoming, C USA
38 J13 **Big Horn Peak** ▲ Arizona, SW USA 33.40N 113.01W
35 V11 **Bighorn River** ≈ Montana/Wyoming, NW USA
16 O5 **Big Island** island Nunavut, NE Canada
41 O16 **Big Koniuji Island** island Shumagin Islands, Alaska, USA
27 N9 **Big Lake** Texas, SW USA 31.11N 101.27W
21 T5 **Big Lake** ◎ Maine, NE USA
32 I3 **Big Manitou Falls** waterfall Wisconsin, N USA 46.32N 92.07W
37 R2 **Big Mountain** ▲ Nevada, W USA 41.18N 119.03W
110 G10 **Bignasco** Ticino, S Switzerland 46.21N 8.37E
31 R16 **Big Nemaha River** ≈ Nebraska, C USA
78 G12 **Bignona** SW Senegal 12.49N 16.16W
Bigorra see Tarbes
Bigosovo see Bihosava
37 S10 **Big Pine** California, W USA 37.09N 118.18W
37 Q14 **Big Pine Mountain** ▲ California, W USA 34.41N 119.37W
29 V6 **Big Piney Creek** ≈ Missouri, C USA
67 M24 **Big Point** headland N Tristan da Cunha
33 P8 **Big Rapids** Michigan, N USA 43.42N 85.28W
32 K6 **Big Rib River** ≈ Wisconsin, N USA
12 L14 **Big Rideau Lake** ◎ Ontario, SE Canada
9 T14 **Big River** Saskatchewan, C Canada 53.48N 106.55W
29 X5 **Big River** ≈ Missouri, C USA
33 N7 **Big Sable Point** headland Michigan, N USA 44.03N 86.30W
35 S7 **Big Sandy** Montana, NW USA 48.08N 110.09W
27 W6 **Big Sandy** Texas, SW USA 32.34N 95.06W
39 V5 **Big Sandy Creek** ≈ Colorado, C USA
31 Q16 **Big Sandy Creek** ≈ Nebraska, C USA
31 V5 **Big Sandy Lake** ◎ Minnesota, N USA
38 J11 **Big Sandy River** ≈ Arizona, SW USA
23 P5 **Big Sandy River** ≈ S USA
25 V6 **Big Satilla Creek** ≈ Georgia, SE USA
31 R12 **Big Sioux River** ≈ Iowa/South Dakota, N USA
37 U7 **Big Smoky Valley** valley Nevada, W USA
27 N7 **Big Spring** Texas, SW USA 32.15N 101.30W
21 Q5 **Big Squaw Mountain** ▲ Maine, NE USA 45.28N 69.42W
23 O7 **Big Stone Gap** Virginia, NE USA 36.52N 82.45W
31 Q8 **Big Stone Lake** ◎ Minnesota/South Dakota, N USA
24 K4 **Big Sunflower River** ≈ Mississippi, S USA
35 T11 **Big Timber** Montana, NW USA 45.50N 109.57W
10 D8 **Big Trout Lake** Ontario, C Canada 53.40N 90.00W
12 I12 **Big Trout Lake** ◎ Ontario, SE Canada
37 O2 **Big Valley Mountains** ▲▲ California, W USA
27 Q13 **Big Wells** Texas, SW USA 28.34N 99.34W
12 F11 **Bigwood** Ontario, S Canada 46.03N 80.37W
114 D11 **Bihać** Federacija Bosna I Hercegovina, NW Bosnia and Herzegovina 44.49N 15.53E
159 P13 **Bihār** prev. Behar. ◈ state N India
Bihār see Bihār Sharīf
83 F20 **Biharamulo** Kagera, NW Tanzania 2.37S 31.19E
159 R13 **Bihārīganj** Bihār, NE India 25.43N 86.58E
159 P14 **Bihār Sharīf** var. Bihār. Bihār, N India 25.13N 85.31E
118 F10 **Bihor** ◈ county NW Romania
172 Q6 **Bihoro** Hokkaidō, NE Japan 43.50N 144.05E
120 K11 **Bihosava** Rus. Bigosovo. Vitsyebskaya Voblasts', NW Belarus 55.50N 27.45E
Bijagos Archipelago see Bijagós, Arquipélago dos
78 G13 **Bijagós, Arquipélago dos** var. Bijagos Archipelago. island group W Guinea-Bissau
161 F16 **Bijāpur** Karnātaka, C India 16.49N 75.42E
148 K5 **Bījār** Kordestān, W Iran 35.54N 47.36E
114 J11 **Bijeljina** Republika Srpska, NE Bosnia and Herzegovina 44.46N 19.13E
115 K15 **Bijelo Polje** NE-Montenegro 43.03N 19.44E
166 I11 **Bijie** Guizhou, S China 27.18N 105.15E
158 J10 **Bijnor** Uttar Pradesh, N India 29.22N 78.09E
158 F11 **Bīkāner** Rājasthān, NW India 28.01N 73.22E
201 V3 **Bikar Atoll** var. Pikaar. atoll Ratak Chain, N Marshall Islands
202 H3 **Bikeman** atoll Tungaru, W Kiribati
202 I3 **Bikenebu** Tarawa, W Kiribati
127 Nn16 **Bikin** Khabarovskiy Kray, SE Russian Federation 46.45N 134.06E
127 Nn16 **Bikin** ≈ SE Russian Federation
201 R3 **Bikini Atoll** var. Pikinni. atoll Ralik Chain, NW Marshall Islands
85 L17 **Bikita** Masvingo, E Zimbabwe 20.04S 31.38E
Bīkkū Bīttī see Bette, Pic
81 I19 **Bikoro** Equateur, W Dem. Rep. Congo 0.45S 18.09E
147 Z9 **Bilād Banī Bū 'Alī** NE Oman 22.01N 59.18E
147 Z9 **Bilād Banī Bū Ḥasan** NE Oman 22.09N 59.13E
147 X9 **Bilād Manaḥ** var. Manaḥ. NE Oman 22.37N 57.27E
79 Q12 **Bilanga** C Burkina 12.35N 0.08W
175 Q7 **Bilang, Teluk** bay Sulawesi, N Indonesia
158 F12 **Bilāra** Rājasthān, N India 26.14N 73.48E
158 K10 **Bilāri** Uttar Pradesh, N India 28.37N 78.48E
144 J5 **Bil'ās, Jabal al** ▲▲ C Syria
160 L11 **Bilāspur** Chhattīsgarh, C India 22.06N 82.08E
158 I8 **Bilāspur** Himāchal Pradesh, N India 31.19N 76.46E
173 G6 **Bila, Sungai** ≈ Sumatera, W Indonesia
143 Y13 **Biläsuvar** Rus. Bilyasuvar; prev. Pushkino. SE Azerbaijan 39.26N 48.33E
119 O5 **Bila Tserkva** Rus. Belaya Tserkov'. Kyyivs'ka Oblast', N Ukraine 49.48N 30.07E
178 H11 **Bilauktaung Range** var. Thanintari Taungdan. ▲▲ Burma/Thailand
107 O2 **Bilbao** Basq. Bilbo. País Vasco, N Spain 43.15N 2.55W
Bilbo see Bilbao
94 H2 **Bíldudalur** Vestfirdhir, NW Iceland 65.40N 23.35W
115 I16 **Bileća** Republika Srpska, S Bosnia and Herzegovina 42.53N 18.27E
142 E12 **Bilecik** Bilecik, NW Turkey 39.59N 29.54E
142 F12 **Bilecik** ◈ province NW Turkey
118 E11 **Biled** Ger. Billed, Hung. Billéd. Timiş, W Romania 45.55N 20.55E
113 O15 **Biłgoraj** Lubelskie, E Poland 50.32N 22.42E
119 P11 **Bilhorod-Dnistrovs'kyy** Rus. Belgorod-Dnestrovskiy, Rom. Cetatea Albă; prev. Akkerman, anc. Tyras. Odes'ka Oblast', SW Ukraine 46.10N 30.18E
81 M16 **Bili** Orientale, N Dem. Rep. Congo 4.07N 25.09E
127 Oo5 **Bilibino** Chukotskiy Avtonomnyy Okrug, NE Russian Federation 67.56N 166.45E
178 Gg8 **Bilin** Mon State, S Burma 17.13N 97.12E
179 Qq12 **Biliran Island** island C Philippines
115 N21 **Bilisht** var. Bilishti. Korçë, SE Albania 40.36N 21.00E
Bilishti see Bilisht
191 N10 **Billabong Creek** var. Moulamein Creek. seasonal river New South Wales, SE Australia
190 G4 **Billa Kalina** South Australia 29.57S 136.13E
207 Q17 **Bill Baileys Bank** undersea feature N Atlantic Ocean 60.34N 10.15W
Billed/Billéd see Biled
159 N14 **Billi** Uttar Pradesh, N India 24.30N 82.58E
99 M15 **Billingham** N England, UK 54.36N 1.16W
35 U11 **Billings** Montana, NW USA 45.47N 108.32W
97 J16 **Billingsfors** Västra Götaland, S Sweden 58.57N 12.14E
Bill of Cape Clear, The see Clear, Cape
30 L9 **Billsburg** South Dakota, N USA 44.22N 101.40W
97 F23 **Billund** Ribe, W Denmark 55.43N 9.07E
38 L11 **Bill Williams Mountain** ▲ Arizona, SW USA 35.12N 112.12W
38 I12 **Bill Williams River** ≈ Arizona, SW USA
79 Y8 **Bilma** Agadez, NE Niger 18.22N 13.01E
79 Y8 **Bilma, Grand Erg de** desert NE Niger
189 Y9 **Biloela** Queensland, E Australia 24.27S 150.31E
114 G8 **Bilo Gora** ▲▲ N Croatia
119 U13 **Bilohirs'k** Rus. Belogorsk; prev. Karasubazar. Respublika Krym, S Ukraine 45.01N 34.45E
118 M3 **Bilokorovychi** Rus. Belokorovichi. Zhytomyrs'ka Oblast', N Ukraine 51.07N 28.02E
119 X5 **Bilokurakine** Luhans'ka Oblast', E Ukraine 49.32N 38.44E
119 T3 **Bilopillya** Rus. Belopol'ye. Sums'ka Oblast', NE Ukraine 51.09N 34.16E
119 Y6 **Bilovods'k** Rus. Belovodsk. Luhans'ka Oblast', E Ukraine 49.10N 39.34E
24 M9 **Biloxi** Mississippi, S USA 30.24N 88.53W
119 R10 **Bilozerka** Khersons'ka Oblast', S Ukraine 46.36N 32.23E
119 W7 **Bilozers'ke** Donets'ka Oblast', E Ukraine 48.29N 37.03E
100 J11 **Bilthoven** Utrecht, C Netherlands 52.07N 5.12E
80 K9 **Biltine** Biltine, E Chad 14.30N 20.52E
80 J9 **Biltine** off. Préfecture de Biltine. ◈ prefecture E Chad
Bilüü see Ulaanhus
Bilwi see Puerto Cabezas
Bilyasuvar see Biläsuvar
119 O11 **Bilyayivka** Odes'ka Oblast', SW Ukraine 46.28N 30.11E
101 K18 **Bilzen** Limburg, NE Belgium 50.52N 5.31E
Bimbéréké see Bembèrèkè
191 R10 **Bimberi Peak** ▲ New South Wales, SE Australia 35.42S 148.46E
79 Q15 **Bimbila** E Ghana 8.54N 0.04E
81 I15 **Bimbo** Ombella-Mpoko, SW Central African Republic 4.19N 18.27E
46 F2 **Bimini Islands** island group W Bahamas
160 I9 **Bīna** Madhya Pradesh, C India 24.09N 78.10E
149 T4 **Bīnālūd, Kūh-e** ▲▲ NE Iran
101 F20 **Binche** Hainaut, S Belgium 50.25N 4.10E
Bindloe Island see Marchena, Isla
85 L16 **Bindura** Mashonaland Central, NE Zimbabwe 17.18S 31.13E
107 T5 **Binefar** Aragón, NE Spain 41.51N 0.16E
85 J16 **Binga** Matabeleland North, W Zimbabwe 17.42S 27.21E
191 T5 **Bingara** New South Wales, SE Australia 29.54S 150.36E
103 F18 **Bingen am Rhein** Rheinland-Pfalz, SW Germany 49.58N 7.54E
28 M11 **Binger** Oklahoma, C USA 35.19N 98.19W
Bingerau see Węgrów
Bin Ghalfān, Jazā'ir see Ḥalāniyāt, Juzur al
21 Q6 **Bingham** Maine, NE USA 45.01N 69.51W
20 H11 **Binghamton** New York, NE USA 42.06N 75.55W
Bin Ghanīmah, Jabal see Bin Ghunaymah, Jabal
77 P11 **Bin Ghunaymah, Jabal** var. Jabal Bin Ghanīmah. ▲▲ C Libya
145 U3 **Bingird** NE Iraq 36.03N 45.03E
Bingmei see Congjiang
143 P14 **Bingöl** Bingöl, E Turkey 38.54N 40.28E
143 P14 **Bingöl** ◈ province E Turkey
167 R6 **Binhai** var. Dongkan. Jiangsu, E China 34.03N 119.46E
178 Kk12 **Binh Đinh** var. An Nhơn. Binh Đinh, C Vietnam 13.52N 109.07E
178 Kk10 **Binh Sơn** var. Châu Ô. Quang Ngai, C Vietnam 15.18N 108.45E
Binimani see Bintimani
173 Ff5 **Binjai** Sumatera, W Indonesia 3.37N 98.30E
191 R6 **Binnaway** New South Wales, SE Australia 31.34S 149.24E
110 E6 **Binningen** Basel-Land, NW Switzerland 47.31N 7.34E
175 R13 **Binongko, Pulau** island Kepulauan Tukangbesi, C Indonesia
174 Gg3 **Bintang, Banjaran** ▲▲ Peninsular Malaysia
174 I7 **Bintan, Pulau** island Kepulauan Riau, W Indonesia
78 J14 **Bintimani** var. Binimani. ▲ NE Sierra Leone 9.21N 11.09W
Bint Jubayl see Bent Jbaïl
174 M5 **Bintulu** Sarawak, East Malaysia 3.12N 113.01E
176 Vv10 **Bintuni** prev. Steenkool. Papua, E Indonesia 2.03S 133.45E
176 Vv10 **Bintuni, Teluk** bay Papua, E Indonesia
169 W8 **Binxian** Heilongjiang, NE China 45.43N 127.24E
166 K14 **Binyang** var. Binzhou. Guangxi Zhuangzu Zizhiqu, S China 23.15N 108.47E
167 Q4 **Binzhou** Shandong, E China 37.22N 118.03E
Binzhou see Binyang
65 G14 **Bío Bío** off. Región del Bío Bío. ◈ region C Chile
65 G14 **Bío Bío, Río** ≈ C Chile
81 C16 **Bioco, Isla de** var. Bioko, Eng. Fernando Po, Sp. Fernando Póo; prev. Macías Nguema Biyogo. island NW Equatorial Guinea
114 D13 **Biograd na Moru** It. Zaravecchia. Zadar, SW Croatia 43.57N 15.27E
Bioko see Bioco, Isla de
115 F14 **Biokovo** ▲▲ S Croatia
Biorra see Birr
Bipontium see Zweibrücken
149 W13 **Bīrag, Kūh-e** ▲▲ SE Iran
77 O10 **Birāk** var. Brak. C Libya 27.31N 14.16E
145 S10 **Bi'r al Islām** C Iraq 32.15N 43.40E
149 U4 **Bīrālūd, Kūh-e** ▲▲ NE Iran
160 N11 **Biramitrapur** Orissa, E India 22.24N 84.42E
145 T11 **Bi'r an Niṣf** S Iraq 31.22N 44.07E
80 L12 **Birao** Vakaga, NE Central African Republic 10.14N 22.49E
152 J10 **Birata** Rus. Darganata, Dargan-Ata. Lebap Welaýaty, NE Turkmenistan 40.30N 62.09E
164 M6 **Biratar Bulak** well NW China 42.00N 90.26E
159 R12 **Birātnagar** Eastern, SE Nepal 26.28N 87.16E
172 Oo6 **Biratori** Hokkaidō, NE Japan 42.35N 142.07E
41 S8 **Birch Creek** Alaska, USA 66.17N 145.54W
40 M11 **Birch Creek** ≈ Alaska, USA
9 T14 **Birch Hills** Saskatchewan, S Canada 52.58N 105.22W
190 M10 **Birchip** Victoria, SE Australia 36.01S 142.55E
31 X4 **Birch Lake** ◎ Minnesota, N USA
9 Q11 **Birch Mountains** ▲▲ Alberta, W Canada
9 V15 **Birch River** Manitoba, S Canada 52.22N 101.03W
46 H12 **Birchs Hill** hill W Jamaica 18.22N 78.05W
41 R11 **Birchwood** Alaska, USA 61.24N 149.28W
196 I5 **Bird Island** island S Northern Mariana Islands
143 N16 **Birecik** Şanlıurfa, S Turkey 37.02N 38.01E
158 M10 **Birendranagar** var. Surkhet. Mid Western, W Nepal 28.35N 81.36E
Bir es Saba see Be'ér Sheva'
76 A12 **Bir-Gandouz** SW Western Sahara 21.35N 16.27W
159 P12 **Birganj** Central, C Nepal 27.03N 84.53E
83 B14 **Biri** ≈ W Sudan
Bi'r Ibn Hirmās see Al Bi'r
176 Yy10 **Biri, Sungai** ≈ Papua, E Indonesia
149 U8 **Bīrjand** Khorāsān-e Janūbī, E Iran 32.54N 59.13E
145 T11 **Birkat Ḥāmid** well S Iraq 31.16N 44.04E
97 F18 **Birkeland** Aust-Agder, S Norway 58.18N 8.13E
103 E19 **Birkenfeld** Rheinland-Pfalz, SW Germany 49.39N 7.09E
99 K18 **Birkenhead** NW England, UK 53.24N 3.01W
111 W7 **Birkfeld** Steiermark, SE Austria 47.21N 15.40E
190 A2 **Birksgate Range** ▲▲ South Australia
Bîrlad see Bârlad
99 K20 **Birmingham** C England, UK 52.30N 1.49W
25 P4 **Birmingham** Alabama, S USA 33.30N 86.47W
99 M20 **Birmingham** ✕ C England, UK 52.27N 1.46W
Bir Moghrein see Bîr Mogreïn
78 J4 **Bîr Mogreïn** var. Bir Moghrein; prev. Fort-Trinquet. Tiris Zemmour, N Mauritania 25.10N 11.34W
203 S4 **Birnie Island** atoll Phoenix Islands, C Kiribati
Birni-Ngaouré see Birnin Gaouré
79 S12 **Birnin Gaouré** var. Birni-Ngaouré. Dosso, SW Niger 12.59N 3.02E
79 S12 **Birnin Kebbi** Kebbi, NW Nigeria 12.28N 4.08E
Birni-Nkonni see Birnin Konni
79 T12 **Birnin Konni** var. Birni-Nkonni. Tahoua, SW Niger 13.50N 5.14E
79 W13 **Birnin Kudu** Jigawa, N Nigeria 11.28N 9.29E
127 N16 **Birobidzhan** Yevreyskaya Avtonomnaya Oblast', SE Russian Federation 48.41N 132.55E
99 D18 **Birr** var. Parsonstown, Ir. Biorra. C Ireland 53.06N 7.54W
191 P4 **Birrie River** ≈ New South Wales/Queensland, SE Australia
110 D7 **Birse** ≈ NW Switzerland
Birsen see Biržai
110 E6 **Birsfelden** Basel-Land, NW Switzerland 47.33N 7.37E
131 U4 **Birsk** Respublika Bashkortostan, W Russian Federation 55.24N 55.33E
121 F14 **Birštonas** Kaunas, C Lithuania 54.37N 24.00E
165 P14 **Biru** Xinjiang Uygur Zizhiqu, W China 31.30N 93.55E
Biruni see Beruniy
126 Ii14 **Biryusa** ≈ C Russian Federation
126 Ii14 **Biryusinsk** Irkutskaya Oblast', C Russian Federation 55.52N 97.48E
120 G10 **Biržai** Ger. Birsen. Panevėžys, NE Lithuania 56.12N 24.47E
123 Jj17 **Birżebbuġa** SE Malta 35.50N 14.32E
Bisanthe see Tekirdağ
175 T9 **Bisa, Pulau** island Maluku, E Indonesia
39 N17 **Bisbee** Arizona, SW USA 31.27N 109.55W
31 O2 **Bisbee** North Dakota, N USA 48.36N 99.21W
Biscaia, Baía de see Biscay, Bay of
104 I13 **Biscarrosse et de Parentis, Étang de** ◎ SW France
106 M1 **Biscay, Bay of** Sp. Golfo de Vizcaya, Port. Baía de Biscaia. bay France/Spain
25 Z16 **Biscayne Bay** bay Florida, SE USA
66 M7 **Biscay Plain** undersea feature SE Bay of Biscay
109 N17 **Bisceglie** Puglia, SE Italy 41.13N 16.31E
Bischoflack see Škofja Loka
Bischofsburg see Biskupiec
111 Q7 **Bischofshofen** Salzburg, NW Austria 47.25N 13.13E
103 P15 **Bischofswerda** Sachsen, E Germany 51.07N 14.13E
105 V5 **Bischwiller** Bas-Rhin, NE France 48.46N 7.52E
23 T10 **Biscoe** North Carolina, SE USA 35.20N 79.46W
204 G5 **Biscoe Islands** island group Antarctica
12 E9 **Biscotasi Lake** ◎ Ontario, S Canada
12 E9 **Biscotasing** Ontario, S Canada 47.16N 82.04W
56 J6 **Biscucuy** Portuguesa, NW Venezuela 9.22N 69.58W
116 K11 **Biser** Khaskovo, S Bulgaria 41.52N 25.58E
115 D15 **Biševo** It. Busi. island SW Croatia
147 N12 **Bīshah, Wādī** dry watercourse C Saudi Arabia
153 U7 **Bishkek** var. Pishpek; prev. Frunze. ● (Kyrgyzstan) Chuyskaya Oblast', N Kyrgyzstan 42.53N 74.26E
153 U7 **Bishkek** ✕ Chuyskaya Oblast', N Kyrgyzstan 42.55N 74.37E
159 R16 **Bishnupur** West Bengal, NE India 23.04N 87.19E
85 J25 **Bisho** Eastern Cape, S South Africa 32.46S 27.21E
37 S9 **Bishop** California, W USA 37.22N 118.24W
27 S15 **Bishop** Texas, SW USA 27.36N 97.49W
99 L15 **Bishop Auckland** N England, UK 54.40N 1.40W
Bishop's Lynn see King's Lynn
99 O21 **Bishop's Stortford** E England, UK 51.45N 0.12E
23 S12 **Bishopville** South Carolina, SE USA 34.13N 80.15W
144 M5 **Bishrī, Jabal** ▲▲ E Syria
169 U4 **Bishui** Heilongjiang, NE China 52.06N 123.42E
83 G17 **Bisina, Lake** prev. Lake Salisbury. ◎ E Uganda
Biskara see Biskra
76 L6 **Biskra** var. Beskra, Biskara. NE Algeria 34.51N 5.44E
112 M8 **Biskupiec** Ger. Bischofsburg. Warmińsko-Mazurskie, NE Poland 53.51N 20.56E
179 Rr15 **Bislig** Mindanao, S Philippines 8.10N 126.18E
29 X6 **Bismarck** Missouri, C USA 37.46N 90.37W
30 M5 **Bismarck** state capital North Dakota, N USA 46.48N 100.46W
194 K9 **Bismarck Archipelago** island group NE PNG
133 Z16 **Bismarck Plate** tectonic feature W Pacific Ocean
194 I12 **Bismarck Range** ▲▲ N PNG
194 J10 **Bismarck Sea** sea W Pacific Ocean
143 P15 **Bismil** Diyarbakır, SE Turkey 37.52N 40.37E
45 N6 **Bismuna, Laguna** lagoon NE Nicaragua
Bisnulok see Phitsanulok
175 T6 **Bisoa, Tanjung** headland Pulau Halmahera, N Indonesia 2.15N 127.57E
30 K7 **Bison** South Dakota, N USA 45.30N 102.25W
95 H17 **Bispfors** Jämtland, C Sweden 63.00N 16.40E
78 G13 **Bissau** ● (Guinea-Bissau) W Guinea-Bissau 11.52N 15.39W
78 G13 **Bissau** ✕ W Guinea-Bissau 11.53N 15.41W
101 M24 **Bissen** Luxembourg, C Luxembourg 49.46N 6.04E
Bissojohka see Børselv
78 G12 **Bissorã** W Guinea-Bissau 12.16N 15.34W
9 O10 **Bistcho Lake** ◎ Alberta, W Canada
24 G5 **Bistineau, Lake** ▣ Louisiana, S USA
Bistrica see Ilirska Bistrica
118 I9 **Bistriţa** Ger. Bistritz, Hung. Beszterce; prev. Nösen. Bistriţa-Năsăud, N Romania 47.10N 24.30E
118 K10 **Bistriţa** Ger. Bistritz. ≈ NE Romania
118 I9 **Bistriţa-Năsăud** ◈ county N Romania
Bistritz see Bistriţa
Bistritz ober Pernstein see Bystřice nad Pernštejnem
158 L11 **Biswān** Uttar Pradesh, N India 27.30N 81.00E
112 M7 **Bisztynek** Warmińsko-Mazurskie, NE Poland 54.05N 20.53E
81 E17 **Bitam** Woleu-Ntem, N Gabon 2.04N 11.30E
103 D18 **Bitburg** Rheinland-Pfalz, SW Germany 49.57N 6.31E
105 U4 **Bitche** Moselle, NE France 49.01N 7.27E
80 I11 **Bitkine** Guéra, C Chad 11.58N 18.13E
143 R15 **Bitlis** Bitlis, SE Turkey 38.22N 42.04E
143 R14 **Bitlis** ◈ province E Turkey
Bitoeng see Bitung
115 N20 **Bitola** Turk. Monastir; prev. Bitolj. S FYR Macedonia 41.01N 21.21E
Bitolj see Bitola
109 O17 **Bitonto** anc. Butuntum. Puglia, SE Italy 41.07N 16.40E
79 Q13 **Bitou** var. Bittou. SE Burkina 11.19N 0.16W
161 C20 **Bitra Island** island Lakshadweep, India, N Indian Ocean
103 M14 **Bitterfeld** Sachsen-Anhalt, E Germany 51.36N 12.18E
34 O9 **Bitterroot Range** ▲▲ Idaho/Montana, NW USA
35 P10 **Bitterroot River** ≈ Montana, NW USA
109 D18 **Bitti** Sardegna, Italy, C Mediterranean Sea 40.30N 9.31E
Bittou see Bitou
175 S7 **Bitung** prev. Bitoeng. Sulawesi, C Indonesia 1.28N 125.13E
62 I12 **Bituruna** Paraná, S Brazil 26.11S 51.34W
79 Y13 **Biu** Borno, E Nigeria 10.35N 12.13E
Biumba see Byumba
171 H14 **Biwa-ko** ◎ Honshū, SW Japan
176 Y13 **Biwarlaut** Papua, E Indonesia 5.44S 138.14E
29 P10 **Bixby** Oklahoma, C USA 35.56N 95.52W
126 H15 **Biya** ≈ S Russian Federation
Biy-Khem see Bol'shoy Yenisey
126 H15 **Biysk** Altayskiy Kray, S Russian Federation 52.34N 85.09E
170 Ff14 **Bizen** Okayama, Honshū, SW Japan 34.43N 134.10E
Bizerta see Bizerte
123 K11 **Bizerte** Ar. Banzart, Eng. Bizerta. N Tunisia 37.18N 9.48E
Bizkaia see Vizcaya
94 G2 **Bjargtangar** headland W Iceland 63.30N 24.28W
Bjärnå see Perniö
97 K22 **Bjärnum** Skåne, S Sweden 56.15N 13.45E
95 I16 **Bjästa** Västernorrland, C Sweden 63.12N 18.30E
115 I14 **Bjelašnica** ▲ SE Bosnia and Herzegovina 43.13N 18.18E
114 C10 **Bjelolasica** ▲ NW Croatia 45.13N 14.56E
114 F8 **Bjelovar** Hung. Belovár. Bjelovar-Bilogora, N Croatia 45.54N 16.49E
114 F8 **Bjelovar-Bilogora** off. Bjelovarsko-Bilogorska Županija. ◈ province NE Croatia
Bjelovarsko-Bilogorska Županija see Bjelovar-Bilogora
94 H10 **Bjerkvik** Nordland, C Norway 68.31N 16.08E
97 G21 **Bjerringbro** Viborg, NW Denmark 56.22N 9.40E
Bjeshkët e Namuna see North Albanian Alps
97 L14 **Björbo** Dalarna, C Sweden 60.28N 14.44E
97 I15 **Bjørkelangen** Akershus, S Norway 59.52N 11.34E
97 O14 **Björklinge** Uppsala, C Sweden 60.03N 17.33E
95 I14 **Björksele** Västerbotten, N Sweden 64.58N 18.30E
95 I16 **Björna** Västernorrland, C Sweden 63.34N 18.38E
97 C14 **Bjørnafjorden** fjord S Norway
97 L16 **Björneborg** Värmland, C Sweden 59.13N 14.15E
Björneborg see Pori
97 E14 **Bjornesfjorden** ◎ S Norway
94 M9 **Bjørnevatn** Finnmark, N Norway 69.40N 29.57E
207 T13 **Bjørnøya** Eng. Bear Island. island N Norway
95 I15 **Bjurholm** Västerbotten, N Sweden 63.57N 19.16E
97 J22 **Bjuv** Skåne, S Sweden 56.04N 12.57E
78 M12 **Bla** Ségou, W Mali 12.58N 5.45W
189 W8 **Blackall** Queensland, E Australia 24.25S 145.31E
31 V2 **Black Bay** lake bay Minnesota, N USA
29 N9 **Black Bear Creek** ≈ Oklahoma, C USA
99 K17 **Blackburn** NW England, UK 53.45N 2.28W
47 W10 **Blackburne** ✕ (Plymouth) E Montserrat 16.45N 62.09W
41 T11 **Blackburn, Mount** ▲ Alaska, USA 61.43N 143.25W
37 N5 **Black Butte Lake** ▣ California, W USA
204 J5 **Black Coast** physical region Antarctica
9 Q16 **Black Diamond** Alberta, SW Canada 50.42N 114.09W
20 K11 **Black Dome** ▲ New York, NE USA 42.16N 74.07W
115 L18 **Black Drin** Alb. Lumi i Drinit të Zi, SCr. Crni Drim. ≈ Albania/FYR Macedonia
10 D6 **Black Duck** ≈ Ontario, C Canada
31 U4 **Blackduck** Minnesota, N USA 47.45N 94.33W
35 R14 **Blackfoot** Idaho, NW USA 43.11N 112.20W
35 P9 **Blackfoot River** ≈ Montana, NW USA
Black Forest see Schwarzwald
30 J10 **Blackhawk** South Dakota, N USA 44.09N 103.18W
30 I10 **Black Hills** ▲▲ South Dakota/Wyoming, N USA
9 T10 **Black Lake** ◎ Saskatchewan, C Canada
33 Q5 **Black Lake** ◎ Michigan, N USA
20 I7 **Black Lake** ◎ New York, NE USA
24 G6 **Black Lake** ▣ Louisiana, S USA
28 F7 **Black Mesa** ▲ Oklahoma, C USA 37.00N 103.07W
23 P10 **Black Mountain** North Carolina, SE USA 35.37N 82.19W
37 P13 **Black Mountain** ▲ California, W USA 35.22N 120.21W
39 Q2 **Black Mountain** ▲ Colorado, C USA 40.47N 107.23W
23 O7 **Black Mountain** ▲ Kentucky, E USA 36.54N 82.53W
98 K1 **Black Mountains** ▲▲ SE Wales, UK
38 H10 **Black Mountains** ▲▲ Arizona, SW USA
35 Q16 **Black Pine Peak** ▲ Idaho, NW USA 42.07N 113.07W
99 K17 **Blackpool** NW England, UK 53.49N 3.03W

◆ Country
● Country Capital
◇ Dependent Territory
○ Dependent Territory Capital
◈ Administrative Region
✕ International Airport
▲ Mountain
▲▲ Mountain Range
⩘ Volcano
≈ River
◎ Lake
▣ Reservoir

39 Q14 **Black Range** ▲ New Mexico, SW USA

46 I12 **Black River** W Jamaica 18.01N 77.52W

12 J14 **Black River** Ontario, SE Canada

133 U12 **Black River** *Chin.* Babian Jiang, Lixian Jiang, *Fr.* Rivière Noire, *Vtn.* Sông Đa. ✍ China/Vietnam

46 I12 **Black River** ✍ W Jamaica

41 T7 **Black River** ✍ Alaska, USA

39 N13 **Black River** ✍ Arizona, SW USA

29 X7 **Black River** ✍ Arkansas/ Missouri, C USA

24 I7 **Black River** ✍ Louisiana, S USA

33 S8 **Black River** ✍ Michigan, N USA

33 Q5 **Black River** ✍ Michigan, N USA

20 I8 **Black River** ✍ New York, NE USA

23 T3 **Black River** ✍ South Carolina, SE USA

32 J7 **Black River** ✍ Wisconsin, N USA

32 J7 **Black River Falls** Wisconsin, N USA 44.18N 90.51W

37 R3 **Black Rock Desert** *desert* Nevada, W USA
Black Sand Desert *see* Garagum

23 S7 **Blacksburg** Virginia, NE USA 37.16N 80.24W

142 H10 **Black Sea** *var.* Euxine Sea, *Bul.* Cherno More, *Rom.* Marea Neagră, *Rus.* Chernoye More, *Turk.* Karadeniz, *Ukr.* Chorne More. *sea* Asia/Europe

119 Q10 **Black Sea Lowland** *Ukr.* Prychornomors'ka Nyzovyna. *depression* SE Europe

35 S17 **Blacks Fork** ✍ Wyoming, C USA

25 V7 **Blackshear** Georgia, SE USA 31.18N 82.14W

25 V7 **Blackshear, Lake** ⊞ Georgia, SE USA

99 A16 **Blacksod Bay** *Ir.* Cuan an Fhóid Duibh. *inlet* W Ireland

23 W7 **Blackstone** Virginia, NE USA 37.04N 78.00W

79 O14 **Black Volta** *var.* Borongo, Mouhoun, Moun Hou, *Fr.* Volta Noire. ✍ W Africa

25 O5 **Black Warrior River** ✍ Alabama, S USA

189 X8 **Blackwater** Queensland, E Australia 23.34S 148.51E

99 D20 **Blackwater** *Ir.* An Abhainn Mhór. ✍ S Ireland

29 T4 **Blackwater River** ✍ Missouri, C USA

23 W7 **Blackwater River** ✍ Virginia, NE USA
Blackwater State *see* Nebraska

29 N8 **Blackwell** Oklahoma, C USA 36.48N 97.16W

27 P7 **Blackwell** Texas, SW USA 32.05N 100.19W

101 J15 **Bladel** Noord-Brabant, S Netherlands 51.22N 5.13E
Bladenmarkt *see* Bălăuseri

116 G11 **Blagoevgrad** *prev.* Gorna Dzhumaya. Blagoevgrad, SW Bulgaria 42.01N 23.04E

116 G11 **Blagoevgrad** ◆ *province* SW Bulgaria

126 Gg14 **Blagoveshchenka** Altayskiy Kray, S Russian Federation 52.49N 79.54E

126 M16 **Blagoveshchensk** Amurskaya Oblast', SE Russian Federation 50.19N 127.30E

131 V4 **Blagoveshchensk** Respublika Bashkortostan, W Russian Federation 55.03N 56.01E

104 I7 **Blain** Loire-Atlantique, NW France 47.26N 1.47W

31 V8 **Blaine** Minnesota, N USA 45.09N 93.13W

34 H6 **Blaine** Washington, NW USA 48.59N 122.45W

9 T15 **Blaine Lake** Saskatchewan, S Canada 52.49N 106.48W

31 S14 **Blair** Nebraska, C USA 41.32N 96.07W

98 J10 **Blairgowrie** C Scotland, UK 56.18N 3.24W

20 C15 **Blairsville** Pennsylvania, NE USA 40.25N 79.12W

118 H11 **Blaj** *Ger.* Blasendorf, *Hung.* Balázsfalva. Alba, SW Romania 46.10N 23.56E

66 F9 **Blake-Bahama Ridge** *undersea feature* W Atlantic Ocean

25 S7 **Blakely** Georgia, SE USA 31.22N 84.55W

66 E10 **Blake Plateau** *var.* Blake Terrace. *undersea feature* W Atlantic Ocean

32 M1 **Blake Point** *headland* Michigan, N USA 48.11N 88.25W
Blake Terrace *see* Blake Plateau

B24 **Blanca, Bahía** *bay* E Argentina

58 C12 **Blanca, Cordillera** ▲ W Peru

107 T12 **Blanca, Costa** *physical region* SE Spain

39 S7 **Blanca Peak** ▲ Colorado, C USA 37.34N 105.29W

26 I9 **Blanca, Sierra** ▲ Texas, SW USA 31.15N 105.26W

123 K11 **Blanc, Cap** *headland* N Tunisia 37.20N 9.41E
Blanc, Cap *see* Nouâdhibou, Râs

33 R12 **Blanchard River** ✍ Ohio, N USA

190 E8 **Blanche, Cape** *headland* South Australia 33.03S 134.10E

195 U15 **Blanche Channel** *channel* NW Solomon Islands

190 J4 **Blanche, Lake** ⊞ South Australia

33 R14 **Blanchester** Ohio, N USA 39.17N 83.59W

190 J9 **Blanchetown** South Australia 34.21S 139.36E

47 U13 **Blanchisseuse** Trinidad, Trinidad and Tobago 10.47N 61.18W

105 T11 **Blanc, Mont** *It.* Monte Bianco. ▲ France/Italy 45.45N 6.51E

27 R11 **Blanco** Texas, SW USA 30.06N 98.25W

54 K14 **Blanco, Cabo** *headland* NW Costa Rica 9.34N 85.06W

34 D14 **Blanco, Cape** *headland* Oregon, NW USA 42.49N 124.33W

64 H10 **Blanco, Río** ✍ W Argentina

27 V5 **Blossom** Texas, SW USA 33.39N 95.23W

64 H10 **Blanco, Río** ✍ NE Peru

13 O9 **Blanc, Réservoir** ⊞ Québec, SE Canada

23 R7 **Bland** Virginia, NE USA 37.06N 81.07W

14 **Bland** ✍ Iceland

39 O7 **Blanding** Utah, W USA 37.37N 109.28W

107 X5 **Blanes** Cataluña, NE Spain 41.40N 2.48E

105 N3 **Blangy-sur-Bresle** Seine-Maritime, N France 49.55N 1.37E

113 C18 **Blanice** *Ger.* Blanitz. ✍ S Czech Republic
Blanitz *see* Blanice

101 C16 **Blankenberge** West-Vlaanderen, NW Belgium 51.19N 3.07E

103 D17 **Blankenheim** Nordrhein-Westfalen, W Germany 50.25N 6.41E

27 R8 **Blanket** Texas, SW USA 31.49N 98.47W

57 O3 **Blanquilla, Isla** *var.* La Blanquilla. *island* N Venezuela
Blanquilla, La *see* Blanquilla, Isla

63 F18 **Blanquillo** Durazno, C Uruguay 32.52S 55.37W

113 G18 **Blansko** *Ger.* Blanz. Jihomoravský Kraj, SE Czech Republic 49.22N 16.39E

85 N15 **Blantyre** *var.* Blantyre-Limbe. Southern, S Malawi 15.45S 35.03E

85 N15 **Blantyre** ✈ Southern, S Malawi 15.34S 35.03E
Blantyre-Limbe *see* Blantyre
Blanz *see* Blansko

100 J10 **Blaricum** Noord-Holland, C Netherlands 52.16N 5.15E
Blasendorf *see* Blaj
Blatnitsa *see* Durankulak

115 F15 **Blato** *It.* Blatta. Dubrovnik-Neretva, S Croatia 42.57N 16.47E
Blatta *see* Blato

113 D17 **Blatten** Valais, SW Switzerland 46.22N 8.00E

103 J22 **Blaufelden** Baden-Württemberg, SW Germany 49.12N 10.01E

97 E23 **Blåvands Huk** *headland* W Denmark 55.33N 8.04E

104 G6 **Blavet** ✍ NW France

104 J11 **Blaye** Gironde, SW France 45.07N 0.36W

191 R8 **Blayney** New South Wales, SE Australia 33.33S 149.13E

67 D25 **Bleaker Island** *island* SE Falkland Islands

111 T10 **Bled** *Ger.* Veldes. NW Slovenia 46.23N 14.06E

101 D20 **Bléharies** Hainaut, SW Belgium 50.30N 3.25E

111 U9 **Bleiburg** *Slvn.* Pliberk. Kärnten, S Austria 46.36N 14.49E

113 L17 **Bleiloch-Stausee** ⊞ C Germany

100 H12 **Bleiswijk** Zuid-Holland, W Netherlands 52.01N 4.31E

97 L22 **Blekinge** ◆ *county* S Sweden

12 D17 **Blenheim** Ontario, S Canada 42.19N 81.58W

193 K15 **Blenheim** Marlborough, South Island, NZ 41.31S 174.00E

101 M15 **Blerick** Limburg, SE Netherlands 51.22N 6.10E
Blesae *see* Blois

9 N15 **Blue River** British Columbia, SW Canada 52.03N 119.21W

27 O12 **Blue River** ✍ Oklahoma, C USA

29 R4 **Blue Springs** Missouri, C USA 39.01N 94.16W

23 R6 **Bluestone Lake** ⊞ West Virginia, NE USA

193 C25 **Bluff** Southland, South Island, NZ 46.36S 168.22E

39 O8 **Bluff** Utah, W USA 37.15N 109.36W

20 P8 **Bluff City** Tennessee, S USA 36.28N 82.15W

67 E24 **Bluff Cove** East Falkland, Falkland Islands 51.44S 58.10W

27 S7 **Bluff Dale** Texas, SW USA 32.18N 98.01W

191 N15 **Bluff Hill Point** *headland* Tasmania, SE Australia 41.03S 144.35E

97 O20 **Blåa** Dalarna, C Sweden 61.00N 15.15E

97 L19 **Bladafors** Jönköping, S Sweden 57.30N 14.40E

126 Kk13 **Bludaybo** Irkutskaya Oblast', S Russian Federation 57.52N 114.04E

24 **Blue**, Bayou *var.* Bodcau Creek. ✍ Louisiana, S USA
Bodcau Creek *see* Bodcau, Bayou

46 D8 **Bodden Town** *var.* Boddentown. Grand Cayman, SW Cayman Islands 19.17N 81.10W

103 K14 **Bode** ✍ C Germany

36 L7 **Bodega Head** *headland* California, W USA 38.16N 123.04W

100 H11 **Bodegraven** Zuid-Holland, C Netherlands 52.04N 4.45E

79 Y16 **Bodélé** *depression* W Chad

94 J13 **Boden** Norrbotten, N Sweden 65.49N 21.43E
Bodensee *see* Constance, Lake, C Europe

67 M15 **Bode Verde Fracture Zone** *tectonic feature* E Atlantic Ocean

161 H14 **Bodhan** Andhra Pradesh, C India 18.40N 77.51E
Bodi *see* Imni

161 H22 **Bodināyakkanūr** Tamil Nādu, SE India 10.01N 77.18E

110 H10 **Bodio** Ticino, S Switzerland 46.23N 8.55E

99 I24 **Bodmin** SW England, UK 50.28N 4.43W

99 I24 **Bodmin Moor** *moorland* SW England, UK

94 E11 **Bodø** Nordland, C Norway 67.18N 14.26E

164 K6 **Bodrum** *var.* Bagrax. Xinjiang Uygur Zizhiqu, NW China 42.00N 86.28E

142 B16 **Bodrum** Muğla, SW Turkey 37.03N 27.28E
Bodzafordulo *see* Intorsura Buzăului

12 F13 **Boat Lake** ⊞ Ontario, S Canada

60 F10 **Boa Vista** *state capital* Roraima, NW Brazil 2.51N 60.43W

60 F10 **Boa Vista** *island* Ilhas de Barlavento, E Cape Verde

78 H9 **Boaz** Alabama, S USA 34.12N 86.10W

166 L15 **Bobai** Guangxi Zhuangzu Zizhiqu, S China 22.09N 109.57E

161 M14 **Bobbili** Andhra Pradesh, E India 18.33N 83.25E

191 R12 **Bombala** New South Wales, SE Australia 36.54S 149.15E
106 F10 **Bombarral** Leiria, C Portugal 39.15N 9.09W
Bombay see Mumbai
176 Vv11 **Bomberai** ≈ Papua, E Indonesia
176 Vv11 **Bomberai, Jazirah** peninsula Papua, E Indonesia
176 Vv11 **Bomberai, Semenanjung** headland Papua, E Indonesia 3.01S 133.25E
83 F18 **Bombo** S Uganda 0.38N 32.31E
168 I8 **Bömbögör** var. Dzadgay. Bayanhongor, C Mongolia 46.12N 99.29E
81 I17 **Bomongo** Equateur, NW Dem. Rep. Congo 2.22N 19.03E
61 I14 **Bom Futuro** Pará, N Brazil 6.27S 54.44W
165 Q15 **Bomi** var. Bowo, Zhamo. Xizang Zizhiqu, W China 29.43N 96.12E
81 N17 **Bomili** Orientale, NE Dem. Rep. Congo 1.45N 27.01E
61 N17 **Bom Jesus da Lapa** Bahia, E Brazil 13.16S 43.22W
62 Q8 **Bom Jesus do Itabapoana** Rio de Janeiro, SE Brazil 21.07S 41.43W
97 C15 **Bømlafjorden** fjord S Norway
97 B15 **Bømlo** island S Norway
126 M14 **Bomnak** Amurskaya Oblast', SE Russian Federation 54.43N 128.50E
81 I17 **Bomongo** Equateur, NW Dem. Rep. Congo 1.22N 18.21E
63 K14 **Bom Retiro** Santa Catarina, S Brazil 27.52S 49.33W
81 L15 **Bomu** var. Mbomou, Mbomu, M'Bomu. ≈ Central African Republic/Dem. Rep. Congo
148 J3 **Bonāb** var. Benāb, Bunab. Āzarbāyjān-e Sharqi, N Iran 37.24N 45.59E
47 Q16 **Bonaire** island E Netherlands Antilles
41 U11 **Bona, Mount** ▲ Alaska, USA 61.22N 141.45W
194 M16 **Bonando** ≈ SE Papau New Guinea
191 Q12 **Bonang** Victoria, SE Australia 37.13S 148.43E
44 L7 **Bonanza** Región Autónoma Atlántico Norte, NE Nicaragua 13.58N 84.37W
39 O4 **Bonanza** Utah, W USA 40.01N 109.12W
47 O9 **Bonao** C Dominican Republic 18.55N 70.25W
188 L3 **Bonaparte Archipelago** island group Western Australia
34 K6 **Bonaparte, Mount** ▲ Washington, NW USA 48.47N 119.07W
41 N11 **Bonasila Dome** ▲ Alaska, USA 62.24N 160.28W
94 H11 **Bonåsjøen** Nordland, C Norway 67.35S 15.39E
47 S15 **Bonasse** Trinidad, Trinidad and Tobago 10.02N 61.48W
13 X7 **Bonaventure** Québec, SE Canada 48.03N 65.30W
13 X7 **Bonaventure** ≈ Québec, SE Canada
11 V11 **Bonavista** Newfoundland and Labrador, SE Canada 48.36N 53.07W
11 U11 **Bonavista Bay** inlet NW Atlantic Ocean
123 Kk11 **Bon, Cap** headland N Tunisia 37.05N 11.04E
81 E19 **Bonda** Ogooué-Lolo, C Gabon 0.50S 12.28E
131 N6 **Bondari** Tambovskaya Oblast', W Russian Federation 52.58N 42.02E
108 G9 **Bondeno** Emilia-Romagna, C Italy 44.53N 11.24E
32 L4 **Bond Falls Flowage** ☒ Michigan, N USA
81 O15 **Bondo** Orientale, N Dem. Rep. Congo 3.51N 23.41E
175 Pp13 **Bondokodi** Pulau Sumba, S Indonesia 9.36S 119.01E
79 O15 **Bondoukou** E Ivory Coast 8.03N 2.45W
Bondoukou/Bondoukuy see Bondoukui
174 Mm15 **Bondowoso** Jawa, C Indonesia 7.54S 113.49E
35 S14 **Bondurant** Wyoming, C USA 43.14N 110.26W
Bône see Annaba, Algeria
Bône see Watampone, Indonesia
32 I5 **Bone Lake** ☒ Wisconsin, N USA
175 Pp14 **Bonelipu** Pulau Buton, C Indonesia 4.42S 123.09E
175 Q14 **Bonerate, Kepulauan** var. Macan. island group C Indonesia
175 Pp15 **Bonerate, Pulau** island Kepulauan Bonerate, C Indonesia
31 O12 **Bonesteel** South Dakota, N USA 43.01N 98.55W
64 I8 **Bonete, Cerro** ▲ N Argentina 27.58S 68.22W
175 Pp11 **Bone, Teluk** bay Sulawesi, C Indonesia
110 D6 **Bonfol** Jura, NW Switzerland 47.28N 7.08E
159 U12 **Bongaigaon** Assam, NE India 26.30N 90.30E
81 K17 **Bonganga** Equateur, NW Dem. Rep. Congo 1.30N 21.03E
80 L13 **Bongo, Massif des** var. Chaîne des Mongos. ▲ NE Central African Republic
80 G12 **Bongor** Mayo-Kébbi, SW Chad 10.18N 15.19E
79 N16 **Bongouanou** E Ivory Coast 6.39N 4.12W
178 Kk11 **Bông Son** var. Hoai Nhon. Binh Dinh, C Vietnam 14.28N 109.00E
25 U7 **Bonham** Texas, SW USA 33.34N 96.10W
Bonhard see Bonyhád
105 U6 **Bonhomme, Col du** pass NE France 48.10N 7.07E
105 Y16 **Bonifacio** Corse, France, C Mediterranean Sea 41.23N 9.09E
Bonifacio, Bocche de/Bonifacio, Bouches de see Bonifacio, Strait of
105 Y16 **Bonifacio, Strait of** Fr. Bouches de Bonifacio, It. Bocche di Bonifacio. strait C Mediterranean Sea

25 Q8 **Bonifay** Florida, SE USA 30.49N 85.42W
Bonin Islands see Ogasawara-shotō
199 N6 **Bonin Trench** undersea feature NW Pacific Ocean
25 W15 **Bonita Springs** Florida, SE USA 26.19N 81.48W
44 I5 **Bonito, Pico** ▲ N Honduras 15.33N 86.55W
103 J21 **Bonn** Nordrhein-Westfalen, W Germany 50.43N 7.06E
12 J12 **Bonnechere** Ontario, SE Canada 45.39N 77.36W
12 J12 **Bonnechere** ≈ Ontario, SE Canada
35 N7 **Bonners Ferry** Idaho, NW USA 48.41N 116.19W
29 R4 **Bonner Springs** Kansas, C USA 39.03N 94.52W
104 I6 **Bonnétable** Sarthe, NW France 48.09N 0.24E
29 X6 **Bonne Terre** Missouri, C USA 37.55N 90.33W
8 J5 **Bonnet Plume** ≈ Yukon Territory, NW Canada
104 M6 **Bonneval** Eure-et-Loir, C France 48.12N 1.23E
105 T10 **Bonneville** Haute-Savoie, E France 46.04N 6.25E
36 J3 **Bonneville Salt Flats** salt flat Utah, W USA
78 V18 **Bonny** Rivers, S Nigeria 4.25N 7.13E
Bonny, Bight of see Biafra, Bight of
39 W4 **Bonny Reservoir** ☒ Colorado, C USA
9 R14 **Bonnyville** Alberta, SW Canada 54.16N 110.46W
109 C18 **Bono** Sardegna, Italy, C Mediterranean Sea 40.24N 9.01E
176 Xx10 **Bonoi** Papua, E Indonesia 1.46S 137.45E
Bononia see Vidin, Bulgaria
Bononia see Boulogne-sur-Mer, France
109 B18 **Bonorva** Sardegna, Italy, C Mediterranean Sea 40.27N 8.46E
32 M15 **Bonpas Creek** ≈ Illinois, N USA
202 J3 **Bonriki** Tarawa, W Kiribati 1.22N 173.09E
191 T4 **Bonshaw** New South Wales, SE Australia 29.06S 151.15E
179 P8 **Bontoc** Luzon, N Philippines 17.04N 120.58E
190 M16 **Bonthe** SW Sierra Leone 7.26N 12.32W
194 M16 **Bonua** ≈ S PNG
27 Y9 **Bon Wier** Texas, SW USA 30.43N 93.40W
113 J25 **Bonyhád** Ger. Bonhard. Tolna, S Hungary 46.17N 18.31E
Bonzabaai see Bonza Bay
85 J25 **Bonza Bay** Afr. Bonzabaai. Eastern Cape, S Africa 32.58S 27.58E
190 D7 **Bookabie** South Australia 31.49S 132.41E
190 H6 **Bookaloo** South Australia 31.56S 137.21E
36 J2 **Book Cliffs** cliff Colorado/Utah, W USA
175 Tr9 **Boo, Kepulauan** island group E Indonesia
27 P1 **Booker** Texas, SW USA 36.27N 100.32W
78 K15 **Boola** S Guinea 8.22N 8.40W
191 O8 **Booligal** New South Wales, SE Australia 33.56S 144.54E
101 G17 **Boom** Antwerpen, N Belgium 51.05N 4.24E
45 N6 **Boom** var. Boon. Región Autónoma Atlántico Norte, NE Nicaragua 14.52N 83.36W
191 S3 **Boomi** New South Wales, SE Australia 28.43S 149.35E
Boon see Boom
31 V13 **Boone** Iowa, C USA 42.04N 93.52W
21 Q8 **Boone** North Carolina, SE USA 36.13N 81.40W
29 S8 **Booneville** Arkansas, C USA 35.08N 93.55W
20 M5 **Booneville** Kentucky, S USA 37.27N 83.41W
22 M3 **Booneville** Mississippi, S USA 34.39N 88.34W
21 V3 **Boonsboro** Maryland, NE USA 39.30N 77.39W
168 H9 **Böön Tsagaan Nuur** ☒ S Mongolia
36 L6 **Boonville** California, W USA 38.58N 123.21W
31 N16 **Boonville** Indiana, N USA 38.03N 87.16W
29 U4 **Boonville** Missouri, C USA 38.58N 92.44W
20 J9 **Boonville** New York, NE USA 43.28N 75.17W
82 M12 **Boorama** Awdal, NW Somalia 9.58N 43.15E
191 O6 **Boorindarra, Mount** hill New South Wales, SE Australia 31.07S 145.20E
191 N9 **Booroorban** New South Wales, SE Australia 34.55S 144.45E
191 R9 **Boorowa** New South Wales, SE Australia 34.28S 148.42E
101 H17 **Boortmeerbeek** Vlaams Brabant, C Belgium 50.58N 4.27E
82 P11 **Boosaaso** var. Bandar Kassim, Bender Qaasim, Bosaso, It. Bender Cassim. Bari, N Somalia 11.26N 49.37E
21 Q8 **Boothbay Harbor** Maine, NE USA 43.52N 69.35W
Boothia Felix see Boothia Peninsula
15 Kk2 **Boothia, Gulf of** gulf Nunavut, NE Canada
15 K2 **Boothia Peninsula** prev. Boothia Felix. peninsula Nunavut, NE Canada
81 E18 **Booué** Ogooué-Ivindo, NE Gabon 0.03S 11.58E
47 O6 **Boquerón** ◊ department W Paraguay
44 M4 **Boquerón** var. Boon. Departamento de Boquerón. ◊ department W Paraguay
45 P15 **Boquete** var. Bajo Boquete. Chiriquí, W Panama 8.45N 82.26W
42 J6 **Boquilla, Presa de la** ☒ N Mexico

42 L5 **Boquillas** var. Boquillas del Carmen. Coahuila de Zaragoza, NE Mexico 29.10N 102.55W
Boquillas del Carmen see Boquillas
126 I11 **Bor** Krasnoyarskiy Kray, C Russian Federation 61.28N 90.09E
83 F15 **Bor** Jonglei, S Sudan 6.12N 31.33E
97 L20 **Bor** Jönköping, S Sweden 57.04N 14.10E
142 J15 **Bor** Niğde, S Turkey 37.48N 34.30E
114 P12 **Bor** Serbia, E Serbia 44.05N 22.06E
203 S10 **Bora-Bora** island Îles Sous le Vent, W French Polynesia
178 Ii10 **Borabu** Maha Sarakham, E Thailand 16.01N 103.06E
35 P13 **Borah Peak** ▲ Idaho, NW USA 44.21N 113.53W
151 U16 **Boraldy** prev. Burunday. Almaty, SE Kazakhstan 43.21N 76.48E
150 G13 **Borankul** prev. Opornyy. Mangistau, SW Kazakhstan 46.09N 54.32E
97 J19 **Borås** Västra Götaland, S Sweden 57.43N 12.55E
149 N11 **Borāzjān** var. Borazjān. Būshehr, S Iran 29.19N 51.12E
Borazjān see Borāzjān
60 G13 **Borba** Amazonas, N Brazil 4.39S 59.34W
106 H11 **Borba** Évora, S Portugal 38.48N 7.28W
Borbetomagus see Worms
57 O7 **Borbón** Bolívar, E Venezuela 7.55N 64.03W
61 Q15 **Borborema, Planalto da** plateau NE Brazil
118 M14 **Borcea, Braţul** ≈ S Romania
Borchalo see Marneuli
205 R13 **Borchgrevink Coast** physical region Antarctica
143 Q11 **Borçka** Artvin, NE Turkey 41.24N 41.37E
100 N12 **Borculo** Gelderland, E Netherlands 52.07N 6.31E
190 G13 **Borda, Cape** headland South Australia 35.45S 136.34E
104 K13 **Bordeaux** anc. Burdigala. Gironde, SW France 44.49N 0.33W
7 T15 **Borden** Saskatchewan, S Canada 52.23N 107.10W
12 D8 **Borden Lake** ☒ Ontario, S Canada
15 L1 **Borden Peninsula** peninsula Baffin Island, Nunavut, NE Canada
190 K1 **Bordertown** South Australia 36.21S 140.48E
94 H2 **Bordheyri** Vestfirdhir, NW Iceland 65.12N 21.09W
94 I7 **Bordhoy** Dan. Bordø Island. Faeroe Islands 62.17N 6.30W
108 B11 **Bordighera** Liguria, NW Italy 43.48N 7.40E
76 K5 **Bordj-Bou-Arreridj** var. Bordj Bou Arreridj, Bordj Bou Arérridj. N Algeria 36.04N 4.45E
123 I10 **Bordj El Bahri, Cap de** headland N Algeria 36.52N 3.13E
76 L10 **Bordj Omar Driss** E Algeria 28.09N 6.52E
149 N13 **Bord Khūn** Hormozgān, S Iran
153 V7 **Bordunskiy** Chuyskaya Oblast', N Kyrgyzstan 42.37N 75.31E
97 M17 **Borensberg** Östergötland, S Sweden 58.33N 15.15E
Borgå see Porvoo
94 L2 **Borgarfjördhur** Austurland, NE Iceland 65.32N 13.46W
94 H3 **Borgarnes** Vesturland, W Iceland 64.33N 21.54W
95 G14 **Børgefjell** ▲ C Norway
100 O7 **Borger** Drenthe, NE Netherlands 52.54N 6.48E
27 N2 **Borger** Texas, SW USA 35.40N 101.24W
97 N20 **Borgholm** Kalmar, S Sweden 56.50N 16.40E
109 N22 **Borgia** Calabria, SW Italy 38.48N 16.28E
101 J18 **Borgloon** Limburg, NE Belgium 50.48N 5.21E
205 P2 **Borg Massif** ▲ Antarctica
24 L9 **Borgne, Lake** ☒ Louisiana, S USA
108 C7 **Borgomanero** Piemonte, NE Italy 45.42N 8.33E
108 G10 **Borgo Panigale** ✗ (Bologna) Emilia-Romagna, C Italy
111 R3 **Borgorose** Lazio, C Italy 42.10N 13.15E
108 A9 **Borgo San Dalmazzo** Piemonte, N Italy 44.19N 7.28E
108 G11 **Borgo San Lorenzo** Toscana, C Italy 43.58N 11.23E
108 F8 **Borgosesia** Piemonte, NE Italy 45.41N 8.21E
108 E9 **Borgo Val di Taro** Emilia-Romagna, C Italy 44.29N 9.48E
108 G6 **Borgo Valsugana** Trentino-Alto Adige, N Italy 46.04N 11.31E
Borhoyn Tal see Dzamīn-Üüd
176 I8 **Borikhan** var. Borikhane. Bolikhamxai, C Laos 18.36N 103.43E
Borikhane see Borikhan
Borislav see Boryslav
131 N8 **Borisoglebsk** Voronezhskaya Oblast', W Russian Federation 51.23N 42.00E
Borisov see Barysaw
Borisovgrad see Pürvomay
Borispol' see Boryspil'
180 I3 **Boriziny** Mahajanga, NW Madagascar 15.31S 47.40E
107 Q5 **Borja** Aragón, NE Spain 41.49N 1.31W
Borjas Blancas see Les Borges Blanques
113 S10 **Borjomi** Rus. Borzhomi. C Georgia 41.50N 43.24E
112 L12 **Borki** Rus. Borkovichi. Vitsyebskaya Voblasts', N Belarus 55.52N 28.20E
103 H16 **Borken** Hessen, C Germany 51.01N 9.16E
103 E14 **Borken** Nordrhein-Westfalen, W Germany 51.51N 6.52E
94 H11 **Borkenes** Troms, N Norway 68.46N 16.10E
80 H7 **Borkou-Ennedi-Tibesti** off. Préfecture du Borkou-Ennedi-Tibesti. ◊ prefecture N Chad
Borkovichi see Borki
103 N12 **Borkum** NW Germany

97 M14 **Borlänge** Dalarna, C Sweden 60.28N 15.25E
108 C9 **Bormida** ≈ NW Italy
108 C8 **Bormio** Lombardia, N Italy
103 M16 **Borna** Sachsen, E Germany 51.07N 12.30E
100 O10 **Borne** Overijssel, E Netherlands 52.18N 6.45E
101 F17 **Bornem** Antwerpen, N Belgium 51.06N 4.13E
174 M6 **Borneo** island Brunei/Indonesia/Malaysia
103 E16 **Bornheim** Nordrhein-Westfalen, W Germany 50.46N 7.06E
97 L24 **Bornholm** county E Denmark
97 L24 **Bornholm** island E Denmark
79 Y13 **Borno** state NE Nigeria
106 K15 **Bornos** Andalucía, S Spain 36.49N 5.42W
168 L7 **Bornuur** Töv, C Mongolia 48.28N 106.15E
119 O4 **Borodyanka** Kyyivs'ka Oblast', N Ukraine 50.40N 29.54E
126 M10 **Borogontsy** Respublika Sakha (Yakutiya), NE Russian Federation 62.42N 131.01E
164 I5 **Borohoro Shan** ▲ NW China
79 O13 **Boromo** SW Burkina 11.46N 2.54W
37 T13 **Boron** California, W USA 35.00N 117.42W
179 R12 **Borongan** Samar, C Philippines 11.26N 125.30E
Borongo see Black Volta
Boron'ki see Baron'ki
Borosjenő see Ineu
Borossebes see Sebiş
78 L15 **Borotou** NW Ivory Coast 8.46N 7.30W
119 W6 **Borova** Kharkivs'ka Oblast', E Ukraine 49.22N 37.39E
116 H8 **Borovan** Vratsa, NW Bulgaria 43.25N 23.45E
128 I14 **Borovichi** Novgorodskaya Oblast', W Russian Federation 58.23N 33.56E
Borovlje see Ferlach
114 J9 **Borovo** Vukovar-Srijem, NE Croatia 45.22N 18.57E
151 Q7 **Borovoye** Kaz. Būrabay. Akmola, N Kazakhstan 53.07N 70.19E
130 K4 **Borovsk** Kaluzhskaya Oblast', W Russian Federation 55.12N 36.22E
125 F12 **Borovskiy** Tyumenskaya Oblast', C Russian Federation 57.04N 65.37E
151 N7 **Borovskoy** Kostanay, N Kazakhstan 53.49N 64.12E
112 M13 **Borovukha** Vitsyebskaya Voblasts', N Belarus 55.27N 14.10E
97 M23 **Borrby** Skåne, S Sweden 55.27N 14.10E
189 R3 **Borroloola** Northern Territory, N Australia 16.09S 136.18E
118 F9 **Borş** Bihor, NW Romania 47.06N 21.47E
118 J10 **Borşa** Hung. Borsa. Maramureş, N Romania 47.40N 24.37E
118 J10 **Borsec** Ger. Bad Borseck, Hung. Borszék. Harghita, C Romania 46.57N 25.32E
94 K8 **Borselv** Lapp. Bissojohka. Finnmark, N Norway 70.18N 25.35E
115 L23 **Borsh** var. Borshi. Vlorë, S Albania 40.04N 19.51E
118 K7 **Borshchev** Pol. Borszczów, Rus. Borshchev. Ternopil's'ka Oblast', W Ukraine 48.48N 26.00E
Borshi see Borsh
113 L20 **Borsod-Abaúj-Zemplén** off. Borsod-Abaúj-Zemplén Megye. ◊ county NE Hungary
101 E15 **Borssele** Zeeland, SW Netherlands 51.26N 3.45E
Borszczów see Borshchiv
Borszék see Borsec
Bortala see Bole
105 O12 **Bort-les-Orgues** Corrèze, C France 45.20N 2.31E
148 L7 **Borüdjerd** var. Burujird, Burujerd. Lorestān, W Iran 33.55N 48.45E
118 H6 **Boryslav** Pol. Boryslaw, Rus. Borislav. L'viv's'ka Oblast', NW Ukraine 49.18N 23.28E
Boryslaw see Boryslav
119 P4 **Boryspil'** Rus. Borispol'. Kyyivs'ka Oblast', N Ukraine 50.20N 30.58E
119 R3 **Borzna** Chernihivs'ka Oblast', NE Ukraine 51.15N 32.25E
127 P16 **Borzya** Chitinskaya Oblast', S Russian Federation 50.18N 116.24E
109 B18 **Bosa** Sardegna, Italy, C Mediterranean Sea 40.18N 8.28E
114 F10 **Bosanska Dubica** var. Kozarska Dubica. Republika Srpska, NW Bosnia and Herzegovina 45.09N 16.47E
114 G10 **Bosanska Gradiška** var. Gradiška. Republika Srpska, N Bosnia and Herzegovina 45.09N 17.14E
114 F10 **Bosanska Kostajnica** var. Srpska Kostajnica. Republika Srpska, NW Bosnia and Herzegovina 45.12N 16.33E
114 E11 **Bosanska Krupa** var. Krupa, Krupa na Uni. Federacija Bosna I Hercegovina, NW Bosnia and Herzegovina 44.52N 16.09E
114 H10 **Bosanski Brod** var. Srpski Brod. Republika Srpska, N Bosnia and Herzegovina 45.07N 17.59E
114 M16 **Bosanski Novi** var. Novi Grad. Republika Srpska, NW Bosnia and Herzegovina 45.03N 16.22E
114 E11 **Bosanski Petrovac** var. Petrovac. Federacija Bosna I Herzegovina, NW Bosnia and Herzegovina 44.34N 16.21E
114 N12 **Bosanski Petrovac** Serbia, E Serbia 44.22N 21.25E
114 I10 **Bosanski Šamac** var. Šamac. N Bosnia and Herzegovina 6.57N 18.18E

114 E12 **Bosansko Grahovo** var. Grahovo, Hrvatsko Grahovo. Federacija Bosna I Hercegovina, W Bosnia and Herzegovina 44.10N 16.22E
Bosaso see Boosaaso
194 G13 **Bosavi, Mount** ▲ W PNG 6.33S 142.50E
166 J14 **Bose** Guangxi Zhuangzu Zizhiqu, S China 23.55N 106.31E
167 Q5 **Boshan** Shandong, E China 36.31N 117.46E
115 P16 **Bosilegrad** prev. Bosiljgrad. Serbia, SE Serbia 42.30N 22.30E
Bosiljgrad see Bosilegrad
Bösing see Pezinok
100 H12 **Boskoop** Zuid-Holland, C Netherlands 52.04N 4.40E
113 G18 **Boskovice** Ger. Boskowitz. Jihomoravský Kraj, SE Czech Republic 49.30N 16.39E
Boskowitz see Boskovice
176 U8 **Bosna** ≈ N Bosnia and Herzegovina
123 J11 **Bosna i Hercegovina, Federacija** ◊ republic Bosnia and Herzegovina
176 X9 **Bosnabraidi** Papua, E Indonesia 0.49S 136.00E
114 H12 **Bosnia and Herzegovina** off. Republic of Bosnia and Herzegovina. ◆ republic SE Europe
81 J16 **Bosobolo** Equateur, NW Dem. Rep. Congo 4.10N 19.55E
171 K17 **Bōsō-hantō** peninsula Honshū, S Japan
Bosora see Buşrá ash Shām
Bosphorus/Bosporus see İstanbul Boğazı
Bosporus Cimmerius see Kerch Strait
Bosporus Thracius see İstanbul Boğazı
Bosra see Buşrá ash Shām
81 H14 **Bossangoa** Ouham, C Central African Republic 6.31N 17.24E
Bossé Bangou see Bossey Bangou
81 I15 **Bossembélé** Ombella-Mpoko, C Central African Republic 5.13N 17.39E
81 H15 **Bossentélé** Ouham-Pendé, W Central African Republic 5.36N 16.37E
79 R12 **Bossey Bangou** var. Bossé Bangou. Tillabéri, SW Niger 13.22N 1.18E
24 G5 **Bossier City** Louisiana, S USA 32.31N 93.43W
85 D20 **Bossiesvlei** Hardap, S Namibia 25.01S 16.45E
79 Y11 **Bosso** Diffa, SE Niger 13.42N 13.18E
63 F15 **Bossoroca** Rio Grande do Sul, S Brazil 28.45S 54.54W
164 J10 **Bostan** Xinjiang Uygur Zizhiqu, W China 39.19N 83.15E
148 K3 **Bostānābād** Āzarbāyjān-e Sharqī, N Iran 37.52N 46.51E
164 K6 **Bosten Hu** var. Bagrax Hu. ☒ NW China
99 O18 **Boston** prev. St.Botolph's Town. E England, UK 52.58N 0.01W
21 O11 **Boston** state capital Massachusetts, NE USA 42.21N 71.03W
152 I9 **Bo'ston** Rus. Bustan. Qoraqalpog'iston Respublikasi, W Uzbekistan 41.49N 60.51E
8 M17 **Boston Bar** British Columbia, SW Canada 49.52N 121.22W
29 T10 **Boston Mountains** ▲ Arkansas, C USA
13 P8 **Bostonnais** ≈ Québec, SE Canada
114 J10 **Bosut** ≈ E Croatia
160 C11 **Botād** Gujarāt, W India 22.12N 71.43E
191 T9 **Botany Bay** inlet New South Wales, SE Australia
85 G19 **Boteti** var. Botletle. ≈ N Botswana
116 J9 **Botev** ▲ C Bulgaria 42.45N 24.57E
116 H9 **Botevgrad** prev. Orkhaniye. Sofiya, W Bulgaria 42.55N 23.47E
85 J16 **Bothaville** Free State, C South Africa 27.25S 26.41E
95 J16 **Bothnia, Gulf of** Fin. Pohjanlahti, Swe. Bottniska Viken. gulf N Baltic Sea
191 P17 **Bothwell** Tasmania, SE Australia 42.24S 147.01E
106 H5 **Boticas** Vila Real, N Portugal 41.40N 7.40W
57 W10 **Boti-Pasi** Sipaliwini, C Surinam 4.08N 55.27W
Botletle see Boteti
131 P16 **Botlikh** Chechenskaya Respublika, SW Russian Federation 42.39N 46.12E
119 N10 **Botna** ≈ E Moldova
153 P13 **Botogo', Tizmasi** Rus. Khrebet Botogo. Tajikistan/Uzbekistan
118 I9 **Botoşani** Hung. Botosány. Botoşani, NE Romania 47.43N 26.40E
118 K8 **Botoşány** ◊ county NE Romania
167 P4 **Botou** prev. Bozhen. Hebei, E China 38.09N 116.37E
101 M20 **Botrange** ▲ E Belgium 50.30N 6.03E
109 O21 **Botricello** Calabria, SW Italy 38.56N 16.51E
85 I23 **Botshabelo** Free State, C South Africa 29.15S 26.51E
85 G19 **Botswana** off. Republic of Botswana. ◆ republic S Africa
25 N2 **Bottineau** North Dakota, N USA 48.49N 100.28W
Bottniska Viken see Bothnia, Gulf of
62 L9 **Botucatu** São Paulo, S Brazil 22.52S 48.30W
61 N16 **Botumirim** Minas Gerais, SE Brazil 16.51S 43.00W
11 W10 **Botwood** Newfoundland, Newfoundland and Labrador, SE Canada 49.06N 55.21W
78 M16 **Bouaflé** C Ivory Coast 7.00N 5.45W
78 M16 **Bouaké** var. Bwake. C Ivory Coast 7.39N 5.01W
81 G14 **Bouar** Nana-Mambéré, W Central African Republic 5.58N 15.38E
76 H7 **Bouârfa** NE Morocco 32.33N 1.54W
78 H7 **Bouarfa** see Buşrá ash Shām
108 D16 **Boucher** ≈ Québec, SE Canada

105 R15 **Bouches-du-Rhône** ◊ department SE France
76 C9 **Bou Craa** var. Bu Craa. NW Western Sahara 26.31N 12.52W
79 O9 **Boû Djébéha** oasis C Mali 18.39N 3.45W
100 C8 **Boudry** Neuchâtel, W Switzerland 46.57N 6.46E
188 L2 **Bougainville, Cape** headland Western Australia 13.53S 126.01E
67 E24 **Bougainville** ✗ East Falkland, Falkland Islands 51.18S 58.28W
195 S13 **Bougainville Island** island N PNG
195 T13 **Bougainville Strait** strait N Solomon Islands
197 B12 **Bougainville Strait** Fr. Détroit de Bougainville. strait C Vanuatu
176 U8 **Bouganville, Selat** strait Papua, E Indonesia
123 J11 **Bougaroun, Cap** headland N Algeria 37.07N 6.18E
79 R8 **Boughessa** Kidal, NE Mali 20.05N 2.13E
78 L13 **Bougouni** Sikasso, SW Mali 11.22N 7.24W
101 J24 **Bouillon** Luxembourg, SE Belgium 49.46N 5.04E
76 K5 **Bouira** N Algeria 36.22N 3.55E
76 D8 **Bou-Izakarn** SW Morocco 29.12N 9.43W
76 B9 **Boujdour** var. Bojador. W Western Sahara 26.06N 14.28W
76 G5 **Boukhalef** ✗ (Tanger) N Morocco 35.35N 5.53W
Boukombé see Boukoumbé
79 R14 **Boukoumbé** var. Boukombé. C Benin 10.13N 1.08E
78 G6 **Boû Lanouâr** Dakhlet Nouâdhibou, W Mauritania 21.16N 16.28W
39 T4 **Boulder** Colorado, C USA 40.01N 105.18W
35 R10 **Boulder** Montana, NW USA 46.14N 112.07W
37 X12 **Boulder City** Nevada, W USA 35.58N 114.49W
189 T7 **Boulia** Queensland, C Australia 23.02S 139.58E
104 J9 **Boulogne** ✈ NW France
Boulogne see Boulogne-sur-Mer
104 L16 **Boulogne-sur-Gesse** Haute-Garonne, S France 43.18N 0.39E
105 N1 **Boulogne-sur-Mer** var. Boulogne; anc. Bononia, Gesoriacum, Gessoriacum. Pas-de-Calais, N France 50.43N 1.37E
81 G16 **Bouloupari** Province Sud, S New Caledonia 21.54S 166.04E
79 Q12 **Boulsa** C Burkina 12.40N 0.28W
79 W11 **Boultoum** Zinder, C Niger 14.43N 10.22E
197 K13 **Bouma** Taveuni, N Fiji 16.49S 179.50W
78 J16 **Bouna** NE Ivory Coast 9.16N 3.00W
117 C17 **Bouméstós** ▲ W Greece 38.48N 20.59E
79 O15 **Bouna** NE Ivory Coast 9.16N 3.00W
21 P4 **Boundary Bald Mountain** ▲ Maine, NE USA 45.45N 70.10W
37 S8 **Boundary Peak** ▲ Nevada, W USA 37.50N 118.21W
78 M14 **Boundiali** N Ivory Coast 9.31N 6.28W
81 H21 **Boundji** Cuvette, C Congo 1.04S 15.18E
79 N14 **Boundoukui** var. Bondoukui, Bondoukuy. W Burkina 11.51N 3.47W
36 L2 **Bountiful** Utah, W USA 40.53N 111.52W
191 T9 **Bounty Bay** inlet New South Wales, SE Australia
203 Q16 **Bounty Bay** bay Pitcairn Island, C Pacific Ocean
199 Jj14 **Bounty Islands** island group S NZ
183 Q13 **Bounty Trough** undersea feature S Pacific Basin
197 I6 **Bourail** Province Sud, C New Caledonia 21.35S 165.29E
29 V5 **Bourbeuse River** ≈ Missouri, C USA
105 Q9 **Bourbon-Lancy** Saône-et-Loire, C France 46.39N 3.48E
33 N11 **Bourbonnais** Illinois, N USA 41.08N 87.52W
105 O10 **Bourbonnais** cultural region C France
105 S7 **Bourbonne-les-Bains** Haute-Marne, N France 48.00N 5.43E
Bourbon Vendée see la Roche-sur-Yon
76 M8 **Bourdj Messaouda** E Algeria 30.18N 9.19E
79 Q10 **Bourem** Gao, C Mali 16.56N 0.21W
101 O10 **Bourg** see Bourg-en-Bresse
105 N11 **Bourganeuf** Creuse, C France 45.57N 1.47E
Bourgas see Burgas
105 S10 **Bourg-en-Bresse** var. Bourg, Bourge-en-Bresse. Ain, E France 46.12N 5.13E
95 J15 **Bourges** anc. Avaricum. Cher, C France 47.06N 2.24E
105 T11 **Bourg-St-Andéol** Ardèche, E France 44.24N 4.36E
105 P8 **Bourgogne** Eng. Burgundy. ◇ region E France
105 S9 **Bourgoin-Jallieu** Isère, E France 45.34N 5.16E
105 T12 **Bourg-St-Maurice** Savoie, E France 45.37N 6.49E
110 C11 **Bourg St.Pierre** Valais, SW Switzerland 45.49N 7.10E
78 H7 **Boû Rjeimât** well W Mauritania 20.33N 15.45W
191 P5 **Bourke** New South Wales, SE Australia 30.07S 145.57E
99 N23 **Bournemouth** S England, UK 50.43N 1.54W
101 M23 **Bourscheid** Diekirch, NE Luxembourg 49.55N 6.04E

76 K6 **Bou Saâda** var. Bou Saada. N Algeria 35.13N 4.09E
38 I13 **Bouse Wash** ≈ Arizona, SW USA
105 N10 **Boussac** Creuse, C France 46.22N 2.12E
104 M16 **Boussens** Haute-Garonne, S France 43.10N 0.58E
80 H12 **Bousso** prev. Fort-Bretonnet. Chari-Baguirmi, S Chad 10.31N 16.45E
78 H9 **Boutilimit** Trarza, SW Mauritania 17.33N 14.42W
67 D21 **Bouvet Island** ◇ Norwegian dependency S Atlantic Ocean
79 U11 **Bouza** Tahoua, S Niger 14.25N 6.09E
111 R10 **Bovec** Ger. Flitsch, It. Plezzo. NW Slovenia 46.20N 13.33E
100 J8 **Bovenkarspel** Noord-Holland, NW Netherlands 52.33N 5.03E
31 V5 **Bovey** Minnesota, N USA 47.18N 93.25W
34 M9 **Bovill** Idaho, NW USA 46.50N 116.24W
26 L4 **Bovina** Texas, SW USA 34.30N 102.52W
109 M17 **Bovino** Puglia, SE Italy 41.14N 15.19E
63 C17 **Bovril** Entre Ríos, E Argentina 31.24S 59.25W
30 L2 **Bowbells** North Dakota, N USA 48.48N 102.15W
9 Q16 **Bow City** Alberta, SW Canada 50.27N 112.16W
31 O8 **Bowdle** South Dakota, N USA 45.27N 99.39W
189 X6 **Bowen** Queensland, NE Australia 20.00S 148.15E
198 B4 **Bowers Ridge** undersea feature N Bering Sea
15 Jj4 **Bowes Point** headland Nunavut, N Canada 67.46N 101.51W
27 S5 **Bowie** Texas, SW USA 33.33N 97.51W
9 R17 **Bow Island** Alberta, SW Canada 49.52N 111.24W
Bowkān see Būkān
22 J7 **Bowling Green** Kentucky, S USA 36.59N 86.26W
29 V3 **Bowling Green** Missouri, C USA 39.20N 91.12W
33 R11 **Bowling Green** Ohio, N USA 41.22N 83.40W
23 W5 **Bowling Green** Virginia, NE USA 38.01N 77.20W
30 J6 **Bowman** North Dakota, N USA 46.10N 103.25W
16 N3 **Bowman Bay** bay NW Atlantic Ocean
204 I5 **Bowman Coast** physical region Antarctica
30 J7 **Bowman-Haley Lake** ☒ North Dakota, N USA
205 Z11 **Bowman Island** island Antarctica
191 S9 **Bowral** New South Wales, SE Australia 34.29S 150.28E
194 K14 **Bowutu Mountains** ▲ C PNG
85 I16 **Bowwood** Southern, S Zambia 17.09S 26.16E
30 I12 **Box Butte Reservoir** ☒ Nebraska, C USA
30 J10 **Box Elder** South Dakota, N USA 44.06N 103.04W
97 M18 **Boxholm** Östergötland, S Sweden 58.12N 15.04E
Bo Xian/Boxian see Bozhou
167 Q4 **Boxing** Shandong, E China 37.06N 118.05E
101 N14 **Boxmeer** Noord-Brabant, SE Netherlands 51.39N 5.57E
101 N14 **Boxtel** Noord-Brabant, S Netherlands 51.36N 5.19E
142 J11 **Boyabat** Sinop, N Turkey 41.27N 34.45E
56 F7 **Boyacá** ◊ province C Colombia
119 O4 **Boyarka** Kyyivs'ka Oblast', N Ukraine 50.19N 30.19E
24 H7 **Boyce** Louisiana, S USA 31.23N 92.40W
35 U11 **Boyd** Montana, NW USA 45.27N 109.03W
27 S6 **Boyd** Texas, SW USA 33.04N 97.34W
23 V8 **Boydton** Virginia, NE USA 36.40N 78.24W
Boyer Ahmadi va Kohkilūyeh see Kohgilūyeh va Būyer Ahmad
31 T13 **Boyer River** ≈ Iowa, C USA
23 W8 **Boykins** Virginia, NE USA 36.35N 77.11W
8 Q16 **Boyle** Alberta, SW Canada 54.38N 112.45W
99 D16 **Boyle** Ir. Mainistir na Búille. C Ireland 53.58N 8.18W
99 F17 **Boyne** Ir. An Bhóinn. ≈ E Ireland
33 Q9 **Boyne City** Michigan, N USA 45.13N 85.00W
25 Z14 **Boynton Beach** Florida, SE USA 26.31N 80.04W
153 O13 **Boysun** Rus. Baysun. Surkhondaryo Viloyati, S Uzbekistan 38.13N 67.07E
Bozan see İntorsura Buzăului
142 B12 **Bozburun** ✈ NW Turkey
143 N16 **Boz Dağları** ▲ W Turkey
35 S11 **Bozeman** Montana, NW USA 45.40N 111.02W
Bozen see Bolzano
81 J16 **Bozene** Equateur, NW Dem. Rep. Congo 2.55N 19.15E
142 H16 **Bozhou** Boxian, Bo Xian. Anhui, E China 33.49N 115.49E
142 K13 **Bozkır** Konya, S Turkey 37.10N 32.15E
142 H16 **Bozkol Yaylası** plateau C Turkey
81 H14 **Bozoum** Ouham-Pendé, W Central African Republic 6.17N 16.26E
143 N16 **Bozova** Şanlıurfa, S Turkey 37.22N 38.33E
Bozrah see Buşrá ash Shām
142 L12 **Bozüyük** Bilecik, NW Turkey 39.55N 30.01E
108 D8 **Bra** Piemonte, NW Italy 44.42N 7.51E
204 L3 **Brabant Island** island Antarctica
101 I20 **Brabant Wallon** ◊ province C Belgium
115 F15 **Brač** var. Brach, It. Brazza; anc. Brattia. island S Croatia
Bracara Augusta see Braga

◆ COUNTRY ◇ DEPENDENT TERRITORY ◈ ADMINISTRATIVE REGION ▲ MOUNTAIN ✈ VOLCANO ☒ LAKE
● COUNTRY CAPITAL ○ DEPENDENT TERRITORY CAPITAL ✗ INTERNATIONAL AIRPORT ▲ MOUNTAIN RANGE ≈ RIVER ☒ RESERVOIR

235

Bracciano – Bryce Canyon

109 H15 **Bracciano** Lazio, C Italy 42.04N 12.12E
109 H14 **Bracciano, Lago di** ◎ C Italy
12 H13 **Bracebridge** Ontario, S Canada 45.01N 79.19W
Brach see Brač
95 G17 **Bräcke** Jämtland, C Sweden 62.42N 15.30E
27 P12 **Brackettville** Texas, SW USA 29.18N 100.25W
99 N22 **Bracknell** S England, UK 51.25N 0.46W
63 K14 **Braço do Norte** Santa Catarina, S Brazil 28.16S 49.11W
118 G11 **Brad** Hung. Brád. Hunedoara, SW Romania 45.52N 23.00E
109 N18 **Bradano** ≈ S Italy
25 V13 **Bradenton** Florida, SE USA 27.30N 82.34W
12 H14 **Bradford** Ontario, S Canada 44.09N 79.34W
99 L17 **Bradford** N England, UK 53.48N 1.45W
29 W10 **Bradford** Arkansas, C USA 35.25N 91.27W
20 D12 **Bradford** Pennsylvania, NE USA 41.57N 78.38W
29 T15 **Bradley** Arkansas, C USA 33.06N 93.39W
27 P7 **Bradshaw** Texas, SW USA 32.06N 99.52W
27 Q9 **Brady** Texas, SW USA 31.07N 99.22W
27 Q9 **Brady Creek** ≈ Texas, SW USA
98 J10 **Braemar** NE Scotland, UK 57.12N 2.52W
118 K8 **Brăești** Botoșani, NW Romania 47.50N 26.26E
106 G5 **Braga** anc. Bracara Augusta. Braga, NW Portugal 41.31N 8.25W
106 G5 **Braga** ◐ district N Portugal
118 J15 **Bragadiru** Teleorman, S Romania 43.43N 25.32E
63 C20 **Bragado** Buenos Aires, E Argentina 35.10S 60.28W
106 J5 **Bragança** Eng. Braganza; anc. Julio Briga. Bragança, NE Portugal 41.46N 6.46W
106 I5 **Bragança** ◐ district N Portugal
62 N9 **Bragança Paulista** São Paulo, S Brazil 22.55S 46.30W
Braganza see Bragança
Bragin see Brahin
31 V7 **Braham** Minnesota, N USA 45.43N 93.10W
Brahe see Brda
Brahestad see Raahe
121 O20 **Brahin** Rus. Bragin. Homyel'skaya Voblasts', SE Belarus 51.46N 30.16E
159 U15 **Brahmanbaria** Chittagong, E Bangladesh 23.58N 91.04E
160 O12 **Brāhmani** ≈ E India
160 N13 **Brahmapur** Orissa, E India 19.21N 84.51E
133 S10 **Brahmaputra** var. Padma, Tsangpo, Ben. Jamuna, Chin. Yarlung Zangbo Jiang, Ind. Bramaputra, Dihang, Siang. ≈ S Asia
99 H19 **Braich y Pwll** headland NW Wales, UK 52.47N 4.46W
191 R10 **Braidwood** New South Wales, SE Australia 35.26S 149.48E
32 M11 **Braidwood** Illinois, N USA 41.16N 88.12W
118 M13 **Brăila** Brăila, E Romania 45.17N 27.57E
118 L13 **Brăila** ◐ county SE Romania
101 G19 **Braine-l'Alleud** Brabant Wallon, C Belgium 50.40N 4.22E
101 F19 **Braine-le-Comte** Hainaut, SW Belgium 50.37N 4.07E
31 U6 **Brainerd** Minnesota, N USA 46.22N 94.10W
101 J19 **Braives** Liège, E Belgium 50.37N 5.09E
85 H23 **Brak** ≈ C South Africa
Brak see Birāk
101 E18 **Brakel** Oost-Vlaanderen, SW Belgium 50.50N 3.48E
100 J13 **Brakel** Gelderland, C Netherlands 51.49N 5.05E
78 H9 **Brakna** ◐ region S Mauritania
97 J17 **Brålanda** Västra Götaland, S Sweden 58.32N 12.18E
Bramaputra see Brahmaputra
97 F23 **Bramming** Ribe, W Denmark 55.28N 8.42E
12 G15 **Brampton** Ontario, S Canada 43.42N 79.46W
102 F12 **Bramsche** Niedersachsen, NW Germany 52.25N 7.58E
118 J12 **Bran** Ger. Törzburg, Hung. Törcsvár. Brașov, S Romania 45.31N 25.23E
31 W8 **Branch** Minnesota, N USA 45.29N 92.57W
23 R14 **Branchville** South Carolina, SE USA 33.15N 80.49W
49 Y6 **Branco, Cabo** headland E Brazil 7.07S 34.45W
60 F11 **Branco, Rio** ≈ N Brazil
110 J8 **Brand** Vorarlberg, W Austria 47.07N 9.45E
85 B18 **Brandberg** ▲ NW Namibia 21.20S 14.22E
97 H14 **Brandbu** Oppland, S Norway 60.24N 10.30E
97 F22 **Brande** Ringkøbing, W Denmark 55.57N 9.07E
Brandebourg see Brandenburg
102 M12 **Brandenburg** var. Brandenburg an der Havel. Brandenburg, NE Germany 52.25N 12.34E
22 K5 **Brandenburg** Kentucky, S USA 37.58N 86.11W
102 N12 **Brandenburg** off. Freie und Hansestadt Hamburg, Fr. Brandebourg. ◐ state NE Germany
Brandenburg an der Havel see Brandenburg
85 I23 **Brandfort** Free State, C South Africa 28.42S 26.28E
9 W16 **Brandon** Manitoba, S Canada 49.49N 99.57W
25 V12 **Brandon** Florida, SE USA 27.56N 82.17W
24 L6 **Brandon** Mississippi, S USA 32.16N 90.01W
99 A20 **Brandon Mountain** Ir. Cnoc Bréanainn. ▲ SW Ireland 52.13N 10.16W
Brandsen see Coronel Brandsen
97 I14 **Brandval** Hedmark, S Norway 60.18N 12.01E
85 F24 **Brandvlei** Northern Cape, W South Africa 30.19S 20.31E
25 U9 **Branford** Florida, SE USA 29.57N 82.54W
112 K7 **Braniewo** Ger. Braunsberg. Warmińsko-Mazurskie, NE Poland 54.24N 19.49E
204 H3 **Bransfield Strait** strait Antarctica
39 U8 **Branson** Colorado, C USA 37.01N 103.52W
29 T8 **Branson** Missouri, C USA 36.38N 93.13W
12 G16 **Brantford** Ontario, S Canada 43.04N 80.21W
104 L12 **Brantôme** Dordogne, SW France 45.21N 0.37E
190 L12 **Branxholme** Victoria, SE Australia 37.51S 141.48E
Brasil see Brazil
61 C16 **Brasiléia** Acre, W Brazil 10.58S 48.45W
61 K18 **Brasília** ● (Brazil) Distrito Federal, C Brazil 15.45S 47.57W
Braslav see Braslaw
120 J12 **Braslaw** Pol. Brasław, Rus. Braslav. Vitsyebskaya Voblasts', N Belarus 55.37N 27.01E
118 J12 **Brașov** Ger. Kronstadt, Hung. Brassó; prev. Orașul Stalin. Brașov, C Romania 45.40N 25.34E
118 I12 **Brașov** ◐ county C Romania
176 W7 **Bras, Pulau** island Kepulauan Mapia, E Indonesia
79 U18 **Brass** Bayelsa, S Nigeria 4.19N 6.21E
101 H16 **Brasschaat** var. Brasschaet. Antwerpen, N Belgium 51.16N 4.30E
Brasschaet see Brasschaat
175 O4 **Brassey, Banjaran** var. Brassey Range. ▲▲ East Malaysia
Brassey Range see Brassey, Banjaran
Brassó see Brașov
25 T1 **Brasstown Bald** ▲ Georgia, SE USA 34.52N 83.48W
115 K22 **Brataj** Vlorë, SW Albania 40.18N 19.37E
116 J10 **Bratan** var. Morozov. ▲ C Bulgaria 42.31N 25.08E
113 F21 **Bratislava** Ger. Pressburg, Hung. Pozsony. ● (Slovakia) Bratislavský Kraj, W Slovakia 48.10N 17.10E
113 H21 **Bratislavský Kraj** ◐ region W Slovakia
116 H10 **Bratiya** ▲ C Bulgaria 42.36N 24.08E
126 J14 **Bratsk** Irkutskaya Oblast', C Russian Federation 56.19N 101.49E
119 Q8 **Brats'ke** Mykolayivs'ka Oblast', S Ukraine 47.52N 31.34E
126 J14 **Bratskoye Vodokhranilishche** Eng. Bratsk Reservoir. ▣ S Russian Federation
Bratsk Reservoir see Bratskoye Vodokhranilishche
Brattia see Brač
96 D9 **Brattvåg** Møre og Romsdal, S Norway 62.36N 6.21E
114 K12 **Bratunac** Republika Srpska, E Bosnia and Herzegovina 44.10N 19.21E
116 J10 **Bratya Daskalovi** prev. Grozdovo. Stara Zagora, C Bulgaria 42.13N 25.21E
111 U2 **Braunau** ≈ N Austria
Braunau see Braunau am Inn
111 Q4 **Braunau am Inn** var. Braunau. Oberösterreich, N Austria 48.16N 13.03E
Braunsberg see Braniewo
102 J13 **Braunschweig** Eng./Fr. Brunswick. Niedersachsen, N Germany 52.16N 10.31E
Brava see Baraawe
107 Y6 **Brava, Costa** coastal region NE Spain
45 V16 **Brava, Punta** headland E Panama 8.21N 78.22W
97 N17 **Bråviken** inlet S Sweden
58 B10 **Bravo, Cerro** ▲ N Peru 5.33S 79.10W
Bravo del Norte, Río/Bravo, Río see Grande, Rio
37 X17 **Brawley** California, W USA 32.58N 115.31W
99 G18 **Bray** Ir. Bré. E Ireland 53.12N 6.06W
61 G16 **Brazil** off. Federative Republic of Brazil, Port. Repùblica Federativa do Brasil, Sp. Brasil; prev. United States of Brazil. ◆ federal republic South America
67 K15 **Brazil Basin** var. Brazilian Basin, Brazil'skaya Kotlovina. undersea feature W Atlantic Ocean
Brazilian Basin see Brazil Basin
Brazilian Highlands see Central, Planalto
Brazil'skaya Kotlovina see Brazil Basin
27 U10 **Brazos River** ≈ Texas, SW USA
176 Yy13 **Brazza** ≈ Papua, E Indonesia
Brazza see Brač
81 G21 **Brazzaville** ● (Congo) Capital District, S Congo 4.13S 15.13E
81 G21 **Brazzaville** ✕ Le Pool, S Congo 4.15S 15.15E
114 J11 **Brčko** Republika Srpska, NE Bosnia and Herzegovina 44.52N 18.49E
112 H8 **Brda** Ger. Brahe. ≈ N Poland
Bré see Bray
193 A23 **Breaksea Sound** sound South Island, NZ
192 L4 **Bream Bay** bay North Island, NZ
192 L4 **Bream Head** headland North Island, NZ 35.51S 174.35E
Bréanainn, Cnoc see Brandon Mountain
47 S6 **Brea, Punta** headland W Puerto Rico 17.56N 66.55W
24 I9 **Breaux Bridge** Louisiana, S USA 30.16N 91.54W
118 J13 **Breaza** Prahova, SE Romania 45.06N 25.44E
174 K14 **Brebes** Jawa, C Indonesia 6.54S 109.00E
98 K10 **Brechin** E Scotland, UK 56.44N 2.38W
101 H15 **Brecht** Antwerpen, N Belgium 51.21N 4.32E
39 S4 **Breckenridge** Colorado, C USA 39.28N 106.02W
31 R6 **Breckenridge** Minnesota, N USA 46.15N 96.35W
27 R6 **Breckenridge** Texas, SW USA 32.45N 98.54W
99 J21 **Brecknock** cultural region SE Wales, UK
65 G25 **Brecknock, Península** headland S Chile 54.39S 71.48W
113 G19 **Břeclav** Ger. Lundenburg. Jihomoravský Kraj, SE Czech Republic 49.04N 16.51E
99 J21 **Brecon** E Wales, UK 51.57N 3.26W
99 J21 **Brecon Beacons** ▲▲ S Wales, UK
101 I14 **Breda** Noord-Brabant, S Netherlands 51.34N 4.46E
97 K20 **Bredaryd** Jönköping, S Sweden 57.10N 13.45E
85 F26 **Bredasdorp** Western Cape, SW South Africa 34.28S 20.03E
95 H16 **Bredbyn** Västernorrland, N Sweden 63.28N 18.04E
125 E13 **Bredy** Chelyabinskaya Oblast', C Russian Federation 52.23N 60.24E
101 K17 **Bree** Limburg, NE Belgium 51.07N 5.36E
69 T15 **Breede** ≈ S South Africa
100 I7 **Breezand** Noord-Holland, NW Netherlands 52.52N 4.47E
115 P18 **Bregalnica** ≈ E FYR Macedonia
110 I6 **Bregenz** anc. Brigantium. Vorarlberg, W Austria 47.31N 9.44E
110 J7 **Bregenzer Wald** ▲▲ W Austria
116 F6 **Bregovo** Vidin, NW Bulgaria 44.07N 22.40E
104 H5 **Bréhat, Île de** island NW France
94 H2 **Breidhafjördhur** bay W Iceland
94 L3 **Breidhdalsvík** Austurland, E Iceland 64.48N 14.02W
110 H9 **Breil** Ger. Brigels. Graubünden, S Switzerland 46.46N 9.04E
94 J8 **Breivikbotn** Finnmark, N Norway 70.36N 22.19E
96 I9 **Brekken** Sør-Trøndelag, S Norway 62.39N 11.49E
96 G7 **Brekstad** Sør-Trøndelag, S Norway 63.42N 9.40E
96 B10 **Bremangerlandet** island S Norway
Brême see Bremen
102 H11 **Bremen** Fr. Brême. Bremen, NW Germany 53.05N 8.48E
25 R3 **Bremen** Georgia, SE USA 33.43N 85.09W
33 O11 **Bremen** Indiana, N USA 41.24N 86.07W
102 H10 **Bremen** off. Freie Hansestadt Bremen, Fr. Brême. ◐ state N Germany
102 G9 **Bremerhaven** Bremen, NW Germany 53.33N 8.34E
Bremersdorp see Manzini
34 G8 **Bremerton** Washington, NW USA 47.34N 122.37W
102 H10 **Bremervörde** Niedersachsen, NW Germany 53.29N 9.06E
27 U9 **Bremond** Texas, SW USA 31.10N 96.40W
27 U10 **Brenham** Texas, SW USA 30.10N 96.24W
110 M8 **Brenner** Tirol, W Austria 47.10N 11.51E
Brenner, Col du/Brennero, Passo del see Brenner Pass
110 M8 **Brenner Pass** var. Brenner Sattel, Fr. Col du Brenner, Ger. Brennerpass, It. Passo del Brennero. pass Austria/Italy 47.00N 11.29E
Brenner Sattel see Brenner Pass
110 G10 **Brenno** ≈ SW Switzerland
108 F7 **Breno** Lombardia, N Italy 45.58N 10.18E
25 O5 **Brent** Alabama, S USA 32.54N 87.10W
108 H7 **Brenta** ≈ NE Italy
99 P21 **Brentwood** E England, UK 51.38N 0.21E
20 L14 **Brentwood** Long Island, New York, NE USA 40.46N 73.12W
108 F7 **Brescia** anc. Brixia. Lombardia, N Italy 45.33N 10.13E
101 D15 **Breskens** Zeeland, SW Netherlands 51.24N 3.33E
Breslau see Dolnośląskie
108 H5 **Bressanone** Ger. Brixen. Trentino-Alto Adige, N Italy 46.43N 11.41E
98 M2 **Bressay** island NE Scotland, UK
104 K9 **Bressuire** Deux-Sèvres, W France 46.50N 0.29W
121 F20 **Brest** Pol. Brześć nad Bugiem, Rus. Brest-Litovsk; prev. Brześć Litewski. Brestskaya Voblasts', SW Belarus 52.06N 23.42E
104 F5 **Brest** Finistère, NW France 48.24N 4.30W
Brest-Litovsk see Brest
114 A10 **Brestova** Istra, NW Croatia 45.09N 14.13E
Brestskaya Oblast' see Brestskaya Voblasts'
121 G19 **Brestskaya Voblasts'** prev. Rus. Brestskaya Oblast'. ◐ province SW Belarus
104 G6 **Bretagne** Eng. Brittany; Lat. Britannia Minor. ◐ region NW France
118 G12 **Bretea-Română** Hung. Oláhbrettye; prev. Bretea-Romînă. Hunedoara, W Romania 45.39N 23.00E
Bretea-Romînă see Bretea-Română
105 O3 **Breteuil** Oise, N France 49.37N 2.18E
104 I10 **Breton, Pertuis** inlet W France
24 L10 **Breton Sound** sound Louisiana, S USA
192 K2 **Brett, Cape** headland North Island, NZ 35.11S 174.21E
103 G21 **Bretten** Baden-Württemberg, SW Germany 49.01N 8.42E
101 K15 **Breugel** Noord-Brabant, S Netherlands 51.30N 5.30E
108 B6 **Breuil-Cervinia** It. Cervinia. Valle d'Aosta, NW Italy 45.57N 7.37E
100 I11 **Breukelen** Utrecht, C Netherlands 52.11N 5.01E
23 P10 **Brevard** North Carolina, SE USA 35.13N 82.43W
40 L9 **Brevig Mission** Alaska, USA 65.19N 166.29W
97 G16 **Brevik** Telemark, S Norway 59.03N 9.40E
191 P5 **Brewarrina** New South Wales, SE Australia 30.01S 146.50E
21 R6 **Brewer** Maine, NE USA 44.46N 68.44W
31 T11 **Brewster** Minnesota, N USA 43.43N 95.28W
31 N14 **Brewster** Nebraska, C USA 41.54N 99.52W
33 U12 **Brewster** Ohio, N USA 40.42N 81.36W
191 O8 **Brewster, Lake** ◎ New South Wales, SE Australia
25 P7 **Brewton** Alabama, S USA 31.06N 87.04W
Brezhnev see Naberezhnyye Chelny
111 W12 **Brežice** Ger. Rann. E Slovenia 45.54N 15.35E
116 G9 **Breznik** Pernik, W Bulgaria 42.45N 22.54E
113 K19 **Brezno** Ger. Bries, Briesen, Hung. Breznóbánya; prev. Brezno nad Hronom. Banskobystrický Kraj, C Slovakia 48.49N 19.40E
Breznóbánya/Brezno nad Hronom see Brezno
118 I12 **Brezoi** Vâlcea, SW Romania 45.18N 24.15E
116 J10 **Brezovo** prev. Abrashlare. Plovdiv, C Bulgaria 42.19N 25.05E
81 K14 **Bria** Haute-Kotto, C Central African Republic 6.30N 22.00E
105 U13 **Briançon** anc. Brigantio. Hautes-Alpes, SE France 44.55N 6.37E
38 K7 **Brian Head** ▲ Utah, W USA 37.40N 112.49W
105 O7 **Briare** Loiret, C France 47.35N 2.46E
191 V2 **Bribie Island** island Queensland, E Australia
45 O14 **Bribrí** Limón, E Costa Rica 9.37N 82.51W
118 L8 **Briceni** var. Brinceni, Rus. Brichany. N Moldova 48.21N 27.02E
Bricgstow see Bristol
Brichany see Briceni
101 M24 **Bridel** Luxembourg, C Luxembourg 49.40N 6.03E
99 J22 **Bridgend** S Wales, UK 51.30N 3.37W
12 I14 **Bridgenorth** Ontario, SE Canada 44.21N 78.22W
25 Q1 **Bridgeport** Alabama, S USA 34.57N 85.42W
37 R8 **Bridgeport** California, W USA 38.14N 119.13W
20 L13 **Bridgeport** Connecticut, NE USA 41.10N 73.12W
33 N15 **Bridgeport** Illinois, N USA 38.42N 87.45W
30 J14 **Bridgeport** Nebraska, C USA 41.37N 103.07W
27 S6 **Bridgeport** Texas, SW USA 33.12N 97.45W
23 S3 **Bridgeport** West Virginia, NE USA 39.17N 80.15W
27 S5 **Bridgeport, Lake** ▣ Texas, SW USA
35 U11 **Bridger** Montana, NW USA 45.16N 108.55W
20 I17 **Bridgeton** New Jersey, NE USA 39.24N 75.10W
188 J14 **Bridgetown** Western Australia 34.01S 116.07E
47 Y14 **Bridgetown** ● (Barbados) SW Barbados 13.05N 59.36W
191 P17 **Bridgewater** Tasmania, SE Australia 42.47S 147.15E
11 P16 **Bridgewater** Nova Scotia, SE Canada 44.19N 64.30W
21 P12 **Bridgewater** Massachusetts, NE USA 41.59N 70.58W
31 Q11 **Bridgewater** South Dakota, N USA 43.33N 97.30W
23 U5 **Bridgewater** Virginia, NE USA 38.22N 78.58W
21 P8 **Bridgton** Maine, NE USA 44.04N 70.43W
99 K23 **Bridgwater** SW England, UK 51.08N 3.00W
99 K22 **Bridgwater Bay** bay SW England, UK
99 O16 **Bridlington** E England, UK 54.04N 0.12W
99 O16 **Bridlington Bay** bay E England, UK
191 P15 **Bridport** Tasmania, SE Australia 41.03S 147.26E
99 K24 **Bridport** S England, UK 50.43N 2.43W
105 O5 **Brie** cultural region N France
Brieg see Brzeg
Briel see Brielle
100 G12 **Brielle** var. Briel, Bril, Eng. The Brill. Zuid-Holland, SW Netherlands 51.54N 4.10E
110 E9 **Brienz** Bern, C Switzerland 46.45N 8.00E
110 E9 **Brienzer See** ◎ SW Switzerland
Bries/Briesen see Brezno
Brietzig see Brzesko
105 S4 **Briey** Meurthe-et-Moselle, NE France 49.15N 5.57E
110 E10 **Brig** Fr. Brigue, It. Briga. Valais, SW Switzerland 46.19N 8.00E
Briga see Brig
103 G24 **Brigach** ≈ S Germany
20 K17 **Brigantine** New Jersey, NE USA 39.23N 74.21W
Brigantio see Briançon
Brigantium see Bregenz
Brigels see Breil
27 S9 **Briggs** Texas, SW USA 30.52N 97.55W
38 L1 **Brigham City** Utah, W USA 41.30N 112.00W
12 J15 **Brighton** Ontario, SE Canada 44.01N 77.44W
99 O23 **Brighton** SE England, UK 50.49N 0.10W
39 T4 **Brighton** Colorado, C USA 39.58N 104.46W
32 K15 **Brighton** Illinois, N USA 39.01N 90.09W
105 T16 **Brignoles** Var, W France 43.25N 6.03E
Brigue see Brig
107 O7 **Brihuega** Castilla-La Mancha, C Spain 40.45N 2.52W
114 A10 **Brijuni** It. Brioni. island group NW Croatia
78 G12 **Brikama** W Gambia 13.13N 16.37W
Bril see Brielle
Brill, The see Brielle
103 G15 **Brilon** Nordrhein-Westfalen, W Germany 51.24N 8.34E
Brinceni see Briceni
109 Q18 **Brindisi** anc. Brundisium, Brundusium. Puglia, SE Italy 40.39N 17.55E
29 W11 **Brinkley** Arkansas, C USA 34.53N 91.11W
Brioni see Brijuni
105 P12 **Brioude** anc. Brivas. Haute-Loire, C France 45.18N 3.22E
Briovera see St-Lô
191 U2 **Brisbane** state capital Queensland, E Australia 27.30S 153.00E
191 V2 **Brisbane** ✕ Queensland, E Australia 27.30S 153.00E
27 P2 **Briscoe** Texas, SW USA 35.34N 100.17W
108 H10 **Brisighella** Emilia-Romagna, C Italy 44.12N 11.45E
110 G11 **Brissago** Ticino, S Switzerland 46.07N 8.40E
99 K22 **Bristol** anc. Bricgstow. SW England, UK 51.27N 2.34W
20 M12 **Bristol** Connecticut, NE USA 41.40N 72.56W
25 R9 **Bristol** Florida, SE USA 30.25N 84.58W
21 N9 **Bristol** New Hampshire, NE USA 43.34N 71.42W
31 Q8 **Bristol** South Dakota, N USA 45.18N 97.45W
23 P8 **Bristol** Tennessee, S USA 36.36N 82.11W
20 M8 **Bristol** Vermont, NE USA 44.07N 73.00W
41 N14 **Bristol Bay** bay Alaska, USA
99 I22 **Bristol Channel** inlet England/Wales, UK
37 W14 **Bristol Lake** ◎ California, W USA
29 P10 **Bristow** Oklahoma, C USA 35.49N 96.23W
88 C10 **Britain** var. Great Britain. island UK
Britannia Minor see Bretagne
8 L12 **British Columbia** Fr. Colombie-Britannique. ◐ province SW Canada
British Guiana see Guyana
British Honduras see Belize
181 Q7 **British Indian Ocean Territory** ◇ UK dependent territory C Indian Ocean
88 B9 **British Isles** island group NW Europe
8 I1 **British Mountains** ▲▲ Yukon Territory, NW Canada
British North Borneo see Sabah
British Solomon Islands Protectorate see Solomon Islands
47 S8 **British Virgin Islands** var. Virgin Islands. ◇ UK dependent territory E West Indies
85 J21 **Brits** North-West, N South Africa 25.39S 27.46E
85 H24 **Britstown** Northern Cape, W South Africa 30.36S 23.30E
12 F12 **Britt** Ontario, S Canada 45.46N 80.34W
31 V12 **Britt** Iowa, C USA 43.06N 93.48W
Brittany see Bretagne
31 Q7 **Britton** South Dakota, N USA 45.47N 97.45W
Briva Curretia see Brive-la-Gaillarde
Briva Isarae see Pontoise
Brivas see Brioude
Brive see Brive-la-Gaillarde
104 M12 **Brive-la-Gaillarde** prev. Brive, anc. Briva Curretia. Corrèze, C France 45.09N 1.31E
107 O4 **Briviesca** Castilla-León, N Spain 42.33N 3.19W
Brixen see Bressanone
Brixia see Brescia
151 S15 **Brlik** prev. Novotroickoje, Novotroitskoye. Zhambyl, SE Kazakhstan 43.39N 73.45E
Brněnský Kraj see Jihomoravský Kraj
113 G18 **Brno** Ger. Brünn. Jihomoravský Kraj, SE Czech Republic 49.10N 16.35E
98 G7 **Broad Bay** bay NW Scotland, UK
27 X8 **Broaddus** Texas, SW USA 31.18N 94.16W
191 O12 **Broadford** Victoria, SE Australia 37.07S 145.04E
98 G9 **Broadford** N Scotland, UK 57.14N 5.54W
98 J13 **Broad Law** ▲ S Scotland, UK 55.30N 3.22W
25 U3 **Broad River** ≈ Georgia, SE USA
23 N8 **Broad River** ≈ North Carolina/South Carolina, SE USA
189 Y8 **Broadsound Range** ▲▲ Queensland, E Australia
35 X11 **Broadus** Montana, NW USA 45.28N 105.22W
23 U4 **Broadway** Virginia, NE USA 38.36N 78.48W
120 E9 **Brocēni** Saldus, SW Latvia 56.41N 22.31E
9 U11 **Brochet** Manitoba, C Canada 57.55N 101.40W
9 U10 **Brochet, Lac** ◎ Manitoba, C Canada
13 S5 **Brochet, Lac au** ◎ Québec, SE Canada
103 K14 **Brocken** ▲ C Germany 51.48N 10.38E
21 O12 **Brockton** Massachusetts, NE USA 42.04N 71.01W
12 L14 **Brockville** Ontario, SE Canada 44.36N 75.42W
20 D13 **Brockway** Pennsylvania, NE USA 41.14N 78.45W
Brod/Bród see Slavonski Brod
15 Kk1 **Brodeur Peninsula** peninsula Baffin Island, Nunavut, NE Canada
98 H13 **Brodick** W Scotland, UK 55.34N 5.09W
Brod na Savi see Slavonski Brod
112 K9 **Brodnica** Ger. Buddenbrock. Kujawski-pomorskie, C Poland 53.15N 19.22E
114 G10 **Brod-Posavina** off. Brodsko-Posavska Županija. ◐ province NE Croatia
118 J5 **Brody** L'vivs'ka Oblast', NW Ukraine 50.04N 25.07E
97 G22 **Brædstrup** Vejle, C Denmark 55.58N 9.37E
100 I10 **Broek-in-Waterland** Noord-Holland, C Netherlands 52.27N 4.58E
34 L13 **Brogan** Oregon, NW USA 44.15N 117.34W
112 N10 **Brok** Mazowieckie, C Poland 52.42N 21.53E
29 P9 **Broken Arrow** Oklahoma, C USA 36.03N 95.47W
191 T9 **Broken Bay** bay New South Wales, SE Australia
31 N15 **Broken Bow** Nebraska, C USA 41.24N 99.38W
29 R13 **Broken Bow** Oklahoma, C USA 34.01N 94.44W
29 R12 **Broken Bow Lake** ▣ Oklahoma, C USA
190 L6 **Broken Hill** New South Wales, SE Australia 31.58S 141.27E
181 S10 **Broken Ridge** undersea feature S Indian Ocean
194 H10 **Broken Water Bay** bay W Bismarck Sea
57 W10 **Brokopondo** Brokopondo, NE Surinam 05.04N 55.00W
57 W10 **Brokopondo** ◐ district C Surinam
Bromberg see Bydgoszcz
97 L22 **Bromölla** Skåne, S Sweden 56.04N 14.28E
99 L20 **Bromsgrove** W England, UK 52.19N 2.03W
97 G20 **Brønderslev** Nordjylland, N Denmark 57.16N 9.58E
108 D8 **Broni** Lombardia, N Italy 45.04N 9.18E
8 K11 **Bronlund Peak** ▲ British Columbia, W Canada 57.27N 126.43W
95 F14 **Brønnøysund** Nordland, C Norway 65.28N 12.13E
25 V10 **Bronson** Florida, SE USA 29.25N 82.38W
33 Q11 **Bronson** Michigan, N USA 41.52N 85.11W
27 X8 **Bronson** Texas, SW USA 31.20N 94.00W
109 L24 **Bronte** Sicilia, Italy, C Mediterranean Sea 37.46N 14.49E
27 P8 **Bronte** Texas, SW USA 31.53N 100.17W
27 Y9 **Brookeland** Texas, SW USA 31.05N 93.57W
179 O15 **Brooke's Point** Palawan, W Philippines 8.54N 117.54E
29 T3 **Brookfield** Missouri, C USA 39.46N 93.04W
24 K7 **Brookhaven** Mississippi, S USA 31.34N 90.26W
34 E16 **Brookings** Oregon, NW USA 42.03N 124.16W
31 R10 **Brookings** South Dakota, N USA 44.15N 96.46W
31 W14 **Brooklyn** Iowa, C USA 41.43N 92.27W
31 U8 **Brooklyn Park** Minnesota, N USA 45.06N 93.18W
23 U7 **Brookneal** Virginia, NE USA 37.03N 78.56W
9 R16 **Brooks** Alberta, SW Canada 50.34N 111.54W
27 V11 **Brookshire** Texas, SW USA 29.47N 95.57W
40 L8 **Brooks Mountain** ▲ Alaska, USA 65.31N 167.24W
40 M11 **Brooks Range** ▲▲ Alaska, USA
33 O12 **Brookston** Indiana, N USA 40.34N 86.53W
25 V11 **Brooksville** Florida, SE USA 28.33N 82.23W
25 N4 **Brooksville** Mississippi, S USA 33.13N 88.34W
188 J13 **Brookton** Western Australia 32.24S 117.04E
33 Q14 **Brookville** Indiana, N USA 39.25N 85.00W
20 D13 **Brookville** Pennsylvania, NE USA 41.07N 79.05W
33 Q14 **Brookville Lake** ▣ Indiana, N USA
188 K5 **Broome** Western Australia 17.58S 122.15E
39 S4 **Broomfield** Colorado, C USA 39.55N 105.05W
Broos see Orăștie
98 J7 **Brora** N Scotland, UK 57.58N 4.00W
98 I7 **Brora** ≈ N Scotland, UK
97 F23 **Brørup** Ribe, W Denmark 55.28N 9.01E
97 L23 **Brösarp** Skåne, S Sweden 55.43N 14.10E
118 J9 **Broșteni** Suceava, NE Romania 47.13N 25.43E
104 M6 **Brou** Eure-et-Loir, C France 48.12N 1.10E
Broucsella see Brussel/Bruxelles
Broughton Bay see Tongjosŏn-man
16 O1 **Broughton Island** Nunavut, NE Canada 67.34N 63.55W
144 G7 **Broummâna** C Lebanon 33.53N 35.39E
24 I9 **Broussard** Louisiana, S USA 30.09N 91.57W
100 E13 **Brouwersdam** dam SW Netherlands 51.46N 3.51E
100 E13 **Brouwershaven** Zeeland, SW Netherlands 51.44N 3.50E
119 P4 **Brovary** Kyyivs'ka Oblast', N Ukraine 50.30N 30.43E
97 G20 **Brovst** Nordjylland, N Denmark 57.06N 9.31E
33 S8 **Brown City** Michigan, N USA 43.12N 82.50W
26 M6 **Brownfield** Texas, SW USA 33.10N 102.16W
35 Q7 **Browning** Montana, NW USA 48.33N 113.00W
35 R6 **Brown, Mount** ▲ Montana, NW USA 48.52N 111.08W
194 K15 **Brown River** ≈ S PNG
(0) M9 **Browns Bank** undersea feature NW Atlantic Ocean
33 O14 **Brownsburg** Indiana, N USA 39.50N 86.24W
20 J16 **Browns Mills** New Jersey, NE USA 39.58N 74.33W
46 J12 **Browns Town** C Jamaica 18.28N 77.22W
33 P15 **Brownstown** Indiana, N USA 38.52N 86.02W
31 R8 **Browns Valley** Minnesota, N USA 45.36N 96.49W
22 K7 **Brownsville** Kentucky, S USA 37.09N 86.13W
22 F9 **Brownsville** Tennessee, S USA 35.34N 89.15W
27 T17 **Brownsville** Texas, SW USA 25.55N 97.28W
57 W10 **Brownsweg** Brokopondo, C Surinam
31 U9 **Brownton** Minnesota, N USA 44.43N 94.21W
21 R5 **Brownville Junction** Maine, NE USA 45.20N 69.04W
27 R8 **Brownwood** Texas, SW USA 31.41N 98.59W
27 R8 **Brownwood Lake** ▣ Texas, SW USA
106 I9 **Brozas** Extremadura, W Spain 39.37N 6.48W
121 M18 **Brozha** Mahilyowskaya Voblasts', E Belarus 52.57N 29.07E
105 O2 **Bruay-en-Artois** Pas-de-Calais, N France 50.31N 2.30E
105 P2 **Bruay-sur-l'Escaut** Nord, N France 50.24N 3.33E
12 F13 **Bruce Peninsula** peninsula Ontario, S Canada
22 H9 **Bruceton** Tennessee, S USA 36.02N 88.14W
27 T9 **Bruceville** Texas, SW USA 31.17N 97.15W
103 G21 **Bruchsal** Baden-Württemberg, SW Germany 49.07N 8.34E
111 Q7 **Bruck** Salzburg, NW Austria 47.18N 12.51E
Bruck see Bruck an der Mur
111 Y4 **Bruck an der Leitha** Niederösterreich, NE Austria 48.02N 16.47E
111 V7 **Bruck an der Mur** var. Bruck. Steiermark, C Austria 47.26N 15.13E
103 M24 **Bruckmühl** Bayern, SE Germany 47.52N 11.54E
173 Dd3 **Brueuh, Pulau** island NW Indonesia
Bruges see Brugge
110 F6 **Brugg** Aargau, NW Switzerland 47.28N 8.13E
101 C16 **Brugge** Fr. Bruges. West-Vlaanderen, NW Belgium 51.13N 3.13E
111 R9 **Bruggen** Kärnten, S Austria 46.46N 13.13E
103 E16 **Brühl** Nordrhein-Westfalen, W Germany 50.49N 6.54E
101 F14 **Bruinisse** Zeeland, SW Netherlands 51.40N 4.04E
174 L5 **Bruit, Pulau** island East Malaysia
12 K10 **Brûlé, Lac** ◎ Québec, SE Canada
32 M4 **Brule River** ≈ Michigan/Wisconsin, N USA
101 H23 **Brûly** Namur, S Belgium 49.55N 4.31E
61 N17 **Brumado** Bahia, E Brazil 14.13S 41.37W
100 M11 **Brummen** Gelderland, E Netherlands 52.04N 6.10E
96 H13 **Brumunddal** Hedmark, S Norway 60.52N 10.55E
25 Q6 **Brundidge** Alabama, S USA 31.43N 85.49W
Brundisium/Brundusium see Brindisi
35 N15 **Bruneau River** ≈ Idaho, NW USA
Bruneck see Brunico
174 Mm4 **Brunei** off. Sultanate of Brunei, Mal. Negara Brunei Darussalam. ◆ monarchy SE Asia
175 N3 **Brunei Bay** var. Teluk Brunei. bay N Brunei
Brunei, Teluk see Brunei Bay
Brunei Town see Bandar Seri Begawan
108 H5 **Brunico** Ger. Bruneck. Trentino-Alto Adige, N Italy 46.49N 11.57E
Brünn see Brno
193 G17 **Brunner, Lake** ◎ South Island, NZ
101 M18 **Brunssum** Limburg, SE Netherlands 50.57N 5.58E
25 W7 **Brunswick** Georgia, SE USA 31.09N 81.30W
21 Q8 **Brunswick** Maine, NE USA 43.54N 69.58W
23 V3 **Brunswick** Maryland, NE USA 39.18N 77.37W
29 T3 **Brunswick** Missouri, C USA 39.25N 93.07W
33 T11 **Brunswick** Ohio, N USA 41.14N 81.50W
Brunswick see Braunschweig
65 H24 **Brunswick, Península** headland S Chile 53.30S 71.27W
113 H17 **Bruntál** Ger. Freudenthal. Moravskoslezský Kraj, E Czech Republic 50.00N 17.27E
205 N3 **Brunt Ice Shelf** ice shelf Antarctica
Brusa see Bursa
39 U3 **Brush** Colorado, C USA 40.15N 103.37W
44 M5 **Brus Laguna** Gracias a Dios, E Honduras 15.46N 84.31W
62 K13 **Brusque** Santa Catarina, S Brazil 27.07S 48.54W
Brussa see Bursa
101 E18 **Brussel** var. Brussels, Fr. Bruxelles, Ger. Brüssel; anc. Broucsella. ● (Belgium) Brussels, C Belgium see also Bruxelles 50.52N 4.21E
Brüssel/Brussels see Brussel/Bruxelles
119 O5 **Brusyliv** Zhytomyrs'ka Oblast', N Ukraine 50.16N 29.31E
191 Q12 **Bruthen** Victoria, SE Australia 37.43S 147.49E
Bruttium see Calabria
Brüx see Most
101 E18 **Bruxelles** var. Brussels, Dut. Brussel, Ger. Brüssel; anc. Broucsella. ● (Belgium) Brussels, C Belgium see also Brussel 50.52N 4.21E
56 J7 **Bruzual** Apure, W Venezuela 7.59N 69.18W
33 Q11 **Bryan** Ohio, N USA 41.28N 84.33W
27 U10 **Bryan** Texas, SW USA 30.40N 96.22W
204 J4 **Bryan Coast** physical region Antarctica
126 I13 **Bryanka** Krasnoyarskiy Kray, C Russian Federation 59.01N 93.13E
119 Y7 **Bryanka** Luhans'ka Oblast', E Ukraine 48.30N 38.45E
190 J8 **Bryan, Mount** ▲ South Australia 33.25S 138.59E
130 I6 **Bryansk** Bryanskaya Oblast', W Russian Federation 53.15N 34.06E
130 H6 **Bryanskaya Oblast'** ◐ province W Russian Federation
204 J5 **Bryant, Cape** headland Antarctica
29 U8 **Bryant Creek** ≈ Missouri, C USA
38 K8 **Bryce Canyon** canyon Utah, W USA

◆ Country
● Country Capital
◇ Dependent Territory
○ Dependent Territory Capital
◐ Administrative Region
✕ International Airport
▲ Mountain
▲▲ Mountain Range
Volcano
≈ River
◎ Lake
▣ Reservoir

121 O15 **Bryli** Rus. Bryli. Mahilyowskaya Voblasts', E Belarus *53.55N 30.31E*
97 C17 **Bryne** Rogaland, S Norway *58.43N 5.37E*
27 R6 **Bryson** Texas, SW USA *33.09N 98.23W*
23 N10 **Bryson City** North Carolina, SE USA *35.33N 83.39W*
12 K11 **Bryson, Lac** ◎ Québec, SE Canada
130 K13 **Bryukhovetskaya** Krasnodarskiy Kray, SW Russian Federation *45.49N 38.01E*
113 H15 **Brzeg** Ger. Brieg; anc. Civitas Altae Ripae. Opolskie, S Poland *50.52N 17.27E*
113 G14 **Brzeg Dolny** Ger. Dyhernfurth. Dolnośląskie, SW Poland *51.15N 16.42E*
Brześć Litewski/Brześć nad Bugiem see Brest
113 L17 **Brzesko** Ger. Brietzig. Małopolskie, S Poland *49.57N 20.35E*
Brzeżany see Berezhany
112 K12 **Brzeziny** Łódzkie, C Poland *51.48N 19.42E*
Brzostowica Wielka see Vyalikaya Byerastavitsa
113 O17 **Brzozów** Podkarpackie, SE Poland *49.38N 22.00E*
Bsharrī/Bsherri see Bcharré
197 I13 **Bua** Vanua Levu, N Fiji *16.48S 178.36E*
97 J20 **Bua** Halland, S Sweden *57.13N 12.07E*
84 M13 **Bua** ≈ C Malawi
Bua see Čiovo
83 L18 **Bu'aale** It. Buale. Jubbada Dhexe, SW Somalia *0.52N 42.37E*
201 Q8 **Buada Lagoon** lagoon Nauru, C Pacific Ocean
195 W14 **Buala** Santa Isabel, E Solomon Islands *8.06S 159.31E*
Buale see Bu'aale
202 H1 **Buariki** atoll Tungaru, W Kiribati
178 I10 **Bua Yai** var. Ban Bua Yai. Nakhon Ratchasima, E Thailand *15.34N 102.25E*
77 P8 **Bu'ayrāt al Ḩasūn** var. Buwayrāt al Hasūn. C Libya *31.22N 15.41E*
78 H13 **Buba** S Guinea-Bissau *11.36N 14.55W*
175 Qq7 **Bubaa** Sulawesi, N Indonesia *0.32N 122.27E*
83 D20 **Bubanza** NW Burundi *3.04S 29.22E*
85 K18 **Bubi** prev. Bubye. ≈ S Zimbabwe
148 L11 **Būbīyan, Jazīrat** island E Kuwait
Bublitz see Bobolice
Bubye see Bubi
197 J13 **Buca** prev. Mbutha. Vanua Levu, N Fiji *16.39S 179.51E*
142 F16 **Bucak** Burdur, SW Turkey *37.26N 30.32E*
56 G8 **Bucaramanga** Santander, N Colombia *7.07N 73.10W*
109 M18 **Buccino** Campania, S Italy *40.37N 15.25E*
118 K9 **Bucecea** Botoşani, NE Romania *47.43N 26.24E*
118 J6 **Buchach** Pol. Buczacz. Ternopil's'ka Oblast', W Ukraine *49.04N 25.22E*
191 Q12 **Buchan** Victoria, SE Australia *37.26S 148.11E*
78 J17 **Buchanan** prev. Grand Bassa. SW Liberia *5.52N 10.03W*
25 R3 **Buchanan** Georgia, SE USA *33.48N 85.11W*
33 O11 **Buchanan** Michigan, N USA *41.49N 86.21W*
23 T6 **Buchanan** Virginia, NE USA *37.31N 79.40W*
27 R10 **Buchanan Dam** Texas, SW USA *30.42N 98.24W*
27 R10 **Buchanan, Lake** ⊠ Texas, SW USA
98 L8 **Buchan Ness** headland NE Scotland, UK *57.28N 1.46W*
11 T12 **Buchans** Newfoundland and Labrador, SE Canada *48.49N 56.44W*
Bucharest see Bucureşti
103 H20 **Buchen** Baden-Württemberg, SW Germany *49.31N 9.18E*
102 I10 **Buchholz in der Nordheide** Niedersachsen, NW Germany *53.19N 9.52E*
110 F7 **Buchs** Aargau, N Switzerland *47.24N 8.03E*
110 I8 **Buchs** Sankt Gallen, NE Switzerland *47.10N 9.26E*
102 H13 **Bückeburg** Niedersachsen, NW Germany *52.16N 9.03E*
38 K14 **Buckeye** Arizona, SW USA *33.22N 112.34W*
Buckeye State see Ohio
23 S4 **Buckhannon** West Virginia, NE USA *38.59N 80.13W*
27 T9 **Buckholts** Texas, SW USA *30.52N 97.07W*
98 K8 **Buckie** NE Scotland, UK *57.39N 2.55W*
12 M12 **Buckingham** Québec, SE Canada *45.34N 75.25W*
23 U6 **Buckingham** Virginia, NE USA *37.33N 78.33W*
99 N21 **Buckinghamshire** cultural region SE England, UK
41 N8 **Buckland** Alaska, USA *65.58N 161.07W*
190 G7 **Buckleboo** South Australia *32.55S 136.11E*
28 K7 **Bucklin** Kansas, C USA *37.33N 99.37W*
29 T3 **Bucklin** Missouri, C USA *39.46N 92.53W*
38 I12 **Buckskin Mountains** ▲▲ Arizona, SW USA
21 R7 **Bucksport** Maine, NE USA *44.34N 68.46W*
84 A9 **Buco Zau** Cabinda, NW Angola *4.47S 12.32E*
Bu Craa see Bou Craa
118 K14 **Bucureşti** Eng. Bucharest, Ger. Bukarest; prev. Altenburg, anc. Cetatea Damboviţei. ● (Romania) Bucureşti, S Romania *44.27N 26.06E*
33 S12 **Bucyrus** Ohio, N USA *40.48N 82.58W*
Buczacz see Buchach
96 E9 **Bud** Møre og Romsdal, S Norway *62.55N 6.55E*
27 S11 **Buda** Texas, SW USA *30.05N 97.50W*
121 O18 **Buda-Kashalyova** Rus. Buda-Koshelëvo. Homyel'skaya Voblasts', SE Belarus *52.43N 30.34E*
Buda-Koshelëvo see Buda-Kashalyova
177 G4 **Budalin** Sagaing, C Burma *22.24N 95.07E*
113 J22 **Budapest** off. Budapest Főváros, SCr. Budimpešta. ● (Hungary) Pest, N Hungary *47.30N 19.03E*
158 K11 **Budaun** Uttar Pradesh, N India *28.01N 79.07E*
147 O9 **Budayyi'ah** oasis C Saudi Arabia *23.04N 43.29E*
205 Y12 **Budd Coast** physical region Antarctica
Buddenbrock see Brodnica
109 C17 **Buddusò** Sardegna, Italy, C Mediterranean Sea *40.37N 9.19E*
99 I23 **Bude** SW England, UK *50.49N 4.33W*
24 J7 **Bude** Mississippi, S USA *31.27N 90.51W*
Budějovický Kraj see Jihočeský Kraj
101 K16 **Budel** Noord-Brabant, SE Netherlands *51.16N 5.34E*
102 I8 **Büdelsdorf** Schleswig-Holstein, N Germany *54.20N 9.40E*
131 O14 **Budënnovsk** Stavropol'skiy Kray, SW Russian Federation *44.46N 44.07E*
118 K14 **Budeşti** Călăraşi, SE Romania *44.13N 26.31E*
Budgewoi see Budgewoi Lake
191 T8 **Budgewoi Lake** var. Budgewoi. New South Wales, SE Australia *33.13S 151.34E*
94 I2 **Búdhardalur** Vesturland, W Iceland *65.07N 21.45W*
Budimpešta see Budapest
81 J16 **Budjala** Equateur, NW Dem. Rep. Congo *2.39N 19.42E*
108 G10 **Budrio** Emilia-Romagna, C Italy *44.33N 11.34E*
Budslav see Budslaw
121 K14 **Budslaw** Rus. Budslav. Minskaya Voblasts', N Belarus *54.46N 27.26E*
Budua see Budva
174 Ll5 **Budu, Tanjung** headland East Malaysia *2.51N 111.42E*
115 J17 **Budva** It. Budua, SW-Montenegro *42.17N 18.49E*
Budweis see České Budějovice
Budyšin see Bautzen
81 D16 **Buea** Sud-Ouest, SW Cameroon *4.09N 9.13E*
105 S13 **Buëch** ≈ SE France
20 J17 **Buena** New Jersey, NE USA *39.30N 74.55W*
64 K12 **Buena Esperanza** San Luis, C Argentina *34.45S 65.15W*
56 C11 **Buenaventura** Valle del Cauca, W Colombia *3.54N 77.01W*
42 I4 **Buenaventura** Chihuahua, N Mexico *29.52N 107.25W*
59 M18 **Buena Vista** Santa Cruz, C Bolivia *17.27S 63.40W*
42 G10 **Buenavista** Baja California Sur, W Mexico *23.39N 109.40W*
39 S5 **Buena Vista** Colorado, C USA *38.50N 106.07W*
25 S5 **Buena Vista** Georgia, SE USA *32.19N 84.31W*
23 T6 **Buena Vista** Virginia, NE USA *37.43N 79.21W*
46 F5 **Buena Vista, Bahia de** bay N Cuba
37 R13 **Buena Vista Lake Bed** ◎ California, W USA
107 P8 **Buendía, Embalse de** ⊠ C Spain
65 F16 **Bueno, Río** ≈ S Chile
64 N12 **Buenos Aires** hist. Santa Maria del Buen Aire. ● (Argentina) Buenos Aires, E Argentina *34.40S 58.30W*
45 O15 **Buenos Aires** Puntarenas, SE Costa Rica *9.09N 83.15W*
63 C20 **Buenos Aires** off. Provincia de Buenos Aires. ◈ province E Argentina
65 H19 **Buenos Aires, Lago** var. Lago General Carrera. ◎ Argentina/Chile
56 C13 **Buesaco** Nariño, SW Colombia *1.22N 77.07W*
31 U8 **Buffalo** Minnesota, N USA *45.10N 93.49W*
28 T6 **Buffalo** Missouri, C USA *37.38N 93.05W*
20 D10 **Buffalo** New York, NE USA *42.53N 78.52W*
29 K8 **Buffalo** Oklahoma, C USA *36.50N 99.37W*
30 J7 **Buffalo** South Dakota, N USA *45.35N 103.32W*
27 V8 **Buffalo** Texas, SW USA *31.25N 96.04W*
35 W12 **Buffalo** Wyoming, C USA *44.21N 106.40W*
31 U11 **Buffalo Center** Iowa, C USA *43.23N 93.57W*
26 M3 **Buffalo Lake** ⊠ Texas, SW USA
32 K7 **Buffalo Lake** ⊠ Wisconsin, N USA
9 S12 **Buffalo Narrows** Saskatchewan, C Canada *55.52N 108.28W*
29 U9 **Buffalo River** ≈ Arkansas, C USA
31 R5 **Buffalo River** ≈ Minnesota, N USA
22 I10 **Buffalo River** ≈ Tennessee, S USA
32 J6 **Buffalo River** ≈ Wisconsin, N USA
46 L12 **Buff Bay** E Jamaica *18.18N 76.40W*
25 T3 **Buford** Georgia, SE USA *34.07N 84.00W*
30 J3 **Buford** North Dakota, N USA *48.00N 103.58W*
35 Y17 **Buford** Wyoming, C USA *41.05N 105.17W*
118 J14 **Buftea** Ilfov, S Romania *44.34N 25.57E*
86 I9 **Bug** Bel. Zakhodni Buh, Eng. Western Bug, Rus. Zapadnyy Bug, Ukr. Zakhidnyy Buh. ≈ E Europe
56 D11 **Buga** Valle del Cauca, W Colombia *3.52N 76.16W*
Buga see Dörvöljin
105 O17 **Bugarach, Pic du** ▲ S France *42.52N 2.23E*
168 F8 **Bugat** var. Bayangol. Govĭ-Altay, SW Mongolia *45.33N 94.22E*
152 B12 **Bugdaýly** Rus. Bugdayly. Balkan Welaýaty, W Turkmenistan *38.42N 54.14E*
Buggs Island Lake see John H.Kerr Reservoir
Bughotu see Santa Isabel
175 Q12 **Bugingkalo** Sulawesi, C Indonesia *4.49S 121.42E*
66 P6 **Bugio** island Madeira, Portugal, NE Atlantic Ocean
94 M8 **Bugøynes** Finnmark, N Norway *69.57N 29.34E*
129 Q3 **Bugrino** Nenetskiy Avtonomnyy Okrug, NW Russian Federation *68.48N 49.12E*
131 T5 **Bugul'ma** Respublika Tatarstan, W Russian Federation *54.31N 52.45E*
Bügür see Luntai
131 T6 **Buguruslan** Orenburgskaya Oblast', W Russian Federation *53.37N 52.30E*
165 R9 **Buh He** ≈ C China
35 O15 **Buhl** Idaho, NW USA *42.36N 114.45W*
103 F22 **Bühl** Baden-Württemberg, SW Germany *48.42N 8.07E*
118 K10 **Buhuşi** Bacău, E Romania *46.34N 26.55E*
Buie d'Istria see Buje
99 J20 **Builth Wells** E Wales, UK *52.07N 3.27W*
195 S13 **Buin** Bougainville Island, NE PNG *6.50S 155.42E*
110 J9 **Buin, Piz** ▲ Austria/Switzerland *46.51N 10.07E*
131 Q4 **Buinsk** Chuvashskaya Respublika, W Russian Federation *55.09N 47.00E*
131 Q4 **Buinsk** Respublika Tatarstan, W Russian Federation *54.58N 48.16E*
169 R8 **Buir Nur** Mong. Buyr Nuur. ◎ China/Mongolia see also Buyr Nuur
100 M5 **Buitenpost** Fris. Bûtenpost. Friesland, N Netherlands *53.15N 6.09E*
Buitenzorg see Bogor
85 F19 **Buitepos** Omaheke, E Namibia *22.17S 19.59E*
107 N7 **Buitrago del Lozoya** Madrid, C Spain *41.00N 3.38W*
Buj see Buy
106 M13 **Bujalance** Andalucía, S Spain *37.54N 4.22W*
115 O17 **Bujanovac** Serbia, SE Serbia *42.29N 21.43E*
107 S6 **Bujaraloz** Aragón, NE Spain *41.28N 0.10W*
114 A9 **Buje** It. Buie d'Istria. Istra, NW Croatia *45.23N 13.40E*
Bujnurd see Bojnūrd
83 D21 **Bujumbura** prev. Usumbura. ● (Burundi) W Burundi *3.25S 29.23E*
83 D20 **Bujumbura** ✕ W Burundi *3.21S 29.19E*
126 L15 **Bukachacha** Chitinskaya Oblast', S Russian Federation *52.49N 116.39E*
165 N11 **Buka Daban** var. Bukadaban Feng. ▲ C China *36.09N 90.52E*
Bukadaban Feng see Buka Daban
195 R11 **Buka Island** island NE PNG
83 F18 **Bukakata** S Uganda *0.18S 31.57E*
81 N24 **Bukama** Katanga, SE Dem. Rep. Congo *9.13S 25.52E*
148 J4 **Būkān** var. Bowkān. Āzarbāyjān-e Gharbī, NW Iran *36.31N 46.14E*
Bukantau, Gory see Bo'kantov Tog'lari
Bukarest see Bucureşti
81 O19 **Bukavu** prev. Costermansville. Sud Kivu, E Dem. Rep. Congo *2.18S 28.49E*
83 F21 **Bukene** Tabora, NW Tanzania *4.15S 32.51E*
147 W8 **Bū Khābī** var. Bakhābī. NW Oman *23.28N 56.06E*
Bukhara see Buxoro
Bukharskaya Oblast' see Buxoro Viloyati
174 I12 **Bukitkemuning** Sumatera, W Indonesia *4.43S 104.27E*
173 G8 **Bukittinggi** prev. Fort de Kock. Sumatera, W Indonesia *0.18S 100.19E*
113 L21 **Bükk** ▲▲ NE Hungary
83 F19 **Bukoba** Kagera, NW Tanzania *1.19S 31.49E*
115 N20 **Bukovo** S FYR Macedonia *40.59N 21.20E*
110 G6 **Bülach** Zürich, NW Switzerland *47.31N 8.30E*
Būlaevo see Bulayevo
Bulag see Möngönmorĭt, Töv, Mongolia
Bulag see Tünel, Hövsgöl, Mongolia
Bulagiyn Denj see Bulgan
191 U7 **Bulahdelah** New South Wales, SE Australia *32.24S 152.13E*
176 Yy15 **Bulaka, Sungai** ≈ Papua, E Indonesia
179 Qq12 **Bulan** Luzon, N Philippines *12.40N 123.55E*
143 N11 **Bulancak** Giresun, N Turkey *40.57N 38.13E*
158 J10 **Bulandshahr** Uttar Pradesh, N India *28.30N 77.49E*
143 R14 **Bulanık** Muş, E Turkey *39.04N 42.16E*
131 V7 **Bulanovo** Orenburgskaya Oblast', W Russian Federation *52.27N 55.08E*
85 J17 **Bulawayo** var. Buluwayo. Bulawayo, SW Zimbabwe *20.08S 28.36E*
85 J17 **Bulawayo** ✕ Matabeleland North, SW Zimbabwe *20.00S 28.36E*
151 Q6 **Bulayevo** Kaz. Būlaevo. Severnyy Kazakhstan, N Kazakhstan *54.55N 70.28E*
142 D15 **Buldan** Denizli, SW Turkey *38.03N 28.49E*
160 G12 **Buldāna** Mahārāshtra, C India *20.31N 76.18E*
40 E16 **Buldir Island** island Aleutian Islands, Alaska, USA
Buldur see Burdur
168 I8 **Bulgan** var. Bulagiyn Denj. Arhangay, C Mongolia *47.14N 100.56E*
168 D7 **Bulgan** var. Jargalant. Bayan-Ölgiy, W Mongolia *46.56N 91.07E*
168 K6 **Bulgan**. Bulgan, N Mongolia *50.31N 101.30E*
168 E8 **Bulgan** var. Burenhayrhan. Hovd, W Mongolia *46.04N 91.34E*
168 J10 **Bulgan** Ömnögovĭ, S Mongolia *44.07N 103.28E*
168 J7 **Bulgan** ◈ province N Mongolia
Bulgan see Bayan-Öndör, Bayanhongor, Mongolia
Bulgan see Darvi, Hovd, Mongolia
Bulgan see Tsagaan-Üür, Hövsgol, Mongolia
116 H10 **Bulgaria** off. Republic of Bulgaria, Bul. Bŭlgariya; prev. People's Republic of Bulgaria. ◆ republic SE Europe
Bŭlgariya see Bulgaria
116 L9 **Bŭlgarka** ▲ E Bulgaria *42.43N 26.19E*
175 T7 **Buli** Pulau Halmahera, E Indonesia *0.56N 128.17E*
175 Tt7 **Buli, Teluk** bay Pulau Halmahera, E Indonesia
166 J13 **Buliu He** ≈ S China
Bullange see Büllingen
Bulla, Ostrov see Xärä Zirä Adası
106 M11 **Bullaque** ≈ C Spain
107 Q13 **Bullas** Murcia, SE Spain *38.01N 1.40W*
82 M12 **Bullaxaar** Woqooyi Galbeed, NW Somalia *10.28N 44.15E*
110 C9 **Bulle** Fribourg, SW Switzerland *46.37N 7.04E*
193 G15 **Buller** ≈ South Island, NZ
191 P12 **Buller, Mount** ▲ Victoria, SE Australia *37.10S 146.31E*
38 H11 **Bullhead City** Arizona, SW USA *35.07N 114.32W*
101 N21 **Büllingen** Fr. Bullange. Liège, E Belgium *50.23N 6.15E*
Bullion State see Missouri
23 T14 **Bull Island** island South Carolina, SE USA
190 M4 **Bulloo River Overflow** wetland New South Wales, SE Australia
192 M12 **Bulls** Manawatu-Wanganui, North Island, NZ *40.10S 175.22E*
23 T14 **Bulls Bay** bay South Carolina, SE USA
29 U9 **Bull Shoals Lake** ⊠ Arkansas/Missouri, C USA
189 Q2 **Bulman** Northern Territory, N Australia *13.39S 134.21E*
168 I6 **Bulnayn Nuruu** ▲▲ N Mongolia
194 J13 **Bulolo** Morobe, C PNG *7.11S 146.34E*
175 Qq7 **Bulowa, Gunung** ▲ Sulawesi, N Indonesia *0.33N 123.39E*
Bulqiza see Bulqizë
115 L19 **Bulqizë** var. Bulqiza. Dibër, C Albania *41.30N 20.16E*
Bulsar see Valsād
175 R7 **Buludawa Keten, Pegunungan** ▲▲ Sulawesi, N Indonesia
175 Pp13 **Bulukumba** prev. Boeloekoemba. Sulawesi, C Indonesia *5.34S 120.13E*
153 O11 **Bulung'ur** Rus. Bulungur; prev. Krasnogvardeysk. Samarqand Viloyati, C Uzbekistan *39.46N 67.18E*
81 I21 **Bulungu** Bandundu, SW Dem. Rep. Congo *4.34S 18.33E*
Bulungur see Bulung'ur
Buluwayo see Bulawayo
81 K17 **Bumba** Equateur, N Dem. Rep. Congo *2.14N 22.25E*
124 O15 **Bumbah, Khalīj al** gulf N Libya
Bumbat see Bayan-Öndör
83 F19 **Bumbire Island** island N Tanzania
175 Oo4 **Bum Bun, Pulau** island East Malaysia
83 J17 **Buna** North Eastern, NE Kenya *2.40N 39.34E*
27 Y10 **Buna** Texas, SW USA *30.25N 94.00W*
Bunab see Bonāb
Bunai see M'bunai
153 S13 **Bunay** S Tajikistan *38.29N 71.41E*
188 I13 **Bunbury** Western Australia *33.24S 115.43E*
99 E14 **Buncrana** Ir. Bun Cranncha. NW Ireland *55.07N 7.27W*
Bun Cranncha see Buncrana
189 Z9 **Bundaberg** Queensland, E Australia *24.49S 152.16E*
191 T5 **Bundarra** New South Wales, SE Australia *30.12S 151.06E*
102 G13 **Bünde** Nordrhein-Westfalen, NW Germany *52.12N 8.34E*
158 H13 **Būndi** Rājasthān, N India *25.28N 75.42E*
194 I12 **Bundi** Madang, N PNG *5.40S 145.10E*
Bun Dobhráin see Bundoran
99 D15 **Bundoran** Ir. Bun Dobhráin. NW Ireland *54.28N 8.16W*
115 K18 **Bunë** SCr. Bojana. ≈ Albania/Montenegro see also Bojana
179 R16 **Bunga** ≈ Mindanao, S Philippines
173 Ff10 **Bungalaut, Selat** strait W Indonesia
178 Ii8 **Bung Kan** Nong Khai, E Thailand *18.19N 103.39E*
189 N4 **Bungle Bungle Range** ▲▲ Western Australia
84 C10 **Bungo** Uíge, NW Angola *7.30S 15.24E*
83 G18 **Bungoma** Western, W Kenya *0.34N 34.34E*
170 Dd15 **Bungo-suidō** strait SW Japan
170 Dd13 **Bungo-Takada** Ōita, Kyūshū, SW Japan *33.36N 131.28E*
102 K8 **Bungsberg** hill N Germany *54.12N 10.45E*
Bungur see Bunyu
81 P17 **Bunia** Orientale, NE Dem. Rep. Congo *1.33N 30.16E*
37 U6 **Bunker Hill** ▲ Nevada, W USA *39.16N 117.06W*
24 I7 **Bunkie** Louisiana, S USA *30.58N 92.12W*
25 X10 **Bunnell** Florida, SE USA *29.28N 81.15W*
107 S10 **Buñol** País Valenciano, E Spain *39.25N 0.46W*
100 K11 **Bunschoten** Utrecht, C Netherlands *52.15N 5.22E*
142 K14 **Bünyan** Kayseri, C Turkey *38.51N 35.49E*
175 Oo5 **Bunyu** var. Bungur. Borneo, N Indonesia *3.33N 117.50E*
175 Oo5 **Bunyu, Pulau** island N Indonesia
Bunzlau see Bolesławiec
Buoddobohki see Patoniva
126 Ll6 **Buorkhaya Guba** bay N Russian Federation
176 Z15 **Bupul** Papua, E Indonesia *7.24S 140.57E*
83 K19 **Bura** Coast, SE Kenya *1.06S 40.01E*
82 P12 **Buraan** Bari, N Somalia *10.03N 49.08E*
Būrabay see Borovoye
Buraida see Buraydah
Buraimi see Al Buraymī
151 Y11 **Buran** Vostochnyy Kazakhstan, E Kazakhstan *48.00N 85.09E*
164 G15 **Burang** Xizang Zizhiqu, W China *30.28N 81.13E*
Burao see Burco
144 H8 **Burāq** Dar'ā, S Syria *33.10N 36.28E*
147 O6 **Buraydah** var. Buraida. Al Qaşīm, N Saudi Arabia *26.50N 44.00E*
37 S15 **Burbank** California, W USA *34.10N 118.19W*
33 N11 **Burbank** Illinois, N USA *41.45N 87.48W*
191 Q8 **Burcher** New South Wales, SE Australia *33.29S 147.16E*
82 N13 **Burco** var. Burao, Bur'o. Togdheer, NW Somalia *9.29N 45.30E*
168 K8 **Bürd** var. Ongon. Övörhangay, C Mongolia *46.58N 103.45E*
152 L13 **Burdalyk** Lebap Welaýaty, E Turkmenistan *38.31N 64.21E*
189 W6 **Burdekin River** ≈ Queensland, NE Australia
29 O7 **Burden** Kansas, C USA *37.18N 96.45W*
Burdigala see Bordeaux
142 E15 **Burdur** var. Buldur. Burdur, SW Turkey *37.43N 30.16E*
142 E15 **Burdur** var. Buldur. ◈ province SW Turkey
142 E15 **Burdur Gölü** salt lake SW Turkey
67 H21 **Burdwood Bank** undersea feature SW Atlantic Ocean
82 I12 **Burē** Amhara, N Ethiopia *10.43N 37.09E*
82 H13 **Burē** Oromo, C Ethiopia *8.13N 35.09E*
95 J15 **Bureå** Västerbotten, N Sweden *64.36N 21.15E*
168 K7 **Büreghangay** var. Darhan. Bulgan, C Mongolia *48.07N 103.54E*
103 G14 **Büren** Nordrhein-Westfalen, W Germany *51.34N 8.34E*
168 L8 **Büren** var. Bayantöhöm. Töv, C Mongolia *46.57N 105.09E*
168 K6 **Bürengiyn Nuruu** ▲▲ N Mongolia
Burenhayrhan see Bulgan
168 I6 **Bürentogtoh** var. Bayan. Hövsgöl, C Mongolia *49.36N 99.36E*
Būrewāla see Mandi Būrewāla
127 N17 **Bureya** ≈ SE Russian Federation
94 J9 **Burfjord** Troms, N Norway *69.55N 21.54E*
102 L13 **Burg** var. Burg an der Ihle, Burg bei Magdeburg. Sachsen-Anhalt, C Germany *52.16N 11.51E*
Burg an der Ihle see Burg
116 N10 **Burgas** var. Bourgas. Burgas, E Bulgaria *42.31N 27.30E*
116 N9 **Burgas** ✕ Burgas, E Bulgaria *42.35N 27.33E*
116 M10 **Burgas** ◈ province E Bulgaria
116 N10 **Burgaski Zaliv** gulf E Bulgaria
116 M10 **Burgasko Ezero** lagoon E Bulgaria
23 V11 **Burgaw** North Carolina, SE USA *34.33N 77.54W*
Burg bei Magdeburg see Burg
110 E8 **Burgdorf** Bern, NW Switzerland *47.03N 7.37E*
111 Y7 **Burgenland** off. Land Burgenland. ◈ state SE Austria
11 S13 **Burgeo** Newfoundland and Labrador, SE Canada *47.42N 57.29W*
85 I24 **Burgersdorp** Eastern Cape, SE South Africa *31.00S 26.20E*
85 K20 **Burgersfort** Mpumalanga, NE South Africa *24.39S 30.18E*
103 N23 **Burghausen** Bayern, SE Germany *48.10N 12.48E*
145 O5 **Burghūth, Sabkhat al** ◎ E Syria
103 M20 **Burglengenfeld** Bayern, SE Germany *49.11N 12.01E*
43 P9 **Burgos** Tamaulipas, C Mexico *24.55N 98.46W*
107 N4 **Burgos** Castilla-León, N Spain *42.21N 3.40W*
107 N4 **Burgos** ◈ province Castilla-León, N Spain
Burgstadlberg see Hradiště
97 P20 **Burgsvik** Gotland, SE Sweden *57.01N 18.18E*
Burgum see Bergum
Burgundy see Bourgogne
165 Q11 **Burhan Budai Shan** ▲▲ C China
142 B12 **Burhaniye** Balıkesir, W Turkey *39.28N 26.58E*
160 G12 **Burhānpur** Madhya Pradesh, C India *21.18N 76.13E*
179 Q11 **Burias Island** island C Philippines
131 W7 **Buribay** Respublika Bashkortostan, W Russian Federation *51.57N 58.11E*
45 O17 **Burica, Punta** headland Costa Rica/Panama *8.02N 82.53W*
178 Ii10 **Buriram** var. Buri Ram, Puriramya. Buri Ram, E Thailand *15.01N 103.06E*
107 S10 **Burjassot** País Valenciano, E Spain *39.33N 0.25W*
83 N16 **Burka Giibi** Hiiraan, C Somalia *3.52N 45.07E*
153 X8 **Burkan** ≈ E Kyrgyzstan
27 R4 **Burkburnett** Texas, SW USA *34.06N 98.34W*
31 O12 **Burke** South Dakota, N USA *43.09N 99.18W*
8 K15 **Burke Channel** channel British Columbia, W Canada
204 J10 **Burke Island** island Antarctica
22 L7 **Burkesville** Kentucky, S USA *36.47N 85.22W*
189 T4 **Burketown** Queensland, NE Australia *17.48S 139.28E*
27 Q8 **Burkett** Texas, SW USA *32.01N 99.17W*
27 Y9 **Burkeville** Texas, SW USA *30.58N 93.41W*
23 V7 **Burkeville** Virginia, NE USA *37.11N 78.12W*
79 O12 **Burkina** off. Burkina Faso; prev. Upper Volta. ◆ republic W Africa
Burkina Faso see Burkina
204 L13 **Burks, Cape** headland Antarctica
12 H12 **Burk's Falls** Ontario, S Canada *45.38N 79.25W*
103 H23 **Burladingen** Baden-Württemberg, S Germany *48.18N 9.05E*
27 T7 **Burleson** Texas, SW USA *32.32N 97.19W*
35 P15 **Burley** Idaho, NW USA *42.32N 113.47W*
150 G8 **Burlin** Zapadnyy Kazakhstan, NW Kazakhstan *51.25N 52.42E*
12 G16 **Burlington** Ontario, S Canada *43.21N 79.45W*
39 W4 **Burlington** Colorado, C USA *39.16N 102.16W*
31 Y15 **Burlington** Iowa, C USA *40.48N 91.05W*
29 P5 **Burlington** Kansas, C USA *38.11N 95.44W*
23 T9 **Burlington** North Carolina, SE USA *36.06N 79.26W*
30 M3 **Burlington** North Dakota, N USA *48.16N 101.25W*
20 L7 **Burlington** Vermont, NE USA *44.28N 73.13W*
32 M9 **Burlington** Wisconsin, N USA *42.38N 88.12W*
29 Q1 **Burlington Junction** Missouri, C USA *40.27N 95.04W*
178 Gg4 **Burma** off. Union of Myanmar, ◆ military dictatorship SE Asia
8 L17 **Burnaby** British Columbia, SW Canada *49.16N 122.58W*
119 O12 **Burnas, Ozero** ◎ SW Ukraine
27 S10 **Burnet** Texas, SW USA *30.45N 98.13W*
37 O3 **Burney** California, W USA *40.52N 121.42W*
191 O16 **Burnie** Tasmania, SE Australia *41.06S 145.52E*
99 L17 **Burnley** NW England, UK *53.48N 2.13W*
Burnoye see Bauyrzhan Momyshuly
159 R15 **Burnpur** West Bengal, NE India *23.39N 86.55E*
34 K14 **Burns** Oregon, NW USA *43.35N 119.03W*
28 K11 **Burns Flat** Oklahoma, C USA *35.21N 99.10W*
22 M7 **Burnside** Kentucky, S USA *36.55N 84.34W*
15 Ii5 **Burnside** ≈ Nunavut, NW Canada
34 L15 **Burns Junction** Oregon, NW USA *42.46N 117.51W*
8 L13 **Burns Lake** British Columbia, SW Canada *54.13N 125.45W*
31 V9 **Burnsville** Minnesota, N USA *44.49N 93.14W*
23 P9 **Burnsville** North Carolina, SE USA *35.55N 82.18W*
23 R4 **Burnsville** West Virginia, NE USA *38.50N 80.39W*
12 I13 **Burnt River** ≈ Ontario, SE Canada
12 I11 **Burntroot Lake** ◎ Ontario, SE Canada
9 W12 **Burntwood** ≈ Manitoba, C Canada
Bur'o see Burco
164 L2 **Burqin** Xinjiang Uygur Zizhiqu, NW China *47.42N 86.49E*
190 J8 **Burra** South Australia *33.41S 138.54E*
191 S9 **Burragorang, Lake** ⊠ New South Wales, SE Australia
98 K5 **Burray** island NE Scotland, UK
115 L19 **Burrel** var. Burreli. Dibër, C Albania *41.36N 20.00E*
Burreli see Burrel
191 R8 **Burrendong Reservoir** ⊠ New South Wales, SE Australia
191 R5 **Burren Junction** New South Wales, SE Australia *30.06S 149.01E*
107 T9 **Burriana** País Valenciano, E Spain *39.54N 0.04W*
191 R10 **Burrinjuck Reservoir** ⊠ New South Wales, SE Australia
38 J12 **Burro Creek** ≈ Arizona, SW USA
42 M5 **Burro, Serranías del** ▲▲ NW Mexico
64 K7 **Burruyacú** Tucumán, N Argentina *26.28S 64.30W*
142 E12 **Bursa** var. Brussa; prev. Brusa, anc. Prusa. Bursa, NW Turkey *40.12N 29.04E*
142 D12 **Bursa** var. Brusa, Brussa. ◈ province NW Turkey
77 Y9 **Bûr Safâga** var. Būr Safājah. E Egypt *26.41N 33.58E*
Būr Safājah see Bûr Safâga
Būr Sa'īd see Port Said
83 O14 **Bur Tinle** Nugaal, C Somalia *7.50N 48.01E*
33 Q5 **Burt Lake** ◎ Michigan, N USA
120 H7 **Burtnieks** var. Burtnieks Ezers. ◎ N Latvia
Burtnieku Ezers see Burtnieks
33 Q9 **Burton** Michigan, N USA *43.00N 84.16W*
Burton on Trent see Burton upon Trent
99 M19 **Burton upon Trent** var. Burton on Trent, Burton-upon-Trent. C England, UK *52.48N 1.36W*
95 J15 **Burträsk** Västerbotten, N Sweden *64.31N 20.40E*
151 S14 **Burubaytal** prev. Burylbaytal. Zhambyl, SE Kazakhstan *45.01N 73.58E*
Burujird see Borūjerd
Burultokay see Fuhai
147 R15 **Burūm** SE Yemen *14.22N 48.53E*
Burunday see Boralday
83 D21 **Burundi** off. Republic of Burundi; prev. Kingdom of Burundi, Urundi. ◆ republic C Africa
175 S11 **Buru, Pulau** prev. Boeroe. island E Indonesia
79 T17 **Burutu** Delta, S Nigeria *5.18N 5.32E*
8 G7 **Burwash Landing** Yukon Territory, W Canada *61.26N 139.12W*
31 O14 **Burwell** Nebraska, C USA *41.46N 99.04W*
99 L17 **Bury** NW England, UK *53.36N 2.16W*
126 K15 **Buryatiya, Respublika** prev. Buryatskaya ASSR. ◈ autonomous republic S Russian Federation
Buryatskaya ASSR see Buryatiya, Respublika
Burylbaytal see Burubaytal
119 S3 **Buryn'** Sums'ka Oblast', NE Ukraine *51.12N 33.49E*
99 P20 **Bury St Edmunds** hist. Beodericsworth. E England, UK *52.15N 0.43E*
116 G8 **Bŭrziya** ≈ NW Bulgaria
108 D9 **Busalla** Liguria, NW Italy *44.35N 8.55E*
179 R17 **Busa, Mount** ▲ Mindanao, S Philippines *6.19N 124.29E*
Busan see Pusan
145 N5 **Buşayrah** Dayr az Zawr, E Syria *35.03N 40.28E*
Buševa see Baba
149 N12 **Būshehr** off. Ostān-e Būshehr. ◈ province SW Iran
Būshehr/Bushire see Bandar-e Būshehr
27 N2 **Bushland** Texas, SW USA *35.11N 102.04W*
32 J12 **Bushnell** Illinois, N USA *40.33N 90.30W*
Busi see Biševo
83 G18 **Busia** SE Uganda *1.20N 34.48E*
Busiasch see Buziaş
81 K16 **Businga** Equateur, NW Dem. Rep. Congo *3.19N 20.52E*
81 J18 **Busira** ≈ NW Dem. Rep. Congo
118 I5 **Bus'k** Rus. Busk. L'vivs'ka Oblast', W Ukraine *49.59N 24.34E*
97 E14 **Buskerud** ◈ county S Norway
115 F14 **Buško Jezero** ⊠ SW Bosnia and Herzegovina
113 M15 **Busko-Zdrój** Świętokrzyskie, C Poland *50.28N 20.43E*
Busra see Al Başrah, Iraq
Buşrá see Buşrá ash Shām, Syria
144 H9 **Buşrá ash Shām** var. Bosora, Bosra, Bozrah, Buşrá. Dar'ā, S Syria *32.31N 36.31E*
188 I13 **Busselton** Western Australia *33.43S 115.15E*
83 C14 **Busseri** ≈ W Sudan
108 E9 **Busseto** Emilia-Romagna, C Italy *45.00N 10.06E*
108 A8 **Bussoleno** Piemonte, NE Italy *45.11N 7.07E*
Bussora see Al Başrah
100 J10 **Bussum** Noord-Holland, C Netherlands *52.16N 5.10E*
43 N7 **Bustamante** Nuevo León, NE Mexico *26.29N 100.30W*
65 I23 **Bustamante, Punta** headland S Argentina *51.34S 68.58W*
Bustan see Bo'ston
118 J12 **Buşteni** Prahova, SE Romania *45.23N 25.31E*
108 D7 **Busto Arsizio** Lombardia, N Italy *45.37N 8.49E*
153 Q10 **Bŭston** Rus. Buston. NW Tajikistan *40.31N 69.21E*
179 P12 **Busuanga Island** island Calamian Group, W Philippines
102 H8 **Büsum** Schleswig-Holstein, N Germany *54.08N 8.52E*
81 M16 **Buta** Orientale, N Dem. Rep. Congo *2.50N 24.41E*
83 E20 **Butare** prev. Astrida. S Rwanda *2.39S 29.44E*
203 O2 **Butaritari** atoll Tungaru, W Kiribati
Butawal see Butwal
98 H13 **Bute** cultural region SW Scotland, UK
168 K6 **Büteeliyn Nuruu** ▲▲ N Mongolia
8 L16 **Bute Inlet** fjord British Columbia, W Canada
98 H12 **Bute, Island of** island SW Scotland, UK
81 P18 **Butembo** Nord Kivu, NE Dem. Rep. Congo *0.09N 29.16E*
Bûtenpost see Buitenpost
109 K25 **Butera** Sicilia, Italy, C Mediterranean Sea *37.12N 14.12E*
101 M20 **Bütgenbach** Liège, E Belgium *50.25N 6.12E*
Butha Qi see Zalantun
177 F5 **Buthidaung** Arakan State, W Burma *20.52N 92.32E*
63 I16 **Butiá** Rio Grande do Sul, S Brazil *30.09S 51.55W*
83 F17 **Butiaba** NW Uganda *1.48N 31.21E*
25 N6 **Butler** Alabama, S USA *32.05N 88.13W*
25 S5 **Butler** Georgia, SE USA *32.33N 84.14W*
33 Q11 **Butler** Indiana, N USA *41.25N 84.52W*
29 R5 **Butler** Missouri, C USA *38.15N 94.19W*
20 B14 **Butler** Pennsylvania, NE USA *40.51N 79.52W*
204 K5 **Butler Island** island Antarctica
23 U8 **Butner** North Carolina, SE USA *36.07N 78.45W*
175 Qq13 **Buton, Pulau** var. Pulau Butung; prev. Boetoeng. island C Indonesia
175 Qq13 **Buton, Selat** strait C Indonesia
Bütow see Bytów
115 L23 **Butrintit, Liqeni i** ◎ S Albania
25 N3 **Buttahatchee River** ≈ Alabama/Mississippi, S USA
35 Q10 **Butte** Montana, NW USA *46.01N 112.33W*
31 O12 **Butte** Nebraska, C USA *42.54N 98.51W*
173 G3 **Butterworth** Pinang, Peninsular Malaysia *5.24N 100.22E*
85 J25 **Butterworth** var. Gcuwa. Eastern Cape, SE South Africa *32.19S 28.09E*
11 O3 **Button Islands** island group Nunavut, NE Canada
37 R13 **Buttonwillow** California, W USA *35.24N 119.26W*
179 R14 **Butuan** off. Butuan City. Mindanao, S Philippines *8.56N 125.32E*
Butung, Pulau see Buton, Pulau
Butuntum see Bitonto
130 M8 **Buturlinovka** Voronezhskaya Oblast', W Russian Federation *50.48N 40.33E*
159 O11 **Butwal** var. Butawal. Western, C Nepal *27.41N 83.28E*
103 G17 **Butzbach** Hessen, W Germany *50.26N 8.40E*
102 L9 **Bützow** Mecklenburg-Vorpommern, N Germany *53.49N 11.58E*
82 N13 **Buuhoodle** Togdheer, N Somalia *8.18N 46.15E*
83 N16 **Buulobarde** var. Buulo Berde. Hiiraan, C Somalia Africa *3.52N 45.36E*

◆ Country
● Country Capital
◇ Dependent Territory
○ Dependent Territory Capital
◈ Administrative Region
✕ International Airport
▲ Mountain
▲▲ Mountain Range
Volcano
≈ River
◎ Lake
⊠ Reservoir

BUULO BERDE – CAMERON MOUNTAINS

Buulo Berde *see* Buulobarde
82 *P12* **Buuraha Cal Miskaat** ▲▲ NE Somalia
83 *L19* **Buur Gaabo** Jubbada Hoose, S Somalia *1.14S 41.48E*
101 *M22* **Buurgplaatz** ▲ N Luxembourg *50.09N 6.02E*
168 *H8* **Buutsagaan** *var.* Buyant. Bayanhongor, C Mongolia *46.07N 98.45E*
Buwayrāt al Hasūn *see* Bu'ayrāt al Ḥasūn
152 *L11* **Buxoro** *var.* Bokhara, ***Rus.*** Bukhara. Buxoro Viloyati, C Uzbekistan *39.50N 64.22E*
152 *J11* **Buxoro Viloyati** ***Rus.*** Bukharskaya Oblast'. ◐ *province* C Uzbekistan
102 *I10* **Buxtehude** Niedersachsen, NW Germany *53.28N 9.42E*
99 *L18* **Buxton** C England, UK *53.18N 1.52W*
128 *M14* **Buy** *var.* Buj. Kostromskaya Oblast', NW Russian Federation *58.27N 41.31E*
Buyanbat *see* Jargalant
168 *D6* **Buyant** Bayan-Ölgiy, W Mongolia *48.31N 89.36E*
Buyant *see* Buutsagaan, Bayanhongor, Mongolia
Buyant *see* Galshar, Hentiy, Mongolia
Buyant *see* Otgon, Dzavhan, Mongolia
169 *N10* **Buyant-Uhaa** Dornogovĭ, SE Mongolia *44.52N 110.12E*
168 *M7* **Buyant Ukha** ✕ (Ulaanbaatar) Töv, N Mongolia
131 *Q16* **Buynaksk** Respublika Dagestan, SW Russian Federation *42.52N 47.03E*
121 *L20* **Buynavichy** ***Rus.*** Buynovichi. Homyel'skaya Voblasts', SE Belarus *51.53N 28.31E*
Buynovichi *see* Buynavichy
78 *L16* **Buyo** SW Ivory Coast *6.23N 7.04W*
78 *L16* **Buyo, Lac de** ▣ W Ivory Coast
169 *R7* **Buyr Nuur** ***var.*** Buir Nur. ◎ China /Mongolia ***see also*** Buir Nur
143 *T13* **Büyükağrı Dağı** ***var.*** Aghri Dagh, Agri Dagi, Koh I Noh, Masis, ***Eng.*** Great Ararat, Mount Ararat. ▲ E Turkey *39.43N 44.19E*
143 *R15* **Büyük Çayı** ≈ NE Turkey
116 *O13* **Büyük Çekmece** İstanbul, NW Turkey *41.02N 28.36E*
116 *N12* **Büyükkarıştıran** Kırklareli, NW Turkey *41.17N 27.33E*
117 *L14* **Büyükkemikli Burnu** *headland* NW Turkey *40.19N 26.14E*
142 *E15* **Büyükmenderes Nehri** ≈ SW Turkey
Büyükzap Suyu *see* Great Zab
104 *M9* **Buzançais** Indre, C France *46.53N 1.25E*
118 *K13* **Buzău** Buzău, SE Romania *45.08N 26.51E*
118 *K13* **Buzău** ◐ *county* SE Romania
118 *L12* **Buzău** ≈ E Romania
77 *S11* **Buzaymah** ***var.*** Bzīmah. SE Libya *24.53N 22.01E*
170 *D13* **Buzen** Fukuoka, Kyūshū, SW Japan *33.30N 131.26E*
118 *F12* **Buziaş** ***Ger.*** Busiasch, ***Hung.*** Buziásfürdő; ***prev.*** Buziás. Timiş, W Romania *45.38N 21.37E*
Buziásfürdő *see* Buziaş
85 *M18* **Búzi, Rio** ≈ C Mozambique
119 *Q10* **Buz'kyy Lyman** *bay* S Ukraine
Büzmeýin *see* Abadan
151 *O8* **Buzuluk** Akmola, C Kazakhstan *51.52N 66.09E*
131 *T6* **Buzuluk** Orenburgskaya Oblast', W Russian Federation *52.47N 52.15E*
131 *N8* **Buzuluk** ≈ SW Russian Federation
21 *P12* **Buzzards Bay** Massachusetts, NE USA *41.45N 70.37W*
21 *P13* **Buzzards Bay** *bay* Massachusetts, NE USA
85 *G16* **Bwabata** Caprivi, NE Namibia *17.52S 22.39E*
195 *P17* **Bwagaoia** Misima Island, SE PNG *10.39S 152.48E*
Bwake *see* Bouaké
197 *C12* **Bwatnapne** Pentecost, C Vanuatu *15.42S 168.07E*
121 *K14* **Byahoml'** ***Rus.*** Begoml'. Vitsyebskaya Voblasts', N Belarus *54.44N 28.03E*
116 *J8* **Byala** Ruse, N Bulgaria *43.32N 27.51E*
116 *N9* **Byala** ***prev.*** Ak-Dere. Varna, E Bulgaria *42.52N 27.53E*
Byala Reka *see* Erythropótamos
116 *H8* **Byala Slatina** Vratsa, NW Bulgaria *43.28N 23.57E*
121 *N15* **Byalynichy** ***Rus.*** Belynichi. Mahilyowskaya Voblasts', E Belarus *53.58N 29.44E*
121 *G19* **Byaroza** ***Pol.*** Bereza Kartuska, ***Rus.*** Berëza. Brestskaya Voblasts', SW Belarus *52.33N 24.58E*
121 *H16* **Byarozawka** ***Rus.*** Berezovka. Hrodzyenskaya Voblasts', W Belarus *53.45N 25.30E*
Bybles *see* Jbaïl
113 *O14* **Bychawa** Lubelskie, SE Poland *51.06N 22.34E*
Bychikha *see* Bychykha
120 *N11* **Bychykha** ***Rus.*** Bychikha. Vitsyebskaya Voblasts', NE Belarus *55.40N 29.58E*
113 *I14* **Byczyna** ***Ger.*** Pitschen. Opolskie, S Poland *51.06N 18.13E*
112 *I10* **Bydgoszcz** ***Ger.*** Bromberg. Kujawski-pomorskie, C Poland *53.16N 18.00E*
121 *H19* **Byelaazyorsk** ***Rus.*** Beloozersk. Brestskaya Voblasts', SW Belarus *52.28N 25.10E*
121 *I17* **Byelaruskaya Hrada** ***Rus.*** Belorusskaya Gryada. *ridge* N Belarus
121 *G18* **Byelavyezhskaya Pushcha** ***Pol.*** Puszcza Białowieska, ***Rus.*** Belovezhskaya Pushcha. *forest* Belarus/Poland ***see also*** Białowieska, Puszcza
121 *H15* **Byenyakoni** ***Rus.*** Benyakoni. Hrodzyenskaya Voblasts', W Belarus *54.15N 25.22E*
121 *M16* **Byerazino** ***Rus.*** Berezino. Minskaya Voblasts', C Belarus *53.49N 28.58E*
120 *L13* **Byerazino** ***Rus.*** Berezino. Vitsyebskaya Voblasts', N Belarus *54.54N 28.12E*
121 *L14* **Byerezino** ***Rus.*** Berezina. ≈ C Belarus
120 *M13* **Byeshankovichy** ***Rus.*** Beshenkovichi. Vitsyebskaya Voblasts', N Belarus *55.03N 29.28E*
33 *U13* **Byesville** Ohio, N USA *39.58N 81.32W*
121 *P18* **Byesyedz'** ***Rus.*** Besed'. ≈ SE Belarus
121 *H19* **Byezdzyezh** ***Rus.*** Bezdezh. Brestskaya Voblasts', SW Belarus *52.18N 25.16E*
95 *J15* **Bygdeå** Västerbotten, N Sweden *64.03N 20.49E*
96 *F12* **Bygdin** ◎ S Norway
95 *J15* **Bygdsiljum** Västerbotten, N Sweden *64.20N 20.31E*
97 *E17* **Bygland** Aust-Agder, S Norway *58.46N 7.50E*
97 *E17* **Byglandsfjord** Aust-Agder, S Norway *58.42N 7.51E*
121 *N16* **Bykhaw** ***Rus.*** Bykhov. Mahilyowskaya Voblasts', E Belarus *53.31N 30.15E*
Bykhov *see* Bykhaw
131 *P9* **Bykovo** Volgogradskaya Oblast', SW Russian Federation *49.52N 45.24E*
126 *L6* **Bykovskiy** Respublika Sakha (Yakutiya), NE Russian Federation *71.57N 129.07E*
205 *R12* **Byrd Glacier** *glacier* Antarctica
12 *K10* **Byrd, Lac** ◎ Québec, SE Canada
191 *P5* **Byrock** New South Wales, SE Australia *30.40S 146.24E*
32 *L10* **Byron** Illinois, N USA *42.06N 89.15W*
191 *V4* **Byron Bay** New South Wales, SE Australia *28.39S 153.34E*
191 *V4* **Byron, Cape** *headland* New South Wales, E Australia *28.37S 153.40E*
65 *F21* **Byron, Isla** *island* S Chile
Byron Island *see* Nikunau
67 *B24* **Byron Sound** *sound* NW Falkland Islands
126 *J5* **Byrranga, Gora** ▲▲ N Russian Federation
95 *J14* **Byske** Västerbotten, N Sweden *64.58N 21.10E*
113 *K18* **Bystrá** ▲ N Slovakia *49.10N 19.49E*
113 *F18* **Bystřice nad Pernštejnem** ***Ger.*** Bistritz ober Pernstein. Vysočina, C Czech Republic *49.30N 16.16E*
Bystrovka *see* Kemin
113 *G16* **Bystrzyca Kłodzka** ***Ger.*** Habelschwerdt. Wałbrzych, SW Poland *50.19N 16.39E*
113 *I18* **Bytča** Žilinský Kraj, N Slovakia *49.15N 18.31E*
121 *L15* **Bytcha** ***Rus.*** Bytcha. Minskaya Voblasts', NE Belarus *54.19N 28.24E*
Byteń/Byten' *see* Bytsyen'
113 *J16* **Bytom** ***Ger.*** Beuthen. Śląskie, S Poland *50.21N 18.51E*
112 *H7* **Bytów** ***Ger.*** Bütow. Pomorskie, N Poland *54.09N 17.30E*
121 *H18* **Bytsyen'** ***Pol.*** Byteń, ***Rus.*** Byten'. Brestskaya Voblasts', SW Belarus *52.53N 25.32E*
83 *E19* **Byumba** ***var.*** Biumba. N Rwanda *1.37S 30.05E*
Byuzmeyin *see* Abadan
121 *O20* **Byval'ki** Homyel'skaya Voblasts', SE Belarus *51.51N 30.37E*
97 *O20* **Byxelkrok** Kalmar, S Sweden *57.18N 17.01E*
Byzantium *see* İstanbul
Bzīmah *see* Buzaymah

C

64 *O6* **Caacupé** Cordillera, S Paraguay *25.22S 57.04W*
64 *P6* **Caaguazú** ***off.*** Departamento de Caaguazú. ◐ *department* C Paraguay
84 *C13* **Caála** ***var.*** Kaala, Robert Williams, ***Port.*** Vila Robert Williams. Huambo, C Angola *12.51S 15.33E*
64 *P7* **Caazapá** Caazapá, S Paraguay *26.09S 56.21W*
64 *P7* **Caazapá** ***off.*** Departamento de Caazapá. ◐ *department* SE Paraguay
83 *P15* **Cabaad, Raas** *headland* C Somalia *6.13N 49.01E*
179 *R14* **Cabadbaran** Mindanao, S Philippines *9.07N 125.34E*
57 *N10* **Cabadisocaña** Amazonas, S Venezuela *4.28N 64.45W*
46 *F5* **Cabaiguán** Sancti Spíritus, C Cuba *22.04N 79.31W*
Caballeria, Cabo *see* Cavalleria, Cap de
39 *Q14* **Caballo Reservoir** ▣ New Mexico, SW USA
42 *L6* **Caballos Mesteños, Llano de los** *plain* N Mexico
106 *L2* **Cabañaquinta** Asturias, N Spain *43.10N 5.37W*
44 *B9* **Cabañas** ◐ *department* E El Salvador
179 *P10* **Cabanatuan** ***off.*** Cabanatuan City. Luzon, N Philippines *15.27N 120.57E*
13 *T8* **Cabano** Québec, SE Canada *47.40N 68.55W*
106 *L11* **Cabeza del Buey** Extremadura, W Spain *38.43N 5.13W*
47 *V5* **Cabezas de San Juan** *headland* E Puerto Rico *18.23N 65.37W*
107 *N2* **Cabezón de la Sal** Cantabria, N Spain *43.19N 4.13W*
Cabhán *see* Cavan
63 *B23* **Cabildo** Buenos Aires, E Argentina *38.28S 61.49W*
Cabillonum *see* Chalon-sur-Saône
56 *H5* **Cabimas** Zulia, NW Venezuela *10.25N 71.27W*
84 *A9* **Cabinda** ***var.*** Kabinda. Cabinda, NW Angola *5.34S 12.12E*
84 *A9* **Cabinda** ***var.*** Kabinda. ◐ *province* NW Angola
35 *N7* **Cabinet Mountains** ▲▲ Idaho/ Montana, NW USA
84 *B11* **Cabiri** Bengo, NW Angola *8.50S 13.42E*
65 *J20* **Cabo Blanco** Santa Cruz, SE Argentina *47.13S 65.43W*
84 *P13* **Cabo Delgado** ***off.*** Província de Capo Delgado. ◐ *province* NE Mozambique
12 *L9* **Cabonga, Réservoir** ▣ Québec, SE Canada
29 *V7* **Cabool** Missouri, C USA *37.07N 92.06W*
191 *V2* **Caboolture** Queensland, E Australia *27.05S 152.56E*
Cabora Bassa, Lake *see* Cahora Bassa, Albufeira de
42 *F3* **Caborca** Sonora, NW Mexico *30.44N 112.06W*
Cabo San Lucas *see* San Lucas
29 *V11* **Cabot** Arkansas, C USA *34.58N 92.01W*
12 *F12* **Cabot Head** *headland* Ontario, S Canada *45.13N 81.17W*
16 *Ss10* **Cabot Strait** *strait* E Canada
Cabo Verde, Ilhas do *see* Cape Verde
106 *M14* **Cabra** Andalucía, S Spain *37.28N 4.28W*
109 *B19* **Cabras** Sardegna, Italy, C Mediterranean Sea *39.55N 8.30E*
196 *A15* **Cabras Island** *island* W Guam
47 *O8* **Cabrera** N Dominican Republic *19.34N 69.55W*
107 *X10* **Cabrera, Illa de** ***anc.*** Capraria. *island* Islas Baleares, Spain, W Mediterranean Sea
106 *J4* **Cabrera** ≈ NW Spain
107 *Q15* **Cabrera, Sierra** ▲▲ S Spain
9 *S16* **Cabri** Saskatchewan, S Canada *50.37N 108.28W*
107 *R10* **Cabriel** ≈ E Spain
56 *M7* **Cabruta** Guárico, C Venezuela *7.39N 66.19W*
179 *Oo8* **Cabugao** Luzon, N Philippines *17.55N 120.29E*
56 *G10* **Cabuyaro** Meta, C Colombia *4.16N 72.47W*
62 *I13* **Caçador** Santa Catarina, S Brazil *26.47S 51.00W*
44 *G8* **Cacaguatique, Cordillera** ***var.*** Cordillera. ▲▲ NE El Salvador
114 *L13* **Čačak** Serbia, C Serbia *43.52N 20.23E*
57 *Y10* **Cacao** NE French Guiana *4.37N 52.28W*
63 *H16* **Caçapava do Sul** Rio Grande do Sul, S Brazil *30.28S 53.28W*
23 *U3* **Cacapon River** ≈ West Virginia, NE USA
109 *J23* **Caccamo** Sicilia, Italy, C Mediterranean Sea *37.55N 13.40E*
109 *A17* **Caccia, Capo** *headland* Sardegna, Italy, C Mediterranean Sea *40.34N 8.09E*
152 *H15* **Çäçe** ***var.*** Chäche, ***Rus.*** Chaacha. Ahal Welaýaty, S Turkmenistan *36.49N 60.33E*
61 *G18* **Cáceres** Mato Grosso, W Brazil *16.04S 57.40W*
106 *J10* **Cáceres** ***Ar.*** Qazris. Extremadura, W Spain *39.28N 6.22W*
106 *J9* **Cáceres** ◐ *province* Extremadura, W Spain
Cachacrou *see* Scotts Head Village
63 *C21* **Cacharí** Buenos Aires, E Argentina *36.24S 59.31W*
28 *L12* **Cache** Oklahoma, C USA *34.37N 98.37W*
8 *M16* **Cache Creek** British Columbia, SW Canada *50.49N 121.19W*
37 *N6* **Cache Creek** ≈ California, W USA
39 *S3* **Cache La Poudre River** ≈ Colorado, C USA
Cacheo *see* Cacheu
29 *W11* **Cache River** ≈ Arkansas, C USA
32 *L17* **Cache River** ≈ Illinois, N USA
78 *G12* **Cacheu** ***var.*** Cacheo. W Guinea-Bissau *12.12N 16.10W*
61 *I15* **Cachimbo** Pará, NE Brazil *9.21S 54.58W*
61 *H15* **Cachimbo, Serra do** ▲▲ C Brazil
84 *D13* **Cachingues** Bié, C Angola *13.05S 16.48E*
56 *G7* **Cáchira** Norte de Santander, N Colombia *7.46N 73.03W*
63 *H16* **Cachoeira do Sul** Rio Grande do Sul, S Brazil *29.58S 52.54W*
61 *O20* **Cachoeiro de Itapemirim** Espírito Santo, SE Brazil *20.51S 41.07W*
84 *E12* **Cacolo** Lunda Sul, NE Angola *10.09S 19.17E*
85 *C14* **Caconda** Huíla, C Angola *13.43S 15.03E*
84 *A9* **Cacongo** Cabinda, NW Angola *5.16S 12.10E*
37 *U9* **Cactus Peak** ▲ Nevada, W USA *37.42N 116.51W*
84 *A11* **Cacuaco** Luanda, NW Angola *8.49S 13.24E*
85 *B14* **Cacula** Huíla, SW Angola *14.31S 14.07E*
69 *R12* **Caculuvar** ≈ SW Angola
61 *O19* **Caçumba, Ilha** *island* SE Brazil
57 *N10* **Cacuri** Amazonas, S Venezuela
83 *N17* **Cadale** Shabeellaha Dhexe, E Somalia *2.48N 46.19E*
107 *X4* **Cadaqués** Cataluña, NE Spain *42.16N 3.16E*
113 *J18* **Čadca** ***Hung.*** Csaca. Žilinský Kraj, N Slovakia *49.27N 18.46E*
29 *P13* **Caddo** Oklahoma, C USA *34.07N 96.15W*
27 *R6* **Caddo** Texas, SW USA *32.42N 98.40W*
27 *X6* **Caddo Lake** ▣ Louisiana/Texas, SW USA
29 *S12* **Caddo Mountains** ▲▲ Arkansas, C USA
43 *O8* **Cadereyta** Nuevo León, NE Mexico *25.35N 99.54W*
99 *J19* **Cader Idris** ▲ NW Wales, United Kingdom *52.43N 3.57W*
190 *F3* **Cadibarrawirracanna, Lake** *salt lake* South Australia
12 *I7* **Cadillac** Québec, SE Canada *48.12N 78.23W*
9 *T17* **Cadillac** Saskatchewan, S Canada *49.43N 107.41W*
104 *K13* **Cadillac** Gironde, SW France *44.37N 0.16W*
33 *P7* **Cadillac** Michigan, N USA *44.16N 85.22W*
107 *V4* **Cadí, Torre de** ▲ NE Spain *42.16N 1.38E*
179 *Q13* **Cadiz** ***off.*** Cadiz City. Negros, C Philippines *10.58N 123.18E*
22 *H7* **Cadiz** Kentucky, S USA *36.53N 87.49W*
33 *U13* **Cadiz** Ohio, N USA *40.16N 81.00W*
106 *J15* **Cádiz** ***anc.*** Gades, Gadier, Gadir, Gadire. Andalucía, SW Spain *36.31N 6.18W*
106 *K15* **Cádiz** ◐ *province* Andalucía, SW Spain
106 *I15* **Cadiz, Bahía de** *bay* SW Spain
Cadiz City *see* Cadiz
106 *H15* **Cádiz, Golfo de** ***Eng.*** Gulf of Cadiz. *gulf* Portugal/Spain
Cadiz, Gulf of *see* Cádiz, Golfo de
37 *X14* **Cadiz Lake** ◎ California, W USA
190 *E2* **Cadney Homestead** South Australia *27.52S 134.03E*
Cadurcum *see* Cahors
85 *F17* **Caecae** North-West, NW Botswana *19.52S 21.04E*
104 *K4* **Caen** Calvados, N France *49.10N 0.19W*
Caene/Caenepolis *see* Qena
Caerdydd *see* Cardiff
Caer Glou *see* Gloucester
Caer Gybi *see* Holyhead
Caerleon *see* Chester
Caer Luel *see* Carlisle
99 *I18* **Caernarfon** ***var.*** Caernarvon, Carnarvon. NW Wales, UK *53.07N 4.16W*
99 *H18* **Caernarfon Bay** *bay* NW Wales, UK
99 *I19* **Caernarvon** *cultural region* NW Wales, UK
Caernarvon *see* Caernarfon
Caesaraugusta *see* Zaragoza
Caesarea Mazaca *see* Kayseri
Caesarobriga *see* Talavera de la Reina
Caesarodunum *see* Tours
Caesaromagus *see* Beauvais
Caesena *see* Cesena
61 *N17* **Caetité** Bahia, E Brazil *14.04S 42.28W*
64 *J6* **Cafayate** Salta, N Argentina *26.02S 66.00W*
179 *Pp9* **Cagayan** ≈ Luzon, N Philippines
179 *R15* **Cagayan de Oro** ***off.*** Cagayan de Oro City. Mindanao, S Philippines *8.28N 124.38E*
179 *Oo17* **Cagayan de Tawi Tawi** *island* S Philippines
179 *Pp14* **Cagayan Islands** *island group* C Philippines
33 *O14* **Cagles Mill Lake** ▣ Indiana, N USA
108 *I12* **Cagli** Marche, C Italy *43.33N 12.39E*
109 *C20* **Cagliari** ***anc.*** Caralis. Sardegna, Italy, C Mediterranean Sea *39.15N 9.06E*
109 *C20* **Cagliari, Golfo di** *gulf* Sardegna, Italy, C Mediterranean Sea
105 *U15* **Cagnes-sur-Mer** Alpes-Maritimes, SE France *43.40N 7.09E*
56 *L5* **Cagua** Aragua, N Venezuela *10.09N 67.27W*
179 *Pp8* **Cagua, Mount** ▲ Luzon, N Philippines *18.10N 122.03E*
56 *F13* **Caguán, Río** ≈ SW Colombia
47 *U6* **Caguas** E Puerto Rico *18.13N 66.02W*
152 *C9* **Çagyl** ***Rus.*** Chagyl. Balkan Welaýaty, NW Turkmenistan *40.48N 55.21E*
25 *P5* **Cahaba River** ≈ Alabama, S USA
44 *E5* **Cahabón, Río** ≈ C Guatemala
85 *B15* **Cahama** Cunene, SW Angola *16.16S 14.19E*
99 *B21* **Caha Mountains** ***Ir.*** An Cheacha. ▲▲ SW Ireland
99 *D20* **Caher** ***Ir.*** An Cathair. S Ireland *52.21N 7.58W*
99 *A21* **Cahersiveen** ***Ir.*** Cathair Saidhbhín. SW Ireland *51.56N 10.12W*
32 *K15* **Cahokia** Illinois, N USA *38.34N 90.11W*
85 *L15* **Cahora Bassa, Albufeira de** ***var.*** Lake Cabora Bassa. ▣ NW Mozambique
99 *G20* **Cahore Point** ***Ir.*** Rinn Chathóir. *headland* SE Ireland *52.33N 6.11W*
104 *M14* **Cahors** ***anc.*** Cadurcum. Lot, S France *44.26N 1.27E*
58 *D9* **Cahuapanas, Río** ≈ N Peru
118 *M12* **Cahul** ***Rus.*** Kagul. S Moldova *45.52N 28.13E*
Cahul, Lacul *see* Kahul, Ozero
85 *N16* **Caia** Sofala, C Mozambique *17.51S 35.22E*
61 *J19* **Caiapó, Serra do** ▲▲ C Brazil
46 *F5* **Caibarién** Villa Clara, C Cuba *22.31N 79.28W*
57 *O5* **Caicara** Monagas, NE Venezuela *9.49N 63.37W*
56 *L5* **Caicara del Orinoco** Bolívar, C Venezuela *7.38N 66.10W*
61 *P14* **Caicó** Rio Grande do Norte, E Brazil *6.25S 37.04W*
46 *M6* **Caicos Islands** *island group* W Turks and Caicos Islands
46 *L5* **Caicos Passage** *strait* Bahamas/ Turks and Caicos Islands
167 *O9* **Caidian** ***prev.*** Hanyang. Hubei, C China *30.33N 114.03E*
Caiffa *see* Ḥefa
188 *M12* **Caiguna** Western Australia *32.14S 125.33E*
Caillí, Ceann *see* Hag's Head
42 *J11* **Caimanero, Laguna del** ***var.*** Laguna del Camaronero. *lagoon* E Pacific Ocean
119 *N10* **Căinari** ***Rus.*** Kaynary. C Moldova *46.43N 29.00E*
59 *L19* **Caine, Río** ≈ C Bolivia
Caiphas *see* Ḥefa
205 *N4* **Caird Coast** *physical region* Antarctica
98 *J9* **Cairn Gorm** ▲ C Scotland, UK *57.07N 3.38W*
98 *J9* **Cairngorm Mountains** ▲▲ C Scotland, UK
41 *P12* **Cairn Mountain** ▲ Alaska, USA *61.07N 155.23W*
189 *W4* **Cairns** Queensland, NE Australia *16.51S 145.43E*
124 *Qq16* **Cairo** ***Ar.*** Al Qāhirah, ***var.*** El Qâhira. ● (Egypt) N Egypt *30.01N 31.18E*
25 *T8* **Cairo** Georgia, SE USA *30.52N 84.12W*
32 *L17* **Cairo** Illinois, N USA *37.00N 89.10W*
77 *V8* **Cairo** ✕ C Egypt *30.06N 31.36E*
Caiseal *see* Cashel
Caisleán an Bharraigh *see* Castlebar
Caisleán na Finne *see* Castlefinn
98 *J6* **Caithness** *cultural region* N Scotland, UK
85 *D15* **Caiundo** Cuando Cubango, S Angola *15.41S 17.28E*
58 *C11* **Cajamarca** ***prev.*** Caxamarca. Cajamarca, NW Peru *7.09S 78.31W*
58 *B11* **Cajamarca** ***off.*** Departamento de Cajamarca. ◐ *department* N Peru
105 *N14* **Cajarc** Lot, S France *44.28N 1.51E*
179 *Q12* **Cajidiocan** Sibuyan Island, C Philippines *12.20N 122.39E*
44 *G6* **Cajón, Represa El** ▣ NW Honduras
60 *N12* **Caju, Ilha do** *island* NE Brazil
Cakaubalavu Reef *see* Kavukavu Reef
165 *R10* **Caka Yanhu** ◎ C China
114 *E7* **Čakovec** ***Ger.*** Csakathurn, ***Hung.*** Csáktornya; ***prev. Ger.*** Tschakathurn. Međimurje, N Croatia *46.24N 16.29E*
79 *V17* **Calabar** Cross River, S Nigeria *4.55N 8.25E*
12 *K13* **Calabogie** Ontario, SE Canada *45.18N 76.43W*
56 *L6* **Calabozo** Guárico, C Venezuela *8.53N 67.28W*
109 *N20* **Calabria** ***anc.*** Bruttium. ◐ *region* SW Italy
106 *M16* **Calaburra, Punta de** *headland* S Spain *36.30N 4.38W*
118 *G14* **Calafat** Dolj, SW Romania *43.55N 23.01E*
Calafate *see* El Calafate
107 *Q4* **Calahorra** La Rioja, N Spain *42.19N 1.58W*
105 *N1* **Calais** Pas-de-Calais, N France *51.00N 1.53E*
21 *T5* **Calais** Maine, NE USA *45.09N 67.15W*
Calais, Pas de *see* Dover, Strait of
Calalen *see* Kallalen
64 *H4* **Calama** Antofagasta, N Chile *22.25S 68.54W*
Calamianes *see* Calamian Group
179 *P13* **Calamian Group** ***var.*** Calamianes. *island group* W Philippines
107 *R7* **Calamocha** Aragón, NE Spain *40.54N 1.18W*
31 *N14* **Calamus River** ≈ Nebraska, C USA
118 *G12* **Călan** ***Ger.*** Kalan, ***Hung.*** Pusztakalán. Hunedoara, SW Romania *45.45N 22.59E*
107 *S7* **Calanda** Aragón, NE Spain *40.55N 0.15W*
173 *E4* **Calang** Sumatera, W Indonesia *4.37N 95.37E*
179 *P11* **Calapan** Mindoro, N Philippines *13.23N 121.08E*
Călăras *see* Călăraşi
118 *M9* **Călăraşi** ***var.*** Călăras, ***Rus.*** Kalarash. C Moldova *47.19N 28.13E*
118 *L14* **Călăraşi** Călăraşi, SE Romania *44.18N 26.52E*
118 *K14* **Călăraşi** ◐ *county* SE Romania
56 *E10* **Calarca** Quindío, W Colombia *4.31N 75.37W*
107 *Q12* **Calasparra** Murcia, SE Spain *38.13N 1.40W*
109 *I23* **Calatafimi** Sicilia, Italy, C Mediterranean Sea *37.54N 12.52E*
107 *Q6* **Calatayud** Aragón, NE Spain *41.21N 1.39W*
179 *Pp11* **Calauag** Luzon, N Philippines *13.57N 122.18E*
37 *P8* **Calaveras River** ≈ California, W USA
179 *Oo11* **Calavite, Cape** *headland* Mindoro, N Philippines *13.25N 120.16E*
179 *Qq12* **Calbayog** ***off.*** Calbayog City. Samar, C Philippines *12.07N 124.35E*
179 *R12* **Calbiga** Samar, C Philippines *11.37N 125.00E*
24 *G9* **Calcasieu Lake** ◎ Louisiana, S USA
24 *H8* **Calcasieu River** ≈ Louisiana, S USA
58 *B6* **Calceta** Manabí, W Ecuador *0.51S 80.09W*
63 *B16* **Calchaquí** Santa Fe, C Argentina *29.55S 60.13W*
64 *J6* **Calchaquí, Río** ≈ NW Argentina
60 *J10* **Calçoene** Amapá, NE Brazil *2.29N 51.01W*
159 *S16* **Calcutta** ✕ West Bengal, N India *22.30N 88.19E*
Calcutta *see* Kolkata
56 *E9* **Caldas** ***off.*** Departamento de Caldas. ◐ *province* W Colombia
106 *F10* **Caldas da Rainha** Leiria, W Portugal *39.24N 9.07W*
106 *G3* **Caldas de Reis** ***var.*** Caldas de Reyes. Galicia, NW Spain *42.36N 8.39W*
Caldas de Reyes *see* Caldas de Reis
60 *F13* **Caldeirão** Amazonas, NW Brazil *3.18S 60.22W*
64 *G7* **Caldera** Atacama, N Chile *27.04S 70.48W*
44 *L14* **Caldera** Puntarenas, W Costa Rica *9.55N 84.42W*
107 *N10* **Calderina** ▲ C Spain *39.18N 3.49W*
143 *T13* **Çaldıran** Van, E Turkey *39.10N 43.52E*
34 *M14* **Caldwell** Idaho, NW USA *43.39N 116.41W*
29 *N8* **Caldwell** Kansas, C USA *37.01N 97.36W*
12 *G15* **Caledon** Ontario, S Canada *43.51N 79.58W*
85 *I23* **Caledon** ***var.*** Mohokare. ≈ Lesotho/South Africa
44 *G1* **Caledonia** Corozal, N Belize *18.13N 88.27W*
12 *G16* **Caledonia** Ontario, S Canada *43.04N 79.57W*
31 *X11* **Caledonia** Minnesota, N USA *43.37N 91.30W*
107 *X5* **Calella** ***var.*** Calella de la Costa. Cataluña, NE Spain *41.37N 2.40E*
Calella de la Costa *see* Calella
25 *P4* **Calera** Alabama, S USA *33.06N 86.45W*
65 *I19* **Caleta Olivia** Santa Cruz, SE Argentina *46.21S 67.37W*
37 *X17* **Calexico** California, W USA *32.39N 115.28W*
99 *H16* **Calf of Man** *island* SW Isle of Man
9 *Q16* **Calgary** Alberta, SW Canada *51.04N 114.04W*
9 *Q16* **Calgary** ✕ Alberta, SW Canada *51.15N 114.03W*
39 *U5* **Calhan** Colorado, C USA *39.00N 104.18W*
66 *O5* **Calheta** Madeira, Portugal, NE Atlantic Ocean *32.42N 17.12W*
25 *R2* **Calhoun** Georgia, SE USA *34.30N 84.57W*
22 *I6* **Calhoun** Kentucky, S USA *37.32N 87.10W*
24 *M3* **Calhoun City** Mississippi, S USA *33.51N 89.18W*
23 *P12* **Calhoun Falls** South Carolina, SE USA *34.05N 82.36W*
56 *D11* **Cali** Valle del Cauca, W Colombia *3.24N 76.30W*
29 *V9* **Calico Rock** Arkansas, C USA *36.07N 92.08W*
161 *F21* **Calicut** ***var.*** Kozhikode. Kerala, SW India *11.17N 75.49E*
37 *Y9* **Caliente** Nevada, W USA *37.37N 114.30W*
29 *U5* **California** Missouri, C USA *38.38N 92.33W*
20 *B15* **California** Pennsylvania, NE USA *40.02N 79.52W*
37 *Q12* **California** ***off.*** State of California; also known as El Dorado, The Golden State. ◐ *state* W USA
37 *P11* **California Aqueduct** *aqueduct* California, W USA
37 *T13* **California City** California, W USA *35.06N 117.55W*
42 *F6* **California, Golfo de** ***Eng.*** Gulf of California; ***prev.*** Sea of Cortez. *gulf* W Mexico
California, Gulf of *see* California, Golfo de
143 *Y13* **Cälilabad** ***Rus.*** Dzhalilabad; ***prev.*** Astrakhan-Bazar. S Azerbaijan *39.15N 48.30E*
118 *I12* **Călimăneşti** Vâlcea, SW Romania *45.13N 24.19E*
118 *J9* **Călimani, Munţii** ▲▲ N Romania
Calinisc *see* Cupcina
37 *X17* **Calipatria** California, W USA *33.07N 115.30W*
Calisia *see* Kalisz
36 *M7* **Calistoga** California, W USA *38.34N 122.37W*
85 *G25* **Calitzdorp** Western Cape, SW South Africa *33.31S 21.40E*
43 *W12* **Calkiní** Campeche, E Mexico *20.21N 90.03W*
190 *K4* **Callabonna Creek** ***var.*** Tilcha Creek. *seasonal river* New South Wales/South Australia
190 *J4* **Callabonna, Lake** ◎ South Australia
104 *G5* **Callac** Côtes d'Armor, NW France *48.28N 3.22W*
37 *U5* **Callaghan, Mount** ▲ Nevada, W USA *39.38N 116.57W*
Callain *see* Callan
99 *E19* **Callan** ***Ir.*** Callain. S Ireland *52.33N 7.22W*
12 *H11* **Callander** Ontario, S Canada *46.12N 79.20W*
98 *I11* **Callander** C Scotland, UK *56.14N 4.16W*
100 *H7* **Callantsoog** Noord-Holland, NW Netherlands *52.51N 4.41E*
59 *D14* **Callao** Callao, W Peru *12.03S 77.09W*
59 *D15* **Callao** ***off.*** Departamento del Callao. ◐ *constitutional province* W Peru
58 *F11* **Callaria, Río** ≈ E Peru
Callatis *see* Mangalia
9 *Q13* **Calling Lake** Alberta, W Canada *55.12N 113.07W*
Callosa de Ensarriá *see* Callosa d'En Sarrià
107 *T11* **Callosa d'En Sarrià** ***var.*** Callosa de Ensarriá. País Valenciano, E Spain *38.40N 0.07W*
107 *S12* **Callosa de Segura** País Valenciano, E Spain *38.07N 0.52W*
31 *X11* **Calmar** Iowa, C USA *43.10N 91.51W*
Calmar *see* Kalmar
45 *R16* **Calobre** Veraguas, C Panama *8.18N 80.49W*
179 *P10* **Caloocan** *municipality* Luzon, N Philippines *14.37N 120.58E*
25 *X14* **Caloosahatchee River** ≈ Florida, SE USA
191 *V2* **Caloundra** Queensland, E Australia *26.48S 153.07E*
Calp *see* Calpe
107 *T11* **Calpe** ***Cat.*** Calp. País Valenciano, E Spain *38.39N 0.03E*
43 *P14* **Calpulalpan** Tlaxcala, S Mexico *19.36N 98.30W*
109 *K25* **Caltagirone** Sicilia, Italy, C Mediterranean Sea *37.13N 14.31E*
109 *J24* **Caltanissetta** Sicilia, Italy, C Mediterranean Sea *37.30N 14.00E*
84 *E11* **Caluango** Lunda Norte, NE Angola *8.16S 19.36E*
84 *C12* **Calucinga** Bié, W Angola *11.18S 16.10E*
84 *B12* **Calulo** Cuanza Sul, NW Angola *9.58S 14.56E*
85 *B14* **Caluquembe** Huíla, W Angola *13.46S 14.40E*
82 *Q11* **Caluula** Bari, NE Somalia *11.55N 50.51E*
104 *K4* **Calvados** ◐ *department* N France
195 *P17* **Calvados Chain, The** *island group* SE PNG
27 *U9* **Calvert** Texas, SW USA *30.58N 96.40W*
22 *H7* **Calvert City** Kentucky, S USA *37.01N 88.21W*
105 *X14* **Calvi** Corse, France, C Mediterranean Sea *42.34N 8.44E*
42 *L12* **Calvillo** Aguascalientes, C Mexico *21.51N 102.42W*
85 *F24* **Calvinia** Northern Cape, W South Africa *31.26S 19.45E*
106 *K8* **Calvitero** ▲ W Spain *40.16N 5.48W*
103 *G22* **Calw** Baden-Württemberg, SW Germany *48.43N 8.43E*
Calydon *see* Kalydón
107 *N11* **Calzada de Calatrava** Castilla-La Mancha, C Spain *38.42N 3.46W*
Cama *see* Kama
84 *C11* **Camabatela** Cuanza Norte, NW Angola *8.13S 15.22E*
66 *Q5* **Camacha** Porto Santo, Madeira, Portugal, NE Atlantic Ocean *32.40N 16.52W*
12 *L8* **Camachigama, Lac** ◎ Québec, SE Canada
42 *M9* **Camacho** Zacatecas, C Mexico *24.23N 102.20W*
84 *D13* **Camacupa** ***var.*** General Machado, ***Port.*** Vila General Machado. Bié, C Angola *11.59S 17.30E*
56 *L7* **Camaguán** Guárico, C Venezuela *8.05N 67.34W*
46 *G6* **Camagüey** ***prev.*** Puerto Príncipe. Camagüey, C Cuba *21.24N 77.54W*
46 *G5* **Camagüey, Archipiélago de** *island group* C Cuba
42 *D5* **Camalli, Sierra de** ▲ NW Mexico *28.21N 113.26W*
59 *G18* **Camana** ***var.*** Camaná. Arequipa, SW Peru *16.37S 72.42W*
31 *Z14* **Camanche** Iowa, C USA *41.47N 90.15W*
37 *P8* **Camanche Reservoir** ▣ California, W USA
63 *I16* **Camaquã** Rio Grande do Sul, S Brazil *30.49S 51.46W*
63 *H16* **Camaquã, Rio** ≈ S Brazil
66 *P6* **Câmara de Lobos** Madeira, Portugal, NE Atlantic Ocean *32.37N 16.58W*
105 *U16* **Camarat, Cap** *headland* SE France *43.12N 6.42E*
43 *O8* **Camargo** Tamaulipas, C Mexico *26.16N 98.49W*
105 *R15* **Camargue** *physical region* SE France
106 *F2* **Camariñas** Galicia, NW Spain *43.07N 9.10W*
Camaronero, Laguna del *see* Caimanero, Laguna del
65 *J18* **Camarones** Chaco, S Argentina *44.48S 65.42W*
65 *J18* **Camarones, Bahía** *bay* S Argentina
106 *J14* **Camas** Andalucía, S Spain *37.24N 6.01W*
178 *J15* **Ca Mau** ***prev.*** Quan Long. Minh Hai, S Vietnam *9.11N 105.09E*
84 *E11* **Camaxilo** Lunda Norte, NE Angola *8.19S 18.52E*
106 *G3* **Cambados** Galicia, NW Spain *42.31N 8.49W*
Cambay, Gulf of *see* Khambhāt, Gulf of
Camberia *see* Chambéry
99 *N22* **Camberley** SE England, UK *51.21N 0.45W*
178 *Ii12* **Cambodia** ***off.*** Kingdom of Cambodia, ***var.*** Democratic Kampuchea, Roat Kampuchea, ***Cam.*** Kampuchea; ***prev.*** People's Democratic Republic of Kampuchea. ◆ *republic* SE Asia
104 *I16* **Cambo-les-Bains** Pyrénées-Atlantiques, SW France *43.22N 1.24W*
105 *P2* **Cambrai** ***Flem.*** Kambryk; ***prev.*** Cambray, ***anc.*** Cameracum. Nord, N France *50.10N 3.13E*
Cambray *see* Cambrai
106 *H2* **Cambre** Galicia, NW Spain *43.18N 8.21W*
37 *O12* **Cambria** California, W USA *35.33N 121.04W*
99 *J20* **Cambrian Mountains** ▲▲ C Wales, UK
12 *G16* **Cambridge** Ontario, S Canada *43.22N 80.16W*
46 *I12* **Cambridge** W Jamaica *18.19N 77.54W*
192 *M8* **Cambridge** Waikato, North Island, NZ *37.53S 175.28E*
99 *O20* **Cambridge** ***Lat.*** Cantabrigia. E England, UK *52.12N 0.07E*
34 *M12* **Cambridge** Idaho, NW USA *44.34N 116.42W*
32 *K11* **Cambridge** Illinois, N USA *41.18N 90.11W*
23 *Y4* **Cambridge** Maryland, NE USA *38.33N 76.04W*
21 *O11* **Cambridge** Massachusetts, NE USA *42.21N 71.05W*
31 *V7* **Cambridge** Minnesota, N USA *45.34N 93.13W*
31 *N16* **Cambridge** Nebraska, C USA *40.18N 100.10W*
33 *U13* **Cambridge** Ohio, NE USA *40.00N 81.34W*
15 *J3* **Cambridge Bay** Victoria Island, Nunavut, NW Canada *68.55N 105.08W*
99 *O20* **Cambridgeshire** *cultural region* E England, UK
107 *U6* **Cambrils de Mar** Cataluña, NE Spain *41.06N 1.02E*
Cambundi-Catembo *see* Nova Gaia
143 *N11* **Çam Burnu** *headland* N Turkey *41.07N 37.48E*
191 *S9* **Camden** New South Wales, SE Australia *34.04S 150.40E*
25 *O6* **Camden** Alabama, S USA *31.59N 87.17W*
29 *U14* **Camden** Arkansas, C USA *33.34N 92.49W*
23 *Y3* **Camden** Delaware, NE USA *39.06N 75.30W*
21 *R7* **Camden** Maine, NE USA *44.12N 69.04W*
20 *I16* **Camden** New Jersey, NE USA *39.55N 75.07W*
20 *I9* **Camden** New York, NE USA *43.21N 75.45W*
23 *R12* **Camden** South Carolina, SE USA *34.15N 80.36W*
22 *H8* **Camden** Tennessee, S USA *36.03N 88.06W*
27 *X9* **Camden** Texas, SW USA *30.55N 94.43W*
41 *S5* **Camden Bay** *bay* S Beaufort Sea
29 *U6* **Camdenton** Missouri, C USA *38.01N 92.44W*
Camellia State *see* Alabama
20 *M7* **Camels Hump** ▲ Vermont, NE USA *44.18N 72.50W*
119 *N8* **Camenca** ***Rus.*** Kamenka. N Moldova *48.01N 28.43E*
Cameracum *see* Cambrai
24 *G9* **Cameron** Louisiana, S USA *29.48N 93.19W*
27 *T9* **Cameron** Texas, SW USA *30.51N 96.58W*
32 *J5* **Cameron** Wisconsin, N USA *45.25N 91.42W*
8 *M12* **Cameron** ≈ British Columbia, W Canada
193 *A24* **Cameron Mountains** ▲▲ South Island, NZ

◆ Country ● Country Capital ◇ Dependent Territory ○ Dependent Territory Capital ◐ Administrative Region ✕ International Airport ▲ Mountain ▲▲ Mountain Range Volcano ≈ River ◎ Lake ▣ Reservoir

Cameroon – Carolina Beach

81 D15 **Cameroon** off. Republic of Cameroon, Fr. Cameroun. ◆ republic W Africa
81 D15 **Cameroon Mountain** ▲ SW Cameroon 4.12N 9.00E
Cameroon Ridge see Camerounaise, Dorsale
Cameroun see Cameroon
81 E14 **Camerounaise, Dorsale** Eng. Cameroon Ridge. ridge NW Cameroon
179 R14 **Camiguin Island** island S Philippines
179 P10 **Camiling** Luzon, N Philippines 15.41N 120.22E
25 T7 **Camilla** Georgia, SE USA 31.13N 84.12W
106 G5 **Caminha** Viana do Castelo, N Portugal 41.52N 8.49W
37 P7 **Camino** California, W USA 38.43N 120.39W
142 B15 **Çamiçi Gölü** ◎ SW Turkey
109 J24 **Cammarata** Sicilia, Italy, C Mediterranean Sea 37.36N 13.39E
44 K10 **Camoapa** Boaco, S Nicaragua 12.24N 85.32W
60 O13 **Camocim** Ceará, E Brazil 2.55S 40.49W
108 D10 **Camogli** Liguria, NW Italy 44.21N 9.10E
189 S5 **Camooweal** Queensland, C Australia 19.57S 138.14E
57 Y11 **Camopi** E French Guiana 3.12N 52.19W
157 Q22 **Camorta** island Nicobar Islands, India, NE Indian Ocean
179 R13 **Camotes Sea** sea C Philippines
44 I6 **Campamento** Olancho, C Honduras 14.33N 86.37W
63 D19 **Campana** Buenos Aires, E Argentina 34.06S 59.04W
65 F21 **Campana, Isla** island S Chile
106 K11 **Campanario** Extremadura, W Spain 38.52N 5.36W
109 L17 **Campania** Eng. Champagne. ⬖ region S Italy
29 Y8 **Campbell** Missouri, C USA 36.29N 90.04W
193 K15 **Campbell, Cape** headland South Island, NZ 41.44S 174.16E
12 J14 **Campbellford** Ontario, SE Canada 44.18N 77.48W
33 R13 **Campbell Hill** hill Ohio, N USA 40.22N 83.43W
199 J14 **Campbell Island** island S NZ
183 P13 **Campbell Plateau** undersea feature SW Pacific Ocean
8 K17 **Campbell River** Vancouver Island, British Columbia, SW Canada 49.58N 125.18W
22 L6 **Campbellsville** Kentucky, S USA 37.20N 85.20W
11 O13 **Campbellton** New Brunswick, SE Canada 48.00N 66.41W
191 P16 **Campbell Town** Tasmania, SE Australia 41.57S 147.30E
191 S9 **Campbelltown** New South Wales, SE Australia 34.04S 150.46E
98 G13 **Campbeltown** W Scotland, UK 55.25N 5.37W
43 W13 **Campeche** Campeche, SE Mexico 19.46N 90.28W
43 W14 **Campeche** ⬖ state SE Mexico
43 T14 **Campeche, Bahía de** Eng. Bay of Campeche. bay E Mexico
Campeche, Banco de see Campeche Bank
66 C11 **Campeche Bank** Sp. Banco de Campeche, Sonda de Campeche. undersea feature S Gulf of Mexico
Campeche, Bay of see Campeche, Bahía de
Campeche, Sonda de see Campeche Bank
46 H7 **Campechuela** Granma, E Cuba 20.11N 77.14W
190 M13 **Camperdown** Victoria, SE Australia 38.16S 143.10E
178 K6 **Câm Pha** Quang Ninh, N Vietnam 21.04N 107.20E
118 H10 **Câmpia Turzii** Ger. Jerischmarkt, Hung. Aranyosgyéres; prev. Cîmpia Turzii, Ghiriş, Gyéres. Cluj, NW Romania 46.33N 23.53E
106 K12 **Campillo de Llerena** Extremadura, W Spain 38.30N 5.48W
106 L15 **Campillos** Andalucía, S Spain 37.04N 4.51W
118 J13 **Câmpina** prev. Cîmpina. Prahova, SE Romania 45.08N 25.44E
61 Q15 **Campina Grande** Paraíba, E Brazil 7.15S 35.49W
62 L9 **Campinas** São Paulo, S Brazil 22.54S 47.06W
40 L10 **Camp Kulowiye** Saint Lawrence Island, Alaska, USA 63.15N 168.45W
81 D17 **Campo** var. Kampo. Sud, SW Cameroon 2.22N 9.49E
Campo see Ntem
61 N15 **Campo Alegre de Lourdes** Bahia, E Brazil 9.28S 43.01W
109 L16 **Campobasso** Molise, C Italy 41.34N 14.40E
109 H24 **Campobello di Mazara** Sicilia, Italy, C Mediterranean Sea 37.37N 12.45E
Campo Criptana see Campo de Criptana
107 O10 **Campo de Criptana** var. Campo Criptana. Castilla-La Mancha, C Spain 39.25N 3.07W
61 I16 **Campo de Diauarum** var. Pôsto Diuarum. Mato Grosso, W Brazil 11.08S 53.16W
56 E5 **Campo de la Cruz** Atlántico, N Colombia 10.22N 74.52W
107 P11 **Campo de Montiel** physical region C Spain
Campo dos Goitacazes see Campos
62 H12 **Campo Erê** Santa Catarina, S Brazil 26.24S 53.04W
64 L7 **Campo Gallo** Santiago del Estero, N Argentina 26.36S 62.50W
61 I20 **Campo Grande** state capital Mato Grosso do Sul, SW Brazil 20.24S 54.34W
62 K12 **Campo Largo** Paraná, S Brazil 25.27S 49.29W
60 N13 **Campo Maior** Piauí, E Brazil 4.49S 42.12W
106 I10 **Campo Maior** Portalegre, C Portugal 39.01N 7.04W
62 H10 **Campo Mourão** Paraná, S Brazil 24.01S 52.24W
62 Q9 **Campos** var. Campo dos Goitacazes. Rio de Janeiro, SE Brazil 21.46S 41.21W
61 L17 **Campos Belos** Goiás, S Brazil 13.11S 46.46W
62 N9 **Campos do Jordão** São Paulo, S Brazil 22.45S 45.36W
62 I13 **Campos Novos** Santa Catarina, S Brazil 27.22S 51.11W
61 O14 **Campos Sales** Ceará, E Brazil 7.01S 40.21W
27 Q9 **Camp San Saba** Texas, SW USA 30.57N 99.16W
23 N6 **Campton** Kentucky, S USA 37.43N 83.28W
118 I13 **Câmpulung** prev. Câmpulung-Muşcel, Cîmpulung. Argeş, S Romania 45.16N 25.03E
118 J9 **Câmpulung Moldovenesc** var. Cîmpulung Moldovenesc, Ger. Kimpolung, Hung. Hosszúmezjő. Suceava, NE Romania 47.31N 25.34E
Câmpulung-Muşcel see Câmpulung
Campus Stellae see Santiago
38 L12 **Camp Verde** Arizona, SW USA 34.33N 111.52W
27 P11 **Camp Wood** Texas, SW USA 29.40N 100.00W
178 Kk13 **Cam Ranh** Khanh Hoa, S Vietnam 11.54N 109.13E
9 Q15 **Camrose** Alberta, SW Canada 53.01N 112.48W
Camulodunum see Colchester
142 B12 **Çan** Çanakkale, NW Turkey 40.01N 26.59E
20 L12 **Canaan** Connecticut, NE USA 42.00N 73.17W
15 Kk13 **Canada** ◆ commonwealth republic N North America
207 P6 **Canada Basin** undersea feature Arctic Ocean
63 B18 **Cañada de Gómez** Santa Fe, C Argentina 32.49S 61.22W
207 P6 **Canada Plain** undersea feature Arctic Ocean
63 A18 **Cañada Rosquín** Santa Fe, C Argentina 32.04S 61.35W
27 P1 **Canadian** Texas, SW USA 35.54N 100.22W
18 Kk11 **Canadian River** ∽ SW USA
15 K12 **Canadian Shield** physical region Canada
65 I18 **Cañadón Grande, Sierra** ▲▲ S Argentina
57 P9 **Canaima** Bolívar, SE Venezuela 9.40N 72.33W
142 B11 **Çanakkale** var. Dardanelli; prev. Chanak, Kale Sultanie. Çanakkale, W Turkey 40.09N 26.25E
142 B12 **Çanakkale** ⬖ province NW Turkey
142 B11 **Çanakkale Boğazı** Eng. Dardanelles. strait NW Turkey
197 I6 **Canala** Province Nord, C New Caledonia 21.31S 165.57E
61 A15 **Canamari** Amazonas, W Brazil 7.37S 72.33W
20 G10 **Canandaigua** New York, NE USA 42.52N 77.14W
20 F10 **Canandaigua Lake** ◎ New York, NE USA
42 G3 **Cananea** Sonora, NW Mexico 30.58N 110.19W
58 B8 **Cañar** ⬖ province C Ecuador
66 N10 **Canarias, Islas** Eng. Canary Islands. ⬖ autonomous community Spain, NE Atlantic Ocean
Canaries Basin see Canary Basin
46 C6 **Canarreos, Archipiélago de los** island group W Cuba
68 K3 **Canary Basin** var. Canaries Basin, Monaco Basin. undersea feature E Atlantic Ocean
Canary Islands see Canarias, Islas
44 L13 **Cañas** Guanacaste, NW Costa Rica 10.25N 85.07W
20 I10 **Canastota** New York, NE USA 43.04N 75.45W
42 K9 **Canatlán** Durango, C Mexico 24.33N 104.45W
106 J9 **Cañaveral** Extremadura, W Spain 39.46N 6.24W
25 Y11 **Canaveral, Cape** headland Florida, SE USA 28.27N 80.31W
61 O18 **Canavieiras** Bahia, E Brazil 15.43S 38.58W
45 R16 **Cañazas** Veraguas, W Panama 8.19N 81.09W
108 H6 **Canazei** Trentino-Alto Adige, N Italy 46.29N 11.50E
191 P6 **Canbelego** New South Wales, SE Australia 31.36S 146.20E
191 R10 **Canberra** ● (Australia) Australian Capital Territory, SE Australia 35.21S 149.08E
191 R10 **Canberra** ✈ Australian Capital Territory, SE Australia 35.19S 149.12E
37 P2 **Canby** California, W USA 41.27N 120.51W
31 S9 **Canby** Minnesota, N USA 44.42N 96.17W
105 N2 **Canche** ∽ N France
104 L13 **Cancon** Lot-et-Garonne, SW France 44.33N 0.37E
43 Z11 **Cancún** Quintana Roo, SE Mexico 21.05N 86.48W
106 K2 **Candás** Asturias, N Spain 43.35N 5.45W
104 J7 **Cande** Maine-et-Loire, NW France 47.33N 1.03W
43 W14 **Candelaria** Campeche, SE Mexico 18.10N 91.00W
26 J11 **Candelaria** Texas, SW USA 30.05N 104.40W
43 W15 **Candelaria, Río** ∽ Guatemala/Mexico
106 L8 **Candeleda** Castilla-León, N Spain 40.10N 5.13W
Candia see Irákleio
43 P8 **Cándido Aguilar** Tamaulipas, C Mexico 25.30N 97.57W
41 N8 **Candle** Alaska, USA 65.54N 161.55W
9 T14 **Candle Lake** Saskatchewan, C Canada 53.43N 105.09W
20 L13 **Candlewood, Lake** ⊠ Connecticut, NE USA
31 O3 **Cando** North Dakota, N USA 48.29N 99.12W
179 P8 **Candon** Luzon, N Philippines 17.15N 120.25E
Canea see Chaniá
47 O12 **Canefield** ✈ (Roseau) SW Dominica 15.20N 61.24W
63 F20 **Canelones** prev. Guadalupe. Canelones, S Uruguay 34.31S 56.16W
63 E20 **Canelones** ⬖ department S Uruguay
Canendiyú see Canindeyú
65 F14 **Cañete** Bío Bío, C Chile 37.48S 73.21W
107 Q9 **Cañete** Castilla-La Mancha, C Spain 40.03N 1.39W
Cañete see San Vicente de Cañete
29 P8 **Caney** Kansas, C USA 37.00N 95.56W
29 P8 **Caney River** ∽ Kansas/Oklahoma, C USA
107 S3 **Canfranc-Estación** Aragón, NE Spain 42.42N 0.31W
85 E14 **Cangamba** Port. Vila de Aljustrel. Moxico, E Angola 13.39S 19.57E
84 C12 **Cangandala** Malanje, NW Angola 9.46S 16.27E
106 G4 **Cangas** Galicia, NW Spain 42.16N 8.46W
106 J2 **Cangas del Narcea** Asturias, N Spain 43.10N 6.31W
106 L2 **Cangas de Onís** Asturias, N Spain 43.21N 5.07W
167 S11 **Cangnan** var. Lingxi. Zhejiang, SE China 27.29N 120.23E
84 C10 **Cangola** Uíge, NW Angola 7.54S 15.57E
85 E14 **Cangombe** Moxico, E Angola 14.27S 20.05E
65 H21 **Cangrejo, Cerro** ▲ S Argentina 49.19S 72.18W
63 H17 **Canguçu** Rio Grande do Sul, S Brazil 31.25S 52.37W
167 P3 **Cangzhou** Hebei, E China 38.19N 116.54E
10 M7 **Caniapiscau** ∽ Québec, E Canada
10 M8 **Caniapiscau, Réservoir de** ⊠ Québec, C Canada
109 J24 **Canicattì** Sicilia, Italy, C Mediterranean Sea 37.22N 13.51E
142 L11 **Canik Dağları** ▲▲ N Turkey
107 P14 **Caniles** Andalucía, S Spain 37.24N 2.41W
61 B16 **Canindé** Acre, W Brazil 10.55S 69.45W
64 P6 **Canindeyú** var. Canendiyú, Canindiyú. ⬖ department E Paraguay
Canindiyú see Canindeyú
204 J10 **Canisteo Peninsula** peninsula Antarctica
20 F11 **Canisteo River** ∽ New York, NE USA
42 M10 **Cañitas** var. Cañitas de Felipe Pescador. Zacatecas, C Mexico 23.35N 102.39W
Cañitas de Felipe Pescador see Cañitas
107 P15 **Canjáyar** Andalucía, S Spain 37.00N 2.45W
142 I12 **Çankırı** var. Chankiri; anc. Gangra, Germanicopolis. Çankın, N Turkey 40.36N 33.35E
142 I11 **Çankırı** var. Chankiri. ⬖ province N Turkey
179 Qq13 **Canlaon Volcano** ⛰ Negros, C Philippines 10.24N 123.05E
9 P16 **Canmore** Alberta, SW Canada 51.07N 115.18W
98 F9 **Canna** island NW Scotland, UK
161 F20 **Cannanore** var. Kananur, Kannur. Kerala, SW India 11.52N 75.22E
33 O17 **Cannelton** Indiana, N USA 37.54N 86.44W
105 U15 **Cannes** Alpes-Maritimes, SE France 43.33N 6.58E
41 R5 **Canning River** ∽ Alaska, USA
108 C6 **Cannobio** Piemonte, NE Italy 46.04N 8.39E
99 L19 **Cannock** C England, UK 52.40N 2.03W
30 M6 **Cannonball River** ∽ North Dakota, N USA
31 W9 **Cannon Falls** Minnesota, N USA 44.30N 92.54W
20 I11 **Cannonsville Reservoir** ⊠ New York, NE USA
191 R12 **Cann River** Victoria, SE Australia 37.34S 149.11E
63 I16 **Canoas** Rio Grande do Sul, S Brazil 29.42S 51.07W
63 I14 **Canoas, Rio** ∽ S Brazil
12 I12 **Canoe Lake** ◎ Ontario, SE Canada
62 J12 **Canoinhas** Santa Catarina, S Brazil 26.12S 50.24W
39 T6 **Canon City** Colorado, C USA 38.25N 105.14W
57 P8 **Caño Negro** Bolívar, SE Venezuela
181 X15 **Canonniers Point** headland N Mauritius
25 W6 **Canoochee River** ∽ Georgia, SE USA
9 V15 **Canora** Saskatchewan, S Canada 51.37N 102.28W
47 Y14 **Canouan** island S Saint Vincent and the Grenadines
11 R15 **Canso** Nova Scotia, SE Canada 45.20N 61.00W
106 M3 **Cantabria** ⬖ autonomous community N Spain
106 K3 **Cantábrica, Cordillera** ▲▲ N Spain
Cantabrigia see Cambridge
105 O12 **Cantal** ⬖ department C France
107 N6 **Cantalejo** Castilla-León, N Spain 41.15N 3.57W
105 O12 **Cantal, Monts du** ▲▲ C France
106 G8 **Cantanhede** Coimbra, C Portugal 40.21N 8.37W
Cantaño see Cataño
57 O6 **Cantaura** Anzoátegui, NE Venezuela 9.18N 64.21W
118 M11 **Cantemir** Rus. Kantemir. S Moldova 46.17N 28.12E
99 Q22 **Canterbury** hist. Cantwaraburh, anc. Durovernum, Lat. Cantuaria. SE England, UK 51.16N 1.04E
193 F19 **Canterbury** off. Canterbury Region. ⬖ region South Island, NZ
193 H20 **Canterbury Bight** bight South Island, NZ
193 H19 **Canterbury Plains** plain South Island, NZ
178 Jj15 **Cân Thơ** Cân Thơ, S Vietnam 10.03N 105.46E
106 K13 **Cantillana** Andalucía, S Spain 37.34N 5.48W
61 N15 **Canto do Buriti** Piauí, NE Brazil 8.07S 43.00W
25 S2 **Canton** Georgia, SE USA 34.14N 84.29W
32 K12 **Canton** Illinois, N USA 40.33N 90.02W
24 L5 **Canton** Mississippi, S USA 32.36N 90.02W
29 V2 **Canton** Missouri, C USA 40.07N 91.31W
20 J7 **Canton** New York, NE USA 44.36N 75.10W
23 O10 **Canton** North Carolina, SE USA 35.31N 82.50W
33 U12 **Canton** Ohio, N USA 40.48N 81.22W
28 L9 **Canton** Oklahoma, C USA 36.03N 98.35W
20 G12 **Canton** Pennsylvania, NE USA 41.38N 76.49W
31 R11 **Canton** South Dakota, N USA 43.19N 96.33W
27 V7 **Canton** Texas, SW USA 32.34N 95.50W
Canton see Guangzhou
Canton Island see Kanton
28 L9 **Canton Lake** ⊠ Oklahoma, C USA
108 D7 **Cantù** Lombardia, N Italy 45.43N 9.07E
Cantuaria/Cantwaraburh see Canterbury
41 R10 **Cantwell** Alaska, USA 63.23N 148.57W
61 O16 **Canudos** Bahia, E Brazil 9.51S 39.07W
49 T7 **Canumã, Rio** ∽ N Brazil
Canusium see Puglia, Canosa di
26 G7 **Canutillo** Texas, SW USA 31.53N 106.34W
27 N3 **Canyon** Texas, SW USA 34.58N 101.55W
35 S12 **Canyon** Wyoming, C USA 44.44N 110.30W
34 K13 **Canyon City** Oregon, NW USA 44.22N 118.58W
35 R10 **Canyon Ferry Lake** ◎ Montana, NW USA
27 S11 **Canyon Lake** ⊠ Texas, SW USA
178 Jj5 **Cao Băng** var. Caobang. Cao Băng, N Vietnam 22.40N 106.16E
166 J12 **Caodu He** ∽ S China
178 J14 **Cao Lanh** Đông Thap, S Vietnam 10.35N 105.25E
84 C11 **Caombo** Malanje, NW Angola 8.42S 16.33E
Caorach, Cuan na g see Sheep Haven
Caozhou see Heze
175 S10 **Capalulu** Pulau Mangole, E Indonesia 1.51S 125.53E
56 K8 **Capanaparo, Río** ∽ Colomiba/Venezuela
60 L12 **Capanema** Pará, NE Brazil 1.07S 47.07W
62 L10 **Capão Bonito** São Paulo, S Brazil 24.01S 48.22W
62 I13 **Capão Doce, Morro do** ▲ S Brazil 26.37S 51.28W
56 I4 **Capatárida** Falcón, N Venezuela 11.10N 70.38W
104 I15 **Capbreton** Landes, SW France 43.40N 1.25W
Cap-Breton, Île du see Cape Breton Island
13 W6 **Cap-Chat** Québec, SE Canada 49.04N 66.43W
13 P11 **Cap-de-la-Madeleine** Québec, SE Canada 46.22N 72.31W
105 N13 **Capdenac** Aveyron, S France 44.35N 2.06E
191 Q15 **Cape Barren Island** island Furneaux Group, Tasmania, SE Australia
67 O18 **Cape Basin** undersea feature S Atlantic Ocean
11 R14 **Cape Breton Island** Fr. Île du Cap-Breton. island Nova Scotia, SE Canada
25 Y11 **Cape Canaveral** Florida, SE USA 28.24N 80.36W
23 Y6 **Cape Charles** Virginia, NE USA 37.16N 76.01W
79 P17 **Cape Coast** prev. Cape Coast Castle. S Ghana 5.10N 1.13W
Cape Coast Castle see Cape Coast
21 Q12 **Cape Cod Bay** bay Massachusetts, NE USA
25 W15 **Cape Coral** Florida, SE USA 26.33N 81.57W
189 R4 **Cape Crawford Roadhouse** Northern Territory, N Australia 16.39S 135.44E
16 N4 **Cape Dorset** Baffin Island, Nunavut, NE Canada 64.12N 76.31W
23 N8 **Cape Fear River** ∽ North Carolina, SE USA
29 Y7 **Cape Girardeau** Missouri, C USA 37.17N 89.31W
23 T14 **Cape Island** island South Carolina, SE USA
194 E11 **Capella** ▲ NW PNG 5.00S 141.09E
100 H12 **Capelle aan den IJssel** Zuid-Holland, SW Netherlands 51.55N 4.36E
85 C15 **Capelongo** Huíla, C Angola 14.45S 15.02E
20 J17 **Cape May** New Jersey, NE USA 38.54N 74.54W
20 J17 **Cape May Court House** New Jersey, NE USA 39.03N 74.46W
Cape Palmas see Harper
15 H2 **Cape Parry** Northwest Territories, N Canada 70.10N 124.33W
67 P19 **Cape Rise** undersea feature SW Indian Ocean
Cape Saint Jacques see Vung Tau
Capesterre see Capesterre-Belle-Eau
47 Y6 **Capesterre-Belle-Eau** var. Capesterre. Basse Terre, S Guadeloupe 16.03N 61.33W
85 D26 **Cape Town** var. Ekapa, Afr. Kaapstad, Kapstad. ● (South Africa-legislative capital) Western Cape, SW South Africa 33.55S 18.28E
85 E26 **Cape Town** ✈ Western Cape, SW South Africa 31.51S 21.06E
78 D9 **Cape Verde** off. Republic of Cape Verde, Port. Cabo Verde, Ilhas do Cabo Verde. ◆ republic E Atlantic Ocean
66 L11 **Cape Verde Basin** undersea feature E Atlantic Ocean
68 K5 **Cape Verde Islands** island group E Atlantic Ocean
66 L10 **Cape Verde Plain** undersea feature E Atlantic Ocean
Cape Verde Plateau/Cape Verde Rise see Cape Verde Terrace
66 L11 **Cape Verde Terrace** var. Cape Verde Plateau, Cape Verde Rise. undersea feature E Atlantic Ocean
189 V2 **Cape York Peninsula** peninsula Queensland, N Australia
46 M8 **Cap-Haïtien** var. Le Cap. N Haiti 19.43N 72.12W
45 T15 **Capira** Panamá, C Panama 8.45N 79.52W
12 K8 **Capitachouane** ∽ Québec, SE Canada
12 L8 **Capitachouane, Lac** ◎ Québec, SE Canada
39 T13 **Capitan** New Mexico, SW USA 33.33N 105.34W
204 G3 **Capitán Arturo Prat** Chilean research station South Shetland Islands, Antarctica 62.24S 59.42W
39 S13 **Capitan Mountains** ▲▲ New Mexico, SW USA
64 M3 **Capitán Pablo Lagerenza** var. Mayor Pablo Lagerenza. Chaco, N Paraguay 19.55S 60.46W
39 T13 **Capitan Peak** ▲ New Mexico, SW USA 33.35N 105.15W
196 H5 **Capitol Hill** Saipan, S Northern Mariana Islands
62 I9 **Capivara, Represa** ⊠ S Brazil
63 J16 **Capivari** Rio Grande do Sul, S Brazil 30.08S 50.32W
115 H15 **Čapljina** Federacija Bosna I Hercegovina, S Bosnia and Herzegovina 43.07N 17.42E
85 M15 **Capoche** var. Kapoche. ∽ Mozambique/Zambia
Capo Delgado, Província de see Cabo Delgado
109 K17 **Capodichino** ✈ (Napoli) Campania, S Italy 40.53N 14.15E
Capodistria see Koper
108 E12 **Capraia, Isola** island Archipelago Toscano, C Italy
109 B16 **Caprara, Punta** var. Punta dello Scorno. headland Isola Asinara, W Italy 41.07N 8.19E
Capraria see Cabrera, Illa de
12 F10 **Capreol** Ontario, S Canada 46.43N 80.55W
109 K18 **Capri** Campania, S Italy 40.33N 14.14E
183 S9 **Capricorn Tablemount** undersea feature W Pacific Ocean 18.34S 172.12W
109 J18 **Capri, Isola di** island S Italy
85 G16 **Caprivi** ⬖ district NE Namibia
Caprivi Concession see Caprivi Strip
85 F16 **Caprivi Strip** Ger. Caprivizipfel; prev. Caprivi Concession. cultural region NE Namibia
Caprivizipfel see Caprivi Strip
27 O5 **Cap Rock Escarpment** cliffs Texas, SW USA
13 R10 **Cap-Rouge** Québec, SE Canada 46.45N 71.18W
Cap Saint-Jacques see Vung Tau
40 F12 **Captain Cook** Hawai'i, USA, C Pacific Ocean 19.30N 155.55W
191 R10 **Captains Flat** New South Wales, SE Australia 35.37S 149.28E
104 K14 **Captieux** Gironde, SW France 44.16N 0.15W
109 K17 **Capua** Campania, S Italy 41.06N 14.13E
56 F14 **Caquetá** off. Departamanto del Caquetá. ⬖ province S Colombia
56 E13 **Caquetá, Río** var. Rio Japurá, Yapurá. ∽ Brazil/Colombia see also Japurá, Rio
CAR see Central African Republic
Cara see Kara
59 I16 **Carabaya, Cordillera** ▲▲ E Peru
56 K5 **Carabobo** off. Estado Carabobo. ⬖ state N Venezuela
118 I14 **Caracal** Olt, S Romania 44.07N 24.18E
60 F10 **Caracaraí** Rondônia, W Brazil 1.46N 61.10W
56 L5 **Caracas** ● (Venezuela) Distrito Federal, N Venezuela 10.28N 66.53W
56 I5 **Carache** Trujillo, N Venezuela 9.40N 70.15W
62 N10 **Caraguatatuba** São Paulo, S Brazil 23.37S 45.24W
50 I7 **Carajás, Serra dos** ▲▲ N Brazil
Caralis see Cagliari
56 E9 **Caramanta** Antioquia, W Colombia 5.36N 75.37W
179 Q11 **Caramoan** Catanduanes Island, N Philippines 13.47N 123.49E
Caramurat see Mihail Kogălniceanu
118 F12 **Caransebeş** Ger. Karansebesch, Hung. Karánsebes. Caraş-Severin, SW Romania 45.23N 22.13E
Carapella see Carapelle
109 M16 **Carapelle** var. Carapella. ∽ SE Italy
57 O9 **Carapo** Bolívar, SE Venezuela
11 P13 **Caraquet** New Brunswick, SE Canada 47.48N 64.58W
Caras see Caraz
118 F12 **Caraşova** Hung. Krassóvár. Caraş-Severin, SW Romania 45.10N 21.51E
118 F12 **Caraş-Severin** ⬖ county SW Romania
44 M5 **Caratasca, Laguna de** lagoon NE Honduras
60 C13 **Carauari** Amazonas, NW Brazil 4.55S 66.57W
Caravaca see Caravaca de la Cruz
107 Q12 **Caravaca de la Cruz** var. Caravaca. Murcia, SE Spain 38.06N 1.51W
108 E7 **Caravaggio** Lombardia, N Italy 45.31N 9.39E
109 C18 **Caravai, Passo di** pass Sardegna, Italy, C Mediterranean Sea 40.06N 9.19E
61 O19 **Caravelas** Bahia, E Brazil 17.45S 39.15W
58 C12 **Caraz** var. Caras. Ancash, W Peru 9.01S 77.48W
63 H14 **Carazinho** Rio Grande do Sul, S Brazil 28.16S 52.46W
44 J11 **Carazo** ⬖ department SW Nicaragua
Carballiño see O Carballiño
106 G2 **Carballo** Galicia, NW Spain 43.12N 8.42W
9 W16 **Carberry** Manitoba, S Canada 49.52N 99.19W
42 F4 **Carbó** Sonora, NW Mexico 29.40N 110.54W
109 C20 **Carbonara, Capo** headland Sardegna, Italy, C Mediterranean Sea 39.06N 9.31E
39 Q5 **Carbondale** Colorado, C USA 39.24N 107.12W
32 L17 **Carbondale** Illinois, N USA 37.43N 89.13W
29 Q4 **Carbondale** Kansas, C USA 38.49N 95.41W
20 I13 **Carbondale** Pennsylvania, NE USA 41.34N 75.30W
11 V12 **Carbonear** Newfoundland and Labrador, SE Canada 47.45N 53.16W
107 Q9 **Carboneras de Guadazaón** var. Carboneras de Guadazón. Castilla-La Mancha, C Spain 39.54N 1.49W
Carboneras de Guadazón see Carboneras de Guadazaón
25 O3 **Carbon Hill** Alabama, S USA 33.53N 87.31W
109 B20 **Carbonia** var. Carbonia Centro. Sardegna, Italy, C Mediterranean Sea 39.10N 8.31E
Carbonia Centro see Carbonia
107 S10 **Carcaixent** País Valenciano, E Spain 39.07N 0.28W
Carcaso see Carcassonne
67 B24 **Carcass Island** island NW Falkland Islands
105 O16 **Carcassonne** anc. Carcaso. Aude, S France 43.13N 2.21E
107 R12 **Carche** ▲ S Spain 38.24N 1.11W
58 A13 **Carchi** ⬖ province N Ecuador
8 I8 **Carcross** Yukon Territory, W Canada 60.10N 134.40W
Cardamomes, Chaîne des see Krâvanh, Chuŏr Phnum
161 G22 **Cardamom Hills** ▲▲ SW India
Cardamom Mountains see Krâvanh, Chuŏr Phnum
106 M12 **Cardeña** Andalucía, S Spain 38.16N 4.19W
46 D4 **Cárdenas** Matanzas, W Cuba 23.01N 81.12W
43 O11 **Cárdenas** San Luis Potosí, C Mexico 22.03N 99.30W
43 U15 **Cárdenas** Tabasco, SE Mexico 18.00N 93.21W
65 H21 **Cardiel, Lago** ◎ S Argentina
99 K22 **Cardiff** Wel. Caerdydd. ◐ S Wales, UK 51.30N 3.13W
99 J22 **Cardiff-Wales** ✈ S Wales, UK 51.24N 3.22W
99 I21 **Cardigan** Wel. Aberteifi. SW Wales, UK 52.06N 4.40W
99 I20 **Cardigan** cultural region W Wales, UK
99 I20 **Cardigan Bay** bay W Wales, UK
21 N8 **Cardigan, Mount** ▲ New Hampshire, NE USA 43.39N 71.52W
12 M13 **Cardinal** Ontario, SE Canada 44.48N 75.22W
107 V5 **Cardona** Cataluña, NE Spain 41.55N 1.40E
63 E19 **Cardona** Soriano, SW Uruguay 33.52S 57.18W
107 V4 **Cardoner** ∽ NE Spain
9 Q17 **Cardston** Alberta, SW Canada 49.13N 113.19W
189 W5 **Cardwell** Queensland, NE Australia 18.24S 146.06E
118 G8 **Carei** Ger. Gross-Karol, Karol, Hung. Nagykároly; prev. Careii-Mari. Satu Mare, NW Romania 47.40N 22.27E
Careii-Mari see Carei
60 F13 **Careiro** Amazonas, NW Brazil 3.39S 60.22W
104 J4 **Carentan** Manche, N France 49.18N 1.15W
106 M2 **Cares** ∽ N Spain
35 P14 **Carey** Idaho, NW USA 43.17N 113.58W
33 S12 **Carey** Ohio, N USA 40.57N 83.22W
27 P4 **Carey** Texas, SW USA 34.28N 100.18W
188 L11 **Carey, Lake** ◎ Western Australia
181 O8 **Cargados Carajos Bank** undersea feature C Indian Ocean
104 G6 **Carhaix-Plouguer** Finistère, NW France 48.16N 3.34W
63 A22 **Carhué** Buenos Aires, E Argentina 37.10S 62.45W
57 O5 **Cariaco** Sucre, NE Venezuela 10.28N 63.33W
109 O20 **Cariati** Calabria, SW Italy 39.30N 16.57E
2 H17 **Caribbean Plate** tectonic feature
46 I11 **Caribbean Sea** sea W Atlantic Ocean
9 N15 **Cariboo Mountains** ▲▲ British Columbia, SW Canada
9 W9 **Caribou** Manitoba, C Canada 59.27N 97.43W
21 S2 **Caribou** Maine, NE USA 46.51N 68.00W
9 P10 **Caribou Mountains** ▲▲ Alberta, SW Canada
Caribrod see Dimitrovgrad
42 I6 **Carichic** Chihuahua, N Mexico 27.57N 107.01W
179 Qq13 **Carigara** Leyte, C Philippines 11.15N 124.43E
105 R3 **Carignan** Ardennes, N France 49.38N 5.08E
191 Q5 **Carinda** New South Wales, SE Australia 30.26S 147.45E
107 R6 **Cariñena** Aragón, NE Spain 41.19N 1.13W
109 I23 **Carini** Sicilia, Italy, C Mediterranean Sea 38.06N 13.09E
109 K17 **Carinola** Campania, S Italy 41.14N 14.03E
Carinthi see Kärnten
57 O5 **Caripe** Monagas, NE Venezuela 10.06N 63.30W
57 P5 **Caripito** Monagas, NE Venezuela 10.03N 63.05W
13 W7 **Carleton** Québec, SE Canada 48.07N 66.07W
33 S10 **Carleton** Michigan, N USA 42.03N 83.23W
11 O14 **Carleton, Mount** ▲ New Brunswick, SE Canada 47.10N 66.54W
12 L13 **Carleton Place** Ontario, SE Canada 45.09N 76.07W
37 V3 **Carlin** Nevada, W USA 40.40N 116.09W
32 K14 **Carlinville** Illinois, N USA 39.16N 89.52W
99 K14 **Carlisle** anc. Caer Luel, Luguvallium, Luguvallum. NW England, UK 54.54N 2.55W
29 V11 **Carlisle** Arkansas, C USA 34.46N 91.45W
33 N15 **Carlisle** Indiana, N USA 38.57N 87.23W
31 V14 **Carlisle** Iowa, C USA 41.30N 93.29W
23 N5 **Carlisle** Kentucky, S USA 38.19N 83.59W
20 F15 **Carlisle** Pennsylvania, NE USA 40.10N 77.10W
23 Q11 **Carlisle** South Carolina, SE USA 34.35N 81.27W
40 J17 **Carlisle Island** island Aleutian Islands, Alaska, USA
29 R7 **Carl Junction** Missouri, C USA 37.10N 94.34W
109 A20 **Carloforte** Sardegna, Italy, C Mediterranean Sea 39.10N 8.17E
Carlopago see Karlobag
63 B21 **Carlos Casares** Buenos Aires, E Argentina 35.39S 61.28W
63 E18 **Carlos Reyles** Durazno, C Uruguay 33.04S 56.28W
63 A21 **Carlos Tejedor** Buenos Aires, E Argentina 35.23S 62.31W
99 F19 **Carlow** Ir. Ceatharlach. SE Ireland 52.49N 6.55W
99 F19 **Carlow** Ir. Cheatharlach. cultural region SE Ireland
98 F7 **Carloway** NW Scotland, UK 58.16N 6.48W
Carlsbad see Karlovy Vary
37 U17 **Carlsbad** California, W USA 33.09N 117.21W
39 U15 **Carlsbad** New Mexico, SW USA 32.24N 104.14W
133 N13 **Carlsberg Ridge** undersea feature S Arabian Sea
Carlsruhe see Karlsruhe
31 W6 **Carlton** Minnesota, N USA 46.39N 92.25W
9 V17 **Carlyle** Saskatchewan, S Canada 49.39N 102.18W
32 L15 **Carlyle** Illinois, N USA 38.36N 89.22W
32 L15 **Carlyle Lake** ⊠ Illinois, N USA
8 H7 **Carmacks** Yukon Territory, W Canada 62.04N 136.21W
108 B9 **Carmagnola** Piemonte, NW Italy 44.50N 7.43E
9 X16 **Carman** Manitoba, S Canada 49.31N 97.58W
Carmana/Carmania see Kermān
99 I21 **Carmarthen** SW Wales, UK 51.52N 4.19W
99 I21 **Carmarthen** cultural region SW Wales, UK
99 I22 **Carmarthen Bay** inlet SW Wales, UK
105 N14 **Carmaux** Tarn, S France 44.03N 2.09E
37 N11 **Carmel** California, W USA 36.32N 121.54W
33 O13 **Carmel** Indiana, N USA 39.58N 86.07W
20 L13 **Carmel** New York, NE USA 41.25N 73.40W
99 H18 **Carmel Head** headland NW Wales, UK 53.24N 4.35W
44 E2 **Carmelita** Petén, N Guatemala 17.33N 90.10W
63 D19 **Carmelo** Colonia, SW Uruguay 34.00S 58.20W
43 V14 **Carmen** var. Ciudad del Carmen. Campeche, SE Mexico 18.37N 91.49W
63 A25 **Carmen de Patagones** Buenos Aires, E Argentina 40.45S 63.00W
42 F8 **Carmen, Isla** island W Mexico
42 M5 **Carmen, Sierra del** ▲▲ NW Mexico
32 M16 **Carmi** Illinois, N USA 38.05N 88.09W
37 O7 **Carmichael** California, W USA 38.36N 121.21W
Carmiel see Karmi'él
27 U11 **Carmine** Texas, SW USA 30.07N 96.40W
106 K14 **Carmona** Andalucía, S Spain 37.28N 5.37W
Carmona see Uíge
Carnaro see Kvarner
12 I13 **Carnarvon** Ontario, SE Canada 45.03N 78.41W
85 G24 **Carnarvon** Northern Cape, W South Africa 30.58S 22.07E
Carnarvon see Caernarfon
188 K9 **Carnarvon Range** ▲▲ Western Australia
188 G9 **Carnarvon** Western Australia 24.57S 113.37E
Carn Domhnach see Carndonagh
98 E13 **Carndonagh** Ir. Carn Domhnach. NW Ireland 55.15N 7.15W
9 V17 **Carnduff** Saskatchewan, S Canada 49.10N 101.49W
28 L11 **Carnegie** Oklahoma, C USA 35.06N 98.36W
188 L9 **Carnegie, Lake** salt lake Western Australia
200 Oo8 **Carnegie Ridge** undersea feature E Pacific Ocean
98 H9 **Carn Eige** ▲ N Scotland, UK 57.18N 5.04W
190 F5 **Carnes** South Australia 30.12S 134.31E
204 J12 **Carney Island** island Antarctica
20 H16 **Carneys Point** New Jersey, NE USA 39.38N 75.29W
Carniche, Alpi see Karnische Alpen
157 Q21 **Car Nicobar** island Nicobar Islands, India, NE Indian Ocean
81 H15 **Carnot** Mambéré-Kadéï, W Central African Republic 4.58N 15.55E
190 F10 **Carnot, Cape** headland South Australia 34.57S 135.39E
98 K11 **Carnoustie** E Scotland, UK 56.29N 2.42W
99 F20 **Carnsore Point** Ir. Ceann an Chairn. headland SE Ireland 52.10N 6.22W
15 Gg4 **Carnwath** ∽ Northwest Territories, NW Canada
33 R8 **Caro** Michigan, N USA 43.29N 83.24W
25 Z15 **Carol City** Florida, SE USA 25.56N 80.15W
61 L14 **Carolina** Maranhão, E Brazil 7.19S 47.25W
47 U5 **Carolina** E Puerto Rico 18.22N 65.57W
23 V12 **Carolina Beach** North Carolina, SE USA 34.02N 77.53W

◆ Country
● Country Capital
◇ Dependent Territory
○ Dependent Territory Capital
⬖ Administrative Region
✈ International Airport
▲ Mountain
▲▲ Mountain Range
⛰ Volcano
∽ River
◎ Lake
⊠ Reservoir

Caroline Island – Central

Caroline Island *see* Millennium Island
201 *N15* **Caroline Islands** *island group* C Micronesia
133 *Z14* **Caroline Plate** *tectonic feature*
199 *H7* **Caroline Ridge** *undersea feature* E Philippine Sea
Carolopois *see* Châlons-en-Champagne
47 *V14* **Caroni Arena Dam** ⊡ Trinidad, Trinidad and Tobago
Caronie, Monti *see* Nebrodi, Monti
57 *P7* **Caroní, Río** ≈ E Venezuela
47 *U14* **Caroni River** ≈ Trinidad, Trinidad and Tobago
Caronium *see* A Coruña
56 *J5* **Carora** Lara, N Venezuela *10.09N 70.06W*
88 *F12* **Carpathian Mountains** *var.* Carpathians, *Cz./Pol.* Karpaty, *Ger.* Karpaten. ▲▲ E Europe
Carpathians *see* Carpathian Mountains
Carpathos/Carpathus *see* Kárpathos
118 *H12* **Carpaţii Meridionali** *var.* Alpi Transilvaniei, Carpaţii Sudici, *Eng.* South Carpathians, Transylvanian Alps, *Ger.* Südkarpaten, Transsylvanische Alpen, *Hung.* Déli-Kárpátok, Erdélyi-Havasok. ▲▲ C Romania
Carpaţii Sudici *see* Carpaţii Meridionali
182 *L7* **Carpentaria, Gulf of** *gulf* N Australia
Carpentoracte *see* Carpentras
105 *R14* **Carpentras** *anc.* Carpentoracte. Vaucluse, SE France *44.03N 5.03E*
108 *F9* **Carpi** Emilia-Romagna, N Italy *44.46N 10.52E*
118 *E11* **Cărpiniş** *Hung.* Gyertyámos. Timiş, W Romania *45.46N 20.51E*
37 *R14* **Carpinteria** California, W USA *34.24N 119.30W*
25 *S9* **Carrabelle** Florida, SE USA *29.51N 84.39W*
Carraig Aonair *see* Fastnet Rock
Carraig Fhearghais *see* Carrickfergus
Carraig Mhachaire Rois *see* Carrickmacross
Carraig na Siúire *see* Carrick-on-Suir
Carrantual *see* Carrauntoohil
108 *E10* **Carrara** Toscana, C Italy *44.04N 10.07E*
63 *F20* **Carrasco** ✕ (Montevideo) Canelones, S Uruguay *34.51S 56.00W*
107 *P9* **Carrascosa del Campo** Castilla-La Mancha, C Spain *40.01N 2.34W*
56 *H4* **Carrasquero** Zulia, NW Venezuela *11.00N 72.01W*
191 *O9* **Carrathool** New South Wales, SE Australia *34.25S 145.30E*
Carrauntohil *see* Carrauntoohil
99 *B21* **Carrauntoohil** *Ir.* Carrantual, Carrauntohil, Corrán Tuathail. ▲ SW Ireland *51.59N 9.45W*
47 *Y15* **Carriacou** *island* N Grenada
99 *G15* **Carrickfergus** *Ir.* Carraig Fhearghais. NE Northern Ireland, UK *54.43N 5.49W*
99 *F16* **Carrickmacross** *Ir.* Carraig Mhachaire Rois. N Ireland *53.58N 6.43W*
99 *D16* **Carrick-on-Shannon** *Ir.* Cora Droma Rúisc. NW Ireland *53.57N 8.04W*
99 *E20* **Carrick-on-Suir** *Ir.* Carraig na Siúire. S Ireland *52.21N 7.25W*
190 *I7* **Carrieton** South Australia *32.27S 138.33E*
42 *L7* **Carrillo** Chihuahua, N Mexico *25.53N 103.54W*
31 *O4* **Carrington** North Dakota, N USA *47.27N 99.07W*
106 *M4* **Carrión** ≈ N Spain
106 *M4* **Carrión de los Condes** Castilla-León, N Spain *42.19N 4.37W*
27 *P13* **Carrizo Springs** Texas, SW USA *28.31N 99.51W*
39 *S13* **Carrizozo** New Mexico, SW USA *33.38N 105.52W*
31 *T13* **Carroll** Iowa, C USA *42.04N 94.52W*
25 *N4* **Carrollton** Alabama, S USA *33.13N 88.05W*
25 *R3* **Carrollton** Georgia, SE USA *33.33N 85.04W*
32 *K14* **Carrollton** Illinois, N USA *39.18N 90.24W*
22 *L4* **Carrollton** Kentucky, S USA *38.40N 85.10W*
33 *R8* **Carrollton** Michigan, N USA *43.27N 83.55W*
29 *T3* **Carrollton** Missouri, C USA *39.21N 93.30W*
33 *U12* **Carrollton** Ohio, N USA *40.34N 81.05W*
27 *T6* **Carrollton** Texas, SW USA *32.57N 96.53W*
9 *U14* **Carrot** ≈ Saskatchewan, S Canada
9 *U14* **Carrot River** Saskatchewan, C Canada *53.18N 103.31W*
20 *J7* **Carry Falls Reservoir** ⊡ New York, NE USA
142 *L11* **Çarşamba** Samsun, N Turkey *41.13N 36.43E*
30 *L6* **Carson** North Dakota, N USA *46.21N 101.33W*
37 *Q6* **Carson City** *state capital* Nevada, W USA *39.10N 119.46W*
37 *R6* **Carson River** ≈ Nevada, W USA
37 *S5* **Carson Sink** *salt flat* Nevada, W USA
9 *Q16* **Carstairs** Alberta, SW Canada *51.34N 114.01W*
Carstensz, Puntjak *see* Jaya, Puncak
56 *E5* **Cartagena** *var.* Cartagena de los Indes. Bolívar, NW Colombia *10.24N 75.33W*
107 *R13* **Cartagena** *anc.* Carthago Nova. Murcia, SE Spain *37.36N 0.58W*
Cartagena de los Indes *see* Cartagena
56 *D10* **Cartago** Valle del Cauca, W Colombia *4.45N 75.55W*
45 *N14* **Cartago** Cartago, C Costa Rica *9.49N 83.53W*
44 *M14* **Cartago** *off.* Provincia de Cartago. ◐ *province* C Costa Rica
27 *O11* **Carta Valley** Texas, SW USA *29.46N 100.37W*
106 *F10* **Cartaxo** Santarém, C Portugal *39.10N 8.46W*
106 *I14* **Cartaya** Andalucía, S Spain *37.16N 7.09W*
Carteret Islands *see* Tulun Islands
31 *S15* **Carter Lake** Iowa, C USA *41.17N 95.55W*
25 *S3* **Cartersville** Georgia, SE USA *34.10N 84.48W*
193 *M14* **Carterton** Wellington, North Island, NZ *41.01S 175.32E*
32 *J13* **Carthage** Illinois, N USA *40.25N 91.09W*
24 *L5* **Carthage** Mississippi, S USA *32.43N 89.31W*
29 *R7* **Carthage** Missouri, C USA *37.10N 94.18W*
20 *I8* **Carthage** New York, NE USA *43.58N 75.36W*
23 *T10* **Carthage** North Carolina, SE USA *35.19N 79.24W*
22 *K8* **Carthage** Tennessee, S USA *36.16N 85.57W*
27 *X7* **Carthage** Texas, SW USA *32.09N 94.20W*
76 *M5* **Carthage** ✕ (Tunis) N Tunisia *36.51N 10.12E*
Carthago Nova *see* Cartagena
12 *E10* **Cartier** Ontario, S Canada *46.40N 81.31W*
56 *E13* **Cartagena de Chaira** Caquetá, S Colombia *1.19N 74.52W*
11 *S8* **Cartwright** Newfoundland and Labrador, E Canada *53.45N 57.00W*
57 *P9* **Caruana de Montaña** Bolívar, SE Venezuela *5.16N 63.12W*
61 *Q15* **Caruaru** Pernambuco, E Brazil *8.15S 35.55W*
57 *P5* **Carúpano** Sucre, NE Venezuela *10.39N 63.13W*
Carusbur *see* Cherbourg
60 *M12* **Carutapera** Maranhão, E Brazil *1.12S 45.57W*
29 *Y9* **Caruthersville** Missouri, C USA *36.07N 89.38W*
105 *O1* **Carvin** Pas-de-Calais, N France *50.31N 3.00E*
60 *E12* **Carvoeiro** Amazonas, NW Brazil *1.24S 61.59W*
106 *E10* **Carvoeiro, Cabo** *headland* C Portugal *39.19N 9.27W*
23 *U9* **Cary** North Carolina, SE USA *35.47N 78.46W*
190 *M3* **Caryapundy Swamp** *wetland* New South Wales/Queensland, SE Australia
67 *E24* **Carysfort, Cape** *headland* East Falkland, Falkland Islands *51.25S 57.49W*
76 *F6* **Casablanca** *Ar.* Dar-el-Beida. NW Morocco *33.39N 7.30W*
62 *M8* **Casa Branca** São Paulo, S Brazil *21.47S 47.05W*
38 *L14* **Casa Grande** Arizona, SW USA *32.52N 111.45W*
108 *C8* **Casale Monferrato** Piemonte, NW Italy *45.07N 8.28E*
108 *E8* **Casalpusterlengo** Lombardia, N Italy *45.10N 9.37E*
56 *H10* **Casanare** *off.* Intendencia de Casanare. ◐ *province* C Colombia
57 *P5* **Casanay** Sucre, NE Venezuela *10.30N 63.25W*
26 *K11* **Casa Piedra** Texas, SW USA *29.43N 104.03W*
109 *Q19* **Casarano** Puglia, SE Italy *40.01N 18.10E*
44 *J11* **Casares** Carazo, W Nicaragua *11.37N 86.19W*
107 *R10* **Casas Ibáñez** Castilla-La Mancha, C Spain *39.16N 1.28W*
63 *I14* **Casca** Rio Grande do Sul, S Brazil *28.39S 51.55W*
180 *I17* **Cascade** Mahé, NE Seychelles *4.39S 55.28E*
35 *N13* **Cascade** Idaho, NW USA *44.31N 116.02W*
31 *Y13* **Cascade** Iowa, C USA *42.18N 91.00W*
35 *R9* **Cascade** Montana, NW USA *47.15N 111.46W*
193 *B20* **Cascade Point** *headland* South Island, NZ *44.00S 168.23E*
34 *G13* **Cascade Range** ▲▲ Oregon/Washington, NW USA
35 *N12* **Cascade Reservoir** ⊡ Idaho, NW USA
(0) *E8* **Cascadia Basin** *undersea feature* NE Pacific Ocean
106 *E11* **Cascais** Lisboa, C Portugal *38.40N 9.25W*
13 *W7* **Cascapédia** ≈ Québec, SE Canada
61 *I22* **Cascavel** Ceará, E Brazil *4.10S 38.15W*
62 *G11* **Cascavel** Paraná, S Brazil *24.55S 53.28W*
108 *I13* **Cascia** Umbria, C Italy *42.45N 13.01E*
108 *F11* **Cascina** Toscana, C Italy *43.40N 10.33E*
21 *Q8* **Casco Bay** *bay* Maine, NE USA
204 *J7* **Case Island** *island* Antarctica
108 *B8* **Caselle** ✕ (Torino) Piemonte, NW Italy *45.06N 7.41E*
109 *K17* **Caserta** Campania, S Italy *41.04N 14.19E*
13 *N8* **Casey** Québec, SE Canada *47.50N 74.09W*
32 *M14* **Casey** Illinois, N USA *39.18N 87.59W*
205 *Y12* **Casey** *Australian research station* Antarctica *65.58S 111.04E*
205 *W3* **Casey Bay** *bay* Antarctica
82 *Q11* **Caseyr, Raas** *headland* NE Somalia *11.51N 51.16E*
99 *D20* **Cashel** *Ir.* Caiseal. S Ireland *52.31N 7.52W*
56 *G6* **Casigua** Zulia, W Venezuela *8.46N 72.30W*
63 *B19* **Casilda** Santa Fe, C Argentina *33.04S 61.10W*
Casim *see* General Toshevo
191 *V4* **Casino** New South Wales, SE Australia *28.49S 153.01E*
Casinum *see* Cassino
113 *E17* **Čáslav** *Ger.* Tschaslau. Střední Čechy, C Czech Republic *49.54N 15.22E*
58 *C13* **Casma** Ancash, C Peru *9.27S 78.21W*
178 *J7* **Ca, Sông** ≈ N Vietnam
109 *K17* **Casoria** Campania, S Italy *40.54N 14.28E*
107 *T6* **Caspe** Aragón, NE Spain *41.13N 0.03W*
35 *X15* **Casper** Wyoming, C USA *42.48N 106.22W*
86 *M10* **Caspian Depression** *Kaz.* Kaspiy Mangy Oypaty, *Rus.* Prikaspiyskaya Nizmennost'. *depression* Kazakhstan/Russian Federation
138 *Kk9* **Caspian Sea** *Az.* Xäzär Dänizi, *Kaz.* Kaspiy Tengizi, *Per.* Baḩr-e Khazar, Daryā-ye Khazar, *Rus.* Kaspiyskoye More. *inland sea* Asia/Europe
85 *L14* **Cassacatiza** Tete, NW Mozambique *14.20S 32.24E*
Cassai *see* Kasai
84 *F13* **Cassamba** Moxico, E Angola *13.07S 20.22E*
109 *N20* **Cassano allo Ionio** Calabria, SE Italy *39.46N 16.16E*
33 *S8* **Cass City** Michigan, N USA *43.36N 83.10W*
Cassel *see* Kassel
12 *M13* **Casselman** Ontario, SE Canada *45.19N 75.04W*
31 *R5* **Casselton** North Dakota, N USA *46.53N 97.10W*
61 *M16* **Cássia** *var.* Santa Rita de Cassia. Bahia, E Brazil *11.03S 44.16W*
8 *J9* **Cassiar** British Columbia, W Canada *59.16N 129.45W*
8 *K10* **Cassiar Mountains** ▲▲ British Columbia, W Canada
85 *C15* **Cassinga** Huíla, SW Angola *15.06S 16.05E*
109 *J16* **Cassino** *prev.* San Germano; *anc.* Casinum. Lazio, C Italy *41.28N 13.49E*
31 *T4* **Cass Lake** Minnesota, N USA *47.22N 94.36W*
31 *T4* **Cass Lake** ◎ Minnesota, N USA
33 *P10* **Cassopolis** Michigan, N USA *41.56N 86.00W*
33 *S8* **Cass River** ≈ Michigan, N USA
29 *S8* **Cassville** Missouri, C USA *36.40N 93.52W*
Castamoni *see* Kastamonu
60 *L12* **Castanhal** Pará, NE Brazil *1.16S 47.55W*
106 *G8* **Castanheira de Pêra** Leiria, C Portugal *40.01N 8.12W*
43 *N7* **Castaños** Coahuila de Zaragoza, NE Mexico *26.48N 101.25W*
110 *I10* **Castasegna** Graubünden, SE Switzerland *46.21N 9.30E*
108 *D8* **Casteggio** Lombardia, N Italy *45.01N 9.10E*
109 *K23* **Castelbuono** Sicilia, Italy, C Mediterranean Sea *37.55N 14.04E*
109 *K15* **Castel di Sangro** Abruzzo, C Italy *41.46N 14.03E*
108 *H7* **Castelfranco Veneto** Veneto, NE Italy *45.40N 11.55E*
104 *K14* **Casteljaloux** Lot-et-Garonne, SW France *44.19N 0.03E*
109 *L18* **Castellabate** *var.* Santa Maria di Castellabate. Campania, S Italy *40.16N 14.57E*
109 *I23* **Castellammare del Golfo** Sicilia, Italy, C Mediterranean Sea *38.01N 12.52E*
109 *H22* **Castellammare, Golfo di** *gulf* Sicilia, Italy, C Mediterranean Sea
105 *U15* **Castellane** Alpes-de-Haute-Provence, SE France *43.49N 6.34E*
109 *O18* **Castellaneta** Puglia, SE Italy *40.37N 16.57E*
108 *E9* **Castel l'Arquato** Emilia-Romagna, C Italy *44.52N 9.51E*
63 *E21* **Castelli** Buenos Aires, E Argentina *36.07S 57.46W*
Castelló de la Plana *see* Castellón de la Plana
107 *S8* **Castellón** ◐ *province* País Valenciano, E Spain
Castellón *see* Castellón de la Plana
107 *T9* **Castellón de la Plana** *var.* Castellón, *Cat.* Castelló de la Plana. País Valenciano, E Spain *39.58N 0.03W*
107 *S7* **Castellote** Aragón, NE Spain *40.46N 0.18W*
105 *N16* **Castelnaudary** Aude, S France *43.18N 1.57E*
104 *L16* **Castelnau-Magnoac** Hautes-Pyrénées, S France *43.18N 0.30E*
108 *F10* **Castelnovo ne' Monti** Emilia-Romagna, C Italy *44.26N 10.24E*
Castelnuovo *see* Herceg-Novi
106 *H9* **Castelo Branco** Castelo Branco, C Portugal *39.49N 7.30W*
106 *H8* **Castelo Branco** ◐ *district* C Portugal
106 *I10* **Castelo de Vide** Portalegre, C Portugal *39.25N 7.27W*
106 *G9* **Castelo do Bode, Barragem do** ⊡ C Portugal
108 *G10* **Castel San Pietro Terme** Emilia-Romagna, C Italy *44.22N 11.34E*
109 *B17* **Castelsardo** Sardegna, Italy, C Mediterranean Sea *40.54N 8.42E*
104 *M14* **Castelsarrasin** Tarn-et-Garonne, S France *44.01N 1.06E*
109 *I24* **Casteltermini** Sicilia, Italy, C Mediterranean Sea *37.33N 13.37E*
109 *H24* **Castelvetrano** Sicilia, Italy, C Mediterranean Sea *37.40N 12.46E*
190 *L12* **Casterton** Victoria, SE Australia *37.37S 141.22E*
104 *J15* **Castets** Landes, SW France *43.55N 1.08W*
108 *H12* **Castiglione del Lago** Umbria, C Italy *43.07N 12.02E*
108 *F13* **Castiglione della Pescaia** Toscana, C Italy *42.46N 10.53E*
108 *F8* **Castiglione delle Stiviere** Lombardia, N Italy *45.24N 10.31E*
106 *M9* **Castilla-La Mancha** ◐ *autonomous community* NE Spain
106 *L5* **Castilla-León** *var.* Castillia y Leon. ◐ *autonomous community* NW Spain
107 *N10* **Castilla Nueva** *cultural region* C Spain
107 *N6* **Castilla Vieja** *cultural region* N Spain
Castillia y Leon *see* Castilla-León
Castillo de Locubim *see* Castillo de Locubín
107 *N14* **Castillo de Locubín** *var.* Castillo de Locubim. Andalucía, S Spain *37.31N 3.55W*
104 *K13* **Castillon-la-Bataille** Gironde, SW France *44.51N 0.01W*
65 *I19* **Castillo, Pampa del** *plain* S Argentina
63 *G19* **Castillos** Rocha, SE Uruguay *34.12S 53.52W*
99 *B16* **Castlebar** *Ir.* Caisleán an Bharraigh. W Ireland *53.52N 9.16W*
99 *F16* **Castleblayney** *Ir.* Baile na Lorgan. N Ireland *54.07N 6.43W*
47 *O11* **Castle Bruce** E Dominica *15.25N 61.15W*
38 *M5* **Castle Dale** Utah, W USA *39.10N 111.02W*
38 *I14* **Castle Dome Peak** ▲ Arizona, SW USA *33.04N 114.08W*
99 *J14* **Castle Douglas** S Scotland, UK *54.56N 3.55W*
99 *E14* **Castlefinn** *Ir.* Caisleán na Finne. NW Ireland *54.48N 7.36W*
99 *M17* **Castleford** N England, UK *53.43N 1.21W*
9 *O17* **Castlegar** British Columbia, SW Canada *49.18N 117.48W*
66 *B12* **Castle Harbour** *inlet* Bermuda, NW Atlantic Ocean
23 *V12* **Castle Hayne** North Carolina, SE USA *34.23N 78.07W*
99 *B20* **Castleisland** *Ir.* Oileán Ciarraí. SW Ireland *52.12N 9.30W*
191 *N12* **Castlemaine** Victoria, SE Australia *37.06S 144.13E*
39 *R5* **Castle Peak** ▲ Colorado, C USA *39.00N 106.51W*
35 *O13* **Castle Peak** ▲ Idaho, NW USA *44.02N 114.42W*
192 *N13* **Castlepoint** Wellington, North Island, NZ *40.54S 176.13E*
99 *D17* **Castlerea** *Ir.* An Caisleán Riabhach. W Ireland *53.45N 8.31W*
99 *G15* **Castlereagh** *Ir.* An Caisleán Riabhach. N Northern Ireland, UK *54.33N 5.53W*
191 *R6* **Castlereagh River** ≈ New South Wales, SE Australia
39 *T5* **Castle Rock** Colorado, C USA *39.22N 104.51W*
32 *K7* **Castle Rock Lake** ⊡ Wisconsin, N USA
67 *G25* **Castle Rock Point** *headland* S Saint Helena *16.01S 5.45W*
99 *I16* **Castletown** SE Isle of Man *54.04N 4.39W*
31 *R9* **Castlewood** South Dakota, N USA *44.43N 97.01W*
9 *R15* **Castor** Alberta, SW Canada *52.13N 111.54W*
12 *M13* **Castor** ≈ Ontario, SE Canada
29 *X7* **Castor River** ≈ Missouri, C USA
Castra Albiensium *see* Castres
Castra Regina *see* Regensburg
105 *N15* **Castres** *anc.* Castra Albiensium. Tarn, S France *43.36N 2.15E*
100 *H9* **Castricum** Noord-Holland, W Netherlands *52.33N 4.40E*
47 *S11* **Castries** ● (Saint Lucia) N Saint Lucia *14.01N 60.59W*
62 *J11* **Castro** Paraná, S Brazil *24.45S 50.58W*
65 *F17* **Castro** Los Lagos, W Chile *42.27S 73.48W*
106 *H7* **Castro Daire** Viseu, N Portugal *40.54N 7.55W*
106 *M13* **Castro del Río** Andalucía, S Spain *37.40N 4.28W*
Castrogiovanni *see* Enna
106 *H14* **Castro Marim** Faro, S Portugal *37.13N 7.25W*
106 *J2* **Castropol** Asturias, N Spain *43.30N 7.01W*
107 *O2* **Castro-Urdiales** *var.* Castro Urdiales. Cantabria, N Spain *43.22N 3.10W*
106 *G13* **Castro Verde** Beja, S Portugal *37.42N 8.04W*
109 *N19* **Castrovillari** Calabria, SW Italy *39.48N 16.12E*
37 *N10* **Castroville** California, W USA *36.46N 121.46W*
27 *R12* **Castroville** Texas, SW USA *29.21N 98.52W*
106 *K11* **Castuera** Extremadura, W Spain *38.43N 5.33W*
63 *F19* **Casupá** Florida, S Uruguay *34.04S 55.39W*
193 *A22* **Caswell Sound** *sound* South Island, NZ
143 *Q13* **Çat** Erzurum, NE Turkey *39.40N 41.03E*
44 *K6* **Catacamas** Olancho, C Honduras *14.50N 85.54W*
58 *A10* **Catacaos** Piura, NW Peru *5.22S 80.40W*
24 *I7* **Catahoula Lake** ◎ Louisiana, S USA
143 *S15* **Çatak** Van, SE Turkey *38.01N 43.04E*
143 *S15* **Çatak Çayi** ≈ SE Turkey
116 *O12* **Çatalca** İstanbul, NW Turkey *41.09N 28.28E*
116 *O12* **Çatalca Yarımadası** *physical region* NW Turkey
64 *H6* **Catalina** Antofagasta, N Chile *25.19S 69.37W*
Catalonia *see* Cataluña
107 *U5* **Cataluña** *Cat.* Catalunya; *Eng.* Catalonia. ◐ *autonomous community* N Spain
Catalunya *see* Cataluña
64 *I7* **Catamarca** *off.* Provincia de Catamarca. ◐ *province* NW Argentina
Catamarca *see* San Fernando del Valle de Catamarca
179 *Pp11* **Catanauan** Luzon, N Philippines *13.36N 122.19E*
85 *M16* **Catandica** Manica, C Mozambique *18.04S 33.10E*
179 *Qq11* **Catanduanes Island** *island* N Philippines
62 *K8* **Catanduva** São Paulo, S Brazil *21.06S 48.57W*
109 *L24* **Catania** Sicilia, Italy, C Mediterranean Sea *37.31N 15.04E*
109 *M24* **Catania, Golfo di** *gulf* Sicilia, Italy, C Mediterranean Sea
47 *U5* **Cataño** *var.* Cantaño. E Puerto Rico *18.26N 66.06W*
109 *O21* **Catanzaro** Calabria, SW Italy *38.53N 16.36E*
109 *O22* **Catanzaro Marina** *var.* Marina di Catanzaro. Calabria, S Italy *38.48N 16.33E*
27 *Q14* **Catarina** Texas, SW USA *28.19N 99.36W*
179 *Qq12* **Catarman** Samar, C Philippines *12.29N 124.34E*
107 *S10* **Catarroja** País Valenciano, E Spain *39.24N 0.24W*
23 *R11* **Catawba River** ≈ North Carolina/South Carolina, SE USA
179 *R12* **Catbalogan** Samar, C Philippines *11.49N 124.55E*
12 *I14* **Catchacoma** Ontario, SE Canada *44.43N 78.19W*
43 *S15* **Catemaco** Veracruz-Llave, SE Mexico *18.28N 95.10W*
Cathair na Mart *see* Westport
Cathair Saidhbhín *see* Cahersiveen
33 *P5* **Cat Head Point** *headland* Michigan, N USA *45.11N 85.37W*
25 *Q2* **Cathedral Caverns** *cave* Alabama, S USA *34.36N 86.11W*
37 *V16* **Cathedral City** California, W USA *33.45N 116.27W*
26 *K10* **Cathedral Mountain** ▲ Texas, SW USA *30.10N 103.39W*
34 *G10* **Cathlamet** Washington, NW USA *46.12N 123.24W*
78 *G13* **Catió** S Guinea-Bissau *11.17N 15.16W*
57 *O10* **Catisimiña** Bolívar, SE Venezuela *4.07N 63.40W*
46 *J3* **Cat Island** *island* C Bahamas
10 *B9* **Cat Lake** Ontario, S Canada *51.47N 91.52W*
23 *P5* **Catlettsburg** Kentucky, S USA *38.24N 82.37W*
193 *D24* **Catlins** ≈ South Island, NZ
37 *R1* **Catnip Mountain** ▲ Nevada, W USA *41.53N 119.19W*
43 *Z11* **Catoche, Cabo** *headland* SE Mexico *21.36N 87.04W*
29 *P9* **Catoosa** Oklahoma, C USA *36.11N 95.45W*
43 *N10* **Catorce** San Luis Potosí, C Mexico *23.42N 100.49W*
65 *I14* **Catriel** Río Negro, C Argentina *37.54S 67.52W*
64 *K13* **Catriló** La Pampa, C Argentina *36.24S 63.25W*
60 *F11* **Catrimani** Roraima, N Brazil *0.24N 61.30W*
60 *E10* **Catrimani, Rio** ≈ N Brazil
20 *K11* **Catskill** New York, NE USA *42.13N 73.52W*
20 *K11* **Catskill Creek** ≈ New York, NE USA
20 *J11* **Catskill Mountains** ▲▲ New York, NE USA
20 *D11* **Cattaraugus Creek** ≈ New York, NE USA
Cattaro *see* Kotor
Cattaro, Bocche di *see* Kotorska, Boka
109 *I24* **Cattolica Eraclea** Sicilia, Italy, C Mediterranean Sea *37.27N 13.24E*
85 *B14* **Catumbela** ≈ W Angola
85 *P14* **Catur** Niassa, N Mozambique *13.50S 35.43E*
84 *C10* **Cauale** ≈ NE Angola
179 *Pp9* **Cauayan** Luzon, N Philippines *16.55N 121.46E*
56 *C12* **Cauca** *off.* Departamento del Cauca. ◐ *province* SW Colombia
49 *P5* **Cauca** ≈ SE Venezuela
60 *P13* **Caucaia** Ceará, E Brazil *3.43S 38.45W*
56 *E7* **Cauca, Río** ≈ N Colombia
56 *E7* **Caucasia** Antioquia, NW Colombia *7.58N 75.13W*
143 *Q8* **Caucasus** *Rus.* Kavkaz. ▲▲ Georgia/Russian Federation
64 *I10* **Caucete** San Juan, W Argentina *31.37S 68.16W*
107 *R11* **Caudete** Castilla-La Mancha, C Spain *38.42N 1.00W*
105 *P2* **Caudry** Nord, N France *50.07N 3.24E*
84 *D11* **Caungula** Lunda Norte, NE Angola *8.22S 18.37E*
64 *G13* **Cauquenes** Maule, C Chile *35.58S 72.22W*
57 *N8* **Caura, Río** ≈ C Venezuela
13 *V7* **Causapscal** Québec, SE Canada *48.22N 67.13W*
119 *N10* **Căuşeni** *Rus.* Kaushany. E Moldova *46.37N 29.21E*
104 *M14* **Caussade** Tarn-et-Garonne, S France *44.10N 1.31E*
104 *K17* **Cauterets** Hautes-Pyrénées, S France *42.53N 0.08W*
8 *J15* **Caution, Cape** *headland* British Columbia, SW Canada *51.10N 127.43W*
46 *H7* **Cauto** ≈ E Cuba
Cauvery *see* Kāveri
104 *L3* **Caux, Pays de** *physical region* N France
109 *L18* **Cava dei Tirreni** Campania, S Italy *40.42N 14.42E*
106 *G6* **Cávado** ≈ N Portugal
Cavaia *see* Kavajë
105 *R15* **Cavaillon** Vaucluse, SE France *43.51N 5.01E*
105 *U16* **Cavalaire-sur-Mer** Var, SE France *43.10N 6.31E*
108 *G6* **Cavalese** *Ger.* Gablös. Trentino-Alto Adige, N Italy *46.18N 11.29E*
31 *Q2* **Cavalier** North Dakota, N USA *48.47N 97.37W*
78 *L17* **Cavalla** *var.* Cavally, Cavally Fleuve. ≈ Ivory Coast/Liberia
107 *Y8* **Cavalleria, Cap de** *var.* Cabo Cabelleria. *headland* Menorca, Spain, W Mediterranean Sea *40.04N 4.06E*
192 *K2* **Cavalli Islands** *island group* N NZ
Cavally/Cavally Fleuve *see* Cavalla
99 *E16* **Cavan** *Ir.* Cabhán. N Ireland *54.00N 7.21W*
99 *E16* **Cavan** *Ir.* An Cabhán. *cultural region* N Ireland
108 *H8* **Cavarzere** Veneto, NE Italy *45.07N 12.04E*
29 *W9* **Cave City** Arkansas, C USA *35.56N 91.33W*
22 *K7* **Cave City** Kentucky, S USA *37.08N 85.57W*
67 *M25* **Cave Point** *headland* S Tristan da Cunha
23 *N5* **Cave Run Lake** ⊡ Kentucky, S USA
60 *K11* **Caviana de Fora, Ilha** *var.* Ilha Caviana. *island* N Brazil
Caviana, Ilha *see* Caviana de Fora, Ilha
115 *I16* **Cavtat** *It.* Ragusavecchia. Dubrovnik-Neretva, SE Croatia *42.36N 18.13E*
Cawnpore *see* Kānpur
Caxamarca *see* Cajamarca
60 *A13* **Caxias** Amazonas, W Brazil *4.27S 71.27W*
60 *N13* **Caxias** Maranhão, E Brazil *4.52S 43.19W*
63 *I15* **Caxias do Sul** Rio Grande do Sul, S Brazil *29.13S 51.10W*
44 *J4* **Caxinas, Punta** *headland* N Honduras *16.01N 86.02W*
84 *B11* **Caxito** Bengo, NW Angola *8.34S 13.37E*
142 *F14* **Çay** Afyon, W Turkey *38.34N 31.01E*
42 *L15* **Cayacal, Punta** *var.* Punta Mongrove. *headland* S Mexico *17.55N 102.09W*
58 *C6* **Cayambe** Pichincha, N Ecuador *0.01N 78.10W*
58 *C6* **Cayambe** ▲ N Ecuador *0.00N 77.58W*
23 *R12* **Cayce** South Carolina, SE USA *33.58N 81.04W*
57 *Y10* **Cayenne** ○ (French Guiana) NE French Guiana *4.55N 52.18W*
57 *Y10* **Cayenne** ✕ NE French Guiana *4.55N 52.18W*
46 *K10* **Cayes** *var.* Les Cayes. SW Haiti *18.10N 73.48W*
47 *U6* **Cayey** C Puerto Rico *18.06N 66.09W*
47 *U6* **Cayey, Sierra de** ▲▲ E Puerto Rico
105 *N14* **Caylus** Tarn-et-Garonne, S France *44.13N 1.42E*
46 *E8* **Cayman Brac** *island* E Cayman Islands
46 *D8* **Cayman Islands** ◇ *UK dependent territory* W West Indies
66 *D11* **Cayman Trench** *undersea feature* NW Caribbean Sea
49 *O3* **Cayman Trough** *undersea feature* NW Caribbean Sea
82 *O13* **Caynabo** Sool, N Somalia *8.55N 46.28E*
44 *F3* **Cayo** ◐ *district* SW Belize
Cayo *see* San Ignacio
45 *N9* **Cayos Guerrero** *reef* E Nicaragua
45 *O9* **Cayos King** *reef* E Nicaragua
46 *E4* **Cay Sal** *islet* SW Bahamas
12 *G16* **Cayuga** Ontario, S Canada *42.57N 79.49W*
27 *V8* **Cayuga** Texas, SW USA *31.55N 95.57W*
20 *G10* **Cayuga Lake** ◎ New York, NE USA
106 *K13* **Cazalla de la Sierra** Andalucía, S Spain *37.56N 5.46W*
118 *L14* **Căzăneşti** Ialomiţa, SE Romania *44.36N 27.02E*
104 *M16* **Cazères** Haute-Garonne, S France *43.15N 1.11E*
114 *E10* **Cazin** Federacija Bosna I Hercegovina, NW Bosnia and Herzegovina *44.58N 15.58E*
84 *G13* **Cazombo** Moxico, E Angola *11.53S 22.52E*
107 *O13* **Cazorla** Andalucía, S Spain *37.55N 3.00W*
Cazza *see* Sušac
106 *L4* **Cea** ≈ NW Spain
Ceadâr-Lunga *see* Ciadîr-Lunga
Ceanannas *see* Kells
Ceann Toirc *see* Kanturk
60 *O13* **Ceará** *off.* Estado do Ceará. ◐ *state* C Brazil
Ceará *see* Fortaleza
Ceara Abyssal Plain *see* Ceará Plain
61 *Q14* **Ceará Mirim** Rio Grande do Norte, E Brazil *5.30S 35.50W*
66 *J13* **Ceará Plain** *var.* Ceara Abyssal Plain. *undersea feature* W Atlantic Ocean
66 *I13* **Ceará Ridge** *undersea feature* C Atlantic Ocean
Ceatharlach *see* Carlow
45 *Q17* **Cébaco, Isla** *island* SW Panama
42 *K7* **Ceballos** Durango, C Mexico *26.33N 104.07W*
63 *G19* **Cebollatí** Rocha, E Uruguay *33.13S 53.49W*
63 *G19* **Cebollatí, Río** ≈ E Uruguay
107 *P5* **Cebollera** ▲ N Spain *42.01N 2.40W*
106 *M8* **Cebreros** Castilla-León, N Spain *40.27N 4.28W*
179 *Qq14* **Cebu** *off.* Cebu City. Cebu, C Philippines *10.16N 123.45E*
179 *Qq13* **Cebu** *island* C Philippines
109 *J16* **Ceccano** Lazio, C Italy *41.34N 13.19E*
Čechy *see* Bohemia
108 *F12* **Cecina** Toscana, C Italy *43.18N 10.31E*
28 *K4* **Cedar Bluff Reservoir** ⊡ Kansas, C USA
32 *M8* **Cedarburg** Wisconsin, N USA *43.18N 87.58W*
38 *J7* **Cedar City** Utah, W USA *37.40N 113.03W*
27 *T11* **Cedar Creek** Texas, SW USA *30.04N 97.30W*
30 *L7* **Cedar Creek** ≈ North Dakota, N USA
27 *U7* **Cedar Creek Reservoir** ⊡ Texas, SW USA
31 *W13* **Cedar Falls** Iowa, C USA *42.31N 92.27W*
33 *N8* **Cedar Grove** Wisconsin, N USA *43.31N 87.48W*
23 *Y6* **Cedar Island** *island* Virginia, NE USA
25 *U11* **Cedar Key** Cedar Keys, Florida, SE USA *29.08N 83.03W*
25 *U11* **Cedar Keys** *island group* Florida, SE USA
9 *V14* **Cedar Lake** ◎ Manitoba, C Canada
12 *I11* **Cedar Lake** ◎ Ontario, SE Canada
26 *M6* **Cedar Lake** ◎ Texas, SW USA
31 *X13* **Cedar Rapids** Iowa, C USA *41.58N 91.39W*
31 *X14* **Cedar River** ≈ Iowa/Minnesota, C USA
31 *O14* **Cedar River** ≈ Nebraska, C USA
33 *P8* **Cedar Springs** Michigan, N USA *43.13N 85.33W*
25 *R3* **Cedartown** Georgia, SE USA *34.00N 85.16W*
29 *O7* **Cedar Vale** Kansas, C USA *37.06N 96.30W*
37 *Q2* **Cedarville** California, W USA *41.30N 120.10W*
106 *H1* **Cedeira** Galicia, NW Spain *43.40N 8.03W*
44 *H8* **Cedeño** Choluteca, S Honduras *13.10N 87.25W*
43 *N10* **Cedral** San Luis Potosí, C Mexico *23.47N 100.40W*
44 *I6* **Cedros** Francisco Morazán, C Honduras *14.38N 87.09W*
42 *M9* **Cedros** Zacatecas, C Mexico *24.39N 101.47W*
42 *B5* **Cedros, Isla** *island* W Mexico
199 *Mm6* **Cedros Trench** *undersea feature* E Pacific Ocean
190 *E7* **Ceduna** South Australia *32.09S 133.43E*
112 *D10* **Cedynia** *Ger.* Zehden. Zachodnio-pomorskie, W Poland *52.54N 14.15E*
82 *P12* **Ceelaayo** Sanaag, N Somalia *11.18N 49.20E*
83 *O16* **Ceel Buur** *It.* El Bur; Galguduud, C Somalia *4.36N 46.33E*
83 *N15* **Ceel Dheere** *var.* Ceel Dher, *It.* El Dere. Galguduud, C Somalia *5.18N 46.07E*
Ceel Dher *see* Ceel Dheere
83 *P14* **Ceel Xamure** Mudug, E Somalia *7.15N 48.55E*
82 *O12* **Ceerigaabo** *var.* Erigabo, Erigavo. Sanaag, N Somalia *10.34N 47.22E*
109 *J23* **Cefalù** *anc.* Cephaloedium. Sicilia, Italy, C Mediterranean Sea *38.01N 14.01E*
107 *N6* **Cega** ≈ N Spain
113 *K23* **Cegléd** *prev.* Czegléd. Pest, C Hungary *47.08N 19.45E*
115 *N18* **Čegrane** W FYR Macedonia *41.50N 20.59E*
107 *Q13* **Cehegín** Murcia, SE Spain *38.04N 1.48W*
142 *K12* **Çekerek** Yozgat, N Turkey *40.04N 35.30E*
152 *B13* **Çekiçler** *Rus.* Chekishlyar, *Turkm.* Chekichler. Balkan Welaýaty, W Turkmenistan *37.35N 53.52E*
109 *J15* **Celano** Abruzzo, C Italy *42.06N 13.33E*
106 *H4* **Celanova** Galicia, NW Spain *42.09N 7.58W*
44 *F6* **Celaque, Cordillera de** ▲▲ W Honduras
43 *N13* **Celaya** Guanajuato, C Mexico *20.31N 100.48W*
Celebes *see* Sulawesi
198 *Ff8* **Celebes Basin** *undersea feature* SE South China Sea
175 *Qq4* **Celebes Sea** *Ind.* Laut Sulawesi. *sea* Indonesia/Philippines
43 *W12* **Celestún** Yucatán, E Mexico *20.49N 90.22W*
33 *Q12* **Celina** Ohio, N USA *40.33N 84.34W*
22 *L8* **Celina** Tennessee, S USA *36.30N 85.30W*
27 *U5* **Celina** Texas, SW USA *33.19N 96.46W*
114 *G11* **Čelinac Donji** Republika Srpska, N Bosnia and Herzegovina *44.43N 17.19E*
111 *V10* **Celje** *Ger.* Cilli. C Slovenia *46.16N 15.14E*
113 *G23* **Celldömölk** Vas, W Hungary *47.16N 17.10E*
102 *J12* **Celle** *var.* Zelle. Niedersachsen, N Germany *52.37N 10.04E*
101 *D19* **Celles** Hainaut, SW Belgium *50.42N 3.25E*
106 *I7* **Celorico da Beira** Guarda, N Portugal *40.37N 7.24W*
Celovec *see* Klagenfurt
66 *M7* **Celtic Sea** *Ir.* An Mhuir Cheilteach. *sea* SW British Isles
66 *N7* **Celtic Shelf** *undersea feature* E Atlantic Ocean
116 *L13* **Çeltik Gölu** ◎ NW Turkey
152 *J17* **Çemenibit** *prev. Rus.* Chemenibit. Mary Welaýaty, S Turkmenistan *35.27N 62.19E*
115 *M14* **Čemerno** ▲ C Serbia
175 *Oo16* **Cempi, Teluk** *bay* Nusa Tenggara, S Indonesia
107 *Q12* **Cenajo, Embalse del** ⊡ S Spain
176 *Ww10* **Cenderawasih, Teluk** *var.* Teluk Irian, Teluk Sarera. *bay* W Pacific Ocean
107 *P4* **Cenicero** La Rioja, N Spain *42.28N 2.37W*
108 *E9* **Ceno** ≈ NW Italy
104 *K13* **Cenon** Gironde, SW France *44.51N 0.33W*
12 *K13* **Centennial Lake** ◎ Ontario, SE Canada
Centennial State *see* Colorado
39 *S7* **Center** Colorado, C USA *37.45N 106.06W*
31 *Q13* **Center** Nebraska, C USA *42.33N 97.51W*
30 *M5* **Center** North Dakota, N USA *47.07N 101.18W*
27 *X8* **Center** Texas, SW USA *31.46N 94.10W*
31 *W8* **Center City** Minnesota, N USA *45.22N 92.46W*
38 *L5* **Centerfield** Utah, W USA *39.07N 111.49W*
22 *K9* **Center Hill Lake** ⊡ Tennessee, S USA
31 *X13* **Center Point** Iowa, C USA *42.11N 91.47W*
27 *R11* **Center Point** Texas, SW USA *29.56N 99.01W*
31 *W16* **Centerville** Iowa, C USA *40.42N 92.49W*
29 *W7* **Centerville** Missouri, C USA *37.27N 91.01W*
31 *R12* **Centerville** South Dakota, N USA *43.07N 96.57W*
22 *I9* **Centerville** Tennessee, S USA *35.43N 87.27W*
27 *V9* **Centerville** Texas, SW USA *31.15N 95.58W*
42 *M5* **Centinela, Picacho del** ▲ NE Mexico *29.07N 102.40W*
108 *G9* **Cento** Emilia-Romagna, N Italy *44.43N 11.16E*
Centrafricaine, République *see* Central African Republic
41 *S8* **Central** Alaska, USA *65.34N 144.48W*
39 *P15* **Central** New Mexico, SW USA *32.46N 108.09W*
85 *H18* **Central** ◐ *district* E Botswana
144 *E10* **Central** ◐ *district* C Israel
83 *I19* **Central** ◐ *province* C Kenya
84 *M13* **Central** ◐ *region* C Malawi
159 *P12* **Central** ◐ *zone* C Nepal
194 *J15* **Central** ◐ *province* S PNG
65 *I21* **Central** ◐ *department* C Paraguay
195 *W15* **Central** *off.* Central Province. ◐ *province* S Solomon Islands
85 *J14* **Central** ◐ *province* C Zambia

◆ Country ● Country Capital ◇ Dependent Territory ○ Dependent Territory Capital ◐ Administrative Region ✕ International Airport ▲ Mountain ▲▲ Mountain Range ⛰ Volcano ≈ River ◎ Lake ⊡ Reservoir

CENTRAL – CHASOVO

119 P11 **Central** ✈ (Odesa) Odes'ka Oblast', SW Ukraine *46.26N 30.41E*
Central *see* Centre
81 H14 **Central African Republic** ***var.*** République Centrafricaine, ***abbrev.*** CAR; ***prev.*** Ubangi-Shari, Oubangui-Chari, Territoire de l'Oubangui-Chari. ◆ *republic* C Africa
198 G6 **Central Basin Trough** *undersea feature* W Pacific Ocean
Central Borneo *see* Kalimantan Tengah
155 P12 **Central Brāhui Range** ▲▲ W Pakistan
Central Celebes *see* Sulawesi Tengah
31 Y13 **Central City** Iowa, C USA *42.12N 91.31W*
22 I6 **Central City** Kentucky, S USA *37.17N 87.07W*
31 P15 **Central City** Nebraska, C USA *41.04N 97.59W*
50 D6 **Central, Cordillera** ▲▲ W Bolivia
56 D11 **Central, Cordillera** ▲▲ W Colombia
44 M13 **Central, Cordillera** ▲▲ C Costa Rica
47 N9 **Central, Cordillera** ▲▲ C Dominican Republic
45 R16 **Central, Cordillera** ▲▲ C Panama
179 P8 **Central, Cordillera** ▲▲ Luzon, N Philippines
47 S6 **Central, Cordillera** ▲▲ Puerto Rico
44 H7 **Central District** ***var.*** Tegucigalpa. ◈ *district* C Honduras
32 L15 **Centralia** Illinois, N USA *38.31N 89.07W*
29 U4 **Centralia** Missouri, C USA *39.12N 92.08W*
34 G9 **Centralia** Washington, NW USA *46.43N 122.57W*
Central Indian Ridge *see* Mid-Indian Ridge
Central Java *see* Jawa Tengah
Central Kalimantan *see* Kalimantan Tengah
154 L14 **Central Makrān Range** ▲▲ W Pakistan
199 J8 **Central Pacific Basin** *undersea feature* C Pacific Ocean
61 M19 **Central, Planalto** ***var.*** Brazilian Highlands. ▲▲ E Brazil
34 F15 **Central Point** Oregon, NW USA *42.22N 122.55W*
161 K25 **Central Province** ◈ *province* C Sri Lanka
Central Provinces and Berar *see* Madhya Pradesh
194 G11 **Central Range** ▲▲ NW PNG
Central Russian Upland *see* Srednerusskaya Vozvyshennost'
Central Siberian Plateau/ Central Siberian Uplands *see* Srednesibirskoye Ploskogor'ye
106 K8 **Central, Sistema** ▲▲ C Spain
Central Sulawesi *see* Sulawesi Tengah
37 N3 **Central Valley** California, W USA *40.39N 122.21W*
37 P8 **Central Valley** *valley* California, W USA
25 Q3 **Centre** Alabama, S USA *34.09N 85.40W*
81 E15 **Centre** ***Eng.*** Central. ◈ *province* C Cameroon
104 M8 **Centre** ◈ *region* N France
181 Y16 **Centre de Flacq** E Mauritius *20.12S 57.43E*
57 Y9 **Centre Spatial Guyanais** *space station* N French Guiana *5.11N 52.42W*
25 O5 **Centreville** Alabama, S USA *32.58N 87.08W*
23 X3 **Centreville** Maryland, NE USA *39.02N 76.04W*
24 J7 **Centreville** Mississippi, S USA *31.05N 91.04W*
Centum Cellae *see* Civitavecchia
166 M14 **Cenxi** Guangxi Zhuangzu Zizhiqu, S China *22.58N 111.00E*
Ceos *see* Tziá
Cephaloedium *see* Cefalu
114 I9 **Čepin** ***Hung.*** Csepén. Osijek-Baranja, E Croatia *45.32N 18.33E*
174 Ll15 **Cepu** ***prev.*** Tjepoe, Tjepu. Jawa, C Indonesia *7.07S 111.34E*
Ceram *see* Seram, Pulau
175 T10 **Ceram Sea** ***Ind.*** Laut Seram. *sea* E Indonesia
198 G9 **Ceram Trough** *undersea feature* W Pacific Ocean
Cerasus *see* Giresun
38 I10 **Cerbat Mountains** ▲▲ Arizona, SW USA
105 P17 **Cerbère, Cap** *headland* S France *42.28N 3.15E*
106 F13 **Cercal do Alentejo** Setúbal, S Portugal *37.48N 8.40W*
113 A18 **Čerchov** ***Ger.*** Czerkow. ▲ W Czech Republic *49.24N 12.47E*
105 O13 **Cère** ≈ C France
63 A16 **Ceres** Santa Fe, C Argentina *29.55S 61.55W*
61 K18 **Ceres** Goiás, C Brazil *15.21S 49.34W*
Ceresio *see* Lugano, Lago di
105 O17 **Céret** Pyrénées-Orientales, S France *42.30N 2.43E*
56 E6 **Cereté** Córdoba, NW Colombia *8.51N 75.48W*
180 I17 **Cerf, Île au** *island* Inner Islands, NE Seychelles
101 G22 **Cerfontaine** Namur, S Belgium *50.08N 4.25E*
Cergy-Pontoise *see* Pontoise
109 N16 **Cerignola** Puglia, SE Italy *41.16N 15.52E*
Cerigo *see* Kýthira
105 O9 **Cérilly** Allier, C France *46.38N 2.51E*
142 I11 **Çerkeş** Çankın, N Turkey *40.51N 32.52E*
142 D10 **Çerkezköy** Tekirdağ, NW Turkey *41.18N 27.58E*
111 T12 **Cerknica** ***Ger.*** Zirknitz. SW Slovenia *45.48N 14.21E*
111 S11 **Cerkno** W Slovenia *46.07N 13.58E*
118 F10 **Cermei** ***Hung.*** Csermő. Arad, W Romania *46.33N 21.50E*
143 O15 **Çermik** Dıyarbakır, SE Turkey *38.09N 39.27E*
114 I10 **Cerna** Vukovar-Srijem, E Croatia *45.10N 18.36E*
Cernăuţi *see* Chernivtsi
118 M14 **Cernavodă** Constanţa, SW Romania *44.19N 28.01E*
105 U7 **Cernay** Haut-Rhin, NE France *47.49N 7.10E*
Černice *see* Schwarzach
43 O8 **Cerralvo** Nuevo León, NE Mexico *26.01N 99.37W*
42 G9 **Cerralvo, Isla** *island* W Mexico
109 L16 **Cerreto Sannita** Campania, S Italy *41.17N 14.39E*
115 L20 **Cërrik** ***var.*** Cerriku. Elbasan, C Albania *41.01N 19.55E*
Cerriku *see* Cërrik
43 O11 **Cerritos** San Luis Potosí, C Mexico *22.25N 100.16W*
62 K11 **Cerro Azul** Paraná, S Brazil *24.48S 49.13W*
63 F18 **Cerro Chato** Treinta y Tres, E Uruguay *33.08S 55.07W*
63 F19 **Cerro Colorado** Florida, S Uruguay *33.52S 55.33W*
58 E13 **Cerro de Pasco** Pasco, C Peru *10.43S 76.15W*
63 G18 **Cerro Largo** ◈ *department* NE Uruguay
63 G14 **Cêrro Largo** Rio Grande do Sul, S Brazil *28.10S 54.43W*
44 E7 **Cerrón Grande, Embalse** ▣ N El Salvador
65 I14 **Cerros Colorados, Embalse** ◎ W Argentina
107 V5 **Cervera** Cataluña, NE Spain *41.40N 1.16E*
106 M3 **Cervera del Pisuerga** Castilla-León, N Spain *42.51N 4.30W*
107 Q5 **Cervera del Río Alhama** La Rioja, N Spain *42.01N 1.58W*
109 H15 **Cerveteri** Lazio, C Italy *42.00N 12.06E*
108 H10 **Cervia** Emilia-Romagna, N Italy *44.14N 12.22E*
108 J7 **Cervignano del Friuli** Friuli-Venezia Giulia, NE Italy *45.49N 13.18E*
109 L17 **Cervinara** Campania, S Italy *41.01N 14.36E*
Cervinia *see* Breuil-Cervinia
108 B6 **Cervino, Monte** ***var.*** Matterhorn. ▲ Italy/Switzerland ***see also*** Matterhorn *46.00N 7.39E*
105 Y14 **Cervione** Corse, France, C Mediterranean Sea *42.22N 9.28E*
106 I1 **Cervo** Galicia, NW Spain *43.39N 7.25W*
56 F5 **Cesar** ***off.*** Departamento del Cesar. ◈ *province* N Colombia
108 H10 **Cesena** ***anc.*** Caesena. Emilia-Romagna, N Italy *44.09N 12.13E*
108 I10 **Cesenatico** Emilia-Romagna, N Italy *44.12N 12.24E*
120 H8 **Cēsis** ***Ger.*** Wenden. Cēsis, C Latvia *57.19N 25.17E*
113 D15 **Česká Lípa** ***Ger.*** Böhmisch-Leipa. Liberecký Kraj, N Czech Republic *50.40N 14.32E*
Česká Republika *see* Czech Republic
113 F17 **Česká Třebová** ***Ger.*** Böhmisch-Trübau. Pardubický Kraj, C Czech Republic *49.54N 16.27E*
113 D19 **České Budějovice** ***Ger.*** Budweis. Jihočeský Kraj, S Czech Republic *48.58N 14.28E*
113 D19 **České Velenice** Jihočeský Kraj, S Czech Republic *48.49N 14.57E*
113 E18 **Českomoravská Vrchovina** ***var.*** Českomoravská Vysočina, ***Eng.*** Bohemian-Moravian Highlands, ***Ger.*** Böhmisch-Mährische Höhe. ▲▲ S Czech Republic
Českomoravská Vysočina *see* Českomoravská Vrchovina
113 C19 **Český Krumlov** ***var.*** Böhmisch-Krumau, ***Ger.*** Krummau. Jihočeský Kraj, S Czech Republic *48.48N 14.18E*
Ceský Les *see* Bohemian Forest
114 F8 **Česma** ≈ N Croatia
142 A14 **Çeşme** İzmir, W Turkey *38.19N 26.19E*
Cess *see* Cestos
191 T8 **Cessnock** New South Wales, SE Australia *32.51S 151.21E*
78 K17 **Cestos** ***var.*** Cess. ≈ S Liberia
120 I9 **Cesvaine** Madona, E Latvia *56.58N 26.15E*
118 G14 **Cetate** Dolj, SW Romania *44.06N 23.03E*
Cetatea Albă *see* Bilhorod-Dnistrovs'kyy
115 J17 **Cetinje** ***It.*** Cettigne, SW-Montenegro *42.23N 18.55E*
109 N20 **Cetraro** Calabria, S Italy *39.30N 15.59E*
Cette *see* Sète
196 A17 **Cetti Bay** *bay* SW Guam
Cettigne *see* Cetinje
106 L17 **Ceuta** ***var.*** Sebta. Ceuta, Spain, N Africa *35.52N 5.19W*
90 C15 **Ceuta** *enclave* Spain, N Africa
108 B9 **Ceva** Piemonte, NE Italy *44.24N 8.01E*
105 P14 **Cévennes** ▲▲ S France
110 G10 **Cevio** Ticino, S Switzerland *46.18N 8.36E*
142 K16 **Ceyhan** Adana, S Turkey *37.01N 35.48E*
142 K17 **Ceyhan Nehri** ≈ S Turkey
143 P17 **Ceylanpınar** Şanlıurfa, SE Turkey *36.53N 40.01E*
Ceylon *see* Sri Lanka
181 R6 **Ceylon Plain** *undersea feature* N Indian Ocean
Ceyre to the Caribs *see* Marie-Galante
105 Q14 **Cèze** ≈ S France
Chaacha *see* Çäçe
131 P6 **Chaadayevka** Penzenskaya Oblast', W Russian Federation *53.07N 45.55E*
178 H12 **Cha-Am** Phetchaburi, SW Thailand *12.48N 99.58E*
149 W15 **Chābahār** ***var.*** Chāh Bahār, Chahbar. Sīstān va Balūchestān, SE Iran *25.21N 60.38E*
63 B19 **Chabas** Santa Fe, C Argentina *33.16S 61.22W*
105 T10 **Chablais** *physical region* E France
63 B20 **Chacabuco** Buenos Aires, E Argentina *34.38S 60.31W*
44 K8 **Chachagón, Cerro** ▲ N Nicaragua *13.18N 85.39W*
58 C10 **Chachapoyas** Amazonas, NW Peru *6.13S 77.54W*
Chäche *see* Çäçe
121 O18 **Chachersk** ***Rus.*** Chechersk. Homyel'skaya Voblasts', SE Belarus *52.54N 30.54E*
121 N16 **Chachevichy** ***Rus.*** Chechevichi. Mahilyowskaya Voblasts', E Belarus *53.31N 29.49E*
63 B14 **Chaco** ***off.*** Provincia de Chaco. ◈ *province* NE Argentina
Chaco *see* Gran Chaco
64 M6 **Chaco Austral** *physical region* N Argentina
64 M3 **Chaco Boreal** *physical region* N Paraguay
64 M6 **Chaco Central** *physical region* N Argentina
41 Y15 **Chacon, Cape** *headland* Prince of Wales Island, Alaska, USA *54.41N 132.00W*
80 H9 **Chad** ***off.*** Republic of Chad, ***Fr.*** Tchad. ◆ *republic* C Africa
126 Hh16 **Chadan** Respublika Tyva, S Russian Federation *51.16N 91.25E*
23 U12 **Chadbourn** North Carolina, SE USA *34.19N 78.49W*
85 L14 **Chadiza** Eastern, E Zambia *14.04S 32.27E*
69 Q7 **Chad, Lake** ***Fr.*** Lac Tchad. ◎ C Africa
126 J13 **Chadobets** ≈ C Russian Federation
30 J12 **Chadron** Nebraska, C USA *42.48N 102.57W*
Chadyr-Lunga *see* Ciadîr-Lunga
169 W14 **Chaeryŏng** SW North Korea *38.22N 125.35E*
107 P17 **Chafarinas, Islas** *island group* S Spain
29 Y7 **Chaffee** Missouri, C USA *37.10N 89.39W*
154 L12 **Chāgai Hills** ***var.*** Chāh Gay. ▲▲ Afghanistan/Pakistan
126 M12 **Chagda** Respublika Sakha (Yakutiya), NE Russian Federation *58.43N 130.38E*
Chaghasarāy *see* Asadābād
155 N5 **Chaghcharān** ***var.*** Chakhcharan, Cheghcheran, Qala Āhangarān. Ghowr, C Afghanistan *34.28N 65.18E*
105 R9 **Chagny** Saône-et-Loire, C France *46.54N 4.45E*
181 Q7 **Chagos Archipelago** ***var.*** Oil Islands. *island group* British Indian Ocean Territory
133 O15 **Chagos Bank** *undersea feature* C Indian Ocean
133 O14 **Chagos-Laccadive Plateau** *undersea feature* N Indian Ocean
181 Q7 **Chagos Trench** *undersea feature* N Indian Ocean
45 T14 **Chagres, Río** ≈ C Panama
47 U14 **Chaguanas** Trinidad, Trinidad and Tobago *10.29N 61.24W*
56 M6 **Chaguaramas** Guárico, N Venezuela *9.21N 66.15W*
Chagyl *see* Çagyl
Chahārmahāl and Bakhtiyāri *see* Chahār Maḩall va Bakhtīārī
148 M9 **Chahār Maḩall va Bakhtīārī** ***off.*** Ostān-e Chahār Maḩall va Bakhtīārī, ***var.*** Chahārmahāl and Bakhtiyāri. ◈ *province* SW Iran
Chāh Bahār/Chahbar *see* Chābahār
149 V13 **Chāh Derāz** Sīstān va Balūchestān, SE Iran
Chāh Gay *see* Chāgai Hills
178 Hh10 **Chai Badan** Lop Buri, C Thailand *15.07N 101.03E*
159 Q16 **Chāībāsa** Jhārkhand, N India *22.34N 85.48E*
81 E19 **Chaillu, Massif du** ▲▲ C Gabon
178 Hh10 **Chai Nat** ***var.*** Chainat, Jainat, Jayanath. Chai Nat, C Thailand *15.12N 100.12E*
67 M14 **Chain Fracture Zone** *tectonic feature* E Atlantic Ocean
181 N5 **Chain Ridge** *undersea feature* W Indian Ocean
Chairn, Ceann an *see* Carnsore Point
164 L5 **Chaiwopu** Xinjiang Uygur Zizhiqu, W China *43.31N 87.55E*
178 I10 **Chaiyaphum** ***var.*** Jayabum. Chaiyaphum, C Thailand *15.49N 102.03E*
64 N10 **Chajarí** Entre Ríos, E Argentina *30.45S 57.57W*
44 C5 **Chajul** Quiché, W Guatemala *15.28N 91.02W*
85 K16 **Chakari** Mashonaland West, N Zimbabwe *18.04S 29.49E*
154 J9 **Chakhānsūr** Nīmrūz, SW Afghanistan *31.11N 62.06E*
Chakhānsūr *see* Nīmrūz
Chakhcharan *see* Chaghcharān
155 V8 **Chak Jhumra** ***var.*** Jhumra. Punjab, E Pakistan *31.33N 73.13E*
152 I16 **Chaknakdysonga** Ahal Welaýaty, S Turkmenistan *35.39N 61.24E*
159 P16 **Chakradharpur** Jhārkhand, N India *22.37N 85.28E*
158 J8 **Chakrāta** Uttaranchal, N India *30.42N 77.52E*
155 U7 **Chakwāl** Punjab, NE Pakistan *32.56N 72.49E*
59 F17 **Chala** Arequipa, SW Peru *15.52S 74.13W*
104 K12 **Chalais** Charente, W France *45.16N 0.02E*
110 D10 **Chalais** Valais, SW Switzerland *46.18N 7.37E*
117 J20 **Chalándri** ***var.*** Halandri; ***prev.*** Khalándrion. *prehistoric site* Sýros, Kykládes, Greece, Aegean Sea *37.28N 24.56E*
196 H6 **Chalan Kanoa** Saipan, S Northern Mariana Islands *15.07S 145.43E*
196 C16 **Chalan Pago** C Guam
Chalap Dalam/Chalap Dalan *see* Chehel Abdālān, Kūh-e
44 F7 **Chalatenango** Chalatenango, N El Salvador *14.03N 88.54W*
44 A9 **Chalatenango** ◈ *department* NW El Salvador
85 P15 **Chalaua** Nampula, NE Mozambique *16.04S 39.08E*
83 I16 **Chalbi Desert** *desert* N Kenya
44 D7 **Chalchuapa** Santa Ana, W El Salvador *13.58N 89.39W*
Chalcidice *see* Chalkidikí
Chalcis *see* Chalkída
Chālderān *see* Sīāh Chashmeh
105 N6 **Châlette-sur-Loing** Loiret, C France *48.01N 2.45E*
13 X8 **Chaleur Bay** ***Fr.*** Baie des Chaleurs. *bay* New Brunswick/ Québec, E Canada
Chaleurs, Baie des *see* Chaleur Bay
59 G16 **Chalhuanca** Apurímac, S Peru *14.21S 73.16W*
160 F12 **Chālisgaon** Mahārāshtra, C India *20.28N 75.10E*
117 N23 **Chálki** *island* Dodekánisa, Greece, Aegean Sea
117 F16 **Chalkiádes** Thessalía, C Greece *39.24N 22.25E*
117 H18 **Chalkída** ***var.*** Halkida; ***prev.*** Khalkís, ***anc.*** Chalcis. Evvoia, E Greece *38.27N 23.37E*
117 G14 **Chalkidikí** ***var.*** Khalkidhikí; ***anc.*** Chalcidice. *peninsula* NE Greece
193 A24 **Chalky Inlet** *inlet* South Island, NZ
41 S7 **Chalkyitsik** Alaska, USA *66.39N 143.43W*
104 I9 **Challans** Vendée, NW France *46.51N 1.52W*
59 K19 **Challapata** Oruro, SW Bolivia *19.02S 66.46W*
199 H7 **Challenger Deep** *undersea feature* W Pacific Ocean
200 Nn12 **Challenger Fracture Zone** *tectonic feature* SE Pacific Ocean
199 Ii13 **Challenger Plateau** *undersea feature* E Tasman Sea
35 P13 **Challis** Idaho, NW USA *44.31N 114.14W*
24 L9 **Chalmette** Louisiana, S USA *29.56N 89.57W*
128 J11 **Chalna** Respublika Kareliya, NW Russian Federation *61.53N 33.59E*
105 Q5 **Châlons-en-Champagne** ***prev.*** Châlons-sur-Marne, ***hist.*** Arcae Remorum, ***anc.*** Carolopois. Marne, NE France *48.58N 4.22E*
Châlons-sur-Marne *see* Châlons-en-Champagne
105 R9 **Chalon-sur-Saône** ***anc.*** Cabillonum. Saône-et-Loire, C France *46.46N 4.51E*
Chaltel, Cerro *see* Fitzroy, Monte
149 N4 **Chālūs** Māzandarān, N Iran *36.40N 51.25E*
104 M11 **Châlus** Haute-Vienne, C France *45.38N 1.00E*
103 N20 **Cham** Bayern, SE Germany *49.13N 12.40E*
110 F7 **Cham** Zug, N Switzerland *47.10N 8.28E*
39 R8 **Chama** New Mexico, SW USA *36.54N 106.34W*
Cha Mai *see* Thung Song
85 E22 **Chamaites** Karas, S Namibia *27.13S 17.55E*
155 O9 **Chaman** Baluchistān, SW Pakistan *30.55N 66.27E*
39 R9 **Chama, Rio** ≈ New Mexico, SW USA
158 I6 **Chamba** Himāchal Pradesh, N India *32.33N 76.10E*
83 I25 **Chamba** Ruvuma, S Tanzania *11.33S 37.01E*
156 H12 **Chambal** ≈ C India
9 U16 **Chamberlain** Saskatchewan, S Canada *50.49N 105.29W*
31 O11 **Chamberlain** South Dakota, N USA *43.48N 99.19W*
21 R3 **Chamberlain Lake** ◎ Maine, NE USA
41 S5 **Chamberlin, Mount** ▲ Alaska, USA *69.16N 144.54W*
39 O11 **Chambers** Arizona, SW USA *35.11N 109.25W*
20 F16 **Chambersburg** Pennsylvania, NE USA *39.54N 77.39W*
33 N5 **Chambers Island** *island* Wisconsin, N USA
105 T11 **Chambéry** ***anc.*** Camberia. Savoie, E France *45.34N 5.55E*
84 L12 **Chambeshi** Northern, NE Zambia *10.55S 31.07E*
84 L12 **Chambeshi** ≈ NE Zambia
76 M6 **Chambi, Jebel** ***var.*** Jabal ash Sha'nabī. ▲ W Tunisia *35.16N 8.39E*
13 Q7 **Chambord** Québec, SE Canada *48.25N 72.02W*
194 G10 **Chambri Lake** ◎ W PNG
145 U11 **Chamcham** S Iraq *31.17N 45.05E*
145 T4 **Chamchamāl** N Iraq *35.31N 44.49E*
42 J14 **Chamela** Jalisco, SW Mexico *19.33N 105.04W*
44 G5 **Chamelecón, Río** ≈ NW Honduras
64 J9 **Chamical** La Rioja, C Argentina *30.21S 66.19W*
117 L23 **Chamilí** *island* Kykládes, Greece, Aegean Sea
178 Ii13 **Châmnar** Kaôh Kông, SW Cambodia *11.45N 103.32E*
158 K9 **Chamoli** Uttaranchal, N India *30.22N 79.19E*
105 U11 **Chamonix-Mont-Blanc** Haute-Savoie, E France *45.55N 6.52E*
160 L11 **Chāmpa** Chhattīsgarh, C India *22.01N 82.42E*
8 H8 **Champagne** Yukon Territory, W Canada *60.48N 136.22W*
105 Q5 **Champagne** *cultural region* N France
Champagne *see* Campania
105 Q5 **Champagne-Ardenne** ◈ *region* N France
105 S9 **Champagnole** Jura, E France *46.43N 5.55E*
32 M13 **Champaign** Illinois, N USA *40.07N 88.14W*
178 Jj11 **Champasak** Champasak, S Laos *14.50N 105.51E*
105 U6 **Champ de Feu** ▲ NE France *48.24N 7.15E*
11 O7 **Champdoré, Lac** ◎ Québec, NE Canada
44 B6 **Champerico** Retalhuleu, SW Guatemala *14.18N 91.54W*
110 C11 **Champéry** Valais, SW Switzerland *46.12N 6.52E*
20 L6 **Champlain** New York, NE USA *44.58N 73.25W*
20 L9 **Champlain Canal** *canal* New York, NE USA
13 P13 **Champlain, Lac** ◎ Quebec, Canada/USA ***see also*** Champlain, Lake
20 L7 **Champlain, Lake** ◎ Canada/ USA ***see also*** Champlain, Lac
105 S7 **Champlitte** Haute-Saône, E France *47.36N 5.31E*
43 W13 **Champotón** Campeche, SE Mexico *19.18N 90.43W*
106 G10 **Chamusca** Santarém, C Portugal *39.21N 8.28W*
121 O20 **Chamyarysy** ***Rus.*** Chemerisy. Homyel'skaya Voblasts', SE Belarus *51.42N 30.26E*
131 P5 **Chamzinka** Respublika Mordoviya, W Russian Federation *54.22N 45.22E*
Chanáil Mhór, An *see* Grand Canal
Chanak *see* Çanakkale
64 G7 **Chañaral** Atacama, N Chile *26.19S 70.34W*
106 H13 **Chança, Rio** ***var.*** Chanza. ≈ Portugal/Spain
59 D14 **Chancay** Lima, W Peru *11.33S 77.16W*
Chan-chiang/Chanchiang *see* Zhanjiang
64 G13 **Chanco** Maule, Chile *35.43S 72.35W*
41 R7 **Chandalar** Alaska, USA *67.30N 148.29W*
41 R6 **Chandalar River** ≈ Alaska, USA
158 L10 **Chandan Chauki** Uttar Pradesh, N India *28.31N 80.43E*
159 S16 **Chandannagar** ***prev.*** Chandernagore. West Bengal, E India *22.52N 88.21E*
158 K10 **Chandausi** Uttar Pradesh, N India *28.27N 78.43E*
24 M10 **Chandeleur Islands** *island group* Louisiana, S USA
24 M9 **Chandeleur Sound** *sound* N Gulf of Mexico
158 I8 **Chandīgarh** Punjab, N India *30.41N 76.51E*
159 Q16 **Chāndil** Jhārkhand, NE India *22.58N 86.04E*
190 D2 **Chandler** South Australia *26.59S 133.22E*
13 Y7 **Chandler** Québec, SE Canada *48.21N 64.40W*
38 L14 **Chandler** Arizona, SW USA *33.18N 111.50W*
29 O10 **Chandler** Oklahoma, C USA *35.42N 96.52W*
27 V7 **Chandler** Texas, SW USA *32.18N 95.28W*
41 Q6 **Chandler River** ≈ Alaska, USA
58 H13 **Chandles, Río** ≈ E Peru
168 H9 **Chandmanĭ** ***var.*** Talshand. Govĭ-Altay, C Mongolia *45.21N 98.00E*
168 E7 **Chandmanĭ** ***var.*** Urdgol. Hovd, W Mongolia *47.39N 92.46E*
Chandmanĭ *see* Altanshiree
12 J13 **Chandos Lake** ◎ Ontario, SE Canada
159 U15 **Chandpur** Chittagong, C Bangladesh *23.13N 90.43E*
160 I13 **Chandrapur** Mahārāshtra, C India *19.58N 79.21E*
85 J15 **Changa** Southern, S Zambia *16.24S 28.27E*
Changan *see* Xi'an, Shaanxi, China
Chang'an *see* Rong'an, Guangxi Zhuangzu Zizhiqu, China
161 G23 **Changanācheri** Kerala, SW India *9.27N 76.34E*
85 M19 **Changane** ≈ S Mozambique
85 M16 **Changara** Tete, NW Mozambique *16.54S 33.15E*
169 X11 **Changbai** ***var.*** Changbai Chosenzu Zizhixian. Jilin, NE China *41.25N 128.08E*
Changbai Chosenzu Zizhixian *see* Changbai
169 X11 **Changbai Shan** ▲▲ NE China
169 V10 **Changchun** ***var.*** Ch'angch'un, Ch'ang-ch'un; ***prev.*** Hsinking. Jilin, NE China *43.52N 125.18E*
166 M10 **Changde** Hunan, S China *29.04N 111.42E*
167 S13 **Changhua** ***Jap.*** Shōka. C Taiwan *24.06N 120.31E*
174 I7 **Changi** ✈ (Singapore) E Singapore *1.22N 103.58E*
164 L5 **Changji** Xinjiang Uygur Zizhiqu, NW China *44.02N 87.12E*
166 L17 **Changjiang** ***var.*** Changjiang Lizu Zizhixian, Shiliu. Hainan, S China *19.16N 109.09E*
163 R11 **Chang Jiang** ***var.*** Yangtze Kiang, ***Eng.*** Yangtze. ≈ C China
167 S8 **Changjiang Kou** *delta* E China
Changjiang Lizu Zizhixian *see* Changjiang
178 I13 **Chang, Ko** *island* S Thailand
167 Q2 **Changli** Hebei, E China *39.43N 119.13E*
169 V10 **Changling** Jilin, NE China *44.15N 124.03E*
Changning *see* Xunwu
167 N11 **Changsha** ***var.*** Ch'angsha, Ch'ang-sha. Hunan, S China *28.10N 113.00E*
167 Q10 **Changshan** Zhejiang, SE China *28.54N 118.26E*
169 V14 **Changshan Qundao** *island group* NE China
167 S8 **Changshu** ***var.*** Ch'ang-shu. Jiangsu, E China *31.36N 120.42E*
169 V11 **Changtu** Liaoning, NE China *42.49N 123.58E*
45 P14 **Changuinola** Bocas del Toro, NW Panama *9.25N 82.31W*
165 N9 **Changweiliang** Qinghai, W China *38.24N 92.07E*
166 K6 **Changwu** ***var.*** Zhaoren. Shaanxi, C China *35.12N 107.45E*
169 U13 **Changxing Dao** *island* N China
166 M9 **Changyang** ***var.*** Longzhouping. Hubei, C China *30.45N 111.13E*
169 W14 **Changyŏn** SW North Korea *38.19N 125.14E*
167 N5 **Changzhi** Shanxi, C China *36.09N 113.01E*
167 R8 **Changzhou** Jiangsu, E China *31.53N 119.50E*
117 H24 **Chaniá** ***var.*** Hania, Khaniá, ***Eng.*** Canea; ***anc.*** Cydonia. Kríti, Greece, E Mediterranean Sea *35.31N 24.01E*
64 J5 **Chañi, Nevado de** ▲ NW Argentina *24.09S 65.44W*
117 H24 **Chanión, Kólpos** *gulf* Kríti, Greece, E Mediterranean Sea
Chankiri *see* Çankırı
32 M11 **Channahon** Illinois, N USA *41.25N 88.13W*
161 H20 **Channapatna** Karnātaka, E India *12.43N 77.13E*
99 K26 **Channel Islands** ***Fr.*** Îles Normandes. *island group* S English Channel
37 R16 **Channel Islands** *island group* California, W USA
11 S13 **Channel-Port aux Basques** Newfoundland and Labrador, SE Canada *47.35N 59.02W*
Channel, The *see* English Channel
99 Q23 **Channel Tunnel** *tunnel* France/ UK
26 M2 **Channing** Texas, SW USA *35.40N 102.19W*
Chantabun/Chantaburi *see* Chanthaburi
106 H3 **Chantada** Galicia, NW Spain *42.36N 7.46W*
178 I12 **Chanthaburi** ***var.*** Chantabun, Chantaburi. Chantaburi, S Thailand *12.34N 102.07E*
105 O4 **Chantilly** Oise, N France *49.12N 2.28E*
15 Kk4 **Chantrey Inlet** *inlet* Nunavut, N Canada
145 V12 **Chanūn as Sa'ūdī** S Iraq *31.04N 46.00E*
29 Q6 **Chanute** Kansas, C USA *37.40N 95.27W*
125 G13 **Chany, Ozero** ◎ C Russian Federation
Chanza *see* Chança, Rio
Ch'ao-an/Chaochow *see* Chaozhou
167 P8 **Chao Hu** ◎ E China
178 Hh11 **Chao Phraya, Mae Nam** ≈ C Thailand
Chaor He *see* Qulin Gol
Chaouèn *see* Chefchaouen
167 P14 **Chaoyang** Guangdong, S China *23.16N 116.30E*
169 T12 **Chaoyang** Liaoning, NE China *41.33N 120.28E*
Chaoyang *see* Huinan, Jilin, China
Chaoyang *see* Jiayin, Heilongjiang, China
167 Q14 **Chaozhou** ***var.*** Chaoan, Chao'an, Ch'ao-an; ***prev.*** Chaochow. Guangdong, SE China *23.39N 116.34E*
60 N13 **Chapadinha** Maranhão, E Brazil *3.45S 43.22W*
10 K12 **Chapais** Québec, SE Canada *49.46N 74.54W*
42 L13 **Chapala** Jalisco, SW Mexico *20.17N 103.13W*
42 L13 **Chapala, Lago de** ◎ C Mexico
152 F13 **Chapan, Gora** ▲ C Turkmenistan *37.48N 58.03E*
59 M18 **Chapare, Río** ≈ C Bolivia
56 E11 **Chaparral** Tolima, C Colombia *3.44N 75.33W*
126 Kk12 **Chapayevo** Respublika Sakha (Yakutiya), NE Russian Federation *60.03N 117.19E*
150 F9 **Chapayev** Zapadnyy Kazakhstan, NW Kazakhstan *50.13N 51.05E*
131 R6 **Chapayevsk** Samarskaya Oblast', W Russian Federation *52.57N 49.41E*
62 H13 **Chapecó** Santa Catarina, S Brazil *27.06S 52.39W*
62 I13 **Chapecó, Rio** ≈ S Brazil
22 J9 **Chapel Hill** Tennessee, S USA *35.38N 86.40W*
46 J12 **Chapelton** C Jamaica *18.04N 77.16W*
12 C8 **Chapleau** Ontario, SE Canada *47.49N 83.24W*
12 D7 **Chapleau** ≈ Ontario, S Canada
9 T16 **Chaplin** Saskatchewan, S Canada *50.27N 106.37W*
130 M6 **Chaplygin** Lipetskaya Oblast', W Russian Federation *53.13N 39.58E*
119 S11 **Chaplynka** Khersons'ka Oblast', S Ukraine *46.20N 33.34E*
15 L3 **Chapman, Cape** *headland* Nunavut, NE Canada *69.15N 89.09W*
27 T15 **Chapman Ranch** Texas, SW USA *27.32N 97.25W*
Chapman's *see* Okwa
23 P5 **Chapmanville** West Virginia, NE USA *37.58N 82.01W*
30 K15 **Chappell** Nebraska, C USA *41.05N 102.28W*
Chapra *see* Chhapra
58 D9 **Chapuli, Río** ≈ N Peru
78 I6 **Châr** *well* N Mauritania *21.31N 12.55W*
126 Kk13 **Chara** Chitinskaya Oblast', S Russian Federation *56.57N 118.05E*
126 Kk13 **Chara** ≈ C Russian Federation
56 G8 **Charala** Santander, C Colombia *6.16N 73.09W*
43 N10 **Charcas** San Luis Potosí, C Mexico *23.09N 101.04W*
27 T13 **Charco** Texas, SW USA *28.42N 97.35E*
204 H7 **Charcot Island** *island* Antarctica
66 M8 **Charcot Seamounts** *undersea feature* E Atlantic Ocean
Chardara *see* Shardara
151 P17 **Chardarinskoye Vodokhranilishche** ▣ S Kazakhstan
33 U11 **Chardon** Ohio, N USA *41.33N 81.10W*
46 K9 **Chardonnières** SW Haiti *18.17N 74.09W*
Chardzhev *see* Türkmenabat
Chardzhevskaya Oblast' *see* Lebap Welaýaty
Chardzhou/Chardzhui *see* Türkmenabat
104 L11 **Charente** ◈ *department* W France
104 J11 **Charente** ≈ W France
104 J10 **Charente-Maritime** ◈ *department* W France
143 U12 **Ch'arents'avan** C Armenia *40.23N 44.41E*
80 I12 **Chari** ***var.*** Shari. ≈ Central African Republic/Chad
80 G11 **Chari-Baguirmi** ***off.*** Préfecture du Chari-Baguirmi. ◈ *prefecture* SW Chad
155 Q4 **Chārīkār** Parvān, NE Afghanistan *35.01N 69.10E*
31 V15 **Chariton** Iowa, C USA *41.00N 93.18W*
29 U3 **Chariton River** ≈ Missouri, C USA
57 T7 **Charity** NW Guyana *7.22N 58.34W*
33 R7 **Charity Island** *island* Michigan, N USA
Chärjew *see* Türkmenabat
Chärjew Oblasty *see* Lebap Welaýaty
Charkhlik/Charkhliq *see* Ruoqiang
101 G20 **Charleroi** Hainaut, S Belgium *50.25N 4.27E*
9 V12 **Charles** Manitoba, C Canada *55.27N 100.58W*
13 R10 **Charlesbourg** Québec, SE Canada *46.49N 71.14W*
23 Y7 **Charles, Cape** *headland* Virginia, NE USA *37.09N 75.57W*
31 W12 **Charles City** Iowa, C USA *43.04N 92.40W*
23 W6 **Charles City** Virginia, NE USA *37.19N 77.01W*
105 O5 **Charles de Gaulle** ✈ (Paris) Seine-et-Marne, N France *49.04N 2.36E*
10 K1 **Charles Island** *island* Nunavut, NE Canada
Charles Island *see* Santa María, Isla
18 Mm5 **Charles-Lindbergh** ✈ (Minneapolis/Saint Paul) Minnesota, N USA *44.47N 93.12W*
32 K9 **Charles Mound** *hill* Illinois, N USA *42.30N 90.14W*
193 A22 **Charles Sound** *sound* South Island, NZ
193 G15 **Charleston** West Coast, South Island, NZ *41.54S 171.25E*
29 S11 **Charleston** Arkansas, C USA *35.18N 94.02W*
32 M14 **Charleston** Illinois, N USA *39.30N 88.10W*
24 L3 **Charleston** Mississippi, S USA *34.00N 90.03W*
29 Z7 **Charleston** Missouri, C USA *36.55N 89.21W*
23 T15 **Charleston** South Carolina, SE USA *32.48N 79.57W*
23 Q5 **Charleston** *state capital* West Virginia, NE USA *38.21N 81.37W*
12 L14 **Charleston Lake** ◎ Ontario, SE Canada
37 W11 **Charleston Peak** ▲ Nevada, W USA *36.16N 115.40W*
47 W10 **Charlestown** Nevis, Saint Kitts and Nevis *17.05N 62.35W*
33 P16 **Charlestown** Indiana, N USA *38.27N 85.40W*
20 M9 **Charlestown** New Hampshire, NE USA *43.14N 72.23W*
23 V3 **Charles Town** West Virginia, NE USA *39.17N 77.51W*
189 W9 **Charleville** Queensland, E Australia *26.24S 146.18E*
105 R3 **Charleville-Mézières** Ardennes, N France *49.45N 4.43E*
33 P5 **Charlevoix** Michigan, N USA *45.19N 85.15W*
33 Q6 **Charlevoix, Lake** ◎ Michigan, N USA
41 T9 **Charley River** ≈ Alaska, USA
66 J6 **Charlie-Gibbs Fracture Zone** *tectonic feature* N Atlantic Ocean
105 Q10 **Charlieu** Loire, E France *46.11N 4.10E*
33 Q9 **Charlotte** Michigan, N USA *42.33N 84.50W*
23 R10 **Charlotte** North Carolina, SE USA *35.13N 80.50W*
22 I8 **Charlotte** Tennessee, S USA *36.11N 87.18W*
27 R13 **Charlotte** Texas, SW USA *28.51N 98.42W*
23 R10 **Charlotte** ✈ North Carolina, SE USA *35.12N 80.54W*
47 T9 **Charlotte Amalie** ***prev.*** Saint Thomas. ○ (Virgin Islands (US)) Saint Thomas, N Virgin Islands (US) *18.22N 64.55W*
23 U7 **Charlotte Court House** Virginia, NE USA *37.04N 78.37W*
25 W14 **Charlotte Harbor** *inlet* Florida, SE USA
Charlotte Island *see* Abaiang
97 J15 **Charlottenberg** Värmland, C Sweden *59.52N 12.16E*
Charlottenhof *see* Aegviidu
23 U5 **Charlottesville** Virginia, NE USA *38.01N 78.28W*
Charlotte Town *see* Roseau, Dominica
Charlotte Town *see* Gouyave, Grenada
11 Q14 **Charlottetown** Prince Edward Island, Prince Edward Island, SE Canada *46.13N 63.09W*
47 Z16 **Charlotteville** Tobago, Trinidad and Tobago *11.16N 60.33W*
190 M11 **Charlton** Victoria, SE Australia *36.18S 143.19E*
10 H10 **Charlton Island** *island* Nunavut, C Canada
105 T6 **Charmes** Vosges, NE France *48.19N 6.19E*
121 F19 **Charnawchytsy** ***Rus.*** Chernavchitsy. Brestskaya Voblasts', SW Belarus *52.13N 23.43E*
13 R10 **Charny** Québec, SE Canada *46.43N 71.14W*
155 T5 **Chārsadda** North-West Frontier Province, NW Pakistan *34.12N 71.46E*
Charshanga/Charshangngy/ Charshangy *see* Köýtendag
Charsk *see* Shar
189 W6 **Charters Towers** Queensland, NE Australia *20.01S 146.19E*
13 R12 **Chartierville** Québec, SE Canada *45.19N 71.13W*
104 M6 **Chartres** ***anc.*** Autricum, Civitas Carnutum. Eure-et-Loir, C France *48.27N 1.27E*
151 W15 **Charyn** ***Kaz.*** Sharyn. Almaty, SE Kazakhstan *43.48N 79.22E*
63 D21 **Chascomús** Buenos Aires, E Argentina *35.34S 58.01W*
9 N16 **Chase** British Columbia, SW Canada *50.49N 119.40W*
23 U7 **Chase City** Virginia, NE USA *36.48N 78.27W*
21 S4 **Chase, Mount** ▲ Maine, NE USA *46.06N 68.30W*
120 M13 **Chashniki** ***Rus.*** Chashniki. Vitsyebskaya Voblasts', N Belarus *54.51N 29.09E*
117 D15 **Chásia** ▲▲ C Greece
31 V9 **Chaska** Minnesota, N USA *44.47N 93.36W*
193 D25 **Chaslands Mistake** *headland* South Island, NZ *46.37S 169.21E*
129 R11 **Chasovo** Respublika Komi, NW Russian Federation *61.58N 50.34E*
Chasovo *see* Vazhgort

◆ COUNTRY ● COUNTRY CAPITAL ◇ DEPENDENT TERRITORY ○ DEPENDENT TERRITORY CAPITAL ◈ ADMINISTRATIVE REGION ✈ INTERNATIONAL AIRPORT ▲ MOUNTAIN ▲▲ MOUNTAIN RANGE VOLCANO ≈ RIVER ◎ LAKE ▣ RESERVOIR

CHASTOVA – CHINCHILLA

128 *H14* **Chastova** Novgorodskaya Oblast', NW Russian Federation *58.37N 32.04E*
149 *R3* **Chāt** Golestān, N Iran *37.52N 55.27E*
Chatak *see* Chhatak
Chatang *see* Zhanang
41 *R9* **Chatanika** Alaska, USA *65.06N 147.28W*
41 *R9* **Chatanika River** ≈ Alaska, USA
153 *T8* **Chat-Bazar** Talasskaya Oblast', NW Kyrgyzstan *42.29N 72.37E*
47 *Y14* **Chateaubelair** Saint Vincent, W Saint Vincent and the Grenadines *13.16N 61.14W*
104 *J7* **Châteaubriant** Loire-Atlantique, NW France *47.43N 1.22W*
105 *Q8* **Château-Chinon** Nièvre, C France *47.04N 3.50E*
110 *C10* **Château d'Oex** Vaud, W Switzerland *46.28N 7.09E*
104 *L7* **Château-du-Loir** Sarthe, NW France *47.40N 0.25E*
104 *M6* **Châteaudun** Eure-et-Loir, C France *48.04N 1.19E*
104 *K7* **Château-Gontier** Mayenne, NW France *47.49N 0.42W*
13 *O13* **Châteauguay** Québec, SE Canada *45.21N 73.46W*
104 *F6* **Châteaulin** Finistère, NW France *48.12N 4.07W*
105 *N9* **Châteaumeillant** Cher, C France *46.33N 2.10E*
104 *K11* **Châteauneuf-sur-Charente** Charente, W France *45.34N 0.33W*
104 *M7* **Château-Renault** Indre-et-Loire, C France *47.34N 0.52E*
105 *N9* **Châteauroux** *prev.* Indreville. Indre, C France *46.50N 1.42E*
105 *T5* **Château-Salins** Moselle, NE France *48.50N 6.29E*
105 *P4* **Château-Thierry** Aisne, N France *49.03N 3.24E*
101 *H21* **Châtelet** Hainaut, S Belgium *50.24N 4.31E*
Châtelherault *see* Châtellerault
104 *L9* **Châtellerault** *var.* Châtelherault. Vienne, W France *46.49N 0.33E*
31 *X10* **Chatfield** Minnesota, N USA *43.51N 92.11W*
11 *O14* **Chatham** New Brunswick, SE Canada *47.01N 65.30W*
12 *D17* **Chatham** Ontario, S Canada *42.24N 82.10W*
99 *P22* **Chatham** SE England, UK *51.22N 0.31E*
32 *K14* **Chatham** Illinois, N USA *39.40N 89.42W*
23 *T7* **Chatham** Virginia, NE USA *36.49N 79.24W*
65 *F22* **Chatham, Isla** *island* S Chile
183 *R12* **Chatham Island** *island* Chatham Islands, NZ
Chatham Island *see* San Cristóbal, Isla
Chatham Island Rise *see* Chatham Rise
199 *Jj14* **Chatham Islands** *island group* NZ, SW Pacific Ocean
183 *Q12* **Chatham Rise** *var.* Chatham Island Rise. *undersea feature* S Pacific Ocean
41 *X13* **Chatham Strait** *strait* Alaska, USA
Chathóir, Rinn *see* Cahore Point
104 *M9* **Châtillon-sur-Indre** Indre, C France *46.58N 1.10E*
105 *Q7* **Châtillon-sur-Seine** Côte d'Or, C France *47.51N 4.30E*
153 *S8* **Chatkal** *Uzb.* Chotqol. ≈ Kyrgyzstan/Uzbekistan
153 *R9* **Chatkal Range** *Rus.* Chatkal'skiy Khrebet. ▲▲ Kyrgyzstan/Uzbekistan
Chatkal'skiy Khrebet *see* Chatkal Range
25 *N7* **Chatom** Alabama, S USA *31.28N 88.15W*
Chatrapur *see* Chhatrapur
149 *S10* **Chatrūd** Kermān, C Iran *30.39N 56.57E*
25 *S2* **Chatsworth** Georgia, SE USA *34.46N 84.46W*
Chāttagām *see* Chittagong
25 *S8* **Chattahoochee** Florida, SE USA *30.40N 84.51W*
25 *R8* **Chattahoochee River** ≈ SE USA
22 *L10* **Chattanooga** Tennessee, S USA *35.05N 85.16W*
153 *V10* **Chatyr-Kël', Ozero** ◎ C Kyrgyzstan
153 *W9* **Chatyr-Tash** Narynskaya Oblast', C Kyrgyzstan *40.54N 76.22E*
13 *R12* **Chaudière** ≈ Québec, SE Canada
178 *J14* **Châu Đôc** *var.* Chauphu, Chau Phu. An Giang, S Vietnam *10.52N 105.07E*
158 *D13* **Chauhtan** *prev.* Chohtan. Rājasthān, NW India *25.27N 71.07E*
117 *Ff5* **Chauk** Magwe, W Burma *20.52N 94.49E*
105 *R6* **Chaumont** *prev.* Chaumont-en-Bassigny. Haute-Marne, N France *48.07N 5.07E*
Chaumont-en-Bassigny *see* Chaumont
127 *O4* **Chaunskaya Guba** *bay* NE Russian Federation
105 *P3* **Chauny** Aisne, N France *49.37N 3.13E*
Châu Ô *see* Binh Sơn
Chau Phu *see* Châu Đôc
104 *I5* **Chausey, Îles** *island group* N France
Chausy *see* Chavusy
20 *C11* **Chautauqua Lake** ◎ New York, NE USA
Châu Thanh *see* Ba Ria
104 *L9* **Chauvigny** Vienne, W France *46.35N 0.37E*
128 *L6* **Chavan'ga** Murmanskaya Oblast', NW Russian Federation *66.07N 37.44E*
12 *K10* **Chavannes, Lac** ◎ Québec, SE Canada
Chavantes, Represa de *see* Xavantes, Represa de
63 *D15* **Chavarría** Corrientes, NE Argentina *28.57S 58.34W*
131 *P4* **Chavash Respubliki** *var.* Chuvashskaya Respublika, *Eng.* Chuvashia. ◈ *autonomous republic* W Russian Federation
106 *I5* **Chaves** *anc.* Aquae Flaviae. Vila Real, N Portugal *41.43N 7.28W*
Chávez, Isla *see* Santa Cruz, Isla
84 *G13* **Chavuma** North Western, NW Zambia *13.04S 22.43E*
121 *O16* **Chavusy** *Rus.* Chausy. Mahilyowskaya Voblasts', E Belarus *53.49N 30.59E*
Chayan *see* Shayan
153 *U8* **Chayek** Narynskaya Oblast', C Kyrgyzstan *41.54N 74.28E*
145 *T6* **Chāy Khānah** E Iraq *34.19N 44.33E*
129 *T16* **Chaykovskiy** Permskaya Oblast', NW Russian Federation *56.45N 54.09E*
178 *K12* **Chbar** Môndól Kiri, E Cambodia *12.46N 107.10E*
25 *Q4* **Cheaha Mountain** ▲ Alabama, S USA *33.29N 85.48W*
Cheatharlach *see* Carlow
23 *S2* **Cheat River** ≈ NE USA
113 *A16* **Cheb** *Ger.* Eger. Karlovarský Kraj, W Czech Republic *50.04N 12.23E*
131 *Q3* **Cheboksary** Chavash Respubliki, W Russian Federation *56.06N 47.14E*
33 *Q5* **Cheboygan** Michigan, N USA *45.40N 84.28W*
Chechaouèn *see* Chefchaouen
Chechenia *see* Chechenskaya Respublika
131 *O15* **Chechenskaya Respublika** *Eng.* Chechenia, Chechnia, *Rus.* Chechnya. ◈ *autonomous republic* SW Russian Federation
69 *N4* **Chech, Erg** *desert* Algeria/Mali
Chechersk *see* Chachersk
Chechevichi *see* Chachevichy
Che-chiang *see* Zhejiang
Chechnia/Chechnya *see* Chechenskaya Respublika
169 *Y15* **Chech'ŏn** *Jap.* Teisen. N South Korea *37.06N 128.15E*
113 *L15* **Chęciny** Świętokrzyskie, S Poland *50.51N 20.31E*
29 *Q10* **Checotah** Oklahoma, C USA *35.28N 95.31W*
11 *R15* **Chedabucto Bay** *inlet* Nova Scotia, E Canada
177 *F7* **Cheduba Island** *island* W Burma
39 *T5* **Cheesman Lake** ⊠ Colorado, C USA
205 *S16* **Cheetham, Cape** *headland* Antarctica *70.25S 162.40E*
76 *G5* **Chefchaouen** *var.* Chaouèn, Chechaouèn, *Sp.* Xauen. N Morocco *35.09N 5.16W*
Chefoo *see* Yantai
40 *M12* **Chefornak** Alaska, USA *60.09N 164.09W*
126 *Mm15* **Chegdomyn** Khabarovskiy Kray, SE Russian Federation *51.09N 132.58E*
78 *M4* **Chegga** Tiris Zemmour, NE Mauritania *25.27N 5.49W*
Cheghcheran *see* Chaghcharān
34 *G9* **Chehalis** Washington, NW USA *46.39N 122.57W*
34 *G9* **Chehalis River** ≈ Washington, NW USA
154 *M6* **Chehel Abdālān, Kūh-e** *var.* Chalap Dalam, *Pash.* Chalap Dalan. ▲▲ C Afghanistan
117 *D14* **Cheimadítida, Límni** *var.* Límni Cheimadítis. ◎ N Greece
Cheimadítis, Límni *see* Cheimadítida, Límni
105 *U15* **Cheiron, Mont** ▲ SE France *43.49N 7.00E*
169 *X17* **Cheju** *Jap.* Saishū. S South Korea *33.31N 126.34E*
169 *Y17* **Cheju** ✈ S South Korea *33.31N 126.28E*
169 *Y17* **Cheju-do** *Jap.* Saishū; *prev.* Quelpart. *island* S South Korea
169 *X17* **Cheju-haehyŏp** *strait* S South Korea
Chekiang *see* Zhejiang
Chekichler/Chekishlyar *see* Çekiçler
196 *F8* **Chelab** Babeldaob, N Palau
153 *N11* **Chelak** *Rus.* Chelek. Samarqand Viloyati, C Uzbekistan *39.55N 66.45E*
34 *J7* **Chelan, Lake** ⊠ Washington, NW USA
Chelek *see* Chelak
Cheleken *see* Hazar
Chélif/Chéliff *see* Chelif, Oued
76 *J5* **Chelif, Oued** *var.* Chélif, Chéliff, Chellif, Shellif. ≈ N Algeria
Chelkar *see* Shalkar
Chelkar, Ozero *see* Shalkar, Ozero
Chellif *see* Chelif, Oued
113 *P14* **Chełm** *Rus.* Kholm. Lubelskie, SE Poland *51.07N 23.28E*
112 *I9* **Chełmno** *Ger.* Culm, Kulm. Kujawski-pomorskie, C Poland *53.21N 18.27E*
117 *E19* **Chelmós** *var.* Ároania. ▲▲ S Greece
12 *F10* **Chelmsford** Ontario, S Canada *46.33N 81.16W*
99 *P21* **Chelmsford** E England, UK *51.43N 0.28E*
112 *J9* **Chełmża** *Ger.* Culmsee, Kulmsee. Kujawski-pomorskie, C Poland *53.12N 18.36E*
29 *Q8* **Chelsea** Oklahoma, C USA *36.32N 95.25W*
20 *M8* **Chelsea** Vermont, NE USA *43.57N 72.24W*
99 *L21* **Cheltenham** C England, UK *51.54N 2.04W*
107 *R9* **Chelva** País Valenciano, E Spain *39.45N 1.00W*
125 *Ee12* **Chelyabinsk** Chelyabinskaya Oblast', C Russian Federation *55.12N 61.25E*
125 *E12* **Chelyabinskaya Oblast'** ◈ *province* C Russian Federation
126 *Jj4* **Chelyuskin, Mys** *headland* N Russian Federation *77.42N 104.13E*
126 *H15* **Chemal** Altayskiy Kray, S Russian Federation *51.22N 85.08E*
43 *Y12* **Chemax** Yucatán, SE Mexico *20.41N 87.54W*
85 *N16* **Chemba** Sofala, C Mozambique *17.10S 34.52E*
84 *J13* **Chembe** Luapula, NE Zambia *11.58S 28.45E*
Chemenibit *see* Çemenibit
Chemerisy *see* Chamyarysy
118 *K7* **Chemerivtsi** Khmel'nyts'ka Oblast', W Ukraine *49.00N 26.21E*
104 *J8* **Chemillé** Maine-et-Loire, NW France *47.15N 0.42W*
181 *X17* **Chemin Grenier** S Mauritius *20.28S 57.28E*
103 *N16* **Chemnitz** *prev.* Karl-Marx-Stadt. Sachsen, E Germany *50.49N 12.55E*
Chemulpo *see* Inch'ŏn
34 *H14* **Chemult** Oregon, NW USA *43.14N 121.48W*
20 *G12* **Chemung River** ≈ New York/Pennsylvania, NE USA
155 *U8* **Chenāb** ≈ India/Pakistan
41 *S9* **Chena Hot Springs** Alaska, USA *65.06N 146.02W*
20 *I11* **Chenango River** ≈ New York, NE USA
174 *Gg3* **Chenderoh, Tasik** ◎ Peninsular Malaysia
13 *Q11* **Chêne, Rivière du** ≈ Québec, SE Canada
34 *L8* **Cheney** Washington, NW USA *47.29N 117.34W*
28 *M6* **Cheney Reservoir** ⊠ Kansas, C USA
Chengchiatun *see* Liaoyuan
Ch'eng-chou/Chengchow *see* Zhengzhou
167 *P1* **Chengde** *var.* Jehol. Hebei, E China *41.00N 117.57E*
166 *I9* **Chengdu** *var.* Chengtu, Ch'eng-tu. Sichuan, C China *30.40N 104.03E*
167 *Q14* **Chenghai** Guangdong, S China *23.33N 116.42E*
Chenghsien *see* Zhengzhou
166 *H13* **Chengjiang** Yunnan, SW China *24.40N 102.55E*
Chengjiang *see* Taihe
166 *L17* **Chengmai** *var.* Jinjiang. Hainan, S China *19.45N 109.56E*
Chengtu/Ch'eng-tu *see* Chengdu
165 *W12* **Chengxian** *var.* Cheng Xian. Gansu, C China *33.42N 105.45E*
Chengyang *see* Juxian
Chengzhong *see* Ningming
Chenkiang *see* Zhenjiang
161 *J19* **Chennai** *prev.* Madras. Tamil Nādu, S India *13.04N 80.18E*
161 *J19* **Chennai** ✈ Tamil Nādu, S India *13.07N 80.13E*
105 *R8* **Chenôve** Côte d'Or, C France *47.16N 5.00E*
Chenstokhov *see* Częstochowa
166 *L11* **Chenxi** *var.* Chenyang. Hunan, S China *28.01N 110.15E*
Chen Xian/Chenxian/Chen Xiang *see* Chenzhou
Chenyang *see* Chenxi
167 *N12* **Chenzhou** *var.* Chenxian, Chen Xian, Chen Xiang. Hunan, S China *25.51N 113.01E*
178 *Kk12* **Cheo Reo** *var.* A Yun Pa. Gia Lai, S Vietnam *13.19N 108.27E*
116 *I11* **Chepelare** Smolyan, S Bulgaria *41.43N 24.40E*
116 *I11* **Chepelarska Reka** ≈ S Bulgaria
58 *B11* **Chepén** La Libertad, C Peru *7.12S 79.24W*
64 *J10* **Chepes** La Rioja, C Argentina *31.23S 66.34W*
167 *O15* **Chep Lap Kok** ✈ (Hong Kong) S China *22.23N 114.11E*
45 *U14* **Chepo** Panamá, C Panama *9.10N 79.05W*
Chepping Wycombe *see* High Wycombe
129 *R14* **Cheptsa** ≈ NW Russian Federation
32 *K3* **Chequamegon Point** *headland* Wisconsin, N USA *46.42N 90.45W*
105 *O8* **Cher** ◈ *department* C France
104 *M8* **Cher** ≈ C France
Cherangani Hills *see* Cherangany Hills
83 *H17* **Cherangany Hills** *var.* Cherangani Hills. ▲▲ W Kenya
23 *S11* **Cheraw** South Carolina, SE USA *34.42N 79.52W*
104 *I3* **Cherbourg** *anc.* Carusbur. Manche, N France *49.39N 1.36W*
131 *R5* **Cherdakly** Ul'yanovskaya Oblast', W Russian Federation *54.21N 48.54E*
129 *U12* **Cherdyn'** Permskaya Oblast', NW Russian Federation *60.21N 56.39E*
128 *J14* **Cherekha** ≈ W Russian Federation
126 *J15* **Cheremkhovo** Irkutskaya Oblast', S Russian Federation *53.16N 102.44E*
126 *Hh15* **Cheremushki** Respublika Khakastya, S Russian Federation *52.48N 91.20E*
Cheren *see* Keren
128 *K14* **Cherepovets** Vologodskaya Oblast', NW Russian Federation *59.09N 37.49E*
129 *O11* **Cherevkovo** Arkhangel'skaya Oblast', NW Russian Federation *61.45N 45.16E*
76 *I6* **Chergui, Chott ech** *salt lake* NW Algeria
Cherikov *see* Cherykaw
119 *P6* **Cherkas'ka Oblast'** *var.* Cherkasy, *Rus.* Cherkasskaya Oblast'. ◈ *province* C Ukraine
Cherkasskaya Oblast' *see* Cherkas'ka Oblast'
Cherkassy *see* Cherkasy
119 *Q6* **Cherkasy** *Rus.* Cherkassy. Cherkas'ka Oblast', C Ukraine *49.25N 32.04E*
Cherkasy *see* Cherkas'ka Oblast'
130 *M15* **Cherkessk** Karachayevo-Cherkesskaya Respublika, SW Russian Federation *44.12N 42.06E*
125 *G13* **Cherlak** Omskaya Oblast', C Russian Federation *54.06N 74.59E*
125 *Ff14* **Cherlakskiy** Omskaya Oblast', C Russian Federation *53.42N 74.23E*
129 *U13* **Chermoz** Permskaya Oblast', NW Russian Federation *58.49N 56.07E*
Chernavchitsy *see* Charnawchytsy
129 *T3* **Chernaya** Nenetskiy Avtonomnyy Okrug, NW Russian Federation *68.36N 56.34E*
129 *T4* **Chernaya** ≈ NW Russian Federation
Chernigov *see* Chernihiv
Chernigovskaya Oblast' *see* Chernihivs'ka Oblast'
119 *Q2* **Chernihiv** *Rus.* Chernigov. Chernihivs'ka Oblast', NE Ukraine *48.18N 25.59E*
Chernihiv *see* Chernihivs'ka Oblast'
119 *V9* **Chernihivka** Zaporiz'ka Oblast', SE Ukraine *47.11N 36.10E*
119 *P2* **Chernihivs'ka Oblast'** *var.* Chernihiv, *Rus.* Chernigovskaya Oblast'. ◈ *province* NE Ukraine
116 *I9* **Cherni Osŭm** ≈ N Bulgaria
118 *J8* **Chernivets'ka Oblast'** *var.* Chernivtsi, *Rus.* Chernovitskaya Oblast'. ◈ *province* W Ukraine
116 *I9* **Cherni Vit** ≈ NW Bulgaria
116 *G10* **Cherni Vrŭkh** ▲ W Bulgaria *42.33N 23.18E*
118 *K8* **Chernivtsi** *Ger.* Czernowitz, *Rom.* Cernăuţi, *Rus.* Chernovtsy. Chernivets'ka Oblast', W Ukraine *48.18N 25.55E*
118 *M7* **Chernivtsi** Vinnyts'ka Oblast', C Ukraine *48.33N 28.06E*
Chernivtsi *see* Chernivets'ka Oblast'
Chernobyl' *see* Chornobyl'
126 *Hh15* **Chernogorsk** Respublika Khakasiya, S Russian Federation *53.48N 91.03E*
Cherno More *see* Black Sea
Chernomorskoye *see* Chornomors'ke
151 *T7* **Chernoretskoye** Pavlodar, NE Kazakhstan *52.51N 76.37E*
Chernovitskaya Oblast' *see* Chernivets'ka Oblast'
Chernovtsy *see* Chernivtsi
151 *U8* **Chernoye** Pavlodar, NE Kazakhstan *51.40N 77.33E*
Chernoye More *see* Black Sea
129 *U16* **Chernushka** Permskaya Oblast', NW Russian Federation *56.30N 56.07E*
119 *N4* **Chernyakhiv** *Rus.* Chernyakhov. Zhytomyrs'ka Oblast', N Ukraine *50.31N 28.38E*
Chernyakhov *see* Chernyakhiv
121 *C14* **Chernyakhovsk** *Ger.* Insterburg. Kaliningradskaya Oblast', W Russian Federation *54.36N 21.49E*
130 *K8* **Chernyanka** Belgorodskaya Oblast', W Russian Federation *50.59N 37.54E*
129 *V5* **Chernyshëva, Gryada** ▲▲ NW Russian Federation
150 *J14* **Chernyshëva, Zaliv** *gulf* SW Kazakhstan
126 *L15* **Chernyshevsk** Chitinskaya Oblast', S Russian Federation *52.28N 116.52E*
126 *K11* **Chernyshevskiy** Respublika Sakha (Yakutiya), NE Russian Federation *62.57N 112.29E*
131 *P13* **Chërnyye Zemli** *plain* SW Russian Federation
Chërnyy Irtysh *see* Ertix He
131 *V7* **Chernyy Otrog** Orenburgskaya Oblast', W Russian Federation *52.03N 56.09E*
31 *T12* **Cherokee** Iowa, C USA *42.45N 95.33W*
28 *M8* **Cherokee** Oklahoma, C USA *36.45N 98.22W*
27 *R9* **Cherokee** Texas, SW USA *30.56N 98.42W*
23 *O8* **Cherokee Lake** ⊠ Tennessee, S USA
Cherokees, Lake O' The *see* Grand Lake O' The Cherokees
46 *H1* **Cherokee Sound** Great Abaco, N Bahamas *26.16N 77.03W*
159 *V13* **Cherrapunji** Meghālaya, NE India *25.16N 91.42E*
30 *L9* **Cherry Creek** ≈ South Dakota, N USA
20 *J16* **Cherry Hill** New Jersey, NE USA *39.55N 75.01W*
29 *Q7* **Cherryvale** Kansas, C USA *37.16N 95.33W*
23 *Q10* **Cherryville** North Carolina, SE USA *35.22N 81.22W*
Cherski Range *see* Cherskogo, Khrebet
127 *O5* **Cherskiy** Respublika Sakha (Yakutiya), NE Russian Federation *68.45N 161.15E*
126 *Mm8* **Cherskogo, Khrebet** *var.* Cherski Range. ▲▲ NE Russian Federation
Cherso *see* Cres
130 *L10* **Chertkovo** Rostovskaya Oblast', SW Russian Federation *49.22N 40.10E*
Cherven' *see* Chervyen'
116 *H8* **Cherven Bryag** Pleven, N Bulgaria *43.17N 24.06E*
118 *M4* **Chervonoarmiys'k** Zhytomyrs'ka Oblast', N Ukraine *50.27N 28.15E*
Chervonograd *see* Chervonohrad
118 *I4* **Chervonohrad** *Rus.* Chervonograd. L'vivs'ka Oblast', NW Ukraine *50.27N 24.11E*
119 *W6* **Chervonooskil's'ke Vodoskhovyshche** *Rus.* Krasnoosol'skoye Vodokhranilishche. ⊠ NE Ukraine
Chervonoye, Ozero *see* Chyrvonaye, Vozyera
119 *S4* **Chervonozavods'ke** Poltavs'ka Oblast', C Ukraine *50.24N 33.22E*
121 *L16* **Chervyen'** *Rus.* Cherven'. Minskaya Voblasts', C Belarus *53.42N 28.23E*
121 *P16* **Cherykaw** *Rus.* Cherikov. Mahilyowskaya Voblasts', E Belarus *53.34N 31.19E*
33 *R9* **Chesaning** Michigan, N USA *43.10N 84.07W*
23 *X5* **Chesapeake Bay** *inlet* NE USA
Cheshevlya *see* Tsyeshawlya
99 *K18* **Cheshire** *cultural region* C England, UK
129 *P5* **Chëshskaya Guba** *var.* Archangel Bay, Chesha Bay, Dvina Bay. *bay* NW Russian Federation
12 *F14* **Chesley** Ontario, S Canada *44.17N 81.06W*
23 *Q10* **Chesnee** South Carolina, SE USA *35.09N 81.51W*
99 *K18* **Chester** *Wel.* Caerleon; *hist.* Legaceaster, *Lat.* Deva, Devana Castra. C England, UK *53.12N 2.54W*
37 *O4* **Chester** California, W USA *40.18N 121.14W*
32 *K16* **Chester** Illinois, N USA *37.54N 89.49W*
35 *S7* **Chester** Montana, NW USA *48.30N 110.59W*
20 *I16* **Chester** Pennsylvania, NE USA *39.51N 75.21W*
23 *R1* **Chester** South Carolina, SE USA *34.42N 81.12W*
27 *X9* **Chester** Texas, SW USA *30.55N 94.36W*
23 *W6* **Chester** Virginia, NE USA *37.22N 77.27W*
23 *R11* **Chester** West Virginia, NE USA *40.34N 80.33W*
99 *M18* **Chesterfield** C England, UK *53.15N 1.25W*
23 *S11* **Chesterfield** South Carolina, SE USA *34.44N 80.05W*
23 *W6* **Chesterfield** Virginia, NE USA *37.22N 77.31W*
199 *I10* **Chesterfield, Îles** *island group* NW New Caledonia
15 *Ll6* **Chesterfield Inlet** Nunavut, NW Canada *63.19N 90.57W*
15 *L6* **Chesterfield Inlet** *inlet* Nunavut, N Canada
23 *Y3* **Chester River** ≈ Delaware/Maryland, NE USA
23 *X3* **Chestertown** Maryland, NE USA *39.12N 76.04W*
21 *R4* **Chesuncook Lake** ◎ Maine, NE USA
32 *J5* **Chetek** Wisconsin, N USA *45.19N 91.37W*
11 *R14* **Chéticamp** Nova Scotia, SE Canada *46.13N 61.19W*
29 *Q8* **Chetopa** Kansas, C USA *37.02N 95.05W*
43 *Y14* **Chetumal** *var.* Payo Obispo. Quintana Roo, SE Mexico *18.32N 88.15W*
Chetumal, Bahia/Chetumal, Bahía de *see* Chetumal Bay
44 *G1* **Chetumal Bay** *var.* Bahia Chetumal, Bahía de Chetumal. *bay* Belize/Mexico
8 *M13* **Chetwynd** British Columbia, W Canada *55.42N 121.36W*
40 *M11* **Chevak** Alaska, USA *61.31N 165.35W*
38 *M12* **Chevelon Creek** ≈ Arizona, SW USA
193 *J17* **Cheviot** Canterbury, South Island, NZ *42.48S 173.17E*
98 *L13* **Cheviot Hills** *hill range* England/Scotland, UK
98 *L13* **Cheviot, The** ▲ NE England, UK *55.28N 2.10W*
12 *M11* **Chevreuil, Lac du** ◎ Québec, SE Canada
83 *I16* **Ch'ew Bahir** *var.* Lake Stefanie. ◎ Ethiopia/Kenya
34 *L7* **Chewelah** Washington, NW USA *48.16N 117.42W*
28 *K10* **Cheyenne** Oklahoma, C USA *35.38N 99.40W*
35 *Z17* **Cheyenne** *state capital* Wyoming, C USA *41.08N 104.45W*
28 *L5* **Cheyenne Bottoms** ◎ Kansas, C USA
18 *Kk6* **Cheyenne River** ≈ South Dakota/Wyoming, N USA
39 *W5* **Cheyenne Wells** Colorado, C USA *38.49N 102.21W*
110 *C9* **Cheyres** Vaud, W Switzerland *46.48N 6.48E*
Chezdi-Oşorheiu *see* Târgu Secuiesc
159 *P13* **Chhapra** *prev.* Chapra. Bihār, N India *25.49N 84.42E*
159 *V13* **Chhatak** *var.* Chatak. Sylhet, NE Bangladesh *25.02N 91.33E*
160 *J9* **Chhatarpur** Madhya Pradesh, C India *24.54N 79.34E*
160 *N13* **Chhatrapur** *prev.* Chatrapur; Orissa, E India *19.25N 85.01E*
160 *L12* **Chhattīsgarh** *plain* C India
160 *K12* **Chhattīsgarh** ◈ *state* E India
160 *I11* **Chhindwāra** Madhya Pradesh, C India *22.04N 78.58E*
159 *T12* **Chhukha** SW Bhutan *27.01N 89.36E*
167 *S14* **Chiai** *var.* Chia-i, Chiayi, Kiayi, Jiayi, *Jap.* Kagi. C Taiwan *23.28N 120.27E*
Chia-mu-ssu *see* Jiamusi
85 *B15* **Chiange** *Port.* Vila de Almoster. Huíla, SW Angola *15.49S 13.52E*
Chiang-hsi *see* Jiangxi
167 *S12* **Chiang Kai-shek** ✈ (T'aipei) N Taiwan *25.09N 121.20E*
178 *I8* **Chiang Khan** Loei, E Thailand *17.51N 101.43E*
178 *H7* **Chiang Mai** *var.* Chiangmai, Chiengmai, Kiangmai. Chiang Mai, NW Thailand *18.48N 98.58E*
178 *H7* **Chiang Mai** ✈ Chiang Mai, NW Thailand *18.44N 98.53E*
178 *Hh6* **Chiang Rai** *var.* Chianpai, Chienrai, Muang Chiang Rai. Chiang Rai, NW Thailand *19.55N 99.51E*
Chiang-su *see* Jiangsu
Chianning/Chian-ning *see* Nanjing
Chianpai *see* Chiang Rai
108 *G12* **Chianti** *cultural region* C Italy
Chiapa *see* Chiapa de Corzo
43 *U16* **Chiapa de Corzo** *var.* Chiapa. Chiapas, SE Mexico *16.42N 92.58W*
43 *V16* **Chiapas** ◈ *state* SE Mexico
108 *J12* **Chiaravalle** Marche, C Italy *43.36N 13.19E*
109 *N22* **Chiaravalle Centrale** Calabria, SW Italy *38.40N 16.25E*
108 *E7* **Chiari** Lombardia, N Italy *45.33N 10.00E*
110 *H12* **Chiasso** Ticino, S Switzerland *45.51N 9.01E*
143 *S9* **Chiat'ura** C Georgia *42.13N 43.11E*
43 *P15* **Chiautla** *var.* Chiautla de Tapia. Puebla, S Mexico *18.16N 98.31W*
Chiautla de Tapia *see* Chiautla
108 *D10* **Chiavari** Liguria, NW Italy *44.19N 9.19E*
108 *E6* **Chiavenna** Lombardia, N Italy *46.19N 9.22E*
Chiayi *see* Chiai
Chiazza *see* Piazza Armerina
172 *Ss12* **Chiba** *var.* Tiba. Chiba, Honshū, S Japan *35.37N 140.05E*
171 *K17* **Chiba** *off.* Chiba-ken, *var.* Tiba. ◈ *prefecture* Honshū, S Japan
85 *M18* **Chibabava** Sofala, C Mozambique *20.16S 33.39E*
167 *O10* **Chibi** *prev.* Puqi. Hubei, C China *24.40N 102.55E*
85 *B15* **Chibia** *Port.* João de Almeida, Vila João de Almeida. Huíla, SW Angola *15.09S 13.45E*
85 *M18* **Chiboma** Sofala, C Mozambique *20.06S 33.54E*
84 *J12* **Chibondo** Luapula, N Zambia *10.42S 28.42E*
84 *K11* **Chibote** Luapula, NE Zambia *9.52S 29.33E*
10 *K12* **Chibougamau** Québec, SE Canada *49.55N 74.24W*
170 *Ff11* **Chiburi-jima** *island* Oki-shotō, SW Japan
85 *M20* **Chibuto** Gaza, S Mozambique *24.40S 33.33E*
33 *N11* **Chicago** Illinois, N USA *41.51N 87.39W*
33 *N11* **Chicago Heights** Illinois, N USA *41.30N 87.38W*
13 *W6* **Chic-Chocs, Monts** *Eng.* Shickshock Mountains. ▲▲ Québec, SE Canada
41 *W13* **Chichagof Island** *island* Alexander Archipelago, Alaska, USA
59 *K20* **Chichas, Cordillera de** ▲▲ SW Bolivia
43 *X12* **Chichén-Itzá, Ruinas** *ruins* Yucatán, SE Mexico *20.35N 88.34W*
99 *N23* **Chichester** SE England, UK *50.49N 0.48W*
171 *Jj16* **Chichibu** *var.* Titibu. Saitama, Honshū, S Japan *35.58N 139.06E*
44 *C5* **Chichicastenango** Quiché, W Guatemala *14.55N 91.06W*
44 *I9* **Chichigalpa** Chinandega, NW Nicaragua *12.34N 87.04W*
Ch'i-ch'i-ha-erh *see* Qiqihar
172 *T16* **Chichijima-rettō** *Eng.* Beechy Group. *island group* SE Japan
56 *K4* **Chichiriviche** Falcón, N Venezuela *10.58N 68.16W*
41 *R11* **Chickaloon** Alaska, USA *61.48N 148.27W*
22 *L10* **Chickamauga Lake** ⊠ Tennessee, S USA
25 *N7* **Chickasawhay River** ≈ Mississippi, S USA
28 *M11* **Chickasha** Oklahoma, C USA *35.03N 97.56W*
41 *T9* **Chicken** Alaska, USA *64.04N 141.56W*
106 *J16* **Chiclana de la Frontera** Andalucía, S Spain *36.25N 6.09W*
58 *B11* **Chiclayo** Lambayeque, NW Peru *6.46S 79.46W*
37 *N5* **Chico** California, W USA *39.42N 121.51W*
85 *L15* **Chicoa** Tete, NW Mozambique *15.45S 32.25E*
85 *M20* **Chicomo** Gaza, S Mozambique *24.29S 34.15E*
20 *M11* **Chicopee** Massachusetts, NE USA *42.08N 72.34W*
65 *I19* **Chico, Río** ≈ SE Argentina
65 *I21* **Chico, Río** ≈ S Argentina
29 *W14* **Chicot, Lake** ◎ Arkansas, C USA
13 *R7* **Chicoutimi** Québec, SE Canada *48.24N 71.04W*
13 *Q8* **Chicoutimi** ≈ Québec, SE Canada
85 *L19* **Chicualacuala** Gaza, SW Mozambique *22.06S 31.42E*
85 *B14* **Chicuma** Benguela, C Angola *13.33S 14.41E*
161 *J21* **Chidambaram** Tamil Nādu, SE India *11.25N 79.42E*
206 *K13* **Chidley, Cape** *headland* Newfoundland and Labrador, E Canada *60.25N 64.39W*
103 *N24* **Chiemsee** ◎ SE Germany
Chiengmai *see* Chiang Mai
Chienrai *see* Chiang Rai
108 *B8* **Chieri** Piemonte, NW Italy *45.01N 7.49E*
108 *F8* **Chiese** ≈ N Italy
109 *K14* **Chieti** *var.* Teate. Abruzzo, C Italy *42.22N 14.10E*
101 *E19* **Chièvres** Hainaut, SW Belgium *50.34N 3.49E*
169 *S12* **Chifeng** *var.* Ulanhad. Nei Mongol Zizhiqu, N China *42.16N 118.55E*
84 *F13* **Chifumage** ≈ E Angola
84 *M13* **Chifunda** Eastern, NE Zambia *11.57S 32.36E*
151 *S14* **Chiganak** *var.* Čiganak. Zhambyl, SE Kazakhstan *45.10N 73.55E*
41 *P15* **Chiginagak, Mount** ▲ Alaska, USA *57.10N 157.00W*
Chigirin *see* Chyhyryn
43 *P13* **Chignahuapan** Puebla, S Mexico *19.52N 98.03W*
41 *O15* **Chignik** Alaska, USA *56.18N 158.24W*
85 *M19* **Chigombe** ≈ S Mozambique
56 *D7* **Chigorodó** Antioquia, NW Colombia *7.42N 76.45W*
85 *M19* **Chigubo** Gaza, S Mozambique *22.50S 33.30E*
Chihertey *see* Altay
Chih-fu *see* Yantai
Chihli *see* Hebei
Chihli, Gulf of *see* Bo Hai
42 *J6* **Chihuahua** Chihuahua, NW Mexico *28.40N 106.06W*
42 *I6* **Chihuahua** ◈ *state* N Mexico
151 *O15* **Chiili** Kzylorda, S Kazakhstan *44.09N 66.44E*
28 *M7* **Chikaskia River** ≈ Kansas/Oklahoma, C USA
161 *H19* **Chik Ballāpur** Karnātaka, W India *13.28N 77.42E*
128 *G15* **Chikhachevo** Pskovskaya Oblast', W Russian Federation *57.17N 29.51E*
161 *F19* **Chikmagalūr** Karnātaka, W India *13.19N 75.46E*
133 *V7* **Chikoy** ≈ C Russian Federation
85 *J15* **Chikumbi** Lusaka, C Zambia *15.16S 28.18E*
84 *M13* **Chikwa** Eastern, NE Zambia *11.39S 32.45E*
Chikwana *see* Chikwawa
85 *N15* **Chikwawa** *var.* Chikwana. Southern, S Malawi *16.01S 34.51E*
161 *J16* **Chilakalūrupet** Andhra Pradesh, E India *16.09N 80.13E*
152 *L14* **Chilan** Lebap Welaýaty, E Turkmenistan *37.57N 64.58E*
Chilapa *see* Chilapa de Alvarez
43 *P16* **Chilapa de Alvarez** *var.* Chilapa. Guerrero, S Mexico *17.36N 99.09W*
161 *J25* **Chilaw** North Western Province, W Sri Lanka *7.34N 79.49E*
59 *D15* **Chilca** Lima, W Peru *12.33S 76.44W*
25 *Q4* **Childersburg** Alabama, S USA *33.16N 86.21W*
27 *P4* **Childress** Texas, SW USA *34.25N 100.13W*
65 *G14* **Chile** *off.* Republic of Chile. ◆ *republic* SW South America
49 *R10* **Chile Basin** *undersea feature* E Pacific Ocean
65 *H20* **Chile Chico** Aisén, W Chile *46.34S 71.43W*
64 *I9* **Chilecito** La Rioja, NW Argentina *29.10S 67.30W*
64 *H12* **Chilecito** Mendoza, W Argentina *33.52S 69.03W*
85 *L14* **Chilembwe** Eastern, E Zambia *13.54S 31.38E*
200 *O13* **Chile Rise** *undersea feature* SE Pacific Ocean
119 *N13* **Chilia Braţul** ≈ SE Romania
Chilia-Nouă *see* Kiliya
151 *V15* **Chilik** Almaty, SE Kazakhstan *43.35N 78.17E*
151 *V15* **Chilik** ≈ SE Kazakhstan
160 *O13* **Chilika Lake** *var.* Chilka Lake. ◎ E India
84 *J13* **Chililabombwe** Copperbelt, C Zambia *12.19S 27.52E*
Chi-lin *see* Jilin
Chilka Lake *see* Chilika Lake
8 *H9* **Chilkoot Pass** *pass* British Columbia, W Canada *59.41N 135.13W*
Chill Ala, Cuan *see* Killala Bay
64 *G13* **Chillán** Bío Bío, C Chile *36.37S 72.10W*
63 *C22* **Chillar** Buenos Aires, E Argentina *37.16S 59.58W*
Chill Chiaráin, Cuan *see* Kilkieran Bay
32 *K12* **Chillicothe** Illinois, N USA *40.55N 89.29W*
29 *S3* **Chillicothe** Missouri, C USA *39.48N 93.33W*
33 *S14* **Chillicothe** Ohio, N USA *39.19N 82.58W*
27 *Q4* **Chillicothe** Texas, SW USA *34.15N 99.31W*
8 *M17* **Chilliwack** British Columbia, SW Canada *49.09N 121.54W*
Chill Mhantáin, Ceann *see* Wicklow Head
Chill Mhantáin, Sléibhte *see* Wicklow Mountains
110 *C10* **Chillon** Vaud, W Switzerland *46.24N 6.56E*
Chil'mamedkum, Peski/Chilmämetgum *see* Çilmämmetgum
65 *F17* **Chiloé, Isla de** *var.* Isla Grande de Chiloé. *island* W Chile
34 *H15* **Chiloquin** Oregon, NW USA *42.33N 121.33W*
43 *O16* **Chilpancingo** *var.* Chilpancingo de los Bravos. Guerrero, S Mexico *17.33N 99.30W*
Chilpancingo de los Bravos *see* Chilpancingo
99 *N21* **Chiltern Hills** *hill range* S England, UK
32 *M7* **Chilton** Wisconsin, N USA *44.04N 88.10W*
84 *F11* **Chiluage** Lunda Sul, NE Angola *9.32S 21.48E*
84 *N12* **Chilumba** *prev.* Deep Bay. Northern, N Malawi *10.27S 34.12E*
167 *T12* **Chilung** *var.* Keelung, *Jap.* Kirun, Kirun'; *prev. Sp.* Santissima Trinidad. N Taiwan *25.10N 121.43E*
85 *N15* **Chilwa, Lake** *var.* Lago Chirua, Lake Shirwa. ◎ SE Malawi
178 *J10* **Chi, Mae Nam** ≈ E Thailand
44 *C6* **Chimaltenango** Chimaltenango, C Guatemala *14.37N 90.48W*
44 *A2* **Chimaltenango** *off.* Departamento de Chimaltenango. ◈ *department* S Guatemala
45 *V15* **Chimán** Panamá, E Panama *8.41N 78.37W*
85 *M17* **Chimanimani** *prev.* Mandidzudzure, Melsetter. Manicaland, E Zimbabwe *19.48S 32.52E*
101 *G22* **Chimay** Hainaut, S Belgium *50.03N 4.19E*
39 *S10* **Chimayo** New Mexico, SW USA *36.00N 105.55W*
Chimbay *see* Chimboy
58 *A13* **Chimborazo** ◈ *province* C Ecuador
58 *C7* **Chimborazo** ⛰ C Ecuador *1.29S 78.50W*
58 *C12* **Chimbote** Ancash, W Peru *9.04S 78.34W*
152 *H7* **Chimboy** *Rus.* Chimbay. Qoraqalpog'iston Respublikasi, NW Uzbekistan *43.03N 59.52E*
194 *H12* **Chimbu** ◈ *province* C PNG
56 *F6* **Chimichagua** Cesar, N Colombia *9.19N 73.51W*
Chimishliya *see* Cimişlia
Chimkent *see* Shymkent
Chimkentskaya Oblast' *see* Yuzhnyy Kazakhstan
30 *I14* **Chimney Rock** *rock* Nebraska, C USA *41.40N 103.21W*
85 *M17* **Chimoio** Manica, C Mozambique *19.07S 33.28E*
84 *K11* **Chimpembe** Northern, NE Zambia *9.33S 29.30E*
43 *O8* **China** Nuevo León, NE Mexico *25.44N 99.09W*
162 *M9* **China** *off.* People's Republic of China, *Chin.* Chung-hua Jen-min Kung-ho-kuo, Zhonghua Renmin Gongheguo; *prev.* Chinese Empire. ◆ *republic* E Asia
21 *Q7* **China Lake** ◎ Maine, NE USA
44 *F8* **Chinameca** San Miguel, E El Salvador *13.28N 88.21W*
Chi-nan/Chinan *see* Jinan
44 *H9* **Chinandega** Chinandega, NW Nicaragua *12.37N 87.07W*
44 *H9* **Chinandega** ◈ *department* NW Nicaragua
China, People's Republic of *see* China
China, Republic of *see* Taiwan
26 *J11* **Chinati Mountains** ▲▲ Texas, SW USA
Chinaz *see* Chinoz
59 *E15* **Chincha Alta** Ica, SW Peru *13.25S 76.08W*
9 *N11* **Chinchaga** ≈ Alberta, SW Canada
Chin-chiang *see* Quanzhou
Chinchilla *see* Chinchilla de Monte Aragón

◆ Country
● Country Capital
◇ Dependent Territory
○ Dependent Territory Capital
◈ Administrative Region
✈ International Airport
▲ Mountain
▲▲ Mountain Range
⛰ Volcano
≈ River
◎ Lake
⊠ Reservoir

◆ COUNTRY ◇ DEPENDENT TERRITORY ◈ ADMINISTRATIVE REGION ▲ MOUNTAIN ▲ VOLCANO ◎ LAKE
● COUNTRY CAPITAL ○ DEPENDENT TERRITORY CAPITAL ✈ INTERNATIONAL AIRPORT ▲ MOUNTAIN RANGE ≈ RIVER ▣ RESERVOIR

◆ COUNTRY ● COUNTRY CAPITAL ◇ DEPENDENT TERRITORY ○ DEPENDENT TERRITORY CAPITAL ◆ ADMINISTRATIVE REGION ✕ INTERNATIONAL AIRPORT ▲ MOUNTAIN ▲ MOUNTAIN RANGE ▲ VOLCANO ≈ RIVER ☒ LAKE ☒ RESERVOIR

COLOMBIE-BRITANNIQUE – CORRYONG

Colombie-Britannique see British Columbia
13 T6 Colombier Québec, SE Canada 48.51N 68.52W
161 J25 Colombo ● (Sri Lanka) Western Province, W Sri Lanka 6.55N 79.52E
161 J25 Colombo ✕ Western Province, SW Sri Lanka 6.50N 79.59E
31 N11 Colome South Dakota, N USA 43.13N 99.42W
63 D18 Colon Entre Ríos, E Argentina 32.13S 58.15W
63 B19 Colón Buenos Aires, E Argentina 33.53S 61.06W
46 D5 Colón Matanzas, C Cuba 22.42N 80.54W
45 T14 Colón prev. Aspinwall. Colón, C Panama 9.04N 80.32W
44 K5 Colón ❖ department NE Honduras
45 S15 Colón off. Provincia de Colón. ❖ province N Panama
59 A16 Colón, Archipiélago de var. Islas de los Galápagos, Eng. Galapagos Islands, Tortoise Islands. island group Ecuador, E Pacific Ocean
46 K5 Colonel Hill Crooked Island, SE Bahamas 22.43N 74.12W
42 B3 Colonet, Cabo headland NW Mexico 30.57N 116.19W
196 G14 Colonia Yap, W Micronesia 9.29N 138.06E
63 D19 Colonia ❖ department SW Uruguay
Colonia see Kolonia, Micronesia
Colonia see Colonia del Sacramento, Uruguay
Colonia Agrippina see Köln
63 D20 Colonia del Sacramento var. Colonia. Colonia, SW Uruguay 34.28S 57.48W
64 L8 Colonia Dora Santiago del Estero, N Argentina 28.34S 62.58W
Colonia Julia Fanestris see Fano
23 W5 Colonial Beach Virginia, NE USA 38.15N 76.57W
23 V6 Colonial Heights Virginia, NE USA 37.15N 77.24W
200 Oo8 Colón Ridge undersea feature E Pacific Ocean
98 F12 Colonsay island W Scotland, UK
59 K22 Colorada, Laguna ◎ SW Bolivia
39 R6 Colorado off. State of Colorado; also known as Centennial State, Silver State. ❖ state C USA
65 H22 Colorado, Cerro ▲ S Argentina 49.58S 71.38W
27 O7 Colorado City Texas, SW USA 32.23N 100.51W
38 M7 Colorado Plateau plateau W USA
63 A24 Colorado, Río ~ E Argentina
45 N12 Colorado, Río ~ NE Costa Rica
Colorado, Río see Colorado River
18 Hh10 Colorado River var. Río Colorado. ~ Mexico/USA
18 L15 Colorado River ~ Texas, SW USA
37 W15 Colorado River Aqueduct aqueduct California, W USA
46 A4 Colorados, Archipiélago de los island group NW Cuba
64 J9 Colorados, Desagües de los ◎ W Argentina
39 T5 Colorado Springs Colorado, C USA 38.49N 104.46W
42 L11 Colotlán Jalisco, SW Mexico 22.07N 103.15W
59 L19 Colquechaca Potosí, C Bolivia 18.39S 66.12W
25 S7 Colquitt Georgia, SE USA 31.10N 84.43W
31 R11 Colton South Dakota, N USA 43.47N 96.55W
34 M10 Colton Washington, NW USA 46.34N 117.10W
37 P8 Columbia California, W USA 38.01N 120.22W
32 K16 Columbia Illinois, N USA 38.26N 90.12W
22 L7 Columbia Kentucky, S USA 37.06N 85.18W
24 I6 Columbia Louisiana, S USA 32.05N 92.03W
23 W3 Columbia Maryland, NE USA 39.11N 76.52W
24 L7 Columbia Mississippi, S USA 31.15N 89.50W
29 U4 Columbia Missouri, C USA 38.55N 92.19W
23 Y9 Columbia North Carolina, SE USA 35.53N 76.16W
20 G16 Columbia Pennsylvania, NE USA 40.01N 76.30W
23 Q12 Columbia state capital South Carolina, SE USA 34.00N 81.00W
22 I9 Columbia Tennessee, S USA 35.37N 87.02W
(0) F9 Columbia ~ Canada/USA
34 K9 Columbia Basin basin Washington, NW USA
207 Q10 Columbia, Cape headland Ellesmere Island, Nunavut, NE Canada
33 Q12 Columbia City Indiana, N USA 41.09N 85.29W
23 W3 Columbia, District of ❖ federal district NE USA
35 P7 Columbia Falls Montana, NW USA 48.22N 114.10W
9 O15 Columbia Icefield icefield Alberta/British Columbia, S Canada
9 O15 Columbia, Mount ▲ Alberta/British Columbia, SW Canada 52.07N 117.30W
9 N15 Columbia Mountains ▲▲ British Columbia, SW Canada
25 P4 Columbiana Alabama, S USA 33.10N 86.36W
33 V12 Columbiana Ohio, N USA 40.53N 80.41W
34 M14 Columbia Plateau plateau Idaho/Oregon, NW USA
31 P7 Columbia Road Reservoir ▣ South Dakota, N USA
67 K16 Columbia Seamount undersea feature C Atlantic Ocean 20.30S 32.00W
85 D25 Columbine, Cape headland SW South Africa 32.50S 17.39E
107 U9 Columbretes, Islas island group E Spain
25 R5 Columbus Georgia, SE USA 32.28N 84.58W
33 P14 Columbus Indiana, N USA 39.12N 85.55W
29 R7 Columbus Kansas, C USA 37.10N 94.50W
25 N4 Columbus Mississippi, S USA 33.30N 88.25W
35 U11 Columbus Montana, NW USA 45.38N 109.15W
31 Q15 Columbus Nebraska, C USA 41.25N 97.22W
39 Q16 Columbus New Mexico, SW USA 31.49N 107.38W
23 P10 Columbus North Carolina, SE USA 35.15N 82.09W
30 K2 Columbus North Dakota, N USA 48.52N 102.47W
33 S13 Columbus state capital Ohio, N USA 39.57N 83.00W
27 U11 Columbus Texas, SW USA 29.42N 96.32W
32 L8 Columbus Wisconsin, N USA 43.21N 89.00W
33 R12 Columbus Grove Ohio, N USA 40.55N 84.03W
31 Y15 Columbus Junction Iowa, C USA 41.16N 91.21W
46 J3 Columbus Point headland Cat Island, C Bahamas 24.07N 75.19W
37 T8 Columbus Salt Marsh salt marsh Nevada, W USA
37 N6 Colusa California, W USA 39.10N 122.03W
34 L7 Colville Washington, NW USA 48.33N 117.54W
192 M5 Colville, Cape headland North Island, NZ 36.28S 175.20E
192 M5 Colville Channel channel North Island, NZ
41 P6 Colville River ~ Alaska, USA
99 J18 Colwyn Bay N Wales, UK 53.18N 3.43W
108 H9 Comacchio var. Commachio; anc. Comactium. Emilia-Romagna, N Italy 44.40N 12.10E
108 H9 Comacchio, Valli di lagoon Adriatic Sea, N Mediterranean Sea
Comactium see Comacchio
43 V17 Comalapa Chiapas, SE Mexico 15.42N 92.06W
43 U15 Comalcalco Tabasco, SE Mexico 18.16N 93.05W
65 H16 Comallo Río Negro, SW Argentina 40.58S 70.13W
28 M12 Comanche Oklahoma, C USA 34.22N 97.57W
27 R8 Comanche Texas, SW USA 31.54N 98.36W
204 H2 Comandante Ferraz Brazilian research station Antarctica 61.57S 58.23W
64 N6 Comandante Fontana Formosa, N Argentina 25.19S 59.42W
65 I22 Comandante Luis Peidra Buena Santa Cruz, S Argentina 50.04S 68.55W
61 O18 Comandatuba Bahia, SE Brazil 15.13S 39.00W
118 K11 Comănești Hung. Kománfalva. Bacău, SW Romania 46.24N 26.27E
59 M19 Comarapa Santa Cruz, C Bolivia 17.52S 64.34W
118 J13 Comarnic Prahova, SE Romania 45.13N 25.36E
44 H6 Comayagua Comayagua, W Honduras 14.33N 87.37W
44 H6 Comayagua ❖ department W Honduras
44 I6 Comayagua, Montañas de ▲▲ C Honduras
23 R15 Combahee River ~ South Carolina, SE USA
64 G10 Combarbalá Coquimbo, C Chile 31.15S 71.03W
105 S7 Combeaufontaine Haute-Saône, E France 47.43N 5.52E
99 G15 Comber Ir. An Comar. E Northern Ireland, UK 54.33N 5.45W
101 K20 Comblain-au-Pont Liège, E Belgium 50.29N 5.36E
104 I6 Combourg Ille-et-Vilaine, NW France 48.21N 1.44W
46 M9 Comendador prev. Elías Piña. W Dominican Republic 18.51N 71.40W
Comer See see Como, Lago di
27 R11 Comfort Texas, SW USA 29.58N 98.54W
159 V15 Comilla Ben. Kumillā. Chittagong, E Bangladesh 23.28N 91.10E
101 B18 Comines Hainaut, W Belgium 50.46N 2.58E
123 J16 Comino Malt. Kemmuna. island C Malta
109 D18 Comino, Capo headland Sardegna, Italy, C Mediterranean Sea 40.32N 9.49E
109 K25 Comiso Sicilia, Italy, C Mediterranean Sea 36.57N 14.37E
43 V16 Comitán var. Comitán de Domínguez. Chiapas, SE Mexico 16.14N 92.06W
Comitán de Domínguez see Comitán
Commachio see Comacchio
Commander Islands see Komandorskiye Ostrova
105 O10 Commentry Allier, C France 46.18N 2.46E
25 T2 Commerce Georgia, SE USA 34.12N 83.27W
29 R8 Commerce Oklahoma, C USA 36.55N 94.52W
27 V5 Commerce Texas, SW USA 33.16N 95.52W
39 T4 Commerce City Colorado, C USA 39.45N 104.54W
105 S5 Commercy Meuse, NE France 48.46N 5.36E
57 W9 Commewijne var. Commewyne. ❖ district NE Surinam
Commewyne see Commewijne
13 P8 Commissaires, Lac des ◎ Québec, SE Canada
66 A12 Commissioner's Point headland W Bermuda
15 L13 Committee Bay bay Nunavut, N Canada
108 D7 Como anc. Comum. Lombardia, N Italy 45.48N 9.04E
65 I19 Comodoro Rivadavia Chubut, SE Argentina 45.49S 67.30W
108 D6 Como, Lago di var. Lario, Eng. Lake Como, Ger. Comer See. ◎ N Italy
Como, Lake see Como, Lago di
42 E7 Comondú Baja California Sur, W Mexico 26.01N 111.50W
118 F12 Comorâşte Hung. Komornok. Caraş-Severin, SW Romania 45.13N 21.34E
Comores, République Fédérale Islamique des see Comoros
161 G24 Comorin, Cape headland SE India 8.00N 77.10E
180 M8 Comoro Basin undersea feature SW Indian Ocean
180 K14 Comoro Islands island group W Indian Ocean
180 H13 Comoros off. Federal Islamic Republic of the Comoros, Fr. République Fédérale Islamique des Comores. ◆ republic W Indian Ocean
8 L17 Comox Vancouver Island, British Columbia, SW Canada 49.40N 124.55W
105 O4 Compiègne Oise, N France 49.25N 2.49E
Complutum see Alcalá de Henares
Compniacum see Cognac
42 K12 Compostela Nayarit, C Mexico 21.14N 104.52W
Compostella see Santiago
62 L11 Comprida, Ilha island S Brazil
119 N11 Comrat Rus. Komrat. S Moldova 46.18N 28.40E
27 O11 Comstock Texas, SW USA 29.39N 101.10W
33 P9 Comstock Park Michigan, N USA 43.00N 85.40W
199 Kk3 Comstock Seamount undersea feature N Pacific Ocean 48.15N 156.55W
Comum see Como
165 N17 Cona Xizang Zizhiqu, W China 27.58N 91.54E
78 H14 Conakry ● (Guinea) SW Guinea 9.31N 13.43W
78 H14 Conakry ✕ SW Guinea 9.37N 13.32W
Conamara see Connemara
Conca see Cuenca
27 Q12 Concan Texas, SW USA 29.27N 99.43W
104 F6 Concarneau Finistère, NW France 47.52N 3.55W
85 O17 Conceição Sofala, C Mozambique 18.47S 36.18E
61 K15 Conceição do Araguaia Pará, NE Brazil 8.15S 49.15W
60 F10 Conceição do Maú Roraima, W Brazil 3.34N 59.52W
63 D14 Concepción var. Concepcion. Corrientes, NE Argentina 28.25S 57.54W
64 J8 Concepción Tucumán, N Argentina 27.19S 65.34W
59 O17 Concepción Santa Cruz, E Bolivia 16.15S 62.07W
64 G13 Concepción Bío Bío, C Chile 36.47S 73.01W
56 E14 Concepción Putumayo, S Colombia 0.03N 75.39W
64 O5 Concepción var. Villa Concepción. Concepción, C Paraguay 23.26S 57.23W
64 O5 Concepción off. Departamento de Concepción. ❖ department E Paraguay
Concepción see La Concepción
Concepción de la Vega see La Vega
43 N9 Concepción del Oro Zacatecas, C Mexico 24.37N 101.25W
63 D18 Concepción del Uruguay Entre Ríos, E Argentina 32.30S 58.15W
44 K11 Concepción, Volcán ▲ SW Nicaragua 11.31N 85.37W
46 J4 Conception Island island C Bahamas
37 P14 Conception, Point headland California, W USA 34.27N 120.28W
56 H6 Concha Zulia, W Venezuela 9.01N 71.45W
62 L9 Conchas São Paulo, S Brazil 23.00S 47.58W
39 U11 Conchas Dam New Mexico, SW USA 35.21N 104.11W
39 U10 Conchas Lake ▣ New Mexico, SW USA
104 M5 Conches-en-Ouche Eure, N France 49.00N 1.00E
39 N12 Concho Arizona, SW USA 34.28N 109.33W
42 J5 Conchos, Río ~ NW Mexico
43 O8 Conchos, Río ~ C Mexico
110 C8 Concise Vaud, W Switzerland 46.52N 6.40E
37 N8 Concord California, W USA 37.58N 122.01W
21 O9 Concord state capital New Hampshire, NE USA 43.10N 71.31W
23 R10 Concord North Carolina, SE USA 35.30N 80.34W
63 D17 Concordia Entre Ríos, E Argentina 31.25S 58.00W
56 D9 Concordia Antioquia, W Colombia 6.03N 75.57W
42 J10 Concordia Sinaloa, C Mexico 23.18N 106.03W
59 I19 Concordia Tacna, SW Peru 18.12S 70.19W
29 N3 Concordia Kansas, C USA 39.34N 97.39W
29 S4 Concordia Missouri, C USA 38.58N 93.34W
62 I13 Concórdia Santa Catarina, S Brazil 27.13S 52.01W
178 J7 Con Cuông Nghê An, N Vietnam 19.02N 104.54E
178 Jj16 Côn Đao var. Con Son. island S Vietnam
Condate see St-Claude, Jura, France
Condate see Rennes, Ille-et-Vilaine, France
Condate see Montereau-Faut-Yonne, Seine-St-Denis, France
31 P8 Conde South Dakota, N USA 45.08N 98.07W
44 J8 Condega Estelí, NW Nicaragua 13.21N 86.23W
105 P2 Condé-sur-l'Escaut Nord, N France 50.27N 3.36E
104 K5 Condé-sur-Noireau Calvados, N France 48.52N 0.31W
Condivincum see Nantes
191 P8 Condobolin New South Wales, SE Australia 33.04S 147.08E
104 L15 Condom Gers, S France 43.56N 0.23E
34 J11 Condon Oregon, NW USA 45.13N 120.11W
56 D9 Condoto Chocó, W Colombia 5.06N 76.37W
25 P7 Conecuh River ~ Alabama/Florida, SE USA
108 H7 Conegliano Veneto, NE Italy 45.52N 12.18E
63 C19 Conesa Buenos Aires, E Argentina 33.36S 60.21W
12 F15 Conestogo ~ Ontario, S Canada
195 O17 Conflict Group island group SE PNG
Confluentes see Koblenz
104 L10 Confolens Charente, W France 46.00N 0.40E
38 J4 Confusion Range ▲▲ Utah, W USA
64 N6 Confuso, Río ~ C Paraguay
23 R12 Congaree River ~ South Carolina, SE USA
Công Hoa Xa Hôi Chu Nghia Viêt Nam see Vietnam
166 K12 Congjiang var. Bingmei. Guizhou, S China 25.48N 108.55E
81 K19 Congo off. Democratic Republic of Congo; prev. Zaire, Belgian Congo, Congo (Kinshasa). ◆ republic C Africa
81 G18 Congo off. Republic of the Congo, Fr. Moyen-Congo; prev. Middle Congo. ◆ republic C Africa
69 T11 Congo var. Kongo, Fr. Zaire. ~ C Africa
Congo see Zaire (province, Angola)
Congo/Congo (Kinshasa) see Congo (Democratic Republic of)
70 G12 Congo Basin drainage basin W Dem. Rep. Congo
69 Q11 Congo Canyon var. Congo Seavalley, Congo Submarine Canyon. undersea feature E Atlantic Ocean
Congo Cone see Congo Fan
67 P15 Congo Fan var. Congo Cone. undersea feature E Atlantic Ocean
Coni see Cuneo
65 H18 Cónico, Cerro ▲ SW Argentina 43.12S 71.42W
Conimbria/Conimbriga see Coimbra
Conjeeveram see Kānchīpuram
9 R13 Conklin Alberta, C Canada 55.36N 111.06W
26 M1 Conlen Texas, SW USA 36.16N 102.10W
Con, Loch see Conn, Lough
Connacht see Connaught
99 B17 Connaught var. Connacht, Ir. Chonnacht, Cúige. cultural region W Ireland
33 V10 Conneaut Ohio, N USA 41.56N 80.32W
20 L13 Connecticut off. State of Connecticut; also known as Blue Law State, Constitution State, Land of Steady Habits, Nutmeg State. ❖ state NE USA
21 N8 Connecticut ~ Canada/USA
21 O6 Connecticut Lakes lakes New Hampshire, NE USA
34 K9 Connell Washington, NW USA 46.39N 118.51W
99 B17 Connemara Ir. Conamara. region W Ireland
33 Q14 Connersville Indiana, N USA 39.38N 85.15W
99 B16 Conn, Lough Ir. Loch Con. ◎ W Ireland
37 X6 Connors Pass pass Nevada, W USA 39.01N 114.37W
189 X7 Connors Range ▲▲ Queensland, E Australia
58 E7 Cononaco, Río ~ E Ecuador
31 W13 Conrad Iowa, C USA 42.13N 92.52W
35 R7 Conrad Montana, NW USA 48.10N 111.58W
27 W10 Conroe Texas, SW USA 30.18N 95.27W
27 V10 Conroe, Lake ▣ Texas, SW USA
63 C17 Conscripto Bernardi Entre Ríos, E Argentina 31.03S 59.04W
61 M20 Conselheiro Lafaiete Minas Gerais, SE Brazil 20.40S 43.48W
Consentia see Cosenza
99 L14 Consett N England, UK 54.49N 1.52W
46 B5 Consolación del Sur Pinar del Río, W Cuba 22.29N 83.31W
Con Son see Côn Đao
9 R15 Consort Alberta, SW Canada 51.58N 110.44W
Constance see Konstanz
110 I6 Constance, Lake Ger. Bodensee. ◎ C Europe
106 G9 Constância Santarém, C Portugal 39.28N 8.22W
119 N14 Constanţa var. Küstendje, Eng. Constanza, Ger. Konstanza, Turk. Küstence. Constanţa, SE Romania 44.09N 28.36E
118 L14 Constanţa ❖ county SE Romania
Constantia see Coutances, France
Constantia see Konstanz, Germany
106 K13 Constantina Andalucía, S Spain 37.54N 5.36W
76 L5 Constantine var. Qacentina, Ar. Qoussantina. NE Algeria 36.22N 6.43E
41 O14 Constantine, Cape headland Alaska, USA 58.23N 158.53W
Constantinople see İstanbul
Constantiola see Olteniţa
Constanz see Konstanz
Constanza see Constanţa
64 G13 Constitución Maule, C Chile 35.25S 72.19W
63 D17 Constitución Salto, N Uruguay 31.05S 57.51W
Constitution State see Connecticut
107 N10 Consuegra Castilla-La Mancha, C Spain 39.28N 3.36W
189 X9 Consuelo Peak ▲ Queensland, E Australia 24.45S 148.01E
58 E11 Contamana Loreto, N Peru 7.19S 75.04W
Contrasto, Colle del see Contrasto, Portella del
109 K23 Contrasto, Portella del var. Colle del Contrasto. pass Sicilia, Italy, C Mediterranean Sea 37.51N 14.22E
56 G8 Contratación Santander, C Colombia 6.18N 73.27W
104 M8 Contres Loir-et-Cher, C France 47.24N 1.30E
109 O17 Conversano Puglia, SE Italy 40.58N 17.07E
29 U11 Conway Arkansas, C USA 35.05N 92.26W
21 O8 Conway New Hampshire, NE USA 43.58N 71.05W
23 U13 Conway South Carolina, SE USA 33.50N 79.03W
27 N2 Conway Texas, SW USA 35.10N 101.23W
29 U11 Conway, Lake ▣ Arkansas, C USA
29 N7 Conway Springs Kansas, C USA 37.23N 97.38W
99 J18 Conwy N Wales, UK 53.16N 3.51W
25 T3 Conyers Georgia, SE USA 33.40N 84.01W
Coo see Kos
190 F4 Coober Pedy South Australia 29.01S 134.46E
189 P2 Cooinda Northern Territory, N Australia 12.54S 132.31E
190 B6 Cook South Australia 30.37S 130.26E
31 W4 Cook Minnesota, N USA 47.51N 92.41W
203 N6 Cook, Baie de bay Moorea, W French Polynesia
8 J16 Cook, Cape headland Vancouver Island, British Columbia, SW Canada 50.04N 127.52W
39 Q15 Cookes Peak ▲ New Mexico, SW USA 32.32N 107.43W
22 L8 Cookeville Tennessee, S USA 36.09N 85.30W
183 P9 Cook Fracture Zone tectonic feature S Pacific Ocean
Cook, Grand Récif de see Cook, Récif de
41 Q12 Cook Inlet inlet Alaska, USA
203 X2 Cook Island island Line Islands, E Kiribati
202 J14 Cook Islands ◇ territory in free association with NZ S Pacific Ocean
Cook, Mount see Aoraki
197 G4 Cook, Récif de var. Grand Récif de Cook. reef S New Caledonia
12 G14 Cookstown Ontario, S Canada 44.12N 79.39W
99 F15 Cookstown Ir. An Chorr Chríochach. C Northern Ireland, UK 54.39N 6.45W
193 K14 Cook Strait var. Raukawa. strait NZ
189 W3 Cooktown Queensland, NE Australia 15.28S 145.15E
191 P6 Coolabah New South Wales, SE Australia 31.03S 146.42E
190 J11 Coola Coola Swamp wetland South Australia
191 S7 Coolah New South Wales, SE Australia 31.49S 149.43E
191 P9 Coolamon New South Wales, SE Australia 34.49S 147.13E
191 T4 Coolatai New South Wales, SE Australia 29.16S 150.45E
188 K12 Coolgardie Western Australia 31.00S 121.12E
38 L14 Coolidge Arizona, SW USA 32.58N 111.29W
27 U8 Coolidge Texas, SW USA 31.45N 96.39W
191 Q11 Cooma New South Wales, SE Australia 36.16S 149.09E
Coomassie see Kumasi
191 R6 Coonabarabran New South Wales, SE Australia 31.19S 149.18E
190 J10 Coonalpyn South Australia 35.43S 139.50E
191 R6 Coonamble New South Wales, SE Australia 30.56S 148.22E
Coondapoor see Kundāpura
161 G21 Coonoor Tamil Nādu, SE India 11.21N 76.46E
31 U14 Coon Rapids Iowa, C USA 41.52N 94.40W
31 V8 Coon Rapids Minnesota, N USA 45.12N 93.18W
27 V5 Cooper Texas, SW USA 33.22N 95.41W
189 U9 Cooper Creek var. Barcoo, Cooper's Creek. seasonal river Queensland/South Australia
41 R12 Cooper Landing Alaska, USA 60.27N 149.59W
23 T14 Cooper River ~ South Carolina, SE USA
Cooper's Creek see Cooper Creek
46 H1 Coopers Town Great Abaco, N Bahamas 26.46N 77.27W
20 J10 Cooperstown New York, NE USA 42.43N 74.55W
31 P4 Cooperstown North Dakota, N USA 47.26N 98.07W
33 P9 Coopersville Michigan, N USA 43.03N 85.55W
190 D7 Coorabie South Australia 31.57S 132.18E
25 Q3 Coosa River ~ Alabama/Georgia, S USA
34 E14 Coos Bay Oregon, NW USA 43.22N 124.13W
191 Q9 Cootamundra New South Wales, SE Australia 34.40S 148.03E
99 E16 Cootehill Ir. Muinchille. N Ireland 54.04N 7.04W
Çop see Chop
59 J17 Copacabana La Paz, W Bolivia 16.11S 69.02W
65 H14 Copahué, Volcán ▲ C Chile 37.56S 71.04W
43 U16 Copainalá Chiapas, SE Mexico 17.04N 93.13W
34 F8 Copalis Beach Washington, NW USA 47.05N 124.11W
44 F6 Copán ❖ department W Honduras
Copán see Copán Ruinas
27 T14 Copano Bay bay NW Gulf of Mexico
44 F6 Copán Ruinas var. Copán. Copán, W Honduras 14.51N 89.07W
Copenhagen see København
109 Q19 Copertino Puglia, SE Italy 40.16N 18.03E
64 H7 Copiapó Atacama, N Chile 27.17S 70.25W
64 G8 Copiapó, Bahía bay N Chile
64 G7 Copiapó, Río ~ N Chile
116 M12 Çöpköy Edirne, NW Turkey 41.14N 26.51E
190 I5 Copley South Australia 30.36S 138.26E
108 H9 Copparo Emilia-Romagna, C Italy 44.53N 11.53E
57 V10 Coppename Rivier var. Koppename. ~ C Surinam
27 S9 Copperas Cove Texas, SW USA 31.07N 97.54W
84 J13 Copperbelt ❖ province C Zambia
41 S11 Copper Center Alaska, USA 61.57N 145.21W
Coppermine see Kugluktuk
15 I5 Coppermine ~ Northwest Territories/Nunavut, N Canada
41 T11 Copper River ~ Alaska, USA
Copper State see Arizona
118 I11 Copşa Mică Ger. Kleinkopisch, Hung. Kiskapus. Sibiu, C Romania 45.48N 24.08E
164 J14 Coqên Xizang Zizhiqu, W China 31.13N 85.12E
Coquilhatville see Mbandaka
34 E14 Coquille Oregon, NW USA 43.10N 124.11W
64 G9 Coquimbo Coquimbo, N Chile 29.59S 71.18W
64 G9 Coquimbo off. Región de Coquimbo. ❖ region C Chile
118 I15 Corabia Olt, S Romania 43.46N 24.31E
59 F17 Coracora Ayacucho, SW Peru 15.07S 73.45W
Cora Droma Rúisc see Carrick-on-Shannon
46 K9 Corail SW Haiti 18.32N 73.54W
191 V4 Coraki New South Wales, SE Australia 29.01S 153.15E
188 G8 Coral Bay Western Australia 23.02S 113.51E
25 Y16 Coral Gables Florida, SE USA 25.43N 80.16W
15 M5 Coral Harbour Southampton Island, Northwest Territories, NE Canada 64.10N 83.15W
199 I10 Coral Sea sea SW Pacific Ocean
182 M7 Coral Sea Basin undersea feature N Coral Sea
199 Hh10 Coral Sea Islands ◇ Australian external territory SW Pacific Ocean
190 M12 Corangamite, Lake ◎ Victoria, SE Australia
Corantijn Rivier see Courantyne River
20 B14 Coraopolis Pennsylvania, NE USA 40.28N 80.08W
109 N17 Corato Puglia, SE Italy 41.09N 16.25E
105 O17 Corbières ▲▲ S France
105 P8 Corbigny Nièvre, C France 47.15N 3.42E
23 N7 Corbin Kentucky, S USA 36.57N 84.06W
106 L14 Corbones ~ SW Spain
Corcaigh see Cork
37 R11 Corcoran California, W USA 36.06N 119.33W
49 T14 Corcovado, Golfo gulf S Chile
65 G18 Corcovado, Volcán ▲ S Chile 43.13S 72.45W
106 F3 Corcubión Galicia, NW Spain 42.55N 9.12W
Corcyra Nigra see Korčula
62 Q9 Cordeiro Rio de Janeiro, SE Brazil 22.01S 42.20W
25 T6 Cordele Georgia, SE USA 31.58N 83.49W
28 L11 Cordell Oklahoma, C USA 35.18N 98.58W
105 N14 Cordes Tarn, S France 44.03N 1.57E
64 O6 Cordillera off. Departamento de la Cordillera. ❖ department C Paraguay
190 K1 Cordillo Downs South Australia 26.44S 140.37E
64 K10 Córdoba Córdoba, C Argentina 31.25S 64.10W
43 R14 Córdoba Veracruz-Llave, E Mexico 18.52N 96.48W
106 M13 Córdoba var. Cordoba, Eng. Cordova; anc. Corduba. Andalucía, SW Spain 37.52N 4.46W
64 K11 Córdoba off. Provincia de Córdoba. ❖ province C Argentina
56 D7 Córdoba off. Departmento de Córdoba. ❖ province NW Colombia
106 L13 Córdoba ❖ province Andalucía, S Spain
64 K10 Córdoba, Sierras de ▲▲ C Argentina
25 O3 Cordova Alabama, S USA 33.45N 87.10W
41 S12 Cordova Alaska, USA 60.32N 145.45W
Cordova/Corduba see Córdoba
Corentyne River see Courantyne River
Corfu see Kérkyra
106 J9 Coria Extremadura, W Spain 39.58N 6.31W
106 J14 Coria del Río Andalucía, S Spain 37.18N 6.04W
191 S8 Coricudgy, Mount ▲ New South Wales, SE Australia 32.49S 150.28E
109 N20 Corigliano Calabro Calabria, SW Italy 39.35N 16.30E
Corinium/Corinium Dobunorum see Cirencester
25 N1 Corinth Mississippi, S USA 34.56N 88.29W
Corinth see Kórinthos
Corinth Canal see Dióryga Korinthou
Corinth, Gulf of/Corinthiacus Sinus see Korinthiakós Kólpos
Corinthus see Kórinthos
44 I9 Corinto Chinandega, NW Nicaragua 12.28N 87.10W
99 C21 Cork Ir. Corcaigh. S Ireland 51.54N 7.06W
99 C21 Cork Ir. Corcaigh. cultural region SW Ireland
99 C21 Cork ✕ SW Ireland 51.52N 8.25W
99 D21 Cork Harbour Ir. Cuan Chorcaí. inlet SW Ireland
109 I23 Corleone Sicilia, Italy, C Mediterranean Sea 37.49N 13.18E
116 N13 Çorlu Tekirdağ, NW Turkey 41.10N 27.48E
116 N12 Çorlu Çayı ~ NW Turkey
Cormaiore see Courmayeur
9 V13 Cormorant Manitoba, C Canada 54.12N 100.33W
25 T2 Cornelia Georgia, SE USA 34.30N 83.31W
62 J10 Cornélio Procópio Paraná, S Brazil 23.07S 50.40W
57 V9 Corneliskondre Sipaliwini, N Surinam 5.21N 56.10W
32 J5 Cornell Wisconsin, N USA 45.09N 91.10W
11 S12 Corner Brook Newfoundland and Labrador, E Canada 48.58N 57.58W
Corner Rise Seamounts see Corner Seamounts
66 I9 Corner Seamounts var. Corner Rise Seamounts. undersea feature NW Atlantic Ocean
118 M9 Corneşti Rus. Korneshty. C Moldova 47.23N 28.00E
Corneto see Tarquinia
Cornhusker State see Nebraska
29 X8 Corning Arkansas, C USA 36.25N 90.35W
37 N5 Corning California, W USA 39.54N 122.12W
31 U15 Corning Iowa, C USA 40.58N 94.46W
20 G11 Corning New York, NE USA 42.08N 77.03W
Corn Islands see Maíz, Islas del
109 J14 Corno Grande ▲ C Italy 42.26N 13.29E
13 N13 Cornwall Ontario, SE Canada 45.01N 74.45W
99 H25 Cornwall cultural region SW England, UK
99 G25 Cornwall, Cape headland SW England, UK 50.11N 5.39W
56 J4 Coro prev. Santa Ana de Coro. Falcón, NW Venezuela 11.27N 69.40W
59 J18 Corocoro La Paz, W Bolivia 17.10S 68.28W
59 K17 Coroico La Paz, W Bolivia 16.09S 67.41W
192 M5 Coromandel Waikato, North Island, NZ 36.47S 175.30E
161 K20 Coromandel Coast coast E India
192 M5 Coromandel Peninsula peninsula North Island, NZ
192 M6 Coromandel Range ▲▲ North Island, NZ
179 P12 Coron Busuanga Island, W Philippines 12.02N 120.10E
37 T15 Corona California, W USA 33.52N 117.34W
39 T12 Corona New Mexico, SW USA 34.15N 105.36W
9 U17 Coronach Saskatchewan, S Canada 49.07N 105.33W
37 U17 Coronado California, W USA 32.41N 117.10W
45 N15 Coronado, Bahía de bay S Costa Rica
9 R15 Coronation Alberta, SW Canada 52.06N 111.25W
15 I4 Coronation Gulf gulf Nunavut, N Canada
204 I1 Coronation Island island Antarctica
41 X14 Coronation Island island Alexander Archipelago, Alaska, USA
63 B18 Coronda Santa Fe, C Argentina 31.58S 60.55W
65 F14 Coronel Bío Bío, C Chile 37.01S 73.07W
63 D20 Coronel Brandsen var. Brandsen. Buenos Aires, E Argentina 35.07S 58.15W
64 K4 Coronel Cornejo Salta, N Argentina 22.46S 63.49W
63 B24 Coronel Dorrego Buenos Aires, E Argentina 38.38S 61.15W
64 P6 Coronel Oviedo Caaguazú, SE Paraguay 25.30S 56.27W
63 B23 Coronel Pringles Buenos Aires, E Argentina 37.58S 61.26W
63 B23 Coronel Suárez Buenos Aires, E Argentina 37.27S 61.57W
63 E22 Coronel Vidal Buenos Aires, E Argentina 37.28S 57.45W
57 V9 Coronie ❖ district NW Surinam
59 G17 Coropuna, Nevado ▲ S Peru 15.31S 72.31W
Çorovoda see Çorovodë
115 L22 Çorovodë var. Çorovoda. Berat, S Albania 40.29N 20.15E
191 P11 Corowa New South Wales, SE Australia 36.01S 146.22E
44 G1 Corozal Corozal, N Belize 18.22N 88.22W
56 E6 Corozal Sucre, NW Colombia 9.18N 75.19W
44 G1 Corozal ❖ district N Belize
27 T14 Corpus Christi Texas, SW USA 27.48N 97.24W
27 T14 Corpus Christi Bay inlet Texas, SW USA
27 R14 Corpus Christi, Lake ▣ Texas, SW USA
65 F16 Corral Los Lagos, C Chile 39.55S 73.30W
107 O9 Corral de Almaguer Castilla-La Mancha, C Spain 39.45N 3.10W
106 K6 Corrales Castilla-León, N Spain 41.22N 5.43W
39 R11 Corrales New Mexico, SW USA 35.11N 106.37W
Corrán Tuathail see Carrauntoohil
108 F9 Correggio Emilia-Romagna, C Italy 44.47N 10.46E
179 P11 Corregidor Island island NW Philippines
61 M16 Corrente Piauí, E Brazil 10.28S 45.10W
61 I19 Correntes, Rio ~ SW Brazil
105 N12 Corrèze ❖ department C France
99 C17 Corrib, Lough Ir. Loch Coirib. ◎ W Ireland
63 C14 Corrientes Corrientes, NE Argentina 27.28S 58.42W
63 D15 Corrientes off. Provincia de Corrientes. ❖ province NE Argentina
46 A5 Corrientes, Cabo headland W Cuba 21.48N 84.30W
42 I13 Corrientes, Cabo headland SW Mexico 20.25N 105.42W
Corrientes, Provincia de see Corrientes
63 C16 Corrientes, Río ~ NE Argentina
58 E8 Corrientes, Río ~ Ecuador/Peru
27 W9 Corrigan Texas, SW USA 31.00N 94.49W
57 U9 Corriverton E Guyana 5.55N 57.09W
Corriza see Korçë
191 Q11 Corryong Victoria, SE Australia 36.14S 147.54E

◆ Country
● Country Capital
◇ Dependent Territory
○ Dependent Territory Capital
❖ Administrative Region
✕ International Airport
▲ Mountain
▲▲ Mountain Range
▲ Volcano
~ River
◎ Lake
▣ Reservoir

CUNJAMBA – DARTMOOR

85 E15 Cunjamba Cuando Cubango, E Angola 15.22S 20.07E
189 V10 Cunnamulla Queensland, E Australia 28.09S 145.43E
Čunusavvon see Junosuando
Cuokkarašša see Čohkarášša
108 B7 Cuorgne Piemonte, NE Italy 45.23N 7.34E
98 K11 Cupar E Scotland, UK 56.19N 3.01W
118 L8 Cupcina Rus. Kupchino; prev. Calinisc, Kalinisk. N Moldova 48.07N 27.22E
56 C8 Cupica Chocó, W Colombia 6.43N 77.31W
56 C8 Cupica, Golfo de gulf W Colombia
114 N13 Ćuprija Serbia, E Serbia 43.57N 21.21E
Cura see Villa de Cura
47 P16 Curaçao island Netherlands Antilles
58 H13 Curanja, Río ≈ E Peru
58 F7 Curaray, Río ≈ Ecuador/Peru
118 K14 Curcani Călărași, SE Romania 44.04N 26.39E
190 H4 Curdimurka South Australia 29.27S 136.56E
105 P7 Cure ≈ C France
181 Y16 Curepipe C Mauritius 20.19S 57.31E
57 R6 Curiapo Delta Amacuro, NE Venezuela 10.03N 63.05W
Curia Rhaetorum see Chur
64 G12 Curicó Maule, C Chile 35.00S 71.15W
Curieta see Krk
180 I15 Curieuse island Inner Islands, NE Seychelles
61 C16 Curitiba Acre, W Brazil 10.08S 69.00W
62 K12 Curitiba prev. Curytiba. state capital Paraná, S Brazil 25.25S 49.25W
62 J13 Curitibanos Santa Catarina, S Brazil 27.18S 50.34W
191 S6 Curlewis New South Wales, SE Australia 31.09S 150.18E
190 J6 Curnamona South Australia 31.39S 139.35E
85 A15 Curoca ≈ SW Angola
191 T6 Currabubula New South Wales, SE Australia 31.17S 150.43E
61 Q14 Currais Novos Rio Grande do Norte, E Brazil 6.12S 36.30W
37 W7 Currant Nevada, W USA 38.43N 115.27W
37 W6 Currant Mountain ▲ Nevada, W USA 38.56N 115.19W
46 H2 Current Eleuthera Island, C Bahamas 25.24N 76.44W
29 W8 Current River ≈ Arkansas/Missouri, C USA
190 M14 Currie Tasmania, SE Australia 39.59S 143.51E
23 Y8 Currituck North Carolina, SE USA 36.27N 76.02W
23 Y8 Currituck Sound sound North Carolina, SE USA
41 R11 Curry Alaska, USA 62.36N 150.00W
Curtbunar see Tervel
118 I13 Curtea de Argeș var. Curtea-de-Arges. Argeș, S Romania 45.06N 24.40E
118 E10 Curtici Ger. Kurtitsch, Hung. Kürtös. Arad, W Romania 46.21N 21.17E
30 M16 Curtis Nebraska, C USA 40.36N 100.27W
106 H2 Curtis-Estación Galicia, NW Spain 43.09N 8.10W
191 O14 Curtis Group island group Tasmania, SE Australia
189 Y8 Curtis Island island Queensland, SE Australia
60 K11 Curuá, Ilha do island NE Brazil
49 U7 Curuá, Rio ≈ N Brazil
61 A14 Curuçá, Rio ≈ NW Brazil
114 L9 Čurug Hung. Csurog. Serbia, N Serbia 45.30N 20.02E
63 D16 Curuzú Cuatiá Corrientes, NE Argentina 29.45S 58.01W
61 M19 Curvelo Minas Gerais, SE Brazil 18.45S 44.27W
20 E14 Curwensville Pennsylvania, NE USA 40.57N 78.29W
32 M3 Curwood, Mount ▲ Michigan, N USA 46.42N 88.14W
Curytiba see Curitiba
Curzola see Korčula
44 A10 Cuscatlán ◐ department C El Salvador
59 H15 Cusco var. Cuzco. Cusco, C Peru 13.34S 72.01W
59 H15 Cusco off. Departamento de Cusco; var. Cuzco. ◐ department C Peru
29 O9 Cushing Oklahoma, C USA 36.01N 96.46W
27 W8 Cushing Texas, SW USA 31.48N 94.50W
42 I6 Cusihuiriachic Chihuahua, N Mexico 28.16N 106.46W
105 P10 Cusset Allier, C France 46.07N 3.27E
25 S6 Cusseta Georgia, SE USA 32.18N 84.46W
30 J10 Custer South Dakota, N USA 43.46N 103.36W
Cüstrin see Kostrzyn
35 Q7 Cut Bank Montana, NW USA 48.37N 112.19W
Cutch, Gulf of see Kachchh, Gulf of
25 S6 Cuthbert Georgia, SE USA 31.46N 84.47W
9 S15 Cut Knife Saskatchewan, S Canada 52.40N 108.54W
25 Y16 Cutler Ridge Florida, SE USA 25.34N 80.21W
24 K10 Cut Off Louisiana, S USA 29.32N 90.20W
65 I15 Cutral-Có Neuquén, C Argentina 38.55S 69.13W
109 O21 Cutro Calabria, SW Italy 39.01N 16.59E
191 O4 Cuttaburra Channels seasonal river New South Wales, SE Australia
160 O12 Cuttack Orissa, E India 20.28N 85.52E
85 C15 Cuvelai Cunene, SW Angola 15.40S 15.48E
81 G18 Cuvette var. Région de la Cuvette. ◐ province C Congo
181 V9 Cuvier Basin undersea feature E Indian Ocean
181 U9 Cuvier Plateau undersea feature E Indian Ocean
84 B12 Cuvo ≈ W Angola
102 H9 Cuxhaven Niedersachsen, NW Germany 53.51N 8.42E
Cuyabá see Cuiabá
179 Pp13 Cuyo East Pass passage C Philippines
179 P13 Cuyo West Pass passage C Philippines
Cuyuni, Río see Cuyuni River
57 S8 Cuyuni River var. Río Cuyuni. ≈ Guyana/Venezuela
Cuzco see Cusco
99 K22 Cwmbran Wel. Cwmbrân. SW Wales, UK 51.39N 3.00W
30 K15 C.W.McConaughy, Lake ⊡ Nebraska, C USA
83 D20 Cyangugu SW Rwanda 2.27S 29.00E
112 D11 Cybinka Ger. Ziebingen. Lubuskie, W Poland 52.11N 14.46E
Cyclades see Kykládes
Cydonia see Chaniá
Cymru see Wales
22 M5 Cynthiana Kentucky, S USA 38.23N 84.17W
9 S17 Cypress Hills ▲▲ Alberta/Saskatchewan, SW Canada
Cypro-Syrian Basin see Cyprus Basin
123 Mm1 Cyprus off. Republic of Cyprus, Gk. Kypros, Turk. Kıbrıs, Kıbrıs Cumhuriyeti. ◆ republic E Mediterranean Sea
86 L14 Cyprus Gk. Kypros, Turk. Kıbrıs. island E Mediterranean Sea
123 Gg10 Cyprus Basin var. Cypro-Syrian Basin. undersea feature E Mediterranean Sea
Cythera see Kýthira
Cythnos see Kýthnos
112 F9 Czaplinek Ger. Tempelburg. Zachodnio-pomorskie, NW Poland 53.33N 16.14E
Czarna Woda see Wda
112 G8 Czarne Pomorskie, N Poland 53.40N 17.00E
112 G10 Czarnków Wielkopolskie, C Poland 52.52N 16.31E
113 E17 Czech Republic Cz. Česká Republika. ◆ republic C Europe
Czegléd see Cegléd
112 G12 Czempiń Wielkolpolskie, C Poland 52.10N 16.46E
Czenstochau see Częstochowa
Czerkow see Čerchov
Czernowitz see Chernivtsi
112 I8 Czersk Pomorskie, N Poland 53.48N 17.58E
113 J15 Częstochowa Ger. Czenstochau, Tschenstochau, Rus. Chenstokhov. Śląskie, S Poland 50.51N 19.09E
112 F10 Człopa Ger. Schloppe. Zachodnio-pomorskie, NW Poland 53.04N 16.04E
112 H8 Człuchów Ger. Schlochau. Pomorskie, NW Poland 53.40N 17.19E

D

169 V9 Da'an var. Dalai. Jilin, NE China 45.28N 124.18E
13 S10 Daaquam Québec, SE Canada 46.36N 70.03W
Daawo, Webi see Dawa Wenz
56 I4 Dabajuro Falcón, NW Venezuela 11.00N 70.41W
79 N15 Dabakala NE Ivory Coast 8.19N 4.24W
169 S11 Daban var. Bairin Youqi. Nei Mongol Zizhiqu, N China 43.33N 118.40E
113 K23 Dabas Pest, C Hungary 47.13N 19.18E
166 L8 Daba Shan ▲▲ C China
Dabba see Daocheng
146 J5 Dabbāgh, Jabal ▲ NW Saudi Arabia 27.52N 35.48E
56 D8 Dabeiba Antioquia, NW Colombia 6.57N 76.13W
160 E11 Dabhoi Gujarāt, W India 22.07N 73.28E
167 P8 Dabie Shan ▲▲ C China
78 J13 Dabola C Guinea 10.48N 11.01W
79 N17 Dabou S Ivory Coast 5.19N 4.22W
168 M15 Dabqig var. Uxin Qi. Nei Mongol Zizhiqu, N China 38.29N 108.48E
112 P8 Dąbrowa Białostocka Podlaskie, NE Poland 53.38N 23.18E
113 M16 Dąbrowa Tarnowska Małopolskie, S Poland 50.10N 21.00E
121 M20 Dabryn' Rus. Dobryn'. Homyel'skaya Voblasts', SE Belarus 51.46N 29.12E
165 P10 Dabsan Hu ◎ C China
167 Q13 Dabu var. Huliao. Guangdong, S China 24.19N 116.07E
118 H15 Dăbuleni Dolj, SW Romania 43.47N 24.05E
Dacca see Dhaka
103 L23 Dachau Bayern, SE Germany 48.16N 11.25E
Dachuan see Dazhou
Dacia Bank see Dacia Seamount
66 M10 Dacia Seamount var. Dacia Bank. undersea feature E Atlantic Ocean 31.10N 13.42W
39 T3 Dacono Colorado, C USA 40.04N 104.56W
Đắc Tô see Đak Tô
Dacura see Dákura
25 W12 Dade City Florida, SE USA 28.21N 82.12W
158 L10 Ḍaḍeldhurā var. Dandeldhura. Far Western, W Nepal 29.12N 80.31E
25 Q5 Dadeville Alabama, S USA 32.49N 85.45W
Dadong see Donggang
105 N15 Dadou ≈ S France
160 D12 Dādra and Nagar Haveli ◐ union territory W India
155 P14 Dādu Sind, SE Pakistan 26.42N 67.48E
178 K11 Đa Du Boloc Kon Tum, C Vietnam 14.06N 107.40E
166 G9 Dadu He ≈ C China
Daegu see Taegu
Daerah Istimewa Aceh see Aceh
179 Q11 Daet Luzon, N Philippines 14.06N 122.57E
166 I11 Dafang Guizhou, S China 27.07N 105.40E
Dafeng see Shanglin
159 W11 Dafla Hills ▲▲ NE India
9 U15 Dafoe Saskatchewan, S Canada 51.46N 104.11W
78 G10 Dagana N Senegal 16.28N 15.35W
Dagana see Dahana, Tajikistan
Dagana see Massakory, Chad
Dagcagoin see Zoigê
120 K11 Dagda Krāslava, SE Latvia 56.06N 27.36E
Dagden see Hiiumaa
Dagden-Sund see Soela Väin
131 P16 Dagestan, Respublika prev. Dagestanskaya ASSR, Eng. Daghestan. ◐ autonomous republic SW Russian Federation
Dagestanskaya ASSR see Dagestan, Respublika
131 R17 Dagestanskiye Ogni Respublika Dagestan, SW Russian Federation 42.09N 48.08E
193 A23 Dagg Sound sound South Island, NZ
Daghestan see Dagestan, Respublika
147 Y8 Daghmar NE Oman 23.09N 59.01E
Dağlıq Qarabağ see Nagorno-Karabakh
Dagö see Hiiumaa
56 D11 Dagua Valle del Cauca, W Colombia 3.37N 76.42W
166 H11 Daguan var. Cuihua. Yunnan, SW China 27.42N 103.51E
179 P9 Dagupan off. Dagupan City. Luzon, N Philippines 16.04N 120.21E
165 N16 Dagzê var. Dêqên. Xizang Zizhiqu, W China 29.38N 91.15E
153 Q13 Dahana Rus. Dagana, Dakhana. SW Tajikistan 38.03N 69.51E
169 V10 Dahei Shan ▲▲ N China
169 T7 Da Hinggan Ling Eng. Great Khingan Range. ▲▲ NE China
Dahlac Archipelago see Dahlak Archipelago
82 K9 Dahlak Archipelago var. Dahlac Archipelago. island group E Eritrea
25 T2 Dahlonega Georgia, SE USA 34.31N 83.59W
103 O14 Dahme Brandenburg, E Germany 52.10N 13.47E
102 O13 Dahme ≈ E Germany
147 O14 Dahm, Ramlat desert NW Yemen
160 E10 Dāhod prev. Dohad. Gujarāt, W India 22.48N 74.18E
Dahomey see Benin
164 G10 Dahongliutan Xinjiang Uygur Zizhiqu, NW China 35.59N 79.12E
Dahra see Dara
145 R2 Dahūk var. Dohuk, Kurd. Dihōk. N Iraq 36.52N 43.01E
118 J15 Daia Giurgiu, S Romania 44.00N 25.59E
171 L15 Daigo Ibaraki, Honshū, S Japan 36.43N 140.22E
169 O13 Dai Hai ◎ N China
Daihoku see T'aipei
195 X14 Dai Island island N Solomon Islands
155 O6 Dāikondī ◐ province C Afghanistan
177 G8 Daik-u Pegu, SW Burma 17.46N 96.40E
144 H9 Dā'īl Dar'ā, S Syria 32.45N 36.07E
178 Kk12 Đai Lanh Khanh Hoa, S Vietnam 12.49N 109.20E
167 Q13 Daimao Shan ▲▲ SE China
107 N11 Daimiel Castilla-La Mancha, C Spain 39.04N 3.37W
117 F22 Daimoniá Pelopónnisos, S Greece 36.38N 22.54E
Dainan see T'ainan
27 W6 Daingerfield Texas, SW USA 33.01N 94.43W
Daingin, Bá an see Dingle Bay
165 R13 Dainkognubma Xizang Zizhiqu, W China 32.25N 97.58E
171 Hh17 Daiō-zaki headland Honshū, SW Japan 34.15N 136.50E
Dairbhre see Valencia Island
63 B22 Daireaux Buenos Aires, E Argentina 36.36S 61.42W
Dairen see Dalian
77 W9 Dairûţ var. Dayrūţ. C Egypt 27.31N 30.46E
170 Ff12 Dai-sen ▲ Kyūshū, SW Japan 35.22N 133.33E
27 X10 Daisetta Texas, SW USA 30.06N 94.38W
199 Gg5 Daitō-jima island group SW Japan
199 Gg5 Daitō Ridge undersea feature N Philippine Sea
167 N3 Daixian var. Dai Xian. Shanxi, C China 39.07N 112.54E
Daiyue see Shanyin
167 Q12 Daiyun Shan ▲▲ SE China
46 M8 Dajabón NW Dominican Republic 19.29N 71.40W
166 G8 Dajin Chuan ≈ C China
154 J6 Dāk ◎ W Afghanistan
78 F11 Dakar ● (Senegal) W Senegal 14.43N 17.27W
78 F11 Dakar ✕ W Senegal 14.42N 17.27W
178 K11 Đak Glây Kon Tum, C Vietnam 15.05N 107.42E
Dakhana see Dahana
159 U16 Dakhin Shahbazpur Island island S Bangladesh
Dakhla see Ad Dakhla
78 F7 Dakhlet Nouâdhibou ◐ region NW Mauritania
Đak Lap see Kiến Đức
Đak Nông see Gia Nghia
79 U11 Dakoro Maradi, S Niger 14.28N 6.45E
31 U12 Dakota City Iowa, C USA 42.42N 94.13W
31 R13 Dakota City Nebraska, C USA 42.25N 96.25W
115 M17 Đakovica var. Djakovica, Alb. Gjakovë. Serbia, S Serbia 42.22N 20.30E
114 I10 Đakovo var. Djakovo, Hung. Diakovár. Osijek-Baranja, E Croatia 45.18N 18.24E
Dakshin see Deccan
178 K11 Đak Tô var. Đắc Tô. Kon Tum, C Vietnam 14.35N 107.55E
45 N7 Dákura var. Dacura. Región Autónoma Atlántico Norte, NE Nicaragua 14.22N 83.13W
97 I14 Dal Akershus, S Norway 60.19N 11.16E
84 E12 Dala Lunda Sul, E Angola 11.03S 20.12E
110 J8 Dalaas Vorarlberg, W Austria 47.08N 10.03E
78 I13 Dalaba W Guinea 10.46N 12.12W
Dalai see Da'an
168 I12 Dalain Hob var. Ejin Qi. Nei Mongol Zizhiqu, N China 41.59N 101.04E
Dalai Nor see Hulun Nur
169 Q11 Dalai Nur salt lake N China
Dala-Jarna see Järna
97 M14 Dalälven ≈ C Sweden
142 C16 Dalaman Muğla, SW Turkey 36.46N 28.46E
142 C16 Dalaman ✕ Muğla, SW Turkey 36.37N 28.51E
142 D16 Dalaman Çayı ≈ SW Turkey
168 K11 Dalandzadgad Ömnögovĭ, S Mongolia 43.35N 104.23E
97 D17 Dalane physical region S Norway
201 Z2 Dalap-Uliga-Djarrit var. Delap-Uliga-Darrit, D-U-D. island group Ratak Chain, SE Marshall Islands
96 J12 Dalarna prev. Kopparberg ◐ county C Sweden
96 L13 Dalarna prev. Eng. Dalecarlia. cultural region C Sweden
97 P16 Dalarö Stockholm, C Sweden 59.07N 18.25E
178 Kk13 Đa Lat Lâm Đồng, S Vietnam 11.55N 108.25E
Dalay see Bayandalay
154 L12 Dālbandīn var. Dāl Bandin. Baluchistān, SW Pakistan 28.48N 64.08E
97 J17 Dalbosjön lake bay S Sweden
189 Y10 Dalby Queensland, E Australia 27.14S 151.16E
96 D13 Dale Hordaland, S Norway 60.34N 5.48E
96 C12 Dale Sogn og Fjordane, S Norway 61.22N 5.24E
34 K12 Dale Oregon, NW USA 44.58N 118.56W
27 T11 Dale Texas, SW USA 29.56N 97.34W
Dalecarlia see Dalarna
23 W4 Dale City Virginia, NE USA 38.38N 77.18W
22 L8 Dale Hollow Lake ⊡ Kentucky/Tennessee, S USA
100 O8 Dalen Drenthe, NE Netherlands 52.42N 6.45E
97 E15 Dalen Telemark, S Norway 59.25N 7.58E
177 F4 Daletme Chin State, W Burma 21.44N 92.48E
25 Q7 Daleville Alabama, S USA 31.18N 85.42W
100 M9 Dalfsen Overijssel, E Netherlands 52.31N 6.16E
26 M1 Dalhart Texas, SW USA 36.04N 102.31W
11 O13 Dalhousie New Brunswick, SE Canada 48.03N 66.22W
158 I6 Dalhousie Himāchal Pradesh, N India 32.31N 76.01E
166 F12 Dali var. Xiaguan. Yunnan, SW China 25.33N 100.10E
Dali see Idálion
169 U14 Dalian var. Dairen, Dalien, Lüda, Ta-lien, Rus. Dalny. Liaoning, NE China 38.53N 121.36E
107 O15 Dalías Andalucía, S Spain 36.49N 2.50W
Dalien see Dalian
Dalijan see Delījān
114 J9 Dalj Hung. Dalja. Osijek-Baranja, E Croatia 45.29N 19.00E
Dalja see Dalj
34 F12 Dallas Oregon, NW USA 44.55N 123.19W
27 U6 Dallas Texas, SW USA 32.46N 96.48W
27 T7 Dallas-Fort Worth ✕ Texas, SW USA 32.37N 97.16W
160 K12 Dalli Rājhara Chhattīsgarh, C India 20.33N 81.06E
41 X15 Dall Island island Alexander Archipelago, Alaska, USA
40 M12 Dall Lake ◎ Alaska, USA
Dállogilli see Korpilombolo
79 S12 Dallol Bosso seasonal river W Niger
147 U7 Dalmā island W UAE
115 E14 Dalmacija Eng. Dalmatia, Ger. Dalmatien, It. Dalmazia. cultural region S Croatia
Dalmatia/Dalmatien/Dalmazia see Dalmacija
127 Nn17 Dal'negorsk Primorskiy Kray, SE Russian Federation 44.27N 135.30E
127 Nn17 Dal'nerechensk Primorskiy Kray, SE Russian Federation 45.57N 133.42E
Dalny see Dalian
78 M16 Daloa C Ivory Coast 6.52N 6.28W
166 J11 Dalou Shan ▲▲ S China
189 X7 Dalrymple Lake ◎ Queensland, E Australia
12 H14 Dalrymple Lake ◎ Ontario, S Canada
189 X7 Dalrymple, Mount ▲ Queensland, E Australia 21.01S 148.34E
95 K20 Dalsbruk Fin. Taalintehdas. Länsi-Suomi, W Finland 60.01N 22.33E
97 K19 Dalsjöfors Västra Götaland, S Sweden 57.43N 13.04E
97 J17 Dals Långed var. Långed. Västra Götaland, S Sweden 58.54N 12.20E
159 O15 Dāltenganj prev. Daltonganj. Jhārkhand, N India 23.59N 84.07E
25 R2 Dalton Georgia, SE USA 34.46N 84.58W
Daltonganj see Dāltenganj
205 X14 Dalton Iceberg Tongue ice feature Antarctica
Dálvvadis see Jokkmokk
94 J1 Dalvík Nordhurland Eystra, N Iceland 65.58N 18.31W
37 N8 Daly City California, W USA 37.44N 122.27W
189 P2 Daly River ≈ Northern Territory, N Australia
189 Q3 Daly Waters Northern Territory, N Australia 16.21S 133.21E
121 F20 Damachava var. Damachova, Pol. Domaczewo, Rus. Domachëvo. Brestskaya Voblasts', SW Belarus 51.45N 23.36E
Damachova see Damachava
79 W11 Damagaram Takaya Zinder, S Niger 14.02N 9.28E
160 D12 Damān Damān and Diu, W India 20.25N 72.58E
160 B12 Damān and Diu ◐ union territory W India
77 V7 Damanhûr anc. Hermopolis Parva. N Egypt 31.02N 30.34E
Damão see Damān
167 O1 Damaqun Shan ▲▲ E China
81 I15 Damara Ombella-Mpoko, S Central African Republic 5.00N 18.45E
85 D18 Damaraland physical region C Namibia
175 T15 Damar, Kepulauan var. Baraf Daja Islands, Kepulauan Barat Daya. island group C Indonesia
174 Gg4 Damar Laut Perak, Peninsular Malaysia 4.13N 100.36E
175 Tt15 Damar, Pulau island Maluku, E Indonesia
Damas see Dimashq
79 Y12 Damasak Borno, NE Nigeria 13.10N 12.40E
Damasco see Dimashq
23 Q8 Damascus Virginia, NE USA 36.37N 81.46W
Damascus see Dimashq
79 X13 Damaturu Yobe, NE Nigeria 11.44N 11.58E
175 Ss4 Damau Pulau Kaburuang, N Indonesia 3.46N 126.49E
149 O5 Damāvand, Qolleh-ye ▲ N Iran 35.59N 52.06E
84 B10 Damba Uíge, NW Angola 6.42S 15.07E
116 M12 Dambaslar Tekirdağ, NW Turkey 41.13N 27.13E
118 J13 Dâmbovița prev. Dîmbovița. ◐ county SE Romania
118 J13 Dâmbovița prev. Dîmbovița. ≈ S Romania
181 Y15 D'Ambre, Île island NE Mauritius
161 K24 Dambulla Central Province, C Sri Lanka 7.51N 80.40E
46 K9 Dame-Marie SW Haiti 18.31N 74.24W
46 J9 Dame Marie, Cap headland SW Haiti 18.37N 74.24W
149 Q4 Dāmghān Semnān, N Iran 36.13N 54.22E
Damietta see Dumyāt
144 G10 Dāmiyā Al Balqā', NW Jordan 32.07N 35.33E
152 G11 Damla Daşoguz Welaýaty, N Turkmenistan 40.05N 59.15E
Dammām see Ad Dammān
102 G12 Damme Niedersachsen, NW Germany 52.31N 8.12E
159 R15 Dāmodar ≈ NE India
160 J9 Damoh Madhya Pradesh, C India 23.52N 79.24E
79 P15 Damongo NW Ghana 9.06N 1.46W
144 G7 Damoûr var. Ad Dāmūr. W Lebanon 33.36N 35.30E
175 Pp7 Dampal, Teluk bay Sulawesi, C Indonesia
188 H7 Dampier Western Australia 20.40S 116.40E
188 H6 Dampier Archipelago island group Western Australia
176 Uu9 Dampier, Selat strait Papua, E Indonesia
194 L12 Dampier Strait strait NE PNG
147 U14 Damqawt var. Damqut. E Yemen 16.35N 52.39E
165 O13 Dam Qu ≈ C China
Damqut see Damqawt
178 Ii13 Dâmrei, Chuŏr Phmun Fr. Chaîne de l'Éléphant. ▲▲ SW Cambodia
110 C7 Damvant Jura, NW Switzerland 47.22N 6.55E
Damwâld see Damwoude
100 L5 Damwoude Fris. Damwâld. Friesland, N Netherlands 53.18N 5.59E
165 N15 Damxung var. Gongtang. Xizang Zizhiqu, W China 30.28N 91.01E
82 K11 Danakil Desert var. Afar Depression, Danakil Plain. desert E Africa
Danakil Plain see Danakil Desert
37 R8 Dana, Mount ▲ California, W USA 37.54N 119.13W
78 L16 Danané W Ivory Coast 7.16N 8.09W
178 Kk10 Đa Năng prev. Tourane. Quang Nam-Đa Năng, C Vietnam 16.04N 108.13E
179 Qq13 Danao var. Danao City. Cebu, C Philippines 10.34N 124.00E
166 G9 Danba var. Zhanggu, Tib. Rongzhag. Sichuan, C China 30.54N 101.49E
Danborg see Daneborg
20 L13 Danbury Connecticut, NE USA 41.21N 73.27W
27 W12 Danbury Texas, SW USA 29.13N 95.20W
37 X15 Danby Lake ◎ California, W USA
204 H4 Danco Coast physical region Antarctica
84 B11 Dande ≈ NW Angola
Dandeldhura see Ḍaḍeldhurā
161 E17 Dandeli Karnātaka, W India 15.18N 74.42E
191 O12 Dandenong Victoria, SE Australia 38.01S 145.13E
169 V13 Dandong var. Tan-tung; prev. An-tung. Liaoning, NE China 40.09N 124.23E
207 Q14 Daneborg var. Danborg. Tunu, N Greenland 74.34N 19.51W
27 V12 Danevang Texas, SW USA 29.03N 96.11W
Dänew see Galkynyş
Danfeng see Shizong
12 L12 Danford Lake Québec, SE Canada 45.55N 76.12W
21 T4 Danforth Maine, NE USA 45.39N 67.54W
39 P3 Danforth Hills ▲▲ Colorado, C USA
Dangara see Danghara
165 V12 Dangchang Gansu, C China 34.01N 104.19E
165 P8 Dangchengwan var. Subei, Subei Mongolzu Zizhixian. Gansu, N China 39.33N 94.50E
84 B10 Dange Uíge, NW Angola 7.55S 15.01E
Dangerous Archipelago see Tuamotu, Îles
85 E26 Danger Point headland SW South Africa 34.37S 19.20E
153 Q13 Danghara Rus. Dangara. SW Tajikistan 38.04N 69.14E
165 P8 Danghe Nanshan ▲▲ W China
82 I12 Dangila var. Dänglā. Amhara, NW Ethiopia 11.08N 36.51E
165 P8 Dangjin Shankou pass N China 39.22N 94.19E
Dangla see Tanggula Shan, China
Dang La see Tanggula Shankou, China
Dänglā see Dangila, Ethiopia
Dangme Chu see Manās
159 Y11 Dāngori Assam, NE India 27.40N 95.34E
Dang Raek, Phanom/Dangrek, Chaîne des see Dângrêk, Chuŏr Phnum
178 Ii11 Dângrêk, Chuŏr Phnum var. Phanom Dang Raek, Phanom Dong Rak, Fr. Chaîne des Dangrek. ▲▲ Cambodia/Thailand
44 G3 Dangriga prev. Stann Creek. Stann Creek, E Belize 16.58N 88.13W
167 P6 Dangshan Anhui, E China 34.28N 116.24E
35 T15 Daniel Wyoming, C USA 42.49N 110.04W
85 H22 Daniëlskuil Northern Cape, N South Africa 28.07S 23.35E
21 N12 Danielson Connecticut, NE USA 41.48N 71.53W
128 M15 Danilov Yaroslavskaya Oblast', W Russian Federation 58.11N 40.11E
131 O9 Danilovka Volgogradskaya Oblast', SW Russian Federation 50.21N 44.03E
Danish West Indies see Virgin Islands (US)
166 L7 Dan Jiang ≈ C China
166 M7 Danjiangkou Shuiku ⊡ C China
147 W8 Ḍank var. Dhank. NW Oman 23.34N 56.16E
158 J7 Dankhar Himāchal Pradesh, N India 32.07N 78.12E
130 L6 Dankov Lipetskaya Oblast', W Russian Federation 53.17N 39.07E
44 J7 Danlí El Paraíso, S Honduras 14.02N 86.34W
Danmark see Denmark
Danmarksstraedet see Denmark Strait
97 O14 Dannemora Uppsala, C Sweden 60.13N 17.49E
20 L6 Dannemora New York, NE USA 44.42N 73.42W
102 K11 Dannenberg Niedersachsen, N Germany 53.05N 11.06E
192 N12 Dannevirke Manawatu-Wanganui, North Island, NZ 40.13S 176.04E
23 U8 Dan River ≈ Virginia, NE USA
178 Hh9 Dan Sai Loei, C Thailand 17.15N 101.04E
20 F10 Dansville New York, NE USA 42.34N 77.40W
Dantzig see Gdańsk
88 E12 Danube Bul. Dunav, Cz. Dunaj, Ger. Donau, Hung. Duna, Rom. Dunărea. ≈ C Europe
Danubian Plain see Dunavska Ravnina
177 Ff8 Danubyu Irrawaddy, SW Burma 17.15N 95.34E
Danum see Doncaster
21 P11 Danvers Massachusetts, NE USA 42.34N 70.54W
29 T11 Danville Arkansas, C USA 35.03N 93.23W
33 N13 Danville Illinois, N USA 40.10N 87.37W
33 O14 Danville Indiana, N USA 39.45N 86.31W
31 Y15 Danville Iowa, C USA 40.52N 91.18W
22 M6 Danville Kentucky, S USA 37.39N 84.46W
20 G14 Danville Pennsylvania, NE USA 40.57N 76.36W
23 T6 Danville Virginia, NE USA 36.35N 79.24W
Danxian/Dan Xian see Danzhou
166 L17 Danzhou prev. Danxian, Dan Xian, Nada. Hainan, S China 19.31N 109.31E
Danzhou see Yichuan
Danzig see Gdańsk
Danziger Bucht see Danzig, Gulf of
112 J6 Danzig, Gulf of var. Gulf of Gdańsk, Ger. Danziger Bucht, Pol. Zakota Gdańska, Rus. Gdan'skaya Bukhta. gulf N Poland
166 F10 Daocheng var. Jinzhu, Tib. Dabba. Sichuan, C China 29.05N 100.14E
Daojiang see Daoxian
Daokou see Huaxian
106 H7 Dão, Rio ≈ N Portugal
Daosa see Dausa
79 Y7 Dao Timmi Agadez, NE Niger 20.31N 13.34E
166 M13 Daoxian var. Daojiang. Hunan, S China 25.30N 111.37E
79 Q14 Dapaong N Togo 10.52N 0.12E
25 N8 Daphne Alabama, S USA 30.36N 87.54W
179 Qq15 Dapitan Mindanao, S Philippines 8.39N 123.25E
165 Q10 Da Qaidam Qinghai, C China 37.49N 95.18E
169 V8 Daqing var. Sartu. Heilongjiang, NE China 46.29N 125.07E
169 O13 Daqing Shan ▲▲ N China
169 T11 Daqin Tal var. Naiman Qi. Nei Mongol Zizhiqu, N China 42.51N 120.41E
Daqm see Duqm
166 G8 Da Qu var. Do Qu. ≈ C China
145 T5 Dāqūq var. Tāwūq. N Iraq 35.07N 44.27E
78 G10 Dara var. Dahra. NW Senegal 15.20N 15.28W
144 H9 Dar'ā var. Der'a, Fr. Déraa. Dar'ā, SW Syria 32.37N 36.06E
144 H8 Dar'ā off. Muḥāfaẓat Dar'ā, var. Darā, Derá, Derrá. ◐ governorate S Syria
149 Q12 Dārāb Fārs, S Iran 28.52N 54.25E
118 K8 Darabani Botoşani, NW Romania 48.10N 26.40E
Daraj see Dirj
148 M8 Dārān Eşfahān, W Iran 33.02N 50.27E
178 Kk12 Đa Răng, Sông var. Ba. ≈ S Vietnam
126 Kk16 Darasun Chitinskaya Oblast', S Russian Federation 51.36N 113.58E
Daraut-Kurgan see Daroot-Korgon
79 W13 Darazo Bauchi, E Nigeria 11.01N 10.27E
145 S3 Darband N Iraq 36.15N 44.17E
145 V4 Darband-i Khān, Sadd dam NE Iraq 35.07N 45.42E
145 N1 Darbāsīyah var. Derbisīye. Al Ḥasakah, N Syria 37.06N 40.42E
120 C11 Darbėnai Klaipėda, NW Lithuania 56.02N 21.16E
159 Q13 Darbhanga Bihār, N India 26.10N 85.54E
40 M9 Darby, Cape headland Alaska, USA 64.19N 162.46W
114 I9 Darda Hung. Dárda. Osijek-Baranja, E Croatia 45.37N 18.41E
29 T11 Dardanelle Arkansas, C USA 35.13N 93.09W
29 S11 Dardanelle, Lake ⊡ Arkansas, C USA
Dardanelles see Çanakkale Boğazı
Dardanelli see Çanakkale
Dardo see Kangding
Dar-el-Beida see Casablanca
142 M14 Darende Malatya, C Turkey 38.33N 37.31E
83 J22 Dar es Salaam Dar es Salaam, E Tanzania 6.51S 39.18E
83 J22 Dar es Salaam ✕ Pwani, E Tanzania 6.57S 39.17E
193 H18 Darfield Canterbury, South Island, NZ 43.28S 172.07E
108 F7 Darfo Lombardia, N Italy 45.54N 10.12E
82 B10 Darfur var. Darfur Massif. cultural region W Sudan
Darfur Massif see Darfur
Darganata/Dargan-Ata see Birata
149 T3 Dargaz var. Darreh Gaz; prev. Moḥammadābād. Khorāsān-Razavī, NE Iran 37.28N 59.08E
145 U4 Dargazayn NE Iraq 35.39N 45.00E
191 P12 Dargo Victoria, SE Australia 37.29S 147.15E
168 L6 Darhan Darhan Uul, N Mongolia 49.24N 105.57E
169 N8 Darhan Hentiy, C Mongolia 46.38N 109.25E
Darhan see Büreghangay
Darhan Muminggan Lianheqi see Bailingmiao
168 L6 Darhan Uul ◐ province N Mongolia
25 W7 Darien Georgia, SE USA 31.22N 81.25W
45 W16 Darién off. Provincia del Darién. ◐ province SE Panama
Darién, Golfo del see Darien, Gulf of
45 X14 Darien, Gulf of Sp. Golfo del Darién. gulf S Caribbean Sea
Darien, Isthmus of see Panamá, Istmo de
44 K9 Dariense, Cordillera ▲▲ C Nicaragua
45 W15 Darién, Serranía del ▲▲ Colombia/Panama
169 P10 Dariganga var. Ovoot. Sühbaatar, SE Mongolia 45.08N 113.51E
Dario see Ciudad Darío
Dariorigum see Vannes
Dariv see Darvi
Darj see Dirj
Darjeeling see Darjiling
159 S12 Darjiling prev. Darjeeling. West Bengal, NE India 27.00N 88.13E
Darkehnen see Ozersk
165 S12 Darlag var. Gümai. Qinghai, C China 33.43N 99.42E
191 T3 Darling Downs hill range Queensland, E Australia
30 M2 Darling, Lake ⊡ North Dakota, N USA
188 I12 Darling Range ▲▲ Western Australia
190 L8 Darling River ≈ New South Wales, SE Australia
99 M15 Darlington N England, UK 54.31N 1.34W
23 T12 Darlington South Carolina, SE USA 34.18N 79.52W
32 K9 Darlington Wisconsin, N USA 42.40N 90.07W
112 G7 Darłowo Zachodnio-pomorskie, NW Poland 54.24N 16.21E
103 G19 Darmstadt Hessen, SW Germany 49.52N 8.39E
77 S7 Darnah var. Dérna. NE Libya 32.46N 22.39E
105 S6 Darney Vosges, NE France 48.06N 5.58E
190 M7 Darnick New South Wales, SE Australia 32.52S 143.38E
205 Y6 Darnley, Cape headland Antarctica 67.36S 70.04E
107 R7 Daroca Aragón, NE Spain 41.07N 1.25W
153 S11 Daroot-Korgon var. Daraut-Kurgan. Oshskaya Oblast', SW Kyrgyzstan 39.34N 72.13E
63 A23 Darragueira var. Darregueira. Buenos Aires, E Argentina 37.40S 63.12W
Darregueira see Darragueira
Darreh Gaz see Dargaz
148 K7 Darreh Shahr var. Darreh-ye Shahr. Īlām, W Iran 33.10N 47.18E
Darreh-ye Shahr see Darreh Shahr
34 I7 Darrington Washington, NW USA 48.15N 121.36W
27 P1 Darrouzett Texas, SW USA 36.27N 100.19W
159 S15 Darsana var. Darshana. Khulna, N Bangladesh 23.31N 88.49E
Darshana see Darsana
102 M7 Darss peninsula NE Germany
102 M7 Darsser Ort headland NE Germany 54.28N 12.31E
99 J24 Dart ≈ SW England, UK
Dartang see Baqên
99 P22 Dartford SE England, UK 51.27N 0.13E
190 L12 Dartmoor Victoria, SE Australia 37.56S 141.18E

◆ Country ● Country Capital ◇ Dependent Territory ○ Dependent Territory Capital ◐ Administrative Region ✕ International Airport ▲ Mountain ▲▲ Mountain Range ⩯ Volcano ≈ River ◎ Lake ⊡ Reservoir

Dartmoor – Derudeb

99 I24 **Dartmoor** moorland SW England, UK
11 Q15 **Dartmouth** Nova Scotia, SE Canada 44.40N 63.34W
99 J24 **Dartmouth** SW England, UK 50.20N 3.34W
13 Y6 **Dartmouth** ≈ Québec, SE Canada
191 Q11 **Dartmouth Reservoir** ◎ Victoria, SE Australia
Dartuch, Cabo see Artrutx, Cap d'
194 G15 **Daru** Western, SW PNG 9.04S 143.12E
114 G9 **Daruvar** *Hung.* Daruvár. Bjelovar-Bilogora, NE Croatia 45.34N 17.12E
Darvaza see Darvoza, Uzbekistan
Darvaza see Derweze, Turkmenistan
Darvazskiy Khrebet see Darvoz, Qatorkŭhi
168 F8 **Darvi** *var.* Dariv. Govĭ-Altay, W Mongolia 46.20N 94.11E
168 F7 **Darvi** *var.* Bulgan. Hovd, W Mongolia 46.57N 93.40E
154 L9 **Darvīshān** *var.* Darweshan, Garmser. Helmand, S Afghanistan 31.01N 64.12E
153 R13 **Darvoz, Qatorkŭhi** *Rus.* Darvazskiy Khrebet. ▲▲ C Tajikistan
153 O10 **Darvoza** *Rus.* Darvaza. Jizzax Viloyati, C Uzbekistan 40.59N 67.19E
Darweshan see Darvīshān
65 J15 **Darwin** Río Negro, S Argentina 39.13S 65.41W
189 O1 **Darwin** *prev.* Palmerston, Port Darwin. territory capital Northern Territory, N Australia 12.27S 130.52E
67 D24 **Darwin** *var.* Darwin Settlement. East Falkland, Falkland Islands 51.51S 58.55W
64 H8 **Darwin, Cordillera** ▲▲ N Chile
59 B17 **Darwin, Volcán** ⛰ Galapagos Islands, Ecuador, E Pacific Ocean 0.12S 91.17W
155 S8 **Darya Khān** Punjab, E Pakistan 31.48N 71.05E
151 O15 **Dar'yalyktakyr, Ravnina** plain S Kazakhstan
149 T11 **Dārzīn** Kermān, S Iran 29.10N 58.09E
Dashennongjia see Shennong Ding
Dashhowuz see Daşoguz
Dashhowuz Welayaty see Daşoguz Welaýaty
168 K7 **Dashinchilen** *var.* Süüj. Bulgan, C Mongolia 47.49N 104.06E
121 O16 **Dashkawka** *Rus.* Dashkovka. Mahilyowskaya Voblasts', E Belarus 53.42N 30.17E
Dashkhovuz see Daşoguz/Daşoguz Welaýaty
Dashkhovuzskiy Velayat see Daşoguz Welaýaty
Dashköpri see Daşköpri
Dashkovka see Dashkawka
154 J15 **Dasht** ≈ SW Pakistan
Dashtidzhum see Dashtijum
153 R13 **Dashtijum** *Rus.* Dashtidzhum. SW Tajikistan 38.06N 70.11E
155 W7 **Daska** Punjab, NE Pakistan 32.21N 74.20E
152 J16 **Daşköpri** *var.* Dashköpri, *Rus.* Tashkepri. Mary Welaýaty, S Turkmenistan 36.15N 62.37E
152 H8 **Daşoguz** *Rus.* Dashkhovuz, *Turkm.* Dashhowuz; *prev.* Tashauz. Daşoguz Welaýaty, N Turkmenistan 41.51N 59.52E
152 E9 **Daşoguz Welaýaty** *var.* Dashhowuz Welayaty, *Rus.* Dashkhovuz, Dashkhovuzskiy Velayat. ◈ province N Turkmenistan
Đa, Sông see Black River
79 R15 **Dassa** *var.* Dassa-Zoumé. S Benin 7.46N 2.15E
Dassa-Zoumé see Dassa
31 U8 **Dassel** Minnesota, N USA 45.06N 94.18W
158 H3 **Dastegil Sar** *var.* Disteghil Sār. ▲ N India
142 C16 **Datça** Muğla, SW Turkey 36.46N 27.40E
172 Nn6 **Date** Hokkaidō, NE Japan 42.28N 140.51E
160 I8 **Datia** *prev.* Duttia. Madhya Pradesh, C India 25.40N 78.28E
Dåtnejaevrie see Tunnsjøen
165 T10 **Datong** *var.* Qiaotou. Qinghai, C China 37.01N 101.33E
167 N2 **Datong** *var.* Tatung, Ta-t'ung. Shanxi, C China 40.09N 113.16E
Datong see Tong'an
165 S9 **Datong He** ≈ C China
165 S9 **Datong Shan** ▲▲ C China
174 Kk6 **Datu, Tanjung** headland Indonesia/Malaysia 2.01N 109.37E
Daua see Dawa Wenz
180 H16 **Dauban, Mount** ▲ Silhouette, NE Seychelles
155 T7 **Dāūd Khel** Punjab, E Pakistan 32.52N 71.34E
121 G15 **Daugai** Alytus, S Lithuania 54.22N 24.20E
Daugava see Western Dvina
120 J11 **Daugavpils** *Ger.* Dünaburg; *prev. Rus.* Dvinsk. municipality Daugvapils, SE Latvia 55.53N 26.33E
Dauka see Dawkah
Daulatabad see Malāyer
103 D18 **Daun** Rheinland-Pfalz, W Germany 50.13N 6.50E
161 E14 **Daund** *prev.* Dhond. Mahārāshtra, W India 18.28N 74.37E
178 Gg12 **Daung Kyun** island S Burma
9 W15 **Dauphin** Manitoba, S Canada 51.09N 100.04W
105 S13 **Dauphiné** cultural region E France
25 N9 **Dauphin Island** island Alabama, S USA
9 X15 **Dauphin River** Manitoba, S Canada 51.55N 98.03W
79 V12 **Daura** Katsina, N Nigeria 13.03N 8.18E
158 H12 **Dausa** *prev.* Daosa. Rājasthān, N India 26.54N 76.18E
Dauwa see Dawwah
143 Y10 **Däväçi** *Rus.* Divichi. NE Azerbaijan 41.15N 48.58E
161 F18 **Dāvangere** Karnātaka, W India 14.30N 75.52E
179 Rr16 **Davao** *off.* Davao City. Mindanao, S Philippines 7.06N 125.35E
179 Rr16 **Davao Gulf** gulf Mindanao, S Philippines
13 Q11 **Daveluyville** Québec, SE Canada 46.12N 72.07W
31 Z14 **Davenport** Iowa, C USA 41.31N 90.34W
34 L8 **Davenport** Washington, NW USA 47.39N 118.09W
45 P16 **David** Chiriquí, W Panama 8.25N 82.25W
13 O11 **David** ≈ Québec, SE Canada
31 R15 **David City** Nebraska, C USA 41.15N 97.07W
David-Gorodok see Davyd-Haradok
9 T16 **Davidson** Saskatchewan, S Canada 51.15N 105.58W
23 R10 **Davidson** North Carolina, SE USA 35.29N 80.49W
28 K12 **Davidson** Oklahoma, C USA 34.15N 99.06W
41 S6 **Davidson Mountains** ▲▲ Alaska, USA
180 M8 **Davie Ridge** undersea feature W Indian Ocean
190 A1 **Davies, Mount** ▲ South Australia 26.14S 129.14E
37 O7 **Davis** California, W USA 38.31N 121.46W
29 N12 **Davis** Oklahoma, C USA 34.30N 97.07W
205 Y7 **Davis** Australian research station Antarctica 68.30S 78.15E
204 H3 **Davis Coast** physical region Antarctica
20 C16 **Davis, Mount** ▲ Pennsylvania, NE USA 39.47N 79.10W
26 K9 **Davis Mountains** ▲▲ Texas, SW USA
205 Z9 **Davis Sea** sea Antarctica
67 O20 **Davis Seamounts** undersea feature S Atlantic Ocean
206 M13 **Davis Strait** strait Baffin Bay/Labrador Sea
131 U5 **Davlekanovo** Respublika Bashkortostan, W Russian Federation 54.13N 55.06E
110 J9 **Davos** *Rmsch.* Tavau. Graubünden, E Switzerland 46.48N 9.50E
121 J20 **Davyd-Haradok** *Pol.* Dawidgródek, *Rus.* David-Gorodok. Brestskaya Voblasts', SW Belarus 52.03N 27.13E
169 U12 **Dawa** Liaoning, NE China 40.55N 122.02E
147 O11 **Dawāsir, Wādī ad** dry watercourse S Saudi Arabia
83 K15 **Dawa Wenz** *var.* Daua, Webi Daawo. ≈ E Africa
Dawaymah, Birkat ad see Umm al Baqar, Hawr
Dawei see Tavoy
121 K14 **Dawhinava** *Rus.* Dolginovo. Minskaya Voblasts', N Belarus 54.39N 27.28E
Dawidgródek see Davyd-Haradok
147 V12 **Dawkah** *var.* Dauka. SW Oman 18.32N 54.03E
Dawlat Qaṭar see Qatar
26 M3 **Dawn** Texas, SW USA 34.54N 102.10W
Dawo see Maqên
146 M11 **Daws** Al Bāḩah, SW Saudi Arabia 20.19N 41.12E
8 H5 **Dawson** *var.* Dawson City. Yukon Territory, NW Canada 64.04N 139.24W
25 S6 **Dawson** Georgia, SE USA 31.46N 84.27W
31 S9 **Dawson** Minnesota, N USA 44.55N 96.03W
Dawson City see Dawson
9 N13 **Dawson Creek** British Columbia, W Canada 55.48N 120.18W
8 H7 **Dawson Range** ▲▲ Yukon Territory, W Canada
189 Y9 **Dawson River** ≈ Queensland, E Australia
8 J15 **Dawsons Landing** British Columbia, SW Canada 51.33N 127.38W
22 I7 **Dawson Springs** Kentucky, S USA 37.10N 87.41W
25 S2 **Dawsonville** Georgia, SE USA 34.28N 84.07W
166 G8 **Dawu** *var.* Xianshui. Sichuan, C China 30.55N 101.08E
Dawu see Maqên
Dawukou see Shizuishan
147 Y10 **Dawwah** *var.* Dauwa. W Oman 20.36N 58.52E
104 J15 **Dax** *var.* Ax; *anc.* Aquae Augustae, Aquae Tarbelicae. Landes, SW France 43.43N 1.03W
Daxian see Dazhou
Daxue see Wencheng
166 G9 **Daxue Shan** ▲▲ C China
Dayan see Lijiang
166 G12 **Dayao** *var.* Jinbi. Yunnan, SW China 25.41N 101.23E
Dayishan see Gaoyou
191 N12 **Daylesford** Victoria, SE Australia 37.24S 144.07E
37 U10 **Daylight Pass** pass California, W USA 36.44N 116.55W
63 D17 **Daymán, Río** ≈ N Uruguay
Dayr see Ad Dayr
144 G10 **Dayr 'Allā** *var.* Deir 'Alla. Al Balqā', N Jordan 32.39N 36.06E
145 N4 **Dayr az Zawr** *var.* Deir ez Zor. Dayr az Zawr, E Syria 35.12N 40.12E
144 M5 **Dayr az Zawr** *off.* Muḩāfaẓat Dayr az Zawr, *var.* Dayr Az-Zor. ◈ governorate E Syria
Dayr Az-Zor see Dayr az Zawr
Dayrūṭ see Dairûṭ
9 Q15 **Daysland** Alberta, SW Canada 52.53N 112.19W
33 R14 **Dayton** Ohio, N USA 39.45N 84.11W
22 L10 **Dayton** Tennessee, S USA 35.30N 85.01W
27 W11 **Dayton** Texas, SW USA 30.03N 94.53W
34 L10 **Dayton** Washington, NW USA 46.19N 117.58W
25 X10 **Daytona Beach** Florida, SE USA 29.12N 81.03W
175 N10 **Dayu** Borneo, C Indonesia 1.58S 115.04E
167 O13 **Dayu Ling** ▲▲ S China
167 R7 **Da Yunhe** *Eng.* Grand Canal. canal E China
167 S11 **Dayu Shan** island SE China
166 K8 **Dazhou** *prev.* Dachuan, Daxian. Sichuan, C China 31.16N 107.31E
166 J9 **Dazhu** *var.* Zhuyang. Sichuan, C China 30.45N 107.10E
166 J9 **Dazu** *var.* Longgang. Chongqing Shi, C China 29.48N 105.46E
85 H24 **De Aar** Northern Cape, C South Africa 30.40S 24.01E
204 K5 **Deacon, Cape** headland Antarctica
41 R5 **Deadhorse** Alaska, USA 70.15N 148.28W
35 T12 **Dead Indian Peak** ▲ Wyoming, C USA 44.36N 109.45W
25 R9 **Dead Lake** ◎ Florida, SE USA
46 J4 **Deadman's Cay** Long Island, C Bahamas 23.09N 75.06W
144 G11 **Dead Sea** *var.* Bahret Lut, Lacus Asphaltites, *Ar.* Al Baḩr al Mayyit, Baḩrat Lūṭ, *Heb.* Yam HaMelaḥ. salt lake Israel/Jordan
30 J9 **Deadwood** South Dakota, N USA 44.22N 103.43W
99 Q22 **Deal** SE England, UK 51.14N 1.22E
85 I22 **Dealesville** Free State, C South Africa 28.40S 25.46E
167 P10 **De'an** *var.* Puting. Jiangxi, S China 29.24N 115.46E
64 K9 **Deán Funes** Córdoba, C Argentina 30.25S 64.22W
204 L12 **Dean Island** island Antarctica
Deanuvuotna see Tanafjorden
33 S10 **Dearborn** Michigan, N USA 42.16N 83.13W
29 R3 **Dearborn** Missouri, C USA 39.31N 94.46W
Deargget see Tärendö
34 K9 **Deary** Idaho, NW USA 46.46N 118.33W
34 M9 **Deary** Washington, NW USA 46.42N 116.36W
8 J10 **Dease** ≈ British Columbia, W Canada
8 J10 **Dease Lake** British Columbia, W Canada 58.28N 130.04W
37 U11 **Death Valley** California, W USA 36.25N 116.50W
37 U11 **Death Valley** valley California, W USA
94 M8 **Deatnu** *Fin.* Tenojoki, *Nor.* Tana. ≈ Finland/Norway *see also* Tenojoki
104 L4 **Deauville** Calvados, N France 49.21N 0.06E
119 X7 **Debal'tseve** *Rus.* Debal'tsevo. Donets'ka Oblast', SE Ukraine 48.21N 38.25E
Debal'tsevo see Debal'tseve
115 M19 **Debar** *Ger.* Dibra, *Turk.* Debre. W FYR Macedonia 41.32N 20.33E
41 O9 **Debauch Mountain** ▲ Alaska, USA 64.31N 159.52W
De Behagle see Laï
27 X7 **De Berry** Texas, SW USA 32.18N 94.09W
131 T2 **Debessy** Udmurtskaya Respublika, NW Russian Federation 57.41N 53.56E
113 N16 **Dębica** Podkarpackie, SE Poland 50.03N 21.24E
De Bildt see De Bilt
100 J11 **De Bilt** *var.* De Bildt. Utrecht, C Netherlands 52.06N 5.10E
127 O9 **Debin** Magadanskaya Oblast', E Russian Federation 62.18N 150.42E
112 N13 **Dęblin** *Rus.* Ivangorod. Lubelskie, E Poland 51.34N 21.49E
112 D10 **Dębno** Zachodnio-pomorskie, NW Poland 52.44N 14.42E
41 S10 **Deborah, Mount** ▲ Alaska, USA 63.38N 147.13W
35 N8 **De Borgia** Montana, NW USA 47.23N 115.24W
Debra Birhan see Debre Birhan
Debra Marcos see Debre Mark'os
Debra Tabor see Debre Tabor
Debre see Debar
82 J13 **Debre Birhan** *var.* Debra Birhan. Amhara, N Ethiopia 9.45N 39.40E
113 N22 **Debrecen** *Ger.* Debreczin, *Rom.* Debreţin; *prev.* Debreczen. Hajdú-Bihar, E Hungary 47.31N 21.37E
Debreczen/Debreczin see Debrecen
82 I12 **Debre Mark'os** *var.* Debra Marcos. Amhara, N Ethiopia 10.18N 37.48E
115 N19 **Debrešte** SW FYR Macedonia 41.29N 21.20E
82 J11 **Debre Tabor** *var.* Debra Tabor. Amhara, N Ethiopia 11.46N 38.06E
Debreţin see Debrecen
82 J13 **Debre Zeyt** Oromo, C Ethiopia 8.41N 39.00E
115 L16 **Dečani** Serbia, S Serbia 42.33N 20.18E
25 P2 **Decatur** Alabama, S USA 34.36N 86.58W
25 S3 **Decatur** Georgia, SE USA 33.46N 84.18W
32 L13 **Decatur** Illinois, N USA 39.50N 88.57W
33 Q12 **Decatur** Indiana, N USA 40.48N 84.55W
24 M5 **Decatur** Mississippi, S USA 32.26N 89.06W
31 S14 **Decatur** Nebraska, C USA 42.00N 96.19W
27 S6 **Decatur** Texas, SW USA 33.14N 97.32W
22 H9 **Decaturville** Tennessee, S USA 35.34N 88.07W
105 O13 **Decazeville** Aveyron, S France 44.34N 2.18E
161 H17 **Deccan** *Hind.* Dakshin. plateau C India
12 J8 **Decelles, Réservoir** ▣ Québec, SE Canada
10 K2 **Déception** Québec, NE Canada 62.06N 74.36W
166 G11 **Dechang** *var.* Dezhou. Sichuan, C China 27.24N 102.09E
113 C15 **Děčín** *Ger.* Tetschen. Ústecký Kraj, NW Czech Republic 50.48N 14.15E
105 P9 **Decize** Nièvre, C France 46.51N 3.25E
100 I6 **De Cocksdorp** Noord-Holland, NW Netherlands 53.09N 4.52E
31 X11 **Decorah** Iowa, C USA 43.18N 91.47W
Dedeagaç/Dedeagach see Alexandroúpoli
196 C15 **Dededo** N Guam 13.30N 144.51E
100 N9 **Dedemsvaart** Overijssel, E Netherlands 52.36N 6.28E
21 O11 **Dedham** Massachusetts, NE USA 42.14N 71.10W
65 H19 **Dedo, Cerro** ▲ SW Argentina 44.46S 71.48W
79 O13 **Dédougou** W Burkina 12.25N 3.27W
128 G15 **Dedovichi** Pskovskaya Oblast', W Russian Federation 57.31N 29.53E
Dedu see Wudalianchi
161 J24 **Deduru Oya** ≈ W Sri Lanka
85 N14 **Dedza** Central, S Malawi 14.24S 34.15E
85 N14 **Dedza Mountain** ▲ C Malawi 14.22S 34.16E
99 J19 **Dee** *Wel.* Afon Dyfrdwy. ≈ England/Wales, UK
98 K9 **Dee** ≈ NE Scotland, UK
Deep Bay see Chilumba
23 T3 **Deep Creek Lake** ▣ Maryland, NE USA
38 J4 **Deep Creek Range** ▲▲ Utah, W USA
29 P10 **Deep Fork** ≈ Oklahoma, C USA
12 J11 **Deep River** Ontario, SE Canada 46.05N 77.28W
23 T10 **Deep River** ≈ North Carolina, SE USA
191 U4 **Deepwater** New South Wales, SE Australia 29.27S 151.52E
33 S14 **Deer Creek Lake** ◎ Ohio, N USA
25 Z15 **Deerfield Beach** Florida, SE USA 26.19N 80.06W
41 N8 **Deering** Alaska, USA 66.04N 162.43W
40 M16 **Deer Island** island Alaska, USA
21 S7 **Deer Isle** island Maine, NE USA
11 S11 **Deer Lake** Newfoundland and Labrador, SE Canada 49.10N 57.18W
101 D18 **Deerlijk** West-Vlaanderen, W Belgium 50.52N 3.21E
35 Q10 **Deer Lodge** Montana, NW USA 46.24N 112.43W
34 L8 **Deer Park** Washington, NW USA 47.55N 117.28W
31 U5 **Deer River** Minnesota, N USA 47.19N 93.47W
Deés see Dej
Defeng see Liping
33 R11 **Defiance** Ohio, N USA 41.16N 84.21W
25 Q8 **De Funiak Springs** Florida, SE USA 30.43N 86.07W
97 L23 **Degeberga** Skåne, S Sweden 55.48N 14.06E
106 H12 **Degebe, Ribeira** ≈ S Portugal
82 M13 **Degeh Bur** Somali, E Ethiopia 8.08N 43.35E
13 U9 **Dégelis** Québec, SE Canada 47.30N 68.38W
79 U17 **Degema** Rivers, S Nigeria 4.46N 6.47E
97 L16 **Degerfors** Örebro, C Sweden 59.13N 14.25E
200 N16 **De Gerlache Seamounts** undersea feature SE Pacific Ocean
103 N21 **Deggendorf** Bayern, SE Germany 48.49N 12.58E
124 Nn2 **Değirmenlik** *Gk.* Kythréa. N Cyprus 35.14N 33.28E
82 I11 **Degoma** Amhara, N Ethiopia 12.22N 37.36E
De Gordyk see Gorredijk
29 T12 **De Gray Lake** ▣ Arkansas, C USA
188 J6 **De Grey River** ≈ Western Australia
130 M10 **Degtevo** Rostovskaya Oblast', SW Russian Federation 49.12N 40.39E
149 X13 **Dehak** Sīstān va Balūchestān, SE Iran 27.10N 62.34E
149 R9 **Deh 'Alī** Kermān, C Iran 31.40N 56.10E
Dehbārez see Rūdān
149 P10 **Deh Bīd** Fārs, C Iran 30.37N 53.11E
148 M10 **Deh Dasht** Kohgīlūyeh va Būyer Aḩmad, SW Iran 30.49N 50.36E
77 N8 **Dehibat** SE Tunisia 31.58N 10.43E
Dehli see Delhi
148 K8 **Dehlorān** Īlām, W Iran 32.40N 47.18E
153 N13 **Dehqonobod** *Rus.* Dekhkanabad. Qashqadaryo Viloyati, S Uzbekistan 38.24N 66.31E
158 J9 **Dehra Dūn** Uttaranchal, N India 30.18N 78.03E
159 O14 **Dehri** Bihār, N India 24.55N 84.10E
154 K10 **Deh Shū** *var.* Deshu. Helmand, S Afghanistan 30.28N 63.21E
169 W9 **Dehui** Jilin, NE China 44.32N 125.42E
101 D17 **Deinze** Oost-Vlaanderen, NW Belgium 50.58N 3.31E
Deir 'Alla see Dayr 'Allā
Deir ez Zor see Dayr az Zawr
Deirgeirt, Loch see Derg, Lough
118 H9 **Dej** *Hung.* Dés; *prev.* Deés. Cluj, NW Romania 47.08N 23.55E
97 K15 **Deje** Värmland, C Sweden 59.34N 13.28E
176 Y14 **De Jongs, Tanjung** headland Papua, SE Indonesia 6.55S 138.31E
De Jouwer see Joure
32 M10 **De Kalb** Illinois, N USA 41.55N 88.45W
24 M5 **De Kalb** Mississippi, S USA 32.46N 88.39W
27 W5 **De Kalb** Texas, SW USA 33.30N 94.34W
Dekéleia see Dhekélia
81 K20 **Dekese** Kasai Occidental, C Dem. Rep. Congo 3.28S 21.24E
Dekhkanabad see Dehqonobod
81 I14 **Dékoa** Kémo, /C Central African Republic 6.17N 19.07E
100 H6 **De Koog** Noord-Holland, NW Netherlands 53.06N 4.43E
32 M9 **Delafield** Wisconsin, N USA 43.03N 88.22W
63 C23 **De La Garma** Buenos Aires, E Argentina 37.58S 60.25W
12 K10 **Delahey, Lac** ◎ Québec, SE Canada
82 E11 **Delami** Southern Kordofan, C Sudan 11.51N 30.30E
25 X11 **De Land** Florida, SE USA 29.01N 81.18W
37 R12 **Delano** California, W USA 35.46N 119.15W
31 V8 **Delano** Minnesota, N USA 45.03N 93.46W
38 K6 **Delano Peak** ▲ Utah, W USA 38.22N 112.21W
Delap-Uliga-Darrit see Dalap-Uliga-Djarrit
154 L7 **Delārām** Nīmrūz, SW Afghanistan 32.10N 63.27E
40 F17 **Delarof Islands** island group Aleutian Islands, Alaska, USA
32 M9 **Delavan** Wisconsin, N USA 42.37N 88.37W
33 S13 **Delaware** Ohio, N USA 40.18N 83.04W
20 I17 **Delaware** *off.* State of Delaware; also known as Blue Hen State, Diamond State, First State. ◈ state NE USA
20 I17 **Delaware Bay** bay NE USA
26 J8 **Delaware Mountains** ▲▲ Texas, SW USA
20 I12 **Delaware River** ≈ NE USA
29 Q3 **Delaware River** ≈ Kansas, C USA
20 J14 **Delaware Water Gap** valley New Jersey/Pennsylvania, NE USA
103 G14 **Delbrück** Nordrhein-Westfalen, W Germany 51.46N 8.34E
9 Q15 **Delburne** Alberta, SW Canada 52.09N 113.11W
180 M12 **Del Cano Rise** undersea feature SW Indian Ocean
115 Q18 **Delčevo** NE FYR Macedonia 41.57N 22.45E
Delcommune, Lac see Nzilo, Lac
100 O10 **Delden** Overijssel, E Netherlands 52.16N 6.40E
191 R12 **Delegate** New South Wales, SE Australia 37.04S 148.57E
De Lemmer see Lemmer
110 D7 **Delémont** *Ger.* Delsberg. Jura, NW Switzerland 47.22N 7.21E
27 R7 **De Leon** Texas, SW USA 32.06N 98.33W
117 F18 **Delfoí** Stereá Ellás, C Greece 38.28N 22.31E
100 G12 **Delft** Zuid-Holland, W Netherlands 52.01N 4.22E
161 J23 **Delft** island NW Sri Lanka
100 O5 **Delfzijl** Groningen, NE Netherlands 53.19N 6.55E
(0) E9 **Delgada Fan** undersea feature NE Pacific Ocean
44 F7 **Delgado** San Salvador, SW El Salvador 13.44N 89.07W
84 Q12 **Delgado, Cabo** headland N Mozambique 10.41S 40.40E
168 G8 **Delger** *var.* Taygan. Govĭ-Altay, C Mongolia 46.20N 97.22E
169 O9 **Delgereh** *var.* Hongor. Dornogovĭ, SE Mongolia 45.49N 111.20E
168 K8 **Delgerhaan** *var.* Hujirt. Töv, C Mongolia 46.41N 104.40E
168 K9 **Delgerhangay** *var.* Hashaat. Dundgovĭ, C Mongolia 45.09N 104.51E
168 L9 **Delgertsogt** *var.* Amardalay. Dundgovĭ, C Mongolia 46.09N 106.24E
82 E6 **Delgo** Northern, N Sudan 20.07N 30.34E
165 R10 **Delhi** *var.* Delingha. Qinghai, C China 37.19N 97.22E
158 I10 **Delhi** *var.* Dehli, *Hind.* Dilli; *hist.* Shahjahanabad. Delhi, N India 28.40N 77.11E
24 J5 **Delhi** Louisiana, S USA 32.28N 91.29W
20 J11 **Delhi** New York, NE USA 42.16N 74.55W
158 I10 **Delhi** ◈ union territory NW India
142 J17 **Deli Burnu** headland S Turkey 36.43N 34.55E
57 X10 **Délices** C French Guiana 4.46N 53.42W
142 J12 **Delice Çayı** ≈ C Turkey
42 J6 **Delicias** *var.* Ciudad Delicias. Chihuahua, N Mexico 28.08N 105.22W
149 N7 **Delījān** *var.* Dalijan, Dilijan. Markazī, W Iran 34.01N 50.39E
114 P12 **Deli Jovan** ▲▲ E Serbia
Déli-Kárpátok see Carpaţii Meridionali
15 H6 **Délįne** *prev.* Fort Franklin. Northwest Territories, NW Canada 65.10N 123.30W
Delingha see Delhi
13 Q7 **Delisle** Québec, SE Canada 48.39N 71.42W
9 T15 **Delisle** Saskatchewan, S Canada 51.54N 107.01W
103 M15 **Delitzsch** Sachsen, E Germany 51.31N 12.19E
35 Q12 **Dell** Montana, NW USA 44.41N 112.42W
26 I7 **Dell City** Texas, SW USA 31.56N 105.12W
105 U7 **Delle** Territoire-de-Belfort, E France 47.30N 7.00E
38 J9 **Dellenbaugh, Mount** ▲ Arizona, SW USA 36.06N 113.32W
31 R11 **Dell Rapids** South Dakota, N USA 43.50N 96.42W
23 Y4 **Delmar** Maryland, NE USA 38.26N 75.32W
20 K11 **Delmar** New York, NE USA 42.37N 73.49W
102 G11 **Delmenhorst** Niedersachsen, NW Germany 53.03N 8.37E
114 C9 **Delnice** Primorje-Gorski Kotar, NW Croatia 45.24N 14.49E
39 R7 **Del Norte** Colorado, C USA 37.40N 106.21W
41 N6 **De Long Mountains** ▲▲ Alaska, USA
191 P16 **Deloraine** Tasmania, SE Australia 41.34S 146.43E
9 W17 **Deloraine** Manitoba, S Canada 49.12N 100.28W
33 O12 **Delphi** Indiana, N USA 40.35N 86.40W
33 Q12 **Delphos** Ohio, N USA 40.49N 84.20W
25 Z15 **Delray Beach** Florida, SE USA 26.27N 80.04W
27 O12 **Del Rio** Texas, SW USA 29.22N 100.55W
Delsberg see Delémont
96 N11 **Delsbo** Gävleborg, C Sweden 61.49N 16.34E
39 P6 **Delta** Colorado, C USA 38.44N 108.04W
38 K5 **Delta** Utah, W USA 39.21N 112.34W
79 T17 **Delta** ◈ state S Nigeria
57 Q6 **Delta Amacuro** *off.* Territorio Delta Amacuro. ◈ federal district NE Venezuela
41 S9 **Delta Junction** Alaska, USA 64.02N 145.43W
25 X11 **Deltona** Florida, SE USA 28.54N 81.15W
191 T5 **Delungra** New South Wales, SE Australia 29.40S 150.49E
168 D6 **Delüün** *var.* Rashaant. Bayan-Ölgiy, W Mongolia 47.48N 90.45E
160 C12 **Delvāda** Gujarāt, W India 20.46N 71.01E
63 B21 **Del Valle** Buenos Aires, E Argentina 35.55S 60.42W
Delvina see Delvinë
117 C15 **Delvináki** *var.* Dhelvinákion; *prev.* Pogónion. Ípeiros, W Greece 39.56N 20.27E
115 L23 **Delvinë** *var.* Delvina, *It.* Delvino. Vlorë, S Albania 39.56N 20.07E
Delvino see Delvinë
118 I7 **Delyatyn** Ivano-Frankivs'ka Oblast', W Ukraine 48.32N 24.38E
131 U5 **Dëma** ≈ W Russian Federation
107 O5 **Demanda, Sierra de la** ▲▲ W Spain
41 T5 **Demarcation Point** headland Alaska, USA 69.40N 141.19W
81 K21 **Demba** Kasai Occidental, C Dem. Rep. Congo 5.24S 22.16E
180 H13 **Dembéni** Grande Comore, NW Comoros 11.49S 43.25E
81 M15 **Dembia** Mbomou, SE Central African Republic 5.08N 24.25E
Dembidollo see Dembī Dolo
82 H13 **Dembī Dolo** *var.* Dembidollo. Oromo, C Ethiopia 8.33N 34.49E
158 K6 **Demchok** *var.* Dêmqog. China/India *see also* Dêmqog 32.30N 79.42E
158 L6 **Demchok** *var.* Dêmqog. disputed region China/India *see also* Dêmqog
100 I12 **De Meern** Utrecht, C Netherlands 52.06N 5.00E
101 I17 **Demer** ≈ C Belgium
66 H12 **Demerara Plain** undersea feature W Atlantic Ocean
66 H12 **Demerara Plateau** undersea feature W Atlantic Ocean
57 T9 **Demerara River** ≈ NE Guyana
130 H3 **Demidov** Smolenskaya Oblast', W Russian Federation 55.15N 31.30E
39 Q15 **Deming** New Mexico, SW USA 32.13N 107.46W
34 H6 **Deming** Washington, NW USA 48.49N 122.13W
60 E10 **Demini, Rio** ≈ NW Brazil
142 D13 **Demirci** Manisa, W Turkey 39.03N 28.40E
115 P19 **Demir Kapija** *prev.* Železna Vrata. SE FYR Macedonia 41.25N 22.15E
116 N11 **Demirköy** Kırklareli, NW Turkey 41.49N 27.47E
102 N9 **Demmin** Mecklenburg-Vorpommern, NE Germany 53.53N 13.03E
25 O5 **Demopolis** Alabama, S USA 32.31N 87.50W
33 N11 **Demotte** Indiana, N USA 41.13N 87.07W
164 F13 **Dêmqog** *var.* Demchok. China/India 32.36N 79.28E *see also* Demchok
158 L6 **Dêmqog** *var.* Demchok. disputed region China/India *see also* Demchok
176 Yy10 **Demta** Papua, E Indonesia 2.19S 140.06E
125 G11 **Dem'yanka** ≈ C Russian Federation
128 H15 **Demyansk** Novgorodskaya Oblast', W Russian Federation 57.39N 32.31E
125 Ff11 **Dem'yanskoye** Tyumenskaya Oblast', C Russian Federation 59.39N 69.15E
105 P2 **Denain** Nord, N France 50.19N 3.24E
41 S10 **Denali** Alaska, USA 63.08N 147.33W
Denali see McKinley, Mount
83 M14 **Denan** Somali, E Ethiopia 6.40N 43.31E
Denau see Denov
99 J18 **Denbigh** *Wel.* Dinbych. NE Wales, UK 53.10N 3.25W
99 J18 **Denbigh** cultural region N Wales, UK
100 I6 **Den Burg** Noord-Holland, NW Netherlands 53.03N 4.46E
101 F18 **Dender** *Fr.* Dendre. ≈ W Belgium
101 F18 **Denderleeuw** Oost-Vlaanderen, NW Belgium 50.52N 4.04E
101 F17 **Dendermonde** *Fr.* Termonde. Oost-Vlaanderen, NW Belgium 51.01N 4.07E
Dendre see Dender
204 I9 **Dendtler Island** island Antarctica
100 P10 **Denekamp** Overijssel, E Netherlands 52.23N 7.00E
79 W12 **Dengas** Zinder, S Niger 13.15N 9.43E
Dêngkagoin see Têwo
168 L13 **Dengkou** *var.* Bayan Gol. Nei Mongol Zizhiqu, N China 40.15N 106.58E
165 Q14 **Dêngqên** *var.* Gyamotang. Xizang Zizhiqu, W China 31.28N 95.28E
Deng Xian see Dengzhou
166 M7 **Dengzhou** *prev.* Deng Xian. Henan, C China 32.43N 112.02E
Dengzhou see Penglai
Den Haag see 's-Gravenhage
100 N9 **Den Ham** Overijssel, E Netherlands 52.30N 6.30E
188 H10 **Denham** Western Australia 25.56S 113.35E
46 J12 **Denham, Mount** ▲ C Jamaica 18.13N 77.33W
24 J8 **Denham Springs** Louisiana, S USA 30.29N 90.57W
100 I7 **Den Helder** Noord-Holland, NW Netherlands 52.54N 4.45E
107 T11 **Dénia** País Valenciano, E Spain 38.51N 0.07E
201 Q8 **Denig** W Nauru
191 N10 **Deniliquin** New South Wales, SE Australia 35.33S 144.58E
31 T14 **Denison** Iowa, C USA 42.00N 95.22W
27 U5 **Denison** Texas, SW USA 33.45N 96.32W
150 L8 **Denisovka** *prev.* Ordzhonikidze. Kostanay, N Kazakhstan 52.24N 61.40E
142 D15 **Denizli** Denizli, SW Turkey 37.46N 29.04E
142 D15 **Denizli** ◈ province SW Turkey
Denjong see Sikkim
191 S7 **Denman** New South Wales, SE Australia 32.24S 150.43E
205 Y10 **Denman Glacier** glacier Antarctica
23 R14 **Denmark** South Carolina, SE USA 33.19N 81.08W
97 G23 **Denmark** *off.* Kingdom of Denmark, *Dan.* Danmark; *anc.* Hafnia. ◆ monarchy N Europe
94 H1 **Denmark Strait** *var.* Danmarksstraedet. strait Greenland/Iceland
47 T11 **Dennery** E Saint Lucia 13.55N 60.53W
100 I7 **Den Oever** Noord-Holland, NW Netherlands 52.56N 5.01E
153 O13 **Denov** *Rus.* Denau. Surkhondaryo Viloyati, S Uzbekistan 38.19N 67.48E
175 N16 **Denpasar** *prev.* Paloe. Bali, C Indonesia 8.40S 115.13E
118 E12 **Denta** Timiş, W Romania 45.18N 21.14E
23 Y3 **Denton** Maryland, NE USA 38.52N 75.49W
27 T6 **Denton** Texas, SW USA 33.10N 97.08W
195 O15 **D'Entrecasteaux Islands** island group SE PNG
39 T4 **Denver** state capital Colorado, C USA 39.44N 105.00W
18 K8 **Denver** ✈ Colorado, C USA 39.57N 104.38W
26 L6 **Denver City** Texas, SW USA 32.57N 102.49W
158 J9 **Deoband** Uttar Pradesh, N India 29.40N 77.40E
Deoghar see Devghar
160 E13 **Deolāli** Mahārāshtra, W India 19.55N 73.49E
160 I10 **Deori** Madhya Pradesh, C India 23.09N 78.39E
159 O12 **Deoria** Uttar Pradesh, N India 26.31N 83.48E
101 A17 **De Panne** West-Vlaanderen, W Belgium 51.06N 2.34E
56 M5 **Dependencia Federal** *off.* Territorio Dependencia Federal. ◈ federal dependency N Venezuela
Dependencia Federal, Territorio see Dependencia Federal
32 M7 **De Pere** Wisconsin, N USA 44.26N 88.03W
20 D10 **Depew** New York, NE USA 42.54N 78.41W
101 E17 **De Pinte** Oost-Vlaanderen, NW Belgium 51.00N 3.37E
27 V5 **Deport** Texas, SW USA 33.31N 95.19W
126 M7 **Deputatskiy** Respublika Sakha (Yakutiya), NE Russian Federation 69.18N 139.48E
Dêqên see Dagzê
29 S13 **De Queen** Arkansas, C USA 34.02N 94.20W
24 G8 **De Quincy** Louisiana, S USA 30.27N 93.25W
83 J20 **Dera** spring/well S Kenya 2.39S 39.52E
Der'a/Derá/Déraa see Dar'ā
155 S10 **Dera Ghāzi Khān** *var.* Dera Ghāzikhān. Punjab, C Pakistan 30.01N 70.37E
155 S8 **Dera Ismāīl Khān** North-West Frontier Province, C Pakistan 31.51N 70.55E
115 L16 **Đeravica** ▲ S Serbia 42.33N 20.08E
118 L6 **Derazhnya** Khmel'nyts'ka Oblast', W Ukraine 49.16N 27.24E
131 R17 **Derbent** Respublika Dagestan, SW Russian Federation 42.01N 48.16E
153 N13 **Derbent** Surkhondaryo Viloyati, S Uzbekistan 38.15N 66.59E
Derbisīye see Darbāsīyah
81 M15 **Derbissaka** Mbomou, SE Central African Republic 5.43N 24.48E
188 L4 **Derby** Western Australia 17.18S 123.36E
99 M19 **Derby** C England, UK 52.55N 1.30W
29 N7 **Derby** Kansas, C USA 37.33N 97.16W
99 L18 **Derbyshire** cultural region C England, UK
114 O11 **Đerdap** physical region E Serbia
Derelí see Gónnoi
168 L9 **Deren** *var.* Tsant. Dundgovĭ, C Mongolia 46.16N 106.55E
176 X11 **Derew** ≈ Papua, E Indonesia
131 R8 **Dergachi** Saratovskaya Oblast', W Russian Federation 51.15N 48.58E
Dergachi see Derhachi
99 C19 **Derg, Lough** *Ir.* Loch Deirgeirt. ◎ W Ireland
119 V5 **Derhachi** *Rus.* Dergachi. Kharkivs'ka Oblast', E Ukraine 50.08N 36.10E
24 G8 **De Ridder** Louisiana, S USA 30.51N 93.18W
143 P16 **Derik** Mardin, SE Turkey 37.22N 40.16E
85 E20 **Derm** Hardap, C Namibia 23.38S 18.12E
150 M14 **Dermentobe** *prev.* Dyurmen'tyube. Kzylorda, S Kazakhstan 45.46N 63.42E
29 W14 **Dermott** Arkansas, C USA 33.31N 91.26W
Dérna see Darnah
Dernberg, Cape see Dolphin Head
24 J11 **Dernieres, Isles** island group Louisiana, S USA
Dernis see Drniš
104 I4 **Déroute, Passage de la** strait Channel Islands/France
Derrá see Dar'ā
Derry see Londonderry
Dertona see Tortona
Dertosa see Tortosa
82 H8 **Derudeb** Red Sea, NE Sudan 17.28N 36.04E

◆ Country
● Country Capital
◇ Dependent Territory
○ Dependent Territory Capital
◈ Administrative Region
✈ International Airport
▲ Mountain
▲▲ Mountain Range
⛰ Volcano
≈ River
◎ Lake
▣ Reservoir

Derventa – Dnistrovs'kyy Lyman

114 H10 **Derventa** Republika Srpska, N Bosnia and Herzegovina 44.57N 17.55E
191 O16 **Derwent Bridge** Tasmania, SE Australia 42.10S 146.13E
191 O17 **Derwent, River** ≈ Tasmania, SE Australia
152 F10 **Derweze** *Rus.* Darvaza. Ahal Welaýaty, C Turkmenistan 40.10N 58.27E
Deržavinsk *see* Derzhavinsk
151 O9 **Derzhavinsk** *var.* Deržavinsk. Akmola, C Kazakhstan 51.04N 66.19E
Dés *see* Dej
59 J18 **Desaguadero** Puno, S Peru 16.31S 69.01W
59 J18 **Desaguadero, Río** ≈ Bolivia/Peru
203 W9 **Désappointement, Îles du** *island group* Îles Tuamotu, C French Polynesia
29 W11 **Des Arc** Arkansas, C USA 34.58N 91.30W
12 C10 **Desbarats** Ontario, S Canada 46.20N 83.52W
64 H13 **Descabezado Grande, Volcán** ☗ C Chile 35.34S 70.40W
42 B2 **Descanso** Baja California, NW Mexico 32.08N 116.51W
104 L9 **Descartes** Indre-et-Loire, C France 46.58N 0.40E
9 T13 **Deschambault Lake** ◎ Saskatchewan, C Canada
Deschnaer Koppe *see* Velká Deštná
34 I11 **Deschutes River** ≈ Oregon, NW USA
82 J12 **Desē** *var.* Desse, *It.* Dessie. Amhara, N Ethiopia 11.01N 39.39E
65 I20 **Deseado, Río** ≈ S Argentina
108 F8 **Desenzano del Garda** Lombardia, N Italy 45.28N 10.31E
38 K3 **Deseret Peak** ▲ Utah, W USA 40.27N 112.37W
66 P6 **Deserta Grande** *island* Madeira, Portugal, NE Atlantic Ocean
66 P6 **Desertas, Ilhas** *island group* Madeira, Portugal, NE Atlantic Ocean
37 X16 **Desert Center** California, W USA 33.42N 115.22W
37 V15 **Desert Hot Springs** California, W USA 33.57N 116.33W
12 K10 **Désert, Lac** ◎ Québec, SE Canada
38 J2 **Desert Peak** ▲ Utah, W USA 41.03N 113.22W
33 R11 **Deshler** Ohio, N USA 41.12N 83.55W
Deshu *see* Deh Shū
Desiderii Fanum *see* St-Dizier
108 D7 **Desio** Lombardia, N Italy 45.37N 9.12E
117 E15 **Deskáti** *var.* Dheskáti. Dytikí Makedonía, N Greece 39.55N 21.49E
30 L2 **Des Lacs River** ≈ North Dakota, N USA
29 X6 **Desloge** Missouri, C USA 37.52N 90.31W
9 Q12 **Desmarais** Alberta, W Canada 55.58N 113.55W
31 Q10 **De Smet** South Dakota, N USA 44.23N 97.33W
31 V14 **Des Moines** *state capital* Iowa, C USA 41.36N 93.36W
19 N8 **Des Moines River** ≈ C USA
119 P4 **Desna** ≈ Russian Federation/Ukraine
118 G14 **Desnățui** ≈ S Romania
65 F24 **Desolación, Isla** *island* S Chile
31 V14 **De Soto** Iowa, C USA 41.31N 94.00W
25 Q4 **De Soto Falls** *waterfall* Alabama, S USA 33.22N 86.12W
85 I25 **Despatch** Eastern Cape, S South Africa 33.48S 25.28E
107 N12 **Despeñaperros, Desfiladero de** *pass* S Spain 38.25N 3.26W
33 N10 **Des Plaines** Illinois, N USA 42.01N 87.52W
117 J21 **Despotikó** *island* Kykládes, Greece, Aegean Sea
114 N12 **Despotovac** Serbia, E Serbia 44.06N 21.25E
103 M14 **Dessau** Sachsen-Anhalt, E Germany 51.51N 12.15E
Desse *see* Desē
101 J16 **Dessel** Antwerpen, N Belgium 51.15N 5.07E
Dessie *see* Desē
Destêrro *see* Florianópolis
25 P9 **Destin** Florida, SE USA 30.23N 86.30W
Deštná *see* Velká Deštná
200 Oo11 **Desventurados, Islas de los** *island group* W Chile
105 N1 **Desvres** Pas-de-Calais, N France 50.41N 1.48E
118 E12 **Deta** *Ger.* Detta. Timiș, W Romania 45.22N 21.13E
103 H14 **Detmold** Nordrhein-Westfalen, W Germany 51.55N 8.52E
33 S10 **Detroit** Michigan, N USA 42.19N 83.03W
27 W5 **Detroit** Texas, SW USA 33.39N 95.16W
33 S10 **Detroit** ≈ Canada/USA
31 S6 **Detroit Lakes** Minnesota, N USA 46.49N 95.49W
33 S10 **Detroit Metropolitan** ✕ Michigan, N USA 42.12N 83.16W
Detta *see* Deta
178 J11 **Det Udom** Ubon Ratchathani, E Thailand 14.54N 105.03E
113 K20 **Detva** *Hung.* Gyeva. Banskobystrický Kraj, C Slovakia 48.34N 19.25E
160 G13 **Deūlgaon Rāja** Mahārāshtra, C India 20.04N 76.08E
101 L15 **Deurne** Noord-Brabant, SE Netherlands 51.28N 5.46E
101 H16 **Deurne** ✕ (Antwerpen) Antwerpen, N Belgium 51.10N 4.28E
Deutsch-Brod *see* Havlíčkův Brod
Deutschendorf *see* Poprad
Deutsch-Eylau *see* Iława
111 Y6 **Deutschkreutz** Burgenland, E Austria 47.36N 16.38E
Deutsch Krone *see* Wałcz
Deutschland/Deutschland, Bundesrepublik *see* Germany
111 V9 **Deutschlandsberg** Steiermark, SE Austria 46.52N 15.13E
Deutsch-Südwestafrika *see* Namibia
111 Y3 **Deutsch-Wagram** Niederösterreich, E Austria 48.19N 16.33E
Deux-Ponts *see* Zweibrücken
12 I11 **Deux Rivieres** Ontario, SE Canada 46.13N 78.16W
104 K9 **Deux-Sèvres** ⬖ *department* W France
118 G11 **Deva** *Ger.* Diemrich, *Hung.* Déva. Hunedoara, W Romania 45.55N 22.54E
Deva *see* Chester
Devana *see* Aberdeen
Devana Castra *see* Chester
Đevđelija *see* Gevgelija
142 L12 **Deveci Dağları** ▲▲ N Turkey
143 P15 **Devegeçidi Barajı** ▣ SE Turkey
142 K15 **Develi** Kayseri, C Turkey 38.22N 35.28E
100 M11 **Deventer** Overijssel, E Netherlands 52.15N 6.10E
13 O10 **Devenyns, Lac** ◎ Québec, SE Canada
98 K8 **Deveron** ≈ NE Scotland, UK
159 R14 **Devghar** *prev.* Deoghar. Jhārkhand, NE India
29 R10 **Devil's Den** *plateau* Arkansas, C USA
37 R7 **Devils Gate** *pass* California, W USA 38.20N 119.23W
32 J2 **Devils Island** *island* Apostle Islands, Wisconsin, N USA
Devil's Island *see* Diable, Île du
31 P3 **Devils Lake** North Dakota, N USA 48.07N 98.49W
33 R10 **Devils Lake** ◎ Michigan, N USA
31 O3 **Devils Lake** ◎ North Dakota, N USA
37 W13 **Devils Playground** *desert* California, W USA
27 O11 **Devils River** ≈ Texas, SW USA
35 Y12 **Devils Tower** ▲ Wyoming, C USA 44.33N 104.45W
116 I11 **Devin** *prev.* Dovlen. Smolyan, SW Bulgaria 41.45N 24.24E
27 R12 **Devine** Texas, SW USA 29.08N 98.54W
158 H13 **Devli** Rājasthān, N India 25.46N 75.22E
Devne *see* Devnya
116 N8 **Devnya** *prev.* Devne. Varna, E Bulgaria 43.13N 27.36E
33 U14 **Devola** Ohio, N USA 39.28N 81.28W
Devoll *see* Devollit, Lumi i
115 M21 **Devollit, Lumi i** *var.* Devoll. ≈ SE Albania
9 Q14 **Devon** Alberta, SW Canada 53.21N 113.47W
99 I23 **Devon** *cultural region* SW England, UK
207 N10 **Devon Island** *prev.* North Devon Island. *island* Parry Islands, Nunavut, NE Canada
191 O16 **Devonport** Tasmania, SE Australia 41.14S 146.20E
142 H11 **Devrek** Zonguldak, N Turkey 41.13N 31.57E
160 G10 **Dewās** Madhya Pradesh, C India 22.58N 76.03E
De Westerein *see* Zwaagwesteinde
29 P8 **Dewey** Oklahoma, C USA 36.48N 95.56W
Dewey *see* Culebra
100 M8 **De Wijk** Drenthe, NE Netherlands 52.41N 6.13E
29 W12 **De Witt** Arkansas, C USA 34.17N 91.20W
31 Z14 **De Witt** Iowa, C USA 41.49N 90.32W
31 R16 **De Witt** Nebraska, C USA 40.23N 96.55W
99 M17 **Dewsbury** N England, UK 53.42N 1.37W
167 Q10 **Dexing** Jiangxi, S China 28.49N 117.37E
29 Y8 **Dexter** Missouri, C USA 36.48N 89.57W
39 U14 **Dexter** New Mexico, SW USA 33.12N 104.25W
166 I8 **Deyang** Sichuan, C China 31.07N 104.22E
190 C4 **Dey-Dey, Lake** *salt lake* South Australia
149 S7 **Deyhūk** Yazd, E Iran 33.18N 57.30E
Deynau *see* Galkynyş
148 L8 **Dezfūl** *var.* Dizful. Khūzestān, SW Iran 32.22N 48.28E
133 X4 **Dezhneva, Mys** *headland* NE Russian Federation 66.07N 69.40W
167 P4 **Dezhou** Shandong, E China 37.28N 116.18E
Dezhou *see* Dechang
Dezh Shāhpūr *see* Marīvān
Dhahran *see* Aẓ Ẓahrān
Dhahran Al Khobar *see* Aẓ Ẓahrān al Khubar
159 U14 **Dhaka** *prev.* Dacca. ● (Bangladesh) Dhaka, C Bangladesh 23.42N 90.22E
159 T15 **Dhaka** ⬖ *division* C Bangladesh
Dhali *see* Idálion
147 O15 **Dhamār** W Yemen 14.31N 44.25E
Dhambul *see* Taraz
160 K12 **Dhamtari** Chhattīsgarh, C India 20.43N 81.36E
159 Q15 **Dhanbād** Jhārkhand, NE India 23.48N 86.27E
158 L10 **Dhangaḍhi** *var.* Dhangarhi. Far Western, W Nepal 28.45N 80.38E
Dhangarhi *see* Dhangaḍhi
Dhank *see* Ḑank
159 R12 **Dhankuṭā** Eastern, E Nepal 27.06N 87.21E
158 I6 **Dhaola Dhār** ▲▲ NE India
160 F10 **Dhār** Madhya Pradesh, C India 22.36N 75.23E
159 R12 **Dharān** *var.* Dharan Bazar. Eastern, E Nepal 26.51N 87.18E
Dharan Bazar *see* Dharān
161 H21 **Dhārāpuram** Tamil Nādu, SE India 10.45N 77.33E
161 H20 **Dharmapuri** Tamil Nādu, SE India 12.10N 78.07E
161 H18 **Dharmavaram** Andhra Pradesh, E India 14.27N 77.43E
160 M11 **Dharmjaygarh** Chhattīsgarh, C India 22.27N 83.16E
Dharmsāla *see* Dharmshāla
158 I7 **Dharmshāla** *prev.* Dharmsāla. Himāchal Pradesh, N India 32.13N 76.24E
161 F17 **Dhārwād** *prev.* Dharwar. Karnātaka, SW India 15.30N 75.04E
Dharwar *see* Dhārwād
Dhaulagiri *see* Dhawalâgiri
159 O10 **Dhawalāgiri** *var.* Dhaulagiri. ▲ C Nepal 28.45N 83.27E
83 L18 **Dheere Laaq** *var.* Lak Dera, *It.* Lach Dera. *seasonal river* Kenya/Somalia
124 O3 **Dhekéleia Sovereign Base Area** *UK military installation* E Cyprus 34.59N 33.45E
124 O3 **Dhekélia** *Eng.* Dhekelia. *Gk.* Dekéleia. *UK air base* SE Cyprus 35.00N 33.45E
Dhelvinákion *see* Delvináki
115 M22 **Dhëmbelit, Majae** ▲ S Albania 40.10N 20.22E
160 O12 **Dhenkānāl** Orissa, E India 20.40N 85.36E
Dheskáti *see* Deskáti
144 G11 **Dhībān** Ma'dabā, NW Jordan 31.30N 35.46E
Dhidhimótikhon *see* Didymóteicho
Dhíkti Ori *see* Díkti
144 I12 **Dhirwah, Wādī adh** *dry watercourse* C Jordan
Dhístomon *see* Dístomo
Dhodhekánisos *see* Dodekánisa
Dhodhóni *see* Dodóni
Dhofar *see* Ẓufār
Dhomokós *see* Domokós
Dhond *see* Daund
161 H17 **Dhone** Andhra Pradesh, C India 15.25N 77.52E
160 B11 **Dhorāji** Gujarāt, W India 21.43N 70.27E
Dhráma *see* Dráma
160 C10 **Dhrāngadhra** Gujarāt, W India 22.58N 71.31E
Dhrepanon, Akrotírio *see* Drépano, Akrotírio
159 T13 **Dhuburi** Assam, NE India 26.06N 89.55E
160 F12 **Dhule** *prev.* Dhulia. Mahārāshtra, C India 20.54N 74.46E
Dhulia *see* Dhule
Dhún Dealgan, Cuan *see* Dundalk Bay
Dhún Droma, Cuan *see* Dundrum Bay
Dhún na nGall, Bá *see* Donegal Bay
Dhū Shaykh *see* Qazānīyah
82 Q13 **Dhuudo** Bari, NE Somalia 9.21N 50.19E
83 N15 **Dhuusa Marreeb** *var.* Dusa Marreb, *It.* Dusa Mareb. Galguduud, C Somalia 5.33N 46.24E
117 J24 **Día** *island* SE Greece
57 Y9 **Diable, Île du** *var.* Devil's Island. *island* N French Guiana
13 N12 **Diable, Rivière du** ≈ Québec, SE Canada
37 N8 **Diablo, Mount** ▲ California, W USA 37.52N 121.57W
37 O9 **Diablo Range** ▲▲ California, W USA
26 I8 **Diablo, Sierra** ▲▲ Texas, SW USA
47 O11 **Diablotins, Morne** ▲ N Dominica 15.30N 61.23W
79 N11 **Diafarabé** Mopti, C Mali 14.12N 5.01W
79 N11 **Diaka** ≈ SW Mali
Diakovár *see* Đakovo
78 I12 **Dialakoto** S Senegal 13.21N 13.19W
63 B18 **Diamante** Entre Ríos, E Argentina 32.04S 60.40W
64 I12 **Diamante, Río** ≈ C Argentina
61 M19 **Diamantina** Minas Gerais, SE Brazil 18.16S 43.37W
61 N17 **Diamantina, Chapada** ▲▲ E Brazil
181 U11 **Diamantina Fracture Zone** *tectonic feature* E Indian Ocean
189 T8 **Diamantina River** ≈ Queensland/South Australia
40 D9 **Diamond Head** *headland* O'ahu, Hawai'i, USA, C Pacific Ocean 21.15N 157.48W
39 P2 **Diamond Peak** ▲ Colorado, C USA 40.56N 108.56W
37 W5 **Diamond Peak** ▲ Nevada, W USA 39.34N 115.46W
Diamond State *see* Delaware
78 J11 **Diamou** Kayes, SW Mali 14.04N 11.16W
97 I23 **Dianalund** Vestsjælland, C Denmark 55.31N 11.30E
67 G25 **Diana's Peak** ▲ C Saint Helena
166 M16 **Dianbai** *var.* Shuidong. Guangdong, S China 21.33N 110.58E
166 G13 **Dian Chi** ▣ SW China
108 B10 **Diano Marina** Liguria, NW Italy 43.55N 8.06E
169 V11 **Diaobingshan** *var.* Tiefa. Liaoning, NE China 42.25N 123.39E
79 R13 **Diapaga** E Burkina 12.04N 1.47E
Diarbekr *see* Diyarbakır
109 J15 **Diavolo, Passo del** *pass* C Italy 41.55N 13.42E
63 B18 **Díaz** Santa Fe, C Argentina 32.22S 61.04W
147 W6 **Dibā al Ḩiṣn** *var.* Dibāh, Dibba. Ash Shāriqah, NE UAE 25.34N 56.16E
145 S3 **Dībaga** N Iraq 35.51N 43.49E
Dibāh *see* Dibā al Ḩiṣn
81 L22 **Dibaya** Kasai Occidental, S Dem. Rep. Congo 6.31S 22.57E
Dibba *see* Dibā al Ḩiṣn
205 W15 **Dibble Iceberg Tongue** *ice feature* Antarctica
115 L19 **Dibër** ⬖ *district* E Albania
85 I20 **Dibete** Central, SE Botswana 23.45S 26.29E
27 W9 **Diboll** Texas, SW USA 31.11N 94.46W
Dibra *see* Debar
159 X11 **Dibrugarh** Assam, NE India 27.29N 94.49E
56 G4 **Dibulla** La Guajira, N Colombia 11.14N 73.22W
27 O5 **Dickens** Texas, SW USA 33.37N 100.50W
21 R2 **Dickey** Maine, NE USA 47.04N 69.05W
32 K9 **Dickeyville** Wisconsin, N USA 42.37N 90.36W
30 K5 **Dickinson** North Dakota, N USA 46.54N 102.48W
(0) E6 **Dickins Seamount** *undersea feature* NE Pacific Ocean
29 O13 **Dickson** Oklahoma, C USA 34.11N 96.58W
22 I9 **Dickson** Tennessee, S USA 36.04N 87.23W
Dicle *see* Tigris
Dicsőszentmárton *see* Târnăveni
100 M12 **Didam** Gelderland, E Netherlands 51.55N 6.07E
169 Y8 **Didao** Heilongjiang, NE China 45.20N 130.54E
78 L12 **Didiéni** Koulikoro, W Mali 13.48N 8.01W
Didimo *see* Dídymo
Didimotiho *see* Didymóteicho
83 K17 **Didimtu** *spring/well* NE Kenya 2.58N 40.07E
69 U9 **Didinga Hills** ▲▲ S Sudan
9 Q16 **Didsbury** Alberta, SW Canada 51.39N 114.09W
158 G11 **Dīdwāna** Rājasthān, N India 27.22N 74.36E
117 G20 **Dídymo** *var.* Didimo. ▲ S Greece 37.28N 23.12E
116 L12 **Didymóteicho** *var.* Dhidhimótikhon, Didimotiho. Anatolikí Makedonía kai Thráki, NE Greece 41.22N 26.28E
105 S13 **Die** Drôme, E France 44.46N 5.21E
79 O13 **Diébougou** SW Burkina 11.00N 3.12W
Diedenhofen *see* Thionville
9 S16 **Diefenbaker, Lake** ▣ Saskatchewan, S Canada
64 H7 **Diego de Almagro** Atacama, N Chile 26.24S 70.10W
65 F23 **Diego de Almagro, Isla** *island* S Chile
63 A20 **Diego de Alvear** Santa Fe, C Argentina 34.24S 62.04W
181 Q7 **Diego Garcia** *island* S British Indian Ocean Territory
Diégo-Suarez *see* Antsirañana
101 M23 **Diekirch** Diekirch, C Luxembourg 49.52N 6.10E
101 L23 **Diekirch** ⬖ *district* N Luxembourg
78 K11 **Diéma** Kayes, W Mali 14.28N 9.10W
103 H15 **Diemel** ≈ W Germany
100 I10 **Diemen** Noord-Holland, C Netherlands 52.21N 4.58E
Diemrich *see* Deva
178 Ii6 **Điên Biên** *var.* Bien Bien, Dien Bien Phu. Lai Châu, N Vietnam 21.22N 103.01E
Dien Bien Phu *see* Điên Biên
178 Jj8 **Diên Châu** Nghê An, N Vietnam 18.54N 105.35E
101 K18 **Diepenbeek** Limburg, NE Belgium 50.54N 5.25E
100 N11 **Diepenheim** Overijssel, E Netherlands 52.10N 6.37E
100 M10 **Diepenveen** Overijssel, E Netherlands 52.18N 6.09E
102 G12 **Diepholz** Niedersachsen, NW Germany 52.36N 8.22E
104 M3 **Dieppe** Seine-Maritime, N France 49.55N 1.04E
100 M12 **Dieren** Gelderland, E Netherlands 52.03N 6.06E
29 S13 **Dierks** Arkansas, C USA 34.07N 94.01W
101 J17 **Diest** Vlaams Brabant, C Belgium 50.58N 5.03E
110 F7 **Dietikon** Zürich, NW Switzerland 47.24N 8.25E
105 R13 **Dieulefit** Drôme, E France 44.30N 5.01E
105 T5 **Dieuze** Moselle, NE France 48.49N 6.41E
121 H15 **Dieveniškės** Vilnius, SE Lithuania 54.12N 25.38E
100 N7 **Diever** Drenthe, NE Netherlands 52.49N 6.19E
103 F17 **Diez** Rheinland-Pfalz, W Germany 50.22N 8.01E
79 Y12 **Diffa** Diffa, SE Niger 13.20N 12.39E
79 Y10 **Diffa** ⬖ *department* SE Niger
101 L25 **Differdange** Luxembourg, SW Luxembourg 49.31N 5.52E
11 O16 **Digby** Nova Scotia, SE Canada 44.37N 65.46W
28 J5 **Dighton** Kansas, C USA 38.28N 100.28W
Dignano d'Istria *see* Vodnjan
105 T14 **Digne** *var.* Digne-les-Bains. Alpes-de-Haute-Provence, SE France 44.04N 6.13E
Digne-les-Bains *see* Digne
Digoel *see* Digul, Sungai
105 Q10 **Digoin** Saône-et-Loire, C France 46.30N 3.59E
179 Rr16 **Digos** Mindanao, S Philippines 6.46N 125.21E
155 Q16 **Digri** Sind, SE Pakistan 25.10N 69.10E
176 Z13 **Digul Barat, Sungai** ≈ Papua, E Indonesia
176 Z14 **Digul, Sungai** *prev.* Digoel. ≈ Papua, E Indonesia
176 Z13 **Digul Timur, Sungai** ≈ Papua, E Indonesia
Dihang *see* Brahmaputra
159 X10 **Dihāng** ≈ NE India
Dihōk *see* Dahūk
83 L17 **Diinsoor** Bay, S Somalia 2.28N 43.00E
Dijlah *see* Tigris
101 H17 **Dijle** ≈ C Belgium
105 R8 **Dijon** *anc.* Dibio. Côte d'Or, C France 47.21N 5.03E
95 H14 **Dikanäs** Västerbotten, N Sweden 65.15N 16.00E
82 L12 **Dikhil** SW Djibouti 11.07N 42.18E
142 B13 **Dikili** İzmir, W Turkey 39.04N 26.52E
101 B17 **Diksmuide** *var.* Dixmuide, *Fr.* Dixmude. West-Vlaanderen, W Belgium 51.01N 2.52E
126 Hh6 **Dikson** Taymyrskiy (Dolgano-Nenetskiy) Avtonomnyy Okrug, N Russian Federation 73.30N 80.35E
117 K25 **Díkti** *var.* Dhíkti Ori. ▲▲ Kríti, Greece, E Mediterranean Sea
79 Z13 **Dikwa** Borno, NE Nigeria 12.00N 13.57E
83 J15 **Dīla** Southern, S Ethiopia 6.19N 38.16E
101 G18 **Dilbeek** Vlaams Brabant, C Belgium 50.51N 4.16E
175 S16 **Dili** *var.* Dilli, Dilly. ● (East Timor) N East Timor 8.33S 125.34E
79 Y11 **Dilia** *var.* Dillia. ≈ SE Niger
Dilijan *see* Delījān
178 K13 **Di Linh** Lâm Đông, S Vietnam 11.34N 108.04E
103 G16 **Dillenburg** Hessen, W Germany 50.45N 8.16E
27 Q13 **Dilley** Texas, SW USA 28.40N 99.10W
Dilli *see* Delhi, India
Dilli *see* Dili, East Timor
Dillia *see* Dilia
82 E11 **Dilling** *var.* Ad Dalanj. Southern Kordofan, C Sudan 12.01N 29.40E
103 D20 **Dillingen** Saarland, SW Germany 49.20N 6.43E
Dillingen *see* Dillingen an der Donau
103 J22 **Dillingen an der Donau** *var.* Dillingen. Bayern, S Germany 48.34N 10.29E
41 O13 **Dillingham** Alaska, USA 59.03N 158.30W
35 Q12 **Dillon** Montana, NW USA 45.13N 112.37W
23 T12 **Dillon** South Carolina, SE USA 34.25N 79.22W
33 T13 **Dillon Lake** ▣ Ohio, N USA
Dilly *see* Dili
Dilman *see* Salmās
81 K24 **Dilolo** Katanga, S Dem. Rep. Congo 10.42S 22.21E
117 J20 **Dílos** *island* Kykládes, Greece, Aegean Sea
147 Y11 **Ḑil', Ra's aḑ** *headland* E Oman 19.12N 57.53E
31 R5 **Dilworth** Minnesota, N USA 46.53N 96.38W
144 H7 **Dimashq** *var.* Ash Shām, Esh Sham, *Eng.* Damascus, *Fr.* Damas, *It.* Damasco. ● (Syria) Dimashq, SW Syria 33.30N 36.19E
144 I8 **Dimashq** *off.* Muḩāfaẓat Dimashq, *var.* Damascus, *Ar.* Ash Sham, Ash Shām, Damasco, Esh Sham, *Fr.* Damas. ⬖ *governorate* S Syria
144 I7 **Dimashq** ✕ Dimashq, S Syria 33.30N 36.19E
81 L21 **Dimbelenge** Kasai Occidental, C Dem. Rep. Congo 5.36S 23.04E
79 N16 **Dimbokro** E Ivory Coast 6.39N 4.43W
190 L11 **Dimboola** Victoria, SE Australia 36.29S 142.03E
Dîmbovița *see* Dâmbovița
Dimitrov *see* Dymytrov
116 K11 **Dimitrovgrad** Khaskovo, S Bulgaria 42.03N 25.36E
131 R5 **Dimitrovgrad** Ul'yanovskaya Oblast', W Russian Federation 54.14N 49.37E
115 Q15 **Dimitrovgrad** *prev.* Caribrod. Serbia, SE Serbia 43.01N 22.46E
Dimitrovo *see* Pernik
Dimlang *see* Vogel Peak
26 M3 **Dimmitt** Texas, SW USA 34.33N 102.18W
116 F7 **Dimovo** Vidin, NW Bulgaria 43.46N 22.46E
61 A16 **Dimpolis** Acre, W Brazil 9.52S 71.51W
117 O23 **Dimyliá** Ródos, Dodekánisa, Greece, Aegean Sea 36.17N 27.59E
179 R13 **Dinagat** Dinagat Island, S Philippines 10.00N 125.36E
179 Rr13 **Dinagat Island** *island* S Philippines
159 S13 **Dinajpur** Rajshahi, NW Bangladesh 25.37N 88.39E
104 I6 **Dinan** Côtes d'Armor, NW France 48.27N 2.01W
101 I21 **Dinant** Namur, S Belgium 50.16N 4.55E
142 E15 **Dinar** Afyon, SW Turkey 38.04N 30.09E
114 F13 **Dinara** ▲ W Croatia 43.49N 16.42E
Dinara *see* Dinaric Alps
104 I5 **Dinard** Ille-et-Vilaine, NW France 48.38N 2.04W
114 F13 **Dinaric Alps** *var.* Dinara. ▲▲ Bosnia and Herzegovina/Croatia
149 N10 **Dīnār, Kūh-e** ▲ C Iran 30.51N 51.36E
Dinbych *see* Denbigh
161 H22 **Dindigul** Tamil Nādu, SE India 10.23N 78.00E
85 M19 **Dindiza** Gaza, S Mozambique 23.22S 33.28E
155 V7 **Dinga** Punjab, E Pakistan 32.37N 73.45E
81 H21 **Dinga** Bandundu, SW Dem. Rep. Congo 5.00S 16.29E
164 L16 **Dinggyê** *var.* Gyangkar. Xizang Zizhiqu, W China 28.18N 88.06E
99 A20 **Dingle** *Ir.* An Daingean. SW Ireland 52.08N 10.16W
99 A20 **Dingle Bay** *Ir.* Bá an Daingin. *bay* SW Ireland
20 I13 **Dingmans Ferry** Pennsylvania, NE USA 41.12N 74.51W
103 N22 **Dingolfing** Bayern, SE Germany 48.37N 12.28E
179 P8 **Dingras** Luzon, N Philippines 18.06N 120.43E
78 J13 **Dinguiraye** N Guinea 11.19N 10.49W
98 I8 **Dingwall** N Scotland, UK 57.36N 4.25W
165 V10 **Dingxi** Gansu, C China 35.36N 104.33E
167 Q7 **Dingyuan** Anhui, E China 32.30N 117.40E
167 O3 **Dingzhou** *prev.* Ding Xian. Hebei, E China 38.31N 114.52E
178 K6 **Đinh Lâp** Lang Sơn, N Vietnam 21.33N 107.03E
178 K14 **Đinh Quan** *var.* Tân Phu. Đông Nai, S Vietnam 11.11N 107.20E
102 E13 **Dinkel** ≈ Germany/Netherlands
103 J21 **Dinkelsbühl** Bayern, S Germany 49.06N 10.18E
103 D14 **Dinslaken** Nordrhein-Westfalen, W Germany 51.34N 6.43E
37 R11 **Dinuba** California, W USA 36.32N 119.23W
23 W7 **Dinwiddie** Virginia, NE USA 37.04N 77.34W
100 N13 **Dinxperlo** Gelderland, E Netherlands 51.51N 6.30E
Dió *see* Díon
Diófás *see* Nucet
78 M12 **Dioïla** Koulikoro, W Mali 12.28N 6.43W
117 F14 **Díon** *var.* Dió; *anc.* Dium. *site of ancient city* Kentrikí Makedonía, N Greece 40.13N 22.30E
117 G19 **Dióryga Korinthou** *Eng.* Corinth Canal. *canal* S Greece
78 G12 **Diouloulou** SW Senegal 13.00N 16.34W
79 N11 **Dioura** Mopti, W Mali 14.48N 5.20W
78 G11 **Diourbel** W Senegal 14.38N 16.12W
158 L10 **Dipāyal** Far Western, W Nepal 29.09N 80.46E
124 Oo2 **Dipkarpaz** *Gk.* Rizokarpaso, Rizokárpason. NE Cyprus 35.36N 34.23E
155 R17 **Diplo** Sind, SE Pakistan 24.29N 69.36E
179 Qq15 **Dipolog** *var.* Dipolog City. Mindanao, S Philippines 8.31N 123.20E
193 C23 **Dipton** Southland, South Island, NZ 45.55S 168.21E
79 O10 **Diré** Tombouctou, C Mali 16.12N 3.31W
82 L13 **Dirē Dawa** Dirē Dawa, E Ethiopia 9.34N 41.53E
Dirfis *see* Dírfys
117 H18 **Dírfys** *var.* Dirfis. ▲▲ Évvioa, C Greece
77 N9 **Dirj** *var.* Daraj, Darj. W Libya 30.09N 10.25E
188 G10 **Dirk Hartog Island** *island* Western Australia
79 Y8 **Dirkou** Agadez, NE Niger 18.45N 13.00E
189 X11 **Dirranbandi** Queensland, E Australia 28.37S 148.13E
83 O16 **Dirri** Galguduud, C Somalia 4.15N 46.31E
Dirschau *see* Tczew
39 N6 **Dirty Devil River** ≈ Utah, W USA
34 E10 **Disappointment, Cape** *headland* Washington, NW USA 46.16N 124.06W
188 L8 **Disappointment, Lake** *salt lake* Western Australia
191 R12 **Disaster Bay** *bay* New South Wales, SE Australia
46 J11 **Discovery Bay** C Jamaica 18.27N 77.23W
190 K13 **Discovery Bay** *inlet* SE Australia
69 Y15 **Discovery II Fracture Zone** *tectonic feature* SW Indian Ocean
Discovery Seamount/Discovery Seamounts *see* Discovery Tablemount
67 O19 **Discovery Tablemount** *var.* Discovery Seamount, Discovery Seamounts. *undersea feature* SW Indian Ocean 42.00S 0.10E
110 G9 **Disentis** *Rmsch.* Mustér. Graubünden, S Switzerland 46.43N 8.52E
41 O10 **Dishna River** ≈ Alaska, USA
205 X4 **Dismal Mountains** ▲▲ Antarctica
30 M14 **Dismal River** ≈ Nebraska, C USA
Disna *see* Dzisna
101 L19 **Dison** Liège, E Belgium 50.37N 5.52E
159 V12 **Dispur** Assam, NE India 26.03N 91.52E
13 R11 **Disraeli** Québec, SE Canada 45.58N 71.21W
117 F18 **Dístomo** *prev.* Dhístomon. Stereá Ellás, C Greece 38.25N 22.40E
Dístos, Límni *see* Dýstos, Límni
61 L18 **Distrito Federal** *Eng.* Federal District. ⬖ *federal district* C Brazil
43 P14 **Distrito Federal** ⬖ *federal district* S Mexico
Distrito Federal, Territorio *see* Distrito Federal
118 J10 **Ditrău** *Hung.* Ditró. Harghita, C Romania 46.47N 25.30E
Ditró *see* Ditrău
160 B12 **Diu** Damān and Diu, W India 20.42N 70.58E
179 Rr14 **Diuata Mountains** ▲▲ Mindanao, S Philippines
Dium *see* Díon
111 S13 **Divača** SW Slovenia 45.40N 13.58E
104 K5 **Dives** ≈ N France
Divichi *see* Däväçi
35 Q11 **Divide** Montana, NW USA 45.44N 112.47W
Divin *see* Dzivin
85 N18 **Divinhe** Sofala, E Mozambique 20.41S 34.46E
61 L20 **Divinópolis** Minas Gerais, SE Brazil 20.07S 44.55W
131 N13 **Divnoye** Stavropol'skiy Kray, SW Russian Federation 45.54N 43.18E
78 M17 **Divo** S Ivory Coast 5.49N 5.22W
Divodurum Mediomatricum *see* Metz
143 N13 **Divriği** Sivas, C Turkey 39.22N 38.06E
Diwaniyah *see* Ad Dīwānīyah
12 J10 **Dix Milles, Lac** ◎ Québec, SE Canada
12 M8 **Dix Milles, Lac des** ◎ Québec, SE Canada
Dixmude/Dixmuide *see* Diksmuide
37 N7 **Dixon** California, W USA 38.19N 121.49W
32 L10 **Dixon** Illinois, N USA 41.51N 89.26W
22 I6 **Dixon** Kentucky, S USA 37.30N 87.39W
29 V6 **Dixon** Missouri, C USA 37.59N 92.05W
39 S9 **Dixon** New Mexico, SW USA 36.10N 105.49W
41 Y15 **Dixon Entrance** *strait* Canada/USA
20 D14 **Dixonville** Pennsylvania, NE USA 40.43N 79.01W
143 T13 **Diyadin** Ağrı, E Turkey 39.33N 43.40E
145 V5 **Diyālá, Nahr** *var.* Rudkhaneh-ye Sīrvān, Sirwan. ≈ Iran/Iraq *see also* Sīrvān, Rudkhaneh-ye
143 P15 **Diyarbakır** *var.* Diarbekr; *anc.* Amida. Dıyarbakır, SE Turkey 37.55N 40.13E
143 P15 **Diyarbakır** *var.* Diarbekr. ⬖ *province* SE Turkey
Dizful *see* Dezfūl
81 F16 **Dja** ≈ SE Cameroon
Djadié *see* Zadié
79 X7 **Djado** Agadez, NE Niger 21.00N 12.11E
79 X6 **Djado, Plateau du** ▲▲ NE Niger
Djailolo *see* Halmahera, Pulau
Djajapura *see* Jayapura
Djakarta *see* Jakarta
Djakovica *see* Đakovica
Djakovo *see* Đakovo
81 G20 **Djambala** Plateaux, C Congo 2.31S 14.43E
Djambi *see* Jambi
Djambi *see* Hari, Batang, Sumatera, W Indonesia
76 M9 **Djanet** E Algeria 28.43N 8.57E
76 M11 **Djanet** *prev.* Fort Charlet. SE Algeria 24.34N 9.33E
Djatiwangi *see* Jatiwangi
Djaul *see* Dyaul Island
Djawa *see* Jawa
Djéblé *see* Jablah
80 I10 **Djédaa** Batha, C Chad 13.31N 18.34E
76 J6 **Djelfa** *var.* El Djelfa. N Algeria 34.42N 3.16E
81 M14 **Djéma** Haut-Mbomou, E Central African Republic 6.03N 25.19E
Djeneponto *see* Jeneponto
79 N12 **Djenné** *var.* Jenné. Mopti, C Mali 13.55N 4.34W
Djérablous *see* Jarābulus
Djerba *see* Jerba, Île de
81 F15 **Djérem** ≈ C Cameroon
Djevdjelija *see* Gevgelija
79 P11 **Djibo** N Burkina 14.09N 1.37W
82 L12 **Djibouti** *var.* Jibuti. ● (Djibouti) E Djibouti 11.32N 42.55E
82 L12 **Djibouti** *off.* Republic of Djibouti, *var.* Jibuti; *prev.* French Somaliland, French Territory of the Afars and Issas, *Fr.* Côte Française des Somalis, Territoire Français des Afars et des Issas. ◆ *republic* E Africa
82 L12 **Djibouti** ✕ C Djibouti 11.29N 42.54E
Djidjel/Djidjelli *see* Jijel
57 W10 **Djoemoe** Sipaliwini, C Surinam 4.00N 55.27W
Djokjakarta *see* Yogyakarta
81 K21 **Djoku-Punda** Kasai Occidental, S Dem. Rep. Congo 5.27S 20.58E
81 K18 **Djolu** Equateur, N Dem. Rep. Congo 0.42N 22.23E
Djorče Petrov *see* Đorče Petrov
81 F17 **Djoua** ≈ Congo/Gabon
79 R14 **Djougou** W Benin 9.42N 1.38E
81 F16 **Djoum** Sud, S Cameroon 2.38N 12.51E
80 I8 **Djourab, Erg du** *dunes* N Chad
81 P17 **Djugu** Orientale, NE Dem. Rep. Congo 1.55N 30.31E
Djumbir *see* Ďumbier
94 L3 **Djúpivogur** Austurland, SE Iceland 64.39N 14.18W
96 L13 **Djura** Dalarna, C Sweden 60.37N 15.00E
Djurdjevac *see* Đurđevac
85 G18 **D'Kar** Ghanzi, NW Botswana 21.31S 21.55E
207 U6 **Dmitriya Lapteva, Proliv** *strait* N Russian Federation
130 J7 **Dmitriyev-L'govskiy** Kurskaya Oblast', W Russian Federation 52.08N 35.09E
Dmitriyevsk *see* Makiyivka
130 K3 **Dmitrov** Moskovskaya Oblast', W Russian Federation 56.23N 37.30E
Dmitrovichi *see* Dzmitravichy
130 J6 **Dmitrovsk-Orlovskiy** Orlovskaya Oblast', W Russian Federation 52.28N 35.01E
119 R3 **Dmytrivka** Chernihivs'ka Oblast', N Ukraine 50.56N 32.57E
Dnepr *see* Dnieper
Dneprodzerzhinsk *see* Dniprodzerzhyns'k
Dneprodzerzhinskoye Vodokhranilishche *see* Dniprodzerzhyns'ke Vodoskhovyshche
Dnepropetrovsk *see* Dnipropetrovs'k
Dnepropetrovskaya Oblast' *see* Dnipropetrovs'ka Oblast'
Dneprorudnoye *see* Dniprorudne
Dneprovskiy Liman *see* Dniprovs'kyy Lyman
Dneprovsko-Bugskiy Kanal *see* Dnyaprowska-Buhski, Kanal
Dnestr *see* Dniester
Dnestrovskiy Liman *see* Dnistrovs'kyy Lyman
88 H11 **Dnieper** *Bel.* Dnyapro, *Rus.* Dnepr, *Ukr.* Dnipro. ≈ E Europe
119 P3 **Dnieper Lowland** *Bel.* Prydnyaprowskaya Nizina, *Ukr.* Prydniprovs'ka Nyzovyna. *lowlands* Belarus/Ukraine
118 M8 **Dniester** *Rom.* Nistru, *Rus.* Dnestr, *Ukr.* Dnister; *anc.* Tyras. ≈ Moldova/Ukraine
Dnipro *see* Dnieper
119 T7 **Dniprodzerzhyns'k** *Rus.* Dneprodzerzhinsk; *prev.* Kamenskoye. Dnipropetrovs'ka Oblast', E Ukraine 48.30N 34.35E
119 T7 **Dniprodzerzhyns'ke Vodoskhovyshche** *Rus.* Dneprodzerzhinskoye Vodokhranilishche. ▣ C Ukraine
119 U7 **Dnipropetrovs'k** *Rus.* Dnepropetrovsk; *prev.* Yekaterinoslav. Dnipropetrovs'ka Oblast', E Ukraine 48.28N 34.59E
119 U8 **Dnipropetrovs'k** ✕ Dnipropetrovs'ka Oblast', S Ukraine 48.20N 35.04E
Dnipropetrovs'k *see* Dnipropetrovs'ka Oblast'
119 T7 **Dnipropetrovs'ka Oblast'** *var.* Dnipropetrovs'k, *Rus.* Dnepropetrovskaya Oblast'. ⬖ *province* E Ukraine
119 U9 **Dniprorudne** *Rus.* Dneprorudnoye. Zaporiz'ka Oblast', SE Ukraine 47.21N 35.00E
119 Q11 **Dniprovs'kyy Lyman** *Rus.* Dneprovskiy Liman. *bay* S Ukraine
Dnister *see* Dniester
119 O11 **Dnistrovs'kyy Lyman** *Rus.* Dnestrovskiy Liman. *inlet* S Ukraine

◆ Country
● Country Capital
◇ Dependent Territory
○ Dependent Territory Capital
⬖ Administrative Region
✕ International Airport
▲ Mountain
▲▲ Mountain Range
☗ Volcano
≈ River
◎ Lake
▣ Reservoir

128 G14 **Dno** Pskovskaya Oblast', W Russian Federation *57.48N 29.58E*
Dnyapro *see* Dnieper
121 H20 **Dnyaprowska-Buhskі, Kanal** *Rus.* Dneprovsko-Bugskiy Kanal. *canal* SW Belarus
11 O14 **Doaktown** New Brunswick, SE Canada *46.34N 66.06W*
80 H13 **Doba** Logone-Oriental, S Chad *8.40N 16.49E*
120 E9 **Dobele** *Ger.* Doblen. Dobele, W Latvia *56.36N 23.14E*
103 N16 **Döbeln** Sachsen, E Germany *51.07N 13.07E*
176 Vv9 **Doberai, Jazirah** *Dut.* Vogelkop. *peninsula* Papua, E Indonesia
112 F10 **Dobiegniew** *Ger.* Lubuskie, W Poland *52.58N 15.43E*
Doblen *see* Dobele
83 K18 **Dobli** *spring/well* SW Somalia *0.24N 41.18E*
176 W13 **Dobo** Pulau Wamar, E Indonesia *5.45S 134.12E*
114 H11 **Doboj** Republika Srpska, N Bosnia and Herzegovina *44.45N 18.03E*
112 L8 **Dobre Miasto** *Ger.* Guttstadt. Warmińsko-Mazurskie, NE Poland *53.59N 20.25E*
116 N7 **Dobrich** *Rom.* Bazargic; *prev.* Tolbukhin. Dobrich, NE Bulgaria *43.34N 27.49E*
116 N7 **Dobrich** ◈ province NE Bulgaria
130 M8 **Dobrinka** Lipetskaya Oblast', W Russian Federation *52.10N 40.30E*
130 M7 **Dobrinka** Volgogradskaya Oblast', SW Russian Federation *50.52N 41.48E*
Dobrla Vas *see* Eberndorf
113 I15 **Dobrodzień** *Ger.* Guttentag. Opolskie, S Poland *50.43N 18.24E*
Dobrogea *see* Dobruja
119 W7 **Dobropillya** *Rus.* Dobropol'ye. Donets'ka Oblast', SE Ukraine *48.29N 37.06E*
Dobropol'ye *see* Dobropillya
119 P8 **Dobrovelychkivka** Kirovohrads'ka Oblast', C Ukraine *48.22N 31.12E*
Dobrudja/Dobrudzha *see* Dobruja
116 O7 **Dobruja** *var.* Dobrudja, *Bul.* Dobrudzha, *Rom.* Dobrogea. *physical region* Bulgaria/Romania
121 P19 **Dobrush** Homyel'skaya Voblasts', SE Belarus *52.25N 31.21E*
129 U14 **Dobryanka** Permskaya Oblast', NW Russian Federation *58.28N 56.27E*
119 P2 **Dobryanka** Chernihivs'ka Oblast', N Ukraine *52.03N 31.09E*
Dobryn' *see* Dabryn'
23 R8 **Dobson** North Carolina, SE USA *36.30N 80.54W*
61 N20 **Doce, Rio** ~ SE Brazil
95 I16 **Docksta** Västernorrland, C Sweden *63.06N 18.22E*
43 N10 **Doctor Arroyo** Nuevo León, NE Mexico *23.40N 100.09W*
64 L4 **Doctor Pedro P. Peña** Boquerón, W Paraguay *22.22S 62.22W*
175 T7 **Dodaga** Pulau Halmahera, E Indonesia *1.06N 128.10E*
161 G21 **Dodda Betta** ▲ S India *11.28N 76.44E*
Dodecanese *see* Dodekánisa
117 M22 **Dodekánisa** *var.* Dodekanisos, Nóties Sporádes, *Eng.* Dodecanese; *prev.* Dhodhekánisos. *island group* SE Greece
Dodekánisos *see* Dodekánisa
28 J6 **Dodge City** Kansas, C USA *37.45N 100.01W*
32 K9 **Dodgeville** Wisconsin, N USA *42.57N 90.07W*
99 H25 **Dodman Point** *headland* SW England, UK *50.13N 4.47W*
83 J14 **Dodola** Oromo, C Ethiopia *7.00N 39.15E*
83 H22 **Dodoma** ● (Tanzania) Dodoma, C Tanzania *6.10S 35.45E*
83 H22 **Dodoma** ◈ *region* C Tanzania
117 C16 **Dodóni** *var.* Dhodhóni. *site of ancient city* Ípeiros, W Greece *39.33N 20.47E*
35 U7 **Dodson** Montana, NW USA *48.25N 108.18W*
27 P3 **Dodson** Texas, SW USA *34.46N 100.01W*
100 M12 **Doesburg** Gelderland, E Netherlands *52.01N 6.07E*
100 N12 **Doetinchem** Gelderland, E Netherlands *51.58N 6.16E*
164 L12 **Dogai Coring** *var.* Lake Montcalm. ◎ W China
143 N15 **Doğanşehir** Malatya, C Turkey *38.06N 37.52E*
86 E9 **Dogger Bank** *undersea feature* C North Sea
25 S10 **Dog Island** *island* Florida, SE USA
12 C7 **Dog Lake** ◎ Ontario, S Canada
108 B9 **Dogliani** Piemonte, NE Italy *44.33N 7.55E*
170 G11 **Dōgo** *island* Oki-shotō, SW Japan
Do Gonbadān *see* Dow Gonbadān
79 S12 **Dogondoutchi** Dosso, SW Niger *13.37N 4.03E*
Dōgo-san *see* Dōgo-yama
170 F13 **Dōgo-yama** *var.* Dōgo-san. ▲ Kyūshū, SW Japan *35.03N 133.12E*
Dogrular *see* Pravda
143 T13 **Doğubayazıt** Ağrı, E Turkey *39.33N 44.07E*
143 P12 **Doğu Karadeniz Dağları** *var.* Anadolu Dağları. ▲▲ NE Turkey
164 K16 **Dogxung Zangbo** ~ W China
Doha *see* Ad Dawḥah
Dohad *see* Dāhod
Dohuk *see* Dahūk
165 N16 **Doilungdêqên** *var.* Namka. Xizang Zizhiqu, W China *29.41N 90.58E*
116 F12 **Doïráni, Límni** *var.* Límni Doïranis, *Bul.* Ezero Doyransko. ◎ N Greece
Doïranis, Límni *see* Doïráni, Límni
Doire *see* Londonderry
101 H22 **Doische** Namur, S Belgium *50.09N 4.43E*
61 P17 **Dois de Julho** ✕ (Salvador) Bahia, NE Brazil *12.04S 38.58W*
62 H12 **Dois Vizinhos** Paraná, S Brazil *25.47S 53.03W*
82 H10 **Doka** Gedaref, E Sudan *13.30N 35.46E*
Doka *see* Kéita, Bahr
145 T3 **Dokan** *var.* Dūkān. E Iraq *35.55N 44.58E*
96 H13 **Dokka** Oppland, S Norway *60.49N 10.04E*
100 L5 **Dokkum** Friesland, N Netherlands *53.20N 6.00E*
100 L5 **Dokkumer Ee** ~ N Netherlands
78 K13 **Doko** NE Guinea *11.46N 8.58W*
Dokshitsy *see* Dokshytsy
120 K13 **Dokshytsy** *Rus.* Dokshitsy. Vitsyebskaya Voblasts', N Belarus *54.54N 27.46E*
119 X8 **Dokuchayevs'k** *var.* Dokuchayevsk. Donets'ka Oblast', SE Ukraine *47.43N 37.40E*
Dolak, Pulau *see* Yos Sudarso, Pulau
31 P9 **Doland** South Dakota, N USA *44.51N 98.06W*
65 J18 **Dolavón** Chaco, S Argentina *43.20S 65.42W*
13 P6 **Dolbeau** Québec, SE Canada *48.52N 72.15W*
104 I5 **Dol-de-Bretagne** Ille-et-Vilaine, NW France *48.33N 1.45W*
66 J13 **Doldrums Fracture Zone** *tectonic feature* W Atlantic Ocean
105 S8 **Dôle** Jura, E France *47.04N 5.30E*
99 J19 **Dolgellau** NW Wales, UK *52.44N 3.54W*
Dolginovo *see* Dawhinava
Dolgi, Ostrov *see* Dolgiy, Ostrov
129 U2 **Dolgiy, Ostrov** *var.* Ostrov Dolgi. *island* NW Russian Federation
168 J9 **Dölgöön** Övörhangay, C Mongolia *45.57N 103.14E*
109 C20 **Dolianova** Sardegna, Italy, C Mediterranean Sea *39.23N 9.08E*
Dolina *see* Dolyna
127 Oo15 **Dolinsk** Ostrov Sakhalin, Sakhalinskaya Oblast', SE Russian Federation *47.20N 142.52E*
Dolinskaya *see* Dolyns'ka
81 F21 **Dolisie** *prev.* Loubomo. Le Niari, S Congo *4.12S 12.40E*
118 G14 **Dolj** ◈ *county* SW Romania
100 P5 **Dollard** *bay* NW Germany
204 J5 **Dolleman Island** *island* Antarctica
116 I8 **Dolni Dŭbnik** Pleven, N Bulgaria *43.24N 24.25E*
116 F8 **Dolni Lom** Vidin, NW Bulgaria *43.31N 22.46E*
Dolnja Lendava *see* Lendava
116 K9 **Dolno Panicherevo** *var.* Panicherevo. Sliven, C Bulgaria *42.36N 25.51E*
113 F14 **Dolnośląskie** ◈ *province* SW Poland
113 K18 **Dolný Kubín** *Hung.* Alsókubin. Zilinský Kraj, N Slovakia *49.13N 19.16E*
108 H8 **Dolo** Veneto, NE Italy *45.25N 12.06E*
Dolomites/Dolomiti *see* Dolomitiche, Alpi
108 H6 **Dolomitiche, Alpi** *var.* Dolomiti, *Eng.* Dolomites. ▲▲ NE Italy
Dolonnur *see* Duolun
Doloon *see* Tsogt-Ovoo
63 E21 **Dolores** Buenos Aires, E Argentina *36.21S 57.39W*
44 E3 **Dolores** Petén, N Guatemala *16.33N 89.25W*
179 R12 **Dolores** Samar, C Philippines *12.01N 125.27E*
107 S12 **Dolores** País Valenciano, E Spain *38.09N 0.45W*
63 D19 **Dolores** Soriano, SW Uruguay *33.34S 58.15W*
43 N12 **Dolores Hidalgo** *var.* Ciudad de Dolores Hidalgo. Guanajuato, C Mexico *21.10N 100.55W*
15 Hh3 **Dolphin and Union Strait** *strait* Northwest Territories/Nunavut, N Canada
67 D23 **Dolphin, Cape** *headland* East Falkland, Falkland Islands *51.15S 58.57W*
46 H12 **Dolphin Head** *hill* W Jamaica *18.21N 78.08W*
85 B21 **Dolphin Head** *var.* Cape Dernberg. *headland* SW Namibia *25.33S 14.36E*
112 G12 **Dolsk** *Ger.* Dolzig. Wielkolpolskie, C Poland *51.59N 17.03E*
178 J8 **Đô Lương** Nghê An, N Vietnam *18.51N 105.19E*
118 I6 **Dolyna** *Rus.* Dolina. Ivano-Frankivs'ka Oblast', W Ukraine *48.58N 24.01E*
119 R8 **Dolyns'ka** *Rus.* Dolinskaya. Kirovohrads'ka Oblast', S Ukraine *48.06N 32.46E*
Dolzig *see* Dolsk
Domachëvo/Domaczewo *see* Damachava
119 P9 **Domanivka** Mykolayivs'ka Oblast', S Ukraine *47.40N 30.56E*
159 S13 **Domar** Rajshahi, N Bangladesh *26.09N 88.49E*
110 I9 **Domat/Ems** Graubünden, SE Switzerland *46.49N 9.28E*
113 A18 **Domažlice** *Ger.* Taus. Plzeňský Kraj, W Czech Republic *49.25N 12.55E*
131 X8 **Dombarovskiy** Orenburgskaya Oblast', W Russian Federation *50.53N 59.18E*
96 G10 **Dombås** Oppland, S Norway *62.04N 9.07E*
85 M17 **Dombe** Manica, C Mozambique *19.59S 33.24E*
84 A13 **Dombe Grande** Benguela, C Angola *12.57S 13.07E*
105 R10 **Dombes** *physical region* E France
176 Xx10 **Dombo** Papua, E Indonesia *1.52S 137.09E*
113 I25 **Dombóvár** Tolna, S Hungary *46.24N 18.09E*
101 D14 **Domburg** Zeeland, SW Netherlands *51.34N 3.30E*
60 L13 **Dom Eliseu** Pará, NE Brazil *4.02S 47.31W*
Domel Island *see* Letsôk-aw Kyun
105 O11 **Dôme, Puy de** ▲ C France *45.46N 3.00E*
38 H13 **Dome Rock Mountains** ▲▲ Arizona, SW USA
Domesnes, Cape *see* Kolkasrags
64 G8 **Domeyko** Atacama, N Chile *28.57S 70.54W*
64 H5 **Domeyko, Cordillera** ▲▲ N Chile
104 K5 **Domfront** Orne, N France *48.35N 0.39W*
176 Xx10 **Dom, Gunung** ▲ Papua, E Indonesia *2.41S 137.00E*
47 X11 **Dominica** *off.* Commonwealth of Dominica. ◆ *republic* E West Indies
49 S3 **Dominica** *island* Dominica
Dominica Channel *see* Martinique Passage
45 N15 **Dominical** Puntarenas, SE Costa Rica *9.16N 83.52W*
47 Q8 **Dominican Republic** ◆ *republic* C West Indies
47 X11 **Dominica Passage** *passage* E Caribbean Sea
101 K14 **Dommel** ~ S Netherlands
83 O14 **Domo** Somali, E Ethiopia *7.53N 46.55E*
130 L4 **Domodedovo** ✕ (Moskva) Moskovskaya Oblast', W Russian Federation *55.19N 37.55E*
108 C6 **Domodossola** Piemonte, NE Italy *46.07N 8.20E*
117 F17 **Domokós** *var.* Dhomokós. Stereá Ellás, C Greece *39.07N 22.18E*
180 I14 **Domoni** Anjouan, SE Comoros *12.15S 44.39E*
63 G16 **Dom Pedrito** Rio Grande do Sul, S Brazil *30.55S 54.39W*
Dompoe *see* Dompu
175 Oo16 **Dompu** *prev.* Dompoe. Sumbawa, C Indonesia *8.30S 118.28E*
Domschale *see* Domžale
64 H13 **Domuyo, Volcán** Ѫ W Argentina *36.36S 70.22W*
111 U11 **Domžale** *Ger.* Domschale. C Slovenia *46.09N 14.33E*
131 O10 **Don** *var.* Duna, Tanais. ~ SW Russian Federation
98 K9 **Don** ~ NE Scotland, UK
190 M11 **Donald** Victoria, SE Australia *36.27S 143.03E*
24 J9 **Donaldsonville** Louisiana, S USA *30.06N 90.59W*
25 S8 **Donalsonville** Georgia, SE USA *31.02N 84.52W*
Donau *see* Danube
103 G23 **Donaueschingen** Baden-Württemberg, SW Germany *47.57N 8.30E*
103 K22 **Donaumoos** *wetland* S Germany
103 K22 **Donauwörth** Bayern, S Germany *48.43N 10.46E*
111 U7 **Donawitz** Steiermark, SE Austria *47.23N 15.00E*
119 X7 **Donbass** *industrial region* Russian Federation/Ukraine
106 K11 **Don Benito** Extremadura, W Spain *38.57N 5.52W*
99 M17 **Doncaster** *anc.* Danum. N England, UK *53.31N 1.07W*
46 K12 **Don Christophers Point** *headland* C Jamaica *18.19N 76.48W*
57 V9 **Donderkamp** Sipaliwini, NW Surinam *5.18N 56.22W*
84 B12 **Dondo** Cuanza Norte, NW Angola *9.40S 14.24E*
175 Q9 **Dondo** Sulawesi, N Indonesia *0.54S 121.33E*
85 N17 **Dondo** Sofala, C Mozambique *19.36S 34.46E*
175 Pp7 **Dondo, Teluk** *bay* Sulawesi, N Indonesia
161 K26 **Dondra Head** *headland* S Sri Lanka *5.57N 80.33E*
Donduşani *see* Donduşeni
118 M8 **Donduşeni** *var.* Donduşani, *Rus.* Dondyushany. N Moldova *48.13N 27.38E*
Dondyushany *see* Donduşeni
99 D15 **Donegal** *Ir.* Dún na nGall. NW Ireland *54.39N 8.06W*
99 D14 **Donegal** *Ir.* Dún na nGall. *cultural region* NW Ireland
99 C15 **Donegal Bay** *Ir.* Bá Dhún na nGall. *bay* NW Ireland
86 K10 **Donets** ~ Russian Federation/Ukraine
119 X8 **Donets'k** *Rus.* Donetsk; *prev.* Stalino. Donets'ka Oblast', E Ukraine *47.58N 37.50E*
119 W8 **Donets'k** ✕ Donets'ka Oblast', E Ukraine *48.03N 37.44E*
Donets'k *see* Donets'ka Oblast'
119 W8 **Donets'ka Oblast'** *var.* Donets'k, *Rus.* Donetskaya Oblast'; *prev. Rus.* Stalinskaya Oblast'. ◈ *province* SE Ukraine
Donetskaya Oblast' *see* Donets'ka Oblast'
69 P8 **Donga** ~ Cameroon/Nigeria
163 O13 **Dongchuan** Yunnan, SW China *26.09N 103.10E*
101 I14 **Dongen** Noord-Brabant, S Netherlands *51.37N 4.55E*
166 K17 **Dongfang** *var.* Basuo. Hainan, S China *19.05N 108.40E*
169 Z7 **Dongfanghong** Heilongjiang, NE China *46.13N 133.13E*
169 W11 **Dongfeng** Jilin, NE China *42.39N 125.33E*
175 P9 **Donggala** Sulawesi, C Indonesia *0.40S 119.43E*
169 V13 **Donggang** *var.* Dadong, *prev.* Donggou. Liaoning, NE China *39.52N 124.07E*
Donggou *see* Donggang
167 O14 **Dongguan** Guangdong, S China *23.03N 113.43E*
178 K9 **Đông Hà** Quang Tri, C Vietnam *16.45N 107.10E*
Dong Hai *see* East China Sea
166 M16 **Donghai Dao** *island* S China
168 I12 **Dong He** *Mong.* Narin Gol. ~ N China
Donghe *see* Wangcang
178 Jj9 **Đông Hơi** Quang Binh, C Vietnam *17.30N 106.34E*
110 H10 **Dongio** Ticino, S Switzerland *46.27N 8.58E*
Dongkan *see* Binhai
166 L11 **Dongkou** Hunan, S China *27.06N 110.34E*
Dongliao *see* Liaoyuan
Dong-nai *see* Đông Nai, Sông
178 K13 **Đông Nai, Sông** *var.* Dong-nai, Dong Noi, Donnai. ~ S Vietnam
167 N14 **Dongnan Qiuling** *plateau* SE China
169 Y9 **Dongning** Heilongjiang, NE China *44.01N 131.03E*
Dong Noi *see* Đông Nai, Sông
85 C14 **Dongo** Huíla, C Angola *14.35S 15.51E*
82 E7 **Dongola** *var.* Dongola, Dunqulah. Northern, N Sudan *19.10N 30.27E*
81 I17 **Dongou** La Likouala, NE Congo *2.04N 18.00E*
Đông Phu *see* Đông Xoai
Dongping *see* Anhua
Dong Rak, Phanom *see* Dângrêk, Chuŏr Phnum
167 Q14 **Dongshan Dao** *island* SE China
Dongsheng *see* Ordos
167 R7 **Dongtai** Jiangsu, E China *32.52N 120.13E*
167 N10 **Dongting Hu** *var.* Tung-t'ing Hu. ◎ S China
167 P10 **Dongxiang** *var.* Xiaogang. Jiangxi, S China *28.17N 116.36E*
178 Jj13 **Đông Xoai** *var.* Đông Phu. Sông Be, S Vietnam *11.31N 106.55E*
167 Q4 **Dongying** Shandong, E China *37.27N 118.01E*
29 X8 **Doniphan** Missouri, C USA *36.37N 90.49W*
Donja Łužyca *see* Niederlausitz
8 G7 **Donjek** ~ Yukon Territory, W Canada
114 E11 **Donji Lapac** Lika-Senj, W Croatia *44.33N 15.58E*
114 H8 **Donji Miholjac** Osijek-Baranja, NE Croatia *45.45N 18.10E*
114 P12 **Donji Milanovac** Serbia, E Serbia *44.27N 22.06E*
114 G12 **Donji Vakuf** *var.* Srbobran. Federacija Bosna I Hercegovina, C Bosnia & Herzegovina *44.08N 17.23E*
100 M6 **Donkerbroek** Friesland, N Netherlands *52.58N 5.15E*
178 Hh11 **Don Muang** ✕ (Krung Thep) Nonthaburi, C Thailand *13.51N 100.40E*
27 S17 **Donna** Texas, SW USA *26.10N 98.03W*
13 Q10 **Donnacona** Québec, SE Canada *46.41N 71.46W*
Donnai *see* Đông Nai, Sông
31 Y16 **Donnellson** Iowa, C USA *40.38N 91.33W*
9 O13 **Donnelly** Alberta, W Canada *55.42N 117.06W*
37 P6 **Donner Pass** *pass* California, W USA *39.19N 120.19W*
103 F19 **Donnersberg** ▲ W Germany *49.37N 7.54E*
Donoso *see* Miguel de la Borda
107 P2 **Donostia-San Sebastián** País Vasco, N Spain *43.19N 1.58W*
117 K21 **Donoúsa** *var.* Donoússa. *island* Kykládes, Greece, Aegean Sea
Donoússa *see* Donoúsa
37 P8 **Don Pedro Reservoir** ⊡ California, W USA
Donqola *see* Dongola
130 L5 **Donskoy** Tul'skaya Oblast', W Russian Federation *54.02N 38.27E*
179 Q11 **Donsol** Luzon, N Philippines *12.56N 123.34E*
83 L16 **Doolow** Somali, E Ethiopia *4.10N 42.04E*
41 Q7 **Doonerak, Mount** ▲ Alaska, USA *67.54N 150.33W*
100 J12 **Doorn** Utrecht, C Netherlands *52.01N 5.21E*
Doornik *see* Tournai
33 N6 **Door Peninsula** *peninsula* Wisconsin, N USA
82 P13 **Dooxo Nugaaleed** *var.* Nogal Valley. *valley* E Somalia
Do Qu *see* Da Qu
108 B7 **Dora Baltea** *anc.* Duria Major. ~ NW Italy
188 K7 **Dora, Lake** *salt lake* Western Australia
108 A8 **Dora Riparia** *anc.* Duria Minor. ~ NW Italy
Dorbiljin *see* Emin
Dorbod/Dorbod Mongolzu Zizhixian *see* Taikang
115 N18 **Đorče Petrov** *var.* Djorče Petrov, Gorče Petrov. N FYR Macedonia *42.01N 21.21E*
12 F16 **Dorchester** Ontario, S Canada *43.00N 81.04W*
99 L24 **Dorchester** *anc.* Durnovaria. S England, UK *50.43N 2.25W*
15 Mm4 **Dorchester, Cape** *headland* Baffin Island, Nunavut, NE Canada *65.25N 77.25W*
85 D19 **Dordabis** Khomas, C Namibia *22.57S 17.39E*
104 L12 **Dordogne** ◈ *department* SW France
105 N12 **Dordogne** ~ W France
100 H13 **Dordrecht** *var.* Dordt, Dort. Zuid-Holland, SW Netherlands *51.48N 4.40E*
Dordt *see* Dordrecht
105 P11 **Dore** ~ C France
9 S13 **Doré Lake** Saskatchewan, C Canada *54.37N 107.36W*
105 O12 **Dore, Monts** ▲▲ C France
103 M23 **Dorfen** Bayern, SE Germany *48.16N 12.06E*
109 D18 **Dorgali** Sardegna, Italy, C Mediterranean Sea *40.18N 9.34E*
165 N11 **Dorgê Co** *var.* Elsen Nur. ◎ C China
168 E6 **Dörgön** *var.* Seer. Hovd, W Mongolia *48.18N 92.37E*
168 F7 **Dörgön Nuur** ◎ NW Mongolia
79 Q12 **Dori** N Burkina *14.03N 0.01W*
85 E24 **Doring** ~ S South Africa
103 E16 **Dormagen** Nordrhein-Westfalen, W Germany *51.06N 6.49E*
105 P4 **Dormans** Marne, N France *49.03N 3.44E*
110 E6 **Dornach** Solothurn, NW Switzerland *47.28N 7.37E*
Dorna Watra *see* Vatra Dornei
110 J7 **Dornbirn** Vorarlberg, W Austria *47.25N 9.46E*
98 I7 **Dornoch** N Scotland, UK *57.52N 4.00W*
98 J7 **Dornoch Firth** *inlet* N Scotland, UK
169 P7 **Dornod** ◈ *province* E Mongolia
169 N10 **Dornogovĭ** ◈ *province* SE Mongolia
79 P10 **Doro** Tombouctou, S Mali *16.07N 0.57W*
118 L14 **Dorobanţu** Călăraşi, S Romania *44.15N 26.55E*
113 J22 **Dorog** Komárom-Esztergom, N Hungary *47.42N 18.44E*
130 I4 **Dorogobuzh** Smolenskaya Oblast', W Russian Federation *54.56N 33.16E*
118 K8 **Dorohoi** Botoşani, NE Romania *47.57N 26.24E*
95 H15 **Dorotea** Västerbotten, N Sweden *64.16N 16.30E*
Dorpat *see* Tartu
188 G10 **Dorre Island** *island* Western Australia
191 U5 **Dorrigo** New South Wales, SE Australia *30.22S 152.43E*
37 N1 **Dorris** California, W USA *41.58N 121.54W*
12 H13 **Dorset** Ontario, SE Canada *45.12N 78.52W*
99 K23 **Dorset** *cultural region* S England, UK
103 E14 **Dorsten** Nordrhein-Westfalen, W Germany *51.40N 6.58E*
Dort *see* Dordrecht
103 F15 **Dortmund** Nordrhein-Westfalen, W Germany *51.31N 7.28E*
102 F12 **Dortmund-Ems-Kanal** *canal* W Germany
142 L17 **Dörtyol** Hatay, S Turkey *36.51N 36.10E*
148 L7 **Do Rūd** *var.* Dow Rūd, Durud. Lorestān, W Iran *33.31N 49.03E*
81 O15 **Doruma** Orientale, N Dem. Rep. Congo *4.35N 27.43E*
13 O12 **Dorval** ✕ (Montréal) Québec, SE Canada *45.27N 73.46W*
168 F7 **Dörvöljin** *var.* Buga. Dzavhan, W Mongolia *47.42N 94.53E*
47 T5 **Dos Bocas, Lago** ◎ C Puerto Rico
106 K14 **Dos Hermanas** Andalucía, S Spain *37.16N 5.55W*
Dospad Dagh *see* Rhodope Mountains
37 P10 **Dos Palos** California, W USA *37.00N 120.39W*
116 I11 **Dospat** Smolyan, S Bulgaria *41.39N 24.10E*
116 H11 **Dospat, Yazovir** ⊡ SW Bulgaria
102 M11 **Dosse** ~ NE Germany
79 S12 **Dosso** Dosso, SW Niger *13.03N 3.13E*
79 S12 **Dosso** ◈ *department* SW Niger
150 G12 **Dossor** Atyrau, SW Kazakhstan *47.32N 52.58E*
153 O10 **Do'stlik** Jizzax Viloyati, C Uzbekistan *40.37N 67.59E*
153 V9 **Dostuk** Narynskaya Oblast', C Kyrgyzstan *41.19N 75.40E*
151 X13 **Dostyk** *prev.* Druzhba. Almaty, SE Kazakhstan *45.15N 82.28E*
25 R7 **Dothan** Alabama, S USA *31.13N 85.23W*
41 T9 **Dot Lake** Alaska, USA *63.39N 144.10W*
120 F12 **Dotnuva** Kaunas, C Lithuania *55.22N 23.52E*
101 D19 **Dottignies** Hainaut, W Belgium *50.43N 3.16E*
105 P2 **Douai** *prev.* Douay, *anc.* Duacum. Nord, N France *50.22N 3.04E*
12 L9 **Douaire, Lac** ◎ Québec, SE Canada
81 D16 **Douala** *var.* Duala. Littoral, W Cameroon *4.04N 9.43E*
81 D16 **Douala** ✕ Littoral, W Cameroon *3.57N 9.48E*
104 F6 **Douarnenez** Finistère, NW France *48.04N 4.19W*
104 E6 **Douarnenez, Baie de** *bay* NW France
Douay *see* Douai
27 O6 **Double Mountain Fork Brazos River** ~ Texas, SW USA
25 O3 **Double Springs** Alabama, S USA *34.09N 87.24W*
105 T8 **Doubs** ◈ *department* E France
110 C8 **Doubs** ~ France/Switzerland
193 A22 **Doubtful Sound** *sound* South Island, NZ
192 J2 **Doubtless Bay** *bay* North Island, NZ
27 X9 **Doucette** Texas, SW USA *30.48N 94.25W*
104 K8 **Doué-la-Fontaine** Maine-et-Loire, NW France *47.12N 0.16W*
79 O11 **Douentza** Mopti, S Mali *14.59N 2.57W*
40 L9 **Douglas** East Falkland, Falkland Islands
99 I16 **Douglas** ○ (Isle of Man) E Isle of Man *54.09N 4.28W*
85 H23 **Douglas** Northern Cape, C South Africa *29.03S 23.46E*
41 X13 **Douglas** Alexander Archipelago, Alaska, USA *58.12N 134.18W*
39 O17 **Douglas** Arizona, SW USA *31.20N 109.32W*
25 U7 **Douglas** Georgia, SE USA *31.30N 82.51W*
35 Y15 **Douglas** Wyoming, C USA *42.48N 105.22W*
23 O7 **Douglas, Cape** *headland* Alaska USA *64.59N 166.41W*
8 J14 **Douglas Channel** *channel* British Columbia, W Canada
190 G3 **Douglas Creek** *seasonal river* South Australia
33 P5 **Douglas Lake** ◎ Michigan, N USA
23 O9 **Douglas Lake** ⊡ Tennessee, S USA
41 Q13 **Douglas, Mount** ▲ Alaska, USA *58.51N 153.31W*
204 I6 **Douglas Range** ▲▲ Alexander Island, Antarctica
105 O2 **Doullens** Somme, N France *50.09N 2.21E*
Douma *see* Dūmā
81 F15 **Doumé** Est, E Cameroon *4.13N 13.27E*
101 E21 **Dour** Hainaut, S Belgium *50.24N 3.46E*
61 K18 **Dourada, Serra** ▲▲ S Brazil
61 I21 **Dourados** Mato Grosso do Sul, S Brazil *22.09S 54.52W*
105 N5 **Dourdan** Essonne, N France *48.33N 1.58E*
106 I6 **Douro** *Sp.* Duero. ~ Portugal/Spain ***see also*** Duero
106 G6 **Douro Litoral** *former province* N Portugal
Douvres *see* Dover
104 K15 **Douze** ~ SW France
191 P17 **Dover** Tasmania, SE Australia *43.19S 147.01E*
99 Q22 **Dover** *Fr.* Douvres; *Lat.* Dubris Portus. SE England, UK *51.08N 3.00W*
19 Rr8 **Dover** *state capital* Delaware, NE USA *39.09N 75.31W*
21 P9 **Dover** New Hampshire, NE USA *43.10N 70.50W*
20 J14 **Dover** New Jersey, NE USA *40.51N 74.33W*
33 U12 **Dover** Ohio, N USA *40.31N 81.28W*
22 H8 **Dover** Tennessee, S USA *36.29N 87.50W*
99 Q23 **Dover, Strait of** *var.* Straits of Dover, *Fr.* Pas de Calais. *strait* England, UK/France
Dover, Straits of *see* Dover, Strait of
Dovlen *see* Devin
96 G11 **Dovre** Oppland, S Norway *61.59N 9.16E*
96 G10 **Dovrefjell** *plateau* S Norway
Dovsk *see* Dowsk
85 M14 **Dowa** Central, C Malawi *13.42S 33.55E*
33 O10 **Dowagiac** Michigan, N USA *41.58N 86.06W*
149 N10 **Dow Gonbadān** *var.* Do Gonbadān, Gonbadān. Kohgīlūyeh va Būyer Aḥmad, SW Iran *30.24N 50.45E*
154 M2 **Dowlatābād** Fāryāb, N Afghanistan *36.30N 64.51E*
99 G16 **Down** *cultural region* SE Northern Ireland, UK
35 R16 **Downey** Idaho, NW USA *42.25N 112.06W*
37 P5 **Downieville** California, W USA *39.33N 120.49W*
99 G16 **Downpatrick** *Ir.* Dún Pádraig. SE Northern Ireland, UK *54.19N 5.43W*
28 M3 **Downs** Kansas, C USA *39.30N 98.33W*
20 J12 **Downsville** New York, NE USA *42.03N 74.59W*
Dow Rūd *see* Do Rūd
31 V12 **Dows** Iowa, C USA *42.39N 93.30W*
121 O17 **Dowsk** *Rus.* Dovsk. Homyel'skaya Voblasts', SE Belarus *53.09N 30.27E*
37 Q4 **Doyle** California, W USA *40.00N 120.06W*
20 I15 **Doylestown** Pennsylvania, NE USA *40.18N 75.07W*
Doyransko, Ezero *see* Doïráni, Límni
116 I8 **Doyrentsi** Lovech, N Bulgaria *43.13N 24.46E*
170 Ff11 **Dōzen** *island* Oki-shotō, SW Japan
12 K9 **Dozois, Réservoir** ⊡ Québec, SE Canada
76 D9 **Drâa** *seasonal river* S Morocco
Drâa, Hammada du *see* Dra, Hamada du
Drabble *see* José Enrique Rodó
119 Q5 **Drabiv** Cherkas'ka Oblast', C Ukraine *49.57N 32.10E*
Drable *see* José Enrique Rodó
105 S13 **Drac** ~ E France
Drač/Drac *see* Durrës
62 I8 **Dracena** São Paulo, S Brazil *21.27S 51.30W*
100 M6 **Drachten** Friesland, N Netherlands *53.07N 6.06E*
94 H11 **Drag** *Lapp.* Ájluokta. Nordland, C Norway *68.02N 16.00E*
118 L14 **Dragalina** Călăraşi, SE Romania *44.25N 27.17E*
118 I14 **Draganesti-Olt** Olt, S Romania *44.06N 25.00E*
118 J14 **Drăgăneşti-Vlaşca** Teleorman, S Romania *44.05N 25.39E*
118 I13 **Drăgăşani** Vâlcea, SW Romania *44.40N 24.16E*
116 G9 **Dragoman** Sofiya, W Bulgaria *42.57N 22.53E*
117 L25 **Dragonáda** *island* SE Greece
Dragonera, Isla *see* Sa Dragonera
47 T14 **Dragon's Mouths, The** *strait* Trinidad and Tobago/Venezuela
97 J23 **Dragør** København, E Denmark *55.36N 12.42E*
116 F10 **Dragovishtsa** Kyustendil, W Bulgaria *42.22N 22.39E*
105 U15 **Draguignan** Var, SE France *43.31N 6.31E*
76 E9 **Dra, Hamada du** *var.* Hammada du Drâa, Haut Plateau du Dra. *plateau* W Algeria
Dra, Haut Plateau du *see* Dra, Hamada du
121 H19 **Drahichyn** *Pol.* Drohiczyn Poleski, *Rus.* Drogichin. Brestskaya Voblasts', SW Belarus *52.10N 25.10E*
31 N4 **Drake** North Dakota, N USA *47.54N 100.23W*
85 K23 **Drakensberg** ▲▲ Lesotho/South Africa
204 F3 **Drake Passage** *passage* Atlantic Ocean/Pacific Ocean
116 L8 **Dralfa** Tŭrgovishte, N Bulgaria *43.17N 26.25E*
116 I12 **Dráma** *var.* Dhráma. Anatolikí Makedonía kai Thráki, NE Greece *41.09N 24.10E*
Dramburg *see* Drawsko Pomorskie
97 H15 **Drammen** Buskerud, S Norway *59.43N 10.12E*
97 H15 **Drammensfjorden** *fjord* S Norway
94 H1 **Drangajökull** ▲ NW Iceland *66.13N 22.18W*
97 F16 **Drangedal** Telemark, S Norway *59.04N 9.01E*
94 I2 **Drangsnes** Vestfirdhir, NW Iceland *65.42N 21.27W*
Drann *see* Dravinja
111 T10 **Drau** *var.* Drava, *Eng.* Drave, *Hung.* Dráva. ~ C Europe ***see also*** Drava
86 I11 **Drava** *var.* Drau, *Eng.* Drave, *Hung.* Dráva. ~ C Europe ***see also*** Drau
Dráva/Drave *see* Drau/Drava
111 W10 **Dravinja** *Ger.* Drann. ~ NE Slovenia
111 V9 **Dravograd** *Ger.* Unterdrauburg; *prev.* Spodnji Dravograd. N Slovenia *46.36N 15.00E*
112 F10 **Drawa** ~ NW Poland
112 F9 **Drawno** Zachodnio-pomorskie, NW Poland *53.12N 15.44E*
112 F9 **Drawsko Pomorskie** *Ger.* Dramburg. Zachodnio-pomorskie, NW Poland *53.31N 15.48E*
31 R3 **Drayton** North Dakota, N USA *48.34N 97.10W*
9 P14 **Drayton Valley** Alberta, SW Canada *53.15N 115.00W*
194 F10 **Dreikikir** East Sepik, NW PNG *3.34S 142.44E*
Dreikirchen *see* Teiuş
100 N7 **Drenthe** ◈ *province* NE Netherlands
117 H15 **Drépano, Akrotírio** *var.* Akra Dhrepanon. *headland* N Greece *39.56N 23.57E*
Drepanum *see* Trapani
12 D17 **Dresden** Ontario, S Canada *42.34N 82.09W*
103 O16 **Dresden** Sachsen, E Germany *51.02N 13.43E*
22 G8 **Dresden** Tennessee, S USA *36.17N 88.42W*
120 M11 **Dretun'** *Rus.* Dretun'. Vitsyebskaya Voblasts', N Belarus *55.42N 29.12E*
104 M5 **Dreux** *anc.* Drocae, Durocasses. Eure-et-Loir, C France *48.43N 1.22E*
96 I11 **Drevsjø** Hedmark, S Norway *61.52N 12.01E*
24 K3 **Drew** Mississippi, S USA *33.48N 90.31W*
112 F10 **Drezdenko** *Ger.* Driesen. Lubuskie, W Poland *52.51N 15.49E*
100 J12 **Driebergen** *var.* Driebergen-Rijsenburg. Utrecht, C Netherlands *52.03N 5.16E*
Driebergen-Rijsenburg *see* Driebergen
Driesen *see* Drezdenko
99 N16 **Driffield** E England, UK *54.00N.28W*
67 D25 **Driftwood Point** *headland* East Falkland, Falkland Islands *52.15S 59.00W*
35 S14 **Driggs** Idaho, NW USA *43.44N 111.06W*
Drin *see* Drinit, Lumi i
114 K12 **Drina** ~ Bosnia and Herzegovina/Serbia
Drin, Gulf of *see* Drinit, Gjiri i
115 K18 **Drinit, Gjiri i** *var.* Pellg i Drinit, *Eng.* Gulf of Drin. *gulf* NW Albania
115 L17 **Drinit, Lumi i** *var.* Drin. ~ NW Albania
Drinit, Pellg i *see* Drinit, Gjiri i
Drinit të Zi, Lumi i *see* Black Drin
115 L22 **Dríno** *var.* Drino, Drínos Pótamos, *Alb.* Lumi i Drinos. ~ Albania/Greece
Drinos, Lumi i/Drínos Pótamos *see* Dríno
27 S11 **Dripping Springs** Texas, SW USA *30.11N 98.04W*
27 S15 **Driscoll** Texas, SW USA *27.40N 97.45W*
24 H5 **Driskill Mountain** ▲ Louisiana, S USA *32.25N 92.54W*
Drissa *see* Drysa
96 G10 **Driva** ~ S Norway
114 E13 **Drniš** *It.* Šibenik-Knin, S Croatia *43.51N 16.10E*
97 H15 **Drøbak** Akershus, S Norway *59.40N 10.37E*
118 G13 **Drobeta-Turnu Severin** *prev.* Turnu Severin. Mehedinţi, SW Romania *44.39N 22.39E*
Drocae *see* Dreux
118 M8 **Drochia** *Rus.* Drokiya. N Moldova *48.02N 27.46E*
99 F17 **Drogheda** *Ir.* Droichead Átha. NE Ireland *53.43N 6.21W*
Drogichin *see* Drahichyn
Drogobych *see* Drohobych
Drohiczyn Poleski *see* Drahichyn
118 H6 **Drohobych** *Pol.* Drohobycz, *Rus.* Drogobych. L'vivs'ka Oblast', NW Ukraine *49.22N 23.34E*
Drohobycz *see* Drohobych
Droichead Átha *see* Drogheda
Droicheadna Bandan *see* Bandon
Droichead na Banna *see* Banbridge
Droim Mór *see* Dromore
Drokiya *see* Drochia
105 R13 **Drôme** ◈ *department* E France
105 S13 **Drôme** ~ E France
99 G15 **Dromore** *Ir.* Droim Mór. SE Northern Ireland, UK *54.25N 6.09W*
108 A9 **Dronero** Piemonte, NE Italy *44.28N 7.25E*
104 L12 **Dronne** ~ SW France
205 Q3 **Dronning Maud Land** *physical region* Antarctica
100 K6 **Dronrijp** *Fris.* Dronryp. Friesland, N Netherlands *53.12N 5.37E*
Dronryp *see* Dronrijp
100 L9 **Dronten** Flevoland, C Netherlands *52.31N 5.40E*
Drontheim *see* Trondheim
104 L13 **Dropt** ~ SW France
155 T4 **Drosh** North-West Frontier Province, NW Pakistan *35.33N 71.48E*
Drossen *see* Ośno Lubuskie
Drug *see* Durg
Drujba *see* Pitnak
120 I12 **Drūkšiai** ◎ NE Lithuania
Druk-yul *see* Bhutan
9 Q16 **Drumheller** Alberta, SW Canada *51.28N 112.42W*
35 Q10 **Drummond** Montana, NW USA *46.39N 113.12W*
33 R4 **Drummond Island** *island* Michigan, N USA
Drummond Island *see* Tabiteuea
23 X7 **Drummond, Lake** ◎ Virginia, NE USA
13 P12 **Drummondville** Québec, SE Canada *45.52N 72.28W*
41 T11 **Drum, Mount** ▲ Alaska, USA *62.11N 144.37W*
29 O9 **Drumright** Oklahoma, C USA *35.59N 96.36W*
101 J14 **Drunen** Noord-Brabant, S Netherlands *51.40N 5.07E*
Druskieniki *see* Druskininkai
121 F15 **Druskininkai** *Pol.* Druskienniki. Alytus, S Lithuania *54.00N 24.00E*
100 K13 **Druten** Gelderland, SE Netherlands *51.52N 5.37E*
120 K11 **Druya** Vitsyebskaya Voblasts', NW Belarus *55.48N 27.27E*
119 S2 **Druzhba** Sums'ka Oblast', NE Ukraine *52.01N 33.56E*
Druzhba *see* Dostyk, Kazakhstan
Druzhba *see* Pitnak, Uzbekistan

◆ Country ● Country Capital ◇ Dependent Territory ○ Dependent Territory Capital ◈ Administrative Region ✕ International Airport ▲ Mountain ▲▲ Mountain Range Ѫ Volcano ~ River ◎ Lake ⊡ Reservoir

Druzhina – East Anglia

126 Mm7 **Druzhina** Respublika Sakha (Yakutiya), NE Russian Federation *68.01N 144.58E*
119 X7 **Druzhkivka** Donets'ka Oblast', E Ukraine *48.38N 37.31E*
114 E12 **Drvar** Federacija Bosna I Hercegovina, Bosnia and Herzegovina *44.21N 16.24E*
115 G15 **Drvenik** Split-Dalmacija, SE Croatia *43.10N 17.13E*
116 K9 **Dryanovo** Gabrovo, N Bulgaria *42.58N 25.28E*
28 G7 **Dry Cimarron River** Kansas/Oklahoma, C USA
10 B11 **Dryden** Ontario, C Canada *49.48N 92.48W*
26 M11 **Dryden** Texas, SW USA *30.01N 102.06W*
205 Q14 **Drygalski Ice Tongue** *ice feature* Antarctica
120 L11 **Drysa** *Rus.* Drissa. N Belarus
25 V17 **Dry Tortugas** *island* Florida, SE USA
81 D15 **Dschang** Ouest, W Cameroon *5.28N 10.01E*
56 J5 **Duaca** Lara, N Venezuela *10.16N 69.12W*
Duacum *see* Douai
Duala *see* Douala
47 N9 **Duarte, Pico** ▲ C Dominican Republic *19.02N 70.57W*
146 J5 **Ḑubā** Tabūk, NW Saudi Arabia *27.25N 35.42E*
Dubai *see* Dubayy
119 N9 **Dubăsari** *Rus.* Dubossary. NE Moldova *47.16N 29.07E*
119 N9 **Dubăsari Reservoir** ◻ NE Moldova
15 Jj8 **Dubawnt** Nunavut, NW Canada
15 K7 **Dubawnt Lake** ◎ Northwest Territories/Nunavut, N Canada
32 L6 **Du Bay, Lake** ◻ Wisconsin, N USA
147 U7 **Dubayy** *Eng.* Dubai. Dubayy, NE UAE *25.10N 55.18E*
147 W7 **Dubayy** *Eng.* Dubai. ✕ Dubayy, NE UAE *25.15N 55.22E*
191 R7 **Dubbo** New South Wales, SE Australia *32.16S 148.40E*
110 G7 **Dübendorf** Zürich, NW Switzerland *47.24N 8.36E*
99 F18 **Dublin** *Ir.* Baile Átha Cliath; *anc.* Eblana. ● (Ireland), E Ireland *53.19N 6.15W*
25 U5 **Dublin** Georgia, SE USA *32.32N 82.54W*
27 R7 **Dublin** Texas, SW USA *32.05N 98.20W*
99 G18 **Dublin** *Ir.* Baile Átha Cliath; *anc.* Eblana. *cultural region* E Ireland
99 G18 **Dublin Airport** ✕ E Ireland *53.25N 6.18W*
201 V12 **Dublon** *var.* Tonoas. *island* Chuuk Islands, C Micronesia
130 K2 **Dubna** Moskovskaya Oblast', W Russian Federation *56.45N 37.09E*
113 G19 **Dubňany** *Ger.* Dubnian. Jihomoravský Kraj, SE Czech Republic *48.54N 17.00E*
Dubnian *see* Dubňany
113 I19 **Dubnica nad Váhom** *Hung.* Máriatölgyes; *prev.* Dubnicz. Trenčiansky Kraj, W Slovakia *48.58N 18.10E*
Dubnicz *see* Dubnica nad Váhom
118 K4 **Dubno** Rivnens'ka Oblast', NW Ukraine *50.27N 25.39E*
20 D13 **Du Bois** Pennsylvania, NE USA *41.07N 78.45W*
35 R13 **Dubois** Idaho, NW USA *44.10N 112.13W*
35 T14 **Dubois** Wyoming, C USA *43.31N 109.37W*
Dubossary *see* Dubăsari
131 O10 **Dubovka** Volgogradskaya Oblast', SW Russian Federation *49.10N 48.49E*
78 H14 **Dubréka** SW Guinea *9.48N 13.31W*
12 B7 **Dubreuilville** Ontario, S Canada *48.21N 84.31W*
Dubris Portus *see* Dover
121 L20 **Dubrova** *Rus.* Dubrova. Homyel'skaya Voblasts', SE Belarus *51.46N 28.13E*
130 I5 **Dubrovka** Bryanskaya Oblast', W Russian Federation *53.44N 33.27E*
115 H16 **Dubrovnik** *It.* Ragusa. Dubrovnik-Neretva, SE Croatia *42.39N 18.06E*
115 I16 **Dubrovnik** ✕ Dubrovnik-Neretva, SE Croatia *42.34N 18.17E*
115 F16 **Dubrovnik-Neretva** *off.* Dubrovačko-Neretvanska Županija. ◆ *province* SE Croatia
Dubrovno *see* Dubrowna
118 L2 **Dubrovytsya** Rivnens'ka Oblast', NW Ukraine *51.34N 26.37E*
121 O14 **Dubrowna** *Rus.* Dubrovno. Vitsyebskaya Voblasts', N Belarus *54.34N 30.40E*
31 Z13 **Dubuque** Iowa, C USA *42.30N 90.39W*
120 E12 **Dubysa** C Lithuania
178 K12 **Đưc Cơ** Gia Lai, C Vietnam *13.48N 107.41E*
203 V12 **Duc de Gloucester, Îles du** *Eng.* Duke of Gloucester Islands. *island group* C French Polynesia
113 C15 **Duchcov** *Ger.* Dux. Ústecký Kraj, NW Czech Republic *50.37N 13.40E*
39 N3 **Duchesne** Utah, W USA *40.09N 110.24W*
203 P17 **Ducie Island** *atoll* E Pitcairn Islands
9 W15 **Duck Bay** Manitoba, S Canada *52.11N 100.08W*
25 X17 **Duck Key** *island* Florida Keys, Florida, SE USA
9 T14 **Duck Lake** Saskatchewan, S Canada *52.52N 106.12W*
9 V15 **Duck Mountain** ▲ Manitoba, S Canada
22 I9 **Duck River** Tennessee, S USA
22 M10 **Ducktown** Tennessee, S USA *35.01N 84.24W*
178 Kk11 **Đưc Phô** Quang Ngai, C Vietnam *14.55N 108.55E*
Đưc Tho *see* Lin Camh
178 Kk13 **Đưc Trong** *var.* Liên Nghia. Lâm Đông, S Vietnam *11.45N 108.24E*
D-U-D *see* Dalap-Uliga-Djarrit
101 M25 **Dudelange** *var.* Forge du Sud, *Ger.* Dudelingen. Luxembourg, S Luxembourg *49.28N 6.04E*
Dudelingen *see* Dudelange
103 J15 **Duderstadt** Niedersachsen, C Germany *51.31N 10.16E*
159 N15 **Dūdhi** Uttar Pradesh, N India *24.13N 83.18E*
126 I8 **Dudinka** Taymyrskiy (Dolgano-Nenetskiy) Avtonomnyy Okrug, N Russian Federation *69.27N 86.13E*
99 L20 **Dudley** C England, UK *52.30N 2.04W*
160 G13 **Dudna** C India
78 L16 **Duékoué** W Ivory Coast *6.45N 7.21W*
106 M5 **Dueñas** Castilla-León, N Spain *41.52N 4.33W*
106 K4 **Duerna** NW Spain
107 O6 **Duero** *Port.* Douro. Portugal/Spain *see also* Douro
Duesseldorf *see* Düsseldorf
23 P12 **Due West** South Carolina, SE USA *34.19N 82.23W*
205 P11 **Dufek Coast** *physical region* Antarctica
101 H17 **Duffel** Antwerpen, C Belgium *51.06N 4.30E*
37 S2 **Duffer Peak** ▲ Nevada, W USA *41.40N 118.45W*
195 X7 **Duff Islands** *island group* E Solomon Islands
Dufour, Pizzo/Dufour, Punta *see* Dufour Spitze
110 E12 **Dufour Spitze** *It.* Pizzo Dufour, Punta Dufour. ▲ Italy/Switzerland *45.54N 7.50E*
114 D9 **Duga Resa** Karlovac, C Croatia *45.25N 15.30E*
24 H5 **Dugdemona River** Louisiana, S USA
160 J12 **Duggipar** Mahārāshtra, C India *21.06N 80.10E*
114 B13 **Dugi Otok** *var.* Isola Grossa, *It.* Isola Lunga. *island* W Croatia
115 F14 **Dugopolje** Split-Dalmacija, S Croatia *43.35N 16.35E*
166 L8 **Du He** C China
56 M11 **Duida, Cerro** ▲ S Venezuela *3.21N 65.45W*
Duinekerke *see* Dunkerque
103 E15 **Duisburg** *prev.* Duisburg-Hamborn. Nordrhein-Westfalen, W Germany *51.24N 6.47E*
Duisburg-Hamborn *see* Duisburg
101 F14 **Duiveland** *island* SW Netherlands
100 M12 **Duiven** Gelderland, E Netherlands *51.57N 6.02E*
145 W10 **Dujaylah, Hawr ad** ◎ S Iraq
166 H9 **Dujiangyan** *var.* Guanxian, Guan Xian. Sichuan, C China *31.01N 103.40E*
83 L18 **Dujuuma** Shabeellaha Hoose, S Somalia *1.04N 42.37E*
Dūkān *see* Dokan
41 Z14 **Duke Island** *island* Alexander Archipelago, Alaska, USA
Dukelský Priesmy/Dukelský Průsmyk *see* Dukla Pass
Duke of Gloucester Islands *see* Duc de Gloucester, Îles du
83 F14 **Duk Faiwil** Jonglei, SE Sudan *7.30N 31.27E*
147 T7 **Dukhān** C Qatar *25.29N 50.48E*
Dukhan Heights *see* Dukhān, Jabal
149 N16 **Dukhān, Jabal** *var.* Dukhan Heights. *hill range* S Qatar
131 Q7 **Dukhovnitskoye** Saratovskaya Oblast', W Russian Federation *52.31N 48.32E*
130 H4 **Dukhovshchina** Smolenskaya Oblast', W Russian Federation *55.15N 32.22E*
Dukielska, Przełęcz *see* Dukla Pass
113 N17 **Dukla** Podkarpackie, SE Poland *49.33N 21.40E*
Duklai Hág *see* Dukla Pass
113 N18 **Dukla Pass** *Cz.* Dukelský Průsmyk, *Ger.* Dukla-Pass, *Hung.* Duklai Hág, *Pol.* Przełęcz Dukielska, *Slvk.* Dukelský Priesmy. *pass* Poland/Slovakia *49.25N 21.42E*
Dukou *see* Panzhihua
120 I12 **Dūkštas** Utena, E Lithuania *55.32N 26.21E*
Dulaan *see* Herlenbayan-Ulaan
165 R10 **Dulan** *var.* Qagan Us. Qinghai, C China *36.11N 97.51E*
39 R8 **Dulce** New Mexico, SW USA *36.55N 107.00W*
45 N16 **Dulce, Golfo** *gulf* S Costa Rica
Dulce, Golfo *see* Izabal, Lago de
44 K6 **Dulce Nombre de Culmí** Olancho, C Honduras *15.04N 85.35W*
64 L9 **Dulce, Río** C Argentina
126 M9 **Dulgalakh** NE Russian Federation
116 M8 **Dŭlgopol** Varna, E Bulgaria *43.05N 27.24E*
159 V14 **Dullabchara** Assam, NE India *24.25N 92.22E*
22 D3 **Dulles** ✕ (Washington DC) Virginia, NE USA *39.00N 77.27W*
103 E14 **Dülmen** Nordrhein-Westfalen, W Germany *51.51N 7.17E*
116 M7 **Dulovo** Silistra, NE Bulgaria *43.50N 27.10E*
31 W5 **Duluth** Minnesota, N USA *46.46N 92.06W*
144 H7 **Dūmā** *Fr.* Douma. Dimashq, SW Syria *33.33N 36.24E*
179 Pp16 **Dumagasa Point** *headland* Mindanao, S Philippines *7.01N 121.54E*
179 Qq14 **Dumaguete** *var.* Dumaguete City. Negros, C Philippines *9.16N 123.17E*
174 Gg6 **Dumai** Sumatera, W Indonesia *1.40N 101.27E*
191 T4 **Dumaresq River** New South Wales/Queensland, SE Australia
29 W13 **Dumas** Arkansas, C USA *33.53N 91.29W*
27 N1 **Dumas** Texas, SW USA *35.51N 101.57W*
144 I7 **Ḑumayr** Dimashq, W Syria *33.36N 36.28E*
98 I12 **Dumbarton** W Scotland, UK *55.57N 4.34W*
98 I12 **Dumbarton** *cultural region* C Scotland, UK
197 J7 **Dumbéa** Province Sud, S New Caledonia *22.11S 166.27E*
113 K19 **Ďumbier** *Ger.* Djumbir, *Hung.* Gyömbér. ▲ C Slovakia *48.54N 19.36E*
118 I11 **Dumbrăveni** *Ger.* Elisabethstedt, *Hung.* Erzsébetváros; *prev.* Ebesfalva, Eppeschdorf, Ibaşfalău. Sibiu, C Romania *45.48N 24.08E*
118 L12 **Dumbrăveni** Vrancea, E Romania *45.30N 27.08E*
99 J14 **Dumfries** S Scotland, UK *55.04N 3.37W*
99 J14 **Dumfries** *cultural region* SW Scotland, UK
159 R15 **Dumka** Jhārkhand, NE India *24.16N 87.15E*
Dümmer *see* Dümmersee
102 G12 **Dümmersee** *var.* Dümmer. ◎ NW Germany
12 J11 **Dumoine** Québec, SE Canada
12 J10 **Dumoine, Lac** ◎ Québec, SE Canada
205 V16 **Dumont d'Urville** *French research station* Antarctica *66.24S 139.38E*
205 W15 **Dumont d'Urville Sea** S Pacific Ocean
12 K11 **Dumont, Lac** ◎ Québec, SE Canada
77 W7 **Dumyāt** *Eng.* Damietta. N Egypt *31.25N 31.48E*
Duna *see* Don, Russian Federation
Duna *see* Danube, C Europe
Düna *see* Western Dvina
Dünaburg *see* Daugavpils
113 J24 **Dunaföldvár** Tolna, C Hungary *46.16N 18.54E*
Dunaj *see* Wien, Austria
Dunaj *see* Danube, C Europe
113 L18 **Dunajec** S Poland
113 H21 **Dunajská Streda** *Hung.* Dunaszerdahely. Trnavský Kraj, W Slovakia *48.00N 17.27E*
Dunapentele *see* Dunaújváros
Dunărea *see* Danube
118 M13 **Dunărea Veche, Braţul** SE Romania
119 N13 **Dunării, Delta** *delta* SE Romania
Dunaszerdahely *see* Dunajská Streda
113 J23 **Dunaújváros** *prev.* Dunapentele, Sztálinváros. Fejér, C Hungary *47.00N 18.55E*
Dunav *see* Danube
116 J8 **Dunavska Ravnina** *Eng.* Danubian Plain. *plain* N Bulgaria
116 G7 **Dunavtsi** Vidin, NW Bulgaria *43.56N 22.49E*
127 N17 **Dunay** Primorskiy Kray, SE Russian Federation *42.53N 132.20E*
Dunayevtsy *see* Dunayivtsi
118 L7 **Dunayivtsi** *Rus.* Dunayevtsy. Khmel'nyts'ka Oblast', NW Ukraine *48.54N 26.51E*
193 F22 **Dunback** Otago, South Island, NZ *45.22S 170.37E*
8 L17 **Duncan** Vancouver Island, British Columbia, SW Canada *48.46N 123.10W*
39 O15 **Duncan** Arizona, SW USA *32.43N 109.06W*
28 M12 **Duncan** Oklahoma, C USA *34.30N 97.57W*
Duncan Island *see* Pinzón, Isla
157 Q20 **Duncan Passage** *strait* Andaman Sea/Bay of Bengal
98 K6 **Duncansby Head** *headland* N Scotland, UK *58.37N 3.01W*
12 G12 **Dunchurch** Ontario, S Canada *45.36N 79.54W*
120 D7 **Dundaga** Talsi, NW Latvia *57.29N 22.19E*
12 G14 **Dundalk** Ontario, S Canada *44.11N 80.22W*
99 F16 **Dundalk** *Ir.* Dún Dealgan. NE Ireland *54.01N 6.25W*
23 X3 **Dundalk** Maryland, NE USA *39.15N 76.31W*
99 F16 **Dundalk Bay** *Ir.* Cuan Dhún Dealgan. *bay* NE Ireland
12 G16 **Dundas** Ontario, S Canada *43.16N 79.55W*
188 L12 **Dundas, Lake** *salt lake* Western Australia
Dundbürd *see* Batnorov
Dún Dealgan *see* Dundalk
13 N13 **Dundee** Québec, SE Canada *45.01N 74.27W*
85 K22 **Dundee** KwaZulu/Natal, E South Africa *28.08S 30.12E*
98 K11 **Dundee** E Scotland, UK *56.28N 3.00W*
33 R10 **Dundee** Michigan, N USA *41.57N 83.39W*
27 R5 **Dundee** Texas, SW USA *33.43N 98.52W*
204 H3 **Dundee Island** *island* Antarctica
168 L9 **Dundgovĭ** ◆ *province* C Mongolia
99 G16 **Dundrum Bay** *Ir.* Cuan Dhún Droma. *inlet* NW Irish Sea
176 Y11 **Dundu** Papua, E Indonesia
9 T15 **Dundurn** Saskatchewan, S Canada *51.43N 106.27W*
Dund-Us *see* Hovd
193 F23 **Dunedin** Otago, South Island, NZ *45.51S 170.31E*
191 R7 **Dunedoo** New South Wales, SE Australia *32.04S 149.23E*
99 D14 **Dunfanaghy** *Ir.* Dún Fionnachaidh. NW Ireland *55.10N 7.58W*
98 J12 **Dunfermline** C Scotland, UK *56.04N 3.28W*
Dún Fionnachaidh *see* Dunfanaghy
155 V10 **Dunga Bunga** Punjab, E Pakistan *29.51N 73.19E*
99 F15 **Dungannon** *Ir.* Dún Geanainn. C Northern Ireland, UK *54.31N 6.46W*
Dun Garbháin *see* Dungarvan
158 F15 **Düngarpur** Rājasthān, N India *23.53N 73.39E*
99 E21 **Dungarvan** *Ir.* Dun Garbháin. S Ireland *52.04N 7.37W*
103 N21 **Dungau** *cultural region* SE Germany
Dún Geanainn *see* Dungannon
99 P23 **Dungeness** *headland* SE England, UK *50.55N 0.58E*
65 I23 **Dungeness, Punta** *headland* S Argentina *52.25S 68.25W*
Dungloe *see* Dunglow
99 D14 **Dunglow** *var.* Dungloe, *Ir.* An Clochán Liath. NW Ireland *54.57N 8.22W*
191 T7 **Dungog** New South Wales, SE Australia *32.24S 151.45E*
81 O16 **Dungu** Orientale, NE Dem. Rep. Congo *3.40N 28.31E*
174 Hh3 **Dungun** *var.* Kuala Dungun. Terengganu, Peninsular Malaysia *4.46N 103.25E*
82 I6 **Dungûnab** Red Sea, NE Sudan *21.06N 37.06E*
13 P13 **Dunham** Québec, SE Canada *45.08N 72.48W*
Dunheved *see* Launceston
Dunholme *see* Durham
169 X10 **Dunhua** Jilin, NE China *43.22N 128.12E*
165 P8 **Dunhuang** Gansu, N China *40.10N 94.43E*
190 L12 **Dunkeld** Victoria, SE Australia *37.41S 142.19E*
105 O1 **Dunkerque** *Eng.* Dunkirk, *Flem.* Duinekerke; *prev.* Dunquerque. Nord, N France *51.06N 2.34E*
99 K23 **Dunkery Beacon** ▲ SW England, UK *51.10N 3.36W*
20 C11 **Dunkirk** New York, NE USA *42.28N 79.19W*
Dunkirk *see* Dunkerque
79 P17 **Dunkwa** SW Ghana *5.58N 1.45W*
99 G18 **Dún Laoghaire** *Eng.* Dunleary; *prev.* Kingstown. E Ireland *53.16N 6.07W*
31 S14 **Dunlap** Iowa, C USA *41.51N 95.36W*
22 L10 **Dunlap** Tennessee, S USA *35.22N 85.23W*
Dunleary *see* Dún Laoghaire
Dún Mánmhaí *see* Dunmanway
99 B21 **Dunmanway** *Ir.* Dún Mánmhaí. SW Ireland *51.43N 9.07W*
20 I13 **Dunmore** Pennsylvania, NE USA *41.25N 75.37W*
23 U10 **Dunn** North Carolina, SE USA *35.18N 78.36W*
Dún na nGall *see* Donegal
25 V11 **Dunnellon** Florida, SE USA *29.03N 82.27W*
98 J6 **Dunnet Head** *headland* N Scotland, UK *58.40N 3.27W*
31 N14 **Dunning** Nebraska, C USA *41.49N 100.04W*
67 B24 **Dunnose Head Settlement** West Falkland, Falkland Islands *51.24S 60.28W*
12 G17 **Dunnville** Ontario, S Canada *42.54N 79.36W*
Dún Pádraig *see* Downpatrick
Dunquerque *see* Dunkerque
Dunqulah *see* Dongola
98 L12 **Duns** SE Scotland, UK *55.46N 2.13W*
31 N2 **Dunseith** North Dakota, N USA *48.48N 100.03W*
37 N2 **Dunsmuir** California, W USA *41.12N 122.19W*
99 N21 **Dunstable** *Lat.* Durocobrivae. E England, UK *51.52N 0.31W*
193 D21 **Dunstan Mountains** ▲ South Island, NZ
105 O9 **Dun-sur-Auron** Cher, C France *46.52N 2.40E*
193 F21 **Duntroon** Canterbury, South Island, NZ *44.52S 170.40E*
155 T10 **Dunyāpur** Punjab, E Pakistan *29.48N 71.48E*
169 U5 **Duobukur He** NE China
169 R12 **Duolun** *var.* Dolonnur. Nei Mongol Zizhiqu, N China *42.11N 116.30E*
178 Ii14 **Dương Đông** Kiên Giang, S Vietnam *10.15N 103.58E*
116 G10 **Dupnitsa** *prev.* Marek, Stanke Dimitrov. Kyustendil, W Bulgaria *42.15N 23.09E*
30 L8 **Dupree** South Dakota, N USA *45.03N 101.36W*
35 Q7 **Dupuyer** Montana, NW USA *48.13N 112.34W*
147 Y11 **Duqm** *var.* Daqm. E Oman *19.42N 57.39E*
65 F23 **Duque de York, Isla** *island* S Chile
189 N4 **Durack Range** ▲ Western Australia
142 K10 **Durağan** Sinop, N Turkey *41.25N 35.03E*
105 S15 **Durance** SE France
33 R9 **Durand** Michigan, N USA *42.54N 83.58W*
32 I6 **Durand** Wisconsin, N USA *44.37N 91.55W*
197 L7 **Durand, Récif** *reef* SE New Caledonia
42 K10 **Durango** *var.* Victoria de Durango. Durango, W Mexico *24.03N 104.37W*
107 P3 **Durango** País Vasco, N Spain *43.10N 2.37W*
39 Q8 **Durango** Colorado, C USA *37.13N 107.51W*
42 J9 **Durango** ◆ *state* C Mexico
116 O7 **Durankulak** *Rom.* Răcari; *prev.* Blatnitsa, Duranulac. Dobrich, NE Bulgaria *43.41N 28.31E*
24 L4 **Durant** Mississippi, S USA *33.04N 89.51W*
29 P13 **Durant** Oklahoma, C USA *33.59N 96.22W*
Duranulac *see* Durankulak
107 N6 **Duratón** N Spain
63 E19 **Durazno** *var.* San Pedro de Durazno. Durazno, C Uruguay *33.24S 56.28W*
63 E19 **Durazno** ◆ *department* C Uruguay
Durazzo *see* Durrës
85 K23 **Durban** *var.* Port Natal. KwaZulu/Natal, E South Africa *29.51S 31.00E*
85 K23 **Durban** ✕ KwaZulu/Natal, E South Africa *29.55S 31.01E*
120 C9 **Durbe** *Ger.* Durben. Liepāja, W Latvia *56.34N 21.22E*
Durben *see* Durbe
101 K21 **Durbuy** Luxembourg, SE Belgium *50.21N 5.27E*
107 N15 **Dúrcal** Andalucía, S Spain *37.00N 3.24W*
114 F8 **Đurđevac** *Ger.* Sankt Georgen, *Hung.* Szentgyörgy; *prev.* Djurdjevac, Gjurgjevac. Koprivnica-Križevci, N Croatia *46.02N 17.03E*
115 K15 **Đurđevica Tara** N-Montenegro *43.09N 19.18E*
99 L24 **Durdle Door** *natural arch* S England, UK
164 L3 **Düre** Xinjiang Uygur Zizhiqu, W China *46.30N 88.26E*
103 D16 **Düren** *anc.* Marcodurum. Nordrhein-Westfalen, W Germany *50.48N 6.28E*
160 K12 **Durg** *prev.* Drug. Chhattīsgarh, C India *21.12N 81.19E*
159 U13 **Durgapur** Dhaka, N Bangladesh *25.10N 90.41E*
159 R15 **Durgāpur** West Bengal, NE India *23.30N 87.19E*
12 F14 **Durham** Ontario, S Canada *44.10N 80.48W*
99 M14 **Durham** *hist.* Dunholme. N England, UK *54.46N 1.34W*
23 U9 **Durham** North Carolina, SE USA *35.59N 78.54W*
99 L15 **Durham** *cultural region* N England, UK
174 Gg7 **Duri** Sumatera, W Indonesia *1.13N 101.13E*
Duria Major *see* Dora Baltea
Duria Minor *see* Dora Riparia
Durlas *see* Thurles
147 P8 **Ḑurmā** Ar Riyāḑ, C Saudi Arabia *24.37N 46.06E*
115 J15 **Durmitor** ▲ N Montenegro *43.06N 19.00E*
98 H6 **Durness** N Scotland, UK *58.34N 4.45W*
111 Y3 **Dürnkrut** Niederösterreich, E Austria *48.28N 16.50E*
Durnovaria *see* Dorchester
Durobrivae *see* Rochester
Durocasses *see* Dreux
Durocobrivae *see* Dunstable
Durocortorum *see* Reims
Durostorum *see* Silistra
Durovernum *see* Canterbury
115 K20 **Durrës** *var.* Durrësi, Dursi, *It.* Durazzo, *SCr.* Drač, *Turk.* Draç. Durrës, W Albania *41.19N 19.25E*
115 K19 **Durrës** ◆ *district* W Albania
Durrësi *see* Durrës
99 A21 **Dursey Island** *Ir.* Oileán Baoi. *island* SW Ireland
Dursi *see* Durrës
Duru *see* Wuchuan
Durud *see* Do Rūd
116 P12 **Durusu** İstanbul, NW Turkey *41.18N 28.41E*
116 O12 **Durusu Gölü** ◎ NW Turkey
144 I9 **Durūz, Jabal ad** ▲ SW Syria *37.00N 32.30E*
192 K13 **D'Urville Island** *island* C NZ
176 Xx9 **D'Urville, Tanjung** *headland* Papua, E Indonesia *1.26S 137.52E*
152 H14 **Duşak** *Rus.* Dushak. Ahal Welaýaty, S Turkmenistan *37.15N 59.57E*
Dusa Mareb/Dusa Marreb *see* Dhuusa Marreeb
120 I11 **Dusetos** Utena, NE Lithuania *55.44N 25.49E*
Dushak *see* Duşak
166 K12 **Dushan** Guizhou, S China *25.45N 107.33E*
153 P13 **Dushanbe** *var.* Dyushambe; *prev.* Stalinabad, *Taj.* Stalinobod. ● (Tajikistan) W Tajikistan *38.35N 68.43E*
153 P13 **Dushanbe** ✕ W Tajikistan *38.31N 68.49E*
143 T9 **Dushet'i** E Georgia *42.07N 44.44E*
20 H13 **Dushore** Pennsylvania, NE USA *41.30N 76.23W*
193 A23 **Dusky Sound** *sound* South Island, NZ
103 E15 **Düsseldorf** *var.* Duesseldorf. Nordrhein-Westfalen, W Germany *51.13N 6.49E*
153 P14 **Dūsti** *Rus.* Dusti. SW Tajikistan *37.22N 68.41E*
204 I9 **Dustin Island** *island* Antarctica
Dutch East Indies *see* Indonesia
Dutch Guiana *see* Surinam
40 L17 **Dutch Harbor** Unalaska Island, Alaska, USA *53.50N 166.33W*
38 J3 **Dutch Mount** ▲ Utah, W USA *40.16N 113.56W*
Dutch New Guinea *see* Papua
Dutch West Indies *see* Netherlands Antilles
85 H20 **Dutlwe** Kweneng, S Botswana *23.56S 23.53E*
151 V16 **Du Toit Fracture Zone** *tectonic feature* SW Indian Ocean
129 U8 **Dutovo** Respublika Komi, NW Russian Federation *63.45N 56.38E*
79 V13 **Dutsan Wai** *var.* Dutsen Wai. Kaduna, C Nigeria *10.49N 8.15E*
79 W13 **Dutse** Jigawa, N Nigeria *11.43N 9.25E*
Dutsen Wai *see* Dutsan Wai
Duttia *see* Datia
12 E17 **Dutton** Ontario, S Canada *42.40N 81.28W*
38 L7 **Dutton, Mount** ▲ Utah, W USA *38.00N 112.10W*
168 E7 **Duut** Hovd, W Mongolia *47.28N 91.52E*
12 K11 **Duval, Lac** ◎ Québec, SE Canada
131 W3 **Duvan** Respublika Bashkortostan, W Russian Federation *55.42N 57.56E*
144 L9 **Duwaykhilat Satiḩ ar Ruwayshid** *seasonal river* SE Jordan
Dux *see* Duchcov
166 J13 **Duyang Shan** ▲ S China
178 Jj15 **Duyên Hai** Tra Vinh, S Vietnam *9.39N 106.28E*
166 K12 **Duyun** Guizhou, S China *26.16N 107.28E*
142 G11 **Düzce** Düzce, NW Turkey *40.51N 31.09E*
142 K14 **Düzce** ◆ *province* NW Turkey
Duzdab *see* Zāhedān
Duzenkyr, Khrebet *see* Duzkyr, Khrebet
152 I16 **Duzkyr, Khrebet** *prev.* Khrebet Duzenkyr. ▲ S Turkmenistan
Dvina Bay *see* Chëshskaya Guba
Dvinsk *see* Daugavpils
128 L7 **Dvinskaya Guba** *bay* NW Russian Federation
114 E10 **Dvor** Sisak-Moslavina, C Croatia *45.05N 16.22E*
119 W5 **Dvorichna** Kharkivs'ka Oblast', E Ukraine *49.52N 37.43E*
113 F16 **Dvůr Králové nad Labem** *Ger.* Königinhof an der Elbe. Královéhradecký Kraj, NE Czech Republic *50.25N 15.48E*
160 A10 **Dwārka** Gujarāt, W India *22.13N 68.58E*
32 M12 **Dwight** Illinois, N USA *41.05N 88.25W*
100 N8 **Dwingeloo** Drenthe, NE Netherlands *52.49N 6.20E*
35 N10 **Dworshak Reservoir** ◻ Idaho, NW USA
Dyal *see* Dyaul Island
Dyanev *see* Galkynyş
Dyatlovo *see* Dzyatlava
195 N9 **Dyaul Island** *var.* Djaul, Dyal. *island* NE PNG
22 G8 **Dyer** Tennessee, S USA *36.04N 88.59W*
16 O1 **Dyer, Cape** *headland* Baffin Island, Nunavut, NE Canada *66.37N 61.13W*
22 F8 **Dyersburg** Tennessee, S USA *36.01N 89.23W*
31 Y13 **Dyersville** Iowa, C USA *42.29N 91.07W*
99 I21 **Dyfed** *cultural region* SW Wales, UK
Dyfrdwy, Afon *see* Dee
Dyhernfurth *see* Brzeg Dolny
113 E19 **Dyje** *var.* Thaya. Austria/Czech Republic *see also* Thaya
119 T5 **Dykanska** Poltavs'ka Oblast', C Ukraine *49.48N 34.33E*
194 L15 **Dyke Ackland Bay** *inlet* E PNG
131 N16 **Dykhtau** ▲ SW Russian Federation *43.01N 42.56E*
113 A16 **Dyleń** *Ger.* Tillenberg. ▲ NW Czech Republic *49.58N 12.31E*
112 K9 **Dylewska Góra** ▲ N Poland *53.33N 19.57E*
119 O4 **Dymer** Kyyivs'ka Oblast', N Ukraine *50.50N 30.21E*
119 W7 **Dymytrov** *Rus.* Dimitrov. Donets'ka Oblast', SE Ukraine *48.18N 37.19E*
113 O17 **Dynów** Podkarpackie, SE Poland *49.49N 22.14E*
31 X13 **Dysart** Iowa, C USA *42.10N 92.18W*
Dysna *see* Dzisna
117 H18 **Dýstos, Límni** *var.* Límni Dístos. ◎ Évvoia, C Greece
117 D18 **Dytikí Elláa** *Eng.* Greece West. ◆ *region* C Greece
117 C14 **Dytikí Makedonía** *Eng.* Macedonia West. ◆ *region* N Greece
Dyurment'yube *see* Dermentobe
131 U4 **Dyurtyuli** Respublika Bashkortostan, W Russian Federation *55.31N 54.49E*
Dyushambe *see* Dushanbe
168 K7 **Dzaamar** *var.* Bat-Öldziyt. Töv, C Mongolia *48.10N 104.49E*
Dzaanhushuu *see* Ihtamir
Dza Chu *see* Mekong
Dzadgay *see* Bömbögör
168 H8 **Dzag** Bayanhongor, C Mongolia *46.54N 99.11E*
Dzalaa *see* Shinejinst
169 O11 **Dzamïn-Üüd** *var.* Borhoyn Tal. Dornogovĭ, SE Mongolia *43.43N 111.53E*
180 J14 **Dzaoudzi** E Mayotte *12.48S 45.18E*
Dzaudzhikau *see* Vladikavkaz
168 G7 **Dzavhan** ◆ *province* NW Mongolia
168 G7 **Dzavhan Gol** NW Mongolia
168 G6 **Dzavhanmandal** *var.* Nuga. Dzavhan, W Mongolia *48.17N 95.07E*
Dzegstey *see* Ögiynuur
168 E7 **Dzereg** *var.* Altanteel. Hovd, W Mongolia *47.05N 92.57E*
131 O3 **Dzerzhinsk** Nizhegorodskaya Oblast', W Russian Federation *56.20N 43.22E*
Dzerzhinsk *see* Dzyarzhynsk, Belarus
Dzerzhinsk *see* Dzerzhyns'k, Ukraine
Dzerzhinskiy *see* Nar'yan-Mar
Dzerzhinskoye *see* Tokzhaylau
119 X7 **Dzerzhyns'k** *Rus.* Dzerzhinsk. Donets'ka Oblast', SE Ukraine *48.21N 37.50E*
118 M5 **Dzerzhyns'k** Zhytomyrs'ka Oblast', N Ukraine *50.07N 27.56E*
Dzhailgan *see* Jayilgan
Dzhalagash *see* Zhalagash
151 N14 **Dzhalagash** *Kaz.* Zhalashash. Kzylorda, S Kazakhstan *45.06N 64.40E*
153 T10 **Dzhalal-Abad** *Kir.* Jalal-Abad. Dzhalal-Abadskaya Oblast', W Kyrgyzstan *40.55N 73.00E*
153 S9 **Dzhalal-Abadskaya Oblast'** *Kir.* Jalal-Abad Oblasty. ◆ *province* W Kyrgyzstan
Dzhalilabad *see* Cälilabad
126 Ll15 **Dzhalinda** Amurskaya Oblast', SE Russian Federation *53.29N 123.53E*
Dzhambeyty *see* Zhympity
Dzhambulskaya Oblast' *see* Zhambyl
Dzhanibek *see* Zhanibek
Dzhankel'dy *see* Jongeldi
119 T12 **Dzhankoy** Respublika Krym, S Ukraine *45.42N 34.24E*
151 V14 **Dzhansugurov** *Kaz.* Zhansūgirov. Almaty, SE Kazakhstan *45.25N 79.23E*
153 R9 **Dzhany-Bazar** *var.* Yangibazar. Dzhalal-Abadskaya Oblast', W Kyrgyzstan *41.40N 70.49E*
Dzhanybek *see* Zhanibek
126 L8 **Dzhardzhan** Respublika Sakha (Yakutiya), NE Russian Federation *68.47N 123.51E*
Dzharkurgan *see* Jarqo'rg'on
119 S11 **Dzharylhats'ka Zatoka** *gulf* S Ukraine
Dzhayilgan *see* Jayilgan
Dzhebel *see* Jebel
153 T14 **Dzhelandy** SE Tajikistan *37.34N 72.34E*
153 Y7 **Dzhergalan** *Kir.* Jyrgalan. Issyk-Kul'skaya Oblast', NE Kyrgyzstan *42.37N 78.55E*
Dzherzinskoye *see* Tokzhaylau
Dzhetygara *see* Zhitikara
Dzhetysay *see* Zhetysay
Dzhezkazgan *see* Zhezkazgan
Dzhigirbent *see* Jigerbent
Dzhirgatal' *see* Jirgatol
Dzhizak *see* Jizzax
Dzhizakskaya Oblast' *see* Jizzax Viloyati
127 N12 **Dzhugdzhur, Khrebet** ▲ E Russian Federation
Dzhul'fa *see* Culfa
Dzhuma *see* Juma
151 W14 **Dzhungarskiy Alatau** ▲ China/Kazakhstan
150 M14 **Dzhusaly** *Kaz.* Zholsaly. Kzylorda, SW Kazakhstan *45.28N 64.04E*
152 J12 **Dzhynlykum, Peski** *desert* E Turkmenistan
112 L9 **Działdowo** Warmińsko-Mazurskie, C Poland *53.13N 20.11E*
113 L16 **Działoszyce** Swiętokrzyskie, C Poland *50.21N 20.19E*
43 X11 **Dzidzantún** Yucatán, E Mexico
113 G15 **Dzierżoniów** *Ger.* Reichenbach. Dolnośląskie, SW Poland *50.43N 16.40E*
43 X11 **Dzilam de Bravo** Yucatán, E Mexico *21.24N 88.52W*
120 L12 **Dzisna** *Rus.* Disna. Vitsyebskaya Voblasts', N Belarus *55.33N 28.13E*
120 K12 **Dzisna** *Lith.* Dysna, *Rus.* Disna. Belarus/Lithuania
121 G20 **Dzivin** *Rus.* Divin. Brestskaya Voblasts', SW Belarus *51.58N 24.33E*
121 M15 **Dzmitravichy** *Rus.* Dmitrovichi. Minskaya Voblasts', C Belarus *53.58N 29.14E*
Dzogsool *see* Bayantsagaan
168 I5 **Dzöölön** *var.* Rinchinlhümbe. Hövsgöl, N Mongolia *51.06N 99.40E*
133 S8 **Dzungaria** *var.* Sungaria, Zungaria. *physical region* W China
Dzungarian Basin *see* Junggar Pendi
Dzür *see* Tes
168 J8 **Dzüünbayan-Ulaan** *var.* Bayan-Ulaan. Övörhangay, C Mongolia *46.38N 102.30E*
Dzüünbulag *see* Matad, Dornod, Mongolia
Dzüünbulag *see* Uulbayan, Sühbaatar, Mongolia
168 L8 **Dzuunmod** Töv, C Mongolia *47.45N 107.00E*
Dzuunmod *see* Ider
Dzüün Soyonï Nuruu *see* Eastern Sayans
Dzüyl *see* Tonhil
Dzvina *see* Western Dvina
121 J16 **Dzyarzhynsk** *Rus.* Dzerzhinsk; *prev.* Kaydanovo. Minskaya Voblasts', C Belarus *53.41N 27.09E*
121 H17 **Dzyatlava** *Pol.* Zdzięcioł, *Rus.* Dyatlovo. Hrodzyenskaya Voblasts', W Belarus *53.27N 25.23E*

E

E *see* Hubei
Éadan Doire *see* Edenderry
39 W6 **Eads** Colorado, C USA *38.28N 102.46W*
39 O13 **Eagar** Arizona, SW USA *34.05N 109.17W*
41 T8 **Eagle** Alaska, USA *64.47N 141.12W*
11 S8 **Eagle** Newfoundland and Labrador, E Canada
8 I3 **Eagle** Yukon Territory, NW Canada
31 T7 **Eagle Bend** Minnesota, N USA *46.10N 95.02W*
30 M8 **Eagle Butte** South Dakota, N USA *44.58N 101.13W*
31 V12 **Eagle Grove** Iowa, C USA *42.39N 93.54W*
21 R2 **Eagle Lake** Maine, NE USA *47.01N 68.35W*
27 U11 **Eagle Lake** Texas, SW USA *29.35N 96.19W*
10 A11 **Eagle Lake** ◎ Ontario, S Canada
37 P3 **Eagle Lake** ◎ California, W USA
21 R3 **Eagle Lake** ◎ Maine, NE USA
31 Y3 **Eagle Mountain** ▲ Minnesota, N USA *47.54N 90.33W*
27 T6 **Eagle Mountain Lake** ◻ Texas, SW USA
39 S9 **Eagle Nest Lake** ◻ New Mexico, SW USA
27 P13 **Eagle Pass** Texas, SW USA *28.43N 100.31W*
67 C25 **Eagle Passage** *passage* SW Atlantic Ocean
37 R8 **Eagle Peak** ▲ California, W USA *38.11N 119.22W*
37 Q2 **Eagle Peak** ▲ California, W USA *41.16N 120.12W*
39 P13 **Eagle Peak** ▲ New Mexico, SW USA *33.39N 109.36W*
8 I4 **Eagle Plain** Yukon Territory, NW Canada *66.23N 136.42W*
34 G15 **Eagle Point** Oregon, NW USA *42.28N 122.48W*
195 N17 **Eagle Point** *headland* SE PNG *10.31S 149.53E*
41 R11 **Eagle River** Alaska, USA *61.18N 149.38W*
32 M2 **Eagle River** Michigan, N USA *47.24N 88.18W*
32 L4 **Eagle River** Wisconsin, N USA *45.55N 89.15W*
23 S6 **Eagle Rock** Virginia, NE USA *37.40N 79.46W*
38 J13 **Eagletail Mountains** ▲ Arizona, SW USA
178 Kk12 **Ea Hleo** Đăc Lăc, S Vietnam *13.09N 108.14E*
178 Kk12 **Ea Kar** Đăc Lăc, S Vietnam *12.47N 108.26E*
Eanjum *see* Anjum
Eanodat *see* Enontekiö
10 B10 **Ear Falls** Ontario, C Canada *50.37N 93.13W*
29 X10 **Earle** Arkansas, C USA *35.16N 90.28W*
37 R12 **Earlimart** California, W USA *35.52N 119.17W*
22 I6 **Earlington** Kentucky, S USA *37.16N 87.30W*
12 H8 **Earlton** Ontario, S Canada *47.41N 79.46W*
31 T13 **Early** Iowa, C USA *42.27N 95.09W*
98 J11 **Earn** N Scotland, UK
193 C21 **Earnslaw, Mount** ▲ South Island, NZ *44.34S 168.26E*
26 M4 **Earth** Texas, SW USA *34.13N 102.24W*
23 P11 **Easley** South Carolina, SE USA *34.49N 82.36W*
East *see* Est
East Açores Fracture Zone *see* East Azores Fracture Zone
99 P19 **East Anglia** *physical region* E England, UK

◆ Country ● Country Capital ◇ Dependent Territory ○ Dependent Territory Capital ◆ Administrative Region ✕ International Airport ▲ Mountain ▲ Mountain Range Volcano River ◎ Lake ◻ Reservoir

13 Q12 **East Angus** Québec, SE Canada 45.29N 71.39W
East Antarctica *see* Greater Antarctica
20 E10 **East Aurora** New York, NE USA 42.44N 78.36W
East Australian Basin *see* Tasman Basin
East Azerbaijan *see* Āzarbāyān-e Sharqī
66 L9 **East Azores Fracture Zone** *var.* East Açores Fracture Zone. *tectonic feature* E Atlantic Ocean
24 M11 **East Bay** *bay* Louisiana, S USA
27 V11 **East Bernard** Texas, SW USA 29.31N 96.04W
31 V8 **East Bethel** Minnesota, N USA 45.24N 93.14W
East Borneo *see* Kalimantan Timur
99 P23 **Eastbourne** SE England, UK 50.46N 0.16E
13 R11 **East-Broughton** Québec, SE Canada 46.13N 71.03W
46 M6 **East Caicos** *island* E Turks and Caicos Islands
192 R7 **East Cape** *headland* North Island, NZ 37.40S 178.31E
182 M4 **East Caroline Basin** *undersea feature* SW Pacific Ocean
198 G5 **East China Sea** *Chin.* Dong Hai. *sea* W Pacific Ocean
99 P19 **East Dereham** E England, UK 52.40N 0.55E
32 J9 **East Dubuque** Illinois, N USA 42.29N 90.38W
9 S17 **Eastend** Saskatchewan, S Canada 49.29N 108.48W
200 Nn11 **Easter Fracture Zone** *tectonic feature* E Pacific Ocean
Easter Island *see* Pascua, Isla de
83 J18 **Eastern** ◈ *province* Kenya
159 Q12 **Eastern** ◈ *zone* E Nepal
84 L13 **Eastern** ◈ *province* E Zambia
85 H24 **Eastern Cape** *off.* Eastern Cape Province, *Afr.* Oos-Kaap. ◈ *province* SE South Africa
Eastern Desert *see* Sahara el Sharqîya
83 F15 **Eastern Equatoria** ◈ *state* SE Sudan
Eastern Euphrates *see* Murat Nehri
161 J17 **Eastern Ghats** ▲▲ SE India
194 I13 **Eastern Highlands** ◈ *province* C PNG
161 K25 **Eastern Province** ◈ *province* E Sri Lanka
Eastern Region *see* Ash Sharqīyah
126 I15 **Eastern Sayans** *Mong.* Dzüün Soyonï Nuruu, *Rus.* Vostochnyy Sayan. ▲▲ Mongolia/Russian Federation
Eastern Scheldt *see* Oosterschelde
Eastern Sierra Madre *see* Madre Oriental, Sierra
Eastern Transvaal *see* Mpumalanga
9 W14 **Easterville** Manitoba, C Canada 53.06N 99.52W
Easterwâlde *see* Oosterwolde
65 M23 **East Falkland** *var.* Isla Soledad. *island* E Falkland Islands
21 P12 **East Falmouth** Massachusetts, NE USA 41.34N 70.31W
East Fayu *see* Fayu
East Flanders *see* Oost Vlaanderen
41 S6 **East Fork Chandalar River** ≈ Alaska, USA
31 U12 **East Fork Des Moines River** ≈ Iowa/Minnesota, C USA
East Frisian Islands *see* Ostfriesische Inseln
20 K10 **East Glenville** New York, NE USA 42.53N 73.55W
31 R4 **East Grand Forks** Minnesota, N USA 47.54N 97.59W
99 O23 **East Grinstead** SE England, UK 51.07N 0.00W
20 M12 **East Hartford** Connecticut, NE USA 41.45N 72.36W
20 M13 **East Haven** Connecticut, NE USA 41.16N 72.52W
181 T9 **East Indiaman Ridge** *undersea feature* E Indian Ocean
133 V16 **East Indies** *island group* SE Asia
East Java *see* Jawa Timur
33 Q6 **East Jordan** Michigan, N USA 45.09N 85.07W
East Kalimantan *see* Kalimantan Timur
East Kazakhstan *see* Vostochnyy Kazakhstan
98 I12 **East Kilbride** S Scotland, UK 55.46N 4.10W
27 R7 **Eastland** Texas, SW USA 32.24N 98.49W
33 Q9 **East Lansing** Michigan, N USA 42.44N 84.28W
37 X11 **East Las Vegas** Nevada, W USA 36.05N 115.02W
99 M23 **Eastleigh** S England, UK 50.58N 1.22W
33 V12 **East Liverpool** Ohio, N USA 40.37N 80.34W
85 J25 **East London** *Afr.* Oos-Londen; *prev.* Emonti, Port Rex. Eastern Cape, S South Africa 33.00S 27.54E
98 K12 **East Lothian** *cultural region* SE Scotland, UK
10 I10 **Eastmain** Québec, E Canada 52.11N 78.27W
10 J10 **Eastmain** ≈ Québec, C Canada
13 P13 **Eastman** Québec, SE Canada 45.19N 72.18W
25 U6 **Eastman** Georgia, SE USA 32.12N 83.10W
183 O3 **East Mariana Basin** *undersea feature* W Pacific Ocean
32 K11 **East Moline** Illinois, N USA 41.30N 90.26W
195 O12 **East New Britain** ◈ *province* E PNG
31 T15 **East Nishnabotna River** ≈ Iowa, C USA
207 V12 **East Novaya Zemlya Trough** *var.* Novaya Zemlya Trough. *undersea feature* W Kara Sea
East Nusa Tenggara *see* Nusa Tenggara Timur
23 X4 **Easton** Maryland, NE USA 38.46N 76.04W
20 I14 **Easton** Pennsylvania, NE USA 40.40N 75.13W
200 N8 **East Pacific Rise** *undersea feature* E Pacific Ocean
East Pakistan *see* Bangladesh
33 V12 **East Palestine** Ohio, N USA 40.49N 80.32W
32 L12 **East Peoria** Illinois, N USA 40.40N 89.34W
25 S3 **East Point** Georgia, SE USA 33.40N 84.26W
21 U6 **Eastport** Maine, NE USA 44.54N 66.59W
29 Z8 **East Prairie** Missouri, C USA 36.46N 89.23W
21 O12 **East Providence** Rhode Island, NE USA 41.48N 71.20W
22 L11 **East Ridge** Tennessee, S USA 35.00N 85.15W
99 N16 **East Riding** *cultural region* N England, UK
20 F9 **East Rochester** New York, NE USA 43.06N 77.29W
32 K15 **East Saint Louis** Illinois, N USA 38.35N 90.07W
67 K21 **East Scotia Basin** *undersea feature* SE Scotia Sea
133 Y8 **East Sea** *var.* Sea of Japan, *Rus.* Yapanskoye More. *sea* NW Pacific Ocean *see also* Japan, Sea of
194 F11 **East Sepik** ◈ *province* NW PNG
181 N4 **East Sheba Ridge** *undersea feature* W Arabian Sea
East Siberian Sea *see* Vostochno-Sibirskoye More
20 I14 **East Stroudsburg** Pennsylvania, NE USA 41.00N 75.10W
East Tasmanian Rise/East Tasmania Plateau/East Tasmania Rise *see* East Tasman Plateau
199 Hh13 **East Tasman Plateau** *var.* East Tasmanian Rise, East Tasmania Plateau, East Tasmania Rise. *undersea feature* SW Tasman Sea
66 L7 **East Thulean Rise** *undersea feature* N Atlantic Ocean
175 S16 **East Timor** *var* Loro Sae prev. Portuguese Timor, Timor Timur ◆ country SE Asia
23 Y6 **Eastville** Virginia, NE USA 37.18N 75.57W
37 R7 **East Walker River** ≈ California/Nevada, W USA
190 D1 **Eateringinna Creek** ≈ South Australia
39 T3 **Eaton** Colorado, C USA 40.31N 104.42W
13 Q12 **Eaton** ≈ Québec, SE Canada
9 S16 **Eatonia** Saskatchewan, S Canada 51.13N 109.22W
33 Q10 **Eaton Rapids** Michigan, N USA 42.30N 84.39W
25 U4 **Eatonton** Georgia, SE USA 33.19N 83.23W
34 H9 **Eatonville** Washington, NW USA 46.51N 122.19W
32 J6 **Eau Claire** Wisconsin, N USA 44.49N 91.30W
Eau Claire, Lac à L' *see* St.Clair, Lake
10 J7 **Eau Claire, Lac à l'** ◎ Québec, SE Canada
32 L6 **Eau Claire River** ≈ Wisconsin, N USA
196 J16 **Eauripik Atoll** *atoll* Caroline Islands, C Micronesia
199 H8 **Eauripik Rise** *undersea feature* W Pacific Ocean
104 K15 **Eauze** Gers, S France 43.52N 0.06E
43 P11 **Ébano** San Luis Potosí, C Mexico 22.13N 98.22W
99 K21 **Ebbw Vale** SE Wales, UK 51.48N 3.13W
81 E17 **Ebebiyin** NE Equatorial Guinea 2.08N 11.15E
97 H22 **Ebeltoft** Århus, C Denmark 56.10N 10.42E
111 X5 **Ebenfurth** Niederösterreich, E Austria 47.51N 16.21E
20 D14 **Ebensburg** Pennsylvania, NE USA 40.28N 78.42W
111 S5 **Ebensee** Oberösterreich, N Austria 47.48N 13.45E
103 H20 **Eberbach** Baden-Württemberg, SW Germany 49.28N 8.58E
124 Q9 **Eber Gölü** *salt lake* C Turkey
111 U9 **Eberndorf** *Slvn.* Dobrla Vas. Kärnten, S Austria 46.33N 14.35E
111 R4 **Eberschwang** Oberösterreich, N Austria 48.09N 13.37E
102 O11 **Eberswalde-Finow** Brandenburg, E Germany 52.49N 13.48E
Ebesfalva *see* Dumbrăveni
172 Oo5 **Ebetsu** *var.* Ebetu. Hokkaidō, NE Japan 43.08N 141.37E
Ebetu *see* Ebetsu
Ebinayon *see* Evinayong
164 I4 **Ebinur Hu** ◎ NW China
144 I3 **Ebla** *Ar.* Tell Mardīkh. *site of ancient city* Idlib, NW Syria
Eblana *see* Dublin
110 H7 **Ebnat** Sankt Gallen, NE Switzerland 47.16N 9.07E
109 L18 **Eboli** Campania, S Italy 40.39N 15.01E
81 E16 **Ebolowa** Sud, S Cameroon 2.55N 11.10E
81 N21 **Ebombo** Kasai Oriental, C Dem. Rep. Congo 5.42S 26.07E
201 T9 **Ebon Atoll** *var.* Epoon. *atoll* Ralik Chain, S Marshall Islands
Ebora *see* Évora
Eboracum *see* York
Eborodunum *see* Yverdon
103 J19 **Ebrach** Bayern, C Germany 49.49N 10.30E
111 X5 **Ebreichsdorf** Niederösterreich, E Austria 47.58N 16.24E
107 S6 **Ebro** ≈ NE Spain
107 N3 **Ebro, Embalse del** ⊡ N Spain
123 Hh8 **Ebro Fan** *undersea feature* W Mediterranean Sea
Eburacum *see* York
Ebusus *see* Eivissa/Ibiza
101 F20 **Écaussinnes-d'Enghien** Hainaut, SW Belgium 50.34N 4.10E
Ecbatana *see* Hamadān
23 Q6 **Eccles** West Virginia, NE USA 37.46N 81.16W
117 L14 **Eceabat** Çanakkale, NW Turkey 40.12N 26.22E
179 P9 **Echague** Luzon, N Philippines 16.42N 121.37E
Ech Cheliff/Ech Chleff *see* Chlef
Echeng *see* Ezhou
171 Kk13 **Echigo-sanmyaku** ▲▲ Honshū, C Japan
117 C18 **Echinádes** *island group* W Greece
116 J12 **Echínos** *var.* Ehinos, Ekhínos. Anatolikí Makedonía kai Thráki, NE Greece 41.16N 25.00E
171 H13 **Echizen-misaki** *headland* Honshū, SW Japan 35.59N 135.57E
Echmiadzin *see* Vagharshapat
15 Hh5 **Echo Bay** Northwest Territories, NW Canada 66.04N 118.00W
37 Y11 **Echo Bay** Nevada, W USA 36.19N 114.27W
38 L9 **Echo Cliffs** *cliff* Arizona, SW USA
12 C10 **Echo Lake** ◎ Ontario, S Canada
37 Q7 **Echo Summit** ▲ California, W USA 38.47N 120.06W
12 L8 **Échouani, Lac** ◎ Québec, SE Canada
101 L17 **Echt** Limburg, SE Netherlands 51.07N 5.52E
103 H22 **Echterdingen** ✈ (Stuttgart) Baden-Württemberg, SW Germany 48.40N 9.13E
101 N24 **Echternach** Grevenmacher, E Luxembourg 49.49N 6.25E
191 N11 **Echuca** Victoria, SE Australia 36.10S 144.46E
106 L14 **Ecija** *anc.* Astigi. Andalucía, SW Spain 37.33N 5.04W
Eckengraf *see* Viesīte
102 I7 **Eckernförde** Schleswig-Holstein, N Germany 54.28N 9.49E
102 J7 **Eckernförder Bucht** *inlet* N Germany
104 L7 **Écommoy** Sarthe, NW France 47.51N 0.15E
12 L10 **Écorce, Lac de l'** ◎ Québec, SE Canada
13 Q8 **Écorces, Rivière aux** ≈ Québec, SE Canada
58 C7 **Ecuador** *off.* Republic of Ecuador. ◆ *republic* NW South America
82 L10 **Ed** *var.* Edd. SE Eritrea 13.54N 41.39E
97 I17 **Ed** Västra Götaland, S Sweden 58.55N 11.55E
100 I9 **Edam** Noord-Holland, C Netherlands 52.31N 5.03E
98 K4 **Eday** *island* NE Scotland, UK
27 S17 **Edcouch** Texas, SW USA 26.17N 97.57W
Edd *see* Ed
82 C11 **Ed Da'ein** Southern Darfur, W Sudan 11.25N 26.07E
82 G11 **Ed Damazin** *var.* Ad Damazīn. Blue Nile, E Sudan 11.45N 34.20E
82 G8 **Ed Damer** *var.* Ad Damar, Ad Dāmir. River Nile, NE Sudan 17.37N 33.58E
82 E8 **Ed Debba** Northern, N Sudan 18.01N 30.55E
82 F10 **Ed Dueim** *var.* Ad Duwaym, Ad Duwēm. White Nile, C Sudan 13.38N 32.36E
191 Q16 **Eddystone Point** *headland* Tasmania, SE Australia 41.01S 148.18E
99 I25 **Eddystone Rocks** *rocks* SW England, UK
31 W15 **Eddyville** Iowa, C USA 41.09N 92.37W
22 H7 **Eddyville** Kentucky, S USA 37.05N 88.04W
100 L12 **Ede** Gelderland, C Netherlands 52.03N 5.40E
79 T16 **Ede** Osun, SW Nigeria 7.40N 4.21E
81 D16 **Edéa** Littoral, SW Cameroon 3.46N 10.07E
113 M20 **Edelény** Borsod-Abaúj-Zemplén, NE Hungary 48.19N 20.44E
191 R12 **Eden** New South Wales, SE Australia 37.04S 149.51E
23 T8 **Eden** North Carolina, SE USA 36.29N 79.46W
27 P9 **Eden** Texas, SW USA 31.13N 99.51W
99 K14 **Eden** ≈ NW England, UK
85 I23 **Edenburg** Free State, C South Africa 29.43S 25.54E
193 D24 **Edendale** Southland, South Island, NZ 46.18S 168.48E
99 E18 **Edenderry** *Ir.* Éadan Doire. C Ireland 53.21N 7.03W
190 L11 **Edenhope** Victoria, SE Australia 37.04S 141.15E
23 X8 **Edenton** North Carolina, SE USA 36.06N 76.46W
103 G16 **Eder** ≈ NW Germany
176 Yy14 **Ederah** ≈ Papua, E Indonesia
103 H15 **Edersee** ◎ W Germany
Edessa *see* Şanlıurfa
116 E13 **Édessa** *var.* Édhessa. Kentrikí Makedonía, N Greece 40.48N 22.03E
Edfu *see* Idfu
31 P16 **Edgar** Nebraska, C USA 40.22N 97.58W
21 P13 **Edgartown** Martha's Vineyard, Massachusetts, NE USA 41.22N 70.30W
41 X13 **Edgecumbe, Mount** ▲ Baranof Island, Alaska, USA 57.03N 135.45W
23 Q13 **Edgefield** South Carolina, SE USA 33.47N 81.55W
31 P6 **Edgeley** North Dakota, N USA 46.19N 98.42W
30 I11 **Edgemont** South Dakota, N USA 43.18N 103.49W
94 O3 **Edgeøya** *island* S Svalbard
29 Q4 **Edgerton** Kansas, C USA 38.45N 95.00W
31 S10 **Edgerton** Minnesota, N USA 43.52N 96.07W
23 X3 **Edgewood** Maryland, NE USA 39.20N 76.21W
27 V6 **Edgewood** Texas, SW USA 32.42N 95.53W
Édhessa *see* Édessa
31 V9 **Edina** Minnesota, N USA 44.53N 93.21W
29 U2 **Edina** Missouri, C USA 40.10N 92.10W
27 S17 **Edinburg** Texas, SW USA 26.18N 98.09W
67 M24 **Edinburgh** *var.* Settlement of Edinburgh. ○ (Tristan da Cunha) NW Tristan da Cunha 37.03S 12.18W
98 J12 **Edinburgh** ◐ S Scotland, UK 55.57N 3.13W
33 P14 **Edinburgh** Indiana, N USA 39.19N 86.00W
98 J12 **Edinburgh** ✈ S Scotland, UK 55.57N 3.22W
118 L8 **Edineț** *var.* Edineți, *Rus.* Yedintsy. NW Moldova 48.10N 27.18E
Edineți *see* Edineț
Edingen *see* Enghien
142 B9 **Edirne** *Eng.* Adrianople; *anc.* Adrianopolis, Hadrianopolis. Edirne, NW Turkey 41.40N 26.34E
142 B11 **Edirne** ◈ *province* NW Turkey
20 K15 **Edison** New Jersey, NE USA 40.31N 74.24W
23 S15 **Edisto Island** South Carolina, SE USA 32.34N 80.17W
23 R14 **Edisto River** ≈ South Carolina, SE USA
35 S10 **Edith, Mount** ▲ Montana, NW USA 46.25N 111.10W
29 N10 **Edmond** Oklahoma, C USA 35.40N 97.27W
34 H8 **Edmonds** Washington, NW USA 47.48N 122.22W
9 Q14 **Edmonton** Alberta, SW Canada 53.34N 113.25W
22 K7 **Edmonton** Kentucky, S USA 36.57N 85.37W
9 Q14 **Edmonton** ✈ Alberta, SW Canada 53.22N 113.43W
31 P3 **Edmore** North Dakota, N USA 48.22N 98.26W
11 N13 **Edmundston** New Brunswick, SE Canada 47.22N 68.19W
27 U12 **Edna** Texas, SW USA 28.58N 96.39W
41 X14 **Edna Bay** Kosciusko Island, Alaska, USA 55.54N 133.40W
79 U16 **Edo** ◈ *state* S Nigeria
108 F6 **Edolo** Lombardia, N Italy 46.12N 10.19E
66 L6 **Edoras Bank** *undersea feature* C Atlantic Ocean
98 G7 **Edrachillis Bay** *bay* NW Scotland, UK
142 B12 **Edremit** Balıkesir, NW Turkey 39.34N 27.01E
142 B12 **Edremit Körfezi** *gulf* NW Turkey
97 P14 **Edsbro** Stockholm, C Sweden 59.54N 18.30E
97 N18 **Edsbruk** Kalmar, S Sweden 58.01N 16.30E
96 M12 **Edsbyn** Gävleborg, C Sweden 61.22N 15.45E
9 O14 **Edson** Alberta, SW Canada 53.36N 116.28W
64 K13 **Eduardo Castex** La Pampa, C Argentina 35.52S 64.15W
60 F12 **Eduardo Gomes** ✈ (Manaus) Amazonas, NW Brazil 5.55S 35.15W
Edwardesabad *see* Bannu
69 U9 **Edward, Lake** *var.* Albert Edward Nyanza, Edward Nyanza, Lac Idi Amin, Lake Rutanzige. ◎ Uganda/Dem. Rep. Congo
Edward Nyanza *see* Edward, Lake
24 K5 **Edwards** Mississippi, S USA 32.19N 90.36W
27 O10 **Edwards Plateau** *plain* Texas, SW USA
32 J11 **Edwards River** ≈ Illinois, N USA
32 K15 **Edwardsville** Illinois, N USA 38.48N 89.57W
205 O13 **Edward VII Peninsula** *peninsula* Antarctica
205 X4 **Edward VIII Gulf** *bay* Antarctica
8 J11 **Edziza, Mount** ▲ British Columbia, W Canada 57.43N 130.39W
25 H16 **Edzo** *prev.* Rae-Edzo. Northwest Territories, NW Canada 62.43N 115.55W
41 N12 **Eek** Alaska, USA 60.13N 162.01W
101 D16 **Eeklo** *var.* Eekloo. Oost-Vlaanderen, NW Belgium 51.10N 3.34E
Eekloo *see* Eeklo
41 N12 **Eek River** ≈ Alaska, USA
100 N6 **Eelde** Drenthe, NE Netherlands 53.07N 6.30E
36 L5 **Eel River** ≈ California, W USA
33 P12 **Eel River** ≈ Indiana, N USA
Eems *see* Ems
100 O4 **Eemshaven** Groningen, NE Netherlands 53.27N 6.50E
100 O5 **Eems Kanaal** *canal* NE Netherlands
100 M11 **Eerbeek** Gelderland, E Netherlands 52.07N 6.04E
101 C17 **Eernegem** West-Vlaanderen, W Belgium 51.08N 3.03E
101 J15 **Eersel** Noord-Brabant, S Netherlands 51.22N 5.19E
Eesti Vabariik *see* Estonia
197 C14 **Efate** *var.* Éfaté, *Fr.* Vaté *prev.* Sandwich Island. *island* C Vanuatu
111 S4 **Eferding** Oberösterreich, N Austria 48.18N 14.00E
32 M15 **Effingham** Illinois, N USA 39.07N 88.32W
119 N15 **Eforie-Nord** Constanța, SE Romania 44.04N 28.37E
119 N15 **Eforie Sud** Constanța, E Romania 44.00N 28.38E
Efyrnwy, Afon *see* Vyrnwy
Eg *see* Batshireet
109 G23 **Egadi, Isole** *island group* S Italy
37 X6 **Egan Range** ▲▲ Nevada, W USA
12 K12 **Eganville** Ontario, SE Canada 45.33N 77.03W
Ege Denizi *see* Aegean Sea
41 O14 **Egegik** Alaska, USA 58.13N 157.22W
113 L21 **Eger** *Ger.* Erlau. Heves, NE Hungary 47.54N 20.21E
Eger *see* Cheb, Czech Republic
Eger *see* Ohre, Czech Republic/Germany
181 P8 **Egeria Fracture Zone** *tectonic feature* W Indian Ocean
97 C17 **Egersund** Rogaland, S Norway 58.27N 6.01E
110 J7 **Egg** Vorarlberg, NW Austria 47.27N 9.55E
103 H14 **Egge-gebirge** ▲▲ C Germany
111 Q4 **Eggelsberg** Oberösterreich, N Austria 48.04N 13.00E
111 W2 **Eggenburg** Niederösterreich, NE Austria 48.36N 15.49E
103 N22 **Eggenfelden** Bayern, SE Germany 48.24N 12.45E
20 J17 **Egg Harbor City** New Jersey, NE USA 39.31N 74.39W
67 G25 **Egg Island** *island* W Saint Helena
191 N14 **Egg Lagoon** Tasmania, SE Australia 39.42S 143.57E
101 I20 **Éghezèe** Namur, C Belgium 50.36N 4.55E
94 L2 **Egilsstadhir** Austurland, E Iceland 65.14N 14.21W
Egina *see* Aígina
Egindibulaq *see* Yegindybulak
Egio *see* Aígio
105 N12 **Égletons** Corrèze, C France 45.24N 2.01E
100 H9 **Egmond aan Zee** Noord-Holland, NW Netherlands 52.37N 4.37E
Egmont *see* Taranaki, Mount
192 J10 **Egmont, Cape** *headland* North Island, NZ 39.18S 173.44E
Egoli *see* Johannesburg
Eğri Palanka *see* Kriva Palanka
97 G23 **Egtved** Vejle, C Denmark 55.34N 9.18E
127 Pp4 **Egvekinot** Chukotskiy Avtonomnyy Okrug, NE Russian Federation 66.13N 178.55W
77 V9 **Egypt** *off.* Arab Republic of Egypt, *Ar.* Jumhūrīyah Mişr al 'Arabīyah; *prev.* United Arab Republic, *anc.* Aegyptus. ◆ *republic* NE Africa
32 L17 **Egypt, Lake Of** ⊡ Illinois, N USA
168 I14 **Ehen Hudag** *var.* Alx Youqi. Nei Mongol Zizhiqu, N China 39.12N 101.40E
170 E15 **Ehime** *off.* Ehime-ken. ◈ *prefecture* Shikoku, SW Japan
103 I23 **Ehingen** Baden-Württemberg, S Germany 48.16N 9.43E
Ehinos *see* Echínos
23 R14 **Ehrhardt** South Carolina, SE USA 33.06N 81.00W
110 L7 **Ehrwald** Tirol, W Austria 47.24N 10.52E
203 W6 **Eiao** *island* Îles Marquises, NE French Polynesia
107 P2 **Eibar** País Vasco, N Spain 43.10N 2.28W
100 O11 **Eibergen** Gelderland, E Netherlands 52.06N 6.39E
111 V9 **Eibiswald** Steiermark, SE Austria 46.40N 15.15E
111 P8 **Eichham** ▲ SW Austria 47.04N 12.24E
103 J15 **Eichsfeld** *hill range* C Germany
103 K21 **Eichstätt** Bayern, SE Germany 48.53N 11.11E
102 H8 **Eider** ≈ N Germany
96 E13 **Eidfjord** Hordaland, S Norway 60.26N 7.05E
96 D13 **Eidfjorden** *fjord* S Norway
96 F9 **Eidsvåg** Møre og Romsdal, S Norway 62.46N 8.00E
97 I14 **Eidsvoll** Akershus, S Norway 60.19N 11.16E
94 N2 **Eidsvollfjellet** ▲ NW Svalbard 79.13N 13.23E
Eier-Berg *see* Suur Munamägi
103 D18 **Eifel** *plateau* W Germany
110 E9 **Eiger** ▲ C Switzerland 46.33N 8.02E
98 G10 **Eigg** *island* W Scotland, UK
161 D24 **Eight Degree Channel** *channel* India/Maldives
46 G1 **Eight Mile Rock** Grand Bahama Island, N Bahamas 26.28N 78.43W
204 J9 **Eights Coast** *physical region* Antarctica
188 K6 **Eighty Mile Beach** *beach* Western Australia
101 L18 **Eijsden** Limburg, SE Netherlands 50.47N 5.41E
97 G15 **Eikeren** ◎ S Norway
Eil *see* Eyl
Eilat *see* Elat
191 O12 **Eildon** Victoria, SE Australia 37.17S 145.57E
191 O12 **Eildon, Lake** ◎ Victoria, SE Australia
82 E8 **Eilei** Northern Kordofan, C Sudan 16.33N 30.54E
103 N15 **Eilenburg** Sachsen, E Germany 51.28N 12.37E
96 H13 **Eina** Oppland, S Norway 60.37N 10.37E
Ein 'Avedat *see* En 'Avedat
103 I14 **Einbeck** Niedersachsen, C Germany 51.49N 9.52E
101 K15 **Eindhoven** Noord-Brabant, S Netherlands 51.25N 5.30E
110 G8 **Einsiedeln** Schwyz, NE Switzerland 47.06N 8.44E
Eipel *see* Ipel'
Éire *see* Ireland, Republic of
Éireann, Muir *see* Irish Sea
Eirik Outer Ridge *see* Eirik Ridge
66 I6 **Eirik Ridge** *var.* Eirik Outer Ridge. *undersea feature* E Labrador Sea
94 I3 **Eiríksjökull** ▲ C Iceland 64.47N 20.23W
61 B14 **Eirunepé** Amazonas, N Brazil 6.37S 69.52W
101 L17 **Eisden** Limburg, NE Belgium 51.05N 5.42E
85 F18 **Eiseb** ≈ Botswana/Namibia
Eisen *see* Yŏngch'ŏn
103 J16 **Eisenach** Thüringen, C Germany 50.58N 10.19E
Eisenburg *see* Vasvár
111 U6 **Eisenerz** Steiermark, SE Austria 47.33N 14.52E
102 Q13 **Eisenhüttenstadt** Brandenburg, E Germany 52.09N 14.36E
111 U10 **Eisenkappel** *Slvn.* Železna Kapela. Kärnten, S Austria 46.27N 14.33E
Eisenmarkt *see* Hunedoara
111 Y5 **Eisenstadt** Burgenland, E Austria 47.49N 16.31E
Eishū *see* Yŏngju
121 H15 **Eišiškės** Vilnius, SE Lithuania 54.10N 24.59E
103 L15 **Eisleben** Sachsen-Anhalt, C Germany 51.31N 11.33E
202 I3 **Eita** Tarawa, W Kiribati 1.21N 173.04E
Eitape *see* Aitape
107 V11 **Eivissa** *var.* Iviza, *Cast.* Ibiza; *anc.* Ebusus. Ibiza, Spain, W Mediterranean Sea 38.54N 1.25E
Eivissa *see* Ibiza
107 R4 **Ejea de los Caballeros** Aragón, NE Spain 42.07N 1.09W
42 E8 **Ejido Insurgentes** Baja California Sur, W Mexico 25.14N 111.45W
Ejin Qi *see* Dalain Hob
Ejmiadzın/Ejmiatsin *see* Vagharshapat
79 P16 **Ejura** C Ghana 7.22N 1.22W
43 R16 **Ejutla** *var.* Ejutla de Crespo. Oaxaca, SE Mexico 16.30N 96.40W
Ejutla de Crespo *see* Ejutla
35 Y10 **Ekalaka** Montana, NW USA 45.52N 104.32W
Ekapa *see* Cape Town
130 **Ekaterinodar** *see* Krasnodar
95 L20 **Ekenäs** *Fin.* Tammisaari. Etelä-Suomi, SW Finland 60.00N 23.30E
152 B13 **Ekerem** *Rus.* Okarem. Balkan Welaýaty, W Turkmenistan 38.06N 53.52E
192 M13 **Eketahuna** Manawatu-Wanganui, North Island, NZ 40.41S 175.40E
Ekhínos *see* Echínos
127 P3 **Ekiatapskiy Khrebet** ▲▲ NE Russian Federation
151 T8 **Ekibastuz** Pavlodar, NE Kazakhstan 51.45N 75.22E
127 N14 **Ekimchan** Amurskaya Oblast', SE Russian Federation 53.04N 132.56E
97 O15 **Ekoln** ◎ C Sweden
82 I7 **Ekowit** Red Sea, NE Sudan 18.46N 37.07E
97 L19 **Eksjö** Jönköping, S Sweden 57.40N 15.00E
95 I15 **Ekträsk** Västerbotten, N Sweden 64.28N 19.49E
41 O13 **Ekuk** Alaska, USA 58.48N 158.25W
10 F9 **Ekwan** ≈ Ontario, C Canada
41 O13 **Ekwok** Alaska, USA 59.21N 157.28W
177 G6 **Ela** Mandalay, C Burma 19.37N 96.15E
El Aaiun *see* El Ayoun
83 N15 **Ēl Ābrēd** Somali, E Ethiopia 5.33N 45.12E
117 F22 **Elafónisos** *island* S Greece
117 F22 **Elafonísou, Porthmós** *strait* S Greece
El-Aïoun *see* El Ayoun
77 U8 **El 'Alamein** *var.* Al 'Alamayn. N Egypt 30.46N 28.58E
43 Q12 **El Alazán** Veracruz-Llave, C Mexico 21.06N 97.43W
59 J18 **El Alto** *var.* La Paz. ✈ (La Paz) La Paz, W Bolivia 16.31S 68.07W
Elam *see* Īlām
El Amparo *see* El Amparo de Apure
56 I8 **El Amparo de Apure** *var.* El Amparo. Apure, C Venezuela 7.03N 70.46W
175 Ss12 **Elara** Pulau Ambelau, E Indonesia 3.49S 127.10E
El Araïch/El Araïche *see* Larache
42 D6 **El Arco** Baja California, NW Mexico 28.03N 113.25W
77 X7 **El 'Arîsh** *var.* Al 'Arīsh. NE Egypt 33.00N 31.00E
117 L25 **Elása** *island* SE Greece
El Asnam *see* Chlef
Elassón *see* Elassóna
117 E15 **Elassóna** *prev.* Elassón. Thessalía, C Greece 39.54N 22.11E
107 N2 **El Astillero** Cantabria, N Spain 43.23N 3.45W
144 F14 **Elat** *var.* Eilat, Elath. Southern, S Israel 29.33N 34.57E
Elat, Gulf of *see* Aqaba, Gulf of
Elath *see* Elat, Israel
Elath *see* Al 'Aqabah, Jordan
117 C17 **Eláti** ▲ Lefkáda, Iónia Nisiá, Greece, C Mediterranean Sea 38.43N 20.38E
196 L16 **Elato Atoll** *atoll* Caroline Islands, C Micronesia
82 C7 **El'Atrun** Northern Darfur, NW Sudan 18.10N 26.40E
76 H6 **El Ayoun** *var.* El Aaiun, El-Aïoun, La Youne. NE Morocco 34.38N 2.28W
143 N14 **Elazığ** *var.* Elâzîğ, Elâziz. Elazığ, E Turkey 38.40N 39.13E
143 O14 **Elazığ** *var.* Elâzîğ, Elâziz. ◈ *province* C Turkey
Elâziz *see* Elazığ
Azraq, Bahr el *see* Blue Nile
25 Q7 **Elba** Alabama, S USA 31.24N 86.04W
108 E13 **Elba, Isola d'** *island* Archipelago Toscano, C Italy
127 Nn15 **El'ban** Khabarovskiy Kray, E Russian Federation 50.03N 136.34E
56 F6 **El Banco** Magdalena, N Colombia 9.00N 74.01W
El Barco *see* O Barco
106 L8 **El Barco de Ávila** Castilla-León, N Spain 40.21N 5.31W
El Barco de Valdeorras *see* O Barco
144 H7 **El Barouk, Jabal** ▲▲ C Lebanon
115 L20 **Elbasan** *var.* Elbasani. Elbasan, C Albania 41.07N 20.04E
115 L20 **Elbasan** ◈ *district* C Albania
Elbasani *see* Elbasan
56 K6 **El Baúl** Cojedes, C Venezuela 8.55N 68.17W
88 D11 **Elbe** *Cz.* Labe. ≈ Czech Republic/Germany
102 L13 **Elbe-Havel-Kanal** *canal* E Germany
102 K9 **Elbe-Lübeck-Kanal** *canal* N Germany
El Beni *see* Beni
144 H7 **El Beqaa** *var.* Al Biqā', Bekaa Valley. *valley* E Lebanon
27 R6 **Elbert** Texas, SW USA 33.15N 98.58W
39 R5 **Elbert, Mount** ▲ Colorado, C USA 39.07N 106.26W
25 U3 **Elberton** Georgia, SE USA 34.06N 82.52W
102 K11 **Elbe-Seiten-Kanal** *canal* N Germany
104 M4 **Elbeuf** Seine-Maritime, N France 49.16N 1.01E
Elbing *see* Elbląg
142 M15 **Elbistan** Kahramanmaraş, S Turkey 38.13N 37.10E
112 K7 **Elbląg** *var.* Elblag, *Ger.* Elbing. Warmińsko-Mazurskie, NE Poland 54.10N 19.25E
45 N10 **El Bluff** Región Autónoma Atlántico Sur, SE Nicaragua 12.01N 83.41W
65 H17 **El Bolsón** Río Negro, W Argentina 41.57S 71.33W
107 P11 **El Bonillo** Castilla-La Mancha, C Spain 38.57N 2.31W
El Bordo *see* Patía
El Boulaida/El Boulaïda *see* Blida
9 T16 **Elbow** Saskatchewan, S Canada 51.07N 106.30W
31 S7 **Elbow Lake** Minnesota, N USA 45.59N 95.58W
131 N16 **El'brus** *var.* Gora El'brus. ▲ SW Russian Federation 43.18N 42.21E
El'brus, Gora *see* El'brus
130 M15 **El'brusskiy** Karachayevo-Cherkesskaya Respublika, SW Russian Federation 43.36N 42.06E
83 D14 **El Buhayrat** *var.* Lakes State. ◈ *state* S Sudan
El Bur *see* Ceel Buur
100 L10 **Elburg** Gelderland, E Netherlands 52.27N 5.46E
107 O6 **El Burgo de Osma** Castilla-León, C Spain 41.36N 3.04W
Elburz Mountains *see* Alborz, Reshteh-ye Kūhhā-ye
37 V17 **El Cajon** California, W USA 32.46N 116.52W
65 H22 **El Calafate** *var.* Calafate. Santa Cruz, S Argentina 50.19S 72.12W
57 Q8 **El Callao** Bolívar, E Venezuela 7.18N 61.48W
27 U12 **El Campo** Texas, SW USA 29.12N 96.16W
56 I7 **El Cantón** Barinas, W Venezuela 7.25N 71.16W
37 Q8 **El Capitan** ▲ California, W USA 37.46N 119.39W
56 H5 **El Carmelo** Zulia, NW Venezuela 10.21N 71.46W
64 J5 **El Carmen** Jujuy, NW Argentina 24.24S 65.16W
56 E5 **El Carmen de Bolívar** Bolívar, NW Colombia 9.45N 75.11W
57 O8 **El Casabe** Bolívar, SE Venezuela 6.25N 63.34W
44 M12 **El Castillo de La Concepción** Río San Juan, SE Nicaragua 10.58N 84.24W
El Cayo *see* San Ignacio
37 X17 **El Centro** California, W USA 32.47N 115.33W
57 N6 **El Chaparro** Anzoátegui, NE Venezuela 9.08N 65.01W
107 S12 **Elche** *Cat.* Elx; *anc.* Ilici, *Lat.* Illicis. País Valenciano, E Spain 38.16N 0.40W
107 Q12 **Elche de la Sierra** Castilla-La Mancha, C Spain 38.27N 2.03W
43 U15 **El Chichonal, Volcán** ✺ SE Mexico 17.20N 93.12W
42 C2 **El Chinero** Baja California, NW Mexico
189 R1 **Elcho Island** *island* Wessel Islands, Northern Territory, N Australia
65 H18 **El Corcovado** Chubut, SW Argentina 43.31S 71.30W
107 R12 **Elda** País Valenciano, E Spain 38.28N 0.46W
102 M10 **Elde** ≈ NE Germany
100 L12 **Elden** Gelderland, E Netherlands 51.57N 5.53E
83 J16 **El Der** *spring/well* S Ethiopia 3.55N 39.48E
El Dere *see* Ceel Dheere
42 E3 **El Desemboque** Sonora, NW Mexico 30.33N 112.59W
56 F5 **El Difícil** *var.* Ariguaní. Magdalena, N Colombia 9.49N 74.16W
126 Mm11 **El'dikan** Respublika Sakha (Yakutiya), NE Russian Federation 60.46N 135.04E
El Djazaïr *see* Alger
El Djelfa *see* Djelfa
31 X15 **Eldon** Iowa, C USA 40.55N 92.13W
29 U5 **Eldon** Missouri, C USA 38.21N 92.34W
56 E13 **El Doncello** Caquetá, S Colombia 1.43N 75.16W
31 W13 **Eldora** Iowa, C USA 42.21N 93.06W
62 G12 **Eldorado** Misiones, NE Argentina 26.22S 54.33W
42 I9 **El Dorado** Sinaloa, C Mexico 24.19N 107.22W
29 U14 **El Dorado** Arkansas, C USA 33.12N 92.40W
32 M17 **Eldorado** Illinois, N USA 37.48N 88.26W
29 O6 **El Dorado** Kansas, C USA 37.49N 96.51W
28 K12 **Eldorado** Oklahoma, C USA 34.28N 99.39W
27 O9 **Eldorado** Texas, SW USA 30.51N 100.36W
57 Q8 **El Dorado** Bolívar, E Venezuela 6.45N 61.37W
56 F10 **El Dorado** ✈ (Bogotá) Cundinamarca, C Colombia 1.15N 71.52W
El Dorado *see* California
29 O6 **El Dorado Lake** ⊡ Kansas, C USA
29 S6 **El Dorado Springs** Missouri, C USA 37.53N 94.01W
83 H18 **Eldoret** Rift Valley, W Kenya 0.31N 35.16E
31 Z14 **Eldridge** Iowa, C USA 41.39N 90.34W
97 J21 **Eldsberga** Halland, S Sweden 56.36N 13.00E
27 R4 **Electra** Texas, SW USA 34.01N 98.55W
39 Q7 **Electra Lake** ⊡ Colorado, C USA
40 B8 **'Ele'ele** *var.* Eleele. Kaua'i, Hawai'i, USA, C Pacific Ocean 21.54N 159.35W
Elefantes *see* Olifants
117 H19 **Elefsína** *prev.* Elevsís. Attikí, C Greece 38.02N 23.33E
117 G19 **Eléftheres** *anc.* Eleutherae. *site of ancient city* Attikí/Stereá Ellás, C Greece 38.12N 23.24E
116 I13 **Eleftheroúpoli** *prev.* Elevtheroúpolis. Anatolikí Makedonía kai Thráki, NE Greece 40.56N 24.16E
76 F10 **El Eglab** ▲▲ SW Algeria
120 F10 **Eleja** Jelgava, C Latvia 56.24N 23.41E
Elek *see* Ilek
121 G14 **Elektrėnai** Vilnius, SE Lithuania 54.47N 24.35E
130 L3 **Elektrostal'** Moskovskaya Oblast', W Russian Federation 55.46N 38.23E
83 H15 **Elemi Triangle** *disputed region* Kenya/Sudan
56 G16 **El Encanto** Amazonas, S Colombia 1.45S 73.12W

◆ Country
● Country Capital
◇ Dependent Territory
○ Dependent Territory Capital
◈ Administrative Region
✈ International Airport
▲ Mountain
▲▲ Mountain Range
✺ Volcano
≈ River
◎ Lake
⊡ Reservoir

ELEPHANT BUTTE RESERVOIR – EPHRATA

39 R14 **Elephant Butte Reservoir** ⊠ New Mexico, SW USA
Éléphant, Chaîne de l' *see* Dâmrei, Chuŏr Phmun
204 G2 **Elephant Island** *island* South Shetland Islands, Antarctica
Elephant River *see* Olifants
El Escorial *see* San Lorenzo de El Escorial
Élesd *see* Aleşd
116 F11 **Eleshnitsa** ≈ W Bulgaria
143 S13 **Eleşkirt** Ağrı, E Turkey 39.22N 42.48E
44 F5 **El Estor** Izabal, E Guatemala 15.31N 89.19W
Eleutherae *see* Eléftheres
46 I2 **Eleuthera Island** *island* N Bahamas
39 S5 **Elevenmile Canyon Reservoir** ⊠ Colorado, C USA
29 W8 **Eleven Point River** ≈ Arkansas/Missouri, C USA
Elevsís *see* Elefsína
Elevtheroúpolis *see* Eleftheroúpoli
77 W8 **El Faiyûm** *var.* Al Fayyūm. N Egypt 29.24N 30.52E
82 B10 **El Fasher** *var.* Al Fāshir. Northern Darfur, W Sudan 13.37N 25.22E
77 W8 **El Fashn** *var.* Al Fashn. C Egypt 28.49N 30.54E
El Ferrol/El Ferrol del Caudillo *see* Ferrol
41 W13 **Elfin Cove** Chichagof Island, Alaska, USA 58.09N 136.16W
107 W4 **El Fluvià** ≈ NE Spain
42 H7 **El Fuerte** Sinaloa, W Mexico 26.28N 108.34W
82 D11 **El Fula** Western Kordofan, C Sudan 11.43N 28.19E
El Gedaref *see* Gedaref
82 A10 **El Geneina** *var.* Ajjinena, Al-Genain, Al Junaynah. Western Darfur, W Sudan 13.27N 22.30E
98 J8 **Elgin** NE Scotland, UK 57.39N 3.19W
32 M10 **Elgin** Illinois, N USA 42.02N 88.16W
31 P14 **Elgin** Nebraska, C USA 41.58N 98.04W
37 Y9 **Elgin** Nevada, W USA 37.19N 114.30W
30 L6 **Elgin** North Dakota, N USA 46.24N 101.51W
28 M12 **Elgin** Oklahoma, C USA 34.46N 98.17W
27 T10 **Elgin** Texas, SW USA 30.21N 97.22W
127 N9 **El'ginskiy** Respublika Sakha (Yakutiya), NE Russian Federation 64.27N 141.57E
77 W8 **El Gîza** *var.* Al Jīzah, Gîza, Gizeh. N Egypt 30.01N 31.13E
76 J8 **El Goléa** *var.* Al Golea. C Algeria 30.35N 2.58E
42 D2 **El Golfo de Santa Clara** Sonora, NW Mexico 31.44N 114.34W
83 G18 **Elgon, Mount** ▲ E Uganda 1.07N 34.29E
107 T4 **El Grado** Aragón, NE Spain 42.09N 0.13E
96 I10 **Elgspiggen** ▲ S Norway 62.13N 11.18E
42 L6 **El Guaje, Laguna** ⊠ NE Mexico
56 H6 **El Guayabo** Zulia, W Venezuela 8.37N 72.19W
79 O6 **El Guettâra** *oasis* N Mali 22.01N 3.00W
78 J6 **El Ḥammâmi** *desert* N Mauritania
78 M5 **El Ḥank** *cliff* N Mauritania
El Haseke *see* Al Ḥasakah
82 H10 **El Hawata** Gedaref, E Sudan 13.25N 34.42E
El Higo *see* Higos
176 Uu16 **Eliase** Pulau Selaru, E Indonesia 8.16S 130.49E
Elías Piña *see* Comendador
27 R6 **Eliasville** Texas, SW USA 32.55N 98.46W
Elichpur *see* Achalpur
39 V13 **Elida** New Mexico, SW USA 33.57N 103.39W
117 F18 **Elikónas** ▲▲ C Greece
69 T10 **Elila** ≈ W Dem. Rep. Congo
41 N9 **Elim** Alaska, USA 64.37N 162.15W
Elimberrum *see* Auch
Eliocroca *see* Lorca
63 B16 **Elisa** Santa Fe, C Argentina 30.42S 61.04W
Elisabethstedt *see* Dumbrăveni
Élisabethville *see* Lubumbashi
131 O13 **Elista** Respublika Kalmykiya, SW Russian Federation 46.17N 44.09E
190 I9 **Elizabeth** South Australia 34.44S 138.39E
23 Q3 **Elizabeth** West Virginia, NE USA 39.03N 81.22W
21 Q9 **Elizabeth, Cape** *headland* Maine, NE USA 43.34N 70.12W
23 Y8 **Elizabeth City** North Carolina, SE USA 36.18N 76.13W
23 P8 **Elizabethton** Tennessee, S USA 36.21N 82.12W
32 M17 **Elizabethtown** Illinois, N USA 37.24N 88.21W
22 K6 **Elizabethtown** Kentucky, S USA 37.41N 85.51W
20 L7 **Elizabethtown** New York, NE USA 44.13N 73.37W
23 U11 **Elizabethtown** North Carolina, SE USA 34.37N 78.36W
20 G15 **Elizabethtown** Pennsylvania, NE USA 40.08N 76.36W
76 E6 **El-Jadida** *prev.* Mazagan. W Morocco 33.15N 8.27W
El Jafr *see* Jafr, Qāʿ al
82 F11 **El Jebelein** White Nile, E Sudan 12.37N 32.51E
112 N8 **Ełk** *Ger.* Lyck. Warmińsko-Mazurskie, NE Poland 53.51N 22.19E
112 O8 **Ełk** ≈ NE Poland
31 Y12 **Elkader** Iowa, C USA 42.51N 91.24W
82 G9 **El Kamlin** Gezira, C Sudan 15.01N 33.02E
35 N11 **Elk City** Idaho, NW USA 45.50N 115.28W
28 K10 **Elk City** Oklahoma, C USA 35.24N 99.24W
29 P7 **Elk City Lake** ⊠ Kansas, C USA
36 M5 **Elk Creek** California, W USA 39.34N 122.34W
30 J10 **Elk Creek** ≈ South Dakota, N USA
76 M5 **El Kef** *var.* Al Kāf, Le Kef. NW Tunisia 36.13N 8.44E
76 F7 **El Kelâa Srarhna** *var.* Kal al Sraghna. C Morocco 32.05N 7.20W
El Kerak *see* Al Karak
9 P17 **Elkford** British Columbia, SW Canada 49.58N 114.57W
El Khalil *see* Hebron
82 E7 **El Khandaq** Northern, N Sudan 18.34N 30.34E
77 W10 **El Khârga** *var.* Al Khārijah. C Egypt 25.31N 30.36E
33 P11 **Elkhart** Indiana, N USA 41.40N 85.58W
28 H7 **Elkhart** Kansas, C USA 37.00N 101.51W
27 V8 **Elkhart** Texas, SW USA 31.37N 95.34W
32 M7 **Elkhart Lake** ◎ Wisconsin, N USA
El Khartûm *see* Khartoum
39 Q3 **Elkhead Mountains** ▲▲ Colorado, C USA
20 I12 **Elk Hill** ▲ Pennsylvania, NE USA 41.42N 75.33W
144 G8 **El Khiyam** *var.* Al Khiyām, Khiam. S Lebanon 33.12N 35.42E
31 S15 **Elkhorn** Nebraska, C USA 41.17N 96.13W
32 M9 **Elkhorn** Wisconsin, N USA 42.40N 88.34W
31 R14 **Elkhorn River** ≈ Nebraska, C USA
131 O16 **El'khotovo** Respublika Severnaya Osetiya, SW Russian Federation 43.18N 44.17E
116 L10 **Elkhovo** *prev.* Kizilagach. Yambol, E Bulgaria 42.12N 26.36E
23 R8 **Elkin** North Carolina, SE USA 36.14N 80.51W
23 S4 **Elkins** West Virginia, NE USA 38.55N 79.51W
205 X3 **Elkins, Mount** ▲ Antarctica 66.25S 53.54E
12 G8 **Elk Lake** Ontario, S Canada 47.44N 80.19W
33 P6 **Elk Lake** ◎ Michigan, N USA
20 F12 **Elkland** Pennsylvania, NE USA 41.59N 77.16W
37 W3 **Elko** Nevada, W USA 40.48N 115.46W
9 R14 **Elk Point** Alberta, SW Canada 53.52N 110.49W
31 R12 **Elk Point** South Dakota, N USA 42.42N 96.37W
31 V8 **Elk River** Minnesota, N USA 45.18N 93.34W
22 J10 **Elk River** ≈ Alabama/Tennessee, S USA
23 R4 **Elk River** ≈ West Virginia, NE USA
22 I7 **Elkton** Kentucky, S USA 36.48N 87.07W
23 Y2 **Elkton** Maryland, NE USA 39.36N 75.49W
31 R10 **Elkton** South Dakota, N USA 44.14N 96.28W
22 I10 **Elkton** Tennessee, S USA 35.01N 86.51W
23 U5 **Elkton** Virginia, NE USA 38.22N 78.35W
El Kuneitra *see* Al Qunayṭirah
83 L15 **El Kure** Somali, E Ethiopia 5.37N 42.05E
82 D12 **El Lagowa** Western Kordofan, C Sudan 11.22N 29.10E
41 S12 **Ellamar** Alaska, USA 60.54N 146.37W
Ellás *see* Greece
25 S6 **Ellaville** Georgia, SE USA 32.14N 84.18W
207 P9 **Ellef Ringnes Island** *island* Nunavut, N Canada
31 V10 **Ellendale** Minnesota, N USA 43.53N 93.19W
31 P7 **Ellendale** North Dakota, N USA 45.57N 98.33W
38 M6 **Ellen, Mount** ▲ Utah, W USA 38.06N 110.48W
34 I9 **Ellensburg** Washington, NW USA 47.00N 124.34W
20 K12 **Ellenville** New York, NE USA 41.43N 74.24W
Ellep *see* Lib
23 T10 **Ellerbe** North Carolina, SE USA 35.04N 79.45W
207 P10 **Ellesmere Island** *island* Queen Elizabeth Islands, Nunavut, N Canada
193 H19 **Ellesmere, Lake** ◎ South Island, NZ
99 K18 **Ellesmere Port** C England, UK 53.16N 2.54W
33 O14 **Ellettsville** Indiana, N USA 39.13N 86.37W
101 E19 **Ellezelles** Hainaut, SW Belgium 50.44N 3.40E
15 Jj4 **Ellice** ≈ Nunavut, NE Canada
Ellice Islands *see* Tuvalu
Ellichpur *see* Achalpur
23 W3 **Ellicott City** Maryland, NE USA 39.16N 76.48W
25 S2 **Ellijay** Georgia, SE USA 34.42N 84.28W
29 W7 **Ellington** Missouri, C USA 37.14N 90.58W
28 L5 **Ellinwood** Kansas, C USA 38.21N 98.34W
85 J24 **Elliot** Eastern Cape, SE South Africa 31.19S 27.51E
12 D10 **Elliot Lake** Ontario, S Canada 46.24N 82.37W
189 X6 **Elliot, Mount** ▲ Queensland, E Australia 19.36S 147.02E
23 T5 **Elliott Knob** ▲ Virginia, NE USA 38.10N 79.18W
28 K4 **Ellis** Kansas, C USA 38.56N 99.33W
190 F8 **Elliston** South Australia 33.39S 134.56E
24 M7 **Ellisville** Mississippi, S USA 31.36N 89.12W
107 V5 **El Llobregat** ≈ NE Spain
98 L9 **Ellon** NE Scotland, UK 57.22N 2.06W
Ellore *see* Elūru
23 S13 **Elloree** South Carolina, SE USA 33.34N 80.37W
28 M4 **Ellsworth** Kansas, C USA 38.43N 98.13W
21 S7 **Ellsworth** Maine, NE USA 44.32N 68.25W
32 I6 **Ellsworth** Wisconsin, N USA 44.43N 92.28W
28 M11 **Ellsworth, Lake** ⊠ Oklahoma, C USA
204 K9 **Ellsworth Land** *physical region* Antarctica
204 L9 **Ellsworth Mountains** ▲▲ Antarctica
103 J21 **Ellwangen** Baden-Württemberg, S Germany 48.58N 10.07E
20 B14 **Ellwood City** Pennsylvania, NE USA 40.49N 80.15W
110 H8 **Elm** Glarus, NE Switzerland 46.55N 9.09E
34 G9 **Elma** Washington, NW USA 47.00N 123.24W
124 Qq15 **El Maḥalla el Kubra** *var.* Al Maḥallah al Kubrá, Mahalla el Kubra. N Egypt 30.58N 31.10E
76 E9 **El Mahbas** *var.* Mahbés. SW Western Sahara 27.25N 9.09W
65 H17 **El Maitén** Chubut, W Argentina 42.03S 71.10W
142 E16 **Elmalı** Antalya, SW Turkey 36.40N 29.54E
82 G10 **El Manaqil** Gezira, C Sudan 14.12N 33.01E
56 M12 **El Mango** Amazonas, S Venezuela 1.55N 66.34W
77 W7 **El Manṣûra** *var.* Al Manṣūrah, Manṣûra. N Egypt 31.02N 31.30E
57 P8 **El Manteco** Bolívar, E Venezuela 7.17N 62.31W
31 O16 **Elm Creek** Nebraska, C USA 40.43N 99.22W
El Mediyya *see* Médéa
79 V9 **Elméki** Agadez, C Niger 17.52N 8.07E
110 K7 **Elmen** Tirol, W Austria 47.22N 10.34E
20 I16 **Elmer** New Jersey, NE USA 39.34N 75.09W
144 G6 **El Mina** *var.* Al Mīnā'. N Lebanon 34.28N 35.49E
77 W9 **El Minya** *var.* Al Minyā, Minya. C Egypt 28.06N 30.40E
12 F15 **Elmira** Ontario, S Canada 43.35N 80.34W
20 G11 **Elmira** New York, NE USA 42.06N 76.49W
38 K13 **El Mirage** Arizona, SW USA 33.36N 112.19W
31 O7 **Elm Lake** ⊠ South Dakota, N USA
El Moján *see* San Rafael
107 N7 **El Molar** Madrid, C Spain 40.43N 3.34W
78 L7 **El Mrâyer** *well* C Mauritania 21.40N 7.50W
78 L5 **El Mreiti** *well* N Mauritania 23.40N 7.23W
78 L8 **El Mreyyé** *desert* E Mauritania
31 P8 **Elm River** ≈ North Dakota/South Dakota, N USA
102 I9 **Elmshorn** Schleswig-Holstein, N Germany 53.45N 9.39E
82 D12 **El Muglad** Western Kordofan, C Sudan 11.01N 27.43E
El Muwaqqar *see* Al Muwaqqar
12 G14 **Elmvale** Ontario, S Canada 44.34N 79.53W
32 K12 **Elmwood** Illinois, N USA 40.46N 89.58W
28 J8 **Elmwood** Oklahoma, C USA 36.37N 100.31W
105 P17 **Elne** *anc.* Illiberis. Pyrénées-Orientales, S France 42.36N 2.58E
56 F11 **El Nevado, Cerro** *elevation* C Colombia 3.56N 74.20W
179 Oo13 **El Nido** Palawan, W Philippines 11.10N 119.25E
64 I12 **El Nihuil** Mendoza, W Argentina 35.07S 68.38W
77 W7 **El Nouzha** ✕ (Alexandria) N Egypt 31.06N 29.58E
82 E10 **El Obeid** *var.* Al Obayyid, Al Ubayyiḍ. Northern Kordofan, C Sudan 13.10N 30.10E
43 O13 **El Oro** México, S Mexico 19.51N 100.07W
58 B8 **El Oro** ◈ *province* SW Ecuador
63 B19 **Elortondo** Santa Fe, C Argentina 33.42S 61.37W
56 J8 **Elorza** Apure, C Venezuela 7.01N 69.30W
El Ouâdi *see* El Oued
76 L7 **El Oued** *var.* Al Oued, El Ouâdi, El Wad. NE Algeria 33.19N 6.52E
38 L15 **Eloy** Arizona, SW USA 32.47N 111.33W
57 Q7 **El Palmar** Bolívar, E Venezuela 8.03N 61.51W
42 K8 **El Palmito** Durango, W Mexico 25.40N 104.58W
57 P7 **El Pao** Bolívar, E Venezuela 8.02N 62.38W
56 K5 **El Pao** Cojedes, N Venezuela 9.42N 68.12W
44 J7 **El Paraíso** El Paraíso, S Honduras 13.52N 86.32W
44 I7 **El Paraíso** ◈ *department* SE Honduras
32 L12 **El Paso** Illinois, N USA 40.44N 89.01W
26 G8 **El Paso** Texas, SW USA 31.45N 106.30W
26 G8 **El Paso** ✕ Texas, SW USA 31.48N 106.24W
107 U7 **El Perello** Cataluña, NE Spain 40.52N 0.43E
57 P5 **El Pilar** Sucre, NE Venezuela 10.33N 63.13W
44 F7 **El Pital, Cerro** ▲ El Salvador/Honduras 14.19N 89.06W
37 Q9 **El Portal** California, W USA 37.40N 119.46W
42 J3 **El Porvenir** Chihuahua, N Mexico 31.13N 105.51W
45 U14 **El Porvenir** San Blas, N Panama 9.33N 78.55W
107 W6 **El Prat de Llobregat** Cataluña, NE Spain 41.19N 2.04E
44 H5 **El Progreso** Yoro, NW Honduras 15.25N 87.49W
44 A2 **El Progreso** *off.* Departamento de El Progreso. ◈ *department* C Guatemala
El Progreso *see* Guastatoya
106 L9 **El Puente del Arzobispo** Castilla-La Mancha, C Spain 39.48N 5.10W
106 J15 **El Puerto de Santa María** Andalucía, S Spain 36.36N 6.13W
64 I8 **El Puesto** Catamarca, NW Argentina 27.57S 67.37W
El Qâhira *see* Cairo
77 V10 **El Qaṣr** *var.* Al Qaṣr. C Egypt 25.39N 28.54E
El Qatrani *see* Al Qaṭrānah
42 I10 **El Quelite** Sinaloa, C Mexico 23.37N 106.26W
64 G9 **Elqui, Río** ≈ N Chile
El Quneitra *see* Al Qunayṭirah
El Quseir *see* Al Quṣayr
El Quweira *see* Al Quwayrah
147 O15 **El-Rahaba** ✕ (Ṣan'ā') W Yemen 15.28N 44.12E
44 M10 **El Rama** Región Autónoma Atlántico Sur, SE Nicaragua 12.12N 84.13W
45 W16 **El Real** *var.* El Real de Santa María. Darién, SE Panama 8.07N 77.42W
El Real de Santa María *see* El Real
28 M10 **El Reno** Oklahoma, C USA 35.31N 97.57W
42 K9 **El Rodeo** Durango, C Mexico 25.08N 104.34W
106 J13 **El Ronquillo** Andalucía, S Spain 37.43N 6.09W
9 S16 **Elrose** Saskatchewan, S Canada 51.07N 107.59W
32 K8 **Elroy** Wisconsin, N USA 43.43N 90.16W
27 S17 **Elsa** Texas, SW USA 26.17N 97.59W
77 W8 **El Ṣaff** *var.* Aṣ Ṣaff. N Egypt 29.26N 31.19E
42 J10 **El Salto** Durango, C Mexico 23.46N 105.22W
44 D8 **El Salvador** *off.* Republica de El Salvador. ◆ *republic* Central America
56 K7 **El Samán de Apure** Apure, C Venezuela 7.51N 68.47W
12 D7 **Elsas** Ontario, S Canada 48.31N 82.53W
42 F3 **El Sásabe** *var.* Aduana del Sásabe. Sonora, NW Mexico 31.27N 111.31W
Elsass *see* Alsace
42 J5 **El Sáuz** Chihuahua, N Mexico 29.03N 106.15W
29 W4 **Elsberry** Missouri, C USA 39.10N 90.46W
47 P9 **El Seibo** *var.* Santa Cruz de El Seibo, Santa Cruz del Seibo. E Dominican Republic 18.45N 69.04W
44 B7 **El Semillero Barra Nahualate** Escuintla, SW Guatemala 14.01N 91.28W
Elsene *see* Ixelles
Elsen Nur *see* Dorgê Co
38 L6 **Elsinore** Utah, W USA 38.40N 112.09W
Elsinore *see* Helsingør
101 L18 **Elsloo** Limburg, SE Netherlands 50.57N 5.46E
62 G13 **El Soberbio** Misiones, NE Argentina 27.15S 54.04W
57 N6 **El Socorro** Guárico, C Venezuela 9.00N 65.42W
56 L6 **El Sombrero** Guárico, N Venezuela 9.25N 67.06W
100 L10 **Elspeet** Gelderland, E Netherlands 52.19N 5.47E
100 L12 **Elst** Gelderland, E Netherlands 51.55N 5.51E
103 O15 **Elsterwerda** Brandenburg, E Germany 51.27N 13.32E
42 J4 **El Sueco** Chihuahua, N Mexico 29.52N 106.23W
El Suweida *see* As Suwaydā'
El Suweis *see* Suez
56 D12 **El Tambo** Cauca, SW Colombia 2.25N 76.49W
183 T13 **Eltanin Fracture Zone** *tectonic feature* SE Pacific Ocean
107 X5 **El Ter** ≈ NE Spain
192 K11 **Eltham** Taranaki, North Island, NZ 39.25S 174.17E
57 O6 **El Tigre** Anzoátegui, NE Venezuela 8.55N 64.15W
El Tigrito *see* San José de Guanipa
56 J5 **El Tocuyo** Lara, N Venezuela 9.47N 69.48W
131 Q10 **El'ton** Volgogradskaya Oblast', SW Russian Federation 49.07N 46.50E
34 K10 **Eltopia** Washington, NW USA 46.33N 118.59W
El Toro *see* Mare de Déu del Toro
63 A18 **El Trébol** Santa Fe, C Argentina 32.12S 61.40W
42 J13 **El Tuito** Jalisco, SW Mexico 20.20N 105.19W
77 X8 **El Ṭûr** *var.* Aṭ Ṭūr. NE Egypt 28.18N 33.37E
161 K16 **Elūru** *prev.* Ellore. Andhra Pradesh, E India 16.45N 81.10E
120 H13 **Elva** *Ger.* Elwa. Tartumaa, SE Estonia 58.13N 26.27E
39 R9 **El Vado Reservoir** ⊠ New Mexico, SW USA
45 S15 **El Valle** Coclé, C Panama 8.39N 80.07W
106 I11 **Elvas** Portalegre, C Portugal 38.52N 7.10W
56 K7 **El Venado** Apure, C Venezuela 7.25N 68.46W
107 V6 **El Vendrell** Cataluña, NE Spain 41.13N 1.31E
96 I13 **Elverum** Hedmark, S Norway 60.52N 11.34E
44 I9 **El Viejo** Chinandega, NW Nicaragua 12.37N 87.09W
56 G7 **El Viejo, Cerro** ▲ C Colombia 7.31N 72.56W
56 H6 **El Vigía** Mérida, NW Venezuela 8.37N 71.39W
107 Q4 **El Villar de Arnedo** La Rioja, N Spain 42.19N 2.05W
61 A14 **Elvira** Amazonas, W Brazil 7.12S 69.56W
Elwa *see* Elva
El Wad *see* El Oued
83 K17 **El Wak** North Eastern, NE Kenya 2.46N 40.57E
35 R7 **Elwell, Lake** ⊠ Montana, NW USA
33 P13 **Elwood** Indiana, N USA 40.16N 85.50W
29 R3 **Elwood** Kansas, C USA 39.43N 94.52W
31 N16 **Elwood** Nebraska, C USA 40.35N 99.51W
Elx *see* Elche
99 O20 **Ely** E England, UK 52.23N 0.15E
31 X4 **Ely** Minnesota, N USA 47.54N 91.52W
37 X6 **Ely** Nevada, W USA 39.15N 114.53W
El Yopal *see* Yopal
33 T11 **Elyria** Ohio, N USA 41.22N 82.06W
47 S9 **El Yunque** ▲ E Puerto Rico 18.15N 65.46W
103 F23 **Elz** ≈ SW Germany
197 C14 **Emae** *island* Shepherd Islands, C Vanuatu
120 I5 **Emajõgi** *Ger.* Embach. ≈ SE Estonia
Emāmrūd *see* Shāhrūd
155 Q2 **Emām Ṣāḥeb** *var.* Emam Saheb, Hazarat Imam. Kondoz, NE Afghanistan 37.10N 68.55E
Emāmshahr *see* Shāhrūd
97 M20 **Emån** ≈ S Sweden
197 D14 **Emao** *island* C Vanuatu
150 J11 **Emba** *Kaz.* Embi. Aktyubinsk, W Kazakhstan 48.49N 58.10E
150 H12 **Emba** *Kaz.* Zhem. ≈ W Kazakhstan
Embach *see* Emajõgi
64 K5 **Embarcación** Salta, N Argentina 23.15S 64.04W
32 M15 **Embarras River** ≈ Illinois, N USA
Embi *see* Emba
83 I19 **Embu** Eastern, C Kenya 0.30N 37.30E
102 E10 **Emden** Niedersachsen, NW Germany 53.22N 7.12E
166 H9 **Emei Shan** ▲ Sichuan, C China 29.32N 103.21E
31 Q4 **Emerado** North Dakota, N USA 47.55N 97.21W
189 X8 **Emerald** Queensland, E Australia 23.33S 148.10E
Emerald Isle *see* Montserrat
59 J15 **Emero, Río** ≈ W Bolivia
9 Y17 **Emerson** Manitoba, S Canada 49.01N 97.07W
31 T15 **Emerson** Iowa, C USA 41.00N 95.22W
31 R13 **Emerson** Nebraska, C USA 42.16N 96.43W
38 M5 **Emery** Utah, W USA 38.54N 111.16W
Emesa *see* Ḥimṣ
142 E13 **Emet** Kütahya, W Turkey 39.21N 29.15E
194 G14 **Emeti** Western, SW PNG 7.51S 143.14E
37 V3 **Emigrant Pass** *pass* Nevada, W USA 40.39N 116.15W
80 I6 **Emi Koussi** ▲ N Chad 19.52N 18.34E
Emilia *see* Emilia-Romagna
43 V15 **Emiliano Zapata** Chiapas, SE Mexico 17.45N 91.45W
108 E9 **Emilia-Romagna** *prev.* Emilia, *anc.* Æmilia. ◈ *region* N Italy
164 J3 **Emin** *var.* Dorbiljin. Xinjiang Uygur Zizhiqu, NW China 46.31N 83.35E
155 W8 **Eminābād** Punjab, E Pakistan 32.01N 73.51E
23 L5 **Eminence** Kentucky, S USA 38.22N 85.10W
29 W7 **Eminence** Missouri, C USA 37.09N 91.21W
116 N9 **Emine, Nos** *headland* E Bulgaria 42.43N 27.53E
164 I3 **Emin He** ≈ NW China
195 N8 **Emirau Island** *island* N PNG
142 F13 **Emirdağ** Afyon, W Turkey 39.01N 31.09E
97 M21 **Emmaboda** Kalmar, S Sweden 56.36N 15.30E
120 E5 **Emmaste** Hiiumaa, W Estonia 58.43N 22.36E
20 I15 **Emmaus** Pennsylvania, NE USA 40.32N 75.28W
191 U4 **Emmaville** New South Wales, SE Australia 29.26S 151.38E
110 E9 **Emme** ≈ W Switzerland
100 L8 **Emmeloord** Flevoland, N Netherlands 52.43N 5.46E
100 O8 **Emmen** Drenthe, NE Netherlands 52.48N 6.57E
110 F8 **Emmen** Luzern, C Switzerland 47.03N 8.14E
103 F23 **Emmendingen** Baden-Württemberg, SW Germany 48.07N 7.51E
100 P8 **Emmer-Compascuum** Drenthe, NE Netherlands 52.47N 7.03E
103 D14 **Emmerich** Nordrhein-Westfalen, W Germany 51.49N 6.16E
31 U12 **Emmetsburg** Iowa, C USA 43.06N 94.40W
34 M14 **Emmett** Idaho, NW USA 43.52N 116.30W
40 M10 **Emmonak** Alaska, USA 62.46N 164.31W
Emona *see* Ljubljana
Emonti *see* East London
26 L12 **Emory Peak** ▲ Texas, SW USA 29.15N 103.18W
42 F6 **Empalme** Sonora, NW Mexico 27.57N 110.49W
85 L23 **Empangeni** KwaZulu/Natal, E South Africa 28.40S 31.57E
63 C14 **Empedrado** Corrientes, NE Argentina 27.57S 58.46W
199 Ii3 **Emperor Seamounts** *undersea feature* NW Pacific Ocean
199 J3 **Emperor Trough** *undersea feature* N Pacific Ocean
37 R4 **Empire** Nevada, W USA 40.26N 119.21W
Empire State of the South *see* Georgia
Emplawas *see* Amplawas
108 F11 **Empoli** Toscana, C Italy 43.43N 10.57E
29 P5 **Emporia** Kansas, C USA 38.24N 96.10W
23 W7 **Emporia** Virginia, NE USA 36.41N 77.32W
20 E13 **Emporium** Pennsylvania, NE USA 41.31N 78.13W
195 S12 **Empress Augusta Bay** *inlet* Bougainville Island, PNG
Empty Quarter *see* Ar Rubʿ al Khālī
102 E10 **Ems** *Dut.* Eems. ≈ NW Germany
102 F13 **Emsdetten** Nordrhein-Westfalen, NW Germany 52.10N 7.31E
Ems-Hunte Canal *see* Küstenkanal
102 F10 **Ems-Jade-Kanal** *canal* NW Germany
102 F11 **Emsland** *cultural region* NW Germany
190 D3 **Emu Junction** South Australia 28.39S 132.13E
169 T3 **Emur He** ≈ NE China
57 R8 **Enachu Landing** NW Guyana 6.09N 60.01W
95 F16 **Enafors** Jämtland, C Sweden 63.16N 12.24E
96 N11 **Enånger** Gävleborg, C Sweden 61.30N 17.10E
98 G7 **Enard Bay** *bay* NW Scotland, UK
Enareträsk *see* Inarijärvi
176 X12 **Enarotali** Papua, E Indonesia 3.55S 136.21E
171 I15 **Ena-san** ▲ Honshū, S Japan 35.27N 137.36E
144 E12 **En 'Avedat** *var.* Ein 'Avedat, *well* S Israel
172 P2 **Enbetsu** Hokkaidō, NE Japan 44.44N 141.47E
63 H16 **Encantadas, Serra das** ▲▲ S Brazil
42 E7 **Encantado, Cerro** ▲ NW Mexico 26.46N 112.33W
64 P7 **Encarnación** Itapúa, S Paraguay 27.19S 55.49W
42 M12 **Encarnación de Díaz** Jalisco, SW Mexico 21.33N 102.13W
79 O17 **Enchi** SW Ghana 5.52N 2.48W
27 Q14 **Encinal** Texas, SW USA 28.02N 99.21W
37 U17 **Encinitas** California, W USA 33.02N 117.17W
27 S16 **Encino** Texas, SW USA 26.58N 98.06W
56 H6 **Encontrados** Zulia, NW Venezuela 9.01N 72.16W
190 I10 **Encounter Bay** *inlet* South Australia
63 F15 **Encruzilhada** Rio Grande do Sul, S Brazil 28.58S 55.31W
63 H16 **Encruzilhada do Sul** Rio Grande do Sul, S Brazil 30.30S 52.31W
113 M20 **Encs** Borsod-Abaúj-Zemplén, NE Hungary 48.21N 21.09E
199 M3 **Endeavour Seamount** *undersea feature* N Pacific Ocean 48.15N 129.04W
189 V1 **Endeavour Strait** *strait* Queensland, NE Australia
175 Q16 **Endeh** Flores, S Indonesia 8.48S 121.37E
97 G23 **Endelave** *island* C Denmark
203 T4 **Enderbury Island** *atoll* Phoenix Islands, C Kiribati
9 N16 **Enderby** British Columbia, SW Canada 50.34N 119.09W
205 W4 **Enderby Land** *physical region* Antarctica
181 N14 **Enderby Plain** *undersea feature* S Indian Ocean
31 Q6 **Enderlin** North Dakota, N USA 46.37N 97.36W
Endersdorf *see* Jędrzejów
30 K16 **Enders Reservoir** ⊠ Nebraska, C USA
20 H11 **Endicott** New York, NE USA 42.06N 76.03W
41 P7 **Endicott Mountains** ▲▲ Alaska, USA
120 I5 **Endla Raba** *wetland* C Estonia
119 T9 **Enerhodar** Zaporiz'ka Oblast', SE Ukraine 47.30N 34.40E
59 F14 **Ene, Río** ≈ C Peru
201 N4 **Enewetak Atoll** *var.* Ānewetak, Eniwetok. *atoll* Ralik Chain, W Marshall Islands
116 L13 **Enez** Edirne, NW Turkey 40.43N 26.04E
23 W8 **Enfield** North Carolina, SE USA 36.10N 77.40W
194 G12 **Enga** ◈ *province* W PNG
47 Q9 **Engaño, Cabo** *headland* E Dominican Republic 18.36N 68.19W
172 Q5 **Engaru** Hokkaidō, NE Japan 44.06N 143.30E
144 F11 **'En Gedi** Southern, E Israel 31.23N 35.21E
110 F9 **Engelberg** Unterwalden, C Switzerland 46.51N 8.25E
23 Y9 **Engelhard** North Carolina, SE USA 35.30N 76.00W
131 P8 **Engel's** Saratovskaya Oblast', W Russian Federation 51.27N 46.09E
103 G24 **Engen** Baden-Württemberg, SW Germany 47.52N 8.46E
Engeten *see* Aiud
174 H13 **Enggano, Pulau** *island* W Indonesia
82 J8 **Enghershatu** ▲ N Eritrea 16.41N 38.21E
101 F19 **Enghien** *Dut.* Edingen. Hainaut, SW Belgium 50.42N 4.03E
29 V12 **England** Arkansas, C USA 34.32N 91.58W
99 M20 **England** *Lat.* Anglia. *national region* UK
15 L2 **Englefield, Cape** *headland* Nunavut, NE Canada 69.51N 85.31W
12 H8 **Englehart** Ontario, S Canada 47.49N 79.52W
39 T4 **Englewood** Colorado, C USA 39.39N 104.59W
33 O16 **English** Indiana, N USA 38.19N 86.28W
41 Q13 **English Bay** Alaska, USA 59.21N 151.55W
English Bazar *see* Ingrāj Bāzār
99 N25 **English Channel** *var.* The Channel, *Fr.* la Manche. *channel* NW Europe
204 J7 **English Coast** *physical region* Antarctica
107 S11 **Enguera** País Valenciano, E Spain 38.58N 0.42W
120 E8 **Engure** Tukums, W Latvia 57.09N 23.13E
120 E8 **Engures Ezers** ◎ NW Latvia
143 R9 **Enguri** *Rus.* Inguri. ≈ NW Georgia
Engyum *see* Gangi
28 M9 **Enid** Oklahoma, C USA 36.24N 97.52W
24 L3 **Enid Lake** ⊠ Mississippi, S USA
201 Y2 **Enigu** *island* Ratak Chain, SE Marshall Islands
Enikale Strait *see* Kerch Strait
153 Z8 **Enil'chek** Issyk-Kul'skaya Oblast', E Kyrgyzstan 42.04N 79.01E
117 F17 **Enipéfs** ≈ C Greece
172 O6 **Eniwa** Hokkaidō, NE Japan 42.54N 141.33E
172 O6 **Eniwa-dake** ✱ Hokkaidō, NE Japan 42.48N 141.15E
Eniwetok *see* Enewetak Atoll
Enjiang *see* Yongfeng
127 Nn11 **Enkan, Mys** *headland* NE Russian Federation 58.29N 141.27E
Enkeldoorn *see* Chivhu
100 J8 **Enkhuizen** Noord-Holland, NW Netherlands 52.34N 5.03E
111 Q4 **Enknach** ≈ N Austria
97 N15 **Enköping** Uppsala, C Sweden 59.39N 17.07E
109 K24 **Enna** *var.* Castrogiovanni, Henna. Sicilia, Italy, C Mediterranean Sea 37.34N 14.18E
82 D11 **En Nahud** Western Kordofan, C Sudan 12.40N 28.28E
144 F8 **En Nâqoûra** *var.* An Nāqūrah. SW Lebanon 33.06N 33.30E
En Nazira *see* Naẕerat
80 K8 **Ennedi** *plateau* E Chad
103 E15 **Ennepetal** Nordrhein-Westfalen, W Germany 51.18N 7.22E
191 P4 **Enngonia** New South Wales, SE Australia 29.19S 145.52E
99 C19 **Ennis** *Ir.* Inis. W Ireland 52.49N 8.58W
35 R11 **Ennis** Montana, NW USA 45.21N 111.45W
27 U7 **Ennis** Texas, SW USA 32.19N 96.37W
99 F20 **Enniscorthy** *Ir.* Inis Córthaidh. SE Ireland 52.30N 6.34W
99 E15 **Enniskillen** *var.* Inniskilling, *Ir.* Inis Ceithleann. SW Northern Ireland, UK 54.21N 7.37W
99 B19 **Ennistimon** *Ir.* Inis Díomáin. W Ireland 52.56N 9.17W
111 T4 **Enns** Oberösterreich, N Austria 48.12N 14.29E
111 T4 **Enns** ≈ C Austria
95 O16 **Eno** Itä-Suomi, E Finland 62.45N 30.15E
26 M5 **Enochs** Texas, SW USA 33.51N 102.46W
95 N17 **Enonkoski** Isä-Suomi, E Finland 62.04N 28.53E
94 K10 **Enontekiö** *Lapp.* Eanodat. Lappi, N Finland 68.25N 23.40E
23 Q11 **Enoree** South Carolina, SE USA 34.39N 81.58W
23 P11 **Enoree River** ≈ South Carolina, SE USA
20 M6 **Enosburg Falls** Vermont, NE USA 44.54N 72.50W
175 P11 **Enrekang** Sulawesi, C Indonesia 3.33S 119.46E
47 N10 **Enriquillo** SW Dominican Republic 17.53N 71.13W
47 N9 **Enriquillo, Lago** ◎ SW Dominican Republic
100 L9 **Ens** Flevoland, N Netherlands 52.39N 5.49E
100 P11 **Enschede** Overijssel, E Netherlands 52.13N 6.55E
42 B2 **Ensenada** Baja California, NW Mexico 31.52N 116.31W
103 E20 **Ensheim** ✕ (Saarbrücken) Saarland, W Germany 49.13N 7.09E
166 L9 **Enshi** Hubei, C China 30.16N 109.25E
171 Hh17 **Enshū-nada** *gulf* SW Japan
25 O8 **Ensley** Florida, SE USA 30.31N 87.16W
Enso *see* Svetogorsk
83 F18 **Entebbe** S Uganda 0.07N 32.29E
83 F18 **Entebbe** ✕ C Uganda 0.04N 32.29E
103 M18 **Entenbühl** ▲ Czech Republic/Germany 50.09N 12.10E
100 N10 **Enter** Overijssel, E Netherlands 52.19N 6.34E
25 Q7 **Enterprise** Alabama, S USA 31.19N 85.50W
34 L11 **Enterprise** Oregon, NW USA 45.25N 117.16W
38 J7 **Enterprise** Utah, W USA 37.33N 113.42W
34 J8 **Entiat** Washington, NW USA 47.39N 120.15W
107 P15 **Entinas, Punta de las** *headland* S Spain 36.40N 2.44W
110 F8 **Entlebuch** Luzern, W Switzerland 47.02N 8.04E
110 F8 **Entlebuch** *valley* C Switzerland
65 I22 **Entrada, Punta** *headland* S Argentina
105 O13 **Entraygues-sur-Truyère** Aveyron, S France 44.39N 2.36E
197 G3 **Entrecasteaux, Récifs d'** *reef* N New Caledonia
63 C17 **Entre Ríos** *off.* Provincia de Entre Ríos. ◈ *province* NE Argentina
44 K7 **Entre Ríos, Cordillera** ▲▲ Honduras/Nicaragua
106 G9 **Entroncamento** Santarém, C Portugal 39.28N 8.28W
176 Z10 **Entrop** Papua, E Indonesia 2.37S 140.43E
79 V16 **Enugu** Enugu, S Nigeria 6.24N 7.24E
79 U16 **Enugu** ◈ *state* SE Nigeria
127 Pp3 **Enurmino** Chukotskiy Avtonomnyy Okrug, NE Russian Federation 66.46N 171.40W
56 E9 **Envigado** Antioquia, W Colombia 6.09N 75.37W
61 B15 **Envira** Amazonas, W Brazil 7.12S 69.58W
Enyélé *see* Enyellé
81 I16 **Enyellé** *var.* Enyélé. La Likouala, NE Congo 2.48N 18.01E
103 H21 **Enz** ≈ SW Germany
171 J16 **Enzan** Yamanashi, Honshū, S Japan 35.42N 138.43E
106 I2 **Eo** ≈ NW Spain
Eochaill *see* Youghal
Eochaille, Cuan *see* Youghal Bay
109 K22 **Eolie, Isole** *var.* Isole Lipari, *Eng.* Aeolian Islands, Lipari Islands. *island group* S Italy
201 U12 **Eot** *island* Chuuk, C Micronesia
Epáno Archánes/Epáno Arkhánai *see* Archánes
117 G14 **Epanomí** Kentrikí Makedonía, N Greece 40.25N 22.55E
100 M10 **Epe** Gelderland, E Netherlands 52.21N 5.58E
79 S16 **Epe** Lagos, S Nigeria 6.37N 4.01E
81 I17 **Epéna** La Likouala, NE Congo 1.27N 17.28E
Eperies/Eperjes *see* Prešov
105 Q4 **Épernay** *anc.* Sparnacum. Marne, N France 49.01N 3.58E
38 L5 **Ephraim** Utah, W USA 39.21N 111.35W
20 H15 **Ephrata** Pennsylvania, NE USA 40.09N 76.08W
34 J8 **Ephrata** Washington, NW USA 47.19N 119.33W

◆ Country
● Country Capital
◇ Dependent Territory
○ Dependent Territory Capital
◈ Administrative Region
✕ International Airport
▲ Mountain
▲▲ Mountain Range
✱ Volcano
≈ River
◎ Lake
⊠ Reservoir

EPI – EZHOU

197 C13 **Epi** *var.* Épi *island* C Vanuatu
107 R6 **Épila** Aragón, NE Spain *41.34N 1.19W*
105 T6 **Épinal** Vosges, NE France *48.10N 6.28E*
Epiphania *see* Ḩamāh
Epirus *see* Ípeiros
124 N4 **Episkopí** SW Cyprus *34.37N 32.53E*
Episkopi Bay *see* Episkopí, Kólpos
124 N4 **Episkopí, Kólpos** *var.* Episkopi Bay. *bay* SE Cyprus
Epitoli *see* Tshwane
Epoon *see* Ebon Atoll
Eporedia *see* Ivrea
Eppeschdorf *see* Dumbrăveni
103 H21 **Eppingen** Baden-Württemberg, SW Germany *49.09N 8.54E*
85 E18 **Epukiro** Omaheke, E Namibia *21.40S 19.09E*
31 Y13 **Epworth** Iowa, C USA *42.27N 90.55W*
149 O10 **Eqlīd** *var.* Iqlid. Fārs, C Iran *30.54N 52.43E*
Equality State *see* Wyoming
81 J18 **Equateur** *off.* Région de l' Equateur. ◈ *region* N Dem. Rep. Congo
157 K22 **Equatorial Channel** *channel* S Maldives
81 B17 **Equatorial Guinea** *off.* Republic of Equatorial Guinea. ◆ *republic* C Africa
194 H14 **Era** ≈ S PNG
124 R13 **Eratosthenes Tablemount** *undersea feature* E Mediterranean Sea *33.48N 32.53E*
Erautini *see* Johannesburg
194 H13 **Erave** Southern Highlands, W PNG *6.36S 143.55E*
142 L12 **Erbaa** Tokat, N Turkey *40.39N 36.37E*
103 E19 **Erbeskopf** ▲ W Germany *49.43N 7.04E*
Erbil *see* Arbīl
124 Nn3 **Ercan** ✕ (Nicosia) N Cyprus *35.07N 33.30E*
Ercegnovi *see* Herceg-Novi
143 T14 **Erçek Gölü** ◎ E Turkey
143 S14 **Erciş** Van, E Turkey *39.02N 43.21E*
142 K14 **Erciyes Dağı** *anc.* Argaeus. ▲ C Turkey *38.35N 35.27E*
113 J22 **Érd** *Ger.* Hanselbeck. Pest, C Hungary *47.22N 18.55E*
169 X11 **Erdaobaihe** *prev.* Baihe. Jilin, NE China *42.24N 128.09E*
165 O12 **Erdaogou** Qinghai, W China *34.30N 92.49E*
169 X11 **Erdao Jiang** ▲▲ NE China
Erdăt-Sângeorz *see* Sângeorgiu de Pădure
142 C11 **Erdek** Balıkesir, NW Turkey *40.25N 27.49E*
Erdély *see* Transylvania
Erdélyi-Havasok *see* Carpaţii Meridionali
142 J17 **Erdemli** Mersin, S Turkey *36.39N 34.18E*
169 O10 **Erdene** *var.* Ulaan-Uul. Dornogovĭ, SE Mongolia *44.21N 111.06E*
168 H9 **Erdene** *var.* Sangiyn Dalay. Govĭ-Altay, C Mongolia *45.12N 97.51E*
168 E6 **Erdenebüren** *var.* Har-Us. Hovd, W Mongolia *48.30N 91.25E*
168 K9 **Erdenedalay** *var.* Sangiyn Dalay. Dundgovĭ, C Mongolia *45.59N 104.58E*
168 G7 **Erdenehayrhan** *var.* Altan. Dzavhan, W Mongolia *48.05N 95.48E*
168 J7 **Erdenemandal** *var.* Öldziyt. Arhangay, C Mongolia *48.30N 101.25E*
168 K6 **Erdenet** Orhon, N Mongolia *49.01N 104.06E*
169 Q9 **Erdenetsagaan** *var.* Chonogol. Sühbaatar, E Mongolia *45.55N 115.19E*
168 I8 **Erdenetsogt** Bayanhongor, C Mongolia *46.27N 100.53E*
Erdenetsogt *see* Bayan-Ovoo
80 K7 **Erdi** *plateau* NE Chad
80 L7 **Erdi Ma** *desert* NE Chad
103 M23 **Erding** Bayern, SE Germany *48.18N 11.54E*
Erdőszáda *see* Ardusat
Erdőszentgyörgy *see* Sângeorgiu de Pădure
104 I7 **Erdre** ≈ NW France
205 R13 **Erebus, Mount** ▲ Ross Island, Antarctica *78.11S 165.09E*
63 H14 **Erechim** Rio Grande do Sul, S Brazil *27.34S 52.15W*
169 O7 **Ereen Davaanï Nuruu** ▲▲ NE Mongolia
169 Q6 **Ereentsav** Dornod, NE Mongolia *49.51N 115.41E*
142 I16 **Ereğli** Konya, S Turkey *37.30N 34.01E*
142 I15 **Ereğli Gölü** ◎ W Turkey
117 A15 **Ereíkoussa** *island* Iónia Nisiá, Greece, C Mediterranean Sea
169 O11 **Erenhot** *var.* Erlian. Nei Mongol Zizhiqu, NE China *43.35N 112.00E*
106 M6 **Eresma** ≈ N Spain
117 K17 **Eresós** *var.* Eressós. Lésvos, E Greece *39.10N 25.57E*
Eressós *see* Eresós
Erevan *see* Yerevan
Ereymentaū *see* Yereymentau
101 K21 **Érezée** Luxembourg, SE Belgium *50.16N 5.34E*
76 G7 **Erfoud** SE Morocco *31.29N 4.18W*
103 D16 **Erft** ≈ W Germany
103 K16 **Erfurt** Thüringen, C Germany *50.59N 11.02E*
143 P15 **Ergani** Dıyarbakır, SE Turkey *38.16N 39.43E*
Ergel *see* Hatanbulag
Ergene Irmağı *see* Ergene Çayı
142 C10 **Ergene Çayı** *var.* Ergene Irmağı. ≈ NW Turkey
120 I9 **Ērgļi** Madona, C Latvia *56.54N 25.37E*
80 H11 **Erguig, Bahr** ≈ SW Chad
169 S5 **Ergun** *var.* Labudalin, *prev.* Ergun Youqi. Nei Mongol Zizhiqu, N China *50.13N 120.09E*
Ergun He *see* Argun
Ergun Youqi *see* Ergun
Ergun Zuoqi *see* Genhe
166 F12 **Er Hai** ▣ SW China
104 G4 **Er, Îles d'** *island group* NW France
106 K4 **Ería** ≈ NW Spain
82 H8 **Eriba** Kassala, NE Sudan *16.37N 36.04E*
98 I6 **Eriboll, Loch** *inlet* NW Scotland, UK
67 Q18 **Erica Seamount** *undersea feature* SW Indian Ocean *38.15S 14.30E*
109 H23 **Erice** Sicilia, Italy, C Mediterranean Sea *38.02N 12.35E*
106 E10 **Ericeira** Lisboa, C Portugal *38.58N 9.25W*
98 H10 **Ericht, Loch** ◎ C Scotland, UK
28 J11 **Erick** Oklahoma, C USA *35.13N 99.52W*
20 B11 **Erie** Pennsylvania, NE USA *42.06N 80.03W*
20 E9 **Erie Canal** *canal* New York, NE USA
Érié, Lac *see* Erie, Lake
33 T10 **Erie, Lake** *Fr.* Lac Érié. ◎ Canada/USA
Erigabo *see* Ceerigaabo
79 N8 **'Erîgât** *desert* N Mali
Erigavo *see* Ceerigaabo
94 P2 **Erik Eriksenstretet** *strait* E Svalbard
9 X15 **Eriksdale** Manitoba, S Canada *50.52N 98.07W*
201 V6 **Erikub Atoll** *var.* Ādkup. *atoll* Ratak Chain, C Marshall Islands
Erimanthos *see* Erýmanthos
172 P8 **Erimo** Hokkaidō, NE Japan *42.01N 143.07E*
172 Oo8 **Erimo-misaki** *headland* Hokkaidō, NE Japan *41.57N 143.12E*
22 H8 **Erin** Tennessee, S USA *36.19N 87.41W*
98 E9 **Eriskay** *island* NW Scotland, UK
Erithraí *see* Erythrés
82 I9 **Eritrea** *off.* State of Eritrea, *Tig.* Ērtra. ◆ *transitional government* E Africa
Erivan *see* Yerevan
103 D16 **Erkelenz** Nordrhein-Westfalen, W Germany *51.04N 6.19E*
97 P15 **Erken** ◎ C Sweden
103 K19 **Erlangen** Bayern, S Germany *49.35N 11.00E*
166 G9 **Erlang Shan** ▲ C China *29.56N 102.24E*
Erlau *see* Eger
111 V5 **Erlauf** ≈ NE Austria
189 Q8 **Erldunda Roadhouse** Northern Territory, N Australia *25.13S 133.13E*
Erlian *see* Erenhot
29 T15 **Erling, Lake** ▣ Arkansas, USA
111 O8 **Erlsbach** Tirol, W Austria *46.54N 12.15E*
Ermak *see* Aksu
100 K10 **Ermelo** Gelderland, C Netherlands *52.18N 5.37E*
85 K21 **Ermelo** Mpumalanga, NE South Africa *26.31S 29.58E*
142 H17 **Ermenek** Karaman, S Turkey *36.37N 32.55E*
Érmihályfalva *see* Valea lui Mihai
117 G20 **Ermióni** Pelopónnisos, S Greece *37.24N 23.15E*
117 J20 **Ermoúpoli** *var.* Hermoupolis; *prev.* Ermoúpolis. Sýros, Kykládes, Greece, Aegean Sea *37.26N 24.55E*
Ermoúpolis *see* Ermoúpoli
Ernabella *see* Pukatja
161 G22 **Ernākulam** Kerala, SW India *10.04N 76.18E*
104 J6 **Ernée** Mayenne, NW France *48.18N 0.54W*
63 H14 **Ernestina, Barragem** ▣ S Brazil
56 E4 **Ernesto Cortissoz** ✕ (Barranquilla) Atlántico, N Colombia
161 H21 **Erode** Tamil Nādu, SE India *11.21N 77.43E*
Eroj *see* Iroj
85 C19 **Erongo** ◈ *district* W Namibia
101 F21 **Erquelinnes** Hainaut, S Belgium *50.18N 4.07E*
76 G7 **Er-Rachidia** *var.* Ksar al Soule. E Morocco *31.58N 4.22W*
82 E11 **Er Rahad** *var.* Ar Rahad. Northern Kordofan, C Sudan *12.42N 30.33E*
Er Ramle *see* Ramla
85 O15 **Errego** Zambézia, NE Mozambique *16.02S 37.12E*
107 Q2 **Errenteria** *Cast.* Rentería. País Vasco, N Spain *43.17N 1.54W*
Er Rif/Er Riff *see* Rif
99 D14 **Errigal Mountain** *Ir.* An Earagail. ▲ N Ireland *55.03N 8.09W*
99 A15 **Erris Head** *Ir.* Ceann Iorrais. *headland* W Ireland *54.18N 10.01W*
197 D15 **Erromango** *island* S Vanuatu
Error Guyot *see* Error Tablemount
181 O4 **Error Tablemount** *var.* Error Guyot. *undersea feature* W Indian Ocean *10.19N 56.04E*
82 G11 **Er Roseires** Blue Nile, E Sudan *11.52N 34.22E*
Erseka *see* Ersekë
115 M22 **Ersekë** *var.* Erseka, Kolonjë. Korçë, SE Albania *40.19N 20.39E*
Érsekújvár *see* Nové Zámky
31 S4 **Erskine** Minnesota, N USA *47.42N 96.00W*
105 V6 **Erstein** Bas-Rhin, NE France *48.24N 7.39E*
110 G9 **Erstfeld** Uri, C Switzerland *46.49N 8.41E*
164 M3 **Ertai** Xinjiang Uygur Zizhiqu, NW China *46.04N 90.06E*
130 M7 **Ertil'** Voronezhskaya Oblast', W Russian Federation *51.51N 40.46E*
Ertis *see* Irtysh, C Asia
Ertis *see* Irtyshsk, Kazakhstan
164 K2 **Ertix He** *Rus.* Chërnyy Irtysh. ≈ China/Kazakhstan
Ērtra *see* Eritrea
23 P9 **Erwin** North Carolina, SE USA *35.19N 78.40W*
Erydropótamos *see* Erythropótamos
117 E19 **Erýmanthos** *var.* Erimanthos. ▲ S Greece *37.57N 21.51E*
117 G19 **Erythrés** *prev.* Erithraí. Stereá Ellás, C Greece *38.19N 23.20E*
116 L12 **Erythropótamos** *var.* Erydropótamos, *Bul.* Byala Reka. ≈ Bulgaria/Greece
166 F12 **Eryuan** *var.* Yuhu. Yunnan, SW China *26.09N 100.01E*
111 U6 **Erzbach** ≈ W Austria
Erzerum *see* Erzurum
103 N17 **Erzgebirge** *Cz.* Krušné Hory, *Eng.* Ore Mountains. ▲▲ Czech Republic/Germany *see also* Krušné Hory
126 I16 **Erzin** Respublika Tyva, S Russian Federation *50.17N 95.03E*
143 O13 **Erzincan** *var.* Erzinjan. Erzincan, E Turkey *39.43N 39.30E*
143 N13 **Erzincan** *var.* Erzinjan. ◈ *province* NE Turkey
Erzinjan *see* Erzincan
Erzsébetváros *see* Dumbrăveni
143 Q13 **Erzurum** *prev.* Erzerum. Erzurum, NE Turkey *39.57N 41.16E*
143 Q12 **Erzurum** *prev.* Erzerum. ◈ *province* NE Turkey
195 N16 **Esa'ala** Normanby Island, SE PNG *9.45S 150.47E*
172 Nn7 **Esan-misaki** *headland* Hokkaidō, N Japan *41.49N 141.12E*
172 Pp3 **Esashi** Hokkaidō, NE Japan *44.57N 142.32E*
171 M11 **Esashi** *var.* Esasi. Iwate, Honshū, C Japan *39.13N 141.08E*
171 Mm6 **Esasho** Hokkaidō, N Japan
Esasi *see* Esashi
97 F23 **Esbjerg** Ribe, W Denmark *55.28N 8.28E*
Esbo *see* Espoo
38 L7 **Escalante** Utah, W USA *37.46N 111.36W*
38 M7 **Escalante River** ≈ Utah, W USA
12 L12 **Escalier, Réservoir l'** ▣ Québec, SE Canada
42 K7 **Escalón** Chihuahua, N Mexico *26.43N 104.20W*
106 M8 **Escalona** Castilla-La Mancha, C Spain *40.10N 4.24W*
25 O8 **Escambia River** ≈ Florida, SE USA
33 N5 **Escanaba** Michigan, N USA *45.45N 87.03W*
33 N4 **Escanaba River** ≈ Michigan, N USA
107 R8 **Escandón, Puerto de** *pass* E Spain *40.17N 0.57W*
43 W14 **Escárcega** Campeche, SE Mexico *18.33N 90.41W*
179 Pp7 **Escarpada Point** *headland* Luzon, N Philippines *18.28N 122.10E*
25 N8 **Escatawpa River** ≈ Alabama/ Mississippi, S USA
105 P2 **Escaut** ≈ N France
Escaut *see* Scheldt
101 M25 **Esch-sur-Alzette** Luxembourg, S Luxembourg *49.30N 5.58E*
103 J15 **Eschwege** Hessen, C Germany *51.10N 10.03E*
103 D16 **Eschweiler** Nordrhein-Westfalen, W Germany *50.48N 6.15E*
Esclaves, Grand Lac des *see* Great Slave Lake
47 O8 **Escocesa, Bahía** *bay* N Dominican Republic
45 W15 **Escocés, Punta** *headland* NE Panama *8.50N 77.37W*
37 U17 **Escondido** California, W USA *33.07N 117.05W*
44 M10 **Escondido, Río** ≈ SE Nicaragua
13 S7 **Escoumins, Rivière des** ≈ Québec, SE Canada
39 O13 **Escudilla Mountain** ▲ Arizona, SW USA *33.57N 109.07W*
42 J11 **Escuinapa** *var.* Escuinapa de Hidalgo. Sinaloa, C Mexico *22.49N 105.46W*
Escuinapa de Hidalgo *see* Escuinapa
44 C6 **Escuintla** Escuintla, S Guatemala *14.16N 90.46W*
43 V17 **Escuintla** Chiapas, SE Mexico *15.15N 92.39W*
44 A2 **Escuintla** *off.* Departamento de Escuintla. ◈ *department* S Guatemala
13 W7 **Escuminac** ≈ Québec, SE Canada
81 D16 **Eséka** Centre, SW Cameroon *3.40N 10.48E*
142 I12 **Esenboğa** ✕ (Ankara) Ankara, C Turkey *40.05N 33.01E*
152 B13 **Esenguly** *Rus.* Gasan-Kuli. Balkan Welaýaty, W Turkmenistan *37.29N 53.56E*
142 D17 **Eşen Çayı** ≈ SW Turkey
107 T4 **Ésera** ≈ NE Spain
149 N8 **Eşfahān** *Eng.* Isfahan; *anc.* Aspadana. Eşfahān, C Iran *32.40N 51.40E*
149 O7 **Eşfahān** *off.* Ostān-e Eşfahān. ◈ *province* C Iran
107 N5 **Esgueva** ≈ N Spain
155 Q3 **Eshkamesh** Takhār, NE Afghanistan *36.25N 69.10E*
155 T2 **Eshkāshem** Badakhshān, NE Afghanistan *36.43N 71.34E*
85 L23 **Eshowe** KwaZulu/Natal, E South Africa *28.49S 31.29E*
149 T5 **'Eshqābād** Khorāsān-Razavī, NE Iran *36.00N 59.01E*
Esh Sham *see* Dimashq
Esh Sharā *see* Ash Sharāh
Esik *see* Yesik
Esil *see* Ishim, Kazakhstan/Russian Federation
Esil *see* Yesil', Kazakhstan
191 V2 **Esk** Queensland, E Australia *27.15S 152.22E*
192 O11 **Eskdale** Hawke's Bay, North Island, NZ *39.24S 176.51E*
Eski Dzhumaya *see* Tŭrgovishte
94 L2 **Eskifjördhur** Austurland, E Iceland *65.04N 14.01W*
145 S3 **Eski Kaļak** *var.* Askī Kalak, Kalak. N Iraq *36.16N 43.40E*
97 N16 **Eskilstuna** Södermanland, C Sweden *59.22N 16.31E*
14 G2 **Eskimo Lakes** *lakes* Northwest Territories, NW Canada
15 L8 **Eskimo Point** *headland* Nunavut, E Canada *61.19N 93.49W*
Eskimo Point *see* Arviat
145 Q2 **Eski Mosul** N Iraq *36.31N 42.45E*
153 T10 **Eski-Nookat** *var.* Iski-Nauket. Oshskaya Oblast', SW Kyrgyzstan *40.18N 72.29E*
142 F12 **Eskişehir** *var.* Eskishehr. Eskişehir, W Turkey *39.46N 30.30E*
142 F13 **Eskişehir** *var.* Eski shehr. ◈ *province* NW Turkey
Eskishehr *see* Eskişehir
106 K5 **Esla** ≈ NW Spain
148 J6 **Eslāmābād** *var.* Eslāmābād-e Gharb; *prev.* Harunabad, Shāhābād. Kermānshāhān, W Iran *34.07N 46.34E*
Eslāmābād-e Gharb *see* Eslāmābād
154 J4 **Eslām Qal'eh** *Pash.* Islam Qala. Herāt, W Afghanistan *34.41N 61.03E*
97 K23 **Eslöv** Skåne, S Sweden *55.49N 13.19E*
149 S12 **Esmā'īlābād** Kermān, S Iran *28.48N 56.39E*
149 U8 **Esmā'īlābād** Khorāsān-e Janūbī, E Iran *35.19N 60.30E*
142 D14 **Eşme** Uşak, W Turkey *38.25N 28.58E*
46 G6 **Esmeralda** Camagüey, E Cuba *21.51N 78.10W*
65 F21 **Esmeralda, Isla** *island* S Chile
58 B5 **Esmeraldas** Esmeraldas, N Ecuador *0.55N 79.40W*
58 B5 **Esmeraldas** ◈ *province* NW Ecuador
Esna *see* Isna
12 B6 **Esnagi Lake** ◎ Ontario, S Canada
149 V14 **Espakeh** Sīstān va Balūchestān, SE Iran *26.54N 60.09E*
105 O13 **Espalion** Aveyron, S France *44.31N 2.45E*
España *see* Spain
12 E11 **Espanola** Ontario, S Canada *46.15N 81.46W*
39 S10 **Espanola** New Mexico, SW USA *35.59N 106.04W*
59 C18 **Española, Isla** *var.* Hood Island. *island* Galapagos Islands, Ecuador, E Pacific Ocean
106 M13 **Espejo** Andalucía, S Spain *37.40N 4.34W*
96 C13 **Espeland** Hordaland, S Norway *60.22N 5.27E*
102 G12 **Espelkamp** Nordrhein-Westfalen, NW Germany *52.22N 8.37E*
40 M8 **Espenberg, Cape** *headland* Alaska, USA *66.33N 163.36W*
188 L13 **Esperance** Western Australia *33.49S 121.52E*
195 W15 **Esperance, Cape** *headland* Guadacanal, C Solomon Islands *9.09S 159.38E*
59 P18 **Esperancita** Santa Cruz, E Bolivia
63 B17 **Esperanza** Santa Fe, C Argentina *31.25S 60.59W*
42 G6 **Esperanza** Sonora, NW Mexico *27.37N 109.51W*
26 H9 **Esperanza** Texas, SW USA *31.09N 105.40W*
204 H3 **Esperanza** *Argentinian research station* Antarctica *63.29S 56.53W*
106 E12 **Espichel, Cabo** *headland* S Portugal *38.25N 9.15W*
56 E10 **Espinal** Tolima, C Colombia *4.09N 74.54W*
50 K10 **Espinhaço, Serra do** ▲▲ SE Brazil
106 G6 **Espinho** Aveiro, N Portugal *41.01N 8.37W*
61 N18 **Espinosa** Minas Gerais, SE Brazil *14.58S 42.49W*
105 O15 **Espinouse** ▲▲ S France
62 Q8 **Espírito Santo** *off.* Estado do Espírito Santo. ◈ *state* E Brazil
197 B12 **Espiritu Santo** *var.* Santo. *island* W Vanuatu
43 Z13 **Espíritu Santo, Bahía del** *bay* SE Mexico
42 F9 **Espíritu Santo, Isla del** *island* W Mexico
43 Y12 **Espita** Yucatán, SE Mexico *21.00N 88.17W*
13 Y7 **Espoir, Cap d'** *headland* Québec, SE Canada *48.24N 64.21W*
Esponsede/Esponsende *see* Esposende
95 L20 **Espoo** *Swe.* Esbo. Etelä-Suomi, S Finland *60.10N 24.42E*
106 G5 **Esposende** *var.* Esponsede, Esponsende. Braga, N Portugal *41.30N 8.46W*
85 M18 **Espungabera** Manica, SW Mozambique *20.27S 32.48E*
65 H17 **Esquel** Chubut, SW Argentina *42.55S 71.19W*
8 L17 **Esquimalt** Vancouver Island, British Columbia, SW Canada *48.25N 123.27W*
63 C16 **Esquina** Corrientes, NE Argentina *30.00S 59.30W*
44 E6 **Esquipulas** Chiquimula, SE Guatemala *14.34N 89.20W*
44 K9 **Esquipulas** Matagalpa, C Nicaragua *12.39N 85.48W*
96 I8 **Essandjøen** ◎ S Norway
76 E7 **Essaouira** *prev.* Mogador. W Morocco *31.33N 9.40W*
Esseg *see* Osijek
Es Semara *see* Smara
101 G15 **Essen** Antwerpen, N Belgium *51.28N 4.28E*
103 E15 **Essen** *var.* Essen an der Ruhr. Nordrhein-Westfalen, W Germany *51.28N 7.01E*
Essen an der Ruhr *see* Essen
76 I5 **Es Senia** ✕ (Oran) NW Algeria *35.34N 0.42W*
57 T8 **Essequibo Islands** *island group* N Guyana
57 T11 **Essequibo River** ≈ C Guyana
12 C18 **Essex** Ontario, S Canada *42.06N 82.52W*
31 T16 **Essex** Iowa, C USA *40.49N 95.18W*
99 P21 **Essex** *cultural region* E England, UK
33 R8 **Essexville** Michigan, N USA *43.37N 83.50W*
103 H22 **Esslingen** *var.* Esslingen am Neckar. Baden-Württemberg, SW Germany *48.45N 9.18E*
Esslingen am Neckar *see* Esslingen
105 N6 **Essonne** ◈ *department* N France
Es Suweida *see* As Suwaydā'
81 F16 **Est** *Eng.* East. ◈ *province* SE Cameroon
106 I1 **Estaca de Bares, Punta da** *point* NW Spain *43.46N 7.40W*
26 M5 **Estacado, Llano** *plain* New Mexico/Texas, SW USA
65 K25 **Estados, Isla de los** *prev. Eng.* Staten Island. *island* S Argentina
149 P12 **Eşţahbān** Fārs, S Iran
12 F11 **Estaire** Ontario, S Canada *46.19N 80.47W*
39 S12 **Estancia** New Mexico, SW USA *34.45N 106.03W*
61 P16 **Estância** Sergipe, E Brazil *11.15S 37.28W*
106 G7 **Estarreja** Aveiro, N Portugal *40.45N 8.34W*
104 M17 **Estats, Pic d'** *Sp.* Pico d'Estats. ▲ France/Spain *42.39N 1.24E*
Estats, Pico d' *see* Estats, Pic d'
85 K23 **Estcourt** KwaZulu/Natal, E South Africa *28.58S 29.54E*
108 H8 **Este** *anc.* Ateste. Veneto, NE Italy *45.14N 11.40E*
44 J9 **Estelí** Estelí, NW Nicaragua *13.04N 86.21W*
44 J9 **Estelí** ◈ *department* NW Nicaragua
107 Q4 **Estella** *Bas.* Lizarra. Navarra, N Spain *42.40N 2.01W*
31 R9 **Estelline** South Dakota, N USA *44.34N 96.54W*
27 P4 **Estelline** Texas, SW USA *34.33N 100.26W*
106 L14 **Estepa** Andalucía, S Spain *37.16N 4.52W*
106 L16 **Estepona** Andalucía, S Spain *36.25N 5.09W*
41 R9 **Ester** Alaska, USA *64.49N 148.03W*
9 V16 **Esterhazy** Saskatchewan, S Canada *50.40N 102.01W*
39 S3 **Estes Park** Colorado, C USA *40.22N 105.31W*
9 V17 **Estevan** Saskatchewan, S Canada *49.07N 103.04W*
31 T11 **Estherville** Iowa, C USA *43.24N 94.49W*
23 R15 **Estill** South Carolina, SE USA *32.45N 81.14W*
105 Q6 **Estissac** Aube, N France *48.17N 3.51E*
13 T9 **Est, Lac de l'** ◎ Québec, SE Canada
Estland *see* Estonia
9 S16 **Eston** Saskatchewan, S Canada *51.09N 108.41W*
120 G5 **Estonia** *off.* Republic of Estonia, *Est.* Eesti Vabariik, *Ger.* Estland, *Latv.* Igaunija; *prev.* Estonian SSR, *Rus.* Estonskaya SSR. ◆ *republic* NE Europe
Estonskaya SSR *see* Estonia
106 E11 **Estoril** Lisboa, W Portugal *38.42N 9.22W*
61 L14 **Estreito** Maranhão, E Brazil *6.34S 47.22W*
106 I8 **Estrela, Serra da** ▲▲ C Portugal
42 D3 **Estrella, Punta** *headland* NW Mexico *30.53N 114.45W*
Estremadura *see* Extremadura
106 F10 **Estremadura** *cultural and historical region* W Portugal
106 H11 **Estremoz** Évora, S Portugal *38.49N 7.34W*
81 D18 **Estuaire** *off.* Province de l'Estuaire, *var.* L'Estuaire. ◈ *province* NW Gabon
Eszék *see* Osijek
113 I22 **Esztergom** *Ger.* Gran; *anc.* Strigonium. Komárom-Esztergom, N Hungary *47.46N 18.44E*
158 K11 **Etah** Uttar Pradesh, N India *27.33N 78.39E*
201 R17 **Etal Atoll** *atoll* Mortlock Islands, C Micronesia
101 K24 **Étalle** Luxembourg, SE Belgium *49.40N 5.36E*
105 N6 **Étampes** Essonne, N France *48.25N 2.10E*
190 J1 **Etamunbanie, Lake** *salt lake* South Australia
105 N1 **Étaples** Pas-de-Calais, N France *50.31N 1.37E*
158 K12 **Etāwah** Uttar Pradesh, N India *26.46N 79.01E*
13 R10 **Etchemin** ≈ Québec, SE Canada
Etchmiadzin *see* Vagharshapat
42 G7 **Etchojoa** Sonora, NW Mexico *26.54N 109.37W*
95 L19 **Etelä-Suomi** ◈ *province* S Finland
85 B16 **Etengua** Kunene, NW Namibia *17.24S 13.05E*
101 K25 **Éthe** Luxembourg, SE Belgium *49.34N 5.32E*
9 W15 **Ethelbert** Manitoba, S Canada *51.30N 100.22W*
82 H12 **Ethiopia** *off.* Federal Democratic Republic of Ethiopia; *prev.* Abyssinia, People's Democratic Republic of Ethiopia. ◆ *republic* E Africa
82 I13 **Ethiopian Highlands** *var.* Ethiopian Plateau. *plateau* N Ethiopia
Ethiopian Plateau *see* Ethiopian Highlands
36 M2 **Etna** California, W USA *41.25N 122.53W*
20 B14 **Etna** Pennsylvania, NE USA *40.29N 79.55W*
96 G12 **Etna** ≈ S Norway
109 L24 **Etna, Monte** *Eng.* Mount Etna. ✶ Sicilia, Italy, C Mediterranean Sea *37.46N 15.00E*
Etna, Mount *see* Etna, Monte
97 C15 **Etne** Hordaland, S Norway *59.40N 5.55E*
Etoliko *see* Aitolikó
41 Y14 **Etolin Island** *island* Alexander Archipelago, Alaska, USA
40 L12 **Etolin Strait** *strait* Alaska, USA
85 C17 **Etosha Pan** *salt lake* N Namibia
81 G18 **Etoumbi** Cuvette-Ouest, NW Congo *0.01N 14.57E*
22 M10 **Etowah** Tennessee, S USA *35.19N 84.31W*
25 S2 **Etowah River** ≈ Georgia, SE USA
152 B13 **Etrek** *var.* Gyzyletrek, *Rus.* Kizyl-Atrek. Balkan Welaýaty, W Turkmenistan *37.40N 54.44E*
152 C13 **Etrek** *Per.* Rūd-e Atrak, *Rus.* Atrak, Atrek. ≈ Iran/ Turkmenistan
104 L3 **Étretat** Seine-Maritime, N France *49.46N 0.23E*
116 H9 **Etropole** Sofiya, W Bulgaria *42.50N 24.00E*
Etsch *see* Adige
Et Tafila *see* Aţ Ţafīlah
101 M23 **Ettelbrück** Diekirch, C Luxembourg *49.51N 6.06E*
201 V12 **Etten** *atoll* Chuuk Islands, C Micronesia
101 H14 **Etten-Leur** Noord-Brabant, S Netherlands *51.34N 4.37E*
78 G7 **Et Tîdra** *var.* Ile Tîdra. *island* Dakhlet Nouâdhibou, NW Mauritania
103 G21 **Ettlingen** Baden-Württemberg, SW Germany *48.57N 8.25E*
104 M2 **Eu** Seine-Maritime, N France *50.01N 1.24E*
200 Rr16 **'Eua** *prev.* Middleburg Island. *island* Tongatapu Group, SE Tonga
200 R15 **Eua Iki** *island* Tongatapu Group, S Tonga
Euboea *see* Évvoia
189 O12 **Eucla** Western Australia *31.40S 128.50E*
33 U11 **Euclid** Ohio, N USA *41.35N 81.31W*
29 W14 **Eudora** Arkansas, C USA *33.06N 91.15W*
29 Q4 **Eudora** Kansas, C USA *38.56N 95.06W*
190 J9 **Eudunda** South Australia *34.11S 139.03E*
25 R6 **Eufaula** Alabama, S USA *31.53N 85.09W*
29 Q11 **Eufaula** Oklahoma, C USA *35.17N 95.34W*
29 Q11 **Eufaula Lake** *var.* Eufaula Reservoir. ▣ Oklahoma, C USA
Eufaula Reservoir *see* Eufaula Lake
34 F13 **Eugene** Oregon, NW USA *44.03N 123.05W*
42 B6 **Eugenia, Punta** *headland* W Mexico *27.48N 115.03W*
191 Q8 **Eugowra** New South Wales, SE Australia *33.28S 148.21E*
106 I2 **Eume** ≈ NW Spain
106 H2 **Eume, Embalse do** ▣ NW Spain
Eumolpias *see* Plovdiv
61 O18 **Eunápolis** Bahia, SE Brazil *16.19S 39.36W*
24 H8 **Eunice** Louisiana, S USA *30.29N 92.25W*
39 W15 **Eunice** New Mexico, SW USA *32.26N 103.09W*
101 M19 **Eupen** Liège, E Belgium *50.37N 6.01E*
138 Jj9 **Euphrates** *Ar.* Al Furāt, *Turk.* Firat Nehri. ≈ SW Asia
144 L3 **Euphrates Dam** *dam* N Syria *35.52N 38.34E*
24 M4 **Eupora** Mississippi, S USA *33.32N 89.16W*
95 K19 **Eura** Länsi-Suomi, W Finland *61.06N 22.12E*
95 K19 **Eurajoki** Länsi-Suomi, W Finland *61.13N 21.44E*
0-1 **Eurasian Plate** *tectonic feature*
104 L4 **Eure** ◈ *department* N France
104 M4 **Eure** ≈ N France
104 M6 **Eure-et-Loir** ◈ *department* C France
36 K3 **Eureka** California, W USA *40.47N 124.12W*
29 P6 **Eureka** Kansas, C USA *37.47N 96.15W*
35 O6 **Eureka** Montana, NW USA *48.52N 115.03W*
37 V5 **Eureka** Nevada, W USA *39.30N 115.58W*
31 O7 **Eureka** South Dakota, N USA *45.46N 99.37W*
38 L4 **Eureka** Utah, W USA *39.57N 112.07W*
34 K10 **Eureka** Washington, NW USA *46.21N 118.41W*
29 S9 **Eureka Springs** Arkansas, C USA *36.25N 93.43W*
190 K6 **Eurinilla Creek** *seasonal river* South Australia
191 O11 **Euroa** Victoria, SE Australia *36.46S 145.35E*
180 M9 **Europa** *island* W Madagascar
106 L3 **Europa, Picos de** ▲▲ N Spain
106 L16 **Europa Point** *headland* S Gibraltar *36.07N 5.20W*
86-87 **Europe** *continent*
100 F12 **Europoort** Zuid-Holland, W Netherlands *51.59N 4.08E*
Euskadi *see* País Vasco
103 D17 **Euskirchen** Nordrhein-Westfalen, W Germany *50.40N 6.47E*
25 W11 **Eustis** Florida, SE USA *28.51N 81.41W*
190 M9 **Euston** New South Wales, SE Australia *34.34S 142.45E*
25 N5 **Eutaw** Alabama, S USA *32.50N 87.53W*
102 K8 **Eutin** Schleswig-Holstein, N Germany *54.07N 10.37E*
8 K14 **Eutsuk Lake** ▣ British Columbia, SW Canada
Euxine Sea *see* Black Sea
85 C16 **Evale** Cunene, SW Angola *16.36S 15.46E*
39 T3 **Evans** Colorado, C USA *40.22N 104.41W*
9 P14 **Evansburg** Alberta, SW Canada *53.34N 114.57W*
31 X13 **Evansdale** Iowa, C USA *42.28N 92.16W*
191 V4 **Evans Head** New South Wales, SE Australia *29.07S 153.27E*
10 J11 **Evans, Lac** ◎ Québec, SE Canada
39 S5 **Evans, Mount** ▲ Colorado, C USA *39.35N 105.38W*
15 Mm6 **Evans Strait** *strait* Nunavut, N Canada
33 N10 **Evanston** Illinois, N USA *42.02N 87.41W*
35 S17 **Evanston** Wyoming, C USA *41.16N 110.57W*
12 D11 **Evansville** Manitoulin Island, Ontario, S Canada *45.48N 82.34W*
33 N16 **Evansville** Indiana, N USA *37.58N 87.33W*
32 L9 **Evansville** Wisconsin, N USA *42.46N 89.16W*
27 S8 **Evant** Texas, SW USA *31.28N 98.09W*
149 P13 **Evaz** Fārs, S Iran *27.48N 53.58E*
31 W4 **Eveleth** Minnesota, N USA *47.27N 92.32W*
190 E3 **Evelyn Creek** *seasonal river* South Australia
189 Q2 **Evelyn, Mount** ▲ Northern Territory, N Australia *13.28S 132.50E*
126 I11 **Evenkiyskiy Avtonomnyy Okrug** ◈ *autonomous district* N Russian Federation
191 R13 **Everard, Cape** *headland* Victoria, SE Australia *37.48S 149.21E*
190 F6 **Everard, Lake** *salt lake* South Australia
190 C2 **Everard Ranges** ▲▲ South Australia
159 R11 **Everest, Mount** *Chin.* Qomolangma Feng, *Nep.* Sagarmāthā. ▲ China/Nepal *27.58N 86.57E*
20 E15 **Everett** Pennsylvania, NE USA *40.00N 78.22W*
34 H7 **Everett** Washington, NW USA *47.58N 122.12W*
101 E17 **Evergem** Oost-Vlaanderen, NW Belgium *51.07N 3.43E*
25 X16 **Everglades City** Florida, SE USA *25.51N 81.22W*
25 Y16 **Everglades, The** *wetland* Florida, SE USA
25 P7 **Evergreen** Alabama, S USA *31.25N 86.55W*
39 T4 **Evergreen** Colorado, C USA *39.37N 105.19W*
Evergreen State *see* Washington
99 L21 **Evesham** C England, UK *52.06N 1.57W*
105 T10 **Évian-les-Bains** Haute-Savoie, E France *46.22N 6.34E*
95 K16 **Evijärvi** Länsi-Suomi, W Finland *63.22N 23.30E*
81 D17 **Evinayong** *var.* Ebinayon, Evinayoung. C Equatorial Guinea *1.28N 10.17E*
Evinayoung *see* Evinayong
117 E18 **Évinos** ≈ C Greece
97 E17 **Evje** Aust-Agder, S Norway *58.34N 7.49E*
Evmolpia *see* Plovdiv
106 H11 **Évora** *anc.* Ebora, *Lat.* Liberalitas Julia. Évora, C Portugal *38.34N 7.54W*
106 G11 **Évora** ◈ *district* S Portugal
104 M4 **Évreux** *anc.* Civitas Eburovicum. Eure, N France *49.01N 1.09E*
104 K6 **Évron** Mayenne, NW France *48.10N 0.24W*
116 L13 **Évros** *Bul.* Maritsa, *Turk.* Meriç; *anc.* Hebrus. ≈ SE Europe *see also* Maritsa/Meriç
117 F21 **Evrótas** ≈ S Greece
105 O5 **Évry** Essonne, N France *48.38N 2.27E*
27 O8 **E.V.Spence Reservoir** ▣ Texas, SW USA
117 I18 **Évvoia** *Lat.* Euboea. *island* C Greece
40 D9 **'Ewa Beach** *var.* Ewa Beach. O'ahu, Hawai'i, USA, C Pacific Ocean *21.19N 158.00W*
34 L9 **Ewan** Washington, NW USA *47.06N 117.46W*
46 K12 **Ewarton** C Jamaica *18.10N 77.04W*
83 J18 **Ewaso Ng'iro** *var.* Nyiro. ≈ C Kenya
194 E13 **Ewe** ≈ W PNG
31 P13 **Ewing** Nebraska, C USA *42.13N 98.20W*
204 J5 **Ewing Island** *island* Antarctica
67 P17 **Ewing Seamount** *undersea feature* E Atlantic Ocean *23.19S 8.45E*
164 L6 **Ewirgol** Xinjiang Uygur Zizhiqu, W China *42.55N 87.39E*
81 G19 **Ewo** Cuvette-Ouest, W Congo *0.55S 14.49E*
29 S3 **Excelsior Springs** Missouri, C USA *39.20N 94.13W*
99 J23 **Exe** ≈ SW England, UK
204 L12 **Executive Committee Range** ▲▲ Antarctica
12 E16 **Exeter** Ontario, S Canada *43.19N 81.26W*
99 J24 **Exeter** *anc.* Isca Damnoniorum. SW England, UK *50.43N 3.31W*
37 R11 **Exeter** California, W USA *36.17N 119.08W*
21 P10 **Exeter** New Hampshire, NE USA *42.57N 70.55W*
Exin *see* Kcynia
31 T14 **Exira** Iowa, C USA *41.36N 94.55W*
99 J23 **Exmoor** *moorland* SW England, UK
23 Y6 **Exmore** Virginia, NE USA *37.31N 75.48W*
188 G8 **Exmouth** Western Australia *22.00S 114.06E*
99 J24 **Exmouth** SW England, UK *50.36N 3.24W*
188 G8 **Exmouth Gulf** *gulf* Western Australia
181 V8 **Exmouth Plateau** *undersea feature* E Indian Ocean
117 J20 **Exompourgo** *ancient monument* Tínos, Kykládes, Greece, Aegean Sea *37.34N 25.12E*
106 I10 **Extremadura** *var.* Estremadura. ◈ *autonomous community* W Spain
80 F12 **Extrême-Nord** *Eng.* Extreme North. ◈ *province* N Cameroon
Extreme North *see* Extrême-Nord
46 I3 **Exuma Cays** *islets* C Bahamas
46 I3 **Exuma Sound** *sound* C Bahamas
83 H20 **Eyasi, Lake** ◎ N Tanzania
97 F17 **Eydehavn** Aust-Agder, S Norway *58.31N 8.52E*
98 L12 **Eyemouth** SE Scotland, UK *55.51N 2.06W*
98 G7 **Eye Peninsula** *peninsula* NW Scotland, UK
82 Q13 **Eyl** *It.* Eil. Nugaal, E Somalia *8.03N 49.49E*
105 N11 **Eymoutiers** Haute-Vienne, C France *45.45N 1.43E*
Eyo (lower course) *see* Uolo, Río
31 X10 **Eyota** Minnesota, N USA *44.00N 92.13W*
190 H2 **Eyre Basin, Lake** *salt lake* South Australia
190 I1 **Eyre Creek** *seasonal river* Northern Territory/South Australia
182 L9 **Eyre, Lake** *salt lake* South Australia
193 C22 **Eyre Mountains** ▲▲ South Island, NZ
190 H3 **Eyre North, Lake** *salt lake* South Australia
190 G7 **Eyre Peninsula** *peninsula* South Australia
190 H4 **Eyre South, Lake** *salt lake* South Australia
97 B18 **Eysturoy** *Dan.* Østerø *Island* Faeroe Islands *62.15N 6.55W*
63 D20 **Ezeiza** ✕ (Buenos Aires) Buenos Aires, E Argentina *34.49S 58.30W*
Ezeres *see* Ezeriş
118 F12 **Ezeriş** *Hung.* Ezeres. Caraş-Severin, W Romania *45.21N 21.55E*
167 O9 **Ezhou** *prev.* Echeng. Hubei, C China *30.22N 114.52E*

◆ COUNTRY
● COUNTRY CAPITAL
◇ DEPENDENT TERRITORY
○ DEPENDENT TERRITORY CAPITAL
◈ ADMINISTRATIVE REGION
✕ INTERNATIONAL AIRPORT
▲ MOUNTAIN
▲▲ MOUNTAIN RANGE
✶ VOLCANO
≈ RIVER
◎ LAKE
▣ RESERVOIR

EZHVA – FICCE

129 R11 **Ezhva** Respublika Komi, NW Russian Federation 61.45N 50.43E
142 B12 **Ezine** Çanakkale, NW Turkey 39.46N 26.19E
Ezo *see* Hokkaidō
Ezra/Ezraa *see* Izra'

F

203 P7 **Faaa** Tahiti, W French Polynesia 17.31S 149.36W
203 P7 **Faaa** ✕ (Papeete) Tahiti, W French Polynesia 17.31S 149.36W
97 H24 **Faaborg** *var.* Fåborg. Fyn, C Denmark 55.06N 10.15E
157 K19 **Faadhippolhu Atoll** *var.* Fadiffolu, Lhaviyani Atoll. *atoll* N Maldives
203 U10 **Faaite** *atoll* Îles Tuamotu, C French Polynesia
203 Q8 **Faaone** Tahiti, W French Polynesia 17.39S 149.18W
26 H8 **Fabens** Texas, SW USA 31.30N 106.09W
96 H12 **Fåberg** Oppland, S Norway 61.15N 10.21E
Fåborg *see* Faaborg
108 I12 **Fabriano** Marche, C Italy 43.19N 15.52E
151 U16 **Fabrichnyy** Almaty, SE Kazakhstan 43.12N 76.19E
56 F10 **Facatativá** Cundinamarca, C Colombia 4.52N 74.27W
79 X9 **Fachi** Agadez, C Niger 18.01N 11.36E
196 B16 **Facpi Point** *headland* W Guam
20 I13 **Factoryville** Pennsylvania, NE USA 41.34N 75.45W
80 K8 **Fada** Borkou-Ennedi-Tibesti, E Chad 17.13N 21.31E
79 Q13 **Fada-Ngourma** E Burkina 12.07N 0.20E
126 Jj4 **Faddeya, Zaliv** *bay* N Russian Federation
126 M4 **Faddeyevskiy, Ostrov** *island* Novosibirskiye Ostrova, NE Russian Federation
147 W12 **Fadhī** S Oman 17.54N 55.30E
108 H10 **Faenza** *anc.* Faventia. Emilia-Romagna, N Italy 44.16N 11.52E
66 M5 **Faeroe-Iceland Ridge** *undersea feature* NW Norwegian Sea
66 M5 **Faeroe Islands** *Dan.* Færøerne, *Faer.* Føroyar. ◇ *Danish external territory* N Atlantic Ocean
88 C8 **Faeroe Islands** *island group* N Atlantic Ocean
Færøerne *see* Faeroe Islands
66 N6 **Faeroe-Shetland Trough** *undersea feature* NE Atlantic Ocean
106 H6 **Fafe** Braga, N Portugal 41.27N 8.10W
82 K13 **Fafen Shet'** ≈ E Ethiopia
200 Qq15 **Fafo** *island* Tongatapu Group, S Tonga
198 Bb8 **Fagaloa Bay** *bay* Upolu, E Samoa
198 B7 **Fagamālo** Savai'i, N Samoa 13.27S 172.22W
118 I12 **Făgăraş** *Ger.* Fogarasch, *Hung.* Fogaras. Braşov, C Romania 45.49N 24.58E
97 M20 **Fagerhult** Kalmar, S Sweden 57.07N 15.40E
96 G13 **Fagernes** Oppland, S Norway 60.58N 9.13E
94 I9 **Fagernes** Troms, N Norway 69.31N 19.16E
97 M14 **Fagersta** Västmanland, C Sweden 59.58N 15.49E
79 W13 **Faggo** *var.* Foggo. Bauchi, N Nigeria 11.22N 9.55E
Faghman *see* Fughmah
Fagibina, Lake *see* Faguibine, Lac
65 J25 **Fagnano, Lago** ◎ S Argentina
101 G22 **Fagne** *hill range* S Belgium
79 N10 **Faguibine, Lac** *var.* Lake Fagibina. ◎ NW Mali
Fahaheel *see* Al Fuḩayḩīl
Fahlun *see* Falun
149 U12 **Fahraj** Kermān, SE Iran 29.03N 58.54E
66 P5 **Faial** Madeira, Portugal, NE Atlantic Ocean 32.46N 16.52W
66 N2 **Faial** *var.* Ilha do Faial. *island* Azores, Portugal, NE Atlantic Ocean
Faial, Ilha do *see* Faial
110 G10 **Faido** Ticino, S Switzerland 46.30N 8.48E
Faifo *see* Hôi An
Failaka Island *see* Faylakah
202 G12 **Faioa, Île** *island* N Wallis and Futuna
189 W8 **Fairbairn Reservoir** ⊠ Queensland, E Australia
41 R9 **Fairbanks** Alaska, USA 64.48N 147.47W
23 U12 **Fair Bluff** North Carolina, SE USA 34.18N 79.02W
33 R14 **Fairborn** Ohio, N USA 39.49N 84.01W
25 S3 **Fairburn** Georgia, SE USA 33.34N 84.34W
32 M12 **Fairbury** Illinois, N USA 40.45N 88.30W
31 Q17 **Fairbury** Nebraska, C USA 40.08N 97.10W
31 T9 **Fairfax** Minnesota, N USA 44.31N 94.43W
29 O8 **Fairfax** Oklahoma, C USA 36.34N 96.42W
23 R14 **Fairfax** South Carolina, SE USA 32.57N 81.14W
37 N8 **Fairfield** California, W USA 38.14N 122.03W
35 O14 **Fairfield** Idaho, NW USA 43.20N 114.45W
32 M16 **Fairfield** Illinois, N USA 38.22N 88.22W
31 X15 **Fairfield** Iowa, C USA 41.00N 91.57W
35 R8 **Fairfield** Montana, NW USA 47.36N 111.59W
33 Q14 **Fairfield** Ohio, N USA 39.21N 84.33W
27 U8 **Fairfield** Texas, SW USA 31.43N 96.10W
29 T7 **Fair Grove** Missouri, C USA 37.22N 93.09W
21 P12 **Fairhaven** Massachusetts, NE USA 41.38N 70.51W
25 N8 **Fairhope** Alabama, S USA 30.31N 87.54W
98 L4 **Fair Isle** *island* NE Scotland, UK
193 F20 **Fairlie** Canterbury, South Island, NZ 44.05S 170.50E
31 U11 **Fairmont** Minnesota, N USA 43.40N 94.27W
31 Q16 **Fairmont** Nebraska, C USA 40.37N 97.36W
23 S3 **Fairmont** West Virginia, NE USA 39.29N 80.08W
33 P13 **Fairmount** Indiana, N USA 40.25N 85.39W
20 H10 **Fairmount** New York, NE USA 43.03N 76.14W
31 R7 **Fairmount** North Dakota, N USA 46.02N 96.36W
39 S5 **Fairplay** Colorado, C USA 39.13N 106.00W
20 F9 **Fairport** New York, NE USA 43.06N 77.26W
9 O12 **Fairview** Alberta, W Canada 56.03N 118.28W
28 L9 **Fairview** Oklahoma, C USA 36.16N 98.28W
38 L4 **Fairview** Utah, W USA 39.37N 111.26W
37 T6 **Fairview Peak** ▲ Nevada, W USA 39.13N 118.09W
196 H14 **Fais** *atoll* Caroline Islands, W Micronesia
155 U8 **Faisalābād** *prev.* Lyallpur. Punjab, NE Pakistan 31.25N 73.06E
Faisaliya *see* Fayşalīyah
30 L8 **Faith** South Dakota, N USA 45.01N 102.02W
159 N12 **Faizābād** Uttar Pradesh, N India 26.46N 82.07E
Faizabad/Faizābād *see* Feyẕābād
47 S9 **Fajardo** E Puerto Rico 18.20N 65.39W
145 R9 **Fajj, Wādī al** *dry watercourse* S Iraq
146 K4 **Fajr, Bi'r** *well* NW Saudi Arabia 28.46N 37.51E
203 W10 **Fakahina** *atoll* Îles Tuamotu, C French Polynesia
202 L10 **Fakaofo Atoll** *island* SE Tokelau
203 U10 **Fakarava** *atoll* Îles Tuamotu, C French Polynesia
131 T2 **Fakel** Udmurtskaya Respublika, NW Russian Federation 57.35N 53.00E
99 P19 **Fakenham** E England, UK 52.50N 0.51E
176 V11 **Fakfak** Papua, E Indonesia 2.55S 132.16E
176 V11 **Fakfak, Pegunungan** ▲▲ Papua, E Indonesia
159 T12 **Fakīragrām** Assam, NE India 26.22N 90.15E
116 M10 **Fakiyska Reka** ≈ SE Bulgaria
97 J24 **Fakse** Storstrøm, SE Denmark 55.16N 12.07E
97 J24 **Fakse Bugt** *bay* SE Denmark
97 J24 **Fakse Ladeplads** Storstrøm, SE Denmark 55.13N 12.10E
169 V11 **Faku** Liaoning, NE China 42.30N 123.27E
78 J14 **Falaba** N Sierra Leone 9.54N 11.22W
104 K5 **Falaise** Calvados, N France 48.52N 0.12W
116 H12 **Falakró** ▲▲ NE Greece
201 T12 **Falalu** *island* Chuuk, C Micronesia
177 Ff4 **Falam** Chin State, W Burma 22.58N 93.45E
149 N8 **Falāvarjān** Eşfahān, C Iran 32.33N 51.28E
118 M11 **Fălciu** Vaslui, E Romania 46.19N 28.10E
56 I4 **Falcón** *off.* Estado Falcón. ◈ *state* NW Venezuela
108 J12 **Falconara Marittima** Marche, C Italy 43.37N 13.22E
Falcone, Capo del *see* Falcone, Punta del
109 A16 **Falcone, Punta del** *var.* Capo del Falcone. *headland* Sardegna, Italy, C Mediterranean Sea 40.57N 8.12E
9 Y16 **Falcon Lake** Manitoba, S Canada 49.43N 95.18W
Falcon Lake *see* Falcón, Presa/Falcon Reservoir
43 O7 **Falcón, Presa** *var.* Falcon Lake, Falcon Reservoir. ⊠ Mexico/USA ***see also*** Falcon Reservoir
27 Q16 **Falcon Reservoir** *var.* Falcon Lake, Presa Falcón. ⊠ Mexico/USA ***see also*** Falcón, Presa
202 L10 **Fale** *island* Fakaofo Atoll, SE Tokelau
198 Aa7 **Faleālupo** Savai'i, NW Samoa 13.30S 172.46W
202 B10 **Falefatu** *island* Funafuti Atoll, C Tuvalu
198 Aa7 **Fālelima** Savai'i, NW Samoa 13.30S 172.40W
97 N18 **Falerum** Östergötland, S Sweden 58.07N 16.15E
Faleshty *see* Făleşti
118 M9 **Făleşti** *Rus.* Faleshty. NW Moldova 47.33N 27.43E
27 S15 **Falfurrias** Texas, SW USA 27.13N 98.08W
9 O13 **Falher** Alberta, W Canada 55.45N 117.18W
Falkenau an der Eger *see* Sokolov
97 J21 **Falkenberg** Halland, S Sweden 56.55N 12.30E
Falkenberg *see* Niemodlin
Falkenburg in Pommern *see* Złocieniec
102 N12 **Falkensee** Brandenburg, NE Germany 52.34N 13.04E
98 J12 **Falkirk** C Scotland, UK 56.00N 3.48W
67 I20 **Falkland Escarpment** *undersea feature* SW Atlantic Ocean
65 K24 **Falkland Islands** *var.* Falklands, Islas Malvinas. ◇ *UK dependent territory* SW Atlantic Ocean
49 W14 **Falkland Islands** *island group* SW Atlantic Ocean
67 I20 **Falkland Plateau** *var.* Argentine Rise. *undersea feature* SW Atlantic Ocean
Falklands *see* Falkland Islands
65 M23 **Falkland Sound** *var.* Estrecho de San Carlos. *strait* C Falkland Islands
Falknov nad Ohří *see* Sokolov
117 H21 **Falkonéra** *island* S Greece
97 K18 **Falköping** Västra Götaland, S Sweden 58.10N 13.31E
145 U8 **Fallāḩ** E Iraq 32.58N 45.09E
37 U16 **Fallbrook** California, W USA 33.22N 117.15W
201 U12 **Falleallej Pass** *passage* Chuuk Islands, C Micronesia
95 J14 **Fällfors** Västerbotten, N Sweden 65.07N 20.46E
204 I6 **Fallières Coast** *physical region* Antarctica
102 I11 **Fallingbostel** Niedersachsen, NW Germany 52.52N 9.42E
35 X9 **Fallon** Montana, NW USA 46.49N 105.07W
37 S5 **Fallon** Nevada, W USA 39.28N 118.46W
21 O12 **Fall River** Massachusetts, NE USA 41.42N 71.09W
29 P6 **Fall River Lake** ⊠ Kansas, C USA
37 O3 **Fall River Mills** California, W USA 41.00N 121.28W
23 W4 **Falls Church** Virginia, NE USA 38.53N 77.11W
31 S17 **Falls City** Nebraska, C USA 40.03N 95.36W
27 S12 **Falls City** Texas, SW USA 28.58N 98.01W
Falluja *see* Al Fallūjah
79 S12 **Falmey** Dosso, SW Niger 12.29N 2.58E
47 W10 **Falmouth** Antigua, Antigua and Barbuda 16.59N 61.48W
46 J11 **Falmouth** W Jamaica 18.28N 77.39W
99 H25 **Falmouth** SW England, UK 50.07N 5.04W
22 M4 **Falmouth** Kentucky, S USA 38.40N 84.19W
21 P13 **Falmouth** Massachusetts, NE USA 41.31N 70.36W
23 W5 **Falmouth** Virginia, NE USA 38.19N 77.28W
201 U12 **Falos** *island* Chuuk, C Micronesia
85 E26 **False Bay** *Afr.* Valsbaai. *bay* SW South Africa
161 K17 **False Divi Point** *headland* E India 15.46N 80.43E
40 M16 **False Pass** Unimak Island, Alaska, USA 54.52N 163.15W
160 P12 **False Point** *headland* E India 20.23N 86.52E
107 U6 **Falset** Cataluña, NE Spain 41.07N 0.49E
97 I25 **Falster** *island* SE Denmark
118 K9 **Fălticeni** *Hung.* Falticsén. Suceava, NE Romania 47.27N 26.18E
Falticsén *see* Fălticeni
96 M13 **Falun** *var.* Fahlun. Dalarna, C Sweden 60.36N 15.36E
Famagusta *see* Gazimağusa
Famagusta Bay *see* Gazimağusa Körfezi
64 I8 **Famatina** La Rioja, NW Argentina 28.53S 67.31W
101 J21 **Famenne** *physical region* SE Belgium
115 D22 **Fan** *var.* Fani. ≈ N Albania
79 X15 **Fan** ≈ E Nigeria
78 M12 **Fana** Koulikoro, SW Mali 12.45N 6.55W
117 K19 **Fána** *ancient harbor* Chíos, SE Greece 38.11N 25.35E
201 V13 **Fanan** *island* Chuuk, C Micronesia
201 U12 **Fanapanges** *island* Chuuk, C Micronesia
117 L20 **Fanári, Akrotírio** *headland* Ikaría, Dodekánisa, Greece, Aegean Sea 37.40N 26.21E
47 Q13 **Fancy** Saint Vincent, Saint Vincent and the Grenadines 13.22N 61.10W
180 I5 **Fandriana** Fianarantsoa, SE Madagascar 20.13S 47.21E
178 H6 **Fang** Chiang Mai, NW Thailand 19.55N 99.13E
82 E13 **Fangak** Jonglei, SE Sudan 9.04N 30.52E
203 W10 **Fangatau** *atoll* Îles Tuamotu, C French Polynesia
203 X12 **Fangataufa** *island* Îles Tuamotu, SE French Polynesia
200 Qq15 **Fanga Uta** *bay* S Tonga
167 N7 **Fangcheng** Henan, C China 33.18N 113.03E
166 K15 **Fangchenggang** *var.* Fangcheng Gezu Zizhixian; *prev.* Fangcheng. Guangxi Zhuangzu Zizhiqu, S China 21.49N 108.21E
167 S15 **Fangshan** S Taiwan 22.19N 120.41E
169 X8 **Fangzheng** Heilongjiang, NE China 45.49N 128.49E
Fani *see* Fan
121 K16 **Fanipal'** *Rus.* Fanipol'. Minskaya Voblasts', C Belarus 53.43N 27.17E
Fanipol' *see* Fanipal'
27 T13 **Fannin** Texas, SW USA 28.41N 97.13W
Fanning Island *see* Tabuaeran
96 G8 **Fannrem** Sør-Trøndelag, S Norway 63.16N 9.48E
108 I11 **Fano** *anc.* Colonia Julia Fanestris, Fanum Fortunae. Marche, C Italy 43.51N 13.01E
97 E23 **Fanø** *island* W Denmark
178 Ii5 **Fan Si Pan** ▲ N Vietnam 22.18N 103.36E
Fanum Fortunae *see* Fano
Fao *see* Al Fāw
147 W7 **Faq'** *var.* Al Faqa. Dubayy, E UAE 24.42N 55.37E
Farab *see* Farap
204 H5 **Faraday** *UK research station* Antarctica 65.35S 64.09W
193 G16 **Faraday, Mount** ▲ South Island, NZ 42.01S 171.37E
81 P16 **Faradje** Orientale, NE Dem. Rep. Congo 3.45N 29.43E
Faradofay *see* Tôlañaro
180 I7 **Farafangana** Fianarantsoa, SE Madagascar 22.49S 47.49E
154 J7 **Farāh** *var.* Farah, Fararud. Farāh, W Afghanistan 32.22N 62.07E
154 K7 **Farāh** ◈ *province* W Afghanistan
154 J7 **Farāh Rūd** ≈ W Afghanistan
196 K7 **Farallon de Medinilla** *island* C Northern Mariana Islands
196 J2 **Farallon de Pajaros** *var.* Uracas. *island* N Northern Mariana Islands
78 J14 **Faranah** S Guinea 10.01N 10.43W
152 K12 **Farap** *Rus.* Farab. Lebap Welaýaty, NE Turkmenistan 39.15N 63.32E
Fararud *see* Farāh
146 M13 **Farasān, Jazā'ir** *island group* SW Saudi Arabia
180 I5 **Faratsiho** Antananarivo, C Madagascar 19.24S 46.57E
196 K15 **Faraulep Atoll** *atoll* Caroline Islands, C Micronesia
101 H20 **Farciennes** Hainaut, S Belgium 50.25N 4.33E
107 O14 **Fardes** ≈ S Spain
203 S10 **Fare** Huahine, W French Polynesia 16.42S 151.01W
99 M23 **Fareham** S England, UK 50.51N 1.10W
41 P11 **Farewell** Alaska, USA 62.35N 153.59W
192 H13 **Farewell, Cape** *headland* South Island, NZ 40.30S 172.39E
Farewell, Cape *see* Nunap Isua
192 I13 **Farewell Spit** *spit* South Island, NZ
97 I17 **Färgelanda** Västra Götaland, S Sweden 58.34N 11.58E
Farghona Valley *see* Fergana Valley
Farghona, Wodii/Farghona Wodiysi *see* Fergana Valley
25 V8 **Fargo** Georgia, SE USA 30.42N 82.33W
31 R5 **Fargo** North Dakota, N USA 46.52N 96.47W
153 S10 **Farg'ona** *Rus.* Fergana; *prev.* Novyy Margilan. Frag'ona Viloyati, E Uzbekistan 40.27N 71.43E
153 R10 **Farg'ona Viloyati** *Rus.* Ferganskaya Oblast'. ◈ *province* E Uzbekistan
31 V10 **Faribault** Minnesota, N USA 44.18N 93.16W
158 J11 **Farīdābād** Haryāna, N India
158 H8 **Farīdkot** Punjab, NW India 30.42N 74.46E
159 T15 **Faridpur** Dhaka, C Bangladesh 23.28N 89.49E
124 N16 **Fārigh, Wādī al** ≈ N Libya
180 I4 **Farihy Alaotra** ◎ C Madagascar
96 M11 **Färila** Gävleborg, C Sweden 61.48N 15.55E
106 E9 **Farilhões** *island* C Portugal
78 G12 **Farim** NW Guinea-Bissau 12.29N 15.14W
Farish *see* Forish
147 T11 **Fāris, Qalamat** *well* SE Saudi Arabia 19.59N 50.57E
97 N21 **Färjestaden** Kalmar, S Sweden 56.37N 16.30E
155 R2 **Farkhār** Takhār, NE Afghanistan 36.39N 69.43E
153 Q14 **Farkhor** *Rus.* Parkhar. SW Tajikistan 37.31N 69.21E
118 F12 **Fârliug** *prev.* Fîrliug, *Hung.* Furluk. Caraş-Severin, SW Romania 45.21N 21.55E
117 M21 **Farmakonísi** *island* Dodekánisa, Greece, Aegean Sea
32 M13 **Farmer City** Illinois, N USA 40.14N 88.38W
33 N14 **Farmersburg** Indiana, N USA 39.14N 87.21W
27 U6 **Farmersville** Texas, SW USA 33.09N 96.21W
24 H5 **Farmerville** Louisiana, S USA 32.46N 92.24W
31 X16 **Farmington** Iowa, C USA 40.37N 91.43W
21 Q6 **Farmington** Maine, NE USA 44.40N 70.09W
31 V9 **Farmington** Minnesota, N USA 44.39N 93.09W
29 X6 **Farmington** Missouri, C USA 37.46N 90.25W
21 O9 **Farmington** New Hampshire, NE USA 43.23N 71.04W
39 P9 **Farmington** New Mexico, SW USA 36.43N 108.13W
38 L2 **Farmington** Utah, W USA 40.58N 111.53W
23 W9 **Farmville** North Carolina, SE USA 35.37N 77.36W
23 U6 **Farmville** Virginia, NE USA 37.18N 78.23W
99 N22 **Farnborough** S England, UK 51.16N 0.46W
99 N22 **Farnham** S England, UK 51.13N 0.49W
8 J7 **Faro** Yukon Territory, W Canada 62.15N 133.30W
106 G14 **Faro** Faro, S Portugal 37.01N 7.55W
106 G14 **Faro** ◈ *district* S Portugal
106 G14 **Faro** ✕ Faro, S Portugal 37.02N 8.01W
80 F13 **Faro** ≈ Cameroon/Nigeria
97 Q18 **Fårö** Gotland, SE Sweden 57.55N 19.10E
Faro, Punta del *see* Peloro, Capo
97 Q18 **Fårösund** Gotland, SE Sweden 57.51N 19.02E
181 N7 **Farquhar Group** *island group* S Seychelles
20 B13 **Farrell** Pennsylvania, NE USA 41.12N 80.28W
158 K11 **Farrukhābād** Uttar Pradesh, N India 27.24N 79.34E
149 P11 **Fārs** *off.* Ostān-e Fārs; *anc.* Persis. ◈ *province* S Iran
117 F16 **Fársala** Thessalía, C Greece 39.18N 22.22E
149 R4 **Fārsīān** Golestān, N Iran
Fars, Khalīj-e *see* Gulf, The
97 G21 **Farsø** Nordjylland, N Denmark 56.46N 9.21E
97 D18 **Farsund** Vest-Agder, S Norway 58.04N 6.48E
147 U14 **Fartak, Ra's** *headland* E Yemen 15.34N 52.19E
62 H13 **Fartura, Serra da** ▲▲ S Brazil
Farvel, Kap *see* Nunap Isua
26 L4 **Farwell** Texas, SW USA 34.22N 103.02W
204 I9 **Farwell Island** *island* Antarctica
158 L9 **Far Western** ◈ *zone* W Nepal
154 M3 **Fāryāb** ◈ *province* N Afghanistan
149 P12 **Fasā** Fārs, S Iran 28.55N 53.39E
147 U12 **Fasad, Ramlat** *desert* SW Oman
109 P17 **Fasano** Puglia, SE Italy 40.49N 17.21E
94 L3 **Fáskrúdhsfjördhur** Austurland, E Iceland 64.55N 14.01W
119 O5 **Fastiv** *Rus.* Fastov. Kyyivs'ka Oblast', NW Ukraine 50.08N 29.59E
99 B22 **Fastnet Rock** *Ir.* Carraig Aonair. *island* SW Ireland
Fastov *see* Fastiv
202 C9 **Fatato** *island* Funafuti Atoll, C Tuvalu
158 K12 **Fatehgarh** Uttar Pradesh, N India 27.22N 79.37E
155 U6 **Fatehjang** Punjab, E Pakistan 33.33N 72.39E
158 G11 **Fatehpur** Rājasthān, N India 27.58N 74.58E
158 L13 **Fatehpur** Uttar Pradesh, N India 25.55N 80.55E
130 J7 **Fatezh** Kurskaya Oblast', W Russian Federation 52.01N 35.51E
78 G11 **Fatick** W Senegal 14.20N 16.29W
106 G9 **Fátima** Santarém, W Portugal 39.37N 8.39W
142 M11 **Fatsa** Ordu, N Turkey 41.01N 37.31E
Fatshan *see* Foshan
202 D12 **Fatua, Pointe** *var.* Pointe Nord. *headland* Île Futuna, S Wallis and Futuna
203 X7 **Fatu Hiva** *island* Îles Marquises, NE French Polynesia
Fatunda *see* Fatundu
81 H21 **Fatundu** *var.* Fatunda. Bandundu, W Dem. Rep. Congo 4.07S 17.13E
31 O8 **Faulkton** South Dakota, N USA 45.02N 99.07W
118 L13 **Făurei** *prev.* Filimon Sîrbu. Brăila, SE Romania 45.04N 27.15E
195 T13 **Fauro** *island* Shortland Islands, NW Solomon Islands
94 G12 **Fauske** Nordland, C Norway 67.15N 15.27E
9 P13 **Faust** Alberta, W Canada 55.19N 115.33W
101 L23 **Fauvillers** Luxembourg, SE Belgium 49.52N 5.40E
109 J24 **Favara** Sicilia, Italy, C Mediterranean Sea 37.19N 13.39E
Faventia *see* Faenza
109 G23 **Favignana, Isola** *island* Isole Egadi, S Italy
10 D8 **Fawn** ≈ Ontario, SE Canada
Faxa Bay *see* Faxaflói
94 H3 **Faxaflói** *Eng.* Faxa Bay. *bay* W Iceland
80 I7 **Faya** *prev.* Faya-Largeau, Largeau. Borkou-Ennedi-Tibesti, N Chad 17.58N 19.06E
Faya-Largeau *see* Faya
197 J5 **Fayaoué** Province des Îles Loyauté, C New Caledonia 20.41S 166.31E
144 M5 **Fayḑāt** *hill range* E Syria
25 O3 **Fayette** Alabama, S USA 33.40N 87.49W
31 X12 **Fayette** Iowa, C USA 42.50N 91.48W
24 J6 **Fayette** Mississippi, S USA 31.42N 91.03W
29 U4 **Fayette** Missouri, C USA 39.09N 92.40W
29 S9 **Fayetteville** Arkansas, C USA 36.03N 94.09W
23 U10 **Fayetteville** North Carolina, SE USA 35.03N 78.52W
22 J10 **Fayetteville** Tennessee, S USA 35.09N 86.34W
27 U11 **Fayetteville** Texas, SW USA 29.52N 96.40W
23 R5 **Fayetteville** West Virginia, NE USA 38.03N 81.06W
147 R4 **Faylakah** *var.* Failaka Island. *island* E Kuwait
145 T10 **Fayşalīyah** *var.* Faisaliya. S Iraq 31.48N 44.36E
201 P15 **Fayu** *var.* East Fayu. *island* Hall Islands, C Micronesia
158 G8 **Fāzilka** Punjab, NW India 30.25N 74.04E
Fdérick *see* Fdérik
78 I6 **Fdérik** *var.* Fdérick, *Fr.* Fort Gouraud. Tiris Zemmour, NW Mauritania 22.40N 12.40W
Feabhail, Loch *see* Foyle, Lough
99 B20 **Feale** ≈ SW Ireland
23 V12 **Fear, Cape** *headland* Bald Head Island, North Carolina, SE USA 33.50N 77.57W
37 O6 **Feather River** ≈ California, W USA
193 M14 **Featherston** Wellington, North Island, NZ 41.07S 175.19E
104 L3 **Fécamp** Seine-Maritime, N France 49.45N 0.22E
Fédala *see* Mohammedia
63 D17 **Federación** Entre Ríos, E Argentina 30.57S 58.04W
63 D17 **Federal** Entre Ríos, E Argentina 30.53S 58.45W
79 T15 **Federal Capital District** ◈ *capital territory* C Nigeria
Federal Capital Territory *see* Australian Capital Territory
Federal District *see* Distrito Federal
23 Y4 **Federalsburg** Maryland, NE USA 38.41N 75.46W
76 M6 **Fedjaj, Chott el** *var.* Chott el Fejaj, Shaţţ al Fijāj. *salt lake* C Tunisia
96 B13 **Fedje** *island* S Norway
150 M7 **Fedorovka** Kostanay, N Kazakhstan 51.12N 52.00E
131 U6 **Fedorovka** Respublika Bashkortostan, W Russian Federation 53.09N 55.07E
Fëdory *see* Fyadory
119 U11 **Fedotova Kosa** *spit* SE Ukraine
201 V13 **Fefan** *atoll* Chuuk Islands, C Micronesia
113 O21 **Fehérgyarmat** Szabolcs-Szatmár-Bereg, E Hungary 47.58N 22.28E
Fehér-Körös *see* Crişul Alb
Fehértemplom *see* Bela Crkva
Fehérvölgy *see* Albac
102 L7 **Fehmarn** *island* N Germany
97 H25 **Fehmarn Belt** *Dan.* Femern Bælt, *Ger.* Fehmarnbelt. *strait* Denmark/Germany ***see also*** Femern Bælt
Fehmarnbelt *see* Fehmarn Belt/Femern Bælt
111 X8 **Fehring** Steiermark, SE Austria 46.56N 16.00E
61 B15 **Feijó** Acre, W Brazil 8.07S 70.27W
192 M12 **Feilding** Manawatu-Wanganui, North Island, NZ 40.14S 175.34E
Feira *see* Feira de Santana
61 O17 **Feira de Santana** *var.* Feira. Bahia, E Brazil 12.16S 38.52W
111 X7 **Feistritz** ≈ SE Austria
Feistritz *see* Ilirska Bistrica
167 P8 **Feixi** *var.* Shangpai; *prev.* Shangpaihe. Anhui, E China 31.40N 117.08E
Fejaj, Chott el *see* Fedjaj, Chott el
113 I23 **Fejér** *off.* Fejér Megye. ◈ *county* W Hungary
97 I24 **Fejø** *island* SE Denmark
142 K15 **Feke** Adana, S Turkey 37.49N 35.55E
Feketehalom *see* Codlea
Fekete-Körös *see* Crişul Negru
107 Y9 **Felanitx** Mallorca, Spain, W Mediterranean Sea 39.28N 3.08E
111 T3 **Feldaist** ≈ N Austria
111 W8 **Feldbach** Steiermark, SE Austria 46.57N 15.52E
103 F24 **Feldberg** ▲ SW Germany 47.52N 8.01E
118 J12 **Feldioara** *Ger.* Marienburg, *Hung.* Földvár. Braşov, C Romania 45.48N 25.37E
110 I7 **Feldkirch** *anc.* Clunia. Vorarlberg, W Austria 47.15N 9.37E
111 S9 **Feldkirchen in Kärnten** *Slvn.* Trg. Kärnten, S Austria 46.42N 14.01E
Félegyháza *see* Kiskunfélegyháza
198 B8 **Feleolo** ✕ (Āpia) Upolu, C Samoa 13.49S 171.59W
106 H6 **Felgueiras** Porto, N Portugal 41.22N 8.12W
Felicitas Julia *see* Lisboa
180 J16 **Félicité** *island* Inner Islands, NE Seychelles
157 K20 **Felidhu Atoll** *atoll* C Maldives
43 Y13 **Felipe Carrillo Puerto** Quintana Roo, SE Mexico 19.33N 88.01W
99 Q21 **Felixstowe** E England, UK 51.58N 1.19E
105 N11 **Felletin** Creuse, C France 45.53N 2.12E
Fellin *see* Viljandi
Felsőbánya *see* Baia Sprie
Felsőmuzslya *see* Mužlja
Felsővisó *see* Vişeu de Sus
37 N10 **Felton** California, W USA 37.03N 122.04W
108 H7 **Feltre** Veneto, NE Italy 46.01N 11.55E
97 H25 **Femern Bælt** *Ger.* Fehmarnbelt, Fehmarn Belt. *strait* Denmark/Germany ***see also*** Fehmarn Belt
97 I24 **Femø** *island* SE Denmark
96 I10 **Femunden** ◎ S Norway
106 H2 **Fene** Galicia, NW Spain 43.28N 8.10W
12 I14 **Fenelon Falls** Ontario, SE Canada 44.34N 78.43W
201 U13 **Feneppi** *atoll* Chuuk Islands, C Micronesia
143 O11 **Fener Burnu** *headland* N Turkey 41.07N 39.26E
117 J14 **Fengári** ▲ Samothráki, E Greece 40.27N 25.37E
169 V13 **Fengcheng** *var.* Feng-cheng, Fenghwangcheng. Liaoning, NE China 40.28N 124.01E
166 K11 **Fenggang** *var.* Longquan. Guizhou, S China 27.57N 107.42E
167 S9 **Fenghua** Zhejiang, SE China 29.38N 121.23E
Fenghwangcheng *see* Fengcheng
Fengjiaba *see* Wangcang
166 L9 **Fengjie** *var.* Yong'an. Chongqing Shi, C China 31.03N 109.29E
166 M14 **Fengkai** *var.* Jiangkou. Guangdong, S China 23.26N 111.28E
167 T13 **Fenglin** *Jap.* Hōrin. C Taiwan 23.52N 121.30E
167 P1 **Fengning** *prev.* Dagezhen. Hebei, E China 41.12N 116.37E
166 E13 **Fengqing** *var.* Fengshan. Yunnan, SW China 24.38N 99.54E
167 O6 **Fengqiu** Henan, C China 35.01N 114.24E
167 Q2 **Fengrun** Hebei, E China 39.49N 118.10E
Fengshan *see* Fengqing, Yunnan, China
Fengshan *see* Luoyuan, Fujian, China
169 T4 **Fengshui Shan** ▲ NE China 52.20N 123.22E
167 P14 **Fengshun** Guangdong, S China 23.51N 116.11E
Fengtien *see* Liaoning, China
Fengtien *see* Shenyang, China
166 J7 **Fengxian** *var.* Feng Xian; *prev.* Shuangshipu. Shaanxi, C China 33.50N 106.33E
Fengxiang *see* Luobei
169 P13 **Fengzhen** Nei Mongol Zizhiqu, N China 40.25N 113.09E
166 M6 **Fen He** ≈ C China
159 V15 **Feni** Chittagong, E Bangladesh 23.00N 91.24E
195 Q10 **Feni Islands** *island group* NE PNG
40 H17 **Fenimore Pass** *strait* Aleutian Islands, Alaska, USA
86 B9 **Feni Ridge** *undersea feature* N Atlantic Ocean
Fennern *see* Vändra
32 J9 **Fennimore** Wisconsin, N USA 42.58N 90.39W
180 J4 **Fenoarivo** Toamasina, E Madagascar 20.52S 46.52E
97 I24 **Fensmark** Storstrøm, SE Denmark 55.16N 11.48E
99 O19 **Fens, The** *wetland* E England, UK
33 R9 **Fenton** Michigan, N USA 42.48N 83.42W
202 K10 **Fenua Fala** *island* SE Tokelau
202 F12 **Fenuafo'ou, Île** *island* E Wallis and Futuna
202 L10 **Fenua Loa** *island* Fakaofo Atoll, E Tokelau
166 M4 **Fenyang** Shanxi, C China 37.14N 111.40E
119 U13 **Feodosiya** *var.* Kefe, *It.* Kaffa; *anc.* Theodosia. Respublika Krym, S Ukraine 45.03N 35.23E
96 I10 **Feragen** ◎ S Norway
76 L5 **Fer, Cap de** *headland* NE Algeria 37.05N 7.10E
33 O16 **Ferdinand** Indiana, N USA 38.13N 86.51W
Ferdinand *see* Montana, Bulgaria
Ferdinand *see* Mihail Kogălniceanu, Romania
Ferdinandsberg *see* Oţelu Roşu
149 T7 **Ferdows** *var.* Firdaus; *prev.* Tūn. Khorāsān-Razavī, E Iran 34.00N 58.09E
105 Q5 **Fère-Champenoise** Marne, N France 48.45N 3.59E
Ferencz-Jósef Csúcs *see* Gerlachovský štít
109 J16 **Ferentino** Lazio, C Italy 41.40N 13.16E
116 L13 **Féres** Anatolikí Makedonía kai Thráki, NE Greece 40.54N 26.12E
Fergana *see* Farg'ona
153 S10 **Fergana Valley** *var.* Farghona Valley, *Rus.* Ferganskaya Dolina, *Taj.* Wodii Farghona, *Uzb.* Farghona Wodiysi. *basin* Tajikistan/Uzbekistan
Ferganskaya Dolina *see* Fergana Valley
Ferganskaya Oblast' *see* Farg'ona Viloyati
153 U9 **Ferganskiy Khrebet** ▲▲ C Kyrgyzstan
12 F15 **Fergus** Ontario, S Canada 43.42N 80.22W
31 S6 **Fergus Falls** Minnesota, N USA 46.15N 96.02W
195 N15 **Fergusson Island** *var.* Kaluwawa. *island* SE PNG
113 K22 **Ferihegy** ✕ (Budapest) Budapest, C Hungary 47.25N 19.13E
Ferizaj *see* Uroševac
79 N14 **Ferkessédougou** N Ivory Coast 9.36N 5.12W
111 T10 **Ferlach** *Slvn.* Borovlje. Kärnten, S Austria 46.31N 14.18E
99 E16 **Fermanagh** *cultural region* SW Northern Ireland, UK
108 J13 **Fermo** *anc.* Firmum Picenum. Marche, C Italy 43.09N 13.43E
106 J6 **Fermoselle** Castilla-León, N Spain 41.19N 6.24W
99 D20 **Fermoy** *Ir.* Mainistir Fhear Maí. SW Ireland 52.07N 8.16W
25 W8 **Fernandina Beach** Amelia Island, Florida, SE USA 30.40N 81.27W
59 A17 **Fernandina, Isla** *var.* Narborough Island. *island* Galapagos Islands, Ecuador, E Pacific Ocean
49 Y5 **Fernando de Noronha** *island* E Brazil
Fernando Po/Fernando Póo *see* Bioco, Isla de
62 J7 **Fernandópolis** São Paulo, S Brazil 20.12S 50.14W
106 M13 **Fernán Núñez** Andalucía, S Spain 37.40N 4.43W
85 Q14 **Fernão Veloso, Baia de** *bay* NE Mozambique
36 K3 **Ferndale** California, W USA 40.34N 124.16W
34 H6 **Ferndale** Washington, NW USA 48.51N 122.35W
9 P17 **Fernie** British Columbia, SW Canada 49.30N 115.00W
37 R5 **Fernley** Nevada, W USA 39.35N 119.15W
Ferozepore *see* Fīrozpur
109 N18 **Ferrandina** Basilicata, S Italy 40.30N 16.25E
108 G9 **Ferrara** *anc.* Forum Alieni. Emilia-Romagna, N Italy 44.49N 11.36E
123 H11 **Ferrat, Cap** *headland* NW Algeria 35.52N 0.24W
109 D20 **Ferrato, Capo** *headland* Sardegna, Italy, C Mediterranean Sea 39.18N 9.37E
106 G12 **Ferreira do Alentejo** Beja, S Portugal 38.04N 8.06W
58 B11 **Ferreñafe** Lambayeque, W Peru 6.37S 79.45W
110 C12 **Ferret** Valais, SW Switzerland 45.57N 7.04E
104 I13 **Ferret, Cap** *headland* W France 44.37N 1.15W
24 I6 **Ferriday** Louisiana, S USA 31.37N 91.33W
Ferro *see* Hierro
109 D16 **Ferro, Capo** *headland* Sardegna, Italy, C Mediterranean Sea 41.09N 9.31E
106 H2 **Ferrol** *var.* El Ferrol; *prev.* El Ferrol del Caudillo. Galicia, NW Spain 43.28N 8.13W
58 B12 **Ferrol, Península de** *peninsula* W Peru
38 M5 **Ferron** Utah, W USA 39.05N 111.07W
23 S7 **Ferrum** Virginia, NE USA 36.54N 80.01W
25 O8 **Ferry Pass** Florida, SE USA 30.30N 87.12W
Ferryville *see* Menzel Bourguiba
31 S4 **Fertile** Minnesota, N USA 47.32N 96.16W
Fertő *see* Neusiedler See
100 L5 **Ferwerd** *Fris.* Ferwert. Friesland, N Netherlands 53.21N 5.46E
Ferwert *see* Ferwerd
76 G6 **Fès** *Eng.* Fez. N Morocco 34.06N 4.57W
81 I22 **Feshi** Bandundu, SW Dem. Rep. Congo 6.07S 18.12E
31 O4 **Fessenden** North Dakota, N USA 47.36N 99.37W
Festenberg *see* Twardogóra
29 X5 **Festus** Missouri, C USA 38.13N 90.24W
118 M14 **Feteşti** Ialomiţa, SE Romania 44.22N 27.51E
142 D17 **Fethiye** Muğla, SW Turkey 36.37N 29.07E
98 M1 **Fetlar** *island* NE Scotland, UK
97 I15 **Fetsund** Akershus, S Norway 59.55N 11.03E
10 L5 **Feuilles, Lac aux** ◎ Québec, E Canada
10 L5 **Feuilles, Rivière aux** ≈ Québec, E Canada
101 M23 **Feulen** Diekirch, C Luxembourg 49.52N 6.03E
105 Q11 **Feurs** Loire, E France 45.44N 4.14E
97 F18 **Fevik** Aust-Agder, S Norway 58.22N 8.40E
126 Mm14 **Fevral'sk** Amurskaya Oblast', SE Russian Federation 52.25N 131.06E
155 S2 **Feyẕābād** *var.* Faizabad, Faizābād, Feyzābād, Fyzabad. Badakhshān, NE Afghanistan 37.06N 70.34E
Fez *see* Fès
99 J19 **Ffestiniog** NW Wales, UK 52.55N 3.54W
Fhóid Duibh, Cuan an *see* Blacksod Bay
64 I8 **Fiambalá** Catamarca, NW Argentina 27.45S 67.37W
180 I6 **Fianarantsoa** Fianarantsoa, C Madagascar 21.27S 47.04E
180 H6 **Fianarantsoa** ◈ *province* SE Madagascar
80 G12 **Fianga** Mayo-Kébbi, SW Chad 9.57N 15.09E
Ficce *see* Fichē

◆ Country
● Country Capital
◇ Dependent Territory
○ Dependent Territory Capital
◈ Administrative Region
✕ International Airport
▲ Mountain
▲▲ Mountain Range
Volcano
≈ River
◎ Lake
⊠ Reservoir

Fichê – Foula

82 J12 **Fichē** *It.* Ficce. Oromo, C Ethiopia 9.48N 38.43E
103 N17 **Fichtelberg** ▲ Czech Republic/Germany 50.26N 12.57E
103 M18 **Fichtelgebirge** ▲▲ SE Germany
103 M19 **Fichtelnaab** ~ SE Germany
108 E9 **Fidenza** Emilia-Romagna, N Italy 44.52N 10.04E
115 K21 **Fier** *var.* Fieri. Fier, SW Albania 40.44N 19.34E
115 K21 **Fier** ◈ *district* W Albania
Fieri *see* Fier
Fierza *see* Fierzë
115 L17 **Fierzë** *var.* Fierza. Shkodër, N Albania 42.15N 20.02E
115 L17 **Fierzës, Liqeni i** ◎ N Albania
110 F10 **Fiesch** Valais, SW Switzerland 46.25N 8.09E
108 G11 **Fiesole** Toscana, C Italy 43.50N 11.18E
144 G12 **Fifah** Aţ Ţafīlah, W Jordan 30.55N 35.25E
98 K11 **Fife** *var.* Kingdom of Fife. *cultural region* E Scotland, UK
98 K11 **Fife Ness** *headland* E Scotland, UK 56.16N 2.35W
Fifteen Twenty Fracture Zone *see* Barracuda Fracture Zone
105 N13 **Figeac** Lot, S France 44.37N 2.01E
97 N19 **Figeholm** Kalmar, SE Sweden 57.12N 16.34E
Figig *see* Figuig
85 J18 **Figtree** Matabeleland South, SW Zimbabwe 20.20S 28.20E
106 F8 **Figueira da Foz** Coimbra, W Portugal 40.09N 8.51W
107 X4 **Figueres** Cataluña, E Spain 42.16N 2.57E
76 H7 **Figuig** *var.* Figig. E Morocco 32.09N 1.13W
Fijāj, Shaţţ al *see* Fedjaj, Chott el
197 J14 **Fiji** *off.* Sovereign Democratic Republic of Fiji, *Fij.* Viti. ◆ *republic* SW Pacific Ocean
197 J13 **Fiji** *island group* SW Pacific Ocean
183 Q8 **Fiji Plate** *tectonic feature*
107 P14 **Filabres, Sierra de los** ▲▲ SE Spain
85 K18 **Filabusi** Matabeleland South, S Zimbabwe 20.31S 29.16E
44 K13 **Filadelfia** Guanacaste, W Costa Rica 10.24N 85.33W
113 K20 **Fil'akovo** *Hung.* Fülek. Banskobystrický Kraj, C Slovakia 48.15N 19.53E
205 N5 **Filchner Ice Shelf** *ice shelf* Antarctica
12 J11 **Fildegrand** ~ Québec, SE Canada
96 E12 **Filefjell** ▲▲ S Norway
35 O15 **Filer** Idaho, NW USA 42.34N 114.36W
Filevo *see* Vŭrbitsa
118 H14 **Filiaşi** Dolj, SW Romania 44.32N 23.30E
117 B16 **Filiátes** Ípeiros, W Greece 39.36N 20.19E
117 D21 **Filiatrá** Pelopónnisos, S Greece 37.10N 21.35E
109 K22 **Filicudi, Isola** *island* Isole Eolie, S Italy
147 Y10 **Filim** E Oman 20.37N 58.11E
Filimon Sîrbu *see* Făurei
79 S11 **Filingué** Tillabéri, W Niger 14.12N 3.16E
Filioúri *see* Líssos
116 I13 **Filippoi** *anc.* Philippi. *site of ancient city* Anatolikí Makedonía kai Thráki, NE Greece 41.01N 24.15E
97 L15 **Filipstad** Värmland, C Sweden 59.43N 14.10E
110 I9 **Filisur** Graubünden, S Switzerland 46.40N 9.43E
37 R14 **Fillmore** California, W USA 34.23N 118.56W
38 K5 **Fillmore** Utah, W USA 38.57N 112.19W
12 J10 **Fils, Lac du** ◎ Québec, SE Canada
142 H11 **Filyos Çayı** ~ N Turkey
205 Q2 **Fimbulheimen** *physical region* Antarctica
205 Q1 **Fimbul Ice Shelf** *ice shelf* Antarctica
108 G9 **Finale Emilia** Emilia-Romagna, C Italy 44.50N 11.17E
108 C10 **Finale Ligure** Liguria, NW Italy 44.11N 8.21E
107 P14 **Fiñana** Andalucía, S Spain 37.09N 2.47W
180 I6 **Finandrahana** Fianarantsoa, SE Madagascar
23 S6 **Fincastle** Virginia, NE USA 37.29N 79.51W
101 M25 **Findel** ✕ (Luxembourg) Luxembourg, C Luxembourg 49.39N 6.16E
98 J9 **Findhorn** ~ N Scotland, UK
33 R12 **Findlay** Ohio, N USA 41.02N 83.39W
20 G11 **Finger Lakes** *lakes* New York, NE USA
85 L14 **Fingoè** Tete, NW Mozambique 15.01S 31.52E
142 E17 **Finike** Antalya, SW Turkey 36.18N 30.07E
104 F6 **Finistère** ◈ *department* NW France
194 J12 **Finisterre, Mount** ▲ C PNG 5.58S 146.30E
194 J12 **Finisterre Range** ▲▲ N PNG
189 Q8 **Finke** Northern Territory, N Australia 25.37S 134.35E
111 S10 **Finkenstein** Kärnten, S Austria 46.34N 13.53E
201 Y15 **Finkol, Mount** *var.* Mount Crozer. ▲ Kosrae, E Micronesia 5.18N 163.00E
95 L17 **Finland** *off.* Republic of Finland, *Fin.* Suomen Tasavalta, Suomi. ◆ *republic* N Europe
128 F12 **Finland, Gulf of** *Est.* Soome Laht, *Fin.* Suomenlahti, *Ger.* Finnischer Meerbusen, *Rus.* Finskiy Zaliv, *Swe.* Finska Viken. *gulf* E Baltic Sea
8 L11 **Finlay** ~ British Columbia, W Canada
191 O10 **Finley** New South Wales, SE Australia 35.41S 145.33E
31 Q4 **Finley** North Dakota, N USA 47.30N 97.50W
Finnischer Meerbusen *see* Finland, Gulf of
94 K9 **Finnmark** ◈ *county* N Norway
94 K9 **Finnmarksvidda** *physical region* N Norway
94 I9 **Finnsnes** Troms, N Norway 69.13N 17.58E
194 K13 **Finschhafen** Morobe, C PNG 6.38S 147.49E
96 E13 **Finse** Hordaland, S Norway 60.35N 7.33E
Finska Viken/Finskiy Zaliv *see* Finland, Gulf of
97 M17 **Finspång** Östergötland, S Sweden 58.42N 15.45E
110 F10 **Finsteraarhorn** ▲ Switzerland 46.33N 8.07E
103 O14 **Finsterwalde** Brandenburg, E Germany 51.37N 13.43E
193 A23 **Fiordland** *physical region* South Island, NZ
108 E9 **Fiorenzuola d'Arda** Emilia-Romagna, C Italy 44.57N 9.53E
Firat Nehri *see* Euphrates
Firdaus *see* Ferdows
20 M14 **Fire Island** *island* New York, NE USA
108 G11 **Firenze** *Eng.* Florence; *anc.* Florentia. Toscana, C Italy 43.46N 11.15E
108 G10 **Firenzuola** Toscana, C Italy 44.07N 11.22E
12 C6 **Fire River** Ontario, S Canada 48.46N 83.34W
Firliug *see* Fârliug
63 B19 **Firmat** Santa Fe, C Argentina 33.28S 61.28W
105 Q12 **Firminy** Loire, E France 45.22N 4.18E
Firmum Picenum *see* Fermo
158 J12 **Fīrozābād** Uttar Pradesh, N India 27.09N 78.24E
158 G8 **Fīrozpur** *var.* Ferozepore. Punjab, NW India 30.55N 74.37E
First State *see* Delaware
149 O12 **Fīrūzābād** Fārs, S Iran 28.51N 52.34E
Fischamend *see* Fischamend Markt
111 Y4 **Fischamend Markt** *var.* Fischamend. Niederösterreich, NE Austria 48.06N 16.37E
111 W6 **Fischbacher Alpen** ▲▲ E Austria
Fischhausen *see* Primorsk
85 D21 **Fish** *var.* Vis. ~ S Namibia
85 F24 **Fish** *Afr.* Vis. ~ SW South Africa
9 X15 **Fisher Branch** Manitoba, S Canada 51.09N 97.34W
9 X15 **Fisher River** Manitoba, S Canada 51.25N 97.23W
21 N13 **Fishers Island** *island* New York, NE USA
39 U8 **Fishers Peak** ▲ Colorado, C USA 37.06N 104.27W
15 M6 **Fisher Strait** *strait* Nunavut, N Canada
99 H21 **Fishguard** *Wel.* Abergwaun. SW Wales, UK 51.58N 4.49W
21 R2 **Fish River Lake** ◎ Maine, NE USA
204 K6 **Fiske, Cape** *headland* Antarctica 74.27S 60.28W
105 P4 **Fismes** Marne, N France 49.19N 3.41E
106 F3 **Fisterra, Cabo** *headland* NW Spain 42.53N 9.16W
21 N11 **Fitchburg** Massachusetts, NE USA 42.34N 71.48W
98 L3 **Fitful Head** *headland* NE Scotland, UK 59.57N 1.24W
97 C14 **Fitjar** Hordaland, S Norway 59.55N 5.19E
198 Bb8 **Fito** ▲ Upolu, C Samoa 13.57S 171.42W
25 U6 **Fitzgerald** Georgia, SE USA 31.42N 83.15W
188 M5 **Fitzroy Crossing** Western Australia 18.10S 125.40E
65 G21 **Fitzroy, Monte** *var.* Cerro Chaltel. ▲ S Argentina 49.18S 73.06W
189 Y8 **Fitzroy River** ~ Queensland, E Australia
188 L5 **Fitzroy River** ~ Western Australia
12 E12 **Fitzwilliam Island** *island* Ontario, S Canada
109 J15 **Fiuggi** Lazio, C Italy 41.47N 13.16E
Fiume *see* Rijeka
109 H15 **Fiumicino** Lazio, C Italy 41.46N 12.13E
Fiumicino *see* Leonardo da Vinci
108 E10 **Fivizzano** Toscana, C Italy 44.13N 10.06E
81 O21 **Fizi** Sud Kivu, E Dem. Rep. Congo 4.15S 28.57E
Fizuli *see* Füzuli
94 I11 **Fjällåsen** Norrbotten, N Sweden 67.31N 20.07E
97 G20 **Fjerritslev** Nordjylland, N Denmark 57.06N 9.16E
F.J.S. *see* Franz Josef Strauss
97 L16 **Fjugesta** Örebro, C Sweden 59.10N 14.50E
Fladstrand *see* Frederikshavn
39 V5 **Flagler** Colorado, C USA 39.17N 103.04W
25 X10 **Flagler Beach** Florida, SE USA 29.28N 81.07W
38 L11 **Flagstaff** Arizona, SW USA 35.12N 111.39W
67 H24 **Flagstaff Bay** *bay* Saint Helena, C Atlantic Ocean
21 P5 **Flagstaff Lake** ◎ Maine, NE USA
96 E13 **Flåm** Sogn og Fjordane, S Norway 60.51N 7.06E
13 O8 **Flamand** ~ Québec, SE Canada
32 J5 **Flambeau River** ~ Wisconsin, N USA
99 O16 **Flamborough Head** *headland* E England, UK 54.06N 0.03W
102 N13 **Fläming** *hill range* NE Germany
18 I17 **Flaming Gorge Reservoir** ▣ Utah/Wyoming, NW USA
176 Xx13 **Flamingo, Teluk** *bay* N Arafura Sea
101 B18 **Flanders** *Dut.* Vlaanderen, *Fr.* Flandre. *cultural region* Belgium/France
Flandre *see* Flanders
31 R10 **Flandreau** South Dakota, N USA 44.03N 96.36W
98 D6 **Flannan Isles** *island group* NW Scotland, UK
30 M6 **Flasher** North Dakota, N USA 46.25N 101.12W
95 G15 **Flåsjön** ◎ N Sweden
41 O11 **Flat** Alaska, USA 62.27N 158.00W
14 G7 **Flat** ~ Northwest Territories, NW Canada
94 H1 **Flateyri** Vestfirdhir, NW Iceland 66.03N 23.28W
35 P8 **Flathead Lake** ◎ Montana, NW USA
181 Y15 **Flat Island** *Fr.* Île Plate. *island* N Mauritius
179 N14 **Flat Island** *island* NE Spratly Islands
27 T11 **Flatonia** Texas, SW USA 29.41N 97.06W
193 M14 **Flat Point** *headland* North Island, NZ 41.12S 176.03E
29 X6 **Flat River** Missouri, C USA 37.51N 90.31W
33 P8 **Flat River** ~ Michigan, N USA
33 P14 **Flatrock River** ~ Indiana, N USA
34 E6 **Flattery, Cape** *headland* Washington, NW USA 48.22N 124.43W
66 B12 **Flatts Village** *var.* The Flatts Village. C Bermuda 32.19N 64.43W
110 H7 **Flawil** Sankt Gallen, NE Switzerland 47.25N 9.12E
99 N22 **Fleet** S England, UK 51.16N 0.49W
99 K16 **Fleetwood** NW England, UK 53.55N 3.01W
20 H15 **Fleetwood** Pennsylvania, NE USA 40.27N 75.49W
97 D18 **Flekkefjord** Vest-Agder, S Norway 58.16N 6.40E
23 N5 **Flemingsburg** Kentucky, S USA 38.25N 83.43W
20 J15 **Flemington** New Jersey, NE USA 40.30N 74.51W
66 I7 **Flemish Cap** *undersea feature* NW Atlantic Ocean
97 N16 **Flen** Södermanland, C Sweden 59.03N 16.37E
102 I6 **Flensburg** Schleswig-Holstein, N Germany 54.46N 9.25E
102 J6 **Flensburger Förde** *inlet* Denmark/Germany
104 K5 **Flers** Orne, N France 48.45N 0.34W
97 C14 **Flesland** ✕ (Bergen) Hordaland, S Norway 60.18N 5.15E
Flessingue *see* Vlissingen
23 P10 **Fletcher** North Carolina, SE USA 35.24N 82.29W
33 R6 **Fletcher Pond** ◎ Michigan, N USA
104 L15 **Fleurance** Gers, S France 43.50N 0.39E
110 B8 **Fleurier** Neuchâtel, W Switzerland 46.55N 6.37E
101 H20 **Fleurus** Hainaut, S Belgium 50.28N 4.33E
105 N7 **Fleury-les-Aubrais** Loiret, C France 47.55N 1.55E
100 K10 **Flevoland** ◈ *province* C Netherlands
Flickertail State *see* North Dakota
110 H9 **Flims** Glarus, NE Switzerland 46.50N 9.16E
190 F8 **Flinders Island** *island* Investigator Group, South Australia
191 P14 **Flinders Island** *island* Furneaux Group, Tasmania, SE Australia
190 I6 **Flinders Ranges** ▲▲ South Australia
189 U5 **Flinders River** ~ Queensland, NE Australia
9 V13 **Flin Flon** Manitoba, C Canada 54.46N 101.51W
99 K18 **Flint** NE Wales, UK 53.15N 3.09W
33 R9 **Flint** Michigan, N USA 43.00N 83.41W
99 J18 **Flint** *cultural region* NE Wales, UK
29 O7 **Flint Hills** *hill range* Kansas, C USA
203 Y6 **Flint Island** *island* Line Islands, E Kiribati
25 S4 **Flint River** ~ Georgia, SE USA
33 R9 **Flint River** ~ Michigan, N USA
201 X12 **Flipper Point** *headland* C Wake Island 19.18N 166.37E
96 I13 **Flisa** Hedmark, S Norway 60.36N 12.01E
96 J13 **Flisa** ~ S Norway
126 Hh4 **Flissingskiy, Mys** *headland* Novaya Zemlya, NW Russian Federation 76.43N 69.01E
Flitsch *see* Bovec
107 U6 **Flix** Cataluña, NE Spain 41.13N 0.32E
97 J19 **Floda** Västra Götaland, S Sweden 57.46N 12.19E
103 O16 **Flöha** ~ E Germany
27 O4 **Flomot** Texas, SW USA 34.13N 100.58W
31 V5 **Floodwood** Minnesota, N USA 46.55N 92.55W
32 M15 **Flora** Illinois, N USA 38.40N 88.29W
105 P14 **Florac** Lozère, S France 44.18N 3.35E
25 Q8 **Florala** Alabama, S USA 31.00N 86.19W
105 S4 **Florange** Moselle, NE France 49.21N 6.06E
Floreana, Isla *see* Santa María, Isla
25 O2 **Florence** Alabama, S USA 34.48N 87.40W
38 L14 **Florence** Arizona, SW USA 33.01N 111.23W
39 T6 **Florence** Colorado, C USA 38.20N 105.06W
29 O5 **Florence** Kansas, C USA 38.13N 96.56W
22 M4 **Florence** Kentucky, S USA 39.00N 84.37W
34 E13 **Florence** Oregon, NW USA 43.58N 124.06W
23 T12 **Florence** South Carolina, SE USA 34.12N 79.45W
27 S9 **Florence** Texas, SW USA 30.50N 97.47W
Florence *see* Firenze
56 E13 **Florencia** Caquetá, S Colombia 1.37N 75.37W
101 H21 **Florennes** Namur, S Belgium 50.15N 4.36E
Florentia *see* Firenze
65 J18 **Florentino Ameghino, Embalse** ▣ S Argentina
101 J24 **Florenville** Luxembourg, SE Belgium 49.42N 5.19E
44 E3 **Flores** Petén, N Guatemala 16.54N 89.55W
63 E19 **Flores** ◈ *department* S Uruguay
175 Pp16 **Flores** *island* Nusa Tenggara, C Indonesia
66 M1 **Flores** *island* Azores, Portugal, NE Atlantic Ocean
Floreshty *see* Floreşti
Flores, Lago de *see* Petén Itzá, Lago
Flores, Laut *see* Flores Sea
175 P15 **Flores Sea** *Ind.* Laut Flores. *sea* C Indonesia
118 M8 **Floreşti** *Rus.* Floreshty. N Moldova 47.52N 28.19E
27 S12 **Floresville** Texas, SW USA 29.07N 98.09W
61 N14 **Floriano** Piauí, E Brazil 6.45S 43.00W
63 K14 **Florianópolis** *prev.* Destêrro. *state capital* Santa Catarina, S Brazil 27.34S 48.31W
46 G6 **Florida** Camagüey, C Cuba 21.31N 78.13W
63 F19 **Florida** Florida, S Uruguay 34.04S 56.13W
63 F19 **Florida** ◈ *department* S Uruguay
25 U9 **Florida** *off.* State of Florida; also known as Peninsular State, Sunshine State. ◈ *state* SE USA
25 Y17 **Florida Bay** *bay* Florida, SE USA
56 G8 **Floridablanca** Santander, N Colombia 7.04N 73.06W
195 X15 **Florida Islands** *island group* C Solomon Islands
25 Y17 **Florida Keys** *island group* Florida, SE USA
39 Q16 **Florida Mountains** ▲▲ New Mexico, SW USA
66 D10 **Florida, Straits of** *strait* Atlantic Ocean/Gulf of Mexico
116 D13 **Flórina** *var.* Phlórina. Dytikí Makedonía, N Greece 40.48N 21.25E
29 X4 **Florissant** Missouri, C USA 38.47N 90.19W
96 C11 **Florø** Sogn og Fjordane, S Norway 61.34N 5.01E
117 L22 **Floúda, Akrotírio** *headland* Astypálaia, Kykládes, Greece, Aegean Sea 36.38N 26.23E
23 S7 **Floyd** Virginia, NE USA 36.53N 80.21W
27 N4 **Floydada** Texas, SW USA 33.58N 101.20W
Flüela Wisshorn *see* Weisshorn
100 K7 **Fluessen** ◎ N Netherlands
107 S5 **Flúmen** ~ NE Spain
109 C20 **Flumendosa** ~ Sardegna, Italy, C Mediterranean Sea
33 R9 **Flushing** Michigan, N USA 43.03N 83.51W
Flushing *see* Vlissingen
27 O6 **Fluvanna** Texas, SW USA 32.54N 101.06W
194 F14 **Fly** ~ Indonesia/PNG
204 I10 **Flying Fish, Cape** *headland* Thurston Island, Antarctica 72.00S 102.25W
Flylân *see* Vlieland
200 Ss13 **Foa** *island* Ha'apai Group, C Tonga
9 U15 **Foam Lake** Saskatchewan, S Canada 51.37N 103.31W
115 J14 **Foča** *var* Srbinje, Republika Srpska, Bosnia and Herzegovina 43.32N 18.45E
118 L12 **Focşani** Vrancea, E Romania 45.45N 27.13E
Fogaras/Fogarasch *see* Făgăraş
109 M16 **Foggia** Puglia, SE Italy 41.28N 15.31E
Foggo *see* Faggo
78 D10 **Fogo** *island* Ilhas de Sotavento, SW Cape Verde
11 U11 **Fogo Island** *island* Newfoundland and Labrador, E Canada
111 U7 **Fohnsdorf** Steiermark, SE Austria 47.13N 14.40E
102 G7 **Föhr** *island* NW Germany
106 F14 **Fóia** ▲ S Portugal 37.19N 8.39W
12 I10 **Foins, Lac aux** ◎ Québec, SE Canada
105 N17 **Foix** Ariège, S France 42.58N 1.39E
130 I5 **Fokino** Bryanskaya Oblast', W Russian Federation 53.22N 34.22E
127 N17 **Fokino** Primorskiy Kray, SE Russian Federation 42.58N 132.25E
Fola, Cnoc *see* Bloody Foreland
96 E13 **Folarskardnuten** ▲ S Norway 60.34N 7.18E
94 G11 **Folda** *fjord* C Norway
95 E14 **Folda** *fjord* C Norway
Földvár *see* Feldioara
95 F14 **Foldereid** Nord-Trøndelag, C Norway 64.58N 12.09E
117 J22 **Folégandros** *island* Kykládes, Greece, Aegean Sea
25 O9 **Foley** Alabama, S USA 30.24N 87.40W
31 U7 **Foley** Minnesota, N USA 45.39N 93.54W
12 E7 **Foleyet** Ontario, S Canada 48.15N 82.25W
97 D14 **Folgefonni** *glacier* S Norway
108 I13 **Foligno** Umbria, C Italy 42.58N 12.40E
99 Q23 **Folkestone** SE England, UK 51.04N 1.10E
25 W8 **Folkston** Georgia, SE USA 30.49N 82.00W
96 H10 **Folldal** Hedmark, S Norway 62.08N 10.00E
27 P1 **Follett** Texas, SW USA 36.25N 100.08W
108 F13 **Follonica** Toscana, C Italy 42.55N 10.45E
23 T15 **Folly Beach** South Carolina, SE USA 32.39N 79.56W
37 O7 **Folsom** California, W USA 38.40N 121.11W
118 M12 **Folteşti** Galaţi, E Romania 45.45N 28.00E
180 H14 **Fomboni** Mohéli, S Comoros 12.18S 43.46E
20 K10 **Fonda** New York, NE USA 42.57N 74.24W
9 S10 **Fond-du-Lac** Saskatchewan, C Canada 59.19N 107.09W
32 M8 **Fond du Lac** Wisconsin, N USA 43.48N 88.27W
9 T10 **Fond-du-Lac** ~ Saskatchewan, C Canada
202 C9 **Fongafale** *var.* Funafuti. ● (Tuvalu) Funafuti Atoll, SE Tuvalu 8.31N 179.11E
202 G8 **Fongafale** *atoll* C Tuvalu
109 C18 **Fonni** Sardegna, Italy, C Mediterranean Sea 40.07N 9.17E
201 V12 **Fono** *island* Chuuk, C Micronesia
56 G4 **Fonseca** La Guajira, N Colombia 10.54N 72.54W
Fonseca, Golfo de *see* Fonseca, Gulf of
44 H8 **Fonseca, Gulf of** *Sp.* Golfo de Fonseca. *gulf* Central America
105 O6 **Fontainebleau** Seine-et-Marne, N France 48.24N 2.42E
65 G19 **Fontana, Lago** ◎ W Argentina
23 N10 **Fontana Lake** ▣ North Carolina, SE USA
109 L24 **Fontanarossa** ✕ (Catania) Sicilia, Italy, C Mediterranean Sea 37.28N 15.04E
9 N11 **Fontas** ~ British Columbia, W Canada
60 D12 **Fonte Boa** Amazonas, N Brazil 2.31S 66.01W
104 J10 **Fontenay-le-Comte** Vendée, NW France 46.28N 0.48W
35 T16 **Fontenelle Reservoir** ▣ Wyoming, C USA
200 Ss12 **Fonualei** *island* Vava'u Group, N Tonga
113 H24 **Fonyód** Somogy, W Hungary 46.43N 17.31E
Foochow *see* Fuzhou
41 Q10 **Foraker, Mount** ▲ Alaska, USA 62.57N 151.24W
197 D14 **Forari** Éfaté, C Vanuatu 17.42S 168.33E
105 U4 **Forbach** Moselle, NE France 49.10N 6.54E
191 Q8 **Forbes** New South Wales, SE Australia 33.24S 148.00E
79 T17 **Forcados** Delta, S Nigeria 5.16N 5.25E
105 S14 **Forcalquier** Alpes-de-Haute-Provence, SE France 43.57N 5.46E
103 K19 **Forchheim** Bayern, SE Germany 49.43N 11.07E
176 V14 **Fordate, Pulau** *island* Kepulauan Tanimbar, E Indonesia
37 R13 **Ford City** California, W USA 35.09N 119.27W
96 D11 **Førde** Sogn og Fjordane, S Norway 61.27N 5.49E
33 N4 **Ford River** ~ Michigan, N USA
191 O4 **Fords Bridge** New South Wales, SE Australia 29.44S 145.25E
22 J6 **Fordsville** Kentucky, S USA 37.36N 86.39W
29 U13 **Fordyce** Arkansas, C USA 33.49N 92.24W
78 I14 **Forécariah** SW Guinea 9.28N 13.06W
207 O14 **Forel, Mont** ▲ SE Greenland 66.55N 36.45W
9 R17 **Foremost** Alberta, SW Canada 49.30N 111.34W
12 D16 **Forest** Ontario, S Canada 43.05N 82.00W
24 L5 **Forest** Mississippi, S USA 32.22N 89.30W
33 S12 **Forest** Ohio, N USA 40.47N 83.26W
31 V11 **Forest City** Iowa, C USA 43.15N 93.38W
23 Q10 **Forest City** North Carolina, SE USA 35.19N 81.52W
34 G11 **Forest Grove** Oregon, NW USA 45.31N 123.06W
191 P17 **Forestier Peninsula** *peninsula* Tasmania, SE Australia
31 V8 **Forest Lake** Minnesota, N USA 45.16N 92.59W
25 S3 **Forest Park** Georgia, SE USA 33.37N 84.22W
31 Q3 **Forest River** ~ North Dakota, N USA
13 T6 **Forestville** Québec, SE Canada 48.45N 69.04W
105 Q11 **Forez, Monts du** ▲▲ C France
98 K10 **Forfar** E Scotland, UK 56.37N 2.54W
28 J8 **Forgan** Oklahoma, C USA 36.54N 100.32W
Forge du Sud *see* Dudelange
103 J24 **Forggensee** ◎ S Germany
153 N10 **Forish** *Rus.* Farish. Jizzax Viloyati, C Uzbekistan 40.33N 66.52E
22 F9 **Forked Deer River** ~ Tennessee, S USA
34 F7 **Forks** Washington, NW USA 47.57N 124.22W
94 N2 **Forlandsundet** *sound* W Svalbard
108 H10 **Forlì** *anc.* Forum Livii. Emilia-Romagna, N Italy 44.13N 12.01E
31 Q7 **Forman** North Dakota, N USA 46.07N 97.39W
99 K17 **Formby** NW England, UK 53.34N 3.04W
107 V11 **Formentera** *anc.* Ophiusa, *Lat.* Frumentum. *island* Illes Baleares, Spain, W Mediterranean Sea
Formentor, Cabo de *see* Formentor, Cap de
107 Y9 **Formentor, Cap de** *var.* Cabo de Formentor, Cape Formentor. *headland* Mallorca, Spain, W Mediterranean Sea 39.57N 3.12E
Formentor, Cape *see* Formentor, Cap de
109 J16 **Formia** Lazio, C Italy 41.16N 13.37E
64 O7 **Formosa** Formosa, NE Argentina 26.07S 58.13W
64 M6 **Formosa** *off.* Provincia de Formosa. ◈ *province* NE Argentina
Formosa/Formo'sa *see* Taiwan
61 I17 **Formosa, Serra** ▲▲ C Brazil
Formosa Strait *see* Taiwan Strait
97 H15 **Fornebu** ✕ (Oslo) Akershus, S Norway 59.54N 10.37E
27 U6 **Forney** Texas, SW USA 32.45N 96.28W
97 H21 **Fornæs** *headland* C Denmark 56.26N 10.57E
108 E9 **Fornovo di Taro** Emilia-Romagna, C Italy 44.42N 10.07E
119 T14 **Foros** Respublika Krym, S Ukraine 44.24N 33.47E
Føroyar *see* Faeroe Islands
98 J8 **Forres** NE Scotland, UK 57.32N 3.37W
29 X11 **Forrest City** Arkansas, C USA 35.01N 90.48W
41 Y15 **Forrester Island** *island* Alexander Archipelago, Alaska, USA
27 N7 **Forsan** Texas, SW USA 32.06N 101.22W
189 V5 **Forsayth** Queensland, NE Australia 18.31S 143.37E
97 L19 **Forserum** Jönköping, S Sweden 57.42N 14.28E
97 K15 **Forshaga** Värmland, C Sweden 59.33N 13.28E
95 L19 **Forssa** Etelä-Suomi, S Finland 60.49N 23.40E
103 Q14 **Forst** *Lus.* Baršć Łužyca. Brandenburg, E Germany 51.43N 14.38E
191 U7 **Forster-Tuncurry** New South Wales, SE Australia 32.13S 152.31E
25 T4 **Forsyth** Georgia, SE USA 33.00N 83.57W
29 T8 **Forsyth** Missouri, C USA 36.41N 93.07W
35 W10 **Forsyth** Montana, NW USA 46.16N 106.40W
155 U11 **Fort Abbās** Punjab, E Pakistan 29.11N 72.54E
10 G10 **Fort Albany** Ontario, C Canada 52.15N 81.34W
58 L13 **Fortaleza** Pando, N Bolivia 9.48S 65.28W
60 P13 **Fortaleza** *prev.* Ceará. *state capital* Ceará, NE Brazil 3.45S 38.34W
61 D16 **Fortaleza** Rondônia, W Brazil 8.45S 64.06W
58 C13 **Fortaleza, Río** ~ W Peru
Fort-Archambault *see* Sarh
23 U3 **Fort Ashby** West Virginia, NE USA 39.30N 78.46W
98 I9 **Fort Augustus** N Scotland, UK 57.13N 4.37W
Fort-Bayard *see* Zhanjiang
35 S8 **Fort Benton** Montana, NW USA 47.49N 110.40W
37 Q1 **Fort Bidwell** California, W USA 41.50N 120.07W
36 L5 **Fort Bragg** California, W USA 39.25N 123.48W
33 N16 **Fort Branch** Indiana, N USA 38.15N 87.34W
Fort-Bretonnet *see* Bousso
35 T17 **Fort Bridger** Wyoming, C USA 41.18N 110.19W
Fort-Cappolani *see* Tidjikja
Fort Charlet *see* Djanet
Fort-Chimo *see* Kuujjuaq
9 R10 **Fort Chipewyan** Alberta, C Canada 58.42N 111.07W
Fort Cobb Lake *see* Fort Cobb Reservoir
28 L11 **Fort Cobb Reservoir** *var.* Fort Cobb Lake. ▣ Oklahoma, C USA
39 T3 **Fort Collins** Colorado, C USA 40.35N 105.04W
12 K12 **Fort-Coulonge** Québec, SE Canada 45.51N 76.43W
Fort-Crampel *see* Kaga Bandoro
Fort-Dauphin *see* Tôlañaro
26 K10 **Fort Davis** Texas, SW USA 30.34N 103.55W
39 O10 **Fort Defiance** Arizona, SW USA 35.44N 109.04W
47 Q12 **Fort-de-France** *prev.* Fort-Royal. ○ (Martinique) W Martinique 14.36N 61.04W
47 P12 **Fort-de-France, Baie de** *bay* W Martinique
Fort de Kock *see* Bukittinggi
25 P6 **Fort Deposit** Alabama, S USA 31.58N 86.34W
31 U13 **Fort Dodge** Iowa, C USA 42.30N 94.10W
11 S10 **Forteau** Quebec, E Canada 51.30N 56.55W
108 E11 **Forte dei Marmi** Toscana, C Italy 43.59N 10.10E
12 H17 **Fort Erie** Ontario, S Canada 42.55N 78.55W
188 H7 **Fortescue River** ~ Western Australia
21 S2 **Fort Fairfield** Maine, NE USA 46.45N 67.51W
Fort-Foureau *see* Kousséri
10 A11 **Fort Frances** Ontario, S Canada 48.37N 93.22W
Fort Franklin *see* Déljne
25 R7 **Fort Gaines** Georgia, SE USA 31.36N 85.03W
39 T8 **Fort Garland** Colorado, C USA 37.22N 105.24W
23 P5 **Fort Gay** West Virginia, NE USA 38.06N 82.35W
Fort George *see* La Grande Rivière
29 Q10 **Fort Gibson** Oklahoma, C USA 35.48N 95.15W
29 Q9 **Fort Gibson Lake** ▣ Oklahoma, C USA
15 Gg5 **Fort Good Hope** *var.* Good Hope. Northwest Territories, NW Canada 66.16N 128.37W
25 V4 **Fort Gordon** Georgia, SE USA 33.25N 82.09W
Fort Gouraud *see* Fdérik
98 I11 **Forth** ~ C Scotland, UK
Fort Hall *see* Murang'a
26 H8 **Fort Hancock** Texas, SW USA 31.18N 105.49W
Fort Hertz *see* Putao
98 K12 **Forth, Firth of** *estuary* E Scotland, UK
12 L14 **Forthton** Ontario, SE Canada 44.43N 75.31W
12 M8 **Fortier** ~ Québec, SE Canada
Fortín General Eugenio Garay *see* General Eugenio A. Garay
Fort Jameson *see* Chipata
Fort Johnston *see* Mangochi
21 R1 **Fort Kent** Maine, NE USA 47.15N 68.33W
Fort-Lamy *see* Ndjamena
25 Z15 **Fort Lauderdale** Florida, SE USA 26.07N 80.08W
23 R11 **Fort Lawn** South Carolina, SE USA 34.43N 80.46W
15 Gg9 **Fort Liard** *var.* Liard. Northwest Territories, W Canada 60.13N 123.28W
46 M8 **Fort-Liberté** NE Haiti 19.37N 71.51W
23 N9 **Fort Loudoun Lake** ▣ Tennessee, S USA
39 T3 **Fort Lupton** Colorado, C USA 40.04N 104.48W
9 R12 **Fort MacKay** Alberta, C Canada 57.12N 111.40W
9 Q17 **Fort Macleod** *var.* MacLeod. Alberta, SW Canada 49.43N 113.24W
31 Y16 **Fort Madison** Iowa, C USA 40.37N 91.15W
Fort Manning *see* Mchinji
27 P9 **Fort McKavett** Texas, SW USA 30.50N 100.07W
9 R12 **Fort McMurray** Alberta, C Canada 56.43N 111.22W
14 Ff3 **Fort McPherson** *var.* McPherson. Northwest Territories, NW Canada 67.28N 134.49W
23 R11 **Fort Mill** South Carolina, SE USA 35.00N 80.57W
Fort-Millot *see* Ngouri
39 U3 **Fort Morgan** Colorado, C USA 40.13N 103.48W
25 W14 **Fort Myers** Florida, SE USA 26.39N 81.52W
25 W15 **Fort Myers Beach** Florida, SE USA 26.27N 81.57W
8 M10 **Fort Nelson** British Columbia, W Canada 58.48N 122.43W
8 M10 **Fort Nelson** ~ British Columbia, W Canada
Fort Norman *see* Tulita.
25 Q2 **Fort Payne** Alabama, S USA 34.23N 85.43W
35 W7 **Fort Peck** Montana, NW USA 48.00N 106.28W
35 V8 **Fort Peck Lake** ▣ Montana, NW USA
25 Y13 **Fort Pierce** Florida, SE USA 27.28N 80.19W
31 N10 **Fort Pierre** South Dakota, N USA 44.21N 100.22W
83 E18 **Fort Portal** SW Uganda 0.39N 30.16E
15 Hh8 **Fort Providence** *var.* Providence. Northwest Territories, W Canada 61.21N 117.39W
9 U16 **Fort Qu'Appelle** Saskatchewan, S Canada 50.49N 103.52W
Fort-Repoux *see* Akjoujt
15 I8 **Fort Resolution** *var.* Resolution. Northwest Territories, W Canada 61.10N 113.39W
35 T13 **Fortress Mountain** ▲ Wyoming, C USA 44.20N 109.51W
Fort Rosebery *see* Mansa
Fort-Rousset *see* Owando
Fort-Royal *see* Fort-de-France
10 I10 **Fort Rupert** *prev.* Rupert House. Québec, SE Canada 51.30N 79.45W
14 G12 **Fort St.James** British Columbia, SW Canada 54.25N 124.15W
9 N12 **Fort St.John** British Columbia, W Canada 56.16N 120.51W
Fort Sandeman *see* Zhob
9 Q14 **Fort Saskatchewan** Alberta, SW Canada 53.42N 113.12W
29 R6 **Fort Scott** Kansas, C USA 37.49N 94.42W
10 E6 **Fort Severn** Ontario, C Canada 56.00N 87.40W
33 R12 **Fort Shawnee** Ohio, N USA 40.41N 84.08W
150 E14 **Fort-Shevchenko** Mangistau, W Kazakhstan 44.28N 50.16E
Fort-Sibut *see* Sibut
15 H8 **Fort Simpson** *var.* Simpson. Northwest Territories, W Canada 61.52N 121.22W
15 I9 **Fort Smith** *district capital* Northwest Territories, W Canada 60.01N 111.55W
29 R10 **Fort Smith** Arkansas, C USA 35.23N 94.24W
39 T13 **Fort Stanton** New Mexico, SW USA 33.28N 105.31W
26 L9 **Fort Stockton** Texas, SW USA 30.54N 102.54W
39 U12 **Fort Sumner** New Mexico, SW USA 34.28N 104.15W
28 K8 **Fort Supply** Oklahoma, C USA 36.34N 99.34W
28 K8 **Fort Supply Lake** ▣ Oklahoma, C USA
31 O10 **Fort Thompson** South Dakota, N USA 44.01N 99.22W
Fort-Trinquet *see* Bîr Mogreïn
107 R12 **Fortuna** Murcia, SE Spain 38.10N 1.07W
36 K3 **Fortuna** California, W USA 40.35N 124.07W
30 J2 **Fortuna** North Dakota, N USA 48.53N 103.46W
25 T5 **Fort Valley** Georgia, SE USA 32.33N 83.53W
9 P11 **Fort Vermilion** Alberta, W Canada 58.22N 115.58W
Fort Victoria *see* Masvingo
33 P13 **Fortville** Indiana, N USA 39.55N 85.51W
25 P9 **Fort Walton Beach** Florida, SE USA 30.24N 86.37W
33 P12 **Fort Wayne** Indiana, N USA 41.07N 85.07W
98 H10 **Fort William** N Scotland, UK 56.49N 5.07W
27 T6 **Fort Worth** Texas, SW USA 32.43N 97.19W
30 M7 **Fort Yates** North Dakota, N USA 46.05N 100.37W
41 S7 **Fort Yukon** Alaska, USA 66.35N 145.05W
Forum Alieni *see* Ferrara
Forum Julii *see* Fréjus
Forum Livii *see* Forlì
149 Q15 **Forūr, Jazīreh-ye** *island* S Iran
96 H7 **Fosen** *physical region* S Norway
167 N14 **Foshan** *var.* Fatshan, Fo-shan, Namhoi. Guangdong, S China 23.03N 113.05E
Fossa Claudia *see* Chioggia
108 B9 **Fossano** Piemonte, NW Italy 44.33N 7.43E
101 H21 **Fosses-la-Ville** Namur, S Belgium 50.24N 4.42E
34 J12 **Fossil** Oregon, NW USA 44.58N 120.15W
Foss Lake *see* Foss Reservoir
108 I11 **Fossombrone** Marche, C Italy 43.42N 12.48E
28 K10 **Foss Reservoir** *var.* Foss Lake. ▣ Oklahoma, C USA
31 S4 **Fosston** Minnesota, N USA 47.34N 95.45W
191 O13 **Foster** Victoria, SE Australia 38.40S 146.15E
9 T12 **Foster Lakes** ◎ Saskatchewan, C Canada
33 S12 **Fostoria** Ohio, N USA 41.09N 83.25W
81 D19 **Fougamou** Ngounié, C Gabon 1.15S 10.37E
104 J6 **Fougères** Ille-et-Vilaine, NW France 48.21N 1.12W
Fou-hsin *see* Fuxin
29 S14 **Fouke** Arkansas, C USA 33.15N 93.53W
98 K2 **Foula** *island* NE Scotland, UK

◆ Country
● Country Capital
◇ Dependent Territory
○ Dependent Territory Capital
◈ Administrative Region
✕ International Airport
▲ Mountain
▲▲ Mountain Range
Volcano
~ River
◎ Lake
▣ Reservoir

Foul Bay – Gabrovo

67 D24 Foul Bay bay East Falkland, Falkland Islands
99 P21 Foulness Island island SE England, UK
193 F15 Foulwind, Cape headland South Island, NZ 41.45S 171.28E
81 E15 Foumban Ouest, NW Cameroon 5.43N 10.49E
180 H13 Foumbouni Grande Comore, NW Comoros 11.49S 43.30E
205 N8 Foundation Ice Stream glacier Antarctica
39 T6 Fountain Colorado, C USA 38.40N 104.42W
38 L4 Fountain Green Utah, W USA 39.37N 111.37W
23 P11 Fountain Inn South Carolina, SE USA 34.41N 82.12W
29 S11 Fourche LaFave River Arkansas, C USA
35 Z13 Four Corners Wyoming, C USA 44.04N 104.08W
105 Q2 Fourmies Nord, N France 50.01N 4.03E
40 J17 Four Mountains, Islands of island group Aleutian Islands, Alaska, USA
181 P17 Fournaise, Piton de la ▲ SE Réunion 21.13S 55.43E
12 J8 Fournière, Lac ◎ Québec, SE Canada
117 L20 Foúrnoi island Dodekánisa, Greece, Aegean Sea
66 K13 Four North Fracture Zone tectonic feature W Atlantic Ocean
Fouron-Saint-Martin see Sint-Martens-Voeren
32 L3 Fourteen Mile Point headland Michigan, N USA 46.59N 89.07W
78 I13 Fouta Djallon var. Futa Jallon. ▲ W Guinea
193 C25 Foveaux Strait strait S NZ
37 Q11 Fowler California, W USA 36.35N 119.40W
39 U6 Fowler Colorado, C USA 38.07N 104.01W
33 N12 Fowler Indiana, N USA 40.36N 87.20W
190 D7 Fowlers Bay bay South Australia
27 R13 Fowlerton Texas, SW USA 28.27N 98.48W
148 M3 Fowman var. Fuman, Fumen. Gīlān, NW Iran 37.15N 49.19E
67 C25 Fox Bay East West Falkland, Falkland Islands
67 C25 Fox Bay West West Falkland, Falkland Islands
12 J14 Foxboro Ontario, SE Canada 44.16N 77.23W
9 O14 Fox Creek Alberta, W Canada 54.25N 116.57W
66 G5 Foxe Basin sea Nunavut, N Canada
66 G5 Foxe Channel channel Nunavut, N Canada
97 I16 Foxen ◎ C Sweden
16 N4 Foxe Peninsula peninsula Baffin Island, Nunavut, NE Canada
193 E19 Fox Glacier West Coast, South Island, NZ 43.28S 170.00E
40 L17 Fox Islands island Aleutian Islands, Alaska, USA
32 M10 Fox Lake Illinois, N USA 42.24N 88.10W
9 V12 Fox Mine Manitoba, C Canada 56.36N 101.48W
37 R3 Fox Mountain ▲ Nevada, W USA 41.01N 119.30W
67 E25 Fox Point headland East Falkland, Falkland Islands 51.55S 58.24W
32 M11 Fox River Illinois/Wisconsin, N USA
32 L7 Fox River Wisconsin, N USA
192 L13 Foxton Manawatu-Wanganui, North Island, NZ 40.30S 175.17E
9 S16 Fox Valley Saskatchewan, S Canada 50.28N 109.28W
9 W16 Foxwarren Manitoba, S Canada 50.30N 101.09W
99 E14 Foyle, Lough Ir. Loch Feabhail. inlet N Ireland
204 H5 Foyn Coast physical region Antarctica
106 I2 Foz Galicia, NW Spain 43.33N 7.16W
62 I12 Foz do Areia, Represa de ▣ S Brazil
61 A16 Foz do Breu Acre, W Brazil 9.21S 72.40W
85 A16 Foz do Cunene Namibe, SW Angola 17.11S 11.52E
62 G12 Foz do Iguaçu Paraná, S Brazil 25.33S 54.31W
60 C12 Foz do Mamoriá Amazonas, NW Brazil 2.28S 66.06W
107 T6 Fraga Aragón, NE Spain 41.31N 0.21E
46 F5 Fragoso, Cayo island C Cuba
63 G18 Fraile Muerto Cerro Largo, NE Uruguay 32.30S 54.30W
101 H21 Fraire Namur, S Belgium 50.16N 4.30E
101 L21 Fraiture, Baraque de hill SE Belgium 50.22N 5.50E
Frakštát see Hlohovec
207 S10 Fram Basin var. Amundsen Basin. undersea feature Arctic Ocean
101 F20 Frameries Hainaut, S Belgium 50.25N 3.40E
21 O11 Framingham Massachusetts, NE USA 42.15N 71.24W
62 L7 Franca São Paulo, S Brazil 20.33S 47.27W
197 G4 Français, Récif des reef W New Caledonia
109 K14 Francavilla al Mare Abruzzo, C Italy 42.25N 14.16E
109 P18 Francavilla Fontana Puglia, SE Italy 40.31N 17.34E
104 M8 France off. French Republic, It./Sp. Francia; prev. Gaul, Gaule, Lat. Gallia. ◆ republic W Europe
47 O8 Francés Viejo, Cabo headland NE Dominican Republic 19.39N 69.57W
81 F19 Franceville var. Massoukou, Masuku. Haut-Ogooué, E Gabon 1.40S 13.31E
81 F19 Franceville ✈ Haut-Ogooué, E Gabon 1.38S 13.24E
Francfort see Frankfurt am Main
105 T8 Franche-Comté ◆ region E France
Francia see France
31 O11 Francis Case, Lake ▣ South Dakota, N USA
62 H12 Francisco Beltrão Paraná, S Brazil 26.04S 53.04W
Francisco I. Madero see Villa Madero
63 A21 Francisco Madero Buenos Aires, E Argentina 35.52S 62.03W
44 H6 Francisco Morazán prev. Tegucigalpa. ◆ department C Honduras
85 J18 Francistown North East, NE Botswana 21.08S 27.31E
Franconian Forest see Frankenwald
Franconian Jura see Fränkische Alb
100 K6 Franeker Fris. Frjentsjer. Friesland, N Netherlands 53.10N 5.33E
Frankenalb see Fränkische Alb
103 H16 Frankenberg Hessen, C Germany 51.04N 8.49E
103 J20 Frankenhöhe hill range C Germany
33 R8 Frankenmuth Michigan, N USA 43.19N 83.44W
103 F20 Frankenstein hill W Germany 49.24N 8.04E
Frankenstein/Frankenstein in Schlesien see Ząbkowice Śląskie
103 G20 Frankenthal Rheinland-Pfalz, W Germany 49.33N 8.21E
103 L18 Frankenwald Eng. Franconian Forest. ▲ C Germany
46 J12 Frankfield C Jamaica 18.07N 77.22W
12 J14 Frankford Ontario, SE Canada 44.12N 77.36W
33 O13 Frankfort Indiana, N USA 40.16N 86.30W
29 O3 Frankfort Kansas, C USA 39.42N 96.25W
22 L5 Frankfort state capital Kentucky, S USA 38.12N 84.52W
Frankfort on the Main see Frankfurt am Main
Frankfurt see Słubice, Poland
Frankfurt see Frankfurt am Main, Germany
103 G18 Frankfurt am Main var. Frankfurt, Fr. Francfort; prev. Eng. Frankfort on the Main. Hessen, SW Germany 50.07N 8.40E
102 Q12 Frankfurt an der Oder Brandenburg, E Germany 52.19N 14.31E
103 L21 Fränkische Alb var. Frankenalb, Eng. Franconian Jura. ▲ S Germany
103 I18 Fränkische Saale C Germany
103 L19 Fränkische Schweiz hill range C Germany
25 R4 Franklin Georgia, SE USA 33.15N 85.06W
33 P14 Franklin Indiana, N USA 39.28N 86.01W
22 J7 Franklin Kentucky, S USA 36.43N 86.34W
24 I9 Franklin Louisiana, S USA 29.48N 91.30W
31 O17 Franklin Nebraska, C USA 40.06N 98.57W
23 N10 Franklin North Carolina, SE USA 35.07N 83.22W
20 C13 Franklin Pennsylvania, NE USA 41.24N 79.49W
22 J9 Franklin Tennessee, S USA 35.55N 86.52W
27 U9 Franklin Texas, SW USA 31.01N 96.29W
23 X7 Franklin Virginia, NE USA 36.40N 76.55W
23 T4 Franklin West Virginia, NE USA 38.39N 79.19W
32 M9 Franklin Wisconsin, N USA 42.53N 88.00W
15 H2 Franklin Bay inlet Northwest Territories, N Canada
34 K7 Franklin D.Roosevelt Lake ▣ Washington, NW USA
37 W4 Franklin Lake ◎ Nevada, W USA
193 B22 Franklin Mountains ▲ South Island, NZ
41 R5 Franklin Mountains ▲ Alaska, USA
41 N4 Franklin, Point headland Alaska, USA 70.54N 158.48W
191 O17 Franklin River Tasmania, SE Australia
15 K2 Franklin Strait strait Nunavut, N Canada
24 K8 Franklinton Louisiana, S USA 30.51N 90.09W
23 U9 Franklinton North Carolina, SE USA 36.06N 78.27W
Frankstadt see Frenštát pod Radhoštěm
27 V7 Frankston Texas, SW USA 32.03N 95.30W
35 U12 Frannie Wyoming, C USA 44.57N 108.37W
13 U5 Franquelin Québec, SE Canada 49.17N 67.52W
13 U5 Franquelin Québec, SE Canada
85 C18 Fransfontein Kunene, NW Namibia 20.10S 15.03E
95 H17 Fränsta Västernorrland, C Sweden 62.30N 16.06E
126 H1 Frantsa-Iosifa, Zemlya Eng. Franz Josef Land. island group N Russian Federation
193 E18 Franz Josef Glacier West Coast, South Island, NZ 43.22S 170.11E
Franz Josef Land see Frantsa-Iosifa, Zemlya
Franz-Josef Spitze see Gerlachovský štít
103 L23 Franz Josef Strauss abbrev. F.J.S. ✈ (München) Bayern, SE Germany 48.07N 11.43E
109 A19 Frasca, Capo della headland Sardegna, Italy, C Mediterranean Sea 39.46N 8.27E
109 I15 Frascati Lazio, C Italy 41.48N 12.40E
9 N14 Fraser British Columbia, SW Canada
85 G24 Fraserburg Western Cape, SW South Africa 31.49S 21.29E
98 L8 Fraserburgh NE Scotland, UK 57.41N 2.19W
189 Z9 Fraser Island var. Great Sandy Island. island Queensland, E Australia
8 L14 Fraser Lake British Columbia, SW Canada 54.00N 124.45W
8 L15 Fraser Plateau plateau British Columbia, SW Canada
192 P10 Frasertown Hawke's Bay, North Island, NZ 38.58S 177.25E
101 E19 Frasnes-lez-Buissenal Hainaut, SW Belgium 50.40N 3.37E
110 I7 Frastanz Vorarlberg, NW Austria 47.13N 9.37E
12 B8 Frater Ontario, S Canada 47.19N 84.28W
Frauenbach see Baia Mare
Frauenburg see Saldus, Latvia
Frauenburg see Frombork, Poland
110 H6 Frauenfeld Thurgau, NE Switzerland 47.34N 8.54E
111 Z5 Frauenkirchen Burgenland, E Austria 47.49N 16.57E
63 D19 Fray Bentos Río Negro, W Uruguay 33.09S 58.14W
63 F19 Fray Marcos Florida, S Uruguay 34.13S 55.43W
31 S6 Frazee Minnesota, N USA 46.42N 95.40W
106 M5 Frechilla Castilla-León, N Spain 42.07N 4.49W
32 I4 Frederic Wisconsin, N USA 45.42N 92.30W
97 G23 Fredericia Vejle, C Denmark 55.34N 9.46E
23 W3 Frederick Maryland, NE USA 39.24N 77.24W
28 L12 Frederick Oklahoma, C USA 34.23N 99.01W
31 P7 Frederick South Dakota, N USA 45.49N 98.31W
31 X12 Fredericksburg Iowa, C USA 42.58N 92.12W
27 R10 Fredericksburg Texas, SW USA 30.16N 98.52W
23 W5 Fredericksburg Virginia, NE USA 38.16N 77.27W
41 X13 Frederick Sound sound Alaska, USA
29 X6 Fredericktown Missouri, C USA 37.33N 90.17W
62 H13 Frederico Westphalen Rio Grande do Sul, S Brazil 27.22S 53.20W
11 O15 Fredericton New Brunswick, SE Canada 45.57N 66.40W
97 I22 Frederiksborg off. Frederiksborgs Amt. ◆ county E Denmark
Frederikshåb see Paamiut
97 H19 Frederikshavn prev. Fladstrand. Nordjylland, N Denmark 57.28N 10.33E
97 J22 Frederikssund Frederiksborg, E Denmark 55.51N 12.04E
47 T9 Frederiksted Saint Croix, S Virgin Islands (US) 17.41N 64.51W
97 I22 Frederiksværk var. Frederiksværk og Hanehoved. Frederiksborg, E Denmark 55.58N 12.01E
Frederiksværk og Hanehoved see Frederiksværk
56 E9 Fredonia Antioquia, W Colombia 5.57N 75.42W
38 K8 Fredonia Arizona, SW USA 36.57N 112.31W
29 P7 Fredonia Kansas, C USA 37.31N 95.49W
20 C11 Fredonia New York, NE USA 42.26N 79.19W
37 P4 Fredonyer Pass pass California, W USA 40.21N 120.52W
95 I15 Fredrika Västerbotten, N Sweden 64.03N 18.25E
97 L14 Fredriksberg Dalarna, C Sweden 60.07N 14.22E
Fredrikshald see Halden
Fredrikshamn see Hamina
97 H16 Fredrikstad Østfold, S Norway 59.12N 10.57E
32 K16 Freeburg Illinois, N USA 38.25N 89.54W
20 K15 Freehold New Jersey, NE USA 40.14N 74.14W
20 H14 Freeland Pennsylvania, NE USA 41.01N 75.54W
190 J5 Freeling Heights ▲ South Australia 30.09S 139.24E
37 Q7 Freel Peak ▲ California, W USA 38.52N 119.52W
16 T7 Freels, Cape headland Newfoundland and Labrador, E Canada 49.16N 53.30W
31 Q11 Freeman South Dakota, N USA 43.21N 97.26W
46 G1 Freeport Grand Bahama Island, N Bahamas 26.28N 78.43W
32 L10 Freeport Illinois, N USA 42.18N 89.37W
27 W12 Freeport Texas, SW USA 28.57N 95.21W
46 G1 Freeport ✈ Grand Bahama Island, N Bahamas 26.31N 78.48W
27 R14 Freer Texas, SW USA 27.52N 98.37W
85 I22 Free State off. Free State Province; prev. Orange Free State, Afr. Oranje Vrystaat. ◆ province C South Africa
Free State see Maryland
78 G15 Freetown ● (Sierra Leone) W Sierra Leone 8.27N 13.16W
180 J16 Frégate island Inner Islands, NE Seychelles
106 J12 Fregenal de la Sierra Extremadura, W Spain 38.10N 6.39W
190 C2 Fregon South Australia 26.44S 132.03E
104 H5 Fréhel, Cap headland NW France 48.41N 2.21W
96 F8 Frei Møre og Romsdal, S Norway 63.02N 7.47E
103 O16 Freiberg Sachsen, E Germany 50.55N 13.21E
103 O16 Freiberger Mulde E Germany
Freiburg see Fribourg, Switzerland
Freiburg see Freiburg im Breisgau, Germany
103 F23 Freiburg im Breisgau var. Freiburg, Fr. Fribourg-en-Brisgau. Baden-Württemberg, SW Germany 48.00N 7.52E
Freiburg in Schlesien see Świebodzice
Freie Hansestadt Bremen see Bremen
Freie und Hansestadt Hamburg see Brandenburg
103 L22 Freising Bayern, SE Germany 48.24N 11.45E
111 T3 Freistadt Oberösterreich, N Austria 48.30N 14.27E
Freistadtl see Hlohovec
103 O16 Freital Sachsen, E Germany 51.00N 13.40E
Freiwaldau see Jeseník
106 J6 Freixo de Espada à Cinta Bragança, N Portugal 41.04N 6.49W
105 U15 Fréjus anc. Forum Julii. Var, SE France 43.25N 6.43E
188 I13 Fremantle Western Australia 32.07S 115.43E
37 N9 Fremont California, W USA 37.32N 121.56W
33 Q11 Fremont Indiana, N USA 41.43N 84.54W
31 W15 Fremont Iowa, C USA 41.12N 92.26W
33 P8 Fremont Michigan, N USA 43.28N 85.56W
31 R15 Fremont Nebraska, C USA 41.25N 96.30W
33 S11 Fremont Ohio, N USA 41.21N 83.07W
35 T14 Fremont Peak ▲ Wyoming, C USA 43.07N 109.37W
38 M6 Fremont River Utah, W USA
23 O9 French Broad River Tennessee, S USA
23 N5 Frenchburg Kentucky, S USA 37.57N 83.41W
20 C12 French Creek Pennsylvania, NE USA
34 K15 Frenchglen Oregon, NW USA 42.49N 118.55W
57 Y10 French Guiana var. Guiana, Guyane. ◇ French overseas department N South America
French Guinea see Guinea
33 O15 French Lick Indiana, N USA 38.33N 86.37W
193 J14 French Pass Marlborough, South Island, NZ 40.57S 173.49E
203 T11 French Polynesia ◇ French overseas territory C Polynesia
French Republic see France
12 F11 French River Ontario, S Canada
French Somaliland see Djibouti
181 P12 French Southern and Antarctic Territories Fr. Terres Australes et Antarctiques Françaises. ◇ French overseas territory S Indian Ocean
French Sudan see Mali
French Territory of the Afars and Issas see Djibouti
French Togoland see Togo
76 J6 Frenda NW Algeria 35.06N 1.03E
113 I18 Frenštát pod Radhoštěm Ger. Frankstadt. Moravskoslezský Kraj E Czech Republic 49.33N 18.10E
78 M17 Fresco S Ivory Coast 5.05N 5.34W
205 U16 Freshfield, Cape headland Antarctica
42 L10 Fresnillo var. Fresnillo de González Echeverría. Zacatecas, C Mexico 23.10N 102.52W
Fresnillo de González Echeverría see Fresnillo
37 Q10 Fresno California, W USA 36.44N 119.48W
Freu, Cabo del see Freu, Cap des
107 Y9 Freu, Cap des var. Cabo del Freu. headland Mallorca, Spain, W Mediterranean Sea 39.44N 3.28E
103 G22 Freudenstadt Baden-Württemberg, SW Germany 48.28N 8.25E
Freudenthal see Bruntál
191 Q17 Freycinet Peninsula peninsula Tasmania, SE Australia
78 H14 Fria W Guinea 10.27N 13.37W
85 A17 Fria, Cape headland NW Namibia 18.32S 12.00E
37 Q10 Friant California, W USA 36.56N 119.44W
64 K8 Frías Catamarca, N Argentina 28.40S 65.00W
110 D9 Fribourg Ger. Freiburg. Fribourg, W Switzerland 46.49N 7.10E
110 C9 Fribourg Ger. Freiburg. ◆ canton W Switzerland
Fribourg-en-Brisgau see Freiburg im Breisgau
34 G7 Friday Harbor San Juan Islands, Washington, NW USA 48.31N 123.01W
Friedau see Ormož
103 K23 Friedberg Bayern, S Germany 48.21N 10.58E
103 H18 Friedberg Hessen, W Germany 50.19N 8.46E
Friedeberg Neumark see Strzelce Krajeńskie
Friedek-Mistek see Frýdek-Místek
Friedland see Pravdinsk
103 I24 Friedrichshafen Baden-Württemberg, S Germany 47.39N 9.28E
Friedrichstadt see Jaunjelgava
31 Q16 Friend Nebraska, C USA 40.37N 97.16W
Friendly Islands see Tonga
57 V9 Friendship Coronie, N Surinam 5.49N 56.16W
32 L7 Friendship Wisconsin, N USA 43.58N 89.48W
111 T8 Friesach Kärnten, S Austria 46.58N 14.24E
Friesche Eilanden see Frisian Islands
103 F22 Friesenheim Baden-Württemberg, SW Germany 48.27N 7.56E
Friesische Inseln see Frisian Islands
100 K6 Friesland ◆ province N Netherlands
62 Q10 Frio, Cabo headland SE Brazil 23.01S 41.59W
26 M3 Friona Texas, SW USA 34.38N 102.43W
44 L12 Frío, Río N Costa Rica
27 R13 Frio River Texas, SW USA
101 M25 Frisange Luxembourg, S Luxembourg 49.31N 6.12E
Frisches Haff see Vistula Lagoon
38 J6 Frisco Peak ▲ Utah, W USA 38.31N 113.17W
86 F9 Frisian Islands Dut. Friesche Eilanden, Ger. Friesische Inseln. island group N Europe
20 L12 Frissell, Mount ▲ Connecticut, NE USA 42.01N 73.25W
97 J19 Fristad Västra Götaland, S Sweden 57.49N 13.01E
27 N2 Fritch Texas, SW USA 35.38N 101.36W
97 J19 Fritsla Västra Götaland, S Sweden 57.33N 12.46E
103 H16 Fritzlar Hessen, C Germany 51.09N 9.16E
108 H6 Friuli-Venezia Giulia ◆ region NE Italy
Frjentsjer see Franeker
206 L13 Frobisher Bay inlet Baffin Island, Nunavut, NE Canada
Frobisher Bay see Iqaluit
9 S12 Frobisher Lake ◎ Saskatchewan, C Canada
96 G7 Frohavet sound C Norway
Frohenbruck see Veselí nad Lužnicí
111 V7 Frohnleiten Steiermark, SE Austria 47.16N 15.19E
101 G22 Froidchapelle Hainaut, S Belgium 50.10N 4.18E
131 O9 Frolovo Volgogradskaya Oblast', SW Russian Federation 49.46N 43.38E
112 K7 Frombork Ger. Frauenburg. Warmińsko-Mazurskie, NE Poland 54.21N 19.40E
99 L22 Frome SW England, UK 51.15N 2.21W
190 I4 Frome Creek seasonal river South Australia
190 J6 Frome Downs South Australia 31.17S 139.48E
190 J5 Frome, Lake salt lake South Australia
Fronicken see Wronki
106 H10 Fronteira Portalegre, C Portugal 39.03N 7.39W
42 M7 Frontera Coahuila de Zaragoza, NE Mexico 26.55N 101.27W
43 U14 Frontera Tabasco, SE Mexico 18.32N 92.35W
42 G3 Fronteras Sonora, NW Mexico 30.51N 109.36W
105 Q16 Frontignan Hérault, S France 43.27N 3.45E
56 D8 Frontino Antioquia, NW Colombia 6.46N 76.10W
23 V4 Front Royal Virginia, NE USA 38.52N 78.09W
109 J16 Frosinone anc. Frusino. Lazio, C Italy 41.37N 13.19E
109 K16 Frosolone Molise, C Italy 41.34N 14.25E
27 U7 Frost Texas, SW USA 32.04N 96.48W
23 U2 Frostburg Maryland, NE USA 39.39N 78.55W
25 X13 Frostproof Florida, SE USA 27.45N 81.31W
Frostviken see Kvarnbergsvattnet
97 M15 Frövi Örebro, C Sweden 59.28N 15.24E
96 F7 Frøya island W Norway
39 P5 Fruita Colorado, C USA 39.10N 108.42W
30 J9 Fruitdale South Dakota, N USA 44.39N 103.38W
25 W11 Fruitland Park Florida, SE USA 28.51N 81.54W
Frumentum see Formentera
153 S11 Frunze Batkenskaya Oblast', SW Kyrgyzstan 40.07N 71.40E
Frunze see Bishkek
119 O9 Frunzivka Odes'ka Oblast', SW Ukraine 47.19N 29.46E
Frusino see Frosinone
110 E9 Frutigen Bern, W Switzerland 46.35N 7.38E
113 I17 Frýdek-Místek Ger. Friedek-Mistek. Moravskoslezský Kraj, E Czech Republic 49.40N 18.22E
200 Qq16 Fua'amotu Tongatapu, S Tonga 21.15S 175.08W
202 A9 Fuafatu island Funafuti Atoll, C Tuvalu
202 A9 Fuagea island Funafuti Atoll, C Tuvalu
202 B8 Fualifeke atoll C Tuvalu
202 A8 Fualopa island Funafuti Atoll, C Tuvalu
157 K22 Fuammulah var. Gnaviyani Atoll. atoll S Maldives
167 R11 Fu'an Fujian, SE China 27.11N 119.42E
Fu-chien see Fujian
Fu-chou see Fuzhou
170 F13 Fuchū var. Hutyû. Hiroshima, Honshū, SW Japan 34.33N 133.16E
166 M13 Fuchuan Guangxi Zhuangzu Zizhiqu, S China 24.56N 111.15E
172 N11 Fudai Iwate, Honshū, C Japan 39.59N 141.50E
167 S11 Fuding var. Tongshan. Fujian, SE China 27.21N 120.10E
83 J20 Fudua spring/well S Kenya 2.13S 39.43E
106 M16 Fuengirola Andalucía, S Spain 36.31N 4.37W
106 J12 Fuente de Cantos Extremadura, W Spain 38.15N 6.18W
106 J11 Fuente del Maestre Extremadura, W Spain 38.31N 6.26W
106 L12 Fuente Obejuna Andalucía, S Spain 38.15N 5.25W
106 L6 Fuentesaúco Castilla-León, N Spain 41.13N 5.30W
64 O3 Fuerte Olimpo var. Olimpo. Alto Paraguay, NE Paraguay 21.01S 57.51W
42 H8 Fuerte, Río C Mexico
66 Q11 Fuerteventura island Islas Canarias, Spain, NE Atlantic Ocean
147 S14 Fughmah var. Faghman, Fugma. C Yemen 16.07N 49.22E
94 M2 Fuglehuken headland W Svalbard 78.54N 10.30E
97 B18 Fugloy Dan. Fuglø Island Faeroe Islands 62.21N 6.16W
207 T15 Fugløya Bank undersea feature E Norwegian Sea
166 E11 Fugong Yunnan, SW China 27.00N 98.48E
Fugma see Fughmah
83 K16 Fugugo spring/well NE Kenya 3.19N 39.39E
164 L2 Fuhai var. Burultokay. Xinjiang Uygur Zizhiqu, NW China 47.15N 87.39E
167 P10 Fu He S China
Fuhkien see Fujian
102 J9 Fuhlsbüttel ✈ (Hamburg) Hamburg, N Germany 53.37N 9.57E
103 L14 Fuhne C Germany
Fu-hsin see Fuxin
Fujairah see Al Fujayrah
171 J17 Fuji var. Huzi. Shizuoka, Honshū, S Japan 35.08N 138.39E
167 Q12 Fujian var. Fu-chien, Fuhkien, Fujian Sheng, Fukien, Min. ◆ province SE China
166 I9 Fu Jiang C China
Fujian Sheng see Fujian
171 Ii17 Fujieda var. Huzieda. Shizuoka, Honshū, S Japan 34.54N 138.15E
Fuji, Mount/Fujiyama see Fuji-san
169 Y7 Fujin Heilongjiang, NE China 47.12N 132.01E
171 J16 Fujinomiya var. Huzinomiya. Shizuoka, Honshū, S Japan 35.19N 138.34E
171 J16 Fuji-san var. Fujiyama, Eng. Mount Fuji. ▲ Honshū, SE Japan 35.23N 138.44E
171 Jj17 Fujisawa var. Huzisawa. Kanagawa, Honshū, S Japan 35.22N 139.28E
171 J16 Fuji-Yoshida var. Huziyosida. Yamanashi, Honshū, S Japan 35.30N 138.48E
172 Oo4 Fukagawa var. Hukagawa. Hokkaidō, NE Japan 43.44N 142.01E
164 L5 Fukang Xinjiang Uygur Zizhiqu, W China 44.07N 87.55E
171 M8 Fukaura Aomori, Honshū, C Japan 40.38N 139.55E
200 R15 Fukave island Tongatapu Group, S Tonga
Fukien see Fujian
171 Gg14 Fukuchiyama var. Hukutiyama. Kyōto, Honshū, SW Japan 35.16N 135.07E
170 B12 Fukue var. Hukue. Nagasaki, Fukue-jima, SW Japan 32.40N 128.46E
170 B12 Fukue-jima island Gotō-rettō, SW Japan
171 Hh13 Fukui var. Hukui. Fukui, Honshū, SW Japan 36.03N 136.12E
171 Hh14 Fukui off. Fukui-ken, var. Hukui. ◆ prefecture Honshū, SW Japan
170 C12 Fukuoka var. Hukuoka; hist. Najima. Fukuoka, Kyūshū, SW Japan 33.36N 130.24E
170 Cc13 Fukuoka off. Fukuoka-ken, var. Hukuoka. ◆ prefecture Kyūshū, SW Japan
171 L13 Fukushima var. Hukusima. Fukushima, Honshū, C Japan 37.46N 140.27E
171 Mm7 Fukushima Hokkaidō, NE Japan 41.27N 140.14E
171 Kk14 Fukushima off. Fukushima-ken, var. Hukusima. ◆ prefecture Honshū, C Japan
170 F14 Fukuyama var. Hukuyama. Hiroshima, Honshū, SW Japan 34.28N 133.23E
78 G13 Fulacunda C Guinea-Bissau 11.46N 15.09W
133 P8 Fūlādī, Kūh-e ▲ E Afghanistan 34.37N 67.31E
197 K16 Fulaga island Lau Group, E Fiji
103 I17 Fulda Hessen, C Germany 50.33N 9.40E
31 S10 Fulda Minnesota, N USA 43.52N 95.36W
103 I16 Fulda C Germany
Fülek see Fil'akovo
Fulin see Hanyuan
166 K10 Fuling Chongqing Shi, C China 29.45N 107.23E
37 T15 Fullerton California, SE USA 33.52N 117.55W
31 P15 Fullerton Nebraska, C USA 41.21N 97.58W
110 M8 Fulpmes Tirol, W Austria 47.11N 11.22E
22 G8 Fulton Kentucky, S USA 36.31N 88.52W
25 N2 Fulton Mississippi, S USA 34.16N 88.24W
29 V4 Fulton Missouri, C USA 38.51N 91.57W
20 H9 Fulton New York, NE USA 43.18N 76.22W
Fuman/Fumen see Fowman
105 R3 Fumay Ardennes, N France 49.58N 4.42E
104 M13 Fumel Lot-et-Garonne, SW France 44.31N 0.58E
171 K17 Funabashi var. Hunabasi. Chiba, Honshū, S Japan 35.40N 139.57E
202 B10 Funafara atoll C Tuvalu
202 C9 Funafuti ✈ Funafuti Atoll, C Tuvalu 8.30S 179.12E
Funafuti see Fongafale
202 F8 Funafuti Atoll atoll C Tuvalu
202 B9 Funangongo atoll C Tuvalu
95 F17 Funäsdalen Jämtland, C Sweden 62.33N 12.33E
66 O6 Funchal Madeira, Portugal, NE Atlantic Ocean 32.40N 16.55W
66 P5 Funchal ✈ Madeira, Portugal, NE Atlantic Ocean 32.37N 16.52W
56 F5 Fundación Magdalena, N Colombia 10.28N 74.10W
106 I8 Fundão var. Fundão. Castelo Branco, C Portugal 40.07N 7.30W
11 O16 Fundy, Bay of bay Canada/USA
Fünen see Fyn
56 C13 Fúnes Nariño, SW Colombia 0.58N 77.27W
Fünfkirchen see Pécs
85 M19 Funhalouro Inhambane, S Mozambique 23.04S 34.24E
167 R6 Funing Jiangsu, E China 33.43N 119.47E
166 I14 Funing var. Xinhua. Yunnan, SW China 23.39N 105.41E
166 M7 Funiu Shan ▲ C China
79 U13 Funtua Katsina, N Nigeria 11.31N 7.19E
167 R12 Fuqing Fujian, SE China 25.40N 119.23E
85 M14 Furancungo Tete, NW Mozambique 14.49S 33.32E
172 P5 Furano var. Hurano. Hokkaidō, NE Japan 43.22N 142.25E
118 I15 Furculeşti Teleorman, S Romania 43.51N 25.07E
Füred see Balatonfüred
172 Qq7 Füren-ko ◎ Hokkaidō, NE Japan
149 R12 Fūrg Fārs, S Iran 28.16N 55.13E
Furluk see Fârliug
Fürmanov/Furmanovka see Moyynkum
Furmanovo see Zhalpaktal
61 L20 Furnas, Represa de ▣ SE Brazil
191 Q14 Furneaux Group island group Tasmania, SE Australia
Furnes see Veurne
166 J10 Furong Jiang S China
144 I5 Furqlus Ḥimṣ, W Syria 34.40N 37.02E
102 F12 Fürstenau Niedersachsen, NW Germany 52.30N 7.40E
111 X8 Fürstenfeld Steiermark, SE Austria 47.03N 16.01E
103 L23 Fürstenfeldbruck Bayern, S Germany 48.10N 11.16E
102 P12 Fürstenwalde Brandenburg, NE Germany 52.22N 14.04E
103 K20 Fürth Bayern, S Germany 49.28N 10.58E
111 W3 Furth bei Göttweig Niederösterreich, NW Austria 48.22N 15.33E
172 O4 Furubira Hokkaidō, NE Japan 43.14N 140.38E
96 L12 Furudal Dalarna, C Sweden 61.10N 15.07E
171 Ii14 Furukawa Gifu, Honshū, SW Japan 36.13N 137.11E
171 M12 Furukawa var. Hurukawa. Miyagi, Honshū, C Japan 38.36N 140.56E
56 F10 Fusagasugá Cundinamarca, C Colombia 4.22N 74.21W
Fusan see Pusan
Fushë-Arëzi/Fushë-Arrësi see Fushë-Arrëz
115 L18 Fushë-Arrëz var. Fushë-Arëzi, Fushë-Arrësi. Shkodër, N Albania 42.05N 20.01E
Fushë-Kruja see Fushë-Krujë
115 K19 Fushë-Krujë var. Fushë-Kruja. Durrës, C Albania 41.30N 19.43E
169 V12 Fushun var. Fou-shan, Fu-shun. Liaoning, NE China 41.49N 123.54E
Fusin see Fuxin
110 G10 Fusio Ticino, S Switzerland 46.27N 8.39E
169 X11 Fusong Jilin, NE China 42.19N 127.16E
103 K24 Füssen Bayern, S Germany 47.34N 10.42E
166 K15 Fusui prev. Funan. Guangxi Zhuangzu Zizhiqu, S China 22.39N 107.49E
Futa Jallon see Fouta Djallon
65 G18 Futaleufú Los Lagos, S Chile 43.12S 71.53W
114 K10 Futog Serbia, NW Serbia 45.15N 19.43E
171 K17 Futtsu var. Huttu. Chiba, Honshū, S Japan 35.11N 139.52E
197 E16 Futuna island S Vanuatu
202 D12 Futuna, Île island S Wallis and Futuna
167 Q11 Futun Xi SE China
166 L5 Fuxian var. Fu Xian. Shaanxi, C China 36.03N 109.19E
Fuxian see Wafangdian
166 G13 Fuxian Hu ▣ SW China
169 U12 Fuxin var. Fou-hsin, Fu-hsin, Fusin. Liaoning, NE China 41.59N 121.39E
Fuxing see Wangmo
167 P7 Fuyang Anhui, E China 32.54N 115.47E
167 O4 Fuyang He E China
169 U7 Fuyu Heilongjiang, NE China 47.48N 124.25E
Fuyu/Fu-yü see Songyuan
169 Z6 Fuyuan Heilongjiang, NE China 48.20N 134.22E
164 M3 Fuyun var. Koktokay. Xinjiang Uygur Zizhiqu, NW China 46.57N 89.29E
113 L22 Füzesabony Heves, E Hungary 47.44N 20.23E
167 R12 Fuzhou var. Foochow, Fu-chou. Fujian, SE China 26.09N 119.16E
167 P11 Fuzhou prev. Linchuan. Jiangxi, S China 27.58N 116.19E
143 W13 Füzuli Rus. Fizuli. SW Azerbaijan 39.33N 47.09E
121 I20 Fyadory Rus. Fëdory. Brestskaya Voblasts', SW Belarus 51.56N 26.21E
97 G24 Fyn off. Fyns Amt, var. Fünen. ◆ county C Denmark
97 G23 Fyn Ger. Fünen. island C Denmark
98 H12 Fyne, Loch inlet W Scotland, UK
97 E16 Fyresvatn ◎ S Norway
FYR Macedonia/FYROM see Macedonia, FYR
Fyzabad see Feyẓābād

G

83 O14 Gaalkacyo var. Galka'yo, It. Galcaio. Mudug, C Somalia 6.42N 47.24E
152 J11 Gabakly Rus. Kabakly. Lebap Welaýaty, NE Turkmenistan 39.45N 62.30E
116 H8 Gabare Vratsa, NW Bulgaria 43.20N 23.57E
104 K15 Gabas SW France
Gabasumdo see Tongde
37 T7 Gabbs Nevada, W USA 38.51N 117.55W
84 B12 Gabela Cuanza Sul, W Angola 10.49S 14.21E
Gaberones see Gaborone
201 X14 Gabert island Caroline Islands, E Micronesia
76 M7 Gabès var. Qābis. E Tunisia 33.53N 10.03E
76 M6 Gabès, Golfe de Ar. Khalīj Qābis. gulf E Tunisia
Gablonz an der Neisse see Jablonec nad Nisou
Gablös see Cavalese
81 E18 Gabon off. Gabonese Republic. ◆ republic C Africa
85 I20 Gaborone prev. Gaberones. ● (Botswana) South East, SE Botswana 24.42S 25.49E
85 I20 Gaborone ✈ South East, SE Botswana 24.45S 25.49E
106 K8 Gabriel y Galán, Embalse de ▣ W Spain
149 U15 Gābrīk, Rūd-e SE Iran
116 J9 Gabrovo Gabrovo, N Bulgaria 42.54N 25.19E

◆ Country ● Country Capital ◇ Dependent Territory ○ Dependent Territory Capital ◆ Administrative Region ✈ International Airport ▲ Mountain ▲ Mountain Range Volcano River ◎ Lake ▣ Reservoir
257

◆ COUNTRY	◇ DEPENDENT TERRITORY	■ ADMINISTRATIVE REGION	▲ MOUNTAIN	▲ VOLCANO	☉ LAKE
● COUNTRY CAPITAL	○ DEPENDENT TERRITORY CAPITAL	✕ INTERNATIONAL AIRPORT	▲ MOUNTAIN RANGE	☒ RIVER	▣ RESERVOIR

GEDSER – GLAMSBJERG

97 I25 **Gedser** Storstrøm, SE Denmark 54.34N 11.57E
101 I16 **Geel** *var.* Gheel. Antwerpen, N Belgium 51.10N 4.58E
191 N13 **Geelong** Victoria, SE Australia 38.09S 144.20E
Ge'e'mu *see* Golmud
101 I14 **Geertruidenberg** Noord-Brabant, S Netherlands 51.43N 4.52E
102 H10 **Geeste** ~ NW Germany
102 J10 **Geesthacht** Schleswig-Holstein, N Germany 53.25N 10.22E
191 P17 **Geeveston** Tasmania, SE Australia 43.12S 146.54E
Gefle *see* Gävle
Gefleborg *see* Gävleborg
164 G13 **Gê'gyai** Xizang Zizhiqu, W China 32.28N 81.03E
79 X12 **Geidam** Yobe, NE Nigeria 12.52N 11.55E
9 T11 **Geikie** ~ Saskatchewan, C Canada
96 F13 **Geilo** Buskerud, S Norway 60.31N 8.13E
96 E10 **Geiranger** Møre og Romsdal, S Norway 62.07N 7.12E
103 I22 **Geislingen** *var.* Geislingen an der Steige. Baden-Württemberg, SW Germany 48.35N 9.52E
Geislingen an der Steige *see* Geislingen
83 F20 **Geita** Mwanza, NW Tanzania 2.52S 32.12E
97 G15 **Geithus** Buskerud, S Norway 59.55N 9.57E
166 H14 **Gejiu** *var.* Kochiu. Yunnan, S China 23.21N 103.07E
Gëkdepe *see* Gökdepe
152 E9 **Geklengkui, Solonchak** *var.* Solonchak Goklenkuy. *salt marsh* NW Turkmenistan
83 D14 **Gel** ~ W Sudan
109 K25 **Gela** *prev.* Terranova di Sicilia. Sicilia, Italy, C Mediterranean Sea 37.04N 14.15E
165 N13 **Géladaindong** ▲ C China 33.24N 91.00E
83 N14 **Geladī** Somali, E Ethiopia 6.58N 46.24E
174 Kk11 **Gelam, Pulau** *var.* Pulau Galam. *island* N Indonesia
Gelaozu Miaozu Zizhixian *see* Wuchuan
100 L11 **Gelderland** *prev. Eng.* Guelders. ◆ *province* E Netherlands
100 J13 **Geldermalsen** Gelderland, C Netherlands 51.52N 5.16E
103 D14 **Geldern** Nordrhein-Westfalen, W Germany 51.31N 6.19E
101 K15 **Geldrop** Noord-Brabant, SE Netherlands 51.25N 5.31E
101 L17 **Geleen** Limburg, SE Netherlands 50.57N 5.49E
130 K14 **Gelendzhik** Krasnodarskiy Kray, SW Russian Federation 44.34N 38.06E
Gelib *see* Jilib
142 B11 **Gelibolu** *Eng.* Gallipoli. Çanakkale, NW Turkey 40.25N 26.40E
117 L14 **Gelibolu Yarımadası** *Eng.* Gallipoli Peninsula. *peninsula* NW Turkey
Gelinting, Teluk *see* Geliting, Teluk
175 Qq16 **Geliting, Teluk** *var.* Teluk Gelinting. *bay* Nusa Tenggara, S Indonesia
83 O14 **Gellinsor** Mudug, C Somalia 6.25N 46.44E
103 H18 **Gelnhausen** Hessen, C Germany 50.12N 9.12E
103 E14 **Gelsenkirchen** Nordrhein-Westfalen, W Germany 51.33N 7.06E
85 C20 **Geluk** Hardap, SW Namibia 24.35S 15.48E
101 H20 **Gembloux** Namur, Belgium 50.34N 4.42E
194 I12 **Gembogl** Chimbu, C PNG 5.52S 145.06E
81 J16 **Gemena** Equateur, NW Dem. Rep. Congo 3.13N 19.49E
101 L14 **Gemert** Noord-Brabant, SE Netherlands 51.33N 5.40E
142 E11 **Gemlik** Bursa, NW Turkey 40.25N 29.10E
Gem of the Mountains *see* Idaho
108 J6 **Gemona del Friuli** Friuli-Venezia Giulia, NE Italy 46.18N 13.11E
Gem State *see* Idaho
Genalē Wenz *see* Juba
174 Ll7 **Genali, Danau** ◎ Borneo, N Indonesia
101 G19 **Genappe** Wallon Brabant, C Belgium 50.39N 4.27E
143 P14 **Genç** Bingöl, E Turkey 38.45N 40.31E
Genck *see* Genk
100 M9 **Genemuiden** Overijssel, E Netherlands 52.38N 6.03E
65 K14 **General Acha** La Pampa, C Argentina 37.24S 64.34W
63 C21 **General Alvear** Buenos Aires, E Argentina 36.03S 60.01W
64 I12 **General Alvear** Mendoza, W Argentina 34.58S 67.40W
63 B20 **General Arenales** Buenos Aires, E Argentina 34.21S 61.19W
63 D21 **General Belgrano** Buenos Aires, E Argentina 35.46S 58.30W
204 H3 **General Bernardo O'Higgins** *Chilean research station* Antarctica 63.09S 57.13W
43 O8 **General Bravo** Nuevo León, NE Mexico 25.47N 99.04W
64 M7 **General Capdevila** Chaco, N Argentina 27.25S 61.30W
General Carrera, Lago *see* Buenos Aires, Lago
43 N9 **General Cepeda** Coahuila de Zaragoza, NE Mexico 25.18N 101.24W
65 K15 **General Conesa** Río Negro, E Argentina 40.07S 64.32W
63 G18 **General Enrique Martínez** Treinta y Tres, E Uruguay 33.13S 53.46W
64 L3 **General Eugenio A. Garay** *var.* Fortín General Eugenio Garay; *prev.* Yrendagüé. Nueva Asunción, NW Paraguay 20.31S 62.09W
63 C18 **General Galarza** Entre Ríos, E Argentina 32.43S 59.24W
63 E22 **General Guido** Buenos Aires, E Argentina 36.36S 57.45W
General José F.Uriburu *see* Zárate
63 E22 **General Juan Madariaga** Buenos Aires, E Argentina 37.02S 57.06W
43 O16 **General Juan N Alvarez** ✕ (Acapulco) Guerrero, S Mexico 16.47N 99.47W
63 B22 **General La Madrid** Buenos Aires, E Argentina 37.13S 61.10W
63 E21 **General Lavalle** Buenos Aires, E Argentina 36.25S 56.55W
General Machado *see* Camacupa
64 I8 **General Manuel Belgrano, Cerro** ▲ W Argentina 29.05S 67.05W
43 O8 **General Mariano Escobero** ✕ (Monterrey) Nuevo León, NE Mexico 25.47N 100.00W
63 B20 **General O'Brien** Buenos Aires, E Argentina 34.54S 60.45W
64 K13 **General Pico** La Pampa, C Argentina 35.40S 63.44W
64 M7 **General Pinedo** Chaco, N Argentina 27.16S 61.19W
63 B20 **General Pinto** Buenos Aires, E Argentina 34.45S 61.49W
63 E22 **General Pirán** Buenos Aires, E Argentina 37.16S 57.46W
45 N15 **General, Río** ~ S Costa Rica
65 I15 **General Roca** Río Negro, C Argentina 39.00S 67.35W
179 Rr17 **General Santos** *off.* General Santos City. Mindanao, S Philippines 6.09N 125.10E
43 O9 **General Terán** Nuevo León, NE Mexico 25.17N 99.37W
116 N7 **General Toshevo** *Rom.* I.G.Duca, *prev.* Casim, Kasimköj. Dobrich, NE Bulgaria 43.43N 28.04E
63 B20 **General Viamonte** Buenos Aires, E Argentina 35.01S 61.00W
63 A20 **General Villegas** Buenos Aires, E Argentina 35.01S 63.01W
Gênes *see* Genova
20 E11 **Genesee River** ~ New York/Pennsylvania, NE USA
32 K11 **Geneseo** Illinois, N USA 41.27N 90.08W
20 F10 **Geneseo** New York, NE USA 42.48N 77.46W
59 L14 **Geneshuaya, Río** ~ N Bolivia
25 Q8 **Geneva** Alabama, S USA 31.01N 85.51W
32 M10 **Geneva** Illinois, N USA 41.53N 88.18W
31 Q16 **Geneva** Nebraska, C USA 40.31N 97.36W
20 G10 **Geneva** New York, NE USA 42.52N 76.58W
33 U10 **Geneva** Ohio, NE USA 41.48N 80.53W
Geneva *see* Genève
110 B10 **Geneva, Lake** *Fr.* Lac de Genève, Lac Léman, le Léman, *Ger.* Genfer See. ◎ France/Switzerland
110 A10 **Genève** *Eng.* Geneva, *Ger.* Genf, *It.* Ginevra. Genève, SW Switzerland 46.13N 6.09E
110 A11 **Genève** *Eng.* Geneva, *Ger.* Genf, *It.* Ginevra. ◆ *canton* SW Switzerland
110 A10 **Genève** *var.* Geneva. ✕ Vaud, SW Switzerland 46.13N 6.06E
Genève, Lac de *see* Geneva, Lake
Genf *see* Genève
Genfer See *see* Geneva, Lake
169 T5 **Genhe** *prev.* Ergun Zuoqi. Nei Mongol Zizhiqu, N China 50.48N 121.30E
169 S5 **Gen He** ~ NE China
Genichesk *see* Heniches'k
106 L14 **Genil** ~ S Spain
101 K18 **Genk** *var.* Genck. Limburg, NE Belgium 50.58N 5.30E
170 Cc12 **Genkai-nada** *gulf* Kyūshū, SW Japan
109 C19 **Gennargentu, Monti del** ▲ Sardegna, Italy, C Mediterranean Sea 40.01N 9.14E
101 M14 **Gennep** Limburg, SE Netherlands 51.43N 5.58E
32 M10 **Genoa** Illinois, N USA 42.06N 88.41W
31 Q15 **Genoa** Nebraska, C USA 41.27N 97.43W
Genoa *see* Genova
Genoa, Gulf of *see* Genova, Golfo di
108 D10 **Genova** *Eng.* Genoa, *Fr.* Gênes; *anc.* Genua. Liguria, NW Italy 44.28N 9.00E
108 D10 **Genova, Golfo di** *Eng.* Gulf of Genoa. *gulf* NW Italy
59 C17 **Genovesa, Isla** *var.* Tower Island. *island* Galapagos Islands, Ecuador, E Pacific Ocean
Genshū *see* Wŏnju
101 E17 **Gent** *Eng.* Ghent, *Fr.* Gand. Oost-Vlaanderen, NW Belgium 51.01N 3.42E
174 J15 **Genteng** Jawa, C Indonesia 7.21S 106.19E
102 M12 **Genthin** Sachsen-Anhalt, E Germany 52.24N 12.10E
29 R9 **Gentry** Arkansas, C USA 36.16N 94.28W
Genua *see* Genova
109 I15 **Genzano di Roma** Lazio, C Italy 41.42N 12.42E
Geokchay *see* Göyçay
Geok-Tepe *see* Gökdepe
126 Gg1 **Georga, Zemlya** *Eng.* George Land. *island* Zemlya Frantsa-Iosifa, N Russian Federation
85 G26 **George** Western Cape, S South Africa 33.51S 22.28E
31 S11 **George** Iowa, C USA 43.20N 96.00W
11 O5 **George** ~ Newfoundland and Labrador/Québec, E Canada
47 T11 **George F L Charles** *prev.* Vigie. ✕ (Castries). NE Saint Lucia 14.01N 60.59W
67 C25 **George Island** *island* S Falkland Islands
191 R10 **George, Lake** ◎ New South Wales, SE Australia
83 E18 **George, Lake** ◎ SW Uganda
25 W10 **George, Lake** ◎ Florida, SE USA
20 L8 **George, Lake** ▣ New York, NE USA
George Land *see* Georga, Zemlya
Georgenburg *see* Jurbarkas
George River *see* Kangiqsualujjuaq
66 G8 **Georges Bank** *undersea feature* W Atlantic Ocean
193 A21 **George Sound** *sound* South Island, NZ
67 F15 **Georgetown** ○ (Ascension Island) NW Ascension Island 17.55S 14.25W
189 V5 **Georgetown** Queensland, NE Australia 18.17S 143.37E
191 P15 **George Town** Tasmania, SE Australia 41.07S 146.50E
46 I4 **George Town** Great Exuma Island, C Bahamas 23.28N 75.47W
46 D8 **George Town** *var.* Georgetown. ○ (Cayman Islands) Grand Cayman, SW Cayman Islands 19.15N 81.22W
78 H12 **Georgetown** E Gambia 13.33N 14.49W
57 T8 **Georgetown** ● (Guyana) N Guyana 6.46N 58.10W
173 Ff3 **George Town** *var.* Penang, Pinang. Pinang, Peninsular Malaysia 5.28N 100.19E
47 Y14 **Georgetown** Saint Vincent, Saint Vincent and the Grenadines 13.14N 61.07W
23 Y4 **Georgetown** Delaware, NE USA 38.39N 75.22W
25 R6 **Georgetown** Georgia, SE USA 31.52N 85.04W
22 M5 **Georgetown** Kentucky, S USA 38.13N 84.33W
23 T13 **Georgetown** South Carolina, SE USA 33.22N 79.17W
27 S10 **Georgetown** Texas, SW USA 30.37N 97.40W
57 T8 **Georgetown** ✕ N Guyana 6.46N 58.10W
205 U16 **George V Coast** *physical region* Antarctica
205 T15 **George V Land** *physical region* Antarctica
204 J7 **George VI Ice Shelf** *ice shelf* Antarctica
204 J6 **George VI Sound** *sound* Antarctica
27 S14 **George West** Texas, SW USA 28.19N 98.07W
143 R9 **Georgia** *off.* Republic of Georgia, *Geor.* Sak'art'velo, *Rus.* Gruzinskaya SSR, Gruziya; *prev.* Georgian SSR. ◆ *republic* SW Asia
25 S5 **Georgia** *off.* State of Georgia; also known as Empire State of the South, Peach State. ◆ *state* SE USA
12 F12 **Georgian Bay** *lake bay* Ontario, S Canada
8 L17 **Georgia, Strait of** *strait* British Columbia, W Canada
Georgi Dimitrov *see* Kostenets
Georgi Dimitrov, Yazovir *see* Koprinka, Yazovir
116 M9 **Georgi Traykov, Yazovir** ▣ NE Bulgaria
Georgiu-Dezh *see* Liski
151 W10 **Georgiyevka** Vostochnyy Kazakhstan, E Kazakhstan 49.19N 81.34E
Georgiyevka *see* Korday
131 N15 **Georgiyevsk** Stavropol'skiy Kray, SW Russian Federation 44.07N 43.22E
102 G13 **Georgsmarienhütte** Niedersachsen, NW Germany 52.12N 8.04E
205 O1 **Georg von Neumayer** *German research station* Antarctica 70.41S 8.18W
103 M16 **Gera** Thüringen, E Germany 50.51N 12.13E
103 K16 **Gera** ~ C Germany
101 E19 **Geraardsbergen** Oost-Vlaanderen, SW Belgium 50.46N 3.52E
117 F21 **Geráki** Pelopónnisos, S Greece 36.56N 22.46E
29 W5 **Gerald** Missouri, C USA 38.24N 91.20W
49 V8 **Geral de Goiás, Serra** ▲ E Brazil
193 G20 **Geraldine** Canterbury, South Island, NZ 44.06S 171.13E
188 H11 **Geraldton** Western Australia 28.47S 114.39E
10 E11 **Geraldton** Ontario, S Canada 49.43N 86.58W
62 J12 **Geral, Serra** ▲ S Brazil
175 P16 **Gerampi** Sumbawa, S Indonesia 8.47S 118.51E
105 U6 **Gérardmer** Vosges, NE France 48.05N 6.54E
Gerasa *see* Jarash
Gerdauen *see* Zheleznodorozhnyy
145 Q11 **Gerdine, Mount** ▲ Alaska, USA 61.40N 152.21W
142 H11 **Gerede** Bolu, N Turkey 40.48N 32.13E
142 H11 **Gerede Çayı** ~ N Turkey
154 M8 **Gereshk** Helmand, SW Afghanistan 31.49N 64.31E
103 L24 **Geretsried** Bayern, S Germany 47.51N 11.28E
107 P14 **Gérgal** Andalucía, S Spain 37.07N 2.34W
194 K13 **Gerhards, Cape** *headland* C PNG 6.43S 147.31E
30 I14 **Gering** Nebraska, C USA 41.49N 103.39W
37 R3 **Gerlach** Nevada, W USA 40.38N 119.21W
Gerlachfalvi Csúcs/Gerlachovka *see* Gerlachovský štít
113 L18 **Gerlachovský štít** *var.* Gerlachovka, *Ger.* Gerlsdorfer Spitze, *Hung.* Gerlachfalvi Csúcs; *prev.* Stalinov Štít, *Ger.* Franz-Josef Spitze, *Hung.* Ferencz-Jósef Csúcs. ▲ N Slovakia 49.12N 20.09E
110 E8 **Gerlafingen** Solothurn, NW Switzerland 47.10N 7.34E
Gerlsdorfer Spitze *see* Gerlachovský štít
145 V3 **Germak** E Iraq 35.49N 46.09E
German East Africa *see* Tanzania
Germanicopolis *see* Çankırı
Germanicum, Mare/German Ocean *see* North Sea
Germanovichi *see* Hyermanavichy
German Southwest Africa *see* Namibia
22 E10 **Germantown** Tennessee, S USA 35.06N 89.51W
103 I15 **Germany** *off.* Federal Republic of Germany, *Ger.* Bundesrepublik Deutschland, Deutschland. ◆ *federal republic* N Europe
103 L23 **Germering** Bayern, SE Germany 48.07N 11.22E
85 J21 **Germiston** *var.* Gauteng. Gauteng, NE South Africa 26.15S 28.10E
Gernika *see* Gernika-Lumo
107 P2 **Gernika-Lumo** *var.* Gernika, Guernica, Guernica y Lumo. País Vasco, N Spain 43.19N 2.40W
171 Ii15 **Gero** Gifu, Honshū, SW Japan 35.48N 137.15E
117 F22 **Geroliménas** Pelopónnisos, S Greece 36.28N 22.25E
Gerona *see* Girona
101 H21 **Gerpinnes** Hainaut, S Belgium 50.20N 4.37E
104 L15 **Gers** ◆ *department* S France
104 L14 **Gers** ~ S France
Gerunda *see* Girona
142 K10 **Gerze** Sinop, N Turkey 41.48N 35.13E
164 I13 **Gêrzê** *var.* Luring. Xizang Zizhiqu, W China 32.19N 84.05E
Gesoriacum/Gessoriacum *see* Boulogne-sur-Mer
101 J21 **Gesves** Namur, SE Belgium 50.24N 5.04E
95 J20 **Geta** Åland, SW Finland 60.22N 19.49E
107 N8 **Getafe** Madrid, C Spain 40.18N 3.43W
97 J21 **Getinge** Halland, S Sweden 56.46N 12.42E
20 F16 **Gettysburg** Pennsylvania, NE USA 39.49N 77.13W
31 N8 **Gettysburg** South Dakota, N USA 45.00N 99.57W
204 K12 **Getz Ice Shelf** *ice shelf* Antarctica
143 S15 **Gevaş** Van, SE Turkey 38.16N 43.04E
Gevgeli *see* Gevgelija
115 Q20 **Gevgelija** *var.* Đevđelija, Djevdjelija, *Turk.* Gevgeli. SE FYR Macedonia 41.09N 22.30E
105 T10 **Gex** Ain, E France 46.21N 6.02E
94 I3 **Geysir** *physical region* SW Iceland
142 F11 **Geyve** Sakarya, NW Turkey 40.31N 30.18E
82 G10 **Gezira** ◆ *state* E Sudan
111 V3 **Gföhl** Niederösterreich, N Austria 48.30N 15.27E
85 H22 **Ghaap Plateau** *Afr.* Ghaapplato. *plateau* C South Africa
Ghaapplato *see* Ghaap Plateau
Ghaba *see* Al Ghābah
144 J8 **Ghāb, Tall** ▲ SE Syria 33.09N 37.48E
145 Q9 **Ghadaf, Wādī al** *dry watercourse* C Iraq
Ghadamès *see* Ghadāmis
76 M9 **Ghadāmis** *var.* Ghadamès, Rhadames. W Libya 30.07N 9.30E
147 Y10 **Ghadan** E Oman 20.20N 57.58E
77 O10 **Ghaddūwah** C Libya 26.36N 14.26E
153 Q11 **Ghafurov** *Rus.* Gafurov; *prev.* Sovetabad. NW Tajikistan 40.13N 69.42E
159 N12 **Ghāghara** ~ S Asia
155 P13 **Ghaibi Dero** Sind, SE Pakistan 27.34N 67.42E
147 Y10 **Ghalat** E Oman 21.06N 58.51E
145 W11 **Ghamūkah, Hawr** ◎ S Iraq
79 P15 **Ghana** *off.* Republic of Ghana. ◆ *republic* W Africa
147 X12 **Ghānah** *spring/well* S Oman 18.35N 56.34E
Ghanongga *see* Ranongga
Ghansi/Ghansiland *see* Ghanzi
85 F18 **Ghanzi** *var.* Khanzi. Ghanzi, W Botswana 21.39S 21.38E
85 G19 **Ghanzi** *var.* Ghansi, Ghansiland, Khanzi. ◆ *district* C Botswana
69 T14 **Ghanzi** *var.* Knanzi. ~ Botswana/South Africa
Ghap'an *see* Kapan
144 F13 **Gharandal** Al 'Aqabah, SW Jordan 30.12N 35.18E
Gharbt, Jabal al *see* Liban, Jebel
76 K7 **Ghardaïa** N Algeria 32.29N 3.44E
145 U14 **Gharībīyah, Sha'īb al** ~ S Iraq
153 R12 **Gharm** *Rus.* Garm. C Tajikistan 39.03N 70.25E
155 P17 **Gharo** Sind, SE Pakistan 24.43N 67.34E
145 W10 **Gharrāf, Shaṭṭ al** ~ S Iraq
Gharvān *see* Gharyān
77 O7 **Gharyān** *var.* Gharvān. NW Libya 32.10N 13.01E
76 M11 **Ghāt** *var.* Gat. SW Libya 24.58N 10.11E
Ghawdex *see* Gozo
147 U8 **Ghayathi** Abū Ẓaby, W UAE 23.51N 53.01E
Ghazāl, Baḥr al *see* Ghazal, Bahr el
80 H9 **Ghazal, Bahr el** *var.* Soro. *seasonal river* C Chad
82 E13 **Ghazal, Bahr el** *var.* Baḥr al Ghazāl. ~ S Sudan
76 H6 **Ghazaouet** NW Algeria 35.05N 1.52W
158 J10 **Ghāziābād** Uttar Pradesh, N India 28.42N 77.28E
159 O13 **Ghāzīpur** Uttar Pradesh, N India 25.38N 83.33E
155 Q6 **Ghaznī** *var.* Ghazni. Ghaznī, E Afghanistan 33.31N 68.24E
155 P7 **Ghaznī** ◆ *province* SE Afghanistan
Ghazzah *see* Gaza
Gheel *see* Geel
Ghelizâne *see* Relizane
Ghent *see* Gent
Gheorghe Brațul *see* Sfântu Gheorghe, Brațul
Gheorghe Gheorghiu-Dej *see* Onești
118 J10 **Gheorgheni** *prev.* Gheorghieni, Sînt-Miclăuș, *Ger.* Niklasmarkt, *Hung.* Gyergyószentmiklós. Harghita, C Romania 46.43N 25.34E
Gheorghieni *see* Gheorgheni
118 H10 **Gherla** *Ger.* Neuschliss, *Hung.* Szamosújvár; *prev.* Armenierstadt. Cluj, NW Romania 47.02N 23.55E
Gheweifat *see* Ghuwayfāt
Ghilan *see* Gīlān
109 C18 **Ghilarza** Sardegna, Italy, C Mediterranean Sea 40.09N 8.50E
Ghilizane *see* Relizane
Ghimbi *see* Gimbi
Ghiriş *see* Câmpia Turzii
105 Y15 **Ghisonaccia** Corse, France, C Mediterranean Sea 42.00N 9.25E
Ghizo *see* Gizo
153 Q11 **Ghonchí** *Rus.* Ganchi. NW Tajikistan 39.57N 69.10E
Ghor *see* Ghowr
159 T13 **Ghoraghat** Rajshahi, NW Bangladesh 25.17N 89.16E
155 R13 **Ghotki** Sind, SE Pakistan 28.00N 69.21E
154 M5 **Ghowr** *var.* Ghor. ◆ *province* C Afghanistan
153 T13 **Ghŭdara** *var.* Gudara, *Rus.* Kudara. SE Tajikistan 38.28N 72.39E
159 R13 **Ghugri** ~ N India
153 S14 **Ghund** *Rus.* Gunt. ~ SE Tajikistan
Ghurdaqah *see* Hurghada
154 J5 **Ghūrīān** Herāt, W Afghanistan 34.19N 61.25E
147 T8 **Ghuwayfāt** *var.* Gheweifat. Abū Ẓaby, W UAE 24.06N 51.40E
123 Mm17 **Ghuzayyil, Sabkhat** *salt lake* N Libya
117 G17 **Giáltra** Évvoia, C Greece 38.21N 22.58E
Giamame *see* Jamaame
178 K13 **Gia Nghia** *var.* Đak Nông. Đắc Lắc, S Vietnam 11.59N 107.42E
116 F13 **Giannitsá** *var.* Yiannitsá. Kentrikí Makedonía, N Greece 40.48N 22.24E
109 F14 **Giannutri, Isola di** *island* Archipelago Toscano, C Italy
98 F13 **Giant's Causeway** *Ir.* Clochán an Aifir. *lava flow* N Northern Ireland, UK
178 J15 **Gia Rai** Minh Hai, S Vietnam 9.16N 105.25E
109 L24 **Giarre** Sicilia, Italy, C Mediterranean Sea 37.43N 15.12E
46 I7 **Gibara** Holguín, E Cuba 21.05N 76.08W
31 O16 **Gibbon** Nebraska, C USA 40.45N 98.50W
34 K11 **Gibbon** Oregon, NW USA 45.40N 118.22W
35 P11 **Gibbonsville** Idaho, NW USA 45.33N 113.55W
66 A13 **Gibb's Hill** *hill* S Bermuda 32.15N 64.51W
94 I9 **Gibostad** Troms, N Norway 69.21N 18.01E
106 I14 **Gibraleón** Andalucía, S Spain 37.22N 6.58W
106 L16 **Gibraltar** ○ (Gibraltar) S Gibraltar 36.08N 5.21W
106 L16 **Gibraltar** ◇ *UK dependent territory* SW Europe
Gibraltar, Détroit de/Gibraltar, Estrecho de *see* Gibraltar, Strait of
106 J17 **Gibraltar, Strait of** *Fr.* Détroit de Gibraltar, *Sp.* Estrecho de Gibraltar. *strait* Atlantic Ocean/Mediterranean Sea
33 S11 **Gibsonburg** Ohio, N USA 41.22N 83.19W
32 M13 **Gibson City** Illinois, N USA 40.27N 88.24W
188 L8 **Gibson Desert** *desert* Western Australia
8 L17 **Gibsons** British Columbia, SW Canada 49.24N 123.31W
155 N12 **Gīdār** Baluchistān, SW Pakistan 28.16N 66.00E
161 I17 **Giddalūr** Andhra Pradesh, E India 15.24N 78.54E
27 U10 **Giddings** Texas, SW USA 30.10N 96.56W
29 Y8 **Gideon** Missouri, C USA 36.27N 89.55W
83 I15 **Gīdolē** Southern, S Ethiopia 5.31N 37.26E
120 H13 **Giedraičiai** Utena, E Lithuania 55.05N 25.16E
105 O7 **Gien** Loiret, C France 47.40N 2.37E
103 G17 **Giessen** Hessen, W Germany 50.34N 8.40E
100 O6 **Gieten** Drenthe, NE Netherlands 53.00N 6.43E
25 Y13 **Gifford** Florida, SE USA 27.40N 80.24W
15 Ll1 **Gifford** ~ Baffin Island, Nunavut, NE Canada
102 J12 **Gifhorn** Niedersachsen, N Germany 52.28N 10.33E
9 P13 **Gift Lake** Alberta, W Canada 55.49N 115.57W
171 Hh15 **Gifu** *var.* Gihu. Gifu, Honshū, SW Japan 35.23N 136.46E
171 I14 **Gifu** *off.* Gifu-ken, *var.* Gihu. ◆ *prefecture* Honshū, SW Japan
130 M13 **Gigant** Rostovskaya Oblast', SW Russian Federation 46.29N 41.18E
42 E8 **Giganta, Sierra de la** ▲ W Mexico
56 E12 **Gigante** Huila, S Colombia 2.24N 75.34W
116 I7 **Gigen** Pleven, N Bulgaria 43.40N 24.31E
Giggiga *see* Jijiga
98 G12 **Gigha Island** *island* SW Scotland, UK
109 E14 **Giglio, Isola del** *island* Archipelago Toscano, C Italy
Gihu *see* Gifu
152 L11 **G'ijduvon** *Rus.* Gizhduvan. Buxoro Viloyati, C Uzbekistan 40.06N 64.38E
106 L2 **Gijón** *var.* Xixón. Asturias, NW Spain 43.31N 5.40W
83 D20 **Gikongoro** SW Rwanda 2.30S 29.32E
38 K14 **Gila Bend** Arizona, SW USA 32.57N 112.43W
38 J14 **Gila Bend Mountains** ▲ Arizona, SW USA
39 N14 **Gila Mountains** ▲ Arizona, SW USA
38 I15 **Gila Mountains** ▲ Arizona, SW USA
148 M4 **Gīlān** *off.* Ostān-e Gīlān; *var.* Ghilan, Guilan. ◆ *province* NW Iran
Gilani *see* Gnjilane
38 L14 **Gila River** ~ Arizona, SW USA
31 W4 **Gilbert** Minnesota, N USA 47.29N 92.27W
Gilbert Islands *see* Tungaru
8 L16 **Gilbert, Mount** ▲ British Columbia, SW Canada 50.49N 124.03W
189 U4 **Gilbert River** ~ Queensland, NE Australia
(0) C6 **Gilbert Seamounts** *undersea feature* NE Pacific Ocean
35 S7 **Gildford** Montana, NW USA 48.34N 110.21W
85 P15 **Gilé** Zambézia, NE Mozambique 16.04S 38.16E
32 K4 **Gile Flowage** ◎ Wisconsin, N USA
190 G7 **Giles, Lake** *salt lake* South Australia
77 U12 **Gilf Kebir Plateau** *Ar.* Haḍabat al Jilf al Kabīr. *plateau* SW Egypt
191 R6 **Gilgandra** New South Wales, SE Australia 31.43S 148.39E
Gilgău *see* Gâlgău
83 I19 **Gilgil** Rift Valley, SW Kenya 0.33S 36.18E
191 S4 **Gil Gil Creek** ~ New South Wales, SE Australia
155 V3 **Gilgit** Jammu and Kashmir, NE Pakistan 35.54N 74.19E
155 V3 **Gilgit** ~ N Pakistan
9 X11 **Gillam** Manitoba, C Canada 56.25N 94.45W
97 J22 **Gilleleje** Frederiksborg, E Denmark 56.05N 12.17E
32 K14 **Gillespie** Illinois, N USA 39.07N 89.49W
29 W13 **Gillett** Arkansas, C USA 34.07N 91.22W
35 X12 **Gillette** Wyoming, C USA 44.17N 105.30W
99 P22 **Gillingham** SE England, UK 51.24N 0.33E
205 X6 **Gillock Island** *island* Antarctica
181 O16 **Gillot** ✕ (St-Denis) N Réunion 20.52S 55.31E
67 H25 **Gill Point** *headland* E Saint Helena 15.58S 5.37W
32 M12 **Gilman** Illinois, N USA 40.44N 87.58W
27 W6 **Gilmer** Texas, SW USA 32.43N 94.56W
Gilolo *see* Halmahera, Pulau
83 G14 **Gilo Wenz** ~ SW Ethiopia
37 O10 **Gilroy** California, W USA 37.00N 121.34W
194 H12 **Giluwe, Mount** ▲ W PNG 6.03S 143.52E
126 M14 **Gilyuy** ~ SE Russian Federation
101 I14 **Gilze** Noord-Brabant, S Netherlands 51.33N 4.55E
172 O14 **Gima** Okinawa, Kume-jima, SW Japan
82 H13 **Gīmbī** *It.* Ghimbi. Oromo, C Ethiopia 9.13N 35.39E
47 T12 **Gimie, Mount** ▲ C Saint Lucia 13.51N 61.00W
9 X16 **Gimli** Manitoba, S Canada 50.39N 97.00W
Gimma *see* Jīma
97 O14 **Gimo** Uppsala, C Sweden 60.10N 18.12E
104 L15 **Gimone** ~ S France
Gimpoe *see* Gimpu
175 Pp9 **Gimpu** *prev.* Gimpoe. Sulawesi, C Indonesia 1.38S 120.00E
190 F5 **Gina** South Australia 29.56S 134.33E
Ginevra *see* Genève
101 J19 **Gingelom** Limburg, NE Belgium 50.46N 5.09E
188 I12 **Gingin** Western Australia 31.22S 115.51E
179 R14 **Gingoog** Mindanao, S Philippines 8.47N 125.05E
83 K14 **Gīnīr** Oromo, C Ethiopia 7.12N 40.43E
Giohar *see* Jawhar
109 O17 **Gioia del Colle** Puglia, SE Italy 40.46N 16.55E
109 M22 **Gioia, Golfo di** *gulf* S Italy
Gióna *see* Giona
117 I16 **Gioúra** *island* Vóreies Sporádes, Greece, Aegean Sea
109 O17 **Giovinazzo** Puglia, SE Italy 41.10N 16.40E
Gipeswic *see* Ipswich
Gipuzkoa *see* Guipúzcoa
Giran *see* Ilan
32 K14 **Girard** Illinois, N USA 39.27N 89.46W
29 R7 **Girard** Kansas, C USA 37.30N 94.50W
27 O6 **Girard** Texas, SW USA 33.18N 100.38W
56 E10 **Girardot** Cundinamarca, C Colombia 4.19N 74.46W
180 M7 **Giraud Seamount** *undersea feature* SW Indian Ocean 9.57S 46.55E
85 A15 **Girául** ~ SW Angola
98 L9 **Girdle Ness** *headland* NE Scotland, UK 57.09N 2.04W
143 N11 **Giresun** *var.* Kerasunt; *anc.* Cerasus, Pharnacia. Giresun, NE Turkey 40.55N 38.34E
143 N12 **Giresun** *var.* Kerasunt. ◆ *province* NE Turkey
143 N12 **Giresun Dağları** ▲ N Turkey
77 X10 **Girga** *var.* Girgeh, Jirjā. C Egypt 26.19N 31.49E
Girgeh *see* Girga
Girgenti *see* Agrigento
194 H10 **Girgir, Cape** *headland* NW PNG 3.48S 144.29E
159 Q15 **Girīdīh** Jhārkhand, NE India 24.10N 86.19E
191 P6 **Girilambone** New South Wales, SE Australia 31.19S 146.57E
Girin *see* Jilin
124 R12 **Girne** *Gk.* Kerýneia, Kyrenia. N Cyprus 35.19N 33.19E
Giron *see* Kiruna
107 X5 **Girona** *var.* Gerona; *anc.* Gerunda. Cataluña, NE Spain 41.58N 2.49E
107 W5 **Girona** *var.* Gerona ◆ *province* Cataluña, NE Spain
104 J12 **Gironde** ◆ *department* SW France
104 J11 **Gironde** *estuary* SW France
107 V5 **Gironella** Cataluña, NE Spain 42.01N 1.52E
105 N15 **Girou** ~ S France
99 H14 **Girvan** W Scotland, UK 55.14N 4.53W
26 M9 **Girvin** Texas, SW USA 31.05N 102.24W
192 Q9 **Gisborne** Gisborne, North Island, NZ 38.41S 178.01E
192 P9 **Gisborne** *off.* Gisborne District. ◆ *unitary authority* North Island, NZ
Giseifu *see* Üijŏngbu
Gisenye *see* Gisenyi
83 D19 **Gisenyi** *var.* Gisenye. NW Rwanda 1.42S 29.18E
97 K20 **Gislaved** Jönköping, S Sweden 57.19N 13.30E
105 N4 **Gisors** Eure, N France 49.18N 1.46E
Gissar *see* Hisor
153 P12 **Gissar Range** *Rus.* Gissarskiy Khrebet. ▲ Tajikistan/Uzbekistan
Gissarskiy Khrebet *see* Gissar Range
101 B16 **Gistel** West-Vlaanderen, W Belgium 51.09N 2.58E
110 F9 **Giswil** Unterwalden, C Switzerland 46.49N 8.11E
117 B16 **Gitánes** *ancient monument* Ípeiros, W Greece 39.34N 20.19E
83 E20 **Gitarama** C Rwanda 2.05S 29.45E
83 E20 **Gitega** C Burundi 3.20S 29.56E
Githio *see* Gýtheio
110 H11 **Giubiasco** Ticino, S Switzerland 46.10N 9.01E
108 K13 **Giulianova** Abruzzo, C Italy 42.45N 13.58E
Giulie, Alpi *see* Julian Alps
Giumri *see* Gyumri
118 M13 **Giurgeni** Ialomița, SE Romania 44.46N 27.51E
118 J15 **Giurgiu** Giurgiu, S Romania 43.54N 25.58E
118 J14 **Giurgiu** ◆ *county* SE Romania
97 F22 **Give** Vejle, C Denmark 55.51N 9.15E
105 R2 **Givet** Ardennes, N France 50.08N 4.50E
105 R11 **Givors** Rhône, E France 45.36N 4.46E
85 K19 **Giyani** Limpopo, NE South Africa 23.19S 30.37E
82 I13 **Giyon** Oromo, C Ethiopia 8.31N 37.56E
Giza/Gizeh *see* El Gîza
77 V8 **Giza, Pyramids of** *ancient monument* N Egypt 29.46N 31.03E
Gizhduvan *see* G'ijduvon
127 Oo8 **Gizhiga** Magadanskaya Oblast', E Russian Federation 61.57N 160.16E
127 Oo8 **Gizhiginskaya Guba** *bay* E Russian Federation
195 T14 **Gizo** Gizo, NW Solomon Islands 8.03S 156.49E
195 T14 **Gizo** *var.* Ghizo. *island* NW Solomon Islands
112 N7 **Giżycko** *Ger.* Warmińsko-Mazurskie, NE Poland 54.03N 21.48E
Gïzymałów *see* Hrymayliv
Gjakovë *see* Đakovica
96 F12 **Gjende** ◎ S Norway
97 F17 **Gjerstad** Aust-Agder, S Norway 58.54N 9.03E
Gjilan *see* Gnjilane
Gjinokastër *see* Gjirokastër
115 L23 **Gjirokastër** *var.* Gjirokastra; *prev.* Gjinokastër, *Gk.* Argyrokastron, *It.* Argirocastro. Gjirokastër, S Albania 40.04N 20.09E
115 L22 **Gjirokastër** ◆ *district* S Albania
15 K3 **Gjoa Haven** King William Island, Nunavut, NW Canada 68.37N 95.57W
96 H13 **Gjøvik** Oppland, S Norway 60.46N 10.40E
115 J22 **Gjuhëzës, Kepi i** *headland* SW Albania 40.25N 19.19E
Gjurgjevac *see* Đurđevac
117 E18 **Gkióna** *var.* Giona. ▲ C Greece
124 Oo3 **Gkréko, Akrotíri** *var.* Cape Greco, Pidálion. *headland* E Cyprus 34.57N 34.06E
101 I18 **Glabbeek-Zuurbemde** Vlaams Brabant, C Belgium 50.54N 4.58E
11 R14 **Glace Bay** Cape Breton Island, Nova Scotia, SE Canada 46.12N 59.57W
9 O16 **Glacier** British Columbia, SW Canada 51.12N 117.33W
41 W12 **Glacier Bay** *inlet* Alaska, USA
34 I7 **Glacier Peak** ▲ Washington, NW USA 48.06N 121.06W
23 Q7 **Glade Spring** Virginia, NE USA 36.47N 81.46W
45 W7 **Gladewater** Texas, SW USA 32.32N 94.57W
189 Y8 **Gladstone** Queensland, E Australia 23.52S 151.16E
190 I8 **Gladstone** South Australia 33.16S 138.21E
9 X16 **Gladstone** Manitoba, S Canada 50.12N 98.56W
33 O5 **Gladstone** Michigan, N USA 45.51N 87.01W
29 R4 **Gladstone** Missouri, C USA 39.12N 94.33W
33 Q7 **Gladwin** Michigan, N USA 43.58N 84.29W
97 J15 **Glafsfjorden** ◎ C Sweden
94 H2 **Gláma** *physical region* NW Iceland
96 I12 **Glåma** *var.* Glommen, Glomma. ~ S Norway
114 F13 **Glamoč** Federacija Bosna I Hercegovina, NE Bosnia and Herzegovina 44.01N 16.51E
99 J22 **Glamorgan** *cultural region* S Wales, UK
97 G24 **Glamsbjerg** Fyn, C Denmark 55.16N 10.07E

◆ Country ● Country Capital ◇ Dependent Territory ○ Dependent Territory Capital ◆ Administrative Region ✕ International Airport ▲ Mountain ▲ Mountain Range ⛰ Volcano ~ River ◎ Lake ▣ Reservoir

179 Rr17 **Glan** Mindanao, S Philippines
5.49N 125.11E
97 M17 **Glan** ✦ S Sweden
111 T9 **Glan** ▲ SE Austria
103 F19 **Glan** ✍ W Germany
Glaris see Glarus
110 H9 **Glarner Alpen** Eng. Glarus Alps.
▲ E Switzerland
110 H8 **Glarus** Glarus, E Switzerland
47.03N 9.04E
110 H9 **Glarus** Fr. Glaris. ◆ canton
C Switzerland
Glarus Alps see Glarner Alpen
29 N3 **Glasco** Kansas, C USA
39.21N 97.50W
98 I12 **Glasgow** Kentucky, S USA
55.52N 4.15W
22 K7 **Glasgow** Missouri, C USA
37.00N 85.54W
29 T4 **Glasgow** Montana, NW USA
39.13N 92.51W
35 W7 **Glasgow** Montana, NW USA
48.12N 106.37W
23 T6 **Glasgow** Virginia, NE USA
37.37N 79.27W
98 I12 **Glasgow** ✈ W Scotland, UK
55.52N 4.27W
9 S14 **Glaslyn** Saskatchewan, S Canada
53.20N 108.18W
20 I16 **Glassboro** New Jersey, NE USA
39.40N 75.05W
26 L10 **Glass Mountains** ▲ Texas,
SW USA
99 K23 **Glastonbury** SW England, UK
51.09N 2.43W
Glatz see Kłodzko
103 N16 **Glauchau** Sachsen, E Germany
50.48N 12.31E
Glavn'a Morava see
Velika Morava
115 N16 **Glavnik** Serbia, S Serbia
42.33N 21.10E
131 T1 **Glazov** Udmurtskaya Respublika,
NW Russian Federation
58.05N 52.38E
Głda see Gwda
111 U8 **Gleinalpe** ▲ SE Austria
111 W8 **Gleisdorf** Steiermark, SE Austria
47.07N 15.43E
Gleiwitz see Gliwice
41 S11 **Glenallen** Alaska, USA
62.06N 145.33W
104 F7 **Glénan, Îles** island group
NW France
193 G21 **Glenavy** Canterbury, South
Island, NZ 44.53S 171.04E
8 I7 **Glenboyle** Yukon Territory,
NW Canada 63.55N 138.43W
23 X3 **Glen Burnie** Maryland, NE USA
39.09N 76.37W
38 L8 **Glen Canyon** canyon Utah,
W USA
38 L8 **Glen Canyon Dam** dam
Arizona, SW USA
36.56N 111.28W
32 K15 **Glen Carbon** Illinois, N USA
38.45N 89.58W
12 E17 **Glencoe** Ontario, S Canada
42.44N 81.42W
85 K22 **Glencoe** KwaZulu/Natal, E South
Africa 28.09S 30.12E
31 U9 **Glencoe** Minnesota, N USA
44.46N 94.09W
98 H10 **Glen Coe** valley N Scotland, UK
38 K13 **Glendale** Arizona, SW USA
33.32N 112.11W
37 S15 **Glendale** California, W USA
34.09N 118.17W
190 G5 **Glendambo** South Australia
30.59S 135.45E
35 Y8 **Glendive** Montana, NW USA
47.07N 104.42W
35 Y15 **Glendo** Wyoming, C USA
42.27N 105.01W
57 S10 **Glendor Mountians** ▲ C Guyana
190 K12 **Glenelg River** ✍ South
Australia/Victoria, SE Australia
31 P4 **Glenfield** North Dakota, N USA
47.25N 98.33W
27 V12 **Glen Flora** Texas, SW USA
29.22N 96.12W
189 P7 **Glen Helen** Northern Territory,
N Australia 23.45S 132.46E
191 U3 **Glen Innes** New South Wales,
SE Australia 29.42S 151.45E
25 P6 **Glen Lake** ✦ Michigan, N USA
8 I7 **Glenlyon Peak** ▲ Yukon
Territory, W Canada
62.32N 134.51W
39 N16 **Glenn, Mount** ▲ Arizona,
SW USA 31.55N 110.00W
35 N15 **Glenns Ferry** Idaho, NW USA
42.57N 115.18W
25 W6 **Glennville** Georgia, SE USA
31.56N 81.55W
8 J10 **Glenora** British Columbia,
W Canada 57.52N 131.16W
190 M7 **Glenorchy** Victoria, SE Australia
36.56S 142.39E
191 V5 **Glenreagh** New South Wales,
SE Australia 30.04S 153.00E
35 X15 **Glenrock** Wyoming, C USA
42.50N 105.52W
98 K11 **Glenrothes** E Scotland, UK
56.11N 3.09W
20 L9 **Glens Falls** New York, NE USA
43.18N 73.38W
99 D14 **Glenties** Ir. Na Gleannta.
NW Ireland 54.46N 8.16W
30 L5 **Glen Ullin** North Dakota, N USA
46.49N 101.49W
23 R4 **Glenville** West Virginia, NE USA
38.55N 80.50W
29 T12 **Glenwood** Arkansas, C USA
34.19N 93.33W
31 S15 **Glenwood** Iowa, C USA
41.03N 95.44W
31 T7 **Glenwood** Minnesota, N USA
45.39N 95.23W
38 L5 **Glenwood** Utah, W USA
38.45N 111.59W
32 I5 **Glenwood City** Wisconsin,
N USA 45.04N 92.11W
37 Q4 **Glenwood Springs** Colorado,
C USA 39.33N 107.21W
110 F10 **Gletsch** Valais, S Switzerland
46.34N 8.21E
Glevum see Gloucester
31 U14 **Glidden** Iowa, C USA
42.03N 94.43W
114 E9 **Glina** Sisak-Moslavina,
NE Croatia 45.19N 16.07E
96 F11 **Glittertind** ▲ S Norway
61.24N 8.19E

113 J16 **Gliwice** Ger. Gleiwitz. Śląskie,
S Poland 50.19N 18.49E
38 M14 **Globe** Arizona, SW USA
33.24N 110.47W
Globino see Hlobyne
110 L9 **Glockturm** ▲ SW Austria
118 L9 **Glodeni** Rus. Glodyany.
N Moldova 47.47N 27.33E
111 S9 **Glödnitz** Kärnten, S Austria
46.57N 14.03E
Glodyany see Glodeni
Glogau see Głogów
111 W6 **Gloggnitz** Niederösterreich,
E Austria 47.41N 15.57E
112 F13 **Głogów** Ger. Glogau, Glogow.
Dolnośląskie, SW Poland
51.39N 16.04E
113 J16 **Głogówek** Ger. Oberglogau.
Opolskie, S Poland 50.21N 17.51E
94 G12 **Glomfjord** Nordland, C Norway
46.81N 13.57E
Glommen see Glåma
95 I14 **Glommersträsk** Norrbotten,
N Sweden 65.16N 19.40E
180 I1 **Glorieuses, Nosy** island group
N Madagascar
67 C25 **Glorious Hill** hill East Falkland,
Falkland Island
40 J12 **Glory of Russia Cape** headland
Saint Matthew Island, Alaska, USA
60.36N 172.57W
24 J7 **Gloster** Mississippi, S USA
31.12N 91.01W
191 U7 **Gloucester** New South Wales,
SE Australia 32.01S 152.00E
194 L12 **Gloucester** New Britain, E PNG
5.28S 148.28E
99 L21 **Gloucester** hist. Caer Glou,
Lat. Glevum. C England, UK
51.52N 2.13W
21 P10 **Gloucester** Massachusetts,
NE USA 42.36N 70.36W
23 X6 **Gloucester** Virginia, NE USA
37.23N 76.30W
99 K21 **Gloucestershire** cultural region
C England, UK
33 T14 **Glouster** Ohio, N USA
39.30N 82.04W
44 H3 **Glovers Reef** reef E Belize
20 K10 **Gloversville** New York, NE USA
43.03N 74.20W
112 K12 **Głowno** Łódź, C Poland
51.58N 19.43E
113 H16 **Głubczyce** Ger. Leobschütz.
Opolskie, S Poland 50.11N 17.49E
130 L11 **Glubokiy** Rostovskaya
Oblast', SW Russian Federation
48.34N 40.16E
151 W9 **Glubokoye** Vostochnyy
Kazakhstan, E Kazakhstan
50.10N 82.16E
113 H16 **Głuchołazy** Ger. Ziegenhals.
Opolskie, S Poland 50.18N 17.22E
102 I9 **Glückstadt** Schleswig-Holstein,
N Germany 53.47N 9.25E
Glukhov see Hlukhiv
Glushkevichi see Hlushkavichy
Glusk/Glussk see Hlusk
Glybokaya see Hlyboka
97 F21 **Glyngøre** Viborg, NW Denmark
56.45N 8.55E
131 Q9 **Gmelinka** Volgogradskaya
Oblast', SW Russian Federation
50.50N 46.51E
111 R8 **Gmünd** Kärnten, S Austria
46.56N 13.32E
111 U2 **Gmünd** Niederösterreich,
N Austria 48.45N 14.57E
Gmünd see Schwäbisch Gmünd
111 S5 **Gmunden** Oberösterreich,
N Austria 47.54N 13.46E
Gmundner See see Traunsee
96 N10 **Gnarp** Gävleborg, C Sweden
62.03N 17.19E
111 W8 **Gnas** Steiermark, SE Austria
46.51N 15.48E
Gnesen see Gniezno
97 O16 **Gnesta** Södermanland, C Sweden
59.02N 17.19E
112 H11 **Gniezno** Ger. Gnesen.
Wielkopolskie, C Poland
52.33N 17.35E
115 O17 **Gnjilane** var. Gilani, Alb. Gjilan.
Serbia, S Serbia 42.27N 21.28E
97 K20 **Gnosjö** Jönköping, S Sweden
57.22N 13.43E
161 E17 **Goa** prev. Old Goa, Vela Goa,
Velha Goa. Goa, W India
15.31N 73.55E
161 E17 **Goa** var. Old Goa. ◆ state W India
Goabddális see Kåbdalis
44 H7 **Goascorán, Río** ✍ El Salvador/
Honduras
79 O16 **Goaso** var. Gawso. W Ghana
6.49N 2.27W
85 K14 **Goba** It. Oromo, S Ethiopia
7.02N 39.58E
85 C20 **Gobabeb** Erongo, W Namibia
23.36S 15.03E
83 E19 **Gobabis** Omaheke, E Namibia
22.24S 18.58E
112 N7 **Gobas** var. Goldap, NE Poland
54.18N 22.23E
147 Q3 **Gobannium** see Abergavenny
86 M7 **Goban Spur** undersea feature
NW Atlantic Ocean
Gobbà see Goba
65 H24 **Gobernador Gregores**
Santa Cruz, S Argentina
48.43S 70.21W
89 F14 **Gobernador Ingeniero**
Virasoro Corrientes,
NE Argentina
158 L12 **Gobi** desert China/Mongolia
170 G16 **Gobō** Wakayama, Honshū,
SW Japan 33.52N 135.09E
103 O14 **Goch** Nordrhein-Westfalen,
W Germany 51.41N 6.10E
83 E19 **Gochas** Hardap, S Namibia
24.54S 18.43E
161 I14 **Godāvari** var. Godavari.
✍ C India
161 L16 **Godāvari, Mouths of the** delta
E India
13 V5 **Godbout** Québec, SE Canada
49.19N 67.37W
13 U5 **Godbout** ✍ Québec, SE Canada
13 U5 **Godbout Est** ✍ Québec,
SE Canada
47 V10 **Godbout West** Oregon, NW USA
12 I12 **Goderich** Ontario, S Canada
43.43N 81.42W
12 E15 **Godhavn** Danish Godhavn.

160 E10 **Godhra** Gujarāt, W India
22.49N 73.40E
Göding see Hodonín
113 K22 **Gödöllő** Pest, N Hungary
47.36N 19.19E
64 H11 **Godoy Cruz** Mendoza,
W Argentina 32.58S 68.49W
9 Y11 **Gods** ✍ Manitoba, C Canada
9 Y13 **Gods Lake** Manitoba, C Canada
54.29N 94.21W
9 X13 **Gods Lake** ✦ Manitoba,
C Canada
Godthaab/Godthåb see Nuuk
143 R11 **Godwin Austen, Mount** see K2
40.46N 42.36E
30 A8 **Goede Hoop, Kaap de** see
Good Hope, Cape of
Goedgegun see Nhlangano
Goeie Hoop, Kaap die see
Good Hope, Cape of
11 O7 **Goélands, Lac aux** ✦ Québec,
SE Canada
100 I13 **Goeree** island SW Netherlands
101 F15 **Goes** Zeeland, SW Netherlands
51.30N 3.55E
Goettingen see Göttingen
21 O10 **Goffstown** New Hampshire,
NE USA 43.01N 71.34W
12 E8 **Gogama** Ontario, S Canada
47.42N 81.43W
170 Ee12 **Gō-gawa** ✍ Honshū, SW Japan
32 L3 **Gogebic, Lake** ✦ Michigan,
N USA
32 K3 **Gogebic Range** hill range
Michigan/Wisconsin, N USA
143 V13 **Gogi, Mount** Arm. Gogi Lerr, Az.
Küküdağ. ▲ Armenia/Azerbaijan
39.33N 45.35E
128 F12 **Gogland, Ostrov** island
NW Russian Federation
113 I15 **Gogolin** Opolskie, S Poland
50.28N 18.04E
79 S14 **Gogonou** see Gogounou
79 S14 **Gogounou** var. Gogonou.
N Benin 10.49N 2.49E
161 K18 **Goianésia** Goiás, C Brazil
15.21S 49.01W
61 K18 **Goiânia** prev. Goyania. state capital
Goiás, C Brazil 16.43S 49.18W
61 J18 **Goiás** off. Estado de Goiás; prev.
Goiaz, Goyaz. ◆ state C Brazil
Goiaz see Goiás
165 R14 **Goinsargoin** Xizang Zizhiqu,
W China 31.15N 98.04E
62 H10 **Goio-Erê** Paraná, SW Brazil
24.08S 53.07W
101 I15 **Goirle** Noord-Brabant,
S Netherlands 51.31N 5.04E
106 I8 **Góis** Coimbra, N Portugal
40.10N 8.06E
Lg16 **Gojō** var. Gozyô. Nara, Honshū,
SW Japan 34.21N 135.42E
171 M10 **Gojōme** Akita, Honshū,
NW Japan 39.55N 140.07E
155 U9 **Gojra** Punjab, E Pakistan
31.09N 72.39E
170 D15 **Gokase-gawa** ✍ Kyūshū,
SW Japan
142 A11 **Gökçeada** var. Imroz Adası, Gk.
Imbros. island NW Turkey
Gökçeada see Imroz
152 F13 **Gökdepe** Rus. Gëkdepe, Geok-
Tepe. Ahal Welaýaty,
C Turkmenistan 38.05N 58.07E
142 I10 **Gökırmak** ✍ N Turkey
Goklenkuy, Solonchak see
Geklengkui, Solonchak
42 C16 **Gökova Körfezi** gulf SW Turkey
142 K15 **Göksu** ✍ S Turkey
142 L15 **Göksun** Kahramanmaraş,
C Turkey 38.03N 36.30E
142 J17 **Göksu Nehri** ✍ S Turkey
85 J16 **Gokwe** Midlands, NW Zimbabwe
18.10S 28.54E
96 F13 **Gol** Buskerud, S Norway
60.42N 8.57E
159 X12 **Golāghāt** Assam, NE India
26.31N 93.54E
112 H10 **Gołańcz** Wielkopolskie, C Poland
52.57N 17.17E
144 G8 **Golan Heights** Ar. Al Jawlān,
Heb. HaGolan. ▲ SW Syria
Golārā see Ārān
Golaya Pristan see Hola Prystan'
149 T11 **Golbāf** Kermān, C Iran
29.51N 57.43E
142 M15 **Gölbaşı** Adıyaman, S Turkey
37.46N 37.40E
111 P9 **Gölbner** ▲ SW Austria
51.16N 12.31E
32 M17 **Golconda** Illinois, N USA
37.18N 88.30W
35 T3 **Golconda** Nevada, W USA
40.56N 117.29W
142 E11 **Gölcük** Kocaeli, NW Turkey
40.42N 29.50E
110 I7 **Goldach** Sankt Gallen,
NE Switzerland 47.28N 9.28E
112 N7 **Goldap** Ger. Goldap.
Warmińsko-Mazurskie, NE Poland
54.18N 22.23E
34 E15 **Gold Beach** Oregon, NW USA
42.24N 124.25W
113 F16 **Goldberg** see Złotoryja
158 M12 **Golden** Uttar Pradesh, N India
27.07N 81.58E
82 I11 **Gondar** see Gonder
82 I11 **Gonder** var. Gondar. Amhara,
N Ethiopia 12.35N 37.27E
160 J12 **Gondia** Mahārāshtra, C India
21.27N 80.12E
106 G6 **Gondomar** Porto, NW Portugal
41.09N 8.32W
142 C12 **Gönen** Balıkesir, W Turkey
40.06N 27.39E
142 C12 **Gönen Çayı** ✍ NW Turkey
165 O15 **Gongbo'gyamda** var. Golinka.
Xizang Zizhiqu, W China
30.03N 93.10E
133 I11 **Golden Grove** E Jamaica
17.55N 76.16E
12 J12 **Golden Lake** ✦ Ontario,
SE Canada
22 K10 **Golden Meadow** Louisiana,
S USA 29.22N 90.15W
47 V10 **Golden Rock** ✈ (Basseterre)
Saint Kitts, Saint Kitts and Nevis
17.16N 62.43W
164 I5 **Golden Valley** Mashonaland
West, N Zimbabwe 18.15S 29.46E

37 U9 **Goldfield** Nevada, W USA
37.40N 117.13W
191 P5 **Gongolgon** New South Wales,
SE Australia 30.19S 146.57E
165 Q6 **Gong Xian** Gansu, N China
34.45N 100.27E
Gongquan see Gongxian
166 I10 **Gongxian** var. Gongquan,
Gong Xian. Sichuan, C China
28.25N 104.51E
163 V10 **Gongzhuling** prev. Huaide. Jilin,
NE China 43.30N 124.48E
165 S14 **Gonjo** Xizang Zizhiqu, W China
30.46N 98.34W
8 K17 **Gold River** Vancouver Island,
British Columbia, SW Canada
49.48N 126.01W
23 V10 **Goldsboro** North Carolina,
SE USA 35.22N 77.59W
26 M8 **Goldsmith** Texas, SW USA
31.58N 102.36W
27 R8 **Goldthwaite** Texas, SW USA
31.27N 98.34W
116 H9 **Golema Ada** see Ostrovo
116 H9 **Golema Planina** ▲ W Bulgaria
116 F9 **Golemi Vrŭkh** ▲ W Bulgaria
42.41N 22.38E
112 D8 **Goleniów** Ger. Gollnow.
Zachodnio-pomorskie, NW Poland
53.33N 14.48E
149 R3 **Golestān** ◆ province N Iran
37 Q14 **Goleta** California, W USA
34.25N 119.51W
45 O16 **Golfito** Puntarenas, SE Costa Rica
8.37N 83.07W
27 T13 **Goliad** Texas, SW USA
28.40N 97.23W
115 L14 **Golija** ▲ SW Serbia
165 O15 **Golinka** see Gongbo'gyamda
142 M12 **Gölköy** Ordu, N Turkey
40.42N 37.37E
111 X3 **Göllersbach** ✍ NE Austria
112 D8 **Gollnow** see Goleniów
Golmo see Golmud
165 P10 **Golmud** var. Ge'e'mu, Golmo,
Chin. Ko-erh-mu. Qinghai,
C China 36.22N 94.56E
105 Y14 **Golo** ✍ Corse, France,
C Mediterranean Sea
Golovanevsk see Holovanivs'k
41 N9 **Golovin** Alaska, USA
64.33N 162.54W
148 M7 **Golpāyegān** var.
Gulpaigan. Eşfahān, W Iran
33.22N 50.18E
98 J7 **Golspie** N Scotland, UK
57.58N 3.55W
114 O11 **Golubac** Serbia, NE Serbia
44.38N 21.36E
112 J9 **Golub-Dobrzyń**
Kujawski-pomorskie, C Poland
53.06N 19.03E
151 S7 **Golubovka** Pavlodar,
N Kazakhstan 53.07N 74.11E
84 B11 **Golungo Alto** Cuanza Norte,
NW Angola 9.10S 14.45E
116 M8 **Golyama Kamchiya**
✍ E Bulgaria
116 L8 **Golyama Reka** ✍ N Bulgaria
116 H11 **Golyama Syutkya**
▲ SW Bulgaria 41.55N 24.03E
116 J12 **Golyam Perelik** ▲ S Bulgaria
41.37N 24.34E
116 J12 **Golyam Persenk** ▲ S Bulgaria
41.50N 24.33E
125 F12 **Golyshmanovo** Tyumenskaya
Oblast', C Russian Federation
56.22N 68.25E
81 P19 **Goma** Nord Kivu, NE Dem. Rep.
Congo 1.36S 29.07E
171 Gg16 **Gomadan-zan** ▲ Honshū,
SW Japan 34.03N 135.34E
79 X14 **Gombe** Gombe, E Nigeria
10.19N 11.02E
69 U10 **Gombe** var. Igombe.
✍ E Tanzania
79 Y14 **Gombi** Adamawa, E Nigeria
10.07N 12.45E
144 I10 **Gombroon** see Bandar-e 'Abbās
Gomel' see Homyel'
Gomel'skaya Oblast' see
Homyel'skaya Voblasts'
66 N11 **Gomera** island Islas Canarias,
Spain, NE Atlantic Ocean
42 I5 **Gómez Farías** Chihuahua,
N Mexico 29.25N 107.46W
42 L8 **Gómez Palacio** Durango,
C Mexico 25.39N 103.30W
164 J13 **Gómon** Xizang Zizhiqu, W China
33.57N 86.40E
175 T11 **Gomumu, Pulau** island Maluku,
E Indonesia
149 T6 **Gonābād** var. Gunabad.
Khorāsān-Razavī, NE Iran
36.21N 58.38E
46 L9 **Gonaïves** var. Les Gonaïves.
N Haiti 19.26N 72.40W
126 M13 **Gonam** ✍ NE Russian
Federation
46 L9 **Gonâve, Canal de la** var. Canal
de Sud. channel N Caribbean Sea
46 K9 **Gonâve, Golfe de la** gulf
N Caribbean Sea
46 K9 **Gonâve, Île de la** island C Haiti
115 J14 **Goražde** Federacija Bosna I
Hercegovina, Bosnia and
Herzegovina 43.39N 18.58E
149 Q3 **Gonbad-e Kāvūs** var.
Gonbad-i-Qawus. Golestān,
N Iran 37.15N 55.10E
82 J13 **Gondey** Moyen-Chari, S Chad
9.07N 19.10E
82 I11 **Gonder** see Gonder *(duplicate - see above)*
166 G9 **Gongga Shan** ▲ C China
29.34N 101.55E
T10 **Gonghe** var. Qabqa. Qinghai,
C China 36.22N 100.44E
164 I5 **Gongliu** vaǧ. Tokkuztara.
Xinjiang Uygur Zizhiqu,
NW China 43.29N 82.16E
12 I12 **Gore Bay** Manitoulin Island,
Ontario, S Canada 45.54N 82.28W
81 I14 **Goré** E Nigeria

27 Q5 **Goree** Texas, SW USA
33.28N 99.31W
143 O11 **Giresun** Giresun, NE Turkey
41.00N 39.00E
21 N6 **Gore Mountain** ▲ Vermont,
NE USA 44.55N 71.47W
41 R13 **Gore Point** headland Alaska, USA
59.12N 150.57W
39 R4 **Gore Range** ▲ Colorado, C USA
99 F19 **Gorey** Ir. Guaire. SE Ireland
52.40N 6.18W
149 P2 **Gorgān** Kermān, N Iran
149 Q4 **Gorgān** var. Astarabad, Astrabad,
Gurgan; prev. Asterābād, anc.
Hyrcania. Golestān, N Iran
36.53N 54.28E
149 Q4 **Gorgān, Rūd-e** ✍ N Iran
108 D12 **Gorgona, Isola di** island
Archipelago Toscano, C Italy
21 P8 **Gorham** Maine, NE USA
43.41N 70.27W
143 T10 **Gori** C Georgia 42.00N 44.07E
100 I13 **Gorinchem** var. Gorkum.
Zuid-Holland, C Netherlands
51.50N 4.59E
143 V13 **Goris** SE Armenia 39.31N 46.20E
128 K16 **Goritsy** Tverskaya Oblast',
W Russian Federation
57.09N 36.44E
108 G13 **Gorj** ◆ county SW Romania
111 W12 **Goritsy** var. Uskočke Planine,
Žumberak, Žumberačko Gorje,
Ger. Uskokengebirge;
prev. Sichelburger Gebirge.
▲ Croatia/Slovenia see also
Žumberačko Gorje
128 J7 **Gorki** see Horki
41 N8 **Gorki** see Horki
85 D26 **Good Hope, Cape of** Afr. Kaap
de Goede Hoop, Kaap die Goeie
Hoop. headland SW South Africa
34.19S 18.25E
8 K10 **Good Hope Lake** British
Columbia, W Canada
59.15N 129.18W
85 E23 **Goodhouse** Northern Cape,
W South Africa 28.54S 18.13E
35 O15 **Gooding** Idaho, NW USA
42.56N 114.42W
28 H3 **Goodland** Kansas, C USA
39.21N 101.42W
181 Y15 **Goodlands** NW Mauritius
20.015 57.39E
22 J8 **Goodlettsville** Tennessee, S USA
36.19N 86.42W
41 N13 **Goodnews** Alaska, USA
59.07N 161.35W
27 O3 **Goodnight** Texas, SW USA
35.00N 101.07W
191 Q4 **Goodooga** New South Wales,
SE Australia 29.09S 147.30E
31 N4 **Goodrich** North Dakota, N USA
47.24N 100.07W
27 W10 **Goodrich** Texas, SW USA
30.36N 94.57W
31 X10 **Goodview** Minnesota, N USA
44.04N 91.42W
28 H8 **Goodwell** Oklahoma, C USA
36.36N 101.38W
99 N17 **Goole** E England, UK
53.42N 0.46W
191 O8 **Goolgowi** New South Wales,
SE Australia 34.00S 145.43E
190 I10 **Goomalling** Western Australia
35.31S 138.43E
189 Y11 **Goombungee** Queensland,
E Australia 28.33S 150.22E
100 O11 **Goor** Overijssel, E Netherlands
52.13N 6.33E
35 V13 **Goose Bay** see Happy Valley-
Goose Bay
23 S14 **Goose Creek** South Carolina,
SE USA 32.58N 80.01W
65 M23 **Goose Green** var. Prado del
Ganso. East Falkland, Falkland
Islands 51.52S 59.00W
17 Q6 **Goose Lake** var. Lago dos
Gansos. ✦ California/Oregon,
W USA
31 Q4 **Goose River** ✍ North Dakota,
N USA
172 T16 **Gopalganj** Dhaka, S Bangladesh
23.03N 89.52E
159 O12 **Gopālganj** Bihār, N India
26.28N 84.25E
103 I22 **Göppingen** Baden-Württemberg,
SW Germany 48.42N 9.39E
112 M12 **Góra Kalwaria** Mazowieckie,
C Poland 52.00N 21.14E
112 G13 **Góra** Ger. Guhrau. Dolnośląskie,
SW Poland 51.40N 16.30E
82 I13 **Goradka** ✍ NE Russian
Federation
Gorakh'an see Harany
153 O13 **Gorakhpur** Uttar Pradesh,
N India 26.45N 83.22E
Gorany see Harany
131 O3 **Gorodets** Nizhegorodskaya
Oblast', NW Russian Federation
56.36N 43.27E
Gorodets see Haradzyets
Gorodeya see Haradzyeya
Gorodishche Penzenskaya
Oblast', W Russian Federation
53.17N 45.39E
131 P6 **Gorodishche** see Horodyshche
Gorodnya see Horodnya
Gorodok see Haradok
Gorodok/Gorodok-
Yagellonski see Horodok
130 M13 **Gorodovikovsk** Respublika
Kalmykiya, SW Russian Federation
46.07N 41.56E
194 I13 **Gordon** ✍ Tasmania, SE
Australia
27 R7 **Gordon** Texas, SW USA
32.32N 98.21W
30 K12 **Gordil** Vakaga, N Central African
Republic 9.37N 21.42E
25 U9 **Gordon** Georgia, SE USA
32.52N 83.19W
30 M12 **Gordon** Nebraska, C USA
42.48N 102.12W
25 R7 **Gordon** Texas, SW USA
32.32N 98.21W *(dup?)*
30 I2 **Gordon Creek** ✍ Nebraska,
C USA
65 I25 **Gordon, Isla** island S Chile
191 O11 **Gordon, Lake** ✦ Tasmania,
SE Australia
191 N11 **Gordon River** ✍ Tasmania,
SE Australia
23 V5 **Gordonsville** Virginia, NE USA
38.09N 78.10W
79 Q11 **Gorom-Gorom** NE Burkina
14.27N 0.13W
176 V12 **Gorong, Kepulauan** island group
E Indonesia
85 M17 **Gorongosa** Sofala,
C Mozambique 18.40S 34.03E
176 Uu12 **Gorong, Pulau** island Kepulauan
Gorong, E Indonesia
175 R8 **Gorontalo** Sulawesi, C Indonesia
7.55N 16.37E
175 Qq7 **Gorontalo** off. Propinsi
Gorontalo. ◆ province N Indonesia

175 Qq8 **Gorontalo, Teluk** bay Sulawesi,
C Indonesia
Gorontalo, Teluk see
Tomini, Gulf of
112 L7 **Górowo Iławeckie** Ger.
Landsberg. Warmińsko-
Mazurskie, NE Poland,
54.18N 20.30E
100 M7 **Gorredijk** Fris. De Gordyk.
Friesland, N Netherlands
53.00N 6.04E
86 C14 **Gorringe Ridge** undersea feature
E Atlantic Ocean
100 M11 **Gorssel** Gelderland,
E Netherlands 52.12N 6.13E
111 T8 **Görtschitz** ✍ S Austria
Goryn see Horyn'
Görz see Gorizia
112 E10 **Gorzów Wielkopolski** Ger.
Landsberg, Landsberg an der
Warthe. Lubuskie, W Poland
52.43N 15.12E
110 I10 **Göschenen** Uri, C Switzerland
46.40N 8.36E
195 N16 **Goschen Strait** strait SE PNG
171 Kk13 **Gosen** Niigata, Honshū, C Japan
37.43N 139.11E
191 T8 **Gosford** New South Wales,
SE Australia 33.25S 151.22E
33 P11 **Goshen** Indiana, N USA
41.34N 85.49W
20 K13 **Goshen** New York, NE USA
41.24N 74.17W
171 Mm8 **Goshoba** see Goşoba
Goshogawara var. Gosyogawara.
Aomori, Honshū, C Japan
40.46N 140.24E
Goshquduq Qum see
Tosquduq Qumlari
103 J14 **Goslar** Niedersachsen, C Germany
51.55N 10.25E
29 Y9 **Gosnell** Arkansas, C USA
35.57N 89.58W
152 B10 **Goşoba** var. Goshoba, Rus.
Koshoba. Balkanskiy Velayat, NW
Turkmenistan 40.28N 54.11E
114 C11 **Gospić** Lika-Senj, C Croatia
44.32N 15.21E
99 N23 **Gosport** S England, UK
50.48N 1.07W
113 M17 **Gorlice** Małopolskie, S Poland
49.37N 21.08E
103 O15 **Görlitz** Sachsen, E Germany
51.09N 14.57E
Görlitz see Zgorzelec
Gorlovka see Horlivka
27 R7 **Gorman** Texas, SW USA
32.12N 98.40W
115 N18 **Gostivar** W FYR Macedonia
41.48N 20.55E
Gostomel' see Hostomel'
112 G12 **Gostyń** var. Gostyn.
Wielkopolskie, C Poland
51.53N 16.59E
112 K11 **Gostynin** Mazowieckie, C Poland
52.25N 19.27E
Gosyogawara see Goshogawara
97 I16 **Göta kanal** canal S Sweden
95 N17 **Göta älv** ✍ S Sweden
97 K18 **Götaland** cultural region S Sweden
97 I16 **Göteborg** Eng. Gothenburg.
Västra Götaland, S Sweden
57.43N 11.58E
79 X16 **Gotel Mountains** ▲ E Nigeria
97 I16 **Götene** Västra Götaland,
S Sweden 58.31N 13.28E
Gotera see San Francisco
103 K16 **Gotha** Thüringen, C Germany
50.57N 10.43E
31 N15 **Gothenburg** Nebraska, C USA
40.57N 100.09W
Gothenburg see Göteborg
79 S14 **Gothèye** Tillabéri, SW Niger
13.52N 1.27E
97 P19 **Gotland** var. Gothland, Gottland.
◆ county SE Sweden
97 O18 **Gotland** island SE Sweden
170 E12 **Gotō-rettō** island group SW Japan
116 H12 **Gotse Delchev** prev. Nevrokop.
Blagoevgrad, SW Bulgaria
41.35S 23.43E
97 Q19 **Gotska Sandön** island SE Sweden
170 Ee12 **Gōtsu** var. Gōtu. Shimane,
Honshū, SW Japan 35.00N 132.13E
103 I15 **Göttingen** var. Goettingen.
Niedersachsen, C Germany
51.33N 9.55E
Gottland see Gotland
95 I16 **Gottne** Västernorrland, C Sweden
63.27N 18.25E
Gottschee see Kočevje
Gottwaldov see Zlín
Gōtu see Gōtsu
152 B11 **Goturdepe** Rus. Koturdepe.
Balkan Velayat, W Turkmenistan
39.32S 53.39E
110 H7 **Götzis** Vorarlberg, NW Austria
47.21N 9.40E
100 I11 **Gouda** Zuid-Holland,
C Netherlands 52.01N 4.42E
78 I12 **Goudiri** var. Goudiry. E Senegal
14.12N 12.40W
Goudiry see Goudiri
79 X12 **Goudoumaria** Diffa, S Niger
13.28N 11.15E
13 R9 **Gouffre, Rivière du** ✍ Québec,
SE Canada
67 M19 **Gough Fracture Zone** tectonic
feature S Atlantic Ocean
67 M19 **Gough Island** island Tristan da
Cunha, S Atlantic Ocean
13 N8 **Gouin, Réservoir** ✦ Québec,
SE Canada
12 B10 **Goulais River** Ontario, S Canada
46.41N 84.22W
191 R9 **Goulburn** New South Wales,
SE Australia 34.45S 149.43E
191 O11 **Goulburn River** ✍ Victoria,
SE Australia
205 O10 **Gould Coast** physical region
Antarctica
78 F13 **Goulimine** see Guelmime
172 I22 **Goumenissa** Kentrikí
Makedonía, N Greece
40.55N 22.27E
79 Q14 **Goundam** Tombouctou, NW Mali
16.25N 3.41W
80 I13 **Goundi** Moyen-Chari, S Chad
9.18N 17.21E
82 I11 **Gounou-Gaya** Mayo-Kébbi,
SW Chad 9.37S 15.30E
79 O14 **Gourci** var. Gourcy. NW Burkina
13.14N 2.22W

Gourcy see Gourci
104 M13 Gourdon Lot, S France 44.45N 1.22E
79 W11 Gouré Zinder, SE Niger 13.58N 10.16E
104 G6 Gourin Morbihan, NW France 48.07N 3.37W
79 P10 Gourma-Rharous Tombouctou, C Mali 16.54N 1.55W
105 N4 Gournay-en-Bray Seine-Maritime, N France 49.29N 1.42E
80 J6 Gouro Borkou-Ennedi-Tibesti, N Chad 19.26N 19.36E
106 H8 Gouveia Guarda, N Portugal 40.28N 7.34W
20 I7 Gouverneur New York, NE USA 44.20N 75.27W
101 L21 Gouvy Luxembourg, E Belgium 50.10N 5.55E
47 R14 Gouyave var. Charlotte Town. NW Grenada 12.10N 61.43W
Goverla, Gora see Hoverla, Hora
61 N20 Governador Valadares Minas Gerais, SE Brazil 18.51S 41.57W
179 Rr16 Governor Generoso Mindanao, S Philippines 6.36N 126.06E
46 I2 Governor's Harbour Eleuthera Island, C Bahamas 25.11N 76.15W
168 F9 Govĭ-Altay ◆ province SW Mongolia
168 I10 Govĭ Altayn Nuruu ▲ S Mongolia
160 L9 Govind Ballabh Pant Sāgar ⊠ C India
158 I7 Govind Sāgar ⊠ NE India
168 M8 Govĭ-Sumber ◆ province C Mongolia
Govurdak see Gowurdak
20 D11 Gowanda New York, NE USA 42.25N 78.55W
154 J10 Gowd-e Zereh, Dasht-e var. Guad-i-Zirreh. marsh SW Afghanistan
12 F8 Gowganda Ontario, S Canada 47.39N 80.43W
12 G8 Gowganda Lake ⊗ Ontario, S Canada
31 U13 Gowrie Iowa, C USA 42.16N 94.17W
153 N14 Gowurdak Rus. Govurdak; prev. Guardak. Lebap Welaýaty, E Turkmenistan 37.50N 66.06E
63 C15 Goya Corrientes, NE Argentina 29.10S 59.15W
Goyania see Goiânia
143 X11 Göyçay Rus. Geokchay. C Azerbaijan 40.38N 47.44E
152 D10 Goymat Rus. Koymat. Balkan Welaýaty, NW Turkmenistan 40.23N 55.45E
152 D10 Goymatdag Rus. Gory Koymatdag. hill range NW Turkmenistan
142 F12 Göynük Bolu, NW Turkey 40.24N 30.45E
172 N12 Goyō-san ▲ Honshū, C Japan 39.12N 141.40E
80 K11 Goz Beïda Ouaddaï, SE Chad 12.06N 21.22E
152 M10 G'ozg'on Rus. Gazgan. Navoiy Viloyati, C Uzbekistan 40.36N 65.29E
164 H11 Gozha Co ⊗ W China
123 J15 Gozo Malt. Ghawdex. island N Malta
82 H9 Gôz Regeb Kassala, NE Sudan 16.03N 35.33E
Gozyô see Gojō
85 H25 Graaff-Reinet Eastern Cape, S South Africa 32.16S 24.31E
Graasten see Gråsten
78 L17 Grabo SW Ivory Coast 4.57N 7.30W
114 P11 Grabovica Serbia, E Serbia 44.30N 22.29E
112 I13 Grabów nad Prosną Wielkopolskie, C Poland 51.30N 18.06E
110 I8 Grabs Sankt Gallen, NE Switzerland 47.10N 9.27E
114 D12 Gračac Zadar, C Croatia 44.18N 15.52E
114 I11 Gračanica Federacija Bosna I Hercegovina, NE Bosnia and Herzegovina 44.41N 18.20E
12 L11 Graceffeld Québec, SE Canada 46.06N 76.03W
101 K19 Grâce-Hollogne Liège, E Belgium 50.38N 5.30E
25 R8 Graceville Florida, SE USA 30.57N 85.31W
31 R8 Graceville Minnesota, N USA 45.34N 96.25W
44 G6 Gracias Lempira, W Honduras 14.34N 88.34W
Gracias see Lempira
44 L5 Gracias a Dios ◆ department E Honduras
45 O6 Gracias a Dios, Cabo de headland Honduras/Nicaragua 15.00N 83.10W
66 O2 Graciosa var. Ilha Graciosa. island Azores, Portugal, NE Atlantic Ocean
66 Q11 Graciosa island Islas Canarias, Spain, NE Atlantic Ocean
Graciosa, Ilha see Graciosa
114 I11 Gradačac Federacija Bosna I Hercegovina, N Bosnia and Herzegovina 44.51N 18.24E
61 J15 Gradaús, Serra dos ▲ C Brazil
106 L3 Gradefes Castilla-León, N Spain 42.37N 5.13W
Gradiška see Bosanska Gradiška
Gradizhsk see Hradyz'k
108 J7 Grado Friuli-Venezia Giulia, NE Italy 45.41N 13.24E
106 K2 Grado Asturias, N Spain 43.22N 6.04W
115 P19 Gradsko C FYR Macedonia 41.34N 21.56E
39 V11 Grady New Mexico, SW USA 34.49N 103.19W
31 T12 Graettinger Iowa, C USA 43.14N 94.45W
103 M23 Grafing Bayern, SE Germany 48.01N 11.57E
27 S6 Graford Texas, SW USA 32.56N 98.15W
191 V5 Grafton New South Wales, SE Australia 29.41S 152.55E
31 Q3 Grafton North Dakota, N USA 48.24N 97.24W
23 S3 Grafton West Virginia, NE USA 39.20N 80.01W
23 T9 Graham North Carolina, SE USA 36.04N 79.24W
27 R6 Graham Texas, SW USA 33.06N 98.34W
Graham Bell Island see Greem-Bell, Ostrov
8 I13 Graham Island island Queen Charlotte Islands, British Columbia, SW Canada
21 S6 Graham Lake ⊗ Maine, NE USA
204 H4 Graham Land physical region Antarctica
39 N15 Graham, Mount ▲ Arizona, SW USA 32.42N 109.52W
Grahamstad see Grahamstown
85 I25 Grahamstown Afr. Grahamstad. Eastern Cape, S South Africa 33.18S 26.31E
Grahovo see Bosansko Grahovo
70 C11 Grain Coast coastal region S Liberia
174 Mm16 Grajagan Jawa, S Indonesia 8.33S 114.13E
174 Mm16 Grajagan, Teluk bay Jawa, S Indonesia
61 L14 Grajaú Maranhão, E Brazil 5.49S 45.12W
60 M13 Grajaú, Rio ↝ NE Brazil
112 O8 Grajewo Podlaskie, NE Poland 53.38N 22.25E
97 F24 Gram Sønderjylland, SW Denmark 55.18N 9.03E
105 N13 Gramat Lot, S France 44.45N 1.45E
24 H5 Grambling Louisiana, S USA 32.31N 92.43W
117 C14 Grámmos ▲ Albania/Greece
98 I9 Grampian Mountains ▲ C Scotland, UK
190 L12 Grampians, The ▲ Victoria, SE Australia
100 O9 Gramsbergen Overijssel, E Netherlands 52.37N 6.39E
115 L21 Gramsh var. Gramshi. Elbasan, C Albania 40.52N 20.12E
Gramshi see Gramsh
Gran see Hron, Slovakia
Gran see Esztergom, N Hungary
56 F11 Granada Meta, C Colombia 3.36N 73.44W
44 J10 Granada Granada, SW Nicaragua 11.55N 85.58W
107 N14 Granada Andalucía, S Spain 37.13N 3.40W
39 W6 Granada Colorado, C USA 38.00N 102.18W
44 J11 Granada ◆ department SW Nicaragua
107 N14 Granada ◆ province Andalucía, S Spain
65 I21 Gran Altiplanicie Central plain S Argentina
99 E17 Granard Ir. Gránard. C Ireland 53.46N 7.30W
65 J20 Gran Bajo basin S Argentina
65 J15 Gran Bajo del Gualicho basin E Argentina
65 I21 Gran Bajo de San Julián basin SE Argentina
27 S7 Granbury Texas, SW USA 32.26N 97.47W
13 P12 Granby Québec, SE Canada 45.24N 72.40W
29 S8 Granby Missouri, C USA 36.55N 94.14W
39 S3 Granby, Lake ⊠ Colorado, C USA
66 O12 Gran Canaria var. Grand Canary. island Islas Canarias, Spain, NE Atlantic Ocean
49 T11 Gran Chaco var. Chaco. lowland plain South America
47 R14 Grand Anse SW Grenada 12.01N 61.45W
Grand-Anse see Portsmouth
46 G1 Grand Bahama Island island N Bahamas
Grand Balé see Tui
105 U7 Grand Ballon Ger. Ballon de Guebwiller. ▲ NE France 47.53N 7.06E
11 T13 Grand Bank Newfoundland and Labrador, SE Canada 47.04N 55.46W
66 I7 Grand Banks of Newfoundland undersea feature NW Atlantic Ocean
Grand Bassa see Buchanan
79 N17 Grand-Bassam var. Bassam. SE Ivory Coast 5.13N 3.46W
12 E16 Grand Bend Ontario, S Canada 43.17N 81.46W
78 L17 Grand-Bérébi var. Grand-Béréby. SW Ivory Coast 4.37N 6.55W
Grand-Béréby see Grand-Bérébi
47 X11 Grand-Bourg Marie-Galante, SE Guadeloupe 15.53N 61.18W
46 M6 Grand Caicos var. Middle Caicos. island C Turks and Caicos Islands
12 K12 Grand Calumet, Île du island Québec, SE Canada
99 E18 Grand Canal Ir. An Chanáil Mhór. canal C Ireland
Grand Canary see Gran Canaria
38 K10 Grand Canyon Arizona, SW USA 36.01N 112.10W
38 J9 Grand Canyon canyon Arizona, SW USA
Grand Canyon State see Arizona
46 D8 Grand Cayman island SW Cayman Islands
9 R14 Grand Centre Alberta, SW Canada 54.25N 110.13W
78 L17 Grand Cess SE Liberia 4.36N 8.12W
110 D12 Grand Combin ▲ S Switzerland 45.58N 7.27E
34 K8 Grand Coulee Washington, NW USA 47.56N 119.00W
34 J8 Grand Coulee valley Washington, NW USA
47 X5 Grand Cul-de-Sac Marin bay N Guadeloupe
Grand Duchy of Luxembourg see Luxembourg
65 I22 Grande, Bahía bay S Argentina
9 N14 Grande Cache Alberta, W Canada 53.52N 119.07W
105 U12 Grande Casse ▲ E France 45.22N 6.50E
180 G12 Grande Comore var. Njazidja, Great Comoro. island NW Comoros
63 G18 Grande, Cuchilla hill range E Uruguay
47 S5 Grande de Añasco, Río ↝ W Puerto Rico
Grande de Chiloé, Isla see Chiloé, Isla de
60 J12 Grande de Gurupá, Ilha river island NE Brazil
59 K21 Grande de Lipez, Río ↝ SW Bolivia
47 U6 Grande de Loíza, Río ↝ E Puerto Rico
47 T5 Grande de Manatí, Río ↝ C Puerto Rico
44 L9 Grande de Matagalpa, Río ↝ C Nicaragua
42 K12 Grande de Santiago, Río var. Santiago. ↝ C Mexico
45 O15 Grande de Térraba, Río var. Río Térraba. ↝ SE Costa Rica
10 J9 Grande Deux, Réservoir la ⊠ Québec, E Canada
62 O10 Grande, Ilha island SE Brazil
9 O13 Grande Prairie Alberta, W Canada 55.10N 118.52W
76 I8 Grand Erg Occidental desert W Algeria
76 L9 Grand Erg Oriental desert Algeria/Tunisia
61 J20 Grande, Rio ↝ S Brazil
2 F15 Grande, Rio var. Río Bravo, Sp. Río Bravo del Norte, Bravo del Norte. ↝ Mexico/USA
59 M18 Grande, Río ↝ C Bolivia
13 Y7 Grande-Rivière Québec, SE Canada 48.27N 64.37W
13 Y6 Grande Rivière ↝ Québec, SE Canada
46 M8 Grande-Rivière-du-Nord N Haiti 19.28N 72.07W
64 K9 Grande, Salina var. Gran Salitral. salt lake C Argentina
13 S7 Grandes-Bergeronnes Québec, SE Canada 48.16N 69.32W
49 W6 Grande, Serra ▲ W Brazil
42 K4 Grande, Sierra ▲ N Mexico
105 S12 Grandes Rousses ▲ E France
65 K17 Grandes, Salinas salt lake E Argentina
47 Y5 Grande Terre island E West Indies
13 X5 Grande-Vallée Québec, SE Canada 49.12N 65.08W
47 Y5 Grande Vigie, Pointe de la headland Grande Terre, N Guadeloupe 16.31N 61.27W
11 N14 Grand Falls New Brunswick, SE Canada 47.01N 67.46W
11 T11 Grand Falls Newfoundland and Labrador, SE Canada 48.57N 55.48W
26 L9 Grandfalls Texas, SW USA 31.20N 102.51W
23 P9 Grandfather Mountain ▲ North Carolina, SE USA 36.06N 81.48W
28 L13 Grandfield Oklahoma, C USA 34.15N 98.40W
9 N17 Grand Forks British Columbia, SW Canada 49.01N 118.30W
31 R4 Grand Forks North Dakota, N USA 47.54N 97.02W
33 O9 Grand Haven Michigan, N USA 43.03N 86.13W
Grandichi see Hrandzichy
31 P15 Grand Island Nebraska, C USA 40.55N 98.20W
33 O3 Grand Island island Michigan, N USA
24 K10 Grand Isle Louisiana, S USA 29.12N 90.00W
67 A23 Grand Jason island Jason Islands, NW Falkland Islands
39 P5 Grand Junction Colorado, C USA 39.03N 108.33W
22 F10 Grand Junction Tennessee, S USA 35.03N 89.11W
12 J9 Grand-Lac-Victoria Québec, SE Canada 47.33N 77.28W
12 J9 Grand lac Victoria ⊗ Québec, SE Canada
79 N17 Grand-Lahou var. Grand Lahu. S Ivory Coast 5.09N 5.01W
Grand Lahu see Grand-Lahou
39 S3 Grand Lake Colorado, C USA 40.15N 105.49W
11 S11 Grand Lake ⊗ Newfoundland and Labrador, E Canada
24 G9 Grand Lake ⊗ Louisiana, S USA
33 R5 Grand Lake ⊗ Michigan, N USA
33 Q13 Grand Lake ⊠ Ohio, N USA
29 R9 Grand Lake O' The Cherokees var. Lake O' The Cherokees. ⊠ Oklahoma, C USA
33 Q9 Grand Ledge Michigan, N USA 42.45N 84.45W
104 I8 Grand-Lieu, Lac de ⊗ NW France
21 U6 Grand Manan Channel channel Canada/USA
11 O15 Grand Manan Island island New Brunswick, SE Canada
31 Y4 Grand Marais Minnesota, N USA 47.45N 90.19W
13 P10 Grand-Mère Quebec, SE Canada 46.36N 72.41W
39 P5 Grand Mesa ▲ Colorado, C USA
110 C10 Grand Muveran ▲ W Switzerland 46.16N 7.12E
106 G12 Grândola Setúbal, S Portugal 38.10N 8.34W
Grand Paradis see Gran Paradiso
197 G4 Grand Passage passage N New Caledonia
79 R16 Grand-Popo S Benin 6.19N 1.49E
31 Z3 Grand Portage Minnesota, N USA 48.00N 89.36W
27 T6 Grand Prairie Texas, SW USA 32.45N 97.00W
9 W14 Grand Rapids Manitoba, C Canada 53.12N 99.19W
33 P9 Grand Rapids Michigan, N USA 42.57N 86.40W
31 V5 Grand Rapids Minnesota, N USA 47.14N 93.31W
197 G5 Grand Récif de Koumac reef W New Caledonia
197 J8 Grand Récif Sud reef S New Caledonia
12 L10 Grand-Remous Québec, SE Canada 46.36N 75.53W
12 F15 Grand River ↝ Ontario, S Canada
33 P9 Grand River ↝ Michigan, N USA
29 T3 Grand River ↝ Missouri, C USA
30 M7 Grand River ↝ South Dakota, N USA
47 Q11 Grand' Rivière N Martinique 14.51N 61.12W
34 F11 Grand Ronde Oregon, NW USA 45.03N 123.43W
34 L11 Grand Ronde River ↝ Oregon/Washington, NW USA
Grand-Saint-Bernard, Col du see Great Saint Bernard Pass
27 V6 Grand Saline Texas, SW USA 32.40N 95.42W
57 X10 Grand-Santi W French Guiana 4.19N 54.24W
Grandsee see Grandson
110 B9 Grandson prev. Grandsee. Vaud, W Switzerland 46.49N 6.39E
180 J16 Grand Sœur island Les Sœurs, NE Seychelles
35 S14 Grand Teton ▲ Wyoming, C USA 43.44N 110.48W
33 P5 Grand Traverse Bay lake bay Michigan, N USA
47 N6 Grand Turk O (Turks and Caicos Islands) Grand Turk Island, S Turks and Caicos Islands 21.24N 71.08W
47 N6 Grand Turk Island island SE Turks and Caicos Islands
105 S13 Grand Veymont ▲ E France 44.51N 5.32E
9 W15 Grandview Manitoba, S Canada 51.10N 100.40W
29 R4 Grandview Missouri, C USA 38.53N 94.31W
38 I10 Grand Wash Cliffs cliff Arizona, SW USA
12 J8 Granet, Lac ⊗ Québec, SE Canada
97 L14 Grangärde Dalarna, C Sweden 60.15N 15.00E
46 H12 Grange Hill W Jamaica 18.18N 78.10W
98 J12 Grangemouth C Scotland, UK 56.01N 3.43W
27 T10 Granger Texas, SW USA 30.43N 97.26W
34 J10 Granger Washington, NW USA 46.20N 120.11W
35 T17 Granger Wyoming, C USA 41.37N 109.58W
Granges see Grenchen
97 L14 Grängesberg Dalarna, C Sweden 60.06N 15.00E
35 N11 Grangeville Idaho, NW USA 45.55N 116.07W
8 K13 Granisle British Columbia, SW Canada 54.55N 126.13W
32 K15 Granite City Illinois, N USA 38.42N 90.09W
31 S9 Granite Falls Minnesota, N USA 44.48N 95.33W
23 Q9 Granite Falls North Carolina, SE USA 35.48N 81.25W
38 K12 Granite Mountain ▲ Arizona, SW USA 34.38N 112.34W
35 T12 Granite Peak ▲ Montana, NW USA 45.09N 109.48W
37 T2 Granite Peak ▲ Nevada, W USA 41.40N 117.35W
38 J3 Granite Peak ▲ Utah, W USA 40.09N 113.18W
Granite State see New Hampshire
109 H24 Granitola, Capo headland Sicilia, Italy, C Mediterranean Sea 37.33N 12.39E
193 H15 Granity West Coast, South Island, NZ 41.37S 171.53E
Gran Lago see Nicaragua, Lago de
65 J18 Gran Laguna Salada ⊗ S Argentina
Gran Malvina, Isla see West Falkland
97 L18 Gränna Jönköping, S Sweden 58.01N 14.30E
107 W5 Granollers var. Granollérs. Cataluña, NE Spain 41.37N 2.18E
108 A7 Gran Paradiso Fr. Grand Paradis. ▲ NW Italy 45.31N 7.13E
Gran Pilastro see Hochfeiler
Gran Salitral see Grande, Salina
Gran San Bernardo, Passo di see Great Saint Bernard Pass
Gran Santiago see Santiago
109 J14 Gran Sasso d'Italia ▲ C Italy
102 N11 Gransee Brandenburg, NE Germany 53.00N 13.10E
30 L15 Grant Nebraska, C USA 40.50N 101.43W
29 R1 Grant City Missouri, C USA 40.29N 94.24W
99 N19 Grantham E England, UK 52.55N 0.39W
67 D24 Grantham Sound sound East Falkland, Falkland Islands
204 K13 Grant Island island Antarctica
47 Z14 Grantley Adams ✕ (Bridgetown) SE Barbados 13.04N 59.29W
37 S7 Grant, Mount ▲ Nevada, W USA 38.34N 118.47W
98 J9 Grantown-on-Spey N Scotland, UK 57.11N 3.52W
37 W8 Grant Range ▲ Nevada, W USA
39 Q11 Grants New Mexico, SW USA 35.09N 107.50W
32 I4 Grantsburg Wisconsin, N USA 45.46N 92.40W
34 F15 Grants Pass Oregon, NW USA 42.26N 123.19W
38 K3 Grantsville Utah, W USA 40.36N 112.27W
23 R4 Grantsville West Virginia, NE USA 38.54N 81.04W
104 I5 Granville Manche, N France 48.49N 1.34W
9 V12 Granville Lake ⊗ Manitoba, C Canada
27 V8 Grapeland Texas, SW USA 31.29N 95.28W
27 T6 Grapevine Texas, SW USA 32.55N 97.04W
85 K20 Graskop Mpumalanga, NE South Africa 24.58S 30.49E
97 P14 Gräsö Uppsala, C Sweden 60.22N 18.30E
95 I19 Gräsö island C Sweden
105 U15 Grasse Alpes-Maritimes, SE France 43.42N 6.52E
20 E14 Grassflat Pennsylvania, NE USA 41.00N 78.04W
35 U9 Grassrange Montana, NW USA 47.02N 108.48W
20 J6 Grass River ↝ New York, NE USA
37 P6 Grass Valley California, W USA 39.12N 121.04W
191 N14 Grassy Tasmania, SE Australia 40.03S 144.04E
30 K4 Grassy Butte North Dakota, N USA 47.20N 103.13W
23 R5 Grassy Knob ▲ West Virginia, NE USA 38.04N 80.31W
97 G24 Gråsten var. Graasten. Sønderjylland, SW Denmark 54.55N 9.37E
97 J18 Grästorp Västra Götaland, S Sweden 58.19N 12.45E
Gratianopolis see Grenoble
111 V8 Gratwein Steiermark, SE Austria 47.06N 15.18E
Gratz see Graz
110 I9 Graubünden Fr. Grisons, It. Grigioni. ◆ canton SE Switzerland
Graudenz see Grudziądz
105 N15 Graulhet Tarn, S France 43.45N 1.58E
107 T4 Graus Aragón, NE Spain 42.11N 0.21E
63 I16 Gravataí Rio Grande do Sul, S Brazil 29.55S 51.00W
100 L13 Grave Noord-Brabant, SE Netherlands 51.45N 5.45E
9 T17 Gravelbourg Saskatchewan, S Canada 49.52N 106.33W
105 N1 Gravelines Nord, N France 51.00N 2.07E
Graven see Grez-Doiceau
12 H13 Gravenhurst Ontario, S Canada 44.55N 79.22W
35 O10 Grave Peak ▲ Idaho, NW USA 46.24N 114.43W
104 I11 Grave, Pointe de headland W France 45.33N 1.24W
191 S4 Gravesend New South Wales, SE Australia 29.37S 150.15E
99 P22 Gravesend SE England, UK 51.27N 0.24E
109 N17 Gravina in Puglia Puglia, SE Italy 40.48N 16.25E
105 S8 Gray Haute-Saône, E France 47.28N 5.34E
25 T4 Gray Georgia, SE USA 33.00N 83.31W
205 V16 Gray, Cape headland Antarctica, 67.30S 143.30E
34 F9 Grayland Washington, NW USA 46.46N 124.07W
41 N10 Grayling Alaska, USA 62.55N 160.07W
33 Q6 Grayling Michigan, N USA 44.40N 84.43W
34 F9 Grays Harbor inlet Washington, NW USA
23 O5 Grayson Kentucky, S USA 38.19N 82.57W
39 S4 Grays Peak ▲ Colorado, C USA 39.37N 105.49W
32 M16 Grayville Illinois, N USA 38.15N 87.59W
111 V8 Graz prev. Gratz. Steiermark, SE Austria 47.04N 15.23E
106 L15 Grazalema Andalucía, S Spain 36.46N 5.22W
115 P15 Grdelica Serbia, SE Serbia 42.54N 22.05E
46 H1 Great Abaco var. Abaco Island. island N Bahamas
Great Admiralty Island see Manus Island
Great Alfold see Great Hungarian Plain
Great Ararat see Büyükağrı Dağı
189 U8 Great Artesian Basin lowlands Queensland, C Australia
197 I15 Great Astrolabe Reef reef Kadavu, SW Fiji
189 O12 Great Australian Bight bight S Australia
66 E11 Great Bahama Bank undersea feature E Gulf of Mexico
192 M4 Great Barrier Island island N NZ
189 X4 Great Barrier Reef reef Queensland, NE Australia
20 L11 Great Barrington Massachusetts, NE USA 42.11N 73.20W
(0) F10 Great Basin basin W USA
15 H5 Great Bear Lake Fr. Grand Lac de l'Ours. ⊗ Northwest Territories, NW Canada
Great Belt see Storebælt
28 L5 Great Bend Kansas, C USA 38.21N 98.45W
Great Bermuda see Bermuda
99 A20 Great Blasket Island Ir. An Blascaod Mór. island SW Ireland
Great Britain see Britain
157 Q23 Great Channel channel Andaman Sea/Indian Ocean
177 F10 Great Coco Island island SW Burma
Great Crosby see Crosby
23 X7 Great Dismal Swamp wetland North Carolina/Virginia, SE USA
35 V16 Great Divide Basin basin Wyoming, C USA
189 W7 Great Dividing Range ▲ NE Australia
12 D12 Great Duck Island island Ontario, S Canada
Great Elder Reservoir see Waconda Lake
205 V8 Greater Antarctica var. East Antarctica. physical region Antarctica
46 G8 Greater Antilles island group West Indies
133 V16 Greater Sunda Islands var. Sunda Islands. island group Indonesia
192 I1 Great Exhibition Bay inlet North Island, NZ
46 H4 Great Exuma Island island C Bahamas
35 R8 Great Falls Montana, NW USA 47.30N 111.18W
23 R11 Great Falls South Carolina, SE USA 34.34N 80.54W
86 F9 Great Fisher Bank undersea feature C North Sea
Great Glen see Mor, Glen
Great Grimsby see Grimsby
46 I4 Great Guana Cay island C Bahamas
66 I5 Great Hellefiske Bank undersea feature N Atlantic Ocean
113 L24 Great Hungarian Plain var. Great Alfold, Plain of Hungary, Hung. Alföld. plain SE Europe
46 L7 Great Inagua var. Inagua Islands. island S Bahamas
Great Indian Desert see Thar Desert
85 G25 Great Karoo var. Great Karroo, High Veld, Afr. Groot Karoo, Hoë Karoo. plateau region S South Africa
Great Karroo see Great Karoo
Great Kei see Groot-Kei
Great Khingan Range see Da Hinggan Ling
12 E11 Great La Cloche Island island Ontario, S Canada
191 P16 Great Lake ⊗ Tasmania, SE Australia
Great Lake see Tônlé Sap
16 O16 Great Lakes lakes Ontario, Canada/USA
Great Lakes State see Michigan
99 L20 Great Malvern W England, UK 52.07N 2.19W
192 M5 Great Mercury Island island N NZ
Great Meteor Seamount see Great Meteor Tablemount
66 K10 Great Meteor Tablemount var. Great Meteor Seamount. undersea feature E Atlantic Ocean 30.00N 28.30W
33 Q14 Great Miami River ↝ Ohio, N USA
157 Q24 Great Nicobar island Nicobar Islands, India, NE Indian Ocean
99 O19 Great Ouse var. Ouse. ↝ E England, UK
191 Q17 Great Oyster Bay bay Tasmania, SE Australia
46 I13 Great Pedro Bluff headland W Jamaica 17.51N 77.44W
23 T12 Great Pee Dee River ↝ North Carolina/South Carolina, SE USA
133 W9 Great Plain of China plain E China
(0) F12 Great Plains var. High Plains. plains Canada/USA
39 W6 Great Plains Reservoirs ⊠ Colorado, C USA
21 Q13 Great Point headland Nantucket Island, Massachusetts, NE USA 41.23N 70.03W
70 I13 Great Rift Valley var. Rift Valley. depression Asia/Africa
83 I23 Great Ruaha ↝ S Tanzania
20 K10 Great Sacandaga Lake ⊠ New York, NE USA
110 C12 Great Saint Bernard Pass Fr. Col du Grand-Saint-Bernard, It. Passo di Gran San Bernardo. pass Italy/Switzerland 45.52N 7.10E
46 F1 Great Sale Cay island N Bahamas
Great Salt Desert see Kavīr, Dasht-e
38 K1 Great Salt Lake salt lake Utah, W USA
38 J3 Great Salt Lake Desert plain Utah, W USA
28 M8 Great Salt Plains Lake ⊠ Oklahoma, C USA
77 T9 Great Sand Sea desert Egypt/Libya
188 L6 Great Sandy Desert desert Western Australia
Great Sandy Desert see Ar Rub' al Khālī
Great Sandy Island see Fraser Island
197 I13 Great Sea Reef reef Vanua Levu, N Fiji
40 H17 Great Sitkin Island island Aleutian Islands, Alaska, USA
15 I8 Great Slave Lake Fr. Grand Lac des Esclaves. ⊗ Northwest Territories, NW Canada
23 O10 Great Smoky Mountains ▲ North Carolina/Tennessee, SE USA
8 L11 Great Snow Mountain ▲ British Columbia, W Canada 57.22N 124.08W
66 A12 Great Sound bay Bermuda, NW Atlantic Ocean
188 M10 Great Victoria Desert desert South Australia/Western Australia
204 H2 Great Wall Chinese research station South Shetland Islands, Antarctica 61.57S 58.23W
21 T7 Great Wass Island island Maine, NE USA
99 Q19 Great Yarmouth var. Yarmouth. E England, UK 52.37N 1.43E
145 S1 Great Zab Ar. Az Zāb al Kabīr, Kurd. Zē-i Bādinān, Turk. Büyükzap Suyu. ↝ Iraq/Turkey
97 I17 Grebbestad Västra Götaland, S Sweden 58.42N 11.15E
Grebenka see Hrebinka
44 M13 Grecia Alajuela, C Costa Rica 10.04N 84.19W
63 E18 Greco Río Negro, W Uruguay 32.49S 57.03W
Greco, Cape see Gkréko, Akrotíri
106 L8 Gredos, Sierra de ▲ W Spain
20 F9 Greece New York, NE USA 43.12N 77.41W
117 E17 Greece off. Hellenic Republic, Gk. Ellás; anc. Hellas. ◆ republic SE Europe
Greece Central see Stereá Ellás
Greece West see Dytikí Ellás
39 T3 Greeley Colorado, C USA 40.21N 104.41W
31 P14 Greeley Nebraska, C USA 41.33N 98.31W
126 Hh1 Greem-Bell, Ostrov Eng. Graham Bell Island. island Zemlya Frantsa-Iosifa, N Russian Federation
32 M6 Green Bay Wisconsin, N USA 44.32N 88.00W
33 N6 Green Bay lake bay Michigan/Wisconsin, N USA
23 S5 Greenbrier River ↝ West Virginia, NE USA
31 S2 Greenbush Minnesota, N USA 48.42N 96.10W
191 R12 Green Cape headland New South Wales, SE Australia 37.15S 150.03E
33 O14 Greencastle Indiana, N USA 39.38N 86.51W
20 F16 Greencastle Pennsylvania, NE USA 39.47N 77.43W
29 T2 Green City Missouri, C USA 40.16N 92.57W
23 O9 Greeneville Tennessee, S USA 36.09N 82.49W
37 O11 Greenfield California, W USA 36.19N 121.15W
33 P14 Greenfield Indiana, N USA 39.47N 85.46W
31 U15 Greenfield Iowa, C USA 41.18N 94.27W
20 M11 Greenfield Massachusetts, NE USA 42.33N 72.34W
29 S7 Greenfield Missouri, C USA 37.25N 93.50W
33 S14 Greenfield Ohio, N USA 39.21N 83.22W
22 G8 Greenfield Tennessee, S USA 36.09N 88.48W
32 M9 Greenfield Wisconsin, N USA 42.55N 87.59W
29 T9 Green Forest Arkansas, C USA 36.19N 93.24W
39 T7 Greenhorn Mountain ▲ Colorado, C USA 37.50N 104.59W
Green Island see Lü Tao
195 R10 Green Islands var. Nissan Islands. island group NE PNG
9 S14 Green Lake Saskatchewan, C Canada 54.15N 107.51W
32 L8 Green Lake ⊗ Wisconsin, N USA
207 O14 Greenland Dan. Grønland, Inuit Kalaallit Nunaat. ◇ Danish external territory NE North America
86 D4 Greenland island NE North America
207 R13 Greenland Plain undersea feature N Greenland Sea
207 R14 Greenland Sea sea Arctic Ocean
39 R4 Green Mountain Reservoir ⊠ Colorado, C USA
20 M8 Green Mountains ▲ Vermont, NE USA
Green Mountain State see Vermont
98 H12 Greenock W Scotland, UK 55.57N 4.45W
41 T5 Greenough, Mount ▲ Alaska, USA 69.15N 141.37W
194 E10 Green River Sandaun, NW PNG 3.46S 141.10E
39 N5 Green River Utah, W USA 39.00N 110.07W
35 U17 Green River Wyoming, C USA 41.33N 109.27W
18 Ii7 Green River ↝ W USA
32 K11 Green River ↝ Illinois, N USA
22 J7 Green River ↝ Kentucky, S USA
30 K5 Green River ↝ North Dakota, N USA
39 N6 Green River ↝ Utah, W USA
35 T16 Green River ↝ Wyoming, C USA
22 L7 Green River Lake ⊠ Kentucky, S USA
25 O5 Greensboro Alabama, S USA 32.42N 87.36W
25 U3 Greensboro Georgia, SE USA 33.34N 83.10W
23 T9 Greensboro North Carolina, SE USA 36.04N 79.47W
33 P14 Greensburg Indiana, N USA 39.20N 85.28W
28 K6 Greensburg Kansas, C USA 37.36N 99.17W
22 L7 Greensburg Kentucky, S USA 37.15N 85.28W
20 C15 Greensburg Pennsylvania, NE USA 40.18N 79.32W
39 O13 Greens Peak ▲ Arizona, SW USA 34.06N 109.34W
23 V12 Green Swamp wetland North Carolina, SE USA
23 O4 Greenup Kentucky, S USA 38.34N 82.49W
38 M16 Green Valley Arizona, SW USA 31.49N 111.00W
78 K17 Greenville var. Sino, Sinoe. SE Liberia 5.01N 9.03W
25 P6 Greenville Alabama, S USA 31.49N 86.37W
25 T8 Greenville Florida, SE USA 30.28N 83.37W
25 S4 Greenville Georgia, SE USA 33.03N 84.42W
32 L15 Greenville Illinois, N USA 38.53N 89.24W
22 I7 Greenville Kentucky, S USA 37.12N 87.10W
21 Q5 Greenville Maine, NE USA 45.26N 69.36W
33 P9 Greenville Michigan, N USA 43.10N 85.15W
24 J4 Greenville Mississippi, S USA 33.24N 91.03W
23 W9 Greenville North Carolina, SE USA 35.36N 77.22W
33 Q13 Greenville Ohio, N USA 40.06N 84.37W
21 O12 Greenville Rhode Island, NE USA 41.52N 71.33W
23 P11 Greenville South Carolina, SE USA 34.51N 82.23W
27 U6 Greenville Texas, SW USA 33.08N 96.06W
33 T12 Greenwich Ohio, N USA 41.01N 82.31W
29 S11 Greenwood Arkansas, C USA 35.13N 94.15W
33 O14 Greenwood Indiana, N USA 39.38N 86.06W
24 K4 Greenwood Mississippi, S USA 33.30N 90.11W
23 P12 Greenwood South Carolina, SE USA 34.12N 82.09W
23 Q12 Greenwood, Lake ⊠ South Carolina, SE USA
23 P11 Greer South Carolina, SE USA 34.56N 82.13W
29 V10 Greers Ferry Lake ⊠ Arkansas, C USA
29 S13 Greeson, Lake ⊠ Arkansas, C USA

◆ Country
● Country Capital
◇ Dependent Territory
○ Dependent Territory Capital
◆ Administrative Region
✕ International Airport
▲ Mountain
▲ Mountain Range
Volcano
↝ River
⊗ Lake
⊠ Reservoir

GREGORY – GULDEN DRAAK SEAMOUNT

31 *O12* **Gregory** South Dakota, N USA 43.11N 99.26W
190 *J3* **Gregory, Lake** *salt lake* South Australia
188 *J9* **Gregory Lake** ◎ Western Australia
189 *V5* **Gregory Range** ▲▲ Queensland, E Australia
Greifenberg/Greifenberg in Pommern *see* Gryfice
Greifenhagen *see* Gryfino
102 *O8* **Greifswald** Mecklenburg-Vorpommern, NE Germany 54.04N 13.23E
102 *O8* **Greifswalder Bodden** *bay* NE Germany
111 *U4* **Grein** Oberösterreich, N Austria 48.14N 14.50E
103 *M17* **Greiz** Thüringen, C Germany 50.40N 12.10E
Gremicha/Gremiha *see* Gremikha
128 *M4* **Gremikha** *var.* Gremicha, Gremiha. Murmanskaya Oblast', NW Russian Federation 68.01N 39.31E
129 *V14* **Gremyachinsk** Permskaya Oblast', NW Russian Federation 58.33N 57.52E
97 *H21* **Grenaa** *var.* Grenå. Århus, C Denmark 56.25N 10.52E
Grenå *see* Grenaa
24 *L3* **Grenada** Mississippi, S USA 33.46N 89.48W
47 *W15* **Grenada** ◆ *commonwealth republic* SE West Indies
49 *S4* **Grenada** *island* Grenada
49 *R4* **Grenada Basin** *undersea feature* W Atlantic Ocean
24 *L3* **Grenada Lake** ⊠ Mississippi, S USA
47 *Y14* **Grenadines, The** *island group* Grenada/St Vincent and the Grenadines
110 *D7* **Grenchen** *Fr.* Granges. Solothurn, NW Switzerland 47.12N 7.30E
191 *Q9* **Grenfell** New South Wales, SE Australia 33.54S 148.09E
9 *V16* **Grenfell** Saskatchewan, S Canada 50.24N 102.55W
94 *J1* **Grenivík** Nordhurland Eystra, N Iceland 65.57N 18.10W
105 *S12* **Grenoble** *anc.* Cularo, Gratianopolis. Isère, E France 45.10N 5.41E
30 *J2* **Grenora** North Dakota, N USA 48.36N 103.57W
94 *N8* **Grense-Jakobselv** Finnmark, N Norway 69.46N 30.39E
47 *S14* **Grenville** E Grenada 12.07N 61.37W
34 *G11* **Gresham** Oregon, NW USA 45.30N 122.25W
Gresk *see* Hresk
108 *B7* **Gressoney-St-Jean** Valle d'Aosta, NW Italy 45.48N 7.49E
24 *K9* **Gretna** Louisiana, S USA 29.54N 90.03W
23 *T7* **Gretna** Virginia, NE USA 36.57N 79.21W
100 *F13* **Grevelingen** *inlet* S North Sea
102 *F13* **Greven** Nordrhein-Westfalen, NW Germany 52.06N 7.37E
117 *D15* **Grevená** Dytikí Makedonía, N Greece 40.06N 21.26E
103 *D16* **Grevenbroich** Nordrhein-Westfalen, W Germany 51.06N 6.34E
101 *N24* **Grevenmacher** Grevenmacher, E Luxembourg 49.40N 6.27E
101 *M24* **Grevenmacher** ◐ *district* E Luxembourg
102 *K9* **Grevesmühlen** Mecklenburg-Vorpommern, N Germany 53.52N 11.12E
193 *H16* **Grey** ≈ South Island, NZ
35 *V12* **Greybull** Wyoming, C USA 44.29N 108.03W
35 *U13* **Greybull River** ≈ Wyoming, C USA
67 *A24* **Grey Channel** *sound* Falkland Islands
Greyerzer See *see* Gruyère, Lac de la
11 *T10* **Grey Islands** *island group* Newfoundland and Labrador, E Canada
20 *L10* **Greylock, Mount** ▲ Massachusetts, NE USA 42.38N 73.09W
193 *G17* **Greymouth** West Coast, South Island, NZ 42.28S 171.13E
189 *U10* **Grey Range** ▲▲ New South Wales/Queensland, E Australia
99 *G18* **Greystones** *Ir.* Na Clocha Liatha. E Ireland 53.07N 6.04W
193 *M14* **Greytown** Wellington, North Island, NZ 41.05S 175.25E
85 *K23* **Greytown** KwaZulu/Natal, E South Africa 29.04S 30.34E
Greytown *see* San Juan del Norte
101 *H19* **Grez-Doiceau** *Dut.* Graven. Wallon Brabant, C Belgium 50.43N 4.41E
117 *J19* **Griá, Akrotírio** *headland* Ándros, Kykládes, Greece, Aegean Sea 37.54N 24.57E
131 *N8* **Gribanovskiy** Voronezhskaya Oblast', W Russian Federation 51.27N 41.53E
80 *I13* **Gribingui** ≈ N Central African Republic
37 *O6* **Gridley** California, W USA 39.21N 121.41W
85 *G23* **Griekwastad** Northern Cape, C South Africa 28.50S 23.16E
25 *S4* **Griffin** Georgia, SE USA 33.15N 84.16W
191 *O9* **Griffith** New South Wales, SE Australia 34.16S 146.01E
12 *F13* **Griffith Island** *island* Ontario, S Canada
23 *W10* **Grifton** North Carolina, SE USA 35.22N 77.26W
Grigioni *see* Graubünden
121 *H14* **Grigiškes** Vilnius, SE Lithuania 54.42N 25.00E
119 *N10* **Grigoriopol** C Moldova 47.09N 29.18E
153 *X7* **Grigor'yevka** Issyk-Kul'skaya Oblast', E Kyrgyzstan 42.43N 77.27E
200 *Oo9* **Grijalva Ridge** *undersea feature* E Pacific Ocean
43 *U15* **Grijalva, Río** *var.* Tabasco. ≈ Guatemala/Mexico
100 *N5* **Grijpskerk** Groningen, NE Netherlands 53.15N 6.18E
85 *C22* **Grillenthal** Karas, SW Namibia 26.55S 15.24E
81 *J15* **Grimari** Ouaka, C Central African Republic 5.44N 20.02E
Grimaylov *see* Hrymayliv
101 *G18* **Grimbergen** Vlaams Brabant, C Belgium 50.55N 4.22E
191 *N15* **Grim, Cape** *headland* Tasmania, SE Australia 40.42S 144.42E
102 *N8* **Grimmen** Mecklenburg-Vorpommern, NE Germany 54.06N 13.03E
12 *G16* **Grimsby** Ontario, S Canada 43.10N 79.34W
99 *O17* **Grimsby** *prev.* Great Grimsby. E England, UK 53.34N 0.04W
94 *J1* **Grímsey** *var.* Grimsey. *island* N Iceland
9 *O12* **Grimshaw** Alberta, W Canada 56.12N 117.37W
97 *F18* **Grimstad** Aust-Agder, S Norway 58.19N 8.34E
94 *H4* **Grindavík** Reykjanes, W Iceland 65.57N 18.10W
110 *F9* **Grindelwald** Bern, S Switzerland 46.37N 8.04E
97 *F23* **Grindsted** Ribe, W Denmark 55.46N 8.55E
31 *W14* **Grinnell** Iowa, C USA 41.44N 92.43W
111 *U10* **Grintovec** ▲ N Slovenia 46.21N 14.31E
190 *H1* **Griselda, Lake** *salt lake* South Australia
Grisons *see* Graubünden
97 *P14* **Grisslehamn** Stockholm, C Sweden 60.04N 18.49E
31 *T15* **Griswold** Iowa, C USA 41.14N 95.08W
104 *M1* **Griz Nez, Cap** *headland* N France 50.51N 1.34E
114 *P13* **Grljan** Serbia, E Serbia 43.52N 22.18E
114 *E11* **Grmeč** ▲▲ NW Bosnia and Herzegovina
101 *H16* **Grobbendonk** Antwerpen, N Belgium 51.12N 4.41E
Grobin *see* Grobiņa
120 *C10* **Grobiņa** *Ger.* Grobin. Liepāja, W Latvia 56.32N 21.12E
85 *K20* **Groblersdal** Mpumalanga, NE South Africa 25.15S 29.25E
85 *G23* **Groblershoop** Northern Cape, W South Africa 28.51S 22.01E
Gródek Jagielloński *see* Horodok
111 *Q6* **Grödig** Salzburg, W Austria 47.42N 13.06E
113 *H15* **Grodków** Opolskie, S Poland 50.42N 17.23E
Grodnenskaya Oblast' *see* Hrodzyenskaya Voblasts'
Grodno *see* Hrodna
112 *L12* **Grodzisk Mazowiecki** Mazowieckie, C Poland 52.07N 20.40E
112 *F12* **Grodzisk Wielkopolski** Wielkolpolskie, C Poland 52.13N 16.21E
Grodzyanka *see* Hradzyanka
100 *O12* **Groenlo** Gelderland, E Netherlands 52.01N 6.36E
85 *E22* **Groenrivier** Karas, SE Namibia 27.27S 18.52E
27 *U8* **Groesbeck** Texas, SW USA 31.31N 96.34W
100 *L13* **Groesbeek** Gelderland, SE Netherlands 51.46N 5.55E
104 *G7* **Groix, Îles de** *island group* NW France
112 *M12* **Grójec** Mazowieckie, C Poland 51.51N 20.52E
67 *K15* **Gröll Seamount** *undersea feature* C Atlantic Ocean 12.54S 33.24W
102 *E13* **Gronau** *var.* Gronau in Westfalen. Nordrhein-Westfalen, NW Germany 52.12N 7.01E
Gronau in Westfalen *see* Gronau
95 *F15* **Grong** Nord-Trøndelag, C Norway 64.29N 12.19E
97 *N22* **Grönhögen** Kalmar, S Sweden 56.16N 16.09E
100 *N5* **Groningen** Groningen, NE Netherlands 53.13N 6.34E
57 *W9* **Groningen** Saramacca, N Surinam 5.45N 55.31W
100 *N5* **Groningen** ◐ *province* NE Netherlands
Grønland *see* Greenland
110 *H11* **Grono** Graubünden, S Switzerland 46.15N 9.07E
97 *M20* **Grönskåra** Kalmar, S Sweden 57.04N 15.45E
27 *O2* **Groom** Texas, SW USA 35.12N 101.06W
37 *W9* **Groom Lake** ◎ Nevada, W USA
85 *H25* **Groot** ≈ S South Africa
189 *S2* **Groote Eylandt** *island* Northern Territory, N Australia
100 *M6* **Grootegast** Groningen, NE Netherlands 53.11N 6.12E
85 *D17* **Grootfontein** Otjozondjupa, N Namibia 19.31S 18.04E
85 *E22* **Groot Karasberge** ▲▲ S Namibia
Groot Karoo *see* Great Karoo
85 *J25* **Groot-Kei** *Eng.* Great Kei. ≈ S South Africa
47 *T10* **Gros Islet** N Saint Lucia 14.04N 60.57W
46 *L8* **Gros-Morne** NW Haiti 19.37N 72.39W
11 *S11* **Gros Morne** ▲ Newfoundland and Labrador, E Canada 49.38N 57.45W
105 *R9* **Grosne** ≈ C France
47 *S12* **Gros Piton** ▲ SW Saint Lucia 13.48N 61.04W
Grossa, Isola *see* Dugi Otok
Grossbetschkerek *see* Zrenjanin
Grosse Isper *see* Grosse Ysper
Grosse Kokel *see* Târnava Mare
103 *M21* **Grosse Laaber** *var.* Grosse Laber. ≈ SE Germany
Grosse Laber *see* Grosse Laaber
Grosse Morava *see* Velika Morava
103 *O15* **Grossenhain** Sachsen, E Germany 51.18N 13.31E
111 *Y4* **Grossenzersdorf** Niederösterreich, NE Austria 48.11N 16.34E
103 *O21* **Grosser Arber** ▲ SE Germany 49.07N 13.10E
103 *K17* **Grosser Beerberg** ▲ C Germany 50.39N 10.45E
103 *G18* **Grosser Feldberg** ▲ W Germany 50.13N 8.28E
111 *O8* **Grosser Löffler** *It.* Monte Lovello. ▲ Austria/Italy 47.02N 11.56E
111 *N8* **Grosser Möseler** *var.* Mesule. ▲ Austria/Italy 47.01N 11.52E
102 *J8* **Grosser Plöner See** ◎ N Germany
103 *O21* **Grosser Rachel** ▲ SE Germany 48.59N 13.23E
Grosser Sund *see* Suur Väin
13 *V6* **Grosses-Roches** Québec, SE Canada 48.55N 67.06W
111 *P8* **Grosses Weiesbachhorn** *var.* Wiesbachhorn. ▲ W Austria 47.09N 12.44E
108 *F13* **Grosseto** Toscana, C Italy 42.45N 11.07E
103 *M22* **Grosse Vils** ≈ SE Germany
111 *U4* **Grosse Ysper** *var.* Grosse Isper. ≈ N Austria
103 *G19* **Gross-Gerau** Hessen, W Germany 49.55N 8.28E
111 *U3* **Gross Gerungs** Niederösterreich, N Austria 48.33N 14.58E
111 *P8* **Grossglockner** ▲ W Austria 47.05N 12.39E
Grosskanizsa *see* Nagykanizsa
Gross-Karol *see* Carei
Grosskikinda *see* Kikinda
111 *W9* **Grossklein** Steiermark, SE Austria 46.43N 15.24E
Grosskoppe *see* Velká Deštná
Grossmeseritsch *see* Velké Meziříčí
Grossmichel *see* Michalovce
103 *H19* **Grossostheim** Bayern, C Germany 49.54N 9.03E
111 *X7* **Grosspetersdorf** Burgenland, SE Austria 47.15N 16.19E
111 *T5* **Grossraming** Oberösterreich, C Austria 47.54N 14.34E
103 *P14* **Grossräschen** Brandenburg, E Germany 51.34N 14.00E
Grossrauschenbach *see* Revúca
Gross-Sankt-Johannis *see* Suure-Jaani
Gross-Schlatten *see* Abrud
111 *V2* **Gross-Siegharts** Niederösterreich, N Austria 48.48N 15.25E
Gross-Skaisgirren *see* Bol'shakovo
Gross-Steffelsdorf *see* Rimavská Sobota
Gross Strehlitz *see* Strzelce Opolskie
111 *O8* **Grossvenediger** ▲ W Austria 47.07N 12.19E
Grosswardein *see* Oradea
Gross Wartenberg *see* Syców
111 *U11* **Grosuplje** C Slovenia 46.00N 14.36E
101 *H17* **Grote Nete** ≈ N Belgium
96 *E10* **Grotli** Oppland, S Norway 62.02N 7.36E
21 *N13* **Groton** Connecticut, NE USA 41.20N 72.03W
31 *P8* **Groton** South Dakota, N USA 45.27N 98.06W
109 *P18* **Grottaglie** Puglia, SE Italy 40.31N 17.25E
109 *L17* **Grottaminarda** Campania, S Italy 41.04N 15.02E
108 *K13* **Grottammare** Marche, C Italy 43.00N 13.52E
23 *U5* **Grottoes** Virginia, NE USA 38.16N 78.49W
Grou *see* Grouw
11 *N10* **Groulx, Monts** ▲▲ Québec, E Canada
12 *E7* **Groundhog** ≈ Ontario, S Canada
38 *J1* **Grouse Creek** Utah, W USA 41.41N 113.52W
38 *J1* **Grouse Creek Mountains** ▲▲ Utah, W USA
100 *L6* **Grouw** *Fris.* Grou. Friesland, N Netherlands 53.07N 5.51E
29 *R8* **Grove** Oklahoma, C USA 36.35N 94.46W
33 *S13* **Grove City** Ohio, N USA 39.52N 83.05W
20 *B13* **Grove City** Pennsylvania, NE USA 41.09N 80.02W
25 *O6* **Grove Hill** Alabama, S USA 31.42N 87.46W
35 *S15* **Grover** Wyoming, C USA 42.48N 110.57W
37 *P13* **Grover City** California, W USA 35.08N 120.37W
27 *Y11* **Groves** Texas, SW USA 29.57N 93.55W
21 *O7* **Groveton** New Hampshire, NE USA 44.35N 71.28W
27 *W9* **Groveton** Texas, SW USA 31.03N 95.07W
38 *J15* **Growler Mountains** ▲▲ Arizona, SW USA
Grozdovo *see* Bratya Daskalovi
131 *P16* **Groznyy** Chechenskaya Respublika, SW Russian Federation 43.20N 45.42E
Grubeshov *see* Hrubieszów
114 *G9* **Grubišno Polje** Bjelovar-Bilogora, NE Croatia 45.42N 17.09E
Grudovo *see* Sredets
112 *J9* **Grudziądz** *Ger.* Graudenz. Kujawsko-pomorskie, C Poland 53.28N 18.45E
27 *R17* **Grulla** *var.* La Grulla. Texas, SW USA 26.15N 98.37W
42 *K14* **Grullo** Jalisco, SW Mexico 19.45N 104.15W
69 *V10* **Grumeti** ≈ N Tanzania
97 *K16* **Grums** Värmland, C Sweden 59.22N 13.10E
111 *S5* **Grünau im Almtal** Oberösterreich, N Austria 47.51N 13.56E
103 *H17* **Grünberg** Hessen, W Germany 50.36N 8.57E
Grünberg/Grünberg in Schlesien *see* Zielona Góra
Grünberg in Schlesien *see* Zielona Góra
94 *H3* **Grundarfjördhur** Vestfirdhir, W Iceland 64.55N 23.15W
23 *P7* **Grundy** Virginia, NE USA 37.16N 82.06W
31 *W13* **Grundy Center** Iowa, C USA 42.21N 92.46W
Grüneberg *see* Zielona Góra
27 *N1* **Gruver** Texas, SW USA 36.16N 101.24W
110 *C9* **Gruyère, Lac de la** *Ger.* Greyerzer See. ◎ SW Switzerland
110 *C9* **Gruyères** Fribourg, W Switzerland 46.34N 7.04E
120 *E11* **Gruzdžiai** Šiauliai, N Lithuania 56.06N 23.15E
Gruzinskaya SSR/Gruziya *see* Georgia
Gryada Akkyr *see* Akgyr Erezi
130 *L7* **Gryazi** Lipetskaya Oblast', W Russian Federation 52.27N 39.56E
128 *M14* **Gryazovets** Vologodskaya Oblast', NW Russian Federation 58.52N 40.12E
113 *M17* **Grybów** Małopolskie, SE Poland 49.35N 20.54E
96 *M13* **Grycksbo** Dalarna, C Sweden 60.40N 15.30E
112 *E8* **Gryfice** *Ger.* Greifenberg, Greifenberg in Pommern. Zachodnio-pomorskie, NW Poland 53.55N 15.10E
112 *D9* **Gryfino** *Ger.* Greifenhagen. Zachodnio-pomorskie, NW Poland 53.15N 14.30E
94 *H9* **Gryllefjord** Troms, N Norway 69.21N 17.07E
97 *L15* **Grythyttan** Örebro, C Sweden 59.52N 14.31E
110 *D10* **Gstaad** Bern, W Switzerland 46.30N 7.16E
45 *P14* **Guabito** Bocas del Toro, NW Panama 9.30N 82.35W
46 *G7* **Guacanayabo, Golfo de** *gulf* S Cuba
42 *I7* **Guachochi** Chihuahua, N Mexico
106 *J11* **Guadajira** ≈ SW Spain
106 *M13* **Guadajoz** ≈ S Spain
42 *L13* **Guadalajara** Jalisco, C Mexico 20.43N 103.23W
107 *O8* **Guadalajara** *Ar.* Wad Al-Hajarah; *anc.* Arriaca. Castilla-La Mancha, C Spain 40.37N 3.10W
107 *O7* **Guadalajara** ◐ *province* Castilla-La Mancha, C Spain
106 *K12* **Guadalcanal** Andalucía, S Spain 38.06N 5.49W
195 *W16* **Guadalcanal** *off.* Guadalcanal Province. ◐ *province* C Solomon Islands
195 *W16* **Guadalcanal** *island* C Solomon Islands
107 *O12* **Guadalén** ≈ S Spain
107 *R13* **Guadalentín** ≈ SE Spain
106 *K15* **Guadalete** ≈ SW Spain
107 *O13* **Guadalimar** ≈ S Spain
107 *P12* **Guadalmena** ≈ S Spain
106 *L11* **Guadalmez** ≈ W Spain
107 *S7* **Guadalope** ≈ E Spain
106 *K13* **Guadalquivir** ≈ W Spain
106 *J14* **Guadalquivir, Marismas del** *var.* Las Marismas. *wetland* SW Spain
42 *M11* **Guadalupe** Zacatecas, C Mexico 22.44N 102.27W
59 *E16* **Guadalupe** Ica, W Peru 13.59S 75.49W
106 *L10* **Guadalupe** Extremadura, W Spain 39.26N 5.18W
38 *L14* **Guadalupe** Arizona, SW USA 33.20N 111.57W
37 *P13* **Guadalupe** California, W USA 34.55N 120.34W
199 *Mm5* **Guadalupe** *island* NW Mexico
Guadalupe *see* Canelones
42 *J3* **Guadalupe Bravos** Chihuahua, N Mexico 31.22N 106.04W
42 *A4* **Guadalupe, Isla** *island* NW Mexico
39 *U15* **Guadalupe Mountains** ▲▲ New Mexico/Texas, SW USA
26 *J8* **Guadalupe Peak** ▲ Texas, SW USA 31.53N 104.51W
27 *R11* **Guadalupe River** ≈ SW USA
106 *K10* **Guadalupe, Sierra de** ▲▲ W Spain
42 *K9* **Guadalupe Victoria** Durango, C Mexico 24.30N 104.03W
42 *I8* **Guadalupe y Calvo** Chihuahua, N Mexico 26.04N 106.58W
107 *N7* **Guadarrama** Madrid, C Spain 40.40N 4.06W
107 *N7* **Guadarrama** ≈ C Spain
106 *M7* **Guadarrama, Puerto de** *pass* C Spain 40.41N 4.14W
107 *N9* **Guadarrama, Sierra de** ▲▲ C Spain
107 *Q9* **Guadazaón** ≈ C Spain
47 *X10* **Guadeloupe** ◇ *French overseas department* E West Indies
49 *S3* **Guadeloupe** *island group* E West Indies
47 *W10* **Guadeloupe Passage** *passage* E Caribbean Sea
106 *H13* **Guadiana** ≈ Portugal/Spain
107 *O13* **Guadiana Menor** ≈ S Spain
107 *Q8* **Guadiela** ≈ C Spain
107 *O14* **Guadix** Andalucía, S Spain 37.19N 3.07W
Guad-i-Zirreh *see* Gowd-e Zereh, Dasht-e
200 *O13* **Guafo Fracture Zone** *tectonic feature* SE Pacific Ocean
65 *F18* **Guafo, Isla** *island* S Chile
44 *I6* **Guaimaca** Francisco Morazán, C Honduras 14.33N 86.49W
56 *J12* **Guainía** *off.* Comisaría del Guainía. ◐ *province* E Colombia
56 *K12* **Guainía, Río** ≈ Colombia/Venezuela
57 *O9* **Guaiquinima, Cerro** *elevation* SE Venezuela 5.45N 63.46W
64 *O7* **Guairá** *off.* Departamento del Guairá. ◐ *department* S Paraguay
62 *G10* **Guaíra** Paraná, S Brazil 24.04S 54.15W
62 *L7* **Guaíra** São Paulo, S Brazil 20.17S 48.21W
Guaire *see* Gorey
65 *F18* **Guaiteca, Isla** *island* S Chile
46 *G6* **Guajaba, Cayo** *headland* C Cuba 21.50N 77.33W
61 *D16* **Guajará-Mirim** Rondônia, W Brazil 10.49S 65.21W
Guajira *see* La Guajira
56 *H3* **Guajira, Península de la** *peninsula* N Colombia
44 *J6* **Gualaco** Olancho, C Honduras 15.00N 86.03W
36 *L7* **Gualala** California, W USA 38.45N 123.33W
44 *E5* **Gualán** Zacapa, C Guatemala 15.06N 89.20W
63 *C19* **Gualeguay** Entre Ríos, E Argentina 33.09S 59.19W
63 *D18* **Gualeguaychú** Entre Ríos, E Argentina 32.58S 58.30W
63 *C18* **Gualeguay, Río** ≈ E Argentina
65 *K16* **Gualicho, Salina del** *salt lake* E Argentina
196 *B15* **Guam** ◇ *US unincorporated territory* W Pacific Ocean
65 *F19* **Guamblin, Isla** *island* Archipiélago de los Chonos, S Chile
63 *A22* **Guaminí** Buenos Aires, E Argentina 37.04S 62.22W
42 *H8* **Guamúchil** Sinaloa, C Mexico 25.23N 108.00W
56 *H4* **Guana** *var.* Misión de Guana. Zulia, NW Venezuela 11.07N 72.17W
46 *C4* **Guanabacoa** La Habana, W Cuba 23.01N 82.12W
44 *K13* **Guanacaste** *off.* Provincia de Guanacaste. ◐ *province* NW Costa Rica
44 *K12* **Guanacaste, Cordillera de** ▲▲ NW Costa Rica
42 *J8* **Guanaceví** Durango, C Mexico 25.55N 105.51W
46 *A5* **Guanahacabibes, Golfo de** *gulf* W Cuba
44 *K4* **Guanaja, Isla de** *island* Islas de la Bahía, N Honduras
46 *C4* **Guanajay** La Habana, W Cuba 22.52N 82.39W
43 *N12* **Guanajuato** Guanajuato, C Mexico 21.00N 101.16W
42 *M12* **Guanajuato** ◐ *state* C Mexico
56 *J6* **Guanare** Portuguesa, N Venezuela 9.04N 69.45W
56 *K7* **Guanare, Río** ≈ W Venezuela
56 *J6* **Guanarito** Portuguesa, NW Venezuela 8.39N 69.12W
166 *M3* **Guancen Shan** ▲▲ C China
64 *I9* **Guandacol** La Rioja, W Argentina 29.31S 68.30W
46 *A5* **Guane** Pinar del Río, W Cuba 22.12N 84.05W
167 *N14* **Guangdong** *var.* Guangdong Sheng, Kuang-tung, Kwangtung, Yue. ◐ *province* S China
Guangdong Sheng *see* Guangdong
Guanghua *see* Laohekou
Guangju *see* Kwangju
166 *I13* **Guangnan** *var.* Liancheng. Yunnan, SW China 24.07N 104.54E
167 *N8* **Guangshui** *prev.* Yingshan. Hubei, C China 31.41N 113.53E
Guangxi *see* Guangxi Zhuangzu Zizhiqu
166 *K14* **Guangxi Zhuangzu Zizhiqu** *var.* Guangxi, Gui, Kuang-hsi, Kwangsi, *Eng.* Kwangsi Chuang Autonomous Region. ◐ *autonomous region* S China
166 *J8* **Guangyuan** *var.* Kuang-yuan, Kwangyuan. Sichuan, C China 32.27N 105.49E
167 *N14* **Guangzhou** *var.* Kuang-chou, Kwangchow, *Eng.* Canton. Guangdong, S China 23.10N 113.19E
61 *N19* **Guanhães** Minas Gerais, SE Brazil 18.46S 42.58W
166 *I12* **Guanling** *var.* Guanling Buyeizu Miaozu Zizhixian. Guizhou, S China 25.56N 105.36E
Guanling Buyeizu Miaozu Zizhixian *see* Guanling
57 *N5* **Guanta** Anzoátegui, NE Venezuela 10.15N 64.37W
46 *J8* **Guantánamo** Guantánamo, SE Cuba 20.06N 75.16W
46 *J8* **Guantánamo, Bahia de** *Eng.* Guantánamo Bay. *US military installation*, SE Cuba 20.06N 75.16W
Guantánamo Bay *see* Bahia de Guantánamo
Guanxian *see* Dujiangyan
167 *Q6* **Guanyun** *var.* Yishan. Jiangsu, E China 34.19N 119.16E
56 *C12* **Guapí** Cauca, SW Colombia 2.36N 77.54W
45 *N13* **Guápiles** Limón, NE Costa Rica 10.11N 83.45W
63 *I15* **Guaporé** Rio Grande do Sul, S Brazil 28.55S 51.53W
49 *S8* **Guaporé, Rio** *var.* Río Iténez. ≈ Bolivia/Brazil *see also* Iténez, Río
58 *B7* **Guaranda** Bolívar, C Ecuador 1.34S 78.58W
62 *H11* **Guaraniaçu** Paraná, S Brazil 25.05S 52.52W
61 *O20* **Guarapari** Espírito Santo, SE Brazil 20.39S 40.31W
62 *I12* **Guarapuava** Paraná, S Brazil 25.22S 51.28W
62 *J8* **Guararapes** São Paulo, S Brazil 21.16S 50.37W
107 *S4* **Guara, Sierra de** ▲▲ NE Spain
62 *N10* **Guaratinguetá** São Paulo, S Brazil 22.44S 45.16W
106 *I7* **Guarda** Guarda, N Portugal 40.31N 7.16W
106 *I7* **Guarda** ◐ *district* N Portugal
Guardak *see* Gowurdak
106 *M3* **Guardo** Castilla-León, N Spain 42.48N 4.49W
106 *K11* **Guareña** Extremadura, W Spain 38.51N 6.06W
62 *J11* **Guaricana, Pico** ▲ S Brazil 25.13S 48.50W
56 *L6* **Guárico** *off.* Estado Guárico. ◐ *state* N Venezuela
46 *J7* **Guarico, Punta** *headland* E Cuba 20.36N 74.43W
56 *L7* **Guárico, Río** ≈ C Venezuela
62 *M10* **Guarujá** São Paulo, SE Brazil 23.50S 46.27W
63 *L22* **Guarulhos** ✈ (São Paulo) São Paulo, S Brazil 23.23S 46.32W
45 *R17* **Guarumal** Veraguas, S Panama 7.48N 81.15W
Guasapa *see* Guasopa
42 *H8* **Guasave** Sinaloa, C Mexico 25.33N 108.28W
56 *I8* **Guasdualito** Apure, C Venezuela 7.13N 70.45W
57 *Q7* **Guasipati** Bolívar, E Venezuela 7.29N 61.54W
195 *Q15* **Guasopa** *var.* Guasapa. Woodlark Island, SE PNG 9.12S 152.55E
108 *F9* **Guastalla** Emilia-Romagna, C Italy 44.54N 10.38E
44 *D6* **Guastatoya** *var.* El Progreso. El Progreso, C Guatemala 14.51N 90.02W
44 *D5* **Guatemala** *off.* Republic of Guatemala. ◆ *republic* Central America
44 *A2* **Guatemala** *off.* Departamento de Guatemala. ◐ *department* S Guatemala
200 *O7* **Guatemala Basin** *undersea feature* E Pacific Ocean
Guatemala City *see* Ciudad de Guatemala
47 *V14* **Guatuaro Point** *headland* Trinidad, Trinidad and Tobago 10.19N 60.58W
194 *G14* **Guavi** ≈ SW PNG
56 *G13* **Guaviare** *off.* Comisaría Guaviare. ◐ *province* S Colombia
56 *J11* **Guaviare, Río** ≈ E Colombia
63 *E15* **Guaviravi** Corrientes, NE Argentina 29.19S 56.49W
56 *G12* **Guayabero, Río** ≈ SW Colombia
47 *U6* **Guayama** E Puerto Rico 17.58N 66.07W
44 *J7* **Guayambre, Río** ≈ S Honduras
Guayanas, Macizo de las *see* Guiana Highlands
47 *V6* **Guayanés, Punta** *headland* E Puerto Rico 18.03N 65.48W
44 *J6* **Guayape, Río** ≈ C Honduras
58 *B7* **Guayaquil** *var.* Santiago de Guayaquil. Guayas, SW Ecuador 2.13S 79.54W
Guayaquil *see* Simon Bolivar
58 *A8* **Guayaquil, Golfo de** *var.* Gulf of Guayaquil. *gulf* SW Ecuador
Guayaquil, Gulf of *see* Guayaquil, Golfo de
58 *A7* **Guayas** ◐ *province* W Ecuador
64 *N7* **Guaycurú, Río** ≈ NE Argentina
42 *F6* **Guaymas** Sonora, NW Mexico 27.56N 110.54W
47 *U5* **Guaynabo** E Puerto Rico 18.19N 66.05W
82 *H12* **Guba** Benishangul, W Ethiopia 11.11N 35.21E
152 *H8* **Gubadag** *Turkm.* Tel'man; *prev.* Tel'mansk. Daşoguz Welaýaty, N Turkmenistan 42.07N 59.55E
129 *T1* **Guba Dolgaya** Nenetskiy Avtonomnyy Okrug, NW Russian Federation 70.16N 58.45E
129 *V13* **Gubakha** Permskaya Oblast', NW Russian Federation 58.52N 57.35E
108 *I12* **Gubbio** Umbria, C Italy 43.27N 12.34E
102 *Q13* **Guben** *var.* Wilhelm-Pieck-Stadt. Brandenburg, E Germany 51.58N 14.42E
Guben *see* Gubin
112 *D12* **Gubin** *Ger.* Guben. Lubuskie, W Poland 51.58N 14.42E
130 *K8* **Gubkin** Belgorodskaya Oblast', W Russian Federation 51.16N 37.32E
168 *J9* **Guchin-Us** *var.* Arguut. Övörhangay, C Mongolia 45.27N 102.25E
Gudara *see* Ghŭdara
107 *S8* **Gúdar, Sierra de** ▲▲ E Spain
143 *P8* **Gudaut'a** NW Georgia 43.06N 40.35E
96 *G12* **Gudbrandsdalen** *valley* S Norway
97 *G21* **Gudenå** *var.* Gudenaa. ≈ C Denmark
Gudenaa *see* Gudenå
131 *P16* **Gudermes** Chechenskaya Respublika, SW Russian Federation 43.23N 46.06E
161 *J18* **Gūdūr** Andhra Pradesh, E India 14.10N 79.51E
152 *B13* **Gudurolum** Balkan Welaýaty, W Turkmenistan 37.28N 54.30E
96 *D13* **Gudvangen** Sogn og Fjordane, S Norway 60.54N 6.49E
105 *U7* **Guebwiller** Haut-Rhin, NE France 47.55N 7.13E
Guéckédou *see* Guékédou
12 *K8* **Guéguen, Lac** ◎ Québec, SE Canada
78 *J15* **Guékédou** *var.* Guéckédou. S Guinea 8.33N 10.08W
43 *R16* **Guelatao** Oaxaca, SE Mexico
Guelders *see* Gelderland
80 *G11* **Guélengdeng** Mayo-Kébbi, W Chad 10.55N 15.31E
76 *L5* **Guelma** *var.* Gâlma. NE Algeria 36.28N 7.25E
76 *D8* **Guelmime** *var.* Goulimime. SW Morocco 28.59N 10.10W
12 *G15* **Guelph** Ontario, S Canada 43.33N 80.12W
104 *I7* **Gueméné-Penfao** Loire-Atlantique, NW France 47.37N 1.49W
104 *I7* **Guer** Morbihan, NW France 47.54N 2.07W
80 *I11* **Guéra** *off.* Préfecture du Guéra. ◐ *prefecture* S Chad
104 *H8* **Guérande** Loire-Atlantique, NW France 47.19N 2.25W
80 *K9* **Guéréda** Biltine, E Chad 14.30N 22.04E
105 *N10* **Guéret** Creuse, C France 46.10N 1.52E
Guernica/Guernica y Lumo *see* Gernika-Lumo
35 *Z15* **Guernsey** Wyoming, C USA 42.16N 104.44W
99 *K25* **Guernsey** *island* Channel Islands, NW Europe
78 *J10* **Guérou** Assaba, S Mauritania 16.48N 11.40W
27 *R16* **Guerra** Texas, SW USA 26.54N 98.53W
43 *O15* **Guerrero** ◐ *state* S Mexico
42 *D6* **Guerrero Negro** Baja California Sur, NW Mexico 27.55N 114.04W
105 *P9* **Gueugnon** Saône-et-Loire, C France 46.36N 4.03E
78 *M17* **Guéyo** S Ivory Coast 5.25N 6.04W
109 *L15* **Guglionesi** Molise, C Italy 41.54N 14.54E
196 *K5* **Guguan** *island* C Northern Mariana Islands
Guhrau *see* Góra
Gui *see* Guangxi Zhuangzu Zizhiqu
Guiana *see* French Guiana
49 *V4* **Guiana Basin** *undersea feature* W Atlantic Ocean
50 *G6* **Guiana Highlands** *var.* Macizo de las Guayanas. ▲▲ N South America
Guiba *see* Juba
104 *I7* **Guichen** Ille-et-Vilaine, NW France 47.57N 1.47W
Guichi *see* Chizhou
63 *E18* **Guichón** Paysandú, W Uruguay 32.21S 57.12W
79 *U12* **Guidan-Roumji** Maradi, S Niger 13.40N 6.41E
Guidder *see* Guider
165 *T10* **Guide** *var.* Heyin. Qinghai, C China 36.06N 101.25E
80 *F12* **Guider** *var.* Guidder. Nord, N Cameroon 9.55N 13.58E
78 *I11* **Guidimaka** ◐ *region* S Mauritania
79 *W12* **Guidimouni** Zinder, S Niger 13.40N 9.31E
78 *G10* **Guier, Lac de** *var.* Lac de Guiers. ◎ N Senegal
166 *L14* **Guigang** *prev.* Guixian, Gui Xian. Guangxi Zhuangzu Zizhiqu, S China 23.06N 109.36E
78 *L16* **Guiglo** W Ivory Coast 6.33N 7.28W
56 *L5* **Güigüe** Carabobo, N Venezuela 10.04N 67.48W
85 *M20* **Guijá** Gaza, S Mozambique 24.30S 33.07E
44 *E7* **Güija, Lago de** ◎ El Salvador/Guatemala
166 *L14* **Gui Jiang** *var.* Gui Shui. ≈ S China
106 *K8* **Guijuelo** Castilla-León, N Spain 40.34N 5.40W
Guilan *see* Gīlān
99 *N22* **Guildford** SE England, UK 51.13N 0.34W
21 *R5* **Guildford** Maine, NE USA 45.10N 69.22W
21 *O7* **Guildhall** Vermont, NE USA 44.34N 71.36W
105 *R13* **Guilherand** Ardèche, E France 44.57N 4.49E
166 *L13* **Guilin** *var.* Kuei-lin, Kweilin. Guangxi Zhuangzu Zizhiqu, S China 25.15N 110.16E
10 *J6* **Guillaume-Delisle, Lac** ◎ Québec, NE Canada
105 *U13* **Guillestre** Hautes-Alpes, SE France 44.41N 6.39E
106 *H6* **Guimarães** *var.* Guimaráes. Braga, N Portugal 41.25N 8.19W
60 *D11* **Guimarães Rosas, Pico** ▲ NW Brazil
25 *N3* **Guin** Alabama, S USA 33.58N 87.54W
Güina *see* Wina
78 *I14* **Guinea** *off.* Republic of Guinea, *var.* Guinée; *prev.* French Guinea, People's Revolutionary Republic of Guinea. ◆ *republic* W Africa
66 *N13* **Guinea Basin** *undersea feature* E Atlantic Ocean
78 *E12* **Guinea-Bissau** *off.* Republic of Guinea-Bissau, *Fr.* Guinée-Bissau, *Port.* Guiné-Bissau; *prev.* Portuguese Guinea. ◆ *republic* W Africa
68 *K7* **Guinea Fracture Zone** *tectonic feature* E Atlantic Ocean
66 *O13* **Guinea, Gulf of** *Fr.* Golfe de Guinée. *gulf* E Atlantic Ocean
Guiné-Bissau *see* Guinea-Bissau
Guinée *see* Guinea
Guinée-Bissau *see* Guinea-Bissau
Guinée, Golfe de *see* Guinea, Gulf of
46 *C4* **Güines** La Habana, W Cuba 22.50N 82.02W
104 *G5* **Guingamp** Côtes d'Armor, NW France 48.34N 3.09W
107 *P3* **Guipúzcoa** *Basq.* Gipuzkoa. ◐ *province* País Vasco, N Spain
46 *C5* **Güira de Melena** La Habana, W Cuba 22.43N 82.31W
76 *G8* **Guir, Hamada du** *desert* Algeria/Morocco
57 *P5* **Güiria** Sucre, NE Venezuela 10.37N 62.21W
Gui Shui *see* Gui Jiang
106 *H2* **Guitiriz** Galicia, NW Spain 43.10N 7.52W
79 *N17* **Guitri** S Ivory Coast 5.31N 5.13W
179 *R13* **Guiuan** Samar, C Philippines 11.02N 125.45E
Gui Xian/Guixian *see* Guigang
166 *J12* **Guiyang** *var.* Kuei-Yang, Kuei-yang, Kueyang, Kweiyang; *prev.* Kweichu. Guizhou, S China 26.33N 106.44E
166 *J12* **Guizhou** *var.* Guizhou Sheng, Kuei-chou, Kweichow, Qian. ◐ *province* S China
Guizhou Sheng *see* Guizhou
104 *J13* **Gujan-Mestras** Gironde, SW France 44.39N 1.04W
160 *B10* **Gujarāt** *var.* Gujerat. ◐ *state* W India
155 *V6* **Gūjar Khān** Punjab, E Pakistan 33.15N 73.18E
Gujerat *see* Gujarāt
155 *V7* **Gujrānwāla** Punjab, NE Pakistan 32.11N 74.08E
155 *V7* **Gujrāt** Punjab, E Pakistan 32.33N 74.03E
152 *B8* **Gulandag** *Rus.* Gory Kulandag. ▲▲ W Turkmenistan
165 *U9* **Gulang** Gansu, C China 37.31N 102.55E
191 *R6* **Gulargambone** New South Wales, SE Australia 31.19S 148.31E
161 *G15* **Gulbarga** Karnātaka, C India 17.22N 76.46E
120 *J8* **Gulbene** *Ger.* Alt-Schwanenburg. Gulbene, NE Latvia 57.10N 26.44E
153 *U10* **Gul'cha** *Kir.* Gülchö. Oshskaya Oblast', SW Kyrgyzstan 40.16N 73.27E
Gülchö *see* Gul'cha
181 *T10* **Gulden Draak Seamount** *undersea feature* E Indian Ocean 33.45S 101.00E

◆ Country
● Country Capital
◇ Dependent Territory
○ Dependent Territory Capital
◐ Administrative Region
✈ International Airport
▲ Mountain
▲▲ Mountain Range
Volcano
≈ River
◎ Lake
⊠ Reservoir

GÜLEK BOĞAZI – HALS

142 J16 **Gülek Boğazı** var. Cilician Gates. pass S Turkey 37.19N 34.49E
194 I14 **Gulf** ◈ province S PNG
25 O9 **Gulf Breeze** Florida, SE USA 30.21N 87.09W
25 V13 **Gulfport** Florida, SE USA 27.45N 82.42W
24 M9 **Gulfport** Mississippi, S USA 30.22N 89.05W
25 O9 **Gulf Shores** Alabama, S USA 30.15N 87.40W
147 T5 **Gulf, The** var. Persian Gulf, Ar. Khalīj al ʿArabī, Per. Khalīj-e Fars. gulf SW Asia
191 R7 **Gulgong** New South Wales, SE Australia 32.22S 149.31E
166 I11 **Gulin** Sichuan, C China 28.06N 105.47E
176 V12 **Gulir** Pulau Kasiui, E Indonesia 4.27S 131.41E
Gulistan see Guliston
153 P10 **Guliston** Rus. Gulistan. Sirdaryo Viloyati, E Uzbekistan 40.28N 68.45E
169 T6 **Guliya Shan** ▲ NE China 49.42N 122.22E
Gulja see Yining
41 S11 **Gulkana** Alaska, USA 62.17N 145.25W
9 S17 **Gull Lake** Saskatchewan, S Canada 50.04N 108.30W
33 P10 **Gull Lake** ◎ Michigan, N USA
31 T6 **Gull Lake** ◎ Minnesota, N USA
97 L16 **Gullspång** Västra Götaland, S Sweden 58.58N 14.04E
142 B15 **Güllük Körfezi** prev. Akbük Limanı. bay W Turkey
158 H5 **Gulmarg** Jammu and Kashmir, NW India 34.04N 74.25E
Gulpaigan see Golpāyegān
101 L18 **Gulpen** Limburg, SE Netherlands 50.48N 5.53E
Gul'shad see Gul'shat
151 S13 **Gul'shat** var. Gul'shad. Karaganda, E Kazakhstan 46.37N 74.21E
83 F17 **Gulu** N Uganda 2.46N 32.21E
116 K10 **Gŭlŭbovo** Stara Zagora, C Bulgaria 42.10N 25.52E
116 I7 **Gulyantsi** Pleven, N Bulgaria 43.37N 24.40E
Gulyaypole see Hulyaypole
Guma see Pishan
Gümai see Darlag
81 K16 **Gumba** Equateur, NW Dem. Rep. Congo 2.58N 21.23E
Gumbinnen see Gusev
83 H24 **Gumbiro** Ruvuma, S Tanzania 10.19S 35.40E
152 B11 **Gumdag** prev. Kum-Dag. Balkan Welaýaty, W Turkmenistan 39.13N 54.35E
79 W12 **Gumel** Jigawa, N Nigeria 12.37N 9.23E
107 N5 **Gumiel de Hizán** Castilla-León, N Spain 41.46N 3.42W
194 I12 **Gumine** var. Gumire. Chimbu, C PNG 6.12S 144.53E
Gumire see Gumine
159 P16 **Gumla** Jhārkhand, N India 23.03N 84.36E
Gumma see Gunma
103 F16 **Gummersbach** Nordrhein-Westfalen, W Germany 51.01N 7.34E
79 T13 **Gummi** Zamfara, NW Nigeria 12.07N 5.07E
Gumpolds see Humpolec
159 N13 **Gumti** var. Gomati. ≈ N India
Gümülcine/Gümüljina see Komotiní
Gümüşane see Gümüşhane
143 O12 **Gümüşhane** var. Gümüşane, Gumushkhane. Gümüşhane, NE Turkey 40.30N 39.27E
143 O12 **Gümüşhane** var. Gümüşane, Gumushkhane. ◈ province NE Turkey
Gumushkhane see Gümüşhane
176 W13 **Gumzai** Pulau Kola, E Indonesia 5.27S 134.38E
160 H9 **Guna** Madhya Pradesh, C India 24.39N 77.21E
Gunabad see Gonābād
Gunan see Qijiang
Gunbad-i-Qawus see Gonbad-e Kāvūs
191 O9 **Gunbar** New South Wales, SE Australia 34.03S 145.32E
191 O9 **Gun Creek** seasonal river New South Wales, SE Australia
191 Q10 **Gundagai** New South Wales, SE Australia 35.06S 148.03E
81 K17 **Gundji** Equateur, N Dem. Rep. Congo 2.13N 21.31E
161 G20 **Gundlupet** Karnātaka, W India 11.48N 76.42E
142 G16 **Gündoğmuş** Antalya, S Turkey 36.52N 32.01E
143 O14 **Güney Doğu Toroslar** ▲▲ SE Turkey
81 J21 **Gungu** Bandundu, SW Dem. Rep. Congo 5.43S 19.19E
131 P17 **Gunib** Respublika Dagestan, SW Russian Federation 42.24N 46.55E
114 J11 **Gunja** Vukovar-Srijem, E Croatia 44.53N 18.51E
33 P9 **Gun Lake** ◎ Michigan, N USA
171 Jj15 **Gunma** off. Gunma-ken, var. Gumma. ◈ prefecture Honshū, S Japan
207 P15 **Gunnbjørn Fjeld** var. Gunnbjörns Bjerge. ▲ C Greenland 69.03N 29.36W
191 S6 **Gunnedah** New South Wales, SE Australia 30.58S 150.15E
181 Y15 **Gunner's Quoin** var. Coin de Mire. island N Mauritius
39 R6 **Gunnison** Colorado, C USA 38.33N 106.55W
38 L5 **Gunnison** Utah, W USA 39.09N 111.49W
39 P5 **Gunnison River** ≈ Colorado, C USA
23 X2 **Gunpowder River** ≈ Maryland, NE USA
Güns see Kőszeg
Gunsan see Kunsan
111 S4 **Gunskirchen** Oberösterreich, N Austria 48.07N 13.54E
Gunt see Ghund
161 H17 **Guntakal** Andhra Pradesh, C India 15.10N 77.24E
25 Q2 **Guntersville** Alabama, S USA 34.21N 86.17W
25 Q2 **Guntersville Lake** ⊠ Alabama, S USA
111 X4 **Guntramsdorf** Niederösterreich, E Austria 48.03N 16.19E
161 J16 **Guntūr** var. Guntur. Andhra Pradesh, SE India 16.19N 80.27E
173 F7 **Gunungsitoli** Pulau Nias, W Indonesia 1.11N 97.35E
161 M14 **Gunupur** Orissa, E India 19.04N 83.52E
103 J23 **Günz** ≈ S Germany
Gunzan see Kunsan
103 J22 **Günzburg** Bayern, S Germany 48.26N 10.18E
103 K21 **Gunzenhausen** Bayern, S Germany 49.07N 10.45E
Guovdageaidnu see Kautokeino
167 P7 **Guoyang** Anhui, E China 33.29N 116.14E
118 G11 **Gurahonț** Hung. Honctő. Arad, W Romania 46.16N 22.20E
Gurahumora see Gura Humorului
118 K9 **Gura Humorului** Ger. Gurahumora. Suceava, NE Romania 47.31N 26.00E
152 H8 **Gurbansoltan Eje** prev. Ýylanly, Rus. Il'yaly. Daşoguz Welaýaty, N Turkmenistan 41.56N 59.42E
164 K4 **Gurbantünggüt Shamo** desert W China
158 H7 **Gurdāspur** Punjab, N India 32.02N 75.23E
29 T13 **Gurdon** Arkansas, C USA 33.55N 93.09W
Gurdzhaani see Gurjaani
Gurgan see Gorgān
158 I10 **Gurgaon** Haryāna, N India 28.24N 76.59E
61 M15 **Gurguéia, Rio** ≈ NE Brazil
57 Q7 **Guri, Embalse de** ⊠ E Venezuela
143 V10 **Gurjaani** Rus. Gurdzhaani. E Georgia 41.42N 45.47E
111 T8 **Gurk** Kärnten, S Austria 46.52N 14.17E
111 T9 **Gurk** Slvn. Krka. ≈ S Austria
Gurkfeld see Krško
116 K9 **Gurkovo** prev. Kolupchii. Stara Zagora, C Bulgaria 42.42N 25.46E
111 S9 **Gurktaler Alpen** ▲▲ S Austria
152 H8 **Gurlan** Rus. Gurlen. Xorazm Viloyati, W Uzbekistan 41.54N 60.18E
Gurlen see Gurlan
85 M16 **Guro** Manica, C Mozambique 17.25S 33.23E
142 M14 **Gürün** Sivas, C Turkey 38.43N 37.15E
61 K16 **Gurupi** Tocantins, C Brazil 11.43S 49.01W
60 L12 **Gurupi, Rio** ≈ NE Brazil
158 E14 **Guru Sikhar** ▲ NW India 24.45N 72.51E
168 H8 **Gurvanbulag** var. Höviyn Am. Bayanhongor, C Mongolia 47.08N 98.41E
168 K7 **Gurvanbulag** var. Avdzaga. Bulgan, C Mongolia 47.43N 103.30E
168 I11 **Gurvantes** var. Urt. Ömnögovĭ, S Mongolia 43.16N 101.00E
Gur'yev/Gur'yevskaya Oblast' see Atyrau
79 U13 **Gusau** Zamfara, NW Nigeria 12.18N 6.27E
130 C3 **Gusev** Ger. Gumbinnen. Kaliningradskaya Oblast', W Russian Federation 54.36N 22.13E
152 J17 **Gushgy** Rus. Kushka. ≈ S Turkmenistan
Gushgy see Serhetabat
Gushiago see Gushiegu
79 Q14 **Gushiegu** var. Gushiago. NE Ghana 9.54N 0.12W
172 P15 **Gushikawa** Okinawa, Okinawa, SW Japan 26.21N 127.49E
115 L16 **Gusinje** E-Montenegro 42.34N 19.51E
126 Jj16 **Gusinoozersk** Respublika Buryatiya, S Russian Federation 51.18N 106.28E
130 M4 **Gus'-Khrustal'nyy** Vladimirskaya Oblast', W Russian Federation 55.39N 40.42E
109 B19 **Guspini** Sardegna, Italy, C Mediterranean Sea 39.33N 8.39E
111 X8 **Güssing** Burgenland, SE Austria 47.04N 16.18E
111 V6 **Gusswerk** Steiermark, E Austria 47.43N 15.18E
94 O2 **Gustav Adolf Land** physical region NE Svalbard
205 X5 **Gustav Bull Mountains** ▲▲ Antarctica
41 W13 **Gustavus** Alaska, USA 58.24N 135.44W
94 O1 **Gustav V Land** physical region NE Svalbard
37 P9 **Gustine** California, W USA 37.14N 121.00W
27 R8 **Gustine** Texas, SW USA 31.51N 98.24W
102 M9 **Güstrow** Mecklenburg-Vorpommern, NE Germany 53.48N 12.11E
97 N18 **Gusum** Östergötland, S Sweden 58.15N 16.30E
Guta/Gúta see Kolárovo
Gutenstein see Ravne na Koroškem
103 G14 **Gütersloh** Nordrhein-Westfalen, W Germany 51.54N 8.22E
29 N10 **Guthrie** Oklahoma, C USA 35.52N 97.25W
27 P5 **Guthrie** Texas, SW USA 33.37N 100.21W
31 U14 **Guthrie Center** Iowa, C USA 41.40N 94.30W
43 Q13 **Gutiérrez Zamora** Veracruz-Llave, E Mexico 20.29N 97.07W
Gutta see Kolárovo
31 Y12 **Guttenberg** Iowa, C USA 42.47N 91.06W
Guttentag see Dobrodzień
Guttstadt see Dobre Miasto
168 G8 **Guulin** Govĭ-Altay, C Mongolia 46.33N 97.21E
159 V12 **Guwāhāti** prev. Gauhāti. Assam, NE India 26.09N 91.42E
145 R3 **Guwēr** var. Al Kuwayr, Al Quwayr, Quwair. N Iraq 36.03N 43.30E
152 A10 **Guwlumaýak** Rus. Kuuli-Mayak. Balkan Welaýaty, NW Turkmenistan 40.14N 52.43E
57 R9 **Guyana** off. Cooperative Republic of Guyana; prev. British Guiana. ◆ republic N South America
23 P5 **Guyandotte River** ≈ West Virginia, NE USA
Guyane see French Guiana
Guyi see Sanjiang
28 H8 **Guymon** Oklahoma, C USA 36.40N 101.28W
152 K12 **Guynuk** Lebap Welaýaty, NE Turkmenistan 39.18N 63.00E
Guyong see Jiangle
23 O9 **Guyot, Mount** ▲ North Carolina/Tennessee, SE USA 35.42N 83.15W
191 U5 **Guyra** New South Wales, SE Australia 30.13S 151.42E
165 W10 **Guyuan** Ningxia, N China 35.57N 106.13E
Guzar see G'uzor
124 N3 **Güzelyurt** Gk. Mórfou, Morphou. W Cyprus 35.11N 33.00E
124 N2 **Güzelyurt Körfezi** var. Morfou Bay, Morphou Bay, Gk. Kólpos Mórfou. bay W Cyprus
Guzhou see Rongjiang
42 I3 **Guzmán** Chihuahua, N Mexico 31.13N 107.27W
153 N13 **G'uzor** Rus. Guzar. Qashqadaryo Viloyati, S Uzbekistan 38.41N 66.12E
121 B14 **Gvardeysk** Ger. Tapaiu. Kaliningradskaya Oblast', W Russian Federation 54.39N 21.02E
Gvardeyskoye see Hvardiys'ke
191 R5 **Gwabegar** New South Wales, SE Australia 30.34S 148.58E
154 J16 **Gwādar** var. Gwadur. Baluchistān, SW Pakistan 25.09N 62.21E
154 J16 **Gwādar East Bay** bay SW Pakistan
154 J16 **Gwādar West Bay** bay SW Pakistan
Gwadur see Gwādar
85 J17 **Gwai** Matabeleland North, W Zimbabwe 19.17S 27.37E
160 I7 **Gwalior** Madhya Pradesh, C India 26.15N 78.12E
85 J18 **Gwanda** Matabeleland South, SW Zimbabwe 20.56S 29.00E
81 N15 **Gwane** Orientale, N Dem. Rep. Congo 4.40N 25.51E
85 I17 **Gwayi** ≈ W Zimbabwe
112 G8 **Gwda** var. Głda, Ger. Küddow. ≈ NW Poland
99 C14 **Gweebarra Bay** Ir. Béal an Bheara. inlet W Ireland
99 D14 **Gweedore** Ir. Gaoth Dobhair. NW Ireland 55.03N 8.13W
Gwelo see Gweru
99 K21 **Gwent** cultural region S Wales, UK
85 K17 **Gweru** prev. Gwelo. Midlands, C Zimbabwe 19.27S 29.49E
31 Q7 **Gwinner** North Dakota, N USA 46.10N 97.42W
79 Y13 **Gwoza** Borno, NE Nigeria 11.07N 13.40E
Gwy see Wye
191 R4 **Gwydir River** ≈ New South Wales, SE Australia
99 I19 **Gwynedd** var. Gwyneth. cultural region NW Wales, UK
Gwyneth see Gwynedd
165 O16 **Gyaca** var. Ngarrab. Xizang Zizhiqu, W China 29.06N 92.37E
Gya'gya see Saga
Gyaijêpozhanggê see Zhidoi
Gyaisi see Jiulong
117 M22 **Gyalí** var. Yialí. island Dodekánisa, Greece, Aegean Sea
Gyamotang see Dêngqên
Gyandzha see Gäncä
Gyangkar see Dinggyê
164 M16 **Gyangzê** Xizang Zizhiqu, W China 28.49N 89.37E
164 L14 **Gyaring Co** ◎ W China
165 Q12 **Gyaring Hu** ◎ C China
117 I20 **Gyáros** var. Yioúra. island Kykládes, Greece, Aegean Sea
126 Hh7 **Gyda** Yamalo-Nenetskiy Avtonomnyy Okrug, N Russian Federation 70.55N 78.34E
126 H7 **Gydanskiy Poluostrov** Eng. Gyda Peninsula. peninsula N Russian Federation
Gyda Peninsula see Gydanskiy Poluostrov
Gyêgu see Yushu
Gyéres see Câmpia Turzii
Gyergyószentmiklós see Gheorgheni
Gyergyótölgyes see Tulgheș
Gyertyámos see Cărpiniș
Gyeva see Detva
Gyigang see Zayü
Gyixong see Gonggar
97 I23 **Gyldenløveshøj** hill range C Denmark
189 Z10 **Gympie** Queensland, E Australia 26.04S 152.40E
177 Ff7 **Gyobingauk** Pegu, SW Burma 18.13N 95.39E
113 M23 **Gyomaendrőd** Békés, SE Hungary 46.55N 20.49E
Gyömbér see Ďumbier
113 L22 **Gyöngyös** Heves, NE Hungary 47.43N 19.48E
113 H22 **Győr** Ger. Raab; Lat. Arrabona. Győr-Moson-Sopron, NW Hungary 47.40N 17.40E
113 G22 **Győr-Moson-Sopron** off. Győr-Moson-Sopron Megye. ◈ county NW Hungary
9 X15 **Gypsumville** Manitoba, S Canada 51.46N 98.37W
10 M4 **Gyrfalcon Islands** island group Nunavut, NE Canada
97 N14 **Gysinge** Gävleborg, C Sweden 60.16N 16.55E
117 F22 **Gýtheio** var. Githio; prev. Yíthion. Pelopónnisos, S Greece 36.46N 22.34E
152 L13 **Gyuichbirleshik** Lebap Welaýaty, E Turkmenistan 38.10N 64.33E
113 N24 **Gyula** Rom. Jula. Békés, SE Hungary 46.37N 21.19E
Gyulafehérvár see Alba Iulia
Gyulovo see Roza
143 T11 **Gyumri** var. Giumri, Rus. Kumayri; prev. Aleksandropol', Leninakan. W Armenia 40.48N 43.51E
152 D13 **Gyunuzyndag, Gora** ▲ W Turkmenistan 38.15N 56.25E
Gyzylarbat see Serdar
152 J15 **Gyzylbaýdak** Rus. Krasnoye Znamya. Mary Welaýaty, S Turkmenistan 36.51N 62.24E
Gyzyletrek see Etrek
152 D10 **Gyzylgaýa** Rus. Kizyl-Kaya. Balkan Welaýaty, NW Turkmenistan 40.37N 55.15E
152 K12 **Gyzylsuw** Rus. Kizyl-Su. Balkan Welaýaty, W Turkmenistan 39.49N 53.00E
130 J3 **Gzhatsk** Smolenskaya Oblast', W Russian Federation 55.33N 35.00E

H

159 T12 **Ha** W Bhutan 27.16N 89.22E
Haabai see Ha'apai Group
101 H17 **Haacht** Vlaams Brabant, C Belgium 50.58N 4.37E
111 T4 **Haag** Niederösterreich, NE Austria 48.07N 14.32E
204 L8 **Haag Nunataks** ▲▲ Antarctica
94 N2 **Haakon VII Land** physical region NW Svalbard
100 O11 **Haaksbergen** Overijssel, E Netherlands 52.09N 6.45E
101 E14 **Haamstede** Zeeland, SW Netherlands 51.43N 3.45E
200 Ss13 **Ha'ano** island Ha'apai Group, C Tonga
200 Ss13 **Ha'apai Group** var. Haabai. island group C Tonga
95 L15 **Haapajärvi** Oulu, C Finland 63.45N 25.19E
95 L17 **Haapamäki** Länsi-Suomi, W Finland 62.11N 24.32E
95 L15 **Haapavesi** Oulu, C Finland 64.09N 25.25E
203 N7 **Haapiti** Moorea, W French Polynesia 17.33S 149.52W
120 F4 **Haapsalu** Ger. Hapsal. Läänemaa, W Estonia 58.57N 23.32E
Ha'Arava see 'Arabah, Wādī al
97 G24 **Haarby** var. Hårby. Fyn, C Denmark 55.13N 10.07E
100 H10 **Haarlem** prev. Harlem. Noord-Holland, W Netherlands 52.22N 4.39E
193 D19 **Haast** West Coast, South Island, NZ 43.53S 169.01E
193 C20 **Haast** ≈ South Island, NZ
193 D20 **Haast Pass** pass South Island, NZ 44.07S 169.18E
200 R16 **Ha'atua** 'Eau, E Tonga 21.23S 174.57W
155 P15 **Hab** ≈ SW Pakistan
147 W7 **Haba** var. Al Haba. Dubayy, NE UAE 25.01N 55.37E
164 K2 **Habahe** var. Kaba. Xinjiang Uygur Zizhiqu, NW China 48.04N 86.20E
147 U13 **Ḩabarūt** var. Habrut. SW Oman 17.19N 52.45E
83 J18 **Habaswein** North Eastern, NE Kenya 1.01N 39.27E
101 L24 **Habay-la-Neuve** Luxembourg, SE Belgium 49.43N 5.38E
145 S8 **Ḩabbānīyah, Buḩayrat** ◎ C Iraq
Habelschwerdt see Bystrzyca Kłodzka
159 V14 **Habiganj** Sylhet, NE Bangladesh 24.22N 91.25E
169 Q12 **Habirag** Nei Mongol Zizhiqu, N China 42.18N 115.40E
97 L19 **Habo** Västra Götaland, S Sweden 57.55N 14.04E
127 P16 **Habomai Islands** island group Kuril'skiye Ostrova, SE Russian Federation
172 P3 **Haboro** Hokkaidō, NE Japan 44.19N 141.42E
159 S16 **Habra** West Bengal, NE India 22.39N 88.17E
Habrut see Ḩabarūt
149 P17 **Ḩabshān** Abū Ẓaby, C UAE 23.51N 53.34E
56 E14 **Hacha** Putumayo, S Colombia 00.02S 75.30W
172 Ss13 **Hachijō** Tōkyō, Hachijō-jima, SE Japan 35.40N 139.19E
172 Ss13 **Hachijō-jima** var. Hatizyô Zima. island Izu-shotō, SE Japan
171 I14 **Hachiman** Gifu, Honshū, SW Japan 35.46N 136.57E
171 M9 **Hachimori** Akita, Honshū, C Japan 40.22N 139.59E
172 N10 **Hachinohe** Aomori, Honshū, C Japan 40.30N 141.28E
171 Jj16 **Hachiōji** var. Hatiôzi. Tōkyō, Honshū, S Japan 35.39N 139.17E
95 G17 **Hackås** Jämtland, C Sweden 62.55N 14.31E
20 K14 **Hackensack** New Jersey, NE USA 40.51N 73.57W
Hadama see Nazrēt
171 J16 **Hadano** Kanagawa, Honshū, S Japan 35.23N 139.13E
147 W13 **Ḩadbaram** S Oman 17.27N 55.13E
145 U13 **Ḩaddānīyah** well S Iraq 30.27N 44.40E
98 K12 **Haddington** SE Scotland, UK 55.59N 2.45W
147 Z8 **Ḩadd, Ra's al** headland NE Oman 22.28N 59.58E
Haded see Xadeed
79 W12 **Hadejia** Jigawa, N Nigeria 12.22N 10.02E
79 W12 **Hadejia** ≈ N Nigeria
144 F9 **Hadera** var. Khadera. Haifa, C Israel 32.25N 34.55E
Hadersleben see Haderslev
97 G24 **Haderslev** Ger. Hadersleben. Sønderjylland, SW Denmark 55.15N 9.30E
157 J21 **Hadhdhunmathi Atoll** var. Haddummati Atoll, Laamu Atoll. atoll S Maldives
Hadhramaut see Ḩaḑramawt
147 W17 **Hadīboh** Suquṭrā, SE Yemen 12.37N 54.04E
164 K9 **Hadilik** Xinjiang Uygur Zizhiqu, W China 37.51N 86.10E
142 H16 **Hadım** Konya, S Turkey 36.58N 32.27E
146 K7 **Hadīyah** Al Madīnah, W Saudi Arabia 25.36N 38.31E
15 J1 **Hadley Bay** bay Victoria Island, Nunavut, N Canada
178 Jj6 **Ha Đông** var. Hadong. Ha Tây, N Vietnam 20.58N 105.46E
147 R15 **Ḩaḑramawt** Eng. Hadhramaut. ▲▲ S Yemen
Hadria see Adria
Hadrianopolis see Edirne
Hadria Picena see Apricena
97 G22 **Hadsten** Århus, C Denmark 56.19N 10.03E
97 G21 **Hadsund** Nordjylland, N Denmark 56.43N 10.07E
119 S4 **Hadyach** Rus. Gadyach. Poltavs'ka Oblast', NE Ukraine 50.21N 34.00E
114 I13 **Hadžići** Federacija Bosna I Hercegovina, SE Bosnia and Herzegovina 43.49N 18.12E
169 W14 **Haeju** S North Korea 38.04N 125.40E
Haerbin/Haerhpin/Ha-erh-pin see Harbin
147 P5 **Ḩafar al Bāţın** Ash Sharqīyah, N Saudi Arabia 28.25N 45.58E
9 T15 **Hafford** Saskatchewan, S Canada 52.43N 107.19W
142 M13 **Hafik** Sivas, N Turkey 39.52N 37.24E
155 V8 **Hāfizābād** Punjab, E Pakistan 32.05N 73.37E
94 H4 **Hafnarfjördhur** Reykjanes, W Iceland 64.03N 21.57W
Hafnia see København, Denmark
Hafnia see Denmark
Hafren see Severn
Hafun see Xaafuun
Hafun, Ras see Xaafuun, Raas
82 G10 **Hag 'Abdullah** Sinnar, E Sudan 13.58N 33.34E
83 K18 **Hagadera** North Eastern, E Kenya 0.06N 40.23E
144 G8 **HaGalil** Eng. Galilee. ▲▲ N Israel
12 G10 **Hagar** Ontario, S Canada 46.27N 80.22W
161 G18 **Hagari** var. Vedāvati. ≈ W India
196 B16 **Hagåtña** var. Agana, Agaña. ○ (Guam) NW Guam 13.27N 144.45E
102 M13 **Hagelberg** hill NE Germany 52.03N 12.33E
41 N14 **Hagemeister Island** island Alaska, USA
103 F15 **Hagen** Nordrhein-Westfalen, W Germany 51.21N 7.27E
102 K10 **Hagenow** Mecklenburg-Vorpommern, N Germany 53.27N 11.10E
8 K15 **Hagensborg** British Columbia, SW Canada 52.24N 126.24W
82 I13 **Hāgere Hiywet** var. Agere Hiywet, Ambo. Oromo, C Ethiopia 9.00N 37.55E
35 O15 **Hagerman** Idaho, NW USA 42.48N 114.53W
39 U14 **Hagerman** New Mexico, SW USA 33.07N 104.19W
23 V2 **Hagerstown** Maryland, NE USA 39.38N 77.43W
12 G16 **Hagersville** Ontario, S Canada 42.58N 80.03W
104 J15 **Hagetmau** Landes, SW France 43.40N 0.36W
97 K14 **Hagfors** Värmland, C Sweden 60.03N 13.45E
95 G16 **Häggenås** Jämtland, C Sweden 63.24N 14.53E
170 Dd12 **Hagi** Yamaguchi, Honshū, SW Japan 34.24N 131.22E
178 J5 **Ha Giang** Ha Giang, N Vietnam 22.49N 104.58E
Hagios Evstrátios see Ágios Efstrátios
HaGolan see Golan Heights
105 T4 **Hagondange** Moselle, NE France 49.15N 6.06E
99 B18 **Hag's Head** Ir. Ceann Caillí. headland W Ireland 52.56N 9.29W
104 I3 **Hague, Cap de la** headland N France 49.43N 1.56W
105 V5 **Haguenau** Bas-Rhin, NE France 48.49N 7.46E
172 T16 **Hahajima-rettō** island group SE Japan
13 R8 **Ha! Ha!, Lac** ◎ Québec, SE Canada
180 H13 **Hahaya** ✕ (Moroni) Grande Comore, NW Comoros
24 K9 **Hahnville** Louisiana, S USA 29.58N 90.24W
85 E22 **Haib** Karas, S Namibia 28.12S 18.19E
Haibak see Āybak
155 N15 **Haibo** ≈ SW Pakistan
Haibowan see Wuhai
169 U12 **Haicheng** Liaoning, NE China 40.52N 122.45E
Haicheng see Haiyuan
Haida see Nový Bor
Haidarabad see Hyderābād
Haidenschaft see Ajdovščina
178 Jj6 **Hai Dương** Hai Hưng, N Vietnam 20.55N 106.21E
144 F9 **Haifa** ◈ district NW Israel
Haifa see Hefa
Haifa, Bay of see Hefa, Mifraz
167 P14 **Haifeng** Guangdong, S China 22.58N 115.16E
Haifong see Hai Phong
167 P3 **Hai He** ≈ E China
Haikang see Leizhou
166 L17 **Haikou** var. Hai-k'ou, Hoihow, Fr. Hoï-Hao. Hainan, S China 20.00N 110.16E
146 M6 **Ḩā'il** Ḩā'il, NW Saudi Arabia 27.00N 42.50E
147 N5 **Ḩā'il** off. Minţaqah Ḩā'il. ◈ province N Saudi Arabia
Hai-la-erh see Hailar
169 S6 **Hailar** var. Hai-la-erh; prev. Hulun. Nei Mongol Zizhiqu, N China 49.15N 119.40E
169 S6 **Hailar He** ≈ NE China
35 P14 **Hailey** Idaho, NW USA 43.31N 114.18W
12 H9 **Haileybury** Ontario, S Canada 47.27N 79.39W
169 X9 **Hailin** Heilongjiang, NE China 44.37N 129.24E
Hā'il, Minţaqah see Ḩā'il
Hailong see Meihekou
95 K14 **Hailuoto** Swe. Karlö. island W Finland
Haima see Haymā'
Haimen see Taizhou
166 M17 **Hainan** var. Hainan Sheng, Qiong. ◈ province S China
166 K17 **Hainan Dao** island S China
Hainan Sheng see Hainan
Hainan Strait see Qiongzhou Haixia
Hainasch see Ainaži
Hainau see Chojnów
101 E20 **Hainaut** ◈ province SW Belgium
Hainburg see Hainburg an der Donau
111 Z4 **Hainburg an der Donau** var. Hainburg. Niederösterreich, NE Austria 48.08N 16.57E
41 W12 **Haines** Alaska, USA 59.13N 135.27W
34 L12 **Haines** Oregon, NW USA 44.53N 117.56W
25 W12 **Haines City** Florida, SE USA 28.06N 81.37W
8 H8 **Haines Junction** Yukon Territory, W Canada 60.45N 137.30W
111 W4 **Hainfeld** Niederösterreich, NE Austria 48.01N 15.45E
103 N16 **Hainichen** Sachsen, E Germany 50.58N 13.07E
Hai Ninh see Mong Cai
178 K6 **Hai Phong** var. Haifong, Haiphong. N Vietnam 20.49N 106.40E
167 S12 **Haitan Dao** island SE China
46 K8 **Haiti** off. Republic of Haiti. ◆ republic C West Indies
37 T11 **Haiwee Reservoir** ⊠ California, W USA
82 I7 **Haiya** Red Sea, NE Sudan 18.16N 36.21E
165 T10 **Haiyan** var. Sanjiaocheng. Qinghai, W China 36.55N 100.54E
166 M13 **Haiyang Shan** ▲▲ S China
165 V10 **Haiyuan** var. Haicheng. Ningxia, N China 36.32N 105.31E
Hajda see Nový Bor
113 M22 **Hajdú-Bihar** off. Hajdú-Bihar Megye. ◈ county E Hungary
113 N22 **Hajdúböszörmény** Hajdú-Bihar, E Hungary 47.39N 21.32E
113 N22 **Hajdúhadház** Hajdú-Bihar, E Hungary 47.40N 21.40E
113 N21 **Hajdúnánás** Hajdú-Bihar, E Hungary 47.49N 21.25E
113 N22 **Hajdúszoboszló** Hajdú-Bihar, E Hungary 47.27N 21.23E
148 I3 **Ḩājī Ebrāhīm, Kūh-e** ▲ Iran/Iraq 36.53N 44.56E
171 Kk11 **Hajiki-zaki** headland Sado, C Japan 38.19N 138.28E
Hajîne see Abū Ḩardān
159 P13 **Hājīpur** Bihār, N India 25.40N 85.13E
147 N14 **Ḩajjah** W Yemen 15.43N 43.33E
145 U11 **Hajjama** S Iraq 31.24N 45.20E
149 R12 **Ḩājjīābād** Hormozgān, C Iran
145 U14 **Ḩājj, Thaqb al** well S Iraq 29.58N 44.32E
115 L16 **Hajla** ▲▲ E-Montenegro
112 P10 **Hajnówka** Ger. Hermhausen. Podlaskie, NE Poland 52.43N 23.37E
177 Ff4 **Haka** Chin State, W Burma 22.42N 93.40E
Hakapehi see Punaauia
Hakâri see Hakkâri
143 T16 **Hakkâri** var. Çölemerik, Hakâri. Hakkâri, SE Turkey 37.36N 43.45E
143 T16 **Hakkâri** var. Hakkari. ◈ province SE Turkey
94 J12 **Hakkas** Norrbotten, N Sweden 66.52N 21.36E
171 Gg16 **Hakken-zan** ▲ Honshū, SW Japan 34.11N 135.57E
172 N9 **Hakkōda-san** ▲ Honshū, C Japan 40.40N 140.49E
172 Pp3 **Hako-dake** ▲ Hokkaidō, NE Japan 44.40N 142.22E
172 N7 **Hakodate** Hokkaidō, NE Japan 41.46N 140.42E
171 Ii12 **Hakui** Ishikawa, Honshū, SW Japan 36.52N 136.45E
202 B16 **Hakupu** SE Niue 19.06S 169.49E
171 I14 **Haku-san** ▲ Honshū, SW Japan 36.07N 136.45E
Hal see Halle
155 Q15 **Hāla** Sind, SE Pakistan 25.46N 68.28E
144 J3 **Ḩalab** Eng. Aleppo, Fr. Alep; anc. Beroea. Ḩalab, NW Syria 36.13N 37.10E
144 J3 **Ḩalab** off. Muḩāfaẓat Ḩalab, var. Aleppo, Halab. ◈ governorate NW Syria
144 J3 **Ḩalab** ✕ Ḩalab, NW Syria 36.12N 37.10E
147 O8 **Ḩalabān** var. Halibān. Ar Riyāḑ, C Saudi Arabia 23.28N 44.19E
145 V4 **Ḩalabja** NE Iraq 35.10N 45.58E
152 L13 **Halaç** Rus. Khalach. Lebap Welaýaty, E Turkmenistan 38.05N 64.46E
202 A16 **Halagigie Point** headland W Niue
77 Z11 **Halaib** SE Egypt 22.10N 36.33E
202 G12 **Halalo** Île Uvea, N Wallis and Futuna 13.21S 176.10W
Halandri see Chalándri
147 X13 **Ḩalāniyāt, Juzur al** var. Jazā'ir Bin Ghalfān, Eng. Kuria Muria Islands. island group S Oman
147 W13 **Ḩalānīyāt, Khalīj al** Eng. Kuria Muria Bay. bay S Oman
Halas see Kiskunhalas
40 G11 **Hālawa** var. Halawa. Hawai'i, USA, C Pacific Ocean 20.13N 155.46W
40 F9 **Hālawa, Cape** var. Cape Halawa. headland Moloka'i, Hawai'i, USA, C Pacific Ocean 21.09N 156.43W
Halban see Tsetserleg
103 K14 **Halberstadt** Sachsen-Anhalt, C Germany 51.54N 11.04E
192 M12 **Halcombe** Manawatu-Wanganui, North Island, NZ 40.09S 175.30E
97 I16 **Halden** prev. Fredrikshald. Østfold, S Norway 59.07N 11.19E
102 L13 **Haldensleben** Sachsen-Anhalt, C Germany 52.18N 11.25E
Háldi see Halti
159 S17 **Haldia** West Bengal, NE India 22.07N 88.06E
158 K10 **Haldwāni** Uttaranchal, N India 29.13N 79.31E
169 P9 **Haldzan** var. Hatavch. Sühbaatar, E Mongolia 46.10N 112.57E
40 F10 **Haleakalā** var. Haleakala crater Maui, Hawai'i, USA, C Pacific Ocean 20.45N 156.12W
27 N4 **Hale Center** Texas, SW USA 34.03N 101.50W
101 J18 **Halen** Limburg, NE Belgium 50.35N 5.08E
25 O2 **Haleyville** Alabama, S USA 34.13N 87.37W
79 O17 **Half Assini** SW Ghana 5.03N 2.57W
37 R8 **Half Dome** ▲ California, W USA 37.46N 119.27W
193 C25 **Halfmoon Bay** var. Oban. Stewart Island, Southland, NZ 46.52S 168.08E
190 E5 **Half Moon Lake** salt lake South Australia
169 R7 **Halhgol** Dornod, E Mongolia 47.57N 118.07E
169 S8 **Halhgol** var. Tsagaannuur. Dornod, E Mongolia 47.30N 118.45E
Haliacmon see Aliákmonas
Halibān see Ḩalabān
12 I13 **Haliburton** Ontario, SE Canada 45.03N 78.32W
12 I12 **Haliburton Highlands** var. Madawaska Highlands. hill range Ontario, SE Canada
11 Q15 **Halifax** Nova Scotia, SE Canada 44.37N 63.34W
99 L17 **Halifax** N England, UK 53.43N 1.52W
23 W8 **Halifax** North Carolina, SE USA 36.18N 77.35W
23 U7 **Halifax** Virginia, NE USA 36.46N 78.55W
11 Q15 **Halifax** ✕ Nova Scotia, SE Canada 44.33N 63.48W
149 T13 **Halīl Rūd** seasonal river SE Iran
144 I6 **Ḩalīmah** ▲ Lebanon/Syria 34.12N 36.37E
168 G8 **Haliun** Govĭ-Altay, W Mongolia 45.55N 96.06E
120 I3 **Haljala** Ger. Halljal. Lääne-Virumaa, N Estonia 59.25N 26.18E
41 Q4 **Halkett, Cape** headland Alaska, USA 70.48N 152.11W
Halkida see Chalkída
98 J6 **Halkirk** N Scotland, UK 58.30N 3.29W
13 X7 **Hall** ≈ Québec, SE Canada
Hall see Schwäbisch Hall
95 H15 **Hälla** Västerbotten, N Sweden 63.55N 17.19E
98 J6 **Halladale** ≈ N Scotland, UK
97 J21 **Halland** ◈ county S Sweden
25 Z15 **Hallandale** Florida, SE USA 25.58N 80.09W
97 K22 **Hallandsås** physical region S Sweden
15 M2 **Hall Beach** Nunavut, N Canada 68.10N 81.55W
101 G19 **Halle** Fr. Hal. Vlaams Brabant, C Belgium 50.43N 4.13E
103 M15 **Halle** var. Halle an der Saale. Sachsen-Anhalt, C Germany 51.28N 11.58E
Halle an der Saale see Halle
37 W3 **Halleck** Nevada, W USA 40.57N 115.27W
97 L15 **Hällefors** Örebro, C Sweden 59.48N 14.27E
97 N16 **Hälleforsnäs** Södermanland, C Sweden 59.10N 16.30E
111 Q6 **Hallein** Salzburg, N Austria 47.40N 13.06E
103 L15 **Halle-Neustadt** Sachsen-Anhalt, C Germany 51.28N 11.54E
27 U12 **Hallettsville** Texas, SW USA 29.27N 96.57W
205 N4 **Halley** UK research station Antarctica 75.42S 26.30W
30 L4 **Halliday** North Dakota, N USA 47.19N 102.19W
39 S2 **Halligan Reservoir** ⊠ Colorado, C USA
102 G7 **Halligen** island group N Germany
96 G13 **Hallingdal** valley S Norway
40 J12 **Hall Island** island Alaska, USA
Hall Island see Maiana
201 P15 **Hall Islands** island group C Micronesia
120 H6 **Halliste** ≈ S Estonia
Halljal see Haljala
95 I15 **Hällnäs** Västerbotten, N Sweden 64.19N 19.41E
31 R2 **Hallock** Minnesota, N USA 48.47N 96.56W
16 Oo3 **Hall Peninsula** peninsula Baffin Island, Nunavut, NE Canada
22 F9 **Halls** Tennessee, S USA 35.52N 89.24W
97 M16 **Hallsberg** Örebro, C Sweden 59.04N 15.07E
189 N5 **Halls Creek** Western Australia 18.17S 127.39E
190 L12 **Halls Gap** Victoria, SE Australia 37.09S 142.30E
97 N15 **Hallstahammar** Västmanland, C Sweden 59.25N 16.16E
111 R6 **Hallstatt** Salzburg, W Austria 47.32N 13.39E
111 R6 **Hallstatter See** ◎ C Austria
97 P14 **Hallstavik** Stockholm, C Sweden 60.12N 18.45E
27 X7 **Hallsville** Texas, SW USA 32.31N 94.30W
105 P1 **Halluin** Nord, N France 50.46N 3.07E
Halmahera, Laut see Halmahera Sea
175 T7 **Halmahera, Pulau** prev. Djailolo, Gilolo, Jailolo. island E Indonesia
175 Tt8 **Halmahera Sea** Ind. Laut Halmahera. sea E Indonesia
97 J21 **Halmstad** Halland, S Sweden 56.41N 12.48E
175 T11 **Halong** Pulau Ambon, E Indonesia 3.39S 128.13E
121 N15 **Halowchyn** Rus. Golovchin. Mahilyowskaya Voblasts', E Belarus 54.03N 29.52E
97 H20 **Hals** Nordjylland, N Denmark 57.00N 10.19E

◆ Country
● Country Capital
◇ Dependent Territory
○ Dependent Territory Capital
◈ Administrative Region
✕ International Airport
▲ Mountain
▲▲ Mountain Range
Volcano
≈ River
◎ Lake
⊠ Reservoir

HALSA – HAUTES FAGNES

96 F8 **Halsa** Møre og Romsdal, S Norway 63.04N 8.13E
121 I15 **Hal'shany** *Rus.* Gol'shany. Hrodzyenskaya Voblasts', W Belarus 54.15N 26.01E
Hälsingborg *see* Helsingborg
31 R5 **Halstad** Minnesota, N USA 47.21N 96.49W
29 N6 **Halstead** Kansas, C USA 38.00N 97.30W
101 G15 **Halsteren** Noord-Brabant, S Netherlands 51.31N 4.16E
95 L16 **Halsua** Länsi-Suomi, W Finland 63.28N 24.10E
103 E14 **Haltern** Nordrhein-Westfalen, W Germany 51.45N 7.10E
94 J9 **Halti** *var.* Haltiatunturi, *Lapp.* Háldi. ▲ Finland/Norway 69.18N 21.19E
Haltiatunturi *see* Halti
118 J6 **Halych** Ivano-Frankivs'ka Oblast', W Ukraine 49.08N 24.44E
Halycus *see* Platani
105 P3 **Ham** Somme, N France 49.46N 3.03E
Hama *see* Ḩamāh
170 Ee12 **Hamada** Shimane, Honshū, SW Japan 34.54N 132.07E
148 L6 **Hamadān** *anc.* Ecbatana. Hamadān, W Iran 34.50N 48.31E
148 L6 **Hamadān** *off.* Ostān-e Hamadān. ◈ *province* W Iran
144 I5 **Ḩamāh** *var.* Hama; *anc.* Epiphania, *Bibl.* Hamath. Ḩamāh, W Syria 35.09N 36.43E
144 I5 **Ḩamāh** *off.* Muḩāfaẓat Ḩamāh, *var.* Hama. ◈ *governorate* C Syria
171 I17 **Hamakita** Shizuoka, Honshū, S Japan 34.46N 137.46E
172 O4 **Hamamasu** Hokkaidō, NE Japan 43.37N 141.24E
171 I17 **Hamamatsu** *var.* Hamamatu. Shizuoka, Honshū, S Japan 34.43N 137.45E
Hamamatu *see* Hamamatsu
172 Qq7 **Hamanaka** Hokkaidō, NE Japan 43.05N 145.05E
171 I17 **Hamana-ko** ◎ Honshū, S Japan
96 I13 **Hamar** *prev.* Storhammer. Hedmark, S Norway 60.48N 11.04E
147 U10 **Ḩamārīr al Kidan, Qalamat** *well* E Saudi Arabia 21.40N 53.13E
170 G12 **Hamasaka** Hyōgo, Honshū, SW Japan 35.37N 134.27E
Hamath *see* Ḩamāh
172 Pp2 **Hamatonbetsu** Hokkaidō, NE Japan 45.07N 142.21E
161 K26 **Hambantota** Southern Province, SE Sri Lanka 6.11N 81.10E
194 G10 **Hambili** 〜 NW PNG
Hambourg *see* Hamburg
102 J9 **Hamburg** Hamburg, N Germany 53.33N 10.02E
29 V14 **Hamburg** Arkansas, C USA 33.13N 91.48W
31 S16 **Hamburg** Iowa, C USA 40.36N 95.39W
20 D10 **Hamburg** New York, NE USA 42.40N 78.49W
102 I10 **Hamburg** *Fr.* Hambourg. ◈ *state* N Germany
154 K5 **Hamdam Āb, Dasht-e** *Pash.* Dasht-i Hamdamab. ▲▲ W Afghanistan
Hamdamab, Dasht-i *see* Hamdam Āb, Dasht-e
20 M13 **Hamden** Connecticut, NE USA 41.22N 72.55W
146 K6 **Ḩamḑ, Wādī al** *dry watercourse* W Saudi Arabia
95 K18 **Hämeenkyrö** Länsi-Suomi, W Finland 61.39N 23.10E
95 L19 **Hämeenlinna** *Swe.* Tavastehus. Etelä-Suomi, S Finland 61.00N 24.25E
HaMelah, Yam *see* Dead Sea
Hamelin *see* Hameln
102 I13 **Hameln** *Eng.* Hamelin. Niedersachsen, N Germany 52.05N 9.21E
188 I8 **Hamersley Range** ▲▲ Western Australia
169 Y12 **Hamgyŏng-sanmaek** ▲▲ N North Korea
169 X13 **Hamhŭng** C North Korea 39.53N 127.31E
165 O6 **Hami** *var.* Ha-mi, *Uigh.* Kumul, Qomul. Xinjiang Uygur Zizhiqu, NW China 42.48N 93.27E
145 X10 **Ḩāmid Amīn** E Iraq 32.06N 46.53E
147 W11 **Hamīdān, Khawr** *oasis* SE Saudi Arabia 20.25N 54.43E
144 H5 **Ḩamīdīyah** *var.* Hamîdîyé. Ţarţūs, W Syria 34.43N 35.58E
116 L12 **Hamidiye** Edirne, NW Turkey 41.09N 26.40E
Hamîdîyé *see* Ḩamīdīyah
190 L12 **Hamilton** Victoria, SE Australia 37.45S 142.04E
66 B12 **Hamilton** ○ (Bermuda) C Bermuda 32.18N 64.48W
12 G16 **Hamilton** Ontario, S Canada 43.15N 79.49W
192 M7 **Hamilton** Waikato, North Island, NZ 37.48S 175.15E
98 I12 **Hamilton** S Scotland, UK 55.46N 4.03W
25 N3 **Hamilton** Alabama, S USA 34.08N 87.59W
40 M10 **Hamilton** Alaska, USA 62.54N 163.53W
32 J13 **Hamilton** Illinois, N USA 40.24N 91.20W
29 S3 **Hamilton** Missouri, C USA 39.44N 94.00W
35 P10 **Hamilton** Montana, NW USA 46.15N 114.09W
27 S8 **Hamilton** Texas, SW USA 31.42N 98.07W
12 G16 **Hamilton** ✕ Ontario, SE Canada 43.12N 79.54W
66 I6 **Hamilton Bank** *undersea feature* SE Labrador Sea
190 E1 **Hamilton Creek** *seasonal river* South Australia
11 R8 **Hamilton Inlet** *inlet* Newfoundland and Labrador, E Canada
29 T12 **Hamilton, Lake** ⊞ Arkansas, C USA
37 W6 **Hamilton, Mount** ▲ Nevada, W USA 39.15N 115.30W
77 S8 **Ḩamīm, Wādī al** 〜 NE Libya
95 N19 **Hamina** *Swe.* Fredrikshamn. Etelä-Suomi, S Finland 60.33N 27.15E
9 W16 **Hamiota** Manitoba, S Canada 50.13N 100.37W
158 L13 **Hamīrpur** Uttar Pradesh, N India 25.57N 80.07E
Hamīs Musait *see* Khamīs Mushayt
23 T11 **Hamlet** North Carolina, SE USA 34.52N 79.41W
27 P6 **Hamlin** Texas, SW USA 32.52N 100.07W
23 P5 **Hamlin** West Virginia, NE USA 38.16N 82.06W
33 O7 **Hamlin Lake** ◎ Michigan, N USA
103 F14 **Hamm** *var.* Hamm in Westfalen. Nordrhein-Westfalen, W Germany 51.39N 7.49E
Ḩammāmāt, Khalīj al *see* Hammamet, Golfe de
77 N5 **Hammamet, Golfe de** *Ar.* Khalīj al Ḩammāmāt. *gulf* NE Tunisia
145 R3 **Ḩammān al 'Alīl** N Iraq 36.07N 43.15E
145 X12 **Ḩammār, Hawr al** ◎ SE Iraq
95 J20 **Hammarland** Åland, SW Finland 60.13N 19.45E
95 H16 **Hammarstrand** Jämtland, C Sweden 63.07N 16.27E
95 O17 **Hammaslahti** Itä-Suomi, E Finland 62.26N 29.58E
101 F17 **Hamme** Oost-Vlaanderen, NW Belgium 51.06N 4.07E
102 H10 **Hamme** 〜 NW Germany
97 G22 **Hammel** Århus, C Denmark 56.15N 9.52E
103 I18 **Hammelburg** Bayern, C Germany 50.06N 9.50E
101 H18 **Hamme-Mille** Wallon Brabant, C Belgium 50.48N 4.42E
102 H10 **Hamme-Oste-Kanal** *canal* NW Germany
95 G16 **Hammerdal** Jämtland, C Sweden 63.34N 15.19E
94 K8 **Hammerfest** Finnmark, N Norway 70.40N 23.40E
103 D14 **Hamminkeln** Nordrhein-Westfalen, W Germany 51.43N 6.36E
Hamm in Westfalen *see* Hamm
28 K10 **Hammon** Oklahoma, C USA 35.37N 99.22W
33 N11 **Hammond** Indiana, N USA 41.35N 87.30W
24 K8 **Hammond** Louisiana, S USA 30.30N 90.27W
101 K20 **Hamoir** Liège, E Belgium 50.28N 5.35E
101 J21 **Hamois** Namur, SE Belgium 50.21N 5.09E
101 K16 **Hamont** Limburg, NE Belgium 51.15N 5.33E
193 F22 **Hampden** Otago, South Island, NZ 45.18S 170.49E
21 R6 **Hampden** Maine, NE USA 44.44N 68.51W
99 M23 **Hampshire** *cultural region* S England, UK
11 O15 **Hampton** New Brunswick, SE Canada 45.30N 65.49W
29 U14 **Hampton** Arkansas, C USA 33.33N 92.28W
31 V12 **Hampton** Iowa, C USA 42.44N 93.12W
21 P10 **Hampton** New Hampshire, NE USA 42.55N 70.48W
23 R14 **Hampton** South Carolina, SE USA 32.52N 81.06W
23 P8 **Hampton** Tennessee, S USA 36.16N 82.10W
23 X7 **Hampton** Virginia, NE USA 37.01N 76.21W
96 L11 **Hamra** Gävleborg, C Sweden 61.40N 15.00E
82 D10 **Hamrat esh Sheikh** Northern Kordofan, C Sudan 14.37N 27.55E
145 S5 **Ḩamrīn, Jabal** ▲▲ N Iraq
123 Jj16 **Hamrun** C Malta 35.53N 14.28E
178 K14 **Ham Thuân Nam** Binh Thuân, S Vietnam 10.49N 107.49E
176 Ww11 **Hamuku** Papua, E Indonesia 3.18S 135.00E
Hāmūn, Daryācheh-ye *see* Şāberī, Hāmūn-e/Sīstān, Daryācheh-ye
Hamwih *see* Southampton
40 G10 **Hāna** *var.* Hana. Maui, Hawai'i, USA, C Pacific Ocean 20.45N 155.59W
23 S14 **Hanahan** South Carolina, SE USA 32.55N 80.01W
40 B8 **Hanalei** Kaua'i, Hawai'i, USA, C Pacific Ocean 22.12N 159.30W
178 Kk10 **Ha Nam** Quang Nam-Đa Nẵng, C Vietnam 15.42N 108.24E
171 Mm11 **Hanamaki** Iwate, Honshū, C Japan 39.25N 141.04E
40 F10 **Hanamanioa, Cape** *headland* Maui, Hawai'i, USA, C Pacific Ocean 20.34N 156.22W
202 B16 **Hanan** ✕ (Alofi) SW Niue
103 H18 **Hanau** Hessen, W Germany 50.06N 8.56E
168 M11 **Hanbogd** *var.* Ih Bulag. Ömnögovĭ, S Mongolia 43.04N 107.43E
15 J7 **Hanbury** 〜 Northwest Territories, NW Canada
Hânceşti *see* Hînceşti
8 M15 **Hanceville** British Columbia, SW Canada 51.54N 122.56W
25 P3 **Hanceville** Alabama, S USA 34.03N 86.46W
Hancewicze *see* Hantsavichy
166 L6 **Hancheng** Shaanxi, C China 35.22N 110.27E
23 V2 **Hancock** Maryland, NE USA 39.42N 78.10W
32 M3 **Hancock** Michigan, N USA 47.07N 88.34W
31 S8 **Hancock** Minnesota, N USA 45.30N 95.47W
20 I12 **Hancock** New York, NE USA 41.57N 75.15W
82 Q12 **Handa** Bari, NE Somalia 10.35N 51.09E
167 O5 **Handan** *var.* Han-tan. Hebei, E China 36.34N 114.28E
97 P16 **Handen** Stockholm, C Sweden 59.12N 18.09E
83 J22 **Handeni** Tanga, E Tanzania 5.25S 38.04E
39 Q7 **Handies Peak** ▲ Colorado, C USA 37.54N 107.30W
113 J19 **Handlová** *Ger.* Krickerhäu, *Hung.* Nyitrabánya; *prev. Ger.* Kriegerhaj. Trenčiansky Kraj, W Slovakia 48.45N 18.45E
171 K17 **Haneda** ✕ (Tōkyō) Tōkyō, Honshū, S Japan 35.33N 139.45E
144 F13 **HaNegev** *Eng.* Negev. *desert* S Israel
Hanfeng *see* Kaixian
37 Q11 **Hanford** California, W USA 36.19N 119.39W
203 V16 **Hanga Roa** Easter Island, Chile, E Pacific Ocean 27.09S 109.25W
168 I7 **Hangay** *var.* Hunt. Arhangay, C Mongolia 47.49N 99.24E
168 H7 **Hangayn Nuruu** ▲▲ C Mongolia
Hang-chou/Hangchow *see* Hangzhou
97 K20 **Hånger** Jönköping, S Sweden 57.06N 13.58E
Hangö *see* Hanko
167 R9 **Hangzhou** *var.* Hang-chou, Hangchow. Zhejiang, SE China 30.18N 120.07E
168 J4 **Hanh** *var.* Turt. Hövsgöl, N Mongolia 51.30N 100.40E
168 F5 **Hanhöhiy Uul** ▲▲ NW Mongolia
168 K10 **Hanhongor** *var.* Ögöömör. Ömnögovĭ, S Mongolia 43.47N 104.31E
152 I14 **Hanhowuz** *Rus.* Khauz-Khan. Ahal Welaýaty, S Turkmenistan 37.15N 61.12E
152 I14 **Hanhowuz Suw Howdany** *Rus.* Khauzkhanskoye Vodokhranilishche. ⊞ S Turkmenistan
143 P15 **Hani** Dıyarbakır, SE Turkey 38.25N 40.22E
Hania *see* Chaniá
147 R11 **Ḩanīsh al Kabīr, Jazīrat al** *island* SW Yemen
Hanka, Lake *see* Khanka, Lake
95 M17 **Hankasalmi** Länsi-Suomi, W Finland 62.25N 26.27E
31 R7 **Hankinson** North Dakota, N USA 46.04N 96.54W
95 K20 **Hanko** *Swe.* Hangö. Etelä-Suomi, SW Finland 59.50N 23.00E
Han-kou/Han-k'ou/Hankow *see* Wuhan
38 M6 **Hanksville** Utah, W USA 38.21N 110.43W
158 K6 **Hanle** Jammu and Kashmir, NW India 32.46N 79.01E
193 I17 **Hanmer Springs** Canterbury, South Island, NZ 42.30S 172.48E
9 R16 **Hanna** Alberta, SW Canada 51.37N 111.55W
29 V3 **Hannibal** Missouri, C USA 39.42N 91.23W
188 M3 **Hann, Mount** ▲ Western Australia 15.53S 125.46E
102 I12 **Hannover** *Eng.* Hanover. Niedersachsen, NW Germany 52.23N 9.43E
101 J19 **Hannut** Liège, C Belgium 50.40N 5.04E
97 L22 **Hanöbukten** *bay* S Sweden
178 Jj6 **Ha Nôi** *Eng.* Hanoi, *Fr.* Ha noï. ● (Vietnam) N Vietnam 21.01N 105.52E
12 F14 **Hanover** Ontario, S Canada 44.22N 81.01W
33 P15 **Hanover** Indiana, N USA 38.42N 85.28W
20 G16 **Hanover** Pennsylvania, NE USA 39.46N 76.57W
23 W6 **Hanover** Virginia, NE USA 37.44N 77.21W
Hanover *see* Hannover
65 G23 **Hanover, Isla** *island* S Chile
Hanselbeck *see* Érd
205 X5 **Hansen Mountains** ▲▲ Antarctica
166 M8 **Han Shui** 〜 C China
158 H10 **Hānsi** Haryāna, NW India 29.07N 75.58E
97 F20 **Hanstholm** Viborg, NW Denmark 57.05N 8.39E
Han-tan *see* Handan
164 H6 **Hantengri Feng** *var.* Pik Khan-Tengri. ▲ China/Kazakhstan *see also* Khan-Tengri, Pik 42.17N 80.11E
121 I18 **Hantsavichy** *Pol.* Hancewicze, *Rus.* Gantsevichi. Brestskaya Voblasts', SW Belarus 52.45N 26.27E
16 N2 **Hantzsch** 〜 Baffin Island, Nunavut, NE Canada
158 G9 **Hanumāngarh** Rājasthān, NW India 29.33N 74.21E
191 O9 **Hanwood** New South Wales, SE Australia 34.19S 146.03E
Hanyang *see* Caidian
Hanyang *see* Wuhan
166 H10 **Hanyuan** *var.* Fulin. Sichuan, C China 29.22N 102.39E
Hanyuan *see* Xihe
166 J7 **Hanzhong** Shaanxi, C China 33.12N 106.59E
203 W11 **Hao** *atoll* Îles Tuamotu, C French Polynesia
159 S16 **Hāora** *prev.* Howrah. West Bengal, NE India 22.34N 88.19E
80 K8 **Haouach, Ouadi** *dry watercourse* E Chad
94 K13 **Haparanda** Norrbotten, N Sweden 65.49N 24.04E
27 N3 **Happy** Texas, SW USA 34.44N 101.51W
36 M1 **Happy Camp** California, W USA 41.48N 123.24W
11 Q9 **Happy Valley-Goose Bay** *prev.* Goose Bay. Newfoundland and Labrador, E Canada 53.19N 60.24W
Hapsal *see* Haapsalu
158 J10 **Hāpur** Uttar Pradesh, N India 28.43N 77.46E
144 F12 **HaQatan, HaMakhtesh** ▲▲ S Israel
146 I4 **Ḩaql** Tabūk, NW Saudi Arabia 29.18N 34.58E
176 Vv13 **Har** Pulau Kai Besar, E Indonesia 5.21S 133.09E
Haraat *see* Tsagaandelger
147 R8 **Ḩaraḑ** *var.* Haradh. Ash Sharqīyah, E Saudi Arabia 24.08N 49.01E
Haradh *see* Ḩaraḑ
120 N12 **Haradok** *Rus.* Gorodok. Vitsyebskaya Voblasts', N Belarus 55.27N 30.00E
94 J13 **Harads** Norrbotten, N Sweden 66.04N 21.04E
121 G19 **Haradzyets** *Rus.* Gorodets. Brestskaya Voblasts', SW Belarus 52.11N 24.41E
121 J17 **Haradzyeya** *Rus.* Gorodeya. Minskaya Voblasts', C Belarus 53.18N 26.33E
203 V10 **Haraiki** *atoll* Îles Tuamotu, C French Polynesia
171 Ll14 **Haramachi** Fukushima, Honshū, E Japan 37.39N 140.55E
120 M12 **Harany** *Rus.* Gorany. Vitsyebskaya Voblasts', N Belarus 55.25N 29.03E
85 L16 **Harare** *prev.* Salisbury. ● (Zimbabwe) Harare, NE Zimbabwe 17.47S 31.03E
85 L16 **Harare** ✕ Mashonaland East, NE Zimbabwe 17.51S 31.06E
80 J10 **Haraz-Djombo** Batha, C Chad 14.10N 19.35E
121 O16 **Harbavichy** *Rus.* Gorbovichi. Mahilyowskaya Voblasts', E Belarus 53.51N 30.42E
78 J16 **Harbel** W Liberia 6.19N 10.19W
169 W8 **Harbin** *var.* Haerbin, Ha-erh-pin, Kharbin; *prev.* Haerhpin, Pingkiang, Pinkiang. Heilongjiang, NE China 45.45N 126.40E
33 S7 **Harbor Beach** Michigan, N USA 43.50N 82.39W
11 T13 **Harbour Breton** Newfoundland and Labrador, E Canada 47.28N 55.49W
67 D25 **Harbours, Bay of** *bay* East Falkland, Falkland Islands
Hårby *see* Haarby
38 I13 **Harcuvar Mountains** ▲▲ Arizona, SW USA
110 I7 **Hard** Vorarlberg, NW Austria 47.28N 9.42E
160 H11 **Harda Khās** Madhya Pradesh, C India 22.22N 77.06E
97 D14 **Hardanger** *physical region* S Norway
97 D14 **Hardangerfjorden** *fjord* S Norway
96 E13 **Hardangerjøkulen** *glacier* S Norway
97 E14 **Hardangervidda** *plateau* S Norway
85 D20 **Hardap** ◈ *district* S Namibia
23 R15 **Hardeeville** South Carolina, SE USA 32.18N 81.04W
100 L5 **Hardegarijp** *Fris.* Hurdegaryp. Friesland, N Netherlands 53.13N 5.57E
100 O9 **Hardenberg** Overijssel, E Netherlands 52.34N 6.37E
191 Q9 **Harden-Murrumburrah** New South Wales, SE Australia 34.33S 148.22E
100 K10 **Harderwijk** Gelderland, C Netherlands 52.21N 5.36E
32 J14 **Hardin** Illinois, N USA 39.10N 90.37W
35 V11 **Hardin** Montana, NW USA 45.43N 107.34W
25 R5 **Harding, Lake** ⊞ Alabama/Georgia, SE USA
22 J6 **Hardinsburg** Kentucky, S USA 37.46N 86.27W
100 I13 **Hardinxveld-Giessendam** Zuid-Holland, C Netherlands 51.52N 4.49E
9 R15 **Hardisty** Alberta, SW Canada 52.42N 111.22W
158 L12 **Hardoi** Uttar Pradesh, N India 27.22N 80.06E
25 U4 **Hardwick** Georgia, SE USA 33.03N 83.13W
29 W9 **Hardy** Arkansas, C USA 36.19N 91.28W
96 D10 **Hareid** Møre og Romsdal, S Norway 62.22N 6.01E
15 Gg5 **Hare Indian** 〜 Northwest Territories, NW Canada
101 D18 **Harelbeke** *var.* Harlebeke. West-Vlaanderen, W Belgium 50.51N 3.19E
Harem *see* Ḩārim
102 E11 **Haren** Niedersachsen, NW Germany 52.47N 7.16E
100 N6 **Haren** Groningen, NE Netherlands 53.09N 6.36E
82 L13 **Hārer** Hārer, E Ethiopia 9.17N 42.18E
97 P14 **Harg** Uppsala, C Sweden 60.13N 18.25E
Hargeisa *see* Hargeysa
82 M13 **Hargeysa** *var.* Hargeisa. Woqooyi Galbeed, NW Somalia 9.31N 44.06E
118 J10 **Harghita** ◈ *county* NE Romania
27 S17 **Hargill** Texas, SW USA 26.26N 98.00W
168 J8 **Harhorin** Övörhangay, C Mongolia 47.13N 102.48E
165 Q9 **Har Hu** ◎ C China
Hariana *see* Haryāna
147 P15 **Ḩarīb** W Yemen 15.08N 45.35E
174 I9 **Hari, Batang** *prev.* Djambi. 〜 Sumatera, W Indonesia
158 J9 **Haridwār** *prev.* Hardwar. Uttaranchal, N India 29.58N 78.09E
161 F18 **Harihar** Karnātaka, W India 14.33N 75.43E
193 F18 **Harihari** West Coast, South Island, NZ 43.09S 170.35E
144 I3 **Ḩārim** *var.* Harem. Idlib, W Syria 36.30N 36.30E
170 G14 **Harima-nada** *sea* S Japan
100 F13 **Haringvliet** *channel* SW Netherlands
100 F13 **Haringvlietdam** *dam* SW Netherlands 51.49N 4.04E
155 U5 **Harīpur** North-West Frontier Province, NW Pakistan 34.00N 73.01E
154 J4 **Harīrūd** *var.* Tedzhen, *Turkm.* Tejen. 〜 Afghanistan/Iran *see also* Tejen
Härjahågnen *see* Østrehogna
95 K18 **Harjavalta** Länsi-Suomi, W Finland 61.17N 22.04E
Härjehågna *see* Østrehogna
120 G4 **Harjumaa** *off.* Harju Maakond. ◈ *province* NW Estonia
23 X11 **Harkers Island** North Carolina, SE USA 34.42N 76.33W
145 S1 **Harki** N Iraq 37.03N 43.39E
31 T14 **Harlan** Iowa, C USA 41.40N 95.19W
23 O7 **Harlan** Kentucky, S USA 36.50N 83.19W
31 N17 **Harlan County Lake** ⊞ Nebraska, C USA
118 L9 **Hârlău** *var.* Hîrlău. Iaşi, NE Romania 47.24N 26.56E
Harlebeke *see* Harelbeke
35 U7 **Harlem** Montana, NW USA 48.31N 108.46W
Harlem *see* Haarlem
97 G22 **Harlev** Århus, C Denmark 56.08N 10.00E
100 K6 **Harlingen** *Fris.* Harns. Friesland, N Netherlands 53.10N 5.25E
27 T17 **Harlingen** Texas, SW USA 26.12N 97.43W
99 O21 **Harlow** E England, UK 51.46N 0.07E
35 T10 **Harlowton** Montana, NW USA 46.26N 109.49W
96 N11 **Harmånger** Gävleborg, C Sweden 61.55N 17.19E
100 I11 **Harmelen** Utrecht, C Netherlands 52.06N 4.58E
31 X11 **Harmony** Minnesota, N USA 43.33N 92.00W
34 J14 **Harney Basin** *basin* Oregon, NW USA
(0) F9 **Harney Basin** ▲▲ Oregon, NW USA
34 J14 **Harney Lake** ◎ Oregon, NW USA
30 J10 **Harney Peak** ▲ South Dakota, N USA 43.52N 103.31W
95 H17 **Härnösand** *var.* Hernösand. Västernorrland, C Sweden 62.37N 17.55E
Harns *see* Harlingen
168 F6 **Har Nuur** ◎ NW Mongolia
107 P4 **Haro** La Rioja, N Spain 42.34N 2.52W
42 F6 **Haro, Cabo** *headland* NW Mexico 27.50N 110.55W
96 D9 **Harøy** *island* S Norway
99 N21 **Harpenden** E England, UK 51.49N 0.22W
78 L18 **Harper** *var.* Cape Palmas. NE Liberia 4.25N 7.43W
28 M7 **Harper** Kansas, C USA 37.17N 98.01W
34 L13 **Harper** Oregon, NW USA 43.51N 117.37W
27 Q10 **Harper** Texas, SW USA 30.18N 99.18W
37 U13 **Harper Lake** *salt flat* California, W USA
41 T9 **Harper, Mount** ▲ Alaska, USA 64.18N 143.54W
97 J21 **Harplinge** Halland, S Sweden 56.45N 12.45E
38 J13 **Harquahala Mountains** ▲▲ Arizona, SW USA
147 T15 **Ḩarrah** SE Yemen 15.02N 50.22E
10 H11 **Harricana** 〜 Québec, SE Canada
22 M9 **Harriman** Tennessee, S USA 35.57N 84.33W
11 R11 **Harrington Harbour** Québec, E Canada 50.34N 59.29W
66 B12 **Harrington Sound** *bay* Bermuda, NW Atlantic Ocean
98 F8 **Harris** *physical region* NW Scotland, UK
29 X10 **Harrisburg** Arkansas, C USA 35.33N 90.43W
32 M17 **Harrisburg** Illinois, N USA 37.44N 88.32W
30 I14 **Harrisburg** Nebraska, C USA 41.31N 103.43W
34 F12 **Harrisburg** Oregon, NW USA 44.16N 123.10W
20 G15 **Harrisburg** *state capital* Pennsylvania, NE USA 40.16N 76.52W
190 F6 **Harris, Lake** ◎ South Australia
25 W11 **Harris, Lake** ◎ Florida, SE USA
85 J22 **Harrismith** Free State, E South Africa 28.16S 29.06E
29 T9 **Harrison** Arkansas, C USA 36.13N 93.06W
33 Q7 **Harrison** Michigan, N USA 44.01N 84.49W
30 I12 **Harrison** Nebraska, C USA 42.39N 103.53W
41 Q5 **Harrison Bay** *inlet* Alaska, USA
24 I6 **Harrisonburg** Louisiana, S USA 31.44N 91.51W
23 U4 **Harrisonburg** Virginia, NE USA 38.27N 78.52W
11 R7 **Harrison, Cape** *headland* Newfoundland and Labrador, E Canada 54.55N 57.48W
29 R5 **Harrisonville** Missouri, C USA 38.39N 94.21W
Harris Ridge *see* Lomonosov Ridge
199 K3 **Harris Seamount** *undersea feature* N Pacific Ocean 46.09N 161.25W
98 F8 **Harris, Sound of** *strait* NW Scotland, UK
33 R6 **Harrisville** Michigan, N USA 44.39N 83.19W
23 R3 **Harrisville** West Virginia, NE USA 39.12N 81.03W
22 M6 **Harrodsburg** Kentucky, S USA 37.45N 84.50W
99 M16 **Harrogate** N England, UK 54.00N 1.33W
27 Q4 **Harrold** Texas, SW USA 34.05N 99.02W
29 S5 **Harry S.Truman Reservoir** ⊞ Missouri, C USA
102 G13 **Harsewinkel** Nordrhein-Westfalen, W Germany 51.58N 8.13E
118 M14 **Hârşova** *prev.* Hîrşova. Constanţa, SE Romania 44.40N 27.58E
94 H10 **Harstad** Troms, N Norway 68.48N 16.31E
33 O8 **Hart** Michigan, N USA 43.43N 86.22W
26 M4 **Hart** Texas, SW USA 34.23N 102.07W
8 I5 **Hart** 〜 Yukon Territory, NW Canada
85 F23 **Hartbees** 〜 C South Africa
111 X7 **Hartberg** Steiermark, SE Austria 47.15N 15.55E
190 I10 **Hart, Cape** *headland* South Australia 35.54S 138.01E
97 E14 **Hårteigen** ▲ S Norway 60.11N 7.01E
25 Q7 **Hartford** Alabama, S USA 31.06N 85.42W
29 R11 **Hartford** Arkansas, C USA 35.01N 94.22W
20 M12 **Hartford** *state capital* Connecticut, NE USA 41.45N 72.41W
22 J6 **Hartford** Kentucky, S USA 37.24N 86.52W
33 P10 **Hartford** Michigan, N USA 42.12N 85.54W
31 R11 **Hartford** South Dakota, N USA 43.37N 96.56W
32 M8 **Hartford** Wisconsin, N USA 43.19N 88.25W
33 P13 **Hartford City** Indiana, N USA 40.27N 85.22W
31 Q13 **Hartington** Nebraska, C USA 42.37N 97.15W
11 N14 **Hartland** New Brunswick, SE Canada 46.18N 67.31W
99 H23 **Hartland Point** *headland* SW England, UK 51.01N 4.33W
99 M15 **Hartlepool** N England, UK 54.40N 1.13W
31 T12 **Hartley** Iowa, C USA 43.10N 95.28W
26 M1 **Hartley** Texas, SW USA 35.52N 102.24W
34 J15 **Hart Mountain** ▲ Oregon, NW USA 42.24N 119.46W
181 U10 **Hartog Ridge** *undersea feature* W Indian Ocean
95 M18 **Hartola** Etelä-Suomi, S Finland 61.34N 26.04E
69 U14 **Harts** *var.* Hartz. 〜 N South Africa
25 P2 **Hartselle** Alabama, S USA 34.26N 86.56W
25 S3 **Hartsfield Atlanta** ✕ Georgia, SE USA 33.38N 84.24W
29 Q11 **Hartshorne** Oklahoma, C USA 34.51N 95.33W
23 S12 **Hartsville** South Carolina, SE USA 34.22N 80.04W
22 K8 **Hartsville** Tennessee, S USA 36.23N 86.10W
29 U7 **Hartville** Missouri, C USA 37.15N 92.30W
25 U2 **Hartwell** Georgia, SE USA 34.21N 82.55W
23 O11 **Hartwell Lake** ⊞ Georgia/South Carolina, SE USA
Hartz *see* Harts
Harunabad *see* Eslāmābād
Har-Us *see* Erdenebüren
168 E6 **Har Us Nuur** ◎ NW Mongolia
32 M10 **Harvard** Illinois, N USA 42.25N 88.36W
31 P16 **Harvard** Nebraska, C USA 40.37N 98.06W
39 R5 **Harvard, Mount** ▲ Colorado, C USA 38.55N 106.19W
33 N11 **Harvey** Illinois, N USA 41.36N 87.39W
31 N4 **Harvey** North Dakota, N USA 47.43N 99.55W
99 Q21 **Harwich** E England, UK 51.55N 1.16E
158 H10 **Haryāna** *var.* Hariana. ◈ *state* N India
147 Y9 **Ḩaryān, Ţawī al** *spring/well* NE Oman 21.56N 58.33E
103 J14 **Harz** ▲▲ C Germany
Hasakah *see* Al Ḩasakah
171 M12 **Hasama** Miyagi, Honshū, C Japan 38.42N 141.09E
142 J15 **Hasan Dağı** ▲ C Turkey 38.09N 34.15E
145 T9 **Ḩasan Ibn Ḩassūn** C Iraq 32.24N 44.13E
155 R6 **Ḩasan Khēl** *var.* Ahmad Khel. Paktīā, SE Afghanistan 33.46N 69.37E
102 F12 **Hase** 〜 NW Germany
Haselberg *see* Krasnoznamensk
102 F12 **Haselünne** Niedersachsen, NW Germany 52.40N 7.28E
Hashaat *see* Delgerhangay
Hashemite Kingdom of Jordan *see* Jordan
145 V8 **Hāshimah** E Iraq 33.22N 45.56E
171 Gg16 **Hashimoto** *var.* Hasimoto. Wakayama, Honshū, SW Japan 34.18N 135.34E
148 K3 **Hashtrūd** *var.* Āzarān. Āžarbāyjān-e Sharqī, N Iran 37.34N 47.10E
147 W13 **Ḩāsik** S Oman 17.22N 55.18E
155 U10 **Hāsilpur** Punjab, E Pakistan 29.44N 72.33E
Hasimoto *see* Hashimoto
29 Q10 **Haskell** Oklahoma, C USA 35.49N 95.40W
27 Q6 **Haskell** Texas, SW USA 33.09N 99.43W
116 M11 **Hasköy** Edirne, NW Turkey 41.37N 26.51E
97 L24 **Hasle** Bornholm, E Denmark 55.12N 14.43E
99 N23 **Haslemere** SE England, UK 51.06N 0.45W
104 I16 **Hasparren** Pyrénées-Atlantiques, SW France 43.22N 1.18W
Hassakeh *see* Al Ḩasakah
161 G19 **Hassan** Karnātaka, W India 13.01N 76.03E
38 J13 **Hassayampa River** 〜 Arizona, SW USA
103 J18 **Hassberge** *hill range* C Germany
96 N10 **Hassela** Gävleborg, C Sweden 62.06N 16.45E
101 J18 **Hasselt** Limburg, NE Belgium 50.55N 5.19E
100 M9 **Hasselt** Overijssel, E Netherlands 52.36N 6.06E
Hassetché *see* Al Ḩasakah
103 J18 **Hassfurt** Bayern, C Germany 50.02N 10.32E
76 L9 **Hassi Bel Guebbour** E Algeria 28.41N 6.29E
76 L8 **Hassi Messaoud** E Algeria 31.41N 6.10E
97 K22 **Hässleholm** Skåne, S Sweden 56.09N 13.45E
Hasta Colonia/Hasta Pompeia *see* Asti
191 O13 **Hastings** Victoria, SE Australia 38.18S 145.12E
192 O11 **Hastings** Hawke's Bay, North Island, NZ 39.39S 176.51E
99 P23 **Hastings** SE England, UK 50.51N 0.36E
33 P9 **Hastings** Michigan, N USA 42.37N 85.16W
31 W9 **Hastings** Minnesota, N USA 44.44N 92.51W
31 P16 **Hastings** Nebraska, C USA 40.35N 98.23W
97 K22 **Hästveda** Skåne, S Sweden 56.16N 13.55E
94 J8 **Hasvik** Finnmark, N Norway 70.29N 22.08E
39 V6 **Haswell** Colorado, C USA 38.27N 103.09W
169 N11 **Hatanbulag** *var.* Ergel. Dornogovĭ, SE Mongolia 43.10N 109.13E
Hatansuudal *see* Bayanlig
Hatavch *see* Haldzan
142 K17 **Hatay** ◈ *province* S Turkey
39 R15 **Hatch** New Mexico, SW USA 32.40N 107.10W
38 K7 **Hatch** Utah, W USA 37.39N 112.25W
22 F9 **Hatchie River** 〜 Tennessee, S USA
118 G12 **Haţeg** *Ger.* Wallenthal, *Hung.* Hátszeg; *prev.* Hatzeg, Hötzing. Hunedoara, SW Romania 45.35N 22.57E
172 Oo17 **Hateruma-jima** *island* Yaeyama-shotō, SW Japan
191 N8 **Hatfield** New South Wales, SE Australia 33.54S 143.43E
168 I5 **Hatgal** Hövsgöl, N Mongolia 50.24N 100.12E
159 V16 **Hathazari** Chittagong, SE Bangladesh 22.30N 91.46E
147 T13 **Hathūt, Hişā'** *oasis* NE Yemen 17.46N 51.14E
178 Ii14 **Ha Tiên** Kiên Giang, S Vietnam 10.24N 104.30E
178 Jj8 **Ha Tinh** Ha Tinh, N Vietnam 18.21N 105.55E
Hatiôzi *see* Hachiōji
144 F12 **Hatira, Haré** *hill range* S Israel
178 J6 **Hat Lot** *var.* Mai Sơn. Sơn La, N Vietnam 21.07N 104.10E
47 P16 **Hato Airport** ✕ (Willemstad) Curaçao, SW Netherlands Antilles 12.10N 68.56W
56 H9 **Hato Corozal** Casanare, C Colombia 6.07N 71.45W
Hato del Volcán *see* Volcán
47 P9 **Hato Mayor** E Dominican Republic 18.44N 69.16W
Hatra *see* Al Ḩaḑr
Hatria *see* Adria
Hátszeg *see* Haţeg
149 R16 **Ḩattá** Dubayy, NE UAE 24.50N 56.06E
190 L9 **Hattah** Victoria, SE Australia 34.49S 142.18E
100 M9 **Hattem** Gelderland, E Netherlands 52.28N 6.04E
23 Z10 **Hatteras** Hatteras Island, North Carolina, SE USA 35.13N 75.39W
23 Rr10 **Hatteras, Cape** *headland* North Carolina, SE USA 35.29N 75.33W
23 Z9 **Hatteras Island** *island* North Carolina, SE USA
66 F10 **Hatteras Plain** *undersea feature* W Atlantic Ocean
95 G14 **Hattfjelldal** Troms, N Norway 65.37N 13.58E
24 M7 **Hattiesburg** Mississippi, S USA 31.19N 89.17W
31 Q4 **Hatton** North Dakota, N USA 47.38N 97.27W
Hatton Bank *see* Hatton Ridge
66 L6 **Hatton Ridge** *var.* Hatton Bank. *undersea feature* N Atlantic Ocean
203 W6 **Hatutu** *island* Îles Marquises, NE French Polynesia
113 K22 **Hatvan** Heves, NE Hungary 47.40N 19.38E
178 H17 **Hat Yai** *var.* Ban Hat Yai. Songkhla, SW Thailand 7.01N 100.27E
Hatzeg *see* Haţeg
Hatzfeld *see* Jimbolia
82 N13 **Haud** *plateau* Ethiopia/Somalia
97 D18 **Hauge** Rogaland, S Norway 58.19N 6.16E
97 C15 **Haugesund** Rogaland, S Norway 59.24N 5.16E
111 X2 **Haugsdorf** Niederösterreich, NE Austria 48.41N 16.04E
192 M9 **Hauhungaroa Range** ▲▲ North Island, NZ
97 E15 **Haukeligrend** Telemark, S Norway 59.45N 7.33E
95 L14 **Haukipudas** Oulu, C Finland 65.11N 25.21E
95 M17 **Haukivesi** ◎ SE Finland
95 M17 **Haukivuori** Isä-Suomi, E Finland 62.02N 27.11E
Hauptkanal *see* Havelländ Grosse
195 Z17 **Hauraha** San Cristobal, SE Solomon Islands 10.47S 162.00E
192 L5 **Hauraki Gulf** *gulf* North Island, NZ
193 B24 **Hauroko, Lake** ◎ South Island, NZ
178 Jj15 **Hâu, Sông** 〜 S Vietnam
94 N12 **Hautajärvi** Lappi, NE Finland 66.30N 29.01E
76 F7 **Haut Atlas** *Eng.* High Atlas. ▲▲ C Morocco
81 M17 **Haut-Congo** *off.* Région du Haut-Congo; *prev.* Haut-Zaïre. ◈ *region* NE Dem. Rep. Congo
105 Y14 **Haute-Corse** ◈ *department* Corse, France, C Mediterranean Sea
104 L16 **Haute-Garonne** ◈ *department* S France
81 K14 **Haute-Kotto** ◈ *prefecture* E Central African Republic
105 P12 **Haute-Loire** ◈ *department* C France
105 R6 **Haute-Marne** ◈ *department* N France
104 M3 **Haute-Normandie** ◈ *region* N France
13 U6 **Hauterive** Québec, SE Canada 49.10N 68.16W
105 T13 **Hautes-Alpes** ◈ *department* SE France
105 S7 **Haute-Saône** ◈ *department* E France
105 T10 **Haute-Savoie** ◈ *department* E France
101 M20 **Hautes Fagnes** *Ger.* Hohes Venn. ▲▲ E Belgium

264

◆ Country ● Country Capital ◇ Dependent Territory ○ Dependent Territory Capital ◈ Administrative Region ✕ International Airport ▲ Mountain ▲▲ Mountain Range Volcano 〜 River ◎ Lake ⊞ Reservoir

HAUTES-PYRÉNÉES – HEZUO

104 K16 Hautes-Pyrénées ◐ department S France
101 L23 Haute Sûre, Lac de la ⊠ NW Luxembourg
104 M11 Haute-Vienne ◐ department C France
21 S8 Haut, Isle au island Maine, NE USA
81 M14 Haut-Mbomou ◐ préfecture SE Central African Republic
105 Q2 Hautmont Nord, N France 50.15N 3.55E
81 F19 Haut-Ogooué off. Province du Haut-Ogooué, var. Le Haut-Ogooué. ◐ province SE Gabon
Haut-Ogooué, Le see Haut-Ogooué
105 U7 Haut-Rhin ◐ department NE France
76 I6 Hauts Plateaux plateau Algeria/Morocco
40 D9 Hau'ula var. Hauula. O'ahu, Hawai'i, USA, C Pacific Ocean 21.36N 157.54W
103 O22 Hauzenberg Bayern, SE Germany 48.39N 13.37E
32 K13 Havana Illinois, N USA 40.18N 90.03W
Havana see La Habana
99 N23 Havant S England, UK 50.51N 0.58W
37 Y14 Havasu, Lake ⊠ Arizona/California, W USA
97 J23 Havdrup Roskilde, E Denmark 55.33N 12.07E
102 N10 Havel ∽ NE Germany
101 J21 Havelange Namur, SE Belgium 50.23N 5.14E
102 M11 Havelberg Sachsen-Anhalt, NE Germany 52.49N 12.05E
155 U5 Haveliān North-West Frontier Province, NW Pakistan 34.07N 73.12E
102 N12 Havelländ Grosse var. Hauptkanal. canal NE Germany
12 J14 Havelock Ontario, SE Canada 44.22N 77.57W
193 J14 Havelock Marlborough, South Island, NZ 41.17S 173.46E
23 X11 Havelock North Carolina, SE USA 34.52N 76.54W
192 O11 Havelock North Hawke's Bay, North Island, NZ 39.40S 176.53E
100 M8 Havelte Drenthe, NE Netherlands 52.46N 6.14E
29 N6 Haven Kansas, C USA 37.54N 97.46W
99 H21 Haverfordwest SW Wales, UK 51.49N 4.57W
99 P20 Haverhill E England, UK 52.04N 0.26E
21 O10 Haverhill Massachusetts, NE USA 42.46N 71.02W
95 G17 Haverö Västernorrland, C Sweden 62.25N 15.04E
113 I17 Havířov Moravskoslezský Kraj, E Czech Republic 49.47N 18.30E
113 E17 Havlíčkův Brod Ger. Deutsch-Brod; prev. Německý Brod. Vysočina, C Czech Republic 49.41N 15.47E
94 K7 Havøysund Finnmark, N Norway 70.59N 24.39E
35 T7 Havre Montana, NW USA 48.33N 109.40W
Havre see le Havre
101 F20 Havré Hainaut, S Belgium 50.28N 4.03E
11 P11 Havre-St-Pierre Québec, E Canada 50.16N 63.36W
142 B10 Havsa Edirne, NW Turkey 41.33N 26.49E
40 D8 Hawai'i off. State of Hawai'i; also known as Aloha State, Paradise of the Pacific var. Hawaii. ◐ state USA, C Pacific Ocean
40 G12 Hawai'i var. Hawaii. island Hawaiian Islands, USA, C Pacific Ocean
199 K5 Hawaiian Islands prev. Sandwich Islands. island group Hawai'i, USA, C Pacific Ocean
199 Jj6 Hawaiian Ridge undersea feature N Pacific Ocean
199 Kk6 Hawaiian Trough undersea feature N Pacific Ocean
31 R12 Hawarden Iowa, C USA 43.00N 96.29W
Hawash see Āwash
145 P6 Hawbayn al Gharbīyah C Iraq 34.24N 42.06E
193 D21 Hawea, Lake ◎ South Island, NZ
192 K11 Hawera Taranaki, North Island, NZ 39.36S 174.16E
22 J5 Hawesville Kentucky, S USA 37.53N 86.44W
40 G11 Hāwī var. Hawi. Hawai'i, USA, C Pacific Ocean 20.13N 155.49W
98 K13 Hawick SE Scotland, UK 55.24N 2.49W
145 S4 Ḩawījah C Iraq 35.15N 43.54E
145 Y10 Ḩawīzah, Hawr al ◎ S Iraq
193 E21 Hawkdun Range ▲▲ South Island, NZ
192 P10 Hawke Bay bay North Island, NZ
190 I6 Hawker South Australia 31.54S 138.25E
192 N11 Hawke's Bay off. Hawkes Bay Region. ◐ region North Island, NZ
155 O16 Hawkes Bay bay SE Pakistan
13 N12 Hawkesbury Ontario, SE Canada 45.35N 74.37W
Hawkeye State see Iowa
25 T5 Hawkinsville Georgia, SE USA 32.16N 83.28W
12 B7 Hawk Junction Ontario, S Canada 48.05N 84.34W
23 N10 Haw Knob ▲ North Carolina/Tennessee, SE USA 35.18N 84.01W
23 Q9 Hawksbill Mountain ▲ North Carolina, SE USA 35.54N 81.53W
35 Z16 Hawk Springs Wyoming, C USA 41.48N 104.17W
Hawlēr see Arbil
31 S5 Hawley Minnesota, N USA 46.53N 96.18W
27 P7 Hawley Texas, SW USA 32.36N 99.47W
147 R14 Ḩawrā' C Yemen 15.39N 48.20E
145 P7 Ḩawrān, Wadi dry watercourse W Iraq
23 T9 Haw River ∽ North Carolina, SE USA
145 U5 Hawshqūrah E Iraq 34.34N 45.33E
37 S7 Hawthorne Nevada, W USA 38.30N 118.38W
39 W3 Haxtun Colorado, C USA 40.36N 102.38W
191 N9 Hay New South Wales, SE Australia 34.31S 144.50E
9 O10 Hay ∽ W Canada
176 U11 Haya Pulau Seram, E Indonesia 3.22S 129.31E
172 N11 Hayachine-san ▲ Honshū, C Japan 39.31N 141.28E
105 S4 Hayange Moselle, NE France 49.19N 6.04E
HaYarden see Jordan
Hayastani Hanrapetut'yun see Armenia
Hayasui-seto see Hōyo-kaikyō
41 N9 Haycock Alaska, USA 65.12N 161.10W
38 M14 Hayden Arizona, SW USA 33.00N 110.46W
39 Q3 Hayden Colorado, C USA 40.29N 107.15W
30 M10 Hayes South Dakota, N USA 44.20N 101.01W
9 X13 Hayes ∽ Manitoba, C Canada
15 Kk11 Hayes ∽ Nunavut, NE Canada
30 M16 Hayes Center Nebraska, C USA 40.28N 101.01W
41 S10 Hayes, Mount ▲ Alaska, USA 63.37N 146.43W
23 N11 Hayesville North Carolina, SE USA 35.15N 84.15W
37 X10 Hayford Peak ▲ Nevada, W USA 36.40N 115.10W
36 M3 Hayfork California, W USA 40.33N 123.10W
Hayir, Qasr al see Ḩayr al Gharbī, Qaşr al
Haylaastay see Sühbaatar
12 I12 Hay Lake ◎ Ontario, SE Canada
147 X11 Haymā' var. Haima. C Oman 19.58N 56.20E
142 H13 Haymana Ankara, C Turkey 39.25N 32.30E
144 J7 Ḩaymūr, Jabal ▲ W Syria
Haynau see Chojnów
24 G4 Haynesville Louisiana, S USA 32.57N 93.08W
25 P6 Hayneville Alabama, S USA 32.13N 86.34W
116 M12 Hayrabolu Tekirdağ, NW Turkey 41.12N 27.08E
142 C10 Hayrabolu Deresi ∽ NW Turkey
144 J6 Ḩayr al Gharbī, Qaşr al var. Qasr al Hayir, Qasr al Hir al Gharbi. ruins Ḩimş, C Syria 34.23N 37.40E
144 L5 Ḩayr ash Sharqī, Qaşr al var. Qasr al Hir Ash Sharqi. ruins Ḩimş, C Syria 35.07N 39.06E
168 J7 Hayrhan var. Uubulan. Arhangay, C Mongolia 48.37N 101.58E
168 J9 Hayrhandulaan var. Mardzad. Övörhangay, C Mongolia 45.58N 102.06E
15 Hh9 Hay River Northwest Territories, W Canada 60.51N 115.42W
28 K4 Hays Kansas, C USA 38.52N 99.19W
30 K12 Hay Springs Nebraska, C USA 42.40N 102.41W
67 H25 Haystack, The ▲ NE Saint Helena 15.55S 5.40W
29 N7 Haysville Kansas, C USA 37.34N 97.21W
119 O7 Haysyn Rus. Gaysin. Vinnyts'ka Oblast', C Ukraine 48.49N 29.29E
29 Y9 Hayti Missouri, C USA 36.13N 89.45W
31 Q9 Hayti South Dakota, N USA 44.39N 97.11W
119 O8 Hayvoron Rus. Gayvorno. Kirovohrads'ka Oblast', C Ukraine 48.19N 29.54E
37 N9 Hayward California, W USA 37.40N 122.07W
32 I4 Hayward Wisconsin, N USA 46.01N 91.25W
99 O23 Haywards Heath SE England, UK 51.00N 0.06W
152 A11 Hazar prev. Rus. Cheleken. Balkan Welaýaty, W Turkmenistan 39.25N 53.07E
149 S11 Hazārān, Kūh-e var. Kūh-e ā Hazr. ▲ SE Iran 29.26N 57.15E
Hazarat Imam see Emām Şāḩeb
23 O7 Hazard Kentucky, S USA 37.15N 83.11W
143 O15 Hazar Gölü ◎ C Turkey
159 P15 Hazārībāg var. Hazāribāgh. Jhārkhand, N India 24.00N 85.23E
Hazāribāgh see Hazārībāg
105 O1 Hazebrouck Nord, N France 50.43N 2.33E
32 K9 Hazel Green Wisconsin, N USA 42.33N 90.26W
199 Ii10 Hazel Holme Bank undersea feature S Pacific Ocean 12.49S 174.30E
8 K13 Hazelton British Columbia, SW Canada 55.15N 127.37W
31 N6 Hazelton North Dakota, N USA 46.27N 100.17W
37 R5 Hazen Nevada, W USA 39.33N 119.02W
30 M5 Hazen North Dakota, N USA 47.18N 101.37W
40 L12 Hazen Bay bay E Bering Sea
145 S5 Hazīm, Bi'r well C Iraq 34.50N 43.25E
25 V6 Hazlehurst Georgia, SE USA 31.51N 82.35W
24 K6 Hazlehurst Mississippi, S USA 31.51N 90.24W
20 K15 Hazlet New Jersey, NE USA 40.24N 74.10W
152 I9 Hazorasp Rus. Khazarosp. Xorazm Viloyati, W Uzbekistan 41.21N 61.01E
153 R13 Hazratishoh, Qatorkŭhi var. Khrebet Khazretishi, Rus. Khrebet Khozretishi. ▲▲ S Tajikistan
Hazr, Kūh-e ā see Hazārān, Kūh-e
155 U6 Hazro Punjab, E Pakistan 33.55N 72.33E
25 R7 Headland Alabama, S USA 31.21N 85.20W
190 C6 Head of Bight headland South Australia 31.33S 131.05E
35 N10 Headquarters Idaho, NW USA 46.38N 115.52W
36 M7 Healdsburg California, W USA 38.36N 122.52W
29 N13 Healdton Oklahoma, C USA 34.13N 97.29W
191 O12 Healesville Victoria, SE Australia 37.41S 145.31E
41 R10 Healy Alaska, USA 63.51N 148.58W
181 R13 Heard and McDonald Islands ◇ Australian external territory S Indian Ocean
181 R13 Heard Island island Heard and McDonald Islands, S Indian Ocean
27 U9 Hearne Texas, SW USA 30.52N 96.35W
10 F12 Hearst Ontario, S Canada 49.42N 83.40W
204 J5 Hearst Island island Antarctica
Heart of Dixie see Alabama
30 L5 Heart River ∽ North Dakota, N USA
33 T13 Heath Ohio, N USA 40.01N 82.26W
191 N11 Heathcote Victoria, SE Australia 36.57S 144.43E
99 N22 Heathrow ✈ (London)SE England, UK 51.28N 0.27W
23 X5 Heathsville Virginia, NE USA 37.54N 76.25W
29 R11 Heavener Oklahoma, C USA 34.53N 94.36W
27 R15 Hebbronville Texas, SW USA 27.18N 98.40W
169 Q13 Hebei var. Hebei Sheng, Hopeh, Hopei, Ji; prev. Chihli. ◐ province E China
Hebei Sheng see Hebei
176 U9 Hebera Papua, E Indonesia 1.08S 129.54E
38 M3 Heber City Utah, W USA 40.29N 111.24W
29 V10 Heber Springs Arkansas, C USA 35.30N 91.58W
167 N5 Hebi Henan, C China 35.57N 114.07E
34 F11 Hebo Oregon, NW USA 45.10N 123.55W
98 F9 Hebrides, Sea of the sea NW Scotland, UK
11 P5 Hebron Newfoundland and Labrador, E Canada 58.15N 62.45W
33 N11 Hebron Indiana, N USA 41.19N 87.12W
31 Q17 Hebron Nebraska, C USA 40.10N 97.35W
30 L5 Hebron North Dakota, N USA 46.54N 102.03W
144 F11 Hebron var. Al Khalil, El Khalil, Heb. Hevron; anc. Kiriath-Arba. S West Bank 31.30N 35.00E
Hebrus see Évros/Maritsa/Meriç
97 N14 Heby Västmanland, C Sweden 59.55N 16.52E
8 I14 Hecate Strait strait British Columbia, W Canada
43 W12 Hecelchakán Campeche, SE Mexico 20.09N 90.04W
166 K13 Hechi var. Jinchengjiang. Guangxi Zhuangzu Zizhiqu, S China 24.40N 108.05E
103 H23 Hechingen Baden-Württemberg, S Germany 48.20N 8.58E
101 K17 Hechtel Limburg, NE Belgium 51.07N 5.24E
166 J9 Hechuan var. Heyang. Chongqing Shi, C China 30.01N 106.15E
31 P7 Hecla South Dakota, N USA 45.52N 98.09W
31 T9 Hector Minnesota, N USA 44.44N 94.43W
95 F17 Hede Jämtland, C Sweden 62.25N 13.33E
97 M14 Hedemora Dalarna, C Sweden 60.18N 15.58E
94 K13 Hedenäset Norrbotten, N Sweden 66.12N 23.40E
97 G23 Hedensted Vejle, C Denmark 55.46N 9.43E
97 N14 Hedesunda Gävleborg, C Sweden 60.25N 17.00E
97 N14 Hedesundafjord ◎ C Sweden
27 O3 Hedley Texas, SW USA 34.52N 100.39W
96 I12 Hedmark ◐ county S Norway
172 Pp14 Hedo-misaki headland Okinawa, SW Japan 26.55N 128.15E
31 X15 Hedrick Iowa, C USA 41.10N 92.18W
101 L16 Heel Limburg, SE Netherlands 51.12N 6.01E
201 Y12 Heel Point point Wake Island 19.18N 166.39E
100 H9 Heemskerk Noord-Holland, W Netherlands 52.31N 4.40E
100 M10 Heerde Gelderland, E Netherlands 52.24N 6.01E
100 L7 Heerenveen Fris. It Hearrenfean. Friesland, N Netherlands 52.57N 5.55E
100 I8 Heerhugowaard Noord-Holland, NW Netherlands 52.40N 4.49E
94 O3 Heer Land physical region C Svalbard
101 M18 Heerlen Limburg, SE Netherlands 50.55N 6.00E
101 J19 Heers Limburg, NE Belgium 50.46N 5.17E
Heerwegen see Polkowice
100 K13 Heesch Noord-Brabant, S Netherlands 51.43N 5.31E
101 K15 Heeze Noord-Brabant, SE Netherlands 51.22N 5.34E
144 F8 Ḩefa var. Haifa; hist. Caiffa, Caiphas, anc. Sycaminum. Haifa, N Israel 32.49N 34.58E
144 F8 Ḩefa, Mifraz Eng. Bay of Haifa. bay N Israel
167 Q8 Hefei var. Hofei; hist. Luchow. Anhui, E China 31.51N 117.20E
25 R3 Heflin Alabama, S USA 33.39N 85.35W
169 X7 Hegang Heilongjiang, NE China 47.18N 130.15E
171 Ii11 Hegura-jima island SW Japan
Heguri-jima see Heigun-tō
Hei see Heilongjiang
102 H8 Heide Schleswig-Holstein, N Germany 54.12N 9.06E
103 G20 Heidelberg Baden-Württemberg, SW Germany 49.24N 8.40E
85 J21 Heidelberg Gauteng, NE South Africa 26.27S 28.21E
24 M6 Heidelberg Mississippi, S USA 31.53N 88.58W
Heidenheim see Heidenheim an der Brenz
103 J22 Heidenheim an der Brenz var. Heidenheim. Baden-Württemberg, S Germany 48.40N 10.09E
111 U2 Heidenreichstein Niederösterreich, N Austria 48.53N 15.07E
170 E14 Heigun-tō var. Heguri-jima. island SW Japan
169 W5 Heihe prev. Ai-hun. Heilongjiang, NE China 50.13N 127.29E
165 S8 Hei He ∽ C China
Hei-ho see Nagqu
85 J22 Heilbron Free State, N South Africa 27.16S 27.58E
103 H21 Heilbronn Baden-Württemberg, SW Germany 49.09N 9.13E
Heiligenbeil see Mamonovo
111 Q8 Heiligenblut Tirol, W Austria 47.04N 12.50E
102 K7 Heiligenhafen Schleswig-Holstein, N Germany 54.22N 10.57E
Heiligenkreuz see Žiar nad Hronom
103 J15 Heiligenstadt Thüringen, C Germany 51.22N 10.09E
Heilong Jiang see Amur
169 W8 Heilongjiang var. Hei, Heilongjiang Sheng, Hei-lung-chiang, Heilungkiang. ◐ province NE China
Heilongjiang Sheng see Heilongjiang
100 H9 Heiloo Noord-Holland, NW Netherlands 52.36N 4.43E
Heilsberg see Lidzbark Warmiński
Hei-lung-chiang/Heilungkiang see Heilongjiang
94 I4 Heimaey var. Heimaæy. island S Iceland
96 H8 Heimdal Sør-Trøndelag, S Norway 63.21N 10.22E
Heinaste see Ainaži
95 M17 Heinävesi Itä-Suomi, E Finland 62.22N 28.42E
101 M22 Heinerscheid Diekirch, N Luxembourg 50.06N 6.04E
100 M10 Heino Overijssel, E Netherlands 52.26N 6.13E
95 M18 Heinola Etelä-Suomi, S Finland 61.13N 26.04E
103 C16 Heinsberg Nordrhein-Westfalen, W Germany 51.02N 6.01E
169 U12 Heishan Liaoning, NE China 41.43N 122.12E
166 H8 Heishui var. Luhua. Sichuan, C China 32.08N 102.54E
101 H17 Heist-op-den-Berg Antwerpen, C Belgium 51.04N 4.43E
Heitō see P'ingtung
176 Y14 Heitske Papua, E Indonesia 7.02S 138.45E
Hejanah see Al Hījānah
Hejaz see Al Ḩijāz
166 M14 He Jiang ∽ S China
Hejiayan see Lüeyang
164 K6 Hejing Xinjiang Uygur Zizhiqu, NW China 42.21N 86.19E
Héjjasfalva see Vânători
Heka see Hoika
143 N14 Hekimhan Malatya, C Turkey 38.49N 37.55E
94 J4 Hekla ▲ S Iceland 63.56N 19.42W
Hekou see Yajiang, Sichuan, China
Hekou see Yanshan, Jiangxi, China
112 J6 Hel Ger. Hela. Pomorskie, N Poland 54.35N 18.48E
Hela see Hel
95 F17 Helagsfjället ▲ C Sweden 62.57N 12.31E
165 W8 Helan var. Xigang. Ningxia, N China 38.33N 106.21E
168 K14 Helan Shan ▲▲ N China
101 M16 Helden Limburg, SE Netherlands 51.20N 6.00E
29 X12 Helena Arkansas, C USA 34.32N 90.34W
35 R10 Helena state capital Montana, NW USA 46.35N 112.02W
98 H12 Helensburgh W Scotland, UK 56.00N 4.45W
192 K5 Helensville Auckland, North Island, NZ 36.42S 174.25E
97 L20 Helgasjön ◎ S Sweden
102 G8 Helgoland Eng. Heligoland. island NW Germany
Helgoland Bay see Helgoländer Bucht
102 G8 Helgoländer Bucht var. Helgoland Bay, Heligoland Bight. bay NW Germany
Heligoland see Helgoland
Heligoland Bight see Helgoländer Bucht
Heliopolis see Baalbek
94 I4 Hella Sudhurland, SW Iceland 63.51N 20.24W
Hellas see Greece
149 N11 Ḩelleh, Rūd-e ∽ S Iran
100 N10 Hellendoorn Overijssel, E Netherlands 52.22N 6.27E
Hellenic Republic see Greece
123 Gg10 Hellenic Trough undersea feature Aegean Sea, C Mediterranean Sea
96 E10 Hellesylt Møre og Romsdal, S Norway 62.06N 6.51E
100 F13 Hellevoetsluis Zuid-Holland, SW Netherlands 51.49N 4.07E
107 Q12 Hellín Castilla-La Mancha, C Spain 38.31N 1.43W
117 H19 Hellinikon ✈ (Athína) Attikí, C Greece 37.53N 23.43E
34 M12 Hells Canyon valley Idaho/Oregon, NW USA
154 L9 Helmand ◐ province S Afghanistan
154 K10 Helmand, Daryā-ye var. Rūd-e Hīrmand. ∽ Afghanistan/Iran see also Hīrmand, Rūd-e
Helmantica see Salamanca
103 K15 Helme ∽ C Germany
101 L15 Helmond Noord-Brabant, S Netherlands 51.28N 5.40E
98 J7 Helmsdale N Scotland, UK 58.06N 3.36W
102 K13 Helmstedt Niedersachsen, N Germany 52.13N 11.01E
169 Y10 Helong Jilin, NE China 42.38N 129.01E
38 M4 Helper Utah, W USA 39.40N 110.52W
102 O10 Helpter Berge hill NE Germany 53.29N 13.37E
97 J22 Helsingborg prev. Hälsingborg. Skåne, S Sweden 55.59N 12.48E
Helsingfors see Helsinki
97 J22 Helsingør Eng. Elsinore. Frederiksborg, E Denmark 56.03N 12.37E
95 M20 Helsinki Swe. Helsingfors. ● (Finland) Etelä-Suomi, S Finland 60.18N 24.58E
99 H25 Helston SW England, UK 50.04N 5.16W
Heltau see Cisnădie
63 C17 Helvecia Santa Fe, C Argentina 31.09S 60.09W
99 K15 Helvellyn ▲ NW England, UK 54.31N 3.00W
Helvetia see Switzerland
77 W8 Helwân var. Hilwân, Hulwan, Hulwân. N Egypt 29.51N 31.19E
99 N21 Hemel Hempstead E England, UK 51.46N 0.28W
37 U16 Hemet California, W USA 33.45N 116.58W
30 J13 Hemingford Nebraska, C USA 42.18N 103.02W
23 T13 Hemingway South Carolina, SE USA 33.45N 79.25W
94 G13 Hemnesberget Nordland, C Norway 66.13N 13.33E
27 Y8 Hemphill Texas, SW USA 31.20N 93.51W
27 V11 Hempstead Texas, SW USA 30.06N 96.04W
97 P20 Hemse Gotland, SE Sweden 57.12N 18.22E
96 F13 Hemsedal valley S Norway
165 T11 Henan var. Henan Mongolzu Zizhixian, Yêgainnyin. Qinghai, C China 34.42N 101.36E
167 N6 Henan var. Henan Sheng, Honan, Yu. ◐ province C China
192 L4 Hen and Chickens island group N NZ
Henan Mongolzu Zizhixian/Henan Sheng see Henan
107 O7 Henares ∽ C Spain
171 M8 Henashi-zaki headland Honshū, C Japan 40.37N 139.51E
104 I16 Hendaye Pyrénées-Atlantiques, SW France 43.22N 1.46W
142 F11 Hendek Sakarya, NW Turkey 40.49N 30.40E
63 B21 Henderson Buenos Aires, E Argentina 36.18S 61.43W
22 I5 Henderson Kentucky, S USA 37.50N 87.35W
37 X11 Henderson Nevada, W USA 36.02N 114.58W
23 V8 Henderson North Carolina, SE USA 36.19N 78.24W
22 G10 Henderson Tennessee, S USA 35.25N 88.37W
27 W7 Henderson Texas, SW USA 32.09N 94.48W
32 J12 Henderson Creek ∽ Illinois, N USA
195 X16 Henderson Field ✈ (Honiara) Guadalcanal, C Solomon Islands 9.28S 160.02E
203 O17 Henderson Island atoll N Pitcairn Islands
23 O10 Hendersonville North Carolina, SE USA 35.19N 82.27W
22 J8 Hendersonville Tennessee, S USA 36.18N 86.37W
149 O14 Hendorābī, Jazīreh-ye island S Iran
57 V10 Hendrik Top var. Hendriktop. elevation C Surinam 4.14N 56.07W
Hendū Kosh see Hindu Kush
12 L12 Heney, Lac ◎ Québec, SE Canada
194 I12 Henganofi Eastern Highlands, C PNG 6.13S 145.31E
Hengchow see Hengyang
167 S15 Hengchun S Taiwan 22.09N 120.43E
165 R16 Hengduan Shan ▲▲ SW China
100 N12 Hengelo Gelderland, E Netherlands 52.02N 6.18E
100 O10 Hengelo Overijssel, E Netherlands 52.15N 6.48E
Hengnan see Hengyang
167 N11 Hengshan Hunan, S China 27.17N 112.51E
166 L4 Hengshan Shaanxi, C China 37.57N 109.17E
167 O4 Hengshui Hebei, E China 37.42N 115.39E
167 N12 Hengyang var. Hengnan, Heng-yang; prev. Hengchow. Hunan, S China 26.54N 112.33E
119 U11 Heniches'k Rus. Genichesk. Khersons'ka Oblast', S Ukraine 46.10N 34.49E
23 Z4 Henlopen, Cape headland Delaware, NE USA 38.48N 75.06W
Henna see Enna
96 M10 Hennan Gävleborg, C Sweden 62.01N 15.55E
104 G7 Hennebont Morbihan, NW France 47.48N 3.16W
32 L11 Hennepin Illinois, N USA 41.13N 89.21W
28 M9 Hennessey Oklahoma, C USA 36.06N 97.54W
102 N12 Hennigsdorf var. Hennigsdorf bei Berlin. Brandenburg, NE Germany 52.37N 13.13E
Hennigsdorf bei Berlin see Hennigsdorf
21 N9 Henniker New Hampshire, NE USA 43.10N 71.47W
27 S5 Henrietta Texas, SW USA 33.49N 98.12W
Henrique de Carvalho see Saurimo
32 L12 Henry Illinois, N USA 41.06N 89.21W
23 Y7 Henry, Cape headland Virginia, NE USA 36.55N 76.01W
29 P10 Henryetta Oklahoma, C USA 35.26N 95.58W
204 M7 Henry Ice Rise ice cap Antarctica
16 N1 Henry Kater, Cape headland Baffin Island, Nunavut, NE Canada 69.09N 66.45W
35 R13 Henrys Fork ∽ Idaho, NW USA
12 E15 Hensall Ontario, S Canada 43.25N 81.28W
102 J9 Henstedt-Ulzburg Schleswig-Holstein, N Germany 53.45N 9.59E
169 N7 Hentiy ◐ province N Mongolia
168 M7 Hentiyn Nuruu ▲▲ N Mongolia
191 P10 Henty New South Wales, SE Australia 35.33S 147.03E
177 Ff8 Henzada Irrawaddy, SW Burma 17.36N 95.25E
Heping see Huishui
103 G19 Heppenheim Hessen, W Germany 49.39N 8.38E
34 J11 Heppner Oregon, NW USA 45.21N 119.33W
166 L15 Hepu var. Lianzhou. Guangxi Zhuangzu Zizhiqu, S China 21.40N 109.12E
94 J2 Heradhsvötn ∽ C Iceland
Herakleion see Irákleio
154 K5 Herāt var. Herat; anc. Aria. Herāt, W Afghanistan 34.22N 62.11E
154 J5 Herāt ◐ province W Afghanistan
105 P14 Hérault ◐ department S France
105 P15 Hérault ∽ S France
9 T16 Herbert Saskatchewan, S Canada 50.27N 107.09W
193 F22 Herbert Otago, South Island, NZ 45.14S 170.48E
40 J17 Herbert Island island Aleutian Islands, Alaska, USA
194 I12 Herbert, Mount ▲ C PNG 5.44S 145.00E
Herbertshöhe see Kokopo
13 Q7 Herbertville Québec, SE Canada 48.22N 71.42W
103 G17 Herborn Hessen, W Germany 50.40N 8.18E
115 I17 Herceg-Novi It. Castelnuovo; prev. Ercegnovi. SW Montenegro 42.28N 18.35E
9 X10 Herchmer Manitoba, C Canada 57.25N 94.12W
194 K14 Hercules Bay bay E PNG
94 K2 Herdhubreidh ▲ C Iceland 65.12N 16.26W
44 M13 Heredia Heredia, C Costa Rica 10.00N 84.06W
44 M12 Heredia off. Provincia de Heredia. ◐ province N Costa Rica
99 K21 Hereford W England, UK 52.04N 2.43W
26 M3 Hereford Texas, SW USA 34.49N 102.25W
13 Q13 Hereford, Mont ▲ Québec, SE Canada 45.04N 71.38W
99 K21 Herefordshire cultural region W England, UK
203 U11 Hereheretue atoll Îles Tuamotu, C French Polynesia
107 N10 Herencia Castilla-La Mancha, C Spain 39.19N 3.19W
101 H18 Herent Vlaams Brabant, C Belgium 50.54N 4.40E
101 I16 Herentals var. Herenthals. Antwerpen, N Belgium 51.10N 4.49E
Herenthals see Herentals
101 H17 Herenthout Antwerpen, N Belgium 51.09N 4.45E
97 J23 Herfølge Roskilde, E Denmark 55.25N 12.09E
102 G13 Herford Nordrhein-Westfalen, NW Germany 52.07N 8.40E
29 O5 Herington Kansas, C USA 38.37N 96.55W
110 H7 Herisau Fr. Hérisau. Appenzell Ausser Rhoden, NE Switzerland 47.22N 9.16E
Héristal see Herstal
101 J18 Herk-de-Stad Limburg, NE Belgium 50.57N 5.12E
Herkulesbad/Herkulesfürdő see Băile Herculane
168 M8 Herlenbayan-Ulaan var. Dulaan. Hentiy, C Mongolia 47.09N 108.48E
Herlen Gol/Herlen He see Kerulen
37 Q4 Herlong California, W USA 40.07N 120.06W
99 L26 Herm island Channel Islands
111 R9 Hermagor Slvn. Šmohor. Kärnten, S Austria 46.37N 13.24E
31 S7 Herman Minnesota, N USA 45.49N 96.08W
98 L1 Herma Ness headland NE Scotland, UK 60.51N 0.55W
29 V4 Hermann Missouri, C USA 38.40N 91.25W
189 Q8 Hermannsburg Northern Territory, N Australia 23.59S 132.55E
Hermannstadt see Sibiu
96 E12 Hermansverk Sogn og Fjordane, S Norway 61.10N 6.52E
144 H6 Hermel var. Hirmil. NE Lebanon 34.23N 36.19E
Hermhausen see Hajnówka
191 P6 Hermidale New South Wales, SE Australia 31.36S 146.42E
57 X9 Herminadorp Sipaliwini, NE Surinam 5.05N 54.22W
34 K11 Hermiston Oregon, NW USA 45.50N 119.17W
29 T6 Hermitage Missouri, C USA 37.57N 93.21W
194 I8 Hermit Islands island group N PNG
27 O7 Hermleigh Texas, SW USA 32.37N 100.44W
144 G7 Hermon, Mount Ar. Jabal ash Shaykh. ▲ S Syria 35.30N 33.30E
Hermopolis Parva see Damanhûr
30 J10 Hermosa South Dakota, N USA 43.49N 103.12W
42 F5 Hermosillo Sonora, NW Mexico 28.58N 110.53W
Hermoupolis see Ermoúpoli
113 N20 Hernád var. Hornád, Ger. Kundert. ∽ Hungary/Slovakia
63 C18 Hernández Entre Ríos, E Argentina 32.21S 60.01W
25 V11 Hernando Florida, SE USA 28.54N 82.22W
24 L1 Hernando Mississippi, S USA 34.49N 89.59W
107 Q2 Hernani País Vasco, N Spain 43.16N 1.58W
101 F19 Herne Vlaams Brabant, C Belgium 50.45N 4.03E
103 E14 Herne Nordrhein-Westfalen, W Germany 51.33N 7.13E
97 F22 Herning Ringkøbing, W Denmark 56.07N 8.58E
Hernösand see Härnösand
124 Q13 Herodotus Basin undersea feature E Mediterranean Sea
124 Nn14 Herodotus Trough undersea feature C Mediterranean Sea
31 T11 Heron Lake Minnesota, N USA 43.48N 95.18W
Herowābād see Khalkhāl
97 G16 Herre Telemark, S Norway 59.06N 9.34E
31 N7 Herreid South Dakota, N USA 45.49N 100.04W
103 H22 Herrenberg Baden-Württemberg, S Germany 48.36N 8.52E
106 L14 Herrera Andalucía, S Spain 37.22N 4.49W
45 R17 Herrera off. Provincia de Herrera. ◐ province S Panama
106 L10 Herrera del Duque Extremadura, W Spain 39.10N 5.03W
106 M4 Herrera de Pisuerga Castilla-León, N Spain 42.34N 4.19W
43 Z13 Herrero, Punta headland SE Mexico 19.15N 87.28W
191 P16 Herrick Tasmania, SE Australia 41.07S 147.53E
32 L17 Herrin Illinois, N USA 37.48N 89.01W
22 M6 Herrington Lake ⊠ Kentucky, S USA
97 K18 Herrljunga Västra Götaland, S Sweden 58.04N 13.01E
105 N16 Hers ∽ S France
8 I1 Herschel Island island Yukon Territory, NW Canada
101 I17 Herselt Antwerpen, C Belgium 51.03N 4.52E
20 G15 Hershey Pennsylvania, NE USA 40.17N 76.39W
101 K19 Herstal Fr. Héristal. Liège, E Belgium 50.40N 5.37E
99 O21 Hertford E England, UK 51.48N 0.04W
23 X8 Hertford North Carolina, SE USA 36.11N 76.28W
99 O21 Hertfordshire cultural region E England, UK
189 Z9 Hervey Bay Queensland, E Australia 25.17S 152.48E
103 O14 Herzberg Brandenburg, E Germany 51.42N 13.15E
101 E18 Herzele Oost-Vlaanderen, NW Belgium 50.52N 3.52E
103 K20 Herzogenaurach Bayern, SE Germany 49.34N 10.52E
111 W4 Herzogenburg Niederösterreich, NE Austria 48.18N 15.43E
Herzogenbusch see 's-Hertogenbosch
105 N2 Hesdin Pas-de-Calais, N France 50.21N 2.00E
166 K14 Heshan Guangxi Zhuangzu Zizhiqu, S China 23.45N 108.58E
165 X10 Heshui var. Xihuachi. Gansu, C China 35.42N 108.06E
101 M25 Hespérange Luxembourg, SE Luxembourg 49.34N 6.10E
37 U14 Hesperia California, W USA 34.25N 117.17W
39 P7 Hesperus Mountain ▲ Colorado, C USA 37.27N 108.05W
8 J6 Hess ∽ Yukon Territory, NW Canada
Hesse see Hessen
103 J21 Hesselberg ▲ S Germany 49.04N 10.32E
97 I22 Hesselø island E Denmark
103 H17 Hessen Eng./Fr. Hesse. ◐ state C Germany
199 Jj6 Hess Tablemount undersea feature C Pacific Ocean 17.49N 174.15W
29 N6 Hesston Kansas, C USA 38.08N 97.25W
95 G15 Hestskjøltoppen ▲ C Norway 64.21N 13.57E
99 K18 Heswall NW England, UK 53.19N 3.06W
159 P12 Hetauḍā Central, C Nepal 27.25N 85.03E
Hétfalu see Săcele
30 K7 Hettinger North Dakota, N USA 46.00N 102.38W
103 L14 Hettstedt Sachsen-Anhalt, C Germany 51.39N 11.31E
94 P3 Heuglin, Kapp headland SE Svalbard 78.15N 22.49E
195 Y16 Heuru San Cristobal, SE Solomon Islands 10.13S 161.25E
101 J17 Heusden Limburg, NE Belgium 51.01N 5.16E
100 J13 Heusden Noord-Brabant, S Netherlands 51.43N 5.05E
104 K3 Hève, Cap de la headland N France 49.28N 0.13W
101 H18 Heverlee Vlaams Brabant, C Belgium 50.52N 4.41E
113 L22 Heves Heves, NE Hungary 47.37N 20.17E
113 L22 Heves off. Heves Megye. ◐ county NE Hungary
Hevron see Hebron
47 Y13 Hewanorra ✈ (Saint Lucia) S Saint Lucia 13.44N 60.57W
Hexian see Hezhou
166 L6 Heyang Shaanxi, C China 35.03N 109.55E
Heyang see Hechuan
Heydebrech see Kędzierzyn-Kozle
Heydekrug see Šilutė
Heyin see Guide
99 K16 Heysham NW England, UK 54.02N 2.54W
167 O14 Heyuan Guangdong, S China 23.50N 114.43E
190 L12 Heywood Victoria, SE Australia 38.09S 141.38E
188 K3 Heywood Islands island group Western Australia
167 O6 Heze var. Caozhou. Shandong, E China 35.16N 115.27E
165 U11 Hezheng Gansu, C China 35.24N 103.21E
166 M13 Hezhou var. Babu; prev. Hexian. Guangxi Zhuangzu Zizhiqu, S China 24.25N 111.31E
165 U11 Hezuo Gansu, C China 34.55N 102.49E

◆ Country ● Country Capital ◇ Dependent Territory ○ Dependent Territory Capital ◐ Administrative Region ✈ International Airport ▲ Mountain ▲▲ Mountain Range Volcano ∽ River ◎ Lake ⊠ Reservoir

HIALEAH – HONGWAN

25 Z16 **Hialeah** Florida, SE USA *25.51N 80.16W*
29 Q3 **Hiawatha** Kansas, C USA *39.48N 95.31W*
38 M4 **Hiawatha** Utah, W USA *39.28N 111.00W*
31 V4 **Hibbing** Minnesota, N USA *47.24N 92.55W*
191 N17 **Hibbs, Point** *headland* Tasmania, SE Australia *42.37S 145.15E*
Hibernia *see* Ireland
170 D12 **Hibiki-nada** *inlet* SW Japan
22 F8 **Hickman** Kentucky, S USA *36.34N 89.11W*
23 Q9 **Hickory** North Carolina, SE USA *35.44N 81.20W*
23 Q9 **Hickory, Lake** ⊚ North Carolina, SE USA
192 Q7 **Hicks Bay** Gisborne, North Island, NZ *37.36S 178.18E*
27 S8 **Hico** Texas, SW USA *31.58N 98.01W*
172 Oo6 **Hidaka** Hokkaidō, NE Japan *42.53N 142.24E*
171 Gg13 **Hidaka** Hyōgo, Honshū, SW Japan *35.27N 134.43E*
172 P7 **Hidaka-sanmyaku** ▲ Hokkaidō, NE Japan
43 O6 **Hidalgo** *var.* Villa Hidalgo. Coahuila de Zaragoza, NE Mexico *27.46N 99.54W*
43 N8 **Hidalgo** Nuevo León, NE Mexico *25.58N 100.27W*
43 O10 **Hidalgo** Tamaulipas, C Mexico *24.17N 99.21W*
43 O13 **Hidalgo** ◆ *state* C Mexico
42 J7 **Hidalgo del Parral** *var.* Parral. Chihuahua, N Mexico *26.58N 105.40W*
171 J14 **Hida-sanmyaku** ▲ Honshū, S Japan
102 N7 **Hiddensee** *island* NE Germany
82 G6 **Hidiglib, Wadi** ∾ NE Sudan
111 U6 **Hieflau** Salzburg, E Austria *47.36N 14.34E*
197 H5 **Hienghène** Province Nord, C New Caledonia *20.43S 164.54E*
Hierosolyma *see* Jerusalem
66 N12 **Hierro** *var.* Ferro. *island* Islas Canarias, Spain, NE Atlantic Ocean
170 Ee13 **Higashi-Hiroshima** *var.* Higasihirosima. Hiroshima, Honshū, SW Japan *34.25N 132.45E*
171 J18 **Higashi-Izu** Shizuoka, Honshū, S Japan *34.43N 138.58E*
171 Ll12 **Higashine** *var.* Higasine. Yamagata, Honshū, C Japan *38.26N 140.23E*
170 C11 **Higashi-suidō** *strait* SW Japan
Higasihirosima *see* Higashi-Hiroshima
Higasine *see* Higashine
27 P1 **Higgins** Texas, SW USA *36.06N 100.01W*
33 P7 **Higgins Lake** ⊚ Michigan, N USA
29 S4 **Higginsville** Missouri, C USA *39.04N 93.43W*
High Atlas *see* Haut Atlas
32 M5 **High Falls Reservoir** ⊡ Wisconsin, N USA
46 K12 **Highgate** C Jamaica *18.15N 76.53W*
27 X11 **High Island** Texas, SW USA *29.35N 94.24W*
33 O5 **High Island** *island* Michigan, N USA
32 K15 **Highland** Illinois, N USA *38.44N 89.40W*
33 N10 **Highland Park** Illinois, N USA *42.10N 87.48W*
23 O10 **Highlands** North Carolina, SE USA *35.04N 83.10W*
9 O11 **High Level** Alberta, W Canada *58.31N 117.07W*
31 O9 **Highmore** South Dakota, N USA *44.29N 99.26W*
179 Oo10 **High Peak** ▲ Luzon, N Philippines *15.28N 120.07E*
High Plains *see* Great Plains
23 S9 **High Point** North Carolina, SE USA *35.58N 80.00W*
20 J13 **High Point** *hill* New Jersey, NE USA *41.19N 74.38W*
9 P13 **High Prairie** Alberta, W Canada *55.27N 116.28W*
9 Q16 **High River** Alberta, SW Canada *50.34N 113.49W*
23 S9 **High Rock Lake** ⊡ North Carolina, SE USA
25 V9 **High Springs** Florida, SE USA *29.49N 82.36W*
High Veld *see* Great Karoo
99 J24 **High Willhays** ▲ SW England, UK *50.39N 3.58W*
99 N22 **High Wycombe** *prev.* Chepping Wycombe, Chipping Wycombe. SE England, UK *51.37N 0.46W*
43 P12 **Higos** *var.* El Higo. Veracruz-Llave, E Mexico *21.47N 98.28W*
104 I16 **Higuer, Cap** *headland* NE Spain *43.23N 1.46W*
47 R5 **Higüero, Punta** *headland* W Puerto Rico *18.21N 67.15W*
47 P9 **Higüey** *var.* Salvaleón de Higüey. E Dominican Republic *18.34N 68.43W*
202 G11 **Hihifo** ✕ (Matā'utu) Île Uvea, N Wallis and Futuna
83 N16 **Hiiraan** *off.* Gobolka Hiiraan. ◆ *region* C Somalia
120 E4 **Hiiumaa** *off.* Hiiumaa Maakond. ◆ *province* W Estonia
120 D4 **Hiiumaa** *Ger.* Dagden, *Swe.* Dagö. *island* W Estonia
Hijanah *see* Al Hījānah
107 S6 **Híjar** Aragón, NE Spain *41.10N 0.27W*
170 E13 **Hikari** Yamaguchi, Honshū, SW Japan *33.55N 131.58E*
170 Ff15 **Hiketa** Kagawa, Shikoku, SW Japan *34.15N 134.20E*
171 Hh15 **Hikone** Shiga, Honshū, SW Japan *35.15N 136.14E*
170 D13 **Hiko-san** ▲ Kyūshū, SW Japan *33.27N 130.55E*
203 V10 **Hikueru** *atoll* Îles Tuamotu, C French Polynesia
192 K3 **Hikurangi** Northland, North Island, NZ *35.37S 174.16E*
192 Q8 **Hikurangi** ▲ North Island, NZ *37.55S 177.59E*
199 J13 **Hikurangi Trench** *var.* Hikurangi Trough. *undersea feature* SW Pacific Ocean
Hikurangi Trough *see* Hikurangi Trench
202 B15 **Hikutavake** NW Niue
124 Nn14 **Hilāl, Ra's al** *headland* N Libya *32.55N 22.09E*
63 A24 **Hilario Ascasubi** Buenos Aires, E Argentina *39.22S 62.39W*
103 K17 **Hildburghausen** Thüringen, C Germany *50.26N 10.44E*
103 E15 **Hilden** Nordrhein-Westfalen, W Germany *51.10N 6.55E*
102 I13 **Hildesheim** Niedersachsen, N Germany *52.09N 9.57E*
35 T9 **Hilger** Montana, NW USA *47.15N 109.18W*
Hili *see* Hilli
Hilla *see* Al Ḥillah
47 O14 **Hillaby, Mount** ▲ N Barbados *13.12N 59.34W*
97 K19 **Hillared** Västra Götaland, S Sweden *57.37N 13.10E*
205 R12 **Hillary Coast** *physical region* Antarctica
44 G2 **Hill Bank** Orange Walk, N Belize *17.36N 88.43W*
35 O14 **Hill City** Idaho, NW USA *43.18N 115.03W*
28 K3 **Hill City** Kansas, C USA *39.21N 99.51W*
31 V5 **Hill City** Minnesota, N USA *46.59N 93.36W*
30 J10 **Hill City** South Dakota, N USA *43.54N 103.33W*
67 C24 **Hill Cove Settlement** West Falkland, Falkland Islands
100 H10 **Hillegom** Zuid-Holland, W Netherlands *52.18N 4.34E*
97 J22 **Hillerød** Frederiksborg, E Denmark *55.55N 12.19E*
38 M7 **Hillers, Mount** ▲ Utah, W USA *37.53N 110.42W*
159 S13 **Hilli** *var.* Hili. Rajshahi, NW Bangladesh *25.17N 89.02E*
31 R11 **Hills** Minnesota, N USA *43.31N 96.21W*
32 L14 **Hillsboro** Illinois, N USA *39.09N 89.29W*
29 N5 **Hillsboro** Kansas, C USA *38.21N 97.12W*
29 X5 **Hillsboro** Missouri, C USA *38.13N 90.33W*
21 N10 **Hillsboro** New Hampshire, NE USA *43.06N 71.52W*
39 Q14 **Hillsboro** New Mexico, SW USA *32.55N 107.33W*
31 R4 **Hillsboro** North Dakota, N USA *47.25N 97.03W*
33 R14 **Hillsboro** Ohio, N USA *39.12N 83.36W*
34 G11 **Hillsboro** Oregon, NW USA *45.31N 122.59W*
27 T8 **Hillsboro** Texas, SW USA *32.01N 97.08W*
32 K8 **Hillsboro** Wisconsin, N USA *43.40N 90.21W*
25 Y14 **Hillsboro Canal** *canal* Florida, SE USA
47 Y15 **Hillsborough** Carriacou, N Grenada *12.28N 61.28W*
99 G15 **Hillsborough** E Northern Ireland, UK *54.27N 6.06W*
23 U9 **Hillsborough** North Carolina, SE USA *36.04N 79.06W*
33 Q10 **Hillsdale** Michigan, N USA *41.55N 84.37W*
191 O8 **Hillston** New South Wales, SE Australia *33.30S 145.33E*
23 R7 **Hillsville** Virginia, NE USA *36.45N 80.44W*
98 L2 **Hillswick** NE Scotland, UK *60.28N 1.37W*
Hill Tippera *see* Tripura
40 H11 **Hilo** Hawai'i, USA, C Pacific Ocean *19.42N 155.04W*
20 F9 **Hilton** New York, NE USA *43.17N 77.47W*
12 C10 **Hilton Beach** Ontario, S Canada *46.14N 83.51W*
23 R16 **Hilton Head Island** South Carolina, SE USA *32.13N 80.45W*
23 R16 **Hilton Head Island** *island* South Carolina, SE USA
101 J15 **Hilvarenbeek** Noord-Brabant, S Netherlands *51.28N 5.07E*
100 J11 **Hilversum** Noord-Holland, C Netherlands *52.13N 5.10E*
Hilwān *see* Helwān
158 J7 **Himāchal Pradesh** ◆ *state* NW India
Himalaya/Himalaya Shan *see* Himalayas
158 M9 **Himalayas** *var.* Himalaya, *Chin.* Himalaya Shan. ▲ S Asia
179 Q14 **Himamaylan** Negros, C Philippines *10.04N 122.52E*
95 K15 **Himanka** Länsi-Suomi, W Finland *64.03N 24.40E*
Himara *see* Himarë
115 L23 **Himarë** *var.* Himara. Vlorë, S Albania *40.06N 19.45E*
144 M2 **Ḥimār, Wādī al** *dry watercourse* N Syria
160 D9 **Himatnagar** Gujarāt, W India *23.37N 73.01E*
111 Y4 **Himberg** Niederösterreich, E Austria *48.03N 16.27E*
171 J14 **Hime-gawa** ∾ Honshū, S Japan
170 G14 **Himeji** *var.* Himezi. Hyōgo, Honshū, SW Japan *34.47N 134.32E*
170 Dd13 **Hime-jima** *island* SW Japan
Himezi *see* Himeji
171 Ii13 **Himi** Toyama, Honshū, SW Japan *36.52N 136.59E*
111 S9 **Himmelberg** Kärnten, S Austria *46.45N 14.01E*
144 I5 **Ḥimṣ** *var.* Homs; *anc.* Emesa. Ḥimṣ, C Syria *34.43N 36.43E*
144 K6 **Ḥimṣ** *off.* Muḥāfaẓat Ḥimṣ, *var.* Homs. ◆ *governorate* C Syria
144 I5 **Ḥimṣ, Buḥayrat** *var.* Buḥayrat Qaṭṭīnah. ⊚ W Syria
179 Rr15 **Hinatuan** Mindanao, S Philippines *8.21N 126.19E*
119 N10 **Hincești** *var.* Hâncești; *prev.* Kotovsk. C Moldova *46.48N 28.33E*
46 M9 **Hinche** C Haiti *19.07N 72.00W*
189 X5 **Hinchinbrook Island** *island* Queensland, NE Australia
41 S12 **Hinchinbrook Island** *island* Alaska, USA
99 M19 **Hinckley** C England, UK *52.33N 1.21W*
31 V7 **Hinckley** Minnesota, N USA *46.01N 92.57W*
38 K5 **Hinckley** Utah, W USA *39.21N 112.39W*
20 J9 **Hinckley Reservoir** ⊡ New York, NE USA
158 I12 **Hindaun** Rājasthān, N India *26.43N 77.01E*
Hindenburg/Hindenburg in Oberschlesien *see* Zabrze
Hindiya *see* Al Hindīyah
23 O6 **Hindman** Kentucky, S USA *37.20N 82.58W*
190 L10 **Hindmarsh, Lake** ⊚ Victoria, SE Australia
193 G19 **Hinds** Canterbury, South Island, NZ *44.00S 171.33E*
193 G19 **Hinds** ∾ South Island, NZ
97 H23 **Hindsholm** *island* C Denmark
155 S4 **Hindu Kush** *Per.* Hendū Kosh. ▲ Afghanistan/Pakistan
161 H19 **Hindupur** Andhra Pradesh, E India *13.46N 77.33E*
9 O12 **Hines Creek** Alberta, W Canada *56.14N 118.36W*
25 W6 **Hinesville** Georgia, SE USA *31.51N 81.36W*
160 I12 **Hinganghāt** Mahārāshtra, C India *20.31N 78.52E*
155 N15 **Hingol** ∾ SW Pakistan
160 H13 **Hingoli** Mahārāshtra, C India *19.45N 77.08E*
143 R13 **Hınıs** Erzurum, E Turkey *39.22N 41.43E*
94 O2 **Hinlopenstretet** *strait* N Svalbard
94 G10 **Hinnøya** *Lapp.* Iinnasuolu. *island* C Norway
170 D15 **Hinokage** Miyazaki, Kyūshū, SW Japan *32.39N 131.20E*
170 F11 **Hino-misaki** *headland* Honshū, SW Japan *35.25N 132.37E*
110 H10 **Hinterrhein** ∾ SW Switzerland
9 O14 **Hinton** Alberta, SW Canada *53.24N 117.34W*
28 M10 **Hinton** Oklahoma, C USA *35.28N 98.21W*
23 R6 **Hinton** West Virginia, NE USA *37.40N 80.53W*
Hios *see* Chíos
43 N8 **Hipolito** Coahuila de Zaragoza, NE Mexico *25.42N 101.22W*
Hipponium *see* Vibo Valentia
170 C12 **Hirado** Nagasaki, Hirado-shima, SW Japan *33.22N 129.32E*
170 C12 **Hirado-shima** *island* SW Japan
171 Gg15 **Hirakata** Ōsaka, Honshū, SW Japan *34.48N 135.37E*
172 P17 **Hirakubo-saki** *headland* Ishigaki-jima, SW Japan *24.36N 124.19E*
160 M11 **Hirākud Reservoir** ⊡ E India
Hir al Gharbi, Qasr al *see* Ḥayr al Gharbī, Qaṣr al
172 N9 **Hiranai** Aomori, Honshū, N Japan *40.56N 140.55E*
172 Pp16 **Hirara** Okinawa, Miyako-jima, SW Japan *24.48N 125.16E*
Qasr al Hir Ash Sharqī *see* Ḥayr ash Sharqī, Qaṣr al
170 F12 **Hirata** Shimane, Honshū, SW Japan *35.26N 132.50E*
171 Jj17 **Hiratsuka** *var.* Hiratuka. Kanagawa, Honshū, S Japan *35.20N 139.20E*
Hiratuka *see* Hiratsuka
142 I13 **Hirfanlı Barajı** ⊡ C Turkey
161 G18 **Hiriyūr** Karnātaka, W India *13.58N 76.33E*
Hirlău *see* Hârlău
154 K10 **Hirmand, Rūd-e** *var.* Daryā-ye Helmand. ∾ Afghanistan/Iran *see also* Helmand, Daryā-ye
Hirmil *see* Hermel
172 P8 **Hiroo** Hokkaidō, NE Japan *42.16N 143.16E*
171 Mm9 **Hirosaki** Aomori, Honshū, C Japan *40.34N 140.28E*
170 E13 **Hiroshima** *var.* Hirosima. Hiroshima, Honshū, SW Japan *34.22N 132.25E*
170 Ee13 **Hiroshima** *off.* Hiroshima-ken, *var.* Hirosima. ◆ *prefecture* Honshū, SW Japan
Hirosima *see* Hiroshima
Hirschberg/Hirschberg im Riesengebirge/Hirschberg in Schlesien *see* Jelenia Góra
105 Q3 **Hirson** Aisne, N France *49.55N 4.04E*
Hirșova *see* Hârșova
97 G19 **Hirtshals** Nordjylland, N Denmark *57.34N 9.58E*
171 H16 **Hisai** Mie, Honshū, SW Japan *34.38N 136.27E*
158 H10 **Hisār** Haryāna, NW India *29.10N 75.45E*
168 K7 **Hishig-Öndör** *var.* Maanĭt. Bulgan, C Mongolia *48.17N 103.29E*
194 J15 **Hisiu** Central, SW PNG *9.01S 146.49E*
153 P13 **Hisor** *Rus.* Gissar. W Tajikistan *38.34N 68.29E*
Hispalis *see* Sevilla
Hispana/Hispania *see* Spain
46 M7 **Hispaniola** *island* Dominion Republic/Haiti
66 F11 **Hispaniola Basin** *var.* Hispaniola Trough. *undersea feature* SW Atlantic Ocean
Hispaniola Trough *see* Hispaniola Basin
Histonium *see* Vasto
145 R7 **Hīt** SW Iraq *33.38N 42.50E*
170 D14 **Hita** Ōita, Kyūshū, SW Japan *33.20N 130.55E*
171 L16 **Hitachi** *var.* Hitati. Ibaraki, Honshū, S Japan *36.40N 140.42E*
171 L15 **Hitachi-Ōta** *var.* Hitatiôta. Ibaraki, Honshū, S Japan *36.31N 140.31E*
Hitati *see* Hitachi
Hitatiôta *see* Hitachi-Ōta
99 O21 **Hitchin** E England, UK *51.57N 0.16W*
203 Q7 **Hitiaa** Tahiti, W French Polynesia *17.34S 149.16W*
170 Cc15 **Hitoyoshi** *var.* Hitoyosi. Kumamoto, Kyūshū, SW Japan *32.12N 130.45E*
Hitoyosi *see* Hitoyoshi
96 F7 **Hitra** *prev.* Hitteren. *island* S Norway
Hitteren *see* Hitra
197 B10 **Hiu** *island* Torres Islands, N Vanuatu
171 K14 **Hiuchiga-take** ▲ Honshū, C Japan *36.57N 139.18E*
170 Ee14 **Hiuchi-nada** *gulf* S Japan
203 X7 **Hiva Oa** *island* Îles Marquises, N French Polynesia
22 M10 **Hiwassee Lake** ⊡ North Carolina, SE USA
22 M10 **Hiwassee River** ∾ SE USA
97 H20 **Hjallerup** Nordjylland, N Denmark *57.10N 10.10E*
97 M16 **Hjälmaren** *Eng.* Lake Hjalmar. ⊚ C Sweden
Hjalmar, Lake *see* Hjälmaren
97 C14 **Hjellestad** Hordaland, S Norway *60.15N 5.13E*
97 D16 **Hjelmeland** Rogaland, S Norway *59.12N 6.07E*
96 G10 **Hjerkinn** Oppland, S Norway *62.13N 9.37E*
97 L18 **Hjo** Västra Götaland, S Sweden *58.16N 14.07E*
97 G19 **Hjørring** Nordjylland, N Denmark *57.28N 9.58E*
178 H1 **Hkakabo Razi** ▲ Burma/China *28.17N 97.28E*
178 H1 **Hkring Bum** ▲ N Burma *27.05N 97.16E*
85 L21 **Hlathikulu** *var.* Hlatikulu. S Swaziland *26.57S 31.19E*
Hlatikulu *see* Hlathikulu
Hliboka *see* Hlyboka
113 F17 **Hlinsko** *var.* Hlinsko v Čechách. Pardubický Kraj, C Czech Republic *49.46N 15.54E*
Hlinsko v Čechách *see* Hlinsko
119 S6 **Hlobyne** *Rus.* Globino. Poltavs'ka Oblast', NE Ukraine *49.24N 33.16E*
113 H20 **Hlohovec** *Ger.* Freistadtl, *Hung.* Galgóc; *prev.* Frakštát. Trnavský Kraj, W Slovakia *48.27N 17.47E*
85 J23 **Hlotse** *var.* Leribe. NW Lesotho *28.55S 28.01E*
113 I17 **Hlučín** *Ger.* Hultschin, *Pol.* Hulczyn. Moravskoslezský Kraj, E Czech Republic *49.54N 18.10E*
119 S2 **Hlukhiv** *Rus.* Glukhov. Sums'ka Oblast', NE Ukraine *51.39N 33.52E*
121 K21 **Hlushkavichy** *Rus.* Glushkevichi. Homyel'skaya Voblasts', SE Belarus *51.33N 27.48E*
121 L18 **Hlusk** *Rus.* Glusk, Glussk. Mahilyowskaya Voblasts', E Belarus *52.54N 28.40E*
118 K8 **Hlyboka** *Ger.* Hliboka, *Rus.* Glybokaya. Chernivets'ka Oblast', W Ukraine *48.04N 25.55E*
120 K13 **Hlybokaye** *Rus.* Glubokoye. Vitsyebskaya Voblasts', N Belarus *55.08N 27.40E*
79 Q16 **Ho** SE Ghana *6.36N 0.28E*
178 Jj6 **Hoa Binh** Hoa Binh, N Vietnam *20.49N 105.19E*
85 E20 **Hoachanas** Hardap, C Namibia *23.52S 18.02E*
Hoai Nhơn *see* Bông Sơn
178 Jj8 **Hoa Lac** Quang Binh, C Vietnam *17.54N 106.24E*
178 J5 **Hoang Liên Sơn** ▲ N Vietnam
85 B17 **Hoanib** ∾ NW Namibia
35 S15 **Hoback Peak** ▲ Wyoming, C USA *43.04N 110.34W*
191 P17 **Hobart** *prev.* Hobarton, Hobart Town. *state capital* Tasmania, SE Australia *42.54S 147.18E*
28 L11 **Hobart** Oklahoma, C USA *35.01N 99.05W*
191 P17 **Hobart** ✕ Tasmania, SE Australia *42.52S 147.28E*
Hobarton/Hobart Town *see* Hobart
39 W14 **Hobbs** New Mexico, SW USA *32.42N 103.08W*
204 L12 **Hobbs Coast** *physical region* Antarctica
25 Z14 **Hobe Sound** Florida, SE USA *27.03N 80.08W*
Hobicaurikány *see* Uricani
56 E12 **Hobo** Huila, S Colombia *2.34N 75.28W*
101 G16 **Hoboken** Antwerpen, N Belgium *51.12N 4.22E*
164 K3 **Hoboksar** *var.* Hoboksar Mongol Zizhixian. Xinjiang Uygur Zizhiqu, NW China *46.48N 85.42E*
Hoboksar Mongol Zizhixian *see* Hoboksar
97 G21 **Hobro** Nordjylland, N Denmark *56.39N 9.51E*
23 X10 **Hobucken** North Carolina, SE USA *35.15N 76.31W*
97 O20 **Hoburgen** *headland* SE Sweden *56.54N 18.07E*
83 P15 **Hobyo** *It.* Obbia. Mudug, E Somalia *5.16N 48.24E*
111 R8 **Hochalmspitze** ▲ SW Austria *47.00N 13.19E*
111 Q4 **Hochburg** Oberösterreich, N Austria *48.10N 12.57E*
110 F8 **Hochdorf** Luzern, N Switzerland *47.10N 8.16E*
111 N8 **Hochfeiler** *It.* Gran Pilastro. ▲ Austria/Italy *46.59N 11.42E*
178 Jj14 **Ho Chi Minh** *var.* Ho Chi Minh City; *prev.* Saigon. S Vietnam *10.46N 106.43E*
Ho Chi Minh City *see* Hô Chi Minh
110 I7 **Höchst** Vorarlberg, NW Austria *47.28N 9.40E*
Höchstadt *see* Höchstadt an der Aisch
103 K19 **Höchstadt an der Aisch** *var.* Höchstadt. Bayern, C Germany *49.43N 10.48E*
110 L9 **Hochwilde** *It.* L'Altissima. ▲ Austria/Italy *46.45N 11.00E*
111 S7 **Hochwildstelle** ▲ C Austria *47.21N 13.53E*
33 T14 **Hocking River** ∾ Ohio, N USA
Hoctúm *see* Hoctún
43 X12 **Hoctún** *var.* Hoctúm. Yucatán, E Mexico *20.48N 89.13W*
Hodeida *see* Al Ḥudaydah
22 K6 **Hodgenville** Kentucky, S USA *37.34N 85.44W*
9 T17 **Hodgeville** Saskatchewan, S Canada *50.06N 106.55W*
78 L9 **Hodh ech Chargui** ◆ *region* E Mauritania
Hodh el Garbi *see* Hodh el Gharbi
78 J10 **Hodh el Gharbi** *var.* Hodh el Garbi. ◆ *region* S Mauritania
113 L25 **Hódmezővásárhely** Csongrád, SE Hungary *46.27N 20.17E*
76 J6 **Hodna, Chott El** *var.* Chott el-Hodna, *Ar.* Shatt al-Hodna. *salt lake* N Algeria
Hodna, Shatt al- *see* Hodna, Chott El
113 G19 **Hodonín** *Ger.* Göding. Jihomoravský Kraj, SE Czech Republic *48.51N 17.07E*
Hödrögö *see* Nömrög
Hodság/Hodschag *see* Odžaci
41 R7 **Hodzana River** ∾ Alaska, USA
Hoei *see* Huy
101 H19 **Hoeilaart** Vlaams Brabant, C Belgium *50.46N 4.28E*
Hoë Karoo *see* Great Karoo
100 F12 **Hoek van Holland** *Eng.* Hook of Holland. Zuid-Holland, W Netherlands *52.00N 4.07E*
100 L11 **Hoenderloo** Gelderland, E Netherlands *52.08N 5.46E*
101 L18 **Hoensbroek** Limburg, SE Netherlands *50.55N 5.55E*
169 Y11 **Hoeryŏng** NE North Korea *42.23N 129.46E*
101 K18 **Hoeselt** Limburg, NE Belgium *50.49N 5.30E*
100 K11 **Hoevelaken** Gelderland, C Netherlands *52.10N 5.27E*
Hoey *see* Huy
103 M18 **Hof** Bayern, SE Germany *50.19N 11.55E*
Höfdhakaupstadhur *see* Skagaströnd
Hofei *see* Hefei
103 G18 **Hofheim am Taunus** Hessen, W Germany *50.04N 8.27E*
Hofmarkt *see* Odorheiu Secuiesc
94 L3 **Höfn** Austurland, SE Iceland *64.14N 15.17W*
96 N13 **Hofors** Gävleborg, C Sweden *60.33N 16.21E*
94 J6 **Hofsjökull** *glacier* C Iceland
94 J1 **Hofsós** Nordhurland Vestra, N Iceland *65.54N 19.25W*
170 Dd13 **Hōfu** Yamaguchi, Honshū, SW Japan *34.01N 131.34E*
Hofuf *see* Al Hufūf
97 J22 **Höganäs** Skåne, S Sweden *56.11N 12.39E*
191 P14 **Hogan Group** *island group* Tasmania, SE Australia
25 R4 **Hogansville** Georgia, SE USA *33.10N 84.55W*
41 P8 **Hogatza River** ∾ Alaska, USA
30 I14 **Hogback Mountain** ▲ Nebraska, C USA *41.40N 103.44W*
97 G14 **Høgevarde** ▲ S Norway *60.19N 9.27E*
Högfors *see* Karkkila
33 P5 **Hog Island** *island* Michigan, N USA
23 Y6 **Hog Island** *island* Virginia, NE USA
Hogoley Islands *see* Chuuk Islands
97 N20 **Högsby** Kalmar, S Sweden *57.10N 16.03E*
38 K1 **Hogup Mountains** ▲ Utah, W USA
103 E17 **Hohe Acht** ▲ W Germany *50.23N 7.00E*
Hohenelbe *see* Vrchlabí
110 I7 **Hohenems** Vorarlberg, W Austria *47.22N 9.43E*
Hohenmauth *see* Vysoké Mýto
Hohensalza *see* Inowrocław
Hohenstadt *see* Zábřeh
Hohenstein in Ostpreussen *see* Olsztynek
22 I9 **Hohenwald** Tennessee, S USA *35.33N 87.33W*
103 L17 **Hohenwarte-Stausee** ⊡ C Germany
Hohes Venn *see* Hautes Fagnes
111 Q8 **Hohe Tauern** ▲ W Austria
169 O13 **Hohhot** *var.* Huhehot, Huhuohaote, *Mong.* Kukukhoto; *prev.* Kweisui, Kwesui. Nei Mongol Zizhiqu, N China *40.49N 111.37E*
168 F7 **Hohmorit** *var.* Sayn-Ust. Govĭ-Altay, W Mongolia *47.23N 94.19E*
105 U6 **Hohneck** ▲ NE France *48.04N 7.01E*
79 Q16 **Hohoe** E Ghana *7.07N 0.31E*
170 D12 **Hōhoku** Yamaguchi, Honshū, SW Japan *34.15N 130.56E*
165 O11 **Hoh Sai Hu** ⊚ C China
165 N11 **Hoh Xil Hu** ⊚ C China
165 L11 **Hoh Xil Shan** ▲ W China
178 Kk10 **Hôi An** *prev.* Faifo. Quang Nam-Đa Nẵng, C Vietnam *15.54N 108.19E*
Hoï-Hao/Hoihow *see* Haikou
165 S11 **Hoika** *prev.* Heka. Qinghai, W China *35.49N 99.49E*
83 F17 **Hoima** W Uganda *1.25N 31.22E*
28 L5 **Hoisington** Kansas, C USA *38.31N 98.46W*
152 D12 **Hojagala** *Rus.* Khodzhakala. Balkan Welaýaty, W Turkmenistan *38.46N 56.14E*
152 M13 **Hojambaz** *Rus.* Khodzhambas. Lebap Welaýaty, E Turkmenistan *38.11N 64.33E*
97 H23 **Højby** Fyn, C Denmark *55.19N 10.27E*
97 F24 **Højer** Sønderjylland, SW Denmark *54.57N 8.43E*
170 Ee14 **Hōjō** *var.* Hôzyô. Ehime, Shikoku, SW Japan *33.58N 132.47E*
192 J3 **Hokianga Harbour** *inlet* SE Tasman Sea
193 F17 **Hokitika** West Coast, South Island, NZ *42.43S 170.58E*
172 P5 **Hokkai-dō** ◆ *territory* Hokkaidō, NE Japan
172 Oo5 **Hokkaidō** *prev.* Ezo, Yeso, Yezo. *island* NE Japan
97 G15 **Hokksund** Buskerud, S Norway *59.46N 9.54E*
149 S4 **Hokmābād** Khorāsān-Razavī, N Iran *36.37N 57.34E*
Hokō *see* P'ohang
Hoko-guntō/Hoko-shotō *see* P'enghu Liehtao
Hoktemberyan *see* Armavir
96 F13 **Hol** Buskerud, S Norway *60.36N 8.18E*
119 R11 **Hola Prystan'** *Rus.* Golaya Pristan. Khersons'ka Oblast', S Ukraine *46.31N 32.31E*
97 I23 **Holbæk** Vestsjælland, E Denmark *55.42N 11.42E*
Holboo *see* Santmargats
191 P10 **Holbrook** New South Wales, SE Australia *35.45S 147.18E*
39 N11 **Holbrook** Arizona, SW USA *34.54N 110.09W*
29 S5 **Holden** Missouri, C USA *38.42N 93.59W*
38 K5 **Holden** Utah, W USA *39.06N 112.16W*
29 O11 **Holdenville** Oklahoma, C USA *35.04N 96.24W*
31 O16 **Holdrege** Nebraska, C USA *40.28N 99.28W*
37 X3 **Hole in the Mountain Peak** ▲ Nevada, W USA *40.54N 115.06W*
161 G20 **Hole Narsipur** Karnātaka, W India *12.46N 76.13E*
113 H18 **Holešov** *Ger.* Holleschau. Zlínský Kraj, E Czech Republic *49.19N 17.34E*
47 N14 **Holetown** *prev.* Jamestown. W Barbados *13.09N 59.37W*
33 Q12 **Holgate** Ohio, N USA *41.12N 84.06W*
46 I7 **Holguín** Holguín, SE Cuba *20.51N 76.16W*
25 V12 **Holiday** Florida, SE USA *28.11N 82.44W*
41 O12 **Holitna River** ∾ Alaska, USA
96 J13 **Höljes** Värmland, C Sweden *60.54N 12.34E*
111 X3 **Hollabrunn** Niederösterreich, NE Austria *48.33N 16.06E*
38 L3 **Holladay** Utah, W USA *40.39N 111.49W*
9 X16 **Holland** Manitoba, S Canada *49.36N 98.52W*
33 O9 **Holland** Michigan, N USA *42.47N 86.06W*
27 T9 **Holland** Texas, SW USA *30.52N 97.24W*
Holland *see* Netherlands
24 K4 **Hollandale** Mississippi, S USA *33.10N 90.51W*
Hollandia *see* Jayapura
Hollandsch Diep *see* Hollands Diep
101 H14 **Hollands Diep** *var.* Hollandsch Diep. *channel* SW Netherlands
Holleschau *see* Holešov
27 R5 **Holliday** Texas, SW USA *33.49N 98.41W*
20 E15 **Hollidaysburg** Pennsylvania, NE USA *40.24N 78.22W*
23 S6 **Hollins** Virginia, NE USA *37.20N 79.56W*
28 J12 **Hollis** Oklahoma, C USA *34.42N 99.54W*
37 O10 **Hollister** California, W USA *36.51N 121.25W*
29 T8 **Hollister** Missouri, C USA *36.37N 93.13W*
95 M19 **Hollola** Etelä-Suomi, S Finland *60.59N 25.31E*
100 K4 **Hollum** Friesland, N Netherlands *53.27N 5.38E*
97 J23 **Höllviksnäs** Skåne, S Sweden *55.25N 12.57E*
39 W6 **Holly** Colorado, C USA *38.03N 102.07W*
33 R9 **Holly** Michigan, N USA *42.47N 83.37W*
23 S14 **Holly Hill** South Carolina, SE USA *33.19N 80.24W*
23 W11 **Holly Ridge** North Carolina, SE USA *34.31N 77.31W*
24 L1 **Holly Springs** Mississippi, S USA *34.46N 89.25W*
25 Z15 **Hollywood** Florida, SE USA *26.00N 80.09W*
15 I2 **Holman** Victoria Island, Northwest Territories, N Canada *70.42N 117.45W*
94 I2 **Hólmavík** Vestfirdhir, NW Iceland *65.42N 21.43W*
32 J7 **Holmen** Wisconsin, N USA *43.57N 91.14W*
25 R8 **Holmes Creek** ∾ Alabama/Florida, SE USA
97 H16 **Holmestrand** Vestfold, S Norway *59.28N 10.19E*
95 J16 **Holmön** *island* N Sweden
97 E22 **Holmsland Klit** *beach* W Denmark
95 J16 **Holmsund** Västerbotten, N Sweden *63.42N 20.25E*
97 Q18 **Holmudden** *headland* SE Sweden *57.59N 19.14E*
194 L15 **Holnicote Bay** *headland* SW PNG *8.30S 148.18E*
144 F10 **Ḥolon** *var.* Kholon. Tel Aviv, C Israel *32.01N 34.46E*
169 P7 **Hölönbuyr** *var.* Bayan. Dornod, E Mongolia *47.56N 112.58E*
119 P8 **Holovanivs'k** *Rus.* Golovanevsk. Kirovohrads'ka Oblast', C Ukraine *48.21N 30.26E*
97 F21 **Holstebro** Ringkøbing, W Denmark *56.22N 8.37E*
97 F23 **Holsted** Ribe, W Denmark *55.30N 8.54E*
31 T13 **Holstein** Iowa, C USA *42.29N 95.32W*
Holsteinborg/Holsteinsborg/Holstenborg/Holstensborg *see* Sisimiut
23 O8 **Holston River** ∾ Tennessee, S USA
33 Q9 **Holt** Michigan, N USA *42.38N 84.31W*
100 N10 **Holten** Overijssel, E Netherlands *52.16N 6.25E*
29 P3 **Holton** Kansas, C USA *39.28N 95.44W*
29 U5 **Holts Summit** Missouri, C USA *38.38N 92.07W*
37 X17 **Holtville** California, W USA *32.48N 115.22W*
100 L5 **Holwerd** *Fris.* Holwert. Friesland, N Netherlands *53.22N 5.51E*
Holwert *see* Holwerd
41 O11 **Holy Cross** Alaska, USA *62.12N 159.46W*
39 R4 **Holy Cross, Mount Of The** ▲ Colorado, C USA *39.28N 106.28W*
99 I18 **Holyhead** *Wel.* Caer Gybi. NW Wales, UK *53.19N 4.37W*
99 H18 **Holy Island** *island* NW Wales, UK
98 L12 **Holy Island** *island* NE England, UK
39 W3 **Holyoke** Colorado, C USA *40.31N 102.18W*
20 M11 **Holyoke** Massachusetts, NE USA *42.12N 72.37W*
103 I14 **Holzminden** Niedersachsen, C Germany *51.49N 9.27E*
83 G19 **Homa Bay** Nyanza, W Kenya *0.31S 34.30E*
Homāyūnshahr *see* Khomeynīshahr
79 P11 **Hombori** Mopti, S Mali *15.13N 1.39W*
103 E20 **Homburg** Saarland, SW Germany *49.19N 7.19E*
16 Nn1 **Home Bay** *bay* Baffin Bay, Nunavut, NE Canada
Homenau *see* Humenné
41 Q13 **Homer** Alaska, USA *59.38N 151.33W*
24 H4 **Homer** Louisiana, S USA *32.47N 93.03W*
20 H10 **Homer** New York, NE USA *42.38N 76.10W*
25 V7 **Homerville** Georgia, SE USA *31.02N 82.45W*
25 Y16 **Homestead** Florida, SE USA *25.28N 80.28W*
29 O9 **Hominy** Oklahoma, C USA *36.24N 96.24W*
96 H8 **Hommelvik** Sør-Trøndelag, S Norway *63.24N 10.46E*
97 C16 **Hommersåk** Rogaland, S Norway *58.55N 5.51E*
161 H15 **Homnābād** Karnātaka, C India *17.46N 77.08E*
24 J7 **Homochitto River** ∾ Mississippi, S USA
85 N20 **Homoine** Inhambane, SE Mozambique *23.51S 35.04E*
114 O12 **Homoljske Planine** ▲ E Serbia
Homonna *see* Humenné
Homs *see* Al Khums, Libya
Homs *see* Ḥimṣ, Syria
121 P19 **Homyel'** *Rus.* Gomel'. Homyel'skaya Voblasts', SE Belarus *52.24N 31.00E*
120 L12 **Homyel'** Vitsyebskaya Voblasts', N Belarus *55.20N 28.52E*
121 L19 **Homyel'skaya Voblasts'** *prev. Rus.* Gomel'skaya Oblast'. ◆ *province* SE Belarus
Honan *see* Henan, China
Honan *see* Luoyang, China
172 Pp6 **Honbetsu** Hokkaidō, NE Japan *43.09N 143.46E*
Honctő *see* Gurahonț
56 E9 **Honda** Tolima, C Colombia *5.12N 74.45W*
85 D24 **Hondeklip** *Afr.* Hondeklipbaai. Northern Cape, W South Africa *30.15S 17.17E*
Hondeklipbaai *see* Hondeklip
9 Q13 **Hondo** Alberta, W Canada *54.43N 113.14W*
170 C14 **Hondo** Kumamoto, Shimo-jima, SW Japan *32.27N 130.10E*
27 Q12 **Hondo** Texas, SW USA *29.21N 99.08W*
44 G1 **Hondo** ∾ Central America
Hondo *see* Honshū
44 G6 **Honduras** *off.* Republic of Honduras. ◆ *republic* Central America
Honduras, Golfo de *see* Honduras, Gulf of
44 H4 **Honduras, Gulf of** *Sp.* Golfo de Honduras. *gulf* W Caribbean Sea
9 V12 **Hone** Manitoba, C Canada *56.13N 101.12W*
23 P12 **Honea Path** South Carolina, SE USA *34.27N 82.23W*
97 H14 **Hønefoss** Buskerud, S Norway *60.10N 10.15E*
33 S12 **Honey Creek** ∾ Ohio, N USA
27 V5 **Honey Grove** Texas, SW USA *33.34N 95.54W*
37 Q4 **Honey Lake** ⊚ California, W USA
104 L4 **Honfleur** Calvados, N France *49.25N 0.13E*
Hon Gai *see* Hông Gai
167 O8 **Hong'an** *prev.* Huang'an. Hubei, C China *31.20N 114.43E*
Hongay *see* Hông Gai
178 K6 **Hông Gai** *var.* Hon Gai, Hongay. Quang Ninh, N Vietnam *20.57N 107.06E*
167 O15 **Honghai Wan** *bay* N South China Sea
Hông Hà, Sông *see* Red River
167 O7 **Hong He** ∾ C China
167 N9 **Hong Hu** ⊚ C China
166 L11 **Hongjiang** Hunan, S China *27.09N 109.58E*
Hongjiang *see* Wangcang
167 O15 **Hong Kong** *Chin.* Xianggang. S China *22.16N 114.09E*
166 L4 **Hongliu He** ∾ C China
165 P8 **Hongliuwan** *var.* Aksay, Aksay Kazakzu Zizhixian. Gansu, N China *39.40N 94.16E*
165 P7 **Hongliuyuan** Gansu, N China *41.01N 95.24E*
Hongor *see* Delgereh
167 S8 **Hongqiao** ✕ (Shanghai) Shanghai Shi, E China *31.28N 121.08E*
166 K14 **Hongshui He** ∾ S China
166 M5 **Hongtong** Shanxi, C China *36.30N 111.42E*
170 G16 **Hongū** Wakayama, Honshū, SW Japan *33.50N 135.42E*
Honguedo, Détroit d' *see* Honguedo Passage
13 Y5 **Honguedo Passage** *var.* Honguedo Strait, *Fr.* Détroit d'Honguedo. *strait* Québec, E Canada
Honguedo Strait *see* Honguedo Passage
Hongwan *see* Hongwansi

◆ Country ● Country Capital ◇ Dependent Territory ○ Dependent Territory Capital ◆ Administrative Region ✕ International Airport ▲ Mountain ▲ Mountain Range ⊼ Volcano ∾ River ⊚ Lake ⊡ Reservoir

HONGWANSI – HULBERT LAKE

165 S8 Hongwansi var. Sunan, Sunan Yugurzu Zizhixian prev. Hongwan. Gansu, N China 38.55N 99.29E
169 X13 Hongwŏn E North Korea 40.03N 127.54E
166 H7 Hongyuan var. Qiongxi, prev. Hurama. Sichuan, C China 32.49N 102.40E
167 Q7 Hongze Hu var. Hung-tse Hu. ⊚ E China
195 W16 Honiara ● (Solomon Islands) Guadalcanal, C Solomon Islands 9.27S 159.55E
171 Ll11 Honjō var. Honzyô. Akita, Honshū, C Japan 39.22N 140.03E
95 K18 Honkajoki Länsi-Suomi, W Finland 62.00N 22.15E
171 Ii16 Honkawane Shizuoka, Honshū, S Japan 35.07N 138.07E
94 K7 Honningsvåg Finnmark, N Norway 70.58N 25.58E
97 I19 Hönö Västra Götaland, S Sweden 57.42N 11.39E
40 G11 Honoka'a var. Honokaa. Hawai'i, USA, C Pacific Ocean 20.04N 155.27W
40 D9 Honolulu ◐ O'ahu, Hawai'i, USA, C Pacific Ocean 21.18N 157.51W
40 H11 Honomū var. Honomu. Hawai'i, USA, C Pacific Ocean 19.51N 155.06W
107 P10 Honrubia Castilla-La Mancha, C Spain 39.36N 2.16W
171 I15 Honshū var. Hondo, Honsyû. island SW Japan
Honsyû see Honshū
Honte see Westerschelde
Honzyô see Honjō
15 Ii5 Hood ≈ Nunavut, NW Canada
Hood Island see Española, Isla
34 H11 Hood, Mount ▲ Oregon, NW USA 45.22N 121.41W
194 K16 Hood Point headland S PNG 10.04S 147.42E
34 H11 Hood River Oregon, NW USA 45.42N 121.31W
100 H10 Hoofddorp Noord-Holland, W Netherlands 52.18N 4.40E
101 G15 Hoogerheide Noord-Brabant, S Netherlands 51.25N 4.19E
100 N8 Hoogeveen Drenthe, NE Netherlands 52.43N 6.30E
100 O6 Hoogezand-Sappemeer Groningen, NE Netherlands 53.10N 6.46E
100 J8 Hoogkarspel Noord-Holland, NW Netherlands 52.42N 4.59E
100 N5 Hoogkerk Groningen, NE Netherlands 53.13N 6.30E
100 G13 Hoogvliet Zuid-Holland, SW Netherlands 51.51N 4.23E
28 I8 Hooker Oklahoma, C USA 36.51N 101.12W
99 E21 Hook Head Ir. Rinn Duáin. headland SE Ireland 52.07N 6.55W
Hook of Holland see Hoek van Holland
Hoolt see Tögrög
41 W13 Hoonah Chichagof Island, Alaska, USA 58.05N 135.21W
40 L11 Hooper Bay Alaska, USA 61.31N 166.06W
33 N13 Hoopeston Illinois, N USA 40.28N 87.40W
97 K22 Höör Skåne, S Sweden 55.55N 13.33E
100 I9 Hoorn Noord-Holland, NW Netherlands 52.37N 5.04E
20 L10 Hoosic River ≈ New York, NE USA
Hoosier State see Indiana
37 Y11 Hoover Dam dam Arizona/Nevada, W USA 36.01N 114.44W
Höövör see Baruunbayan-Ulaan
143 Q11 Hopa Artvin, NE Turkey 41.23N 41.27E
20 J14 Hopatcong New Jersey, NE USA 40.55N 74.39W
8 M17 Hope British Columbia, SW Canada 49.21N 121.28W
41 R12 Hope Alaska, USA 60.55N 149.38W
29 T14 Hope Arkansas, C USA 33.40N 93.35W
33 P14 Hope Indiana, N USA 39.18N 85.46W
31 Q5 Hope North Dakota, N USA 47.18N 97.42W
11 Q7 Hopedale Newfoundland and Labrador, NE Canada 55.25N 60.14W
Hopeh/Hopei see Hebei
188 K13 Hope, Lake salt lake Western Australia
43 X13 Hopelchén Campeche, SE Mexico 19.44N 89.52W
23 U11 Hope Mills North Carolina, SE USA 34.58N 78.57W
191 O7 Hope, Mount New South Wales, SE Australia 32.49S 145.55E
94 P4 Hopen island SE Svalbard
207 Q4 Hope, Point headland Alaska, USA
10 M3 Hopes Advance, Cap headland Québec, NE Canada 61.07N 69.30W
190 L10 Hopetoun Victoria, SE Australia 35.46S 142.23E
85 H23 Hopetown Northern Cape, W South Africa 29.38S 24.06E
23 W6 Hopewell Virginia, NE USA 37.16N 77.15W
111 O7 Hopfgarten-im-Brixental Tirol, W Austria 47.28N 12.14E
189 N8 Hopkins Lake salt lake Western Australia
190 M12 Hopkins River ≈ Victoria, SE Australia
22 I7 Hopkinsville Kentucky, S USA 36.52N 87.29W
36 M6 Hopland California, W USA 38.58N 123.09W
97 G24 Hoptrup Sønderjylland, SW Denmark 55.09N 9.27E
Hoqin Zuoyi Zhongji see Baokang
34 F9 Hoquiam Washington, NW USA 46.58N 123.53W
31 R6 Horace North Dakota, N USA 46.44N 96.54W
143 R12 Horasan Erzurum, NE Turkey 40.03N 42.10E
103 G22 Horb am Neckar Baden-Württemberg, S Germany 48.27N 8.42E
97 K23 Hörby Skåne, S Sweden 55.50N 13.42E
45 P16 Horconcitos Chiriquí, W Panama 8.17N 82.10W
97 C14 Hordaland ◆ county S Norway
118 H13 Horezu Vâlcea, SW Romania 45.06N 24.00E
110 G7 Horgen Zürich, N Switzerland 47.16N 8.36E
Horgo see Tariat
Hōrin see Fenglin
169 O13 Horinger Nei Mongol Zizhiqu, N China 40.23N 111.48E
Horiult see Bogd
9 U17 Horizon Saskatchewan, S Canada 49.33N 105.05W
199 J10 Horizon Bank undersea feature S Pacific Ocean
199 Jj11 Horizon Deep undersea feature W Pacific Ocean
97 L14 Hörken Örebro, S Sweden 60.03N 14.55E
121 O15 Horki Rus. Gorki. Mahilyowskaya Voblasts', E Belarus 54.17N 30.59E
205 O10 Horlick Mountains ▲▲ Antarctica
119 X7 Horlivka Rom. Adâncata, Rus. Gorlovka. Donets'ka Oblast', E Ukraine 48.19N 38.04E
149 V11 Ḩormak Sīstān va Balūchestān, SE Iran 30.00N 60.50E
149 R13 Hormozgān off. Ostān-e Hormozgān. ◆ province S Iran
Hormoz, Tangeh-ye see Hormuz, Strait of
147 W6 Hormuz, Strait of var. Strait of Ormuz, Per. Tangeh-ye Hormoz. strait Iran/Oman
111 W2 Horn Niederösterreich, NE Austria 48.39N 15.37E
97 M18 Horn Östergötland, S Sweden 57.54N 15.49E
15 Hh8 Horn ≈ Northwest Territories, NW Canada
Hornád see Hernád
15 H3 Hornaday ≈ Northwest Territories, NW Canada
94 H13 Hornavan ⊚ N Sweden
67 C24 Hornby Mountains hill range West Falkland, Falkland Islands
Horn, Cape see Hornos, Cabo de
99 O18 Horncastle E England, UK 53.12N 0.07W
97 N14 Horndal Dalarna, C Sweden 60.16N 16.25E
95 I16 Hörnefors Västerbotten, N Sweden 63.37N 19.54E
20 F11 Hornell New York, NE USA 42.19N 77.38W
Horné Nové Mesto see Kysucké Nové Mesto
10 F12 Hornepayne Ontario, S Canada 49.13N 84.48W
96 D10 Hornindalsvatnet ⊚ S Norway
103 G22 Hornisgrinde ▲ SW Germany 48.37N 8.13E
24 M9 Horn Island island Mississippi, S USA
Hornja Łužica see Oberlausitz
65 J26 Hornos, Cabo de Eng. Cape Horn. headland S Chile 55.52S 67.00W
119 S10 Hornostayivka Khersons'ka Oblast', S Ukraine 47.00N 33.42E
191 T9 Hornsby New South Wales, SE Australia 33.44S 151.08E
99 O16 Hornsea E England, UK 53.54N 0.09W
96 O11 Hornslandet peninsula C Sweden
97 H22 Hornslet Århus, C Denmark 56.19N 10.19E
94 O4 Hornsundtind ▲ S Svalbard 76.54N 16.07E
Horochów see Horokhiv
118 J7 Horodenka Rus. Gorodenka. Ivano-Frankivs'ka Oblast', W Ukraine 48.41N 25.28E
119 Q2 Horodnya Rus. Gorodnya. Chernihivs'ka Oblast', NE Ukraine 51.54N 31.30E
118 K6 Horodok Khmel'nyts'ka Oblast', W Ukraine 49.10N 26.34E
118 H5 Horodok Pol. Gródek Jagielloński, Rus. Gorodok, Gorodok Yagellonski. L'vivs'ka Oblast', NW Ukraine 49.48N 23.39E
119 Q6 Horodyshche Rus. Gorodishche. Cherkas'ka Oblast', C Ukraine 49.18N 31.27E
172 P4 Horokanai Hokkaidō, NE Japan 44.02N 142.08E
118 J4 Horokhiv Pol. Horochów, Rus. Gorokhov. Volyns'ka Oblast', NW Ukraine 50.31N 24.50E
172 P7 Horoshiri-dake var. Horosiri Dake. ▲ Hokkaidō, N Japan 42.43N 142.41E
Horosiri Dake see Horoshiri-dake
113 C17 Hořovice Ger. Horowitz. Středočeský Kraj, W Czech Republic 49.49N 13.53E
Horowitz see Hořovice
Horqin Zuoyi Houqi see Ganjig
Horqin Zuoyi Zhongji see Bayan Huxu
64 O5 Horqueta Concepción, C Paraguay 23.23S 57.04W
57 O12 Horqueta Minas Amazonas, S Venezuela 2.19N 63.31W
97 J20 Horred Västra Götaland, S Sweden 57.22N 12.25E
157 J19 Horsburgh Atoll atoll N Maldives
22 K7 Horse Cave Kentucky, S USA 37.10N 85.54W
39 V6 Horse Creek ≈ Colorado, C USA
29 S6 Horse Creek ≈ Missouri, C USA
20 G11 Horseheads New York, NE USA 42.10N 76.49W
39 P13 Horse Mount ▲ New Mexico, SW USA 33.58N 108.10W
97 G22 Horsens Vejle, C Denmark 55.52N 9.52E
67 F25 Horse Pasture Point headland W Saint Helena 15.57S 5.46W
35 N13 Horseshoe Bend Idaho, NW USA 43.55N 116.11W
38 L13 Horseshoe Reservoir ⊡ Arizona, SW USA
66 M9 Horseshoe Seamounts undersea feature E Atlantic Ocean
190 L11 Horsham Victoria, SE Australia 36.44S 142.13E
99 O23 Horsham SE England, UK 51.01N 0.21W
101 M15 Horst Limburg, SE Netherlands 51.29N 6.04E
66 N2 Horta Faial, Azores, Portugal, NE Atlantic Ocean 38.31N 28.39W
97 H16 Horten Vestfold, S Norway 59.25N 10.24E
113 M23 Hortobágy-Berettyó ≈ E Hungary
29 Q3 Horton Kansas, C USA 39.39N 95.31W
15 H3 Horton ≈ Northwest Territories, NW Canada
97 I23 Hørve Vestsjælland, E Denmark 55.46N 11.28E
97 L22 Hörvik Blekinge, S Sweden 56.01N 14.45E
144 E11 Horvot Haluza var. Khorvot Khalutsa. ruins Southern, S Israel 30.49N 34.50E
12 E7 Horwood Lake ⊚ Ontario, S Canada
118 K4 Horyn' Rus. Goryn. ≈ NW Ukraine
83 I14 Hosa'ina var. Hosseina, It. Hosanna. Southern, S Ethiopia 7.38N 37.58E
Hosanna see Hosa'ina
103 H18 Hösbach Bayern, C Germany 50.00N 9.12E
Hose Mountains see Hose, Pegunungan
174 Mm6 Hose, Pegunungan var. Hose Mountains. ▲▲ East Malaysia
154 L15 Hoshāb Baluchistān, SW Pakistan 26.01N 63.51E
160 H10 Hoshangābād Madhya Pradesh, C India 22.43N 77.45E
118 L4 Hoshcha Rivnens'ka Oblast', NW Ukraine 50.37N 26.38E
158 I7 Hoshiārpur Punjab, NW India 31.35N 75.57E
Höshööt see Öldziyt
101 M23 Hosingen Diekirch, NE Luxembourg 50.01N 6.04E
195 N12 Hoskins New Britain, E PNG 5.28S 150.25E
161 G17 Hospet Karnātaka, C India 15.16N 76.19E
106 K4 Hospital de Orbigo Castilla-León, N Spain 42.27N 5.52W
Hospitalet see L'Hospitalet de Llobregat
94 N13 Hossa Oulu, E Finland 65.28N 29.36E
Hosseina see Hosa'ina
Hosszúmezjő see Câmpulung Moldovenesc
65 I25 Hoste, Isla island S Chile
119 O4 Hostomel' Rus. Gostomel'. Kyyivs'ka Oblast', N Ukraine 50.40N 30.15E
161 H20 Hosūr Tamil Nādu, SE India 12.45N 77.51E
178 H8 Hot Chiang Mai, NW Thailand 18.14N 98.35E
164 G10 Hotan var. Khotan, Chin. Ho-t'ien. Xinjiang Uygur Zizhiqu, NW China 37.10N 79.51E
164 H9 Hotan He ≈ NW China
85 G22 Hotazel Northern Cape, N South Africa 27.12S 22.58E
39 Q5 Hotchkiss Colorado, C USA 38.47N 107.43W
37 V7 Hot Creek Range ▲▲ Nevada, W USA
Hote see Hoti
176 U11 Hoti var. Hote. Pulau Seram, E Indonesia 2.58S 130.19E
Ho-t'ien see Hotan
Hotin see Khotyn
95 H15 Hoting Jämtland, C Sweden 64.07N 16.14E
168 L14 Hotong Qagan Nur ⊚ N China
168 J8 Hotont Arhangay, C Mongolia 47.21N 102.27E
29 T12 Hot Springs Arkansas, C USA 34.30N 93.03W
30 J11 Hot Springs South Dakota, N USA 43.25N 103.28W
23 S5 Hot Springs Virginia, NE USA 38.00N 79.50W
37 Q4 Hot Springs Peak ▲ California, W USA 40.23N 120.06W
29 T12 Hot Springs Village Arkansas, C USA 34.39N 93.03W
Hotspur Bank see Hotspur Seamount
67 J16 Hotspur Seamount var. Hotspur Bank. undersea feature C Atlantic Ocean 18.00S 35.00W
15 Hh6 Hottah Lake ⊚ Northwest Territories, NW Canada
46 K9 Hotte, Massif de la ▲▲ SW Haiti
101 K21 Hotton Luxembourg, SE Belgium 50.18N 5.25E
Hötzing see Haţeg
197 I6 Houaïlou Province Nord, C New Caledonia 21.17S 165.37E
76 K5 Houari Boumediène ✕ (Alger) N Algeria 36.38N 3.15E
178 Hh6 Houayxay var. Ban Houayxay, Ban Houei Sai. Bokèo, N Laos 20.16N 100.27E
105 N5 Houdan Yvelines, N France 48.48N 1.36E
101 F20 Houdeng-Goegnies var. Houdeng-Gœgnies. Hainaut, S Belgium 50.28N 4.10E
104 K14 Houeillès Lot-et-Garonne, SW France 44.15N 0.02E
101 L22 Houffalize Luxembourg, SE Belgium 50.08N 5.47E
32 M3 Houghton Michigan, N USA 41.55N 84.37W
33 Q7 Houghton Lake Michigan, N USA 44.18N 84.45W
33 Q7 Houghton Lake ⊚ Michigan, N USA
21 T3 Houlton Maine, NE USA 46.09N 67.49W
166 M5 Houma Shanxi, C China 35.33N 111.19E
200 Q15 Houma 'Eua, C Tonga 21.10S 175.17W
200 R16 Houma Tongatapu, S Tonga 21.18S 174.55W
24 J10 Houma Louisiana, S USA 29.34N 90.43W
200 Qq16 Houma Taloa headland Tongatapu, S Tonga 21.16S 175.07W
79 O13 Houndé SW Burkina 11.34N 3.31W
104 J12 Hourtin-Carcans, Lac d' ⊚ SW France
38 J5 House Range ▲▲ Utah, W USA
8 K13 Houston British Columbia, SW Canada 54.24N 126.39W
41 R11 Houston Alaska, USA 61.37N 149.50W
31 X10 Houston Minnesota, N USA 43.45N 91.34W
24 M3 Houston Mississippi, S USA 33.54N 89.00W
29 V7 Houston Missouri, C USA 37.19N 91.57W
27 W11 Houston Texas, SW USA 29.45N 95.21W
27 W11 Houston ✕ Texas, SW USA 30.03N 95.18W
100 J12 Houten Utrecht, C Netherlands 52.01N 5.10E
101 K17 Houthalen Limburg, NE Belgium 51.01N 5.22E
101 I22 Houyet Namur, SE Belgium 50.10N 5.00E
97 H22 Hov Århus, C Denmark 55.54N 10.13E
97 L17 Hova Västra Götaland, S Sweden 58.52N 14.13E
168 E6 Hovd var. Dund-Us. Hovd, W Mongolia 48.06N 91.22E
168 E6 Hovd var. Khovd, Kobdo; prev. Jirgalanta. Hovd, W Mongolia 47.58N 91.40E
168 E7 Hovd ◆ province W Mongolia
Hovd see Bogd
168 C5 Hovd Gol ≈ NW Mongolia
99 O23 Hove SE England, UK 50.49N 0.10W
31 N8 Hoven South Dakota, N USA 45.12N 99.47W
118 I8 Hoverla, Hora Rus. Gora Goverla. ▲ W Ukraine 48.09N 24.30E
Höviyn Am see Gurvanbulag
97 M21 Hovmantorp Kronoberg, S Sweden 56.46N 15.07E
169 N11 Hövsgöl Dornogovĭ, SE Mongolia 43.35N 109.40E
168 I5 Hövsgöl ◆ province N Mongolia
Hovsgol, Lake see Hövsgöl Nuur
168 J5 Hövsgöl Nuur var. Lake Hovsgol. ⊚ N Mongolia
80 L9 Howa, Ouadi var. Wādi Howar. ≈ Chad/Sudan see also Howar, Wādi
29 P7 Howard Kansas, C USA 37.28N 96.15W
31 Q10 Howard South Dakota, N USA 43.58N 97.31W
27 N10 Howard Draw valley Texas, SW USA
31 U8 Howard Lake Minnesota, N USA 45.03N 94.03W
82 B8 Howar, Wādi var. Ouadi Howa. ≈ Chad/Sudan see also Howa, Ouadi
27 U5 Howe Texas, SW USA 33.29N 96.38W
191 R12 Howe, Cape headland New South Wales/Victoria, SE Australia 37.30S 149.58E
33 R9 Howell Michigan, N USA 42.36N 83.55W
30 L9 Howes South Dakota, N USA 44.34N 102.03W
85 K23 Howick KwaZulu/Natal, E South Africa 29.29S 30.13E
Howrah see Hāora
29 W9 Hoxie Arkansas, C USA 36.03N 90.58W
28 J3 Hoxie Kansas, C USA 39.21N 100.26W
103 I14 Höxter Nordrhein-Westfalen, W Germany 51.46N 9.22E
164 K6 Hoxud Xinjiang Uygur Zizhiqu, NW China 42.18N 86.51E
98 J5 Hoy island N Scotland, UK
45 S17 Hoya, Cerro ▲ S Panama 7.22N 80.38W
96 D12 Høyanger Sogn og Fjordane, S Norway 61.13N 6.04E
103 P15 Hoyerswerda Lus. Wojerecy. Sachsen, E Germany 51.27N 14.17E
170 Dd15 Hōyo-kaikyō var. Hayasui-seto. strait SW Japan
106 J8 Hoyos Extremadura, W Spain 40.10N 6.43W
31 W4 Hoyt Lakes Minnesota, N USA 47.31N 92.08W
89 V2 Hoyvík Streymoy, N Faeroe Islands
143 O14 Hozat Tunceli, E Turkey 39.09N 39.13E
Hôzyô see Hōjō
113 F16 Hradec Králové Ger. Königgrätz. Královéhradecký Kraj, N Czech Republic 50.13N 15.49E
Hradecký Kraj see Královéhradecký Kraj
113 B16 Hradiště Ger. Burgstadlberg. ▲ NW Czech Republic 50.12N 13.04E
119 R6 Hradyz'k Rus. Gradizhsk. Poltavs'ka Oblast', NE Ukraine 49.12N 33.08E
121 M16 Hradzyanka Rus. Grodzyanka. Mahilyowskaya Voblasts', E Belarus 53.36N 28.47E
121 F16 Hrandzichy Rus. Grandichi. Hrodzyenskaya Voblasts', W Belarus 53.43N 23.50E
113 H18 Hranice Ger. Mährisch-Weisskirchen. Olomoucký Kraj, E Czech Republic 49.34N 17.45E
114 I13 Hrasnica Federacija Bosna I Hercegovina, SE Bosnia and Herzegovina 43.48N 18.19E
111 V11 Hrastnik C Slovenia 46.09N 15.08E
143 U12 Hrazdan Rus. Razdan. C Armenia 40.30N 44.50E
143 T12 Hrazdan var. Zanga, Rus. Razdan. ≈ C Armenia
119 R5 Hrebinka Rus. Grebenka. Poltavs'ka Oblast', NE Ukraine 50.08N 32.27E
121 K17 Hresk Rus. Gresk. Minskaya Voblasts', C Belarus 53.10N 27.28E
Hrisoupoli see Chrysoúpoli
121 F16 Hrodna Pol. Grodno. Hrodzyenskaya Voblasts', W Belarus 53.40N 23.50E
121 F16 Hrodzyenskaya Voblasts' prev. Rus. Grodnenskaya Oblast'. ◆ province W Belarus
113 J21 Hron Ger. Gran, Hung. Garam. ≈ C Slovakia
113 Q14 Hrubieszów Rus. Grubeshov. Lubelskie, E Poland 50.48N 23.54E
114 F13 Hrvace Split-Dalmacija, SE Croatia 43.46N 16.35E
Hrvatska see Croatia
114 F10 Hrvatska Kostajnica var. Kostajnica. Sisak-Moslavina, C Croatia 45.14N 16.35E
Hrvatsko Grahovo see Bosansko Grahovo
118 K6 Hrymayliv Pol. Gízymałów, Rus. Grimaylov. Ternopil's'ka Oblast', W Ukraine 49.18N 26.02E
178 H4 Hsenwi Shan State, E Burma 23.20N 97.59E
Hsia-men see Xiamen
Hsiang-t'an see Xiangtan
Hsi Chiang see Xi Jiang
178 Gg6 Hsihseng Shan State, C Burma 20.07N 97.16E
167 S13 Hsinchu municipality N Taiwan 24.51N 121.01E
Hsing-k'ai Hu see Khanka, Lake
Hsi-ning/Hsining see Xining
Hsinking see Changchun
Hsin-yang see Xinyang
167 S14 Hsinying var. Sinying, Jap. Shinei. C Taiwan 23.12N 120.15E
178 Gg4 Hsipaw Shan State, C Burma 22.36N 97.16E
Hsu-chou see Xuzhou
167 S13 Hsüeh Shan ▲ N Taiwan
Hu see Shanghai Shi
85 B18 Huab ≈ W Namibia
59 M21 Huacaya Chuquisaca, S Bolivia 20.55S 63.24W
59 J19 Huachacalla Oruro, SW Bolivia 19.01S 68.22W
165 X9 Huachi var. Rouyuanchengzi. Gansu, C China 36.24N 107.58E
59 N16 Huachi, Laguna ⊚ N Bolivia
59 D14 Huacho Lima, W Peru 11.09S 77.37W
169 Y7 Huachuan Heilongjiang, NE China 46.57N 130.48E
169 P12 Huade Nei Mongol Zizhiqu, N China 41.52N 113.58E
169 W10 Huadian Jilin, NE China 42.58N 126.37E
58 E13 Huagaruncho, Cordillera ▲▲ C Peru
Hua Hin see Ban Hua Hin
203 S10 Huahine island Îles Sous le Vent, W French Polynesia
Huahua, Rio see Wawa, Río
178 Ii9 Huai ≈ E Thailand
167 Q7 Huai'an var. Qingjiang; prev. Huaiyin. Jiangsu, E China 33.33N 119.03E
167 P6 Huaibei Anhui, E China 34.00N 116.48E
Huaide see Gongzhuling
163 T10 Huai He ≈ C China
166 L11 Huaihua Hunan, S China 27.36N 109.56E
167 N14 Huaiji Guangdong, S China 23.54N 112.12E
167 O2 Huailai var. Shacheng. Hebei, E China 40.22N 115.34E
167 P7 Huainan var. Huai-nan, Hwainan. Anhui, E China 32.36N 116.56E
167 N2 Huairen Shanxi, C China 35.28N 110.29E
167 O7 Huaiyang Henan, C China 33.39N 114.34E
Huaiyin see Huai'an
178 Gg16 Huai Yot Trang, SW Thailand 7.45N 99.36E
43 Q15 Huajuapan var. Huajuapan de León. Oaxaca, SE Mexico 17.49N 97.48W
Huajuapan de León see Huajuapan
43 O9 Hualahuises Nuevo León, NE Mexico 24.55N 99.44W
38 I11 Hualapai Mountains ▲▲ Arizona, SW USA
38 I11 Hualapai Peak ▲ Arizona, SW USA 35.04N 113.54W
64 J7 Hualfin Catamarca, N Argentina 27.15S 66.52W
167 T13 Hualien var. Hwalien, Jap. Karen. C Taiwan 23.58N 121.34E
58 E10 Huallaga, Río ≈ N Peru
58 C11 Huamachuco La Libertad, C Peru 7.50S 78.03W
43 Q14 Huamantla Tlaxcala, S Mexico 19.18N 97.57W
84 C13 Huambo Port. Nova Lisboa. Huambo, C Angola 12.48S 15.45E
84 B13 Huambo ◆ province C Angola
43 P15 Huamuxtitlán Guerrero, S Mexico 17.49N 98.34W
169 Y8 Huanan Heilongjiang, NE China 46.21N 130.43E
65 H17 Huancache, Sierra ▲▲ SW Argentina
59 I17 Huancané Puno, SE Peru 15.15S 69.47W
59 F16 Huancapi Ayacucho, C Peru 13.36S 74.09W
59 E15 Huancavelica Huancavelica, SW Peru 12.45S 75.03W
59 E15 Huancavelica off. Departamento de Huancavelica. ◆ department W Peru
59 E14 Huancayo Junín, C Peru 12.03S 75.13W
59 K20 Huanchaca, Cerro ▲ S Bolivia 20.12S 66.35W
58 C12 Huandoy, Nevado ▲ W Peru 8.48S 77.33W
167 O8 Huangchuan Henan, C China 32.08N 115.03E
167 O9 Huanggang Hubei, C China 30.27N 114.48E
Huang Hai see Yellow Sea
163 Q8 Huang He var. Yellow River. ≈ C China
167 Q4 Huanghe Kou delta E China
166 L5 Huangling Shaanxi, C China 35.34N 109.12E
169 P13 Huangqi Hai ⊚ N China
167 Q9 Huang Shan ▲ Anhui, E China 29.43N 118.19E
167 Q9 Huangshan var. Tunxi. Anhui, E China 29.48N 118.17E
167 O9 Huangshi var. Huang-shih, Hwangshih. Hubei, C China 30.14N 115.00E
Huang-shih see Huangshi
166 L5 Huangtu Gaoyuan plateau C China
63 B22 Huanguelén Buenos Aires, E Argentina 37.01S 61.57W
167 S10 Huangyan Zhejiang, SE China 28.42N 121.13E
165 T10 Huangyuan Qinghai, C China 36.40N 101.12E
165 T10 Huangzhong var. Lushar. Qinghai, C China 36.31N 101.32E
169 W12 Huanren var. Huanren Manzu Zizhixian. Liaoning, NE China 41.16N 125.25E
Huanren Manzu Zizhixian see Huanren
59 F15 Huanta Ayacucho, C Peru 12.54S 74.13W
58 E13 Huánuco Huánuco, C Peru 9.57S 76.15W
58 D13 Huánuco off. Departamento de Huánuco. ◆ department C Peru
59 K19 Huanuni Oruro, W Bolivia 18.15S 66.54W
165 X9 Huanxian Gansu, C China 36.30N 107.20E
167 S12 Huap'ing Yu island N Taiwan
64 H3 Huara Tarapacá, N Chile 19.59S 69.42W
59 D14 Huaral Lima, W Peru 11.28S 77.12W
Huarás see Huaraz
58 D13 Huaraz var. Huarás. Ancash, W Peru 9.30S 77.31W
59 I16 Huari Huari, Río ≈ S Peru
58 C13 Huarmey Ancash, W Peru 10.03S 78.09W
42 H4 Huásabas Sonora, NW Mexico 29.46N 109.18W
58 D8 Huasaga, Río ≈ Ecuador/Peru
178 H16 Hua Sai Nakhon Si Thammarat, SW Thailand 8.01N 100.18E
58 D12 Huascarán, Nevado ▲ W Peru 9.01S 77.27W
64 G8 Huasco Atacama, N Chile 28.28S 71.12W
64 G8 Huasco, Río ≈ C Chile
165 S11 Huashikia Qinghai, W China
42 G7 Huatabampo Sonora, NW Mexico 26.49N 109.40W
165 W10 Huating Gansu, C China 35.13N 106.39E
178 Jj7 Huatt, Phou ▲ N Vietnam 19.45N 104.48E
43 Q14 Huatusco var. Huatusco de Chicuellar. Veracruz-Llave, C Mexico 19.13N 96.57W
Huatusco de Chicuellar see Huatusco
43 P13 Huauchinango Puebla, S Mexico 20.12N 98.03W
Huaunta see Wounta
43 R15 Huautla var. Huautla de Jiménez. Oaxaca, SE Mexico 18.10N 96.51W
Huautla de Jiménez see Huautla
167 O5 Huaxian var. Daokou, Hua Xian. Henan, C China 35.33N 114.30E
Huazangsi see Tianzhu
31 V13 Hubbard Iowa, C USA 42.18N 93.18W
27 U8 Hubbard Texas, SW USA 31.52N 96.43W
27 Q6 Hubbard Creek Lake ⊚ Texas, SW USA
33 R6 Hubbard Lake ⊚ Michigan, N USA
166 M9 Hubei var. E, Hubei Sheng, Hupeh, Hupei. ◆ province C China
Hubei Sheng see Hubei
111 P8 Huben Tirol, W Austria 46.55N 12.35E
33 R13 Huber Heights Ohio, N USA 39.50N 84.07W
161 F17 Hubli Karnātaka, SW India 15.19N 75.13E
169 X12 Huch'ang N North Korea 41.24N 127.04E
99 M18 Hucknall C England, UK 53.01N 1.10W
99 L17 Huddersfield N England, UK 53.39N 1.46W
97 O16 Huddinge Stockholm, C Sweden 59.15N 17.57E
96 N11 Hudiksvall Gävleborg, C Sweden 61.45N 17.12E
31 W13 Hudson Iowa, C USA 42.24N 92.27W
21 O11 Hudson Massachusetts, NE USA 42.24N 71.34W
33 Q11 Hudson Michigan, N USA 41.51N 84.21W
32 H6 Hudson Wisconsin, N USA 44.58N 92.43W
9 V14 Hudson Bay Saskatchewan, S Canada 58.13N 90.48W
10 G6 Hudson Bay bay NE Canada
205 T16 Hudson, Cape headland Antarctica 68.15S 154.00E
Hudson, Détroit d' see Hudson Strait
29 Q9 Hudson, Lake ⊡ Oklahoma, C USA
20 K9 Hudson River ≈ New Jersey/New York, NE USA
8 M12 Hudson's Hope British Columbia, W Canada 56.03N 121.58W
10 L2 Hudson Strait Fr. Détroit d'Hudson. strait Nunavut/Québec, NE Canada
Hudūd ash Shamālīyah, Minţaqat al see Al Ḩudūd ash Shamālīyah
Hudur see Xuddur
178 K9 Huê Thưa Thiên-Huê, C Vietnam 16.28N 107.34E
106 J7 Huebra ≈ W Spain
26 H8 Hueco Mountains ▲▲ Texas, SW USA
118 G10 Huedin Hung. Bánffyhunyad. Cluj, NW Romania 46.51N 23.01E
42 J10 Huehuento, Cerro ▲ C Mexico 24.04N 105.42W
44 B5 Huehuetenango Huehuetenango, W Guatemala 15.19N 91.25W
44 B4 Huehuetenango off. Departamento de Huehuetenango. ◆ department W Guatemala
42 L11 Huejuquilla Jalisco, SW Mexico 22.40N 103.52W
43 P12 Huejutla var. Huejutla de Reyes. Hidalgo, C Mexico 21.08N 98.16W
Huejutla de Reyes see Huejutla
104 G6 Huelgoat Finistère, NW France 48.22N 3.45W
107 O13 Huelma Andalucía, S Spain 37.39N 3.28W
106 I14 Huelva anc. Onuba. Andalucía, SW Spain 37.15N 6.55W
106 I13 Huelva ◆ province Andalucía, SW Spain
106 J13 Huelva ≈ SW Spain
107 Q14 Huercal-Overa Andalucía, S Spain 37.22N 1.55W
39 Q9 Huerfano Mountain ▲ New Mexico, SW USA 36.25N 107.50W
39 T7 Huerfano River ≈ Colorado, C USA
107 S12 Huertas, Cabo headland SE Spain 38.21N 0.25W
107 R6 Huerva ≈ N Spain
107 S4 Huesca anc. Osca. Aragón, NE Spain 42.07N 0.25W
107 T4 Huesca ◆ province Aragón, NE Spain
107 P13 Huéscar Andalucía, S Spain 37.39N 2.31W
43 N15 Huetamo var. Huetamo de Núñez. Michoacán de Ocampo, SW Mexico 18.37N 100.53W
Huetamo de Núñez see Huetamo
107 P8 Huete Castilla-La Mancha, C Spain 40.07N 2.40W
25 P4 Hueytown Alabama, S USA 33.27N 87.00W
30 L16 Hugh Butler Lake ⊡ Nebraska, C USA
189 V6 Hughenden Queensland, NE Australia 20.56S 144.15E
190 A6 Hughes South Australia 30.41S 129.31E
41 P8 Hughes Alaska, USA 66.03N 154.15W
29 X11 Hughes Arkansas, C USA 34.57N 90.28W
27 W6 Hughes Springs Texas, SW USA 33.00N 94.37W
39 V5 Hugo Colorado, C USA 39.08N 103.28W
29 Q13 Hugo Oklahoma, C USA 34.01N 95.31W
29 Q13 Hugo Lake ⊡ Oklahoma, C USA
28 H7 Hugoton Kansas, C USA 37.10N 101.21W
Huhehot/Huhuohaote see Hohhot
Huhttán see Kvikkjokk
167 R13 Hui'an var. Luocheng. Fujian, SE China 25.06N 118.45E
192 O9 Huiarau Range ▲▲ North Island, NZ
85 D22 Huib-Hoch Plateau plateau S Namibia
43 O13 Huichapán Hidalgo, C Mexico 20.22N 99.42W
Huicheng see Shexian
169 W13 Hŭich'ŏn C North Korea 40.09N 126.17E
56 E12 Huila off. Departamento del Huila. ◆ province S Colombia
85 B15 Huíla ◆ province SW Angola
56 D11 Huila, Nevado del elevation C Colombia 2.56N 75.59W
85 B15 Huíla Plateau plateau S Angola
166 G12 Huili Sichuan, C China 26.39N 102.13E
167 P4 Huimin Shandong, E China 37.28N 117.30E
169 W11 Huinan var. Chaoyang. Jilin, NE China 42.40N 126.03E
64 K12 Huinca Renancó Córdoba, C Argentina 34.51S 64.22W
165 V10 Huining var. Huishi. Gansu, C China 35.42N 105.01E
Huishi see Huining
166 J12 Huishui var. Heping. Guizhou, S China 26.07N 106.39E
104 L6 Huisne ≈ NW France
100 L12 Huissen Gelderland, SE Netherlands 51.57N 5.57E
165 N11 Huiten Nur ⊚ C China
95 K19 Huittinen Länsi-Suomi, W Finland 61.10N 22.40E
43 O15 Huitzuco var. Huitzuco de los Figueroa. Guerrero, S Mexico 18.18N 99.22W
Huitzuco de los Figueroa see Huitzuco
165 W11 Huixian var. Hui Xian. Gansu, C China 33.48N 106.02E
43 V17 Huixtla Chiapas, SE Mexico 15.07N 92.29W
166 H12 Huize var. Zhongping. Yunnan, SW China 26.28N 103.18E
100 J10 Huizen Noord-Holland, C Netherlands 52.16N 5.15E
167 O14 Huizhou Guangdong, S China 23.05N 114.22E
168 J6 Hujirt Arhangay, C Mongolia 48.49N 101.20E
Hujirt see Delgerhaan, Töv, Mongolia
Hujirt see Tsetserleg, Övörhangay, Mongolia
Hukagawa see Fukagawa
Hŭksan-chedo see Hŭksan-gundo
169 W17 Hŭksan-gundo var. Hŭksan-chedo. island group SW South Korea
Hukue see Fukue
Hukui see Fukui
85 G20 Hukuntsi Kgalagadi, SW Botswana 23.58S 21.43E
Hukuoka see Fukuoka
Hukusima see Fukushima
Hukutiyama see Fukuchiyama
Hukuyama see Fukuyama
169 W8 Hulan Heilongjiang, NE China 45.58N 126.37E
169 W8 Hulan He ≈ NE China
33 Q4 Hulbert Lake ⊚ Michigan, N USA

◆ Country
● Country Capital
◇ Dependent Territory
○ Dependent Territory Capital
◆ Administrative Region
✕ International Airport
▲ Mountain
▲▲ Mountain Range
Volcano
≈ River
⊚ Lake
⊡ Reservoir

267

I

◆ COUNTRY ◇ DEPENDENT TERRITORY ◆ ADMINISTRATIVE REGION ▲ MOUNTAIN ⊠ VOLCANO
◆ COUNTRY CAPITAL ◇ DEPENDENT TERRITORY CAPITAL ✕ INTERNATIONAL AIRPORT ▲ MOUNTAIN RANGE ⟿ RIVER ⊚ LAKE ⊞ RESERVOIR

ILLINTSI – ISELIN SEAMOUNT

119 N6 **Illintsi** Vinnyts'ka Oblast', C Ukraine 49.07N 29.13E
Illiturgis see Andújar
76 M10 **Illizi** SE Algeria 26.30N 8.28E
29 Y7 **Illmo** Missouri, C USA 37.13N 89.30W
Illur co see Lorca
Illuro see Mataró
Illyrisch-Feistritz see Ilirska Bistrica
103 K16 **Ilm** ≈ C Germany
103 K17 **Ilmenau** Thüringen, C Germany 50.40N 10.55E
128 H14 **Il'men', Ozero** ◎ NW Russian Federation
59 H18 **Ilo** Moquegua, SW Peru 17.39S 71.22W
179 Q13 **Iloilo** off. Iloilo City. Panay Island, C Philippines 10.42N 122.34E
114 K10 **Ilok** Hung. Újlak. Serbia, NW Serbia 45.12N 19.22E
95 O16 **Ilomantsi** Itä-Suomi, E Finland 62.40N 30.55E
44 F8 **Ilopango, Lago de** volcanic lake C El Salvador
79 T15 **Ilorin** Kwara, W Nigeria 8.32N 4.34E
119 X8 **Ilovays'k** Rus. Ilovaysk. Donets'ka Oblast', SE Ukraine 47.54N 38.13E
131 O10 **Ilovlya** Volgogradskaya Oblast', SW Russian Federation 49.45N 44.18E
131 O10 **Ilovlya** ≈ SW Russian Federation
127 P8 **Il'pyrskoye** Koryakskiy Avtonomnyy Okrug, E Russian Federation 60.00N 164.16E
130 K14 **Il'skiy** Krasnodarskiy Kray, SW Russian Federation 44.52N 38.26E
190 B2 **Iltur** South Australia 27.33S 130.31E
176 Y11 **Ilugwa** Papua, E Indonesia 3.42S 139.09E
İluh see Batman
120 I11 **Ilūkste** Daugvapils, SE Latvia 55.58N 26.21E
176 Uu12 **Ilur** Pulau Gorong, E Indonesia 4.00S 131.25E
34 F10 **Ilwaco** Washington, NW USA 46.19N 124.03W
Il'yaly see Gurbansoltan Eje
İlyasbaba Burnu see Tekke Burnu
129 U9 **Ilych** ≈ NW Russian Federation
103 O21 **Ilz** ≈ SE Germany
113 M14 **Iłża** Radom, SE Poland 51.09N 21.15E
170 Ee14 **Imabari** var. Imaharu. Ehime, Shikoku, SW Japan 34.04N 132.58E
172 N5 **Imagane** Hokkaidō, NE Japan 42.26N 140.00E
Imaharu see Imabari
171 K15 **Imaichi** var. Imaiti. Tochigi, Honshū, S Japan 36.43N 139.40E
Imaiti see Imaichi
171 Hh14 **Imajō** Fukui, Honshū, SW Japan 35.45N 136.10E
145 R9 **Imām Ibn Hāshim** C Iraq 32.46N 43.21E
145 T11 **Imān 'Abd Allāh** S Iraq 31.36N 44.34E
128 J4 **Imandra, Ozero** ◎ NW Russian Federation
170 E16 **Imano-yama** ▲ Shikoku, SW Japan 32.51N 132.48E
170 C13 **Imari** Saga, Kyūshū, SW Japan 33.16N 129.51E
Imarssuak Mid-Ocean Seachannel see Imarssuak Seachannel
66 J6 **Imarssuak Seachannel** var. Imarssuak Mid-Ocean Seachannel. channel N Atlantic Ocean
95 N18 **Imatra** Etelä-Suomi, S Finland 61.13N 28.49E
171 H14 **Imazu** Shiga, Honshū, SW Japan 35.25N 136.00E
58 C6 **Imbabura** ◈ province N Ecuador
57 R9 **Imbaimadai** W Guyana 5.44N 60.23W
63 K14 **Imbituba** Santa Catarina, S Brazil 28.15S 48.43W
29 W9 **Imboden** Arkansas, C USA 36.12N 91.10W
Imbros see Gökçeada
Imeni 26 Bakinskikh Komissarov see 26 Bakı Komissarı/Uzboý
129 N13 **Imeni Babushkina** Vologodskaya Oblast', NW Russian Federation 59.40N 43.04E
130 J7 **Imeni Karla Libknekhta** Kurskaya Oblast', W Russian Federation 51.36N 35.28E
Imeni Mollanepesa see Mollanepes Adyndaky
127 N14 **Imeni Poliny Osipenko** Khabarovskiy Kray, SE Russian Federation 52.21N 136.17E
Imeni S.A.Niyazova see S.A.Nyýazow Adyndaky
Imeni Sverdlova Rudnik see Sverdlovs'k
196 E9 **Imeong** Babeldaob, N Palau
83 L14 **Īmī** Somali, E Ethiopia 6.27N 42.10E
117 M21 **Imia** Turk. Kardak. island Dodekánisa, Greece, Aegean Sea
Imishli see İmişli
143 X12 **İmişli** Rus. Imishli. C Azerbaijan 39.54N 48.04E
169 X14 **Imjin-gang** ≈ North Korea/South Korea
37 S3 **Imlay** Nevada, W USA 40.39N 118.10W
33 S9 **Imlay City** Michigan, N USA 43.01N 83.04W
25 X15 **Immokalee** Florida, SE USA 26.24N 81.25W
79 U17 **Imo** ◈ state SE Nigeria
108 G10 **Imola** Emilia-Romagna, N Italy 44.22N 11.43E
194 E9 **Imonda** Sandaun, NW PNG 3.19S 141.10E
Imoschi see Imotski
115 G14 **Imotski** It. Imoschi. Split-Dalmacija, SE Croatia 43.28N 17.13E
61 L14 **Imperatriz** Maranhão, NE Brazil 5.31S 47.28W
108 B10 **Imperia** Liguria, NW Italy 43.52N 8.03E
59 E15 **Imperial** Lima, W Peru 13.04S 76.20W
37 X17 **Imperial** California, W USA 32.51N 115.34W
30 L16 **Imperial** Nebraska, C USA 40.30N 101.37W
26 M9 **Imperial** Texas, SW USA 31.15N 102.40W
37 Y17 **Imperial Dam** dam California, W USA 32.52N 114.27W
81 I17 **Impfondo** La Likouala, NE Congo 1.40N 18.02E
159 X14 **Imphāl** Manipur, NE India 24.46N 93.55E
105 P9 **Imphy** Nièvre, C France 46.55N 3.16E
108 G11 **Impruneta** Toscana, C Italy 43.42N 11.16E
117 K15 **İmroz** var. Gökçeada. Çanakkale, NW Turkey 40.11N 25.53E
Imroz Adası see Gökçeada
110 L7 **Imst** Tirol, W Austria 47.13N 10.40E
42 F3 **Imuris** Sonora, NW Mexico 30.48N 110.52W
179 P11 **Imus** Luzon, N Philippines 14.27N 120.55E
171 J15 **Ina** Nagano, Honshū, S Japan 35.55N 137.59E
67 M18 **Inaccessible Island** island W Tristan da Cunha
117 F20 **Ínachos** ≈ S Greece
196 H6 **I Naftan, Puntan** headland Saipan, S Northern Mariana Islands
Inagua Islands see Great Inagua/Little Inagua
193 H15 **Inangahua** West Coast, South Island, NZ 41.51S 171.58E
176 V10 **Inanwatan** Papua, E Indonesia 2.06S 132.07E
59 I14 **Iñapari** Madre de Dios, E Peru 11.00S 69.34W
196 B17 **Inarajan** SE Guam 13.16N 144.45E
94 L10 **Inari** Lapp. Anár, Aanaar. Lappi, N Finland 68.54N 27.06E
94 L10 **Inarijärvi** Lapp. Aanaarjävri, Swe. Enareträsk. ◎ N Finland
94 L9 **Inarijoki** Lapp. Anárjohka. ≈ Finland/Norway
Inău see Ineu
171 L14 **Inawashiro-ko** var. Inawasiro Ko. ◎ Honshū, C Japan
Inawasiro Ko see Inawashiro-ko
107 X9 **Inca** Mallorca, Spain, W Mediterranean Sea 39.43N 2.54E
64 H7 **Inca de Oro** Atacama, N Chile 26.45S 69.54W
117 J15 **İnce Burnu** headland NW Turkey 40.08N 25.39E
142 K9 **İnce Burnu** headland N Turkey 42.06N 34.57E
142 I17 **İncekum Burnu** headland S Turkey 36.13N 33.57E
78 G7 **Inchiri** ◈ region NW Mauritania
169 X15 **Inch'ŏn** off. Inch'ŏn-gwangyŏksi, Jap. Jinsen; prev. Chemulpo. NW South Korea 37.27N 126.40E
169 X15 **Inch'on** ✕ (Sŏul) NW South Korea 37.37N 126.42E
85 M17 **Inchope** Manica, C Mozambique 19.09S 33.54E
Incoronata see Kornat
105 Y15 **Incudine, Monte** ▲ Corse, France, C Mediterranean Sea 41.52N 9.13E
62 M10 **Indaiatuba** São Paulo, S Brazil 23.03S 47.14W
95 H17 **Indal** Västernorrland, C Sweden 62.36N 17.06E
95 H17 **Indalsälven** ≈ C Sweden
42 K8 **Inde** Durango, C Mexico 25.55N 105.10W
Indefatigable Island see Santa Cruz, Isla
37 S10 **Independence** California, W USA 36.48N 118.12W
31 X13 **Independence** Iowa, C USA 42.28N 91.53W
29 P7 **Independence** Kansas, C USA 37.13N 95.42W
22 M4 **Independence** Kentucky, S USA 38.56N 84.32W
29 R4 **Independence** Missouri, C USA 39.05N 94.25W
23 R8 **Independence** Virginia, NE USA 36.37N 81.09W
32 J7 **Independence** Wisconsin, N USA 44.21N 91.25W
207 R12 **Independence Fjord** fjord N Greenland
Independence Island see Malden Island
37 W2 **Independence Mountains** ▲▲ Nevada, W USA
59 K18 **Independencia** Cochabamba, C Bolivia 17.07S 66.52W
59 E16 **Independencia, Bahía de la** bay W Peru
Independencia, Monte see Adam, Mount
118 M12 **Independența** Galați, SE Romania 45.27N 27.45E
Inderagiri see Indragiri, Sungai
Inderbor see Inderborskiy
150 F11 **Inderborskiy** Kaz. Inderbor. Atyrau, W Kazakhstan 48.35N 51.45E
157 I14 **India** off. Republic of India, var. Indian Union, Union of India, Hind. Bhārat. ◆ republic S Asia
India see Inđija
20 D14 **Indiana** Pennsylvania, NE USA 40.37N 79.09W
33 N13 **Indiana** off. State of Indiana; also known as The Hoosier State. ◈ state N USA
33 O14 **Indianapolis** state capital Indiana, N USA 39.46N 86.09W
9 O10 **Indian Cabins** Alberta, W Canada 59.51N 117.06W
44 G1 **Indian Church** Orange Walk, N Belize 17.47N 88.39W
Indian Desert see Thar Desert
9 U16 **Indian Head** Saskatchewan, S Canada 50.31N 103.40W
33 O4 **Indian Lake** ◎ Michigan, N USA
20 K9 **Indian Lake** ◎ New York, NE USA
33 R13 **Indian Lake** ▣ Ohio, N USA
180-181 **Indian Ocean** ocean
31 V15 **Indianola** Iowa, C USA 41.21N 93.33W
24 K4 **Indianola** Mississippi, S USA 33.27N 90.39W
38 J6 **Indian Peak** ▲ Utah, W USA 38.18N 113.52W
25 Y13 **Indian River** lagoon Florida, SE USA
37 W10 **Indian Springs** Nevada, W USA 36.33N 115.40W
25 Y14 **Indiantown** Florida, SE USA 27.01N 80.29W
61 K19 **Indiara** Goiás, S Brazil 17.12S 50.09W
129 Q4 **Indiga** Nenetskiy Avtonomnyy Okrug, NW Russian Federation 67.40N 49.01E
126 Mm6 **Indigirka** ≈ NE Russian Federation
114 L10 **Inđija** Hung. India; prev. Indjija. Serbia, N Serbia 45.03N 20.04E
37 V16 **Indio** California, W USA 33.42N 116.13W
44 M12 **Indio, Río** ≈ SE Nicaragua
158 I10 **Indira Gandhi International** ✕ (Delhi) Delhi, N India
157 Q23 **Indira Point** headland Andaman and Nicobar Islands, India, NE Indian Ocean 6.54N 93.54E
195 X15 **Indispensable Strait** strait C Solomon Islands
Indjija see Inđija
133 Q13 **Indo-Australian Plate** tectonic feature
181 N11 **Indomed Fracture Zone** tectonic feature SW Indian Ocean
175 Nn12 **Indonesia** off. Republic of Indonesia, Ind. Republik Indonesia; prev. Dutch East Indies, Netherlands East Indies, United States of Indonesia. ◆ republic SE Asia
Indonesian Borneo see Kalimantan
160 G10 **Indore** Madhya Pradesh, C India 22.42N 75.50E
174 Hh8 **Indragiri, Sungai** var. Batang Kuantan, Inderagiri. ≈ Sumatera, W Indonesia
Indramajoe/Indramaju see Indramayu
174 K14 **Indramayu** prev. Indramajoe, Indramaju. Jawa, C Indonesia 6.22S 108.19E
161 K14 **Indrāvati** ≈ S India
105 N9 **Indre** ◈ department C France
104 M8 **Indre** ≈ C France
96 D13 **Indre Ålvik** Hordaland, S Norway 60.26N 6.27E
104 L8 **Indre-et-Loire** ◈ department C France
Indreville see Châteauroux
158 G3 **Indus** Chin. Yindu He; prev. Yin-tu Ho. ≈ S Asia
Indus Cone see Indus Fan
181 P3 **Indus Fan** var. Indus Cone. undersea feature N Arabian Sea
155 P17 **Indus, Mouths of the** delta S Pakistan
85 I24 **Indwe** Eastern Cape, SE South Africa 31.28S 27.19E
142 I10 **İnebolu** Kastamonu, N Turkey 41.57N 33.45E
79 P8 **I-n-Échaï** oasis C Mali 20.04N 2.00W
116 M13 **İnecik** Tekirdağ, NW Turkey 40.55N 27.16E
142 E12 **İnegöl** Bursa, NW Turkey 40.06N 29.31E
Inessa see Biancavilla
118 F10 **Ineu** Hung. Borosjenő; prev. Inău. Arad, W Romania 46.25N 21.50E
Ineul/Ineu, Vîrful see Ineu, Vârful
118 J9 **Ineu, Vârful** var. Ineul; prev. Vîrful Ineu. ▲ N Romania 47.31N 24.52E
23 P6 **Inez** Kentucky, S USA 37.53N 82.33W
76 E8 **Inezgane** ✕ (Agadir) W Morocco 30.35N 9.27W
43 T17 **Inferior, Laguna** lagoon S Mexico
42 M15 **Infiernillo, Presa del** ▣ S Mexico
106 L2 **Infiesto** Asturias, N Spain 43.21N 5.21W
95 L20 **Ingå** Fin. Inkoo. Etelä-Suomi, S Finland 60.01N 24.05E
79 U10 **Ingal** var. I-n-Gall. Agadez, C Niger 16.52N 6.57E
I-n-Gall see Ingal
101 C18 **Ingelmunster** West-Vlaanderen, W Belgium 50.12N 3.15E
81 I18 **Ingende** Equateur, W Dem. Rep. Congo 0.15S 18.58E
64 L5 **Ingeniero Guillermo Nueva Juárez** Formosa, N Argentina 23.55S 61.49W
65 H16 **Ingeniero Jacobacci** Río Negro, C Argentina 41.21S 69.46W
12 F16 **Ingersoll** Ontario, S Canada 43.03N 80.52W
Ingettolgoy see Selenge
189 W5 **Ingham** Queensland, NE Australia 18.34S 146.12E
152 M11 **Ingichka** Samarqand Viloyati, C Uzbekistan 39.46N 65.56E
99 L16 **Ingleborough** ▲ N England, UK 54.07N 2.22W
27 T14 **Ingleside** Texas, SW USA 27.52N 97.12W
192 K10 **Inglewood** Taranaki, North Island, NZ 39.10S 174.12E
37 S15 **Inglewood** California, W USA 33.57N 118.21W
126 Kk16 **Ingoda** ≈ S Russian Federation
103 L21 **Ingolstadt** Bayern, S Germany 48.46N 11.25E
35 V9 **Ingomar** Montana, NW USA 46.34N 107.21W
11 R14 **Ingonish Beach** Cape Breton Island, Nova Scotia, SE Canada 46.42N 60.22W
159 S14 **Ingrāj Bāzār** prev. English Bazar. West Bengal, NE India 25.00N 88.10E
27 Q11 **Ingram** Texas, SW USA 30.04N 99.14W
205 X7 **Ingrid Christensen Coast** physical region Antarctica
76 K14 **I-n-Guezzam** S Algeria 19.35N 5.49E
Ingulets see Inhulets'
Inguri see Enguri
Ingushetia/Ingushetiya, Respublika see Ingushskaya Respublika
131 O15 **Ingushskaya Respublika** var. Respublika Ingushetiya, Eng. Ingushetia. ◈ autonomous republic SW Russian Federation
85 N20 **Inhambane** Inhambane, SE Mozambique 23.52S 35.31E
85 M20 **Inhambane** off. Província de Inhambane. ◈ province S Mozambique
85 N17 **Inhaminga** Sofala, C Mozambique 18.22S 35.02E
85 N20 **Inharrime** Inhambane, SE Mozambique 24.28S 35.01E
85 M18 **Inhassoro** Inhambane, E Mozambique 21.31S 35.13E
119 S9 **Inhulets'** Rus. Ingulets. Dnipropetrovs'ka Oblast', E Ukraine 47.40N 33.15E
119 R10 **Inhulets'** Rus. Ingulets. ≈ S Ukraine
107 Q10 **Iniesta** Castilla-La Mancha, C Spain 39.27N 1.45W
I-ning see Yining
56 K11 **Inírida, Río** ≈ E Colombia
Inis see Ennis
Inis Ceithleann see Enniskillen
Inis Córthaidh see Enniscorthy
Inis Díomáin see Ennistimon
99 A17 **Inishbofin** Ir. Inis Bó Finne. island W Ireland
99 B18 **Inisheer** var. Inishere, Ir. Inis Oírr. island W Ireland
Inishere see Inisheer
99 B18 **Inishmaan** Ir. Inis Meáin. island W Ireland
99 A18 **Inishmore** Ir. Árainn. island W Ireland
98 E13 **Inishtrahull** Ir. Inis Trá Tholl. island NW Ireland
99 A17 **Inishturk** Ir. Inis Toirc. island W Ireland
Inkoo see Ingå
193 J16 **Inland Kaikoura Range** ▲▲ South Island, NZ
Inland Sea see Seto-naikai
23 P11 **Inman** South Carolina, SE USA 35.03N 82.05W
110 L7 **Inn** ≈ C Europe
207 O11 **Innaanganeq** var. Kap York. headland NW Greenland 75.54N 66.27W
190 K2 **Innamincka** South Australia 27.47S 140.45E
94 G12 **Inndyr** Nordland, C Norway 67.01N 14.00E
44 G3 **Inner Channel** inlet SE Belize
98 F11 **Inner Hebrides** island group W Scotland, UK
180 H15 **Inner Islands** var. Central Group. island group NE Seychelles
Inner Mongolia/Inner Mongolian Autonomous Region see Nei Mongol Zizhiqu
98 G8 **Inner Sound** strait NW Scotland, UK
102 J13 **Innerste** ≈ C Germany
189 W5 **Innisfail** Queensland, NE Australia 17.29S 146.03E
9 Q15 **Innisfail** Alberta, SW Canada 52.01N 113.58W
Inniskilling see Enniskillen
41 O11 **Innoko River** ≈ Alaska, USA
170 F14 **Innoshima** var. Innosima. Hiroshima, SW Japan 34.18N 133.09E
Innosima see Innoshima
Innsbruch see Innsbruck
110 M7 **Innsbruck** var. Innsbruch. Tirol, W Austria 47.16N 11.25E
81 I19 **Inongo** Bandundu, W Dem. Rep. Congo 1.55S 18.19E
Inoucdjouac see Inukjuak
Inowrazlaw see Inowrocław
112 I10 **Inowrocław** Ger. Hohensalza; prev. Inowrazlaw. Kujawski-pomorskie, C Poland 52.47N 18.15E
59 K18 **Inquisivi** La Paz, W Bolivia 17.01S 67.03W
Inrin see Yüanlin
79 O8 **I-n-Sâkâne, 'Erg** desert N Mali
76 J10 **I-n-Salah** var. In Salah. C Algeria 27.10N 2.31E
131 O5 **Insar** Respublika Mordoviya, W Russian Federation 53.52N 44.26E
201 X15 **Insiaf** Kosrae, E Micronesia
96 L13 **Insjön** Dalarna, C Sweden 60.40N 15.05E
Insterburg see Chernyakhovsk
Insula see Lille
118 L13 **Însurăţei** Brăila, SE Romania 44.55N 27.40E
129 V6 **Inta** Respublika Komi, NW Russian Federation 66.00N 60.09E
79 R9 **I-n-Tebezas** Kidal, E Mali 17.58N 1.51E
Interamna see Teramo
Interamna Nahars see Terni
30 L11 **Interior** South Dakota, N USA 43.42N 101.57W
110 E9 **Interlaken** Bern, SW Switzerland 46.40N 7.51E
31 V2 **International Falls** Minnesota, N USA 48.37N 93.25W
178 Gg7 **Inthanon, Doi** ▲ NW Thailand 18.33N 98.29E
44 G7 **Intibucá** ◈ department SW Honduras
44 G8 **Intipucá** La Unión, SE El Salvador 13.10N 88.03W
63 B15 **Intiyaco** Santa Fe, C Argentina 28.43S 60.04W
118 K12 **Întorsura Buzăului** Ger. Bozau, Hung. Bodzafordulő. Covasna, E Romania 45.49N 26.10E
24 H9 **Intracoastal Waterway** inland waterway system Louisiana, S USA
27 V13 **Intracoastal Waterway** inland waterway system Texas, SW USA
110 G11 **Intragna** Ticino, S Switzerland 46.12N 8.42E
171 Kk17 **Inubō-zaki** headland Honshū, S Japan 35.42N 140.51E
170 D14 **Inukai** Ōita, Kyūshū, SW Japan 33.05N 131.37E
10 I5 **Inukjuak** var. Inoucdjouac; prev. Port Harrison. Québec, NE Canada 58.28N 77.58W
65 I24 **Inútil, Bahía** bay S Chile
Inuuvik see Inuvik
14 G3 **Inuvik** var. Inuuvik. Northwest Territories, NW Canada 68.25N 133.34W
171 I15 **Inuyama** Aichi, Honshū, SW Japan 35.22N 136.55E
58 G13 **Inuya, Río** ≈ E Peru
129 U13 **In'va** ≈ NW Russian Federation
98 H11 **Inveraray** W Scotland, UK 56.13N 5.04W
193 C24 **Invercargill** Southland, South Island, NZ 46.25S 168.22E
191 T5 **Inverell** New South Wales, SE Australia 29.49S 151.07E
98 I8 **Invergordon** N Scotland, UK 57.42N 4.01W
9 P16 **Invermere** British Columbia, SW Canada 50.30N 116.00W
11 R14 **Inverness** Cape Breton Island, Nova Scotia, SE Canada 46.13N 61.19W
98 I8 **Inverness** N Scotland, UK 57.27N 4.15W
25 V11 **Inverness** Florida, SE USA 28.50N 82.19W
98 I9 **Inverness** cultural region NW Scotland, UK
98 K9 **Inverurie** NE Scotland, UK 57.13N 2.13W
190 F8 **Investigator Group** island group South Australia
181 T7 **Investigator Ridge** undersea feature E Indian Ocean
190 H10 **Investigator Strait** strait South Australia
31 R11 **Inwood** Iowa, C USA 43.16N 96.25W
126 H16 **Inya** Respublika Altay, S Russian Federation 50.27N 86.45E
127 Nn10 **Inya** ≈ E Russian Federation
Inyanga see Nyanga
85 M16 **Inyangani** ▲ NE Zimbabwe 18.22S 32.57E
85 J17 **Inyathi** Matabeleland North, SW Zimbabwe 19.36S 28.52E
37 T12 **Inyokern** California, W USA 35.37N 117.48W
37 T10 **Inyo Mountains** ▲▲ California, W USA
131 P6 **Inza** Ul'yanovskaya Oblast', W Russian Federation 53.51N 46.21E
131 W5 **Inzer** Respublika Bashkortostan, W Russian Federation 54.11N 57.37E
131 N7 **Inzhavino** Tambovskaya Oblast', W Russian Federation 52.18N 42.28E
117 C16 **Ioánnina** var. Janina, Yannina. Ípeiros, W Greece 39.39N 20.52E
170 B17 **Iō-jima** var. Iwojima. island Nansei-shotō, SW Japan
128 L4 **Iokan'ga** ≈ NW Russian Federation
29 Q6 **Iola** Kansas, C USA 37.55N 95.24W
Iolcus see Iolkós
117 G16 **Iolkós** anc. Iolcus. site of ancient city Thessalía, C Greece 39.24N 22.56E
Iolotan' see Ýolöten
85 A16 **Iona** Namibe, SW Angola 16.54S 12.39E
98 F11 **Iona** island W Scotland, UK
118 M15 **Ion Corvin** Constanța, SE Romania 44.06N 27.49E
37 P7 **Ione** California, W USA 38.21N 120.55W
118 I13 **Ionești** Vâlcea, SW Romania 44.51N 24.12E
33 Q9 **Ionia** Michigan, N USA 42.59N 85.04W
Ionia Basin see Ionian Basin
123 Mm12 **Ionian Basin** var. Ionia Basin. undersea feature Ionian Sea, C Mediterranean Sea
117 B17 **Iónia Nisiá** var. Iónioi Nísoi, Eng. Ionian Islands. island group W Greece
Ionian Islands see Iónia Nisiá/Iónioi Nísoi
123 Mm11 **Ionian Sea** Gk. Iónio Pélagos, It. Mar Ionio. sea C Mediterranean Sea
117 B17 **Iónioi Nísoi** Eng. Ionian Islands. ◈ region W Greece
Iónioi Nísoi see Iónia Nisiá
Ionio, Mar/Iónio Pélagos see Ionian Sea
Iordan see Yordan
143 U10 **Iori** var. Qabırrı. ≈ Azerbaijan/Georgia
Iorrais, Ceann see Erris Head
117 J22 **Íos** var. Nio. island Kykládes, Greece, Aegean Sea
Íos see Chóra
117 I20 **Ioulís** prev. Kéa. Tziá, Kykládes, Greece, Aegean Sea 37.22N 24.21E
24 G9 **Iowa** Louisiana, S USA 30.12N 93.00W
31 V13 **Iowa** off. State of Iowa; also known as The Hawkeye State. ◈ state C USA
31 Y14 **Iowa City** Iowa, C USA 41.39N 91.31W
31 V13 **Iowa Falls** Iowa, C USA 42.31N 93.15W
27 R4 **Iowa Park** Texas, SW USA 33.57N 98.40W
31 Y14 **Iowa River** ≈ Iowa, C USA
121 M19 **Ipa** Rus. Ipa. ≈ SE Belarus
61 N20 **Ipatinga** Minas Gerais, SE Brazil 19.31S 42.30W
131 N13 **Ipatovo** Stavropol'skiy Kray, SW Russian Federation 45.40N 42.51E
117 C16 **Ípeiros** Eng. Epirus. ◈ region W Greece
Ipek see Peć
113 J21 **Ipel'** var. Ipoly, Ger. Eipel. ≈ Hungary/Slovakia
56 C13 **Ipiales** Nariño, SW Colombia 0.50N 77.42W
201 V14 **Ipis** atoll Chuuk Islands, C Micronesia
61 A14 **Ipixuna** Amazonas, W Brazil 6.57S 71.42W
174 Gg4 **Ipoh** Perak, Peninsular Malaysia 4.36N 101.01E
Ipoly see Ipel'
197 D15 **Ipota** Erromango, S Vanuatu 18.54S 169.19E
81 K14 **Ippy** Ouaka, C Central African Republic 6.17N 21.13E
116 L13 **İpsala** Edirne, NW Turkey 40.55N 26.24E
Ipsario see Ypsário
191 V3 **Ipswich** Queensland, E Australia 27.36S 152.49E
99 Q20 **Ipswich** hist. Gipeswic. E England, UK 52.05N 1.08E
31 O8 **Ipswich** South Dakota, N USA 45.24N 99.00W
Iput' see Iputs'
121 P18 **Iputs'** Rus. Iput'. ≈ Belarus/Russian Federation
16 O3 **Iqaluit** prev. Frobisher Bay. Baffin Island, Nunavut, NE Canada 63.43N 68.28W
165 P9 **Iqe** Qinghai, W China 38.03N 94.45E
165 P9 **Iqe He** ≈ C China
Iqlid see Eqlīd
64 G3 **Iquique** Tarapacá, N Chile 20.15S 70.07W
58 G8 **Iquitos** Loreto, N Peru 3.51S 73.13W
27 N9 **Iraan** Texas, SW USA 30.52N 101.52W
81 K14 **Ira Banda** Haute-Kotto, E Central African Republic 5.57N 22.05E
172 Pp16 **Irabu-jima** island Miyako-shotō, SW Japan
57 Y9 **Iracoubo** N French Guiana 5.28N 53.15W
171 Hh17 **Irago-misaki** headland Honshū, SW Japan 34.35N 137.00E
62 H13 **Iraí** Rio Grande do Sul, S Brazil 27.15S 53.16W
116 G12 **Irákleia** Kentrikí Makedonía, N Greece 41.09N 23.16E
117 J21 **Irákleia** island Kykládes, Greece, Aegean Sea
117 J25 **Irákleio** var. Herakleion, Eng. Candia; prev. Iráklion. Kríti, Greece, E Mediterranean Sea 35.19N 25.07E
117 J25 **Irákleio** ✕ Kríti, Greece, E Mediterranean Sea 35.20N 25.10E
117 F15 **Irákleio** anc. Heracleum. castle Kentrikí Makedonía, N Greece 40.02N 22.34E
Iráklion see Irákleio
149 O7 **Iran** off. Islamic Republic of Iran; prev. Persia. ◆ republic SW Asia
60 F13 **Iranduba** Amazonas, NW Brazil 3.19S 60.09W
87 P13 **Iranian Plate** tectonic feature
149 Q9 **Iranian Plateau** var. Plateau of Iran. plateau N Iran
175 N6 **Iran, Pegunungan** var. Iran Mountains. ▲▲ Indonesia/Malaysia
Iran, Plateau of see Iranian Plateau
149 W13 **Īrānshahr** Sīstān va Balūchestān, SE Iran 27.14N 60.40E
57 P5 **Irapa** Sucre, NE Venezuela 10.33N 62.37W
43 N13 **Irapuato** Guanajuato, C Mexico 20.40N 101.22W
145 R7 **Iraq** off. Republic of Iraq, Ar. 'Irāq. ◆ republic SW Asia
62 J12 **Irati** Paraná, S Brazil 25.25S 50.37W
107 R3 **Irati** ≈ N Spain
129 T8 **Irayël'** Respublika Komi, NW Russian Federation 64.28N 55.20E
45 N13 **Irazú, Volcán** △ C Costa Rica 9.57N 83.52W
Irbenskiy Zaliv/Irbes Šaurums see Irbe Strait
120 D7 **Irbe Strait** Est. Kura Kurk, Latv. Irbes Šaurums, Rus. Irbenskiy Zaliv; prev. Est. Irbe Väin. strait Estonia/Latvia
Irbe Väin see Irbe Strait
144 G9 **Irbid** Irbid, N Jordan 32.33N 35.51E
144 G9 **Irbid** off. Muḩāfaẓat Irbid. ◈ governorate N Jordan
Irbīl see Arbīl
125 F11 **Irbit** Sverdlovskaya Oblast', C Russian Federation 57.37N 63.10E
111 S6 **Irdning** Steiermark, SE Austria 47.29N 14.04E
81 I18 **Irebu** Equateur, W Dem. Rep. Congo 0.32S 17.44E
86 C9 **Ireland** Lat. Hibernia. island Ireland/UK
99 D17 **Ireland** off. Ireland, var. Republic of Ireland, Ir. Éire. ◆ republic NW Europe
66 A12 **Ireland Island North** island W Bermuda
66 A12 **Ireland Island South** island W Bermuda
Ireland, Republic of see Ireland
129 V15 **Iren'** ≈ NW Russian Federation
193 A22 **Irene, Mount** ▲ South Island, NZ 45.04S 167.24E
Irgalem see Yirga 'Alem
150 L11 **Irgiz** Aktyubinsk, C Kazakhstan 48.37N 61.12E
Irian see New Guinea
Irian Barat see Papua
176 V10 **Irian Jaya Barat** off. Propinsi Irian Jaya Barat, Eng. West Irian Jaya. ◈ province E Indonesia
Irian, Teluk see Cenderawasih, Teluk
80 K9 **Iriba** Biltine, NE Chad 15.10N 22.10E
179 Q11 **Iriga** Luzon, N Philippines 13.25N 123.24E
131 X7 **Iriklinskoye Vodokhranilishche** ▣ W Russian Federation
83 H23 **Iringa** Iringa, C Tanzania 7.49S 35.39E
83 H23 **Iringa** ◈ region S Tanzania
172 O17 **Iriomote-jima** island Sakishima-shotō, SW Japan
44 L4 **Iriona** Colón, NE Honduras 15.53N 85.08W
49 U7 **Iriri** ≈ N Brazil
60 I13 **Iriri, Rio** ≈ C Brazil
Iris see Yeşilırmak
37 W9 **Irish, Mount** ▲ Nevada, W USA 37.39N 115.22W
99 H17 **Irish Sea** Ir. Muir Éireann. sea C British Isles
145 U12 **Irjal ash Shaykhīyah** S Iraq 30.49N 44.58E
153 U11 **Irkeshtam** Oshskaya Oblast', SW Kyrgyzstan 39.39N 73.49E
126 J16 **Irkut** ≈ S Russian Federation
126 Jj16 **Irkutsk** Irkutskaya Oblast', S Russian Federation 52.18N 104.15E
126 Jj13 **Irkutskaya Oblast'** ◈ province S Russian Federation
Irlir, Gora see Irlir Toghi
152 K8 **Irlir Tog'I** var. Gora Irlir. ▲ N Uzbekistan 42.43N 63.24E
Irminger Basin see Reykjanes Basin
23 R12 **Irmo** South Carolina, SE USA 34.05N 81.10W
104 E6 **Iroise** sea NW France
201 X2 **Iroj** var. Eroj. island Ratak Chain, SE Marshall Islands
190 H7 **Iron Baron** South Australia 33.01S 137.13E
195 X15 **Iron Bottom Sound** sound C Solomon Islands
12 C10 **Iron Bridge** Ontario, S Canada 46.16N 83.12W
22 H10 **Iron City** Tennessee, S USA 35.01N 87.34W
12 I13 **Irondale** ≈ Ontario, SE Canada
190 H7 **Iron Knob** South Australia 32.46S 137.08E
32 M5 **Iron Mountain** Michigan, N USA 45.51N 88.03W
32 M4 **Iron River** Michigan, N USA 46.05N 88.38W
32 J3 **Iron River** Wisconsin, N USA 46.34N 91.22W
29 X6 **Ironton** Missouri, C USA 37.36N 90.37W
33 S15 **Ironton** Ohio, N USA 38.32N 82.40W
32 K4 **Ironwood** Michigan, N USA 46.27N 90.10W
10 H12 **Iroquois Falls** Ontario, S Canada 48.46N 80.40W
33 N12 **Iroquois River** ≈ Illinois/Indiana, N USA
171 Ii18 **Irō-zaki** headland Honshū, S Japan 34.36N 138.49E
Irpen' see Irpin'
119 O4 **Irpin'** Rus. Irpen'. Kyyivs'ka Oblast', N Ukraine 50.31N 30.15E
119 O4 **Irpin'** Rus. Irpen'. ≈ N Ukraine
147 Q16 **'Irqah** SW Yemen 13.42N 47.21E
177 Ff8 **Irrawaddy** var. Ayeyarwady. ◈ division SW Burma
177 G6 **Irrawaddy** var. Ayeyarwady. ≈ W Burma
177 Ff9 **Irrawaddy, Mouths of the** delta SW Burma
119 N4 **Irsha** ≈ N Ukraine
118 H7 **Irshava** Zakarpats'ka Oblast', W Ukraine 48.19N 23.03E
109 N18 **Irsina** Basilicata, S Italy 40.42N 16.18E
Irtish see Irtysh
133 R5 **Irtysh** var. Irtish, Kaz. Ertis. ≈ C Asia
151 S7 **Irtyshsk** Kaz. Ertis. Pavlodar, NE Kazakhstan 53.21N 75.27E
81 P17 **Irumu** Orientale, E Dem. Rep. Congo 1.27N 29.52E
107 Q2 **Irun** Cast. Irún. País Vasco, N Spain 43.19N 1.48W
Iruña see Pamplona
107 Q3 **Irurtzun** Navarra, N Spain 42.55N 1.49W
98 I13 **Irvine** W Scotland, UK 55.37N 4.40W
23 N6 **Irvine** Kentucky, S USA 37.42N 83.58W
27 T6 **Irving** Texas, SW USA 32.48N 96.57W
22 K5 **Irvington** Kentucky, S USA 37.52N 86.16W
Isaak see Iisaku
30 L8 **Isabel** South Dakota, N USA 45.21N 101.25W
195 W14 **Isabel** off. Isabel Province. ◈ province N Solomon Islands
179 Q17 **Isabela** Basilan Island, SW Philippines 6.41N 122.00E
47 S5 **Isabela** W Puerto Rico 18.30N 67.01W
47 N8 **Isabela, Cabo** headland NW Dominican Republic 19.54N 71.03W
59 A18 **Isabela, Isla** var. Albemarle Island. island Galapagos Islands, Ecuador, E Pacific Ocean
42 I12 **Isabela, Isla** island C Mexico
44 K9 **Isabella, Cordillera** ▲▲ NW Nicaragua
37 S12 **Isabella Lake** ▣ California, W USA
33 N2 **Isabelle, Point** headland Michigan, N USA 47.20N 87.56W
Isabel Segunda see Vieques
118 M13 **Isaccea** Tulcea, E Romania 45.16N 28.28E
94 H1 **Ísafjarðardjúp** inlet NW Iceland
94 H1 **Ísafjördhur** Vestfirdhir, NW Iceland 66.04N 23.09W
170 C13 **Isahaya** Nagasaki, Kyūshū, SW Japan 32.51N 130.04E
155 S7 **Īsa Khel** Punjab, E Pakistan 32.39N 71.12E
180 H7 **Isalo** var. Massif de L'Isalo. ▲▲ SW Madagascar
Isalo, Massif de L' see Isalo
81 K20 **Isandja** Kasai Occidental, C Dem. Rep. Congo 3.03S 21.57E
197 D16 **Isangel** Tanna, S Vanuatu 19.34S 169.17E
81 M18 **Isangi** Orientale, C Dem. Rep. Congo 0.46N 24.15E
103 L24 **Isar** ≈ Austria/Germany
103 M23 **Isar-Kanal** canal SE Germany
Isbarta see İsparta
Isca Damnoniorum see Exeter
109 K18 **Ischia** var. Isola d'Ischia; anc. Aenaria. Campania, S Italy 40.43N 13.57E
109 J18 **Ischia, Isola d'** island S Italy
56 B12 **Iscuandé** var. Santa Bárbara. Nariño, SW Colombia 2.31N 78.04W
171 Hh16 **Ise** Mie, Honshū, SW Japan 34.28N 136.42E
102 J12 **Ise** ≈ N Germany
97 I23 **Isefjord** fjord E Denmark
Iseghem see Izegem
199 Jj17 **Iselin Seamount** undersea feature S Pacific Ocean 72.30S 179.00W

◆ Country
● Country Capital
◇ Dependent Territory
○ Dependent Territory Capital
◈ Administrative Region
✕ International Airport
▲ Mountain
▲▲ Mountain Range
△ Volcano
≈ River
◎ Lake
▣ Reservoir
269

Isenhof – Jamaica

Isenhof *see* Püssi
108 *E7* **Iseo** Lombardia, N Italy *45.40N 10.03E*
105 *U12* **Iseran, Col de l'** *pass* E France *45.26N 7.00E*
105 *S11* **Isère** ◈ *department* E France
105 *S12* **Isère** 〰 E France
103 *F15* **Iserlohn** Nordrhein-Westfalen, W Germany *51.22N 7.42E*
109 *K16* **Isernia** *var.* Æsernia. Molise, C Italy *41.34N 14.13E*
171 *Jj15* **Isesaki** Gunma, Honshū, S Japan *36.19N 139.10E*
133 *Q5* **Iset'** 〰 C Russian Federation
171 *Hh16* **Ise-wan** *bay* S Japan
79 *S15* **Iseyin** Oyo, W Nigeria *7.56N 3.33E*
Isfahan *see* Eşfahān
153 *Q11* **Isfana** Batkenskaya Oblast', SW Kyrgyzstan *39.51N 69.31E*
153 *R11* **Isfara** N Tajikistan *40.06N 70.34E*
155 *O4* **Isfi Maidān** Ghowr, N Afghanistan *35.09N 66.16E*
94 *O3* **Isfjorden** *fjord* W Svalbard
Isha Baydhabo *see* Baydhabo
129 *V11* **Isherim, Gora** ▲ NW Russian Federation *61.06N 59.09E*
131 *Q5* **Isheyevka** Ul'yanovskaya Oblast', W Russian Federation *54.27N 48.18E*
172 *Oo17* **Ishigaki** Okinawa, Ishigaki-jima, SW Japan *24.19N 124.09E*
172 *P17* **Ishigaki-jima** *var.* Isigaki Zima. *island* Sakishima-shotō, SW Japan
172 *O5* **Ishikari** Hokkaidō, NE Japan *43.12N 141.21E*
172 *Oo5* **Ishikari-gawa** *var.* Isikari Gawa. 〰 Hokkaidō, NE Japan
172 *O4* **Ishikari-wan** *bay* Hokkaidō, NE Japan
171 *L14* **Ishikawa** Fukushima, Honshū, C Japan *37.08N 140.26E*
172 *Oo14* **Ishikawa** *var.* Isikawa. Okinawa, Okinawa, SW Japan *26.25N 127.46E*
171 *I13* **Ishikawa** *off.* Ishikawa-ken, *var.* Isikawa. ◈ *prefecture* Honshū, SW Japan
125 *Ff12* **Ishim** Tyumenskaya Oblast', C Russian Federation *56.12N 69.25E*
133 *R6* **Ishim** *Kaz.* Esil. 〰 Kazakhstan/Russian Federation
131 *V6* **Ishimbay** Respublika Bashkortostan, W Russian Federation *53.21N 56.03E*
151 *O9* **Ishimskoye** Akmola, C Kazakhstan *51.22N 67.07E*
171 *M13* **Ishinomaki** *var.* Isinomaki. Miyagi, Honshū, C Japan *38.25N 141.16E*
171 *Kk16* **Ishioka** *var.* Isioka. Ibaraki, Honshū, S Japan *36.12N 140.18E*
170 *Ee15* **Ishizuchi-san** ▲ Shikoku, SW Japan *33.44N 133.07E*
Ishkashim *see* Ishkoshim
Ishkashimskiy Khrebet *see* Ishkoshim, Qatorkŭhi
153 *S15* **Ishkoshim** *Rus.* Ishkashim. S Tajikistan *36.46N 71.35E*
153 *S15* **Ishkoshim, Qatorkŭhi** *Rus.* Ishkashimskiy Khrebet. ⛰ SE Tajikistan
33 *N4* **Ishpeming** Michigan, N USA *46.29N 87.40W*
153 *N11* **Ishtixon** *Rus.* Ishtykhan. Samarqand Viloyati, C Uzbekistan *39.59N 66.28E*
Ishtykhan *see* Ishtixon
159 *T15* **Ishurdi** *var.* Iswardi. Rajshahi, W Bangladesh *24.10N 89.04E*
63 *G17* **Isidoro Noblia** Cerro Largo, NE Uruguay *31.58S 54.09W*
104 *J4* **Isigny-sur-Mer** Calvados, N France *49.20N 1.06W*
Isikari Gawa *see* Ishikari-gawa
Isikawa *see* Ishikawa
142 *C11* **Işıklar Dağı** ⛰ NW Turkey
109 *C19* **Isili** Sardegna, Italy, C Mediterranean Sea *39.46N 9.06E*
125 *Ff13* **Isil'kul'** Omskaya Oblast', C Russian Federation *54.52N 71.07E*
Isinomaki *see* Ishinomaki
Isioka *see* Ishioka
83 *I18* **Isiolo** Eastern, C Kenya *0.21N 37.33E*
81 *O16* **Isiro** Orientale, NE Dem. Rep. Congo *2.51N 27.46E*
94 *P2* **Isispynten** *headland* NE Svalbard *79.51N 26.44E*
126 *Ll11* **Isit** Respublika Sakha (Yakutiya), NE Russian Federation *60.53N 125.32E*
155 *O2* **Iskabad Canal** *canal* N Afghanistan
153 *Q9* **Iskandar** *Rus.* Iskander. Toshkent Viloyati, E Uzbekistan *41.32N 69.46E*
Iskander *see* Iskandar
Iskăr *see* Iskŭr
124 *O2* **İskele** *var.* Trikomo, *Gk.* Tríkomon. E Cyprus *35.16N 33.54E*
142 *K17* **İskenderun** *Eng.* Alexandretta. Hatay, S Turkey *36.34N 36.10E*
144 *H2* **İskenderun Körfezi** *Eng.* Gulf of Alexandretta. *gulf* S Turkey
142 *J11* **İskilip** Çorum, N Turkey *40.45N 34.28E*
Iski-Nauket *see* Eski-Nookat
126 *Gg14* **Iskitim** Novosibirskaya Oblast', C Russian Federation *54.36N 83.05E*
116 *J11* **Iskra** *prev.* Popovo. Kŭrdzhali, S Bulgaria *41.55N 25.12E*
116 *G10* **Iskŭr** *var.* Iskăr. 〰 NW Bulgaria
116 *H10* **Iskŭr, Yazovir** *prev.* Yazovir Stalin. ⊠ W Bulgaria
43 *S15* **Isla** Veracruz-Llave, SE Mexico *18.01N 95.30W*
121 *J15* **Islach** *Rus.* Isloch'. 〰 C Belarus
106 *H14* **Isla Cristina** Andalucía, S Spain *37.12N 7.19W*
Isla de León *see* San Fernando
155 *U6* **Islāmābād** ● (Pakistan) Federal Capital Territory Islāmābād, NE Pakistan *33.40N 73.07E*
155 *V6* **Islāmābād** ✕ Federal Capital Territory Islāmābād, NE Pakistan *33.40N 73.07E*
Islamabad *see* Anantnāg
155 *R17* **Islāmkot** Sind, SE Pakistan *24.37N 70.04E*
25 *Y17* **Islamorada** Florida Keys, Florida, SE USA *24.55N 80.37W*
159 *P14* **Islāmpur** Bihār, N India *25.09N 85.13E*
Islam Qala *see* Eslām Qal'eh
Island/Ísland *see* Iceland
20 *K16* **Island Beach** *spit* New Jersey, NE USA
21 *S4* **Island Falls** Maine, NE USA *45.59N 68.16W*
190 *H6* **Island Lagoon** ◎ South Australia
9 *Y13* **Island Lake** ◎ Manitoba, C Canada
31 *W5* **Island Lake Reservoir** ⊠ Minnesota, N USA
35 *R13* **Island Park** Idaho, NW USA *44.27N 111.21W*
21 *N6* **Island Pond** Vermont, NE USA *44.48N 71.51W*
192 *K2* **Islands, Bay of** *inlet* North Island, NZ
105 *R7* **Is-sur-Tille** Côte d'Or, C France *47.34N 5.03E*
44 *J3* **Islas de la Bahía** ◈ *department* N Honduras
67 *L20* **Islas Orcadas Rise** *undersea feature* S Atlantic Ocean
98 *F12* **Islay** *island* SW Scotland, UK
118 *I15* **Islaz** Teleorman, S Romania *43.43N 24.52E*
31 *V7* **Isle** Minnesota, N USA *46.08N 93.28W*
104 *M12* **Isle** 〰 W France
99 *I16* **Isle of Man** ◇ *UK crown dependency* NW Europe
23 *X7* **Isle of Wight** Virginia, NE USA *36.54N 76.41W*
99 *M24* **Isle of Wight** *cultural region* S England, UK
203 *Y3* **Isles Lagoon** ◎ Kiritimati, E Kiribati
39 *R11* **Isleta Pueblo** New Mexico, SW USA *34.54N 106.40W*
Isloch' *see* Islach
63 *E19* **Ismael Cortinas** Flores, S Uruguay *33.57S 57.04W*
Ismailia *see* Ismâ'ilîya
77 *W7* **Ismâ'ilîya** *var.* Ismailia. N Egypt *30.31N 32.13E*
Ismailly *see* İsmayıllı
143 *X11* **İsmayıllı** *Rus.* Ismailly. C Azerbaijan *40.47N 48.09E*
Ismid *see* İzmit
77 *X10* **Isna** *var.* Esna. SE Egypt *25.16N 32.24E*
95 *K18* **Isojoki** Länsi-Suomi, W Finland *62.07N 22.00E*
84 *M12* **Isoka** Northern, NE Zambia *10.07S 32.42E*
Isola d'Ischia *see* Ischia
Isola d'Istria *see* Izola
Isonzo *see* Soča
13 *U4* **Isoukustouc** 〰 Québec, SE Canada
142 *F15* **İsparta** *var.* Isbarta. İsparta, SW Turkey *37.46N 30.31E*
142 *F15* **İsparta** *var.* Isbarta. ◈ *province* SW Turkey
116 *M7* **Isperikh** *prev.* Kemanlar. Razgrad, N Bulgaria *43.43N 26.49E*
109 *L26* **Ispica** Sicilia, Italy, C Mediterranean Sea *36.46N 14.55E*
154 *J14* **Ispikān** Baluchistān, SW Pakistan *26.21N 62.15E*
143 *Q12* **İspir** Erzurum, NE Turkey *40.28N 41.01E*
144 *E12* **Israel** *off.* State of Israel, *var.* Medinat Israel, *Heb.* Yisrael, Yisra'el. ◆ *republic* SW Asia
Issa *see* Vis
57 *S9* **Issano** C Guyana *5.49N 59.28W*
78 *M16* **Issia** SW Ivory Coast *6.33N 6.33W*
Issiq Köl *see* Issyk-Kul', Ozero
105 *P11* **Issoire** Puy-de-Dôme, C France *45.33N 3.15E*
105 *N9* **Issoudun** *anc.* Uxellodunum. Indre, C France *46.57N 1.58E*
83 *H22* **Issuna** Singida, C Tanzania *5.24S 34.48E*
Issyk *see* Yesik
Issyk-Kul' *see* Balykchy
153 *X7* **Issyk-Kul', Ozero** *var.* Issiq Köl, *Kir.* Ysyk-Köl. ◎ E Kyrgyzstan
153 *X7* **Issyk-Kul'skaya Oblast'** *Kir.* Ysyk-Köl Oblasty. ◈ *province* E Kyrgyzstan
155 *Q7* **Istādeh-ye Moqor, Āb-e-** *var.* Āb-i-Istāda. ◎ SE Afghanistan
142 *D11* **İstanbul** *Bul.* Tsarigrad, *Eng.* Istanbul; *prev.* Constantinople, *anc.* Byzantium. İstanbul, NW Turkey *41.01N 28.57E*
116 *P12* **İstanbul** ◈ *province* NW Turkey
116 *P12* **İstanbul Boğazı** *var.* Bosporus Thracius, *Eng.* Bosphorus, Bosporus, *Turk.* Karadeniz Boğazı. *strait* NW Turkey
Istarska Županija *see* Istra
117 *G19* **Ísthmia** *var.* Isthmía. Pelopónnisos, S Greece *37.55N 23.02E*
117 *G17* **Istiaía** Évvoia, C Greece *38.57N 23.09E*
56 *D9* **Istmina** Chocó, W Colombia *5.09N 76.42W*
25 *W13* **Istokpoga, Lake** ◎ Florida, SE USA
114 *A9* **Istra** *off.* Istarska županija. ◈ *province* NW Croatia
114 *I10* **Istra** *Eng.* Istria, *Ger.* Istrien. *cultural region* NW Croatia
105 *R15* **Istres** Bouches-du-Rhône, SE France *43.30N 4.58E*
Istria/Istrien *see* Istra
179 *R16* **Isulan** Mindanao, S Philippines *6.36N 124.36E*
194 *I11* **Isumrud Strait** *strait* NE PNG
Iswardi *see* Ishurdi
131 *V7* **Isyangulovo** Respublika Bashkortostan, W Russian Federation *52.10N 56.38E*
64 *O6* **Itá** Central, S Paraguay *25.28S 57.21W*
61 *O17* **Itaberaba** Bahia, E Brazil *12.34S 40.21W*
61 *M20* **Itabira** *prev.* Presidente Vargas. Minas Gerais, SE Brazil *19.39S 43.13W*
61 *O18* **Itabuna** Bahia, E Brazil *14.48S 39.18W*
61 *J18* **Itacaiu** Mato Grosso, S Brazil *14.49S 51.21W*
60 *G12* **Itacoatiara** Amazonas, N Brazil *3.06S 58.22W*
56 *D9* **Itagüí** Antioquia, W Colombia *6.12N 75.40W*
62 *D13* **Itá Ibaté** Corrientes, NE Argentina *27.27S 57.24W*
62 *G11* **Itaipú, Represa de** ⊠ Brazil/Paraguay
60 *H13* **Itaituba** Pará, NE Brazil *4.15S 55.55W*
62 *K13* **Itajaí** Santa Catarina, S Brazil *26.49S 48.39W*
Italia/Italiana, Republica/Italian Republic, The *see* Italy
Italian Somaliland *see* Somalia
27 *T7* **Italy** Texas, SW USA *32.10N 96.52W*
108 *G12* **Italy** *off.* The Italian Republic, *It.* Italia, Republica Italiana. ◆ *republic* S Europe
61 *O19* **Itamaraju** Bahia, E Brazil *16.58S 39.31W*
61 *C14* **Itamarati** Amazonas, W Brazil *6.12S 68.16W*
61 *M19* **Itambé, Pico de** ▲ SE Brazil *18.22S 43.21W*
171 *Gg15* **Itami** ✕ (Ōsaka) Ōsaka, Honshū, SW Japan *34.47N 135.24E*
117 *H15* **Ítamos** ▲ N Greece *40.06N 23.51E*
159 *W11* **Itānagar** Arunāchal Pradesh, NE India *27.09N 93.35E*
Itany *see* Litani
61 *N19* **Itaobim** Minas Gerais, SE Brazil *16.34S 41.27W*
61 *P15* **Itaparica, Represa de** ⊠ E Brazil
60 *M13* **Itapecuru-Mirim** Maranhão, E Brazil *3.24S 44.19W*
62 *Q8* **Itaperuna** Rio de Janeiro, SE Brazil *21.13S 41.51W*
61 *O18* **Itapetinga** Bahia, E Brazil *15.16S 40.16W*
62 *L10* **Itapetininga** São Paulo, S Brazil *23.33S 48.03W*
62 *K10* **Itapeva** São Paulo, S Brazil *23.58S 48.54W*
49 *W6* **Itapicuru, Rio** 〰 NE Brazil
60 *O13* **Itapipoca** Ceará, E Brazil *3.28S 39.34W*
62 *M9* **Itapira** São Paulo, S Brazil *22.25S 46.46W*
62 *K8* **Itápolis** São Paulo, S Brazil *21.36S 48.43W*
62 *K10* **Itaporanga** São Paulo, S Brazil *23.43S 49.28W*
64 *P7* **Itapúa** *off.* Departamento de Itapúa. ◈ *department* SE Paraguay
61 *E15* **Itapuã do Oeste** Rondônia, W Brazil *9.21S 63.07W*
63 *E15* **Itaqui** Rio Grande do Sul, S Brazil *29.10S 56.28W*
62 *K10* **Itararé** São Paulo, S Brazil *24.07S 49.16W*
62 *K10* **Itararé, Rio** 〰 S Brazil
160 *H11* **Itārsi** Madhya Pradesh, C India *22.42N 77.55E*
27 *T7* **Itasca** Texas, SW USA *32.09N 97.09W*
Itassi *see* Vieille Case
95 *N17* **Itä-Suomi** ◈ *province* E Finland
62 *D13* **Itatí** Corrientes, NE Argentina *27.16S 58.15W*
62 *K10* **Itatinga** São Paulo, S Brazil *23.08S 48.36W*
117 *F18* **Itéas, Kólpos** *gulf* C Greece
59 *N15* **Iténez, Río** *var.* Rio Guaporé. 〰 Bolivia/Brazil *see also* Guaporé, Rio
56 *H11* **Iteviate, Río** 〰 C Colombia
102 *I13* **Ith** *hill range* C Germany
33 *Q8* **Ithaca** Michigan, N USA *43.17N 84.36W*
20 *H11* **Ithaca** New York, NE USA *42.25N 76.30W*
117 *C18* **Itháki** *island* Iónia Nisiá, Greece, C Mediterranean Sea
Itháki *see* Vathý
It Hearrenfean *see* Heerenveen
Itihara *see* Ichihara
81 *L17* **Itimbiri** 〰 N Dem. Rep. Congo
Itinomiya *see* Ichinomiya
Itinoseki *see* Ichinoseki
41 *Q5* **Itkilik River** 〰 Alaska, USA
171 *J17* **Itō** Shizuoka, Honshū, S Japan *34.59N 139.03E*
171 *J13* **Itoigawa** Niigata, Honshū, C Japan *37.01N 137.52E*
13 *R6* **Itomamo, Lac** ◎ Québec, SE Canada
172 *Oo15* **Itoman** Okinawa, SW Japan *26.04N 127.40E*
104 *M5* **Iton** 〰 N France
59 *M16* **Itonamas Río** 〰 NE Bolivia
Itoupé, Mont *see* Sommet Tabulaire
Itseqqortoormiit *see* Ittoqqortoormiit
24 *K4* **Itta Bena** Mississippi, S USA *33.30N 90.19W*
109 *B17* **Ittiri** Sardegna, Italy, C Mediterranean Sea *40.36N 8.34E*
207 *Q14* **Ittoqqortoormiit** *var.* Itseqqortoormiit, *Dan.* Scoresbysund, *Eng.* Scoresby Sound. Tunu, C Greenland *70.33N 21.52W*
62 *M10* **Itu** São Paulo, S Brazil *23.17S 47.16W*
178 *Mm14* **Itu Aba Island** *island* W Spratly Islands
56 *D8* **Ituango** Antioquia, NW Colombia *7.06N 75.51W*
61 *A14* **Ituí, Rio** 〰 NW Brazil
81 *O20* **Itula** Sud Kivu, E Dem. Rep. Congo *3.30S 27.49E*
61 *K19* **Itumbiara** Goiás, C Brazil *18.25S 49.15W*
57 *T9* **Ituni** E Guyana *5.24N 58.18W*
43 *X13* **Iturbide** Campeche, SE Mexico *19.41N 89.29W*
Ituri *see* Aruwimi
127 *Pp16* **Iturup, Ostrov** *island* Kuril'skiye Ostrova, SE Russian Federation
62 *L7* **Ituverava** São Paulo, S Brazil *20.22S 47.48W*
61 *C15* **Ituxi, Rio** 〰 W Brazil
63 *E14* **Ituzaingó** Corrientes, NE Argentina *27.34S 56.43W*
103 *K18* **Itz** 〰 C Germany
102 *I9* **Itzehoe** Schleswig-Holstein, N Germany *53.55N 9.31E*
25 *N2* **Iuka** Mississippi, S USA *34.48N 88.11W*
62 *I11* **Ivaiporã** Paraná, S Brazil *24.16S 51.46W*
62 *I11* **Ivaí, Rio** 〰 S Brazil
94 *L10* **Ivalo** *Lapp.* Avveel, Avvil. Lappi, N Finland *68.34N 27.29E*
94 *L10* **Ivalojoki** *Lapp.* Avreel. 〰 N Finland
121 *H20* **Ivanava** *Pol.* Janów, Janów Poleski, *Rus.* Ivanovo. Brestskaya Voblasts', SW Belarus *52.07N 25.31E*
Ivangorod *see* Dęblin
Ivangrad *see* Berane
191 *N7* **Ivanhoe** New South Wales, SE Australia *32.54S 144.20E*
31 *S9* **Ivanhoe** Minnesota, N USA *44.27N 96.15W*
12 *D8* **Ivanhoe** 〰 Ontario, S Canada
114 *E8* **Ivanić-Grad** Sisak-Moslavina, N Croatia *45.43N 16.23E*
119 *T10* **Ivanivka** Khersons'ka Oblast', S Ukraine *46.43N 34.28E*
119 *P10* **Ivanivka** Odes'ka Oblast', SW Ukraine *46.57N 30.26E*
115 *L14* **Ivanjica** Serbia, C Serbia *43.36N 20.14E*
114 *G11* **Ivanjska** *var.* Potkozarje. Republika Srpska, NW Bosnia & Herzegovina *44.54N 17.04E*
113 *H21* **Ivanka** ✕ (Bratislava) Bratislavský Kraj, W Slovakia *48.10N 17.13E*
119 *O3* **Ivankiv** *Rus.* Ivankov. Kyyivs'ka Oblast', N Ukraine *50.55N 29.53E*
Ivankov *see* Ivankiv
41 *O15* **Ivanof Bay** Alaska, USA *55.55N 159.28W*
118 *J7* **Ivano-Frankivs'k** *Ger.* Stanislau, *Pol.* Stanisławów, *Rus.* Ivano-Frankovsk; *prev.* Stanislav. Ivano-Frankivs'ka Oblast', W Ukraine *48.55N 24.45E*
Ivano-Frankivs'k *see* Ivano-Frankivs'ka Oblast'
118 *I7* **Ivano-Frankivs'ka Oblast'** *var.* Ivano-Frankivs'k, *Rus.* Ivano-Frankovskaya Oblast'; *prev.* Stanislavskaya Oblast'. ◈ *province* W Ukraine
Ivano-Frankovsk *see* Ivano-Frankivs'k
Ivano-Frankovskaya Oblast' *see* Ivano-Frankivs'ka Oblast'
128 *M16* **Ivanovo** Ivanovskaya Oblast', W Russian Federation *57.01N 40.58E*
Ivanovo *see* Ivanava
125 *A16* **Ivanovskaya Oblast'** ◈ *province* W Russian Federation
37 *X12* **Ivanpah Lake** ◎ California, W USA
114 *E7* **Ivanščica** ⛰ NE Croatia
116 *M8* **Ivanski** Shumen, NE Bulgaria *43.09N 27.02E*
131 *R7* **Ivanteyevka** Saratovskaya Oblast', W Russian Federation *52.13N 49.06E*
Ivantsevichi/Ivatsevichi *see* Ivatsevichy
118 *I4* **Ivanychi** Volyns'ka Oblast', NW Ukraine *50.37N 24.22E*
121 *H18* **Ivatsevichy** *Pol.* Iwacewicze, *Rus.* Ivantsevichi, Ivatsevichi. Brestskaya Voblasts', SW Belarus *52.43N 25.21E*
116 *L12* **Ivaylovgrad** Khaskovo, S Bulgaria *41.32N 26.06E*
116 *K11* **Ivaylovgrad, Yazovir** ⊠ S Bulgaria
125 *F10* **Ivdel'** Sverdlovskaya Oblast', C Russian Federation *60.42N 60.07E*
Ivenets *see* Ivyanyets
118 *L12* **Iveşti** Galaţi, E Romania *45.27N 28.00E*
Ivgovuotna *see* Lyngen
Ivigtut *see* Ivittuut
81 *F18* **Ivindo** 〰 Congo/Gabon
61 *I21* **Ivinheima** Mato Grosso do Sul, SW Brazil *22.16S 53.52W*
206 *M15* **Ivittuut** *var.* Ivigtut. Kitaa, S Greenland *61.28N 48.33W*
Iviza *see* Eivissa/Ibiza
180 *I6* **Ivohibe** Fianarantsoa, SE Madagascar *22.28S 46.52E*
Ivoire, Côte d' *see* Ivory Coast
194 *I14* **Ivori** 〰 S PNG
78 *L15* **Ivory Coast** *off.* Republic of the Ivory Coast, *Fr.* Côte d'Ivoire, République de la Côte d'Ivoire. ◆ *republic* W Africa
70 *C11* **Ivory Coast** *Fr.* Côte d'Ivoire. *coastal region* S Ivory Coast
97 *L22* **Ivösjön** ◎ S Sweden
108 *B7* **Ivrea** *anc.* Eporedia. Piemonte, NW Italy *45.28N 7.52E*
10 *J2* **Ivujivik** Québec, NE Canada *62.25N 77.49W*
121 *J16* **Ivyanyets** *Rus.* Ivenets. Minskaya Voblasts', C Belarus *53.52N 26.45E*
Iv'ye *see* Iwye
Iwacewicze *see* Ivatsevichy
172 *N11* **Iwaizumi** Iwate, Honshū, NE Japan *39.48N 141.46E*
171 *Ll15* **Iwaki** Fukushima, Honshū, N Japan *37.01N 140.52E*
171 *Mm9* **Iwaki-san** ▲ Honshū, C Japan *40.39N 140.20E*
170 *E13* **Iwakuni** Yamaguchi, Honshū, SW Japan *34.07N 132.06E*
172 *Oo5* **Iwamizawa** Hokkaidō, NE Japan *43.11N 141.43E*
172 *Nn5* **Iwanai** Hokkaidō, NE Japan *42.51N 140.21E*
171 *Ll13* **Iwanuma** Miyagi, Honshū, C Japan *38.07N 140.49E*
171 *I17* **Iwata** Shizuoka, Honshū, S Japan *34.42N 137.49E*
172 *N10* **Iwate** Iwate, Honshū, N Japan *40.02N 141.12E*
171 *Mm11* **Iwate** *off.* Iwate-ken. ◈ *prefecture* Honshū, C Japan
171 *Mm10* **Iwate-san** ▲ Honshū, C Japan *39.52N 140.59E*
Iwje *see* Iwye
79 *S16* **Iwo** Oyo, SW Nigeria *7.21N 3.58E*
Iwojima *see* Iō-jima
121 *I16* **Iwye** *Pol.* Iwje, *Rus.* Iv'ye. Hrodzyenskaya Voblasts', W Belarus *53.55N 25.46E*
44 *C4* **Ixcán, Río** 〰 Guatemala/Mexico
101 *G18* **Ixelles** *Dut.* Elsene. Brussels, C Belgium *50.49N 4.21E*
59 *J16* **Ixiamas** La Paz, NW Bolivia *13.43S 68.10W*
43 *O13* **Ixmiquilpan** *var.* Ixmiquilpán. Hidalgo, C Mexico *20.28N 99.11W*
85 *K23* **Ixopo** KwaZulu/Natal, E South Africa *30.07S 30.03E*
Ixtaccíhuatal, Volcán *see* Iztaccíhuati, Volcán
42 *M16* **Ixtapa** Guerrero, S Mexico *17.37N 101.29W*
43 *S16* **Ixtepec** Oaxaca, SE Mexico *16.32N 95.03W*
42 *K12* **Ixtlán** *var.* Ixtlán del Río. Nayarit, C Mexico *21.03N 104.23W*
Ixtlán del Río *see* Ixtlán
125 *F12* **Iyevlevo** Tyumenskaya Oblast', C Russian Federation *57.36N 67.20E*
170 *E14* **Iyo** Ehime, Shikoku, SW Japan *33.44N 132.42E*
170 *F15* **Iyomishima** *var.* Iyomisima. Ehime, Shikoku, SW Japan *33.58N 133.31E*
Iyomisima *see* Iyomishima
170 *Dd14* **Iyo-nada** *sea* S Japan
44 *E4* **Izabal** *off.* Departamento de Izabal. ◈ *department* E Guatemala
44 *F5* **Izabal, Lago de** *prev.* Golfo Dulce. ◎ E Guatemala
149 *O9* **Īzad Khvāst** Fārs, C Iran *31.31N 52.08E*
43 *X12* **Izamal** Yucatán, SE Mexico *20.58N 89.00W*
131 *Q16* **Izberbash** Respublika Dagestan, SW Russian Federation *42.32N 47.51E*
101 *C18* **Izegem** *prev.* Iseghem. West-Vlaanderen, W Belgium *50.55N 3.13E*
148 *M9* **Īzeh** Khūzestān, SW Iran *31.48N 49.52E*
172 *P14* **Izena-jima** *island* Nansei-shotō, SW Japan
116 *N10* **Izgrev** Burgas, E Bulgaria *42.09N 27.49E*
131 *T2* **Izhevsk** *prev.* Ustinov. Udmurtskaya Respublika, NW Russian Federation *56.48N 53.12E*
129 *S7* **Izhma** Respublika Komi, NW Russian Federation *64.56N 53.52E*
129 *S7* **Izhma** 〰 NW Russian Federation
147 *X8* **Izkī** NE Oman *22.45N 57.35E*
Izmail *see* Izmayil
119 *N13* **Izmayil** *Rus.* Izmail. Odes'ka Oblast', SW Ukraine *45.19N 28.48E*
142 *B14* **İzmir** *prev.* Smyrna. İzmir, W Turkey *38.25N 27.10E*
142 *C14* **İzmir** *prev.* Smyrna. ◈ *province* W Turkey
142 *E11* **İzmit** *var.* Ismid; *anc.* Astacus. Kocaeli, NW Turkey *40.46N 29.55E*
106 *M14* **Iznájar** Andalucía, S Spain *37.17N 4.16W*
106 *M14* **Iznajar, Embalse de** ⊠ S Spain
107 *N14* **Iznalloz** Andalucía, S Spain *37.23N 3.31W*
142 *E11* **İznik** Bursa, NW Turkey *40.27N 29.43E*
142 *E12* **İznik Gölü** ◎ NW Turkey
130 *M14* **Izobil'nyy** Stavropol'skiy Kray, SW Russian Federation *45.22N 41.40E*
111 *S13* **Izola** *It.* Isola d'Istria. SW Slovenia *45.31N 13.40E*
144 *H9* **Izra'** *var.* Ezra, Ezraa. Dar'ā, S Syria *32.52N 36.15E*
43 *P14* **Iztaccíhuati, Volcán** *var.* Volcán Ixtaccíhuatal. ⩚ S Mexico *19.07N 98.37W*
44 *C7* **Iztapa** Escuintla, SE Guatemala *13.55N 90.45W*
Izúcar de Matamoros *see* Matamoros
171 *J17* **Izu-hantō** *peninsula* Honshū, S Japan
170 *C11* **Izuhara** Nagasaki, Tsushima, SW Japan *34.11N 129.16E*
170 *C15* **Izumi** Kagoshima, Kyūshū, SW Japan *32.05N 130.22E*
171 *Gg15* **Izumiōtsu** Ōsaka, Honshū, SW Japan *34.29N 135.25E*
171 *Gg15* **Izumi-Sano** Ōsaka, Honshū, SW Japan *34.24N 135.19E*
170 *F12* **Izumo** Shimane, Honshū, SW Japan *35.22N 132.45E*
Izu Shichito *see* Izu-shotō
172 *Ss13* **Izu-shotō** *var.* Izu Shichito. *island group* S Japan
199 *H4* **Izu Trench** *undersea feature* NW Pacific Ocean
126 *I4* **Izvestiy TsIK, Ostrova** *island* N Russian Federation
116 *G10* **Izvor** Pernik, W Bulgaria *42.27N 22.53E*
118 *L5* **Izyaslav** Khmel'nyts'ka Oblast', W Ukraine *50.08N 26.53E*
119 *W6* **Izyum** Kharkivs'ka Oblast', E Ukraine *49.12N 37.18E*

J

95 *M18* **Jaala** Etelä-Suomi, S Finland *61.04N 26.30E*
146 *J5* **Jabal ash Shifā** *desert* NW Saudi Arabia
147 *U8* **Jabal aẓ Ẓannah** *var.* Jebel Dhanna. Abū Ẓaby, W UAE *24.10N 52.36E*
144 *E11* **Jabalīya** *var.* Jabāliyah. NE Gaza Strip *31.30N 34.25E*
Jabāliyah *see* Jabalīya
107 *N11* **Jabalón** 〰 C Spain
160 *J10* **Jabalpur** *prev.* Jubbulpore. Madhya Pradesh, C India *23.10N 79.58E*
147 *N15* **Jabal Zuqar, Jazīrat** *var.* Az Zuqur. *island* SW Yemen
Jabat *see* Jabwot
144 *J3* **Jabbūl, Sabkhat al** *salt flat* NW Syria
189 *P1* **Jabiru** Northern Territory, N Australia *12.44S 132.48E*
144 *H4* **Jablah** *var.* Jeble, *Fr.* Djéblé. Al Lādhiqīyah, W Syria *35.00N 36.00E*
114 *C11* **Jablanac** Lika-Senj, W Croatia *44.43N 14.54E*
115 *H14* **Jablanica** Federacija Bosna I Hercegovina, SW Bosnia and Herzegovina *43.39N 17.43E*
115 *M20* **Jablanica** *Alb.* Mali i Jabllanicës, *var.* Malet e Jabllanicës. ⛰ Albania/FYR Macedonia *see also* Jabllanicës, Mali i
Jabllanicës, Malet e *see* Jablanica/Jabllanicës, Mali i
115 *M20* **Jabllanicës, Mali i** *var.* Malet e Jabllanicës, *Mac.* Jablanica. ⛰ Albania/FYR Macedonia *see also* Jablanica
113 *E15* **Jablonec nad Nisou** *Ger.* Gablonz an der Neisse. Liberecký Kraj, N Czech Republic *50.43N 15.10E*
Jabłonków/Jablunkau *see* Jablunkov
112 *J9* **Jabłonowo Pomorskie** Kujawski-pomorskie, C Poland *53.24N 19.08E*
113 *J17* **Jablunkov** *Ger.* Jablunkau, *Pol.* Jabłonków. Moravskoslezský Kraj, E Czech Republic *49.34N 18.45E*
61 *Q15* **Jaboatão** Pernambuco, E Brazil *08.05S 35.00W*
62 *L8* **Jaboticabal** São Paulo, S Brazil *21.15S 48.16W*
201 *U7* **Jabwot** *var.* Jabat, Jebat, Jōwat. *island* Ralik Chain, S Marshall Islands
107 *S4* **Jaca** Aragón, NE Spain *42.34N 0.33W*
44 *B4* **Jacaltenango** Huehuetenango, W Guatemala *15.39N 91.46W*
61 *G14* **Jacaré-a-Canga** Pará, NE Brazil *5.58S 57.31W*
62 *N10* **Jacareí** São Paulo, S Brazil *23.18S 45.55W*
61 *I18* **Jaciara** Mato Grosso, W Brazil *15.58S 54.57W*
61 *E15* **Jaciparaná** Rondônia, W Brazil *9.20S 64.27W*
21 *P5* **Jackman** Maine, NE USA *45.35N 70.14W*
37 *X1* **Jackpot** Nevada, W USA *41.57N 114.41W*
22 *M8* **Jacksboro** Tennessee, S USA *36.19N 84.10W*
27 *S6* **Jacksboro** Texas, SW USA *33.13N 98.10W*
25 *N7* **Jackson** Alabama, S USA *31.30N 87.53W*
37 *P7* **Jackson** California, W USA *38.19N 120.46W*
23 *O6* **Jackson** Kentucky, S USA *37.30N 83.22W*
24 *J8* **Jackson** Louisiana, S USA *30.50N 91.13W*
33 *Q10* **Jackson** Michigan, N USA *42.15N 84.24W*
31 *T11* **Jackson** Minnesota, N USA *43.38N 95.00W*
24 *K5* **Jackson** *state capital* Mississippi, S USA *32.19N 90.12W*
29 *Y7* **Jackson** Missouri, C USA *37.22N 89.40W*
23 *W8* **Jackson** North Carolina, SE USA *36.24N 77.22W*
33 *T15* **Jackson** Ohio, NE USA *39.03N 82.40W*
22 *G9* **Jackson** Tennessee, S USA *35.37N 88.46W*
35 *S14* **Jackson** Wyoming, C USA *43.28N 110.45W*
193 *C19* **Jackson Bay** *bay* South Island, NZ
194 *K16* **Jackson Field** ✕ (Port Moresby) Central/National Capital District, S PNG *9.28S 147.12E*
193 *C20* **Jackson Head** *headland* South Island, NZ *43.57S 168.38E*
25 *S8* **Jackson, Lake** ◎ Florida, SE USA
35 *S13* **Jackson Lake** ◎ Wyoming, C USA
204 *J6* **Jackson, Mount** ▲ Antarctica *71.43S 63.45W*
39 *U3* **Jackson Reservoir** ◎ Colorado, C USA
25 *Q3* **Jacksonville** Alabama, S USA *33.48N 85.45W*
29 *V11* **Jacksonville** Arkansas, C USA *34.52N 92.06W*
25 *W8* **Jacksonville** Florida, SE USA *30.19N 81.39W*
32 *K14* **Jacksonville** Illinois, N USA *39.43N 90.13W*
23 *W11* **Jacksonville** North Carolina, SE USA *34.45N 77.25W*
27 *W7* **Jacksonville** Texas, SW USA *31.57N 95.16W*
25 *X9* **Jacksonville Beach** Florida, SE USA *30.17N 81.23W*
46 *L9* **Jacmel** *var.* Jaquemel. S Haiti *18.13N 72.33W*
Jacob *see* Nkayi
155 *Q12* **Jacobābād** Sind, SE Pakistan *28.16N 68.30E*
57 *T11* **Jacobs Ladder Falls** *waterfall* S Guyana *2.57N 58.06W*
47 *O11* **Jaco, Pointe** *headland* N Dominica *15.38N 61.25W*
13 *Q9* **Jacques-Cartier** 〰 Québec, SE Canada
11 *P11* **Jacques-Cartier, Détroit de** *var.* Jacques-Cartier Passage. *strait* Gulf of St. Lawrence/St. Lawrence River
13 *W6* **Jacques-Cartier, Mont** ▲ Québec, SE Canada *48.58N 66.00W*
Jacques-Cartier Passage *see* Jacques-Cartier, Détroit de
195 *O12* **Jacquinot Bay** *inlet* New Britain, PNG
63 *H16* **Jacuí, Rio** 〰 S Brazil
62 *L11* **Jacupiranga** São Paulo, S Brazil *24.42S 48.00W*
102 *G10* **Jade** 〰 NW Germany
102 *G10* **Jadebusen** *bay* NW Germany
Jadotville *see* Likasi
Jadransko More/Jadransko Morje *see* Adriatic Sea
107 *O7* **Jadraque** Castilla-La Mancha, C Spain *40.55N 2.55W*
58 *C10* **Jaén** Cajamarca, N Peru *5.43S 78.46W*
107 *N13* **Jaén** Andalucía, SW Spain *37.46N 3.48W*
107 *N13* **Jaén** ◈ *province* Andalucía, S Spain
161 *J23* **Jaffna** Northern Province, N Sri Lanka *9.42N 80.03E*
161 *K23* **Jaffna Lagoon** *lagoon* N Sri Lanka
21 *N10* **Jaffrey** New Hampshire, NE USA *42.46N 72.00W*
144 *H13* **Jafr, Qā' al** *var.* El Jafr. *salt pan* S Jordan
158 *J9* **Jagādhri** Haryāna, N India *30.10N 77.18E*
120 *H4* **Jägala** *var.* Jägala Jõgi, *Ger.* Jaggowal. 〰 NW Estonia
Jägala Jõgi *see* Jägala
Jagannath *see* Puri
161 *L14* **Jagdalpur** Chhattīsgarh, C India *19.07N 82.04E*
169 *U5* **Jagdaqi** Nei Mongol Zizhiqu, N China *50.25N 124.02E*
Jägerndorf *see* Krnov
Jaggowal *see* Jägala
145 *O2* **Jaghjaghah, Nahr** 〰 N Syria
179 *Qq14* **Jagna** Bohol, C Philippines *9.37N 124.16E*
114 *N13* **Jagodina** *prev.* Svetozarevo. Serbia, C Serbia *43.59N 21.15E*
114 *K12* **Jagodnja** ⛰ W Serbia
103 *I20* **Jagst** 〰 SW Germany
161 *I14* **Jagtiāl** Andhra Pradesh, C India *18.49N 78.53E*
63 *H18* **Jaguarão** Rio Grande do Sul, S Brazil *32.32S 53.20W*
63 *H18* **Jaguarão, Rio** *var.* Río Yaguarón. 〰 Brazil/Uruguay
62 *K11* **Jaguariaíva** Paraná, S Brazil *24.15S 49.43W*
46 *D5* **Jagüey Grande** Matanzas, W Cuba *22.31N 81.09W*
159 *P14* **Jahānābād** Bihār, N India *25.13N 84.58E*
Jahra *see* Al Jahrā'
149 *P12* **Jahrom** *var.* Jahrum. Fārs, S Iran *28.34N 53.32E*
Jahrum *see* Jahrom
Jailolo *see* Halmahera, Pulau
175 *Tt8* **Jailolo, Selat** *strait* E Indonesia
Jainat *see* Chai Nat
Jainti *see* Jayanti
158 *H12* **Jaipur** *prev.* Jeypore. Rājasthān, N India *26.54N 75.46E*
159 *T14* **Jaipur Hat** Rajshahi, NW Bangladesh *25.04N 89.03E*
158 *D11* **Jaisalmer** Rājasthān, NW India *26.55N 70.56E*
160 *O12* **Jājapur** Orissa, E India *18.54N 82.36E*
149 *R4* **Jājarm** Khorāsān-e Shemālī, NE Iran *36.58N 56.25E*
114 *G12* **Jajce** Federacija Bosna I Hercegovina, W Bosnia and Herzegovina *44.20N 17.16E*
Jajı *see* 'Alī Kheyl
85 *D17* **Jakalsberg** Otjozondjupa, N Namibia *19.22S 17.28E*
174 *J14* **Jakarta** *prev.* Djakarta, *Dut.* Batavia. ● (Indonesia) Jawa, C Indonesia *6.07S 106.45E*
8 *I8* **Jakes Corner** Yukon Territory, W Canada *60.18N 134.00W*
158 *H9* **Jākhal** Haryāna, NW India *29.46N 75.51E*
Jakobeny *see* Iacobeni
95 *K16* **Jakobstad** *Fin.* Pietarsaari. Länsi-Suomi, W Finland *63.40N 22.40E*
Jakobstadt *see* Jēkabpils
115 *O18* **Jakupica** ⛰ C FYR Macedonia
39 *W15* **Jal** New Mexico, SW USA *32.07N 103.10W*
147 *P7* **Jalājil** *var.* Ğalāğıl. Ar Riyāḍ, C Saudi Arabia *25.42N 45.22E*
Jalal-Abad *see* Dzhalal-Abad, Dzhalal-Abadskaya Oblast', W Kyrgyzstan
155 *S5* **Jalālābād** *var.* Jalalabad, Jelalabad. Nangarhār, E Afghanistan *34.25N 70.28E*
Jalal-Abad Oblasty *see* Dzhalal-Abadskaya Oblast'
155 *V7* **Jalālpur** Punjab, E Pakistan *32.39N 74.10E*
155 *T11* **Jalālpur Pīrwāla** Punjab, E Pakistan *29.30N 71.19E*
158 *H8* **Jalandhar** *prev.* Jullundur. Punjab, N India *31.19N 75.36E*
44 *J7* **Jalán, Río** 〰 S Honduras
44 *E6* **Jalapa** Jalapa, C Guatemala *14.39N 89.58W*
44 *J7* **Jalapa** Nueva Segovia, NW Nicaragua *13.57N 86.09W*
44 *A3* **Jalapa** *off.* Departamento de Jalapa. ◈ *department* SE Guatemala
44 *E6* **Jalapa, Río** 〰 SE Guatemala
149 *X13* **Jālaq** Sīstān va Balūchestān, SE Iran
95 *K17* **Jalasjärvi** Länsi-Suomi, W Finland *62.30N 22.49E*
155 *O8* **Jaldak** Zābol, SE Afghanistan *32.00N 66.45E*
62 *J7* **Jales** São Paulo, S Brazil *20.15S 50.34W*
160 *P11* **Jaleshwar** *var.* Jaleswar. Orissa, NE India *21.51N 87.15E*
Jaleswar *see* Jaleshwar
160 *F12* **Jalgaon** Mahārāshtra, C India *21.01N 75.34E*
145 *W12* **Jalībah** S Iraq *30.37N 46.31E*
145 *W13* **Jalīb Shahāb** S Iraq *30.25N 46.08E*
79 *X15* **Jalingo** Taraba, E Nigeria *8.54N 11.22E*
42 *K13* **Jalisco** ◈ *state* SW Mexico
160 *G13* **Jālna** Mahārāshtra, W India *19.52N 75.55E*
Jalomitsa *see* Ialomiţa
107 *R5* **Jalón** 〰 N Spain
158 *E13* **Jālor** Rājasthān, N India *25.21N 72.43E*
114 *K11* **Jalovik** Serbia, W Serbia *44.37N 19.48E*
42 *L12* **Jalpa** Zacatecas, C Mexico *21.40N 103.00W*
159 *S12* **Jalpāiguri** West Bengal, NE India *26.43N 88.24E*
43 *O12* **Jalpán** *var.* Jalpan. Querétaro de Arteaga, C Mexico *21.13N 99.28W*
69 *P2* **Jalta** *island* N Tunisia
77 *S9* **Jālū** *var.* Jūlā. NE Libya *29.01N 21.33E*
201 *U8* **Jaluit Atoll** *var.* Jālwōj. *atoll* Ralik Chain, S Marshall Islands
Jālwōj *see* Jaluit Atoll
83 *L18* **Jamaame** *It.* Giamame; *prev.* Margherita. Jubbada Hoose, S Somalia *0.00N 42.43E*
79 *W13* **Jamaare** 〰 NE Nigeria
46 *G9* **Jamaica** ◆ *commonwealth republic* W West Indies
49 *P3* **Jamaica** *island* W West Indies

◆ Country
● Country Capital
◇ Dependent Territory
○ Dependent Territory Capital
◈ Administrative Region
✕ International Airport
▲ Mountain
⛰ Mountain Range
⩚ Volcano
〰 River
◎ Lake
⊠ Reservoir

JAMAICA CHANNEL – JIUSUO

46 I9 **Jamaica Channel** *channel* Haiti/Jamaica
159 T14 **Jamalpur** Dhaka, N Bangladesh 24.54N 89.57E
159 Q14 **Jamālpur** Bihār, NE India 25.19N 86.30E
174 I6 **Jamaluang** *var.* Jemaluang. Johor, Peninsular Malaysia 2.13N 103.48E
61 I14 **Jamanxim, Rio** ≈ C Brazil
58 B8 **Jambeli, Canal de** *channel* S Ecuador
101 I20 **Jambes** Namur, SE Belgium 50.26N 4.51E
174 Hh9 **Jambi** *var.* Telanaipura; *prev.* Djambi. Sumatera, W Indonesia 1.34S 103.37E
174 H9 **Jambi** *off.* Propinsi Jambi, *var.* Djambi. ◈ *province* W Indonesia
Jamdena *see* Yamdena, Pulau
10 H8 **James Bay** *bay* Ontario/Québec, E Canada
65 F19 **James, Isla** *island* Archipiélago de los Chonos, S Chile
189 Q8 **James Ranges** ▲▲ Northern Territory, C Australia
31 P8 **James River** ≈ North Dakota/South Dakota, N USA
23 X7 **James River** ≈ Virginia, NE USA
204 H4 **James Ross Island** *island* Antarctica
190 I8 **Jamestown** South Australia 33.13S 138.36E
67 G25 **Jamestown** ○ (Saint Helena) NW Saint Helena 15.55S 5.43W
37 P8 **Jamestown** California, W USA 37.57N 120.25W
22 L7 **Jamestown** Kentucky, S USA 36.58N 85.03W
20 D11 **Jamestown** New York, NE USA 42.04N 79.15W
31 P5 **Jamestown** North Dakota, N USA 46.54N 98.42W
22 L8 **Jamestown** Tennessee, S USA 36.25N 84.57W
Jamestown *see* Holetown
13 N10 **Jamet** ≈ Québec, SE Canada
43 Q17 **Jamiltepec** *var.* Santiago Jamiltepec. Oaxaca, SE Mexico 16.16N 97.50W
97 F20 **Jammerbugten** *bay* Skagerrak, E North Sea
158 H6 **Jammu** *prev.* Jummoo. Jammu and Kashmir, NW India 32.43N 74.54E
158 I5 **Jammu and Kashmir** *var.* Jammu-Kashmir, Kashmir. ◈ *state* NW India
155 V4 **Jammu and Kashmir** *disputed region* India/Pakistan
160 B10 **Jāmnagar** *prev.* Navanagar. Gujarāt, W India 22.28N 70.06E
155 S11 **Jāmpur** Punjab, E Pakistan 29.39N 70.34E
95 L18 **Jämsä** Länsi-Suomi, W Finland 61.51N 25.10E
95 L18 **Jämsänkoski** Länsi-Suomi, W Finland 61.54N 25.10E
159 Q16 **Jamshedpur** Jhārkhand, NE India 22.46N 86.12E
96 K9 **Jämtland** ◈ *county* C Sweden
159 Q14 **Jamūi** Bihār, NE India 24.57N 86.13E
159 T14 **Jamuna** ≈ N Bangladesh
Jamuna *see* Brahmaputra
Jamundá *see* Nhamundá, Rio
56 D11 **Jamundí** Valle del Cauca, SW Colombia 3.16N 76.31W
159 Q12 **Janakpur** Central, C Nepal 26.45N 85.55E
61 N18 **Janaúba** Minas Gerais, SE Brazil 15.46S 43.16W
60 K11 **Janaucu, Ilha** *island* NE Brazil
149 Q7 **Jandaq** Eşfahān, C Iran 34.04N 54.25E
66 Q11 **Jandia, Punta de** *headland* Fuerteventura, Islas Canarias, Spain, NE Atlantic Ocean 28.03N 14.31W
61 B14 **Jandiatuba, Rio** ≈ NW Brazil
107 N12 **Jándula** ≈ S Spain
31 V10 **Janesville** Minnesota, N USA 44.07N 93.43W
32 L9 **Janesville** Wisconsin, N USA 42.42N 89.01W
155 N13 **Jangal** Baluchistān, SW Pakistan 28.00N 65.48E
85 N20 **Jangamo** Inhambane, SE Mozambique 24.04S 35.25E
161 J14 **Jangaon** Andhra Pradesh, C India 18.47N 79.25E
159 S14 **Jangīpur** West Bengal, NE India 24.31N 88.03E
Janina *see* Ioánnina
Janischken *see* Joniškis
114 J11 **Janja** Republika Srpska, NE Bosnia and Herzegovina 44.40N 19.15E
Jankovac *see* Jánoshalma
207 Q15 **Jan Mayen** ◇ *Norwegian dependency* N Atlantic Ocean
86 D5 **Jan Mayen** *island* N Atlantic Ocean
207 R15 **Jan Mayen Fracture Zone** *tectonic feature* Greenland Sea/Norwegian Sea
207 R15 **Jan Mayen Ridge** *undersea feature* Greenland Sea/Norwegian Sea
42 H3 **Janos** Chihuahua, N Mexico 30.45N 108.21W
113 K25 **Jánoshalma** *SCr.* Jankovac. Bács-Kiskun, S Hungary 46.18N 19.16E
Janow/Janów *see* Jonava, Lithuania
Janów *see* Ivanava, Belarus
112 H10 **Janowiec Wielkopolski** *Ger.* Janowitz. Kujawski-pomorskie, C Poland 52.47N 17.30E
Janowitz *see* Janowiec Wielkopolski
113 O15 **Janów Lubelski** Lubelskie, E Poland 50.43N 22.24E
Janów Poleski *see* Ivanava
85 H25 **Jansenville** Eastern Cape, S South Africa 32.55S 24.40E
176 W12 **Jantan** Papua, E Indonesia 3.53S 134.20E
61 M18 **Januária** Minas Gerais, SE Brazil 15.28S 44.22W
Janūbīyah, Al Bādiyah al *see* Ash Shāmīyah
104 I7 **Janzé** Ille-et-Vilaine, NW France 47.55N 1.28W
160 F10 **Jaora** Madhya Pradesh, C India 23.40N 75.10E
171 H12 **Japan** *var.* Nippon, *Jap.* Nihon. ◆ *monarchy* E Asia
133 Y9 **Japan** *island group* E Asia
199 H3 **Japan Basin** *undersea feature* N Sea of Japan
133 Y8 **Japan, Sea of** *var.* East Sea, *Rus.* Yapanskoye More. *sea* NW Pacific Ocean *see also* East Sea
199 H4 **Japan Trench** *undersea feature* NW Pacific Ocean
Japen *see* Yapen, Pulau
61 A15 **Japiim** *var.* Máncio Lima. Acre, W Brazil 8.00S 73.39W
60 D12 **Japurá** Amazonas, N Brazil 1.43S 66.14W
60 C12 **Japurá, Rio** *var.* Río Caquetá, Yapurá. ≈ Brazil/Colombia *see also* Caquetá, Río
45 W17 **Jaqué** Darién, SE Panama 7.30N 78.09W
Jaquemel *see* Jacmel
Jarablos *see* Jarābulus
144 K2 **Jarābulus** *var.* Jarablos, Jerablus, *Fr.* Djérablous. Ḥalab, N Syria 36.51N 38.02E
62 K13 **Jaraguá do Sul** Santa Catarina, S Brazil 26.28S 49.07W
106 K9 **Jaraicejo** Extremadura, W Spain 39.40N 5.49W
106 K9 **Jaráiz de la Vera** Extremadura, W Spain 40.04N 5.45W
107 O7 **Jarama** ≈ C Spain
65 J20 **Jaramillo** Santa Cruz, SE Argentina 47.10S 67.07W
Jarandilla de la Vega *see* Jarandilla de la Vera
106 K8 **Jarandilla de la Vera** *var.* Jarandilla de la Vega. Extremadura, W Spain 40.07N 5.39W
155 V9 **Jarānwāla** Punjab, E Pakistan 31.19N 73.25E
144 G9 **Jarash** *var.* Jerash; *anc.* Gerasa. Irbid, NW Jordan 32.16N 35.54E
Jarbah, Jazīrat *see* Jerba, Île de
96 N13 **Järbo** Gävleborg, C Sweden 60.43N 16.40E
Jardan *see* Yordan
46 F7 **Jardines de la Reina, Archipiélago de los** *island group* C Cuba
168 I8 **Jargalant** Bayanhongor, C Mongolia 47.14N 99.43E
168 K6 **Jargalant** Bulgan, N Mongolia 49.09N 104.19E
168 G7 **Jargalant** *var.* Buyanbat. Govĭ-Altay, W Mongolia 47.00N 95.57E
168 I6 **Jargalant** *var.* Orgil. Hövsgöl, C Mongolia 48.31N 99.19E
Jargalant *see* Battsengel, Arhangay, Mongolia
Jargalant *see* Biger, Govĭ-Altay, Mongolia
Jargalant *see* Bulgan, Bayan-Olgiy, Mongolia
Jarīd, Shaṭṭ al *see* Jerid, Chott el
60 I11 **Jari, Rio** *var.* Jary. ≈ N Brazil
147 N7 **Jarīr, Wādī al** *dry watercourse* C Saudi Arabia
Jarja *see* Yur'ya
96 L13 **Järna** *var.* Dala-Jarna. Dalarna, C Sweden 60.31N 14.22E
97 O16 **Järna** Stockholm, C Sweden 59.04N 17.34E
104 K11 **Jarnac** Charente, W France 45.41N 0.10W
112 H12 **Jarocin** Wielkopolskie, C Poland 51.58N 17.30E
113 F16 **Jaroměř** *Ger.* Jermer. Královéhradecký Kraj, N Czech Republic 50.22N 15.55E
Jaroslau *see* Jarosław
113 O16 **Jarosław** *Ger.* Jaroslau, *Rus.* Yaroslav. Podkarpackie, SE Poland 50.01N 22.41E
95 F16 **Järpen** Jämtland, C Sweden 63.21N 13.30E
153 O14 **Jarqo'rg'on** *Rus.* Dzharkurgan. Surkhondaryo Viloyati, S Uzbekistan 37.31N 67.20E
145 P2 **Jarrāh, Wadi** *dry watercourse* NE Syria
Jars, Plain of *see* Xiangkhoang, Plateau de
168 K14 **Jartai Yanchi** ◎ N China
61 E16 **Jaru** Rondônia, W Brazil 10.24S 62.45W
Jarud Qi *see* Lubei
120 I4 **Järva-Jaani** *Ger.* Sankt-Johannis. Järvamaa, N Estonia 59.02N 25.52E
120 G5 **Järvakandi** *Ger.* Jerwakant. Raplamaa, NW Estonia 58.47N 24.49E
120 H4 **Järvamaa** *off.* Järva Maakond. ◈ *province* N Estonia
95 L19 **Järvenpää** Etelä-Suomi, S Finland 60.28N 25.03E
12 G17 **Jarvis** Ontario, S Canada 42.53N 80.06W
185 R8 **Jarvis Island** ◇ *US unincorporated territory* C Pacific Ocean
96 M11 **Järvsö** Gävleborg, C Sweden 61.43N 16.25E
Jary *see* Jari, Rio
114 M9 **Jaša Tomić** Serbia, NE Serbia 45.27N 20.51E
114 D12 **Jasenice** Zadar, SW Croatia 44.15N 15.33E
144 I11 **Jashshat al 'Adlah, Wādī al** *dry watercourse* C Jordan
79 Q16 **Jasikan** E Ghana 7.24N 0.28E
Jāsk *see* Bandar-e Jāsk
152 F6 **Jasliq** *Rus.* Zhaslyk. Qoraqalpog'iston Respublikasi, NW Uzbekistan 43.57N 57.30E
113 N17 **Jasło** Podkarpackie, SE Poland 49.45N 21.28E
9 U16 **Jasmin** Saskatchewan, S Canada 51.11N 103.34W
67 A23 **Jason Islands** *island group* NW Falkland Islands
204 I4 **Jason Peninsula** *peninsula* Antarctica
33 N15 **Jasonville** Indiana, N USA 39.09N 87.12W
9 O15 **Jasper** Alberta, SW Canada 52.55N 118.04W
12 L13 **Jasper** Ontario, SE Canada 44.50N 75.57W
25 O3 **Jasper** Alabama, S USA 33.49N 87.16W
29 T9 **Jasper** Arkansas, C USA 36.00N 93.11W
25 U8 **Jasper** Florida, SE USA 30.31N 82.57W
33 N16 **Jasper** Indiana, N USA 38.22N 86.57W
31 R11 **Jasper** Minnesota, N USA 43.51N 96.24W
29 S7 **Jasper** Missouri, C USA 37.20N 94.18W
22 K10 **Jasper** Tennessee, S USA 35.04N 85.37W
27 Y9 **Jasper** Texas, SW USA 30.55N 94.00W
9 O15 **Jasper National Park** *national park* Alberta/British Columbia, SW Canada
Jassy *see* Iaşi
115 N14 **Jastrebac** ▲▲ SE Serbia
114 D9 **Jastrebarsko** Zagreb, N Croatia 45.40N 15.40E
Jastrow *see* Jastrowie
112 G9 **Jastrowie** *Ger.* Jastrow. Wielkopolskie, C Poland 53.25N 16.48E
113 J17 **Jastrzębie-Zdrój** Śląskie, S Poland 49.58N 18.34E
113 L22 **Jászapáti** Jász-Nagykun-Szolnok, E Hungary 47.31N 20.09E
113 L22 **Jászberény** Jász-Nagykun-Szolnok, E Hungary 47.30N 19.54E
113 L23 **Jász-Nagykun-Szolnok** *off.* Jász-Nagykun-Szolnok Megye. ◈ *county* E Hungary
61 J19 **Jataí** Goiás, C Brazil 17.58S 51.45W
60 G12 **Jatapu, Serra do** ▲▲ N Brazil
43 W16 **Jatate, Río** ≈ SE Mexico
155 P17 **Jāti** Sind, SE Pakistan 24.19N 68.18E
46 F6 **Jatibonico** Sancti Spíritus, C Cuba 21.55N 79.12W
174 Jj14 **Jatiluhur, Danau** ◎ Jawa, S Indonesia
Jativa *see* Xátiva
174 K14 **Jatiwangi** *prev.* Djatiwangi. Jawa, C Indonesia 6.45S 108.12E
155 S11 **Jattoi** Punjab, E Pakistan 29.22N 70.55E
62 L9 **Jaú** São Paulo, S Brazil 22.17S 48.32W
60 F11 **Jauaperi, Rio** ≈ N Brazil
101 I19 **Jauche** Wallon Brabant, C Belgium 50.42N 4.55E
Jauer *see* Jawor
Jauf *see* Al Jawf
155 U7 **Jauharābād** Punjab, E Pakistan 32.19N 72.15E
59 E14 **Jauja** Junín, C Peru 11.44S 75.30W
43 O10 **Jaumave** Tamaulipas, C Mexico 23.28N 99.22W
120 H10 **Jaunjelgava** *Ger.* Friedrichstadt. Aizkraukle, S Latvia 56.38N 25.03E
Jaunlatgale *see* Pytalovo
120 I8 **Jaunpiebalga** Gulbene, NE Latvia 57.10N 26.02E
120 E9 **Jaunpils** Tukums, C Latvia 56.45N 23.03E
159 N13 **Jaunpur** Uttar Pradesh, N India 25.43N 82.40E
31 N8 **Java** South Dakota, N USA 45.29N 99.54W
Java *see* Jawa
107 R9 **Javalambre** ▲ E Spain 40.02N 1.06W
181 V7 **Java Ridge** *undersea feature* E Indian Ocean
61 A14 **Javari, Rio** *var.* Yavarí. ≈ Brazil/Peru
Javarthushuu *see* Bayan-Uul
174 Kk13 **Java Sea** *Ind.* Laut Jawa. *sea* W Indonesia
181 U7 **Java Trench** *var.* Sunda Trench. *undersea feature* E Indian Ocean
149 Q10 **Javazm** *var.* Jowzam. Kermān, C Iran
107 T11 **Jávea** *Cat.* Xàbia. País Valenciano, E Spain 38.48N 0.10E
Javhlant *see* Bayan-Ovoo
65 G20 **Javier, Isla** *island* S Chile
115 L14 **Javor** ▲▲ Bosnia and Herzegovina/Serbia
113 K20 **Javorie** *Hung.* Jávoros. ▲ S Slovakia 48.26N 19.16E
Jávoros *see* Javorie
95 J14 **Jävre** Norrbotten, N Sweden 65.07N 21.31E
174 K14 **Jawa** *Eng.* Java; *prev.* Djawa. *island* C Indonesia
174 J15 **Jawa Barat** *off.* Propinsi Jawa Barat, *Eng.* West Java. ◈ *province* S Indonesia
Jawa, Laut *see* Java Sea
145 R3 **Jawān** NW Iraq 35.57N 43.03E
174 Kk15 **Jawa Tengah** *off.* Propinsi Jawa Tengah, *Eng.* Central Java. ◈ *province* S Indonesia
174 Ll15 **Jawa Timur** *off.* Propinsi Jawa Timur, *Eng.* East Java. ◈ *province* S Indonesia
83 N17 **Jawhar** *var.* Jowhar, *It.* Giohar. Shabeellaha Dhexe, S Somalia 2.36N 45.30E
113 F14 **Jawor** *Ger.* Jauer. Dolnośląskie, SW Poland 51.01N 16.10E
Jaworów *see* Yavoriv
113 J16 **Jaworzno** Śląskie, S Poland 50.13N 19.07E
Jaxartes *see* Syr Darya
29 R9 **Jay** Oklahoma, C USA 36.25N 94.48W
Jayabum *see* Chaiyaphum
Jayanath *see* Chai Nat
159 T12 **Jayanti** *prev.* Jainti. West Bengal, NE India 26.43N 89.43E
176 Xx12 **Jaya, Puncak** *prev.* Puntjak Carstensz, Puntjak Sukarno. ▲ Papua, E Indonesia 4.00S 137.10E
176 Z10 **Jayapura** *var.* Djajapura, *Dut.* Hollandia; *prev.* Kotabaru, Sukarnapura. Papua, E Indonesia 2.37S 140.39E
176 Y12 **Jayawijaya, Pegunungan** ▲▲ Papua, E Indonesia
Jay Dairen *see* Dalian
Jayhawker State *see* Kansas
153 S12 **Jayilgan** *Rus.* Dzhailgan, Dzhayilgan. C Tajikistan 39.17N 71.32E
161 L14 **Jaypur** *var.* Jeypore, Jeypur. Orissa, E India 18.54N 82.36E
27 O6 **Jayton** Texas, SW USA 33.15N 100.34W
149 U13 **Jaz Mūrīān, Hāmūn-e** ◎ SE Iran
144 M4 **Jazrah** Ar Raqqah, C Syria 35.56N 39.02E
144 G6 **Jbaïl** *var.* Jebeil, Jubayl, Jubeil; *anc.* Biblical Gebal, Bybles. W Lebanon 34.00N 35.45E
27 O7 **J.B.Thomas, Lake** ⊡ Texas, SW USA
Jdaïdé *see* Judaydah
37 X12 **Jean** Nevada, W USA 35.45N 115.20W
24 I9 **Jeanerette** Louisiana, S USA 29.54N 91.39W
46 L8 **Jean-Rabel** NW Haiti 19.49N 73.12W
149 T12 **Jebāl Bārez, Kūh-e** ▲▲ SE Iran
Jebat *see* Jabwot
79 T15 **Jebba** Kwara, W Nigeria 9.04N 4.50E
Jebeil *see* Jbaïl
118 E12 **Jebel** *Hung.* Széphely; *prev. Hung.* Zsebely. Timiş, W Romania 45.33N 21.13E
152 B11 **Jebel** *Rus.* Dzhebel. Balkan Welaýaty, W Turkmenistan 39.42N 54.10E
Jebel, Bahr el *see* White Nile
Jebel Dhanna *see* Jabal az̧ Z̧annah
Jeble *see* Jablah
98 K13 **Jedburgh** SE Scotland, UK 55.28N 2.34W
Jedda *see* Jiddah
113 L15 **Jędrzejów** *Ger.* Endersdorf. Świętokrzyskie, C Poland 50.39N 20.18E
102 K12 **Jeetze** *var.* Jeetzel. ≈ C Germany
Jeetzel *see* Jeetze
31 U14 **Jefferson** Iowa, C USA 42.01N 94.22W
23 Q8 **Jefferson** North Carolina, SE USA 36.24N 81.33W
27 X6 **Jefferson** Texas, SW USA 32.45N 94.21W
32 M9 **Jefferson** Wisconsin, N USA 43.01N 88.48W
29 U5 **Jefferson City** *state capital* Missouri, C USA 38.33N 92.12W
35 R10 **Jefferson City** Montana, NW USA 46.24N 112.01W
23 N9 **Jefferson City** Tennessee, S USA 36.07N 83.29W
37 U7 **Jefferson, Mount** ▲ Nevada, W USA 38.49N 116.54W
34 H12 **Jefferson, Mount** ▲ Oregon, NW USA 44.40N 121.48W
22 L5 **Jeffersontown** Kentucky, S USA 38.11N 85.33W
33 P16 **Jeffersonville** Indiana, N USA 38.16N 85.45W
35 V15 **Jeffrey City** Wyoming, C USA 42.29N 107.49W
79 T13 **Jega** Kebbi, NW Nigeria 12.15N 4.21E
Jehol *see* Chengde
64 P5 **Jejui-Guazú, Río** ≈ E Paraguay
120 I10 **Jēkabpils** *Ger.* Jakobstadt. Jēkabpils, S Latvia 56.30N 25.56E
25 W7 **Jekyll Island** *island* Georgia, SE USA
174 L11 **Jelai, Sungai** ≈ Borneo, N Indonesia
Jelalabad *see* Jalālābād
113 H14 **Jelcz-Laskowice** Dolnośląskie, SW Poland 51.01N 17.24E
113 E14 **Jelenia Góra** *Ger.* Hirschberg, Hirschberg im Riesengebirge, Hirschberg in Riesengebirge, Hirschberg in Schlesien. Dolnośląskie, SW Poland 50.54N 15.48E
159 S11 **Jelep La** *pass* N India 27.24N 88.51E
120 F9 **Jelgava** *Ger.* Mitau. Jelgava, C Latvia 56.38N 23.47E
114 L13 **Jelica** ▲▲ C Serbia
22 M8 **Jellico** Tennessee, S USA 36.33N 84.06W
97 G23 **Jelling** Vejle, C Denmark 55.45N 9.24E
174 Ii5 **Jemaja, Pulau** *island* W Indonesia
Jemaluang *see* Jamaluang
101 E20 **Jemappes** Hainaut, S Belgium 50.27N 3.52E
174 M16 **Jember** *prev.* Djember. Jawa, C Indonesia 8.07S 113.45E
101 I20 **Jemeppe-sur-Sambre** Namur, S Belgium 50.27N 4.41E
39 R10 **Jemez Pueblo** New Mexico, SW USA 35.36N 106.43W
164 K2 **Jeminay** Xinjiang Uygur Zizhiqu, NW China 47.28N 85.49E
201 U5 **Jemo Island** *atoll* Ratak Chain, C Marshall Islands
175 Nn8 **Jempang, Danau** ◎ Borneo, N Indonesia
103 L16 **Jena** Thüringen, C Germany 50.55N 11.34E
24 I6 **Jena** Louisiana, S USA 31.40N 92.07W
110 I8 **Jenaz** Graubünden, SE Switzerland 46.56N 9.43E
111 N7 **Jenbach** Tirol, W Austria 47.23N 11.47E
175 P13 **Jeneponto** *prev.* Djeneponto. Sulawesi, C Indonesia 5.40S 119.42E
144 F9 **Jenīn** N West Bank 32.28N 35.17E
23 P7 **Jenkins** Kentucky, S USA 37.10N 82.37W
29 P9 **Jenks** Oklahoma, C USA 36.01N 95.58W
Jenné *see* Djenné
111 X8 **Jennersdorf** Burgenland, SE Austria 46.57N 16.08E
24 H9 **Jennings** Louisiana, S USA 30.13N 92.39W
15 Jj4 **Jenny Lind Island** *island* Nunavut, N Canada
25 Y13 **Jensen Beach** Florida, SE USA 27.15N 80.13W
15 M2 **Jens Munk Island** *island* Nunavut, NE Canada
61 O17 **Jequié** Bahia, E Brazil 13.52S 40.06W
61 O18 **Jequitinhonha, Rio** ≈ E Brazil
Jerablus *see* Jarābulus
76 H6 **Jerada** NE Morocco 34.16N 2.07W
Jerash *see* Jarash
77 N7 **Jerba, Île de** *var.* Djerba, Jazīrat Jarbah. *island* E Tunisia
46 K9 **Jérémie** SW Haiti 18.38N 74.10W
Jerez *see* Jeréz de la Frontera, Spain
Jeréz *see* Jerez de García Salinas, Mexico
42 L11 **Jerez de García Salinas** *var.* Jeréz. Zacatecas, C Mexico 22.40N 103.00W
106 J15 **Jeréz de la Frontera** *var.* Jerez; *prev.* Xeres. Andalucía, SW Spain 36.40N 6.07W
106 I12 **Jeréz de los Caballeros** Extremadura, W Spain 38.19N 6.45W
Jergucati *see* Jorgucat
144 G10 **Jericho** *Ar.* Arīḩā, *Heb.* Yeriẖo. E West Bank 31.51N 35.27E
76 M7 **Jerid, Chott el** *var.* Shaṭṭ al Jarīd. *salt lake* SW Tunisia
191 O10 **Jerilderie** New South Wales, SE Australia 35.24S 145.43E
Jerischmarkt *see* Câmpia Turzii
94 K11 **Jerisjärvi** ◎ NW Finland
Jermentau *see* Yereymentau
Jermer *see* Jaroměř
38 K11 **Jerome** Arizona, SW USA 34.45N 112.06W
35 O15 **Jerome** Idaho, NW USA 42.43N 114.31W
99 L26 **Jersey** *island* Channel Islands, NW Europe
20 K14 **Jersey City** New Jersey, NE USA 40.42N 74.01W
20 F13 **Jersey Shore** Pennsylvania, NE USA 41.12N 77.13W
32 K14 **Jerseyville** Illinois, N USA 39.07N 90.19W
106 K8 **Jerte** ≈ W Spain
144 F10 **Jerusalem** *Ar.* Al Quds, Al Quds ash Sharīf, *Heb.* Yerushalayim; *anc.* Hierosolyma. ● (Israel) Jerusalem, NE Israel 31.46N 35.13E
144 G10 **Jerusalem** ◈ *district* E Israel
191 S10 **Jervis Bay** New South Wales, SE Australia 35.09S 150.42E
191 S10 **Jervis Bay Territory** ◈ *territory* SE Australia
Jerwakant *see* Järvakandi
111 S10 **Jesenice** *Ger.* Assling. NW Slovenia 46.26N 14.00E
113 H16 **Jeseník** *Ger.* Freiwaldau. Olomoucký Kraj, E Czech Republic 50.14N 17.12E
Jesi *see* Iesi
108 I8 **Jesolo** *var.* Iesolo. Veneto, NE Italy 45.32N 12.37E
Jesselton *see* Kota Kinabalu
97 I14 **Jessheim** Akershus, S Norway 60.07N 11.10E
159 T15 **Jessore** Khulna, W Bangladesh 23.10N 89.12E
25 W6 **Jesup** Georgia, SE USA 31.36N 81.54W
43 S15 **Jesús Carranza** Veracruz-Llave, SE Mexico 17.30N 95.01W
64 K10 **Jesús María** Córdoba, C Argentina 30.58S 64.04W
28 K6 **Jetmore** Kansas, C USA 38.04N 99.53W
105 Q2 **Jeumont** Nord, N France 50.18N 4.06E
97 H14 **Jevnaker** Oppland, S Norway 60.13N 10.22E
Jewe *see* Jõhvi
27 V9 **Jewett** Texas, SW USA 31.21N 96.08W
21 N12 **Jewett City** Connecticut, NE USA 41.36N 71.58W
Jewish Autonomous Oblast *see* Yevreyskaya Avtonomnaya Oblast'
Jeypore/Jeypur *see* Jaypur, Orissa, India
Jeypore *see* Jaipur, Rājasthān, India
115 L17 **Jezercës, Maja e** ▲ N Albania 42.27N 19.49E
113 B18 **Jezerní Hora** ▲ SW Czech Republic 49.10N 13.11E
160 F10 **Jhābua** Madhya Pradesh, C India 22.47N 74.36E
158 H14 **Jhālāwār** Rājasthān, N India 24.33N 76.10E
Jhang/Jhang Sadar *see* Jhang Sadr
155 U9 **Jhang Sadr** *var.* Jhang, Jhang Sadar. Punjab, NE Pakistan 31.16N 72.19E
158 J13 **Jhānsi** Uttar Pradesh, N India 25.27N 78.34E
159 O16 **Jhārkhand** ◈ *state* NE India
160 M11 **Jhārsuguda** Orissa, E India 21.54N 84.09E
155 V7 **Jhelum** Punjab, NE Pakistan 32.55N 73.42E
133 P9 **Jhelum** ≈ E Pakistan
Jhenaidaha *see* Jhenida
159 T15 **Jhenida** *var.* Jhenaidaha. Dhaka, W Bangladesh 23.34N 89.39E
155 P16 **Jhimpīr** Sind, SE Pakistan 25.01N 67.59E
Jhind *see* Jīnd
155 R16 **Jhudo** Sind, SE Pakistan 24.58N 69.23E
Jhumra *see* Chak Jhumra
158 H11 **Jhunjhunūn** Rājasthān, N India 28.07N 75.21E
Ji *see* Hebei, China
Ji *see* Jilin, China
Jiading *see* Xinfeng
159 S14 **Jiāganj** West Bengal, NE India 24.18N 88.07E
166 J7 **Jialing Jiang** ≈ C China
169 Y7 **Jiamusi** *var.* Chia-mu-ssu, Kiamusze. Heilongjiang, NE China 46.45N 130.19E
167 O11 **Ji'an** Jiangxi, S China 27.06N 114.57E
169 W12 **Ji'an** Jilin, NE China 41.04N 126.07E
169 T13 **Jianchang** Liaoning, NE China 40.48N 119.51E
Jianchang *see* Nancheng
Jiancheng *see* Jianyang
166 F11 **Jianchuan** *var.* Jinhuan. Yunnan, SW China 26.28N 99.49E
164 M4 **Jiangjunmiao** Xinjiang Uygur Zizhiqu, W China 44.42N 90.06E
166 K11 **Jiangkou** *var.* Shuangjiang. Guizhou, S China 27.46N 108.53E
Jiangkou *see* Fengkai
167 Q12 **Jiangle** *var.* Guyong. Fujian, SE China 26.44N 117.26E
167 N15 **Jiangmen** Guangdong, S China 22.34N 113.01E
Jiangna *see* Yanshan
167 Q10 **Jiangshan** Zhejiang, SE China 28.41N 118.33E
167 Q7 **Jiangsu** *var.* Chiang-su, Jiangsu Sheng, Kiangsu, Su. ◈ *province* E China
Jiangsu Sheng *see* Jiangsu
167 O11 **Jiangxi** *var.* Chiang-hsi, Gan, Jiangxi Sheng, Kiangsi. ◈ *province* S China
Jiangxi Sheng *see* Jiangxi
166 I8 **Jiangyou** *prev.* Zhongba. Sichuan, C China 31.52N 104.52E
167 N9 **Jianli** *var.* Rongcheng. Hubei, C China 29.48N 112.45E
167 Q11 **Jian'ou** Fujian, SE China 27.04N 118.19E
169 S12 **Jianping** *var.* Yebaishou. Liaoning, NE China 41.13N 119.37E
Jianshe *see* Baiyü
166 L9 **Jianshi** *var.* Yezhou. Hubei, C China 30.37N 109.42E
133 V11 **Jian Xi** ≈ SE China
167 Q11 **Jianyang** Fujian, SE China 27.24N 118.06E
166 I9 **Jianyang** *var.* Jiancheng. Sichuan, C China 30.22N 104.31E
169 X10 **Jiaohe** Jilin, NE China 43.41N 127.20E
Jiaojiang *see* Taizhou
Jiaoxian *see* Jiaozhou
167 R5 **Jiaozhou** *prev.* Jiaoxian. Shandong, E China 36.17N 120.00E
167 N6 **Jiaozuo** Henan, C China 35.13N 113.13E
Jiashan *see* Mingguang
164 F8 **Jiashi** *var.* Payzawat. Xinjiang Uygur Zizhiqu, NW China 39.27N 76.45E
160 L9 **Jiāwān** Madhya Pradesh, C India 24.19N 82.16E
167 S9 **Jiaxing** Zhejiang, SE China 30.43N 120.46E
Jiayi *see* Chiai
169 X6 **Jiayin** *var.* Chaoyang. Heilongjiang, NE China 48.51N 130.24E
165 R8 **Jiayuguan** Gansu, N China 39.49N 98.27E
Jibhalanta *see* Uliastay
144 M4 **Jibli** Ar Raqqah, C Syria 35.49N 39.23E
118 H9 **Jibou** *Hung.* Zsibó. Sălaj, NW Romania 47.13N 23.17E
147 Z9 **Jibsh, Ra's al** *headland* E Oman 21.20N 59.23E
Jibuti *see* Djibouti
113 E15 **Jičín** *Ger.* Jitschin. Královéhradecký Kraj, N Czech Republic 50.27N 15.20E
146 K10 **Jiddah** *Eng.* Jedda. ● (Saudi Arabia) Makkah, W Saudi Arabia 21.33N 39.13E
147 W11 **Jiddat al Ḥarāsīs** *desert* C Oman
Jiesjavrre *see* Iešjávri
166 M4 **Jiexiu** Shanxi, C China 37.00N 111.50E
167 P14 **Jieyang** Guangdong, S China 23.33N 116.21E
121 F14 **Jieznas** Kaunas, S Lithuania 54.37N 24.10E
Jīfa', Bi'r *see* Jif'īyah, Bi'r
147 P15 **Jif'īyah, Bi'r** *var.* Bi'r Jīfa'. *well* C Yemen 14.48N 46.00E
79 W13 **Jigawa** ◈ *state* N Nigeria
152 J10 **Jigerbent** *Rus.* Dzhigirbent. Lebap Welaýaty, NE Turkmenistan 40.44N 61.56E
46 I7 **Jiguaní** Granma, E Cuba 20.24N 76.25W
165 T12 **Jigzhi** *var.* Chugqênsumdo. Qinghai, C China 33.23N 101.25E
Jih-k'a-tse *see* Xigazê
113 E18 **Jihlava** *Ger.* Iglau, *Pol.* Igława. Vysočina, C Czech Republic 49.22N 15.36E
113 E18 **Jihlava** *var.* Igel, *Ger.* Iglawa. ≈ S Czech Republic
Jihlavský Kraj *see* Vysočina
113 C18 **Jihočeský Kraj** *prev.* Budějovický Kraj. ◈ *region* S Czech Republic
113 G19 **Jihomoravský Kraj** *prev.* Brněnský Kraj. ◈ *region* SE Czech Republic
76 L5 **Jijel** *var.* Djidjel; *prev.* Djidjelli. NE Algeria 36.49N 5.43E
118 L9 **Jijia** ≈ N Romania
82 L13 **Jijiga** *It.* Giggiga. Somali, E Ethiopia 9.21N 42.53E
107 S12 **Jijona** *var.* Xixona. País Valenciano, E Spain 38.34N 0.29W
Jilf al Kabīr, Haḑabat al *see* Gilf Kebir Plateau
83 L18 **Jilib** *It.* Gelib. Jubbada Dhexe, S Somalia 0.18N 42.48E
169 W10 **Jilin** *var.* Chi-lin, Girin, Kirin; *prev.* Yungki, Yunki. Jilin, NE China 43.46N 126.31E
169 W10 **Jilin** *var.* Chi-lin, Girin, Ji, Jilin Sheng, Kirin. ◈ *province* NE China
169 W11 **Jilin Hada Ling** ▲▲ NE China
Jilin Sheng *see* Jilin
169 S4 **Jiliu He** ≈ NE China
107 Q6 **Jiloca** ≈ N Spain
83 I14 **Jīma** *var.* Jimma, *It.* Gimma. Oromo, C Ethiopia 7.41N 36.51E
46 M9 **Jimaní** W Dominican Republic 18.27N 71.51W
118 E11 **Jimbolia** *Ger.* Hatzfeld, *Hung.* Zsombolya. Timiş, W Romania 45.47N 20.43E
106 K16 **Jimena de la Frontera** Andalucía, S Spain 36.27N 5.28W
42 K7 **Jiménez** Chihuahua, N Mexico 27.09N 104.54W
43 N5 **Jiménez** Coahuila de Zaragoza, NE Mexico 29.04N 100.43W
43 P9 **Jiménez** *var.* Santander Jiménez. Tamaulipas, C Mexico 24.11N 98.29W
42 L10 **Jiménez del Teul** Zacatecas, C Mexico 23.13N 103.46W
79 Y14 **Jimeta** Adamawa, E Nigeria 9.16N 12.25E
Jimma *see* Jīma
164 M5 **Jimsar** Xinjiang Uygur Zizhiqu, NW China 44.05N 88.48E
20 I14 **Jim Thorpe** Pennsylvania, NE USA 40.51N 75.43W
Jin *see* Shanxi, China
Jin *see* Tianjin Shi, China
167 P5 **Jinan** *var.* Chinan, Chi-nan, Tsinan. Shandong, E China 36.42N 116.57E
Jin'an *see* Songpan
Jinbi *see* Dayao
165 T8 **Jinchang** Gansu, N China 38.31N 102.07E
167 N5 **Jincheng** Shanxi, C China 35.33N 112.51E
Jincheng *see* Wuding
Jinchengjiang *see* Hechi
158 I9 **Jīnd** *prev.* Jhind. Haryāna, NW India 29.25N 76.14E
191 Q11 **Jindabyne** New South Wales, SE Australia 36.28S 148.36E
113 O18 **Jindřichův Hradec** *Ger.* Neuhaus. Jihočeský Kraj, S Czech Republic 49.09N 15.01E
Jing *see* Beijing Shi, China
Jing *see* Jinghe, China
165 X10 **Jingchuan** Gansu, C China 35.19N 107.23E
167 Q10 **Jingdezhen** Jiangxi, S China 29.18N 117.18E
167 O12 **Jinggangshan** Jiangxi, S China 26.36N 114.11E
167 P3 **Jinghai** Tianjin Shi, E China 38.53N 116.45E
166 K6 **Jing He** ≈ C China
164 I4 **Jinghe** *var.* Jing. Xinjiang Uygur Zizhiqu, NW China 44.35N 82.55E
166 F15 **Jinghong** *var.* Yunjinghong. Yunnan, SW China 22.03N 100.55E
166 M9 **Jingmen** Hubei, C China 30.58N 112.09E
169 X10 **Jingpo Hu** ◎ NE China
166 M8 **Jing Shan** ▲▲ C China
165 V9 **Jingtai** *var.* Yitiaoshan. Gansu, C China 37.12N 104.06E
166 J14 **Jingxi** *var.* Xinjing. Guangxi Zhuangzu Zizhiqu, S China 23.10N 106.22E
Jing Xian *see* Jingzhou, Hunan
169 W11 **Jingyu** Jilin, NE China 42.23N 126.48E
165 V10 **Jingyuan** Gansu, C China 36.34N 104.43E
166 M9 **Jingzhou** *prev.* Shashi, Sha-shih, Shasi. Hubei, C China 30.21N 112.09E
166 L12 **Jingzhou** *var.* Jing Xian, Jingzhou Miaozu Dongzu Zizhixian, Quyang. Hunan, S China 26.34N 109.40E
Jingzhou Miaozu Dongzu Zizhixian *see* Jingzhou, Hunan
Jinhe *see* Jinping
167 R10 **Jinhua** Zhejiang, SE China 29.15N 119.36E
Jinhuan *see* Jianchuan
169 P13 **Jining** Nei Mongol Zizhiqu, N China 40.58N 113.08E
167 P5 **Jining** Shandong, E China 35.25N 116.35E
83 G18 **Jinja** S Uganda 0.27N 33.13E
167 R13 **Jinjiang** *var.* Qingyang. Fujian, SE China 24.45N 118.35E
167 O11 **Jin Jiang** ≈ S China
Jinjiang *see* Chengmai
176 W14 **Jin, Kepulauan** *island group* E Indonesia
Jinmen Dao *see* Chinmen Tao
44 J9 **Jinotega** Jinotega, NW Nicaragua 13.03N 85.59W
44 K7 **Jinotega** ◈ *department* N Nicaragua
44 J11 **Jinotepe** Carazo, SW Nicaragua 11.49N 86.11W
166 L13 **Jinping** *var.* Sanjiang. Guizhou, S China 26.42N 109.13E
166 H14 **Jinping** *var.* Jinhe. Yunnan, SW China 22.47N 103.12E
Jinsen *see* Inch'ŏn
166 J11 **Jinsha** Guizhou, S China 27.24N 106.16E
163 N12 **Jinsha Jiang** *Eng.* Yangtze. ≈ SW China
166 M10 **Jinshi** Hunan, S China 29.42N 111.46E
Jinshi *see* Xinning
168 I9 **Jinst** *var.* Bodĭ. Bayanhongor, C Mongolia 45.25N 100.33E
165 R7 **Jinta** Gansu, N China 40.01N 98.57E
179 Q12 **Jintotolo Channel** *channel* C Philippines
167 Q12 **Jin Xi** ≈ SE China
Jinxi *see* Huludao
Jinxian *see* Jinzhou
167 P6 **Jinxiang** Shandong, E China 35.07N 116.19E
167 P8 **Jinzhai** *var.* Meishan. Anhui, E China 31.42N 115.47E
167 N4 **Jinzhong** *var.* Yuci. Shanxi, C China 37.34N 112.45E
169 U14 **Jinzhou** *prev.* Jinxian. Liaoning, NE China 39.04N 121.45E
169 T12 **Jinzhou** *var.* Chin-chou, Chinchow; *prev.* Chinhsien. Liaoning, NE China 41.07N 121.06E
Jinzhu *see* Daocheng
144 H12 **Jinz, Qā' al** ◎ C Jordan
49 S8 **Jiparaná, Rio** ≈ W Brazil
58 A7 **Jipijapa** Manabí, W Ecuador 1.22S 80.34W
44 F8 **Jiquilisco** Usulután, S El Salvador 13.19N 88.34W
Jirgalanta *see* Hovd
153 S12 **Jirgatol** *Rus.* Dzhirgatal'. C Tajikistan 39.13N 71.09E
Jirjā *see* Girga
113 B15 **Jirkov** *Ger.* Görkau. Ústecký Kraj, NW Czech Republic 50.30N 13.28E
Jiroft *see* Sabzvārān
166 L11 **Jishou** Hunan, S China 28.20N 109.43E
Jisr ash Shadadi *see* Ash Shadādah
118 I14 **Jitaru** Olt, S Romania 44.27N 24.32E
Jitschin *see* Jičín
118 H14 **Jiu** *Ger.* Schil, Schyl, *Hung.* Zsil, Zsily. ≈ S Romania
167 R11 **Jiufeng Shan** ▲▲ SE China
167 P9 **Jiujiang** Jiangxi, S China 29.45N 115.58E
167 O10 **Jiuling Shan** ▲▲ S China
166 G10 **Jiulong** *var.* Garba, *Tib.* Gyaisi. Sichuan, C China 29.00N 101.30E
167 Q13 **Jiulong Jiang** ≈ SE China
167 Q12 **Jiulong Xi** ≈ SE China
165 R8 **Jiuquan** *var.* Suzhou. Gansu, N China 39.42N 98.36E
166 K17 **Jiusuo** Hainan, S China 18.25N 109.55E

◆ Country
● Country Capital
◇ Dependent Territory
○ Dependent Territory Capital
◈ Administrative Region
✕ International Airport
▲ Mountain
▲▲ Mountain Range
Volcano
≈ River
◎ Lake
⊡ Reservoir

169 *W10* **Jiutai** Jilin, NE China *44.01N 125.51E*
166 *K13* **Jiuwan Dashan** ▲▲ S China
166 *I7* **Jiuzhaigou** ***prev.*** Nanping. Sichuan, C China *33.25N 104.05E*
154 *I16* **Jīwani** Baluchistān, SW Pakistan *25.05N 61.46E*
169 *Y8* **Jixi** Heilongjiang, NE China *45.16N 131.01E*
169 *Y7* **Jixian** Heilongjiang, NE China *46.43N 131.10E*
166 *M5* **Jixian** ***var.*** Ji Xian. Shanxi, C China *36.15N 110.41E*
Jiza *see* Al Jīzah
147 *N13* **Jīzān** ***var.*** Qīzān. Jīzān, SW Saudi Arabia *17.49N 42.49E*
147 *N13* **Jīzān** ***var.*** Minṭaqat Jīzān. ◆ *province* SW Saudi Arabia
146 *K6* **Jizl, Wādī al** *dry watercourse* W Saudi Arabia
170 *Ff12* **Jizō-zaki** *headland* Honshū, SW Japan *35.34N 133.16E*
147 *U14* **Jiz', Wādī al** *dry watercourse* E Yemen
153 *O11* **Jizzax** ***Rus.*** Dzhizak. Jizzax Viloyati, C Uzbekistan *40.07N 67.47E*
153 *N10* **Jizzax Viloyati** ***Rus.*** Dzhizakskaya Oblast'. ◆ *province* C Uzbekistan
62 *I13* **Joaçaba** Santa Catarina, S Brazil *27.08S 51.30W*
Joal *see* Joal-Fadiout
78 *F11* **Joal-Fadiout** ***prev.*** Joal. W Senegal *14.16N 16.51W*
78 *E10* **João Barrosa** Boa Vista, E Cape Verde *16.01N 22.44W*
João Belo *see* Xai-Xai
João de Almeida *see* Chibia
61 *Q15* **João Pessoa** ***prev.*** Paraíba. *state capital* Paraíba, E Brazil *7.06S 34.52W*
27 *X7* **Joaquin** Texas, SW USA *31.58N 94.03W*
64 *K6* **Joaquín V.González** Salta, N Argentina *25.03S 64.06W*
Joazeiro *see* Juazeiro
Jo'burg *see* Johannesburg
111 *O7* **Jochberger Ache** ≈ W Austria
Jo-ch'iang *see* Ruoqiang
94 *K12* **Jock** Norrbotten, N Sweden *66.40N 22.45E*
44 *I5* **Jocón** Yoro, N Honduras *15.17N 86.55W*
107 *O13* **Jódar** Andalucía, S Spain *37.51N 3.18W*
158 *F12* **Jodhpur** Rājasthān, NW India *26.16N 73.01E*
101 *I19* **Jodoigne** Wallon Brabant, C Belgium *50.43N 4.52E*
97 *I22* **Jægerspris** Frederiksborg, E Denmark *55.52N 11.58E*
95 *O16* **Joensuu** Itä-Suomi, E Finland *62.36N 29.45E*
97 *C17* **Jæren** *physical region* S Norway
39 *W4* **Joes** Colorado, C USA *39.36N 102.40W*
203 *Z3* **Joe's Hill** *hill* Kiritimati, NE Kiribati *1.48N 157.19W*
171 *Jj13* **Jōetsu** ***var.*** Zyôetu. Niigata, Honshū, C Japan *37.09N 138.13E*
85 *M18* **Jofane** Inhambane, S Mozambique *21.16S 34.21E*
159 *R12* **Jogbani** Bihār, NE India *26.22N 87.16E*
120 *I5* **Jõgeva** ***Ger.*** Laisholm. Jõgevamaa, E Estonia *58.46N 26.23E*
120 *I4* **Jõgevamaa** ***off.*** Jõgeva Maakond. ◆ *province* E Estonia
161 *E18* **Jog Falls** *waterfall* Karnātaka, W India *14.16N 74.44E*
149 *S4* **Joghatāy** Khorāsān-Razavī, NE Iran *36.34N 57.00E*
159 *U12* **Jogīghopa** Assam, NE India *26.13N 90.34E*
158 *I7* **Jogindarnagar** Himāchal Pradesh, N India *31.55N 76.55E*
Jogjakarta *see* Yogyakarta
171 *Ii13* **Jōhana** Toyama, Honshū, SW Japan *36.30N 136.53E*
85 *J21* **Johannesburg** ***var.*** Egoli, Erautini, Gauteng, ***abbrev.*** Jo'burg. Gauteng, NE South Africa *26.10S 28.01E*
37 *T13* **Johannesburg** California, W USA *35.20N 117.37W*
85 *I21* **Johannesburg** ✕ Gauteng, NE South Africa *26.08S 28.01E*
Johannisburg *see* Pisz
155 *P14* **Johi** Sind, SE Pakistan *26.46N 67.28E*
57 *T13* **Johi Village** S Guyana *1.48N 58.33W*
34 *K13* **John Day** Oregon, NW USA *44.25N 118.57W*
34 *I11* **John Day River** ≈ Oregon, NW USA
20 *L14* **John F Kennedy** ✕ (New York) Long Island, New York, NE USA *40.39N 73.45W*
23 *V8* **John H.Kerr Reservoir** ***var.*** Buggs Island Lake, Kerr Lake. ⊠ North Carolina/Virginia, SE USA
39 *V6* **John Martin Reservoir** ⊠ Colorado, C USA
98 *K6* **John o'Groats** N Scotland, UK *58.37N 3.03W*
29 *P5* **John Redmond Reservoir** ⊠ Kansas, C USA
41 *Q7* **John River** ≈ Alaska, USA
28 *H6* **Johnson** Kansas, C USA *37.33N 101.46W*
20 *M7* **Johnson** Vermont, NE USA *44.39N 72.40W*
20 *D13* **Johnsonburg** Pennsylvania, NE USA *41.28N 78.37W*
20 *H11* **Johnson City** New York, NE USA *42.06N 75.54W*
23 *P8* **Johnson City** Tennessee, S USA *36.18N 82.21W*
27 *R10* **Johnson City** Texas, SW USA *30.16N 98.24W*
37 *S12* **Johnsondale** California, W USA *35.58N 118.32W*
8 *I8* **Johnsons Crossing** Yukon Territory, W Canada *60.30N 133.15W*
23 *T13* **Johnsonville** South Carolina, SE USA *33.50N 79.26W*
23 *Q13* **Johnston** South Carolina, SE USA *33.49N 81.48W*
199 *K6* **Johnston Atoll** ◇ *US unincorporated territory* C Pacific Ocean
183 *Q3* **Johnston Atoll** *atoll* C Pacific Ocean
32 *L17* **Johnston City** Illinois, N USA *37.49N 88.55W*
188 *K12* **Johnston, Lake** *salt lake* Western Australia
33 *S13* **Johnstown** Ohio, N USA *40.08N 82.39W*
20 *D15* **Johnstown** Pennsylvania, NE USA *40.19N 78.55W*
174 *Hh6* **Johor** ***var.*** Johore. ◆ *state* Peninsular Malaysia
Johor Baharu *see* Johor Bahru
174 *I6* **Johor Bahru** ***var.*** Johor Baharu, Johore Bahru. Johor, Peninsular Malaysia *1.28N 103.43E*
Johore *see* Johor
Johore Bahru *see* Johor Bahru
120 *K3* **Jõhvi** ***Ger.*** Jewe. Ida-Virumaa, NE Estonia *59.21N 27.25E*
105 *P7* **Joigny** Yonne, C France *47.58N 3.24E*
Joinvile *see* Joinville
62 *K12* **Joinville** ***var.*** Joinvile. Santa Catarina, S Brazil *26.19S 48.55W*
105 *R6* **Joinville** Haute-Marne, N France *48.26N 5.07E*
204 *H3* **Joinville Island** *island* Antarctica
43 *O15* **Jojutla** ***var.*** Jojutla de Juárez. Morelos, S Mexico *18.36N 99.11W*
Jojutla de Juárez *see* Jojutla
94 *I12* **Jokkmokk** ***Lapp.*** Dálvvadis. Norrbotten, N Sweden *66.35N 19.56E*
94 *L2* **Jökulsá á Dal** ≈ E Iceland
94 *K2* **Jökulsá á Fjöllum** ≈ NE Iceland
Jokyakarta *see* Yogyakarta
32 *M11* **Joliet** Illinois, N USA *41.33N 88.04W*
13 *O11* **Joliette** Québec, SE Canada *46.01N 73.27W*
179 *Pp17* **Jolo** Jolo Island, SW Philippines *6.02N 121.00E*
96 *D11* **Jølstravatnet** ◎ S Norway
174 *Ll15* **Jombang** ***prev.*** Djombang. Jawa, S Indonesia *7.33S 112.13E*
165 *R14* **Jomda** Xizang Zizhiqu, W China *31.26N 98.09E*
120 *G13* **Jonava** ***Ger.*** Janow, ***Pol.*** Janów. Kaunas, C Lithuania *55.04N 24.19E*
152 *L11* **Jondor** ***Rus.*** Zhondor. Buxoro Viloyati, C Uzbekistan *39.46N 64.11E*
165 *V11* **Jonê** Gansu, C China *34.36N 103.39E*
152 *K10* **Jongeldi** ***Rus.*** Dzhankel'dy. Buxoro Viloyati, C Uzbekistan *40.50N 63.16E*
29 *X9* **Jonesboro** Arkansas, C USA *35.50N 90.42W*
25 *S4* **Jonesboro** Georgia, SE USA *33.31N 84.21W*
32 *L17* **Jonesboro** Illinois, N USA *37.25N 89.19W*
24 *H5* **Jonesboro** Louisiana, S USA *32.14N 92.43W*
23 *P8* **Jonesboro** Tennessee, S USA *36.17N 82.28W*
21 *T6* **Jonesport** Maine, NE USA *44.33N 67.35W*
(0) *J4* **Jones Sound** *channel* Nunavut, N Canada
24 *I6* **Jonesville** Louisiana, S USA *31.37N 91.49W*
33 *Q10* **Jonesville** Michigan, N USA *41.58N 84.39W*
23 *Q11* **Jonesville** South Carolina, SE USA *34.49N 81.38W*
83 *F14* **Jonglei** Jonglei, SE Sudan *6.54N 31.19E*
83 *F14* **Jonglei** ***var.*** Gongoleh State. ◆ *state* SE Sudan
83 *F14* **Jonglei Canal** *canal* S Sudan
120 *F11* **Joniškėlis** Panevėžys, N Lithuania *56.02N 24.10E*
120 *F10* **Joniškis** ***Ger.*** Janischken. Šiauliai, N Lithuania *56.15N 23.36E*
97 *L19* **Jönköping** Jönköping, S Sweden *57.45N 14.10E*
97 *K20* **Jönköping** ◆ *county* S Sweden
13 *Q7* **Jonquière** Québec, SE Canada *48.25N 71.16W*
43 *V15* **Jonuta** Tabasco, SE Mexico *18.04N 92.03W*
104 *K12* **Jonzac** Charente-Maritime, W France *45.26N 0.25W*
29 *R7* **Joplin** Missouri, C USA *37.04N 94.30W*
35 *W8* **Jordan** Montana, NW USA *47.18N 106.54W*
144 *H12* **Jordan** ***off.*** Hashemite Kingdom of Jordan, ***Ar.*** Al Mamlakah al Urdunīyah al Hāshimīyah, Al Urdunn; ***prev.*** Transjordan. ◆ *monarchy* SW Asia
144 *G9* **Jordan** ***Ar.*** Urdunn, ***Heb.*** HaYarden. ≈ SW Asia
Jordan Lake *see* B.Everett Jordan Reservoir
113 *K17* **Jordanów** Małopolskie, S Poland *49.39N 19.51E*
34 *M15* **Jordan Valley** Oregon, NW USA *42.59N 117.03W*
144 *G9* **Jordan Valley** *valley* N Israel
59 *D15* **Jorge Chávez International** ***var.*** Lima. ✕ (Lima) Lima, W Peru *12.07S 77.01W*
115 *L23* **Jorgucat** ***var.*** Jergucati, Jorgucati. Gjirokastër, S Albania *39.57N 20.14E*
Jorgucati *see* Jorgucat
159 *X12* **Jorhāt** Assam, NE India *26.45N 94.09E*
95 *J14* **Jörn** Västerbotten, N Sweden *65.02N 20.04E*
39 *R14* **Jornada Del Muerto** *valley* New Mexico, SW USA
95 *N17* **Joroinen** Isä-Suomi, E Finland *62.10N 27.49E*
97 *C16* **Jørpeland** Rogaland, S Norway *59.01N 6.01E*
79 *W14* **Jos** Plateau, C Nigeria *9.58N 8.57E*
179 *Rr17* **Jose Abad Santos** ***var.*** Trinidad. Mindanao, S Philippines *5.51N 125.35E*
63 *F19* **José Batlle y Ordóñez** ***var.*** Batlle y Ordóñez. Florida, C Uruguay *33.28S 55.07W*
65 *H18* **José de San Martín** Chubut, S Argentina *44.03S 70.27W*
63 *E19* **José Enrique Rodó** ***var.*** Rodó, José E.Rodo; ***prev.*** Drabble, Drable. Soriano, SW Uruguay *33.43S 57.33W*
José E.Rodo *see* José Enrique Rodó
Josefsdorf *see* Žabalj
46 *C4* **José Martí** ✕ (La Habana) Cuidad de La Habana, N Cuba *23.03N 82.22W*
63 *F19* **José Pedro Varela** ***var.*** José P.Varela. Lavalleja, S Uruguay *33.30S 54.28W*
189 *N2* **Joseph Bonaparte Gulf** *gulf* N Australia
39 *N11* **Joseph City** Arizona, SW USA *34.56N 110.18W*
11 *O9* **Joseph, Lake** ◎ Newfoundland and Labrador, E Canada
12 *G13* **Joseph, Lake** ◎ Ontario, S Canada
194 *I11* **Josephstaal** Madang, N PNG *4.42S 144.59E*
José P.Varela *see* José Pedro Varela
61 *J14* **José Rodrigues** Pará, N Brazil *5.45S 51.19W*
158 *K9* **Joshīmath** Uttaranchal, N India *30.33N 79.34E*
27 *T7* **Joshua** Texas, SW USA *32.27N 97.23W*
37 *V15* **Joshua Tree** California, W USA *34.07N 116.18W*
79 *V14* **Jos Plateau** *plateau* C Nigeria
104 *H6* **Josselin** Morbihan, NW France *47.57N 2.35W*
Jos Sudarso *see* Yos Sudarso, Pulau
96 *E11* **Jostedalsbreen** *glacier* S Norway
96 *F12* **Jotunheimen** ▲▲ S Norway
144 *G7* **Joûnié** ***var.*** Juniyah. W Lebanon *33.54N 33.36E*
27 *R13* **Jourdanton** Texas, SW USA *28.55N 98.33W*
100 *L7* **Joure** ***Fris.*** De Jouwer. Friesland, N Netherlands *52.58N 5.48E*
95 *M18* **Joutsa** Länsi-Suomi, W Finland *61.46N 26.09E*
95 *N18* **Joutseno** Etelä-Suomi, S Finland *61.06N 28.30E*
94 *M12* **Joutsijärvi** Lappi, NE Finland *66.40N 28.00E*
110 *A9* **Joux, Lac de** ◎ W Switzerland
46 *D5* **Jovellanos** Matanzas, W Cuba *22.49N 81.14W*
159 *V13* **Jowai** Meghālaya, NE India *25.25N 92.21E*
Jōwat *see* Jabwot
Jowhar *see* Jawhar
149 *O12* **Jowkān** Fārs, S Iran
Jowzam *see* Javazm
155 *N2* **Jowzjān** ◆ *province* N Afghanistan
Józseffalva *see* Žabalj
J.Storm Thurmond Reservoir *see* Clark Hill Lake
47 *T6* **Juana Díaz** C Puerto Rico *18.03N 66.30W*
42 *L9* **Juan Aldama** Zacatecas, C Mexico *24.18N 103.23W*
(0) *E9* **Juan de Fuca Plate** *tectonic feature*
34 *F7* **Juan de Fuca, Strait of** *strait* Canada/USA
Juan Fernandez Islands *see* Juan Fernández, Islas
200 *Oo12* **Juan Fernández, Islas** ***Eng.*** Juan Fernandez Islands. *island group* W Chile
57 *O4* **Juangriego** Nueva Esparta, NE Venezuela *11.03N 63.58W*
58 *D11* **Juanjuí** ***var.*** Juanjuy. San Martín, N Peru *7.12S 76.45W*
Juanjuy *see* Juanjuí
95 *N16* **Juankoski** Itä-Suomi, C Finland *63.01N 28.24E*
Juan Lacaze *see* Juan L.Lacaze
63 *E20* **Juan L.Lacaze** ***var.*** Juan Lacaze, Puerto Sauce; ***prev.*** Sauce. Colonia, SW Uruguay *34.25S 57.25W*
64 *L5* **Juan Solá** Salta, N Argentina *23.30S 62.42W*
65 *F21* **Juan Stuven, Isla** *island* S Chile
61 *H16* **Juará** Mato Grosso, W Brazil *11.10S 57.28W*
43 *N7* **Juárez** ***var.*** Villa Juárez. Coahuila de Zaragoza, NE Mexico *27.39N 100.43W*
42 *C2* **Juárez, Sierra de** ▲▲ NW Mexico
61 *O15* **Juazeiro** ***prev.*** Joazeiro. Bahia, E Brazil *9.25S 40.30W*
61 *P14* **Juazeiro do Norte** Ceará, E Brazil *7.10S 39.18W*
83 *F15* **Juba** ***var.*** Jūbā. Bahr el Gabel, S Sudan *4.49N 31.34E*
83 *L17* **Juba** ***Amh.*** Genalē Wenz, ***It.*** Guiba, ***Som.*** Ganaane, Webi Jubba. ≈ Ethiopia/Somalia
204 *H2* **Jubany** *Argentinian research station* Antarctica *61.57S 58.23W*
Jubayl *see* Jbaïl
83 *L18* **Jubbada Dhexe** ***off.*** Gobolka Jubbada Dhexe. ◆ *region* SW Somalia
83 *K18* **Jubbada Hoose** ◆ *region* SW Somalia
Jubba, Webi *see* Juba
Jubbulpore *see* Jabalpur
Jubeil *see* Jbaïl
76 *B9* **Juby, Cap** *headland* SW Morocco *27.58N 12.56W*
107 *R10* **Júcar** ***var.*** Jucar. ≈ C Spain
42 *L12* **Juchipila** Zacatecas, C Mexico *21.25N 103.06W*
43 *S16* **Juchitán** ***var.*** Juchitán de Zaragosa. Oaxaca, SE Mexico *16.27N 95.00W*
Juchitán de Zaragosa *see* Juchitán
144 *G11* **Judaea** *cultural region* Israel/West Bank
144 *F11* **Judaean Hills** ***Heb.*** Haré Yehuda. *hill range* E Israel
144 *H8* **Judaydah** ***Fr.*** Jdaïdé. Dimashq, W Syria *33.17N 36.15E*
145 *P11* **Judayyidat Hāmir** S Iraq *31.29N 41.25E*
111 *U8* **Judenburg** Steiermark, C Austria *47.09N 14.42E*
35 *T8* **Judith River** ≈ Montana, NW USA
29 *V11* **Judsonia** Arkansas, C USA *35.16N 91.38W*
147 *P14* **Jufrah, Wādī al** *dry watercourse* NW Yemen
Jugar *see* Sêrxü
Jugoslavija/Jugoslavija, Savezna Republika *see* Serbia
44 *K10* **Juigalpa** Chontales, S Nicaragua *12.04N 85.21W*
167 *T13* **Juishui** C Taiwan *23.43N 121.28E*
102 *E9* **Juist** *island* NW Germany
61 *M21* **Juiz de Fora** Minas Gerais, SE Brazil *21.46S 43.22W*
64 *J5* **Jujuy** ***off.*** Provincia de Jujuy. ◆ *province* N Argentina
Jujuy *see* San Salvador de Jujuy
94 *J11* **Jukkasjärvi** ***Lapp.*** Čohkkiras. Norrbotten, N Sweden *67.52N 20.39E*
Jula *see* Gyula, Hungary
Jūlā *see* Jālū, Libya
39 *W2* **Julesburg** Colorado, C USA *40.59N 102.15W*
Julia Beterrae *see* Béziers
59 *I17* **Juliaca** Puno, SE Peru *15.32S 70.10W*
189 *U6* **Julia Creek** Queensland, C Australia *20.40S 141.49E*
37 *V17* **Julian** California, W USA *33.04N 116.36W*
100 *H7* **Julianadorp** Noord-Holland, NW Netherlands *52.53N 4.43E*
111 *S11* **Julian Alps** ***Ger.*** Julische Alpen, ***It.*** Alpi Giulie, ***Slvn.*** Julijske Alpe. ▲▲ Italy/Slovenia
57 *V11* **Juliana Top** ▲ C Surinam *3.39N 56.36W*
Julianehåb *see* Qaqortoq
Julijske Alpe *see* Julian Alps
42 *J6* **Julimes** Chihuahua, N Mexico *28.29N 105.21W*
Julio Briga *see* Bragança, Portugal
Juliobriga *see* Logroño, Spain
63 *G15* **Júlio de Castilhos** Rio Grande do Sul, S Brazil *29.14S 53.42W*
Juliomagus *see* Angers
Julische Alpen *see* Julian Alps
Jullundur *see* Jalandhar
153 *N11* **Juma** ***Rus.*** Dzhuma. Samarqand Viloyati, C Uzbekistan *39.43N 66.37E*
167 *O3* **Juma He** ≈ E China
83 *L18* **Jumboo** Jubbada Hoose, S Somalia *0.12S 42.34E*
37 *Y11* **Jumbo Peak** ▲ Nevada, W USA *36.12N 114.09W*
107 *R12* **Jumilla** Murcia, SE Spain *38.28N 1.19W*
159 *N10* **Jumlā** Mid Western, NW Nepal *29.22N 82.13E*
Jummoo *see* Jammu
Jumna *see* Yamuna
Jumporn *see* Chumphon
32 *K5* **Jump River** ≈ Wisconsin, N USA
160 *B11* **Jūnāgadh** ***var.*** Junagarh. Gujarāt, W India *21.31N 70.31E*
Junagarh *see* Jūnāgadh
167 *Q6* **Junan** ***prev.*** Shizilu. Shandong, E China *35.11N 118.47E*
64 *G11* **Juncal, Cerro** ▲ C Chile *33.03S 70.02W*
27 *Q10* **Junction** Texas, SW USA *30.29N 99.46W*
38 *K6* **Junction** Utah, W USA *38.14N 112.13W*
29 *O4* **Junction City** Kansas, C USA *39.01N 96.49W*
34 *F13* **Junction City** Oregon, NW USA *44.13N 123.12W*
62 *M10* **Jundiaí** São Paulo, S Brazil *23.10S 46.54W*
194 *E13* **June** ≈ W PNG
41 *X12* **Juneau** *state capital* Alaska, USA *58.13N 134.11W*
32 *M8* **Juneau** Wisconsin, N USA *43.22N 88.42W*
107 *U6* **Juneda** Cataluña, NE Spain *41.33N 0.49E*
191 *Q9* **Junee** New South Wales, SE Australia *34.51S 147.33E*
37 *R8* **June Lake** California, W USA *37.46N 119.04W*
Jungbunzlau *see* Mladá Boleslav
164 *L4* **Junggar Pendi** ***Eng.*** Dzungarian Basin. *basin* NW China
101 *N24* **Junglinster** Grevenmacher, C Luxembourg *49.43N 6.15E*
20 *F14* **Juniata River** ≈ Pennsylvania, NE USA
63 *B20* **Junín** Buenos Aires, E Argentina *34.36S 61.01W*
59 *E14* **Junín** Junín, C Peru *11.13S 76.01W*
59 *F14* **Junín** ***off.*** Departamento de Junín. ◆ *department* C Peru
65 *H15* **Junín de los Andes** Neuquén, W Argentina *39.57S 71.04W*
59 *D14* **Junín, Lago de** ◎ C Peru
Junīyah *see* Joûnié
Junkseylon *see* Phuket
166 *I11* **Junlian** Sichuan, C China *28.11N 104.31E*
27 *O11* **Juno** Texas, SW USA *30.09N 101.07W*
94 *J11* **Junosuando** ***Lapp.*** Čunusavvon. Norrbotten, N Sweden *67.25N 22.28E*
95 *H16* **Junsele** Västernorrland, C Sweden *63.42N 16.54E*
Junten *see* Sunch'ŏn
34 *L14* **Juntura** Oregon, NW USA *43.43N 118.05W*
95 *N14* **Juntusranta** Oulu, E Finland *65.12N 29.30E*
120 *H11* **Juodupė** Panevėžys, NE Lithuania *56.07N 25.37E*
121 *H14* **Juozapinės Kalnas** ▲ SE Lithuania *54.29N 25.27E*
101 *K19* **Juprelle** Liège, E Belgium *50.43N 5.31E*
82 *D13* **Jur** ≈ C Sudan
105 *S9* **Jura** ◆ *department* E France
110 *C7* **Jura** ◆ *canton* NW Switzerland
110 *B8* **Jura** ***var.*** Jura Mountains. ▲▲ France/Switzerland
98 *G12* **Jura** *island* SW Scotland, UK
Juraciszki *see* Yuratsishki
56 *C8* **Juradó** Chocó, NW Colombia *7.07N 77.45W*
Jura Mountains *see* Jura
98 *G12* **Jura, Sound of** *strait* W Scotland, UK
145 *V15* **Juraybīyāt, Bi'r** *well* S Iraq *29.13N 45.28E*
120 *E13* **Jurbarkas** ***Ger.*** Georgenburg, Jurburg. Tauragė, W Lithuania *55.04N 22.45E*
101 *F20* **Jurbise** Hainaut, SW Belgium *50.33N 3.54E*
Jurburg *see* Jurbarkas
120 *F9* **Jūrmala** Rīga, C Latvia *56.56N 23.42E*
176 *Ww13* **Jursian, Pulau** *island* E Indonesia
60 *D13* **Juruá** Amazonas, NW Brazil *3.08S 65.59W*
50 *F7* **Juruá, Rio** ***var.*** Río Yuruá. ≈ Brazil/Peru
61 *G16* **Juruena** Mato Grosso, W Brazil *10.32S 58.38W*
61 *G16* **Juruena** ≈ W Brazil
171 *Mm8* **Jūsan-ko** ◎ Honshū, C Japan
27 *O6* **Justiceburg** Texas, SW USA *32.57N 101.07W*
Justinianopolis *see* Kirşehir
64 *K11* **Justo Daract** San Luis, C Argentina *33.52S 65.12W*
61 *C14* **Jutaí** Amazonas, W Brazil *5.10S 68.45W*
60 *C13* **Jutaí, Rio** ≈ NW Brazil
102 *N13* **Jüterbog** Brandenburg, E Germany *51.58N 13.06E*
44 *E6* **Jutiapa** Jutiapa, S Guatemala *14.18N 89.52W*
44 *A3* **Jutiapa** ***off.*** Departamento de Jutiapa. ◆ *department* SE Guatemala
44 *J6* **Juticalpa** Olancho, C Honduras *14.39N 86.12W*
84 *I13* **Jutila** North Western, NW Zambia *12.33S 26.09E*
Jutland *see* Jylland
86 *F8* **Jutland Bank** *undersea feature* SE North Sea
95 *N16* **Juuka** Itä-Suomi, E Finland *63.12N 29.16E*
95 *N17* **Juva** Isä-Suomi, SE Finland *61.55N 27.54E*
Juvavum *see* Salzburg
46 *A6* **Juventud, Isla de la** ***var.*** Isla de Pinos, ***Eng.*** Isle of Youth; ***prev.*** The Isle of the Pines. *island* W Cuba
167 *Q5* **Juxian** ***var.*** Chengyang, Ju Xian. Shandong, E China *35.33N 118.45E*
167 *P6* **Juye** Shandong, E China *35.25N 116.04E*
115 *O15* **Južna Morava** ***Ger.*** Südliche Morava. ≈ SE Serbia
85 *H20* **Jwaneng** Southern, S Botswana *24.35S 24.45E*
97 *I23* **Jyderup** Vestsjælland, E Denmark *55.40N 11.25E*
97 *F22* **Jylland** ***Eng.*** Jutland. *peninsula* W Denmark
Jyrgalan *see* Dzhergalan
95 *M17* **Jyväskylä** Länsi-Suomi, W Finland *62.07N 25.47E*

K

155 *X3* **K2** ***Chin.*** Qogir Feng, ***Eng.*** Mount Godwin Austen. ▲ China/Pakistan *35.55N 76.30E*
40 *D9* **Ka'a'awa** ***var.*** Kaaawa. O'ahu, Hawai'i, USA, C Pacific Ocean *21.33N 157.51W*
83 *G16* **Kaabong** NE Uganda *3.30N 34.07E*
Kaaden *see* Kadaň
57 *V9* **Kaaimanston** Sipaliwini, N Surinam *5.06N 56.04W*
Kaakhka *see* Kaka
Kaala *see* Caála
197 *H5* **Kaala-Gomen** Province Nord, W New Caledonia *20.40S 164.24E*
94 *L9* **Kaamanen** ***Lapp.*** Gámas. Lappi, N Finland *69.04N 27.16E*
Kaapstad *see* Cape Town
Kaarasjoki *see* Karasjok
Kaaresuanto *see* Karesuando
94 *J10* **Kaaresuvanto** ***Lapp.*** Gárassavon. Lappi, N Finland *68.28N 22.29E*
95 *K19* **Kaarina** Länsi-Suomi, W Finland *60.24N 22.25E*
101 *I14* **Kaatsheuvel** Noord-Brabant, S Netherlands *51.39N 5.01E*
95 *N16* **Kaavi** Itä-Suomi, C Finland *62.58N 28.30E*
Ka'a'wa *see* Kaaawa
176 *Y15* **Kaba** Papua, E Indonesia *7.34S 138.27E*
Kaba *see* Habahe
175 *Q13* **Kabaena, Pulau** *island* C Indonesia
175 *Q13* **Kabaena, Selat** *strait* Sulawesi, C Indonesia
Kabakly *see* Gabakly
78 *J14* **Kabala** N Sierra Leone *9.40N 11.36W*
83 *E19* **Kabale** SW Uganda *1.15S 29.58E*
57 *U10* **Kabalebo Rivier** ≈ W Surinam
81 *N22* **Kabalo** Katanga, SE Dem. Rep. Congo *6.01S 26.55E*
151 *W13* **Kabanbay** ***Kaz.*** Qabanbay ***prev.*** Andreyevka, ***Kaz.*** Andreevka. Almaty, SE Kazakhstan *45.49N 80.34E*
81 *O21* **Kabambare** Maniema, E Dem. Rep. Congo *4.40S 27.40E*
197 *K15* **Kabara** ***prev.*** Kambara. *island* Lau Group, E Fiji
Kabardino-Balkaria *see* Kabardino-Balkarskaya Respublika
130 *M15* **Kabardino-Balkarskaya Respublika** ***Eng.*** Kabardino-Balkaria. ◆ *autonomous republic* SW Russian Federation
81 *O19* **Kabare** Sud Kivu, E Dem. Rep. Congo *2.13S 28.40E*
176 *Uu8* **Kabarei** Papua, E Indonesia *0.01S 130.58E*
179 *Q16* **Kabasalan** Mindanao, S Philippines *7.46N 122.49E*
79 *U15* **Kabba** Kogi, S Nigeria *7.48N 6.07E*
94 *I13* **Kåbdalis** ***Lapp.*** Goabddális. Norrbotten, N Sweden *66.08N 20.03E*
144 *M6* **Kabd aş Şārim** *hill range* E Syria
12 *B7* **Kabenung Lake** ◎ Ontario, S Canada
31 *W3* **Kabetogama Lake** ◎ Minnesota, N USA
Kabia, Pulau *see* Kabin, Pulau
81 *M22* **Kabinda** Kasai Oriental, SE Dem. Rep. Congo *6.09S 24.28E*
Kabinda *see* Cabinda
175 *P13* **Kabin, Pulau** ***var.*** Pulau Kabia. *island* W Indonesia
175 *Rr16* **Kabir** Pulau Pantar, S Indonesia *8.15S 124.12E*
155 *T10* **Kabīrwāla** Punjab, E Pakistan *30.24N 71.51E*
176 *U8* **Kable Bet** Papua, E Indonesia *0.24S 129.54E*
80 *I13* **Kabo** Ouham, NW Central African Republic *7.43N 18.38E*
155 *Q5* **Kābol** ***var.*** Kabul, ***Pash.*** Kābul. ● (Afghanistan) Kābol, E Afghanistan *34.34N 69.07E*
155 *Q5* **Kābol** ***Eng.*** Kabul, ***Pash.*** Kābul. ◆ *province* E Afghanistan
155 *Q5* **Kābol** ✕ Kābol, E Afghanistan *34.31N 69.10E*
85 *H14* **Kabompo** North Western, W Zambia *13.36S 24.10E*
85 *H14* **Kabompo** ≈ W Zambia
81 *M22* **Kabongo** Katanga, SE Dem. Rep. Congo *7.19S 25.34E*
123 *Kk12* **Kaboudia, Rass** *headland* E Tunisia *35.13N 11.09E*
149 *U4* **Kabūd Gonbad** Khorāsān-Razavī, NE Iran *37.01N 59.46E*
148 *L5* **Kabūd Rāhang** Hamadān, W Iran *35.12N 48.43E*
84 *L12* **Kabuko** Northern, NE Zambia *11.31S 31.16E*
155 *R5* **Kabul** ***var.*** Daryā-ye Kābul. ≈ Afghanistan/Pakistan ***see also*** Kābul, Daryā-ye
Kābul *see* Kābol
155 *S5* **Kābul, Daryā-ye** ***var.*** Kabul. ≈ Afghanistan/Pakistan ***see also*** Kabul
81 *O25* **Kabunda** Katanga, SE Dem. Rep. Congo *12.21S 29.14E*
175 *Ss4* **Kaburuang, Pulau** *island* Kepulauan Talaud, N Indonesia
82 *G8* **Kabushiya** River Nile, NE Sudan *16.54N 33.40E*
85 *J14* **Kabwe** Central, C Zambia *14.28S 28.25E*
194 *K12* **Kabwum** Morobe, C PNG *6.07S 147.11E*
115 *N17* **Kačanik** Serbia, S Serbia *42.13N 21.16E*
176 *U8* **Kacepi** Pulau Gebe, E Indonesia *0.05S 129.30E*
120 *F13* **Kačerginė** Kaunas, C Lithuania *54.55N 23.40E*
119 *S13* **Kacha** Respublika Krym, S Ukraine *44.46N 33.33E*
160 *A10* **Kachchh, Gulf of** ***var.*** Gulf of Cutch, Gulf of Kutch. *gulf* W India
160 *I11* **Kachchhīdhāna** Madhya Pradesh, C India *21.33N 78.54E*
155 *Q11* **Kachchh, Rann of** ***var.*** Rann of Kachh, Rann of Kutch. *salt marsh* India/Pakistan
41 *Q13* **Kachemak Bay** *bay* Alaska, USA
Kachh, Rann of *see* Kachchh, Rann of
79 *V14* **Kachia** Kaduna, C Nigeria *9.52N 8.00E*
178 *Gg2* **Kachin State** ◆ *state* N Burma
151 *T7* **Kachiry** Pavlodar, NE Kazakhstan *53.04N 76.05E*
126 *Jj15* **Kachug** Irkutskaya Oblast', S Russian Federation *53.52N 105.54E*
143 *Q11* **Kaçkar Dağları** ▲▲ NE Turkey
161 *C21* **Kadamatt Island** *island* Lakshadweep, India, N Indian Ocean
113 *B15* **Kadaň** ***Ger.*** Kaaden.Ústecký Kraj, NW Czech Republic *50.22N 13.14E*
178 *Gg12* **Kadan Kyun** ***prev.*** King Island. *island* Mergui Archipelago, S Burma
197 *I16* **Kadavu** ***prev.*** Kandavu. *island* S Fiji
197 *I15* **Kadavu Passage** *channel* S Fiji
81 *G16* **Kadéï** ≈ Cameroon/Central African Republic
Kadhimain *see* Al Kāẓimīyah
Kadijica *see* Kadiytsa
116 *M13* **Kadıköy Barajı** ⊠ NW Turkey
190 *I8* **Kadina** South Australia *33.59S 137.43E*
142 *H15* **Kadınhanı** Konya, C Turkey *38.15N 32.13E*
78 *M14* **Kadiolo** Sikasso, S Mali *10.30N 5.43W*
142 *L16* **Kadirli** Osmaniye, S Turkey *37.22N 36.04E*
116 *G11* **Kadiytsa** ***Mac.*** Kadijica. ▲ Bulgaria/FYR Macedonia *41.48N 22.58E*
30 *L10* **Kadoka** South Dakota, N USA *43.49N 101.30W*
131 *N5* **Kadom** Ryazanskaya Oblast', W Russian Federation *54.35N 42.27E*
85 *K16* **Kadoma** ***prev.*** Gatooma. Mashonaland West, C Zimbabwe *18.18S 29.55E*
82 *E12* **Kadugli** Southern Kordofan, S Sudan *11.00N 29.44E*
79 *V14* **Kaduna** Kaduna, C Nigeria *10.32N 7.25E*
79 *V14* **Kaduna** ◆ *state* C Nigeria
79 *V15* **Kaduna** ≈ N Nigeria
128 *K14* **Kaduy** Vologodskaya Oblast', NW Russian Federation *59.10N 37.11E*
160 *E13* **Kadwa** ≈ W India
127 *Nn9* **Kadykchan** Magadanskaya Oblast', E Russian Federation *62.54N 146.53E*
Kadzharan *see* K'ajaran
129 *T7* **Kadzherom** Respublika Komi, NW Russian Federation *64.42N 55.51E*
153 *X8* **Kadzhi-Say** ***Kir.*** Kajisay. Issyk-Kul'skaya Oblast', NE Kyrgyzstan *42.07N 77.10E*
78 *I10* **Kaédi** Gorgol, S Mauritania *16.12N 13.31W*
80 *G12* **Kaélé** Extrême-Nord, N Cameroon *10.09N 14.25E*
40 *C9* **Ka'ena Point** ***var.*** Kaena Point *headland* O'ahu, Hawai'i, USA, C Pacific Ocean *21.34N 158.16W*
192 *J2* **Kaeo** Northland, North Island, NZ *35.03S 173.40E*
169 *X14* **Kaesŏng** ***var.*** Kaesŏng-si. S North Korea *37.57N 126.30E*
Kaesŏng-si *see* Kaesŏng
Kaewieng *see* Kavieng
81 *L24* **Kafakumba** Katanga, S Dem. Rep. Congo *9.39S 23.43E*
Kafan *see* Kapan
79 *V14* **Kafanchan** Kaduna, C Nigeria *9.32N 8.18E*
Kaffa *see* Feodosiya
78 *G11* **Kaffrine** C Senegal *14.07N 15.27W*
Kafiau *see* Kofiau, Pulau
Kafiréas, Akrotírio *see* Ntóro, Kávo
117 *I19* **Kafiréos, Stenó** *strait* Évvoia/Kykládes, Greece, Aegean Sea
Kafirnigan *see* Kofarnihon
Kafo *see* Kafu
Kafr ash Shaykh/Kafrel Sheik *see* Kafr el Sheikh
77 *W7* **Kafr el Sheikh** ***var.*** Kafr ash Shaykh, Kafrel Sheik. N Egypt *31.08N 30.58E*
83 *F17* **Kafu** ***var.*** Kafo. ≈ W Uganda
85 *J15* **Kafue** Lusaka, SE Zambia *15.43S 28.10E*
85 *I14* **Kafue** ≈ C Zambia
69 *T13* **Kafue Flats** *plain* C Zambia
171 *I13* **Kaga** Ishikawa, Honshū, SW Japan *36.18N 136.19E*
81 *J14* **Kaga Bandoro** ***prev.*** Fort-Crampel. Nana-Grébizi, C Central African Republic *6.54N 19.09E*
83 *E18* **Kagadi** W Uganda *0.57N 30.52E*
40 *H17* **Kagalaska Island** *island* Aleutian Islands, Alaska, USA
Kagan *see* Kogon
Kaganovichabad *see* Kolkhozobod
Kagarlyk *see* Kaharlyk
170 *F15* **Kagawa** ***off.*** Kagawa-ken. ◆ *prefecture* Shikoku, SW Japan
160 *J13* **Kagaznagar** Andhra Pradesh, C India *19.25N 79.30E*
95 *J14* **Kåge** Västerbotten, N Sweden *64.49N 21.00E*
83 *E19* **Kagera** ***var.*** Ziwa Magharibi, ***Eng.*** West Lake. ◆ *region* NW Tanzania
83 *E19* **Kagera** ***var.*** Akagera. ≈ Rwanda/Tanzania ***see also*** Akagera
78 *L5* **Kâgheṭ** ***var.*** Karet. *physical region* N Mauritania
Kagi *see* Chiai
143 *S12* **Kağızman** Kars, NE Turkey *40.08N 43.10E*
196 *I6* **Kagman Point** *headland* Saipan, S Northern Mariana Islands
170 *Bb15* **Kagoshima** ***var.*** Kagosima. Kagoshima, Kyūshū, SW Japan *31.36N 130.33E*
172 *Qq14* **Kagoshima** ***off.*** Kagoshima-ken, ***var.*** Kagosima. ◆ *prefecture* Kyūshū, SW Japan
170 *Bb16* **Kagoshima-wan** *bay* SW Japan
Kagosima *see* Kagoshima
194 *H12* **Kagua** Southern Highlands, W PNG *6.25S 143.48E*
Kagul *see* Cahul
Kagul, Ozero *see* Kahul, Ozero
40 *B8* **Kahala Point** *headland* Kaua'i, Hawai'i, USA, C Pacific Ocean *22.08N 159.17W*
83 *F21* **Kahama** Shinyanga, NW Tanzania *3.48S 32.36E*
119 *P5* **Kaharlyk** ***Rus.*** Kagarlyk. Kyyivs'ka Oblast', N Ukraine *49.49N 30.49E*
174 *Mm10* **Kahayan, Sungai** ≈ Borneo, C Indonesia
81 *I22* **Kahemba** Bandundu, SW Dem. Rep. Congo *7.20S 19.00E*
193 *A23* **Kaherekoau Mountains** ▲▲ South Island, NZ
149 *W14* **Kahīrī** ***var.*** Kūhīrī. Sīstān va Balūchestān, SE Iran *26.55N 61.04E*
103 *L16* **Kahla** Thüringen, C Germany *50.49N 11.33E*
103 *G15* **Kahler Asten** ▲ W Germany *51.11N 8.32E*
155 *Q4* **Kahmard, Daryā-ye** ***prev.*** Darya-i-Surkhab. ≈ NE Afghanistan
149 *T13* **Kahnūj** Kermān, SE Iran *27.59N 57.40E*
29 *V1* **Kahoka** Missouri, C USA *40.25N 91.43W*
40 *E10* **Kaho'olawe** ***var.*** Kahoolawe *island* Hawai'i, USA, C Pacific Ocean
142 *M16* **Kahramanmaraş** ***var.*** Kahraman Maraş, Maraş, Marash. Kahramanmaraş, S Turkey *37.34N 36.54E*
142 *L15* **Kahramanmaraş** ***var.*** Kahraman Maraş, Maraş, Marash. ◆ *province* C Turkey
Kahror/Kahror Pakka *see* Karor Pacca
143 *N15* **Kâhta** Adıyaman, S Turkey *37.48N 38.34E*
40 *D8* **Kahuku** O'ahu, Hawai'i, USA, C Pacific Ocean *21.40N 157.57W*
40 *D8* **Kahuku Point** *headland* O'ahu, Hawai'i, USA, C Pacific Ocean *21.42N 157.59W*
118 *M12* **Kahul, Ozero** ***var.*** Lacul Cahul, ***Rus.*** Ozero Kagul. ◎ Moldova/Ukraine
149 *V11* **Kahūrak** Sīstān va Balūchestān, SE Iran *29.25N 59.37E*
192 *G13* **Kahurangi Point** *headland* South Island, NZ *40.41S 171.57E*
155 *V6* **Kahūta** Punjab, E Pakistan *33.34N 73.22E*
79 *S14* **Kaiama** Kwara, W Nigeria *9.37N 3.58E*
194 *J12* **Kaiapit** Morobe, C PNG *6.16S 146.13E*
193 *I18* **Kaiapoi** Canterbury, South Island, NZ *43.22S 172.39E*
38 *K9* **Kaibab Plateau** *plain* Arizona, SW USA
171 *Gg14* **Kaibara** Hyōgo, Honshū, SW Japan *35.06N 135.03E*
176 *Vv13* **Kai Besar, Pulau** *island* Kepulauan Kai, E Indonesia
38 *L9* **Kaibito Plateau** *plain* Arizona, SW USA
164 *K6* **Kaidu He** ***var.*** Karaxahar. ≈ NW China
57 *S10* **Kaieteur Falls** *waterfall* C Guyana *5.04N 59.32W*
167 *O6* **Kaifeng** Henan, C China *34.46N 114.19E*
192 *J3* **Kaihu** Northland, North Island, NZ *35.47S 173.39E*
Kaihua *see* Wenshan
176 *V13* **Kai Kecil, Pulau** *island* Kepulauan Kai, E Indonesia

◆ Country
● Country Capital
◇ Dependent Territory
○ Dependent Territory Capital
◆ Administrative Region
✕ International Airport
▲ Mountain
▲▲ Mountain Range
Volcano
≈ River
◎ Lake
⊠ Reservoir

Kai, Kepulauan – Kangmar

176 V14 **Kai, Kepulauan** *prev.* Kei Islands. *island group* Maluku, SE Indonesia
192 J3 **Kaikohe** Northland, North Island, NZ *35.25S 173.48E*
193 J16 **Kaikoura** Canterbury, South Island, NZ *42.21S 173.40E*
193 J16 **Kaikoura Peninsula** *peninsula* South Island, NZ
Kailas Range *see* Gangdisê Shan
166 K12 **Kaili** Guizhou, S China *26.34N 107.58E*
40 F10 **Kailua** Maui, Hawai'i, USA, C Pacific Ocean *20.53N 156.13W*
Kailua *see* Kalaoa
40 G11 **Kailua-Kona** *var.* Kona. Hawai'i, USA, C Pacific Ocean *19.43N 155.58W*
194 E13 **Kaim** ↝ W PNG
176 Y13 **Kaima** Papua, E Indonesia *5.36S 138.39E*
192 M7 **Kaimai Range** ⛰ North Island, NZ
116 E13 **Kaïmaktsalán** ▲ Greece/FYR Macedonia *40.57N 21.48E*
193 C20 **Kaimanawa Mountains** ⛰ North Island, NZ
120 E4 **Käina** *Ger.* Keinis; *prev.* Keina. Hiiumaa, W Estonia *58.49N 22.45E*
111 V7 **Kainach** ↝ SE Austria
170 G16 **Kainan** Tokushima, Shikoku, SW Japan *33.36N 134.20E*
170 Ff16 **Kainan** Wakayama, Honshū, SW Japan *34.10N 135.11E*
194 J12 **Kainantu** Eastern Highlands, C PNG *6.16S 145.49E*
153 U7 **Kaindy** *Kir.* Kayyngdy. Chuyskaya Oblast', N Kyrgyzstan *42.48N 73.39E*
79 T14 **Kainji Dam** *dam* W Nigeria *9.52N 4.36E*
Kainji Lake *see* Kainji Reservoir
79 T14 **Kainji Reservoir** *var.* Kainji Lake. ⊠ W Nigeria
194 J14 **Kaintiba** *var.* Kamina. Gulf, S PNG *7.29S 146.04E*
94 K12 **Kainulaisjärvi** Norrbotten, N Sweden *67.00N 22.31E*
192 K5 **Kaipara Harbour** *harbor* North Island, NZ
158 I10 **Kairāna** Uttar Pradesh, N India *29.24N 77.10E*
194 G9 **Kairiru Island** *island* NW PNG
76 M6 **Kairouan** *var.* Al Qayrawān. E Tunisia *35.45N 10.11E*
Kaisaria *see* Kayseri
103 F20 **Kaiserslautern** Rheinland-Pfalz, SW Germany *49.27N 7.46E*
120 G13 **Kaišiadorys** Kaunas, S Lithuania *54.51N 24.27E*
192 I2 **Kaitaia** Northland, North Island, NZ *35.07S 173.13E*
193 E24 **Kaitangata** Otago, South Island, NZ *46.15S 169.49E*
158 I9 **Kaithal** Haryāna, NW India *29.46N 76.20E*
Kaitong *see* Tongyu
174 J11 **Kait, Tanjung** *headland* Sumatera, W Indonesia *3.13S 106.03E*
40 E9 **Kaiwi Channel** *channel* Hawai'i, USA, C Pacific Ocean
166 K9 **Kaixian** *var.* Hanfeng. Sichuan, C China *31.13N 108.25E*
169 V11 **Kaiyuan** *var.* K'ai-yüan. Liaoning, NE China *42.36N 124.03E*
166 H14 **Kaiyuan** Yunnan, SW China *23.42N 103.13E*
41 O9 **Kaiyuh Mountains** ⛰ Alaska, USA
95 M15 **Kajaani** *Swe.* Kajana. Oulu, C Finland *64.16N 27.46E*
155 N7 **Kajakī, Band-e** ◎ C Afghanistan
Kajan *see* Kayan, Sungai
Kajana *see* Kajaani
143 V13 **K'ajaran** *Rus.* Kadzharan. SE Armenia *39.10N 46.09E*
Kajisay *see* Kadzhi-Say
115 O20 **Kajmakčalan** ▲ S FYR Macedonia *40.57N 21.48E*
Kajnar *see* Kaynar
155 N6 **Kajrān** Dāikondī, C Afghanistan *33.12N 65.28E*
155 N5 **Kaj Rūd** ↝ C Afghanistan
152 G14 **Kaka** *Rus.* Kaakhka. Ahal Welaýaty, S Turkmenistan *37.19N 59.36E*
10 C12 **Kakabeka Falls** Ontario, S Canada *48.24N 89.40W*
85 F23 **Kakamas** Northern Cape, W South Africa *28.45S 20.33E*
83 H18 **Kakamega** Western, W Kenya *0.13N 34.43E*
114 H13 **Kakanj** Federacija Bosna I Hercegovina, Bosnia and Herzegovina *44.06N 18.07E*
193 F22 **Kakanui Mountains** ⛰ South Island, NZ
192 K11 **Kakaramea** Taranaki, North Island, NZ *39.42S 174.27E*
78 J16 **Kakata** C Liberia *6.34N 10.19W*
192 M11 **Kakatahi** Manawatu-Wanganui, North Island, NZ *39.40S 175.20E*
115 M23 **Kakavi** Gjirokastër, S Albania *39.55N 20.19E*
153 O14 **Kakaydi** Surkhondaryo Viloyati, S Uzbekistan *37.37N 67.30E*
170 Ee13 **Kake** Hiroshima, Honshū, SW Japan *34.37N 132.17E*
41 X13 **Kake** Kupreanof Island, Alaska, USA *56.58N 133.57W*
175 R12 **Kakea** Pulau Wowoni, C Indonesia *4.09S 123.06E*
171 Ii17 **Kakegawa** Shizuoka, Honshū, S Japan *34.58N 138.21E*
172 Qq13 **Kakeromajima** Kagoshima, SW Japan
149 T6 **Kākhak** *var.* Kākhk. Khorāsān-Razavī, E Iran
120 L11 **Kakhanavichy** *Rus.* Kokhanovichi. Vitsyebskaya Voblasts', N Belarus *55.57N 28.06E*
41 P13 **Kakhonak** Alaska, USA *59.26N 154.48W*
119 S10 **Kakhovka** Khersons'ka Oblast', S Ukraine *46.48N 33.30E*
119 U9 **Kakhovs'ka Vodoskhovyshche** *Rus.* Kakhovskoye Vodokhranilishche. ⊠ SE Ukraine
Kakhovskoye Vodokhranilishche *see* Kakhovs'ka Vodoskhovyshche
119 T11 **Kakhovs'kyy Kanal** *canal* S Ukraine
Kakia *see* Khakhea
161 L16 **Kākināda** *prev.* Cocanada. Andhra Pradesh, E India *16.55N 82.13E*
Käkisalmi *see* Priozersk
170 G14 **Kakogawa** Hyōgo, Honshū, SW Japan *34.49N 134.52E*
83 F18 **Kakoge** C Uganda *1.03N 32.30E*
151 O7 **Kak, Ozero** ◎ N Kazakhstan
Ka-Krem *see* Malyy Yenisey
Kakshaal-Too, Khrebet *see* Kokshaal-Tau
41 S5 **Kaktovik** Alaska, USA *70.07N 143.37W*
171 Ll13 **Kakuda** Miyagi, Honshū, C Japan *37.59N 140.47E*
171 M11 **Kakunodate** Akita, Honshū, C Japan *39.36N 140.38E*
Kalaallit Nunaat *see* Greenland
155 T7 **Kālābāgh** Punjab, E Pakistan *32.58N 71.30E*
175 Rr16 **Kalabahi** Pulau Alor, S Indonesia *8.13S 124.31E*
196 I5 **Kalabera** Saipan, S Northern Mariana Islands
85 G14 **Kalabo** Western, W Zambia *14.52S 22.33E*
130 M9 **Kalach** Voronezhskaya Oblast', W Russian Federation *50.24N 41.00E*
125 G13 **Kalachinsk** Omskaya Oblast', C Russian Federation *55.03N 74.30E*
131 N10 **Kalach-na-Donu** Volgogradskaya Oblast', SW Russian Federation *48.45N 43.29E*
177 F5 **Kaladan** ↝ W Burma
12 K14 **Kaladar** Ontario, SE Canada *44.38N 77.06W*
40 G13 **Ka Lae** *var.* South Cape, South Point. *headland* Hawai'i, USA, C Pacific Ocean *18.54N 155.40W*
85 G19 **Kalahari Desert** *desert* Southern Africa
40 B8 **Kalāheo** *var.* Kalaheo. Kaua'i, Hawai'i, USA, C Pacific Ocean *21.55N 159.31W*
Kalaikhum *see* Qal'aikhum
Kala-i-Mor *see* Galaýmor
95 K15 **Kalajoki** Oulu, W Finland *64.15N 24.00E*
Kalak *see* Eski Kaļak
Kal al Sraghna *see* El Kelâa Srarhna
34 G10 **Kalama** Washington, NW USA *46.00N 122.50W*
Kalámai *see* Kalámata
117 G14 **Kalamariá** Kentrikí Makedonía, N Greece *40.36N 22.58E*
117 C15 **Kalamás** *prev.* Thiamis, Thýamis. *var.* Thiamis. ↝ W Greece
117 E21 **Kalámata** *prev.* Kalámai. Pelopónnisos, S Greece *37.01N 22.07E*
33 P10 **Kalamazoo** Michigan, N USA *42.17N 85.35W*
33 P9 **Kalamazoo River** ↝ Michigan, N USA
Kalambaka *see* Kalampáka
119 S13 **Kalamits'ka Zatoka** *Rus.* Kalamitskiy Zaliv. *gulf* S Ukraine
Kalamitskiy Zaliv *see* Kalamits'ka Zatoka
117 H18 **Kálamos** Attikí, C Greece *38.16N 23.51E*
117 C18 **Kálamos** *island* Iónia Nisiá, Greece, C Mediterranean Sea
117 D15 **Kalampáka** *var.* Kalambaka. Thessalía, C Greece *39.43N 21.36E*
Kalan *see* Călan, Romania
Kalan *see* Tunceli, Turkey
119 S11 **Kalanchak** Khersons'ka Oblast', S Ukraine *46.14N 33.19E*
40 G11 **Kalaoa** *var.* Kailua. Hawai'i, USA, C Pacific Ocean *19.43N 155.58W*
175 Pp15 **Kalao, Pulau** *island* Kepulauan Bonerate, W Indonesia
175 Q15 **Kalaotoa, Pulau** *island* W Indonesia
161 J24 **Kala Oya** ↝ NW Sri Lanka
Kalarash *see* Călărași
95 H17 **Kälarne** Jämtland, C Sweden *63.00N 16.10E*
149 V15 **Kalar Rūd** ↝ SE Iran
178 Ii9 **Kalasin** *var.* Muang Kalasin. Kalasin, E Thailand *16.28N 103.31E*
155 O11 **Kālat** *var.* Kelat, Khelat. Baluchistān, SW Pakistan *29.02N 66.34E*
Kalāt *see* Qalāt
117 J14 **Kalathriá, Akrotírio** *headland* Samothráki, NE Greece *40.24N 25.34E*
200 R17 **Kalau** *island* Tongatapu Group, SE Tonga
40 E9 **Kalaupapa** Moloka'i, Hawai'i, USA, C Pacific Ocean *21.11N 156.59W*
131 N13 **Kalaus** ↝ SW Russian Federation
Kalávrita *see* Kalávryta
117 E19 **Kalávryta** *var.* Kalávrita. Dytikí Ellás, S Greece *38.01N 22.06E*
147 Y10 **Kalbān** W Oman *20.19N 58.40E*
188 H11 **Kalbarri** Western Australia *27.43S 114.08E*
151 X10 **Kalbinskiy Khrebet** *Kaz.* Qalba Zhotasy. ⛰ E Kazakhstan
150 G10 **Kaldygayty** ↝ W Kazakhstan
142 I12 **Kalecik** Ankara, N Turkey *40.08N 33.27E*
175 R13 **Kaledupa, Pulau** *island* Kepulauan Tukangbesi, C Indonesia
81 O19 **Kalehe** Sud Kivu, E Dem. Rep. Congo *2.04S 28.52E*
81 P22 **Kalemie** *prev.* Albertville. Katanga, SE Dem. Rep. Congo *5.55S 29.09E*
177 Ff3 **Kalemyo** Sagaing, W Burma *23.11N 94.03E*
84 H12 **Kalene Hill** North Western, NW Zambia *11.10S 24.12E*
Kale Sultanie *see* Çanakkale
128 I7 **Kalevala** Respublika Kareliya, NW Russian Federation *65.12N 31.16E*
177 Ff3 **Kalewa** Sagaing, C Burma *23.15N 94.19E*
Kalgan *see* Zhangjiakou
41 Q12 **Kalgin Island** *island* Alaska, USA
188 L12 **Kalgoorlie** Western Australia *30.51S 121.27E*
Kali *see* Sārda
117 E17 **Kaliakoúda** ▲ C Greece *38.47N 21.42E*
116 O8 **Kaliakra, Nos** *headland* NE Bulgaria *43.22N 28.28E*
117 F19 **Kaliánoi** Pelopónnisos, S Greece *37.55N 22.28E*
179 Q13 **Kalibo** Panay Island, C Philippines *11.40N 122.21E*
117 N24 **Kalí Límni** ▲ Kárpathos, SE Greece *35.34N 27.08E*
81 N20 **Kalima** Maniema, E Dem. Rep. Congo *2.33S 26.27E*
174 M8 **Kalimantan** *Eng.* Indonesian Borneo. *geopolitical region* Borneo, C Indonesia
174 L8 **Kalimantan Barat** *off.* Propinsi Kalimantan Barat, *Eng.* West Borneo, West Kalimantan. ◐ *province* N Indonesia
174 Mm11 **Kalimantan Selatan** *off.* Propinsi Kalimantan Selatan, *Eng.* South Borneo, South Kalimantan. ◐ *province* N Indonesia
174 M9 **Kalimantan Tengah** *off.* Propinsi Kalimantan Tengah, *Eng.* Central Borneo, Central Kalimantan. ◐ *province* N Indonesia
175 N7 **Kalimantan Timur** *off.* Propinsi Kalimantan Timur, *Eng.* East Borneo, East Kalimantan. ◐ *province* N Indonesia
Kálimnos *see* Kálymnos
159 S12 **Kālimpang** West Bengal, NE India *27.05N 88.25E*
Kalinin *see* Tver', Russian Federation
Kalinin *see* Boldumsaz, Turkmenistan
Kalininabad *see* Kalininobod
130 B3 **Kaliningrad** Kaliningradskaya Oblast', W Russian Federation *54.48N 21.33E*
Kaliningrad *see* Kaliningradskaya Oblast'
130 A3 **Kaliningradskaya Oblast'** *var.* Kaliningrad. ◐ *province and enclave* W Russian Federation
Kalinino *see* Tashir
153 P14 **Kalininobod** *Rus.* Kalininabad. SW Tajikistan *37.49N 68.55E*
131 O8 **Kalininsk** Saratovskaya Oblast', W Russian Federation *51.31N 44.25E*
Kalininsk *see* Boldumsaz
Kalinisk *see* Cupcina
121 M19 **Kalinkavichy** *Rus.* Kalinkovichi. Homyel'skaya Voblasts', SE Belarus *52.07N 29.19E*
Kalinkovichi *see* Kalinkavichy
83 G18 **Kaliro** SE Uganda *0.54N 33.30E*
Kalisch/Kalish *see* Kalisz
35 O7 **Kalispell** Montana, NW USA *48.12N 114.18W*
112 I13 **Kalisz** *Ger.* Kalisch, *Rus.* Kalish; *anc.* Calisia. Wielkopolskie, C Poland *51.46N 18.04E*
112 F9 **Kalisz Pomorski** *Ger.* Kallies. Zachodnio-pomorskie, NW Poland *53.55N 15.55E*
130 M10 **Kalitva** ↝ SW Russian Federation
83 F21 **Kaliua** Tabora, C Tanzania *5.03S 31.48E*
94 K13 **Kalix** Norrbotten, N Sweden *65.51N 23.13E*
94 J11 **Kalixfors** Norrbotten, N Sweden *67.45N 20.20E*
151 T8 **Kalkaman** Pavlodar, NE Kazakhstan *51.57N 75.58E*
Kalkandelen *see* Tetovo
189 O4 **Kalkarindji** Northern Territory, N Australia *17.31S 130.40E*
33 P6 **Kalkaska** Michigan, N USA *44.43N 85.12W*
95 F16 **Kall** Jämtland, C Sweden *63.30N 13.15E*
201 X2 **Kallalen** *var.* Calalen. *island* Ratak Chain, SE Marshall Islands
120 J5 **Kallaste** *Ger.* Krasnogor. Tartumaa, SE Estonia *58.37N 27.12E*
95 N16 **Kallavesi** ◎ SE Finland
117 F17 **Kallídromo** ⛰ C Greece
Kallies *see* Kalisz Pomorski
97 M22 **Kallinge** Blekinge, S Sweden *56.13N 15.16E*
117 L16 **Kalloní** Lésvos, E Greece *39.14N 26.15E*
95 F16 **Kallsjön** ◎ C Sweden
97 N21 **Kalmar** *var.* Calmar. Kalmar, S Sweden *56.40N 16.22E*
97 M19 **Kalmar** *var.* Calmar. ◐ *county* S Sweden
97 N20 **Kalmarsund** *strait* S Sweden
154 L16 **Kalmat, Khor** *Eng.* Kalmat Lagoon. *lagoon* SW Pakistan
Kalmat Lagoon *see* Kalmat, Khor
119 X9 **Kal'mius** ↝ E Ukraine
101 H15 **Kalmthout** Antwerpen, N Belgium *51.24N 4.27E*
Kalmykia/Kalmykiya-Khal'mg Tangch, Respublika *see* Kalmykiya, Respublika
131 O12 **Kalmykiya, Respublika** *var.* Respublika Kalmykiya-Khal'mg Tangch, *Eng.* Kalmykia; *prev.* Kalmytskaya ASSR. ◐ *autonomous republic* SW Russian Federation
Kalmytskaya ASSR *see* Kalmykiya, Respublika
120 F9 **Kalnciems** Jelgava, C Latvia *56.46N 23.37E*
116 L10 **Kalnitsa** ↝ SE Bulgaria
113 J24 **Kalocsa** Bács-Kiskun, S Hungary *46.31N 19.00E*
116 J9 **Kalofer** Plovdiv, C Bulgaria *42.36N 25.00E*
40 E10 **Kalohi Channel** *channel* Hawai'i, USA, C Pacific Ocean
85 I16 **Kalomo** Southern, S Zambia *17.04S 26.27E*
31 X14 **Kalona** Iowa, C USA *41.28N 91.42W*
117 K22 **Kalotási, Akrotírio** *headland* Amorgós, Kykládes, Greece, Aegean Sea *36.47N 25.45E*
158 J8 **Kalpa** Himāchal Pradesh, N India *31.33N 78.16E*
117 C15 **Kalpáki** Ípeiros, W Greece *39.53N 20.38E*
161 C22 **Kalpeni Island** *island* Lakshadweep, India, N Indian Ocean
158 K13 **Kālpi** Uttar Pradesh, N India *26.07N 79.43E*
164 G7 **Kalpin** Xinjiang Uygur Zizhiqu, NW China *40.35N 78.52E*
155 P16 **Kalri Lake** ◎ SE Pakistan
149 R5 **Kāl Shūr** N Iran
41 N11 **Kalskag** Alaska, USA *61.32N 160.15W*
97 B18 **Kalsoy** *Dan.* Kalsø *Island* Faeroe Islands *62.20N 6.46W*
41 O9 **Kaltag** Alaska, USA *64.19N 158.43W*
110 H7 **Kaltbrunn** Sankt Gallen, NE Switzerland *47.11N 9.00E*
Kaltdorf *see* Pruszków
79 X14 **Kaltungo** Gombe, E Nigeria *9.49N 11.22E*
130 K4 **Kaluga** Kaluzhskaya Oblast', W Russian Federation *54.31N 36.16E*
161 J26 **Kalu Ganga** ↝ S Sri Lanka
84 J13 **Kalulushi** Copperbelt, C Zambia *12.52S 28.06E*
188 M2 **Kalumburu** Western Australia *14.11S 126.40E*
97 H23 **Kalundborg** Vestsjælland, E Denmark *55.42N 11.06E*
84 K11 **Kalungwishi** ↝ N Zambia
155 T8 **Kalūr Kot** Punjab, E Pakistan *32.07N 71.19E*
118 I6 **Kalush** *Pol.* Kałusz. Ivano-Frankivs'ka Oblast', W Ukraine *49.01N 24.21E*
Kałusz *see* Kalush
112 N11 **Kałuszyn** Mazowieckie, C Poland *52.12N 21.43E*
161 J26 **Kalutara** Western Province, SW Sri Lanka *6.34N 79.58E*
Kaluwawa *see* Fergusson Island
130 I5 **Kaluzhskaya Oblast'** ◐ *province* W Russian Federation
121 E14 **Kalvarija** *Pol.* Kalwaria. Marijampolė, S Lithuania *54.25N 23.13E*
95 K15 **Kälviä** Länsi-Suomi, W Finland *63.50N 23.31E*
111 U6 **Kalwang** Steiermark, E Austria *47.25N 14.48E*
Kalwaria *see* Kalvarija
160 D13 **Kalyān** Mahārāshtra, W India *19.16N 73.10E*
128 K16 **Kalyazin** Tverskaya Oblast', W Russian Federation *57.15N 37.53E*
117 D18 **Kalydón** *anc.* Calydon. *site of ancient city* Dytikí Ellás, C Greece *38.24N 21.31E*
117 M21 **Kálymnos** *var.* Kálimnos. Kálymnos, Dodekánisa, Greece, Aegean Sea *36.57N 26.58E*
117 M21 **Kálymnos** *var.* Kálimnos. *island* Dodekánisa, Greece, Aegean Sea
119 O5 **Kalynivka** Kyyivs'ka Oblast', N Ukraine *50.14N 30.16E*
119 N6 **Kalynivka** Vinnyts'ka Oblast', C Ukraine *49.27N 28.32E*
44 M10 **Kama** *var.* Cama. Región Autónoma Atlántico Sur, SE Nicaragua *12.06N 83.55W*
125 E9 **Kama** ↝ NW Russian Federation
172 N12 **Kamaishi** *var.* Kamaisi. Iwate, Honshū, C Japan *39.17N 141.51E*
Kamaisi *see* Kamaishi
120 H11 **Kamajai** Panevėžys, NE Lithuania *55.16N 25.30E*
120 H13 **Kamajai** Utena, E Lithuania *55.49N 25.30E*
171 Jj17 **Kamakura** Kanagawa, Honshū, S Japan *35.17N 139.31E*
155 U9 **Kamālia** Punjab, NE Pakistan *30.43N 72.39E*
85 I14 **Kamalondo** North Western, NW Zambia *13.42S 25.38E*
142 I13 **Kaman** Kirşehir, C Turkey *39.22N 33.43E*
81 O20 **Kamanyola** Sud Kivu, E Dem. Rep. Congo *2.54S 29.04E*
147 N14 **Kamarān** *island* W Yemen
57 R9 **Kamarang** W Guyana *5.49N 60.38W*
Kāmāreddi/Kamareddy *see* Rāmāreddi
Kama Reservoir *see* Kamskoye Vodokhranilishche
154 K13 **Kamarod** Baluchistān, SW Pakistan *27.34N 63.36E*
175 R13 **Kamaru** Pulau Buton, C Indonesia *5.10S 123.03E*
79 S13 **Kamba** Kebbi, NW Nigeria *11.50N 3.44E*
Kambaeng Petch *see* Kamphaeng Phet
188 L12 **Kambalda** Western Australia *31.15S 121.33E*
155 P13 **Kambar** *var.* Qambar. Sind, SE Pakistan *27.34N 68.03E*
Kambara *see* Kabara
78 I14 **Kambia** W Sierra Leone *9.09N 12.52W*
175 S16 **Kambing, Pulau** *island* W East Timor
Kambos *see* Kámpos
81 N25 **Kambove** Katanga, SE Dem. Rep. Congo *10.49S 26.39E*
Kambryk *see* Cambrai
127 Pp10 **Kamchatka** ↝ E Russian Federation
Kamchatka *see* Kamchatka, Poluostrov
Kamchatka Basin *see* Komandorskaya Basin
127 P11 **Kamchatka, Poluostrov** *Eng.* Kamchatka. *peninsula* E Russian Federation
127 Pp11 **Kamchatskaya Oblast'** ◐ *province* E Russian Federation
127 Pp10 **Kamchatskiy Zaliv** *gulf* E Russian Federation
116 N9 **Kamchiya** ↝ E Bulgaria
116 L9 **Kamchiya, Yazovir** ◎ E Bulgaria
Kamdesh *see* Kāmdeysh
155 T4 **Kāmdeysh** *var.* Kamdesh. Nūrestān, E Afghanistan *35.25N 71.25E*
170 Ee14 **Kamega-mori** ▲ Shikoku, SW Japan *33.45N 133.12E*
120 M13 **Kamen'** *Rus.* Kamen'. Vitsyebskaya Voblasts', N Belarus *55.01N 28.52E*
Kamenets *see* Kamyanyets
Kamenets-Podol'skaya Oblast' *see* Khmel'nyts'ka Oblast'
Kamenets-Podol'skiy *see* Kam"yanets'-Podil's'kyy
115 Q18 **Kamenica** NE FYR Macedonia *42.03N 22.34E*
114 A11 **Kamenjak, Rt** *headland* NW Croatia
150 F8 **Kamenka** Zapadnyy Kazakhstan, NW Kazakhstan *51.06N 51.16E*
129 O6 **Kamenka** Arkhangel'skaya Oblast', NW Russian Federation *65.55N 44.01E*
130 06 **Kamenka** Penzenskaya Oblast', W Russian Federation *53.12N 44.00E*
131 L8 **Kamenka** Voronezhskaya Oblast', W Russian Federation *50.44N 39.31E*
Kamenka *see* Camenca, Moldova
Kamenka *see* Kam"yanka, Ukraine
Kamenka-Bugskaya *see* Kam"yanka-Buz'ka
Kamenka Dneprovskaya *see* Kam"yanka-Dniprovs'ka
Kamen Kashirskiy *see* Kamin'-Kashyrs'kyy
126 Gg14 **Kamen'-na-Obi** Altayskiy Kray, S Russian Federation *53.42N 81.04E*
130 L15 **Kamennomostskiy** Respublika Adygeya, SW Russian Federation *44.13N 40.12E*
130 L11 **Kamenolomni** Rostovskaya Oblast', SW Russian Federation *47.36N 40.18E*
131 P8 **Kamenskiy** Saratovskaya Oblast', W Russian Federation *50.56N 45.32E*
127 P7 **Kamenskoye** Koryakskiy Avtonomnyy Okrug, E Russian Federation *62.29N 166.16E*
Kamenskoye *see* Dniprodzerzhyns'k
130 L11 **Kamensk-Shakhtinskiy** Rostovskaya Oblast', SW Russian Federation *48.18N 40.16E*
125 Ee11 **Kamensk-Ural'skiy** Sverdlovskaya Oblast', C Russian Federation *56.30N 61.45E*
103 P15 **Kamenz** Sachsen, E Germany *51.15N 14.06E*
171 Gg14 **Kameoka** Kyōto, Honshū, SW Japan *35.02N 135.35E*
130 M3 **Kameshkovo** Vladimirskaya Oblast', W Russian Federation *56.21N 41.01E*
171 H15 **Kameyama** Mie, Honshū, SW Japan *34.52N 136.25E*
170 Cc10 **Kami-Agata** Nagasaki, Tsushima, SW Japan *34.40N 129.27E*
35 N10 **Kamiah** Idaho, NW USA *46.13N 116.01W*
Kamień Koszyrski *see* Kamin'-Kashyrs'kyy
112 H9 **Kamień Krajeński** *Ger.* Kamin in Westpreussen. Kujawsko-pomorskie, C Poland *53.31N 17.31E*
113 F15 **Kamienna Góra** *Ger.* Landeshut, Landeshut in Schlesien. Dolnośląskie, SW Poland *50.48N 16.00E*
112 D8 **Kamień Pomorski** *Ger.* Cummin in Pommern. Zachodnio-pomorskie, NW Poland *53.57N 14.44E*
172 N7 **Kamiiso** Hokkaidō, NE Japan *41.50N 140.38E*
81 L22 **Kamiji** Kasai Oriental, S Dem. Rep. Congo *6.35S 23.18E*
172 Pp5 **Kamikawa** Hokkaidō, NE Japan *43.51N 142.47E*
170 Bb15 **Kami-Koshiki-jima** *island* SW Japan
81 M23 **Kamina** Katanga, S Dem. Rep. Congo *8.42S 25.01E*
Kamina *see* Kaintiba
44 C6 **Kaminaljuyú** *ruins* Guatemala, C Guatemala *14.34N 90.36W*
Kamin in Westpreussen *see* Kamień Krajeński
118 J2 **Kamin'-Kashyrs'kyy** *Pol.* Kamień Koszyrski, *Rus.* Kamen Kashirskiy. Volyns'ka Oblast', NW Ukraine *51.39N 24.59E*
172 N6 **Kaminokuni** Hokkaidō, NE Japan *41.48N 140.05E*
171 Ll13 **Kaminoyama** Yamagata, Honshū, C Japan *38.09N 140.15E*
171 Ii14 **Kamioka** Gifu, Honshū, SW Japan *36.20N 137.18E*
41 Q13 **Kamishak Bay** *bay* Alaska, USA
172 Pp6 **Kami-Shihoro** Hokkaidō, NE Japan *43.14N 143.18E*
Kamishli *see* Al Qāmishlī
Kamissar *see* Kamsar
170 Cc10 **Kami-Tsushima** Nagasaki, Tsushima, SW Japan *34.40N 129.27E*
81 O20 **Kamituga** Sud Kivu, E Dem. Rep. Congo *3.07S 28.10E*
170 B17 **Kamiyaku** Kagoshima, Yaku-shima, SW Japan *30.24N 130.32E*
9 N16 **Kamloops** British Columbia, SW Canada *50.39N 120.24W*
109 G25 **Kamma** Sicilia, Italy, C Mediterranean Sea *36.46N 12.03E*
199 Ii4 **Kammu Seamount** *undersea feature* N Pacific Ocean *32.09N 173.00E*
111 U11 **Kamnik** *Ger.* Stein. C Slovenia *46.13N 14.34E*
Kamniške Alpe *see* Kamniško-Savinjske Alpe
111 T10 **Kamniško-Savinjske Alpe** *var.* Kamniške Alpe, Sanntaler Alpen, *Ger.* Steiner Alpen. ⛰ N Slovenia
171 Kk13 **Kamo** Niigata, Honshū, C Japan *37.42N 139.03E*
Kamo *see* Gavarr
171 K17 **Kamogawa** Chiba, Honshū, S Japan *35.05N 140.04E*
155 W8 **Kāmoke** Punjab, E Pakistan *31.58N 74.13E*
84 L13 **Kamoto** Eastern, E Zambia *13.16S 32.04E*
111 V3 **Kamp** ↝ N Austria
83 F18 **Kampala** ● (Uganda) S Uganda *0.21N 32.28E*
174 H8 **Kampar, Sungai** ↝ Sumatera, W Indonesia
174 Ii10 **Kampa, Teluk** *bay* Pulau Bangka, W Indonesia
100 L9 **Kampen** Overijssel, E Netherlands *52.33N 5.55E*
81 N20 **Kampene** Maniema, E Dem. Rep. Congo *3.34S 26.40E*
31 Q9 **Kampeska, Lake** ◎ South Dakota, N USA
178 Gg9 **Kamphaeng Phet** *var.* Kambaeng Petch. Kamphaeng Phet, W Thailand *16.28N 99.31E*
Kampo *see* Campo, Cameroon
Kampo *see* Ntem, Cameroon/Equatorial Guinea
178 J13 **Kâmpóng Cham** *prev.* Kompong Cham. Kâmpóng Cham, C Cambodia *12.00N 105.27E*
178 J13 **Kâmpóng Chhnăng** *prev.* Kompong. Kâmpóng Chhnăng, C Cambodia *12.15N 104.40E*
178 Ii12 **Kâmpóng Khleăng** *prev.* Kompong Kleang. Siĕmréab, NW Cambodia *13.04N 104.07E*
178 I14 **Kâmpóng Saôm** *prev.* Kompong Som, Sihanoukville. Kâmpóng Saôm, SW Cambodia *10.37N 103.30E*
178 J13 **Kâmpóng Spoe** *prev.* Kompong Speu. Kâmpóng Spœ, S Cambodia *11.28N 104.29E*
124 N3 **Kámpos** *var.* Kambos. NW Cyprus *35.03N 32.44E*
178 Ii14 **Kâmpôt** Kâmpôt, SW Cambodia *10.37N 104.10E*
Kamptee *see* Kāmthi
79 O14 **Kampti** SW Burkina *10.07N 3.22W*
Kampuchea *see* Cambodia
174 Ll5 **Kampung Sirik** Sarawak, East Malaysia *2.42N 111.28E*
176 Y13 **Kampung, Sungai** ↝ Papua, E Indonesia
176 Vv12 **Kamrau, Teluk** *bay* Papua, E Indonesia
9 V15 **Kamsack** Saskatchewan, S Canada *51.34N 101.51W*
78 H13 **Kamsar** *var.* Kamissar. W Guinea *10.36N 14.34W*
131 R4 **Kamskoye Ust'ye** Respublika Tatarstan, W Russian Federation *55.13N 49.11E*
129 U14 **Kamskoye Vodokhranilishche** *var.* Kama Reservoir. ⊠ NW Russian Federation
160 I12 **Kāmthi** *prev.* Kamptee. Mahārāshtra, C India *21.19N 79.11E*
Kamuela *see* Waimea
172 Nn5 **Kamuenai** Hokkaidō, NE Japan *43.07N 140.25E*
172 P7 **Kamui-dake** 🌋 Hokkaidō, NE Japan *42.24N 142.57E*
172 Nn4 **Kamui-misaki** *headland* Hokkaidō, NE Japan *43.20N 140.20E*
45 O15 **Kámuk, Cerro** ▲ SE Costa Rica *9.15N 83.01W*
176 Vv9 **Kamundan, Sungai** ↝ Papua, E Indonesia
176 X12 **Kamura, Sungai** ↝ Papua, E Indonesia
118 K7 **Kam"yanets'-Podil's'kyy** *Rus.* Kamenets-Podol'skiy. Khmel'nyts'ka Oblast', W Ukraine *48.42N 26.36E*
119 Q6 **Kam"yanka** *Rus.* Kamenka. Cherkas'ka Oblast', C Ukraine *49.03N 32.06E*
118 I5 **Kam"yanka-Buz'ka** *Rus.* Kamenka-Bugskaya. L'vivs'ka Oblast', NW Ukraine *50.03N 24.20E*
119 T9 **Kam"yanka-Dniprovs'ka** *Rus.* Kamenka Dneprovskaya. Zaporiz'ka Oblast', SE Ukraine *47.28N 34.24E*
121 F19 **Kamyanyets** *Rus.* Kamenets. Brestskaya Voblasts', SW Belarus *52.24N 23.50E*
131 P9 **Kamyshin** Volgogradskaya Oblast', SW Russian Federation *50.06N 45.20E*
125 Ee11 **Kamyshlov** Sverdlovskaya Oblast', C Russian Federation *56.55N 62.37E*
131 Q13 **Kamyzyak** Astrakhanskaya Oblast', SW Russian Federation *46.07N 48.03E*
10 K8 **Kanaaupscow** ↝ Québec, C Canada
38 K8 **Kanab** Utah, W USA *37.03N 112.31W*
38 K9 **Kanab Creek** ↝ Arizona/Utah, SW USA
197 J13 **Kanacea** *prev.* Kanathea. Taveuni, N Fiji *16.59S 179.54E*
197 K14 **Kanacea** *island* Lau Group, E Fiji
40 G17 **Kanaga Island** *island* Aleutian Islands, Alaska, USA
40 G17 **Kanaga Volcano** ▲ Kanaga Island, Alaska, USA *51.55N 177.09W*
171 J17 **Kanagawa** *off.* Kanagawa-ken. ◐ *prefecture* Honshū, S Japan
11 Q8 **Kanairiktok** ↝ Newfoundland and Labrador, E Canada
Kanaky *see* New Caledonia
81 K22 **Kananga** *prev.* Luluabourg. Kasai Occidental, S Dem. Rep. Congo *5.51S 22.22E*
Kananur *see* Cannanore
Kanara *see* Karnātaka
38 J7 **Kanarraville** Utah, W USA *37.32N 113.10W*
131 Q4 **Kanash** Chuvashskaya Respubliki, W Russian Federation *55.30N 47.27E*
Kanathea *see* Kanacea
23 Q4 **Kanawha River** ↝ West Virginia, NE USA
171 I15 **Kanayama** Gifu, Honshū, SW Japan *35.46N 137.15E*
171 I12 **Kanazawa** Ishikawa, Honshū, SW Japan *36.34N 136.40E*
177 G4 **Kanbalu** Sagaing, C Burma *23.10N 95.31E*
177 Ff8 **Kanbe** Yangon, SW Burma *16.40N 96.01E*
178 H11 **Kanchanaburi** Kanchanaburi, W Thailand *14.01N 99.31E*
Kanchanjańghā/Kānchenjunga *see* Kangchenjunga
151 V11 **Kanchingiz, Khrebet** ⛰ E Kazakhstan
161 J19 **Kānchīpuram** *prev.* Conjeeveram. Tamil Nādu, SE India *12.49N 79.43E*
155 N8 **Kandahār** *Per.* Qandahār. Kandahār, S Afghanistan *31.36N 65.48E*
155 N9 **Kandahār** *Per.* Qandahār. ◐ *province* SE Afghanistan
Kandalakša *see* Kandalaksha
128 I5 **Kandalaksha** *var.* Kandalakša, *Fin.* Kantalahti. Murmanskaya Oblast', NW Russian Federation *67.09N 32.13E*
Kandalaksha Gulf / Kandalakshskaya Guba *see* Kandalakshskiy Zaliv
128 K6 **Kandalakshskiy Zaliv** *var.* Kandalakshskaya Guba, *Eng.* Kandalaksha Gulf. *bay* NW Russian Federation
Kandalangodi *see* Kandalangoti
85 G17 **Kandalangoti** *var.* Kandalangodi. North-West, NW Botswana *19.25S 22.12E*
175 N10 **Kandangan** Borneo, C Indonesia *2.49S 115.15E*
Kandau *see* Kandava
120 E8 **Kandava** *Ger.* Kandau. Tukums, W Latvia *57.02N 22.48E*
Kandavu *see* Kadavu
79 R14 **Kandé** *var.* Kanté. NE Togo *9.55N 1.01E*
103 F23 **Kandel** ▲ SW Germany *48.03N 8.00E*
194 G12 **Kandep** Enga, W PNG *5.50S 143.26E*
155 R12 **Kandh Kot** Sind, SE Pakistan *28.15N 69.18E*
79 S13 **Kandi** N Benin *11.04N 2.58E*
155 P14 **Kandiāro** Sind, SE Pakistan *27.01N 68.16E*
142 F11 **Kandıra** Kocaeli, NW Turkey *41.04N 30.07E*
191 S8 **Kandos** New South Wales, SE Australia *32.52S 149.58E*
154 M16 **Kandrāch** *var.* Kanrach. Baluchistān, SW Pakistan *25.26N 65.28E*
180 I4 **Kandreho** Mahajanga, C Madagascar *17.27S 46.06E*
194 M12 **Kandrian** New Britain, E PNG *6.10S 149.33E*
Kandukur *see* Kondukūr
161 K25 **Kandy** Central Province, C Sri Lanka *7.16N 80.40E*
150 I10 **Kandyagash** *Kaz.* Qandyaghash; *prev.* Oktyabr'sk. Aktyubinsk, W Kazakhstan *49.25N 57.24E*
20 D12 **Kane** Pennsylvania, NE USA *41.39N 78.47W*
66 I11 **Kane Fracture Zone** *tectonic feature* NW Atlantic Ocean
Kanëka *see* Kanëvka
80 G9 **Kanem** *off.* Préfecture du Kanem. ◐ *prefecture* W Chad
40 D9 **Kāne'ohe** *var.* Kaneohe. O'ahu, Hawai'i, USA, C Pacific Ocean *21.25N 157.48W*
Kanestron, Akrotírio *see* Palioúri, Akrotírio
Kanëv *see* Kaniv
128 M5 **Kanëvka** *var.* Kanëka. Murmanskaya Oblast', NW Russian Federation *67.07N 39.43E*
130 K13 **Kanevskaya** Krasnodarskiy Kray, SW Russian Federation *46.07N 38.57E*
Kanevskoye Vodokhranilishche *see* Kanivs'ke Vodoskhovyshche
171 Ll12 **Kaneyama** Yamagata, Honshū, C Japan *38.54N 140.20E*
85 G20 **Kang** Kgalagadi, C Botswana *23.40S 22.49E*
78 L13 **Kangaba** Koulikoro, SW Mali *11.57N 8.24W*
142 M13 **Kangal** Sivas, C Turkey *39.15N 37.22E*
Kangān *see* Bandar-e Kangān
149 S15 **Kangān** Hormozgān, SE Iran *27.49N 52.04E*
173 G2 **Kangar** Perlis, Peninsular Malaysia *6.28N 100.10E*
78 L13 **Kangaré** Sikasso, S Mali *11.39N 8.10W*
190 F10 **Kangaroo Island** *island* South Australia
95 M17 **Kangasniemi** Itä-Suomi, E Finland *61.58N 26.36E*
148 K6 **Kangāvar** *var.* Kangāwar. Kermānshāh, W Iran *34.30N 47.53E*
Kangāwar *see* Kangāvar
159 S11 **Kangchenjunga** *var.* Kānchenjunga, *Nep.* Kanchanjańghā. ▲ NE India *27.36N 88.06E*
166 G9 **Kangding** *var.* Lucheng, *Tib.* Dardo. Sichuan, C China *30.03N 101.56E*
175 Nn14 **Kangean, Kepulauan** *island group* S Indonesia
175 N14 **Kangean, Pulau** *island* Kepulauan Kangean, S Indonesia
69 U8 **Kangen** *var.* Kengen. ↝ SE Sudan
207 N14 **Kangerlussuaq** *Dan.* Sondre Strømfjord ✕ Kitaa, W Greenland *66.59N 50.28W*
207 Q15 **Kangertittivaq** *Dan.* Scoresby Sund. *fjord* E Greenland
178 H2 **Kangfang** Kachin State, N Burma *26.09N 98.36E*
176 Z13 **Kanggup** Papua, E Indonesia *5.56S 140.49E*
169 X12 **Kanggye** N North Korea *40.57N 126.37E*
207 P15 **Kangikajik** *var.* Kap Brewster. *headland* E Greenland *70.10N 22.00W*
11 N5 **Kangiqsualujjuaq** *prev.* George River, Port-Nouveau-Québec. Quebec, E Canada *58.34N 65.58W*
10 L2 **Kangiqsujuaq** *prev.* Maricourt, Wakeham Bay. Québec, NE Canada *61.35N 72.00W*
10 M4 **Kangirsuk** *prev.* Bellin, Payne. Québec, E Canada *60.00N 70.01W*
Kangle *see* Wanzai
164 J15 **Kangmar** Xizang Zizhiqu, W China *30.45N 85.43E*
164 M16 **Kangmar** Xizang Zizhiqu, W China *28.34N 89.40E*

◆ Country
● Country Capital
◇ Dependent Territory
○ Dependent Territory Capital
◐ Administrative Region
✕ International Airport
▲ Mountain
⛰ Mountain Range
🌋 Volcano
↝ River
◎ Lake
⊠ Reservoir

169 Y14 **Kangnŭng** *Jap.* Kōryō. NE South Korea 37.47N 128.51E
81 D18 **Kango** Estuaire, NW Gabon 0.17N 10.00E
158 I7 **Kāngra** Himāchal Pradesh, NW India 32.04N 76.16E
159 Q16 **Kangsabati Reservoir** ⊠ N India
165 O17 **Kangto** ▲ China/India 27.54N 92.33E
165 W12 **Kangxian** *var.* Kang Xian, Zuitai, Zuitaizi. Gansu, C China 33.21N 105.40E
177 Ff4 **Kani** Sagaing, C Burma 22.24N 94.55E
78 M15 **Kani** NW Ivory Coast 8.24N 6.38W
81 M23 **Kaniama** Katanga, S Dem. Rep. Congo 7.31S 24.10E
Kanibadam *see* Konibodom
175 O2 **Kanibongan** Sabah, East Malaysia 6.40N 117.12E
193 F17 **Kaniere** West Coast, South Island, NZ 42.45S 171.00E
193 G17 **Kaniere, Lake** ◎ South Island, NZ
196 E17 **Kanifaay** Yap, W Micronesia
129 O4 **Kanin Kamen'** ▲▲ NW Russian Federation
129 N3 **Kanin Nos** Nenetskiy Avtonomnyy Okrug, NW Russian Federation 68.38N 43.19E
129 N3 **Kanin Nos, Mys** *headland* NW Russian Federation 68.39N 43.14E
129 O5 **Kanin, Poluostrov** *peninsula* NW Russian Federation
145 V8 **Kānī Sakht** E Iraq 33.19N 46.04E
145 T3 **Kānī Sulaymān** N Iraq 35.54N 44.35E
172 N8 **Kanita** Aomori, Honshū, C Japan 41.04N 140.36E
119 Q5 **Kaniv** *Rus.* Kanëv. Cherkas'ka Oblast', C Ukraine 49.46N 31.28E
190 K11 **Kaniva** Victoria, SE Australia 36.25S 141.13E
119 Q5 **Kanivs'ke Vodoskhovyshche** *Rus.* Kanevskoye Vodokhranilishche. ⊠ C Ukraine
114 L8 **Kanjiža** *Ger.* Altkanischa, *Hung.* Magyarkanizsa, Ókanizsa; *prev.* Stara Kanjiža. Serbia, N Serbia 46.03N 20.03E
95 K18 **Kankaanpää** Länsi-Suomi, W Finland 61.46N 22.25E
32 M12 **Kankakee** Illinois, N USA 41.07N 87.51W
33 O11 **Kankakee River** ≈ Illinois/Indiana, N USA
78 K14 **Kankan** E Guinea 10.25N 9.19W
160 K13 **Kānker** Chhattīsgarh, C India 20.19N 81.29E
78 J10 **Kankossa** Assaba, S Mauritania 15.54N 11.31W
178 Gg13 **Kanmaw Kyun** *var.* Kisseraing, Kithareng. *island* Mergui Archipelago, S Burma
170 E13 **Kanmuri-yama** ▲ Kyūshū, SW Japan 34.28N 132.03E
23 R10 **Kannapolis** North Carolina, SE USA 35.29N 80.37W
95 L16 **Kannonkoski** Länsi-Suomi, W Finland 62.58N 25.19E
Kannur *see* Cannanore
95 K15 **Kannus** Länsi-Suomi, W Finland 63.51N 23.55E
79 V13 **Kano** Kano, N Nigeria 11.56N 8.30E
79 V13 **Kano** ◈ *state* N Nigeria
79 V13 **Kano** ✈ Kano, N Nigeria 11.56N 8.26E
170 F14 **Kan'onji** *var.* Kanonzi. Kagawa, Shikoku, SW Japan 34.10N 133.38E
Kanonzi *see* Kan'onji
28 M5 **Kanopolis Lake** ⊠ Kansas, C USA
38 K5 **Kanosh** Utah, W USA 38.48N 112.26W
174 Ll6 **Kanowit** Sarawak, East Malaysia 2.03N 112.15E
170 Bb17 **Kanoya** Kagoshima, Kyūshū, SW Japan 31.21N 130.49E
158 L13 **Kānpur** *Eng.* Cawnpore. Uttar Pradesh, N India 26.28N 80.21E
Kanrach *see* Kandrāch
171 Gg15 **Kansai** ✈ (Ōsaka) Ōsaka, Honshū, SW Japan 34.25N 135.13E
29 R9 **Kansas** Oklahoma, C USA 36.14N 94.46W
28 L5 **Kansas** *off.* State of Kansas; also known as Jayhawker State, Sunflower State. ◈ *state* C USA
29 R4 **Kansas City** Kansas, C USA 39.06N 94.37W
29 R4 **Kansas City** Missouri, C USA 39.06N 94.34W
29 R3 **Kansas City** ✈ Missouri, C USA 39.18N 94.45W
29 P4 **Kansas River** ≈ Kansas, C USA
126 I14 **Kansk** Krasnoyarskiy Kray, S Russian Federation 56.11N 95.32E
Kansu *see* Gansu
153 V7 **Kant** Chuyskaya Oblast', N Kyrgyzstan 42.54N 74.47E
Kantalahti *see* Kandalaksha
178 Gg16 **Kantang** *var.* Ban Kantang. Trang, SW Thailand 7.25N 99.30E
117 H25 **Kántanos** Kríti, Greece, E Mediterranean Sea 35.20N 23.42E
79 R12 **Kantchari** E Burkina 12.28N 1.31E
Kanté *see* Kandé
Kantemir *see* Cantemir
130 L9 **Kantemirovka** Voronezhskaya Oblast', W Russian Federation 49.43N 39.53E
178 J11 **Kantharalak** Si Sa Ket, E Thailand 14.32N 104.37E
Kantipur *see* Kathmandu
41 Q9 **Kantishna River** ≈ Alaska, USA
171 K16 **Kantō** *physical region* Honshū, SW Japan
203 S3 **Kanton** *var.* Abariringa, Canton Island; *prev.* Mary Island. *atoll* Phoenix Islands, C Kiribati
171 Jj15 **Kantō-sanchi** ▲▲ Honshū, S Japan
99 C20 **Kanturk** *Ir.* Ceann Toirc. SW Ireland 52.12N 8.54W
57 T11 **Kanuku Mountains** ▲▲ S Guyana
171 Kk15 **Kanuma** Tochigi, Honshū, S Japan 36.36N 139.46E
85 H20 **Kanye** Southern, SE Botswana 24.54S 25.14E
85 H17 **Kanyu** North-West, C Botswana 20.07S 24.36E
177 G7 **Kanyutkwin** Pegu, C Burma 18.19N 96.30E
81 M24 **Kanzenze** Katanga, SE Dem. Rep. Congo 10.33S 25.28E
200 Ss13 **Kao** *island* Kotu Group, W Tonga
167 S14 **Kaohsiung** *var.* Gaoxiong, *Jap.* Takao, Takow. S Taiwan 22.36N 120.16E
167 S14 **Kaohsiung** ✈ S Taiwan 22.26N 120.32E
Kaokaona *see* Kirakira
85 B17 **Kaoko Veld** ▲▲ N Namibia
78 G11 **Kaolack** *var.* Kaolak. W Senegal 14.09N 16.07W
Kaolak *see* Kaolack
Kaolan *see* Lanzhou
195 W15 **Kaolo** San Jorge, N Solomon Islands 8.24S 159.35E
85 H14 **Kaoma** Western, W Zambia 14.43S 24.46E
40 B8 **Kapa'a** *var.* Kapaa. Kaua'i, Hawai'i, USA, C Pacific Ocean 22.04N 159.19W
115 J16 **Kapa Moračka** ▲ C-Montenegro 42.53N 19.01E
143 V13 **Kapan** *Rus.* Kafan; *prev.* Ghap'an. SE Armenia 39.13N 46.25E
84 L13 **Kapandashila** Northern, NE Zambia 12.43S 31.00E
81 L23 **Kapanga** Katanga, S Dem. Rep. Congo 8.22S 22.37E
151 U15 **Kapchagay** *Kaz.* Kapshaghay. Almaty, SE Kazakhstan 43.52N 77.05E
151 V15 **Kapchagayskoye Vodokhranilishche** *Kaz.* Qapshagay Böyeni. ⊠ SE Kazakhstan
101 F15 **Kapelle** Zeeland, SW Netherlands 51.28N 3.58E
101 G16 **Kapellen** Antwerpen, N Belgium 51.19N 4.25E
97 P15 **Kapellskär** Stockholm, C Sweden 59.43N 19.03E
83 H18 **Kapenguria** Rift Valley, W Kenya 1.13N 35.07E
111 V6 **Kapfenberg** Steiermark, C Austria 47.27N 15.15E
85 J14 **Kapiri Mposhi** Central, C Zambia 13.54S 28.40E
155 R4 **Kāpīsā** ◈ *province* E Afghanistan
10 G10 **Kapiskau** ≈ Ontario, C Canada
192 K13 **Kapiti Island** *island* C NZ
80 K9 **Kapka, Massif du** ▲▲ E Chad
Kaplamada *see* Kaubalatmada, Gunung
24 H9 **Kaplan** Louisiana, S USA 30.00N 92.16W
Kaplangky, Plato *see* Gaplaňgyr Platosy
113 D19 **Kaplice** *Ger.* Kaplitz. Jihočeský Kraj , S Czech Republic 48.42N 14.27E
Kaplitz *see* Kaplice
Kapoche *see* Capoche
176 U10 **Kapocol** Papua, E Indonesia 1.59S 130.11E
178 Gg14 **Kapoe** Ranong, SW Thailand 9.33N 98.37E
Kapoeas *see* Kapuas, Sungai
83 G15 **Kapoeta** Eastern Equatoria, SE Sudan 4.49N 33.34E
113 I25 **Kapos** ≈ S Hungary
113 H25 **Kaposvár** Somogy, SW Hungary 46.22N 17.54E
96 H13 **Kapp** Oppland, S Norway 60.42N 10.49E
102 I7 **Kappeln** Schleswig-Holstein, N Germany 54.40N 9.56E
Kaproncza *see* Koprivnica
111 P7 **Kaprun** Salzburg, C Austria 47.15N 12.48E
Kapshaghay *see* Kapchagay
Kapstad *see* Cape Town
Kapsukas *see* Marijampolė
176 Yy10 **Kaptiau** Papua, E Indonesia 2.23S 139.51E
121 L19 **Kaptsevichy** *Rus.* Koptsevichi. Homyel'skaya Voblasts', SE Belarus 52.13N 28.19E
Kapuas Hulu, Banjaran/ Kapuas Hulu, Pegunungan *see* Kapuas Mountains
174 M7 **Kapuas Mountains** *Ind.* Banjaran Kapuas Hulu, Pegunungan Kapuas Hulu. ▲▲ Indonesia/Malaysia
174 Kk8 **Kapuas, Sungai** ≈ Borneo, N Indonesia
175 N10 **Kapuas, Sungai** *prev.* Kapoeas. ≈ Borneo, C Indonesia
190 J9 **Kapunda** South Australia 34.23S 138.51E
158 H8 **Kapūrthala** Punjab, N India 31.22N 75.15E
174 L14 **Kapur Utara, Pegugungan** ▲▲ Jawa, S Indonesia
10 G12 **Kapuskasing** Ontario, S Canada 49.25N 82.25W
12 D6 **Kapuskasing** ≈ Ontario, S Canada
131 P11 **Kapustin Yar** Astrakhanskaya Oblast', SW Russian Federation 48.36N 45.49E
84 K11 **Kaputa** Northern, NE Zambia 8.27S 29.35E
113 G22 **Kapuvár** Győr-Moson-Sopron, NW Hungary 47.35N 17.01E
Kapydzhik, Gora *see* Qazangödağ
121 J17 **Kapyl'** *Rus.* Kopyl'. Minskaya Voblasts', C Belarus 53.09N 27.04E
45 N9 **Kara** *var.* Cara. Región Autónoma Atlántico Sur, E Nicaragua 12.52N 83.35W
79 R14 **Kara** *var.* Lama-Kara. NE Togo 9.36N 1.12E
79 Q14 **Kara** ≈ N Togo
153 U7 **Kara-Balta** Chuyskaya Oblast', N Kyrgyzstan 42.50N 73.51E
150 L7 **Karabalyk** *prev.* Komsomol, Komsomolets. Kostanay, N Kazakhstan 53.48N 61.58E
150 G11 **Karabau** Atyrau, W Kazakhstan 48.29N 53.05E
152 E7 **Karabaur', Uval** *Kaz.* Korabavur Pastligi, *Uzb.* Qorabowur Kirlari. *physical region* Kazakhstan/Uzbekistan
Karabekaul *see* Garabekewül
Karabil', Vozvyshennost' *see* Garabil Belentligi
Kara-Bogaz-Gol *see* Garabogazköl
Kara-Bogaz-Gol, Zaliv *see* Garabogaz Aylagy
151 R15 **Karaboget** *Kaz.* Qaraböget. Zhambyl, S Kazakhstan 44.36N 72.03E
142 H11 **Karabük** Karabük, NW Turkey 41.12N 32.36E
142 H11 **Karabük** ◈ *province* NW Turkey
126 Ii13 **Karabula** Krasnoyarskiy Kray, C Russian Federation 58.01N 97.17E
151 V14 **Karabulak** *Kaz.* Qarabulaq. Almaty, SE Kazakhstan 44.54N 78.29E
151 Y11 **Karabulak** *Kaz.* Qarabulaq. Vostochnyy Kazakhstan, E Kazakhstan 47.33N 84.38E
151 Q17 **Karabulak** *Kaz.* Qarabulaq. Yuzhnyy Kazakhstan, S Kazakhstan 42.31N 69.46E
142 C17 **Kara Burnu** *headland* SW Turkey 36.34N 28.00E
150 K10 **Karabutak** *Kaz.* Qarabutaq. Aktyubinsk, W Kazakhstan 49.58N 60.06E
142 D12 **Karacabey** Bursa, NW Turkey 40.13N 28.22E
116 O12 **Karacaköy** İstanbul, NW Turkey 41.24N 28.21E
116 M12 **Karacaoğlan** Kırklareli, NW Turkey 41.30N 27.06E
Karachay-Cherkessia *see* Karachayevo-Cherkesskaya Respublika
130 L15 **Karachayevo-Cherkesskaya Respublika** *Eng.* Karachay-Cherkessia. ◈ *autonomous republic* SW Russian Federation
130 M15 **Karachayevsk** Karachayevo-Cherkesskaya Respublika, SW Russian Federation 43.43N 41.53E
130 J6 **Karachev** Bryanskaya Oblast', W Russian Federation 53.07N 35.56E
155 O16 **Karāchi** Sind, SE Pakistan 24.51N 67.01E
155 O16 **Karāchi** ✈ Sind, S Pakistan 24.51N 67.01E
Karácsonkő *see* Piatra-Neamț
161 E15 **Karād** Mahārāshtra, W India 17.19N 74.15E
142 H16 **Karadağ** ▲ S Turkey 37.00N 33.00E
153 T10 **Karadar'ya** *Uzb.* Qoradaryo. ≈ Kyrgyzstan/Uzbekistan
Karadeniz *see* Black Sea
Karadeniz Boğazı *see* İstanbul Boğazı
152 B13 **Karadepe** Balkan Welaýaty, W Turkmenistan 38.04N 54.01E
Karadzhar *see* Qorajar
Karaferiye *see* Véroia
Karagan *see* Garagan
151 R10 **Karaganda** *Kaz.* Qaraghandy. Karaganda, C Kazakhstan 49.52N 73.07E
151 R10 **Karaganda** *off.* Karagandinskaya Oblast', *Kaz.* Qaraghandy Oblysy. ◈ *province* C Kazakhstan
Karagandinskaya Oblast' *see* Karaganda
151 T10 **Karagayly** *Kaz.* Qaraghayly. Karaganda, C Kazakhstan 49.25N 75.31E
Karagel' *see* Garagöl
127 Pp8 **Karaginskiy, Ostrov** *island* E Russian Federation
207 T1 **Karaginskiy Zaliv** *bay* E Russian Federation
143 P13 **Karagöl Dağları** ▲▲ NE Turkey
116 L13 **Karahisar** Edirne, NW Turkey 40.47N 26.34E
131 V3 **Karaidel'** Respublika Bashkortostan, W Russian Federation 55.50N 56.55E
131 V3 **Karaidel'skiy** Respublika Bashkortostan, W Russian Federation 55.51N 57.09E
116 L13 **Karaidemir Barajı** ⊠ NW Turkey
161 J21 **Kāraikāl** Pondicherry, SE India 10.58N 79.49E
161 I22 **Kāraikkudi** Tamil Nādu, SE India 10.04N 78.46E
151 Y11 **Kara Irtysh** *Rus.* Chërnyy Irtysh. ≈ NE Kazakhstan
149 N5 **Karaj** Tehrān, N Iran 35.43N 51.25E
174 H5 **Karak** Pahang, Peninsular Malaysia 3.24N 101.58E
Karak *see* Al Karak
153 T11 **Kara-Kabak** Oshskaya Oblast', SW Kyrgyzstan 39.40N 72.45E
Kara-Kala *see* Magtymguly
Karakala *see* Oqqal'a
Karakalpakstan, Respublika *see* Qoraqalpog'iston Respublikasi
Karakalpakya *see* Qoraqalpog'iston
Karakax *see* Moyu
164 G10 **Karakax He** ≈ NW China
124 S9 **Karakaya Barajı** ⊠ C Turkey
175 Ss4 **Karakelang, Pulau** *island* N Indonesia
Karakılısse *see* Ağrı
Karak, Muḥāfaẓat al *see* Al Karak
Kara-Köl *see* Kara-Kul'
153 Y7 **Karakol** *prev.* Przheval'sk. Issyk-Kul'skaya Oblast', NE Kyrgyzstan 42.31N 78.20E
153 X8 **Karakol** *var.* Karakolka. Issyk-Kul'skaya Oblast', NE Kyrgyzstan 41.30N 77.18E
Karakolka *see* Karakol
155 W2 **Karakoram Highway** *road* China/Pakistan
155 Z3 **Karakoram Pass** *Chin.* Karakoram Shankou. *pass* C Asia 35.23N 77.45E
158 I3 **Karakoram Range** ▲▲ C Asia
Karakoram Shankou *see* Karakoram Pass
Karaköse *see* Ağrı
151 P14 **Karakoyyn, Ozero** *Kaz.* Qaraqoyyn. ◎ C Kazakhstan
85 F19 **Karakubis** Ghanzi, W Botswana 22.03S 20.36E
153 T9 **Kara-Kul'** *Kir.* Kara-Köl. Dzhalal-Abadskaya Oblast', W Kyrgyzstan 40.35N 73.36E
Karakul' *see* Qorako'l, Uzbekistan
Karakul' *see* Qarokŭl, Tajikistan
153 U10 **Kara-Kul'dzha** Oshskaya Oblast', SW Kyrgyzstan 40.32N 73.50E
131 T3 **Karakulino** Udmurtskaya Respublika, NW Russian Federation 56.02N 53.45E
Karakul', Ozero *see* Qarokŭl
Kara Kum *see* Garagum
Kara Kum Canal/ Karakumskiy Kanal *see* Garagum Kanaly
Karakumy, Peski *see* Garagum
85 E17 **Karakuwisa** Okavango, NE Namibia 18.55S 19.40E
126 Jj14 **Karam** Irkutskaya Oblast', S Russian Federation 55.07N 107.21E
Karamai *see* Karamay
175 N13 **Karamain, Pulau** *island* N Indonesia
142 I16 **Karaman** Karaman, S Turkey 37.10N 33.13E
142 H16 **Karaman** ◈ *province* S Turkey
116 M8 **Karamandere** ≈ NE Bulgaria
164 J4 **Karamay** *var.* Karamai, Kelamayi, *prev. Chin.* K'o-la-ma-i. Xinjiang Uygur Zizhiqu, NW China 45.33N 84.45E
175 Nn11 **Karambu** Borneo, N Indonesia 3.48S 116.06E
193 H14 **Karamea** West Coast, South Island, NZ 41.15S 172.07E
193 H14 **Karamea** ≈ South Island, NZ
193 G15 **Karamea Bight** *gulf* South Island, NZ
Karamet-Niyaz *see* Garamätnyýaz
164 K10 **Karamiran He** ≈ NW China
176 Yy11 **Karamor, Pengunungan** ▲▲ Papua, E Indonesia
153 S11 **Karamyk** Oshskaya Oblast', SW Kyrgyzstan 39.28N 71.45E
175 Nn16 **Karangasem** Bali, S Indonesia 8.24S 115.40E
160 H12 **Kāranja** Mahārāshtra, C India 20.30N 77.26E
Karanpur *see* Karanpura
158 F9 **Karanpura** *var.* Karanpur. Rājasthān, NW India 29.46N 73.30E
Karánsebes/Karansebesch *see* Caransebeș
151 T14 **Karaoy** *Kaz.* Qaraoy. Almaty, SE Kazakhstan 45.52N 74.44E
116 N7 **Karapelit** *Rom.* Stejarul. Dobrich, NE Bulgaria 43.40N 27.33E
142 I15 **Karapınar** Konya, C Turkey 37.43N 33.34E
85 D22 **Karas** ◈ *district* S Namibia
153 Y8 **Kara-Say** Issyk-Kul'skaya Oblast', NE Kyrgyzstan 41.34N 77.55E
85 E22 **Karasburg** Karas, S Namibia 27.59S 18.45E
Kara Sea *see* Karskoye More
94 K9 **Kárášjohka** *var.* Karašjokka. ≈ N Norway
94 L9 **Karasjok** *Fin.* Kaarasjoki, *Lapp.* Kárášjohka. Finnmark, N Norway 69.27N 25.28S
Kárášjohka *see* Karasjok
Karašjokka *see* Kárášjohka
Kara Strait *see* Karskiye Vorota, Proliv
Kara Su *see* Mesta/Néstos
151 N8 **Karasu** *Kaz.* Qarasū. Kostanay, N Kazakhstan 52.43N 65.28E
142 F11 **Karasu** Sakarya, NW Turkey 41.03N 30.39E
Karasubazar *see* Bilohirs'k
125 G14 **Karasuk** Novosibirskaya Oblast', C Russian Federation 53.41N 78.04E
151 U13 **Karatal** *Kaz.* Qaratal. ≈ SE Kazakhstan
142 K17 **Karataş** Adana, S Turkey 36.37N 35.24E
151 Q16 **Karatau** *Kaz.* Qarataū. Zhambyl, S Kazakhstan 43.09N 70.28E
Karatau *see* Karatau, Khrebet
151 P16 **Karatau, Khrebet** *var.* Karatau, *Kaz.* Qarataū. ▲▲ S Kazakhstan
150 G13 **Karaton** *Kaz.* Qaraton. Atyrau, W Kazakhstan 46.33N 53.31E
170 C12 **Karatsu** *var.* Karatu. Saga, Kyūshū, SW Japan 33.27N 129.55E
Karatu *see* Karatsu
126 Hh7 **Karaul** Taymyrskiy (Dolgano-Nenetskiy) Avtonomnyy Okrug, N Russian Federation 70.07N 83.12E
Karaulbazar *see* Qorovulbozor
Karauzyak *see* Qorao'zak
117 D16 **Karáva** ▲ C Greece 39.19N 21.33E
Karavanke *see* Karawanken
117 F22 **Karavás** Kýthira, S Greece 36.21N 22.57E
115 J20 **Karavastasë, Laguna e** *var.* Kënet' e Karavastas, Kravasta Lagoon. *lagoon* W Albania
Karavastas, Kënet' e *see* Karavastasë, Laguna e
120 I5 **Karavere** Tartumaa, E Estonia 58.25N 26.29E
117 L23 **Karavonísia** *island* Kykládes, Greece, Aegean Sea
174 Jj14 **Karawang** *prev.* Krawang. Jawa, C Indonesia 6.13S 107.16E
111 T10 **Karawanken** *Slvn.* Karavanke. ▲▲ Austria/Serbia
Karaxahar *see* Kaidu He
143 R13 **Karayazı** Erzurum, NE Turkey 39.40N 42.09E
151 Q12 **Karazhal** Karaganda, C Kazakhstan 48.02N 70.52E
145 S9 **Karbalā'** *var.* Kerbala, Kerbela. S Iraq 32.37N 44.03E
96 L11 **Kårböle** Gävleborg, C Sweden 61.59N 15.16E
113 M23 **Karcag** Jász-Nagykun-Szolnok, E Hungary 47.21N 20.51E
Kardak *see* Imia
116 N7 **Kardam** Dobrich, NE Bulgaria 43.45N 28.06E
Kardamila *see* Kardámyla
117 L18 **Kardámyla** *var.* Kardamila, Kardhámila. Chíos, E Greece 38.33N 26.04E
Kardeljevo *see* Ploče
Kardh *see* Qardho
Kardhámila *see* Kardámyla
Kardhítsa *see* Kardítsa
117 E16 **Kardítsa** *var.* Kardhítsa. Thessalía, C Greece 39.22N 21.55E
120 E4 **Kärdla** *Ger.* Kertel. Hiiumaa, W Estonia 59.00N 22.42E
Karelia *see* Kareliya, Respublika
121 I16 **Karelichy** *Pol.* Korelicze, *Rus.* Korelichi. Hrodzyenskaya Voblasts', W Belarus 53.34N 26.07E
128 I10 **Kareliya, Respublika** *prev.* Karel'skaya ASSR, *Eng.* Karelia. ◈ *autonomous republic* NW Russian Federation
Karel'skaya ASSR *see* Kareliya, Respublika
83 E22 **Karema** Rukwa, W Tanzania 6.49S 30.25E
Karen *see* Hualien
85 I14 **Karenda** Central, C Zambia 14.42S 26.52E
178 Gg8 **Karen State** *var.* Kawthule State, Kayin State. ◈ *state* S Burma
94 J10 **Karesuando** *Fin.* Kaaresuanto, *Lapp.* Gárasavvon. Norrbotten, N Sweden 68.25N 22.28E
Karet *see* Kâgheț
Kareyz-e-Elyās/Kārez Iliās *see* Kārīz-e Elyās
126 Gg12 **Kargasok** Tomskaya Oblast', C Russian Federation 59.01N 80.34E
126 Gg14 **Kargat** Novosibirskaya Oblast', C Russian Federation 55.07N 80.19E
142 J11 **Kargı** Çorum, N Turkey 41.09N 34.31E
158 I5 **Kargil** Jammu and Kashmir, NW India 34.34N 76.06E
Kargilik *see* Yecheng
128 L11 **Kargopol'** Arkhangel'skaya Oblast', NW Russian Federation 61.30N 38.53E
112 F12 **Kargowa** *Ger.* Unruhstadt. Lubuskie, W Poland 52.05N 15.50E
79 X13 **Kari** Bauchi, E Nigeria 11.13N 10.34E
85 J15 **Kariba** Mashonaland West, N Zimbabwe 16.28S 28.47E
85 J16 **Kariba, Lake** ⊠ Zambia/Zimbabwe
172 Nn5 **Kariba-yama** ▲ Hokkaidō, NE Japan 42.36N 139.55E
85 C19 **Karibib** Erongo, C Namibia 21.56S 15.51E
Karies *see* Karyés
94 L9 **Karigasniemi** *Lapp.* Garegegasnjárga. Lappi, N Finland 69.24N 25.52E
172 P6 **Karikachi-tōge** *pass* Hokkaidō, NE Japan 43.08N 142.46E
192 J2 **Karikari, Cape** *headland* North Island, NZ 34.47S 173.24E
Karīmābād *see* Hunza
174 K10 **Karimata, Kepulauan** *island group* N Indonesia
174 K9 **Karimata, Pulau** *island* Kepulauan Karimata, N Indonesia
174 K10 **Karimata, Selat** *strait* W Indonesia
161 I14 **Karīmnagar** Andhra Pradesh, C India 18.28N 79.09E
194 I13 **Karimui** Chimbu, C PNG 6.19S 144.48E
174 L13 **Karimunjawa, Pulau** *island* S Indonesia
82 N12 **Karin** Sahil, N Somalia 10.48N 45.46E
Kariot *see* Ikaría
95 L20 **Karis** *Fin.* Karjaa. Etelä-Suomi, SW Finland 60.05N 23.39E
Káristos *see* Kárystos
154 J4 **Kārīz-e Elyās** *var.* Kareyz-e-Elyās, Kārez Iliās. Herāt, NW Afghanistan 35.26N 61.24E
Karjaa *see* Karis
151 T10 **Karkaralinsk** *Kaz.* Qarqaraly. Karaganda, E Kazakhstan 49.31N 75.53E
194 J11 **Karkar Island** *island* N PNG
149 N7 **Karkas, Kūh-e** ▲▲ C Iran
148 K8 **Karkheh, Rūd-e** ≈ SW Iran
117 L20 **Karkinágri** *var.* Karkinágrio. Ikaría, Dodekánisa, Greece, Aegean Sea 37.31N 26.01E
Karkinágrio *see* Karkinágri
119 R12 **Karkinits'ka Zatoka** *Rus.* Karkinitskiy Zaliv. *gulf* S Ukraine
Karkinitskiy Zaliv *see* Karkinits'ka Zatoka
95 L19 **Karkkila** *Swe.* Högfors. Etelä-Suomi, S Finland 60.31N 24.10E
95 M19 **Kärkölä** Etelä-Suomi, S Finland 60.52N 25.17E
190 G9 **Karkoo** South Australia 34.03S 135.45E
Karkūk *see* Kirkūk
120 D5 **Kärla** *Ger.* Kergel. Saaremaa, W Estonia 58.19N 22.15E
Karleby *see* Kokkola
112 F7 **Karlino** *Ger.* Körlin an der Persante. Zachodnio-pomorskie, NW Poland 54.02N 15.52E
143 Q13 **Karlıova** Bingöl, E Turkey 39.16N 41.01E
119 U6 **Karlivka** Poltavs'ka Oblast', C Ukraine 49.27N 35.08E
Karl-Marx-Stadt *see* Chemnitz
Karlö *see* Hailuoto
114 C11 **Karlobag** *It.* Carlopago. Lika-Senj, W Croatia 44.31N 15.06E
114 D9 **Karlovac** *Ger.* Karlstadt, *Hung.* Károlyváros. Karlovac, C Croatia 45.28N 15.31E
114 C10 **Karlovac** *off.* Karlovačka Županija. ◈ *province* C Croatia
Karlovačka Županija *see* Karlovac
113 A16 **Karlovarský Kraj** ◈ W Czech Republic
117 M19 **Karlovási** *var.* Néon Karlovási, Néon Karlovásion. Sámos, Dodekánisa, Greece, Aegean Sea 37.48N 26.42E
116 J9 **Karlovo** *prev.* Levskigrad. Plovdiv, C Bulgaria 42.39N 24.49E
113 A16 **Karlovy Vary** *Ger.* Karlsbad; *prev. Eng.* Carlsbad. Karlovarský Kraj, W Czech Republic 50.13N 12.51E
Karlsbad *see* Karlovy Vary
97 L17 **Karlsborg** Västra Götaland, S Sweden 58.31N 14.31E
Karlsburg *see* Alba Iulia
97 L22 **Karlshamn** Blekinge, S Sweden 56.10N 14.49E
97 L16 **Karlskoga** Örebro, C Sweden 59.19N 14.33E
97 M22 **Karlskrona** Blekinge, S Sweden 56.11N 15.38E
103 G21 **Karlsruhe** *var.* Carlsruhe. Baden-Württemberg, SW Germany 49.01N 8.24E
97 K16 **Karlstad** Värmland, C Sweden 59.22N 13.36E
31 R3 **Karlstad** Minnesota, N USA 48.34N 96.31W
103 I18 **Karlstadt** Bayern, C Germany 49.58N 9.46E
Karlstadt *see* Karlovac
41 Q14 **Karluk** Kodiak Island, Alaska, USA 57.34N 154.27W
Karluk *see* Qarluq
121 O17 **Karma** *Rus.* Korma. Homyel'skaya Voblasts', SE Belarus 53.07N 30.48E
161 F14 **Karmāla** Mahārāshtra, W India 18.26N 75.08E
152 M11 **Karmana** Navoiy Viloyati, C Uzbekistan 40.09N 65.18E
144 G8 **Karmi'él** *var.* Carmiel. Northern, N Israel 32.55N 35.21E
97 B16 **Karmøy** *island* S Norway
158 I9 **Karnāl** Haryāna, N India 29.40N 76.58E
159 W15 **Karnaphuli Reservoir** ⊠ NE India
161 F17 **Karnātaka** *var.* Kanara; *prev.* Maisur, Mysore. ◈ *state* W India
27 S13 **Karnes City** Texas, SW USA 28.52N 97.54W
111 P9 **Karnische Alpen** *It.* Alpi Carniche. ▲▲ Austria/Italy
116 M9 **Karnobat** Burgas, E Bulgaria 42.39N 26.58E
111 Q9 **Kärnten** *off.* Land Kärnten, *Eng.* Carinthi, *Slvn.* Koroška. ◈ *state* S Austria
Karnul *see* Kurnool
85 K16 **Karoi** Mashonaland West, N Zimbabwe 16.49S 29.40E
Karol *see* Carei
Károly-Fehérvár *see* Alba Iulia
Károlyváros *see* Karlovac
179 Qq15 **Karomatan** Mindanao, S Philippines 7.47N 123.48E
84 M12 **Karonga** Northern, N Malawi 9.56S 33.54E
153 W10 **Karool-Tëbë** Narynskaya Oblast', C Kyrgyzstan 40.33N 75.52E
190 J9 **Karoonda** South Australia 35.04S 139.58E
155 S9 **Karor Lāl Esan** Punjab, E Pakistan 31.15N 70.54E
155 T11 **Karor Pacca** *var.* Kahror, Kahror Pakka. Punjab, E Pakistan 29.37N 71.58E
Karosa *see* Karossa
175 P10 **Karossa** *var.* Karosa. Sulawesi, C Indonesia 1.38S 119.21E
Karpasía/Karpas Peninsula *see* Kırpaşa
Karpaten *see* Carpathian Mountains
117 L22 **Karpáthio Pélagos** *sea* Dodekánisa, Greece, Aegean Sea
117 N24 **Kárpathos** Kárpathos, SE Greece 35.30N 27.13E
117 N24 **Kárpathos** *It.* Scarpanto; *anc.* Carpathos, Carpathus. *island* SE Greece
Karpathos Strait *see* Karpathou, Stenó
117 N24 **Karpathou, Stenó** *var.* Karpathos Strait, Scarpanto Strait. *strait* Dodekánisa, Greece, Aegean Sea
Karpaty *see* Carpathian Mountains
117 E17 **Karpenísi** *prev.* Karpenísion. Stereá Ellás, C Greece 38.55N 21.45E
Karpenísion *see* Karpenísi
Karpilovka *see* Aktsyabrski
129 O8 **Karpogory** Arkhangel'skaya Oblast', NW Russian Federation 64.01N 44.22E
188 I7 **Karratha** Western Australia 20.43S 116.52E
143 S12 **Kars** *var.* Qars. Kars, NE Turkey 40.34N 43.04E
143 S12 **Kars** *var.* Qars. ◈ *province* NE Turkey
151 O12 **Karsakpay** *Kaz.* Qarsaqbay. Karaganda, C Kazakhstan 47.51N 66.42E
95 L15 **Kärsämäki** Oulu, C Finland 63.58N 25.49E
Karsau *see* Kārsava
120 K9 **Kārsava** *Ger.* Karsau; *prev. Rus.* Korsovka. Ludza, E Latvia 56.46N 27.39E
Karshi *see* Garşy, Turkmenistan
Karshi *see* Qarshi, Uzbekistan
Karshinskaya Step *see* Qarshi Cho'li
Karshinskiy Kanal *see* Qarshi Kanali
86 I5 **Karskiye Vorota, Proliv** *Eng.* Kara Strait. *strait* N Russian Federation
126 Gg5 **Karskoye More** *Eng.* Kara Sea. *sea* Arctic Ocean
95 L17 **Karstula** Länsi-Suomi, W Finland 62.52N 24.48E
131 Q5 **Karsun** Ul'yanovskaya Oblast', W Russian Federation 54.12N 47.00E
125 E12 **Kartaly** Chelyabinskaya Oblast', C Russian Federation 53.02N 60.42E
20 E13 **Karthaus** Pennsylvania, NE USA 41.06N 78.03W
112 I7 **Kartuzy** Pomorskie, NW Poland 54.21N 18.10E
172 N10 **Karumai** Iwate, Honshū, C Japan 40.19N 141.27E
189 U4 **Karumba** Queensland, NE Australia 17.31S 140.51E
148 L10 **Kārūn** *var.* Rūd-e Kārūn. ≈ SW Iran
94 K13 **Karungi** Norrbotten, N Sweden 66.03N 23.55E
94 K13 **Karunki** Lappi, N Finland 66.01N 24.06E
Kārūn, Rūd-e *see* Kārūn
161 H21 **Karūr** Tamil Nādu, SE India 10.58N 78.03E
95 K17 **Karvia** Länsi-Suomi, W Finland 62.07N 22.34E
113 J17 **Karviná** *Ger.* Karwin, *Pol.* Karwina; *prev.* Nová Karvinná. Moravskoslezský Kraj, E Czech Republic 49.51N 18.33E
161 E17 **Kārwār** Karnātaka, W India 14.49N 74.09E
110 M7 **Karwendelgebirge** ▲▲ Austria/Germany
Karwin/Karwina *see* Karviná
117 I14 **Karyés** *var.* Karies. Ágion Óros, N Greece 40.15N 24.15E
126 Kk16 **Karymskoye** Chitinskaya Oblast', S Russian Federation 51.36N 114.02E
117 I19 **Kárystos** *var.* Káristos. Évvoia, C Greece 38.01N 24.25E
142 E17 **Kaş** Antalya, SW Turkey 36.12N 29.37E
41 Y14 **Kasaan** Prince of Wales Island, Alaska, USA 55.32N 132.24W
170 G14 **Kasai** Hyōgo, Honshū, SW Japan 34.56N 134.49E
81 K21 **Kasai** *var.* Cassai, Kassai. ≈ Angola/Dem. Rep. Congo
81 K22 **Kasai Occidental** *off.* Région Kasai Occidental. ◈ *region* S Dem. Rep. Congo
81 L21 **Kasai Oriental** *off.* Région Kasai Oriental. ◈ *region* C Dem. Rep. Congo
81 L24 **Kasaji** Katanga, S Dem. Rep. Congo 10.22S 23.29E
171 Kk16 **Kasama** Ibaraki, Honshū, S Japan 36.21N 140.15E
84 L12 **Kasama** Northern, N Zambia 10.13S 31.12E
Kasan *see* Koson
85 H16 **Kasane** North-West, NE Botswana 17.48S 25.06E
83 E23 **Kasanga** Rukwa, W Tanzania 8.27S 31.10E
81 G21 **Kasangulu** Bas-Congo, W Dem. Rep. Congo 4.33S 15.12E
Kasansay *see* Kosonsoy
Kasargen *see* Kasari
161 E20 **Kāsaragod** Kerala, SW India 12.30N 75.01E
120 P13 **Kasari** *var.* Kasari Jōgi, *Ger.* Kasargen. ≈ W Estonia
Kasari Jōgi *see* Kasari
15 K9 **Kasba Lake** ◎ Northwest Territories/Nunavut, N Canada
Kaschau *see* Košice
170 Bb16 **Kaseda** Kagoshima, Kyūshū, SW Japan 31.23N 130.18E
85 I14 **Kasempa** North Western, NW Zambia 13.27S 25.49E
81 O24 **Kasenga** Katanga, SE Dem. Rep. Congo 10.22S 28.37E
81 P17 **Kasenye** *var.* Kasenyi. Orientale, NE Dem. Rep. Congo 1.22N 30.25E
Kasenyi *see* Kasenye
83 E18 **Kasese** SW Uganda 0.10N 30.06E
81 O19 **Kasese** Maniema, E Dem. Rep. Congo 1.36S 27.31E
158 J11 **Kāsganj** Uttar Pradesh, N India 27.48N 78.36E
149 U4 **Kashaf Rūd** ≈ NE Iran
149 N7 **Kāshān** Eşfahān, C Iran 33.57N 51.30E
130 M10 **Kashary** Rostovskaya Oblast', SW Russian Federation 49.02N 40.58E
41 O12 **Kashegelok** Alaska, USA 60.57N 157.46W
Kashgar *see* Kashi
164 E7 **Kashi** *Chin.* Kaxgar, K'o-shih, *Uigh.* Kashgar. Xinjiang Uygur Zizhiqu, NW China 39.32N 75.58E
171 Gg16 **Kashihara** *var.* Kasihara. Nara, Honshū, SW Japan 34.31N 135.49E
171 Kk17 **Kashima** Ibaraki, Honshū, S Japan 35.59N 140.37E
170 C13 **Kashima** *var.* Kasima. Saga, Kyūshū, SW Japan 33.09N 130.07E
171 L16 **Kashima-nada** *gulf* S Japan
128 K15 **Kashin** Tverskaya Oblast', W Russian Federation 57.20N 37.34E
158 K10 **Kāshīpur** Uttaranchal, N India 29.13N 78.58E
130 L4 **Kashira** Moskovskaya Oblast', W Russian Federation 54.53N 38.13E
171 K17 **Kashiwa** *var.* Kasiwa. Chiba, Honshū, S Japan 35.50N 139.59E
171 Jj13 **Kashiwazaki** *var.* Kasiwazaki. Niigata, Honshū, C Japan 37.22N 138.33E
Kashkadar'inskaya Oblast' *see* Qashqadaryo Viloyati
149 T5 **Kāshmar** *var.* Turshiz; *prev.* Solṭānābād, Torshiz. Khorāsān-Razavī, NE Iran 35.15N 58.28E
Kashmir *see* Jammu and Kashmir
155 R12 **Kashmor** Sind, SE Pakistan 28.23N 69.43E
155 S5 **Kashmūnd Ghar** *Eng.* Kashmund Range. ▲▲ E Afghanistan
Kashmund Range *see* Kashmūnd Ghar
Kasi *see* Vārānasi
159 O12 **Kasia** Uttar Pradesh, N India 26.45N 83.55E
41 N12 **Kasigluk** Alaska, USA 60.54N 162.31W
Kasihara *see* Kashihara
41 R12 **Kasilof** Alaska, USA 60.20N 151.16W
Kasima *see* Kashima
Kasimköj *see* General Toshevo
130 M4 **Kasimov** Ryazanskaya Oblast', W Russian Federation 54.59N 41.22E
81 P18 **Kasindi** Nord Kivu, E Dem. Rep. Congo 0.07N 29.41E
175 Ss8 **Kasiruta, Pulau** *island* Kepulauan Bacan, E Indonesia
84 M12 **Kasitu** ≈ N Malawi
176 V12 **Kasiui, Pulau** *island* Kepulauan Watubela, E Indonesia
Kasiwa *see* Kashiwa
Kasiwazaki *see* Kashiwazaki
32 L14 **Kaskaskia River** ≈ Illinois, N USA
95 J17 **Kaskinen** *Swe.* Kaskö. Länsi-Suomi, W Finland 62.19N 21.15E
Kaskö *see* Kaskinen
Kas Kong *see* Kŏng, Kaôh
9 O17 **Kaslo** British Columbia, SW Canada 49.54N 116.57W
Käsmark *see* Kežmarok
174 M10 **Kasongan** Borneo, C Indonesia 2.01S 113.21E

◆ Country
● Country Capital
◇ Dependent Territory
○ Dependent Territory Capital
◈ Administrative Region
✈ International Airport
▲ Mountain
▲▲ Mountain Range
Volcano
≈ River
◎ Lake
⊠ Reservoir

Kasongo – Kerchens'kyy Pivostriv

81 N21 **Kasongo** Maniema, E Dem. Rep. Congo *4.22S 26.42E*
81 H22 **Kasongo-Lunda** Bandundu, SW Dem. Rep. Congo *6.30S 16.51E*
117 M24 **Kásos** *island* S Greece
Kasos Strait *see* Kasou, Stenó
117 M25 **Kasou, Stenó** *var.* Kasos Strait. *strait* Dodekánisos/Kríti, Greece, Aegean Sea
143 T10 **Kaspi** C Georgia *41.54N 44.25E*
116 M8 **Kaspichan** Shumen, NE Bulgaria *43.18N 27.09E*
Kaspīy Mangy Oypaty *see* Caspian Depression
131 Q16 **Kaspiysk** Respublika Dagestan, SW Russian Federation *42.52N 47.40E*
Kaspiyskiy *see* Lagan'
Kaspiyskoye More/Kaspiy Tengizi *see* Caspian Sea
Kassa *see* Košice
Kassai *see* Kasai
82 I9 **Kassala** Kassala, E Sudan *15.24N 36.25E*
82 H9 **Kassala** ◈ *state* NE Sudan
117 G15 **Kassándra** *prev.* Pallíni; *anc.* Pallene. *peninsula* NE Greece
117 G15 **Kassándras, Akrotírio** *headland* N Greece *39.58N 23.22E*
117 H15 **Kassándras, Kólpos** *var.* Kólpos Toronaíos. *gulf* N Greece
145 Y11 **Kassārah** E Iraq *31.21N 47.25E*
103 I15 **Kassel** *prev.* Cassel. Hessen, C Germany *51.19N 9.30E*
76 M6 **Kasserine** *var.* Al Qaşrayn. W Tunisia *35.15N 8.52E*
12 J14 **Kasshabog Lake** ◎ Ontario, SE Canada
145 O5 **Kassīr, Sabkhat al** ◎ E Syria
31 W10 **Kasson** Minnesota, N USA *44.00N 92.42W*
117 C17 **Kassópeia** *var.* Kassópi. *site of ancient city* Ípeiros, W Greece *39.08N 20.38E*
Kassópi *see* Kassópeia
117 N24 **Kastállou, Akrotírio** *headland* Kárpathos, SE Greece *35.24N 27.08E*
142 I11 **Kastamonu** *var.* Castamoni, Kastamuni. Kastamonu, N Turkey *41.22N 33.46E*
142 I10 **Kastamonu** *var.* Kastamuni. ◈ *province* N Turkey
Kastamuni *see* Kastamonu
117 E14 **Kastaneá** Kentrikí Makedonía, N Greece *40.25N 22.09E*
Kastélli *see* Kíssamos
Kastellórizon *see* Megísti
97 N21 **Kastlösa** Kalmar, S Sweden *56.25N 16.25E*
117 D14 **Kastoría** Dytikí Makedonía, N Greece *40.30N 21.16E*
130 K7 **Kastornoye** Kurskaya Oblast', W Russian Federation *51.49N 38.07E*
117 I21 **Kástro** Sífnos, Kykládes, Greece, Aegean Sea *36.58N 24.45E*
97 J23 **Kastrup** ✕ (København) København, E Denmark *55.36N 12.39E*
121 Q17 **Kastsyukovichy** *Rus.* Kostyukovichi. Mahilyowskaya Voblasts', E Belarus *53.19N 32.03E*
121 O18 **Kastsyukowka** *Rus.* Kostyukovka. Homyel'skaya Voblasts', SE Belarus *52.32N 30.54E*
170 Cc12 **Kasuga** Fukuoka, Kyūshū, SW Japan *33.31N 130.27E*
171 I15 **Kasugai** Aichi, Honshū, SW Japan *35.15N 136.57E*
83 E21 **Kasulu** Kigoma, W Tanzania *4.33S 30.06E*
171 Gg13 **Kasumi** Hyōgo, Honshū, SW Japan *35.36N 134.37E*
171 Kk16 **Kasumiga-ura** ◎ Honshū, S Japan
131 R17 **Kasumkent** Respublika Dagestan, SW Russian Federation *41.39N 48.09E*
84 M13 **Kasungu** Central, C Malawi *13.01S 33.30E*
155 W9 **Kasūr** Punjab, E Pakistan *31.07N 74.30E*
85 G15 **Kataba** Western, W Zambia *15.28S 23.25E*
21 R4 **Katahdin, Mount** ▲ Maine, NE USA *45.55N 68.52W*
81 M20 **Katako-Kombe** Kasai Oriental, C Dem. Rep. Congo *3.24S 24.25E*
41 T12 **Katalla** Alaska, USA *60.12N 144.31W*
Katana *see* Qaţanā
81 L24 **Katanga** *off.* Région du Katanga; *prev.* Shaba. ◈ *region* SE Dem. Rep. Congo
126 J12 **Katanga** ∽ C Russian Federation
160 J11 **Katangi** Madhya Pradesh, C India *21.46N 79.49E*
188 J13 **Katanning** Western Australia *33.44S 117.33E*
189 P8 **Kata Tjuta** *var.* Mount Olga ▲ Northern Territory, C Australia *25.20S 130.47E*
Katawaz *see* Zarghūn Shahr
157 Q22 **Katchall Island** *island* Nicobar Islands, India, NE Indian Ocean
117 F14 **Kateríni** Kentrikí Makedonía, N Greece *40.17N 22.30E*
119 P7 **Katerynopil'** Cherkas'ka Oblast', C Ukraine *49.00N 30.59E*
178 Gg3 **Katha** Sagaing, N Burma *24.10N 96.19E*
189 P2 **Katherine** Northern Territory, N Australia *14.28S 132.19E*
160 B11 **Kāthiāwār Peninsula** *peninsula* W India
159 P11 **Kathmandu** *Nep.* Kāṭhmāṇḍu; *prev.* Kantipur. ● (Nepal) Central, C Nepal *27.46N 85.16E*
158 H7 **Kathua** Jammu and Kashmir, NW India *32.24N 75.33E*
78 L12 **Kati** Koulikoro, SW Mali *12.45N 8.06W*
159 R13 **Katihār** Bihār, NE India *25.33N 87.34E*
192 N7 **Katikati** Bay of Plenty, North Island, NZ *37.33S 175.55E*
85 H16 **Katima Mulilo** Caprivi, NE Namibia *17.31S 24.19E*
79 N15 **Katiola** C Ivory Coast *8.12N 5.04W*
203 V10 **Katiu** *atoll* Îles Tuamotu, C French Polynesia
119 N12 **Katlabukh, Ozero** ◎ SW Ukraine
41 P14 **Katmai, Mount** ▲ Alaska, USA *58.16N 154.57W*
160 J9 **Katni** Madhya Pradesh, C India *23.46N 80.28E*
117 D19 **Káto Achaïa** *var.* Kato Ahaia, Káto Akhaía. Dytikí Ellás, S Greece *38.08N 21.35E*
Kato Ahaia/Káto Akhaía *see* Káto Achaïa
124 Nn3 **Kato Lakatámeia** *var.* Kato Lakatamia. C Cyprus *35.07N 33.20E*
Kato Lakatamia *see* Kato Lakatámeia
81 N22 **Katompi** Katanga, SE Dem. Rep. Congo *6.10S 26.19E*
85 K14 **Katondwe** Lusaka, C Zambia *15.08S 30.10E*
116 H12 **Káto Nevrokópi** *prev.* Káto Nevrokópion. Anatolikí Makedonía kai Thráki, NE Greece *41.21N 23.52E*
Káto Nevrokópion *see* Káto Nevrokópi
83 E18 **Katonga** ∽ S Uganda
117 F15 **Káto Ólympos** ▲▲ C Greece
117 D17 **Katoúna** Dytikí Ellás, C Greece *38.46N 21.07E*
117 E19 **Káto Vlasiá** Dytikí Makedonía, S Greece *38.02N 21.54E*
113 J16 **Katowice** *Ger.* Kattowitz. Śląskie, S Poland *50.14N 19.00E*
159 S15 **Kātoya** West Bengal, NE India *23.39N 88.10E*
142 E16 **Katrançik Dağı** ▲▲ SW Turkey
97 N16 **Katrineholm** Södermanland, C Sweden *58.58N 16.15E*
98 I11 **Katrine, Loch** ◎ C Scotland, UK
79 V12 **Katsina** Katsina, N Nigeria *12.58N 7.33E*
79 U12 **Katsina** ◈ *state* N Nigeria
69 P8 **Katsina Ala** ∽ S Nigeria
170 C11 **Katsumoto** Nagasaki, Iki, SW Japan *33.49N 129.42E*
171 L16 **Katsuta** *var.* Katuta. Ibaraki, Honshū, S Japan *36.24N 140.31E*
171 K17 **Katsuura** *var.* Katuura. Chiba, Honshū, S Japan *35.09N 140.16E*
171 I14 **Katsuyama** *var.* Katuyama. Fukui, Honshū, SW Japan *36.03N 136.28E*
170 Ff13 **Katsuyama** Okayama, Honshū, SW Japan *35.06N 133.43E*
Kattakurgan *see* Kattaqo'rg'on
153 N11 **Kattaqo'rg'on** *Rus.* Kattakurgan. Samarqand Viloyati, C Uzbekistan *39.55N 66.11E*
117 O23 **Kattavía** Ródos, Dodekánisa, Greece, Aegean Sea *35.56N 27.47E*
97 I21 **Kattegat** *Dan.* Kattegatt. *strait* N Europe
Kattegatt *see* Kattegat
97 P19 **Katthammarsvik** Gotland, SE Sweden *57.27N 18.54E*
Kattowitz *see* Katowice
127 N17 **Katun'** ∽ S Russian Federation
Katuta *see* Katsuta
Katuura *see* Katsuura
Katuyama *see* Katsuyama
Katwijk *see* Katwijk aan Zee
100 G11 **Katwijk aan Zee** *var.* Katwijk. Zuid-Holland, W Netherlands *52.12N 4.24E*
40 B8 **Kaua'i** *var.* Kauai. *island* Hawaiian Islands, Hawai'i, USA, C Pacific Ocean
40 C8 **Kaua'i Channel** *var.* Kauai Channel *channel* Hawai'i, USA, C Pacific Ocean
175 Ss11 **Kaubalatmada, Gunung** *var.* Kaplamada. ▲ Pulau Buru, E Indonesia *3.16S 126.17E*
203 U10 **Kauehi** *atoll* Îles Tuamotu, C French Polynesia
Kauen *see* Kaunas
103 K24 **Kaufbeuren** Bayern, S Germany *47.52N 10.37E*
27 U7 **Kaufman** Texas, SW USA *32.35N 96.18W*
103 I15 **Kaufungen** Hessen, C Germany *51.16N 9.39E*
95 K17 **Kauhajoki** Länsi-Suomi, W Finland *62.24N 22.12E*
95 K16 **Kauhava** Länsi-Suomi, W Finland *63.06N 23.07E*
32 M7 **Kaukauna** Wisconsin, N USA *44.18N 88.18W*
94 L11 **Kaukonen** Lappi, N Finland *67.28N 24.49E*
40 A8 **Kaulakahi Channel** *channel* Hawai'i, USA, C Pacific Ocean
40 E9 **Kaunakakai** Moloka'i, Hawai'i, USA, C Pacific Ocean *21.05N 157.01W*
40 F12 **Kaunā Point** *var.* Kauna Point *headland* Hawai'i, USA, C Pacific Ocean *19.02N 155.52W*
120 F13 **Kaunas** *Ger.* Kauen, *Pol.* Kowno; *prev. Rus.* Kovno. Kaunas, C Lithuania *54.54N 23.57E*
120 F13 **Kaunas** ◈ *province* C Lithuania
194 H10 **Kaup** East Sepik, NW PNG *3.48S 143.56E*
79 U12 **Kaura Namoda** Zamfara, NW Nigeria *12.43N 6.17E*
Kaushany *see* Căuşeni
95 K16 **Kaustinen** Länsi-Suomi, W Finland *63.33N 23.40E*
175 T7 **Kau, Teluk** *bay* Pulau Halmahera, E Indonesia
101 M23 **Kautenbach** Diekirch, NE Luxembourg *49.57N 6.01E*
94 K10 **Kautokeino** *Lapp.* Guovdageaidnu. Finnmark, N Norway *69.00N 23.01E*
Kavadar *see* Kavadarci
115 P19 **Kavadarci** *Turk.* Kavadar. C FYR Macedonia *41.25N 22.00E*
Kavaja *see* Kavajë
115 K20 **Kavajë** *It.* Cavaia, Kavaja. Tiranë, W Albania *41.11N 19.33E*
116 M13 **Kavak Çayı** ∽ NW Turkey
Kavakli *see* Topolovgrad
116 I13 **Kavála** *prev.* Kavála. Anatolikí Makedonía kai Thráki, NE Greece *40.57N 24.25E*
116 I13 **Kaválas, Kólpos** *gulf* Aegean Sea, NE Mediterranean Sea
127 Nn17 **Kavalerovo** Primorskiy Kray, SE Russian Federation *44.17N 135.06E*
161 J17 **Kāvali** Andhra Pradesh, E India *15.04N 80.02E*
Kaválla *see* Kavála
Kavango *see* Cubango/Okavango
161 C21 **Kavaratti** Lakshadweep, SW India *10.33N 72.37E*
116 O8 **Kavarna** Dobrich, NE Bulgaria *43.26N 28.21E*
120 G12 **Kavarskas** Utena, E Lithuania *55.27N 24.55E*
78 I13 **Kavendou** ▲ C Guinea *10.49N 12.14W*
Kavengo *see* Cubango/Okavango
161 F20 **Kāveri** *var.* Cauvery. ∽ S India
195 N9 **Kavieng** *var.* Kaewieng. NE PNG *2.34S 150.48E*
85 H16 **Kavimba** North-West, NE Botswana *18.03S 24.30E*
85 I15 **Kavingu** Southern, S Zambia *15.39S 26.03E*
149 Q6 **Kavīr, Dasht-e** *var.* Great Salt Desert. *salt pan* N Iran
Kavirondo Gulf *see* Winam Gulf
Kavkaz *see* Caucasus
97 K23 **Kävlinge** Skåne, S Sweden *55.46N 13.04E*
197 I15 **Kavukavu Reef** *var.* Beqa Barrier Reef, Cakaubalavu Reef. *reef* Viti Levu, SW Fiji
84 G12 **Kavungo** Moxico, E Angola *11.31S 22.59E*
171 M10 **Kawabe** Akita, Honshū, C Japan *39.39N 140.14E*
171 K15 **Kawagoe** Saitama, Honshū, S Japan *35.55N 139.30E*
171 K16 **Kawaguchi** *var.* Kawaguti. Saitama, Honshū, S Japan *35.49N 139.40E*
Kawaguti *see* Kawaguchi
172 N11 **Kawai** Iwate, Honshū, C Japan *39.36N 141.40E*
40 A8 **Kawaihoa Point** *headland* Ni'ihau, Hawai'i, USA, C Pacific Ocean *21.47N 160.12W*
192 K3 **Kawakawa** Northland, North Island, NZ *35.23S 174.03E*
84 I13 **Kawama** North Western, NW Zambia *13.04S 25.59E*
84 K11 **Kawambwa** Luapula, N Zambia *9.48S 29.04E*
170 F14 **Kawanoe** Ehime, Shikoku, SW Japan *34.01N 133.32E*
160 K11 **Kawardha** Chhattīsgarh, C India *21.59N 81.12E*
12 I14 **Kawartha Lakes** ◎ Ontario, SE Canada
171 K17 **Kawasaki** Kanagawa, Honshū, S Japan *35.33N 139.40E*
175 T9 **Kawassi** Pulau Obi, E Indonesia *1.32S 127.25E*
172 N8 **Kawauchi** Aomori, Honshū, C Japan *41.11N 141.00E*
192 L5 **Kawau Island** *island* N NZ
192 N10 **Kaweka Range** ▲▲ North Island, NZ
Kawelecht *see* Puhja
176 Z13 **Kawentinkim** Papua, E Indonesia *5.04S 140.55E*
192 O8 **Kawerau** Bay of Plenty, North Island, NZ *38.06S 176.42E*
192 L8 **Kawhia** Waikato, North Island, NZ *38.04S 174.49E*
192 K8 **Kawhia Harbour** *inlet* North Island, NZ
37 V8 **Kawich Peak** ▲ Nevada, W USA *38.00N 116.27W*
37 V9 **Kawich Range** ▲▲ Nevada, W USA
12 G12 **Kawigamog Lake** ◎ Ontario, S Canada
175 Rr3 **Kawio, Kepulauan** *island group* N Indonesia
178 Gg9 **Kawkareik** Karen State, S Burma *16.34N 98.14E*
29 O8 **Kaw Lake** ⊠ Oklahoma, C USA
177 G3 **Kawlin** Sagaing, N Burma *23.48N 95.40E*
Kawm Umbū *see* Kôm Ombo
Kawthule State *see* Karen State
Kaxgar *see* Kashi
164 D7 **Kaxgar He** ∽ NW China
164 J5 **Kax He** ∽ NW China
79 P12 **Kaya** C Burkina *13.04N 1.09W*
178 Gg7 **Kayah State** ◈ *state* C Burma
126 J7 **Kayak** Taymyrskiy (Dolgano-Nenetskiy) Avtonomnyy Okrug, N Russian Federation *71.27N 103.21E*
41 T12 **Kayak Island** *island* Alaska, USA
116 M11 **Kayalıköy Barajı** ⊠ NW Turkey
161 G23 **Kāyamkulam** Kerala, SW India *9.10N 76.31E*
177 G8 **Kayan** Yangon, SW Burma *16.54N 96.34E*
175 N6 **Kayan, Sungai** *prev.* Kajan. ∽ Borneo, C Indonesia
150 F14 **Kaydak, Sor** *salt flat* SW Kazakhstan
Kaydanovo *see* Dzyarzhynsk
39 N9 **Kayenta** Arizona, SW USA *36.43N 110.15W*
78 J11 **Kayes** Kayes, W Mali *14.25N 11.21W*
78 J11 **Kayes** ◈ *region* SW Mali
Kayin State *see* Karen State
151 U10 **Kaynar** *var.* Kajnar. Vostochnyy Kazakhstan, E Kazakhstan *49.13N 77.27E*
Kaynary *see* Căinari
85 H15 **Kayoya** Western, W Zambia *16.13S 24.09E*
Kayrakkum *see* Qayroqqum
Kayrakkumskoye Vodokhranilishche *see* Qayroqqum, Obanbori
142 K14 **Kayseri** *var.* Kaisaria; *anc.* Caesarea Mazaca, Mazaca. Kayseri, C Turkey *38.42N 35.28E*
142 K14 **Kayseri** *var.* Kaisaria. ◈ *province* C Turkey
38 L2 **Kaysville** Utah, W USA *41.10N 111.55W*
126 Hh8 **Kayyerkan** Taymyrskiy (Dolgano-Nenetskiy) Avtonomnyy Okrug, N Russian Federation *69.26N 87.31E*
Kayyngdy *see* Kaindy
12 L11 **Kazabazua** Québec, SE Canada *45.58N 76.00W*
12 L12 **Kazabazua** ∽ Québec, SE Canada
126 M7 **Kazach'ye** Respublika Sakha (Yakutiya), NE Russian Federation *70.38N 135.54E*
Kazakdar'ya *see* Qozoqdaryo
152 E9 **Kazakhlyshor, Solonchak** *var.* Solonchak Shorkazakhly. *salt marsh* NW Turkmenistan
Kazakhskaya SSR/Kazakh Soviet Socialist Republic *see* Kazakhstan
151 R9 **Kazakhskiy Melkosopochnik** *Eng.* Kazakh Uplands, Kirghiz Steppe, *Kaz.* Saryarqa. *uplands* C Kazakhstan
150 L12 **Kazakhstan** *off.* Republic of Kazakhstan, *var.* Kazakstan, *Kaz.* Qazaqstan, Qazaqstan Respublikasy; *prev.* Kazakh Soviet Socialist Republic, *Rus.* Kazakhskaya SSR. ◆ *republic* C Asia
Kazakh Uplands *see* Kazakhskiy Melkosopochnik
Kazakstan *see* Kazakhstan
150 L14 **Kazalinsk** Kzylorda, S Kazakhstan *45.51N 62.08E*
131 R4 **Kazan'** Respublika Tatarstan, W Russian Federation *55.43N 49.07E*
131 R4 **Kazan'** ✕ Respublika Tatarstan, W Russian Federation *55.46N 49.21E*
15 K8 **Kazan** ∽ Nunavut, NW Canada
Kazandzhik *see* Bereket
119 R8 **Kazanka** Mykolayivs'ka Oblast', S Ukraine *47.49N 32.50E*
Kazanketken *see* Qozonketkan
Kazanlik *see* Kazanlŭk
116 J9 **Kazanlŭk** *prev.* Kazanlik. Stara Zagora, C Bulgaria *42.38N 25.24E*
172 T17 **Kazan-rettō** *Eng.* Volcano Islands. *island group* SE Japan
125 F12 **Kazanskoye** Tyumenskaya Oblast', C Russian Federation *55.39N 69.06E*
119 V12 **Kazantip, Mys** *headland* S Ukraine *45.27N 35.50E*
153 U9 **Kazarman** Narynskaya Oblast', C Kyrgyzstan *41.21N 74.03E*
Kazatin *see* Kozyatyn
Kazbegi *see* Kazbek
Kazbegi *see* Qazbegi
143 T9 **Kazbek** *var.* Kazbegi, *Geor.* Mqinvartsveri. ▲ N Georgia *42.43N 44.28E*
84 M13 **Kazembe** Eastern, NE Zambia *12.06S 32.45E*
149 N11 **Kāzerūn** Fārs, S Iran *29.40N 51.38E*
129 R12 **Kazhym** Respublika Komi, NW Russian Federation *60.19N 51.26E*
Kazi Ahmad *see* Qāzi Ahmad
Kazi Magomed *see* Qazimämmäd
142 H16 **Kâzımkarabekir** Karaman, S Turkey *37.13N 32.58E*
113 M20 **Kazincbarcika** Borsod-Abaúj-Zemplén, NE Hungary *48.15N 20.40E*
121 H17 **Kazlowshchyna** *Pol.* Kozlowszczyzna, *Rus.* Kozlovshchina. Hrodzyenskaya Voblasts', W Belarus *53.19N 25.18E*
121 E14 **Kazlų Rūda** Marijampolė, S Lithuania *54.45N 23.28E*
150 E9 **Kaztalovka** Zapadnyy Kazakhstan, W Kazakhstan *49.47N 48.40E*
81 K22 **Kazumba** Kasai Occidental, S Dem. Rep. Congo *6.19S 21.57E*
171 Mm10 **Kazuno** Akita, Honshū, C Japan *40.08N 140.47E*
Kazvin *see* Qazvīn
120 J12 **Kaz'yany** *Rus.* Koz'yany. Vitsyebskaya Voblasts', NW Belarus *55.19N 26.52E*
125 Ff9 **Kazym** ∽ N Russian Federation
112 H10 **Kcynia** *Ger.* Exin. Kujawsko-pomorskie, C Poland *53.00N 17.29E*
Kéa *see* Ioulís/Tziá
40 H11 **Kea'au** *var.* Keaau. Hawai'i, USA, C Pacific Ocean *19.36N 155.01W*
40 F11 **Keāhole Point** *var.* Keahole Point *headland* Hawai'i, USA, C Pacific Ocean *19.43N 156.03W*
40 G12 **Kealakekua** Hawai'i, USA, C Pacific Ocean *19.31N 155.55W*
40 H11 **Kea, Mauna** ▲ Hawai'i, USA, C Pacific Ocean *19.50N 155.30W*
39 N10 **Keams** Arizona, SW USA *35.47N 110.09W*
Kéamu *see* Aneityum
31 O16 **Kearney** Nebraska, C USA *40.42N 99.06W*
38 L3 **Kearns** Utah, W USA *40.39N 112.00W*
117 H20 **Kéas, Stenó** *strait* SE Greece
143 O14 **Keban Barajı** *dam* C Turkey *38.49N 38.46E*
143 O14 **Keban Barajı** ⊠ C Turkey
79 S13 **Kebbi** ◈ *state* NW Nigeria
78 G10 **Kébémèr** NW Senegal *15.24N 16.25W*
76 M7 **Kebili** *var.* Qibilī. C Tunisia *33.42N 9.06E*
144 H4 **Kebir, Nahr el** ∽ NW Syria
82 A10 **Kebkabiya** Northern Darfur, W Sudan *13.39N 24.04E*
94 I11 **Kebnekaise** ▲ N Sweden *68.01N 18.24E*
83 M14 **K'ebrī Dehar** Somali, E Ethiopia *6.43N 44.15E*
154 K15 **Kech** ∽ SW Pakistan
8 K10 **Kechika** ∽ British Columbia, W Canada
113 K23 **Kecskemét** Bács-Kiskun, C Hungary *46.54N 19.41E*
174 Gg2 **Kedah** ◈ *state* Peninsular Malaysia
120 F12 **Kėdainiai** Kaunas, C Lithuania *55.19N 24.00E*
Kedder *see* Kehra
11 N13 **Kedgwick** New Brunswick, SE Canada *47.37N 67.21W*
174 Ll15 **Kediri** Jawa, C Indonesia *7.45S 112.01E*
176 Y10 **Kedir Sarmi** Papua, E Indonesia *2.00S 139.01E*
169 V7 **Kedong** Heilongjiang, NE China *48.00N 126.15E*
78 I12 **Kédougou** SE Senegal *12.34N 12.09W*
126 Gg13 **Kedrovyy** Tomskaya Oblast', C Russian Federation *57.31N 79.45E*
113 H16 **Kędzierzyn-Koźle** *Ger.* Heydebrech. Opolskie, S Poland *50.20N 18.12E*
14 G6 **Keele** ∽ Northwest Territories, NW Canada
8 K6 **Keele Peak** ▲ Yukon Territory, NW Canada *63.31N 130.21W*
Keelung *see* Chilung
21 N10 **Keene** New Hampshire, NE USA *42.56N 72.14W*
101 H17 **Keerbergen** Vlaams Brabant, C Belgium *51.01N 4.39E*
85 E21 **Keetmanshoop** Karas, S Namibia *26.36S 18.07E*
10 A11 **Keewatin** Ontario, S Canada *49.46N 94.30W*
31 V4 **Keewatin** Minnesota, N USA *47.24N 93.04W*
Kefallinía *see* Kefalloniá
117 B18 **Kefalloniá** *var.* Kefallinía. *island* Iónia Nisiá, Greece, C Mediterranean Sea
117 M22 **Kéfalos** Kos, Dodekánisa, Greece, Aegean Sea *36.44N 26.58E*
175 Rr17 **Kefamenanu** Timor, C Indonesia *9.31S 124.28E*
144 F10 **Kefar Sava** *var.* Kfar Saba. Central, C Israel *32.12N 34.58E*
Kefe *see* Feodosiya
79 V15 **Keffi** Nassarawa, C Nigeria *8.52N 7.54E*
94 H4 **Keflavík** ✕ (Reykjavík) Reykjanes, W Iceland *63.58N 22.37W*
94 H4 **Keflavík** Reykjanes, W Iceland *64.01N 22.35W*
Kegalee *see* Kegalla
161 J25 **Kegalla** *var.* Kegalee, Kegalle. Sabaragamuwa Province, C Sri Lanka *7.13N 80.21E*
Kegalle *see* Kegalla
Kegayli *see* Kegeyli
Kegel *see* Keila
151 W16 **Kegen** Almaty, SE Kazakhstan *42.57N 79.15E*
152 H7 **Kegeyli** *prev.* Kegayli. Qoraqalpog'iston Respublikasi, W Uzbekistan *42.46N 59.49E*
103 F22 **Kehl** Baden-Württemberg, SW Germany *48.34N 7.49E*
120 H3 **Kehra** *Ger.* Kedder. Harjumaa, NW Estonia *59.19N 25.22E*
119 U6 **Kehychivka** Kharkivs'ka Oblast', E Ukraine *49.18N 35.46E*
99 L17 **Keighley** N England, UK *53.51N 1.53W*
Kei Islands *see* Kai, Kepulauan
Keijō *see* Sŏul
120 G3 **Keila** *Ger.* Kegel. Harjumaa, NW Estonia *59.19N 24.28E*
Keilberg *see* Klínovec
85 F23 **Keimoes** Northern Cape, W South Africa *28.41S 20.57E*
Keina/Keinis *see* Käina
176 Yy14 **Keisak** Papua, E Indonesia *7.01S 140.02E*
Keishū *see* Kyŏngju
79 T11 **Keïta** Tahoua, C Niger *14.43N 5.45E*
80 J12 **Kéita, Bahr** *var.* Doka. ∽ S Chad
190 K10 **Keith** South Australia *36.01S 140.22E*
98 K8 **Keith** NE Scotland, UK *57.33N 2.57W*
28 K3 **Keith Sebelius Lake** ⊠ Kansas, C USA
34 G11 **Keizer** Oregon, NW USA *44.59N 123.01W*
40 A8 **Kekaha** Kaua'i, Hawai'i, USA, C Pacific Ocean *21.58N 159.43W*
153 U10 **Këk-Art** *prev.* Alaykel', Alay-Kuu. Oshskaya Oblast', SW Kyrgyzstan *40.15N 74.21E*
153 W10 **Këk-Aygyr** *var.* Keyaygyr. Narynskaya Oblast', C Kyrgyzstan *40.42N 75.37E*
153 V9 **Këk-Dzhar** Narynskaya Oblast', C Kyrgyzstan *41.28N 74.48E*
12 L8 **Kekek** ∽ Québec, SE Canada
193 K15 **Kekerengu** Canterbury, South Island, NZ *41.55S 174.05E*
113 L21 **Kékes** ▲ N Hungary *47.53N 19.59E*
175 Rr17 **Kekneno, Gunung** ▲ Timor, S Indonesia
153 S9 **Këk-Tash** *Kir.* Kök-Tash. Dzhalal-Abadskaya Oblast', W Kyrgyzstan *41.08N 72.25E*
83 M15 **K'elafo** Somali, E Ethiopia *5.36N 44.12E*
175 O6 **Kelai, Sungai** ∽ Borneo, N Indonesia
Kelamayi *see* Karamay
Kelang *see* Klang
174 H3 **Kelantan** ◈ *state* Peninsular Malaysia
Kelantan *see* Kelantan, Sungai
174 H3 **Kelantan, Sungai** *var.* Kelantan. ∽ Peninsular Malaysia
Kelat *see* Kālat
Këlcyra *see* Këlcyrë
115 L22 **Këlcyrë** *var.* Këlcyra. Gjirokastër, S Albania *40.19N 20.10E*
Kelifskiy Uzboy *see* Kelif Uzboýy
152 L14 **Kelif Uzboýy** *Rus.* Kelifskiy Uzboy. *salt marsh* E Turkmenistan
143 O12 **Kelkit** Gümüşhane, NE Turkey *40.05N 39.25E*
142 M12 **Kelkit Çayı** ∽ N Turkey
81 G18 **Kéllé** Cuvette-Ouest, W Congo *0.04S 14.33E*
79 W11 **Kellé** Zinder, S Niger *14.10N 10.10E*
151 P7 **Kellerovka** Severnyy Kazakhstan, N Kazakhstan *53.51N 69.15E*
15 H1 **Kellett, Cape** *headland* Banks Island, Northwest Territories, NW Canada *71.57N 125.55W*
33 S11 **Kelleys Island** *island* Ohio, N USA
35 N8 **Kellogg** Idaho, NW USA *47.30N 116.07W*
94 M12 **Kelloselkä** Lappi, N Finland *66.55N 28.52E*
99 F17 **Kells** *Ir.* Ceanannas. E Ireland *53.43N 6.52W*
120 E12 **Kelmė** Šiauliai, C Lithuania *55.39N 22.57E*
101 M19 **Kelmis** *var.* La Calamine. Liège, E Belgium *50.43N 6.01E*
80 H12 **Kélo** Tandjilé, SW Chad *9.21N 15.49E*
85 I14 **Kelongwa** North Western, NW Zambia *13.41S 26.19E*
9 N17 **Kelowna** British Columbia, SW Canada *49.49N 119.28W*
9 X12 **Kelsey** Manitoba, C Canada *56.02N 96.31W*
36 M6 **Kelseyville** California, W USA *38.58N 122.51W*
98 K13 **Kelso** SE Scotland, UK *55.36N 2.27W*
34 G10 **Kelso** Washington, NW USA *46.09N 122.54W*
205 W15 **Keltie, Cape** *headland* Antarctica
Keltsy *see* Kielce
174 Hh6 **Keluang** *var.* Kluang. Johor, Peninsular Malaysia *2.01N 103.18E*
174 I8 **Kelume** Pulau Lingga, W Indonesia *0.12S 104.27E*
9 U15 **Kelvington** Saskatchewan, S Canada *52.10N 103.30W*
128 J7 **Kem'** Respublika Kareliya, NW Russian Federation *64.55N 34.17E*
128 I7 **Kem'** ∽ NW Russian Federation
143 O13 **Kemah** Erzincan, E Turkey *39.34N 39.01E*
143 N13 **Kemaliye** Erzincan, C Turkey *39.17N 38.30E*
Kemaman *see* Cukai
Kemanlar *see* Isperikh
8 K14 **Kemano** British Columbia, SW Canada *53.39N 127.58W*
Kemarat *see* Khemmarat
175 Qq9 **Kembani** Pulau Peleng, N Indonesia *1.32S 122.57E*
142 F17 **Kemer** Antalya, SW Turkey *36.39N 30.33E*
126 H14 **Kemerovo** *prev.* Shcheglovsk. Kemerovskaya Oblast', C Russian Federation *55.25N 86.04E*
126 H14 **Kemerovskaya Oblast'** ◈ *province* S Russian Federation
94 L13 **Kemi** Lappi, NW Finland *65.46N 24.34E*
94 M12 **Kemijärvi** *Swe.* Kemiträsk. Lappi, N Finland *66.41N 27.24E*
94 M12 **Kemijärvi** ◎ N Finland
94 L13 **Kemijoki** ∽ NW Finland
153 V7 **Kemin** *prev.* Bystrovka. Chuyskaya Oblast', N Kyrgyzstan
94 L13 **Keminmaa** Lappi, NW Finland *65.49N 24.34E*
Kemins Island *see* Nikumaroro
Kemiö *see* Kimito
Kemiträsk *see* Kemijärvi
131 P5 **Kemlya** Respublika Mordoviya, W Russian Federation *54.42N 45.16E*
101 B18 **Kemmel** West-Vlaanderen, W Belgium *50.42N 2.51E*
35 S16 **Kemmerer** Wyoming, C USA *41.47N 110.32W*
Kemmuna *see* Comino
81 I14 **Kémo** ◈ *prefecture* S Central African Republic
27 U7 **Kemp** Texas, SW USA *32.26N 96.13W*
95 L14 **Kempele** Oulu, C Finland *64.55N 25.25E*
103 D15 **Kempen** Nordrhein-Westfalen, W Germany *51.22N 6.25E*
27 Q5 **Kemp, Lake** ◎ Texas, SW USA
205 W5 **Kemp Land** *physical region* Antarctica
27 S9 **Kempner** Texas, SW USA *31.03N 98.01W*
46 H3 **Kemp's Bay** Andros Island, W Bahamas *24.02N 77.32W*
191 U6 **Kempsey** New South Wales, SE Australia *31.04S 152.49E*
103 J24 **Kempten** Bayern, S Germany *47.43N 10.19E*
13 N9 **Kempt, Lac** ◎ Québec, SE Canada
191 P17 **Kempton** Tasmania, SE Australia *42.34S 147.13E*
160 J9 **Ken** ∽ C India
41 R12 **Kenai** Alaska, USA *60.33N 151.15W*
(0) D5 **Kenai Mountains** ▲▲ Alaska, USA
41 R12 **Kenai Peninsula** *peninsula* Alaska, USA
23 V11 **Kenansville** North Carolina, SE USA *34.57N 77.54W*
152 A10 **Kenar** *prev. Rus.* Ufra. Balkan Welaýaty, NW Turkmenistan *40.00N 53.05E*
124 Pp15 **Kenâyis, Râs el-** *headland* N Egypt *31.13N 27.53E*
99 K16 **Kendal** NW England, UK *54.19N 2.45W*
25 Y16 **Kendall** Florida, SE USA *25.39N 80.18W*
15 Ll6 **Kendall, Cape** *headland* Nunavut, E Canada *63.31N 87.09W*
20 J15 **Kendall Park** New Jersey, NE USA *40.25N 74.33W*
33 Q11 **Kendallville** Indiana, N USA *41.24N 85.10W*
175 Qq12 **Kendari** Sulawesi, C Indonesia *3.57S 122.36E*
174 L10 **Kendawangan** Borneo, C Indonesia *2.31S 110.13E*
174 Ll15 **Kendeng, Pegunungan** ▲▲ Jawa, S Indonesia
160 O12 **Kendrāpāra** *var.* Kendrāparha. Orissa, E India *20.29N 86.25E*
Kendrāparha *see* Kendrāpāra
160 O11 **Kendujhargarh** *prev.* Keonjihargarh. Orissa, E India *21.42N 85.36E*
27 S13 **Kenedy** Texas, SW USA *28.49N 97.51W*
Kënekesir *see* Könekesir
78 J15 **Kenema** SE Sierra Leone *7.55N 11.12W*
31 P16 **Kenesaw** Nebraska, C USA *40.37N 98.39W*
Këneurgench *see* Köneürgenç
81 H21 **Kenge** Bandundu, SW Dem. Rep. Congo *4.52S 16.58E*
Kengen *see* Kangen
178 Hh5 **Keng Tung** *var.* Kentung. Shan State, E Burma *21.18N 99.36E*
85 F23 **Kenhardt** Northern Cape, W South Africa *29.20S 21.10E*
78 J12 **Kéniéba** Kayes, W Mali *12.47N 11.16W*
Kenimekh *see* Konimex
175 Nn3 **Keningau** Sabah, East Malaysia *5.21N 116.10E*
76 F6 **Kénitra** *prev.* Port-Lyautey. NW Morocco *34.19N 6.29W*
23 V9 **Kenly** North Carolina, SE USA *35.39N 78.16W*
99 B21 **Kenmare** *Ir.* Neidín. S Ireland *51.52N 9.34W*
30 L2 **Kenmare** North Dakota, N USA *48.40N 102.04W*
99 A21 **Kenmare River** *Ir.* An Ribhéar. *inlet* NE Atlantic Ocean
20 D10 **Kenmore** New York, NE USA *42.58N 78.52W*
27 W8 **Kennard** Texas, SW USA *31.21N 95.10W*
31 N10 **Kennebec** South Dakota, N USA *43.53N 99.52W*
21 Q7 **Kennebec River** ∽ Maine, NE USA
21 P9 **Kennebunk** Maine, NE USA *43.22N 70.33W*
41 R13 **Kennedy Entrance** *strait* Alaska, USA
177 Ff3 **Kennedy Peak** ▲ W Burma *23.18N 93.52E*
24 K9 **Kenner** Louisiana, S USA *29.57N 90.15W*
188 I8 **Kenneth Range** ▲▲ Western Australia
29 Y9 **Kennett** Missouri, C USA *36.14N 90.03W*
20 I16 **Kennett Square** Pennsylvania, NE USA *39.50N 75.40W*
34 K10 **Kennewick** Washington, NW USA *46.12N 119.08W*
10 E11 **Kenogami** ∽ Ontario, S Canada
13 Q7 **Kénogami, Lac** ◎ Québec, SE Canada
12 G8 **Kenogami Lake** Ontario, S Canada *48.04N 80.10W*
12 F7 **Kenogamissi Lake** ◎ Ontario, S Canada
8 I6 **Keno Hill** Yukon Territory, NW Canada *63.54N 135.18W*
10 A11 **Kenora** Ontario, S Canada *49.46N 94.25W*
33 N9 **Kenosha** Wisconsin, N USA *42.34N 87.49W*
11 P14 **Kensington** Prince Edward Island, SE Canada *46.25N 63.39W*
28 L3 **Kensington** Kansas, C USA *39.46N 99.01W*
34 I11 **Kent** Oregon, NW USA *45.14N 120.43W*
26 J9 **Kent** Texas, SW USA *31.03N 104.13W*
34 H8 **Kent** Washington, NW USA *47.22N 122.13W*
99 P22 **Kent** *cultural region* SE England, UK
151 P16 **Kentau** Yuzhnyy Kazakhstan, S Kazakhstan *43.28N 68.40E*
191 P14 **Kent Group** *island group* Tasmania, SE Australia
33 N12 **Kentland** Indiana, N USA *40.46N 87.25W*
33 R12 **Kenton** Ohio, N USA *40.39N 83.36W*
15 J4 **Kent Peninsula** *peninsula* Nunavut, N Canada
117 F14 **Kentrikí Makedonía** *Eng.* Macedonia Central. ◈ *region* N Greece
22 J6 **Kentucky** *off.* Commonwealth of Kentucky; also known as The Bluegrass State. ◈ *state* C USA
22 H8 **Kentucky Lake** ⊠ Kentucky/Tennessee, S USA
Kentung *see* Keng Tung
11 P15 **Kentville** Nova Scotia, SE Canada *45.04N 64.30W*
24 K8 **Kentwood** Louisiana, S USA *30.56N 90.30W*
33 P9 **Kentwood** Michigan, N USA *42.52N 85.33W*
83 H17 **Kenya** *off.* Republic of Kenya. ◆ *republic* E Africa
Kenya, Mount *see* Kirinyaga
174 Hh3 **Kenyir, Tasik** *var.* Tasek Kenyir. ◎ Peninsular Malaysia
31 W10 **Kenyon** Minnesota, N USA *44.16N 92.59W*
31 Y16 **Keokuk** Iowa, C USA *40.24N 91.22W*
Keonjihargarh *see* Kendujhargarh
Kéos *see* Tziá
31 X16 **Keosauqua** Iowa, C USA *40.43N 91.58W*
31 X15 **Keota** Iowa, C USA *41.21N 91.57W*
23 O11 **Keowee, Lake** ⊠ South Carolina, SE USA
128 I7 **Kepa** *var.* Kepe. Respublika Kareliya, NW Russian Federation *65.09N 32.15E*
Kepe *see* Kepa
201 O13 **Kepirohi Falls** *waterfall* Pohnpei, E Micronesia
193 B22 **Kepler Mountains** ▲▲ South Island, NZ
113 I14 **Kępno** Wielkopolskie, C Poland *51.17N 17.56E*
67 C24 **Keppel Island** *island* N Falkland Islands
Keppel Island *see* Niuatoputapu
67 C23 **Keppel Sound** *sound* N Falkland Islands
142 D12 **Kepsut** Balıkesir, NW Turkey *39.40N 28.09E*
174 J6 **Kepulauan Riau** *off.* Propinsi Kepulauan Riau. ◈ *province* NW Indonesia
176 W12 **Kerai** Papua, E Indonesia *3.53S 134.30E*
Kerak *see* Al Karak
161 F22 **Kerala** ◈ *state* S India
194 H10 **Keram** ∽ N PNG
172 O14 **Kerama-rettō** *island group* SW Japan
191 N10 **Kerang** Victoria, SE Australia *35.46S 144.01E*
Kerasunt *see* Giresun
117 H19 **Keratéa** *var.* Keratea. Attikí, C Greece *37.48N 23.58E*
95 M19 **Kerava** *Swe.* Kervo. Etelä-Suomi, S Finland *60.22N 25.01E*
Kerbala/Kerbela *see* Karbalā'
34 F15 **Kerby** Oregon, NW USA *42.10N 123.39W*
119 W12 **Kerch** *Rus.* Kerch'. Respublika Krym, SE Ukraine *45.22N 36.30E*
Kerchens'ka Protska/Kerchenskiy Proliv *see* Kerch Strait
119 V13 **Kerchens'kyy Pivostriv** *peninsula* S Ukraine

◆ Country
● Country Capital
◇ Dependent Territory
○ Dependent Territory Capital
◈ Administrative Region
✕ International Airport
▲ Mountain
▲▲ Mountain Range
⛰ Volcano
∽ River
◎ Lake
⊠ Reservoir

KERCH STRAIT – KIL

124 R4 **Kerch Strait** *var.* Bosporus Cimmerius, Enikale Strait, *Rus.* Kerchenskiy Proliv, *Ukr.* Kerchens'ka Protska. *strait* Black Sea/Sea of Azov
158 K8 **Kerdārnāth** Uttaranchal, N India 30.43N 79.03E
Kerdilio *see* Kerdýlio
116 H13 **Kerdýlio** *var.* Kerdilio. ▲ N Greece 40.46N 23.37E
194 J14 **Kerema** Gulf, S PNG 7.58S 145.46E
Keremitlik *see* Lyulyakovo
142 I9 **Kerempe Burnu** *headland* N Turkey 42.01N 33.20E
82 J9 **Keren** *var.* Cheren. C Eritrea 15.45N 38.22E
27 U7 **Kerens** Texas, SW USA 32.07N 96.13W
192 M6 **Kerepehi** Waikato, North Island, NZ 37.18S 175.33E
151 P10 **Kerey, Ozero** ◎ C Kazakhstan
Kergel *see* Kärla
181 Q12 **Kerguelen** *island* C French Southern and Antarctic Territories
181 Q13 **Kerguelen Plateau** *undersea feature* S Indian Ocean
117 C20 **Kerí** Zákynthos, Iónia Nisiá, Greece, C Mediterranean Sea 37.40N 20.48E
83 H19 **Kericho** Rift Valley, W Kenya 0.21S 35.16E
192 K2 **Kerikeri** Northland, North Island, NZ 35.13S 173.57E
95 O17 **Kerimäki** Isä-Suomi, E Finland 61.55N 29.18E
174 Gg10 **Kerinci, Danau** ◎ Sumatera, W Indonesia
174 Gg9 **Kerinci, Gunung** ▲ Sumatera, W Indonesia 2.00S 101.40E
Keriya *see* Yutian
164 H9 **Keriya He** ∽ NW China
100 J9 **Kerkbuurt** Noord-Holland, C Netherlands 52.29N 5.08E
100 J13 **Kerkdriel** Gelderland, C Netherlands 51.46N 5.21E
77 N6 **Kerkenah, Îles de** *var.* Kerkenna Islands, *Ar.* Juzur Qarqannah. *island group* E Tunisia
Kerkenna Islands *see* Kerkenah, Îles de
117 M20 **Kerketévs** ▲ Sámos, Dodekánisa, Greece, Aegean Sea 37.44N 26.39E
31 T8 **Kerkhoven** Minnesota, N USA 45.12N 95.18W
Kerki *see* Atamyrat
Kerkichi *see* Kerkiçi
152 M14 **Kerkiçi** *Rus.* Kerkichi. Lebap Welaýaty, E Turkmenistan 37.46N 65.18E
117 F16 **Kerkíneo** *prehistoric site* Thessalía, C Greece 39.32N 22.42E
116 G12 **Kerkíni, Límni** *var.* Límni Kerkinitis. ◎ N Greece
Kerkinitis, Límni *see* Kerkíni, Límni
Kérkira *see* Kérkyra
101 M18 **Kerkrade** Limburg, SE Netherlands 50.52N 6.04E
Kerkuk *see* Kirkūk
117 B16 **Kérkyra** *var.* Kérkira, *Eng.* Corfu. Kérkyra, Iónia Nisiá, Greece, C Mediterranean Sea 39.36N 19.55E
117 B16 **Kerkyra** ✈ Kérkyra, Iónia Nisiá, Greece, C Mediterranean Sea 39.36N 19.55E
117 A16 **Kérkyra** *var.* Kérkira, *Eng.* Corfu. *island* Iónia Nisiá, Greece, C Mediterranean Sea
199 Jj12 **Kermadec Islands** *island group* NZ, SW Pacific Ocean
183 R10 **Kermadec Ridge** *undersea feature* SW Pacific Ocean
183 R11 **Kermadec Trench** *undersea feature* SW Pacific Ocean
149 S10 **Kermān** *var.* Kirman; *anc.* Carmana. Kermān, C Iran 30.18N 57.04E
149 R11 **Kermān** *off.* Ostān-e Kermān, *var.* Kirman; *anc.* Carmania. ◐ *province* SE Iran
149 U12 **Kermān, Biābān-e** *var.* Kerman Desert. *desert* SE Iran
148 K6 **Kermānshāh** *var.* Qahremānshahr, *prev.* Bākhtarān. Kermānshāh, W Iran 34.19N 47.04E
149 Q9 **Kermānshāh** Yazd, C Iran 34.19N 47.04E
148 J6 **Kermānshāh** *off.* Ostān-e Kermānshāh; *prev.* Bākhtarān, Kermānshāhān. ◐ *province* W Iran
Kermānshāhān *see* Kermānshāh
116 L10 **Kermen** Sliven, C Bulgaria 42.30N 26.12E
26 L8 **Kermit** Texas, SW USA 31.51N 103.05W
23 P6 **Kermit** West Virginia, NE USA 37.51N 82.24W
23 S9 **Kernersville** North Carolina, SE USA 36.12N 80.13W
37 S12 **Kern River** ∽ California, W USA
37 S12 **Kernville** California, W USA 35.44N 118.25W
117 K21 **Kéros** *island* Kykládes, Greece, Aegean Sea
78 K14 **Kérouané** SE Guinea 9.16N 9.00W
103 D16 **Kerpen** Nordrhein-Westfalen, W Germany 50.51N 6.40E
152 I11 **Kerpichli** Lebap Welaýaty, NE Turkmenistan 40.12N 61.09E
26 M1 **Kerrick** Texas, SW USA 36.29N 102.14W
Kerr Lake *see* John H.Kerr Reservoir
9 S15 **Kerrobert** Saskatchewan, S Canada 51.55N 109.09W
27 Q11 **Kerrville** Texas, SW USA 30.03N 99.06W
99 B20 **Kerry** *Ir.* Ciarraí. *cultural region* SW Ireland
23 S11 **Kershaw** South Carolina, SE USA 34.33N 80.34W
Kertel *see* Kärdla
97 H23 **Kerteminde** Fyn, C Denmark 55.27N 10.40E
169 Q7 **Kerulen** *Chin.* Herlen He, *Mong.* Herlen Gol. ∽ China/Mongolia
Kervo *see* Kerava
Kerýneia *see* Girne
10 H11 **Kesagami Lake** ◎ Ontario, SE Canada
95 O17 **Kesälahti** Itä-Suomi, E Finland 61.54N 29.49E
142 B11 **Keşan** Edirne, NW Turkey 40.52N 26.38E
171 Mm12 **Kesennuma** Miyagi, Honshū, C Japan 38.54N 141.34E
169 V7 **Keshan** Heilongjiang, NE China 48.00N 125.46E
32 M6 **Keshena** Wisconsin, N USA 44.54N 88.37W
142 I13 **Keskin** Kırıkkale, C Turkey 39.40N 33.36E
Késmárk *see* Kežmarok
128 I6 **Kesten'ga** *var.* Kest Enga. Respublika Kareliya, NW Russian Federation 65.53N 31.47E
100 K12 **Kesteren** Gelderland, C Netherlands 51.55N 5.34E
12 H14 **Keswick** Ontario, S Canada 44.15N 79.26W
99 K15 **Keswick** NW England, UK 54.30N 3.03W
113 H24 **Keszthely** Zala, SW Hungary 46.46N 17.16E
126 Hh13 **Ket'** ∽ C Russian Federation
79 R17 **Keta** SE Ghana 5.54N 1.02E
174 Kk10 **Ketapang** Borneo, C Indonesia 1.49S 109.58E
131 O12 **Ketchenery** *prev.* Sovetskoye. Respublika Kalmykiya, SW Russian Federation 47.18N 44.31E
41 Y14 **Ketchikan** Revillagigedo Island, Alaska, USA 55.20N 131.39W
35 O14 **Ketchum** Idaho, NW USA 43.40N 114.24W
Kete/Kete Krakye *see* Kete-Krachi
79 Q15 **Kete-Krachi** *var.* Kete, Kete Krakye. E Ghana 7.49N 0.03W
100 L9 **Ketelmeer** *channel* E Netherlands
155 P17 **Keti Bandar** Sind, SE Pakistan 23.55N 67.31E
151 W16 **Ketmen', Khrebet** ⛰ SE Kazakhstan
79 S16 **Kétou** SE Benin 7.25N 2.36E
112 M7 **Kętrzyn** *Ger.* Rastenburg. Warmińsko-Mazurskie, NE Poland, 54.03N 21.22E
99 N20 **Kettering** C England, UK 52.24N 0.43W
33 R14 **Kettering** Ohio, N USA 39.41N 84.10W
20 F13 **Kettle Creek** ∽ Pennsylvania, NE USA
34 L7 **Kettle Falls** Washington, NW USA 48.36N 118.03W
12 D16 **Kettle Point** *headland* Ontario, S Canada 43.12N 82.01W
31 V6 **Kettle River** ∽ Minnesota, N USA
194 E12 **Ketu** ∽ W PNG
20 G10 **Keuka Lake** ◎ New York, NE USA
Keupriya *see* Primorsko
95 L17 **Keuruu** Länsi-Suomi, W Finland 62.15N 24.34E
Kevevára *see* Kovin
94 L9 **Kevo** *Lapp.* Geavvú. Lappi, N Finland 69.42N 27.08E
46 M6 **Kew** North Caicos, N Turks and Caicos Islands 21.52N 71.57W
32 K11 **Kewanee** Illinois, N USA 41.15N 89.55W
33 N7 **Kewaunee** Wisconsin, N USA 44.27N 87.31W
32 M3 **Keweenaw Bay** ◎ Michigan, N USA
33 N2 **Keweenaw Peninsula** *peninsula* Michigan, N USA 47.15N 88.19W
33 N2 **Keweenaw Point** *headland* Michigan, N USA 47.24N 87.42W
31 N12 **Keya Paha River** ∽ Nebraska/South Dakota, N USA
Keyaygyr *see* Këk-Aygyr
25 Z16 **Key Biscayne** Florida, SE USA 25.41N 80.09W
28 G8 **Keyes** Oklahoma, C USA 36.48N 102.15W
25 Y17 **Key Largo** Key Largo, Florida, SE USA 25.06N 80.24W
23 U3 **Keyser** West Virginia, NE USA 39.26N 78.58W
29 O9 **Keystone Lake** ⊡ Oklahoma, C USA
38 L16 **Keystone Peak** ▲ Arizona, SW USA 31.52N 111.12W
Keystone State *see* Pennsylvania
23 U7 **Keysville** Virginia, NE USA 37.02N 78.28W
29 T3 **Keytesville** Missouri, C USA 39.25N 92.56W
25 W17 **Key West** Florida Keys, Florida, SE USA 24.34N 81.48W
131 T1 **Kez** Udmurtskaya Respublika, NW Russian Federation 57.55N 53.42E
Kezdivásárhely *see* Târgu Secuiesc
126 J13 **Kezhma** Krasnoyarskiy Kray, C Russian Federation 58.57N 101.00E
113 L18 **Kežmarok** *Ger.* Käsmark, *Hung.* Késmárk. Prešovský Kraj, E Slovakia 49.09N 20.25E
Kfar Saba *see* Kefar Sava
85 F20 **Kgalagadi** ◐ *district* SW Botswana
85 I20 **Kgatleng** ◐ *district* SE Botswana
196 F8 **Kgkeklau** Babeldaob, N Palau
129 R6 **Khabarikha** *var.* Chabaricha. Respublika Komi, NW Russian Federation 65.52N 52.19E
127 N16 **Khabarovsk** Khabarovskiy Kray, SE Russian Federation 48.31N 135.07E
126 Mm12 **Khabarovskiy Kray** ◐ *territory* E Russian Federation
147 W7 **Khabb** Abū Ẓaby, E UAE 24.39N 55.43E
Khabour, Nahr al *see* Khābūr, Nahr al
Khabura *see* Al Khābūrah
145 N2 **Khābūr, Nahr al** *var.* Nahr al Khabour. ∽ Syria/Turkey
Khachmas *see* Xaçmaz
82 B12 **Khadari** ∽ W Sudan
Khadera *see* Ḥadera
147 X12 **Khādhil** *var.* Khudal. SE Oman 18.48N 56.48E
161 E14 **Khadki** *prev.* Kirkee. Mahārāshtra, W India 18.34N 73.52E
130 L14 **Khadyzhensk** Krasnodarskiy Kray, SW Russian Federation 44.26N 39.31E
116 N9 **Khadzhiyska Reka** ∽ E Bulgaria
119 P10 **Khadzhybeys'kyy Lyman** ◎ SW Ukraine
144 K3 **Khafsah** Ḥalab, N Syria 36.16N 38.03E
158 M13 **Khāga** Uttar Pradesh, N India 25.46N 81.04E
159 Q13 **Khagaria** Bihār, NE India 25.31N 86.27E
155 Q13 **Khairpur** Sind, SE Pakistan 27.30N 68.49E
126 Hh15 **Khakasiya, Respublika** *prev.* Khakasskaya Avtonomnaya Oblast', *Eng.* Khakassia. ◐ *autonomous republic* C Russian Federation
Khakassia/Khakasskaya Avtonomnaya Oblast' *see* Khakasiya, Respublika
178 H9 **Kha Khaeng, Khao** ▲ W Thailand 16.13N 99.03E
85 G20 **Khakhea** *var.* Kakia. Southern, S Botswana 24.40S 23.28E
Khalach *see* Halaç
Khalándrion *see* Chalándri
131 W7 **Khalilovo** Orenburgskaya Oblast', W Russian Federation 51.25N 58.13E
Khalkabad *see* Xalqobod
148 L3 **Khalkhāl** *prev.* Herowābād. Ardabīl, NW Iran 37.36N 48.34E
Khalkidhikí *see* Chalkidikí
Khalkís *see* Chalkída
129 W3 **Khal'mer-Yu** Respublika Komi, NW Russian Federation 68.00N 64.45E
121 M14 **Khalopyenichy** *Rus.* Kholopenichi. Minskaya Voblasts', NE Belarus 54.31N 28.58E
Khalturin *see* Orlov
147 Y10 **Khalūf** *var.* Al Khaluf. E Oman 20.27N 57.58E
160 K10 **Khamaria** Madhya Pradesh, C India 23.07N 80.54E
160 D11 **Khambhāt** Gujarāt, W India 22.19N 72.39E
160 C12 **Khambhāt, Gulf of** *Eng.* Gulf of Cambay. *gulf* W India
178 K10 **Khâm Đức** *var.* Phước Sơn. Quang Nam-Đa Năng, C Vietnam 15.28N 107.49E
160 G12 **Khāmgaon** Mahārāshtra, C India 20.40N 76.34E
147 O14 **Khamir** *var.* Khamr. W Yemen 16.00N 43.56E
147 N12 **Khamīs Mushayt** *var.* Hamīs Musait. 'Asīr, SW Saudi Arabia 18.19N 42.41E
126 L10 **Khampa** Respublika Sakha (Yakutiya), NE Russian Federation 63.43N 123.02E
Khamr *see* Khamir
85 C19 **Khan** ∽ W Namibia
155 Q2 **Khānābād** Kondoz, NE Afghanistan 36.42N 69.07E
Khân Abou Châmâte/Khan Abou Ech Cham *see* Khān Abū Shāmāt
144 I7 **Khān Abū Shāmāt** *var.* Khân Abou Châmâte, Khan Abou Ech Cham. Dimashq, W Syria 33.43N 36.56E
Khān al Baghdādī *see* Al Baghdādī
Khān al Maḥāwīl *see* Al Maḥāwīl
145 T7 **Khān al Mashāhidah** C Iraq 33.40N 44.15E
145 T10 **Khān al Muṣallá** S Iraq 32.09N 44.19E
145 U6 **Khānaqīn** E Iraq 34.22N 45.22E
145 T11 **Khān ar Ruḥbah** S Iraq 31.42N 44.18E
145 P2 **Khān as Sūr** N Iraq 36.28N 41.36E
145 T8 **Khān Āzād** C Iraq 33.07N 44.21E
160 N13 **Khandaparha** *prev.* Khandpara. Orissa, E India 20.15N 85.10E
Khandpara *see* Khandaparha
155 T2 **Khandūd** *var.* Khandud, Wakhan. Badakhshān, NE Afghanistan 36.57N 72.19E
160 G11 **Khandwa** Madhya Pradesh, C India 21.49N 76.22E
126 Mm10 **Khandyga** Respublika Sakha (Yakutiya), NE Russian Federation 62.39N 135.30E
155 T10 **Khānewāl** Punjab, NE Pakistan 30.18N 71.55E
155 S10 **Khāngarh** Punjab, E Pakistan 29.56N 71.10E
Khanh Hung *see* Soc Trăng
Khaniá *see* Chaniá
Khanka *see* Xonqa
169 Z8 **Khanka, Lake** *var.* Hsing-k'ai Hu, Lake Hanka, *Chin.* Xingkai Hu, *Rus.* Ozero Khanka. ◎ China/Russian Federation
Khanka, Ozero *see* Khanka, Lake
Khankendi *see* Xankändi
Khanlar *see* Xanlar
126 Kk10 **Khannya** ∽ NE Russian Federation
155 S12 **Khānpur** Punjab, SE Pakistan 23.37N 70.40E
155 S12 **Khānpur** Punjab, E Pakistan 28.31N 70.30E
144 I4 **Khān Shaykhūn** *var.* Khan Sheikhun. Idlib, NW Syria 35.27N 36.37E
Khan Sheikhun *see* Khān Shaykhūn
151 S15 **Khantau** Zhambyl, S Kazakhstan 44.13N 73.47E
151 W16 **Khan Tengri, Pik** ▲ SE Kazakhstan 42.13N 80.13E
178 J9 **Khanthabouli** *prev.* Savannakhét. Savannakhét, S Laos 16.37N 104.48E
125 Ff10 **Khanty-Mansiysk** *prev.* Ostyako-Voguls'k. Khanty-Mansiyskiy Avtonomnyy Okrug, C Russian Federation 61.01N 69.00E
129 V8 **Khanty-Mansiyskiy Avtonomnyy Okrug** ◐ *autonomous district* C Russian Federation
145 R4 **Khānūqah** C Iraq 35.25N 43.15E
144 E11 **Khān Yūnis** *var.* Khān Yūnus. S Gaza Strip 31.23N 34.19E
Khān Yūnus *see* Khān Yūnis
Khanzi *see* Ghanzi
145 U5 **Khān Zūr** E Iraq 35.03N 45.08E
178 H10 **Khao Laem Reservoir** ⊡ W Thailand
126 Kk17 **Khapcheranga** Chitinskaya Oblast', S Russian Federation 49.46N 112.21E
131 Q12 **Kharabali** Astrakhanskaya Oblast', SW Russian Federation 47.28N 47.14E
159 R16 **Kharagpur** West Bengal, NE India 22.30N 87.19E
145 V11 **Kharā'ib 'Abd al Karīm** S Iraq 31.07N 45.33E
149 Q8 **Kharānaq** Yazd, C Iran 31.54N 54.21E
Kharbin *see* Harbin
152 H13 **Khardzhagaz** Ahal Welaýaty, C Turkmenistan 37.54N 60.10E
Khārga Oasis *see* Great Oasis, The
160 F11 **Khargon** Madhya Pradesh, C India 21.49N 75.39E
155 V7 **Khāriān** Punjab, NE Pakistan 32.52N 73.52E
119 X8 **Kharisyz'k** Donets'ka Oblast', E Ukraine 48.01N 38.10E
119 V5 **Kharkiv** *Rus.* Khar'kov. Kharkivs'ka Oblast', NE Ukraine 50.00N 36.14E
119 V5 **Kharkiv** ✈ Kharkivs'ka Oblast', E Ukraine 49.54N 36.20E
Kharkiv *see* Kharkivs'ka Oblast'
119 U5 **Kharkivs'ka Oblast'** *var.* Kharkiv, *Rus.* Khar'kovskaya Oblast'. ◐ *province* E Ukraine
Khar'kov *see* Kharkiv
Khar'kovskaya Oblast' *see* Kharkivs'ka Oblast'
128 L3 **Kharlovka** Murmanskaya Oblast', NW Russian Federation 68.47N 37.09E
116 K11 **Kharmanli** Khaskovo, S Bulgaria 41.55N 25.54E
116 K11 **Kharmanliyska Reka** ∽ S Bulgaria
128 M13 **Kharovsk** Vologodskaya Oblast', NW Russian Federation 59.57N 40.05E
82 F9 **Khartoum** *var.* El Khartûm, Khartum. ● (Sudan) Khartoum, C Sudan 15.33N 32.31E
82 F9 **Khartoum** ◐ *state* NE Sudan
82 F9 **Khartoum** ✈ Khartoum, C Sudan 15.36N 32.37E
82 F9 **Khartoum North** Khartoum, C Sudan 15.37N 32.33E
119 X8 **Khartsyz'k** *Rus.* Khartsyzsk. Donets'ka Oblast', SE Ukraine 48.01N 38.10E
Khartsyzsk *see* Khartsyz'k
Khartum *see* Khartoum
Khasab *see* Al Khaṣab
127 N18 **Khasan** Primorskiy Kray, SE Russian Federation 42.24N 130.45E
131 P16 **Khasavyurt** Respublika Dagestan, SW Russian Federation 43.16N 46.33E
149 W12 **Khāsh** *prev.* Vāsht. Sīstān va Balūchestān, SE Iran 28.15N 61.11E
154 K8 **Khāsh, Dasht-e** *Eng.* Khash Desert. *desert* SW Afghanistan
Khash Desert *see* Khāsh, Dasht-e
Khashim Al Qirba/Khashm al Qirbah *see* Khashm el Girba
82 H9 **Khashm el Girba** *var.* Khashim Al Qirba, Khashm al Qirbah. Kassala, E Sudan 15.00N 35.59E
144 G14 **Khashsh, Jabal al** ⛰ S Jordan
143 S10 **Khashuri** C Georgia 41.59N 43.36E
159 V13 **Khāsi Hills** *hill range* NE India
116 K11 **Khaskovo** Khaskovo, S Bulgaria 41.56N 25.34E
116 K11 **Khaskovo** ◐ *province* S Bulgaria
126 J7 **Khatanga** Taymyrskiy (Dolgano-Nenetskiy) Avtonomnyy Okrug, N Russian Federation 71.55N 102.17E
126 J7 **Khatanga** ∽ N Russian Federation
Khatanga, Gulf of *see* Khatangskiy Zaliv
126 Jj6 **Khatangskiy Zaliv** *var.* Gulf of Khatanga. *bay* N Russian Federation
147 W7 **Khatmat al Malāḥah** N Oman 24.56N 56.22E
149 S16 **Khaṭmat al Malāḥah** Ash Shāriqah, E UAE
127 Q6 **Khatyrka** Chukotskiy Avtonomnyy Okrug, NE Russian Federation 62.03N 175.09E
Khauz-Khan *see* Hanhowuz
Khauzkhanskoye Vodokhranilishche *see* Hanhowuz Suw Howdany
Khavaling *see* Khovaling
Khavast *see* Xovos
145 W10 **Khawrah, Nahr al** ∽ S Iraq
Khawr Barakah *see* Baraka
147 W7 **Khawr Fakkān** *var.* Khor Fakkan. Ash Shāriqah, NE UAE 25.21N 56.19E
146 L6 **Khaybar** Al Madīnah, NW Saudi Arabia 25.52N 39.15E
Khaybar, Kowtal-e *see* Khyber Pass
153 S11 **Khaydarkan** *var.* Khaydarken. Batkenskaya Oblast', SW Kyrgyzstan 39.56N 71.16E
Khaydarken *see* Khaydarkan
129 U2 **Khaypudyrskaya Guba** *bay* NW Russian Federation
145 S1 **Khayrūzuk** E Iraq 36.58N 44.19E
Khazar, Baḥr-e/Khazar, Daryā-ye *see* Caspian Sea
Khazarosp *see* Hazorasp
Khazretishi, Khrebet *see* Hazratishoh, Qatorkŭhi
Khelat *see* Kālat
76 F6 **Khemisset** NW Morocco 33.52N 6.04W
178 J10 **Khemmarat** *var.* Kemarat. Ubon Ratchathani, E Thailand 16.03N 105.10E
76 L6 **Khenchela** *var.* Khenchla. NE Algeria 35.22N 7.09E
Khenchla *see* Khenchela
76 G7 **Khénifra** C Morocco 32.59N 5.37W
Khersān, Rūd-e *see* Garm, Āb-e
119 R10 **Kherson** Khersons'ka Oblast', S Ukraine 46.39N 32.37E
Kherson *see* Khersons'ka Oblast'
119 S14 **Khersones, Mys** *Rus.* Mys Khersonesskiy. *headland* S Ukraine 44.34N 33.24E
Khersonesskiy, Mys *see* Khersones, Mys
119 R10 **Khersons'ka Oblast'** *var.* Kherson, *Rus.* Khersonskaya Oblast'. ◐ *province* S Ukraine
Khersonskaya Oblast' *see* Khersons'ka Oblast'
126 J7 **Kheta** Taymyrskiy (Dolgano-Nenetskiy) Avtonomnyy Okrug, N Russian Federation 71.33N 99.40E
126 J7 **Kheta** ∽ N Russian Federation
178 Jj8 **Khe Ve** Quang Binh, C Vietnam 17.52N 105.49E
155 U7 **Khewra** Punjab, E Pakistan 32.40N 73.04E
Khiam *see* El Khiyam
128 J4 **Khibiny** ⛰ NW Russian Federation
126 K16 **Khilok** Chitinskaya Oblast', S Russian Federation 51.26N 110.25E
126 K16 **Khilok** ∽ S Russian Federation
130 K3 **Khimki** Moskovskaya Oblast', W Russian Federation 55.57N 37.48E
153 S12 **Khingov** *Rus.* Obi-Khingou. ∽ C Tajikistan
Khíos *see* Chíos
155 R15 **Khipro** Sind, SE Pakistan 25.50N 69.18E
145 S10 **Khirr, Wādī al** *dry watercourse* S Iraq
116 I10 **Khisarya** Plovdiv, C Bulgaria 42.33N 24.43E
Khiva/Khiwa *see* Xiva
178 H9 **Khlong Khlung** Kamphaeng Phet, W Thailand 16.15N 99.41E
178 Gg16 **Khlong Thom** Krabi, SW Thailand 7.55N 99.09E
178 I12 **Khlung** Chantaburi, S Thailand 12.25N 102.12E
Khmel'nik *see* Khmil'nyk
Khmel'nitskaya Oblast' *see* Khmel'nyts'ka Oblast'
Khmel'nitskiy *see* Khmel'nyts'kyy
118 K5 **Khmel'nyts'ka Oblast'** *var.* Khmel'nyts'kyy, *Rus.* Khmel'nitskaya Oblast'; *prev.* Kamenets-Podol'skaya Oblast'. ◐ *province* NW Ukraine
118 L6 **Khmel'nyts'kyy** *Rus.* Khmel'nitskiy; *prev.* Proskurov. Khmel'nyts'ka Oblast', W Ukraine 49.24N 26.59E
Khmel'nyts'kyy *see* Khmel'nyts'ka Oblast'
118 M6 **Khmil'nyk** *Rus.* Khmel'nik. Vinnyts'ka Oblast', C Ukraine 49.36N 27.59E
150 I10 **Khobda** *prev.* Novoalekseyevka. Aktyubinsk, W Kazakhstan 50.10N 55.39E
143 R9 **Khobi** W Georgia 42.20N 41.54E
121 P15 **Khodasy** *Rus.* Khodosy. Mahilyowskaya Voblasts', E Belarus 53.56N 31.28E
118 I6 **Khodoriv** *Pol.* Chodorów, *Rus.* Khodorov. L'vivs'ka Oblast', NW Ukraine 49.19N 24.19E
Khodorov *see* Khodoriv
Khodosy *see* Khodasy
Khodzhakala *see* Hojagala
Khodzhambas *see* Hojambaz
Khodzhent *see* Khŭjand
Khodzheyli *see* Xo'jayli
Khoi *see* Khvoy
Khojend *see* Khŭjand
Khokand *see* Qo'qon
130 L8 **Khokhol'skiy** Voronezhskaya Oblast', W Russian Federation 51.33N 38.43E
178 Hh10 **Khok Samrong** Lop Buri, C Thailand 15.03N 100.43E
155 P2 **Kholm** *var.* Tashqurghan, *Pash.* Khulm. Balkh, N Afghanistan 36.42N 67.40E
128 H15 **Kholm** Novgorodskaya Oblast', W Russian Federation 57.10N 31.06E
Kholm *see* Chełm
Kholmech' *see* Kholmyech
127 Oo16 **Kholmsk** Ostrov Sakhalin, Sakhalinskaya Oblast', SE Russian Federation 46.57N 142.10E
121 O19 **Kholmyech** *Rus.* Kholmech'. Homyel'skaya Voblasts', SE Belarus 52.09N 30.37E
Kholon *see* Ḥolon
Kholopenichi *see* Khalopyenichy
85 D19 **Khomas** ◐ *district* C Namibia
85 D19 **Khomas Hochland** *var.* Khomasplato. *plateau* C Namibia
Khomasplato *see* Khomas Hochland
Khomein *see* Khomeyn
148 M7 **Khomeyn** *var.* Khomein, Khumain. Markazī, W Iran 33.37N 50.03E
149 N8 **Khomeynīshahr** *prev.* Homāyūnshahr. Eṣfahān, C Iran 32.39N 51.34E
Khoms *see* Al Khums
Khong Sedone *see* Muang Khôngxédôn
178 I9 **Khon Kaen** *var.* Muang Khon Kaen. Khon Kaen, E Thailand 16.25N 102.49E
Khonqa *see* Xonqa
178 I9 **Khon San** Khon Kaen, E Thailand 16.40N 101.51E
127 N8 **Khonuu** Respublika Sakha (Yakutiya), NE Russian Federation 66.24N 143.15E
131 N8 **Khopër** *var.* Khoper. ∽ SW Russian Federation
127 Nn16 **Khor** Khabarovskiy Kray, SE Russian Federation 47.43N 134.48E
127 Nn16 **Khor** ∽ SE Russian Federation
149 U9 **Khorāsān-e Janūbī** *off.* Ostān-e Khorāsān-e Janūbī. ◐ *province* E Iran
149 S3 **Khorāsān-e Shemālī** *off.* Ostān-e Khorāsān-e Shemālī. ◐ *province* NE Iran
149 U5 **Khorāsān-Razavī** *off.* Ostān-e Khorāsān-Razavī. ◐ *province* NE Iran
Khorat *see* Nakhon Ratchasima
160 O13 **Khordha** *prev.* Khurda. Orissa, E India 20.13N 85.39E
129 U4 **Khorey-Ver** Nenetskiy Avtonomnyy Okrug, NW Russian Federation 67.25N 58.05E
Khorezmskaya Oblast' *see* Xorazm Viloyati
Khor Fakkan *see* Khawr Fakkān
151 W15 **Khorgos** Almaty, SE Kazakhstan 44.13N 80.22E
126 K16 **Khorinsk** Respublika Buryatiya, S Russian Federation 52.13N 109.52E
85 C18 **Khorixas** Kunene, NW Namibia 20.22S 14.55E
147 O17 **Khormaksar** *var.* Aden. ✈ ('Adan) SW Yemen 12.56N 45.00E
Khormal *see* Khurmāl
Khormuj *see* Khvormūj
Khorog *see* Khorugh
119 S5 **Khorol** Poltavs'ka Oblast', NE Ukraine 49.49N 33.16E
148 L7 **Khorramābād** *var.* Khurramabad. Lorestān, W Iran 33.28N 48.21E
148 K10 **Khorramshahr** *var.* Khurramshahr, Muhammerah; *prev.* Mohammerah. Khūzestān, SW Iran 30.29N 48.09E
153 S14 **Khorugh** *Rus.* Khorog. S Tajikistan 37.29N 71.31E
131 Q12 **Khosheutovo** Astrakhanskaya Oblast', SW Russian Federation 47.04N 47.49E
Khotan *see* Hotan
Khorvot Khalutsa *see* Ḥorvot Haluẕa
Khotimsk *see* Khotsimsk
Khotin *see* Khotyn
121 R16 **Khotsimsk** *Rus.* Khotimsk. Mahilyowskaya Voblasts', E Belarus 53.24N 32.34E
118 K7 **Khotyn** *Rom.* Hotin, *Rus.* Khotin. Chernivets'ka Oblast', W Ukraine 48.29N 26.30E
76 F7 **Khouribga** C Morocco 32.54N 6.51W
153 Q13 **Khovaling** *Rus.* Khavaling. SW Tajikistan 38.22N 69.54E
Khovd *see* Hovd
155 R6 **Khowst** Khowst, E Afghanistan 33.22N 69.57E
155 S6 **Khowst** ◐ *province* E Afghanistan
Khoy *see* Khvoy
121 N20 **Khoyniki** *Rus.* Khoyniki. Homyel'skaya Voblasts', SE Belarus 51.53N 29.58E
Khozretishi, Khrebet *see* Hazratishoh, Qatorkŭhi
Khrisoúpolis *see* Chrysoúpoli
126 Mm6 **Khroma** ∽ NE Russian Federation
150 J10 **Khromtau** *Kaz.* Khromtaū. Aktyubinsk, W Kazakhstan 50.14N 58.22E
Khrysokhou Bay *see* Chrysochoú, Kólpos
119 O7 **Khrystynivka** Cherkas'ka Oblast', C Ukraine 48.49N 29.55E
178 J10 **Khuang Nai** Ubon Ratchathani, E Thailand 15.22N 104.33E
Khudal *see* Khādhil
Khudat *see* Xudat
155 W9 **Khudiān** Punjab, E Pakistan 30.58N 74.19E
Khudzhand *see* Khŭjand
153 O13 **Khufar** Surkhondaryo Viloyati, S Uzbekistan 38.31N 67.45E
85 G21 **Khuis** Kgalagadi, SW Botswana 26.37S 21.50E
153 Q11 **Khŭjand** *var.* Khodzhent, Khojend, *Rus.* Khudzhand; *prev.* Leninabad, *Taj.* Leninobod. N Tajikistan 40.16N 69.37E
178 I11 **Khukhan** Si Sa Ket, E Thailand 14.38N 104.12E
Khulm *see* Kholm
159 T16 **Khulna** Khulna, SW Bangladesh 22.48N 89.31E
159 T16 **Khulna** ◐ *division* SW Bangladesh
Khumain *see* Khomeyn
Khums *see* Al Khums
155 W2 **Khunjerāb Pass** *Chin.* Kunjirap Daban. *pass* China/Pakistan *see also* Kunjirap Daban 36.46N 75.16E
159 P16 **Khunti** Jhārkhand, N India 23.01N 85.19E
178 Gg7 **Khun Yuam** Mae Hong Son, NW Thailand 18.54N 97.54E
Khurais *see* Khurayṣ
147 R7 **Khurayṣ** *var.* Khurais. Ash Sharqīyah, C Saudi Arabia 25.06N 48.02E
Khurda *see* Khordha
158 J11 **Khurja** Uttar Pradesh, N India 28.15N 77.51E
145 V4 **Khurmāl** *var.* Khormal. NE Iraq 35.19N 46.06E
Khurramabad *see* Khorramābād
Khurramshahr *see* Khorramshahr
155 U7 **Khushāb** Punjab, NE Pakistan 32.16N 72.18E
118 H8 **Khust** *Cz.* Chust, Husté, *Hung.* Huszt. Zakarpats'ka Oblast', W Ukraine 48.10N 23.19E
82 D11 **Khuwei** Western Kordofan, C Sudan 13.01N 29.13E
155 O13 **Khuzdār** Baluchistān, SW Pakistan 27.49N 66.33E
148 L9 **Khūzestān** *off.* Ostān-e Khūzestān, *var.* Khuzistan; *prev.* Arabistan, *anc.* Susiana. ◐ *province* SW Iran
126 Jj15 **Khuzhir** Respublika Buryatiya, S Russian Federation 53.10N 107.18E
Khuzistan *see* Khūzestān
155 R2 **Khvājeh Ghār** *var.* Khwajaghar, Khwaja-i-Ghar. Takhār, NE Afghanistan 37.05N 69.28E
131 Q7 **Khvalynsk** Saratovskaya Oblast', W Russian Federation 52.30N 48.06E
149 N12 **Khvormūj** *var.* Khormuj. Būshehr, S Iran 28.32N 51.22E
148 I2 **Khvoy** *var.* Khoi, Khoy. Āžarbāyjān-e Gharbī, NW Iran 38.36N 45.03E
Khwajaghar/Khwaja-i-Ghar *see* Khvājeh Ghār
155 S5 **Khyber Pass** *var.* Kowtal-e Khaybar. *pass* Afghanistan/Pakistan 34.07N 71.05E
195 V14 **Kia** Santa Isabel, N Solomon Islands 7.34S 158.31E
191 S10 **Kiama** New South Wales, SE Australia 34.40S 150.49E
179 R17 **Kiamba** Mindanao, S Philippines 5.59N 124.36E
81 O22 **Kiambi** Katanga, SE Dem. Rep. Congo 7.15S 28.01E
29 Q12 **Kiamichi Mountains** ⛰ Oklahoma, C USA
29 Q12 **Kiamichi River** ∽ Oklahoma, C USA
12 M10 **Kiamika, Réservoir** ⊡ Québec, SE Canada
Kiamusze *see* Jiamusi
41 N7 **Kiana** Alaska, USA 66.58N 160.25W
Kiangmai *see* Chiang Mai
Kiang-ning *see* Nanjing
Kiangsi *see* Jiangxi
Kiangsu *see* Jiangsu
95 M14 **Kiantajärvi** ◎ E Finland
117 F19 **Kiáto** *prev.* Kiáton. Pelopónnisos, S Greece 38.01N 22.45E
Kiáton *see* Kiáto
Kiayi *see* Chiai
69 T9 **Kibali** *var.* Uele (upper course). ∽ NE Dem. Rep. Congo
81 E20 **Kibangou** Le Niari, SW Congo 3.27S 12.21E
Kibarty *see* Kybartai
94 M8 **Kiberg** Finnmark, N Norway 70.17N 30.47E
97 F22 **Kibæk** Ringkøbing, W Denmark 56.03N 8.52E
81 N20 **Kibombo** Maniema, E Dem. Rep. Congo 3.52S 25.59E
83 E20 **Kibondo** Kigoma, NW Tanzania 3.34S 30.40E
83 J15 **Kibre Mengist** *var.* Adola. Oromo, C Ethiopia 5.50N 39.06E
Kıbrıs/Kıbrıs Cumhuriyeti *see* Cyprus
83 E20 **Kibungo** *var.* Kibungu. SE Rwanda 2.09S 30.30E
Kibungu *see* Kibungo
115 N19 **Kičevo** SW FYR Macedonia 41.31N 20.57E
129 P13 **Kichmengskiy Gorodok** Vologodskaya Oblast', NW Russian Federation 60.00N 45.52E
32 J8 **Kickapoo River** ∽ Wisconsin, N USA
9 P16 **Kicking Horse Pass** *pass* Alberta/British Columbia, SW Canada 51.27N 116.13W
79 R9 **Kidal** Kidal, C Mali 18.22N 1.21E
79 Q8 **Kidal** ◐ *region* NE Mali
179 R16 **Kidapawan** Mindanao, S Philippines 7.02N 125.04E
99 L20 **Kidderminster** C England, UK 52.22N 2.13W
78 I11 **Kidira** E Senegal 14.27N 12.18W
192 O11 **Kidnappers, Cape** *headland* North Island, NZ 41.13S 175.15E
102 J8 **Kiel** Schleswig-Holstein, N Germany 54.21N 10.04E
113 L15 **Kielce** *Rus.* Keltsy. Świętokrzyskie, C Poland 50.52N 20.39E
102 K7 **Kieler Bucht** *bay* N Germany
102 J7 **Kieler Förde** *inlet* N Germany
178 K13 **Kiên Đức** *var.* Dak Lap. Dắc Lắc, S Vietnam 11.59N 107.30E
81 N24 **Kienge** Katanga, SE Dem. Rep. Congo 10.33S 27.33E
195 S12 **Kieta** Bougainville Island, NE PNG 6.13S 155.39E
102 Q12 **Kietz** Brandenburg, NE Germany 52.33N 14.36E
Kiev *see* Kyyiv
Kiev Reservoir *see* Kyyivs'ke Vodoskhovyshche
78 J10 **Kiffa** Assaba, S Mauritania 16.37N 11.22W
117 H19 **Kifisiá** Attikí, C Greece 38.04N 23.49E
117 F18 **Kifisós** ∽ C Greece
145 U5 **Kifrī** N Iraq 34.43N 44.58E
83 D20 **Kigali** ● (Rwanda) C Rwanda 1.58S 30.02E
83 E20 **Kigali** ✈ C Rwanda 1.43S 30.01E
143 P13 **Kiğı** Bingöl, E Turkey 39.19N 40.19E
83 E21 **Kigoma** Kigoma, W Tanzania 4.52S 29.36E
83 E21 **Kigoma** ◐ *region* W Tanzania
40 F10 **Kihei** *var.* Kihei. Maui, Hawai'i, USA, C Pacific Ocean 20.47N 156.28W
95 K17 **Kihniö** Länsi-Suomi, W Finland 62.10N 23.10E
120 F6 **Kihnu** *var.* Kihnu Saar, *Ger.* Kühnö. *island* SW Estonia
Kihnu Saar *see* Kihnu
40 A8 **Kii Landing** Ni'ihau, Hawai'i, USA, C Pacific Ocean 21.58N 160.03W
95 L14 **Kiiminki** Oulu, C Finland 65.05N 25.46E
171 H16 **Kii-Nagashima** *var.* Nagashima. Mie, Honshū, SW Japan 34.10N 136.18E
171 Gg16 **Kii-sanchi** ⛰ Honshū, SW Japan
94 L11 **Kiistala** Lappi, N Finland 67.52N 25.19E
170 Ff16 **Kii-suidō** *strait* S Japan
172 R14 **Kikai-shima** *var.* Kikaiga-shima. *island* Nansei-shotō, SW Japan
114 M8 **Kikinda** *Ger.* Grosskikinda, *Hung.* Nagykikinda; *prev.* Velika Kikinda. Serbia, N Serbia 45.48N 20.29E
Kikládhes *see* Kykládes
172 N7 **Kikonai** Hokkaidō, NE Japan 41.40N 140.25E
194 H14 **Kikori** Gulf, S PNG 7.31S 144.16E
194 G13 **Kikori** ∽ W PNG
170 Cc14 **Kikuchi** *var.* Kikuti. Kumamoto, Kyūshū, SW Japan 33.00N 130.49E
Kikuti *see* Kikuchi
131 N8 **Kikvidze** Volgogradskaya Oblast', SW Russian Federation 50.47N 42.58E
12 I10 **Kikwissi, Lac** ◎ Québec, SE Canada
81 I21 **Kikwit** Bandundu, W Dem. Rep. Congo 4.59S 18.53E
97 K15 **Kil** Värmland, C Sweden 59.30N 13.19E

276

◆ Country ● Country Capital ◇ Dependent Territory ○ Dependent Territory Capital ◐ Administrative Region ✈ International Airport ▲ Mountain ⛰ Mountain Range Volcano ∽ River ◎ Lake ⊡ Reservoir

◆ COUNTRY   ◇ DEPENDENT TERRITORY   ◆ ADMINISTRATIVE REGION   ▲ MOUNTAIN   ▼ VOLCANO   ◎ LAKE
● COUNTRY CAPITAL   ○ DEPENDENT TERRITORY CAPITAL   ✕ INTERNATIONAL AIRPORT   ▲ MOUNTAIN RANGE   ✍ RIVER   ⊟ RESERVOIR

KLINTEHAMN – KOPILI

97 P19 **Klintehamn** Gotland, SE Sweden *57.22N 18.15E*
131 R8 **Klintsovka** Saratovskaya Oblast', W Russian Federation *51.42N 49.17E*
130 H6 **Klintsy** Bryanskaya Oblast', W Russian Federation *52.46N 32.20E*
97 K22 **Klippan** Skåne, S Sweden *56.07N 13.10E*
94 G13 **Klippen** Västerbotten, N Sweden *65.50N 15.07E*
124 Nn3 **Klírou** W Cyprus *35.01N 33.11E*
116 I9 **Klisura** Plovdiv, C Bulgaria *42.42N 24.28E*
97 F20 **Klitmøller** Viborg, NW Denmark *57.01N 8.29E*
114 F11 **Ključ** Federacija Bosna I Hercegovina, NW Bosnia and Herzegovina *44.32N 16.46E*
113 J14 **Kłobuck** Śląskie, S Poland *50.55N 18.54E*
112 J11 **Kłodawa** Wielkopolskie, C Poland *52.14N 18.55E*
113 G16 **Kłodzko** *Ger.* Glatz. Dolnośląskie, SW Poland *50.27N 16.37E*
97 I14 **Kløfta** Akershus, S Norway *60.04N 11.09E*
114 P12 **Klokočevac** Serbia, E Serbia *44.19N 22.11E*
120 G3 **Klooga** *Ger.* Lodensee. Harjumaa, NW Estonia *59.18N 24.15E*
101 F15 **Kloosterzande** Zeeland, SW Netherlands *51.22N 4.01E*
115 L19 **Klos** *var.* Klosi. Dibër, C Albania *41.30N 20.07E*
Klosi *see* Klos
Klösterle an der Eger *see* Klášterec nad Ohří
111 X3 **Klosterneuburg** Niederösterreich, NE Austria *48.19N 16.19E*
110 J9 **Klosters** Graubünden, SE Switzerland *46.54N 9.52E*
110 G7 **Kloten** Zürich, N Switzerland *47.27N 8.34E*
110 G7 **Kloten** ✕ (Zürich) Zürich, N Switzerland *47.25N 8.36E*
102 K12 **Klötze** Sachsen-Anhalt, C Germany *52.37N 11.09E*
10 K3 **Klotz, Lac** ⊚ Québec, NE Canada
103 O15 **Klotzsche** ✕ (Dresden) Sachsen, E Germany *51.06N 13.44E*
8 H7 **Kluane Lake** ⊚ Yukon Territory, W Canada
Kluang *see* Keluang
113 I14 **Kluczbork** *Ger.* Kreuzburg, Kreuzburg in Oberschlesien. Opolskie, S Poland *50.59N 18.13E*
41 W12 **Klukwan** Alaska, USA *59.24N 135.49W*
Klyastitsy *see* Klyastsitsy
120 L11 **Klyastsitsy** *Rus.* Klyastitsy. Vitsyebskaya Voblasts', N Belarus *55.54N 28.38E*
131 T5 **Klyavlino** Samarskaya Oblast', W Russian Federation *54.21N 52.12E*
86 K9 **Klyaz'in** ≈ W Russian Federation
131 N3 **Klyaz'ma** ≈ W Russian Federation
121 J17 **Klyetsk** *Pol.* Kleck, *Rus.* Kletsk. Minskaya Voblasts', SW Belarus *53.04N 26.38E*
153 S8 **Klyuchevka** Talasskaya Oblast', NW Kyrgyzstan *42.33N 71.45E*
127 Pp10 **Klyuchevskaya Sopka, Vulkan** ⛰ E Russian Federation *56.03N 160.37E*
127 Pp10 **Klyuchi** Kamchatskaya Oblast', E Russian Federation *56.18N 160.44E*
97 D17 **Knaben** Vest-Agder, S Norway *58.46N 7.04E*
Knanzi *see* Ghanzi
97 K21 **Knäred** Halland, S Sweden *56.30N 13.21E*
99 M16 **Knaresborough** N England, UK *54.01N 1.35W*
116 H8 **Knezha** Vratsa , NW Bulgaria *43.29N 24.04E*
27 O9 **Knickerbocker** Texas, SW USA *31.18N 100.35W*
30 K5 **Knife River** ≈ North Dakota, N USA
8 K16 **Knight Inlet** *inlet* British Columbia, W Canada
41 S12 **Knight Island** *island* Alaska, USA
99 K20 **Knighton** E Wales, UK *52.20N 3.00W*
37 O7 **Knights Landing** California, W USA *38.47N 121.43W*
114 E13 **Knin** Šibenik-Knin, S Croatia *44.03N 16.12E*
27 Q12 **Knippal** Texas, SW USA
111 U7 **Knittelfeld** Steiermark, C Austria *47.13N 14.51E*
97 O15 **Knivsta** Uppsala, C Sweden *59.43N 17.49E*
115 P14 **Knjaževac** Serbia, E Serbia *43.34N 22.16E*
29 S4 **Knob Noster** Missouri, C USA *38.47N 93.33W*
101 D15 **Knokke-Heist** West-Vlaanderen, NW Belgium *51.21N 3.19E*
97 H20 **Knøsen** *hill* N Denmark *57.09N 10.15E*
Knosós *see* Knossos
117 J25 **Knossos** *Gk.* Knosós. *prehistoric site* Kríti, Greece, E Mediterranean Sea *35.17N 25.10E*
27 N7 **Knott** Texas, SW USA *32.21N 101.35W*
204 K5 **Knowles, Cape** *headland* Antarctica *71.45S 60.19W*
33 O11 **Knox** Indiana, N USA *41.16N 86.37W*
31 O3 **Knox** North Dakota, N USA *48.19N 99.43W*
20 C13 **Knox** Pennsylvania, NE USA *41.13N 79.33W*
201 X8 **Knox Atoll** *var.* Ņadikdik, Narikrik. *atoll* Ratak Chain, SE Marshall Islands
8 H13 **Knox, Cape** *headland* Graham Island, British Columbia, SW Canada *54.05N 133.02W*
27 P5 **Knox City** Texas, SW USA *33.25N 99.49W*
205 Y11 **Knox Coast** *physical region* Antarctica
33 T12 **Knox Lake** ⊠ Ohio, N USA
25 T5 **Knoxville** Georgia, SE USA *32.44N 83.58W*
32 K12 **Knoxville** Illinois, N USA *40.54N 90.16W*
31 W15 **Knoxville** Iowa, C USA *41.19N 93.06W*
23 N9 **Knoxville** Tennessee, S USA *35.57N 83.55W*
207 P11 **Knud Rasmussen Land** *physical region* N Greenland
Knüll *see* Knüllgebirge
103 I16 **Knüllgebirge** *var.* Knüll. ▲▲ C Germany
Knyazhevo *see* Sredishte
Knyazhitsy *see* Knyazhytsy
121 O15 **Knyazhytsy** *Rus.* Knyazhitsy. Mahilyowskaya Voblasts', E Belarus *54.10N 30.27E*
85 G26 **Knysna** Western Cape, SW South Africa *34.01S 23.05E*
176 V10 **Koagas** Papua, E Indonesia *2.40S 132.16E*
Koartac *see* Quaqtaq
174 J10 **Koba** Pulau Bangka, W Indonesia *2.29S 106.22E*
170 C16 **Kobayashi** *var.* Kobayasi. Miyazaki, Kyūshū, SW Japan *32.01N 130.55E*
Kobayasi *see* Kobayashi
Kobdo *see* Hovd
171 Gg14 **Kōbe** Hyōgo, Honshū, SW Japan *34.39N 135.10E*
Kobelyaki *see* Kobelyaky
119 T6 **Kobelyaky** *Rus.* Kobelyaki. Poltavs'ka Oblast', NE Ukraine *49.10N 34.13E*
97 J22 **København** *Eng.* Copenhagen; *anc.* Hafnia. ● (Denmark) Sjælland, København, E Denmark *55.43N 12.34E*
97 J23 **København** *off.* Københavns Amt. ◈ *county* E Denmark
78 K10 **Kobenni** Hodh el Gharbi, S Mauritania *15.58N 9.24W*
176 U11 **Kobi** Pulau Seram, E Indonesia *2.56S 129.53E*
103 F17 **Koblenz** *prev.* Coblenz, *Fr.* Coblence, *anc.* Confluentes. Rheinland-Pfalz, W Germany *50.21N 7.36E*
110 F6 **Koblenz** Aargau, N Switzerland *47.34N 8.16E*
176 Ww11 **Kobowre, Pegunungan** ▲▲ Papua, E Indonesia
128 J14 **Kobozha** Novgorodskaya Oblast', W Russian Federation *58.48N 35.00E*
Kobrin *see* Kobryn
176 W14 **Kobroor, Pulau** *island* Kepulauan Aru, E Indonesia
121 G19 **Kobryn** *Pol.* Kobryn, *Rus.* Kobrin. Brestskaya Voblasts', SW Belarus *52.13N 24.21E*
41 O7 **Kobuk** Alaska, USA *66.54N 156.52W*
41 O7 **Kobuk River** ≈ Alaska, USA
143 Q10 **K'obulet'i** W Georgia *41.47N 41.46E*
126 Ll10 **Kobyay** Respublika Sakha (Yakutiya), NE Russian Federation *63.36N 126.33E*
142 E11 **Kocaeli** ◈ *province* NW Turkey
115 P18 **Kočani** NE FYR Macedonia *41.55N 22.25E*
114 K12 **Koceljevo** Serbia, W Serbia *44.28N 19.49E*
111 U12 **Kočevje** *Ger.* Gottschee. S Slovenia *45.41N 14.47E*
159 T12 **Koch Bihār** West Bengal, NE India *26.19N 89.25E*
126 J10 **Kochechum** ≈ N Russian Federation
103 I20 **Kocher** ≈ SW Germany
129 T13 **Kochevo** Permskaya Oblast', NW Russian Federation *59.37N 54.16E*
170 Ee15 **Kōchi** *var.* Kôti. Kōchi, Shikoku, SW Japan *33.31N 133.30E*
170 Ee15 **Kōchi** *off.* Kōchi-ken, *var.* Kôti. ◈ *prefecture* Shikoku, SW Japan
Kochi *see* Cochin
Kochiu *see* Gejiu
Kochkor *see* Kochkorka
153 V8 **Kochkorka** *Kir.* Kochkor. Narynskaya Oblast', C Kyrgyzstan *42.09N 75.42E*
129 V5 **Kochmes** Respublika Komi, NW Russian Federation *66.10N 60.46E*
131 P15 **Kochubey** Respublika Dagestan, SW Russian Federation *44.25N 46.33E*
117 I17 **Kochýlas** ▲ Skýros, Vóreies Sporádes, Greece, Aegean Sea *38.50N 24.35E*
112 O13 **Kock** Lubelskie, E Poland *51.39N 22.26E*
83 J19 **Kodacho** *spring/well* S Kenya *1.52S 39.22E*
161 K24 **Koddiyar Bay** *bay* NE Sri Lanka
41 Q14 **Kodiak** Kodiak Island, Alaska, USA *57.47N 152.24W*
41 Q14 **Kodiak Island** *island* Alaska, USA
160 B12 **Kodīnār** Gujarāt, W India *20.43N 70.46E*
128 M9 **Kodino** Arkhangel'skaya Oblast', NW Russian Federation *63.36N 39.54E*
126 Ii13 **Kodinsk** Krasnoyarskiy Kray, C Russian Federation *58.37N 99.18E*
82 F12 **Kodok** Upper Nile, SE Sudan *9.51N 32.07E*
119 N8 **Kodyma** Odes'ka Oblast', SW Ukraine *48.05N 29.09E*
101 B17 **Koekelare** West-Vlaanderen, W Belgium *51.07N 2.58E*
Koeln *see* Köln
Koepang *see* Kupang
Ko-erh-mu *see* Golmud
101 J17 **Koersel** Limburg, NE Belgium *51.04N 5.17E*
85 E21 **Koës** Karas, SE Namibia *25.57S 19.04E*
Koetai *see* Mahakam, Sungai
Koetaradja *see* Bandaaceh
38 I14 **Kofa Mountains** ▲▲ Arizona, SW USA
176 Z15 **Kofarau** Papua, E Indonesia *7.29S 140.28E*
153 P13 **Kofarnihon** *Rus.* Kofarnikhon; *prev.* Ordzhonikidzeabad, *Taj.* Orjonikidzeobod, Yangi-Bazar. W Tajikistan *38.32N 68.56E*
153 P14 **Kofarnihon** *Rus.* Kafirnigan. ≈ SW Tajikistan
Kofarnikhon *see* Kofarnihon
116 M11 **Kofçaz** Kırklareli, NW Turkey *41.57N 27.07E*
176 U9 **Kofiau, Pulau** *var.* Kafiau. *island* Kepulauan Raja Ampat, E Indonesia
117 J25 **Kófinas** ▲ Kríti, Greece, E Mediterranean Sea *34.58N 25.03E*
124 Nn4 **Kofínou** *var.* Kophinou. S Cyprus *34.49N 33.24E*
111 V8 **Köflach** Steiermark, SE Austria *47.04N 15.04E*
79 Q17 **Koforidua** SE Ghana *6.04N 0.17W*
170 Ff12 **Kōfu** Tottori, Honshū, SW Japan *35.16N 133.31E*
171 J15 **Kōfu** *var.* Kôhu. Yamanashi, Honshū, S Japan *35.40N 138.33E*
171 K16 **Koga** Ibaraki, Honshū, S Japan *36.12N 139.42E*
83 F22 **Koga** Tabora, C Tanzania *6.08S 32.20E*
Kogălniceanu *see* Mihail Kogălniceanu
11 P6 **Kogaluk** ≈ Newfoundland and Labrador, E Canada
10 J4 **Kogaluk** ≈ Québec, NE Canada
126 Gg10 **Kogalym** Khanty-Mansiyskiy Avtonomnyy Okrug, C Russian Federation *62.13N 74.34E*
97 J23 **Køge** Roskilde, E Denmark *55.28N 12.12E*
97 J23 **Køge Bugt** *bay* E Denmark
79 U16 **Kogi** ◈ *state* C Nigeria
152 L11 **Kogon** *Rus.* Kagan. Buxoro Viloyati, C Uzbekistan *39.46N 64.28E*
169 Y17 **Kōgŭm-do** *island* S South Korea
Kőhalom *see* Rupea
155 T6 **Kohāt** North-West Frontier Province, NW Pakistan *33.37N 71.30E*
120 G4 **Kohila** *Ger.* Koil. Raplamaa, NW Estonia *59.07N 24.46E*
159 X13 **Kohīma** Nāgāland, E India *25.40N 94.07E*
Koh I Noh *see* Büyükağrı Dağı
148 L10 **Kohgīlūyeh va Būyer Aḩmad** *off.* Ostān-e Kohgīlūyeh va Būyer Aḩmad, *var.* Boyer Ahmadī va Kohkīlūyeh. ◈ *province* SW Iran
Kohsān *see* Kūhestān
120 J3 **Kohtla-Järve** Ida-Virumaa, NE Estonia *59.22N 27.21E*
Kôhu *see* Kōfu
119 N10 **Kohyl'nyk** *Rom.* Cogîlnic. ≈ Moldova/Ukraine
171 K13 **Koide** Niigata, Honshū, C Japan *37.13N 138.58E*
8 G7 **Koidern** Yukon Territory, W Canada *61.55N 140.22W*
78 J15 **Koidu** E Sierra Leone *8.39N 11.01W*
120 I4 **Koigi** Järvamaa, C Estonia *58.51N 25.45E*
Koil *see* Kohila
180 H13 **Koimbani** Grande Comore, NW Comoros *11.37S 43.22E*
145 T3 **Koi Sanjaq** *var.* Koysanjaq, Kūysanjaq. N Iraq *36.04N 44.37E*
95 O16 **Koitere** ⊚ E Finland
Koivisto *see* Primorsk
169 Z16 **Kōje-do** *Jap.* Kyōsai-tō. *island* S South Korea
82 J13 **K'ok'a Hāyk'** ⊚ C Ethiopia
Kokand *see* Qo'qon
190 F6 **Kokatha** South Australia *31.17S 135.16E*
Kokcha *see* Ko'kcha
152 M10 **Ko'kcha** *Rus.* Kokcha. Buxoro Viloyati, C Uzbekistan *40.30N 64.58E*
Kokchetav *see* Kokshetau
95 K18 **Kokemäenjoki** ≈ SW Finland
176 X12 **Kokenau** *var.* Kokonau. Papua, E Indonesia *4.38S 136.24E*
85 E22 **Kokerboom** Karas, SE Namibia *28.10S 19.25E*
121 N14 **Kokhanava** *Rus.* Kokhanovo. Vitsyebskaya Voblasts', NE Belarus *54.28N 29.58E*
Kokhanovichi *see* Kakhanavichy
Kokhanovo *see* Kokhanava
Kök-Janggak *see* Kok-Yangak
95 K16 **Kokkola** *Swe.* Karleby; *prev. Swe.* Gamlakarleby. Länsi-Suomi, W Finland *63.49N 23.10E*
164 L3 **Kok Kuduk** *well* N China *46.03N 87.34E*
120 H9 **Koknese** Aizkraukle, C Latvia *56.38N 25.27E*
79 T13 **Koko** Kebbi, W Nigeria *11.25N 4.33E*
194 K15 **Kokoda** Northern, S PNG *8.51S 147.37E*
78 K12 **Kokofata** Kayes, W Mali *12.48N 9.56W*
41 N6 **Kokolik River** ≈ Alaska, USA
33 O13 **Kokomo** Indiana, N USA *40.29N 86.07W*
Kokonau *see* Kokenau
Koko Nor *see* Qinghai Hu, China
Koko Nor *see* Qinghai, China
195 P10 **Kokopo** *var.* Kopopo; *prev.* Herbertshöhe. New Britain, E PNG *4.19S 152.13E*
151 X10 **Kokpekti** *Kaz.* Kökpekti. Vostochnyy Kazakhstan, E Kazakhstan *48.45N 82.24E*
151 X11 **Kokpekti** ≈ E Kazakhstan
41 P9 **Kokrines** Alaska, USA *64.57N 154.42W*
41 P9 **Kokrines Hills** ▲▲ Alaska, USA
151 P17 **Koksaray** Yuzhnyy Kazakhstan, S Kazakhstan *42.40N 68.09E*
153 X9 **Kokshaal-Tau** *Rus.* Khrebet Kakshaal-Too. ▲▲ China/Kyrgyzstan
151 P7 **Kokshetau** *Kaz.* Kökshetaū; *prev.* Kokchetav. Akmola, N Kazakhstan *53.18N 69.25E*
101 A17 **Koksijde** West-Vlaanderen, W Belgium *51.07N 2.39E*
10 M5 **Koksoak** ≈ Québec, E Canada
85 K24 **Kokstad** KwaZulu/Natal, E South Africa *30.23S 29.22E*
151 V14 **Koksu** *Kaz.* Köksu; *prev.* Rudnichnyy. Almaty, SE Kazakhstan *44.39N 78.57E*
151 W15 **Koktal** *Kaz.* Köktal. Almaty, SE Kazakhstan *44.04N 79.43E*
151 Q12 **Koktas** ≈ C Kazakhstan
Kök-Tash *see* Këk-Tash
Koktokay *see* Fuyun
170 C16 **Kokubu** Kagoshima, Kyūshū, SW Japan *31.44N 130.44E*
126 L15 **Kokuy** Chitinskaya Oblast', S Russian Federation *52.13N 117.18E*
153 T9 **Kok-Yangak** *Kir.* Kök-Janggak. Dzhalal-Abadskaya Oblast', W Kyrgyzstan *41.02N 73.11E*
164 F9 **Kokyar** Xinjiang Uygur Zizhiqu, W China *37.24N 77.15E*
155 O13 **Kolāchi** *var.* Kulachi. ≈ SW Pakistan
78 J15 **Kolahun** N Liberia *8.24N 10.01W*
175 Q12 **Kolaka** Sulawesi, C Indonesia *4.04S 121.37E*
Kolam *see* Quilon
K'o-la-ma-i *see* Karamay
Kola Peninsula *see* Kol'skiy Poluostrov
161 H19 **Kolār** Karnātaka, E India *13.10N 78.10E*
161 H19 **Kolār Gold Fields** Karnātaka, E India *12.56N 78.16E*
94 K11 **Kolari** Lappi, NW Finland *67.19N 23.51E*
113 I21 **Kolárovo** *Ger.* Gutta; *prev.* Guta, *Hung.* Gúta. Nitriansky Kraj, SW Slovakia *47.54N 18.00E*
115 K16 **Kolašin** C-Montenegro *42.49N 19.32E*
158 F11 **Kolāyat** Rājasthān, NW India *27.55N 73.01E*
97 N15 **Kolbäck** Västmanland, C Sweden *59.33N 16.15E*
Kolbcha *see* Kowbcha
207 Q15 **Kolbeinsey Ridge** *undersea feature* Denmark Strait/Norwegian Sea
Kolberg *see* Kołobrzeg
97 H15 **Kolbotn** Akershus, S Norway *62.15N 10.24E*
113 N16 **Kolbuszowa** Podkarpackie, SE Poland *50.12N 22.07E*
130 L3 **Kol'chugino** Vladimirskaya Oblast', W Russian Federation *56.19N 39.24E*
78 H12 **Kolda** S Senegal *12.58N 14.58W*
97 G23 **Kolding** Vejle, C Denmark *55.28N 9.30E*
81 M17 **Kole** Orientale, N Dem. Rep. Congo *2.09N 25.17E*
81 K20 **Kole** Kasai Oriental, SW Dem. Rep. Congo *3.27S 22.28E*
Kōle *see* Kili Island
86 F6 **Kölen** *Nor.* Kjølen. ▲▲ Norway/Sweden
Kolepom, Pulau *see* Yos Sudarso, Pulau
120 H3 **Kolga Laht** *Ger.* Kolko-Wiek. *bay* N Estonia
129 Q3 **Kolguyev, Ostrov** *island* NW Russian Federation
161 E16 **Kolhāpur** Mahārāshtra, SW India *16.42N 74.13E*
157 K21 **Kolhumadulu Atoll** *var.* Kolumadulu Atoll, Thaa Atoll. *atoll* S Maldives
95 O16 **Koli** *var.* Kolinkylä. Itä-Suomi, E Finland *63.06N 29.45E*
41 O13 **Koliganek** Alaska, USA *59.43N 157.16W*
113 E16 **Kolín** *Ger.* Kolin. Středočeský Kraj, C Czech Republic *50.01N 15.10E*
Kolinkylä *see* Koli
202 E12 **Koliu** Île Futuna, W Wallis and Futuna
120 E7 **Kolka** Talsi, NW Latvia *57.43N 22.33E*
120 E7 **Kolkasrags** *prev. Eng.* Cape Domesnes. *headland* NW Latvia *57.45N 22.35E*
159 S16 **Kolkata** *var.* Calcutta. West Bengal, NE India *22.30N 88.19E*
Kolkhozabad *see* Kolkhozobod
153 P14 **Kolkhozobod** *Rus.* Kolkhozabad; *prev.* Kaganovichabad, Tugalan. SW Tajikistan *37.33N 68.34E*
Kolki/Kołki *see* Kolky
Kolko-Wiek *see* Kolga Laht
118 K3 **Kolky** *Pol.* Kołki, *Rus.* Kolki. Volyns'ka Oblast', NW Ukraine *51.05N 25.40E*
Kollam *see* Quilon
161 G20 **Kollegāl** Karnātaka, W India *12.07N 77.06E*
100 M5 **Kollum** Friesland, N Netherlands *53.16N 6.09E*
Kolmar *see* Colmar
103 E16 **Köln** *var.* Koeln, *Eng./Fr.* Cologne; *prev.* Cöln, *anc.* Colonia Agrippina, Oppidum Ubiorum. Nordrhein-Westfalen, W Germany *50.57N 6.57E*
112 N9 **Kolno** Podlaskie, NE Poland *53.24N 21.57E*
112 J12 **Koło** Wielkopolskie, C Poland *52.10N 18.39E*
40 B8 **Kōloa** *var.* Koloa. Kaua'i, Hawai'i, USA, C Pacific Ocean *21.54N 159.28W*
112 E7 **Kołobrzeg** *Ger.* Kolberg. Zachodnio-pomorskie, NW Poland *54.10N 15.33E*
130 H4 **Kolodnya** Smolenskaya Oblast', W Russian Federation *54.57N 32.22E*
202 E13 **Kolofau, Mont** ⛰ Île Alofi, S Wallis and Futuna *14.21S 178.01W*
129 O14 **Kologriv** Kostromskaya Oblast', NW Russian Federation *58.49N 44.22E*
78 L12 **Kolokani** Koulikoro, W Mali *13.34N 8.01W*
79 N13 **Koloko** W Burkina *11.06N 5.18W*
195 U14 **Kolombangara** *var.* Kilimbangara, Nduke. *island* New Georgia Islands, NW Solomon Islands
Kolomea *see* Kolomyya
130 L4 **Kolomna** Moskovskaya Oblast', W Russian Federation *55.02N 38.52E*
118 J7 **Kolomyya** *Ger.* Kolomea. Ivano-Frankivs'ka Oblast', W Ukraine *48.31N 25.00E*
78 M13 **Kolondiéba** Sikasso, SW Mali *11.04N 6.55W*
200 R15 **Kolonga** Tongatapu, S Tonga *21.07S 175.04W*
201 U16 **Kolonia** *var.* Colonia. Pohnpei, E Micronesia *6.57N 158.12E*
Kolonja *see* Kolonjë
115 K21 **Kolonjë** *var.* Kolonja. Fier, C Albania *40.49N 19.37E*
Kolonjë *see* Ersekë
Kolotambu *see* Avuavu
200 Q15 **Kolovai** Tongatapu, S Tonga *21.05S 175.20W*
175 R13 **Kolowanawatobo, Teluk** *bay* Pulau Buton, C Indonesia
Kolozsvár *see* Cluj-Napoca
114 C9 **Kolpa** *Ger.* Kulpa, *SCr.* Kupa. ≈ Croatia/Slovenia
126 H12 **Kolpashevo** Tomskaya Oblast', C Russian Federation *58.21N 82.44E*
128 H13 **Kolpino** Leningradskaya Oblast', NW Russian Federation *59.43N 30.39E*
102 M10 **Kölpinsee** ⊚ NE Germany
152 K8 **Ko'lquduq** *Rus.* Kulkuduk. Navoiy Viloyati, N Uzbekistan *42.36N 63.24E*
128 K5 **Kol'skiy Poluostrov** *Eng.* Kola Peninsula. *peninsula* NW Russian Federation
131 T6 **Koltubanovskiy** Orenburgskaya Oblast', W Russian Federation *53.00N 52.00E*
114 L11 **Kolubara** ≈ C Serbia
Kolupchii *see* Gurkovo
112 K13 **Koluszki** Łodzkie, C Poland *51.43N 19.49E*
129 T6 **Kolva** ≈ NW Russian Federation
95 E14 **Kolvereid** Nord-Trøndelag, W Norway *64.47N 11.22E*
154 L15 **Kolwa** Baluchistān, SW Pakistan *26.03N 64.00E*
81 M24 **Kolwezi** Katanga, S Dem. Rep. Congo *10.43S 25.29E*
127 Nn7 **Kolyma** ≈ NE Russian Federation
Kolyma Lowland *see* Kolymskaya Nizmennost'
Kolyma Range/Kolymskiy, Khrebet *see* Kolymskoye Nagor'ye
127 Nn6 **Kolymskaya Nizmennost'** *Eng.* Kolyma Lowland. *lowlands* NE Russian Federation
127 Nn6 **Kolymskoye** Respublika Sakha (Yakutiya), NE Russian Federation *68.42N 158.46E*
127 N17 **Kolymskoye Nagor'ye** *var.* Khrebet Kolymskiy, *Eng.* Kolyma Range. ▲▲ E Russian Federation
127 N17 **Kolyuchinskaya Guba** *bay* NE Russian Federation
151 W15 **Kol'zhat** Almaty, SE Kazakhstan *43.30N 80.37E*
116 G8 **Kom** ▲ NW Bulgaria *43.10N 23.02E*
82 I13 **Koma** Oromo, C Ethiopia *8.19N 36.48E*
79 X12 **Komadugu Gana** ≈ NE Nigeria
171 Ii15 **Komagane** Nagano, Honshū, S Japan *35.46N 137.56E*
81 P17 **Komanda** Orientale, NE Dem. Rep. Congo *1.23N 29.44E*
207 U1 **Komandorskaya Basin** *var.* Kamchatka Basin. *undersea feature* SW Bering Sea
129 Pp9 **Komandorskiye Ostrova** *Eng.* Commander Islands. *island group* E Russian Federation
Komárnfalva *see* Comănești
113 I22 **Komárno** *Ger.* Komorn, *Hung.* Komárom. Nitriansky Kraj, SW Slovakia *47.46N 18.07E*
113 I22 **Komárom** Komárom-Esztergom, NW Hungary *47.44N 18.06E*
Komárom *see* Komárno
113 I22 **Komárom-Esztergom** *off.* Komárom-Esztergom Megye. ◈ *county* N Hungary
171 I13 **Komatsu** *var.* Komatu. Ishikawa, Honshū, SW Japan *36.24N 136.27E*
170 Ff15 **Komatsushima** Tokushima, Shikoku, SW Japan *34.00N 134.36E*
Komatu *see* Komatsu
85 D17 **Kombat** Otjozondjupa, N Namibia *19.42S 17.45E*
Kombissiguiri *see* Kombissiri
79 P13 **Kombissiri** *var.* Kombissiguiri. C Burkina *12.03N 1.14W*
196 E10 **Komebail Lagoon** *lagoon* N Palau
83 F20 **Kome Island** *island* N Tanzania
Komeyo *see* Wandai
176 W13 **Komfane** Pulau Wokam, E Indonesia *5.36S 134.42E*
119 P10 **Kominternivs'ke** Odes'ka Oblast', SW Ukraine *46.52N 30.56E*
129 R8 **Komi, Respublika** ◈ *autonomous republic* NW Russian Federation
113 I25 **Komló** Baranya, SW Hungary *46.11N 18.19E*
Kommunarsk *see* Alchevs'k
153 S12 **Kommunizm, Qullai** ▲ E Tajikistan
194 G12 **Komo** Southern Highlands, W PNG *6.06S 142.52E*
175 P16 **Komodo** Pulau Komodo, S Indonesia *8.35S 119.27E*
175 P16 **Komodo, Pulau** *island* Nusa Tenggara, S Indonesia
79 N15 **Komoé** *var.* Komoé Fleuve. ≈ E Ivory Coast
Komoé Fleuve *see* Komoé
77 X11 **Kôm Ombo** *var.* Kawm Umbū. SE Egypt *24.23N 32.58E*
81 F20 **Komono** La Lékoumou, SW Congo *3.15S 13.13E*
176 Y16 **Komoran** Papua, E Indonesia *8.14S 138.51E*
176 Y16 **Komoran, Pulau** *island* E Indonesia
Komorn *see* Komárno
Komornok *see* Comorâşte
171 J14 **Komoro** Nagano, Honshū, S Japan *36.22N 138.25E*
Komosolabad *see* Komsomolobod
Komotau *see* Chomutov
116 K13 **Komotiní** *var.* Gümüljina, *Turk.* Gümülcine. Anatolikí Makedonía kai Thráki, NE Greece *41.06N 25.27E*
115 K16 **Komovi** ▲▲ SE-Montenegro
119 R8 **Kompaniyivka** Kirovohrads'ka Oblast', C Ukraine *48.16N 32.12E*
194 H12 **Kompiam** Enga, W PNG *5.23S 143.54E*
Kompong *see* Kâmpóng Chhnăng
Kompong Cham *see* Kâmpóng Cham
Kompong Kleang *see* Kâmpóng Khleăng
Kompong Som *see* Kâmpóng Saôm
Kompong Speu *see* Kâmpóng Spoe
Komrat *see* Comrat
Komsomol *see* Komsomol'skiy, Atyrau, Kazakhstan
Komsomol/Komsomolets *see* Karabalyk, Kostanay, Kazakhstan
126 Ii2 **Komsomolets, Ostrov** *island* Severnaya Zemlya, N Russian Federation
150 F13 **Komsomolets, Zaliv** *lake gulf* SW Kazakhstan
153 Q12 **Komsomolobod** *Rus.* Komosolabad. C Tajikistan *38.51N 69.54E*
128 M16 **Komsomol'sk** Ivanovskaya Oblast', W Russian Federation *56.58N 40.15E*
119 S6 **Komsomol's'k** Poltavs'ka Oblast', C Ukraine *49.01N 33.37E*
152 M11 **Komsomol'sk** Navoiy Viloyati, N Uzbekistan *40.14N 65.10E*
150 G12 **Komsomol'skiy** *Kaz.* Komsomol. Atyrau, W Kazakhstan *47.18N 53.37E*
129 W4 **Komsomol'skiy** Respublika Komi, NW Russian Federation *67.33N 64.00E*
127 Nn15 **Komsomol'sk-na-Amure** Khabarovskiy Kray, SE Russian Federation *50.31N 136.58E*
Komsomol'sk-na-Ustyurte *see* Kubla-Ustyurt
150 K10 **Komsomol'skoye** Aktyubinsk, NW Kazakhstan
131 Q8 **Komsomol'skoye** Saratovskaya Oblast', W Russian Federation *50.45N 47.00E*
151 P10 **Kon** ≈ C Kazakhstan
Kona *see* Kailua-Kona
128 K16 **Konakovo** Tverskaya Oblast', W Russian Federation *56.42N 36.44E*
155 S4 **Konar** *var.* Konarhā, *Pash.* Kunar. ◈ *province* E Afghanistan
149 V15 **Konārak** Sīstān va Balūchestān, SE Iran *25.26N 60.22E*
Konarhā *see* Konar
29 O11 **Konawa** Oklahoma, C USA *34.57N 96.45W*
176 V9 **Konda** Papua, E Indonesia *1.34S 131.58E*
125 Ff11 **Konda** ≈ C Russian Federation
160 L13 **Kondagaon** Chhattīsgarh, C India *19.38N 81.41E*
12 K10 **Kondiaronk, Lac** ⊚ Québec, SE Canada
188 J13 **Kondinin** Western Australia *32.31S 118.15E*
83 H21 **Kondoa** Dodoma, C Tanzania *4.54S 35.46E*
131 P6 **Kondol'** Penzenskaya Oblast', W Russian Federation *52.49N 45.03E*
116 N10 **Kondolovo** Burgas, E Bulgaria *42.07N 27.43E*
176 Z16 **Kondomirat** Papua, E Indonesia *8.57S 140.55E*
128 J10 **Kondopoga** Respublika Kareliya, NW Russian Federation *62.12N 34.16E*
155 Q2 **Kondoz** *var.* Kondūz, Qondūz *Pash.* Kunduz, Kundūz. Kondoz, NE Afghanistan *36.48N 68.50E*
155 Q2 **Kondoz** *Pash.* Kunduz. ◈ *province* NE Afghanistan
161 J17 **Kondukūr** *var.* Kandukur. Andhra Pradesh, E India *15.17N 79.49E*
Kondūz *see* Kondoz
197 H6 **Koné** Province Nord, W New Caledonia *21.04S 164.51E*
152 E13 **Könekesir** *Rus.* Kënekesir. Balkan Welaýaty, W Turkmenistan *38.16N 56.51E*
152 G8 **Köneürgenç** *var.* Köneürgench, *Rus.* Këneurgench; *prev.* Kunya-Urgench. Daşoguz Welaýaty, N Turkmenistan *42.20N 59.09E*
Köneürgench *see* Köneürgenç
79 N15 **Kong** N Ivory Coast *9.06N 4.34W*
41 S5 **Kongakut River** ≈ Alaska, USA
207 O14 **Kong Christian IX Land** *Eng.* King Christian IX Land. *physical region* SE Greenland
207 P13 **Kong Christian X Land** *Eng.* King Christian X Land. *physical region* E Greenland
207 N13 **Kong Frederik IX Land** *Eng.* King Frederik IX Land. *physical region* SW Greenland
207 Q12 **Kong Frederik VIII Land** *Eng.* King Frederik VIII Land. *physical region* NE Greenland
207 N15 **Kong Frederik VI Kyst** *Eng.* King Frederik VI Coast. *physical region* SE Greenland
178 I13 **Kŏng, Kaôh** *prev.* Kas Kong. *island* SW Cambodia
94 P2 **Kong Karls Land** *Eng.* King Charles Islands. *island group* SE Svalbard
83 G14 **Kong Kong** ≈ SE Sudan
Kongo *see* Congo (river)
85 G16 **Kongola** Caprivi, NE Namibia *17.47S 23.24E*
81 N21 **Kongolo** Katanga, E Dem. Rep. Congo *5.20S 26.57E*
83 F14 **Kongor** Jonglei, SE Sudan *7.09N 31.44E*
207 Q14 **Kong Oscar Fjord** *fjord* E Greenland
79 P12 **Kongoussi** N Burkina *13.19N 1.31W*
97 G15 **Kongsberg** Buskerud, S Norway *59.39N 9.37E*
94 Q2 **Kongsøya** *island* Kong Karls Land, E Svalbard
97 I14 **Kongsvinger** Hedmark, S Norway *60.10N 12.00E*
Kongtong *see* Pingliang
178 Jj11 **Kông, Tônle** *Lao.* Xê Kong. ≈ Cambodia/Laos
164 E8 **Kongur Shan** ▲ NW China *38.39N 75.21E*
83 I22 **Kongwa** Dodoma, C Tanzania *6.13S 36.28E*
Kong, Xê *see* Kông, Tônle
Konia *see* Konya
153 R11 **Konibodom** *Rus.* Kanibadam. N Tajikistan *40.16N 70.20E*
113 K15 **Koniecpol** Śląskie, S Poland *50.47N 19.45E*
Konieh *see* Konya
Königgrätz *see* Hradec Králové
Königinhof an der Elbe *see* Dvůr Králové nad Labem
103 K23 **Königsbrunn** Bayern, S Germany *48.16N 10.52E*
Königshütte *see* Chorzów
103 O24 **Königssee** ⊚ SE Germany
111 S8 **Königstuhl** ▲ S Austria *46.57N 13.47E*
111 U3 **Konigswiesen** Oberösterreich, N Austria *48.25N 14.48E*
103 E17 **Königswinter** Nordrhein-Westfalen, W Germany *50.40N 7.12E*
152 M11 **Konimex** *Rus.* Kenimekh. Navoiy Viloyati, N Uzbekistan *40.14N 65.10E*
112 I12 **Konin** *Ger.* Kuhnau. Wielkopolskie, C Poland *52.13N 18.16E*
Koninkrijk der Nederlanden *see* Netherlands
115 L24 **Konispol** *var.* Konispoli. Vlorë, S Albania *39.40N 20.10E*
Konispoli *see* Konispol
117 C15 **Kónitsa** Ípeiros, W Greece *40.04N 20.48E*
Konitz *see* Chojnice
110 D8 **Köniz** Bern, W Switzerland *46.55N 7.26E*
115 H14 **Konjic** Federacija Bosna I Hercegovina, C Bosnia and Herzegovina *43.39N 17.55E*
94 J10 **Könkämäälven** ≈ Finland/Sweden
161 D14 **Konkan** W India
85 D22 **Konkiep** ≈ S Namibia
78 I14 **Konkouré** ≈ W Guinea
79 O11 **Konna** Mopti, S Mali *14.58N 3.49W*
195 P10 **Konogaiang, Mount** ▲ New Ireland, NE PNG *4.05S 152.43E*
195 P10 **Konogogo** New Ireland, NE PNG *3.25S 152.09E*
110 E9 **Konolfingen** Bern, W Switzerland *46.53N 7.36E*
79 P16 **Konongo** C Ghana *6.39N 1.06W*
195 O9 **Konos** New Ireland, NE PNG *3.07S 151.43E*
128 M12 **Konosha** Arkhangel'skaya Oblast', NW Russian Federation *60.58N 40.09E*
119 R3 **Konotop** Sums'ka Oblast', NE Ukraine *51.15N 33.13E*
164 L7 **Konqi He** ≈ NW China
113 L14 **Końskie** Świętokrzyskie, C Poland *51.12N 20.26E*
Konstantinovka *see* Kostyantynivka
130 M11 **Konstantinovsk** Rostovskaya Oblast', SW Russian Federation *47.37N 41.07E*
103 H24 **Konstanz** *var.* Constanz, *Eng.* Constance; *hist.* Kostnitz, *anc.* Constantia. Baden-Württemberg, S Germany *47.40N 9.10E*
Konstanza *see* Constanța
79 T14 **Kontagora** Niger, W Nigeria *10.25N 5.29E*
80 E13 **Kontcha** Nord, N Cameroon *8.00N 12.13E*
101 G17 **Kontich** Antwerpen, N Belgium *51.07N 4.27E*
95 O16 **Kontiolahti** Itä-Suomi, E Finland *62.46N 29.51E*
95 M15 **Kontiomäki** Oulu, C Finland *64.20N 28.09E*
178 K11 **Kon Tum** *var.* Kontum. Kon Tum, C Vietnam *14.23N 108.00E*
Konur *see* Sulakyurt
142 H15 **Konya** *var.* Konieh; *prev.* Konia, *anc.* Iconium. Konya, C Turkey *37.51N 32.30E*
142 H15 **Konya** *var.* Konia, Konieh. ◈ *province* C Turkey
151 T13 **Konyrat** *var.* Kounradskiy, *Kaz.* Qongyrat. Karaganda, C Kazakhstan *46.58N 74.54E*
151 W15 **Konyrolen** Almaty, SE Kazakhstan *44.16N 79.18E*
83 I19 **Konza** Eastern, S Kenya *1.44S 37.07E*
100 I9 **Koog aan den Zaan** Noord-Holland, C Netherlands *52.28N 4.49E*
190 E7 **Koonibba** South Australia *31.55S 133.23E*
33 O11 **Koontz Lake** Indiana, N USA *41.25N 86.24W*
176 V8 **Koor** Papua, E Indonesia *0.21S 132.28E*
191 R9 **Koorawatha** New South Wales, SE Australia *34.03S 148.33E*
120 J5 **Koosa** Tartumaa, E Estonia *58.31N 27.06E*
35 N7 **Kootenai** *var.* Kootenay. ≈ Canada/USA *see also* Kootenay
9 P17 **Kootenay** *var.* Kootenai. ≈ Canada/USA *see also* Kootenai
85 F24 **Kootjieskolk** Northern Cape, W South Africa *31.16S 20.21E*
115 M15 **Kopaonik** ▲▲ S Serbia
Kopar *see* Koper
94 K1 **Kópasker** Nordhurland Eystra, N Iceland *66.15N 16.23W*
94 H4 **Kópavogur** Reykjanes, W Iceland *64.06N 21.47W*
151 U13 **Kopbirlik** *prev.* Kīrov, Kirova. Almaty, SE Kazakhstan *46.24N 77.16E*
111 S13 **Koper** *It.* Capodistria; *prev.* Kopar. SW Slovenia *45.32N 13.42E*
97 C16 **Kopervik** Rogaland, S Norway *59.16N 5.18E*
Köpetdag Gershi/Kopetdag, Khrebet *see* Koppeh Dāgh
125 Ee12 **Kopeysk** Kurganskaya Oblast', C Russian Federation *55.06N 61.31E*
Kophinou *see* Kofínou
190 G8 **Kopi** South Australia *33.24S 135.40E*
Kopiago *see* Lake Copiago
159 W12 **Kopili** ≈ NE India

◆ COUNTRY ● COUNTRY CAPITAL ◇ DEPENDENT TERRITORY ○ DEPENDENT TERRITORY CAPITAL ◈ ADMINISTRATIVE REGION ✕ INTERNATIONAL AIRPORT ▲ MOUNTAIN ▲▲ MOUNTAIN RANGE ⛰ VOLCANO ≈ RIVER ⊚ LAKE ⊠ RESERVOIR

97 M15 **Köping** Västmanland, C Sweden 59.31N 16.00E
115 K17 **Koplik** var. Kopliku. Shkodër, NW Albania 42.12N 19.26E
Kopliku see Koplik
Kopopo see Kokopo
96 I11 **Koppang** Hedmark, S Norway 61.34N 11.01E
Kopparberg see Dalarna
149 S3 **Koppeh Dāgh** Rus. Khrebet Kopetdag, Turkm. Köpetdag Gershi. ▲▲ Iran/Turkmenistan
Koppename see Coppename Rivier
97 J15 **Koppom** Värmland, C Sweden 59.42N 12.07E
Kopreinitz see Koprivnica
116 K9 **Koprinka, Yazovir** prev. Yazovir Georgi Dimitrov. ⊞ C Bulgaria
114 F7 **Koprivnica** Ger. Kopreinitz, Hung. Kaproncza. Koprivnica-Križevci, N Croatia 46.10N 16.49E
114 F8 **Koprivnica-Križevci** off. Koprivničko-Križevačka Županija. ◈ province N Croatia
113 I17 **Kopřivnice** Ger. Nesselsdorf. Moravskoslezský Kraj, E Czech Republic 49.36N 18.09E
Köprülü see Veles
Koptsevichi see Kaptsevichy
Kopyl' see Kapyl'
121 O14 **Kopys'** Rus. Kopys'. Vitsyebskaya Voblasts', NE Belarus 54.21N 30.21E
115 M18 **Korab** ▲ Albania/FYR Macedonia 41.48N 20.33E
Korabavur Pastligi see Karabaur', Uval
83 M14 **K'orahē** Somali, E Ethiopia 6.36N 44.21E
117 L16 **Kórakas, Akrotírio** headland Lésvos, E Greece 39.20N 26.20E
114 D9 **Korana** ≈ C Croatia
161 L14 **Korāput** Orissa, E India 18.49N 82.43E
Korat see Nakhon Ratchasima
178 Ii9 **Korat Plateau** plateau E Thailand
145 T1 **Kōrāwa, Sar-i** ▲ NE Iraq 37.07N 44.39E
160 L11 **Korba** Chhattīsgarh, C India 22.25N 82.43E
103 H15 **Korbach** Hessen, C Germany 51.16N 8.52E
Korça see Korçë
115 M21 **Korçë** var. Korça, Gk. Korytsa, It. Corriza; prev. Koritsa. Korçë, SE Albania 40.37N 20.46E
115 M21 **Korçë** ◈ district SE Albania
115 G15 **Korčula** It. Curzola. Dubrovnik-Neretva, S Croatia 42.57N 17.08E
115 F15 **Korčula** It. Curzola; anc. Corcyra Nigra. island S Croatia
115 F15 **Korčulanski Kanal** channel S Croatia
151 T6 **Korday** prev. Georgiyevka. Zhambyl, SE Kazakhstan 43.06N 74.42E
148 J5 **Kordestān** off. Ostān-e Kordestān, var. Kurdestan. ◈ province W Iran
149 P4 **Kord Kūy** var. Kurd Kui. Golestān, N Iran 36.49N 54.04E
169 V13 **Korea Bay** bay China/North Korea
Korea, Democratic People's Republic of see North Korea
176 Uu15 **Koreare** Pulau Yamdena, E Indonesia 7.33S 131.13E
Korea, Republic of see South Korea
169 Z17 **Korea Strait** Jap. Chōsen-kaikyō, Kor. Taehan-haehyŏp. channel Japan/South Korea
Korelichi/Korelicze see Karelichy
82 J11 **Korem** Tigray, N Ethiopia 12.32N 39.29E
79 U11 **Korén Adoua** ≈ C Niger
130 I7 **Korenevo** Kurskaya Oblast', W Russian Federation 51.21N 34.53E
130 L13 **Korenovsk** Krasnodarskiy Kray, SW Russian Federation 45.28N 39.25E
118 L4 **Korets'** Pol. Korzec, Rus. Korets. Rivnens'ka Oblast', NW Ukraine 50.38N 27.12E
127 Pp8 **Korf** Koryakskiy Avtonomnyy Okrug, E Russian Federation 60.20N 165.37E
204 L7 **Korff Ice Rise** ice cap Antarctica
151 Q10 **Korgalzhyn** var. Kurgal'dzhino, Kurgal'dzhinsky, Kaz. Qorgazhyn. Akmola, C Kazakhstan 50.33N 69.58E
94 G13 **Korgen** Troms, N Norway 66.04N 13.51E
153 R9 **Korgon-Dëbë** Dzhalal-Abadskaya Oblast', W Kyrgyzstan 41.51N 70.52E
78 M14 **Korhogo** N Ivory Coast 9.28N 5.38W
117 F19 **Korinthiakós Kólpos** Eng. Gulf of Corinth; anc. Corinthiacus Sinus. gulf C Greece
117 F19 **Kórinthos** Eng. Corinth; anc. Corinthus. Pelopónnisos, S Greece 37.55N 22.55E
115 M18 **Koritnik** ▲ S Serbia 42.06N 20.34E
Koritsa see Korçë
171 L14 **Kōriyama** Fukushima, Honshū, C Japan 37.25N 140.20E
142 E16 **Korkuteli** Antalya, SW Turkey 37.04N 30.12E
164 K6 **Korla** Chin. K'u-erh-lo. Xinjiang Uygur Zizhiqu, NW China 41.48N 86.10E
126 H11 **Korliki** Khanty-Mansiyskiy Avtonomnyy Okrug, C Russian Federation 61.28N 82.12E
Körlin an der Persante see Karlino
Korma see Karma
12 D8 **Kormak** Ontario, S Canada 47.38N 83.00W
Kormakíti, Akrotíri/Kormakiti, Cape/Kormakítis see Koruçam Burnu
113 G23 **Körmend** Vas, W Hungary 47.01N 16.34E
145 T5 **Kōrmōr** E Iraq 35.06N 44.47E
114 C13 **Kornat** It. Incoronata. island W Croatia
Korneshty see Corneşti
111 X3 **Korneuburg** Niederösterreich, NE Austria 48.22N 16.20E
151 P7 **Korneyevka** Severnyy Kazakhstan, N Kazakhstan 54.01N 68.30E
97 I17 **Kornsjø** Østfold, S Norway 58.55N 11.40E
79 O11 **Koro** Mopti, S Mali 14.05N 3.06W
197 J14 **Koro** island C Fiji
194 F12 **Koroba** Southern Highlands, W PNG 5.46S 142.48E
130 K8 **Korocha** Belgorodskaya Oblast', W Russian Federation 50.49N 37.08E
142 H12 **Köroğlu Dağları** ▲▲ C Turkey
191 V6 **Korogoro Point** headland New South Wales, SE Australia 31.03S 153.04E
83 J21 **Korogwe** Tanga, E Tanzania 5.12S 38.26E
190 L13 **Koroit** Victoria, SE Australia 38.17S 142.22E
197 H15 **Korolevu** Viti Levu, W Fiji 18.12S 177.44E
202 I17 **Koromiri** island S Cook Islands
179 R16 **Koronadal** Mindanao, S Philippines 6.23N 124.54E
116 G13 **Koróneia, Límni** var. Límni Korónia. ◎ N Greece
117 E22 **Koróni** Pelopónnisos, S Greece 36.46N 21.57E
Korónia, Límni see Koróneia, Límni
112 I9 **Koronowo** Ger. Krone an der Brahe. Kujawski-pomorskie, C Poland 53.18N 17.56E
119 R2 **Korop** Chernihivs'ka Oblast', N Ukraine 51.35N 32.57E
117 H19 **Koropí** Attikí, C Greece 37.54N 23.52E
196 C8 **Koror** var. Oreor. ● (Palau) Oreor, N Palau 7.21N 134.28E
Koror see Oreor
Kőrös see Križevci
113 L23 **Körös** ≈ E Hungary
Körösbánya see Baia de Criş
197 J14 **Koro Sea** sea C Fiji
Koroška see Kärnten
119 N3 **Korosten'** Zhytomyrs'ka Oblast', NW Ukraine 50.56N 28.39E
Korostyshev see Korostyshiv
119 N4 **Korostyshiv** Rus. Korostyshev. Zhytomyrs'ka Oblast', N Ukraine 50.18N 29.04E
129 V3 **Korotaikha** ≈ NW Russian Federation
126 H9 **Korotchayevo** Yamalo-Nenetskiy Avtonomnyy Okrug, N Russian Federation 66.00N 78.11E
80 I8 **Koro Toro** Borkou-Ennedi-Tibesti, N Chad 16.01N 18.27E
41 N16 **Korovin Island** island Shumagin Islands, Alaska, USA
197 I14 **Korovou** Viti Levu, W Fiji 17.48S 178.32E
95 M17 **Korpilahti** Länsi-Suomi, W Finland 62.01N 25.34E
94 K12 **Korpilombolo** Lapp. Dállogilli. Norrbotten, N Sweden 66.51N 23.00E
127 Oo16 **Korsakov** Ostrov Sakhalin, Sakhalinskaya Oblast', SE Russian Federation 46.41N 142.45E
95 J16 **Korsholm** Fin. Mustasaari. Länsi-Suomi, W Finland 63.07N 21.45E
97 I23 **Korsør** Vestsjælland, E Denmark 55.19N 11.09E
Korsovka see Kārsava
119 P6 **Korsun'-Shevchenkivs'kyy** Rus. Korsun'-Shevchenkovskiy. Cherkas'ka Oblast', C Ukraine 49.25N 31.15E
Korsun'-Shevchenkovskiy see Korsun'-Shevchenkivs'kyy
101 C17 **Kortemark** West-Vlaanderen, W Belgium 51.03N 3.03E
101 H18 **Kortenberg** Vlaams Brabant, C Belgium 50.52N 4.33E
101 K18 **Kortessem** Limburg, NE Belgium 50.52N 5.22E
101 E14 **Kortgene** Zeeland, SW Netherlands 51.34N 3.48E
82 F8 **Korti** Northern, N Sudan 18.06N 31.33E
101 C18 **Kortrijk** Fr. Courtrai. West-Vlaanderen, W Belgium 50.49N 3.16E
124 N2 **Koruçam Burnu** var. Cape Kormakiti, Kormakítis, Gk. Akrotíri Kormakíti. headland N Cyprus 35.24N 32.55E
191 O13 **Korumburra** Victoria, SE Australia 38.27S 145.48E
Koryak Range see Koryakskoye Nagor'ye
127 P8 **Koryakskiy Avtonomnyy Okrug** ◈ autonomous district E Russian Federation
Koryakskiy Khrebet see Koryakskoye Nagor'ye
127 Pp7 **Koryakskoye Nagor'ye** var. Koryakskiy Khrebet, Eng. Koryak Range. ▲▲ NE Russian Federation
129 P11 **Koryazhma** Arkhangel'skaya Oblast', NW Russian Federation 61.16N 47.06E
Kōryō see Kangnŭng
Korytsa see Korçë
119 Q2 **Koryukivka** Chernihivs'ka Oblast', N Ukraine 51.45N 32.16E
Korzec see Korets'
117 N21 **Kos** Kos, Dodekánisa, Greece, Aegean Sea 36.53N 27.18E
117 M21 **Kos** It. Coo; anc. Cos. island Dodekánisa, Greece, Aegean Sea
129 T12 **Kosa** Permskaya Oblast', NW Russian Federation 59.55N 54.54E
129 T13 **Kosa** ≈ NW Russian Federation
170 C11 **Kō-saki** headland Nagasaki, Tsushima, SW Japan 34.06N 129.13E
169 X13 **Kosan** SE North Korea 38.50N 127.26E
121 H18 **Kosava** Rus. Kosovo. Brestskaya Voblasts', SW Belarus 52.45N 25.16E
Kosch see Kose
150 G12 **Koschagyl** Kaz. Qosshaghyl. Atyrau, W Kazakhstan 46.52N 53.46E
112 G12 **Kościan** Ger. Kosten. Wielkopolskie, C Poland 52.04N 16.37E
112 I7 **Kościerzyna** Pomorskie, NW Poland 54.06N 17.55E
24 L4 **Kosciusko** Mississippi, S USA 33.03N 89.35W
Kosciusko, Mount see Kosciuszko, Mount
191 R11 **Kosciuszko, Mount** prev. Mount Kosciusko ▲ New South Wales, SE Australia 36.28S 148.15E
120 H4 **Kose** Ger. Kosch. Harjumaa, NW Estonia 59.10N 25.10E
116 G6 **Koshava** Vidin, NW Bulgaria 44.03N 23.00E
153 U9 **Kosh-Dëbë** var. Koshtebë. Narynskaya Oblast', C Kyrgyzstan 41.03N 74.08E
171 K16 **Koshigaya** var. Kosigaya. Saitama, Honshū, S Japan 35.54N 139.46E
K'o-shih see Kashi
170 B15 **Koshikijima-rettō** var. Kosikizima Rettô. island group SW Japan
151 W13 **Koshkarkol', Ozero** ◎ SE Kazakhstan
32 L9 **Koshkonong, Lake** ◎ Wisconsin, N USA
Koshoba see Goşoba
171 J14 **Kōshoku** var. Kôsyoku. Nagano, Honshū, S Japan 36.31N 138.07E
Koshtebë see Kosh-Dëbë
Kōshū see Kwangju
113 N19 **Košice** Ger. Kaschau, Hung. Kassa. Košický Kraj, E Slovakia 48.43N 21.15E
113 M20 **Košický Kraj** ◈ region E Slovakia
Kosigaya see Koshigaya
Kosikizima Rettô see Koshikijima-retto
159 R12 **Kosi Reservoir** ⊞ E Nepal
118 J8 **Kosiv** Ivano-Frankivs'ka Oblast', W Ukraine 48.19N 25.04E
151 O11 **Koskol'** Karaganda, C Kazakhstan 49.34N 67.03E
129 Q9 **Koslan** Respublika Komi, NW Russian Federation 63.27N 48.52E
Köslin see Koszalin
152 M12 **Koson** Rus. Kasan. Qashqadaryo Viloyati, S Uzbekistan 39.03N 65.34E
169 Y13 **Kosŏng** SE North Korea 38.40N 128.13E
153 S9 **Kosonsoy** Rus. Kasansay. Namangan Viloyati, E Uzbekistan 41.15N 71.28E
115 M16 **Kosovo** prev. Autonomous Province of Kosovo and Metohija. region S Serbia
Kosovo see Kosava
Kosovo and Metohija, Autonomous Province of see Kosovo
115 N16 **Kosovo Polje** Serbia, S Serbia 42.40N 21.07E
115 O16 **Kosovska Kamenica** Serbia, SE Serbia 42.37N 21.33E
115 M16 **Kosovska Mitrovica** Alb. Mitrovicë; prev. Mitrovica, Titova Mitrovica. Serbia, S Serbia 42.54N 20.52E
201 X17 **Kosrae** ◈ state E Micronesia
201 Y14 **Kosrae** prev. Kusaie. island Caroline Islands, E Micronesia
27 U9 **Kosse** Texas, SW USA 31.16N 96.38W
111 P6 **Kössen** Tirol, W Austria 47.40N 12.24E
78 M16 **Kossou, Lac de** ◎ C Ivory Coast
Kossukavak see Krumovgrad
Kostajnica see Hrvatska Kostajnica
150 M7 **Kostanay** var. Kustanay, Kaz. Qostanay. N Kazakhstan 53.15N 63.34E
150 L8 **Kostanay** var. Kostanayskaya Oblast, Kaz. Qostanay Oblysy. ◈ province N Kazakhstan
Kostanayskaya Oblast see Kostanay
Kostamus see Kostomuksha
Kosten see Kościan
116 H10 **Kostenets** prev. Georgi Dimitrov. Sofiya, W Bulgaria 42.17N 23.52E
82 F10 **Kosti** White Nile, C Sudan 13.10N 32.37E
Kostnitz see Konstanz
128 H7 **Kostomuksha** Fin. Kostamus. Respublika Kareliya, NW Russian Federation 64.33N 30.28E
118 K3 **Kostopil'** Rus. Kostopol'. Rivnens'ka Oblast', NW Ukraine 50.20N 26.28E
Kostopol' see Kostopil'
128 M15 **Kostroma** Kostromskaya Oblast', NW Russian Federation 57.46N 40.59E
129 N14 **Kostroma** ≈ NW Russian Federation
129 N14 **Kostromskaya Oblast'** ◈ province NW Russian Federation
112 D11 **Kostrzyn** Ger. Cüstrin, Küstrin. Lubuskie, W Poland 52.35N 14.39E
112 H11 **Kostrzyn** Wielkolpolskie, C Poland 52.23N 17.13E
119 X7 **Kostyantynivka** Rus. Konstantinovka. Donets'ka Oblast', SE Ukraine 48.30N 37.45E
Kostyukovichi see Kastsyukovichy
Kostyukovka see Kastsyukowka
Kôsyoku see Kōshoku
129 U6 **Kos'yu** Respublika Komi, NW Russian Federation 65.39N 59.01E
129 U6 **Kos'yu** ≈ NW Russian Federation
112 F7 **Koszalin** Ger. Köslin. Zachodnio-pomorskie, NW Poland 54.11N 16.10E
113 F22 **Kőszeg** Ger. Güns. Vas, W Hungary 47.24N 16.33E
158 H13 **Kota** prev. Kotah. Rājasthān, N India 25.13N 75.51E
174 H9 **Kota Baru** Sumatera, W Indonesia 1.07S 101.43E
175 Nn11 **Kotabaru** Pulau Laut, C Indonesia 3.15S 116.15E
Kotabaru see Jayapura
174 H2 **Kota Bharu** var. Kota Baharu, Kota Bahru. Kelantan, Peninsular Malaysia 6.07N 102.15E
Kotaboemi see Kotabumi
174 Ii12 **Kotabumi** prev. Kotaboemi. Sumatera, W Indonesia 4.49S 104.54E
155 S10 **Kot Addu** Punjab, E Pakistan 30.25N 70.54E
Kotah see Kota
175 Nn2 **Kota Kinabalu** prev. Jesselton. Sabah, East Malaysia 5.58N 116.04E
175 Nn2 **Kota Kinabalu** ✈ Sabah, East Malaysia 5.58N 116.04E
94 M12 **Kotala** Lappi, N Finland 67.01N 29.00E
Kotamobagoe see Kotamobagu
175 Rr7 **Kotamobagu** prev. Kotamobagoe. Sulawesi, C Indonesia 0.46N 124.21E
161 L14 **Kotapad** var. Kotapārh. Orissa, E India 19.10N 82.23E
Kotapārh see Kotapad
178 Gg17 **Ko Ta Ru Tao** island SW Thailand
174 L11 **Kotawaringin, Teluk** bay Borneo, C Indonesia
155 Q13 **Kot Dīji** Sind, SE Pakistan 27.16N 68.43E
158 K9 **Kotdwāra** Uttaranchal, N India 29.43N 78.33E
129 Q14 **Kotel'nich** Kirovskaya Oblast', NW Russian Federation 58.19N 48.12E
131 N12 **Kotel'nikovo** Volgogradskaya Oblast', SW Russian Federation 47.37N 43.07E
126 Ll4 **Kotel'nyy, Ostrov** island Novosibirskiye Ostrova, N Russian Federation
119 T5 **Kotel'va** Poltavs'ka Oblast', C Ukraine 50.04N 34.46E
103 M14 **Köthen** var. Cöthen. Sachsen-Anhalt, C Germany 51.46N 11.58E
Kôti see Kōchi
83 G17 **Kotido** NE Uganda 3.03N 34.07E
95 N19 **Kotka** Etelä-Suomi, S Finland 60.28N 26.54E
129 P11 **Kotlas** Arkhangel'skaya Oblast', NW Russian Federation 61.13N 46.43E
40 M10 **Kotlik** Alaska, USA 63.01N 163.33W
79 Q17 **Kotoka** ✈ (Accra) S Ghana 5.41N 0.10W
Kotonu see Cotonou
115 J17 **Kotor** It. Cattaro, SW-Montenegro 42.25N 18.47E
Kotor see Kotoriba
114 F7 **Kotoriba** Hung. Kotor. Međimurje, N Croatia 46.20N 16.47E
115 I17 **Kotorska, Boka** It. Bocche di Cattaro. bay SW-Montenegro
114 H11 **Kotorsko** Republika Srpska, N Bosnia and Herzegovina 44.50N 18.03E
114 G11 **Kotor Varoš** Republika Srpska, N Bosnia and Herzegovina 44.37N 17.24E
Koto Sho/Kotosho see Lan Yü
130 M7 **Kotovsk** Tambovskaya Oblast', W Russian Federation 52.39N 41.31E
119 O9 **Kotovs'k** Rus. Kotovsk. Odes'ka Oblast', SW Ukraine 47.42N 29.30E
Kotovsk see Hînceşti
121 G16 **Kotra** Rus. Kotra. ≈ W Belarus
155 P16 **Kotri** Sind, SE Pakistan 25.22N 68.16E
111 Q9 **Kötschach** Kärnten, S Austria 46.41N 12.57E
161 K15 **Kottagūdem** Andhra Pradesh, E India 17.36N 80.40E
161 F21 **Kottappadi** Kerala, SW India 11.38N 76.03E
161 G23 **Kottayam** Kerala, SW India 9.37N 76.31E
Kottbus see Cottbus
Kotte see Sri Jayawardanapura
81 K15 **Kotto** ≈ Central African Republic/Dem. Rep. Congo
200 S13 **Kotu Group** island group W Tonga
Koturdepe see Goturdepe
126 J9 **Kotuy** ≈ N Russian Federation
85 M16 **Kotwa** Mashonaland East, NE Zimbabwe 16.58S 32.46E
41 N7 **Kotzebue** Alaska, USA 66.54N 162.36W
40 M7 **Kotzebue Sound** inlet Alaska, USA
Kotzenan see Chocianów
Kotzman see Kitsman'
79 R14 **Kouandé** NW Benin 10.19N 1.42E
81 J15 **Kouango** Ouaka, S Central African Republic 5.00N 20.01E
79 O13 **Koudougou** C Burkina 12.15N 2.22W
100 K7 **Koudum** Friesland, N Netherlands 52.55N 5.26E
117 L25 **Koufonísi** island SE Greece
117 K21 **Koufonísi** island Kykládes, Greece, Aegean Sea
40 M8 **Kougarok Mountain** ▲ Alaska, USA 65.41N 165.29W
81 E20 **Kouilou** ≈ S Congo
16 N3 **Koukdjuak** ≈ Baffin Island, Nunavut, NE Canada
124 N4 **Koúklia** SW Cyprus 34.42N 32.35E
81 E19 **Koulamoutou** Ogooué-Lolo, C Gabon 1.06S 12.26E
78 L12 **Koulikoro** Koulikoro, SW Mali 12.55N 7.35W
78 L11 **Koulikoro** ◈ region SW Mali
197 H5 **Koumac** Province Nord, W New Caledonia 20.34S 164.18E
171 J15 **Koumi** Nagano, Honshū, S Japan 36.06N 138.27E
80 I13 **Koumra** Moyen-Chari, S Chad 8.55N 17.31E
Kounadougou see Koundougou
78 M15 **Kounahiri** C Ivory Coast 7.47N 5.51W
78 I12 **Koundâra** NW Guinea 12.28N 13.15W
79 N13 **Koundougou** var. Kounadougou. C Burkina 11.43N 4.40W
78 H11 **Koungheul** C Senegal 14.00N 14.48W
Kounradskiy see Konyrat
27 X10 **Kountze** Texas, SW USA 30.22N 94.18W
79 Q13 **Koupéla** C Burkina 12.09N 0.23W
79 N13 **Kouri** Sikasso, SW Mali 12.09N 4.46W
57 Y9 **Kourou** N French Guiana 5.07N 52.37W
116 J12 **Kouroú** ≈ NE Greece
78 K14 **Kouroussa** C Guinea 10.40N 9.49W
Kousseir see Al Quşayr
80 G11 **Kousséri** prev. Fort-Foureau. Extrême-Nord, NE Cameroon 12.01N 15.03E
Kouteifé see Al Quṭayfah
78 M13 **Koutiala** Sikasso, S Mali 12.24N 5.30W
78 M14 **Kouto** NW Ivory Coast 9.51N 6.25W
95 M19 **Kouvola** Etelä-Suomi, S Finland 60.50N 26.48E
81 G18 **Kouyou** ≈ C Congo
114 M10 **Kovačica** Hung. Antafalva; prev. Kovacsicza. Serbia, N Serbia 45.08N 20.36E
Kovacsicza see Kovačica
Kővárhosszúfalu see Satulung
Kovászna see Covasna
128 I4 **Kovdor** Murmanskaya Oblast', NW Russian Federation 67.32N 30.27E
128 I5 **Kovdozero, Ozero** ◎ NW Russian Federation
118 J3 **Kovel'** Pol. Kowel. Volyns'ka Oblast', NW Ukraine 51.13N 24.42E
114 M11 **Kovin** Hung. Kevevára; prev. Temes-Kubin. Serbia, NE Serbia 44.45N 20.59E
Kovno see Kaunas
131 N3 **Kovrov** Vladimirskaya Oblast', W Russian Federation 56.24N 41.21E
131 O5 **Kovylkino** Respublika Mordoviya, W Russian Federation 54.03N 43.52E
112 J11 **Kowal** Kujawsko-pomorskie, C Poland 52.31N 19.08E
112 J9 **Kowalewo Pomorskie** Ger. Schönsee. Kujawsko-pomorskie, C Poland 53.07N 18.48E
Kowasna see Covasna
121 M16 **Kowbcha** Rus. Kolbcha. Mahilyowskaya Voblasts', E Belarus 53.40N 29.13E
Koweit see Kuwait
Kowel see Kovel'
193 F17 **Kowhitirangi** West Coast, South Island, NZ 42.54S 171.01E
167 O15 **Kowloon** Chin. Jiulong. Hong Kong, S China
Kowno see Kaunas
165 N7 **Kox Kuduk** well NW China 40.32N 92.30E
142 D16 **Köyceğiz** Muğla, SW Turkey 36.58N 28.38E
129 N6 **Koyda** Arkhangel'skaya Oblast', NW Russian Federation 66.22N 42.42E
Koymat see Goymat
Koymatdag, Gory see Goymatdag
Koyna Reservoir see Shivāji Sāgar
171 M11 **Koyoshi-gawa** ≈ Honshū, C Japan
Koysanjaq see Koi Sanjaq
Koytash see Qo'ytosh
152 M14 **Köýtendag** prev. Rus. Charshanga, Charshangy, Turkm. Charshangngy. Lebap Welaýaty, E Turkmenistan 37.31N 65.58E
41 N9 **Koyuk** Alaska, USA 64.55N 161.09W
41 N9 **Koyuk River** ≈ Alaska, USA
41 O9 **Koyukuk** Alaska, USA 64.52N 157.42W
41 O9 **Koyukuk River** ≈ Alaska, USA
142 J13 **Kozaklı** Nevşehir, C Turkey 39.13N 34.51E
170 F13 **Kōzan** Hiroshima, Honshū, SW Japan 34.35N 133.02E
142 K16 **Kozan** Adana, S Turkey 37.27N 35.46E
117 E14 **Kozáni** Dytikí Makedonía, N Greece 40.18N 21.48E
114 F10 **Kozara** ▲▲ NW Bosnia and Herzegovina
Kozarska Dubica see Bosanska Dubica
119 P3 **Kozelets'** Rus. Kozelets. Chernihivs'ka Oblast', NE Ukraine 50.54N 31.09E
119 S6 **Kozel'shchyna** Poltavs'ka Oblast', C Ukraine 49.13N 33.49E
130 J5 **Kozel'sk** Kaluzhskaya Oblast', W Russian Federation 54.04N 35.51E
Kozhikode see Calicut
129 V9 **Kozhimiz, Gora** ▲ NW Russian Federation 63.13N 58.54E
128 L9 **Kozhozero, Ozero** ◎ NW Russian Federation
129 T7 **Kozhva** var. Kozya. Respublika Komi, NW Russian Federation 65.06N 57.00E
129 T7 **Kozhva** ≈ NW Russian Federation
129 U6 **Kozhim** Respublika Komi, NW Russian Federation 65.43N 59.25E
112 N13 **Kozienice** Mazowieckie, C Poland 51.37N 21.30E
111 S13 **Kozina** SW Slovenia 45.36N 13.56E
116 H7 **Kozloduy** Vratsa, NW Bulgaria 43.47N 23.42E
131 Q3 **Kozlovka** Chavash Respubliki, W Russian Federation 55.53N 48.07E
Kozlovshchina/Kozlowszczyzna see Kazlowshchyna
131 P3 **Koz'modem'yansk** Respublika Mariy El, W Russian Federation 56.19N 46.33E
118 J6 **Kozova** Ternopil's'ka Oblast', W Ukraine 49.25N 25.09E
115 P20 **Kožuf** ▲ S FYR Macedonia 41.10N 22.14E
172 S13 **Kōzu-shima** island E Japan
Kozya see Kozhva
Koz'yany see Kaz'yany
119 N5 **Kozyatyn** Rus. Kazatin. Vinnyts'ka Oblast', C Ukraine 49.40N 28.48E
79 Q16 **Kpalimé** var. Palimé. SW Togo 6.54N 0.37E
79 Q16 **Kpandu** E Ghana 7.00N 0.18E
101 F15 **Krabbendijke** Zeeland, SW Netherlands 51.25N 4.07E
178 Gg16 **Krabi** var. Muang Krabi. Krabi, SW Thailand 8.04N 98.52E
178 Gg14 **Kra Buri** Ranong, SW Thailand 10.25N 98.48E
178 Jj13 **Krâchéh** prev. Kratie. Krâchéh, E Cambodia 12.28N 106.01E
97 G17 **Kragerø** Telemark, S Norway 58.53N 9.22E
114 M13 **Kragujevac** Serbia, C Serbia 44.01N 20.54E
Krainburg see Kranj
178 Gg14 **Kra, Isthmus of** isthmus Malaysia/Thailand
114 D12 **Krajina** cultural region SW Croatia
Krakatau, Pulau see Rakata, Pulau
Krakau see Małopolskie
113 L16 **Kraków** Eng. Cracow, Ger. Krakau; anc. Cracovia. Małopolskie, S Poland 50.03N 19.57E
102 L9 **Krakower See** ◎ NE Germany
178 Ii12 **Krâlănh** Siĕmréab, NW Cambodia 13.35N 103.27E
47 Q16 **Kralendijk** Bonaire, E Netherlands Antilles 12.07N 68.13W
114 B10 **Kraljevica** It. Porto Re. Primorje-Gorski Kotar, NW Croatia 45.15N 14.36E
114 M13 **Kraljevo** prev. Rankovićevo. Serbia, C Serbia 43.44N 20.40E
113 E16 **Královéhradecký Kraj** prev. Hradecký Kraj. ◈ region N Czech Republic
Kralup an der Moldau see Kralupy nad Vltavou
113 C16 **Kralupy nad Vltavou** Ger. Kralup an der Moldau. Středočeský Kraj, NW Czech Republic 50.13N 14.17E
119 W7 **Kramators'k** Rus. Kramatorsk. Donets'ka Oblast', SE Ukraine 48.43N 37.34E
95 H17 **Kramfors** Västernorrland, C Sweden 62.55N 17.49E
Kranéa see Kraniá
110 M7 **Kranebitten** ✈ (Innsbruck) Tirol, W Austria 47.18N 11.21E
117 D15 **Kraniá** var. Kranéa. Dytikí Makedonía, N Greece 39.54N 21.21E
117 G20 **Kranídi** Pelopónnisos, S Greece 37.21N 23.09E
111 T11 **Kranj** Ger. Krainburg. NW Slovenia 46.16N 14.16E
117 F16 **Krannón** battleground Thessalía, C Greece 39.32N 22.20E
Kranz see Zelenogradsk
114 D7 **Krapina** Krapina-Zagorje, N Croatia 46.12N 15.52E
114 E8 **Krapina** ≈ N Croatia
114 D8 **Krapina-Zagorje** off. Krapinsko-Zagorska Županija. ◈ province N Croatia
116 L7 **Krapinets** ≈ NE Bulgaria
113 I15 **Krapkowice** Ger. Krappitz. Opolskie, S Poland 50.28N 17.55E
Krappitz see Krapkowice
129 O12 **Krasavino** Vologodskaya Oblast', NW Russian Federation 60.56N 46.27E
125 Ff5 **Krasino** Novaya Zemlya, Arkhangel'skaya Oblast', N Russian Federation 70.45N 54.16E
127 N18 **Kraskino** Primorskiy Kray, SE Russian Federation 42.40N 130.51E
120 J11 **Krāslava** Krāslava, SE Latvia 55.56N 27.08E
121 M14 **Krasnaluki** Rus. Krasnoluki. Vitsyebskaya Voblasts', N Belarus 54.37N 28.49E
121 P17 **Krasnapollye** Rus. Krasnopol'ye. Mahilyowskaya Voblasts', E Belarus 53.19N 31.24E
130 L15 **Krasnaya Polyana** Krasnodarskiy Kray, SW Russian Federation 43.40N 40.13E
Krasnaya Slabada/Krasnaya Sloboda see Chyrvonaya Slabada
121 J15 **Krasnaye** Rus. Krasnoye. Minskaya Voblasts', C Belarus 54.13N 27.04E
113 O14 **Kraśnik** Ger. Kratznick. Lubelskie, E Poland 50.55N 22.13E
119 O9 **Krasni Okny** Odes'ka Oblast', SW Ukraine 47.33N 29.28E
151 P7 **Krasnoarmeysk** Severnyy Kazakhstan, N Kazakhstan 53.52N 69.51E
131 P8 **Krasnoarmeysk** Saratovskaya Oblast', W Russian Federation 51.01N 45.42E
Krasnoarmeysk see Krasnoarmiys'k/Tayynsha
127 Oo4 **Krasnoarmeyskiy** Chukotskiy Avtonomnyy Okrug, NE Russian Federation 69.30N 171.44E
119 W7 **Krasnoarmiys'k** Rus. Krasnoarmeysk. Donets'ka Oblast', SE Ukraine 48.16N 37.13E
129 P11 **Krasnoborsk** Arkhangel'skaya Oblast', NW Russian Federation 61.31N 45.57E
130 K14 **Krasnodar** prev. Ekaterinodar, Yekaterinodar. Krasnodarskiy Kray, SW Russian Federation 45.02N 39.00E
130 K13 **Krasnodarskiy Kray** ◈ territory SW Russian Federation
119 Z7 **Krasnodon** Luhans'ka Oblast', E Ukraine 48.16N 39.45E
Krasnogor see Kallaste
131 T2 **Krasnogorskoye** Latv. Sarkaņi. Udmurtskaya Respublika, NW Russian Federation 57.42N 52.29E
Krasnograd see Krasnohrad
Krasnogvardeysk see Bulung'ur
130 M13 **Krasnogvardeyskoye** Stavropol'skiy Kray, SW Russian Federation 45.49N 41.31E
Krasnogvardeyskoye see Krasnohvardiys'ke
119 U6 **Krasnohrad** Rus. Krasnograd. Kharkivs'ka Oblast', E Ukraine 49.22N 35.27E
119 S12 **Krasnohvardiys'ke** Rus. Krasnogvardeyskoye. Respublika Krym, S Ukraine 45.30N 34.19E
126 L16 **Krasnokamensk** Chitinskaya Oblast', S Russian Federation 50.03N 118.01E
129 U14 **Krasnokamsk** Permskaya Oblast', W Russian Federation 58.07N 55.48E
131 U8 **Krasnokholm** Orenburgskaya Oblast', W Russian Federation 51.34N 54.11E
119 U5 **Krasnokuts'k** Rus. Krasnokutsk. Kharkivs'ka Oblast', E Ukraine 50.01N 35.03E
130 L7 **Krasnolesnyy** Voronezhskaya Oblast', W Russian Federation 51.53N 39.37E
Krasnoluki see Krasnaluki
Krasnoosol'skoye Vodokhranilishche see Chervonooskil's'ke Vodoskhovyshche
119 S11 **Krasnoperekops'k** Rus. Krasnoperekopsk. Respublika Krym, S Ukraine 45.56N 33.46E
119 U4 **Krasnopillya** Sums'ka Oblast', NE Ukraine 50.46N 35.17E
Krasnopol'ye see Krasnapollye
126 H9 **Krasnosel'kup** Yamalo-Nenetskiy Avtonomnyy Okrug, N Russian Federation 65.46N 82.11E
128 L5 **Krasnoshchel'ye** Murmanskaya Oblast', NW Russian Federation 67.22N 37.03E
131 O5 **Krasnoslobodsk** Respublika Mordoviya, W Russian Federation 54.24N 43.51E
131 T2 **Krasnoslobodsk** Volgogradskaya Oblast', SW Russian Federation 48.41N 44.34E
Krasnostav see Krasnystaw
125 F10 **Krasnotur'insk** Sverdlovskaya Oblast', C Russian Federation 59.45N 60.19E
125 E11 **Krasnoufimsk** Sverdlovskaya Oblast', C Russian Federation 56.43N 57.39E
125 Ee10 **Krasnoural'sk** Sverdlovskaya Oblast', C Russian Federation 58.24N 59.44E
131 V5 **Krasnousol'skiy** Respublika Bashkortostan, W Russian Federation 53.55N 56.22E
129 U12 **Krasnovishersk** Permskaya Oblast', NW Russian Federation 60.22N 57.04E
Krasnovodsk see Türkmenbaşy
Krasnovodskiy Zaliv see Türkmenbaşy Aylagy
152 B10 **Krasnovodskoye Plato** Turkm. Krasnowodsk Platosy. plateau NW Turkmenistan
Krasnowodsk Aylagy see Türkmenbaşy Aylagy
Krasnowodsk Platosy see Krasnovodskoye Plato
126 Hh14 **Krasnoyarsk** Krasnoyarskiy Kray, S Russian Federation 56.04N 92.46E
131 X7 **Krasnoyarskiy** Orenburgskaya Oblast', W Russian Federation 51.56N 59.54E
126 I12 **Krasnoyarskiy Kray** ◈ territory C Russian Federation
126 I14 **Krasnoyarskoye Vodokhranilishche** ⊞ S Russian Federation
Krasnoye see Krasnaye
Krasnoye Znamya see Gyzylbaýdak
129 R11 **Krasnozatonskiy** Respublika Komi, NW Russian Federation 61.39N 51.00E
120 D13 **Krasnoznamensk** prev. Lasdehnen, Ger. Haselberg. Kaliningradskaya Oblast', W Russian Federation 54.57N 22.28E
130 K3 **Krasnoznamensk** Moskovskaya Oblast', W Russian Federation 55.40N 37.05E
119 R11 **Krasnoznam"yans'kyy Kanal** canal S Ukraine
113 P14 **Krasnystaw** Rus. Krasnostav. Lubelskie, SE Poland 51.00N 23.10E
130 H4 **Krasnyy** Smolenskaya Oblast', W Russian Federation 54.36N 31.27E
131 P2 **Krasnyye Baki** Nizhegorodskaya Oblast', W Russian Federation 57.07N 45.12E
131 Q13 **Krasnyye Barrikady** Astrakhanskaya Oblast', SW Russian Federation 46.14N 47.48E
128 K15 **Krasnyy Kholm** Tverskaya Oblast', W Russian Federation 58.04N 37.05E
131 Q8 **Krasnyy Kut** Saratovskaya Oblast', W Russian Federation 50.54N 46.58E
Krasnyy Liman see Krasnyy Lyman
119 Y7 **Krasnyy Luch** prev. Krindachevka. Luhans'ka Oblast', E Ukraine 48.08N 38.52E
119 X6 **Krasnyy Lyman** Rus. Krasnyy Liman. Donets'ka Oblast', SE Ukraine 49.00N 37.50E
131 R3 **Krasnyy Steklovar** Respublika Mariy El, W Russian Federation 56.14N 48.49E
131 P8 **Krasnyy Tekstil'shchik** Saratovskaya Oblast', W Russian Federation 51.35N 45.49E
131 R13 **Krasnyy Yar** Astrakhanskaya Oblast', SW Russian Federation 46.33N 48.21E
Krassóvár see Caraşova
118 L5 **Krasyliv** Khmel'nyts'ka Oblast', W Ukraine 49.38N 26.59E
113 O21 **Kraszna** Rom. Crasna. ≈ Hungary/Romania
Kratie see Krâchéh
194 I13 **Kratke Range** ▲▲ C PNG
115 P17 **Kratovo** NE FYR Macedonia 42.04N 22.08E
Kratznick see Kraśnik
176 Yy11 **Krau** Papua, E Indonesia 3.15S 140.07E
178 Ii13 **Krâvanh, Chuŏr Phnum** Eng. Cardamom Mountains, Fr. Chaîne des Cardamomes. ▲▲ W Cambodia
Kravasta Lagoon see Karavastasë, Laguna e
Krawang see Karawang
Kraxatau see Rakata, Pulau
131 Q15 **Kraynovka** Respublika Dagestan, SW Russian Federation 43.58N 47.24E
120 D12 **Kražiai** Šiauliai, C Lithuania 55.36N 22.41E
29 P11 **Krebs** Oklahoma, C USA 34.55N 95.43W

◆ Country ● Country Capital ◇ Dependent Territory ○ Dependent Territory Capital ◈ Administrative Region ✈ International Airport ▲ Mountain ▲▲ Mountain Range Volcano ≈ River ◎ Lake ⊞ Reservoir

103 D15 **Krefeld** Nordrhein-Westfalen,
W Germany 51.19N 6.34E
Kreisstadt see Krosno
Odrzańskie
117 D17 **Kremastón, Technití Límni**
◆ C Greece
Kremenchug see Kremenchuk
Kremenchugskoye
Vodokhranilishche/
Kremenchuk Reservoir see
Kremenchuts'ke Vodoskhovyshche
119 S6 **Kremenchuk** Rus. Kremenchug.
Poltavs'ka Oblast', NE Ukraine
49.03N 33.27E
119 R6 **Kremenchuts'ke**
Vodoskhovyshche Eng.
Kremenchuk Reservoir,
Rus. Kremenchugskoye
Vodokhranilishche. ◙
C Ukraine
118 K5 **Kremenets'** Pol. Krzemieniec,
Rus. Kremenets. Ternopil's'ka
Oblast', W Ukraine 50.05N 25.43E
Kremennaya see Kreminna
119 X6 **Kreminna** Rus. Kremennaya.
Luhans'ka Oblast', E Ukraine
49.03N 38.14E
39 R4 **Kremmling** Colorado, C USA
40.03N 106.23W
111 V3 **Krems** see NE Austria
Krems see Krems an der Donau
111 W3 **Krems an der Donau** var.
Krems. Niederösterreich, N Austria
48.25N 15.34E
Kremsier see Kroměříž
111 S4 **Kremsmünster** Oberösterreich,
N Austria 48.04N 14.08E
40 M17 **Krenitzin Islands** island Aleutian
Islands, Alaska, USA
Kresena see Kresna
116 G11 **Kresna** var. Kresena. Blagoevgrad,
SW Bulgaria 41.43N 23.12E
114 O12 **Krespolin** Serbia, E Serbia
44.37N 21.36E
27 N4 **Kress** Texas, SW USA
34.21N 101.43W
127 Pp4 **Kresta, Zaliv** bay E Russian
Federation
117 D20 **Kréstena** prev. Selinoús. Dytikí
Ellás, S Greece 37.36N 21.36E
128 H14 **Kresttsy** Novgorodskaya
Oblast', W Russian Federation
58.15N 32.28E
126 Kk11 **Krestyakh** Respublika Sakha
(Yakutiya), NE Russian Federation
62.10N 116.24E
Kretikon Delagos see
Kritikó Pélagos
120 C11 **Kretinga** Ger. Krottingen.
Klaipėda, NW Lithuania
55.53N 21.13E
Kreutz see Cristuru Secuiesc
Kreuz see Križevci, Croatia
Kreuz see Risti, Estonia
Kreuzburg/Kreuzburg in
Oberschlesien see Kluczbork
Kreuzingen see Bol'shakovo
110 H6 **Kreuzlingen** Thurgau,
NE Switzerland 47.37N 9.10E
103 K25 **Kreuzspitze** ▲ S Germany
47.30N 10.55E
103 F16 **Kreuztal** Nordrhein-Westfalen,
W Germany 50.58N 8.00E
121 I15 **Kreva** Rus. Krevo. Hrodzyenskaya
Voblasts', W Belarus 54.19N 26.16E
Krevo see Kreva
Kría see Krýa Vrýsi
81 D16 **Kribi** Sud, SW Cameroon
2.53N 9.57E
Krichëv see Krychaw
Krickerhäu/Kriegerhaj see
Handlová
111 W6 **Krieglach** Steiermark, E Austria
47.33N 15.37E
110 F8 **Kriens** Luzern, W Switzerland
47.01N 8.16E
Krimmitschau see Crimmitschau
100 H12 **Krimpen aan den IJssel**
Zuid-Holland, SW Netherlands
51.56N 4.39E
Krindachevka see Krasnyy Luch
117 G25 **Kriós, Akrotírio** headland Kríti,
Greece, E Mediterranean Sea
35.17N 23.31E
161 J16 **Krishna** prev. Kistna. ◙ C India
114 H20 **Krishnagiri** Tamil Nādu,
SE India 12.33N 78.10E
161 K17 **Krishna, Mouths of the** delta
SE India
159 S15 **Krishnanagar** West Bengal,
N India 23.22N 88.31E
161 G20 **Krishnarājāsāgara Reservoir**
◙ W India
119 N9 **Kristdala** Kalmar, S Sweden
57.24N 16.12E
Kristiania see Oslo
97 E18 **Kristiansand** var. Christiansand.
Vest-Agder, S Norway 58.07N 7.52E
97 L22 **Kristianstad** Skåne, S Sweden
56.01N 14.10E
96 F8 **Kristiansund** var. Christiansund.
Møre og Romsdal, S Norway
63.07N 7.45E
Kristiinankaupunki see
Kristinestad
95 I14 **Kristineberg** Västerbotten,
N Sweden 65.07N 18.36E
97 L16 **Kristinehamn** Värmland,
C Sweden 59.16N 14.09E
95 J17 **Kristinestad** Fin.
Kristiinankaupunki. Länsi-Suomi,
W Finland 62.15N 21.24E
Kristyor see Crișcior
117 J25 **Kríti** Eng. Crete. ◆ region Greece,
Aegean Sea
117 I24 **Kríti** Eng. Crete. island Greece,
Aegean Sea
117 J23 **Kritikó Pélagos** var. Kretikon
Delagos, Eng. Sea of Crete; anc.
Mare Creticum. sea Greece,
Aegean Sea
Kriulyany see Criuleni
114 I12 **Krivaja** ◙ NE Bosnia and
Herzegovina
Krivaja see Mali Idoš
115 P17 **Kriva Palanka** Turk. Eğri
Palanka. NE FYR Macedonia
42.13N 22.19E
Krivichi see Kryvichy
113 H8 **Krivodol** Vratsa, NW Bulgaria
43.23N 23.30E
130 M10 **Krivorozh'ye** Rostovskaya
Oblast', SW Russian Federation
48.51N 40.49E
Krivoshin see Kryvoshyn

114 F7 **Krivoy Rog** see Kryvyy Rih
114 F7 **Križevci** Ger. Kreuz, Hung. Kőrös.
Varaždin, NE Croatia 46.02N 16.32E
114 B10 **Krk** It. Veglia. Primorje-Gorski
Kotar, NW Croatia 45.01N 14.36E
114 B10 **Krk** It. Veglia; anc. Curieta. island
NW Croatia
111 V12 **Krka** ◙ SE Slovenia
111 V13 **Krka** see Gurk
113 H16 **Krn** ▲ NW Slovenia 46.15N 13.37E
113 H16 **Krnov** Ger. Jägerndorf.
Moravskoslezský Kraj, E Czech
Republic 50.05N 17.42E
Kroatien see Croatia
97 G14 **Krøderen** Buskerud, S Norway
60.06N 9.48E
97 G14 **Krøderen** ◙ S Norway
Kroi see Krui
97 N17 **Krokek** Östergötland, S Sweden
58.40N 16.25E
Krokodil see Crocodile
95 G16 **Krokom** Jämtland, C Sweden
63.19N 14.30E
119 S2 **Krolevets'** Rus. Krolevets.
Sums'ka Oblast', NE Ukraine
51.34N 33.24E
Królewska Huta see Chorzów
113 H18 **Kroměříž** Ger. Kremsier. Zlínský
Kraj, E Czech Republic
49.18N 17.24E
100 I9 **Krommenie** Noord-Holland,
C Netherlands 52.30N 4.46E
130 J6 **Kromy** Orlovskaya Oblast',
W Russian Federation
52.41N 35.45E
103 L18 **Kronach** Bayern, E Germany
50.14N 11.19E
Krone an der Brahe see
Koronowo
178 J13 **Krŏng Kaôh Kŏng** Kaôh Kŏng,
SW Cambodia 11.37N 102.58E
97 K21 **Kronoberg** ◆ county S Sweden
127 Pp11 **Kronotskiy Zaliv** bay E Russian
Federation
205 O2 **Kronprinsesse Märtha Kyst**
physical region Antarctica
205 V3 **Kronprins Olav Kyst** physical
region Antarctica
113 J14 **Kronshtadt** Leningradskaya
Oblast', NW Russian Federation
60.01N 29.42E
128 G12 **Kronstadt** see Brașov
85 I22 **Kroonstad** Free State, C South
Africa 27.40S 27.15E
126 Kk13 **Kropotkin** Irkutskaya Oblast',
C Russian Federation
58.30N 115.21E
130 L14 **Kropotkin** Krasnodarskiy
Kray, SW Russian Federation
45.28N 40.30E
112 J11 **Krośniewice** Łódzkie, C Poland
52.14N 19.10E
130 N17 **Krosno** Ger. Krossen.
Podkarpackie, SE Poland
49.40N 21.46E
112 E12 **Krosno Odrzańskie** Ger.
Crossen, Kreisstadt. Lubuskie,
W Poland 52.02N 15.06E
Krossen see Krosno
112 H13 **Krotoszyn** Ger. Krotoschin.
Wielkopolskie, C Poland
51.43N 17.24E
Krottingen see Kretinga
Krousón see Krousónas
117 J25 **Krousónas** prev. Krousón,
Krousoún. Kríti, Greece,
E Mediterranean Sea 35.13N 24.58E
Krousoún see Krousónas
Krraba see Krrabë
115 L20 **Krrabë** var. Krraba. Tiranë,
C Albania 41.15N 19.56E
115 L17 **Krrabit, Mali i** ▲ N Albania
111 W12 **Krško** Ger. Gurkfeld; prev. Videm-
Krško. E Slovenia 45.57N 15.31E
85 K19 **Kruger National Park** national
park Northern, N South Africa
85 J21 **Krugersdorp** Gauteng, NE South
Africa 26.04S 27.46E
40 D16 **Krugloi Point** headland Agattu
Island, Alaska, USA 52.30N 173.46E
Krugloye see Kruhlaye
121 N15 **Kruhlaye** Rus. Krugloye.
Mahilyowskaya Voblasts', E Belarus
54.15N 29.48E
114 I13 **Krui** var. Kroi. Sumatera,
SW Indonesia 5.11S 103.55E
116 G16 **Kruibeke** Oost-Vlaanderen,
N Belgium 51.10N 4.18E
85 G25 **Kruidfontein** Western Cape,
SW South Africa 32.50S 21.59E
101 F15 **Kruininigen** Zeeland,
SW Netherlands 51.28N 4.01E
115 L19 **Krujë** var. Kruja. It. Croia. Durrës,
C Albania 41.30N 19.48E
Kruja see Krujë
27 T6 **Krum** Texas, SW USA
33.15N 97.14W
103 J23 **Krumbach** Bayern, S Germany
48.12N 10.21E
115 M17 **Krumë** Kukës, NE Albania
42.11N 20.25E
Krummau see Český Krumlov
116 K12 **Krumovgrad** prev. Kossukavak.
Kürdzhali, S Bulgaria 41.29N 25.40E
116 K12 **Krumovitsa** ◙ S Bulgaria
116 L10 **Krumovo** Yambol, E Bulgaria
42.16N 26.25E
178 Hh11 **Krung Thep, Ao** var. Bight of
Bangkok. bay S Thailand
● (Thailand) Bangkok, C Thailand
13.43N 100.30E
178 Hh12 **Krung Thep, Ao** var. Bight of
Bangkok. bay S Thailand
Krung Thep Mahanakhon see
Krung Thep
Krupa/Krupa na Uni see
Bosanska Krupa
121 M15 **Krupki** Rus. Krupki. Minskaya
Voblasts', C Belarus 54.19N 29.07E
97 G14 **Kruså** var. Krusaa. Sønderjylland,
SW Denmark 54.50N 9.25E
Krusaa see Kruså
5 I4 **Krusenstern, Cape** headland
Nunavut, NW Canada
68.17N 114.00W
115 N14 **Kruševac** Serbia, C Serbia
43.36N 21.19E

115 N19 **Kruševo** SW FYR Macedonia
41.22N 21.15E
113 A15 **Krušné Hory** Eng. Ore
Mountains, Ger. Erzgebirge.
▲ Czech Republic/Germany see
also Erzgebirge
41 W13 **Kruzof Island** island Alexander
Archipelago, Alaska, USA
116 F13 **Krýa Vrýsi** var. Kría Vrísi.
Kentrikí Makedonía, N Greece
40.40N 22.18E
121 P16 **Krychaw** Rus. Krichëv.
Mahilyowskaya Voblasts', E Belarus
53.42N 31.43E
66 K11 **Krylov Seamount** undersea
feature E Atlantic Ocean
17.34N 30.07W
Krym see Krym, Respublika
119 O9 **Krym, Respublika** var. Krym,
Eng. Crimea, Crimean Oblast; prev.
Rus. Krymskaya ASSR, Krymskaya
Oblast'. ◆ province SE Ukraine
122 D11 **Kuğuk Çekmece** İstanbul,
NW Turkey 41.01N 28.46E
170 Dd13 **Kudamatsu** var. Kudamatu.
Yamaguchi, Honshū, SW Japan
34.00N 131.53E
119 T13 **Kryms'ki Hory** ▲ S Ukraine
119 T13 **Kryms'kyy Pivostriv** peninsula
S Ukraine
113 M18 **Krynica** Ger. Tannenhof.
Małopolskie, S Poland
49.26N 20.57E
119 P8 **Kryve Ozero** Odes'ka Oblast',
SW Ukraine 47.54N 30.19E
121 I18 **Kryvoshyn** Rus. Krivoshin.
Brestskaya Voblasts', SW Belarus
52.52N 26.07E
121 K14 **Kryvychy** Rus. Krivichi.
Minskaya Voblasts', C Belarus
54.43N 27.16E
119 S8 **Kryvyy Rih** Rus. Krivoy
Rog. Dnipropetrovs'ka Oblast',
SE Ukraine 47.53N 33.24E
119 N8 **Kryzhopil'** Vinnyts'ka Oblast',
C Ukraine 48.22N 28.51E
Krzemieniec see Kremenets'
113 J14 **Krzepice** Śląskie, S Poland
50.58N 18.42E
112 F10 **Krzyż Wielkopolski**
Wielkopolskie, C Poland
52.52N 16.03E
76 J5 **Ksar al Kabir** see Ksar-el-Kebir
Ksar al Soule see Er-Rachidia
76 G5 **Ksar El Boukhari** N Algeria
35.53N 2.45E
Ksar-el-Kebir var. Alcázar,
Ksar al Kabir, Ksar-el-Kébir, Ar.
Al-Ksar al-Kabir, Al-Qsar al-Kbir,
Sp. Alcazarquivir. NW Morocco
35.04N 5.55W
113 H12 **Książ Wielkopolski** Ger.
Xions. Wielkopolskie, C Poland
52.03N 17.10E
131 O3 **Kstovo** Nizhegorodskaya
Oblast', W Russian Federation
56.07N 44.12E
Mm4 **Kuala Belait** W Brunei
4.48N 114.12E
178 H13 **Kuala Dungun** see Dungun
174 M7 **Kualakapuas** Borneo, C Indonesia
174 M10 **Kualakuayan** Borneo,
C Indonesia 2.01S 112.34E
174 H4 **Kuala Lipis** Pahang, Peninsular
Malaysia 04.11N 102.00E
174 H5 **Kuala Lumpur** ● (Malaysia)
Kuala Lumpur, Peninsular Malaysia
3.07N 101.42E
174 H5 **Kuala Lumpur International**
✈ Selangor, Peninsular Malaysia
2.51N 101.45E
Kuala Pelabohan Kelang see
Pelabuhan Klang
115 Nn3 **Kuala Penyu** Sabah, East
Malaysia 5.37N 115.36E
40 E9 **Kualapu'u** var. Kualapuu.
Moloka'i, Hawai'i, USA, C Pacific
Ocean 21.09N 157.02W
174 H4 **Kuala, Sungai** ◙ Sumatera,
W Indonesia
178 Hh3 **Kuala Terengganu** var. Kuala
Trengganu. Terengganu, Peninsular
Malaysia 5.19N 103.07E
174 H9 **Kualatungkal** Sumatera,
W Indonesia 0.49S 103.22E
175 O3 **Kuamut, Sungai** ◙
East Malaysia
175 Qq7 **Kuandang** Sulawesi, N Indonesia
0.50N 122.55E
175 Qq7 **Kuandang, Teluk** bay Sulawesi,
N Indonesia
169 V12 **Kuandian** var. Kuandian Manzu
Zizhixian. Liaoning, NE China
40.41N 124.46E
Kuandian Manzu Zizhixian
see Kuandian
82 C11 **Kuando-Kubango** see Cuando
Cubango
Kuang-chou see Guangzhou
Kuang-hsi see Guangxi Zhuangzu
Zizhiqu
Kuang-tung see Guangdong
Kuang-yuan see Guangyuan
174 Hh4 **Kuantan** Pahang, Peninsular
Malaysia 3.49N 103.19E
Kuantan, Batang see
Indragiri, Sungai
Kuanza Norte see Cuanza Norte
Kuanza Sul see Cuanza Sul
Kuanzhou, see Qingjian
Kuba see Quba
95 H16 **Kubbe** Västernorrland, C Sweden
63.31N 18.04E
82 A11 **Kubbum** Southern Darfur,
W Sudan 11.46N 23.48E
128 L13 **Kubenskoye, Ozero**
◙ NW Russian Federation
152 G6 **Kubla-Ustyurt** Aus.
Komsomol'sk-na-Ustyurte.
Qoraqalpog'iston Respublikasi,
NW Uzbekistan 44.06N 58.14E
115 Ee16 **Kubokawa** Kōchi, Shikoku,
SW Japan 33.22N 133.11E
174 L7 **Kubor, Mount** ▲ C PNG
N Bulgaria 43.48N 26.31E
5 I4 **Kubrat** prev. Balbunar. Razgrad,
NE Bulgaria 43.48N 26.31E
114 O13 **Kučajske Planine** ▲ E Serbia
114 Pp2 **Kuccharo-ko** ◙ Hokkaidō,
NE Japan 43.36N 144.20E

114 O11 **Kuchan** see Qūchān
44.29N 21.42E
174 L6 **Kuching** prev. Sarawak. Sarawak,
East Malaysia 1.31N 110.19E
174 L7 **Kuching** ✈ Sarawak, East
Malaysia 1.31N 110.19E
170 Aa17 **Kuchinoerabu-jima** island
Nansei-shotō, SW Japan
170 C13 **Kuchinotsu** Nagasaki, Kyūshū,
SW Japan 32.36N 130.11E
171 Q6 **Kuchl** Salzburg, NW Austria
47.37N 13.12E
154 L9 **Kuchnay Darweyshān**
Helmand, S Afghanistan
31.01N 64.09E
Kuchurgan see Kuchurhan
119 O10 **Kuchurhan** Rus. Kuchurgan.
◙ NE Ukraine
115 L21 **Kuçovë** var. Kuçova; prev.
Qyteti Stalin. Berat, C Albania
40.48N 19.55E
170 A12 **Kudamatu** see Kudamatsu
175 O1 **Kudat** Sabah, East Malaysia
6.54N 116.46E
161 G17 **Kūdligi** Karnātaka, W India
14.58N 76.24E
113 F16 **Kudowa** see Kudowa-Zdrój
113 F16 **Kudowa-Zdrój** Ger. Kudowa.
Dolnośląskie, SW Poland
50.27N 16.13E
119 P9 **Kudryavtsivka** Mykolayivs'ka
Oblast', S Ukraine
47.18N 31.02E
174 L14 **Kudus** Prev. Koedoes. Jawa,
C Indonesia 6.46S 110.48E
129 T13 **Kudymkar** Permskaya
Oblast', NW Russian Federation
59.01N 54.40E
Kudzir see Cugir
Kuei-chou see Guizhou
Kuei-lin see Guilin
Kuei-yang see Guiyang
K'u-erh-lo see Korla
Kueyang see Guiyang
Kufa see Al Kūfah
161 L19 **Kūfstein** Tirol, W Austria
47.36N 12.10E
111 O6 **Kufstein** Tirol, W Austria
47.36N 12.10E
151 V14 **Kugaly** Kaz. Qoghaly. Almaty,
SE Kazakhstan 44.38N 78.40E
I4 **Kugluktuk** var. Qurlurtuuq
prev. Coppermine. Nunavut, NW
Canada 67.49N 115.12W
149 Y13 **Kūhak** Sīstān va Balūchestān,
SE Iran 27.10N 63.15E
149 R9 **Kūhbonān** Kermān, C Iran
31.22N 56.16E
154 J5 **Kūhestān** var. Kohsān. Herāt,
W Afghanistan 34.40N 61.10E
95 N15 **Kuhmo** Oulu, E Finland
64.04N 29.34E
95 L18 **Kuhmoinen** Länsi-Suomi,
W Finland 61.32N 25.09E
Kuhnau see Konin
Kühnō see Kihnu
149 O8 **Kūhpāyeh** Eşfahān, C Iran
32.42N 52.25E
178 H13 **Kui Buri** var. Ban Kui Nua.
Prachuap Khiri Khan, SW Thailand
12.10N 99.49E
Kuibyshev see Kuybyshevskoye
Vodokhranilishche
84 D13 **Kuito** Port. Silva Porto. Bié,
C Angola 12.21S 16.54E
41 X14 **Kuiu Island** island Alexander
Archipelago, Alaska, USA
94 L13 **Kuivaniemi** Oulu, C Finland
65.34N 25.13E
79 V14 **Kujama** Kaduna, C Nigeria
10.27N 7.39E
112 I10 **Kujawsko-pomorskie**
◆ province C Poland
172 N10 **Kuji** var. Kuzi. Iwate, Honshū,
C Japan 40.12N 141.47E
172 N10 **Kujto, Ozero** see Kuyto, Ozero
170 D14 **Kujū-renzan** var. Kujū-
renzan. ▲ Kyūshū, SW Japan
30.07N 131.13E
175 O3 **Kukalaya, Rio** var. Rio Cuculaya,
Rio Kukulaya. ◙ NE Nicaragua
115 O16 **Kukavica** var. Vlajna. ▲ SE Serbia
42.46N 21.58E
115 M18 **Kukës** var. Kukësi. Kukës,
NE Albania 42.04N 20.25E
115 L18 **Kukës** ◆ district NE Albania
Kukësi see Kukës
194 J14 **Kukipi** Gulf, S PNG
8.10S 146.09E
131 S3 **Kukmor** Respublika Tatarstan,
W Russian Federation
56.11N 50.56E
176 Vv11 **Kukudu** see Shaogguan
41 N6 **Kukpowruk River** ◙
Alaska, USA
40 M6 **Kukpuk River** ◙
Alaska, USA
Kukukhoto see Hohhot
Kukulaya, Rio see
Kukalaya, Rio
174 Hh7 **Kukup** Johor, Peninsular Malaysia
1.18N 103.27E
201 W12 **Kuku Point** headland NW Wake
Island 19.19N 166.36E
152 G11 **Kukurtli** Ahal Welaýaty,
C Turkmenistan 39.58N 58.47E
131 V6 **Kül, Rüd-e** ◙ N Bulgaria
98 L9 **Kül, Rüd-e** ◙
114 F7 **Kula** Vidin, NW Bulgaria
43.54N 22.30E
142 D14 **Kula** Manisa, W Turkey
38.33N 28.38E
114 K9 **Kula** Serbia, NW Serbia
45.37N 19.31E
35 R4 **Kumiva Peak** ▲ Nevada, W USA
40.24N 119.16W
154 N7 **Kum Kuduk** well NW China
40.21N 91.43E
158 N7 **Kulachi** see Kolāchi
150 F11 **Kulagino** Kaz. Külagino. Atyrau,
W Kazakhstan 48.30N 51.33E
154 L7 **Kulāl, Mount** ▲ NW Kenya
95 M16 **Kumla** Örebro, C Sweden
59.06N 15.09E
144 H7 **Kulak** ◙ SW Russian Federation
159 M7 **Kula Kangri** var. Kulhakangri.
▲ Bhutan/China 28.06N 90.19E
150 E13 **Kulaly, Ostrov** island
W Kazakhstan

151 S16 **Kulan** Kaz. Qulan; prev. Lugovoy,
Lugovoye. Zhambyl, S Kazakhstan
42.55N 72.49E
178 H1 **Kumon Range** ▲ N Burma
126 K14 **Kumora** Respublika
Buryatiya, S Russian Federation
55.43N 110.47E
85 F22 **Kums** Karas, SE Namibia
28.07S 19.40E
159 V14 **Kulaura** Sylhet, NE Bangladesh
24.31N 92.01E
120 D9 **Kuldīga** Ger. Goldingen. Kuldīga,
W Latvia 56.57N 21.59E
Kuldja see Yining
131 N4 **Kulebaki** Nizhegorodskaya
Oblast', W Russian Federation
55.25N 42.32E
40 H12 **Kumukahi, Cape** headland
Hawai'i, USA, C Pacific Ocean
19.31N 154.48W
131 Q17 **Kumukh** Respublika Dagestan,
SW Russian Federation
42.10N 47.07E
114 E11 **Kulen Vakuf** var. Spasovo,
Federacija Bosna I Hercegovina,
NW Bosnia and Herzegovina
44.33N 16.03E
Kumul see Hami
131 N9 **Kumylzhenskaya**
Volgogradskaya Oblast',
SW Russian Federation
50.07N 11.27E
189 Q9 **Kulgera Roadhouse**
Northern Territory, N Australia
25.49S 133.30E
147 W6 **Kumzär** N Oman 26.19N 56.26E
Kunar see Konar
158 J14 **Kulhakangri** see Kula Kangri
131 T1 **Kuliga** Udmurtskaya Respublika,
NW Russian Federation
58.14N 53.49E
127 P16 **Kunashir, Ostrov** var. Kunashiri.
island Kuril'skiye Ostrova,
SE Russian Federation
120 G4 **Kullamaa** Läänemaa, W Estonia
58.14N 24.24E
207 O12 **Kullorsuaq** var. Kuvdlorssuak.
Kitaa, C Greenland
74.57N 57.07W
31 O6 **Kulm** North Dakota, N USA
46.18N 98.57W
152 D12 **Kul'mach** prev. Turkm. Isgender.
Balkan Welaýaty, W Turkmenistan
39.04N 55.49E
103 L18 **Kulmbach** Bayern, SE Germany
50.07N 11.27E
Kulmsee see Chełmża
174 Hh7 **Kundur, Pulau** island
W Indonesia
153 Q14 **Kŭlob** Rus. Kulyab. SW Tajikistan
37.55N 68.46E
94 M13 **Kuloharju** Lappi, N Finland
65.51N 28.10E
129 N7 **Kuloy** Arkhangel'skaya Oblast',
NW Russian Federation
64.55N 43.35E
129 N7 **Kuloy** ◙ NW Russian Federation
143 Q14 **Külp** Diyarbakır, SE Turkey
38.31N 41.01E
79 P14 **Kulpawn** ◙ N Ghana
149 R13 **Kūl, Rūd-e** var. Kūl.
◙ S Iran
150 G12 **Kul'sary** Kaz. Qulsary. Atyrau,
W Kazakhstan 46.58N 53.58E
99 R15 **Kulti** West Bengal, NE India
23.45N 86.49E
95 O13 **Kultsjön** ◙ N Sweden
142 I14 **Kulu** Konya, W Turkey
39.06N 33.01E
127 Nn10 **Kulu** ◙ E Russian Federation
125 G14 **Kulunda** Altayskiy Kray,
S Russian Federation 52.33N 79.04E
151 T7 **Kulunda Steppe** Kaz. Qulyndy
Zhazyghy, Rus. Kulundinskaya
Ravnina. grassland Kazakhstan/
Russian Federation
125 V15 **Kulundinskaya Ravnina** see
Kulunda Steppe
119 W13 **Kulykivka** Chernihivs'ka Oblast',
N Ukraine 51.23N 31.39E
Kum see Qom
170 Ee15 **Kuma** Ehime, Shikoku, SW Japan
33.36N 132.53E
131 P14 **Kuma** ◙ SW Russian Federation
171 K15 **Kumagaya** Saitama, Honshū,
S Japan 36.10N 139.22E
172 N6 **Kumaishi** Hokkaidō, NE Japan
171 Ll11 **Kumai, Teluk** bay Borneo,
C Indonesia
174 M8 **Kumak** Orenburgskaya Oblast',
W Russian Federation
51.16N 60.06E
176 Y9 **Kumamba, Kepulauan** island
group E Indonesia
170 C14 **Kumamoto** Kumamoto, Kyūshū,
SW Japan 32.49N 130.40E
170 C14 **Kumamoto off.** Kumamoto-ken.
◆ prefecture Kyūshū, SW Japan
171 Gg17 **Kumano** Mie, Honshū, SW Japan
33.54N 136.03E
115 O17 **Kumanova** see Kumanovo
115 O17 **Kumanovo** Turk. Kumanova.
N FYR Macedonia 42.07N 21.42E
193 G17 **Kumara** West Coast, South Island,
NZ 42.39S 171.12E
188 J8 **Kumarina Roadhouse** Western
Australia 24.46S 119.39E
194 J14 **Kumarkhali** Khulna,
W Bangladesh 23.52N 89.13E
79 P16 **Kumasi** prev. Coomassie.
C Ghana 6.40N 1.39W
81 D15 **Kumba** Sud-Ouest, W Cameroon
4.39N 9.25E
116 N13 **Kumbağ** Tekirdağ, NW Turkey
62.54N 27.41E
161 J21 **Kumbakonam** Tamil Nādu,
SE India 10.58N 79.24E
176 Z16 **Kumbe, Sungai** ◙ Papua,
E Indonesia
81 E15 **Kumbo** Nord-Ouest, W Cameroon
5.38N 10.03E
175 R17 **Kumbu, Pulau** island
E Indonesia 10.13S 123.37E
170 O14 **Kume-jima** island Nansei-shotō,
SW Japan
41 Q5 **Kumhwa** ◙ Alaska, USA
171 I4 **Kumi** S South Korea 36.14N 128.21E
131 V6 **Kumertau** Respublika
Bashkortostan, W Russian
Federation 52.48N 55.48E
125 F11 **Kuminskiy** Khanty-Mansiyskiy
Avtonomnyy Okrug, C Russian
Federation 58.42N 65.56E
125 G14 **Kupino** Novosibirskaya Oblast',
C Russian Federation 54.22N 77.09E
120 H11 **Kupiškis** Panevėžys,
NE Lithuania 55.51N 24.58E
115 N7 **Kumla** Örebro, C Sweden
59.51N 16.40E
142 F12 **Kumluca** Antalya, SW Turkey
36.23N 30.17E
116 L13 **Küplü** Edirne, NW Turkey
81 H11 **Kumo** Gombe, E Nigeria
10.03N 11.13E
142 G17 **Kumlu** Hatay, S Turkey

119 O13 **Kumola** ◙ C Kazakhstan
126 K14 **Kumora** Respublika
Buryatiya, S Russian Federation
55.43N 110.47E
85 F22 **Kums** Karas, SE Namibia
28.05S 19.40E
143 W11 **Kura** Az. Kür, Geor. Mtkvari, Turk.
Kura Nehri. ◙ SW Asia
57 R8 **Kurasia** NW Guyana
6.52N 60.13W
170 Ee13 **Kurahashi-jima** island
SW Japan
Kura Kurk see Irbe Strait
153 Q10 **Kurama Range** Rus.
Kuraminskiy Khrebet.
▲ Tajikistan/Uzbekistan
Kuraminskiy Khrebet see
Kurama Range
131 N9 **Kura Nehri** see Kura
Kurashiki var. Kurasiki.
Okayama, Honshū, SW Japan
34.35N 133.44E
160 L10 **Kurasia** Chhattīsgarh, C India
23.11N 82.16E
Kurasiki see Kurashiki
170 F14 **Kurayoshi** var. Kurayosi. Tottori,
Honshū, SW Japan 35.25N 133.51E
Kurayosi see Kurayoshi
169 X6 **Kurčin He** ◙ NE China
151 X10 **Kurchum** Kaz. Kürshim.
Vostochnyy Kazakhstan,
E Kazakhstan 48.35N 83.37E
151 Y10 **Kurchum** ◙ E Kazakhstan
143 X11 **Kürdämir** Rus. Kyurdamir.
C Azerbaijan 40.21N 48.08E
145 S1 **Kurdistan** cultural region SW Asia
Kurd Kui see Kord Küy
161 F15 **Kurduvādi** Mahārāshtra, W India
18.06N 75.31E
116 J11 **Kürdzhali** var. Kurdzhali.
Kürdzhali, S Bulgaria 41.39N 25.23E
116 K11 **Kürdzhali** ◆ province S Bulgaria
116 J11 **Kürdzhali, Yazovir**
◙ S Bulgaria
170 Ee13 **Kure** Hiroshima, Honshū,
SW Japan 34.15N 132.33E
199 J5 **Kure Atoll** var. Ocean Island. atoll
Hawaiian Islands, Hawaii, USA,
C Pacific Ocean
142 J10 **Küre Dağları** ▲ N Turkey
152 C11 **Kurenets** Rus. Gora Kyuren.
▲ W Turkmenistan 39.05N 55.09E
Kurenets see Kuranyets
120 G6 **Kuressaare** Ger. Arensburg; prev.
Kingissepp. Saaremaa, W Estonia
58.14N 22.27E
126 I9 **Kureyka** Krasnoyarskiy Kray,
N Russian Federation 66.22N 87.21E
126 I9 **Kureyka** ◙ N Russian Federation
Kurgal'dzhino/
Kurgal'dzhinskiy see
Korgalzhyn
129 V15 **Kurgan** Permskaya Oblast',
NW Russian Federation
57.24N 56.56E
125 F12 **Kurgan** Kurganskaya Oblast',
C Russian Federation 55.30N 65.19E
130 L14 **Kurganinsk** Krasnodarskiy
Kray, SW Russian Federation
44.52N 40.45E
125 Ee12 **Kurganskaya Oblast'** ◆ province
C Russian Federation
Kurgan-Tyube see Qürghonteppa
203 O2 **Kuria** prev. Woodle Island. island
Tungaru, W Kiribati
Kuria Muria Bay see
Ḥalāniyāt, Khalīj al
Kuria Muria Islands see
Ḥalāniyāt, Juzur al
159 T13 **Kurigram** Rajshahi,
N Bangladesh 25.49N 89.37E
176 Yy16 **Kurik** Papua, E Indonesia
8.12S 140.15E
95 K17 **Kurikka** Länsi-Suomi, W Finland
62.36N 22.25E
171 M12 **Kurikoma-yama** ▲ Honshū,
C Japan 38.57N 140.44E
199 Hh3 **Kurile Basin** undersea feature
NW Pacific Ocean
Kurile Islands see Kuril'skiye
Ostrova
Kurile-Kamchatka
Depression see Kuril Trench
199 Hh3 **Kuril Trench** var. Kurile-
Kamchatka Depression. undersea
feature NW Pacific Ocean
131 Q9 **Kurilovka** Saratovskaya
Oblast', SW Russian Federation
50.39N 48.02E
127 P15 **Kuril'sk** Kuril'skiye Ostrova,
Sakhalinskaya Oblast', SE Russian
Federation 45.10N 147.51E
127 Pp15 **Kuril'skiye Ostrova** Eng. Kurile
Islands. island group SE Russian
Federation

119 W5 **Kup"yans'k-Vuzlovyy**
Kharkivs'ka Oblast', E Ukraine
49.40N 37.41E
164 I6 **Kuqa** Xinjiang Uygur Zizhiqu,
NW China 41.43N 82.58E
Kür see Kura
143 W11 **Kura** Az. Kür, Geor. Mtkvari, Turk.
Kura Nehri. ◙ SW Asia
170 Ee13 **Kurahashi-jima** island
SW Japan
153 Q10 **Kurama Range** Rus.
Kuraminskiy Khrebet.
▲ Tajikistan/Uzbekistan
Kuraminskiy Khrebet see
Kurama Range
Kura Nehri see Kura
176 Ww10 **Kuran, Kepulauan** island group
E Indonesia
121 J14 **Kuranyets** Rus. Kurenets.
Minskaya Voblasts', C Belarus
54.34N 26.58E
170 Ff14 **Kurashiki** var. Kurasiki.
Okayama, Honshū, SW Japan
34.35N 133.44E
120 I3 **Kunda** Lääne-Virumaa,
NE Estonia 59.31N 26.32E
158 M13 **Kunda** Uttar Pradesh, N India
25.43N 81.31E
161 E19 **Kundāpura** var. Coondapoor.
Karnātaka, W India
13.39N 74.41E
81 O24 **Kundelungu, Monts** ▲ S Dem.
Rep. Congo
194 I12 **Kundiawa** Chimbu, W PNG
06.00S 144.57E
174 Hh7 **Kundla** see Sāvarkundla
103 L18 **Kulmbach** Bayern, SE Germany
50.07N 11.27E
152 F5 **Kunya-Urgench** see Köneürgenç
Kunene var. Cunene. ◙ Angola/
Namibia see also Cunene
Kunene see Xinyuan
97 I19 **Kungälv** Västra Götaland,
S Sweden 57.54N 12.00E
153 W7 **Kungei Ala-Tau** Rus. Khrebet
Kyungöy Ala-Too, Kir. Küngöy Ala-
Too. ▲ Kazakhstan/Kyrgyzstan
Küngöy Ala-Too see
Kungei Ala-Tau
Kungrad see Qo'ng'irot
97 J19 **Kungsbacka** Halland, S Sweden
57.30N 12.04E
97 J19 **Kungshamn** Västra Götaland,
S Sweden 58.21N 11.15E
97 M16 **Kungsör** Västmanland, C Sweden
59.26N 16.04E
81 J16 **Kungu** Equateur, NW Dem. Rep.
Congo 2.46N 19.12E
125 F12 **Kungur** Permskaya Oblast',
NW Russian Federation 57.24N 56.56E
177 G9 **Kungyangon** Yangon, SW Burma
16.27N 96.00E
113 M22 **Kunhegyes** Jász-Nagykun-
Szolnok, E Hungary 47.23N 20.37E
178 H5 **Kunhing** Shan State, E Burma
21.17N 98.26E
170 C15 **Kunimi-dake** ▲ Kyūshū,
SW Japan 32.31N 131.01E
170 Ee15 **Kunijirap Daban** var. Khūnjerāb
Pass. pass China/Pakistan
36.46N 75.16E see also
Khūnjerāb Pass
131 P14 **Kuma** ◙ SW Russian Federation
164 D9 **Kunlun Shan** Eng. Kunlun
Mountains. ▲ NW China
164 H10 **Kunlun Shan** pass C China
8.12S 140.15E
165 P11 **Kunlun Shankou** pass C China
35.45N 93.59E
166 G13 **Kunming** var. K'un-ming; prev.
Yunnan. Yunnan, SW China
25.04N 102.40E
172 N6 **Kunnui** Hokkaidō, NE Japan
42.06N 140.18E
97 B18 **Kunoy** Dan. Kunø Island Faeroe
Islands 62.18N 6.40W
169 X16 **Kunsan** var. Gunsan, Jap. Gunzan.
W South Korea 35.58N 126.42E
171 Gg17 **Kunszentmárton** Jász-Nagykun-
Szolnok, E Hungary 46.49N 20.15E
113 L24 **Kunszentmárton** Jász-Nagykun-
Szolnok, E Hungary 46.49N 20.15E
113 J23 **Kunszentmiklós** Bács-Kiskun,
C Hungary 47.02N 19.05E
189 N3 **Kununurra** Western Australia
15.49S 128.43E
Kunya-Urgench see Köneürgenç
Kunyang see Pingyang
Kunya-Urgench see Köneürgenç
103 J20 **Künzelsau** Baden-Württemberg,
S Germany 49.22N 9.43E
167 S10 **Kuocang Shan** ▲ SE China
128 H5 **Kuoloyarvi** var. Luolajarvi.
Murmanskaya Oblast', NW Russian
Federation 66.58N 29.14E
95 N16 **Kuopio** Itä-Suomi, C Finland
62.54N 27.41E
95 N16 **Kuortane** Länsi-Suomi,
W Finland 62.48N 23.31E
95 M18 **Kuortti** Itä-Suomi, E Finland
61.25N 26.25E
95 K17 **Kupa** see Kolpa
57 R17 **Kupang** prev. Koepang. Timor,
C Indonesia 10.13S 123.37E
174 Mm8 **Kupang** Central, S PNG
10.04S 148.16E
188 M4 **Kupingarri** Western Australia
16.65 125.57E
120 H11 **Kupiškis** Panevėžys,
NE Lithuania 55.51N 24.58E
119 W5 **Kup"yans'k** Rus. Kupyansk.
Kharkiv's'ka Oblast', E Ukraine
49.42N 37.36E

119 W5 **Kup"yans'k-Vuzlovyy**
Kharkivs'ka Oblast', E Ukraine
49.40N 37.41E
164 I6 **Kuqa** Xinjiang Uygur Zizhiqu,
NW China 41.43N 82.58E
Kür see Kura
143 W11 **Kura** Az. Kür, Geor. Mtkvari, Turk.
Kura Nehri. ◙ SW Asia
57 R8 **Kurasia** NW Guyana
6.52N 60.13W
170 Ee13 **Kurahashi-jima** island
SW Japan
Kura Kurk see Irbe Strait
153 Q10 **Kurama Range** Rus.
Kuraminskiy Khrebet.
▲ Tajikistan/Uzbekistan
Kuraminskiy Khrebet see
Kurama Range
Kura Nehri see Kura
170 Ee13 **Kurashiki** var. Kurasiki.
Okayama, Honshū, SW Japan
34.35N 133.44E
160 L10 **Kurasia** Chhattīsgarh, C India
23.11N 82.16E
Kurasiki see Kurashiki
170 F14 **Kurayoshi** var. Kurayosi. Tottori,
Honshū, SW Japan 35.25N 133.51E
Kurayosi see Kurayoshi
169 X6 **Kurčin He** ◙ NE China
151 X10 **Kurchum** Kaz. Kürshim.
Vostochnyy Kazakhstan,
E Kazakhstan 48.35N 83.37E
151 Y10 **Kurchum** ◙ E Kazakhstan
143 X11 **Kürdämir** Rus. Kyurdamir.
C Azerbaijan 40.21N 48.08E
145 S1 **Kurdistan** cultural region SW Asia
Kurd Kui see Kord Küy
161 F15 **Kurduvādi** Mahārāshtra, W India
18.06N 75.31E
116 J11 **Kürdzhali** var. Kurdzhali.
Kürdzhali, S Bulgaria 41.39N 25.23E
116 K11 **Kürdzhali** ◆ province S Bulgaria
116 J11 **Kürdzhali, Yazovir**
◙ S Bulgaria
170 Ee13 **Kure** Hiroshima, Honshū,
SW Japan 34.15N 132.33E
199 J5 **Kure Atoll** var. Ocean Island. atoll
Hawaiian Islands, Hawaii, USA,
C Pacific Ocean
142 J10 **Küre Dağları** ▲ N Turkey
152 C11 **Kurenets** Rus. Gora Kyuren.
▲ W Turkmenistan 39.05N 55.09E
Kurenets see Kuranyets
120 G6 **Kuressaare** Ger. Arensburg; prev.
Kingissepp. Saaremaa, W Estonia
58.14N 22.27E
126 I9 **Kureyka** Krasnoyarskiy Kray,
N Russian Federation 66.22N 87.21E
126 I9 **Kureyka** ◙ N Russian Federation
Kurgal'dzhino/
Kurgal'dzhinskiy see
Korgalzhyn
125 F12 **Kurgan** Kurganskaya Oblast',
C Russian Federation 55.30N 65.19E
130 L14 **Kurganinsk** Krasnodarskiy
Kray, SW Russian Federation
44.52N 40.45E
125 Ee12 **Kurganskaya Oblast'** ◆ province
C Russian Federation
Kurgan-Tyube see Qürghonteppa
203 O2 **Kuria** prev. Woodle Island. island
Tungaru, W Kiribati
Kuria Muria Bay see
Ḥalāniyāt, Khalīj al
Kuria Muria Islands see
Ḥalāniyāt, Juzur al
159 T13 **Kurigram** Rajshahi,
N Bangladesh 25.49N 89.37E
176 Yy16 **Kurik** Papua, E Indonesia
8.12S 140.15E
95 K17 **Kurikka** Länsi-Suomi, W Finland
62.36N 22.25E
171 M12 **Kurikoma-yama** ▲ Honshū,
C Japan 38.57N 140.44E
199 Hh3 **Kurile Basin** undersea feature
NW Pacific Ocean
Kurile Islands see Kuril'skiye
Ostrova
Kurile-Kamchatka
Depression see Kuril Trench
199 Hh3 **Kuril Trench** var. Kurile-
Kamchatka Depression. undersea
feature NW Pacific Ocean
131 Q9 **Kurilovka** Saratovskaya
Oblast', SW Russian Federation
50.39N 48.02E
127 P15 **Kuril'sk** Kuril'skiye Ostrova,
Sakhalinskaya Oblast', SE Russian
Federation 45.10N 147.51E
127 Pp15 **Kuril'skiye Ostrova** Eng. Kurile
Islands. island group SE Russian
Federation
44 M9 **Kurinwas, Rio** ◙ E Nicaragua
Kurisches Haff see Courland
Lagoon
Kurkund see Kilingi-Nõmme
82 G12 **Kurmuk** Blue Nile, SE Sudan
10.36N 34.16E
Kurna see Al Qurnah
161 J21 **Kurnool** var. Karnul. Andhra
Pradesh, S India 15.51N 78.01E
171 J13 **Kurobe** Toyama, Honshū,
SW Japan 36.52N 137.24E
170 C13 **Kurogi** Fukuoka, Kyūshū,
SW Japan 33.09N 130.45E
171 Mm9 **Kuroishi** var. Kuroisi. Aomori,
Honshū, C Japan 40.40N 140.34E
Kuroisi see Kuroishi
171 Kk14 **Kuroiso** Tochigi, Honshū, S Japan
36.58N 140.01E
172 N5 **Kuromatsunai** Hokkaidō,
NE Japan
170 Oo17 **Kuro-shima** SW Japan
171 H16 **Kurono-yama** ▲ Honshū,
SW Japan 34.31N 136.10E
193 F21 **Kurow** Canterbury, South Island,
NZ 44.44S 170.29E
174 Uu13 **Kur, Pulau** island E Indonesia
131 N15 **Kursavka** Stavropol'skiy
Kray, SW Russian Federation
44.28N 42.31E
120 E11 **Kuršėnai** Šiauliai, N Lithuania
56.00N 22.56E
Kürshim see Kurchum
Kurshskaya Kosa/Kuršių
Nerija see Courland Spit

Kursk – Lagonegro

130 J7 **Kursk** Kurskaya Oblast', W Russian Federation 51.43N 36.46E
130 I7 **Kurskaya Oblast'** ◆ province W Russian Federation
Kurskiy Zaliv see Courland Lagoon
115 N15 **Kuršumlija** Serbia, S Serbia 43.09N 21.16E
143 R15 **Kurtalan** Siirt, SE Turkey 37.56N 41.43E
125 Ee12 **Kurtamysh** Kurganskaya Oblast', C Russian Federation 54.51N 64.46E
Kurtbunar see Tervel
Kurt-Dere see Vŭlchidol
Kurtitsch/Kürtös see Curtici
Kurtty see Kurty
151 U15 **Kurty** var. Kurtty. SE Kazakhstan
95 L18 **Kuru** Länsi-Suomi, W Finland 61.51N 23.46E
82 C13 **Kuru** W Sudan
116 M13 **Kuru Dağı** ▲ NW Turkey
164 L7 **Kuruktag** ▲ NW China
85 G22 **Kuruman** Northern Cape, N South Africa 27.28S 23.27E
69 T14 **Kuruman** W South Africa
170 Cc13 **Kurume** Fukuoka, Kyūshū, SW Japan 33.15N 130.27E
126 K15 **Kurumkan** Respublika Buryatiya, S Russian Federation 54.13N 110.21E
161 J25 **Kurunegala** North Western Province, C Sri Lanka 7.28N 80.22E
57 T10 **Kurupukari** C Guyana 4.39N 58.39W
129 U10 **Kur"ya** Respublika Komi, NW Russian Federation 61.38N 57.12E
150 E15 **Kuryk** prev. Yeraliyev. Mangistau, SW Kazakhstan 43.12N 51.43E
142 B15 **Kuşadası** Aydın, SW Turkey 37.51N 27.15E
117 M19 **Kuşadası Körfezi** gulf SW Turkey
170 Aa16 **Kusagaki-guntō** island SW Japan
Kusaie see Kosrae
151 T12 **Kusak** C Kazakhstan
Kusary see Qusar
178 Hh8 **Ku Sathan, Doi** ▲ NW Thailand 18.22N 100.31E
171 H15 **Kusatsu** var. Kusatu. Shiga, Honshū, SW Japan 35.02N 135.58E
Kusatu see Kusatsu
144 F11 **Kuseifa** Southern, C Israel 31.15N 35.01E
142 C12 **Kuş Gölü** ◎ NW Turkey
130 L12 **Kushchevskaya** Krasnodarskiy Kray, SW Russian Federation 46.35N 39.40E
171 H16 **Kushida-gawa** Honshū, SW Japan
170 Bb15 **Kushikino** var. Kusikino. Kagoshima, Kyūshū, SW Japan 31.42N 130.13E
170 C17 **Kushima** var. Kusima. Miyazaki, Kyūshū, SW Japan 31.27N 131.11E
170 G17 **Kushimoto** Wakayama, Honshū, SW Japan 33.28N 135.45E
172 Q7 **Kushiro** var. Kusiro. Hokkaidō, NE Japan 42.58N 144.24E
154 K4 **Kūshk** Herāt, W Afghanistan 34.54N 62.09E
Kushka see Gushgy/Serhetabat
151 N8 **Kushmurun** Kaz. Qusmuryn. Kostanay, N Kazakhstan 52.27N 64.31E
151 N8 **Kushmurun, Ozero** Kaz. Qusmuryn. ◎ N Kazakhstan
131 U4 **Kushnarenkovo** Respublika Bashkortostan, W Russian Federation 55.07N 55.24E
Kushrabat see Qo'shrabot
159 T15 **Kushtia** var. Kustia. Khulna, W Bangladesh 23.54N 89.07E
125 Ee10 **Kushva** Sverdlovskaya Oblast', C Russian Federation 58.14N 59.36E
Kusikino see Kushikino
Kusima see Kushima
Kusiro see Kushiro
40 M13 **Kuskokwim Bay** bay Alaska, USA
41 P11 **Kuskokwim Mountains** ▲ Alaska, USA
41 N12 **Kuskokwim River** Alaska, USA
110 G7 **Küsnacht** Zürich, N Switzerland 47.21N 8.32E
172 Qq6 **Kussharo-ko** var. Kussyaro. ◎ Hokkaidō, NE Japan
Küssnacht see Küssnacht am Rigi
110 F8 **Küssnacht am Rigi** var. Küssnacht. Schwyz, C Switzerland 47.03N 8.25E
Kussyaro see Kussharo-ko
Kustanay see Kostanay
Küstence/Küstendje see Constanța
102 F11 **Küstenkanal** var. Ems-Hunte Canal. canal NW Germany
Küstrin see Kostrzyn
Kustia see Kushtia
175 T7 **Kusu** Pulau Halmahera, E Indonesia 0.51N 127.41E
175 Nn16 **Kuta** Pulau Lombok, S Indonesia 8.52S 116.15E
145 T4 **Kutabān** N Iraq 35.21N 44.45E
142 E13 **Kütahya** prev. Kutaia. Kütahya, W Turkey 39.25N 29.55E
142 E13 **Kütahya** var. Kutaia. ◆ province W Turkey
Kutai see Mahakam, Sungai
Kutaia see Kütahya
143 R9 **K'ut'aisi** W Georgia 42.15N 42.42E
Kūt al 'Amārah see Al Kūt
Kut al Hai/Kūt al Ḩayy see Al Ḩayy
Kut al Imara see Al Kūt
126 M12 **Kutana** Respublika Sakha (Yakutiya), NE Russian Federation 59.05N 131.43E
Kutaradja/Kutaraja see Bandaaceh
172 Nn5 **Kutchan** Hokkaidō, NE Japan 42.54N 140.46E
Kutch, Gulf of see Kachchh, Gulf of
Kutch, Rann of see Kachchh, Rann of
114 F9 **Kutina** Sisak-Moslavina, NE Croatia 45.29N 16.45E
114 H9 **Kutjevo** Požega-Slavonija, NE Croatia 45.26N 17.54E
113 E17 **Kutná Hora** Ger. Kuttenberg. Středočeský Kraj, C Czech Republic 49.57N 15.15E
112 K12 **Kutno** Łódzkie, C Poland 52.13N 19.23E
Kuttenberg see Kutná Hora
81 I20 **Kutu** Bandundu, W Dem. Rep. Congo 2.42S 18.07E
159 V17 **Kutubdia Island** island SE Bangladesh
82 B10 **Kutum** Northern Darfur, W Sudan 14.10N 24.40E
153 Y7 **Kuturgu** Issyk-Kul'skaya Oblast', E Kyrgyzstan 42.45N 78.04E
10 M5 **Kuujjuaq** prev. Fort-Chimo. Québec, E Canada 58.10N 68.15W
10 I7 **Kuujjuarapik** Québec, C Canada 55.07N 78.09W
Kuuli-Mayak see Guwlumaýak
120 I6 **Kuulse magi** ▲ S Estonia
94 N13 **Kuusamo** Oulu, E Finland 65.57N 29.15E
95 M19 **Kuusankoski** Etelä-Suomi, S Finland 60.51N 26.40E
131 W7 **Kuvandyk** Orenburgskaya Oblast', W Russian Federation 51.27N 57.18E
Kuvango see Cubango
Kuvasay see Quwasoy
Kuvdlorssuak see Kullorsuaq
128 I16 **Kuvshinovo** Tverskaya Oblast', W Russian Federation 57.03N 34.09E
147 Q4 **Kuwait** off. State of Kuwait, var. Dawlat al Kuwait, Koweit, Kuweit. ◆ monarchy SW Asia
Kuwait see Al Kuwayt
Kuwait Bay see Kuwayt, Jūn al
Kuwait City see Al Kuwayt
Kuwait, Dawlat al see Kuwait
Kuwajleen see Kwajalein Atoll
171 H15 **Kuwana** Mie, Honshū, SW Japan 35.03N 136.40E
176 V9 **Kuwawin** Papua, E Indonesia 1.10S 132.40E
145 X9 **Kuwayt** E Iraq 32.26N 47.12E
148 K11 **Kuwayt, Jūn al** var. Kuwait Bay. bay E Kuwait
Kuweit see Kuwait
119 P10 **Kuyal'nyts'kyy Lyman** ◎ SW Ukraine
125 G13 **Kuybyshev** Novosibirskaya Oblast', C Russian Federation 55.28N 77.55E
Kuybyshev see Bolgar, Respublika Tatarstan, Russian Federation
Kuybyshev see Samara
119 W9 **Kuybysheve** Rus. Kuybyshevo. Zaporiz'ka Oblast', SE Ukraine 47.20N 36.41E
Kuybyshevo see Kuybysheve
Kuybyshev Reservoir see Kuybyshevskoye Vodokhranilishche
Kuybyshevskaya Oblast' see Samarskaya Oblast'
Kuybyshevskiy see Novoishimskiy
131 R4 **Kuybyshevskoye Vodokhranilishche** var. Kuibyshev, Eng. Kuybyshev Reservoir. ▣ W Russian Federation
127 N9 **Kuydusun** Respublika Sakha (Yakutiya), NE Russian Federation 63.15N 143.10E
129 U16 **Kuyeda** Permskaya Oblast', NW Russian Federation 56.23N 55.19E
Küysanjaq see Koi Sanjaq
128 I7 **Kuyto, Ozero** var. Ozero Kujto. ◎ NW Russian Federation
164 J4 **Kuytun** Xinjiang Uygur Zizhiqu, NW China 44.25N 84.55E
126 J15 **Kuytun** Irkutskaya Oblast', S Russian Federation 54.18N 101.28E
126 Ii12 **Kuyumba** Evenkiyskiy Avtonomnyy Okrug, C Russian Federation 61.00N 97.07E
57 S12 **Kuyuwini Landing** S Guyana 2.06N 59.14W
Kuzi see Kuji
40 M9 **Kuzitrin River** Alaska, USA
131 P6 **Kuznetsk** Penzenskaya Oblast', W Russian Federation 53.06N 46.27E
118 K3 **Kuznetsovs'k** Rivnens'ka Oblast', NW Ukraine 51.21N 25.51E
128 K6 **Kuzomen'** Murmanskaya Oblast', NW Russian Federation 66.16N 36.47E
170 N12 **Kuzumaki** Iwate, Honshū, C Japan 40.04N 141.26E
94 H9 **Kvaløya** island N Norway
94 K8 **Kvalsund** Finnmark, N Norway 70.30N 23.56E
96 G11 **Kvam** Oppland, S Norway 61.42N 9.43E
131 X7 **Kvarkeno** Orenburgskaya Oblast', W Russian Federation 52.09N 59.44E
95 G15 **Kvarnbergsvattnet** var. Frostviken. ◎ N Sweden
114 A11 **Kvarner** var. Carnaro, It. Quarnero. gulf W Croatia
114 B11 **Kvarnerić** channel W Croatia
41 O14 **Kvichak Bay** bay Alaska, USA
94 H12 **Kvikkjokk** Lapp. Huhttán. Norrbotten, N Sweden 66.58N 17.45E
97 D17 **Kvina** S Norway
94 Q1 **Kvitøya** island NE Svalbard
97 F16 **Kviteseid** Telemark, S Norway 59.23N 8.31E
97 H24 **Kværndrup** Fyn, C Denmark 55.10N 10.31E
81 H20 **Kwa** W Dem. Rep. Congo
79 Q15 **Kwadwokurom** C Ghana 7.49N 0.15W
195 X14 **Kwailibesi** Malaita, N Solomon Islands 8.25S 160.48E
201 S6 **Kwajalein Atoll** var. Kuwajleen. atoll Ralik Chain, C Marshall Islands
57 W9 **Kwakoegron** Brokopondo, N Surinam 5.13N 55.19W
83 J21 **Kwale** Coast, S Kenya 4.11S 39.30E
79 U17 **Kwale** Delta, S Nigeria 5.51N 6.29E
81 H20 **Kwamouth** Bandundu, W Dem. Rep. Congo 3.10S 16.16E
Kwando see Cuando
Kwangchow see Guangzhou
Kwangchu see Kwangju
169 X16 **Kwangju** off. Kwangju-gwangyŏksi, var. Guangju, Kwangchu, Jap. Kōshū. SW South Korea 35.09N 126.52E
81 H20 **Kwango** Port. Cuango. Angola/Dem. Rep. Congo see also Cuango
Kwangsi/Kwangsi Chuang Autonomous Region see Guangxi Zhuangzu Zizhiqu
Kwangtung see Guangdong
Kwangyuan see Guangyuan
83 F17 **Kwania, Lake** ◎ C Uganda
Kwanza see Cuanza
79 S15 **Kwara** ◆ state SW Nigeria
176 Ww11 **Kwatisore** Papua, E Indonesia 3.14S 134.57E
85 K22 **KwaZulu/Natal** off. KwaZulu/Natal Province; prev. Natal. ◆ province E South Africa
Kweichow see Guizhou
Kweichu see Guiyang
Kweilin see Guilin
Kweisui see Hohhot
Kweiyang see Guiyang
85 K17 **Kwekwe** prev. Que Que. Midlands, C Zimbabwe 18.55S 29.48E
85 G20 **Kweneng** ◆ district S Botswana
Kwesui see Hohhot
41 N12 **Kwethluk** Alaska, USA 60.48N 161.26W
41 N12 **Kwethluk River** Alaska, USA
112 J8 **Kwidzyń** Ger. Marienwerder. Pomorskie, N Poland 53.44N 18.55E
40 M13 **Kwigillingok** Alaska, USA 59.51N 163.07W
194 K16 **Kwikila** Central, S PNG 9.48S 147.37E
81 I20 **Kwilu** W Dem. Rep. Congo
Kwito see Cuito
176 V8 **Kwoka, Gunung** ▲ Papua, E Indonesia 0.34S 132.25E
80 I12 **Kyabé** Moyen-Chari, S Chad 9.28N 18.54E
191 O11 **Kyabram** Victoria, SE Australia 36.21S 145.04E
178 Gg9 **Kyaikkami** prev. Amherst. Mon State, S Burma 16.02N 97.36E
177 Ff9 **Kyaiklat** Irrawaddy, SW Burma 16.25N 95.42E
177 G8 **Kyaikto** Mon State, S Burma 17.16N 97.01E
126 Jj16 **Kyakhta** Respublika Buryatiya, S Russian Federation 50.24N 106.12E
190 G8 **Kyancutta** South Australia 33.10S 135.33E
177 Ff7 **Kyangin** Irrawaddy, SW Burma 18.19N 95.15E
178 Jj8 **Ky Anh** Ha Tinh, N Vietnam 18.05N 106.16E
177 Ff5 **Kyaukpadaung** Mandalay, C Burma 20.49N 95.07E
177 F6 **Kyaukpyu** Arakan State, W Burma 19.27N 93.33E
177 G5 **Kyaukse** Mandalay, C Burma 21.34N 96.12E
177 Ff8 **Kyaunggon** Irrawaddy, SW Burma 17.04N 95.12E
121 E14 **Kybartai** Pol. Kibarty. Marijampolė, S Lithuania 54.37N 22.44E
158 I7 **Kyelang** Himāchal Pradesh, NW India 32.33N 77.03E
113 G19 **Kyjov** Ger. Gaya. Jihomoravský Kraj, SE Czech Republic 49.00N 17.07E
117 J21 **Kykládes** var. Kikládhes, Eng. Cyclades. island group SE Greece
27 S11 **Kyle** Texas, SW USA 29.59N 97.52W
98 G9 **Kyle of Lochalsh** N Scotland, UK 57.17N 5.39W
103 D18 **Kyll** W Germany
117 F19 **Kyllíni** var. Killini. ▲ S Greece
95 M19 **Kymijoki** S Finland
117 H18 **Kými, Akrotírio** headland Évvoia, C Greece 38.39N 24.08E
129 W14 **Kyn** Permskaya Oblast', NW Russian Federation 57.48N 58.38E
191 N12 **Kyneton** Victoria, SE Australia 37.14S 144.28E
83 G17 **Kyoga, Lake** var. Lake Kioga. ◎ C Uganda
171 H13 **Kyōga-misaki** headland Honshū, SW Japan 35.46N 135.13E
191 V4 **Kyogle** New South Wales, SE Australia 28.37S 153.00E
169 W15 **Kyŏnggi-man** bay NW South Korea
169 Z16 **Kyŏngju** Jap. Keishū. SE South Korea 35.49N 129.09E
Kyŏngsŏng see Sŏul
Kyōsai-tō see Kŏje-do
83 F19 **Kyotera** S Uganda 0.37S 31.34E
171 H15 **Kyōto** Kyōto, Honshū, SW Japan 35.01N 135.46E
171 H14 **Kyōto** off. Kyōto-fu, var. Kyôto Hu. ◆ urban prefecture Honshū, SW Japan
Kyōto-fu/Kyōto Hu see Kyōto
117 D21 **Kyparissía** var. Kiparissia. Pelopónnisos, S Greece 37.13N 21.39E
117 D20 **Kyparissiakós Kólpos** gulf S Greece
Kyperounda see Kyperoúnta
124 N3 **Kyperoúnta** var. Kyperounda. C Cyprus 34.57N 33.02E
Kypros see Cyprus
117 H16 **Kyrá Panagía** island Vóreies Sporádes, Greece, Aegean Sea
Kyrenia see Girne
Kyrenia Mountains see Beşparmak Dağları
Kyrgyz Republic see Kyrgyzstan
153 U9 **Kyrgyzstan** off. Kyrgyz Republic, var. Kirghizia; prev. Kirgizskaya SSR, Kirghiz SSR, Republic of Kyrgyzstan. ◆ republic C Asia
102 M11 **Kyritz** Brandenburg, NE Germany 52.56N 12.24E
Kyrkslätt see Kirkkonummi
96 G8 **Kyrksæterøra** Sør-Trøndelag, S Norway 63.16N 9.04E
129 U8 **Kyrta** Respublika Komi, NW Russian Federation 64.03N 57.41E
125 Ee12 **Kyshtym** Chelyabinskaya Oblast', S Russian Federation 55.39N 60.31E
113 J18 **Kysucké Nové Mesto** prev. Horné Nové Mesto, Ger. Kisutzaneustadtl, Oberneustadtl, Hung. Kiszucaújhely. Žilinský Kraj, N Slovakia 49.19N 18.47E
119 N12 **Kytay, Ozero** ◎ SW Ukraine
117 F23 **Kýthira** var. Kíthira, It. Cerigo; Lat. Cythera. Kýthira, S Greece 36.09N 22.58E
117 F23 **Kýthira** var. Kíthira, It. Cerigo; Lat. Cythera. island S Greece
117 I20 **Kýthnos** Kýthnos, Kykládes, Greece, Aegean Sea 37.24N 24.28E
117 I20 **Kýthnos** var. Kíthnos, Thermiá, It. Termia; anc. Cythnos. island Kykládes, Greece, Aegean Sea
117 I20 **Kýthnou, Stenó** strait Kykládes, Greece, Aegean Sea
Kythréa see Değirmenlik
Kyungëy Ala-Too, Khrebet see Kungei Ala-Tau
Kyurdamir see Kürdämir
Kyuren, Gora see Kürendag
172 C15 **Kyūshū** var. Kyûsyû. island SW Japan
199 Gg6 **Kyushu-Palau Ridge** var. Kyusyu-Palau Ridge. undersea feature W Pacific Ocean
170 Cc15 **Kyūshū-sanchi** ▲ Kyūshū, SW Japan
116 F10 **Kyustendil** anc. Pautalia. Kyustendil, W Bulgaria 42.17N 22.42E
116 G11 **Kyustendil** ◆ province W Bulgaria
Kyûsyû see Kyūshū
Kyusyu-Palau Ridge see Kyushu-Palau Ridge
126 L7 **Kyusyur** Respublika Sakha (Yakutiya), NE Russian Federation 70.36N 127.19E
191 P10 **Kywong** New South Wales, SE Australia 34.59S 146.42E
119 P4 **Kyyiv** Eng. Kiev, Rus. Kiyev. ● (Ukraine) Kyyivs'ka Oblast', N Ukraine 50.26N 30.31E
Kyyiv see Kyyivs'ka Oblast'
119 O4 **Kyyivs'ka Oblast'** var. Kyyiv, Rus. Kiyevskaya Oblast'. ◆ province N Ukraine
119 P3 **Kyyivs'ke Vodoskhovyshche** Eng. Kiev Reservoir, Rus. Kiyevskoye Vodokhranilishche. ▣ N Ukraine
95 L16 **Kyyjärvi** Länsi-Suomi, W Finland 63.01N 24.34E
126 I16 **Kyzyl** Respublika Tyva, C Russian Federation 51.45N 94.28E
153 S8 **Kyzyl-Adyr** prev. Kirovskoye. Talasskaya Oblast', NW Kyrgyzstan 42.37N 71.34E
151 V14 **Kyzylagash** Almaty, SE Kazakhstan 45.19N 78.45E
152 C13 **Kyzylbair** Balkan Welaýaty, W Turkmenistan 38.13N 55.38E
Kyzyl-Dzhiik, Pereval see Uzbel Shankou
151 S7 **Kyzylkak, Ozero** ◎ NE Kazakhstan
151 X11 **Kyzylkesek** Vostochnyy Kazakhstan, E Kazakhstan 47.55N 82.01E
153 S10 **Kyzyl-Kiya** Kir. Kyzyl-Kyya. Batkenskaya Oblast', SW Kyrgyzstan 40.15N 72.07E
150 L11 **Kyzylkol', Ozero** ◎ C Kazakhstan
151 N15 **Kyzylorda** var. Kzyl-Orda, Qizil Orda Kaz. Qyzylorda; prev. Perovsk. Kyzylorda, S Kazakhstan 44.54N 65.30E
150 L14 **Kyzylorda** off. Kyzylordinskaya Oblast' Kaz. Qyzylorda Oblysy. ◆ province S Kazakhstan
138 L9 **Kyzyl Kum** var. Kizil Kum, Qizil Qum, Uzb. Qizilqum. desert Kazakhstan/Uzbekistan
Kyzyl-Kyya see Kyzyl-Kiya
Kyzylrabat see Qizilravote
Kyzylrabot see Qizilrabot
Kyzylsu see Kyzyl-Suu
153 X7 **Kyzyl-Suu** prev. Pokrovka. Issyk-Kul'skaya Oblast', NE Kyrgyzstan 42.19N 77.55E
153 S12 **Kyzyl-Suu** var. Kyzylsu. Kyrgyzstan/Tajikistan
153 X8 **Kyzyl-Tuu** Issyk-Kul'skaya Oblast', E Kyrgyzstan 42.06N 76.54E
151 Q12 **Kyzylzhar** Kaz. Qyzylzhar. Karaganda, C Kazakhstan 48.22N 70.00E
Kzyl-Orda see Kyzylorda
Kzylordinskaya Oblast' see Kyzylorda
Kzyltu see Kishkenekol'

L

111 X2 **Laa an der Thaya** Niederösterreich, NE Austria 48.42N 16.22E
65 K15 **La Adela** La Pampa, SE Argentina 38.57S 64.02W
Laagen see Numedalslågen
111 S5 **Laakirchen** Oberösterreich, N Austria 47.59N 13.49E
Laaland see Lolland
106 I11 **La Albuera** Extremadura, W Spain 38.43N 6.49W
107 O7 **La Alcarria** physical region C Spain
106 K14 **La Algaba** Andalucía, S Spain 37.27N 6.01W
107 P9 **La Almarcha** Castilla-La Mancha, C Spain 39.40N 2.22W
107 R6 **La Almunia de Doña Godina** Aragón, NE Spain 41.28N 1.22W
43 N5 **La Amistad, Presa** ▣ NW Mexico
120 F4 **Läänemaa** off. Lääne Maakond. ◆ province NW Estonia
120 I3 **Lääne-Virumaa** off. Lääne-Viru Maakond. ◆ province NE Estonia
64 J9 **La Antigua, Salina** salt lake W Argentina
101 E17 **Laarne** Oost-Vlaanderen, NW Belgium 51.03N 3.49E
82 O13 **Laas Caanood** Sool, N Somalia 8.33N 47.44E
43 O9 **La Ascensión** Nuevo León, NE Mexico 24.15N 99.53W
82 N12 **Laas Dhaareed** Sanaag, N Somalia 10.12N 46.09E
57 O4 **La Asunción** Nueva Esparta, NE Venezuela 11.06N 63.53W
Laatokka see Ladozhskoye Ozero
102 I13 **Laatzen** Niedersachsen, NW Germany 52.19N 9.46E
40 E9 **Lā'au Point** var. Laau Point headland Moloka'i, Hawai'i, USA, C Pacific Ocean 21.06N 157.18W
44 D6 **La Aurora** ✕ (Ciudad de Guatemala) Guatemala, C Guatemala 14.33N 90.30W
76 C9 **Laâyoune** var. Aaiún. ○ (Western Sahara) NW Western Sahara 27.10N 13.10W
130 L14 **Laba** SW Russian Federation
42 M6 **La Babia** Coahuila de Zaragoza, NE Mexico 28.36N 102.04W
13 R7 **La Baie** Québec, SE Canada 48.20N 70.54W
175 R16 **Labala** Pulau Lomblen, S Indonesia 8.30S 123.27E
64 K8 **La Banda** Santiago del Estero, N Argentina 27.43S 64.13W
La Banda Oriental see Uruguay
106 K4 **La Bañeza** Castilla-León, N Spain 42.18N 5.54W
42 M13 **La Barca** Jalisco, SW Mexico 20.18N 102.30W
42 K14 **La Barra de Navidad** Jalisco, C Mexico 19.12N 104.38W
197 J13 **Labasa** prev. Lambasa. Vanua Levu, N Fiji 16.25S 179.24E
179 Q15 **Labason** Mindanao, S Philippines 8.03N 122.31E
104 H8 **la Baule-Escoublac** Loire-Atlantique, NW France 47.16N 2.24W
Labe see Elbe
78 I13 **Labé** NW Guinea 11.19N 12.16W
25 X14 **La Belle** Florida, SE USA 26.45N 81.26W
13 N11 **Labelle** Québec, SE Canada 46.15N 74.43W
8 H7 **Laberge, Lake** ◎ Yukon Territory, W Canada
Labes see Łobez
Labiau see Polessk
114 A10 **Labin** It. Albona. Istra, NW Croatia 45.05N 14.07E
130 L14 **Labinsk** Krasnodarskiy Kray, SW Russian Federation 44.39N 40.43E
107 X5 **La Bisbal d'Empordà** Cataluña, NE Spain 41.58N 3.01E
121 P16 **Labkovichy** Rus. Lobkovichi. Mahilyowskaya Voblasts', E Belarus 53.49N 31.43E
13 S4 **La Blache, Lac de** ◎ Québec, SE Canada
179 Q11 **Labo** Luzon, N Philippines 14.10N 122.47E
Laboehanbadjo see Labuhanbajo
Laborca see Laborec
113 N18 **Laborec** Hung. Laborca. E Slovakia
110 D11 **La Borgne** S Switzerland
47 T12 **Laborie** SW Saint Lucia 13.45N 61.00W
81 F21 **La Bouenza** ◆ province S Congo
104 J14 **Labouheyre** Landes, SW France 44.12N 0.55W
64 L12 **Laboulaye** Córdoba, C Argentina 34.05S 63.20W
11 Q7 **Labrador** cultural region Newfoundland and Labrador, SW Canada
66 I6 **Labrador Basin** var. Labrador Sea Basin. undersea feature Labrador Sea
11 N9 **Labrador City** Newfoundland and Labrador, E Canada 52.55N 66.52W
11 Q5 **Labrador Sea** sea NW Atlantic Ocean
Labrador Sea Basin see Labrador Basin
Labrang see Xiahe
56 G9 **Labranzagrande** Boyacá, C Colombia 5.30N 72.33W
47 U15 **La Brea** Trinidad, Trinidad and Tobago 10.13N 61.36W
61 D14 **Lábrea** Amazonas, N Brazil 7.19S 64.46W
13 S6 **Labrieville** Québec, SE Canada 49.15N 69.31W
104 K14 **Labrit** Landes, SW France 44.03N 0.29W
110 C9 **La Broye** SW Switzerland
105 N15 **Labruguière** Tarn, S France 43.31N 2.15E
174 I8 **Labu** Pulau Singkep, W Indonesia 0.34S 104.24E
175 N3 **Labuan** var. Victoria. Labuan, East Malaysia 5.19N 115.13E
175 N3 **Labuan** ◆ federal territory East Malaysia
Labuan see Labuan, Pulau
175 N3 **Labuan, Pulau** var. Labuan. island East Malaysia
Labudalin see Ergun
175 Pp16 **Labuhanbajo** prev. Laboehanbadjo. Flores, S Indonesia 8.29S 119.54E
173 G6 **Labuhanbilik** Sumatera, N Indonesia 2.33N 100.09E
173 Ee5 **Labuhanhaji** Sumatera, W Indonesia 3.31N 97.00E
Labuk see Labuk, Sungai
Labuk Bay see Labuk, Teluk
175 O2 **Labuk, Sungai** var. Labuk. East Malaysia
175 Oo2 **Labuk, Teluk** var. Labuk Bay, Telukan Labuk. bay S Sulu Sea
Labuk, Telukan see Labuk, Teluk
177 Ff9 **Labutta** Irrawaddy, SW Burma 16.07N 94.45E
125 G8 **Labytnangi** Yamalo-Nenetskiy Avtonomnyy Okrug, N Russian Federation 66.39N 66.26E
80 F10 **Lac** off. Préfecture du Lac. ◆ prefecture W Chad
115 K19 **Laç** var. Laci. Lezhë, C Albania 41.37N 19.37E
59 K19 **Lacajahuira, Rio** W Bolivia
La Calamine see Kelmis
64 G11 **La Calera** Valparaíso, C Chile 32.48S 71.13W
11 P11 **Lac-Allard** Québec, E Canada 50.37N 63.26W
106 L13 **La Campana** Andalucía, S Spain 37.35N 5.24W
104 J12 **Lacanau** Gironde, SW France 44.59N 1.04W
44 C2 **Lacandón, Sierra del** ▲ Guatemala/Mexico
La Cañiza see A Cañiza
43 W16 **Lacantún, Río** SE Mexico
105 Q3 **la Capelle** Aisne, N France 49.58N 3.55E
114 K10 **Laćarak** Serbia, NW Serbia 45.00N 19.34E
64 L11 **La Carlota** Córdoba, C Argentina 33.27S 63.16W
179 Q13 **La Carlota** Negros, S Philippines 10.21N 122.55E
106 L13 **La Carlota** Andalucía, S Spain 37.40N 4.55W
107 N12 **La Carolina** Andalucía, S Spain 38.15N 3.37W
105 O15 **Lacaune** Tarn, S France 43.42N 2.42E
13 P7 **Lac-Bouchette** Québec, SE Canada 48.14N 72.11W
Laccadive Islands/Laccadive Minicoy and Amindivi Islands, the see Lakshadweep
9 Y16 **Lac du Bonnet** Manitoba, S Canada 50.13N 96.04W
32 L4 **Lac du Flambeau** Wisconsin, N USA 45.58N 89.51W
13 P8 **Lac-Édouard** Québec, SE Canada 47.39N 72.16W
44 I4 **La Ceiba** Atlántida, N Honduras 15.45N 86.28W
56 E9 **La Ceja** Antioquia, W Colombia 6.08N 75.21W
190 J11 **Lacepede Bay** bay South Australia
34 G9 **Lacey** Washington, NW USA 47.01N 122.49W
105 P12 **la Chaise-Dieu** Haute-Loire, C France 45.19N 3.41E
116 G13 **Lachanás** Kentrikí Makedonía, N Greece 40.57N 23.15E
128 L11 **Lacha, Ozero** ◎ NW Russian Federation
105 O8 **la Charité-sur-Loire** Nièvre, C France 47.10N 2.59E
105 N9 **la Châtre** Indre, C France 46.34N 1.58E
110 C8 **La Chaux-de-Fonds** Neuchâtel, W Switzerland 47.07N 6.51E
Lach Dera see Dheere Laaq
110 G8 **Lachen** Schwyz, C Switzerland 47.11N 8.49E
191 Q8 **Lachlan River** New South Wales, SE Australia
45 T15 **La Chorrera** Panamá, C Panama 8.51N 79.46W
13 V7 **Lac-Humqui** Québec, SE Canada 48.21N 67.32W
13 N12 **Lachute** Québec, SE Canada 45.39N 74.21W
Lachyn see Laçın
Laci see Laç
143 W13 **Laçın** Rus. Lachyn. SW Azerbaijan 39.36N 46.34E
105 S16 **la Ciotat** anc. Citharista. Bouches-du-Rhône, SE France 43.10N 5.36E
20 D10 **Lackawanna** New York, NE USA 42.49N 78.49W
9 Q13 **Lac La Biche** Alberta, SW Canada 54.46N 111.58W
Lac La Martre see Wha Ti
13 R12 **Lac-Mégantic** var. Mégantic. Québec, SE Canada 45.34N 70.52W
Lacobriga see Lagos
42 G5 **La Colorada** Sonora, NW Mexico 28.46N 110.29W
9 Q15 **Lacombe** Alberta, SW Canada 52.30N 113.42W
32 L12 **Lacon** Illinois, N USA 41.01N 89.24W
45 P16 **La Concepción** var. Concepción. Chiriquí, W Panama 8.30N 82.37W
56 H5 **La Concepción** Zulia, NW Venezuela 10.22N 71.46W
56 H5 **La Concepción** Zulia, NW Venezuela 10.37N 71.51W
109 C19 **Laconi** Sardegna, Italy, C Mediterranean Sea 39.52N 9.02E
21 O9 **Laconia** New Hampshire, NE USA 43.31N 71.28W
63 H19 **La Coronilla** Rocha, E Uruguay 33.54S 53.32W
La Coruña see A Coruña
105 O11 **la Courtine** Creuse, C France 45.42N 2.18E
104 J16 **Lacq** Pyrénées-Atlantiques, SW France 43.25N 0.37W
13 P9 **La Croche** Québec, SE Canada 47.38N 72.42W
31 X3 **la Croix, Lac** ◎ Canada/USA
28 K5 **La Crosse** Kansas, C USA 38.31N 99.18W
23 V7 **La Crosse** Virginia, NE USA 36.41N 78.03W
34 L9 **La Crosse** Washington, NW USA 46.48N 117.51W
32 J7 **La Crosse** Wisconsin, N USA 43.45N 91.12W
56 C13 **La Cruz** Nariño, SW Colombia 1.31N 77.01W
44 K12 **La Cruz** Guanacaste, NW Costa Rica 11.04N 85.37W
42 I10 **La Cruz** Sinaloa, W Mexico 23.52N 106.52W
63 F19 **La Cruz** Florida, S Uruguay 33.54S 56.10W
44 M9 **La Cruz de Río Grande** Región Autónoma Atlántico Sur, E Nicaragua 13.04N 84.07W
56 J4 **La Cruz de Taratara** Falcón, N Venezuela 11.03N 69.43W
13 Q10 **Lac-St-Charles** Québec, SE Canada 46.56N 71.24W
42 M6 **La Cuesta** Coahuila de Zaragoza, NE Mexico 28.43N 102.33W
59 A17 **La Cumbra, Volcán** ⚠ Galapagos Islands, Ecuador, E Pacific Ocean 0.21S 91.30W
158 J5 **Ladākh Range** ▲ NE India
28 I5 **Ladder Creek** Kansas, C USA
47 X10 **la Désirade** atoll E Guadeloupe
Lādhiqīyah, Muḩāfaẓat al see Al Lādhiqīyah
85 F25 **Ladismith** Western Cape, SW South Africa 33.27S 21.15E
158 G11 **Lādnūn** Rājasthān, NW India 27.36N 74.25E
Ladoga, Lake see Ladozhskoye Ozero
117 E19 **Ládon** S Greece
56 E9 **La Dorada** Caldas, C Colombia 5.28N 74.40W
128 H11 **Ladozhskoye Ozero** Eng. Lake Ladoga, Fin. Laatokka. ◎ NW Russian Federation
39 R12 **Ladron Peak** ▲ New Mexico, SW USA 34.25N 107.04W
128 J11 **Ladva-Vetka** Respublika Kareliya, NW Russian Federation 61.18N 34.24E
191 Q15 **Lady Barron** Tasmania, SE Australia 40.12S 148.12E
12 G9 **Lady Evelyn Lake** ◎ Ontario, S Canada
25 W11 **Lady Lake** Florida, SE USA 28.55N 81.55W
8 L17 **Ladysmith** Vancouver Island, British Columbia, SW Canada 48.55N 123.45W
85 J22 **Ladysmith** KwaZulu/Natal, E South Africa 28.34S 29.46E
32 J5 **Ladysmith** Wisconsin, N USA 45.27N 91.07W
151 P9 **Ladyzhenka** Akmola, C Kazakhstan 50.58N 68.44E
194 K13 **Lae** Morobe, W PNG 6.45S 146.55E
201 R6 **Lae Atoll** atoll Ralik Chain, W Marshall Islands
42 C3 **La Encantada, Cerro de** ▲ NW Mexico 31.03N 115.25W
96 E12 **Lærdalsøyri** Sogn og Fjordane, S Norway 61.04N 7.24E
57 N11 **La Esmeralda** Amazonas, S Venezuela 3.10N 65.33W
44 G7 **La Esperanza** Intibucá, SW Honduras 14.18N 88.10W
32 K8 **La Farge** Wisconsin, N USA 43.36N 90.39W
25 R5 **Lafayette** Alabama, S USA 32.54N 85.24W
39 T4 **Lafayette** Colorado, C USA 39.59N 105.06W
25 R2 **La Fayette** Georgia, SE USA 34.42N 85.16W
33 O13 **Lafayette** Indiana, N USA 40.25N 86.52W
24 I9 **Lafayette** Louisiana, S USA 30.13N 92.01W
22 K8 **Lafayette** Tennessee, S USA 36.31N 86.01W
21 N7 **Lafayette, Mount** ▲ New Hampshire, NE USA 44.09N 71.37W
La Fe see Santa Fé
105 P3 **la Fère** Aisne, N France 49.41N 3.20E
104 L6 **la Ferté-Bernard** Sarthe, NW France 48.13N 0.40E
104 K5 **la Ferté-Macé** Orne, N France 48.35N 0.21W
105 N7 **la Ferté-St-Aubin** Loiret, C France 47.42N 1.57E
105 P5 **la Ferté-sous-Jouarre** Seine-et-Marne, N France 48.57N 3.07E
79 V15 **Lafia** Nassarawa, C Nigeria 8.29N 8.34E
79 T15 **Lafiagi** Kwara, W Nigeria 8.52N 5.25E
9 T17 **Lafleche** Saskatchewan, S Canada 49.40N 106.28W
104 K7 **la Flèche** Sarthe, NW France 47.42N 0.04W
111 X7 **Lafnitz** Hung. Lapines. Austria/Hungary
197 I6 **La Foa** Province Sud, S New Caledonia 21.46S 165.49E
22 M8 **La Follette** Tennessee, S USA 36.22N 84.07W
13 N12 **Lafontaine** Québec, SE Canada 45.52N 74.01W
24 K10 **Lafourche, Bayou** Louisiana, S USA
64 K6 **La Fragua** Santiago del Estero, N Argentina 26.06S 64.06W
56 H7 **La Fría** Táchira, NW Venezuela 8.13N 72.15W
106 J7 **La Fuente de San Esteban** Castilla-León, N Spain 40.48N 6.14W
194 G11 **Lagaip** W PNG
63 B15 **La Gallareta** Santa Fe, C Argentina 29.34S 60.22W
131 Q14 **Lagan'** prev. Kaspiyskiy. Respublika Kalmykiya, SW Russian Federation 45.25N 47.19E
97 L20 **Lagan** Kronoberg, S Sweden 56.55N 14.01E
97 K21 **Lågan** S Sweden
94 L2 **Lagarfljót** var. Lögurinn. ◎ E Iceland
39 R7 **La Garita Mountains** ▲ Colorado, C USA
179 P9 **Lagawe** Luzon, N Philippines 16.46N 121.06E
80 F13 **Lagdo** Nord, N Cameroon 9.12N 13.43E
80 F13 **Lagdo, Lac de** ◎ N Cameroon
102 H13 **Lage** Nordrhein-Westfalen, W Germany 52.00N 8.48E
96 H12 **Lågen** S Norway
63 J14 **Lages** Santa Catarina, S Brazil 27.44S 50.16W
Lágesvuotna see Laksefjorden
155 R4 **Laghmān** ◆ province E Afghanistan
76 J6 **Laghouat** N Algeria 33.49N 2.59E
107 Q10 **La Gineta** Castilla-La Mancha, C Spain 39.08N 2.00W
117 E21 **Lagkáda** var. Langada. Pelopónnisos, S Greece 36.49N 22.19E
116 G13 **Lagkadás** var. Langades, Langadhás. Kentrikí Makedonía, N Greece 40.45N 23.04E
117 E20 **Lagkádia** var. Langádhia, Langadia. Pelopónnisos, S Greece 37.39N 22.03E
56 F6 **La Gloria** Cesar, N Colombia 8.37N 73.49W
43 O7 **La Gloria** Nuevo León, NE Mexico
94 N3 **Lågneset** headland W Svalbard 77.46N 13.44E
106 G14 **Lagoa** Faro, S Portugal 37.07N 8.27W
La Goagira see La Guajira
Lago Agrio see Nueva Loja
63 I14 **Lagoa Vermelha** Rio Grande do Sul, S Brazil 28.13S 51.31W
143 V10 **Lagodekhi** SE Georgia 41.49N 46.15E
44 C7 **La Gomera** Escuintla, S Guatemala 14.04N 91.03W
Lagone see Logone
109 M19 **Lagonegro** Basilicata, S Italy 40.06N 15.42E

◆ Country ● Country Capital ◇ Dependent Territory ○ Dependent Territory Capital ◆ Administrative Region ✕ International Airport ▲ Mountain ▲ Mountain Range ⚠ Volcano River ◎ Lake ▣ Reservoir

Lago Ranco – La Paragua

65 G16 Lago Ranco Los Lagos, S Chile 40.21S 72.29W
79 S16 Lagos Lagos, SW Nigeria 6.24N 3.16E
106 F14 Lagos anc. Lacobriga. Faro, S Portugal 37.04N 8.40W
79 S16 Lagos ◆ state SW Nigeria
42 M12 Lagos de Moreno Jalisco, SW Mexico 21.21N 101.55W
Lagosta see Lastovo
76 A12 Lagouira SW Western Sahara 20.55N 17.04W
94 O1 Lågøya island N Svalbard
34 L11 La Grande Oregon, NW USA 45.21N 118.04W
105 Q14 la Grande-Combe Gard, S France 44.13N 4.01E
10 K9 La Grande Rivière var. Fort George. ≈ Québec, SE Canada
25 R4 La Grange Georgia, SE USA 33.01N 85.01W
33 P11 Lagrange Indiana, N USA 41.38N 85.25W
22 L5 La Grange Kentucky, S USA 38.22N 85.07W
29 V2 La Grange Missouri, C USA 40.00N 91.31W
23 V10 La Grange North Carolina, SE USA 35.18N 77.47W
27 U11 La Grange Texas, SW USA 29.54N 96.52W
107 N7 La Granja Castilla-León, N Spain 40.53N 4.01W
57 Q9 La Gran Sabana grassland E Venezuela
56 H7 La Grita Táchira, NW Venezuela 8.09N 71.58W
La Grulla see Grulla
13 R11 La Guadeloupe Québec, SE Canada 45.57N 70.56W
56 L5 La Guaira Vargas, N Venezuela 10.35N 66.52W
56 G4 La Guajira off. Departamento de La Guajira, var. Guajira, La Goagira. ◆ province NE Colombia
196 I4 Lagua Lichan, Punta headland Saipan, S Northern Mariana Islands
20 K14 La Guardia ✕ (New York) Long Island, New York, NE USA 40.44N 73.51W
La Guardia/Laguardia see A Guarda
107 P4 Laguardia Basq. Biasteri. País Vasco, N Spain 42.32N 2.31W
La Gudiña see A Gudiña
105 O9 la Guerche-sur-l'Aubois Cher, C France 46.55N 3.00E
105 O13 Laguiole Aveyron, S France 34.49S 20.01E
85 F26 L'Agulhas var. Agulhas. W Cape, SW South Africa 33.32N 117.46W
63 K14 Laguna Santa Catarina, S Brazil 28.28S 48.45W
39 Q11 Laguna New Mexico, SW USA 35.03N 107.30W
37 T16 Laguna Beach California, W USA 33.32N 117.46W
37 Y17 Laguna Dam dam Arizona/California, W USA 32.49N 114.30W
42 L7 Laguna El Rey Coahuila de Zaragoza, N Mexico
37 V17 Laguna Mountains ▲ California, W USA
63 B17 Laguna Paiva Santa Fe, C Argentina 31.21S 60.40W
64 H3 Lagunas Tarapacá, N Chile 21.01S 69.36W
58 E9 Lagunas Loreto, N Peru 5.16S 75.40W
59 M20 Lagunillas Santa Cruz, SE Bolivia 19.37S 63.39W
56 H6 Lagunillas Mérida, NW Venezuela 8.31N 71.24W
46 C4 La Habana var. Havana. ● (Cuba) Ciudad de La Habana, W Cuba 23.07N 82.25W
175 Oo3 Lahad Datu Sabah, East Malaysia 5.01N 118.19E
175 Oo3 Lahad Datu, Teluk var. Telukan Lahad Datu, Teluk Darvel, Teluk Datu; prev. Darvel Bay. bay Sabah, East Malaysia
40 F10 Lahaina Maui, Hawai'i, USA, C Pacific Ocean 20.52N 156.40W
174 Hh12 Lahat Sumatera, W Indonesia 3.46S 103.31E
La Haye see 's-Gravenhage
Lahej see Laḥij
64 G9 La Higuera Coquimbo, N Chile 29.33S 71.15W
147 S13 Laḥī, Ḥisā' al spring/well NE Yemen 17.28N 50.05E
147 O16 Laḥij var. Laḥj, Eng. Lahej. SW Yemen 13.03N 44.55E
148 M3 Lāhījān Gīlān, NW Iran 37.15N 50.03E
121 I19 Lahishyn Pol. Lohiszyn, Rus. Logishin. Brestskaya Voblasts', SW Belarus 52.19N 25.59E
Laḥj see Laḥij
103 F18 Lahn ≈ W Germany
Lähn see Wleń
97 J21 Laholm Halland, S Sweden 56.30N 13.04E
97 J21 Laholmsbukten bay S Sweden
37 R6 Lahontan Reservoir ⊠ Nevada, W USA
155 W8 Lahore Punjab, NE Pakistan 31.35N 74.18E
155 W8 Lahore ✕ Punjab, E Pakistan 31.34N 74.22E
57 Q6 La Horqueta Delta Amacuro, NE Venezuela 9.13N 62.02W
121 K15 Lahoysk Rus. Logoysk. Minskaya Voblasts', C Belarus 54.12N 27.53E
103 F22 Lahr Baden-Württemberg, S Germany 48.21N 7.51E
95 M19 Lahti Swe. Lahtis. Etelä-Suomi, S Finland 61.00N 25.40E
Lahtis see Lahti
42 M14 La Huacana Michoacán de Ocampo, SW Mexico 18.56N 101.52W
42 K14 La Huerta Jalisco, SW Mexico 19.28N 104.40W
80 H12 Laï prev. Behagle, De Behagle. Tandjilé, S Chad 9.22N 16.13E
194 G12 Laiagam Enga, W PNG 5.31S 143.28E
Laibach see Ljubljana
178 Ii5 Lai Châu Lai Châu, N Vietnam 22.04N 103.10E
40 D9 Lā'ie var. Laie. O'ahu, Hawai'i, USA, C Pacific Ocean 21.39N 157.55W
104 L5 l'Aigle Orne, N France 48.46N 0.37E
105 Q7 Laignes Côte d'Or, C France 47.51N 4.24E
95 K17 Laihia Länsi-Suomi, W Finland 62.58N 22.00E
Laila see Laylā
85 F25 Laingsburg Western Cape, SW South Africa 33.09S 20.48E
111 U2 Lainsitz Cz. Lužnice. ≈ Austria/Czech Republic
98 I7 Lairg N Scotland, UK 58.02N 4.22W
83 I17 Laisamis Eastern, N Kenya 1.35N 37.49E
Laisberg see Leisi
131 R4 Laishevo Respublika Tatarstan, W Russian Federation 55.26N 49.27E
Laisholm see Jõgeva
94 H13 Laisvall Norrbotten, N Sweden 66.07N 17.10E
95 K19 Laitila Länsi-Suomi, W Finland 60.52N 21.40E
167 P5 Laiwu Shandong, E China 36.12N 117.36E
167 R4 Laixi var. Shuiji. Shandong, E China 36.53N 120.33E
167 R4 Laiyang Shandong, E China 37.03N 120.48E
167 O3 Laiyuan Hebei, E China 39.19N 114.43E
167 R4 Laizhou var. Ye Xian. Shandong, E China 37.12N 120.01E
167 Q4 Laizhou Wan var. Laichow Bay. bay E China
39 S8 La Jara Colorado, C USA 37.16N 105.57W
63 I15 Lajeado Rio Grande do Sul, S Brazil 29.28S 52.00W
114 L12 Lajkovac Serbia, C Serbia 44.22N 20.12E
113 K23 Lajosmizse Bács-Kiskun, C Hungary 47.03N 19.29E
Lajta see Leitha
42 I6 La Junta Chihuahua, N Mexico 28.27N 107.21W
39 V7 La Junta Colorado, C USA 37.58N 103.34W
94 J13 Lakatrāsk Norrbotten, N Sweden 66.16N 21.10E
Lak Dera see Dheere Laaq
Lakeamu see Lakekamu
31 P12 Lake Andes South Dakota, N USA 43.08N 98.33W
24 H9 Lake Arthur Louisiana, S USA 30.04N 92.40W
197 L15 Lakeba prev. Lakemba. island Lau Group, E Fiji
197 L14 Lakeba Passage channel E Fiji
31 S10 Lake Benton Minnesota, N USA 44.15N 96.17W
25 V9 Lake Butler Florida, SE USA 30.01N 82.20W
191 P8 Lake Cargelligo New South Wales, SE Australia 33.21S 146.25E
24 G9 Lake Charles Louisiana, S USA 30.13N 93.13W
29 X9 Lake City Arkansas, C USA 35.49N 90.25W
39 Q7 Lake City Colorado, C USA 38.01N 107.18W
25 V9 Lake City Florida, SE USA 30.12N 82.39W
31 U13 Lake City Iowa, C USA 42.16N 94.43W
33 P7 Lake City Michigan, N USA 44.18N 85.13W
31 W9 Lake City Minnesota, N USA 44.27N 92.16W
23 T13 Lake City South Carolina, SE USA 33.52N 79.45W
31 Q7 Lake City South Dakota, N USA 45.42N 97.22W
22 M8 Lake City Tennessee, S USA 36.13N 84.09W
194 F12 Lake Copiago var. Kopiago. Southern Highlands, W PNG 5.28S 142.30E
8 L17 Lake Cowichan Vancouver Island, British Columbia, SW Canada 48.49N 124.04W
31 U10 Lake Crystal Minnesota, N USA 44.07N 94.13W
27 T6 Lake Dallas Texas, SW USA 33.06N 97.01W
99 K15 Lake District physical region NW England, UK
20 D10 Lake Erie Beach New York, NE USA 42.37N 79.04W
31 T11 Lakefield Minnesota, N USA 43.40N 95.10W
27 V6 Lake Fork Reservoir ⊠ Texas, SW USA
32 M9 Lake Geneva Wisconsin, N USA 42.36N 88.25W
20 L9 Lake George New York, NE USA 43.25N 73.45W
16 O4 Lake Harbour Baffin Island, Nunavut, NE Canada 62.48N 69.49W
38 I12 Lake Havasu City Arizona, SW USA 34.26N 114.20W
27 W12 Lake Jackson Texas, SW USA 29.01N 95.25W
194 J14 Lakekamu var. Lakeamu. ≈ S PNG
188 K13 Lake King Western Australia 33.09S 119.46E
194 F12 Lake Kutubu ⊚ W PNG
25 V12 Lakeland Florida, SE USA 28.03N 81.57W
25 U7 Lakeland Georgia, SE USA 31.02N 83.04W
189 W4 Lakeland Downs Queensland, NE Australia 15.54S 144.54E
9 P16 Lake Louise Alberta, SW Canada 51.25N 116.10W
Lakemba see Lakeba
31 V11 Lake Mills Iowa, C USA 43.25N 93.31W
41 Q10 Lake Minchumina Alaska, USA 63.55N 152.25W
Lakemti see Nek'emtē
194 E13 Lake Murray Western, SW PNG 6.45S 141.25E
82 F5 Lake Nasser var. Buhayrat Nasir, Buḥayrat Nāṣir, Buḥeiret Nâṣir. ⊚ Egypt/Sudan
33 R9 Lake Orion Michigan, N USA 42.46N 83.14W
202 B16 Lakepa NE Niue 18.58S 169.48E
31 T11 Lake Park Iowa, C USA 43.27N 95.19W
20 K7 Lake Placid New York, NE USA 44.16N 73.57W
20 K9 Lake Pleasant New York, NE USA 43.27N 74.24W
36 M6 Lakeport California, W USA 39.03N 122.55W
31 Q10 Lake Preston South Dakota, N USA 44.21N 97.22W
24 J5 Lake Providence Louisiana, S USA 32.48N 91.10W
193 E20 Lake Pukaki Canterbury, South Island, NZ 44.12S 170.10E
191 Q12 Lakes Entrance Victoria, SE Australia 37.52S 147.58E
39 N12 Lakeside Arizona, SW USA 34.09N 109.58W
37 V17 Lakeside California, W USA 32.50N 116.55W
25 S9 Lakeside Florida, SE USA 30.22N 84.18W
30 K13 Lakeside Nebraska, C USA 42.01N 102.27W
34 E13 Lakeside Oregon, NW USA 43.34N 124.10W
23 W6 Lakeside Virginia, NE USA 37.36N 77.28W
Lakes State see El Buhayrat
Lake State see Michigan
193 F20 Lake Tekapo Canterbury, South Island, NZ 44.01S 170.29E
23 O10 Lake Toxaway North Carolina, SE USA 35.06N 82.57W
31 T13 Lake View Iowa, C USA 42.18N 95.04W
34 I16 Lakeview Oregon, NW USA 42.13N 120.21W
27 O3 Lakeview Texas, SW USA 34.38N 100.36W
29 W14 Lake Village Arkansas, C USA 33.19N 91.16W
25 W12 Lake Wales Florida, SE USA 27.54N 81.35W
39 T4 Lakewood Colorado, C USA 39.38N 105.07W
20 K15 Lakewood New Jersey, NE USA 40.04N 74.11W
20 C11 Lakewood New York, NE USA 42.03N 79.19W
33 T11 Lakewood Ohio, N USA 41.28N 81.48W
25 Y13 Lakewood Park Florida, SE USA 27.32N 80.24W
25 Z14 Lake Worth Florida, SE USA 26.37N 80.03W
158 H4 Lake Wular ⊚ NE India
128 H11 Lakhdenpokh'ya Respublika Kareliya, NW Russian Federation 61.25N 30.05E
158 L11 Lakhīmpur Uttar Pradesh, N India 27.57N 80.46E
160 J11 Lakhnādon Madhya Pradesh, C India 22.36N 79.36E
Lakhnau see Lucknow
160 A9 Lakhpat Gujarāt, W India 23.49N 68.54E
121 K19 Lakhva Rus. Lakhva. Brestskaya Voblasts', SW Belarus 52.13N 27.15E
28 I6 Lakin Kansas, C USA 37.56N 101.18W
155 S7 Lakki Marwat North-West Frontier Province, NW Pakistan 32.36N 70.55E
117 F21 Lakonía historical region S Greece
117 F22 Lakonikós Kólpos gulf S Greece
78 M17 Lakota S Ivory Coast 5.52N 5.42W
31 U11 Lakota Iowa, C USA 43.22N 94.04W
31 P3 Lakota North Dakota, N USA 48.02N 98.20W
Lak Sao see Ban Lakxao
94 L8 Lakselfjorden Lapp. Lágesvuotna. fjord N Norway
94 K8 Lakselv Lapp. Leavdnja. Finnmark, N Norway 70.01N 24.57E
161 B21 Lakshadweep prev. the Laccadive, Minicoy and Amindivi Islands. ◆ union territory India, N Indian Ocean
161 C22 Lakshadweep Eng. Laccadive Islands. island group India, N Indian Ocean
159 S17 Lakshmikāntapur West Bengal, NE India 22.04N 88.19E
114 G11 Laktaši Republika Srpska, N Bosnia and Herzegovina 44.54N 17.16E
155 V7 Lāla Mūsa Punjab, NE Pakistan 32.40N 74.01E
la Laon see Laon
116 M11 Lalapaşa Edirne, NW Turkey 41.52N 26.43E
85 P14 Lalaua Nampula, N Mozambique 14.21S 38.16E
107 S9 L'Alcora var. Alcora. País Valenciano, E Spain 40.04N 0.13W
107 S10 L'Alcúdia var. L'Alcudia. País Valenciano, E Spain 39.10N 0.30W
82 J11 Lalibela Amhara, N Ethiopia, 12.01N 39.05E
159 T12 Lalmanirhat Rajshahi, N Bangladesh 25.51N 89.34E
81 F20 La Lékoumou ◆ province SW Congo
44 E8 La Libertad La Libertad, SW El Salvador 13.28N 89.17W
44 E3 La Libertad Petén, N Guatemala 16.46N 90.07W
44 H6 La Libertad Comayagua, SW Honduras 14.44N 87.37W
42 E4 La Libertad var. Puerto Libertad. Sonora, NW Mexico 29.52N 112.39W
44 K10 La Libertad Chontales, S Nicaragua 12.14N 85.15W
44 A9 La Libertad ◆ department SW El Salvador
58 B11 La Libertad off. Departamento de La Libertad. ◆ department W Peru
64 G11 La Ligua Valparaíso, C Chile 32.23S 71.16W
145 U5 La'li Khān E Iraq 34.58N 45.36E
81 H16 La Likouala ◆ province NE Congo
106 H3 Lalín Galicia, NW Spain 42.40N 8.06W
104 L13 Lalinde Dordogne, SW France 44.52N 0.42E
106 K16 La Línea var. La Línea de la Concepción. Andalucía, S Spain 36.10N 5.21W
La Línea de la Concepción see La Línea
158 J14 Lalitpur Uttar Pradesh, N India 24.42N 78.24E
159 P11 Lalitpur Central, C Nepal 27.45N 85.17E
158 K10 Lālkua Uttaranchal, N India 29.04N 79.31E
9 R12 La Loche Saskatchewan, C Canada 56.31N 109.27W
104 M6 la Loupe Eure-et-Loir, C France 48.30N 1.04E
101 G20 La Louvière Hainaut, S Belgium 50.28N 4.15E
L'Altissima see Hochwilde
106 L14 La Luisiana Andalucía, S Spain 37.30N 5.14W
39 S14 La Luz New Mexico, SW USA 32.58N 105.56W
109 D16 La Maddalena Sardegna, Italy, C Mediterranean Sea 41.13N 9.25E
64 J7 La Madrid Tucumán, N Argentina 27.37S 65.16W
Lama-Kara see Kara
175 R16 Lamakera, Selat strait Nusa Tenggara, S Indonesia
13 S8 La Malbaie Québec, SE Canada 47.39N 70.10W
178 Jj10 Lamam Xékong, S Laos 15.22N 106.40E
107 P10 La Mancha physical region C Spain
la Manche see English Channel
197 C13 Lamap Malekula, C Vanuatu 16.26S 167.47E
39 W6 Lamar Colorado, C USA 38.03N 102.36W
29 S7 Lamar Missouri, C USA 37.30N 94.16W
23 S12 Lamar South Carolina, SE USA 34.10N 80.03W
109 C19 La Marmora, Punta ▲ Sardegna, Italy, C Mediterranean Sea 39.58N 9.20E
15 H7 La Martre, Lac ⊚ Northwest Territories, NW Canada
58 D10 Lamas San Martín, N Peru 6.27S 76.32W
44 I5 La Masica Atlántida, NW Honduras 15.37N 87.04W
105 R12 Lamastre Ardèche, E France 45.00N 4.32E
La Matepec see Santa Ana, Volcán de
46 I7 La Maya Santiago de Cuba, E Cuba 20.09N 75.40W
111 S5 Lambach Oberösterreich, N Austria 48.06N 13.52E
173 Ff8 Lambak Pulau Pini, W Indonesia 0.08N 98.36E
104 H5 Lamballe Côtes d'Armor, NW France 48.28N 2.31W
81 D18 Lambaréné Moyen-Ogooué, W Gabon 0.40S 10.13E
Lambasa see Labasa
175 Q12 Lambasina Besar, Pulau island C Indonesia
58 B11 Lambayeque Lambayeque, W Peru 6.39S 79.54W
58 A10 Lambayeque off. Departamento de Lambayeque. ◆ department NW Peru
99 G17 Lambay Island Ir. Reachrainn. island E Ireland
195 O10 Lambert, Cape headland New Britain, E PNG 4.15S 151.31E
205 W6 Lambert Glacier glacier Antarctica
31 T10 Lamberton Minnesota, N USA 44.14N 95.15W
29 X4 Lambert-Saint Louis ✕ Missouri, C USA 38.43N 90.19W
33 R11 Lambertville Michigan, N USA 41.46N 83.37W
20 J15 Lambertville New Jersey, NE USA 40.20N 74.55W
175 Pp9 Lambogo Sulawesi, N Indonesia 0.57S 120.23E
108 D8 Lambro ≈ N Italy
15 H2 Lambton, Cape headland Banks Island, Northwest Territories, NW Canada 71.04N 123.07W
35 W11 Lame Deer Montana, NW USA 45.37N 106.37W
106 H6 Lamego Viseu, N Portugal 41.04N 7.49W
197 C13 Lamen Bay Épi, C Vanuatu 16.36S 168.10E
47 X6 Lamentin Basse Terre, N Guadeloupe 16.16N 61.37W
Lamentin see le Lamentin
190 K10 Lameroo South Australia 35.22S 140.30E
56 F10 La Mesa Cundinamarca, C Colombia 4.39N 74.24W
37 U17 La Mesa California, W USA 32.44N 117.00W
39 R16 La Mesa New Mexico, SW USA 32.03N 106.41W
27 N6 Lamesa Texas, SW USA 32.43N 101.57W
109 N21 Lamezia Terme Calabria, SE Italy 38.54N 16.13E
197 I15 Lami Viti Levu, C Fiji 18.07S 178.25E
117 F17 Lamía Stereá Ellás, C Greece 38.54N 22.26E
179 Q17 Lamitan Basilan Island, SW Philippines 6.40N 122.07E
197 H13 Lamiti Gau, C Fiji 18.00S 179.20E
176 Uu8 Lamlam Papua, E Indonesia 0.03S 130.46E
196 B16 Lamlam, Mount ▲ SW Guam 13.19N 144.40E
111 Q6 Lammer ≈ E Austria
193 E23 Lammerlaw Range ▲ South Island, NZ
97 L20 Lammhult Kronoberg, S Sweden 57.09N 14.34E
95 L18 Lammi Etelä-Suomi, S Finland 61.06N 25.00E
201 U11 Lamoil island Chuuk, C Micronesia
37 W3 Lamoille Nevada, W USA 40.47N 115.37W
20 M7 Lamoille River ≈ Vermont, NE USA
32 J13 La Moine River ≈ Illinois, N USA
179 Pp10 Lamon Bay bay Luzon, N Philippines
31 V16 Lamoni Iowa, C USA 40.37N 93.56W
37 R13 Lamont California, W USA 35.15N 118.54W
29 N8 Lamont Oklahoma, C USA 36.41N 97.33W
56 E13 La Montañita var. Montañita. Caquetá, S Colombia 1.22N 75.28W
45 N8 La Mosquitia var. Miskito Coast, Eng. Mosquito Coast. coastal region E Nicaragua
104 I9 la Mothe-Achard Vendée, NW France 46.37N 1.37W
196 L15 Lamotrek Atoll atoll Caroline Islands, C Micronesia
31 P6 La Moure North Dakota, N USA 46.21N 98.17W
178 H8 Lampang var. Muang Lampang. Lampang, NW Thailand 18.16N 99.30E
178 Ii9 Lam Pao Reservoir ⊠ E Thailand
27 S9 Lampasas Texas, SW USA 31.03N 98.10W
27 S9 Lampasas River ≈ Texas, SW USA
43 N7 Lampazos var. Lampazos de Naranjo. Nuevo León, NE Mexico 27.00N 100.28W
Lampazos de Naranjo see Lampazos
117 E19 Lámpeia Dytikí Ellás, S Greece 37.51N 21.48E
103 G19 Lampertheim Hessen, W Germany 49.36N 8.28E
99 I20 Lampeter SW Wales, UK 52.07N 4.03W
178 H7 Lamphun var. Lampun, Muang Lamphun. Lamphun, NW Thailand 18.36N 99.01E
9 X10 Lamprey Manitoba, C Canada 58.18N 94.06W
Lampun see Lamphun
174 I13 Lampung off. Propinsi Lampung. ◆ province SW Indonesia
174 Ii13 Lampung, Teluk bay Sumatera, SW Indonesia
130 K6 Lamskoye Lipetskaya Oblast', W Russian Federation 52.57N 38.04E
83 K20 Lamu Coast, SE Kenya 2.17S 40.49E
45 N14 La Muerte, Cerro ▲ C Costa Rica 9.33N 83.47W
105 S13 la Mure Isère, E France 44.54N 5.48E
39 S10 Lamy New Mexico, SW USA 35.27N 105.52W
121 J18 Lan' Rus. Lan'. ≈ C Belarus
40 E10 Lāna'i var. Lanai. island Hawai'i, USA, C Pacific Ocean
40 E10 Lāna'i City var. Lanai City. Lāna'i, Hawai'i, USA, C Pacific Ocean 20.49N 156.55W
101 L18 Lanaken Limburg, NE Belgium 50.52N 5.39E
179 R15 Lanao, Lake var. Lake Sultan Alonto. ⊚ Mindanao, S Philippines
98 J12 Lanark S Scotland, UK 55.38N 4.24W
98 I13 Lanark cultural region S Scotland, UK
106 L9 La Nava de Ricomalillo Castilla-La Mancha, C Spain 39.40N 4.58W
178 Gg13 Lanbi Kyun prev. Sullivan Island. island Mergui Archipelago, S Burma
Lancang Jiang see Mekong
99 K17 Lancashire cultural region NW England, UK
13 N13 Lancaster Ontario, SE Canada 45.10N 74.31W
99 K16 Lancaster NW England, UK 54.03N 2.48W
37 T14 Lancaster California, W USA 34.42N 118.08W
22 M6 Lancaster Kentucky, S USA 37.35N 84.34W
29 U1 Lancaster Missouri, C USA 40.30N 92.31W
21 O7 Lancaster New Hampshire, NE USA 44.28N 71.34W
20 D10 Lancaster New York, NE USA 42.54N 78.40W
33 T14 Lancaster Ohio, N USA 39.42N 82.36W
20 H16 Lancaster Pennsylvania, NE USA 40.03N 76.18W
23 R11 Lancaster South Carolina, SE USA 34.43N 80.46W
27 U7 Lancaster Texas, SW USA 32.35N 96.45W
23 X5 Lancaster Virginia, NE USA 37.45N 76.25W
32 J9 Lancaster Wisconsin, N USA 42.52N 90.43W
207 N10 Lancaster Sound sound Nunavut, N Canada
Lan-chou/Lan-chow/Lanchow see Lanzhou
109 K14 Lanciano Abruzzo, C Italy 42.15N 14.22E
113 O16 Łańcut Podkarpackie, SE Poland 50.04N 22.13E
174 Kk8 Landak, Sungai ≈ Borneo, N Indonesia
Landao see Lantau Island
Landau see Landau an der Isar, Bayern, Germany
Landau see Landau in der Pfalz, Rheinland-Pfalz, Germany
103 N22 Landau an der Isar var. Landau. Bayern, SE Germany 48.40N 12.41E
103 F20 Landau in der Pfalz var. Landau. Rheinland-Pfalz, SW Germany 49.12N 8.07E
Land Burgenland see Burgenland
110 K8 Landeck Tirol, W Austria 47.09N 10.34E
101 J19 Landen Vlaams Brabant, C Belgium 50.45N 5.04E
35 U15 Lander Wyoming, C USA 42.49N 108.43W
104 F5 Landerneau Finistère, NW France 48.27N 4.16W
97 K20 Landeryd Halland, S Sweden 57.04N 13.15E
104 J15 Landes ◆ department SW France
Landeshut/Landeshut in Schlesien see Kamienna Góra
107 R9 Landete Castilla-La Mancha, C Spain 39.54N 1.22W
101 M18 Landgraaf Limburg, SE Netherlands 50.55N 6.04E
104 F5 Landivisiau Finistère, NW France 48.31N 4.03W
Land of Enchantment see New Mexico
Land of Opportunity see Arkansas
Land of Steady Habits see Connecticut
Land of the Midnight Sun see Alaska
110 I8 Landquart Graubünden, SE Switzerland 46.58N 9.35E
110 J9 Landquart ≈ Austria/Switzerland
23 P10 Landrum South Carolina, SE USA 35.10N 82.11W
Landsberg see Górowo Iławeckie, Warmińsko-Mazurskie, NE Poland
Landsberg see Gorzów Wielkopolski, Gorzów, Poland
103 K23 Landsberg am Lech Bayern, S Germany 48.03N 10.52E
Landsberg an der Warthe see Gorzów Wielkopolski
99 G25 Land's End headland SW England, UK 50.02N 5.41W
103 M22 Landshut Bayern, SE Germany 48.31N 12.09E
Landskron see Lanškroun
97 J22 Landskrona Skåne, S Sweden 55.52N 12.52E
100 I10 Landsmeer Noord-Holland, C Netherlands 52.25N 4.55E
97 J19 Landvetter ✕ (Göteborg) Västra Götaland, S Sweden 57.39N 12.22E
Landwarów see Lentvaris
25 R5 Lanett Alabama, S USA 32.52N 85.11W
110 C8 La Neuveville var. Neuveville, Ger. Neuenstadt. Neuchâtel, W Switzerland 47.05N 7.03E
97 G21 Langå var. Langaa. Århus, C Denmark 56.22N 9.55E
Langaa see Langå
164 G14 La'nga Co ⊚ W China
Langada see Lagkáda
Langades/Langadhás see Lagkadás
Langádhia/Langadia see Lagkádia
153 T14 Langar Rus. Lyangar. SE Tajikistan 37.04N 72.39E
152 M10 Langar Rus. Lyangar. Navoiy Viloyati, C Uzbekistan 40.27N 65.54E
148 M3 Langarūd Gīlān, NW Iran 37.12N 50.10E
9 V16 Langbank Saskatchewan, S Canada 50.01N 102.16W
31 P2 Langdon North Dakota, N USA 48.45N 98.22W
105 P12 Langeac Haute-Loire, C France 45.06N 3.31E
104 L8 Langeais Indre-et-Loire, C France 47.22N 0.27E
82 I8 Langeb, Wadi ≈ NE Sudan
Långed see Dals Långed
97 G25 Langeland island S Denmark
101 B18 Langemark West-Vlaanderen, W Belgium 50.55N 2.55E
103 G18 Langen Hessen, W Germany 49.58N 8.40E
103 J22 Langenau Baden-Württemberg, S Germany 48.30N 10.08E
9 V16 Langenburg Saskatchewan, S Canada 50.49N 101.43W
103 E16 Langenfeld Nordrhein-Westfalen, W Germany 51.06N 6.57E
110 L8 Längenfeld Tirol, W Austria 47.04N 10.59E
102 I12 Langenhagen Niedersachsen, N Germany 52.25N 9.43E
102 I12 Langenhagen ✕ (Hannover) Niedersachsen, NW Germany 52.28N 9.40E
111 W3 Langenlois Niederösterreich, NE Austria 48.28N 15.42E
110 E7 Langenthal Bern, NW Switzerland 47.13N 7.46E
111 W6 Langenwang Steiermark, E Austria 47.34N 15.39E
111 X3 Langenzersdorf Niederösterreich, E Austria 48.19N 16.22E
102 F9 Langeoog island NW Germany
126 Gg11 Langepas Khanty-Mansiyskiy Avtonomnyy Okrug, C Russian Federation 61.12N 75.24E
97 H23 Langeskov Fyn, C Denmark 55.22N 10.36E
97 G16 Langesund Telemark, S Norway 59.00N 9.43E
97 G17 Langesundsfjorden fjord S Norway
96 D10 Langevåg Møre og Romsdal, S Norway 62.25N 6.13E
167 P3 Langfang Hebei, E China 39.30N 116.39E
96 E9 Langfjorden fjord S Norway
31 Q8 Langford South Dakota, N USA 45.36N 97.48W
173 G6 Langgapayung Sumatera, W Indonesia 1.42N 99.57E
108 E9 Langhirano Emilia-Romagna, C Italy 44.37N 10.16E
99 K14 Langholm S Scotland, UK 55.13N 3.11W
94 I3 Langjökull glacier C Iceland
173 Ff2 Langkawi, Pulau island Peninsular Malaysia
175 R13 Langkesi, Kepulauan island group C Indonesia
178 Gg15 Langkha Tuk, Khao ▲ SW Thailand 9.19N 98.39E
12 L8 Langlade Québec, SE Canada 48.13N 75.58W
8 M17 Langley British Columbia, SW Canada 49.07N 122.39W
178 Jj7 Lang Mô Thanh Hoa, N Vietnam 19.36N 105.30E
Langnau see Langnau im Emmental
110 E8 Langnau im Emmental var. Langnau. Bern, W Switzerland 46.57N 7.46E
105 Q13 Langogne Lozère, S France 44.40N 3.52E
104 K13 Langon Gironde, SW France 47.43N 1.49W
La Ngounié see Ngounié
94 G10 Langøya island C Norway
164 G14 Langqên Zangbo ≈ China/India
106 K2 Langreo var. Sama de Langreo. Asturias, N Spain 43.18N 5.40W
105 S7 Langres Haute-Marne, N France 47.53N 5.20E
105 R8 Langres, Plateau de plateau C France
173 F4 Langsa Sumatera, W Indonesia 4.29N 97.53E
95 H16 Långsele Västernorrland, C Sweden 63.10N 17.04E
168 L12 Lang Shan ▲ N China
97 M14 Långshyttan Dalarna, C Sweden 60.25N 16.01E
178 K5 Lang Sơn var. Langson. Lang Sơn, N Vietnam 21.49N 106.45E
178 Gg14 Lang Suan Chumphon, SW Thailand 9.52N 99.03E
95 J14 Långträsk Norrbotten, N Sweden 65.22N 20.19E
27 N11 Langtry Texas, SW USA 29.46N 101.25W
105 P16 Languedoc cultural region S France
105 P15 Languedoc-Roussillon ◆ region S France
29 X10 L'Anguille River ≈ Arkansas, C USA
95 I16 Långviksmon Västernorrland, N Sweden 63.39N 18.45E
103 K22 Langweid Bayern, S Germany 48.29N 10.50E
166 J8 Langzhong Sichuan, C China 31.46N 105.55E
Lan Hsü see Lan Yü
9 U15 Lanigan Saskatchewan, S Canada 51.49N 105.01W
118 K5 Lanivtsi Ternopil's'ka Oblast', W Ukraine 49.52N 26.05E
143 Y13 Länkäran Rus. Lenkoran'. S Azerbaijan 38.46N 48.50E
104 L16 Lannemezan Hautes-Pyrénées, S France 43.07N 0.22E
104 G5 Lannion Côtes d'Armor, NW France 48.43N 3.27W
12 M11 L'Annonciation Québec, SE Canada 46.22N 74.51W
107 V5 L'Anoia ≈ NE Spain
20 I15 Lansdale Pennsylvania, NE USA 40.14N 75.13W
12 L14 Lansdowne Ontario, SE Canada 44.25N 76.00W
158 K9 Lansdowne Uttaranchal, N India 29.49N 78.42E
32 M3 L'Anse Michigan, N USA 46.45N 88.27W
13 S7 L'Anse-St-Jean Québec, SE Canada 48.14N 70.13W
95 K18 Länsi-Suomi ◆ province W Finland
31 Y11 Lansing Iowa, C USA 43.22N 91.11W
29 R4 Lansing Kansas, C USA 39.15N 94.54W
33 Q9 Lansing state capital Michigan, N USA 42.44N 84.33W
94 J12 Lansjärv Norrbotten, N Sweden 66.39N 22.10E
113 G17 Lanškroun Ger. Landskron. Pardubický Kraj, C Czech Republic 49.53N 16.34E
178 Gg16 Lanta, Ko island S Thailand
167 O15 Lantau Island Cant. Tai Yue Shan, Chin. Landao. island Hong Kong, S China
Lan-ts'ang Chiang see Mekong
175 Q7 Lanu Sulawesi, N Indonesia 1.00N 121.33E
109 D19 Lanusei Sardegna, Italy, C Mediterranean Sea 39.55N 9.31E
104 H7 Lanvaux, Landes de physical region NW France
169 W8 Lanxi Heilongjiang, NE China 46.18N 126.49E
167 R10 Lanxi Zhejiang, SE China 29.13N 119.30E
La Nyanga see Nyanga
167 T15 Lan Yü var. Huoshao Tao, var. Hungt'ou, Lan Hsü, Lanyü, Eng. Orchid Island; prev. Kotosho, Koto Sho. island SE Taiwan
66 P11 Lanzarote island Islas Canarias, Spain, NE Atlantic Ocean
165 V10 Lanzhou var. Lan-chou, Lanchow, Lan-chow; prev. Kaolan. Gansu, C China 36.01N 103.52E
108 B8 Lanzo Torinese Piemonte, NE Italy 45.18N 7.26E
179 P8 Laoag Luzon, N Philippines 18.11N 120.34E
179 R12 Laoang Samar, C Philippines 12.29N 125.01E
178 J5 Lao Cai Lao Cai, N Vietnam 22.29N 104.00E
Laodicea/Laodicea ad Mare see Al Lādhiqīyah
Laoet see Laut, Pulau
169 T11 Laoha He ≈ NE China
166 M8 Laohekou prev. Guanghua. Hubei, C China 32.21N 111.40E
Laoi, An see Lee
99 E19 Laois prev. Leix, Queen's County. cultural region C Ireland
Laojunmiao see Yumen
169 W12 Lao Ling ▲ NE China
66 Q11 La Oliva var. Oliva. Fuerteventura, Islas Canarias, Spain, NE Atlantic Ocean 28.36N 13.52W
Lao, Loch see Belfast Lough
Laolong see Longchuan
Lao Mangnai see Mangnai
105 P3 Laon var. la Laon; anc. Laudunum. Aisne, N France 49.34N 3.37E
Lao People's Democratic Republic see Laos
56 M3 La Orchila, Isla island N Venezuela
66 O11 La Orotava Tenerife, Islas Canarias, Spain, NE Atlantic Ocean 28.22N 16.31W
59 E14 La Oroya Junín, C Peru 11.29S 75.57W
178 Ii7 Laos off. Lao People's Democratic Republic. ◆ republic SE Asia
167 R5 Laoshan Wan bay E China
169 Y10 Laoye Ling ▲ NE China
62 J12 Lapa Paraná, S Brazil 25.46S 49.43W
105 P10 Lapalisse Allier, C France 46.13N 3.39E
56 F9 La Palma Cundinamarca, C Colombia 5.22N 74.24W
44 F7 La Palma Chalatenango, N El Salvador 14.19N 89.10W
45 W16 La Palma Darién, SE Panama 8.24N 78.09W
66 N11 La Palma island Islas Canarias, Spain, NE Atlantic Ocean
106 J14 La Palma del Condado Andalucía, S Spain 37.22N 6.33W
63 F18 La Paloma Durazno, C Uruguay 34.37S 54.07W
63 G20 La Paloma Rocha, E Uruguay 34.37S 54.07W
63 A21 La Pampa off. Provincia de La Pampa. ◆ province C Argentina
57 P8 La Paragua Bolívar, E Venezuela 6.53N 63.16W

◆ Country
● Country Capital
◇ Dependent Territory
○ Dependent Territory Capital
◆ Administrative Region
✕ International Airport
▲ Mountain
▲ Mountain Range
⩀ Volcano
≈ River
⊚ Lake
⊠ Reservoir

Lapatsichy – Leeds

121 O16 **Lapatsichy** *Rus.* Lopatichi. Mahilyowskaya Voblasts', E Belarus 53.34N 30.53E
63 C16 **La Paz** Entre Ríos, E Argentina 30.45S 59.36W
64 I11 **La Paz** Mendoza, C Argentina 33.27S 67.35W
59 J18 **La Paz** *var.* La Paz de Ayacucho. ● (Bolivia-legislative and administrative capital) La Paz, W Bolivia 16.30S 68.12W
44 H6 **La Paz** La Paz, SW Honduras 14.27N 87.41W
42 F9 **La Paz** Baja California Sur, NW Mexico 24.06N 110.18W
63 F20 **La Paz** Canelones, S Uruguay 34.46S 56.13W
59 J16 **La Paz** ◐ *department* W Bolivia
44 B9 **La Paz** ◐ *department* S El Salvador
44 G7 **La Paz** ◐ *department* SW Honduras
La Paz *see* El Alto, Bolivia
La Paz *see* Robles, Colombia
La Paz *see* La Paz Centro, Nicaragua
42 F9 **La Paz, Bahía de** *bay* W Mexico
44 I10 **La Paz Centro** *var.* La Paz. León, W Nicaragua 12.19N 86.40W
La Paz de Ayacucho *see* La Paz
56 J15 **La Pedrera** Amazonas, SE Colombia 1.19S 69.31W
33 S9 **Lapeer** Michigan, N USA 43.03N 83.19W
42 K6 **La Perla** Chihuahua, N Mexico 28.11N 104.28W
172 Pp1 **La Perouse Strait** *Jap.* Sōya-kaikyō, *Rus.* Proliv Laperuza. *strait* Japan/Russian Federation
65 I14 **La Perra, Salitral de** *salt lake* C Argentina
Laperuza, Proliv *see* La Perouse Strait
43 Q10 **La Pesca** Tamaulipas, C Mexico 23.49N 97.45W
42 M13 **La Piedad Cavadas** Michoacán de Ocampo, C Mexico 20.19N 102.01W
Lapines *see* Lafnitz
95 M16 **Lapinlahti** Itä-Suomi, C Finland 63.21N 27.25E
Lápithos *see* Lapta
24 K9 **Laplace** Louisiana, S USA 30.04N 90.28W
47 X12 **La Plaine** SE Dominica 15.19N 61.15W
181 P16 **la Plaine-des-Palmistes** C Réunion
94 K11 **Lapland** *Fin.* Lappi, *Swe.* Lappland. *cultural region* N Europe
30 M8 **La Plant** South Dakota, N USA 45.06N 100.40W
63 D20 **La Plata** Buenos Aires, E Argentina 34.56S 57.55W
56 D12 **La Plata** Huila, SW Colombia 2.25N 75.47W
23 W4 **La Plata** Maryland, NE USA 38.28N 76.55W
La Plata *see* Sucre
47 U6 **la Plata, Río de** ≈ C Puerto Rico
107 W4 **La Pobla de Lillet** Cataluña, NE Spain 42.15N 1.57E
107 U4 **La Pobla de Segur** Cataluña, NE Spain 42.15N 0.58E
13 S9 **La Pocatière** Québec, SE Canada 47.17N 70.04W
106 L3 **La Pola de Gordón** Castilla-León, N Spain 42.50N 5.38W
33 O11 **La Porte** Indiana, N USA 41.36N 86.43W
20 H13 **Laporte** Pennsylvania, NE USA 41.25N 76.28W
31 X13 **La Porte City** Iowa, C USA 42.19N 92.11W
64 J8 **La Posta** Catamarca, C Argentina 27.59S 65.32W
42 E8 **La Poza Grande** Baja California Sur, W Mexico 25.45N 111.58W
95 K16 **Lappajärvi** Länsi-Suomi, W Finland 63.11N 23.37E
95 L16 **Lappajärvi** ◎ W Finland
95 N18 **Lappeenranta** *Swe.* Villmanstrand. Etelä-Suomi, S Finland 61.04N 28.15E
95 J17 **Lappfjärd** *Fin.* Lapväärtti. Länsi-Suomi, W Finland 62.13N 21.34E
94 L12 **Lappi** *Swe.* Lappland. ◐ *province* N Finland
Lappi/Lappland *see* Lapland
Lappo *see* Lapua
63 C23 **Laprida** Buenos Aires, E Argentina 37.33S 60.46W
27 P13 **La Pryor** Texas, SW USA 28.56N 99.51W
142 B11 **Lâpseki** Çanakkale, NW Turkey 40.17N 26.36E
124 Nn2 **Lapta** *Gk.* Lápithos. NW Cyprus 35.19N 33.11E
Laptev Sea *see* Laptevykh, More
126 Kk5 **Laptevykh, More** *Eng.* Laptev Sea. *sea* Arctic Ocean
95 K16 **Lapua** *Swe.* Lappo. Länsi-Suomi, W Finland 62.57N 23.00E
107 P3 **La Puebla de Arganzón** País Vasco, N Spain 42.45N 2.49W
106 L14 **La Puebla de Cazalla** Andalucía, S Spain 37.13N 5.18W
106 M9 **La Puebla de Montalbán** Castilla-La Mancha, C Spain 39.52N 4.22W
56 I6 **La Puerta** Trujillo, NW Venezuela 9.09N 70.44W
179 Qq13 **Lapu-Lapu** C Philippines 10.18N 123.58E
Lapurdum *see* Bayonne
42 E7 **La Purísima** Baja California Sur, W Mexico 26.10N 112.04W
Lapväärtti *see* Lappfjärd
112 O10 **Łapy** Podlaskie, NE Poland 53.00N 22.50E
82 D6 **Laqiya Arba'in** Northern, NW Sudan 20.01N 28.01E
64 J4 **La Quiaca** Jujuy, N Argentina 22.12S 65.36W
109 J14 **L'Aquila** *var.* Aquila, Aquila degli Abruzzo. Abruzzo, C Italy 42.21N 13.24E
149 Q13 **Lār** Fārs, S Iran 27.42N 54.19E
56 J5 **Lara** *off.* Estado Lara. ◐ *state* NW Venezuela
106 G2 **Laracha** Galicia, NW Spain 43.14N 8.34W
76 G5 **Larache** *var.* al Araïch, El Araïch, El Araïche, *anc.* Lixus. NW Morocco 35.16N 6.07W
105 T14 **Laragne-Montéglin** Hautes-Alpes, SE France 44.21N 5.46E
106 M13 **La Rambla** Andalucía, S Spain 37.37N 4.44W
35 Y17 **Laramie** Wyoming, C USA 41.18N 105.35W
35 X15 **Laramie Mountains** ▲▲ Wyoming, C USA
35 Y16 **Laramie River** ≈ Wyoming, C USA
62 H12 **Laranjeiras do Sul** Paraná, S Brazil 25.22S 52.22W
Larantoeka *see* Larantuka
175 Qq16 **Larantuka** *prev.* Larantoeka. Flores, C Indonesia 8.20S 123.00E
176 V15 **Larat** Pulau Larat, E Indonesia 7.07S 131.46E
176 V15 **Larat, Pulau** *island* Kepulauan Tanimbar, E Indonesia
97 P19 **Lärbro** Gotland, SE Sweden 57.46N 18.49E
108 A9 **Larche, Col de** *pass* France/Italy 44.26N 6.54E
12 H8 **Larder Lake** Ontario, S Canada 48.06N 79.43W
107 O2 **Laredo** Cantabria, N Spain 43.22N 3.22W
27 Q15 **Laredo** Texas, SW USA 27.30N 99.30W
42 H9 **La Reforma** Sinaloa, W Mexico 25.04N 108.03W
100 N11 **Laren** Gelderland, E Netherlands 52.12N 6.22E
100 J11 **Laren** Noord-Holland, C Netherlands 52.15N 5.13E
104 K13 **la Réole** Gironde, SW France 44.34N 0.00W
La Réunion *see* Réunion
Largeau *see* Faya
105 U13 **l'Argentière-la-Bessée** Hautes-Alpes, SE France 44.49N 6.34E
155 O4 **Lar Gerd** *var.* Largird. Balkh, N Afghanistan 35.36N 66.48E
Largird *see* Lar Gerd
25 V12 **Largo** Florida, SE USA 27.54N 82.47W
39 Q9 **Largo, Canon** *valley* New Mexico, SW USA
46 D6 **Largo, Cayo** *island* W Cuba
25 Z17 **Largo, Key** *island* Florida Keys, Florida, SE USA
98 H12 **Largs** W Scotland, UK 55.47N 4.50W
104 I16 **la Rhune** *var.* Larrún. ▲ France/Spain *see also* Larrún 43.19N 1.36W
la Riege *see* Ariège
31 Q4 **Larimore** North Dakota, N USA 47.54N 97.37W
109 L15 **Larino** Molise, C Italy 41.46N 14.50E
Lario *see* Como, Lago di
64 J9 **La Rioja** La Rioja, NW Argentina 29.25S 66.49W
64 I9 **La Rioja** *off.* Provincia de La Rioja. ◐ *province* NW Argentina
107 O4 **La Rioja** ◐ *autonomous community* N Spain
117 F16 **Lárisa** *var.* Larissa. Thessalía, C Greece 39.38N 22.27E
Larissa *see* Lárisa
155 Q13 **Lārkāna** *var.* Larkhana. Sind, SE Pakistan 27.31N 68.18E
Larkhana *see* Lārkāna
Larnaca *see* Lárnaka
124 Nn3 **Lárnaka** *var.* Larnaca, Larnax. SE Cyprus 34.54N 33.38E
124 Nn3 **Lárnaka** ✕ SE Cyprus 34.52N 33.38E
Larnax *see* Lárnaka
99 G14 **Larne** *Ir.* Latharna. E Northern Ireland, UK 54.51N 5.49W
28 L5 **Larned** Kansas, C USA 38.10N 99.06W
106 L3 **La Robla** Castilla-León, N Spain 42.48N 5.37W
106 J10 **La Roca de la Sierra** Extremadura, W Spain 39.06N 6.41W
101 K22 **La Roche-en-Ardenne** Luxembourg, SE Belgium 50.11N 5.35E
104 L11 **la Rochefoucauld** Charente, W France 45.43N 0.23E
104 J10 **la Rochelle** *anc.* Rupella. Charente-Maritime, W France 46.09N 1.07W
104 I9 **la Roche-sur-Yon** *prev.* Bourbon Vendée, Napoléon-Vendée. Vendée, NW France 46.40N 1.25W
107 Q10 **La Roda** Castilla-La Mancha, C Spain 39.13N 2.10W
106 L14 **La Roda de Andalucía** Andalucía, S Spain 37.12N 4.45W
47 P9 **La Romana** E Dominican Republic 18.25N 69.00W
9 T13 **La Ronge** Saskatchewan, C Canada 55.07N 105.18W
9 U13 **La Ronge, Lac** ◎ Saskatchewan, C Canada
24 K10 **Larose** Louisiana, S USA 29.34N 90.22W
44 M7 **La Rosita** Región Autónoma Atlántico Norte, NE Nicaragua 13.55N 84.23W
189 Q3 **Larrimah** Northern Territory, N Australia 15.30S 133.12E
64 N11 **Larroque** Entre Ríos, E Argentina 33.05S 59.06W
107 Q2 **Larrún** *Fr.* la Rhune. ▲ France/Spain *see also* la Rhune 43.18N 1.35W
205 X6 **Lars Christensen Coast** *physical region* Antarctica
41 Q14 **Larsen Bay** Kodiak Island, Alaska, USA 57.32N 153.58W
204 I5 **Larsen Ice Shelf** *ice shelf* Antarctica
15 K3 **Larsen Sound** *sound* Nunavut, N Canada
La Rúa *see* A Rúa de Valdeorras
104 K16 **Laruns** Pyrénées-Atlantiques, SW France 43.00N 0.25W
97 G16 **Larvik** Vestfold, S Norway 59.03N 10.01E
126 H11 **Lar'yak** Khanty-Mansiyskiy Avtonomnyy Okrug, C Russian Federation 61.09N 80.01E
La-sa *see* Lhasa
175 Tt11 **Lasahata** Pulau Seram, E Indonesia 2.52S 128.27E
Lasahau *see* Lasihao
39 O6 **La Sal** Utah, W USA 38.19N 109.14W
12 C17 **La Salle** Ontario, S Canada 42.13N 83.05W
32 L11 **La Salle** Illinois, N USA 41.19N 89.06W
47 O9 **Las Americas** ✕ (Santo Domingo) S Dominican Republic 18.24N 69.38W
81 G17 **La Sangha** ◐ *province* N Congo
39 V6 **Las Animas** Colorado, C USA 38.04N 103.13W
110 D10 **La Sarine** *var.* Sarine. ≈ SW Switzerland
110 B9 **La Sarraz** Vaud, W Switzerland 46.40N 6.32E
10 H12 **La Sarre** Québec, SE Canada 48.49N 79.12W
56 L3 **Las Aves, Islas** *var.* Islas de Aves. *island group* N Venezuela
57 N7 **Las Bonitas** Bolívar, C Venezuela 7.50N 65.40W
106 K15 **Las Cabezas de San Juan** Andalucía, S Spain 36.58N 5.55W
63 G19 **Lascano** Rocha, E Uruguay 33.40S 54.12W
64 I5 **Lascar, Volcán** ▲ N Chile 23.22S 67.33W
43 T15 **Las Choapas** *var.* Choapas. Veracruz-Llave, SE Mexico 17.51N 94.00W
39 R15 **Las Cruces** New Mexico, SW USA 32.19N 106.49W
Lasdehnen *see* Krasnoznamensk
107 V4 **La See d'Urgel** *var.* La Seu d'Urgell, Seo de Urgel. Cataluña, NE Spain 42.22N 1.27E
La Selle *see* Selle, Pic de la
64 G9 **La Serena** Coquimbo, C Chile 29.54S 71.18W
106 K11 **La Serena** *physical region* W Spain
La Seu d'Urgell *see* La See d'Urgel
105 T16 **la Seyne-sur-Mer** Var, SE France 43.07N 5.52E
63 D21 **Las Flores** Buenos Aires, E Argentina 36.03S 59.07W
64 H9 **Las Flores** San Juan, W Argentina 30.14S 69.10W
9 S14 **Lashburn** Saskatchewan, S Canada 53.09N 109.37W
64 I11 **Las Heras** Mendoza, W Argentina 32.46S 68.51W
178 Gg4 **Lashio** Shan State, E Burma 22.58N 97.48E
154 M8 **Lashkar Gāh** *var.* Lash-Kar-Gar'. Helmand, S Afghanistan 31.34N 64.21E
Lash-Kar-Gar' *see* Lashkar Gāh
175 Qq13 **Lasihao** *var.* Lasahau. Pulau Muna, C Indonesia 5.01S 122.23E
109 N21 **La Sila** ▲▲ SW Italy
65 H23 **La Silueta, Cerro** ▲ S Chile 52.22S 72.09W
44 L9 **La Sirena** Región Autónoma Atlántico Sur, E Nicaragua 12.58N 84.42W
112 J13 **Łask** Łódzkie, C Poland 51.36N 19.06E
111 V11 **Laško** *Ger.* Tüffer. C Slovenia 46.08N 15.13E
65 H14 **Las Lajas** Neuquén, W Argentina 38.31S 70.22W
65 H15 **Las Lajas, Cerro** ▲ W Argentina 38.49S 70.42W
64 M6 **Las Lomitas** Formosa, N Argentina 24.44S 60.34W
43 V16 **Las Margaritas** Chiapas, SE Mexico 16.15N 91.58W
Las Marismas *see* Guadalquivir, Marismas del
56 M6 **Las Mercedes** Guárico, N Venezuela 9.06N 66.22W
44 F6 **Las Minas, Cerro** ▲ W Honduras 14.33N 88.41W
107 O11 **La Solana** Castilla-La Mancha, C Spain 38.55N 3.13W
47 Q14 **La Soufrière** ※ Saint Vincent, Saint Vincent and the Grenadines 13.20N 61.11W
104 M10 **la Souterraine** Creuse, C France 46.15N 1.28E
64 N7 **Las Palmas** Chaco, N Argentina 27.07S 58.45W
45 Q16 **Las Palmas** Veraguas, W Panama 8.09N 81.28W
66 P12 **Las Palmas** *var.* Las Palmas de Gran Canaria. Gran Canaria, Islas Canarias, Spain, NE Atlantic Ocean 28.07N 15.27W
66 P12 **Las Palmas** ◐ *province* Islas Canarias, Spain, NE Atlantic Ocean
66 Q12 **Las Palmas** ✕ Gran Canaria, Islas Canarias, Spain, NE Atlantic Ocean
Las Palmas de Gran Canaria *see* Las Palmas
42 D6 **Las Palomas** Baja California Sur, W Mexico 31.43N 107.37W
107 P10 **Las Pedroñeras** Castilla-La Mancha, C Spain 39.27N 2.40W
108 E10 **La Spezia** Liguria, NW Italy 44.07N 9.49E
63 F20 **Las Piedras** Canelones, S Uruguay 34.42S 56.13W
65 J18 **Las Plumas** Chubut, S Argentina 43.46S 67.15W
63 B18 **Las Rosas** Santa Fe, C Argentina 32.27S 61.30W
Lassa *see* Lhasa
37 O4 **Lassen Peak** ▲ California, W USA 40.27N 121.28W
204 K6 **Lassiter Coast** *physical region* Antarctica
111 V9 **Lassnitz** ≈ SE Austria
13 O12 **L'Assomption** Québec, SE Canada 45.48N 73.27W
13 N11 **L'Assomption** ≈ Québec, SE Canada
45 S17 **Las Tablas** Los Santos, S Panama 7.45N 80.17W
Lastarria, Volcán *see* Azufre, Volcán
39 V4 **Last Chance** Colorado, C USA 39.41N 103.34W
Last Frontier, The *see* Alaska
9 U16 **Last Mountain Lake** ◎ Saskatchewan, S Canada
64 H9 **Las Tórtolas, Cerro** ▲ W Argentina 29.57S 69.49W
63 C14 **Las Toscas** Santa Fe, C Argentina 28.22S 59.19W
81 F19 **Lastoursville** Ogooué-Lolo, E Gabon 0.49S 12.43E
115 F16 **Lastovo** *It.* Lagosta. *island* SW Croatia
115 F16 **Lastovski Kanal** *channel* SW Croatia
42 E6 **Las Tres Vírgenes, Volcán** ※ W Mexico 27.27N 112.34W
42 F4 **Las Trincheras** Sonora, NW Mexico 30.21N 111.27W
57 N8 **Las Trincheras** Bolívar, E Venezuela 6.57N 64.49W
46 H7 **Las Tunas** *var.* Victoria de las Tunas. Las Tunas, E Cuba 20.58N 76.58W
La Suisse *see* Switzerland
42 I5 **Las Varas** Chihuahua, N Mexico 29.35N 108.01W
42 J12 **Las Varas** Nayarit, C Mexico 21.11N 105.09W
64 L10 **Las Varillas** Córdoba, E Argentina 31.54S 62.45W
37 X11 **Las Vegas** Nevada, W USA 36.09N 115.10W
39 T10 **Las Vegas** New Mexico, SW USA 35.35N 105.15W
195 W8 **Lata** Nendö, Solomon Islands 10.45S 165.43E
11 R10 **La Tabatière** Québec, E Canada 50.51N 58.58W
58 C6 **Latacunga** Cotopaxi, C Ecuador 0.58S 78.36W
204 I7 **Latady Island** *island* Antarctica
56 E14 **La Tagua** Putumayo, S Colombia 0.04S 74.39W
Latakia *see* Al Lādhiqīyah
94 J10 **Lätäseno** ≈ NW Finland
12 H9 **Latchford** Ontario, S Canada 47.20N 79.45W
12 J13 **Latchford Bridge** Ontario, SE Canada 45.16N 77.29W
200 Ss12 **Late** *island* Vava'u Group, N Tonga
159 P15 **Lātehār** Jhārkhand, N India 23.48N 84.28E
13 R7 **Laterrière** Québec, SE Canada 48.17N 71.10W
104 J13 **la Teste** Gironde, SW France 44.37N 1.04W
27 V8 **Latexo** Texas, SW USA 31.24N 95.28W
20 L10 **Latham** New York, NE USA 42.45N 73.45W
Latharna *see* Larne
110 B9 **La Thielle** *var.* Thièle. ≈ W Switzerland
29 R3 **Lathrop** Missouri, C USA 39.33N 94.19W
109 I16 **Latina** *prev.* Littoria. Lazio, C Italy 41.28N 12.52E
43 R14 **La Tinaja** Veracruz-Llave, S Mexico
108 J7 **Latisana** Friuli-Venezia Giulia, NE Italy 45.47N 13.01E
Latium *see* Lazio
117 K25 **Lató** *site of ancient city* Kríti, Greece, E Mediterranean Sea 35.09N 25.40E
197 J7 **La Tontouta** ✕ (Noumea) Province Sud, S New Caledonia 22.06S 166.12E
57 N4 **La Tortuga, Isla** *var.* Isla Tortuga. *island* N Venezuela
110 C10 **La Tour-de-Peilz** *var.* La Tour de Peilz. Vaud, SW Switzerland 46.28N 6.52E
105 S11 **la Tour-du-Pin** Isère, E France 45.34N 5.25E
104 J11 **la Tremblade** Charente-Maritime, W France 45.45N 1.07W
104 L10 **la Trimouille** Vienne, W France 46.27N 1.02E
44 J9 **La Trinidad** Estelí, NW Nicaragua 12.57N 86.13W
179 P9 **La Trinidad** Luzon, N Philippines 16.30N 120.39E
43 V16 **La Trinitaria** Chiapas, SE Mexico 16.02N 92.00W
47 Q11 **la Trinité** E Martinique 14.43N 60.57W
13 U7 **La Trinité-des-Monts** Québec, SE Canada 48.07N 68.31W
20 C15 **Latrobe** Pennsylvania, NE USA 40.18N 79.19W
191 P13 **La Trobe River** ≈ Victoria, SE Australia
Lattakia/Lattaquié *see* Al Lādhiqīyah
175 Tt11 **Latu** Pulau Seram, E Indonesia 3.24S 128.37E
13 P9 **La Tuque** Québec, SE Canada 47.25N 72.46W
161 G14 **Lātūr** Mahārāshtra, C India 18.24N 76.34E
120 G8 **Latvia** *off.* Republic of Latvia, *Ger.* Lettland, *Latv.* Latvija, Latvijas Republika; *prev.* Latvian SSR, *Rus.* Latviyskaya SSR. ◆ *republic* NE Europe
Latvian SSR/Latvija/Latvijas Republika/Latviyskaya SSR *see* Latvia
195 O12 **Lau** New Britain, E PNG 5.46S 151.21E
183 R9 **Lau Basin** *undersea feature* S Pacific Ocean
103 O15 **Lauchhammer** Brandenburg, E Germany 51.27N 13.32E
Laudunum *see* Laon
Laudus *see* St-Lô
Lauenburg/Lauenburg in Pommern *see* Lębork
103 L20 **Lauf an der Pegnitz** Bayern, SE Germany 49.31N 11.16E
110 D7 **Laufen** Basel, NW Switzerland 47.25N 7.31E
111 P5 **Lauffen** Salzburg, NW Austria 47.54N 12.57E
94 I2 **Laugarbakki** Nordhurland Vestra, N Iceland 65.18N 20.51W
94 I4 **Laugarvatn** Sudhurland, SW Iceland 64.09N 20.43W
33 O3 **Laughing Fish Point** *headland* Michigan, N USA 46.31N 87.01W
197 L14 **Lau Group** *island group* E Fiji
Lauis *see* Lugano
95 M17 **Laukaa** Länsi-Suomi, W Finland 62.27N 25.58E
120 D12 **Laukuva** Tauragė, W Lithuania 55.37N 22.12E
Laun *see* Louny
191 P16 **Launceston** Tasmania, SE Australia 41.25S 147.07E
99 I24 **Launceston** *anc.* Dunheved. SW England, UK 50.37N 4.21W
56 C13 **La Unión** Nariño, SW Colombia 1.34N 77.09W
44 H8 **La Unión** La Unión, SE El Salvador 13.19N 87.52W
44 I6 **La Unión** Olancho, C Honduras 15.02N 86.40W
42 M15 **La Unión** Guerrero, S Mexico 17.59N 101.48W
43 Y14 **La Unión** Quintana Roo, E Mexico 18.00N 101.48W
107 S13 **La Unión** Murcia, SE Spain 37.37N 0.53W
56 L7 **La Unión** Barinas, C Venezuela 8.12N 67.46W
44 B10 **La Unión** ◐ *department* E El Salvador
40 H11 **Laupāhoehoe** *var.* Laupahoehoe. Hawai'i, USA, C Pacific Ocean 20.00N 155.15W
103 I23 **Laupheim** Baden-Württemberg, S Germany 48.13N 9.54E
189 W3 **Laura** Queensland, NE Australia 15.37S 144.34E
201 X2 **Laura** *atoll* Majuro Atoll, SE Marshall Islands
Laurana *see* Lovran
56 L8 **La Urbana** Bolívar, C Venezuela 7.05N 66.58W
23 Y4 **Laurel** Delaware, NE USA 38.33N 75.34W
25 V14 **Laurel** Florida, SE USA 27.07N 82.27W
23 W3 **Laurel** Maryland, NE USA 39.06N 76.51W
24 M6 **Laurel** Mississippi, S USA 31.41N 89.10W
35 U11 **Laurel** Montana, NW USA 45.40N 108.46W
31 R13 **Laurel** Nebraska, C USA 42.25N 97.04W
20 H15 **Laureldale** Pennsylvania, NE USA 40.24N 75.52W
20 C16 **Laurel Hill** *ridge* Pennsylvania, NE USA
31 T12 **Laurens** Iowa, C USA 42.51N 94.51W
23 P11 **Laurens** South Carolina, SE USA 34.29N 82.01W
Laurentian Highlands *see* Laurentian Mountains
13 P10 **Laurentian Mountains** *var.* Laurentian Highlands, *Fr.* Les Laurentides. *plateau* Newfoundland and Labrador/Québec, Canada
13 O12 **Laurentides** Québec, SE Canada 45.51N 73.49W
Laurentides, Les *see* Laurentian Mountains
109 M19 **Lauria** Basilicata, S Italy 40.03N 15.49E
204 I1 **Laurie Island** *island* Antarctica
23 T11 **Laurinburg** North Carolina, SE USA 34.51N 79.40W
32 M2 **Laurium** Michigan, N USA 47.14N 88.26W
Lauru *see* Choiseul
110 B9 **Lausanne** *It.* Losanna. Vaud, SW Switzerland 46.31N 6.39E
103 Q16 **Lausche** *Cz.* Luže. ▲ Czech Republic/Germany *see also* Luže 50.52N 14.39E
103 Q16 **Lausitzer Bergland** *var.* Lausitzer Gebirge, *Cz.* Gory Lużyckie, Lužické Hory, *Eng.* Lusatian Mountains. ▲▲ E Germany
Lausitzer Gebirge *see* Lausitzer Bergland
Lausitzer Neisse *see* Neisse
105 T12 **Lautaret, Col du** *pass* SE France 45.03N 6.23E
65 G15 **Lautaro** Araucanía, C Chile 38.31S 72.27W
103 F21 **Lauter** ≈ W Germany
110 I7 **Lauterach** Vorarlberg, NW Austria 47.28N 9.43E
103 I17 **Lauterbach** Hessen, C Germany 50.37N 9.24E
110 E9 **Lauterbrunnen** Bern, C Switzerland 46.36N 7.52E
175 Nn12 **Laut Kecil, Kepulauan** *island group* N Indonesia
197 H14 **Lautoka** Viti Levu, W Fiji 17.40S 177.25E
175 Nn11 **Laut, Pulau** *prev.* Laoet. *island* Borneo, C Indonesia
174 Jj4 **Laut, Pulau** *island* Kepulauan Natuna, W Indonesia
175 Nn11 **Laut, Selat** *strait* Borneo, C Indonesia
173 F4 **Laut Tawar, Danau** ◎ Sumatera, NW Indonesia
201 V14 **Lauvergne Island** *island* Chuuk, C Micronesia
100 M5 **Lauwers Meer** ◎ N Netherlands
100 M4 **Lauwersoog** Groningen, NE Netherlands 53.25N 6.14E
104 M14 **Lauzerte** Tarn-et-Garonne, S France 44.15N 1.08E
27 U13 **Lavaca Bay** *bay* Texas, SW USA
27 U12 **Lavaca River** ≈ Texas, SW USA
13 O12 **Laval** Québec, SE Canada 45.32N 73.44W
104 J6 **Laval** Mayenne, NW France 48.04N 0.46W
13 T6 **Laval** ≈ Québec, SE Canada
107 S9 **La Vall d'Uixó** *var.* Vall d'Uxo. País Valenciano, E Spain 39.49N 0.15W
63 F19 **Lavalleja** ◐ *department* S Uruguay
13 O12 **Lavaltrie** Québec, SE Canada 45.56N 73.14W
195 X17 **Lavanggu** Rennell, S Solomon Islands 11.39S 160.13E
149 O14 **Lāvān, Jazīreh-ye** *island* S Iran
111 U8 **Lavant** ≈ S Austria
120 G5 **Lavassaare** *Ger.* Lawassaar. Pärnumaa, SW Estonia 58.31N 24.22E
106 L3 **La Vecilla de Curueño** Castilla-León, N Spain 42.51N 5.24W
47 N8 **La Vega** *var.* Concepción de la Vega. C Dominican Republic 19.15N 70.32W
La Vela *see* La Vela de Coro
56 J4 **La Vela de Coro** *var.* La Vela. Falcón, N Venezuela 11.26N 69.35W
105 N17 **Lavelanet** Ariège, S France 42.55N 1.49E
109 M17 **Lavello** Basilicata, S Italy 41.03N 15.48E
38 J8 **La Verkin** Utah, W USA 37.12N 113.16W
28 J8 **Laverne** Oklahoma, C USA 36.42N 99.53W
27 S12 **La Vernia** Texas, SW USA 29.19N 98.07W
95 K18 **Lavia** Länsi-Suomi, W Finland 61.36N 22.34E
12 I12 **Lavieille, Lake** ◎ Ontario, SE Canada
96 C12 **Lavik** Sogn og Fjordane, S Norway 61.06N 5.25E
La Vila Joíosa *see* Villajoyosa
35 U10 **Lavina** Montana, NW USA 46.18N 108.55W
204 H5 **Lavoisier Island** *island* Antarctica
25 U2 **Lavonia** Georgia, SE USA 34.26N 83.06W
105 R13 **la Voulte-sur-Rhône** Ardèche, E France 44.49N 4.46E
127 Q3 **Lavrentiya** Chukotskiy Avtonomnyy Okrug, NE Russian Federation 65.33N 171.12W
117 H20 **Lávrio** *prev.* Lávrion. Attikí, C Greece 37.43N 24.03E
Lávrion *see* Lávrio
85 L22 **Lavumisa** *prev.* Gollel. SE Swaziland 27.20S 31.51E
155 T4 **Lawarai Pass** *pass* N Pakistan 35.22N 71.48E
Lawassaar *see* Lavassaare
147 P16 **Lawdar** SW Yemen 13.49N 45.54E
27 Q7 **Lawn** Texas, SW USA 32.07N 99.45W
205 Y4 **Law Promontory** *headland* Antarctica
79 O14 **Lawra** NW Ghana 10.40N 2.55W
193 E23 **Lawrence** Otago, South Island, NZ 45.53S 169.43E
33 P14 **Lawrence** Indiana, N USA 39.49N 86.01W
29 Q4 **Lawrence** Kansas, C USA 38.58N 95.14W
21 O10 **Lawrence** Massachusetts, NE USA 42.42N 71.09W
22 L5 **Lawrenceburg** Kentucky, S USA 38.02N 84.54W
22 I10 **Lawrenceburg** Tennessee, S USA 35.14N 87.19W
25 T3 **Lawrenceville** Georgia, SE USA 33.57N 83.59W
33 N15 **Lawrenceville** Illinois, N USA 38.43N 87.40W
23 V7 **Lawrenceville** Virginia, NE USA 36.45N 77.51W
29 S3 **Lawson** Missouri, C USA 39.26N 94.12W
28 L12 **Lawton** Oklahoma, C USA 34.35N 98.19W
146 I4 **Lawz, Jabal al** ▲ NW Saudi Arabia 28.45N 35.20E
97 L16 **Laxå** Örebro, C Sweden 59.00N 14.37E
129 T5 **Laya** ≈ NW Russian Federation
59 I19 **La Yarada** Tacna, SW Peru 18.14S 70.30W
147 S15 **Layjūn** C Yemen 15.27N 49.16E
147 Q9 **Laylā** *var.* Laila. Ar Riyāḍ, C Saudi Arabia 22.13N 46.39E
25 P4 **Lay Lake** ⊠ Alabama, S USA
47 P14 **Layou** Saint Vincent, Saint Vincent and the Grenadines 13.11N 61.16W
La Youne *see* El Ayoun
199 Jj5 **Laysan Island** *island* Hawaiian Islands, Hawaii, USA, C Pacific Ocean
38 L2 **Layton** Utah, W USA 41.03N 112.00W
36 L5 **Laytonville** California, N USA 39.39N 123.30W
180 H17 **Lazare, Pointe** *headland* Mahé, NE Seychelles 4.46S 55.28E
127 O14 **Lazarev** Khabarovskiy Kray, SE Russian Federation 52.11N 141.18E
114 L12 **Lazarevac** Serbia, C Serbia 44.25N 20.17E
67 N22 **Lazarev Sea** *sea* Antarctica
42 M15 **Lázaro Cárdenas** Michoacán de Ocampo, SW Mexico 17.55N 102.12W
121 F15 **Lazdijai** Alytus, S Lithuania 54.13N 23.33E
109 H15 **Lazio** *anc.* Latium. ◐ *region* C Italy
113 A16 **Lázně Kynžvart** *Ger.* Bad Königswart. Karlovarský Kraj, W Czech Republic 50.00N 12.40E
Lazovsk *see* Sîngerei
178 Ii13 **Leach** Poŭthĭsăt, W Cambodia 12.19N 103.45E
29 X9 **Leachville** Arkansas, C USA 35.56N 90.15W
30 I9 **Lead** South Dakota, N USA 44.21N 103.45W
9 S16 **Leader** Saskatchewan, S Canada 50.55N 109.31W
21 S6 **Lead Mountain** ▲ Maine, NE USA 44.53N 68.07W
39 R5 **Leadville** Colorado, C USA 39.15N 106.17W
9 V12 **Leaf Rapids** Manitoba, C Canada 56.30N 100.01W
24 M7 **Leaf River** ≈ Mississippi, S USA
27 W11 **League City** Texas, SW USA 29.30N 95.05W
94 K8 **Leaibevuotna** *Nor.* Olderfjord. Finnmark, N Norway 70.29N 24.58E
25 N7 **Leakesville** Mississippi, S USA 31.09N 88.33W
27 Q11 **Leakey** Texas, SW USA 29.43N 99.45W
Leal *see* Lihula
85 G15 **Lealui** Western, W Zambia 15.12S 22.58E
Leamhcán *see* Lucan
12 C18 **Leamington** Ontario, S Canada 42.03N 82.34W
Leamington/Leamington Spa *see* Royal Leamington Spa
Leammi *see* Lemmenjoki
27 S10 **Leander** Texas, SW USA 30.34N 97.51W
62 F13 **Leandro N.Alem** Misiones, NE Argentina 27.34S 55.15W
99 A20 **Leane, Lough** *Ir.* Loch Léin. ◎ SW Ireland
188 G8 **Learmouth** Western Australia 22.17S 114.03E
Leau *see* Zoutleeuw
L'Eau d'Heure *see* Plate Taille, Lac de la
202 D12 **Leava** Île Futuna, S Wallis and Futuna
Leavdnja *see* Lakselv
29 R3 **Leavenworth** Kansas, C USA 39.17N 94.55W
34 I8 **Leavenworth** Washington, NW USA 47.36N 120.39W
94 L8 **Leavvajohka** *var.* Levajok, Lœvvajok. Finnmark, N Norway 69.57N 26.18E
29 R4 **Leawood** Kansas, C USA 38.57N 94.37W
112 H6 **Łeba** *Ger.* Leba. Pomorskie, N Poland 54.45N 17.31E
112 I6 **Łeba** *Ger.* Leba. ≈ N Poland
103 D20 **Lebach** Saarland, SW Germany 49.25N 6.54E
Łeba, Jezioro *see* Łebsko, Jezioro
179 R17 **Lebak** Mindanao, S Philippines 6.28N 124.03E
175 Oo11 **Lebani, Teluk** *bay* Sulawesi, C Indonesia
33 O13 **Lebanon** Indiana, N USA 40.03N 86.28W
22 L6 **Lebanon** Kentucky, S USA 37.34N 85.15W
29 U6 **Lebanon** Missouri, C USA 37.40N 92.39W
21 N9 **Lebanon** New Hampshire, NE USA 43.40N 72.15W
34 G12 **Lebanon** Oregon, NW USA 44.32N 122.54W
20 H15 **Lebanon** Pennsylvania, NE USA 40.20N 76.24W
22 J8 **Lebanon** Tennessee, S USA 36.13N 86.16W
23 P7 **Lebanon** Virginia, NE USA 36.54N 82.04W
144 G6 **Lebanon** *off.* Republic of Lebanon, *Ar.* Al Lubnān, *Fr.* Liban. ◆ *republic* SW Asia
22 K6 **Lebanon Junction** Kentucky, S USA 37.49N 85.43W
Lebanon, Mount *see* Liban, Jebel
152 J10 **Lebap** Lebapskiy Velayat, NE Turkmenistan 41.04N 61.49E
Lebapskiy Velayat *see* Lebap Welaýaty
152 H11 **Lebap Welaýaty** *Rus.* Lebapskiy Velayat; *prev.* *Rus.* Chardzhevskaya Oblast', *Turkm.* Chärjew Oblasty. ◐ *province* E Turkmenistan
Lebasee *see* Łebsko, Jezioro
101 F17 **Lebbeke** Oost-Vlaanderen, NW Belgium 51.00N 4.08E
37 S14 **Lebec** California, W USA 34.51N 118.52W
Lebedin *see* Lebedyn
126 Ll12 **Lebedinyy** Respublika Sakha (Yakutiya), NE Russian Federation 58.23N 125.24E
130 L6 **Lebedyan'** Lipetskaya Oblast', W Russian Federation 53.00N 39.11E
119 T4 **Lebedyn** *Rus.* Lebedin. Sums'ka Oblast', NE Ukraine 50.36N 34.30E
10 I12 **Lebel-sur-Quévillon** Québec, SE Canada 49.01N 76.55W
94 L8 **Lebesby** Finnmark, N Norway 70.31N 27.00E
104 M9 **le Blanc** Indre, C France 46.38N 1.04E
29 P5 **Lebo** Kansas, C USA 38.22N 95.50W
81 L15 **Lebo** Orientale, N Dem. Rep. Congo 4.30N 23.58E
112 H6 **Lębork** *var.* Lębórk, *Ger.* Lauenburg, Lauenburg in Pommern. Pomorskie, N Poland 54.31N 17.43E
105 O17 **le Boulou** Pyrénées-Orientales, S France 42.31N 2.49E
110 A9 **Le Brassus** Vaud, W Switzerland 46.35N 6.14E
106 J15 **Lebrija** Andalucía, S Spain 36.55N 6.04W
112 G6 **Łebsko, Jezioro** *Ger.* Lebasee; *prev.* Jezioro Łeba. ◎ N Poland
65 F14 **Lebu** Bío Bío, C Chile 37.34S 73.37W
Lebyazh'ye *see* Akku
106 F6 **Leça da Palmeira** Porto, N Portugal 41.12N 8.43W
105 U15 **le Cannet** Alpes-Maritimes, SE France 43.35N 7.00E
Le Cap *see* Cap-Haïtien
105 P2 **le Cateau-Cambrésis** Nord, N France 50.05N 3.32E
109 Q18 **Lecce** Puglia, SE Italy 40.22N 18.10E
108 D7 **Lecco** Lombardia, N Italy 45.49N 9.27E
31 V10 **Le Center** Minnesota, N USA 44.23N 93.43W
110 J7 **Lech** Vorarlberg, W Austria 47.14N 10.10E
103 K22 **Lech** ≈ Austria/Germany
117 D19 **Lechainá** *var.* Lehena, Lekhainá. Dytikí Ellás, S Greece 37.56N 21.16E
104 J11 **le Château d'Oléron** Charente-Maritime, W France 45.53N 1.12W
105 R3 **le Chesne** Ardennes, N France 49.33N 4.42E
105 R13 **le Cheylard** Ardèche, E France 44.55N 4.27E
110 K7 **Lechtaler Alpen** ▲▲ W Austria
102 H6 **Leck** Schleswig-Holstein, N Germany 54.45N 9.00E
12 L9 **Lecointre, Lac** ◎ Québec, SE Canada
24 H7 **Lecompte** Louisiana, S USA 31.05N 92.24W
105 Q9 **le Creusot** Saône-et-Loire, C France 46.48N 4.25E
Lecumberri *see* Lekunberri
112 P13 **Łęczna** Lubelskie, E Poland 51.18N 22.51E
112 J12 **Łęczyca** *Ger.* Lentschiza, *Rus.* Lenchitsa. Łódzkie, C Poland 52.03N 19.10E
102 F10 **Leda** ≈ NW Germany
111 Y9 **Ledava** ≈ NE Slovenia
101 F17 **Lede** Oost-Vlaanderen, NW Belgium 50.58N 3.58E
106 K6 **Ledesma** Castilla-León, N Spain 41.05N 6.00W
47 Q12 **le Diamant** SW Martinique 14.28N 61.02W
180 J16 **Le Digue** *island* Inner Islands, NE Seychelles
105 Q10 **le Donjon** Allier, C France 46.19N 3.50E
104 M10 **le Dorat** Haute-Vienne, C France 46.14N 1.05E
Ledo Salinarius *see* Lons-le-Saunier
9 Q14 **Leduc** Alberta, SW Canada 53.16N 113.30W
127 Pp7 **Ledyanaya, Gora** ▲ E Russian Federation 61.51N 171.03E
99 C21 **Lee** *Ir.* An Laoi. ≈ SW Ireland
31 U5 **Leech Lake** ◎ Minnesota, N USA
28 K10 **Leedey** Oklahoma, C USA 35.54N 99.21W
99 M17 **Leeds** N England, UK 53.49N 1.34W
25 P4 **Leeds** Alabama, S USA 33.33N 86.32W

◆ Country ◇ Dependent Territory ◐ Administrative Region ▲ Mountain ※ Volcano ◎ Lake
● Country Capital ○ Dependent Territory Capital ✕ International Airport ▲▲ Mountain Range ≈ River ⊠ Reservoir

31 O3 **Leeds** North Dakota, N USA 48.19N 99.43W

100 N6 **Leek** Groningen, NE Netherlands 53.10N 6.24E

101 K15 **Leende** Noord-Brabant, SE Netherlands 51.21N 5.34E

102 F10 **Leer** Niedersachsen, NW Germany 53.14N 7.25E

100 J13 **Leerdam** Zuid-Holland, C Netherlands 51.54N 5.06E

100 K12 **Leersum** Utrecht, C Netherlands 52.01N 5.25E

25 W11 **Leesburg** Florida, SE USA 28.48N 81.52W

23 V3 **Leesburg** Virginia, NE USA 39.07N 77.33W

29 R4 **Lees Summit** Missouri, C USA 38.55N 94.21W

24 G7 **Leesville** Louisiana, S USA 31.08N 93.15W

27 S12 **Leesville** Texas, SW USA 29.22N 97.45W

33 U13 **Leesville Lake** ▣ Ohio, N USA
Leesville Lake see Smith Mountain Lake

191 P9 **Leeton** New South Wales, SE Australia 34.33S 146.24E

100 L6 **Leeuwarden** Fris. Ljouwert. Friesland, N Netherlands 53.15N 5.48E

188 I14 **Leeuwin, Cape** headland Western Australia 34.18S 115.03E

37 R8 **Lee Vining** California, W USA 37.57N 119.07W

47 V8 **Leeward Islands** island group E West Indies
Leeward Islands see Vent, Îles Sous le, W French Polynesia
Leeward Islands see Sotavento, Ilhas de, Cape Verde

81 G20 **Léfini** ≈ SE Congo 53.22N 6.31W

117 C17 **Lefká** prev. Levkás. Lefkáda, Iónia Nisiá, Greece, C Mediterranean Sea 38.50N 20.43E

117 B17 **Lefkáda** It. Santa Maura; prev. Levkás, anc. Leucas. island Iónia Nisiá, Greece, C Mediterranean Sea

117 H25 **Lefká Óri** ▲ Kríti, Greece, E Mediterranean Sea

124 N3 **Lefke** Gk. Léfka. W Cyprus 35.06N 32.52E

117 B16 **Lefkímmi** var. Levkímmi. Kérkyra, Iónia Nisiá, Greece, C Mediterranean Sea 39.25N 20.03E
Lefkonico/Lefkónikon see Geçitkale
Lefkoşa/Lefkosía see Nicosia

27 O2 **Lefors** Texas, SW USA 35.26N 100.48W

47 R12 **le François** E Martinique 14.36N 60.54W

188 L12 **Lefroy, Lake** salt lake Western Australia
Legaceaster see Chester

107 N8 **Leganés** Madrid, C Spain 40.19N 3.46W
Legaspi see Legazpi City

179 Q11 **Legazpi City** var. Legaspi. Luzon, N Philippines 13.06N 123.43E
Leghorn see Livorno

112 M11 **Legionowo** Mazowieckie, C Poland 52.23N 20.55E

101 K24 **Léglise** Luxembourg, SE Belgium 49.48N 5.31E

108 G8 **Legnago** Lombardia, NE Italy 45.13N 11.18E

108 D7 **Legnano** Veneto, NE Italy 45.36N 8.54E

113 F14 **Legnica** Ger. Liegnitz. Dolnośląskie, SW Poland 51.12N 16.11E

37 Q9 **Le Grand** California, W USA 37.12N 120.15W

105 Q15 **le Grau-du-Roi** Gard, S France 43.33N 4.10E

191 U3 **Legume** New South Wales, SE Australia 28.24S 152.20E

104 L4 **le Havre** Eng. Havre; prev. le Havre-de-Grâce. Seine-Maritime, N France 49.30N 0.07E
le Havre-de-Grâce see le Havre
Lehena see Lechainá

38 L3 **Lehi** Utah, W USA 40.23N 111.51W

20 I14 **Lehighton** Pennsylvania, NE USA 40.49N 75.42W

31 O6 **Lehr** North Dakota, N USA 46.15N 99.21W

40 A8 **Lehua Island** island Hawaiian Islands, Hawai'i, USA, C Pacific Ocean

155 S9 **Leiah** Punjab, NE Pakistan 30.57N 70.53E

111 W9 **Leibnitz** Steiermark, SE Austria 46.48N 15.33E

99 M19 **Leicester** Lat. Batae Coritanorum. C England, UK 52.37N 1.04W

99 M19 **Leicestershire** cultural region C England, UK
Leicheng see Leizhou

100 H11 **Leiden** prev. Leyden, anc. Lugdunum Batavorum. Zuid-Holland, C Netherlands 52.09N 4.30E

100 H11 **Leiderdorp** Zuid-Holland, W Netherlands 52.07N 4.31E

100 G11 **Leidschendam** Zuid-Holland, W Netherlands 52.04N 4.24E

101 D18 **Leie** Fr. Lys. ≈ Belgium/France
Leifear see Lifford

192 L4 **Leigh** Auckland, North Island, NZ 36.17S 174.48E

99 K17 **Leigh** NW England, UK 53.30N 2.33W

190 I5 **Leigh Creek** South Australia 30.27S 138.25E

25 O2 **Leighton** Alabama, S USA 34.42N 87.31W

99 M21 **Leighton Buzzard** E England, UK 51.55N 0.40W
Léim an Bhradáin see Leixlip
Léim an Mhadaidh see Limavady
Léime, Ceann see Loop Head, Ireland
Léime, Ceann see Slyne Head, Ireland

103 G20 **Leimen** Baden-Württemberg, SW Germany 49.21N 8.40E

102 I13 **Leine** ≈ NW Germany

103 J15 **Leinefelde** Thüringen, C Germany 51.22N 10.19E
Léin, Loch see Leane, Lough

99 D19 **Leinster** Ir. Cúige Laighean. cultural region E Ireland

99 F19 **Leinster, Mount** Ir. Stua Laighean. ▲ SE Ireland 52.36N 6.45W

121 T15 **Leipalingis** Alytus, S Lithuania 54.21N 23.54E

94 J12 **Leipojärvi** Norrbotten, N Sweden 67.03N 21.15E

33 R12 **Leipsic** Ohio, N USA 41.06N 83.58W
Leipsic see Leipzig

117 M20 **Leipsoí** island Dodekánisa, Greece, Aegean Sea

103 M15 **Leipzig** Pol. Lipsk; hist. Leipsic, anc. Lipsia. Sachsen, E Germany 51.19N 12.24E

103 M15 **Leipzig Halle** ✈ Sachsen, E Germany 51.26N 12.14E

106 G9 **Leiria** anc. Collipo. Leiria, C Portugal 39.45N 8.49W

106 F9 **Leiria** ◆ district C Portugal

97 C15 **Leirvik** Hordaland, S Norway 59.48N 5.26E

120 E5 **Leisi** Ger. Laisberg. Saaremaa, W Estonia 58.35N 22.42E

106 J3 **Leitariegos, Puerto de** pass NW Spain 43.02N 6.26W

22 J6 **Leitchfield** Kentucky, S USA 37.28N 86.17W

111 Y5 **Leitha** Hung. Lajta. ≈ Austria/Hungary
Leitir Ceanainn see Letterkenny
Leitmeritz see Litoměřice
Leitomischl see Litomyšl

99 D16 **Leitrim** Ir. Liatroim. cultural region NW Ireland
Leivádia see Livádeia
Leix see Laois

99 F18 **Leixlip** Eng. Salmon Leap, Ir. Léim an Bhradáin. E Ireland 53.22N 6.31W

66 N8 **Leixões** Porto, N Portugal 41.10N 8.40W

167 N12 **Leiyang** Hunan, S China 58.57N 94.43W

162 L16 **Leizhou** var. Haikang, Leicheng. Guangdong, S China 20.54N 110.04E

166 L16 **Leizhou Bandao** var. Luichow Peninsula. peninsula S China

100 H13 **Lek** ≈ SW Netherlands

116 I13 **Lekánis** ▲ NE Greece

180 H13 **Le Kartala** ▲ Grande Comore, NW Comoros

81 G20 **Lékéti, Monts de la** ▲ S Congo
Lekhainá see Lechainá

116 H8 **Lekhchevo** Montana, NW Bulgaria 43.32N 23.31E

94 G11 **Leknes** Nordland, C Norway 68.07N 13.36E

81 E21 **Le Kouilou** ◆ province SW Congo

96 L13 **Leksand** Dalarna, C Sweden 60.44N 15.00E

128 H8 **Leksozero, Ozero** ⊚ NW Russian Federation

107 Q3 **Lekunberri** var. Lecumberri. Navarra, N Spain 43.00N 1.54W

175 T6 **Lelai, Tanjung** headland Pulau Halmahera, N Indonesia 1.31N 128.43E

47 Q12 **Le Lamentin** var. Lamentin. C Martinique 14.37N 61.01W

47 Q12 **Le Lamentin** ✈ (Fort-de-France) C Martinique 14.34N 61.00W

33 P6 **Leland** Michigan, N USA 44.59N 85.45W

24 J4 **Leland** Mississippi, S USA 33.24N 90.54W

97 J16 **Lelång** var. Lelången. ⊚ S Sweden
Lelången see Lelång
Lel'chitsy see Lyel'chytsy
le Léman see Geneva, Lake
Leli see Tianlin

27 O3 **Lelia Lake** Texas, SW USA 34.52N 100.42W

115 I14 **Lelija** ▲ SE Bosnia and Herzegovina 43.25N 18.31E

110 C8 **Le Locle** Neuchâtel, W Switzerland 47.04N 6.45E

201 Y14 **Lelu** Kosrae, E Micronesia

201 Y14 **Lelu Island** var. Lelu. island Kosrae, E Micronesia

57 W9 **Lelydorp** Wanica, N Surinam 5.36N 55.04W

100 K9 **Lelystad** Flevoland, C Netherlands 52.30N 5.25E

65 K25 **Le Maire, Estrecho de** strait S Argentina

174 Hh7 **Lemang** Pulau Rangsang, W Indonesia 1.04N 102.44E

195 R11 **Lemanaia** Buka Island, NE PNG 5.04S 154.37E
Léman, Lac see Geneva, Lake

104 L6 **Le Mans** Sarthe, NW France 48.00N 0.12E

31 S12 **Le Mars** Iowa, C USA 42.47N 96.10W

174 I11 **Lematang, Air** ≈ Sumatera, W Indonesia

111 S3 **Lembach im Mühlkreis** Oberösterreich, N Austria 48.23N 13.53E

103 G23 **Lemberg** ▲ SW Germany 48.09N 8.47E
Lemberg see L'viv
Lemdiyya see Médéa

124 Qq12 **Lemesós** var. Limassol. SW Cyprus 34.40N 33.02E

102 H13 **Lemgo** Nordrhein-Westfalen, W Germany 52.02N 8.54E

35 P13 **Lemhi Range** ▲ Idaho, NW USA

16 Oo2 **Lemieux Islands** island group Nunavut, NE Canada

175 Q7 **Lemito** Sulawesi, N Indonesia 0.25N 121.40E

94 L10 **Lemmenjoki** Lapp. Leammi. ≈ NE Finland

100 L7 **Lemmer** Fris. De Lemmer. Friesland, N Netherlands 52.49N 5.43E

30 L7 **Lemmon** South Dakota, N USA 45.54N 102.08W

38 M15 **Lemmon, Mount** ▲ Arizona, SW USA 32.26N 110.47W

37 S14 **Lemoncove** California, W USA 36.23N 119.01W

201 T13 **Lemotol Bay** bay Chuuk Islands, C Micronesia

47 Y5 **le Moule** var. Moule. Grande Terre, NE Guadeloupe 16.20N 61.20W
Lemovices see Limoges
Le-Moyen-Ogooué see Moyen-Ogooué

10 M6 **le Moyne, Lac** ⊚ Québec, E Canada

95 L18 **Lempäälä** Länsi-Suomi, W Finland 61.13N 23.46E

44 F7 **Lempa, Río** ≈ Central America

44 F7 **Lempira** prev. Gracias. ◆ department SW Honduras
Lemsalu see Limbaži

46 J9 **Le Murge** ▲ SE Italy

109 N17 **Lemva** ≈ NW Russian Federation

31 O7 **Leola** South Dakota, N USA 45.41N 98.58W

99 K20 **Leominster** W England, UK 52.09N 2.18W

21 N11 **Leominster** Massachusetts, NE USA 42.29N 71.43W

32 V16 **Leon** Iowa, C USA 40.44N 93.45W

42 M12 **León** var. León de los Aldamas. Guanajuato, C Mexico 21.05N 101.43W

44 I10 **León** León, NW Nicaragua 12.24N 86.52W

106 I4 **León** Castilla-León, NW Spain 42.34N 5.33W

44 J9 **León** ◆ department W Nicaragua

106 K4 **León** ◆ province Castilla-León, NW Spain
León see Cotopaxi

104 I15 **Léon** Landes, S France 43.54N 1.17W

27 V9 **Leona** Texas, SW USA 31.09N 95.58W

188 K11 **Leonara** Western Australia 28.52S 121.16E

27 U5 **Leonard** Texas, SW USA 33.22N 96.15W
Leonard Murray Mountains see Murray Range

109 J9 **Leonardo da Vinci** prev. Fiumicino. ✈ (Roma) Lazio, C Italy 41.48N 12.15E

23 X5 **Leonardtown** Maryland, NE USA 38.17N 76.35W

109 Q23 **Leona River** ≈ Texas, SW USA

43 Z11 **Leona Vicario** Quintana Roo, SE Mexico 20.57N 87.06W

64 M3 **Leon, Cerro** ▲ NW Paraguay 20.21S 60.16W

111 T4 **Leonding** Oberösterreich, N Austria 48.17N 14.15E

109 I14 **Leonessa** Lazio, C Italy 42.33N 12.57E

109 K24 **Leonforte** Sicilia, Italy, C Mediterranean Sea 37.37N 14.22E

191 O13 **Leongatha** Victoria, SE Australia 38.30S 145.56E
Leonídi see Leonídio

117 F21 **Leonídio** var. Leonídi. Pelopónnisos, S Greece 37.10N 22.50E

106 J4 **León, Montes de** ▲ NW Spain

27 S8 **Leon River** ≈ Texas, SW USA
Leontini see Lentini
Léopold II, Lac see Mai-Ndombe, Lac

101 J17 **Leopoldsburg** Limburg, NE Belgium 51.07N 5.16E
Léopoldville see Kinshasa

28 S5 **Leoti** Kansas, C USA 38.28N 101.21W

118 M11 **Leova** Rus. Leovo. SW Moldova 46.31N 28.16E
Leovo see Leova

104 G8 **le Palais** Morbihan, NW France 47.20N 3.08W

29 X10 **Lepanto** Arkansas, C USA 35.34N 90.21W

174 J11 **Lepar, Pulau** island W Indonesia

106 I14 **Lepe** Andalucía, S Spain 37.15N 7.12W
Lepel' see Lyepyel'

85 I19 **Lephephe** Kweneng, SE Botswana 23.17S 25.48E

167 Q10 **Leping** Jiangxi, S China 29.01N 117.07E

124 J12 **le Plessis-Belleville** ✈ N France

117 S7 **Lepsoi** var. Lessach. ≈ E Austria
Léssach see Lessach

Lépontiennes, Alpes/Lepontine, Alpi see Lepontine Alps

110 G10 **Lepontine Alps** Fr. Alpes Lépontiennes, It. Alpi Lepontine. ▲ Italy/Switzerland

81 E20 **Le Pool** ◆ province S Congo

181 O16 **Le Port** NW Réunion

105 N1 **le Portel** Pas-de-Calais, N France 50.42N 1.34E

95 N17 **Leppävirta** Itä-Suomi, C Finland 62.30N 27.49E

47 Q11 **le Prêcheur** NW Martinique 14.48N 61.13W
Lepsi see Lepsy

151 V13 **Lepsa** Kaz. Lepsi. Almaty, SE Kazakhstan 46.13N 78.55E

151 V13 **Lepsy** Kaz. Lepsi. ≈ SE Kazakhstan 46.13N 79.02E
Le Puglie see Puglia

105 Q12 **le Puy** prev. le Puy-en-Velay, hist. Anicium, Podium Anicensis. Haute-Loire, C France 45.03N 3.52E
le Puy-en-Velay see le Puy

47 X11 **le Raizet** var. Le Raizet. ✈ (Pointe-à-Pitre) Grande Terre, C Guadeloupe 16.16N 61.31W

12 G15 **Léré** Mayo-Kébbi, SW Chad 9.40N 14.16E
Leribe see Hlotse

109 E10 **Lerici** Liguria, NW Italy 44.06N 9.53E

56 I14 **Lérida** Vaupés, SE Colombia 0.01S 70.28W
Lérida see Lleida

107 N5 **Lerma** Castilla-León, N Spain 42.02N 3.45W

42 M13 **Lerma, Río** ≈ C Mexico
Lérni see Lérni

117 F20 **Lérni** var. Lérna. prehistoric site Pelopónnisos, S Greece 37.31N 22.43E

95 N14 **Lentiira** Oulu, E Finland 64.22N 29.52E

109 L25 **Lentini** anc. Leontini. Sicilia, Italy, C Mediterranean Sea 37.17N 15.00E
Lentium see Lens
Lentschiza see Łęczyca

95 N15 **Lentua** ⊚ E Finland

121 H14 **Lentvaris** Pol. Landwarów. Vilnius, SE Lithuania 54.39N 24.58E

110 F7 **Lenzburg** Aargau, N Switzerland 47.24N 8.09E

111 R5 **Lenzing** Oberösterreich, N Austria 47.58N 13.34E

79 P13 **Léo** SW Burkina 11.09N 2.04W

111 V7 **Leoben** Steiermark, C Austria 47.22N 15.06E
Leobschütz see Głubczyce

46 J9 **Léogâne** S Haiti 18.28N 72.39W

175 Q7 **Leok** Sulawesi, N Indonesia 1.10N 121.20E

104 M4 **les Abymes** var. Abymes. Grande Terre, C Guadeloupe 16.16N 61.30W
les Albères see Albères, Chaîne des

104 M2 **les Andelys** Eure, N France 49.15N 1.27E

47 Q12 **les Anses-d'Arlets** SW Martinique 14.29N 61.05W

107 U6 **Les Borges Blanques** var. Borjas Blancas. Cataluña, NE Spain 41.31N 0.52E

33 Q4 **Les Cheneaux Islands** island Michigan, N USA

107 T8 **Les Coves de Vinromà** Cast. Cuevas de Vinromá. País Valenciano, E Spain 40.18N 0.07E

110 C10 **le Sépey** Vaud, W Switzerland 46.21N 7.04E

13 T7 **Les Escoumins** Québec, SE Canada 48.21N 69.25W
Les Gonaïves see Gonaïves

166 H9 **Leshan** Sichuan, C China 29.42N 103.43E

110 D11 **Les Haudères** Valais, SW Switzerland 46.02N 7.27E

104 J9 **les Herbiers** Vendée, NW France 46.52N 1.01W

129 Q8 **Leshukonskoye** Arkhangel'skaya Oblast', NW Russian Federation 64.54N 45.48E
Lesina see Hvar

109 M15 **Lesina, Lago di** ⊚ SE Italy

116 K13 **Lesítse** ▲ NE Greece

96 G10 **Lesja** Oppland, S Norway 62.07N 8.56E

97 L15 **Lesjöfors** Värmland, C Sweden 59.57N 14.12E

113 O18 **Lesko** Podkarpackie, SE Poland 49.28N 22.19E

115 O15 **Leskovac** Serbia, SE Serbia 43.00N 21.58E

115 M22 **Leskovik** var. Leskoviku. Korçë, S Albania 40.09N 20.39E
Leskoviku see Leskovik

26 M5 **Lesley** Texas, SW USA 33.35N 100.22W

129 S13 **Lesnoy** Kirovskaya Oblast', NW Russian Federation 59.49N 52.07E

128 I13 **Lesosibirsk** Krasnoyarskiy Kray, C Russian Federation 58.12N 92.22E

85 J23 **Lesotho** off. Kingdom of Lesotho; prev. Basutoland. ◆ monarchy S Africa

127 Nn17 **Lesozavodsk** Primorskiy Kray, SE Russian Federation 45.23N 133.15E

104 J12 **Lesparre-Médoc** Gironde, SW France 45.18N 0.57W

110 C8 **Les Ponts-de-Martel** Neuchâtel, W Switzerland 47.00N 6.45E

104 I14 **Les Sables-d'Olonne** Vendée, NW France 46.30N 1.46W

13 R10 **Lévis** var. Levis. Québec, SE Canada 46.46N 71.10W

105 P1 **Lesquin** ✈ Nord, N France 50.34N 3.07E

23 P6 **Levisa Fork** ≈ Kentucky/Virginia, S USA

117 L21 **Levítha** island Kykládes, Greece, Aegean Sea

47 W11 **les Saintes** var. Îles des Saintes. island group S Guadeloupe

76 L5 **Les Salines** ✈ (Annaba) NE Algeria 36.45N 7.57E

20 J15 **Levittown** Pennsylvania, NE USA 40.09N 74.50W
Levkás see Lefkáda
Levkímmi see Lefkímmi

115 L19 **Levski** Pleven, N Bulgaria 43.22N 25.10E
Levskigrad see Karlovo

130 L6 **Lev Tolstoy** Lipetskaya Oblast', W Russian Federation 53.12N 39.28E

197 I14 **Levuka** Ovalau, C Fiji 17.42S 178.49E

177 G6 **Lewe** Mandalay, C Burma 19.40N 96.04E

99 O23 **Lewes** SE England, UK 50.52N 0.01E

23 Z4 **Lewes** Delaware, NE USA 38.46N 75.08W

31 Q12 **Lewis and Clark Lake** ⊚ Nebraska/South Dakota, C USA

20 G14 **Lewisburg** Pennsylvania, NE USA 40.57N 76.52W

117 M21 **Léros** island Dodekánisa, Greece, Aegean Sea

32 L13 **Le Roy** Illinois, N USA 40.21N 88.45W

29 Q6 **Le Roy** Kansas, C USA 38.04N 95.37W

31 W11 **Le Roy** Minnesota, N USA 43.30N 92.30W

20 E10 **Le Roy** New York, NE USA 42.58N 77.58W
Lerrnayin Gharabakh see Nagorno-Karabakh

97 J19 **Lerum** Västra Götaland, S Sweden 57.46N 12.12E

105 N1 **le Touquet-Paris-Plage** Pas-de-Calais, N France 50.31N 1.34E

177 G8 **Letpadan** Pegu, SW Burma 17.22N 94.10E

177 Ff6 **Letpan** Arakan State, W Burma 19.22N 94.11E

47 Y6 **le Tréport** Seine-Maritime, N France 50.03N 1.21E

178 Gg13 **Letsôk-aw Kyun** var. Letsutan Island; prev. Domel Island. island Mergui Archipelago, S Burma
Letsutan Island see Letsôk-aw Kyun

99 E14 **Letterkenny** Ir. Leitir Ceanainn. NW Ireland 54.57N 7.43W
Lettland see Latvia

118 M6 **Letychiv** Khmel'nyts'ka Oblast', W Ukraine 49.22N 27.39E
Letzebuerg see Luxembourg

118 H14 **Leu** Dolj, SW Romania 44.10N 24.01E
Leucas see Lefkáda

105 P17 **Leucate** Aude, S France 42.55N 3.03E

105 P17 **Leucate, Étang de** ⊚ S France

110 E10 **Leuk** Valais, SW Switzerland 46.18N 7.46E

110 E10 **Leukerbad** Valais, SW Switzerland 46.22N 7.47E

100 K11 **Leusden-Centrum** var. Leusden. Utrecht, C Netherlands 52.07N 5.25E

104 J14 **Leuven** Fr. Louvain, Ger. Löwen. Vlaams Brabant, C Belgium 50.52N 4.42E

101 H18 **Leuze** Namur, C Belgium 50.33N 4.55E

101 I20 **Leuze** Namur, C Belgium 50.33N 4.55E

101 E19 **Leuze-en-Hainaut** var. Leuze. Hainaut, SW Belgium 50.36N 3.37E
Léva see Levice
Levádhia see Livádeia

131 Q17 **Levashi** Respublika Dagestan, SW Russian Federation 42.27N 47.19E

38 L4 **Levan** Utah, W USA 39.33N 111.51W

95 E16 **Levanger** Nord-Trøndelag, C Norway 63.45N 11.18E

124 P14 **Levantine Basin** undersea feature E Mediterranean Sea

108 D10 **Levanto** Liguria, W Italy 44.09N 9.33E

109 H23 **Levanzo, Isola di** island Isole Egadi, S Italy

131 Q17 **Levashi** Respublika Dagestan, SW Russian Federation 42.27N 47.19E

113 J21 **Levice** Ger. Lewentz, Lewenz, Hung. Léva. Nitriansky Kraj, SW Slovakia 48.13N 18.37E

108 G6 **Levico Terme** Trentino-Alto Adige, N Italy 46.02N 11.19E

117 E20 **Levídi** Pelopónnisos, S Greece 37.39N 22.13E

105 P14 **le Vigan** Gard, S France 43.00N 3.36E

192 L13 **Levin** Manawatu-Wanganui, North Island, NZ 40.37S 175.17E

13 R10 **Lévis** var. Levis. Québec, SE Canada 46.46N 71.10W

23 P6 **Levisa Fork** ≈ Kentucky/Virginia, S USA

117 L21 **Levítha** island Kykládes, Greece, Aegean Sea

20 L14 **Levittown** Long Island, New York, NE USA 40.42N 73.29W

20 J15 **Levittown** Pennsylvania, NE USA 40.09N 74.50W
Levkás see Lefkáda
Levkímmi see Lefkímmi

116 J8 **Levski** Pleven, N Bulgaria 43.22N 25.10E
Levskigrad see Karlovo

130 L6 **Lev Tolstoy** Lipetskaya Oblast', W Russian Federation 53.12N 39.28E

197 I14 **Levuka** Ovalau, C Fiji 17.42S 178.49E

177 G6 **Lewe** Mandalay, C Burma 19.40N 96.04E

177 S16 **les Stes-Maries-de-la-Mer** Bouches-du-Rhône, SE France 43.27N 4.26E

99 O23 **Lewes** SE England, UK 50.52N 0.01E

23 Z4 **Lewes** Delaware, NE USA 38.46N 75.08W

31 Q12 **Lewis and Clark Lake** ⊚ Nebraska/South Dakota, C USA

20 G14 **Lewisburg** Pennsylvania, NE USA 40.57N 76.52W

23 S6 **Lewisburg** West Virginia, NE USA 37.48N 80.27W

98 F6 **Lewis, Butt of** headland NW Scotland, UK 58.31N 6.18W

98 F7 **Lewis, Isle of** island NW Scotland, UK

37 U4 **Lewis, Mount** ▲ Nevada, W USA 40.22N 116.50W

193 H16 **Lewis Pass** pass South Island, NZ 42.23S 172.21E

35 P7 **Lewis Range** ▲ Montana, NW USA

25 O3 **Lewis Smith Lake** ▣ Alabama, S USA

9 Q17 **Lethbridge** Alberta, SW Canada 49.43N 112.48W

57 S11 **Lethem** S Guyana 3.24N 59.45W

85 H18 **Letiahau** ≈ W Botswana

56 J18 **Leticia** Amazonas, S Colombia 4.09S 69.57W

175 T15 **Leti, Kepulauan** island group E Indonesia

85 I18 **Letlhakane** Central, C Botswana 21.28S 25.03E

85 H20 **Letlhakeng** Kweneng, SE Botswana 24.04S 25.03E

116 J8 **Letnitsa** Lovech, N Bulgaria 43.19N 25.02E

105 N1 **le Touquet** Pas-de-Calais, N France 50.31N 1.34E

177 G8 **Letpadan** Pegu, SW Burma 17.22N 94.10E

177 Ff6 **Letpan** Arakan State, W Burma 19.22N 94.11E

104 M2 **le Tréport** Seine-Maritime, N France 50.03N 1.21E

47 Q12 **les Anses-d'Arlets** SW Martinique 14.29N 61.05W

178 Gg13 **Letsôk-aw Kyun** var. Letsutan Island; prev. Domel Island. island Mergui Archipelago, S Burma

99 E14 **Letterkenny** Ir. Leitir Ceanainn. NW Ireland 54.57N 7.43W

118 M6 **Letychiv** Khmel'nyts'ka Oblast', W Ukraine 49.22N 27.39E

118 H14 **Leu** Dolj, SW Romania 44.10N 24.01E

105 T12 **les Écrins** ▲ E France 44.54N 6.25E

110 C10 **le Sépey** Vaud, W Switzerland 46.21N 7.04E

13 T7 **Les Escoumins** Québec, SE Canada 48.21N 69.25W

105 P17 **Leucate, Étang de** ⊚ S France

166 H9 **Leukerbad** Valais, SW Switzerland 46.22N 7.47E

100 K11 **Leusden-Centrum** var. Leusden. Utrecht, C Netherlands 52.07N 5.25E

104 J9 **les Herbiers** Vendée, NW France 46.52N 1.01W

129 Q8 **Leshukonskoye** Arkhangel'skaya Oblast', NW Russian Federation 64.54N 45.48E

109 M15 **Lesina, Lago di** ⊚ SE Italy

116 K13 **Lesítse** ▲ NE Greece

96 G10 **Lesja** Oppland, S Norway 62.07N 8.56E

97 L15 **Lesjöfors** Värmland, C Sweden 59.57N 14.12E

113 O18 **Lesko** Podkarpackie, SE Poland 49.28N 22.19E

115 O15 **Leskovac** Serbia, SE Serbia 43.00N 21.58E

115 M22 **Leskovik** var. Leskoviku. Korçë, S Albania 40.09N 20.39E

38 L4 **Levan** Utah, W USA 39.33N 111.51W

95 E16 **Levanger** Nord-Trøndelag, C Norway 63.45N 11.18E

124 P14 **Levantine Basin** undersea feature E Mediterranean Sea

108 D10 **Levanto** Liguria, W Italy 44.09N 9.33E

109 H23 **Levanzo, Isola di** island Isole Egadi, S Italy

113 J21 **Levice** Ger. Lewentz, Lewenz, Hung. Léva. Nitriansky Kraj, SW Slovakia 48.13N 18.37E

117 E20 **Levídi** Pelopónnisos, S Greece 37.39N 22.13E

105 P14 **le Vigan** Gard, S France 43.00N 3.36E

192 L13 **Levin** Manawatu-Wanganui, North Island, NZ 40.37S 175.17E

13 R10 **Lévis** var. Levis. Québec, SE Canada 46.46N 71.10W

117 L21 **Levítha** island Kykládes, Greece, Aegean Sea

116 J8 **Levski** Pleven, N Bulgaria 43.22N 25.10E

130 L6 **Lev Tolstoy** Lipetskaya Oblast', W Russian Federation 53.12N 39.28E

197 I14 **Levuka** Ovalau, C Fiji 17.42S 178.49E

177 G6 **Lewe** Mandalay, C Burma 19.40N 96.04E

105 N9 **Lévroux** Indre, C France 47.00N 1.37E

166 L15 **Lianjiang** var. Liancheng. Guangdong, China 21.41N 110.12E

167 O13 **Lianping** var. Yuanshan. Guangdong, China 24.22N 114.23E

Lianshan see Huludao

167 N13 **Lian Xian** var. Linxian; prev. Lian Xian. Guangdong, S China 24.48N 112.20E

Lianzhou see Hepu

Liao see Liaoning

167 S3 **Liaocheng** Shandong, E China 36.31N 115.59E

169 U11 **Liaodong Bandao** var. Liaotung Peninsula, Gulf of Liaotung. peninsula NE China

169 U11 **Liaodong Wan** Eng. Gulf of Lantung, Gulf of Liaotung. gulf NE China

131 U9 **Liao He** ≈ NE China

169 U12 **Liaoning** var. Liao, Liaoning Sheng, Shengjing; hist. Fengtien, Shenking. ◆ province NE China

Liaoning Sheng see Liaoning

Liaotung, Gulf of see Liaodong Wan

Liaotung Peninsula see Liaodong Bandao

169 U12 **Liaoyang** var. Liao-yang. Liaoning, NE China 41.16N 123.12E

34 M10 **Lewiston** Idaho, NW USA 46.25N 117.01W

21 P7 **Lewiston** Maine, NE USA 44.07N 70.13W

31 X10 **Lewiston** Minnesota, N USA 43.58N 91.52W

20 D9 **Lewiston** New York, NE USA 43.10N 79.02W

38 L1 **Lewiston** Utah, W USA 41.58N 111.52W

32 K13 **Lewiston** Illinois, N USA 40.23N 90.09W

35 T9 **Lewistown** Montana, NW USA 47.04N 109.25W

29 T14 **Lewisville** Arkansas, C USA 33.21N 93.34W

27 T6 **Lewisville** Texas, SW USA 33.00N 96.57W

27 T6 **Lewisville, Lake** ▣ Texas, SW USA
Le Woleu-Ntem see Woleu-Ntem

25 U3 **Lexington** Georgia, SE USA 33.51N 83.04W

22 M5 **Lexington** Kentucky, S USA 38.03N 84.30W

24 L4 **Lexington** Mississippi, S USA 33.06N 90.03W

29 S4 **Lexington** Missouri, C USA 39.10N 93.52W

31 N16 **Lexington** Nebraska, C USA 40.46N 99.44W

22 S9 **Lexington** North Carolina, SE USA 35.49N 80.15W

29 N11 **Lexington** Oklahoma, C USA 35.00N 97.20W

23 R12 **Lexington** South Carolina, SE USA 33.58N 81.14W

22 G9 **Lexington** Tennessee, S USA 35.39N 88.23W

27 T10 **Lexington** Texas, SW USA 30.25N 97.00W

23 T6 **Lexington** Virginia, NE USA 37.47N 79.26W

23 X5 **Lexington Park** Maryland, NE USA 38.16N 76.27W

104 J14 **Leyre** ≈ SW France

179 R13 **Leyte** island C Philippines

179 R13 **Leyte Gulf** gulf E Philippines

113 O16 **Leżajsk** Podkarpackie, SE Poland 50.15N 22.24E

115 K18 **Lezhë** var. Lezha; prev. Lesh, Leshi. Lezhë, NW Albania 41.46N 19.40E

115 K18 **Lezhë** ◆ district NW Albania

105 O16 **Lézignan-Corbières** Aude, S France 43.12N 2.46E

130 J7 **L'gov** Kurskaya Oblast', W Russian Federation 51.38N 35.17E

165 P15 **Lhari** Xizang Zizhiqu, W China 30.34N 93.40E

165 N16 **Lhasa** var. La-sa, Lassa. Xizang Zizhiqu, W China 29.41N 91.10E

165 O15 **Lhasa He** ≈ W China

165 K16 **Lhazê** var. Quxar. Xizang Zizhiqu, W China 29.07N 87.32E

164 K14 **Lhazhong** Xizang Zizhiqu, W China 31.58N 86.43E

173 F3 **Lhoksukon** Sumatera, W Indonesia 5.04N 97.19E

165 Q15 **Lhorong** var. Zito. Xizang Zizhiqu, W China 30.51N 95.41E

107 W6 **L'Hospitalet de Llobregat** var. Hospitalet. Cataluña, NE Spain 41.21N 2.06E

159 R11 **Lhotse** ▲ China/Nepal 28.00N 86.55E

165 N17 **Lhozhag** var. Garbo. Xizang Zizhiqu, W China 28.21N 90.47E

165 O16 **Lhünzê** var. Xingba. Xizang Zizhiqu, W China 28.25N 92.30E

165 N15 **Lhünzhub** var. Ganqu. Xizang Zizhiqu, W China 29.58N 91.20E

178 H8 **Li** Lamphun, NW Thailand 17.46N 98.54E

117 L21 **Liádi** var. Livádi. island Kykládes, Greece, Aegean Sea

167 P12 **Liancheng** var. Lianfeng. Fujian, SE China 25.47N 116.42E
Liancheng see Guangnan, Yunnan, China
Liancheng see Qinglong, Guizhou, China

117 L21 **Liádi** var. Livádi. island Kykládes, Greece, Aegean Sea

179 Rr14 **Lianga** Mindanao, S Philippines 8.36N 126.04E

166 K9 **Liangping** var. Liangshan. Chongqing Shi, C China 30.40N 107.46E

167 O9 **Liangzhou** see Wuwei

167 R12 **Lianjiang** Fujian, SE China 26.13N 119.33E

166 L15 **Lianjiang** var. Liancheng. Guangdong, China 21.41N 110.12E

167 O13 **Lianping** var. Yuanshan. Guangdong, China 24.22N 114.23E

117 M21 **Léros** island Dodekánisa, Greece, Aegean Sea

105 R14 **Lévézou** ≈ S France

105 N9 **Lévroux** Indre, C France 47.00N 1.37E

166 L15 **Lévy, Cap** headland N France 49.41N 1.28W

99 O23 **Lewes** SE England, UK 50.52N 0.01E

167 O13 **Lianjiang** var. Liancheng. Guangdong, China 21.41N 110.12E

167 N13 **Lian Xian** var. Linxian; prev. Lian Xian. Guangdong, S China 24.48N 112.20E
Lianzhou see Hepu
Liao see Liaoning

167 S3 **Liaocheng** Shandong, E China 36.31N 115.59E

169 U11 **Liaodong Bandao** var. Liaotung Peninsula, Gulf of Liaotung. peninsula NE China

169 U11 **Liaodong Wan** Eng. Gulf of Lantung, Gulf of Liaotung. gulf NE China

131 U9 **Liao He** ≈ NE China

169 U12 **Liaoning** var. Liao, Liaoning Sheng, Shengjing; hist. Fengtien, Shenking. ◆ province NE China
Liaoning Sheng see Liaoning
Liaotung, Gulf of see Liaodong Wan
Liaotung Peninsula see Liaodong Bandao

169 U12 **Liaoyang** var. Liao-yang. Liaoning, NE China 41.16N 123.12E

◆ Country ● Country Capital ◇ Dependent Territory ○ Dependent Territory Capital ◈ Administrative Region ✕ International Airport ▲ Mountain ▲ Mountain Range ▲ Volcano ≈ River ⊚ Lake ▣ Reservoir

Liaoyuan – Liuwa Plain

169 V11 **Liaoyuan** *var.* Dongliao, Shuangliao, *Jap.* Chengchiatun. Jilin, NE China 42.51N 125.09E
169 U12 **Liaozhong** Liaoning, NE China 41.33N 122.54E
Liaqatabad *see* Piplān
8 M10 **Liard** ≈ W Canada
Liard *see* Fort Liard
8 L10 **Liard River** British Columbia, W Canada 59.22N 126.04W
155 O15 **Liāri** Baluchistān, SW Pakistan 25.43N 66.28E
Liatroim *see* Leitrim
201 S6 **Lib** *var.* Ellep. *island* Ralik Chain, C Marshall Islands
Liban *see* Lebanon
144 H6 **Liban, Jebel** *Ar.* Jabal al Gharbt, Jabal Lubnān, *Eng.* Mount Lebanon. ▲▲ C Lebanon
Libau *see* Liepāja
35 N7 **Libby** Montana, NW USA 48.25N 115.33W
81 I16 **Libenge** Equateur, NW Dem. Rep. Congo 3.39N 18.39E
28 I7 **Liberal** Kansas, C USA 37.01N 100.55W
29 R7 **Liberal** Missouri, C USA 37.33N 94.31W
Liberalitas Julia *see* Évora
113 D15 **Liberec** *Ger.* Reichenberg. Liberecký Kraj, N Czech Republic 50.44N 15.04E
113 D15 **Liberecký Kraj** ◈ *region* N Czech Republic
44 K12 **Liberia** Guanacaste, NW Costa Rica 10.36N 85.26W
78 K17 **Liberia** *off.* Republic of Liberia. ◆ *republic* W Africa
63 D16 **Libertad** Corrientes, NE Argentina 30.01S 57.51W
63 E20 **Libertad** San José, S Uruguay 34.37S 56.39W
56 I7 **Libertad** Barinas, NW Venezuela 8.21N 69.39W
56 K6 **Libertad** Cojedes, N Venezuela 9.19N 68.43W
64 G12 **Libertador** *off.* Región del Libertador General Bernardo O'Higgins. ◈ *region* C Chile
Libertador General San Martín *see* Ciudad de Libertador General San Martín
22 L6 **Liberty** Kentucky, S USA 37.19N 84.54W
24 J7 **Liberty** Mississippi, S USA 31.09N 90.49W
29 R4 **Liberty** Missouri, C USA 39.15N 94.22W
20 J12 **Liberty** New York, NE USA 41.48N 74.45W
23 T9 **Liberty** North Carolina, SE USA 35.49N 79.34W
Libian Desert *see* Libyan Desert
101 J23 **Libin** Luxembourg, SE Belgium 50.01N 5.13E
166 K13 **Libo** *var.* Yuping. Guizhou, S China 25.28N 107.52E
Libohova *see* Libohovë
115 L23 **Libohovë** *var.* Libohova. Gjirokastër, S Albania 40.03N 20.13E
83 K18 **Liboi** North Eastern, E Kenya 0.23N 40.55E
104 K13 **Libourne** Gironde, SW France 44.55N 0.13W
101 K23 **Libramont** Luxembourg, SE Belgium 49.55N 5.21E
115 M20 **Librazhd** *var.* Librazhdi. Elbasan, E Albania 41.10N 20.22E
Librazhdi *see* Librazhd
81 C18 **Libreville** ● (Gabon) Estuaire, NW Gabon 0.25N 9.29E
179 Rr15 **Libuganon** ≈ Mindanao, S Philippines
77 P10 **Libya** *off.* Socialist People's Libyan Arab Jamahiriya, *Ar.* Al Jamāhīrīyah al 'Arabīyah al Lībīyah ash Sha'bīyah al Ishtirākīyah; *prev.* Libyan Arab Republic. ◆ *Islamic state* N Africa
77 T11 **Libyan Desert** *var.* Libian Desert, *Ar.* Aş Şahrā' al Lībīyah. *desert* N Africa
77 T8 **Libyan Plateau** *var.* Aḍ Ḍiffah. *plateau* Egypt/Libya
Lībīyah, Aş Şahrā' al *see* Libyan Desert
64 G12 **Licantén** Maule, C Chile 35.00S 72.00W
109 J25 **Licata** *anc.* Phintias. Sicilia, Italy, C Mediterranean Sea 37.07N 13.56E
143 P14 **Lice** Dıyarbakır, SE Turkey 38.28N 40.39E
99 L19 **Lichfield** C England, UK 52.42N 1.48W
85 N14 **Lichinga** Niassa, N Mozambique 13.17S 35.15E
111 V3 **Lichtenau** Niederösterreich, N Austria 48.29N 15.24E
85 I21 **Lichtenburg** North-West, N South Africa 26.06S 26.08E
103 K18 **Lichtenfels** Bayern, SE Germany 50.09N 11.03E
100 O12 **Lichtenvoorde** Gelderland, E Netherlands 51.58N 6.34E
Lichtenwald *see* Sevnica
101 C17 **Lichtervelde** West-Vlaanderen, W Belgium 51.01N 3.09E
166 L9 **Lichuan** Hubei, C China 30.19N 108.55E
29 V7 **Licking** Missouri, C USA 37.30N 91.51W
22 M4 **Licking River** ≈ Kentucky, S USA
114 C11 **Lički Osik** Lika-Senj, C Croatia 44.36N 15.24E
Ličko-Senjska Županija *see* Lika-Senj
109 K19 **Licosa, Punta** *headland* S Italy 40.15N 14.54E
121 H16 **Lida** *Rus.* Lida. Hrodzyenskaya Voblasts', W Belarus 53.53N 25.19E
95 H17 **Liden** Västernorrland, C Sweden 62.43N 16.49E
31 R7 **Lidgerwood** North Dakota, N USA 46.04N 97.09W
Lidhorikíon *see* Lidoríki
97 K21 **Lidhult** Kronoberg, S Sweden 56.49N 13.25E
97 P16 **Lidingö** Stockholm, C Sweden 59.22N 18.10E
97 K17 **Lidköping** Västra Götaland, S Sweden 58.30N 13.10E
Lido di Iesolo *see* Lido di Jesolo
108 I8 **Lido di Jesolo** *var.* Lido di Iesolo. Veneto, NE Italy 45.30N 12.37E
109 H15 **Lido di Ostia** Lazio, C Italy 41.42N 12.19E
Lidokhorikion *see* Lidoríki
117 E18 **Lidoríki** *prev.* Lidhorikíon, Lidokhorikion. Stereá Ellás, C Greece 38.31N 22.12E
112 K9 **Lidzbark** Warmińsko-Mazurskie, NE Poland 53.15N 19.49E
112 L7 **Lidzbark Warmiński** *Ger.* Heilsberg. Warmińsko-Mazurskie, NE Poland, 54.07N 20.34E
111 U3 **Liebenau** Oberösterreich, N Austria 48.33N 14.48E
189 P7 **Liebig, Mount** ▲ Northern Territory, C Australia 23.19S 131.30E
111 V8 **Lieboch** Steiermark, SE Austria 47.00N 15.21E
110 I8 **Liechtenstein** *off.* Principality of Liechtenstein. ◆ *principality* C Europe
101 F18 **Liedekerke** Vlaams Brabant, C Belgium 50.51N 4.05E
101 K19 **Liège** *Dut.* Luik, *Ger.* Lüttich. Liège, E Belgium 50.37N 5.34E
101 K20 **Liège** *Dut.* Luik. ◈ *province* E Belgium
Liegnitz *see* Legnica
95 O16 **Lieksa** Itä-Suomi, E Finland 63.20N 30.00E
120 F10 **Lielupe** ≈ Latvia/Lithuania
120 G9 **Lielvārde** Ogre, C Latvia 56.45N 24.48E
178 Kk14 **Liên Hương** *var.* Tuy Phong. Binh Thuân, S Vietnam 11.13N 108.40E
Liên Nghia *see* Đưc Trong
111 P9 **Lienz** Tirol, W Austria 46.49N 12.45E
120 B10 **Liepāja** *Ger.* Libau. Liepāja, W Latvia 56.31N 21.02E
101 H17 **Lier** *Fr.* Lierre. Antwerpen, N Belgium 51.07N 4.34E
97 H15 **Lierbyen** Buskerud, S Norway 59.46N 10.13E
101 L21 **Lierneux** Liège, E Belgium 50.12N 5.51E
Lierre *see* Lier
103 D18 **Lieser** ≈ W Germany
111 U7 **Liesing** ≈ E Austria
110 E6 **Liestal** Basel-Land, N Switzerland 47.28N 7.43E
Lietuva *see* Lithuania
Lievenhof *see* Līvāni
105 O2 **Liévin** Pas-de-Calais, N France 50.25N 2.48E
12 M9 **Lièvre, Rivière du** ≈ Québec, SE Canada
111 T6 **Liezen** Steiermark, C Austria 47.34N 14.12E
99 E14 **Lifford** *Ir.* Leifear. NW Ireland 54.49N 7.28W
197 K5 **Lifou** *island* Îles Loyauté, E New Caledonia
200 Ss13 **Lifuka** *island* Ha'apai Group, C Tonga
179 Q11 **Ligao** Luzon, N Philippines 13.16N 123.30E
Liger *see* Loire
44 H2 **Lighthouse Reef** *reef* E Belize
191 Q4 **Lightning Ridge** New South Wales, SE Australia 29.29S 148.00E
105 N9 **Lignières** Cher, C France 46.45N 2.10E
105 S5 **Ligny-en-Barrois** Meuse, NE France 48.42N 5.22E
85 P15 **Ligonha** ≈ NE Mozambique
33 P11 **Ligonier** Indiana, N USA 41.25N 85.33W
83 I25 **Ligunga** Ruvuma, S Tanzania 10.51S 37.10E
108 D9 **Ligure, Appennino** *Eng.* Ligurian Mountains. ▲▲ NW Italy
Ligure, Mar *see* Ligurian Sea
108 C9 **Liguria** ◈ *region* NW Italy
Ligurian Mountains *see* Ligure, Appennino
123 K6 **Ligurian Sea** *Fr.* Mer Ligurienne, *It.* Mar Ligure. *sea* N Mediterranean Sea
Ligurienne, Mer *see* Ligurian Sea
195 P9 **Lihir Group** *island group* NE PNG
195 P9 **Lihir Island** *island* Lihir Group, N PNG
40 B8 **Līhu'e** *var.* Lihue. Kaua'i, Hawai'i, USA, C Pacific Ocean 21.58N 159.22W
120 F5 **Lihula** *Ger.* Leal. Läänemaa, W Estonia 58.43N 23.52E
128 I2 **Liinakhamari** *var.* Linacmamari. Murmanskaya Oblast', NW Russian Federation 69.40N 31.27E
Liivi Laht *see* Riga, Gulf of
166 F11 **Lijiang** *var.* Dayan, Lijiang Naxizu Zizhixian. Yunnan, SW China 26.52N 100.10E
Lijiang Naxizu Zizhixian *see* Lijiang
114 C11 **Lika-Senj** *off.* Ličko-Senjska Županija. ◈ *province* W Croatia
81 N25 **Likasi** *prev.* Jadotville. Katanga, SE Dem. Rep. Congo 11.01S 26.51E
81 L16 **Likati** Orientale, N Dem. Rep. Congo 3.28N 23.45E
8 M15 **Likely** British Columbia, SW Canada 52.40N 121.34W
159 Y11 **Likhapāni** Assam, NE India 27.24N 95.51E
128 J16 **Likhoslavl'** Tverskaya Oblast', W Russian Federation 57.08N 35.27E
201 U5 **Likiep Atoll** *atoll* Ratak Chain, C Marshall Islands
97 D18 **Liknes** Vest-Agder, S Norway 58.19N 6.58E
81 H18 **Likouala** ≈ N Congo
81 H18 **Likouala aux Herbes** ≈ E Congo
202 B16 **Liku** E Niue 19.01S 169.46E
Likupang, Selat *see* Bangka, Selat
29 Y8 **Lilbourn** Missouri, C USA 36.35N 89.37W
105 X14 **l'Île-Rousse** Corse, France, C Mediterranean Sea 42.39N 8.59E
111 W5 **Lilienfeld** Niederösterreich, NE Austria 48.01N 15.36E
167 N11 **Liling** Hunan, S China 27.42N 113.49E
97 J18 **Lilla Edet** Västra Götaland, S Sweden 58.07N 12.07E
105 P1 **Lille** *var.* l'Isle, *Dut.* Rijssel, *Flem.* Ryssel; *prev.* Lisle, *anc.* Insula. Nord, N France 50.37N 3.04E
97 G24 **Lillebælt** *var.* Lille Bælt, *Eng.* Little Belt. *strait* S Denmark
104 L3 **Lillebonne** Seine-Maritime, N France 49.30N 0.34E
96 H12 **Lillehammer** Oppland, S Norway 61.07N 10.28E
105 O1 **Lillers** Pas-de-Calais, N France 50.34N 2.26E
97 F18 **Lillesand** Aust-Agder, S Norway 58.13N 8.22E
97 I15 **Lillestrøm** Akershus, S Norway 59.58N 11.04E
95 F18 **Lillhärdal** Jämtland, C Sweden 61.51N 14.04E
23 U10 **Lillington** North Carolina, SE USA 35.24N 78.49W
107 O9 **Lillo** Castilla-La Mancha, C Spain 39.43N 3.19W
8 M16 **Lillooet** British Columbia, SW Canada 50.40N 121.58W
85 M14 **Lilongwe** ● (Malawi) Central, W Malawi 13.58S 33.48E
85 M14 **Lilongwe** ✕ Central, W Malawi 13.46S 33.44E
85 M14 **Lilongwe** ≈ W Malawi
179 Q15 **Liloy** Mindanao, S Philippines 8.04N 122.42E
Lilybaeum *see* Marsala
190 J7 **Lilydale** South Australia 32.57S 140.00E
191 P16 **Lilydale** Tasmania, SE Australia 41.17S 147.13E
115 J14 **Lim** ≈ Bosnia and Herzegovina/Serbia
59 D15 **Lima** ● (Peru) Lima, W Peru 12.05S 78.00W
96 K13 **Lima** Dalarna, C Sweden 60.55N 13.19E
33 R12 **Lima** Ohio, NE USA 40.43N 84.06W
59 D14 **Lima** ◈ *department* W Peru
Lima *see* Jorge Chávez International
106 G5 **Lima, Rio** *Sp.* Limia ≈ Portugal / Spain *see also* Limia
113 L17 **Limanowa** Małopolskie, S Poland 49.43N 20.25E
174 I8 **Limas** Pulau Sebangka, W Indonesia 0.09N 104.31E
Limassol *see* Lemesós
99 F14 **Limavady** *Ir.* Léim an Mhadaidh. NW Northern Ireland, UK 55.03N 6.57W
65 J14 **Limay Mahuida** La Pampa, C Argentina 37.09S 66.40W
65 H15 **Limay, Río** ≈ W Argentina
103 N16 **Limbach-Oberfrohna** Sachsen, E Germany 50.52N 12.46E
83 F22 **Limba Limba** ≈ C Tanzania
109 C17 **Limbara, Monte** ▲ Sardegna, Italy, C Mediterranean Sea 40.50N 9.10E
120 G7 **Limbaži** *Est.* Lemsalu. Limbaži, N Latvia 57.33N 24.46E
46 M8 **Limbé** N Haiti 19.40N 72.25W
175 Qq7 **Limboto, Danau** ◎ Sulawesi, N Indonesia
101 L19 **Limbourg** Liège, E Belgium 50.37N 5.55E
101 K17 **Limburg** ◈ *province* NE Belgium
101 L16 **Limburg** ◈ *province* SE Netherlands
103 F17 **Limburg an der Lahn** Hessen, W Germany 50.22N 8.04E
96 K13 **Limedsforsen** Dalarna, C Sweden 60.52N 13.25E
62 L9 **Limeira** São Paulo, S Brazil 22.34S 47.25W
99 C19 **Limerick** *Ir.* Luimneach. SW Ireland 52.40N 8.37W
99 C20 **Limerick** *Ir.* Luimneach. *cultural region* SW Ireland
21 S2 **Limestone** Maine, NE USA 46.52N 67.49W
27 U9 **Limestone, Lake** ◎ Texas, SW USA
41 P12 **Lime Village** Alaska, USA 61.21N 155.26W
97 F20 **Limfjorden** *fjord* N Denmark
97 J23 **Limhamn** Skåne, S Sweden 55.34N 12.57E
106 H5 **Limia** *Port.* Rio Lima ≈ Portugal/ Spain *see also* Lima, Rio
95 L14 **Liminka** Oulu, C Finland 64.48N 25.19E
Limín Vathéos *see* Sámos
117 G17 **Límni** Évvoia, C Greece 38.46N 23.20E
117 J15 **Límnos** *anc.* Lemnos. *island* E Greece
104 M11 **Limoges** *anc.* Augustoritum Lemovicensium, Lemovices. Haute-Vienne, C France 45.50N 1.16E
39 U5 **Limon** Colorado, C USA 39.15N 103.41W
45 O13 **Limón** *var.* Puerto Limón. Limón, E Costa Rica 9.59N 83.02W
44 K4 **Limón** Colón, NE Honduras 15.51N 85.30W
45 N13 **Limón** *off.* Provincia de Limón. ◈ *province* E Costa Rica
108 A10 **Limone Piemonte** Piemonte, NE Italy 44.12N 7.37E
Limones *see* Valdéz
Limonum *see* Poitiers
105 N11 **Limousin** ◈ *region* C France
105 N16 **Limoux** Aude, S France 43.03N 2.13E
85 L19 **Limpopo** *var.* Crocodile. ≈ S Africa
85 J20 **Limpopo** *off.* Limpopo Province; *prev.* Northern, Northern Transvaal. ◈ *province* NE South Africa
166 K17 **Limu Ling** ▲▲ S China
115 M20 **Lin** *var.* Lini. Elbasan, E Albania 41.03N 20.37E
Linacmamari *see* Liinakhamari
179 P13 **Linapacan Island** *island* W Philippines
64 G13 **Linares** Maule, C Chile 35.49S 71.37W
56 C13 **Linares** Nariño, SW Colombia 1.23N 77.33W
43 O9 **Linares** Nuevo León, NE Mexico 24.50N 99.33W
107 N12 **Linares** Andalucía, S Spain 38.04N 3.37W
109 G15 **Linaro, Capo** *headland* C Italy 42.01N 11.49E
108 D8 **Linate** ✕ (Milano) Lombardia, N Italy 45.27N 9.18E
178 Jj8 **Lin Camh** *prev.* Đưc Tho. Ha Tinh, N Vietnam 18.30N 105.36E
166 F13 **Lincang** Yunnan, SW China 23.55N 100.03E
Lincheng *see* Lingao
Linchuan *see* Fuzhou
63 B20 **Lincoln** Buenos Aires, E Argentina 34.50S 61.32W
193 H19 **Lincoln** Canterbury, South Island, NZ 43.37S 172.30E
99 N18 **Lincoln** *anc.* Lindum, Lindum Colonia. E England, UK 53.13N 0.33W
37 O6 **Lincoln** California, W USA 38.52N 121.18W
32 L13 **Lincoln** Illinois, N USA 40.09N 89.21W
28 M4 **Lincoln** Kansas, C USA 39.03N 98.09W
21 S5 **Lincoln** Maine, NE USA 45.22N 68.30W
29 T5 **Lincoln** Missouri, C USA 38.23N 93.19W
31 R16 **Lincoln** *state capital* Nebraska, C USA 40.46N 96.42W
34 F11 **Lincoln City** Oregon, NW USA 44.57N 124.01W
178 M10 **Lincoln Island** *island* E Paracel Islands
207 Q11 **Lincoln Sea** *sea* Arctic Ocean
99 N18 **Lincolnshire** *cultural region* E England, UK
23 R10 **Lincolnton** North Carolina, SE USA 35.28N 81.15W
27 V7 **Lindale** Texas, SW USA 32.31N 95.24W
103 I25 **Lindau** *var.* Lindau am Bodensee. Bayern, S Germany 47.33N 9.40E
Lindau am Bodensee *see* Lindau
126 L9 **Linde** ≈ NE Russian Federation
57 T9 **Linden** E Guyana 5.58N 58.11W
25 O6 **Linden** Alabama, S USA 32.18N 87.48W
22 H9 **Linden** Tennessee, S USA 35.37N 87.50W
27 X6 **Linden** Texas, SW USA 33.01N 94.22W
20 J16 **Lindenwold** New Jersey, NE USA 39.47N 74.58W
97 M15 **Lindesberg** Örebro, C Sweden 59.36N 15.15E
97 D18 **Lindesnes** *headland* S Norway 57.58N 7.03E
Líndhos *see* Líndos
83 K24 **Lindi** Lindi, SE Tanzania 10.00S 39.41E
83 J24 **Lindi** ◈ *region* SE Tanzania
81 N17 **Lindi** ≈ NE Dem. Rep. Congo
169 V7 **Lindian** Heilongjiang, NE China 47.10N 124.51E
193 E21 **Lindis Pass** *pass* South Island, NZ 44.33S 169.40E
85 J22 **Lindley** Free State, C South Africa 27.48S 27.57E
97 J19 **Lindome** Västra Götaland, S Sweden 57.34N 12.04E
169 S10 **Lindong** *var.* Bairin Zuoqi. Nei Mongol Zizhiqu, N China 43.59N 119.24E
117 O23 **Líndos** *var.* Líndhos. Ródos, Dodekánisa, Greece, Aegean Sea 36.04N 28.04E
12 I14 **Lindsay** Ontario, SE Canada 44.21N 78.43W
37 R11 **Lindsay** California, W USA 36.11N 119.06W
35 X8 **Lindsay** Montana, NW USA 47.13N 105.10W
29 N11 **Lindsay** Oklahoma, C USA 34.50N 97.37W
29 N5 **Lindsborg** Kansas, C USA 38.34N 97.39W
97 N21 **Lindsdal** Kalmar, S Sweden 56.43N 16.18E
175 Pp9 **Lindu, Danau** ◎ Sulawesi, N Indonesia
Lindum/Lindum Colonia *see* Lincoln
203 W3 **Line Islands** *island group* E Kiribati
Linëvo *see* Linova
166 M5 **Linfen** *var.* Lin-fen. Shanxi, C China 36.07N 111.34E
161 F18 **Linganamakki Reservoir** ▣ SW India
166 L17 **Lingao** *var.* Lincheng. Hainan, S China 19.44N 109.23E
179 Oo9 **Lingayen** Luzon, N Philippines 16.00N 120.12E
179 Oo9 **Lingayen Gulf** *gulf* Luzon, N Philippines
166 M6 **Lingbao** *var.* Guolüezhen. Henan, C China 34.34N 110.50E
96 N12 **Lingbo** Gävleborg, C Sweden 61.04N 16.45E
Lingcheng *see* Beiliu, Guangxi, China
Lingcheng *see* Lingshan, Guangxi, China
Lingeh *see* Bandar-e Langeh
102 E12 **Lingen** *var.* Lingen an der Ems. Niedersachsen, NW Germany 52.31N 7.19E
Lingen an der Ems *see* Lingen
174 Ii8 **Lingga, Kepulauan** *island group* W Indonesia
174 I8 **Lingga, Pulau** *island* Kepulauan Lingga, W Indonesia
12 J14 **Lingham Lake** ◎ Ontario, SE Canada
96 M13 **Linghed** Dalarna, C Sweden 60.48N 15.55E
35 Z15 **Lingle** Wyoming, C USA 42.07N 104.21W
20 G15 **Linglestown** Pennsylvania, NE USA 40.20N 76.46W
81 K18 **Lingomo II** Equateur, NW Dem. Rep. Congo 0.42N 21.59E
166 L15 **Lingshan** *var.* Lingcheng. Guangxi Zhuangzu Zizhiqu, S China 22.28N 109.19E
166 L17 **Lingshui** *var.* Lingshui Lizu Zizhixian. Hainan, S China 18.35N 110.03E
Lingshui Lizu Zizhixian *see* Lingshui
161 G16 **Lingsugūr** Karnātaka, C India 16.13N 76.33E
109 L23 **Linguaglossa** Sicilia, Italy, C Mediterranean Sea 37.51N 15.06E
78 H10 **Linguère** N Senegal 15.24N 15.06W
165 W8 **Lingwu** Ningxia, N China 38.04N 106.21E
Lingxi *see* Yongshun, Hunan, China
Lingxi *see* Cangnan, Zhejiang, China
Lingxian/Ling Xian *see* Yanling
169 S12 **Lingyuan** Liaoning, NE China 41.09N 119.24E
169 U4 **Linhai** Heilongjiang, NE China 51.30N 124.18E
167 S10 **Linhai** *var.* Taizhou. Zhejiang, SE China 28.53N 121.10E
61 O20 **Linhares** Espírito Santo, SE Brazil 19.22S 40.04W
168 M13 **Linhe** Nei Mongol Zizhiqu, N China 40.46N 107.27E
Lini *see* Lin
145 S1 **Līnik, Chiyā-ē** ▲▲ N Iraq
97 M18 **Linköping** Östergötland, S Sweden 58.25N 15.37E
169 Y8 **Linkou** Heilongjiang, NE China 45.18N 130.16E
120 F11 **Linkuva** Šiauliai, N Lithuania 56.06N 23.58E
29 V5 **Linn** Missouri, C USA 38.29N 91.51W
27 S16 **Linn** Texas, SW USA 26.32N 98.06W
29 T2 **Linneus** Missouri, C USA 39.53N 93.10W
98 H10 **Linnhe, Loch** *inlet* W Scotland, UK
121 G19 **Linova** *Rus.* Linëvo. Brestskaya Voblasts', SW Belarus 52.28N 24.33E
167 O5 **Linqing** Shandong, E China 36.49N 115.39E
62 K8 **Lins** São Paulo, S Brazil 21.40S 49.43W
95 F17 **Linsell** Jämtland, C Sweden 62.10N 14.00E
166 J9 **Linshui** Sichuan, C China 30.24N 106.54E
46 K12 **Linstead** C Jamaica 18.07N 77.01W
165 U11 **Lintan** Gansu, N China 34.43N 101.27E
165 V11 **Lintao** Gansu, C China 35.23N 103.54E
13 S12 **Lintère** ≈ Québec, SE Canada
110 H8 **Linth** ≈ NW Switzerland
110 H8 **Linthal** Glarus, NE Switzerland 46.59N 8.57E
33 N15 **Linton** Indiana, N USA 39.01N 87.10W
31 N6 **Linton** North Dakota, N USA 46.16N 100.13W
169 R11 **Linxi** Nei Mongol Zizhiqu, N China 43.29N 117.59E
165 U11 **Linxia** *var.* Linxia Huizu Zizhizhou. Gansu, C China 35.33N 103.08E
Linxia Huizu Zizhizhou *see* Linxia
Linxian *see* Lianzhou
167 Q6 **Linyi** Shandong, S China 37.12N 116.54E
167 P4 **Linyi** Shandong, E China 37.13N 116.50E
166 M6 **Linyi** Shanxi, C China 35.10N 110.45E
111 T4 **Linz** *anc.* Lentia. Oberösterreich, N Austria 48.19N 14.18E
165 S8 **Linze** *var.* Shahepu. Gansu, N China 39.06N 100.03E
46 J13 **Lionel Town** C Jamaica 17.49N 77.13W
105 Q16 **Lion, Golfe du** *Eng.* Gulf of Lion, Gulf of Lions; *anc.* Sinus Gallicus. *gulf* S France
Lion, Gulf of/Lions, Gulf of *see* Lion, Golfe du
85 K16 **Lions Den** Mashonaland West, N Zimbabwe 17.16S 30.00E
12 F13 **Lion's Head** Ontario, S Canada 44.59N 81.16W
Lios Ceannúir, Bá *see* Liscannor Bay
Lios Mór *see* Lismore
Lios na gCearrbhach *see* Lisburn
Lios Tuathail *see* Listowel
81 G17 **Liouesso** La Sangha, N Congo 1.01N 15.43E
Liozno *see* Lyozna
179 P11 **Lipa** *off.* Lipa City. Luzon, N Philippines 13.57N 121.10E
27 S7 **Lipan** Texas, SW USA 32.31N 98.03W
Lipari Islands/Lipari, Isole *see* Eolie, Isole
109 L22 **Lipari, Isola** *island* Isole Eolie, S Italy
118 L8 **Lipcani** *Rus.* Lipkany. N Moldova 48.16N 26.47E
95 N17 **Liperi** Itä-Suomi, E Finland 62.30N 29.25E
130 L7 **Lipetsk** Lipetskaya Oblast', W Russian Federation 52.37N 39.37E
130 K6 **Lipetskaya Oblast'** ◈ *province* W Russian Federation
59 K22 **Lipez, Cordillera de** ▲▲ SW Bolivia
112 E10 **Lipiany** *Ger.* Lippehne. Zachodnio-pomorskie, W Poland 53.00N 14.58E
114 G9 **Lipik** Požega-Slavonija, NE Croatia 45.24N 17.08E
128 L12 **Lipin Bor** Vologodskaya Oblast', NW Russian Federation 60.12N 38.04E
166 L12 **Liping** *var.* Defeng. Guizhou, S China 26.16N 109.07E
Lipkany *see* Lipcani
121 H15 **Lipnishki** *Rus.* Lipnishki. Hrodzyenskaya Voblasts', W Belarus 54.01N 25.39E
112 J10 **Lipno** Kujawsko-pomorskie, C Poland 52.51N 19.11E
118 F11 **Lipova** *Hung.* Lippa. Arad, W Romania 46.06N 21.40E
Lipovets *see* Lypovets'
Lippa *see* Lipova
103 E14 **Lippe** ≈ W Germany
Lippehne *see* Lipiany
103 G14 **Lippstadt** Nordrhein-Westfalen, W Germany 51.40N 8.21E
27 P1 **Lipscomb** Texas, SW USA 36.12N 100.13W
Lipsia/Lipsk *see* Leipzig
Liptau-Sankt-Nikolaus/Liptószentmiklós *see* Liptovský Mikuláš
113 K19 **Liptovský Mikuláš** *Ger.* Liptau-Sankt-Nikolaus, *Hung.* Liptószentmiklós. Žilinský Kraj, N Slovakia 49.06N 19.36E
191 O13 **Liptrap, Cape** *headland* Victoria, SE Australia 38.55S 145.58E
166 L13 **Lipu** Guangxi Zhuangzu Zizhiqu, S China 24.29N 110.24E
147 X12 **Liqbi** S Oman 18.27N 56.37E
83 G17 **Lira** N Uganda 2.15N 32.55E
59 F15 **Lircay** Huancavelica, C Peru 12.58S 74.43W
109 J15 **Liri** ≈ C Italy
150 M8 **Lisakovsk** Kostanay, NW Kazakhstan 52.37N 62.34E
81 K17 **Lisala** Equateur, N Dem. Rep. Congo 2.10N 21.28E
106 F11 **Lisboa** *Eng.* Lisbon; *anc.* Felicitas Julia, Olisipo. ● (Portugal) Lisboa, W Portugal 38.43N 9.07W
106 F10 **Lisboa** ◈ *Eng.* Lisbon. *district* C Portugal
21 N7 **Lisbon** New Hampshire, NE USA 44.11N 71.52W
31 Q6 **Lisbon** North Dakota, N USA 46.27N 97.42W
Lisbon *see* Lisboa
21 Q8 **Lisbon Falls** Maine, NE USA 44.00N 70.03W
99 G15 **Lisburn** *Ir.* Lios na gCearrbhach. E Northern Ireland, UK 54.31N 6.03W
40 L6 **Lisburne, Cape** *headland* Alaska, USA 68.52N 166.13W
99 B19 **Liscannor Bay** *Ir.* Bá Lios Ceannúir. *inlet* W Ireland
115 Q18 **Lisec** ▲ E FYR Macedonia 41.46N 22.30E
166 F13 **Lishe Jiang** ≈ SW China
Lishi *see* Lüliang
169 V10 **Lishu** Jilin, NE China 43.25N 124.19E
167 R10 **Lishui** Zhejiang, SE China 28.27N 119.25E
199 Jj5 **Lisianski Island** *island* Hawaiian Islands, Hawaii, USA, C Pacific Ocean
Lisichansk *see* Lysychans'k
104 L4 **Lisieux** *anc.* Noviomagus. Calvados, N France 49.09N 0.13E
130 L8 **Liski** *prev.* Georgiu-Dezh. Voronezhskaya Oblast', W Russian Federation 51.00N 39.36E
Lisle/l'Isle *see* Lille
105 N4 **l'Isle-Adam** Val-d'Oise, N France 49.07N 2.13E
105 R15 **l'Isle-sur-la-Sorgue** Vaucluse, SE France 43.55N 5.03E
13 S9 **L'Islet** Québec, SE Canada 47.07N 70.18W
190 M12 **Lismore** Victoria, SE Australia 37.59S 143.18E
99 D20 **Lismore** *Ir.* Lios Mór. S Ireland 52.10N 7.10W
Lissa *see* Vis, Croatia
Lissa *see* Leszno, Poland
100 H11 **Lisse** Zuid-Holland, W Netherlands 52.15N 4.33E
116 K13 **Líssos** *var.* Filiourí. ≈ NE Greece
97 D18 **Lista** *peninsula* S Norway
97 D18 **Listafjorden** *fjord* S Norway
205 R13 **Lister, Mount** ▲ Antarctica 78.12S 161.46E
130 M8 **Listopadovka** Voronezhskaya Oblast', W Russian Federation 51.54N 41.08E
12 F15 **Listowel** Ontario, S Canada 43.44N 80.57W
99 B20 **Listowel** *Ir.* Lios Tuathail. SW Ireland 52.27N 9.28W
166 L14 **Litang** Guangxi Zhuangzu Zizhiqu, S China 23.09N 109.07E
166 F9 **Litang** *var.* Gaocheng. Sichuan, C China 30.03N 100.12E
166 F10 **Litang Qu** ≈ C China
57 X12 **Litani** *var.* Itany. ≈ French Guiana/Surinam
144 G8 **Lītani, Nahr el** *var.* Nahr al Litant. ≈ C Lebanon
Litant, Nahr al *see* Lītani, Nahr el
Litauen *see* Lithuania
32 K14 **Litchfield** Illinois, N USA 39.17N 89.52W
31 U8 **Litchfield** Minnesota, N USA 45.09N 94.31W
38 K13 **Litchfield Park** Arizona, SW USA 33.29N 112.21W
191 S8 **Lithgow** New South Wales, SE Australia 33.30S 150.09E
117 I26 **Líthino, Akrotírio** *headland* Kríti, Greece, E Mediterranean Sea 34.55N 24.43E
120 D12 **Lithuania** *off.* Republic of Lithuania, *Ger.* Litauen, *Lith.* Lietuva, *Pol.* Litwa, *Rus.* Litva; *prev.* Lithuanian SSR, *Rus.* Litovskaya SSR. ◆ *republic* NE Europe
Lithuanian SSR *see* Lithuania
111 U11 **Litija** *Ger.* Littai. C Slovenia 46.03N 14.50E
20 H15 **Lititz** Pennsylvania, NE USA 40.09N 76.18W
117 F15 **Litóchoro** *var.* Litohoro, Litókhoron. Kentrikí Makedonía, N Greece 40.06N 22.30E
Litohoro/Litókhoron *see* Litóchoro
113 C15 **Litoměřice** *Ger.* Ústecký Kraj, NW Czech Republic 50.32N 14.09E
113 F17 **Litomyšl** *Ger.* Pardubický Kraj, C Czech Republic 49.52N 16.16E
113 G17 **Litovel** *Ger.* Littau. Olomoucký Kraj, E Czech Republic 49.42N 17.04E
127 Nn15 **Litovko** Khabarovskiy Kray, SE Russian Federation 49.22N 135.10E
Litovskaya SSR *see* Lithuania
Littai *see* Litija
Littau *see* Litovel
46 G1 **Little Abaco** *var.* Abaco Island. *island* N Bahamas
113 I21 **Little Alföld** *Ger.* Kleines Ungarisches Tiefland, *Hung.* Kisalföld, *Slvk.* Podunajská Rovina. *plain* Hungary/Slovakia
157 Q20 **Little Andaman** *island* Andaman Islands, India, NE Indian Ocean
28 M5 **Little Arkansas River** ≈ Kansas, C USA
192 L4 **Little Barrier Island** *island* N NZ
Little Belt *see* Lillebælt
40 M11 **Little Black River** ≈ Alaska, USA
29 O2 **Little Blue River** ≈ Kansas/Nebraska, C USA
46 D8 **Little Cayman** *island* E Cayman Islands
9 X11 **Little Churchill** ≈ Manitoba, C Canada
177 Ee10 **Little Coco Island** *island* SW Burma
38 L10 **Little Colorado River** ≈ Arizona, SW USA
12 E11 **Little Current** Manitoulin Island, Ontario, S Canada 45.57N 81.55W
10 E11 **Little Current** ≈ Ontario, S Canada
40 L8 **Little Diomede Island** *island* Alaska, USA
46 I4 **Little Exuma** *island* C Bahamas
31 U7 **Little Falls** Minnesota, N USA 45.59N 94.21W
20 J10 **Little Falls** New York, NE USA 43.02N 74.51W
26 M5 **Littlefield** Texas, SW USA 33.55N 102.19W
31 V3 **Littlefork** Minnesota, N USA 48.24N 93.33W
31 V3 **Little Fork River** ≈ Minnesota, N USA
9 N16 **Little Fort** British Columbia, SW Canada 51.27N 120.15W
9 Y14 **Little Grand Rapids** Manitoba, C Canada 52.06N 95.29W
99 N23 **Littlehampton** SE England, UK 50.48N 0.33W
37 T2 **Little Humboldt River** ≈ Nevada, W USA
46 K6 **Little Inagua** *var.* Inagua Islands. *island* S Bahamas
23 Q4 **Little Kanawha River** ≈ West Virginia, NE USA
85 F25 **Little Karoo** *plateau* S South Africa
41 O16 **Little Koniuji Island** *island* Shumagin Islands, Alaska, USA
46 H12 **Little London** W Jamaica 18.14N 78.13W
11 R10 **Little Mecatina** *Fr.* Rivière du Petit Mécatina. ≈ Newfoundland and Labrador/Québec, E Canada
98 F8 **Little Minch, The** *strait* NW Scotland, UK
29 T13 **Little Missouri River** ≈ Arkansas, USA
30 J7 **Little Missouri River** ≈ NW USA
30 J3 **Little Muddy River** ≈ North Dakota, N USA
157 Q22 **Little Nicobar** *island* Nicobar Islands, India, NE Indian Ocean
29 R6 **Little Osage River** ≈ Missouri, C USA
99 P20 **Little Ouse** ≈ E England, UK
155 V2 **Little Pamir** *Pash.* Pāmīr-e Khord, *Rus.* Malyy Pamir. ▲▲ Afghanistan/Tajikistan
23 U12 **Little Pee Dee River** ≈ North Carolina/South Carolina, SE USA
29 V10 **Little Red River** ≈ Arkansas, C USA
Little Rhody *see* Rhode Island
193 I19 **Little River** Canterbury, South Island, NZ 43.45S 172.49E
23 U12 **Little River** South Carolina, SE USA 33.52N 78.36W
29 Y9 **Little River** ≈ Arkansas/Missouri, C USA
29 R13 **Little River** ≈ Arkansas/Oklahoma, USA
25 T7 **Little River** ≈ Georgia, SE USA
24 H6 **Little River** ≈ Louisiana, S USA
27 T10 **Little River** ≈ Texas, SW USA
29 V12 **Little Rock** *state capital* Arkansas, C USA 34.45N 92.17W
33 N8 **Little Sable Point** *headland* Michigan, N USA 43.38N 86.32W
105 U11 **Little Saint Bernard Pass** *Fr.* Col du Petit St-Bernard, *It.* Colle di Piccolo San Bernardo. *pass* France/Italy 45.41N 6.54E
38 K7 **Little Salt Lake** ◎ Utah, W USA
188 K8 **Little Sandy Desert** *desert* Western Australia
31 S13 **Little Sioux River** ≈ Iowa, C USA
40 E17 **Little Sitkin Island** *island* Aleutian Islands, Alaska, USA
9 O13 **Little Smoky** Alberta, W Canada 54.35N 117.06W
9 O14 **Little Smoky** ≈ Alberta, W Canada
39 P3 **Little Snake River** ≈ Colorado, C USA
66 A12 **Little Sound** *bay* Bermuda, NW Atlantic Ocean
39 T4 **Littleton** Colorado, C USA 39.36N 105.01W
21 N7 **Littleton** New Hampshire, NE USA 44.18N 71.46W
20 D11 **Little Valley** New York, NE USA 42.15N 78.46W
32 M15 **Little Wabash River** ≈ Illinois, N USA
12 D10 **Little White River** ≈ Ontario, S Canada
30 M12 **Little White River** ≈ South Dakota, N USA
27 R5 **Little Wichita River** ≈ Texas, SW USA
148 I4 **Little Zab** *Ar.* Nahraz Zāb aş Şaghīr, *Kurd.* Zē-i Kōya, *Per.* Rūdkhāneh-ye Zāb-e Kūchek. ≈ Iran/Iraq
81 D15 **Littoral** ◈ *province* W Cameroon
Littoria *see* Latina
Litva/Litwa *see* Lithuania
113 B15 **Litvínov** *Ger.* Ústecký Kraj, NW Czech Republic 50.37N 13.37E
118 M6 **Lityn** Vinnyts'ka Oblast', C Ukraine 49.19N 28.06E
Liu-chou/Liuchow *see* Liuzhou
169 W11 **Liuhe** Jilin, NE China 42.15N 125.49E
Liukang Tenggaya, Kepulauan *see* Sabalana, Kepulauan
85 Q15 **Liúpo** Nampula, NE Mozambique 15.36S 39.57E
85 G14 **Liuwa Plain** *plain* W Zambia

◆ Country
● Country Capital
◇ Dependent Territory
○ Dependent Territory Capital
◈ Administrative Region
✕ International Airport
▲ Mountain
▲▲ Mountain Range
⋀ Volcano
≈ River
◎ Lake
▣ Reservoir

Liuzhou – Loto

166 L13 Liuzhou var. Liu-chou, Liuchow. Guangxi Zhuangzu Zizhiqu, S China 24.08N 108.54E
118 H8 Livada Hung. Sárköz. Satu Mare, NW Romania 47.52N 23.03E
117 J20 Liváda, Akrotírio headland Tínos, Kykládes, Greece, Aegean Sea 37.36N 25.15E
117 F18 Livadeiá prev. Leivádia; prev. Levádhia. Stereá Ellás, C Greece 38.24N 22.51E
Livádi see Liádi
Livanátai see Livanátes
117 G18 Livanátes prev. Livanátai. Stereá Ellás, C Greece 38.43N 23.01E
120 I10 Līvāni Ger. Lievenhof. Preiļi, SE Latvia 56.22N 26.12E
67 E25 Lively Island island SE Falkland Islands
67 D25 Lively Sound sound SE Falkland Islands
41 R8 Livengood Alaska, USA 65.31N 148.32W
108 I7 Livenza ~ NE Italy
37 O6 Live Oak California, W USA 39.17N 121.41W
25 U9 Live Oak Florida, SE USA 30.18N 82.59W
37 O9 Livermore California, W USA 37.40N 121.46W
22 I6 Livermore Kentucky, S USA 37.31N 87.08W
21 Q7 Livermore Falls Maine, NE USA 44.30N 70.09W
26 J10 Livermore, Mount ▲ Texas, SW USA 30.37N 104.10W
11 P16 Liverpool Nova Scotia, SE Canada 44.03N 64.43W
99 K17 Liverpool NW England, UK 53.25N 2.55W
191 S7 Liverpool Range ▲▲ New South Wales, SE Australia
98 J12 Livingston C Scotland, UK 55.51N 3.31W
25 N5 Livingston Alabama, S USA 32.34N 88.12W
37 P9 Livingston California, W USA 37.22N 120.45W
24 J8 Livingston Louisiana, S USA 30.30N 90.45W
35 S11 Livingston Montana, NW USA 45.40N 110.33W
22 L8 Livingston Tennessee, S USA 36.22N 85.19W
27 W9 Livingston Texas, SW USA 30.42N 94.55W
44 F4 Livingston Izabal, E Guatemala 15.49N 88.46W
85 I16 Livingstone var. Maramba. Southern, S Zambia 17.51S 25.48E
193 B22 Livingstone Mountains ▲▲ South Island, NZ
82 K13 Livingstone Mountains ▲▲ S Tanzania
84 N12 Livingstonia Northern, N Malawi 10.29S 34.06E
204 G4 Livingston Island island Antarctica
27 W9 Livingston, Lake ▣ Texas, SW USA
114 F13 Livno Federacija Bosna I Hercegovina, SW Bosnia and Herzegovina 43.49N 17.00E
130 K7 Livny Orlovskaya Oblast', W Russian Federation 52.25N 37.42E
95 M14 Livojoki ~ C Finland
33 R10 Livonia Michigan, N USA 42.22N 83.22W
108 E11 Livorno Eng. Leghorn. Toscana, C Italy 43.31N 10.18E
Livramento see Santana do Livramento
147 U8 Līwā var. Al Liwā'. oasis region S UAE
83 I24 Liwale Lindi, SE Tanzania 9.46S 37.55E
165 W9 Liwangbu Ningxia, N China 36.42N 106.04E
85 N15 Liwonde Southern, S Malawi 15.04S 35.12E
165 V11 Lixian var. Li Xian. Gansu, C China 34.15N 105.07E
166 H8 Lixian var. Li Xian, Zagunao. Sichuan, C China 31.27N 103.06E
Lixian Jiang see Black River
117 B18 Lixoúri prev. Lixoúrion. Kefallonía, Iónia Nisiá, Greece, C Mediterranean Sea 38.12N 20.25E
Lixoúrion see Lixoúri
Lixus see Larache
Lizarra see Estella
35 U15 Lizard Head Peak ▲ Wyoming, C USA 42.47N 109.12W
99 H25 Lizard Point headland SW England, UK 49.57N 5.12W
114 L12 Ljig Serbia, C Serbia 44.14N 20.16E
Ljouwert see Leeuwarden
Ljubelj see Loibl Pass
111 U11 Ljubljana Ger. Laibach, It. Lubiana; anc. Aemona, Emona. ● (Slovenia) C Slovenia 46.03N 14.28E
111 T11 Ljubljana ✕ C Slovenia 46.14N 14.26E
115 N17 Ljuboten ▲ S Serbia 42.12N 21.06E
97 P19 Ljugarn Gotland, SE Sweden 57.23N 18.45E
86 G7 Ljungan ~ N Sweden
95 F17 Ljungan ~ C Sweden
97 K21 Ljungby Kronoberg, S Sweden 56.49N 13.55E
97 M17 Ljungsbro Östergötland, S Sweden 58.31N 15.30E
97 I18 Ljungskile Västra Götaland, S Sweden 58.13N 11.55E
96 M11 Ljusdal Gävleborg, C Sweden 61.49N 16.10E
96 M11 Ljusnan ~ C Sweden
96 N12 Ljusne Gävleborg, C Sweden 61.11N 17.07E
97 P15 Ljusterö Stockholm, C Sweden 59.31N 18.40E
111 X9 Ljutomer Ger. Luttenberg. NE Slovenia 46.31N 16.12E
65 G15 Llaima, Volcán ▲ S Chile 39.01S 71.38W
107 X4 Llançà var. Llansá. Cataluña, NE Spain 42.23N 3.08E
99 J21 Llandovery C Wales, UK 52.01N 3.47W
99 J20 Llandrindod Wells E Wales, UK 52.15N 3.22W
99 J18 Llandudno N Wales, UK 53.19N 3.49W
99 I21 Llanelli prev. Llanelly. SW Wales, UK 51.41N 4.11W
Llanelly see Llanelli
106 M2 Llanes Asturias, N Spain 43.24N 4.46W
99 K19 Llangollen NE Wales, UK 52.58N 3.10W
27 R10 Llano Texas, SW USA 30.45N 98.40W
27 Q10 Llano River ~ Texas, SW USA
56 I9 Llanos physical region Colombia/Venezuela
65 G16 Llanquihue, Lago ◎ S Chile
Llansá see Llançà
107 U5 Lleida Cast. Lérida; anc. Ilerda. Cataluña, NE Spain 41.37N 0.36E
107 U5 Lleida Cast. Lérida ⬖ province Cataluña, NE Spain
106 K12 Llerena Extremadura, W Spain 38.13N 6.00W
107 S9 Llíria País Valenciano, E Spain 39.37N 0.36W
107 W4 Llivia Cataluña, NE Spain 42.27N 2.00E
107 O3 Llodio País Vasco, N Spain 43.07N 2.58W
107 X5 Lloret de Mar Cataluña, NE Spain 41.42N 2.51E
Llorri see Tossal de l'Orri
8 L11 Lloyd George, Mount ▲ British Columbia, W Canada 57.46N 124.57W
9 R14 Lloydminster Alberta/Saskatchewan, SW Canada 53.18N 110.00W
107 X9 Llucmajor Mallorca, Spain, W Mediterranean Sea 39.30N 2.55E
38 L6 Loa Utah, W USA 38.24N 111.38W
174 Mm4 Loagan Bunut ◎ East Malaysia
178 Mm14 Loaita Island island W Spratly Islands
40 G12 Loa, Mauna ▲ Hawai'i, USA, C Pacific Ocean 19.28N 155.39W
Loanda see Luanda
81 J22 Loange ~ S Dem. Rep. Congo
81 E21 Loango Le Kouilou, S Congo 4.37S 11.49E
108 B10 Loano Liguria, NW Italy 44.07N 8.15E
64 H4 Loa, Río ~ N Chile
85 I20 Lobatse var. Lobatsi. Kgatleng, SE Botswana 25.10S 25.40E
Lobatsi see Lobatse
103 Q15 Löbau Sachsen, E Germany 51.06N 14.39E
81 H16 Lobaye ⬖ prefecture SW Central African Republic
81 I16 Lobaye ~ SW Central African Republic
101 G21 Lobbes Hainaut, S Belgium 50.21N 4.16E
63 D23 Lobería Buenos Aires, E Argentina 38.07S 58.48W
112 F8 Łobez Ger. Labes. Zachodnio-pomorskie, NW Poland 53.29N 15.39E
84 A13 Lobito Benguela, W Angola 12.19S 13.34E
Lobkovichi see Labkovichy
Lob Nor see Lop Nur
176 W11 Lobo Papua, E Indonesia 3.41S 134.06E
106 J11 Lobón Extremadura, W Spain 38.51N 6.37W
63 D20 Lobos Buenos Aires, E Argentina 35.10S 59.07W
42 E4 Lobos, Cabo headland NW Mexico 29.53N 112.43W
42 F6 Lobos, Isla island NW Mexico
Lobositz see Lovosice
Lobsens see Łobżenica
Loburi see Lop Buri
112 H9 Łobżenica Ger. Lobsens. Wielkopolskie, C Poland 53.19N 17.11E
110 G11 Locarno Ger. Luggarus. Ticino, S Switzerland 46.10N 8.47E
98 E9 Lochboisdale NW Scotland, UK 57.08N 7.17W
100 N11 Lochem Gelderland, E Netherlands 52.10N 6.25E
104 M8 Loches Indre-et-Loire, C France 47.08N 1.00E
Loch Garman see Wexford
98 H12 Lochgilphead W Scotland, UK 56.02N 5.27W
98 H7 Lochinver N Scotland, UK 58.10N 5.14W
98 F8 Lochmaddy NW Scotland, UK 57.35N 7.10W
98 J10 Lochnagar ▲ C Scotland, UK 56.58N 3.09W
101 E17 Lochristi Oost-Vlaanderen, NW Belgium 51.07N 3.49E
98 H9 Lochy, Loch ◎ N Scotland, UK
190 G8 Lock South Australia 33.37S 135.45E
99 J14 Lockerbie S Scotland, UK 55.10N 3.27W
29 S13 Lockesburg Arkansas, C USA 33.58N 94.10W
191 P10 Lockhart New South Wales, SE Australia 35.15S 146.43E
27 S11 Lockhart Texas, SW USA 29.52N 97.40W
20 F13 Lock Haven Pennsylvania, NE USA 41.08N 77.27W
27 N4 Lockney Texas, SW USA 34.06N 101.27W
102 O12 Löcknitz ~ NE Germany
20 E9 Lockport New York, NE USA 43.09N 78.40W
178 Jj13 Lôc Ninh Sông Be, S Vietnam 11.51N 106.34E
109 N23 Locri Calabria, SW Italy 38.16N 16.16E
Locse see Levoča
29 T2 Locust Creek ~ Missouri, C USA
25 P3 Locust Fork ~ Alabama, S USA
29 Q9 Locust Grove Oklahoma, C USA 36.12N 95.10W
96 E11 Lodalskåpa ▲ S Norway 61.47N 7.10E
191 N10 Loddon River ~ Victoria, SE Australia
Lodensee see Klooga
105 P15 Lodève anc. Luteva. Hérault, S France 43.43N 3.19E
128 I12 Lodeynoye Pole Leningradskaya Oblast', NW Russian Federation 60.41N 33.29E
35 V11 Lodge Grass Montana, NW USA 45.19N 107.20W
30 J15 Lodgepole Creek ~ Nebraska/Wyoming, C USA
155 T11 Lodhrān Punjab, E Pakistan 29.36N 71.34E
108 D8 Lodi Lombardia, NW Italy 45.15N 9.36E
37 O8 Lodi California, W USA 38.07N 121.17W
33 T12 Lodi Ohio, N USA 41.00N 82.01W
94 H10 Lødingen Nordland, C Norway 68.24N 15.55E
81 L20 Lodja Kasai Oriental, C Dem. Rep. Congo 3.28S 23.24E
39 O3 Lodore, Canyon of canyon Colorado, C USA
107 Q4 Lodosa Navarra, N Spain 42.25N 2.04W
83 H16 Lodwar Rift Valley, NW Kenya 3.06N 35.38E
112 K13 Łódź Rus. Lodz. Łódź, C Poland 51.51N 19.26E
112 J13 Łódzkie ⬖ province C Poland 51.51N 19.26E
178 I8 Loei var. Loey, Muang Loei. Loei, C Thailand 17.28N 101.42E
100 I11 Loenen Utrecht, C Netherlands 52.13N 5.01E
178 J9 Loeng Nok Tha Yasothon, E Thailand 16.12N 104.31E
85 F24 Loeriesfontein Northern Cape, W South Africa 30.53S 19.28E
97 H20 Læsø island N Denmark
Loewoek see Luwuk
Loey see Loei
78 J16 Lofa ~ N Liberia
111 P6 Lofer Salzburg, C Austria 47.37N 12.42E
94 F11 Lofoten var. Lofoten Islands. island group C Norway
Lofoten Islands see Lofoten
97 N18 Loftahammar Kalmar, S Sweden 57.55N 16.45E
131 O10 Log Volgogradskaya Oblast', SW Russian Federation 49.32N 43.52E
79 S12 Loga Dosso, SW Niger 13.33N 3.18E
31 S14 Logan Iowa, C USA 41.38N 95.47W
28 K3 Logan Kansas, C USA 39.39N 99.34W
33 T14 Logan Ohio, N USA 39.32N 82.24W
38 L1 Logan Utah, W USA 41.45N 111.50W
23 P6 Logan West Virginia, NE USA 37.51N 81.59W
37 Y10 Logandale Nevada, W USA 36.36N 114.28W
21 O11 Logan International ✕ (Boston) Massachusetts, NE USA 42.22N 71.00W
9 N16 Logan Lake British Columbia, SW Canada 50.28N 120.42W
25 Q4 Logan Martin Lake ▣ Alabama, S USA
8 G8 Logan, Mount ▲ Yukon Territory, W Canada 60.32N 140.34W
34 I7 Logan, Mount ▲ Washington, NW USA 48.32N 120.57W
35 P7 Logan Pass pass Montana, NW USA 48.43N 113.44W
33 O12 Logansport Indiana, N USA 40.44N 86.25W
24 F6 Logansport Louisiana, S USA 31.58N 94.00W
Logar see Lowgar
69 R11 Loge ~ NW Angola
Logishin see Lahishyn
Log na Coille see Lugnaquillia Mountain
80 G11 Logone var. Lagone. ~ Cameroon/Chad
80 G13 Logone-Occidental off. Préfecture du Logone-Occidental. ⬖ prefecture SW Chad
80 H13 Logone Occidental ~ SW Chad
80 G13 Logone-Oriental off. Préfecture du Logone-Oriental. ⬖ prefecture SW Chad
80 H13 Logone Oriental ~ SW Chad
Logone Oriental see Pendé
L'Ogooué-Ivindo see Ogooué-Ivindo
L'Ogooué-Lolo see Ogooué-Lolo
L'Ogooué-Maritime see Ogooué-Maritime
Logoysk see Lahoysk
107 P4 Logroño anc. Vareia, Lat. Juliobriga. La Rioja, N Spain 42.28N 2.25W
106 L10 Logrosán Extremadura, W Spain 39.21N 5.28W
97 G20 Løgstør Nordjylland, N Denmark 56.57N 9.19E
97 H22 Løgten Århus, C Denmark 56.16N 10.19E
97 F24 Løgumkloster Sønderjylland, SW Denmark 55.04N 8.58E
Lögurinn see Lagarfljót
197 B10 Loh island Torres Islands, N Vanuatu
159 P15 Lohārdaga Jhārkhand, N India 23.27N 84.42E
158 H10 Lohāru Haryāna, N India 28.27N 75.53E
103 D15 Lohausen ✕ (Düsseldorf) Nordrhein-Westfalen, W Germany 51.18N 6.51E
201 O14 Lohd Pohnpei, E Micronesia
194 I14 Lohiki ~ S PNG
94 L12 Lohiniva Lappi, N Finland 67.09N 25.04E
Lohiszyn see Lahishyn
95 L20 Lohja var. Lojo. Etelä-Suomi, S Finland 60.14N 24.07E
175 O8 Lohjanan Borneo, C Indonesia
27 Q9 Lohn Texas, SW USA 31.15N 99.22W
102 G12 Lohne Niedersachsen, NW Germany 52.40N 8.13E
Lohr see Lohr am Main
103 I18 Lohr am Main var. Lohr. Bayern, C Germany 50.00N 9.30E
111 T10 Loibl Pass Ger. Loiblpass, Slvn. Ljubelj. pass Austria/Slovenia 46.25N 14.15E
178 Gg6 Loi-Kaw Kayah State, C Burma 19.40N 97.12E
95 K19 Loimaa Länsi-Suomi, W Finland 60.51N 23.03E
105 O6 Loing ~ C France
178 I6 Loi, Phou ▲ N Laos 20.18N 103.14E
104 L7 Loir ~ C France
105 Q11 Loire ⬖ department E France
104 M7 Loire var. Liger. ~ C France
104 I8 Loire-Atlantique ⬖ department NW France
105 O7 Loiret ⬖ department C France
104 M8 Loir-et-Cher ⬖ department C France
103 L24 Loisach ~ SE Germany
58 B9 Loja Loja, S Ecuador 3.58S 79.16W
106 M14 Loja Andalucía, S Spain 37.10N 4.09W
58 B9 Loja ⬖ province S Ecuador
Lojo see Lohja
118 J4 Lokachi Volyns'ka Oblast', NW Ukraine 50.44N 24.39E
81 M20 Lokandu Maniema, C Dem. Rep. Congo 2.34S 25.43E
94 M11 Lokan Tekojärvi ◎ NE Finland
143 Z11 Lökbatan Rus. Lokbatan. E Azerbaijan 40.21N 49.43E
101 F17 Lokeren Oost-Vlaanderen, NW Belgium 51.06N 3.58E
Lokhvitsa see Lokhvytsya
119 S4 Lokhvytsya Rus. Lokhvitsa. Poltavs'ka Oblast', NE Ukraine 50.21N 33.15E
83 H17 Lokichar Rift Valley, NW Kenya 2.22N 35.40E
83 G16 Lokichokio Rift Valley, NW Kenya 4.16N 34.22E
83 H16 Lokitaung Rift Valley, NW Kenya 4.15N 35.45E
94 M11 Lokka Lappi, N Finland 67.47N 27.40E
96 G8 Løkken Verk Sør-Trøndelag, S Norway 63.07N 9.40E
128 G16 Loknya Pskovskaya Oblast', W Russian Federation 56.48N 30.08E
79 V15 Loko Nassarawa, C Nigeria 8.00N 7.48E
79 U15 Lokoja Kogi, C Nigeria 7.47N 6.44E
125 E12 Lokomotivnyy Chelyabinskaya Oblast', C Russian Federation 53.00N 60.35E
83 H17 Lokori Rift Valley, W Kenya 1.55N 36.03E
79 R16 Lokossa S Benin 6.37N 1.43E
120 I3 Loksa Ger. Loxa. Harjumaa, NW Estonia 59.36N 25.43E
16 P3 Loks Land island Nunavut, NE Canada
82 C13 Lol ~ S Sudan
78 K15 Lola SE Guinea 7.52N 8.28W
37 Q5 Lola, Mount ▲ California, W USA 39.27N 120.20W
83 H20 Loliondo Arusha, NE Tanzania 2.03S 35.46E
97 H25 Lolland prev. Laaland. island S Denmark
195 O11 Lolobau Island island E PNG
175 T6 Loloda Utara, Kepulauan island group E Indonesia
81 E16 Lolodorf Sud, SW Cameroon 3.16N 10.49E
116 G7 Lom prev. Lom-Palanka. Oblast Montana, NW Bulgaria 43.48N 23.16E
116 G7 Lom ~ Montana, NW Bulgaria
81 M19 Lomami ~ C Dem. Rep. Congo
59 F17 Lomas Arequipa, SW Peru 15.29S 74.54W
65 I23 Lomas, Bahía bay S Chile
63 D20 Lomas de Zamora Buenos Aires, E Argentina 34.52S 58.26W
63 D20 Loma Verde Buenos Aires, E Argentina 35.16S 58.24W
188 K4 Lombadina Western Australia 16.39S 122.54E
108 E6 Lombardia Eng. Lombardy. ⬖ region N Italy
Lombardy see Lombardia
104 M15 Lombez Gers, S France 43.28N 0.54E
175 R15 Lomblen, Pulau island Nusa Tenggara, S Indonesia
181 W7 Lombok Basin undersea feature E Indian Ocean
175 Nn16 Lombok, Pulau island Nusa Tenggara, C Indonesia
175 Nn16 Lombok, Selat strait S Indonesia
79 Q16 Lomé ● (Togo) S Togo 6.08N 1.13E
79 Q16 Lomé ✕ S Togo 6.08N 1.13E
81 L19 Lomela Kasai Oriental, C Dem. Rep. Congo 2.19S 23.15E
27 R9 Lometa Texas, SW USA 31.13N 98.23W
81 F16 Lomié Est, SE Cameroon 3.09N 13.34E
32 M8 Lomira Wisconsin, N USA 43.36N 88.26W
97 K23 Lomma Skåne, S Sweden 55.40N 13.04E
101 J16 Lommel Limburg, N Belgium 51.13N 5.19E
98 I11 Lomond, Loch ◎ C Scotland, UK
207 R9 Lomonosov Ridge var. Harris Ridge, Rus. Khrebet Lomonsova. undersea feature Arctic Ocean
Lomonsova, Khrebet see Lomonosov Ridge
Lom-Palanka see Lom
Lomphat see Lumphăt
37 P14 Lompoc California, W USA 34.39N 120.29W
178 Hh9 Lom Sak var. Muang Lom Sak. Phetchabun, C Thailand 16.45N 101.12E
112 N9 Łomża Rus. Lomzha. Podlaskie, NE Poland 53.10N 22.04E
Lomzha see Łomża
161 D14 Lonāvale prev. Lonauli. Mahārāshtra, W India 18.45N 73.27E
65 G15 Loncoche Araucanía, C Chile 39.21S 72.34W
65 H14 Loncopue Neuquén, W Argentina 38.06S 70.36W
101 G17 Londerzeel Vlaams Brabant, C Belgium 51.00N 4.19E
Londinium see London
12 E16 London Ontario, S Canada 42.59N 81.13W
203 Y2 London Kiritimati, E Kiribati 02.00N 157.28W
99 O22 London anc. Augusta, Lat. Londinium. ● (UK) SE England, UK 51.30N 0.10W
23 N7 London Kentucky, S USA 37.06N 84.03W
33 S13 London Ohio, NE USA 39.52N 83.27W
27 Q10 London Texas, SW USA 30.40N 99.33W
99 O22 London City ✕ SE England, UK 51.31N 0.07E
99 E14 Londonderry var. Derry, Ir. Doire. NW Northern Ireland, UK 55.00N 7.19W
99 F14 Londonderry cultural region NW Northern Ireland, UK
188 M2 Londonderry, Cape headland Western Australia 13.46S 126.56E
65 H25 Londonderry, Isla island S Chile
45 O7 Londres, Cayos reef NE Nicaragua
62 I10 Londrina Paraná, S Brazil 23.18S 51.13W
29 N13 Lone Grove Oklahoma, C USA 34.11N 97.15W
12 E12 Lonely Island island Ontario, S Canada
37 T8 Lone Mountain ▲ Nevada, W USA 38.01N 117.28W
27 V6 Lone Oak Texas, SW USA 33.02N 95.58W
37 T11 Lone Pine California, W USA 36.36N 118.04W
Lone Star State see Texas
85 D14 Longa Cuando Cubango, C Angola 14.37S 18.27E
84 B12 Longa ~ W Angola
85 E15 Longa ~ SE Angola
Long'an see Pingwu
207 S4 Longa, Proliv Eng. Long Strait. strait NE Russian Federation
46 J13 Long Bay bay W Jamaica
23 V13 Long Bay bay North Carolina/South Carolina, E USA
37 T16 Long Beach California, W USA 33.46N 118.11W
24 M9 Long Beach Mississippi, S USA 30.21N 89.09W
20 L14 Long Beach Long Island, New York, NE USA 40.34N 73.38W
34 F9 Long Beach Washington, NW USA 46.21N 124.03W
20 K16 Long Beach Island island New Jersey, NE USA
67 M25 Longbluff headland SW Tristan da Cunha
25 U13 Longboat Key island Florida, SE USA
20 K15 Long Branch New Jersey, NE USA 40.18N 73.59W
46 J5 Long Cay island SE Bahamas
Longcheng see Xiaoxian
167 P14 Longchuan var. Laolong. Guangdong, S China 24.07N 115.10E
Longchuan see Nanhua
Longchuan Jiang see Shweli
34 K12 Long Creek Oregon, NW USA 44.40N 119.07W
165 W10 Longde Ningxia, N China 35.37N 106.07E
191 P16 Longford Tasmania, SE Australia 41.41S 147.03E
99 D17 Longford Ir. An Longfort. C Ireland 53.44N 7.49W
99 E17 Longford Ir. An Longfort. cultural region C Ireland
Longgang see Dazu
169 W11 Longgang Shan ▲▲ NE China
167 P1 Longhua Hebei, E China 41.18N 117.43E
175 Nn8 Longiram Borneo, C Indonesia 0.01S 115.36E
46 J4 Long Island island C Bahamas
10 H8 Long Island island Nunavut, C Canada
194 K11 Long Island var. Arop Island. island N PNG
20 L14 Long Island island New York, NE USA
Long Island see Bermuda
20 M14 Long Island Sound sound NE USA
166 K13 Long Jiang ~ S China
169 U7 Longjiang Heilongjiang, NE China 47.20N 123.09E
169 Y10 Longjing var. Yanji. Jilin, NE China 42.48N 129.26E
167 R4 Longkou Shandong, E China 37.40N 120.21E
10 E11 Longlac Ontario, S Canada 49.46N 86.34W
21 S1 Long Lake ◎ Maine, NE USA
33 O6 Long Lake ◎ Michigan, N USA
33 R5 Long Lake ◎ Michigan, N USA
31 N6 Long Lake ◎ North Dakota, N USA
32 J4 Long Lake ▣ Wisconsin, N USA
101 K23 Longlier Luxembourg, SE Belgium 49.51N 5.27E
166 I13 Longlin var. Longlin Gezu Zizhixian, Xinzhou. Guangxi Zhuangzu Zizhiqu, S China 24.46N 105.19E
39 T3 Longmont Colorado, C USA 40.09N 105.07W
163 P10 Longnan var. Wudu. Gansu, C China 33.22N 105.01E
31 N13 Long Pine Nebraska, C USA 42.32N 99.42W
Longping see Luodian
12 F17 Long Point headland Ontario, S Canada 42.33N 80.15W
12 K15 Long Point headland Ontario, SE Canada 43.56N 76.53W
192 P10 Long Point headland North Island, NZ 39.07S 177.41E
32 L2 Long Point headland Michigan, N USA 47.50N 89.09W
12 G17 Long Point Bay lake bay Ontario, S Canada
31 T7 Long Prairie Minnesota, N USA 45.58N 94.52W
Longquan see Fenggang
11 S11 Long Range Mountains hill range Newfoundland and Labrador, E Canada
67 H25 Long Range Point headland SE Saint Helena 16.00S 05.41W
189 V8 Longreach Queensland, E Australia 23.31S 144.18E
166 H7 Longriba Sichuan, C China 32.32N 102.20E
166 L10 Longshan var. Min'an. Hunan, S China 29.25N 109.28E
39 S3 Longs Peak ▲ Colorado, C USA 40.15N 105.37W
Long Strait see Longa, Proliv
104 K8 Longué Maine-et-Loire, NW France 47.23N 0.07W
11 P11 Longue-Pointe Québec, E Canada 50.20N 64.13W
105 S4 Longuyon Meurthe-et-Moselle, NE France 49.25N 5.37E
27 W7 Longview Texas, SW USA 32.30N 94.44W
34 G10 Longview Washington, NW USA 46.08N 122.56W
67 H25 Longwood C Saint Helena
27 P7 Longworth Texas, SW USA 32.37N 100.20W
105 S3 Longwy Meurthe-et-Moselle, NE France 49.31N 5.46E
165 V11 Longxi Gansu, C China 35.00N 104.34E
Longxian see Wengyuan
178 J14 Long Xuyên var. Longxuyen. An Giang, S Vietnam 10.22N 105.25E
167 Q13 Longyan Fujian, SE China 25.06N 117.01E
94 O3 Longyearbyen ○ (Svalbard) Spitsbergen, W Svalbard 78.12N 15.39E
166 J15 Longzhou Guangxi Zhuangzu Zizhiqu, S China 22.22N 106.46E
Longzhouping see Changyang
102 F12 Löningen Niedersachsen, NW Germany 52.43N 7.42E
29 V11 Lonoke Arkansas, C USA 34.46N 91.54W
97 L21 Lönsboda Skåne, S Sweden 56.24N 14.19E
105 S9 Lons-le-Saunier anc. Ledo Salinarius. Jura, E France 46.40N 5.31E
33 O15 Loogootee Indiana, N USA 38.40N 86.54W
33 Q9 Looking Glass River ~ Michigan, N USA
23 X11 Lookout, Cape headland North Carolina, SE USA 34.36N 76.31W
41 O6 Lookout Ridge ridge Alaska, USA
189 N11 Loongana Western Australia 30.53S 127.15E
101 I14 Loon op Zand Noord-Brabant, S Netherlands 51.37N 5.04E
99 A19 Loop Head Ir. Ceann Léime. headland W Ireland 52.55N 10.33W
111 V4 Loosdorf Niederösterreich, NE Austria 48.13N 15.25E
164 G10 Lop Xinjiang Uygur Zizhiqu, NW China 37.06N 80.12E
114 J11 Lopare Republika Srpska, NE Bosnia and Herzegovina 44.39N 18.49E
Lopatichi see Lapatsichy
131 Q15 Lopatin Respublika Dagestan, SW Russian Federation 43.52N 47.40E
131 P7 Lopatino Penzenskaya Oblast', W Russian Federation 52.38N 45.46E
178 Hh10 Lop Buri var. Loburi. Lop Buri, C Thailand 14.46N 100.40E
27 R16 Lopeno Texas, SW USA 26.42N 99.06W
197 D13 Lopevi var. Ulveah. island C Vanuatu
81 C18 Lopez, Cap headland W Gabon 0.39S 8.44E
100 I12 Lopik Utrecht, C Netherlands 51.58N 4.57E
Lop Nor see Lop Nur
164 M7 Lop Nur var. Lob Nor, Lop Nor, Lo-pu Po. seasonal lake NW China
Lopnur see Yuli
81 K17 Lopori ~ NW Dem. Rep. Congo
100 O5 Loppersum Groningen, NE Netherlands 53.19N 6.45E
94 I8 Lopphavet sound N Norway
Lo-pu Po see Lop Nur
Lora see Lowrah
190 F3 Lora Creek seasonal river South Australia
106 K13 Lora del Río Andalucía, S Spain 37.39N 5.31W
154 M11 Lora, Hāmūn-i wetland SW Pakistan
33 T11 Lorain Ohio, N USA 41.27N 82.10W
27 O7 Loraine Texas, SW USA 32.24N 100.42W
33 R13 Loramie, Lake ▣ Ohio, N USA
107 Q13 Lorca Ar. Lurka; anc. Eliocroca, Lat. Illur co. Murcia, S Spain 37.40N 1.40W
199 I12 Lord Howe Island island E Australia
Lord Howe Island see Ontong Java Atoll
183 O10 Lord Howe Rise undersea feature SW Pacific Ocean
199 I12 Lord Howe Seamounts undersea feature W Pacific Ocean
39 P15 Lordsburg New Mexico, SW USA 32.19N 108.42W
194 K8 Lorengau var. Lorungau. Manus Island, N PNG 2.03S 147.16E
27 N5 Lorenzo Texas, SW USA 33.40N 101.31W
148 K7 Lorestān off. Ostān-e Lorestān, var. Luristan. ⬖ province W Iran
59 M17 Loreto Beni, N Bolivia 15.19S 64.40W
108 J12 Loreto Marche, C Italy 43.25N 13.37E
42 F8 Loreto Baja California Sur, W Mexico 25.59N 111.21W
42 M11 Loreto Zacatecas, C Mexico 22.15N 102.00W
58 E9 Loreto off. Departamento de Loreto. ⬖ department NE Peru
83 K18 Lorian Swamp swamp E Kenya
56 E6 Lorica Córdoba, NW Colombia 9.13N 75.49W
104 G7 Lorient prev. l'Orient. Morbihan, NW France 47.45N 3.22W
113 K22 Lőrinci Heves, NE Hungary 47.43N 19.39E
12 G11 Loring Ontario, S Canada 45.55N 79.59W
35 V6 Loring Montana, NW USA 48.49N 107.48W
105 R13 Loriol-sur-Drôme Drôme, E France 44.46N 4.51E
23 U12 Loris South Carolina, SE USA 34.03N 78.53W
59 I18 Loriscota, Laguna ◎ S Peru
191 N13 Lorne Victoria, SE Australia 38.33S 143.57E
98 G11 Lorn, Firth of inlet W Scotland, UK
Loro Sae see East Timor
103 F24 Lörrach Baden-Württemberg, S Germany 47.37N 7.40E
105 T5 Lorraine ⬖ region NE France
Lorungau see Lorengau
96 L11 Los Gävleborg, C Sweden 61.42N 15.15E
37 P14 Los Alamos California, W USA 34.44N 120.16W
39 S10 Los Alamos New Mexico, SW USA 35.52N 106.17W
44 F5 Los Amates Izabal, E Guatemala 15.16N 89.07W
37 S15 Los Angeles California, W USA 34.03N 118.14W
37 S15 Los Angeles ✕ California, W USA 33.54N 118.24W
65 G14 Los Ángeles Bío Bío, C Chile 37.29S 72.18W
37 T13 Los Angeles Aqueduct aqueduct California, W USA
Losanna see Lausanne
65 H20 Los Antiguos Santa Cruz, SW Argentina 46.36S 71.31W
201 Q16 Losap Atoll atoll C Micronesia
37 P10 Los Banos California, W USA 37.00N 120.39W
106 K16 Los Barrios Andalucía, S Spain 36.10N 5.30W
64 L5 Los Blancos Salta, N Argentina 23.39S 62.36W
44 L12 Los Chiles Alajuela, NW Costa Rica 11.00N 84.42W
107 O2 Los Corrales de Buelna Cantabria, N Spain 43.15N 4.04W
27 T17 Los Fresnos Texas, SW USA 26.03N 97.28W
37 N9 Los Gatos California, W USA 37.13N 121.58W
112 O11 Łosice Mazowieckie, E Poland 52.13N 22.42E
114 B11 Lošinj Ger. Lussin, It. Lussino. island W Croatia
Los Jardines see Ngetik Atoll
65 G15 Los Lagos Los Lagos, C Chile 39.52S 72.52W
65 F17 Los Lagos off. Región de los Lagos. ⬖ region C Chile
Loslau see Wodzisław Śląski
66 N11 Los Llanos var. Los Llanos de Aridane. La Palma, Islas Canarias, Spain, NE Atlantic Ocean 28.39N 17.54W
Los Llanos de Aridane see Los Llanos
39 R11 Los Lunas New Mexico, SW USA 34.48N 106.43W
65 I16 Los Menucos Río Negro, C Argentina 40.52S 68.07W
42 H8 Los Mochis Sinaloa, C Mexico 25.48N 108.57W
37 N4 Los Molinos California, W USA 40.00N 122.05W
106 M9 Los Navalmorales Castilla-La Mancha, C Spain 39.43N 4.37W
27 S15 Los Olmos Creek ~ Texas, SW USA
Losonc/Losontz see Lučenec
178 Jj5 Lô, Sông Chin. Panlong Jiang. ~ China/Vietnam
46 B5 Los Palacios Pinar del Río, W Cuba 22.30N 83.19W
106 K14 Los Palacios y Villafranca Andalucía, S Spain 37.10N 5.55W
175 Ss16 Lospalos E East Timor 8.28S 126.56E
39 R12 Los Pinos Mountains ▲▲ New Mexico, SW USA
39 R11 Los Ranchos De Albuquerque New Mexico, SW USA 35.09N 106.37W
42 M14 Los Reyes Michoacán de Ocampo, SW Mexico 19.36N 102.29W
58 B7 Los Ríos ⬖ province C Ecuador
66 O11 Los Rodeos ✕ (Santa Cruz de Tenerife) Tenerife, Islas Canarias, Spain, NE Atlantic Ocean 28.27N 16.19W
56 L4 Los Roques, Islas island group N Venezuela
45 S17 Los Santos Los Santos, S Panama 7.55N 80.25W
45 S17 Los Santos off. Provincia de Los Santos. ⬖ province S Panama
Los Santos see Los Santos de Maimona
106 J12 Los Santos de Maimona var. Los Santos. Extremadura, W Spain 38.27N 6.22W
100 P10 Losser Overijssel, E Netherlands 52.16N 7.01E
98 J8 Lossiemouth NE Scotland, UK 57.43N 3.18W
63 B14 Los Tábanos Santa Fe, C Argentina 28.27S 59.57W
56 J4 Los Taques Falcón, N Venezuela 11.49N 70.16W
12 G11 Lost Channel Ontario, S Canada 45.54N 80.20W
56 L5 Los Teques Miranda, N Venezuela 10.23N 67.01W
37 Q12 Lost Hills California, W USA 35.35N 119.40W
38 I7 Lost Peak ▲ Utah, W USA 37.30N 113.57W
35 P11 Lost Trail Pass pass Montana, NW USA 45.40N 113.58W
195 N15 Losuia Kiriwina Island, SE PNG 8.30S 151.04E
64 G10 Los Vilos Coquimbo, C Chile 31.52S 71.28W
107 N10 Los Yébenes Castilla-La Mancha, C Spain 39.34N 3.52W
105 N13 Lot ⬖ department S France
105 N13 Lot ~ S France
65 F14 Lota Bío Bío, C Chile 37.08S 73.07W
83 G15 Lotagipi Swamp wetland Kenya/Sudan
104 L14 Lot-et-Garonne ⬖ department SW France
85 K21 Lothair Mpumalanga, NE South Africa 26.22S 30.25E
35 R7 Lothair Montana, NW USA 48.28N 111.15W
81 L20 Loto Kasai Oriental, C Dem. Rep. Congo 2.48S 22.30E

◆ Country ● Country Capital ◇ Dependent Territory ○ Dependent Territory Capital ⬖ Administrative Region ✕ International Airport ▲ Mountain ▲▲ Mountain Range Volcano ~ River ◎ Lake ▣ Reservoir

LOTOFAGĀ – LUXEMBOURG

198 B8 **Lotofagā** Upolu, SE Samoa 13.57S 171.51W
110 E10 **Lötschbergtunnel** tunnel Valais, SW Switzerland
27 T9 **Lott** Texas, SW USA 31.12N 97.02W
128 H3 **Lotta** var. Lutto. ≈ Finland/Russian Federation
192 Q7 **Lottin Point** headland North Island, NZ 37.26S 178.07E
Lötzen see Giżycko
Loualaba see Lualaba
178 I6 **Louangnamtha** var. Luong Nam Tha. Louang Namtha, N Laos 20.55N 101.24E
178 I7 **Louangphabang** var. Louangphrabang, Luang Prabang. Louangphabang, N Laos 19.51N 102.08E
Louangphrabang see Louangphabang
204 H5 **Loubet Coast** physical region Antarctica
Loubomo see Dolisie
Louch see Loukhi
104 H6 **Loudéac** Côtes d'Armor, NW France 48.10N 2.45W
166 M11 **Loudi** Hunan, S China 27.51N 111.58E
81 F21 **Loudima** La Bouenza, S Congo 4.06S 13.04E
22 M9 **Loudon** Tennessee, S USA 35.43N 84.19W
33 T12 **Loudonville** Ohio, N USA 40.38N 82.13W
104 L8 **Loudun** Vienne, W France 47.01N 0.04E
104 K7 **Loué** Sarthe, NW France 48.00N 0.14W
78 G10 **Louga** NW Senegal 15.36N 16.14W
99 M19 **Loughborough** C England, UK 52.46N 1.10W
99 C18 **Loughrea** Ir. Baile Locha Riach. W Ireland 53.12N 8.34W
105 S9 **Louhans** Saône-et-Loire, C France 46.38N 5.12E
23 P5 **Louisa** Kentucky, S USA 38.06N 82.40W
23 V5 **Louisa** Virginia, NE USA 38.02N 78.00W
23 V9 **Louisburg** North Carolina, SE USA 36.05N 78.18W
27 U12 **Louise** Texas, SW USA 29.07N 96.22W
13 P11 **Louiseville** Québec, SE Canada 46.15N 72.54W
195 Q17 **Louisiade Archipelago** island group SE PNG
29 W3 **Louisiana** Missouri, C USA 39.25N 91.03W
24 G8 **Louisiana** off. State of Louisiana; also known as Creole State, Pelican State. ⬖ state S USA
194 K9 **Lou Island** island N PNG
85 K19 **Louis Trichardt** Limpopo, NE South Africa 23.06S 29.55E
25 V4 **Louisville** Georgia, SE USA 33.00N 82.24W
32 M15 **Louisville** Illinois, N USA 38.46N 88.32W
22 K5 **Louisville** Kentucky, S USA 38.15N 85.45W
24 M4 **Louisville** Mississippi, S USA 33.07N 89.03W
31 S15 **Louisville** Nebraska, C USA 41.00N 96.09W
199 Jj12 **Louisville Ridge** undersea feature S Pacific Ocean
128 J6 **Loukhi** var. Louch. Respublika Kareliya, NW Russian Federation 66.05N 33.04E
81 H19 **Loukoléla** Cuvette, E Congo 1.04S 17.10E
106 G14 **Loulé** Faro, S Portugal 37.07N 8.01W
113 C16 **Louny** Ger. Laun. Ústecký kraj NW Czech Republic 50.22N 13.49E
31 O15 **Loup City** Nebraska, C USA 41.16N 98.58W
31 P15 **Loup River** ≈ Nebraska, C USA
13 S9 **Loup, Rivière du** ≈ Québec, SE Canada
10 K7 **Loups Marins, Lacs des** lakes Québec, NE Canada
104 K16 **Lourdes** Hautes-Pyrénées, S France 43.06N 0.03W
Lourenço Marques see Maputo
106 F11 **Loures** Lisboa, C Portugal 38.49N 9.10W
106 F10 **Lourinhã** Lisboa, C Portugal 39.13N 9.19W
117 C16 **Loúros** ≈ W Greece
106 G8 **Lousã** Coimbra, N Portugal 40.07N 8.15W
166 M10 **Lou Shui** ≈ C China
191 O5 **Louth** New South Wales, SE Australia 30.34S 145.07E
99 O18 **Louth** E England, UK 53.18N 0.00W
99 F17 **Louth** Ir. Lú. cultural region NE Ireland
117 H15 **Loutrá** Kentrikí Makedonía, N Greece 39.55N 23.37E
117 G19 **Loutráki** Pelopónnisos, S Greece 37.55N 22.55E
Louvain see Leuven
101 H19 **Louvain-la Neuve** Walloon Brabant, C Belgium 50.39N 4.36E
12 J8 **Louvicourt** Québec, SE Canada 48.04N 77.22W
104 M4 **Louviers** Eure, N France 49.13N 1.10E
32 K14 **Lou Yaeger, Lake** ⊠ Illinois, N USA
95 J15 **Lövånger** Västerbotten, N Sweden 64.22N 21.19E
128 J14 **Lovat'** ≈ NW Russian Federation
115 J17 **Lovćen** ▲ SW-Montenegro 42.22N 18.49E
116 J8 **Lovech** Lovech, N Bulgaria 43.09N 24.42E
116 J9 **Lovech** ⬖ province N Bulgaria
27 V9 **Lovelady** Texas, SW USA 31.07N 95.27W
39 T3 **Loveland** Colorado, C USA 40.24N 105.04W
35 U12 **Lovell** Wyoming, C USA 44.50N 108.23W
Lovello, Monte see Grosser Löffler
37 S4 **Lovelock** Nevada, W USA 40.11N 118.30W
108 E7 **Lovere** Lombardia, N Italy 45.51N 10.06E
32 L10 **Loves Park** Illinois, N USA 42.19N 89.03W
28 M2 **Lovewell Reservoir** ⊠ Kansas, C USA
95 M19 **Loviisa** Swe. Lovisa. Etelä-Suomi, S Finland 60.27N 26.15E
39 V15 **Loving** New Mexico, SW USA 32.17N 104.06W
23 U6 **Lovingston** Virginia, NE USA 37.45N 78.47W
39 V14 **Lovington** New Mexico, SW USA 32.56N 103.21W
Lovisa see Loviisa
113 C15 **Lovosice** Ger. Lobositz. Ústecký Kraj, NW Czech Republic 50.29N 14.01E
128 K4 **Lovozero** Murmanskaya Oblast', NW Russian Federation 68.00N 35.03E
128 K4 **Lovozero, Ozero** ◎ NW Russian Federation
114 B9 **Lovran** It. Laurana. Primorje-Gorski Kotar, NW Croatia 45.16N 14.15E
118 E11 **Lovrin** Ger. Lowrin. Timiş, W Romania 45.58N 20.48E
84 E10 **Lóvua** Lunda Norte, NE Angola 7.21S 20.09E
84 G12 **Lóvua** Moxico, E Angola 11.33S 23.35E
67 D25 **Low Bay** bay East Falkland, Falkland Islands
15 M6 **Low, Cape** headland Nunavut, E Canada 63.05N 85.27W
35 N10 **Lowell** Idaho, NW USA 46.07N 115.36W
21 O10 **Lowell** Massachusetts, NE USA 42.37N 71.19W
Löwen see Leuven
Löwenberg in Schlesien see Lwówek Śląski
Lower Austria see Niederösterreich
Lower Bann see Bann
Lower California see Baja California
Lower Danube see Niederösterreich
193 L14 **Lower Hutt** Wellington, North Island, NZ 41.13S 174.51E
41 N11 **Lower Kalskag** Alaska, USA 61.30N 160.28W
37 O1 **Lower Klamath Lake** ◎ California, W USA
37 Q2 **Lower Lake** ◎ California/Nevada, W USA
99 E15 **Lower Lough Erne** ◎ SW Northern Ireland, UK
Lower Lusatia see Niederlausitz
Lower Normandy see Basse-Normandie, France
8 K9 **Lower Post** British Columbia, W Canada 59.53N 128.19W
31 T4 **Lower Red Lake** ◎ Minnesota, N USA
Lower Rhine see Neder Rijn
Lower Saxony see Niedersachsen
Lower Tunguska see Nizhnyaya Tunguska
99 Q19 **Lowestoft** E England, UK 52.28N 1.45E
155 Q5 **Lowgar** var. Logar. ⬖ province E Afghanistan
190 H7 **Low Hill** South Australia 32.17S 136.46E
112 K12 **Łowicz** Łódzkie, C Poland 52.06N 19.55E
35 N13 **Lowman** Idaho, NW USA 44.04N 115.37W
155 P8 **Lowrah** var. Lora. ≈ SE Afghanistan
Lowrin see Lovrin
191 N17 **Low Rocky Point** headland Tasmania, SE Australia 42.59S 145.28E
20 I8 **Lowville** New York, NE USA 43.47N 75.29W
Loxa see Loksa
190 K9 **Loxton** South Australia 34.30S 140.36E
83 G21 **Loya** Tabora, C Tanzania 4.57S 33.53E
32 K6 **Loyal** Wisconsin, N USA 44.45N 90.30W
20 G13 **Loyalsock Creek** ≈ Pennsylvania, NE USA
37 Q5 **Loyalton** California, W USA 39.39N 120.16W
Lo-yang see Luoyang
197 J6 **Loyauté, Îles** island group S New Caledonia
Loyev see Loyew
121 O20 **Loyew** Rus. Loyev. Homyel'skaya Voblasts', SE Belarus 51.55N 30.48E
129 S13 **Loyno** Kirovskaya Oblast', NW Russian Federation 59.44N 52.42E
105 P13 **Lozère** ⬖ department S France
105 Q14 **Lozère, Mont** ▲ S France 44.27N 3.44E
114 J11 **Loznica** Serbia, W Serbia 44.32N 19.13E
119 V7 **Lozova** Rus. Lozovaya. Kharkivs'ka Oblast', E Ukraine 48.54N 36.22E
Lozovaya see Lozova
107 N7 **Lozoyuela** Madrid, C Spain 40.55N 3.36W
Lœvvajok see Leavvajohka
Lu see Shandong, China
Lú see Louth, Ireland
84 F12 **Luacano** Moxico, E Angola 11.19S 21.30E
81 N21 **Lualaba** Fr. Loualaba. ≈ SE Dem. Rep. Congo
85 H14 **Luampa** Western, NW Zambia 15.02S 24.27E
85 H15 **Luampa Kuta** Western, W Zambia 15.22S 24.40E
167 P8 **Lu'an** Anhui, E China 31.46N 116.31E
106 K2 **Luanco** Asturias, N Spain 43.36N 5.48W
84 A11 **Luanda** var. Loanda, Port. São Paulo de Loanda. ● (Angola) Luanda, NW Angola 8.48S 13.17E
84 A11 **Luanda** ⬖ province NW Angola
84 A11 **Luanda** ✕ Luanda, NW Angola 8.49S 13.16E
84 D12 **Luando** ≈ C Angola
Luang see Tapi, Mae Nam
85 G14 **Luanginga** var. Luanguinga. ≈ Angola/Zambia
178 Gg15 **Luang, Khao** ▲ SW Thailand 8.21N 99.46E
Luang Prabang see Louangphabang
178 I8 **Luang Prabang Range** Th. Thiukhaoluang Phrahang. ▲▲ Laos/Thailand
178 H16 **Luang, Thale** lagoon S Thailand
Luangua, Rio see Luangwa
84 E11 **Luangue** ≈ NE Angola
Luanguinga see Luanginga
85 K15 **Luangwa** var. Aruângua. Lusaka, C Zambia 15.34S 30.23E
85 K14 **Luangwa** var. Aruângua, Rio Luangua. ≈ Mozambique/Zambia
167 Q2 **Luan He** ≈ E China
202 G11 **Luaniva, Île** island E Wallis and Futuna
167 P2 **Luanping** var. Anjiangying. Hebei, E China 40.55N 117.19E
84 J13 **Luanshya** Copperbelt, C Zambia 13.09S 28.24E
64 K13 **Luan Toro** La Pampa, C Argentina 36.14S 65.08W
167 Q2 **Luanxian** var. Luan Xian. Hebei, E China 39.47N 118.46E
84 J12 **Luapula** ⬖ province N Zambia
81 O25 **Luapula** ≈ Dem. Rep. Congo/Zambia
106 J2 **Luarca** Asturias, N Spain 43.33N 6.31W
174 Ll7 **Luar, Danau** ◎ Borneo, N Indonesia
81 L25 **Luashi** Katanga, S Dem. Rep. Congo 10.54S 23.55E
84 G12 **Luau** Port. Vila Teixeira de Sousa. Moxico, NE Angola 10.43S 22.07E
81 C16 **Luba** prev. San Carlos. Isla de Bioco, NW Equatorial Guinea 3.26N 8.36E
44 F4 **Lubaantun** ruins Toledo, S Belize 16.18N 88.57W
113 P16 **Lubaczów** var. Lŭbaczów. Podkarpackie, SE Poland 50.09N 23.08E
Lubale see Lubalo
84 E11 **Lubalo** Lunda Norte, NE Angola 9.02S 19.11E
84 E11 **Lubalo** var. Lubale. ≈ Angola/Zaire
120 J9 **Lubāna** Madona, E Latvia 56.55N 29.43E
Lubānas Ezers see Lubāns
179 P11 **Lubang Island** island N Philippines
85 B15 **Lubango** Port. Sá da Bandeira. Huíla, SW Angola 14.54S 13.33E
120 J9 **Lubāns** var. Lubānas Ezers. ◎ E Latvia
81 M21 **Lubao** Kasai Oriental, C Dem. Rep. Congo 5.21S 25.42E
112 O13 **Lubartów** Ger. Qumälisch. Lubelskie, E Poland 51.26N 22.36E
102 G13 **Lübbecke** Nordrhein-Westfalen, NW Germany 52.18N 8.37E
102 O13 **Lübben** Brandenburg, E Germany 51.55N 13.51E
103 P14 **Lübbenau** Brandenburg, E Germany 51.52N 13.57E
27 N5 **Lubbock** Texas, SW USA 33.34N 101.51W
Lubcz see Lyubcha
21 U6 **Lubec** Maine, NE USA 44.49N 67.00W
102 K9 **Lübeck** Schleswig-Holstein, N Germany 53.52N 10.40E
102 K8 **Lübecker Bucht** bay N Germany
81 M21 **Lubefu** Kasai Oriental, C Dem. Rep. Congo 4.43S 24.25E
169 T10 **Lubei** var. Jarud Qi. Nei Mongol Zizhiqu, N China 44.25N 121.12E
113 O14 **Lubelska, Wyżyna** plateau SE Poland
113 O14 **Lubelskie** ⬖ province E Poland
Lubembe see Luembe
Lüben see Lubin
150 H9 **Lubenka** Zapadnyy Kazakhstan, W Kazakhstan 50.27N 54.07E
81 P18 **Lubero** Nord Kivu, E Dem. Rep. Congo 0.10S 29.12E
81 L22 **Lubi** ≈ S Dem. Rep. Congo
Lubiana see Ljubljana
112 J11 **Lubień Kujawski** Kujawsko-pomorskie, C Poland 52.25N 19.10E
69 T11 **Lubilandji** ≈ S Dem. Rep. Congo
112 F13 **Lubin** Ger. Lüben. Dolnośląskie, SW Poland 51.22N 16.12E
113 O14 **Lublin** Rus. Lyublin. Lubelskie, E Poland 51.15N 22.33E
113 J15 **Lubliniec** Śląskie, S Poland 50.40N 18.40E
Lubnān, Jabal see Liban, Jebel
119 R5 **Lubny** Poltavs'ka Oblast', NE Ukraine 50.00N 33.00E
Luboml see Lyuboml'
112 G11 **Luboń** Ger. Peterhof. Wielkolpolskie, C Poland 52.22N 16.54E
112 D12 **Lubsko** Ger. Sommerfeld. Lubuskie, W Poland 51.46N 14.56E
81 N24 **Lubudi** Katanga, SE Dem. Rep. Congo 9.57S 25.58E
174 Hh11 **Lubuklinggau** Sumatera, W Indonesia 3.15S 102.51E
81 N25 **Lubumbashi** prev. Élisabethville. Katanga, SE Dem. Rep. Congo 11.39S 27.31E
85 I14 **Lubungu** Central, C Zambia 14.28S 26.30E
112 E12 **Lubuskie** ⬖ province W Poland
81 N18 **Lubutu** Maniema, E Dem. Rep. Congo 0.42S 26.31E
Luca see Lucca
84 C11 **Lucala** ≈ W Angola
12 E16 **Lucan** Ontario, S Canada 43.10N 81.22W
99 F18 **Lucan** Ir. Leamhcán. E Ireland 53.22N 6.27W
Lucanian Mountains see Lucano, Appennino
109 M18 **Lucano, Appennino** Eng. Lucanian Mountains. ▲▲ S Italy
84 F11 **Lucapa** var. Lukapa. Lunda Norte, NE Angola 8.23S 20.42E
31 V15 **Lucas** Iowa, C USA 41.01N 93.26W
63 C18 **Lucas González** Entre Ríos, E Argentina 32.25S 59.33W
67 C25 **Lucas Point** headland West Falkland, Falkland Islands 52.10S 60.22W
33 S15 **Lucasville** Ohio, N USA 38.52N 83.00W
108 F11 **Lucca** anc. Luca. Toscana, C Italy 43.50N 10.30E
46 H12 **Lucea** W Jamaica 18.26N 78.10W
99 H15 **Luce Bay** inlet SW Scotland, UK
24 M8 **Lucedale** Mississippi, S USA 30.55N 88.35W
179 Pp11 **Lucena** off. Lucena City. Luzon, N Philippines 13.57N 121.38E
106 M14 **Lucena** Andalucía, S Spain 37.25N 4.28W
107 S8 **Lucena del Cid** País Valenciano, E Spain 40.07N 0.15W
113 D15 **Lučenec** Ger. Losontz, Hung. Losonc. Banskobystrický Kraj, C Slovakia 48.21N 19.36E
Lucentum see Alicante
109 M16 **Lucera** Puglia, SE Italy 41.30N 15.19E
Lucerna/Lucerne see Luzern
Lucerne, Lake of see Vierwaldstätter See
42 J4 **Lucero** Chihuahua, N Mexico 30.51N 106.27W
127 Nn17 **Luchegorsk** Primorskiy Kray, SE Russian Federation 46.26N 134.10E
107 Q13 **Luchena** ≈ SE Spain
Lucheng see Kangding
84 N13 **Lucheringo** var. Luchulingo. ≈ N Mozambique
Luchesa see Luchosa
Luchin see Luchyn
120 N13 **Luchosa** Rus. Luchesa. ≈ N Belarus
Luchow see Hefei
102 K11 **Lüchow** Mecklenburg-Vorpommern, N Germany 52.57N 11.10E
Luchulingo see Lucheringo
121 N17 **Luchyn** Rus. Luchin. Homyel'skaya Voblasts', SE Belarus 53.01N 30.01E
57 U11 **Lucie Rivier** ≈ W Surinam
190 K11 **Lucindale** South Australia 36.57S 140.20E
175 T13 **Lucipara, Kepulauan** island group E Indonesia
85 A14 **Lucira** Namibe, SW Angola 13.51S 12.35E
Łuck see Luts'k
103 O14 **Luckau** Brandenburg, E Germany 51.50N 13.42E
102 N13 **Luckenwalde** Brandenburg, E Germany 52.06N 13.11E
12 E15 **Lucknow** Ontario, S Canada 43.58N 81.30W
158 L12 **Lucknow** var. Lakhnau. Uttar Pradesh, N India 26.49N 80.54E
104 J10 **Luçon** Vendée, NW France 46.27N 1.10W
46 I7 **Lucrecia, Cabo** headland E Cuba 21.00N 75.34W
84 F13 **Lucusse** Moxico, E Angola 12.32S 20.46E
Lüda see Dalian
116 M9 **Luda Kamchiya** ≈ E Bulgaria
Ludasch see Luduş
116 I10 **Luda Yana** ≈ C Bulgaria
114 F7 **Ludbreg** Varaždin, N Croatia 46.15N 16.36E
31 P7 **Ludden** North Dakota, N USA 45.58N 98.07W
103 F15 **Lüdenscheid** Nordrhein-Westfalen, W Germany 51.13N 7.37E
85 C21 **Lüderitz** prev. Angra Pequena. Karas, SW Namibia 26.37S 15.10E
158 H8 **Ludhiāna** Punjab, N India 30.55N 75.52E
33 O7 **Ludington** Michigan, N USA 43.58N 86.27W
99 K20 **Ludlow** W England, UK 52.19N 2.27W
37 W14 **Ludlow** California, W USA 34.43N 116.07W
30 J7 **Ludlow** South Dakota, N USA 45.48N 103.21W
20 M9 **Ludlow** Vermont, NE USA 43.24N 72.39W
116 L7 **Ludogorie** physical region NE Bulgaria
25 W6 **Ludowici** Georgia, SE USA 31.42N 81.44W
Ludsan see Ludza
118 I10 **Luduş** Ger. Ludasch, Hung. Marosludas. Mureş, C Romania 46.27N 24.04E
97 M14 **Ludvika** Dalarna, C Sweden 60.07N 15.13E
103 H21 **Ludwigsburg** Baden-Württemberg, SW Germany 48.54N 9.12E
102 O13 **Ludwigsfelde** Brandenburg, NE Germany 52.17N 13.15E
103 G20 **Ludwigshafen** var. Ludwigshafen am Rhein. Rheinland-Pfalz, W Germany 49.28N 8.24E
Ludwigshafen am Rhein see Ludwigshafen
103 L20 **Ludwigskanal** canal SE Germany
102 L10 **Ludwigslust** Mecklenburg-Vorpommern, N Germany 53.19N 11.28E
120 K10 **Ludza** Ger. Ludsan. Ludza, E Latvia 56.32N 27.41E
81 K21 **Luebo** Kasai Occidental, SW Dem. Rep. Congo 5.19S 21.21E
27 Q6 **Lueders** Texas, SW USA 32.46N 99.38W
81 N20 **Lueki** Maniema, C Dem. Rep. Congo 3.25S 25.49E
84 F10 **Luembe** var. Lubembe. ≈ Angola/Dem. Rep. Congo
84 E13 **Luena** var. Lwena, Port. Luso. Moxico, E Angola 11.46S 19.52E
81 M24 **Luena** Katanga, SE Dem. Rep. Congo 9.28S 25.45E
84 K12 **Luena** Northern, NE Zambia 10.31S 30.12E
84 F13 **Luena** ≈ E Angola
85 F16 **Luengue** ≈ SE Angola
69 V13 **Luenha** ≈ W Mozambique
85 G15 **Lueti** ≈ Angola/Zambia
166 J7 **Lüeyang** var. Hejiayan. Shaanxi, C China 33.12N 106.31E
167 P14 **Lufeng** Guangdong, S China 22.58N 115.36E
81 N24 **Lufira** ≈ SE Dem. Rep. Congo
81 N25 **Lufira, Lac de Retenue de la** var. Lac Tshangalele. ◎ SE Dem. Rep. Congo
27 W8 **Lufkin** Texas, SW USA 31.20N 94.43W
84 L11 **Lufubu** ≈ N Zambia
128 G14 **Luga** Leningradskaya Oblast', NW Russian Federation 58.43N 29.46E
128 G13 **Luga** ≈ NW Russian Federation
Luganer See see Lugano, Lago di
110 H11 **Lugano** Ger. Lauis. Ticino, S Switzerland 46.01N 8.57E
110 H12 **Lugano, Lago di** var. Ceresio, Ger. Luganer See. ◎ S Switzerland
Lugansk see Luhans'k
197 B12 **Luganville** Espiritu Santo, C Vanuatu 15.31S 167.12E
Lugdunum see Lyon
Lugdunum Batavorum see Leiden
85 O15 **Lugela** Zambézia, NE Mozambique 16.27S 36.47E
85 O16 **Lugela** ≈ C Mozambique
84 P13 **Lugenda, Rio** ≈ N Mozambique
Luggarus see Locarno
Lugh Ganana see Luuq
99 G19 **Lugnaquillia Mountain** Ir. Log na Coille. ▲ E Ireland 52.58N 6.27W
108 H10 **Lugo** Emilia-Romagna, N Italy 44.25N 11.52E
106 I3 **Lugo** anc. Lugus Augusti. Galicia, NW Spain 43.00N 7.33W
106 I3 **Lugo** ⬖ province Galicia, NW Spain
23 R12 **Lugoff** South Carolina, SE USA 34.13N 80.41W
118 F12 **Lugoj** Ger. Lugosch, Hung. Lugos. Timiş, W Romania 45.40N 21.56E
Lugos/Lugosch see Lugoj
Lugovoy/Lugovoye see Kulan
164 I13 **Lugu** Xizang Zizhiqu, W China 33.26N 84.10E
Lugus Augusti see Lugo
Luguvallium/Luguvallum see Carlisle
119 Y7 **Luhans'k** Rus. Lugansk; prev. Voroshilovgrad. Luhans'ka Oblast', E Ukraine 48.32N 39.21E
119 Y7 **Luhans'k** ✕ Luhans'ka Oblast', E Ukraine 48.25N 39.24E
119 X6 **Luhans'ka Oblast'** var. Luhans'k; prev. Voroshilovgrad, Rus. Voroshilovgradskaya Oblast'. ⬖ province E Ukraine
167 Q7 **Luhe** Jiangsu, E China 32.22N 118.51E
175 T11 **Luhu** Pulau Seram, E Indonesia 3.20S 127.58E
Luhua see Heishui
166 G8 **Luhuo** var. Xindu, Tib. Zhaggo. Sichuan, C China 31.25N 100.39E
118 M3 **Luhyny** Zhytomyrs'ka Oblast', N Ukraine 51.06N 28.24E
85 G15 **Lui** ≈ W Zambia
85 G16 **Luiana** ≈ SE Angola
85 L15 **Luia, Rio** var. Ruya. ≈ Mozambique/Zimbabwe
Luichow Peninsula see Leizhou Bandao
Luik see Liège
84 C13 **Luimbale** Huambo, C Angola 12.15S 15.19E
Luimneach see Limerick
108 D6 **Luino** Lombardia, N Italy 46.00N 8.45E
84 E13 **Luio** ≈ E Angola
94 L11 **Luiro** ≈ NE Finland
81 N25 **Luishia** Katanga, SE Dem. Rep. Congo 11.18S 27.08E
61 M19 **Luislândia do Oeste** Minas Gerais, SE Brazil 17.59S 45.35W
42 K5 **Luis L.León, Presa** ⊠ N Mexico
Luis Muñoz Marin see San Juan
205 N5 **Luitpold Coast** physical region Antarctica
81 K22 **Luiza** Kasai Occidental, S Dem. Rep. Congo 7.10S 22.27E
63 D20 **Luján** Buenos Aires, E Argentina 34.34S 59.07W
81 N24 **Lukafu** Katanga, SE Dem. Rep. Congo 10.28S 27.31E
Lukapa see Lucapa
114 I11 **Lukavac** Federacija Bosna I Hercegovina, NE Bosnia and Herzegovina 44.33N 18.31E
81 I20 **Lukenie** ≈ C Dem. Rep. Congo
81 H19 **Lukolela** Equateur, W Dem. Rep. Congo 1.03S 17.07E
121 M14 **Lukoml'skaye, Vozyera** Rus. Ozero Lukoml'skoye. ◎ N Belarus
Lukoml'skoye, Ozero see Lukoml'skaye, Vozyera
116 I8 **Lukovit** Lovech, N Bulgaria 43.13N 24.10E
112 O12 **Łuków** Ger. Bogendorf. Lubelskie, E Poland 51.57N 22.22E
131 O4 **Lukoyanov** Nizhegorodskaya Oblast', W Russian Federation 55.02N 44.26E
81 N22 **Lukuga** ≈ SE Dem. Rep. Congo
81 F21 **Lukula** Bas-Congo, SW Dem. Rep. Congo 5.22S 12.57E
85 G14 **Lukulu** Western, NW Zambia 14.24S 23.12E
201 R17 **Lukunor Atoll** atoll Mortlock Islands, C Micronesia
84 J12 **Lukwesa** Luapula, NE Zambia 10.03S 28.42E
95 K14 **Luleå** Norrbotten, N Sweden 65.34N 22.10E
94 J13 **Luleälven** ≈ N Sweden
142 C10 **Lüleburgaz** Kırklareli, NW Turkey 41.25N 27.22E
166 M4 **Lüliang** var. Lishi. Shanxi, C China 37.27N 111.05E
166 M4 **Lüliang Shan** ▲ C China
81 O21 **Lulimba** Maniema, E Dem. Rep. Congo 4.42S 28.37E
24 K9 **Luling** Louisiana, S USA 29.55N 90.22W
27 T11 **Luling** Texas, SW USA 29.40N 97.39W
81 I18 **Lulonga** ≈ NW Dem. Rep. Congo
81 K22 **Lulua** ≈ S Dem. Rep. Congo
Luluabourg see Kananga
198 Dd8 **Luma** Ta'ū, E American Samoa 14.15S 169.30W
174 M16 **Lumajang** Jawa, C Indonesia 8.06S 113.13E
164 G13 **Lumajangdong Co** ◎ W China
84 G13 **Lumbala Kaquengue** Moxico, E Angola 12.40S 22.34E
85 F14 **Lumbala N'Guimbo** var. Nguimbo, Port. Gago Coutinho, Vila Gago Coutinho. Moxico, E Angola 14.04S 21.25E
23 T11 **Lumber River** ≈ North Carolina/South Carolina, SE USA
Lumber State see Maine
24 L8 **Lumberton** Mississippi, S USA 31.00N 89.27W
23 U11 **Lumberton** North Carolina, SE USA 34.37N 79.00W
107 R4 **Lumbier** Navarra, N Spain 42.39N 1.19W
85 Q15 **Lumbo** Nampula, NE Mozambique 15.00S 40.40E
128 M4 **Lumbovka** Murmanskaya Oblast', NW Russian Federation 67.41N 40.31E
106 J7 **Lumbrales** Castilla-León, N Spain 40.57N 6.43W
159 W13 **Lumding** Assam, NE India 25.46N 93.10E
84 F12 **Lumege** var. Lumeje. Moxico, E Angola 11.30S 20.57E
Lumeje see Lumege
194 F10 **Lumi** Sandaun, NW PNG 3.30S 142.04E
101 J17 **Lummen** Limburg, NE Belgium 50.58N 5.12E
95 J20 **Lumparland** Åland, SW Finland 60.06N 20.15E
178 K12 **Lumphăt** prev. Lomphat. Rôtânôkiri, NE Cambodia 13.32N 106.57E
9 U16 **Lumsden** Saskatchewan, S Canada 50.39N 104.52W
193 C23 **Lumsden** Southland, South Island, NZ 45.43S 168.26E
174 J11 **Lumut, Tanjung** headland Sumatera, W Indonesia 3.47S 105.55E
163 P4 **Lün** Töv, C Mongolia 47.51N 105.11E
118 I13 **Lunca Corbului** Argeş, S Romania 44.41N 24.46E
97 K23 **Lund** Skåne, S Sweden 55.42N 13.10E
37 X6 **Lund** Nevada, W USA 38.50N 115.00W
84 D11 **Lunda Norte** ⬖ province NE Angola
84 E12 **Lunda Sul** ⬖ province NE Angola
84 M13 **Lundazi** Eastern, NE Zambia 12.19S 33.10E
97 G16 **Lunde** Telemark, S Norway 61.31N 6.37E
Lundenburg see Břeclav
97 C17 **Lundevatnet** ◎ S Norway
Lundi see Runde
99 I23 **Lundy** island SW England, UK
102 J10 **Lüneburg** Niedersachsen, N Germany 53.15N 10.25E
102 J11 **Lüneburger Heide** heathland NW Germany
105 Q15 **Lunel** Hérault, S France 43.40N 4.08E
103 F14 **Lünen** Nordrhein-Westfalen, W Germany 51.37N 7.31E
11 P16 **Lunenburg** Nova Scotia, SE Canada 44.22N 64.21W
23 V7 **Lunenburg** Virginia, NE USA 36.56N 78.15W
105 T5 **Lunéville** Meurthe-et-Moselle, NE France 48.34N 6.30E
85 I14 **Lunga** ≈ C Zambia
Lunga, Isola see Dugi Otok
164 H12 **Lungdo** Xizang Zizhiqu, W China 33.45N 82.09E
164 I14 **Lunggar** Xizang Zizhiqu, W China 31.10N 84.01E
78 I15 **Lungi** ✕ (Freetown) W Sierra Leone 8.36N 13.10W
Lungkiang see Qiqihar
Lungleh see Lunglei
159 W15 **Lunglei** prev. Lungleh. Mizoram, NE India 22.55N 92.49E
164 L15 **Lungsang** Xizang Zizhiqu, W China 29.49N 88.27E
84 E13 **Lungué-Bungo** var. Lungwebungu. ≈ Angola/Zambia see also Lungwebungu
85 G14 **Lungwebungu** var. Lungué-Bungo. ≈ Angola/Zambia see also Lungué-Bungo
158 F12 **Lūni** Rājasthān, N India 26.03N 73.00E
158 F12 **Lūni** ≈ N India
Luninets see Luninyets
37 S7 **Luning** Nevada, W USA 38.29N 118.10W
Łuniniec see Luninyets
131 P6 **Lunino** Penzenskaya Oblast', W Russian Federation 53.35N 45.12E
121 J19 **Luninyets** Pol. Łuniniec, Rus. Luninets. Brestskaya Voblasts', SW Belarus 52.15N 26.49E
158 F10 **Lūnkaransar** Rājasthān, NW India 28.31N 73.49E
121 G17 **Lunna** Pol. Łunna, Rus. Lunna. Hrodzyenskaya Voblasts', W Belarus 53.27N 24.16E
78 I15 **Lunsar** W Sierra Leone 8.40N 12.31W
85 K14 **Lunsemfwa** ≈ C Zambia
164 J6 **Luntai** var. Bügür. Xinjiang Uygur Zizhiqu, NW China 41.48N 84.14E
100 K11 **Lunteren** Gelderland, C Netherlands 52.04N 5.37E
175 O16 **Lunyuk** Sumbawa, S Indonesia 8.56S 117.15E
111 U5 **Lunz am See** Niederösterreich, C Austria 47.54N 15.01E
169 Y7 **Luobei** var. Fengxiang. Heilongjiang, NE China 47.35N 130.51E
Luocheng see Hui'an, Fujian, China
Luocheng see Luoding, Guangdong, China
166 J13 **Luodian** var. Longping. Guizhou, S China 25.25N 106.49E
166 M15 **Luoding** var. Luocheng. Guangdong, S China 22.44N 111.28E
166 M6 **Luo He** ≈ C China
166 L5 **Luo He** ≈ C China
167 N7 **Luohe** Henan, C China 33.37N 114.00E
Luolajarvi see Kuoloyarvi
Luong Nam Tha see Louangnamtha
166 L13 **Luoqing Jiang** ≈ S China
167 O8 **Luoshan** Henan, C China 32.12N 114.30E
167 O12 **Luoxiao Shan** ▲ S China
167 N6 **Luoyang** var. Honan, Lo-yang. Henan, C China 34.40N 112.25E
167 R12 **Luoyuan** var. Fengshan. Fujian, SE China 26.29N 119.32E
81 F21 **Luozi** Bas-Congo, W Dem. Rep. Congo 4.57S 14.07E
85 J17 **Lupane** Matabeleland North, W Zimbabwe 18.46S 27.47E
166 I12 **Lupanshui** prev. Shuicheng. Guizhou, S China 26.38N 104.49E
174 Ll7 **Lupar, Batang** ≈ East Malaysia
Lupatia see Altamura
118 G12 **Lupeni** Hung. Lupény. Hunedoara, SW Romania 45.20N 23.07E
Lupény see Lupeni
84 N13 **Lupiliche** Niassa, N Mozambique 11.36S 35.15E
85 E14 **Lupire** Cuando Cubango, E Angola 14.39S 19.39E
179 Rr16 **Lupon** Mindanao, S Philippines 6.53N 126.00E
81 L22 **Luputa** Kasai Oriental, S Dem. Rep. Congo 7.07S 23.43E
123 Jj17 **Luqa** ✕ (Valletta) S Malta 35.53N 14.27E
165 U11 **Luqu** var. Ma'ai. Gansu, C China 34.34N 102.27E
47 U5 **Luquillo, Sierra de** ▲▲ E Puerto Rico
28 L4 **Luray** Kansas, C USA 39.06N 98.41W
23 U4 **Luray** Virginia, NE USA 38.40N 78.27W
105 T7 **Lure** Haute-Saône, E France 47.42N 6.30E
84 D11 **Luremo** Lunda Norte, NE Angola 8.32S 17.55E
99 F15 **Lurgan** Ir. An Lorgain. S Northern Ireland, UK 54.28N 6.19W
59 K18 **Luribay** La Paz, W Bolivia 17.09S 67.39W
Luring see Gêrzê
85 Q14 **Lúrio** Nampula, NE Mozambique 13.32S 40.33E
85 P14 **Lúrio, Rio** ≈ NE Mozambique
Luristan see Lorestān
Lurka see Lorca
85 J15 **Lusaka** ● (Zambia) Lusaka, SE Zambia 15.23S 28.16E
85 J15 **Lusaka** ⬖ province C Zambia
85 J15 **Lusaka** ✕ Lusaka, C Zambia 15.10S 28.22E
81 L21 **Lusambo** Kasai Oriental, C Dem. Rep. Congo 4.54S 23.25E
195 N14 **Lusancay Islands and Reefs** island group SE PNG
81 I21 **Lusanga** Bandundu, SW Dem. Rep. Congo 4.55S 18.40E
81 N21 **Lusangi** Maniema, E Dem. Rep. Congo 4.39S 27.10E
Lusatian Mountains see Lausitzer Bergland
Lushar see Huangzhong
Lushnja see Lushnjë
115 K21 **Lushnjë** var. Lushnja. Fier, C Albania 40.54N 19.43E
83 J21 **Lushoto** Tanga, E Tanzania 4.48S 38.19E
104 L10 **Lusignan** Vienne, W France 46.25N 0.06E
35 Z15 **Lusk** Wyoming, C USA 42.45N 104.27W
Luso see Luena
104 L10 **Lussac-les-Châteaux** Vienne, W France 46.23N 0.44E
Lussin/Lussino see Lošinj
Lussinpiccolo see Mali Lošinj
110 I7 **Lustenau** Vorarlberg, W Austria 47.26N 9.39E
167 T14 **Lü Tao** var. Huoshao Dao, Lütao, Eng. Green Island. island SE Taiwan
Lūt, Baḩrat/Lut, Bahret see Dead Sea
24 K9 **Lutcher** Louisiana, S USA 30.02N 90.42W
149 T9 **Lūt, Dasht-e** var. Kavīr-e Lūt. desert E Iran
85 F14 **Lutembo** Moxico, E Angola 13.30S 21.21E
Lutetia/Lutetia Parisiorum see Paris
Luteva see Lodève
12 G15 **Luther Lake** ◎ Ontario, S Canada
195 U13 **Luti** Choiseul Island, NW Solomon Islands 7.13S 157.01E
Lūt, Kavīr-e see Lūt, Dasht-e
99 N21 **Luton** SE England, UK 51.52N 0.25W
99 N21 **Luton** ✕ (London) SE England, UK 51.54N 0.24W
110 B10 **Lutry** Vaud, SW Switzerland 46.31N 6.31E
15 I18 **Łutselk'e** prev. Snowdrift. Northwest Territories, W Canada 62.24N 110.42W
31 Y4 **Lutsen** Minnesota, N USA 47.39N 90.37W
118 J4 **Luts'k** Pol. Łuck, Rus. Lutsk. Volyns'ka Oblast', NW Ukraine 50.45N 25.22E
Luttenberg see Ljutomer
Lüttich see Liège
85 G25 **Luttig** Western Cape, SW South Africa 32.33S 22.13E
Lutto see Lotta
84 E13 **Lutuai** Moxico, E Angola 12.38S 20.06E
119 Y7 **Lutuhyne** Luhans'ka Oblast', E Ukraine 48.24N 39.12E
176 Ww13 **Lutur, Pulau** island Kepulauan Aru, E Indonesia
25 V12 **Lutz** Florida, SE USA 28.09N 82.27W
Lutzow-Holm Bay see Lützow Holmbukta
205 V2 **Lützow Holmbukta** var. Lutzow-Holm Bay. bay Antarctica
83 L16 **Luuq** It. Lugh Ganana. Gedo, SW Somalia 3.42N 42.34E
94 M12 **Luusua** Lappi, NE Finland 66.28N 27.16E
25 Q6 **Luverne** Alabama, S USA 31.43N 86.15W
31 S11 **Luverne** Minnesota, N USA 43.39N 96.12W
81 O22 **Luvua** ≈ SE Dem. Rep. Congo
84 F13 **Luvuei** Moxico, E Angola 13.08S 21.09E
83 H24 **Luwego** ≈ S Tanzania
84 K12 **Luwingu** Northern, NE Zambia 10.13S 29.55E
175 Qq9 **Luwuk** prev. Loewoek. Sulawesi, C Indonesia 0.55S 122.46E
25 N3 **Luxapallila Creek** ≈ Alabama/Mississippi, S USA
101 M25 **Luxembourg** ● (Luxembourg) Luxembourg, S Luxembourg 49.37N 6.07E
101 M25 **Luxembourg** off. Grand Duchy of Luxembourg, var. Lëtzebuerg, Luxemburg. ◆ monarchy NW Europe
101 J23 **Luxembourg** ⬖ province SE Belgium

◆ Country ● Country Capital ◇ Dependent Territory ○ Dependent Territory Capital ⬖ Administrative Region ✕ International Airport ▲ Mountain ▲▲ Mountain Range Volcano ≈ River ◎ Lake ⊠ Reservoir
287

LUXEMBOURG – MAHĀD

101 L24 **Luxembourg** ◈ district S Luxembourg
33 N6 **Luxemburg** Wisconsin, N USA 44.32N 87.42W
Luxemburg see Luxembourg
105 U7 **Luxeuil-les-Bains** Haute-Saône, E France 47.49N 6.22E
166 E13 **Luxi** prev. Mangshi. Yunnan, SW China 24.27N 98.31E
84 E10 **Luxico** ≈ Angola/Dem. Rep. Congo
77 X10 **Luxor** Ar. Al Uqşur. E Egypt 25.39N 32.39E
77 X10 **Luxor** ✕ C Egypt 25.39N 32.48E
166 M4 **Luya Shan** ▲▲ C China
104 J15 **Luy de Béarn** ≈ SW France
104 J15 **Luy de France** ≈ SW France
129 P12 **Luza** Kirovskaya Oblast', NW Russian Federation 60.37N 47.13E
129 Q12 **Luza** ≈ NW Russian Federation
106 I16 **Luz, Costa de la** coastal region SW Spain
113 K20 **Luže** var. Lausche. ▲ Czech Republic/Germany see also Lausche 50.51N 14.40E
110 F8 **Luzern** Fr. Lucerne, It. Lucerna. Luzern, C Switzerland 47.03N 8.16E
110 E8 **Luzern** Fr. Lucerne. ◈ canton C Switzerland
166 L13 **Luzhai** Guangxi Zhuangzu Zizhiqu, S China 24.33N 109.46E
120 K12 **Luzhki** Rus. Luzhki. Vitsyebskaya Voblasts', N Belarus 55.20N 27.54E
166 I10 **Luzhou** Sichuan, C China 28.55N 105.28E
Lužická Nisa see Neisse
Lužické Hory see Lausitzer Bergland
Lužnice see Lainsitz
179 Pp9 **Luzon** island N Philippines
179 Oo6 **Luzon Strait** strait Philippines/Taiwan
118 I5 **L'viv** Ger. Lemberg, Pol. Lwów, Rus. L'vov. L'vivs'ka Oblast', W Ukraine 49.48N 24.04E
L'viv see L'vivs'ka Oblast'
118 I4 **L'vivs'ka Oblast'** var. L'viv, Rus. L'vovskaya Oblast'. ◈ province NW Ukraine
L'vov see L'viv
L'vovskaya Oblast' see L'vivs'ka Oblast'
Lwena see Luena
Lwów see L'viv
112 F11 **Lwówek** Ger. Neustadt bei Pinne. Wielkolpolskie, C Poland 52.27N 16.10E
113 E14 **Lwówek Śląski** Ger. Löwenberg in Schlesien. Dolnośląskie, SW Poland 51.06N 15.35E
121 I18 **Lyakhavichy** Rus. Lyakhovichi. Brestskaya Voblasts', SW Belarus 53.01N 26.15E
Lyakhovichi see Lyakhavichy
193 B22 **Lyall, Mount** ▲ South Island, NZ 45.14S 167.31E
Lyallpur see Faisalābād
125 G10 **Lyamin** ≈ C Russian Federation
Lyangar see Langar
125 G10 **Lyantor** Khanty-Mansiyskiy Avtonomnyy Okrug, C Russian Federation 61.40N 72.21E
128 H11 **Lyaskelya** Respublika Kareliya, NW Russian Federation 61.42N 31.06E
121 I18 **Lyasnaya** Rus. Lesnaya. Brestskaya Voblasts', SW Belarus 52.58N 25.46E
121 F19 **Lyasnaya** Pol. Leśna, Rus. Lesnaya. ≈ SW Belarus
128 H15 **Lychkovo** Novgorodskaya Oblast', W Russian Federation 57.55N 32.24E
Lyck see Ełk
95 I15 **Lycksele** Västerbotten, N Sweden 64.34N 18.40E
20 G13 **Lycoming Creek** ≈ Pennsylvania, NE USA
Lycopolis see Asyût
205 N3 **Lyddan Island** island Antarctica
85 K20 **Lydenburg** Mpumalanga, NE South Africa 25.01S 30.27E
121 L20 **Lyel'chytsy** Rus. Lel'chitsy. Homyel'skaya Voblasts', SE Belarus 51.46N 28.19E
121 P14 **Lyenina** Rus. Lenino. Mahilyowskaya Voblasts', E Belarus 54.26N 31.07E
120 L13 **Lyepyel'** Rus. Lepel'. Vitsyebskaya Voblasts', N Belarus 54.54N 28.43E
27 S17 **Lyford** Texas, SW USA 26.24N 97.47W
97 E17 **Lygna** ≈ S Norway
20 G14 **Lykens** Pennsylvania, NE USA 40.33N 76.42W
117 E21 **Lykódimo** ▲ S Greece 36.56N 21.49E
99 K24 **Lyme Bay** bay S England, UK
99 K24 **Lyme Regis** S England, UK 50.44N 2.55W
112 L7 **Łyna** Ger. Alle. ≈ N Poland
31 P12 **Lynch** Nebraska, C USA 42.49N 98.27W
22 J10 **Lynchburg** Tennessee, S USA 35.15N 86.22W
23 T6 **Lynchburg** Virginia, NE USA 37.24N 79.08W
23 T12 **Lynches River** ≈ South Carolina, SE USA
34 H6 **Lynden** Washington, NW USA 48.57N 122.27W
190 I5 **Lyndhurst** South Australia 30.19S 138.20E
29 Q5 **Lyndon** Kansas, C USA 38.37N 95.40W
21 N7 **Lyndonville** Vermont, NE USA 44.31N 71.58W
97 D18 **Lyngdal** Vest-Agder, S Norway 58.07N 7.04E
94 I9 **Lyngen** Lapp. Ivgovuotna. inlet Arctic Ocean
97 G17 **Lyngør** Aust-Agder, S Norway 58.38N 9.05E
94 I9 **Lyngseidet** Troms, N Norway 69.36N 20.07E
21 P11 **Lynn** Massachusetts, NE USA 42.28N 70.57W
Lynn see King's Lynn
25 R9 **Lynn Haven** Florida, SE USA 30.15N 85.39W
9 V11 **Lynn Lake** Manitoba, C Canada 56.51N 101.01W
Lynn Regis see King's Lynn
120 I13 **Lyntupy** Rus. Lyntupy. Vitsyebskaya Voblasts', NW Belarus 55.03N 26.19E
105 R11 **Lyon** Eng. Lyons; anc. Lugdunum. Rhône, E France 45.46N 4.49E
15 H3 **Lyon, Cape** headland Northwest Territories, NW Canada 69.47N 123.10W
20 K6 **Lyon Mountain** ▲ New York, NE USA 44.42N 73.52W
105 Q11 **Lyonnais, Monts du** ▲▲ C France
67 N25 **Lyon Point** headland SE Tristan da Cunha 37.06S 12.13W
190 E5 **Lyons** South Australia 30.40S 133.50E
39 T3 **Lyons** Colorado, C USA 40.13N 105.16W
25 V6 **Lyons** Georgia, SE USA 32.12N 82.19W
28 M5 **Lyons** Kansas, C USA 38.21N 98.12W
31 R14 **Lyons** Nebraska, C USA 41.56N 96.28W
20 G10 **Lyons** New York, NE USA 43.03N 76.58W
Lyons see Lyon
120 O13 **Lyozna** Rus. Liozno. Vitsyebskaya Voblasts', NE Belarus 55.01N 30.48E
119 S4 **Lypova Dolyna** Sums'ka Oblast', NE Ukraine 50.36N 33.50E
119 N6 **Lypovets'** Rus. Lipovets. Vinnyts'ka Oblast', C Ukraine 49.13N 29.06E
Lys see Leie
113 I18 **Lysá Hora** ▲ E Czech Republic 49.31N 18.27E
97 D16 **Lysefjorden** fjord S Norway
97 I18 **Lysekil** Västra Götaland, S Sweden 58.16N 11.25E
Lýsi see Akdoğan
35 V14 **Lysite** Wyoming, C USA 43.16N 107.42W
131 P3 **Lyskovo** Nizhegorodskaya Oblast', W Russian Federation 56.04N 45.01E
110 D8 **Lyss** Bern, W Switzerland 47.04N 7.19E
97 H22 **Lystrup** Århus, C Denmark 56.13N 10.13E
129 V14 **Lys'va** Permskaya Oblast', NW Russian Federation 58.04N 57.48E
119 P6 **Lysyanka** Cherkas'ka Oblast', C Ukraine 49.15N 30.50E
119 X6 **Lysychans'k** Rus. Lisichansk. Luhans'ka Oblast', E Ukraine 48.52N 38.27E
99 K17 **Lytham St Anne's** NW England, UK 53.45N 3.01W
193 I19 **Lyttelton** Canterbury, South Island, NZ 43.35S 172.44E
8 M17 **Lytton** British Columbia, SW Canada 50.12N 121.34W
121 L18 **Lyuban'** Rus. Lyuban'. Minskaya Voblasts', S Belarus 52.48N 28.00E
121 L18 **Lyubanskaye Vodaskhovishcha** ▣ C Belarus
118 M5 **Lyubar** Zhytomyrs'ka Oblast', N Ukraine 49.54N 27.48E
Lyubashëvka see Lyubashivka
119 O8 **Lyubashivka** Rus. Lyubashëvka. Odes'ka Oblast', SW Ukraine 47.49N 30.18E
121 I16 **Lyubcha** Pol. Lubcz, Rus. Lyubcha. Hrodzyenskaya Voblasts', W Belarus 53.46N 26.04E
130 L4 **Lyubertsy** Moskovskaya Oblast', W Russian Federation 55.37N 38.02E
118 K2 **Lyubeshiv** Volyns'ka Oblast', NW Ukraine 51.46N 25.33E
128 M14 **Lyubim** Yaroslavskaya Oblast', NW Russian Federation 58.21N 40.46E
116 K11 **Lyubimets** Khaskovo, S Bulgaria 41.51N 26.03E
Lyublin see Lublin
118 I3 **Lyuboml'** Pol. Luboml. Volyns'ka Oblast', NW Ukraine 51.12N 24.01E
Lyubotin see Lyubotyn
119 U5 **Lyubotyn** Rus. Lyubotin. Kharkivs'ka Oblast', E Ukraine 49.57N 35.57E
130 I5 **Lyudinovo** Kaluzhskaya Oblast', W Russian Federation 53.52N 34.28E
131 T2 **Lyuk** Udmurtskaya Respublika, NW Russian Federation 56.55N 52.45E
116 M9 **Lyulyakovo** prev. Keremitlik. Burgas, E Bulgaria 42.53N 27.05E
121 I18 **Lyusina** Rus. Lyusino. Brestskaya Voblasts', SW Belarus 52.37N 26.31E
Lyusino see Lyusina

M

144 G9 **Ma'ād** Irbid, N Jordan 32.37N 35.36E
Ma'ai see Luqu
Maalahti see Malax
Maale see Male'
144 G13 **Ma'ān** Ma'ān, SW Jordan 30.10N 35.45E
144 H13 **Ma'ān** off. Muḩāfaz̧at Ma'ān, var. Ma'an, Ma'ān. ◈ governorate S Jordan
95 M16 **Maaninka** Itä-Suomi, C Finland 63.10N 27.19E
Maanĭt see Bayan, Töv, Mongolia
Maanĭt see Hishig-Öndör, Bulgan, Mongolia
95 N15 **Maanselkä** Oulu, C Finland 63.53N 28.27E
167 Q8 **Ma'anshan** Anhui, E China 31.45N 118.31E
196 F16 **Maap** island Caroline Islands, W Micronesia
120 H3 **Maardu** Ger. Maart. Harjumaa, NW Estonia 59.28N 25.01E
Ma'aret-en-Nu'man see Ma'arrat an Nu'mān
101 K16 **Maarheeze** Noord-Brabant, SE Netherlands 51.19N 5.37E
Maarianhamina see Mariehamn
144 I4 **Ma'arrat an Nu'mān** var. Ma'aret-en-Nu'man, Fr. Maarret enn Naamâne. Idlib, NW Syria 35.40N 36.40E
Maarret enn Naamâne see Ma'arrat an Nu'mān
100 I11 **Maarssen** Utrecht, C Netherlands 52.07N 5.03E
Maart see Maardu
101 L17 **Maas** Fr. Meuse. ≈ W Europe see also Meuse
101 M15 **Maasbree** Limburg, SE Netherlands 51.22N 6.03E
101 L17 **Maaseik** prev. Maeseyck. Limburg, NE Belgium 51.04N 5.48E
179 R13 **Maasin** Leyte, C Philippines 10.10N 124.55E
101 L17 **Maasmechelen** Limburg, NE Belgium 50.58N 5.42E
100 G12 **Maassluis** Zuid-Holland, SW Netherlands 51.55N 4.15E
101 L18 **Maastricht** var. Maestricht; anc. Traietum ad Mosam, Traiectum Tungorum. Limburg, SE Netherlands 50.51N 5.42E
191 N18 **Maatsuyker Group** island group Tasmania, SE Australia
Maba see Qujiang
85 L20 **Mabalane** Gaza, S Mozambique 23.43S 32.37E
27 V7 **Mabank** Texas, SW USA 32.22N 96.06W
172 N10 **Mabechi-gawa** var. Mabuchi-gawa. ≈ Honshū, C Japan
99 O18 **Mablethorpe** E England, UK 53.20N 0.14E
176 W9 **Maboi** Papua, E Indonesia 1.00S 134.02E
85 M19 **Mabote** Inhambane, S Mozambique 22.03S 34.09E
34 J10 **Mabton** Washington, NW USA 46.13N 120.00W
Mabuchi-gawa see Mabechi-gawa
85 H20 **Mabutsane** Southern, S Botswana 24.22S 23.34E
65 G19 **Macá, Cerro** ▲ S Chile 45.07S 73.11W
62 Q9 **Macaé** Rio de Janeiro, SE Brazil 22.21S 41.48W
84 N13 **Macaloge** Niassa, N Mozambique 12.30S 35.25E
Macan see Bonerate, Kepulauan
167 N15 **Macao** Chin. Aomen, Port. Macau. S China
106 H9 **Mação** Santarém, C Portugal 39.33N 8.00W
60 J11 **Macapá** state capital Amapá, N Brazil 0.04N 51.04W
45 S17 **Macaracas** Los Santos, S Panama 7.43N 80.33W
57 P6 **Macare, Caño** ≈ NE Venezuela
57 Q6 **Macareo, Caño** ≈ NE Venezuela
Macarsca see Makarska
MacArthur see Ormoc
190 L12 **Macarthur** Victoria, SE Australia 38.04S 142.02E
58 C7 **Macas** Morona Santiago, SE Ecuador 2.22S 78.07W
Macassar see Makassar
61 Q14 **Macau** Rio Grande do Norte, E Brazil 5.04S 36.37W
Macau see Macao
Macău see Makó, Hungary
67 E24 **Macbride Head** headland East Falkland, Falkland Islands 51.25S 57.55W
25 V9 **Macclenny** Florida, SE USA 30.16N 82.07W
99 L18 **Macclesfield** C England, UK 53.16N 2.07W
198 F6 **Macclesfield Bank** undersea feature N South China Sea
MacCluer Gulf see Berau, Teluk
189 N7 **Macdonald, Lake** salt lake Western Australia
189 Q7 **Macdonnell Ranges** ▲▲ Northern Territory, C Australia
98 K8 **Macduff** NE Scotland, UK 57.39N 2.28W
106 I6 **Macedo de Cavaleiros** Bragança, N Portugal 41.31N 6.57W
Macedonia Central see Kentrikí Makedonía
Macedonia East and Thrace see Anatolikí Makedonía kai Thráki
115 O19 **Macedonia, FYR** off. the Former Yugoslav Republic of Macedonia, var. Macedonia, Mac. Makedonija, abbrev. FYR Macedonia, FYROM. ◆ republic SE Europe
Macedonia West see Dytikí Makedonía
61 Q16 **Maceió** state capital Alagoas, E Brazil 9.40S 35.43W
78 K15 **Macenta** SE Guinea 8.31N 9.31W
108 J12 **Macerata** Marche, C Italy 43.19N 13.28E
9 S11 **MacFarlane** ≈ Saskatchewan, C Canada
190 H7 **Macfarlane, Lake** var. Lake Mcfarlane. ◎ South Australia
Macgillicuddy's Reeks Mountains see Macgillycuddy's Reeks
99 B21 **Macgillycuddy's Reeks** var. Macgillicuddy's Reeks Mountains, Ir. Na Cruacha Dubha. ▲▲ SW Ireland
9 X16 **MacGregor** Manitoba, S Canada 49.58N 98.49W
155 O10 **Mach** Baluchistān, SW Pakistan 29.52N 67.19E
58 C6 **Machachi** Pichincha, C Ecuador 0.33S 78.34W
85 M19 **Machaila** Gaza, S Mozambique 22.15S 32.57E
Machaire Fíolta see Magherafelt
Machaire Rátha see Maghera
83 I19 **Machakos** Eastern, S Kenya 1.33S 37.17E
58 B8 **Machala** El Oro, SW Ecuador 3.19S 79.57W
Machali see Madoi
85 J19 **Machaneng** Central, SE Botswana 23.12S 27.28E
85 M18 **Machanga** Sofala, E Mozambique 20.55S 35.03E
82 G13 **Machar Marshes** wetland SE Sudan
104 I8 **Machecoul** Loire-Atlantique, NW France 46.59N 1.51W
167 O8 **Macheng** Hubei, C China 31.10N 115.00E
161 J16 **Mācherla** Andhra Pradesh, C India 16.28N 79.25E
159 O11 **Māchhāpuchhre** ▲ C Nepal 28.30N 83.57E
21 T6 **Machias** Maine, NE USA 44.43N 67.28W
21 R3 **Machias River** ≈ Maine, NE USA
21 T6 **Machias River** ≈ Maine, NE USA
66 P5 **Machico** Madeira, Portugal, NE Atlantic Ocean 32.43N 16.46W
161 K16 **Machilīpatnam** var. Bandar Masulipatnam. Andhra Pradesh, E India 16.12N 81.10E
56 G5 **Machiques** Zulia, NW Venezuela 10.01N 72.40W
59 G15 **Machupicchu** Cusco, C Peru 13.07S 72.30W
85 M20 **Macia** var. Vila de Macia. Gaza, S Mozambique 25.01S 33.05E
Macías Nguema Biyogo see Bioco, Isla de
118 M13 **Măcin** Tulcea, SE Romania 45.15N 28.09E
191 T4 **Macintyre River** ≈ New South Wales/Queensland, SE Australia
189 Y7 **Mackay** Queensland, NE Australia 21.10S 149.10E
189 O7 **Mackay, Lake** salt lake Northern Territory/Western Australia
8 M13 **Mackenzie** British Columbia, W Canada 55.18N 123.09W
15 Gg6 **Mackenzie** ≈ Northwest Territories, NW Canada
205 Y6 **Mackenzie Bay** bay Antarctica
8 J1 **Mackenzie Bay** bay NW Canada
2 D9 **Mackenzie Delta** delta Northwest Territories, NW Canada
207 P8 **Mackenzie King Island** island Queen Elizabeth Islands, Northwest Territories, N Canada
14 G5 **Mackenzie Mountains** ▲▲ Northwest Territories, NW Canada
33 Q5 **Mackinac, Straits of** ◎ Michigan, N USA
204 K5 **Mackintosh, Cape** headland Antarctica 72.52S 60.00W
9 R15 **Macklin** Saskatchewan, S Canada 52.19N 109.51W
191 V6 **Macksville** New South Wales, SE Australia 30.39S 152.54E
191 V5 **Maclean** New South Wales, SE Australia 29.30S 153.15E
85 J24 **Maclear** Eastern Cape, SE South Africa 31.04S 28.22E
191 U6 **Macleay River** ≈ New South Wales, SE Australia
MacLeod see Fort Macleod
188 G9 **Macleod, Lake** ◎ Western Australia
8 I6 **Macmillan** ≈ Yukon Territory, NW Canada
32 J12 **Macomb** Illinois, N USA 40.27N 90.40W
109 B18 **Macomer** Sardegna, Italy, C Mediterranean Sea 40.14N 8.46E
84 Q13 **Macomia** Cabo Delgado, NE Mozambique 12.15S 40.06E
25 T5 **Macon** Georgia, SE USA 32.48N 83.41W
25 N4 **Macon** Mississippi, S USA 33.06N 88.33W
29 U3 **Macon** Missouri, C USA 39.44N 92.28W
105 R10 **Mâcon** anc. Matisco, Matisco Ædourum. Saône-et-Loire, C France 46.19N 4.48E
24 J6 **Macon, Bayou** ≈ Arkansas/Louisiana, S USA
84 G13 **Macondo** Moxico, E Angola 12.31S 23.45E
85 M16 **Macossa** Manica, C Mozambique 17.51S 33.54E
9 T12 **Macoun Lake** ◎ Saskatchewan, C Canada
32 K14 **Macoupin Creek** ≈ Illinois, N USA
Macouria see Tonate
85 N18 **Macovane** Inhambane, SE Mozambique 21.30S 35.07E
191 N17 **Macquarie Harbour** inlet Tasmania, SE Australia
199 Ii15 **Macquarie Island** island NZ, SW Pacific Ocean
191 T8 **Macquarie, Lake** lagoon New South Wales, SE Australia
191 Q6 **Macquarie Marshes** wetland New South Wales, SE Australia
183 O13 **Macquarie Ridge** undersea feature SW Pacific Ocean
191 Q6 **Macquarie River** ≈ New South Wales, SE Australia
191 P17 **Macquarie River** ≈ Tasmania, SE Australia
205 V5 **Mac. Robertson Land** physical region Antarctica
99 C21 **Macroom** Ir. Maigh Chromtha. SW Ireland 51.54N 8.57W
44 G5 **Macuelizo** Santa Bárbara, NW Honduras 15.21N 88.31W
190 G2 **Macumba River** ≈ South Australia
59 I16 **Macusani** Puno, S Peru 14.07S 70.27W
58 E8 **Macusari, Río** ≈ N Peru
43 U15 **Macuspana** Tabasco, SE Mexico 17.43N 92.36W
144 G10 **Ma'dabā** var. Mādabā, Madeba; anc. Medeba. Ma'dabā, NW Jordan 31.43N 35.48E
144 G11 **Ma'dabā** off. Muḩāfaz̧at Ma'dabā. ◈ governorate C Jordan
180 G2 **Madagascar** off. Democratic Republic of Madagascar, Malg. Madagasikara; prev. Malagasy Republic. ◆ republic W Indian Ocean
180 I5 **Madagascar** island W Indian Ocean
132 L17 **Madagascar Basin** undersea feature W Indian Ocean
132 L16 **Madagascar Plain** undersea feature W Indian Ocean
69 Y14 **Madagascar Plateau** var. Madagascar Ridge, Madagascar Rise, Rus. Madagaskarskiy Khrebet. undersea feature W Indian Ocean
Madagascar Ridge/Madagascar Rise see Madagascar Plateau
Madagasikara see Madagascar
Madagaskarskiy Khrebet see Madagascar Plateau
66 N2 **Madalena** Pico, Azores, Portugal, NE Atlantic Ocean 38.31N 28.15W
79 Y6 **Madama** Agadez, NE Niger 21.54N 13.43E
116 J12 **Madan** Smolyan, S Bulgaria 41.30N 24.58E
161 I19 **Madanapalle** Andhra Pradesh, E India 13.33N 78.31E
194 I11 **Madang** Madang, N PNG 5.09S 145.48E
194 I11 **Madang** ◈ province N PNG
152 G7 **Madaniyat** Rus. Madeniyet. Qoraqalpog'iston Respublikasi, W Uzbekistan 42.48N 59.00E
Madanīyīn see Médenine
79 U11 **Madaoua** Tahoua, SW Niger 14.06N 6.01E
Madaras see Vtáčnik
159 U15 **Madaripur** Dhaka, C Bangladesh 23.09N 90.10E
79 U12 **Madarounfa** Maradi, S Niger 13.16N 7.07E
Mađarska see Hungary
Madau see Madaw
195 P15 **Madau Island** island SE PNG
152 B13 **Madaw** Rus. Madau. Balkan Welaýaty, W Turkmenistan 38.11N 54.46E
21 S1 **Madawaska** Maine, NE USA 47.19N 68.19W
12 J13 **Madawaska** ≈ Ontario, SE Canada
Madawaska Highlands see Haliburton Highlands
177 G4 **Madaya** Mandalay, C Burma 22.12N 96.04E
109 K17 **Maddaloni** Campania, S Italy 41.03N 14.22E
31 O3 **Maddock** North Dakota, N USA 47.57N 99.31W
101 I14 **Made** Noord-Brabant, S Netherlands 51.40N 4.48E
Madeba see Ma'dabā
66 L9 **Madeira** var. Ilha de Madeira. island Madeira, Portugal, NE Atlantic Ocean
Madeira, Ilha de see Madeira
66 O5 **Madeira Islands** Port. Região Autoónoma da Madeira. ◈ autonomous region Madeira, Portugal, NE Atlantic Ocean
66 L9 **Madeira Plain** undersea feature E Atlantic Ocean
66 L9 **Madeira Ridge** undersea feature E Atlantic Ocean
61 F14 **Madeira, Rio** Sp. Río Madera. ≈ Bolivia/Brazil see also Madera, Río
103 J25 **Mädelegabel** ▲ Austria/Germany 47.18N 10.19E
13 X6 **Madeleine** ≈ Québec, SE Canada
13 X5 **Madeleine, Cap de la** headland Québec, SE Canada 49.13N 65.20W
11 Q13 **Madeleine, Îles de la** Eng. Magdalen Islands. island group Québec, E Canada
31 U10 **Madelia** Minnesota, N USA 44.03N 94.26W
37 P3 **Madeline** California, W USA 41.02N 120.28W
32 K3 **Madeline Island** island Apostle Islands, Wisconsin, N USA
143 O15 **Maden** Elaziğ, SE Turkey 38.24N 39.42E
151 V12 **Madeniyet** Vostochnyy Kazakhstan, E Kazakhstan 47.51N 78.37E
Madeniyet see Madaniyat
42 H5 **Madera** Chihuahua, N Mexico 29.10N 108.10W
37 Q10 **Madera** California, W USA 36.57N 120.02W
58 L13 **Madera, Río** Port. Rio Madeira. ≈ Bolivia/Brazil see also Madeira, Rio
108 D6 **Madesimo** Lombardia, N Italy 46.20N 9.26E
147 O14 **Madhāb, Wādī** dry watercourse NW Yemen
159 R13 **Madhepura** prev. Madhipure. Bihār, NE India 25.55N 86.48E
Madhipure see Madhepura
159 Q13 **Madhubani** Bihār, N India 26.21N 86.04E
159 Q15 **Madhupur** Jhārkhand, NE India 24.16N 86.37E
160 I10 **Madhya Pradesh** prev. Central Provinces and Berar. ◈ state C India
59 K15 **Madidi, Río** ≈ W Bolivia
161 F20 **Madikeri** prev. Mercara. Karnātaka, W India 12.28N 75.40E
29 O13 **Madill** Oklahoma, C USA 34.05N 96.46W
81 G21 **Madimba** Bas-Congo, SW Dem. Rep. Congo 4.58S 15.07E
144 M4 **Ma'dīn** Ar Raqqah, C Syria 35.45N 39.36E
Madīnah, Minţaqat al see Al Madīnah
78 M14 **Madinani** NW Ivory Coast 9.37N 6.57W
147 O17 **Madīnat ash Sha'b** prev. Al Ittiḩād. SW Yemen 12.52N 44.55E
144 K3 **Madīnat ath Thawrah** var. Ath Thawrah. Ar Raqqah, N Syria Asia 35.36N 39.00E
181 O6 **Madingley Rise** undersea feature W Indian Ocean
81 E21 **Madingo-Kayes** Le Kouilou, S Congo 4.22S 11.40E
81 F21 **Madingou** La Bouenza, S Congo 4.10S 13.33E
Madioen see Madiun
25 U8 **Madison** Florida, SE USA 30.27N 83.24W
25 T3 **Madison** Georgia, SE USA 33.37N 83.28W
33 P15 **Madison** Indiana, N USA 38.44N 85.22W
29 P6 **Madison** Kansas, C USA 38.08N 96.08W
21 Q6 **Madison** Maine, NE USA 44.48N 69.52W
31 S9 **Madison** Minnesota, N USA 45.00N 96.12W
24 K5 **Madison** Mississippi, S USA 32.27N 90.07W
31 Q14 **Madison** Nebraska, C USA 41.49N 97.27W
31 R10 **Madison** South Dakota, N USA 44.00N 97.06W
23 V5 **Madison** Virginia, NE USA 38.24N 78.12W
23 Q5 **Madison** West Virginia, NE USA 38.04N 81.49W
32 L9 **Madison** state capital Wisconsin, N USA 43.04N 89.22W
23 T6 **Madison Heights** Virginia, NE USA 37.25N 79.07W
22 I6 **Madisonville** Kentucky, S USA 37.19N 87.30W
22 M10 **Madisonville** Tennessee, S USA 35.31N 84.21W
27 V9 **Madisonville** Texas, SW USA 30.57N 95.54W
174 Ll15 **Madiun** prev. Madioen. Jawa, C Indonesia 7.37S 111.33E
Madjene see Majene
12 J14 **Madoc** Ontario, SE Canada 44.31N 77.27W
Madoera see Madura, Pulau
83 J18 **Mado Gashi** North Eastern, E Kenya 0.40N 39.09E
165 R11 **Madoi** var. Machali. Qinghai, C China 34.53N 98.07E
201 O13 **Madolenihmw** Pohnpei, E Micronesia
120 I9 **Madona** Ger. Modohn. Madona, E Latvia 56.51N 26.10E
109 J23 **Madonie** ▲▲ Sicilia, Italy, C Mediterranean Sea
147 Y11 **Madrakah, Ra's** headland E Oman 18.56N 57.54E
34 I12 **Madras** Oregon, NW USA 44.37N 121.07W
Madras see Chennai
59 H14 **Madre de Dios** off. Departamento de Madre de Dios. ◈ department E Peru
65 F22 **Madre de Dios, Isla** island S Chile
59 J14 **Madre de Dios, Río** ≈ Bolivia/Peru
27 T16 **Madre, Laguna** ◎ Texas, SW USA
43 Q9 **Madre, Laguna** lagoon NE Mexico
39 Q12 **Madre Mount** ▲ New Mexico, SW USA 34.18N 107.54W
107 N8 **Madrid** ● (Spain) Madrid, C Spain 40.25N 3.43W
31 V14 **Madrid** Iowa, C USA 41.52N 93.49W
107 N7 **Madrid** ◈ autonomous community C Spain
107 N10 **Madridejos** Castilla-La Mancha, C Spain 39.28N 3.31W
106 L7 **Madrigal de las Altas Torres** Castilla-León, N Spain 41.05N 5.00W
106 K10 **Madrigalejo** Extremadura, W Spain 39.08N 5.36W
36 L3 **Mad River** ≈ California, W USA
44 J8 **Madriz** ◈ department NW Nicaragua
106 K10 **Madroñera** Extremadura, W Spain 39.25N 5.46W
189 N12 **Madura** Western Australia 31.52S 127.01E
Madura see Madurai
161 H22 **Madurai** prev. Madura, Mathurai. Tamil Nādu, S India 9.55N 78.07E
174 M15 **Madura, Pulau** prev. Madoera. island C Indonesia
174 Mm15 **Madura, Selat** strait C Indonesia
131 Q17 **Madzhalis** Respublika Dagestan, SW Russian Federation 42.12N 47.46E
116 K12 **Madzharovo** Khaskovo, S Bulgaria 41.36N 25.52E
85 M14 **Madzimoyo** Eastern, E Zambia 13.39S 32.31E
171 K15 **Maebashi** var. Maebasi, Mayebashi. Gunma, Honshū, S Japan 36.24N 139.01E
Maebasi see Maebashi
178 Hh6 **Mae Chan** Chiang Rai, NW Thailand 20.13N 99.52E
178 Gg7 **Mae Hong Son** var. Maehongson, Muai To. Mae Hong Son, NW Thailand 19.16N 97.55E
Mae Nam Khong see Mekong
178 Hh7 **Mae Nam Nan** ≈ NW Thailand
178 H10 **Mae Nam Tha Chin** ≈ W Thailand
178 Hh7 **Mae Nam Yom** ≈ W Thailand
178 H7 **Mae Sariang** Mae Hong Son, NW Thailand 18.07N 97.57E
39 O3 **Maeser** Utah, W USA 40.28N 109.35W
Maeseyck see Maaseik
178 Gg9 **Mae Sot** var. Ban Mae Sot. Tak, W Thailand 16.43N 98.31E
Maestricht see Maastricht
178 H7 **Mae Suai** var. Ban Mae Suai. Chiang Rai, NW Thailand 19.36N 99.32E
178 H7 **Mae Tho, Doi** ▲ NW Thailand 18.56N 99.20E
180 I4 **Maevatanana** Mahajanga, C Madagascar 16.57S 46.49E
197 C12 **Maéwo** prev. Aurora. island C Vanuatu
175 T8 **Mafa** Pulau Halmahera, E Indonesia 0.01N 127.49E
85 I23 **Mafeteng** W Lesotho 29.48S 27.15E
101 J21 **Maffe** Namur, SE Belgium 50.21N 5.19E
176 Y10 **Maffin** Papua, E Indonesia 1.57S 138.48E
191 P12 **Maffra** Victoria, SE Australia 37.59S 147.03E
83 K23 **Mafia** island E Tanzania
83 J23 **Mafia Channel** sea waterway E Tanzania
85 I21 **Mafikeng** North-West, N South Africa 25.52S 25.39E
62 J12 **Mafra** Santa Catarina, S Brazil 26.07S 49.46W
106 F10 **Mafra** Lisboa, C Portugal 38.57N 9.19W
149 Q17 **Mafraq** Abū Z̧aby, C UAE 24.21N 54.33E
Mafraq/Mafraq, Muḩāfaz̧at al see Al Mafraq
127 O10 **Magadan** Magadanskaya Oblast', E Russian Federation 59.37N 150.49E
127 Nn8 **Magadanskaya Oblast'** ◈ province E Russian Federation
110 G11 **Magadino** Ticino, S Switzerland 46.09N 8.50E
65 G23 **Magallanes** off. Región de Magallanes y de la Antártica Chilena. ◈ region S Chile
Magallanes see Punta Arenas
Magallanes, Estrecho de see Magellan, Strait of
12 I10 **Maganasipi, Lac** ◎ Québec, SE Canada
56 F6 **Magangué** Bolívar, N Colombia 9.13N 74.46W
Magareva see Mangareva
79 V12 **Magaria** Zinder, S Niger 13.00N 8.55E
194 M16 **Magarida** Central, SW PNG 10.13S 149.17E
179 Pp9 **Magat** ≈ Luzon, N Philippines
29 T11 **Magazine Mountain** ▲ Arkansas, C USA 35.10N 93.38W
78 I15 **Magburaka** C Sierra Leone 8.43N 11.57W
126 M14 **Magdagachi** Amurskaya Oblast', SE Russian Federation 53.25N 125.41E
64 O12 **Magdalena** Buenos Aires, E Argentina 35.04S 57.30W
59 M15 **Magdalena** Beni, N Bolivia 13.22S 64.07W
42 F4 **Magdalena** Sonora, NW Mexico 30.37N 110.58W
39 Q13 **Magdalena** New Mexico, SW USA 34.07N 107.14W
56 F5 **Magdalena** off. Departamento del Magdalena. ◈ province N Colombia
42 E9 **Magdalena, Bahía** bay W Mexico
65 G19 **Magdalena, Isla** island Archipiélago de los Chonos, S Chile
42 D8 **Magdalena, Isla** island W Mexico
49 P6 **Magdalena, Río** ≈ C Colombia
42 F4 **Magdalena, Río** ≈ NW Mexico
Magdalen Islands see Madeleine, Îles de la
102 L13 **Magdeburg** Sachsen-Anhalt, C Germany 52.07N 11.39E
24 L6 **Magee** Mississippi, S USA 31.52N 89.43W
174 Kk15 **Magelang** Jawa, C Indonesia 7.28S 110.10E
199 J7 **Magellan Rise** undersea feature C Pacific Ocean
65 H24 **Magellan, Strait of** Sp. Estrecho de Magallanes. strait Argentina/Chile
108 D7 **Magenta** Lombardia, NW Italy 45.28N 8.52E
Magerøy see Magerøya
94 K7 **Magerøya** var. Magerøy, Lapp. Máhkarávju. island N Norway
170 B17 **Mage-shima** island Nansei-shotō, SW Japan
110 G11 **Maggia** Ticino, S Switzerland 46.15N 8.42E
110 G10 **Maggia** ≈ SW Switzerland
Maggiore, Lago see Maggiore, Lake
108 C6 **Maggiore, Lake** It. Lago Maggiore. ◎ Italy/Switzerland
46 I12 **Maggotty** W Jamaica 18.09N 77.46W
78 I10 **Maghama** Gorgol, S Mauritania 15.31N 12.49W
99 F14 **Maghera** Ir. Machaire Rátha. C Northern Ireland, UK 54.51N 6.40W
99 F15 **Magherafelt** Ir. Machaire Fíolta. C Northern Ireland, UK 54.45N 6.36W
196 H6 **Magicienne Bay** bay Saipan, S Northern Mariana Islands
107 O13 **Magina** ▲ S Spain 37.43N 3.24W
83 H24 **Magingo** Ruvuma, S Tanzania 9.57S 35.23E
126 Jj14 **Magistral'nyy** Irkutskaya Oblast', S Russian Federation 56.18N 107.27E
114 H11 **Maglaj** Federacija Bosna I Hercegovina, N Bosnia and Herzegovina 44.32N 18.03E
109 Q19 **Maglie** Puglia, SE Italy 40.07N 18.18E
38 L2 **Magna** Utah, W USA 40.42N 112.06W
Magnesia see Manisa
12 G12 **Magnetawan** ≈ Ontario, S Canada
125 Dd12 **Magnitogorsk** Chelyabinskaya Oblast', C Russian Federation 53.28N 59.06E
29 T14 **Magnolia** Arkansas, C USA 33.16N 93.14W
24 K7 **Magnolia** Mississippi, S USA 31.08N 90.27W
27 V10 **Magnolia** Texas, SW USA 30.12N 95.46W
Magnolia State see Mississippi
97 J15 **Magnor** Hedmark, S Norway 59.57N 12.14E
197 K14 **Mago** prev. Mango. island Lau Group, E Fiji
85 L15 **Màgoé** Tete, NW Mozambique 15.51S 31.49E
13 Q13 **Magog** Québec, SE Canada 45.16N 72.09W
85 J15 **Magoye** Southern, S Zambia 16.01S 27.37E
43 Q12 **Magozal** Veracruz-Llave, C Mexico 21.33N 97.57W
12 B7 **Magpie** ≈ Ontario, S Canada
9 Q17 **Magrath** Alberta, SW Canada 49.27N 112.52W
107 R10 **Magro** ≈ E Spain
78 I9 **Magţa' Laḩjar** var. Magta Lahjar, Magta' Lahjar, Magtá Lahjar. Brakna, SW Mauritania 17.27N 13.07W
152 D12 **Magtymguly** prev. Garrygala, Rus. Kara-Kala. Balkan Welaýaty, W Turkmenistan 38.27N 56.15E
85 L20 **Magude** Maputo, S Mozambique 25.01S 32.40E
79 Y12 **Magumeri** Borno, NE Nigeria 12.07N 12.48E
201 O14 **Magur Islands** island group Caroline Islands, C Micronesia
Magway see Magwe
177 Ff6 **Magwe** var. Magway. Magwe, W Burma 20.07N 94.59E
177 Ff6 **Magwe** var. Magway. ◈ division C Burma
Magyar-Becse see Bečej
Magyarkanizsa see Kanjiža
Magyarország see Hungary
Magyarzsombor see Zimbor
148 J4 **Mahābād** var. Mehabad; prev. Sāūjbulāgh. Āz̄arbāyjān-e Gharbī, NW Iran 36.43N 45.43E
180 H5 **Mahabo** Toliara, W Madagascar 20.22S 44.39E
Maha Chai see Samut Sakhon
161 D14 **Mahād** Mahārāshtra, W India 18.04N 73.21E

◆ Country ● Country Capital ◇ Dependent Territory ○ Dependent Territory Capital ◈ Administrative Region ✕ International Airport ▲ Mountain ▲▲ Mountain Range Volcano ≈ River ◎ Lake ▣ Reservoir

MAHADDAY WEYNE – MANAMA

83 N17 **Mahadday Weyne** Shabeellaha Dhexe, C Somalia 2.55N 45.30E
81 Q17 **Mahagi** Orientale, NE Dem. Rep. Congo 2.16N 30.58E
Mahāil see Muhāyil
180 I4 **Mahajamba** seasonal river NW Madagascar
158 G10 **Mahājan** Rājasthān, NW India 28.46N 73.49E
180 I3 **Mahajanga** var. Majunga. Mahajanga, NW Madagascar 15.40S 46.19E
180 I3 **Mahajanga** ◐ province W Madagascar
180 I3 **Mahajanga** ✕ Mahajanga, NW Madagascar 15.40S 46.19E
175 N7 **Mahakam, Sungai** var. Koetai, Kutai. ≈ Borneo, C Indonesia
85 I19 **Mahalapye** var. Mahalatswe. Central, SE Botswana 23.01S 26.52E
Mahalatswe see Mahalapye
Mahalla el Kubra see El Mahalla el Kubra
175 Q10 **Mahalona** Sulawesi, C Indonesia 2.37S 121.26E
Mahameru see Semeru, Gunung
149 S11 **Mahān** Kermān, E Iran 30.07N 57.15E
160 N12 **Mahānadi** ≈ E India
180 J5 **Mahanoro** Toamasina, E Madagascar 19.52S 48.48E
159 P13 **Mahārājganj** Bihār, N India 26.07N 84.31E
160 G13 **Mahārāshtra** ◐ state W India
180 I4 **Mahavavy** seasonal river N Madagascar
161 K24 **Mahaweli Ganga** ≈ C Sri Lanka
Mahbés see El Mahbas
161 J15 **Mahbūbābād** Andhra Pradesh, E India 17.35N 80.00E
161 H16 **Mahbūbnagar** Andhra Pradesh, C India 16.45N 78.01E
146 M8 **Mahd adh Dhahab** Al Madīnah, W Saudi Arabia 23.33N 40.56E
57 S9 **Mahdia** C Guyana 5.16N 59.08W
77 N6 **Mahdia** var. Al Mahdīyah, Mehdia. NE Tunisia 35.14N 11.06E
161 F20 **Mahe** Fr. Mahé; prev. Mayyali. Pondicherry, SW India 11.44N 75.33E
180 I16 **Mahé** ✕ Mahé, NE Seychelles 4.37S 55.27E
180 H16 **Mahé** island Inner Islands, NE Seychelles
181 Y17 **Mahebourg** SE Mauritius 20.24S 57.42E
158 L10 **Mahendranagar** Far Western, W Nepal 28.58N 80.13E
83 I23 **Mahenge** Morogoro, SE Tanzania 8.40S 36.40E
193 F22 **Maheno** Otago, South Island, NZ 45.10S 170.51E
160 D9 **Mahesāna** Gujarāt, W India 23.37N 72.28E
160 F11 **Maheshwar** Madhya Pradesh, C India 22.12N 75.40E
157 F14 **Mahi** ≈ N India
192 Q10 **Mahia Peninsula** peninsula North Island, NZ
121 O16 **Mahilyow** Rus. Mogilëv. Mahilyowskaya Voblasts', E Belarus 53.54N 30.23E
121 M16 **Mahilyowskaya Voblasts'** prev. Rus. Mogilëvskaya Oblast'. ◐ province E Belarus
203 P7 **Mahina** Tahiti, W French Polynesia 17.28S 149.27W
193 E23 **Mahinerangi, Lake** ◎ South Island, NZ
Máhkarávju see Magerøya
85 L22 **Mahlabatini** KwaZulu/Natal, E South Africa 28.10S 31.27E
177 G5 **Mahlaing** Mandalay, C Burma 21.03N 95.43E
111 X8 **Mahldorf** Steiermark, SE Austria 46.54N 15.55E
Mahmūd-e 'Erāqī see Maḩmūd-e Rāqī
155 R4 **Maḩmūd-e Rāqī** var. Mahmūd-e 'Erāqī. Kāpīsā, NE Afghanistan 35.01N 69.19E
Mahmudiya see Al Maḩmūdīyah
31 S5 **Mahnomen** Minnesota, N USA 47.19N 95.58W
158 K14 **Mahoba** Uttar Pradesh, N India 25.18N 79.52E
107 Z9 **Mahón** Cat. Maó, Eng. Port Mahon; anc. Portus Magonis. Menorca, Spain, W Mediterranean Sea 39.54N 4.15E
20 D14 **Mahoning Creek Lake** ⊠ Pennsylvania, NE USA
107 Q10 **Mahora** Castilla-La Mancha, C Spain 39.13N 1.43W
Mähren see Moravia
Mährisch-Budwitz see Moravské Budějovice
Mährisch-Kromau see Moravský Krumlov
Mährisch-Neustadt see Uničov
Mährisch-Schönberg see Šumperk
Mährisch-Trübau see Moravská Třebová
Mährisch-Weisskirchen see Hranice
Māh-Shahr see Bandar-e Māhshahr
81 N19 **Mahulu** Maniema, E Dem. Rep. Congo 1.04S 27.10E
160 C12 **Mahuva** Gujarāt, W India 21.06N 71.46E
116 N11 **Mahya Dağı** ▲ NW Turkey 41.47N 27.34E
107 T6 **Maials** var. Mayals. Cataluña, NE Spain 41.22N 0.30E
203 O2 **Maiana** prev. Hall Island. atoll Tungaru, W Kiribati
203 S11 **Maiao** var. Tapuaemanu, Tubuai-Manu. island Îles du Vent, W French Polynesia
56 H4 **Maicao** La Guajira, N Colombia 11.25N 72.15W
Mai Ceu/Mai Chio see Maych'ew
105 U8 **Maîche** Doubs, E France 47.15N 6.43E
99 N22 **Maidenhead** S England, UK 51.31N 0.43W
9 S15 **Maidstone** Saskatchewan, S Canada 53.06N 109.21W
99 P22 **Maidstone** SE England, UK 51.16N 0.31E
79 Y13 **Maiduguri** Borno, NE Nigeria 11.51N 13.09E
110 I8 **Maienfeld** Sankt Gallen, NE Switzerland 47.01N 9.30E
118 J12 **Măieruș** Hung. Szászmagyarós. Brașov, C Romania 45.55N 25.30E
Maigh Chromtha see Macroom
Maigh Eo see Mayo
57 N9 **Maigualida, Sierra** ▲▲ S Venezuela
160 K9 **Maihar** Madhya Pradesh, C India 24.18N 80.46E
160 K11 **Maikala Range** ▲▲ C India
69 T10 **Maiko** ≈ W Dem. Rep. Congo
Mailand see Milano
158 L11 **Mailāni** Uttar Pradesh, N India 28.16N 80.19E
155 U10 **Māilsi** Punjab, E Pakistan 29.46N 72.15E
153 R8 **Maimak** Talasskaya Oblast', NW Kyrgyzstan 42.40N 71.12E
Maimāna see Meymaneh
Maimansingh see Mymensingh
176 Vv11 **Maimawa** Papua, E Indonesia 3.21S 133.36E
Maimuna see Al Maymūnah
103 G18 **Main** ≈ C Germany
117 F22 **Maïna** ancient monument Pelopónnisos, S Greece 36.24N 22.28E
117 E20 **Maïnalo** ▲▲ S Greece
103 L22 **Mainburg** Bayern, SE Germany 48.40N 11.48E
Main Camp see Banana
12 E12 **Main Channel** lake channel Ontario, S Canada
81 I20 **Mai-Ndombe, Lac** prev. Lac Léopold II. ◎ W Dem. Rep. Congo
103 K20 **Main-Donau-Kanal** canal SE Germany
21 R6 **Maine** off. State of Maine; also known as Lumber State, Pine Tree State. ◐ state NE USA
104 K6 **Maine** cultural region NW France
104 J7 **Maine-et-Loire** ◐ department NW France
21 Q9 **Maine, Gulf of** gulf NE USA
79 X12 **Maïné-Soroa** Diffa, SE Niger 13.13N 12.05E
178 Gg1 **Maingkwan** var. Mungkawn. Kachin State, N Burma 26.19N 96.37E
Main Island see Bermuda
Mainistir Fhear Maí see Fermoy
Mainistirna Búille see Boyle
Mainistir na Corann see Midleton
Mainistir na Féile see Abbeyfeale
98 J5 **Mainland** island Orkney, N Scotland, UK
98 L2 **Mainland** island Shetland, NE Scotland, UK
165 P16 **Mainling** var. Tungdor. Xizang Zizhiqu, W China 29.12N 94.06E
158 K12 **Mainpuri** Uttar Pradesh, N India 27.13N 79.01E
105 N5 **Maintenon** Eure-et-Loir, C France 48.35N 1.34E
180 H4 **Maintirano** Mahajanga, W Madagascar 18.01S 44.03E
95 M15 **Mainua** Oulu, C Finland 64.05N 27.28E
103 G18 **Mainz** Fr. Mayence. Rheinland-Pfalz, SW Germany 50.00N 8.16E
78 I9 **Maio** var. Vila do Maio. Maio, S Cape Verde 15.07N 23.12W
78 E10 **Maio** var. Mayo. island Ilhas de Sotavento, SE Cape Verde
64 G12 **Maipo, Río** ≈ C Chile
64 H12 **Maipo, Volcán** ▲ W Argentina 34.09S 69.51W
63 E22 **Maipú** Buenos Aires, E Argentina 36.52S 57.52W
64 I11 **Maipú** Mendoza, E Argentina 33.00S 68.46W
64 H11 **Maipú** Santiago, C Chile 33.30S 70.52W
110 I10 **Maira** It. Mera. ≈ Italy/Switzerland
108 A9 **Maira** ≈ NW Italy
159 V12 **Mairābari** Assam, NE India 26.28N 92.22E
46 K7 **Maisí** Guantánamo, E Cuba 20.13N 74.08W
120 H13 **Maišiagala** Vilnius, SE Lithuania 54.52N 25.03E
159 V17 **Maiskhal Island** island SE Bangladesh
178 Gg13 **Mai Sombun** Chumphon, SW Thailand 10.49N 99.13E
Mai Sơn see Hat Lot
Maisur see Karnātaka, India
Maisur see Mysore, India
191 T8 **Maitland** New South Wales, SE Australia 32.47S 151.31E
190 I9 **Maitland** South Australia 34.21S 137.42E
12 F15 **Maitland** ≈ Ontario, S Canada
205 R1 **Maitri** Indian research station Antarctica 70.03S 8.59E
165 N15 **Maizhokunggar** Xizang Zizhiqu, W China 29.49N 91.40E
45 O10 **Maíz, Islas del** var. Corn Islands. island group SE Nicaragua
171 H14 **Maizuru** Kyōto, Honshū, SW Japan 35.28N 135.21E
56 F6 **Majagual** Sucre, N Colombia 8.36N 74.30W
43 Z13 **Majahual** Quintana Roo, E Mexico 18.43N 87.43W
Majardah, Wādī see Medjerda, Oued/Mejerda
Mājeej see Mejit Island
175 P11 **Majene** prev. Madjene. Sulawesi, C Indonesia 3.33S 118.58E
45 V15 **Majé, Serranía de** ▲▲ E Panama
114 I11 **Majevica** ▲▲ NE Bosnia and Herzegovina
83 H15 **Maji** Southern, S Ethiopia 6.11N 35.32E
147 X7 **Majis** NW Oman 24.25N 56.34E
Majorca see Mallorca
107 X9 **Major, Puig** ▲ Mallorca, Spain, W Mediterranean Sea 39.50N 2.50E
Mājro see Majuro Atoll
Majunga see Mahajanga
201 Y3 **Majuro** ✕ Majuro Atoll, SE Marshall Islands 7.04N 171.07E
201 Y2 **Majuro Atoll** var. Mājro. atoll Ratak Chain, SE Marshall Islands
201 X2 **Majuro Lagoon** lagoon Majuro Atoll, SE Marshall Islands
78 H11 **Maka** C Senegal 13.39N 14.25W
81 F20 **Makabana** Le Niari, SW Congo 3.28S 12.36E
40 D9 **Mākaha** var. Makaha. O'ahu, Hawai'i, USA, C Pacific Ocean 21.28N 158.13W
40 B8 **Makahū'ena Point** var. Makahuena Point. headland Kaua'i, Hawai'i, USA, C Pacific Ocean 21.52N 159.28W
40 D9 **Makakilo City** O'ahu, Hawai'i, USA, C Pacific Ocean 21.21N 158.05W
85 H18 **Makalamabedi** Central, C Botswana 20.18S 23.52E
Makale see Mek'elē
164 K17 **Makalu** Chin. Makaru Shan. ▲ China/Nepal 27.53N 87.09E
83 G23 **Makampi** Mbeya, S Tanzania 8.00S 33.17E
151 X12 **Makanchi** Kaz. Maqanshy. Vostochnyy Kazakhstan, E Kazakhstan 46.47N 82.00E
44 M8 **Makantaka** Región Autónoma Atlántico Norte, NE Nicaragua 13.13N 84.04W
202 B16 **Makapu Point** headland W Niue 18.58S 169.55E
193 C24 **Makarewa** Southland, South Island, NZ 46.17S 168.16E
119 O4 **Makariv** Kyyivs'ka Oblast', N Ukraine 50.28N 29.49E
193 D20 **Makarora** ≈ South Island, NZ
127 Oo15 **Makarov** Ostrov Sakhalin, Sakhalinskaya Oblast', SE Russian Federation 48.24N 142.37E
207 R9 **Makarov Basin** undersea feature Arctic Ocean
199 Hh4 **Makarov Seamount** undersea feature W Pacific Ocean 29.30N 153.30E
115 F15 **Makarska** It. Macarsca. Split-Dalmacija, SE Croatia 43.18N 17.00E
Makaru Shan see Makalu
129 O15 **Makar'yev** Kostromskaya Oblast', NW Russian Federation 57.52N 43.46E
84 L11 **Makasa** Northern, NE Zambia 9.42S 31.54E
Makasar see Makassar
Makasar, Selat see Makassar Straits
175 P13 **Makassar** var. Macassar, Makasar; prev. Ujungpandang. Sulawesi, C Indonesia 5.09S 119.28E
198 Ff8 **Makassar Straits** Ind. Selat Makasar. strait C Indonesia
150 G12 **Makat** Kaz. Maqat. Atyrau, SW Kazakhstan 47.41N 53.24E
203 T10 **Makatea** island Îles Tuamotu, C French Polynesia
145 U7 **Makātū** E Iraq 33.55N 45.25E
180 H6 **Makay** var. Massif du Makay. ▲▲ SW Madagascar
116 J12 **Makaza** pass Bulgaria/Greece 41.16N 25.26E
176 Uu9 **Makbon** Papua, E Indonesia 0.43S 131.30E
Makedonija see Macedonia, FYR
202 B16 **Makefu** W Niue 18.58S 169.55W
203 V10 **Makemo** atoll Îles Tuamotu, C French Polynesia
78 I15 **Makeni** C Sierra Leone 8.57N 12.01W
Makenzen see Orlyak
Makeyevka see Makiyivka
131 Q16 **Makhachkala** prev. Petrovsk-Port. Respublika Dagestan, SW Russian Federation 42.58N 47.30E
150 F11 **Makhambet** Atyrau, W Kazakhstan 47.35N 51.35E
Makharadze see Ozurget'i
145 W13 **Makhfar Al Buşayyah** S Iraq 30.09N 46.09E
145 R4 **Makhmūr** N Iraq 35.46N 43.31E
144 I11 **Makhrūq, Wadi al** dry watercourse E Jordan
145 R4 **Makḩūl, Jabal** ▲ C Iraq
147 R13 **Makhyah, Wādī** dry watercourse N Yemen
176 W11 **Maki** Papua, E Indonesia 3.00S 134.10E
175 Ss8 **Makian, Pulau** island Maluku, E Indonesia
193 G21 **Makikihi** Canterbury, South Island, NZ 44.36S 171.09E
203 O2 **Makin** prev. Pitt Island. atoll Tungaru, W Kiribati
83 I20 **Makindu** Eastern, S Kenya 2.15S 37.49E
151 Q8 **Makinsk** Akmola, N Kazakhstan 52.37N 70.26E
195 Y17 **Makira** off. Makira Province. ◐ province SE Solomon Islands
Makira see San Cristobal
119 X8 **Makiyivka** Rus. Makeyevka; prev. Dmitriyevsk. Donets'ka Oblast', E Ukraine 47.57N 37.47E
146 L10 **Makkah** Eng. Mecca. Makkah, W Saudi Arabia 21.27N 39.50E
146 M10 **Makkah** var. Minţaqat Makkah. ◐ province W Saudi Arabia
11 R7 **Makkovik** Newfoundland and Labrador, NE Canada 55.06N 59.06W
100 K6 **Makkum** Friesland, N Netherlands 53.03N 5.25E
Mako see Makung
113 M25 **Makó** Rom. Macău. Csongrád, SE Hungary 46.14N 20.28E
12 G9 **Makobe Lake** ◎ Ontario, S Canada
197 I14 **Makogai** island C Fiji
81 F18 **Makokou** Ogooué-Ivindo, NE Gabon 0.37N 12.46E
83 G23 **Makongolosi** Mbeya, S Tanzania 8.24S 33.09E
83 E19 **Makota** SW Uganda 0.37S 30.12E
81 G18 **Makoua** Cuvette, C Congo 0.01S 15.40E
112 M10 **Maków Mazowiecki** Mazowieckie, C Poland 52.51N 21.06E
113 K17 **Maków Podhalański** Małopolskie, S Poland 49.43N 19.40E
149 V14 **Makran** cultural region Iran/Pakistan
158 G12 **Makrāna** Rājasthān, N India 27.01N 74.43E
149 U15 **Makran Coast** coastal region SE Iran
121 F20 **Makrany** Rus. Mokrany. Brestskaya Voblasts', SW Belarus 51.49N 24.15E
Makrinoros see Makrynóros
117 H20 **Makrónisosi** island Kykládes, Greece, Aegean Sea
117 D17 **Makrynóros** var. Makrinoros. ▲▲ C Greece
117 G19 **Makryplági** ▲ C Greece 38.00N 23.06E
Maksamaa see Maxmo
128 J15 **Maksatikha** var. Maksatha, Maksaticha. Tverskaya Oblast', W Russian Federation 57.49N 35.46E
160 G10 **Maksi** Madhya Pradesh, C India 23.18N 76.09E
148 I1 **Mākū** Āžarbāyjān-e Gharbī, NW Iran 39.16N 44.33E
159 Y11 **Mākum** Assam, NE India 27.28N 95.28E
Makun see Makung
167 R14 **Makung** prev. Mako, Makun. W Taiwan 23.34N 119.34E
170 Bb16 **Makurazaki** Kagoshima, Kyūshū, SW Japan 31.15N 130.15E
79 V15 **Makurdi** Benue, C Nigeria 7.41N 8.35E
125 F12 **Makushino** Kurganskaya Oblast', C Russian Federation 55.11N 67.16E
40 L17 **Makushin Volcano** ▲ Unalaska Island, Alaska, USA 53.53N 166.55W
85 K16 **Makwiro** Mashonaland West, N Zimbabwe 17.52S 30.24E
59 D15 **Mala** Lima, W Peru 12.45S 76.38W
Mala see Mallow, Ireland
Mala see Malaita, Solomon Islands
95 I14 **Malå** Västerbotten, N Sweden 65.12N 18.45E
202 G12 **Mala'atoli** Île Uvea, E Wallis and Futuna
179 Qq15 **Malabang** E Mindanao, S Philippines 7.37N 124.04E
161 E21 **Malabār Coast** coast SW India
81 C16 **Malabo** prev. Santa Isabel. ● (Equatorial Guinea) Isla de Bioco, NW Equatorial Guinea 3.43N 8.51E
81 C16 **Malabo** ✕ Isla de Bioco, N Equatorial Guinea 3.44N 8.51E
Malaca see Málaga
Malacca see Melaka
173 G4 **Malacca, Strait of** Ind. Selat Malaka. strait Indonesia/Malaysia
Malacka see Malacky
113 G20 **Malacky** Hung. Malacka. Bratislavský Kraj, W Slovakia 48.25N 17.01E
35 R16 **Malad City** Idaho, NW USA 42.10N 112.16W
119 Q4 **Mala Divytsya** Chernihivs'ka Oblast', N Ukraine 50.40N 32.13E
121 J15 **Maladzyechna** Pol. Molodeczno, Rus. Molodechno. Minskaya Voblasts', C Belarus 54.19N 26.51E
202 D12 **Malaee** Île Futuna, N Wallis and Futuna
39 V15 **Malaga** New Mexico, SW USA 32.10N 104.04W
56 G8 **Málaga** Santander, C Colombia 6.42N 72.43W
106 M15 **Málaga** anc. Malaca. Andalucía, S Spain 36.43N 4.25W
106 L15 **Málaga** ◐ province Andalucía, S Spain
106 M15 **Málaga** ✕ Andalucía, S Spain 36.38N 4.36W
Malagasy Republic see Madagascar
107 N10 **Malagón** Castilla-La Mancha, C Spain 39.10N 3.51W
99 G18 **Malahide** Ir. Mullach Íde. E Ireland 53.27N 6.09W
195 Y14 **Malaita** off. Malaita Province. ◐ province N Solomon Islands
195 Y15 **Malaita** var. Mala. island N Solomon Islands
82 F13 **Malakal** Upper Nile, S Sudan 9.31N 31.40E
114 C10 **Mala Kapela** ▲▲ NW Croatia
27 V7 **Malakoff** Texas, SW USA 32.10N 96.00W
Malakula see Malekula
155 V7 **Malakwāl** var. Mālikwāla. Punjab, E Pakistan 32.32N 73.18E
194 J12 **Malalamai** Madang, W PNG 5.47S 146.40E
194 J14 **Malalaua** Gulf, S PNG 8.04S 146.09E
175 Q11 **Malamala** Sulawesi, C Indonesia 3.21S 120.58E
174 M15 **Malang** Jawa, C Indonesia 7.58S 112.45E
85 O14 **Malanga** Niassa, N Mozambique 13.27S 36.05E
Malange see Malanje
94 I9 **Malangen** sound N Norway
84 C11 **Malanje** var. Malange. Malanje, NW Angola 9.33S 16.25E
84 C11 **Malanje** var. Malange. ◐ province N Angola
154 M16 **Malān, Rās** headland SW Pakistan 25.13N 63.31E
79 S13 **Malanville** NE Benin 11.49N 3.22E
Malapane see Ozimek
161 F21 **Malappuram** Kerala, SW India 11.00N 76.02E
45 T17 **Mala, Punta** headland S Panama 7.28N 79.58W
97 N16 **Mälaren** ◎ C Sweden
64 H13 **Malargüe** Mendoza, W Argentina 35.31S 69.34W
12 J8 **Malartic** Québec, SE Canada 48.09N 78.09W
121 F20 **Malaryta** Pol. Maloryta, Rus. Malorita. Brestskaya Voblasts', SW Belarus 51.46N 24.04E
65 J19 **Malaspina** Chubut, SE Argentina 44.56S 66.52W
41 U12 **Malaspina Glacier** glacier Alaska, USA
143 N15 **Malatya** anc. Melitene. Malatya, SE Turkey 38.22N 38.18E
142 M14 **Malatya** ◐ province C Turkey
119 Q7 **Mala Vyska** Rus. Malaya Viska. Kirovohrads'ka Oblast', S Ukraine 48.37N 31.36E
85 M14 **Malawi** off. Republic of Malaŵi; prev. Nyasaland, Nyasaland Protectorate. ◆ republic S Africa
Malawi, Lake see Nyasa, Lake
95 J17 **Malax** Fin. Maalahti. Länsi-Suomi, W Finland 62.55N 21.30E
128 H14 **Malaya Vishera** Novgorodskaya Oblast', W Russian Federation 58.52N 32.12E
Malaya Viska see Mala Vyska
179 R15 **Malaybalay** Mindanao, S Philippines 8.10N 125.08E
148 L6 **Malāyer** prev. Daulatabad. Hamadān, W Iran 34.19N 48.46E
174 Gg3 **Malay Peninsula** peninsula Malaysia/Thailand
174 I3 **Malaysia** var. Federation of Malaysia; prev. the separate territories of Federation of Malaya, Sarawak and Sabah (North Borneo) and Singapore. ◆ monarchy SE Asia
143 R14 **Malazgirt** Muş, E Turkey 39.09N 42.30E
13 R8 **Malbaie** ≈ Québec, SE Canada
79 T12 **Malbaza** Tahoua, S Niger 13.57N 5.32E
112 J7 **Malbork** Ger. Marienburg, Marienburg in Westpreussen. Pomorskie, N Poland 54.01N 19.02E
102 N9 **Malchin** Mecklenburg-Vorpommern, N Germany 53.43N 12.46E
102 M9 **Malchiner See** ◎ NE Germany
101 D16 **Maldegem** Oost-Vlaanderen, NW Belgium 51.12N 3.27E
100 L13 **Malden** Gelderland, SE Netherlands 51.46N 5.51E
21 O11 **Malden** Massachusetts, NE USA 42.25N 71.04W
29 Y8 **Malden** Missouri, C USA 36.33N 89.58W
203 X4 **Malden Island** prev. Independence Island. atoll E Kiribati
181 Q6 **Maldives** off. Maldivian Divehi, Republic of Maldives. ◆ republic N Indian Ocean
Maldivian Divehi see Maldives
99 P21 **Maldon** E England, UK 51.43N 0.40E
63 G20 **Maldonado** Maldonado, S Uruguay 34.57S 54.58W
63 G20 **Maldonado** ◐ department S Uruguay
43 P17 **Maldonado, Punta** headland S Mexico 16.18N 98.31W
157 K19 **Male'** Div. Maale ● (Maldives) Male' Atoll, C Maldives 4.10N 73.29E
108 G6 **Malè** Trentino-Alto Adige, N Italy 46.21N 10.51E
78 K13 **Maléa** var. Maléya. NE Guinea 11.46N 9.43W
Maléas, Ákra see Agriliá, Akrotírio
117 G22 **Maléas, Akrotírio** headland S Greece 36.25N 23.11E
157 K19 **Male' Atoll** var. Kaafu Atoll. atoll C Maldives
Malebo, Pool see Stanley Pool
160 E12 **Mālegaon** Mahārāshtra, W India 20.33N 74.31E
83 F15 **Malek** Jonglei, S Sudan 6.04N 31.36E
197 B13 **Malekula** var. Malakula; prev. Mallicolo. island W Vanuatu
201 Y15 **Malem** Kosrae, E Micronesia 5.16N 163.01E
85 O15 **Malema** Nampula, N Mozambique 14.57S 37.28E
81 N23 **Malemba-Nkulu** Katanga, SE Dem. Rep. Congo 8.01S 26.48E
195 Q10 **Malendok Island** island Tanga Islands, NE PNG
128 K9 **Malen'ga** Respublika Kareliya, NW Russian Federation 63.50N 36.21E
97 M20 **Målerås** Kalmar, S Sweden 56.55N 15.34E
105 O6 **Malesherbes** Loiret, C France 48.18N 2.25E
117 G18 **Malesína** Stereá Ellás, E Greece 38.37N 23.15E
Maléya see Maléa
131 O15 **Malgobek** Chechenskaya Respublika, SW Russian Federation 43.34N 44.34E
107 X5 **Malgrat de Mar** Cataluña, NE Spain 41.39N 2.45E
82 C9 **Malha** Northern Darfur, W Sudan 15.07N 26.00E
145 Q5 **Malḩāt** C Iraq 34.44N 42.41E
34 K14 **Malheur Lake** ◎ Oregon, NW USA
34 L14 **Malheur River** ≈ Oregon, NW USA
78 I13 **Mali** NW Guinea 12.07N 12.28W
79 O9 **Mali** off. Republic of Mali, Fr. République du Mali; prev. French Sudan, Sudanese Republic. ◆ republic W Africa
175 S16 **Maliana** W East Timor 8.57S 125.25E
178 H1 **Mali Hka** ≈ N Burma
Mali Idjoš see Mali Iđoš
114 K8 **Mali Iđoš** var. Mali Idjoš, Hung. Kishegyes; prev. Krivaja. Serbia, N Serbia 45.43N 19.40E
114 K9 **Mali Kanal** canal N Serbia
175 R8 **Maliku** Sulawesi, N Indonesia 0.36S 123.13E
Malik, Wadi al see Milk, Wadi el
Mālikwāla see Malakwāl
178 Gg12 **Mali Kyun** var. Tavoy Island. island Mergui Archipelago, S Burma
97 M19 **Målilla** Kalmar, S Sweden 57.24N 15.49E
114 B11 **Mali Lošinj** It. Lussinpiccolo. Primorje-Gorski Kotar, W Croatia 44.31N 14.28E
Malin see Malyn
179 Q15 **Malindang, Mount** ▲ Mindanao, S Philippines 8.12N 123.37E
83 K20 **Malindi** Coast, SE Kenya 3.13S 40.04E
Malines see Mechelen
98 E13 **Malin Head** Ir. Cionn Mhálanna. headland NW Ireland 55.37N 7.37W
175 Pp7 **Malino, Gunung** ▲ Sulawesi, N Indonesia 0.44N 120.45E
115 M21 **Maliq** var. Maliqi. Korçë, SE Albania 40.45N 20.45E
Maliqi see Maliq
179 Rr16 **Malita** Mindanao, S Philippines 6.13N 125.39E
160 G12 **Malkāpur** Mahārāshtra, C India 20.52N 76.18E
142 B10 **Malkara** Tekirdağ, NW Turkey 40.55N 26.56E
121 J19 **Mal'kavichy** Rus. Mal'kovichi. Brestskaya Voblasts', SW Belarus 52.28N 26.39E
Malkiye see Al Mālikīyah
116 L11 **Malko Sharkovo, Yazovir** ⊠ SE Bulgaria
116 N11 **Malko Tŭrnovo** Burgas, E Bulgaria 42.00N 27.33E
Mal'kovichi see Mal'kavichy
191 R12 **Mallacoota** Victoria, SE Australia 37.34S 149.45E
98 G10 **Mallaig** N Scotland, UK 57.03N 5.48W
190 I9 **Mallala** South Australia 34.29S 138.30E
77 W9 **Mallawi** C Egypt 27.49N 30.43E
107 R5 **Mallén** Aragón, NE Spain 41.52N 1.25W
108 F5 **Malles Venosta** Ger. Mals im Vinschgau. Trentino-Alto Adige, N Italy 46.40N 10.37E
Mallicolo see Malekula
111 Q8 **Mallnitz** Salzburg, S Austria 46.58N 13.09E
107 W9 **Mallorca** Eng. Majorca; anc. Baleares Major. island Illes Balears, Spain, W Mediterranean Sea
99 C20 **Mallow** Ir. Mala. SW Ireland 52.07N 8.39W
95 E15 **Malm** Nord-Trøndelag, C Norway 64.04N 11.12E
97 L19 **Malmbäck** Jönköping, S Sweden 57.34N 14.30E
94 J12 **Malmberget** Lapp. Malmivaara. Norrbotten, N Sweden 67.09N 20.39E
101 M20 **Malmédy** Liège, E Belgium 50.25N 6.01E
85 E25 **Malmesbury** Western Cape, SW South Africa 33.28S 18.43E
Malmivaara see Malmberget
97 N16 **Malmköping** Södermanland, C Sweden 59.07N 16.49E
97 K23 **Malmö** Skåne, S Sweden 55.35N 13.00E
97 K23 **Malmo** ✕ Skåne, S Sweden 55.33N 13.23E
47 Q16 **Malmok** headland Bonaire, S Netherlands Antilles 12.16N 68.21W
97 M18 **Malmslätt** Östergötland, S Sweden 58.25N 15.30E
129 R16 **Malmyzh** Kirovskaya Oblast', NW Russian Federation 56.30N 50.37E
197 B12 **Malo** island W Vanuatu
130 J7 **Maloarkhangel'sk** Orlovskaya Oblast', W Russian Federation 52.25N 36.37E
Maloelap see Maloelap Atoll
201 V6 **Maloelap Atoll** var. Maloelap. atoll E Marshall Islands
Maloenda see Malunda
110 I10 **Maloja** Graubünden, S Switzerland 46.25N 9.42E
84 L12 **Malole** Northern, NE Zambia 10.05S 31.37E
197 H13 **Malolo** island Mamanuca Group, W Fiji
197 H13 **Malolo Barrier Reef** var. Ro Ro Reef. reef W Fiji
179 P10 **Malolos** Luzon, N Philippines 14.51N 120.49E
20 K6 **Malone** New York, NE USA 44.51N 74.18W
81 K25 **Malonga** Katanga, S Dem. Rep. Congo 10.30S 23.06E
113 K17 **Małopolskie** ◐ province S Poland
Malorita/Maloryta see Malaryta
128 K9 **Maloshuyka** Arkhangel'skaya Oblast', NW Russian Federation 63.43N 37.20E
116 G10 **Mal'ovitsa** ▲ W Bulgaria 42.12N 23.19E
151 V15 **Malovodnoye** Almaty, SE Kazakhstan 43.31N 77.42E
96 C10 **Måløy** Sogn og Fjordane, S Norway 61.55N 5.06E
130 K4 **Maloyaroslavets** Kaluzhskaya Oblast', W Russian Federation 55.03N 36.31E
125 F6 **Malozemel'skaya Tundra** physical region NW Russian Federation
106 J10 **Malpartida de Cáceres** Extremadura, W Spain 39.25N 6.30W
106 K9 **Malpartida de Plasencia** Extremadura, W Spain 39.58N 6.03W
108 C7 **Malpensa** ✕ (Milano) Lombardia, N Italy 45.41N 8.40E
78 J6 **Malqteïr** desert N Mauritania
Mals im Vinschgau see Malles Venosta
120 J10 **Malta** Rēzekne, SE Latvia 56.19N 27.11E
35 V7 **Malta** Montana, NW USA 48.21N 107.52W
123 Jj14 **Malta** off. Republic of Malta. ◆ republic C Mediterranean Sea
111 R8 **Malta** var. Maltabach. ≈ S Austria
123 L11 **Malta** island Malta, C Mediterranean Sea
Maltabach see Malta
Malta, Canale di see Malta Channel
123 L12 **Malta Channel** It. Canale di Malta. strait Italy/Malta
85 D20 **Maltahöhe** Hardap, SW Namibia 24.49S 16.58E
99 N16 **Malton** N England, UK 54.07N 0.49W
175 T11 **Maluku** off. Propinsi Maluku, Dut. Molukken, Eng. Moluccas. ◐ province E Indonesia
175 Ss9 **Maluku** Dut. Molukken, Eng. Moluccas; prev. Spice Islands. island group E Indonesia
Maluku, Laut see Molucca Sea
175 Ss8 **Maluku Utara** off. Propinsi Maluku Utara. ◐ province E Indonesia
79 V13 **Malumfashi** Katsina, N Nigeria 11.51N 7.39E
175 P11 **Malunda** prev. Maloenda. Sulawesi, C Indonesia 2.58S 118.52E
96 K13 **Malung** Dalarna, C Sweden 60.40N 13.45E
96 K13 **Malungsfors** Dalarna, C Sweden 60.43N 13.34E
195 X14 **Maluu** var. Malu'u. Malaita, N Solomon Islands 8.22S 160.39E
161 D16 **Mālvan** Mahārāshtra, W India 16.05N 73.28E
Malventum see Benevento
29 U12 **Malvern** Arkansas, C USA 34.21N 92.48W
31 S15 **Malvern** Iowa, C USA 40.59N 95.36W
46 I13 **Malvern** ▲ W Jamaica 17.59N 77.42W
Malvinas, Islas see Falkland Islands
119 N4 **Malyn** Rus. Malin. Zhytomyrs'ka Oblast', N Ukraine 50.46N 29.14E
127 O5 **Malyy Anyuy** ≈ NE Russian Federation
131 O11 **Malyye Derbety** Respublika Kalmykiya, SW Russian Federation 47.57N 44.39E
Malyy Kavkaz see Lesser Caucasus
126 M5 **Malyy Lyakhovskiy, Ostrov** island NE Russian Federation
Malyy Pamir see Little Pamir
126 Jj4 **Malyy Taymyr, Ostrov** island Severnaya Zemlya, N Russian Federation
150 E10 **Malyy Uzen'** Kaz. Kishiözen. ≈ Kazakhstan/Russian Federation
126 I16 **Malyy Yenisey** var. Ka-Krem. ≈ S Russian Federation
126 K13 **Mama** Irkutskaya Oblast', C Russian Federation 58.13N 112.45E
131 S3 **Mamadysh** Respublika Tatarstan, W Russian Federation 55.46N 51.22E
119 N14 **Mamaia** Constanța, E Romania 44.13N 28.37E
197 G14 **Mamanuca Group** island group Yasawa Group, W Fiji
152 L13 **Mamash** Lebap Welaýaty, E Turkmenistan 38.24N 64.12E
176 W11 **Mamasiware** Papua, E Indonesia 2.46S 134.26E
194 L14 **Mambare** ≈ S PNG
81 O17 **Mambasa** Orientale, NE Dem. Rep. Congo 1.22N 29.02E
176 Xx10 **Mamberamo, Sungai** ≈ Papua, E Indonesia
81 G15 **Mambéré** ≈ SW Central African Republic
81 G15 **Mambéré-Kadéï** ◐ prefecture SW Central African Republic
176 X9 **Mambetaloi** Papua, E Indonesia 1.38S 136.12E
Mambij see Manbij
81 H18 **Mambili** ≈ W Congo
85 N18 **Mambone** var. Nova Mambone. Inhambane, E Mozambique 20.59S 35.04E
179 P11 **Mamburao** Mindoro, N Philippines 13.16N 120.36E
180 I16 **Mamelles** island Inner Islands, NE Seychelles
101 M25 **Mamer** Luxembourg, SW Luxembourg 49.37N 6.01E
104 L6 **Mamers** Sarthe, NW France 48.21N 0.22E
81 D15 **Mamfe** Sud-Ouest, W Cameroon 5.46N 9.18E
151 P6 **Mamlyutka** Severnyy Kazakhstan, N Kazakhstan 54.55N 68.31E
38 M15 **Mammoth** Arizona, SW USA 32.43N 110.38W
35 S12 **Mammoth Hot Springs** Wyoming, C USA 44.57N 110.40W
Mamoedjoe see Mamuju
121 A14 **Mamonovo** Ger. Heiligenbeil. Kaliningradskaya Oblast', W Russian Federation 54.28N 19.57E
59 L14 **Mamoré, Rio** ≈ Bolivia/Brazil
78 I14 **Mamou** W Guinea 10.34N 12.45W
24 H8 **Mamou** Louisiana, S USA 30.37N 92.25W
180 I14 **Mamoudzou** ○ (Mayotte) C Mayotte 12.48S 45.00E
180 I3 **Mampikony** Mahajanga, N Madagascar 16.03S 47.39E
79 P16 **Mampong** C Ghana 7.01N 1.36W
112 M7 **Mamry, Jezioro** Ger. Mauersee. ◎ NE Poland
175 P10 **Mamuju** prev. Mamoedjoe. Sulawesi, S Indonesia 2.40S 118.51E
175 Oo10 **Mamuju, Teluk** bay Sulawesi, C Indonesia
85 F19 **Mamuno** Ghanzi, W Botswana 22.15S 20.01E
115 K19 **Mamuras** var. Mamurasi, Mamurras. Lezhë, C Albania 41.34N 19.42E
Mamurasi/Mamurras see Mamuras
78 L16 **Man** W Ivory Coast 7.24N 7.33W
57 X9 **Mana** NW French Guiana 5.40N 53.49W
58 A6 **Manabí** ◐ province W Ecuador
44 G4 **Manabique, Punta** var. Cabo Tres Puntas. headland E Guatemala 15.57N 88.37W
56 G11 **Manacacías, Río** ≈ C Colombia
60 F13 **Manacapuru** Amazonas, N Brazil 3.16S 60.37W
107 Y9 **Manacor** Mallorca, Spain, W Mediterranean Sea 39.35N 3.12E
175 Rr6 **Manado** prev. Menado. Sulawesi, C Indonesia 1.31N 124.55E
196 H5 **Managaha** island S Northern Mariana Islands
101 G20 **Manage** Hainaut, S Belgium 50.30N 4.13E
44 J10 **Managua** ● (Nicaragua) Managua, W Nicaragua 12.07N 86.15W
44 J10 **Managua** ◐ department W Nicaragua
44 J10 **Managua** ✕ Managua, W Nicaragua 12.07N 86.11W
44 J10 **Managua, Lago de** var. Xolotlán. ◎ W Nicaragua
Manaḩ see Bilād Manaḩ
20 K16 **Manahawkin** New Jersey, NE USA 39.39N 74.12W
192 K11 **Manaia** Taranaki, North Island, NZ 39.32S 174.04E
180 J6 **Manakara** Fianarantsoa, SE Madagascar 22.09S 48.00E
158 J7 **Manāli** Himāchal Pradesh, NW India 32.18N 77.12E
133 U12 **Ma, Nam** Vtn. Sông Mã. ≈ Laos/Vietnam
Manama see Al Manāmah

◆ Country ● Country Capital ◇ Dependent Territory ○ Dependent Territory Capital ◐ Administrative Region ✕ International Airport ▲ Mountain ▲▲ Mountain Range ▲ Volcano ≈ River ◎ Lake ⊠ Reservoir

Manam Island – Margherita Peak

194 *I10* **Manam Island** *island* N PNG
69 *Y13* **Mananara** ≈ SE Madagascar
190 *M9* **Manangatang** Victoria, SE Australia *35.04S 142.53E*
180 *J6* **Mananjary** Fianarantsoa, SE Madagascar *21.13S 48.19E*
78 *L14* **Manankoro** Sikasso, SW Mali *10.33N 7.25W*
78 *J12* **Manantali, Lac de** ⊠ W Mali
Manáos *see* Manaus
193 *B23* **Manapouri** Southland, South Island, NZ *45.33S 167.38E*
193 *B23* **Manapouri, Lake** ◎ South Island, NZ
60 *F13* **Manaquiri** Amazonas, NW Brazil *3.27S 60.37W*
Manar *see* Mannar
164 *K5* **Manas** Xinjiang Uygur Zizhiqu, NW China *44.16N 86.12E*
159 *U12* **Manās** *var.* Dangme Chu. ≈ Bhutan/India
153 *R8* **Manas, Gora** ▲ Kyrgyzstan/Uzbekistan *42.17N 71.04E*
159 *P10* **Manāsalu** *var.* Manaslu. ▲ C Nepal *28.33N 84.33E*
164 *K3* **Manas Hu** ◎ NW China
Manaslu *see* Manāsalu
39 *S8* **Manassa** Colorado, C USA *37.10N 105.56W*
23 *W4* **Manassas** Virginia, NE USA *38.45N 77.28W*
47 *T5* **Manatí** C Puerto Rico *18.26N 66.29W*
175 *S16* **Manatuto** N East Timor *8.31S 126.00E*
194 *L14* **Manau** Northern, S PNG *8.05S 147.57E*
56 *H4* **Manaure** La Guajira, N Colombia *11.46N 72.28W*
60 *F12* **Manaus** *prev.* Manáos. *state capital* Amazonas, NW Brazil *03.06S 60.00W*
142 *G17* **Manavgat** Antalya, SW Turkey *36.46N 31.28E*
192 *M13* **Manawatu** ≈ North Island, NZ
192 *L11* **Manawatu-Wanganui** *off.* Manawatu-Wanganui Region. ◈ *region* North Island, NZ
176 *Uu12* **Manawoka, Pulau** *island* Kepulauan Gorong, E Indonesia
179 *Rr16* **Manay** Mindanao, S Philippines *7.12N 126.29E*
144 *K2* **Manbij** *var.* Mambij, *Fr.* Membidj. Ḥalab, N Syria *36.31N 37.55E*
107 *N13* **Mancha Real** Andalucía, S Spain *37.46N 3.37W*
104 *I4* **Manche** ◈ *department* N France
99 *L17* **Manchester** *Lat.* Mancunium. NW England, UK *53.30N 2.15W*
25 *S5* **Manchester** Georgia, SE USA *32.51N 84.37W*
31 *Y13* **Manchester** Iowa, C USA *42.28N 91.27W*
23 *N7* **Manchester** Kentucky, S USA *37.10N 83.40W*
21 *O10* **Manchester** New Hampshire, NE USA *42.58N 71.25W*
22 *K10* **Manchester** Tennessee, S USA *35.28N 86.05W*
20 *M9* **Manchester** Vermont, NE USA *43.09N 73.03W*
99 *L18* **Manchester** ✕ NW England, UK *53.21N 2.16W*
155 *P15* **Manchhar Lake** ◎ SE Pakistan
Man-chou-li *see* Manzhouli
133 *X7* **Manchurian Plain** *plain* NE China
Máncio Lima *see* Japiim
Mancunium *see* Manchester
154 *J15* **Mand** Baluchistān, SW Pakistan *26.06N 61.58E*
Mand *see* Mand, Rūd-e
83 *H25* **Manda** Iringa, SW Tanzania *10.25S 34.38E*
180 *H6* **Mandabe** Toliara, W Madagascar *21.01S 44.55E*
168 *M10* **Mandah** *var.* Töhöm. Dornogovĭ, SE Mongolia *44.25N 108.18E*
97 *E18* **Mandal** Vest-Agder, S Norway *58.01N 7.27E*
Mandal *see* Arbulag, Hövsgöl, Mongolia
Mandal *see* Batsümber, Töv, Mongolia
177 *G5* **Mandalay** Mandalay, C Burma *21.57N 96.04E*
177 *G6* **Mandalay** ◈ *division* C Burma
168 *L9* **Mandalgovĭ** Dundgovĭ, C Mongolia *45.47N 106.18E*
145 *V7* **Mandalī** E Iraq *33.43N 45.33E*
168 *K10* **Mandal-Ovoo** *var.* Sharhulsan. Ömnögovĭ, S Mongolia *44.43N 104.06E*
97 *E18* **Mandalselva** ≈ S Norway
169 *P11* **Mandalt** *var.* Sonid Zuoqi. Nei Mongol Zizhiqu, N China *43.49N 113.36E*
30 *M5* **Mandan** North Dakota, N USA *46.49N 100.53W*
Mandargiri Hill *see* Mandār Hill
159 *R14* **Mandār Hill** *prev.* Mandargiri Hill. Bihār, NE India *24.51N 87.03E*
175 *P11* **Mandar, Teluk** *bay* Sulawesi, C Indonesia
109 *C19* **Mandas** Sardegna, Italy, C Mediterranean Sea *39.40N 9.07E*
Mandasor *see* Mandsaur
83 *L16* **Mandera** North Eastern, NE Kenya *3.55N 41.52E*
35 *V13* **Manderson** Wyoming, C USA *44.13N 107.55W*
46 *J12* **Mandeville** C Jamaica *18.01N 77.31W*
24 *K9* **Mandeville** Louisiana, S USA *30.21N 90.04W*
158 *I7* **Mandi** Himāchal Pradesh, NW India *31.40N 76.58E*
78 *K14* **Mandiana** E Guinea *10.37N 8.39W*
155 *U10* **Mandi Būrewāla** *var.* Būrewāla. Punjab, E Pakistan *30.04N 72.46E*
158 *G9* **Mandi Dabwāli** Haryāna, NW India *29.55N 74.40E*
Mandidzudzure *see* Chimanimani
85 *M15* **Mandié** Manica, NW Mozambique *16.27S 33.28E*
85 *N14* **Mandimba** Niassa, N Mozambique *14.21S 35.40E*
175 *Ss9* **Mandioli, Pulau** *island* Kepulauan Bacan, E Indonesia
59 *Q19* **Mandioré, Laguna** ◎ E Bolivia
160 *J10* **Mandla** Madhya Pradesh, C India *22.39N 80.21E*
85 *M20* **Mandlakazi** *var.* Manjacaze. Gaza, S Mozambique *24.43S 33.57E*
97 *E24* **Mandø** *var.* Manø. *island* W Denmark
176 *Ww9* **Mandori** Papua, E Indonesia *1.01S 134.58E*
Mandoúdhion/Mandoudi *see* Mantoúdi
117 *G19* **Mándra** Attikí, C Greece *38.04N 23.31E*
180 *I7* **Mandrare** ≈ S Madagascar
116 *M10* **Mandra, Yazovir** *salt lake* SE Bulgaria
109 *L23* **Mandrazzi, Portella** *pass* Sicilia, Italy, C Mediterranean Sea *37.57N 15.02E*
180 *J3* **Mandritsara** Mahajanga, N Madagascar *15.49S 48.49E*
149 *O13* **Mand, Rūd-e** *var.* Mand. ≈ S Iran
160 *F9* **Mandsaur** *prev.* Mandasor. Madhya Pradesh, C India *24.05N 75.04E*
160 *F11* **Māndu** Madhya Pradesh, C India *22.22N 75.24E*
175 *Oo5* **Mandul, Pulau** *island* N Indonesia
85 *G15* **Mandundu** Western, W Zambia *16.34S 22.18E*
188 *I13* **Mandurah** Western Australia *32.31S 115.40E*
109 *P18* **Manduria** Puglia, SE Italy *40.24N 17.37E*
161 *G20* **Mandya** Karnātaka, C India *12.34N 76.55E*
79 *P12* **Mané** C Burkina *12.59N 1.21W*
108 *E8* **Manerbio** Lombardia, NW Italy *45.22N 10.09E*
Manevichi *see* Manevychi
118 *K3* **Manevychi** *Pol.* Maniewicze, *Rus.* Manevichi. Volyns'ka Oblast', NW Ukraine *51.18N 25.29E*
109 *N16* **Manfredonia** Puglia, SE Italy *41.38N 15.54E*
109 *N16* **Manfredonia, Golfo di** *gulf* Adriatic Sea, N Mediterranean Sea
79 *P13* **Manga** C Burkina *11.40N 1.04W*
61 *L16* **Mangabeiras, Chapada das** ▲▲ E Brazil
81 *J20* **Mangai** Bandundu, W Dem. Rep. Congo *3.57S 19.32E*
202 *L17* **Mangaia** *island group* S Cook Islands
192 *M9* **Mangakino** Waikato, North Island, NZ *38.22S 175.45E*
118 *M15* **Mangalia** *anc.* Callatis. Constanța, SE Romania *43.46N 28.34E*
80 *J11* **Mangalmé** Guéra, SE Chad *12.25N 19.37E*
161 *E19* **Mangalore** Karnātaka, W India *12.54N 74.51E*
203 *Y13* **Mangareva** *var.* Magareva. *island* Îles Tuamotu, SE French Polynesia
85 *I23* **Mangaung** Free State, C South Africa *29.10S 26.19E*
Mangaung *see* Bloemfontein
160 *K9* **Mangawān** Madhya Pradesh, C India *24.39N 81.33E*
192 *M11* **Mangaweka** Manawatu-Wanganui, North Island, NZ *39.49S 175.47E*
192 *N11* **Mangaweka** ▲ North Island, NZ *39.51S 176.06E*
81 *P17* **Mangbwalu** Orientale, NE Dem. Rep. Congo *2.06N 30.04E*
103 *L24* **Mangfall** ≈ SE Germany
174 *K11* **Manggar** Pulau Belitung, W Indonesia *2.51S 108.14E*
176 *Vv12* **Manggawitu** Papua, E Indonesia *4.11S 133.28E*
177 *G2* **Mangin Range** ▲▲ N Burma
145 *R1* **Mangish** N Iraq *37.03N 43.04E*
150 *F15* **Mangistau** *Kaz.* Mangqystaū Oblysy; *prev.* Mangyshlaskaya. ◈ *province* SW Kazakhstan
Mangit *see* Mang'it
152 *H8* **Mang'it** *Rus.* Mangit. Qoraqalpog'iston Respublikasi, W Uzbekistan *42.06N 60.02E*
56 *A13* **Manglares, Cabo** *headland* SW Colombia *1.36N 79.01W*
155 *V6* **Mangla Reservoir** ⊠ NE Pakistan
165 *N9* **Mangnai** *var.* Lao Mangnai. Qinghai, C China *37.52N 91.39E*
Mango *see* Mago, Fiji
Mango *see* Sansanné-Mango, Togo
Mangoche *see* Mangochi
85 *N14* **Mangochi** *var.* Mangoche; *prev.* Fort Johnston. Southern, SE Malawi *14.27S 35.15E*
79 *N14* **Mangodara** SW Burkina *9.49N 4.22W*
180 *H6* **Mangoky** ≈ W Madagascar
175 *S10* **Mangole, Pulau** *island* Kepulauan Sula, E Indonesia
192 *J2* **Mangonui** Northland, North Island, NZ *35.00S 173.30E*
Mangqystaū Oblysy *see* Mangistau
Mangqystaū Shyghanaghy *see* Mangyshlakskiy Zaliv
106 *H7* **Mangualde** Viseu, N Portugal *40.36N 7.46W*
63 *H18* **Mangueira, Lagoa** ◎ S Brazil
79 *X6* **Manguéni, Plateau du** ▲▲ NE Niger
169 *T4* **Mangui** Nei Mongol Zizhiqu, N China *52.02N 122.13E*
28 *K11* **Mangum** Oklahoma, C USA *34.52N 99.30W*
81 *O18* **Manguredjipa** Nord Kivu, E Dem. Rep. Congo *0.28N 28.33E*
85 *L16* **Mangwendi** Mashonaland East, E Zimbabwe *18.22S 31.24E*
150 *F15* **Mangyshlak, Plato** *plateau* SW Kazakhstan
150 *E14* **Mangyshlakskiy Zaliv** *Kaz.* Mangqystaū Shyghanaghy. *gulf* SW Kazakhstan
Mangyshlaskaya *see* Mangistau
168 *E7* **Manhan** *var.* Tögrög. Hovd, W Mongolia *47.24N 92.06E*
Manhan *see* Alag-Erdene
29 *O4* **Manhattan** Kansas, C USA *39.11N 96.33W*
101 *L21* **Manhay** Luxembourg, SE Belgium *50.13N 5.43E*
85 *L21* **Manhiça** *prev.* Vila de Manhiça. Maputo, S Mozambique *25.20S 32.49E*
85 *L21* **Manhoca** Maputo, S Mozambique *26.47S 32.37E*
61 *N20* **Manhuaçu** Minas Gerais, SE Brazil *20.16S 42.01W*
149 *R11* **Mānī** Kermān, C Iran
56 *H10* **Maní** Casanare, C Colombia *4.49N 72.15W*
85 *M17* **Manica** *var.* Vila de Manica. Manica, W Mozambique *18.51S 32.50E*
85 *M17* **Manica** *off.* Província de Manica. ◈ *province* W Mozambique
85 *L17* **Manicaland** ◈ *province* E Zimbabwe
13 *U5* **Manic Deux, Réservoir** ⊠ Québec, SE Canada
Manich *see* Manych
61 *F14* **Manicoré** Amazonas, N Brazil *5.48S 61.16W*
11 *N11* **Manicouagan** Québec, SE Canada *50.40N 68.46W*
11 *N11* **Manicouagan** ≈ Québec, SE Canada
13 *U6* **Manicouagan, Péninsule de** *peninsula* Québec, SE Canada
11 *N11* **Manicouagan, Réservoir** ◎ Québec, E Canada
13 *T4* **Manic Trois, Réservoir** ⊠ Québec, SE Canada
81 *M20* **Maniema** *off.* Région du Maniema. ◈ *region* E Dem. Rep. Congo
Maniewicze *see* Manevychi
166 *F8* **Maniganggo** Sichuan, C China *32.01N 99.04E*
9 *Y15* **Manigotagan** Manitoba, S Canada *51.06N 96.18W*
159 *R13* **Manihāri** Bihār, N India *25.21N 87.37E*
203 *U9* **Manihi** *island* Îles Tuamotu, C French Polynesia
202 *L13* **Manihiki** *atoll* N Cook Islands
183 *U8* **Manihiki Plateau** *undersea feature* C Pacific Ocean
206 *M14* **Maniitsoq** *var.* Manîtsoq, *Dan.* Sukkertoppen. Kita, S Greenland *65.12N 52.05W*
159 *T15* **Manikganj** Dhaka, C Bangladesh *23.52N 90.00E*
158 *M14* **Mānikpur** Uttar Pradesh, N India *25.04N 81.06E*
179 *P11* **Manila** *off.* City of Manila. ● (Philippines) Luzon, N Philippines *14.34N 120.58E*
29 *Y9* **Manila** Arkansas, C USA *35.52N 90.10W*
201 *N16* **Manila Reef** *reef* W Micronesia
191 *T6* **Manilla** New South Wales, SE Australia *30.44S 150.43E*
200 *Qq14* **Maniloa** *island* Tongatapu Group, S Tonga
127 *P7* **Manily** Koryakskiy Avtonomnyy Okrug, E Russian Federation *62.33N 165.03E*
176 *Ww9* **Manim, Pulau** *island* E Indonesia
173 *Ff8* **Maninjau, Danau** ◎ Sumatera, W Indonesia
159 *W13* **Manipur** ◈ *state* NE India
159 *X14* **Manipur Hills** *hill range* E India
142 *C14* **Manisa** *var.* Manissa; *prev.* Saruhan, *anc.* Magnesia. Manisa, W Turkey *38.36N 27.28E*
142 *C13* **Manisa** *var.* Manissa. ◈ *province* W Turkey
Manissa *see* Manisa
33 *O7* **Manistee** Michigan, N USA *44.14N 86.19W*
33 *P7* **Manistee River** ≈ Michigan, N USA
33 *O4* **Manistique** Michigan, N USA *45.57N 86.15W*
33 *P4* **Manistique Lake** ◎ Michigan, N USA
9 *W13* **Manitoba** ◈ *province* S Canada
9 *X16* **Manitoba, Lake** ◎ Manitoba, S Canada
9 *X17* **Manitou** Manitoba, S Canada *49.12N 98.28W*
33 *N2* **Manitou Island** *island* Michigan, N USA
12 *H11* **Manitou Lake** ◎ Ontario, SE Canada
10 *G15* **Manitoulin Island** *island* Ontario, S Canada
39 *T5* **Manitou Springs** Colorado, C USA *38.51N 104.56W*
12 *G12* **Manitouwabing Lake** ◎ Ontario, S Canada
10 *E12* **Manitouwadge** Ontario, S Canada *49.13N 85.51W*
10 *G15* **Manitowaning** Manitoulin Island, Ontario, S Canada *45.43N 81.49W*
12 *B7* **Manitowik Lake** ◎ Ontario, S Canada
33 *N7* **Manitowoc** Wisconsin, N USA *44.04N 87.40W*
Manîtsoq *see* Maniitsoq
145 *O7* **Mānī', Wādī al** *dry watercourse* W Iraq
10 *J14* **Maniwaki** Québec, SE Canada *46.24N 75.58W*
176 *X11* **Maniwori** Papua, E Indonesia *2.49S 136.00E*
56 *E10* **Manizales** Caldas, W Colombia *5.03N 73.52W*
114 *F11* **Manjača** ▲▲ NW Bosnia and Herzegovina
Manjacaze *see* Mandlakazi
188 *J14* **Manjimup** Western Australia *34.18S 116.14E*
111 *V4* **Mank** Niederösterreich, C Austria *48.06N 15.13E*
81 *I17* **Mankanza** Equateur, NW Dem. Rep. Congo *1.40N 19.08E*
159 *N12* **Mankāpur** Uttar Pradesh, N India *27.03N 82.12E*
28 *M3* **Mankato** Kansas, C USA *39.45N 98.10W*
31 *U10* **Mankato** Minnesota, N USA *44.10N 94.00W*
119 *O7* **Man'kivka** Cherkas'ka Oblast', C Ukraine *48.58N 30.10E*
78 *M15* **Mankono** C Ivory Coast *8.06N 6.07W*
9 *T17* **Mankota** Saskatchewan, S Canada *49.25N 107.04W*
161 *K23* **Mankulam** Northern Province, N Sri Lanka *9.09N 80.27E*
168 *L10* **Manlay** *var.* Üydzen. Ömnögovĭ, S Mongolia *44.08N 106.48E*
41 *Q9* **Manley Hot Springs** Alaska, USA *65.00N 150.37W*
20 *H10* **Manlius** New York, NE USA *43.00N 75.58W*
107 *W5* **Manlleu** Cataluña, NE Spain *41.58N 2.16E*
31 *V11* **Manly** Iowa, C USA *43.17N 93.12W*
160 *E13* **Manmād** Mahārāshtra, W India *20.15N 74.28E*
190 *J7* **Mannahill** South Australia *32.29S 139.58E*
161 *J23* **Mannar** *var.* Manar. Northern Province, NW Sri Lanka *9.01N 79.53E*
161 *I24* **Mannar, Gulf of** *gulf* India/Sri Lanka
161 *J23* **Mannar Island** *island* N Sri Lanka
Mannersdorf *see* Mannersdorf am Leithagebirge
111 *Y5* **Mannersdorf am Leithagebirge** *var.* Mannersdorf. Niederösterreich, E Austria *47.58N 16.36E*
111 *Y6* **Mannersdorf an der Rabnitz** Burgenland, E Austria *47.25N 16.32E*
103 *G20* **Mannheim** Baden-Württemberg, SW Germany *49.28N 8.29E*
9 *O12* **Manning** Alberta, W Canada *56.52N 117.39W*
31 *T14* **Manning** Iowa, C USA *41.54N 95.03W*
30 *K5* **Manning** North Dakota, N USA *47.13N 102.46W*
23 *S13* **Manning** South Carolina, SE USA *33.42N 80.12W*
203 *Y2* **Manning, Cape** *headland* Kiritimati, NE Kiribati *2.01N 157.25W*
195 *V13* **Manning Strait** *strait* NW Solomon Islands
23 *S3* **Mannington** West Virginia, NE USA *39.31N 80.20W*
190 *A1* **Mann Ranges** ▲▲ South Australia
109 *C19* **Mannu** ≈ Sardegna, Italy, C Mediterranean Sea
9 *R14* **Mannville** Alberta, SW Canada *53.19N 111.08W*
78 *J15* **Mano** ≈ Liberia/Sierra Leone
Manø *see* Mandø
41 *O13* **Manokotak** Alaska, USA *59.00N 158.58W*
176 *W9* **Manokwari** Papua, E Indonesia *0.49S 134.04E*
81 *N22* **Manono** Shabo, SE Dem. Rep. Congo *7.18S 27.25E*
27 *T10* **Manor** Texas, SW USA *30.20N 97.33W*
99 *D16* **Manorhamilton** *Ir.* Cluainín. NW Ireland *54.18N 8.10W*
105 *S15* **Manosque** Alpes-de-Haute-Provence, SE France *43.49N 5.46E*
10 *L11* **Manouane, Lac** ◎ Québec, SE Canada
169 *W12* **Manp'o** *var.* Manp'ojin. NW North Korea *41.10N 126.24E*
Manp'ojin *see* Manp'o
203 *T4* **Manra** *prev.* Sydney Island. *atoll* Phoenix Islands, C Kiribati
107 *V5* **Manresa** Cataluña, NE Spain *41.44N 1.52E*
158 *H9* **Mānsa** Punjab, NW India *30.00N 75.25E*
84 *J12* **Mansa** *prev.* Fort Rosebery. Luapula, N Zambia *11.13S 28.55E*
78 *G12* **Mansa Konko** C Gambia *13.26N 15.29W*
13 *Q11* **Manseau** Québec, SE Canada *46.23N 71.59W*
155 *U5* **Mānsehra** North-West Frontier Province, NW Pakistan *34.22N 73.18E*
15 *Mm6* **Mansel Island** *island* Nunavut, NE Canada
191 *O12* **Mansfield** Victoria, SE Australia *37.04S 146.06E*
99 *M18* **Mansfield** C England, UK *53.09N 1.10W*
29 *S11* **Mansfield** Arkansas, C USA *35.03N 94.15W*
24 *G6* **Mansfield** Louisiana, S USA *32.02N 93.42W*
21 *O12* **Mansfield** Massachusetts, NE USA *42.00N 71.11W*
33 *T12* **Mansfield** Ohio, N USA *40.45N 82.31W*
20 *G12* **Mansfield** Pennsylvania, NE USA *41.46N 77.02W*
20 *M7* **Mansfield, Mount** ▲ Vermont, NE USA *44.31N 72.49W*
61 *M16* **Mansidão** Bahia, E Brazil *10.46S 44.03W*
104 *L11* **Mansle** Charente, W France *45.52N 0.11E*
78 *G12* **Mansôa** C Guinea-Bissau *12.07N 15.18W*
49 *V8* **Manso, Rio** ≈ C Brazil
Manṣûra *see* El Manṣûra
Mansurabad *see* Mehrān, Rūd-e
58 *A6* **Manta** Manabí, W Ecuador *0.57S 80.39W*
58 *A6* **Manta, Bahía de** *bay* W Ecuador
59 *F14* **Mantaro, Río** ≈ C Peru
37 *O8* **Manteca** California, W USA *37.48N 121.13W*
56 *J7* **Mantecal** Apure, C Venezuela *7.34N 69.07W*
33 *N11* **Manteno** Illinois, N USA *41.15N 87.49W*
23 *Y9* **Manteo** Roanoke Island, North Carolina, SE USA *35.53N 75.39W*
Mantes-Gassicourt *see* Mantes-la-Jolie
105 *N5* **Mantes-la-Jolie** *prev.* Mantes-Gassicourt, Mantes-sur-Seine, *anc.* Medunta. Yvelines, N France *48.58N 1.42E*
Mantes-sur-Seine *see* Mantes-la-Jolie
38 *L5* **Manti** Utah, W USA *39.16N 111.38W*
Mantinea *see* Mantíneia
117 *F20* **Mantíneia** *anc.* Mantinea. *site of ancient city* Pelopónnisos, S Greece *37.36N 22.22E*
61 *M21* **Mantiqueira, Serra da** ▲▲ S Brazil
31 *W10* **Mantorville** Minnesota, N USA *44.04N 92.45W*
117 *G17* **Mantoúdi** *var.* Mandoudi; *prev.* Mandoúdhion. Évvoia, C Greece *38.46N 23.28E*
Mantoue *see* Mantova
108 *F8* **Mantova** *Eng.* Mantua, *Fr.* Mantoue. Lombardia, NW Italy *45.10N 10.46E*
95 *M19* **Mäntsälä** Etelä-Suomi, S Finland *60.38N 25.21E*
95 *L17* **Mänttä** Länsi-Suomi, W Finland *62.00N 24.36E*
Mantua *see* Mantova
129 *O14* **Manturovo** Kostromskaya Oblast', NW Russian Federation *58.19N 44.42E*
95 *M18* **Mäntyharju** Ita-Suomi, SE Finland *61.25N 26.52E*
94 *M13* **Mäntyjärvi** Lappi, N Finland *66.00N 27.35E*
202 *L16* **Manuae** *island* S Cook Islands
203 *Q10* **Manuae** *atoll* Îles Sous le Vent, W French Polynesia
198 *Dd8* **Manua Islands** *island group* E American Samoa
42 *L5* **Manuel Benavides** Chihuahua, N Mexico *29.07N 103.52W*
63 *D21* **Manuel J.Cobo** Buenos Aires, E Argentina *35.49S 57.54W*
60 *M12* **Manuel Luís, Recife** *reef* E Brazil
63 *F15* **Manuel Viana** Rio Grande do Sul, S Brazil *29.33S 55.28W*
61 *I14* **Manuel Zinho** Pará, N Brazil *7.21S 54.47W*
203 *V11* **Manuhangi** *atoll* Îles Tuamotu, C French Polynesia
193 *E22* **Manuherikia** ≈ South Island, NZ
175 *R11* **Manui, Pulau** *island* N Indonesia
Manukau *see* Manurewa
192 *L6* **Manukau Harbour** *harbor* North Island, NZ
174 *K14* **Manuk, Ci** ≈ Jawa, S Indonesia
176 *U12* **Manuk, Pulau** *island* Maluku, E Indonesia
203 *Z2* **Manulu Lagoon** ◎ Kiritimati, E Kiribati
190 *J7* **Manunda Creek** *seasonal river* South Australia
59 *K15* **Manupari, Río** ≈ N Bolivia
192 *L6* **Manurewa** *var.* Manukau. Auckland, North Island, NZ *37.03S 174.55E*
59 *K15* **Manurimi, Río** ≈ NW Bolivia
194 *I8* **Manus** ◈ *province* N PNG
194 *J8* **Manus Island** *var.* Great Admiralty Island. *island* N PNG
176 *U15* **Manuwui** Pulau Babar, E Indonesia *7.47S 129.39E*
31 *Q3* **Manvel** North Dakota, N USA *48.07N 97.15W*
35 *Z14* **Manville** Wyoming, C USA *42.45N 104.38W*
24 *G6* **Many** Louisiana, S USA *31.34N 93.28W*
83 *H21* **Manyara, Lake** ◎ NE Tanzania
130 *L12* **Manych** *var.* Manich. ≈ SW Russian Federation
131 *N13* **Manych-Gudilo, Ozero** *salt lake* SW Russian Federation
85 *H14* **Manyinga** North Western, NW Zambia *13.28S 24.18E*
107 *O11* **Manzanares** Castilla-La Mancha, C Spain *39.00N 3.23W*
46 *H7* **Manzanillo** Granma, E Cuba *20.21N 77.07W*
42 *K14* **Manzanillo** Colima, SW Mexico *19.00N 104.18W*
42 *K14* **Manzanillo, Bahía** *bay* SW Mexico
39 *S11* **Manzano Mountains** ▲▲ New Mexico, SW USA
39 *R12* **Manzano Peak** ▲ New Mexico, SW USA *34.35N 106.27W*
169 *R6* **Manzhouli** *var.* Man-chou-li. Nei Mongol Zizhiqu, N China *49.36N 117.28E*
Manzil Bū Ruqaybah *see* Menzel Bourguiba
145 *X9* **Manzilīyah** E Iraq *32.26N 47.01E*
85 *L21* **Manzini** *prev.* Bremersdorp. C Swaziland *26.30S 31.33E*
85 *L21* **Manzini** ✕ (Mbabane) C Swaziland *26.36S 31.25E*
80 *G10* **Mao** Kanem, W Chad *14.06N 15.16E*
47 *N8* **Mao** NW Dominican Republic *19.33N 71.09W*
Maó *see* Mahón
Maoemere *see* Maumere
165 *W9* **Maojing** Gansu, N China *36.25N 106.36E*
176 *Xx12* **Maoke, Pegunungan** *Dut.* Sneeuw-gebergte, *Eng.* Snow Mountains. ▲▲ Papua, E Indonesia
Maol Réidh, Caoc *see* Mweelrea
166 *M15* **Maoming** Guangdong, S China *21.45N 110.50E*
166 *H8* **Maoxian** *var.* Mao Xian; *prev.* Fengyizhen. Sichuan, C China *31.42N 103.48E*
85 *L19* **Mapai** Gaza, SW Mozambique *22.52S 32.00E*
164 *H15* **Mapam Yumco** ◎ W China
85 *I15* **Mapanza** Southern, S Zambia *16.16S 26.54E*
56 *J4* **Mapararí** Falcón, N Venezuela *10.47N 69.26W*
43 *U17* **Mapastepec** Chiapas, SE Mexico *15.24N 92.55W*
175 *O5* **Mapat, Pulau** *island* N Indonesia
176 *Yy14* **Mapi** Papua, E Indonesia *7.02S 139.24E*
176 *Vv7* **Mapia, Kepulauan** *island group* E Indonesia
42 *L8* **Mapimí** Durango, C Mexico *25.50N 103.50W*
85 *N19* **Mapinhane** Inhambane, SE Mozambique *22.14S 35.07E*
57 *N7* **Mapire** Monagas, NE Venezuela *7.48N 64.40W*
9 *S17* **Maple Creek** Saskatchewan, S Canada *49.55N 109.28W*
33 *Q9* **Maple River** ≈ Michigan, N USA
31 *P7* **Maple River** ≈ North Dakota/South Dakota, N USA
31 *S13* **Mapleton** Iowa, C USA *42.10N 95.47W*
31 *U10* **Mapleton** Minnesota, N USA *43.55N 93.57W*
31 *R5* **Mapleton** North Dakota, N USA *46.51N 97.04W*
34 *F13* **Mapleton** Oregon, NW USA *44.01N 123.56W*
38 *L3* **Mapleton** Utah, W USA *40.07N 111.37W*
199 *Ii5* **Mapmaker Seamounts** *undersea feature* N Pacific Ocean
194 *G10* **Maprik** East Sepik, NW PNG *3.35S 143.03E*
85 *L21* **Maputo** *prev.* Lourenço Marques. ● (Mozambique) Maputo, S Mozambique *25.58S 32.34E*
85 *L21* **Maputo** ◈ *province* S Mozambique
85 *L21* **Maputo** ✕ Maputo, S Mozambique *25.47S 32.36E*
69 *V14* **Maputo** ≈ S Mozambique
Maqanshy *see* Makanchi
Maqat *see* Makat
115 *K19* **Maqë** ≈ NW Albania
115 *M19* **Maqellarë** Dibër, C Albania *41.36N 20.29E*
165 *S12* **Maqên** *var.* Dawo; *prev.* Dawu. Qinghai, C China *34.32N 100.17E*
165 *S11* **Maqen Kangri** ▲ C China *34.44N 99.25E*
165 *U12* **Maqu** *var.* Nyinma. Gansu, C China *34.02N 102.00E*
106 *M9* **Maqueda** Castilla-La Mancha, C Spain *40.04N 4.22W*
84 *B9* **Maquela do Zombo** Uíge, NW Angola *6.03S 15.05E*
65 *I16* **Maquinchao** Río Negro, C Argentina *41.19S 68.46W*
31 *Z13* **Maquoketa** Iowa, C USA *42.03N 90.42W*
31 *Y13* **Maquoketa River** ≈ Iowa, C USA
12 *F13* **Mar** Ontario, S Canada *44.48N 81.12W*
97 *F14* **Mår** ◎ S Norway
83 *G19* **Mara** ◈ *region* N Tanzania
203 *P8* **Maraa** Tahiti, W French Polynesia *17.43S 149.34W*
60 *D12* **Maraã** Amazonas, NW Brazil *1.48S 65.21W*
203 *O8* **Maraa, Pointe** *headland* Tahiti, W French Polynesia *17.43S 149.34W*
61 *K14* **Marabá** Pará, NE Brazil *5.22S 49.10W*
56 *H5* **Maracaibo** Zulia, NW Venezuela *10.39N 71.39W*
Maracaibo, Gulf of *see* Venezuela, Golfo de
56 *H5* **Maracaibo, Lago de** *var.* Lake Maracaibo. *inlet* NW Venezuela
Maracaibo, Lake *see* Maracaibo, Lago de
60 *K10* **Maracá, Ilha de** *island* NE Brazil
61 *H20* **Maracaju, Serra de** ▲▲ S Brazil
60 *I11* **Maracanaquará, Planalto** ▲▲ NE Brazil
56 *L5* **Maracay** Aragua, N Venezuela *10.15N 67.36W*
Marada *see* Marādah
77 *R9* **Marādah** *var.* Marada. N Libya *29.15N 19.28E*
79 *U12* **Maradi** Maradi, S Niger *13.30N 7.05E*
79 *U11* **Maradi** ◈ *department* S Niger
83 *E21* **Maragarazi** *var.* Muragarazi. ≈ Burundi/Tanzania
Maragha *see* Marāgheh
148 *J3* **Marāgheh** *var.* Maragha. Āžarbāyjān-e Sharqī, NW Iran *37.21N 46.13E*
147 *P7* **Marāh** *var.* Marrāt. Ar Riyāḑ, C Saudi Arabia *25.04N 45.30E*
57 *N11* **Marahuaca, Cerro** ▲ S Venezuela *3.37N 65.25W*
29 *R5* **Marais des Cygnes River** ≈ Kansas/Missouri, C USA
60 *L11* **Marajó, Baía de** *bay* N Brazil
61 *K12* **Marajó, Ilha de** *island* N Brazil
203 *O2* **Marakei** *atoll* Tungaru, W Kiribati
Marakesh *see* Marrakech
83 *I18* **Maralal** Rift Valley, C Kenya *1.04N 36.42E*
85 *G21* **Maralaleng** Kgalagadi, S Botswana *25.42S 22.39E*
151 *U8* **Maraldy, Ozero** ◎ NE Kazakhstan
190 *C5* **Maralinga** South Australia *30.16S 131.35E*
179 *R15* **Maramag** Mindanao, S Philippines *7.45N 124.58E*
Máramarossziget *see* Sighetu Marmației
195 *Y16* **Maramasike** *var.* Small Malaita. *island* N Solomon Islands
Maramba *see* Livingstone
204 *H3* **Marambio** *Argentinian research station* Antarctica *64.22S 57.18W*
118 *H9* **Maramureş** ◈ *county* NW Romania
38 *L15* **Marana** Arizona, SW USA *32.24N 111.12W*
107 *P7* **Maranchón** Castilla-La Mancha, C Spain *41.01N 2.10W*
148 *J2* **Marand** *var.* Merend. Āžarbāyjān-e Sharqī, NW Iran *38.23N 45.48E*
Marandellas *see* Marondera
60 *L13* **Maranhão** *off.* Estado do Maranhão. ◈ *state* E Brazil
106 *H10* **Maranhão, Barragem do** ⊠ C Portugal
155 *O11* **Mārān, Koh-i** ▲ SW Pakistan *29.24N 66.50E*
108 *J7* **Marano, Laguna di** *lagoon* NE Italy
58 *E9* **Marañón, Río** ≈ N Peru
104 *J10* **Marans** Charente-Maritime, W France *46.19N 0.58W*
85 *M20* **Marão** Inhambane, S Mozambique *24.15S 34.09E*
193 *B23* **Mararoa** ≈ South Island, NZ
Maraş/Marash *see* Kahramanmaraş
109 *M19* **Maratea** Basilicata, S Italy *39.57N 15.44E*
106 *G11* **Marateca** Setúbal, S Portugal *38.34N 8.40W*
117 *B20* **Marathiá, Akrotírio** *headland* Zákynthos, Iónia Nisiá, Greece, C Mediterranean Sea *37.39N 20.49E*
10 *E12* **Marathon** Ontario, S Canada *48.43N 86.22W*
25 *Y17* **Marathon** Florida Keys, Florida, SE USA *24.42N 81.05W*
26 *L10* **Marathon** Texas, SW USA *30.10N 103.14W*
Marathón *see* Marathónas
117 *H19* **Marathónas** *prev.* Marathón. Attikí, C Greece *38.09N 23.58E*
175 *Oo6* **Maratua, Pulau** *island* N Indonesia
61 *O18* **Maraú** Bahia, SE Brazil *14.07S 39.02W*
149 *R3* **Marāveh Tappeh** Golestān, N Iran *37.52N 55.57E*
26 *L11* **Maravillas Creek** ≈ Texas, SW USA
194 *J13* **Marawaka** Eastern Highlands, C PNG *6.56S 145.54E*
179 *R15* **Marawi** Mindanao, S Philippines *7.58N 124.16E*
143 *Y11* **Märäzä** *Rus.* Maraza. E Azerbaijan *40.32N 48.56E*
Marbat *see* Mirbāṭ
106 *L16* **Marbella** Andalucía, S Spain *36.31N 4.49W*
188 *J7* **Marble Bar** Western Australia *21.13S 119.48E*
38 *L9* **Marble Canyon** *canyon* Arizona, SW USA
27 *S10* **Marble Falls** Texas, SW USA *30.34N 98.16W*
29 *Y7* **Marble Hill** Missouri, C USA *37.18N 89.58W*
35 *T15* **Marbleton** Wyoming, C USA *45.31N 110.06W*
Marburg *see* Maribor
Marburg *see* Marburg an der Lahn, Germany
103 *H16* **Marburg an der Lahn** *hist.* Marburg. Hessen, W Germany *50.49N 8.46E*
113 *H23* **Marcal** ≈ W Hungary
44 *G7* **Marcala** La Paz, SW Honduras *14.13N 88.02W*
113 *H24* **Marcali** Somogy, SW Hungary *46.33N 17.24E*
85 *A16* **Marca, Ponta da** *headland* SW Angola *16.31S 11.42E*
61 *I16* **Marcelândia** Mato Grosso, W Brazil *11.18S 54.49W*
29 *T3* **Marceline** Missouri, C USA *39.42N 92.57W*
62 *I13* **Marcelino Ramos** Rio Grande do Sul, S Brazil *27.31S 51.57W*
57 *Y12* **Marcel, Mont** ▲ S French Guiana *2.32N 53.00W*
99 *O19* **March** E England, UK *52.37N 0.13E*
111 *Z3* **March** *var.* Morava. ≈ C Europe *see also* Morava
108 *I12* **Marche** *Eng.* Marches. ◈ *region* C Italy
105 *N11* **Marche** *cultural region* C France
101 *J21* **Marche-en-Famenne** Luxembourg, SE Belgium *50.13N 5.21E*
106 *K14* **Marchena** Andalucía, S Spain *37.19N 5.24W*
59 *B17* **Marchena, Isla** *var.* Bindloe Island. *island* Galapagos Islands, Ecuador, E Pacific Ocean
Marches *see* Marche
101 *J20* **Marchin** Liège, E Belgium *50.30N 5.17E*
189 *S1* **Marchinbar Island** *island* Wessel Islands, Northern Territory, N Australia
64 *L9* **Mar Chiquita, Laguna** ◎ C Argentina
105 *Q10* **Marcigny** Saône-et-Loire, C France *46.16N 4.04E*
25 *W16* **Marco** Florida, SE USA *25.56N 81.43W*
Marcodurum *see* Düren
61 *O15* **Marcolândia** Pernambuco, E Brazil *7.21S 40.40W*
108 *I8* **Marco Polo** ✕ (Venezia) Veneto, NE Italy *45.30N 12.21E*
Marcq *see* Mark
118 *M8* **Mărculeşti** *Rus.* Markuleshty. N Moldova *47.54N 28.14E*
31 *S12* **Marcus** Iowa, C USA *42.49N 95.48W*
41 *S11* **Marcus Baker, Mount** ▲ Alaska, USA *61.26N 147.45W*
199 *Hh5* **Marcus Island** *var.* Minami Tori Shima. *island* E Japan
20 *K8* **Marcy, Mount** ▲ New York, NE USA *44.06N 73.55W*
155 *T5* **Mardān** North-West Frontier Province, N Pakistan *34.13N 71.59E*
65 *N14* **Mar del Plata** Buenos Aires, E Argentina *37.59S 57.31W*
143 *Q16* **Mardin** Mardin, SE Turkey *37.19N 40.43E*
143 *Q16* **Mardin** ◈ *province* SE Turkey
143 *Q16* **Mardin Dağları** ▲▲ SE Turkey
Mardzad *see* Hayrhandulaan
197 *L6* **Maré** *island* Îles Loyauté, E New Caledonia
Marea Neagră *see* Black Sea
107 *Z8* **Mare de Déu del Toro** *var.* El Toro. ▲ Menorca, Spain, W Mediterranean Sea *39.59N 4.06E*
189 *W4* **Mareeba** Queensland, NE Australia *17.03S 145.30E*
98 *G8* **Maree, Loch** ◎ N Scotland, UK
Mareeq *see* Mereeg
Marek *see* Dupnitsa
78 *J11* **Maréna** Kayes, W Mali *14.36N 10.57W*
202 *I2* **Marenanuka** *atoll* Tungaru, W Kiribati
31 *X14* **Marengo** Iowa, C USA *41.48N 92.04W*
104 *J11* **Marennes** Charente-Maritime, W France *45.47N 1.04W*
109 *G23* **Marettimo, Isola** *island* Isole Egadi, S Italy
26 *K10* **Marfa** Texas, SW USA *30.18N 104.01W*
59 *P17* **Marfíl, Laguna** ◎ E Bolivia
Marganets *see* Marhanets'
27 *Q4* **Margaret** Texas, SW USA *34.00N 99.38W*
188 *I14* **Margaret River** Western Australia *33.58S 115.10E*
194 *G12* **Margarima** Southern Highlands, W PNG *5.57S 143.22E*
57 *N4* **Margarita, Isla de** *island* N Venezuela
117 *I25* **Margarítes** Kríti, Greece, E Mediterranean Sea *35.19N 24.40E*
99 *Q22* **Margate** *prev.* Mergate. SE England, UK *51.24N 1.24E*
25 *Z15* **Margate** Florida, SE USA *26.14N 80.12W*
Margelan *see* Marg'ilon
105 *P13* **Margeride, Montagnes de la** ▲▲ C France
Margherita *see* Jamaame
109 *N16* **Margherita di Savoia** Puglia, SE Italy *41.22N 16.09E*
Margherita, Lake *see* Ābaya Hāyk'
83 *E18* **Margherita Peak** *Fr.* Pic Marguerite. ▲ Uganda/Dem. Rep. Congo *0.28N 29.58E*

◆ Country ● Country Capital ◇ Dependent Territory ○ Dependent Territory Capital ◈ Administrative Region ✕ International Airport ▲ Mountain ▲▲ Mountain Range Volcano ≈ River ◎ Lake ⊠ Reservoir

MARGHĪ – MATANUSKA RIVER

155 O4 Marghī Bāmīān, N Afghanistan 35.10N 66.26E
118 G9 Marghita Hung. Margitta. Bihor, NW Romania 47.20N 22.19E
Marghitan see Marg'ilon
118 K8 Marginea Suceava, NE Romania 47.49N 25.47E
Margitta see Marghita
153 S10 Marg'ilon var. Margelan, Rus. Margilan. Farg'ona Viloyati, E Uzbekistan 40.29N 71.43E
154 K9 Märgow, Dasht-e desert SW Afghanistan
101 L18 Margraten Limburg, SE Netherlands 50.49N 5.49E
8 M15 Marguerite British Columbia, SW Canada 52.17N 122.10W
13 V3 Marguerite ≈ Québec, SE Canada
204 I6 Marguerite Bay bay Antarctica
Marguerite, Pic see Margherita Peak
119 T9 Marhanets' Rus. Marganets. Dnipropetrovs'ka Oblast', E Ukraine 47.34N 34.37E
194 E15 Mari Western, SW PNG 9.10S 141.39E
203 R12 Maria island Îles Australes, SW French Polynesia
203 Y12 Maria atoll Groupe Actéon, SE French Polynesia
42 I12 María Cleofas, Isla island C Mexico
64 H4 María Elena var. Oficina María Elena. Antofagasta, N Chile 22.18S 69.40W
97 G21 Mariager Århus, C Denmark 56.39N 9.58E
63 C22 María Ignacia Buenos Aires, E Argentina 37.24S 59.30W
191 P17 Maria Island island Tasmania, SE Australia
42 H12 María Madre, Isla island C Mexico
42 I12 María Magdalena, Isla island C Mexico
199 H6 Mariana Islands island group Guam/Northern Mariana Islands
183 N3 Mariana Trench var. Challenger Deep. undersea feature W Pacific Ocean
159 X12 Mariāni Assam, NE India 26.39N 94.18E
29 X11 Marianna Arkansas, C USA 34.46N 90.45W
25 R8 Marianna Florida, SE USA 30.46N 85.13W
180 J16 Marianne island Inner Islands, NE Seychelles
97 M19 Mariannelund Jönköping, S Sweden 57.37N 15.33E
63 D15 Mariano I.Loza Corrientes, NE Argentina 29.22S 58.12W
Mariano Machado see Ganda
113 A16 Mariánské Lázně Ger. Marienbad. Karlovarský Kraj, W Czech Republic 49.57N 12.42E
Máriaradna see Radna
35 S7 Marias River ≈ Montana, NW USA
Maria-Theresiopel see Subotica
Máriatölgyes see Dubnica nad Váhom
192 H1 Maria van Diemen, Cape headland North Island, NZ 34.27S 172.38E
111 V5 Mariazell Steiermark, E Austria 47.45N 15.17E
147 P15 Mar'ib W Yemen 15.28N 45.25E
97 I25 Maribo Storstrøm, S Denmark 54.46N 11.30E
111 W9 Maribor Ger. Marburg. NE Slovenia 46.33N 15.40E
Marica see Maritsa
37 R13 Maricopa California, W USA 35.03N 119.24W
Maricourt see Kangiqsujuaq
83 D15 Maridi Western Equatoria, SW Sudan 4.55N 29.30E
204 M11 Marie Byrd Land physical region Antarctica
199 L16 Marie Byrd Seamount undersea feature N Amundsen Sea 70.00S 118.00W
47 X11 Marie-Galante var. Ceyre to the Caribs. island SE Guadeloupe
47 Y6 Marie-Galante, Canal de channel S Guadeloupe
95 J20 Mariehamn Fin. Maarianhamina. Åland, SW Finland 60.04N 19.55E
46 C4 Mariel La Habana, W Cuba 22.58N 82.49W
101 H22 Mariembourg Namur, S Belgium 50.07N 4.30E
Marienbad see Mariánské Lázně
Marienburg see Alūksne, Latvia
Marienburg see Malbork, Poland
Marienburg see Feldioara, Romania
Marienburg in Westpreussen see Malbork
Marienhausen see Viļaka
85 D20 Mariental Hardap, SW Namibia 24.35S 17.55E
20 D13 Marienville Pennsylvania, NE USA 41.27N 79.07W
Marienwerder see Kwidzyń
60 C12 Marié, Rio ≈ NW Brazil
97 K17 Mariestad Västra Götaland, S Sweden 58.42N 13.49E
25 S3 Marietta Georgia, SE USA 33.57N 84.34W
33 U14 Marietta Ohio, N USA 39.25N 81.27W
29 N13 Marietta Oklahoma, C USA 33.56N 97.07W
83 H18 Marigat Rift Valley, W Kenya 0.28S 35.58E
105 S16 Marignane Bouches-du-Rhône, SE France 43.25N 5.12E
Marignano see Melegnano
47 O11 Marigot NE Dominica 15.31N 61.17W
126 Hh14 Mariinsk Kemerovskaya Oblast', S Russian Federation 56.13N 87.27E
131 Q3 Mariinskiy Posad Respublika Mariy El, W Russian Federation 56.07N 47.44E
121 E14 Marijampolė prev. Kapsukas. Marijampolė, S Lithuania 54.33N 23.21E
121 E14 Marijampolė ◆ province SW Lithuania
116 G12 Marikostenovo Blagoevgrad, SW Bulgaria 41.25N 23.21E
62 J9 Marília São Paulo, S Brazil 22.13S 49.58W
84 D11 Marimba Malanje, NW Angola 8.18S 16.58E
145 T1 Mārī Mīlā E Iraq 36.58N 44.42E
106 G4 Marín Galicia, NW Spain 42.22N 8.42W
37 N10 Marina California, W USA 36.40N 121.48W
Marina di Catanzaro see Catanzaro Marina
Mar"ina Gorka see Mar"ina Horka
121 L17 Mar"ina Horka Rus. Mar'ina Gorka. Minskaya Voblasts', C Belarus 53.30N 28.09E
179 Pp11 Marinduque island C Philippines
33 S9 Marine City Michigan, N USA 42.43N 82.29W
33 N6 Marinette Wisconsin, N USA 45.06N 87.37W
62 I10 Maringá Paraná, S Brazil 23.25S 51.55W
85 N16 Maringuè Sofala, C Mozambique 17.57S 34.23E
106 F9 Marinha Grande Leiria, C Portugal 39.45N 8.55W
109 I15 Marino Lazio, C Italy 41.46N 12.40E
61 A15 Mário Lobão Acre, W Brazil 8.21S 72.58W
25 O5 Marion Alabama, S USA 32.37N 87.19W
29 Y11 Marion Arkansas, C USA 35.12N 90.12W
32 L17 Marion Illinois, N USA 37.43N 88.55W
33 P13 Marion Indiana, N USA 40.31N 85.40W
31 X13 Marion Iowa, C USA 42.01N 91.36W
29 O5 Marion Kansas, C USA 38.21N 97.01W
22 H6 Marion Kentucky, S USA 37.19N 88.04W
23 P9 Marion North Carolina, SE USA 35.43N 82.00W
33 S12 Marion Ohio, N USA 40.34N 83.07W
23 T12 Marion South Carolina, SE USA 34.10N 79.24W
23 Q7 Marion Virginia, NE USA 36.49N 81.31W
29 O5 Marion Lake ▣ Kansas, C USA
23 S13 Marion, Lake ▣ South Carolina, SE USA
29 S8 Marionville Missouri, C USA 37.00N 93.38W
57 N7 Maripa Bolívar, E Venezuela 7.27N 65.10W
57 X11 Maripasoula W French Guiana 3.43N 54.04W
37 Q9 Mariposa California, W USA 37.28N 119.59W
63 G19 Mariscala Lavalleja, S Uruguay 34.03S 54.46W
64 M4 Mariscal Estigarribia Boquerón, NW Paraguay 22.02S 60.39W
58 C6 Mariscal Sucre var. Quito. ✕ (Quito) Pichincha, C Ecuador 0.21S 78.37W
32 K16 Marissa Illinois, N USA 38.15N 89.45W
105 U14 Maritime Alps Fr. Alpes Maritimes, It. Alpi Marittime. ▲ France/Italy
Maritimes, Alpes see Maritime Alps
Maritime Territory see Primorskiy Kray
116 K11 Maritsa var. Marica, Gk. Évros, Turk. Meriç; anc. Hebrus. ≈ SW Europe see also Évros/Meriç
Maritsa see Simeonovgrad
Marittime, Alpi see Maritime Alps
Maritzburg see Pietermaritzburg
119 X9 Mariupol' prev. Zhdanov. Donets'ka Oblast', SE Ukraine 47.06N 37.34E
57 Q6 Mariusa, Caño ≈ NE Venezuela
148 J5 Marīvān prev. Dezh Shāhpūr. Kordestān, W Iran 35.30N 46.09E
125 A16 Mariy El, Respublika prev. Mariyskaya ASSR. ◆ autonomous republic W Russian Federation
131 R3 Mariyets Respublika Mariy El, W Russian Federation 56.31N 49.48E
Mariyskaya ASSR see Mariy El, Respublika
120 G4 Märjamaa Ger. Merjama. Raplamaa, NW Estonia 58.53N 24.24E
101 I15 Mark Fr. Marcq. ≈ Belgium/Netherlands
83 N17 Marka var. Merca. Shabeellaha Hoose, S Somalia 1.43N 44.45E
151 Z10 Markakol', Ozero Kaz. Marqaköl. ◎ E Kazakhstan
78 M12 Markala Ségou, W Mali 13.38N 6.07W
165 S15 Markam var. Gartog. Xizang Zizhiqu, W China 29.40N 98.33E
97 K21 Markaryd Kronoberg, S Sweden 56.25N 13.34E
148 L7 Markazī off. Ostān-e Markazī. ◆ province W Iran
12 F14 Markdale Ontario, S Canada 44.19N 80.37W
29 X10 Marked Tree Arkansas, C USA 35.31N 90.25W
100 N11 Markelo Overijssel, E Netherlands 52.15N 6.30E
100 J9 Markermeer ◎ C Netherlands
99 N20 Market Harborough C England, UK 52.30N 0.57W
99 N18 Market Rasen E England, UK 53.23N 0.21W
126 Kk10 Markha ≈ NE Russian Federation
10 H16 Markham Ontario, S Canada 43.53N 79.13W
27 V12 Markham Texas, SW USA 28.57N 96.04W
194 J13 Markham ≈ C PNG
205 Q11 Markham, Mount ▲ Antarctica 82.58S 163.30E
112 M11 Marki Mazowieckie, C Poland 52.19N 21.07E
164 F8 Markit Xinjiang Uygur Zizhiqu, NW China 38.55N 77.40E
119 Y5 Markivka Rus. Markovka. Luhans'ka Oblast', E Ukraine 49.34N 39.35E
37 Q7 Markleeville California, W USA 38.41N 119.47W
100 L8 Marknesse Flevoland, N Netherlands 52.44N 5.54E
81 H14 Markounda var. Marcounda. Ouham, NW Central African Republic 7.37N 17.00E
Markovka see Markivka
127 P6 Markovo Chukotskiy Avtonomnyy Okrug, NE Russian Federation 64.43N 170.13E
131 P8 Marks Saratovskaya Oblast', W Russian Federation 51.40N 46.44E
24 K2 Marks Mississippi, S USA 34.15N 90.16W
24 I7 Marksville Louisiana, S USA 31.07N 92.04W
103 I19 Marktheidenfeld Bayern, C Germany 49.50N 9.36E
103 J24 Marktoberdorf Bayern, S Germany 47.45N 10.36E
103 M18 Marktredwitz Bayern, E Germany 50.00N 12.04E
Markt-Übelbach see Übelbach
29 V3 Mark Twain Lake ▣ Missouri, C USA
Markulesthy see Mărculeşti
103 E14 Marl Nordrhein-Westfalen, W Germany 51.40N 7.06E
190 E2 Marla South Australia 27.19S 133.35E
189 Y8 Marlborough Queensland, E Australia 22.55S 150.07E
99 M22 Marlborough S England, UK 51.25N 1.44W
193 I15 Marlborough off. Marlborough District. ◆ unitary authority South Island, NZ
105 P3 Marle Aisne, N France 49.54N 3.48E
33 S8 Marlette Michigan, N USA 43.20N 83.05W
27 T9 Marlin Texas, SW USA 31.18N 96.54W
23 S5 Marlinton West Virginia, NE USA 38.13N 80.05W
28 M12 Marlow Oklahoma, C USA 34.39N 97.57W
161 E17 Marmagao Goa, W India 15.22N 73.53E
Marmanda see Marmande
104 L13 Marmande anc. Marmanda. Lot-et-Garonne, SW France 44.30N 0.10E
142 C11 Marmara Balıkesir, NW Turkey 40.36N 27.34E
142 D11 Marmara Denizi Eng. Sea of Marmara. sea NW Turkey
116 N13 Marmaraereğlisi Tekirdağ, NW Turkey 40.58N 27.57E
Marmara, Sea of see Marmara Denizi
142 C16 Marmaris Muğla, SW Turkey 36.52N 28.16E
30 J6 Marmarth North Dakota, N USA 46.17N 103.55W
23 Q5 Marmet West Virginia, NE USA 38.12N 81.31W
108 H5 Marmolada, Monte ▲ N Italy 46.36N 11.58E
106 M13 Marmolejo Andalucía, S Spain 38.03N 4.10W
12 J14 Marmora Ontario, SE Canada 44.28N 77.40W
41 Q14 Marmot Bay bay Alaska, USA
105 Q4 Marne ◆ department N France
105 Q4 Marne ≈ N France
143 U10 Marneuli prev. Borchalo, Sarvani. S Georgia 41.28N 44.45E
80 I13 Maro Moyen-Chari, S Chad 8.25N 18.46E
56 L12 Maroa Amazonas, S Venezuela 2.40N 67.33W
180 J3 Maroantsetra Toamasina, NE Madagascar 15.22S 49.43E
203 W11 Marokau atoll Îles Tuamotu, C French Polynesia
180 J5 Marolambo Toamasina, E Madagascar 20.03S 48.07E
180 J2 Maromokotro ▲ N Madagascar
85 L16 Marondera prev. Marandellas. Mashonaland East, NE Zimbabwe 18.10S 31.33E
57 X9 Maroni Dut. Marowijne. ≈ French Guiana/Surinam
191 V2 Maroochydore-Mooloolaba Queensland, E Australia 26.36S 153.04E
175 P13 Maros Sulawesi, C Indonesia 4.58S 119.34E
118 H11 Maros var. Mureş, Mureşul, Ger. Marosch, Mieresch. ≈ Hungary/Romania see also Mureş
Marosch see Maros/Mureş
Maroshévíz see Topliţa
Marosillye see Ilia
Marosludas see Luduş
Marosújvár/Marosújvárakna see Ocna Mureş
Marosvásárhely see Târgu Mureş
203 V14 Marotiri var. Îlots de Bass, Morotiri. island group Îles Australes, SW French Polynesia
80 G12 Maroua Extrême-Nord, N Cameroon 10.34N 14.19E
57 X12 Marouini Rivier ≈ SE Surinam
180 I3 Marovoay Mahajanga, NW Madagascar 16.04S 46.40E
57 W9 Marowijne ◆ district NE Surinam
Marowijne see Maroni
Marqaköl see Markakol', Ozero
199 M9 Marquesas Fracture Zone tectonic feature E Pacific Ocean
Marquesas Islands see Marquises, Îles
25 W17 Marquesas Keys island group Florida, SE USA
31 Y12 Marquette Iowa, C USA 43.02N 91.10W
33 N3 Marquette Michigan, N USA 46.32N 87.24W
105 N1 Marquise Pas-de-Calais, N France 50.49N 1.42E
203 X7 Marquises, Îles Eng. Marquesas Islands. island group N French Polynesia
191 Q6 Marra Creek ≈ New South Wales, SE Australia
82 B10 Marra Hills plateau W Sudan
82 B11 Marra, Jebel ▲ W Sudan 12.59N 24.16E
76 E7 Marrakech var. Marakesh, Eng. Marrakesh; prev. Morocco. W Morocco 31.39N 7.57W
Marrakesh see Marrakech
Marrāt see Marāh
191 N15 Marrawah Tasmania, SE Australia 40.55S 144.41E
190 I4 Marree South Australia 29.39S 138.06E
83 L17 Marrehan ▲ SW Somalia
85 N17 Marromeu Sofala, C Mozambique 18.18S 35.58E
106 J17 Marroquí, Punta headland SW Spain 36.01N 5.39W
191 N8 Marrowie Creek seasonal river New South Wales, SE Australia
85 O14 Marrupa Niassa, N Mozambique 13.13S 37.30E
190 D1 Marryat South Australia 26.22S 133.22E
77 Y10 Marsa 'Alam SE Egypt 25.01N 34.52E
77 R8 Marsá al Burayqah var. Al Burayqah. N Libya 30.21N 19.37E
83 J17 Marsabit Eastern, N Kenya 2.19N 37.58E
109 H23 Marsala anc. Lilybaeum. Sicilia, Italy, C Mediterranean Sea 37.48N 12.26E
123 Jj17 Marsaxlokk Bay bay SE Malta
67 G15 Mars Bay bay Ascension Island, C Atlantic Ocean
103 H15 Marsberg Nordrhein-Westfalen, W Germany 51.28N 8.51E
9 R15 Marsden Saskatchewan, S Canada 52.50N 109.45W
100 H7 Marsdiep strait NW Netherlands
105 R16 Marseille Eng. Marseilles; anc. Massilia. Bouches-du-Rhône, SE France 43.19N 5.21E
Marseille-Marignane see Provence
32 M11 Marseilles Illinois, N USA 41.19N 88.42W
Marseilles see Marseille
78 J16 Marshall W Liberia 6.10N 10.22W
41 N11 Marshall Alaska, USA 61.52N 162.04W
29 U9 Marshall Arkansas, C USA 35.54N 92.37W
33 N14 Marshall Illinois, N USA 39.23N 87.41W
33 Q10 Marshall Michigan, N USA 42.16N 84.57W
31 S9 Marshall Minnesota, N USA 44.26N 95.48W
29 T4 Marshall Missouri, C USA 39.07N 93.12W
23 O9 Marshall North Carolina, SE USA 35.49N 82.41W
27 X6 Marshall Texas, SW USA 32.32N 94.22W
201 S4 Marshall Islands off. Republic of the Marshall Islands. ◆ republic W Pacific Ocean
183 Q3 Marshall Islands island group W Pacific Ocean
199 I7 Marshall Seamounts undersea feature SW Pacific Ocean
31 W13 Marshalltown Iowa, C USA 42.01N 92.54W
21 P12 Marshfield Massachusetts, NE USA 42.04N 70.40W
29 T7 Marshfield Missouri, C USA 37.20N 92.54W
32 K6 Marshfield Wisconsin, N USA 44.41N 90.12W
46 H1 Marsh Harbour Great Abaco, W Bahamas 26.31N 77.03W
21 S3 Mars Hill Maine, NE USA 46.31N 67.51W
23 P9 Mars Hill North Carolina, SE USA 35.49N 82.33W
24 H10 Marsh Island island Louisiana, S USA
23 S11 Marshville North Carolina, SE USA 34.59N 80.22W
13 W5 Marsoui Québec, SE Canada 49.12N 65.58W
13 R8 Mars, Rivière à ≈ Québec, SE Canada
97 O15 Märsta Stockholm, C Sweden 59.37N 17.52E
97 H24 Marstal Fyn, C Denmark 54.52N 10.31E
97 I19 Marstrand Västra Götaland, S Sweden 57.54N 11.31E
27 U8 Mart Texas, SW USA 31.32N 96.49W
178 Gg9 Martaban var. Moktama. Mon State, S Burma 16.31N 97.34E
177 G9 Martaban, Gulf of gulf S Burma
109 Q19 Martano Puglia, SE Italy 40.12N 18.19E
Martapoera see Martapura
175 N11 Martapura prev. Martapoera. Borneo, C Indonesia 3.25S 114.51E
101 L23 Martelange Luxembourg, SE Belgium 49.50N 5.43E
116 L7 Marten Ruse, N Bulgaria 43.57N 26.08E
12 H10 Marten River Ontario, S Canada 46.43N 79.45W
9 T15 Martensville Saskatchewan, S Canada 52.15N 106.42W
Marteskirch see Târnăveni
Martes Tolosane see Martres-Tolosane
117 K25 Mártha Kríti, Greece, E Mediterranean Sea 35.03N 25.22E
191 Q6 Marthaguy Creek ≈ New South Wales, SE Australia
21 P13 Martha's Vineyard island Massachusetts, NE USA
110 C11 Martigny Valais, SW Switzerland 46.04N 7.03E
105 R16 Martigues Bouches-du-Rhône, SE France 43.24N 5.03E
113 J19 Martin Ger. Sankt Martin, Hung. Turócszentmárton; prev. Turčianský Svätý Martin. Žilinský Kraj, N Slovakia 49.03N 18.54E
30 L11 Martin South Dakota, N USA 43.10N 101.43W
22 G8 Martin Tennessee, S USA 36.20N 88.51W
107 S7 Martín ≈ E Spain
109 P18 Martina Franca Puglia, SE Italy 40.42N 17.19E
193 M14 Martinborough Wellington, North Island, NZ 41.15S 175.28E
27 S11 Martindale Texas, SW USA 29.49N 97.49W
37 N8 Martinez California, W USA 38.00N 122.12W
25 V3 Martinez Georgia, SE USA 33.31N 82.04W
43 Q13 Martínez de La Torre Veracruz-Llave, E Mexico 20.06N 97.03W
47 Y12 Martinique ◇ French overseas department E West Indies
1 O15 Martinique island E West Indies
Martinique Channel see Martinique Passage
47 X12 Martinique Passage var. Dominica Channel, Martinique Channel. channel Dominica/Martinique
25 Q5 Martin Lake ▣ Alabama, S USA
117 G18 Martíno prev. Martínon. Stereá Ellás, C Greece 38.34N 23.13E
Martínon see Martíno
204 J11 Martin Peninsula peninsula Antarctica
41 S5 Martin Point headland Alaska, USA 70.06N 143.04W
111 V3 Martinsberg Niederösterreich, NE Austria 48.23N 15.09E
23 V3 Martinsburg West Virginia, NE USA 39.25N 77.55W
33 V13 Martins Ferry Ohio, N USA 40.06N 80.43W
Martinskirch see Târnăveni
33 O14 Martinsville Indiana, N USA 39.25N 86.25W
23 S8 Martinsville Virginia, NE USA 36.41N 79.52W
67 K16 Martin Vaz, Ilhas island group E Brazil
Martök see Martuk
192 M12 Marton Manawatu-Wanganui, North Island, NZ 40.05S 175.22E
107 N13 Martos Andalucía, S Spain 37.43N 3.58W
104 M16 Martres-Tolosane var. Martes Tolosane. Haute-Garonne, S France 43.13N 1.00E
94 M11 Martti Lappi, NE Finland 67.28N 28.19E
150 I9 Martuk Kaz. Martök. Aktyubinsk, NW Kazakhstan 50.45N 56.30E
143 U12 Martuni E Armenia 40.07N 45.20E
60 L11 Marudá Pará, E Brazil 5.25S 49.04W
175 O2 Marudu, Teluk bay East Malaysia
155 O8 Ma'rūf Kandahār, SE Afghanistan 31.37N 67.08E
170 F14 Marugame Kagawa, Shikoku, SW Japan 34.16N 133.46E
193 H16 Maruia ≈ South Island, NZ
100 M6 Marum Groningen, NE Netherlands 53.07N 6.16E
197 C13 Marum, Mount ▲ Ambrym, C Vanuatu 16.15S 168.07E
81 P23 Marungu ▲ SE Dem. Rep. Congo
203 Y12 Marutea atoll Groupe Actéon, C French Polynesia
149 O11 Marv Dasht var. Mervdasht. Fārs, S Iran 29.51N 52.44E
105 P13 Marvejols Lozère, S France 44.35N 3.16E
29 X12 Marvell Arkansas, C USA 34.33N 90.52W
38 L6 Marvine, Mount ▲ Utah, W USA 38.40N 111.38W
145 Q7 Marwānīyah C Iraq 33.58N 42.31E
158 F13 Mārwār var. Marwar Junction. Rājasthān, N India 25.43N 73.39E
Marwar Junction see Mārwār
9 R14 Marwayne Alberta, SW Canada 53.30N 110.25W
152 I14 Mary prev. Merv. Mary Welaýaty, S Turkmenistan 37.24N 61.48E
Mary see Mary Welaýaty
189 Z9 Maryborough Queensland, E Australia 25.31S 152.36E
190 M11 Maryborough Victoria, SE Australia 37.04S 143.43E
Maryborough see Port Laoise
85 G23 Marydale Northern Cape, W South Africa 29.25S 22.06E
119 W8 Mar"yinka Donets'ka Oblast', E Ukraine 47.57N 37.27E
Mary Island see Kanton
23 W4 Maryland off. State of Maryland; also known as America in Miniature, Cockade State, Free State, Old Line State. ◆ state NE USA
27 P7 Maryneal Texas, SW USA 32.12N 100.25W
99 J15 Maryport NW England, UK 54.44N 3.28W
11 U13 Marystown Newfoundland and Labrador, SE Canada 47.10N 55.10W
38 K6 Marysvale Utah, W USA 38.26N 112.14W
37 O6 Marysville California, W USA 39.07N 121.35W
29 O3 Marysville Kansas, C USA 39.48N 96.37W
33 S13 Marysville Michigan, N USA 42.54N 82.29W
33 S9 Marysville Ohio, N USA 40.13N 83.22W
34 H7 Marysville Washington, NW USA 48.03N 122.10W
29 R2 Maryville Missouri, C USA 40.20N 94.52W
23 N9 Maryville Tennessee, S USA 35.45N 83.58W
152 I15 Mary Welaýaty var. Mary, Rus. Maryyskiy Velayat. ◆ province S Turkmenistan
Maryyskiy Velayat see Mary Welaýaty
Marzūq see Murzuq
176 V11 Mas Papua, E Indonesia 3.28S 132.40E
44 J11 Masachapa var. Puerto Masachapa. Managua, W Nicaragua 11.47N 86.31W
83 G19 Masai Mara National Reserve reserve C Kenya
83 I21 Masai Steppe grassland NW Tanzania
83 F19 Masaka SW Uganda 0.19S 31.46E
175 N13 Masalembo Besar, Pulau island S Indonesia
143 Y13 Masallı Rus. Masally. S Azerbaijan 39.03N 48.39E
Masally see Masallı
175 Pp10 Masamba Sulawesi, C Indonesia 2.33S 120.19E
Masampo see Masan
169 Y16 Masan prev. Masampo. S South Korea 35.10N 128.36E
Masandam Peninsula see Musandam Peninsula
83 J25 Masasi Mtwara, SE Tanzania 10.43S 38.48E
Masawa see Massawa
44 J10 Masaya Masaya, W Nicaragua 11.58N 86.06W
44 J10 Masaya ◆ department W Nicaragua
179 Q12 Masbate Masbate, N Philippines 12.21N 123.34E
179 Qq12 Masbate island C Philippines
76 I6 Mascara var. Mouaskar. NW Algeria 35.25N 0.10E
181 O7 Mascarene Basin undersea feature W Indian Ocean
181 O9 Mascarene Islands island group W Indian Ocean
181 N9 Mascarene Plain undersea feature W Indian Ocean
181 O7 Mascarene Plateau undersea feature W Indian Ocean
204 H5 Mascart, Cape headland Adelaide Island, Antarctica
64 J10 Mascasín, Salinas de salt lake C Argentina
42 K13 Mascota Jalisco, C Mexico 20.31N 104.46W
13 O12 Mascouche Québec, SE Canada 45.46N 73.37W
128 J9 Masel'gskaya Respublika Kareliya, NW Russian Federation 63.09N 34.22E
85 J23 Maseru ● (Lesotho) W Lesotho 29.21S 27.34E
85 J23 Maseru ✕ W Lesotho 29.27S 27.37E
Mashaba see Mashava
166 K14 Mashan var. Baishan. Guangxi Zhuangzu Zizhiqu, S China 23.40N 108.10E
85 K17 Mashava prev. Mashaba. Masvingo, SE Zimbabwe 20.03S 30.28E
149 U4 Mashhad var. Meshed. Khorāsān-Razavī, NE Iran 36.16N 59.34E
172 Oo4 Mashike Hokkaidō, NE Japan 43.51N 141.30E
Mashiz see Bardsīr
155 N14 Mashkai ≈ SW Pakistan
149 X13 Māshkel var. Rūd-i Māshkel, Rūd-e Māshkīd. ≈ Iran/Pakistan
154 K12 Māshkel, Hāmūn-i salt marsh SW Pakistan
Māshkel, Rūd-i/Māshkīd, Rūd-e see Māshkel
85 K15 Mashonaland Central ◆ province N Zimbabwe
85 K16 Mashonaland East ◆ province NE Zimbabwe
85 J16 Mashonaland West ◆ province NW Zimbabwe
Mashtagi see Maştağa
172 Qq6 Mashū-ko var. Masyû Ko. ◎ Hokkaidō, NE Japan
147 S14 Masīlah, Wādī al dry watercourse SE Yemen
81 I21 Masi-Manimba Bandundu, SW Dem. Rep. Congo 4.44S 17.56E
83 F17 Masindi W Uganda 1.40N 31.45E
83 I19 Masinga Reservoir ▣ S Kenya
179 Oo10 Masinloc Luzon, N Philippines 15.35N 119.57E
Masira see Maşīrah, Jazīrat
Masira, Gulf of see Maşīrah, Khalīj
147 Y10 Maşīrah, Jazīrat var. Masīra. island E Oman
147 Y10 Maşīrah, Khalīj var. Gulf of Masira. bay E Oman
Masis see Büyükağrı Dağı
81 O19 Masisi Nord Kivu, E Dem. Rep. Congo 1.25S 28.50E
176 U11 Masiwang ≈ Pulau Seram, E Indonesia
Masjed-e Soleymān see Masjed Soleymān
148 L9 Masjed Soleymān var. Masjed-e Soleymān, Masjid-i Sulaiman. Khūzestān, SW Iran 31.58N 49.17E
Masjid-i Sulaiman see Masjed Soleymān
Maskat see Masqaţ
145 Q7 Maskhān C Iraq 33.41N 42.46E
147 X8 Maskin var. Miskin. NW Oman 23.28N 56.46E
99 B17 Mask, Lough Ir. Loch Measca. ◎ W Ireland
116 N10 Maslen Nos headland E Bulgaria 42.19N 27.47E
180 K3 Masoala, Tanjona headland NE Madagascar 15.58N 50.13E
Masohi see Amahai
33 Q9 Mason Michigan, N USA 42.33N 84.25W
33 R14 Mason Ohio, N USA 39.21N 84.18W
27 Q10 Mason Texas, SW USA 30.44N 99.15W
23 P4 Mason West Virginia, NE USA 39.01N 82.01W
193 B25 Mason Bay bay Stewart Island, NZ
32 K13 Mason City Illinois, N USA 40.12N 89.42W
31 V12 Mason City Iowa, C USA 43.09N 93.12W
Mă, Sông see Ma, Nam
20 B16 Masontown Pennsylvania, NE USA 39.49N 79.53W
147 Y8 Masqaţ var. Maskat, Eng. Muscat. ● (Oman) NE Oman 23.34N 58.36E
108 E10 Massa Toscana, C Italy 44.01N 10.07E
20 M11 Massachusetts off. Commonwealth of Massachusetts; also known as Bay State, Old Bay State, Old Colony State. ◆ state NE USA
21 P11 Massachusetts Bay bay Massachusetts, NE USA
37 R2 Massacre Lake ◎ Nevada, W USA
109 O18 Massafra Puglia, SE Italy 40.35N 17.05E
110 G11 Massagno Ticino, S Switzerland 46.01N 8.55E
80 G11 Massaguet Chari-Baguirmi, W Chad 12.28N 15.25E
Massakori see Massakory
80 G10 Massakory var. Massakori; prev. Dagana. Chari-Baguirmi, W Chad 13.01N 15.43E
80 H11 Massalassef Chari-Baguirmi, SW Chad 11.37N 17.09E
108 F13 Massa Marittima Toscana, C Italy 43.03N 10.55E
84 B11 Massangano Cuanza Norte, NW Angola 9.36S 14.19E
85 M18 Massangena Gaza, S Mozambique 21.34S 32.57E
82 J9 Massawa var. Masawa, Amh. Mits'iwa. E Eritrea 15.37N 39.27E
82 K9 Massawa Channel channel E Eritrea
20 J6 Massena New York, NE USA 44.55N 74.53W
80 H11 Massenya Chari-Baguirmi, SW Chad 11.21N 16.09E
8 I13 Masset Graham Island, British Columbia, SW Canada 54.00N 132.09W
104 L16 Masseube Gers, S France 43.26N 0.33E
12 E11 Massey Ontario, S Canada 46.13N 82.06W
105 P12 Massiac Cantal, C France 45.16N 3.13E
105 P12 Massif Central plateau C France
Massilia see Marseille
33 U12 Massillon Ohio, N USA 40.48N 81.31W
79 N12 Massina Ségou, W Mali 13.58N 5.24W
85 N19 Massinga Inhambane, SE Mozambique 23.16S 35.23E
85 L20 Massingir Gaza, SW Mozambique 23.57S 32.12E
205 Z10 Masson Island island Antarctica
Massoukou see Franceville
143 Z11 Maştağa Rus. Mashtagi, Mastaga. E Azerbaijan 40.31N 50.01E
Mastanli see Momchilgrad
192 M13 Masterton Wellington, North Island, NZ 40.56S 175.39E
20 M14 Mastic Long Island, New York, NE USA 40.48N 72.50W
155 O10 Mastung Baluchistān, SW Pakistan 29.46N 66.48E
121 J20 Mastva Rus. Mostva. ≈ SW Belarus
121 G17 Masty Rus. Mosty. Hrodzyenskaya Voblasts', W Belarus 53.25N 24.30E
170 E12 Masuda Shimane, Honshū, SW Japan 34.40N 131.50E
94 J11 Masugnsbyn Norrbotten, N Sweden 67.28N 22.01E
Masuku see Franceville
85 K17 Masvingo prev. Fort Victoria, Nyanda, Victoria. Masvingo, SE Zimbabwe 20.04S 30.49E
85 K18 Masvingo prev. Victoria. ◆ province SE Zimbabwe
176 W10 Maswaar, Pulau island Irian Jaya, E Indonesia
144 H5 Maşyāf Fr. Misiaf. Ḩamāh, C Syria 35.04N 36.21E
Masyû Ko see Mashū-ko
112 E9 Maszewo Zachodniopomorskie, NW Poland 53.29N 15.01E
85 I17 Matabeleland North ◆ province W Zimbabwe
85 J18 Matabeleland South ◆ province S Zimbabwe
84 O13 Mataca Niassa, N Mozambique 12.27S 36.13E
197 G13 Matacawa Levu island Yasawa Group, NW Fiji
12 G8 Matachewan Ontario, S Canada 47.58N 80.39W
169 Q8 Matad var. Dzüünbulag. Dornod, E Mongolia 46.48N 115.21E
81 F22 Matadi Bas-Congo, W Dem. Rep. Congo 5.49S 13.31E
27 O4 Matador Texas, SW USA 34.01N 100.50W
44 J9 Matagalpa Matagalpa, C Nicaragua 12.53N 85.55W
44 K9 Matagalpa ◆ department W Nicaragua
10 I12 Matagami Québec, S Canada 49.46N 77.37W
27 U13 Matagorda Texas, SW USA 28.40N 96.57W
27 U13 Matagorda Bay inlet Texas, SW USA
27 U14 Matagorda Island island Texas, SW USA
27 V13 Matagorda Peninsula headland Texas, SW USA 28.34N 96.01W
203 Q8 Mataiea Tahiti, W French Polynesia 17.46S 149.25W
203 T9 Mataiva atoll Îles Tuamotu, C French Polynesia
191 O7 Matakana New South Wales, SE Australia 32.59S 145.53E
192 N7 Matakana Island island NE NZ
85 C15 Matala Huíla, SW Angola 14.45S 15.01E
202 G12 Matala'a Pointe headland Île Uvea, N Wallis and Futuna 13.19S 176.07W
161 K25 Matale Central Province, C Sri Lanka 7.28N 80.37E
202 E12 Matalesina, Pointe headland Île Alofi, W Wallis and Futuna
78 I10 Matam NE Senegal 15.40N 13.18W
192 M8 Matamata Waikato, North Island, NZ 37.49S 175.45E
79 V12 Matamey Zinder, S Niger 13.27N 8.27E
42 L8 Matamoros Coahuila de Zaragoza, NE Mexico 25.34N 103.12W
43 P15 Matamoros var. Izúcar de Matamoros. Puebla, S Mexico 18.36N 98.30W
43 Q8 Matamoros Tamaulipas, C Mexico 25.49N 97.31W
175 Q10 Matana, Danau ◎ Sulawesi, C Indonesia
77 S13 Ma'ţan as Sārah SE Libya 21.45N 21.55E
84 J12 Matanda Luapula, N Zambia 11.24S 28.25E
83 J24 Matandu ≈ S Tanzania
13 V6 Matane Québec, SE Canada 48.48N 67.31W
13 V6 Matane ≈ Québec, SE Canada
79 S12 Matankari Dosso, SW Niger 13.39N 4.03E
41 R11 Matanuska River ≈ Alaska, USA

◆ Country ● Country Capital ◇ Dependent Territory ○ Dependent Territory Capital ◆ Administrative Region ✕ International Airport ▲ Mountain ▲ Mountain Range ▲ Volcano ≈ River ◎ Lake ▣ Reservoir

MATANZA – MEDINA DEL CAMPO

56 G7 **Matanza** Santander, N Colombia 7.22N 73.01W
46 D4 **Matanzas** Matanzas, NW Cuba 23.00N 81.32W
13 V7 **Matapédia** ≈ Québec, SE Canada
13 V6 **Matapédia, Lac** ⊚ Québec, SE Canada
202 B17 **Mata Point** *headland* SE Niue 19.07S 169.51E
202 D12 **Matapu, Pointe** *headland* Île Futuna, W Wallis and Futuna
64 G12 **Mataquito, Río** ≈ C Chile
161 K26 **Matara** Southern Province, S Sri Lanka 5.57N 80.33E
117 D18 **Matarágka** *var.* Mataránga. Dytikí Ellás, C Greece 38.31N 21.32E
175 Nn16 **Mataram** Pulau Lombok, C Indonesia 8.36S 116.07E
Mataránga *see* Matarágka
189 Q3 **Mataranka** Northern Territory, N Australia 14.55S 133.03E
107 W6 **Mataró** *anc.* Illuro. Cataluña, E Spain 41.31N 2.27E
192 O8 **Matata** Bay of Plenty, North Island, NZ 37.54S 176.45E
198 Cc8 **Matātula, Cape** *headland* Tutuila, W American Samoa 14.15S 170.34W
193 D24 **Mataura** Southland, South Island, NZ 46.11S 168.53E
193 D24 **Mataura** ≈ South Island, NZ
Mata Uta *see* Matā'utu
202 G11 **Matā'utu** *var.* Mata Uta. ○ (Wallis and Futuna) Île Uvea, Wallis and Futuna 13.22S 176.12W
198 B8 **Matāutu** Upolu, C Samoa 13.57S 171.55W
202 G12 **Matā'utu, Baie de** *bay* Île Uvea, Wallis and Futuna
203 P7 **Mataval, Baie de** *bay* Tahiti, W French Polynesia
202 I16 **Matavera** Rarotonga, S Cook Islands 21.13S 159.43W
203 V16 **Mataveri** Easter Island, Chile, E Pacific Ocean 27.10S 109.27W
203 V17 **Mataveri** ✕ (Easter Island) Easter Island, Chile, E Pacific Ocean 27.10S 109.27W
192 P9 **Matawai** Gisborne, North Island, NZ 38.23S 177.31E
13 O10 **Matawin** ≈ Québec, SE Canada
151 V13 **Matay** Almaty, SE Kazakhstan 45.52N 78.45E
12 K8 **Matchi-Manitou, Lac** ⊚ Québec, SE Canada
43 O10 **Matehuala** San Luis Potosí, C Mexico 23.40N 100.37W
47 V13 **Matelot** Trinidad, Trinidad and Tobago 10.48N 61.06W
85 M15 **Matenge** Tete, NW Mozambique 15.22S 33.47E
109 O18 **Matera** Basilicata, S Italy 40.39N 16.34E
113 O21 **Mátészalka** Szabolcs-Szatmár-Bereg, E Hungary 47.57N 22.16E
176 Y10 **Matewar** Papua, E Indonesia 1.44S 138.26E
95 H17 **Matfors** Västernorrland, C Sweden 62.22N 16.59E
104 K11 **Matha** Charente-Maritime, W France 45.50N 0.13W
(0) F15 **Mathematicians Seamounts** *undersea feature* E Pacific Ocean
23 X6 **Mathews** Virginia, NE USA 37.24N 76.17W
27 S14 **Mathis** Texas, SW USA 28.05N 97.49W
158 J11 **Mathura** *prev.* Muttra. Uttar Pradesh, N India 27.30N 77.42E
Mathurai *see* Madurai
179 Rr16 **Mati** Mindanao, S Philippines 6.58N 126.11E
Matianus *see* Orūmīyeh, Daryācheh-ye
Matiara *see* Matiāri
155 Q15 **Matiāri** *var.* Matiara. Sind, SE Pakistan 25.37N 68.28E
43 S16 **Matías Romero** Oaxaca, SE Mexico 16.52N 94.57W
45 O13 **Matina** Limón, E Costa Rica 10.02N 83.15W
12 D10 **Matinenda Lake** ⊚ Ontario, S Canada
21 R8 **Matinicus Island** *island* Maine, NE USA
Matisco/Matisco Ædourum *see* Mâcon
155 Q16 **Mātli** Sind, SE Pakistan 25.06N 68.37E
99 M18 **Matlock** C England, UK 53.07N 1.31W
61 F18 **Mato Grosso** *prev.* Vila Bela da Santissima Trindade. Mato Grosso, W Brazil 14.52S 59.58W
61 G17 **Mato Grosso** *off.* Estado de Mato Grosso; *prev.* Matto Grosso. ◈ *state* W Brazil
62 H8 **Mato Grosso do Sul** *off.* Estado de Mato Grosso do Sul. ◈ *state* S Brazil
61 I18 **Mato Grosso, Planalto de** *plateau* C Brazil
85 L21 **Matola** Maputo, S Mozambique 25.57S 32.27E
106 G6 **Matosinhos** *prev.* Matozinhos. Porto, NW Portugal 41.10N 8.42W
Matou *see* Pingguo
57 Z10 **Matoury** NE French Guiana 4.49N 52.17W
Matozinhos *see* Matosinhos
113 L21 **Mátra** ▲▲ N Hungary
147 Y8 **Maṭraḥ** *var.* Mutrah. NE Oman 23.35N 58.30E
118 L12 **Mătrașești** Vrancea, E Romania 45.52N 27.13E
110 M8 **Matrei Am Brenner** Tirol, W Austria 47.09N 11.28E
111 P8 **Matrei in Osttirol** Tirol, W Austria 47.04N 12.31E
78 I15 **Matru** SW Sierra Leone 7.37N 12.07W
77 U7 **Maṭrûḥ** *var.* Mersa Maṭrûḥ; *anc.* Paraetonium. NW Egypt 31.20N 27.15E
172 Q13 **Matsubara** *var.* Matubara. Kagoshima, Tokuno-shima, SW Japan 32.58N 129.55E
171 K16 **Matsudo** *var.* Matudo. Chiba, Honshū, S Japan 35.45N 139.49E
170 F11 **Matsue** *var.* Matsuye, Matue. Shimane, Honshū, SW Japan 35.27N 133.03E
171 Mm7 **Matsumae** Hokkaidō, NE Japan 41.27N 140.04E
171 J14 **Matsumoto** *var.* Matumoto. Nagano, Honshū, S Japan 36.18N 137.58E
171 H16 **Matsusaka** *var.* Matsuzaka, Matusaka. Mie, Honshū, SW Japan 34.34N 136.30E
167 S12 **Matsu Tao** *Chin.* Mazu Dao. *island* NW Taiwan
Matsutō *see* Mattō
170 C12 **Matsuura** *var.* Matuura. Nagasaki, Kyūshū, SW Japan 33.21N 129.40E
170 Ee14 **Matsuyama** *var.* Matuyama. Ehime, Shikoku, SW Japan 33.49N 132.46E
Matsuye *see* Matsue
Matsuzaka *see* Matsusaka
171 J17 **Matsuzaki** Shizuoka, Honshū, S Japan 34.43N 138.45E
12 F8 **Mattagami** ≈ Ontario, S Canada
12 F8 **Mattagami Lake** ⊚ Ontario, S Canada
64 K12 **Mattaldi** Córdoba, C Argentina 34.32S 64.18W
23 Y9 **Mattamuskeet, Lake** ⊚ North Carolina, SE USA
23 W6 **Mattaponi River** ≈ Virginia, NE USA
12 I11 **Mattawa** Ontario, SE Canada 46.19N 78.42W
12 I11 **Mattawa** ≈ Ontario, SE Canada
21 S5 **Mattawamkeag** Maine, NE USA 45.30N 68.20W
21 S4 **Mattawamkeag Lake** ⊚ Maine, NE USA
110 D11 **Matterhorn** *It.* Monte Cervino. ▲ Italy/Switzerland 45.58N 7.36E *see also* Cervino, Monte
37 W1 **Matterhorn** ▲ Nevada, W USA 41.48N 115.22W
34 L12 **Matterhorn** *var.* Sacajawea Peak. ▲ Oregon, NW USA 45.12N 117.18W
37 R8 **Matterhorn Peak** ▲ California, W USA 38.06N 119.19W
111 Y5 **Mattersburg** Burgenland, E Austria 47.44N 16.23E
110 E11 **Matter Vispa** ≈ S Switzerland
57 R7 **Matthews Ridge** N Guyana 7.30N 60.07W
46 K7 **Matthew Town** Great Inagua, S Bahamas 20.56N 73.40W
111 Q4 **Mattighofen** Oberösterreich, NW Austria 48.07N 13.09E
109 N16 **Mattinata** Puglia, SE Italy 41.41N 16.01E
147 T9 **Maṭṭī, Sabkhat** *salt flat* Saudi Arabia/UAE
20 M14 **Mattituck** Long Island, New York, NE USA 40.59N 72.31W
171 I13 **Mattō** *var.* Matsutō. Ishikawa, Honshū, SW Japan 36.31N 136.34E
Matto Grosso *see* Mato Grosso
32 M14 **Mattoon** Illinois, N USA 39.28N 88.22W
59 L16 **Mattos, Río** ≈ C Bolivia
Mattu *see* Metu
174 Ll5 **Matu** Sarawak, East Malaysia 2.39N 111.31E
59 E14 **Matucana** Lima, W Peru 11.53S 76.23W
Matudo *see* Matsudo
Matue *see* Matsue
197 J16 **Matuku** *island* S Fiji
114 B9 **Matulji** Primorje-Gorski Kotar, NW Croatia 45.21N 14.18E
Matumoto *see* Matsumoto
57 P5 **Maturín** Monagas, NE Venezuela 9.45N 63.10W
Matusaka *see* Matsusaka
Matuura *see* Matsuura
Matuyama *see* Matsuyama
130 K11 **Matveyev Kurgan** Rostovskaya Oblast', SW Russian Federation 47.31N 38.55E
131 O8 **Matyshevo** Volgogradskaya Oblast', SW Russian Federation 50.53N 44.09E
159 O13 **Mau** *var.* Maunāth Bhanjan. Uttar Pradesh, N India 25.57N 83.33E
85 O14 **Maúa** Niassa, N Mozambique 13.54S 37.13E
104 M17 **Maubermé, Pic de** *var.* Tuc de Moubermé, *Sp.* Pico Mauberme; *prev.* Tuc de Maubermé. ▲ France/Spain 42.48N 0.54E *see also* Moubermé, Tuc de
Mauberme, Pico *see* Maubermé, Pic de/Moubermé, Tuc de
Maubermé, Tuc de *see* Maubermé, Pic de/ Moubermé, Tuc de
105 Q2 **Maubeuge** Nord, N France 50.16N 4.00E
177 Ff8 **Maubin** Irrawaddy, SW Burma 16.43N 95.37E
158 L13 **Maudaha** Uttar Pradesh, N India 25.40N 80.07E
191 N9 **Maude** New South Wales, SE Australia 34.30S 144.20E
205 P3 **Maudheimvidda** *physical region* Antarctica
67 N22 **Maud Rise** *undersea feature* S Atlantic Ocean
111 Q4 **Mauerkirchen** Oberösterreich, NW Austria 48.10N 13.07E
Mauersee *see* Mamry, Jezioro
196 K2 **Maug Islands** *island group* N Northern Mariana Islands
105 Q15 **Mauguio** Hérault, S France 43.37N 4.01E
199 Kk6 **Maui** *island* Hawai'i, USA, C Pacific Ocean
202 M16 **Mauke** *atoll* S Cook Islands
64 G13 **Maule** *off.* Región del Maule. ◈ *region* C Chile
104 J9 **Mauléon** Deux-Sèvres, W France 46.55N 0.45W
104 J16 **Mauléon-Licharre** Pyrénées-Atlantiques, SW France 43.14N 0.51W
64 G13 **Maule, Río** ≈ C Chile
65 G17 **Maullín** Los Lagos, S Chile 41.37S 73.34W
Maulmain *see* Moulmein
33 R11 **Maumee** Ohio, N USA 41.34N 83.40W
33 Q12 **Maumee River** ≈ Indiana/Ohio, N USA
29 U11 **Maumelle** Arkansas, C USA 34.51N 92.24W
29 T11 **Maumelle, Lake** ⊠ Arkansas, C USA
175 Qq16 **Maumere** *prev.* Maoemere. Flores, S Indonesia 8.34S 122.13E
85 G17 **Maun** North-West, C Botswana 20.00S 23.25E
Maunāth Bhanjan *see* Mau
Maunawai *see* Waimea
202 H16 **Maungaroa** ▲ Rarotonga, S Cook Islands 21.13S 159.48W
192 K3 **Maungatapere** Northland, North Island, NZ 35.46S 174.10E
192 K4 **Maungaturoto** Northland, North Island, NZ 36.06S 174.21E
203 R10 **Maupiti** *var.* Maurua. *island* Îles Sous le Vent, W French Polynesia
158 K14 **Mau Rānīpur** Uttar Pradesh, N India 25.13N 79.07E
24 K9 **Maurepas, Lake** ⊚ Louisiana, S USA
105 T16 **Maures** ▲▲ SE France
105 O12 **Mauriac** Cantal, C France 45.13N 2.21E
Maurice *see* Mauritius
67 J20 **Maurice Ewing Bank** *undersea feature* SW Atlantic Ocean
190 C4 **Maurice, Lake** *salt lake* South Australia
20 I17 **Maurice River** ≈ New Jersey, NE USA
27 Y10 **Mauriceville** Texas, SW USA 30.13N 93.52W
100 K12 **Maurik** Gelderland, C Netherlands 51.57N 5.25E
78 H8 **Mauritania** *off.* Islamic Republic of Mauritania, *Ar.* Mūrītānīyah. ◆ *republic* W Africa
181 W15 **Mauritius** *off.* Republic of Mauritius, *Fr.* Maurice. ◆ *republic* W Indian Ocean
132 M17 **Mauritius** *island* W Indian Ocean
181 N9 **Mauritius Trench** *undersea feature* W Indian Ocean
104 H6 **Mauron** Morbihan, NW France 48.06N 2.16W
105 N13 **Maurs** Cantal, C France 44.45N 2.12E
Maurua *see* Maupiti
Maury Mid-Ocean Channel *see* Maury Seachannel
66 L6 **Maury Seachannel** *var.* Maury Mid-Ocean Channel. *undersea feature* N Atlantic Ocean
32 K8 **Mauston** Wisconsin, N USA 43.45N 90.01W
111 R8 **Mauterndorf** Salzburg, NW Austria 47.09N 13.39E
111 T4 **Mauthausen** Oberösterreich, N Austria 48.13N 14.30E
111 Q9 **Mauthen** Kärnten, S Austria 46.39N 12.58E
85 F15 **Mavinga** Cuando Cubango, SE Angola 15.49S 20.23E
85 M17 **Mavita** Manica, W Mozambique 19.31S 33.09E
117 K22 **Mavrópetra, Akrotírio** *headland* Santoríni, Kykládes, Greece, Aegean Sea 36.28N 25.22E
117 F16 **Mavrovoúni** ▲ C Greece 39.37N 22.45E
192 Q8 **Mawhai Point** *headland* North Island, NZ 38.08S 178.24E
177 Ff3 **Mawlaik** Sagaing, C Burma 23.40N 94.25E
Mawlamyine *see* Moulmein
147 N14 **Mawr, Wādī** *dry watercourse* NW Yemen
205 X5 **Mawson** *Australian research station* Antarctica 67.24S 63.16E
205 X5 **Mawson Coast** *physical region* Antarctica
30 M4 **Max** North Dakota, N USA 47.48N 101.18W
43 W12 **Maxcanú** Yucatán, SE Mexico 20.35N 90.00W
Maxesibebi *see* Mount Ayliff
111 Q5 **Maxglan** ✕ (Salzburg) Salzburg, W Austria 47.46N 13.00E
95 K16 **Maxmo** *Fin.* Maksamaa. Länsi-Suomi, W Finland 63.13N 22.04E
23 T11 **Maxton** North Carolina, SE USA 34.47N 79.34W
27 R8 **May** Texas, SW USA 31.58N 98.54W
194 E10 **May** ≈ NW PNG
127 N17 **Maya** ≈ E Russian Federation
157 Q19 **Māyābandar** Andaman and Nicobar Islands, India, E Indian Ocean 12.43N 92.52E
Mayadin *see* Al Mayādīn
46 L5 **Mayaguana** *island* SE Bahamas
46 L5 **Mayaguana Passage** *passage* SE Bahamas
47 S6 **Mayagüez** W Puerto Rico 18.12N 67.08W
47 R6 **Mayagüez, Bahía de** *bay* W Puerto Rico
Mayals *see* Maials
81 G20 **Mayama** Le Pool, SE Congo 3.49S 14.52E
39 V8 **Maya, Mesa De** ▲ Colorado, C USA 37.06N 103.30W
149 R4 **Mayamey** Semnān, N Iran 36.26N 55.49E
44 F3 **Maya Mountains** *Sp.* Montañas Mayas. ▲▲ Belize/Guatemala
46 I7 **Mayarí** Holguín, E Cuba 20.40N 75.42W
Mayas, Montañas *see* Maya Mountains
20 I17 **May, Cape** *headland* New Jersey, NE USA 38.55N 74.57W
82 J11 **Maych'ew** *var.* Mai Chio, *It.* Mai Ceu, Tigray, N Ethiopia 12.55N 39.30E
144 I2 **Maydān Ikbiz** Ḥalab, N Syria 36.51N 36.40E
Maydān Shahr *see* Meydān Shahr
82 O12 **Maydh** Sanaag, N Somalia 10.57N 47.07E
Maydī *see* Mīdī
Mayebashi *see* Maebashi
Mayence *see* Mainz
104 K6 **Mayenne** Mayenne, NW France 48.18N 0.37W
104 J6 **Mayenne** ◈ *department* NW France
104 J7 **Mayenne** ≈ N France
38 K12 **Mayer** Arizona, SW USA 34.25N 112.15W
24 J4 **Mayersville** Mississippi, S USA 32.54N 91.04W
9 P14 **Mayerthorpe** Alberta, SW Canada 53.58N 115.06W
23 S12 **Mayesville** South Carolina, SE USA 34.00N 80.10W
193 G19 **Mayfield** Canterbury, South Island, NZ 43.50S 171.24E
35 N14 **Mayfield** Idaho, NW USA 43.24N 115.56W
22 G7 **Mayfield** Kentucky, S USA 36.44N 88.38W
38 L5 **Mayfield** Utah, W USA 39.06N 111.42W
Mayhan *see* Sant
39 T14 **Mayhill** New Mexico, SW USA 32.52N 105.28W
151 T9 **Maykain** *Kaz.* Mayqayyng. Pavlodar, NE Kazakhstan 51.24N 75.46E
130 L14 **Maykop** Respublika Adygeya, SW Russian Federation 44.36N 40.06E
Maylibash *see* Maylybas
Mayli-Say *see* Mayluu-Suu
153 T9 **Mayluu-Suu** *prev.* Mayli-Say, *Kir.* Mayly-Say. Dzhalal-Abadskaya Oblast', W Kyrgyzstan 41.16N 72.27E
150 L14 **Maylybas** *prev.* Maylibash. Kyzylorda, S Kazakhstan 45.51N 62.37E
Mayly-Say *see* Mayluu-Suu
Maymana *see* Meymaneh
178 Gg5 **Maymyo** Mandalay, C Burma 22.03N 96.30E
127 P6 **Mayn** ≈ NE Russian Federation
131 Q5 **Mayna** Ul'yanovskaya Oblast', W Russian Federation 54.04N 47.20E
23 N8 **Maynardville** Tennessee, S USA 36.15N 83.48W
12 J13 **Maynooth** Ontario, SE Canada 45.14N 77.54W
8 I6 **Mayo** Yukon Territory, NW Canada 63.37N 135.48W
25 U9 **Mayo** Florida, SE USA 30.03N 83.10W
99 B16 **Mayo** *Ir.* Maigh Eo. *cultural region* W Ireland
Mayo *see* Maio
80 G12 **Mayo-Kébbi** *off.* Préfecture du Mayo-Kébbu, *var.* Mayo-Kébi. ◈ *prefecture* SW Chad
Mayo-Kébi *see* Mayo-Kébbi
81 F19 **Mayoko** Le Niari, SW Congo 2.18S 12.45E
179 Q11 **Mayon Volcano** ⩓ Luzon, N Philippines 13.15N 123.40E
63 A24 **Mayor Buratovich** Buenos Aires, E Argentina 39.12S 62.41W
106 L4 **Mayorga** Castilla-León, N Spain 42.10N 5.16W
192 N6 **Mayor Island** *island* NE NZ
Mayor Pablo Lagerenza *see* Capitán Pablo Lagerenza
181 I14 **Mayotte** ◇ *French territorial collectivity* E Africa
Mayoumba *see* Mayumba
46 J13 **May Pen** C Jamaica 17.58N 77.15W
Mayqayyng *see* Maykain
179 P7 **Mayraira Point** *headland* Luzon, N Philippines 18.36N 120.47E
111 N8 **Mayrhofen** Tirol, W Austria 47.09N 11.52E
194 F10 **May River** East Sepik, NW PNG 4.10S 141.51E
126 Mm15 **Mayskiy** Amurskaya Oblast', SE Russian Federation 52.13N 129.30E
131 O15 **Mayskiy** Kabardino-Balkarskaya Respublika, SW Russian Federation 43.37N 44.04E
151 U9 **Mayskoye** Pavlodar, NE Kazakhstan 50.55N 78.11E
20 J17 **Mays Landing** New Jersey, NE USA 39.27N 74.43W
23 N4 **Maysville** Kentucky, S USA 38.39N 83.44W
29 R2 **Maysville** Missouri, C USA 39.53N 94.21W
176 Y14 **Mayu** *channel* Papua, E Indonesia
81 D20 **Mayumba** *var.* Mayoumba. Nyanga, S Gabon 3.22S 10.37E
175 Ss7 **Mayu, Pulau** *island* Maluku, E Indonesia
33 S8 **Mayville** Michigan, N USA 43.18N 83.16W
20 C11 **Mayville** New York, NE USA 42.15N 79.31W
31 Q4 **Mayville** North Dakota, N USA 47.27N 97.17W
126 M11 **Mayya** Respublika Sakha (Yakutiya), NE Russian Federation 61.45N 130.16E
Mayyali *see* Mahe
Mayyit, Al Baḥr al *see* Dead Sea
85 J15 **Mazabuka** Southern, S Zambia 15.52S 27.46E
Mazaca *see* Kayseri
Mazagan *see* El-Jadida
34 J7 **Mazama** Washington, NW USA 48.34N 120.26W
105 O15 **Mazamet** Tarn, S France 43.30N 2.21E
149 O4 **Māzandarān** *off.* Ostān-e Māzandarān. ◈ *province* N Iran
162 F7 **Mazar** Xinjiang Uygur Zizhiqu, NW China 36.31N 76.59E
109 H24 **Mazara del Vallo** Sicilia, Italy, C Mediterranean Sea 37.39N 12.36E
155 O2 **Mazār-e Sharīf** *var.* Mazār-i Sharif. Balkh, N Afghanistan 36.44N 67.06E
Mazār-i Sharif *see* Mazār-e Sharīf
107 R13 **Mazarrón** Murcia, SE Spain 37.36N 1.19W
107 R14 **Mazarrón, Golfo de** *gulf* SE Spain
57 S9 **Mazaruni River** ≈ N Guyana
44 B6 **Mazatenango** Suchitepéquez, SW Guatemala 14.31N 91.28W
42 I10 **Mazatlán** Sinaloa, C Mexico 23.15N 106.24W
38 L12 **Mazatzal Mountains** ▲▲ Arizona, SW USA
120 D10 **Mažeikiai** Telšiai, NW Lithuania 56.19N 22.21E
120 D7 **Mazirbe** Talsi, NW Latvia 57.39N 22.16E
42 G5 **Mazocahui** Sonora, NW Mexico 29.34N 110.07W
59 I18 **Mazocruz** Puno, S Peru 16.41S 69.42W
Mazoe, Rio *see* Mazowe
81 N21 **Mazomeno** Maniema, E Dem. Rep. Congo 4.54S 27.13E
165 Q6 **Mazong Shan** ▲ N China 41.40N 97.10E
85 L16 **Mazowe** *var.* Rio Mazoe. ≈ Mozambique/Zimbabwe
112 L11 **Mazowieckie** ◈ *province* C Poland
Mazra'a *see* Al Mazra'ah
144 G6 **Mazraat Kfar Debiâne** C Lebanon 34.00N 35.51E
120 H7 **Mazsalaca** *Est.* Väike-Salatsi, *Ger.* Salisburg. Valmiera, N Latvia 57.52N 25.03E
112 L9 **Mazury** *physical region* NE Poland
121 M20 **Mazyr** *Rus.* Mozyr'. Homyel'skaya Voblasts', SE Belarus 52.03N 29.14E
109 K25 **Mazzarino** Sicilia, Italy, C Mediterranean Sea 37.18N 14.13E
Mba *see* Ba
85 L21 **Mbabane** ● (Swaziland) NW Swaziland 26.24S 31.13E
Mbacké *see* Mbaké
79 N16 **Mbahiakro** E Ivory Coast 7.25N 4.18W
81 I16 **Mbaïki** *var.* M'Baiki. Lobaye, SW Central African Republic 3.52N 17.58E
81 F14 **Mbakaou, Lac de** ⊚ C Cameroon
78 G11 **Mbaké** *var.* Mbacké. W Senegal 14.50N 15.52W
84 L11 **Mbala** *prev.* Abercorn. Northern, NE Zambia 8.49S 31.22E
85 J18 **Mbalabala** *prev.* Balla Balla. Matabeleland South, SW Zimbabwe 20.27S 29.03E
83 G18 **Mbale** E Uganda 1.04N 34.12E
81 E16 **Mbalmayo** *var.* M'Balmayo. Centre, S Cameroon 3.30N 11.31E
83 H25 **Mbamba Bay** Ruvuma, S Tanzania 11.15S 34.44E
81 I18 **Mbandaka** *prev.* Coquilhatville. Equateur, NW Dem. Rep. Congo 0.07N 18.11E
84 B9 **M'Banza Congo** *var.* Mbanza Congo; *prev.* São Salvador, São Salvador do Congo. Zaire, NW Angola 6.10S 14.16E
81 G21 **Mbanza-Ngungu** Bas-Congo, W Dem. Rep. Congo 5.19S 14.45E
69 V11 **Mbarangandu** ≈ E Tanzania
83 E19 **Mbarara** SW Uganda 0.36S 30.40E
81 L15 **Mbari** ≈ SE Central African Republic
83 I24 **Mbarika Mountains** ▲▲ S Tanzania
85 J24 **Mbashe** ≈ S South Africa
Mbatiki *see* Batiki
80 F13 **Mbé** Nord, N Cameroon 7.51N 13.36E
83 J24 **Mbemkuru** *var.* Mbwemkuru. ≈ S Tanzania
Mbengga *see* Beqa
180 H13 **Mbéni** Grande Comore, NW Comoros
85 K18 **Mberengwa** Midlands, S Zimbabwe 20.25S 29.57E
83 G24 **Mbeya** Mbeya, SW Tanzania 8.54S 33.28E
83 G23 **Mbeya** ◈ *region* S Tanzania
81 E19 **Mbigou** Ngounié, C Gabon 01.54S 12.00E
Mbilua *see* Vella Lavella
81 F19 **Mbinda** Le Niari, SW Congo 2.07S 12.52E
81 D17 **Mbini** W Equatorial Guinea 1.34N 9.39E
Mbini *see* Uolo, Río
85 L18 **Mbizi** Masvingo, SE Zimbabwe 21.21S 30.58E
83 G23 **Mbogo** Mbeya, W Tanzania 7.24S 33.26E
81 N15 **Mboki** Haut-Mbomou, SE Central African Republic 5.18N 25.52E
81 G18 **Mbomo** Cuvette-Ouest, NW Congo 0.25N 14.42E
81 L15 **Mbomou** ◈ *prefecture* SE Central African Republic
Mbomou/M'Bomu/Mbomu *see* Bomu
78 F11 **Mbour** W Senegal 14.24N 16.58W
78 I10 **Mbout** Gorgol, S Mauritania 16.01N 12.37W
81 J14 **Mbrès** *var.* Mbrés. Nana-Grébizi, C Central African Republic 6.40N 19.46E
81 L22 **Mbuji-Mayi** *prev.* Bakwanga. Kasai Oriental, S Dem. Rep. Congo 6.04S 23.30E
194 J9 **M'buke Islands** *island group* N PNG
83 H21 **Mbulu** Manyara, N Tanzania 3.45S 35.33E
194 K8 **M'bunai** *var.* Bunai. Manus Island, N PNG 2.09S 147.11E
64 N8 **Mburucuyá** Corrientes, NE Argentina 28.03S 58.15W
Mbutha *see* Buca
Mbwemkuru *see* Mbemkuru
83 G21 **Mbwikwe** Singida, C Tanzania 5.19S 34.09E
11 O15 **McAdam** New Brunswick, SE Canada 45.34N 67.19W
27 O5 **McAdoo** Texas, SW USA 33.41N 100.58W
37 V2 **McAfee Peak** ▲ Nevada, W USA 41.31N 115.57W
29 P11 **McAlester** Oklahoma, C USA 34.55N 95.46W
27 S17 **McAllen** Texas, SW USA 26.12N 98.13W
23 S11 **McBee** South Carolina, SE USA 34.30N 80.12W
9 N14 **McBride** British Columbia, SW Canada 53.21N 120.19W
26 M9 **McCamey** Texas, SW USA 31.08N 102.13W
35 R15 **McCammon** Idaho, NW USA 42.38N 112.10W
37 X11 **McCarran** ✕ (Las Vegas) Nevada, W USA 36.04N 115.07W
41 T11 **McCarthy** Alaska, USA 61.25N 142.55W
32 M5 **McCaslin Mountain** *hill* Wisconsin, N USA 45.24N 88.24W
27 O2 **McClellan Creek** ≈ Texas, SW USA
23 T14 **McClellanville** South Carolina, SE USA 33.07N 79.27W
15 Jj2 **McClintock Channel** *channel* Nunavut, N Canada
205 R12 **McClintock, Mount** ▲ Antarctica 80.09S 156.42E
37 N2 **McCloud** California, W USA 41.15N 122.09W
37 N3 **McCloud River** ≈ California, W USA
37 Q9 **McClure, Lake** ⊠ California, W USA
207 O8 **McClure Strait** *strait* Northwest Territories, N Canada
31 N4 **McClusky** North Dakota, N USA 47.27N 100.25W
23 T11 **McColl** South Carolina, SE USA 34.40N 79.33W
24 K7 **McComb** Mississippi, S USA 31.14N 90.27W
20 E16 **McConnellsburg** Pennsylvania, NE USA 39.56N 78.00W
33 T14 **McConnelsville** Ohio, N USA 39.39N 81.51W
30 M17 **McCook** Nebraska, C USA 40.12N 100.37W
23 P13 **McCormick** South Carolina, SE USA 33.54N 82.17W
9 W16 **McCreary** Manitoba, S Canada 50.48N 99.34W
29 W11 **McCrory** Arkansas, C USA 35.15N 91.12W
27 T10 **McDade** Texas, SW USA 30.15N 97.15W
25 O8 **McDavid** Florida, SE USA 30.51N 87.18W
37 T1 **McDermitt** Nevada, W USA 41.57N 117.43W
25 S4 **McDonough** Georgia, SE USA 33.27N 84.09W
38 L12 **McDowell Mountains** ▲▲ Arizona, SW USA
22 H8 **McEwen** Tennessee, S USA 36.06N 87.37W
37 R12 **McFarland** California, W USA 35.41N 119.14W
Mcfarlane, Lake *see* Macfarlane, Lake
29 P12 **McGee Creek Lake** ⊠ Oklahoma, C USA
29 W13 **McGehee** Arkansas, C USA 33.37N 91.24W
37 X5 **Mcgill** Nevada, W USA 39.24N 114.46W
12 K11 **McGillivray, Lac** ⊚ Québec, SE Canada
41 P10 **Mcgrath** Alaska, USA 62.57N 155.36W
27 T8 **McGregor** Texas, SW USA 31.26N 97.24W
35 O12 **McGuire, Mount** ▲ Idaho, NW USA 45.10N 114.36W
85 M14 **Mchinji** *prev.* Fort Manning. Central, W Malawi 13.47S 32.51E
30 M7 **McIntosh** South Dakota, N USA 45.52N 101.19W
16 O3 **McKeand** ≈ Baffin Island, Nunavut, NE Canada
203 R4 **McKean Island** *island* Phoenix Islands, C Kiribati
32 J13 **McKee Creek** ≈ Illinois, N USA
20 C15 **Mckeesport** Pennsylvania, NE USA 40.18N 79.48W
23 V7 **McKenney** Virginia, NE USA 36.57N 77.42W
22 G8 **McKenzie** Tennessee, S USA 36.07N 88.31W
193 B20 **McKerrow, Lake** ⊚ South Island, NZ
41 Q10 **McKinley, Mount** *var.* Denali. ▲ Alaska, USA 63.04N 151.00W
41 R10 **McKinley Park** Alaska, USA 63.42N 149.01W
36 K3 **McKinleyville** California, W USA 40.56N 124.06W
27 U6 **McKinney** Texas, SW USA 33.12N 96.37W
28 I5 **McKinney, Lake** ⊚ Kansas, C USA
30 M7 **McLaughlin** South Dakota, N USA 45.48N 100.48W
27 O2 **McLean** Texas, SW USA 35.13N 100.36W
32 M16 **Mcleansboro** Illinois, N USA 38.05N 88.32W
9 O13 **McLennan** Alberta, W Canada 55.42N 116.49W
12 L9 **McLennan, Lac** ⊚ Québec, SE Canada
8 M13 **McLeod Lake** British Columbia, W Canada 55.03N 123.02W
29 N10 **McLoud** Oklahoma, C USA 35.26N 97.05W
34 G15 **McLoughlin, Mount** ▲ Oregon, NW USA 42.27N 122.18W
39 U15 **McMillan, Lake** ⊠ New Mexico, SW USA
34 G11 **McMinnville** Oregon, NW USA 45.13N 123.12W
22 K9 **McMinnville** Tennessee, S USA 35.42N 85.46W
205 R13 **McMurdo** *US research station* Antarctica 77.40S 167.16E
26 H9 **McNary** Texas, SW USA 31.15N 105.46W
39 N13 **Mcnary** Arizona, SW USA 34.04N 109.51W
29 N5 **McPherson** Kansas, C USA 38.22N 97.39W
McPherson *see* Fort McPherson
25 U6 **McRae** Georgia, SE USA 32.04N 82.54W
31 P4 **McVille** North Dakota, N USA 47.45N 98.10W
85 J25 **Mdantsane** Eastern Cape, SE South Africa 32.54S 27.39E
178 Jj6 **Me** Ninh Binh, N Vietnam 20.21N 105.49E
28 J7 **Meade** Kansas, C USA 37.14N 100.20W
41 O5 **Meade River** ≈ Alaska, USA
37 Y11 **Mead, Lake** ⊠ Arizona/Nevada, W USA
26 M5 **Meadow** Texas, SW USA 33.20N 102.12W
9 S14 **Meadow Lake** Saskatchewan, C Canada 55.08N 108.25W
37 Y10 **Meadow Valley Wash** ≈ Nevada, W USA
24 J7 **Meadville** Mississippi, S USA 31.28N 90.51W
20 B12 **Meadville** Pennsylvania, NE USA 41.38N 80.09W
12 F14 **Meaford** Ontario, S Canada 44.35N 80.35W
Meáin, Inis *see* Inishmaan
106 G8 **Mealhada** Aveiro, N Portugal 40.22N 8.27W
11 R8 **Mealy Mountains** ▲▲ Newfoundland and Labrador, E Canada
9 O10 **Meander River** Alberta, W Canada 59.01N 117.42W
34 E11 **Meares, Cape** *headland* Oregon, NW USA 45.29N 123.59W
49 V6 **Mearim, Rio** ≈ NE Brazil
Measca, Loch *see* Mask, Lough
99 F17 **Meath** *Ir.* An Mhí. *cultural region* E Ireland
9 T14 **Meath Park** Saskatchewan, S Canada 53.25N 105.18W
105 O5 **Meaux** Seine-et-Marne, N France 48.58N 2.54E
23 T9 **Mebane** North Carolina, SE USA 36.06N 79.16W
176 W9 **Mebo, Gunung** ▲ Papua, E Indonesia 1.10S 133.53E
96 I8 **Mebonden** Sør-Trøndelag, S Norway 63.13N 11.00E
84 A10 **Mebridege** ≈ NW Angola
37 W16 **Mecca** California, W USA 33.34N 116.04W
Mecca *see* Makkah
31 Y14 **Mechanicsville** Iowa, C USA 41.54N 91.15W
20 L10 **Mechanicville** New York, NE USA 42.54N 73.41W
101 H17 **Mechelen** *Eng.* Mechlin, *Fr.* Malines. Antwerpen, C Belgium 51.01N 4.28E
196 C8 **Mecherchar** *var.* Eil Malk. *island* Palau Islands, Palau
103 D17 **Mechernich** Nordrhein-Westfalen, W Germany 50.36N 6.39E
130 L12 **Mechetinskaya** Rostovskaya Oblast', SW Russian Federation 46.46N 40.30E
116 J11 **Mechka** ≈ S Bulgaria
Mechlin *see* Mechelen
63 D23 **Mechongué** Buenos Aires, E Argentina 38.09S 58.13W
117 L14 **Mecidiye** Edirne, NW Turkey 40.39N 26.33E
103 I24 **Meckenbeuren** Baden-Württemberg, S Germany 47.42N 9.34E
102 L8 **Mecklenburger Bucht** *bay* N Germany
102 M10 **Mecklenburgische Seenplatte** *wetland* NE Germany
102 L9 **Mecklenburg-Vorpommern** ◈ *state* NE Germany
85 Q15 **Meconta** Nampula, NE Mozambique 15.01S 39.52E
113 I25 **Mecsek** ▲▲ SW Hungary
85 P14 **Mecubúri** ≈ N Mozambique
85 Q14 **Mecúfi** Cabo Delgado, NE Mozambique 13.18S 40.33E
84 O13 **Mecula** Niassa, N Mozambique 12.03S 37.37E
173 Ff5 **Medan** Sumatera, E Indonesia 3.34N 98.39E
63 A24 **Médanos** *var.* Medanos. Buenos Aires, E Argentina 38.51S 62.44W
63 C19 **Médanos** Entre Ríos, E Argentina 33.25S 59.03W
161 K24 **Medawachchiya** North Central Province, N Sri Lanka 8.32N 80.30E
108 C8 **Mede** Lombardia, N Italy 45.06N 8.43E
76 J5 **Médéa** *var.* El Mediyya, Lemdiyya. N Algeria 36.24N 2.42E
Medeba *see* Ma'dabā
56 E8 **Medellín** Antioquia, NW Colombia 6.15N 75.36W
102 H9 **Medem** ≈ NW Germany
100 J8 **Medemblik** Noord-Holland, NW Netherlands 52.46N 5.06E
77 N7 **Médenine** *var.* Madanīyīn. SE Tunisia 33.23N 10.30E
78 G9 **Mederdra** Trarza, SW Mauritania 16.55N 15.40W
Medeshamstede *see* Peterborough
44 F4 **Medesto Mendez** Izabal, NE Guatemala 15.54N 89.13W
21 O11 **Medford** Massachusetts, NE USA 42.25N 71.08W
29 N8 **Medford** Oklahoma, C USA 36.49N 97.45W
34 G15 **Medford** Oregon, NW USA 42.19N 122.52W
32 K6 **Medford** Wisconsin, N USA 45.07N 90.22W
41 P10 **Medfra** Alaska, USA 63.06N 154.42W
118 M14 **Medgidia** Constanța, SE Romania 44.16N 28.13E
Medgyes *see* Mediaș
45 O5 **Media Luna, Arrecifes de la** *reef* E Honduras
62 G11 **Medianeira** Paraná, S Brazil 25.15S 54.07W
31 Y15 **Mediapolis** Iowa, C USA 41.00N 91.09W
118 I11 **Mediaș** *Ger.* Mediasch, *Hung.* Medgyes. Sibiu, C Romania 46.09N 24.20E
43 S15 **Medias Aguas** Veracruz-Llave, SE Mexico 17.40N 95.01W
Mediasch *see* Mediaș
108 G10 **Medicina** Emilia-Romagna, C Italy 44.29N 11.41E
35 X16 **Medicine Bow** Wyoming, C USA 41.52N 106.11W
39 S2 **Medicine Bow Mountains** ▲▲ Colorado/Wyoming, C USA
35 X16 **Medicine Bow River** ≈ Wyoming, C USA
9 R17 **Medicine Hat** Alberta, SW Canada 50.03N 110.40W
28 L7 **Medicine Lodge** Kansas, C USA 37.14N 98.33W
28 L7 **Medicine Lodge River** ≈ Kansas/Oklahoma, C USA
114 E7 **Međimurje** *off.* Međimurska Županija. ◈ *province* N Croatia
Međimurska Županija *see* Međimurje
56 G10 **Medina** Cundinamarca, C Colombia 4.31N 73.21W
20 E9 **Medina** New York, NE USA 43.13N 78.23W
31 O5 **Medina** North Dakota, N USA 46.53N 99.18W
33 T11 **Medina** Ohio, N USA 41.08N 81.51W
27 Q11 **Medina** Texas, SW USA 29.46N 99.14W
Medina *see* Al Madīnah
123 Ll12 **Medina Bank** *undersea feature* C Mediterranean Sea
107 P6 **Medinaceli** Castilla-León, N Spain 41.10N 2.25W
106 L6 **Medina del Campo** Castilla-León, N Spain 41.18N 4.55W

◆ Country
● Country Capital
◇ Dependent Territory
○ Dependent Territory Capital
◈ Administrative Region
✕ International Airport
▲ Mountain
▲▲ Mountain Range
⩓ Volcano
≈ River
⊚ Lake
⊠ Reservoir

MÉDINA DE RIOSECO – METU

106 L5 **Medina de Ríoseco** Castilla-León, N Spain 41.52N 5.03W
Médina Gonassé see Médina Gounas
78 H12 **Médina Gounas** var. Médina Gonassé. S Senegal 13.06N 13.49W
27 S12 **Medina River** ∽ Texas, SW USA
106 K16 **Medina Sidonia** Andalucía, S Spain 36.28N 5.55W
Medinat Israel see Israel
121 H14 **Medininkai** Vilnius, SE Lithuania 54.31N 25.39E
159 R16 **Medinīpur** West Bengal, NE India 22.27N 87.19E
Mediolanum see Saintes, France
Mediolanum see Milano, Italy
Mediomatrica see Metz
124 O13 **Mediterranean Ridge** undersea feature C Mediterranean Sea
123 L11 **Mediterranean Sea** Fr. Mer Méditerranée. sea Africa/Asia/Europe
Méditerranée, Mer see Mediterranean Sea
81 N17 **Medje** Orientale, NE Dem. Rep. Congo 2.27N 27.14E
123 K11 **Medjerda, Oued** var. Mejerda, Wādī Majardah. ∽ Algeria/Tunisia see also Mejerda
116 G7 **Medkovets** Montana, NW Bulgaria 43.39N 23.22E
95 J15 **Medle** Västerbotten, N Sweden 64.45N 20.45E
131 W7 **Mednogorsk** Orenburgskaya Oblast', W Russian Federation 51.24N 57.37E
127 Qq9 **Mednyy, Ostrov** island E Russian Federation
104 J12 **Médoc** cultural region SW France
165 Q16 **Mêdog** Xizang Zizhiqu, W China 29.25N 95.25E
30 J5 **Medora** North Dakota, N USA 46.52N 103.32W
81 E17 **Médouneu** Woleu-Ntem, N Gabon 0.58N 10.49E
108 I7 **Meduna** ∽ NE Italy
Medunta see Mantes-la-Jolie
Medvedica see Medveditsa
128 J16 **Medveditsa** var. Medvedica. ∽ W Russian Federation
131 O9 **Medveditsa** ∽ SW Russian Federation
114 E8 **Medvednica** ▲▲ NE Croatia
129 R15 **Medvedok** Kirovskaya Oblast', NW Russian Federation 57.23N 50.01E
127 Nn5 **Medvezh'i, Ostrova** island group NE Russian Federation
128 J9 **Medvezh'yegorsk** Respublika Kareliya, NW Russian Federation 62.56N 34.26E
111 T11 **Medvode** Ger. Zwischenwässern. NW Slovenia 46.09N 14.21E
130 J4 **Medyn'** Kaluzhskaya Oblast', W Russian Federation 54.59N 35.52E
188 J10 **Meekatharra** Western Australia 26.36S 118.34E
39 Q4 **Meeker** Colorado, C USA 40.02N 107.54W
11 T12 **Meelpaeg Lake** ◎ Newfoundland and Labrador, E Canada
Meenen see Menen
103 M16 **Meerane** Sachsen, E Germany 50.49N 12.28E
103 D15 **Meerbusch** Nordrhein-Westfalen, W Germany 51.19N 6.43E
100 I12 **Meerkerk** Zuid-Holland, C Netherlands 51.55N 5.00E
101 L18 **Meerssen** var. Mersen. Limburg, SE Netherlands 50.52N 5.45E
158 J10 **Meerut** Uttar Pradesh, N India 29.01N 77.40E
35 U13 **Meeteetse** Wyoming, C USA 44.10N 108.53W
101 K17 **Meeuwen** Limburg, NE Belgium 51.04N 5.36E
83 J16 **Mēga** Oromo, C Ethiopia 4.03N 38.15E
83 J16 **Mēga Escarpment** escarpment S Ethiopia
Megála Kalívia see Megála Kalývia
117 E16 **Megála Kalývia** var. Megála Kalívia. Thessalía, C Greece 39.30N 21.48E
117 H14 **Megáli Panagiá** var. Megáli Panayía. Kentrikí Makedonía, N Greece 40.24N 23.42E
Megáli Panayía see Megáli Panagiá
Megáli Préspa, Límni see Prespa, Lake
116 K12 **Megálo Livádi** ▲ Bulgaria/Greece 41.18N 25.51E
117 E20 **Megalópoli** prev. Megalópolis. Pelopónnisos, S Greece 37.23N 22.08E
Megalópolis see Megalópoli
176 V9 **Megamo** Papua, E Indonesia 0.55S 131.46E
117 C18 **Meganísi** island Iónia Nisiá, Greece, C Mediterranean Sea
Meganom, Mys see Mehanom, Mys
Mégantic see Lac-Mégantic
13 R12 **Mégantic, Mont** ▲ Québec, SE Canada 45.27N 71.09W
117 G19 **Mégara** Attikí, C Greece 38.00N 23.20E
27 R5 **Megargel** Texas, SW USA 33.27N 98.55W
100 K13 **Megen** Noord-Brabant, S Netherlands 51.49N 5.34E
159 U13 **Meghālaya** ◈ state NE India
159 U16 **Meghna** ∽ S Bangladesh
143 V14 **Meghri** Rus. Megri. SE Armenia 38.57N 46.15E
126 Gg11 **Megion** Khanty-Mansiyskiy Avtonomnyy Okrug, C Russian Federation 61.01N 76.15E
117 Q23 **Megísti** var. Kastellórizon. island SE Greece
Megri see Meghri
Mehabad see Mahābād
118 F13 **Mehadia** Hung. Mehádia. Caraş-Severin, SW Romania 44.53N 22.20E
94 L7 **Mehamn** Finnmark, N Norway 71.01N 27.46E
119 U13 **Mehanom, Mys** Rus. Mys Meganom. headland S Ukraine 44.48N 35.04E
155 P14 **Mehar** Sind, SE Pakistan 27.10N 67.56E
188 J8 **Meharry, Mount** ▲ Western Australia 23.17S 118.48E
Mehdia see Mahdia
118 G14 **Mehedinţi** ◈ county SW Romania
159 S15 **Meherpur** Khulna, W Bangladesh 23.46N 88.40E
23 W8 **Meherrin River** ∽ North Carolina/Virginia, SE USA
Meheso see Mī'ēso
203 T11 **Mehetia** island Îles du Vent, W French Polynesia
120 K6 **Mehikoorma** Tartumaa, E Estonia 58.14N 27.29E
Me Hka see Nmai Hka
149 N5 **Mehrabad** ✕ (Tehrān) Tehrān, N Iran 35.46N 51.07E
148 J7 **Mehrān** Īlām, W Iran 33.07N 46.10E
149 Q14 **Mehrān, Rūd-e** prev. Mansurabad. ∽ W Iran
149 Q9 **Mehrīz** Yazd, C Iran 31.31N 54.28E
155 R5 **Mehtar Lām** var. Mehtarlām, Meterlam, Methariam, Metharlam. Laghmān, E Afghanistan 34.39N 70.10E
105 N8 **Mehun-sur-Yèvre** Cher, C France 47.09N 2.15E
81 G14 **Meiganga** Adamaoua, NE Cameroon 6.31N 14.07E
166 H10 **Meigu** var. Bapu. Sichuan, C China 28.22N 103.07E
169 W11 **Meihekou** var. Hailong. Jilin, NE China 42.31N 125.40E
101 L15 **Meijel** Limburg, SE Netherlands 51.22N 5.52E
Meijiang see Ningdu
177 G5 **Meiktila** Mandalay, C Burma 20.52N 95.54E
Meilbhe, Loch see Melvin, Lough
110 G7 **Meilen** Zürich, N Switzerland 47.16N 8.39E
Meilu see Wuchuan
167 T12 **Meinhua Yu** island N Taiwan
103 J17 **Meiningen** Thüringen, C Germany 50.34N 10.25E
110 F9 **Meiringen** Bern, S Switzerland 46.42N 8.13E
Meishan see Jinzhai
103 O15 **Meissen** var. Meißen. Sachsen, E Germany 51.10N 13.28E
103 I15 **Meissner** ▲ C Germany 51.13N 9.52E
101 K25 **Meix-devant-Virton** Luxembourg, SE Belgium 49.36N 5.27E
Mei Xian see Meizhou
Meixing see Xinjin
167 P13 **Meizhou** var. Meixian, Mei Xian. Guangdong, S China 24.21N 116.05E
69 P2 **Mejerda** var. Oued Medjerda, Wādī Majardah. ∽ Algeria/Tunisia see also Medjerda, Oued
44 F7 **Mejicanos** San Salvador, C El Salvador 13.50N 89.13W
Méjico see Mexico
64 G5 **Mejillones** Antofagasta, N Chile 23.03S 70.25W
201 V5 **Mejit Island** var. Mājeej. island Ratak Chain, NE Marshall Islands
81 F17 **Mékambo** Ogooué-Ivindo, NE Gabon 1.03N 13.49E
82 J10 **Mek'elē** var. Makale. Tigray, N Ethiopia 13.36N 39.28E
76 I10 **Mekerrhane, Sebkha** var. Sebkha Meqerghane, Sebkra Mekerrhane. salt flat C Algeria
Mekerrhane, Sebkra see Mekerrhane, Sebkha
78 G10 **Mékhé** NW Senegal 15.08N 16.42W
152 G14 **Mekhinli** Ahal Welaýaty, C Turkmenistan 37.28N 59.20E
13 P9 **Mékinac, Lac** ◎ Québec, SE Canada
Meklong see Samut Songhram
76 G6 **Meknès** N Morocco 33.54N 5.27W
133 U12 **Mekong** var. Lan-ts'ang Chiang, Cam. Mékôngk, Chin. Lancang Jiang, Lao. Mènam Khong, Th. Mae Nam Khong, Tib. Dza Chu, Vtn. Sông Tiên Giang. ∽ SE Asia
Mekongga, Pegunungan see Mengkoka, Pegunungan
Mékôngk see Mekong
178 K15 **Mekong, Mouths of the** delta S Vietnam
40 L12 **Mekoryuk** Nunivak Island, Alaska, USA 60.23N 166.11W
79 R14 **Mékrou** ∽ N Benin
174 H6 **Melaka** var. Malacca. Melaka, Peninsular Malaysia 2.13N 102.13E
174 H6 **Melaka** var. Malacca. ◈ state Peninsular Malaysia
Melaka, Selat see Malacca, Strait of
183 O6 **Melanesia** island group W Pacific Ocean
183 P5 **Melanesian Basin** undersea feature W Pacific Ocean
175 Ss4 **Melanguane** Pulau Karakelang, N Indonesia 4.02N 126.43E
174 Ll8 **Melawi, Sungai** ∽ Borneo, N Indonesia
191 N12 **Melbourne** state capital Victoria, SE Australia 37.51S 144.56E
29 V9 **Melbourne** Arkansas, C USA 36.03N 91.54W
25 Y12 **Melbourne** Florida, SE USA 28.04N 80.36W
31 W14 **Melbourne** Iowa, C USA 41.57N 93.07W
94 G10 **Melbu** Nordland, C Norway 68.30N 14.46E
Melchor de Mencos see Ciudad Melchor de Mencos
65 F19 **Melchor, Isla** island Archipiélago de los Chonos, S Chile
42 M9 **Melchor Ocampo** Zacatecas, C Mexico 24.45N 101.38W
12 C11 **Meldrum Bay** Manitoulin Island, Ontario, S Canada 45.55N 83.06W
Meleda see Mljet
108 D8 **Melegnano** prev. Marignano. Lombardia, N Italy 45.22N 9.19E
196 F9 **Melekeok** var. Melekeiok. Babeldaob, N Palau 7.30N 134.39E
114 L9 **Melenci** Hung. Melencze. Serbia, N Serbia 45.32N 20.18E
Melencze see Melenci
131 N4 **Melenki** Vladimirskaya Oblast', W Russian Federation 55.21N 41.37E
131 V6 **Meleuz** Respublika Bashkortostan, W Russian Federation 52.55N 55.54E
10 L6 **Mélèzes, Rivière aux** ∽ Québec, C Canada
80 I11 **Melfi** Guéra, S Chad 11.04N 17.57E
109 M17 **Melfi** Basilicata, S Italy 41.00N 15.33E
9 U14 **Melfort** Saskatchewan, S Canada 52.52N 104.37W
106 H4 **Melgaço** Viana do Castelo, N Portugal 42.07N 8.15W
107 N4 **Melgar de Fernamental** Castilla-León, N Spain 42.24N 4.15W
76 L6 **Melghir, Chott** var. Chott Melrhir. salt lake E Algeria
96 H8 **Melhus** Sør-Trøndelag, S Norway 63.16N 10.16E
106 H3 **Melide** Galicia, NW Spain 42.54N 8.01W
Meligalá see Meligalás
117 E21 **Meligalás** prev. Meligalá. Pelopónnisos, S Greece 37.13N 21.58E
62 L12 **Mel, Ilha do** island S Brazil
122 G11 **Melilla** anc. Rusaddir, Russadir. Melilla, Spain, N Africa 35.18N 2.55W
73 N1 **Melilla** enclave Spain, N Africa
65 G18 **Melimoyu, Monte** ▲ S Chile 44.06S 72.49W
175 N8 **Melintang, Danau** ◎ Borneo, N Indonesia
119 U7 **Melioratyvne** Dnipropetrovs'ka Oblast', E Ukraine 48.35N 35.18E
64 G11 **Melipilla** Santiago, C Chile 33.33S 71.34W
117 I25 **Mélissa, Akrotírio** headland Kríti, Greece, E Mediterranean Sea 35.06N 24.33E
15 Kk16 **Melita** Manitoba, S Canada 49.16N 100.58W
Melita see Mljet
Melitene see Malatya
109 M23 **Melito di Porto Salvo** Calabria, SW Italy 37.55N 15.48E
119 U10 **Melitopol'** Zaporiz'ka Oblast', SE Ukraine 46.49N 35.22E
111 V4 **Melk** Niederösterreich, NE Austria 48.12N 15.20E
97 K15 **Mellan-Fryken** ◎ C Sweden
101 E17 **Melle** Oost-Vlaanderen, NW Belgium 51.00N 3.48E
102 G13 **Melle** Niedersachsen, NW Germany 52.12N 8.19E
97 J17 **Mellerud** Västra Götaland, S Sweden 58.42N 12.27E
104 K10 **Melle-sur-Bretonne** Deux-Sèvres, W France 46.13N 0.07W
31 P8 **Mellette** South Dakota, N USA 45.07N 98.29W
123 J16 **Mellieha** E Malta 35.58N 14.21E
82 B10 **Mellit** Northern Darfur, W Sudan 14.07N 25.34E
77 N7 **Mellita** ✕ SE Tunisia 33.47N 10.51E
65 G21 **Mellizo Sur, Cerro** ▲ S Chile 48.27S 73.10W
102 G9 **Mellum** island NW Germany
85 L22 **Melmoth** KwaZulu/Natal, E South Africa 28.30S 31.23E
113 D16 **Mělník** Ger. Melnik. Středočeský Kraj, NW Czech Republic 50.21N 14.30E
126 H13 **Mel'nikovo** Tomskaya Oblast', C Russian Federation 56.35N 84.11E
63 G18 **Melo** Cerro Largo, NE Uruguay 32.22S 54.10W
Melodunum see Melun
Melrhir, Chott see Melghir, Chott
191 P7 **Melrose** New South Wales, SE Australia 32.41S 146.58E
190 I7 **Melrose** South Australia 32.52S 138.16E
31 T7 **Melrose** Minnesota, N USA 45.40N 94.46W
35 Q11 **Melrose** Montana, NW USA 45.33N 112.41W
39 V12 **Melrose** New Mexico, SW USA 34.25N 103.37W
110 I8 **Mels** Sankt Gallen, NE Switzerland 47.03N 9.25E
Melsetter see Chimanimani
35 V9 **Melstone** Montana, NW USA 46.37N 107.49W
103 I16 **Melsungen** Hessen, C Germany 51.07N 9.33E
94 L12 **Meltaus** Lappi, NW Finland 66.54N 25.18E
99 N19 **Melton Mowbray** C England, UK 52.46N 1.03W
84 Q13 **Meluco** Cabo Delgado, NE Mozambique 12.39S 39.35E
105 O5 **Melun** anc. Melodunum. Seine-et-Marne, N France 48.31N 2.40E
82 F12 **Melut** Upper Nile, SE Sudan 10.27N 32.13E
29 P5 **Melvern Lake** ▣ Kansas, C USA
9 V16 **Melville** Saskatchewan, S Canada 50.57N 102.49W
Melville Bay/Melville Bugt see Qimusseriarsuaq
47 O11 **Melville Hall** ✕ (Dominica) NE Dominica 15.33N 61.19W
189 O1 **Melville Island** island Northern Territory, N Australia
207 O8 **Melville Island** island Parry Islands, Northwest Territories, NW Canada
16 R7 **Melville, Lake** ◎ Newfoundland and Labrador, E Canada
15 Ll2 **Melville Peninsula** peninsula Nunavut, NE Canada
Melville Sound see Viscount Melville Sound
27 Q9 **Melvin** Texas, SW USA 31.12N 99.34W
99 D15 **Melvin, Lough** Ir. Loch Meilbhe. ◎ S Northern Ireland, UK/Ireland
174 M9 **Memala** Borneo, C Indonesia 1.43S 112.36E
115 L22 **Memaliaj** Gjirokastër, S Albania 40.21N 19.56E
85 Q14 **Memba** Nampula, NE Mozambique 14.07S 40.33E
85 Q14 **Memba, Baia de** inlet NE Mozambique
Membidj see Manbij
Memel see Neman, NE Europe
Memel see Klaipėda, Lithuania
103 J23 **Memmingen** Bayern, S Germany 47.58N 10.10E
29 U1 **Memphis** Missouri, C USA 40.27N 92.10W
22 E10 **Memphis** Tennessee, S USA 35.09N 90.03W
27 P3 **Memphis** Texas, SW USA 34.43N 100.31W
22 E10 **Memphis** ✕ Tennessee, S USA 35.02N 89.57W
13 Q13 **Memphrémagog, Lac** var. Lake Memphremagog. ◎ Canada/USA see also Memphremagog, Lake
21 N6 **Memphremagog, Lake** var. Lac Memphrémagog. ◎ Canada/USA see also Memphrémagog, Lac
119 Q2 **Mena** Chernihivs'ka Oblast', NE Ukraine 51.30N 32.15E
29 S12 **Mena** Arkansas, C USA 34.35N 94.14W
Menaam see Menaldum
Menado see Manado
108 D6 **Menaggio** Lombardia, N Italy 46.03N 9.14E
31 T6 **Menahga** Minnesota, N USA 46.45N 95.06W
79 R10 **Ménaka** Goa, E Mali 15.54N 2.25E
100 K5 **Menaldum** Fris. Menaam. Friesland, N Netherlands 53.13N 5.37E
Mènam Khong see Mekong
76 E7 **Menara** ✕ (Marrakech) C Morocco 31.36N 8.00W
27 Q9 **Menard** Texas, SW USA 30.55N 99.47W
199 M14 **Menard Fracture Zone** tectonic feature E Pacific Ocean
32 M7 **Menasha** Wisconsin, N USA 44.13N 88.25W
Mencezi Garagum see Merkezi Garagumy
200 O10 **Mendaña Fracture Zone** tectonic feature E Pacific Ocean
174 M10 **Mendawai, Sungai** ∽ Borneo, C Indonesia
105 P13 **Mende** anc. Mimatum. Lozère, S France 44.31N 3.30E
83 J14 **Mendebo** ▲▲ C Ethiopia
82 J9 **Mendefera** prev. Adi Ugri. S Eritrea 14.53N 38.51E
207 S7 **Mendeleyev Ridge** undersea feature Arctic Ocean
131 T3 **Mendeleyevsk** Respublika Tatarstan, W Russian Federation 55.54N 52.19E
103 F15 **Menden** Nordrhein-Westfalen, W Germany 51.25N 7.48E
24 L6 **Mendenhall** Mississippi, S USA 31.57N 89.52W
40 L13 **Mendenhall, Cape** headland Nunivak Island, Alaska, USA 59.45N 166.10W
43 P9 **Méndez** var. Villa de Méndez. Tamaulipas, C Mexico 25.06N 98.32W
82 H13 **Mendī** Oromo, C Ethiopia 9.43N 35.07E
194 G12 **Mendi** Southern Highlands, W PNG 6.07S 143.39E
99 K22 **Mendip Hills** var. Mendips. hill range S England, UK
Mendips see Mendip Hills
36 L6 **Mendocino** California, W USA 39.18N 123.48W
36 J3 **Mendocino, Cape** headland California, W USA 40.26N 124.24W
(0) B8 **Mendocino Fracture Zone** tectonic feature NE Pacific Ocean
37 P10 **Mendota** California, W USA 36.44N 120.24W
32 L11 **Mendota** Illinois, N USA 41.32N 89.04W
32 K8 **Mendota, Lake** ◎ Wisconsin, N USA
64 I11 **Mendoza** Mendoza, W Argentina 33.00S 68.47W
64 I12 **Mendoza** off. Provincia de Mendoza. ◈ province W Argentina
110 H12 **Mendrisio** Ticino, S Switzerland 45.52N 8.58E
174 Hh7 **Mendung** Pulau Mendol, W Indonesia 0.33N 103.09E
56 I5 **Mene de Mauroa** Falcón, NW Venezuela 10.39N 71.04W
56 I5 **Mene Grande** Zulia, NW Venezuela 9.51N 70.57W
142 B14 **Menemen** İzmir, W Turkey 38.34N 27.03E
101 C18 **Menen** var. Meenen, Fr. Menin. West-Vlaanderen, W Belgium 50.48N 3.07E
169 Q8 **Menengiyn Tal** plain E Mongolia
201 R9 **Meneng Point** headland SW Nauru 0.33S 166.57E
94 L10 **Menesjärvi** Lapp. Menešjávri. Lappi, N Finland 68.39N 26.22E
Menešjávri see Menesjärvi
109 I24 **Menfi** Sicilia, Italy, C Mediterranean Sea 37.34N 12.58E
167 P7 **Mengcheng** Anhui, E China 33.17N 116.31E
166 F15 **Menghai** Yunnan, SW China 22.02N 100.18E
175 Q11 **Mengkoka, Pegunungan** var. Pegunungan Mekongga. ▲▲ Sulawesi, C Indonesia
166 F15 **Mengla** Yunnan, SW China 21.30N 101.33E
67 F24 **Menguera Point** headland East Falkland, Falkland Islands
166 M13 **Mengzhu Ling** ▲▲ S China
166 H14 **Mengzi** Yunnan, SW China 23.20N 103.32E
116 H13 **Meníkio** var. Menoíkio. ▲▲ NE Greece
Menin see Menen
190 L7 **Menindee** New South Wales, SE Australia 32.24S 142.25E
190 L7 **Menindee Lake** ◎ New South Wales, SE Australia
190 J10 **Meningie** South Australia 35.43S 139.20E
105 O5 **Mennecy** Essonne, N France 48.34N 2.25E
31 Q12 **Menno** South Dakota, N USA 43.14N 97.34W
Menoíkio see Meníkio
33 N5 **Menominee** Michigan, N USA 45.06N 87.36W
32 M5 **Menominee River** ∽ Michigan/Wisconsin, N USA
32 M8 **Menomonee Falls** Wisconsin, N USA 43.11N 88.09W
32 I6 **Menomonie** Wisconsin, N USA 44.52N 91.55W
85 D14 **Menongue** var. Vila Serpa Pinto, Port. Serpa Pinto. Cuando Cubango, C Angola 14.38S 17.38E
123 Ii8 **Menorca** Eng. Minorca; anc. Balearis Minor. island Illes Balears, Spain, W Mediterranean Sea
107 S13 **Menor, Mar** lagoon SE Spain
41 S10 **Mentasta Lake** ◎ Alaska, USA
41 S10 **Mentasta Mountains** ▲▲ Alaska, USA
173 Ff10 **Mentawai, Kepulauan** island group W Indonesia
173 G10 **Mentawai, Selat** strait W Indonesia
174 Ii10 **Mentok** Pulau Bangka, W Indonesia 2.01S 105.10E
105 V15 **Menton** It. Mentone. Alpes-Maritimes, SE France 43.46N 7.30E
26 K8 **Mentone** Texas, SW USA 31.42N 103.36W
Mentone see Menton
33 U11 **Mentor** Ohio, N USA 41.40N 81.20W
175 Nn7 **Menyapa, Gunung** ▲ Borneo, N Indonesia 1.04N 116.01E
165 T9 **Menyuan** var. Menyuan Huizu Zizhixian. Qinghai, C China 37.27N 101.33E
Menyuan Huizu Zizhixian see Menyuan
76 M5 **Menzel Bourguiba** var. Manzil Bū Ruqaybah; prev. Ferryville. N Tunisia 37.09N 9.51E
142 M15 **Menzelet Barajı** ▣ C Turkey
131 T4 **Menzelinsk** Respublika Tatarstan, W Russian Federation 55.44N 53.00E
188 K11 **Menzies** Western Australia 29.42S 121.04E
205 V6 **Menzies, Mount** ▲ Antarctica 73.32S 61.02E
42 J6 **Meoqui** Chihuahua, N Mexico 28.19N 105.30W
85 N14 **Meponda** Niassa, NE Mozambique 13.19S 34.52E
100 M8 **Meppel** Drenthe, NE Netherlands 52.42N 6.12E
102 E12 **Meppen** Niedersachsen, NW Germany 52.42N 7.18E
Meqerghane, Sebkha see Mekerrhane, Sebkha
107 T6 **Mequinenza, Embalse de** ▣ NE Spain
32 M8 **Mequon** Wisconsin, N USA 43.13N 87.57W
Mera see Maira
190 D3 **Meramangye, Lake** salt lake South Australia
29 W5 **Meramec River** ∽ Missouri, C USA
Meran see Merano
174 H10 **Merangin** ∽ Sumatera, W Indonesia
108 G5 **Merano** Ger. Meran. Trentino-Alto Adige, N Italy 46.40N 11.10E
174 H4 **Merapuh Lama** Pahang, Peninsular Malaysia 4.37N 101.58E
108 D7 **Merate** Lombardia, N Italy 45.42N 9.26E
175 Nn11 **Meratus, Pegunungan** ▲▲ Borneo, N Indonesia
176 Z16 **Merauke** Papua, E Indonesia 8.28S 140.28E
176 Z16 **Merauke, Sungai** ∽ Papua, E Indonesia
190 L9 **Merbein** Victoria, SE Australia 34.11S 142.03E
101 F21 **Merbes-le-Château** Hainaut, S Belgium 50.19N 4.09E
Merca see Marka
56 C13 **Mercaderes** Cauca, SW Colombia 1.47N 77.10W
Mercara see Madikeri
37 P9 **Merced** California, W USA 37.17N 120.30W
63 C20 **Mercedes** Buenos Aires, E Argentina 34.42S 59.30W
63 D15 **Mercedes** Corrientes, NE Argentina 29.09S 58.04W
64 J11 **Mercedes** prev. Villa Mercedes. San Luis, C Argentina 33.40S 65.24W
63 D19 **Mercedes** Soriano, SW Uruguay 33.16S 58.01W
27 S17 **Mercedes** Texas, SW USA 26.09N 97.54W
37 R9 **Merced Peak** ▲ California, W USA 37.34N 119.30W
37 P9 **Merced River** ∽ California, W USA
20 B13 **Mercer** Pennsylvania, NE USA 41.13N 80.13W
101 G18 **Merchtem** Vlaams Brabant, C Belgium 50.57N 4.13E
13 O13 **Mercier** Québec, SE Canada 45.15N 73.45W
27 Q9 **Mercury** Texas, SW USA 31.23N 99.09W
192 M5 **Mercury Islands** island group N NZ
21 O9 **Meredith** New Hampshire, NE USA 43.36N 71.28W
67 B25 **Meredith, Cape** var. Cabo Belgrano headland West Falkland, Falkland Islands 52.15S 60.40W
39 V6 **Meredith, Lake** ◎ Colorado, C USA
27 N2 **Meredith, Lake** ▣ Texas, SW USA
83 O16 **Mereeg** var. Mareeq, It. Meregh. Galguduud, E Somalia 3.47N 47.19E
119 V5 **Merefa** Kharkivs'ka Oblast', E Ukraine 49.48N 36.04E
Meregh see Mereeg
197 C11 **Mere Lava** island Banks Islands, N Vanuatu
101 E17 **Merelbeke** Oost-Vlaanderen, NW Belgium 51.00N 3.45E
Merend see Marand
127 Oo9 **Merenga** Magadanskaya Oblast', E Russian Federation 61.43N 156.02E
178 K12 **Mereuch** Môndól Kiri, E Cambodia 13.01N 107.26E
Mergate see Margate
178 Gg12 **Mergui** Tenasserim, S Burma 12.25N 98.34E
177 G12 **Mergui Archipelago** island group S Burma
116 L12 **Meriç** Edirne, NW Turkey 41.12N 26.24E
116 L12 **Meriç** Bul. Maritsa, Gk. Évros; anc. Hebrus. ∽ SE Europe see also Évros/Maritsa
43 X12 **Mérida** Yucatán, SW Mexico 20.58N 89.35W
106 J11 **Mérida** anc. Augusta Emerita. Extremadura, W Spain 38.55N 6.19W
56 I6 **Mérida** Mérida, W Venezuela 8.36N 71.07W
56 H7 **Mérida** off. Estado Mérida. ◈ state W Venezuela
20 M13 **Meriden** Connecticut, NE USA 41.32N 72.48W
24 M5 **Meridian** Mississippi, S USA 32.24N 88.43W
27 S8 **Meridian** Texas, SW USA 31.55N 97.39W
104 J13 **Mérignac** Gironde, SW France 44.50N 0.39W
104 J13 **Mérignac** ✕ (Bordeaux) Gironde, SW France 44.51N 0.44W
95 J18 **Merikarvia** Länsi-Suomi, W Finland 61.51N 21.30E
191 R12 **Merimbula** New South Wales, SE Australia 36.52S 149.51E
190 L9 **Meringur** Victoria, SE Australia 34.26S 141.19E
Merín, Laguna see Mirim Lagoon
99 I19 **Merioneth** cultural region W Wales, UK
196 A11 **Merir** island Palau Islands, N Palau
196 B17 **Merizo** SW Guam 13.15N 144.40E
Merjama see Märjamaa
151 S16 **Merke** Zhambyl, S Kazakhstan 42.52N 73.09E
27 P7 **Merkel** Texas, SW USA 32.28N 100.00W
152 E12 **Merkezi Garagumy** var. Mencezi Garagum, Rus. Tsentral'nyye Nizmennyye Garagumy. desert C Turkmenistan
121 F15 **Merkinė** Alytus, S Lithuania 54.09N 24.11E
101 G16 **Merksem** Antwerpen, N Belgium 51.17N 4.26E
101 I15 **Merksplas** Antwerpen, N Belgium 51.22N 4.54E
Merkulovichi see Myerkulavichy
121 G15 **Merkys** ∽ S Lithuania
34 F15 **Merlin** Oregon, NW USA 42.34N 123.23W
63 C20 **Merlo** Buenos Aires, E Argentina 34.39S 58.45W
144 G8 **Meron, Haré** ▲ N Israel 35.06N 33.00E
76 K6 **Merouane, Chott** salt lake NE Algeria
82 F7 **Merowe** Northern, N Sudan 18.28N 31.49E
188 J12 **Merredin** Western Australia 31.31S 118.18E
99 I14 **Merrick** ▲ S Scotland, UK 55.09N 4.28W
34 H16 **Merrill** Oregon, NW USA 42.00N 121.37W
32 L5 **Merrill** Wisconsin, N USA 45.12N 89.43W
33 N11 **Merrillville** Indiana, N USA 41.28N 87.19W
21 O10 **Merrimack River** ∽ Massachusetts/New Hampshire, NE USA
30 L12 **Merriman** Nebraska, C USA 42.54N 101.42W
9 N17 **Merritt** British Columbia, SW Canada 50.09N 120.49W
25 Y12 **Merritt Island** Florida, SE USA 28.21N 80.42W
25 Y11 **Merritt Island** island Florida, SE USA
30 M12 **Merritt Reservoir** ▣ Nebraska, C USA
191 S7 **Merriwa** New South Wales, SE Australia 32.09S 150.24E
191 O8 **Merriwagga** New South Wales, SE Australia 33.51S 145.38E
24 G8 **Merryville** Louisiana, S USA 30.45N 93.32W
82 K9 **Mersa Fatma** E Eritrea 14.52N 40.16E
104 M7 **Mer St-Aubin** Loir-et-Cher, C France 47.42N 1.31E
Mersa Maṭrûḥ see Maṭrûḥ
101 M24 **Mersch** Luxembourg, C Luxembourg 49.45N 6.06E
103 M15 **Merseburg** Sachsen-Anhalt, C Germany 51.22N 12.00E
Mersen see Meerssen
99 K18 **Mersey** ∽ NW England, UK
142 J17 **Mersin** Mersin, S Turkey 36.49N 34.39E
142 I17 **Mersin** prev. İçel, Ichili. ◈ province S Turkey
174 I6 **Mersing** Johor, Peninsular Malaysia 2.25N 103.49E
120 E8 **Mērsrags** Talsi, NW Latvia 57.21N 23.05E
158 G12 **Merta** var. Merta City. Rājasthān, N India 26.40N 74.04E
Merta City see Merta
158 F12 **Merta Road** Rājasthān, N India 26.45N 73.59E
99 J21 **Merthyr Tydfil** S Wales, UK 51.46N 3.22W
106 H13 **Mértola** Beja, S Portugal 37.37N 7.40W
150 G14 **Mertvyy Kultuk, Sor** salt flat SW Kazakhstan
205 V16 **Mertz Glacier** glacier Antarctica
101 M24 **Mertzig** Diekirch, C Luxembourg 49.50N 6.00E
27 O9 **Mertzon** Texas, SW USA 31.15N 100.49W
83 I18 **Meru** Eastern, C Kenya 0.03N 37.37E
105 N4 **Méru** Oise, N France 49.15N 2.07E
83 I20 **Meru, Mount** ▲ NE Tanzania 3.12S 36.45E
Merv see Mary
Mervdasht see Marv Dasht
142 K11 **Merzifon** Amasya, N Turkey 40.52N 35.28E
103 D20 **Merzig** Saarland, SW Germany 49.27N 6.39E
38 L14 **Mesa** Arizona, SW USA 33.25N 111.49W
31 V4 **Mesabi Range** ▲▲ Minnesota, N USA
56 H6 **Mesa Bolívar** Mérida, NW Venezuela 8.30N 71.37W
109 Q18 **Mesagne** Puglia, SE Italy 40.33N 17.49E
41 P12 **Mesa Mountain** ▲ Alaska, USA 60.26N 155.14W
117 J25 **Mesará** lowland Kríti, Greece, E Mediterranean Sea
39 S14 **Mescalero** New Mexico, SW USA 33.09N 105.46W
103 G15 **Meschede** Nordrhein-Westfalen, W Germany 51.21N 8.16E
143 Q12 **Mescit Dağları** ▲▲ NE Turkey
201 V13 **Mesegon** island Chuuk, C Micronesia
Meseritz see Międzyrzecz
56 F11 **Mesetas** Meta, C Colombia 3.14N 74.09W
Meshchera Lowland see Meshcherskaya Nizina
130 M4 **Meshcherskaya Nizina** Eng. Meshchera Lowland. basin W Russian Federation
130 J5 **Meshchovsk** Kaluzhskaya Oblast', W Russian Federation 54.21N 35.23E
129 R9 **Meshchura** Respublika Komi, NW Russian Federation 63.18N 50.56E
Meshed see Mashhad
Meshed-i-Sar see Bābolsar
82 E13 **Meshra'er Req** Warab, S Sudan 8.30N 29.27E
39 R15 **Mesilla** New Mexico, SW USA 32.15N 106.49W
110 H10 **Mesocco** Ger. Misox. Ticino, S Switzerland 46.18N 9.13E
117 D18 **Mesolóngi** prev. Mesolóngion. Dytikí Ellás, W Greece 38.22N 21.26E
Mesolóngion see Mesolóngi
12 E8 **Mesomikenda Lake** ◎ Ontario, S Canada
63 D15 **Mesopotamia** var. Mesopotamia Argentina. physical region NE Argentina
Mesopotamia Argentina see Mesopotamia
37 Y10 **Mesquite** Nevada, W USA 36.47N 114.04W
84 Q13 **Messalo, Rio** var. Mualo. ∽ NE Mozambique
Messana/Messene see Messina
101 L25 **Messancy** Luxembourg, SE Belgium 49.36N 5.49E
109 M23 **Messina** var. Messana, Messene; anc. Zancle. Sicilia, Italy, C Mediterranean Sea 38.11N 15.33E
Messina see Musina
Messina, Strait of see Messina, Stretto di
109 M23 **Messina, Stretto di** Eng. Strait of Messina. strait SW Italy
117 E21 **Messíni** Pelopónnisos, S Greece 37.03N 22.00E
117 E21 **Messinía** peninsula S Greece
117 E22 **Messiniakós Kólpos** gulf S Greece
126 H8 **Messoyakha** ∽ N Russian Federation
116 H11 **Mesta** Gk. Néstos, Turk. Kara Su. ∽ Bulgaria/Greece see also Néstos
Mestghanem see Mostaganem
143 R8 **Mestia** var. Mestiya. N Georgia 43.03N 42.49E
Mestiya see Mestia
117 K18 **Mestón, Akrotírio** headland Chíos, E Greece 38.15N 25.52E
108 H8 **Mestre** Veneto, NE Italy 45.30N 12.13E
61 M16 **Mestre, Espigão** ▲▲ E Brazil
174 Ii11 **Mesuji** ∽ Sumatera, W Indonesia
Mesule see Grosser Möseler
8 J10 **Meszah Peak** ▲ British Columbia, W Canada 58.31N 131.28W
56 G11 **Meta** off. Departamento del Meta. ◈ province C Colombia
13 Q8 **Metabetchouane** ∽ Québec, SE Canada
16 O4 **Meta Incognita Peninsula** peninsula Baffin Island, Nunavut, NE Canada
24 K9 **Metairie** Louisiana, S USA 29.58N 90.09W
34 M6 **Metaline Falls** Washington, NW USA 48.51N 117.21W
64 K6 **Metán** Salta, N Argentina 25.25S 64.52W
84 N13 **Metangula** Niassa, N Mozambique 12.40S 34.49E
44 E7 **Metapán** Santa Ana, NW El Salvador 14.19N 89.30W
56 K9 **Meta, Río** ∽ Colombia/Venezuela
108 I11 **Metauro** ∽ C Italy
82 H11 **Metema** Amhara, N Ethiopia 12.53N 36.10E
117 D15 **Metéora** religious building Thessalía, C Greece 39.45N 21.37E
67 O20 **Meteor Rise** undersea feature SW Indian Ocean
195 N9 **Meteran** New Hanover, NE PNG 2.36S 150.09E
Meterlam see Mehtar Lām
117 G20 **Methanon** peninsula S Greece
Methariam/Metharlam see Mehtar Lām
34 J6 **Methow River** ∽ Washington, NW USA
21 O10 **Methuen** Massachusetts, NE USA 42.43N 71.10W
193 G19 **Methven** Canterbury, South Island, NZ 43.37S 171.38E
Metis see Metz
115 G15 **Metković** Dubrovnik-Neretva, SE Croatia 43.02N 17.37E
41 Y14 **Metlakatla** Annette Island, Alaska, USA 55.07N 131.34W
111 V13 **Metlika** Ger. Möttling. SE Slovenia 45.38N 15.18E
111 T8 **Metnitz** Kärnten, S Austria 46.58N 14.09E
29 W12 **Meto, Bayou** ∽ Arkansas, C USA
174 Ii13 **Metro** Sumatera, W Indonesia 5.05S 105.17E
32 M17 **Metropolis** Illinois, N USA 37.09N 88.43W
Metropolitan see Santiago
37 N8 **Metropolitan Oakland** ✕ California, W USA 37.42N 122.13W
117 D15 **Métsovo** prev. Métsovon. Ípeiros, C Greece 39.47N 21.12E
Métsovon see Métsovo
25 V5 **Metter** Georgia, SE USA 32.24N 82.03W
101 H21 **Mettet** Namur, S Belgium 50.19N 4.43E
103 D20 **Mettlach** Saarland, SW Germany 49.28N 6.37E
Mettu see Metu
82 H13 **Metu** var. Mattu, Mettu. Oromo, C Ethiopia 8.18N 35.39E

◆ Country
● Country Capital
◇ Dependent Territory
○ Dependent Territory Capital
◈ Administrative Region
✕ International Airport
▲ Mountain
▲▲ Mountain Range
Volcano
∽ River
◎ Lake
▣ Reservoir

175 N7 **Metulang** Borneo, N Indonesia 1.28N 114.40E
144 G8 **Metulla** Northern, N Israel 33.16N 35.35E
105 T4 **Metz** anc. Divodurum Mediomatricum, Mediomatrica, Metis. Moselle, NE France 49.07N 6.09E
103 H22 **Metzingen** Baden-Württemberg, S Germany 48.31N 9.16E
173 E4 **Meulaboh** Sumatera, W Indonesia 4.10N 96.09E
101 D18 **Meulebeke** West-Vlaanderen, W Belgium 50.57N 3.18E
105 U6 **Meurthe** ~ NE France
105 S5 **Meurthe-et-Moselle** ◊ department NE France
105 S4 **Meuse** ◊ department NE France
86 F10 **Meuse** Dut. Maas. ~ W Europe see also Maas
195 O11 **Mevelo** ~ New Britain, C Papau New Guinea
Mexcala, Río see Balsas, Río
27 U8 **Mexia** Texas, SW USA 31.40N 96.28W
60 K11 **Mexiana, Ilha** island NE Brazil
42 C1 **Mexicali** Baja California, NW Mexico 32.34N 115.26W
29 V4 **Mexico** Missouri, C USA 39.10N 91.52W
20 H9 **Mexico** New York, NE USA 43.27N 76.14W
42 L7 **Mexico** off. United Mexican States, var. Méjico, México, Sp. Estados Unidos Mexicanos. ◆ federal republic N Central America
43 O14 **Mexico** var. Ciudad de México, Eng. Mexico City. ● (Mexico) México, C Mexico 19.24N 99.04W
43 O13 **Mexico** ◊ state S Mexico
(0) J13 **Mexico Basin** var. Sigsbee Deep. undersea feature C Gulf of Mexico
Mexico City see México
México, Golfo de see Mexico, Gulf of
46 B4 **Mexico, Gulf of** Sp. Golfo de México. gulf W Atlantic Ocean
Meyadine see Al Mayādīn
155 Q5 **Meydān Shahr** var. Maydān Shahr. Vardak, E Afghanistan 34.27N 68.48E
41 Y14 **Meyers Chuck** Etolin Island, Alaska, USA 55.44N 132.15W
154 M3 **Meymaneh** var. Maimāna, Maymana. Fāryāb, NW Afghanistan 35.57N 64.48E
149 N7 **Meymeh** Eşfahān, C Iran 33.28N 51.09E
127 Pp6 **Meynypil'gyno** Chukotskiy Avtonomnyy Okrug, NE Russian Federation 62.33N 177.00E
110 A10 **Meyrin** Genève, SW Switzerland 46.13N 6.04E
177 Ff8 **Mezaligon** Irrawaddy, SW Burma 17.53N 95.12E
43 O15 **Mezcala** Guerrero, S Mexico 17.55N 99.34W
116 H8 **Mezdra** Vratsa, NW Bulgaria 43.09N 23.44E
105 P16 **Mèze** Hérault, S France 43.25N 3.37E
129 O6 **Mezen'** Arkhangel'skaya Oblast', NW Russian Federation 65.54N 44.10E
129 P2 **Mezen'** ~ NW Russian Federation
Mezen, Bay of see Mezenskaya Guba
105 Q13 **Mézenc, Mont** ▲ C France 44.57N 4.15E
129 O8 **Mezenskaya Guba** var. Bay of Mezen. bay NW Russian Federation
125 Bb7 **Mezha** ~ NW Russian Federation
Mezha see Myazha
126 Hh15 **Mezhdurechensk** Kemerovskaya Oblast', S Russian Federation 53.37N 87.59E
125 F4 **Mezhdusharskiy, Ostrov** island Novaya Zemlya, N Russian Federation
Mezhëvo see Myezhava
Mezhgor'ye see Mizhhir"ya
131 W5 **Mezhgor'ye** var. Respublika Bashkortostan, W Russian Federation 54.10N 57.55E
119 V8 **Mezhova** Dnipropetrovs'ka Oblast', E Ukraine 48.15N 36.44E
8 J12 **Meziadin Junction** British Columbia, W Canada 56.06N 129.15W
113 G16 **Mezilesské sedlo** var. Przełęcz Międzyleska. pass Czech Republic/Poland 50.05N 16.40E
104 L14 **Mézin** Lot-et-Garonne, SW France 44.03N 0.16E
113 M24 **Mezőberény** Békés, SE Hungary 46.49N 21.00E
113 M24 **Mezőhegyes** Békés, SE Hungary 46.19N 20.51E
113 M23 **Mezőkovácsháza** Békés, SE Hungary 46.25N 20.52E
113 M23 **Mezőkövesd** Borsod-Abaúj-Zemplén, NE Hungary 47.48N 20.34E
Mezőtelegd see Tileagd
113 M23 **Mezőtúr** Jász-Nagykun-Szolnok, E Hungary 47.00N 20.37E
42 K10 **Mezquital** Durango, C Mexico 23.29N 104.24W
108 G6 **Mezzolombardo** Trentino-Alto Adige, N Italy 46.13N 11.08E
84 L13 **Mfuwe** Northern, N Zambia 13.00S 31.45E
123 J16 **Mgarr** Gozo, N Malta 36.01N 14.18E
130 H6 **Mglin** Bryanskaya Oblast', W Russian Federation 53.01N 32.54E
Mhálanna, Cionn see Malin Head
160 G10 **Mhow** Madhya Pradesh, C India 22.36N 75.47E
Miadzioł Nowy see Myadzyel
179 Q13 **Miagao** Panay Island, C Philippines 10.40N 122.15E
43 R17 **Miahuatlán** var. Miahuatlán de Porfirio Díaz. Oaxaca, SE Mexico 16.21N 96.36W
Miahuatlán de Porfirio Díaz see Miahuatlán
106 K10 **Miajadas** Extremadura, W Spain 39.10N 5.54W
Miajlar see Myājlār

38 M14 **Miami** Arizona, SW USA 33.23N 110.53W
25 Z16 **Miami** Florida, SE USA 25.46N 80.11W
29 R8 **Miami** Oklahoma, C USA 36.52N 94.52W
27 O2 **Miami** Texas, SW USA 35.41N 100.38W
25 Z16 **Miami** ✈ Florida, SE USA 25.47N 80.16W
25 Z16 **Miami Beach** Florida, SE USA 25.47N 80.07W
25 Y15 **Miami Canal** canal Florida, SE USA
23 R14 **Miamisburg** Ohio, N USA 39.38N 84.17W
155 U10 **Miǎn Channún** Punjab, E Pakistan 31.25N 72.24E
148 J4 **Miāndowāb** var. Mianduab, Mīyāndoāb. Āžarbāyjān-e Gharbī, NW Iran 36.58N 46.06E
180 H5 **Miandrivazo** Toliara, C Madagascar 19.31S 45.28E
Mianduab see Miāndowāb
148 K3 **Miāneh** var. Miyāneh. Āžarbāyjān-e Sharqī, NW Iran 37.25N 47.43E
155 O16 **Miāni Hōr** lagoon S Pakistan
166 G10 **Mianning** Sichuan, C China 28.34N 102.12E
155 T7 **Miānwāli** Punjab, NE Pakistan 32.31N 71.33E
166 J7 **Mianxian** var. Mian Xian. Shaanxi, C China 33.12N 106.36E
166 I8 **Mianyang** Sichuan, C China 31.28N 104.43E
Mianyang see Xiantao
167 R3 **Miaodao Qundao** island group E China
167 S13 **Miaoli** N Taiwan 24.33N 120.48E
125 E12 **Miass** Chelyabinskaya Oblast', C Russian Federation 55.00N 59.55E
112 G8 **Miastko** Ger. Rummelsburg in Pommern. Pomorskie, N Poland 54.00N 16.58E
Miava see Myjava
9 O15 **Mica Creek** British Columbia, SW Canada 51.58N 118.29W
166 J7 **Micang Shan** ▲ C China
194 I12 **Michael, Mount** ▲ C PNG 6.24S 145.18E
Mi Chai see Nong Khai
113 O19 **Michalovce** Ger. Grossmichel, Hung. Nagymihály. Košický Kraj, E Slovakia 48.46N 21.54E
101 M20 **Michel, Baraque** hill E Belgium 50.38N 6.09E
41 S5 **Michelson, Mount** ▲ Alaska, USA 69.19N 144.16W
47 P9 **Miches** E Dominican Republic 18.56N 69.04W
32 M4 **Michigamme, Lake** ⊚ Michigan, N USA
32 M4 **Michigamme Reservoir** ⊠ Michigan, N USA
32 M4 **Michigamme River** ~ Michigan, N USA
33 N8 **Michigan** off. State of Michigan; also known as Great Lakes State, Lake State, Wolverine State. ◊ state N USA
33 O11 **Michigan City** Indiana, N USA 41.43N 86.52W
33 O8 **Michigan, Lake** ⊚ N USA
33 P2 **Michipicoten Bay** lake bay Ontario, N Canada
12 A8 **Michipicoten Island** island Ontario, S Canada
12 B7 **Michipicoten River** Ontario, S Canada 47.56N 84.48W
Michurin see Tsarevo
130 M6 **Michurinsk** Tambovskaya Oblast', W Russian Federation 52.56N 40.30E
Mico, Punta/Mico, Punto see Monkey Point
44 L10 **Mico, Río** ~ SE Nicaragua
47 T12 **Micoud** SE Saint Lucia 13.49N 60.54W
201 N16 **Micronesia** off. Federated States of Micronesia. ◆ federation W Pacific Ocean
183 P4 **Micronesia** island group W Pacific Ocean
174 Jj5 **Midai, Pulau** island Kepulauan Natuna, W Indonesia 3.00N 107.47E
Mid-Atlantic Cordillera see Mid-Atlantic Ridge
67 M17 **Mid-Atlantic Ridge** var. Mid-Atlantic Cordillera, Mid-Atlantic Rise, Mid-Atlantic Swell. undersea feature Atlantic Ocean
Mid-Atlantic Rise/ Mid-Atlantic Swell see Mid-Atlantic Ridge
101 E15 **Middelburg** Zeeland, SW Netherlands 51.30N 3.36E
85 H24 **Middelburg** Eastern Cape, S South Africa 31.30S 25.01E
85 K21 **Middelburg** Mpumalanga, NE South Africa 25.46S 29.28E
97 G23 **Middelfart** Fyn, C Denmark 55.30N 9.43E
100 G13 **Middelharnis** Zuid-Holland, SW Netherlands 51.45N 4.10E
101 B16 **Middelkerke** West-Vlaanderen, W Belgium 51.11N 2.51E
100 I9 **Middenbeemster** Noord-Holland, C Netherlands 52.33N 4.55E
100 I8 **Middenmeer** Noord-Holland, NW Netherlands 52.48N 4.58E
37 Q2 **Middle Alkali Lake** ⊚ California, W USA
200 Nn6 **Middle America Trench** undersea feature E Pacific Ocean
151 P19 **Middle Andaman** island Andaman Islands, India, NE Indian Ocean
Middle Atlas see Moyen Atlas
23 R3 **Middlebourne** West Virginia, NE USA 39.29N 80.54W
25 W9 **Middleburg** Florida, SE USA 30.03N 81.55W
Middleburg Island see 'Eua
Middle Caicos see Grand Caicos
27 N8 **Middle Concho River** ~ Texas, SW USA
Middle Congo see Congo (Republic of)
41 R6 **Middle Fork Chandalar River** ~ Alaska, USA
41 Q7 **Middle Fork Koyukuk River** ~ Alaska, USA

35 O12 **Middle Fork Salmon River** ~ Idaho, NW USA
9 T15 **Middle Lake** Saskatchewan, S Canada 52.31N 105.16W
30 L13 **Middle Loup River** ~ Nebraska, C USA
193 E22 **Middlemarch** Otago, South Island, NZ 45.30S 170.07E
33 T15 **Middleport** Ohio, N USA 39.00N 82.03W
31 U14 **Middle Raccoon River** ~ Iowa, C USA
31 R3 **Middle River** ~ Minnesota, N USA
23 N8 **Middlesboro** Kentucky, S USA 36.37N 83.42W
99 M15 **Middlesbrough** N England, UK 54.34N 1.13W
44 G3 **Middlesex** Stann Creek, C Belize 17.00N 88.31W
19 N22 **Middlesex** cultural region SE England, UK
13 P15 **Middleton** Nova Scotia, SE Canada 44.54N 65.01W
22 F10 **Middleton** Tennessee, S USA 35.05N 88.57W
32 L9 **Middleton** Wisconsin, N USA 43.06N 89.30W
41 S16 **Middleton Island** island Alaska, USA
41 S13 **Middletown** California, W USA 38.44N 122.39W
36 M7 **Middletown** Delaware, NE USA 39.25N 75.39W
23 Y2 **Middletown** New Jersey, NE USA 40.22N 74.07W
20 K15 **Middletown** New York, NE USA 41.27N 74.25W
33 R14 **Middletown** Ohio, N USA 39.33N 84.19W
20 G15 **Middletown** Pennsylvania, NE USA 40.11N 76.42W
147 N14 **Midi** var. Maydī. NW Yemen 16.18N 42.51E
105 O16 **Midi, Canal du** canal S France
104 K17 **Midi de Bigorre, Pic du** ▲ S France 42.57N 0.08E
104 K17 **Midi d'Ossau, Pic du** ▲ SW France 42.51N 0.27W
181 R7 **Mid-Indian Basin** undersea feature N Indian Ocean
181 P7 **Mid-Indian Ridge** var. Central Indian Ridge. undersea feature C Indian Ocean
27 N8 **Midkiff** Texas, SW USA 31.35N 101.51W
112 M8 **Midland** Ontario, S Canada 44.43N 79.51W
33 R8 **Midland** Michigan, N USA 43.37N 84.15W
29 M10 **Midland** South Dakota, N USA 44.04N 101.07W
26 M8 **Midland** Texas, SW USA 32.00N 102.04W
85 K17 **Midlands** ◊ province C Zimbabwe
99 D21 **Midleton** Ir. Mainistir na Corann. SW Ireland 51.55N 8.10W
27 T7 **Midlothian** Texas, SW USA 32.28N 96.59W
98 K12 **Midlothian** cultural region S Scotland, UK
180 I7 **Midongy** Fianarantsoa, S Madagascar 21.58S 47.46E
104 K15 **Midou** ~ SW France
199 Ii6 **Mid-Pacific Mountains** var. Mid-Pacific Seamounts. undersea feature NW Pacific Ocean
Mid-Pacific Seamounts see Mid-Pacific Mountains
179 R16 **Midsayap** Mindanao, S Philippines 7.12N 124.31E
38 L3 **Midvale** Utah, W USA 40.36N 111.28W
119 Jj5 **Midway Islands** ◇ US territory C Pacific Ocean
35 X14 **Midwest** Wyoming, C USA 43.24N 106.15W
29 N10 **Midwest City** Oklahoma, C USA 35.27N 97.24W
158 M10 **Mid Western** ◊ zone W Nepal
100 P5 **Midwolda** Groningen, NE Netherlands 53.12N 7.00E
143 O16 **Midyat** Mardin, SE Turkey 37.25N 41.19E
116 F18 **Midžor** SCr. Midžor. ▲ Bulgaria/Serbia 43.24N 22.41E see also Midžor
171 H16 **Mie** off. Mie-ken. ◊ prefecture Honshū, SW Japan
113 L16 **Miechów** Małopolskie, S Poland 50.20N 20.00E
112 F11 **Międzychód** Ger. Mitteldorf. Wielkopolskie, C Poland 52.36N 15.52E
112 J7 **Międzyrzec Podlaski** Lubelskie, E Poland 52.00N 22.47E
112 E11 **Międzyrzecz** Ger. Meseritz. Lubelskie, W Poland 52.26N 15.33E
Mie-ken see Mie
104 L16 **Miélan** Gers, S France 43.25N 0.18E
113 N16 **Mielec** Podkarpackie, SE Poland 50.18N 21.27E
97 L21 **Mien** ⊚ S Sweden
43 O8 **Mier** Tamaulipas, C Mexico 26.25N 99.10W
118 J11 **Miercurea-Ciuc** Ger. Szeklerburg, Hung. Csíkszereda. Harghita, C Romania 46.23N 25.47E
Mieresch see Maros/Mureş
189 Y10 **Mieres** var. Mieres del Camín. Asturias, NW Spain 43.15N 5.46W
Mieres del Camín see Mieres
101 K15 **Mierlo** Noord-Brabant, SE Netherlands 51.27N 5.37E
26 K13 **Mi'ēso** var. Meheso, Oromo. C Ethiopia 9.13N 40.47E
Miesso see Mi'ēso
113 J11 **Mieszkowice** Ger. Bärwalde Neumark. Zachodnio-pomorskie, W Poland 52.45N 14.24E
20 G14 **Mifflinburg** Pennsylvania, NE USA 40.55N 77.03W
20 F14 **Mifflintown** Pennsylvania, NE USA 40.32N 77.23W

43 R15 **Miguel Alemán, Presa** ⊠ SE Mexico
42 L9 **Miguel Asua** var. Miguel Auza. Zacatecas, C Mexico 24.16N 103.28W
Miguel Auza see Miguel Asua
45 S15 **Miguel de la Borda** var. Donoso. Colón, C Panama 9.06N 80.19W
43 N13 **Miguel Hidalgo** ✈ (Guadalajara) Jalisco, SW Mexico 20.52N 101.09W
42 H7 **Miguel Hidalgo, Presa** ⊠ W Mexico
118 J14 **Mihăilești** Giurgiu, S Romania 44.19N 25.54E
118 M14 **Mihail Kogălniceanu** var. Kogălniceanu; prev. Caramurat, Ferdinand. Constanţa, SE Romania 44.37N 28.26E
119 N14 **Mihai Viteazu** Constanţa, SE Romania 44.37N 28.41E
142 G12 **Mihalıççık** Eskişehir, NW Turkey 39.52N 31.30E
170 Ee13 **Mihara** Hiroshima, Honshū, SW Japan 34.24N 133.03E
171 Jj17 **Mihara-yama** ▲ Miyako-jima, SW Japan
107 S8 **Mijares** ~ E Spain
100 I11 **Mijdrecht** Utrecht, C Netherlands 52.12N 4.52E
172 Oo5 **Mikasa** Hokkaidō, NE Japan 43.19N 141.54E
121 K19 **Mikashevichy** Pol. Mikaszewicze. Rus. Mikashevichi. Brestskaya Voblasts', SW Belarus 52.13N 27.28E
Mikaszewicze see Mikashevichy
171 Hh16 **Mikawa-wan** bay S Japan
130 L5 **Mikhaylov** Ryazanskaya Oblast', W Russian Federation 54.13N 39.03E
Mikhaylovgrad see Montana
205 Z8 **Mikhaylov Island** island Antarctica
151 T6 **Mikhaylovka** Pavlodar, N Kazakhstan 53.49N 76.31E
131 N9 **Mikhaylovka** Volgogradskaya Oblast', SW Russian Federation 50.06N 43.17E
Mikhaylovka see Mykhaylivka
127 Pp11 **Mil'kovo** Kamchatskaya Oblast', E Russian Federation 54.39N 158.35E
9 R7 **Milk River** Alberta, SW Canada 49.10N 112.06W
46 J13 **Milk River** C Jamaica
35 W7 **Milk River** ~ Montana, NW USA
82 D9 **Milk, Wadi el** var. Wadi al Malik. ~ C Sudan
112 E10 **Mikkeli** Swe. Sankt Michel. Itä-Suomi, E Finland 61.41N 27.14E
112 M8 **Mikołajki** Ger. Nikolaiken. Warmińsko-Mazurskie, NE Poland 53.49N 21.31E
Mikonos see Mýkonos
116 I9 **Mikre** Lovech, N Bulgaria 43.37N 24.32E
116 C13 **Mikri Préspa, Límni** ⊚ N Greece
129 P4 **Mikulkin, Mys** headland NW Russian Federation 67.50N 46.36E
83 I23 **Mikumi** Morogoro, SE Tanzania 7.22S 37.00E
129 R10 **Mikun'** Respublika Komi, NW Russian Federation 62.20N 50.02E
171 Hh13 **Mikuni** Fukui, Honshū, SW Japan 36.12N 136.09E
171 Jj14 **Mikuni-tōge** pass Honshū, C Japan 36.46N 138.47E
172 S13 **Mikura-jima** island E Japan
31 V7 **Milaca** Minnesota, N USA 45.45N 93.39W
64 J10 **Milagro** La Rioja, C Argentina 31.00S 66.01W
58 B7 **Milagro** Guayas, SW Ecuador 2.08S 79.34W
33 P4 **Milakokia Lake** ⊚ Michigan, N USA
32 J1 **Milan** Illinois, N USA 41.27N 90.33W
33 R10 **Milan** Michigan, N USA 42.05N 83.40W
29 W7 **Milan** Missouri, C USA 40.12N 93.07W
22 H7 **Milan** Tennessee, S USA 35.55N 88.45W
Milan see Milano
97 F15 **Miland** Telemark, S Norway 59.57N 8.44E
85 N15 **Milange** Zambézia, NE Mozambique 16.08S 35.51E
108 D8 **Milano** Eng. Milan, Ger. Mailand; anc. Mediolanum. Lombardia, N Italy 45.28N 9.10E
142 C15 **Milas** Muğla, SW Turkey 37.16N 27.46E
121 K21 **Milashevichy** Rus. Milashevichi. Homyel'skaya Voblasts', SE Belarus 51.38N 27.54E
121 J18 **Milavidy** Rus. Milovidy. Brestskaya Voblasts', SW Belarus 52.53N 25.24E
Milavidy see Milovidy
109 L23 **Milazzo** anc. Mylae. Sicilia, Italy, C Mediterranean Sea 38.13N 15.15E
31 R8 **Milbank** South Dakota, N USA 45.12N 96.36W
21 T7 **Milbridge** Maine, NE USA 44.32N 67.52W
102 L11 **Milde** ~ C Germany
12 F14 **Mildmay** Ontario, S Canada 44.03N 81.07W
190 L9 **Mildura** Victoria, SE Australia 34.13S 142.09E
143 X12 **Mil Düzü** Rus. Mil'skaya Ravnina, Mil'skaya Step'. physical region SW Azerbaijan
166 H13 **Mile** var. Miyang. Yunnan, SW China 24.28N 103.25E
Mile see Mili Atoll
189 Y10 **Mileto** Calabria, SW Italy 38.35N 16.03E
27 P8 **Miles** Texas, SW USA 31.36N 100.10W
35 X9 **Miles City** Montana, NW USA 46.25N 105.48W
9 U17 **Milestone** Saskatchewan, S Canada 50.00N 104.24W
109 K16 **Miletto, Monte** ▲ C Italy 41.27N 14.24E
12 G15 **Milford** Ontario, SE Canada 43.57N 77.09W

23 Y3 **Milford** var. Milford City. Delaware, NE USA 38.54N 75.25W
31 T11 **Milford** Iowa, C USA 43.19N 95.09W
21 S6 **Milford** Maine, NE USA 44.57N 68.37W
31 R16 **Milford** Nebraska, C USA 40.46N 97.03W
21 O10 **Milford** New Hampshire, NE USA 42.49N 71.38W
20 J13 **Milford** Pennsylvania, NE USA 41.19N 74.48W
27 T7 **Milford** Texas, SW USA 32.07N 96.57W
38 K6 **Milford** Utah, W USA 38.22N 112.57W
Milford see Milford Haven
Milford City see Milford
99 H21 **Milford Haven** prev. Milford. SW Wales, UK 51.43N 5.01W
29 O4 **Milford Lake** ⊠ Kansas, C USA
193 B21 **Milford Sound** Southland, South Island, NZ 44.40S 167.57E
193 B21 **Milford Sound** inlet South Island, NZ
Milhau see Millau
Milḩ, Baḩr al see Razāzah, Buḩayrat ar
145 T10 **Milḩ, Wādī al** dry watercourse S Iraq
Min see Fujian
201 W8 **Mili Atoll** var. Mile. atoll Ratak Chain, SE Marshall Islands
112 H13 **Milicz** Dolnośląskie, SW Poland 51.31N 17.18E
109 L25 **Militello in Val di Catania** Sicilia, Italy, C Mediterranean Sea 37.16N 14.46E
Mil'kovo see Mil'kovo
101 L14 **Mill** Noord-Brabant, SE Netherlands 51.42N 5.46E
105 P14 **Millau** var. Milhau; anc. Æmilianum. Aveyron, S France 44.06N 3.04E
12 I14 **Millbrook** Ontario, SE Canada 44.09N 78.26W
95 N18 **Milledgeville** Georgia, SE USA 33.04N 83.13W
12 C12 **Mille Lacs, Lac des** ⊚ Ontario, S Canada
31 V6 **Mille Lacs Lake** ⊚ Minnesota, N USA
25 V4 **Millen** Georgia, SE USA 32.50N 81.56W
203 Y5 **Millennium Island** prev. Caroline Island, Thornton Island. atoll Line Islands, E Kiribati
29 O4 **Miller** South Dakota, N USA 44.24N 98.00W
32 K5 **Miller Dam Flowage** ⊠ Wisconsin, N USA
41 U12 **Miller, Mount** ▲ Alaska, USA 60.29N 142.25W
130 L10 **Millerovo** Rostovskaya Oblast', SW Russian Federation 48.57N 40.25E
39 N17 **Miller Peak** ▲ Arizona, SW USA 31.23N 110.17W
33 T12 **Millersburg** Ohio, N USA 40.33N 81.55W
20 G15 **Millersburg** Pennsylvania, NE USA 40.31N 76.56W
27 Q8 **Millersview** Texas, SW USA 31.26N 99.44W
108 B10 **Millesimo** Piemonte, NE Italy 44.24N 8.09E
105 N11 **Millevaches, Plateau de** plateau C France
190 K12 **Millicent** South Australia 37.37S 140.21E
27 Q13 **Millett** Texas, SW USA 28.33N 99.10W
100 M13 **Millingen aan den Rijn** Gelderland, SE Netherlands 51.52N 6.02E
22 E10 **Millington** Tennessee, S USA 35.20N 89.54W
21 R4 **Millinocket** Maine, NE USA 45.38N 68.45W
21 R4 **Millinocket Lake** ⊚ Maine, NE USA
205 Z11 **Mill Island** island Antarctica
191 T3 **Millmerran** Queensland, E Australia 27.52S 151.15E
111 R9 **Millstatt** Kärnten, S Austria
99 B19 **Milltown Malbay** Ir. Sráid na Cathrach. W Ireland 52.51N 9.23W
20 J23 **Millville** New Jersey, NE USA 39.24N 75.01W
29 S3 **Millwood Lake** ⊠ Arkansas, C USA
Milne Bank see Milne Seamounts
195 O17 **Milne Bay** ◊ province SE PNG
195 N17 **Milne Bay** bay SE PNG
66 J8 **Milne Seamounts** var. Milne Bank. undersea feature N Atlantic Ocean
31 R8 **Milnor** North Dakota, N USA 46.15N 97.27W
21 R5 **Milo** Maine, NE USA 45.15N 68.59W
117 I22 **Milos** island Kykládes, Greece, Aegean Sea
Milos see Plāka
112 H11 **Miłosław** Wielkopolskie, C Poland 52.13N 17.28E
115 K19 **Milot** var. Miloti. C Albania 41.42N 19.43E
Miloti see Milot
189 Y10 **Milove** Luhans'ka Oblast', E Ukraine 49.22N 40.09E
Milovidy see Milavidy
190 L7 **Milparinka** New South Wales, SE Australia 29.45S 141.57E
37 N9 **Milpitas** California, W USA 37.25N 121.54W
Mil'skaya Ravnina/Mil'skaya Step' see Mil Düzü
12 I13 **Milton** Ontario, S Canada 43.31N 79.52W
193 E24 **Milton** Otago, South Island, NZ 46.07S 169.59E
25 P8 ... **Milton** var. Milton City. Delaware, NE USA 38.48N 75.21W
25 P8 **Milton** Florida, SE USA 30.37N 87.02W
20 G14 **Milton** Pennsylvania, NE USA 41.01N 76.49W
20 L7 **Milton** Vermont, NE USA 44.37N 73.04W
34 K11 **Milton-Freewater** Oregon, NW USA 45.55N 118.24W
99 N21 **Milton Keynes** SE England, UK 52.00N 0.43W
29 N3 **Miltonvale** Kansas, C USA 39.21N 97.27W
167 N10 **Miluo** Hunan, S China 28.53N 113.00E
32 M9 **Milwaukee** Wisconsin, N USA 43.03N 87.55W
Milyang see Miryang
Mimatum see Mende
39 Q15 **Mimbres Mountains** ▲ New Mexico, SW USA
190 D2 **Mimili** South Australia 27.01S 132.33E
104 J14 **Mimizan** Landes, SW France 44.12N 1.12W
81 E19 **Mimongo** Ngounié, C Gabon 1.36S 11.43E
33 V13 **Mina Junction** Ohio, N USA 40.19N 80.36W
Mingora see Mingâora

177 G8 **Mingaladon** ✈ (Yangon) Yangon, SW Burma 16.55N 96.11E
25 P8 **Mingan** Québec, E Canada 50.19N 64.01W
155 U5 **Mingâora** var. Mingora, Mingora. North-West Frontier Province, N Pakistan 34.46N 72.22E
Mingbuloq Rus. Mynbulak. Navoiy Viloyati, N Uzbekistan 42.18N 62.53E
152 K9 **Mingbuloq Botig'i** Rus. Vpadina Mynbulak. depression N Uzbekistan
Mingechaur/Mingechevir see Mingäçevir
Mingechaurskoye Vodokhranilishche/ Mingechevirskoye Vodokhranilishche see Mingäçevir Su Anbarı
167 Q7 **Mingguang** prev. Jiashan. Anhui, S China 32.45N 117.58E
177 Ff4 **Mingin** Sagaing, C Burma 22.51N 94.30E
107 Q10 **Minglanilla** Castilla-La Mancha, C Spain 39.31N 1.36W
33 V13 **Mingo Junction** Ohio, N USA 40.19N 80.36W
169 V7 **Mingshui** Heilongjiang, NE China 47.10N 125.52E
85 G14 **Minguri** Nampula, NE Mozambique 14.30S 40.37E
165 U10 **Minhe** var. Shangchuankou. Qinghai, C China 36.21N 102.40E
177 Ff6 **Minhla** Magwe, W Burma 19.57N 94.58E
178 J15 **Minh Lương** Kiên Giang, S Vietnam 9.52N 105.10E
106 G5 **Minho, Rio** Sp. Miño. ~ Portugal/Spain
106 G5 **Minho** former province N Portugal
Minho see also Miño
161 C24 **Minicoy Island** island SW India
35 P15 **Minidoka** Idaho, NW USA 42.45N 113.29W
120 C11 **Minija** ~ W Lithuania
188 G9 **Minilya** Western Australia 23.45S 114.03E
12 E8 **Minisinakwa Lake** ⊚ Ontario, S Canada
47 T12 **Ministre Point** headland S Saint Lucia 13.42N 60.57W
9 V15 **Minitonas** Manitoba, S Canada 52.07N 101.02W
Minius see Miño
167 R14 **Min Jiang** ~ SE China
166 H10 **Min Jiang** ~ C China
190 H9 **Minlaton** South Australia 34.52S 137.33E
172 M8 **Minmaya** var. Mimmaya. Aomori, Honshū, C Japan 41.10N 140.24E
79 U14 **Minna** Niger, C Nigeria 9.33N 6.33E
172 Pp16 **Minna-jima** island Sakishima-shotō, SW Japan
29 N4 **Minneapolis** Kansas, C USA 39.07N 97.42W
31 V9 **Minneapolis** Minnesota, N USA 44.58N 93.15W
31 V9 **Minneapolis-Saint Paul** ✈ Minnesota, N USA 44.53N 93.13W
15 Kk15 **Minnedosa** Manitoba, S Canada 50.13N 99.49W
28 J7 **Minneola** Kansas, C USA 37.26N 100.00W
31 S7 **Minnesota** off. State of Minnesota; also known as Gopher State, New England of the West, North Star State. ◊ state N USA
31 S9 **Minnesota River** ~ Minnesota/ South Dakota, N USA
31 V9 **Minnetonka** Minnesota, N USA 44.55N 93.28W
31 Q3 **Minnewaukan** North Dakota, N USA 48.03N 99.15W
190 F7 **Minnipa** South Australia 32.52S 135.07E
106 G5 **Miño** Galicia, NW Spain 43.21N 8.12W
106 G5 **Miño** var. Mino, Minius, Port. Rio Minho. ~ Portugal/Spain
171 Ii16 **Minobu** Yamanashi, Honshū, S Japan 35.22N 138.30E
32 L4 **Minocqua** Wisconsin, N USA 45.53N 89.42W
171 I15 **Minokamo** Gifu, Honshū, SW Japan 35.24N 136.57E
32 L12 **Minonk** Illinois, N USA 40.54N 89.01W
Minorca see Menorca
30 M3 **Minot** North Dakota, N USA 48.15N 101.19W
165 U9 **Minqin** Gansu, N China 38.35N 103.07E
121 I16 **Minsk** ● (Belarus) Minskaya Voblasts', C Belarus 53.52N 27.34E
121 L16 **Minsk** ✈ Minskaya Voblasts', C Belarus 53.08N 27.58E
121 K16 **Minskaya Voblasts'** prev. Rus. Minskaya Oblast'. ◊ province C Belarus
121 I15 **Minskaya Wzvyshsha** ▲ C Belarus
112 N12 **Mińsk Mazowiecki** var. Nowo-Minsk. Mazowieckie, C Poland 52.11N 21.33E
33 Q13 **Minster** Ohio, N USA 40.23N 84.22W
81 F15 **Minta** Centre, C Cameroon 4.34N 12.54E
155 V7 **Mintaka Pass** Chin. Mingteke Daban. pass China/Pakistan 36.59N 75.04E
117 D20 **Minthi** ~ S Greece
Minthun see Minden
11 O14 **Minto** New Brunswick, SE Canada 46.04N 66.04W
8 H6 **Minto** Yukon Territory, W Canada 62.33N 136.45W
41 R9 **Minto** Alaska, USA 65.07N 149.22W
31 Q3 **Minto** North Dakota, N USA 48.17N 97.22W
13 Q3 **Minto, Lac** ⊚ Québec, C Canada
205 R16 **Minto, Mount** ▲ Antarctica 71.38S 169.11E

◆ Country | ● Country Capital | ◇ Dependent Territory | ○ Dependent Territory Capital | ◊ Administrative Region | ✈ International Airport | ▲ Mountain | ▲ Mountain Range | ⊙ Volcano | ~ River | ⊚ Lake | ⊠ Reservoir

MINTON – MONASTERZYSKA

9 U17 **Minton** Saskatchewan, S Canada 49.12N 104.33W
201 R15 **Minto Reef** atoll Caroline Islands, C Micronesia
39 R4 **Minturn** Colorado, C USA 39.34N 106.21W
109 J16 **Minturno** Lazio, C Italy 41.15N 13.47E
126 Hh15 **Minusinsk** Krasnoyarskiy Kray, S Russian Federation 53.37N 91.49E
110 G11 **Minusio** Ticino, S Switzerland 46.11N 8.47E
81 E17 **Minvoul** Woleu-Ntem, N Gabon 2.07N 12.12E
147 R13 **Minwakh** N Yemen 16.54N 48.04E
165 V11 **Minxian** var. Min Xian. Gansu, C China 34.22N 104.02E
Minya see El Minya
33 R6 **Mio** Michigan, N USA 44.40N 84.09W
Mionn Ard see Mine Head
176 Ww9 **Mios Num, Selat** strait Papua, E Indonesia
164 L5 **Miquan** Xinjiang Uygur Zizhiqu, NW China 44.04N 87.40E
121 I17 **Mir** Hrodzyenskaya Voblasts', W Belarus 53.25N 26.28E
108 H8 **Mira** Veneto, NE Italy 45.25N 12.07E
106 G13 **Mira, Rio** ≈ S Portugal
10 K15 **Mirabel** var. Montreal. ✈ (Montréal) Québec, SE Canada 45.27N 73.47W
62 Q8 **Miracema** Rio de Janeiro, SE Brazil 21.24S 42.10W
56 G9 **Miraflores** Boyacá, C Colombia 5.07N 73.09W
42 G10 **Miraflores** Baja California Sur, W Mexico 23.24N 109.45W
46 L9 **Miragoâne** S Haiti 18.25N 73.07W
161 E16 **Miraj** Mahārāshtra, W India 16.51N 74.42E
63 E23 **Miramar** Buenos Aires, E Argentina 38.15S 57.49W
105 R15 **Miramas** Bouches-du-Rhône, SE France 43.34N 4.58E
104 K12 **Mirambeau** Charente-Maritime, W France 45.23N 0.33W
104 L13 **Miramont-de-Guyenne** Lot-et-Garonne, SW France 44.34N 0.20E
117 L25 **Mirampéllou, Kólpos** gulf Krití, Greece, E Mediterranean Sea
164 L8 **Miran** Xinjiang Uygur Zizhiqu, NW China 39.13N 88.58E
56 M5 **Miranda** off. Estado Miranda. ◈ state N Venezuela
Miranda de Corvo see Miranda do Corvo
107 O3 **Miranda de Ebro** La Rioja, N Spain 42.40N 2.57W
106 G8 **Miranda do Corvo** var. Miranda de Corvo. Coimbra, N Portugal 40.04N 8.19W
106 J6 **Miranda do Douro** Bragança, N Portugal 41.30N 6.16W
104 L15 **Mirande** Gers, S France 43.31N 0.25E
106 I6 **Mirandela** Bragança, N Portugal 41.28N 7.10W
27 R15 **Mirando City** Texas, SW USA 27.24N 99.00W
108 G9 **Mirandola** Emilia-Romagna, N Italy 44.52N 11.04E
62 I8 **Mirandópolis** São Paulo, S Brazil 21.10S 51.03W
62 K8 **Mirassol** São Paulo, S Brazil 20.50S 49.30W
106 J3 **Miravalles** ▲ NW Spain 42.52N 6.45W
44 L12 **Miravalles, Volcán** 🌋 NW Costa Rica 10.43N 85.07W
147 W13 **Mirbāṭ** var. Marbat. S Oman 17.03N 54.44E
46 M9 **Mirebalais** C Haiti 18.46N 72.03W
105 T6 **Mirecourt** Vosges, NE France 48.19N 6.04E
105 N16 **Mirepoix** Ariège, S France 43.04N 1.52E
Mirgorod see Myrhorod
145 W10 **Mīr Ḩājī Khalīl** E Iraq 32.11N 46.19E
174 Mm4 **Miri** Sarawak, East Malaysia 4.22N 113.58E
79 W12 **Miria** Zinder, S Niger 13.39N 9.15E
190 F5 **Mirikata** South Australia 29.56S 135.13E
56 K4 **Mirimire** Falcón, N Venezuela 11.07N 68.36W
63 H18 **Mirim Lagoon** var. Lake Mirim, Sp. Laguna Merín. lagoon Brazil/Uruguay
Mirim, Lake see Mirim Lagoon
Mírina see Mýrina
180 H14 **Miringoni** Mohéli, S Comoros 12.16S 93.39E
149 W11 **Mīrjāveh** Sīstān va Balūchestān, SE Iran 29.04N 61.23E
205 Z9 **Mirny** Russian research station Antarctica 66.25S 93.09E
128 M10 **Mirnyy** Arkhangel'skaya Oblast', NW Russian Federation 62.50N 40.20E
126 Kk11 **Mirnyy** Respublika Sakha (Yakutiya), NE Russian Federation 62.30N 113.58E
Mironovka see Myronivka
112 F9 **Mirosławiec** Zachodnio-pomorskie, NW Poland 53.21N 16.04E
Mirovo see Vrattsa
102 N10 **Mirow** Mecklenburg-Vorpommern, N Germany 53.16N 12.48E
158 G6 **Mīrpur** Jammu and Kashmir, NW India 33.06N 73.49E
Mīrpur see New Mīrpur
155 P17 **Mīrpur Batoro** Sind, SE Pakistan 24.40N 68.15E
155 Q16 **Mīrpur Khās** Sind, SE Pakistan 25.31N 69.00E
155 P17 **Mīrpur Sakro** Sind, SE Pakistan 24.31N 67.37E
149 T14 **Mīr Shahdād** Hormozgān, S Iran 26.15N 58.28E
Mirtoan Sea see Mirtóo Pélagos
117 G21 **Mirtóo Pélagos** Eng. Mirtoan Sea; anc. Myrtoum Mare. sea S Greece
169 Z16 **Miryang** var. Milyang, Jap. Mitsuō. SE South Korea 35.30N 128.46E
Mirzachirla see Murzechirla
170 Dd14 **Misaki** Ehime, Shikoku, SW Japan 33.22N 132.04E
43 Q13 **Misantla** Veracruz-Llave, E Mexico 19.54N 96.51W
172 N9 **Misawa** Aomori, Honshū, C Japan 40.41N 141.22E
59 G14 **Mishagua, Río** ≈ C Peru
169 Z8 **Mishan** Heilongjiang, NE China 45.30N 131.53E
33 O11 **Mishawaka** Indiana, N USA 41.40N 86.10W
41 N6 **Misheguk Mountain** ▲ Alaska, USA 68.13N 161.11W
171 Jj17 **Mishima** var. Misima. Shizuoka, Honshū, S Japan 35.07N 138.55E
170 Dd11 **Mi-shima** island SW Japan
131 V4 **Mishkino** Respublika Bashkortostan, W Russian Federation 55.31N 55.57E
159 Y10 **Mishmi Hills** hill range NE India
167 N11 **Mi Shui** ≈ S China
Misiaf see Maşyāf
109 J23 **Misilmeri** Sicilia, Italy, C Mediterranean Sea 38.03N 13.27E
Misima see Mishima
195 P17 **Misima Island** island SE PNG
Misión de Guana see Guana
62 F13 **Misiones** off. Provincia de Misiones. ◈ province NE Argentina
64 P8 **Misiones** off. Departamento de las Misiones. ◈ department S Paraguay
Misión San Fernando see San Fernando
Miskin see Maskin
Miskito Coast see La Mosquitia
45 O7 **Miskitos, Cayos** island group NE Nicaragua
113 M21 **Miskolc** Borsod-Abaúj-Zemplén, NE Hungary 48.04N 20.46E
175 Tt10 **Misool, Pulau** island Maluku, E Indonesia
Misox see Mesocco
31 Y3 **Misquah Hills** hill range Minnesota, N USA
77 P7 **Mişrātah** var. Misurata. NW Libya 32.22N 15.06E
123 Ll15 **Mişrātah, Râs** headland N Libya 32.22N 15.16E
12 C7 **Missanabie** Ontario, S Canada 48.18N 84.04W
60 E10 **Missão Catrimani** Roraima, N Brazil 1.25N 62.05W
12 D6 **Missinaibi** ≈ Ontario, S Canada
12 C7 **Missinaibi Lake** ◎ Ontario, S Canada
9 T13 **Missinipe** Saskatchewan, C Canada 55.36N 104.45W
30 M11 **Mission** South Dakota, N USA 43.16N 100.38W
27 S17 **Mission** Texas, SW USA 26.13N 98.19W
10 F10 **Missisa Lake** ◎ Ontario, C Canada
20 M6 **Missisquoi Bay** lake bay Canada/USA
12 C10 **Mississagi** ≈ Ontario, S Canada
12 G15 **Mississauga** Ontario, S Canada 43.36N 79.34W
33 P12 **Mississinewa Lake** ⊠ Indiana, N USA
33 P12 **Mississinewa River** ≈ Indiana/Ohio, N USA
24 K4 **Mississippi** off. State of Mississippi; also known as Bayou State, Magnolia State. ◈ state SE USA
12 K13 **Mississippi** ≈ Ontario, SE Canada
24 M10 **Mississippi Delta** delta Louisiana, S USA
49 N1 **Mississippi Fan** undersea feature N Gulf of Mexico
12 L13 **Mississippi Lake** ◎ Ontario, SE Canada
(0) J11 **Mississippi River** ≈ C USA
24 M9 **Mississippi Sound** sound Alabama/Mississippi, S USA
35 P9 **Missoula** Montana, NW USA 46.54N 114.03W
29 T5 **Missouri** off. State of Missouri; also known as Bullion State, Show Me State. ◈ state C USA
27 V11 **Missouri City** Texas, SW USA 29.37N 95.32W
(0) J10 **Missouri River** ≈ C USA
13 Q6 **Mistassibi** ≈ Québec, SE Canada
13 P6 **Mistassini** Québec, SE Canada 48.54N 72.13W
13 P6 **Mistassini** ≈ Québec, SE Canada
10 J11 **Mistassini, Lac** ◎ Québec, SE Canada
111 Y3 **Mistelbach an der Zaya** Niederösterreich, NE Austria 48.33N 16.33E
109 L24 **Misterbianco** Sicilia, Italy, C Mediterranean Sea 37.31N 15.01E
97 N19 **Misterhult** Kalmar, S Sweden 57.28N 16.34E
59 H17 **Misti, Volcán** ▲ S Peru 16.20S 71.22W
Mistras see Mystrás
109 K23 **Mistretta** anc. Amestratus. Sicilia, Italy, C Mediterranean Sea 37.55N 14.22E
170 C14 **Misumi** Kumamoto, Kyūshū, SW Japan 32.37N 130.29E
170 Ee12 **Misumi** Shimane, Honshū, SW Japan 34.47N 132.00E
Misurata see Mişrātah
85 O14 **Mitande** Niassa, N Mozambique 14.06S 36.03E
42 J13 **Mita, Punta de** headland C Mexico 20.46N 105.31W
57 W12 **Mitaraka, Massif du** ▲ NE South America 2.18N 54.31W
Mitau see Jelgava
189 X9 **Mitchell** Queensland, E Australia 26.29S 148.00E
12 E15 **Mitchell** Ontario, S Canada 43.28N 81.11W
30 I13 **Mitchell** Nebraska, C USA 41.56N 103.48W
34 J12 **Mitchell** Oregon, NW USA 44.34N 120.09W
31 P11 **Mitchell** South Dakota, N USA 43.42N 98.01W
25 P5 **Mitchell Lake** ⊠ Alabama, S USA
33 P7 **Mitchell, Lake** ◎ Michigan, N USA
23 P9 **Mitchell, Mount** ▲ North Carolina, SE USA 35.46N 82.16W
189 V3 **Mitchell River** ≈ Queensland, NE Australia
99 D20 **Mitchelstown** Ir. Baile Mhistéala. SW Ireland 52.19N 8.16W
12 M9 **Mitchinamécus, Lac** ◎ Québec, SE Canada
Mitèmboni see Mitemele, Río
81 D17 **Mitemele, Río** var. Mitèmboni, Temboni, Utamboni. ≈ S Equatorial Guinea
155 S12 **Mithānkot** Punjab, E Pakistan 28.57N 70.21E
155 T7 **Mitha Tiwāna** Punjab, E Pakistan 32.16N 72.07E
155 R17 **Mithi** Sind, SE Pakistan 24.43N 69.52E
Míthimna see Míthymna
Mi Tho see My Tho
117 L16 **Míthymna** var. Míthimna. Lésvos, E Greece 39.22N 26.11E
202 L16 **Mitiaro** island S Cook Islands
Mitilíni see Mytilíni
13 U7 **Mitis** ≈ Québec, SE Canada
43 R16 **Mitla** Oaxaca, SE Mexico 16.55N 96.19W
171 Kk16 **Mito** Ibaraki, Honshū, S Japan 36.21N 140.25E
94 N2 **Mitra, Kapp** headland W Svalbard 79.07N 11.11E
192 M13 **Mitre** ▲ North Island, NZ 40.46S 175.27E
193 B21 **Mitre Peak** ▲ South Island, NZ 44.37S 167.45E
41 O15 **Mitrofania Island** island Alaska, USA
Mitrovica/Mitrowitz see Sremska Mitrovica, Serbia, Serbia
Mitrovica/Mitrovicë see Kosovska Mitrovica, Serbia, Serbia
180 H12 **Mitsamiouli** Grande Comore, NW Comoros 11.22S 43.19E
180 I3 **Mitsinjo** Mahajanga, NW Madagascar 16.00S 45.52E
Mits'iwa see Massawa
180 H13 **Mitsoudjé** Grande Comore, NW Comoros
Mitspe Ramon see Mizpé Ramon
172 Oo7 **Mitsuishi** Hokkaidō, NE Japan 42.12N 142.40E
171 K13 **Mitsuke** var. Mituke. Niigata, Honshū, C Japan 37.33N 138.57E
Mitsuō see Miryang
170 Cc10 **Mitsushima** Nagasaki, Tsushima, SW Japan 34.16N 129.18E
102 G12 **Mittelandkanal** canal NW Germany
110 J7 **Mittelberg** Vorarlberg, NW Austria 47.19N 10.09E
Mitteldorf see Międzychód
Mittelstadt see Baia Sprie
Mitterburg see Pazin
111 P7 **Mittersill** Salzburg, NW Austria 47.16N 12.27E
103 N16 **Mittweida** Sachsen, E Germany 50.59N 12.57E
56 J13 **Mitú** Vaupés, SE Colombia 1.07N 70.04W
Mituke see Mitsuke
Mitumba, Chaîne des/Mitumba Range see Mitumba, Monts
81 O22 **Mitumba, Monts** var. Chaîne des Mitumba, Mitumba Range. ▲▲ E Dem. Rep. Congo
81 N23 **Mitwaba** Katanga, SE Dem. Rep. Congo 8.37S 27.19E
81 E18 **Mitzic** Woleu-Ntem, N Gabon 0.48N 11.30E
84 K11 **Miueru Wantipa, Lake** ◎ N Zambia
171 Jj17 **Miura** Kanagawa, Honshū, S Japan 35.07N 139.37E
171 M13 **Miyagi** off. Miyagi-ken. ◈ prefecture Honshū, C Japan
144 M7 **Miyāh, Wādī al** dry watercourse E Syria
172 Ss13 **Miyake** Tōkyō, Miyako-jima, SE Japan 34.34N 135.33E
172 N11 **Miyako** Iwate, Honshū, C Japan 39.39N 141.57E
172 Q16 **Miyako-jima** island Sakishima-shotō, SW Japan
170 C16 **Miyakonojō** var. Miyakonzyô. Miyazaki, Kyūshū, SW Japan 31.42N 131.03E
Miyakonzyô see Miyakonojō
172 Pp16 **Miyako-shotō** island group SW Japan
150 G11 **Miyaly** Atyrau, W Kazakhstan 48.52N 53.55E
Miyāndoāb see Mīāndowāb
Miyāneh see Mīāneh
Miyang see Mile
170 C15 **Miyanojō** Kagoshima, Kyūshū, SW Japan 31.55N 130.29E
170 Cc16 **Miyazaki** Miyazaki, Kyūshū, SW Japan 31.55N 131.23E
170 C15 **Miyazaki** off. Miyazaki-ken. ◈ prefecture Kyūshū, SW Japan
171 H13 **Miyazu** Kyōto, Honshū, SW Japan 35.28N 135.21E
Miyory see Myory
170 F13 **Miyoshi** var. Miyosi. Hiroshima, Honshū, SW Japan 34.48N 132.51E
Miyosi see Miyoshi
Miza see Mizë
83 H14 **Mīzan Teferī** Southern, S Ethiopia 6.57N 35.30E
Mizda see Mizdah
77 O8 **Mizdah** var. Mizda. NW Libya 31.25N 12.58E
115 K20 **Mizë** var. Miza. Fier, W Albania 40.58N 19.32E
99 A22 **Mizen Head** Ir. Carn Uí Néid. headland SW Ireland 51.26N 9.50W
118 H7 **Mizhhir"ya** Rus. Mezhgor'ye. Zakarpats'ka Oblast', W Ukraine 48.28N 23.31E
166 L4 **Mizhi** Shaanxi, C China 37.43N 110.13E
118 K13 **Mizil** Prahova, SE Romania 45.00N 26.29E
116 H7 **Miziya** Vratsa, NW Bulgaria 43.42N 23.52E
159 W15 **Mizo Hills** hill range E India
159 W15 **Mizoram** ◈ state NE India
144 F12 **Mizpé Ramon** var. Mitspe Ramon. Southern, S Israel 30.37N 34.46E
59 L19 **Mizque** Cochabamba, C Bolivia 17.58S 65.18W
59 M19 **Mizque, Río** ≈ C Bolivia
171 I15 **Mizunami** Gifu, Honshū, SW Japan 35.19N 137.12E
171 Mm12 **Mizusawa** Iwate, Honshū, C Japan 39.09N 141.07E
97 M18 **Mjölby** Östergötland, S Sweden 58.19N 15.10E
97 G15 **Mjøndalen** Buskerud, S Norway 59.45N 9.58E
97 J19 **Mjörn** ◎ S Sweden
96 I13 **Mjøsa** var. Mjøsen. ◎ S Norway
Mjøsen see Mjøsa
83 G21 **Mkalama** Singida, C Tanzania 4.09S 34.34E
82 K13 **Mkata** ≈ C Tanzania
85 K14 **Mkushi** Central, C Zambia 13.37S 29.27E
85 L22 **Mkuze** KwaZulu/Natal, E South Africa 27.40S 32.05E
83 J22 **Mkwaja** Tanga, E Tanzania 5.42S 38.48E
113 D16 **Mladá Boleslav** Ger. Jungbunzlau. Středočeský Kraj, N Czech Republic 50.24N 14.55E
114 M12 **Mladenovac** Serbia, C Serbia 44.27N 20.42E
116 L11 **Mladinovo** Khaskovo, S Bulgaria 41.57N 26.13E
115 O17 **Mlado Nagoričane** N FYR Macedonia 42.11N 21.49E
Mlanje see Mulanje
114 N12 **Mlava** ≈ E Serbia
112 L9 **Mława** Mazowieckie, C Poland 53.07N 20.23E
115 G16 **Mljet** It. Meleda; anc. Melita. island S Croatia
118 K4 **Mlyniv** Rivnens'ka Oblast', NW Ukraine 50.31N 25.36E
85 I21 **Mmabatho** North-West, N South Africa 25.51S 25.37E
85 I19 **Mmashoro** Central, E Botswana 21.56S 26.39E
46 J7 **Moa** Holguín, E Cuba 20.38N 74.36W
78 J15 **Moa** ≈ Guinea/Sierra Leone
39 O6 **Moab** Utah, W USA 38.34N 109.34W
189 V1 **Moa Island** island Queensland, NE Australia
197 J15 **Moala** island S Fiji
85 L21 **Moamba** Maputo, SW Mozambique 25.33S 32.15E
81 F19 **Moanda** var. Mouanda. Haut-Ogooué, SE Gabon 1.31S 13.07E
175 T16 **Moa, Pulau** island Kepulauan Leti, E Indonesia
85 M15 **Moatize** Tete, NW Mozambique 16.03S 33.49E
81 P22 **Moba** Katanga, E Dem. Rep. Congo 7.03S 29.51E
171 K17 **Mobara** Chiba, Honshū, S Japan 35.25N 140.19E
Mobay see Montego Bay
81 K15 **Mobaye** Basse-Kotto, S Central African Republic 4.19N 21.17E
81 K15 **Mobayi-Mbongo** Equateur, NW Dem. Rep. Congo 4.19N 21.18E
27 P2 **Mobeetie** Texas, SW USA 35.33N 100.25W
29 U3 **Moberly** Missouri, C USA 39.25N 92.26W
25 N8 **Mobile** Alabama, S USA 30.41N 88.02W
25 N9 **Mobile Bay** bay Alabama, S USA
25 N8 **Mobile River** ≈ Alabama, S USA
31 N8 **Mobridge** South Dakota, N USA 45.32N 100.25W
Mobutu Sese Seko, Lac see Albert, Lake
47 N8 **Moca** N Dominican Republic 19.23N 70.31W
Moçâmedes see Namibe
178 J6 **Môc Châu** Sơn La, N Vietnam 20.52N 104.38E
197 L15 **Moce** island Lau Group, E Fij
85 Q15 **Moçambique** Nampula, NE Mozambique 15.00S 40.44E
Mocha see Al Mukhā
200 Oo13 **Mocha Fracture Zone** tectonic feature SE Pacific Ocean
65 F14 **Mocha, Isla** island C Chile
58 C12 **Moche, Río** ≈ W Peru
178 J14 **Môc Hoa** Long An, S Vietnam 10.46N 105.55E
85 I20 **Mochudi** Kgatleng, SE Botswana 24.25S 26.07E
84 Q13 **Mocímboa da Praia** var. Vila de Mocímboa da Praia. Cabo Delgado, N Mozambique 11.16S 40.21E
96 L13 **Mockfjärd** Dalarna, C Sweden 60.30N 14.57E
23 R9 **Mocksville** North Carolina, SE USA 35.53N 80.33W
34 F8 **Moclips** Washington, NW USA 47.11N 124.13W
84 C13 **Môco** var. Morro de Môco. ▲ W Angola 12.36S 15.09E
56 D13 **Mocoa** Putumayo, SW Colombia 1.07N 76.37W
62 M8 **Mococa** São Paulo, S Brazil 21.30S 47.00W
Môco, Morro de see Môco
42 H8 **Mocorito** Sinaloa, C Mexico 25.24N 107.55W
42 J4 **Moctezuma** Chihuahua, N Mexico 30.10N 106.24W
43 N11 **Moctezuma** San Luis Potosí, C Mexico 22.44N 101.04W
42 G4 **Moctezuma** Sonora, NW Mexico 29.49N 109.40W
43 P12 **Moctezuma, Río** ≈ C Mexico
Mó, Cuan see Clew Bay
85 O16 **Mocuba** Zambézia, NE Mozambique 16.49S 37.01E
105 U12 **Modane** Savoie, E France 45.14N 6.41E
108 F9 **Modena** anc. Mutina. Emilia-Romagna, N Italy 44.39N 10.55E
38 I7 **Modena** Utah, W USA 37.46N 113.54W
37 O9 **Modesto** California, W USA 37.38N 121.01W
109 L25 **Modica** anc. Motyca. Sicilia, Italy, C Mediterranean Sea 36.52N 14.45E
85 J20 **Modimolle** prev. Nylstroom. Limpopo, NE South Africa 24.39S 28.23E
81 K17 **Modjamboli** Equateur, N Dem. Rep. Congo 2.27N 22.03E
111 X4 **Mödling** Niederösterreich, NE Austria 48.07N 16.15E
Modohn see Madona
Modot see Tsenhermandal
176 W12 **Modowi** Papua, E Indonesia 4.05S 134.39E
114 I12 **Modračko Jezero** ⊠ NE Bosnia and Herzegovina
114 I10 **Modriča** Republika Srpska, N Bosnia and Herzegovina 44.57N 18.17E
191 O13 **Moe** Victoria, SE Australia 38.10S 146.18E
Moearatewe see Muaratewe
Moei, Mae Nam see Thaungyin
96 H13 **Moelv** Hedmark, S Norway 60.55N 10.47E
94 I10 **Moen** Troms, N Norway 69.08N 18.35E
Moen see Weno, Micronesia
Möen see Møn, Denmark
Moena see Muna, Pulau
38 M10 **Moenkopi Wash** ≈ Arizona, SW USA
193 F22 **Moeraki Point** headland South Island, NZ 45.23S 170.52E
101 F16 **Moerbeke** Oost-Vlaanderen, NW Belgium 51.11N 3.57E
101 H14 **Moerdijk** Noord-Brabant, S Netherlands 51.42N 4.37E
Moero, Lac see Mweru, Lake
103 D15 **Moers** var. Mörs. Nordrhein-Westfalen, W Germany 51.27N 6.37E
Moesi see Musi, Air
Moeskroen see Mouscron
98 J13 **Moffat** S Scotland, UK 55.28N 3.36W
193 C22 **Moffat Peak** ▲ South Island, NZ 44.57S 168.10E
158 H8 **Moga** Punjab, N India 30.49N 75.13E
81 N19 **Moga** Sud Kivu, E Dem. Rep. Congo 2.16S 26.54E
Mogadiscio/Mogadishu see Muqdisho
Mogador see Essaouira
106 J6 **Mogadouro** Bragança, N Portugal 41.19N 6.43W
171 Ll12 **Mogami-gawa** ≈ Honshū, C Japan
178 Gg2 **Mogaung** Kachin State, N Burma 25.19N 96.54E
112 L13 **Mogielnica** Mazowieckie, C Poland 51.40N 20.42E
Mogilëv see Mahilyow
Mogilev-Podol'skiy see Mohyliv-Podil's'kyy
Mogilëvskaya Oblast' see Mahilyowskaya Voblasts'
112 I11 **Mogilno** Kujawsko-pomorskie, C Poland 52.39N 17.58E
62 L9 **Mogi-Mirim** var. Moji-Mirim. São Paulo, S Brazil 22.26S 46.55W
85 Q15 **Mogincual** Nampula, NE Mozambique 15.33S 40.28E
116 E13 **Moglenítsas** ≈ N Greece
108 H8 **Mogliano Veneto** Veneto, NE Italy 45.34N 12.13E
115 M21 **Moglicë** Korçë, SE Albania 40.43N 20.22E
126 L15 **Mogocha** Chitinskaya Oblast', S Russian Federation 53.39N 119.47E
126 H13 **Mogochin** Tomskaya Oblast', C Russian Federation 57.42N 83.24E
82 F13 **Mogogh** Jonglei, SE Sudan 8.25N 31.19E
176 Vv10 **Mogoi** Papua, E Indonesia 1.44S 133.13E
178 Gg4 **Mogok** Mandalay, C Burma 22.55N 96.28E
39 P14 **Mogollon Mountains** ▲▲ New Mexico, SW USA
38 M12 **Mogollon Rim** cliff Arizona, SW USA
63 E23 **Mogotes, Punta** headland E Argentina 38.03S 57.31W
44 J8 **Mogotón** ▲ NW Nicaragua 13.45N 86.22W
106 I14 **Moguer** Andalucía, S Spain 37.15N 6.52W
113 J26 **Mohács** Baranya, SW Hungary 46.00N 18.40E
193 C20 **Mohaka** ≈ North Island, NZ
30 M2 **Mohall** North Dakota, N USA 48.45N 101.30W
Moḩammadābād see Dargaz
76 F6 **Mohammedia** prev. Fédala. NW Morocco 33.46N 7.16W
76 F6 **Mohammed V** ✈ (Casablanca) W Morocco 33.07N 8.28W
Mohammerah see Khorramshahr
38 H10 **Mohave, Lake** ⊠ Arizona/Nevada, W USA
38 I12 **Mohave Mountains** ▲▲ Arizona, SW USA
38 I15 **Mohawk Mountains** ▲▲ Arizona, SW USA
20 J10 **Mohawk River** ≈ New York, NE USA
169 T3 **Mohe** var. Xilinji. Heilongjiang, NE China 53.00N 122.33E
97 L20 **Moheda** Kronoberg, S Sweden 57.00N 14.34E
180 H13 **Mohéli** var. Mwali, Mohilla, Mohila, Fr. Moili. island S Comoros
158 I11 **Mohendergarh** Haryāna, N India 28.16N 76.13E
40 K12 **Mohican, Cape** headland Nunivak Island, Alaska, USA 60.12N 167.25W
Mohn see Muhu
103 G15 **Möhne** ≈ W Germany
103 G15 **Möhne-Stausee** ⊠ W Germany
94 P2 **Mohn, Kapp** headland NW Svalbard 79.26N 25.44E
207 S14 **Mohns Ridge** undersea feature Greenland Sea/Norwegian Sea
59 I17 **Moho** Puno, SW Peru 15.21S 69.32W
Mohokare see Caledon
97 L17 **Moholm** Västra Götaland, S Sweden 58.37N 14.04E
38 J11 **Mohon Peak** ▲ Arizona, SW USA 34.55N 113.07W
83 J23 **Mohoro** Pwani, E Tanzania 8.09S 39.10E
Mohra see Moravice
Mohrungen see Morąg
118 M7 **Mohyliv-Podil's'kyy** Rus. Mogilev-Podol'skiy. Vinnyts'ka Oblast', C Ukraine 48.28N 27.49E
97 D17 **Moi** Rogaland, S Norway 58.27N 6.31E
197 I6 **Moindou** Province Sud, C New Caledonia 21.42S 165.40E
118 K11 **Moinești** Hung. Mojnest. Bacău, E Romania 46.27N 26.31E
Móinteach Mílic see Mountmellick
12 J14 **Moira** ≈ Ontario, SE Canada
94 G13 **Mo i Rana** Nordland, C Norway 66.19N 14.10E
159 X14 **Moirāng** Manipur, NE India 24.28N 93.45E
117 J25 **Moíres** Kríti, Greece, E Mediterranean Sea 35.03N 24.51E
120 H6 **Mõisaküla** Ger. Moiseküll. Viljandimaa, S Estonia 58.05N 25.11E
Moiseküll see Mõisaküla
13 W4 **Moisie** Québec, E Canada 50.12N 66.06W
13 W3 **Moisie** ≈ Québec, SE Canada
104 M14 **Moissac** Tarn-et-Garonne, S France 44.07N 1.04E
80 I13 **Moïssala** Moyen-Chari, S Chad 8.21N 17.46E
57 O7 **Moitaco** Bolívar, E Venezuela 8.00N 64.22W
97 P15 **Möja** Stockholm, C Sweden 59.25N 18.55E
107 Q14 **Mojácar** Andalucía, S Spain 37.09N 1.49W
37 T13 **Mojave** California, W USA 35.03N 118.10W
37 V13 **Mojave Desert** plain California, W USA
37 V13 **Mojave River** ≈ California, W USA
Moji-Mirim see Mogi-Mirim
115 K15 **Mojkovac** E-Montenegro 42.57N 19.34E
Mojnest see Moinești
174 Ll15 **Mojokerto** prev. Modjokerto. Jawa, C Indonesia 7.25S 112.31E
Mōka see Mooka
159 Q13 **Mokāma** prev. Mokameh, Mukama. Bihār, N India 25.24N 85.55E
81 O25 **Mokambo** Katanga, SE Dem. Rep. Congo 12.23S 28.21E
Mokameh see Mokāma
40 D9 **Mōkapu Point** var. Mokapu Point headland O'ahu, Hawai'i, USA, C Pacific Ocean 21.27N 157.43W
192 L9 **Mokau** Waikato, North Island, NZ 38.42S 174.37E
192 L9 **Mokau** ≈ North Island, NZ
37 P7 **Mokelumne River** ≈ California, W USA
85 J23 **Mokhotlong** NE Lesotho 29.19S 29.06E
Mokil Atoll see Mwokil Atoll
97 N14 **Möklinta** Västmanland, C Sweden 60.04N 16.34E
192 L4 **Mokohinau Islands** island group N NZ
159 X12 **Mokokchūng** Nāgāland, NE India 26.19N 94.30E
80 F12 **Mokolo** Extrême-Nord, N Cameroon 10.49N 13.54E
193 D24 **Mokoreta** ≈ South Island, NZ
85 J20 **Mokopane** prev. Potgietersrus. Limpopo, NE South Africa 24.09S 28.58E
169 X17 **Mokp'o** Jap. Moppo. SW South Korea 34.49N 126.26E
115 L16 **Mokra Gora** ▲▲ S Serbia
Mokrany see Makrany
131 O5 **Moksha** ≈ W Russian Federation
Moktama see Martaban
79 T14 **Mokwa** Niger, W Nigeria 9.19N 5.01E
101 J16 **Mol** prev. Moll. Antwerpen, N Belgium 51.10N 5.07E
109 O17 **Mola di Bari** Puglia, SE Italy 41.03N 17.04E
Molai see Moláoi
43 P13 **Molango** Hidalgo, C Mexico 20.48N 98.43W
117 F22 **Moláoi** var. Molai. Pelopónnisos, S Greece 36.47N 22.50E
43 Z12 **Molas del Norte, Punta** var. Punta Molas. headland SE Mexico 20.34N 86.43W
Molas, Punta see Molas del Norte, Punta
107 R11 **Molatón** ▲ C Spain 38.58N 1.19W
99 K18 **Mold** NE Wales, UK 53.10N 3.07W
Moldau see Moldova
Moldau see Vltava, Czech Republic
Moldavia see Moldova
Moldavian SSR/Moldavskaya SSR see Moldova
96 E9 **Molde** Møre og Romsdal, S Norway 62.43N 7.07E
Moldotau, Khrebet see Moldo-Too, Khrebet
153 V9 **Moldo-Too, Khrebet** prev. Khrebet Moldotau. ▲▲ C Kyrgyzstan
118 K9 **Moldova** ≈ N Romania
118 K9 **Moldova** Eng. Moldavia, Ger. Moldau. former province NE Romania
118 L9 **Moldova** off. Republic of Moldova, var. Moldavia; prev. Moldavian SSR, Rus. Moldavskaya SSR. ◆ republic SE Europe
118 F13 **Moldova Nouă** Ger. Neumoldowa, Hung. Újmoldova. Caraş-Severin, SW Romania 44.45N 21.39E
118 F13 **Moldova Veche** Ger. Altmoldowa, Hung. Ómoldova. Caraş-Severin, SW Romania 44.45N 21.13E
Moldoveanul see Vârful Moldoveanu
85 I20 **Molepolole** Kweneng, SE Botswana 24.25S 25.30E
46 L8 **Môle-St-Nicolas** NW Haiti 19.46N 73.19W
120 H13 **Molėtai** Utena, E Lithuania 55.14N 25.25E
109 O17 **Molfetta** Puglia, SE Italy 41.12N 16.34E
175 R8 **Molibagu** Sulawesi, N Indonesia 0.25N 123.57E
64 G12 **Molina** Maule, C Chile 35.06S 71.18W
107 Q7 **Molina de Aragón** Castilla-La Mancha, C Spain 40.49N 1.54W
107 R13 **Molina de Segura** Murcia, SE Spain 38.03N 1.10W
32 J11 **Moline** Illinois, N USA 41.30N 90.31W
29 P7 **Moline** Kansas, C USA 37.21N 96.18W
81 P23 **Moliro** Katanga, SE Dem. Rep. Congo 8.10S 30.31E
109 K16 **Molise** ◈ region S Italy
97 K15 **Molkom** Värmland, C Sweden 59.36N 13.43E
Moll see Mol
111 Q9 **Möll** ≈ S Austria
152 I14 **Mollanepes Adyndaky** Rus. Imeni Mollanepesa. Mary Welaýaty, S Turkmenistan 37.36N 61.54E
97 J22 **Mölle** Skåne, S Sweden 56.15N 12.19E
59 H18 **Mollendo** Arequipa, SW Peru 17.01S 72.01W
107 U5 **Mollerussa** Cataluña, NE Spain 41.37N 0.52E
110 H8 **Mollis** Glarus, NE Switzerland 47.05N 9.03E
97 J19 **Mölndal** Västra Götaland, S Sweden 57.39N 12.05E
97 J19 **Mölnlycke** Västra Götaland, S Sweden 57.42N 12.19E
119 U9 **Molochans'k** Rus. Molochansk. Zaporiz'ka Oblast', SE Ukraine 47.10N 35.38E
119 U10 **Molochna** Rus. Molochnaya. ≈ S Ukraine
Molochnaya see Molochna
119 U10 **Molochnyy Lyman** bay N Black Sea
Molodechno/Molodeczno see Maladzyechna
205 V3 **Molodezhnaya** Russian research station Antarctica 67.33S 46.12E
128 J14 **Mologa** ≈ NW Russian Federation
40 E9 **Moloka'i** var. Molokai. island Hawai'i, USA, C Pacific Ocean
183 X3 **Molokai Fracture Zone** tectonic feature NE Pacific Ocean
128 K15 **Molokovo** Tverskaya Oblast', W Russian Federation 58.10N 36.43E
129 Q14 **Moloma** ≈ NW Russian Federation
191 R8 **Molong** New South Wales, SE Australia 33.07S 148.52E
85 H21 **Molopo** seasonal river Botswana/South Africa
117 F17 **Mólos** Stereá Ellás, C Greece 38.48N 22.40E
175 Q7 **Molosipat** Sulawesi, N Indonesia 0.28N 121.08E
Molotov see Severodvinsk, Arkhangel'skaya Oblast', Russian Federation
Molotov see Perm', Permskaya Oblast', Russian Federation
81 G17 **Moloundou** Est, SE Cameroon 2.03N 15.13E
105 U5 **Molsheim** Bas-Rhin, NE France 48.33N 7.30E
15 L12 **Molson Lake** ◎ Manitoba, C Canada
Moluccas see Maluku
175 Rr8 **Molucca Sea** Ind. Laut Maluku. sea E Indonesia
Molukken see Maluku
85 O15 **Molumbo** Zambézia, N Mozambique 15.33S 36.19E
176 Uu14 **Molu, Pulau** island Maluku, E Indonesia
85 P16 **Moma** Nampula, NE Mozambique 16.42S 39.12E
176 Xx13 **Momats** ≈ Papua, E Indonesia
44 J11 **Mombacho, Volcán** 🌋 SW Nicaragua 11.49N 85.58W
83 K21 **Mombasa** Coast, SE Kenya 4.04N 39.40E
83 J21 **Mombasa** ✈ Coast, SE Kenya 4.01S 39.31E
Mombetsu see Monbetsu
176 Y16 **Mombum** Papua, E Indonesia 8.16S 138.51E
116 J12 **Momchilgrad** prev. Mastanli. Kŭrdzhali, S Bulgaria 41.33N 25.25E
101 F23 **Momignies** Hainaut, S Belgium 50.02N 4.10E
56 E6 **Momil** Córdoba, NW Colombia 9.15N 75.40W
44 I10 **Momotombo, Volcán** 🌋 W Nicaragua 12.25N 86.33W
58 B5 **Mompiche, Ensenada de** bay NW Ecuador
81 K18 **Mompono** Equateur, NW Dem. Rep. Congo 0.11N 21.31E
56 F6 **Mompós** Bolívar, NW Colombia 9.10N 74.21W
97 J24 **Møn** prev. Möen. island SE Denmark
38 L4 **Mona** Utah, W USA 39.49N 111.52W
Mona, Canal de la see Mona Passage
98 E8 **Monach Islands** island group NW Scotland, UK
105 V14 **Monaco** var. Monaco-Ville; anc. Monoecus. ● (Monaco) S Monaco 43.46N 7.22E
105 V14 **Monaco** off. Principality of Monaco. ◆ monarchy W Europe
Monaco see München
Monaco Basin see Canary Basin
Monaco-Ville see Monaco
98 I9 **Monadhliath Mountains** ▲▲ N Scotland, UK
57 O6 **Monagas** off. Estado Monagas. ◈ state NE Venezuela
99 F16 **Monaghan** Ir. Muineachán. N Ireland 54.15N 6.58W
99 E16 **Monaghan** Ir. Muineachán. cultural region N Ireland
45 S16 **Monagrillo** Herrera, S Panama 7.58N 80.23W
26 L8 **Monahans** Texas, SW USA 31.33N 102.52W
47 Q9 **Mona, Isla** island W Puerto Rico
47 Q9 **Mona Passage** Sp. Canal de la Mona. channel Dominican Republic/Puerto Rico
45 O14 **Mona, Punta** headland E Costa Rica 9.44N 82.48W
161 K25 **Monaragala** Uva Province, SE Sri Lanka 6.52N 81.22E
35 S9 **Monarch** Montana, NW USA 47.04N 110.51W
14 Ff14 **Monarch Mountain** ▲ British Columbia, SW Canada 51.59N 125.56W
Monasterio see Monesterio
Monasterzyska see Monastyrys'ka

◆ Country
● Country Capital
◇ Dependent Territory
○ Dependent Territory Capital
◈ Administrative Region
✈ International Airport
▲ Mountain
▲▲ Mountain Range
🌋 Volcano
≈ River
◎ Lake
⊠ Reservoir

MONASTIR – MOROCCO

Monastir *see* Bitola
Monastyriska *see* Monastyrys'ka
119 O7 **Monastyryshche** Cherkas'ka Oblast', C Ukraine 48.59N 29.47E
118 J6 **Monastyrys'ka** *Pol.* Monasterzyska, *Rus.* Monastyriska. Ternopil's'ka Oblast', W Ukraine 49.04N 25.10E
81 E15 **Monatélé** Centre, SW Cameroon 4.16N 11.12E
172 Q4 **Monbetsu** *var.* Mombetsu, Monbetu. Hokkaidō, NE Japan 44.22N 143.22E
Monbetu *see* Monbetsu
108 B8 **Moncalieri** Piemonte, NW Italy 45.00N 7.41E
106 G4 **Monção** Viana do Castelo, N Portugal 42.03N 8.29W
107 Q5 **Moncayo** ▲ N Spain 41.43N 1.51W
107 Q5 **Moncayo, Sierra del** ▲▲ N Spain
128 J4 **Monchegorsk** Murmanskaya Oblast', NW Russian Federation 67.55N 32.46E
103 D15 **Mönchengladbach** *prev.* München-Gladbach. Nordrhein-Westfalen, W Germany 51.12N 6.25E
106 F14 **Monchique** Faro, S Portugal 37.19N 8.33W
106 G14 **Monchique, Serra de** ▲▲ S Portugal
23 S14 **Moncks Corner** South Carolina, SE USA 33.12N 80.00W
43 N7 **Monclova** Coahuila de Zaragoza, NE Mexico 26.55N 101.25W
Moncorvo *see* Torre de Moncorvo
11 P14 **Moncton** New Brunswick, SE Canada 46.04N 64.49W
106 F8 **Mondego, Cabo** *headland* N Portugal 40.10N 8.58W
106 G8 **Mondego, Rio** ≈ N Portugal
106 I2 **Mondoñedo** Galicia, NW Spain 43.25N 7.22W
101 N25 **Mondorf-les-Bains** Grevenmacher, SE Luxembourg 49.30N 6.16E
104 M7 **Mondoubleau** Loir-et-Cher, C France 48.00N 0.49E
32 J6 **Mondovi** Wisconsin, N USA 44.34N 91.40W
108 B9 **Mondovì** Piemonte, NW Italy 44.22N 7.55E
Mondragón *see* Arrasate
109 J17 **Mondragone** Campania, S Italy 41.07N 13.52E
111 R5 **Mondsee** ◎ N Austria
126 J16 **Mondy** Respublika Buryatiya, S Russian Federation 51.41N 101.03E
117 G22 **Monemvasiá** *var.* Monemvasía. Pelopónnisos, S Greece 36.22N 23.03E
20 B15 **Monessen** Pennsylvania, NE USA 40.07N 79.51W
106 J12 **Monesterio** *var.* Monasterio. Extremadura, W Spain 38.04N 6.16W
12 L8 **Monet** Québec, SE Canada 48.09N 75.37W
29 S8 **Monett** Missouri, C USA 36.55N 93.55W
29 X9 **Monette** Arkansas, C USA 35.53N 90.20W
12 G11 **Monetville** Ontario, S Canada 46.08N 80.24W
108 J7 **Monfalcone** Friuli-Venezia Giulia, NE Italy 45.49N 13.31E
106 H10 **Monforte** Portalegre, C Portugal 39.03N 7.25W
106 I4 **Monforte de Lemos** Galicia, NW Spain 42.31N 7.30W
83 I24 **Monga** Lindi, SE Tanzania 9.05S 37.51E
81 L16 **Monga** Orientale, N Dem. Rep. Congo 4.12N 22.49E
83 F15 **Mongalla** Bahr el Gabel, S Sudan 5.12N 31.42E
159 U11 **Mongar** E Bhutan 27.16N 91.07E
178 K6 **Mong Cai** *var.* Hai Ninh. Quang Ninh, N Vietnam 21.33N 107.56E
188 I11 **Mongers Lake** *salt lake* Western Australia
195 U14 **Mongga** Kolombangara, NW Solomon Islands 7.51S 157.00E
178 Hh6 **Möng Hpayak** Shan State, E Burma 20.56N 100.00E
Monghyr *see* Munger
108 B10 **Mongioie** ▲ NW Italy 44.13N 7.46E
178 Gg5 **Möng Küng** Shan State, E Burma 21.39N 97.31E
Mongla *see* Mungla
196 C15 **Mongmong** C Guam
178 Gg6 **Möng Nai** Shan State, E Burma 20.28N 97.51E
80 I11 **Mongo** Guéra, C Chad 12.11N 18.39E
78 I14 **Mongo** ≈ N Sierra Leone
169 I8 **Mongolia** *Mong.* Mongol Uls. ◆ *republic* E Asia
133 V8 **Mongolia, Plateau of** *plateau* E Mongolia
Mongolküre *see* Zhaosu
Mongol Uls *see* Mongolia
81 E17 **Mongomo** E Equatorial Guinea 1.39N 11.18E
168 M7 **Möngönmorït** *var.* Bulag. Töv, C Mongolia 48.09N 108.33E
79 Y12 **Mongonu** *var.* Monguno. Borno, NE Nigeria 12.42N 13.37E
Mongora *see* Mingāora
80 K11 **Mongororo** Ouaddaï, SE Chad 12.03N 22.26E
Mongos, Chaîne des *see* Bongo, Massif des
81 I16 **Mongoumba** Lobaye, SW Central African Republic 3.39N 18.30E
Mongrove, Punta *see* Cayacal, Punta
85 G15 **Mongu** Western, W Zambia 15.13S 23.09E
78 I10 **Mônguel** Gorgol, SW Mauritania 16.25N 13.07W
Monguno *see* Mongonu
178 H4 **Möng Yai** Shan State, E Burma 22.25N 98.02E
178 Hh5 **Möng Yang** Shan State, E Burma 21.52N 99.31E
178 H3 **Möng Yu** Shan State, E Burma 24.00N 97.57E
Mönhbulag *see* Yösöndzüyl
169 O8 **Mönhhaan** *var.* Bayasgalant. Sühbaatar, E Mongolia 46.55N 112.11E
168 E7 **Mönhhayrhan** *var.* Tsenher. Hovd, W Mongolia 47.07N 92.04E
Mönh Sarïdag *see* Munku-Sardyk, Gora
194 L15 **Moni** ≈ S Papau New Guinea
117 I15 **Moní Megístis Lávras** *monastery* Kentrikí Makedonía, N Greece 40.10N 24.22E
117 F18 **Moní Osíou Loúkas** *monastery* Stereá Ellás, C Greece 38.22N 22.42E
56 F9 **Moniquirá** Boyacá, C Colombia 5.57N 73.35W
105 Q12 **Monistrol-sur-Loire** Haute-Loire, C France 45.19N 4.12E
37 V7 **Monitor Range** ▲▲ Nevada, W USA
117 I14 **Moní Vatopedíou** *monastery* Kentrikí Makedonía, N Greece 40.19N 24.13E
179 Rr15 **Monkayo** Mindanao, S Philippines 7.45N 125.58E
Monkchester *see* Newcastle upon Tyne
85 N14 **Monkey Bay** Southern, SE Malawi 14.09S 34.53E
45 N11 **Monkey Point** *var.* Punta Mico, Punte Mono, Punto Mico. *headland* SE Nicaragua 11.37N 83.39W
Monkey River *see* Monkey River Town
44 G3 **Monkey River Town** *var.* Monkey River. Toledo, SE Belize 16.22N 88.28W
12 M13 **Monkland** Ontario, SE Canada 45.11N 74.51W
81 J19 **Monkoto** Equateur, NW Dem. Rep. Congo 1.35S 20.43E
99 K21 **Monmouth** *Wel.* Trefynwy. SE Wales, UK 51.49N 2.43W
32 J12 **Monmouth** Illinois, N USA 40.54N 90.39W
34 F12 **Monmouth** Oregon, NW USA 44.51N 123.13W
99 K21 **Monmouth** *cultural region* SE Wales, UK
100 I10 **Monnickendam** Noord-Holland, C Netherlands 52.28N 5.01E
79 R15 **Mono** ≈ C Togo
Monoecus *see* Monaco
37 R8 **Mono Lake** ◎ California, W USA
117 O23 **Monólithos** Ródos, Dodekánisa, Greece, Aegean Sea 36.08N 27.45E
21 Q12 **Monomoy Island** *island* Massachusetts, NE USA
33 O12 **Monon** Indiana, N USA 40.52N 86.54W
31 Y12 **Monona** Iowa, C USA 43.03N 91.23W
32 L9 **Monona** Wisconsin, N USA 43.03N 89.18W
20 B15 **Monongahela** Pennsylvania, NE USA 40.10N 79.54W
20 B16 **Monongahela River** ≈ NE USA
109 P17 **Monopoli** Puglia, SE Italy 40.57N 17.18E
Mono, Punte *see* Monkey Point
113 K23 **Monor** Pest, C Hungary 47.19N 19.28E
Monostor *see* Beli Manastir
80 K8 **Monou** Borkou-Ennedi-Tibesti, NE Chad 16.22N 22.15E
107 S12 **Monovar** *Cat.* Monover. País Valenciano, E Spain 38.25N 0.49W
Monover *see* Monovar
107 R7 **Monreal del Campo** Aragón, NE Spain 40.46N 1.19W
109 I23 **Monreale** Sicilia, Italy, C Mediterranean Sea 38.04N 13.16E
25 T3 **Monroe** Georgia, SE USA 33.47N 83.42W
31 W14 **Monroe** Iowa, C USA 41.31N 93.06W
24 I5 **Monroe** Louisiana, S USA 32.31N 92.06W
33 S10 **Monroe** Michigan, N USA 41.55N 83.24W
20 K13 **Monroe** New York, NE USA 41.18N 74.09W
23 S11 **Monroe** North Carolina, SE USA 34.59N 80.33W
38 L6 **Monroe** Utah, W USA 38.37N 112.07W
34 H7 **Monroe** Washington, NW USA 47.51N 121.58W
32 L9 **Monroe** Wisconsin, N USA 42.34N 89.39W
29 V3 **Monroe City** Missouri, C USA 39.39N 91.43W
33 O15 **Monroe Lake** ⊠ Indiana, N USA
25 O7 **Monroeville** Alabama, S USA 31.31N 87.19W
20 C15 **Monroeville** Pennsylvania, NE USA 40.24N 79.44W
78 J16 **Monrovia** ● (Liberia) W Liberia 6.18N 10.48W
78 J16 **Monrovia** ✕ W Liberia 6.22N 10.50W
107 T7 **Monroyo** Aragón, NE Spain 40.46N 0.03W
101 F20 **Mons** *Dut.* Bergen. Hainaut, S Belgium 50.28N 3.58E
106 I8 **Monsanto** Castelo Branco, C Portugal 40.01N 7.07W
108 H8 **Monselice** Veneto, NE Italy 45.15N 11.47E
178 Gg9 **Mon State** ◈ *state* S Burma
100 G12 **Monster** Zuid-Holland, W Netherlands 52.01N 4.10E
97 N20 **Mönsterås** Kalmar, S Sweden 57.03N 16.27E
103 F17 **Montabaur** Rheinland-Pfalz, W Germany 50.25N 7.48E
108 G8 **Montagnana** Veneto, NE Italy 45.14N 11.31E
37 N1 **Montague** California, W USA 41.43N 122.31W
27 S5 **Montague** Texas, SW USA 33.39N 97.41W
191 S11 **Montague Island** *island* New South Wales, SE Australia
41 S12 **Montague Island** *island* Alaska, USA
41 S13 **Montague Strait** *strait* N Gulf of Alaska
104 J8 **Montaigu** Vendée, NW France 46.58N 1.18W
Montaigu *see* Scherpenheuvel
107 S7 **Montalbán** Aragón, NE Spain 40.49N 0.48W
108 G13 **Montalcino** Toscana, C Italy 43.01N 11.34E
106 H5 **Montalegre** Vila Real, N Portugal 41.49N 7.48W
116 G8 **Montana** *prev.* Ferdinand, Mikhaylovgrad. Montana, NW Bulgaria 43.25N 23.14E
110 D10 **Montana** Valais, SW Switzerland 46.23N 7.29E
41 R11 **Montana** Alaska, USA 62.06N 150.03W
116 G8 **Montana** ◈ *province* NW Bulgaria
35 T9 **Montana** *off.* State of Montana; also known as Mountain State, Treasure State. ◈ *state* NW USA
106 J10 **Montánchez** Extremadura, W Spain 39.15N 6.07W
Montañita *see* La Montañita
13 Q8 **Mont-Apica** Québec, SE Canada 47.57N 71.24W
106 G10 **Montargil** Portalegre, C Portugal 39.04N 8.10W
106 G10 **Montargil, Barragem de** ⊠ C Portugal
105 O7 **Montargis** Loiret, C France 48.00N 2.43E
105 O4 **Montataire** Oise, N France 49.16N 2.24E
104 M14 **Montauban** Tarn-et-Garonne, S France 44.01N 1.19E
21 N14 **Montauk** Long Island, New York, NE USA 41.01N 71.58W
21 N14 **Montauk Point** *headland* Long Island, New York, NE USA 41.04N 71.51W
105 Q7 **Montbard** Côte d'Or, C France 47.35N 4.25E
105 U7 **Montbéliard** Doubs, E France 47.31N 6.49E
27 W11 **Mont Belvieu** Texas, SW USA 29.51N 94.53W
107 U6 **Montblanc** *var.* Montblanch. Cataluña, NE Spain 41.22N 1.10E
Montblanch *see* Montblanc
105 Q11 **Montbrison** Loire, E France 45.37N 4.04E
Montcalm, Lake *see* Dogai Coring
105 Q9 **Montceau-les-Mines** Saône-et-Loire, C France 46.40N 4.19E
105 U12 **Mont Cenis, Col du** *pass* E France 45.16N 6.54E
104 K15 **Mont-de-Marsan** Landes, SW France 43.54N 0.30W
105 O3 **Montdidier** Somme, N France 49.39N 2.34E
197 J7 **Mont-Dore** Province Sud, S New Caledonia 22.18S 166.34E
22 K10 **Monteagle** Tennessee, S USA 35.15N 85.47W
59 M20 **Monteagudo** Chuquisaca, S Bolivia 19.48S 63.57W
43 R16 **Monte Albán** *ruins* Oaxaca, S Mexico 17.01N 96.46W
107 R11 **Montealegre del Castillo** Castilla-La Mancha, C Spain 38.48N 1.18W
61 N18 **Monte Azul** Minas Gerais, SE Brazil 15.13S 42.52W
12 M12 **Montebello** Québec, SE Canada 45.40N 74.55W
108 H7 **Montebelluna** Veneto, NE Italy 45.46N 12.03E
62 G13 **Montecarlo** Misiones, NE Argentina 26.37S 54.45W
63 D16 **Monte Caseros** Corrientes, NE Argentina 30.15S 57.39W
62 J13 **Monte Castelo** Santa Catarina, S Brazil 26.34S 50.12W
108 F11 **Montecatini Terme** Toscana, C Italy 43.52N 10.46E
44 H7 **Montecillos, Cordillera de** ▲▲ W Honduras
64 I12 **Monte Comén** Mendoza, W Argentina 34.34S 67.52W
46 M8 **Monte Cristi** *var.* San Fernando de Monte Cristi. NW Dominican Republic 19.52N 71.39W
60 C13 **Monte Cristo** Amazonas, W Brazil 3.13S 68.00W
109 E14 **Montecristo, Isola di** *island* Archipelago Toscano, C Italy
Monte Croce Carnico, Passo di *see* Plöcken Pass
60 J12 **Monte Dourado** Pará, NE Brazil 0.48S 52.32W
42 L11 **Monte Escobedo** Zacatecas, C Mexico 22.19N 103.30W
108 I13 **Montefalco** Umbria, C Italy 42.54N 12.40E
109 H14 **Montefiascone** Lazio, C Italy 42.33N 12.01E
107 N14 **Montefrío** Andalucía, S Spain 37.19N 4.00W
46 I11 **Montego Bay** *var.* Mobay. W Jamaica 18.28N 77.55W
Montego Bay *see* Sangster
106 J8 **Montehermoso** Extremadura, W Spain 40.04N 6.19W
106 F10 **Montejunto, Serra de** ▲ C Portugal 39.10N 9.01W
Monteleone di Calabria *see* Vibo Valentia
56 E7 **Montelíbano** Córdoba, NW Colombia 7.58N 75.24W
105 R13 **Montélimar** *anc.* Acunum Acusio, Montilium Adhemari. Drôme, E France 44.33N 4.45E
106 K15 **Montellano** Andalucía, S Spain 37.00N 5.34W
37 Y2 **Montello** Nevada, W USA 41.18N 114.10W
32 L8 **Montello** Wisconsin, N USA 43.46N 89.19W
65 J18 **Montemayor, Meseta de** *plain* SE Argentina
43 O9 **Montemorelos** Nuevo León, NE Mexico 25.10N 99.51W
106 G11 **Montemor-o-Novo** Évora, S Portugal 38.37N 8.13W
106 G8 **Montemor-o-Velho** *var.* Montemor-o-Vélho. Coimbra, N Portugal 40.10N 8.40W
106 H7 **Montemuro, Serra de** ▲ N Portugal 40.59N 7.59W
104 K12 **Montendre** Charente-Maritime, W France 45.17N 0.24W
63 I15 **Montenegro** Rio Grande do Sul, S Brazil 29.40S 51.32W
115 J16 **Montenegro** *Serb.* Crna Gora. ◆ *republic* SE-Europe
64 G10 **Monte Patria** Coquimbo, N Chile 30.40S 71.00W
47 O9 **Monte Plata** E Dominican Republic 18.46N 69.43W
85 P14 **Montepuez** Cabo Delgado, N Mozambique 13.11S 38.59E
85 P14 **Montepuez** ≈ N Mozambique
108 G13 **Montepulciano** Toscana, C Italy 43.02N 11.51E
64 L6 **Monte Quemado** Santiago del Estero, N Argentina 25.46S 62.51W
105 O6 **Montereau-Faut-Yonne** *anc.* Condate. Seine-St-Denis, N France 48.22N 2.57E
37 N11 **Monterey** California, W USA 36.36N 121.53W
22 L9 **Monterey** Tennessee, S USA 36.09N 85.16W
23 T5 **Monterey** Virginia, NE USA 38.24N 79.33W
Monterey *see* Monterrey
37 N10 **Monterey Bay** *bay* California, W USA
56 D6 **Montería** Córdoba, NW Colombia 8.45N 75.54W
59 N18 **Montero** Santa Cruz, C Bolivia 17.19S 63.15W
64 J7 **Monteros** Tucumán, C Argentina 27.12S 65.30W
106 I5 **Monterrei** Galicia, NW Spain 41.55N 7.27W
43 O8 **Monterrey** *var.* Monterey. Nuevo León, NE Mexico 25.40N 100.16W
34 F9 **Montesano** Washington, NW USA 46.58N 123.37W
109 M19 **Montesano sulla Marcellana** Campania, S Italy 40.15N 15.41E
109 N16 **Monte Sant' Angelo** Puglia, SE Italy 41.43N 15.58E
61 O16 **Monte Santo** Bahia, E Brazil 10.25S 39.18W
109 D18 **Monte Santu, Capo di** *headland* Sardegna, Italy, C Mediterranean Sea 40.05N 9.43E
61 M19 **Montes Claros** Minas Gerais, SE Brazil 16.45S 43.52W
109 K14 **Montesilvano Marina** Abruzzo, C Italy 42.28N 14.07E
25 P4 **Montevallo** Alabama, S USA 33.06N 86.51W
108 G12 **Montevarchi** Toscana, C Italy 43.31N 11.34E
31 S9 **Montevideo** Minnesota, N USA 44.56N 95.43W
63 F20 **Montevideo** ● (Uruguay) Montevideo, S Uruguay 34.55S 56.10W
39 S7 **Monte Vista** Colorado, C USA 37.33N 106.08W
25 T5 **Montezuma** Georgia, SE USA 32.18N 84.01W
31 W14 **Montezuma** Iowa, C USA 41.35N 92.31W
28 J6 **Montezuma** Kansas, C USA 37.33N 100.25W
105 U12 **Montgenèvre, Col de** *pass* France/Italy 44.56N 6.45E
99 K20 **Montgomery** E Wales, UK 52.37N 3.05W
25 Q5 **Montgomery** *state capital* Alabama, S USA 32.22N 86.18W
31 V9 **Montgomery** Minnesota, N USA 44.26N 93.34W
20 G13 **Montgomery** Pennsylvania, NE USA 41.08N 76.52W
23 Q5 **Montgomery** West Virginia, NE USA 38.07N 81.19W
99 K19 **Montgomery** *cultural region* E Wales, UK
Montgomery *see* Sāhīwāl
29 V4 **Montgomery City** Missouri, C USA 38.58N 91.30W
37 S8 **Montgomery Pass** *pass* Nevada, W USA 37.57N 118.21W
104 K12 **Montguyon** Charente-Maritime, W France 45.12N 0.13W
110 C10 **Monthey** Valais, SW Switzerland 46.15N 6.55E
29 V13 **Monticello** Arkansas, C USA 33.37N 91.44W
25 T4 **Monticello** Florida, SE USA 30.33N 83.52W
25 T8 **Monticello** Georgia, SE USA 33.18N 83.40W
32 M13 **Monticello** Illinois, N USA 40.01N 88.34W
33 O12 **Monticello** Indiana, N USA 40.45N 86.46W
31 Y13 **Monticello** Iowa, C USA 42.14N 91.11W
22 L7 **Monticello** Kentucky, S USA 36.51N 84.51W
31 V8 **Monticello** Minnesota, N USA 45.19N 93.45W
24 K7 **Monticello** Mississippi, S USA 31.33N 90.06W
29 V2 **Monticello** Missouri, C USA 40.07N 91.42W
20 J12 **Monticello** New York, NE USA 41.39N 74.41W
39 O7 **Monticello** Utah, W USA 37.52N 109.20W
108 F8 **Montichiari** Lombardia, N Italy 45.24N 10.27E
104 M12 **Montignac** Dordogne, SW France 45.24N 0.54E
101 G21 **Montignies-le-Tilleul** *var.* Montigny-le-Tilleul. Hainaut, S Belgium 50.22N 4.22E
12 J8 **Montigny, Lac de** ◎ Québec, SE Canada
105 S6 **Montigny-le-Roi** Haute-Marne, N France 48.02N 5.28E
Montigny-le-Tilleul *see* Montignies-le-Tilleul
45 R16 **Montijo** Veraguas, S Panama 7.58N 81.12W
106 F11 **Montijo** Setúbal, W Portugal 38.42N 8.58W
106 J11 **Montijo** Extremadura, W Spain 38.55N 6.37W
Montilium Adhemari *see* Montélimar
106 M13 **Montilla** Andalucía, S Spain 37.36N 4.39W
104 L3 **Montivilliers** Seine-Maritime, N France 49.31N 0.10E
13 U7 **Mont-Joli** Québec, SE Canada 48.33N 68.12W
12 M10 **Mont-Laurier** Québec, SE Canada 46.33N 75.31W
13 X5 **Mont-Louis** Québec, SE Canada 49.13N 65.44W
105 N17 **Mont-Louis** *var.* Mont Louis. Pyrénées-Orientales, S France 42.30N 2.07E
105 O10 **Montluçon** Allier, C France 46.21N 2.37E
13 R10 **Montmagny** Québec, SE Canada 47.00N 70.31W
105 S3 **Montmédy** Meuse, NE France 49.31N 5.21E
105 P5 **Montmirail** Marne, N France 48.53N 3.31E
13 R9 **Montmorency** ≈ Québec, SE Canada
104 M10 **Montmorillon** Vienne, W France 46.25N 0.52E
109 J14 **Montorio al Vomano** Abruzzo, C Italy 42.31N 13.39E
106 M13 **Montoro** Andalucía, S Spain 38.00N 4.21W
35 S16 **Montpelier** Idaho, NW USA 42.19N 111.18W
31 P6 **Montpelier** North Dakota, N USA 46.40N 98.34W
20 M7 **Montpelier** *state capital* Vermont, NE USA 44.15N 72.32W
105 Q15 **Montpellier** Hérault, S France 43.37N 3.52E
104 L12 **Montpon-Ménestérol** Dordogne, SW France 45.01N 0.10E
10 K15 **Montréal** *Eng.* Montreal. Québec, SE Canada 45.30N 73.36W
12 C8 **Montreal** ≈ Ontario, S Canada
12 G8 **Montreal** ≈ Ontario, S Canada
Montreal *see* Mirabel
9 T14 **Montreal Lake** ◎ Saskatchewan, C Canada
12 B9 **Montreal River** Ontario, S Canada 47.13N 84.36W
105 N2 **Montreuil** Pas-de-Calais, N France 50.28N 1.46E
104 K8 **Montreuil-Bellay** Maine-et-Loire, NW France 47.07N 0.10W
110 C10 **Montreux** Vaud, SW Switzerland 46.27N 6.55E
110 B9 **Montricher** Vaud, W Switzerland 46.37N 6.24E
98 K10 **Montrose** E Scotland, UK 56.43N 2.28W
29 W14 **Montrose** Arkansas, C USA 33.18N 91.29W
39 Q6 **Montrose** Colorado, C USA 38.28N 107.52W
31 Y16 **Montrose** Iowa, C USA 40.31N 91.24W
20 H12 **Montrose** Pennsylvania, NE USA 41.49N 75.52W
23 X5 **Montross** Virginia, NE USA 38.04N 76.50W
13 O12 **Mont-St-Hilaire** Québec, SE Canada 45.34N 73.10W
105 S3 **Mont-St-Martin** Meurthe-et-Moselle, NE France 49.31N 5.51E
47 V10 **Montserrat** *var.* Emerald Isle. ◇ *UK dependent territory* E West Indies
107 V5 **Montserrat** ▲ NE Spain 41.39N 1.44E
106 M7 **Montuenga** Castilla-León, N Spain 41.04N 4.37W
101 M19 **Montzen** Liège, E Belgium 50.42N 5.59E
39 N8 **Monument Valley** *valley* Arizona/Utah, SW USA
177 G4 **Monywa** Sagaing, C Burma 22.04N 95.12E
108 D7 **Monza** Lombardia, N Italy 45.34N 9.16E
85 J15 **Monze** Southern, S Zambia 16.19S 27.29E
107 T5 **Monzón** Aragón, NE Spain 41.54N 0.12E
27 T9 **Moody** Texas, SW USA 31.18N 97.21W
100 L13 **Mook** Limburg, SE Netherlands 51.45N 5.52E
171 Kk15 **Mooka** *var.* Mōka. Tochigi, Honshū, S Japan 36.28N 140.01E
190 K3 **Moomba** South Australia 28.07S 140.12E
12 G13 **Moon** ≈ Ontario, S Canada
Moon *see* Muhu
189 Y10 **Moonie** Queensland, E Australia 27.45S 150.22E
198 B10 **Moonless Mountains** *undersea feature* E Pacific Ocean
190 L13 **Moonlight Head** *headland* Victoria, SE Australia 38.47S 143.12E
Moon-Sund *see* Väinameri
190 H8 **Moonta** South Australia 34.03S 137.36E
Moor *see* Mór
188 I12 **Moora** Western Australia 30.22S 116.04E
100 H12 **Moordrecht** Zuid-Holland, C Netherlands 51.58N 4.40E
35 T9 **Moore** Montana, NW USA 47.00N 109.40W
29 N11 **Moore** Oklahoma, C USA 35.20N 97.29W
27 R12 **Moore** Texas, SW USA 29.03N 99.01W
203 S10 **Moorea** *island* Îles du Vent, W French Polynesia
23 U3 **Moorefield** West Virginia, NE USA 39.03N 78.58W
25 X14 **Moore Haven** Florida, SE USA 26.49N 81.05W
188 J11 **Moore, Lake** ◎ Western Australia
21 N7 **Moore Reservoir** ⊠ New Hampshire/Vermont, NE USA
46 G1 **Moores Island** *island* N Bahamas
23 R10 **Mooresville** North Carolina, SE USA 35.34N 80.48W
31 R5 **Moorhead** Minnesota, N USA 46.51N 96.43W
24 K4 **Moorhead** Mississippi, S USA 33.27N 90.30W
176 Ww10 **Moor, Kepulauan** *island group* E Indonesia
101 F18 **Moorsel** Oost-Vlaanderen, C Belgium 50.58N 4.06E
101 C18 **Moorslede** West-Vlaanderen, W Belgium 50.53N 3.03E
20 L8 **Moosalamoo, Mount** ▲ Vermont, NE USA 43.55N 73.03W
103 M22 **Moosburg an der Isar** Bayern, SE Germany 48.28N 11.55E
35 S14 **Moose** Wyoming, C USA 43.38N 110.42W
10 H11 **Moose** ≈ Ontario, S Canada
10 H10 **Moose Factory** Ontario, S Canada 51.16N 80.31W
21 Q4 **Moosehead Lake** ◎ Maine, NE USA
9 U16 **Moose Jaw** Saskatchewan, S Canada 50.25N 105.29W
9 V14 **Moose Lake** Manitoba, C Canada 53.42N 100.22W
31 W6 **Moose Lake** Minnesota, N USA 46.28N 92.46W
21 P6 **Mooselookmeguntic Lake** ◎ Maine, NE USA
41 R12 **Moose Pass** Alaska, USA 60.28N 149.21W
21 P5 **Moose River** ≈ Maine, NE USA
20 J9 **Moose River** ≈ New York, NE USA
9 V16 **Moosomin** Saskatchewan, S Canada 50.09N 101.40W
10 H10 **Moosonee** Ontario, SE Canada 51.18N 80.40W
21 N12 **Moosup** Connecticut, NE USA 41.42N 71.51W
85 N16 **Mopeia** Zambézia, NE Mozambique 17.58S 35.43E
85 H18 **Mopipi** Central, C Botswana 21.10S 24.54E
Moppo *see* Mokp'o
79 N11 **Mopti** Mopti, C Mali 14.30N 4.15W
79 O11 **Mopti** ◈ *region* S Mali
59 H18 **Moquegua** Moquegua, SE Peru 17.12S 70.55W
59 H18 **Moquegua** *off.* Departamento de Moquegua. ◈ *department* S Peru
113 I23 **Mór** *Ger.* Moor. Fejér, C Hungary 47.21N 18.13E
80 G11 **Mora** Extrême-Nord, N Cameroon 11.01N 14.07E
106 G11 **Mora** Évora, S Portugal 38.55N 8.10W
107 N9 **Mora** Castilla-La Mancha, C Spain 39.40N 3.46W
96 L12 **Mora** Dalarna, C Sweden 61.00N 14.30E
31 V7 **Mora** Minnesota, N USA 45.52N 93.18W
39 T10 **Mora** New Mexico, SW USA 35.56N 105.16W
115 J17 **Morača** ≈ S-Montenegro
158 K10 **Morādābād** Uttar Pradesh, N India 28.49N 78.45E
107 U6 **Móra d'Ebre** *var.* Mora de Ebro. Cataluña, NE Spain 41.04N 0.37E
Mora de Ebro *see* Móra d'Ebre
107 S8 **Mora de Rubielos** Aragón, NE Spain 40.15N 0.45W
180 H4 **Morafenobe** Mahajanga, W Madagascar 17.49S 44.54E
112 K8 **Morąg** *Ger.* Mohrungen. Warmińsko-Mazurskie, NE Poland 53.55N 19.55E
113 L25 **Mórahalom** Csongrád, S Hungary 46.13N 19.51E
107 N11 **Moral de Calatrava** Castilla-La Mancha, C Spain 38.49N 3.34W
65 G19 **Moraleda, Canal** *strait* SE Pacific Ocean
56 J3 **Morales** Bolívar, N Colombia 8.16N 73.52W
56 D12 **Morales** Cauca, SW Colombia 2.43N 76.36W
44 F5 **Morales** Izabal, E Guatemala 15.29N 88.46W
180 J5 **Moramanga** Toamasina, E Madagascar 18.57S 48.13E
29 Q6 **Moran** Kansas, C USA 37.55N 95.10W
27 Q7 **Moran** Texas, SW USA 32.33N 99.10W
189 X7 **Moranbah** Queensland, NE Australia 22.01S 148.07E
46 L13 **Morant Bay** E Jamaica 17.52N 76.24W
98 G10 **Morar, Loch** ◎ N Scotland, UK
Morata *see* Goodenough Island
107 Q12 **Moratalla** Murcia, SE Spain 38.10N 1.52W
110 C8 **Morat, Lac de** *Ger.* Murtensee. ◎ W Switzerland
86 I11 **Morava** *var.* March. ≈ C Europe *see also* March
Morava *see* Moravia, Czech Republic
Morava *see* Velika Morava, Serbia
31 W15 **Moravia** Iowa, C USA 40.53N 92.49W
113 F18 **Moravia** *Cz.* Morava, *Ger.* Mähren. *cultural region* E Czech Republic
113 H17 **Moravice** *Ger.* Mohra. ≈ NE Czech Republic
118 E12 **Moraviţa** Timiş, SW Romania 45.15N 21.17E
113 G17 **Moravská Třebová** *Ger.* Mährisch-Trübau. Pardubický Kraj, C Czech Republic 49.45N 16.40E
113 E19 **Moravské Budějovice** *Ger.* Mährisch-Budwitz. Vysočina, C Czech Republic 49.03N 15.48E
113 H17 **Moravskoslezský Kraj** *prev.* Ostravský Kraj. ◈ *region* E Czech Republic
113 F19 **Moravský Krumlov** *Ger.* Mährisch-Kromau. Jihomoravský Kraj, SE Czech Republic 48.58N 16.30E
98 J8 **Moray** *cultural region* N Scotland, UK
98 J8 **Moray Firth** *inlet* N Scotland, UK
44 B10 **Morazán** ◈ *department* NE El Salvador
160 C10 **Morbi** Gujarāt, W India 22.51N 70.49E
104 G7 **Morbihan** ◈ *department* NW France
Mörbisch *see* Mörbisch am See
111 Y5 **Mörbisch am See** *var.* Mörbisch. Burgenland, E Austria 47.43N 16.40E
97 N21 **Mörbylånga** Kalmar, S Sweden 56.31N 16.25E
104 J14 **Morcenx** Landes, SW France 44.04N 0.55W
Morcheh Khort *see* Mürcheh Khvort
169 T5 **Mordaga** Nei Mongol Zizhiqu, N China 51.15N 120.47E
15 L16 **Morden** Manitoba, S Canada 49.12N 98.04W
Mordovskaya ASSR/Mordvinia *see* Mordoviya, Respublika
131 N5 **Mordoviya, Respublika** *prev.* Mordovskaya ASSR, *Eng.* Mordovia, Mordvinia. ◈ *autonomous republic* W Russian Federation
130 M7 **Mordovo** Tambovskaya Oblast', W Russian Federation 52.05N 40.49E
Morea *see* Pelopónnisos
30 K8 **Moreau River** ≈ South Dakota, N USA
99 K16 **Morecambe** NW England, UK 54.04N 2.52W
99 K16 **Morecambe Bay** *inlet* NW England, UK
191 S4 **Moree** New South Wales, SE Australia 29.28S 149.52E
194 E15 **Morehead** Western, SW PNG 8.42S 141.37E
23 N5 **Morehead** Kentucky, S USA 38.13N 83.25W
194 E15 **Morehead** ≈ SW PNG
23 X11 **Morehead City** North Carolina, SE USA 34.43N 76.43W
29 Y8 **Morehouse** Missouri, C USA 36.51N 89.41W
110 E10 **Mörel** Valais, SW Switzerland 46.22N 8.03E
56 D13 **Morelia** Caquetá, S Colombia 1.27N 75.46W
43 N14 **Morelia** Michoacán de Ocampo, S Mexico 19.40N 101.10W
107 T7 **Morella** País Valenciano, E Spain 40.37N 0.06W
42 I7 **Morelos** Chihuahua, N Mexico 26.37N 107.37W
43 O15 **Morelos** ◈ *state* S Mexico
160 H7 **Morena** Madhya Pradesh, C India 26.35N 77.59E
106 L12 **Morena, Sierra** ▲▲ S Spain
39 O14 **Morenci** Arizona, SW USA 33.05N 109.21W
33 R11 **Morenci** Michigan, N USA 41.43N 84.13W
118 J13 **Moreni** Dâmboviţa, S Romania 44.58N 25.39E
96 D9 **Møre og Romsdal** ◈ *county* S Norway
14 Ee12 **Moresby Island** *island* Queen Charlotte Islands, British Columbia, SW Canada
191 W2 **Moreton Island** *island* Queensland, E Australia
105 O3 **Moreuil** Somme, N France 49.47N 2.28E
37 V7 **Morey Peak** ▲ Nevada, W USA 38.40N 116.16W
129 U4 **More-Yu** ≈ NW Russian Federation
105 T9 **Morez** Jura, E France 46.33N 6.01E
Mórfou *see* Güzelyurt
Morfou Bay/Mórfou, Kólpos *see* Güzelyurt Körfezi
190 J8 **Morgan** South Australia 34.02S 139.39E
25 S7 **Morgan** Georgia, SE USA 31.31N 84.34W
27 S8 **Morgan** Texas, SW USA 32.01N 97.36W
24 J10 **Morgan City** Louisiana, S USA 29.42N 91.12W
22 H6 **Morganfield** Kentucky, S USA 37.40N 87.55W
37 O10 **Morgan Hill** California, W USA 37.05N 121.38W
23 Q9 **Morganton** North Carolina, SE USA 35.45N 81.41W
22 J7 **Morgantown** Kentucky, S USA 37.13N 86.40W
23 S2 **Morgantown** West Virginia, NE USA 39.37N 79.57W
110 B10 **Morges** Vaud, SW Switzerland 46.30N 6.24E
154 M4 **Morghāb, Daryā-ye** *Rus.* Murgab, Murghab, *Turkm.* Murgap, Murgap Deryasy. ≈ Afghanistan/Turkmenistan *see also* Murgap
98 I9 **Mor, Glen** *var.* Glen Albyn, Great Glen. *valley* N Scotland, UK
105 T5 **Morhange** Moselle, NE France 48.56N 6.37E
164 M5 **Mori** *var.* Mori Kazak Zizhixian. Xinjiang Uygur Zizhiqu, NW China 43.48N 90.21E
172 Nn6 **Mori** Hokkaidō, NE Japan 42.04N 140.35E
37 Y6 **Moriah, Mount** ▲ Nevada, W USA 39.16N 114.10W
39 S11 **Moriarty** New Mexico, SW USA 34.59N 106.03W
56 J12 **Morichal** Guaviare, E Colombia 2.18N 69.54W
194 H14 **Morigio Island** *island* S PNG
Mori Kazak Zizhixian *see* Mori
Morin Dawa Daurzu Zizhiqi *see* Nirji
15 I13 **Morinville** Alberta, SW Canada 53.48N 113.37W
171 Mm11 **Morioka** Iwate, Honshū, C Japan 39.42N 141.08E
191 T8 **Morisset** New South Wales, SE Australia 33.07S 151.32E
171 Mm10 **Moriyoshi-yama** ▲ Honshū, C Japan 39.58N 140.32E
94 K13 **Morjärv** Norrbotten, N Sweden 66.03N 22.45E
131 R3 **Morki** Respublika Mariy El, W Russian Federation 56.27N 49.01E
126 K10 **Morkoka** ≈ NE Russian Federation
104 F5 **Morlaix** Finistère, NW France 48.34N 3.49W
97 M20 **Mörlunda** Kalmar, S Sweden 57.19N 15.52E
109 N19 **Mormanno** Calabria, SW Italy 39.54N 15.58E
38 L11 **Mormon Lake** ◎ Arizona, SW USA
37 Y10 **Mormon Peak** ▲ Nevada, W USA 36.59N 114.25W
Mormon State *see* Utah
47 Y5 **Morne-à-l'Eau** Grande Terre, N Guadeloupe 16.20N 61.28W
31 Y15 **Morning Sun** Iowa, C USA 41.06N 91.15W
200 O14 **Mornington Abyssal Plain** *undersea feature* SE Pacific Ocean
65 F22 **Mornington, Isla** *island* S Chile
189 T4 **Mornington Island** *island* Wellesley Islands, Queensland, N Australia
117 E18 **Mórnos** ≈ C Greece
155 P14 **Moro** Sind, SE Pakistan 26.36N 67.58E
34 I11 **Moro** Oregon, NW USA 45.28N 120.44W
194 K14 **Morobe** Morobe, C PNG 7.46S 147.35E
194 J14 **Morobe** ◈ *province* C PNG
33 N12 **Morocco** Indiana, N USA 40.57N 87.27W

◆ Country ● Country Capital ◇ Dependent Territory ○ Dependent Territory Capital ◈ Administrative Region ✕ International Airport ▲ Mountain ▲▲ Mountain Range ⋀ Volcano ≈ River ◎ Lake ⊠ Reservoir

MOROCCO– MUHU

76 E8 Morocco off. Kingdom of Morocco, Ar. Al Mamlakah. ◆ monarchy N Africa
Morocco see Marrakech
83 I22 Morogoro Morogoro, E Tanzania 6.49S 37.40E
83 H24 Morogoro ◆ region SE Tanzania
179 Qq16 Moro Gulf gulf S Philippines
43 N13 Moroleón Guanajuato, C Mexico 20.00N 101.13W
180 H6 Morombe Toliara, W Madagascar 21.46S 43.21E
46 G5 Morón Ciego de Ávila, C Cuba 22.04N 78.39W
56 K5 Morón Carabobo, N Venezuela 10.28N 68.10W
Morón see Morón de la Frontera
169 N8 Mörön Hentiy, C Mongolia 47.21N 110.21E
168 I6 Mörön Hövsgöl, N Mongolia 49.38N 100.07E
58 D8 Morona, Río ~ N Peru
58 C8 Morona Santiago ◆ province E Ecuador
180 H5 Morondava Toliara, W Madagascar 20.19S 44.16E
106 K14 Morón de la Frontera var. Morón. Andalucía, S Spain 37.07N 5.27W
180 G13 Moroni ● (Comoros) Grande Comore, NW Comoros 11.40S 43.16E
175 T16 Morotai, Pulau island Maluku, E Indonesia
175 T6 Morotai, Selat strait Maluku, E Indonesia
Morotiri see Marotiri
83 H17 Moroto NE Uganda 2.31N 34.40E
Morozov see Bratan
130 M11 Morozovsk Rostovskaya Oblast', SW Russian Federation 48.21N 41.54E
99 L14 Morpeth N England, UK 55.10N 1.40W
Morphou see Güzelyurt
Morphou Bay see Güzelyurt Körfezi
30 I13 Morrill Nebraska, C USA 41.57N 103.55W
29 U11 Morrilton Arkansas, C USA 35.09N 92.44W
9 Q16 Morrin Alberta, SW Canada 51.40N 112.45W
192 M7 Morrinsville Waikato, North Island, NZ 37.40S 175.32E
9 X16 Morris Manitoba, S Canada 49.21N 97.21W
32 M11 Morris Illinois, N USA 41.21N 88.25W
31 S8 Morris Minnesota, N USA 45.31N 95.52W
12 M13 Morrisburg Ontario, SE Canada 44.55N 75.07W
207 R11 Morris Jesup, Kap headland N Greenland 83.33N 32.40W
190 B1 Morris, Mount ▲ South Australia 26.04S 131.03E
32 K10 Morrison Illinois, N USA 41.48N 89.58W
38 K13 Morristown Arizona, SW USA 33.48N 112.34W
20 J14 Morristown New Jersey, NE USA 40.48N 74.28W
23 O8 Morristown Tennessee, S USA 36.12N 83.18W
44 L11 Morrito Río San Juan, SW Nicaragua 11.37N 85.03W
37 P13 Morro Bay California, W USA 35.21N 120.51W
97 L22 Mörrum Blekinge, S Sweden 56.10N 14.45E
85 N16 Morrumbala Zambézia, NE Mozambique 17.16S 35.34E
85 N20 Morrumbene Inhambane, SE Mozambique 23.38S 35.22E
97 F21 Mors island NW Denmark
Mörs see Moers
27 N1 Morse Texas, SW USA 36.03N 101.28W
131 N6 Morshansk Tambovskaya Oblast', W Russian Federation 53.27N 41.46E
104 L5 Mortagne-au-Perche Orne, N France 48.32N 0.31E
104 J8 Mortagne-sur-Sèvre Vendée, NW France 47.00N 0.57W
106 G8 Mortágua Viseu, N Portugal 40.24N 8.13W
104 J5 Mortain Manche, N France 48.39N 0.51W
108 C8 Mortara Lombardia, N Italy 45.15N 8.43E
61 J17 Mortes, Rio das ~ C Brazil
190 M12 Mortlake Victoria, SE Australia 38.06S 142.48E
Mortlock Group see Takuu Islands
201 Q17 Mortlock Islands prev. Nomoi Islands. island group C Micronesia
31 T9 Morton Minnesota, N USA 44.33N 94.58W
24 L5 Morton Mississippi, S USA 32.21N 89.39W
26 M5 Morton Texas, SW USA 33.40N 102.45W
34 H9 Morton Washington, NW USA 46.33N 122.16W
(0) D7 Morton Seamount undersea feature NE Pacific Ocean 50.15N 142.45W
47 U15 Moruga Trinidad, Trinidad and Tobago 10.04N 61.16W
191 P9 Morundah New South Wales, SE Australia 34.57S 146.18E
Moruroa see Mururoa
191 S11 Moruya New South Wales, SE Australia 35.55S 150.04E
105 Q8 Morvan physical region C France
193 G21 Morven Canterbury, South Island, NZ 44.51S 171.07E
191 O13 Morwell Victoria, SE Australia 38.13S 146.25E
129 N6 Morzhovets, Ostrov island NW Russian Federation
130 J4 Mosal'sk Kaluzhskaya Oblast', W Russian Federation 54.30N 34.55E
103 H20 Mosbach Baden-Württemberg, SW Germany 49.21N 9.06E
97 E18 Mosby Vest-Agder, S Norway 58.12N 7.55E
35 V9 Mosby Montana, NW USA 46.58N 107.53W
34 M9 Moscow Idaho, NW USA 46.43N 117.00W
22 F10 Moscow Tennessee, S USA 35.04N 89.27W
Moscow see Moskva
103 D19 Mosel Fr. Moselle. ~ W Europe see also Moselle
105 T4 Moselle ◆ department NE France
105 T6 Moselle Ger. Mosel. ~ W Europe see also Mosel
34 K9 Moses Lake ◎ Washington, NW USA
85 I18 Mosetse Central, E Botswana 20.40S 26.37E
94 H4 Mosfellsbær Sudhurland, SW Iceland 65.09N 21.43W
193 F23 Mosgiel Otago, South Island, NZ 45.51S 170.21E
128 M11 Mosha ~ NW Russian Federation
83 I20 Moshi Kilimanjaro, NE Tanzania 3.21S 37.19E
112 G12 Mosina Wielkolpolskie, C Poland 52.13N 16.48E
32 L6 Mosinee Wisconsin, N USA 44.45N 89.39W
94 F13 Mosjøen Nordland, C Norway 65.49N 13.12E
127 Nn13 Moskal'vo Ostrov Sakhalin, Sakhalinskaya Oblast', SE Russian Federation 53.36N 142.31E
94 I13 Moskosel Norrbotten, N Sweden 65.52N 19.30E
130 K4 Moskovskaya Oblast' ◆ province W Russian Federation
Moskovskiy see Moskva
130 J3 Moskva Eng. Moscow. ● (Russian Federation) Gorod Moskva, W Russian Federation 55.45N 37.42E
153 Q14 Moskva Rus. Moskovskiy; prev. Chubek. SW Tajikistan 37.41N 69.33E
130 L4 Moskva ~ W Russian Federation
85 I20 Mosomane Kgatleng, SE Botswana 24.03S 26.16E
Moson and Magyaróvár see Mosonmagyaróvár
113 H21 Mosoni-Duna Ger. Kleine Donau. ~ NW Hungary
113 H21 Mosonmagyaróvár Ger. Wieselburg-Ungarisch-Altenburg; prev. Moson and Magyaróvár, Ger. Wieselburg and Ungarisch-Altenburg. Győr-Moson-Sopron, NW Hungary 47.51N 17.15E
Mospino see Mospyne
119 X8 Mospyne Rus. Mospino. Donets'ka Oblast', E Ukraine 47.53N 38.03E
56 B12 Mosquera Nariño, SW Colombia 2.31N 78.24W
39 U10 Mosquero New Mexico, SW USA 35.46N 103.57W
Mosquito Coast see La Mosquitia
33 U11 Mosquito Creek Lake ▣ Ohio, N USA
Mosquito Gulf see Mosquitos, Golfo de los
25 X11 Mosquito Lagoon wetland Florida, SE USA
45 N10 Mosquito, Punta headland E Nicaragua 12.18N 83.38W
45 W14 Mosquito, Punta headland NE Panama 9.06N 77.52W
45 Q15 Mosquitos, Golfo de los Eng. Mosquito Gulf. gulf N Panama
97 H16 Moss Østfold, S Norway 59.25N 10.40E
Mossâmedes see Namibe
24 G8 Moss Bluff Louisiana, S USA 30.18N 93.11W
193 C23 Mossburn Southland, South Island, NZ 45.40S 168.15E
85 G26 Mosselbaai var. Mosselbai, Eng. Mossel Bay. Western Cape, SW South Africa 34.10S 22.07E
Mosselbai/Mossel Bay see Mosselbaai
81 F20 Mossendjo Le Niari, SW Congo 2.57S 12.39E
191 N8 Mossgiel New South Wales, SE Australia 33.16S 144.34E
103 H22 Mössingen Baden-Württemberg, S Germany 48.22N 9.01E
189 W4 Mossman Queensland, NE Australia 16.34S 145.27E
61 P14 Mossoró Rio Grande do Norte, NE Brazil 5.10S 37.19W
25 N9 Moss Point Mississippi, S USA 30.24N 88.31W
191 S9 Moss Vale New South Wales, SE Australia 34.33S 150.22E
34 G9 Mossyrock Washington, NW USA 46.32N 122.30W
113 B15 Most Ger. Brüx. Ústecký Kraj, NW Czech Republic 50.30N 13.37E
168 E7 Möst var. Ulaantolgoy. Hovd, W Mongolia 46.39N 92.50E
123 Jj16 Mosta var. Musta. C Malta 35.54N 14.25E
76 I5 Mostaganem var. Mestghanem. NW Algeria 35.55N 0.08E
115 H14 Mostar Federacija Bosna I Hercegovina, S Bosnia and Herzegovina 43.20N 17.47E
63 J17 Mostardas Rio Grande do Sul, S Brazil 31.06S 50.52W
118 K14 Mostiştea ~ S Romania
Mostva see Mastva
Mosty see Masty
118 H5 Mostys'ka L'vivs'ka Oblast', W Ukraine 49.47N 23.09E
Mosul see Al Mawşil
97 F15 Møsvatnet ◎ S Norway
82 J12 Mot'a Amhara, N Ethiopia 11.03N 38.03E
197 C10 Mota island Banks Islands, N Vanuatu
81 H16 Motaba ~ N Congo
107 O10 Mota del Cuervo Castilla-La Mancha, C Spain 39.30N 2.52W
106 L5 Mota del Marqués Castilla-León, N Spain 41.37N 5.10W
44 F5 Motagua, Río ~ Guatemala/Honduras
121 H19 Motal' Brestskaya Voblasts', SW Belarus 52.13N 25.34E
97 L17 Motala Östergötland, S Sweden 58.33N 15.05E
197 C10 Mota Lava island Banks Islands, N Vanuatu
203 X7 Motane var. Mohotani. island Îles Marquises, NE French Polynesia
158 K13 Moth Uttar Pradesh, N India 25.43N 78.55E
Mother of Presidents/Mother of States see Virginia
98 I12 Motherwell C Scotland, UK 55.48N 4.00W
159 P12 Motīhāri Bihār, N India 26.40N 84.55E
107 Q10 Motilla del Palancar Castilla-La Mancha, C Spain 39.34N 1.55W
192 N7 Motiti Island island NE NZ
67 E25 Motley Island island SE Falkland Islands
85 J19 Motloutse ~ E Botswana
43 V17 Motozintla de Mendoza Chiapas, SE Mexico 15.22N 92.11W
107 N15 Motril Andalucía, S Spain 36.45N 3.29W
118 G13 Motru Gorj, SW Romania 44.49N 22.55E
171 Mm5 Motsuta-misaki headland Hokkaidō, NE Japan 42.36N 139.48E
30 L6 Mott North Dakota, N USA 46.21N 102.17W
Möttling see Metlika
109 O18 Mottola Puglia, SE Italy 40.37N 17.01E
192 P8 Motu ~ North Island, NZ
193 I14 Motueka Tasman, South Island, NZ 41.08S 173.01E
193 I14 Motueka ~ South Island, NZ
Motu Iti see Tupai
43 X12 Motul var. Motul de Felipe Carrillo Puerto. Yucatán, SE Mexico 21.06N 89.16W
Motul de Felipe Carrillo Puerto see Motul
203 U17 Motu Nui island Easter Island, Chile, E Pacific Ocean
203 Q10 Motu One var. Bellingshausen. atoll Îles Sous le Vent, W French Polynesia
202 I16 Motutapu island E Cook Islands
200 R15 Motu Tapu island Tongatapu Group, S Tonga
192 L5 Motutapu Island island N NZ
Motyca see Modica
126 I13 Motygino Krasnoyarskiy Kray, C Russian Federation 58.09N 94.35E
Mouanda see Moanda
Mouaskar see Mascara
107 U3 Moubermé, Tuc de Fr. Pic de Maubermé, Sp. Pico Mauberme; prev. Tuc de Maubermé. ▲ France/Spain 42.48N 0.57E see also Maubermé, Pic de
47 N7 Mouchoir Passage passage SE Turks and Caicos Islands
78 I9 Moudjéria Tagant, SW Mauritania 17.52N 12.19W
110 C9 Moudon Vaud, W Switzerland 46.41N 6.49E
Mouhoun see Black Volta
81 E19 Mouila Ngounié, C Gabon 1.49S 11.01E
81 K14 Mouka Haute-Kotto, C Central African Republic 7.12N 21.52E
Moukden see Shenyang
191 N10 Moulamein New South Wales, SE Australia 35.06S 144.03E
Moulamein Creek see Billabong Creek
76 F6 Moulay-Bousselham NW Morocco 34.54N 6.15W
Moule see le Moule
82 M11 Moulhoulé N Djibouti 12.34N 43.06E
105 P9 Moulins Allier, C France 46.34N 3.19E
178 Gg9 Moulmein var. Maulmain, Mawlamyine. Mon State, S Burma 16.30N 97.39E
177 F9 Moulmeingyun Irrawaddy, SW Burma 16.24N 95.15E
76 G6 Moulouya var. Mulucha, Muluya, Mulwiya. seasonal river NE Morocco
25 O2 Moulton Alabama, S USA 34.28N 87.16W
31 W16 Moulton Iowa, C USA 40.41N 92.40W
27 T11 Moulton Texas, SW USA 29.34N 97.08W
25 T7 Moultrie Georgia, SE USA 31.10N 83.47W
23 S14 Moultrie, Lake ▣ South Carolina, SE USA
24 K3 Mound Bayou Mississippi, S USA 33.52N 90.43W
32 L17 Mound City Illinois, N USA 37.06N 89.09W
29 R6 Mound City Kansas, C USA 38.08N 94.48W
29 Q2 Mound City Missouri, C USA 40.07N 95.13W
31 N7 Mound City South Dakota, N USA 45.42N 100.04W
80 H13 Moundou Logone-Occidental, SW Chad 8.34N 16.01E
29 P10 Mounds Oklahoma, C USA 35.52N 96.03W
23 R2 Moundsville West Virginia, NE USA 39.55N 80.44W
178 Ii12 Moŭng Roessei Bătdâmbâng, W Cambodia 12.46N 103.28E
Moun Hou see Black Volta
14 G5 Mountain ~ Northwest Territories, NW Canada
39 S12 Mountainair New Mexico, SW USA 34.31N 106.14W
37 V1 Mountain City Nevada, W USA 41.48N 115.58W
23 Q8 Mountain City Tennessee, S USA 36.28N 81.48W
29 U7 Mountain Grove Missouri, C USA 37.07N 92.15W
29 U9 Mountain Home Arkansas, C USA 36.19N 92.24W
35 N15 Mountain Home Idaho, NW USA 43.07N 115.42W
27 Q11 Mountain Home Texas, SW USA 30.11N 99.19W
31 W4 Mountain Iron Minnesota, N USA 47.31N 92.37W
31 T10 Mountain Lake Minnesota, N USA 43.57N 94.54W
25 S3 Mountain Park Georgia, SE USA 34.04N 84.24W
37 W12 Mountain Pass pass California, W USA 35.28N 115.31W
29 T12 Mountain Pine Arkansas, C USA 34.34N 93.10W
41 Y14 Mountain Point Annette Island, Alaska, USA 55.17N 131.31W
Mountain State see Montana, USA
Mountain State see West Virginia, USA
29 V7 Mountain View Arkansas, C USA 35.52N 92.07W
40 H12 Mountain View Hawai'i, USA, C Pacific Ocean 19.31N 155.03W
29 V10 Mountain View Missouri, C USA 37.00N 91.42W
40 M11 Mountain Village Alaska, USA 62.06N 163.42W
23 R8 Mount Airy North Carolina, SE USA 36.30N 80.36W
85 K24 Mount Ayliff Xh. Maxesibebi. Eastern Cape, SE South Africa 30.48S 29.22E
31 U16 Mount Ayr Iowa, C USA 40.42N 94.14W
190 J9 Mount Barker South Australia 35.06S 138.52E
188 J14 Mount Barker Western Australia 34.42S 117.40E
191 P11 Mount Beauty Victoria, SE Australia 36.47S 147.12E
12 E16 Mount Brydges Ontario, S Canada 42.54N 81.29W
33 N16 Mount Carmel Illinois, N USA 38.23N 87.46W
32 K10 Mount Carroll Illinois, N USA 42.04N 89.58W
33 S9 Mount Clemens Michigan, N USA 42.36N 82.52W
193 E19 Mount Cook Canterbury, South Island, NZ 43.46S 170.06E
85 L16 Mount Darwin Mashonaland Central, NE Zimbabwe 16.45S 31.32E
21 S7 Mount Desert Island island Maine, NE USA
25 W11 Mount Dora Florida, SE USA 28.48N 81.38W
190 G5 Mount Eba South Australia 30.11S 135.40E
27 W8 Mount Enterprise Texas, SW USA 31.53N 94.40W
190 J4 Mount Fitton South Australia 29.55S 139.26E
85 J24 Mount Fletcher Eastern Cape, SE South Africa 30.40S 28.30E
12 F15 Mount Forest Ontario, S Canada 43.58N 80.43W
190 K12 Mount Gambier South Australia 37.47S 140.48E
189 W5 Mount Garnet Queensland, NE Australia 17.41S 145.07E
23 P6 Mount Gay West Virginia, NE USA 37.49N 82.00W
33 S12 Mount Gilead Ohio, N USA 40.33N 82.49W
194 H12 Mount Hagen Western Highlands, C PNG 5.53S 144.12E
20 J16 Mount Holly New Jersey, NE USA 39.59N 74.46W
23 R10 Mount Holly North Carolina, SE USA 35.18N 81.01W
29 T12 Mount Ida Arkansas, C USA 34.33N 93.37W
189 T6 Mount Isa Queensland, C Australia 20.48S 139.32E
23 U4 Mount Jackson Virginia, NE USA 38.45N 78.38W
20 D12 Mount Jewett Pennsylvania, NE USA 41.43N 78.37W
20 L13 Mount Kisco New York, NE USA 41.12N 73.42W
20 B15 Mount Lebanon Pennsylvania, NE USA 40.21N 80.03W
190 J8 Mount Lofty Ranges ▲ South Australia
188 J10 Mount Magnet Western Australia 28.09S 117.52E
192 N7 Mount Maunganui Bay of Plenty, North Island, NZ 37.39S 176.11E
99 E18 Mountmellick Ir. Móinteach Mílic. C Ireland 53.07N 7.19W
32 L10 Mount Morris Illinois, N USA 42.03N 89.25W
33 R9 Mount Morris Michigan, N USA 43.07N 83.42W
20 F10 Mount Morris New York, NE USA 42.43N 77.51W
20 B16 Mount Morris Pennsylvania, NE USA 39.43N 80.06W
32 K15 Mount Olive Illinois, N USA 39.04N 89.43W
23 V10 Mount Olive North Carolina, SE USA 35.12N 78.03W
23 N4 Mount Olivet Kentucky, S USA 38.32N 84.01W
31 Y15 Mount Pleasant Iowa, C USA 40.57N 91.33W
33 Q8 Mount Pleasant Michigan, N USA 43.36N 84.46W
20 C15 Mount Pleasant Pennsylvania, NE USA 40.07N 79.33W
23 T14 Mount Pleasant South Carolina, SE USA 32.47N 79.51W
22 I9 Mount Pleasant Tennessee, S USA 35.32N 87.11W
27 W6 Mount Pleasant Texas, SW USA 33.10N 94.49W
38 L4 Mount Pleasant Utah, W USA 39.33N 111.27W
65 N23 Mount Pleasant ✕ (Stanley) East Falkland, Falkland Islands
99 G25 Mount's Bay inlet SW England, UK
37 N2 Mount Shasta California, W USA 41.18N 122.19W
32 J13 Mount Sterling Illinois, N USA 39.59N 90.44W
23 N5 Mount Sterling Kentucky, S USA 38.03N 83.56W
20 E15 Mount Union Pennsylvania, NE USA 40.21N 77.51W
25 V6 Mount Vernon Georgia, SE USA 32.10N 82.35W
32 L16 Mount Vernon Illinois, N USA 38.19N 88.54W
22 M6 Mount Vernon Kentucky, S USA 37.22N 84.22W
29 S7 Mount Vernon Missouri, C USA 37.06N 93.49W
33 T13 Mount Vernon Ohio, N USA 40.23N 82.29W
34 K13 Mount Vernon Oregon, NW USA 44.22N 119.07W
27 W6 Mount Vernon Texas, SW USA 33.11N 95.13W
34 H7 Mount Vernon Washington, NW USA 48.25N 122.19W
22 L5 Mount Washington Kentucky, S USA 38.03N 85.33W
190 F8 Mount Wedge South Australia 33.29S 135.08E
32 L14 Mount Zion Illinois, N USA 39.46N 88.52W
189 Y9 Moura Queensland, NE Australia 24.34S 149.57E
60 F12 Moura Amazonas, NW Brazil 1.32S 61.43W
106 H12 Moura Beja, S Portugal 38.07N 7.27W
106 I12 Mourão Évora, S Portugal 38.22N 7.19W
78 L11 Mourdiah Koulikoro, W Mali 14.28N 7.31W
80 K7 Mourdi, Dépression du desert lowland Chad/Sudan
104 J16 Mourenx Pyrénées-Atlantiques, SW France 43.24N 0.37W
Mourgana see Mourgkána
117 C15 Mourgkána var. Mourgana. ▲ Albania/Greece 39.48N 20.24E
99 G16 Mourne Mountains Ir. Beanna Boirche. ▲ SE Northern Ireland, UK
117 I15 Moúrtzeflos, Akrotírio headland Límnos, E Greece 40.00N 25.02E
101 C19 Mouscron Dut. Moeskroen. Hainaut, W Belgium 50.43N 3.13E
Mouse River see Souris River
80 H10 Moussoro Kanem, W Chad 13.40N 16.31E
105 T11 Moûtiers Savoie, E France 45.28N 6.31E
180 J14 Moutsamoudou var. Mutsamudu. Anjouan, SE Comoros 12.10S 44.25E
76 K11 Mouydir, Monts de ▲ S Algeria
81 F20 Mouyondzi La Bouenza, S Congo 3.58S 13.57E
117 E16 Mouzáki prev. Mouzákion. Thessalía, C Greece 39.25N 21.40E
Mouzákion see Mouzáki
31 S13 Moville Iowa, C USA 42.30N 96.04W
84 E13 Moxico ◆ province E Angola
180 I14 Moya Anjouan, SE Comoros 12.18S 44.27E
42 L12 Moyahua Zacatecas, C Mexico 21.19N 103.10W
83 J16 Moyalē Oromo, C Ethiopia 3.34N 38.58E
78 I15 Moyamba W Sierra Leone 8.04N 12.30W
76 G7 Moyen Atlas Eng. Middle Atlas. ▲ N Morocco
80 H13 Moyen-Chari off. Préfecture du Moyen-Chari. ◆ prefecture S Chad
Moyen-Congo see Congo (Republic of)
85 J24 Moyeni var. Quthing. SW Lesotho 30.25S 27.43E
81 D18 Moyen-Ogooué off. Province du Moyen-Ogooué, var. Le Moyen-Ogooué. ◆ province C Gabon
105 S4 Moyeuvre-Grande Moselle, NE France 49.15N 6.03E
35 N7 Moyie Springs Idaho, NW USA 48.43N 116.15W
152 G6 Mo'ynoq Rus. Muynak. Qoraqalpog'iston Respublikasi, NW Uzbekistan 43.45N 59.03E
83 F16 Moyo NW Uganda 3.37N 31.43E
58 D10 Moyobamba San Martín, NW Peru 6.04S 76.55W
175 O16 Moyo, Pulau island S Indonesia
80 H10 Moyto Chari-Baguirmi, W Chad 12.34N 16.33E
164 G9 Moyu var. Karakax. Xinjiang Uygur Zizhiqu, NW China 37.16N 79.39E
126 Jj9 Moyyero ~ N Russian Federation
151 S15 Moyynkum var. Furmanovka, Kaz. Fūrmanov. Zhambyl, S Kazakhstan 44.15N 72.55E
151 Q15 Moyynkum, Peski Kaz. Moyynqum. desert S Kazakhstan
Moyynqum see Moyynkum, Peski
151 S12 Moyynty Karaganda, C Kazakhstan 47.10N 73.24E
151 S12 Moyynty ~ C Kazakhstan
Mozambika, Lakandranon' i see Mozambique Channel
85 M18 Mozambique off. Republic of Mozambique; prev. People's Republic of Mozambique, Portuguese East Africa. ◆ republic S Africa
Mozambique Basin see Natal Basin
Mozambique, Canal de see Mozambique Channel
85 P17 Mozambique Channel Fr. Canal de Mozambique, Mal. Lakandranon' i Mozambika. strait W Indian Ocean
180 L11 Mozambique Escarpment var. Mozambique Scarp. undersea feature SW Indian Ocean
180 L10 Mozambique Plateau var. Mozambique Rise. undersea feature SW Indian Ocean
Mozambique Rise see Mozambique Plateau
Mozambique Scarp see Mozambique Escarpment
131 O15 Mozdok Respublika Severnaya Osetiya, SW Russian Federation 43.48N 44.42E
59 K17 Mozetenes, Serranías de ▲ C Bolivia
130 J4 Mozhaysk Moskovskaya Oblast', W Russian Federation 55.31N 36.01E
131 T3 Mozhga Udmurtskaya Respublika, NW Russian Federation 56.24N 52.13E
Mozyr' see Mazyr
81 P22 Mpala Katanga, E Dem. Rep. Congo 6.43S 29.28E
81 G19 Mpama ~ C Congo
83 E22 Mpanda Rukwa, W Tanzania 6.21S 31.01E
84 L11 Mpande Northern, NE Zambia 9.13S 31.42E
85 J18 Mphoengs Matabeleland South, SW Zimbabwe 21.04S 27.56E
83 F18 Mpigi S Uganda 0.13N 32.19E
84 L13 Mpika Northern, NE Zambia 11.49S 31.27E
85 J14 Mpima Central, C Zambia 14.25S 28.34E
84 J13 Mpongwe Copperbelt, C Zambia 13.25S 28.13E
84 K11 Mporokoso Northern, N Zambia 9.22S 30.06E
81 H20 Mpouya Plateaux, SE Congo 2.39S 16.12E
79 P16 Mpraeso C Ghana 6.46N 0.41W
84 L11 Mpulungu Northern, N Zambia 8.47S 31.09E
85 K21 Mpumalanga prev. Eastern Transvaal, Afr. Oos-Transvaal. ◆ province NE South Africa
85 D16 Mpungu Okavango, N Namibia 17.36S 18.16E
83 I22 Mpwapwa Dodoma, C Tanzania 6.21S 36.28E
Mqinvartsveri see Kazbek
112 M8 Mrągowo Ger. Sensburg. Warmińsko-Mazurskie, NE Poland 53.52N 21.19E
131 V6 Mrakovo Respublika Bashkortostan, W Russian Federation 52.43N 56.36E
180 I13 Mramani Anjouan, E Comoros 12.18S 44.39E
114 F12 Mrkonjić Grad Republika Srpska, W Bosnia and Herzegovina 44.25N 17.04E
112 H9 Mrocza Kujawsko-pomorskie, NW Poland 53.15N 17.38E
128 I14 Msta ~ NW Russian Federation
Mstislavl' see Mstsislaw
121 P15 Mstsislaw Rus. Mstislavl'. Mahilyowskaya Voblasts', E Belarus 54.01N 31.43E
Mtkvari see Kura
Mtoko see Mutoko
130 K6 Mtsensk Orlovskaya Oblast', W Russian Federation 53.17N 36.34E
83 K24 Mtwara Mtwara, SE Tanzania 10.16S 40.11E
83 J25 Mtwara ◆ region SE Tanzania
106 G14 Mu ▲ S Portugal 37.24N 8.04W
200 Qq15 Mu'a Tongatapu, S Tonga 21.11S 175.07W
Muai To see Mae Hong Son
85 P16 Mualama Zambézia, NE Mozambique 16.51S 38.21E
Mualo see Messalo, Rio
81 E22 Muanda Bas-Congo, SW Dem. Rep. Congo 5.53S 12.17E
Muang Chiang Rai see Chiang Rai
178 J6 Muang Ham Houaphan, N Laos 20.19N 104.00E
178 J9 Muang Hinboun Khammouan, C Laos 17.37N 104.37E
Muang Kalasin see Kalasin
Muang Khammouan see Thakhèk
178 Jj11 Muang Không Champasak, S Laos 14.08N 105.48E
178 Jj10 Muang Khôngxédôn var. Khong Sedone. Salavan, S Laos 15.34N 105.46E
Muang Khon Kaen see Khon Kaen
178 Ii6 Muang Khoua Phôngsali, N Laos 21.07N 102.31E
Muang Krabi see Krabi
Muang Lampang see Lampang
Muang Lamphun see Lamphun
Muang Loei see Loei
Muang Lom Sak see Lom Sak
Muang Nakhon Sawan see Nakhon Sawan
178 I6 Muang Namo Oudômxai, N Laos 20.58N 101.46E
Muang Nan see Nan
178 Ii6 Muang Ngoy Louangphabang, N Laos 20.43N 102.42E
178 I5 Muang Ou Tai Phôngsali, N Laos 22.06N 101.59E
Muang Pak Lay see Pak Lay
Muang Pakxan see Pakxan
178 Jj10 Muang Pakxong Champasak, S Laos 15.10N 106.17E
178 Jj9 Muang Phalan var. Muang Phalane. Savannakhét, S Laos 16.40N 105.33E
Muang Phalane see Muang Phalan
Muang Phan see Phan
Muang Phayao see Phayao
Muang Phichit see Phichit
178 Jj9 Muang Phin Savannakhét, S Laos 16.31N 106.01E
Muang Phitsanulok see Phitsanulok
Muang Phrae see Phrae
Muang Roi Et see Roi Et
Muang Sakon Nakhon see Sakon Nakhon
Muang Samut Prakan see Samut Prakan
178 I6 Muang Sing Louang Namtha, N Laos 21.12N 101.09E
Muang Ubon see Ubon Ratchathani
Muang Uthai Thani see Uthai Thani
178 I7 Muang Vangviang Viangchan, C Laos 18.53N 102.27E
Muang Xaignabouri see Xaignabouli
Muang Xay see Xai
178 Jj9 Muang Xépôn var. Sepone. Savannakhét, S Laos 16.40N 106.15E
174 H6 Muar var. Bandar Maharani. Johor, Peninsular Malaysia 2.01N 102.34E
173 Ff6 Muara Sumatera, W Indonesia 2.18N 98.54E
174 Hh11 Muarabeliti Sumatera, W Indonesia 3.13S 103.00E
174 H9 Muarabungo Sumatera, W Indonesia 1.36S 103.37E
174 I11 Muaraenim Sumatera, W Indonesia 3.36S 103.43E
174 Mm8 Muarajuloi Borneo, C Indonesia 0.12S 114.03E
175 Nn9 Muarakaman Borneo, C Indonesia 0.09S 116.43E
173 Ff9 Muarasigep Pulau Siberut, W Indonesia 1.01S 98.48E
174 Hh9 Muaratembesi Sumatera, W Indonesia 1.42S 103.07E
175 N9 Muaratewe var. Muarateweh; prev. Moearatewe. Borneo, C Indonesia 0.58S 114.52E
Muarateweh see Muaratewe
175 O7 Muarawahau Borneo, N Indonesia 1.03N 116.48E
144 G13 Mubārak, Jabal ▲ S Jordan 29.19N 35.13E
159 N13 Mubārakpur Uttar Pradesh, N India 26.05N 83.19E
Mubarek see Muborak
83 F18 Mubende SW Uganda 0.34N 31.24E
79 Y14 Mubi Adamawa, NE Nigeria 10.15N 13.18E
152 M12 Muborak Rus. Mubarek. Qashqadaryo Viloyati, S Uzbekistan 39.17N 65.10E
176 Vv9 Mubrani Papua, E Indonesia 0.42S 133.25E
69 U12 Muchinga Escarpment escarpment NE Zambia
131 N7 Muchkapskiy Tambovskaya Oblast', W Russian Federation 51.51N 42.25E
98 G10 Muck island W Scotland, UK
84 Q13 Mucojo Cabo Delgado, N Mozambique 12.04S 40.30E
84 F12 Muconda Lunda Sul, NE Angola 10.37S 21.19E
56 I10 Muco, Río ~ E Colombia
85 O16 Mucubela Zambézia, NE Mozambique 16.51S 37.48E
44 J5 Mucupina, Monte ▲ N Honduras 15.07N 86.36W
142 J14 Mucur Kirşehir, C Turkey 39.04N 34.25E
149 U8 Mūd Khorāsān-e Janūbī, E Iran 32.40N 59.30E
169 Y9 Mudanjiang var. Mu-tan-chiang. Heilongjiang, NE China 44.33N 129.40E
169 Y9 Mudan Jiang ~ NE China
142 D11 Mudanya Bursa, NW Turkey 40.22N 28.52E
30 K8 Mud Butte South Dakota, N USA 45.00N 102.51W
161 G16 Muddebihāl Karnātaka, C India 16.26N 76.07E
29 P12 Muddy Boggy Creek ~ Oklahoma, C USA
38 M6 Muddy Creek ~ Utah, W USA
39 V7 Muddy Creek Reservoir ▣ Colorado, C USA
35 W15 Muddy Gap Wyoming, C USA 42.21N 107.27W
37 Y11 Muddy Peak ▲ Nevada, W USA 36.17N 114.40W
191 R7 Mudgee New South Wales, SE Australia 32.37S 149.34E
31 S3 Mud Lake ◎ Minnesota, N USA
31 P7 Mud Lake Reservoir ▣ South Dakota, N USA
178 Gg9 Mudon Mon State, S Burma 16.14N 97.46E
83 O14 Mudug off. Gobolka Mudug. ◆ region NE Somalia
83 O14 Mudug var. Mudugh. plain N Somalia
Mudugh see Mudug
85 Q15 Muecate Nampula, NE Mozambique 14.56S 39.38E
84 Q13 Mueda Cabo Delgado, NE Mozambique 11.40S 39.36E
44 L10 Muelle de los Bueyes Región Autónoma Atlántico Sur, SE Nicaragua 12.03N 84.34W
Muenchen see München
85 M14 Muende Tete, NW Mozambique 14.22S 33.00E
27 T5 Muenster Texas, SW USA 33.39N 97.22W
Muenster see Münster
45 O6 Muerto, Cayo reef NE Nicaragua
43 T17 Muerto, Mar lagoon SE Mexico
66 F11 Muertos Trough undersea feature N Caribbean Sea
85 H14 Mufaya Kuta Western, NW Zambia 14.30S 24.18E
84 J13 Mufulira Copperbelt, C Zambia 12.33S 28.15E
167 O10 Mufu Shan ▲ C China
Mugalzhar Taŭlary see Mugodzhary, Gory
143 Y12 Muğan Düzü Rus. Muganskaya Ravnina, Muganskaya Step'. physical region S Azerbaijan
Muganskaya Ravnina/Muganskaya Step' see Muğan Düzü
108 K8 Muggia Friuli-Venezia Giulia, NE Italy 45.36N 13.48E
159 N14 Mughal Sarāi Uttar Pradesh, N India 25.18N 83.07E
Mughla see Muğla
147 W11 Mughshin var. Muqshin. S Oman 19.25N 54.38E
153 S12 Mughsu Rus. Muksu. ~ C Tajikistan
170 Ff16 Mugi Tokushima, Shikoku, SW Japan 33.39N 134.24E
142 C16 Muğla var. Mughla. Muğla, SW Turkey 37.13N 28.22E
142 C16 Muğla var. Mughla. ◆ province SW Turkey
150 J11 Mugodzhary, Gory Kaz. Mugalzhar Taŭlary. ▲ W Kazakhstan
85 O15 Mugulama Zambézia, NE Mozambique 16.01S 37.33E
145 U9 Muḩammad E Iraq 32.46N 45.14E
145 R8 Muḩammadīyah C Iraq 33.22N 42.48E
82 I6 Muhammad Qol Red Sea, NE Sudan 20.52N 37.09E
77 Y9 Muhammad, Rās headland E Egypt 27.45N 34.18E
Muhammerah see Khorramshahr
146 M12 Muhāyil var. Mahāil. 'Asir, SW Saudi Arabia 18.34N 42.01E
145 O7 Muḩaywīr W Iraq 33.34N 41.06E
103 H21 Mühlacker Baden-Württemberg, SW Germany 48.57N 8.51E
Mühlbach see Sebeş
Mühldorf see Mühldorf am Inn
103 N23 Mühldorf am Inn var. Mühldorf. Bayern, SE Germany 48.14N 12.32E
103 J15 Mühlhausen var. Mühlhausen in Thüringen. Thüringen, C Germany 51.13N 10.28E
Mühlhausen in Thüringen see Mühlhausen
205 Q2 Mühlig-Hofmann Mountains ▲ Antarctica
95 L14 Muhos Oulu, C Finland 64.48N 26.00E
144 K6 Mūḩ, Sabkhat al ◎ C Syria
120 E5 Muhu Ger. Mohn, Moon. island W Estonia

◆ Country ● Country Capital ◇ Dependent Territory ○ Dependent Territory Capital ◆ Administrative Region ✕ International Airport ▲ Mountain ▲ Mountain Range Volcano ~ River ◎ Lake ▣ Reservoir

83 *F19* **Muhutwe** Kagera, NW Tanzania *1.31S 31.40E*
Muhu Väin *see* Väinameri
100 *J10* **Muiden** Noord-Holland, C Netherlands *52.19N 5.04E*
200 *R15* **Mui Hopohoponga** *headland* Tongatapu, S Tonga *21.09S 175.01W*
171 *K14* **Muika** ***var.*** Muikamachi. Niigata, Honshū, C Japan *37.04N 138.53E*
Muikamachi *see* Muika
Muinchille *see* Cootehill
Muineachán *see* Monaghan
99 *F19* **Muine Bheag** ***Eng.*** Bagenalstown. SE Ireland *52.42N 6.57W*
58 *B5* **Muisne** Esmeraldas, NW Ecuador *0.34N 79.58W*
85 *P14* **Muite** Nampula, NE Mozambique *14.02S 39.06E*
43 *Z11* **Mujeres, Isla** *island* E Mexico
118 *G7* **Mukacheve** ***Hung.*** Munkács, ***Rus.*** Mukachevo. Zakarpats'ka Oblast', W Ukraine *48.26N 22.44E*
Mukachevo *see* Mukacheve
174 *Ll5* **Mukah** Sarawak, East Malaysia *2.55N 112.01E*
Mukalla *see* Al Mukallā
Mukama *see* Mokāma
Mukāshafa/Mukashshafah *see* Mukayshīfah
172 *Oo6* **Mu-kawa** ≈ Hokkaidō, NE Japan
145 *S6* **Mukayshīfah** ***var.*** Mukāshafa, Mukashshafah. N Iraq *34.24N 43.44E*
178 *J9* **Mukdahan** Mukdahan, E Thailand *16.31N 104.43E*
Mukden *see* Shenyang
172 *Ss16* **Mukojima-rettō** ***Eng.*** Parry group. *island group* SE Japan
152 *M14* **Mukry** Lebap Welaýaty, E Turkmenistan *37.39N 65.37E*
Muksu *see* Mughsu
159 *U14* **Muktagacha** ***var.*** Muktagachha Dhaka, N Bangladesh *24.46N 90.16E*
Muktagachha *see* Muktagacha
84 *K13* **Mukuku** Central, C Zambia *12.10S 29.50E*
84 *K11* **Mukupa Kaoma** Northern, NE Zambia *9.55S 30.19E*
83 *I18* **Mukutan** Rift Valley, W Kenya *1.06N 36.16E*
85 *F16* **Mukwe** Caprivi, NE Namibia *18.01S 21.24E*
107 *R13* **Mula** Murcia, SE Spain *38.01N 1.28W*
157 *K20* **Mulaku Atoll** ***var.*** Meemu Atoll. *atoll* C Maldives
85 *J15* **Mulalika** Lusaka, C Zambia *15.37S 28.48E*
169 *X8* **Mulan** Heilongjiang, NE China *45.57N 128.00E*
85 *N15* **Mulanje** ***var.*** Mlanje. Southern, S Malawi *16.04S 35.35E*
42 *H5* **Mulatos** Sonora, NW Mexico *28.42N 108.44W*
25 *P3* **Mulberry Fork** ≈ Alabama, S USA
41 *P12* **Mulchatna River** ≈ Alaska, USA
129 *W4* **Mul'da** Respublika Komi, NW Russian Federation *67.29N 63.55E*
103 *M14* **Mulde** ≈ E Germany
29 *R10* **Muldrow** Oklahoma, C USA *35.25N 94.34W*
42 *E7* **Mulegé** Baja California Sur, W Mexico *26.54N 112.00W*
110 *I10* **Mulegns** Graubünden, S Switzerland *46.30N 9.36E*
81 *M21* **Mulenda** Kasai Oriental, C Dem. Rep. Congo *4.19S 24.55E*
26 *M4* **Muleshoe** Texas, SW USA *34.13N 102.43W*
85 *O15* **Mulevala** Zambézia, NE Mozambique *16.18S 37.40E*
191 *P5* **Mulgoa Creek** *seasonal river* New South Wales, SE Australia
107 *O15* **Mulhacén** ***var.*** Cerro de Mulhacén. ▲ S Spain *37.07N 3.11W*
Mulhacén, Cerro de *see* Mulhacén
Mülhausen *see* Mulhouse
103 *E24* **Mülheim** Baden-Württemberg, SW Germany *47.49N 7.36E*
103 *E15* **Mülheim** ***var.*** Mulheim an der Ruhr. Nordrhein-Westfalen, W Germany *51.25N 6.52E*
Mulheim an der Ruhr *see* Mülheim
105 *U7* **Mulhouse** ***Ger.*** Mülhausen. Haut-Rhin, NE France *47.45N 7.19E*
166 *G11* **Muli** ***var.*** Qiaowa, Muli Zangzu Zizhixian. Sichuan, C China *27.49N 101.10E*
176 *Y15* **Muli** *channel* Papua, E Indonesia
169 *Y9* **Muling** Heilongjiang, NE China *44.54N 130.35E*
Mullach Íde *see* Malahide
Mullaitivu *see* Mullaittivu
161 *K23* **Mullaittivu** ***var.*** Mullaitivu. Northern Province, N Sri Lanka *9.15N 80.48E*
35 *N8* **Mullan** Idaho, NW USA *47.28N 115.48W*
30 *M13* **Mullen** Nebraska, C USA *42.02N 101.01W*
191 *Q6* **Mullengudgery** New South Wales, SE Australia *31.42S 147.24E*
23 *Q6* **Mullens** West Virginia, NE USA *37.34N 81.22W*
Müller-gerbergte *see* Muller, Pegunungan
174 *Mm7* **Muller, Pegunungan** ***Dut.*** Müller-gerbergte. ▲▲ Borneo, C Indonesia
194 *F12* **Muller Range** ▲▲ W PNG
33 *Q5* **Mullett Lake** ◎ Michigan, N USA
20 *J16* **Mullica River** ≈ New Jersey, NE USA
27 *R8* **Mullin** Texas, SW USA *31.33N 98.40W*
99 *E17* **Mullingar** ***Ir.*** An Muileann gCearr. C Ireland *53.31N 7.19W*
23 *T12* **Mullins** South Carolina, SE USA *34.12N 79.15W*
98 *G11* **Mull, Isle of** *island* W Scotland, UK
131 *R5* **Mullovka** Ul'yanovskaya Oblast', W Russian Federation *54.13N 49.19E*
97 *K19* **Mullsjö** Västra Götaland, S Sweden *57.55N 13.55E*
191 *V4* **Mullumbimby** New South Wales, SE Australia *28.34S 153.28E*
85 *H15* **Mulobezi** Western, SW Zambia *16.48S 25.10E*
85 *C15* **Mulondo** Huíla, SW Angola *15.41S 15.09E*
85 *G15* **Mulonga Plain** *plain* W Zambia
81 *N23* **Mulongo** Katanga, SE Dem. Rep. Congo *7.44S 26.57E*
155 *T10* **Multān** Punjab, E Pakistan *30.12N 71.29E*
95 *L17* **Multia** Länsi-Suomi, W Finland *62.27N 24.49E*
Mulucha *see* Moulouya
85 *J14* **Mulungushi** Central, C Zambia *14.15S 28.27E*
85 *K14* **Mulungwe** Central, C Zambia *13.57S 29.51E*
Muluya *see* Moulouya
29 *N7* **Mulvane** Kansas, C USA *37.28N 97.14W*
191 *O10* **Mulwala** New South Wales, SE Australia *35.59S 146.00E*
Mulwiya *see* Moulouya
190 *K6* **Mulyungarie** South Australia *31.29S 140.45E*
160 *D13* **Mumbai** ***prev.*** Bombay. Mahārāshtra, W India *18.55N 72.51E*
160 *D13* **Mumbai** ✈ Mahārāshtra, W India *19.10N 72.51E*
85 *D14* **Mumbué** Bié, C Angola *13.52S 17.15E*
194 *J13* **Mumeng** Morobe, C PNG *6.57S 146.37E*
176 *W9* **Mumi** Papua, E Indonesia *1.33S 134.09E*
Muminabad/Mŭ'minobod *see* Leningrad
131 *Q13* **Mumra** Astrakhanskaya Oblast', SW Russian Federation *45.46N 47.46E*
43 *X12* **Muna** Yucatán, SE Mexico *20.28N 89.45W*
126 *Kk9* **Muna** ≈ NE Russian Federation
158 *C12* **Munābāo** Rājasthān, NW India *25.46N 70.19E*
Munamägi *see* Suur Munamägi
175 *Qq13* **Muna, Pulau** ***prev.*** Moena. *island* C Indonesia
175 *Qq13* **Muna, Selat** *strait* Sulawesi, C Indonesia
103 *L18* **Münchberg** Bayern, E Germany *50.10N 11.49E*
103 *L23* **München** ***var.*** Muenchen, ***Eng.*** Munich, ***It.*** Monaco. Bayern, SE Germany *48.08N 11.34E*
München-Gladbach *see* Mönchengladbach
110 *E6* **Münchenstein** Basel-Land, NW Switzerland *47.31N 7.37E*
8 *L10* **Muncho Lake** British Columbia, W Canada *58.52N 125.40W*
33 *P13* **Muncie** Indiana, N USA *40.10N 85.22W*
20 *G13* **Muncy** Pennsylvania, NE USA *41.10N 76.46W*
195 *U14* **Munda** New Georgia, NW Solomon Islands *8.15S 157.15E*
9 *Q14* **Mundare** Alberta, SW Canada *53.34N 112.20W*
27 *Q5* **Munday** Texas, SW USA *33.27N 99.37W*
33 *N10* **Mundelein** Illinois, N USA *42.15N 88.00W*
103 *I15* **Münden** Niedersachsen, C Germany *52.16N 8.54E*
107 *Q12* **Mundo** ≈ S Spain
194 *L11* **Mundua Island** *island* Witu Islands, C PNG
84 *B12* **Munenga** Cuanza Sul, NW Angola *10.05S 14.35E*
107 *P11* **Munera** Castilla-La Mancha, C Spain *39.03N 2.28W*
22 *E9* **Munford** Tennessee, S USA *35.27N 89.49W*
22 *K7* **Munfordville** Kentucky, S USA *37.15N 85.53W*
190 *D5* **Mungala** South Australia *30.36S 132.57E*
85 *M16* **Mungári** Manica, C Mozambique *17.09S 33.33E*
81 *O16* **Mungbere** Orientale, NE Dem. Rep. Congo *2.37N 28.30E*
159 *Q13* **Munger** ***prev.*** Monghyr. Bihār, NE India *25.22N 86.28E*
190 *I2* **Mungeranie** South Australia *28.02S 138.42E*
Mu Nggava *see* Rennell
174 *K6* **Mungguresak, Tanjung** *headland* Borneo, N Indonesia *1.57N 109.19E*
Mungiki *see* Bellona
191 *R4* **Mungindi** New South Wales, SE Australia *28.59S 149.00E*
Mungkawn *see* Maingkwan
159 *T16* **Mungla** ***var.*** Mongla. Khulna, S Bangladesh *22.18N 89.34E*
84 *C13* **Mungo** Huambo, W Angola *11.46S 16.13E*
196 *F16* **Munguuy Bay** *bay* Yap, W Micronesia
84 *E13* **Munhango** Bié, C Angola *12.12S 18.34E*
197 *L14* **Munia** *island* Lau Group, E Fiji
Munich *see* München
107 *S7* **Muniesa** Aragón, NE Spain *41.01N 0.49W*
33 *O4* **Munising** Michigan, N USA *46.24N 86.39W*
Munkács *see* Mukacheve
97 *I17* **Munkedal** Västra Götaland, S Sweden *58.28N 11.37E*
97 *K15* **Munkfors** Värmland, C Sweden *59.49N 13.34E*
126 *J16* **Munku-Sardyk, Gora** ***var.*** Mönh Sarĭdag. ▲ Mongolia/ Russian Federation *51.45N 100.22E*
101 *E18* **Munkzwalm** Oost-Vlaanderen, NW Belgium *50.53N 3.44E*
178 *J10* **Mun, Mae Nam** ≈ E Thailand
159 *U15* **Munshiganj** Dhaka, C Bangladesh *23.31N 90.31E*
110 *D8* **Münsingen** Bern, W Switzerland *46.52N 7.36E*
105 *U6* **Munster** Haut-Rhin, NE France *48.03N 7.09E*
102 *J11* **Munster** Niedersachsen, NW Germany *52.58N 10.06E*
99 *B20* **Munster** ***Ir.*** Cúige Mumhan. *cultural region* S Ireland
102 *F13* **Münster** ***var.*** Muenster, Münster in Westfalen. Nordrhein-Westfalen, W Germany *51.58N 7.37E*
110 *F10* **Münster** Valais, S Switzerland *46.31N 8.18E*
Münsterberg in Schlesien *see* Ziębice
Münster in Westfalen *see* Münster
102 *E13* **Münsterland** *cultural region* NW Germany
102 *F13* **Münster-Osnabruck** ✈ Nordrhein-Westfalen, NW Germany *52.08N 7.41E*
33 *R4* **Munuscong Lake** ◎ Michigan, N USA
85 *K17* **Munyati** ≈ C Zimbabwe
111 *R3* **Münzkirchen** Oberösterreich, N Austria *48.29N 13.37E*
94 *K11* **Muodoslompolo** Norrbotten, N Sweden *67.57N 23.31E*
94 *M13* **Muojärvi** ◎ NE Finland
178 *J6* **Mương Khên** Hoa Binh, N Vietnam *20.34N 105.18E*
Muong Sai *see* Xai
178 *I7* **Muong Xiang Ngeun** ***var.*** Xieng Ngeun. Louangphabang, N Laos *19.43N 102.09E*
94 *K11* **Muonio** Lappi, N Finland *67.58N 23.40E*
Muonioälv/Muoniojoki *see* Muonionjoki
94 *K11* **Muonionjoki** ***var.*** Muoniojoki, ***Swe.*** Muonioälv. ≈ Finland/ Sweden
85 *N17* **Mupa** ≈ C Mozambique
85 *E16* **Mupini** Okavango, NE Namibia *17.55S 19.34E*
82 *F8* **Muqaddam, Wadi** ≈ N Sudan
144 *K9* **Muqāţ** Al Mafraq, E Jordan *32.28N 38.04E*
147 *X7* **Muqaz** N Oman *24.13N 56.48E*
83 *N17* **Muqdisho** ***Eng.*** Mogadishu, ***It.*** Mogadiscio. ● (Somalia) Banaadir, S Somalia *2.06N 45.27E*
83 *N17* **Muqdisho** ✈ Banaadir, E Somalia *1.58N 45.18E*
Muqshin *see* Mughshin
111 *T8* **Mur** ***SCr.*** Mura. ≈ C Europe
Mura *see* Mur
111 *X9* **Mura** ≈ NE Slovenia
143 *T14* **Muradiye** Van, E Turkey *39.00N 43.44E*
Muragarazi *see* Maragarazi
171 *L12* **Murakami** Niigata, Honshū, C Japan *38.13N 139.28E*
65 *G22* **Murallón, Cerro** ▲ S Argentina *49.49S 73.25W*
83 *E20* **Muramvya** C Burundi *3.18S 29.41E*
83 *I19* **Murang'a** ***prev.*** Fort Hall. Central, SW Kenya *0.43S 37.10E*
83 *H16* **Murangering** Rift Valley, NW Kenya *3.48N 35.29E*
Murapara *see* Murupara
146 *M5* **Murār, Bi'r al** *well* NW Saudi Arabia *27.20N 40.21E*
129 *Q13* **Murashi** Kirovskaya Oblast', NW Russian Federation *59.27N 48.02E*
105 *O12* **Murat** Cantal, C France *45.07N 2.52E*
116 *N12* **Muratlı** Tekirdağ, NW Turkey *41.12N 27.30E*
143 *R14* **Murat Nehri** ***var.*** Eastern Euphrates; ***anc.*** Arsanias. ≈ NE Turkey
109 *D20* **Muravera** Sardegna, Italy, C Mediterranean Sea *39.24N 9.34E*
171 *Ll12* **Murayama** Yamagata, Honshū, C Japan *38.29N 140.21E*
124 *Oo15* **Muraysah, Ra's al** *headland* N Libya *31.58N 25.00E*
106 *I6* **Murça** Vila Real, N Portugal *41.24N 7.28W*
82 *Q11* **Murcanyo** Bari, NE Somalia *11.39N 50.27E*
149 *N8* **Mūrcheh Khvort** ***var.*** Morcheh Khort. Eşfahān, C Iran *33.07N 51.26E*
193 *H15* **Murchison** Tasman, South Island, NZ *41.48S 172.19E*
193 *B22* **Murchison Mountains** ▲▲ South Island, NZ
188 *I10* **Murchison River** ≈ Western Australia
107 *R13* **Murcia** Murcia, SE Spain *37.58N 1.07W*
107 *Q13* **Murcia** ⬖ *autonomous community* SE Spain
105 *O13* **Mur-de-Barrez** Aveyron, S France *44.48N 2.39E*
190 *G8* **Murdinga** South Australia *33.46S 135.46E*
30 *M10* **Murdo** South Dakota, N USA *43.53N 100.42W*
13 *X6* **Murdochville** Québec, SE Canada *48.57N 65.30W*
111 *W9* **Mureck** Steiermark, SE Austria *46.42N 15.46E*
116 *M13* **Mürefte** Tekirdağ, NW Turkey *40.40N 27.15E*
118 *I10* **Mureş** ⬖ *county* N Romania
86 *J11* **Mureş** ***var.*** Maros, Mureşul, ***Ger.*** Marosch, Mieresch. ≈ Hungary/ Romania *see also* Maros
Mureşul *see* Maros/Mureş
104 *M16* **Muret** Haute-Garonne, S France *43.28N 1.19E*
29 *T13* **Murfreesboro** Arkansas, C USA *34.03N 93.41W*
23 *W8* **Murfreesboro** North Carolina, SE USA *36.26N 77.06W*
22 *J9* **Murfreesboro** Tennessee, S USA *35.51N 86.23W*
Murgab *see* Morghāb, Daryā-ye/ Murgap/Murghob
152 *I14* **Murgap** ***Rus.*** Murgap. Mary Welaýaty, S Turkmenistan *37.19N 61.48E*
152 *J16* **Murgap** ***var.*** Murgap Deryasy, Murghab, ***Pash.*** Daryā-ye Morghāb, ***Rus.*** Murgab. ≈ Afghanistan/Turkmenistan *see also* Morghāb, Daryā-ye
Murgap Deryasy *see* Morghāb, Daryā-ye/Murgap
116 *H9* **Murgash** ▲ W Bulgaria *42.51N 23.58E*
Murghab Morghāb, Daryā-ye/ Murgap
153 *U13* **Murghob** ***Rus.*** Murgab. SE Tajikistan *38.11N 73.59E*
153 *U13* **Murghob** ***Rus.*** Murgab. ≈ SE Tajikistan
189 *Z10* **Murgon** Queensland, E Australia *26.07S 152.03E*
202 *I16* **Muri** Rarotonga, S Cook Islands *21.15S 159.43W*
110 *F7* **Muri** Aargau, W Switzerland *47.16N 8.21E*
110 *D8* **Muri** ***var.*** Muri bei Bern. Bern, W Switzerland *46.55N 7.30E*
106 *K3* **Murias de Paredes** Castilla-León, N Spain *42.51N 6.11W*
Muri bei Bern *see* Muri
84 *F11* **Muriege** Lunda Sul, NE Angola *9.55S 21.12E*
201 *P14* **Murilo Atoll** *atoll* Hall Islands, C Micronesia
Mūrītānīyah *see* Mauritania
102 *N10* **Müritz** ***var.*** Müritzee. ◎ NE Germany
Müritzee *see* Müritz
102 *L10* **Müritz-Elde-Kanal** *canal* N Germany
192 *K6* **Muriwai Beach** Auckland, North Island, NZ *36.56S 174.28E*
94 *J13* **Murjek** Norrbotten, N Sweden *66.27N 20.54E*
128 *J3* **Murmansk** Murmanskaya Oblast', NW Russian Federation *68.58N 33.07E*
128 *I4* **Murmanskaya Oblast'** ⬖ *province* NW Russian Federation
207 *V14* **Murmansk Rise** *undersea feature* SW Barents Sea
128 *J3* **Murmashi** Murmanskaya Oblast', NW Russian Federation *68.49N 32.42E*
130 *M5* **Murmino** Ryazanskaya Oblast', W Russian Federation *54.31N 40.01E*
103 *K24* **Murnau** Bayern, SE Germany *47.41N 11.12E*
105 *X16* **Muro, Capo di** *headland* Corse, France, C Mediterranean Sea *41.45N 8.40E*
109 *M18* **Muro Lucano** Basilicata, S Italy *40.48N 15.33E*
131 *N4* **Murom** Vladimirskaya Oblast', W Russian Federation *55.33N 42.03E*
125 *G13* **Muromtsevo** Omskaya Oblast', C Russian Federation *56.18N 75.15E*
172 *Nn6* **Muroran** Hokkaidō, NE Japan *42.19N 140.58E*
106 *G3* **Muros** Galicia, NW Spain *42.46N 9.03W*
106 *F3* **Muros e Noia, Ría de** *estuary* NW Spain
170 *F16* **Muroto** Kōchi, Shikoku, SW Japan *33.18N 134.07E*
170 *F16* **Muroto-zaki** *headland* Shikoku, SW Japan *33.15N 134.09E*
118 *L7* **Murovani Kurylivtsi** Vinnyts'ka Oblast', C Ukraine *48.43N 27.31E*
112 *G11* **Murowana Goślina** Wielkolpolskie, C Poland *52.33N 16.59E*
34 *M14* **Murphy** Idaho, NW USA *43.14N 116.36W*
23 *N10* **Murphy** North Carolina, SE USA *35.05N 84.01W*
37 *P8* **Murphys** California, W USA *38.07N 120.27W*
32 *L17* **Murphysboro** Illinois, N USA *37.45N 89.20W*
31 *V15* **Murray** Iowa, C USA *41.03N 93.56W*
22 *H8* **Murray** Kentucky, S USA *36.36N 88.18W*
190 *J10* **Murray Bridge** South Australia *35.06S 139.15E*
183 *X2* **Murray Fracture Zone** *tectonic feature* NE Pacific Ocean
194 *E13* **Murray, Lake** ◎ SW PNG
23 *P12* **Murray, Lake** ⊠ South Carolina, SE USA
8 *K8* **Murray, Mount** ▲ Yukon Territory, NW Canada *60.49N 128.57W*
194 *H13* **Murray Range** ***var.*** Leonard Murray Mountains. ▲▲ W PNG
Murray Range *see* Murray Ridge
181 *O3* **Murray Ridge** ***var.*** Murray Range. *undersea feature* N Arabian Sea
191 *N10* **Murray River** ≈ SE Australia
190 *K10* **Murrayville** Victoria, SE Australia *35.17S 141.12E*
155 *U5* **Murree** Punjab, E Pakistan *33.55N 73.25E*
103 *I21* **Murrhardt** Baden-Württemberg, S Germany *49.00N 9.34E*
191 *O9* **Murrumbidgee River** ≈ New South Wales, SE Australia
85 *P15* **Murrupula** Nampula, NE Mozambique *15.26S 38.46E*
191 *T7* **Murrurundi** New South Wales, SE Australia *31.47S 150.51E*
111 *X9* **Murska Sobota** ***Ger.*** Olsnitz. NE Slovenia *46.40N 16.09E*
160 *G12* **Murtajāpur** ***prev.*** Murtazapur. Mahārāshtra, C India *20.43N 77.28E*
79 *S16* **Murtala Muhammed** ✈ (Lagos) Ogun, SW Nigeria *6.31N 3.12E*
Murtazapur *see* Murtajāpur
110 *C8* **Murten** Neuchâtel, W Switzerland *46.55N 7.06E*
Murtensee *see* Morat, Lac de
190 *L11* **Murtoa** Victoria, SE Australia *36.39S 142.27E*
94 *N13* **Murtovaara** Oulu, E Finland *65.40N 29.25E*
Murua Island *see* Woodlark Island
161 *D14* **Murud** Mahārāshtra, W India *18.27N 72.56E*
192 *O9* **Murupara** ***var.*** Murapara. Bay of Plenty, North Island, NZ *38.27S 176.40E*
203 *X12* **Mururoa** ***var.*** Moruroa. *atoll* Îles Tuamotu, SE French Polynesia
Murviedro *see* Sagunto
160 *J9* **Murwāra** Madhya Pradesh, N India *23.50N 80.23E*
191 *V4* **Murwillumbah** New South Wales, SE Australia *28.19S 153.24E*
152 *H11* **Murzechirla** ***prev.*** Mirzachirla. Ahal Welaýaty, C Turkmenistan *39.33N 60.02E*
Murzuk *see* Murzuq
77 *O11* **Murzuq** ***var.*** Marzūq, Murzuk. SW Libya *25.55N 13.55E*
Murzuq, Edeyin *see* Murzuq, Idhān
77 *N11* **Murzuq, Ḩamādat** *plateau* W Libya
77 *O11* **Murzuq, Idhān** ***var.*** Edeyin Murzuq. *desert* SW Libya
111 *W6* **Mürzzuschlag** Steiermark, E Austria *47.34N 15.40E*
143 *Q14* **Muş** ***var.*** Mush. Muş, E Turkey *38.45N 41.30E*
143 *Q14* **Muş** ***var.*** Mush. ⬖ *province* E Turkey
194 *L16* **Musa** ≈ S PNG
120 *G11* **Mūša** ≈ Latvia/Lithuania
77 *X8* **Mûsa, Gebel** ▲ NE Egypt *28.33N 33.51E*
Musaiyib *see* Al Musayyib
Musa Khel *see* Mūsā Khel Bazār
155 *R9* **Mūsā Khel Bazār** ***var.*** Musa Khel. Baluchistān, SW Pakistan *30.52N 69.46E*
116 *H10* **Musala** ▲ W Bulgaria *42.12N 23.36E*
173 *F6* **Musala, Pulau** *island* W Indonesia
85 *I15* **Musale** Southern, S Zambia *15.27S 26.50E*
147 *Y9* **Muşalla** NE Oman *22.19N 58.03E*
147 *W6* **Musandam Peninsula** ***Ar.*** Masandam Peninsula. *peninsula* N Oman
Musay'īd *see* Umm Sa'īd
Muscat *see* Masqaţ
Muscat and Oman *see* Oman
31 *Y14* **Muscatine** Iowa, C USA *41.25N 91.03W*
Muscat Sīb Airport *see* Seeb
33 *O15* **Muscatuck River** ≈ Indiana, N USA
194 *G10* **Muschu Island** *island* NW PNG
32 *K8* **Muscoda** Wisconsin, N USA *43.11N 90.27W*
193 *F19* **Musgrave, Mount** ▲ South Island, NZ *43.48S 170.43E*
189 *P9* **Musgrave Ranges** ▲▲ South Australia
Mush *see* Muş
144 *H12* **Mushayyish, Qaşr al** *castle* Ma'ān, C Jordan *30.58N 36.41E*
81 *H20* **Mushie** Bandundu, W Dem. Rep. Congo *3.00S 16.55E*
174 *I11* **Musi, Air** ***prev.*** Moesi. ≈ Sumatera, W Indonesia
199 *K5* **Musicians Seamounts** *undersea feature* N Pacific Ocean
85 *K19* **Musina** ***prev.*** Messina. Limpopo, NE South Africa *22.18S 30.02E*
56 *D8* **Musinga, Alto** ▲ NW Colombia *6.49N 76.24W*
31 *T2* **Muskeg Bay** *lake bay* Minnesota, N USA
33 *O8* **Muskegon** Michigan, N USA *43.13N 86.15W*
33 *O8* **Muskegon Heights** Michigan, N USA *43.12N 86.14W*
33 *P8* **Muskegon River** ≈ Michigan, N USA
33 *T14* **Muskingum River** ≈ Ohio, N USA
97 *P16* **Muskö** Stockholm, C Sweden *58.58N 18.10E*
Muskogean *see* Tallahassee
29 *Q10* **Muskogee** Oklahoma, C USA *35.45N 95.22W*
12 *H13* **Muskoka, Lake** ◎ Ontario, S Canada
82 *H8* **Musmar** Red Sea, NE Sudan *18.13N 35.40E*
85 *K14* **Musofu** Central, C Zambia *13.31S 29.03E*
83 *G19* **Musoma** Mara, N Tanzania *1.31S 33.49E*
84 *L13* **Musoro** Central, C Zambia *13.21S 31.04E*
194 *M8* **Mussau Island** *island* NE PNG
100 *P7* **Musselkanaal** Groningen, NE Netherlands *52.55N 7.01E*
35 *V9* **Musselshell River** ≈ Montana, NW USA
84 *C12* **Mussende** Cuanza Sul, NW Angola *10.33S 16.01E*
104 *L12* **Mussidan** Dordogne, SW France *45.03N 0.22E*
101 *L25* **Musson** Luxembourg, SE Belgium *49.33N 5.42E*
158 *J9* **Mussoorie** Uttaranchal, N India *30.25N 78.04E*
Musta *see* Mosta
158 *M13* **Mustafābād** Uttar Pradesh, N India *25.54N 81.16E*
142 *D12* **Mustafakemalpaşa** Bursa, NW Turkey *40.03N 28.25E*
Mustafa-Pasha *see* Svilengrad
83 *M15* **Mustahīl** Somali, E Ethiopia *5.18N 44.34E*
26 *M7* **Mustang Draw** *valley* Texas, SW USA
27 *T14* **Mustang Island** *island* Texas, SW USA
Mustasaari *see* Korsholm
Mustér *see* Disentis
65 *I19* **Musters, Lago** ◎ S Argentina
47 *Y14* **Mustique** *island* C Saint Vincent and the Grenadines
120 *I6* **Mustla** Viljandimaa, S Estonia *58.12N 25.51E*
120 *J4* **Mustvee** ***Ger.*** Tschorna. Jõgevamaa, E Estonia *58.51N 26.57E*
44 *L9* **Musún, Cerro** ▲ NE Nicaragua *13.01N 85.02W*
191 *T7* **Muswellbrook** New South Wales, SE Australia *32.16S 150.55E*
113 *M18* **Muszyna** Małopolskie, SE Poland *49.21N 20.54E*
77 *V10* **Mût** ***var.*** Mut. C Egypt *25.34N 28.58E*
142 *I17* **Mut** Mersin, S Turkey *36.37N 33.27E*
111 *V9* **Muta** N Slovenia *46.37N 15.09E*
202 *B15* **Mutalau** N Niue *18.55S 169.49E*
Mu-tan-chiang *see* Mudanjiang
84 *I13* **Mutanda** North Western, NW Zambia *12.22S 26.15E*
61 *O17* **Mutá, Ponta do** *headland* E Brazil *13.54S 38.54W*
85 *L17* **Mutare** ***var.*** Mutari; ***prev.*** Umtali. Manicaland, E Zimbabwe *18.54S 32.36E*
Mutari *see* Mutare
56 *D8* **Mutatá** Antioquia, NW Colombia *7.16N 76.31W*
Mutina *see* Modena
176 *Z15* **Muting** Papua, E Indonesia *7.10S 140.41E*
85 *L16* **Mutoko** ***prev.*** Mtoko. Mashonaland East, NE Zimbabwe *17.24S 32.13E*
83 *J20* **Mutomo** Eastern, S Kenya *1.49S 38.13E*
126 *J12* **Mutoray** Evenkiyskiy Avtonomnyy Okrug, C Russian Federation *61.30N 101.00E*
Mutrah *see* Maţraḩ
81 *M24* **Mutshatsha** Katanga, S Dem. Rep. Congo *10.40S 24.25E*
172 *Nn8* **Mutsu** ***var.*** Mutu. Aomori, Honshū, N Japan *41.18N 141.11E*
172 *N8* **Mutsu-wan** *bay* N Japan
110 *E6* **Muttenz** Basel-Land, NW Switzerland *47.31N 7.39E*
193 *A26* **Muttonbird Islands** *island group* SW NZ
Mutu *see* Mutsu
85 *O15* **Mutuáli** Nampula, N Mozambique *14.51S 37.01E*
84 *D13* **Mutumbo** Bié, C Angola *13.10S 17.22E*
201 *Y14* **Mutunte, Mount** ***var.*** Mount Buache. ▲ Kosrae, E Micronesia *5.21N 163.00E*
161 *K24* **Mutur** Eastern Province, E Sri Lanka *8.27N 81.15E*
94 *L13* **Muurola** Lappi, NW Finland *66.21N 25.19E*
168 *M14* **Mu Us Shadi** ***var.*** Ordos Desert, ***prev.*** Mu Us Shamo. *desert* N China
Mu Us Shamo *see* Mu Us Shadi
84 *B11* **Muxima** Bengo, NW Angola *9.27S 13.58E*
128 *I8* **Muyezerskiy** Respublika Kareliya, NW Russian Federation *63.54N 32.00E*
83 *E20* **Muyinga** NE Burundi *2.54S 30.19E*
44 *K9* **Muy Muy** Matagalpa, C Nicaragua *12.43N 85.37W*
Muynak *see* Mo'ynoq
81 *N22* **Muyumba** Katanga, SE Dem. Rep. Congo *7.13S 27.02E*
155 *V5* **Muzaffarābād** Jammu and Kashmir, NE Pakistan *34.24N 73.30E*
155 *S10* **Muzaffargarh** Punjab, E Pakistan *30.04N 71.10E*
158 *J9* **Muzaffarnagar** Uttar Pradesh, N India *29.28N 77.42E*
159 *P13* **Muzaffarpur** Bihār, N India *26.07N 85.22E*
164 *H6* **Muzat He** ≈ W China
85 *L15* **Muze** Tete, NW Mozambique *15.05S 31.16E*
125 *Ff8* **Muzhi** Yamalo-Nenetskiy Avtonomnyy Okrug, N Russian Federation *65.25N 64.28E*
104 *H7* **Muzillac** Morbihan, NW France *47.34N 2.30W*
Muzkol, Khrebet *see* Muzqŭl, Qatorkŭhi
114 *L9* **Mužlja** ***Hung.*** Felsőmuzslya; ***prev.*** Gornja Mužlja. Serbia, N Serbia *45.21N 20.25E*
56 *F9* **Muzo** Boyacá, C Colombia *5.34N 74.07W*
85 *J15* **Muzoka** Southern, S Zambia *16.39S 27.21E*
41 *Y15* **Muzon, Cape** *headland* Dall Island, Alaska, USA *54.39N 132.41W*
42 *M6* **Múzquiz** Coahuila de Zaragoza, NE Mexico *27.52N 101.31W*
153 *U13* **Muzqŭl, Qatorkŭhi** ***Rus.*** Khrebet Muzkol. ▲▲ SE Tajikistan
164 *G10* **Muztag** ▲ NW China *36.02N 80.13E*
164 *K10* **Muz Tag** ▲ W China *36.26N 87.15E*
164 *D8* **Muztagata** ▲ NW China *38.16N 75.03E*
85 *K17* **Mvuma** ***prev.*** Umvuma. Midlands, C Zimbabwe *19.16S 30.31E*
84 *L13* **Mwanya** Eastern, E Zambia *12.40S 32.15E*
83 *G20* **Mwanza** Mwanza, NW Tanzania *2.31S 32.55E*
81 *N23* **Mwanza** Katanga, SE Dem. Rep. Congo *7.49S 26.49E*
83 *F20* **Mwanza** ⬖ *region* N Tanzania
84 *M13* **Mwase Lundazi** Eastern, E Zambia *12.26S 33.20E*
99 *B17* **Mweelrea** ***Ir.*** Caoc Maol Réidh. ▲ W Ireland *53.37N 9.47W*
81 *K21* **Mweka** Kasai Occidental, C Dem. Rep. Congo *4.51S 21.37E*
84 *K12* **Mwenda** Luapula, N Zambia *10.25S 29.10E*
81 *L22* **Mwene-Ditu** Kasai Oriental, S Dem. Rep. Congo *7.05S 23.33E*
85 *L18* **Mwenezi** ≈ S Zimbabwe
81 *O20* **Mwenga** Sud Kivu, E Dem. Rep. Congo *3.00S 28.28E*
84 *K11* **Mweru, Lake** ***var.*** Lac Moero. ◎ Dem. Rep. Congo/Zambia
84 *H13* **Mwinilunga** North Western, NW Zambia *11.43S 24.24E*
201 *V16* **Mwokil Atoll** ***var.*** Mokil Atoll. *atoll* Caroline Islands, E Micronesia
Myadel' *see* Myadzyel
120 *J13* **Myadzyel** ***Pol.*** Miadzioł Nowy, ***Rus.*** Myadel'. Minskaya Voblasts', N Belarus *54.51N 26.51E*
158 *C12* **Myājlār** ***var.*** Miajlar. Rājasthān, NW India *26.16N 70.21E*
127 *O9* **Myakit** Magadanskaya Oblast', E Russian Federation *61.23N 151.58E*
25 *W13* **Myakka River** ≈ Florida, SE USA
128 *L14* **Myaksa** Vologodskaya Oblast', NW Russian Federation *58.54N 38.15E*
191 *U8* **Myall Lake** ◎ New South Wales, SE Australia
177 *Ff7* **Myanaung** Irrawaddy, SW Burma *18.16N 95.19E*
Myanmar *see* Burma
177 *F9* **Myaungmya** Irrawaddy, SW Burma *16.33N 94.55E*
120 *N11* **Myazha** ***Rus.*** Mezha. Vitsyebskaya Voblasts', NE Belarus *55.40N 30.25E*
121 *O18* **Myerkulavichy** ***Rus.*** Merkulovichi. Homyel'skaya Voblasts', SE Belarus *52.57N 30.33E*
121 *N14* **Myezhava** ***Rus.*** Mezhëvo. Vitsyebskaya Voblasts', NE Belarus *54.39N 30.18E*
177 *Ff5* **Myingyan** Mandalay, C Burma *21.25N 95.19E*
177 *G5* **Myinmu** Sagaing, C Burma *21.58N 95.34E*
178 *Gg2* **Myitkyina** Kachin State, N Burma *25.24N 97.25E*
177 *G5* **Myittha** Mandalay, C Burma *21.21N 96.06E*
113 *H19* **Myjava** ***Hung.*** Miava. Trenčiansky Kraj, W Slovakia *48.48N 17.31E*
Myjeldino *see* Myyëldino
119 *U9* **Mykhaylivka** ***Rus.*** Mikhaylovka. Zaporiz'ka Oblast', SE Ukraine *47.16N 35.14E*
97 *A18* **Mykines** ***Dan.*** Myggenaes *Island* Faeroe Islands *62.07N 7.38W*
118 *I5* **Mykolayiv** L'vivs'ka Oblast', W Ukraine *49.34N 23.58E*
119 *Q10* **Mykolayiv** ***Rus.*** Nikolayev. Mykolayivs'ka Oblast', S Ukraine *46.57N 31.58E*
119 *Q10* **Mykolayiv** ✈ Mykolayivs'ka Oblast', S Ukraine *47.02N 31.54E*
Mykolayiv *see* Mykolayivs'ka Oblast'
119 *P9* **Mykolayivka** Odes'ka Oblast', SW Ukraine *47.34N 30.48E*
119 *S13* **Mykolayivka** Respublika Krym, S Ukraine *44.58N 33.37E*
119 *P9* **Mykolayivs'ka Oblast'** ***var.*** Mykolayiv, ***Rus.*** Nikolayevskaya Oblast'. ⬖ *province* S Ukraine
117 *J20* **Mýkonos** Mýkonos, Kykládes, Greece, Aegean Sea *37.27N 25.20E*
117 *K20* **Mýkonos** ***var.*** Míkonos. *island* Kykládes, Greece, Aegean Sea
129 *R7* **Myla** Respublika Komi, NW Russian Federation *65.24N 50.51E*
Mylae *see* Milazzo
95 *M19* **Myllykoski** Etelä-Suomi, S Finland *60.45N 26.52E*
Mymensing *see* Mymensingh
159 *U14* **Mymensingh** ***var.*** Maimansingh, Mymensing; ***prev.*** Nasirābād. Dhaka, N Bangladesh *24.45N 90.22E*
95 *K19* **Mynämäki** Länsi-Suomi, W Finland *60.41N 22.00E*
151 *S14* **Mynaral** ***Kaz.*** Myngaral. Zhambyl, S Kazakhstan *45.25N 73.37E*
Mynbulak *see* Mingbuloq
Mynbulak, Vpadina *see* Mingbuloq Botig'I
Myngaral *see* Mynaral
177 *F5* **Myohaung** Arakan State, W Burma *20.34N 93.12E*
169 *W13* **Myohyang-sanmaek** ▲▲ C North Korea
171 *Jj13* **Myōkō-san** ▲ Honshū, S Japan *36.54N 138.05E*
85 *J15* **Myooye** Central, C Zambia *15.10S 27.24E*
120 *K12* **Myory** ***prev.*** Miyory. Vitsyebskaya Voblasts', N Belarus *55.39N 27.39E*
94 *J4* **Mýrdalsjökull** *glacier* S Iceland
94 *G10* **Myre** Nordland, C Norway *68.54N 15.04E*
119 *S5* **Myrhorod** ***Rus.*** Mirgorod. Poltavs'ka Oblast', NE Ukraine *49.57N 33.36E*
117 *J15* **Mýrina** ***var.*** Mírina. Límnos, SE Greece *39.52N 25.04E*
119 *P5* **Myronivka** ***Rus.*** Mironovka. Kyyivs'ka Oblast', N Ukraine *49.40N 30.58E*
23 *U13* **Myrtle Beach** South Carolina, SE USA *33.41N 78.53W*
34 *F14* **Myrtle Creek** Oregon, NW USA *43.01N 123.19W*
191 *P11* **Myrtleford** Victoria, SE Australia *36.34S 146.45E*
34 *E14* **Myrtle Point** Oregon, NW USA *43.04N 124.08W*
117 *K25* **Mýrtos** Kríti, Greece, E Mediterranean Sea *35.00N 25.34E*
Myrtoum Mare *see* Mirtóo Pélagos
95 *G17* **Myrviken** Jämtland, C Sweden *62.59N 14.19E*
97 *I15* **Mysen** Østfold, S Norway *59.33N 11.19E*
128 *L15* **Myshkin** Yaroslavskaya Oblast', NW Russian Federation *57.47N 38.28E*
113 *K17* **Myślenice** Małopolskie, S Poland *49.49N 19.55E*
112 *D10* **Myślibórz** Zachodnio-pomorskie, NW Poland *52.55N 14.51E*
161 *G20* **Mysore** ***var.*** Maisur. Karnātaka, W India *12.18N 76.37E*
Mysore *see* Karnātaka
117 *F21* **Mystrás** ***var.*** Mistras. Pelopónnisos, S Greece *37.03N 22.22E*
129 *T12* **Mysy** Permskaya Oblast', NW Russian Federation *60.40N 53.59E*
113 *K15* **Myszków** Śląskie, S Poland *50.35N 19.16E*
178 *Jj14* **My Tho** ***var.*** Mi Tho. Tiên Giang, S Vietnam *10.21N 106.21E*
Mytilene *see* Mytilíni
117 *L17* **Mytilíni** ***var.*** Mitilíni; ***anc.*** Mytilene. Lésvos, E Greece *39.05N 26.33E*
130 *K3* **Mytishchi** Moskovskaya Oblast', W Russian Federation *56.00N 37.51E*
39 *N3* **Myton** Utah, W USA *40.11N 110.03W*
94 *K2* **Mývatn** ◎ C Iceland
129 *T11* **Myyëldino** ***var.*** Myjeldino. Respublika Komi, NW Russian Federation *61.46N 54.48E*
84 *M13* **Mzimba** Northern, NW Malawi *11.56S 33.36E*
84 *M12* **Mzuzu** Northern, N Malawi *11.23S 34.03E*

N

103 *M19* **Naab** ≈ SE Germany
100 *G12* **Naaldwijk** Zuid-Holland, W Netherlands *52.00N 4.13E*
40 *G12* **Nā'ālehu** ***var.*** Naalehu. Hawai'i, USA, C Pacific Ocean *19.04N 155.36W*
95 *K19* **Naantali** ***Swe.*** Nådendal. Länsi-Suomi, W Finland *60.25N 22.10E*
100 *J10* **Naarden** Noord-Holland, C Netherlands *52.18N 5.10E*
111 *U4* **Naarn** ≈ N Austria
99 *F18* **Naas** ***Ir.*** An Nás, Nás na Ríogh. C Ireland *53.13N 6.39W*
94 *M9* **Näätämöjoki** ***Lapp.*** Njávdám. ≈ NE Finland
85 *E23* **Nababeep** ***var.*** Nababiep. Northern Cape, W South Africa *29.36S 17.46E*

◆ Country
● Country Capital
◇ Dependent Territory
○ Dependent Territory Capital
⬖ Administrative Region
✈ International Airport
▲ Mountain
▲▲ Mountain Range
Volcano
≈ River
◎ Lake
⊠ Reservoir

Nababiep – Naruto

Nababiep see Nababeep
Nabadwip see Navadwip
171 H16 **Nabari** Mie, Honshū, SW Japan 34.37N 136.06E
Nabatié see Nabatîyé
144 G8 **Nabatîyé** var. An Nabaṭīyah at Taḥtā, Nabatié, Nabatiyet et Tahta. SW Lebanon 33.18N 35.36E
Nabatiyet et Tahta see Nabatîyé
197 I13 **Nabavatu** Vanua Levu, N Fiji 16.35S 178.55E
202 I2 **Nabeina** island Tungaru, W Kiribati
131 T4 **Naberezhnyye Chelny** prev. Brezhnev. Respublika Tatarstan, W Russian Federation 55.43N 52.21E
41 T10 **Nabesna** Alaska, USA 62.22N 143.00W
41 T10 **Nabesna River** ≈ Alaska, USA
77 N5 **Nabeul** var. Nābul. NE Tunisia 36.32N 10.45E
158 I9 **Nābha** Punjab, NW India 30.22N 76.12E
176 Ww11 **Nabire** Papua, E Indonesia 3.22S 135.31E
147 O15 **Nabī Shu'ayb, Jabal an** ▲ W Yemen 15.24N 44.04E
197 I13 **Nabiti** Vanua Levu, N Fiji 16.37S 178.54E
144 F10 **Nablus** var. Nābulus, Heb. Shekhem; anc. Neapolis, Bibl. Shechem. N West Bank 32.14N 35.16E
197 I13 **Nabouwalu** Vanua Levu, N Fiji 17.00S 178.43E
Nābul see Nabeul
Nābulus see Nablus
197 I13 **Nabuna** Vanua Levu, N Fiji 16.13S 179.46E
179 Rr15 **Nabunturan** Mindanao, S Philippines 7.34N 125.54E
85 Q14 **Nacala** Nampula, NE Mozambique 14.30S 40.37E
44 H8 **Nacaome** Valle, S Honduras 13.30N 87.31W
Na Cealla Beaga see Killybegs
Na-ch'ii see Nagqu
171 Gg17 **Nachikatsuura** var. Nachi-Katsuura. Wakayama, Honshū, SE Japan 33.37N 135.54E
83 J24 **Nachingwea** Lindi, SE Tanzania 10.21S 38.46E
113 F16 **Náchod** Královéhradecký Kraj, N Czech Republic 50.25N 16.09E
Na Clocha Liatha see Greystones
42 G3 **Naco** Sonora, NW Mexico 31.16N 109.56W
27 X8 **Nacogdoches** Texas, SW USA 31.36N 94.40W
42 G4 **Nacozari de García** Sonora, NW Mexico 30.27N 109.43W
197 H13 **Nacula** prev. Nathula. island Yasawa Group, NW Fiji
Nada see Danzhou
79 O14 **Nadawli** NW Ghana 10.30N 2.40W
106 I3 **Nadela** Galicia, NW Spain 42.58N 7.33W
Nådendal see Naantali
150 M7 **Nadezhdinka** prev. Nadezhdinskiy. Kostanay, N Kazakhstan 53.46N 63.43E
Nadezhdinskiy see Nadezhdinka
Nadgan see Nadqān, Qalamat
197 H14 **Nadi** prev. Nandi. Viti Levu, W Fiji 17.48S 177.25E
197 H14 **Nadi** prev. Nandi. ✕ Viti Levu, W Fiji 17.46S 177.28E
160 D10 **Nadiād** Gujarāt, W India 22.42N 72.54E
Nadikdik see Knox Atoll
118 E11 **Nădlac** Ger. Nadlak, Hung. Nagylak. Arad, W Romania 46.10N 20.47E
Nadlak see Nădlac
76 H6 **Nador** prev. Villa Nador. NE Morocco 35.15N 2.56W
147 S9 **Nadqān, Qalamat** var. Nadgan. well E Saudi Arabia 23.10N 50.08E
113 N22 **Nádudvar** Hajdú-Bihar, E Hungary 47.26N 21.09E
123 J16 **Nadur** Gozo, N Malta 36.03N 14.18E
197 J13 **Naduri** prev. Nanduri. Vanua Levu, N Fiji 16.27S 179.10E
118 I7 **Nadvirna** Pol. Nadwórna, Rus. Nadvornaya. Ivano-Frankivs'ka Oblast', W Ukraine 48.27N 24.30E
128 J8 **Nadvoitsy** Respublika Kareliya, NW Russian Federation 63.52N 34.17E
Nadvornaya/Nadwórna see Nadvirna
126 Gg9 **Nadym** Yamalo-Nenetskiy Avtonomnyy Okrug, N Russian Federation 65.25N 72.40E
126 Gg9 **Nadym** ≈ C Russian Federation
194 J13 **Nadzab** Morobe, C PNG 6.36S 146.45E
79 X13 **Nafada** Gombe, E Nigeria 11.02N 11.18E
110 H8 **Näfels** Glarus, NE Switzerland 47.06N 9.04E
117 E18 **Náfpaktos** var. Návpaktos. Dytikí Ellás, C Greece 38.22N 21.49E
117 F20 **Náfplio** prev. Návplion. Pelopónnisos, S Greece 37.33N 22.50E
145 U6 **Naft Khāneh** E Iraq 34.01N 45.26E
155 N13 **Nāg** Baluchistān, SW Pakistan 27.43N 65.31E
179 Q11 **Naga** off. Naga City; prev. Nueva Caceres. Luzon, N Philippines 13.36N 123.10E
Nagaarzê see Nagarzê
10 F11 **Nagagami** ≈ Ontario, S Canada
170 E14 **Nagahama** Ehime, Shikoku, SW Japan 33.36N 132.29E
171 Hh14 **Nagahama** Shiga, Honshū, SW Japan 35.22N 136.16E
159 X12 **Nāga Hills** ▲▲ NE India
171 Ll13 **Nagai** Yamagata, Honshū, C Japan 38.07N 140.02E
Na Gaibhlte see Galty Mountains
41 N16 **Nagai Island** island Shumagin Islands, Alaska, USA
159 X12 **Nāgāland** ◐ state NE India
171 Jj13 **Nagano** Nagano, Honshū, S Japan 36.39N 138.10E
171 J14 **Nagano** off. Nagano-ken. ◐ prefecture Honshū, S Japan
171 K13 **Nagaoka** Niigata, Honshū, C Japan 37.26N 138.48E
159 W12 **Nagaon** prev. Nowgong. Assam, NE India 26.21N 92.41E
161 J21 **Nāgappattinam** var. Negapatam, Negapattinam. Tamil Nādu, SE India 10.45N 79.49E
Nagara Nayok see Nakhon Nayok
Nagara Panom see Nakhon Phanom
Nagara Pathom see Nakhon Pathom
Nagara Sridharmaraj see Nakhon Si Thammarat
Nagara Svarga see Nakhon Sawan
161 H16 **Nāgārjuna Sāgar** ▣ E India
44 I10 **Nagarote** León, SW Nicaragua 12.16N 86.33W
164 M16 **Nagarzê** var. Nagaarzê. Xizang Zizhiqu, W China 28.57N 90.25E
170 Bb13 **Nagasaki** Nagasaki, Kyūshū, SW Japan 32.45N 129.52E
170 Bb12 **Nagasaki** off. Nagasaki-ken. ◐ prefecture Kyūshū, SW Japan
170 Bb14 **Naga-shima** island SW Japan
170 Dd13 **Naga-shima** island SW Japan
Nagashima see Kii-Nagashima
170 Dd12 **Nagato** Yamaguchi, Honshū, SW Japan 34.22N 131.10E
158 F11 **Nāgaur** Rājasthān, NW India 27.12N 73.43E
160 F10 **Nāgda** Madhya Pradesh, C India 23.28N 75.27E
100 L8 **Nagele** Flevoland, N Netherlands 52.39N 5.43E
161 H24 **Nāgercoil** Tamil Nādu, SE India 8.10N 77.30E
159 X12 **Nāginimāra** Nāgāland, NE India 26.43N 94.51E
Na Gleannta see Glenties
172 P14 **Nago** Okinawa, Okinawa, SW Japan 26.36N 127.58E
160 K9 **Nāgod** Madhya Pradesh, C India 24.36N 80.35E
161 J26 **Nagoda** Southern Province, S Sri Lanka 6.13N 80.13E
103 G22 **Nagold** Baden-Württemberg, SW Germany 48.33N 8.43E
Nagorno-Karabakhskaya Avtonomnaya Oblast see Nagorno-Karabakh
126 Ll13 **Nagornyy** Respublika Sakha (Yakutiya), NE Russian Federation 55.53N 124.58E
143 V12 **Nagorno-Karabakh** var. Nagorno-Karabakhskaya Avtonomnaya Oblast , Arm. Lerrnayin Gharabakh, Az. Dağliq Qarabağ, Rus. Nagornyy Karabakh. former autonomous region SW Azerbaijan
Nagornyy Karabakh see Nagorno-Karabakh
129 R13 **Nagorsk** Kirovskaya Oblast', NW Russian Federation 59.18N 50.49E
171 Hh15 **Nagoya** Aichi, Honshū, SW Japan 35.10N 136.52E
160 I12 **Nāgpur** Mahārāshtra, C India 21.09N 79.06E
162 K10 **Nagqu** Chin. Na-ch'ii; prev. Hei-ho. Xizang Zizhiqu, W China 31.30N 91.57E
158 J8 **Nāg Tibba Range** ▲▲ N India
47 O8 **Nagua** NE Dominican Republic 19.18N 69.48W
113 H25 **Nagyatád** Somogy, SW Hungary 46.14N 17.19E
Nagybánya see Baia Mare
Nagybecskerek see Zrenjanin
Nagydisznód see Cisnădie
Nagyenyed see Aiud
113 N21 **Nagykálló** Szabolcs-Szatmár-Bereg, E Hungary 47.49N 21.47E
113 G25 **Nagykanizsa** Ger. Grosskanizsa. Zala, SW Hungary 46.27N 17.00E
Nagykároly see Carei
113 K22 **Nagykáta** Pest, C Hungary 47.24N 19.43E
Nagykikinda see Kikinda
113 K23 **Nagykőrös** Pest, C Hungary 47.04N 19.45E
Nagy-Küküllő see Târnava Mare
Nagylak see Nădlac
Nagymihály see Michalovce
Nagyrőce see Revúca
Nagysomkút see Şomcuta Mare
Nagysurány see Šurany
Nagyszalonta see Salonta
Nagyszeben see Sibiu
Nagyszentmiklós see Sânnicolau Mare
Nagyszöllös see Vynohradiv
Nagyszombat see Trnava
Nagytapolcsány see Topoľčany
Nagyvárad see Oradea
172 Oo15 **Naha** Okinawa, Okinawa, SW Japan 26.10N 127.40E
158 J8 **Nāhan** Himāchal Pradesh, NW India 30.33N 77.18E
Nahang, Rūd-e see Nihing
Nahariya see Nahariyya
144 F8 **Nahariyya** var. Nahariya. Northern, N Israel 33.01N 35.04E
148 L6 **Nahāvand** var. Nehavend. Hamadān, W Iran 34.13N 48.21E
103 F19 **Nahe** ≈ SW Germany
Na h-Iarmhidhe see Westmeath
201 O13 **Nahnalaud** ▲ Pohnpei, E Micronesia
Nahoi, Cape see Cumberland, Cape
Nahtavárr see Nattavaara
65 H16 **Nahuel Huapi, Lago** ◎ W Argentina
25 W7 **Nahunta** Georgia, SE USA 31.11N 81.58W
42 J6 **Naica** Chihuahua, N Mexico 27.53N 105.30W
9 U15 **Naicam** Saskatchewan, S Canada 52.26N 104.30W
Naiman Qi see Daqin Tal
164 M4 **Naimin Bulak** spring NW China 44.57N 90.29E
11 P6 **Nain** Newfoundland and Labrador, NE Canada 56.33N 61.45W
149 P8 **Nā'īn** Eşfahān, C Iran 32.52N 53.04E
158 K10 **Naini Tāl** Uttaranchal, N India 29.22N 79.25E
160 J11 **Nainpur** Madhya Pradesh, C India 22.25N 80.10E
197 J14 **Nairai** island C Fiji
98 J8 **Nairn** N Scotland, UK 57.36N 3.51W
98 I8 **Nairn** cultural region NE Scotland, UK
83 I19 **Nairobi** ● (Kenya) Nairobi Area, S Kenya 1.16S 36.49E
83 I19 **Nairobi** ✕ Nairobi Area, S Kenya 1.21S 37.01E
84 P13 **Nairoto** Cabo Delgado, NE Mozambique 12.22S 39.05E
120 G3 **Naissaar** island N Estonia
Naissus see Niš
197 K13 **Naitaba** var. Naitauba; prev. Naitamba. island Lau Group, E Fiji
Naitamba/Naitauba see Naitaba
83 I19 **Naivasha** Rift Valley, SW Kenya 0.43S 36.25E
83 H19 **Naivasha, Lake** ◎ SW Kenya
Najaf see An Najaf
149 N8 **Najafābād** var. Nejafabad. Eşfahān, C Iran 32.37N 51.22E
147 N7 **Najd** var. Nejd. cultural region C Saudi Arabia
107 O4 **Nájera** La Rioja, N Spain 42.25N 2.45W
107 P4 **Najerilla** ≈ N Spain
169 U7 **Naji** var. Arun Qi. Nei Mongol Zizhiqu, N China 48.05N 123.28E
158 J9 **Najībābād** Uttar Pradesh, N India 29.37N 78.19E
Najima see Fukuoka
169 Y11 **Najin** NE North Korea 42.13N 130.15E
145 T9 **Najm al Ḩassūn** C Iraq 32.24N 44.13E
147 O13 **Najrān** var. Abā as Su'ūd. Najrān, S Saudi Arabia 17.31N 44.08E
147 P12 **Najrān** off. Minţaqat al Najrān. ◐ province S Saudi Arabia
170 Bb12 **Nakadōri-jima** island Gotō-rettō, SW Japan
172 Pp3 **Nakagawa** Hokkaidō, NE Japan 44.49N 142.04E
171 Kk15 **Naka-gawa** ≈ Honshū, S Japan
40 F9 **Nākālele Point** var. Nakalele Point headland Maui, Hawai'i, USA, C Pacific Ocean 21.01N 156.35W
170 D12 **Nakama** Fukuoka, Kyūshū, SW Japan 33.49N 130.42E
Nakambé see White Volta
Nakamti see Nek'emtē
170 E15 **Nakamura** Kōchi, Shikoku, SW Japan 33.00N 132.54E
195 O12 **Nakanai Mountains** ▲▲ New Britain, E PNG
171 Jj14 **Nakano** Nagano, Honshū, S Japan 36.43N 138.22E
170 Ff11 **Nakano-shima** island Oki-shotō, SW Japan
170 Ff12 **Nakano-umi** var. Naka-umi. ◎ Honshū, SW Japan
171 Mm8 **Nakasato** Aomori, Honshū, C Japan 40.58N 140.26E
172 P7 **Nakasatsunai** Hokkaidō, NE Japan 42.42N 143.09E
172 Qq7 **Nakashibetsu** Hokkaidō, NE Japan 43.31N 144.58E
83 F18 **Nakasongola** C Uganda 1.19N 32.28E
172 Pp3 **Nakatonbetsu** Hokkaidō, NE Japan 44.58N 142.18E
170 D13 **Nakatsu** var. Nakatu. Ōita, Kyūshū, SW Japan 33.34N 131.12E
171 I15 **Nakatsugawa** var. Nakatugawa. Gifu, Honshū, SW Japan 35.30N 137.29E
Nakatu see Nakatsu
Nakatugawa see Nakatsugawa
Naka-umi see Nakano-umi
172 O5 **Nakayama-tōge** pass Hokkaidō, NE Japan 42.51N 141.05E
Nakdong see Naktong-gang
Nakel see Nakło nad Notecią
82 J8 **Nakfa** N Eritrea 16.38N 38.26E
Nakhichevan' see Naxçıvan
127 Nn18 **Nakhodka** Primorskiy Kray, SE Russian Federation 42.46N 132.47E
126 H8 **Nakhodka** Yamalo-Nenetskiy Avtonomnyy Okrug, N Russian Federation 67.48N 77.48E
Nakhon Navok see Nakhon Nayok
178 Hh11 **Nakhon Nayok** var. Nagara Nayok, Nakhon Navok. Nakhon Nayok, C Thailand 14.12N 101.08E
178 H11 **Nakhon Pathom** var. Nagara Pathom, Nakorn Pathom. Nakhon Pathom, W Thailand 13.49N 100.06E
178 J9 **Nakhon Phanom** var. Nagara Panom. Nakhon Phanom, E Thailand 17.22N 104.46E
178 Hh10 **Nakhon Ratchasima** var. Khorat, Korat. Nakhon Ratchasima, E Thailand 15.00N 102.06E
178 H10 **Nakhon Sawan** var. Muang Nakhon Sawan, Nagara Svarga. Nakhon Sawan, W Thailand 15.42N 100.06E
178 H15 **Nakhon Si Thammarat** var. Nagara Sridharmaraj, Nakhon Sithammaraj. Nakhon Si Thammarat, SW Thailand 8.24N 99.58E
Nakhon Sithammaraj see Nakhon Si Thammarat
145 Y11 **Nakhrash** SE Iraq 31.13N 47.24E
8 I9 **Nakina** British Columbia, W Canada 59.12N 132.48W
112 H9 **Nakło nad Notecią** Ger. Nakel. Kujawsko-pomorskie, C Poland 53.07N 17.34E
41 P13 **Naknek** Alaska, USA 58.45N 157.01W
158 H8 **Nakodar** Punjab, NW India 31.06N 75.31E
84 M11 **Nakonde** Northern, NE Zambia 9.22S 32.45E
Nakorn Pathom see Nakhon Pathom
97 H24 **Nakskov** Storstrøm, SE Denmark 54.50N 11.05E
169 Y15 **Naktong-gang** var. Nakdong, Jap. Rakutō-kō. ≈ C South Korea
83 H18 **Nakuru** Rift Valley, SW Kenya 0.16S 36.04E
83 H19 **Nakuru, Lake** ◎ Rift Valley, C Kenya
9 O17 **Nakusp** British Columbia, SW Canada 50.13N 117.48W
155 N15 **Nāl** ≈ W Pakistan
167 M7 **Nalayh** Töv, C Mongolia 47.48N 107.17E
159 V12 **Nalbāri** Assam, NE India 26.36N 91.49E
65 G19 **Nalcayec, Isla** island Archipiélago de los Chonos, S Chile
131 N15 **Nal'chik** Kabardino-Balkarskaya Respublika, SW Russian Federation 43.29N 43.39E
161 I16 **Nalgonda** Andhra Pradesh, C India 17.04N 79.15E
159 S14 **Nalhāti** West Bengal, NE India 24.19N 87.52E
159 U14 **Nalitabari** Dhaka, N Bangladesh 25.06N 90.10E
161 I17 **Nallamala Hills** ▲▲ E India
142 G12 **Nallıhan** Ankara, NW Turkey 40.12N 31.22E
106 K2 **Nalón** ≈ NW Spain
178 Gg3 **Nalong** Kachin State, N Myanmar 24.42N 97.27E
77 N8 **Nālūt** NW Libya 31.52N 10.58E
176 Uu12 **Nama** Pulau Manawoka, E Indonesia 4.07S 131.22E
201 Q16 **Nama** island C Micronesia
85 O16 **Namacurra** Zambézia, NE Mozambique 17.31S 37.03E
196 F9 **Namai Bay** bay Babeldaob, N Palau
31 W2 **Namakan Lake** ◎ Canada/USA
149 O6 **Namak, Daryācheh-ye** marsh N Iran
149 T6 **Namak, Kavīr-e** salt pan NE Iran
178 H6 **Namaklwe** Shan State, E Myanmar 19.45N 99.01E
Namaksār, Kowl-e/Namakzār, Daryācheh-ye see Namakzar
154 I5 **Namakzar** Pash. Daryācheh-ye Namakzār, Kowl-e Namaksār. marsh Afghanistan/Iran
176 W13 **Namalau** Pulau Jursian, E Indonesia 5.50S 134.43E
83 I20 **Namanga** Rift Valley, S Kenya 2.33S 36.48E
153 S10 **Namangan** Namangan Viloyati, E Uzbekistan 40.59N 71.33E
Namanganskaya Oblast' see Namangan Viloyati
153 R10 **Namangan Viloyati** Rus. Namanganskaya Oblast'. ◐ province E Uzbekistan
85 Q14 **Namapa** Nampula, NE Mozambique 13.43S 39.48E
85 C21 **Namaqualand** physical region S Namibia
83 G18 **Namasagali** C Uganda 1.01N 32.58E
195 P10 **Namatanai** New Ireland, NE PNG 3.42S 152.28E
85 I14 **Nambala** Central, C Zambia 15.06S 27.03E
83 J23 **Nambanje** Lindi, SE Tanzania 8.37S 38.21E
176 Ww9 **Namber** Papua, E Indonesia 0.58S 134.51E
85 G16 **Nambiya** North-West, N Botswana 18.09S 23.08E
191 V2 **Nambour** Queensland, E Australia 26.43S 152.54E
191 V6 **Nambucca Heads** New South Wales, SE Australia 30.37S 153.00E
165 N15 **Nam Co** ◎ W China
178 Ii5 **Nâm Cum** Lai Châu, N Vietnam 22.37N 103.12E
Namdik see Namorik Atoll
178 Jj6 **Nam Đinh** Nam Ha, N Vietnam 20.25N 106.12E
175 Tt11 **Namea, Tanjung** headland Pulau Seram, SE Indonesia
101 I20 **Namêche** Namur, SE Belgium 50.29N 5.02E
32 J4 **Namekagon Lake** ◎ Wisconsin, N USA
196 F10 **Namekakl Passage** passage Babeldaob, N Palau
Namen see Namur
85 P15 **Nametil** Nampula, NE Mozambique 15.46S 39.21E
169 X14 **Nam-gang** ≈ C North Korea
169 Y16 **Nam-gang** ≈ S South Korea
169 Y17 **Namhae-do** Jap. Nankai-tō. island S South Korea
Namhoi see Foshan
85 C19 **Namib Desert** desert W Namibia
85 A15 **Namibe** Port. Moçâmedes, Mossâmedes. Namibe, SW Angola 15.10S 12.09E
85 A15 **Namibe** ◐ province SE Angola
85 C18 **Namibia** off. Republic of Namibia, var. South West Africa, Afr. Suidwes-Afrika, Ger. Deutsch-Südwestafrika; prev. German Southwest Africa, South-West Africa. ◆ republic S Africa
67 O17 **Namibia Plain** undersea feature S Atlantic Ocean
171 Ll14 **Namie** Fukushima, Honshū, C Japan 37.29N 140.58E
171 Mm8 **Namioka** Aomori, Honshū, C Japan 40.43N 140.34E
42 I5 **Namiquipa** Chihuahua, N Mexico 29.15N 107.25W
165 P15 **Namjagbarwa Feng** ▲ W China 29.39N 95.00E
Namka see Doilungdêqên
175 Ss11 **Namlea** Pulau Buru, E Indonesia 3.12S 127.06E
164 L16 **Namling** Xizang Zizhiqu, W China 29.40N 88.58E
Namnetes see Nantes
178 Ii8 **Nam Ngum** ≈ C Laos
Namo see Namu Atoll
191 R5 **Namoi River** ≈ New South Wales, SE Australia
201 Q17 **Namoluk Atoll** atoll Mortlock Islands, C Micronesia
201 O15 **Namonuito Atoll** atoll Caroline Islands, C Micronesia
201 T9 **Namorik Atoll** var. Namdik. atoll Ralik Chain, S Marshall Islands
178 Ii6 **Nam Ou** ≈ N Laos
34 M14 **Nampa** Idaho, NW USA 43.32N 116.33W
78 M11 **Nampala** Ségou, W Mali 15.21N 5.32W
169 W14 **Namp'o** SW North Korea 38.45N 125.25E
85 P15 **Nampula** Nampula, NE Mozambique 15.09S 39.13E
85 P15 **Nampula** off. Província de Nampula. ◐ province NE Mozambique
169 W13 **Namsan-ni** NW North Korea 40.25N 125.01E
Namslau see Namysłów
95 E15 **Namsos** Nord-Trøndelag, C Norway 64.28N 11.31E
95 F14 **Namsskogan** Nord-Trøndelag, C Norway 64.57N 13.04E
178 H6 **Nam Teng** ≈ E Burma
178 I6 **Nam Tha** ≈ N Laos
126 M10 **Namtsy** Respublika Sakha (Yakutiya), NE Russian Federation 62.42N 129.30E
178 Gg4 **Namtu** Shan State, E Burma 23.04N 97.25E
8 J15 **Namu** British Columbia, SW Canada 51.46N 127.49W
201 T7 **Namu Atoll** var. Namo. atoll Ralik Chain, C Marshall Islands
197 K15 **Namuka-i-lau** island Lau Group, E Fiji
85 O15 **Namuli, Mont** ▲ NE Mozambique 15.15S 37.33E
85 P14 **Namuno** Cabo Delgado, N Mozambique 13.36S 38.52E
101 I20 **Namur** Dut. Namen. Namur, SE Belgium 50.28N 4.52E
101 H21 **Namur** Dut. Namen. ◐ province S Belgium
85 D17 **Namutoni** Kunene, N Namibia 18.47S 16.48E
169 Y16 **Namwŏn** Jap. Nangen. S South Korea 35.24N 127.20E
178 Mm14 **Namyit Island** island S Spratly Islands
113 H14 **Namysłów** Ger. Namslau. Opolskie, S Poland 51.05N 17.41E
178 Hh7 **Nan** var. Muang Nan. Nan, NW Thailand 18.47N 100.46E
81 G15 **Nana** ≈ W Central African Republic
172 Nn7 **Nanae** Hokkaidō, NE Japan 41.55N 140.40E
81 I14 **Nana-Grébizi** ◐ prefecture N Central African Republic
8 L17 **Nanaimo** Vancouver Island, British Columbia, SW Canada 49.07N 123.58W
40 C9 **Nānākuli** var. Nanakuli. O'ahu, Hawai'i, USA, C Pacific Ocean 21.23N 158.09W
81 G15 **Nana-Mambéré** ◐ prefecture W Central African Republic
167 R13 **Nan'an** Fujian, SE China 24.57N 118.22E
191 U2 **Nanango** Queensland, E Australia 26.42S 151.58E
171 Ii12 **Nanao** Ishikawa, Honshū, SW Japan 37.02N 136.57E
167 Q14 **Nan'ao Dao** island S China
171 Ii11 **Nanatsu-shima** island SW Japan
58 F8 **Nanay, Río** ≈ NE Peru
166 J8 **Nanbu** Sichuan, C China 31.19N 106.02E
169 X7 **Nancha** Heilongjiang, NE China 47.09N 129.16E
167 P10 **Nanchang** var. Nan-ch'ang, Nanch'ang-hsien. Jiangxi, S China 28.38N 115.57E
Nanch'ang-hsien see Nanchang
167 P11 **Nancheng** var. Jianchang. Jiangxi, S China 27.37N 116.37E
Nan-ching see Nanjing
166 J9 **Nanchong** Sichuan, C China 30.46N 106.03E
166 J10 **Nanchuan** Chongqing Shi, C China 29.06N 107.13E
105 T5 **Nancy** Meurthe-et-Moselle, NE France 48.40N 6.10E
193 A22 **Nancy Sound** sound South Island, NZ
158 L9 **Nanda Devi** ▲ NW India 30.27N 80.00E
44 J11 **Nandaime** Granada, SW Nicaragua 11.46N 86.03W
166 K13 **Nandan** Guangxi Zhuangzu Zizhiqu, S China 25.03N 107.31E
161 H14 **Nānded** Mahārāshtra, C India 19.10N 77.21E
170 G15 **Nanden** Hyōgo, Awaji-shima, SW Japan 34.19N 134.53E
191 S5 **Nandewar Range** ▲▲ New South Wales, SE Australia
Nandi see Nadi
166 E13 **Nanding He** ≈ China/Vietnam
Nándorhgy see Oţelu Roşu
160 E11 **Nandurbār** Mahārāshtra, W India 21.22N 74.18E
Nanduri see Naduri
161 I17 **Nandyāl** Andhra Pradesh, E India 15.30N 78.28E
167 P11 **Nanfeng** var. Qincheng. Jiangxi, S China 27.15N 116.30E
Nang see Nangxian
81 E15 **Nanga Eboko** Centre, C Cameroon 4.37N 12.21E
155 W4 **Nanga Parbat** ▲ India/Pakistan 35.15N 74.36E
174 L8 **Nangapinoh** Borneo, C Indonesia 0.21S 111.43E
155 R5 **Nangarhār** ◐ province E Afghanistan
174 M8 **Nangaserawai** var. Nangah Serawai. Borneo, C Indonesia 0.19S 112.25E
174 L9 **Nangatayap** Borneo, C Indonesia 1.30S 110.33E
Nangen see Namwŏn
105 P5 **Nangis** Seine-et-Marne, N France 48.36N 3.02E
169 X13 **Nangnim-sanmaek** ▲▲ C North Korea
167 O4 **Nangong** Hebei, E China 37.24N 115.24E
165 Q14 **Nangqên** var. Xangda. Qinghai, C China 32.05N 96.28E
178 I11 **Nang Rong** Buri Ram, E Thailand 14.37N 102.48E
165 O16 **Nangxian** var. Nang. Xizang Zizhiqu, W China 29.04N 93.03E
Nan Hai see South China Sea
166 L8 **Nan He** ≈ C China
166 F12 **Nanhua** var. Longchuan. Yunnan, SW China 25.15N 101.15E
Naniwa see Ōsaka
161 G20 **Nanjangūd** Karnātaka, W India 12.07N 76.40E
167 Q8 **Nanjing** var. Nan-ching, Nanking; prev. Chianning, Chian-ning, Kiang-ning. Jiangsu, E China 32.03N 118.46E
Nankai-tō see Namhae-do
167 O12 **Nankang** var. Rongjiang. Jiangxi, S China 25.40N 114.40E
Nanking see Nanjing
170 F15 **Nankoku** Kōchi, Shikoku, SW Japan 33.34N 133.37E
167 N13 **Nan Ling** ▲▲ S China
166 L15 **Nanliu Jiang** ≈ S China
201 P13 **Nan Madol** ruins Temwen Island, E Micronesia
166 K15 **Nanning** var. Nan-ning; prev. Yung-ning. Guangxi Zhuangzu Zizhiqu, S China 22.49N 108.19E
206 M15 **Nanortalik** Kitaa, S Greenland 60.12N 44.53W
Nanouki see Aranuka
166 H13 **Nanpan Jiang** ≈ S China
158 M11 **Nānpāra** Uttar Pradesh, N India 27.51N 81.30E
167 Q12 **Nanping** var. Nan-p'ing; prev. Yenping. Fujian, SE China 26.40N 118.07E
Nanping see Jiuzhaigou
Nanpu see Pucheng
167 R12 **Nanri Dao** island SE China
172 Q13 **Nansei-shotō** Eng. Ryukyu Islands. island group SW Japan
Nansei Syotō Trench see Ryukyu Trench
207 T10 **Nansen Basin** undersea feature Arctic Ocean
207 T10 **Nansen Cordillera** var. Arctic-Mid Oceanic Ridge, Nansen Ridge. undersea feature Arctic Ocean
Nansen Ridge see Nansen Cordillera
133 T9 **Nan Shan** ▲▲ C China
179 Nn14 **Nanshan Island** island E Spratly Islands
Nansha Qundao see Spratly Islands
10 K3 **Nantais, Lac** ◎ Québec, NE Canada
105 N5 **Nanterre** Hauts-de-Seine, N France 48.52N 2.13E
104 I8 **Nantes** Bret. Naoned; anc. Condivincum, Namnetes. Loire-Atlantique, NW France 47.12N 1.31W
12 G17 **Nanticoke** Ontario, S Canada 42.49N 80.04W
20 H13 **Nanticoke** Pennsylvania, NE USA 41.12N 76.00W
23 Y4 **Nanticoke River** ≈ Delaware/Maryland, NE USA
9 Q17 **Nanton** Alberta, SW Canada 50.21N 113.46W
167 S8 **Nantong** Jiangsu, E China 32.00N 120.52E
167 S13 **Nant'ou** W Taiwan 23.54N 120.33E
105 S10 **Nantua** Ain, E France 46.10N 5.34E
21 Q13 **Nantucket** Nantucket Island, Massachusetts, NE USA 41.15N 70.05W
21 Q13 **Nantucket Island** island Massachusetts, NE USA
21 Q13 **Nantucket Sound** sound Massachusetts, NE USA
84 P13 **Nantulo** Cabo Delgado, N Mozambique 12.30S 39.03E
201 O12 **Nanuh** Pohnpei, E Micronesia
197 K13 **Nanuku Passage** channel NE Fiji
202 D6 **Nanumaga** var. Nanumanga. atoll NW Tuvalu
Nanumanga see Nanumaga
202 D5 **Nanumea Atoll** atoll NW Tuvalu
61 O19 **Nanuque** Minas Gerais, SE Brazil 17.49S 40.21W
175 Ss4 **Nanusa, Kepulauan** island group N Indonesia
169 U4 **Nanweng He** ≈ NE China
166 I10 **Nanxi** Sichuan, C China 28.54N 104.58E
167 N10 **Nanxian** var. Nan Xian, Nanzhou. Hunan, S China 29.23N 112.18E
167 N7 **Nanyang** var. Nan-yang. Henan, C China 32.58N 112.29E
167 P6 **Nanyang Hu** ◎ E China
171 L13 **Nan'yō** Yamagata, Honshū, C Japan 38.05N 140.07E
83 I18 **Nanyuki** Central, C Kenya 0.01N 37.04E
166 M8 **Nanzhang** Hubei, C China 31.47N 111.48E
Nanzhou see Nanxian
107 T11 **Nao, Cabo de La** headland E Spain 38.43N 0.13E
10 M9 **Naococane, Lac** ◎ Québec, E Canada
159 S14 **Naogaon** Rajshahi, NW Bangladesh 24.49N 88.58E
Naokot see Naukot
197 C12 **Naone** Maewo, C Vanuatu 15.03S 168.06E
Naoned see Nantes
117 E14 **Náousa** Kentrikí Makedonía, N Greece 40.38N 22.06E
37 N8 **Napa** California, W USA 38.15N 122.17W
41 O11 **Napaimiut** Alaska, USA 61.32N 158.46W
41 N12 **Napakiak** Alaska, USA 60.42N 161.57W
126 H7 **Napalkovo** Yamalo-Nenetskiy Avtonomnyy Okrug, N Russian Federation 70.06N 73.43E
10 I16 **Napanee** Ontario, SE Canada 44.13N 76.57W
176 Ww11 **Napanwainami** Papua, E Indonesia 3.01S 135.51E
176 W11 **Napan-Yaur** Papua, E Indonesia 2.55S 134.50E
41 N12 **Napaskiak** Alaska, USA 60.42N 161.46W
178 Jj5 **Na Phac** Cao Bâng, N Vietnam 22.24N 105.54E
176 Ww9 **Napido** Papua, E Indonesia 0.41S 135.27E
192 O11 **Napier** Hawke's Bay, North Island, NZ 39.30S 176.55E
205 X3 **Napier Mountains** ▲▲ Antarctica
13 O13 **Napierville** Québec, SE Canada 45.12N 73.25W
25 W15 **Naples** Florida, SE USA 26.08N 81.48W
27 W5 **Naples** Texas, SW USA 33.12N 94.40W
Naples see Napoli
166 I14 **Napo** Guangxi Zhuangzu Zizhiqu, S China 23.21N 105.47E
58 C6 **Napo** ◐ province NE Ecuador
31 O6 **Napoleon** North Dakota, N USA 46.30N 99.46W
33 R11 **Napoleon** Ohio, N USA 41.23N 84.07W
Napoléon-Vendée see la Roche-sur-Yon
24 J9 **Napoleonville** Louisiana, S USA 29.55N 91.01W
109 K17 **Napoli** Eng. Naples, Ger. Neapel; anc. Neapolis. Campania, S Italy 40.52N 14.15E
109 J18 **Napoli, Golfo di** gulf S Italy
59 F7 **Napo, Río** ≈ Ecuador/Peru
203 W9 **Napuka** island Îles Tuamotu, C French Polynesia
148 J3 **Naqadeh** Āżarbāyjān-e Gharbī, NW Iran 36.57N 45.24E
145 U6 **Naqnah** E Iraq 34.13N 45.33E
Nar see Nera
171 H15 **Nara** Nara, Honshū, SW Japan 34.40N 135.49E
78 L11 **Nara** Koulikoro, W Mali 15.04N 7.19W
171 Gg16 **Nara** off. Nara-ken. ◐ prefecture Honshū, SW Japan
155 R14 **Nāra Canal** irrigation canal S Pakistan
190 K11 **Naracoorte** South Australia 37.01S 140.45E
191 P8 **Naradhan** New South Wales, SE Australia 33.37S 146.19E
Naradhivas see Narathiwat
58 B8 **Naranjal** Guayas, W Ecuador 2.39S 79.34W
59 Q19 **Naranjos** Santa Cruz, E Bolivia
43 Q12 **Naranjos** Veracruz-Llave, E Mexico 21.20N 97.42W
165 Q6 **Naran Sebstein Bulag** spring NW China 42.40N 96.58E
149 X12 **Narānū** Sīstān va Balūchestān, SE Iran
170 Bb12 **Narao** Nagasaki, Nakadōri-jima, SW Japan 32.40N 129.03E
161 J16 **Narasaraopet** Andhra Pradesh, E India 16.16N 80.06E
164 J5 **Narat** Xinjiang Uygur Zizhiqu, W China 43.19N 84.01E
178 Hh17 **Narathiwat** var. Naradhivas. Narathiwat, SW Thailand 6.25N 101.48E
39 V10 **Nara Visa** New Mexico, SW USA 35.35N 103.06W
Nārāyāni see Gandak
Narbada see Narmada
Narbo Martius see Narbonne
105 P16 **Narbonne** anc. Narbo Martius. Aude, S France 43.11N 3.00E
Narborough Island see Fernandina, Isla
106 J2 **Narcea** ≈ NW Spain
158 J9 **Narendranagar** Uttaranchal, N India 30.10N 78.21E
Nares Abyssal Plain see Nares Plain
66 G11 **Nares Plain** var. Nares Abyssal Plain. undersea feature NW Atlantic Ocean
207 P10 **Nares Strait** Dan. Nares Stræde. strait Canada/Greenland
Nares Stræde see Nares Strait
112 O9 **Narew** ≈ E Poland
161 F17 **Nargund** Karnātaka, W India 15.43N 75.23E
85 D20 **Narib** Hardap, S Namibia 24.10S 17.46E
Narikrik see Knox Atoll
Narin Gol see Dong He
56 B13 **Nariño** off. Departamento de Nariño. ◐ province SW Colombia
171 Kk17 **Narita** Chiba, Honshū, S Japan 35.46N 140.17E
171 Kk17 **Narita** ✕ (Tōkyō) Chiba, Honshū, S Japan 35.45N 140.23E
Nariya see An Nu'ayrīyah
168 F5 **Nariyn Gol** ≈ Mongolia/Russian Federation
168 J8 **Nariynteel** var. Tsagaan-Ovoo. Övörhangay, C Mongolia 45.57N 101.25E
158 J8 **Nārkanda** Himāchal Pradesh, NW India 31.13N 77.27E
94 L13 **Narkaus** Lappi, NW Finland 66.13N 26.09E
160 E11 **Narmada** var. Narbada. ≈ C India
158 H11 **Narnaul** var. Nārnaul. Haryāna, N India 28.05N 76.12E
109 I14 **Narni** Umbria, C Italy 42.31N 12.31E
109 J24 **Naro** Sicilia, Italy, C Mediterranean Sea 37.18N 13.48E
Narodichi see Narodychi
129 V7 **Narodnaya, Gora** ▲ NW Russian Federation 65.04N 60.12E
119 N3 **Narodychi** Rus. Narodichi. Zhytomyrs'ka Oblast', N Ukraine 51.11N 29.01E
130 J4 **Naro-Fominsk** Moskovskaya Oblast', W Russian Federation 55.25N 36.41E
83 H19 **Narok** Rift Valley, SW Kenya 1.04S 35.54E
106 H2 **Narón** Galicia, NW Spain 43.31N 8.08W
191 S11 **Narooma** New South Wales, SE Australia 36.16S 150.08E
Narova see Narva
Narovlya see Narowlya
155 W8 **Nārowāl** Punjab, E Pakistan 32.04N 74.54E
121 N20 **Narowlya** Rus. Narovlya. Homyel'skaya Voblasts', SE Belarus 51.49N 29.30E
95 J17 **Närpes** Fin. Närpiö. Länsi-Suomi, W Finland 62.28N 21.19E
Närpiö see Närpes
191 S5 **Narrabri** New South Wales, SE Australia 30.21S 149.48E
191 P9 **Narrandera** New South Wales, SE Australia 34.46S 146.32E
191 Q4 **Narran Lake** ◎ New South Wales, SE Australia
191 Q4 **Narran River** ≈ New South Wales/Queensland, SE Australia
188 J13 **Narrogin** Western Australia 32.52S 117.16E
191 Q7 **Narromine** New South Wales, SE Australia 32.16S 148.15E
23 R6 **Narrows** Virginia, NE USA 37.19N 80.48W
206 M15 **Narsarsuaq** ✕ Kitaa, S Greenland 61.07N 45.03W
160 I10 **Narsimhapur** Madhya Pradesh, C India 22.58N 79.15E
Narsingdi see Narsinghdi
159 U15 **Narsinghdi** var. Narsingdi. Dhaka, C Bangladesh 23.55N 90.40E
160 H9 **Narsinghgarh** Madhya Pradesh, C India 23.42N 77.04E
169 Q11 **Nart** Nei Mongol Zizhiqu, N China 42.54N 115.55E
Nartës, Gjol i/Nartës, Laguna e see Nartës, Liqeni i
115 J22 **Nartës, Liqeni i** var. Gjol i Nartës, Laguna e Nartës. ◎ SW Albania
117 F17 **Narthákí** ▲ C Greece 39.12N 22.24E
131 O15 **Nartkala** Kabardino-Balkarskaya Respublika, SW Russian Federation 43.34N 43.55E
170 Ff15 **Naruto** Tokushima, Shikoku, SW Japan 34.09N 134.34E

◆ Country ● Country Capital ◇ Dependent Territory ○ Dependent Territory Capital ◐ Administrative Region ✕ International Airport ▲ Mountain ▲▲ Mountain Range Volcano ≈ River ◎ Lake ▣ Reservoir

NARVA – NEUKUHREN

120 *K3* **Narva** Ida-Virumaa, NE Estonia *59.22N 28.12E*
120 *K4* **Narva** ***prev.*** Narova. ≈ Estonia/Russian Federation
120 *J3* **Narva Bay** ***Est.*** Narva Laht, ***Ger.*** Narwa-Bucht, ***Rus.*** Narvskiy Zaliv. *bay* Estonia/Russian Federation
Narva Laht *see* Narva Bay
128 *F13* **Narva Reservoir** ***Est.*** Narva Veehoidla, ***Rus.*** Narvskoye Vodokhranilishche. ▣ Estonia/Russian Federation
Narva Veehoidla *see* Narva Reservoir
94 *H10* **Narvik** Nordland, C Norway *68.25N 17.24E*
Narvskiy Zaliv *see* Narva Bay
Narvskoye Vodokhranilishche *see* Narva Reservoir
Narwa-Bucht *see* Narva Bay
158 *I9* **Narwāna** Haryāna, NW India *29.40N 76.10E*
129 *R4* **Nar'yan-Mar** ***prev.*** Beloshchel'ye, Dzerzhinskiy. Nenetskiy Avtonomnyy Okrug, NW Russian Federation *67.38N 53.00E*
126 *H12* **Narym** Tomskaya Oblast', C Russian Federation *58.59N 81.20E*
151 *Y10* **Narymskiy Khrebet** ***Kaz.*** Naryn Zhotasy. ▲▲ E Kazakhstan
153 *W9* **Naryn** Narynskaya Oblast', C Kyrgyzstan *41.24N 75.59E*
153 *U8* **Naryn** ≈ Kyrgyzstan/Uzbekistan
151 *W16* **Narynkol** ***Kaz.*** Narynqol. Almaty, SE Kazakhstan *42.41N 80.10E*
Naryn Oblasty *see* Narynskaya Oblast'
Narynqol *see* Narynkol
153 *V9* **Narynskaya Oblast'** ***Kir.*** Naryn Oblasty. ◈ *province* C Kyrgyzstan
Naryn Zhotasy *see* Narymskiy Khrebet
130 *J6* **Naryshkino** Orlovskaya Oblast', W Russian Federation *53.00N 35.41E*
97 *L14* **Nås** Dalarna, C Sweden *60.28N 14.30E*
94 *G13* **Nasafjellet** ***Lapp.*** Násávárre. ▲ C Norway *66.29N 15.23E*
95 *H16* **Näsåker** Västernorrland, C Sweden *63.27N 16.55E*
197 *J14* **Nasau** Koro, C Fiji *17.20S 179.26E*
118 *I9* **Năsăud** ***Ger.*** Nussdorf, ***Hung.*** Naszód. Bistrița-Năsăud, N Romania *47.16N 24.24E*
Násávárre *see* Nasafjellet
105 *P13* **Nasbinals** Lozère, S France *44.40N 3.03E*
Na Sceirí *see* Skerries
Nase *see* Naze
193 *E22* **Naseby** Otago, South Island, NZ *45.02S 170.09E*
149 *R10* **Nāṣerīyeh** Kermān, C Iran
27 *X5* **Nash** Texas, SW USA *33.26N 94.04W*
160 *E13* **Nāshik** ***prev.*** Nāsik. Mahārāshtra, W India *20.04N 73.48E*
58 *E7* **Nashiño, Río** ≈ Ecuador/Peru
31 *W12* **Nashua** Iowa, C USA *42.57N 92.32W*
35 *W7* **Nashua** Montana, NW USA *48.06N 106.16W*
21 *O10* **Nashua** New Hampshire, NE USA *42.45N 71.26W*
29 *S13* **Nashville** Arkansas, C USA *33.57N 93.51W*
25 *U7* **Nashville** Georgia, SE USA *31.12N 83.15W*
32 *L16* **Nashville** Illinois, N USA *38.20N 89.22W*
33 *O14* **Nashville** Indiana, N USA *39.13N 86.15W*
23 *V9* **Nashville** North Carolina, SE USA *35.58N 77.58W*
22 *J8* **Nashville** *state capital* Tennessee, S USA *36.10N 86.48W*
22 *J9* **Nashville** ✕ Tennessee, S USA *36.06N 86.44W*
66 *H10* **Nashville Seamount** *undersea feature* NW Atlantic Ocean *30.00N 57.20W*
114 *H9* **Našice** Osijek-Baranja, E Croatia *45.29N 18.05E*
112 *M11* **Nasielsk** Mazowieckie, C Poland *52.33N 20.46E*
95 *K18* **Näsijärvi** ◎ SW Finland
Nāsik *see* Nāshik
82 *G13* **Nasir** Upper Nile, SE Sudan *8.37N 33.06E*
155 *Q12* **Nasīrābād** Baluchistān, SW Pakistan *28.29N 68.24E*
154 *K15* **Nasīrābād** Baluchistān, SW Pakistan *28.25N 68.28E*
Nasīrābād *see* Mymensingh
Nasir, Buhayrat/Nâşir, Buḥeiret *see* Nasser, Lake
Nāsiri *see* Ahvāz
Nasiriya *see* An Nāṣirīyah
Nás na Ríogh *see* Naas
109 *L23* **Naso** Sicilia, Italy, C Mediterranean Sea *38.07N 14.46E*
Nasratabad *see* Zābol
8 *J11* **Nass** ≈ British Columbia, SW Canada
79 *V15* **Nassarawa** Nassarawa, C Nigeria *8.33N 7.42E*
46 *H2* **Nassau** ● (Bahamas) New Providence, N Bahamas *25.03N 77.20W*
46 *H2* **Nassau** ✕ New Providence, C Bahamas *25.00N 77.26W*
202 *J13* **Nassau** *island* N Cook Islands
25 *W8* **Nassau Sound** *sound* Florida, SE USA
110 *L7* **Nassereith** Tirol, W Austria *47.19N 10.51E*
97 *L19* **Nässjö** Jönköping, S Sweden *57.39N 14.40E*
101 *K22* **Nassogne** Luxembourg, SE Belgium *50.08N 5.19E*
10 *J6* **Nastapoka Islands** *island group* Nunavut, C Canada
95 *M19* **Nastola** Etelä-Suomi, S Finland *60.57N 25.55E*
171 *L14* **Nasu-dake** ▲ Honshū, S Japan *37.07N 139.57E*
179 *P11* **Nasugbu** Luzon, N Philippines *14.03N 120.39E*
96 *N11* **Näsviken** Gävleborg, C Sweden *61.46N 16.55E*
Naszód *see* Năsăud
85 *I17* **Nata** Central, NE Botswana *20.10S 26.10E*
56 *E11* **Natagaima** Tolima, C Colombia *3.30N 75.06W*
61 *Q14* **Natal** Rio Grande do Norte, E Brazil *5.46S 35.15W*
173 *Ff8* **Natal** Sumatera, N Indonesia *0.25N 99.09E*
Natal *see* KwaZulu/Natal
181 *L10* **Natal Basin** ***var.*** Mozambique Basin. *undersea feature* W Indian Ocean
27 *R12* **Natalia** Texas, SW USA *29.11N 98.51W*
69 *W15* **Natal Valley** *undersea feature* SW Indian Ocean
Natanya *see* Netanya
149 *O7* **Naṭanz** Eṣfahān, C Iran *33.31N 51.55E*
11 *Q11* **Natashquan** Québec, E Canada *50.10N 61.49W*
11 *Q10* **Natashquan** ≈ Newfoundland and Labrador/Québec, E Canada
24 *J7* **Natchez** Mississippi, S USA *31.33N 91.24W*
24 *G6* **Natchitoches** Louisiana, S USA *31.45N 93.05W*
110 *E10* **Naters** Valais, S Switzerland *46.22N 8.00E*
Nathanya *see* Netanya
94 *O3* **Nathorst Land** *physical region* W Svalbard
Nathula *see* Nacula
194 *J15* **National Capital District** ◈ *province* S PNG
37 *U17* **National City** California, W USA *32.40N 117.06W*
192 *M10* **National Park** Manawatu-Wanganui, North Island, NZ *39.11S 175.22E*
79 *R14* **Natitingou** NW Benin *10.21N 1.25E*
42 *B5* **Natividad, Isla** *island* W Mexico
171 *M13* **Natori** Miyagi, Honshū, C Japan *38.11N 140.52E*
20 *C14* **Natrona Heights** Pennsylvania, NE USA *40.37N 79.42W*
83 *H20* **Natron, Lake** ◎ Kenya/Tanzania
Natsrat *see* Naẕerat
177 *Ff7* **Nattalin** Pegu, C Burma *18.25N 95.34E*
94 *J12* **Nattavaara** ***Lapp.*** Nahtavárr. Norrbotten, N Sweden *66.45N 20.58E*
111 *S3* **Natternbach** Oberösterreich, N Austria *48.26N 13.44E*
97 *M22* **Nättraby** Blekinge, S Sweden *56.12N 15.30E*
174 *K4* **Natuna Besar, Pulau** *island* Kepulauan Natuna, W Indonesia
174 **Natuna Islands** *see* Natuna, Kepulauan
174 *Jj5* **Natuna, Kepulauan** ***var.*** Natuna Islands. *island group* W Indonesia
174 *J6* **Natuna, Laut** *sea* W Indonesia
23 *N6* **Natural Bridge** *tourist site* Kentucky, C USA *37.44N 83.37W*
181 *V11* **Naturaliste Fracture Zone** *tectonic feature* E Indian Ocean
182 *J10* **Naturaliste Plateau** *undersea feature* E Indian Ocean
Nau *see* Nov
105 *O14* **Naucelle** Aveyron, S France *44.10N 2.19E*
85 *D20* **Nauchas** Hardap, C Namibia *23.36S 16.21E*
110 *K9* **Nauders** Tirol, W Austria *46.52N 10.31E*
Naugard *see* Nowogard
120 *F12* **Naujamiestis** Panevėžys, C Lithuania *55.42N 24.10E*
120 *E10* **Naujoji Akmenė** Šiauliai, NW Lithuania *56.20N 22.57E*
155 *R16* **Naukot** ***var.*** Naokot. Sind, SE Pakistan *24.52N 69.27E*
103 *L16* **Naumburg** ***var.*** Naumburg an der Saale. Sachsen-Anhalt, C Germany *51.09N 11.48E*
Naumburg am Queis *see* Nowogrodziec
Naumburg an der Saale *see* Naumburg
203 *W15* **Naunau** *ancient monument* Easter Island, Chile, E Pacific Ocean
144 *G10* **Nā'ūr** 'Ammān, W Jordan *31.52N 35.49E*
201 *Q8* **Nauru** ***off.*** Republic of Nauru; ***prev.*** Pleasant Island. ◆ *republic* W Pacific Ocean
183 *P5* **Nauru** *island* W Pacific Ocean
201 *Q9* **Nauru International** ✕ S Nauru
Nausari *see* Navsāri
21 *Q12* **Nauset Beach** *beach* Massachusetts, NE USA
Naushahra *see* Nowshera
155 *P14* **Naushahro Fīroz** Sind, SE Pakistan *26.53N 68.12E*
Naushara *see* Nowshera
197 *I14* **Nausori** Viti Levu, W Fiji *17.48S 177.35E*
58 *F9* **Nauta** Loreto, N Peru *4.31S 73.35W*
159 *O12* **Nautanwa** Uttar Pradesh, N India *27.25N 83.25E*
43 *R13* **Nautla** Veracruz-Llave, E Mexico *20.12N 96.46W*
Nauzad *see* Now Zād
43 *N6* **Nava** Coahuila de Zaragoza, NE Mexico *28.28N 100.45W*
Navabad *see* Navobod
106 *L6* **Nava del Rey** Castilla-León, N Spain *41.19N 5.04W*
159 *S15* **Navadwīp** ***prev.*** Nabadwip. West Bengal, NE India *23.24N 88.22E*
197 *J14* **Navaga** Koro, W Fiji *17.21S 179.22E*
106 *M9* **Navahermosa** Castilla-La Mancha, C Spain *39.39N 4.25W*
121 *I16* **Navahrudak** ***Pol.*** Nowogródek, ***Rus.*** Novogrudok. Hrodzyenskaya Voblasts', W Belarus *53.34N 25.54E*
121 *I16* **Navahrudskaye Wzvyshsha** ▲▲ W Belarus
38 *M8* **Navajo Mount** ▲ Utah, W USA *37.00N 110.52W*
39 *Q9* **Navajo Reservoir** ▣ New Mexico, SW USA
179 *Qq12* **Naval** Biliran Island, C Philippines *11.32N 124.26E*
106 *K9* **Navalmoral de la Mata** Extremadura, W Spain *39.54N 5.33W*
106 *K10* **Navalvillar de Pelea** Extremadura, W Spain *39.05N 5.27W*
99 *F17* **Navan** ***Ir.*** An Uaimh. E Ireland *53.39N 6.40W*
Navanagar *see* Jāmnagar
120 *L12* **Navapolatsk** ***Rus.*** Novopolotsk. Vitsyebskaya Voblasts', N Belarus *55.33N 28.34E*
155 *P6* **Nāvar, Dasht-e** ***Pash.*** Dasht-i-Nawar. *desert* C Afghanistan
127 *Q5* **Navarin, Mys** *headland* NE Russian Federation *62.18N 179.06E*
65 *I25* **Navarino, Isla** *island* S Chile
107 *Q4* **Navarra** ***Eng./Fr.*** Navarre. ◈ *autonomous community* N Spain
Navarre *see* Navarra
107 *P4* **Navarrete** La Rioja, N Spain *42.25N 2.34W*
63 *C20* **Navarro** Buenos Aires, E Argentina *35.01S 59.18W*
107 *O12* **Navas de San Juan** Andalucía, S Spain *38.10N 3.19W*
27 *V10* **Navasota** Texas, SW USA *30.23N 96.05W*
27 *U9* **Navasota River** ≈ Texas, SW USA
46 *I9* **Navassa Island** ◇ *US unincorporated territory* C West Indies
121 *L19* **Navasyolki** ***Rus.*** Novosëlki. Homyel'skaya Voblasts', SE Belarus *52.24N 28.27E*
121 *H17* **Navayel'nya** ***Pol.*** Nowojelnia, ***Rus.*** Novoyel'nya. Hrodzyenskaya Voblasts', W Belarus *53.26N 25.36E*
176 *Yy11* **Naver** Papua, E Indonesia *3.27S 139.45E*
120 *H5* **Navesti** ≈ C Estonia
106 *J2* **Navia** Asturias, N Spain *43.33N 6.43W*
106 *J2* **Navia** ≈ NW Spain
61 *I21* **Naviraí** Mato Grosso do Sul, SW Brazil *23.01S 54.09W*
197 *G14* **Naviti** *island* Yasawa Group, NW Fiji
130 *I6* **Navlya** Bryanskaya Oblast', W Russian Federation *52.47N 34.28E*
197 *J13* **Navoalevu** Vanua Levu, N Fiji *16.22S 179.28E*
153 *R12* **Navobod** ***Rus.*** Navabad, Novabad. C Tajikistan *39.00N 70.06E*
153 *P13* **Navobod** ***Rus.*** Navabad. W Tajikistan *38.37N 68.42E*
Navoi *see* Navoiy
152 *M11* **Navoiy** ***Rus.*** Navoi. Navoiy Viloyati, C Uzbekistan *40.05N 65.22E*
Navoiyskaya Oblast' *see* Navoiy Viloyati
152 *K8* **Navoiy Viloyati** ***Rus.*** Navoiyskaya Oblast'. ◈ *province* N Uzbekistan
42 *G7* **Navojoa** Sonora, NW Mexico *27.04N 109.28W*
Navolat *see* Navolato
42 *H9* **Navolato** ***var.*** Navolat. Sinaloa, C Mexico *24.46N 167.42W*
197 *C12* **Navonda** Ambae, C Vanuatu *15.21S 167.58E*
Návpaktos *see* Náfpaktos
Návplion *see* Náfplio
79 *P14* **Navrongo** N Ghana *10.54N 1.03W*
160 *D12* **Navsāri** ***var.*** Nausari. Gujarāt, W India *20.55N 72.55E*
197 *I15* **Navua** Viti Levu, W Fiji *18.13S 178.10E*
144 *H8* **Nawá** Dar'ā, S Syria *32.52N 36.03E*
Nawabashah *see* Nawābshāh
159 *S14* **Nawabganj** Rajshahi, NW Bangladesh *24.36N 88.17E*
159 *S14* **Nawābganj** Uttar Pradesh, N India *26.52N 82.09E*
155 *Q15* **Nawābshāh** ***var.*** Nawabashah. Sind, S Pakistan *26.15N 68.25E*
159 *P14* **Nawāda** Bihār, N India *24.54N 85.33E*
158 *H11* **Nawalgarh** Rājasthān, N India *27.51N 75.16E*
Nawāl, Sabkhat an *see* Noual, Sebkhet en
Nawar, Dasht-i- *see* Nāvar, Dasht-e
178 *Gg4* **Nawnghkio** ***var.*** Nawngkio. Shan State, C Burma *22.21N 96.48E*
Nawngkio *see* Nawnghkio
143 *U13* **Naxçıvan** ***Rus.*** Nakhichevan'. SW Azerbaijan *39.13N 45.24E*
166 *I10* **Naxi** Sichuan, C China *28.48N 105.25E*
117 *K21* **Náxos** ***var.*** Naxos. Náxos, Kykládes, Greece, Aegean Sea *37.06N 25.22E*
117 *K21* **Náxos** *island* Kykládes, Greece, Aegean Sea
42 *J11* **Nayarit** ◈ *state* C Mexico
197 *K14* **Nayau** *island* Lau Group, E Fiji
149 *S8* **Nāy Band** Yazd, E Iran *32.26N 57.30E*
172 *Pp4* **Nayoro** Hokkaidō, NE Japan *44.21N 142.27E*
106 *F9* **Nazaré** ***var.*** Nazare. Leiria, C Portugal *39.36N 9.04W*
26 *M4* **Nazareth** Texas, SW USA *34.32N 102.06W*
Nazareth *see* Naẕerat
181 *O8* **Nazareth Bank** *undersea feature* W Indian Ocean
126 *Hh14* **Nazarovo** Krasnoyarskiy Kray, S Russian Federation *56.00N 89.33E*
42 *K9* **Nazas** Durango, C Mexico *25.16N 104.04W*
59 *F16* **Nazca** Ica, S Peru *14.52S 75.01W*
(0) *L17* **Nazca Plate** *tectonic feature*
200 *Oo11* **Nazca Ridge** *undersea feature* E Pacific Ocean
172 *R13* **Naze** ***var.*** Nase. Kagoshima, Amami-ōshima, SW Japan *28.21N 129.30E*
144 *G9* **Naẕerat** ***var.*** Natsrat, ***Ar.*** En Nazira, ***Eng.*** Nazareth. Northern, N Israel *32.42N 35.18E*
143 *R14* **Nazik Gölü** ◎ E Turkey
142 *C15* **Nazilli** Aydın, SW Turkey *37.55N 28.19E*
143 *P14* **Nazimiye** Tunceli, E Turkey *39.12N 39.51E*
126 *Gg11* **Nazino** Tomskaya Oblast', C Russian Federation *60.02N 78.51E*
Nazinon *see* Red Volta
8 *L15* **Nazko** British Columbia, SW Canada *52.57N 123.44W*
131 *O16* **Nazran'** Ingushskaya Respublika, SW Russian Federation *43.15N 44.52E*
82 *J13* **Nazrēt** ***var.*** Adama, Hadama. Oromo, C Ethiopia *8.31N 39.20E*
Nazwāh *see* Nizwá
125 *Ff13* **Nazyvayevsk** Omskaya Oblast', C Russian Federation *55.35N 71.13E*
84 *J13* **Nchanga** Copperbelt, C Zambia *12.30S 27.52E*
84 *J11* **Nchelenge** Luapula, N Zambia *9.24S 28.45E*
Ncheu *see* Ntcheu
Ndaghamcha, Sebkra de *see* Te-n-Dghâmcha, Sebkhet
83 *G21* **Ndala** Tabora, C Tanzania *4.45S 33.15E*
84 *B11* **N'Dalatando** ***Port.*** Salazar, Vila Salazar. Cuanza Norte, NW Angola *9.18S 14.48E*
79 *S14* **Ndali** C Benin *9.52N 2.44E*
83 *E18* **Ndeke** SW Uganda *0.11S 30.04E*
80 *J13* **Ndélé** Bamingui-Bangoran, N Central African Republic *8.24N 20.40E*
81 *E19* **Ndendé** Ngounié, S Gabon *2.21S 11.19E*
81 *E20* **Ndindi** Nyanga, S Gabon *3.46S 11.06E*
80 *G11* **Ndjamena** ***var.*** N'Djamena; ***prev.*** Fort-Lamy. ● (Chad) Chari-Baguirmi, W Chad *12.08N 15.01E*
80 *G11* **Ndjamena** ✕ Chari-Baguirmi, W Chad *12.09N 15.00E*
81 *D18* **Ndjolé** Moyen-Ogooué, W Gabon *0.07S 10.45E*
84 *J13* **Ndola** Copperbelt, C Zambia *12.58S 28.35E*
Ndrhamcha, Sebkha de *see* Te-n-Dghâmcha, Sebkhet
81 *L15* **Ndu** Orientale, N Dem. Rep. Congo *4.46N 22.54E*
83 *H21* **Nduguti** Singida, C Tanzania *4.19S 34.40E*
195 *X16* **Nduindui** Guadalcanal, C Solomon Islands *9.46S 159.54E*
Nduke *see* Kolombangara
117 *F16* **Néa Anchiálos** ***var.*** Nea Anhialos, Néa Ankhíalos. Thessalía, C Greece *39.18N 22.49E*
Nea Anhialos/Néa Ankhíalos *see* Néa Anchiálos
117 *H18* **Néa Artáki** Évvoia, C Greece *38.31N 23.39E*
99 *F15* **Neagh, Lough** ◎ E Northern Ireland, UK
34 *F7* **Neah Bay** Washington, NW USA *48.21N 124.39W*
117 *J22* **Nea Kaméni** *island* Kykládes, Greece, Aegean Sea
189 *O8* **Neale, Lake** ◎ Northern Territory, C Australia
190 *G2* **Neales River** *seasonal river* South Australia
117 *G14* **Néa Moudaniá** ***var.*** Néa Moudanía, Néa Moudhaniá. Kentrikí Makedonía, N Greece *40.15N 23.19E*
Néa Moudhaniá *see* Néa Moudaniá
118 *K10* **Neamț** ◈ *county* NE Romania
Neapel *see* Napoli
117 *D14* **Neápoli** ***prev.*** Neápolis. Dytikí Makedonía, N Greece *40.18N 21.23E*
117 *K25* **Neápoli** Kríti, Greece, E Mediterranean Sea *35.15N 25.37E*
117 *G22* **Neápoli** Pelopónnisos, S Greece *36.29N 23.05E*
Neapolis *see* Napoli, Italy
Neapolis *see* Nablus, West Bank
Neápolis *see* Neápoli, Greece
40 *D16* **Near Islands** *island group* Aleutian Islands, Alaska, USA
99 *J21* **Neath** S Wales, UK *51.39N 3.48W*
116 *H13* **Néa Zíchni** ***var.*** Néa Zíkhni; ***prev.*** Néa Zíkhna. Kentrikí Makedonía, NE Greece *41.02N 23.51E*
Néa Zíkhna/Néa Zíkhni *see* Néa Zíchni
44 *C5* **Nebaj** Quiché, W Guatemala *15.25N 91.05W*
79 *P13* **Nebbou** S Burkina *11.22N 1.49W*
Nebitdag *see* Balkanabat
56 *M13* **Neblina, Pico da** ▲ NW Brazil *0.49N 66.31W*
128 *I13* **Nebolchi** Novgorodskaya Oblast', W Russian Federation *59.08N 33.19E*
38 *L4* **Nebo, Mount** ▲ Utah, W USA *39.47N 111.46W*
30 *L14* **Nebraska** ***off.*** State of Nebraska; also known as Blackwater State, Cornhusker State, Tree Planters State. ◈ *state* C USA
31 *S16* **Nebraska City** Nebraska, C USA *40.38N 95.52W*
109 *K23* **Nebrodi, Monti** ***var.*** Monti Caronie. ▲▲ Sicilia, Italy, C Mediterranean Sea
8 *L14* **Nechako** ≈ British Columbia, SW Canada
31 *Q2* **Neche** North Dakota, N USA *48.57N 97.33W*
27 *V8* **Neches** Texas, SW USA *31.51N 95.28W*
27 *W8* **Neches River** ≈ Texas, SW USA
103 *H20* **Neckar** ≈ SW Germany
103 *H20* **Neckarsulm** Baden-Württemberg, SW Germany *49.12N 9.13E*
199 *K5* **Necker Island** *island* C British Virgin Islands
183 *U3* **Necker Ridge** *undersea feature* N Pacific Ocean
63 *D23* **Necochea** Buenos Aires, E Argentina *38.33S 58.42W*
106 *H2* **Neda** Galicia, NW Spain *43.28N 8.09W*
117 *E20* **Néda** ***var.*** Nédas. ≈ S Greece
Nédas *see* Néda
27 *Y11* **Nederland** Texas, SW USA *29.58N 93.59W*
Nederland *see* Netherlands
100 *K12* **Neder Rijn** ***Eng.*** Lower Rhine. ≈ C Netherlands
101 *L16* **Nederweert** Limburg, SE Netherlands *51.16N 5.45E*
97 *G16* **Nedre Tokke** ◎ S Norway
Nedrigaylov *see* Nedryhayliv
119 *S3* **Nedryhayliv** ***Rus.*** Nedrigaylov. Sums'ka Oblast', NE Ukraine *50.51N 33.52E*
100 *O11* **Neede** Gelderland, E Netherlands *52.07N 6.36E*
35 *T13* **Needle Mountain** ▲ Wyoming, C USA *44.03N 109.33W*
37 *Y14* **Needles** California, W USA *34.50N 114.37W*
99 *M24* **Needles, The** *rocks* Isle of Wight, S England, UK
64 *O7* **Ñeembucú** ***off.*** Departamento de Ñeembucú. ◈ *department* SW Paraguay
32 *M7* **Neenah** Wisconsin, N USA *44.09N 88.26W*
9 *W16* **Neepawa** Manitoba, S Canada *50.13N 99.28W*
101 *K16* **Neerpelt** Limburg, NE Belgium *51.13N 5.25E*
76 *M6* **Nefta** ✕ W Tunisia *34.03N 8.05E*
130 *L15* **Neftegorsk** Krasnodarskiy Kray, SW Russian Federation *44.21N 39.40E*
131 *U3* **Neftekamsk** Respublika Bashkortostan, W Russian Federation *56.06N 54.12E*
131 *O14* **Neftekumsk** Stavropol'skiy Kray, SW Russian Federation *44.45N 45.00E*
125 *G11* **Nefteyugansk** Khanty-Mansiyskiy Avtonomnyy Okrug, C Russian Federation *61.07N 72.18E*
Neftezavodsk *see* Seýdi
84 *C10* **Negage** ***var.*** N'Gage. Uíge, NW Angola *7.46S 15.27E*
Negapatam/Negapattinam *see* Nāgappattinam
175 *N16* **Negara** Bali, Indonesia *8.21S 114.34E*
175 *N10* **Negara** Borneo, C Indonesia *2.40S 115.04E*
Negara Brunei Darussalam *see* Brunei
33 *N4* **Negaunee** Michigan, N USA *46.30N 87.36W*
83 *J15* **Negēlē** ***var.*** Negelli, ***It.*** Neghelli. Oromo, C Ethiopia *5.13N 39.43E*
Negelli *see* Negēlē
Negeri Pahang Darul Makmur *see* Pahang
Negeri Selangor Darul Ehsan *see* Selangor
174 *H5* **Negeri Sembilan** ***var.*** Negri Sembilan. ◈ *state* Peninsular Malaysia
94 *P3* **Negerpynten** *headland* S Svalbard *77.15N 22.40E*
Negev *see* HaNegev
Neghelli *see* Negēlē
118 *I12* **Negoiu** ***var.*** Negoiul. ▲ S Romania *45.34N 24.34E*
Negoiul *see* Negoiu
84 *P13* **Negomane** ***var.*** Negomano. Cabo Delgado, N Mozambique *11.22S 38.32E*
Negomano *see* Negomane
161 *J25* **Negombo** Western Province, SW Sri Lanka *7.13N 79.51E*
Negoreloye *see* Nyeharelaye
114 *P12* **Negotin** Serbia, E Serbia *44.13N 22.31E*
115 *P19* **Negotino** C FYR Macedonia *41.29N 22.04E*
58 *A10* **Negra, Punta** *headland* NW Peru *6.03S 81.08W*
106 *G3* **Negreira** Galicia, NW Spain *42.54N 8.46W*
118 *L10* **Negrești** Vaslui, E Romania *46.49N 27.28E*
Negrești *see* Negrești-Oaș
118 *H8* **Negrești-Oaș** ***Hung.*** Avasfelsőfalu; ***prev.*** Negrești. Satu Mare, NE Romania *47.56N 23.21E*
46 *H12* **Negril** W Jamaica *18.16N 78.21W*
Negri Sembilan *see* Negeri Sembilan
65 *K15* **Negro, Río** ≈ E Argentina
64 *N7* **Negro, Río** ≈ NE Argentina
59 *N17* **Negro, Río** ≈ E Bolivia
64 *O5* **Negro, Río** ≈ C Paraguay
50 *F6* **Negro, Río** ≈ N South America
63 *E18* **Negro, Río** ≈ Brazil/Uruguay
Negro, Río *see* Sico Tinto, Río, Honduras
Negro, Río *see* Chixoy, Río, Guatemala/Mexico
179 *Q14* **Negros** *island* C Philippines
118 *M15* **Negru Vodă** Constanța, SE Romania *43.47N 28.10E*
11 *P13* **Neguac** New Brunswick, SE Canada *47.16N 65.04W*
12 *B7* **Negwazu, Lake** ◎ Ontario, S Canada
Négyfalu *see* Săcele
34 *F10* **Nehalem** Oregon, NW USA *45.42N 123.55W*
34 *F10* **Nehalem River** ≈ Oregon, NW USA
Nehavend *see* Nahāvand
149 *V9* **Nehbandān** Khorāsān-e Janūbī, E Iran *31.33N 60.01E*
169 *V6* **Nehe** Heilongjiang, NE China *48.28N 124.52E*
200 *Ss12* **Neiafu** 'Uta Vava'u, N Tonga *18.36S 173.58W*
47 *N9* **Neiba** ***var.*** Neyba. SW Dominican Republic *18.27N 71.28W*
Néid, Carn Uí *see* Mizen Head
94 *M9* **Neiden** Finnmark, N Norway *69.40N 29.22E*
Neidín *see* Kenmare
Néifinn *see* Nephin
105 *S10* **Neige, Crêt de la** ▲ E France *46.18N 5.58E*
181 *O16* **Neiges, Piton des** ▲ C Réunion *21.04S 55.28E*
13 *R9* **Neiges, Rivière des** ≈ Québec, SE Canada
166 *I10* **Neijiang** Sichuan, C China *29.31N 105.03E*
32 *K6* **Neillsville** Wisconsin, N USA *44.34N 90.36W*
Nei Monggol Zizhiqu/Nei Mongol *see* Nei Mongol Zizhiqu
169 *Q10* **Nei Mongol Gaoyuan** *plateau* NE China
169 *O12* **Nei Mongol Zizhiqu** ***var.*** Nei Mongol, ***Eng.*** Inner Mongolia, Inner Mongolian Autonomous Region; ***prev.*** Nei Monggol Zizhiqu. ◈ *autonomous region* N China
167 *O4* **Neiqiu** Hebei, E China *37.22N 114.34E*
Neiriz *see* Neyrīz
103 *Q16* **Neisse** ***Cz.*** Lužická Nisa, ***Ger.*** Lausitzer Neisse, ***Pol.*** Nisa, Nysa Łużycka. ≈ C Europe
Neisse *see* Nysa
56 *E11* **Neiva** Huila, S Colombia *2.58N 75.15W*
166 *M7* **Neixiang** Henan, C China *33.07N 111.49E*
Nejafabad *see* Najafābād
9 *V9* **Nejanilini Lake** ◎ Manitoba, C Canada
Nejd *see* Najd
82 *I13* **Nek'emtē** ***var.*** Lakemti, Nakamti. Oromo, C Ethiopia *9.06N 36.31E*
130 *M9* **Nekhayevskiy** Volgogradskaya Oblast', SW Russian Federation *50.25N 41.44E*
32 *K7* **Nekoosa** Wisconsin, N USA *44.19N 89.54W*
117 *C16* **Nekromanteíon** *ancient monument* Ípeiros, W Greece *39.13N 20.31E*
Neksø *see* Nexo
106 *H7* **Nelas** Viseu, N Portugal *40.31N 7.52W*
128 *H16* **Nelidovo** Tverskaya Oblast', W Russian Federation *56.13N 32.45E*
31 *P13* **Neligh** Nebraska, C USA *42.07N 98.01W*
127 *N12* **Nel'kan** Khabarovskiy Kray, E Russian Federation *57.44N 136.09E*
94 *M10* **Nellim** ***var.*** Nellimö, ***Lapp.*** Njellim. Lappi, N Finland *68.49N 28.18E*
Nellimö *see* Nellim
161 *J18* **Nellore** Andhra Pradesh, E India *14.29N 80.00E*
127 *O16* **Nel'ma** Khabarovskiy Kray, SE Russian Federation *47.43N 139.08E*
63 *B17* **Nelson** Santa Fe, C Argentina *31.16S 60.45W*
9 *O17* **Nelson** British Columbia, SW Canada *49.29N 117.13W*
193 *I14* **Nelson** Nelson, South Island, NZ *41.16S 173.16E*
99 *L17* **Nelson** NW England, UK *53.51N 2.13W*
31 *P17* **Nelson** Nebraska, C USA *40.12N 98.04W*
193 *J14* **Nelson** ◈ *unitary authority* South Island, NZ
9 *X12* **Nelson** ≈ Manitoba, C Canada
191 *U8* **Nelson Bay** New South Wales, SE Australia *32.45S 152.09E*
190 *K13* **Nelson, Cape** *headland* Victoria, SE Australia *38.25S 141.33E*
194 *M15* **Nelson, Cape** *headland* S PNG *8.57S 149.19E*
65 *G23* **Nelson, Estrecho** *strait* SE Pacific Ocean
9 *W12* **Nelson House** Manitoba, C Canada *55.49N 98.51W*
32 *J4* **Nelson Lake** ◎ Wisconsin, N USA
33 *T14* **Nelsonville** Ohio, N USA *39.27N 82.13W*
29 *S2* **Nelsoon River** ≈ Iowa/Missouri, C USA
85 *K21* **Nelspruit** Mpumalanga, NE South Africa *25.28S 30.58E*
78 *L10* **Néma** Hodh ech Chargui, SE Mauritania *16.31N 7.12W*
120 *D13* **Neman** ***Ger.*** Ragnit. Kaliningradskaya Oblast', W Russian Federation *55.01N 22.00E*
86 *I9* **Neman** ***Bel.*** Nyoman, ***Ger.*** Memel, ***Lith.*** Nemunas, ***Pol.*** Niemen, ***Rus.*** Neman. ≈ NE Europe
Nemausus *see* Nîmes
117 *F19* **Neméa** Pelopónnisos, S Greece *37.49N 22.40E*
Německý Brod *see* Havlíčkův Brod
12 *D7* **Nemegosenda** ≈ Ontario, S Canada
12 *D8* **Nemegosenda Lake** ◎ Ontario, S Canada
121 *H14* **Nemencinė** Vilnius, SE Lithuania *54.50N 25.29E*
Nemetocenna *see* Arras
Nemirov *see* Nemyriv
105 *O6* **Nemours** Seine-et-Marne, N France *48.16N 2.40E*
Nemunas *see* Neman
172 *R7* **Nemuro** Hokkaidō, NE Japan *43.19N 145.34E*
172 *R7* **Nemuro-hantō** *peninsula* Hokkaidō, NE Japan
172 *R6* **Nemuro-kaikyō** *strait* Japan/Russian Federation
172 *R7* **Nemuro-wan** *bay* N Japan
118 *H5* **Nemyriv** ***Rus.*** Nemirov. L'vivs'ka Oblast', NW Ukraine *50.07N 23.27E*
119 *N7* **Nemyriv** ***Rus.*** Nemirov. Vinnyts'ka Oblast', C Ukraine *48.57N 28.51E*
99 *D19* **Nenagh** ***Ir.*** An tAonach. C Ireland *52.52N 8.12W*
41 *R9* **Nenana** Alaska, USA *64.33N 149.05W*
41 *R9* **Nenana River** ≈ Alaska, USA
195 *W8* **Nendö** ***var.*** Swallow Island. *island* Santa Cruz Islands, E Solomon Islands
99 *O19* **Nene** ≈ E England, UK
129 *R4* **Nenetskiy Avtonomnyy Okrug** ◈ *autonomous district* NW Russian Federation
203 *W11* **Nengonengo** *atoll* Îles Tuamotu, C French Polynesia
169 *U6* **Nen Jiang** ***var.*** Nonni. ≈ NE China
169 *V6* **Nenjiang** Heilongjiang, NE China *49.10N 125.18E*
201 *P16* **Neoch** *atoll* Caroline Islands, C Micronesia
117 *D18* **Neochóri** Dytikí Ellás, C Greece *38.23N 21.14E*
29 *Q7* **Neodesha** Kansas, C USA *37.25N 95.40W*
31 *S14* **Neola** Iowa, C USA *41.27N 95.40W*
117 *E16* **Néo Monastíri** ***var.*** Néon Monastíri. Thessalía, C Greece *39.22N 21.55E*
Néon Karlovási/Néon Karlovásion *see* Karlovási
Néon Monastíri *see* Néo Monastíri
29 *R8* **Neosho** Missouri, C USA *36.52N 94.22W*
29 *Q7* **Neosho River** ≈ Kansas/Oklahoma, C USA
127 *N17* **Nepa** ≈ C Russian Federation
159 *N10* **Nepal** ***off.*** Kingdom of Nepal. ◆ *monarchy* S Asia
158 *M11* **Nepālganj** Mid Western, SW Nepal *28.04N 81.37E*
12 *L13* **Nepean** Ontario, SE Canada *45.19N 75.53W*
38 *L4* **Nephi** Utah, W USA *39.43N 111.49W*
99 *B16* **Nephin** ***Ir.*** Néifinn. ▲ W Ireland *54.00N 9.21W*
69 *T9* **Nepoko** ≈ NE Dem. Rep. Congo
20 *K15* **Neptune** New Jersey, NE USA *40.10N 74.03W*
190 *G10* **Neptune Islands** *island group* South Australia
109 *I14* **Nera** ***anc.*** Nar. ≈ C Italy
104 *L14* **Nérac** Lot-et-Garonne, SW France *44.07N 0.21E*
113 *D16* **Neratovice** ***Ger.*** Neratowitz. Středočeský Kraj, C Czech Republic *50.16N 14.31E*
Neratowitz *see* Neratovice
126 *L15* **Nercha** ≈ S Russian Federation
126 *L15* **Nerchinsk** Chitinskaya Oblast', S Russian Federation *52.01N 116.25E*
126 *L16* **Nerchinskiy Zavod** Chitinskaya Oblast', S Russian Federation *51.13N 119.25E*
128 *M15* **Nerekhta** Kostromskaya Oblast', NW Russian Federation *57.27N 40.33E*
120 *H10* **Nereta** Aizkraukle, S Latvia *56.12N 25.18E*
108 *K13* **Nereto** Abruzzo, C Italy *42.49N 13.50E*
115 *H15* **Neretva** ≈ Bosnia and Herzegovina/Croatia
117 *C17* **Nerikós** *ruins* Lefkáda, Iónia Nisiá, Greece, C Mediterranean Sea *38.48N 20.43E*
85 *F15* **Neriquinha** Cuando Cubango, SE Angola *15.44S 21.34E*
120 *I13* **Neris** ***Bel.*** Viliya, ***Pol.*** Wilia; ***prev.*** ***Pol.*** Wilja. ≈ Belarus/Lithuania
Neris *see* Viliya
107 *N15* **Nerja** Andalucía, S Spain *36.45N 3.34W*
128 *L16* **Nerl'** ≈ W Russian Federation
176 *Vv13* **Nerong, Selat** *strait* Kepulauan Kai, E Indonesia
107 *P12* **Nerpio** Castilla-La Mancha, C Spain *38.08N 2.18W*
106 *J13* **Nerva** Andalucía, S Spain *37.39N 6.31W*
126 *Ll13* **Neryungri** Respublika Sakha (Yakutiya), NE Russian Federation *56.37N 124.19E*
100 *L4* **Nes** Friesland, N Netherlands *53.28N 5.46E*
96 *G13* **Nesbyen** Buskerud, S Norway *60.34N 9.34E*
94 *L2* **Neskaupstadhur** Austurland, E Iceland *65.08N 13.45W*
94 *F13* **Nesna** Nordland, C Norway *66.11N 12.54E*
28 *K5* **Ness City** Kansas, C USA *38.27N 99.54W*
Nesselsdorf *see* Kopřivnice
110 *H7* **Nesslau** Sankt Gallen, NE Switzerland *47.13N 9.12E*
98 *I9* **Ness, Loch** ◎ N Scotland, UK
Nesterov *see* Zhovkva
116 *I12* **Néstos** ***Bul.*** Mesta, ***Turk.*** Kara Su. ≈ Bulgaria/Greece ***see also*** Mesta
97 *C14* **Nesttun** Hordaland, S Norway *60.19N 5.16E*
Nesvizh *see* Nyasvizh
144 *F9* **Netanya** ***var.*** Natanya, Nathanya. Central, C Israel *32.19N 34.51E*
100 *I9* **Netherlands** ***off.*** Kingdom of the Netherlands, ***var.*** Holland, ***Dut.*** Koninkrijk der Nederlanden, Nederland. ◆ *monarchy* NW Europe
47 *S9* **Netherlands Antilles** ***prev.*** Dutch West Indies. ◇ *Dutch autonomous region* S Caribbean Sea
Netherlands East Indies *see* Indonesia
Netherlands Guiana *see* Surinam
Netherlands New Guinea *see* Papua
118 *L4* **Netishyn** Khmel'nyts'ka Oblast', W Ukraine *50.20N 26.38E*
144 *E11* **Netivot** Southern, S Israel *31.25N 34.36E*
109 *O21* **Neto** ≈ S Italy
16 *N2* **Nettilling Lake** ◎ Baffin Island, Nunavut, N Canada
31 *V3* **Nett Lake** ◎ Minnesota, N USA
109 *I16* **Nettuno** Lazio, C Italy *41.26N 12.40E*
Netum *see* Noto
43 *U16* **Netzahualcóyotl, Presa** ▣ SE Mexico
Netze *see* Noteć
Neu Amerika *see* Puławy
Neubetsche *see* Novi Bečej
Neubidschow *see* Nový Bydžov
Neubistritz *see* Nová Bystřice
102 *N9* **Neubrandenburg** Mecklenburg-Vorpommern, NE Germany *53.33N 13.16E*
103 *K22* **Neuburg an der Donau** Bayern, S Germany *48.43N 11.10E*
110 *C8* **Neuchâtel** ***Ger.*** Neuenburg. Neuchâtel, W Switzerland *46.58N 6.55E*
110 *C8* **Neuchâtel** ***Ger.*** Neuenburg. ◈ *canton* W Switzerland
110 *C8* **Neuchâtel, Lac de** ***Ger.*** Neuenburger See. ◎ W Switzerland
Neudorf *see* Spišská Nová Ves
102 *L10* **Neue Elde** *canal* N Germany
Neuenburg *see* Neuchâtel
Neuenburg an der Elbe *see* Nymburk
Neuenburger See *see* Neuchâtel, Lac de
110 *F7* **Neuenhof** Aargau, N Switzerland *47.27N 8.17E*
102 *H11* **Neuenland** ✕ (Bremen) Bremen, NW Germany *53.03N 8.46E*
Neuenstadt *see* La Neuveville
103 *C18* **Neuerburg** Rheinland-Pfalz, W Germany *50.01N 6.13E*
101 *K24* **Neufchâteau** Luxembourg, SE Belgium *49.49N 5.25E*
105 *S6* **Neufchâteau** Vosges, NE France *48.21N 5.42E*
104 *M3* **Neufchâtel-en-Bray** Seine-Maritime, N France *49.44N 1.26E*
111 *S3* **Neufelden** Oberösterreich, N Austria *48.27N 14.01E*
Neugradisk *see* Nova Gradiška
Neuhaus *see* Jindřichův Hradec
Neuhäusel *see* Nové Zámky
110 *G6* **Neuhausen** ***var.*** Neuhausen am Rheinfall. Schaffhausen, N Switzerland *47.24N 8.37E*
Neuhausen am Rheinfall *see* Neuhausen
103 *I17* **Neuhof** Hessen, C Germany *50.26N 9.34E*
Neuhof *see* Zgierz
Neukuhren *see* Pionerskiy

◆ Country
● Country Capital
◇ Dependent Territory
○ Dependent Territory Capital
◈ Administrative Region
✕ International Airport
▲ Mountain
▲▲ Mountain Range
Volcano
≈ River
◎ Lake
▣ Reservoir

NEU-LANGENBURG – NIKOLAINKAUPUNKI

Neu-Langenburg *see* Tukuyu
111 *W4* **Neulengbach** Niederösterreich, NE Austria *48.10N 15.53E*
115 *G15* **Neum** Federacija Bosna I Hercegovina, S Bosnia and Herzegovina *42.57N 17.33E*
Neumark *see* Nowy Targ, Nowy Sącz, Poland
Neumark *see* Nowe Miasto Lubawskie, Toruń, Poland
Neumarkt *see* Neumarkt im Hausruckkreis, Oberösterreich, Austria
Neumarkt *see* Neumarkt Am Wallersee, Salzburg, Austria
Neumarkt *see* Środa Śląska, Wrocław, Poland
Neumarkt *see* Târgu Secuiesc, Covasna, Romania
Neumarkt *see* Târgu Mureş, Mureş, Romania
111 *Q5* **Neumarkt am Wallersee** *var.* Neumarkt. Salzburg, NW Austria *47.55N 13.16E*
111 *R4* **Neumarkt im Hausruckkreis** *var.* Neumarkt. Oberösterreich, N Austria *48.16N 13.40E*
103 *L20* **Neumarkt in der Oberpfalz** Bayern, SE Germany *49.16N 11.28E*
Neumarktl *see* Tržič
Neumoldowa *see* Moldova Nouă
102 *J8* **Neumünster** Schleswig-Holstein, N Germany *54.04N 9.58E*
111 *X5* **Neunkirchen** *var.* Neunkirchen am Steinfeld. Niederösterreich, E Austria *47.43N 16.04E*
103 *E20* **Neunkirchen** Saarland, SW Germany *49.21N 7.10E*
Neunkirchen am Steinfeld *see* Neunkirchen
Neuoderberg *see* Bohumín
65 *I15* **Neuquén** Neuquén, SE Argentina *39.03S 68.36W*
65 *H14* **Neuquén** *off.* Provincia de Neuquén. ◆ *province* W Argentina
65 *H14* **Neuquén, Río** ~ W Argentina
Neurode *see* Nowa Ruda
102 *N11* **Neuruppin** Brandenburg, NE Germany *52.55N 12.49E*
Neusalz an der Oder *see* Nowa Sól
Neu Sandec/Neusandez *see* Małopolskie
103 *K22* **Neusäss** Bayern, S Germany *48.24N 10.49E*
Neusatz *see* Novi Sad
Neuschliss *see* Gherla
23 *N8* **Neuse River** ~ North Carolina, SE USA
111 *Z5* **Neusiedl am See** Burgenland, E Austria *47.56N 16.51E*
113 *G22* **Neusiedler See** *Hung.* Fertő. ◎ Austria/Hungary
Neusohl *see* Banská Bystrica
103 *D15* **Neuss** *anc.* Novaesium, Novesium. Nordrhein-Westfalen, W Germany *51.12N 6.40E*
Neuss *see* Nyon
Neustadt *see* Neustadt an der Aisch, Bayern, Germany
Neustadt *see* Neustadt bei Coburg, Bayern, Germany
Neustadt *see* Prudnik, Opole, Poland
Neustadt *see* Baia Mare, Maramureş, Romania
102 *I12* **Neustadt am Rübenberge** Niedersachsen, N Germany *52.30N 9.28E*
103 *J19* **Neustadt an der Aisch** *var.* Neustadt. Bayern, C Germany *49.34N 10.36E*
Neustadt an der Haardt *see* Neustadt an der Weinstrasse
103 *F20* **Neustadt an der Weinstrasse** *prev.* Neustadt an der Haardt, *hist.* Niewenstat, *anc.* Nova Civitas. Rheinland-Pfalz, SW Germany *49.21N 8.09E*
103 *K18* **Neustadt bei Coburg** *var.* Neustadt. Bayern, C Germany *50.19N 11.06E*
Neustadt bei Pinne *see* Lwówek
Neustadt in Oberschlesien *see* Prudnik
Neustadtl *see* Novo mesto
Neustadtl in Mähren *see* Nové Město na Moravě
Neustettin *see* Szczecinek
110 *M8* **Neustift im Stubaital** *var.* Stubaital. Tirol, W Austria *47.07N 11.26E*
102 *N10* **Neustrelitz** Mecklenburg-Vorpommern, NE Germany *53.22N 13.04E*
Neutitschein *see* Nový Jičín
Neutra *see* Nitra
103 *J22* **Neu-Ulm** Bayern, S Germany *48.23N 10.01E*
Neuveville *see* La Neuveville
105 *N12* **Neuvic** Corrèze, C France *45.23N 2.16E*
Neuwarp *see* Nowe Warpno
102 *G9* **Neuwerk** *island* NW Germany
103 *E17* **Neuwied** Rheinland-Pfalz, W Germany *50.25N 7.28E*
Neuzen *see* Terneuzen
128 *H12* **Neva** ~ NW Russian Federation
31 *V14* **Nevada** Iowa, C USA *42.01N 93.27W*
29 *R6* **Nevada** Missouri, C USA *37.50N 94.21W*
37 *R5* **Nevada** *off.* State of Nevada; also known as Battle Born State, Sagebrush State, Silver State. ◆ *state* W USA
37 *P6* **Nevada City** California, W USA *39.15N 121.02W*
128 *G16* **Nevel'** Pskovskaya Oblast', W Russian Federation *56.01N 29.54E*
127 *Oo16* **Nevel'sk** Ostrov Sakhalin, Sakhalinskaya Oblast', SE Russian Federation *46.41N 141.54E*
126 *Ll14* **Never** Amurskaya Oblast', SE Russian Federation *53.58N 124.04E*
131 *Q6* **Neverkino** Penzenskaya Oblast', W Russian Federation *52.53N 46.46E*
105 *P9* **Nevers** *anc.* Noviodunum. Nièvre, C France *47.00N 3.09E*
20 *J12* **Neversink River** ~ New York, NE USA
191 *Q6* **Nevertire** New South Wales, SE Australia *31.52S 147.42E*
115 *H15* **Nevesinje** Republika Srpska, S Bosnia and Herzegovina *43.15N 18.09E*
120 *G12* **Nevėžis** ~ C Lithuania
130 *M14* **Nevinnomyssk** Stavropol'skiy Kray, SW Russian Federation *44.39N 41.57E*
47 *W10* **Nevis** *island* Saint Kitts and Nevis
Nevoso, Monte *see* Veliki Snežnik
Nevrokop *see* Gotse Delchev
142 *J14* **Nevşehir** *var.* Nevshehr. Nevşehir, C Turkey *38.37N 34.43E*
142 *J14* **Nevşehir** *var.* Nevshehr. ◆ *province* C Turkey
Nevshehr *see* Nevşehir
125 *Ee11* **Nev'yansk** Sverdlovskaya Oblast', C Russian Federation *57.26N 60.15E*
83 *J25* **Newala** Mtwara, SE Tanzania *10.58S 39.18E*
33 *P16* **New Albany** Indiana, N USA *38.16N 85.49W*
24 *M2* **New Albany** Mississippi, S USA *34.29N 89.00W*
31 *Y11* **New Albin** Iowa, C USA *43.30N 91.17W*
57 *U8* **New Amsterdam** E Guyana *6.17N 57.30W*
191 *Q4* **New Angledool** New South Wales, SE Australia *29.06S 147.54E*
23 *Y2* **Newark** Delaware, NE USA *39.40N 75.45W*
20 *K14* **Newark** New Jersey, NE USA *40.42N 74.12W*
20 *G10* **Newark** New York, NE USA *43.01N 77.04W*
33 *T13* **Newark** Ohio, N USA *40.03N 82.24W*
Newark *see* Newark-on-Trent
37 *W5* **Newark Lake** ◎ Nevada, W USA
99 *N18* **Newark-on-Trent** *var.* Newark. C England, UK *53.04N 0.49W*
24 *M7* **New Augusta** Mississippi, S USA *31.12N 89.03W*
21 *P12* **New Bedford** Massachusetts, NE USA *41.37N 70.55W*
34 *G11* **Newberg** Oregon, NW USA *45.18N 122.58W*
23 *X10* **New Bern** North Carolina, SE USA *35.07N 77.03W*
22 *F8* **Newbern** Tennessee, S USA *36.06N 89.15W*
33 *P4* **Newberry** Michigan, N USA *46.21N 85.30W*
23 *Q12* **Newberry** South Carolina, SE USA *34.16N 81.37W*
20 *F15* **New Bloomfield** Pennsylvania, NE USA *40.24N 77.08W*
27 *X5* **New Boston** Texas, SW USA *33.27N 94.25W*
27 *S11* **New Braunfels** Texas, SW USA *29.43N 98.09W*
33 *Q13* **New Bremen** Ohio, N USA *40.26N 84.22W*
99 *F18* **Newbridge** *Ir.* An Droichead Nua. C Ireland *53.10N 6.48W*
20 *B14* **New Brighton** Pennsylvania, NE USA *40.44N 80.18W*
20 *M12* **New Britain** Connecticut, NE USA *41.37N 72.45W*
195 *N13* **New Britain** *island* E PNG
199 *Hh9* **New Britain Trench** *undersea feature* W Pacific Ocean
20 *J15* **New Brunswick** New Jersey, NE USA *40.29N 74.27W*
13 *V8* **New Brunswick** *Fr.* Nouveau-Brunswick. ◆ *province* SE Canada
20 *K13* **Newburgh** New York, NE USA *41.30N 74.00W*
99 *M22* **Newbury** S England, UK *51.25N 1.19W*
21 *P10* **Newburyport** Massachusetts, NE USA *42.49N 70.53W*
79 *T14* **New Bussa** Niger, W Nigeria *9.50N 4.32E*
197 *J4* **New Caledonia** *var.* Kanaky, *Fr.* Nouvelle-Calédonie. ◇ *French overseas territory* SW Pacific Ocean
197 *H5* **New Caledonia** *island* SW Pacific Ocean
183 *O10* **New Caledonia Basin** *undersea feature* W Pacific Ocean
191 *T8* **Newcastle** New South Wales, SE Australia *32.55S 151.46E*
11 *O14* **Newcastle** New Brunswick, SE Canada *47.01N 65.36W*
12 *I15* **Newcastle** Ontario, SE Canada *43.55N 78.35W*
99 *C20* **Newcastle** *Ir.* An Caisleán Nua. SW Ireland *52.25N 9.04W*
85 *K22* **Newcastle** KwaZulu/Natal, E South Africa *27.45S 29.59E*
99 *G16* **Newcastle** *Ir.* An Caisleán Nua. SE Northern Ireland, UK *54.12N 5.54W*
33 *P13* **New Castle** Indiana, N USA *39.55N 85.21W*
22 *L5* **New Castle** Kentucky, S USA *38.22N 85.09W*
29 *N11* **Newcastle** Oklahoma, C USA *35.15N 97.36W*
20 *B13* **New Castle** Pennsylvania, NE USA *40.59N 80.19W*
27 *R6* **Newcastle** Texas, SW USA *33.11N 98.44W*
38 *J7* **Newcastle** Utah, W USA *37.40N 113.31W*
23 *S6* **New Castle** Virginia, NE USA *37.29N 80.06W*
35 *Z13* **Newcastle** Wyoming, C USA *43.52N 104.13W*
47 *W10* **Newcastle** ✕ Nevis, Saint Kitts and Nevis *17.08N 62.36W*
99 *L14* **Newcastle** ✕ NE England, UK *55.03N 1.42W*
Newcastle *see* Newcastle upon Tyne
99 *L18* **Newcastle-under-Lyme** C England, UK *53.00N 2.14W*
99 *M14* **Newcastle upon Tyne** *var.* Newcastle; *hist.* Monkchester, *Lat.* Pons Aelii. NE England, UK *54.58N 1.34W*
189 *Q4* **Newcastle Waters** Northern Territory, N Australia *17.20S 133.26E*
Newchwang *see* Yingkou
20 *K13* **New City** New York, NE USA *41.08N 73.57W*
33 *U13* **Newcomerstown** Ohio, N USA *40.16N 81.36W*
20 *G15* **New Cumberland** Pennsylvania, NE USA *40.13N 76.52W*
23 *R1* **New Cumberland** West Virginia, NE USA *40.30N 80.35W*
158 *I10* **New Delhi** ● (India) Delhi, N India *28.34N 77.14E*
9 *O17* **New Denver** British Columbia, SW Canada *49.58N 117.21W*
30 *J9* **Newell** South Dakota, N USA *44.42N 103.25W*
23 *Q13* **New Ellenton** South Carolina, SE USA *33.25N 81.41W*
24 *J6* **Newellton** Louisiana, S USA *32.04N 91.14W*
30 *K6* **New England** North Dakota, N USA *46.32N 102.52W*
21 *P8* **New England** *cultural region* NE USA
New England of the West *see* Minnesota
191 *U5* **New England Range** ▲ New South Wales, SE Australia
66 *G9* **New England Seamounts** *var.* Bermuda-New England Seamount Arc. *undersea feature* W Atlantic Ocean
40 *M14* **Newenham, Cape** *headland* Alaska, USA *58.39N 162.10W*
144 *F11* **Newé Zohar** Southern, E Israel *31.07N 35.23E*
20 *D9* **Newfane** New York, NE USA *43.16N 78.40W*
99 *M23* **New Forest** *physical region* S England, UK
16 *S8* **Newfoundland** *Fr.* Terre-Neuve. *island* Newfoundland and Labrador, SE Canada
11 *R9* **Newfoundland and Labrador** *Fr.* Terre Neuve. ◆ *province* E Canada
67 *J8* **Newfoundland Basin** *undersea feature* NW Atlantic Ocean
66 *I8* **Newfoundland Ridge** *undersea feature* NW Atlantic Ocean
66 *J8* **Newfoundland Seamounts** *undersea feature* N Sargasso Sea
20 *G16* **New Freedom** Pennsylvania, NE USA *39.43N 76.41W*
195 *U14* **New Georgia** *island* New Georgia Islands, NW Solomon Islands
195 *T15* **New Georgia Islands** *island group* NW Solomon Islands
195 *U14* **New Georgia Sound** *var.* The Slot. *sound* E Solomon Sea
32 *L9* **New Glarus** Wisconsin, N USA *42.50N 89.38W*
11 *Q15* **New Glasgow** Nova Scotia, SE Canada *45.36N 62.37W*
New Goa *see* Panaji
194 *D11* **New Guinea** *Dut.* Nieuw Guinea, *Ind.* Irian. *island* Indonesia/PNG
199 *H9* **New Guinea Trench** *undersea feature* SW Pacific Ocean
34 *I6* **Newhalem** Washington, NW USA *48.40N 121.18W*
41 *P13* **Newhalen** Alaska, USA *59.43N 154.54W*
31 *X13* **Newhall** Iowa, C USA *42.00N 91.58W*
12 *F16* **New Hamburg** Ontario, S Canada *43.24N 80.37W*
21 *N9* **New Hampshire** *off.* State of New Hampshire; also known as The Granite State. ◆ *state* NE USA
31 *W12* **New Hampton** Iowa, C USA *43.03N 92.19W*
195 *N9* **New Hanover** *island* NE PNG
20 *M13* **New Haven** Connecticut, NE USA *41.18N 72.55W*
33 *Q12* **New Haven** Indiana, N USA *41.02N 84.59W*
29 *W5* **New Haven** Missouri, C USA *38.34N 91.15W*
99 *P23* **Newhaven** SE England, UK *50.48N 0.00W*
8 *K13* **New Hazelton** British Columbia, SW Canada *55.15N 127.30W*
New Hebrides *see* Vanuatu
183 *P9* **New Hebrides Trench** *undersea feature* N Coral Sea
20 *H15* **New Holland** Pennsylvania, NE USA *40.06N 76.05W*
24 *I9* **New Iberia** Louisiana, S USA *30.00N 91.51W*
195 *N10* **New Ireland** ◆ *province* NE PNG
195 *P10* **New Ireland** *island* NE PNG
67 *A24* **New Island** *island* W Falkland Islands
20 *J15* **New Jersey** *off.* State of New Jersey; also known as The Garden State. ◆ *state* NE USA
20 *C14* **New Kensington** Pennsylvania, NE USA *40.33N 79.45W*
23 *W6* **New Kent** Virginia, NE USA *37.31N 76.58W*
29 *O8* **Newkirk** Oklahoma, C USA *36.52N 97.03W*
23 *Q9* **Newland** North Carolina, SE USA *36.04N 81.50W*
30 *L6* **New Leipzig** North Dakota, N USA *46.21N 101.54W*
12 *H9* **New Liskeard** Ontario, S Canada *47.31N 79.40W*
24 *G7* **Newllano** Louisiana, S USA *31.06N 93.16W*
21 *N13* **New London** Connecticut, NE USA *41.21N 72.04W*
31 *Y15* **New London** Iowa, C USA *40.55N 91.24W*
31 *T8* **New London** Minnesota, N USA *45.18N 94.56W*
29 *V3* **New London** Missouri, C USA *39.35N 91.24W*
32 *M7* **New London** Wisconsin, N USA *44.25N 88.44W*
29 *Y8* **New Madrid** Missouri, C USA *36.35N 89.31W*
188 *J8* **Newman** Western Australia *23.18S 119.45E*
204 *M13* **Newman Island** *island* Antarctica
12 *H15* **Newmarket** Ontario, S Canada *44.03N 79.26W*
99 *P20* **Newmarket** E England, UK *52.18N 0.28E*
21 *P10* **Newmarket** New Hampshire, NE USA *43.04N 70.53W*
23 *U4* **New Market** Virginia, NE USA *38.39N 78.40W*
23 *R2* **New Martinsville** West Virginia, NE USA *39.39N 80.48W*
33 *U14* **New Matamoras** Ohio, N USA *39.32N 81.04W*
34 *M12* **New Meadows** Idaho, NW USA *44.57N 116.16W*
28 *R12* **New Mexico** *off.* State of New Mexico; also known as Land of Enchantment, Sunshine State. ◆ *state* SW USA
155 *V6* **New Mirpur** *var.* Mirpur. Sind, SE Pakistan *33.09N 73.42E*
157 *T17* **New Moore Island** *island* E India
25 *S4* **Newnan** Georgia, SE USA *33.22N 84.48W*
191 *P17* **New Norfolk** Tasmania, SE Australia *42.46S 147.01E*
24 *K9* **New Orleans** Louisiana, S USA *30.00N 90.00W*
24 *K9* **New Orleans** ✕ Louisiana, S USA *29.59N 90.17W*
20 *K12* **New Paltz** New York, NE USA *41.44N 74.04W*
33 *U12* **New Philadelphia** Ohio, N USA *40.29N 81.27W*
192 *K10* **New Plymouth** Taranaki, North Island, NZ *39.04S 174.06E*
99 *M24* **Newport** S England, UK *50.42N 1.18W*
99 *K22* **Newport** SE Wales, UK *51.35N 3.00W*
29 *W10* **Newport** Arkansas, C USA *35.36N 91.16W*
33 *N13* **Newport** Indiana, N USA *39.52N 87.24W*
22 *M3* **Newport** Kentucky, S USA *39.05N 84.30W*
31 *W9* **Newport** Minnesota, N USA *44.52N 93.00W*
34 *F12* **Newport** Oregon, NW USA *44.38N 124.03W*
21 *O13* **Newport** Rhode Island, NE USA *41.29N 71.17W*
23 *O9* **Newport** Tennessee, S USA *35.58N 83.11W*
21 *N6* **Newport** Vermont, NE USA *44.55N 72.13W*
34 *M7* **Newport** Washington, NW USA *48.08N 117.05W*
23 *X7* **Newport News** Virginia, NE USA *36.58N 76.25W*
99 *N20* **Newport Pagnell** SE England, UK *52.04N 0.43W*
25 *U12* **New Port Richey** Florida, SE USA *28.14N 82.42W*
31 *V9* **New Prague** Minnesota, N USA *44.32N 93.34W*
46 *H3* **New Providence** *island* N Bahamas
99 *H24* **Newquay** SW England, UK *50.27N 5.03W*
99 *I20* **New Quay** SW Wales, UK *52.13N 4.22W*
31 *V10* **New Richland** Minnesota, N USA *43.53N 93.29W*
13 *X7* **New-Richmond** Québec, SE Canada *48.10N 65.54W*
33 *R15* **New Richmond** Ohio, N USA *38.57N 84.16W*
32 *I5* **New Richmond** Wisconsin, N USA *45.09N 92.31W*
44 *G1* **New River** ~ N Belize
57 *T12* **New River** ~ SE Guyana
23 *R6* **New River** ~ West Virginia, NE USA
44 *G1* **New River Lagoon** ◎ N Belize
24 *J8* **New Roads** Louisiana, S USA *30.42N 91.26W*
20 *L14* **New Rochelle** New York, NE USA *40.55N 73.44W*
31 *O4* **New Rockford** North Dakota, N USA *47.40N 99.08W*
99 *P23* **New Romney** SE England, UK *50.58N 0.57E*
99 *F20* **New Ross** *Ir.* Ros Mhic Thriúin. SE Ireland *52.24N 6.55W*
99 *F16* **Newry** *Ir.* An tIúr. SE Northern Ireland, UK *54.10N 6.19W*
30 *M5* **New Salem** North Dakota, N USA *46.51N 101.24W*
New Sarum *see* Salisbury
31 *W14* **New Sharon** Iowa, C USA *41.28N 92.39W*
New Siberian Islands *see* Novosibirskiye Ostrova
25 *X11* **New Smyrna Beach** Florida, SE USA *29.01N 80.55W*
191 *O7* **New South Wales** ◆ *state* SE Australia
41 *O13* **New Stuyahok** Alaska, USA *59.27N 95.18W*
23 *N8* **New Tazewell** Tennessee, S USA *36.26N 83.36W*
40 *M12* **Newtok** Alaska, USA *60.56N 164.37W*
25 *S7* **Newton** Georgia, SE USA *31.18N 84.20W*
31 *W14* **Newton** Iowa, C USA *41.42N 93.03W*
29 *N6* **Newton** Kansas, C USA *38.03N 97.20W*
21 *O11* **Newton** Massachusetts, NE USA *42.19N 71.10W*
24 *M5* **Newton** Mississippi, S USA *32.19N 89.09W*
20 *J14* **Newton** New Jersey, NE USA *41.03N 74.45W*
23 *R9* **Newton** North Carolina, SE USA *35.40N 81.13W*
27 *Y9* **Newton** Texas, SW USA *30.51N 93.45W*
99 *J24* **Newton Abbot** SW England, UK *50.33N 3.34W*
98 *K13* **Newton St Boswells** SE Scotland, UK *55.34N 2.40W*
99 *I14* **Newton Stewart** S Scotland, UK *54.58N 4.30W*
94 *O2* **Newtontoppen** ▲ C Svalbard *78.57N 17.34E*
30 *K3* **New Town** North Dakota, N USA *47.58N 102.30W*
99 *J20* **Newtown** E Wales, UK *52.31N 3.19W*
99 *G15* **Newtownabbey** *Ir.* Baile na Mainistreach. E Northern Ireland, UK *54.40N 5.57W*
99 *G15* **Newtownards** *Ir.* Baile Nua na hArda. SE Northern Ireland, UK *54.36N 5.40W*
31 *U10* **New Ulm** Minnesota, N USA *44.20N 94.28W*
30 *K10* **New Underwood** South Dakota, N USA *44.05N 102.46W*
27 *V10* **New Waverly** Texas, SW USA *30.32N 95.28W*
20 *K14* **New York** New York, NE USA *40.44N 73.57W*
20 *G10* **New York** ◆ *state* NE USA
37 *X13* **New York Mountains** ▲ California, W USA
192 *K12* **New Zealand** *abbrev.* NZ. ◆ *commonwealth republic* SW Pacific Ocean
97 *M24* **Nexø** *var.* Neksø. Bornholm, E Denmark *55.04N 15.05E*
129 *O15* **Neya** Kostromskaya Oblast', NW Russian Federation *58.19N 43.51E*
Neyba *see* Neiba
149 *Q12* **Neyrīz** *var.* Neiriz, Niriz. Fārs, S Iran *29.13N 54.18E*
149 *T4* **Neyshābūr** *var.* Nishapur. Khorāsān-Razavī, NE Iran *36.14N 58.46E*
161 *J21* **Neyveli** Tamil Nādu, SE India *11.36N 79.25E*
Nezhin *see* Nizhyn
35 *N10* **Nezperce** Idaho, NW USA *46.14N 116.15W*
24 *H8* **Nezpique, Bayou** ~ Louisiana, S USA
176 *W14* **Ngabordamlu, Tanjung** *headland* Pulau Trangan, SE Indonesia *6.58S 134.13E*
79 *Y13* **Ngadda** ~ NE Nigeria
N'Gage *see* Negage
193 *G16* **Ngahere** West Coast, South Island, NZ *42.22S 171.29E*
79 *Z12* **Ngala** Borno, NE Nigeria *12.19N 14.11E*
164 *K16* **Ngamring** Xizang Zizhiqu, W China *29.16N 87.10E*
83 *K19* **Ngangerabeli Plain** *plain* SE Kenya
164 *I14* **Ngangla Ringco** ◎ W China
164 *G13* **Nganglong Kangri** ▲ W China *32.55N 81.00E*
164 *K15* **Ngangzê Co** ◎ W China
81 *F14* **Ngaoundéré** *var.* N'Gaoundéré. Adamaoua, N Cameroon *7.19N 13.34E*
83 *E20* **Ngara** Kagera, NW Tanzania *2.30S 30.40E*
196 *F8* **Ngardmau Bay** *bay* Babeldaob, N Palau
196 *F7* **Ngaregur** *island* Palau Islands, N Palau
Ngarrab *see* Gyaca
192 *L7* **Ngaruawahia** Waikato, North Island, NZ *37.41S 175.09E*
192 *N11* **Ngaruroro** ~ North Island, NZ
202 *I16* **Ngatangiia** Rarotonga, S Cook Islands *21.13S 159.43W*
192 *M6* **Ngatea** Waikato, North Island, NZ *37.16S 175.29E*
177 *F8* **Ngathainggyaung** Irrawaddy, SW Burma *17.22N 95.04E*
Ngatik *see* Ngetik Atoll
Ngau *see* Gau
174 *Ll15* **Ngawi** Jawa, S Indonesia *7.22S 111.22E*
196 *C7* **Ngcheangel** *var.* Kayangel Islands. *island* Palau Islands, N Palau
196 *E10* **Ngchemiangel** Babeldaob, N Palau
196 *C8* **Ngeaur** *var.* Angaur. *island* Palau Islands, S Palau
196 *E10* **Ngerkeai** Babeldaob, N Palau
196 *F9* **Ngermechau** Babeldaob, N Palau *7.34N 134.39E*
196 *C8* **Ngeruktabel** *prev.* Urukthapel. *island* Palau Islands, S Palau
196 *F8* **Ngetbong** Babeldaob, N Palau *7.37N 134.34E*
201 *T17* **Ngetik Atoll** *var.* Ngatik; *prev.* Los Jardines. *atoll* Caroline Islands, E Micronesia
196 *E10* **Ngetkip** Babeldaob, N Palau
Nggamea *see* Qamea
195 *V15* **Nggatokae** *island* New Georgia Islands, NW Solomon Islands
Nghia Dan *see* Thai Hoa
85 *C16* **N'Giva** *var.* Ondjiva, *Port.* Vila Pereira de Eça. Cunene, S Angola *17.01S 15.41E*
81 *G20* **Ngo** Plateaux, SE Congo *2.28S 15.43E*
178 *Jj7* **Ngoc Lac** Thanh Hoa, N Vietnam *20.06N 105.21E*
81 *G17* **Ngoko** ~ Cameroon/Congo
176 *W14* **Ngoni, Tanjung** *headland* Maluku, Kepulauan Aru, SE Indonesia *6.10S 134.04E*
83 *H19* **Ngorengore** Rift Valley, SW Kenya *1.01S 35.26E*
165 *Q11* **Ngoring Hu** ◎ C China
Ngorolaka *see* Banifing
83 *H20* **Ngorongoro Crater** *crater* N Tanzania *3.10S 35.34E*
81 *D19* **Ngounié** *off.* Province de la Ngounié, *var.* La Ngounié. ◆ *province* S Gabon
81 *D19* **Ngounié** ~ Congo/Gabon
80 *H10* **Ngoura** *var.* NGoura. Chari-Baguirmi, W Chad *12.52N 16.27E*
80 *G10* **Ngouri** *var.* NGouri; *prev.* Fort-Millot. Lac, W Chad *13.40N 15.24E*
79 *Y10* **Ngourti** Diffa, E Niger *15.22N 13.13E*
79 *Y11* **Nguigmi** *var.* N'Guigmi. Diffa, SE Niger *14.16N 13.07E*
Nguimbo *see* Lumbala N'Guimbo
196 *F15* **Ngulu Atoll** *atoll* Caroline Islands, W Micronesia
197 *C14* **Nguna** *island* C Vanuatu
N'Gunza *see* Sumbe
175 *N16* **Ngurah Rai** ✕ (Bali) Bali, S Indonesia
79 *W12* **Nguru** Yobe, NE Nigeria *12.55N 10.30E*
Ngwaketze *see* Southern
85 *I16* **Ngweze** ~ S Zambia
85 *M17* **Nhamatanda** Sofala, C Mozambique *19.16S 34.10E*
60 *G12* **Nhamundá, Rio** *var.* Jamundá, Yamundá. ~ N Brazil
62 *J7* **Nhandeara** São Paulo, S Brazil *20.40S 50.03W*
N'Harea *see* Nharêa
84 *D12* **Nharêa** *var.* N'Harea, Nhareia. Bié, W Angola *11.28S 16.57E*
Nhareia *see* Nharêa
178 *Kk13* **Nha Trang** Khanh Hoa, S Vietnam *12.15N 109.10E*
190 *L11* **Nhill** Victoria, SE Australia *36.21S 141.38E*
85 *L22* **Nhlangano** *prev.* Goedgegun. SW Swaziland *27.01S 31.11E*
189 *S1* **Nhulunbuy** Northern Territory, N Australia *12.15S 136.46E*
79 *N10* **Niafounké** Tombouctou, W Mali *15.54N 3.58W*
33 *N5* **Niagara** Wisconsin, N USA *45.45N 87.57W*
12 *H16* **Niagara** ~ Ontario, S Canada
12 *G15* **Niagara Escarpment** *hill range* Ontario, S Canada
12 *H16* **Niagara Falls** Ontario, S Canada *43.04N 79.06W*
20 *D9* **Niagara Falls** New York, NE USA *43.06N 79.04W*
16 *Pp17* **Niagara Falls** *waterfall* Canada/USA *43.04N 79.04W*
78 *K12* **Niagassola** *var.* Nyagassola. NE Guinea *12.22N 9.07W*
79 *R12* **Niamey** ● (Niger) Niamey, SW Niger *13.28N 2.03E*
79 *R12* **Niamey** ✕ Niamey, SW Niger *13.28N 2.14E*
79 *R14* **Niamtougou** N Togo *9.49N 1.07E*
81 *O16* **Niangara** Orientale, NE Dem. Rep. Congo *3.45N 27.54E*
79 *O10* **Niangay, Lac** ◎ E Mali
79 *N14* **Niangoloko** SW Burkina *10.15N 4.53W*
29 *U6* **Niangua River** ~ Missouri, C USA
81 *O17* **Nia-Nia** Orientale, NE Dem. Rep. Congo *1.26N 27.38E*
21 *N13* **Niantic** Connecticut, NE USA *41.19N 72.11W*
169 *U7* **Nianzishan** Heilongjiang, NE China *47.31N 122.52E*
173 *F7* **Nias, Pulau** *island* W Indonesia
84 *O13* **Niassa** *off.* Província do Niassa. ◆ *province* N Mozambique
203 *U10* **Niau** *island* Îles Tuamotu, C French Polynesia
97 *G20* **Nibe** Nordjylland, N Denmark *56.58N 9.39E*
201 *Q8* **Nibok** N Nauru *0.31S 166.55E*
120 *C10* **Nīca** Liepāja, W Latvia *56.21N 21.03E*
Nicaea *see* Nice
44 *J9* **Nicaragua** *off.* Republic of Nicaragua. ◆ *republic* Central America
44 *K11* **Nicaragua, Lago de** *var.* Cocibolca, Gran Lago, *Eng.* Lake Nicaragua. ◎ S Nicaragua
Nicaragua, Lake *see* Nicaragua, Lago de
66 *D11* **Nicaraguan Rise** *undersea feature* NW Caribbean Sea
Nicaria *see* Ikaría
109 *N21* **Nicastro** Calabria, SW Italy *38.58N 16.19E*
105 *V15* **Nice** *It.* Nizza; *anc.* Nicaea. Alpes-Maritimes, SE France *43.43N 7.13E*
Nice *see* Côte d'Azur
Nicephorium *see* Ar Raqqah
10 *M9* **Nichicun, Lac** ◎ Québec, E Canada
170 *C17* **Nichinan** *var.* Nitinan. Miyazaki, Kyūshū, SW Japan *31.36N 131.22E*
46 *E4* **Nicholas Channel** *channel* N Cuba
Nicholas II Land *see* Severnaya Zemlya
155 *U2* **Nicholas Range** *Pash.* Selseleh-ye Kūh-e Vākhān, *Taj.* Qatorkūhi Vakhon. ▲▲ Afghanistan/Tajikistan
22 *M6* **Nicholasville** Kentucky, S USA *37.52N 84.34W*
46 *G2* **Nicholls Town** Andros Island, NW Bahamas *25.07N 78.01W*
23 *U12* **Nichols** South Carolina, SE USA *34.13N 79.09W*
57 *U9* **Nickerie** ◆ *district* NW Surinam
57 *V9* **Nickerie Rivier** ~ NW Surinam
157 *P22* **Nicobar Islands** *island group* India, E Indian Ocean
118 *L9* **Nicolae Bălcescu** Botoşani, NE Romania *47.33N 26.52E*
13 *P11* **Nicolet** Québec, SE Canada *46.13N 72.37W*
13 *Q12* **Nicolet** ~ Québec, SE Canada
33 *Q4* **Nicolet, Lake** ◎ Michigan, N USA
31 *U10* **Nicollet** Minnesota, N USA *44.16N 94.11W*
63 *F19* **Nico Pérez** Florida, S Uruguay *33.30S 55.10W*
Nicopolis *see* Nikopol, Bulgaria
Nicopolis *see* Nikópoli, Greece
124 *R12* **Nicosia** *Gk.* Lefkosía, *Turk.* Lefkoşa. ● (Cyprus) C Cyprus *35.10N 33.22E*
109 *K24* **Nicosia** Sicilia, Italy, C Mediterranean Sea *37.45N 14.24E*
109 *N22* **Nicotera** Calabria, SW Italy *38.33N 15.55E*
44 *K13* **Nicoya** Guanacaste, W Costa Rica *10.06N 85.26W*
44 *L14* **Nicoya, Golfo de** *gulf* W Costa Rica
44 *L14* **Nicoya, Península de** *peninsula* NW Costa Rica
Nictheroy *see* Niterói
120 *B12* **Nida** *Ger.* Nidden. Klaipėda, SW Lithuania *55.19N 21.00E*
113 *L15* **Nida** ~ S Poland
Nidaros *see* Trondheim
110 *D8* **Nidau** Bern, W Switzerland *47.07N 7.15E*
103 *H17* **Nidda** ~ W Germany
Nidden *see* Nida
97 *F17* **Nidelva** ~ S Norway
126 *J10* **Nidym** Evenkiyskiy Avtonomnyy Okrug, N Russian Federation *64.08N 99.52E*
112 *L9* **Nidzica** *Ger.* Niedenburg. Warmińsko-Mazurskie, NE Poland, *53.22N 20.27E*
102 *H6* **Niebüll** Schleswig-Holstein, N Germany *54.47N 8.51E*
Niedenburg *see* Nidzica
101 *N25* **Niederanven** Luxembourg, C Luxembourg *49.39N 6.15E*
105 *V4* **Niederbronn-les-Bains** Bas-Rhin, NE France *48.57N 7.37E*
Niederdonau *see* Niederösterreich
111 *S7* **Niedere Tauern** ▲ C Austria
103 *P14* **Niederlausitz** *Eng.* Lower Lusatia, *Lus.* Donja Łužyca. *physical region* E Germany
111 *U5* **Niederösterreich** *off.* Land Niederösterreich, *Eng.* Lower Austria, *Ger.* Niederdonau; *prev.* Lower Danube. ◆ *state* NE Austria
102 *G12* **Niedersachsen** *Eng.* Lower Saxony, *Fr.* Basse-Saxe. ◆ *state* NW Germany
81 *D17* **Niefang** *var.* Sevilla de Niefang. NW Equatorial Guinea *1.52N 10.12E*
85 *G23* **Niekerkshoop** Northern Cape, W South Africa *29.21S 22.49E*
101 *G17* **Niel** Antwerpen, N Belgium *51.07N 4.19E*
Niélé *see* Niellé
78 *M14* **Niellé** *var.* Niélé. N Ivory Coast *10.12N 5.37W*
81 *O22* **Niemba** Katanga, E Dem. Rep. Congo *5.58S 28.24E*
113 *G15* **Niemcza** *Ger.* Nimptsch. Dolnośląskie, SW Poland *50.45N 16.52E*
Niemen *see* Neman
94 *J13* **Niemisel** Norrbotten, N Sweden *66.00N 22.00E*
113 *H15* **Niemodlin** *Ger.* Falkenberg. Opolskie, S Poland *50.37N 17.45E*
78 *M13* **Niéna** Sikasso, SW Mali *11.24N 6.20W*
102 *H12* **Nienburg** Niedersachsen, N Germany *52.37N 9.12E*
102 *N13* **Nieplitz** ~ NE Germany
113 *L16* **Niepołomice** Małopolskie, S Poland *50.02N 20.12E*
103 *D14* **Niers** ~ Germany/Netherlands
103 *Q15* **Niesky** *Lus.* Niska. Sachsen, E Germany *51.16N 14.49E*
Nieśwież *see* Nyasvizh
Nieuport *see* Nieuwpoort
100 *O8* **Nieuw-Amsterdam** Drenthe, NE Netherlands *52.43N 6.52E*
57 *W9* **Nieuw Amsterdam** Commewijne, NE Surinam *5.52N 55.04W*
101 *M14* **Nieuw-Bergen** Limburg, SE Netherlands *51.36N 6.04E*
100 *O7* **Nieuw-Buinen** Drenthe, NE Netherlands *52.57N 6.55E*
100 *J12* **Nieuwegein** Utrecht, C Netherlands *52.03N 5.06E*
100 *P6* **Nieuwe Pekela** Groningen, NE Netherlands *53.04N 6.58E*
100 *P5* **Nieuweschans** Groningen, NE Netherlands *53.10N 7.10E*
Nieuw Guinea *see* New Guinea
100 *I11* **Nieuwkoop** Zuid-Holland, C Netherlands *52.09N 4.46E*
100 *M9* **Nieuwleusen** Overijssel, S Netherlands *52.34N 6.16E*
100 *J11* **Nieuw-Loosdrecht** Noord-Holland, C Netherlands *52.12N 5.07E*
57 *U9* **Nieuw Nickerie** Nickerie, NW Surinam *05.52N 57.00W*
100 *P5* **Nieuwolda** Groningen, NE Netherlands *53.15N 6.58E*
101 *B17* **Nieuwpoort** *var.* Nieuport. West-Vlaanderen, W Belgium *51.07N 2.45E*
101 *G14* **Nieuw-Vossemeer** Noord-Brabant, S Netherlands *51.34N 4.13E*
100 *P7* **Nieuw-Weerdinge** Drenthe, NE Netherlands *52.51N 7.00E*
42 *L10* **Nieves** Zacatecas, C Mexico *24.00N 102.57W*
66 *O11* **Nieves, Pico de las** ▲ Gran Canaria, Islas Canarias, Spain, NE Atlantic Ocean *27.58N 15.34W*
105 *P8* **Nièvre** ◆ *department* C France
Niewenstat *see* Neustadt an der Weinstrasse
142 *J15* **Niğde** Niğde, C Turkey *37.58N 34.42E*
142 *J15* **Niğde** ◆ *province* C Turkey
85 *J21* **Nigel** Gauteng, NE South Africa *26.25S 28.28E*
79 *V10* **Niger** *off.* Republic of Niger. ◆ *republic* W Africa
79 *T14* **Niger** ◆ *state* C Nigeria
69 *P8* **Niger** ~ W Africa
Niger Cone *see* Niger Fan
69 *P9* **Niger Delta** *delta* S Nigeria
69 *P9* **Niger Fan** *var.* Niger Cone. *undersea feature* E Atlantic Ocean
79 *T13* **Nigeria** *off.* Federal Republic of Nigeria. ◆ *federal republic* W Africa
79 *T17* **Niger, Mouths of the** *delta* S Nigeria
193 *C24* **Nightcaps** Southland, South Island, NZ *45.58S 168.03E*
12 *F7* **Night Hawk Lake** ◎ Ontario, S Canada
67 *M19* **Nightingale Island** *island* S Tristan da Cunha, S Atlantic Ocean
40 *M12* **Nightmute** Alaska, USA *60.28N 164.43W*
116 *G13* **Nigríta** Kentrikí Makedonía, NE Greece *40.54N 23.28E*
154 *J15* **Nihing** *Per.* Rūd-e Nahang. ~ Iran/Pakistan
203 *V10* **Nihiru** *atoll* Îles Tuamotu, C French Polynesia
Nihommatsu *see* Nihonmatsu
Nihon *see* Japan
171 *L13* **Nihonmatsu** *var.* Nihommatsu, Nihonmatu. Fukushima, Honshū, C Japan *37.35N 140.22E*
Nihonmatu *see* Nihonmatsu
64 *I12* **Nihuil, Embalse del** ⊠ W Argentina
171 *K12* **Niigata** Niigata, Honshū, C Japan *37.55N 139.01E*
171 *K13* **Niigata** *off.* Niigata-ken. ◆ *prefecture* Honshū, C Japan
170 *F15* **Niihama** Ehime, Shikoku, SW Japan *33.57N 133.15E*
40 *A8* **Ni'ihau** *var.* Niihau. *island* Hawai'i, USA, C Pacific Ocean
172 *Ss13* **Nii-jima** *island* E Japan
170 *Ff13* **Niimi** Okayama, Honshū, SW Japan *35.00N 133.27E*
171 *Kk13* **Niitsu** *var.* Niitu. Niigata, Honshū, C Japan *37.48N 139.06E*
Niitu *see* Niitsu
107 *P15* **Níjar** Andalucía, S Spain *36.57N 2.13W*
100 *K11* **Nijkerk** Gelderland, C Netherlands *52.13N 5.30E*
101 *H16* **Nijlen** Antwerpen, N Belgium *51.10N 4.40E*
100 *L13* **Nijmegen** *Ger.* Nimwegen; *anc.* Noviomagus. Gelderland, SE Netherlands *51.49N 5.52E*
100 *N10* **Nijverdal** Overijssel, E Netherlands *52.22N 6.28E*
202 *G16* **Nikao** Rarotonga, S Cook Islands
Nikaria *see* Ikaría
128 *I2* **Nikel'** Murmanskaya Oblast', NW Russian Federation *69.24N 30.12E*
175 *Rr17* **Nikiniki** Timor, S Indonesia *10.00S 124.30E*
133 *Q15* **Nikitin Seamount** *undersea feature* E Indian Ocean *5.48S 84.48E*
79 *S14* **Nikki** E Benin *9.55N 3.12E*
171 *Kk15* **Nikkō** *var.* Nikko. Tochigi, Honshū, S Japan *36.45N 139.37E*
Niklasmarkt *see* Gheorgheni
41 *P10* **Nikolai** Alaska, USA *63.00N 154.22W*
Nikolaiken *see* Mikołajki
Nikolainkaupunki *see* Länsi-Suomi

◆ Country
● Country Capital
◇ Dependent Territory
○ Dependent Territory Capital
◆ Administrative Region
✕ International Airport
▲ Mountain
▲▲ Mountain Range
Volcano
~ River
◎ Lake
⊠ Reservoir

NIKOLAYEV – NORTH EAST POINT

Nikolayev see Mykolayiv
151 O6 Nikolayevka Severnyy Kazakhstan, N Kazakhstan
Nikolayevka see Zhetigen
131 P9 Nikolayevsk Volgogradskaya Oblast', SW Russian Federation 50.03N 45.30E
Nikolayevskaya Oblast' see Mykolayivs'ka Oblast'
127 Nn14 Nikolayevsk-na-Amure Khabarovskiy Kray, SE Russian Federation 53.04N 140.39E
131 P6 Nikol'sk Penzenskaya Oblast', W Russian Federation 53.46N 46.03E
129 O13 Nikol'sk Vologodskaya Oblast', NW Russian Federation 59.35N 45.31E
Nikol'sk see Ussuriysk
40 K17 Nikolski Umnak Island, Alaska, USA 52.56N 168.52W
Nikol'skiy see Satpayev
131 V7 Nikol'skoye Orenburgskaya Oblast', W Russian Federation 52.01N 55.48E
Nikol'sk-Ussuriyskiy see Ussuriysk
116 J7 Nikopol anc. Nicopolis. Pleven, N Bulgaria 43.43N 24.55E
119 S9 Nikopol' Dnipropetrovs'ka Oblast', SE Ukraine 47.34N 34.23E
117 C17 Nikópoli anc. Nicopolis. site of ancient city Ípeiros, W Greece 39.01N 20.43E
142 M12 Niksar Tokat, N Turkey 40.36N 36.54E
149 V14 Nīkshahr Sīstān va Balūchestān, SE Iran 26.15N 60.10E
115 J16 Nikšić C Montenegro 42.46N 18.56E
203 R4 Nikumaroro prev. Gardner Island, Kemins Island. atoll Phoenix Islands, C Kiribati
203 P3 Nikunau var. Nukunau; prev. Byron Island. atoll Tungaru, W Kiribati
161 G21 Nilambūr Kerala, SW India 11.16N 76.15E
37 X16 Niland California, W USA 33.14N 115.31W
69 T3 Nile Ar. Nahr an Nīl. ~ N Africa
82 G8 Nile former province NW Uganda
77 W7 Nile Delta delta N Egypt
69 T3 Nile Fan undersea feature E Mediterranean Sea
33 O11 Niles Michigan, N USA 41.49N 86.15W
33 V11 Niles Ohio, N USA 41.10N 80.46W
161 F20 Nīleswaram Kerala, SW India 12.18N 75.07E
12 K10 Nilgaut, Lac ◎ Québec, SE Canada
155 O6 Nīlī Dāikondī, C Afghanistan 33.43N 66.07E
164 I5 Nilka Xinjiang Uygur Zizhiqu, NW China 43.46N 82.33E
Nīl, Nahr an see Nile
95 N16 Nilsiä Itä-Suomi, C Finland 63.13N 28.00E
160 F9 Nīmach Madhya Pradesh, C India 24.30N 74.51E
158 G14 Nimbāhera Rājasthān, N India 24.37N 74.45E
78 L15 Nimba, Monts var. Nimba Mountains. ▲▲ W Africa
Nimba Mountains see Nimba, Monts
Nimburg see Nymburk
105 Q15 Nîmes anc. Nemausus, Nismes. Gard, S France 43.49N 4.19E
158 H11 Nīm ka Thāna Rājasthān, N India 27.44N 75.44E
191 R11 Nimmitabel New South Wales, SE Australia 36.34S 149.18E
Nimptsch see Niemcza
205 R11 Nimrod Glacier glacier Antarctica
Nimroze see Nīmrūz
154 K8 Nīmrūz var. Nimroze; prev. Chakhānsūr. ◆ province SW Afghanistan
83 F16 Nimule Eastern Equatoria, S Sudan 3.33N 32.06E
Nimwegen see Nijmegen
161 C23 Nine Degree Channel channel India/Maldives
20 G9 Ninemile Point headland New York, NE USA 43.31N 76.22W
181 S8 Ninetyeast Ridge undersea feature E Indian Ocean
191 P13 Ninety Mile Beach beach Victoria, SE Australia
192 I2 Ninety Mile Beach beach North Island, NZ
23 P12 Ninety Six South Carolina, SE USA 34.10N 82.01W
169 Y9 Ning'an Heilongjiang, NE China 44.20N 129.28E
167 S9 Ningbo var. Ning-po, Yin-hsien; prev. Ninghsien. Zhejiang, SE China 29.54N 121.33E
167 U12 Ningde Fujian, SE China 26.48N 119.33E
167 P12 Ningdu var. Meijiang. Jiangxi, S China 26.28N 115.58E
Ning'er see Pu'er
194 E12 Ningerum Western, SW PNG 5.43S 141.09E
167 R9 Ningguo Anhui, E China 30.33N 118.58E
167 S9 Ninghai Zhejiang, SE China 29.19N 121.22E
Ning-hsia see Ningxia
Ninghsien see Ningbo
166 J15 Ningming var. Chengzhong. Guangxi Zhuangzu Zizhiqu, S China 22.07N 106.43E
166 H11 Ningnan var. Pisha. Sichuan, C China 26.59N 102.49E
Ning-po see Ningbo
Ningsia/Ningsia Hui/Ningsia Hui Autonomous Region see Ningxia
166 J5 Ningxia off. Ningxia Huizu Zizhiqu, var. Ning-hsia, Ningsia, Eng. Ningsia Hui, Ningsia Hui Autonomous Region. ◆ autonomous region N China
165 X10 Ningxian Gansu, N China 35.30N 108.04E
178 Jj7 Ninh Binh Ninh Binh, N Vietnam 20.12N 105.58E
178 Kk13 Ninh Hoa Khanh Hoa, S Vietnam 12.28N 109.07E
194 H7 Ninigo Group island group N PNG
41 Q12 Ninilchik Alaska, USA 60.03N 151.40W
29 N7 Ninnescah River ~ Kansas, C USA
205 U16 Ninnis Glacier glacier Antarctica
172 N10 Ninohe Iwate, Honshū, C Japan 40.17N 141.18E
101 F18 Ninove Oost-Vlaanderen, C Belgium 50.49N 4.01E
179 P11 Ninoy Aquino ✕ (Manila) Luzon, N Philippines 14.26N 121.00E
Nio see Íos
31 P12 Niobrara Nebraska, C USA 42.43N 97.59W
30 M12 Niobrara River ~ Nebraska/Wyoming, C USA
81 I20 Nioki Bandundu, W Dem. Rep. Congo 2.44S 17.42E
78 M11 Niono Ségou, C Mali 14.15N 5.57W
78 K11 Nioro var. Nioro du Sahel. Kayes, W Mali 15.13N 9.38W
78 G11 Nioro du Rip SW Senegal 13.44N 15.48W
Nioro du Sahel see Nioro
104 K10 Niort Deux-Sèvres, W France 46.21N 0.24W
180 H14 Nioumachoua Mohéli, S Comoros 12.21S 43.43E
194 G12 Nipa Southern Highlands, W PNG 6.12S 143.29E
9 U14 Nipawin Saskatchewan, S Canada 53.21N 103.55W
10 D12 Nipigon Ontario, S Canada 49.01N 88.15W
10 D11 Nipigon, Lake ◎ Ontario, S Canada
9 S13 Nipin ~ Saskatchewan, C Canada
12 G11 Nipissing, Lake ◎ Ontario, S Canada
37 P13 Nipomo California, W USA 35.02N 120.28W
Nippon see Japan
144 K6 Niqniqīyah, Jabal an ▲ C Syria
64 I9 Niquivil San Juan, W Argentina 30.25S 68.42W
176 Yy10 Nirabotong Papua, E Indonesia 2.35S 140.08E
171 J16 Nirasaki Yamanashi, Honshū, S Japan 35.43N 138.24E
Niriz see Neyrīz
169 U7 Nirji var. Morin Dawa Daurzu Zizhiqu. Nei Mongol Zizhiqu, N China 48.21N 124.32E
161 I14 Nirmal Andhra Pradesh, C India 19.04N 78.21E
159 Q13 Nirmāli Bihār, NE India 26.18N 86.34E
115 O14 Niš Eng. Nish, Ger. Nisch; anc. Naissus. Serbia, SE Serbia 43.20N 21.52E
106 H9 Nisa Portalegre, C Portugal 39.31N 7.39W
Nisa see Neisse
147 P4 Nişab Al Ḥudūd ash Shamālīyah, N Saudi Arabia 29.10N 44.43E
147 Q15 Nişāb var. Anşāb. SW Yemen 14.24N 46.47E
115 P14 Nišava Bul. Nishava. ~ Bulgaria/Serbia see also Nishava
109 K25 Niscemi Sicilia, Italy, C Mediterranean Sea 37.09N 14.22E
Nisch/Nish see Niš
172 Nn5 Niseko Hokkaidō, NE Japan 42.50N 140.43E
Nishapur see Neyshābūr
116 G9 Nishava var. Nišava. ~ Bulgaria/Serbia see also Nišava
120 L11 Nishcha Rus. Nishcha. ~ N Belarus
172 Qq7 Nishibetsu-gawa ~ Hokkaidō, NE Japan
170 E13 Nishi-gawa ~ Honshū, SW Japan
170 Ee13 Nishi-Nōmi-jima var. Nōmi-jima. island SW Japan
170 Bb17 Nishinoomote Kagoshima, Tanega-shima, SW Japan 30.42N 130.59E
172 Ss16 Nishino-shima Eng. Rosario. island Ogasawara-shotō, SE Japan
171 Hh16 Nishio var. Nisio. Aichi, Honshū, SW Japan 34.52N 137.01E
170 C13 Nishi-Sonogi-hantō peninsula Kyūshū, SW Japan
171 Gg14 Nishiwaki var. Nisiwaki. Hyōgo, Honshū, SW Japan 35.02N 134.57E
147 U14 Nishtūn SE Yemen 15.47N 52.08E
Nisiros see Nísyros
Nisiwaki see Nishiwaki
Niska see Niesky
115 O14 Niška Banja Serbia, SE Serbia 43.18N 22.01E
10 D6 Niskibi ~ Ontario, C Canada
113 O15 Nisko Podkarpackie, SE Poland 50.31N 22.09E
8 H7 Nisling ~ Yukon Territory, W Canada
101 H22 Nismes Namur, S Belgium 50.04N 4.31E
Nismes see Nîmes
118 M10 Nisporeni Rus. Nisporeny. W Moldova 47.04N 28.10E
Nisporeny see Nisporeni
97 K20 Nissan ~ S Sweden
195 R11 Nissan Island island Green Islands, NE PNG
Nissan Islands see Green Islands
97 F16 Nisser ◎ S Norway
97 E21 Nissum Bredning inlet NW Denmark
31 U6 Nisswa Minnesota, N USA 46.31N 94.17W
Nistru see Dniester
117 M22 Nísyros var. Nisiros. island Dodekánisa, Greece, Aegean Sea
120 H8 Nītaure Cēsis, C Latvia 57.05N 25.12E
62 P10 Niterói prev. Nictheroy. Rio de Janeiro, SE Brazil 22.54S 43.06W
12 F16 Nith ~ Ontario, S Canada
98 J13 Nith ~ S Scotland, UK
Nitinan see Nichinan
113 I21 Nitra Ger. Neutra, Hung. Nyitra. Nitriansky Kraj, SW Slovakia 48.19N 18.04E
113 I20 Nitra Ger. Neutra, Hung. Nyitra. ~ W Slovakia
113 I21 Nitriansky Kraj ◆ region SW Slovakia
23 Q5 Nitro West Virginia, NE USA 38.24N 81.50W
125 F11 Nitsa ~ C Russian Federation
97 H14 Nittedal Akershus, S Norway 60.08N 10.45E
Niuatobutabu see Niuatoputapu
200 S11 Niuatoputapu var. Niuatobutabu; prev. Keppel Island. island N Tonga
200 Q15 Niu'Aunofa headland Tongatapu, S Tonga 21.03S 175.19W
Niuchwang see Yingkou
202 B16 Niue ◇ self-governing territory in free association with NZ S Pacific Ocean
202 F10 Niulakita var. Nurakita. atoll S Tuvalu
202 E6 Niutao atoll NW Tuvalu
95 L15 Nivala Oulu, C Finland 63.56N 25.00E
104 I15 Nive ~ SW France
101 G19 Nivelles Wallon Brabant, C Belgium 50.36N 4.04E
105 P8 Nivernais cultural region C France
13 N8 Niverville, Lac ◎ Québec, SE Canada
29 T7 Nixa Missouri, C USA 37.02N 93.17W
37 R5 Nixon Nevada, W USA 39.48N 119.24W
27 S12 Nixon Texas, SW USA 29.16N 97.45W
Niya see Minfeng
Niyazov see Nyýazow
161 H14 Nizāmābād Andhra Pradesh, C India 18.40N 78.04E
161 H15 Nizām Sāgar ◎ C India
129 N16 Nizhegorodskaya Oblast' ◆ province W Russian Federation
126 K14 Nizhneangarsk Respublika Buryatiya, S Russian Federation 55.47N 109.39E
Nizhnegorskiy see Nyzhn'ohirs'kyy
131 S4 Nizhnekamsk Respublika Tatarstan, W Russian Federation 55.36N 51.45E
131 U3 Nizhnekamskoye Vodokhranilishche ▣ W Russian Federation
127 O5 Nizhnekolymsk Respublika Sakha (Yakutiya), NE Russian Federation 68.32N 161.00E
127 N16 Nizhneleninskoye Yevreyskaya Avtonomnaya Oblast', SE Russian Federation 47.50N 132.30E
126 Ii14 Nizhneudinsk Irkutskaya Oblast', S Russian Federation 54.48N 98.51E
126 Gg11 Nizhnevartovsk Khanty-Mansiyskiy Avtonomnyy Okrug, C Russian Federation 60.57N 76.40E
126 Ll6 Nizhneyansk Respublika Sakha (Yakutiya), NE Russian Federation 71.25N 135.59E
131 Q11 Nizhniy Baskunchak Astrakhanskaya Oblast', SW Russian Federation 48.15N 46.49E
126 M11 Nizhniy Bestyakh Respublika Sakha (Yakutiya), NE Russian Federation 61.55N 130.07E
131 O6 Nizhniy Lomov Penzenskaya Oblast', W Russian Federation 53.32N 43.39E
131 P3 Nizhniy Novgorod prev. Gor'kiy. Nizhegorodskaya Oblast', W Russian Federation 56.17N 43.59E
129 T8 Nizhniy Odes Respublika Komi, NW Russian Federation 63.42N 54.58E
Nizhniy Pyandzh see Panji Poyon
125 Ee11 Nizhniy Tagil Sverdlovskaya Oblast', C Russian Federation 57.57N 59.51E
129 T9 Nizhnyaya-Omra Respublika Komi, NW Russian Federation 62.46N 55.54E
129 P5 Nizhnyaya Pesha Nenetskiy Avtonomnyy Okrug, NW Russian Federation 66.54N 47.37E
125 F11 Nizhnyaya Tavda Tyumenskaya Oblast', C Russian Federation 57.41N 65.54E
126 Jj12 Nizhnyaya Tunguska Eng. Lower Tunguska. ~ N Russian Federation
119 Q3 Nizhyn Rus. Nezhin. Chernihivs'ka Oblast', NE Ukraine 51.03N 31.54E
142 M17 Nizip Gaziantep, S Turkey 37.01N 37.46E
147 X8 Nizwá var. Nazwāh. NE Oman 22.50N 57.27E
Nizza see Nice
108 C9 Nizza Monferrato Piemonte, NE Italy 44.47N 8.22E
Njávdám see Näätämöjoki
Njellim see Nellim
83 H24 Njombe Iringa, S Tanzania 9.19S 34.46E
83 G23 Njombe ~ C Tanzania
94 I10 Njunis ▲ N Norway 68.47N 19.24E
95 H17 Njurunda Västernorrland, C Sweden 62.15N 17.24E
96 N11 Njutånger Gävleborg, C Sweden 61.37N 17.04E
81 D14 Nkambe Nord-Ouest, NW Cameroon 6.34N 10.43E
Nkata Bay see Nkhata Bay
81 F21 Nkayi prev. Jacob. La Bouenza, S Congo 4.10S 13.17E
85 J17 Nkayi Matabeleland North, W Zimbabwe 19.02S 28.55E
84 N13 Nkhata Bay var. Nkata Bay. Northern, N Malawi 11.36S 34.16E
83 E22 Nkonde Kigoma, N Tanzania 6.16S 30.17E
81 D15 Nkongsamba var. N'Kongsamba. Littoral, W Cameroon 4.58N 9.52E
85 E16 Nkurenkuru Okavango, N Namibia 17.39S 18.37E
79 Q15 Nkwanta E Ghana 8.18N 0.27E
178 H1 Nmai Hka var. Me Hka. ~ N Burma
Noardwâlde see Noordwolde
41 N7 Noatak Alaska, USA 67.34N 162.58W
41 N7 Noatak River ~ Alaska, USA
Nobeji see Noheji
170 D15 Nobeoka Miyazaki, Kyūshū, SW Japan 32.34N 131.37E
29 N11 Noble Oklahoma, C USA 35.08N 97.23W
33 P13 Noblesville Indiana, N USA 40.03N 86.00W
172 O6 Noboribetsu var. Noboribetu. Hokkaidō, NE Japan 42.27N 141.08E
Noboribetu see Noboribetsu
61 H18 Nobres Mato Grosso, W Brazil 14.43S 56.15W
109 N21 Nocera Terinese Calabria, S Italy 39.03N 16.10E
43 Q16 Nochixtlán var. Asunción Nochixtlán. Oaxaca, SE Mexico 17.28N 97.18W
27 S5 Nocona Texas, SW USA 33.47N 97.43W
65 K21 Nodales, Bahía de los bay S Argentina
29 Q2 Nodaway River ~ Iowa/Missouri, C USA
29 R8 Noel Missouri, C USA 36.33N 94.29W
97 C17 Nærbø Rogaland, S Norway 58.40N 5.39E
97 I24 Næstved Storstrøm, SE Denmark 55.12N 11.47E
42 H3 Nogales Chihuahua, NW Mexico 18.49N 97.12W
42 F3 Nogales Sonora, NW Mexico 31.16N 110.52W
38 M17 Nogales Arizona, SW USA 31.20N 110.55W
Nogal Valley see Dooxo Nugaaleed
104 K15 Nogaro Gers, S France 43.46N 0.01W
112 J7 Nogat ~ N Poland
170 D12 Nōgata Fukuoka, Kyūshū, SW Japan 33.42N 130.43E
131 P15 Nogayskaya Step' steppe SW Russian Federation
104 M6 Nogent-le-Rotrou Eure-et-Loir, C France 48.19N 0.49E
105 O4 Nogent-sur-Oise Oise, N France 49.16N 2.28E
105 P6 Nogent-sur-Seine Aube, N France 48.30N 3.31E
126 I10 Noginsk Evenkiyskiy Avtonomnyy Okrug, N Russian Federation 64.28N 91.09E
130 L3 Noginsk Moskovskaya Oblast', W Russian Federation 55.51N 38.23E
127 O14 Nogliki Ostrov Sakhalin, Sakhalinskaya Oblast', SE Russian Federation 51.44N 143.14E
171 I14 Nōgōhaku-san ▲ Honshū, SW Japan 35.46N 136.30E
168 D5 Nogoonnuur Bayan-Ölgiy, NW Mongolia 49.31N 89.48E
63 C18 Nogoyá Entre Ríos, E Argentina 32.25S 59.49W
113 K21 Nógrád off. Nógrád Megye. ◆ county N Hungary
107 U5 Noguera Pallaresa ~ NE Spain
107 U4 Noguera Ribagorçana ~ NE Spain
172 N9 Noheji var. Nobeji. Aomori, Honshū, C Japan 40.51N 141.07E
103 E19 Nohfelden Saarland, SW Germany 49.35N 7.08E
40 A8 Nohili Point headland Kaua'i, Hawai'i, USA, C Pacific Ocean 22.03N 159.48W
106 G3 Noia Galicia, NW Spain 42.48N 8.52W
105 N16 Noire, Montagne ▲▲ S France
13 P12 Noire, Rivière ~ Québec, SE Canada
12 J10 Noire, Rivière ~ Québec, SE Canada
Noire, Rivière see Black River
104 G6 Noires, Montagnes ▲▲ NW France
104 H8 Noirmoutier-en-l'Île Vendée, NW France 47.00N 2.15W
104 H8 Noirmoutier, Île de island NW France
171 Jj17 Nojima-zaki headland Honshū, S Japan 34.54N 139.54E
195 W8 Noka Nendö, E Solomon Islands 10.42S 165.57E
85 G17 Nokaneng North-West, NW Botswana 19.40S 22.12E
95 L18 Nokia Länsi-Suomi, W Finland 61.28N 23.30E
154 K11 Nok Kundi Baluchistān, SW Pakistan 28.49N 62.39E
32 L14 Nokomis Illinois, N USA 39.18N 89.17W
32 K5 Nokomis, Lake ▣ Wisconsin, N USA
80 G9 Nokou Kanem, W Chad 14.36N 14.45E
197 B12 Nokuku Espiritu Santo, W Vanuatu 14.56S 166.34E
97 J18 Nol Västra Götaland, S Sweden 57.55N 12.03E
81 H16 Nola Sangha-Mbaéré, SW Central African Republic 3.28N 16.05E
27 P7 Nolan Texas, SW USA 32.15N 100.15W
129 R15 Nolinsk Kirovskaya Oblast', NW Russian Federation 57.34N 49.54E
97 B19 Nólsoy Dan. Nolsø Island Faeroe Islands 61.59N 6.39W
194 F12 Nomad Western, SW Papau New Guinea 6.11S 142.13E
170 B15 Noma-zaki headland Kyūshū, SW Japan 31.24N 130.07E
42 K10 Nombre de Dios Durango, C Mexico 23.51N 104.13W
44 I5 Nombre de Dios, Cordillera ▲▲ N Honduras
40 M9 Nome Alaska, USA 64.30N 165.24W
31 Q6 Nome North Dakota, N USA 46.39N 97.49W
40 M9 Nome, Cape headland Alaska, USA 64.25N 165.00W
168 K11 Nomgon var. Sangiyn Dalay. Ömnögovĭ, S Mongolia 42.50N 105.04E
Nōmi-jima see Nishi-Nōmi-jima
12 M11 Nominingue, Lac ◎ Québec, SE Canada
Nomoi Islands see Mortlock Islands
170 Bb13 Nomo-zaki headland Kyūshū, SW Japan 32.34N 129.45E
168 G6 Nömrög var. Hödrögö. Dzavhan, N Mongolia 48.51N 96.48E
200 S13 Nomuka island Nomuka Group, C Tonga
200 S14 Nomuka Group island group W Tonga
201 Q15 Nomwin Atoll atoll Hall Islands, C Micronesia
15 I8 Nonacho Lake ◎ Northwest Territories, NW Canada
Nondaburi see Nonthaburi
41 P12 Nondalton Alaska, USA 59.58N 154.51W
169 V10 Nong'an Jilin, NE China 44.23N 125.04E
178 I10 Nong Bua Khok Nakhon Ratchasima, C Thailand 15.23N 101.51E
178 I9 Nong Bua Lamphu Udon Thani, E Thailand 17.11N 102.27E
178 J7 Nông Hèt Xiangkhoang, N Laos 19.27N 104.02E
Nongkaya see Nong Khai
178 I8 Nong Khai var. Mi Chai, Nongkaya. Nong Khai, E Thailand 17.52N 102.43E
178 Gg15 Nong Met Surat Thani, SW Thailand 9.27N 99.09E
85 L22 Nongoma KwaZulu/Natal, E South Africa 27.54S 31.40E
178 Hh10 Nong Phai Phetchabun, C Thailand 15.58N 101.02E
159 U13 Nongstoin Meghālaya, NE India 25.24N 91.19E
85 C19 Nonidas Erongo, N Namibia 22.36S 14.40E
Nonni see Nen Jiang
42 I7 Nonoava Chihuahua, N Mexico 27.24N 106.18W
203 O3 Nonouti prev. Sydenham Island. atoll Tungaru, W Kiribati
178 Hh11 Nonthaburi var. Nondaburi, Nontha Buri. Nonthaburi, C Thailand 13.48N 100.33E
104 L11 Nontron Dordogne, SW France 45.34N 0.41E
189 P1 Noonamah Northern Territory, N Australia 12.46S 131.08E
30 K2 Noonan North Dakota, N USA 48.51N 102.57W
101 E14 Noord-Beveland var. North Beveland. island SW Netherlands
101 I14 Noord-Brabant Eng. North Brabant. ◆ province S Netherlands
100 H7 Noorder Haaks spit NW Netherlands
100 H9 Noord-Holland Eng. North Holland. ◆ province NW Netherlands
Noordhollandsch Kanaal see Noordhollands Kanaal
100 H8 Noordhollands Kanaal var. Noordhollandsch Kanaal. canal NW Netherlands
Noord-Kaap see Northern Cape
100 L8 Noordoostpolder island N Netherlands
47 P16 Noordpunt headland Curaçao, C Netherlands Antilles 12.21N 69.08W
100 I8 Noord-Scharwoude Noord-Holland, NW Netherlands 52.42N 4.48E
Noordwes see North-West
100 G11 Noordwijk aan Zee Zuid-Holland, W Netherlands 52.15N 4.25E
100 H11 Noordwijkerhout Zuid-Holland, W Netherlands 52.16N 4.30E
100 M7 Noordwolde Fris. Noardwâlde. Friesland, N Netherlands 52.54N 6.10E
Noordzee see North Sea
100 H10 Noordzee-Kanaal canal NW Netherlands
95 K18 Noormarkku Swe. Norrmark. Länsi-Suomi, W Finland 61.34N 21.54E
41 N8 Noorvik Alaska, USA 66.50N 161.01W
8 J17 Nootka Sound inlet British Columbia, W Canada
84 A9 Nóqui Zaire, NW Angola 5.53S 13.26E
97 L15 Nora Örebro, C Sweden 59.31N 15.01E
153 Q13 Norak Rus. Nurek. W Tajikistan 38.23N 69.13E
16 P14 Noranda Quebec, SE Canada 48.16N 79.03W
31 W12 Nora Springs Iowa, C USA 43.08N 93.00W
97 M14 Norberg Västmanland, C Sweden 60.04N 15.34E
12 K13 Norcan Lake ◎ Ontario, SE Canada
207 R12 Nord Avannaarsua, N Greenland 81.38N 12.51W
80 F13 Nord Eng. North. ◆ province N Cameroon
105 P2 Nord ◆ department N France
94 P1 Nordaustlandet island NE Svalbard
97 G24 Nordborg Ger. Nordburg. Sønderjylland, SW Denmark 55.04N 9.40E
Nordburg see Nordborg
97 F23 Nordby Ribe, W Denmark 55.27N 8.25E
9 P15 Nordegg Alberta, SW Canada 52.27N 116.06W
102 E9 Norden Niedersachsen, NW Germany 53.36N 7.12E
102 G10 Nordenham Niedersachsen, NW Germany 53.28N 8.27E
126 Ii4 Nordenshel'da, Arkhipelag island group N Russian Federation
94 O3 Nordenskiold Land physical region W Svalbard
102 E9 Norderney island NW Germany
102 J9 Norderstedt Schleswig-Holstein, N Germany 53.42N 9.58E
96 C11 Nordfjord physical region S Norway
96 D11 Nordfjord fjord S Norway
96 D11 Nordfjordeid Sogn og Fjordane, S Norway 61.54N 6.01E
94 G11 Nordfold Nordland, C Norway 67.48N 15.16E
Nordfriesische Inseln see North Frisian Islands
102 H7 Nordfriesland cultural region N Germany
103 K15 Nordhausen Thüringen, C Germany 51.31N 10.48E
27 T13 Nordheim Texas, SW USA 28.55N 97.36W
96 C13 Nordhordland physical region S Norway
102 E12 Nordhorn Niedersachsen, NW Germany 52.25N 7.04E
94 I1 Nordhurfjördhur Vestfirdhir, NW Iceland 66.01N 21.33W
94 J1 Nordhurland Eystra ◆ region N Iceland
94 I2 Nordhurland Vestra ◆ region N Iceland
180 H16 Nord, Île du island Inner Islands, NE Seychelles
97 F20 Nordjylland off. Nordjyllands Amt. ◆ county N Denmark
94 K7 Nordkapp Eng. North Cape. headland N Norway 71.10N 25.42E
94 O1 Nordkapp headland N Svalbard 80.31N 19.58E
94 L7 Nordkinn headland N Norway 71.07N 27.40E
81 N19 Nord Kivu off. Région du Nord Kivu. ◆ region E Dem. Rep. Congo
94 G12 Nordland ◆ county C Norway
103 J21 Nördlingen Bayern, S Germany 48.49N 10.28E
95 I16 Nordmaling Västerbotten, N Sweden 63.34N 19.30E
97 K15 Nordmark Värmland, C Sweden 59.52N 14.04E
Nord, Mer du see North Sea
96 F8 Nordmøre physical region S Norway
102 I8 Nord-Ostee-Kanal canal N Germany
(0) J3 Nordostrundingen headland NE Greenland 83.00N 10.00W
81 D14 Nord-Ouest Eng. North-West. ◆ province NW Cameroon
Nord-Ouest, Territoires du see Northwest Territories
105 N2 Nord-Pas-de-Calais ◆ region N France
103 F19 Nordpfälzer Bergland ▲▲ W Germany
Nord, Pointe see Fatua, Pointe
197 H5 Nord, Province ◆ province C New Caledonia
103 D14 Nordrhein-Westfalen Eng. North Rhine-Westphalia, Fr. Rhénanie du Nord-Westphalie. ◆ state W Germany
Nordsee/Nordsjøen/Nordsøen see North Sea
102 H7 Nordstrand island N Germany
95 E15 Nord-Trøndelag ◆ county C Norway
99 E19 Nore Ir. An Fheoir. ~ S Ireland
31 Q14 Norfolk Nebraska, C USA 42.01N 97.25W
23 X7 Norfolk Virginia, NE USA 36.51N 76.17W
99 P19 Norfolk cultural region E England, UK
199 Ii11 Norfolk Island ◇ Australian external territory SW Pacific Ocean
183 P9 Norfolk Ridge undersea feature W Pacific Ocean
29 U8 Norfork Lake ▣ Arkansas/Missouri, C USA
100 N6 Norg Drenthe, NE Netherlands 53.04N 6.28E
Norge see Norway
97 D14 Norheimsund Hordaland, S Norway 60.22N 6.09E
27 S16 Norias Texas, SW USA 26.47N 97.45W
171 J14 Norikura-dake ▲ Honshū, S Japan 36.06N 137.33E
126 I8 Noril'sk Taymyrskiy (Dolgano-Nenetskiy) Avtonomnyy Okrug, N Russian Federation 69.21N 88.01E
12 I13 Norland Ontario, SE Canada 44.46N 78.48W
23 V8 Norlina North Carolina, SE USA 36.26N 78.11W
32 L13 Normal Illinois, N USA 40.30N 88.59W
29 N11 Norman Oklahoma, C USA 35.13N 97.27W
Norman see Tulita
195 O16 Normanby Island island SE PNG
Normandes, Îles see Channel Islands
60 G9 Normandia Roraima, N Brazil 3.57N 59.39W
104 L5 Normandie Eng. Normandy. cultural region N France
104 J5 Normandie, Collines de hill range NW France
Normandy see Normandie
27 V9 Normangee Texas, SW USA 31.01N 96.06W
23 Q10 Norman, Lake ▣ North Carolina, SE USA
46 K13 Norman Manley ✕ (Kingston) E Jamaica 17.55N 76.46W
189 U5 Norman River ~ Queensland, NE Australia
189 U4 Normanton Queensland, NE Australia 17.48S 141.07E
15 Gg5 Norman Wells Northwest Territories, NW Canada 65.18N 126.42W
10 H12 Normétal Québec, S Canada 48.58N 79.22W
169 O7 Norovlin var. Uldz. Hentiy, NE Mongolia 48.47N 112.01E
9 V15 Norquay Saskatchewan, S Canada 51.51N 102.04W
96 N11 Norra Dellen ◎ C Sweden
95 G15 Norråker Jämtland, C Sweden 64.25N 15.40E
96 N12 Norrala Gävleborg, C Sweden 61.22N 17.04E
Norra Ny see Stöllet
94 G13 Norra Storfjället ▲ N Sweden 65.57N 15.15E
94 I13 Norrbotten ◆ county N Sweden
97 G23 Nørre Aaby var. Nørre Åby. Fyn, C Denmark 55.28N 9.52E
Nørre Åby see Nørre Aaby
97 I24 Nørre Alslev Storstrøm, SE Denmark 54.54N 11.52E
97 E23 Nørre Nebel Ribe, W Denmark 55.45N 8.16E
97 G20 Nørresundby Nordjylland, N Denmark 57.05N 9.55E
23 N8 Norris Lake ▣ Tennessee, S USA
20 I15 Norristown Pennsylvania, NE USA 40.07N 75.20W
97 N17 Norrköping Östergötland, S Sweden 58.34N 16.10E
Norrmark see Noormarkku
96 N13 Norrsundet Gävleborg, C Sweden 60.55N 17.09E
97 P15 Norrtälje Stockholm, C Sweden 59.45N 18.42E
188 L12 Norseman Western Australia 32.16S 121.45E
95 I14 Norsjö Västerbotten, N Sweden 64.55N 19.30E
97 G16 Norsjø ◎ S Norway
126 Mm15 Norsk Amurskaya Oblast', SE Russian Federation 52.20N 129.57E
Norske Havet see Norwegian Sea
197 C13 Norsup Malekula, C Vanuatu 16.05S 167.24E
203 V15 Norte, Cabo headland Easter Island, Chile, E Pacific Ocean 27.03S 109.24W
56 F7 Norte de Santander off. Departamento de Norte de Santander. ◆ province N Colombia
63 E21 Norte, Punta headland E Argentina 36.17S 56.46W
23 R13 North South Carolina, SE USA 33.37N 81.06W
North see Nord
20 L10 North Adams Massachusetts, NE USA 42.40N 73.06W
115 L17 North Albanian Alps Alb. Bjeshkët e Namuna, SCr. Prokletije. ▲▲ Albania/Montenegro
99 M15 Northallerton N England, UK 54.19N 1.25W
188 J12 Northam Western Australia 31.40S 116.40E
85 J20 Northam Northern, N South Africa 24.56S 27.18E
1 North America continent
1 N12 North American Basin undersea feature W Sargasso Sea
(0) C5 North American Plate tectonic feature
20 M11 North Amherst Massachusetts, NE USA 42.24N 72.31W
99 N20 Northampton C England, UK 52.13N 0.54W
99 M20 Northamptonshire cultural region C England, UK
157 P18 North Andaman island Andaman Islands, India, NE Indian Ocean
67 D25 North Arm East Falkland, Falkland Islands 52.06S 59.21W
23 Q13 North Augusta South Carolina, SE USA 33.30N 81.58W
181 W8 North Australian Basin Fr. Bassin Nord de l' Australie. undersea feature E Indian Ocean
33 R11 North Baltimore Ohio, N USA 41.10N 83.40W
9 T15 North Battleford Saskatchewan, S Canada 52.46N 108.19W
12 H11 North Bay Ontario, S Canada 46.19N 79.28W
10 H6 North Belcher Islands island group Belcher Islands, Nunavut, C Canada
31 R15 North Bend Nebraska, C USA 41.27N 96.46W
34 E14 North Bend Oregon, NW USA 43.24N 124.13W
98 K12 North Berwick SE Scotland, UK 56.03N 2.44W
North Beveland see Noord-Beveland
North Borneo see Sabah
191 P5 North Bourke New South Wales, SE Australia 30.03S 145.56E
North Brabant see Noord-Brabant
190 F2 North Branch Neales seasonal river South Australia
46 M6 North Caicos island NW Turks and Caicos Islands
28 L10 North Canadian River ~ Oklahoma, C USA
33 U12 North Canton Ohio, N USA 40.52N 81.24W
11 R13 North, Cape headland Cape Breton Island, Nova Scotia, SE Canada 47.06N 60.24W
192 I1 North Cape headland North Island, NZ 34.23S 173.02E
195 N9 North Cape headland New Ireland, NE PNG 2.33S 150.48E
North Cape see Nordkapp
20 J17 North Cape May New Jersey, NE USA 38.59N 74.55W
10 C9 North Caribou Lake ◎ Ontario, C Canada
23 U10 North Carolina off. State of North Carolina; also known as Old North State, Tar Heel State, Turpentine State. ◆ state SE USA
North Celebes see Sulawesi Utara
161 J24 North Central Province ◆ province N Sri Lanka
33 S4 North Channel lake channel Canada/USA
99 G14 North Channel strait Northern Ireland/Scotland, UK
23 S14 North Charleston South Carolina, SE USA 32.51N 79.58W
33 N10 North Chicago Illinois, N USA 42.19N 87.50W
205 Y10 Northcliffe Glacier glacier Antarctica
33 Q14 North College Hill Ohio, N USA 39.13N 84.33W
27 O8 North Concho River ~ Texas, SW USA
21 O8 North Conway New Hampshire, NE USA 44.03N 71.06W
29 V14 North Crossett Arkansas, C USA 33.10N 91.56W
30 L4 North Dakota off. State of North Dakota; also known as Flickertail State, Peace Garden State, Sioux State. ◆ state N USA
North Devon Island see Devon Island
99 O22 North Downs hill range SE England, UK
20 C11 North East Pennsylvania, NE USA 42.13N 79.49W
85 I18 North East ◆ district NE Botswana
67 G15 North East Bay bay Ascension Island, C Atlantic Ocean
40 L10 Northeast Cape headland Saint Lawrence Island, Alaska, USA 63.16N 168.50W
178 Mm13 Northeast Cay island NW Spratly Islands
83 J17 North Eastern ◆ province Kenya
North East Frontier Agency/North East Frontier Agency of Assam see Arunāchal Pradesh
67 E25 North East Island island E Falkland Islands
201 V11 Northeast Island island Chuuk, C Micronesia
46 L12 North East Point headland E Jamaica 18.09N 76.19W

◆ Country ● Country Capital ◇ Dependent Territory ○ Dependent Territory Capital ◆ Administrative Region ✕ International Airport ▲ Mountain ▲▲ Mountain Range Volcano ~ River ◎ Lake ▣ Reservoir

Northeast Point – Nsimalen

46 L6 **Northeast Point** *headland* Great Inagua, S Bahamas 21.18N 73.01W
46 K5 **Northeast Point** *headland* Acklins Island, SE Bahamas 22.43N 73.50W
203 Z2 **Northeast Point** *headland* Kiritimati, E Kiribati 10.22S 105.45E
46 H2 **Northeast Providence Channel** *channel* N Bahamas
103 J14 **Northeim** Niedersachsen, C Germany 51.42N 10.00E
31 X14 **North English** Iowa, C USA 41.30N 92.04W
144 G8 **Northern** ◐ *district* N Israel
84 M12 **Northern** ◐ *region* N Malawi
194 L15 **Northern** ◐ *province* S PNG
82 D7 **Northern** ◐ *state* N Sudan
84 K12 **Northern** ◐ *province* NE Zambia
Northern *see* Limpopo
82 B13 **Northern Bahr el Ghazal** ◐ *state* SW Sudan
Northern Border Region *see* Al Ḥudūd ash Shamālīyah
85 F24 **Northern Cape** *off.* Northern Cape Province, *Afr.* Noord-Kaap. ◐ *province* W South Africa
202 K14 **Northern Cook Islands** *island group* N Cook Islands
82 B8 **Northern Darfur** ◐ *state* NW Sudan
Northern Dvina *see* Severnaya Dvina
99 F14 **Northern Ireland** *var.* The Six Counties. *political division* UK
82 D9 **Northern Kordofan** ◐ *state* C Sudan
197 K14 **Northern Lau Group** *island group* Lau Group, NE Fiji
196 K3 **Northern Mariana Islands** ◇ *US commonwealth territory* W Pacific Ocean
161 J23 **Northern Province** ◐ *province* N Sri Lanka
Northern Rhodesia *see* Zambia
Northern Sporades *see* Vóreies Sporádes
190 D1 **Northern Territory** ◐ *territory* N Australia
Northern Transvaal *see* Limpopo
Northern Ural Hills *see* Severnyye Uvaly
86 I9 **North European Plain** *plain* N Europe
29 V2 **North Fabius River** ≈ Missouri, C USA
67 D24 **North Falkland Sound** *sound* N Falkland Islands
31 V9 **Northfield** Minnesota, N USA 44.27N 93.10W
21 O9 **Northfield** New Hampshire, NE USA 43.26N 71.34W
183 Q8 **North Fiji Basin** *undersea feature* N Coral Sea
99 Q22 **North Foreland** *headland* SE England, UK 51.22N 1.26E
37 P6 **North Fork American River** ≈ California, W USA
41 R7 **North Fork Chandalar River** ≈ Alaska, USA
30 K7 **North Fork Grand River** ≈ North Dakota/South Dakota, N USA
23 O6 **North Fork Kentucky River** ≈ Kentucky, S USA
41 Q7 **North Fork Koyukuk River** ≈ Alaska, USA
41 Q10 **North Fork Kuskokwim River** ≈ Alaska, USA
28 K11 **North Fork Red River** ≈ Oklahoma/Texas, SW USA
28 K3 **North Fork Solomon River** ≈ Kansas, C USA
25 W14 **North Fort Myers** Florida, SE USA 26.40N 81.52W
33 P5 **North Fox Island** *island* Michigan, N USA
102 G6 **North Frisian Islands** *var.* Nordfriesische Inseln. *island group* N Germany
207 N9 **North Geomagnetic Pole** *pole* Arctic Ocean 78.30N 69.00W
20 M13 **North Haven** Connecticut, NE USA 41.25N 72.51W
192 J5 **North Head** *headland* North Island, NZ 36.23S 174.01E
20 L6 **North Hero** Vermont, NE USA 44.49N 73.14W
37 O7 **North Highlands** California, W USA 38.40N 121.25W
North Holland *see* Noord-Holland
83 I16 **North Horr** Eastern, N Kenya 3.17N 37.08E
157 K21 **North Huvadhu Atoll** *var.* Gaafu Alifu Atoll. *atoll* S Maldives
67 A24 **North Island** *island* W Falkland Islands
192 N9 **North Island** *island* N NZ
23 U14 **North Island** *island* South Carolina, SE USA
33 O11 **North Judson** Indiana, N USA 41.12N 86.44W
North Kazakhstan *see* Severnyy Kazakhstan
33 V10 **North Kingsville** Ohio, N USA 41.54N 80.41W
169 Y13 **North Korea** *off.* Democratic People's Republic of Korea, *Kor.* Chosŏn-minjujuŭi-inmin-kanghwaguk. ◆ *republic* E Asia
159 X11 **North Lakhimpur** Assam, NE India 27.10N 94.00E
192 J3 **Northland** *off.* Northland Region. ◐ *region* North Island, NZ
199 J12 **Northland Plateau** *undersea feature* S Pacific Ocean
37 X11 **North Las Vegas** Nevada, W USA 36.12N 115.07W
33 O11 **North Liberty** Indiana, N USA 41.36N 86.22W
31 X14 **North Liberty** Iowa, C USA 41.45N 91.36W
29 V12 **North Little Rock** Arkansas, C USA 34.46N 92.15W
30 M13 **North Loup River** ≈ Nebraska, C USA
157 K18 **North Maalhosmadulu Atoll** *var.* North Malosmadulu Atoll, Raa Atoll. *atoll* N Maldives
33 U10 **North Madison** Ohio, N USA 41.48N 81.03W
33 P12 **North Manchester** Indiana, N USA 41.00N 85.45W
33 P6 **North Manitou Island** *island* Michigan, N USA
31 U10 **North Mankato** Minnesota, N USA 44.11N 94.03W
25 Z15 **North Miami** Florida, SE USA 25.54N 80.11W
157 K18 **North Miladummadulu Atoll** *atoll* N Maldives
North Minch *see* Minch, The
25 W15 **North Naples** Florida, SE USA 26.13N 81.47W
183 P8 **North New Hebrides Trench** *undersea feature* N Coral Sea
25 Y15 **North New River Canal** ≈ Florida, SE USA
157 K20 **North Nilandhe Atoll** *var.* Faafu Atoll. *atoll* C Maldives
38 L2 **North Ogden** Utah, W USA 41.18N 111.57W
North Ossetia *see* Severnaya Osetiya-Alaniya, Respublika
37 S10 **North Palisade** ▲ California, W USA 37.06N 118.31W
201 U11 **North Pass** *passage* Chuuk Islands, C Micronesia
30 M15 **North Platte** Nebraska, C USA 41.07N 100.46W
35 X17 **North Platte River** ≈ C USA
67 G14 **North Point** *headland* Ascension Island, C Atlantic Ocean
180 I16 **North Point** *headland* Mahé, NE Seychelles 4.22S 55.28E
33 S6 **North Point** *headland* Michigan, N USA 45.01N 83.16W
33 R5 **North Point** *headland* Michigan, N USA 45.21N 83.30W
41 S9 **North Pole** Alaska, USA 64.42N 147.09W
207 R9 **North Pole** *pole* Arctic Ocean 90.00N 0.00W
25 O4 **Northport** Alabama, S USA 33.13N 87.34W
25 W14 **North Port** Florida, SE USA 27.03N 82.15W
34 L6 **Northport** Washington, NW USA 48.54N 117.48W
34 L12 **North Powder** Oregon, NW USA 45.00N 117.56W
31 U13 **North Raccoon River** ≈ Iowa, C USA
North Rhine-Westphalia *see* Nordrhein-Westfalen
99 M16 **North Riding** *cultural region* N England, UK
98 G5 **North Rona** *island* NW Scotland, UK
98 K4 **North Ronaldsay** *island* NE Scotland, UK
38 L2 **North Salt Lake** Utah, W USA 40.51N 111.54W
9 P15 **North Saskatchewan** ≈ Alberta/Saskatchewan, S Canada
37 X5 **North Schell Peak** ▲ Nevada, W USA 39.25N 114.34W
North Scotia Ridge *see* South Georgia Ridge
88 D10 **North Sea** *Dan.* Nordsøen, *Dut.* Noordzee, *Fr.* Mer du Nord, *Ger.* Nordsee, *Nor.* Nordsjøen; *prev.* German Ocean, *Lat.* Mare Germanicum. *sea* NW Europe
37 T6 **North Shoshone Peak** ▲ Nevada, W USA 39.08N 117.28W
North Siberian Lowland/ North Siberian Plain *see* Severo-Sibirskaya Nizmennost'
31 R13 **North Sioux City** South Dakota, N USA 42.31N 96.28W
98 K4 **North Sound, The** *sound* N Scotland, UK
191 T4 **North Star** New South Wales, SE Australia 28.55S 150.25E
North Star State *see* Minnesota
191 V3 **North Stradbroke Island** *island* Queensland, E Australia
North Sulawesi *see* Sulawesi Utara
North Sumatra *see* Sumatera Utara
12 D17 **North Sydenham** ≈ Ontario, S Canada
20 H9 **North Syracuse** New York, NE USA 43.07N 76.07W
192 K9 **North Taranaki Bight** *gulf* North Island, NZ
10 H9 **North Twin Island** *island* Nunavut, C Canada
98 E8 **North Uist** *island* NW Scotland, UK
99 L14 **Northumberland** *cultural region* N England, UK
189 Y7 **Northumberland Isles** *island group* Queensland, NE Australia
11 Q14 **Northumberland Strait** *strait* SE Canada
34 G14 **North Umpqua River** ≈ Oregon, NW USA
47 Q13 **North Union** Saint Vincent, Saint Vincent and the Grenadines 13.15N 61.07W
8 L17 **North Vancouver** British Columbia, SW Canada 49.21N 123.04W
20 K9 **Northville** New York, NE USA 43.13N 74.08W
99 Q19 **North Walsham** E England, UK 52.49N 1.22E
41 T10 **Northway** Alaska, USA 62.57N 141.56W
85 G17 **North-West** ◐ *district* NW Botswana
85 G21 **North-West** *off.* North-West Province, *Afr.* Noordwes. ◐ *province* N South Africa
North-West *see* Nord-Ouest
66 I6 **Northwest Atlantic Mid-Ocean Canyon** *undersea feature* N Atlantic Ocean
188 G8 **North West Cape** *headland* Western Australia 21.48S 114.10E
40 J9 **Northwest Cape** *headland* Saint Lawrence Island, Alaska, USA 63.46N 171.45W
84 H13 **North Western** ◐ *province* W Zambia
161 J24 **North Western Province** ◐ *province* W Sri Lanka
155 U4 **North-West Frontier Province** ◐ *province* NW Pakistan
98 H8 **North West Highlands** ▲ N Scotland, UK
199 Hh4 **Northwest Pacific Basin** *undersea feature* NW Pacific Ocean
203 Y2 **Northwest Point** *headland* Kiritimati, E Kiribati 10.25S 105.34E
46 G1 **Northwest Providence Channel** *channel* N Bahamas
11 Q8 **North West River** Newfoundland and Labrador, E Canada 53.30N 60.10W
15 I15 **Northwest Territories** *Fr.* Territoires du Nord-Ouest. ◐ *territory* NW Canada
99 K18 **Northwich** C England, UK 53.16N 2.31W
27 Q5 **North Wichita River** ≈ Texas, SW USA
20 J17 **North Wildwood** New Jersey, NE USA 39.00N 74.48W
23 R9 **North Wilkesboro** North Carolina, SE USA 36.09N 81.09W
21 P8 **North Windham** Maine, NE USA 43.51N 70.25W
207 Q6 **Northwind Plain** *undersea feature* Arctic Ocean
31 V11 **Northwood** Iowa, C USA 43.26N 93.13W
31 Q4 **Northwood** North Dakota, N USA 47.43N 97.34W
99 M15 **North York Moors** *moorland* N England, UK
27 V9 **North Zulch** Texas, SW USA 30.54N 96.06W
28 K2 **Norton** Kansas, C USA 39.49N 99.53W
33 S13 **Norton** Ohio, N USA 40.25N 83.04W
23 P7 **Norton** Virginia, NE USA 36.55N 82.37W
41 N9 **Norton Bay** *bay* Alaska, USA
Norton de Matos *see* Balombo
33 O9 **Norton Shores** Michigan, N USA 43.10N 86.15W
40 M10 **Norton Sound** *inlet* Alaska, USA
29 Q3 **Nortonville** Kansas, C USA 39.25N 95.19W
104 I8 **Nort-sur-Erdre** Loire-Atlantique, NW France 47.27N 1.30W
205 N2 **Norvegia, Cape** *headland* Antarctica 71.16S 12.25W
20 L13 **Norwalk** Connecticut, NE USA 41.08N 73.28W
31 V14 **Norwalk** Iowa, C USA 41.28N 93.40W
33 S11 **Norwalk** Ohio, N USA 41.14N 82.37W
21 P7 **Norway** Maine, NE USA 44.13N 70.30W
33 N5 **Norway** Michigan, N USA 45.47N 87.54W
95 E17 **Norway** *off.* Kingdom of Norway, *Nor.* Norge. ◆ *monarchy* N Europe
9 X13 **Norway House** Manitoba, C Canada 53.58N 97.49W
207 R16 **Norwegian Basin** *undersea feature* NW Norwegian Sea
86 D6 **Norwegian Sea** *Nor.* Norske Havet. *sea* NE Atlantic Ocean
207 S17 **Norwegian Trench** *undersea feature* NE North Sea
12 F16 **Norwich** Ontario, S Canada 42.57N 80.37W
99 Q19 **Norwich** E England, UK 52.37N 1.18E
21 N13 **Norwich** Connecticut, NE USA 41.30N 72.02W
20 I11 **Norwich** New York, NE USA 42.31N 75.31W
31 U9 **Norwood** Minnesota, N USA 44.46N 93.55W
33 Q15 **Norwood** Ohio, N USA 39.07N 84.27W
12 H11 **Nosbonsing, Lake** ⊛ Ontario, S Canada
Nösen *see* Bistriţa
172 P1 **Noshappu-misaki** *headland* Hokkaidō, NE Japan 45.26N 141.38E
171 M9 **Noshiro** *var.* Nosiro; *prev.* Noshirominato. Akita, Honshū, C Japan 40.10N 140.01E
Noshirominato/Nosiro *see* Noshiro
119 Q3 **Nosivka** *Rus.* Nosovka. Chernihivs'ka Oblast', NE Ukraine 50.55N 31.37E
69 T14 **Nosop** *var.* Nossob, Nossop. ≈ Botswana/Namibia
129 S4 **Nosovaya** Nenetskiy Avtonomnyy Okrug, NW Russian Federation 68.12N 54.33E
Nosovka *see* Nosivka
149 V11 **Noşratābād** Sīstān va Balūchestān, E Iran 29.53N 59.57E
97 J18 **Nossebro** Västra Götaland, S Sweden 58.12N 12.42E
98 K6 **Noss Head** *headland* N Scotland, UK 58.29N 3.03W
Nossi-Bé *see* Be, Nosy
85 E20 **Nossob** ≈ E Namibia
Nossob/Nossop *see* Nosop
180 J2 **Nosy Be** ✕ Antsiranana, N Madagascar 23.36S 47.36E
180 J6 **Nosy Varika** Fianarantsoa, SE Madagascar 20.36S 48.31E
12 L10 **Notawassi** ≈ Québec, SE Canada
12 M9 **Notawassi, Lac** ⊛ Québec, SE Canada
38 J5 **Notch Peak** ▲ Utah, W USA 39.08N 113.24W
112 G10 **Noteć** *Ger.* Netze. ≈ NW Poland
Nóties Sporádes *see* Dodekánisa
117 J22 **Nótion Aigaíon** *Eng.* Aegean South. ◐ *region* E Greece
117 H18 **Nótios Evvoïkós Kólpos** *gulf* E Greece
117 B16 **Nótio Stenó Kérkyras** *strait* W Greece
109 L25 **Noto** *anc.* Netum. Sicilia, Italy, C Mediterranean Sea 36.52N 15.04E
171 J12 **Noto** Ishikawa, Honshū, SW Japan 37.18N 137.11E
97 G15 **Notodden** Telemark, S Norway 59.33N 9.15E
109 L25 **Noto, Golfo di** *gulf* Sicilia, Italy, C Mediterranean Sea
171 J12 **Noto-hantō** *peninsula* Honshū, SW Japan
171 J12 **Noto-jima** *island* SW Japan
172 Qq5 **Notoro-ko** ⊛ Hokkaidō, NE Japan
11 T11 **Notre Dame Bay** *bay* Newfoundland, E Canada
13 P6 **Notre-Dame-de-Lorette** Québec, SE Canada 49.05N 72.24W
12 L11 **Notre-Dame-de-Pontmain** Québec, SE Canada 46.18N 75.37W
13 T8 **Notre-Dame-du-Lac** Québec, SE Canada 47.36N 68.48W
13 Q6 **Notre-Dame-du-Rosaire** Québec, SE Canada 48.48N 71.27W
13 U8 **Notre-Dame, Monts** ▲ Québec, S Canada
79 R16 **Notsé** S Togo 6.53N 1.09E
172 R7 **Notsuke-suidō** *strait* Japan/ Russian Federation
172 R7 **Notsuke-zaki** *headland* Hokkaidō, NE Japan 43.33N 145.18E
12 G14 **Nottawasaga** ≈ Ontario, S Canada
12 G14 **Nottawasaga Bay** *lake bay* Ontario, S Canada
10 I11 **Nottaway** ≈ Québec, SE Canada
25 S1 **Nottely Lake** ⊠ Georgia, SE USA
97 H16 **Nøtterøy** *island* S Norway
99 M19 **Nottingham** C England, UK 52.58N 1.10W
16 N5 **Nottingham Island** *island* Nunavut, NE Canada
99 N18 **Nottinghamshire** *cultural region* C England, UK
23 V7 **Nottoway** Virginia, NE USA 37.07N 78.03W
23 V7 **Nottoway River** ≈ Virginia, NE USA
78 G7 **Nouâdhibou** *prev.* Port-Étienne. Dakhlet Nouâdhibou, W Mauritania 20.54N 17.01W
78 G7 **Nouâdhibou** ✕ Dakhlet Nouâdhibou, W Mauritania 20.59N 17.02W
78 F7 **Nouâdhibou, Dakhlet** *prev.* Baie du Lévrier. *bay* W Mauritania
78 F7 **Nouâdhibou, Râs** *prev.* Cap Blanc. *headland* NW Mauritania 20.48N 17.03W
78 G9 **Nouakchott** ● (Mauritania) Nouakchott District, SW Mauritania 18.09N 15.58W
78 G9 **Nouakchott** ✕ Trarza, SW Mauritania 18.18N 15.54W
123 K13 **Noual, Sebkhet en** *var.* Sabkhat an Nawāl. *salt flat* C Tunisia
78 G8 **Nouâmghâr** *var.* Nouamrhar. Dakhlet Nouâdhibou, W Mauritania 19.22N 16.31W
Nouamrhar *see* Nouâmghâr
Nouă Sulița *see* Novoselytsya
197 I7 **Nouméa** ○ (New Caledonia) Province Sud, S New Caledonia 22.13S 166.29E
81 E15 **Noun** ≈ C Cameroon
79 N12 **Nouna** W Burkina 12.43N 3.54W
85 H24 **Noupoort** Northern Cape, C South Africa 31.10S 24.57E
Nouveau-Brunswick *see* New Brunswick
Nouveau-Comptoir *see* Wemindji
13 T4 **Nouvel, Lacs** ⊛ Québec, SE Canada
13 W7 **Nouvelle** Québec, SE Canada 48.07N 66.16W
13 W7 **Nouvelle** ≈ Québec, SE Canada
Nouvelle-Calédonie *see* New Caledonia
Nouvelle Écosse *see* Nova Scotia
105 R3 **Nouzonville** Ardennes, N France 49.49N 4.45E
153 Q11 **Nov** *Rus.* Nau. NW Tajikistan 40.10N 69.16E
61 I21 **Nova Alvorada** Mato Grosso do Sul, SW Brazil 21.25S 54.19W
Novabad *see* Navobod
113 D19 **Nová Bystřice** *Ger.* Neubistritz. Jihočeský Kraj, S Czech Republic 48.59N 15.05E
118 H13 **Novaci** Gorj, SW Romania 45.08N 23.39E
Nova Civitas *see* Neustadt an der Weinstrasse
Novaesium *see* Neuss
62 H10 **Nova Esperança** Paraná, S Brazil 23.09S 52.13W
108 H11 **Novafeltria** Marche, C Italy 43.54N 12.18E
62 Q9 **Nova Friburgo** Rio de Janeiro, SE Brazil 22.16S 42.34W
84 D12 **Nova Gaia** *var.* Cambundi-Catembo. Malanje, NE Angola 10.03S 17.31E
111 S12 **Nova Gorica** W Slovenia 45.57N 13.40E
114 G10 **Nova Gradiška** *Ger.* Neugradisk, *Hung.* Újgradiska. Brod-Posavina, NE Croatia 45.15N 17.23E
62 K7 **Nova Granada** São Paulo, S Brazil 20.33S 49.19W
62 O10 **Nova Iguaçu** Rio de Janeiro, SE Brazil 22.31S 44.04W
119 S10 **Nova Kakhovka** *Rus.* Novaya Kakhovka. Khersons'ka Oblast', SE Ukraine 46.45N 33.19E
Nová Karvinná *see* Karviná
Nova Lamego *see* Gabú
Nova Lisboa *see* Huambo
114 C11 **Novalja** Lika-Senj, W Croatia 44.33N 14.53E
121 M14 **Novalukoml'** *Rus.* Novolukoml'. Vitsyebskaya Voblasts', N Belarus 54.40N 29.09E
Nova Mambone *see* Mambone
85 P16 **Nova Nabúri** Zambézia, NE Mozambique 16.47S 38.55E
119 Q9 **Nova Odesa** *var.* Novaya Odessa. Mykolayivs'ka Oblast', S Ukraine 47.18N 31.45E
62 H10 **Nova Olímpia** Paraná, S Brazil 23.28S 53.12W
63 I15 **Nova Prata** Rio Grande do Sul, S Brazil 28.45S 51.37W
12 H12 **Novar** Ontario, S Canada 45.26N 79.14W
108 C7 **Novara** *anc.* Novaria. Piemonte, NW Italy 45.27N 8.36E
Novaria *see* Novara
11 P15 **Nova Scotia** *Fr.* Nouvelle Écosse. ◐ *province* SE Canada
(0) M9 **Nova Scotia** *physical region* SE Canada
36 M8 **Novato** California, W USA 38.06N 122.35W
199 Jj8 **Nova Trough** *undersea feature* W Pacific Ocean
118 L7 **Nova Ushtsya** Khmel'nyts'ka Oblast', W Ukraine 48.50N 27.16E
85 M17 **Nova Vanduzi** Manica, C Mozambique 18.54S 33.18E
119 U5 **Nova Vodolaha** *Rus.* Novaya Vodolaga. Kharkivs'ka Oblast', E Ukraine 49.42N 35.48E
126 L13 **Novaya Chara** Chitinskaya Oblast', S Russian Federation 56.45N 117.58E
126 J14 **Novaya Igirma** Irkutskaya Oblast', C Russian Federation 57.08N 103.52E
Novaya Kakhovka *see* Nova Kakhovka
150 E10 **Novaya Kazanka** Zapadnyy Kazakhstan, W Kazakhstan 48.57N 49.34E
128 I12 **Novaya Ladoga** Leningradskaya Oblast', NW Russian Federation 60.03N 32.15E
125 Ee10 **Novaya Lyalya** Sverdlovskaya Oblast, C Russian Federation 59.01N 60.37E
131 R5 **Novaya Malykla** Ul'yanovskaya Oblast', W Russian Federation 54.13N 49.55E
Novaya Odessa *see* Nova Odesa
126 M4 **Novaya Sibir', Ostrov** *island* Novosibirskiye Ostrova, NE Russian Federation
Novaya Vodolaga *see* Nova Vodolaha
121 P17 **Novaya Yel'nya** *Rus.* Novaya Yel'nya. Mahilyowskaya Voblasts', E Belarus 53.16N 31.13E
125 G4 **Novaya Zemlya** *island group* N Russian Federation
Novaya Zemlya Trough *see* East Novaya Zemlya Trough
116 K10 **Nova Zagora** Sliven, C Bulgaria 42.29N 26.00E
107 S12 **Novelda** País Valenciano, E Spain 38.24N 0.45W
113 H19 **Nové Mesto nad Váhom** *Ger.* Waagneustadtl, *Hung.* Vágújhely. Trenčiansky Kraj, W Slovakia 48.48N 17.50E
113 F17 **Nové Město na Moravě** *Ger.* Neustadt in Mähren. Vysočina, C Czech Republic 49.34N 16.04E
Novesium *see* Neuss
113 I21 **Nové Zámky** *Ger.* Neuhäusel, *Hung.* Érsekújvár. Nitriansky Kraj, SW Slovakia 49.00N 18.10E
Novgorod *see* Velikiy Novgorod
Novgorod-Severskiy *see* Novhorod-Sivers'kyy
125 C6 **Novgorodskaya Oblast'** ◐ *province* W Russian Federation
119 R8 **Novhorodka** Kirovohrads'ka Oblast', C Ukraine 48.21N 32.38E
119 R2 **Novhorod-Sivers'kyy** *Rus.* Novgorod-Severskiy. Chernihivs'ka Oblast', NE Ukraine 52.00N 33.15E
33 R10 **Novi** Michigan, N USA 42.28N 83.28W
Novi *see* Novi Vinodolski
114 L9 **Novi Bečej** *prev.* Új-Becse, Vološinovo, *Ger.* Neubetsche, *Hung.* Törökbecse. Serbia, N Serbia 45.36N 20.09E
27 Q8 **Novice** Texas, SW USA 32.00N 99.38W
114 A9 **Novigrad** Istra, NW Croatia 45.19N 13.33E
Novi Grad *see* Bosanski Novi
116 G9 **Novi Iskŭr** Sofiya-Grad, W Bulgaria 42.46N 23.19E
108 C9 **Novi Ligure** Piemonte, NW Italy 44.46N 8.46E
101 L22 **Noville** Luxembourg, SE Belgium 50.04N 5.46E
204 I10 **Noville Peninsula** *peninsula* Thurston Island, Antarctica
Noviodunum *see* Soissons, Aisne, France
Noviodunum *see* Nevers, Nièvre, France
Noviodunum *see* Nyon, Vaud, Switzerland
Noviomagus *see* Lisieux, France
Noviomagus *see* Nijmegen, Netherlands
116 M8 **Novi Pazar** Shumen, NE Bulgaria 43.21N 27.13E
115 M15 **Novi Pazar** *Turk.* Yenipazar. Serbia, S Serbia 43.09N 20.31E
114 K10 **Novi Sad** *Ger.* Neusatz, *Hung.* Újvidék. Serbia, N Serbia 45.16N 19.49E
119 T6 **Novi Sanzhary** Poltavs'ka Oblast', C Ukraine 49.21N 34.18E
114 H12 **Novi Travnik** *prev.* Pučarevo. Federacija Bosna I Hercegovina, C Bosnia and Herzegovina 44.12N 17.39E
114 B10 **Novi Vinodolski** *var.* Novi. Primorje-Gorski Kotar, NW Croatia 45.08N 14.46E
60 F12 **Novo Airão** Amazonas, N Brazil 2.06S 61.19W
131 N14 **Novoaleksandrovsk** Stavropol'skiy Kray, SW Russian Federation 44.41N 43.01E
Novoalekseyevka *see* Khobda
126 H14 **Novoaltaysk** Altayskiy Kray, S Russian Federation 53.22N 83.58E
131 N9 **Novoanninskiy** Volgogradskaya Oblast', SW Russian Federation 50.31N 42.43E
60 F13 **Novo Aripuanã** Amazonas, N Brazil 5.04S 60.19W
119 Y6 **Novoaydar** Luhans'ka Oblast', E Ukraine 49.00N 39.00E
119 X9 **Novoazovs'k** *Rus.* Novoazovsk. Donets'ka Oblast', E Ukraine 47.07N 38.06E
126 Mm16 **Novobureyskiy** Amurskaya Oblast', SE Russian Federation 49.42N 129.46E
131 Q3 **Novocheboksarsk** Chavash Respubliki, W Russian Federation 56.07N 47.32E
131 R5 **Novocheremshansk** Ul'yanovskaya Oblast', W Russian Federation 54.23N 50.08E
130 L12 **Novocherkassk** Rostovskaya Oblast', SW Russian Federation 47.23N 40.00E
131 R6 **Novodevich'ye** Samarskaya Oblast', W Russian Federation 53.33N 48.51E
128 M8 **Novodvinsk** Arkhangel'skaya Oblast', NW Russian Federation 64.22N 40.48E
Novograd-Volynskiy *see* Novohrad-Volyns'kyy
Novogrudok *see* Navahrudak
63 I15 **Novo Hamburgo** Rio Grande do Sul, S Brazil 29.42S 51.07W
61 H16 **Novo Horizonte** Mato Grosso, W Brazil 11.19S 57.11W
62 K8 **Novo Horizonte** São Paulo, S Brazil 21.27S 49.14W
118 M4 **Novohrad-Volyns'kyy** *Rus.* Novograd-Volynskiy. Zhytomyrs'ka Oblast', N Ukraine 50.33N 27.31E
151 O7 **Novoishimskiy** *prev.* Kuybyshevskiy. Severnyy Kazakhstan, N Kazakhstan 53.16N 66.53E
150 L14 **Novokazalinsk** *see* Ayteke Bi
130 M8 **Novokhopersk** Voronezhskaya Oblast', W Russian Federation 51.09N 41.34E
131 R6 **Novokuybyshevsk** Samarskaya Oblast', W Russian Federation 53.06N 49.56E
126 H14 **Novokuznetsk** *prev.* Stalinsk. Kemerovskaya Oblast', S Russian Federation 53.45N 87.12E
205 R1 **Novolazarevskaya** *Russian research station* Antarctica 70.42S 11.31E
Novolukoml' *see* Novalukoml'
111 V12 **Novo mesto** *Ger.* Rudolfswert; *prev. Ger.* Neustadtl. SE Slovenia 45.48N 15.09E
130 K15 **Novomikhaylovskiy** Krasnodarskiy Kray, SW Russian Federation 44.18N 38.49E
114 L8 **Novo Miloševo** Serbia, N Serbia 45.43N 20.20E
Novomirgorod *see* Novomyrhorod
130 L5 **Novomoskovsk** Tul'skaya Oblast', W Russian Federation 54.04N 38.22E
119 U7 **Novomoskovs'k** *Rus.* Novomoskovsk. Dnipropetrovs'ka Oblast', E Ukraine 48.37N 35.13E
119 V8 **Novomykolayivka** Zaporiz'ka Oblast', SE Ukraine 47.58N 35.54E
119 Q7 **Novomyrhorod** *Rus.* Novomirgorod. Kirovohrads'ka Oblast', S Ukraine 48.46N 31.39E
126 I12 **Novonazimovo** Krasnoyarskiy Kray, C Russian Federation 59.30N 90.45E
131 N8 **Novonikolayevskiy** Volgogradskaya Oblast', SW Russian Federation 50.55N 42.24E
131 P10 **Novonikol'skoye** Volgogradskaya Oblast', SW Russian Federation 49.23N 45.06E
131 X7 **Novoorsk** Orenburgskaya Oblast', W Russian Federation 51.21N 59.03E
130 M13 **Novopokrovskaya** Krasnodarskiy Kray, SW Russian Federation 45.58N 40.43E
Novopolotsk *see* Navapolatsk
119 Y5 **Novopskov** Luhans'ka Oblast', E Ukraine 49.33N 39.07E
Novoradomsk *see* Radomsko
Novo Redondo *see* Sumbe
131 R8 **Novorepnoye** Saratovskaya Oblast', W Russian Federation 51.04N 48.34E
130 K14 **Novorossiysk** Krasnodarskiy Kray, SW Russian Federation 44.49N 37.38E
Novorossiyskiy/ Novorossiyskoye *see* Akzhar
126 Jj6 **Novorybnaya** Taymyrskiy (Dolgano-Nenetskiy) Avtonomnyy Okrug, N Russian Federation 72.48N 105.49E
128 F15 **Novorzhev** Pskovskaya Oblast', W Russian Federation 57.01N 29.19E
Novoselitsa *see* Novoselytsya
119 S12 **Novoselivs'ke** Respublika Krym, S Ukraine 45.26N 33.37E
Novosël'ki *see* Navasyolki
116 G6 **Novo Selo** Vidin, NW Bulgaria 44.08N 22.48E
115 M14 **Novo Selo** Serbia, C Serbia 43.39N 20.54E
118 K8 **Novoselytsya** *Rom.* Nouă Sulița, *Rus.* Novoselitsa. Chernivets'ka Oblast', W Ukraine 48.13N 26.18E
131 U7 **Novosergiyevka** Orenburgskaya Oblast', W Russian Federation 52.04N 53.40E
130 L11 **Novoshakhtinsk** Rostovskaya Oblast', SW Russian Federation 47.48N 39.51E
126 Gg14 **Novosibirsk** Novosibirskaya Oblast', C Russian Federation 55.04N 83.04E
125 G13 **Novosibirskaya Oblast'** ◐ *province* C Russian Federation
126 M4 **Novosibirskiye Ostrova** *Eng.* New Siberian Islands. *island group* N Russian Federation
130 K6 **Novosil'** Orlovskaya Oblast', W Russian Federation 53.00N 37.59E
128 G16 **Novosokol'niki** Pskovskaya Oblast', W Russian Federation 56.21N 30.07E
131 Q6 **Novospasskoye** Ul'yanovskaya Oblast', W Russian Federation 53.08N 47.48E
131 X8 **Novotroitsk** Orenburgskaya Oblast', W Russian Federation 51.09N 58.18E
Novotroitskoye *see* Brlik, Kazakhstan
Novotroitskoye *see* Novotroyits'ke, Ukraine
119 T11 **Novotroyits'ke** *Rus.* Novotroitskoye. Khersons'ka Oblast', S Ukraine 46.21N 34.21E
Novoukrainka *see* Novoukrayinka
119 Q8 **Novoukrayinka** *Rus.* Novoukrainka. Kirovohrads'ka Oblast', C Ukraine 48.19N 31.33E
131 Q5 **Novoul'yanovsk** Ul'yanovskaya Oblast', W Russian Federation 54.10N 48.19E
125 Ee10 **Novoural'skoe** Sverdlovskaya Oblast', W Russian Federation 56.58N 59.50E
131 W8 **Novouralets** Orenburgskaya Oblast', W Russian Federation 51.19N 56.57E
Novo-Urgench *see* Urganch
118 I4 **Novovolyns'k** *Rus.* Novovolynsk. Volyns'ka Oblast', NW Ukraine 50.46N 24.09E
119 S9 **Novovorontsovka** Khersons'ka Oblast', S Ukraine 47.28N 33.55E
153 Y7 **Novovoznesenovka** Issyk-Kul'skaya Oblast', E Kyrgyzstan 42.36N 78.44E
129 R14 **Novovyatsk** Kirovskaya Oblast', NW Russian Federation 58.30N 49.42E
Novoyel'nya *see* Navayel'nya
128 I7 **Novoye Yushkozero** Respublika Kareliya, NW Russian Federation 64.46N 32.13E
119 O6 **Novozhyvotiv** Vinnyts'ka Oblast', C Ukraine 49.16N 29.31E
130 H6 **Novozybkov** Bryanskaya Oblast', W Russian Federation 52.36N 31.58E
114 F9 **Novska** Sisak-Moslavina, NE Croatia 45.20N 16.58E
Nový Bohumín *see* Bohumín
113 D15 **Nový Bor** *Ger.* Haida; *prev.* Bor u České Lípy, Hajda. Liberecký Kraj, N Czech Republic 50.46N 14.32E
113 E16 **Nový Bydžov** *Ger.* Neubidschow. Královéhradecký Kraj, N Czech Republic 50.15N 15.27E
121 G18 **Novy Dvor** *Rus.* Novyy Dvor. Hrodzyenskaya Voblasts', W Belarus 52.49N 24.22E
113 I17 **Nový Jičín** *Ger.* Neutitschein. Moravskoslezský Kraj, E Czech Republic 49.36N 18.00E
120 K12 **Novy Pahost** *Rus.* Novyy Pogost. Vitsyebskaya Voblasts', NW Belarus 55.30N 27.28E
Novyy Bug *see* Novyy Buh
119 R9 **Novyy Buh** *Rus.* Novyy Bug. Mykolayivs'ka Oblast', S Ukraine 47.39N 32.31E
119 Q4 **Novyy Bykiv** Chernihivs'ka Oblast', N Ukraine 50.36N 31.39E
Novyy Dvor *see* Novy Dvor
Novyye Aneny *see* Anenii Noi
131 P7 **Novyye Burasy** Saratovskaya Oblast', W Russian Federation 52.10N 46.00E
Novyy Margilan *see* Farghona
130 K8 **Novyy Oskol** Belgorodskaya Oblast', W Russian Federation 50.43N 37.55E
Novyy Pogost *see* Novy Pahost
131 R2 **Novyy Tor"yal** Respublika Mariy El, W Russian Federation 56.59N 48.53E
126 K14 **Novyy Uoyan** Respublika Buryatiya, S Russian Federation 56.06N 111.27E
126 Gg9 **Novyy Urengoy** Yamalo-Nenetskiy Avtonomnyy Okrug, N Russian Federation 66.06N 76.25E
127 N15 **Novyy Urgal** Khabarovskiy Kray, E Russian Federation 51.02N 132.45E
Novyy Uzen' *see* Zhanaozen
125 G12 **Novyy Vasyugan** Tomskaya Oblast', C Russian Federation 58.28N 76.19E
113 N16 **Nowa Dęba** Podkarpackie, SE Poland 50.31N 21.53E
113 G15 **Nowa Ruda** *Ger.* Neurode. Dolnośląskie, SW Poland 50.34N 16.30E
112 F12 **Nowa Sól** *var.* Nowasól, *Ger.* Neusalz an der Oder. Lubuskie, W Poland 51.47N 15.42E
29 Q8 **Nowata** Oklahoma, C USA 36.42N 95.38W
148 M6 **Nowbarān** Markazī, W Iran 35.07N 49.51E
112 J8 **Nowe** Kujawski-pomorskie, C Poland 53.39N 18.44E
112 K9 **Nowe Miasto Lubawskie** *Ger.* Neumark. Warmińsko-Mazurskie, NE Poland 53.24N 19.36E
112 L13 **Nowe Miasto nad Pilicą** Mazowieckie, C Poland 51.37N 20.34E
112 D8 **Nowe Warpno** *Ger.* Neuwarp. Zachodnio-pomorskie, NW Poland 53.52N 14.12E
Nowgong *see* Nagaon
112 E8 **Nowogard** *var.* Nowógard, *Ger.* Naugard. Zachodnio-pomorskie, NW Poland 53.41N 15.09E
112 N9 **Nowogród** Podlaskie, NE Poland 53.14N 21.52E
Nowogródek *see* Navahrudak
113 E14 **Nowogrodziec** *Ger.* Naumburg am Queis. Dolnośląskie, SW Poland 51.12N 15.24E
Nowojelnia *see* Navayel'nya
Nowo-Minsk *see* Mińsk Mazowiecki
35 V13 **Nowood River** ≈ Wyoming, C USA
Nowo-Święciany *see* Švenčionėliai
191 S10 **Nowra-Bomaderry** New South Wales, SE Australia 34.51S 150.41E
155 T5 **Nowshera** *var.* Naushahra, Naushara. North-West Frontier Province, NE Pakistan 34.00N 72.00E
112 J7 **Nowy Dwór Gdański** *Ger.* Tiegenhof. Pomorskie, N Poland 54.12N 19.03E
112 L11 **Nowy Dwór Mazowiecki** Mazowieckie, C Poland 52.25N 20.43E
113 M17 **Nowy Sącz** *Ger.* Neu Sandec. Małopolskie, S Poland 49.36N 20.41E
113 L18 **Nowy Targ** *Ger.* Neumark. Małopolskie, S Poland 49.28N 20.00E
112 F11 **Nowy Tomyśl** *var.* Nowy Tomysl. Wielkolpolskie, C Poland 52.18N 16.07E
154 M7 **Now Zād** *var.* Nauzad. Helmand, S Afghanistan 32.22N 64.31E
25 N4 **Noxubee River** ≈ Alabama/ Mississippi, S USA
126 Gg10 **Noyabr'sk** Yamalo-Nenetskiy Avtonomnyy Okrug, N Russian Federation 63.08N 75.19E
104 L8 **Noyant** Maine-et-Loire, NW France 47.28N 0.08W
41 X14 **Noyes Island** *island* Alexander Archipelago, Alaska, USA
105 O3 **Noyon** Oise, N France 49.35N 3.00E
104 I7 **Nozay** Loire-Atlantique, NW France 47.34N 1.36W
84 L12 **Nsando** Northern, NE Zambia 10.22S 31.14E
85 N16 **Nsanje** Southern, S Malawi 16.57S 35.10E
79 P17 **Nsawam** SE Ghana 5.46N 0.19W
81 E16 **Nsimalen** ✕ Centre, C Cameroon 19.15N 81.22W

◆ Country ● Country Capital ◇ Dependent Territory ○ Dependent Territory Capital ◐ Administrative Region ✕ International Airport ▲ Mountain ▲ Mountain Range ⩕ Volcano ≈ River ⊛ Lake ⊠ Reservoir

Nsombo – Ōgaki

84 K12 Nsombo Northern, NE Zambia 10.35S 29.58E
84 H13 Ntambu North Western, NW Zambia 12.22S 24.57E
85 N14 Ntcheu var. Ncheu. Central, S Malawi 14.49S 34.37E
81 D17 Ntem prev. Campo, Kampo. ~ Cameroon/Equatorial Guinea
85 I14 Ntemwa North Western, NW Zambia 14.03S 26.13E
Ntlenyana, Mount see Thabana Ntlenyana
81 I19 Ntomba, Lac var. Lac Tumba. ◎ NW Dem. Rep. Congo
117 I19 Ntóro, Kávo prev. Akrotírio Kafiréas. headland Évvoia, C Greece 38.10N 24.35E
83 E19 Ntungamo SW Uganda 0.54S 30.16E
83 E18 Ntusi SW Uganda 0.03N 31.11E
85 H18 Ntwetwe Pan salt lake NE Botswana
95 M15 Nuasjärvi ◎ C Finland
82 F11 Nuba Mountains ▲ C Sudan
70 I9 Nubian Desert desert NE Sudan
118 G10 Nucet Hung. Diófás. Bihor, W Romania 46.28N 22.34E
Nu Chiang see Salween
151 U9 Nuclear Testing Ground nuclear site Pavlodar, E Kazakhstan
58 E9 Nucuray, Río ~ N Peru
27 R14 Nueces River ~ Texas, SW USA
9 V9 Nueltin Lake ◎ Manitoba/Nunavut, C Canada
101 K15 Nuenen Noord-Brabant, S Netherlands 51.29N 5.36E
64 G6 Nuestra Señora, Bahía bay N Chile
63 D14 Nuestra Señora Rosario de Caa Catí Corrientes, NE Argentina 27.48S 57.42W
56 J9 Nueva Antioquia Vichada, E Colombia 6.04N 69.30W
Nueva Caceres see Naga
43 O7 Nueva Ciudad Guerrera Tamaulipas, C Mexico 26.32N 99.13W
57 N4 Nueva Esparta off. Estado Nueva Esparta. ◆ state NE Venezuela
46 C5 Nueva Gerona Isla de la Juventud, S Cuba 21.49N 82.49W
44 H8 Nueva Guadalupe San Miguel, E El Salvador 13.30N 88.21W
44 M11 Nueva Guinea Región Autónoma Atlántico Sur, SE Nicaragua 11.40N 84.22W
63 D19 Nueva Helvecia Colonia, SW Uruguay 34.16S 57.52W
65 J25 Nueva, Isla island S Chile
42 M14 Nueva Italia Michoacán de Ocampo, SW Mexico 19.01N 102.06W
58 D6 Nueva Loja var. Lago Agrio. Sucumbíos, NE Ecuador
44 F6 Nueva Ocotepeque prev. Ocotepeque. Ocotepeque, W Honduras 14.25N 89.11W
63 D19 Nueva Palmira Colonia, SW Uruguay 33.52S 58.25W
43 N6 Nueva Rosita Coahuila de Zaragoza, NE Mexico 27.58N 101.10W
44 E7 Nueva San Salvador prev. Santa Tecla. La Libertad, SW El Salvador 13.42N 89.18W
44 J8 Nueva Segovia ◆ department NW Nicaragua
Nueva Tabarca see Plana, Isla
Nueva Villa de Padilla see Nuevo Padilla
63 B21 Nueve de Julio Buenos Aires, E Argentina 35.29S 60.52W
46 H6 Nuevitas Camagüey, E Cuba 21.34N 77.18W
63 D18 Nuevo Berlín Río Negro, W Uruguay 32.58S 58.03W
42 I4 Nuevo Casas Grandes Chihuahua, N Mexico 30.23N 107.53W
45 T14 Nuevo Chagres Colón, C Panama 9.13N 80.03W
43 W15 Nuevo Coahuila Campeche, E Mexico 17.52N 90.46W
65 K17 Nuevo, Golfo gulf S Argentina
43 O7 Nuevo Laredo Tamaulipas, NE Mexico 27.27N 99.31W
43 N8 Nuevo León ◆ state NE Mexico
43 P10 Nuevo Padilla var. Nueva Villa de Padilla. Tamaulipas, C Mexico 24.01N 98.48W
58 E6 Nuevo Rocafuerte Orellana, E Ecuador 0.55S 75.25W
Nuga see Dzavhanmandal
82 O13 Nugaal off. Gobolka Nugaal. ◆ region N Somalia
193 E24 Nugget Point headland South Island, NZ 46.26S 169.49E
195 R9 Nuguria Islands island group E PNG
192 P10 Nuhaka Hawke's Bay, North Island, NZ 39.03S 177.43E
144 M10 Nuhaydayn, Wādī an dry watercourse W Iraq
202 E7 Nui Atoll atoll W Tuvalu
Nu Jiang see Salween
Nûk see Nuuk
190 G7 Nukey Bluff hill South Australia 32.34S 135.36E
Nukha see Şäki
127 O9 Nukh Yablonevyy, Gora ▲ E Russian Federation 60.26N 151.45E
195 T13 Nukiki Choiseul Island, NW Solomon Islands 6.45S 94.30E
194 F10 Nuku Sandaun, NW PNG 3.40S 142.29E
200 R15 Nuku island Tongatapu Group, NE Tonga
200 Qq15 Nuku'alofa Tongatapu, S Tonga 21.09S 175.13W
200 Qq15 Nuku'alofa ● (Tonga) Tongatapu, S Tonga 21.07S 175.13W
202 G12 Nukuatea island N Wallis and Futuna
202 F7 Nukufetau Atoll atoll C Tuvalu
202 G12 Nukuhifala island E Wallis and Futuna
203 W7 Nuku Hiva island Îles Marquises, NE French Polynesia
199 I19 Nuku Hiva Island island Îles Marquises, N French Polynesia
202 F9 Nukulaelae Atoll var. Nukulailai. atoll E Tuvalu
Nukulailai see Nukulaelae Atoll
202 G11 Nukuloa island N Wallis and Futuna
195 W10 Nukumanu Islands prev. Tasman Group. island group NE PNG
Nukunau see Nikunau
202 J9 Nukunonu Atoll island C Tokelau
202 J9 Nukunonu Village Nukunonu Atoll, C Tokelau
201 S18 Nukuoro Atoll atoll Caroline Islands, S Micronesia
152 H8 Nukus Qoraqalpog'iston Respublikasi, W Uzbekistan 42.28N 59.32E
202 G11 Nukutapu island N Wallis and Futuna
41 O9 Nulato Alaska, USA 64.43N 158.06W
41 O10 Nulato Hills ▲ Alaska, USA
107 T9 Nules País Valenciano, E Spain 39.52N 0.10W
Nuling see Sultan Kudarat
190 C6 Nullarbor South Australia 31.28S 130.57E
188 M11 Nullarbor Plain plateau South Australia/Western Australia
169 S12 Nulu'erhu Shan ▲ N China
79 X14 Numan Adamawa, E Nigeria 9.26N 11.58E
171 K14 Numata Gunma, Honshū, S Japan 36.39N 139.00E
172 Oo4 Numata Hokkaidō, NE Japan 43.48N 141.55E
83 C15 Numatinna ~ W Sudan
171 J17 Numazu Shizuoka, Honshū, S Japan 35.05N 138.52E
97 F14 Numedalen valley S Norway
97 G14 Numedalslågen var. Laagen. ~ S Norway
95 L19 Nummela Etelä-Suomi, S Finland 60.21N 24.19E
125 G9 Numto Khanty-Mansiyskiy Avtonomnyy Okrug, N Russian Federation 63.33N 70.53E
191 O11 Numurkah Victoria, SE Australia 36.04S 145.28E
206 L16 Nunap Isua var. Uummannarsuaq, Dan. Kap Farvel, Eng. Cape Farewell. headland S Greenland 59.57N 44.27W
15 K5 Nunavut ◆ Territory N Canada
56 H9 Nunchia Casanare, C Colombia 5.37N 72.13W
99 M20 Nuneaton C England, UK 52.31N 1.28W
159 W14 Nungba Manipur, NE India 24.46N 93.25E
40 L12 Nunivak Island island Alaska, USA
158 I5 Nun Kun ▲ NW India 34.01N 76.04E
100 L10 Nunspeet Gelderland, E Netherlands 52.21N 5.45E
109 C18 Nuoro Sardegna, Italy, C Mediterranean Sea 40.19N 9.19E
77 R12 Nuqayy, Jabal hill range S Libya
56 C9 Nuquí Chocó, W Colombia 5.43N 77.16W
149 O4 Nūr Māzandarān, N Iran 36.34N 52.01E
151 Q9 Nura ~ N Kazakhstan
149 N11 Nūrābād Fārs, C Iran 30.07N 51.30E
Nurakita see Niulakita
Nurata see Nurota
Nuratau, Khrebet see Nurota Tizmasi
142 L17 Nur Dağları ▲ S Turkey
Nurek see Norak
Nuremberg see Nürnberg
155 S4 Nūrestān ◆ province C Afghanistan
142 M15 Nurhak Kahramanmaraş, S Turkey 37.57N 37.21E
190 J9 Nuriootpa South Australia 34.28S 139.00E
131 S5 Nurlat Respublika Tatarstan, W Russian Federation 54.26N 50.48E
95 N15 Nurmes Itä-Suomi, E Finland 63.31N 29.10E
103 K20 Nürnberg Eng. Nuremberg. Bayern, S Germany 49.27N 11.04E
103 K20 Nürnberg ✕ Bayern, SE Germany 49.29N 11.04E
152 M10 Nurota Rus. Nurata. Navoiy Viloyati, C Uzbekistan 40.40N 65.43E
153 N10 Nurota Tizmasi Rus. Khrebet Nuratau. ▲ C Uzbekistan
155 T8 Nūrpur Punjab, E Pakistan 31.54N 71.55E
191 P6 Nurri, Mount hill New South Wales, SE Australia 31.42S 146.03E
27 T13 Nursery Texas, SW USA 28.55N 97.04W
175 P16 Nusa Tenggara Eng. Lesser Sunda Islands. island group East Timor/ Indonesia
175 O15 Nusa Tenggara Barat off. Propinsi Nusa Tenggara Barat, Eng. West Nusa Tenggara. ◆ province S Indonesia
175 Q17 Nusa Tenggara Timur off. Propinsi Nusa Tenggara Timur, Eng. East Nusa Tenggara. ◆ province S Indonesia
176 Vv12 Nusawulan Papua, E Indonesia 4.03S 132.56E
143 Q16 Nusaybin var. Nisibin. Manisa, SE Turkey 37.07N 41.10E
41 O14 Nushagak Bay bay Alaska, USA
41 O13 Nushagak Peninsula headland Alaska, USA 58.39N 159.03W
41 O13 Nushagak River ~ Alaska, USA
166 E11 Nu Shan ▲ SW China
155 N11 Nushki Baluchistān, SW Pakistan 29.33N 66.01E
Nussdorf see Năsăud
114 J9 Nuštar Vukovar-Srijem, E Croatia 45.20N 18.48E
101 L18 Nuth Limburg, SE Netherlands 50.55N 5.52E
102 N13 Nuthe ~ NE Germany
Nutmeg State see Connecticut
41 T10 Nutzotin Mountains ▲ Alaska, USA
66 I5 Nuuk var. Nûk, Dan. Godthaab, Godthåb. ○ (Greenland). Kitaa, SW Greenland 64.15N 51.34W
94 L13 Nuupas Lappi, NW Finland 66.01N 26.19E
203 O7 Nuupere, Pointe headland Moorea, W French Polynesia 17.34S 149.46W
203 O7 Nuuroa, Pointe headland Tahiti, W French Polynesia
Nüürst see Baganuur
Nuwara see Nuwara Eliya
161 K25 Nuwara Eliya var. Nuwara. Central Province, S Sri Lanka 6.58N 80.46E
190 E7 Nuyts Archipelago island group South Australia
85 F17 Nxaunxau North-West, NW Botswana 18.57S 21.18E
41 N12 Nyac Alaska, USA 61.00N 159.56W
125 Ff10 Nyagan' Khanty-Mansiyskiy Avtonomnyy Okrug, N Russian Federation 62.10N 65.32E
Nyagassola see Niagassola
Nyagquka see Yajiang
83 I18 Nyahururu Central, W Kenya 0.04N 36.22E
190 M10 Nyah West Victoria, SE Australia 35.14S 143.18E
164 M15 Nyainqêntanglha Feng ▲ W China 30.20N 90.28E
165 N15 Nyainqêntanglha Shan ▲ W China
82 B11 Nyala Southern Darfur, W Sudan 12.01N 24.49E
85 M16 Nyamapanda Mashonaland East, NE Zimbabwe 16.57S 32.51E
83 H25 Nyamtumbo Ruvuma, S Tanzania 10.33S 36.07E
Nyanda see Masvingo
128 M11 Nyandoma Arkhangel'skaya Oblast', NW Russian Federation 61.39N 40.09E
85 M16 Nyanga prev. Inyanga. Manicaland, E Zimbabwe 18.14S 32.42E
81 D20 Nyanga off. Province de la Nyanga, var. La Nyanga. ◆ province SW Gabon
81 E20 Nyanga ~ Congo/Gabon
83 F20 Nyantakara Kagera, NW Tanzania 3.04S 31.22E
83 G19 Nyanza ◆ province W Kenya
83 E21 Nyanza-Lac S Burundi 4.16S 29.38E
70 J14 Nyasa, Lake var. Lake Malawi; prev. Lago Nyassa. ◎ E Africa
Nyasaland/Nyasaland Protectorate see Malawi
Nyassa, Lago see Nyasa, Lake
121 J17 Nyasvizh Pol. Nieśwież, Rus. Nesvizh. Minskaya Voblasts', C Belarus 53.13N 26.40E
177 G8 Nyaunglebin Pegu, SW Burma 17.58N 96.43E
177 G5 Nyaung-u Magwe, C Burma 21.03N 95.43E
97 H24 Nyborg Fyn, C Denmark 55.19N 10.48E
97 N21 Nybro Kalmar, S Sweden 56.45N 15.54E
121 J16 Nyeharelaye Rus. Negoreloye. Minskaya Voblasts', C Belarus 53.36N 27.05E
205 W3 Nye Mountains ▲ Antarctica
83 I19 Nyeri Central, C Kenya 0.25S 36.55E
120 M11 Nyeshcharda, Vozyera ◎ N Belarus
94 O2 Ny-Friesland physical region N Svalbard
97 L14 Nyhammar Dalarna, C Sweden 60.19N 14.55E
166 F7 Nyikog Qu ~ C China
164 L14 Nyima Xizang Zizhiqu, W China 31.53N 87.50E
85 L14 Nyimba Eastern, E Zambia 14.33S 30.49E
165 P16 Nyingchi var. Pula. Xizang Zizhiqu, W China 29.34N 94.22E
Nyinma see Maqu
113 O21 Nyírbátor Szabolcs-Szatmár-Bereg, E Hungary 47.49N 22.06E
113 N21 Nyíregyháza Szabolcs-Szatmár-Bereg, NE Hungary 47.57N 21.43E
Nyiro see Ewaso Ng'iro
Nyitra see Nitra
Nyitrabánya see Handlová
95 K16 Nykarleby Fin. Uusikaarlepyy. Länsi-Suomi, W Finland 63.22N 22.30E
97 I25 Nykøbing Storstrøm, SE Denmark 54.46N 11.52E
97 J22 Nykøbing Vestsjælland, C Denmark 55.55N 11.40E
97 F21 Nykøbing Viborg, NW Denmark 56.48N 8.52E
97 N17 Nyköping Södermanland, S Sweden 58.45N 17.03E
97 L15 Nykroppa Värmland, C Sweden 59.37N 14.18E
Nylstroom see Modimolle
191 P7 Nymagee New South Wales, SE Australia 32.06S 146.19E
191 V5 Nymboida New South Wales, SE Australia 29.57S 152.45E
191 U5 Nymboida River ~ New South Wales, SE Australia
113 D16 Nymburk var. Neuenburg an der Elbe, Ger. Nimburg. Středočeský Kraj, C Czech Republic 50.12N 15.00E
97 O16 Nynäshamn Stockholm, C Sweden 58.54N 17.55E
191 Q6 Nyngan New South Wales, SE Australia 31.36S 147.07E
Nyoman see Neman
110 A10 Nyon Ger. Neuss; anc. Noviodunum. Vaud, SW Switzerland 46.22N 6.15E
81 D16 Nyong ~ SW Cameroon
105 S14 Nyons Drôme, E France 44.22N 5.06E
81 D14 Nyos, Lac Eng. Lake Nyos. ◎ NW Cameroon
Nyos, Lake see Nyos, Lac
129 U11 Nyrob var. Nyrov. Permskaya Oblast', NW Russian Federation 60.41N 56.42E
Nyrov see Nyrob
113 H15 Nysa Ger. Neisse. Opolskie, S Poland 50.28N 17.20E
Nysa Łużycka see Neisse
Nyslott see Savonlinna
34 M13 Nyssa Oregon, NW USA 43.52N 116.59W
Nystad see Uusikaupunki
97 I25 Nysted Storstrøm, SE Denmark 54.40N 11.41E
129 U14 Nytva Permskaya Oblast', NW Russian Federation 57.56N 55.22E
171 L19 Nyūdō-zaki headland Honshū, C Japan 39.59N 139.40E
129 P9 Nyukhcha Arkhangel'skaya Oblast', NW Russian Federation 63.24N 46.34E
128 H8 Nyuk, Ozero var. Ozero Njuk. ◎ NW Russian Federation
129 O12 Nyuksenitsa var. Njuksenica. Vologodskaya Oblast', NW Russian Federation 60.25N 44.12E
81 O22 Nyunzu Katanga, SE Dem. Rep. Congo 5.55S 28.00E
126 Kk11 Nyurba Respublika Sakha (Yakutiya), NE Russian Federation 63.17N 118.14E
126 Kk12 Nyuya Respublika Sakha (Yakutiya), NE Russian Federation 60.33N 116.10E
126 K12 Nyuya ~ NE Russian Federation
152 K12 Nyýazow Rus. Niyazov. Lebap Welaýaty, NE Turkmenistan 39.13N 63.16E
119 T10 Nyzhni Sirohozy Khersons'ka Oblast', S Ukraine 46.49N 34.21E
119 U12 Nyzhn'ohirs'kyy Rus. Nizhnegorskiy. Respublika Krym, S Ukraine 45.26N 34.42E
83 G21 Nzega Tabora, C Tanzania 4.13S 33.10E
78 K15 Nzérékoré SE Guinea 7.45N 8.49W
84 A10 N'Zeto prev. Ambrizete. Zaire, NW Angola 7.13S 12.52E
81 M24 Nzilo, Lac prev. Lac Delcommune. ◎ SE Dem. Rep. Congo

O

31 O11 Oacoma South Dakota, N USA 43.49N 99.25W
31 N9 Oahe Dam dam South Dakota, N USA 44.27N 100.24W
30 M9 Oahe, Lake ⊟ North Dakota/ South Dakota, N USA
40 C9 O'ahu var. Oahu island Hawai'i, USA, C Pacific Ocean
172 Qq6 O-Akan-dake ▲ Hokkaidō, NE Japan 43.26N 144.09E
190 K8 Oakbank South Australia 33.07S 140.36E
21 P13 Oak Bluffs Martha's Vineyard, New York, NE USA 41.25N 70.32W
38 K4 Oak City Utah, W USA 39.22N 112.19W
39 R3 Oak Creek Colorado, C USA 40.16N 106.57W
37 P8 Oakdale California, W USA 37.46N 120.51W
24 H8 Oakdale Louisiana, S USA 30.49N 92.39W
31 P7 Oakes North Dakota, N USA 46.08N 98.05W
24 J4 Oak Grove Louisiana, S USA 32.51N 91.25W
99 N19 Oakham C England, UK 52.40N 0.45W
34 H7 Oak Harbor Washington, NW USA 48.17N 122.38W
23 R5 Oak Hill West Virginia, NE USA 37.59N 81.09W
37 N8 Oakland California, W USA 37.48N 122.16W
31 T15 Oakland Iowa, C USA 41.18N 95.22W
21 Q7 Oakland Maine, NE USA 44.32N 69.43W
23 T3 Oakland Maryland, NE USA 39.24N 79.24W
31 R14 Oakland Nebraska, C USA 41.50N 96.28W
33 N11 Oak Lawn Illinois, N USA 41.43N 87.45W
35 P16 Oakley Idaho, NW USA 42.13N 113.54W
28 I4 Oakley Kansas, C USA 39.06N 100.51W
33 N10 Oak Park Illinois, N USA 41.53N 87.46W
9 X16 Oak Point Manitoba, S Canada 50.23N 97.00W
34 G13 Oakridge Oregon, NW USA 43.45N 122.27W
22 M9 Oak Ridge Tennessee, S USA 36.01N 84.12W
192 K10 Oakura Taranaki, North Island, NZ 39.07S 173.58E
24 L7 Oak Vale Mississippi, S USA 31.26N 89.57W
12 G16 Oakville Ontario, S Canada 43.27N 79.40W
27 V8 Oakwood Texas, SW USA 31.34N 95.51W
193 F22 Oamaru Otago, South Island, NZ 45.10S 170.51E
98 F13 Oa, Mull of headland W Scotland, UK 55.35N 6.20W
175 Q7 Oan Sulawesi, N Indonesia 1.16N 121.25E
193 J17 Oaro Canterbury, South Island, NZ 42.29S 173.30E
37 X2 Oasis Nevada, W USA 41.01N 114.29W
205 S15 Oates Land physical region Antarctica
191 P17 Oatlands Tasmania, SE Australia 42.21S 147.23E
38 I11 Oatman Arizona, SW USA 35.03N 114.19W
43 R16 Oaxaca var. Oaxaca de Juárez; prev. Antequera. Oaxaca, SE Mexico 17.04N 96.40W
43 Q16 Oaxaca ◆ state SE Mexico
Oaxaca de Juárez see Oaxaca
125 G8 Ob' ~ C Russian Federation
12 G9 Obabika Lake ◎ Ontario, S Canada
Obagan see Ubagan
120 M12 Obal' Rus. Obol'. Vitsyebskaya Voblasts', N Belarus 55.22N 29.16E
81 E16 Obala Centre, SW Cameroon 4.09N 11.31E
12 C6 Oba Lake ◎ Ontario, S Canada
171 H14 Obama Fukui, Honshū, SW Japan 35.29N 135.42E
98 H11 Oban W Scotland, UK 56.25N 5.29W
Oban see Halfmoon Bay
171 Ll12 Obanazawa Yamagata, Honshū, C Japan 38.40N 140.21E
Obando see Puerto Inírida
106 I4 O Barco var. El Barco, El Barco de Valdeorras, O Barco de Valdeorras. Galicia, NW Spain 42.24N 7.00W
O Barco de Valdeorras see O Barco
Obbia see Hobyo
95 J16 Obbola Västerbotten, N Sweden 63.42N 20.18E
Obbrovazzo see Obrovac
Obchuga see Abchuha
Obdorsk see Salekhard
Óbecse see Bečej
120 I11 Obeliai Panevėžys, NE Lithuania 55.57N 25.47E
62 F13 Oberá Misiones, NE Argentina 27.28S 55.07W
110 E8 Oberburg Bern, W Switzerland 47.00N 7.37E
111 Q9 Oberdrauburg Salzburg, S Austria 46.45N 12.59E
Oberglogau see Głogówek
111 W4 Ober Grafendorf Niederösterreich, NE Austria 48.09N 15.33E
103 E15 Oberhausen Nordrhein-Westfalen, W Germany 51.28N 6.52E
Oberhollabrunn see Tulln
Oberlaibach see Vrhnika
103 Q15 Oberlausitz Lus. Hornja Łužica. physical region E Germany
28 J2 Oberlin Kansas, C USA 39.48N 100.31W
24 H8 Oberlin Louisiana, S USA 30.37N 92.45W
33 T11 Oberlin Ohio, N USA 41.17N 82.13W
105 U5 Obernai Bas-Rhin, NE France 48.28N 7.30E
111 R4 Obernberg-am-Inn Oberösterreich, N Austria 48.19N 13.20E
Oberndorf see Oberndorf am Neckar
103 G23 Oberndorf am Neckar var. Oberndorf. Baden-Württemberg, SW Germany 48.18N 8.32E
111 Q5 Oberndorf bei Salzburg Salzburg, W Austria 47.57N 12.57E
Oberneustadtl see Kysucké Nové Mesto
191 S8 Oberon New South Wales, SE Australia 33.42S 149.50E
111 Q4 Oberösterreich off. Land Oberösterreich, Eng. Upper Austria. ◆ state NW Austria
Oberpahlen see Põltsamaa
103 M19 Oberpfälzer Wald ▲ SE Germany
111 Y6 Oberpullendorf Burgenland, E Austria 47.32N 16.30E
Oberradkersburg see Gornja Radgona
103 G18 Oberursel Hessen, W Germany 50.12N 8.34E
111 Q8 Obervellach Salzburg, S Austria 46.56N 13.10E
111 X7 Oberwart Burgenland, SE Austria 47.18N 16.12E
Oberwischau see Vişeu de Sus
111 T7 Oberwölz var. Oberwölz-Stadt. Steiermark, SE Austria 47.12N 14.20E
Oberwölz-Stadt see Oberwölz
33 S13 Obetz Ohio, N USA 39.52N 82.57W
Ob', Gulf of see Obskaya Guba
56 G8 Obia Santander, C Colombia 6.16N 73.18W
60 H12 Óbidos Pará, NE Brazil 1.52S 55.30W
106 F10 Óbidos Leiria, C Portugal 39.21N 9.09W
Obidovichi see Abidavichy
153 Q13 Obigarm W Tajikistan 38.42N 69.34E
172 P7 Obihiro Hokkaidō, NE Japan 42.55N 143.09E
Obi-Khingou see Khingov
153 P13 Obikiik SW Tajikistan 38.07N 68.36E
115 N16 Obilić Serbia, S Serbia 42.50N 20.57E
131 O12 Obil'noye Respublika Kalmykiya, SW Russian Federation 47.31N 44.24E
22 F8 Obion Tennessee, S USA 36.15N 89.11W
22 F8 Obion River ~ Tennessee, S USA
175 T9 Obi, Pulau island Maluku, E Indonesia
172 Oo4 Obira Hokkaidō, NE Japan 44.01N 141.39E
175 T9 Obi, Selat strait Maluku, E Indonesia
131 N11 Oblivskaya Rostovskaya Oblast', SW Russian Federation 48.34N 42.31E
127 N16 Obluch'ye Yevreyskaya Avtonomnaya Oblast', SE Russian Federation 48.59N 131.18E
130 K4 Obninsk Kaluzhskaya Oblast', W Russian Federation 55.06N 36.40E
116 J8 Obnova Pleven, N Bulgaria 43.26N 25.04E
81 N15 Obo Haut-Mbomou, E Central African Republic 5.20N 26.28E
165 T9 Obo Qinghai, C China 37.57N 101.03E
82 M11 Obock E Djibouti 11.57N 43.09E
Obol' see Obal'
Obolyanka see Abalyanka
176 Vv11 Obome Papua, E Indonesia 3.42S 133.21E
112 G11 Oborniki Wielkolpolskie, C Poland 52.38N 16.48E
81 G19 Obouya Cuvette, C Congo 0.55S 15.40E
130 J8 Oboyan' Kurskaya Oblast', W Russian Federation 51.12N 36.15E
128 M9 Obozerskiy Arkhangel'skaya Oblast', NW Russian Federation 63.26N 40.20E
114 L11 Obrenovac Serbia, N Serbia 44.39N 20.12E
114 D12 Obrovac It. Obbrovazzo. Zadar, SW Croatia 44.12N 15.40E
Obrovo see Abrova
37 Q3 Observation Peak ▲ California, W USA 40.48N 120.07W
126 H7 Obskaya Guba Eng. Gulf of Ob'. gulf N Russian Federation
181 N13 Ob' Tablemount undersea feature S Indian Ocean 50.16S 51.59E
181 T10 Ob' Trench undersea feature E Indian Ocean
79 P16 Obuasi S Ghana 6.15N 1.36W
119 P5 Obukhiv Rus. Obukhov. Kyyivs'ka Oblast', N Ukraine 50.05N 30.37E
Obukhov see Obukhiv
129 U14 Obva ~ NW Russian Federation
119 V10 Obytichna Kosa spit SE Ukraine
119 V10 Obytichna Zatoka gulf SE Ukraine
107 O3 Oca ~ N Spain
25 W10 Ocala Florida, SE USA 29.11N 82.08W
42 M7 Ocampo Coahuila de Zaragoza, NE Mexico 27.18N 102.24W
56 G7 Ocaña Norte de Santander, N Colombia 8.16N 73.21W
107 N9 Ocaña Castilla-La Mancha, C Spain 39.57N 3.30W
106 H4 O Carballiño Cast. Carballiño Galicia, NW Spain 42.25N 8.04W
39 T9 Ocate New Mexico, SW USA 36.09N 105.03W
Ocavango see Okavango
56 D14 Occidental, Cordillera ▲ W Colombia
59 D14 Occidental, Cordillera ▲ W S America
23 Q6 Oceana West Virginia, NE USA 37.41N 81.37W
23 Z4 Ocean City Maryland, NE USA 38.20N 75.05W
20 J17 Ocean City New Jersey, NE USA 39.15N 74.33W
8 K15 Ocean Falls British Columbia, SW Canada 52.24N 127.42W
Ocean Island see Kure Atoll
Ocean Island see Banaba
66 J9 Oceanographer Fracture Zone tectonic feature NW Atlantic Ocean
37 U17 Oceanside California, W USA 33.12N 117.22W
24 M9 Ocean Springs Mississippi, S USA 30.24N 88.49W
Ocean State see Rhode Island
27 O9 O C Fisher Lake ⊟ Texas, SW USA
119 Q10 Ochakiv Rus. Ochakov. Mykolayivs'ka Oblast', S Ukraine 46.36N 31.33E
Ochakov see Ochakiv
Ochamchira see Och'amch'ire
143 Q9 Och'amch'ire Rus. Ochamchira. W Georgia 42.45N 41.30E
Ochansk see Okhansk
129 T15 Ocher Permskaya Oblast', NW Russian Federation 57.54N 54.40E
117 I19 Óchi ▲ Évvoia, C Greece 38.03N 24.27E
172 R8 Ochiishi-misaki headland Hokkaidō, NE Japan 43.10N 145.29E
25 S9 Ochlockonee River ~ Florida/ Georgia, SE USA
46 K12 Ocho Rios C Jamaica 18.24N 77.06W
Ochrida see Ohrid
Ochrida, Lake see Ohrid, Lake
103 J19 Ochsenfurt Bayern, C Germany 49.39N 10.03E
25 U7 Ocilla Georgia, SE USA 31.35N 83.15W
96 N13 Ockelbo Gävleborg, C Sweden 60.51N 16.46E
Ocker see Oker
97 I19 Öckerö Västra Götaland, S Sweden 57.43N 11.39E
25 U6 Ocmulgee River ~ Georgia, SE USA
118 H11 Ocna Mureş Hung. Marosújvár; prev. Ocna Mureşului; prev. Hung. Marosújvárakna. Alba, C Romania 46.25N 23.52E
Ocna Mureşului see Ocna Mureş
118 H11 Ocna Sibiului Ger. Salzburg, Hung. Vizakna. Sibiu, C Romania 45.52N 23.59E
118 H13 Ocnele Mari prev. Vioara. Vâlcea, S Romania 45.03N 24.18E
118 L7 Ocniţa Rus. Oknitsa. N Moldova 48.25N 27.30E
25 U4 Oconee, Lake ⊟ Georgia, SE USA
25 U5 Oconee River ~ Georgia, SE USA
32 M9 Oconomowoc Wisconsin, N USA 43.06N 88.29W
32 M6 Oconto Wisconsin, N USA 44.55N 87.52W
32 M6 Oconto Falls Wisconsin, N USA 44.52N 88.06W
32 M6 Oconto River ~ Wisconsin, N USA
106 I3 O Corgo Galicia, NW Spain 42.55N 7.25W
43 V16 Ocosingo Chiapas, SE Mexico 16.51N 92.06W
44 J8 Ocotal Nueva Segovia, NW Nicaragua 13.38N 86.27W
44 F6 Ocotepeque ◆ department W Honduras
Ocotepeque see Nueva Ocotepeque
42 L13 Ocotlán Jalisco, SW Mexico 20.18N 102.45W
43 R16 Ocotlán var. Ocotlán de Morelos. Oaxaca, SE Mexico 16.49N 96.49W
Ocotlán de Morelos see Ocotlán
43 U16 Ocozocuautla Chiapas, SE Mexico 16.43N 93.19W
23 Y10 Ocracoke Island island North Carolina, SE USA
104 I3 Octeville Manche, N France 49.37N 1.39W
October Revolution Island see Oktyabr'skoy Revolyutsii, Ostrov
45 R17 Ocú Herrera, S Panama 7.55N 80.47W
85 Q14 Ocua Cabo Delgado, NE Mozambique 13.37S 39.44E
Ocumare see Ocumare del Tuy
56 M5 Ocumare del Tuy var. Ocumare. Miranda, N Venezuela 10.07N 66.46W
79 P17 Oda SE Ghana 5.54N 1.01W
170 F12 Ōda var. Oda. Shimane, Honshū, SW Japan 35.09N 132.31E
94 K3 Ódádhahraun lava flow C Iceland
176 Y14 Odammun ~ Papua, E Indonesia
171 Mm9 Ōdate Akita, Honshū, C Japan 40.18N 140.34E
171 J16 Odawara Kanagawa, Honshū, S Japan 35.13N 139.07E
97 D14 Odda Hordaland, S Norway 60.03N 6.34E
97 G22 Odder Århus, C Denmark 55.58N 10.10E
Oddur see Xuddur
31 T13 Odebolt Iowa, C USA 42.18N 95.15W
106 H14 Odeleite Faro, S Portugal 37.01N 7.28W
27 Q4 Odell Texas, SW USA 34.19N 99.24W
27 T14 Odem Texas, SW USA 27.57N 97.34W
106 F13 Odemira Beja, S Portugal 37.34N 8.37W
142 C14 Ödemiş İzmir, SW Turkey 38.10N 27.58E
Ödenburg see Sopron
85 I22 Odendaalsrus Free State, C South Africa 27.52S 26.42E
Odenpäh see Otepää
97 H23 Odense Fyn, C Denmark 55.24N 10.22E
103 H19 Odenwald ▲ W Germany
86 H10 Oder Cz./Pol. Odra. ~ C Europe
Oderberg see Bohumín
102 P11 Oderbruch wetland Germany/ Poland
Oderhaff see Szczeciński, Zalew
102 O11 Oder-Havel-Kanal canal NE Germany
Oderhellen see Odorheiu Secuiesc
102 P13 Oder-Spree-Kanal canal NE Germany
Odertal see Zdzieszowice
108 I7 Oderzo Veneto, NE Italy 45.48N 12.33E
124 Pp4 Odesa Rus. Odessa. Odes'ka Oblast', SW Ukraine 46.28N 30.43E
Odesa see Odes'ka Oblast'
97 L18 Ödeshög Östergötland, S Sweden 58.13N 14.40E
119 O9 Odes'ka Oblast' var. Odesa, Rus. Odesskaya Oblast'. ◆ province SW Ukraine
26 M8 Odessa Texas, SW USA 31.51N 102.22W
34 K8 Odessa Washington, NW USA 47.19N 118.41W
Odessa see Odesa
Odesskaya Oblast' see Odes'ka Oblast'
125 Ff13 Odesskoye Omskaya Oblast', C Russian Federation 54.15N 72.45E
Odessus see Varna
104 F6 Odet ~ NW France
106 I14 Odiel ~ SW Spain
78 L14 Odienné NW Ivory Coast 9.32N 7.34W
179 Pp12 Odiongan Tablas Island, C Philippines 12.23N 122.01E
118 L12 Odobeşti Vrancea, E Romania 45.46N 27.06E
112 H13 Odolanów Ger. Adelnau. Wielkopolskie, C Poland 51.35N 17.42E
178 J13 Ôdôngk Kâmpóng Spoe, S Cambodia 11.48N 104.45E
27 N6 O'donnell Texas, SW USA 32.57N 101.49W
100 O7 Odoorn Drenthe, NE Netherlands 52.52N 6.49E
Odorhei see Odorheiu Secuiesc
118 J11 Odorheiu Secuiesc Ger. Oderhellen, Hung. Vámosudvarhely; prev. Odorhei; Ger. Hofmarkt. Harghita, C Romania 46.18N 25.17E
Odra see Oder
114 J9 Odžaci Ger. Hodschag, Hung. Hodság. Serbia, NW Serbia 45.31N 19.15E
61 N14 Oeiras Piauí, E Brazil 7.00S 42.07W
106 F11 Oeiras Lisboa, C Portugal 38.40N 9.18W
103 G14 Oelde Nordrhein-Westfalen, W Germany 51.49N 8.09E
30 J11 Oelrichs South Dakota, N USA 43.08N 103.13W
Oels/Oels in Schlesien see Oleśnica
103 M17 Oelsnitz Sachsen, E Germany 50.22N 12.12E
31 X12 Oelwein Iowa, C USA 42.40N 91.54W
Oeniadae see Oiniádes
203 N17 Oeno Island atoll Pitcairn Islands, C Pacific Ocean
Oesel see Saaremaa
110 L7 Oetz var. Ötz. Tirol, W Austria 47.15N 10.56E
143 P11 Of Trabzon, NE Turkey 40.57N 40.16E
32 K15 O'Fallon Illinois, N USA 38.35N 89.54W
29 W4 O'Fallon Missouri, C USA 38.54N 90.31W
109 N16 Ofanto ~ S Italy
99 D18 Offaly Ir. Ua Uíbh Fhailí; prev. King's County. cultural region C Ireland
103 H18 Offenbach var. Offenbach am Main. Hessen, W Germany 50.06N 8.46E
Offenbach am Main see Offenbach
103 F22 Offenburg Baden-Württemberg, SW Germany 48.28N 7.57E
190 C2 Officer Creek seasonal river South Australia
Oficina María Elena see María Elena
Oficina Pedro de Valdivia see Pedro de Valdivia
117 K22 Ofidoússa island Kykládes, Greece, Aegean Sea
Ofiral see Sharm el Sheikh
94 H10 Ofotfjorden fjord N Norway
198 D8 Ofu island Manua Islands, E American Samoa
171 Mm12 Ōfunato Iwate, Honshū, C Japan 39.04N 141.41E
171 M10 Oga Akita, Honshū, C Japan 39.54N 139.48E
Ogaadeen see Ogadēn
171 M11 Ogachi Akita, Honshū, C Japan 39.03N 140.26E
171 M11 Ogachi-tōge pass Honshū, C Japan 39.00N 140.20E
83 N14 Ogadēn Som. Ogaadeen. plateau Ethiopia/Somalia
171 M10 Oga-hantō peninsula Honshū, C Japan
171 Hh14 Ōgaki Gifu, Honshū, SW Japan 35.21N 136.35E

◆ Country ● Country Capital ◇ Dependent Territory ○ Dependent Territory Capital ◆ Administrative Region ✕ International Airport ▲ Mountain ▲ Mountain Range ⧗ Volcano ~ River ◎ Lake ⊟ Reservoir

OGALLALA – ONSALA

30 L15 **Ogallala** Nebraska, C USA *41.09N 101.43W*
174 I12 **Ogan, Air** ≈ Sumatera, W Indonesia
172 T16 **Ogasawara-shotō** *Eng.* Bonin Islands. *island group* SE Japan
12 I9 **Ogascanane, Lac** ◎ Québec, SE Canada
172 N9 **Ogawara-ko** ◎ Honshū, C Japan
79 T15 **Ogbomosho** *var.* Ogmoboso. Oyo, W Nigeria *8.10N 4.16E*
Ogbomoso *see* Ogbomosho
31 U13 **Ogden** Iowa, C USA *42.03N 94.01W*
38 L2 **Ogden** Utah, W USA *41.09N 111.58W*
20 I6 **Ogdensburg** New York, NE USA *44.42N 75.25W*
197 L16 **Ogea Driki** *island* Lau Group, E Fiji
197 L16 **Ogea Levu** *island* Lau Group, E Fiji
25 W5 **Ogeechee River** ≈ Georgia, SE USA
Oger *see* Ogre
171 K12 **Ogi** Niigata, Sado, C Japan *37.49N 138.16E*
8 H5 **Ogilvie** Yukon Territory, NW Canada *63.34N 139.43W*
8 H4 **Ogilvie** ≈ Yukon Territory, NW Canada
8 H5 **Ogilvie Mountains** ▲▲ Yukon Territory, NW Canada
Oginskiy Kanal *see* Ahinski Kanal
168 J7 **Ögiynuur** *var.* Dzegstey. Arhangay, C Mongolia *47.38N 102.31E*
152 F6 **Og'iyon Sho'rxogi** *wetland* NW Uzbekistan
152 B10 **Oglanly** Balkan Welaýaty, W Turkmenistan *39.56N 54.25E*
25 T5 **Oglethorpe** Georgia, SE USA *32.17N 84.03W*
25 T2 **Oglethorpe, Mount** ▲ Georgia, SE USA *34.29N 84.19W*
108 F7 **Oglio** *anc.* Ollius. ≈ N Italy
105 T8 **Ognon** ≈ E France
175 Pp7 **Ogoamas, Pegunungan** ▲▲ Sulawesi, N Indonesia
127 N14 **Ogodzha** Amurskaya Oblast', S Russian Federation *52.51N 132.49E*
79 W16 **Ogoja** Cross River, S Nigeria *6.37N 8.48E*
10 C10 **Ogoki** ≈ Ontario, S Canada
10 D11 **Ogoki Lake** ◎ Ontario, C Canada
Ögöömör *see* Hanhongor
81 F19 **Ogooué** ≈ Congo/Gabon
81 E18 **Ogooué-Ivindo** *off.* Province de l'Ogooué-Ivindo, *var.* L'Ogooué-Ivindo. ◐ *province* N Gabon
81 E19 **Ogooué-Lolo** *off.* Province de l'Ogooué-Lolo, *var.* L'Ogooué-Lolo. ◐ *province* C Gabon
81 C19 **Ogooué-Maritime** *off.* Province de l'Ogooué-Maritime, *var.* L'Ogooué-Maritime. ◐ *province* W Gabon
170 Cc13 **Ogōri** Fukuoka, Kyūshū, SW Japan *33.25N 130.30E*
170 Dd13 **Ogōri** Yamaguchi, Honshū, SW Japan *34.05N 131.20E*
116 H7 **Ogosta** ≈ NW Bulgaria
114 Q9 **Ogražden** *Bul.* Ograzhden. ▲▲ Bulgaria/FYR Macedonia ***see also*** Ograzhden
116 G12 **Ograzhden** | Mac. Orgražden. ▲▲ Bulgaria/FYR Macedonia ***see also*** Ogražden
120 G9 **Ogre** *Ger.* Oger. Ogre, C Latvia *56.49N 24.36E*
120 H9 **Ogre** ≈ C Latvia
114 C10 **Ogulin** Karlovac, NW Croatia *45.15N 15.13E*
79 S16 **Ogun** ◐ *state* SW Nigeria
Ogurdzhaly, Ostrov *see* Ogurjaly Adasy
152 A12 **Ogurjaly Adasy** *Rus.* Ogurdzhaly, Ostrov. *island* W Turkmenistan
79 U16 **Ogwashi-Uku** Delta, S Nigeria *6.08N 6.38E*
193 B23 **Ohai** Southland, South Island, NZ *45.56S 167.59E*
153 Q10 **Ohangaron** *Rus.* Akhangaran. Toshkent Viloyati, E Uzbekistan *40.56N 69.37E*
153 Q10 **Ohangaron** *Rus.* Akhangaran. ≈ E Uzbekistan
85 C16 **Ohangwena** ◐ *district* N Namibia
171 K17 **Ōhara** Chiba, Honshū, S Japan *35.14N 140.19E*
32 M10 **O'Hare** ✕ (Chicago) Illinois, N USA *41.59N 87.56W*
172 Nn8 **Ōhata** Aomori, Honshū, C Japan *41.23N 141.09E*
192 L13 **Ohau** Manawatu-Wanganui, North Island, NZ *40.40S 175.15E*
193 E20 **Ohau, Lake** ◎ South Island, NZ
Ohcejohka *see* Utsjoki
101 J20 **Ohey** Namur, SE Belgium *50.26N 5.07E*
203 X15 **O'Higgins, Cabo** *headland* Easter Island, Chile, E Pacific Ocean *27.04S 109.15W*
O'Higgins, Lago *see* San Martín, Lago
33 S12 **Ohio** *off.* State of Ohio; also known as The Buckeye State. ◐ *state* N USA
(0) L10 **Ohio River** ≈ N USA
Ohlau *see* Oława
103 H16 **Ohm** ≈ C Germany
200 R16 **Ohonua** 'Eua, E Tonga *21.20S 174.57W*
25 V5 **Ohoopee River** ≈ Georgia, SE USA
102 L12 **Ohre** *Ger.* Eger. ≈ Czech Republic/Germany
Ohri *see* Ohrid
115 M20 **Ohrid** *Turk.* Ochrida, Ohri. SW FYR Macedonia *41.07N 20.48E*
115 M20 **Ohrid, Lake** *var.* Lake Ochrida, *Alb.* Liqeni i Ohrit, Mac. Ohridsko Ezero. ◎ Albania/FYR Macedonia
Ohridsko Ezero/ Ohrit, Liqeni i *see* Ohrid, Lake
192 L9 **Ohura** Manawatu-Wanganui, North Island, NZ *38.51S 174.58E*
60 J9 **Oiapoque** Amapá, E Brazil *3.54N 51.46W*
60 J10 **Oiapoque, Rio** *var.* Fleuve l'Oyapok, Oyapock. ≈ Brazil/French Guiana ***see also*** Oyapok, Fleuve l'
13 O9 **Oies, Île aux** *island* Québec, SE Canada
94 L13 **Oijärvi** Oulu, C Finland *65.37N 26.04E*
94 L12 **Oikarainen** Lappi, N Finland *66.30N 25.46E*
196 F10 **Oikuul** Babeldaob, N Palau
20 C13 **Oil City** Pennsylvania, NE USA *41.25N 79.42W*
20 C12 **Oil Creek** ≈ Pennsylvania, NE USA
37 R13 **Oildale** California, W USA *35.25N 119.01W*
Oileán Ciarral *see* Castleisland
Oil Islands *see* Chagos Archipelago
117 D18 **Oiniádes** *anc.* Oeniadae. *site of ancient city* Dytikí Ellás, W Greece *38.23N 21.13E*
117 L18 **Oinoússes** *island* E Greece
Oírr, Inis *see* Inisheer
101 J15 **Oirschot** Noord-Brabant, S Netherlands *51.30N 5.18E*
105 N4 **Oise** ◐ *department* N France
105 P3 **Oise** ≈ N France
101 J14 **Oisterwijk** Noord-Brabant, S Netherlands *51.34N 5.12E*
47 O14 **Oistins** S Barbados *13.04N 59.33W*
170 D14 **Ōita** Ōita, Kyūshū, SW Japan *33.15N 131.34E*
170 D14 **Ōita** *off.* Ōita-ken. ◐ *prefecture* Kyūshū, SW Japan
117 E17 **Oíti** ▲ C Greece *38.48N 22.12E*
172 Oo6 **Oiwake** Hokkaidō, NE Japan *42.54N 141.49E*
37 R14 **Ojai** California, W USA *34.25N 119.15W*
96 K13 **Öje** Dalarna, C Sweden *60.49N 13.54E*
95 J14 **Öjebyn** Norrbotten, N Sweden *65.20N 21.26E*
170 Bb12 **Ojika-jima** *island* SW Japan
42 K5 **Ojinaga** Chihuahua, N Mexico *29.30N 104.25W*
171 K13 **Ojiya** *var.* Oziya. Niigata, Honshū, C Japan *37.18N 138.47E*
42 M11 **Ojo Caliente** *var.* Ojocaliente. Zacatecas, C Mexico *22.39N 102.17W*
42 D6 **Ojo de Liebre, Laguna** *var.* Laguna Scammon, Scammon Lagoon. *lagoon* W Mexico
64 I7 **Ojos del Salado, Cerro** ▲ W Argentina *27.04S 68.34W*
107 R7 **Ojos Negros** Aragón, NE Spain *40.43N 1.30W*
42 M12 **Ojuelos de Jalisco** Aguascalientes, C Mexico *21.52N 101.40W*
131 N4 **Oka** ≈ W Russian Federation
85 D19 **Okahandja** Otjozondjupa, C Namibia *21.58S 16.55E*
192 L9 **Okahukura** Manawatu-Wanganui, North Island, NZ *38.48S 175.13E*
192 J3 **Okaihau** Northland, North Island, NZ *35.18S 173.44E*
85 D18 **Okakarara** Otjozondjupa, N Namibia *20.34S 17.24E*
11 P5 **Okak Islands** *island group* Newfoundland and Labrador, E Canada
8 M17 **Okanagan** ≈ British Columbia, SW Canada
9 N17 **Okanagan Lake** ◎ British Columbia, SW Canada
Ókanizsa *see* Kanjiža
85 C16 **Okankolo** Otjikoto, N Namibia *17.57S 16.28E*
34 K6 **Okanogan River** ≈ Washington, NW USA
194 I13 **Okapa** Eastern Highlands, C PNG *6.22S 145.29E*
85 D18 **Okaputa** Otjozondjupa, N Namibia *20.09S 16.55E*
155 V9 **Okāra** Punjab, E Pakistan *30.49N 73.31E*
28 M10 **Okarche** Oklahoma, C USA *35.43N 97.58W*
Okarem *see* Ekerem
201 X14 **Okat Harbor** *harbor* Kosrae, E Micronesia
24 M5 **Okatibbee Creek** ≈ Mississippi, S USA
85 C17 **Okaukuejo** Kunene, N Namibia *19.09S 15.57E*
Okavanggo *see* Cubango/Okavango
85 E17 **Okavango** ◐ *district* NW Namibia
85 G17 **Okavango** *var.* Cubango, Kavango, Kavengo, Kubango, Okavanggo, *Port.* Ocavango. ≈ S Africa ***see also*** Cubango
85 G17 **Okavango Delta** *wetland* N Botswana
171 J15 **Okaya** Nagano, Honshū, S Japan *36.04N 138.02E*
170 Ff14 **Okayama** Okayama, Honshū, SW Japan *34.40N 133.54E*
170 F13 **Okayama** *off.* Okayama-ken. ◐ *prefecture* Honshū, SW Japan
171 I16 **Okazaki** Aichi, Honshū, C Japan *34.58N 137.10E*
112 M12 **Okęcie** ✕ (Warszawa) Mazowieckie, C Poland *52.08N 20.57E*
25 Y13 **Okeechobee** Florida, SE USA *27.14N 80.49W*
25 Y14 **Okeechobee, Lake** ◎ Florida, SE USA
28 M9 **Okeene** Oklahoma, C USA *36.07N 98.19W*
25 V8 **Okefenokee Swamp** *wetland* Georgia, SE USA
99 J24 **Okehampton** SW England, UK *50.44N 4.00W*
29 P10 **Okemah** Oklahoma, C USA *35.25N 96.18W*
79 U16 **Okene** Kogi, S Nigeria *7.31N 6.15E*
102 K13 **Oker** *var.* Ocker. ≈ NW Germany
103 J14 **Oker-Stausee** ◎ C Germany
127 O13 **Okha** Ostrov Sakhalin, Sakhalinskaya Oblast', SE Russian Federation *53.33N 142.55E*
129 U15 **Okhansk** *var.* Ochansk. Permskaya Oblast', NW Russian Federation *57.44N 55.20E*
127 N10 **Okhota** ≈ E Russian Federation
127 Nn11 **Okhotsk** Khabarovskiy Kray, E Russian Federation *59.21N 143.14E*
199 I2 **Okhotsk, Sea of** *sea* NW Pacific Ocean
119 T4 **Okhtyrka** *Rus.* Akhtyrka. Sums'ka Oblast', NE Ukraine *50.19N 34.54E*
199 Gg6 **Oki-Daitō Ridge** *undersea feature* W Pacific Ocean
85 E23 **Okiep** Northern Cape, W South Africa *29.39S 17.53E*
Oki-guntō *see* Oki-shotō
170 Ff11 **Oki-kaikyō** *strait* SW Japan
172 P15 **Okinawa** Okinawa, SW Japan *26.19N 127.46E*
172 Oo14 **Okinawa** *off.* Okinawa-ken. ◐ *prefecture* Okinawa, SW Japan
172 Oo14 **Okinawa** *island* SW Japan
172 Q14 **Okinoerabu-jima** *island* Nansei-shotō, SW Japan
170 Dd15 **Okino-shima** *island* SW Japan
170 Ff11 **Oki-shotō** *var.* Oki-guntō. *island group* SW Japan
79 T16 **Okitipupa** Ondo, SW Nigeria *6.33N 4.43E*
177 G8 **Okkan** Pegu, SW Burma *17.31N 95.51E*
29 N10 **Oklahoma** *off.* State of Oklahoma; also known as The Sooner State. ◐ *state* C USA
29 N11 **Oklahoma City** *state capital* Oklahoma, C USA *35.28N 97.31W*
27 Q4 **Oklaunion** Texas, SW USA *34.07N 99.07W*
25 W10 **Oklawaha River** ≈ Florida, SE USA
29 P10 **Okmulgee** Oklahoma, C USA *35.37N 95.57W*
Oknitsa *see* Ocniţa
24 M3 **Okolona** Mississippi, S USA *34.00N 88.45W*
172 Q4 **Okoppe** Hokkaidō, NE Japan *44.27N 143.06E*
9 Q16 **Okotoks** Alberta, SW Canada *50.46N 113.57W*
82 H6 **Oko, Wadi** ≈ NE Sudan
81 G19 **Okoyo** Cuvette, W Congo *1.28S 15.04E*
79 S15 **Okpara** ≈ Benin/Nigeria
94 J8 **Øksfjord** Finnmark, N Norway *70.13N 22.22E*
176 Z12 **Oksibil** Papua, E Indonesia *4.52S 140.32E*
129 R4 **Oksino** Nenetskiy Avtonomnyy Okrug, NW Russian Federation *67.33N 52.15E*
94 G13 **Oksskolten** ▲ C Norway *66.00N 14.18E*
Oksu *see* Oqsu
150 M8 **Oktaybr'skiy** Kostanay, N Kazakhstan
194 E11 **Ok Tedi** Western, W PNG
Oktemberyan *see* Armavir
177 G7 **Oktwin** Pegu, C Burma *18.46N 96.21E*
131 R6 **Oktyabr'sk** Samarskaya Oblast', W Russian Federation *53.13N 48.36E*
Oktyabr'sk *see* Kandyagash
129 N12 **Oktyabr'skiy** Arkhangel'skaya Oblast', NW Russian Federation *61.03N 43.16E*
127 Pp12 **Oktyabr'skiy** Kamchatskaya Oblast', E Russian Federation *52.35N 94.18E*
131 T5 **Oktyabr'skiy** Respublika Bashkortostan, W Russian Federation *54.28N 53.29E*
131 O11 **Oktyabr'skiy** Volgogradskaya Oblast', SW Russian Federation *48.00N 43.35E*
Oktyabr'skiy *see* Aktsyabrski
131 V7 **Oktyabr'skoye** Orenburgskaya Oblast', W Russian Federation *52.22N 55.39E*
126 J3 **Oktyabr'skoy Revolyutsii, Ostrov** *Eng.* October Revolution Island. *island* Severnaya Zemlya, N Russian Federation
170 C15 **Ōkuchi** *var.* Ôkuti. Kagoshima, Kyūshū, SW Japan *32.03N 130.36E*
Okulovka *see* Uglovka
171 Mm5 **Okushiri-tō** *var.* Okusiri Tô. *island* NE Japan
Okusiri Tô *see* Okushiri-tō
79 S15 **Okuta** Kwara, W Nigeria *9.18N 3.09E*
Ôkuti *see* Ōkuchi
85 F19 **Okwa** *var.* Chapman's. ≈ Botswana/Namibia
127 O10 **Ola** Magadanskaya Oblast', E Russian Federation *59.36N 151.18E*
29 T11 **Ola** Arkansas, C USA *35.01N 93.13W*
Ola *see* Ala
37 T11 **Olacha Peak** ▲ California, W USA *36.15N 118.07W*
94 J1 **Ólafsfjördhur** Nordhurland Eystra, N Iceland *66.04N 18.36W*
94 H3 **Ólafsvík** Vesturland, W Iceland *64.52N 23.45W*
Oláhbrettye *see* Bretea-Română
Oláhszentgyőrgy *see* Sângeorz-Băi
Oláh-Toplicza *see* Topliţa
37 T11 **Olancha** California, W USA *36.16N 118.00W*
44 J5 **Olanchito** Yoro, C Honduras *15.27N 86.37W*
44 J6 **Olancho** ◐ *department* E Honduras
97 O20 **Öland** *island* S Sweden
97 O19 **Ölands norra udde** *headland* S Sweden *57.21N 17.06E*
97 N22 **Ölands södra udde** *headland* S Sweden *56.12N 16.26E*
190 K7 **Olary** South Australia *32.18S 140.16E*
29 R4 **Olathe** Kansas, C USA *38.52N 94.49W*
63 C22 **Olavarría** Buenos Aires, E Argentina *36.57S 60.19W*
94 O2 **Olav V Land** *physical region* C Svalbard
113 H14 **Oława** *Ger.* Ohlau. Dolnośląskie, SW Poland *50.57N 17.18E*
109 D17 **Olbia** *prev.* Terranova Pausania. Sardegna, Italy, C Mediterranean Sea *40.55N 9.30E*
46 G5 **Old Bahama Channel** *channel* Bahamas/Cuba
Old Bay State/Old Colony State *see* Massachusetts
8 H2 **Old Crow** Yukon Territory, NW Canada *67.34N 139.55W*
Old Dominion *see* Virginia
Oldeberkeap *see* Oldeberkoop
100 M7 **Oldeberkoop** *Fris.* Oldeberkeap. Friesland, N Netherlands *52.55N 6.07E*
100 L10 **Oldebroek** Gelderland, E Netherlands *52.27N 5.54E*
100 L8 **Oldemarkt** Overijssel, N Netherlands *52.49N 5.58E*
96 E11 **Olden** Sogn og Fjordane, C Norway *61.52N 6.44E*
102 G10 **Oldenburg** Niedersachsen, NW Germany *53.09N 8.13E*
102 K8 **Oldenburg** *var.* Oldenburg in Holstein. Schleswig-Holstein, N Germany *54.17N 10.55E*
Oldenburg in Holstein *see* Oldenburg
100 P10 **Oldenzaal** Overijssel, E Netherlands *52.19N 6.52E*
Olderfjord *see* Leaibevuotna
20 J8 **Old Forge** New York, NE USA *43.42N 74.59W*
Old Goa *see* Goa
99 L17 **Oldham** NW England, UK *53.36N 2.00W*
41 Q14 **Old Harbor** Kodiak Island, Alaska, USA *57.12N 153.18W*
46 J13 **Old Harbour** C Jamaica *17.55N 77.06W*
99 C22 **Old Head of Kinsale** *Ir.* An Seancheann. *headland* SW Ireland *51.37N 8.33W*
22 J8 **Old Hickory Lake** ⊟ Tennessee, S USA
Old Line State *see* Maryland
Old North State *see* North Carolina
83 I17 **Ol Doinyo Lengeyo** ▲▲ C Kenya
9 Q16 **Olds** Alberta, SW Canada *51.49N 114.06W*
21 O7 **Old Speck Mountain** ▲ Maine, NE USA *44.34N 70.55W*
21 S6 **Old Town** Maine, NE USA *44.55N 68.39W*
9 T17 **Old Wives Lake** ◎ Saskatchewan, S Canada
168 J7 **Öldziyt** *var.* Höshööt. Arhangay, C Mongolia *48.06N 102.34E*
168 I8 **Öldziyt** *var.* Ulaan-Uul. Bayanhongor, C Mongolia *46.03N 100.52E*
168 L10 **Öldziyt** *var.* Rashaant. Dundgovĭ, C Mongolia *44.54N 106.32E*
168 K8 **Öldziyt** *var.* Sangiyn Dalay. Övörhangay, C Mongolia *46.35N 103.18E*
Öldziyt *see* Erdenemandal, Arhangay, Mongolia
Öldziyt *see* Sayhandulaan, Dornogovĭ, Mongolia
196 H6 **Oleai** *var.* San Jose. Saipan, S Northern Mariana Islands
20 E11 **Olean** New York, NE USA *42.04N 78.24W*
112 O7 **Olecko** *Ger.* Treuburg. Warmińsko-Mazurskie, NE Poland *54.01N 22.28E*
108 C7 **Oleggio** Piemonte, NE Italy *45.36N 8.37E*
126 L13 **Olëkma** Amurskaya Oblast', SE Russian Federation *57.00N 120.27E*
126 L13 **Olëkma** ≈ C Russian Federation
126 L12 **Olëkminsk** Respublika Sakha (Yakutiya), NE Russian Federation *60.25N 120.25E*
119 W7 **Oleksandrivka** Donets'ka Oblast', E Ukraine *48.42N 36.56E*
119 R7 **Oleksandrivka** *Rus.* Aleksandrovka. Kirovohrads'ka Oblast', C Ukraine *48.58N 32.13E*
119 Q9 **Oleksandrivka** Mykolayivs'ka Oblast', S Ukraine *47.42N 31.17E*
119 S7 **Oleksandriya** *Rus.* Aleksandriya. Kirovohrads'ka Oblast', C Ukraine *48.42N 33.07E*
95 B20 **Ølen** Hordaland, S Norway *59.36N 5.48E*
128 J4 **Olenegorsk** Murmanskaya Oblast', NW Russian Federation *68.06N 33.15E*
126 K8 **Olenëk** Respublika Sakha (Yakutiya), NE Russian Federation *68.28N 112.18E*
126 Jj9 **Olenëk** ≈ NE Russian Federation
126 Kk6 **Olenëkskiy Zaliv** *bay* N Russian Federation
128 K6 **Olenitsa** Murmanskaya Oblast', NW Russian Federation *66.27N 35.21E*
104 I11 **Oléron, Île d'** *island* W France
113 H14 **Oleśnica** *Ger.* Oels, Oels in Schlesien. Dolnośląskie, SW Poland *51.13N 17.19E*
113 I15 **Olesno** *Ger.* Rosenberg. Opolskie, S Poland *50.53N 18.23E*
118 M3 **Olevs'k** *Rus.* Olevsk. Zhytomyrs'ka Oblast', N Ukraine *51.12N 27.38E*
127 Nn18 **Ol'ga** Primorskiy Kray, SE Russian Federation *43.41N 135.06E*
Olga, Mount *see* Kata Tjuta
94 P2 **Olgastretet** *strait* E Svalbard
168 D5 **Ölgiy** Bayan-Ölgiy, W Mongolia *48.57N 89.59E*
97 F23 **Ølgod** Ribe, W Denmark *55.43N 8.37E*
106 H14 **Olhão** Faro, S Portugal *37.01N 7.49W*
95 L14 **Olhava** Oulu, C Finland *65.28N 25.25E*
114 B12 **Olib** *It.* Ulbo. *island* W Croatia
85 B16 **Olifa** Kunene, NW Namibia *17.25S 14.27E*
85 E20 **Olifants** *var.* Elephant River. ≈ E Namibia
85 E25 **Olifants** *var.* Elefantes. ≈ SW South Africa
85 G22 **Olifantshoek** Northern Cape, N South Africa *27.52S 22.46E*
196 L15 **Olimarao Atoll** *atoll* Caroline Islands, C Micronesia
Ólimbos *see* Ólympos
Olimpo *see* Fuerte Olimpo
61 Q15 **Olinda** Pernambuco, E Brazil *08.00S 34.51W*
Olinthos *see* Ólynthos
85 I20 **Oliphants Drift** Kgatleng, SE Botswana *24.13S 26.52E*
Olisipo *see* Lisboa
Olita *see* Alytus
107 Q4 **Olite** Navarra, N Spain *42.28N 1.40W*
64 K10 **Oliva** Córdoba, C Argentina *32.03S 63.34W*
107 T11 **Oliva** País Valenciano, E Spain *38.55N 0.09W*
106 I12 **Oliva de la Frontera** Extremadura, W Spain *38.16N 6.54W*
Olivares *see* Olivares de Júcar
64 H9 **Olivares, Cerro de** ▲ N Chile *30.25S 69.52W*
107 P9 **Olivares de Júcar** *var.* Olivares. Castilla-La Mancha, C Spain *39.45N 2.21W*
24 L1 **Olive Branch** Mississippi, S USA *34.58N 89.49W*
23 O5 **Olive Hill** Kentucky, S USA *38.18N 83.10W*
37 O6 **Olivehurst** California, W USA *39.05N 121.33W*
106 G7 **Oliveira de Azeméis** Aveiro, N Portugal *40.49N 8.28W*
106 I11 **Olivenza** Extremadura, W Spain *38.40N 7.06W*
9 N17 **Oliver** British Columbia, SW Canada *49.10N 119.37W*
105 N7 **Olivet** Loiret, C France *47.52N 1.53E*
31 Q12 **Olivet** South Dakota, N USA *43.13N 97.40W*
31 T9 **Olivia** Minnesota, N USA *44.46N 94.59W*
193 C20 **Olivine Range** ▲▲ South Island, NZ
110 H10 **Olivone** Ticino, S Switzerland *46.32N 8.55E*
Ölkeyek *see* Ul'kayak
131 O9 **Ol'khovka** Volgogradskaya Oblast', SW Russian Federation *49.54N 44.36E*
113 K16 **Olkusz** Małopolskie, S Poland *50.16N 19.31E*
24 I6 **Olla** Louisiana, S USA *31.54N 92.14W*
64 I4 **Ollagüe, Volcán** *var.* Oyahue, Volcán Oyahue. ▲ N Chile *21.25S 68.10W*
201 U13 **Ollan** *island* Chuuk, C Micronesia
196 F7 **Ollei** Babeldaob, N Palau *7.43N 134.37E*
Ollius *see* Oglio
110 C10 **Ollon** Vaud, W Switzerland *46.19N 7.00E*
153 Q10 **Olmaliq** *Rus.* Almalyk. Toshkent Viloyati, E Uzbekistan *40.51N 69.39E*
106 M6 **Olmedo** Castilla-León, N Spain *41.16N 4.40W*
58 B10 **Olmos** Lambayeque, W Peru *6.00S 79.43W*
Olmütz *see* Olomouc
32 M15 **Olney** Illinois, N USA *38.43N 88.05W*
27 R5 **Olney** Texas, SW USA *33.22N 98.45W*
97 L22 **Olofström** Blekinge, S Sweden *56.16N 14.33E*
195 Y15 **Olomburi** Malaita, N Solomon Islands *9.00S 161.09E*
113 H17 **Olomouc** *Ger.* Olmütz, *Pol.* Ołomuniec. Olomoucký Kraj, E Czech Republic *49.36N 17.13E*
113 H18 **Olomoucký Kraj** ◐ region E Czech Republic
Ołomuniec *see* Olomouc
125 Cc6 **Olonets** Respublika Kareliya, NW Russian Federation *60.58N 33.01E*
179 P10 **Olongapo** *off.* Olongapo City. Luzon, N Philippines *14.52N 120.16E*
104 J16 **Oloron-Ste-Marie** Pyrénées-Atlantiques, SW France *43.12N 0.34W*
198 Dd8 **Olosega** *island* Manua Islands, E American Samoa
107 W4 **Olot** Cataluña, NE Spain *42.10N 2.30E*
152 K12 **Olot** *Rus.* Alat. Buxoro Viloyati, C Uzbekistan *39.22N 63.42E*
114 I12 **Olovo** Federacija Bosna I Hercegovina, E Bosnia and Herzegovina *44.08N 18.35E*
126 Kk16 **Olovyannaya** Chitinskaya Oblast', S Russian Federation *50.58N 115.24E*
127 Oo6 **Oloy** ≈ NE Russian Federation
103 F16 **Olpe** Nordrhein-Westfalen, W Germany *51.01N 7.51E*
111 N8 **Olperer** ▲ SW Austria *47.03N 11.36E*
Olshanka *see* Vil'shanka
Ol'shany *see* Al'shany
Olsnitz *see* Murska Sobota
100 M10 **Olst** Overijssel, E Netherlands *52.19N 6.06E*
112 L8 **Olsztyn** *Ger.* Allenstein. Warmińsko-Mazurskie, NE Poland, *53.46N 20.28E*
112 L8 **Olsztynek** *Ger.* Hohenstein in Ostpreussen. Warmińsko-Mazurskie, NE Poland, *53.34N 20.16E*
118 I14 **Olt** ◐ *county* SW Romania
118 I14 **Olt** *var.* Oltul, *Ger.* Alt. ≈ S Romania
110 E7 **Olten** Solothurn, NW Switzerland *47.20N 7.51E*
118 K14 **Olteniţa** *prev. Eng.* Oltenitsa, *anc.* Constantiola. Călăraşi, SE Romania *44.04N 26.40E*
Oltenitsa *see* Olteniţa
118 H14 **Olteţ** ≈ S Romania
26 M4 **Olton** Texas, SW USA *34.10N 102.07W*
143 R12 **Oltu** Erzurum, NE Turkey *40.34N 41.58E*
Oltul *see* Olt
152 G7 **Oltynko'l** Qoraqalpog'iston Respublikasi, NW Uzbekistan *43.04N 58.51E*
167 S15 **Oluan Pi** *Eng.* Cape Olwanpi. *headland* S Taiwan *21.57N 120.48E*
Ólubló *see* Stará L'ubovňa
143 R11 **Olur** Erzurum, NE Turkey *40.49N 42.07E*
106 L15 **Olvera** Andalucía, S Spain *36.55N 5.15W*
Ol'viopol' *see* Pervomays'k
Olwanpi, Cape *see* Oluan Pi
17 G2 **Olympia** *state capital* Washington, NW USA *47.02N 122.54W*
117 D20 **Olympía** Dytikí Ellás, S Greece *37.39N 21.36E*
190 H5 **Olympic Dam** South Australia *30.25S 136.56E*
34 F7 **Olympic Mountains** ▲▲ Washington, NW USA
124 R12 **Ólympos** *var.* Troodos, *Eng.* Mount Olympus. ▲ C Cyprus *34.55N 32.49E*
117 F15 **Ólympos** *var.* Ólimbos, *Eng.* Mount Olympus. ▲ N Greece *40.04N 22.24E*
117 L17 **Ólympos** ▲ Lésvos, E Greece *39.03N 26.20E*
17 G1 **Olympus, Mount** ▲ Washington, NW USA *47.48N 123.42W*
Olympus, Mount *see* Ólympos
117 G14 **Ólynthos** *var.* Olinthos; *anc.* Olynthus. *site of ancient city* Kentrikí Makedonía, N Greece *40.16N 23.21E*
Olynthus *see* Ólynthos
119 Q3 **Olyshivka** Chernihivs'ka Oblast', N Ukraine *51.13N 31.19E*
127 Q7 **Olyutorskiy, Mys** *headland* E Russian Federation *59.56N 170.22E*
127 Pp8 **Olyutorskiy Zaliv** *bay* E Russian Federation
194 F11 **Om** ≈ W PNG
133 S6 **Om'** ≈ N Russian Federation
164 I13 **Oma** Xizang Zizhiqu, W China *32.30N 83.13E*
172 N8 **Ōma** Aomori, Honshū, C Japan *41.31N 140.54E*
129 P6 **Oma** ≈ NW Russian Federation
171 J14 **Ōmachi** *var.* Ômati. Nagano, Honshū, S Japan *36.33N 137.49E*
171 Ii17 **Omae-zaki** *headland* Honshū, S Japan *34.36N 138.12E*
171 M11 **Ōmagari** Akita, Honshū, C Japan *39.27N 140.28E*
99 E15 **Omagh** *Ir.* An Ómaigh. W Northern Ireland, UK *54.36N 7.18W*
31 S15 **Omaha** Nebraska, C USA *41.14N 95.57W*
85 E19 **Omaheke** ◐ *district* W Namibia
147 W10 **Oman** *off.* Sultanate of Oman, *Ar.* Salṭanat 'Umān; *prev.* Muscat and Oman. ◆ *monarchy* SW Asia
133 O10 **Oman Basin** *var.* Bassin d'Oman. *undersea feature* N Indian Ocean
Oman, Bassin d' *see* Oman Basin
133 N10 **Oman, Gulf of** *Ar.* Khalīj 'Umān. *gulf* N Arabian Sea
192 J3 **Omapere** Northland, North Island, NZ *35.32S 173.24E*
193 E20 **Omarama** Canterbury, South Island, NZ *44.29S 169.57E*
114 F11 **Omarska** Republika Sprska, NW Bosnia and Herzegovina *44.53N 16.52E*
85 C18 **Omaruru** Erongo, NW Namibia *21.25S 15.57E*
85 C19 **Omaruru** ≈ W Namibia
85 E17 **Omatako** ≈ NE Namibia
Ômati *see* Ōmachi
85 E18 **Omawewozonyanda** Omaheke, E Namibia *21.30S 19.34E*
172 N7 **Oma-zaki** *headland* Honshū, C Japan *41.32N 140.53E*
Omba *see* Ambae
Ombai *see* Alor, Pulau
175 Rr16 **Ombai, Selat** *strait* Nusa Tenggara, S Indonesia
85 C16 **Ombalantu** Omusati, N Namibia *17.33S 14.58E*
81 H15 **Ombella-Mpoko** ◐ *prefecture* S Central African Republic
Ombetsu *see* Onbetsu
85 B17 **Ombombo** Kunene, NW Namibia *18.43S 13.55E*
81 D19 **Omboué** Ogooué-Maritime, W Gabon *1.37S 9.19E*
108 G13 **Ombrone** ≈ C Italy
82 F9 **Omdurman** *var.* Umm Durmān. Khartoum, C Sudan *15.37N 32.28E*
171 Jj16 **Ōme** Tōkyō, Honshū, S Japan *35.48N 139.10E*
108 C6 **Omegna** Piemonte, NE Italy *45.54N 8.25E*
191 P12 **Omeo** Victoria, SE Australia *37.09S 147.36E*
144 F11 **'Omer** Southern, C Israel *31.16N 34.51E*
43 P16 **Ometepec** Guerrero, S Mexico *16.39N 98.22W*
44 K11 **Ometepe, Isla de** *island* S Nicaragua
Om Hager *see* Om Hajer
82 I10 **Om Hajer** *var.* Om Hager. SW Eritrea *14.19N 36.46E*
171 H14 **Ōmi-Hachiman** *var.* Ōmihachiman. Shiga, Honshū, SW Japan *35.09N 136.04E*
8 L12 **Omineca Mountains** ▲▲ British Columbia, W Canada
115 F14 **Omiš** *It.* Almissa. Split-Dalmacija, S Croatia *43.27N 16.41E*
114 B10 **Omišalj** Primorje-Gorski Kotar, NW Croatia *45.10N 14.33E*
170 Dd12 **Ōmi-shima** *island* SW Japan
85 D19 **Omitara** Khomas, C Namibia *22.18S 18.01E*
43 O16 **Omitlán, Río** ≈ S Mexico
41 X14 **Ommaney, Cape** *headland* Baranof Island, Alaska, USA *56.10N 134.40W*
100 N9 **Ommen** Overijssel, E Netherlands *52.31N 6.25E*
169 N7 **Ömnödelger** *var.* Bayanbulag. Hentiy, C Mongolia *47.54N 109.51E*
168 K11 **Ömnögovĭ** ◐ *province* S Mongolia
203 X7 **Omoa** Fatu Hira, NE French Polynesia *10.30S 138.40E*
Omo Botego *see* Omo Wenz
Ómoldova *see* Moldova Veche
127 O6 **Omolon** Chukotskiy Avtonomnyy Okrug, NE Russian Federation *65.11N 96.33E*
127 O7 **Omolon** ≈ NE Russian Federation
126 Ll8 **Omoloy** ≈ NE Russian Federation
171 M10 **Omono-gawa** ≈ Honshū, C Japan
83 I14 **Omo Wenz** *var.* Omo Botego. ≈ Ethiopia/Kenya
125 Ff13 **Omsk** Omskaya Oblast', C Russian Federation *55.00N 73.22E*
125 Ff12 **Omskaya Oblast'** ◐ *province* C Russian Federation
127 O8 **Omsukchan** Magadanskaya Oblast', E Russian Federation *62.25N 155.22E*
172 Q4 **Ōmu** Hokkaidō, NE Japan *44.36N 142.55E*
112 M9 **Omulew** ≈ NE Poland
118 J12 **Omul, Vârful** *prev.* Vîrful Omu. ▲ C Romania *45.24N 25.26E*
85 D16 **Omundaungilo** Ohangwena, N Namibia *17.28S 16.39E*
170 C13 **Ōmura** Nagasaki, Kyūshū, SW Japan *32.55N 129.54E*
85 B17 **Omusati** ◐ *district* N Namibia
170 Cc13 **Ōmuta** Fukuoka, Kyūshū, SW Japan *33.02N 130.26E*
129 S14 **Omutninsk** Kirovskaya Oblast', NW Russian Federation *58.37N 52.08E*
Omu, Vîrful *see* Omul, Vârful
31 V7 **Onamia** Minnesota, N USA *46.04N 93.40W*
23 Y5 **Onancock** Virginia, NE USA *37.42N 75.45W*
12 E10 **Onaping Lake** ◎ Ontario, S Canada
32 M12 **Onarga** Illinois, N USA *40.39N 88.00W*
13 R6 **Onatchiway, Lac** ◎ Québec, SE Canada
31 S14 **Onawa** Iowa, C USA *42.01N 96.06W*
172 Pp7 **Onbetsu** *var.* Ombetsu. Hokkaidō, NE Japan *42.52N 143.54E*
85 B16 **Oncócua** Cunene, SW Angola *16.37S 13.23E*
107 S9 **Onda** País Valenciano, E Spain *39.58N 0.17W*
113 N18 **Ondava** ≈ NE Slovakia
Ondjiva *see* N'Giva
79 T16 **Ondo** Ondo, SW Nigeria *7.07N 4.50E*
79 T16 **Ondo** ◐ *state* SW Nigeria
169 N8 **Öndörhaan** *var.* Undur Khan; *prev.* Tsetsen Khan. Hentiy, E Mongolia *47.20N 110.42E*
168 M9 **Öndörshil** *var.* Böhöt. Dundgovĭ, C Mongolia *45.13N 108.12E*
168 L8 **Öndörshireet** *var.* Bayshint. Töv, C Mongolia *47.22N 105.04E*
168 I7 **Öndör-Ulaan** *var.* Teel. Arhangay, C Mongolia *48.01N 100.30E*
85 D18 **Ondundazongonda** Otjozondjupa, N Namibia *20.28S 18.00E*
157 K21 **One and Half Degree Channel** *channel* S Maldives
197 L15 **Oneata** *island* Lau Group, E Fiji
128 L9 **Onega** Arkhangel'skaya Oblast', NW Russian Federation *63.54N 37.58E*
125 Dd6 **Onega** ≈ NW Russian Federation
Onega Bay *see* Onezhskaya Guba
Onega, Lake *see* Onezhskoye Ozero
20 I10 **Oneida** New York, NE USA *43.05N 75.39W*
22 M8 **Oneida** Tennessee, S USA *36.30N 84.30W*
20 H9 **Oneida Lake** ◎ New York, NE USA
31 P13 **O'Neill** Nebraska, C USA *42.28N 98.37W*
127 Pp13 **Onekotan, Ostrov** *island* Kuril'skiye Ostrova, SE Russian Federation
25 P3 **Oneonta** Alabama, S USA *33.57N 86.28W*
20 J11 **Oneonta** New York, NE USA *42.27N 75.03W*
202 I16 **Oneroa** *island* S Cook Islands
118 K11 **Oneşti** *Hung.* Onyest; *prev.* Gheorghe Gheorghiu-Dej. Bacău, E Romania *46.13N 26.46E*
200 Qq15 **Onevai** *island* Tongatapu Group, S Tonga
110 A11 **Onex** Genève, SW Switzerland *46.11N 6.04E*
128 K8 **Onezhskaya Guba** *Eng.* Onega Bay. *bay* NW Russian Federation
125 D6 **Onezhskoye Ozero** *Eng.* Lake Onega. ◎ NW Russian Federation
85 C16 **Ongandjera** Omusati, N Namibia *17.49S 15.06E*
192 N12 **Ongaonga** Hawke's Bay, North Island, NZ *39.57S 176.21E*
Ongi *see* Sayhan-Ovoo, Dundgovĭ, Mongolia
Ongi *see* Uyanga, Övörhangay, Mongolia
169 W14 **Ongjin** SW North Korea *37.55N 125.21E*
161 J17 **Ongole** Andhra Pradesh, E India *15.33N 80.03E*
Ongon *see* Bürd
Ongtüstik Qazaqstan Oblysy *see* Yuzhnyy Kazakhstan
101 I21 **Onhaye** Namur, S Belgium *50.15N 4.51E*
177 G8 **Onhne** Pegu, SW Burma *17.02N 96.28E*
143 S9 **Oni** N Georgia *42.36N 43.13E*
31 N9 **Onida** South Dakota, N USA *44.42N 100.03W*
170 E15 **Onigajō-yama** ▲ Shikoku, SW Japan *33.10N 132.37E*
180 H7 **Onilahy** ≈ S Madagascar
79 U16 **Onitsha** Anambra, S Nigeria *6.09N 6.48E*
171 Gg14 **Ono** Hyōgo, Honshū, SW Japan *34.51N 134.56E*
197 I15 **Ono** *island* SW Fiji
171 I14 **Ōno** Fukui, Honshū, SW Japan *35.59N 136.29E*
170 D12 **Onoda** Yamaguchi, Honshū, SW Japan *33.59N 131.10E*
197 L17 **Ono-i-lau** *island* SE Fiji
170 Cc13 **Ōnojō** *var.* Ônozyô. Fukuoka, Kyūshū, SW Japan *33.30N 130.30E*
126 K16 **Onokhoy** Respublika Buryatiya, S Russian Federation *51.51N 108.17E*
170 F14 **Onomichi** *var.* Onomiti. Hiroshima, Honshū, SW Japan *34.25N 133.13E*
Onomiti *see* Onomichi
169 O7 **Onon Gol** ≈ N Mongolia
Ononte *see* Orontes
57 N6 **Onoto** Anzoátegui, NE Venezuela *9.36N 65.10W*
203 O3 **Onotoa** *prev.* Clerk Island. *atoll* Tungaru, W Kiribati
Ônozyô *see* Ōnojō
97 I19 **Onsala** Halland, S Sweden *57.25N 12.00E*

◆ Country
● Country Capital
◇ Dependent Territory
○ Dependent Territory Capital
◐ Administrative Region
✕ International Airport
▲ Mountain
▲▲ Mountain Range
☒ Volcano
≈ River
◎ Lake
⊟ Reservoir

◆ COUNTRY ○ DEPENDENT TERRITORY ◆ ADMINISTRATIVE REGION ▲ MOUNTAIN ▲ VOLCANO ◎ LAKE
● COUNTRY CAPITAL ○ DEPENDENT TERRITORY CAPITAL × INTERNATIONAL AIRPORT ▲ MOUNTAIN RANGE ≈ RIVER ⊞ RESERVOIR

Ostrava – País Valenciano

113 I17 **Ostrava** Moravskoslezský Kraj, E Czech Republic 49.49N 18.15E
Ostravský Kraj see Moravskoslezský Kraj
96 J11 **Østrehogna** Swe. Härjahågnen, Härjehågna. ▲ Norway/Sweden 61.43N 12.07E
112 K8 **Ostróda** Ger. Osterode, Osterode in Ostpreussen. Warmińsko-Mazurskie, NE Poland 53.42N 19.58E
Ostrog/Ostróg see Ostroh
130 L8 **Ostrogozhsk** Voronezhskaya Oblast', W Russian Federation 50.52N 39.00E
118 L4 **Ostroh** Pol. Ostróg, Rus. Ostrog. Rivnens'ka Oblast', NW Ukraine 50.19N 26.30E
112 N9 **Ostrołęka** Ger. Wiesenhof, Rus. Ostrolenka. Mazowieckie, C Poland 53.06N 21.33E
113 A16 **Ostrov** Ger. Schlackenwerth. Karlovarský Kraj, W Czech Republic 50.18N 12.53E
128 F15 **Ostrov** Latv. Austrava. Pskovskaya Oblast', W Russian Federation 57.21N 28.18E
Ostrovets see Ostrowiec Świętokrzyski
115 M21 **Ostrovicës, Mali i** ▲ SE Albania 40.36N 20.25E
172 T6 **Ostrov Iturup** island NE Russian Federation
128 M4 **Ostrovnoy** Murmanskaya Oblast', NW Russian Federation 68.00N 39.40E
116 L7 **Ostrovo** prev. Golema Ada. Razgrad, N Bulgaria 43.40N 26.37E
129 N15 **Ostrovskoye** Kostromskaya Oblast', NW Russian Federation 57.46N 42.18E
Ostrów see Ostrów Wielkopolski
Ostrowiec see Ostrowiec Świętokrzyski
113 M14 **Ostrowiec Świętokrzyski** var. Ostrowiec, Rus. Ostrovets. Świętokrzyskie, C Poland 50.54N 21.22E
112 P13 **Ostrów Lubelski** Lubelskie, E Poland 51.29N 22.57E
112 N10 **Ostrów Mazowiecka** var. Ostrów Mazowiecki. Mazowieckie, C Poland 52.48N 21.53E
Ostrów Mazowiecki see Ostrów Mazowiecka
Ostrowo see Ostrów Wielkopolski
112 H13 **Ostrów Wielkopolski** var. Ostrów, Ger. Ostrowo. Wielkopolskie, C Poland 51.40N 17.47E
Ostryna see Astryna
112 I13 **Ostrzeszów** Wielkopolskie, C Poland 51.26N 17.54E
109 P18 **Ostuni** Puglia, SE Italy 40.43N 17.34E
Ostyako-Voguls'k see Khanty-Mansiysk
Osum see Osumit, Lumi i
116 I9 **Osŭm** ⁂ N Bulgaria
170 Bb17 **Ōsumi-hantō** ▲ Kyūshū, SW Japan
170 Bb17 **Ōsumi-kaikyō** strait SW Japan
115 L22 **Osumit, Lumi i** var. Osum. ⁂ SE Albania
79 T16 **Osun** var. Oshun. ◆ state SW Nigeria
106 L14 **Osuna** Andalucía, S Spain 37.13N 5.06W
62 J8 **Osvaldo Cruz** São Paulo, S Brazil 21.49S 50.52W
Osveya see Asvyeya
20 J7 **Oswegatchie River** ⁂ New York, NE USA
29 Q7 **Oswego** Kansas, C USA 37.08N 95.07W
20 H9 **Oswego** New York, NE USA 43.27N 76.13W
99 K19 **Oswestry** W England, UK 52.50N 3.06W
113 J16 **Oświęcim** Ger. Auschwitz. Małopolskie, S Poland 50.02N 19.11E
171 K15 **Ōta** Gunma, Honshū, S Japan 36.17N 139.20E
193 E22 **Otago** off. Otago Region. ◆ region South Island, NZ
193 F23 **Otago Peninsula** peninsula South Island, NZ
170 E13 **Ōtake** Hiroshima, Honshū, SW Japan 34.13N 132.13E
192 L13 **Otaki** Wellington, North Island, NZ 40.46S 175.08E
171 L14 **Ōtakine-yama** ▲ Honshū, C Japan 37.23N 140.42E
95 M15 **Otanmäki** Oulu, C Finland 64.07N 27.04E
151 T15 **Otar** Zhambyl, SE Kazakhstan 43.34N 75.13E
172 O5 **Otaru** Hokkaidō, NE Japan 43.13N 140.58E
193 C24 **Otatara** Southland, South Island, NZ 46.26S 168.18E
193 C24 **Otautau** Southland, South Island, NZ 46.10S 168.01E
95 M18 **Otava** Isä-Suomi, E Finland 61.37N 27.07E
113 B18 **Otava** Ger. Wottawa. ⁂ SW Czech Republic
58 C6 **Otavalo** Imbabura, N Ecuador 0.13N 78.15W
85 D17 **Otavi** Otjozondjupa, N Namibia 19.34S 17.25E
171 Kk15 **Ōtawara** Tochigi, Honshū, S Japan 36.52N 140.01E
85 B16 **Otchinjau** Cunene, SW Angola 16.31S 13.54E
118 F12 **Oţelu Roşu** Ger. Ferdinandsberg, Hung. Nándorhgy. Caras-Severin, SW Romania 45.30N 22.22E
193 E21 **Otematata** Canterbury, South Island, NZ 44.37S 170.12E
120 I6 **Otepää** Ger. Odenpäh. Valgamaa, SE Estonia 58.04N 26.31E
168 H7 **Otgon** var. Buyant. Dzavhan, C Mongolia 47.14N 97.14E
34 K9 **Othello** Washington, NW USA 46.49N 119.10W
117 A15 **Othonoí** island Iónia Nisiá, Greece, C Mediterranean Sea
Othris see Óthrys
117 F17 **Óthrys** var. Othris. ▲ C Greece
79 Q14 **Oti** ⁂ N Togo
42 K10 **Otinapa** Durango, C Mexico 24.01N 104.58W
193 G17 **Otira** West Coast, South Island, NZ 42.51S 171.32E
39 V3 **Otis** Colorado, C USA 40.09N 102.57W
10 L10 **Otish, Monts** ▲ Québec, E Canada
85 C17 **Otjikondo** Kunene, N Namibia 19.48S 15.28E
85 C17 **Otjikoto** var. Oshikoto. ◆ district N Namibia
85 E18 **Otjinene** Omaheke, NE Namibia 21.10S 18.43E
85 D18 **Otjiwarongo** Otjozondjupa, N Namibia 20.28S 16.36E
85 D18 **Otjosondu** var. Otjosundu. Otjozondjupa, C Namibia 21.19S 17.51E
Otjosundu see Otjosondu
85 D18 **Otjozondjupa** ◆ district C Namibia
114 C11 **Otočac** Lika-Senj, W Croatia 44.52N 15.13E
172 Pp6 **Otofuke-gawa** ⁂ Hokkaidō, NE Japan
Otog Qi see Ulan
172 Pp3 **Otoineppu** Hokkaidō, NE Japan 44.43N 142.13E
114 J10 **Otok** Vukovar-Srijem, E Croatia 45.10N 18.52E
118 K14 **Otopeni** ✈ (Bucureşti) Ilfov, S Romania 44.34N 26.09E
192 L8 **Otorohanga** Waikato, North Island, NZ 38.10S 175.13E
10 D9 **Otoskwin** ⁂ Ontario, C Canada
170 F15 **Ōtoyo** Kōchi, Shikoku, SW Japan 33.45N 133.42E
97 E16 **Otra** ⁂ S Norway
109 R19 **Otranto** Puglia, SE Italy 40.08N 18.28E
Otranto, Canale d' see Otranto, Strait of
109 Q18 **Otranto, Strait of** It. Canale d'Otranto. strait Albania/Italy
113 H18 **Otrokovice** Ger. Otrokowitz. Zlínský Kraj, E Czech Republic 49.13N 17.32E
Otrokowitz see Otrokovice
33 P10 **Otsego** Michigan, N USA 42.27N 85.42W
33 Q6 **Otsego Lake** ◎ Michigan, N USA
20 I11 **Otselic River** ⁂ New York, NE USA
171 H15 **Ōtsu** var. Ōtu. Shiga, Honshū, SW Japan 35.03N 135.49E
171 Jj16 **Ōtsuki** var. Otuki. Yamanashi, Honshū, S Japan 35.35N 138.53E
96 G11 **Otta** Oppland, S Norway 61.46N 9.31E
201 U13 **Otta** island Chuuk, C Micronesia
96 F11 **Otta** ⁂ S Norway
201 U13 **Otta Pass** passage Chuuk Islands, C Micronesia
97 J22 **Ottarp** Skåne, S Sweden 55.55N 12.55E
12 L12 **Ottawa** ● (Canada) Ontario, SE Canada 45.24N 75.40W
32 L11 **Ottawa** Illinois, N USA 41.21N 88.50W
29 Q5 **Ottawa** Kansas, C USA 38.37N 95.16W
33 R12 **Ottawa** Ohio, N USA 41.01N 84.03W
12 L12 **Ottawa** var. Uplands. ✈ Ontario, SE Canada 45.19N 75.39W
12 M12 **Ottawa** Fr. Outaouais. ⁂ Ontario/Québec, SE Canada
10 I4 **Ottawa Islands** island group Nunavut, C Canada
20 L8 **Otter Creek** ⁂ Vermont, NE USA
38 L6 **Otter Creek Reservoir** ⊠ Utah, W USA
100 L11 **Otterlo** Gelderland, E Netherlands 52.06N 5.46E
96 D9 **Otterøya** island S Norway
31 S6 **Otter Tail Lake** ◎ Minnesota, N USA
31 R7 **Otter Tail River** ⁂ Minnesota, C USA
97 H23 **Otterup** Fyn, C Denmark 55.31N 10.25E
101 H19 **Ottignies** Wallon Brabant, C Belgium 50.40N 4.34E
103 L23 **Ottobrunn** Bayern, SE Germany 48.02N 11.40E
194 I12 **Otto, Mount** ▲ C PNG 5.54S 145.24E
31 X15 **Ottumwa** Iowa, C USA 41.00N 92.24W
Ōtu see Ōtsu
85 B16 **Otuazuma** Kunene, NW Namibia 17.52S 13.16E
Otuki see Ōtsuki
79 V16 **Oturkpo** Benue, S Nigeria 7.12N 8.06E
200 Ss14 **Otu Tolu Group** island group SE Tonga
190 M13 **Otway, Cape** headland Victoria, SE Australia 38.52S 143.31E
65 H24 **Otway, Seno** inlet S Chile
Ötz see Oetz
110 L8 **Ötztaler Ache** ⁂ W Austria
110 L9 **Ötztaler Alpen** It. Alpi Venoste. ▲ SW Austria
29 T12 **Ouachita, Lake** ⊠ Arkansas, C USA
29 R11 **Ouachita Mountains** ▲ Arkansas/Oklahoma, C USA
29 U13 **Ouachita River** ⁂ Arkansas/Louisiana, C USA
Ouadaï see Ouaddaï
78 J7 **Ouadâne** var. Ouadane. Adrar, C Mauritania 20.57N 11.34W
80 K13 **Ouadda** Haute-Kotto, N Central African Republic 8.02N 22.22E
80 J10 **Ouaddaï** off. Préfecture du Ouaddaï, var. Ouadaï, Wadai. ◆ prefecture SE Chad
79 P13 **Ouagadougou** var. Wagadugu. ● (Burkina) C Burkina 12.20N 1.31W
79 P13 **Ouagadougou** ✕ C Burkina 12.21N 1.27W
79 O12 **Ouahigouya** NW Burkina 13.31N 2.19W
Ouahran see Oran
81 J14 **Ouaka** ◆ prefecture C Central African Republic
81 J15 **Ouaka** ⁂ S Central African Republic
Oualam see Ouallam
78 M9 **Oualâta** var. Oualata. Hodh ech Chargui, SE Mauritania 17.18N 7.00W
79 R11 **Ouallam** var. Oualam. Tillabéri, W Niger 14.13N 2.07E
180 H14 **Ouanani** Mohéli, S Comoros 12.19S 94.37E
57 Z10 **Ouanary** E French Guiana 4.10N 51.40W
80 L13 **Ouanda Djallé** Vakaga, NE Central African Republic 8.53N 22.47E
81 N14 **Ouando** Haut-Mbomou, SE Central African Republic 5.57N 25.57E
81 L15 **Ouango** Mbomou, S Central African Republic 4.19N 22.30E
79 N14 **Ouangolodougou** var. Wangolodougou. N Ivory Coast 9.58N 5.09W
180 I13 **Ouani** Anjouan, SE Comoros
81 M15 **Ouara** ⁂ E Central African Republic
78 K7 **Ouarâne** desert C Mauritania
13 O11 **Ouareau** ⁂ Québec, SE Canada
76 K7 **Ouargla** var. Wargla. NE Algeria 32.00N 5.16E
76 F8 **Ouarzazate** S Morocco 30.54N 6.55W
79 Q11 **Ouatagouna** Gao, E Mali 15.06N 0.41E
76 G6 **Ouazzane** var. Ouezzane, Ar. Wazan, Wazzan. N Morocco 34.52N 5.34W
Oubangui see Ubangi
Oubangui-Chari see Central African Republic
Oubari, Edeyen d' see Awbāri, Idhān
100 G13 **Oud-Beijerland** Zuid-Holland, SW Netherlands 51.49N 4.25E
100 F13 **Ouddorp** Zuid-Holland, SW Netherlands 51.49N 3.55E
79 P9 **Oudeïka** oasis C Mali 17.16N 1.42W
100 G13 **Oude Maas** ⁂ SW Netherlands
101 E18 **Oudenaarde** Fr. Audenarde. Oost-Vlaanderen, SW Belgium 50.49N 3.37E
101 H14 **Oudenbosch** Noord-Brabant, S Netherlands 51.34N 4.31E
100 P6 **Oude Pekela** Groningen, NE Netherlands 53.06N 7.00E
Ouderkerk see Ouderkerk aan den Amstel
100 I10 **Ouderkerk aan den Amstel** var. Ouderkerk. Noord-Holland, C Netherlands 52.18N 4.54E
100 I6 **Oudeschild** Noord-Holland, NW Netherlands 53.01N 4.51E
101 G14 **Oude-Tonge** Zuid-Holland, SW Netherlands 51.40N 4.13E
100 I12 **Oudewater** Utrecht, C Netherlands 52.01N 4.54E
Oudjda see Oujda
100 L5 **Oudkerk** Friesland, N Netherlands 53.16N 5.52E
104 J7 **Oudon** ⁂ NW France
100 I9 **Oudorp** Noord-Holland, NW Netherlands 52.39N 4.46E
85 G25 **Oudtshoorn** Western Cape, SW South Africa 33.32S 22.12E
101 I16 **Oud-Turnhout** Antwerpen, N Belgium 51.19N 5.01E
76 F7 **Oued-Zem** C Morocco 32.53N 6.30W
197 H5 **Ouégoa** Province Nord, C New Caledonia 20.22S 164.25E
78 L13 **Ouéléssébougou** var. Ouolosségbougou. Koulikoro, SW Mali 11.58N 7.51W
79 N16 **Ouellé** E Ivory Coast 7.18N 4.01W
79 R16 **Ouémé** ⁂ C Benin
197 J7 **Ouen, Île** island S New Caledonia
79 O13 **Ouessa** S Burkina 11.02N 2.44W
104 D5 **Ouessant, Île d'** Eng. Ushant. island NW France
81 H17 **Ouésso** La Sangha, NW Congo 1.37N 16.03E
81 D15 **Ouest** Eng. West. ◆ province W Cameroon
202 G11 **Ouest, Baie de l'** bay Îles Wallis, Wallis and Futuna
13 Y7 **Ouest, Pointe de l'** headland Québec, SE Canada 48.08N 64.57W
Ouezzane see Ouazzane
101 K20 **Ouffet** Liège, E Belgium 50.30N 5.31E
81 H14 **Ouham** ◆ prefecture NW Central African Republic
80 I13 **Ouham** ⁂ Central African Republic/Chad
81 G14 **Ouham-Pendé** ◆ prefecture W Central African Republic
79 R16 **Ouidah** Eng. Whydah, Wida. S Benin 6.22N 2.07E
76 H6 **Oujda** Ar. Oudjda, Ujda. NE Morocco 34.45N 1.53W
78 I7 **Oujeft** Adrar, C Mauritania 20.05N 13.00W
95 L15 **Oulainen** Oulu, C Finland 64.14N 24.50E
Ould Yanja see Ould Yenjé
78 J10 **Ould Yenjé** var. Ould Yanja. Guidimaka, S Mauritania 15.33N 11.43W
95 L14 **Oulu** Swe. Uleåborg. Oulu, C Finland 65.01N 25.28E
95 M14 **Oulu** Swe. Uleåborg. ◆ province N Finland
95 L15 **Oulujärvi** Swe. Uleträsk. ◎ C Finland
95 M14 **Oulujoki** Swe. Uleälv. ⁂ C Finland
95 L14 **Oulunsalo** Oulu, C Finland 64.55N 25.19E
108 A8 **Oulx** Piemonte, NE Italy 45.05N 6.41E
80 J9 **Oum-Chalouba** Borkou-Ennedi-Tibesti, NE Chad 15.48N 20.46E
78 M16 **Oumé** C Ivory Coast 6.23N 5.25W
76 F7 **Oum er Rbia** ⁂ C Morocco
80 J10 **Oum-Hadjer** Batha, E Chad 13.18N 19.40E
94 K10 **Ounasjoki** ⁂ N Finland
80 J7 **Ounianga Kébir** Borkou-Ennedi-Tibesti, N Chad 19.06N 20.28E
Ouolossébougou see Ouéléssébougou
Oup see Auob
101 K19 **Oupeye** Liège, E Belgium 50.42N 5.37E
101 N21 **Our** ⁂ NW Europe
39 Q7 **Ouray** Colorado, C USA 38.01N 107.40W
105 R7 **Ource** ⁂ C France
106 G9 **Ourém** Santarém, C Portugal 39.40N 8.32W
106 H4 **Ourense** Cast. Orense; Lat. Aurium. Galicia, NW Spain 42.19N 7.52W
106 I4 **Ourense** Cast. Orense ◆ province Galicia, NW Spain
61 O15 **Ouricuri** Pernambuco, E Brazil 7.51S 40.04W
62 J9 **Ourinhos** São Paulo, S Brazil 22.58S 49.52W
106 G13 **Ourique** Beja, S Portugal 37.37N 8.13W
61 M20 **Ouro Preto** Minas Gerais, NE Brazil 20.25S 43.30W
Ours, Grand Lac de l' see Great Bear Lake
101 K20 **Ourthe** ⁂ E Belgium
171 Mm11 **Ōu-sanmyaku** ▲ Honshū, C Japan
99 M17 **Ouse** ⁂ N England, UK
Ouse see Great Ouse
104 H7 **Oust** ⁂ NW France
Outaouais see Ottawa
13 T4 **Outardes Quatre, Réservoir** ⊠ Québec, SE Canada
13 T5 **Outardes, Rivière aux** ⁂ Québec, SE Canada
98 E8 **Outer Hebrides** var. Western Isles. island group NW Scotland, UK
32 K3 **Outer Island** island Apostle Islands, Wisconsin, N USA
37 S16 **Outer Santa Barbara Passage** passage California, SW USA
106 G3 **Outes** Galicia, NW Spain 42.50N 8.54W
85 C18 **Outjo** Kunene, N Namibia 20.06S 16.06E
9 T16 **Outlook** Saskatchewan, S Canada 51.30N 107.03W
95 N16 **Outokumpu** Itä-Suomi, E Finland 62.43N 29.04E
98 M2 **Out Skerries** island group NE Scotland, UK
197 J5 **Ouvéa** island Îles Loyauté, NE New Caledonia
105 S14 **Ouvèze** ⁂ SE France
190 L9 **Ouyen** Victoria, SE Australia 35.06S 142.18E
41 Q14 **Ouzinkie** Kodiak Island, Alaska, USA 57.54N 152.27W
143 O13 **Ovacık** Tunceli, E Turkey 39.22N 39.13E
108 C9 **Ovada** Piemonte, NE Italy 44.41N 8.39E
197 I14 **Ovalau** island C Fiji
64 G9 **Ovalle** Coquimbo, N Chile 30.33S 71.16W
85 C17 **Ovamboland** physical region N Namibia
56 L10 **Ovana, Cerro** ▲ S Venezuela 4.41N 66.54W
106 G7 **Ovar** Aveiro, N Portugal 40.52N 8.37W
116 L10 **Ovcharitsa, Yazovir** ⊠ SE Bulgaria
56 E6 **Ovejas** Sucre, NW Colombia 9.30N 75.15W
103 E16 **Overath** Nordrhein-Westfalen, W Germany 50.55N 7.16E
100 F13 **Overflakkee** island SW Netherlands
101 H19 **Overijse** Vlaams Brabant, C Belgium 50.46N 4.31E
100 N10 **Overijssel** ◆ province E Netherlands
100 M9 **Overijssels Kanaal** canal E Netherlands
94 K13 **Överkalix** Norrbotten, N Sweden 66.19N 22.49E
29 R4 **Overland Park** Kansas, C USA 38.57N 94.40W
101 L14 **Overloon** Noord-Brabant, SE Netherlands 51.35N 5.54E
101 K16 **Overpelt** Limburg, NE Belgium 51.13N 5.24E
37 Y10 **Overton** Nevada, W USA 36.32N 114.25W
27 W7 **Overton** Texas, SW USA 32.16N 94.58W
94 K13 **Övertorneå** Norrbotten, N Sweden 66.22N 23.38E
97 N18 **Överum** Kalmar, S Sweden 57.58N 16.19E
94 G13 **Överuman** ◎ N Sweden
Övgödiy see Telmen
119 P11 **Ovidiopol'** Odes'ka Oblast', SW Ukraine 46.15N 30.27E
118 M14 **Ovidiu** Constanţa, SE Romania 44.16N 28.34E
47 N10 **Oviedo** SW Dominican Republic 17.46N 71.22W
106 K2 **Oviedo** anc. Asturias. Asturias, NW Spain 43.21N 5.49W
106 K2 **Oviedo** ✕ Asturias, N Spain 43.21N 5.49W
Ovilava see Wels
120 D7 **Oviši** Ventspils, W Latvia 57.34N 21.43E
152 K10 **Ovminzatovo Tog'lari** Rus. Gory Auminzatau. ▲ N Uzbekistan
Ovoot see Darīganga
163 O4 **Övörhangay** ◆ province C Mongolia
96 E12 **Øvre Årdal** Sogn og Fjordane, S Norway 61.17N 7.44E
97 J14 **Övre Fryken** ◎ C Sweden
94 J11 **Övre Soppero** Lapp. Badje-Sohppar. Norrbotten, N Sweden 68.07N 21.40E
119 N3 **Ovruch** Zhytomyrs'ka Oblast', N Ukraine 51.19N 28.50E
Övt see Bat-Öldziy
193 E24 **Owaka** Otago, South Island, NZ 46.27S 169.42E
81 H18 **Owando** prev. Fort-Rousset. Cuvette, C Congo 0.28S 15.55E
171 Gg17 **Owase** Mie, Honshū, SW Japan 34.04N 136.10E
29 P9 **Owasso** Oklahoma, C USA 36.16N 95.51W
31 V10 **Owatonna** Minnesota, N USA 44.04N 93.13W
181 O4 **Owen Fracture Zone** tectonic feature W Arabian Sea
193 H15 **Owen, Mount** ▲ South Island, NZ 41.32S 172.33E
193 H15 **Owen River** Tasman, South Island, NZ 41.40S 172.28E
46 D8 **Owen Roberts** ✕ Grand Cayman, Cayman Islands 19.15N 81.22W
22 I6 **Owensboro** Kentucky, S USA 37.46N 87.06W
37 T11 **Owens Lake** salt flat California, W USA
12 F14 **Owen Sound** Ontario, S Canada 44.34N 80.55W
12 F13 **Owen Sound** ◎ Ontario, S Canada
37 T10 **Owens River** ⁂ California, W USA
194 K15 **Owen Stanley Range** ▲ S PNG
29 V5 **Owensville** Missouri, C USA 38.21N 91.30W
22 M4 **Owenton** Kentucky, S USA 38.33N 84.51W
79 U17 **Owerri** Imo, S Nigeria 5.19N 7.07E
192 M10 **Owhango** Manawatu-Wanganui, North Island, NZ 39.01S 175.22E
23 N5 **Owingsville** Kentucky, S USA 38.10N 83.42W
79 T16 **Owo** Ondo, SW Nigeria 7.10N 5.31E
33 R9 **Owosso** Michigan, N USA 43.00N 84.10W
37 V1 **Owyhee** Nevada, W USA 41.57N 116.07W
34 L14 **Owyhee, Lake** ◎ Oregon, NW USA
34 L15 **Owyhee River** ⁂ Idaho/Oregon, NW USA
94 K1 **Öxarfjördhur** var. Axarfjördhur. fjord N Iceland
96 K12 **Oxberg** Dalarna, C Sweden 61.07N 14.10E
9 V17 **Oxbow** Saskatchewan, S Canada 49.16N 102.12W
97 O17 **Oxelösund** Södermanland, S Sweden 58.40N 17.10E
193 H18 **Oxford** Canterbury, South Island, NZ 43.18S 172.10E
99 M21 **Oxford** Lat. Oxonia. S England, UK 51.46N 1.15W
25 Q3 **Oxford** Alabama, S USA 33.36N 85.50W
24 L2 **Oxford** Mississippi, S USA 34.23N 89.30W
31 N16 **Oxford** Nebraska, C USA 40.15N 99.37W
20 I11 **Oxford** New York, NE USA 42.21N 75.39W
23 U8 **Oxford** North Carolina, SE USA 36.18N 78.35W
33 Q14 **Oxford** Ohio, N USA 39.30N 84.45W
20 H16 **Oxford** Pennsylvania, NE USA 39.46N 75.57W
9 X12 **Oxford House** Manitoba, C Canada 54.55N 95.13W
31 Y13 **Oxford Junction** Iowa, C USA 41.58N 90.57W
9 X12 **Oxford Lake** ◎ Manitoba, C Canada
99 M21 **Oxfordshire** cultural region S England, UK
Oxia see Oxyá
43 X12 **Oxkutzcab** Yucatán, SE Mexico 20.14N 89.20W
37 R15 **Oxnard** California, W USA 34.12N 119.10W
Oxonia see Oxford
12 I12 **Oxtongue** ⁂ Ontario, SE Canada
Oxus see Amu Darya
117 E15 **Oxyá** var. Oxia. ▲ C Greece 39.46N 21.56E
171 Ii13 **Oyabe** Toyama, Honshū, SW Japan 36.41N 136.53E
Oyahue/Oyahue, Volcán see Ollagüe, Volcán
171 K16 **Oyama** Tochigi, Honshū, S Japan 36.19N 139.46E
49 U5 **Oyapock** ⁂ E French Guiana
Oyapock see Oiapoque, Rio
57 Z10 **Oyapok, Baie de L'** bay Brazil/French Guiana
57 Z11 **Oyapok, Fleuve l'** var. Oyapock, Rio Oiapoque. ⁂ Brazil/French Guiana see also Oiapoque, Rio
81 E17 **Oyem** Woleu-Ntem, N Gabon 1.34N 11.31E
9 R16 **Oyen** Alberta, SW Canada 51.19N 110.28W
97 I15 **Øyeren** ◎ S Norway
Oygon see Tüdevtey
98 I7 **Oykel** ⁂ N Scotland, UK
127 N9 **Oymyakon** Respublika Sakha (Yakutiya), NE Russian Federation 63.28N 142.22E
81 H19 **Oyo** Cuvette, C Congo 1.05S 15.55E
79 S15 **Oyo** Oyo, W Nigeria 7.51N 3.57E
79 S15 **Oyo** ◆ state SW Nigeria
58 D13 **Oyón** Lima, C Peru 10.39S 76.46W
105 S10 **Oyonnax** Ain, E France 46.16N 5.39E
152 L10 **Oyoqog'itma** Rus. Ayakagytma. Buxoro Viloyati, C Uzbekistan 40.37N 64.26E
152 M9 **Oyoqquduq** Rus. Ayakkuduk. Navoiy Viloyati, N Uzbekistan 41.16N 65.12E
34 F9 **Oysterville** Washington, NW USA 46.33N 124.03W
97 D14 **Øystese** Hordaland, S Norway 60.22N 6.13E
153 U10 **Oy-Tal** Oshskaya Oblast', SW Kyrgyzstan 40.23N 74.04E
153 T10 **Oy-Tal** ⁂ SW Kyrgyzstan
151 S16 **Oytal** Zhambyl, S Kazakhstan 42.50N 73.21E
Oyyl see Uil
179 Qq15 **Ozamiz** Mindanao, S Philippines 8.09N 123.51E
Ozarichi see Azarychy
25 R7 **Ozark** Alabama, S USA 31.27N 85.38W
29 S10 **Ozark** Arkansas, C USA 35.29N 93.49W
29 T8 **Ozark** Missouri, C USA 37.01N 93.12W
29 T8 **Ozark Plateau** plain Arkansas/Missouri, C USA
29 T6 **Ozarks, Lake of the** ⊠ Missouri, C USA
199 Jj11 **Ozbourn Seamount** undersea feature W Pacific Ocean 26.00S 174.49W
113 L20 **Ózd** Borsod-Abaúj-Zemplén, NE Hungary 48.14N 20.18E
114 D11 **Ozeblin** ▲ C Croatia 44.37N 15.52E
127 Pp12 **Ozernovskiy** Kamchatskaya Oblast', E Russian Federation 51.28N 156.32E
150 M7 **Ozërnoye** var. Ozërnyy. Kostanay, N Kazakhstan 53.27N 63.10E
Ozërnyy see Ozërnoye
128 I15 **Ozërnyy** Tverskaya Oblast', W Russian Federation 57.55N 33.45E
117 D18 **Ozerós, Límni** ◎ W Greece
121 D14 **Ozersk** prev. Darkehnen, Ger. Angerapp. Kaliningradskaya Oblast', W Russian Federation 54.23N 21.59E
124 Ee11 **Ozërsk** Chelyabinskaya Oblast', C Russian Federation 55.44N 60.59E
130 L4 **Ozery** Moskovskaya Oblast', W Russian Federation 54.51N 38.37E
Özgön see Uzgen
109 C17 **Ozieri** Sardegna, Italy, C Mediterranean Sea 40.34N 9.01E
113 I15 **Ozimek** Ger. Malapane. Opolskie, S Poland 50.41N 18.16E
131 R8 **Ozinki** Saratovskaya Oblast', W Russian Federation 51.16N 49.45E
Oziya see Ojiya
27 O10 **Ozona** Texas, SW USA 30.42N 101.12W
Ozorkov see Ozorków
112 J12 **Ozorków** Rus. Ozorkov. Łódź, C Poland 51.58N 19.16E
170 E14 **Ōzu** Ehime, Shikoku, SW Japan 33.31N 132.31E
143 R10 **Ozurget'i** prev. Makharadze. W Georgia 41.57N 42.01E

P

101 J17 **Paal** Limburg, NE Belgium 51.03N 5.08E
197 C13 **Paama** island C Vanuatu
206 M14 **Paamiut** var. Pâmiut, Dan. Frederikshåb. Kitaa, S Greenland 62.22N 49.52W
178 Gg9 **Pa-an** Karen State, S Burma 16.51N 97.37E
103 L22 **Paar** ⁂ SE Germany
85 E26 **Paarl** Western Cape, SW South Africa 33.45S 18.58E
95 L15 **Paavola** Oulu, C Finland 64.34N 25.15E
98 E8 **Pabbay** island NW Scotland, UK
175 P12 **Pabbiring, Kepulauan** island group C Indonesia
159 T15 **Pabna** Rajshahi, W Bangladesh 24.02N 89.15E
111 U4 **Pabneukirchen** Oberösterreich, N Austria 48.19N 14.49E
120 H13 **Pabradė** Pol. Podbrodzie. Vilnius, SE Lithuania 54.58N 25.43E
58 L13 **Pacahuaras, Río** ⁂ N Bolivia
Pacaraima, Sierra/Pacaraim, Serra see Pakaraima Mountains
58 B11 **Pacasmayo** La Libertad, W Peru 7.27S 79.34W
44 D6 **Pacaya, Volcán de** ※ S Guatemala 14.19N 90.36W
117 K23 **Pachia** var. Pachía. island Kykládes, Greece, Aegean Sea
Pachía see Pacheía
109 L26 **Pachino** Sicilia, Italy, C Mediterranean Sea 36.43N 15.06E
58 F12 **Pachitea, Río** ⁂ C Peru
160 I11 **Pachmarhi** Madhya Pradesh, C India 22.36N 78.18E
124 N4 **Páchna** var. Pakhna. SW Cyprus 34.47N 32.48E
117 H25 **Páchnes** ▲ Kríti, Greece, E Mediterranean Sea 35.19N 24.00E
56 F9 **Pacho** Cundinamarca, C Colombia 5.07N 74.11W
160 F12 **Pāchora** Mahārāshtra, C India 20.52N 75.28E
43 P13 **Pachuca** var. Pachuca de Soto. Hidalgo, C Mexico 20.05N 98.46W
Pachuca de Soto see Pachuca
29 W5 **Pacific** Missouri, C USA 38.28N 90.44W
199 Jj15 **Pacific-Antarctic Ridge** undersea feature S Pacific Ocean
34 F8 **Pacific Beach** Washington, NW USA 47.09N 124.12W
37 N10 **Pacific Grove** California, W USA 36.35N 121.54W
31 S15 **Pacific Junction** Iowa, C USA 41.01N 95.48W
198-199 **Pacific Ocean** ocean
133 Z10 **Pacific Plate** tectonic feature
115 J15 **Pačir** ▲ N-Montenegro 43.19N 19.07E
190 L5 **Packsaddle** New South Wales, SE Australia 30.42S 141.55E
34 H9 **Packwood** Washington, NW USA 46.37N 121.38W
Padalung see Phatthalung
175 Q12 **Padamarang, Pulau** island C Indonesia
173 G9 **Padang** Sumatera, W Indonesia 01.00S 100.21E
174 Hh5 **Padang Endau** Pahang, Peninsular Malaysia 2.38N 103.37E
Padangpandjang see Padangpanjang
173 G8 **Padangpanjang** prev. Padangpandjang. Sumatera, W Indonesia 0.30S 100.25E
173 Ff7 **Padangsidempuan** prev. Padangsidimpoean. Sumatera, W Indonesia 1.22N 99.14E
Padangsidimpoean see Padangsidempuan
128 I9 **Padany** Respublika Kareliya, NW Russian Federation 63.18N 33.20E
95 M18 **Padasjoki** Etelä-Suomi, S Finland 61.20N 25.20E
59 M22 **Padcaya** Tarija, S Bolivia 21.52S 64.46W
103 H14 **Paderborn** Nordrhein-Westfalen, NW Germany 51.43N 8.45E
Padeşul/Padeş, Vîrful see Padeş, Vârful
118 F12 **Padeş, Vârful** var. Padeşul; prev. Vîrful Padeş. ▲ W Romania 45.39N 22.19E
114 L10 **Padinska Skela** Serbia, N Serbia 44.58N 20.25E
Padma see Brahmaputra
159 S14 **Padma** var. Ganges. ⁂ Bangladesh/India see also Ganges
108 H8 **Padova** Eng. Padua; anc. Patavium. Veneto, NE Italy 45.24N 11.52E
84 A10 **Padrão, Ponta do** headland NW Angola 6.06S 12.18E
27 T16 **Padre Island** island Texas, SW USA
106 G3 **Padrón** Galicia, NW Spain 42.43N 8.40W
120 K13 **Padsvillye** Rus. Podsvil'ye. Vitsyebskaya Voblasts', N Belarus 55.10N 27.58E
190 K11 **Padthaway** South Australia 36.39S 140.30E
Padua see Padova
22 G7 **Paducah** Kentucky, S USA 37.09N 88.52W
27 P4 **Paducah** Texas, SW USA 33.59N 100.19W
107 N15 **Padul** Andalucía, S Spain 37.01N 3.37W
203 P8 **Paea** Tahiti, W French Polynesia 17.40S 149.34W
193 L14 **Paekakariki** Wellington, North Island, NZ 41.00S 174.58E
169 X11 **Paektu-san** var. Baitou Shan. ▲ China/North Korea 42.00N 128.03W
169 V15 **Paengnyŏng-do** island NW South Korea
192 M7 **Paeroa** Waikato, North Island, NZ 37.22S 175.39E
56 D12 **Páez** Cauca, SW Colombia 2.37N 76.00W
123 Mm4 **Páfos** var. Paphos. W Cyprus 34.46N 32.25E
123 Mm4 **Páfos** ✕ SW Cyprus 34.46N 32.25E
85 L19 **Pafúri** Gaza, SW Mozambique 22.24S 31.27E
114 C12 **Pag** It. Pago. Lika-Senj, W Croatia 44.26N 15.01E
114 B11 **Pag** It. Pago. island Zadar, SW Croatia
179 Qq16 **Pagadian** Mindanao, S Philippines 7.47N 123.22E
173 G11 **Pagai Selatan, Pulau** island Kepulauan Mentawai, W Indonesia
173 Ff10 **Pagai Utara, Pulau** island Kepulauan Mentawai, W Indonesia
196 K4 **Pagan** island C Northern Mariana Islands
117 G16 **Pagasitikós Kólpos** gulf E Greece
38 L8 **Page** Arizona, SW USA 36.54N 111.28W
31 Q5 **Page** North Dakota, N USA 47.09N 97.33W
120 D13 **Pagėgiai** Ger. Pogegen. Tauragė, SW Lithuania 55.08N 21.54E
23 S11 **Pageland** South Carolina, SE USA 34.46N 80.23W
83 G16 **Pager** ⁂ NE Uganda
155 Q5 **Paghmān** Kābol, E Afghanistan 34.33N 68.55E
Pago see Pag
196 C16 **Pago Bay** bay E Guam, W Pacific Ocean
117 M20 **Pagóndas** var. Pagóndhas. Sámos, Dodekánisa, Greece, Aegean Sea 37.40N 26.49E
Pagóndhas see Pagóndas
198 C8 **Pago Pago** ○ (American Samoa) Tutuila, W American Samoa 14.16S 170.43W
39 R8 **Pagosa Springs** Colorado, C USA 37.13N 107.01W
40 H12 **Pāhala** var. Pahala. Hawai'i, USA, C Pacific Ocean 19.12N 155.28W
174 H4 **Pahang** off. Negeri Pahang Darul Makmur. ◆ state Peninsular Malaysia
Pahang see Pahang, Sungai
174 Hh5 **Pahang, Sungai** var. Pahang, Sungei Pahang. ⁂ Peninsular Malaysia
155 S8 **Pahārpur** North-West Frontier Province, NW Pakistan 32.06N 71.00E
193 B24 **Pahia Point** headland South Island, NZ 46.19S 167.42E
192 M13 **Pahiatua** Manawatu-Wanganui, North Island, NZ 40.30S 175.48E
40 H12 **Pāhoa** var. Pahoa. Hawai'i, USA, C Pacific Ocean 19.28N 154.55W
25 Y14 **Pahokee** Florida, SE USA 26.49N 80.40W
37 X9 **Pahranagat Range** ▲ Nevada, W USA
37 W11 **Pahrump** Nevada, W USA 36.11N 115.58W
Pahsien see Chongqing
37 V9 **Pahute Mesa** ▲ Nevada, W USA
178 H7 **Pai** Mae Hong Son, NW Thailand 19.24N 98.25E
40 F10 **Pā'ia** var. Paia. Maui, Hawai'i, USA, C Pacific Ocean 20.54N 94.22W
Pai-ch'eng see Baicheng
120 H4 **Paide** Ger. Weissenstein. Järvamaa, N Estonia 58.54N 25.36E
99 J24 **Paignton** SW England, UK 50.25N 3.34W
192 K3 **Paihia** Northland, North Island, NZ 35.18S 174.06E
95 M18 **Päijänne** ◎ S Finland
116 F13 **Páïko** ▲ N Greece
59 M17 **Paila, Río** ⁂ C Bolivia
178 I12 **Pailin** Bătdâmbâng, W Cambodia 12.51N 102.34E
Pailing see Chun'an
56 F6 **Pailitas** Cesar, N Colombia 8.58N 73.37W
40 F9 **Pailolo Channel** channel Hawai'i, USA, C Pacific Ocean
95 K19 **Paimio** Swe. Pemar. Länsi-Suomi, W Finland 60.27N 22.42E
172 O17 **Paimi-saki** var. Yaeme-saki. headland Iriomote-jima, SW Japan 24.18N 123.40E
104 G5 **Paimpol** Côtes d'Armor, NW France 48.46N 3.03W
174 Gg9 **Painan** Sumatera, W Indonesia 1.22S 100.33E
65 G23 **Paine, Cerro** ▲ S Chile 51.01S 72.57W
33 U11 **Painesville** Ohio, N USA 41.43N 81.15W
33 S14 **Paint Creek** ⁂ Ohio, N USA
38 L10 **Painted Desert** desert Arizona, SW USA
Paint Hills see Wemindji
32 M4 **Paint River** ⁂ Michigan, N USA
27 P8 **Paint Rock** Texas, SW USA 31.30N 99.55W
23 O6 **Paintsville** Kentucky, S USA 37.48N 82.48W
Paisance see Piacenza
98 I12 **Paisley** W Scotland, UK 55.49N 4.25W
34 I15 **Paisley** Oregon, NW USA 42.40N 120.31W
107 R10 **País Valenciano** var. Valencia, Cat. València; anc. Valentia. ◆ autonomous community NE Spain

◆ Country
● Country Capital
◇ Dependent Territory
○ Dependent Territory Capital
◆ Administrative Region
✕ International Airport
▲ Mountain
▲ Mountain Range
※ Volcano
⁂ River
◎ Lake
⊠ Reservoir
307

País Vasco – Paris

107 O3 **País Vasco** Basq. Euskadi, Eng. The Basque Country, Sp. Provincias Vascongadas. ◐ autonomous community N Spain
58 A9 **Paita** Piura, NW Peru 5.07S 81.07W
197 J7 **Païta** Province Sud, S New Caledonia 22.06S 166.18E
175 O1 **Paitan, Teluk** bay Sabah, East Malaysia
106 H7 **Paiva, Rio** ≈ N Portugal
94 K12 **Pajala** Norrbotten, N Sweden 67.12N 23.19E
106 K3 **Pajares, Puerto de** pass NW Spain 43.00N 5.53W
56 G9 **Pajarito** Boyacá, C Colombia 5.18N 72.43W
56 G4 **Pájaro** La Guajira, S Colombia 11.41N 72.37W
Pakanbaru see Pekanbaru
57 Q10 **Pakaraima Mountains** var. Serra Pacaraim, Sierra Pacaraima. ▲▲ N South America
178 Hh11 **Pak Chong** Nakhon Ratchasima, C Thailand 14.38N 101.22E
127 Pp7 **Pakhachi** Koryakskiy Avtonomnyy Okrug, E Russian Federation 60.36N 168.59E
Pakhna see Páchna
201 U16 **Pakin Atoll** atoll Caroline Islands, E Micronesia
155 Q12 **Pakistan** off. Islamic Republic of Pakistan, var. Islami Jamhuriya e Pakistan. ◆ republic S Asia
Pakistan, Islami Jamhuriya e see Pakistan
178 I8 **Pak Lay** var. Muang Pak Lay. Xaignabouli, C Laos 18.06N 101.21E
Paknam see Samut Prakan
177 Ff5 **Pakokku** Magwe, C Burma 21.19N 95.04E
112 I10 **Pakość** Ger. Pakosch. Kujawski-pomorskie, C Poland 52.47N 18.03E
Pakosch see Pakość
155 V10 **Pākpattan** Punjab, E Pakistan 30.19N 73.27E
178 H16 **Pak Phanang** var. Ban Pak Phanang. Nakhon Si Thammarat, SW Thailand 8.19N 100.10E
114 G9 **Pakrac** Hung. Pakrácz. Požega-Slavonija, NE Croatia 45.26N 17.09E
Pakrácz see Pakrac
120 F11 **Pakruojis** Šiauliai, N Lithuania 55.59N 23.50E
113 J24 **Paks** Tolna, S Hungary 46.37N 18.51E
Pak Sane see Pakxan
Paksé see Pakxé
178 I11 **Pak Thong Chai** Nakhon Ratchasima, C Thailand 14.43N 102.01E
155 R6 **Paktīā** ◐ province SE Afghanistan
155 Q7 **Paktīkā** ◐ province SE Afghanistan
175 Pp9 **Pakuli** Sulawesi, C Indonesia 1.14S 119.55E
83 F17 **Pakwach** NW Uganda 2.28N 31.28E
178 Ii8 **Pakxan** var. Muang Pakxan, Pak Sane. Bolikhamxai, C Laos 18.27N 103.38E
178 Jj10 **Pakxé** var. Paksé. Champasak, S Laos 15.09N 105.49E
80 G12 **Pala** Mayo-Kébbi, SW Chad 9.22N 14.54E
63 A17 **Palacios** Santa Fe, C Argentina 30.43S 61.37W
27 V13 **Palacios** Texas, SW USA 28.42N 96.13W
107 X5 **Palafrugell** Cataluña, NE Spain 41.55N 3.10E
109 L24 **Palagonia** Sicilia, Italy, C Mediterranean Sea 37.19N 14.45E
115 E17 **Palagruža** It. Pelagosa. island SW Croatia
117 G20 **Palaiá Epídavros** Pelopónnisos, S Greece 37.38N 23.09E
124 Nn3 **Palaichóri** var. Palekhori. C Cyprus 34.55N 33.06E
117 H25 **Palaiochóra** Kríti, Greece, E Mediterranean Sea 35.14N 23.37E
117 A15 **Palaiokastrítsa** religious building Kerkýra, Iónia Nisiá, Greece, C Mediterranean Sea 39.41N 19.42E
117 J19 **Palaiópoli** Ándros, Kykládes, Greece, Aegean Sea 37.49N 24.49E
105 N5 **Palaiseau** Essonne, N France 48.40N 2.13E
Palakkad see Pālghāt
160 N11 **Pāla Laharha** Orissa, E India 21.27N 85.14E
85 G19 **Palamakoloi** Ghanzi, C Botswana 23.10S 22.22E
117 E16 **Palamás** Thessalía, C Greece 39.28N 22.04E
107 X5 **Palamós** Cataluña, NE Spain 41.51N 3.06E
120 J5 **Palamuse** Ger. Sankt-Bartholomäi. Jõgevamaa, E Estonia 58.40N 26.34E
191 Q14 **Palana** Tasmania, SE Australia 39.48S 147.54E
127 P9 **Palana** Koryakskiy Avtonomnyy Okrug, E Russian Federation 59.04N 159.58E
120 C11 **Palanga** Ger. Polangen. Klaipėda, NW Lithuania 5.54N 21.05E
149 V10 **Palangān, Kūh-e** ▲▲ E Iran
Palangkaraja see Palangkaraya
174 Mm10 **Palangkaraya** prev. Palangkaraja. Borneo, C Indonesia 2.16S 113.55E
161 H22 **Palani** Tamil Nādu, SE India 10.30N 77.24E
Palanka see Bačka Palanka
160 D9 **Pālanpur** Gujarāt, W India 24.12N 72.28E
Palantia see Palencia
85 I19 **Palapye** Central, SE Botswana 22.37S 27.06E
161 J19 **Pālār** ≈ SE India
106 H3 **Palas de Rei** Galicia, NW Spain 42.52N 7.51W
127 O10 **Palatka** Magadanskaya Oblast', E Russian Federation 60.09N 150.33E
25 W10 **Palatka** Florida, SE USA 29.39N 81.38W
196 B9 **Palau** var. Belau. ◆ republic W Pacific Ocean
133 Y14 **Palau Islands** var. Palau. island group N Palau
198 Aa8 **Palauli Bay** bay Savai'i, Samoa, C Pacific Ocean
178 Gg12 **Palaw** Tenasserim, S Burma 12.57N 98.39E
179 Oo15 **Palawan** island W Philippines
179 Oo15 **Palawan Passage** passage W Philippines
198 F7 **Palawan Trough** undersea feature S South China Sea
179 P10 **Palayan City** Luzon, N Philippines 15.34N 121.34E
161 H23 **Pālayankottai** Tamil Nādu, SE India 8.44N 77.45E
109 L25 **Palazzolo Acreide** anc. Acrae. Sicilia, Italy, C Mediterranean Sea 37.04N 14.54E
120 G3 **Paldiski** prev. Baltiski, Eng. Baltic Port, Ger. Baltischport. Harjumaa, NW Estonia 59.20N 24.04E
114 I13 **Pale** Republika Srpska, E Bosnia and Herzegovina 43.49N 18.35E
Palekhori see Palaichóri
175 Q7 **Paleleh, Pegunungan** ▲▲ Sulawesi, N Indonesia
175 Qq7 **Paleleh, Teluk** bay Sulawesi, N Indonesia
174 I11 **Palembang** Sumatera, W Indonesia 2.58S 104.45E
65 G18 **Palena** Los Lagos, S Chile 43.40S 71.49W
65 G18 **Palena, Río** ≈ S Chile
106 M5 **Palencia** anc. Palantia, Pallantia. Castilla-León, NW Spain 41.01N 4.31W
106 M3 **Palencia** ◐ province Castilla-León, N Spain
37 X15 **Palen Dry Lake** ◎ California, W USA
43 V15 **Palenque** Chiapas, SE Mexico 17.37N 92.03W
43 V15 **Palenque** var. Ruinas de Palenque. ruins Chiapas, SE Mexico 17.31N 91.58W
47 O9 **Palenque, Punta** headland S Dominican Republic 18.13N 70.08W
Palenque, Ruinas de see Palenque
Palerme see Palermo
109 I23 **Palermo** Fr. Palerme; anc. Panhormus, Panormus. Sicilia, Italy, C Mediterranean Sea 38.07N 13.22E
27 V8 **Palestine** Texas, SW USA 31.44N 95.38W
27 V7 **Palestine, Lake** ⊟ Texas, SW USA
109 I15 **Palestrina** Lazio, C Italy 41.49N 12.53E
177 F5 **Paletwa** Chin State, W Burma 21.21N 92.51E
161 G21 **Pālghāt** var. Palakkad; prev. Pulicat. Kerala, SW India 10.46N 76.42E
158 F13 **Pāli** Rājasthān, N India 25.48N 73.21E
178 Gg16 **Palian** Trang, SW Thailand
201 O12 **Palikir** ● (Micronesia) Pohnpei, E Micronesia 6.58N 158.13E
179 R17 **Palimbang** Mindanao, S Philippines 6.16N 124.10E
Palimé see Kpalimé
109 L19 **Palinuro, Capo** headland S Italy 40.02N 15.16E
117 H15 **Palioúri, Akrotírio** var. Akra Kanestron. headland N Greece 39.55N 23.45E
35 R14 **Palisades Reservoir** ⊟ Idaho, NW USA
101 J23 **Paliseul** Luxembourg, SE Belgium 49.55N 5.09E
160 C11 **Pālitāna** Gujarāt, W India 21.30N 71.49E
120 F4 **Palivere** Läänemaa, W Estonia 58.59N 23.58E
43 V14 **Palizada** Campeche, SE Mexico 18.15N 92.03W
95 L18 **Pälkäne** Länsi-Suomi, W Finland 61.21N 24.15E
161 J22 **Palk Strait** strait India/Sri Lanka
161 J23 **Pallai** Northern Province, NW Sri Lanka 9.34N 80.19E
Pallantia see Palencia
108 C6 **Pallanza** Piemonte, NE Italy 45.57N 8.32E
131 Q9 **Pallasovka** Volgogradskaya Oblast', SW Russian Federation 50.06N 46.52E
Pallene/Pallíni see Kassándra
193 L15 **Palliser Bay** bay North Island, NZ
193 L15 **Palliser, Cape** headland North Island, NZ 41.37S 175.16E
203 U9 **Palliser, Îles** island group Îles Tuamotu, C French Polynesia
107 X9 **Palma** var. Palma de Mallorca. Mallorca, Spain, W Mediterranean Sea 39.34N 2.39E
107 X9 **Palma** ✕ Mallorca, Spain, W Mediterranean Sea
84 Q12 **Palma** Cabo Delgado, N Mozambique 10.46S 40.30E
107 X10 **Palma, Badia de** bay Mallorca, Spain, W Mediterranean Sea
106 L13 **Palma del Río** Andalucía, S Spain 37.42N 5.16W
Palma de Mallorca see Palma
109 J25 **Palma di Montechiaro** Sicilia, Italy, C Mediterranean Sea 37.12N 13.46E
108 J7 **Palmanova** Friuli-Venezia Giulia, NE Italy 45.54N 13.20E
56 J7 **Palmarito** Apure, C Venezuela 7.36N 70.11W
45 N15 **Palmar Sur** Puntarenas, SE Costa Rica 8.54N 83.27W
62 I12 **Palmas** Paraná, S Brazil 26.29S 52.00W
61 K16 **Palmas** var. Palmas do Tocantins, C Brazil 10.24S 48.19W
78 L18 **Palmas, Cape** Fr. Cap des Palmès headland SW Ivory Coast 4.18N 7.31W
Palmas do Tocantins see Palmas
56 D11 **Palmaseca** ✕ (Cali) Valle del Cauca, SW Colombia 3.31N 76.27W
109 B21 **Palmas, Golfo di** gulf Sardegna, Italy, C Mediterranean Sea
46 I7 **Palma Soriano** Santiago de Cuba, E Cuba 20.10N 76.00W
25 Y12 **Palm Bay** Florida, SE USA 28.01N 80.35W
37 T14 **Palmdale** California, W USA 34.34N 118.07W
63 H14 **Palmeira das Missões** Rio Grande do Sul, S Brazil 27.54S 53.19W
84 A11 **Palmeirinhas, Ponta das** headland NW Angola 9.04S 13.02E
41 R11 **Palmer** Alaska, USA 61.36N 149.06W
21 N11 **Palmer** Massachusetts, NE USA 42.09N 72.19W
27 U7 **Palmer** Texas, SW USA 32.25N 96.40W
204 H4 **Palmer** US research station Antarctica 64.37S 64.01W
13 R11 **Palmer** ≈ Québec, SE Canada
39 T5 **Palmer Lake** Colorado, C USA 39.07N 104.55W
204 J6 **Palmer Land** physical region Antarctica
12 F15 **Palmerston** Ontario, SE Canada 43.51N 80.49W
193 F22 **Palmerston** Otago, South Island, NZ 45.27S 170.42E
202 K15 **Palmerston** island S Cook Islands
Palmerston see Darwin
192 M12 **Palmerston North** Manawatu-Wanganui, North Island, NZ 40.19S 175.52E
Palmés, Cap des see Palmas, Cape
25 V13 **Palmetto** Florida, SE USA 27.31N 82.34W
Palmetto State see South Carolina
109 M22 **Palmi** Calabria, SW Italy 38.21N 15.51E
56 D11 **Palmira** Valle del Cauca, W Colombia 3.33N 76.16W
58 F8 **Palmira, Río** ≈ N Peru
63 D19 **Palmitas** Soriano, SW Uruguay 33.27S 57.48W
Palmnicken see Yantarnyy
37 V15 **Palm Springs** California, W USA 33.48N 116.33W
29 V2 **Palmyra** Missouri, C USA 39.47N 91.31W
20 G10 **Palmyra** New York, NE USA 43.02N 77.13W
20 G15 **Palmyra** Pennsylvania, NE USA 40.18N 76.35W
23 V5 **Palmyra** Virginia, NE USA 37.53N 78.15W
Palmyra see Tudmur
199 K7 **Palmyra Atoll** ◇ US privately owned unincorporated territory C Pacific Ocean
160 P12 **Palmyras Point** headland E India 20.46N 87.00E
37 N9 **Palo Alto** California, W USA 37.26N 122.08W
27 O1 **Palo Duro Creek** ≈ Texas, SW USA
Paloe see Palu
Paloe see Denpasar, Bali, C Indonesia
174 Hh6 **Paloh** Johor, Peninsular Malaysia 2.10N 103.10E
82 F12 **Paloich** Upper Nile, SE Sudan 10.28N 32.31E
42 I3 **Palomas** Chihuahua, N Mexico 31.45N 107.38W
109 I15 **Palombara Sabina** Lazio, C Italy 42.04N 12.45E
107 S13 **Palos, Cabo de** headland SE Spain 37.38N 0.42W
106 I14 **Palos de la Frontera** Andalucía, S Spain 37.13N 6.52W
62 G11 **Palotina** Paraná, S Brazil 24.16S 53.49W
34 M9 **Palouse** Washington, NW USA 46.54N 117.04W
34 L9 **Palouse River** ≈ Washington, NW USA
37 Y16 **Palo Verde** California, W USA 33.25N 114.43W
59 E16 **Palpa** Ica, W Peru 14.33S 75.09W
97 M16 **Pålsboda** Örebro, C Sweden 59.04N 15.21E
95 M15 **Paltamo** Oulu, C Finland 64.25N 27.49E
175 Pp9 **Palu** prev. Paloe. Sulawesi, C Indonesia 0.54S 119.52E
143 P14 **Palu** Elazığ, E Turkey 38.43N 39.55E
175 Q16 **Palu, Pulau** island S Indonesia
175 P8 **Palu, Teluk** bay Sulawesi, C Indonesia
158 I11 **Palwal** Haryāna, N India 28.15N 77.18E
127 Oo4 **Palyavaam** ≈ NE Russian Federation
79 Q13 **Pama** SE Burkina 11.13N 0.46E
180 J14 **Pamandzi** ✕ (Mamoudzou) Petite-Terre, E Mayotte
Pamangkat see Pemangkat
149 R11 **Pā Mazār** Kermān, C Iran
85 N19 **Pambarra** Inhambane, SE Mozambique 21.57S 35.06E
176 Xx10 **Pamdai** Papua, E Indonesia 1.58S 137.19E
176 X10 **Pami** Papua, E Indonesia 2.45S 136.02E
105 N16 **Pamiers** Ariège, S France 43.07N 1.36E
153 T14 **Pamir** var. Daryā-ye Pāmīr, Taj. Dar"yoi Pomir. ≈ Afghanistan/Tajikistan see also Pāmīr, Daryā-ye
Pamir/Pāmīr, Daryā-ye see Pamirs
155 U1 **Pāmīr, Daryā-ye** var. Pamir, Taj. Dar"yoi Pomir. ≈ Afghanistan/Tajikistan see also Pamir
Pāmīr-e Khord see Little Pamir
133 Q8 **Pamirs** Pash. Daryā-ye Pāmīr, Rus. Pamir. ▲▲ C Asia
Pâmiut see Paamiut
23 X10 **Pamlico River** ≈ North Carolina, SE USA
23 Y10 **Pamlico Sound** sound North Carolina, SE USA
27 O2 **Pampa** Texas, SW USA 35.31N 100.58W
Pampa Aullagas, Lago see Poopó, Lago
63 B21 **Pampa Húmeda** grassland E Argentina
58 A10 **Pampa las Salinas** salt lake NW Peru
59 F15 **Pampas** Huancavelica, C Peru 12.22S 74.52W
64 K13 **Pampas** plain C Argentina
57 O4 **Pampatar** Nueva Esparta, NE Venezuela 10.58N 63.49W
Pampeluna see Pamplona
106 H8 **Pampilhosa da Serra** var. Pampilhosa de Serra. Coimbra, N Portugal 40.03N 7.58W
181 Y15 **Pamplemousses** N Mauritius 20.06S 57.34E
56 G7 **Pamplona** Norte de Santander, N Colombia 7.24N 72.37W
107 Q3 **Pamplona** Basq. Iruña; prev. Pampeluna, anc. Pompaelo. Navarra, N Spain 42.49N 1.39W
116 I11 **Pamporovo** prev. Vasil Kolarov. Smolyan, S Bulgaria 41.39N 24.45E
142 D15 **Pamukkale** Denizli, W Turkey 37.51N 29.13E
23 W5 **Pamunkey River** ≈ Virginia, NE USA
158 K5 **Pamzal** Jammu and Kashmir, NW India 34.16N 78.49E
32 L14 **Pana** Illinois, N USA 39.23N 89.04W
43 Y11 **Panabá** Yucatán, SE Mexico 21.18N 88.15W
37 Y8 **Panaca** Nevada, W USA 37.47N 114.24W
117 E19 **Panachaikó** ▲▲ S Greece
12 F11 **Panache Lake** ◎ Ontario, S Canada
116 I10 **Panagyurishte** Pazardzhik, C Bulgaria 42.30N 24.10E
174 I14 **Panaitan, Pulau** island S Indonesia
174 Ii14 **Panaitan, Selat** strait Jawa, SW Indonesia
117 D18 **Panaitolikó** ▲▲ C Greece
161 E17 **Panaji** var. Pangim, Panjim, New Goa. Goa, W India 15.31N 73.52E
45 T14 **Panama** off. Republic of Panama. ◆ republic Central America
45 T15 **Panamá** var. Ciudad de Panamá, Eng. Panama City. ● (Panama) Panamá, C Panama 8.57N 79.33W
45 U14 **Panamá** off. Provincia de Panamá. ◐ province E Panama
45 U15 **Panamá, Bahía de** bay N Gulf of Panama
200 Oo8 **Panama Basin** undersea feature E Pacific Ocean
45 T15 **Panama Canal** canal E Panama
25 R9 **Panama City** Florida, SE USA 30.09N 85.39W
45 T14 **Panama City** ✕ Panamá, C Panama 9.02N 79.24W
Panama City see Panamá
25 Q9 **Panama City Beach** Florida, SE USA 30.10N 85.48W
45 T17 **Panamá, Golfo de** var. Gulf of Panama. gulf S Panama
Panama, Gulf of see Panamá, Golfo de
Panama, Isthmus of see Panamá, Istmo de
45 T15 **Panamá, Istmo de** Eng. Isthmus of Panama; prev. Isthmus of Darien. isthmus E Panama
37 U11 **Panamint Range** ▲▲ California, W USA
109 L22 **Panarea, Isola** island Isole Eolie, S Italy
108 G9 **Panaro** ≈ N Italy
179 Q14 **Panay Gulf** gulf C Philippines
179 Pp13 **Panay Island** island C Philippines
37 W7 **Pancake Range** ▲▲ Nevada, W USA
114 M11 **Pančevo** Ger. Pantschowa, Hung. Pancsova. Serbia, N Serbia 44.52N 20.39E
115 M15 **Pančićev Vrh** ▲ SW Serbia 43.16N 20.49E
118 L12 **Panciu** Vrancea, E Romania 45.54N 27.07E
118 F10 **Pâncota** Hung. Pankota; prev. Pîncota. Arad, W Romania 46.19N 21.45E
Pancsova see Pančevo
85 N20 **Panda** Inhambane, SE Mozambique 24.04S 34.44E
176 X9 **Pandaidori, Kepulauan** island group E Indonesia
27 N11 **Pandale** Texas, SW USA 30.09N 101.34W
174 H7 **Pandang, Pulau** island W Indonesia
174 Kk9 **Pandang Tikar, Pulau** island N Indonesia
63 F20 **Pan de Azúcar** Maldonado, S Uruguay 34.45S 55.13W
120 H11 **Pandėlys** Panevėžys, NE Lithuania 56.04N 25.18E
161 F15 **Pandharpur** Mahārāshtra, W India 17.42N 75.24E
190 J1 **Pandie Pandie** South Australia 26.06S 139.26E
175 Pp9 **Pandiri** Sulawesi, C Indonesia 1.32S 120.47E
63 F20 **Pando** Canelones, S Uruguay 34.43S 55.58W
59 J14 **Pando** ◐ department N Bolivia
199 Ii10 **Pandora Bank** undersea feature W Pacific Ocean
97 G20 **Pandrup** Nordjylland, N Denmark 57.13N 9.42E
159 V12 **Pandu** Assam, NE India 26.08N 91.37E
81 J15 **Pandu** Equateur, NW Dem. Rep. Congo 5.03N 19.14E
Paneas see Bāniyās
61 F15 **Panelas** Mato Grosso, W Brazil 9.06S 60.41W
120 G12 **Panevėžys** Panevėžys, C Lithuania 55.44N 24.21E
120 G11 **Panevėžys** ◐ province NE Lithuania
Panfilov see Zharkent
131 N9 **Panfilovo** Volgogradskaya Oblast', SW Russian Federation 50.25N 42.55E
81 N17 **Panga** Orientale, N Dem. Rep. Congo 1.52N 26.18E
200 Ss13 **Pangai** Lifuka, C Tonga 19.49S 174.22W
116 H13 **Pangaío** ▲▲ N Greece
81 G20 **Pangala** Le Pool, S Congo 3.26S 14.38E
83 J22 **Pangani** Tanga, E Tanzania 5.27S 39.00E
83 I21 **Pangani** ≈ NE Tanzania
195 U13 **Panggoe** Choiseul Island, NW Solomon Islands 7.00S 95.05E
81 N20 **Pangi** Maniema, E Dem. Rep. Congo 3.12S 26.39E
194 H12 **Pangia** Southern Highlands, W PNG 6.18S 144.12E
Pangim see Panaji
173 F4 **Pangkalanbrandan** Sumatera, W Indonesia 4.00N 98.15E
Pangkalanbun see Pangkalanbuun
174 Ll10 **Pangkalanbuun** var. Pangkalanbun. Borneo, C Indonesia 2.43S 111.37E
174 J10 **Pangkalpinang** Pulau Bangka, W Indonesia 2.04S 106.09E
9 U17 **Pangman** Saskatchewan, S Canada 49.37N 104.33W
Pang-Nga see Phang-Nga
16 Nn2 **Pangnirtung** Baffin Island, Nunavut, NE Canada 66.04N 65.45W
158 K6 **Pangong Tso** var. Bangong Co. ◎ China/India see also Bangong Co
38 K7 **Panguitch** Utah, W USA 37.49N 112.26W
195 S12 **Panguna** Bougainville Island, NE PNG 6.22S 155.19E
179 Pp17 **Pangutaran Group** island group Sulu Archipelago, SW Philippines
27 N2 **Panhandle** Texas, SW USA 35.18N 101.23W
Panhormus see Palermo
176 X12 **Paniai, Danau** ◎ Papua, E Indonesia
81 L21 **Pania-Mutombo** Kasai Oriental, C Dem. Rep. Congo 5.09S 23.49E
Panicherevo see Dolno Panicherevo
197 H5 **Panié, Mont** ▲ C New Caledonia 20.33S 164.41E
158 I10 **Pānīpat** Haryāna, N India 29.18N 77.00E
153 Q14 **Panj** Rus. Pyandzh; prev. Kirovabad. SW Tajikistan 37.39N 69.55E
153 P15 **Panj** Rus. Pyandzh. ≈ Afghanistan/Tajikistan
155 O5 **Panjāb** Bāmiān, C Afghanistan 34.21N 67.00E
153 O12 **Panjakent** Rus. Pendzhikent. W Tajikistan 39.28N 67.33E
154 L14 **Panjgūr** Baluchistān, SW Pakistan 26.58N 64.05E
Panjim see Panaji
169 U12 **Panjin** Liaoning, NE China 41.11N 122.05E
153 P14 **Panji Poyon** Rus. Nizhniy Pyandzh. SW Tajikistan 37.14N 68.32E
155 S4 **Panjshīr** ◐ province NE Afghanistan
155 Q4 **Panjshīr** ≈ E Afghanistan
Pankota see Pâncota
79 W14 **Pankshin** Plateau, C Nigeria 9.21N 9.27E
169 Y10 **Pan Ling** ▲▲ N China
Panlong Jiang see Lô, Sông
160 J9 **Panna** Madhya Pradesh, C India 24.43N 80.10E
101 M16 **Panningen** Limburg, SE Netherlands 51.19N 5.58E
155 R13 **Pāno Āqil** Sind, SE Pakistan 27.56N 69.16E
124 Nn3 **Páno Léfkara** S Cyprus 34.52N 33.18E
124 N3 **Páno Panagiá** var. Pano Panayia. W Cyprus 34.55N 32.38E
Pano Panayia see Páno Panagiá
Panopolis see Akhmîm
31 U14 **Panora** Iowa, C USA 41.41N 94.21W
62 I8 **Panorama** São Paulo, S Brazil 21.22S 51.51W
117 I24 **Pánormos** Kríti, Greece, E Mediterranean Sea 35.24N 24.42E
Panormus see Palermo
169 W11 **Panshi** Jilin, NE China 42.50N 126.06E
61 H19 **Pantanal** var. Pantanalmato-Grossense. swamp SW Brazil
Pantanalmato-Grossense see Pantanal
63 H16 **Pântano Grande** Rio Grande do Sul, S Brazil 30.12S 52.24W
175 R16 **Pantar, Pulau** island Kepulauan Alor, S Indonesia
23 X9 **Pantego** North Carolina, SE USA 35.34N 76.39E
109 G25 **Pantelleria** anc. Cossyra, Cosyra. Sicilia, Italy, C Mediterranean Sea 36.47N 12.00E
109 G25 **Pantelleria, Isola di** island SW Italy
Pante Macassar/Pante Makassar see Pante Makasar
175 Rr17 **Pante Makasar** var. Pante Macassar, Pante Makassar. W East Timor 9.10S 124.27E
158 K10 **Pantnagar** Uttaranchal, N India 29.00N 79.28E
117 A15 **Pantokrátoras** ▲ Kérkyra, Iónia Nisiá, Greece, C Mediterranean Sea 39.45N 19.51E
Pantschowa see Pančevo
179 Rr16 **Pantukan** Mindanao, S Philippines 7.10N 125.55E
43 P11 **Pánuco** Veracruz-Llave, E Mexico 22.01N 98.10W
43 P11 **Pánuco, Río** ≈ C Mexico
166 I12 **Panxian** Guizhou, S China 25.45N 104.28E
173 G7 **Panyabungan** Sumatera, N Indonesia 0.55N 99.30E
79 W14 **Panyam** Plateau, C Nigeria 9.28N 9.13E
163 N13 **Panzhihua** prev. Dukou, Tu-k'ou. Sichuan, C China 26.35N 101.41E
81 I22 **Panzi** Bandundu, SW Dem. Rep. Congo 7.10S 17.55E
44 E5 **Panzós** Alta Verapaz, E Guatemala 15.21N 89.40W
Pao-chi/Paoki see Baoji
Pao-king see Shaoyang
109 N20 **Paola** Calabria, SW Italy 39.21N 16.03E
123 Jj17 **Paola** E Malta 35.52N 14.30E
29 R5 **Paola** Kansas, C USA 38.34N 94.52W
33 O15 **Paoli** Indiana, N USA 38.31N 86.26W
197 D14 **Paonangisu** Éfaté, C Vanuatu 17.33S 168.23E
175 Tt11 **Paoni** var. Pauni. Pulau Seram, E Indonesia 2.48S 129.03E
39 Q5 **Paonia** Colorado, C USA 38.52N 107.35W
203 O7 **Paopao** Moorea, W French Polynesia 17.28S 149.48W
Pao-shan see Baoshan
Pao-ting see Baoding
Pao-t'ou/Paotow see Baotou
81 H14 **Paoua** Ouham-Pendé, W Central African Republic 7.22N 16.25E
Pap see Pop
113 H23 **Pápa** Veszprém, W Hungary 47.19N 17.27E
44 J12 **Papagayo, Golfo de** gulf NW Costa Rica
40 H11 **Pāpa'ikou** var. Papaikou. Hawai'i, USA, C Pacific Ocean 19.45N 155.06W
43 R15 **Papaloapan, Río** ≈ S Mexico
192 L6 **Papakura** Auckland, North Island, NZ 37.03S 174.57E
43 Q13 **Papantla** var. Papantla de Olarte. Veracruz-Llave, E Mexico 20.27N 97.21W
Papantla de Olarte see Papantla
203 P8 **Papara** Tahiti, W French Polynesia 17.45S 149.33W
192 K4 **Paparoa** Northland, North Island, NZ 36.06S 174.12E
193 G16 **Paparoa Range** ▲▲ South Island, NZ
117 K20 **Pápas, Akrotirio** headland Ikaría, Dodekánisa, Greece, Aegean Sea 37.31N 25.58E
98 L2 **Papa Stour** island NE Scotland, UK
192 L6 **Papatoetoe** Auckland, North Island, NZ 36.58S 174.52E
193 E25 **Papatowai** Otago, South Island, NZ 46.33S 169.33E
98 K4 **Papa Westray** island NE Scotland, UK
203 T10 **Papeete** ○ (French Polynesia) Tahiti, W French Polynesia 17.31S 149.34W
102 F11 **Papenburg** Niedersachsen, NW Germany 53.04N 7.24E
100 H13 **Papendrecht** Zuid-Holland, SW Netherlands 51.49N 4.42E
203 Q7 **Papenoo** Tahiti, W French Polynesia 17.28S 149.25W
203 Q7 **Papenoo Rivière** ≈ Tahiti, W French Polynesia
203 N7 **Papetoai** Moorea, W French Polynesia 17.28S 149.52W
94 L3 **Papey** island E Iceland
Paphos see Páfos
42 H5 **Papigochic, Río** ≈ NW Mexico
120 E10 **Papilė** Šiauliai, NW Lithuania 56.08N 22.51E
31 S15 **Papillion** Nebraska, C USA 41.09N 96.02W
13 T5 **Papinachois** ≈ Québec, SE Canada
176 Y13 **Papua** var. Irian Barat, West Irian, West New Guinea, West Papua ; prev. Dutch New Guinea, Irian Jaya, Netherlands New Guinea. ◐ province E Indonesia
194 I15 **Papua, Gulf of** gulf S PNG
194 H13 **Papua New Guinea** off. Independent State of Papua New Guinea; prev. Territory of Papua and New Guinea, abbrev. PNG. ◆ commonwealth republic NW Melanesia
199 H10 **Papua Plateau** undersea feature N Coral Sea
114 G9 **Papuk** ▲▲ NE Croatia
177 G8 **Papun** Karen State, S Burma 18.04N 97.25E
44 L14 **Paquera** Puntarenas, W Costa Rica 9.52N 84.55W
57 V9 **Para** ◐ district N Surinam
60 I13 **Pará** off. Estado do Pará. ◐ state NE Brazil
Pará see Belém
126 H12 **Parabel'** Tomskaya Oblast', C Russian Federation 58.54N 80.45E
188 I8 **Paraburdoo** Western Australia 23.07S 117.40E
59 E16 **Paracas, Península de** peninsula W Peru
61 L19 **Paracatu** Minas Gerais, NE Brazil 17.13S 46.52W
198 F7 **Paracel Islands** ◇ disputed territory SE Asia
190 I6 **Parachilna** South Australia 31.09S 138.23E
155 R6 **Pārachinār** North-West Frontier Province, NW Pakistan 33.55N 70.04E
114 N13 **Paraćin** Serbia, C Serbia 43.51N 21.25E
12 K8 **Paradis** Québec, SE Canada 48.13N 76.36W
41 N11 **Paradise** var. Paradise Hill. Alaska, USA 62.28N 96.09W
37 O5 **Paradise** California, W USA 39.42N 121.39W
37 X11 **Paradise** Nevada, W USA 36.05N 115.10W
Paradise Hill see Paradise
39 R11 **Paradise Hills** New Mexico, SW USA 35.12N 106.42W
Paradise of the Pacific see Hawaii
38 L13 **Paradise Valley** Arizona, SW USA 33.31N 111.56W
37 T2 **Paradise Valley** Nevada, W USA 41.30N 117.30W
117 O22 **Paradisi** ✕ (Ródos) Ródos, Dodekánisa, Greece, Aegean Sea 36.24N 28.08E
176 X10 **Paradoi** Papua, E Indonesia 2.10S 136.25E
160 P12 **Pārādwīp** Orissa, E India 20.18N 86.39E
Paraetonium see Maṭrûḥ
119 R4 **Parafiyivka** Chernihivs'ka Oblast', N Ukraine 50.53N 32.40E
38 K7 **Paragonah** Utah, W USA 37.53N 112.46W
29 X9 **Paragould** Arkansas, C USA 36.03N 90.30W
49 X8 **Paraguaçu** var. Paraguassú. ≈ E Brazil
62 J9 **Paraguaçu Paulista** São Paulo, S Brazil 22.22S 50.35W
56 H4 **Paraguaipoa** Zulia, NW Venezuela 11.21N 71.58W
64 O6 **Paraguarí** Paraguarí, S Paraguay 25.38S 57.09W
64 O7 **Paraguarí** off. Departamento de Paraguarí. ◐ department S Paraguay
57 O8 **Paragua, Río** ≈ SE Venezuela
59 O16 **Paraguá, Río** ≈ NE Bolivia
Paraguassú see Paraguaçu
64 N5 **Paraguay** ◆ republic C South America
49 U10 **Paraguay** var. Río Paraguay. ≈ C South America
Parahiba/Parahyba see Paraíba
61 P15 **Paraíba** off. Estado da Paraíba; prev. Parahiba, Parahyba. ◐ state E Brazil
Paraíba see João Pessoa
62 P9 **Paraíba do Sul, Rio** ≈ SE Brazil
Parainen see Pargas
45 N14 **Paraíso** Cartago, C Costa Rica 9.50N 83.51W
43 U14 **Paraíso** Tabasco, SE Mexico 18.23N 93.03W
59 O17 **Paraiso, Río** ≈ E Bolivia
Parajd see Praid
79 S14 **Parakou** C Benin 9.22N 2.40E
117 F20 **Paralía Tyroú** Pelopónnisos, S Greece 37.17N 22.50E
124 O3 **Paralimni** E Cyprus 35.01N 34.01E
117 G18 **Paralímni, Límni** ◎ C Greece
194 G15 **Parama Island** island SW PNG
57 W8 **Paramaribo** ● (Surinam) Paramaribo, N Surinam 5.52N 55.13W
57 W9 **Paramaribo** ◐ district N Surinam
57 W9 **Paramaribo** ✕ Paramaribo, N Surinam 5.52N 55.13W
Paramithiá see Paramythiá
58 C13 **Paramonga** Lima, W Peru 10.40S 77.51W
127 Pp13 **Paramushir, Ostrov** island SE Russian Federation
117 C16 **Paramythiá** var. Paramithiá. Ípeiros, W Greece 39.28N 20.31E
64 M10 **Paraná** Entre Ríos, E Argentina 31.48S 60.29W
62 H11 **Paraná** off. Estado do Paraná. ◐ state S Brazil
49 U11 **Paraná** var. Alto Paraná. ≈ C South America
62 K12 **Paranaguá** Paraná, S Brazil 25.31S 48.36W
61 J20 **Paranaíba, Rio** ≈ E Brazil
63 C19 **Paraná Ibicuy, Río** ≈ E Argentina
61 H15 **Paranaíta** Mato Grosso, W Brazil 9.35S 57.01W
62 H9 **Paranapanema, Rio** ≈ S Brazil
62 K11 **Paranapiacaba, Serra do** ▲▲ S Brazil
62 H9 **Paranavaí** Paraná, S Brazil 23.03S 52.25W
149 N5 **Parandak** Markazī, W Iran 35.19N 50.40E
116 I12 **Paranésti** var. Paranéstio. Anatolikí Makedonía kai Thráki, NE Greece 41.16N 24.31E
Paranéstio see Paranésti
203 W11 **Paraoa** atoll Îles Tuamotu, C French Polynesia
192 L13 **Paraparaumu** Wellington, North Island, NZ 40.55S 175.01E
59 N20 **Parapeti, Río** ≈ SE Bolivia
56 L10 **Paraque, Cerro** ▲ W Venezuela 6.00S 67.00W
160 I11 **Parasiya** Madhya Pradesh, C India 22.11N 78.47E
117 M23 **Paraspóri, Akrotírio** headland Kárpathos, SE Greece 35.54N 27.15E
62 O10 **Parati** Rio de Janeiro, SE Brazil 23.15S 44.42W
61 K14 **Parauapebas** Pará, N Brazil 6.03S 49.48W
105 Q10 **Paray-le-Monial** Saône-et-Loire, C France 46.27N 4.07E
Parbatsar see Parvatsar
160 G13 **Parbhani** Mahārāshtra, C India 19.16N 76.51E
102 L10 **Parchim** Mecklenburg-Vorpommern, N Germany 53.25N 11.51E
Parchwitz see Prochowice
112 P13 **Parczew** Lubelskie, E Poland 51.39N 22.59E
62 L8 **Pardo, Rio** ≈ S Brazil
113 E16 **Pardubice** Ger. Pardubitz. Pardubický Kraj, C Czech Republic 50.01N 15.46E
113 E17 **Pardubický Kraj** ◐ region C Czech Republic
Pardubitz see Pardubice
121 F16 **Parechcha** Pol. Porzecze, Rus. Porech'ye. Hrodzyenskaya Voblasts', W Belarus 53.51N 24.07E
61 F17 **Parecis, Chapada dos** var. Serra dos Parecis. ▲▲ W Brazil
Parecis, Serra dos see Parecis, Chapada dos
106 M4 **Paredes de Nava** Castilla-León, N Spain 42.09N 4.42W
201 U12 **Parem** island Chuuk, C Micronesia
201 O12 **Parem Island** island E Micronesia
192 I1 **Parengarenga Harbour** inlet North Island, NZ
13 N8 **Parent** Québec, SE Canada 47.55N 74.36W
104 J14 **Parentis-en-Born** Landes, SW France 44.22N 1.04W
Parenzo see Poreč
193 G20 **Pareora** Canterbury, South Island, NZ 44.28S 171.12E
175 P12 **Parepare** Sulawesi, C Indonesia 4.00S 119.40E
117 B16 **Párga** Ípeiros, W Greece 39.18N 20.19E
95 K20 **Pargas** Swe. Parainen. Länsi-Suomi, W Finland 60.18N 22.19E
66 O5 **Pargo, Ponta do** headland Madeira, Portugal, NE Atlantic Ocean 32.48N 17.16W
Paria, Golfo de see Paria, Gulf of
57 N6 **Pariaguán** Anzoátegui, NE Venezuela 8.51N 64.43W
47 X17 **Paria, Gulf of** var. Golfo de Paria. gulf Trinidad and Tobago/Venezuela
59 I15 **Pariamanu, Río** ≈ E Peru
38 L8 **Paria River** ≈ Utah, W USA
Parichi see Parychy
42 M14 **Paricutín, Volcán** 🌋 C Mexico 19.25N 102.20W
45 P16 **Parida, Isla** island SW Panama
57 T8 **Parika** NE Guyana 6.51N 58.25W
95 O18 **Parikkala** Etelä-Suomi, S Finland 61.33N 29.33E
60 E10 **Parima, Serra** var. Sierra Parima. ▲▲ Brazil/Venezuela see also Parima, Sierra
57 N11 **Parima, Sierra** var. Serra Parima. ▲▲ Brazil/Venezuela see also Parima, Serra
59 F17 **Parinacochas, Laguna** ◎ SW Peru
58 A9 **Pariñas, Punta** headland NW Peru 4.45S 81.22W
60 H12 **Parintins** Amazonas, N Brazil 2.37S 56.45W
105 O5 **Paris** anc. Lutetia, Lutetia Parisiorum, Parisii. ● (France) Paris, N France 48.52N 2.19E
203 Y2 **Paris** Kiritimati, E Kiribati 1.55N 95.30W
29 S11 **Paris** Arkansas, C USA 35.17N 93.43W
35 S16 **Paris** Idaho, NW USA 42.14N 111.24W

◆ Country ● Country Capital ◇ Dependent Territory ○ Dependent Territory Capital ◐ Administrative Region ✕ International Airport ▲ Mountain ▲▲ Mountain Range 🌋 Volcano ≈ River ◎ Lake ⊟ Reservoir

Paris – Pembroke

33 N14 **Paris** Illinois, N USA 39.36N 87.42W
22 M5 **Paris** Kentucky, S USA 38.12N 84.15W
29 V3 **Paris** Missouri, C USA 39.28N 92.00W
22 H8 **Paris** Tennessee, S USA 36.18N 88.19W
27 V5 **Paris** Texas, SW USA 33.40N 95.33W
Parisii see Paris
45 S16 **Parita** Herrera, S Panama 7.59N 80.31W
45 S16 **Parita, Bahía de** bay S Panama
Parkan/Párkány see Štúrovo
95 K18 **Parkano** Länsi-Suomi, W Finland 62.03N 23.00E
29 N6 **Park City** Kansas, C USA 37.48N 97.19W
38 L3 **Park City** Utah, W USA 40.39N 111.30W
38 I12 **Parker** Arizona, SW USA 34.07N 114.16W
25 R9 **Parker** Florida, SE USA 30.07N 85.36W
31 R11 **Parker** South Dakota, N USA 43.24N 97.08W
37 Z14 **Parker Dam** California, W USA 34.17N 114.08W
31 W13 **Parkersburg** Iowa, C USA 42.34N 92.47W
23 Q3 **Parkersburg** West Virginia, NE USA 39.15N 81.33W
31 T7 **Parkers Prairie** Minnesota, N USA 46.09N 95.19W
179 R17 **Parker Volcano** ▲ Mindanao, S Philippines 6.09N 124.52E
189 W13 **Parkes** New South Wales, SE Australia 33.09S 148.10E
32 K4 **Park Falls** Wisconsin, N USA 45.57N 90.25W
Parkhar see Farkhor
12 E16 **Parkhill** Ontario, S Canada 43.11N 81.39W
31 T5 **Park Rapids** Minnesota, N USA 46.55N 95.03W
31 Q3 **Park River** North Dakota, N USA 48.24N 97.44W
31 Q11 **Parkston** South Dakota, N USA 43.24N 97.58W
8 L17 **Parksville** Vancouver Island, British Columbia, SW Canada 49.13N 124.13W
39 S3 **Parkview Mountain** ▲ Colorado, C USA 40.19N 106.08W
107 N8 **Parla** Madrid, C Spain 40.13N 3.48W
31 S8 **Parle, Lac qui** ⊠ Minnesota, N USA
161 G14 **Parli Vaijnāth** Mahārāshtra, C India 18.52N 76.36E
108 F9 **Parma** Emilia-Romagna, N Italy 44.49N 10.19E
33 T11 **Parma** Ohio, N USA 41.24N 81.43W
Parnahyba see Parnaíba
60 N13 **Parnaíba** var. Parnahyba. Piauí, E Brazil 2.58S 41.46W
67 J14 **Parnaíba Ridge** undersea feature C Atlantic Ocean
60 N13 **Parnaíba, Rio** ∽ NE Brazil
117 F18 **Parnassós** ▲ C Greece
193 J17 **Parnassus** Canterbury, South Island, NZ 42.41S 173.18E
190 H10 **Parndana** South Australia 35.48S 137.13E
117 H19 **Párnitha** ▲ C Greece
Párnon see Párnonas
117 F21 **Párnonas** var. Párnon. ▲ S Greece
120 G5 **Pärnu** Ger. Pernau, Latv. Pērnava; prev. Rus. Pernov. Pärnumaa, SW Estonia 58.23N 24.31E
120 G6 **Pärnu** var. Parnu Jõgi, Ger. Pernau. ∽ SW Estonia
120 G5 **Pärnu-Jaagupi** Ger. Sankt-Jakobi. Pärnumaa, SW Estonia 58.36N 24.30E
Parnu Jõgi see Pärnu
120 G5 **Pärnu Laht** Ger. Pernauer Bucht. bay SW Estonia
120 F5 **Pärnumaa** off. Pärnu Maakond. ◆ province SW Estonia
159 T11 **Paro** W Bhutan 27.22N 89.31E
159 T11 **Paro** ✕ (Thimphu) W Bhutan 27.22N 89.31E
193 G17 **Paroa** West Coast, South Island, NZ 42.31S 171.10E
169 X14 **P'aro-ho** var. Hwach'ŏn-chŏsuji. ⊠ N South Korea
117 J21 **Paroikiá** prev. Páros. Páros, Kykládes, Greece, Aegean Sea 37.04N 25.09E
191 N6 **Paroo River** seasonal river New South Wales/Queensland, SE Australia
Paropamisus Range see Sefidkūh, Selseleh-ye
117 J21 **Páros** island Kykládes, Greece, Aegean Sea
Páros see Paroikiá
38 K7 **Parowan** Utah, W USA 37.50N 112.49W
105 U13 **Parpaillon** ▲ SE France
110 I9 **Parpan** Graubünden, S Switzerland 46.46N 9.32E
64 G13 **Parral** Maule, C Chile 36.07S 71.47W
Parral see Hidalgo del Parral
191 T9 **Parramatta** New South Wales, SE Australia 33.49S 150.58E
23 Y6 **Parramore Island** island Virginia, NE USA
42 M8 **Parras** var. Parras de la Fuente. Coahuila de Zaragoza, NE Mexico 25.26N 102.07W
Parras de la Fuente see Parras
44 M14 **Parrita** Puntarenas, S Costa Rica 9.33N 84.20W
12 G13 **Parry Island** island Ontario, S Canada
207 O9 **Parry Islands** island group Nunavut, NW Canada
12 G12 **Parry Sound** Ontario, S Canada 45.21N 80.03W
112 F7 **Parsęta** Ger. Persante. ∽ NW Poland
30 L3 **Parshall** North Dakota, N USA 47.57N 102.07W
29 Q7 **Parsons** Kansas, C USA 37.20N 95.15W
22 H9 **Parsons** Tennessee, S USA 35.39N 88.07W
23 T3 **Parsons** West Virginia, NE USA 39.06N 79.40W
Parsonstown see Birr
102 P11 **Parsteiner See** ◎ NE Germany
109 L24 **Partanna** Sicilia, Italy, C Mediterranean Sea 37.43N 12.54E
110 I8 **Partenen** Graubünden, E Switzerland 46.58N 10.01E
104 K9 **Parthenay** Deux-Sèvres, W France 46.39N 0.13W
97 J19 **Partille** Västra Götaland, S Sweden 57.43N 12.12E
109 I23 **Partinico** Sicilia, Italy, C Mediterranean Sea 38.03N 13.07E
113 I20 **Partizánske** prev. Šimonovany; Hung. Simony. Trenčiansky Kraj, W Slovakia 48.39N 18.22E
60 H11 **Paru de Oeste, Rio** ∽ N Brazil
190 K9 **Paruna** South Australia 34.45S 140.43E
60 I11 **Paru, Rio** ∽ N Brazil
155 Q5 **Parvān** Pash. Parwān. ◆ province E Afghanistan
161 M14 **Pārvatīpuram** Andhra Pradesh, E India 17.01N 81.47E
158 G12 **Parvatsar** prev. Parbatsar. Rājasthān, N India 26.52N 74.49E
Parwān see Parvān
164 I15 **Paryang** Xizang Zizhiqu, W China 30.04N 83.28E
121 M18 **Parychy** Rus. Parichi. Homyel'skaya Voblasts', SE Belarus 52.48N 29.25E
85 J21 **Parys** Free State, C South Africa 26.51S 27.28E
37 T15 **Pasadena** California, W USA 34.09N 118.08W
27 W11 **Pasadena** Texas, SW USA 29.41N 95.12W
58 B8 **Pasaje** El Oro, SW Ecuador 3.17S 79.45W
143 T9 **P'asanauri** N Georgia 42.21N 44.40E
173 G10 **Pasapuat** Pulau Pagai Utara, W Indonesia 2.36S 99.58E
178 Gg7 **Pasawng** Kayah State, C Burma 18.50N 97.16E
116 L13 **Paşayiğit** Edirne, NW Turkey 40.58N 26.38E
25 N9 **Pascagoula** Mississippi, S USA 30.21N 88.31W
24 M8 **Pascagoula River** ∽ Mississippi, S USA
118 F12 **Paşcani** Hung. Páskán. Iaşi, NE Romania 47.13N 26.46E
111 T4 **Pasching** Oberösterreich, N Austria 48.16N 14.10E
34 K10 **Pasco** Washington, NW USA 46.13N 119.06W
58 E13 **Pasco** off. Departamento de Pasco. ◆ department C Peru
203 N11 **Pascua, Isla de** var. Rapa Nui, Eng. Easter Island. island E Pacific Ocean
65 G21 **Pascua, Río** ∽ S Chile
105 N1 **Pas-de-Calais** ◆ department N France
102 P10 **Pasewalk** Mecklenburg-Vorpommern, NE Germany 53.30N 13.58E
9 T10 **Pasfield Lake** ◎ Saskatchewan, C Canada
Pa-shih Hai-hsia see Bashi Channel
Pashkeni see Bolyarovo
Pashmakli see Smolyan
179 P10 **Pasig** Luzon, N Philippines 14.34N 121.04E
159 X10 **Pāsighāt** Arunāchel Pradesh, NE India 28.08N 95.13E
143 Q12 **Pasinler** Erzurum, NE Turkey 39.58N 41.40E
Pasi Oloy, Qatorkŭhi see Zaalayskiy Khrebet
44 E3 **Pasión, Río de la** ∽ N Guatemala
174 Gg10 **Pasirganting** Sumatera, W Indonesia 2.04S 100.51E
Pasirpangarayan see Bagansiapiapi
174 H2 **Pasir Puteh** var. Pasir Putih. Kelantan, Peninsular Malaysia 5.49N 102.24E
174 L6 **Pasir, Tanjung** headland East Malaysia 2.24N 111.12E
97 N20 **Påskallavik** Kalmar, S Sweden 57.10N 16.25E
Páskán see Paşcani
Paskevicha, Zaliv see Tushchybas, Zaliv
112 K7 **Pasłęk** Ger. Preußisch Holland. Warmińsko-Mazurskie, NE Poland 54.03N 19.39E
112 K7 **Pasłęka** Ger. Passarge. ∽ N Poland
154 K16 **Pasni** Baluchistān, SW Pakistan 25.13N 63.30E
65 I18 **Paso de Indios** Chubut, S Argentina 43.52S 69.06W
56 L7 **Paso del Caballo** Guárico, N Venezuela 8.19N 67.07W
63 E15 **Paso de los Libres** Corrientes, NE Argentina 29.39S 57.04W
63 E18 **Paso de los Toros** Tacuarembó, C Uruguay 32.45S 56.30W
37 P12 **Paso Robles** California, W USA 35.37N 120.42W
13 Y7 **Paspébiac** Québec, SE Canada 48.03N 65.10W
9 U14 **Pasquia Hills** ▲ Saskatchewan, S Canada
155 W7 **Pasrūr** Punjab, E Pakistan 32.12N 74.42E
32 M1 **Passage Island** island Michigan, N USA
67 B24 **Passage Islands** island group W Falkland Islands
15 I1 **Passage Point** headland Banks Island, Northwest Territories, NW Canada 73.31N 115.12W
Passarge see Pasłęka
117 C15 **Passarón** ancient monument Ípeiros, W Greece 39.41N 20.43E
Passarowitz see Požarevac
103 O22 **Passau** Bayern, SE Germany 48.34N 13.28E
24 M9 **Pass Christian** Mississippi, S USA 30.19N 89.15W
109 L26 **Passero, Capo** headland Sicilia, Italy, C Mediterranean Sea 36.40N 15.09E
179 Q13 **Passi** Panay Island, C Philippines 11.05N 122.37E
63 H14 **Passo Fundo** Rio Grande do Sul, S Brazil 28.16S 52.19W
62 H13 **Passo Fundo, Barragem de** ⊠ S Brazil
63 H15 **Passo Real, Barragem de** ⊠ S Brazil
61 L20 **Passos** Minas Gerais, NE Brazil 20.45S 46.37W
178 M11 **Passu Keah** island S Paracel Islands
120 J13 **Pastavy** Pol. Postawy, Rus. Postavy. Vitsyebskaya Voblasts', NW Belarus 55.07N 26.50E
58 D7 **Pastaza** ◆ province E Ecuador
58 D9 **Pastaza, Río** ∽ Ecuador/Peru
63 A21 **Pasteur** Buenos Aires, E Argentina 35.10S 62.13W
13 V3 **Pasteur** ∽ Québec, SE Canada
153 Q12 **Pastigav** Rus. Pastigov. W Tajikistan 39.27N 69.16E
Pastigov see Pastigav
56 C13 **Pasto** Nariño, SW Colombia 1.12N 77.16W
40 M10 **Pastol Bay** bay Alaska, USA
39 O8 **Pastora Peak** ▲ Arizona, SW USA 36.48N 109.10W
107 O8 **Pastrana** Castilla-La Mancha, C Spain 40.24N 2.55W
174 M15 **Pasuruan** prev. Pasoeroean. Jawa, C Indonesia 7.37S 112.43E
120 F11 **Pasvalys** Panevėžys, N Lithuania 56.03N 24.24E
113 K21 **Pásztó** Nógrád, N Hungary 47.57N 19.41E
201 U12 **Pata** var. Patta. atoll Chuuk Islands, C Micronesia
38 M16 **Patagonia** Arizona, SW USA 31.32N 110.45W
65 H20 **Patagonia** physical region Argentina/Chile
Patalung see Phatthalung
160 D9 **Pātan** Gujarāt, W India 23.51N 72.10E
160 J10 **Pātan** Madhya Pradesh, C India 23.19N 79.41E
175 T18 **Patani** Pulau Halmahera, E Indonesia 0.19N 128.46E
Patani see Pattani
13 V7 **Patapédia Est** ∽ Québec, SE Canada
118 K13 **Pătârlagele** prev. Pătîrlagele. Buzău, SE Romania 45.19N 26.21E
Patavium see Padova
190 I5 **Patawarta Hill** ▲ South Australia 30.57S 138.42E
190 L10 **Patchewollock** Victoria, SE Australia 35.24S 142.11E
192 K11 **Patea** Taranaki, North Island, NZ 39.48S 174.35E
192 K11 **Patea** ∽ North Island, NZ
79 U15 **Pategi** Kwara, C Nigeria 8.39N 5.46E
83 K20 **Pate Island** var. Patta Island. island SE Kenya
107 S10 **Paterna** País Valenciano, E Spain 39.30N 0.24W
111 R9 **Paternion** Slvn. Špatrjan. Kärnten, S Austria 46.40N 13.43E
109 L24 **Paternò** anc. Hybla, Hybla Major. Sicilia, Italy, C Mediterranean Sea 37.34N 14.55E
34 J7 **Pateros** Washington, NW USA 48.01N 119.55W
20 J14 **Paterson** New Jersey, NE USA 40.54N 74.11W
34 J10 **Paterson** Washington, NW USA 45.56N 119.37W
193 C25 **Paterson Inlet** inlet Stewart Island, NZ
100 N6 **Paterswolde** Drenthe, NE Netherlands 53.07N 6.32E
158 H7 **Pathānkot** Himāchal Pradesh, N India 32.16N 75.43E
Pathein see Bassein
35 W15 **Pathfinder Reservoir** ⊠ Wyoming, C USA
178 Hh11 **Pathum Thani** var. Patumdhani, Prathum Thani. Pathum Thani, C Thailand 14.03N 100.28E
174 L14 **Pati** Jawa, C Indonesia 6.45S 111.00E
56 C12 **Patía** var. El Bordo. Cauca, SW Colombia 2.06N 77.02W
158 I9 **Patiāla** var. Puttiala. Punjab, NW India 30.21N 76.27E
56 B12 **Patía, Río** ∽ SW Colombia
175 T8 **Patinti, Selat** strait Maluku, E Indonesia
196 D15 **Pati Point** headland NE Guam 13.36N 144.39E
Pătîrlagele see Pătârlagele
58 C13 **Pativilca** Lima, W Peru 10.40S 77.52W
178 Gg1 **Pātkai Bum** var. Patkai Range. ▲ Burma/India
Patkai Range see Pātkai Bum
117 L20 **Pátmos** Pátmos, Dodekánisa, Greece, Aegean Sea 37.18N 26.32E
117 L20 **Pátmos** island Dodekánisa, Greece, Aegean Sea
159 P13 **Patna** var. Azimabad. Bihār, N India 25.36N 85.11E
160 M12 **Patnāgarh** Orissa, E India 20.42N 83.12E
179 Pp13 **Patnongon** Panay Island, C Philippines 10.56N 122.03E
143 S13 **Patnos** Ağrı, E Turkey 39.13N 42.52E
62 H12 **Pato Branco** Paraná, S Brazil 26.15S 52.40W
33 O16 **Patoka Lake** ◎ Indiana, N USA
94 L9 **Patoniva** Lapp. Buoddobohki. Lappi, N Finland 69.44N 27.01E
115 K21 **Patos** var. Patosi. Fier, SW Albania 40.40N 19.37E
Patos see Patos de Minas
61 K19 **Patos de Minas** var. Patos. Minas Gerais, NE Brazil 18.34S 46.31W
Patosi see Patos
63 I17 **Patos, Lagoa dos** lagoon S Brazil
64 J9 **Patquía** La Rioja, C Argentina 30.01S 66.54W
117 E19 **Pátra** Eng. Patras; prev. Pátrai. Dytikí Ellás, S Greece 38.13N 21.45E
Pátrai/Patras see Pátra
117 D18 **Patraïkós Kólpos** gulf S Greece
94 G2 **Patreksfjördhur** Vestfirdhir, W Iceland 65.33N 23.54W
26 M7 **Patricia** Texas, SW USA 32.34N 102.00W
65 F21 **Patricio Lynch, Isla** island S Chile
Patta see Pata
Patta Island see Pate Island
178 Hh17 **Pattani** var. Patani. Pattani, SW Thailand 6.50N 101.18E
178 Hh12 **Pattaya** Chon Buri, S Thailand 12.55N 100.55E
21 S4 **Patten** Maine, NE USA 45.58N 68.27W
37 O9 **Patterson** California, W USA 37.27N 121.07W
24 J10 **Patterson** Louisiana, S USA 29.41N 91.18W
37 R7 **Patterson, Mount** ▲ California, W USA 38.27N 119.16W
33 P4 **Patterson, Point** headland Michigan, N USA 45.58N 85.39W
109 L23 **Patti** Sicilia, Italy, C Mediterranean Sea 38.07N 14.58E
109 L23 **Patti, Golfo di** gulf Sicilia, Italy, C Mediterranean Sea
95 L14 **Pattijoki** Oulu, W Finland 64.41N 24.40E
199 Mm5 **Patton Escarpment** undersea feature E Pacific Ocean
29 S2 **Pattonsburg** Missouri, C USA 40.03N 94.08W
(0) D6 **Patton Seamount** undersea feature NE Pacific Ocean 54.40N 150.30W
8 J12 **Pattullo, Mount** ▲ British Columbia, W Canada 56.18N 129.43W
159 U16 **Patuakhali** var. Patukhali. Barisal, S Bangladesh 22.19N 90.19E
44 M5 **Patuca, Río** ∽ E Honduras
Patukhali see Patuakhali
Patumdhani see Pathum Thani
42 M14 **Pátzcuaro** Michoacán de Ocampo, SW Mexico 19.30N 101.36W
44 C6 **Patzicía** Chimaltenango, S Guatemala 14.37N 90.54W
104 K16 **Pau** Pyrénées-Atlantiques, SW France 43.18N 0.22W
104 J12 **Pauillac** Gironde, SW France 45.12N 0.44W
177 Ff5 **Pauk** Magwe, W Burma 21.25N 94.30E
15 H3 **Paulatuk** Northwest Territories, NW Canada 69.23N 124.00W
44 K5 **Paulaya, Río** ∽ NE Honduras
24 M6 **Paulding** Mississippi, S USA 32.01N 89.01W
33 Q12 **Paulding** Ohio, N USA 41.08N 84.34W
31 S12 **Paullina** Iowa, C USA 42.58N 95.41W
61 P15 **Paulo Afonso** Bahia, E Brazil 9.21S 38.13W
40 M16 **Pauloff Harbor** var. Pavlor Harbour. Sanak Island, Alaska, USA 54.26N 162.43W
29 N12 **Pauls Valley** Oklahoma, C USA 34.44N 97.13W
177 Ff7 **Paungde** Pegu, C Burma 18.30N 95.30E
Pauni see Paoni
158 K9 **Pauri** Uttaranchal, N India 30.07N 78.48E
Pautalia see Kyustendil
176 Z11 **Pauwasi** ∽ Papua, E Indonesia
148 J5 **Pāveh** Kermānshāh, NW Iran 35.01N 46.15E
130 L5 **Pavelets** Ryazanskaya Oblast', W Russian Federation 53.47N 39.22E
108 D8 **Pavia** anc. Ticinum. Lombardia, N Italy 45.10N 9.10E
120 C9 **Pāvilosta** Liepāja, W Latvia 56.52N 21.12E
129 P14 **Pavino** Kostromskaya Oblast', NW Russian Federation 59.10N 46.09E
116 J8 **Pavlikeni** Veliko Tŭrnovo, N Bulgaria 43.15N 25.20E
151 T8 **Pavlodar** Pavlodar, NE Kazakhstan 52.21N 76.58E
151 S9 **Pavlodar** off. Pavlodarskaya Oblast', Kaz. Pavlodar Oblysy. ◆ province NE Kazakhstan
Pavlodar Oblysy/Pavlodarskaya Oblast' see Pavlodar
Pavlograd see Pavlohrad
119 U7 **Pavlohrad** Rus. Pavlograd. Dnipropetrovs'ka Oblast', E Ukraine 48.32N 35.50E
Pavlor Harbour see Pauloff Harbor
151 R9 **Pavlovka** Akmola, C Kazakhstan 51.22N 72.35E
131 V4 **Pavlovka** Respublika Bashkortostan, W Russian Federation 55.28N 56.36E
131 Q7 **Pavlovka** Ul'yanovskaya Oblast', W Russian Federation 52.40N 47.08E
131 N3 **Pavlovo** Nizhegorodskaya Oblast', W Russian Federation 55.59N 43.03E
130 L9 **Pavlovsk** Voronezhskaya Oblast', W Russian Federation 50.26N 40.08E
130 L13 **Pavlovskaya** Krasnodarskiy Kray, SW Russian Federation 46.06N 39.52E
119 S7 **Pavlysh** Kirovohrads'ka Oblast', C Ukraine 48.54N 33.20E
108 F10 **Pavullo nel Frignano** Emilia-Romagna, C Italy 44.19N 10.52E
29 P8 **Pawhuska** Oklahoma, C USA 36.40N 96.20W
23 U13 **Pawleys Island** South Carolina, SE USA 33.27N 79.07W
178 Gg6 **Pawn** ∽ C Burma
32 K14 **Pawnee** Illinois, N USA 39.35N 89.34W
29 O9 **Pawnee** Oklahoma, C USA 36.18N 96.47W
39 U2 **Pawnee Buttes** ▲ Colorado, C USA 40.49N 103.58W
31 S17 **Pawnee City** Nebraska, C USA 40.06N 96.09W
28 K5 **Pawnee River** ∽ Kansas, C USA
33 O10 **Paw Paw** Michigan, N USA 42.12N 86.09W
33 O10 **Paw Paw Lake** Michigan, N USA 42.12N 86.16W
21 O12 **Pawtucket** Rhode Island, NE USA 41.52N 71.22W
Pax Augusta see Badajoz
117 I25 **Paximádia** island SE Greece
Pax Julia see Beja
117 B16 **Paxoí** island Iónia Nisiá, Greece, C Mediterranean Sea
41 S10 **Paxson** Alaska, USA 62.58N 145.27W
153 O11 **Paxtakor** Jizzax Viloyati, C Uzbekistan 40.21N 67.54E
32 M13 **Paxton** Illinois, N USA 40.27N 88.06W
128 J11 **Pay** Respublika Kareliya, NW Russian Federation 61.10N 34.24E
177 G8 **Payagyi** Pegu, SW Burma 17.28N 96.31E
110 C9 **Payerne** Ger. Peterlingen. Vaud, W Switzerland 46.49N 6.57E
34 M13 **Payette** Idaho, NW USA 44.04N 116.55W
34 M13 **Payette River** ∽ Idaho, NW USA
129 V2 **Pay-Khoy, Khrebet** ▲ NW Russian Federation
Payne see Kangirsuk
10 K4 **Payne, Lac** ◎ Québec, NE Canada
31 T8 **Paynesville** Minnesota, N USA 45.22N 94.42W
174 M4 **Payong, Tanjung** headland East Malaysia 3.46N 113.27E
Payo Obispo see Chetumal
63 D18 **Paysandú** Paysandú, W Uruguay 32.21S 58.04W
63 D17 **Paysandú** ◆ department W Uruguay
104 I7 **Pays de la Loire** ◆ region NW France
38 L12 **Payson** Arizona, SW USA 34.13N 111.19W
38 L4 **Payson** Utah, W USA 40.02N 111.43W
129 W4 **Payyer, Gora** ▲ NW Russian Federation 66.49N 64.33E
Payzawat see Jiashi
143 Q11 **Pazar** Rize, NE Turkey 41.10N 40.52E
142 F10 **Pazarbaşı Burnu** headland NW Turkey 41.12N 30.18E
142 M16 **Pazarcık** Kahramanmaraş, S Turkey 37.31N 37.19E
116 I10 **Pazardzhik** prev. Tatar Pazardzhik. Pazardzhik, C Bulgaria 42.11N 24.21E
66 H11 **Pazardzhik** ◆ province C Bulgaria 42.11N 24.21E
56 H9 **Paz de Ariporo** Casanare, E Colombia 5.51N 71.52W
114 A10 **Pazin** Ger. Mitterburg, It. Pisino. Istra, NW Croatia 45.14N 13.56E
44 D7 **Paz, Río** ∽ El Salvador/Guatemala
115 O18 **Pčinja** ∽ N FYR Macedonia
200 Qq15 **Pea** Tongatapu, S Tonga 21.10S 175.14W
29 O6 **Peabody** Kansas, C USA 38.10N 97.06W
9 O12 **Peace** ∽ Alberta/British Columbia, W Canada
Peace Garden State see North Dakota
9 Q10 **Peace Point** Alberta, C Canada 59.11N 112.12W
9 O12 **Peace River** Alberta, W Canada 56.15N 117.18W
25 W13 **Peace River** ∽ Florida, SE USA
9 N17 **Peachland** British Columbia, SW Canada 49.49N 119.48W
38 J10 **Peach Springs** Arizona, SW USA 35.33N 113.27W
Peach State see Georgia
25 S4 **Peachtree City** Georgia, SE USA 33.24N 84.36W
201 Y13 **Peacock Point** point SE Wake Island 19.16N 166.39E
99 M18 **Peak District** physical region C England, UK
191 Q7 **Peak Hill** New South Wales, SE Australia 32.39S 148.12E
67 G15 **Peak, The** ▲ C Ascension Island
107 O13 **Peal de Becerro** Andalucía, S Spain 37.55N 3.07W
201 X11 **Peale Island** island N Wake Island
39 O6 **Peale, Mount** ▲ Utah, W USA 38.26N 109.13W
41 O4 **Peard Bay** bay Alaska, USA
25 Q7 **Pea River** ∽ Alabama/Florida, S USA
27 W11 **Pearland** Texas, SW USA 29.33N 95.17W
40 D9 **Pearl City** O'ahu, Hawai'i, USA, C Pacific Ocean 21.24N 95.58W
40 D9 **Pearl Harbor** inlet O'ahu, Hawai'i, USA, C Pacific Ocean
Pearl Islands see Perlas, Archipiélago de las
Pearl Lagoon see Perlas, Laguna de
24 M5 **Pearl River** ∽ Louisiana/Mississippi, S USA
27 Q13 **Pearsall** Texas, SW USA 28.53N 99.05W
25 U7 **Pearson** Georgia, SE USA 31.18N 82.51W
27 P4 **Pease River** ∽ Texas, SW USA
10 F7 **Peawanuk** Ontario, C Canada 54.55N 85.31W
85 P16 **Pebane** Zambézia, NE Mozambique 17.13S 38.10E
67 C23 **Pebble Island** island N Falkland Islands
67 C23 **Pebble Island Settlement** Pebble Island, N Falkland Islands 51.19S 59.40W
115 L16 **Peć** Alb. Pejë, Turk. Ipek. Serbia, S Serbia 42.40N 20.19E
27 R8 **Pecan Bayou** ∽ Texas, SW USA
24 H10 **Pecan Island** Louisiana, S USA 29.39N 92.26W
62 L12 **Peças, Ilha das** island S Brazil
32 L10 **Pecatonica River** ∽ Illinois/Wisconsin, N USA
110 G10 **Peccia** Ticino, S Switzerland 46.24N 8.39E
Pechenegi see Pechenihy
Pechenezhskoye Vodokhranilishche see Pecheniz'ke Vodoskhovyshche
128 I2 **Pechenga** Fin. Petsamo. Murmanskaya Oblast', NW Russian Federation 69.34N 31.14E
119 V5 **Pechenihy** Rus. Pechenegi. Kharkivs'ka Oblast', E Ukraine 49.49N 36.57E
119 V5 **Pecheniz'ke Vodoskhovyshche** Rus. Pechenezhskoye Vodokhranilishche. ⊠ E Ukraine
129 U7 **Pechora** Respublika Komi, NW Russian Federation 65.08N 57.09E
129 R6 **Pechora** ∽ NW Russian Federation
Pechora Bay see Pechorskaya Guba
Pechora Sea see Pechorskoye More
129 S3 **Pechorskaya Guba** Eng. Pechora Bay. bay NW Russian Federation
125 Ff6 **Pechorskoye More** Eng. Pechora Sea. sea NW Russian Federation
118 E11 **Pecica** Ger. Petschka, Hung. Ópécska. Arad, W Romania 46.09N 21.06E
26 K8 **Pecos** Texas, SW USA 31.25N 103.30W
27 N11 **Pecos River** ∽ New Mexico/Texas, SW USA
113 I25 **Pécs** Ger. Fünfkirchen; Lat. Sopianae. Baranya, SW Hungary 46.04N 18.11E
45 T17 **Pedasí** Los Santos, S Panama 7.30N 80.02W
Pedde see Pedja
191 O17 **Pedder, Lake** ◎ Tasmania, SE Australia
46 M10 **Pedernales** SW Dominican Republic 17.59N 71.42W
57 Q5 **Pedernales** Delta Amacuro, NE Venezuela 9.58N 62.15W
27 R10 **Pedernales River** ∽ Texas, SW USA
64 H6 **Pedernales, Salar de** salt lake N Chile
Pedhoulas see Pedoulás
57 X11 **Pédima** var. Malavate. SW French Guiana 3.15N 54.07W
190 F1 **Pedirka** South Australia 26.41S 135.11E
175 T7 **Pediwang** Pulau Halmahera, E Indonesia 1.29N 127.57E
120 I5 **Pedja** var. Pedja Jõgi, Ger. Pedde. ∽ E Estonia
Pedja Jõgi see Pedja
124 N3 **Pedoulás** var. Pedhoulas. W Cyprus 34.58N 32.51E
61 N18 **Pedra Azul** Minas Gerais, NE Brazil 16.01S 41.16W
106 I3 **Pedrafita, Porto de** var. Puerto de Piedrafita. pass NW Spain 42.43N 7.01W
78 E9 **Pedra Lume** Sal, NE Cape Verde 16.46N 22.54W
45 P16 **Pedregal** Chiriquí, W Panama 8.21N 82.26W
56 J4 **Pedregal** Falcón, N Venezuela 11.01N 70.06W
42 L9 **Pedriceña** Durango, C Mexico 25.08N 103.46W
62 L11 **Pedro Barros** São Paulo, S Brazil 24.12S 47.22W
41 Q13 **Pedro Bay** Alaska, USA 59.47N 154.06W
64 H4 **Pedro de Valdivia** var. Oficina Pedro de Valdivia. Antofagasta, N Chile 22.33S 69.37W
64 P4 **Pedro Juan Caballero** Amambay, E Paraguay 22.33S 55.40W
65 L15 **Pedro Luro** Buenos Aires, E Argentina 39.26S 62.40W
107 O10 **Pedro Muñoz** Castilla-La Mancha, C Spain 39.25N 2.55W
161 J22 **Pedro, Point** headland NW Sri Lanka 9.54N 80.08E
190 K9 **Peebinga** South Australia 34.56S 140.56E
98 J13 **Peebles** SE Scotland, UK 55.39N 3.14W
33 S15 **Peebles** Ohio, N USA 38.57N 83.23W
98 J12 **Peebles** cultural region SE Scotland, UK
20 K13 **Peekskill** New York, NE USA 41.17N 73.54W
99 I16 **Peel** W Isle of Man 54.13N 4.04W
14 Ff4 **Peel** ∽ Northwest Territories/Yukon Territory, NW Canada
15 I1 **Peel Point** headland Victoria Island, Northwest Territories, NW Canada 73.22N 114.33W
15 K1 **Peel Sound** passage Nunavut, N Canada
102 N9 **Peene** ∽ NE Germany
101 K17 **Peer** Limburg, NE Belgium 51.08N 5.28E
12 H14 **Pefferlaw** Ontario, S Canada 44.18N 79.11W
193 I18 **Pegasus Bay** bay South Island, NZ
123 Mm3 **Pégeia** var. Peyia. SW Cyprus 34.52N 32.24E
111 V7 **Peggau** Steiermark, SE Austria 47.10N 15.20E
103 L19 **Pegnitz** Bayern, SE Germany 49.45N 11.33E
103 L19 **Pegnitz** ∽ SE Germany
107 T11 **Pego** País Valenciano, E Spain 38.51N 0.07W
177 G8 **Pegu** var. Bago. Pegu, SW Burma 17.18N 96.31E
177 G7 **Pegu** ◆ division S Burma
176 W7 **Pegun, Pulau** island Kepulauan Mapia, E Indonesia
201 N13 **Pehleng** Pohnpei, E Micronesia
116 M12 **Pehlivanköy** Kırklareli, NW Turkey 41.21N 26.56E
79 R14 **Péhonko** C Benin 10.14N 1.57E
63 B21 **Pehuajó** Buenos Aires, E Argentina 35.48S 61.52W
Pei-ching see Beijing/Beijing Shi
102 J13 **Peine** Niedersachsen, C Germany 52.19N 10.13E
Pei-p'ing see Beijing/Beijing Shi
Peipsi Järv/Peipus-See see Peipus, Lake
120 J5 **Peipus, Lake** Est. Peipsi Järv, Ger. Peipus-See, Rus. Chudskoye Ozero. ◎ Estonia/Russian Federation
117 H19 **Peiraías** prev. Piraiévs, Eng. Piraeus. Attikí, C Greece 37.56N 23.39E
Peisern see Pyzdry
62 I8 **Peixe, Rio do** ∽ S Brazil
61 I16 **Peixoto de Azevedo** Mato Grosso, W Brazil 10.18S 55.03W
174 J8 **Pejantan, Pulau** island W Indonesia
Pejë see Peć
114 N11 **Pek** ∽ E Serbia
178 I7 **Pèk** var. Xieng Khouang; prev. Xiangkhoang. Xiangkhoang, N Laos 19.19N 103.23E
174 Kk14 **Pekalongan** Jawa, C Indonesia 6.54S 109.37E
174 Gg7 **Pekanbaru** var. Pakanbaru. Sumatera, W Indonesia 0.31N 101.27E
32 L12 **Pekin** Illinois, N USA 40.34N 89.38W
Peking see Beijing/Beijing Shi
Pelabohan Kelang/Pelabuhan Kelang see Pelabuhan Klang
173 G5 **Pelabuhan Klang** var. Kuala Pelabohan Kelang, Pelabohan Kelang, Pelabuhan Kelang, Port Klang, Port Swettenham. Selangor, Peninsular Malaysia 2.57N 101.24E
174 J15 **Pelabuhan Ratu, Teluk** bay Jawa, SW Indonesia
123 L12 **Pelagie, Isole** island group SW Italy
Pelagosa see Palagruža
24 L5 **Pelahatchie** Mississippi, S USA 32.19N 89.48W
175 N11 **Pelaihari** var. Pleihari. Borneo, C Indonesia 3.48S 114.45E
105 U14 **Pelat, Mont** ▲ SE France 44.16N 6.46E
118 F12 **Peleaga, Vârful** prev. Vîrful Peleaga. ▲ W Romania 45.23N 22.52E
Peleaga, Vîrful see Peleaga, Vârful
126 K12 **Peleduy** Respublika Sakha (Yakutiya), NE Russian Federation 59.39N 112.36E
12 C18 **Pelee Island** island Ontario, S Canada
47 Q11 **Pelée, Montagne** ▲ N Martinique 14.47N 61.10W
12 D18 **Pelee, Point** headland Ontario, S Canada 41.56N 82.30W
175 R9 **Pelei** Pulau Peleng, N Indonesia 1.26S 123.27E
Peleliu see Beliliou
175 R9 **Peleng, Pulau** island Kepulauan Banggai, N Indonesia
175 Qq9 **Peleng, Selat** strait Sulawesi, C Indonesia
25 T7 **Pelham** Georgia, SE USA 31.07N 84.09W
113 E18 **Pelhřimov** Ger. Pilgram. Vysočina, C Czech Republic 49.25N 15.13E
41 W13 **Pelican** Chichagof Island, Alaska, USA 57.52N 136.05W
203 Z3 **Pelican Lagoon** ◎ Kiritimati, E Kiribati
31 U6 **Pelican Lake** ◎ Minnesota, N USA
31 V3 **Pelican Lake** ◎ Minnesota, N USA
32 L5 **Pelican Lake** ◎ Wisconsin, N USA
46 G1 **Pelican Point** Grand Bahama Island, N Bahamas 26.39N 78.09W
85 B19 **Pelican Point** headland W Namibia 22.55S 14.25E
31 S6 **Pelican Rapids** Minnesota, N USA 46.34N 96.04W
Pelican State see Louisiana
9 U13 **Pelikan Narrows** Saskatchewan, C Canada 55.11N 102.51W
117 L18 **Pelinaío** ▲ Chíos, E Greece 38.31N 26.01E
Pelinnaeum see Pelinnaío
117 E16 **Pelinnaío** anc. Pelinnaeum. ruins Thessalía, C Greece 39.33N 21.45E
115 N20 **Pelister** ▲ SW FYR Macedonia 41.00N 21.12E
115 G15 **Pelješac** peninsula S Croatia
94 M12 **Pelkosenniemi** Lappi, NE Finland 67.06N 27.30E
31 W15 **Pella** Iowa, C USA 41.24N 92.55W
116 F13 **Pélla** site of ancient city Kentrikí Makedonía, N Greece 40.46N 22.35E
25 Q3 **Pell City** Alabama, S USA 33.35N 86.17W
63 A22 **Pellegrini** Buenos Aires, E Argentina 36.16S 63.07W
94 K12 **Pello** Lappi, NW Finland 66.47N 24.00E
102 G7 **Pellworm** island N Germany
8 H6 **Pelly** ∽ Yukon Territory, NW Canada
15 L3 **Pelly Bay** Nunavut, N Canada 68.37N 89.45W
8 I8 **Pelly Mountains** ▲ Yukon Territory, W Canada
Pélmonostor see Beli Manastir
39 P13 **Pelona Mountain** ▲ New Mexico, SW USA 33.40N 108.06W
Peloponnese/Peloponnesus see Pelopónnisos
117 E20 **Pelopónnisos** Eng. Peloponnese. ◆ region S Greece
117 E20 **Pelopónnisos** var. Morea, Eng. Peloponnese; anc. Peloponnesus. peninsula S Greece
109 L23 **Peloritani, Monti** anc. Pelorus and Neptunius. ▲ Sicilia, Italy, C Mediterranean Sea
109 M22 **Peloro, Capo** var. Punta del Faro. headland S Italy 38.15N 15.39E
Pelorus and Neptunius see Peloritani, Monti
63 H17 **Pelotas** Rio Grande do Sul, S Brazil 31.45S 52.19W
63 I14 **Pelotas, Rio** ∽ S Brazil
94 K10 **Peltovuoma** Lapp. Bealdovuopmi. Lappi, N Finland 68.23N 24.11E
125 F10 **Pelym** ∽ C Russian Federation
21 R4 **Pemadumcook Lake** ◎ Maine, NE USA
174 Kk14 **Pemalang** Jawa, C Indonesia 6.52S 109.07E
174 K7 **Pemangkat** var. Pamangkat. Borneo, C Indonesia 1.11N 109.00E
Pemar see Paimio
173 Ff5 **Pematangsiantar** Sumatera, W Indonesia 2.58N 99.01E
85 Q14 **Pemba** prev. Port Amelia, Porto Amélia. Cabo Delgado, NE Mozambique 13.00S 40.30E
83 J22 **Pemba** ◆ region E Tanzania
83 K21 **Pemba** island E Tanzania
85 Q14 **Pemba, Baia de** inlet NE Mozambique
83 J21 **Pemba Channel** channel E Tanzania
188 J14 **Pemberton** Western Australia 34.27S 116.09E
8 M16 **Pemberton** British Columbia, SW Canada 50.19N 122.49W
31 Q2 **Pembina** North Dakota, N USA 48.58N 97.14W
31 Q2 **Pembina** ∽ Canada/USA
9 P15 **Pembina** ∽ Alberta, SW Canada
176 Xx15 **Pembre** Papua, E Indonesia 7.49S 138.01E
12 K12 **Pembroke** Ontario, SE Canada 45.49N 77.07W
99 H21 **Pembroke** SW Wales, UK 51.40N 4.55W

◆ Country ● Country Capital ◇ Dependent Territory ○ Dependent Territory Capital ◆ Administrative Region ✕ International Airport ▲ Mountain ▲ Mountain Range ▲ Volcano ∽ River ◎ Lake ⊠ Reservoir
309

25 W6 **Pembroke** Georgia, SE USA *32.09N 81.35W*
23 U11 **Pembroke** North Carolina, SE USA *34.40N 79.12W*
23 R7 **Pembroke** Virginia, NE USA *37.19N 80.38W*
99 H21 **Pembroke** *cultural region* SW Wales, UK
Pembuang, Sungai *see* Seruyan, Sungai
45 S15 **Peña Blanca, Cerro** ▲ C Panama *8.39N 80.39W*
106 K8 **Peña de Francia, Sierra de la** ▲ W Spain
106 G6 **Penafiel** *var.* Peñafiel. Porto, N Portugal *41.12N 8.16W*
107 N6 **Peñafiel** Castilla-León, N Spain *41.36N 4.07W*
107 S8 **Peñagolosa** ▲ E Spain *40.10N 0.15W*
107 N7 **Peñalara, Pico de** ▲ C Spain *40.52N 3.55W*
175 Nn5 **Penambo, Banjaran** *var.* Banjaran Tama Abu, Penambo Range. ▲ Indonesia/Malaysia
Penambo Range *see* Penambo, Banjaran
43 O10 **Peña Nevada, Cerro** ▲ C Mexico *23.46N 99.52W*
Penang *see* Pinang, Pulau, Peninsular Malaysia
Penang *see* Pinang
Penang *see* George Town
62 J8 **Penápolis** São Paulo, S Brazil *21.23S 50.02W*
106 L7 **Peñaranda de Bracamonte** Castilla-León, N Spain *40.54N 5.13W*
107 S8 **Peñarroya** ▲ E Spain *40.24N 0.42W*
106 L12 **Peñarroya-Pueblonuevo** Andalucía, S Spain *38.21N 5.18W*
99 K22 **Penarth** S Wales, UK *51.27N 3.10W*
106 K1 **Peñas, Cabo de** *headland* N Spain *43.39N 5.52W*
65 F20 **Penas, Golfo de** *gulf* S Chile
Pen-ch'i *see* Benxi
81 H14 **Pendé** *var.* Logone Oriental. ≈ Central African Republic/Chad
78 I14 **Pendembu** E Sierra Leone *9.06N 12.12W*
31 R13 **Pender** Nebraska, C USA *42.06N 96.42W*
Penderma *see* Bandırma
34 K11 **Pendleton** Oregon, NW USA *45.40N 118.47W*
34 M7 **Pend Oreille, Lake** ◎ Idaho, NW USA
34 M7 **Pend Oreille River** ≈ Idaho/Washington, NW USA
Pendzhikent *see* Panjakent
Peneius *see* Pineiós
106 G8 **Penela** Coimbra, N Portugal *40.01N 8.22W*
12 G13 **Penetanguishene** Ontario, S Canada *44.45N 79.55W*
157 H15 **Penganga** ≈ C India
167 T12 **P'engchia Yu** *island* N Taiwan
81 M21 **Penge** Kasai Oriental, C Dem. Rep. Congo *5.29S 24.38E*
Penghu Archipelago/P'enghu Ch'üntao/Penghu Islands *see* P'enghu Liehtao
167 R14 **P'enghu Liehtao** *var.* P'enghu Ch'üntao, Penghu Islands, *Eng.* Penghu Archipelago, Pescadores, *Jap.* Hoko-guntō, Hoko-shotō. *island group* W Taiwan
Penghu Shuidao/P'enghu Shuitao *see* Pescadores Channel
167 R4 **Penglai** *var.* Dengzhou. Shandong, E China *37.48N 120.43E*
Peng-pu *see* Bengbu
Penhsihu *see* Benxi
Penibético, Sistema *see* Béticos, Sistemas
106 F10 **Peniche** Leiria, W Portugal *39.21N 9.22W*
175 Nn16 **Penida, Nusa** *island* S Indonesia
Peninsular State *see* Florida
107 T8 **Peñíscola** País Valenciano, E Spain *40.22N 0.24E*
42 M13 **Pénjamo** Guanajuato, C Mexico *20.20N 101.35W*
Penki *see* Benxi
104 F7 **Penmarch, Pointe de** *headland* NW France *47.46N 4.34W*
109 L15 **Penna, Punta della** *headland* C Italy *42.10N 14.43E*
109 K14 **Penne** Abruzzo, C Italy *42.28N 13.57E*
Penner *see* Penneru
161 J18 **Penneru** *var.* Penner. ≈ C India
190 I10 **Penneshaw** South Australia *35.45S 137.57E*
20 C14 **Penn Hills** Pennsylvania, NE USA *40.28N 79.52W*
Penninae, Alpes/Pennine, Alpi *see* Pennine Alps
110 D11 **Pennine Alps** *Fr.* Alpes Pennines, *It.* Alpi Pennine; *Lat.* Alpes Penninae. ▲ Italy/Switzerland
Pennine Chain *see* Pennines
99 L15 **Pennines** *var.* Pennine Chain. ▲ N England, UK
Pennines, Alpes *see* Pennine Alps
23 O8 **Pennington Gap** Virginia, NE USA *36.45N 83.01W*
20 I16 **Penns Grove** New Jersey, NE USA *39.42N 75.27W*
20 I16 **Pennsville** New Jersey, NE USA *39.37N 75.29W*
20 E14 **Pennsylvania** *off.* Commonwealth of Pennsylvania; also known as The Keystone State. ◆ *state* NE USA
20 G10 **Penn Yan** New York, NE USA *42.39N 77.02W*
128 H16 **Peno** Tverskaya Oblast', W Russian Federation *56.55N 32.44E*
21 R7 **Penobscot Bay** *bay* Maine, NE USA
21 S5 **Penobscot River** ≈ Maine, NE USA
190 K12 **Penola** South Australia *37.24S 140.50E*
42 K9 **Peñón Blanco** Durango, C Mexico *25.12N 100.50W*
190 E7 **Penong** South Australia *31.57S 133.01E*
45 S16 **Penonomé** Coclé, C Panama *8.29N 80.21W*
202 L13 **Penrhyn** *atoll* N Cook Islands
199 Kk10 **Penrhyn Basin** *undersea feature* C Pacific Ocean
191 S9 **Penrith** New South Wales, SE Australia *33.45S 150.48E*
99 K15 **Penrith** NW England, UK *54.40N 2.43W*
25 O9 **Pensacola** Florida, SE USA *30.25N 87.13W*
25 O9 **Pensacola Bay** *bay* Florida, SE USA
205 N7 **Pensacola Mountains** ▲ Antarctica
190 L12 **Penshurst** Victoria, SE Australia *37.54S 142.19E*
197 C12 **Pentecost** *Fr.* Pentecôte. *island* C Vanuatu
13 V4 **Pentecôte** ≈ Québec, SE Canada
Pentecôte *see* Pentecost
13 V4 **Pentecôte, Lac** ◎ Québec, SE Canada
15 Gg16 **Penticton** British Columbia, SW Canada *49.28N 119.37W*
98 J6 **Pentland Firth** *strait* N Scotland, UK
98 J12 **Pentland Hills** *hill range* S Scotland, UK
175 Rr10 **Penu** Pulau Taliabu, E Indonesia *1.43S 125.09E*
161 H18 **Penukonda** Andhra Pradesh, E India *14.04N 77.38E*
177 G7 **Penwegon** Pegu, C Burma *18.13N 96.34E*
26 M8 **Penwell** Texas, SW USA *31.45N 102.32W*
99 J21 **Pen y Fan** ▲ SE Wales, UK *51.52N 3.25W*
99 L16 **Pen-y-ghent** ▲ N England, UK *54.11N 2.15W*
175 T12 **Penyu, Kepulauan** *island group* E Indonesia
131 O6 **Penza** Penzenskaya Oblast', W Russian Federation *53.11N 45.00E*
99 G25 **Penzance** SW England, UK *50.07N 5.33W*
131 N6 **Penzenskaya Oblast'** ◆ *province* W Russian Federation
127 P7 **Penzhina** ≈ E Russian Federation
127 N17 **Penzhinskaya Guba** *bay* E Russian Federation
Penzig *see* Pieńsk
38 K13 **Peoria** Arizona, SW USA *33.34N 112.14W*
32 L12 **Peoria** Illinois, N USA *40.41N 89.35W*
32 L12 **Peoria Heights** Illinois, N USA *40.45N 89.34W*
33 N11 **Peotone** Illinois, N USA *41.19N 87.47W*
20 J11 **Pepacton Reservoir** ⊠ New York, NE USA
78 I15 **Pepel** W Sierra Leone *8.39N 13.04W*
32 I6 **Pepin, Lake** ◎ Minnesota/Wisconsin, N USA
101 L20 **Pepinster** Liège, E Belgium *50.34N 5.49E*
115 L20 **Peqin** *var.* Peqini. Elbasan, C Albania *41.03N 19.46E*
Peqini *see* Peqin
42 D7 **Pequeña, Punta** *headland* W Mexico *26.13N 112.34W*
174 I11 **Perabumulih** *var.* Prabumulih. Sumatera, W Indonesia *3.27S 104.15E*
174 Gg4 **Perak** ◆ *state* Peninsular Malaysia
174 Gg4 **Perak, Sungai** ≈ Peninsular Malaysia
107 R7 **Perales del Alfambra** Aragón, NE Spain *40.38N 1.00W*
117 C15 **Pérama** *var.* Perama. Ípeiros, W Greece *39.42N 20.51E*
94 M13 **Perä-Posio** Lappi, NE Finland *66.10N 27.56E*
13 Z6 **Percé** Québec, SE Canada *48.31N 64.15W*
13 Z6 **Percé, Rocher** *island* Québec, S Canada
104 L5 **Perche, Collines de** ▲ N France
111 X4 **Perchtoldsdorf** Niederösterreich, NE Austria *48.06N 16.16E*
188 L6 **Percival Lakes** *lakes* Western Australia
107 T3 **Perdido, Monte** ▲ NE Spain *42.41N 0.01E*
25 O8 **Perdido River** ≈ Alabama/Florida, S USA
Perece Vela Basin *see* West Mariana Basin
118 G7 **Perechyn** Zakarpats'ka Oblast', W Ukraine *48.45N 22.28E*
56 E10 **Pereira** Risaralda, W Colombia *4.52N 75.48W*
62 I7 **Pereira Barreto** São Paulo, S Brazil *20.37S 51.07W*
61 G15 **Pereirinha** Pará, N Brazil *8.18S 57.30W*
131 N10 **Perelazovskiy** Volgogradskaya Oblast', SW Russian Federation *49.10N 42.30E*
131 S7 **Perelyub** Saratovskaya Oblast', W Russian Federation *51.52N 50.19E*
33 P7 **Pere Marquette River** ≈ Michigan, N USA
Peremyshl *see* Przemyśl
118 I5 **Peremyshlyany** L'vivs'ka Oblast', W Ukraine *49.42N 24.33E*
Pereshchepino *see* Pereshchepyne
118 L9 **Pereshchepyne** *Rus.* Pereshchepino. Dnipropetrovs'ka Oblast', E Ukraine *48.59N 35.21E*
128 L16 **Pereslavl'-Zalesskiy** Yaroslavskaya Oblast', W Russian Federation *56.42N 38.45E*
119 Y7 **Pereval's'k** Luhans'ka Oblast', E Ukraine *48.28N 38.54E*
131 U7 **Perevolotskiy** Orenburgskaya Oblast', W Russian Federation *51.54N 54.05E*
127 Nn16 **Pereyaslavka** Khabarovskiy Kray, SE Russian Federation *47.49N 134.56E*
Pereyaslav-Khmel'nitskiy *see* Pereyaslav-Khmel'nyts'kyy
119 Q5 **Pereyaslav-Khmel'nyts'kyy** *Rus.* Pereyaslav-Khmel'nitskiy. Kyyivs'ka Oblast', N Ukraine *50.04N 31.28E*
111 U4 **Perg** Oberösterreich, N Austria *48.15N 14.39E*
63 B19 **Pergamino** Buenos Aires, E Argentina *33.55S 60.38W*
108 G6 **Pergine Valsugana** *Ger.* Persen. Trentino-Alto Adige, N Italy *46.04N 11.13E*
31 S6 **Perham** Minnesota, N USA *46.35N 95.34W*
95 L16 **Perho** Länsi-Suomi, W Finland *63.15N 24.25E*
118 E11 **Periam** *Ger.* Perjamosch, *Hung.* Perjámos. Timiş, W Romania *46.01N 20.54E*
13 Q6 **Péribonca** ≈ Québec, SE Canada
10 L11 **Péribonca, Lac** ◎ Québec, SE Canada
13 Q6 **Péribonca, Petite Rivière** ≈ Québec, SE Canada
13 Q7 **Péribonka** Québec, SE Canada *48.45N 72.01W*
42 I9 **Pericos** Sinaloa, C Mexico *25.04N 107.40W*
174 Kk7 **Perigi** Borneo, C Indonesia
104 L12 **Périgueux** *anc.* Vesuna. Dordogne, SW France *45.12N 0.41E*
56 G5 **Perijá, Serranía de** ▲ Columbia/Venezuela
117 H17 **Peristéra** *island* Vóreies Sporádes, Greece, Aegean Sea
65 H20 **Perito Moreno** Santa Cruz, S Argentina *46.35S 71.00W*
161 G22 **Periyāl** *var.* Periyār. ≈ SW India
Periyār *see* Periyāl
161 G23 **Periyār Lake** ◎ S India
Perjámos/Perjamosch *see* Periam
29 O9 **Perkins** Oklahoma, C USA *35.58N 97.01W*
118 L7 **Perkivtsi** Chernivets'ka Oblast', W Ukraine *48.28N 26.48E*
45 U15 **Perlas, Archipiélago de las** *Eng.* Pearl Islands. *island group* SE Panama
45 O10 **Perlas, Cayos de** *reef* SE Nicaragua
45 N9 **Perlas, Laguna de** *Eng.* Pearl Lagoon. *lagoon* E Nicaragua
45 N10 **Perlas, Punta de** *headland* E Nicaragua *12.22N 83.30W*
102 L11 **Perleberg** Brandenburg, N Germany *53.04N 11.51E*
Perlepe *see* Prilep
173 G2 **Perlis** ◆ *state* Peninsular Malaysia
129 U14 **Perm'** *prev.* Molotov. Permskaya Oblast', NW Russian Federation *58.01N 56.10E*
115 M22 **Përmet** *var.* Përmeti, Prëmet. Gjirokastër, S Albania *40.12N 20.24E*
Përmeti *see* Përmet
129 U15 **Permskaya Oblast'** ◆ *province* NW Russian Federation
61 P15 **Pernambuco** *off.* Estado de Pernambuco. ◆ *state* E Brazil
Pernambuco *see* Recife
Pernambuco Abyssal Plain *see* Pernambuco Plain
49 Y6 **Pernambuco Plain** *var.* Pernambuco Abyssal Plain. *undersea feature* E Atlantic Ocean
67 K15 **Pernambuco Seamounts** *undersea feature* C Atlantic Ocean
190 H6 **Pernatty Lagoon** *salt lake* South Australia
Pernau *see* Pärnu
Pernauer Bucht *see* Pärnu Laht
Pērnava *see* Pärnu
116 G9 **Pernik** *prev.* Dimitrovo. Pernik, W Bulgaria *42.36N 23.01E*
116 G10 **Pernik** ◆ *province* W Bulgaria
95 K20 **Perniö** *Swe.* Bjärnå. Länsi-Suomi, W Finland *60.13N 23.10E*
111 X5 **Pernitz** Niederösterreich, E Austria *47.54N 15.58E*
Pernov *see* Pärnu
105 O3 **Péronne** Somme, N France *49.55N 2.57E*
12 L8 **Péronne, Lac** ◎ Québec, SE Canada
108 A8 **Perosa Argentina** Piemonte, NE Italy *45.02N 7.10E*
43 Q14 **Perote** Veracruz-Llave, E Mexico *19.31N 97.16W*
Pérouse *see* Perugia
203 W15 **Pérouse, Bahía de la** *bay* Easter Island, Chile, E Pacific Ocean
Perovsk *see* Kyzylorda
105 O17 **Perpignan** Pyrénées-Orientales, S France *42.40N 2.52E*
115 M20 **Përrenjas** *var.* Përrenjasi, Prenjas, Prenjasi. Elbasan, E Albania *41.04N 20.34E*
Përrenjasi *see* Përrenjas
94 O2 **Perriertoppen** ▲ C Svalbard *79.10N 17.01E*
27 S6 **Perrin** Texas, SW USA *32.59N 98.03W*
25 Y16 **Perrine** Florida, SE USA *25.36N 80.21W*
39 S12 **Perro, Laguna del** ◎ New Mexico, SW USA
104 G5 **Perros-Guirec** Côtes d'Armor, NW France *48.49N 3.28W*
25 T9 **Perry** Florida, SE USA *30.07N 83.34W*
25 T5 **Perry** Georgia, SE USA *32.27N 83.43W*
31 U14 **Perry** Iowa, C USA *41.50N 94.06W*
20 E10 **Perry** New York, NE USA *42.43N 78.00W*
29 N9 **Perry** Oklahoma, C USA *36.17N 97.17W*
29 Q3 **Perry Lake** ⊠ Kansas, C USA
33 R11 **Perrysburg** Ohio, N USA *41.33N 83.37W*
27 O1 **Perryton** Texas, SW USA *36.24N 100.48W*
41 O15 **Perryville** Alaska, USA *55.55N 159.08W*
29 U11 **Perryville** Arkansas, C USA *35.00N 92.48W*
29 Y6 **Perryville** Missouri, C USA *37.43N 89.51W*
Persante *see* Parsęta
Persen *see* Pergine Valsugana
Pershay *see* Pyarshai
119 V7 **Pershotravens'k** Dnipropetrovs'ka Oblast', E Ukraine *48.19N 36.22E*
119 W9 **Pershotravneve** Donets'ka Oblast', E Ukraine *47.03N 37.20E*
Persia *see* Iran
Persian Gulf *see* Gulf, The
Persis *see* Fārs
97 K22 **Perstorp** Skåne, S Sweden *56.07N 13.22E*
143 O14 **Pertek** Tunceli, C Turkey *38.52N 39.19E*
191 P16 **Perth** Tasmania, SE Australia *41.39S 147.11E*
188 I13 **Perth** *state capital* Western Australia *31.58S 115.49E*
12 L13 **Perth** Ontario, SE Canada *44.54N 76.15W*
98 J11 **Perth** C Scotland, UK *56.24N 3.28W*
188 I12 **Perth** ✕ Western Australia *31.51S 116.06E*
98 J10 **Perth** *cultural region* C Scotland, UK
181 V10 **Perth Basin** *undersea feature* SE Indian Ocean
105 S15 **Pertuis** Vaucluse, SE France *43.42N 5.30E*
105 Y16 **Pertusato, Capo** *headland* Corse, France, C Mediterranean Sea *41.22N 9.10E*
32 L11 **Peru** Illinois, N USA *41.18N 89.09W*
33 P12 **Peru** Indiana, N USA *40.45N 86.04W*
59 E13 **Peru** *off.* Republic of Peru. ◆ *republic* W South America
Peru *see* Beru
200 Oo10 **Peru Basin** *undersea feature* E Pacific Ocean
200 Oo9 **Peru-Chile Trench** *undersea feature* E Pacific Ocean
114 F13 **Perućko Jezero** ◎ S Croatia
108 H13 **Perugia** *Fr.* Pérouse; *anc.* Perusia. Umbria, C Italy *43.06N 12.24E*
Perugia, Lake of *see* Trasimeno, Lago
63 D15 **Perugorría** Corrientes, NE Argentina *29.21S 58.34W*
62 M11 **Peruíbe** São Paulo, S Brazil *24.18S 47.01W*
161 B21 **Perumalpār** *reef* India, N Indian Ocean
Perusia *see* Perugia
101 D20 **Péruwelz** Hainaut, SW Belgium *50.30N 3.34E*
143 R15 **Pervari** Siirt, SE Turkey *37.58N 42.30E*
131 O4 **Pervomaysk** Nizhegorodskaya Oblast', W Russian Federation *54.52N 43.49E*
119 X7 **Pervomays'k** Luhans'ka Oblast', E Ukraine *48.37N 38.36E*
119 P8 **Pervomays'k** *prev.* Ol'viopol'. Mykolayivs'ka Oblast', S Ukraine *48.01N 30.51E*
119 S12 **Pervomays'ke** Respublika Krym, S Ukraine *45.43N 33.49E*
129 R14 **Pervomayskiy** Kirovskaya Oblast', NW Russian Federation *59.15N 49.20E*
131 V7 **Pervomayskiy** Orenburgskaya Oblast', W Russian Federation *51.32N 54.58E*
130 M6 **Pervomayskiy** Tambovskaya Oblast', W Russian Federation *53.15N 40.20E*
119 V6 **Pervomays'kyy** Kharkivs'ka Oblast', E Ukraine *49.24N 36.12E*
125 E10 **Pervoural'sk** Sverdlovskaya Oblast', C Russian Federation *56.58N 59.50E*
127 Pp12 **Pervyy Kuril'skiy Proliv** *strait* E Russian Federation
101 I19 **Perwez** Walloon Brabant, C Belgium *50.39N 4.49E*
108 I11 **Pesaro** *anc.* Pisaurum. Marche, C Italy *43.55N 12.52E*
37 N9 **Pescadero** California, W USA *37.15N 122.23W*
Pescadores *see* P'enghu Liehtao
167 S14 **Pescadores Channel** *var.* Penghu Shuidao, P'enghu Shuitao. *channel* W Taiwan
109 K14 **Pescara** *anc.* Aternum, Ostia Aterni. Abruzzo, C Italy *42.28N 14.13E*
109 K15 **Pescara** ≈ C Italy
108 F11 **Pescia** Toscana, C Italy *43.54N 10.40E*
110 C8 **Peseux** Neuchâtel, W Switzerland *46.58N 6.52E*
129 P6 **Pesha** ≈ NW Russian Federation
155 T5 **Peshāwar** North-West Frontier Province, N Pakistan *34.00N 71.33E*
155 T6 **Peshāwar** ✕ North-West Frontier Province, N Pakistan *34.01N 71.40E*
115 M19 **Peshkopi** *var.* Peshkopia, Peshkopija. Dibër, NE Albania *41.40N 20.25E*
Peshkopia/Peshkopija *see* Peshkopi
116 I11 **Peshtera** Pazardzhik, C Bulgaria *42.01N 24.18E*
33 N6 **Peshtigo** Wisconsin, N USA *45.04N 87.43W*
33 N6 **Peshtigo River** ≈ Wisconsin, N USA
Peski *see* Pyeski
129 S13 **Peskovka** Kirovskaya Oblast', NW Russian Federation *59.04N 52.17E*
105 S8 **Pesmes** Haute-Saône, E France *47.17N 5.33E*
106 H6 **Peso da Régua** *var.* Pêso da Regua. Vila Real, N Portugal *41.10N 7.46W*
42 F5 **Pesqueira** Sonora, NW Mexico *29.22N 110.52W*
104 J13 **Pessac** Gironde, SW France *44.46N 0.42W*
113 J23 **Pest** *off.* Pest Megye. ◆ *county* C Hungary
128 J14 **Pestovo** Novgorodskaya Oblast', W Russian Federation *58.37N 35.48E*
42 M15 **Petacalco, Bahía** *bay* W Mexico
Petach-Tikva/Petah Tiqva *see* Petah Tiqwa
144 F10 **Petah Tiqwa** *var.* Petach-Tikva, Petah Tiqva, Petakh Tikva. Tel Aviv, C Israel *32.04N 34.52E*
Petakh Tikva *see* Petah Tiqwa
95 L17 **Petäjävesi** Länsi-Suomi, W Finland *62.16N 25.10E*
24 M7 **Petal** Mississippi, S USA *31.21N 89.15W*
117 I19 **Petalioí** *island* C Greece
117 H19 **Petalión, Kólpos** *gulf* E Greece
117 J19 **Pétalo** ▲ Ándros, Kykládes, Greece, Aegean Sea *37.51N 24.50E*
36 M8 **Petaluma** California, W USA *38.15N 122.37W*
101 L25 **Pétange** Luxembourg, SW Luxembourg *49.33N 5.52E*
56 M5 **Petare** Miranda, N Venezuela *10.29N 66.47W*
43 N16 **Petatlán** Guerrero, S Mexico *17.31N 101.16W*
85 L14 **Petauke** Eastern, E Zambia *14.12S 31.16E*
12 J12 **Petawawa** Ontario, SE Canada *45.53N 77.16W*
12 J11 **Petawawa** ≈ Ontario, SE Canada
Petchaburi *see* Phetchaburi
44 D2 **Petén** *off.* Departamento del Petén. ◆ *department* N Guatemala
44 D2 **Petén Itzá, Lago** *var.* Lago de Flores. ◎ N Guatemala
32 K7 **Petenwell Lake** ⊠ Wisconsin, N USA
12 D6 **Peterbell** Ontario, S Canada *48.34N 83.19W*
190 I7 **Peterborough** South Australia *32.59S 138.50E*
12 I14 **Peterborough** Ontario, SE Canada *44.19N 78.19W*
99 N20 **Peterborough** *prev.* Medeshamstede. E England, UK *52.34N 0.15W*
21 N10 **Peterborough** New Hampshire, NE USA *42.51N 71.54W*
98 L8 **Peterhead** NE Scotland, UK *57.30N 1.46W*
Peterhof *see* Luboń
199 Mm16 **Peter I Island** ◇ *Norwegian dependency* Antarctica
204 H9 **Peter I Island** *var.* Peter I øy. *island* Antarctica
Peter I øy *see* Peter I Island
99 M14 **Peterlee** N England, UK *54.45N 1.18W*
Peterlingen *see* Payerne
207 P14 **Petermann Bjerg** ▲ C Greenland *73.16N 27.59W*
9 S12 **Peter Pond Lake** ◎ Saskatchewan, C Canada
41 X13 **Petersburg** Mytkof Island, Alaska, USA *56.43N 132.51W*
32 K13 **Petersburg** Illinois, N USA *40.01N 89.52W*
33 N16 **Petersburg** Indiana, N USA *38.30N 87.16W*
31 Q3 **Petersburg** North Dakota, N USA *47.59N 97.59W*
27 N5 **Petersburg** Texas, SW USA *33.52N 101.36W*
23 V7 **Petersburg** Virginia, NE USA *37.13N 77.24W*
23 T4 **Petersburg** West Virginia, NE USA *38.59N 79.07W*
102 H12 **Petershagen** Nordrhein-Westfalen, NW Germany *52.22N 8.58E*
57 S9 **Peters Mine** *var.* Peter's Mine. N Guyana *6.13N 59.18W*
109 O21 **Petilia Policastro** Calabria, SW Italy *39.07N 16.48E*
46 M9 **Pétionville** S Haiti *18.29N 72.16W*
47 X6 **Petit-Bourg** Basse Terre, C Guadeloupe *16.11N 61.34W*
13 Y5 **Petit-Cap** Québec, SE Canada *49.00N 64.26W*
47 Y6 **Petit Cul-de-Sac Marin** *bay* C Guadeloupe
46 M9 **Petite-Rivière-de-l'Artibonite** C Haiti *19.06N 72.28W*
181 X16 **Petite Rivière Noire, Piton de la** ▲ C Mauritius
13 R9 **Petite-Rivière-St-François** Québec, SE Canada *47.18N 70.34W*
46 L9 **Petit-Goâve** S Haiti *18.23N 72.51W*
Petitjean *see* Sidi-Kacem
11 N10 **Petit Lac Manicouagan** ◎ Québec, E Canada
21 T7 **Petit Manan Point** *headland* Maine, NE USA *44.23N 67.54W*
Petit Mécatina, Rivière du *see* Little Mecatina
9 N10 **Petitot** ≈ Alberta/British Columbia, W Canada
47 S12 **Petit Piton** ▲ SW Saint Lucia *13.49N 61.03W*
Petit-Popo *see* Aného
Petit St-Bernard, Col du *see* Little Saint Bernard Pass
11 O8 **Petitsikapau Lake** ◎ Newfoundland and Labrador, E Canada
94 L11 **Petkula** Lappi, N Finland *67.40N 26.43E*
43 X12 **Peto** Yucatán, SE Mexico *20.09N 88.55W*
64 G10 **Petorca** Valparaíso, C Chile *32.13S 70.49W*
33 Q5 **Petoskey** Michigan, N USA *45.51N 88.03W*
144 G14 **Petra** *archaeological site* Ma'ān, W Jordan *30.19N 35.25E*
Petra *see* Wādī Mūsā
117 F14 **Pétras, Sténa** *pass* N Greece *40.12N 22.15E*
127 Nn18 **Petra Velikogo, Zaliv** *bay* SE Russian Federation
Petrel *see* Petrer
12 K15 **Petre, Point** *headland* Ontario, SE Canada *43.49N 77.07W*
107 S12 **Petrer** *var.* Petrel. País Valenciano, E Spain *38.28N 0.46W*
129 U11 **Petretsovo** Permskaya Oblast', NW Russian Federation *61.22N 57.21E*
116 G12 **Petrich** Blagoevgrad, SW Bulgaria *41.24N 23.12E*
197 H3 **Petrie, Récif** *reef* N New Caledonia
39 N11 **Petrified Forest** *prehistoric site* Arizona, SW USA *35.10N 109.49W*
Petrikau *see* Piotrków Trybunalski
Petrikov *see* Pyetrykaw
118 H12 **Petrila** *Hung.* Petrilla. Hunedoara, W Romania *45.27N 23.25E*
Petrilla *see* Petrila
114 E9 **Petrinja** Sisak-Moslavina, C Croatia *45.27N 16.14E*
Petroaleksandrovsk *see* To'rtkok'l
Petrőcz *see* Bački Petrovac
128 G12 **Petrodvorets** *Fin.* Pietarhovi. Leningradskaya Oblast', NW Russian Federation *59.52N 29.52E*
Petrograd *see* Sankt-Peterburg
Petrokov *see* Piotrków Trybunalski
56 G6 **Petrólea** Norte de Santander, NE Colombia *8.30N 72.34W*
12 D16 **Petrolia** Ontario, S Canada *42.54N 82.07W*
27 S4 **Petrolia** Texas, SW USA *34.00N 98.13W*
61 O15 **Petrolina** Pernambuco, E Brazil *9.22S 40.30W*
47 T6 **Petrona, Punta** *headland* C Puerto Rico *17.57N 66.23W*
Petropavl *see* Petropavlovsk
119 V7 **Petropavlivka** Dnipropetrovs'ka Oblast', E Ukraine *48.28N 36.28E*
151 P6 **Petropavlovsk** *Kaz.* Petropavl. Severnyy Kazakhstan, N Kazakhstan *54.46N 69.06E*
127 Pp11 **Petropavlovsk-Kamchatskiy** Kamchatskaya Oblast', E Russian Federation *53.03N 158.43E*
62 P9 **Petrópolis** Rio de Janeiro, SE Brazil *22.30S 43.28W*
118 H12 **Petroşani** *var.* Petroşeni, *Ger.* Petroschen, *Hung.* Petrozsény. Hunedoara, W Romania *45.25N 23.22E*
Petroschen/Petroşeni *see* Petroşani
Petroskoi *see* Petrozavodsk
Petrovac/Petrovácz *see* Bački Petrovac
115 J17 **Petrovac na Moru** S Montenegro *42.11N 19.00E*
119 S8 **Petrove** Kirovohrads'ka Oblast', C Ukraine *48.22N 33.12E*
115 O18 **Petrovec** C FYR Macedonia *41.57N 21.37E*
Petrovgrad *see* Zrenjanin
131 P7 **Petrovsk** Saratovskaya Oblast', W Russian Federation *52.20N 45.23E*
128 J9 **Petrovskiy Yam** Respublika Kareliya, NW Russian Federation *63.19N 35.14E*
Petrovsk-Port *see* Makhachkala
126 K16 **Petrovsk-Zabaykal'skiy** Chitinskaya Oblast', S Russian Federation *51.15N 108.36E*
131 P9 **Petrov Val** Volgogradskaya Oblast', SW Russian Federation *50.10N 45.16E*
128 J11 **Petrozavodsk** *Fin.* Petroskoi. Respublika Kareliya, NW Russian Federation *61.46N 34.19E*
Petrozsény *see* Petroşani
85 D20 **Petrusdal** Hardap, C Namibia *23.42S 17.23E*
119 T7 **Petrykivka** Dnipropetrovs'ka Oblast', E Ukraine *48.44N 34.42E*
Petsamo *see* Pechenga
Petschka *see* Pecica
Pettau *see* Ptuj
111 S5 **Pettenbach** Oberösterreich, C Austria *47.58N 14.03E*
27 S13 **Pettus** Texas, SW USA *28.34N 97.49W*
125 F13 **Petukhovo** Kurganskaya Oblast', C Russian Federation *55.04N 67.49E*
Petuna *see* Songyuan
111 R4 **Peuerbach** Oberösterreich, N Austria *48.19N 13.45E*
64 G12 **Peumo** Libertador, C Chile *34.22S 71.58W*
173 Ee3 **Peusangan, Krueng** ≈ Sumatera, NW Indonesia
127 O4 **Pevek** Chukotskiy Avtonomnyy Okrug, NE Russian Federation *69.40N 170.19E*
29 X5 **Pevely** Missouri, C USA *38.16N 90.24W*
Peyia *see* Pégeia
104 J15 **Peyrehorade** Landes, SW France *43.33N 1.04W*
128 J14 **Peza** ≈ NW Russian Federation
105 P16 **Pézenas** Hérault, S France *43.28N 3.25E*
113 H20 **Pezinok** *Ger.* Bösing, *Hung.* Bazin. Bratislavský Kraj, W Slovakia *48.16N 17.16E*
103 L22 **Pfaffenhofen an der Ilm** Bayern, SE Germany *48.31N 11.30E*
110 G7 **Pfäffikon** Schwyz, C Switzerland *47.11N 8.46E*
103 F20 **Pfälzer Wald** *hill range* W Germany
103 N22 **Pfarrkirchen** Bayern, SE Germany *48.25N 12.56E*
103 G21 **Pforzheim** Baden-Württemberg, SW Germany *48.52N 8.42E*
103 H24 **Pfullendorf** Baden-Württemberg, S Germany *47.55N 9.16E*
110 K8 **Pfunds** Tirol, W Austria *46.56N 10.30E*
103 G19 **Pfungstadt** Hessen, W Germany *49.48N 8.36E*
85 L20 **Phalaborwa** Limpopo, NE South Africa *23.50S 31.08E*
158 E11 **Phalodi** Rājasthān, NW India *27.06N 72.22E*
158 E12 **Phalsund** Rājasthān, NW India *26.22N 71.55E*
161 E15 **Phaltan** Mahārāshtra, W India *18.01N 74.31E*
178 Hh7 **Phan** *var.* Muang Phan. Chiang Rai, NW Thailand *19.34N 99.43E*
178 H14 **Phangan, Ko** *island* SW Thailand
178 Gg15 **Phang-Nga** *var.* Pang-Nga, Phangnga. Phangnga, SW Thailand *8.28N 98.31E*
Phan Rang/Phanrang *see* Phan Rang-Thap Cham
178 Kk13 **Phan Rang-Thap Cham** *var.* Phanrang, Phan Rang, Phan Rang Thap Cham. Ninh Thuân, S Vietnam *11.34N 109.00E*
178 Kk14 **Phan Ri** Binh Thuân, S Vietnam *11.11N 108.31E*
178 K14 **Phan Thiêt** Binh Thuân, S Vietnam *10.55N 108.06E*
Pharnacia *see* Giresun
27 S17 **Pharr** Texas, SW USA *26.11N 98.10W*
Pharus *see* Hvar
178 H16 **Phatthalung** *var.* Padalung, Patalung. Phatthalung, SW Thailand *7.37N 100.04E*
178 Hh7 **Phayao** *var.* Muang Phayao. Phayao, NW Thailand *19.10N 99.55E*
9 U10 **Phelps Lake** ◎ Saskatchewan, C Canada
23 X9 **Phelps Lake** ◎ North Carolina, SE USA
25 R5 **Phenix City** Alabama, S USA *32.28N 85.00W*
178 Jj8 **Pheo** Quang Binh, C Vietnam *17.42N 105.58E*
Phet Buri *see* Phetchaburi
178 H12 **Phetchaburi** *var.* Bejraburi, Petchaburi, Phet Buri. Phetchaburi, SW Thailand *13.04N 99.58E*
178 Hh9 **Phichit** *var.* Bichitra, Muang Phichit, Pichit. Phichit, C Thailand *16.28N 100.21E*
24 M5 **Philadelphia** Mississippi, S USA *32.45N 89.06W*
20 I7 **Philadelphia** New York, NE USA *44.10N 75.40W*
20 I16 **Philadelphia** Pennsylvania, NE USA *40.00N 75.10W*
20 I16 **Philadelphia** ✕ Pennsylvania, NE USA *39.51N 75.13W*
Philadelphia *see* 'Ammān
30 L10 **Philip** South Dakota, N USA *44.02N 101.39W*
101 H22 **Philippeville** Namur, S Belgium *50.12N 4.33E*
Philippeville *see* Skikda
23 S3 **Philippi** West Virginia, NE USA *39.09N 80.02W*
Philippi *see* Fílippoi
205 Y9 **Philippi Glacier** *glacier* Antarctica
198 G7 **Philippine Basin** *undersea feature* W Pacific Ocean
133 X12 **Philippine Plate** *tectonic feature*
179 Q13 **Philippines** *off.* Republic of the Philippines. ◆ *republic* SE Asia
133 X13 **Philippines** *island group* W Pacific Ocean
179 S12 **Philippine Sea** *sea* W Pacific Ocean
198 G7 **Philippine Trench** *undersea feature* W Philippine Sea
85 H23 **Philippolis** Free State, C South Africa *30.16S 25.16E*
Philippopolis *see* Plovdiv, Bulgaria
Philippopolis *see* Shahbā', Syria
47 V9 **Philipsburg** Sint Maarten, N Netherlands Antilles *17.58N 63.02W*
35 P10 **Philipsburg** Montana, NW USA *46.19N 113.17W*
41 R6 **Philip Smith Mountains** ▲ Alaska, USA
158 H8 **Phillaur** Punjab, N India *31.01N 75.49E*
191 N13 **Phillip Island** *island* Victoria, SE Australia
27 N2 **Phillips** Texas, SW USA *35.39N 101.21W*
32 K5 **Phillips** Wisconsin, N USA *45.42N 90.22W*
28 K3 **Phillipsburg** Kansas, C USA *39.45N 99.19W*
20 I14 **Phillipsburg** New Jersey, NE USA *40.39N 75.09W*
23 S7 **Philpott Lake** ⊠ Virginia, NE USA
Phintias *see* Licata
178 Hh9 **Phitsanulok** *var.* Bisnulok, Muang Phitsanulok, Pitsanulok. Phitsanulok, C Thailand *16.49N 100.15E*
Phlórina *see* Flórina
Phnom Penh *see* Phnum Penh
178 J13 **Phnum Penh** *var.* Phnom Penh. ● (Cambodia) Phnum Penh, S Cambodia *11.34N 104.55E*
178 J12 **Phnum Tbêng Meanchey** Preăh Vihéar, N Cambodia *13.45N 104.58E*
38 K13 **Phoenix** *state capital* Arizona, SW USA *33.27N 112.04W*
Phoenix Island *see* Rawaki
203 R3 **Phoenix Islands** *island group* C Kiribati
20 I15 **Phoenixville** Pennsylvania, NE USA *40.07N 75.31W*
85 K22 **Phofung** *var.* Mont-aux-Sources. ▲ N Lesotho *28.47S 28.52E*
178 I10 **Phon** Khon Kaen, E Thailand *15.47N 102.35E*
178 I5 **Phôngsali** *var.* Phong Saly. Phôngsali, N Laos *21.40N 102.04E*
Phong Saly *see* Phôngsali
178 I8 **Phônhông** C Laos *18.29N 102.26E*
178 J5 **Phô Rang** *var.* Bao Yên. Lao Cai, N Vietnam *22.12N 104.27E*
Phort Láirge, Cuan *see* Waterford Harbour
178 Gg10 **Phra Chedi Sam Ong** Kanchanaburi, W Thailand *15.18N 98.26E*
178 Hh8 **Phrae** *var.* Muang Prae, Prae. Phrae, NW Thailand *18.07N 100.09E*
Phra Nakhon Si Ayutthaya *see* Ayutthaya
177 G15 **Phra Thong, Ko** *island* SW Thailand
Phu Cường *see* Thu Dâu Môt
177 G16 **Phuket** *var.* Bhuket, Puket, *Mal.* Ujung Salang; *prev.* Junkseylon, Salang. Phuket, SW Thailand *7.52N 98.22E*
177 G16 **Phuket** ✕ Phuket, SW Thailand *8.03N 98.16E*
177 G16 **Phuket, Ko** *island* SW Thailand
160 N12 **Phulabāni** *prev.* Phulbani. Orissa, E India *20.30N 84.18E*
Phulbani *see* Phulabāni
178 K10 **Phu Lôc** Th,a Thiên-Huê, C Vietnam *16.13N 107.53E*
178 J14 **Phumĭ Banam** Prey Vêng, S Cambodia *11.14N 105.18E*
178 Ii13 **Phumĭ Chŏam** Kâmpóng Spœ, SW Cambodia *11.42N 103.58E*
178 Jj11 **Phumĭ Kalêng** Stœng Trêng, NE Cambodia *13.57N 106.17E*
178 J12 **Phumĭ Kâmpóng Trâbêk** *prev.* Phum Kompong Trabek. Kâmpóng Thum, C Cambodia *13.06N 105.16E*
178 Ii12 **Phumĭ Koŭk Kduŏch** Bătdâmbâng, NW Cambodia *13.16N 103.08E*
178 K12 **Phumĭ Labăng** Rôtânôkiri, NE Cambodia *13.51N 107.01E*
178 J11 **Phumĭ Mlu Prey** Preăh Vihéar, N Cambodia *13.48N 105.16E*
178 Ii11 **Phumĭ Moŭng** Siĕmréab, NW Cambodia *13.45N 103.35E*
178 Ii13 **Phumĭ Prâmaôy** Poŭthĭsăt, W Cambodia *12.13N 103.05E*
178 I14 **Phumĭ Samĭt** Kaôh Kông, SW Cambodia *10.54N 103.09E*
178 Ii11 **Phumĭ Sâmraông** *prev.* Phum Samrong. Siĕmréab, NW Cambodia *14.09N 103.30E*
178 Jj12 **Phumĭ Siĕmbok** Stœng Trêng, N Cambodia *13.28N 105.59E*
178 Jj12 **Phumĭ Thalabârĭvăt** Stœng Trêng, N Cambodia *13.34N 105.57E*
178 Ii14 **Phumĭ Veal Renh** Kâmpôt, SW Cambodia *10.43N 103.49E*

178 I13 Phumĭ Yeay Sên Kaôh Kông, SW Cambodia 11.09N 103.09E
Phum Kompong Trabek see Phumĭ Kâmpóng Trâbêk
Phum Samrong see Phumĭ Sâmraông
178 Kk11 Phu My Binh Đinh, C Vietnam 14.07N 109.05E
178 J15 Phung Hiêp Cân Thơ, S Vietnam 9.49N 105.48E
159 T12 Phuntsholing SW Bhutan 26.52N 89.25E
178 J15 Phước Long Minh Hai, S Vietnam 9.27N 105.25E
Phước Sơn see Khâm Đưc
178 Ii14 Phu Quôc, Đao var. Phu Quoc Island. island S Vietnam
Phu Quoc Island see Phu Quôc, Đao
178 J6 Phu Tho Vinh Phu, N Vietnam 21.22N 105.13E
Phu Vinh see Tra Vinh
201 T13 Piaanu Pass passage Chuuk Islands, C Micronesia
108 E8 Piacenza Fr. Paisance; anc. Placentia. Emilia-Romagna, N Italy 45.01N 9.42E
109 K14 Pianella Abruzzo, C Italy 42.23N 14.04E
109 M15 Pianosa, Isola island Archipelago Toscano, C Italy
176 Vv11 Piar Papua, E Indonesia 2.49S 132.46E
47 U14 Piarco var. Port of Spain. ✈ (Port-of-Spain) Trinidad, Trinidad and Tobago 10.36N 61.21W
112 M12 Piaseczno Mazowieckie, C Poland 52.04N 21.05E
118 I15 Piatra Teleorman, S Romania 43.49N 25.10E
118 L10 Piatra-Neamţ Hung. Karácsonkő. Neamţ, NE Romania 46.54N 26.23E
Piauhy see Piauí
61 N15 Piauí off. Estado do Piauí; prev. Piauhy. ◈ state E Brazil
108 I7 Piave ∼ NE Italy
109 K24 Piazza Armerina var. Chiazza. Sicilia, Italy, C Mediterranean Sea 37.22N 14.22E
83 G14 Pībor Amh. Pībor Wenz. ∼ Ethiopia/Sudan
83 G14 Pibor Post Jonglei, SE Sudan 6.49N 33.06E
Pībor Wenz see Pibor
Pibrans see Příbram
38 K11 Picacho Butte ▲ Arizona, SW USA 35.12N 112.44W
42 D4 Picachos, Cerro ▲ NW Mexico 29.15N 114.04W
105 O4 Picardie Eng. Picardy. ◈ region N France
Picardy see Picardie
24 L8 Picayune Mississippi, S USA 30.31N 89.40W
Piccolo San Bernardo, Colle di see Little Saint Bernard Pass
64 K5 Pichanal Salta, N Argentina 23.22S 64.11W
153 P12 Pichandar W Tajikistan 38.44N 68.51E
29 R8 Picher Oklahoma, C USA 36.59N 94.49W
64 G12 Pichilemu Libertador, C Chile 34.25S 72.00W
42 F9 Pichilingue Baja California Sur, W Mexico 24.19N 110.16W
58 B6 Pichincha ◈ province N Ecuador
58 C6 Pichincha ▲ N Ecuador 0.12S 78.39W
Pichit see Phichit
43 U15 Pichucalco Chiapas, SE Mexico 17.32N 93.07W
24 L5 Pickens Mississippi, S USA 32.52N 89.58W
23 O11 Pickens South Carolina, SE USA 34.52N 82.42W
12 G11 Pickerel ∼ Ontario, S Canada
12 H15 Pickering Ontario, S Canada 43.50N 79.03W
99 N16 Pickering N England, UK 54.14N 0.46W
33 S13 Pickerington Ohio, N USA 39.52N 82.45W
10 C10 Pickle Lake Ontario, C Canada 51.30N 90.10W
31 P12 Pickstown South Dakota, N USA 43.02N 98.31W
27 V6 Pickton Texas, SW USA 33.01N 95.19W
25 N1 Pickwick Lake ⊞ S USA
66 N2 Pico var. Ilha do Pico. island Azores, Portugal, NE Atlantic Ocean
65 J19 Pico de Salamanca Chubut, SE Argentina 45.26S 67.26W
1 P9 Pico Fracture Zone tectonic feature NW Atlantic Ocean
Pico, Ilha do see Pico
61 O14 Picos Piauí, E Brazil 7.04S 41.24W
65 I20 Pico Truncado Santa Cruz, SE Argentina 46.49S 68.01W
191 S9 Picton New South Wales, SE Australia 34.12S 150.36E
12 K15 Picton Ontario, SE Canada 43.59N 77.09W
193 K14 Picton Marlborough, South Island, NZ 41.18S 174.00E
65 H15 Picún Leufú, Arroyo ∼ SW Argentina
Pidálion see Gkréko, Akrotíri
161 K25 Pidurutalagala ▲ S Sri Lanka 7.03N 80.47E
118 K6 Pidvolochys'k Ternopil's'ka Oblast', W Ukraine 49.31N 26.09E
109 K16 Piedimonte Matese Campania, S Italy 41.20N 14.30E
29 X7 Piedmont Missouri, C USA 37.09N 90.42W
23 P11 Piedmont South Carolina, SE USA 34.42N 82.27W
19 Q12 Piedmont escarpment E USA
Piedmont see Piemonte
33 U13 Piedmont Lake ⊞ Ohio, N USA
106 M11 Piedrabuena Castilla-La Mancha, C Spain 39.01N 4.10W
Piedrafita, Puerto de see Pedrafita, Porto de
106 L8 Piedrahita Castilla-León, N Spain 40.27N 5.19W
43 N6 Piedras Negras var. Ciudad Porfirio Díaz. Coahuila de Zaragoza, NE Mexico 28.40N 100.31W
63 E21 Piedras, Punta headland E Argentina 35.27S 57.04W
59 I14 Piedras, Río de las ∼ E Peru
113 J16 Piekary Śląskie Śląskie, S Poland 50.23N 19.01E
95 M17 Pieksämäki Itä-Suomi, E Finland 62.18N 27.10E
111 V5 Pielach ∼ NE Austria
95 M16 Pielavesi Itä-Suomi, C Finland 63.13N 26.45E
95 M16 Pielavesi ◎ C Finland
95 N16 Pielinen var. Pielisjärvi. ◎ E Finland
Pielisjärvi see Pielinen
108 A8 Piemonte Eng. Piedmont. ◈ region NW Italy
113 L18 Pieniny ⛰ Poland/Slovakia
113 E14 Pieńsk Ger. Penzig. Dolnośląskie, SW Poland 51.14N 15.03E
31 Q13 Pierce Nebraska, C USA 42.12N 97.31W
9 R14 Pierceland Saskatchewan, C Canada
117 E14 Piéria ⛰ N Greece
31 N10 Pierre state capital South Dakota, N USA 44.22N 100.21W
104 K16 Pierrefitte-Nestalas Hautes-Pyrénées, S France 42.58N 0.04W
105 R14 Pierrelatte Drôme, E France 44.22N 4.40E
13 P11 Pierreville Québec, SE Canada 46.05N 72.48W
13 O7 Pierriche ∼ Québec, SE Canada
113 H20 Piešťany Ger. Pistyan, Hung. Pöstyén. Trnavský, W Slovakia 48.36N 17.48E
111 X5 Piesting ∼ E Austria
Pietarhovi see Petrodvorets
Pietari see Sankt-Peterburg
Pietarsaari see Jakobstad
85 K23 Pietermaritzburg var. Maritzburg. KwaZulu/Natal, E South Africa 29.34S 30.23E
Pietersburg see Polokwane
109 K24 Pietraperzia Sicilia, Italy, C Mediterranean Sea 37.25N 14.07E
109 N22 Pietra Spada, Passo della pass SW Italy 38.30N 16.20E
85 K22 Piet Retief Mpumalanga, E South Africa 27.00S 30.49E
118 I9 Pietrosul, Vârful prev. Virful Pietrosu. ▲ N Romania 47.36N 24.39E
118 J10 Pietrosul, Vârful prev. Virful Pietrosu. ▲ N Romania 47.06N 25.09E
Pietrosu, Virful see Pietrosul, Vârful
108 I6 Pieve di Cadore Veneto, NE Italy 46.27N 12.22E
12 C18 Pigeon Bay lake bay Ontario, S Canada
29 X8 Piggott Arkansas, C USA 36.22N 90.11W
85 L21 Piggs Peak NW Swaziland 25.58S 31.16E
Pigs, Bay of see Cochinos, Bahía de
63 A23 Pigüé Buenos Aires, E Argentina 37.37S 62.24W
43 O12 Piguícas ▲ C Mexico 21.08N 99.37W
200 Qq15 Piha Passage passage S Tonga
Pihkva Järv see Pskov, Lake
95 N18 Pihlajavesi ◎ SE Finland
95 J18 Pihlava Länsi-Suomi, W Finland 61.33N 21.36E
95 L16 Pihtipudas Länsi-Suomi, W Finland 63.20N 25.37E
42 L14 Pihuamo Jalisco, SW Mexico 19.16N 103.21W
201 U11 Piis Moen var. Pis. atoll Chuuk Islands, C Micronesia
43 U17 Pijijiapán Chiapas, SE Mexico 15.39N 93.13W
100 G12 Pijnacker Zuid-Holland, W Netherlands 52.01N 4.25E
44 H5 Pijol, Pico ▲ NW Honduras 15.07N 87.39W
Pikaar see Bikar Atoll
128 I13 Pikalevo Leningradskaya Oblast', NW Russian Federation 59.33N 34.04E
196 M15 Pikelot island Caroline Islands, C Micronesia
32 M5 Pike River ∼ Wisconsin, N USA
39 T5 Pikes Peak ▲ Colorado, C USA 38.51N 105.06W
23 P6 Pikeville Kentucky, S USA 37.28N 82.31W
22 L9 Pikeville Tennessee, S USA 35.36N 85.11W
Pikinni see Bikini Atoll
81 H18 Pikounda La Sangha, C Congo 0.30N 16.43E
112 G9 Piła Ger. Schneidemühl. Wielkopolskie, C Poland 53.09N 16.43E
64 N6 Pilagá, Riacho ∼ NE Argentina
63 D20 Pilar Buenos Aires, E Argentina 34.28S 58.55W
64 N7 Pilar var. Villa del Pilar. Ñeembucú, S Paraguay 26.55S 58.19W
64 N6 Pilcomayo, Río ∼ C South America
153 R12 Pildon Rus. Pil'don. C Tajikistan 39.10N 71.00E
Piles see Pylés
Pilgram see Pelhřimov
179 Q11 Pili Luzon, N Philippines 13.31N 123.15E
158 L10 Pīlībhīt Uttar Pradesh, N India 28.37N 79.48E
112 M13 Pilica ∼ C Poland
117 G16 Pílio ⛰ C Greece
113 J22 Pilisvörösvár Pest, N Hungary 47.37N 18.55E
67 G15 Pillar Bay bay Ascension Island, C Atlantic Ocean
191 P17 Pillar, Cape headland Tasmania, SE Australia 43.13S 147.58E
Pillau see Baltiysk
191 R5 Pilliga New South Wales, SE Australia 30.22S 148.53E
46 H8 Pilón Granma, E Cuba 19.54N 77.20W
Pilos see Pýlos
9 W17 Pilot Mound Manitoba, S Canada 49.12N 98.49W
23 S8 Pilot Mountain North Carolina, SE USA 36.23N 80.28W
41 O14 Pilot Point Alaska, USA 57.33N 95.34W
27 T5 Pilot Point Texas, SW USA 33.24N 96.57W
34 K11 Pilot Rock Oregon, NW USA 45.28N 118.49W
40 M11 Pilot Station Alaska, USA 61.56N 162.52W
Pilsen see Plzeň
113 K18 Pilsko ▲ N Slovakia 49.31N 19.21E
Pilten see Piltene
120 D8 Piltene Ger. Pilten. Ventspils, W Latvia 57.14N 21.41E
113 M16 Pilzno Podkarpackie, SE Poland 49.58N 21.18E
Pilzno see Plzeň
39 N14 Pima Arizona, SW USA 32.49N 109.50W
60 H13 Pimenta Pará, N Brazil 4.32S 56.17W
61 F16 Pimenta Bueno Rondônia, W Brazil 11.40S 61.13W
58 B11 Pimentel Lambayeque, W Peru 6.51S 79.52W
107 S6 Pina Aragón, NE Spain 41.28N 0.31W
121 I20 Pina Rus. Pina. ∼ SW Belarus
42 E2 Pinacate, Sierra del ▲ NW Mexico 31.49N 113.30W
65 H22 Pináculo, Cerro ▲ S Argentina 50.46S 72.07W
203 X11 Pinaki atoll Îles Tuamotu, E French Polynesia
39 N15 Pinaleno Mountains ⛰ Arizona, SW USA
179 Pp12 Pinamalayan Mindoro, N Philippines 13.00N 121.30E
174 Kk8 Pinang Borneo, C Indonesia 0.36N 109.10W
173 G3 Pinang var. Penang. ◈ state Peninsular Malaysia
Pinang see Pinang, Pulau, Peninsular Malaysia
Pinang see George Town
173 G3 Pinang, Pulau var. Penang, Pinang; prev. Prince of Wales Island. island Peninsular Malaysia
46 B5 Pinar del Río Pinar del Río, W Cuba 22.23N 83.42W
116 N11 Pınarhisar Kırklareli, NW Turkey 41.37N 27.30E
179 P10 Pinatubo, Mount Ѫ Luzon, N Philippines 15.07N 120.21E
9 Y16 Pinawa Manitoba, S Canada 50.09N 95.52W
9 Q17 Pincher Creek Alberta, SW Canada 49.31N 113.52W
32 L16 Pinckneyville Illinois, N USA 38.04N 89.22W
Pińcota see Pâncota
113 L15 Pińczów Świętokrzyskie, C Poland 50.30N 20.31E
155 U7 Pind Dādan Khān Punjab, E Pakistan 32.36N 73.07E
Píndhos/Píndhos Óros see Píndos
155 V8 Pindi Bhattiān Punjab, E Pakistan 31.54N 73.19E
155 U6 Pindi Gheb Punjab, E Pakistan 33.15N 72.16E
117 D15 Píndos var. Píndhos Óros, Eng. Pindus Mountains; prev. Píndhos. ⛰ C Greece
Pindus Mountains see Píndos
20 J16 Pine Barrens physical region New Jersey, NE USA
29 V12 Pine Bluff Arkansas, C USA 34.13N 92.01W
25 X11 Pine Castle Florida, SE USA 28.28N 81.22W
31 V7 Pine City Minnesota, N USA 45.49N 92.55W
189 P2 Pine Creek Northern Territory, N Australia 13.51S 131.51E
37 V4 Pine Creek ∼ Nevada, W USA
20 F13 Pine Creek ∼ Pennsylvania, NE USA
29 Q13 Pine Creek Lake ⊞ Oklahoma, C USA
35 T15 Pinedale Wyoming, C USA 42.52N 109.51W
9 X15 Pine Dock Manitoba, S Canada 51.34N 96.47W
9 Y16 Pine Falls Manitoba, S Canada 50.29N 96.12W
37 R10 Pine Flat Lake ⊞ California, W USA
129 N8 Pinega Arkhangel'skaya Oblast', NW Russian Federation 64.40N 43.24E
129 N8 Pinega ∼ NW Russian Federation
13 N12 Pine Hill Québec, SE Canada 45.44N 74.30W
9 T12 Pinehouse Lake ◎ Saskatchewan, C Canada
23 T10 Pinehurst North Carolina, SE USA 35.12N 79.28W
117 D19 Pineiós ∼ S Greece
117 E16 Pineiós var. Piniós; anc. Peneius. ∼ C Greece
31 W10 Pine Island Minnesota, N USA 44.12N 92.39W
25 V15 Pine Island island Florida, SE USA
204 K10 Pine Island Glacier glacier Antarctica
27 X9 Pineland Texas, SW USA 31.15N 93.58W
25 V13 Pinellas Park Florida, SE USA 27.50N 82.42W
8 M13 Pine Pass pass British Columbia, W Canada 55.21N 122.43W
15 I9 Pine Point Northwest Territories, W Canada 60.52N 114.30W
30 K12 Pine Ridge South Dakota, N USA 43.01N 102.33W
31 U6 Pine River Minnesota, N USA 46.43N 94.24W
33 Q8 Pine River ∼ Michigan, N USA
32 M4 Pine River ∼ Wisconsin, N USA
108 A8 Pinerolo Piemonte, NE Italy 44.56N 7.21E
117 I15 Pines, Akrotírio var. Akrotírio Pínnes. headland N Greece 40.06N 24.19E
27 W6 Pines, Lake O' the ⊞ Texas, SW USA
Pines, The Isle of the see Juventud, Isla de la
Pine Tree State see Maine
23 N7 Pineville Kentucky, S USA 36.45N 83.42W
24 H7 Pineville Louisiana, S USA 31.19N 92.25W
29 R8 Pineville Missouri, C USA 36.35N 94.22W
23 R10 Pineville North Carolina, SE USA 35.04N 80.53W
23 Q6 Pineville West Virginia, NE USA 37.34N 81.32W
35 V8 Piney Buttes physical region Montana, NW USA
166 H14 Pingbian var. Pingbian Miaozu Zizhixian, Yuping. Yunnan, SW China 22.51N 103.28E
Pingbian Miaozu Zizhixian see Pingbian
163 S9 Pingdingshan Henan, C China 33.52N 113.19E
167 R4 Pingdu Shandong, E China 36.48N 119.56E
201 W16 Pingelap Atoll atoll Caroline Islands, E Micronesia
166 K14 Pingguo var. Matou. Guangxi Zhuangzu Zizhiqu, S China 23.22N 107.34E
167 Q13 Pinghe var. Xiaoxi. Fujian, SE China 24.30N 117.19E
P'ing-hsiang see Pingxiang
167 N10 Pingjiang Hunan, S China 28.44N 113.33E
Pingkiang see Harbin
166 L8 Pingli Shaanxi, C China 32.24N 109.17E
165 W10 Pingliang var. Kongtong, P'ing-liang. Gansu, C China 35.31N 106.46E
165 W8 Pingluo Ningxia, N China 38.55N 106.31E
Pingma see Tiandong
178 H9 Ping, Mae Nam ∼ W Thailand
167 Q1 Pingquan Hebei, E China 41.01N 118.34E
31 P5 Pingree North Dakota, N USA 47.07N 98.54W
169 W9 Pingshan Jilin, NE China 44.36N 127.13E
Pingsiang see Pingxiang
167 S14 P'ingtung Jap. Heitō. S Taiwan 22.43N 120.26E
166 I8 Pingwu var. Long'an. Sichuan, C China 32.33N 104.32E
166 J15 Pingxiang Guangxi Zhuangzu Zizhiqu, S China 22.03N 106.43E
167 O11 Pingxiang var. P'ing-hsiang; prev. Pingsiang. Jiangxi, S China 27.42N 113.49E
167 S11 Pingyang var. Kunyang. Zhejiang, SE China 27.46N 120.37E
167 P5 Pingyi Shandong, E China 35.30N 117.37E
167 P5 Pingyin Shandong, E China 36.18N 116.24E
62 H13 Pinhalzinho Santa Catarina, S Brazil 26.53S 52.57W
62 I12 Pinhão Paraná, S Brazil 25.46S 51.32W
63 H17 Pinheiro Machado Rio Grande do Sul, S Brazil 31.34S 53.22W
106 I7 Pinhel Guarda, N Portugal 40.46N 7.03W
Piniós see Pineiós
195 R10 Pinipel Island island Green Islands, NE PNG
173 F8 Pini, Pulau island Kepulauan Batu, W Indonesia
111 Y7 Pinka ∼ SE Austria
111 X7 Pinkafeld Burgenland, SE Austria 47.18N 16.09E
Pinkiang see Harbin
8 M12 Pink Mountain British Columbia, W Canada 57.01N 122.36W
177 G3 Pinlebu Sagaing, N Burma 24.02N 95.21E
40 J12 Pinnacle Island island Alaska, USA
188 I12 Pinnacles, The tourist site Western Australia
190 K10 Pinnaroo South Australia 35.17S 140.54E
Pinne see Pniewy
102 I9 Pinneberg Schleswig-Holstein, N Germany 53.40N 9.48E
Pínnes, Akrotírio see Pines, Akrotírio
Pinos, Isla de see Juventud, Isla de la
37 R14 Pinos, Mount ▲ California, W USA 34.48N 119.09W
107 R12 Pinoso País Valenciano, E Spain 38.25N 1.01W
107 N14 Pinos-Puente Andalucía, S Spain 37.16N 3.46W
43 Q17 Pinotepa Nacional var. Santiago Pinotepa Nacional. Oaxaca, SE Mexico 16.19N 98.02W
116 F13 Pínovo ▲ N Greece 41.06N 22.19E
197 K7 Pins, Île des var. Kunyé. island E New Caledonia
121 I20 Pinsk Pol. Pińsk. Brestskaya Voblasts', SW Belarus 52.07N 26.07E
12 D18 Pins, Pointe aux headland Ontario, S Canada 42.14N 81.53W
59 B16 Pinta, Isla var. Abingdon. island Galapagos Islands, Ecuador, E Pacific Ocean
129 Q12 Pinyug Kirovskaya Oblast', NW Russian Federation 60.12N 47.45E
59 B17 Pinzón, Isla var. Duncan Island. island Galapagos Islands, Ecuador, E Pacific Ocean
37 Y8 Pioche Nevada, W USA 37.54N 114.27W
108 F13 Piombino Toscana, C Italy 42.54N 10.30E
(0) C9 Pioneer Fracture Zone tectonic feature NE Pacific Ocean
126 Ii2 Pioner, Ostrov island Severnaya Zemlya, N Russian Federation
120 A13 Pionerskiy Ger. Neukuhren. Kaliningradskaya Oblast', W Russian Federation 54.57N 20.16E
112 N13 Pionki Mazowieckie, C Poland 51.28N 21.27E
192 L9 Piopio Waikato, North Island, NZ 38.27S 175.00E
112 K13 Piotrków Trybunalski Ger. Petrikau, Rus. Petrokov. Lodzkie, C Poland 51.25N 19.42E
158 F12 Pīpār Road Rājasthān, N India 26.25N 73.28E
117 I16 Pipéri island Vóreies Sporádes, Greece, Aegean Sea
31 S10 Pipestone Minnesota, N USA 44.00N 96.19W
10 C9 Pipestone ∼ Ontario, C Canada
63 E21 Pipinas Buenos Aires, E Argentina 35.31S 57.19W
155 T7 Piplān prev. Liaqatabad. Punjab, E Pakistan 32.19N 71.21E
13 R5 Pipmuacan, Réservoir ⊞ Québec, SE Canada
Piqan see Shanshan
33 R13 Piqua Ohio, N USA 40.08N 84.14W
107 P5 Piqueras, Puerto de pass N Spain 42.04N 2.35W
62 H11 Piquiri, Rio ∼ S Brazil
62 L9 Piracicaba São Paulo, S Brazil 22.44S 47.33W
Piraeus/Piraiévs see Peiraías
62 K10 Piraju São Paulo, S Brazil 23.12S 49.24W
62 K9 Pirajuí São Paulo, S Brazil 21.58S 49.27W
65 G21 Pirámide, Cerro ▲ S Chile 49.06S 73.32W
Piramiva see Pyramíva
111 R13 Piran It. Pirano. SW Slovenia 45.31N 13.36E
64 N6 Piranè Formosa, N Argentina 25.42S 59.06W
61 J18 Piranhas Goiás, S Brazil 16.24S 51.51W
Pirano see Piran
148 I4 Pīrānshahr Āzarbāyjān-e Gharbī, NW Iran 36.46N 45.10E
61 M19 Pirapora Minas Gerais, NE Brazil 17.19S 44.54W
62 I9 Pirapòzinho São Paulo, S Brazil 22.17S 51.31W
63 G19 Piraraja Lavalleja, S Uruguay 33.43S 54.45W
62 L9 Pirassununga São Paulo, S Brazil 21.58S 47.23W
47 V6 Pirata, Monte ▲ E Puerto Rico 18.06N 65.33W
62 I13 Piratuba Santa Catarina, S Brazil 27.26S 51.47W
116 I9 Pirdop prev. Srednogorie. Sofiya, W Bulgaria 42.44N 24.09E
203 P7 Pirea Tahiti, W French Polynesia
61 K18 Pirenópolis Goiás, S Brazil 15.48S 49.00W
159 S13 Pirganj Rajshahi, NW Bangladesh 25.51N 88.25E
Pirgi see Pyrgí
Pírgos see Pýrgos
63 F20 Piriápolis Maldonado, S Uruguay 34.51S 55.15W
116 G11 Pirin ⛰ SW Bulgaria
Pirineos see Pyrenees
60 N13 Piripiri Piauí, E Brazil 4.15S 41.46W
120 H4 Pirita var. Pirita Jõgi. ∼ NW Estonia
Pirita Jõgi see Pirita
56 J6 Píritu Portuguesa, N Venezuela 9.21N 69.16W
95 L18 Pirkkala Länsi-Suomi, W Finland 61.27N 23.47E
103 F20 Pirmasens Rheinland-Pfalz, SW Germany 49.12N 7.36E
103 P16 Pirna Sachsen, E Germany 50.57N 13.56E
Piroe see Piru
115 Q15 Pirot Serbia, SE Serbia 43.12N 22.34E
158 H6 Pīr Panjāl Range ⛰ NE India
45 W16 Pirre, Cerro ▲ SE Panama 7.54N 77.42W
143 Y11 Pirsaat Rus. Pirsagat. ∼ E Azerbaijan
Pirsagat see Pirsaat
149 V11 Pīr Shūrān, Selseleh-ye ⛰ SE Iran
94 M12 Pirttikoski Lappi, N Finland 66.20N 27.08E
Pirttikylä see Pörtom
175 T11 Piru prev. Piroe. Pulau Seram, E Indonesia 3.01S 128.10E
Piryatin see Pyryatyn
Pis see Piis Moen
108 F11 Pisa var. Pisae. Toscana, C Italy 43.43N 10.22E
Pisae see Pisa
176 Uu10 Pisang, Kepulauan island group E Indonesia
176 Xx11 Pisapa Papua, E Indonesia 3.25S 137.04E
201 V12 Pisar atoll Chuuk Islands, C Micronesia
Pisaurum see Pesaro
12 M10 Piscatosine, Lac ◎ Québec, SE Canada
111 W7 Pischeldorf Steiermark, SE Austria 47.11N 15.48E
Pischk see Simeria
109 L19 Pisciotta Campania, S Italy 40.07N 15.13E
59 E16 Pisco Ica, SW Peru 13.46S 76.12W
118 G9 Pişcolt Hung. Piskolt. Satu Mare, NW Romania 47.34N 22.18E
59 E16 Pisco, Río ∼ E Peru
113 C18 Písek Budějovický Kraj, S Czech Republic 49.18N 14.07E
33 R14 Pisgah Ohio, N USA 39.19N 84.22W
Pisha see Ningnan
164 F9 Pishan var. Guma. Xinjiang Uygur Zizhiqu, NW China 37.36N 78.45E
119 N8 Pishchanka Vinnyts'ka Oblast', C Ukraine 48.12N 28.52E
115 K21 Pishë Fier, SW Albania 40.40N 19.22E
149 X14 Pīshīn Sīstān va Balūchestān, SE Iran 26.05N 61.46E
155 O9 Pishin North-West Frontier Province, NW Pakistan 30.39N 66.52E
155 N11 Pishin Lora var. Psein Lora, Pash. Pseyn Bowr. ∼ SW Pakistan
Pishma see Pizhma
Pishpek see Bishkek
175 Q13 Pising Pulau Kabaena, C Indonesia 5.07S 121.50E
Pisino see Pazin
Piski see Simeria
Piskolt see Pişcolt
153 Q9 Piskom Rus. Pskem. ∼ E Uzbekistan
Piskom Tizmasi see Pskemskiy Khrebet
37 P13 Pismo Beach California, W USA 35.08N 120.38W
79 P12 Pissila C Burkina 13.07N 0.51W
64 H8 Pissis, Monte ▲ N Argentina 27.45S 68.43W
43 X12 Piste Yucatán, E Mexico 20.40N 88.34W
109 O18 Pisticci Basilicata, S Italy 40.22N 16.33E
108 F11 Pistoia anc. Pistoria, Pistoriæ. Toscana, C Italy 43.57N 10.52E
34 E15 Pistol River Oregon, NW USA 42.13N 124.23W
Pistoria/Pistoriæ see Pistoia
13 U5 Pistuacanis ∼ Québec, SE Canada
Pistyan see Piešťany
106 M5 Pisuerga ∼ N Spain
112 N8 Pisz Ger. Johannisburg. Warmińsko-Mazurskie, NE Poland 53.37N 21.49E
78 I13 Pita NW Guinea 11.04N 12.15W
56 D12 Pitalito Huila, S Colombia 1.51N 76.01W
62 I11 Pitanga Paraná, S Brazil 24.45S 51.43W
190 M9 Pitarpunga Lake salt lake New South Wales, SE Australia
199 M11 Pitcairn Island island S Pitcairn Islands
199 M11 Pitcairn Islands ◇ UK dependent territory C Pacific Ocean
95 J14 Piteå Norrbotten, N Sweden 65.19N 21.30E
94 I13 Piteälven ∼ N Sweden
118 I13 Piteşti Argeş, S Romania 44.53N 24.49E
Pithagorio see Pythagóreio
188 I12 Pithara Western Australia 30.31S 116.38E
105 N6 Pithiviers Loiret, C France 48.10N 2.15E
158 L9 Pithorāgarh Uttaranchal, N India 29.34N 80.12E
196 B16 Piti W Guam 13.28N 144.42E
108 G13 Pitigliano Toscana, C Italy 42.38N 11.40E
42 F3 Pitiquito Sonora, NW Mexico 30.39N 112.00W
Pitkäranta see Pitkyaranta
40 M11 Pitkas Point Alaska, USA 62.01N 163.17W
128 H11 Pitkyaranta Fin. Pitkäranta. Respublika Kareliya, NW Russian Federation 61.34N 31.27E
98 J10 Pitlochry C Scotland, UK 56.46N 3.48W
20 I16 Pitman New Jersey, NE USA 39.43N 75.06W
152 I9 Pitnak Var. Drujba, Rus. Druzhba. Xorazm Viloyati, W Uzbekistan 41.14N 61.13E
114 G8 Pitomača Virovitica-Podravina, NE Croatia 45.57N 17.14E
37 O2 Pit River ∼ California, W USA
65 G15 Pitrufquén Araucanía, S Chile 38.58S 72.40W
Pitsanulok see Phitsanulok
Pitschen see Byczyna
Pitsunda see Bichvint'a
111 X6 Pitten ∼ E Austria
8 J14 Pitt Island island British Columbia, W Canada
Pitt Island see Makin
24 M3 Pittsboro Mississippi, S USA 33.55N 89.20W
23 T9 Pittsboro North Carolina, SE USA 35.46N 79.21W
29 R7 Pittsburg Kansas, C USA 37.24N 94.42W
27 W6 Pittsburg Texas, SW USA 33.00N 94.58W
20 B14 Pittsburgh Pennsylvania, NE USA 40.26N 80.00W
32 J14 Pittsfield Illinois, N USA 39.36N 90.48W
21 R6 Pittsfield Maine, NE USA 44.46N 69.22W
20 L11 Pittsfield Massachusetts, NE USA 42.27N 73.15W
191 U3 Pittsworth Queensland, E Australia 27.43S 151.36E
64 I8 Pituil La Rioja, NW Argentina 28.33S 67.24W
58 A10 Piura Piura, NW Peru 5.11S 80.41W
58 A9 Piura off. Departamento de Piura. ◈ department NW Peru
37 S13 Piute Peak ▲ California, W USA 35.27N 118.24W
115 J15 Piva ∼ N-Montenegro
119 V5 Pivdenne Kharkivs'ka Oblast', E Ukraine 49.52N 36.04E
119 P8 Pivdennyy Buh Rus. Yuzhnyy Bug. ∼ S Ukraine
56 F5 Pivijay Magdalena, N Colombia 10.28N 74.37W
111 T13 Pivka prev. Šent Peter, Ger. Sankt Peter, It. San Pietro del Carso. SW Slovenia 45.41N 14.12E
119 U13 Pivnichno-Kryms'kyy Kanal canal S Ukraine
115 J15 Pivsko Jezero ◎ N-Montenegro
113 M18 Piwniczna Małopolskie, S Poland 49.26N 20.43E
37 R12 Pixley California, W USA 35.58N 119.18W
129 Q15 Pizhma var. Pishma. ∼ NW Russian Federation
11 U13 Placentia Newfoundland and Labrador, SE Canada 47.12N 53.58W
Placentia see Piacenza
11 U13 Placentia Bay inlet Newfoundland and Labrador, SE Canada
179 Qq12 Placer Masbate, N Philippines 11.54N 123.54E
37 P7 Placerville California, W USA 38.42N 120.48W
46 F5 Placetas Villa Clara, C Cuba 22.18N 79.40W
115 Q18 Plačkovica ⛰ E FYR Macedonia
38 L2 Plain City Utah, W USA 41.18N 112.05W
24 G4 Plain Dealing Louisiana, S USA 32.54N 93.42W
33 O14 Plainfield Indiana, N USA 39.42N 86.18W
20 K14 Plainfield New Jersey, NE USA 40.37N 74.25W
35 O8 Plains Montana, NW USA 47.27N 114.52W
26 L6 Plains Texas, SW USA 33.11N 102.49W
31 X10 Plainview Minnesota, N USA 44.10N 92.10W
31 Q13 Plainview Nebraska, C USA 42.21N 97.47W
27 N4 Plainview Texas, SW USA 34.12N 101.43W
28 K4 Plainville Kansas, C USA 39.13N 99.18W
117 I22 Pláka prev. Mílos. Mílos, Kykládes, Greece, Aegean Sea 36.45N 24.26E
117 J15 Pláka, Akrotírio headland Límnos, E Greece 40.02N 25.25E
115 N19 Plakenska Planina ⛰ SW FYR Macedonia
46 K5 Plana Cays islets SE Bahamas
107 S12 Plana, Isla var. Nueva Tabarca. island E Spain
61 L18 Planaltina Goiás, S Brazil 15.34S 47.27W
85 O14 Planalto Moçambicano plateau N Mozambique
114 N10 Plandište Serbia, NE Serbia 45.13N 21.07E
102 N13 Plane ∼ NE Germany
56 E6 Planeta Rica Córdoba, NW Colombia 8.24N 75.39W
31 P11 Plankinton South Dakota, N USA 43.43N 98.28W
32 M11 Plano Illinois, N USA 41.39N 88.32W
27 U6 Plano Texas, SW USA 33.01N 96.42W
25 W12 Plant City Florida, SE USA 28.01N 82.06W
24 J9 Plaquemine Louisiana, S USA 30.17N 91.13W
106 K9 Plasencia Extremadura, W Spain 40.01N 6.04W
112 P7 Płaska Podlaskie, NE Poland 53.55N 23.18E
114 C10 Plaški Karlovac, C Croatia 45.04N 15.21E
115 N19 Plasnica SW FYR Macedonia 41.28N 21.07E
125 E12 Plast Chelyabinskaya Oblast', C Russian Federation 54.24N 60.51E
11 N14 Plaster Rock New Brunswick, SE Canada 46.55N 67.24W
109 J24 Platani anc. Halycus. ∼ Sicilia, Italy, C Mediterranean Sea
117 G17 Plataniá Thessalía, C Greece 39.09N 23.15E
117 G24 Plátanos Kríti, Greece, E Mediterranean Sea 35.27N 23.34E
67 H18 Plata, Río de la var. River Plate. estuary Argentina/Uruguay
79 V15 Plateau ◈ state C Nigeria
81 G19 Plateaux var. Région des Plateaux. ◈ province C Congo
94 P1 Platen, Kapp headland NE Svalbard 80.30N 22.46E
Plate, River see Plata, Río de la
101 G22 Plate Taille, Lac de la var. L'Eau d'Heure. ◎ SE Belgium
Plathe see Płoty
41 N13 Platinum Alaska, USA 59.00N 161.49W
56 F5 Plato Magdalena, N Colombia 9.47N 74.46W
31 O11 Platte South Dakota, N USA 43.20N 98.51W
29 R3 Platte City Missouri, C USA 39.22N 94.46W
Plattensee see Balaton
29 R3 Platte River ∼ Iowa/Missouri, USA
31 Q15 Platte River ∼ Nebraska, C USA
39 T3 Platteville Colorado, C USA 40.13N 104.49W
32 K9 Platteville Wisconsin, N USA 42.44N 90.27W
103 N21 Plattling Bayern, SE Germany 48.45N 12.52E
29 R3 Plattsburg Missouri, C USA 39.34N 94.27W
20 L6 Plattsburgh New York, NE USA 44.42N 73.28W
31 S15 Plattsmouth Nebraska, C USA 41.00N 95.52W
103 M17 Plauen var. Plauen im Vogtland. Sachsen, E Germany 50.30N 12.08E
Plauen im Vogtland see Plauen
102 M10 Plauer See ◎ NE Germany
115 L16 Plav SE-Montenegro 42.36N 19.57E
120 I10 Pļaviņas Ger. Stockmannshof. Aizkraukle, S Latvia 56.37N 25.40E
130 K5 Plavsk Tul'skaya Oblast', W Russian Federation 53.42N 37.21E
43 Z12 Playa del Carmen Quintana Roo, E Mexico 20.37N 87.04W
42 J12 Playa Los Corchos Nayarit, SW Mexico 22.31N 105.28W
39 P16 Playas Lake ◎ New Mexico, SW USA
43 S15 Playa Vicenté Veracruz-Llave, SE Mexico 17.42N 95.01W
178 K11 Plây Cu var. Pleiku. Gia Lai, C Vietnam 13.57N 108.01E
30 L3 Plaza North Dakota, N USA 48.00N 102.00W
65 I15 Plaza Huincul Neuquén, C Argentina 38.54S 69.10W
38 L3 Pleasant Grove Utah, W USA 40.21N 111.44W
31 V14 Pleasant Hill Iowa, C USA 41.34N 93.31W
29 R4 Pleasant Hill Missouri, C USA 38.47N 94.16W
Pleasant Island see Nauru
38 K13 Pleasant, Lake ⊞ Arizona, SW USA
21 P8 Pleasant Mountain ▲ Maine, NE USA 44.01N 70.47W
29 R5 Pleasanton Kansas, C USA 38.09N 94.43W
27 R12 Pleasanton Texas, SW USA 28.58N 98.28W
193 G20 Pleasant Point Canterbury, South Island, NZ 44.16S 171.09E
21 R5 Pleasant River ∼ Maine, NE USA
20 J17 Pleasantville New Jersey, NE USA 39.22N 74.31W
105 N12 Pléaux Cantal, C France 45.08N 2.10E
113 B19 Plechý Ger. Plöckenstein. ▲ Austria/Czech Republic 48.45N 13.50E
Pleebo see Plibo
Pleihari see Pelaihari
Pleiku see Plây Cu
103 M16 Pleisse ∼ E Germany
Plencia see Plentzia
192 O7 Plenty, Bay of bay North Island, NZ
35 Y6 Plentywood Montana, NW USA 48.46N 104.33W
107 O2 Plentzia var. Plencia. País Vasco, N Spain 43.25N 2.56W

◆ Country
● Country Capital
◇ Dependent Territory
○ Dependent Territory Capital
◈ Administrative Region
✈ International Airport
▲ Mountain
⛰ Mountain Range
Ѫ Volcano
∼ River
◎ Lake
⊞ Reservoir

104 H5 **Plérin** Côtes d'Armor, NW France 48.33N 2.46W
128 M10 **Plesetsk** Arkhangel'skaya Oblast', NW Russian Federation 62.40N 40.14E
Pleshchenitsy see Plyeshchanitsy
Pleskau see Pskov
Pleskauer See see Pskov, Lake
Pleskava see Pskov
114 E8 **Pleso International** ✈ (Zagreb) Zagreb, NW Croatia 45.45N 16.00E
Pless see Pszczyna
13 Q11 **Plessisville** Québec, SE Canada 46.14N 71.45W
112 H12 **Pleszew** Wielkopolskie, C Poland 51.54N 17.46E
10 L10 **Plétipi, Lac** ◎ Québec, SE Canada
103 F15 **Plettenberg** Nordrhein-Westfalen, W Germany 51.13N 7.52E
116 I8 **Pleven** prev. Plevna. Pleven, N Bulgaria 43.25N 24.36E
116 I8 **Pleven** ◈ province N Bulgaria
Plevlja/Plevlje see Pljevlja
Plevna see Pleven
Plezzo see Bovec
Pliberk see Bleiburg
78 L17 **Plibo** var. Pleebo. SE Liberia 4.37N 7.40W
124 Oo13 **Pliny Trench** undersea feature C Mediterranean Sea
120 K13 **Plisa** Rus. Plissa. Vitsyebskaya Voblasts', N Belarus 55.12N 27.58E
Plissa see Plisa
114 D11 **Plitvica Selo** Lika-Senj, W Croatia 44.53N 15.36E
114 D11 **Plješevica** ▲▲ C Croatia
115 K14 **Pljevlja** prev. Plevlja, Plevlje, N-Montenegro 43.21N 19.21E
Ploça see Ploçë
Plocce see Ploče
115 G15 **Ploče** It. Plocce; prev. Kardeljevo. Dubrovnik-Neretva, SE Croatia 43.02N 17.25E
115 K22 **Ploçë** var. Ploça. Vlorë, SW Albania 40.24N 19.41E
112 K11 **Płock** Ger. Plozk. Mazowieckie, C Poland 52.31N 19.40E
111 Q10 **Plöcken Pass** Ger. Plöckenpass, It. Passo di Monte Croce Carnico. pass SW Austria 46.36N 12.55E
Plöckenstein see Plechý
101 B19 **Ploegsteert** Hainaut, W Belgium 50.45N 2.52E
104 H6 **Ploërmel** Morbihan, NW France 47.57N 2.24W
Ploești see Ploiești
118 K13 **Ploiești** prev. Ploești. Prahova, SE Romania 44.56N 26.03E
117 L17 **Plomári** prev. Plomárion. Lésvos, E Greece 38.58N 26.24E
Plomárion see Plomári
105 O12 **Plomb du Cantal** ▲ C France 45.03N 2.48E
191 V6 **Plomer, Point** headland New South Wales, SE Australia 31.19S 153.00E
102 J8 **Plön** Schleswig-Holstein, N Germany 54.10N 10.25E
112 L11 **Płońsk** Mazowieckie, C Poland 52.37N 20.22E
121 J20 **Plotnitsa** Rus. Plotnitsa. Brestskaya Voblasts', SW Belarus 52.03N 26.39E
112 E8 **Płoty** Ger. Plathe. Zachodnio-pomorskie, NW Poland 53.48N 15.16E
104 G7 **Plouay** Morbihan, NW France 47.54N 3.14W
113 D15 **Ploučnice** Ger. Polzen. ≈ NE Czech Republic
116 I10 **Plovdiv** prev. Eumolpias, anc. Evmolpia, Philippopolis, Lat. Trimontium. Plovdiv, C Bulgaria 42.08N 24.47
116 J11 **Plovdiv** ◈ province C Bulgaria
32 L6 **Plover** Wisconsin, N USA 44.30N 89.33W
Plozk see Płock
29 U11 **Plumerville** Arkansas, C USA 35.09N 92.38W
21 P10 **Plum Island** island Massachusetts, NE USA
34 M9 **Plummer** Idaho, NW USA 47.19N 116.54W
85 J18 **Plumtree** Matabeleland South, SW Zimbabwe 20.27S 27.49E
120 D11 **Plungė** Telšiai, W Lithuania 55.55N 21.53E
115 J15 **Plužine** NW-Montenegro 43.08N 18.49E
121 K14 **Plyeshchanitsy** Rus. Pleshchenitsy. Minskaya Voblasts', N Belarus 54.25N 27.49E
47 V10 **Plymouth** ○ (Montserrat) SW Montserrat 16.39N 62.11W
99 I24 **Plymouth** SW England, UK 50.22N 4.10W
33 O11 **Plymouth** Indiana, N USA 41.19N 86.19W
21 P12 **Plymouth** Massachusetts, NE USA 41.57N 70.40W
21 N8 **Plymouth** New Hampshire, NE USA 43.43N 71.39W
23 X9 **Plymouth** North Carolina, SE USA 35.52N 76.45W
32 M8 **Plymouth** Wisconsin, N USA 43.48N 87.58W
99 J20 **Plynlimon** ▲ C Wales, UK 52.27N 3.48W
128 G14 **Plyussa** Pskovskaya Oblast', W Russian Federation 58.27N 29.21E
113 B17 **Plzeň** Ger. Pilsen, Pol. Pilzno. Plzeňský Kraj, W Czech Republic 49.44N 13.22E
113 B17 **Plzeňský Kraj** ◈ region W Czech Republic
112 F11 **Pniewy** Ger. Pinne. Wielkolpolskie, C Poland 52.31N 16.14E
108 D8 **Po** ≈ N Italy
79 P13 **Pô** S Burkina 11.10N 1.10W
44 M13 **Poás, Volcán** 🌋 NW Costa Rica 10.12N 84.12W
79 S16 **Pobè** S Benin 7.00N 2.41E
127 N8 **Pobeda, Gora** ▲ NE Russian Federation 65.28N 145.44E
Pobeda Peak see Pobedy, Pik/Tomür Feng
153 Z7 **Pobedy, Pik** Chin. Tomür Feng. ▲ China/Kazakhstan 42.02N 80.02E see also Tomür Feng
112 H11 **Pobiedziska** Ger. Pudewitz. Wielkolpolskie, C Poland 52.30N 17.19E
Po, Bocche del see Po, Foci del
29 W9 **Pocahontas** Arkansas, C USA 36.15N 90.58W
31 U12 **Pocahontas** Iowa, C USA 42.44N 94.40W
35 Q15 **Pocatello** Idaho, NW USA 42.52N 112.27W
178 J13 **Pochentong** ✈ (Phnum Penh) Phnum Penh, S Cambodia 11.24N 104.52E
130 I6 **Pochep** Bryanskaya Oblast', W Russian Federation 52.56N 33.20E
130 H4 **Pochinok** Smolenskaya Oblast', W Russian Federation 54.20N 32.29E
43 R17 **Pochutla** var. San Pedro Pochutla. Oaxaca, SE Mexico 15.44N 96.27W
64 I6 **Pocitos, Salar** var. Salar Quiróm. salt lake NW Argentina
103 O22 **Pocking** Bayern, SE Germany 48.22N 13.17E
195 R17 **Pocklington Reef** reef SE PNG
199 Hh9 **Pocklington Trough** undersea feature W Pacific Ocean
61 P15 **Poço da Cruz, Açude** ⊡ E Brazil
29 R11 **Pocola** Oklahoma, C USA 35.13N 94.28W
23 Y5 **Pocomoke City** Maryland, NE USA 38.04N 75.34W
61 L21 **Poços de Caldas** Minas Gerais, NE Brazil 21.48S 46.33W
128 H14 **Podberez'ye** Novgorodskaya Oblast', NW Russian Federation 58.42N 31.22E
Podbrodzie see Pabradė
129 U8 **Podcher'ye** Respublika Komi, NW Russian Federation 63.55N 57.34E
113 E16 **Poděbrady** Ger. Podiebrad. Středočeský Kraj, C Czech Republic 50.09N 15.06E
176 Yy10 **Podena, Kepulauan** island group E Indonesia
130 L9 **Podgorenskiy** Voronezhskaya Oblast', W Russian Federation 50.22N 39.43E
115 J17 **Podgorica** ● prev. Titograd, S-Montenegro 42.25N 19.16E
115 K17 **Podgorica** ✈ S-Montenegro 42.22N 19.16E
111 T13 **Podgrad** SW Slovenia 45.31N 14.09E
Podiebrad see Poděbrady
118 M5 **Podil's'ka Vysochina** plateau W Ukraine
Podium Anicensis see le Puy
126 Ii11 **Podkamennaya Tunguska** Eng. Stony Tunguska. ≈ C Russian Federation
113 N17 **Podkarpackie** ◈ province SE Poland
Pod Klošter see Arnoldstein
112 O9 **Podlaskie** ◈ province NE Poland
131 Q8 **Podlesnoye** Saratovskaya Oblast', W Russian Federation 51.51N 47.03E
130 K4 **Podol'sk** Moskovskaya Oblast', W Russian Federation 55.24N 37.30E
78 H10 **Podor** N Senegal 16.40N 14.57W
129 P12 **Podosinovets** Kirovskaya Oblast', NW Russian Federation 60.15N 47.06E
128 I12 **Podporozh'ye** Leningradskaya Oblast', NW Russian Federation 60.52N 34.00E
Podravska Slatina see Slatina, Croatia
114 J13 **Podromanlja** Republika Srpska, SE Bosnia & Herzegovina 43.55N 18.46E
Podsvil'ye see Padsvillye
118 L9 **Podu Iloaiei** prev. Podul Iloaiei. Iași, NE Romania 47.13N 27.16E
115 N15 **Podujevo** Serbia, S Serbia 42.56N 21.13E
Podul Iloaiei see Podu Iloaiei
Podunajská Rovina see Little Alföld
128 M12 **Podyuga** Arkhangel'skaya Oblast', NW Russian Federation 61.04N 40.46E
58 A9 **Poechos, Embalse** ◎ NW Peru
57 W10 **Poeketi** Sipaliwini, E Surinam
102 L8 **Poel** island N Germany
85 M20 **Poelela, Lagoa** ◎ S Mozambique
Poerwodadi see Purwodadi
Poetovio see Ptuj
85 E23 **Pofadder** Northern Cape, W South Africa 29.03S 19.25E
108 I9 **Po, Foci del** var. Bocche del Po. ≈ NE Italy
118 E12 **Pogăniș** ≈ W Romania
Pogegen see Pagėgiai
108 G12 **Poggibonsi** Toscana, C Italy 43.28N 11.09E
109 I14 **Poggio Mirteto** Lazio, C Italy 42.17N 12.42E
111 V4 **Pöggstall** Niederösterreich, N Austria 48.19N 15.10E
118 L13 **Pogoanele** Buzău, SE Romania 44.55N 27.00E
Pogónion see Delvináki
115 M21 **Pogradec** var. Pogradeci. Korçë, SE Albania 40.54N 20.40E
Pogradeci see Pogradec
127 N18 **Pogranichnyy** Primorskiy Kray, SE Russian Federation 44.18N 131.33E
40 M16 **Pogromni Volcano** ▲ Unimak Island, Alaska, USA 54.34N 164.41W
169 Z15 **P'ohang** Jap. Hokō. E South Korea 36.01N 129.20E
13 T9 **Pohénégamook, Lac** ◎ Québec, SE Canada
95 L20 **Pohja** Swe. Pojo. Etelä-Suomi, SW Finland 60.07N 23.30E
Pohjanlahti see Bothnia, Gulf of
201 U16 **Pohnpei** ◈ state E Micronesia
201 O12 **Pohnpei** ✈ Pohnpei, E Micronesia
201 O12 **Pohnpei** prev. Ponape Ascension Island. island E Micronesia
113 F19 **Pohořelice** Ger. Pohrlitz. Jihomoravský Kraj, SE Czech Republic 48.58N 16.30E
111 V10 **Pohorje** Ger. Bacher. ▲▲ N Slovenia
119 N6 **Pohrebyshche** Vinnyts'ka Oblast', C Ukraine 49.31N 29.16E
Pohrlitz see Pohořelice
175 Qq9 **Poh, Teluk** bay Sulawesi, C Indonesia
167 P9 **Po Hu** ⊡ E China
118 G15 **Poiana Mare** Dolj, S Romania 43.55N 23.01E
Poictiers see Poitiers
131 N6 **Poim** Penzenskaya Oblast', W Russian Federation 53.03N 43.11E
197 I6 **Poindimié** Province Nord, C New Caledonia 20.55S 165.18E
165 N15 **Poindo** Xizang Zizhiqu, W China 29.58N 91.20E
205 Y13 **Poinsett, Cape** headland Antarctica 65.35S 113.00E
31 R9 **Poinsett, Lake** ◎ South Dakota, N USA
24 I10 **Point Au Fer Island** island Louisiana, S USA
41 X14 **Point Baker** Prince of Wales Island, Alaska, USA 56.19N 133.31W
27 U13 **Point Comfort** Texas, SW USA 28.40N 96.33W
Point de Galle see Galle
46 K10 **Pointe à Gravois** headland SW Haiti 18.00N 73.53W
24 L10 **Pointe a la Hache** Louisiana, S USA 29.34N 89.48W
47 Y6 **Pointe-à-Pitre** Grande Terre, C Guadeloupe 16.15N 61.31W
13 U7 **Pointe-au-Père** Québec, SE Canada 48.31N 68.27W
13 V5 **Pointe-aux-Anglais** Québec, SE Canada 49.40N 67.09W
47 T10 **Pointe du Cap** headland N Saint Lucia 14.06N 60.56W
81 E21 **Pointe-Noire** Le Kouilou, S Congo 4.46S 11.52E
47 X6 **Pointe Noire** Basse Terre, W Guadeloupe 16.13N 61.47W
81 E21 **Pointe-Noire** ✈ Le Kouilou, S Congo 4.45S 11.55E
47 U15 **Point Fortin** Trinidad, Trinidad and Tobago 10.09N 61.41W
40 M6 **Point Hope** Alaska, USA 68.21N 166.48W
41 N5 **Point Lay** Alaska, USA 69.42N 162.57W
20 B16 **Point Marion** Pennsylvania, NE USA 39.44N 79.53W
20 K16 **Point Pleasant** New Jersey, NE USA 40.04N 74.00W
23 P4 **Point Pleasant** West Virginia, NE USA 38.50N 82.08W
47 R14 **Point Salines** ✈ (St.George's) SW Grenada 12.00N 61.47W
104 L9 **Poitiers** prev. Poictiers, anc. Limonum. Vienne, W France 46.34N 0.19E
104 K9 **Poitou** cultural region W France
104 K10 **Poitou-Charentes** ◈ region W France
105 N3 **Poix-de-Picardie** Somme, N France 49.47N 1.58E
Pojo see Pohja
39 S10 **Pojoaque** New Mexico, SW USA 35.52N 106.01W
158 E11 **Pokaran** Rājasthān, NW India 26.55N 71.55E
191 R4 **Pokataroo** New South Wales, SE Australia 29.37S 148.43E
121 P18 **Pokats'** Rus. Pokot'. ≈ SE Belarus
31 V5 **Pokegama Lake** ◎ Minnesota, N USA
192 L6 **Pokeno** Waikato, North Island, NZ 37.15S 175.01E
159 O11 **Pokharā** Western, C Nepal 28.13N 84.00E
131 T6 **Pokhvistnevo** Samarskaya Oblast', W Russian Federation 53.38N 52.07E
57 W10 **Pokigron** Sipaliwini, C Surinam 4.25N 55.24W
94 L10 **Pokka** Lapp. Bohkká. Lappi, N Finland 68.10N 25.45E
81 N16 **Poko** Orientale, NE Dem. Rep. Congo 3.07N 26.51E
Pokot' see Pokats'
Po-ko-to Shan see Bogda Shan
153 S7 **Pokrovka** Talasskaya Oblast', NW Kyrgyzstan 42.45N 71.33E
Pokrovka see Kyzyl-Suu
126 M11 **Pokrovsk** Respublika Sakha (Yakutiya), NE Russian Federation 61.40N 129.25E
119 V8 **Pokrovs'ke** Rus. Pokrovskoye. Dnipropetrovs'ka Oblast', E Ukraine 47.58N 36.15E
Pokrovskoye see Pokrovs'ke
Pola see Pula
39 N10 **Polacca** Arizona, SW USA 35.49N 110.21W
106 L2 **Pola de Laviana** Asturias, N Spain 43.15N 5.33W
106 K2 **Pola de Lena** Asturias, N Spain 43.10N 5.49W
106 L2 **Pola de Siero** Asturias, N Spain 43.24N 5.39W
203 Y3 **Poland** Kiritimati, E Kiribati 1.52N 95.33W
112 H12 **Poland** off. Republic of Poland, var. Polish Republic, Pol. Polska, Rzeczpospolita Polska; prev. Pol. Polska Rzeczpospolita Ludowa, Polish People's Republic. ◆ republic C Europe
Polangen see Palanga
112 G7 **Polanów** Ger. Pollnow. Zachodnio-pomorskie, NW Poland 54.07N 16.38E
142 H13 **Polatlı** Ankara, C Turkey 39.34N 32.07E
120 L12 **Polatsk** Rus. Polotsk. Vitsyebskaya Voblasts', N Belarus 55.28N 28.46E
112 F8 **Połczyn-Zdrój** Ger. Bad Polzin. Zachodnio-pomorskie, NW Poland 53.43N 16.02E
155 R5 **Pol-e 'Alam** Lowgar, E Afghanistan 33.58N 69.02E
Polekhatum see Pulhatyn
155 Q3 **Pol-e Khomrī** var. Pul-i-Khumri. Baghlān, NE Afghanistan 35.55N 68.45E
207 S10 **Pole Plain** undersea feature Arctic Ocean
149 P5 **Pol-e Safīd** var. Pol-e-Sefid, Pul-i-Sefid. Māzandarān, N Iran 36.10N 53.03E
Pol-e-Sefid see Pol-e Safīd
120 B13 **Polessk** Ger. Labiau. Kaliningradskaya Oblast', W Russian Federation 54.52N 21.06E
Polesskoye see Polis'ke
175 P11 **Polewali** Sulawesi, C Indonesia 3.25S 119.22E
116 G11 **Polezhan** ▲ SW Bulgaria 41.42N 23.28E
80 F13 **Poli** Nord, N Cameroon 8.42N 13.09E
Poli see Pólis
109 M19 **Policastro, Golfo di** gulf S Italy
112 D8 **Police** Ger. Politz. Zachodniopomorskie, NW Poland 53.34N 14.34E
180 I17 **Police, Pointe** headland Mahé, NE Seychelles 4.48S 55.31E
117 L17 **Polichnítos** var. Polihnitos, Políkhnitos. Lésvos, E Greece 39.04N 26.10E
Poligiros see Polýgyros
109 P17 **Polignano a Mare** Puglia, SE Italy 40.58N 17.13E
105 S9 **Poligny** Jura, E France 46.51N 5.42E
Polihnitos see Polichnítos
Polikastro/Políkastron see Polýkastro
Políkhnitos see Polichnítos
116 K8 **Polikrayshte** Veliko Tŭrnovo, N Bulgaria 43.12N 25.38E
179 Pp10 **Polillo Islands** island group N Philippines
111 Q9 **Polinik** ▲ SW Austria 46.54N 13.10E
117 J15 **Políochni** var. Polýochni. site of ancient city Límnos, E Greece 39.51N 25.21E
123 Mm3 **Pólis** var. Poli. W Cyprus 35.02N 32.27E
Polish People's Republic see Poland
Polish Republic see Poland
119 O3 **Polis'ke** Rus. Polesskoye. Kyyivs'ka Oblast', N Ukraine 51.15N 29.27E
109 N22 **Polistena** Calabria, SW Italy 38.25N 16.04E
Politz see Police
Políyiros see Polýgyros
31 V14 **Polk City** Iowa, C USA 41.46N 93.42W
112 F13 **Polkowice** Ger. Heerwegen. Dolnośląskie, SW Poland 51.31N 16.04E
161 G22 **Pollāchi** Tamil Nādu, SE India 10.38N 77.00E
111 W7 **Pöllau** Steiermark, SE Austria 47.18N 15.46E
201 T13 **Polle** atoll Chuuk Islands, C Micronesia
107 X9 **Pollença** Mallorca, Spain, W Mediterranean Sea 39.54N 3.05E
Pollnow see Polanów
31 N7 **Pollock** South Dakota, N USA 45.53N 100.15W
94 L8 **Polmak** Finnmark, N Norway 70.01N 28.04E
32 L10 **Polo** Illinois, N USA 41.59N 89.34W
200 Qq15 **Poloa** island Tongatapu Group, N Tonga
44 E5 **Polochic, Río** ≈ C Guatemala
Pologi see Polohy
119 V9 **Polohy** Rus. Pologi. Zaporiz'ka Oblast', SE Ukraine 47.29N 36.18E
85 K20 **Polokwane** prev. Pietersburg. Limpopo, NE South Africa 23.54S 29.22E
12 M10 **Polonais, Lac des** ◎ Québec, SE Canada
63 G20 **Polonio, Cabo** headland E Uruguay 34.22S 53.46W
161 K24 **Polonnaruwa** North Central Province, C Sri Lanka 7.55N 81.01E
118 L5 **Polonne** Rus. Polonnoye. Khmel'nyts'ka Oblast', NW Ukraine 50.10N 27.30E
Polonnoye see Polonne
Polotsk see Polatsk
111 T7 **Pöls** var. Pölsbach. ≈ E Austria
Pölsbach see Pöls
Polska/Polska, Rzeczpospolita/Polska Rzeczpospolita Ludowa see Poland
116 L10 **Polski Gradets** Stara Zagora, C Bulgaria 42.12N 26.06E
116 K8 **Polsko Kosovo** Ruse, N Bulgaria 43.26N 25.40E
35 P8 **Polson** Montana, NW USA 47.41N 114.09W
119 T6 **Poltava** Poltavs'ka Oblast', NE Ukraine 49.33N 34.32E
Poltava see Poltavs'ka Oblast'
119 R5 **Poltavs'ka Oblast'** var. Poltava, Rus. Poltavskaya Oblast'. ◈ province NE Ukraine
Poltavskaya Oblast' see Poltavs'ka Oblast'
Poltoratsk see Aşgabat
120 I5 **Põltsamaa** Ger. Oberpahlen. Jõgevamaa, E Estonia 58.40N 25.58E
120 I4 **Põltsamaa** var. Põltsamaa Jõgi. ≈ C Estonia
Põltsamaa Jõgi see Põltsamaa
125 F10 **Polunochnoye** Sverdlovskaya Oblast', C Russian Federation 60.56N 60.15E
125 G8 **Poluy** ≈ N Russian Federation
120 J6 **Põlva** Ger. Pölwe. Põlvamaa, SE Estonia 58.03N 27.05E
95 N16 **Polvijärvi** Itä-Suomi, E Finland 62.52N 29.19E
Pölwe see Põlva
117 I22 **Polýaigos** island Kykládes, Greece, Aegean Sea
117 I22 **Polyaígou Folégandrou, Stenó** strait Kykládes, Greece, Aegean Sea
128 J3 **Polyarnyy** Murmanskaya Oblast', NW Russian Federation 69.10N 33.21E
129 W5 **Polyarnyy Ural** ▲▲ NW Russian Federation
117 G14 **Polýgyros** var. Poligiros, Políyiros. Kentrikí Makedonía, N Greece 40.21N 23.27E
116 F13 **Polýkastro** var. Polikastro; prev. Políkastron. Kentrikí Makedonía, N Greece 41.01N 22.33E
199 Kk9 **Polynesia** island group C Pacific Ocean
Polýochni see Políochni
43 Y13 **Polyuc** Quintana Roo, E Mexico
111 V10 **Polzela** C Slovenia 46.18N 15.04E
Polzen see Ploučnice
176 Ww9 **Pom** Papua, E Indonesia 1.34S 135.39E
58 D12 **Pomabamba** Ancash, C Peru 8.51S 77.13W
193 D23 **Pomahaka** ≈ South Island, NZ
108 F12 **Pomarance** Toscana, C Italy 43.19N 10.53E
106 G9 **Pombal** Leiria, C Portugal 39.55N 8.37W
78 D9 **Pombas** Santo Antão, NW Cape Verde 17.09N 25.02W
85 N19 **Pomene** Inhambane, SE Mozambique 22.57S 35.34E
112 G8 **Pomerania** cultural region Germany/Poland
112 D7 **Pomeranian Bay** Ger. Pommersche Bucht, Pol. Zatoka Pomorska. bay Germany/Poland
33 T15 **Pomeroy** Ohio, N USA 39.01N 82.01W
34 L10 **Pomeroy** Washington, NW USA 46.28N 117.36W
119 Q8 **Pomichna** Kirovohrads'ka Oblast', C Ukraine 48.07N 31.25E
195 O12 **Pomio** New Britain, E PNG 5.28S 151.29E
Pomir, Dar"yoi see Pamir/Pāmīr, Daryā-ye
29 T6 **Pomme de Terre Lake** ⊡ Missouri, C USA
31 S8 **Pomme de Terre River** ≈ Minnesota, N USA
Pommersche Bucht see Pomeranian Bay
37 T15 **Pomona** California, W USA 34.03N 117.45W
116 N9 **Pomorie** Burgas, E Bulgaria 42.31N 27.39E
Pomorska, Zatoka see Pomeranian Bay
112 H8 **Pomorskie** ◈ province N Poland
129 Q4 **Pomorskiy Proliv** strait NW Russian Federation
129 T10 **Pomozdino** Respublika Komi, NW Russian Federation 62.11N 54.13E
Pompaelo see Pamplona
175 Q9 **Pompangeo, Pegunungan** ▲▲ Sulawesi, C Indonesia
25 Z15 **Pompano Beach** Florida, SE USA 26.14N 80.06W
109 K18 **Pompei** Campania, S Italy 40.45N 14.27E
35 V10 **Pompeys Pillar** Montana, NW USA 45.58N 107.55W
Ponape Ascension Island see Pohnpei
31 R13 **Ponca** Nebraska, C USA 42.34N 96.42W
29 O8 **Ponca City** Oklahoma, C USA 36.42N 97.05W
47 T6 **Ponce** C Puerto Rico 18.01N 66.36W
25 X10 **Ponce de Leon Inlet** inlet Florida, SE USA
24 K8 **Ponchatoula** Louisiana, S USA 30.26N 90.26W
28 M8 **Pond Creek** Oklahoma, C USA 36.40N 97.48W
161 J20 **Pondicherry** var. Puduchcheri, Fr. Pondichéry. Pondicherry, SE India 11.58N 79.49E
157 I20 **Pondicherry** var. Puduchcheri, Fr. Pondichéry. ◈ union territory India
Pondichéry see Pondicherry
207 N11 **Pond Inlet** Baffin Island, Nunavut, NE Canada 72.37N 77.56W
197 I6 **Ponérihouen** Province Nord, C New Caledonia 21.04S 165.24E
106 J4 **Ponferrada** Castilla-León, NW Spain 42.33N 6.34W
192 N13 **Pongaroa** Manawatu-Wanganui, North Island, NZ 40.36S 176.08E
178 I12 **Pong Nam Ron** Chantaburi, S Thailand 12.55N 102.15E
83 C14 **Pongo** ≈ S Sudan
158 I7 **Pong Reservoir** ⊡ N India
113 N14 **Poniatowa** Lubelskie, E Poland 51.10N 22.04E
178 J13 **Pônley** Kâmpóng Chhnăng, C Cambodia 12.26N 104.25E
161 I20 **Ponnaiyār** ≈ SE India
9 Q15 **Ponoka** Alberta, SW Canada 52.42N 113.33W
131 U6 **Ponomarevka** Orenburgskaya Oblast', W Russian Federation 53.16N 54.10E
174 L15 **Ponorogo** Jawa, C Indonesia 7.51S 111.30E
128 M5 **Ponoy** Murmanskaya Oblast', NW Russian Federation 67.00N 41.06E
125 E5 **Ponoy** ≈ NW Russian Federation
104 K11 **Pons** Charente-Maritime, W France 45.31N 0.31W
Pons see Ponts
Pons Aelii see Newcastle upon Tyne
Pons Vetus see Pontevedra
101 G20 **Pont-à-Celles** Hainaut, S Belgium 50.31N 4.21E
104 K16 **Pontacq** Pyrénées-Atlantiques, SW France 43.10N 0.07W
66 P3 **Ponta Delgada** São Miguel, Azores, Portugal, NE Atlantic Ocean 37.28N 25.40W
66 P3 **Ponta Delgado** ✈ São Miguel, Azores, Portugal, NE Atlantic Ocean
66 N2 **Ponta do Pico** ▲ Pico, Azores, Portugal, NE Atlantic Ocean 38.28N 28.25W
62 J11 **Ponta Grossa** Paraná, S Brazil 25.07S 50.09W
105 S5 **Pont-à-Mousson** Meurthe-et-Moselle, NE France 48.55N 6.03E
105 T9 **Pontarlier** Doubs, E France 46.54N 6.19E
108 G11 **Pontassieve** Toscana, C Italy 43.46N 11.28E
104 L4 **Pont-Audemer** Eure, N France 49.22N 0.31E
24 K9 **Pontchartrain, Lake** ◎ Louisiana, S USA
104 I8 **Pontchâteau** Loire-Atlantique, NW France 47.26N 2.04W
105 R10 **Pont-de-Vaux** Ain, E France 46.25N 4.57E
106 G4 **Ponteareas** Galicia, NW Spain 42.10N 8.29W
108 J6 **Pontebba** Friuli-Venezia Giulia, NE Italy 46.32N 13.18E
106 G4 **Ponte Caldelas** Galicia, NW Spain 42.22N 8.30W
109 J16 **Pontecorvo** Lazio, C Italy 41.27N 13.40E
106 G5 **Ponte da Barca** Viana do Castelo, N Portugal 41.48N 8.25W
106 G5 **Ponte de Lima** Viana do Castelo, N Portugal 41.46N 8.34W
108 F11 **Pontedera** Toscana, C Italy 43.40N 10.37E
106 H10 **Ponte de Sor** Portalegre, C Portugal 39.15N 8.01W
106 H2 **Pontedeume** Galicia, NW Spain 43.22N 8.09W
108 F6 **Ponte di Legno** Lombardia, N Italy 46.16N 10.31E
9 T17 **Ponteix** Saskatchewan, S Canada 49.43N 107.22W
61 N20 **Ponte Nova** Minas Gerais, NE Brazil 20.25S 42.54W
61 G18 **Pontes e Lacerda** Mato Grosso, W Brazil 15.13S 59.21W
106 G4 **Pontevedra** anc. Pons Vetus. Galicia, NW Spain 42.25N 8.39W
106 G3 **Pontevedra** ◈ province Galicia, NW Spain
106 G4 **Pontevedra, Ría de** estuary NW Spain
32 M12 **Pontiac** Illinois, N USA 40.51N 88.37W
33 R9 **Pontiac** Michigan, N USA 42.38N 83.17W
174 Kk8 **Pontianak** Borneo, C Indonesia 0.04S 109.16E
109 I16 **Pontino, Agro** plain C Italy
Pontisarae see Pontoise
104 H6 **Pontivy** Morbihan, NW France 48.04N 2.58W
104 F6 **Pont-l'Abbé** Finistère, NW France 47.52N 4.13W
105 N4 **Pontoise** anc. Briva Isarae, Cergy-Pontoise, Pontisarae. Val-d'Oise, N France 49.03N 2.04E
9 W13 **Ponton** Manitoba, C Canada 54.36N 99.02W
104 J5 **Pontorson** Manche, N France 48.33N 1.31W
24 M2 **Pontotoc** Mississippi, S USA 34.15N 89.00W
27 R9 **Pontotoc** Texas, SW USA 30.52N 98.57W
108 E10 **Pontremoli** Toscana, C Italy 44.24N 9.55E
110 J10 **Pontresina** Graubünden, S Switzerland 46.29N 9.52E
107 U5 **Ponts** var. Pons. Cataluña, NE Spain 41.55N 1.12E
105 R14 **Pont-St-Esprit** Gard, S France 44.15N 4.37E
99 K21 **Pontypool** Wel. Pontypŵl. SE Wales, UK 51.43N 3.01W
99 J22 **Pontypridd** S Wales, UK 51.37N 3.22W
Pontypŵl see Pontypool
45 R17 **Ponuga** Veraguas, SE Panama 7.50N 80.58W
192 L6 **Ponui Island** island N NZ
121 K14 **Ponya** Rus. Ponya. ≈ N Belarus
109 I17 **Ponza, Isola di** island Isole Ponziane, S Italy
109 I17 **Ponziane, Isole** island C Italy
190 F7 **Poochera** South Australia 32.45S 134.51E
99 L24 **Poole** S England, UK 50.43N 1.58W
27 S6 **Poolville** Texas, SW USA 33.00N 97.55W
Poona see Pune
190 M8 **Pooncarie** New South Wales, SE Australia 33.26S 142.37E
191 N6 **Poopelloe Lake** seasonal lake New South Wales, SE Australia
59 K19 **Poopó** Oruro, C Bolivia 18.22S 66.58W
59 K19 **Poopó, Lago** var. Lago Pampa Aullagas. ◎ W Bolivia
192 L3 **Poor Knights Islands** island N NZ
41 P10 **Poorman** Alaska, USA 64.05N 155.34W
190 E3 **Pootnoura** South Australia 28.31S 134.09E
153 R10 **Pop** Rus. Pap. Namangan Viloyati, E Uzbekistan 40.49N 71.06E
119 X7 **Popasna** Rus. Popasnaya. Luhans'ka Oblast', E Ukraine 48.37N 38.24E
Popasnaya see Popasna
56 D12 **Popayán** Cauca, SW Colombia 2.27N 76.31W
101 B18 **Poperinge** West-Vlaanderen, W Belgium 50.52N 2.43E
126 K7 **Popigay** Taymyrskiy (Dolgano-Nenetskiy) Avtonomnyy Okrug, N Russian Federation 71.54N 110.45E
126 Jj7 **Popigay** ≈ N Russian Federation
119 O5 **Popil'nya** Zhytomyrs'ka Oblast', N Ukraine 49.57N 29.24E
190 K8 **Popiltah Lake** seasonal lake New South Wales, SE Australia
35 X7 **Poplar** Montana, NW USA 48.06N 105.12W
9 Y14 **Poplar** ≈ Manitoba, C Canada
29 X8 **Poplar Bluff** Missouri, C USA 36.45N 90.23W
35 X6 **Poplar River** ≈ Montana, NW USA
43 P14 **Popocatépetl** 🌋 S Mexico 18.59N 98.37W
174 Ll16 **Popoh** Jawa, S Indonesia 8.13S 111.50E
81 H21 **Popokabaka** Bandundu, SW Dem. Rep. Congo 5.43S 16.35E
109 J15 **Popoli** Abruzzo, C Italy 42.09N 13.51E
195 X16 **Popomanaseu, Mount** ▲ Guadalcanal, C Solomon Islands 9.40S 96.01E
194 L15 **Popondetta** Northern, S PNG 8.45S 148.15E
114 F9 **Popovača** Sisak-Moslavina, NE Croatia 45.35N 16.37E
116 J10 **Popovitsa** Tŭrgovishte, C Bulgaria 42.08N 25.04E
116 L8 **Popovo** Tŭrgovishte, N Bulgaria 43.19N 26.13E
Popovo see Iskra
Popper see Poprad
32 M5 **Popple River** ≈ Wisconsin, N USA
113 L19 **Poprad** Ger. Deutschendorf, Hung. Poprád. Prešovský Kraj, E Slovakia 49.03N 20.16E
113 L18 **Poprad** Ger. Popper, Hung. Poprád. ≈ Poland/Slovakia
113 L19 **Poprad-Tatry** ✈ (Poprad) Prešovský Kraj, E Slovakia 49.04N 20.21E
23 X7 **Poquoson** Virginia, NE USA 37.07N 76.21W
155 O15 **Porāli** ≈ SW Pakistan
192 N12 **Porangahau** Hawke's Bay, North Island, NZ 40.19S 176.36E
61 K17 **Porangatu** Goiás, C Brazil 13.28S 49.13W
121 G18 **Porazava** Pol. Porozow, Rus. Porozovo. Hrodzyenskaya Voblasts', W Belarus 52.57N 24.24E
160 A11 **Porbandar** Gujarāt, W India 21.40N 69.40E
8 I13 **Porcher Island** island British Columbia, SW Canada
106 M13 **Porcuna** Andalucía, S Spain 37.52N 4.12W
12 F7 **Porcupine** Ontario, S Canada 48.31N 81.07W
66 M6 **Porcupine Bank** undersea feature N Atlantic Ocean
9 V15 **Porcupine Hills** ▲▲ Manitoba/Saskatchewan, S Canada
32 L3 **Porcupine Mountains** hill range Michigan, N USA
66 M7 **Porcupine Plain** undersea feature E Atlantic Ocean
14 F4 **Porcupine River** ≈ Canada/USA
108 I7 **Pordenone** anc. Portenau. Friuli-Venezia Giulia, NE Italy 45.58N 12.39E
56 H9 **Pore** Casanare, E Colombia 5.42N 71.58W
114 A9 **Poreč** It. Parenzo. Istra, NW Croatia 45.16N 13.36E
62 I9 **Porecatu** Paraná, S Brazil 22.46S 51.22W
Porech'ye see Parechcha
131 P4 **Poretskoye** Chavash Respubliki, W Russian Federation 55.12N 46.20E
79 Q13 **Porga** N Benin 11.04N 0.58E
194 G12 **Porgera** Enga, W PNG 5.27S 143.09E
95 K18 **Pori** Swe. Björneborg. Länsi-Suomi, W Finland 61.28N 21.49E
193 L14 **Porirua** Wellington, North Island, NZ 41.08S 174.50E
94 I12 **Porjus** Lapp. Bårjås. Norrbotten, N Sweden 66.55N 19.55E
128 G14 **Porkhov** Pskovskaya Oblast', W Russian Federation 57.46N 29.26E
57 O4 **Porlamar** Nueva Esparta, NE Venezuela 10.56N 63.53W
104 I8 **Pornic** Loire-Atlantique, NW France 47.07N 2.07W
194 G12 **Poroma** Southern Highlands, W PNG 6.15S 143.34E
127 Oo15 **Poronaysk** Ostrov Sakhalin, Sakhalinskaya Oblast', SE Russian Federation 49.15N 143.00E
117 G20 **Póros** Póros, S Greece 37.30N 23.29E
117 C19 **Póros** Kefalloniá, Iónia Nisiá, Greece, C Mediterranean Sea 38.09N 20.45E
117 G20 **Póros** island S Greece
83 G24 **Poroto Mountains** ▲▲ SW Tanzania
114 B10 **Porozina** Primorje-Gorski Kotar, NW Croatia 45.07N 14.17E
Porozovo/Porozow see Porazava
205 X15 **Porpoise Bay** bay Antarctica
67 G15 **Porpoise Point** headland NE Ascension Island 7.54S 14.22W
67 C25 **Porpoise Point** headland East Falkland, Falkland Islands 52.19S 59.18W
110 C6 **Porrentruy** Jura, NW Switzerland 47.25N 7.06E
108 F10 **Porretta Terme** Emilia-Romagna, C Italy 44.10N 11.01E
Porriño see O Porriño
94 L7 **Porsangerfjorden** Lapp. Porsángguvuotna. fjord N Norway
94 K8 **Porsangerhalvøya** peninsula N Norway
Porsángguvuotna see Porsangerfjorden
97 G16 **Porsgrunn** Telemark, S Norway 59.07N 9.37E
142 E13 **Porsuk Çayı** ≈ C Turkey
Porsy see Boldumsaz
59 N18 **Portachuelo** Santa Cruz, C Bolivia 17.20S 63.24W
190 I9 **Port Adelaide** South Australia 34.49S 138.31E
99 F15 **Portadown** Ir. Port An Dúnáin. S Northern Ireland, UK 54.25N 6.27W
33 P10 **Portage** Michigan, N USA 42.12N 85.34W
20 D15 **Portage** Pennsylvania, NE USA 40.23N 78.40W
32 K8 **Portage** Wisconsin, N USA 43.33N 89.28W
32 M3 **Portage Lake** ◎ Michigan, N USA
9 X16 **Portage la Prairie** Manitoba, S Canada 49.58N 98.19W
33 R11 **Portage River** ≈ Ohio, N USA
29 Y8 **Portageville** Missouri, C USA 36.25N 89.42W
30 L2 **Portal** North Dakota, N USA 48.57N 102.33W
8 L17 **Port Alberni** Vancouver Island, British Columbia, SW Canada 49.10N 124.49W
12 E15 **Port Albert** Ontario, S Canada 43.51N 81.42W
106 I10 **Portalegre** anc. Ammaia, Amoea. Portalegre, E Portugal 39.16N 7.25W
106 H10 **Portalegre** ◈ district C Portugal
39 V12 **Portales** New Mexico, SW USA 34.11N 103.19W
41 X14 **Port Alexander** Baranof Island, Alaska, USA 56.15N 134.38W
85 I25 **Port Alfred** Eastern Cape, S South Africa 33.30S 26.55E
8 J16 **Port Alice** Vancouver Island, British Columbia, SW Canada 50.22N 127.24W
24 J8 **Port Allen** Louisiana, S USA 30.27N 91.12W
Port Amelia see Pemba
Port An Dúnáin see Portadown
34 G7 **Port Angeles** Washington, NW USA 48.07N 123.25W
46 L12 **Port Antonio** NE Jamaica 18.10N 76.27W
117 D16 **Pórta Panagiá** religious building Thessalía, C Greece 39.28N 21.37E
27 T14 **Port Aransas** Texas, SW USA 27.49N 97.03W
99 E18 **Portarlington** Ir. Cúil an tSúdaire. C Ireland 53.10N 7.10W

◆ Country
● Country Capital
◇ Dependent Territory
○ Dependent Territory Capital
◈ Administrative Region
✈ International Airport
▲ Mountain
▲▲ Mountain Range
🌋 Volcano
≈ River
◎ Lake
⊡ Reservoir

PORT ARTHUR – PRIMOŠTEN

191 P17 **Port Arthur** Tasmania, SE Australia *43.09S 147.51E*
27 Y11 **Port Arthur** Texas, SW USA *29.55N 93.55W*
98 G12 **Port Askaig** W Scotland, UK *55.51N 6.06W*
190 I7 **Port Augusta** South Australia *32.29S 137.43E*
46 M9 **Port-au-Prince** ● (Haiti) C Haiti *18.33N 72.19W*
46 M9 **Port-au-Prince** ✕ E Haiti *18.38N 72.13W*
24 I8 **Port Barre** Louisiana, S USA *30.33N 91.57W*
157 Q19 **Port Blair** Andaman and Nicobar Islands, SE India *11.40N 92.43E*
27 X12 **Port Bolivar** Texas, SW USA *29.21N 94.45W*
107 X4 **Portbou** Cataluña, NE Spain *42.26N 3.10E*
79 N17 **Port Bouet** ✕ (Abidjan) SE Ivory Coast *5.17N 3.55W*
190 I8 **Port Broughton** South Australia *33.39S 137.55E*
12 F17 **Port Burwell** Ontario, S Canada *42.37N 80.47W*
10 G17 **Port Burwell** Québec, NE Canada *60.25N 64.49W*
190 M13 **Port Campbell** Victoria, SE Australia *38.37S 143.00E*
13 V4 **Port-Cartier** Québec, SE Canada *50.00N 66.55W*
193 F23 **Port Chalmers** Otago, South Island, NZ *45.46S 170.37E*
25 W14 **Port Charlotte** Florida, SE USA *27.00N 82.07W*
40 L9 **Port Clarence** Alaska, USA *65.15N 166.51W*
8 I13 **Port Clements** Graham Island, British Columbia, SW Canada *53.37N 132.12W*
33 S11 **Port Clinton** Ohio, N USA *41.30N 82.56W*
12 H17 **Port Colborne** Ontario, S Canada *42.51N 79.16W*
13 Y7 **Port-Daniel** Québec, SE Canada *48.10N 64.58W*
Port Darwin *see* Darwin
191 O17 **Port Davey** *headland* Tasmania, SE Australia *43.19S 145.54E*
46 K8 **Port-de-Paix** NW Haiti *19.53N 72.50W*
189 W4 **Port Douglas** Queensland, NE Australia *16.32S 145.27E*
8 J13 **Port Edward** British Columbia, SW Canada *54.10N 130.16W*
85 K24 **Port Edward** KwaZulu/Natal, SE South Africa *31.03S 30.13E*
60 J12 **Portel** Pará, NE Brazil *1.58S 50.45W*
106 H12 **Portel** Évora, S Portugal *38.18N 7.42W*
12 E14 **Port Elgin** Ontario, S Canada *44.26N 81.22W*
47 Y14 **Port Elizabeth** Bequia, Saint Vincent and the Grenadines *13.01N 61.15W*
85 I26 **Port Elizabeth** Eastern Cape, S South Africa *33.58S 25.36E*
98 G13 **Port Ellen** W Scotland, UK *55.37N 6.12W*
Portenau *see* Pordenone
99 H16 **Port Erin** SW Isle of Man *54.05N 4.47W*
47 Q13 **Porter Point** *headland* Saint Vincent, Saint Vincent and the Grenadines *13.22N 61.10W*
193 G18 **Porters Pass** *pass* South Island, NZ *43.18S 171.45E*
85 E25 **Porterville** Western Cape, SW South Africa *33.03S 19.00E*
37 R12 **Porterville** California, W USA *36.03N 119.03W*
Port-Étienne *see* Nouâdhibou
190 L13 **Port Fairy** Victoria, SE Australia *38.24S 142.13E*
192 M4 **Port Fitzroy** Great Barrier Island, Auckland, NE NZ *36.10S 175.21E*
Port Florence *see* Kisumu
Port-Francqui *see* Ilebo
81 C18 **Port-Gentil** Ogooué-Maritime, W Gabon *0.40S 8.49E*
190 I7 **Port Germein** South Australia *33.02S 138.01E*
24 J6 **Port Gibson** Mississippi, S USA *31.57N 90.58W*
41 Q13 **Port Graham** Alaska, USA *59.21N 151.49W*
79 U17 **Port Harcourt** Rivers, S Nigeria *4.43N 7.02E*
8 J16 **Port Hardy** Vancouver Island, British Columbia, SW Canada *50.40N 127.30W*
Port Harrison *see* Inukjuak
11 R14 **Port Hawkesbury** Cape Breton Island, Nova Scotia, SE Canada *45.36N 61.22W*
188 I6 **Port Hedland** Western Australia *20.22S 118.40E*
41 O15 **Port Heiden** Alaska, USA *56.54N 158.40W*
99 I19 **Porthmadog** *var.* Portmadoc. NW Wales, UK *52.55N 4.07W*
12 I15 **Port Hope** Ontario, SE Canada *43.56N 78.16W*
11 S9 **Port Hope Simpson** Newfoundland and Labrador, E Canada *52.30N 56.18W*
67 C24 **Port Howard Settlement** West Falkland, Falkland Islands
33 T9 **Port Huron** Michigan, N USA *42.58N 82.25W*
109 K17 **Portici** Campania, S Italy *40.48N 14.19E*
143 Y13 **Port-İliç** *Rus.* Port Il'ich. SE Azerbaijan *38.54N 48.49E*
Port Il'ich *see* Port-İliç
106 G14 **Portimão** *var.* Vila Nova de Portimão. Faro, S Portugal *37.07N 8.31W*
27 T17 **Port Isabel** Texas, SW USA *26.04N 97.13W*
20 J13 **Port Jervis** New York, NE USA *41.22N 74.39W*
57 S7 **Port Kaituma** NW Guyana *7.42N 59.52W*
130 K12 **Port-Katon** Rostovskaya Oblast', SW Russian Federation *46.52N 38.46E*
191 S9 **Port Kembla** New South Wales, SE Australia *34.29S 150.53E*
190 F8 **Port Kenny** South Australia *33.09S 134.38E*
Port Klang *see* Pelabuhan Klang
Port Láirge *see* Waterford
191 S8 **Portland** New South Wales, SE Australia *33.24S 150.00E*
190 L13 **Portland** Victoria, SE Australia *38.21S 141.37E*
192 K4 **Portland** Northland, North Island, NZ *35.48S 174.19E*
33 Q13 **Portland** Indiana, N USA *40.25N 84.58W*
21 P8 **Portland** Maine, NE USA *43.40N 70.16W*
33 Q9 **Portland** Michigan, N USA *42.51N 84.52W*
31 Q4 **Portland** North Dakota, N USA *47.28N 97.22W*
34 G11 **Portland** Oregon, NW USA *45.31N 122.40W*
22 J8 **Portland** Tennessee, S USA *36.34N 86.31W*
27 T14 **Portland** Texas, SW USA *27.52N 97.19W*
34 G11 **Portland** ✕ Oregon, NW USA *45.36N 122.34W*
190 L13 **Portland Bay** *bay* Victoria, SE Australia
46 K13 **Portland Bight** *bay* S Jamaica
99 L24 **Portland Bill** *var.* Bill of Portland. *headland* S England, UK *50.31N 2.28W*
Portland, Bill of *see* Portland Bill
191 P15 **Portland, Cape** *headland* Tasmania, SE Australia *40.46S 147.58E*
8 J12 **Portland Inlet** *inlet* British Columbia, W Canada
192 P11 **Portland Island** *island* E NZ
67 F15 **Portland Point** *headland* SW Ascension Island
46 J13 **Portland Point** *headland* C Jamaica *17.42N 77.10W*
105 P16 **Port-la-Nouvelle** Aude, S France *43.01N 3.04E*
Portlaoighise *see* Port Laoise
99 E18 **Port Laoise** *var.* Portlaoise, *Ir.* Portlaoighise; *prev.* Maryborough. C Ireland *53.01N 7.16W*
27 U13 **Port Lavaca** Texas, SW USA *28.36N 96.39W*
190 G9 **Port Lincoln** South Australia *34.43S 135.49E*
41 Q14 **Port Lions** Kodiak Island, Alaska, USA *57.55N 152.48W*
78 I15 **Port Loko** W Sierra Leone *8.49N 12.49W*
67 E24 **Port Louis** East Falkland, Falkland Islands *51.31S 58.07W*
47 Y5 **Port-Louis** Grande Terre, N Guadeloupe *16.25N 61.31W*
181 X16 **Port Louis** ● (Mauritius) NW Mauritius *20.10S 57.30E*
Port Louis *see* Scarborough
Port-Lyautey *see* Kénitra
190 K12 **Port MacDonnell** South Australia *38.04S 140.40E*
191 U7 **Port Macquarie** New South Wales, SE Australia *31.25S 152.55E*
Portmadoc *see* Porthmadog
Port Mahon *see* Mahón
46 K12 **Port Maria** C Jamaica *18.21N 76.53W*
8 K16 **Port McNeill** Vancouver Island, British Columbia, SW Canada *50.34N 127.06W*
11 P11 **Port-Menier** Île d'Anticosti, Québec, E Canada *49.49N 64.19W*
41 N15 **Port Moller** Alaska, USA *56.00N 96.31W*
46 L13 **Port Morant** E Jamaica *17.52N 76.19W*
46 K13 **Portmore** C Jamaica *17.58N 76.52W*
194 I16 **Port Moresby** ● (PNG) Central/National Capital District, SW PNG *9.28S 147.11E*
Port Natal *see* Durban
27 Y11 **Port Neches** Texas, SW USA *29.59N 93.57W*
190 G9 **Port Neill** South Australia *34.06S 136.19E*
13 S6 **Portneuf** ≈ Québec, SE Canada
13 R6 **Portneuf, Lac** ◎ Québec, SE Canada
85 D23 **Port Nolloth** Northern Cape, W South Africa *29.18S 16.58E*
20 J17 **Port Norris** New Jersey, NE USA *39.13N 75.00W*
Port-Nouveau-Québec *see* Kangiqsualujjuaq
106 G6 **Porto** *Eng.* Oporto; *anc.* Portus Cale. Porto, NW Portugal *41.09N 8.37W*
106 G6 **Porto** *var.* Pôrto. ⬖ *district* N Portugal
106 G6 **Porto** ✕ Porto, W Portugal *41.15N 8.45W*
63 I16 **Porto Alegre** *var.* Pôrto Alegre. *state capital* Rio Grande do Sul, S Brazil *30.03S 51.10W*
Porto Alexandre *see* Tombua
84 B12 **Porto Amboim** Cuanza Sul, NW Angola *10.43S 13.49E*
Porto Amélia *see* Pemba
Porto Bello *see* Portobelo
45 T14 **Portobelo** *var.* Porto Bello, Puerto Bello. Colón, N Panama *9.32N 79.40W*
62 G10 **Pôrto Camargo** Paraná, S Brazil *23.23S 53.47W*
27 U13 **Port O'Connor** Texas, SW USA *28.26N 96.26W*
Pôrto de Mós *see* Porto de Moz
60 J12 **Porto de Moz** *var.* Pôrto de Mós. Pará, NE Brazil *1.45S 52.15W*
66 O5 **Porto do Moniz** Madeira, Portugal, NE Atlantic Ocean
61 H16 **Porto dos Gaúchos** Mato Grosso, W Brazil *11.31S 57.16W*
Porto Edda *see* Sarandë
109 J24 **Porto Empedocle** Sicilia, Italy, C Mediterranean Sea *37.16N 13.31E*
61 H20 **Porto Esperança** Mato Grosso do Sul, SW Brazil *19.36S 57.24W*
108 E13 **Portoferraio** Toscana, C Italy *42.48N 10.18E*
98 G6 **Port of Ness** NW Scotland, UK *58.29N 6.15W*
47 U14 **Port-of-Spain** ● (Trinidad and Tobago) Trinidad, Trinidad and Tobago *10.39N 61.30W*
Port of Spain *see* Piarco
105 X15 **Porto, Golfe de** *gulf* Corse, France, C Mediterranean Sea
Porto Grande *see* Mindelo
108 I7 **Portogruaro** Veneto, NE Italy *45.46N 12.49E*
37 P5 **Portola** California, W USA *39.48N 120.28W*
197 B12 **Port-Olry** Espiritu Santo, C Vanuatu *15.03S 167.04E*
95 J17 **Pörtom** *Fin.* Pirttikylä. Länsi-Suomi, W Finland *62.42N 21.40E*
Port Omna *see* Portumna
61 G21 **Porto Murtinho** Mato Grosso do Sul, SW Brazil *21.42S 57.52W*
61 K16 **Porto Nacional** Tocantins, C Brazil *10.40S 48.19W*
79 S16 **Porto-Novo** ● (Benin) S Benin *6.28N 2.37E*
25 X10 **Port Orange** Florida, SE USA *29.06N 80.59W*
34 G8 **Port Orchard** Washington, NW USA *47.32N 122.38W*
Porto Re *see* Kraljevica
34 E15 **Port Orford** Oregon, NW USA *42.45N 124.30W*
Porto Rico *see* Puerto Rico
108 J13 **Porto San Giorgio** Marche, C Italy *43.10N 13.47E*
109 F14 **Porto San Stefano** Toscana, C Italy *42.26N 11.09E*
66 P5 **Porto Santo** *var.* Vila Baleira. Porto Santo, Madeira, Portugal, NE Atlantic Ocean *33.04N 16.19W*
66 Q5 **Porto Santo** ✕ Porto Santo, Madeira, Portugal, NE Atlantic Ocean *33.04N 16.19W*
66 P5 **Porto Santo** *var.* Ilha do Porto Santo. *island* Madeira, Portugal, NE Atlantic Ocean
62 H9 **Porto São José** Paraná, S Brazil *22.43S 53.10W*
61 O19 **Porto Seguro** Bahia, E Brazil *16.25S 39.07W*
109 B17 **Porto Torres** Sardegna, Italy, C Mediterranean Sea *40.49N 8.22E*
61 J23 **Porto União** Santa Catarina, S Brazil *26.15S 51.04W*
105 Y16 **Porto-Vecchio** Corse, France, C Mediterranean Sea *41.35N 9.17E*
61 E15 **Porto Velho** *var.* Velho. *state capital* Rondônia, W Brazil *8.45S 63.54W*
58 A6 **Portoviejo** *var.* Puertoviejo. Manabí, W Ecuador *1.02S 80.31W*
193 B26 **Port Pegasus** *bay* Stewart Island, NZ
12 H15 **Port Perry** Ontario, SE Canada *44.08N 78.57W*
191 N12 **Port Phillip Bay** *harbor* Victoria, SE Australia
190 I8 **Port Pirie** South Australia *33.10S 138.01E*
98 G9 **Portree** N Scotland, UK *57.25N 6.11W*
Port Rex *see* East London
Port Rois *see* Portrush
46 K13 **Port Royal** E Jamaica *17.56N 76.49W*
23 R15 **Port Royal** South Carolina, SE USA *32.22N 80.41W*
23 R15 **Port Royal Sound** *inlet* South Carolina, SE USA
99 F14 **Portrush** *Ir.* Port Rois. N Northern Ireland, UK *55.12N 6.40W*
77 W7 **Port Said** *Ar.* Būr Sa'īd. N Egypt *31.16N 32.18E*
25 R9 **Port Saint Joe** Florida, SE USA *29.49N 85.18W*
25 Y11 **Port Saint John** Florida, SE USA *28.28N 80.46W*
85 K24 **Port St.Johns** Eastern Cape, SE South Africa *31.34S 29.30E*
105 R16 **Port-St-Louis-du-Rhône** Bouches-du-Rhône, SE France *43.22N 4.48E*
46 K10 **Port Salut** SW Haiti *18.04N 73.55W*
67 E24 **Port Salvador** *inlet* East Falkland, Falkland Islands
67 D24 **Port San Carlos** East Falkland, Falkland Islands *51.30S 58.58W*
11 S10 **Port Saunders** Newfoundland and Labrador, SE Canada *50.40N 57.17W*
85 K24 **Port Shepstone** KwaZulu/Natal, E South Africa *30.40S 30.24E*
47 O11 **Portsmouth** *var.* Grand-Anse. NW Dominica *15.33N 61.27W*
99 N24 **Portsmouth** S England, UK *50.48N 1.04W*
21 P10 **Portsmouth** New Hampshire, NE USA *43.04N 70.46W*
33 S15 **Portsmouth** Ohio, N USA *38.43N 83.00W*
23 X7 **Portsmouth** Virginia, NE USA *36.50N 76.18W*
12 E17 **Port Stanley** Ontario, S Canada *42.39N 81.12W*
67 B25 **Port Stephens** *inlet* West Falkland, Falkland Islands
67 B25 **Port Stephens Settlement** West Falkland, Falkland Islands
99 F14 **Portstewart** *Ir.* Port Stíobhaird. N Northern Ireland, UK *55.10N 6.43W*
Port Stíobhaird *see* Portstewart
82 I7 **Port Sudan** Red Sea, NE Sudan *19.37N 37.13E*
24 L10 **Port Sulphur** Louisiana, S USA *29.28N 89.41W*
Port Swettenham *see* Klang/Pelabuhan Klang
99 J22 **Port Talbot** S Wales, UK *51.36N 3.46W*
94 L11 **Porttipahdan Tekojärvi** ◎ N Finland
34 G7 **Port Townsend** Washington, NW USA *48.07N 122.45W*
106 H9 **Portugal** *off.* Republic of Portugal. ◆ *republic* SW Europe
107 O2 **Portugalete** País Vasco, N Spain *43.19N 3.01W*
56 J6 **Portuguesa** *off.* Estado Portuguesa. ⬖ *state* N Venezuela
Portuguese East Africa *see* Mozambique
Portuguese Guinea *see* Guinea-Bissau
Portuguese Timor *see* East Timor
Portuguese West Africa *see* Angola
99 D18 **Portumna** *Ir.* Port Omna. W Ireland *53.06N 8.13W*
Portus Cale *see* Porto
Portus Magnus *see* Almería
Portus Magonis *see* Mahón
105 P17 **Port-Vendres** *var.* Port Vendres. Pyrénées-Orientales, S France *42.31N 3.06E*
190 H9 **Port Victoria** South Australia *34.34S 137.31E*
197 C14 **Port-Vila** *var.* Vila. ● (Vanuatu) Éfaté, C Vanuatu *17.45S 168.21E*
190 I9 **Port Wakefield** South Australia *34.13S 138.10E*
33 N8 **Port Washington** Wisconsin, N USA *43.22N 87.54W*
59 J14 **Porvenir** Pando, NW Bolivia *11.15S 68.43W*
65 I24 **Porvenir** Magallanes, S Chile *53.18S 70.22W*
63 D18 **Porvenir** Paysandú, W Uruguay *32.22S 57.58W*
95 M19 **Porvoo** *Swe.* Borgå. Etelä-Suomi, S Finland *60.25N 25.40E*
Porzecze *see* Parechcha
106 M10 **Porzuna** Castilla-La Mancha, C Spain *39.10N 4.10W*
63 E14 **Posadas** Misiones, NE Argentina *27.27S 55.52W*
106 L13 **Posadas** Andalucía, S Spain *37.48N 5.06W*
Poschega *see* Požega
110 J11 **Poschiavino** ≈ Italy/Switzerland
110 J10 **Poschiavo** *Ger.* Puschlav. Graubünden, S Switzerland *46.19N 10.02E*
114 D12 **Posedarje** Zadar, SW Croatia *44.12N 15.27E*
Posen *see* Poznań
128 L14 **Poshekhon'ye** Yaroslavskaya Oblast', W Russian Federation *58.31N 39.07E*
94 M13 **Posio** Lappi, NE Finland *66.06N 28.16E*
Poskam *see* Zepu
Posnania *see* Poznań
175 Pp9 **Poso** Sulawesi, C Indonesia *1.22S 120.45E*
175 Pp10 **Poso, Danau** ◎ Sulawesi, C Indonesia
143 R10 **Posof** Ardahan, NE Turkey *41.31N 42.44E*
175 Pp9 **Poso, Sungai** ≈ Sulawesi, C Indonesia
27 R6 **Possum Kingdom Lake** ⊠ Texas, SW USA
27 N6 **Post** Texas, SW USA *33.11N 101.22W*
Postavy/Postawy *see* Pastavy
10 I7 **Poste-de-la-Baleine** Québec, NE Canada *55.13N 77.54W*
101 M17 **Posterholt** Limburg, SE Netherlands *51.07N 6.01E*
85 G22 **Postmasburg** Northern Cape, N South Africa *28.19S 23.04E*
Pôsto Diuarum *see* Campo de Diauarum
61 I16 **Pôsto Jacaré** Mato Grosso, W Brazil *11.59S 53.27W*
111 T12 **Postojna** *Ger.* Adelsberg, *It.* Postumia. SW Slovenia *45.48N 14.12E*
Postumia *see* Postojna
31 X12 **Postville** Iowa, C USA *43.04N 91.34W*
Pöstyén *see* Piešťany
115 G14 **Posušje** Federacija Bosna I Herzegovina, SE Bosnia & Herzegovina *43.28N 17.20E*
175 Pp16 **Pota** Flores, C Indonesia *8.21S 120.49E*
117 G23 **Potamós** Antikýthira, S Greece *35.53N 23.17E*
57 S9 **Potaru River** ≈ C Guyana
85 I21 **Potchefstroom** North-West, N South Africa *26.42S 27.06E*
29 R11 **Poteau** Oklahoma, C USA *35.03N 94.37W*
27 R12 **Poteet** Texas, SW USA *29.02N 98.34W*
117 G14 **Poteídaia** *site of ancient city* Kentrikí Makedonía, N Greece *40.12N 23.21E*
Potentia *see* Potenza
109 M18 **Potenza** *anc.* Potentia. Basilicata, S Italy *40.40N 15.49E*
193 A24 **Poteriteri, Lake** ◎ South Island, NZ
106 M2 **Potes** Cantabria, N Spain *43.10N 4.40W*
Potgietersrus *see* Mokopane
27 S12 **Poth** Texas, SW USA *29.04N 98.04W*
34 J9 **Potholes Reservoir** ⊠ Washington, NW USA
143 Q9 **P'ot'i** W Georgia *42.10N 41.42E*
79 X13 **Potiskum** Yobe, NE Nigeria *11.38N 11.07E*
Potkozarje *see* Ivanjska
34 M9 **Potlatch** Idaho, NW USA *46.55N 116.51W*
35 N9 **Pot Mountain** ▲ Idaho, NW USA *46.44N 115.24W*
115 H14 **Potoci** Federacija Bosna I Hercegovina, SE Bosnia & Herzegovina *43.24N 17.52E*
23 V3 **Potomac River** ≈ NE USA
29 W6 **Potosi** Missouri, C USA *37.56N 90.47W*
59 L20 **Potosí** Potosí, S Bolivia *19.34S 65.51W*
44 H9 **Potosí** Chinandega, NW Nicaragua *12.58N 87.30W*
59 K21 **Potosí** ⬖ *department* SW Bolivia
64 H7 **Potrerillos** Atacama, N Chile *26.25S 70.09W*
44 H5 **Potrerillos** Cortés, NW Honduras *15.12N 87.57W*
64 H8 **Potro, Cerro del** ▲ N Chile *28.22S 69.34W*
102 N12 **Potsdam** Brandenburg, NE Germany *52.24N 13.04E*
20 J7 **Potsdam** New York, NE USA *44.40N 74.58W*
111 X5 **Pottendorf** Niederösterreich, E Austria *47.53N 16.22E*
111 X5 **Pottenstein** Niederösterreich, E Austria *47.55N 16.06E*
197 G4 **Pott, Île** *island* Îles Belep, W New Caledonia
20 I15 **Pottstown** Pennsylvania, NE USA *40.15N 75.39W*
20 H14 **Pottsville** Pennsylvania, NE USA *40.40N 76.10W*
161 L25 **Pottuvil** Eastern Province, SE Sri Lanka *6.52N 81.49E*
155 U6 **Potwar Plateau** *plateau* NE Pakistan
104 J7 **Pouancé** Maine-et-Loire, W France *47.46N 1.11W*
197 H5 **Pouébo** Province Nord, C New Caledonia *20.40S 164.02E*
197 H6 **Pouembout** Province Nord, W New Caledonia *21.09S 164.52E*
13 R6 **Poulin de Courval, Lac** ◎ Québec, SE Canada
20 L9 **Poultney** Vermont, NE USA *43.31N 73.12W*
197 H5 **Poum** Province Nord, W New Caledonia *20.15S 164.03E*
61 L21 **Pouso Alegre** Minas Gerais, NE Brazil *22.13S 45.55W*
198 Bb8 **Poutasi** Upolu, SE Samoa *14.00S 171.43W*
178 Ii12 **Poŭthĭsăt** *prev.* Pursat. Poŭthĭsăt, W Cambodia *12.31N 103.55E*
178 Ii13 **Poŭthĭsăt, Stœ̆ng** *prev.* Pursat. ≈ W Cambodia
104 J9 **Pouzauges** Vendée, NW France *46.47N 0.54W*
Po, Valle del *see* Po Valley
108 F8 **Po Valley** *It.* Valle del Po. *valley* N Italy
113 I19 **Považská Bystrica** *Ger.* Waagbistritz, *Hung.* Vágbeszterce. Trenčiansky Kraj, W Slovakia *49.07N 18.26E*
128 J10 **Povenets** Respublika Kareliya, NW Russian Federation *62.50N 34.47E*
192 Q9 **Poverty Bay** *inlet* North Island, NZ
114 K12 **Povlen** ▲▲ W Serbia
106 G6 **Póvoa de Varzim** Porto, NW Portugal *41.22N 8.46W*
131 N8 **Povorino** Voronezhskaya Oblast', W Russian Federation *51.10N 42.16E*
Povungnituk *see* Puvirnituq
10 J3 **Povungnituk, Rivière de** ≈ Québec, NE Canada
12 H11 **Powassan** Ontario, S Canada *46.04N 79.21W*
37 U17 **Poway** California, W USA *32.57N 117.02W*
35 W14 **Powder River** Wyoming, C USA *43.01N 106.57W*
35 Y10 **Powder River** ≈ Montana/Wyoming, NW USA
34 L12 **Powder River** ≈ Oregon, NW USA
35 W13 **Powder River Pass** *pass* Wyoming, C USA *44.08N 107.03W*
35 U12 **Powell** Wyoming, C USA *44.45N 108.45W*
67 I22 **Powell Basin** *undersea feature* NW Weddell Sea
38 M8 **Powell, Lake** ◎ Utah, W USA
39 R4 **Powell, Mount** ▲ Colorado, C USA *39.25N 106.20W*
8 L17 **Powell River** British Columbia, SW Canada *49.54N 124.34W*
33 N5 **Powers** Michigan, N USA *45.40N 87.29W*
30 K2 **Powers Lake** North Dakota, N USA *48.33N 102.37W*
23 V6 **Powhatan** Virginia, NE USA *37.32N 77.55W*
33 V13 **Powhatan Point** Ohio, N USA *39.49N 80.49W*
99 J20 **Powys** *cultural region* E Wales, UK
197 I6 **Poya** Province Nord, C New Caledonia *21.19S 165.07E*
167 P10 **Poyang Hu** ◎ S China
126 Mm16 **Poyarkovo** Amurskaya Oblast', SE Russian Federation *49.37N 128.40E*
32 L7 **Poygan, Lake** ◎ Wisconsin, N USA
111 Y2 **Poysdorf** Niederösterreich, NE Austria *48.40N 16.37E*
114 N11 **Požarevac** *Ger.* Passarowitz. Serbia, NE Serbia *44.37N 21.11E*
43 Q13 **Poza Rica** *var.* Poza Rica de Hidalgo. Veracruz-Llave, E Mexico *20.33N 97.27W*
Poza Rica de Hidalgo *see* Poza Rica
114 L13 **Požega** *Prev.* Slavonska Požega; *Ger.* Poschega, *Hung.* Pozsega. Požega-Slavonija, NE Croatia *43.19N 17.42E*
114 H9 **Požega-Slavonija** *off.* Požeško-Slavonska Županija. ⬖ *province* NE Croatia
129 U13 **Pozhva** Permskaya Oblast', NW Russian Federation *59.07N 56.04E*
112 G11 **Poznań** *Ger.* Posen, Posnania. Wielkolpolskie, C Poland *52.24N 16.56E*
107 O13 **Pozo Alcón** Andalucía, S Spain *37.43N 2.55W*
64 H3 **Pozo Almonte** Tarapacá, N Chile *20.13S 69.48W*
106 L12 **Pozoblanco** Andalucía, S Spain *38.22N 4.47W*
107 Q11 **Pozo Cañada** Castilla-La Mancha, C Spain *38.49N 1.45W*
64 N5 **Pozo Colorado** Presidente Hayes, C Paraguay *23.25S 58.51W*
65 J20 **Pozos, Punta** *headland* S Argentina *47.55S 65.46W*
Pozsega *see* Požega
Pozsony *see* Bratislava
57 N5 **Pozuelos** Anzoátegui, NE Venezuela *10.10N 64.39W*
109 L26 **Pozzallo** Sicilia, Italy, C Mediterranean Sea *36.43N 14.51E*
109 K17 **Pozzuoli** *anc.* Puteoli. Campania, S Italy *40.49N 14.07E*
79 P17 **Pra** ≈ S Ghana
Prabumulih *see* Perabumulih
113 C19 **Prachatice** *Ger.* Prachatitz. Jihočeský Kraj, S Czech Republic *49.01N 14.00E*
Prachatitz *see* Prachatice
178 Hh11 **Prachin Buri** *var.* Prachinburi. Prachin Buri, C Thailand *14.05N 101.19E*
Prachuab Girikhand *see* Prachuap Khiri Khan
178 H13 **Prachuap Khiri Khan** *var.* Prachuab Girikhand. Prachuap Khiri Khan, SW Thailand *11.50N 99.45E*
113 H16 **Praděd** *Ger.* Altvater. ▲ NE Czech Republic *50.06N 17.14E*
56 D11 **Pradera** Valle del Cauca, SW Colombia *3.24N 76.19W*
105 O17 **Prades** Pyrénées-Orientales, S France *42.36N 2.22E*
61 O19 **Prado** Bahia, SE Brazil *17.13S 39.15W*
56 E11 **Prado** Tolima, C Colombia *3.38N 74.57W*
Prado del Ganso *see* Goose Green
Prae *see* Phrae
Prag/Praga/Prague *see* Praha
29 O10 **Prague** Oklahoma, C USA *35.29N 96.40W*
113 D16 **Praha** *Eng.* Prague, *Ger.* Prag, *Pol.* Praga. ● (Czech Republic) Středočeský Kraj, NW Czech Republic *50.06N 14.25E*
118 J13 **Prahova** ⬖ *county* SE Romania
118 J13 **Prahova** ≈ S Romania
78 E10 **Praia** ● (Cape Verde) Santiago, S Cape Verde *14.55N 23.31W*
85 M21 **Praia do Bilene** Gaza, S Mozambique *25.18S 33.10E*
85 M20 **Praia do Xai-Xai** Gaza, S Mozambique *25.04S 33.43E*
118 J10 **Praid** *Hung.* Parajd. Harghita, C Romania *46.33N 25.06E*
28 J3 **Prairie Dog Creek** ≈ Kansas/Nebraska, C USA
32 J9 **Prairie du Chien** Wisconsin, N USA *43.01N 91.07W*
29 S9 **Prairie Grove** Arkansas, C USA *35.58N 94.19W*
33 P10 **Prairie River** ≈ Michigan, N USA
Prairie State *see* Illinois
27 V11 **Prairie View** Texas, SW USA *30.05N 95.59W*
178 Ii11 **Prakhon Chai** Buri Ram, E Thailand *14.36N 103.04E*
111 R4 **Pram** ≈ N Austria
111 S4 **Prambachkirchen** Oberösterreich, N Austria *48.18N 13.50E*
120 H2 **Prangli** *island* N Estonia
160 J13 **Prānhita** ≈ C India
180 I15 **Praslin** *island* Inner Islands, NE Seychelles
117 O23 **Prasonísi, Akrotírio** *headland* Ródos, Dodekánisa, Greece, Aegean Sea *35.53N 27.46E*
113 I14 **Praszka** Opolskie, S Poland *51.05N 18.29E*
121 M18 **Pratasy** *Rus.* Protasy. Homyel'skaya Voblasts', SE Belarus *52.48N 29.04E*
178 I10 **Prathai** Nakhon Ratchasima, E Thailand *15.31N 102.42E*
Prathet Thai *see* Thailand
Prathum Thani *see* Pathum Thani
65 F21 **Prat, Isla** *island* S Chile
108 G11 **Prato** Toscana, C Italy *43.52N 11.04E*
105 O17 **Prats-de-Mollo-la-Preste** Pyrénées-Orientales, S France *42.25N 2.28E*
28 L6 **Pratt** Kansas, C USA *37.38N 98.44W*
110 E6 **Pratteln** Basel-Land, NW Switzerland *47.31N 7.42E*
199 L2 **Pratt Seamount** *undersea feature* N Pacific Ocean *56.09N 142.30W*
25 P5 **Prattville** Alabama, S USA *32.27N 86.27W*
Praust *see* Pruszcz Gdański
116 M7 **Pravda** *prev.* Dogrular. Silistra, NE Bulgaria *43.53N 26.58E*
121 B14 **Pravdinsk** *Ger.* Friedland. Kaliningradskaya Oblast', W Russian Federation *54.26N 21.01E*
106 K2 **Pravia** Asturias, N Spain *43.29N 6.06W*
120 L12 **Prazaroki** *Rus.* Prozoroki. Vitsyebskaya Voblasts', N Belarus *55.16N 28.11E*
Prázsmár *see* Prejmer
178 J11 **Preăh Vihéar** Preăh Vihéar, N Cambodia *13.57N 104.48E*
118 J12 **Predeal** *Hung.* Predeál. Brașov, C Romania *45.30N 25.31E*
111 S8 **Predlitz** Steiermark, SE Austria *47.04N 13.54E*
9 V15 **Preeceville** Saskatchewan, S Canada *51.58N 102.40W*
Preenkuln *see* Priekule
104 K6 **Pré-en-Pail** Mayenne, NW France *48.27N 0.15W*
111 T4 **Pregarten** Oberösterreich, N Austria *48.21N 14.31E*
56 H7 **Pregonero** Táchira, NW Venezuela *8.01N 71.45W*
120 J10 **Preiļi** *Ger.* Preli. Preiļi, SE Latvia *56.17N 26.52E*
118 J12 **Prejmer** *Ger.* Tartlau, *Hung.* Prázsmár. Brașov, S Romania *45.42N 25.49E*
115 J16 **Prekornica** ▲▲ C-Montenegro
Preli *see* Preiļi
Prëmet *see* Përmet
102 M12 **Premnitz** Brandenburg, NE Germany *52.33N 12.22E*
27 S15 **Premont** Texas, SW USA *27.21N 98.07W*
115 H14 **Prenj** ▲▲ S Bosnia and Herzegovina
Prenjas/Prenjasi *see* Përrenjas
24 L7 **Prentiss** Mississippi, S USA *31.36N 89.52W*
Preny *see* Prienai
102 O10 **Prenzlau** Brandenburg, NE Germany *53.19N 13.52E*
126 Jj12 **Preobrazhenka** Irkutskaya Oblast', C Russian Federation *60.01N 108.00E*
177 Ee9 **Preparis Island** *island* SW Burma
Prerau *see* Přerov
113 H18 **Přerov** *Ger.* Prerau. Olomoucký Kraj, E Czech Republic *49.27N 17.27E*
Preschau *see* Prešov
12 M14 **Prescott** Ontario, SE Canada *44.43N 75.33W*
38 K12 **Prescott** Arizona, SW USA *34.33N 112.26W*
29 T13 **Prescott** Arkansas, C USA *33.48N 93.22W*
34 L10 **Prescott** Washington, NW USA *46.17N 118.21W*
32 H6 **Prescott** Wisconsin, N USA *44.46N 92.45W*
193 A24 **Preservation Inlet** *inlet* South Island, NZ
114 O7 **Preševo** Serbia, SE Serbia *42.20N 21.38E*
31 N10 **Presho** South Dakota, N USA *43.54N 100.03W*
60 M13 **Presidente Dutra** Maranhão, E Brazil *5.16S 44.30W*
62 I8 **Presidente Epitácio** São Paulo, S Brazil *21.45S 52.07W*
64 N5 **Presidente Hayes** *off.* Departamento de Presidente Hayes. ⬖ *department* C Paraguay
62 I9 **Presidente Prudente** São Paulo, S Brazil *22.09S 51.24W*
Presidente Stroessner *see* Ciudad del Este
Presidente Vargas *see* Itabira
62 I8 **Presidente Venceslau** São Paulo, S Brazil *21.52S 51.51W*
199 L11 **President Thiers Seamount** *undersea feature* C Pacific Ocean *24.39S 145.50W*
26 J11 **Presidio** Texas, SW USA *29.33N 104.22W*
Preslav *see* Veliki Preslav
113 M19 **Prešov** *var.* Preschau, *Ger.* Eperies, *Hung.* Eperjes. Prešovský Kraj, E Slovakia *49.00N 21.13E*
113 M19 **Prešovský Kraj** ⬖ *region* E Slovakia
115 N20 **Prespa, Lake** *Alb.* Liqen i Prespës, *Gk.* Límni Megáli Préspa, Limni Prespa, Mac. Prespansko Ezero, *Serb.* Prespansko Jezero. ◎ SE Europe
Prespa, Limni/Prespansko Ezero/Prespansko Jezero/Prespës, Liqen i *see* Prespa, Lake
21 S2 **Presque Isle** Maine, NE USA *46.40N 68.01W*
20 B11 **Presque Isle** *headland* Pennsylvania, NE USA *42.09N 80.06W*
Pressburg *see* Bratislava
79 P17 **Prestea** SW Ghana *5.22N 2.07W*
113 B17 **Přeštice** *Ger.* Pschestitz. Plzeňský Kraj, W Czech Republic *49.36N 13.19E*
99 K17 **Preston** NW England, UK *53.46N 2.42W*
25 S6 **Preston** Georgia, SE USA *32.08N 84.35W*
35 R16 **Preston** Idaho, NW USA *42.06N 111.52W*
31 Z13 **Preston** Iowa, C USA *42.03N 90.24W*
31 X11 **Preston** Minnesota, N USA *43.41N 92.06W*
23 O6 **Prestonsburg** Kentucky, S USA *37.40N 82.46W*
98 I13 **Prestwick** W Scotland, UK *55.30N 4.39W*
Pretoria *see* Tshwane
Pretoria-Witwatersrand-Vereeniging *see* Gauteng
Pretusha *see* Pretushë
115 M21 **Pretushë** *var.* Pretusha. Korçë, SE Albania *40.50N 20.45E*
Preussisch Eylau *see* Bagrationovsk
Preussisch-Stargard *see* Starogard Gdański
Preußisch Holland *see* Pasłęk
117 C17 **Préveza** Ípeiros, W Greece *38.58N 20.43E*
39 V3 **Prewitt Reservoir** ⊠ Colorado, C USA
178 J13 **Prey Vêng** Prey Vêng, S Cambodia *11.30N 105.19E*
150 M12 **Priaral'skiye Karakumy, Peski** *desert* SW Kazakhstan
126 L16 **Priargunsk** Chitinskaya Oblast', S Russian Federation *50.25N 119.12E*
40 K14 **Pribilof Islands** *island group* Alaska, USA
115 K14 **Priboj** Serbia, W Serbia *43.34N 19.33E*
113 C17 **Příbram** *Ger.* Pibrans. Středočeský Kraj, W Czech Republic *49.40N 14.01E*
38 M4 **Price** Utah, W USA *39.34N 110.48W*
39 N5 **Price River** ≈ Utah, W USA
25 N8 **Prichard** Alabama, S USA *30.44N 88.04W*
27 R8 **Priddy** Texas, SW USA *31.39N 98.30W*
107 P8 **Priego** Castilla-La Mancha, C Spain *40.25N 2.19W*
106 M14 **Priego de Córdoba** Andalucía, S Spain *37.27N 4.12W*
120 C10 **Priekule** *Ger.* Preenkuln. Liepāja, SW Latvia *56.26N 21.36E*
120 C12 **Priekulė** *Ger.* Prökuls. Klaipėda, W Lithuania *55.36N 21.16E*
121 F14 **Prienai** *Pol.* Preny. Kaunas, S Lithuania *54.37N 23.56E*
85 G23 **Prieska** Northern Cape, C South Africa *29.40S 22.45E*
34 M7 **Priest Lake** ⊠ Idaho, NW USA
34 M7 **Priest River** Idaho, NW USA *48.10N 117.02W*
106 M3 **Prieta, Peña** ▲ N Spain *43.01N 4.42W*
42 J10 **Prieto, Cerro** ▲ C Mexico *24.10N 105.21W*
113 J19 **Prievidza** *var.* Priewitz, *Ger.* Priwitz, *Hung.* Privigye. Trenčiansky Kraj, C Slovakia *48.48N 18.37E*
Priewitz *see* Prievidza
114 F10 **Prijedor** Republika Srpska, NW Bosnia & Herzegovina *45.00N 16.43E*
115 K14 **Prijepolje** Serbia, W Serbia *43.24N 19.39E*
Prikaspiyskaya Nizmennost' *see* Caspian Depression
115 O19 **Prilep** *Turk.* Perlepe. S FYR Macedonia *41.21N 21.33E*
110 B9 **Prilly** Vaud, SW Switzerland *46.32N 6.36E*
Priluki *see* Pryluky
64 L10 **Primero, Río** ≈ C Argentina
31 S12 **Primghar** Iowa, C USA *43.05N 95.37W*
114 B9 **Primorje-Gorski Kotar** *off.* Primorsko-Goranska Županija. ⬖ *province* NW Croatia
120 A13 **Primorsk** *Ger.* Fischhausen. Kaliningradskaya Oblast', W Russian Federation *54.45N 20.00E*
128 G12 **Primorsk** *Fin.* Koivisto. Leningradskaya Oblast', NW Russian Federation *60.20N 28.39E*
Primorsk/Primorskoye *see* Prymors'k
127 Nn17 **Primorskiy Kray** *prev. Eng.* Maritime Territory. ⬖ *territory* SE Russian Federation
116 N10 **Primorsko** *prev.* Keupriya. Burgas, E Bulgaria *42.15N 27.45E*
130 K13 **Primorsko-Akhtarsk** Krasnodarskiy Kray, SW Russian Federation *46.03N 38.44E*
119 U13 **Primors'kyy** Respublika Krym, S Ukraine *45.09N 35.33E*
115 D14 **Primošten** Šibenik-Knin, S Croatia *43.34N 15.57E*

◆ Country
● Country Capital
◇ Dependent Territory
○ Dependent Territory Capital
⬖ Administrative Region
✕ International Airport
▲ Mountain
▲▲ Mountain Range
Volcano
≈ River
◎ Lake
⊠ Reservoir

Primrose Lake – Putten

9 R13 **Primrose Lake** ◎ Saskatchewan, C Canada
9 T14 **Prince Albert** Saskatchewan, S Canada *53.08N 105.43W*
85 G25 **Prince Albert** Western Cape, SW South Africa *33.13S 22.03E*
15 I1 **Prince Albert Peninsula** *peninsula* Victoria Island, Northwest Territories, NW Canada
15 I3 **Prince Albert Sound** *inlet* Northwest Territories, N Canada
15 Mm2 **Prince Charles Island** *island* Nunavut, NE Canada
205 W6 **Prince Charles Mountains** ⛰ Antarctica
Prince-Édouard, Île-du *see* Prince Edward Island
180 M13 **Prince Edward Fracture Zone** *tectonic feature* SW Indian Ocean
11 P14 **Prince Edward Island** ***Fr.*** Île-du Prince-Édouard. ◈ *province* SE Canada
11 Q14 **Prince Edward Island** ***Fr.*** Île-du Prínce-Édouard. *island* SE Canada
181 M12 **Prince Edward Islands** *island group* S South Africa
23 X4 **Prince Frederick** Maryland, NE USA *38.32N 76.33W*
8 M14 **Prince George** British Columbia, SW Canada *53.55N 122.49W*
23 W6 **Prince George** Virginia, NE USA *37.13N 77.13W*
207 O8 **Prince Gustaf Adolf Sea** *sea* Nunavut, N Canada
207 Q3 **Prince of Wales, Cape** *headland* Alaska, USA *65.39N 168.12W*
189 V1 **Prince of Wales Island** *island* Queensland, E Australia
15 Jj1 **Prince of Wales Island** *island* Queen Elizabeth Islands, Nunavut, NW Canada
41 Y14 **Prince of Wales Island** *island* Alexander Archipelago, Alaska, USA
Prince of Wales Island *see* Pinang, Pulau
15 I1 **Prince of Wales Strait** *strait* Northwest Territories, N Canada
207 O8 **Prince Patrick Island** *island* Parry Islands, Northwest Territories, NW Canada
15 Kk1 **Prince Regent Inlet** *channel* Nunavut, N Canada
8 J13 **Prince Rupert** British Columbia, SW Canada *54.18N 130.16W*
Prince's Island *see* Príncipe
23 Y5 **Princess Anne** Maryland, NE USA *38.12N 75.48W*
205 R1 **Princess Astrid Kyst** *physical region* Antarctica
189 W2 **Princess Charlotte Bay** *bay* Queensland, NE Australia
205 W7 **Princess Elizabeth Land** *physical region* Antarctica
8 J14 **Princess Royal Island** *island* British Columbia, SW Canada
47 U15 **Princes Town** Trinidad, Trinidad and Tobago *10.16N 61.22W*
9 N17 **Princeton** British Columbia, SW Canada *49.25N 120.34W*
32 L11 **Princeton** Illinois, N USA *41.22N 89.27W*
33 N16 **Princeton** Indiana, N USA *38.21N 87.33W*
31 Z14 **Princeton** Iowa, C USA *41.40N 90.21W*
22 H7 **Princeton** Kentucky, S USA *37.06N 87.52W*
31 V8 **Princeton** Minnesota, N USA *45.34N 93.34W*
29 S1 **Princeton** Missouri, C USA *40.24N 93.34W*
20 J15 **Princeton** New Jersey, NE USA *40.21N 74.39W*
23 R6 **Princeton** West Virginia, NE USA *37.22N 81.06W*
41 S12 **Prince William Sound** *inlet* Alaska, USA
69 P9 **Príncipe** ***var.*** Príncipe Island, ***Eng.*** Prince's Island. *island* N Sao Tome and Principe
Príncipe Island *see* Príncipe
34 I13 **Prineville** Oregon, NW USA *44.18N 120.50W*
30 J11 **Pringle** South Dakota, N USA *43.34N 103.34W*
27 N1 **Pringle** Texas, SW USA *35.55N 101.28W*
101 H14 **Prinsenbeek** Noord-Brabant, S Netherlands *51.36N 4.42E*
100 L6 **Prinses Margriet Kanaal** *canal* N Netherlands
205 T2 **Prinsesse Ragnhild Kyst** *physical region* Antarctica
205 U2 **Prins Harald Kyst** *physical region* Antarctica
94 N2 **Prins Karls Forland** *island* W Svalbard
45 N8 **Prinzapolka** Región Autónoma Atlántico Norte, NE Nicaragua *13.19N 83.34W*
44 L8 **Prinzapolka, Río** ≈ NE Nicaragua
125 Ff9 **Priob'ye** Khanty-Mansiyskiy Avtonomnyy Okrug, N Russian Federation *62.25N 65.36E*
106 H1 **Prior, Cabo** *headland* NW Spain *43.33N 8.21W*
31 V9 **Prior Lake** Minnesota, N USA *44.42N 93.25W*
128 H11 **Priozersk** ***Fin.*** Käkisalmi. Leningradskaya Oblast', NW Russian Federation *61.02N 30.07E*
121 J20 **Pripet** ***Bel.*** Prypyats', ***Ukr.*** Pryp"yat'. ≈ Belarus/Ukraine
121 J20 **Pripet Marshes** *wetland* Belarus/Ukraine
Prishtinë *see* Priština
130 J8 **Pristen'** Kurskaya Oblast', W Russian Federation *51.15N 36.47E*
115 N16 **Priština** ***Alb.*** Prishtinë. Serbia, S Serbia *42.39N 21.09E*
102 M10 **Pritzwalk** Brandenburg, NE Germany *53.10N 12.11E*
105 R13 **Privas** Ardèche, E France *44.45N 4.34E*
109 I16 **Priverno** Lazio, C Italy *41.28N 13.10E*
Privigye *see* Prievidza
114 C12 **Privlaka** Zadar, SW Croatia *44.15N 15.07E*
128 M15 **Privolzhsk** Ivanovskaya Oblast', NW Russian Federation *57.24N 41.16E*
131 P7 **Privolzhskaya Vozvyshennost'** ***var.*** Volga Uplands. ⛰ W Russian Federation
131 P8 **Privolzhskoye** Saratovskaya Oblast', W Russian Federation *51.08N 45.57E*
Priwitz *see* Prievidza
131 N13 **Priyutnoye** Respublika Kalmykiya, SW Russian Federation *46.08N 43.33E*
115 M17 **Prizren** ***Alb.*** Prizreni. Serbia, S Serbia *42.13N 20.46E*
Prizreni *see* Prizren
109 I24 **Prizzi** Sicilia, Italy, C Mediterranean Sea *37.43N 13.25E*
115 P18 **Probištip** NE FYR Macedonia *42.00N 22.06E*
174 M15 **Probolinggo** Jawa, C Indonesia *7.45S 113.12E*
Probstberg *see* Wyszków
113 F14 **Prochowice** ***Ger.*** Parchwitz. Dolnośląskie, SW Poland *51.15N 16.22E*
31 W5 **Proctor** Minnesota, N USA *46.46N 92.13W*
27 R8 **Proctor** Texas, SW USA *31.57N 98.25W*
27 R8 **Proctor Lake** ▣ Texas, SW USA
161 I18 **Proddatūr** Andhra Pradesh, E India *14.46N 78.39E*
106 H9 **Proença-a-Nova** Castelo Branco, C Portugal *39.45N 7.55W*
97 I24 **Præstø** Storstrøm, SE Denmark *55.07N 12.03E*
101 I21 **Profondeville** Namur, SE Belgium *50.22N 4.52E*
43 W11 **Progreso** Yucatán, SE Mexico *21.14N 89.40W*
126 Mm16 **Progress** Amurskaya Oblast', SE Russian Federation *49.40N 129.30E*
131 O15 **Prokhladnyy** Kabardino-Balkarskaya Respublika, SW Russian Federation *43.48N 44.02E*
Prokletije *see* North Albanian Alps
126 H14 **Prokop'yevsk** Kemerovskaya Oblast', S Russian Federation *53.56N 86.48E*
Prökuls *see* Priekulė
115 O15 **Prokuplje** Serbia, SE Serbia *43.15N 21.35E*
128 H14 **Proletariy** Novgorodskaya Oblast', W Russian Federation *58.24N 31.40E*
130 M12 **Proletarsk** Rostovskaya Oblast', SW Russian Federation *46.42N 41.48E*
130 J8 **Proletarskiy** Belgorodskaya Oblast', W Russian Federation *50.48N 35.46E*
177 Ff7 **Prome** ***var.*** Pyè. Pegu, C Burma *18.49N 95.13E*
62 J8 **Promissão** São Paulo, S Brazil *21.33S 49.51W*
62 J8 **Promissão, Represa de** ▣ S Brazil
129 V4 **Promyshlennyy** Respublika Komi, NW Russian Federation *67.36N 63.59E*
121 O16 **Pronya** ***Rus.*** Pronya. ≈ E Belarus
8 M11 **Prophet River** British Columbia, W Canada *58.07N 122.39W*
32 K11 **Prophetstown** Illinois, N USA *41.40N 89.56W*
61 P16 **Propriá** Sergipe, E Brazil *10.15S 36.51W*
105 X16 **Propriano** Corse, France, C Mediterranean Sea *41.41N 8.54E*
Prościejów *see* Prostějov
Proskurov *see* Khmel 'nyts'kyy
116 H12 **Prosotsáni** Anatolikí Makedonía kai Thráki, NE Greece *41.10N 23.58E*
179 Rr15 **Prosperidad** Mindanao, S Philippines *8.36N 125.54E*
34 J10 **Prosser** Washington, NW USA *46.12N 119.46W*
Prossnitz *see* Prostějov
113 G18 **Prostějov** ***Ger.*** Prossnitz, ***Pol.*** Prościejów. Olomoucký Kraj, E Czech Republic *49.28N 17.07E*
119 V8 **Prosyana** Dnipropetrovs'ka Oblast', E Ukraine *48.07N 36.22E*
113 L16 **Proszowice** Małopolskie, S Poland *50.12N 20.15E*
Protasy *see* Pratasy
180 J11 **Protea Seamount** *undersea feature* SW Indian Ocean *36.49S 18.04E*
117 D21 **Próti** *island* S Greece
116 N8 **Provadiya** Varna, E Bulgaria *43.10N 27.28E*
105 S15 **Provence** ***prev.*** Marseille-Marignane. ✈ (Marseille) Bouches-du-Rhône, SE France *43.25N 5.15E*
105 T14 **Provence** *cultural region* SE France
105 T14 **Provence-Alpes-Côte d'Azur** ◈ *region* SE France
22 H6 **Providence** Kentucky, S USA *37.23N 87.47W*
21 N12 **Providence** *state capital* Rhode Island, NE USA *41.50N 71.26W*
38 L1 **Providence** Utah, W USA *41.42N 111.49W*
Providence *see* Fort Providence
69 X10 **Providence Atoll** ***var.*** Providence. *atoll* S Seychelles
12 D12 **Providence Bay** Manitoulin Island, Ontario, S Canada *45.39N 82.16W*
25 R6 **Providence Canyon** *valley* Alabama/Georgia, S USA
24 I5 **Providence, Lake** ◎ Louisiana, S USA
37 X13 **Providence Mountains** ⛰ California, W USA
46 L6 **Providenciales** *island* W Turks and Caicos Islands
127 Q4 **Provideniya** Chukotskiy Avtonomnyy Okrug, NE Russian Federation *64.22N 173.14W*
21 Q12 **Provincetown** Massachusetts, NE USA *42.01N 70.10W*
105 P5 **Provins** Seine-et-Marne, N France *48.34N 3.18E*
38 L3 **Provo** Utah, W USA *40.13N 111.39W*
9 R15 **Provost** Alberta, SW Canada *52.24N 110.16W*
114 G13 **Prozor** Federacija Bosna I Hercegovina, SW Bosnia & Herzegovina *43.46N 17.38E*
Prozoroki *see* Prazaroki
62 I11 **Prudentópolis** Paraná, S Brazil *25.12S 50.58W*
41 R5 **Prudhoe Bay** Alaska, USA *70.16N 148.18W*
41 R4 **Prudhoe Bay** *bay* Alaska, USA
113 H16 **Prudnik** ***Ger.*** Neustadt, Neustadt in Oberschlesien. Opolskie, S Poland *50.19N 17.34E*
121 J16 **Prudy** ***Rus.*** Prudy. Minskaya Voblasts', C Belarus *53.48N 26.32E*
103 D18 **Prüm** Rheinland-Pfalz, W Germany *50.15N 6.27E*
103 D18 **Prüm** ≈ W Germany
Prusa *see* Bursa
112 J7 **Pruszcz Gdański** ***Ger.*** Praust. Pomorskie, N Poland *54.16N 18.36E*
112 M12 **Pruszków** ***Ger.*** Kaltdorf. Mazowieckie, C Poland *52.09N 20.49E*
118 K8 **Prut** ***Ger.*** Pruth. ≈ E Europe
Pruth *see* Prut
110 L8 **Prutz** Tirol, W Austria *47.07N 10.42E*
Pružana *see* Pruzhany
121 G19 **Pruzhany** ***Pol.*** Pružana. Brestskaya Voblasts', SW Belarus *52.33N 24.28E*
128 I11 **Pryazha** Respublika Kareliya, NW Russian Federation *61.42N 33.39E*
119 U10 **Pryazovs'ke** Zaporiz'ka Oblast', SE Ukraine *46.43N 35.39E*
Prychornomors'ka Nyzovyna *see* Black Sea Lowland
Prydniprovs'ka Nyzovyna/ Prydnyaprowskaya Nizina *see* Dnieper Lowland
205 Y7 **Prydz Bay** *bay* Antarctica
119 R4 **Pryluky** ***Rus.*** Priluki. Chernihivs'ka Oblast', NE Ukraine *50.34N 32.23E*
119 V10 **Prymors'k** ***Rus.*** Primorsk; ***prev.*** Primorskoye. Zaporiz'ka Oblast', SE Ukraine *46.43N 36.19E*
29 Q9 **Pryor** Oklahoma, C USA *36.18N 95.18W*
35 U11 **Pryor Creek** ≈ Montana, NW USA
Pryp"yat'/Prypyats' *see* Pripet
112 M10 **Przasnysz** Mazowieckie, C Poland *53.01N 20.53E*
113 K14 **Przedbórz** Łodzkie, S Poland *51.04N 19.51E*
113 P17 **Przemyśl** ***Rus.*** Peremyshl. Podkarpackie, SE Poland *49.46N 22.46E*
113 O16 **Przeworsk** Podkarpackie, SE Poland *50.04N 22.30E*
Przheval'sk *see* Karakol
112 L13 **Przysucha** Mazowieckie, SE Poland *51.22N 20.36E*
117 H18 **Psachná** ***var.*** Psahna, Psakhná. Évvoia, C Greece *38.34N 23.40E*
Psahna/Psakhná *see* Psachná
117 K18 **Psará** *island* E Greece
117 I16 **Psathoúra** *island* Vóreies Sporádes, Greece, Aegean Sea
Pschestitz *see* Přeštice
Psein Lora *see* Pishin Lora
119 S5 **Psël** ≈ Russian Federation/Ukraine
117 M21 **Psérimos** *island* Dodekánisa, Greece, Aegean Sea
Pseyn Bowr *see* Pishin Lora
Pskem *see* Piskom
153 R8 **Pskemskiy Khrebet** ***Uzb.*** Piskom Tizmasi. ⛰ Kyrgyzstan/Uzbekistan
128 F14 **Pskov** ***Ger.*** Pleskau, ***Latv.*** Pleskava. Pskovskaya Oblast', W Russian Federation *58.31N 31.15E*
120 K6 **Pskov, Lake** ***Est.*** Pihkva Järv, ***Ger.*** Pleskauer See, ***Rus.*** Pskovskoye Ozero. ◎ Estonia/Russian Federation
128 F15 **Pskovskaya Oblast'** ◈ *province* W Russian Federation
Pskovskoye Ozero *see* Pskov, Lake
114 G9 **Psunj** ⛰ NE Croatia
113 J17 **Pszczyna** ***Ger.*** Pless. Śląskie, S Poland *49.58N 18.56E*
Ptačnik/Ptacsnik *see* Vtáčnik
117 D17 **Ptéri** ▲ C Greece *39.08N 21.32E*
Ptich' *see* Ptsich
117 E14 **Ptolemaïda** ***prev.*** Ptolemaïs. Dytikí Makedonía, N Greece *40.31N 21.40E*
Ptolemaïs *see* Ptolemaïda, Greece
Ptolemaïs *see* 'Akko, Israel
123 Gg10 **Ptolemy Seamounts** *undersea feature* C Mediterranean Sea
121 M19 **Ptsich** ***Rus.*** Ptich'. Homyel'skaya Voblasts', SE Belarus *52.10N 28.49E*
121 M18 **Ptsich** ***Rus.*** Ptich'. ≈ SE Belarus
111 X10 **Ptuj** ***Ger.*** Pettau; ***anc.*** Poetovio. NE Slovenia *46.26N 15.53E*
194 E9 **Pua** ≈ NW PNG
63 A23 **Puán** Buenos Aires, E Argentina *37.34S 62.45W*
198 B7 **Pu'apu'a** Savai'i, C Samoa *13.31S 172.09W*
198 A7 **Puava, Cape** *headland* Savai'i, NW Samoa
58 F12 **Pucallpa** Ucayali, C Peru *8.21S 74.33W*
59 J17 **Pucarani** La Paz, NW Bolivia *16.18S 68.28W*
Pučarevo *see* Novi Travnik
163 U12 **Pucheng** ***var.*** Nanpu. Fujian, SE China *27.54N 118.34E*
166 L6 **Pucheng** Shaanxi, C China *34.55N 109.28E*
129 N16 **Puchezh** Ivanovskaya Oblast', W Russian Federation *56.58N 41.08E*
113 I19 **Púchov** ***Hung.*** Puhó. Trenčiansky Kraj, W Slovakia *49.06N 18.19E*
118 J13 **Pucioasa** Dâmbovița, S Romania *45.04N 25.22E*
112 I6 **Puck** Pomorskie, N Poland *54.43N 18.24E*
32 L8 **Puckaway Lake** ◎ Wisconsin, N USA
65 G15 **Pucón** Araucanía, S Chile *39.18S 71.52W*
95 M14 **Pudasjärvi** Oulu, C Finland *65.19N 27.01E*
154 L8 **Pūdeh Tal, Shelleh-ye** ≈ SW Afghanistan
131 S1 **Pudem** Udmurtskaya Respublika, NW Russian Federation *58.18N 52.08E*
Pudewitz *see* Pobiedziska
128 K11 **Pudozh** Respublika Kareliya, NW Russian Federation *61.48N 36.30E*
99 M17 **Pudsey** N England, UK *53.48N 1.40W*
Puduchcheri *see* Pondicherry
157 H21 **Pudukkottai** Tamil Nādu, SE India *10.22N 78.46E*
176 Z10 **Pue** Papua, E Indonesia *2.42S 140.36E*
43 P14 **Puebla** ***var.*** Puebla de Zaragoza. Puebla, S Mexico *19.02N 98.12W*
43 P15 **Puebla** ◈ *state* S Mexico
106 L11 **Puebla de Alcocer** Extremadura, W Spain *38.58N 5.13W*
Puebla de Don Fabrique *see* Puebla de Don Fadrique
107 P13 **Puebla de Don Fadrique** ***var.*** Puebla de Don Fabrique. Andalucía, S Spain *37.58N 2.25W*
106 J11 **Puebla de la Calzada** Extremadura, W Spain *38.54N 6.37W*
106 J5 **Puebla de Sanabria** Castilla-León, N Spain *42.04N 6.37W*
Puebla de Trives *see* A Pobla de Trives
Puebla de Zaragoza *see* Puebla
39 T6 **Pueblo** Colorado, C USA *38.15N 104.36W*
39 N10 **Pueblo Colorado Wash** *valley* Arizona, SW USA
63 C16 **Pueblo Libertador** Corrientes, NE Argentina *30.13S 59.22W*
42 J10 **Pueblo Nuevo** Durango, C Mexico *23.24N 105.21W*
44 J8 **Pueblo Nuevo** Estelí, NW Nicaragua *13.24N 86.26W*
56 J3 **Pueblo Nuevo** Falcón, N Venezuela *11.58N 69.57W*
44 B6 **Pueblo Nuevo Tiquisate** ***var.*** Tiquisate. Escuintla, SW Guatemala *14.16N 91.21W*
43 Q11 **Pueblo Viejo, Laguna de** *lagoon* E Mexico
65 J14 **Puelches** La Pampa, C Argentina *38.08S 65.56W*
106 L14 **Puente-Genil** Andalucía, S Spain *37.23N 4.45W*
107 Q3 **Puente la Reina** ***Bas.*** Gares. Navarra, N Spain *42.40N 1.49W*
106 L12 **Puente Nuevo, Embalse de** ▣ S Spain
59 D14 **Puente Piedra** Lima, W Peru *11.49S 77.01W*
166 F14 **Pu'er** ***var.*** Ning'er. Yunnan, SW China *23.09N 100.57E*
47 V6 **Puerca, Punta** *headland* E Puerto Rico *18.13N 65.36W*
39 R12 **Puerco, Rio** ≈ New Mexico, SW USA
59 J17 **Puerto Acosta** La Paz, W Bolivia *15.33S 69.15W*
65 G19 **Puerto Aisén** Aisén, S Chile *45.24S 72.42W*
43 R17 **Puerto Ángel** Oaxaca, SE Mexico *15.39N 96.29W*
Puerto Argentino *see* Stanley
43 T17 **Puerto Arista** Chiapas, SE Mexico *15.55N 93.47W*
45 O16 **Puerto Armuelles** Chiriquí, SW Panama *8.16N 82.51W*
Puerto Arrecife *see* Arrecife
56 D14 **Puerto Asís** Putumayo, SW Colombia *0.27N 76.27W*
56 L9 **Puerto Ayacucho** Amazonas, SW Venezuela *5.44N 67.36W*
59 C18 **Puerto Ayora** Galapagos Islands, Ecuador, E Pacific Ocean *0.45S 90.19W*
59 C18 **Puerto Baquerizo Moreno** ***var.*** Baquerizo Moreno. Galapagos Islands, Ecuador, E Pacific Ocean *0.54S 89.37W*
44 G4 **Puerto Barrios** Izabal, E Guatemala *15.42N 88.34W*
Puerto Bello *see* Portobelo
56 F8 **Puerto Berrío** Antioquia, C Colombia *6.25N 74.27W*
56 F9 **Puerto Boyaca** Boyacá, C Colombia *5.58N 74.36W*
56 K4 **Puerto Cabello** Carabobo, N Venezuela *10.27N 68.02W*
45 N7 **Puerto Cabezas** ***var.*** Bilwi. Región Autónoma Atlántico Norte, NE Nicaragua *14.04N 83.22W*
56 L9 **Puerto Carreño** Vichada, E Colombia *6.08N 67.30W*
56 E4 **Puerto Colombia** Atlántico, N Colombia *10.58N 74.57W*
44 H4 **Puerto Cortés** Cortés, NW Honduras *15.49N 87.55W*
56 J4 **Puerto Cumarebo** Falcón, N Venezuela *11.28N 69.21W*
Puerto de Cabras *see* Puerto del Rosario
57 Q5 **Puerto de Hierro** Sucre, NE Venezuela *10.40N 62.03W*
66 O11 **Puerto de la Cruz** Tenerife, Islas Canarias, Spain, NE Atlantic Ocean *28.24N 16.33W*
66 Q11 **Puerto del Rosario** ***var.*** Puerto de Cabras. Fuerteventura, Islas Canarias, Spain, NE Atlantic Ocean *28.28N 13.52W*
65 J20 **Puerto Deseado** Santa Cruz, SE Argentina *47.46S 65.52W*
42 F8 **Puerto Escondido** Baja California Sur, W Mexico *25.49N 111.20W*
43 R17 **Puerto Escondido** Oaxaca, SE Mexico *15.48N 96.57W*
62 G12 **Puerto Esperanza** Misiones, NE Argentina *26.01S 54.39W*
58 D6 **Puerto Francisco de Orellana** ***var.*** Coca. Orellana, N Ecuador *0.27S 76.57W*
56 H10 **Puerto Gaitán** Meta, C Colombia *4.19N 72.07W*
Puerto Gallegos *see* Río Gallegos
62 G12 **Puerto Iguazú** Misiones, NE Argentina *25.39S 54.34W*
58 F12 **Puerto Inca** Huánuco, N Peru *9.21S 74.55W*
56 L11 **Puerto Inírida** ***var.*** Obando. Guainía, E Colombia *3.48N 67.54W*
44 K13 **Puerto Jesús** Guanacaste, NW Costa Rica *10.08N 85.26W*
43 Z11 **Puerto Juárez** Quintana Roo, SE Mexico *21.06N 86.46W*
57 N5 **Puerto La Cruz** Anzoátegui, NE Venezuela *10.13N 64.40W*
56 E14 **Puerto Leguízamo** Putumayo, S Colombia *0.07S 74.51W*
45 N5 **Puerto Lempira** Gracias a Dios, E Honduras *15.13N 83.48W*
Puerto Libertad *see* La Libertad
56 I11 **Puerto Limón** Meta, E Colombia *4.00N 71.09W*
56 D13 **Puerto Limón** Putumayo, SW Colombia *1.01N 76.30W*
Puerto Limón *see* Limón
107 N11 **Puertollano** Castilla-La Mancha, C Spain *38.40N 4.07W*
65 K17 **Puerto Lobos** Chubut, SE Argentina *42.00S 64.58W*
56 I3 **Puerto López** La Guajira, N Colombia *11.54N 71.21W*
107 Q14 **Puerto Lumbreras** Murcia, SE Spain *37.34N 1.49W*
43 V17 **Puerto Madero** Chiapas, SE Mexico *14.43N 92.25W*
65 K17 **Puerto Madryn** Chubut, S Argentina *42.45S 65.01W*
Puerto Magdalena *see* Bahía Magdalena
59 J15 **Puerto Maldonado** Madre de Dios, E Peru *12.37S 69.10W*
Puerto Masachapa *see* Masachapa
Puerto México *see* Coatzacoalcos
65 G17 **Puerto Montt** Los Lagos, C Chile *41.28S 72.57W*
43 Z12 **Puerto Morelos** Quintana Roo, SE Mexico *20.47N 86.54W*
56 L10 **Puerto Nariño** Vichada, E Colombia *4.57N 67.51W*
65 H23 **Puerto Natales** Magallanes, S Chile *51.42S 72.28W*
45 X15 **Puerto Obaldía** San Blas, NE Panama *8.37N 77.25W*
46 H6 **Puerto Padre** Las Tunas, E Cuba *21.13N 76.34W*
56 L9 **Puerto Páez** Apure, C Venezuela *6.10N 67.30W*
42 E3 **Puerto Peñasco** Sonora, NW Mexico *31.21N 113.32W*
57 N5 **Puerto Píritu** Anzoátegui, NE Venezuela *10.02N 65.02W*
47 N8 **Puerto Plata** ***var.*** San Felipe de Puerto Plata. N Dominican Republic *19.46N 70.42W*
47 N8 **Puerto Plata** ✈ N Dominican Republic *19.43N 70.43W*
Puerto Presidente Stroessner *see* Ciudad del Este
179 Oo14 **Puerto Princesa** ***off.*** Puerto Princesa City. Palawan, W Philippines *9.48N 118.43E*
Puerto Princesa City *see* Puerto Princesa
Puerto Príncipe *see* Camagüey
Puerto Quellón *see* Quellón
62 F13 **Puerto Rico** Misiones, NE Argentina *26.48S 54.58W*
59 K14 **Puerto Rico** Pando, N Bolivia *11.09S 67.28W*
56 E12 **Puerto Rico** Caquetá, S Colombia *1.53N 75.08W*
47 U5 **Puerto Rico** ***off.*** Commonwealth of Puerto Rico; ***prev.*** Porto Rico. ◇ *US commonwealth territory* C West Indies
66 F11 **Puerto Rico** *island* C West Indies
66 G11 **Puerto Rico Trench** *undersea feature* NE Caribbean Sea
56 I8 **Puerto Rondón** Arauca, E Colombia *6.16N 71.05W*
Puerto San José *see* San José
65 J21 **Puerto San Julián** ***var.*** San Julián. Santa Cruz, SE Argentina *49.14S 67.40W*
65 I22 **Puerto Santa Cruz** ***var.*** Santa Cruz. Santa Cruz, SE Argentina *50.05S 68.31W*
Puerto Sauce *see* Juan L.Lacaze
59 Q20 **Puerto Suárez** Santa Cruz, E Bolivia *18.58S 57.47W*
56 D13 **Puerto Umbría** Putumayo, SW Colombia *0.52N 76.31W*
42 J13 **Puerto Vallarta** Jalisco, SW Mexico *20.36N 105.15W*
65 G16 **Puerto Varas** Los Lagos, C Chile *41.24S 72.55W*
44 M13 **Puerto Viejo** Heredia, NE Costa Rica *10.27N 84.00W*
Puertoviejo *see* Portoviejo
59 B18 **Puerto Villamil** ***var.*** Villamil. Galapagos Islands, Ecuador, E Pacific Ocean *0.57S 91.00W*
56 F8 **Puerto Wilches** Santander, N Colombia *7.19N 73.55W*
65 H20 **Pueyrredón, Lago** ***var.*** Lago Cochrane. ◎ S Argentina
131 R7 **Pugachëv** Saratovskaya Oblast', W Russian Federation *52.06N 48.50E*
131 T3 **Pugachëvo** Udmurtskaya Respublika, NW Russian Federation *56.38N 53.03E*
34 H8 **Puget Sound** *sound* Washington, NW USA
109 O17 **Puglia** ***var.*** Le Puglie, ***Eng.*** Apulia. ◈ *region* SE Italy
109 N17 **Puglia, Canosa di** ***anc.*** Canusium. Puglia, SE Italy *41.13N 16.04E*
120 I6 **Puhja** ***Ger.*** Kawelecht. Tartumaa, SE Estonia *58.19N 26.19E*
Puhó *see* Púchov
107 V4 **Puigcerdà** Cataluña, NE Spain *42.25N 1.53E*
Puigmal *see* Puigmal d'Err
105 N17 **Puigmal d'Err** ***var.*** Puigmal. ▲ S France *42.24N 2.07E*
78 I16 **Pujehun** S Sierra Leone *7.22N 11.43W*
Puka *see* Pukë
193 E20 **Pukaki, Lake** ◎ South Island, NZ
40 F10 **Pukalani** Maui, Hawai'i, USA, C Pacific Ocean *20.50N 94.20W*
202 J13 **Pukapuka** *atoll* N Cook Islands
203 X9 **Pukapuka** *atoll* Îles Tuamotu, E French Polynesia
Pukari Neem *see* Purekkari Neem
203 X11 **Pukarua** ***var.*** Pukaruha. *atoll* Îles Tuamotu, E French Polynesia
Pukaruha *see* Pukarua
12 A7 **Pukaskwa** ≈ Ontario, S Canada
9 V12 **Pukatawagan** Manitoba, C Canada *55.46N 101.13W*
203 X16 **Pukatikei, Maunga** Ѫ Easter Island, Chile, E Pacific Ocean
190 C1 **Pukatja** ***var.*** Ernabella. South Australia *26.18S 132.13E*
169 Y12 **Pukch'ŏng** E North Korea *40.13N 128.19E*
115 L18 **Pukë** ***var.*** Puka. Shkodër, N Albania *42.03N 19.53E*
192 L6 **Pukekohe** Auckland, North Island, NZ *37.12S 174.54E*
192 L7 **Pukemiro** Waikato, North Island, NZ *37.37S 175.02E*
202 D12 **Puke, Mont** ▲ Île Futuna, W Wallis and Futuna
Puket *see* Phuket
193 C20 **Puketeraki Range** ⛰ South Island, NZ
192 N13 **Puketoi Range** ⛰ North Island, NZ
193 F21 **Pukeuri Junction** Otago, South Island, NZ *45.01S 171.01E*
121 L16 **Pukhavichy** ***Rus.*** Pukhovichi. Minskaya Voblasts', C Belarus *53.30N 28.15E*
Pukhovichi *see* Pukhavichy
128 M10 **Puksoozero** Arkhangel'skaya Oblast', NW Russian Federation *62.37N 40.29E*
114 A10 **Pula** ***It.*** Pola; ***prev.*** Pulj. Istra, NW Croatia *44.53N 13.51E*
Pula *see* Nyingchi
169 U14 **Pulandian** ***var.*** Xinjin. Liaoning, NE China *39.25N 121.58E*
169 T14 **Pulandian Wan** *bay* NE China
179 Rr15 **Pulangi** ≈ Mindanao, S Philippines
201 O15 **Pulap Atoll** *atoll* Caroline Islands, C Micronesia
20 H9 **Pulaski** New York, NE USA *43.34N 76.06W*
22 I10 **Pulaski** Tennessee, S USA *35.11N 87.00W*
23 R7 **Pulaski** Virginia, NE USA *37.03N 80.46W*
176 Yy13 **Pulau, Sungai** ≈ Papua, E Indonesia
112 N13 **Puławy** ***Ger.*** Neu Amerika. Lubelskie, E Poland *51.25N 21.56E*
152 I16 **Pulhatyn** ***Rus.*** Polekhatum; ***prev.*** Pul'-I-Khatum. Ahal Welaýaty, S Turkmenistan *36.01N 61.08E*
103 E16 **Pulheim** Nordrhein-Westfalen, W Germany *51.00N 6.48E*
Pulicat *see* Pālghāt
161 J19 **Pulicat Lake** *lagoon* SE India
194 M12 **Pulie** ≈ New Britain, C PNG
Pul'-I-Khatum *see* Pulhatyn
Pul-i-Khumri *see* Pol-e Khomrī
Pul-i-Sefid *see* Pol-e Safīd
Pulj *see* Pula
111 W2 **Pulkau** ≈ NE Austria
95 L15 **Pulkkila** Oulu, C Finland *64.14N 25.52E*
125 Cc6 **Pul'kovo** ✈ (Sankt-Peterburg) Leningradskaya Oblast', NW Russian Federation *60.06N 30.23E*
34 M9 **Pullman** Washington, NW USA *46.43N 117.10W*
110 B10 **Pully** Vaud, SW Switzerland *46.31N 6.40E*
42 F7 **Púlpita, Punta** *headland* W Mexico *26.30N 111.28W*
112 M10 **Pułtusk** Mazowieckie, C Poland *52.41N 21.04E*
164 H10 **Pulu** Xinjiang Uygur Zizhiqu, W China *36.10N 81.28E*
143 P13 **Pülümür** Tunceli, E Turkey *39.30N 39.54E*
201 N16 **Pulusuk** *island* Caroline Islands, C Micronesia
201 N16 **Puluwat Atoll** *atoll* Caroline Islands, C Micronesia
27 N11 **Pumpville** Texas, SW USA *39.55N 101.43W*
203 P7 **Punaauia** ***var.*** Hakapehi. Tahiti, W French Polynesia *17.37S 149.37W*
58 B8 **Puná, Isla** *island* SW Ecuador
193 G16 **Punakaiki** West Coast, South Island, NZ *42.07S 171.21E*
159 T11 **Punakha** C Bhutan *27.37N 89.49E*
59 L18 **Punata** Cochabamba, C Bolivia *17.33S 65.52W*
161 E14 **Pune** ***prev.*** Poona. Mahārāshtra, W India *18.31N 73.52E*
85 M17 **Pungoè, Rio** ***var.*** Púnguè, Pungwe. ≈ C Mozambique
23 X10 **Pungo River** ≈ North Carolina, SE USA
Púnguè/Pungwe *see* Pungoè, Rio
81 N19 **Punia** Maniema, E Dem. Rep. Congo *1.28S 26.25E*
64 H8 **Punilla, Sierra de la** ⛰ W Argentina
167 P14 **Puning** Guangdong, S China *23.18N 116.12E*
64 G10 **Punitaqui** Coquimbo, C Chile *30.49S 71.13W*
158 H8 **Punjab** ◈ *state* NW India
155 T9 **Punjab** ***prev.*** West Punjab, Western Punjab. ◈ *province* E Pakistan
133 Q9 **Punjab Plains** *plain* N India
95 O17 **Punkaharju** ***var.*** Punkasalmi. Isä-Suomi, E Finland *61.45N 29.21E*
Punkasalmi *see* Punkaharju
59 I17 **Puno** Puno, SE Peru *15.52S 70.03W*
59 H17 **Puno** ***off.*** Departamento de Puno. ◈ *department* S Peru
63 B24 **Punta Alta** Buenos Aires, E Argentina *38.53S 62.00W*
65 H24 **Punta Arenas** ***prev.*** Magallanes. Magallanes, S Chile *53.10S 70.55W*
47 T6 **Punta, Cerro de** ▲ C Puerto Rico *18.10N 66.36W*
45 T15 **Punta Chame** Panamá, C Panama *8.39N 79.42W*
59 G17 **Punta Colorada** Arequipa, SW Peru *16.17S 72.31W*
42 F9 **Punta Coyote** Baja California Sur, W Mexico
64 G8 **Punta de Díaz** Atacama, N Chile *28.03S 70.36W*
63 G20 **Punta del Este** Maldonado, S Uruguay *34.58S 54.58W*
65 K17 **Punta Delgada** Chubut, SE Argentina *42.46S 63.40W*
57 O5 **Punta de Mata** Monagas, NE Venezuela *9.43N 63.39W*
57 O4 **Punta de Piedras** Nueva Esparta, NE Venezuela *10.54N 64.06W*
44 F4 **Punta Gorda** Toledo, SE Belize *16.07N 88.47W*
45 N11 **Punta Gorda** Región Autónoma Atlántico Sur, SE Nicaragua *11.31N 83.46W*
25 W14 **Punta Gorda** Florida, SE USA *26.55N 82.03W*
44 M11 **Punta Gorda, Río** ≈ SE Nicaragua
64 H6 **Punta Negra, Salar de** *salt lake* N Chile
42 D5 **Punta Prieta** Baja California, NW Mexico *28.55N 114.10W*
44 L13 **Puntarenas** Puntarenas, W Costa Rica *9.57N 84.49W*
44 L13 **Puntarenas** ***off.*** Provincia de Puntarenas. ◈ *province* W Costa Rica
82 P13 **Puntland** *cultural region* NE Somalia
56 J4 **Punto Fijo** Falcón, N Venezuela *11.42N 70.13W*
107 S4 **Puntón de Guara** ▲ N Spain *42.18N 0.13W*
20 D14 **Punxsutawney** Pennsylvania, NE USA *40.55N 78.57W*
95 M14 **Puolanka** Oulu, C Finland *64.51N 27.42E*
59 J17 **Pupuya, Nevado** ▲ W Bolivia *15.04S 69.01W*
Puqi *see* Chibi
59 F16 **Puquio** Ayacucho, S Peru *14.43S 74.06W*
126 H9 **Pur** ≈ N Russian Federation
194 I13 **Purari** ≈ S PNG
29 N11 **Purcell** Oklahoma, C USA *35.00N 97.21W*
9 O16 **Purcell Mountains** ⛰ British Columbia, SW Canada
107 P14 **Purchena** Andalucía, S Spain *37.21N 2.21W*
29 S8 **Purdy** Missouri, C USA *36.49N 93.55W*
120 I2 **Purekkari Neem** ***prev.*** Pukari Neem. *headland* N Estonia *59.33N 24.49E*
39 U7 **Purgatoire River** ≈ Colorado, C USA
Purgstall *see* Purgstall an der Erlauf
111 V5 **Purgstall an der Erlauf** ***var.*** Purgstall. Niederösterreich, NE Austria *48.01N 15.08E*
160 O13 **Puri** ***var.*** Jagannath. Orissa, E India *19.52N 85.49E*
Puriramya *see* Buriram
111 X4 **Purkersdorf** Niederösterreich, NE Austria *48.13N 16.12E*
100 I9 **Purmerend** Noord-Holland, C Netherlands *52.30N 4.55E*
157 G16 **Pūrna** ≈ C India
Purnea *see* Pūrnia
159 R13 **Pūrnia** ***prev.*** Purnea. Bihār, NE India *25.46N 87.28E*
Pursat *see* Poŭthĭsăt, Poŭthĭsăt, W Cambodia
Pursat *see* Poŭthĭsăt, Stœng, W Cambodia
Purulia *see* Puruliya
156 L13 **Puruliya** ***prev.*** Purulia. West Bengal, NE India *23.19N 86.24E*
49 G7 **Purus, Rio** ***Sp.*** Río Purús. ≈ Brazil/Peru
194 G15 **Purutu Island** *island* SW PNG
95 N17 **Puruvesi** ◎ SE Finland
24 L7 **Purvis** Mississippi, S USA *31.08N 89.24W*
116 J11 **Pŭrvomay** ***prev.*** Borisovgrad. Plovdiv, C Bulgaria *42.06N 25.14E*
174 J14 **Purwakarta** ***prev.*** Poerwakarta. Jawa, C Indonesia *6.30S 107.25E*
174 L15 **Purwodadi** ***prev.*** Poerwodadi. Jawa, C Indonesia *7.04S 110.52E*
174 K15 **Purwokerto** ***prev.*** Poerwokerto. Jawa, C Indonesia *7.25S 109.13E*
174 Kk15 **Purworejo** ***prev.*** Poerworedjo. Jawa, C Indonesia *7.45S 110.04E*
22 H8 **Puryear** Tennessee, S USA *36.25N 88.21W*
160 H13 **Pusad** Mahārāshtra, C India *19.56N 77.40E*
169 Z16 **Pusan** ***off.*** Pusan-gwangyŏksi, ***var.*** Busan, ***Jap.*** Fusan. SE South Korea *35.11N 129.04E*
173 Ee4 **Pusatgajo, Pegunungan** ⛰ Sumatera, NW Indonesia
Puschlav *see* Poschiavo
Pushkin *see* Tsarskoye Selo
131 Q8 **Pushkino** Saratovskaya Oblast', W Russian Federation *51.09N 47.00E*
Pushkino *see* Biläsuvar
113 M22 **Püspökladány** Hajdú-Bihar, E Hungary *47.19N 21.04E*
120 J3 **Püssi** ***Ger.*** Isenhof. Ida-Virumaa, NE Estonia *59.21N 27.05E*
118 I5 **Pustomyty** L'vivs'ka Oblast', W Ukraine *49.43N 23.55E*
128 F16 **Pustoshka** Pskovskaya Oblast', W Russian Federation *56.21N 29.16E*
Pusztakalán *see* Călan
178 H1 **Putao** ***prev.*** Fort Hertz. Kachin State, N Burma *27.22N 97.24E*
192 M8 **Putaruru** Waikato, North Island, NZ *38.02S 175.46E*
Puteoli *see* Pozzuoli
167 R12 **Putian** Fujian, SE China *25.28N 119.01E*
109 O17 **Putignano** Puglia, SE Italy *40.51N 17.07E*
Puting *see* De'an
Putivl' *see* Putyvl'
43 Q16 **Putla** ***var.*** Putla de Guerrero. Oaxaca, SE Mexico *16.54N 97.55W*
Putla de Guerrero *see* Putla
21 N12 **Putnam** Connecticut, NE USA *41.56N 71.52W*
27 Q7 **Putnam** Texas, SW USA *32.22N 99.11W*
20 M10 **Putney** Vermont, NE USA *42.59N 72.30W*
113 L20 **Putnok** Borsod-Abaúj-Zemplén, NE Hungary *48.18N 20.25E*
Putorana, Gory/Putorana Mountains *see* Putorana, Plato
126 Ii8 **Putorana, Plato** ***var.*** Gory Putorana, ***Eng.*** Putorana Mountains. ⛰ N Russian Federation
174 H5 **Putrajaya** ● (Malaysia), Kuala Lumpur, Peninsular Malaysia *2.57N 101.42E*
64 H2 **Putre** Tarapacá, N Chile *18.11S 69.30W*
161 J24 **Puttalam** North Western Province, W Sri Lanka *8.01N 79.54E*
161 J24 **Puttalam Lagoon** *lagoon* W Sri Lanka
101 H17 **Putte** Antwerpen, C Belgium *51.04N 4.39E*
96 E10 **Puttegga** ▲ S Norway *62.13N 7.40E*
100 K11 **Putten** Gelderland, C Netherlands *52.15N 5.36E*

◆ Country
● Country Capital
◇ Dependent Territory
○ Dependent Territory Capital
◈ Administrative Region
✈ International Airport
▲ Mountain
⛰ Mountain Range
Ѫ Volcano
≈ River
◎ Lake
▣ Reservoir

PUTTGARDEN – QUSEIR

102 K7 **Puttgarden** Schleswig-Holstein, N Germany *54.30N 11.12E*
Puttiala *see* Patiāla
103 D20 **Püttlingen** Saarland, SW Germany *49.16N 6.52E*
56 D14 **Putumayo** *off.* Intendencia del Putumayo. ◈ *province* S Colombia
50 E7 **Putumayo, Río** *var.* Rio Içá. ≈ NW South America **see also** Içá, Rio
174 K8 **Putus, Tanjung** *headland* Borneo, N Indonesia *0.27S 109.04E*
118 J8 **Putyla** Chernivets'ka Oblast', W Ukraine *47.59N 25.04E*
119 S3 **Putyvl'** *Rus.* Putivl'. Sums'ka Oblast', NE Ukraine *51.21N 33.52E*
95 M18 **Puula** ◎ SE Finland
95 N18 **Puumala** Isä-Suomi, E Finland *61.31N 28.12E*
120 I5 **Puurmani** *Ger.* Talkhof. Jõgevamaa, E Estonia *58.36N 26.17E*
101 G17 **Puurs** Antwerpen, N Belgium *51.04N 4.16E*
40 F10 **Pu'u 'Ula'ula** *var.* Red Hill. ▲ Maui, Hawai'i, USA, C Pacific Ocean *20.42N 94.16W*
40 A8 **Pu'uwai** *var.* Puuwai. Ni'ihau, Hawai'i, USA, C Pacific Ocean *21.54N 96.11W*
10 J4 **Puvirnituq** *prev.* Povungnituk. Québec, NE Canada *60.10N 77.19W*
34 H8 **Puyallup** Washington, NW USA *47.11N 122.17W*
167 O5 **Puyang** Henan, C China *35.42N 115.03E*
167 R9 **Puyang Jiang** *var.* Tsien Tang. ≈ SE China
105 O11 **Puy-de-Dôme** ◈ *department* C France
105 N15 **Puylaurens** Tarn, S France *43.33N 2.01E*
104 M13 **Puy-l'Evêque** Lot, S France *44.31N 1.10E*
105 N17 **Puymorens, Col de** *pass* S France *42.33N 1.50E*
58 C7 **Puyo** Pastaza, C Ecuador *1.30S 77.58W*
193 A24 **Puysegur Point** *headland* South Island, NZ *46.09S 166.38E*
154 J8 **Pūzak, Hāmūn-e** *Pash.* Hāmūn-i-Puzak. ◎ SW Afghanistan
Puzak, Hāmūn-i- *see* Pūzak, Hāmūn-e
83 J23 **Pwani** *Eng.* Coast. ◈ *region* E Tanzania
81 O23 **Pweto** Katanga, SE Dem. Rep. Congo *8.29S 28.57E*
99 I19 **Pwllheli** NW Wales, UK *52.53N 4.22W*
201 O14 **Pwok** Pohnpei, E Micronesia
126 Gg10 **Pyakupur** ≈ N Russian Federation
128 M6 **Pyalitsa** Murmanskaya Oblast', NW Russian Federation *66.16N 39.55E*
128 K10 **Pyal'ma** Respublika Kareliya, NW Russian Federation *62.24N 35.56E*
Pyandzh *see* Panj
128 I6 **Pyaozero, Ozero** ◎ NW Russian Federation
177 Ff9 **Pyapon** Irrawaddy, SW Burma *16.15N 95.40E*
121 J15 **Pyarshai** *Rus.* Pershay. Minskaya Voblasts', C Belarus *54.02N 26.44E*
126 I6 **Pyasina** ≈ N Russian Federation
116 I10 **Pyasŭchnik, Yazovir** ⊠ C Bulgaria
125 B13 **Pyatigorsk** Stavropol'skiy Kray, SW Russian Federation *44.01N 43.06E*
Pyatikhatki *see* P"yatykhatky
119 S7 **P"yatykhatky** *Rus.* Pyatikhatki. Dnipropetrovs'ka Oblast', E Ukraine *48.22N 33.43E*
177 G6 **Pyawbwe** Mandalay, C Burma *20.39N 96.04E*
131 T3 **Pychas** Udmurtskaya Respublika, NW Russian Federation *56.30N 52.33E*
Pyè *see* Prome
177 F6 **Pyechin** Chin State, W Burma *20.01N 93.36E*
121 G17 **Pyeski** *Rus.* Peski. Hrodzyenskaya Voblasts', W Belarus *53.22N 24.37E*
121 L19 **Pyetrykaw** *Rus.* Petrikov. Homyel'skaya Voblasts', SE Belarus *52.07N 28.30E*
95 M16 **Pyhajärvi** ◎ C Finland
95 O17 **Pyhäjärvi** ◎ SE Finland
95 L15 **Pyhäjoki** Oulu, W Finland *64.28N 24.15E*
95 L15 **Pyhäjoki** ≈ W Finland
95 M15 **Pyhäntä** Oulu, C Finland *64.07N 26.19E*
95 M16 **Pyhäsalmi** Oulu, C Finland *63.38N 26.00E*
95 O17 **Pyhäselkä** ◎ SE Finland
95 M19 **Pyhtää** *Swe.* Pyttis. Etelä-Suomi, S Finland *60.29N 26.40E*
177 G6 **Pyinmana** ● (Burma) Mandalay, C Burma *19.45N 96.12E*
117 N24 **Pylés** *var.* Piles. Kárpathos, SE Greece *35.31N 27.08E*
117 D21 **Pýlos** *var.* Pilos. Pelopónnisos, S Greece *36.55N 21.42E*
20 B12 **Pymatuning Reservoir** ⊠ Ohio/Pennsylvania, NE USA
169 X15 **P'yŏngt'aek** NW South Korea *37.00N 127.04E*
169 V14 **P'yŏngyang** *var.* P'yŏngyang-si, *Eng.* Pyongyang. ● (North Korea) SW North Korea *39.04N 125.46E*
P'yŏngyang-si *see* P'yŏngyang
37 Q4 **Pyramid Lake** ◎ Nevada, W USA
39 P15 **Pyramid Mountains** ▲▲ New Mexico, SW USA
39 R5 **Pyramid Peak** ▲ Colorado, C USA *39.04N 106.57W*
117 D17 **Pyramíva** *var.* Piramiva. ▲ C Greece *39.08N 21.18E*
Pyrenaei Montes *see* Pyrenees
88 B12 **Pyrenees** *Fr.* Pyrénées, *Sp.* Pirineos; *anc.* Pyrenaei Montes. ▲▲ SW Europe
104 J16 **Pyrénées-Atlantiques** ◈ *department* SW France
105 N17 **Pyrénées-Orientales** ◈ *department* S France
117 L19 **Pyrgí** *var.* Pirgi. Chíos, E Greece *38.13N 26.01E*
117 D20 **Pýrgos** *var.* Pírgos. Dytikí Ellás, S Greece *37.40N 21.27E*
Pyritz *see* Pyrzyce
117 E19 **Pýrros** ≈ S Greece
119 R4 **Pyryatyn** *Rus.* Piryatin. Poltavs'ka Oblast', NE Ukraine *50.13N 32.31E*
112 D9 **Pyrzyce** *Ger.* Pyritz. Zachodnio-pomorskie, NW Poland *53.09N 14.52E*
128 F15 **Pytalovo** *Latv.* Abrene; *prev.* Jaunlatgale. Pskovskaya Oblast', W Russian Federation *57.06N 27.55E*
117 M20 **Pythagóreio** *var.* Pithagorio. Sámos, Dodekánisa, Greece, Aegean Sea *37.42N 26.57E*
12 L11 **Pythonga, Lac** ◎ Québec, SE Canada
Pyttis *see* Pyhtää
177 G7 **Pyu** Pegu, C Burma *18.28N 96.25E*
177 G8 **Pyuntaza** Pegu, SW Burma *17.51N 96.43E*
159 N11 **Pyuthān** Mid Western, W Nepal *28.09N 82.50E*
112 H12 **Pyzdry** *Ger.* Peisern. Wielkopolskie, C Poland *52.10N 17.42E*

Q

144 H13 **Qā' al Jafr** ◎ S Jordan
207 O11 **Qaanaaq** *var.* Qânâq, *Dan.* Thule. Avannaarsua, N Greenland *77.34N 69.44W*
144 G7 **Qabb Eliâs** E Lebanon *33.46N 35.49E*
Qabil *see* Al Qābil
Qabırrı *see* Iori
Qābis *see* Gabès
Qābis, Khalīj *see* Gabès, Golfe de
Qabqa *see* Gonghe
147 S14 **Qabr Hūd** C Yemen *16.02N 49.36E*
Qacentina *see* Constantine
154 L4 **Qādes** Bādghīs, NW Afghanistan *34.52N 63.25E*
145 T11 **Qādisīyah** S Iraq *31.43N 44.28E*
149 O4 **Qā'emshahr** *prev.* 'Alīābad, Shāhī. Māzandarān, N Iran *36.31N 52.49E*
149 U7 **Qā'en** *var.* Qain, Qāyen. Khorāsān-Razavī, E Iran *33.43N 59.07E*
147 U13 **Qafa** *spring/well* SW Oman *17.46N 52.55E*
Qafṣah *see* Gafsa
169 Q12 **Qagan Nur** *var.* Xulun Hobot Qagan, Zhengxiangbai Qi. Nei Mongol Zizhiqu, N China *42.10N 114.57E*
169 V9 **Qagan Nur** ◎ NE China
169 Q11 **Qagan Nur** ◎ N China
Qagan Us *see* Dulan
164 H13 **Qagcaka** Xizang Zizhiqu, W China *32.31N 81.52E*
Qagcheng *see* Xiangcheng
Qahremānshahr *see* Kermānshāh
165 Q10 **Qaidam He** ≈ C China
162 L8 **Qaidam Pendi** *basin* C China
Qain *see* Qā'en
Qala Āhangarān *see* Chaghcharān
145 U3 **Qaḷā Diza** *var.* Qal 'at Dīzah. NE Iraq *36.10N 45.07E*
Qal'ah Sālih *see* Qal'at Şāliḩ
153 R13 **Qal'aikhum** *Rus.* Kalaikhum. S Tajikistan *38.28N 70.49E*
Qala Nau *see* Qal'eh-ye Now
147 V17 **Qalansīyah** Suquṭrā, W Yemen *12.40N 53.30E*
Qala Panja *see* Qal'eh-ye Panjeh
Qala Shāhar *see* Qal'eh Shahr
155 O8 **Qalāt** *Pash.* Kalāt. Zābol, S Afghanistan *32.10N 66.54E*
145 W9 **Qal'at Aḥmad** E Iraq *32.24N 46.46E*
147 N11 **Qal'at Bīshah** 'Asīr, SW Saudi Arabia *19.59N 42.38E*
144 H4 **Qal'at Burzay** Ḥamāh, W Syria *35.37N 36.16E*
Qal 'at Dīzah *see* Qaḷā Diza
145 W9 **Qal'at Ḥusayh** E Iraq *32.19N 46.46E*
145 V10 **Qal'at Majnūnah** S Iraq *31.39N 45.44E*
145 X11 **Qal'at Şāliḩ** *var.* Qal'ah Sālih. E Iraq *31.30N 47.24E*
145 V10 **Qal'at Sukkar** SE Iraq *31.52N 46.04E*
Qalba Zhotasy *see* Kalbinskiy Khrebet
149 Q12 **Qal'eh Biābān** Fārs, S Iran
155 N4 **Qal'eh Shahr** *Pash.* Qala Shāhar. Sar-e Pol, N Afghanistan *35.34N 65.38E*
154 L4 **Qal'eh-ye Now** *var.* Qala Nau. Bādghīs, NW Afghanistan *34.59N 63.07E*
155 T2 **Qal'eh-ye Panjeh** *var.* Qala Panja. Badakhshān, NE Afghanistan *36.56N 72.15E*
Qamar Bay *see* Qamar, Ghubbat al
147 U14 **Qamar, Ghubbat al** *Eng.* Qamar Bay. *bay* Oman/Yemen
147 V13 **Qamar, Jabal al** ▲▲ SW Oman
153 N12 **Qamashi** Qashqadaryo Viloyati, S Uzbekistan *38.52N 66.30E*
Qambar *see* Kambar
165 R14 **Qamdo** Xizang Zizhiqu, W China *31.09N 97.09E*
197 K13 **Qamea** *prev.* Nggamea. *island* N Fiji
77 R7 **Qamīnis** NE Libya *31.48N 20.04E*
Qamishly *see* Al Qāmishlī
Qânâq *see* Qaanaaq
Qandahār *see* Kandahār
82 Q11 **Qandala** Bari, NE Somalia *11.30N 50.00E*
Qandyaghash *see* Kandyagash
144 L2 **Qanṭārī** Ar Raqqah, N Syria *36.24N 39.16E*
Qapiciğ Dağı *see* Qazangödağ
164 H5 **Qapqal** *var.* Qapqal Xibe Zizhixian. Xinjiang Uygur Zizhiqu, NW China *43.46N 81.09E*
Qapqal Xibe Zizhixian *see* Qapqal
Qapshagay Böyeni *see* Kapchagayskoye Vodokhranilishche
Qapugtang *see* Zadoi
206 M15 **Qaqortoq** *Dan.* Julianehåb. Kitaa, S Greenland *60.51N 46.01W*
77 U8 **Qâra** *var.* Qārah. NW Egypt *29.34N 26.28E*
145 T4 **Qara Anjīr** N Iraq *35.30N 44.37E*
Qarabāgh *see* Qarah Bāgh
Qaraböget *see* Karaboget
Qarabulaq *see* Karabulak
Qarabutaq *see* Karabutak
Qaraghandy/Qaraghandy Oblysy *see* Karaganda
Qaraghayly *see* Karagayly
145 U4 **Qara Gol** NE Iraq *35.21N 45.38E*
Qārah *see* Qâra
154 J4 **Qarah Bāgh** *var.* Qarabāgh. Herāt, NW Afghanistan *35.06N 61.33E*
144 G7 **Qaraoun, Lac de** *var.* Buḩayrat al Qir'awn. ◎ S Lebanon
Qaraoy *see* Karaoy
Qaraqoyyn *see* Karakoyyn, Ozero
Qara Qum *see* Garagum
Qarasū *see* Karasu
Qaratal *see* Karatal
Qarataū *see* Karatau, Khrebet, Kazakhstan
Qarataū *see* Karatau, Zhambyl, Kazakhstan
Qaraton *see* Karaton
82 P13 **Qardho** *var.* Kardh, *It.* Gardo. Bari, N Somalia *9.34N 49.30E*
148 M6 **Qareh Chāy** ≈ N Iran
148 K2 **Qareh Sū** ≈ NW Iran
Qariateïne *see* Al Qaryatayn
Qarkilik *see* Ruoqiang
153 O13 **Qarluq** *Rus.* Karluk. Surkhondaryo Viloyati, S Uzbekistan *38.17N 67.39E*
153 U12 **Qarokŭl** *Rus.* Karakul'. E Tajikistan *39.07N 73.33E*
153 T12 **Qarokŭl** *Rus.* Ozero Karakul'. ◎ E Tajikistan
Qarqan *see* Qiemo
164 K9 **Qarqan He** ≈ NW China
Qarqannah, Juzur *see* Kerkenah, Îles de
Qarqaraly *see* Karkaralinsk
155 O1 **Qarqīn** Jowzjān, N Afghanistan *37.25N 66.03E*
Qars *see* Kars
Qarsaqbay *see* Karsakpay
152 M12 **Qarshi** *Rus.* Karshi; *prev.* Bek-Budi. Qashqadaryo Viloyati, S Uzbekistan *38.54N 65.48E*
152 L12 **Qarshi Cho'li** *Rus.* Karshinskaya Step. *grassland* S Uzbekistan
152 M13 **Qarshi Kanali** *Rus.* Karshinskiy Kanal. *canal* Turkmenistan/Uzbekistan
Qaryatayn *see* Al Qaryatayn
152 M12 **Qashqadaryo Viloyati** *Rus.* Kashkadar'inskaya Oblast'. ◈ *province* S Uzbekistan
Qasigianguit *see* Qasigiannguit
207 N13 **Qasigiannguit** *var.* Qasigianguit, *Dan.* Christianshåb. Kitaa, C Greenland *68.42N 50.49W*
Qaşīm, Minṭaqat *see* Al Qaşīm
145 P8 **Qaşr 'Amīj** C Iraq *33.30N 41.52E*
145 R9 **Qaşr Darwīshāh** C Iraq *32.36N 43.27E*
148 J6 **Qaşr-e Shīrīn** Kermānshāh, W Iran *34.33N 45.37E*
77 V10 **Qasr Farâfra** W Egypt *27.00N 27.58E*
Qassim *see* Al Qaşīm
147 O16 **Qa'ṭabah** SW Yemen *13.51N 44.42E*
144 H7 **Qaṭanā** *var.* Katana. Dimashq, S Syria *33.27N 36.04E*
149 N15 **Qatar** *off.* State of Qatar, *Ar.* Dawlat Qaṭar. ◆ *monarchy* SW Asia
Qatrana *see* Al Qaṭrānah
149 Q12 **Qaṭrūyeh** Fārs, S Iran
Qattara Depression/Qaṭṭārah, Munkhafaḍ al *see* Qaṭṭâra, Monkhafad el
77 U8 **Qaṭṭâra, Monkhafad el** *var.* Munkhafaḍ al Qaṭṭārah, *Eng.* Qattara Depression. *desert* NW Egypt
Qaṭṭīnah, Buḩayrat *see* Ḩimş, Buḩayrat
Qaydār *see* Qeydār
Qāyen *see* Qā'en
153 Q11 **Qayroqqum** *Rus.* Kayrakkum. NW Tajikistan *40.16N 69.46E*
153 Q10 **Qayroqqum, Obanbori** *Rus.* Kayrakkumskoye Vodokhranilishche. ⊠ NW Tajikistan
143 V13 **Qazangödağ** *Rus.* Gora Kapydzhik, *Turk.* Qapiciğ Dağı. ▲ SW Azerbaijan *39.18N 46.00E*
145 U7 **Qazānīyah** *var.* Dhū Shaykh. E Iraq *33.39N 45.33E*
Qazaqstan/Qazaqstan Respublikasy *see* Kazakhstan
143 T9 **Qazbegi** *Rus.* Kazbegi. NE Georgia *42.39N 44.36E*
155 P15 **Qāzi Ahmad** *var.* Kazi Ahmad. Sind, SE Pakistan *26.19N 68.06E*
143 Y12 **Qazimämmäd** *Rus.* Kazi Magomed. SE Azerbaijan *40.03N 48.56E*
Qazris *see* Cáceres
148 M4 **Qazvīn** *var.* Kazvin. Qazvīn, N Iran *36.16N 50.00E*
148 M5 **Qazvīn** ◈ *province* N Iran
197 K12 **Qelelevu Lagoon** *lagoon* NE Fiji
77 X10 **Qena** *var.* Qinā; *anc.* Caene, Caenepolis. E Egypt *26.12N 32.49E*
115 L23 **Qeparo** Vlorë, S Albania *40.04N 19.49E*
Qeqertarssuaq *see* Qeqertarsuaq
207 N13 **Qeqertarsuaq** *var.* Qeqertarssuaq, *Dan.* Godhavn. Kitaa, Greenland *69.27N 52.54W*
206 M13 **Qeqertarsuaq** *island* W Greenland
207 N13 **Qeqertarsuup Tunua** *Dan.* Disko Bugt. *inlet* W Greenland
Qerveh *see* Qorveh
149 S14 **Qeshm** Hormozgān, S Iran *26.58N 56.16E*
149 R14 **Qeshm** *var.* Jazīreh-ye Qeshm, Qeshm Island. *island* S Iran
Qeshm Island/Qeshm, Jazīreh-ye *see* Qeshm
148 L4 **Qeydār** *var.* Qaydār. Zanjān, NW Iran *36.50N 47.40E*
148 K5 **Qezel Owzan, Rūd-e** *var.* Ki Zil Uzen, Qi Zil Uzun. ≈ NW Iran
Qian *see* Guizhou
167 Q2 **Qian'an** Hebei, E China *40.01N 118.43E*
Qiandaohu *see* Chun'an
Qiandao Hu *see* Xin'anjiang Shuiku
Qian Gorlo/ Qian Gorlos/ Qian Gorlos Mongolzu Zizhixian/Qianguozhen *see* Qianguo
169 V9 **Qianguo** *var.* Qian Gorlo, Qian Gorlos, Qian Gorlos Mongolzu Zizhixian, Qianguozhen. Jilin, NE China *45.06N 124.48E*
167 N9 **Qianjiang** Hubei, C China *30.26N 112.55E*
166 K10 **Qianjiang** Sichuan, C China *29.30N 108.45E*
166 L14 **Qian Jiang** ≈ S China
166 G9 **Qianning** *var.* Gartar. Sichuan, C China *30.33N 101.22E*
169 U13 **Qian Shan** ▲▲ NE China
166 H10 **Qianwei** *var.* Yujin. Sichuan, C China *29.15N 103.52E*
166 J11 **Qianxi** Guizhou, S China *27.00N 106.01E*
Qiaotou *see* Datong
Qiaowa *see* Muli
165 Q7 **Qiaowan** Gansu, N China *40.37N 96.43E*
Qibilī *see* Kebili
164 K9 **Qiemo** *var.* Qarqan. Xinjiang Uygur Zizhiqu, NW China *38.09N 85.30E*
166 J10 **Qijiang** *var.* Gunan. Chongqing Shi, C China *29.06N 106.35E*
165 N5 **Qijiaojing** Xinjiang Uygur Zizhiqu, NW China *43.28N 91.34E*
Qike *see* Xunke
155 P9 **Qila Saifullāh** Baluchistān, SW Pakistan *30.45N 68.08E*
165 S9 **Qilian** *var.* Babao. Qinghai, C China *38.09N 100.08E*
139 Nn10 **Qilian Shan** *var.* Kilien Mountains. ▲▲ N China
207 O11 **Qimusseriarsuaq** *Dan.* Melville Bugt, *Eng.* Melville Bay. *bay* NW Greenland
Qinā *see* Qena
165 W11 **Qin'an** Gansu, C China *34.49N 105.50E*
Qincheng *see* Nanfeng
Qing *see* Qinghai
169 W7 **Qing'an** Heilongjiang, NE China *46.53N 127.29E*
167 R5 **Qingdao** *var.* Ching-Tao, Ch'ing-tao, Tsingtao, Tsintao, *Ger.* Tsingtau. Shandong, E China *36.30N 120.55E*
169 V8 **Qinggang** Heilongjiang, NE China *46.40N 126.04E*
Qinggil *see* Qinghe
165 P11 **Qinghai** *var.* Chinghai, Koko Nor, Qing, Qinghai Sheng, Tsinghai. ◈ *province* C China
165 S10 **Qinghai Hu** *var.* Ch'ing Hai, Tsing Hai, *Mong.* Koko Nor. ◎ C China
Qinghai Sheng *see* Qinghai
164 M3 **Qinghe** *var.* Qinggil. Xinjiang Uygur Zizhiqu, NW China *46.42N 90.19E*
166 L4 **Qingjian** *var.* Kuanzhou; *prev.* Xiuyan. Shaanxi, C China *37.10N 110.09E*
166 L9 **Qing Jiang** ≈ C China
Qingjiang *see* Huai'an
Qingkou *see* Ganyu
166 I12 **Qinglong** *var.* Liancheng. Guizhou, S China *25.49N 105.10E*
167 Q2 **Qinglong** Hebei, E China *40.24N 118.57E*
Qingshan *see* Wudalianchi
165 R12 **Qingshuihe** Qinghai, C China *33.08N 97.19E*
165 X10 **Qingyang** *var.* Xifeng. Gansu, C China *35.46N 107.35E*
Qingyang *see* Jinjiang
167 N14 **Qingyuan** Guangdong, S China *23.42N 113.02E*
169 V11 **Qingyuan** *var.* Qingyuan Manzu Zizhixian. Liaoning, NE China *42.08N 124.55E*
Qingyuan Manzu Zizhixian *see* Qingyuan
164 L13 **Qingzang Gaoyuan** *var.* Xizang Gaoyuan, *Eng.* Plateau of Tibet. *plateau* W China
167 Q4 **Qingzhou** *prev.* Yidu. Shandong, E China *36.46N 118.23E*
163 R9 **Qin He** ≈ C China
167 Q2 **Qinhuangdao** Hebei, E China *39.57N 119.31E*
166 K7 **Qin Ling** ▲▲ C China
Qin Xian *see* Qinxian
167 N5 **Qinxian** *var.* Qin Xian. Shanxi, C China *36.46N 112.42E*
167 N6 **Qinyang** Henan, C China *35.04N 112.55E*
166 K15 **Qinzhou** Guangxi Zhuangzu Zizhiqu, S China *22.09N 108.36E*
Qiong *see* Hainan
166 L17 **Qionghai** *prev.* Jiaji. Hainan, S China *19.12N 110.26E*
166 H9 **Qionglai** Sichuan, C China *30.24N 103.28E*
166 H8 **Qionglai Shan** ▲▲ C China
Qiongxi *see* Hongyuan
166 L17 **Qiongzhou Haixia** *var.* Hainan Strait. *strait* S China
169 U7 **Qiqihar** *var.* Ch'i-ch'i-ha-erh, Tsitsihar; *prev.* Lungkiang. Heilongjiang, NE China *47.23N 124.00E*
Qīr *see* Qīr-va-Kārzīn
164 H10 **Qira** Xinjiang Uygur Zizhiqu, NW China *37.04N 80.45E*
Qir'awn, Buḩayrat al *see* Qaraoun, Lac de
149 P12 **Qīr-va-Kārzīn** *var.* Qīr. Fārs, S Iran *28.27N 53.04E*
144 F11 **Qiryat Gat** *var.* Kiryat Gat. Southern, C Israel *31.37N 34.46E*
144 G8 **Qiryat Shemona** Northern, N Israel *33.13N 35.34E*
Qishlaq *see* Garmsār
147 U14 **Qishn** SE Yemen *15.28N 51.43E*
144 G9 **Qishon, Nahal** ≈ N Israel
Qita Ghazzah *see* Gaza Strip
162 K5 **Qitai** Xinjiang Uygur Zizhiqu, NW China *44.00N 89.33E*
169 Y8 **Qitaihe** Heilongjiang, NE China *45.45N 130.53E*
147 W12 **Qitbīt, Wādī** *dry watercourse* S Oman
167 O5 **Qixian** *var.* Qi Xian, Zhaoge. Henan, C China *35.34N 114.10E*
Qīzān *see* Jīzān
Qizil Orda *see* Kyzylorda
Qizil Qum/Qizilqum *see* Kyzyl Kum
153 V14 **Qizilrabot** *Rus.* Kyzylrabot. SE Tajikistan *37.28N 74.43E*
152 J10 **Qizilravot** *Rus.* Kyzylrabat. Buxoro Viloyati, C Uzbekistan *40.35N 62.09E*
Qi Zil Uzun *see* Qezel Owzan, Rūd-e
145 S4 **Qizil Yār** N Iraq *35.26N 44.12E*
Qoghaly *see* Kugaly
Qogir Feng *see* K2
149 N6 **Qom** *var.* Kum, Qum. Qom, N Iran *34.43N 50.53E*
149 N6 **Qom** ◈ *province* N Iran
Qomisheh *see* Shahreẕā
Qomolangma Feng *see* Everest, Mount
148 M7 **Qom, Rūd-e** ≈ C Iran
Qomsheh *see* Shahreẕā
Qomul *see* Hami
Qondūz *see* Kondoz
152 G7 **Qo'ng'irot** *Rus.* Kungrad. Qoraqalpog'iston Respublikasi, NW Uzbekistan *43.01N 58.49E*
Qongyrat *see* Konyrat
Qoqek *see* Tacheng
153 R10 **Qo'qon** *var.* Khokand, *Rus.* Kokand. Farg'ona Viloyati, E Uzbekistan *40.34N 70.55E*
Qorabowur Kirlari *see* Karabaur', Uval
Qoradaryo *see* Karadar'ya
152 G6 **Qorajar** *Rus.* Karadzhar. Qoraqalpog'iston Respublikasi, NW Uzbekistan *43.34N 58.35E*
152 K12 **Qorako'l** *Rus.* Karakul'. Buxoro Viloyati, C Uzbekistan *39.27N 63.45E*
152 E5 **Qoraqalpog'iston** *Rus.* Karakalpakya. Qoraqalpog'iston Respublikasi, NW Uzbekistan *44.45N 56.06E*
152 G7 **Qoraqalpog'iston Respublikasi** *Rus.* Respublika Karakalpakstan. ◈ *autonomous republic* NW Uzbekistan
152 H7 **Qorao'zak** *Rus.* Karauzyak. Qoraqalpog'iston Respublikasi, NW Uzbekistan *43.07N 60.03E*
Qorgazhyn *see* Korgalzhyn
144 H6 **Qornet es Saouda** ▲ NE Lebanon *36.06N 34.06E*
152 L12 **Qorovulbozor** *Rus.* Karaulbazar. Buxoro Viloyati, C Uzbekistan *39.28N 64.49E*
148 K5 **Qorveh** *var.* Qerveh, Qurveh. Kordestān, W Iran *35.13N 47.46E*
153 N11 **Qo'shrabot** *Rus.* Kushrabat. Samarqand Viloyati, C Uzbekistan *40.15N 66.40E*
Qosshaghyl *see* Koschagyl
Qostanay/Qostanay Oblysy *see* Kostanay
149 P12 **Qoṭbābād** Fārs, S Iran *28.52N 53.40E*
149 R13 **Qoṭbābād** Hormozgān, S Iran *27.49N 56.00E*
144 H6 **Qoubaïyât** *var.* Al Qubayyāt. N Lebanon *37.00N 34.30E*
Qoussantîna *see* Constantine
164 K16 **Qowowuyag** *see* Cho Oyu
153 O11 **Qo'ytosh** *Rus.* Koytash. Jizzax Viloyati, C Uzbekistan *40.13N 67.19E*
152 G7 **Qozonketkan** *Rus.* Kazanketken. Qoraqalpog'iston Respublikasi, W Uzbekistan *42.59N 59.21E*
152 H6 **Qozoqdaryo** *Rus.* Kazakdar'ya. Qoraqalpog'iston Respublikasi, NW Uzbekistan *43.26N 59.47E*
21 N11 **Quabbin Reservoir** ⊠ Massachusetts, NE USA
102 F12 **Quakenbrück** Niedersachsen, NW Germany *52.41N 7.57E*
20 I15 **Quakertown** Pennsylvania, NE USA *40.26N 75.17W*
190 M10 **Quambatook** Victoria, SE Australia *35.52S 143.28E*
27 Q4 **Quanah** Texas, SW USA *34.19N 99.45W*
178 Kk11 **Quang Ngai** *var.* Quangngai, Quang Nghia. Quang Ngai, C Vietnam *15.09N 108.49E*
Quang Nghia *see* Quang Ngai
178 K9 **Quang Tri** *var.* Triêu Hai. Quang Tri, C Vietnam *16.42N 107.15E*
Quanjiang *see* Suichuan
Quan Long *see* Ca Mau
158 L4 **Quanshuigou** China/India *35.40N 79.28E*
167 R13 **Quanzhou** *var.* Ch'uan-chou, Tsinkiang; *prev.* Chin-chiang. Fujian, SE China *24.56N 118.31E*
166 M12 **Quanzhou** Guangxi Zhuangzu Zizhiqu, S China *25.59N 111.01E*
9 V16 **Qu'Appelle** ≈ Saskatchewan, S Canada
10 M3 **Quaqtaq** *prev.* Koartac. Québec, NE Canada *60.49N 69.30W*
63 E16 **Quaraí** Rio Grande do Sul, S Brazil *30.24S 56.24W*
61 H24 **Quaraí, Rio** *Sp.* Río Cuareim. ≈ Brazil/Uruguay **see also** Cuareim, Río
175 P10 **Quarles, Pegunungan** ▲▲ Sulawesi, C Indonesia
Quarnero *see* Kvarner
109 C20 **Quartu Sant' Elena** Sardegna, Italy, C Mediterranean Sea *39.15N 9.12E*
31 X13 **Quasqueton** Iowa, C USA *42.23N 91.45W*
181 X16 **Quatre Bornes** W Mauritius *20.15S 57.28E*
180 I17 **Quatre Bornes** Mahé, NE Seychelles
143 X10 **Quba** *Rus.* Kuba. N Azerbaijan *41.22N 48.30E*
Qubba *see* Ba'qūbah
149 T3 **Qūchān** *var.* Kuchan. Khorāsān-Razavī, NE Iran *37.12N 58.28E*
191 R10 **Queanbeyan** New South Wales, SE Australia *35.24S 149.16E*
13 Q10 **Québec** *var.* Quebec. Québec, SE Canada *46.49N 71.15W*
12 K10 **Québec** *var.* Quebec. ◈ *province* SE Canada
63 D17 **Quebracho** Paysandú, W Uruguay *31.58S 57.52W*
103 K14 **Quedlinburg** Sachsen-Anhalt, C Germany *51.48N 11.09E*
144 H10 **Queen Alia** ✕ ('Ammān) 'Ammān, C Jordan
8 L16 **Queen Bess, Mount** ▲ British Columbia, SW Canada *51.15N 124.29W*
8 I14 **Queen Charlotte** British Columbia, SW Canada *53.18N 132.04W*
67 B24 **Queen Charlotte Bay** *bay* West Falkland, Falkland Islands
8 H14 **Queen Charlotte Islands** *Fr.* Îles de la Reine-Charlotte. *island group* British Columbia, SW Canada
8 I15 **Queen Charlotte Sound** *sea area* British Columbia, W Canada
8 J16 **Queen Charlotte Strait** *strait* British Columbia, W Canada
29 U1 **Queen City** Missouri, C USA *40.24N 92.34W*
27 X5 **Queen City** Texas, SW USA *33.09N 94.09W*
207 O9 **Queen Elizabeth Islands** *Fr.* Îles de la Reine-Élisabeth. *island group* Nunavut, N Canada
205 Y10 **Queen Mary Coast** *physical region* Antarctica
67 N24 **Queen Mary's Peak** ▲ C Tristan da Cunha
206 M8 **Queen Maud Gulf** *gulf* Arctic Ocean
205 P11 **Queen Maud Mountains** ▲▲ Antarctica
Queen's County *see* Laois
189 U7 **Queensland** ◈ *state* N Australia
199 Hh10 **Queensland Plateau** *undersea feature* N Coral Sea
191 O16 **Queenstown** Tasmania, SE Australia *42.06S 145.33E*
193 C22 **Queenstown** Otago, South Island, NZ *45.03S 168.41E*
85 I24 **Queenstown** Eastern Cape, S South Africa *31.52S 26.50E*
Queenstown *see* Cobh
34 F8 **Queets** Washington, NW USA *47.31N 124.19W*
63 D18 **Queguay Grande, Río** ≈ W Uruguay
61 O16 **Queimadas** Bahia, E Brazil *10.58S 39.37W*
84 D11 **Quela** Malanje, NW Angola *9.18S 17.07E*
85 O16 **Quelimane** *var.* Kilimane, Kilmain, Quilimane. Zambézia, NE Mozambique *17.52S 36.51E*
65 G18 **Quellón** *var.* Puerto Quellón. Los Lagos, S Chile *43.05S 73.38W*
Quelpart *see* Cheju-do
39 P12 **Quemado** New Mexico, SW USA *34.18N 108.29W*
27 O12 **Quemado** Texas, SW USA *28.58N 100.36W*
46 K7 **Quemado, Punta de** *headland* E Cuba *20.13N 74.07W*
Quemoy *see* Chinmen Tao
64 K13 **Quemú Quemú** La Pampa, E Argentina *36.03S 63.30W*
161 E17 **Quepem** Goa, W India *15.13N 74.03E*
44 M14 **Quepos** Puntarenas, S Costa Rica *9.28N 84.10W*
Que Que *see* Kwekwe
63 D23 **Quequén** Buenos Aires, E Argentina *38.30S 58.43W*
63 D23 **Quequén Grande, Río** ≈ E Argentina
63 C23 **Quequén Salado, Río** ≈ E Argentina
Quera *see* Chur
43 N13 **Querétaro** Querétaro de Arteaga, C Mexico *20.36N 100.24W*
42 F4 **Querobabi** Sonora, NW Mexico *30.03N 111.02W*
44 M13 **Quesada** *var.* Ciudad Quesada, San Carlos. Alajuela, N Costa Rica *10.17N 84.24W*
107 O13 **Quesada** Andalucía, S Spain *37.52N 3.05W*
167 O7 **Queshan** Henan, C China *32.48N 114.03E*
8 M15 **Quesnel** British Columbia, SW Canada *52.58N 122.30W*
39 S9 **Questa** New Mexico, SW USA *36.41N 105.37W*
104 H7 **Questembert** Morbihan, NW France *47.39N 2.24W*
59 K22 **Quetena, Río** ≈ SW Bolivia
155 O10 **Quetta** Baluchistān, SW Pakistan *30.15N 67.00E*
Quetzalcoalco *see* Coatzacoalcos
Quetzaltenango *see* Quezaltenango
58 B6 **Quevedo** Los Ríos, C Ecuador *1.01S 79.27W*
44 B6 **Quezaltenango** *var.* Quetzaltenango. Quezaltenango, W Guatemala *14.48N 91.27W*
44 A2 **Quezaltenango** *off.* Departamento de Quezaltenango, *var.* Quetzaltenango. ◈ *department* SW Guatemala
44 E6 **Quezaltepeque** Chiquimula, SE Guatemala *14.38N 89.25W*
179 O15 **Quezon** Palawan, W Philippines *9.13N 118.01E*
179 P10 **Quezon City** Luzon, N Philippines *14.39N 121.01E*
167 P5 **Qufu** Shandong, E China *35.37N 117.05E*
84 B12 **Quibala** Cuanza Sul, NW Angola *10.44S 14.58E*
84 B11 **Quibaxe** *var.* Quibaxi. Cuanza Norte, NW Angola *8.30S 14.36E*
Quibaxi *see* Quibaxe
56 D9 **Quibdó** Chocó, W Colombia *5.40N 76.37W*
104 G7 **Quiberon** Morbihan, NW France *47.30N 3.07W*
104 G7 **Quiberon, Baie de** *bay* NW France
56 J5 **Quíbor** Lara, N Venezuela *9.55N 69.34W*
44 C4 **Quiché** *off.* Departamento del Quiché. ◈ *department* W Guatemala
101 E21 **Quiévrain** Hainaut, S Belgium *50.25N 3.40E*
42 I9 **Quila** Sinaloa, C Mexico *24.24N 107.11W*
85 B14 **Quilengues** Huíla, SW Angola *14.03S 14.03E*
Quilimane *see* Quelimane
59 G15 **Quillabamba** Cusco, C Peru *12.48S 72.42W*
59 L18 **Quillacollo** Cochabamba, C Bolivia *17.23S 66.15W*
64 H4 **Quillagua** Antofagasta, N Chile *21.33S 69.32W*
105 N17 **Quillan** Aude, S France *42.52N 2.10E*
9 U15 **Quill Lakes** ◎ Saskatchewan, S Canada
64 G11 **Quillota** Valparaíso, C Chile *32.54S 71.16W*
161 G23 **Quilon** *var.* Kolam, Kollam. Kerala, SW India *8.57N 76.36E*
189 V9 **Quilpie** Queensland, C Australia *26.39S 144.15E*
155 O4 **Quil-Qala** Bāmīān, N Afghanistan *35.13N 67.02E*
64 L7 **Quimilí** Santiago del Estero, C Argentina *27.38S 62.25W*
59 O19 **Quimome** Santa Cruz, E Bolivia *17.45S 61.15W*
104 F6 **Quimper** *anc.* Quimper Corentin. Finistère, NW France *48.00N 4.05W*
Quimper Corentin *see* Quimper
104 G7 **Quimperlé** Finistère, NW France *47.52N 3.33W*
34 F8 **Quinault** Washington, NW USA *47.27N 123.53W*
34 F8 **Quinault River** ≈ Washington, NW USA
37 P5 **Quincy** California, W USA *39.55N 120.57W*
25 S8 **Quincy** Florida, SE USA *30.35N 84.34W*
32 I13 **Quincy** Illinois, N USA *39.56N 91.24W*
21 O11 **Quincy** Massachusetts, NE USA *42.15N 71.00W*
34 J9 **Quincy** Washington, NW USA *47.13N 119.51W*
56 E10 **Quindío** *off.* Departamento del Quindío. ◈ *province* C Colombia
56 E10 **Quindío, Nevado del** ▲ C Colombia *4.42N 75.25W*
64 J10 **Quines** San Luis, C Argentina *32.15S 65.46W*
41 N13 **Quinhagak** Alaska, USA *59.45N 161.55W*
78 G13 **Quinhámel** W Guinea-Bissau *11.52N 15.52W*
Qui Nhon/Quinhon *see* Quy Nhơn
Quinindé *see* Rosa Zárate
27 U6 **Quinlan** Texas, SW USA *32.54N 96.08W*
63 H17 **Quinta** Rio Grande do Sul, S Brazil *32.05S 52.18W*
107 O10 **Quintanar de la Orden** Castilla-La Mancha, C Spain *39.36N 3.03W*
43 X13 **Quintana Roo** ◈ *state* SE Mexico
107 S6 **Quinto** Aragón, NE Spain *41.25N 0.31W*
110 G10 **Quinto** Ticino, S Switzerland *46.32N 8.44E*
29 Q11 **Quinton** Oklahoma, C USA *35.07N 95.22W*
64 K12 **Quinto, Río** ≈ C Argentina
84 A10 **Quinzau** Zaire, NW Angola *6.50S 12.48E*
12 H8 **Quinze, Lac des** ◎ Québec, SE Canada
85 B15 **Quipungo** Huíla, C Angola *14.49S 14.29E*
64 G13 **Quirihue** Bío Bío, C Chile *36.15S 72.34W*
84 D12 **Quirima** Malanje, NW Angola *10.51S 18.06E*
191 T6 **Quirindi** New South Wales, SE Australia *31.29S 150.40E*
57 P5 **Quiriquire** Monagas, NE Venezuela *9.58N 63.13W*
12 D10 **Quirke Lake** ◎ Ontario, S Canada
63 B21 **Quiroga** Buenos Aires, E Argentina *35.18S 61.22W*
106 I4 **Quiroga** Galicia, NW Spain *42.28N 7.15W*
Quiróm, Salar *see* Pocitos, Salar
58 B9 **Quiroz, Río** ≈ NW Peru
84 Q13 **Quissanga** Cabo Delgado, NE Mozambique *12.21S 40.31E*
85 M20 **Quissico** Inhambane, S Mozambique *24.42S 34.43E*
27 O4 **Quitaque** Texas, SW USA *34.22N 101.03W*
84 Q13 **Quiterajo** Cabo Delgado, NE Mozambique *11.37S 40.22E*
25 T6 **Quitman** Georgia, SE USA *30.46N 83.33W*
24 M6 **Quitman** Mississippi, S USA *32.02N 88.43W*
27 V6 **Quitman** Texas, SW USA *32.48N 95.27W*
58 C6 **Quito** ● (Ecuador) Pichincha, N Ecuador *0.13S 78.30W*
Quito *see* Mariscal Sucre
60 P13 **Quixadá** Ceará, E Brazil *4.57S 39.04W*
85 Q15 **Quixaxe** Nampula, NE Mozambique *15.15S 40.07E*
166 J9 **Qu Jiang** ≈ C China
167 R10 **Qu Jiang** ≈ SE China
167 N13 **Qujiang** *var.* Maba. Guangdong, S China *24.47N 113.34E*
166 H12 **Qujing** Yunnan, SW China *25.39N 103.52E*
Qulan *see* Kulan
169 T8 **Qulin Gol** *prev.* Chaor He. ≈ N China
152 L10 **Quljuqtov Tog'lari** *Rus.* Gory Kul'dzhuktau. ▲▲ C Uzbekistan
Qulsary *see* Kul'sary
Qulyndy Zhazyghy *see* Kulunda Steppe
Qum *see* Qom
Qumälisch *see* Lubartów
165 P11 **Qumar He** ≈ C China
165 Q12 **Qumarlêb** *var.* Yuegaitan. Qinghai, C China *34.06N 95.54E*
Qumisheh *see* Shahreẕā
153 O14 **Qumqo'rg'on** *Rus.* Kumkurgan. Surkhondaryo Viloyati, S Uzbekistan *37.54N 67.31E*
Qunaytirah/Qunayṭirah, Muḩāfaẓat al/Qunaytra *see* Al Qunayṭirah
201 V12 **Quoi** *island* Chuuk, C Micronesia
15 Kk6 **Quoich** ≈ Nunavut, NE Canada
85 E26 **Quoin Point** *headland* SW South Africa *34.48S 19.39E*
190 I7 **Quorn** South Australia *32.22S 138.03E*
Qurein *see* Al Kuwayt
153 P14 **Qŭrghonteppa** *Rus.* Kurgan-Tyube. SW Tajikistan *37.51N 68.42E*
Qurlurtuuq *see* Kugluktuk
Qurveh *see* Qorveh
Qusair *see* Quseir
143 X10 **Qusar** *Rus.* Kusary. NE Azerbaijan *41.26N 48.27E*
Quşayr *see* Al Quşayr
77 Y10 **Quseir** *var.* Al Quşayr, Qusair. E Egypt *26.05N 34.16E*

◆ Country
● Country Capital
◇ Dependent Territory
○ Dependent Territory Capital
◈ Administrative Region
✕ International Airport
▲ Mountain
▲▲ Mountain Range
Volcano
≈ River
◎ Lake
⊠ Reservoir

QŪSHCHĪ – RAYMOND

148 I2 **Qūshchī** Āžarbāyjān-e Gharbī, N Iran 37.58N 45.04E
Qusmuryn see Kushmurun, Kostanay, Kazakhstan
Qusmuryn see Kushmurun, Ozero, Kazakhstan
Quṭayfah/Qutayfe/Quteife see Al Quṭayfah
Quthing see Moyeni
153 S10 **Quvasoy** Rus. Kuvasay. Farg'ona Viloyati, E Uzbekistan 40.17N 71.53E
Quwair see Guwēr
Quxar see Lhazê
Qu Xian see Quzhou
165 N16 **Qüxü** var. Xoi. Xizang Zizhiqu, W China 29.25N 90.48E
Quyang see Jingzhou, Hunan
178 Kk13 **Quy Chanh** Ninh Thuân, S Vietnam 11.28N 108.53E
178 Kk12 **Quy Nhơn** var. Quinhon, Qui Nhon. Binh Đinh, C Vietnam 13.46N 109.10E
167 R10 **Quzhou** var. Qu Xian. Zhejiang, SE China 28.55N 118.54E
Qyteti Stalin see Kuçovë
Qyzylorda/Qyzylorda Oblysy see Kyzylorda
Qyzyltū see Kishkenekol'
Qyzylzhar see Kyzylzhar

R

111 R4 **Raab** Oberösterreich, N Austria 48.19N 13.40E
111 X8 **Raab** Hung. Rába. ~ Austria/Hungary see also Rába
Raab see Győr
111 V2 **Raabs an der Thaya** Niederösterreich, E Austria 48.51N 15.28E
95 L14 **Raahe** Swe. Brahestad. Oulu, W Finland 64.42N 24.30E
100 M10 **Raalte** Overijssel, E Netherlands 52.22N 6.16E
101 I14 **Raamsdonksveer** Noord-Brabant, S Netherlands 51.42N 4.54E
94 L12 **Raanujärvi** Lappi, NW Finland 66.39N 24.40E
98 G9 **Raasay** island NW Scotland, UK
120 H3 **Raasiku** Ger. Rasik. Harjumaa, NW Estonia 59.22N 25.12E
114 B11 **Rab** It. Arbe. Primorje-Gorski Kotar, NW Croatia 44.46N 14.46E
114 B11 **Rab** It. Arbe. island NW Croatia
175 P16 **Raba** Sumbawa, S Indonesia 8.30S 118.46E
113 G22 **Rába** Ger. Raab. ~ Austria/Hungary see also Raab
114 A10 **Rabac** Istra, NW Croatia 45.03N 14.09E
106 I2 **Rábade** Galicia, NW Spain 42.07N 7.37W
82 F10 **Rabak** White Nile, C Sudan 13.12N 32.43E
194 M16 **Rabaraba** Milne Bay, SE PNG 10.02S 149.53E
104 K16 **Rabastens-de-Bigorre** Hautes-Pyrénées, S France 43.22N 0.10E
123 Jj17 **Rabat** W Malta 35.51N 14.25E
76 F6 **Rabat** var. al Dar al Baida. ● (Morocco) NW Morocco 34.01N 6.51W
Rabat see Victoria
195 P10 **Rabaul** New Britain, E PNG 4.13S 152.10E
Rabbah Ammon/Rabbath Ammon see 'Ammān
30 K8 **Rabbit Creek** ~ South Dakota, N USA
12 H10 **Rabbit Lake** ◎ Ontario, S Canada
197 K13 **Rabi** prev. Rambi. island N Fiji
146 K9 **Rābigh** Makkah, W Saudi Arabia 22.51N 39.00E
44 D5 **Rabinal** Baja Verapaz, C Guatemala 15.05N 90.23W
173 Ee6 **Rabi, Pulau** island NW Indonesia, East Indies
113 L17 **Rabka** Małopolskie, S Poland 49.37N 20.00E
161 F16 **Rabkavi** Karnātaka, W India 16.40N 75.03E
Râbniṭa see Rîbniṭa
111 Y6 **Rabnitz** ~ E Austria
128 J7 **Rabocheostrovsk** Respublika Kareliya, NW Russian Federation 64.58N 34.46E
25 U1 **Rabun Bald** ▲ Georgia, SE USA 34.58N 83.18W
77 S11 **Rabyānah** SE Libya 24.07N 21.58E
77 S11 **Rabyānah, Ramlat** var. Rebiana Sand Sea, Ṣaḥrā' Rabyānah. desert SE Libya
Rabyānah, Ṣaḥrā' see Rabyānah, Ramlat
118 L11 **Răcăciuni** Bacău, E Romania 46.20N 27.00E
Racaka see Riwoqê
109 J24 **Racalmuto** Sicilia, Italy, C Mediterranean Sea 37.25N 13.43E
118 J14 **Răcari** Dâmboviṭa, SE Romania 44.37N 25.43E
Răcari see Durankulak
118 F13 **Răcăşdia** Hung. Rakasd. Caraş-Severin, SW Romania 44.58N 21.36E
108 B9 **Racconigi** Piemonte, NE Italy 44.45N 7.41E
33 T15 **Raccoon Creek** ~ Ohio, N USA
11 V13 **Race, Cape** headland Newfoundland and Labrador, E Canada 46.40N 53.05W
24 K10 **Raceland** Louisiana, S USA 29.43N 90.36W
21 Q12 **Race Point** headland Massachusetts, NE USA 42.03N 70.14W
178 J15 **Rach Gia** Kiên Giang, S Vietnam 10.01N 105.04E
178 J14 **Rach Gia, Vinh** bay S Vietnam
78 J8 **Rachid** Tagant, C Mauritania 18.48N 11.40W
112 L10 **Raciąż** Mazowieckie, C Poland 52.46N 20.04E
113 I16 **Racibórz** Ger. Ratibor. Śląskie, S Poland 50.06N 18.13E
33 N9 **Racine** Wisconsin, N USA 42.42N 87.49W
12 D7 **Racine Lake** ◎ Ontario, S Canada
113 J23 **Ráckeve** Pest, C Hungary 47.07N 18.57E
Rácz-Becse see Bečej
147 O15 **Radā'** var. Ridā'. W Yemen 14.24N 44.49E
115 O15 **Radan** ▲ SE Serbia 42.59N 21.31E
65 J19 **Rada Tilly** Chubut, SE Argentina 45.54S 67.33W
118 K8 **Rădăuṭi** Ger. Radautz, Hung. Rádóc. Suceava, N Romania 47.49N 25.58E
118 L8 **Rădăuṭi-Prut** Botoşani, NE Romania 48.14N 26.47E
Radautz see Rădăuṭi
Radbusa see Radbuza
113 A17 **Radbuza** Ger. Radbusa. ~ SE Czech Republic
22 K6 **Radcliff** Kentucky, S USA 37.50N 85.57W
145 O2 **Radd, Wādī ar** dry watercourse N Syria
97 H16 **Råde** Østfold, S Norway 59.21N 10.52E
111 V11 **Radeče** Ger. Ratschach. C Slovenia 46.01N 15.10E
Radein see Radenci
118 J4 **Radekhiv** Pol. Radziechów, Rus. Radekhov. L'vivs'ka Oblast', W Ukraine 50.17N 24.39E
Radekhov see Radekhiv
111 X9 **Radenci** Ger. Radein; prev. Radinci. NE Slovenia 46.36N 16.02E
111 S9 **Radenthein** Kärnten, S Austria 46.48N 13.42E
23 R7 **Radford** Virginia, NE USA 37.07N 80.34W
160 C9 **Rādhanpur** Gujarāt, W India 23.52N 71.49E
Radinci see Radenci
131 Q6 **Radishchevo** Ul'yanovskaya Oblast', W Russian Federation 52.49N 47.54E
10 I9 **Radisson** Québec, E Canada 53.47N 77.35W
9 P16 **Radium Hot Springs** British Columbia, SW Canada 50.39N 116.09W
118 F11 **Radna** Hung. Máriaradna. Arad, W Romania 46.04N 21.40E
116 K10 **Radnevo** Stara Zagora, C Bulgaria 42.18N 25.57E
99 J20 **Radnor** cultural region E Wales, UK
Radnót see Iernut
Rádóc see Rădăuṭi
103 H24 **Radolfzell am Bodensee** Baden-Württemberg, S Germany 47.43N 8.58E
112 M13 **Radom** Mazowieckie, C Poland 51.23N 21.07E
118 I14 **Radomireşti** Olt, S Romania 44.06N 25.00E
113 K14 **Radomsko** Rus. Novoradomsk. Łodzkie, C Poland 51.04N 19.25E
119 N4 **Radomyshl'** Zhytomyrs'ka Oblast', N Ukraine 50.30N 29.16E
115 P19 **Radoviš** prev. Radovište. E FYR Macedonia 41.39N 22.26E
Radovište see Radoviš
96 B13 **Radøy** island S Norway
111 R7 **Radstadt** Salzburg, NW Austria 47.24N 13.31E
190 E8 **Radstock, Cape** headland South Australia 33.11S 134.18E
121 G15 **Radun'** Rus. Radun'. Hrodzyenskaya Voblasts', W Belarus 54.03N 25.00E
126 Gg11 **Raduzhnyy** Khanty-Mansiyskiy Avtonomnyy Okrug, C Russian Federation 62.03N 77.28E
130 M3 **Raduzhnyy** Vladimirskaya Oblast', W Russian Federation 55.59N 40.15E
120 F11 **Radviliškis** Šiauliai, N Lithuania 55.48N 23.32E
9 U17 **Radville** Saskatchewan, S Canada 49.28N 104.19W
146 K7 **Raḍwá, Jabal** ▲ W Saudi Arabia 24.31N 38.21E
113 P16 **Radymno** Podkarpackie, SE Poland 49.57N 22.49E
118 J5 **Radyvyliv** Rivnens'ka Oblast', NW Ukraine 50.07N 25.12E
Radziechów see Radekhiv
112 I11 **Radziejów** Kujawsko-pomorskie, C Poland 52.36N 18.33E
112 O12 **Radzyń Podlaski** Lubelskie, E Poland 51.48N 22.36E
15 Hh4 **Rae** ~ Nunavut, NW Canada
158 M13 **Rāe Bareli** Uttar Pradesh, N India 26.13N 81.13E
Rae-Edzo see Edzo
23 T11 **Raeford** North Carolina, SE USA 34.58N 79.13W
101 M19 **Raeren** Liège, E Belgium 50.42N 6.06E
15 Kk3 **Rae Strait** strait Nunavut, N Canada
192 L11 **Raetihi** Manawatu-Wanganui, North Island, NZ 39.28S 175.16E
203 U13 **Raevavae** var. Raivavae. island Îles Australes, SW French Polynesia
Rafa see Rafah
64 M10 **Rafaela** Santa Fe, E Argentina 31.16S 61.25W
144 E11 **Rafah** var. Rafa, Rafaḥ, Heb. Rafiaḥ, Raphiah. SW Gaza Strip 31.17N 34.18E
81 L15 **Rafaï** Mbomou, SE Central African Republic 5.01N 23.51E
147 O4 **Rafḥah** Al Ḥudūd ash Shamālīyah, N Saudi Arabia 29.40N 43.28E
Rafiaḥ see Rafah
149 R10 **Rafsanjān** Kermān, C Iran 30.25N 56.00E
82 B13 **Raga** Western Bahr el Ghazal, SW Sudan 8.28N 25.40E
21 S8 **Ragged Island** island Maine, NE USA
46 I5 **Ragged Island Range** island group S Bahamas
192 L7 **Raglan** Waikato, North Island, NZ 37.49S 174.52E
24 G8 **Ragley** Louisiana, S USA 30.31N 93.13W
Ragnit see Neman
109 K25 **Ragusa** Sicilia, Italy, C Mediterranean Sea 36.55N 14.42E
Ragusa see Dubrovnik
Ragusavecchia see Cavtat
175 Qq12 **Raha** Pulau Muna, C Indonesia 4.49S 122.43E
121 N17 **Rahachow** Rus. Rogachëv. Homyel'skaya Voblasts', SE Belarus 53.03N 30.04E
69 U6 **Rahad** var. Nahr ar Rahad. ~ W Sudan
Rahad, Nahr ar see Rahad
Rahaeng see Tak
144 F11 **Rahat** Southern, C Israel 31.20N 34.43E
146 L8 **Rahaṭ, Ḥarrat** lavaflow W Saudi Arabia
155 S12 **Rahīmyār Khān** Punjab, SE Pakistan 28.27N 70.21E
97 I14 **Råholt** Akershus, S Norway 60.16N 11.10E
Rahovec see Orahovac
203 S10 **Raiatea** island Îles Sous le Vent, W French Polynesia
161 H16 **Rāichūr** Karnātaka, C India 16.15N 77.19E
Raidestos see Tekirdağ
159 S13 **Rāiganj** West Bengal, NE India 25.37N 88.10E
160 M11 **Raigarh** Chhattīsgarh, C India 21.55N 83.24E
175 Q18 **Raijua, Selat** strait Nusa Tenggara, S Indonesia
191 O16 **Railton** Tasmania, SE Australia 41.24S 146.28E
38 L8 **Rainbow Bridge** natural arch Utah, W USA
25 Q3 **Rainbow City** Alabama, S USA 33.57N 86.02W
9 N11 **Rainbow Lake** Alberta, W Canada 58.30N 119.24W
23 R5 **Rainelle** West Virginia, NE USA 37.57N 80.46W
34 G10 **Rainier** Oregon, NW USA 46.05N 122.55W
34 H9 **Rainier, Mount** ◬ Washington, NW USA 46.51N 121.45W
25 Q2 **Rainsville** Alabama, S USA 34.29N 85.51W
10 B11 **Rainy Lake** ◎ Canada/USA
10 A11 **Rainy River** Ontario, C Canada 48.43N 94.33W
Raippaluoto see Replot
160 K12 **Raipur** Chhattīsgarh, C India 21.16N 81.42E
160 H10 **Raisen** Madhya Pradesh, C India 23.21N 77.49E
13 N13 **Raisin** ~ Ontario, SE Canada
33 R11 **Raisin, River** ~ Michigan, N USA
Raivavae see Raevavae
155 W9 **Rāiwind** Punjab, E Pakistan 31.13N 74.10E
176 U9 **Raja Ampat, Kepulauan** island group E Indonesia
161 L16 **Rājahmundry** Andhra Pradesh, E India 17.05N 81.42E
161 I18 **Rājampet** Andhra Pradesh, E India 14.09N 79.10E
Rajang see Rajang, Batang
174 Mm6 **Rajang, Batang** var. Rajang. ~ East Malaysia
155 S11 **Rājanpur** Punjab, E Pakistan 29.07N 70.19E
161 H23 **Rājapālaiyam** Tamil Nādu, SE India 9.25N 77.36E
158 E12 **Rājasthān** ◈ state NW India
159 T15 **Rajbari** Dhaka, C Bangladesh 23.46N 89.39E
159 R12 **Rājbirāj** Eastern, E Nepal 26.34N 86.52E
160 G9 **Rājgarh** Madhya Pradesh, C India 24.01N 76.42E
158 H10 **Rājgarh** Rājasthān, NW India 28.37N 75.25E
159 P14 **Rājgīr** Bihār, N India 25.01N 85.25E
112 O8 **Rajgród** Podlaskie, NE Poland 53.43N 22.40E
160 L12 **Rājim** Chhattīsgarh, C India 20.57N 81.58E
114 C11 **Rajinac, Mali** ▲ W Croatia 44.47N 15.04E
160 B10 **Rājkot** Gujarāt, W India 22.18N 70.46E
159 R14 **Rājmahal** Jhārkhand, NE India 25.03N 87.49E
159 Q14 **Rājmahāl Hills** hill range N India
160 K12 **Rāj Nāndgaon** Chhattīsgarh, C India 21.06N 81.01E
158 I8 **Rājpura** Punjab, NW India 30.30N 76.36E
159 S14 **Rajshahi** prev. Rampur Boalia. Rajshahi, W Bangladesh 24.24N 88.40E
159 S13 **Rajshahi** ◈ division NW Bangladesh
202 K13 **Rakahanga** atoll N Cook Islands
193 H19 **Rakaia** Canterbury, South Island, NZ 43.45S 172.02E
193 G19 **Rakaia** ~ South Island, NZ
158 H3 **Rakaposhi** ▲ N India 36.06N 74.31E
Rakasd see Răcăşdia
174 Ii14 **Rakata, Pulau** var. Pulau Krakatau. island S Indonesia
147 U10 **Rakbah, Qalamat ar** well SE Saudi Arabia 20.37N 52.45E
Rakhine State see Arakan State
118 I8 **Rakhiv** Zakarpats'ka Oblast', W Ukraine 48.05N 24.15E
147 V13 **Rakhyūt** SW Oman 16.41N 53.09E
197 I14 **Rakiraki** Viti Levu, W Fiji 17.21S 178.11E
Rakka see Ar Raqqah
120 I4 **Rakke** Lääne-Virumaa, NE Estonia 58.58N 26.14E
97 I16 **Rakkestad** Østfold, S Norway 59.25N 11.19E
112 F12 **Rakoniewice** Ger. Rakwitz. Wielkolpolskie, C Poland 52.09N 16.10E
Rakonitz see Rakovník
85 H18 **Rakops** Central, C Botswana 21.01S 24.23E
113 C16 **Rakovník** Ger. Rakonitz. Středočeský Kraj, W Czech Republic 50.07N 13.43E
116 J10 **Rakovski** Plovdiv, C Bulgaria 42.16N 24.58E
Rakutō-kō see Naktong-gang
120 I3 **Rakvere** Ger. Wesenberg. Lääne-Virumaa, N Estonia 59.21N 26.19E
Rakwitz see Rakoniewice
24 L6 **Raleigh** Mississippi, S USA 32.01N 89.30W
23 U9 **Raleigh** state capital North Carolina, SE USA 35.46N 78.38W
23 Y11 **Raleigh Bay** bay North Carolina, SE USA
23 U9 **Raleigh-Durham** ✕ North Carolina, SE USA 35.54N 78.45W
201 S6 **Ralik Chain** island group Ralik Chain, W Marshall Islands
27 N5 **Ralls** Texas, SW USA 33.40N 101.23W
20 G13 **Ralston** Pennsylvania, NE USA 41.29N 76.57W
147 O16 **Ramādah** W Yemen 13.35N 43.50E
Ramadi see Ar Ramādī
107 N2 **Ramales de la Victoria** Cantabria, N Spain 43.15N 3.28W
144 F10 **Ramallah** C West Bank 31.53N 34.49E
63 C19 **Ramallo** Buenos Aires, E Argentina 33.30S 60.01W
161 H20 **Rāmanagaram** Karnātaka, E India 12.45N 77.16E
161 I23 **Rāmanāthapuram** Tamil Nādu, SE India 9.22N 78.52E
160 N12 **Rāmapur** Orissa, E India 21.48N 84.00E
161 I14 **Rāmāreddi** var. Kāmāreddi, Kamareddy. Andhra Pradesh, C India 18.19N 78.23E
144 F10 **Ramat Gan** Tel Aviv, W Israel 32.04N 34.48E
105 T6 **Rambervillers** Vosges, NE France 48.15N 6.50E
Rambi see Rabi
105 N5 **Rambouillet** Yvelines, N France 48.39N 1.49E
194 L8 **Rambutyo Island** island N PNG
159 Q12 **Rāmechhāp** Central, C Nepal 27.19N 86.04E
191 R12 **Rame Head** headland Victoria, SE Australia 37.48S 149.30E
130 L4 **Ramenskoye** Moskovskaya Oblast', W Russian Federation 55.31N 38.24E
128 J15 **Rameshki** Tverskaya Oblast', W Russian Federation 57.21N 36.05E
159 P14 **Rāmgarh** Jhārkhand, N India 23.37N 85.31E
158 D11 **Rāmgarh** Rājasthān, NW India 27.26N 70.35E
148 M9 **Rāmhormoz** var. Ram Hormuz, Ramuz. Khūzestān, SW Iran 31.17N 49.37E
Ram Hormuz see Rāmhormoz
Ram, Jebel see Ramm, Jabal
144 F10 **Ramla** var. Ramle, Ramleh, Ar. Er Ramle. Central, C Israel 31.55N 34.52E
Ramle/Ramleh see Ramla
144 F14 **Ramm, Jabal** var. Jebel Ram. ▲ SW Jordan 29.34N 35.24E
158 K10 **Rāmnagar** Uttaranchal, N India 29.22N 79.07E
97 N15 **Ramnäs** Västmanland, C Sweden 59.46N 16.16E
Râmnicul-Sărat see Râmnicu Sărat
118 L12 **Râmnicu Sărat** prev. Râmnicul-Sărat, Rîmnicu-Sărat. Buzău, E Romania 45.24N 27.06E
118 I13 **Râmnicu Vâlcea** prev. Rîmnicu Vîlcea. Vâlcea, C Romania 45.04N 24.32E
Ramokgwebana see Ramokgwebane
85 J18 **Ramokgwebane** var. Ramokgwebana. Central, NE Botswana 20.36S 27.39E
130 L7 **Ramon'** Voronezhskaya Oblast', W Russian Federation 51.51N 39.18E
37 V17 **Ramona** California, W USA 33.02N 116.52W
58 A10 **Ramón, Laguna** ◎ NW Peru
12 G7 **Ramore** Ontario, S Canada 48.26N 80.19W
42 M11 **Ramos** San Luis Potosí, C Mexico 22.48N 101.55W
43 N8 **Ramos Arizpe** Coahuila de Zaragoza, NE Mexico 25.34N 100.58W
42 J9 **Ramos, Río de** ~ C Mexico
85 I21 **Ramotswa** South East, S Botswana 24.51S 25.51E
41 R8 **Rampart** Alaska, USA 65.30N 150.10W
14 G5 **Ramparts** ~ Northwest Territories, NW Canada
158 K10 **Rāmpur** Uttar Pradesh, N India 28.48N 79.03E
160 F9 **Rāmpura** Madhya Pradesh, C India 24.34N 75.25E
Rampur Boalia see Rajshahi
177 F6 **Ramree Island** island W Burma
147 W6 **Rams** var. Ar Rams. Ra's al Khaymah, NE UAE 25.52N 56.01E
149 N4 **Rāmsar** prev. Sakhtsar. Māzandarān, N Iran 36.55N 50.39E
95 H16 **Ramsele** Västernorrland, N Sweden 63.33N 16.35E
23 T9 **Ramseur** North Carolina, SE USA 35.43N 79.39W
99 I16 **Ramsey** NE Isle of Man 54.19N 4.24W
99 I16 **Ramsey Bay** bay NE Isle of Man
12 E9 **Ramsey Lake** ◎ Ontario, S Canada
99 Q22 **Ramsgate** SE England, UK 51.19N 1.25E
96 M10 **Ramsjö** Gävleborg, C Sweden 62.10N 15.40E
160 I12 **Rāmtek** Mahārāshtra, C India 21.28N 79.28E
Ramtha see Ar Ramthā
194 H11 **Ramu** ~ N PNG
Ramuz see Rāmhormoz
120 G12 **Ramygala** Panevėžys, C Lithuania 55.30N 24.18E
158 H14 **Rāna Pratāp Sāgar** ◎ N India
175 O2 **Ranau** Sabah, East Malaysia 5.55N 116.43E
174 I12 **Ranau, Danau** ◎ Sumatera, W Indonesia
64 H12 **Rancagua** Libertador, C Chile 34.10S 70.45W
101 G22 **Rance** Hainaut, S Belgium 50.09N 4.16E
104 H6 **Rance** ~ NW France
62 J9 **Rancharia** São Paulo, S Brazil 22.13S 50.53W
159 P15 **Rānchi** Jhārkhand, N India 23.22N 85.19E
63 D21 **Ranchos** Buenos Aires, E Argentina 35.31S 58.22W
39 S9 **Ranchos De Taos** New Mexico, SW USA 36.21N 105.36W
65 G16 **Ranco, Lago** ◎ C Chile
97 C16 **Randaberg** Rogaland, S Norway 59.00N 5.38E
31 U7 **Randall** Minnesota, N USA 46.05N 94.30W
109 L23 **Randazzo** Sicilia, Italy, C Mediterranean Sea 37.52N 14.57E
97 G21 **Randers** Århus, C Denmark 56.28N 10.03E
94 I12 **Randijaure** ◎ N Sweden
23 T9 **Randleman** North Carolina, SE USA 35.49N 79.48W
21 O11 **Randolph** Massachusetts, NE USA 42.09N 71.02W
31 Q13 **Randolph** Nebraska, C USA 42.25N 97.05W
38 M1 **Randolph** Utah, W USA 41.40N 111.10W
102 P9 **Randow** ~ NE Germany
97 H14 **Randsfjorden** ◎ S Norway
94 K13 **Råneå** Norrbotten, N Sweden 65.52N 22.17E
94 G12 **Ranelva** ~ C Norway
95 F15 **Ranemsletta** Nord-Trøndelag, C Norway 64.36N 11.55E
78 H10 **Ranérou** C Senegal 15.17N 14.00W
Råneś see Ringvassøya
193 E22 **Ranfurly** Otago, South Island, NZ 45.07S 170.06E
178 Hh17 **Rangae** Narathiwat, SW Thailand 6.19N 101.45E
159 V16 **Rangamati** Chittagong, SE Bangladesh 22.40N 92.10E
192 I2 **Rangaunu Bay** bay North Island, NZ
21 P6 **Rangeley** Maine, NE USA 44.58N 70.37W
39 O4 **Rangely** Colorado, C USA 40.05N 108.48W
27 R7 **Ranger** Texas, SW USA 32.28N 98.40W
12 C9 **Ranger Lake** Ontario, S Canada 46.51N 83.34W
12 C9 **Ranger Lake** ◎ Ontario, S Canada
159 V12 **Rangia** Assam, NE India 26.27N 91.34E
193 I18 **Rangiora** Canterbury, South Island, NZ 43.19S 172.33E
203 T9 **Rangiroa** atoll Îles Tuamotu, W French Polynesia
192 N9 **Rangitaiki** ~ North Island, NZ
193 F19 **Rangitata** ~ South Island, NZ
192 M12 **Rangitikei** ~ North Island, NZ
192 L6 **Rangitoto Island** island N NZ
Rangkasbitoeng see Rangkasbitung
174 Ii14 **Rangkasbitung** prev. Rangkasbitoeng. Jawa, SW Indonesia 6.21S 106.12E
178 Hh9 **Rang, Khao** ▲ C Thailand 16.13N 99.03E
153 V13 **Rangkŭl** Rus. Rangkul'. SE Tajikistan 38.30N 74.24E
Rangkul' see Rangkŭl
Rangoon see Yangon
159 T13 **Rangpur** Rajshahi, N Bangladesh 25.46N 89.20E
174 Hh7 **Rangsang, Pulau** island W Indonesia
161 F18 **Rānībennur** Karnātaka, W India 14.36N 75.39E
159 R15 **Rāniganj** West Bengal, NE India 23.34N 87.13E
155 Q13 **Rānīpur** Sind, SE Pakistan 27.16N 68.34E
Rāniyah see Ŗānya
27 N9 **Rankin** Texas, SW USA 31.12N 101.56W
15 L7 **Rankin Inlet** Nunavut, C Canada 62.52N 92.13W
191 P8 **Rankins Springs** New South Wales, SE Australia 33.51S 146.16E
Rankovićevo see Kraljevo
110 I7 **Rankweil** Vorarlberg, W Austria 47.16N 9.40E
Rann see Brežice
131 T8 **Ranneye** Orenburgskaya Oblast', W Russian Federation 51.28N 52.29E
98 I10 **Rannoch, Loch** ◎ C Scotland, UK
203 U17 **Rano Kau** var. Rano Kao. crater Easter Island, Chile, E Pacific Ocean 27.10S 109.25W
178 Gg14 **Ranong** Ranong, SW Thailand 9.58N 98.40E
195 T14 **Ranongga** var. Ghanongga. island NW Solomon Islands
203 W16 **Rano Raraku** ancient monument Easter Island, Chile, E Pacific Ocean 27.07S 109.18W
176 W9 **Ransiki** Papua, E Indonesia 1.27S 134.12E
94 K12 **Rantajärvi** Norrbotten, N Sweden 66.45N 23.39E
95 N17 **Rantasalmi** Isä-Suomi, SE Finland 62.02N 28.22E
175 N11 **Rantau** Borneo, C Indonesia 2.55S 115.09E
174 Hh7 **Rantau, Pulau** var. Pulau Tebingtinggi. island W Indonesia
175 Pp11 **Rantepao** Sulawesi, C Indonesia 2.58S 119.58E
32 M13 **Rantoul** Illinois, N USA 40.19N 88.08W
95 L15 **Rantsila** Oulu, C Finland 64.31N 25.40E
94 L13 **Ranua** Lappi, NW Finland 65.55N 26.34E
145 T3 **Ŗānya** var. Rāniyah. NE Iraq 36.15N 44.52E
163 X3 **Raohe** Heilongjiang, NE China 46.49N 134.00E
76 H9 **Raoui, Erg er** desert W Algeria
199 L11 **Rapa** island Îles Australes, S French Polynesia
203 V14 **Rapa Iti** island Îles Australes, SW French Polynesia
108 D10 **Rapallo** Liguria, NW Italy 44.21N 9.13E
Rapa Nui see Pascua, Isla de
Raphiah see Rafah
23 V5 **Rapidan River** ~ Virginia, NE USA
30 J10 **Rapid City** South Dakota, N USA 44.04N 103.13W
13 P8 **Rapide-Blanc** Québec, SE Canada 47.48N 72.57W
12 I8 **Rapide-Deux** Québec, SE Canada 47.56N 78.33W
120 K6 **Räpina** Ger. Rappin. Põlvamaa, SE Estonia 58.06N 27.27E
120 G4 **Rapla** Ger. Rappel. Raplamaa, NW Estonia 59.00N 24.46E
120 G4 **Raplamaa** off. Rapla Maakond. ◈ province NW Estonia
23 X6 **Rappahonnock River** ~ Virginia, NE USA
Rappel see Rapla
110 G7 **Rapperswil** Sankt Gallen, NE Switzerland 47.13N 8.49E
Rappin see Räpina
159 N12 **Rāpti** ~ N India
59 K16 **Rapulo, Río** ~ E Bolivia
Raqqah/Raqqah, Muḥāfaẓat al see Ar Raqqah
20 J8 **Raquette Lake** ◎ New York, NE USA
20 J6 **Raquette River** ~ New York, NE USA
203 V10 **Raraka** atoll Îles Tuamotu, C French Polynesia
203 V10 **Raroia** atoll Îles Tuamotu, C French Polynesia
202 H15 **Rarotonga** ✕ Rarotonga, S Cook Islands, C Pacific Ocean 21.15S 159.45W
202 H16 **Rarotonga** island S Cook Islands, C Pacific Ocean
153 P12 **Rarz** W Tajikistan 39.23N 68.43E
Ras al 'Ain see Ra's al 'Ayn
145 N2 **Ra's al 'Ayn** var. Ras al'Ain. Al Ḥasakah, N Syria 36.52N 40.04E
144 H3 **Ra's al Basīṭ** Al Lādhiqīyah, W Syria 35.57N 35.55E
Ra's al-Hafgī see Ra's al Khafjī
147 R5 **Ra's al Khafjī** var. Ra's al-Hafgī. Ash Sharqīyah, NE Saudi Arabia 28.22N 48.29E
Ras al-Khaimah/Ras al Khaimah see Ra's al Khaymah
149 R15 **Ra's al Khaymah** var. Ras al Khaimah. Ra's al Khaymah, NE UAE 25.44N 55.54E
149 R15 **Ra's al Khaymah** var. Ras al-Khaimah. ✕ Ra's al Khaymah, NE UAE 25.37N 55.51E
144 G13 **Ra's an Naqb** Ma'ān, S Jordan 30.00N 35.29E
63 B26 **Rasa, Punta** headland E Argentina 40.50S 62.15W
176 W10 **Rasawi** Papua, E Indonesia 2.04S 134.02E
Râşcani see Rîşcani
82 J10 **Ras Dashen Terara** ▲ N Ethiopia 13.12N 38.09E
157 K19 **Rasdu Atoll** atoll C Maldives
120 E12 **Raseiniai** Kaunas, C Lithuania 55.23N 23.06E
77 X8 **Râs Ghârib** E Egypt 28.16N 33.01E
168 J6 **Rashaant** Hövsgöl, N Mongolia 49.08N 101.27E
Rashaant see Delüün, Bayan-Ölgiy, Mongolia
Rashaant see Öldziyt, Dundgovĭ, Mongolia
145 Y11 **Rashīd** E Iraq 31.15N 47.31E
77 V7 **Rashîd** Eng. Rosetta. N Egypt 31.24N 30.25E
148 M3 **Rasht** var. Resht. Gīlān, NW Iran 37.18N 49.37E
145 S2 **Rashwān** N Iraq 36.28N 43.54E
Rasik see Raasiku
115 M15 **Raška** Serbia, C Serbia 43.18N 20.37E
121 P15 **Rasna** Rus. Ryasna. Mahilyowskaya Voblasts', E Belarus 54.01N 31.12E
118 J12 **Râşnov** prev. Rîşno, Rozsnyó, Hung. Barcarozsnyó. Braşov, C Romania 45.34N 25.27E
120 L11 **Rasony** Rus. Rossony. Vitsyebskaya Voblasts', N Belarus 55.55N 28.51E
Ra's Shamrah see Ugarit
131 N7 **Rasskazovo** Tambovskaya Oblast', W Russian Federation 52.42N 41.45E
121 O16 **Rasta** ~ E Belarus
Rastadt see Rastatt
Rastâne see Ar Rastān
147 S6 **Ra's Tannūrah** Eng. Ras Tanura. Ash Sharqīyah, NE Saudi Arabia 26.44N 50.04E
Ras Tanura see Ra's Tannūrah
103 G21 **Rastatt** var. Rastadt. Baden-Württemberg, SW Germany 48.52N 8.12E
Rastenburg see Kętrzyn
155 V7 **Rasūlnagar** Punjab, E Pakistan 32.19N 73.51E
201 U6 **Ratak Chain** island group Ratak Chain, E Marshall Islands
121 K15 **Ratamka** Rus. Ratomka. Minskaya Voblasts', C Belarus 53.57N 27.23E
95 G17 **Rätan** Jämtland, C Sweden 62.28N 14.34E
158 G11 **Ratangarh** Rājasthān, NW India 28.01N 74.39E
Rat Buri see Ratchaburi
178 H11 **Ratchaburi** var. Rat Buri. Ratchaburi, W Thailand 13.30N 99.49E
31 W15 **Rathbun Lake** ▣ Iowa, C USA
Ráth Caola see Rathkeale
177 F5 **Rathedaung** Arakan State, W Burma 20.30N 92.48E
102 M12 **Rathenow** Brandenburg, NE Germany 52.34N 12.20E
99 C19 **Rathkeale** Ir. Ráth Caola. SW Ireland 52.31N 8.55W
98 F13 **Rathlin Island** Ir. Reachlainn. island N Northern Ireland, UK
99 C20 **Ráthluirc** Ir. An Ráth. SW Ireland 52.22N 8.44W
Ratibor see Racibórz
Ratisbon/Ratisbona/Ratisbonne see Regensburg
Rätische Alpen see Rhaetian Alps
40 E17 **Rat Island** island Aleutian Islands, Alaska, USA
40 E17 **Rat Islands** island group Aleutian Islands, Alaska, USA
160 F10 **Ratlām** prev. Rutlam. Madhya Pradesh, C India 23.23N 75.03E
161 D15 **Ratnāgiri** Mahārāshtra, W India 17.00N 73.20E
161 K26 **Ratnapura** Sabaragamuwa Province, S Sri Lanka 6.40N 80.25E
118 J2 **Ratne** Rus. Ratno. Volyns'ka Oblast', NW Ukraine 51.40N 24.33E
Ratno see Ratne
Ratomka see Ratamka
39 U8 **Raton** New Mexico, SW USA 36.54N 104.27W
145 O7 **Ratqah, Wādī ar** dry watercourse W Iraq
Ratschach see Radeče
178 H17 **Rattaphum** Songkhla, SW Thailand 7.07N 100.16E
28 L6 **Rattlesnake Creek** ~ Kansas, C USA
96 L13 **Rättvik** Dalarna, C Sweden 60.53N 15.12E
102 K9 **Ratzeburg** Mecklenburg-Vorpommern, N Germany 53.41N 10.48E
102 K9 **Ratzeburger See** ◎ N Germany
8 J10 **Ratz, Mount** ▲ British Columbia, SW Canada 57.22N 132.17W
63 D22 **Rauch** Buenos Aires, E Argentina 36.47S 59.06W
43 U16 **Raudales** Chiapas, SE Mexico
Raudhatain see Ar Rawḍatayn
Raudnitz an der Elbe see Roudnice nad Labem
94 K1 **Raufarhöfn** Nordhurland Eystra, NE Iceland 66.26N 15.57W
96 H13 **Raufoss** Oppland, S Norway 60.43N 10.36E
Raukawa see Cook Strait
192 Q8 **Raukumara** ▲ North Island, NZ 37.46S 178.07E
199 J12 **Raukumara Plain** undersea feature N Coral Sea
192 P8 **Raukumara Range** ▲▲ North Island, NZ
160 N11 **Rāulakela** var. Raurkela; prev. Rourkela. Orissa, E. India 22.13N 84.52E
97 F15 **Rauland** Telemark, S Norway 59.41N 7.57E
95 J19 **Rauma** Swe. Raumo. Länsi-Suomi, W Finland 61.09N 21.30E
96 F10 **Rauma** ~ S Norway
Raumo see Rauma
120 H8 **Rauna** Cēsis, C Latvia 57.19N 25.34E
174 Mm16 **Raung, Gunung** ▲ Jawa, S Indonesia 8.00S 114.07E
Raurkela see Rāulakela
97 J22 **Raus** Skåne, S Sweden 56.01N 12.48E
172 R6 **Rausu** Hokkaidō, NE Japan 44.00N 145.06E
172 R6 **Rausu-dake** ▲ Hokkaidō, NE Japan 44.06N 145.04E
95 M17 **Rautalampi** Itä-Suomi, C Finland 62.37N 26.48E
95 N16 **Rautavaara** Itä-Suomi, C Finland 63.30N 28.19E
118 M9 **Răutel** ~ C Moldova
95 O18 **Rautjärvi** Etelä-Suomi, S Finland 61.21N 29.20E
Rautu see Sosnovo
203 V11 **Ravahere** atoll Îles Tuamotu, C French Polynesia
109 J25 **Ravanusa** Sicilia, Italy, C Mediterranean Sea 37.16N 13.57E
149 S9 **Rāvar** Kermān, C Iran 31.15N 56.51E
153 Q11 **Ravat** Batkenskaya Oblast', SW Kyrgyzstan 39.54N 70.06E
20 K11 **Ravena** New York, NE USA 42.28N 73.49W
108 H10 **Ravenna** Emilia-Romagna, N Italy 44.28N 12.15E
31 O15 **Ravenna** Nebraska, C USA 41.01N 98.54W
33 U11 **Ravenna** Ohio, N USA 41.09N 81.14W
103 I24 **Ravensburg** Baden-Württemberg, S Germany 47.46N 9.37E
189 W4 **Ravenshoe** Queensland, NE Australia 17.29S 145.28E
188 K13 **Ravensthorpe** Western Australia 33.37S 120.03E
23 Q4 **Ravenswood** West Virginia, NE USA 38.57N 81.45W
155 U9 **Rāvi** ~ India/Pakistan
114 C9 **Ravna Gora** Primorje-Gorski Kotar, NW Croatia 45.20N 14.54E
111 U10 **Ravne na Koroškem** Ger. Gutenstein. N Slovenia 46.33N 14.57E
145 P6 **Rāwah** W Iraq 34.32N 41.54E
203 T4 **Rawaki** prev. Phoenix Island. atoll Phoenix Islands, C Kiribati
155 U6 **Rāwalpindi** Punjab, NE Pakistan 33.38N 73.06E
112 L13 **Rawa Mazowiecka** Łódzkie, C Poland 51.46N 20.15E
145 T2 **Ŗawāndiz** var. Rawandoz, Rawāndūz. N Iraq 36.37N 44.31E
Rawandoz/Rawāndūz see Ŗawāndiz
176 Vv9 **Rawarra** ~ Papua, E Indonesia
176 V9 **Rawas** Papua, E Indonesia 1.07S 132.12E
145 O4 **Rawḍah** ◎ E Syria
112 G13 **Rawicz** Ger. Rawitsch. Wielkopolskie, C Poland 51.37N 16.51E
Rawitsch see Rawicz
188 M11 **Rawlinna** Western Australia 31.00S 125.35E
35 W16 **Rawlins** Wyoming, C USA 41.47N 107.14W
65 K17 **Rawson** Chubut, SE Argentina 43.22S 65.01W
165 R16 **Rawu** Xizang Zizhiqu, W China 29.30N 96.42E
159 P12 **Raxaul** Bihār, N India 26.58N 84.51E
30 K3 **Ray** North Dakota, N USA 48.19N 103.11W
174 M9 **Raya, Bukit** ▲ Borneo, C Indonesia 0.40S 112.40E
161 I18 **Rāyachoti** Andhra Pradesh, E India 14.03N 78.43E
Rāyadrug see Rāyagarha
161 M14 **Rāyagarha** prev. Rāyadrug. Orissa, E India 19.11N 83.22E
144 H7 **Rayak** var. Rayaq, Riyāq. E Lebanon 33.51N 36.03E
Rayaq see Rayak
145 T2 **Ŗāyat** E Iraq 36.39N 44.56E
174 J10 **Raya, Tanjung** headland Pulau Bangka, W Indonesia 1.49S 106.04E
11 R13 **Ray, Cape** headland Newfoundland and Labrador, E Canada 47.38N 59.15W
126 Mm16 **Raychikhinsk** Amurskaya Oblast', SE Russian Federation 49.47N 129.19E
131 U5 **Rayevskiy** Respublika Bashkortostan, W Russian Federation 54.04N 54.58E
9 Q17 **Raymond** Alberta, SW Canada 49.30N 112.40W
24 K6 **Raymond** Mississippi, S USA 32.15N 90.25W
34 F9 **Raymond** Washington, NW USA 46.41N 123.43W

◆ Country ● Country Capital ◇ Dependent Territory ○ Dependent Territory Capital ◈ Administrative Region ✕ International Airport ▲ Mountain ▲▲ Mountain Range ◬ Volcano ~ River ◎ Lake ▣ Reservoir

RAYMOND TERRACE – RIETI

191 T8 **Raymond Terrace** New South Wales, SE Australia *32.46S 151.45E*
27 T17 **Raymondville** Texas, SW USA *26.27N 97.45W*
9 U16 **Raymore** Saskatchewan, S Canada *51.24N 104.34W*
41 Q8 **Ray Mountains** ⛰ Alaska, USA
24 H9 **Rayne** Louisiana, S USA *30.13N 92.15W*
43 O12 **Rayón** San Luis Potosí, C Mexico *21.54N 99.33W*
42 G4 **Rayón** Sonora, NW Mexico *29.45N 110.33W*
178 Hh12 **Rayong** Rayong, S Thailand *12.42N 101.16E*
27 T5 **Ray Roberts, Lake** ◎ Texas, SW USA
20 E15 **Raystown Lake** ⊠ Pennsylvania, NE USA
147 V13 **Raysūt** SW Oman *16.58N 54.01E*
29 R4 **Raytown** Missouri, C USA *39.00N 94.27W*
24 I5 **Rayville** Louisiana, S USA *32.29N 91.45W*
148 L5 **Razan** Hamadān, W Iran *35.22N 48.58E*
145 S9 **Razāzah, Buḩayrat ar** *var.* Baḩr al Milḩ. ◎ C Iraq
116 L9 **Razboyna** ▲ E Bulgaria *42.54N 26.31E*
Razdan *see* Hrazdan
Razdolnoye *see* Rozdol'ne
Razelm, Lacul *see* Razim, Lacul
145 U2 **Ŗazga** E Iraq *36.25N 45.06E*
116 L8 **Razgrad** Razgrad, N Bulgaria *43.33N 26.31E*
116 L8 **Razgrad** ◈ *province* N Bulgaria
119 N13 **Razim, Lacul** *prev.* Lacul Razelm. *lagoon* NW Black Sea
116 G11 **Razlog** Blagoevgrad, SW Bulgaria *41.52N 23.28E*
120 K10 **Rāznas Ezers** ◎ SE Latvia
104 E6 **Raz, Pointe du** *headland* NW France *48.06N 4.52W*
Reachlainn *see* Rathlin Island
Reachrainn *see* Lambay Island
99 N22 **Reading** S England, UK *51.28N 0.58W*
20 H15 **Reading** Pennsylvania, NE USA *40.19N 75.55W*
50 C7 **Real, Cordillera** ⛰ C Ecuador
64 K12 **Realicó** La Pampa, C Argentina *35.01S 64.13W*
27 R15 **Realitos** Texas, SW USA *27.26N 98.31W*
110 G9 **Realp** Uri, C Switzerland *46.36N 8.32E*
178 Ii12 **Reăng Kesei** Bătdâmbâng, W Cambodia *12.57N 103.15E*
203 Y11 **Reao** *atoll* Îles Tuamotu, E French Polynesia
Reate *see* Rieti
188 L11 **Rebecca, Lake** ◎ Western Australia
Rebiana Sand Sea *see* Rabyānah, Ramlat
128 H8 **Reboly** Respublika Kareliya, NW Russian Federation *63.51N 30.49E*
172 P1 **Rebun** Rebun-tō, NE Japan *45.19N 141.02E*
172 P1 **Rebun-suidō** *strait* E Sea of Japan
172 P1 **Rebun-tō** *island* NE Japan
108 J12 **Recanati** Marche, C Italy *43.23N 13.34E*
Rechitsa *see* Rechytsa
111 Y7 **Rechnitz** Burgenland, SE Austria *47.18N 16.26E*
121 J20 **Rechytsa** *Rus.* Rechitsa. Brestskaya Voblasts', SW Belarus *51.51N 26.49E*
121 O19 **Rechytsa** *Rus.* Rechitsa. Homyel'skaya Voblasts', SE Belarus *52.22N 30.22E*
61 Q15 **Recife** *prev.* Pernambuco. *state capital* Pernambuco, E Brazil *8.06S 34.52W*
85 I26 **Recife, Cape** *Afr.* Kaap Recife. *headland* S South Africa *34.03S 25.37E*
Recife, Kaap *see* Recife, Cape
180 I16 **Récifs, Îles aux** *island* Inner Islands, NE Seychelles
103 E14 **Recklinghausen** Nordrhein-Westfalen, W Germany *51.37N 7.12E*
102 M8 **Recknitz** ≈ NE Germany
101 K23 **Recogne** Luxembourg, SE Belgium *49.56N 5.20E*
63 C15 **Reconquista** Santa Fe, C Argentina *29.10S 59.41W*
205 O6 **Recovery Glacier** *glacier* Antarctica
61 G15 **Recreio** Mato Grosso, W Brazil *8.13S 58.15W*
29 X9 **Rector** Arkansas, C USA *36.15N 90.17W*
112 E9 **Recz** *Ger.* Reetz Neumark. Zachodnio-pomorskie, NW Poland *53.16N 15.32E*
101 L24 **Redange** *var.* Redange-sur-Attert. Diekirch, W Luxembourg *49.46N 5.52E*
Redange-sur-Attert *see* Redange
20 C13 **Redbank Creek** ≈ Pennsylvania, NE USA
11 S9 **Red Bay** Quebec, E Canada *51.40N 56.37W*
25 N2 **Red Bay** Alabama, S USA *34.26N 88.08W*
37 N4 **Red Bluff** California, W USA *40.09N 122.14W*
26 J8 **Red Bluff Reservoir** ◎ New Mexico/Texas, SW USA
32 K16 **Red Bud** Illinois, N USA *38.12N 89.59W*
32 J5 **Red Cedar River** ≈ Wisconsin, N USA
9 R17 **Redcliff** Alberta, SW Canada *50.06N 110.48W*
85 K17 **Redcliff** Midlands, C Zimbabwe *19.01S 29.43E*
190 L9 **Red Cliffs** Victoria, SE Australia *34.21S 142.12E*
31 P17 **Red Cloud** Nebraska, C USA *40.05N 98.31W*
24 L8 **Red Creek** ≈ Mississippi, S USA
9 P15 **Red Deer** Alberta, SW Canada *52.15N 113.48W*
9 Q16 **Red Deer** ≈ Alberta, SW Canada
41 O11 **Red Devil** Alaska, USA *61.45N 95.18W*
37 N3 **Redding** California, W USA *40.33N 122.26W*
99 L20 **Redditch** W England, UK *52.19N 1.55W*
31 P9 **Redfield** South Dakota, N USA *44.51N 98.31W*
26 J12 **Redford** Texas, SW USA *29.31N 104.19W*
47 V13 **Redhead** Trinidad, Trinidad and Tobago *10.48N 60.56W*
190 I8 **Red Hill** South Australia *33.34S 138.13E*
Red Hill *see* Pu'u 'Ula'ula
28 K7 **Red Hills** *hill range* Kansas, C USA
11 T12 **Red Indian Lake** ◎ Newfoundland and Labrador, E Canada
128 J16 **Redkino** Tverskaya Oblast', W Russian Federation *56.41N 36.07E*
10 A10 **Red Lake** Ontario, C Canada *51.00N 93.55W*
38 I10 **Red Lake** *salt flat* Arizona, SW USA
31 S4 **Red Lake Falls** Minnesota, N USA *47.52N 96.16W*
31 R4 **Red Lake River** ≈ Minnesota, N USA
37 U15 **Redlands** California, W USA *34.03N 117.10W*
20 G16 **Red Lion** Pennsylvania, NE USA *39.53N 76.36W*
35 U11 **Red Lodge** Montana, NW USA *45.11N 109.15W*
34 H13 **Redmond** Oregon, NW USA *44.16N 121.10W*
38 L5 **Redmond** Utah, W USA *39.00N 111.51W*
34 H8 **Redmond** Washington, NW USA *47.40N 122.07W*
Rednitz *see* Regnitz
31 T15 **Red Oak** Iowa, C USA *41.00N 95.10W*
20 K12 **Red Oaks Mill** New York, NE USA *41.39N 73.52W*
104 I7 **Redon** Ille-et-Vilaine, NW France *47.39N 2.04W*
47 W10 **Redonda** *island* SW Antigua and Barbuda
106 G4 **Redondela** Galicia, NW Spain *42.16N 8.36W*
106 H11 **Redondo** Évora, S Portugal *38.37N 7.31W*
41 Q12 **Redoubt Volcano** ▲ Alaska, USA *60.29N 152.44W*
9 Y16 **Red River** ≈ Canada/USA
133 U12 **Red River** *var.* Yuan, *Chin.* Yuan Jiang, *Vtn.* Sông Hông Hà. ≈ China/Vietnam
27 W4 **Red River** ≈ S USA
24 H7 **Red River** ≈ Louisiana, S USA
32 M6 **Red River** ≈ Wisconsin, N USA
Red Rock, Lake *see* Red Rock Reservoir
31 W14 **Red Rock Reservoir** *var.* Lake Red Rock. ⊠ Iowa, C USA
194 J15 **Redscar Bay** *bay* S PNG
82 H7 **Red Sea** ◈ *state* NE Sudan
77 Y9 **Red Sea** *anc.* Sinus Arabicus. *sea* Africa/Asia
23 T11 **Red Springs** North Carolina, SE USA *34.49N 79.10W*
15 Gg6 **Redstone** ≈ Northwest Territories, NW Canada
9 V17 **Redvers** Saskatchewan, S Canada *49.31N 101.33W*
79 P13 **Red Volta** *var.* Nazinon, *Fr.* Volta Rouge. ≈ Burkina/Ghana
9 Q14 **Redwater** Alberta, SW Canada *53.57N 113.06W*
30 M16 **Red Willow Creek** ≈ Nebraska, C USA
31 W9 **Red Wing** Minnesota, N USA *44.33N 92.31W*
37 N9 **Redwood City** California, W USA *37.29N 122.13W*
31 T9 **Redwood Falls** Minnesota, N USA *44.33N 95.07W*
198 Ff7 **Reed Bank** *undersea feature* C South China Sea
33 P7 **Reed City** Michigan, N USA *43.52N 85.30W*
30 K6 **Reeder** North Dakota, N USA *46.03N 102.55W*
37 R11 **Reedley** California, W USA *36.35N 119.27W*
35 T11 **Reedpoint** Montana, NW USA *45.41N 109.33W*
32 K8 **Reedsburg** Wisconsin, N USA *43.33N 90.03W*
34 E13 **Reedsport** Oregon, NW USA *43.42N 124.06W*
195 X8 **Reef Islands** *island group* Santa Cruz Islands, E Solomon Islands
193 H16 **Reefton** West Coast, South Island, NZ *42.07S 171.52E*
22 F8 **Reelfoot Lake** ◎ Tennessee, S USA
99 D17 **Ree, Lough** *Ir.* Loch Rí. ◎ C Ireland
Reengus *see* Rīngas
37 U4 **Reese River** ≈ Nevada, W USA
100 M8 **Reest** ≈ E Netherlands
Reetz Neumark *see* Recz
Reevhtse *see* Rossvatnet
143 N13 **Refahiye** Erzincan, C Turkey *39.54N 38.45E*
25 N4 **Reform** Alabama, S USA *33.22N 88.01W*
97 K20 **Reftele** Jönköping, S Sweden *57.10N 13.34E*
27 T14 **Refugio** Texas, SW USA *28.18N 97.16W*
112 E8 **Rega** ≈ NW Poland
Regar *see* Tursunzoda
103 O21 **Regen** Bayern, SE Germany *48.57N 13.10E*
103 M20 **Regen** ≈ SE Germany
103 M21 **Regensburg** *Eng.* Ratisbon, *Fr.* Ratisbonne; *hist.* Ratisbona, *anc.* Castra Regina, Reginum. Bayern, SE Germany *49.01N 12.06E*
103 M21 **Regenstauf** Bayern, SE Germany *49.06N 12.07E*
76 I10 **Reggane** C Algeria *26.45N 0.10E*
100 N9 **Regge** ≈ E Netherlands
Reggio *see* Reggio nell' Emilia
Reggio Calabria *see* Reggio di Calabria
109 M23 **Reggio di Calabria** *var.* Reggio Calabria, *Gk.* Rhegion; *anc.* Regium, Rhegium. Calabria, SW Italy *38.06N 15.39E*
Reggio Emilia *see* Reggio nell' Emilia
108 F9 **Reggio nell' Emilia** *var.* Reggio Emilia, *abbrev.* Reggio; *anc.* Regium Lepidum. Emilia-Romagna, N Italy *44.42N 10.37E*
118 I10 **Reghin** *Ger.* Sächsisch-Reen, *Hung.* Szászrégen; *prev.* Reghinul Săsesc, *Ger.* Sächsisch-Regen. Mureş, C Romania *46.46N 24.40E*
Reghinul Săsesc *see* Reghin
9 U16 **Regina** Saskatchewan, S Canada *50.25N 104.39W*
9 U16 **Regina** ✈ Saskatchewan, S Canada *50.21N 104.43W*
57 Z10 **Régina** E French Guiana *4.19N 52.07W*
9 U16 **Regina Beach** Saskatchewan, S Canada *50.44N 105.03W*
Reginum *see* Regensburg
Registan *see* Rīgestān
62 L11 **Registro** São Paulo, S Brazil *24.30S 47.49W*
Regium *see* Reggio di Calabria
Regium Lepidum *see* Reggio nell' Emilia
103 K19 **Regnitz** *var.* Rednitz. ≈ SE Germany
42 K10 **Regocijo** Durango, W Mexico *23.34N 105.10W*
106 H12 **Reguengos de Monsaraz** Évora, S Portugal *38.25N 7.31W*
103 M18 **Rehau** Bayern, E Germany *50.15N 12.03E*
85 D19 **Rehoboth** Hardap, C Namibia *23.18S 17.03E*
Rehoboth/Rehovoth *see* Reḥovot
23 Z4 **Rehoboth Beach** Delaware, NE USA *38.42N 75.03W*
144 F10 **Reḥovot** *var.* Rehoboth, Rekhovot, Rehovoth. Central, C Israel *31.54N 34.49E*
83 J20 **Rei** *spring/well* S Kenya *3.24S 39.18E*
Reichenau *see* Rychnov nad Kněžnou, Czech Republic
Reichenau *see* Bogatynia, Poland
103 M17 **Reichenbach** *var.* Reichenbach im Vogtland. Sachsen, E Germany *50.36N 12.18E*
Reichenbach *see* Dzierżoniów
Reichenbach im Vogtland *see* Reichenbach
Reichenberg *see* Liberec
189 O11 **Reid** Western Australia *30.48S 128.24E*
25 V6 **Reidsville** Georgia, SE USA *32.05N 82.07W*
23 T8 **Reidsville** North Carolina, SE USA *36.21N 79.39W*
Reifnitz *see* Ribnica
99 O22 **Reigate** SE England, UK *51.13N 0.13W*
Reikjavik *see* Reykjavík
104 I10 **Ré, Île de** *island* W France
39 N15 **Reiley Peak** ▲ Arizona, SW USA *32.24N 110.09W*
105 Q4 **Reims** *Eng.* Rheims; *anc.* Durocortorum, Remi. Marne, N France *49.16N 4.01E*
65 G23 **Reina Adelaida, Archipiélago** *island group* S Chile
47 O16 **Reina Beatrix** ✈ (Oranjestad) C Aruba *12.30N 69.57W*
110 F7 **Reinach** Aargau, W Switzerland *47.15N 8.12E*
110 E6 **Reinach** Basel-Land, NW Switzerland *47.30N 7.36E*
66 O11 **Reina Sofía** ✈ (Tenerife) Tenerife, Islas Canarias, Spain, NE Atlantic Ocean
31 W13 **Reinbeck** Iowa, C USA *42.19N 92.36W*
102 J10 **Reinbek** Schleswig-Holstein, N Germany *53.31N 10.15E*
9 U12 **Reindeer** ≈ Saskatchewan, C Canada
9 U11 **Reindeer Lake** ◎ Manitoba/Saskatchewan, C Canada
Reine-Charlotte, Îles de la *see* Queen Charlotte Islands
Reine-Élisabeth, Îles de la *see* Queen Elizabeth Islands
96 F13 **Reineskarvet** ▲ S Norway *60.38N 7.48E*
192 H1 **Reinga, Cape** *headland* North Island, NZ *34.24S 172.40E*
107 N3 **Reinosa** Cantabria, N Spain *43.01N 4.09W*
111 R8 **Reisseck** ▲ S Austria *46.57N 13.21E*
23 W3 **Reisterstown** Maryland, NE USA *39.27N 76.46W*
Reisui *see* Yŏsu
100 N5 **Reitdiep** ≈ NE Netherlands
203 V10 **Reitoru** *atoll* Îles Tuamotu, C French Polynesia
97 M17 **Rejmyre** Östergötland, S Sweden *58.49N 15.55E*
Reka *see* Rijeka
Reka Ili *see* Ile/Ili He
97 N16 **Rekarne** Västmanland, C Sweden *59.25N 16.04*
Rekhovot *see* Reḥovot
15 Ii7 **Reliance** Northwest Territories, C Canada *62.45N 109.07W*
35 U16 **Reliance** Wyoming, C USA *41.42N 109.13W*
76 I5 **Relizane** *var.* Ghelîzâne, Ghilizane. NW Algeria *35.45N 0.39E*
190 I7 **Remarkable, Mount** ▲ South Australia *32.46S 138.08E*
56 E8 **Remedios** Antioquia, N Colombia *7.01N 74.42W*
45 Q16 **Remedios** Veraguas, W Panama *8.12N 81.49W*
44 D8 **Remedios, Punta** *headland* SW El Salvador *13.31N 89.48W*
Remi *see* Reims
101 N25 **Remich** Grevenmacher, SE Luxembourg *49.33N 6.22E*
101 J19 **Remicourt** Liège, E Belgium *50.40N 5.19E*
12 H8 **Rémigny, Lac** ◎ Québec, SE Canada
57 Z10 **Rémire** NE French Guiana *4.52N 52.16W*
131 N13 **Remontnoye** Rostovskaya Oblast', SW Russian Federation *46.35N 43.38E*
176 V13 **Remoon** Pulau Kur, E Indonesia *5.18S 131.59E*
101 L20 **Remouchamps** Liège, E Belgium *50.29N 5.43E*
105 R15 **Remoulins** Gard, S France *43.56N 4.34E*
181 X16 **Rempart, Mont du** *var.* Mount Rempart. *hill* W Mauritius
103 E15 **Remscheid** Nordrhein-Westfalen, W Germany *51.10N 7.10E*
31 S12 **Remsen** Iowa, C USA *42.48N 95.58W*
96 I12 **Rena** Hedmark, S Norway *61.07N 11.21E*
96 I11 **Renåa** ≈ S Norway
Renaix *see* Ronse
120 H7 **Rencēni** Valmiera, N Latvia *57.43N 25.25E*
120 D9 **Renda** Kuldīga, W Latvia *57.04N 22.18E*
109 N20 **Rende** Calabria, SW Italy *39.19N 16.10E*
101 K21 **Rendeux** Luxembourg, SE Belgium *50.15N 5.28E*
Rendina *see* Rentína
32 L16 **Rend Lake** ⊠ Illinois, N USA
195 U15 **Rendova** *island* New Georgia Islands, NW Solomon Islands
102 I8 **Rendsburg** Schleswig-Holstein, N Germany *54.18N 9.40E*
110 B9 **Renens** Vaud, SW Switzerland *46.31N 6.36E*
12 K12 **Renfrew** Ontario, SE Canada *45.28N 76.42W*
98 I12 **Renfrew** *cultural region* SW Scotland, UK
174 H8 **Rengat** Sumatera, W Indonesia *0.25S 102.38E*
159 W12 **Rengma Hills** ⛰ NE India
64 H12 **Rengo** Libertador, C Chile *34.26S 70.53W*
118 M12 **Reni** Odes'ka Oblast', SW Ukraine *45.30N 28.24E*
82 F11 **Renk** Upper Nile, E Sudan *11.48N 32.49E*
95 L19 **Renko** Etelä-Suomi, S Finland *60.52N 24.16E*
100 L12 **Renkum** Gelderland, SE Netherlands *51.58N 5.43E*
190 K9 **Renmark** South Australia *34.12S 140.43E*
195 W17 **Rennell** *var.* Mu Nggava. *island* S Solomon Islands
189 Q4 **Renner Springs Roadhouse** Northern Territory, N Australia *18.12S 133.48E*
104 I6 **Rennes** *Bret.* Roazon; *anc.* Condate. Ille-et-Vilaine, NW France *48.07N 1.40W*
205 S16 **Rennick Glacier** *glacier* Antarctica
9 Y16 **Rennie** Manitoba, S Canada *49.51N 95.28W*
37 Q5 **Reno** Nevada, W USA *39.31N 119.48W*
108 H10 **Reno** ≈ N Italy
37 Q5 **Reno-Cannon** ✈ Nevada, W USA *39.26N 119.42W*
85 F24 **Renoster** ≈ SW South Africa
13 T5 **Renouard, Lac** ◎ Québec, SE Canada
20 F13 **Renovo** Pennsylvania, NE USA *41.19N 77.42W*
167 O3 **Renqiu** Hebei, E China *38.49N 116.02E*
166 I9 **Renshou** Sichuan, C China *29.58N 104.06E*
33 N12 **Rensselaer** Indiana, N USA *40.55N 87.10W*
20 L11 **Rensselaer** New York, NE USA *42.38N 73.44W*
Rentería *see* Errenteria
117 E17 **Rentína** *var.* Rendina. Thessalía, C Greece *39.04N 21.58E*
31 T9 **Renville** Minnesota, N USA *44.48N 95.13W*
79 O13 **Réo** W Burkina *12.19N 2.28W*
13 O12 **Repentigny** Québec, SE Canada *45.42N 73.28W*
152 K13 **Repetek** Lebap Welaýaty, E Turkmenistan *38.40N 63.12E*
95 J16 **Replot** *Fin.* Raippaluoto. *island* W Finland
Reppen *see* Rzepin
Reps *see* Rupea
29 T7 **Republic** Missouri, C USA *37.07N 93.28W*
34 K7 **Republic** Washington, NW USA *48.39N 118.44W*
29 N3 **Republican River** ≈ Kansas/Nebraska, C USA
15 Ll4 **Repulse Bay** Northwest Territories, N Canada *66.34N 86.19W*
58 F9 **Requena** Loreto, NE Peru *5.02S 73.47W*
107 R10 **Requena** País Valenciano, E Spain *39.28N 1.07W*
105 O14 **Réquista** Aveyron, S France *44.00N 2.31E*
142 M12 **Reşadiye** Tokat, N Turkey *40.24N 37.19E*
Reschenpass *see* Resia, Passo di
Reschitza *see* Reşiţa
115 N20 **Resen** *Turk.* Resne. SW FYR Macedonia *41.07N 21.00E*
62 J11 **Reserva** Paraná, S Brazil *24.40S 50.52W*
9 V15 **Reserve** Saskatchewan, S Canada *52.24N 102.37W*
39 P13 **Reserve** New Mexico, SW USA *33.42N 108.45W*
Reshetilovka *see* Reshetylivka
119 S6 **Reshetylivka** *Rus.* Reshetilovka. Poltavs'ka Oblast', NE Ukraine *49.34N 34.04E*
Resht *see* Rasht
108 F5 **Resia, Passo di** *Ger.* Reschenpass. *pass* Austria/Italy *46.51N 10.32E*
Resicabánya *see* Reşiţa
64 N7 **Resistencia** Chaco, NE Argentina *27.27S 58.55W*
118 F12 **Reşiţa** *Ger.* Reschitza, *Hung.* Resicabánya. Caraş-Severin, W Romania *45.13N 21.58E*
Resne *see* Resen
207 N9 **Resolute** Cornwallis Island, Nunavut, N Canada *74.40N 94.54W*
Resolution *see* Fort Resolution
16 P4 **Resolution Island** *island* Nunavut, NE Canada
193 A23 **Resolution Island** *island* SW NZ
13 W7 **Restigouche** Québec, SE Canada *48.01N 66.42W*
9 W17 **Reston** Manitoba, S Canada *49.33N 101.03W*
12 H11 **Restoule Lake** ◎ Ontario, S Canada
56 F10 **Restrepo** Meta, C Colombia *4.20N 73.29W*
44 B6 **Retalhuleu** Retalhuleu, SW Guatemala *14.30N 91.41W*
44 A1 **Retalhuleu** *off.* Departamento de Retalhuleu. ◈ *department* SW Guatemala
99 N18 **Retford** C England, UK *53.18N 0.52W*
105 Q3 **Rethel** Ardennes, N France *49.31N 4.22E*
Rethimno/Réthimnon *see* Réthymno
117 I25 **Réthymno** *var.* Rethimno; *prev.* Réthimnon. Kríti, Greece, E Mediterranean Sea *35.21N 24.28E*
Retiche, Alpi *see* Rhaetian Alps
101 J16 **Retie** Antwerpen, N Belgium *51.18N 5.05E*
113 J21 **Rétság** Nógrád, N Hungary *47.57N 19.07E*
111 W2 **Retz** Niederösterreich, NE Austria *48.46N 15.58E*
181 N15 **Réunion** *off.* La Réunion. ◇ *French overseas department* W Indian Ocean
132 L17 **Réunion** *island* W Indian Ocean
107 U6 **Reus** Cataluña, E Spain *41.10N 1.06E*
101 J15 **Reusel** Noord-Brabant, S Netherlands *51.21N 5.10E*
110 F7 **Reuss** ≈ NW Switzerland
Reuţel *see* Ciuhuru
103 H22 **Reutlingen** Baden-Württemberg, S Germany *48.30N 9.13E*
110 L7 **Reutte** Tirol, W Austria *47.30N 10.43E*
101 M16 **Reuver** Limburg, SE Netherlands *51.16N 6.04E*
30 K7 **Reva** South Dakota, N USA *45.30N 103.03W*
Reval/Revel' *see* Tallinn
128 J4 **Revda** Murmanskaya Oblast', NW Russian Federation *67.57N 34.29E*
125 Ee11 **Revda** Sverdlovskaya Oblast', C Russian Federation *56.48N 59.42E*
105 N16 **Revel** Haute-Garonne, S France *43.27N 1.58E*
9 O16 **Revelstoke** British Columbia, SW Canada *51.01N 118.12W*
45 N13 **Reventazón, Río** ≈ E Costa Rica
108 G9 **Revere** Lombardia, N Italy *45.03N 11.07E*
41 Y14 **Revillagigedo Island** *island* Alexander Archipelago, Alaska, USA
199 Mm7 **Revillagigedo Islands** *island group* NW Mexico
105 R3 **Revin** Ardennes, N France *49.57N 4.39E*
94 O3 **Revnosa** *headland* C Svalbard *78.03N 18.52E*
Revolyutsii, Pik *see* Revolyutsiya, Qullai
153 T13 **Revolyutsiya, Qullai** *Rus.* Pik Revolyutsii. ▲ SE Tajikistan *38.40N 72.26E*
113 L19 **Revúca** *Ger.* Grossrauschenbach, *Hung.* Nagyrőce. Banskobystrický Kraj, C Slovakia *48.40N 20.10E*
160 K9 **Rewa** Madhya Pradesh, C India *24.31N 81.18E*
158 I11 **Rewāri** Haryāna, N India *28.13N 76.37E*
35 R14 **Rexburg** Idaho, NW USA *43.49N 111.47W*
80 G13 **Rey Bouba** Nord, NE Cameroon *8.40N 14.10E*
94 L3 **Reydharfjördhur** Austurland, E Iceland *65.02N 14.12W*
59 K16 **Reyes** Beni, NW Bolivia *14.17S 67.18W*
36 L8 **Reyes, Point** *headland* California, W USA *37.58N 123.01W*
56 B12 **Reyes, Punta** *headland* SW Colombia *2.43N 78.07W*
142 L17 **Reyhanlı** Hatay, S Turkey *36.16N 36.33E*
45 U16 **Rey, Isla del** *island* Archipiélago de las Perlas, SE Panama
94 H2 **Reykhólar** Vestfirdhir, W Iceland *65.28N 22.12W*
94 K2 **Reykjahlídh** Nordhurland Eystra, NE Iceland *65.37N 16.54W*
94 I4 **Reykjanes** ◈ *region* SW Iceland
207 O16 **Reykjanes Basin** *var.* Irminger Basin. *undersea feature* N Atlantic Ocean
207 N17 **Reykjanes Ridge** *undersea feature* N Atlantic Ocean
94 H4 **Reykjavík** *var.* Reikjavik. ● (Iceland) Höfudhborgarsvaedhi, W Iceland *64.07N 21.54W*
20 D13 **Reynoldsville** Pennsylvania, NE USA *41.04N 78.51W*
43 P8 **Reynosa** Tamaulipas, C Mexico *26.03N 98.19W*
Reẕā'īyeh *see* Orūmīyeh
Reẕā'īyeh, Daryācheh-ye *see* Orūmīyeh, Daryācheh-ye
104 I8 **Rezé** Loire-Atlantique, NW France *47.10N 1.36W*
120 K10 **Rēzekne** *Ger.* Rositten; *prev. Rus.* Rezhitsa. Rēzekne, SE Latvia *56.31N 27.22E*
Rezhitsa *see* Rēzekne
119 N9 **Rezina** NE Moldova *47.44N 28.58E*
116 N11 **Rezovo** *Turk.* Rezve. Burgas, E Bulgaria *42.00N 28.00E*
116 N11 **Rezovska Reka** *Turk.* Rezve Deresi. ≈ Bulgaria/Turkey *see also* Rezve Deresi
Rezve *see* Rezovo
116 N11 **Rezve Deresi** *Bul.* Rezovska Reka. ≈ Bulgaria/Turkey *see also* Rezovska Reka
Rhadames *see* Ghadāmis
Rhaedestus *see* Tekirdağ
110 J10 **Rhaetian Alps** *Fr.* Alpes Rhétiques, *Ger.* Rätische Alpen, *It.* Alpi Retiche. ⛰ C Europe
110 I8 **Rhätikon** ⛰ C Europe
103 G14 **Rheda-Wiedenbrück** Nordrhein-Westfalen, W Germany *51.51N 8.19E*
100 M12 **Rheden** Gelderland, E Netherlands *52.01N 6.03E*
Rhegion/Rhegium *see* Reggio di Calabria
Rheims *see* Reims
Rhein *see* Rhine
103 E17 **Rheinbach** Nordrhein-Westfalen, W Germany *50.37N 6.57E*
102 F13 **Rheine** *var.* Rheine in Westfalen. Nordrhein-Westfalen, NW Germany *52.16N 7.27E*
Rheine in Westfalen *see* Rheine
Rheinfeld *see* Rheinfelden
103 F24 **Rheinfelden** Baden-Württemberg, S Germany *47.34N 7.46E*
110 E6 **Rheinfelden** *var.* Rheinfeld. Aargau, N Switzerland *47.33N 7.46E*
103 E17 **Rheinisches Schiefergebirge** *var.* Rhine State Uplands, *Eng.* Rhenish Slate Mountains. ⛰ W Germany
103 D18 **Rheinland-Pfalz** *Eng.* Rhineland-Palatinate, *Fr.* Rhénanie-Palatinat. ◈ *state* W Germany
103 G18 **Rhein/Main** ✈ (Frankfurt am Main) Hessen, W Germany *50.03N 8.33E*
Rhénanie du Nord-Westphalie *see* Nordrhein-Westfalen
Rhénanie-Palatinat *see* Rheinland-Pfalz
100 K12 **Rhenen** Utrecht, C Netherlands *51.57N 5.34E*
Rhenish Slate Mountains *see* Rheinisches Schiefergebirge
Rhétiques, Alpes *see* Rhaetian Alps
102 N10 **Rhin** ≈ NE Germany
Rhin *see* Rhine
86 F10 **Rhine** *Dut.* Rijn, *Fr.* Rhin, *Ger.* Rhein. ≈ W Europe
32 L5 **Rhinelander** Wisconsin, N USA *45.39N 89.22W*
Rhineland-Palatinate *see* Rheinland-Pfalz
Rhine State Uplands *see* Rheinisches Schiefergebirge
102 N11 **Rhinkanal** *canal* NE Germany
83 F17 **Rhino Camp** NW Uganda *2.58N 31.24E*
76 D7 **Rhir, Cap** *headland* W Morocco *30.40N 9.54W*
108 D7 **Rho** Lombardia, N Italy *45.31N 9.01E*
21 N12 **Rhode Island** *off.* State of Rhode Island and Providence Plantations; also known as Little Rhody, Ocean State. ◈ *state* NE USA
21 O13 **Rhode Island** *island* Rhode Island, NE USA
21 O13 **Rhode Island Sound** *sound* Maine/Rhode Island, NE USA
Rhodes *see* Ródos
Rhode-Saint-Genèse *see* Sint-Genesius-Rode
86 L14 **Rhodes Basin** *undersea feature* E Mediterranean Sea
Rhodesia *see* Zimbabwe
116 I12 **Rhodope Mountains** *var.* Rodhópi Óri, *Bul.* Rhodope Planina, Rodopi, *Gk.* Orosirá Rodhópis, *Turk.* Dospad Dagh. ⛰ Bulgaria/Greece
Rhodope Planina *see* Rhodope Mountains
Rhodos *see* Ródos
103 I18 **Rhön** ⛰ C Germany
105 Q10 **Rhône** ◈ *department* E France
88 C12 **Rhône** ≈ France/Switzerland
105 R12 **Rhône-Alpes** ◈ *region* E France
123 J6 **Rhône Fan** *undersea feature* W Mediterranean Sea
100 G13 **Rhoon** Zuid-Holland, SW Netherlands *51.52N 4.25E*
98 G9 **Rhum** *var.* Rum. *island* W Scotland, UK
Rhuthun *see* Ruthin
99 J18 **Rhyl** NE Wales, UK *53.19N 3.28W*
61 K18 **Rialma** Goiás, S Brazil *15.22S 49.35W*
106 L3 **Riaño** Castilla-León, N Spain *42.59N 5.00W*
107 O9 **Riansáres** ≈ C Spain
158 H6 **Riāsi** Jammu and Kashmir, NW India *33.03N 74.51E*
174 Gg7 **Riau** *off.* Propinsi Riau. ◈ *province* W Indonesia
Riau Archipelago *see* Riau, Kepulauan
174 I8 **Riau, Kepulauan** *var.* Riau Archipelago, *Dut.* Riouw-Archipel. *island group* W Indonesia
107 O6 **Riaza** Castilla-León, N Spain *41.17N 3.29W*
107 N6 **Riaza** ≈ N Spain
83 K17 **Riba** *spring/well* NE Kenya *1.56N 40.38E*
106 H4 **Ribadavia** Galicia, NW Spain *42.16N 8.07W*
106 J2 **Ribadeo** Galicia, NW Spain *43.31N 7.04W*
106 L2 **Ribadesella** Asturias, N Spain *43.27N 5.04W*
106 G10 **Ribatejo** *former province* C Portugal
85 P15 **Ribáuè** Nampula, N Mozambique *14.56S 38.19E*
99 K17 **Ribble** ≈ NW England, UK
97 F23 **Ribe** Ribe, W Denmark *55.19N 8.46E*
97 F23 **Ribe** *off.* Ribe Amt, *var.* Ripen. ◈ *county* W Denmark
106 G3 **Ribeira** Galicia, NW Spain *42.33N 9.01W*
66 O5 **Ribeira Brava** Madeira, Portugal, NE Atlantic Ocean *32.39N 17.04W*
66 P3 **Ribeira Grande** São Miguel, Azores, Portugal, NE Atlantic Ocean *37.34N 25.31W*
62 L8 **Ribeirão Preto** São Paulo, S Brazil *21.09S 47.48W*
62 L11 **Ribeira, Rio** ≈ S Brazil
109 I24 **Ribera** Sicilia, Italy, C Mediterranean Sea *37.31N 13.16E*
59 L14 **Riberalta** Beni, N Bolivia *11.00S 66.04W*
107 W4 **Ribes de Freser** Cataluña, NE Spain *42.18N 2.11E*
32 L6 **Rib Mountain** ▲ Wisconsin, N USA *44.55N 89.41W*
111 U12 **Ribnica** *Ger.* Reifnitz. S Slovenia *45.46N 14.40E*
119 N9 **Rîbniţa** *var.* Râbniţa, *Rus.* Rybnitsa. NE Moldova *47.46N 29.01E*
102 M8 **Ribnitz-Damgarten** Mecklenburg-Vorpommern, NE Germany *54.14N 12.25E*
113 D16 **Říčany** *Ger.* Ritschan. Středočeský Kraj, W Czech Republic *49.58N 14.39E*
31 U7 **Rice** Minnesota, N USA *45.42N 94.10W*
32 J5 **Rice Lake** Wisconsin, N USA *45.33N 91.43W*
12 I15 **Rice Lake** ◎ Ontario, SE Canada
12 E8 **Rice Lake** ◎ Ontario, S Canada
25 V3 **Richard B.Russell Lake** ⊠ Georgia, SE USA
27 U6 **Richardson** Texas, SW USA *32.57N 96.43W*
9 R11 **Richardson** ≈ Alberta, C Canada
8 I3 **Richardson Mountains** ⛰ Yukon Territory, NW Canada
193 C21 **Richardson Mountains** ⛰ South Island, NZ
44 F3 **Richardson Peak** ▲ SE Belize *16.34N 88.46W*
78 G10 **Richard Toll** N Senegal *16.27N 15.44W*
30 L5 **Richardton** North Dakota, N USA *46.52N 102.19W*
12 F13 **Rich, Cape** *headland* Ontario, S Canada *44.42N 80.37W*
104 L8 **Richelieu** Indre-et-Loire, C France *47.01N 0.18E*
35 P15 **Richfield** Idaho, NW USA *43.03N 114.11W*
38 K5 **Richfield** Utah, W USA *38.46N 112.06W*
20 J10 **Richfield Springs** New York, NE USA *42.52N 74.57W*
20 M6 **Richford** Vermont, NE USA *44.59N 72.37W*
29 R6 **Rich Hill** Missouri, C USA *38.06N 94.22W*
11 P14 **Richibucto** New Brunswick, SE Canada *46.42N 64.54W*
110 G8 **Richisau** Glarus, NE Switzerland *47.00N 8.54E*
25 S6 **Richland** Georgia, SE USA *32.05N 84.40W*
29 U6 **Richland** Missouri, C USA *37.51N 92.24W*
27 U8 **Richland** Texas, SW USA *31.55N 96.25W*
34 K10 **Richland** Washington, NW USA *46.17N 119.16W*
32 K8 **Richland Center** Wisconsin, N USA *43.18N 90.22W*
23 W11 **Richlands** North Carolina, SE USA *34.52N 77.33W*
23 Q7 **Richlands** Virginia, NE USA *37.05N 81.47W*
27 R9 **Richland Springs** Texas, SW USA *31.16N 98.56W*
191 S8 **Richmond** New South Wales, SE Australia *33.36S 150.43E*
8 L17 **Richmond** British Columbia, SW Canada *49.07N 123.09W*
12 L13 **Richmond** Ontario, SE Canada *45.12N 75.49W*
13 Q12 **Richmond** Québec, SE Canada *45.39N 72.07W*
193 I14 **Richmond** Tasman, South Island, NZ *41.24S 173.04E*
37 N8 **Richmond** California, W USA *37.57N 122.22W*
33 Q14 **Richmond** Indiana, N USA *39.48N 84.52W*
22 M6 **Richmond** Kentucky, S USA *37.45N 84.17W*
29 S4 **Richmond** Missouri, C USA *39.16N 93.58W*
27 V11 **Richmond** Texas, SW USA *29.34N 95.45W*
38 L1 **Richmond** Utah, W USA *41.55N 111.51W*
23 W6 **Richmond** *state capital* Virginia, NE USA *37.33N 77.27W*
12 H15 **Richmond Hill** Ontario, S Canada *43.51N 79.24W*
193 J15 **Richmond Range** ⛰ South Island, NZ
29 S12 **Rich Mountain** ▲ Arkansas, C USA *34.37N 94.17W*
33 S13 **Richwood** Ohio, N USA *40.25N 83.18W*
23 R5 **Richwood** West Virginia, NE USA *38.13N 80.31W*
106 K5 **Ricobayo, Embalse de** ⊠ NW Spain
Ricomagus *see* Riom
Ridā' *see* Radā'
100 H13 **Ridderkerk** Zuid-Holland, SW Netherlands *51.52N 4.34E*
35 N16 **Riddle** Idaho, NW USA *42.07N 116.09W*
34 F14 **Riddle** Oregon, NW USA *42.57N 123.21W*
12 L13 **Rideau** ≈ Ontario, SE Canada
37 T12 **Ridgecrest** California, W USA *35.37N 117.40W*
20 L13 **Ridgefield** Connecticut, NE USA *41.16N 73.30W*
24 K5 **Ridgeland** Mississippi, S USA *32.25N 90.07W*
23 R15 **Ridgeland** South Carolina, SE USA *32.28N 80.58W*
22 F8 **Ridgely** Tennessee, S USA *36.15N 89.29W*
12 D17 **Ridgetown** Ontario, S Canada *42.27N 81.52W*
Ridgeway *see* Ridgway
23 R12 **Ridgeway** South Carolina, SE USA *34.17N 80.56W*
20 D13 **Ridgway** *var.* Ridgeway. Pennsylvania, NE USA *41.24N 78.40W*
9 W16 **Riding Mountain** ⛰ Manitoba, S Canada
Ried *see* Ried im Innkreis
111 R4 **Ried im Innkreis** *var.* Ried. Oberösterreich, NW Austria *48.13N 13.28E*
111 X8 **Riegersburg** Steiermark, SE Austria *47.03N 15.52E*
110 E6 **Riehen** Basel-Stadt, NW Switzerland *47.34N 7.39E*
94 J9 **Riehppegáisá** *var.* Rieppe. ▲ N Norway *69.38N 21.31E*
101 K18 **Riemst** Limburg, NE Belgium *50.49N 5.35E*
Rieppe *see* Riehppegáisá
103 O15 **Riesa** Sachsen, E Germany *51.18N 13.18E*
65 H24 **Riesco, Isla** *island* S Chile
109 K25 **Riesi** Sicilia, Italy, C Mediterranean Sea *37.16N 14.04E*
85 F25 **Riet** ≈ SW South Africa
85 I23 **Riet** ≈ SW South Africa
120 D11 **Rietavas** Telšiai, W Lithuania *55.43N 21.56E*
85 F19 **Rietfontein** Omaheke, E Namibia *21.54S 20.57E*
109 I14 **Rieti** *anc.* Reate. Lazio, C Italy *42.22N 12.49E*

◆ COUNTRY ● COUNTRY CAPITAL ◇ DEPENDENT TERRITORY ○ DEPENDENT TERRITORY CAPITAL ◈ ADMINISTRATIVE REGION ✈ INTERNATIONAL AIRPORT ▲ MOUNTAIN ⛰ MOUNTAIN RANGE ▲ VOLCANO ≈ RIVER ◎ LAKE ⊠ RESERVOIR

86 D14 **Rif** var. Er Rif, Er Riff, Riff. ▲▲ N Morocco
Riff see Rif
39 Q4 **Rifle** Colorado, C USA 39.30N 107.46W
33 R7 **Rifle River** ≈ Michigan, N USA
83 H18 **Rift Valley** ◈ province Kenya
Rift Valley see Great Rift Valley
120 F9 **Rīga** Eng. Riga. ● (Latvia) Rīga, C Latvia 56.57N 24.07E
Rigaer Bucht see Riga, Gulf of
120 F6 **Riga, Gulf of** Est. Liivi Laht, Ger. Rigaer Bucht, Latv. Rīgas Jūras Līcis, Rus. Rizhskiy Zaliv; prev. Est. Riia Laht. gulf Estonia/Latvia
149 U12 **Rīgān** Kermān, SE Iran 28.39N 59.01E
Rīgas Jūras Līcis see Riga, Gulf of
13 N12 **Rigaud** ≈ Ontario/Québec, SE Canada
35 R14 **Rigby** Idaho, NW USA 43.40N 111.54W
154 M10 **Rīgestān** var. Registan. desert region S Afghanistan
34 M11 **Riggins** Idaho, NW USA 45.24N 116.18W
11 R8 **Rigolet** Newfoundland and Labrador, NE Canada 51.10N 58.25W
80 G9 **Rig-Rig** Kanem, W Chad 14.19N 14.19E
120 F4 **Riguldi** Läänemaa, W Estonia 59.07N 23.34E
Riia Laht see Riga, Gulf of
95 L19 **Riihimäki** Etelä-Suomi, S Finland 60.45N 24.45E
205 O2 **Riiser-Larsen Ice Shelf** ice shelf Antarctica
205 U2 **Riiser-Larsen Peninsula** peninsula Antarctica
67 P22 **Riiser-Larsen Sea** sea Antarctica
42 D2 **Riíto** Sonora, NW Mexico 32.06N 114.57W
114 B9 **Rijeka** Ger. Sankt Veit am Flaum, It. Fiume, Slvn. Reka; anc. Tarsatica. Primorje-Gorski Kotar, NW Croatia 45.20N 14.25E
101 I14 **Rijen** Noord-Brabant, S Netherlands 51.34N 4.55E
101 H15 **Rijkevorsel** Antwerpen, N Belgium 51.23N 4.43E
Rijn see Rhine
100 G11 **Rijnsburg** Zuid-Holland, W Netherlands 52.12N 4.27E
Rijssel see Lille
100 N10 **Rijssen** Overijssel, E Netherlands 52.19N 6.30E
100 G12 **Rijswijk** Eng. Ryswick. Zuid-Holland, W Netherlands 52.04N 4.22E
94 I10 **Riksgränsen** Norrbotten, N Sweden 68.24N 18.15E
172 Q6 **Rikubetsu** Hokkaidō, NE Japan 43.30N 143.43E
171 Mm12 **Rikuzen-Takata** Iwate, Honshū, C Japan 39.01N 141.37E
29 O4 **Riley** Kansas, C USA 39.18N 96.49W
101 I17 **Rillaar** Vlaams Brabant, C Belgium 50.58N 4.58E
Rí, Loch see Ree, Lough
116 G11 **Rilska Reka** ≈ W Bulgaria
79 T12 **Rima** ≈ N Nigeria
147 N7 **Rimah, Wādī ar** var. Wādī ar Rummah. dry watercourse C Saudi Arabia
Rimaszombat see Rimavská Sobota
203 R12 **Rimatara** island Îles Australes, SW French Polynesia
113 L20 **Rimavská Sobota** Ger. Gross-Steffelsdorf, Hung. Rimaszombat. Banskobystrický Kraj, C Slovakia 48.24N 20.01E
9 Q15 **Rimbey** Alberta, SW Canada 52.39N 114.10W
97 P15 **Rimbo** Stockholm, C Sweden 59.43N 18.21E
97 M18 **Rimforsa** Östergötland, S Sweden 58.06N 15.40E
108 I11 **Rimini** anc. Ariminum. Emilia-Romagna, N Italy 44.03N 12.33E
Rîmnicu-Sărat see Râmnicu Sărat
Rîmnicu Vîlcea see Râmnicu Vâlcea
155 Y3 **Rimo Muztāgh** ▲▲ India/Pakistan
13 U7 **Rimouski** Québec, SE Canada 48.25N 68.31W
164 M16 **Rinbung** Xizang Zizhiqu, W China 29.15N 89.40E
Rinchinlhümbe see Dzöölön
64 I5 **Rincón, Cerro** ▲ N Chile 24.01S 67.19W
106 M15 **Rincón de la Victoria** Andalucía, S Spain 36.43N 4.18W
Rincón del Bonete, Lago Artificial de see Río Negro, Embalse del
107 Q4 **Rincón de Soto** La Rioja, N Spain 42.15N 1.49W
96 G8 **Rindal** Møre og Romsdal, S Norway 63.02N 9.09E
117 J20 **Ríneia** island Kykládes, Greece, Aegean Sea
158 H11 **Rīngas** prev. Reengus, Rīngus. Rājasthān, N India 27.18N 75.27E
97 H24 **Ringe** Fyn, C Denmark 55.13N 10.30E
96 H11 **Ringebu** Oppland, S Norway 61.31N 10.09E
Ringen see Rõngu
195 U14 **Ringgi** Kolombangara, NW Solomon Islands 8.03S 95.08E
25 R1 **Ringgold** Georgia, SE USA 34.55N 85.06W
24 G5 **Ringgold** Louisiana, S USA 32.19N 93.16W
27 S5 **Ringgold** Texas, SW USA 33.47N 97.56W
97 E22 **Ringkøbing** Ringkøbing, W Denmark 56.04N 8.22E
97 E21 **Ringkøbing** off. Ringkøbing Amt. ◈ county W Denmark
97 E22 **Ringkøbing Fjord** fjord W Denmark
35 S10 **Ringling** Montana, NW USA 46.15N 110.48W
29 N13 **Ringling** Oklahoma, C USA 34.12N 97.35W
96 H13 **Ringsaker** Hedmark, S Norway 60.54N 10.45E
97 I23 **Ringsted** Vestsjælland, E Denmark 55.28N 11.48E
Rīngus see Rīngas
94 I9 **Ringvassøya** Lapp. Ráneš. island N Norway
20 K13 **Ringwood** New Jersey, NE USA 41.06N 74.15W
Rinn Duáin see Hook Head
102 H13 **Rinteln** Niedersachsen, NW Germany 52.10N 9.04E
Rio see Rio de Janeiro
117 E18 **Río** Dytikí Ellás, S Greece 38.18N 21.48E
58 C7 **Riobamba** Chimborazo, C Ecuador 1.38S 78.40W
62 P9 **Rio Bonito** Rio de Janeiro, SE Brazil 22.42S 42.38W
61 C16 **Rio Branco** state capital Acre, W Brazil 9.58S 67.49W
63 H18 **Río Branco** Cerro Largo, NE Uruguay 32.34S 53.21W
Rio Branco, Território de see Roraima
43 P8 **Río Bravo** Tamaulipas, C Mexico 25.57N 98.03W
65 G16 **Río Bueno** Los Lagos, C Chile 40.19S 72.55W
57 P5 **Río Caribe** Sucre, NE Venezuela 10.40N 63.07W
56 M5 **Río Chico** Miranda, N Venezuela 10.18N 66.00W
65 H18 **Río Cisnes** Aisén, S Chile 44.29S 71.15W
62 L9 **Rio Claro** São Paulo, S Brazil 22.22S 47.31W
47 V14 **Rio Claro** Trinidad, Trinidad and Tobago 10.18N 61.10W
56 J5 **Río Claro** Lara, N Venezuela 9.54N 69.22W
65 K15 **Río Colorado** Río Negro, E Argentina 39.04S 64.04W
64 K11 **Río Cuarto** Córdoba, C Argentina 33.06S 64.20W
62 P10 **Rio de Janeiro** var. Rio. state capital Rio de Janeiro, SE Brazil 22.52S 43.16W
62 P9 **Rio de Janeiro** off. Estado do Rio de Janeiro. ◈ state SE Brazil
45 R17 **Río de Jesús** Veraguas, S Panama 7.57N 81.09W
36 K3 **Rio Dell** California, W USA 40.30N 124.07W
62 K13 **Rio do Sul** Santa Catarina, S Brazil 27.15S 49.37W
65 I23 **Río Gallegos** var. Gallegos, Puerto Gallegos. Santa Cruz, S Argentina 51.39S 69.21W
63 I18 **Rio Grande** var. São Pedro do Rio Grande do Sul. Rio Grande do Sul, S Brazil 32.03S 52.07W
26 I9 **Rio Grande** ≈ Texas, SW USA
65 J24 **Río Grande** Tierra del Fuego, S Argentina 53.45S 67.46W
42 L10 **Río Grande** Zacatecas, C Mexico 23.48N 103.03W
44 J9 **Río Grande** León, NW Nicaragua 12.57N 86.31W
47 V5 **Río Grande** E Puerto Rico 18.22N 65.49W
27 R17 **Rio Grande City** Texas, SW USA 26.22N 98.49W
61 P14 **Rio Grande do Norte** off. Estado do Rio Grande do Norte. ◈ state E Brazil
63 G15 **Rio Grande do Sul** off. Estado do Rio Grande do Sul. ◈ state S Brazil
67 M17 **Rio Grande Fracture Zone** tectonic feature C Atlantic Ocean
67 J18 **Rio Grande Gap** undersea feature S Atlantic Ocean
Rio Grande Plateau see Rio Grande Rise
67 J18 **Rio Grande Rise** var. Rio Grande Plateau. undersea feature SW Atlantic Ocean
56 G4 **Ríohacha** La Guajira, N Colombia 11.22N 72.46W
45 S16 **Río Hato** Coclé, C Panama 8.22N 80.09W
27 T17 **Rio Hondo** Texas, SW USA 26.14N 97.34W
58 D10 **Rioja** San Martín, N Peru 6.03S 77.05W
43 Y11 **Río Lagartos** Yucatán, SE Mexico 21.34N 88.07W
105 P11 **Riom** anc. Ricomagus. Puy-de-Dôme, C France 45.54N 3.06E
106 F10 **Rio Maior** Santarém, C Portugal 39.19N 8.55W
105 O12 **Riom-ès-Montagnes** Cantal, C France 45.15N 2.39E
62 J12 **Rio Negro** Paraná, S Brazil 26.06S 49.46W
65 I15 **Río Negro** off. Provincia de Río Negro. ◈ province C Argentina
63 D18 **Río Negro** ◈ department W Uruguay
49 V12 **Río Negro, Embalse del** var. Lago Artificial de Rincón del Bonete. ⊠ C Uruguay
109 M17 **Rionero in Vulture** Basilicata, S Italy 40.55N 15.40E
143 S9 **Rioni** ≈ W Georgia
107 P12 **Riópar** Castilla-La Mancha, C Spain 38.31N 2.27W
63 H16 **Rio Pardo** Rio Grande do Sul, S Brazil 29.41S 52.25W
39 R11 **Rio Rancho Estates** New Mexico, SW USA 35.14N 106.40W
44 L11 **Río San Juan** ◈ department S Nicaragua
56 E9 **Ríosucio** Caldas, W Colombia 5.25N 75.43W
56 C7 **Ríosucio** Chocó, NW Colombia 7.24N 77.09W
64 K10 **Río Tercero** Córdoba, C Argentina 32.12S 64.03W
56 J5 **Río Tocuyo** Lara, N Venezuela 10.12N 69.58W
Riouw-Archipel see Riau, Kepulauan
61 J19 **Rio Verde** Goiás, C Brazil 17.49S 50.55W
43 O12 **Río Verde** var. Rioverde. San Luis Potosí, C Mexico 21.58N 100.00W
37 O8 **Rio Vista** California, W USA 38.09N 121.42W
114 M11 **Ripanj** Serbia, N Serbia 44.37N 20.30E
108 J13 **Ripatransone** Marche, C Italy 43.00N 13.45E
Ripen see Ribe
24 M2 **Ripley** Mississippi, S USA 34.43N 88.57W
33 R15 **Ripley** Ohio, N USA 38.45N 83.51W
22 F9 **Ripley** Tennessee, S USA 35.45N 89.31W
23 Q4 **Ripley** West Virginia, NE USA 38.49N 81.42W
107 W4 **Ripoll** Cataluña, NE Spain 42.12N 2.12E
99 M16 **Ripon** N England, UK 54.07N 1.31W
32 M7 **Ripon** Wisconsin, N USA 43.52N 88.48W
109 L24 **Riposto** Sicilia, Italy, C Mediterranean Sea 37.43N 15.13E
101 L14 **Rips** Noord-Brabant, SE Netherlands 51.31N 5.49E
56 D9 **Risaralda** off. Departamento de Risaralda. ◈ province C Colombia
118 L8 **Rîşcani** var. Râşcani, Rus. Ryshkany. NW Moldova 47.55N 27.31E
158 J9 **Rishikesh** Uttaranchal, N India 30.06N 78.16E
172 P2 **Rishiri-suidō** strait E Sea of Japan
172 Oo2 **Rishiri-tō** var. Risiri Tô. island NE Japan
172 P2 **Rishiri-yama** ⛰ Rishiri-tō, NE Japan 45.11N 141.11E
27 R7 **Rising Star** Texas, SW USA 32.06N 98.57W
33 Q15 **Rising Sun** Indiana, N USA 38.58N 84.52W
Risiri Tô see Rishiri-tō
104 L4 **Risle** ≈ N France
Rîşno see Râşnov
29 V13 **Rison** Arkansas, C USA 33.57N 92.11W
97 G17 **Risør** Aust-Agder, S Norway 58.43N 9.13E
94 H10 **Risøyhamn** Nordland, C Norway 69.00N 15.37E
103 I23 **Riss** ≈ S Germany
120 G4 **Risti** Ger. Kreuz. Läänemaa, W Estonia 59.03N 24.11E
13 V8 **Ristigouche** ≈ Québec, SE Canada
95 N18 **Ristiina** Isä-Suomi, E Finland 61.31N 27.15E
95 N14 **Ristijärvi** Oulu, C Finland 64.30N 28.15E
196 C14 **Ritidian Point** headland N Guam 13.39N 144.51E
Ritschan see Říčany
37 R9 **Ritter, Mount** ▲ California, W USA 37.40N 119.10W
33 T12 **Rittman** Ohio, N USA 40.58N 81.46W
34 L9 **Ritzville** Washington, NW USA 47.07N 118.22W
Riva see Riva del Garda
63 A21 **Rivadavia** Buenos Aires, E Argentina 35.28S 62.58W
108 F7 **Riva del Garda** var. Riva Trentino-Alto Adige, N Italy 45.54N 10.50E
108 B8 **Rivarolo Canavese** Piemonte, W Italy 45.21N 7.42E
44 K11 **Rivas** Rivas, SW Nicaragua 11.25N 85.49W
44 J11 **Rivas** ◈ department SW Nicaragua
105 R11 **Rive-de-Gier** Loire, E France 45.31N 4.36E
63 A22 **Rivera** Buenos Aires, E Argentina 37.13S 63.13W
63 F16 **Rivera** Rivera, NE Uruguay 30.54S 55.31W
63 F17 **Rivera** ◈ department NE Uruguay
37 P9 **Riverbank** California, W USA 37.43N 120.59W
78 K17 **River Cess** SW Liberia 5.28N 9.31W
30 M4 **Riverdale** North Dakota, N USA 47.29N 101.22W
32 I6 **River Falls** Wisconsin, N USA 44.52N 92.38W
9 T16 **Riverhurst** Saskatchewan, S Canada 50.52N 106.49W
191 O10 **Riverina** physical region New South Wales, SE Australia
82 G8 **River Nile** ◈ state NE Sudan
65 F19 **Rivero, Isla** island Archipiélago de los Chonos, S Chile
9 W16 **Rivers** Manitoba, S Canada 50.01N 100.13W
79 U17 **Rivers** ◈ state S Nigeria
193 D23 **Riversdale** Southland, South Island, NZ 45.54S 168.44E
85 F26 **Riversdale** Western Cape, SW South Africa 34.04S 21.15E
37 U15 **Riverside** California, W USA 33.57N 117.24W
27 W9 **Riverside** Texas, SW USA 30.51N 95.24W
39 U3 **Riverside Reservoir** ⊠ Colorado, C USA
8 K15 **Rivers Inlet** British Columbia, SW Canada 51.43N 127.19W
8 K15 **Rivers Inlet** inlet British Columbia, SW Canada
9 X15 **Riverton** Manitoba, S Canada 51.00N 97.00W
193 C24 **Riverton** Southland, South Island, NZ 46.19S 168.02E
32 L13 **Riverton** Illinois, N USA 39.50N 89.31W
38 L3 **Riverton** Utah, W USA 40.32N 111.57W
35 V15 **Riverton** Wyoming, C USA 43.01N 108.22W
12 G10 **River Valley** Ontario, S Canada 46.36N 80.09W
11 P14 **Riverview** New Brunswick, SE Canada 46.03N 64.46W
105 O17 **Rivesaltes** Pyrénées-Orientales, S France 42.46N 2.48E
38 H11 **Riviera** Arizona, SW USA 35.06N 114.36W
27 S15 **Riviera** Texas, SW USA 27.15N 97.48W
25 Z14 **Riviera Beach** Florida, SE USA 26.46N 80.03W
13 Q10 **Rivière-à-Pierre** Québec, SE Canada 46.59N 72.12W
13 T9 **Rivière-Bleue** Québec, SE Canada 47.25N 69.01W
13 T8 **Rivière-du-Loup** Québec, SE Canada 47.49N 69.31W
181 Y15 **Rivière du Rempart** NE Mauritius 20.06S 57.40E
47 R12 **Rivière-Pilote** S Martinique 14.29N 60.54W
181 O17 **Rivière St-Etienne, Point de la** headland SW Réunion
11 S10 **Rivière-St-Paul** Québec, E Canada 51.26N 57.52W
Rivière Sèche see Bel Air
118 K4 **Rivne** Pol. Równe, Rus. Rovno. Rivnens'ka Oblast', NW Ukraine 50.37N 26.15E
Rivne see Rivnens'ka Oblast'
118 K3 **Rivnens'ka Oblast'** var. Rivne, Rus. Rovenskaya Oblast'. ◈ province NW Ukraine
108 B8 **Rivoli** Piemonte, NW Italy 45.04N 7.31E
165 Q14 **Riwoqê** var. Racaka. Xizang Zizhiqu, W China 31.10N 96.25E
101 H19 **Rixensart** Wallon Brabant, C Belgium 50.43N 4.31E
Riyadh/Riyāḍ, Minṭaqat ar see Ar Riyāḍ
Riyāq see Rayak
Rizaiyeh see Orūmīyeh
143 P11 **Rize** Rize, NE Turkey 41.02N 40.33E
143 P11 **Rize** prev. Çoruh. ◈ province NE Turkey
167 R5 **Rizhao** Shandong, E China 35.23N 119.31E
Rizhskiy Zaliv see Riga, Gulf of
Rizokarpaso/Rizokárpason see Dipkarpaz
109 O21 **Rizzuto, Capo** headland S Italy 38.54N 17.05E
97 F15 **Rjukan** Telemark, S Norway 59.52N 8.37E
97 D16 **Rjuven** ▲▲ S Norway
78 H9 **Rkîz** Trarza, W Mauritania 16.49N 15.19W
117 Q23 **Ro** prev. Ágios Geórgios. island SE Greece
97 H14 **Roa** Oppland, S Norway 60.16N 10.38E
107 N5 **Roa** Castilla-León, N Spain 41.42N 3.55W
47 T9 **Road Town** ○ (British Virgin Islands) Tortola, C British Virgin Islands 18.24N 64.38W
98 F6 **Roag, Loch** inlet NW Scotland, UK
39 O5 **Roan Cliffs** cliff Colorado/Utah, W USA
23 P9 **Roan High Knob** var. Roan Mountain. ▲ North Carolina/Tennessee, SE USA 36.09N 82.07W
Roan Mountain see Roan High Knob
105 Q10 **Roanne** anc. Rodunma. Loire, E France 46.03N 4.04E
25 R4 **Roanoke** Alabama, S USA 33.09N 85.22W
23 S7 **Roanoke** Virginia, NE USA 37.16N 79.56W
23 Z9 **Roanoke Island** island North Carolina, SE USA
23 W8 **Roanoke Rapids** North Carolina, SE USA 36.27N 77.39W
23 X9 **Roanoke River** ≈ North Carolina/Virginia, SE USA
39 O4 **Roan Plateau** plain Utah, W USA
39 R5 **Roaring Fork River** ≈ Colorado, C USA
27 O5 **Roaring Springs** Texas, SW USA 33.54N 100.51W
44 J4 **Roatán** var. Coxen Hole, Coxin Hole. Islas de la Bahía, N Honduras 16.18N 86.32W
44 I4 **Roatán, Isla de** island Islas de la Bahía, N Honduras
Roat Kampuchea see Cambodia
Roazon see Rennes
149 T7 **Robāṭ-e Chāh Gonbad** Yazd, E Iran
149 R7 **Robāṭ-e Khān** Yazd, C Iran 33.24N 56.04E
149 T7 **Robāṭ-e Khvosh Āb** Yazd, E Iran
149 R8 **Robāṭ-e Posht-e Bādām** Yazd, NE Iran 33.01N 55.34E
149 Q8 **Robaṭ-e Rizāb** Yazd, C Iran
183 S8 **Robbie Ridge** undersea feature W Pacific Ocean
23 T10 **Robbins** North Carolina, SE USA 35.25N 79.35W
191 N15 **Robbins Island** island Tasmania, SE Australia
23 N10 **Robbinsville** North Carolina, SE USA 35.19N 83.48W
190 J12 **Robe** South Australia 37.11S 139.48E
23 W9 **Robersonville** North Carolina, SE USA 35.49N 77.15W
27 P8 **Robert Lee** Texas, SW USA 31.54N 100.26W
37 V5 **Roberts Creek Mountain** ▲ Nevada, W USA 39.52N 116.16W
95 J15 **Robertsfors** Västerbotten, N Sweden 64.12N 20.49E
29 R11 **Robert S.Kerr Reservoir** ⊠ Oklahoma, C USA
40 L12 **Roberts Mountain** ▲ Nunivak Island, Alaska, USA 60.01N 166.15W
85 F26 **Robertson** Western Cape, SW South Africa 33.48S 19.52E
204 H4 **Robertson Island** island Antarctica
78 J16 **Robertsport** W Liberia 6.45N 11.15W
190 J8 **Robertstown** South Australia 34.00S 139.04E
Robert Williams see Caála
13 P7 **Roberval** Québec, SE Canada 48.31N 72.16W
33 N15 **Robinson** Illinois, N USA 39.00N 87.44W
200 Oo12 **Róbinson Crusoe, Isla** island Islas Juan Fernández, Chile, E Pacific Ocean
188 J9 **Robinson Range** ▲▲ Western Australia
194 L16 **Robinson River** Central, S PNG 10.06S 148.51E
190 M9 **Robinvale** Victoria, SE Australia 34.37S 142.45E
107 P11 **Robledo** Castilla-La Mancha, C Spain 38.45N 2.27W
56 G5 **Robles** var. La Paz, Robles La Paz. Cesar, N Colombia 10.24N 73.10W
Robles La Paz see Robles
9 V15 **Roblin** Manitoba, S Canada 51.15N 101.19W
195 U13 **Rob Roy** island NW Solomon Islands
9 S17 **Robsart** Saskatchewan, S Canada 49.22N 109.15W
9 N15 **Robson, Mount** ▲ British Columbia, SW Canada 53.09N 119.16W
27 T14 **Robstown** Texas, SW USA 27.47N 97.40W
27 P6 **Roby** Texas, SW USA 32.43N 100.22W
106 E11 **Roca, Cabo da** headland C Portugal 38.47N 9.32W
Rocadas see Xangongo
43 S14 **Roca Partida, Punta** headland C Mexico 18.43N 95.11W
49 X6 **Rocas, Atol das** island E Brazil
109 L18 **Roccadaspide** var. Rocca d'Aspide. Campania, S Italy 40.25N 15.12E
109 K15 **Roccaraso** Abruzzo, C Italy 41.49N 14.01E
108 H10 **Rocca San Casciano** Emilia-Romagna, C Italy 44.06N 11.51E
108 G13 **Roccastrada** Toscana, C Italy 43.00N 11.09E
63 G20 **Rocha** Rocha, E Uruguay 34.30S 54.22W
63 G19 **Rocha** ◈ department E Uruguay
99 L17 **Rochdale** NW England, UK 53.37N 2.09W
104 L11 **Rochechouart** Haute-Vienne, C France 45.49N 0.49E
101 J22 **Rochefort** Namur, SE Belgium 50.10N 5.13E
104 J11 **Rochefort** var. Rochefort sur Mer. Charente-Maritime, W France 45.57N 0.58W
Rochefort sur Mer see Rochefort
129 N10 **Rochegda** Arkhangel'skaya Oblast', NW Russian Federation 62.37N 43.21E
32 L10 **Rochelle** Illinois, N USA 41.54N 89.03W
27 Q9 **Rochelle** Texas, SW USA 31.13N 99.10W
13 V3 **Rochers Ouest, Rivière aux** ≈ Québec, SE Canada
99 O22 **Rochester** anc. Durobrivae. SE England, UK 51.24N 0.30E
33 O12 **Rochester** Indiana, N USA 41.03N 86.13W
31 W10 **Rochester** Minnesota, N USA 44.01N 92.28W
21 O9 **Rochester** New Hampshire, NE USA 43.18N 70.58W
20 F9 **Rochester** New York, NE USA 43.09N 77.37W
27 P5 **Rochester** Texas, SW USA 33.19N 99.51W
33 S9 **Rochester Hills** Michigan, N USA 42.39N 83.04W
Rocheuses, Montagnes/Rockies see Rocky Mountains
66 M6 **Rockall** island UK, N Atlantic Ocean
66 L6 **Rockall Bank** undersea feature N Atlantic Ocean
86 B8 **Rockall Rise** undersea feature N Atlantic Ocean
86 C9 **Rockall Trough** undersea feature N Atlantic Ocean
37 U2 **Rock Creek** ≈ Nevada, W USA
27 T10 **Rockdale** Texas, SW USA 30.39N 96.58W
205 N12 **Rockefeller Plateau** plateau Antarctica
32 K11 **Rock Falls** Illinois, N USA 41.46N 89.41W
25 Q5 **Rockford** Alabama, S USA 32.53N 86.11W
32 L10 **Rockford** Illinois, N USA 42.16N 89.05W
13 Q12 **Rock Forest** Québec, SE Canada 45.21N 71.58W
9 T17 **Rockglen** Saskatchewan, S Canada 49.10N 105.57W
189 Y8 **Rockhampton** Queensland, E Australia 23.31S 150.31E
23 R11 **Rock Hill** South Carolina, SE USA 34.55N 80.59W
188 I13 **Rockingham** Western Australia 32.16S 115.21E
23 T11 **Rockingham** North Carolina, SE USA 34.56N 79.46W
32 J11 **Rock Island** Illinois, N USA 41.30N 90.34W
27 U12 **Rock Island** Texas, SW USA 29.31N 96.33W
12 C10 **Rock Lake** Ontario, S Canada 46.25N 83.49W
31 O2 **Rock Lake** North Dakota, N USA 48.45N 99.12W
12 I12 **Rock Lake** ◎ Ontario, SE Canada
12 M12 **Rockland** Ontario, SE Canada 45.33N 75.16W
21 R7 **Rockland** Maine, NE USA 44.08N 69.06W
190 L11 **Rocklands Reservoir** ⊠ Victoria, SE Australia
37 O7 **Rocklin** California, W USA 38.48N 121.13W
25 R3 **Rockmart** Georgia, SE USA 34.00N 85.02W
33 N16 **Rockport** Indiana, N USA 37.52N 87.04W
29 Q1 **Rock Port** Missouri, C USA 40.26N 95.30W
27 T14 **Rockport** Texas, SW USA 28.01N 97.03W
34 I7 **Rockport** Washington, NW USA 48.28N 121.36W
31 S11 **Rock Rapids** Iowa, C USA 43.25N 96.10W
32 K11 **Rock River** ≈ Illinois/Wisconsin, N USA
46 I3 **Rock Sound** Eleuthera Island, C Bahamas 24.51N 76.09W
35 U17 **Rock Springs** Wyoming, C USA 41.35N 109.12W
27 P11 **Rocksprings** Texas, SW USA 30.01N 100.12W
57 T9 **Rockstone** C Guyana 5.58N 58.33W
31 S12 **Rock Valley** Iowa, C USA 43.12N 96.17W
33 N14 **Rockville** Indiana, N USA 39.45N 87.13W
23 W3 **Rockville** Maryland, NE USA 39.04N 77.04W
27 U6 **Rockwall** Texas, SW USA 32.55N 96.27W
31 U13 **Rockwell City** Iowa, C USA 42.24N 94.37W
33 S10 **Rockwood** Michigan, N USA 42.04N 83.15W
22 M9 **Rockwood** Tennessee, S USA 35.52N 84.41W
27 Q8 **Rockwood** Texas, SW USA 31.29N 99.23W
39 U6 **Rocky Ford** Colorado, C USA 38.03N 103.45W
12 D9 **Rocky Island Lake** ◎ Ontario, S Canada
23 V9 **Rocky Mount** North Carolina, SE USA 35.56N 77.47W
23 S7 **Rocky Mount** Virginia, NE USA 37.00N 79.53W
35 Q8 **Rocky Mountain** ▲ Montana, NW USA 47.45N 112.46W
9 P15 **Rocky Mountain House** Alberta, SW Canada 52.24N 114.52W
39 T3 **Rocky Mountain National Park** national park Colorado, C USA
2 E12 **Rocky Mountains** var. Rockies, Fr. Montagnes Rocheuses. ▲▲ Canada/USA
44 H1 **Rocky Point** headland NE Belize 18.21N 88.04W
85 A17 **Rocky Point** headland NW Namibia 19.01S 12.27E
97 F14 **Rødberg** Buskerud, S Norway 60.16N 9.00E
97 I25 **Rødby** Storstrøm, SE Denmark 54.42N 11.24E
97 I25 **Rødbyhavn** Storstrøm, SE Denmark 54.39N 11.24E
11 T10 **Roddickton** Newfoundland and Labrador, SE Canada 50.51N 56.03W
97 F23 **Rødding** Sønderjylland, SW Denmark 55.22N 9.04E
97 M22 **Rödeby** Blekinge, S Sweden 56.16N 15.34E
100 N6 **Roden** Drenthe, NE Netherlands 53.07N 6.25E
64 H9 **Rodeo** San Juan, W Argentina 30.12S 69.06W
105 O14 **Rodez** anc. Segodunum. Aveyron, S France 44.21N 2.34E
Rodholívos see Rodolívos
Rodhópi Óri see Rhodope Mountains
Ródhos/Rodi see Ródos
109 N15 **Rodi Garganico** Puglia, SE Italy 41.54N 15.51E
103 N20 **Roding** Bayern, SE Germany 49.12N 12.30E
115 J19 **Rodinit, Kepi i** headland W Albania 41.35N 19.27E
118 I9 **Rodnei, Munții** ▲▲ N Romania
192 L4 **Rodney, Cape** headland North Island, NZ 36.16S 174.48E
40 L9 **Rodney, Cape** headland Alaska, USA 64.39N 166.24W
128 M16 **Rodniki** Ivanovskaya Oblast', W Russian Federation 57.04N 41.45E
121 Q16 **Rodnya** Rus. Rodnya. Mahilyowskaya Voblasts', E Belarus 53.30N 32.12E
Rodó see José Enrique Rodó
116 H13 **Rodolívos** var. Rodholívos. Kentrikí Makedonía, NE Greece 40.55N 23.59E
Rodopi see Rhodope Mountains
117 O22 **Ródos** var. Ródhos, Eng. Rhodes, It. Rodi. Ródos, Dodekánisa, Greece, Aegean Sea 36.25N 28.13E
117 O22 **Ródos** var. Ródhos, Eng. Rhodes, It. Rodi; anc. Rhodos. island Dodekánisa, Greece, Aegean Sea
Rodosto see Tekirdağ
61 A14 **Rodrigues** Amazonas, W Brazil 6.50S 73.45W
181 P8 **Rodrigues** var. Rodriquez. island E Mauritius
Rodriquez see Rodrigues
Rodunma see Roanne
188 I7 **Roebourne** Western Australia 20.49S 117.04E
85 J20 **Roedtan** Limpopo, NE South Africa 24.37S 29.04E
100 H11 **Roelofarendsveen** Zuid-Holland, W Netherlands 52.12N 4.37E
Roepat see Rupat, Pulau
Roer see Rur
101 M16 **Roermond** Limburg, SE Netherlands 51.12N 6.00E
101 C18 **Roeselare** Fr. Roulers; prev. Rousselaere. West-Vlaanderen, W Belgium 50.57N 3.07E
15 Ll5 **Roes Welcome Sound** strait Nunavut, N Canada
Roeteng see Ruteng
Rofreit see Rovereto
Rogachëv see Rahachow
59 L15 **Rogagua, Laguna** ◎ NW Bolivia
97 C16 **Rogaland** ◈ county S Norway
27 Y9 **Roganville** Texas, SW USA 30.49N 93.54W
111 W11 **Rogaška Slatina** Ger. Rohitsch-Sauerbrunn; prev. Rogatec-Slatina. E Slovenia 46.13N 15.38E
Rogatec-Slatina see Rogaška Slatina
114 J13 **Rogatica** Republica Srpska, SE Bosnia & Herzegovina 43.50N 18.55E
Rogatin see Rohatyn
95 F17 **Rogen** ◎ C Sweden
29 S9 **Rogers** Arkansas, C USA 36.19N 94.07W
31 P5 **Rogers** North Dakota, N USA 47.03N 98.12W
27 T9 **Rogers** Texas, SW USA 30.53N 97.10W
33 R5 **Rogers City** Michigan, N USA 45.25N 83.49W
Roger Simpson Island see Abemama
37 T14 **Rogers Lake** salt flat California, W USA
23 Q8 **Rogers, Mount** ▲ Virginia, NE USA 36.39N 81.32W
35 O16 **Rogerson** Idaho, NW USA 42.11N 114.36W
9 O16 **Rogers Pass** pass British Columbia, SW Canada 51.18N 117.36W
23 O8 **Rogersville** Tennessee, S USA 36.26N 83.01W
101 L16 **Roggel** Limburg, SE Netherlands 51.16N 5.55E
Roggeveen see Roggewein, Cabo
200 Nn12 **Roggeveen Basin** undersea feature E Pacific Ocean
203 X16 **Roggewein, Cabo** var. Roggeveen. headland Easter Island, Chile, E Pacific Ocean 27.07S 109.15W
105 Y13 **Rogliano** Corse, France, C Mediterranean Sea 42.58N 9.25E
109 N21 **Rogliano** Calabria, SW Italy 39.09N 16.18E
94 G12 **Rognan** Nordland, C Norway 67.04N 15.21E
102 K10 **Rögnitz** ≈ N Germany
Rogozhina/Rogozhinë see Rrogozhinë
112 G10 **Rogoźno** Wielkopolskie, C Poland 52.46N 16.57E
34 E15 **Rogue River** ≈ Oregon, NW USA
118 I6 **Rohatyn** Rus. Rogatin. Ivano-Frankivs'ka Oblast', W Ukraine 49.25N 24.35E
201 O14 **Rohi** Pohnpei, E Micronesia
Rohitsch-Sauerbrunn see Rogaška Slatina
155 Q13 **Rohri** Sind, SE Pakistan 27.40N 68.52E
158 I10 **Rohtak** Haryāna, N India 28.55N 76.32E
Roi Ed see Roi Et
178 Ii10 **Roi Et** var. Muang Roi Et, Roi Ed. Roi Et, E Thailand 16.04N 103.37E
203 U9 **Roi Georges, Îles du** island group Îles Tuamotu, C French Polynesia
159 Y10 **Roing** Arunāchal Pradesh, NE India 28.06N 95.46E
120 E7 **Roja** Talsi, NW Latvia 57.31N 22.44E
63 B20 **Rojas** Buenos Aires, E Argentina 34.13S 60.41W
155 R12 **Rojhān** Punjab, E Pakistan 28.44N 70.01E
43 Q12 **Rojo, Cabo** headland C Mexico 21.33N 97.19W
47 Q10 **Rojo, Cabo** headland W Puerto Rico 17.57N 67.10W
173 G7 **Rokan Kanan, Sungai** ≈ Sumatera, W Indonesia
173 G7 **Rokan Kiri, Sungai** ≈ Sumatera, W Indonesia
120 I11 **Rokiškis** Panevėžys, NE Lithuania 55.58N 25.34E
172 Nn9 **Rokkasho** Aomori, Honshū, C Japan 40.59N 141.22E
113 B17 **Rokycany** Ger. Rokytzan. Plzeňský Kraj, NW Czech Republic 49.45N 13.36E
119 P6 **Rokytne** Kyyivs'ka Oblast', N Ukraine 49.40N 30.29E
118 L3 **Rokytne** Rivnens'ka Oblast', NW Ukraine 51.19N 27.09E
Rokytzan see Rokycany
164 L11 **Rola Co** ◎ W China
31 V13 **Roland** Iowa, C USA 42.10N 93.30W
97 D15 **Røldal** Hordaland, S Norway 59.52N 6.49E
100 O7 **Rolde** Drenthe, NE Netherlands 52.58N 6.39E
31 O2 **Rolette** North Dakota, N USA 48.39N 99.50W
29 V6 **Rolla** Missouri, C USA 37.57N 91.46W
31 O2 **Rolla** North Dakota, N USA 48.51N 99.37W
110 A10 **Rolle** Vaud, W Switzerland 46.27N 6.19E
189 X8 **Rolleston** Queensland, E Australia 24.30S 148.36E
193 H19 **Rolleston** Canterbury, South Island, NZ 43.34S 172.24E
193 G18 **Rolleston Range** ▲▲ South Island, NZ
12 H8 **Rollet** Québec, SE Canada 47.56N 79.14W
24 J4 **Rolling Fork** Mississippi, S USA 32.54N 90.52W
22 L6 **Rolling Fork** ≈ Kentucky, S USA
12 J11 **Rolphton** Ontario, SE Canada 46.09N 77.43W
Röm see Rømø
189 X10 **Roma** Queensland, E Australia 26.36S 148.53E
109 I15 **Roma** Eng. Rome. ● (Italy) Lazio, C Italy 41.52N 12.30E
97 P19 **Roma** Gotland, SE Sweden 57.31N 18.28E
23 T14 **Romain, Cape** headland South Carolina, SE USA 33.00N 79.21W
11 P11 **Romaine** ≈ Newfoundland and Labrador/Québec, E Canada
27 R17 **Roma Los Saenz** Texas, SW USA 26.24N 99.01W
116 H8 **Roman** Vratsa, NW Bulgaria 43.09N 23.56E
118 L10 **Roman** Hung. Románvásár. Neamț, NE Romania 46.46N 26.55E
66 M13 **Romanche Fracture Zone** tectonic feature E Atlantic Ocean
63 C15 **Romang** Santa Fe, C Argentina 29.30S 59.46W
175 T15 **Romang, Pulau** var. Pulau Roma. island Kepulauan Damar, E Indonesia
175 Ss15 **Romang, Selat** strait Nusa Tenggara, S Indonesia
118 J11 **Romania** Bul. Rumŭniya, Ger. Rumänien, Hung. Románia, Rom. România, SCr. Rumunjska, Ukr. Rumuniya; prev. Republica Socialistă România, Roumania, Rumania, Socialist Republic of Romania, Rom. Romînia. ◆ republic SE Europe
119 T14 **Roman-Kash** ▲ S Ukraine 44.37N 34.13E
25 W16 **Romano, Cape** headland Florida, SE USA 25.51N 81.40W
46 G5 **Romano, Cayo** island C Cuba
126 Kk15 **Romanovka** Respublika Buryatiya, S Russian Federation 53.10N 112.34E
131 N8 **Romanovka** Saratovskaya Oblast', W Russian Federation 51.45N 42.45E
110 I6 **Romanshorn** Thurgau, NE Switzerland 47.33N 9.21E
105 R12 **Romans-sur-Isère** Drôme, E France 45.03N 5.03E
201 U12 **Romanum** island Chuuk, C Micronesia
Románvásár see Roman
41 S5 **Romanzof Mountains** ▲▲ Alaska, USA
Roma, Pulau see Romang, Pulau
105 S4 **Rombas** Moselle, NE France 49.15N 6.04E
176 Xx10 **Rombebai, Danau** ◎ Papua, E Indonesia
25 R2 **Rome** Georgia, SE USA 34.01N 85.01W
20 I9 **Rome** New York, NE USA 43.13N 75.28W
Rome see Roma
33 S9 **Romeo** Michigan, N USA 42.48N 83.00W
Römerstadt see Rýmařov
Rometan see Romiton
105 P5 **Romilly-sur-Seine** Aube, N France 48.31N 3.43E

◆ Country
● Country Capital
◇ Dependent Territory
○ Dependent Territory Capital
◈ Administrative Region
✕ International Airport
▲ Mountain
▲▲ Mountain Range
⛰ Volcano
≈ River
◎ Lake
⊠ Reservoir

ROMÎNIA – RUSTAQ

Romînia *see* Romania
152 *L11* **Romiton** *Rus.* Rometan. Buxoro Viloyati, C Uzbekistan *39.56N 64.21E*
23 *U3* **Romney** West Virginia, NE USA *39.20N 78.45W*
119 *S4* **Romny** Sums'ka Oblast', NE Ukraine *50.45N 33.30E*
97 *E24* **Rømø** *Ger.* *Röm. island* SW Denmark
119 *S5* **Romodan** Poltavs'ka Oblast', NE Ukraine *50.00N 33.20E*
131 *P5* **Romodanovo** Respublika Mordoviya, W Russian Federation *54.25N 45.24E*
Romorantin *see* Romorantin-Lanthenay
105 *N8* **Romorantin-Lanthenay** *var.* Romorantin. Loir-et-Cher, C France *47.22N 1.43E*
174 *Hh5* **Rompin, Sungai** Peninsular Malaysia
96 *F9* **Romsdal** *physical region* S Norway
96 *F10* **Romsdalen** *valley* S Norway
96 *E9* **Romsdalsfjorden** *fjord* S Norway
35 *P8* **Ronan** Montana, NW USA *47.31N 114.06W*
61 *M14* **Roncador** Maranhão, E Brazil *5.48S 45.08W*
195 *W12* **Roncador Reef** *reef* N Solomon Islands
61 *J17* **Roncador, Serra do** C Brazil
23 *S6* **Ronceverte** West Virginia, NE USA *37.45N 80.27W*
109 *H14* **Ronciglione** Lazio, C Italy *42.16N 12.15E*
106 *L15* **Ronda** Andalucía, S Spain *36.45N 5.10W*
96 *G11* **Rondane** S Norway
106 *L15* **Ronda, Serranía de** S Spain
97 *H22* **Rønde** Århus, C Denmark *56.18N 10.28E*
Rōndik *see* Rongrik Atoll
61 *E16* **Rondônia** *off.* Estado de Rondônia; *prev.* Território de Rondônia. *state* W Brazil
61 *I18* **Rondonópolis** Mato Grosso, W Brazil *16.28S 54.37W*
96 *G11* **Rondslottet** S Norway *61.54N 9.48E*
97 *P20* **Ronehamn** Gotland, SE Sweden *57.10N 18.30E*
166 *L13* **Rong'an** *var.* Chang'an, Rongan. Guangxi Zhuangzu Zizhiqu, S China *25.13N 109.19E*
Rongcheng *see* Jianli, Hubei, China
Rongcheng *see* Rongxian, Guangxi, China
201 *R4* **Rongelap Atoll** *var.* Rōnļap. *atoll* Ralik Chain, NW Marshall Islands
Rongerik *see* Rongerik Atoll
166 *K12* **Rongjiang** *var.* Guzhou. Guizhou, S China *25.59N 108.27E*
166 *L13* **Rong Jiang** S China
Rongjiang *see* Nankang
Rong, Kas *see* Rŭng, Kaôh
178 *Hh8* **Rong Kwang** Phrae, NW Thailand *18.19N 100.18E*
201 *T4* **Rongrik Atoll** *var.* Rōndik, Rongerik. *atoll* Ralik Chain, N Marshall Islands
201 *X2* **Rongrong** *island* SE Marshall Islands
166 *L13* **Rongshui** *var.* Rongshui Miaozu Zizhixian. Guangxi Zhuangzu Zizhiqu, S China *25.08N 109.15E*
Rongshui Miaozu Zizhixian *see* Rongshui
120 *I6* **Rõngu** *Ger.* Ringen. Tartumaa, SE Estonia *58.10N 26.17E*
Rongwo *see* Tongren
166 *L15* **Rongxian** *var.* Rongcheng. Guangxi Zhuangzu Zizhiqu, S China *22.52N 110.33E*
Rongzhag *see* Danba
Roniu *see* Ronui, Mont
201 *N13* **Ronkiti** Pohnpei, E Micronesia *6.48N 158.10E*
Rōnļap *see* Rongelap Atoll
97 *L24* **Rønne** Bornholm, E Denmark *55.07N 14.43E*
97 *M22* **Ronneby** Blekinge, S Sweden *56.12N 15.18E*
204 *J7* **Ronne Entrance** *inlet* Antarctica
204 *L6* **Ronne Ice Shelf** *ice shelf* Antarctica
101 *E19* **Ronse** *Fr.* Renaix. Oost-Vlaanderen, SW Belgium *50.45N 3.36E*
203 *R8* **Ronui, Mont** *var.* Roniu. Tahiti, W French Polynesia *17.49S 149.12W*
32 *K14* **Roodhouse** Illinois, N USA *39.28N 90.22W*
85 *C19* **Rooibank** Erongo, W Namibia *23.04S 14.34E*
Rooke Island *see* Umboi Island
67 *N24* **Rookery Point** *headland* NE Tristan da Cunha *37.03S 12.15W*
176 *W10* **Roon, Pulau** *island* E Indonesia
181 *V7* **Roo Rise** *undersea feature* E Indian Ocean
158 *J9* **Roorkee** Uttaranchal, N India *29.51N 77.54E*
101 *H15* **Roosendaal** Noord-Brabant, S Netherlands *51.31N 4.28E*
27 *P10* **Roosevelt** Texas, SW USA *30.28N 100.06W*
39 *N3* **Roosevelt** Utah, W USA *40.18N 109.59W*
49 *T8* **Roosevelt** W Brazil
205 *O13* **Roosevelt Island** *island* Antarctica
8 *L10* **Roosevelt, Mount** British Columbia, W Canada *58.28N 125.22W*
9 *P17* **Roosville** British Columbia, SW Canada *48.59N 115.03W*
31 *X10* **Root River** Minnesota, N USA
113 *N16* **Ropczyce** Podkarpackie, SE Poland *50.03N 21.36E*
189 *Q3* **Roper Bar** Northern Territory, N Australia *14.45S 134.30E*
26 *M5* **Ropesville** Texas, SW USA *33.24N 102.09W*
104 *K14* **Roquefort** Landes, SW France *44.01N 0.18W*
63 *C21* **Roque Pérez** Buenos Aires, E Argentina *35.25S 59.24W*
60 *E10* **Roraima** *off.* Estado de Roraima; *prev.* Território de Rio Branco, Território de Roraima. *state* N Brazil
60 *F9* **Roraima, Mount** N South America *5.10N 60.36W*
176 *X10* **Rori** Papua, E Indonesia *1.44S 136.49E*
Ro Ro Reef *see* Malolo Barrier Reef
96 *I9* **Røros** Sør-Trøndelag, S Norway *62.37N 11.25E*
110 *I7* **Rorschach** Sankt Gallen, NE Switzerland *47.28N 9.30E*
95 *E14* **Rørvik** Nord-Trøndelag, C Norway *64.52N 11.13E*
121 *G17* **Ros'** *Rus.* Ross'. Hrodzyenskaya Voblasts', W Belarus *53.20N 24.25E*
121 *G17* **Ros'** *Rus.* Ross'. W Belarus
119 *O6* **Ros'** N Ukraine
46 *K7* **Rosa, Lake** Great Inagua, S Bahamas
34 *M9* **Rosalia** Washington, NW USA *47.14N 117.22W*
203 *W15* **Rosalia, Punta** *headland* Easter Island, Chile, E Pacific Ocean *27.04S 109.19W*
47 *P12* **Rosalie** E Dominica *15.22N 61.15W*
37 *T14* **Rosamond** California, W USA *34.51N 118.09W*
37 *S14* **Rosamond Lake** *salt flat* California, W USA
63 *B18* **Rosario** Santa Fe, C Argentina *32.56S 60.38W*
42 *J11* **Rosario** Sinaloa, C Mexico *23.00N 105.51W*
42 *G6* **Rosario** Sonora, NW Mexico *27.53N 109.18W*
64 *O6* **Rosario** San Pedro, C Paraguay *24.26S 57.06W*
63 *E20* **Rosario** Colonia, SW Uruguay *34.19S 57.18W*
56 *H5* **Rosario** Zulia, NW Venezuela *10.18N 72.19W*
Rosario *see* Rosarito
42 *B4* **Rosario, Bahía del** *bay* NW Mexico
64 *K6* **Rosario de la Frontera** Salta, N Argentina *25.50S 65.00W*
63 *C18* **Rosario del Tala** Entre Ríos, E Argentina *32.19S 59.10W*
63 *F16* **Rosário do Sul** Rio Grande do Sul, S Brazil *30.15S 54.55W*
61 *H18* **Rosário Oeste** Mato Grosso, W Brazil *14.49S 56.25W*
42 *E7* **Rosarito** Baja California, NW Mexico *26.27N 111.37W*
42 *B1* **Rosarito** *var.* Rosario. Baja California, NW Mexico *32.25N 117.03W*
42 *E7* **Rosarito** Baja California Sur, W Mexico *26.28N 111.40W*
106 *L9* **Rosarito, Embalse del** W Spain
109 *N22* **Rosarno** Calabria, SW Italy *38.28N 15.58E*
58 *B5* **Rosa Zárate** *var.* Quinindé. Esmeraldas, SW Ecuador *0.18N 79.28W*
Roscianum *see* Rossano
31 *O8* **Roscoe** South Dakota, N USA *45.24N 99.19W*
27 *P7* **Roscoe** Texas, SW USA *32.27N 100.32W*
104 *F5* **Roscoff** Finistère, NW France *48.43N 4.00W*
Ros Comáin *see* Roscommon
99 *C17* **Roscommon** *Ir.* Ros Comáin. C Ireland *53.37N 8.10W*
33 *Q7* **Roscommon** Michigan, N USA *44.30N 84.34W*
99 *C17* **Roscommon** *Ir.* Ros Comáin. *cultural region* C Ireland
Ros. Cré *see* Roscrea
99 *D19* **Roscrea** *Ir.* Ros. Cré. C Ireland *52.57N 7.46W*
47 *X12* **Roseau** *prev.* Charlotte Town. (Dominica) SW Dominica *15.16N 61.22W*
31 *S2* **Roseau** Minnesota, N USA *48.51N 95.45W*
181 *Y16* **Rose Belle** SE Mauritius *20.24S 57.36E*
191 *O16* **Rosebery** Tasmania, SE Australia *41.51S 145.33E*
23 *U11* **Roseboro** North Carolina, SE USA *34.58N 78.31W*
27 *T9* **Rosebud** Texas, SW USA *31.04N 96.58W*
35 *W10* **Rosebud Creek** Montana, NW USA
34 *F14* **Roseburg** Oregon, NW USA *43.13N 123.20W*
24 *J3* **Rosedale** Mississippi, S USA *33.51N 91.01W*
101 *H21* **Rosée** Namur, S Belgium *50.15N 4.43E*
57 *U8* **Rose Hall** E Guyana *6.14N 57.30W*
181 *X16* **Rose Hill** W Mauritius *20.13S 57.28E*
82 *H12* **Roseires, Reservoir** *var.* Lake Rusayris. E Sudan
Rosenau *see* Rožnov pod Radhoštěm, Czech Republic
Rosenau *see* Rožňava, Slovakia
27 *V11* **Rosenberg** Texas, SW USA *29.33N 95.48W*
Rosenberg *see* Olesno, Poland
Rosenberg *see* Ružomberok, Slovakia
102 *I10* **Rosengarten** Niedersachsen, N Germany *53.24N 9.53E*
103 *M24* **Rosenheim** Bayern, S Germany *47.51N 12.07E*
Rosenhof *see* Zilupe
107 *X4* **Roses** Cataluña, NE Spain *42.15N 3.10E*
107 *X4* **Roses, Golf de** *gulf* NE Spain
109 *K14* **Roseto degli Abruzzi** Abruzzo, C Italy *42.39N 14.01E*
9 *S16* **Rosetown** Saskatchewan, S Canada *51.34N 107.58W*
Rosetta *see* Rashid
37 *O7* **Roseville** California, W USA *38.44N 121.16W*
32 *J12* **Roseville** Illinois, N USA *40.42N 90.40W*
31 *V8* **Roseville** Minnesota, N USA *45.00N 93.09W*
31 *R7* **Rosholt** South Dakota, N USA *45.51N 96.42W*
108 *F12* **Rosignano Marittimo** Toscana, C Italy *43.24N 10.28E*
118 *I14* **Roşiori de Vede** Teleorman, S Romania *44.06N 25.00E*
116 *K8* **Rositsa** N Bulgaria
Rositten *see* Rēzekne
97 *J23* **Roskilde** Roskilde, E Denmark *55.39N 12.07E*
97 *I23* **Roskilde** *off.* Roskilde Amt. *county* E Denmark
Ros Láir *see* Rosslare
130 *H5* **Roslavl'** Smolenskaya Oblast', W Russian Federation *53.59N 32.57E*
34 *I8* **Roslyn** Washington, NW USA *47.13N 120.52W*
101 *K14* **Rosmalen** Noord-Brabant, S Netherlands *51.43N 5.21E*
Ros Mhic Thriúin *see* New Ross
115 *P19* **Rosoman** C FYR Macedonia *41.31N 21.55E*
104 *F6* **Rosporden** Finistère, NW France *47.58N 3.54W*
193 *F17* **Ross** West Coast, South Island, NZ *42.54S 170.51E*
8 *J7* **Ross** Yukon Territory, W Canada
Ross' *see* Ros'
98 *H8* **Ross and Cromarty** *cultural region* N Scotland, UK
109 *O20* **Rossano** *anc.* Roscianum. Calabria, SW Italy *39.34N 16.37E*
24 *L5* **Ross Barnett Reservoir** Mississippi, S USA
9 *W16* **Rossburn** Manitoba, S Canada *50.42N 100.49W*
12 *H13* **Rosseau** Ontario, S Canada *45.15N 79.38W*
12 *H13* **Rosseau, Lake** Ontario, S Canada
195 *R17* **Rossel Island** *prev.* Yela Island. *island* SE PNG
205 *P12* **Ross Ice Shelf** *ice shelf* Antarctica
11 *P16* **Rossignol, Lake** Nova Scotia, SE Canada
85 *C19* **Rössing** Erongo, W Namibia *22.27S 14.52E*
205 *Q14* **Ross Island** *island* Antarctica
Rossitten *see* Rybachiy
Rossiyskaya Federatsiya *see* Russian Federation
9 *N17* **Rossland** British Columbia, SW Canada *49.03N 117.49W*
99 *F20* **Rosslare** *Ir.* Ros Láir. Wexford, SE Ireland *52.15N 6.22W*
99 *F20* **Rosslare Harbour** Wexford, SE Ireland *52.15N 6.19W*
103 *M14* **Rosslau** Sachsen-Anhalt, E Germany *51.52N 12.15E*
78 *G10* **Rosso** Trarza, SW Mauritania *16.36N 15.49W*
105 *X14* **Rosso, Cap** *headland* Corse, France, C Mediterranean Sea *42.25N 8.22E*
95 *H16* **Rossön** Jämtland, C Sweden *63.54N 16.21E*
99 *K21* **Ross-on-Wye** W England, UK *51.55N 2.34W*
Rossony *see* Rasony
130 *L9* **Rossosh'** Voronezhskaya Oblast', W Russian Federation *50.09N 39.34E*
189 *Q7* **Ross River** Northern Territory, N Australia *23.36S 134.30E*
8 *J7* **Ross River** Yukon Territory, W Canada *61.57N 132.26W*
205 *O15* **Ross Sea** *sea* Antarctica
94 *G13* **Røssvatnet** *Lapp.* Reevhtse. C Norway
25 *R1* **Rossville** Georgia, SE USA *34.59N 85.22W*
Rostak *see* Ar Rustāq
149 *P14* **Rostāq** Hormozgān, S Iran *26.48N 53.50E*
119 *N5* **Rostavytsya** N Ukraine
9 *T15* **Rosthern** Saskatchewan, S Canada *52.40N 106.19W*
102 *M8* **Rostock** Mecklenburg-Vorpommern, NE Germany *54.04N 12.07E*
128 *L16* **Rostov** Yaroslavskaya Oblast', W Russian Federation *57.11N 39.19E*
Rostov *see* Rostov-na-Donu
130 *L12* **Rostov-na-Donu** *var.* Rostov, *Eng.* Rostov-on-Don. Rostovskaya Oblast', SW Russian Federation *47.16N 39.45E*
Rostov-on-Don *see* Rostov-na-Donu
130 *L10* **Rostovskaya Oblast'** *province* SW Russian Federation
95 *J14* **Rosvik** Norrbotten, N Sweden *65.26N 21.48E*
25 *S3* **Roswell** Georgia, SE USA *34.01N 84.21W*
39 *U14* **Roswell** New Mexico, SW USA *33.23N 104.31W*
96 *K12* **Rot** Dalarna, C Sweden *61.16N 14.04E*
103 *I23* **Rot** S Germany
106 *J15* **Rota** Andalucía, S Spain *36.39N 6.20W*
196 *K9* **Rota** *island* S Northern Mariana Islands
27 *P6* **Rotan** Texas, SW USA *32.51N 100.28W*
Rotcher Island *see* Tamana
102 *I11* **Rotenburg** Niedersachsen, NW Germany *53.06N 9.25E*
Rotenburg *see* Rotenburg an der Fulda
103 *I16* **Rotenburg an der Fulda** *var.* Rotenburg. Thüringen, C Germany *51.00N 9.43E*
103 *L18* **Roter Main** E Germany
103 *K20* **Roth** Bayern, SE Germany *49.15N 11.06E*
103 *G16* **Rothaargebirge** W Germany
Rothenburg *see* Rothenburg ob der Tauber
103 *J20* **Rothenburg ob der Tauber** *var.* Rothenburg. Bayern, S Germany *49.23N 10.10E*
204 *H6* **Rothera** *UK research station* Antarctica *67.28S 68.31W*
193 *I17* **Rotherham** Canterbury, South Island, NZ *42.42S 172.56E*
99 *M17* **Rotherham** N England, UK *53.25N 1.19W*
98 *H12* **Rothesay** W Scotland, UK *55.49N 5.03W*
110 *E7* **Rothrist** Aargau, N Switzerland *47.18N 7.54E*
204 *H6* **Rothschild Island** *island* Antarctica
175 *Qq18* **Roti, Pulau** *island* S Indonesia
175 *R18* **Roti, Selat** *strait* Nusa Tenggara, S Indonesia
191 *O8* **Roto** New South Wales, SE Australia *33.04S 145.27E*
192 *N8* **Rotoiti, Lake** North Island, NZ
Rotomagus *see* Rouen
109 *N19* **Rotondella** Basilicata, S Italy *40.12N 16.30E*
105 *X15* **Rotondo, Monte** Corse, France, C Mediterranean Sea *42.15N 9.03E*
193 *I15* **Rotoroa, Lake** South Island, NZ
192 *N8* **Rotorua** Bay of Plenty, North Island, NZ *38.09S 176.13E*
192 *N8* **Rotorua, Lake** North Island, NZ
103 *N22* **Rott** SE Germany
110 *F10* **Rotten** S Switzerland
111 *T6* **Rottenmann** Steiermark, E Austria *47.31N 14.18E*
100 *H12* **Rotterdam** Zuid-Holland, SW Netherlands *51.55N 4.30E*
20 *K10* **Rotterdam** New York, NE USA *42.46N 73.57W*
97 *M21* **Rottnen** S Sweden
100 *N4* **Rottumeroog** *island* Waddeneilanden, NE Netherlands
100 *N4* **Rottumerplaat** *island* Waddeneilanden, NE Netherlands
103 *G23* **Rottweil** Baden-Württemberg, S Germany *48.10N 8.37E*
203 *O7* **Rotui, Mont** Moorea, W French Polynesia *17.30S 149.49W*
105 *P1* **Roubaix** Nord, N France *50.42N 3.10E*
113 *C15* **Roudnice nad Labem** *Ger.* Raudnitz an der Elbe. Ústecký Kraj, NW Czech Republic *50.25N 14.13E*
104 *M4* **Rouen** *anc.* Rotomagus. Seine-Maritime, N France *49.25N 1.04E*
176 *Y11* **Rouffaer Reserves** *reserve* Papua, E Indonesia
13 *N10* **Rouge, Rivière** Québec, SE Canada
22 *J6* **Rough River** Kentucky, S USA
22 *J6* **Rough River Lake** Kentucky, S USA
Rouhaïbé *see* Ar Ruḩaybah
104 *K11* **Rouillac** Charente, W France *45.46N 0.04W*
Roulers *see* Roeselare
Roumania *see* Romania
181 *Y15* **Round Island** *var.* Île Ronde. *island* NE Mauritius
12 *J12* **Round Lake** Ontario, SE Canada
37 *U7* **Round Mountain** Nevada, W USA *38.42N 117.04W*
27 *R10* **Round Mountain** Texas, SW USA *30.25N 98.20W*
191 *U5* **Round Mountain** New South Wales, SE Australia *30.22S 152.13E*
27 *S10* **Round Rock** Texas, SW USA *30.30N 97.40W*
35 *U10* **Roundup** Montana, NW USA *46.27N 108.32W*
57 *Y10* **Roura** NE French Guiana *4.45N 52.18W*
Rourkela *see* Rāulakela
98 *J4* **Rousay** *island* N Scotland, UK
Rousselaere *see* Roeselare
105 *O17* **Roussillon** *cultural region* S France
13 *V7* **Routhierville** Québec, SE Canada *48.09N 67.07W*
101 *K25* **Rouvroy** Luxembourg, SE Belgium *49.33N 5.28E*
12 *I7* **Rouyn-Noranda** Québec, SE Canada *48.16N 79.01W*
Rouyuanchengzi *see* Huachi
94 *L12* **Rovaniemi** Lappi, N Finland *66.28N 25.40E*
108 *E7* **Rovato** Lombardia, N Italy *45.34N 10.03E*
129 *N11* **Rovdino** Arkhangel'skaya Oblast', NW Russian Federation *61.36N 42.28E*
Roven'ki *see* Roven'ky
119 *Y8* **Roven'ky** *var.* Roven'ki. Luhans'ka Oblast', E Ukraine *48.04N 39.19E*
Rovenskaya Oblast' *see* Rivnens'ka Oblast'
Rovenskaya Sloboda *see* Rovyenskaya Slabada
108 *G7* **Rovereto** *Ger.* Rofreit. Trentino-Alto Adige, N Italy *45.52N 11.03E*
178 *J12* **Rôviĕng Tbong** Preăh Vihéar, N Cambodia *13.18N 105.06E*
Rovigno *see* Rovinj
108 *H8* **Rovigo** Veneto, NE Italy *45.04N 11.48E*
114 *A10* **Rovinj** *It.* Rovigno. Istra, NW Croatia *45.06N 13.39E*
56 *E10* **Rovira** Tolima, C Colombia *4.15N 75.15W*
Rovno *see* Rivne
131 *P9* **Rovnoye** Saratovskaya Oblast', W Russian Federation *50.43N 46.03E*
84 *Q12* **Rovuma, Rio** *var.* Ruvuma. Mozambique/Tanzania *see also* Ruvuma
121 *O19* **Rovyenskaya Slabada** *Rus.* Rovenskaya Sloboda. Homyel'skaya Voblasts', SE Belarus *52.12N 30.19E*
191 *R5* **Rowena** New South Wales, SE Australia *29.51S 148.55E*
23 *T11* **Rowland** North Carolina, SE USA *34.32N 79.17W*
15 *M1* **Rowley** Baffin Island, Nunavut, NE Canada
15 *M2* **Rowley Island** *island* Nunavut, NE Canada
181 *W8* **Rowley Shoals** *reef* NW Australia
179 *Pp12* **Roxas** Mindoro, N Philippines *12.36N 121.29E*
179 *Q13* **Roxas City** Panay Island, C Philippines *11.33N 122.43E*
23 *U8* **Roxboro** North Carolina, SE USA *36.23N 78.58W*
193 *D23* **Roxburgh** Otago, South Island, NZ *45.32S 169.18E*
98 *K13* **Roxburgh** *cultural region* SE Scotland, UK
190 *H5* **Roxby Downs** South Australia *30.29S 136.56E*
97 *M17* **Roxen** S Sweden
27 *V5* **Roxton** Texas, SW USA *33.33N 95.43W*
13 *P12* **Roxton-Sud** Québec, SE Canada *45.30N 72.35W*
35 *U8* **Roy** Montana, NW USA *47.19N 108.55W*
39 *U10* **Roy** New Mexico, SW USA *35.56N 104.12W*
99 *E17* **Royal Canal** *Ir.* An Chanáil Ríoga. *canal* C Ireland
32 *L1* **Royale, Isle** *island* Michigan, N USA
39 *S6* **Royal Gorge** *valley* Colorado, C USA
99 *M20* **Royal Leamington Spa** *var.* Leamington, Leamington Spa. C England, UK *52.18N 1.31W*
99 *O23* **Royal Tunbridge Wells** *var.* Tunbridge Wells. SE England, UK *51.07N 0.16E*
26 *L9* **Royalty** Texas, SW USA *31.21N 102.51W*
104 *J11* **Royan** Charente-Maritime, W France *45.37N 1.01W*
67 *B24* **Roy Cove Settlement** West Falkland, Falkland Islands *51.31S 60.22W*
105 *O3* **Roye** Somme, N France *49.42N 2.46E*
97 *H15* **Røyken** Buskerud, S Norway *59.47N 10.21E*
95 *F14* **Røyrvik** Nord-Trøndelag, C Norway *64.53N 13.30E*
27 *U6* **Royse City** Texas, SW USA *32.58N 96.19W*
99 *O21* **Royston** E England, UK *52.05N 0.01W*
25 *U2* **Royston** Georgia, SE USA *34.17N 83.06W*
116 *L10* **Roza** *prev.* Gyulovo. Yambol, E Bulgaria *42.29N 26.30E*
115 *L16* **Rožaje** E Montenegro *42.51N 20.11E*
112 *M10* **Różan** Mazowieckie, C Poland *52.36N 21.27E*
119 *O10* **Rozdil'na** Odes'ka Oblast', SW Ukraine *46.51N 30.03E*
119 *S12* **Rozdol'ne** *Rus.* Razdolnoye. Respublika Krym, S Ukraine *45.45N 33.27E*
151 *Q9* **Rozhdestvenka** Akmola, C Kazakhstan *50.51N 71.25E*
118 *I6* **Rozhnyativ** Ivano-Frankivs'ka Oblast', W Ukraine *48.58N 24.07E*
118 *J3* **Rozhyshche** Volyns'ka Oblast', NW Ukraine *50.54N 25.16E*
Roznau am Radhost *see* Rožnov pod Radhoštěm
113 *L19* **Rožňava** *Ger.* Rosenau, *Hung.* Rozsnyó. Košický Kraj, E Slovakia *48.40N 20.31E*
118 *K10* **Roznov** Neamţ, NE Romania *46.46N 26.33E*
113 *I18* **Rožnov pod Radhoštěm** *Ger.* Rosenau, Roznau am Radhost. Zlínský Kraj, E Czech Republic *49.28N 18.09E*
Rózsahegy *see* Ružomberok
Rozsnyó *see* Râşnov, Romania
Rozsnyó *see* Rožňava, Slovakia
115 *K18* **Rranxë** Shkodër, NW Albania *41.58N 19.27E*
115 *L18* **Rrëshen** *var.* Rresheni, Rrshen. Lezhë, C Albania *41.46N 19.54E*
Rresheni *see* Rrëshen
Rrogozhina *see* Rrogozhinë
115 *K20* **Rrogozhinë** *var.* Rogozhina, Rogozhinë, Rrogozhina. Tiranë, W Albania *41.04N 19.40E*
Rrshen *see* Rrëshen
114 *O13* **Rtanj** E Serbia *43.45N 21.54E*
131 *O7* **Rtishchevo** Saratovskaya Oblast', W Russian Federation *52.16N 43.46E*
192 *N12* **Ruahine Range** *var.* Ruarine. North Island, NZ
193 *L14* **Ruamahanga** North Island, NZ
Ruanda *see* Rwanda
192 *M10* **Ruapehu, Mount** North Island, NZ *39.15S 175.33E*
193 *C25* **Ruapuke Island** *island* SW NZ
Ruarine *see* Ruahine Range
192 *O9* **Ruatahuna** Bay of Plenty, North Island, NZ *38.38S 176.56E*
192 *Q8* **Ruatoria** Gisborne, North Island, NZ *37.54S 178.18E*
192 *K4* **Ruawai** Northland, North Island, NZ *36.08S 174.03E*
13 *N8* **Ruban** Québec, SE Canada
83 *I22* **Rubeho Mountains** C Tanzania
172 *Q5* **Rubeshibe** Hokkaidō, NE Japan *43.49N 143.37E*
Rubezhnoye *see* Rubizhne
115 *L18* **Rubik** Lezhë, C Albania *41.46N 19.48E*
56 *H7* **Rubio** Táchira, W Venezuela *7.42N 72.22W*
119 *X6* **Rubizhne** *Rus.* Rubezhnoye. Luhans'ka Oblast', E Ukraine *49.01N 38.22E*
83 *F20* **Rubondo Island** *island* N Tanzania
126 *Gg15* **Rubtsovsk** Altayskiy Kray, S Russian Federation *51.34N 81.10E*
41 *P9* **Ruby** Alaska, USA *64.44N 155.29W*
37 *W3* **Ruby Dome** Nevada, W USA *40.35N 115.25W*
37 *W4* **Ruby Lake** Nevada, W USA
37 *W4* **Ruby Mountains** Nevada, W USA
35 *Q12* **Ruby Range** Montana, NW USA
120 *C10* **Rucava** Liepāja, SW Latvia *56.09N 21.10E*
149 *S13* **Rūdān** *var.* Dehbārez. Hormozgān, S Iran *27.30N 57.10E*
Rudelstadt *see* Ciechanowiec
Rudensk *see* Rudzyensk
121 *G14* **Rūdiškės** Vilnius, S Lithuania *54.31N 24.49E*
97 *H24* **Rudkøbing** Fyn, C Denmark *54.57N 10.43E*
127 *Nn17* **Rudnaya Pristan'** Primorskiy Kray, SE Russian Federation *44.19N 135.42E*
129 *S13* **Rudnichnyy** Kirovskaya Oblast', NW Russian Federation *59.37N 52.28E*
Rudnichnyy *see* Koksu
116 *N9* **Rudnik** Varna, E Bulgaria *42.57N 27.46E*
Rudny *see* Rudnyy
130 *H4* **Rudnya** Smolenskaya Oblast', W Russian Federation *54.55N 31.10E*
131 *O8* **Rudnya** Volgogradskaya Oblast', SW Russian Federation *50.54N 44.27E*
150 *M7* **Rudnyy** *var.* Rudny. Kostanay, N Kazakhstan *53.00N 63.05E*
126 *Hh1* **Rudol'fa, Ostrov** *island* Zemlya Frantsa-Iosifa, NW Russian Federation
Rudolf, Lake *see* Lake Turkana
Rudolfswert *see* Novo mesto
103 *L17* **Rudolstadt** Thüringen, C Germany *50.43N 11.19E*
33 *Q4* **Rudyard** Michigan, N USA *46.15N 84.36W*
35 *S7* **Rudyard** Montana, NW USA *48.33N 110.37W*
121 *K16* **Rudzyensk** *Rus.* Rudensk. Minskaya Voblasts', C Belarus *53.36N 27.52E*
106 *L6* **Rueda** Castilla-León, N Spain *41.24N 4.58W*
116 *F10* **Ruen** Bulgaria/FYR Macedonia *42.10N 22.31E*
82 *G10* **Rufa'a** Gezira, C Sudan *14.49N 33.21E*
104 *L10* **Ruffec** Charente, W France *46.01N 0.10E*
23 *R14* **Ruffin** South Carolina, SE USA *33.00N 80.48W*
83 *J23* **Rufiji** E Tanzania
63 *A20* **Rufino** Santa Fe, C Argentina *34.15S 62.40W*
78 *F11* **Rufisque** W Senegal *14.44N 17.18W*
85 *K14* **Rufunsa** Lusaka, C Zambia *15.03S 29.36E*
120 *J9* **Rugāji** Balvi, E Latvia *57.01N 27.07E*
167 *R7* **Rugao** Jiangsu, E China *32.25N 120.39E*
99 *M20* **Rugby** C England, UK *52.22N 1.18W*
31 *N3* **Rugby** North Dakota, N USA *48.24N 100.00W*
102 *N7* **Rügen** *headland* NE Germany *54.25N 13.21E*
Ruhaybeh *see* Ar Ruḩaybah
83 *E19* **Ruhengeri** NW Rwanda *1.39S 29.16E*
Ruhja *see* Rūjiena
102 *M10* **Ruhner Berg** *hill* N Germany *53.17N 12.00E*
120 *F7* **Ruhnu** *var.* Ruhnu Saar, *Swe.* Runö. *island* SW Estonia
Ruhnu Saar *see* Ruhnu
103 *G15* **Ruhr** W Germany
93 *W6* **Ruhr Valley** *industrial region* W Germany
167 *S11* **Rui'an** *var.* Rui an. Zhejiang, SE China *27.48N 120.36E*
167 *P10* **Ruichang** Jiangxi, S China *29.46N 115.37E*
26 *J11* **Ruidosa** Texas, SW USA *30.00N 104.40W*
39 *S14* **Ruidoso** New Mexico, SW USA *33.19N 105.40W*
167 *P12* **Ruijin** Jiangxi, S China *25.52N 116.01E*
166 *D13* **Ruili** Yunnan, SW China *24.04N 97.49E*
100 *N8* **Ruinen** Drenthe, NE Netherlands *52.46N 6.19E*
101 *D17* **Ruiselede** West-Vlaanderen, W Belgium *51.03N 3.21E*
66 *P5* **Ruivo de Santana, Pico** Madeira, Portugal, NE Atlantic Ocean *32.46N 16.57W*
42 *J12* **Ruiz** Nayarit, SW Mexico *22.00N 105.09W*
56 *E10* **Ruiz, Nevado del** W Colombia *4.52N 75.22W*
144 *J9* **Rujaylah, Ḩarrat ar** *salt lake* N Jordan
Rujen *see* Rūjiena
120 *H7* **Rūjiena** *Est.* Ruhja, *Ger.* Rujen. Valmiera, N Latvia *57.54N 25.22E*
81 *I18* **Ruki** W Dem. Rep. Congo (Zaire)
83 *E22* **Rukwa** *region* SW Tanzania
83 *F23* **Rukwa, Lake** SE Tanzania
27 *P6* **Rule** Texas, SW USA *33.10N 99.53W*
24 *K3* **Ruleville** Mississippi, S USA *33.43N 90.33W*
Rum *see* Rhum
114 *K10* **Ruma** Serbia, N Yugoslavia *45.02N 19.51E*
Rumadiya *see* Ar Ramādī
147 *Q7* **Rumāḩ** Ar Riyāḑ, C Saudi Arabia *25.35N 47.09E*
Rumaitha *see* Ar Rumaythah
Rumania/Rumänien *see* Romania
Rumänisch-Sankt-Georgen *see* Sângeorz-Băi
145 *Y13* **Rumaylah** SE Iraq *30.16N 47.22E*
145 *P2* **Rumaylah, Wādī** *dry watercourse* NE Syria
176 *V10* **Rumbati** Papua, E Indonesia *2.44S 132.04E*
83 *E14* **Rumbek** El Buhayrat, S Sudan *6.49N 29.42E*
176 *W10* **Rumberpon, Pulau** *island* E Indonesia
Rumburg *see* Rumburk
113 *D14* **Rumburk** *Ger.* Rumburg. Ústecký Kraj, NW Czech Republic *50.59N 14.31E*
46 *J4* **Rum Cay** *island* C Bahamas
101 *M26* **Rumelange** Luxembourg, S Luxembourg *49.28N 6.01E*
101 *D20* **Rumes** Hainaut, SW Belgium *50.33N 3.19E*
21 *P7* **Rumford** Maine, NE USA *44.31N 70.31W*
112 *I6* **Rumia** Pomorskie, N Poland *54.35N 18.21E*
115 *J17* **Rumija** S Montenegro
105 *T11* **Rumilly** Haute-Savoie, E France *45.52N 5.57E*
145 *O6* **Rūmiyah** W Iraq *34.28N 41.17E*
Rummah, Wādī ar *see* Rimah, Wādī ar
Rummelsburg in Pommern *see* Miastko
172 *Oo4* **Rumoi** Hokkaidō, NE Japan *43.55N 141.37E*
84 *M12* **Rumphi** *var.* Rumpi. Northern, N Malawi *11.00S 33.51E*
Rumpi *see* Rumphi
31 *V7* **Rum River** Minnesota, N USA
196 *F16* **Rumung** *island* Caroline Islands, W Micronesia
Rumuniya/Rumŭniya/Rumunjska *see* Romania
193 *G16* **Runanga** West Coast, South Island, NZ *42.24S 171.15E*
192 *P7* **Runaway, Cape** *headland* North Island, NZ *37.33S 177.59E*
99 *K18* **Runcorn** C England, UK *53.19N 2.43W*
120 *K10* **Rundāni** Ludza, E Latvia *56.19N 27.51E*
85 *L18* **Runde** *var.* Lundi. SE Zimbabwe
85 *E16* **Rundu** *var.* Runtu. Okavango, NE Namibia *17.55S 19.45E*
95 *I16* **Rundvik** Västerbotten, N Sweden *63.31N 19.22E*
83 *G20* **Runere** Mwanza, N Tanzania *3.06S 33.18E*
27 *S13* **Runge** Texas, SW USA *28.52N 97.42W*
178 *I14* **Rŭng, Kaôh** *prev.* Kas Rong. *island* SW Cambodia
81 *O16* **Rungu** Orientale, NE Dem. Rep. Congo (Zaire) *3.09N 27.58E*
83 *F23* **Rungwa** Rukwa, W Tanzania *7.18S 31.40E*
83 *G22* **Rungwa** Singida, C Tanzania *6.54S 33.33E*
96 *M13* **Runn** C Sweden
26 *M4* **Running Water Draw** *valley* New Mexico/Texas, SW USA
Runö *see* Ruhnu
Runtu *see* Rundu
201 *V12* **Ruo** *island* Caroline Islands, C Micronesia
164 *L9* **Ruoqiang** *var.* Jo-ch'iang, *Uigh.* Charkhlik, Charkhliq, Qarkilik. Xinjiang Uygur Zizhiqu, NW China *38.59N 88.07E*
165 *S7* **Ruo Shui** N China
94 *L8* **Ruostekfielbmá** *var.* Rustefjelbma Finnmark, N Norway *70.25N 28.10E*
95 *L18* **Ruovesi** Länsi-Suomi, W Finland *61.58N 24.04E*
114 *B9* **Rupa** Primorje-Gorski Kotar, NW Croatia *45.29N 14.15E*
190 *M11* **Rupanyup** Victoria, SE Australia *36.38S 142.37E*
174 *H6* **Rupat, Pulau** *prev.* Roepat. *island* W Indonesia
174 *Gg6* **Rupat, Selat** *strait* Sumatera, W Indonesia
118 *J11* **Rupea** *Ger.* Reps, *Hung.* Kőhalom; *prev.* Cohalm. Braşov, C Romania *46.01N 25.13E*
101 *G17* **Rupel** N Belgium
Rupella *see* la Rochelle
35 *P15* **Rupert** Idaho, NW USA *42.37N 113.40W*
23 *R5* **Rupert** West Virginia, NE USA *37.57N 80.40W*
Rupert House *see* Fort Rupert
10 *J10* **Rupert, Rivière de** Québec, C Canada
204 *M13* **Ruppert Coast** *physical region* Antarctica
102 *N11* **Ruppiner Kanal** *canal* NE Germany
57 *S11* **Rupununi River** S Guyana
103 *D16* **Rur** *Dut.* Roer. Germany/Netherlands
60 *H13* **Rurópolis Presidente Medici** Pará, N Brazil *4.05S 55.26W*
203 *S12* **Rurutu** *island* Îles Australes, SW French Polynesia
Rusaddir *see* Melilla
85 *L17* **Rusape** Manicaland, E Zimbabwe *18.31S 32.07E*
Rusayris, Lake *see* Roseires, Reservoir
Ruschuk/Rusçuk *see* Ruse
116 *K7* **Ruse** *var.* Ruschuk, Rustchuk, *Turk.* Rusçuk. Ruse, N Bulgaria *43.49N 25.58E*
116 *L7* **Ruse** *province* N Bulgaria
111 *W10* **Ruše** NE Slovenia *46.31N 15.30E*
116 *K7* **Rusenski Lom** N Bulgaria
99 *G17* **Rush** *Ir.* An Ros. E Ireland *53.31N 6.06W*
167 *S4* **Rushan** *var.* Xiacun. Shandong, E China *36.57N 121.33E*
Rushan *see* Rŭshon
Rushanskiy Khrebet *see* Rushon, Qatorkŭhi
31 *V7* **Rush City** Minnesota, N USA *45.41N 92.56W*
39 *V5* **Rush Creek** Colorado, C USA
31 *X10* **Rushford** Minnesota, N USA *43.48N 91.45W*
160 *N13* **Rushikulya** E India
12 *D8* **Rush Lake** Ontario, S Canada
32 *M7* **Rush Lake** Wisconsin, N USA
30 *J10* **Rushmore, Mount** South Dakota, N USA *43.52N 103.27W*
153 *S13* **Rŭshon** *Rus.* Rushan. S Tajikistan *37.58N 71.31E*
153 *S14* **Rushon, Qatorkŭhi** *Rus.* Rushanskiy Khrebet. SE Tajikistan
28 *M12* **Rush Springs** Oklahoma, C USA *34.46N 97.57W*
47 *V15* **Rushville** Trinidad, Trinidad and Tobago *10.07N 61.03W*
32 *J13* **Rushville** Illinois, N USA *40.07N 90.33W*
30 *K12* **Rushville** Nebraska, C USA *42.41N 102.28W*
191 *O11* **Rushworth** Victoria, SE Australia *36.36S 145.03E*
27 *W8* **Rusk** Texas, SW USA *31.48N 95.09W*
95 *I14* **Rusksele** Västerbotten, N Sweden *64.49N 18.55E*
120 *C12* **Rusnė** Klaipėda, W Lithuania *55.18N 21.19E*
116 *M10* **Rusokastrenska Reka** E Bulgaria
Russadir *see* Melilla
111 *X3* **Russbach** NE Austria
9 *V16* **Russell** Manitoba, S Canada *50.46N 101.16W*
192 *K2* **Russell** Northland, North Island, NZ *35.17S 174.07E*
28 *L4* **Russell** Kansas, C USA *38.54N 98.51W*
23 *O4* **Russell** Kentucky, S USA *38.30N 82.43W*
195 *W15* **Russell Islands** *island group* C Solomon Islands
22 *L7* **Russell Springs** Kentucky, S USA *37.02N 85.03W*
25 *O2* **Russellville** Alabama, S USA *34.30N 87.43W*
29 *T11* **Russellville** Arkansas, C USA *35.16N 93.07W*
22 *J7* **Russellville** Kentucky, S USA *36.51N 86.53W*
103 *G18* **Rüsselsheim** Hessen, W Germany *50.00N 8.25E*
Russia *see* Russian Federation
Russian America *see* Alaska
127 *N17* **Russian Federation** *off.* Russian Federation, *var.* Russia, *Latv.* Krievija, *Rus.* Rossiyskaya Federatsiya. *republic* Asia/Europe
41 *N11* **Russian Mission** Alaska, USA *61.48N 161.23W*
36 *M7* **Russian River** California, W USA
204 *L13* **Russkaya** *Russian research station* Antarctica *74.45S 135.24W*
126 *H3* **Russkaya Gavan'** Novaya Zemlya, Arkhangel'skaya Oblast', N Russian Federation *76.13N 62.48E*
126 *J4* **Russkiy, Ostrov** *island* N Russian Federation
111 *Y5* **Rust** Burgenland, E Austria *47.48N 16.42E*
Rustaq *see* Ar Rustāq

◆ Country
● Country Capital
◇ Dependent Territory
○ Dependent Territory Capital
◆ Administrative Region
✈ International Airport
▲ Mountain
▲ Mountain Range
Volcano
River
Lake
Reservoir

Rust'avi – St-Hilarion

143 U10 Rust'avi SE Georgia 41.36N 45.00E
23 T7 Rustburg Virginia, NE USA 37.16N 79.04W
Rustchuk see Ruse
Rustefjelbma see Ruostekfielbmá
85 I21 Rustenburg North-West, N South Africa 25.40S 27.15E
24 H5 Ruston Louisiana, S USA 32.31N 92.38W
83 E21 Rutana SE Burundi 4.01S 30.01E
64 I4 Rutana, Volcán ▲ N Chile 22.43S 67.52W
Rutanzige, Lake see Edward, Lake
Rutba see Ar Ruṭbah
106 M14 Rute Andalucía, S Spain 37.19N 4.22W
175 Pp16 Ruteng prev. Roeteng. Flores, C Indonesia 8.34S 120.28E
204 L8 Rutford Ice Stream ice feature Antarctica
37 X6 Ruth Nevada, W USA 39.15N 115.00W
103 G15 Rüthen Nordrhein-Westfalen, W Germany 51.30N 8.28E
12 D17 Rutherford Ontario, S Canada 42.39N 82.06W
23 Q10 Rutherfordton North Carolina, SE USA 35.22N 81.57W
99 J18 Ruthin Wel. Rhuthun. NE Wales, UK 53.05N 3.18W
110 G7 Rüti Zürich, N Switzerland 47.16N 8.51E
Rutlam see Ratlām
20 M9 Rutland Vermont, NE USA 43.37N 72.58W
99 N19 Rutland cultural region C England, UK
23 N8 Rutledge Tennessee, S USA 36.16N 83.31W
164 G12 Rutög var. Rutog, Rutok. Xizang Zizhiqu, W China 33.27N 79.43E
Rutok see Rutög
81 P19 Rutshuru Nord Kivu, E Dem. Rep. Congo (Zaire) 1.13S 29.27E
100 L8 Rutten Flevoland, N Netherlands 52.49N 5.44E
131 Q17 Rutul Respublika Dagestan, SW Russian Federation 41.35N 47.30E
95 L14 Ruukki Oulu, C Finland 64.40N 25.35E
100 N11 Ruurlo Gelderland, E Netherlands 52.04N 6.27E
149 S15 Ru'ūs al Jibāl headland Oman/UAE 26.13N 56.23E
144 I7 Ru'ūs aṭ Ṭiwāl, Jabal ▲ W Syria
83 H23 Ruvuma ◆ region SE Tanzania
83 I25 Ruvuma var. Rio Rovuma. ∽ Mozambique/Tanzania see also Rovuma, Rio
Ruwais see Ar Ruways
144 L9 Ruwayshid, Wadi ar dry watercourse NE Jordan
147 Z10 Ruways, Ra's ar headland E Oman 20.58N 59.00E
81 P18 Ruwenzori ▲ Uganda/Dem. Rep. Congo (Zaire)
147 Y8 Ruwī NE Oman 23.33N 58.31E
116 F9 Ruy ▲ Bulgaria/Yugoslavia 42.52N 22.35E
Ruya see Luia, Rio
83 E20 Ruyigi E Burundi 3.28S 30.19E
131 P5 Ruzayevka Respublika Mordoviya, W Russian Federation 54.04N 44.56E
121 G18 Ruzhany Rus. Ruzhany. Brestskaya Voblasts', SW Belarus 52.52N 24.52E
116 I10 Rŭzhevo Konare var. Rŭzhevo Konare. Plovdiv, C Bulgaria 42.16N 24.58E
Ruzhin see Ruzhyn
116 G7 Ruzhintsi Vidin, NW Bulgaria 43.38N 22.50E
167 N6 Ruzhou Henan, C China 34.12N 112.45E
119 N5 Ruzhyn Rus. Ruzhin. Zhytomyrs'ka Oblast', N Ukraine 49.42N 29.01E
113 K19 Ružomberok Ger. Rosenberg, Hung. Rózsahegy. Žilinský Kraj, N Slovakia 49.03N 19.18E
113 C16 Ruzyně ✕ (Praha) Praha, C Czech Republic 50.06N 14.16E
83 D19 Rwanda off. Rwandese Republic; prev. Ruanda. ◆ republic C Africa
Rwandese Republic see Rwanda
97 G22 Ry Århus, C Denmark 56.06N 9.46E
Ryasna see Rasna
130 L5 Ryazan' Ryazanskaya Oblast', W Russian Federation 54.37N 39.37E
130 L5 Ryazanskaya Oblast' ◆ province W Russian Federation
130 M6 Ryazhsk Ryazanskaya Oblast', W Russian Federation 53.42N 40.09E
120 B13 Rybachiy Ger. Rossitten. Kaliningradskaya Oblast', W Russian Federation 55.09N 20.49E
128 J2 Rybachiy, Poluostrov peninsula NW Russian Federation
Rybach'ye see Balykchy
128 L15 Rybinsk prev. Andropov. Yaroslavskaya Oblast', W Russian Federation 58.03N 38.52E
128 K14 Rybinskoye Vodokhranilishche Eng. Rybinsk Reservoir, Rybinsk Sea. ▣ W Russian Federation
Rybinsk Reservoir/Rybinsk Sea see Rybinskoye Vodokhranilishche
113 I16 Rybnik Śląskie, S Poland 50.05N 18.30E
Rybnitsa see Rîbniţa
113 F16 Rychnov nad Kněžnou Ger. Reichenau. Královéhradecký Kraj, N Czech Republic 50.09N 16.15E
112 I12 Rychwał Wielkolpolskie, C Poland 52.04N 18.09E
9 O13 Rycroft Alberta, W Canada 55.45N 118.42W
97 L21 Ryd Kronoberg, S Sweden 56.27N 14.44E
97 L20 Rydaholm Jönköping, S Sweden 56.57N 14.19E
204 I8 Rydberg Peninsula peninsula Antarctica
99 P23 Rye SE England, UK 50.57N 0.42E
35 T10 Ryegate Montana, NW USA 46.21N 109.12W
37 S3 Rye Patch Reservoir ▣ Nevada, W USA
97 D15 Ryfylke physical region S Norway
97 H16 Rygge Østfold, S Norway 59.22N 10.45E
112 N13 Ryki Lubelskie, E Poland 51.37N 21.57E
Rykovo see Yenakiyeve
130 I7 Ryl'sk Kurskaya Oblast', W Russian Federation 51.34N 34.41E
191 S8 Rylstone New South Wales, SE Australia 32.48S 149.58E
113 H17 Rýmařov Ger. Römerstadt. Moravskoslezský Kraj, E Czech Republic 49.57N 17.13E
150 E11 Ryn-Peski desert W Kazakhstan
171 K12 Ryōtsu var. Ryôtu. Niigata, Sado, C Japan 38.02N 138.23E
Ryôtu see Ryōtsu
112 K10 Rypin Kujawsko-pomorskie, C Poland 53.03N 19.25E
Ryshkany see Rîşcani
Ryssel see Lille
Ryswick see Rijswijk
97 M24 Rytterknægten hill E Denmark 55.07N 14.53E
171 Kk16 Ryūgasaki Ibaraki, Honshū, S Japan 35.54N 140.11E
198 G5 Ryukyu Trench var. Nansei Syotō Trench. undersea feature S East China Sea
112 D11 Rzepin Ger. Reppen. Lubuskie, W Poland 52.20N 14.48E
113 N16 Rzeszów Podkarpackie, SE Poland 50.04N 22.00E
128 I16 Rzhev Tverskaya Oblast', W Russian Federation 56.16N 34.21E
Rzhishchev see Rzhyshchiv
119 P5 Rzhyshchiv Rus. Rzhishchev. Kyyivs'ka Oblast', N Ukraine 49.58N 31.01E

S

144 E11 Sa'ad Southern, W Israel 31.27N 34.31E
111 P7 Saalach ∽ W Austria
103 L14 Saale ∽ C Germany
103 L17 Saalfeld var. Saalfeld an der Saale. Thüringen, C Germany 50.39N 11.22E
Saalfeld see Zalewo
Saalfeld an der Saale see Saalfeld
110 C8 Saane ∽ W Switzerland
103 D19 Saar Fr. Sarre. ∽ France/Germany
103 E20 Saarbrücken Fr. Sarrebruck. Saarland, SW Germany 49.13N 7.01E
Saarburg see Sarrebourg
Saare see Saaremaa
120 D6 Sääre var. Sjar. Saaremaa, W Estonia 57.55N 22.03E
120 D5 Saaremaa off. Saare Maakond. ◆ province W Estonia
120 E6 Saaremaa Ger. Oesel, Ösel; prev. Saare. island W Estonia
94 L12 Saarenkylä Lappi, N Finland 66.31N 25.51E
Saargemund see Sarreguemines
95 L17 Saarijärvi Länsi-Suomi, W Finland 62.42N 25.16E
Saar in Mähren see Žďár nad Sázavou
94 M10 Saariselkä Lapp. Suoločielgi. Lappi, N Finland 68.26N 27.28E
94 L10 Saariselkä hill range NE Finland
103 D20 Saarland Fr. Sarre. ◆ state SW Germany
Saarlautern see Saarlouis
103 D20 Saarlouis prev. Saarlautern. Saarland, SW Germany 49.18N 6.49E
110 E11 Saaser Vispa ∽ S Switzerland
143 X12 Saatlı Rus. Saatly. C Azerbaijan 39.57N 48.24E
Saatly see Saatlı
Saaz see Žatec
176 X9 Saba Papua, E Indonesia 1.04S 136.15E
47 V9 Saba island N Netherlands Antilles
144 J7 Sab' Ābār var. Sab'a Biyar, Sa'b Bi'ār. Ḥimş, C Syria 33.46N 37.40E
Sab'a Biyar see Sab' Ābār
114 K11 Šabac Serbia, W Yugoslavia 44.45N 19.42E
107 W5 Sabadell Cataluña, E Spain 41.33N 2.07E
171 Hh13 Sabae Fukui, Honshū, SW Japan 36.00N 136.12E
175 O3 Sabah prev. British North Borneo, North Borneo. ◆ state East Malaysia
174 Gg4 Sabak var. Sabak Bernam. Selangor, Peninsular Malaysia 3.45N 100.58E
Sabak Bernam see Sabak
40 D16 Sabak, Cape headland Agattu Island, Alaska, USA 52.21N 173.43E
83 J20 Sabaki ∽ S Kenya
175 P14 Sabalana, Kepulauan var. Kepulauan Liukang Tenggaya. island group C Indonesia
148 L2 Sabalān, Kuhhā-ye ▲ NW Iran 38.21N 47.47E
160 H7 Sabalgarh Madhya Pradesh, C India 26.18N 77.28E
46 E4 Sabana, Archipiélago de island group C Cuba
44 H7 Sabanagrande var. Sabana Grande. Francisco Morazán, S Honduras 13.48N 87.15W
56 E5 Sabanalarga Atlántico, N Colombia 10.37N 74.55W
43 W14 Sabancuy Campeche, SE Mexico 18.56N 91.08W
47 N8 Sabaneta NW Dominican Republic 19.27N 71.22W
56 J4 Sabaneta Falcón, N Venezuela 11.15N 70.04W
196 H4 Sabaneta, Puntan prev. Ushi Point. headland Saipan, S Northern Mariana Islands 15.17N 145.49E
176 Y12 Sabang Papua, E Indonesia 4.33S 138.42E
118 L10 Săbăoani Neamţ, NE Romania 47.01N 26.51E
161 J26 Sabaragamuwa Province ◆ province C Sri Lanka
Sabaria see Szombathely
160 D10 Sābarmati ∽ NW India
175 T6 Sabatai Pulau Morotai, E Indonesia 2.04N 128.23E
147 Q15 Sab'atayn, Ramlat as desert C Yemen
109 I16 Sabaudia Lazio, C Italy 41.17N 13.02E
59 J19 Sabaya Oruro, S Bolivia 19.09S 68.20W
Sa'b Bi'ār see Sab' Ābār
Sabbioncello see Orebić
154 I8 Şāberī, Hāmūn-e var. Daryācheh-ye Hāmūn, Daryācheh-ye Sīstān. ◎ Afghanistan/Iran see also Sīstān, Daryācheh-ye
29 P2 Sabetha Kansas, C USA 39.54N 95.48W
77 P10 Sabhā C Libya 27.01N 14.25E
69 V13 Sabi var. Rio Save. ∽ Mozambique/Zimbabwe see also Save, Rio
120 E8 Sabile Ger. Zabeln. Talsi, NW Latvia 57.03N 22.33E
33 R14 Sabina Ohio, N USA 39.29N 83.38W
42 I3 Sabinal Chihuahua, N Mexico 30.59N 107.29W
27 Q12 Sabinal Texas, SW USA 29.19N 99.28W
27 Q11 Sabinal River ∽ Texas, SW USA
107 S4 Sabiñánigo Aragón, NE Spain 42.31N 0.22W
43 N6 Sabinas Coahuila de Zaragoza, NE Mexico 27.52N 101.04W
43 O8 Sabinas Hidalgo Nuevo León, NE Mexico 26.28N 100.08W
43 N6 Sabinas, Río ∽ NE Mexico
24 F9 Sabine Lake ◎ Louisiana/Texas, S USA
94 O3 Sabine Land physical region C Svalbard
27 W7 Sabine River ∽ Louisiana/Texas, SW USA
143 X12 Sabirabad C Azerbaijan 40.00N 48.27E
Sabkha see As Sabkhah
179 P12 Sablayan Mindoro, N Philippines 12.48N 120.48E
11 P16 Sable, Cape headland Newfoundland and Labrador, SE Canada 43.21N 65.40W
25 X17 Sable, Cape headland Florida, SE USA 25.12N 81.06W
11 R16 Sable Island island Nova Scotia, SE Canada
12 L11 Sables, Lac des ◎ Québec, SE Canada
12 E10 Sables, Rivière aux ∽ Ontario, S Canada
104 K7 Sable-sur-Sarthe Sarthe, NW France 47.49N 0.19W
129 U7 Sablya, Gora ▲ NW Russian Federation 64.46N 58.52E
79 U14 Sabon Birnin Gwari Kaduna, C Nigeria 10.43N 6.39E
79 V11 Sabon Kafi Zinder, C Niger 14.37N 8.46E
106 I6 Sabor, Rio ∽ N Portugal
12 J8 Sabourin, Lac ◎ Québec, SE Canada
104 J14 Sabres Landes, SW France 44.07N 0.46W
205 X13 Sabrina Coast physical region Antarctica
146 M11 Sabt al Ulayā 'Asīr, SW Saudi Arabia 19.33N 41.58E
106 I8 Sabugal Guarda, N Portugal 40.19N 7.04W
31 Z13 Sabula Iowa, C USA 42.04N 90.10W
147 N13 Şabyā Jīzān, SW Saudi Arabia 17.49N 42.49E
Sabzawar see Sabzevār
Sabzawaran see Sabzvārān
149 S4 Sabzevār var. Sabzawar. Khorāsān-Razavī, NE Iran 36.13N 57.38E
149 T12 Sabzvārān var. Sabzawaran; prev. Jiroft. Kermān, SE Iran 28.40N 57.40E
Sacajawea Peak see Matterhorn
84 C9 Sacandica Uíge, NW Angola 6.01S 15.57E
44 A2 Sacatepéquez off. Departamento de Sacatepéquez. ◆ department S Guatemala
106 F11 Sacavém Lisboa, W Portugal 38.46N 9.06W
31 T13 Sac City Iowa, C USA 42.25N 94.59W
107 P8 Sacedón Castilla-La Mancha, C Spain 40.28N 2.43W
118 J12 Săcele Ger. Vierdörfer, Hung. Négyfalu; prev. Ger. Sieben Dörfer, Hung. Hétfalu. Braşov, C Romania 45.36N 25.40E
10 C8 Sachigo Ontario, C Canada 53.52N 92.16W
10 C7 Sachigo ∽ Ontario, C Canada
10 C8 Sachigo Lake ◎ Ontario, C Canada
169 Y16 Sach'ŏn Jap. Sansenhō; prev. Samch'ŏnpŏ. S South Korea 34.55N 128.07E
103 O15 Sachsen Eng. Saxony, Fr. Saxe. ◆ state E Germany
103 K14 Sachsen-Anhalt Eng. Saxony-Anhalt. ◆ state C Germany
111 R9 Sachsenburg Salzburg, S Austria 46.49N 13.23E
Sachsenfeld see Žalec
15 H1 Sachs Harbour Banks Island, Northwest Territories, N Canada 72.00N 125.13W
Sächsisch-Reen/Sächsisch-Regen see Reghin
20 H8 Sackets Harbor New York, NE USA 43.57N 76.06W
11 P14 Sackville New Brunswick, SE Canada 45.54N 64.22W
21 P9 Saco Maine, NE USA 43.32N 70.25W
21 P8 Saco River ∽ Maine/New Hampshire, NE USA
37 O7 Sacramento state capital California, W USA 38.34N 121.29W
39 T14 Sacramento Mountains ▲ New Mexico, SW USA
37 N6 Sacramento River ∽ California, W USA
37 N4 Sacramento Valley valley California, W USA
38 I10 Sacramento Wash valley Arizona, SW USA
107 N15 Sacratif, Cabo headland S Spain 36.41N 3.30W
118 F9 Săcueni prev. Săcuieni, Hung. Székelyhid. Bihor, W Romania 47.19N 22.04E
Săcuieni see Săcueni
107 R4 Sádaba Aragón, NE Spain 42.15N 1.16W
Sá da Bandeira see Lubango
144 I6 Şadad Ḥimş, W Syria 34.19N 36.52E
147 O13 Şa'dah NW Yemen 16.59N 43.45E
170 Dd14 Sadamisaki-hantō peninsula Shikoku, SW Japan
175 P12 Sadang, Sungai ∽ Sulawesi, C Indonesia
178 H17 Sadao Songkhla, SW Thailand 6.34N 100.22E
148 L8 Sadd-e Dez, Daryācheh-ye ◎ W Iran
21 S3 Saddleback Mountain hill Maine, NE USA 46.25N 68.00W
21 P6 Saddleback Mountain ▲ Maine, NE USA 44.57N 70.27W
178 J114 Sa Dec Đông Thap, S Vietnam 10.19N 105.45E
147 W13 Sadḥ S Oman 17.10N 55.07E
78 J11 Sadiola Kayes, W Mali 13.48N 11.47W
155 R12 Sādiqābād Punjab, E Pakistan 28.16N 70.10E
159 Y10 Sadiya Assam, NE India 27.49N 95.37E
145 W9 Sa'dīyah, Hawr as ◎ E Iraq
171 K12 Sado var. Sadoga-shima. island C Japan
Sadoga-shima see Sado
106 F12 Sado, Rio ∽ S Portugal
116 I8 Sadovets Pleven, N Bulgaria 43.19N 24.21E
131 O11 Sadovoye Respublika Kalmykiya, SW Russian Federation 47.51N 44.34E
107 W9 Sa Dragonera var. Isla Dragonera. island Illes Balears, Spain, W Mediterranean Sea
97 H20 Sæby Nordjylland, N Denmark 57.19N 10.33E
107 P9 Saelices Castilla-La Mancha, C Spain 39.55N 2.49W
Saena Julia see Siena
Saetabicula see Alzira
116 O12 Safaalan Tekirdağ, NW Turkey 41.26N 28.07E
Safad see Ẕefat
Şafāqis see Sfax
198 B8 Safata Bay bay Upolo, Samoa, C Pacific Ocean
Safed see Ẕefat
Safed, Āb-i- see Sefid, Darya-ye
145 X11 Şaffāf, Ḩawr aş wetland S Iraq
97 J16 Säffle Värmland, C Sweden 59.07N 12.55E
39 N15 Safford Arizona, SW USA 32.46N 109.41W
76 E7 Safi W Morocco 32.19N 9.14W
149 V9 Safīdābeh Khorāsān-e Janūbī, E Iran 31.04N 60.30E
148 M4 Safīd, Rūd-e ∽ NW Iran
130 I4 Safonovo Smolenskaya Oblast', W Russian Federation 55.05N 33.12E
142 H11 Safranbolu Karabük, N Turkey 41.16N 32.40E
145 Y13 Safwān SE Iraq 30.06N 47.43E
164 J16 Saga var. Gya'gya. Xizang Zizhiqu, W China 29.22N 85.19E
170 Cc13 Saga Saga, Kyūshū, SW Japan 33.14N 130.16E
170 Cc13 Saga off. Saga-ken. ◆ prefecture Kyūshū, SW Japan
171 Ll12 Sagae Yamagata, Honshū, C Japan 38.22N 140.13E
177 G5 Sagaing Sagaing, C Burma 21.55N 95.55E
177 G3 Sagaing ◆ division N Burma
171 Jj16 Sagamihara Kanagawa, Honshū, S Japan 35.32N 139.23E
171 Jj17 Sagami-nada inlet SW Japan
171 Jj17 Sagami-wan bay SW Japan
Sagan see Żagań
31 Y3 Saganaga Lake ◎ Minnesota, N USA
161 F18 Sāgar Karnātaka, W India 14.09N 75.02E
160 I9 Sāgar prev. Saugor. Madhya Pradesh, C India 23.52N 78.46E
13 S8 Sagard Québec, SE Canada 48.01N 70.03W
Sagarmāthā see Everest, Mount
179 Qq13 Sagay Negros, C Philippines 10.54N 123.26E
Sagebrush State see Nevada
149 V11 Sāghand Yazd, C Iran 32.33N 55.12E
21 N14 Sag Harbor Long Island, New York, NE USA 40.59N 72.15W
Saghez see Saqqez
33 R8 Saginaw Michigan, N USA 43.25N 83.57W
33 R8 Saginaw Bay lake bay Michigan, N USA
150 H11 Sagiz Atyrau, W Kazakhstan 48.12N 54.55E
66 H6 Saglek Bank undersea feature W Labrador Sea
11 P5 Saglek Bay bay SW Labrador Sea
Saglouc/Sagluk see Salluit
105 X15 Sagone, Golfe de gulf Corse, France, C Mediterranean Sea
107 P13 Sagra ▲ S Spain 37.59N 2.33W
106 F14 Sagres Faro, S Portugal 37.01N 8.55W
39 S7 Saguache Colorado, C USA 38.05N 106.05W
46 J7 Sagua de Tánamo Holguín, E Cuba 20.34N 75.14W
46 E5 Sagua la Grande Villa Clara, C Cuba 22.48N 80.06W
13 R7 Saguenay ∽ Québec, SE Canada
76 C9 Saguia al Hamra var. Saqia al Hamra. ∽ N Western Sahara
Sagunt/Saguntum see Sagunto
107 S9 Sagunto Cat. Sagunt, Ar. Murviedro; anc. Saguntum. País Valenciano, E Spain 39.40N 0.16W
144 H10 Saḥāb 'Ammān, NW Jordan 31.52N 36.00E
56 E6 Sahagún Córdoba, NW Colombia 8.57N 75.26W
106 L4 Sahagún Castilla-León, N Spain 42.22N 5.01W
147 X8 Saḥam N Oman 24.06N 56.52E
70 F9 Sahara desert Libya/Algeria
77 U9 Sahara el Gharbîya var. Aş Şaḥrā' al Gharbīyah, Eng. Western Desert. desert C Egypt
77 X9 Sahara el Sharqîya var. Aş Şaḥrā' ash Sharqīyah, Eng. Arabian Desert, Eastern Desert. desert E Egypt
Saharan Atlas see Atlas Saharien
158 J9 Sahāranpur Uttar Pradesh, N India 29.58N 77.33E
66 L10 Saharan Seamounts var. Saharian Seamounts. undersea feature E Atlantic Ocean 25.00N 20.00W
159 Q13 Saharsa Bihār, NE India 25.54N 86.36E
69 O7 Sahel physical region C Africa
159 R14 Sāhibganj Jhārkhand, NE India 25.15N 87.40E
82 N12 Sahil off. Gobolka Sahil. ◆ region N Somalia
145 Q7 Sāhilīyah C Iraq 33.43N 42.42E
144 H4 Sāḥilīyah, Jibāl as ▲ NW Syria
116 M13 Şahin Tekirdağ, NW Turkey 41.01N 26.51E
155 U8 Sāhīwāl Punjab, E Pakistan 31.57N 72.22E
155 U9 Sāhīwāl prev. Montgomery. Punjab, E Pakistan 30.40N 73.04E
147 W11 Şaḥmah, Ramlat as desert C Oman
145 T13 Şaḥrā' al Ḥijārah desert S Iraq
42 H5 Sahuaripa Sonora, NW Mexico 29.02N 109.14W
38 M16 Sahuarita Arizona, SW USA 31.24N 110.55W
42 L13 Sahuayo var. Sahuayo de José María Morelos; prev. Sahuayo de Díaz, Sahuayo de Porfirio Díaz. Michoacán de Ocampo, SW Mexico 20.04N 102.44W
Sahuayo de Díaz/Sahuayo de José María Morelos/Sahuayo de Porfirio Díaz see Sahuayo
181 W8 Sahul Shelf undersea feature N Timor Sea
178 Hh17 Sai Buri Pattani, SW Thailand 6.42N 101.37E
76 I6 Saïda NW Algeria 34.49N 0.10E
144 G7 Saïda var. Şaydā, Sayida; anc. Sidon. W Lebanon 33.20N 35.24E
Sa'īdābād see Sīrjān
82 B13 Sa'id Bundas Western Bahr el Ghazal, SW Sudan 8.24N 24.53E
194 J12 Saidor Madang, N PNG 5.37S 146.28E
159 S13 Saidpur var. Syedpur. Rajshahi, NW Bangladesh 25.48N 89.00E
110 C7 Saignelégier Jura, NW Switzerland 47.18N 7.03E
170 G11 Saigō Shimane, Dōgo, SW Japan 36.12N 133.18E
Saigon see Hô Chi Minh
169 P11 Saihan Tal var. Sonid Youqi. Nei Mongol Zizhiqu, N China 42.45N 112.36E
168 I12 Saihan Toroi Nei Mongol Zizhiqu, N China 41.44N 100.29E
Sai Hun see Syr Darya
94 M11 Saija Lappi, NE Finland 67.07N 28.46E
170 Ee14 Saijō Ehime, Shikoku, SW Japan 33.55N 133.10E
170 Dd15 Saiki Ōita, Kyūshū, SW Japan 32.57N 131.52E
176 Uu9 Saileen Papua, E Indonesia 1.14S 130.56E
95 N18 Saimaa ◎ SE Finland
95 N18 Saimaa Canal Fin. Saimaan Kanava, Rus. Saymenskiy Kanal. canal Finland/Russian Federation
Saimaan Kanava see Saimaa Canal
42 L10 Saín Alto Zacatecas, C Mexico 23.38N 103.13W
98 L12 St Abb's Head headland SE Scotland, UK 55.54N 2.07W
9 Y16 St.Adolphe Manitoba, S Canada 49.39N 96.55W
105 O15 St-Affrique Aveyron, S France 43.57N 2.52E
13 Q10 St-Agapit Québec, SE Canada 46.33N 71.25W
99 O21 St Albans anc. Verulamium. E England, UK 51.46N 0.21W
20 L6 Saint Albans Vermont, NE USA 44.49N 73.07W
23 Q5 Saint Albans West Virginia, NE USA 38.21N 81.47W
St Alban's Head see St.Aldhelm's Head
9 Q14 St.Albert Alberta, SW Canada 53.37N 113.37W
99 M24 St. Aldhelm's Head var. St.Alban's Head. headland S England, UK 50.34N 2.04W
13 S8 St-Alexandre Québec, SE Canada 47.39N 69.36W
13 O11 St-Alexis-des-Monts Québec, SE Canada 46.30N 73.08W
105 P2 St-Amand-les-Eaux Nord, N France 50.27N 3.25E
105 O9 St-Amand-Montrond var. St-Amand-Mont-Rond. Cher, C France 46.43N 2.28E
13 Q7 St-Ambroise Québec, SE Canada 48.35N 71.19W
181 P16 St-André NE Réunion
12 M12 St-André-Avellin Québec, SE Canada 45.45N 75.04W
104 K12 St-André-de-Cubzac Gironde, SW France 45.01N 0.26W
98 K11 St Andrews E Scotland, UK 56.20N 2.48W
25 Q9 Saint Andrews Bay bay Florida, SE USA
25 W7 Saint Andrew Sound sound Georgia, SE USA
Saint Anna Trough see Svyataya Anna Trough
46 J11 St.Ann's Bay C Jamaica 18.25N 77.12W
11 T10 St.Anthony Newfoundland and Labrador, SE Canada 51.21N 55.34W
35 R13 Saint Anthony Idaho, NW USA 43.56N 111.38W
190 M11 Saint Arnaud Victoria, SE Australia 36.39S 143.15E
193 I15 St.Arnaud Range ▲ South Island, NZ
13 T8 St-Arsène Québec, SE Canada 47.55N 69.21W
11 R10 St-Augustin Québec, E Canada 51.13N 58.39W
25 X9 Saint Augustine Florida, SE USA 29.54N 81.19W
99 H24 St Austell SW England, UK 50.21N 4.46W
105 T4 St-Avold Moselle, NE France 49.06N 6.43E
105 N17 St-Barthélemy ▲ S France
104 L17 St-Béat Haute-Garonne, S France 42.55N 0.39E
99 I15 St Bees Head headland NW England, UK 54.30N 3.39W
181 P16 St-Benoît E Réunion
105 T13 St-Bonnet Hautes-Alpes, SE France 44.41N 6.04E
St.Botolph's Town see Boston
99 G21 St Brides Bay inlet SW Wales, UK
104 H5 St-Brieuc Côtes d'Armor, NW France 48.31N 2.45W
104 H5 St-Brieuc, Baie de bay NW France
104 L7 St-Calais Sarthe, NW France 47.55N 0.48E
13 Q10 St-Casimir Québec, SE Canada 46.40N 72.05W
12 H16 St.Catharines Ontario, S Canada 43.10N 79.15W
47 S14 St.Catherine, Mount ▲ N Grenada 12.10N 61.41W
66 C11 St Catherine Point headland E Bermuda
25 X6 Saint Catherines Island island Georgia, SE USA
99 M24 St Catherine's Point headland S England, UK 50.34N 1.17W
105 N13 St-Céré Lot, S France 44.52N 1.53E
110 A10 St.Cergue Vaud, W Switzerland 46.25N 6.10E
105 R11 St-Chamond Loire, E France 45.28N 4.31E
35 S16 Saint Charles Idaho, NW USA 42.05N 111.23W
29 X4 Saint Charles Missouri, C USA 38.48N 90.28W
105 P13 St-Chély-d'Apcher Lozère, S France 44.51N 3.16E
Saint Christopher-Nevis see Saint Kitts and Nevis
33 S9 Saint Clair Michigan, N USA 42.49N 82.29W
12 D17 St.Clair ∽ Canada/USA
191 O17 St.Clair, Lake ◎ Tasmania, SE Australia
12 C17 St.Clair, Lake var. Lac à L'eau Claire. ◎ Canada/USA
33 S10 Saint Clair Shores Michigan, N USA 42.30N 82.53W
105 S10 St-Claude anc. Condate. Jura, E France 46.22N 5.52E
47 X6 St-Claude Basse Terre, SW Guadeloupe 16.01N 61.41W
25 X12 Saint Cloud Florida, SE USA 28.15N 81.15W
31 U8 Saint Cloud Minnesota, N USA 45.33N 94.09W
47 T9 Saint Croix island S Virgin Islands (US)
32 J4 Saint Croix Flowage ▣ Wisconsin, N USA
21 T5 Saint Croix River ∽ Canada/USA
31 W7 Saint Croix River ∽ Minnesota/Wisconsin, N USA
47 S14 St.David's SE Grenada 12.01N 61.40W
99 H21 St David's SW Wales, UK 51.53N 5.16W
99 G21 St David's Head headland SW Wales, UK 51.54N 5.19W
66 C12 St David's Island island E Bermuda
181 O16 St-Denis ○ (Réunion) NW Réunion 20.55S 14.33E
105 U6 St-Dié Vosges, NE France 48.16N 6.57E
105 R5 St-Dizier anc. Desiderii Fanum. Haute-Marne, N France 48.39N 5.00E
13 N11 St-Donat Québec, SE Canada 46.16N 74.12W
13 N11 Ste-Adèle Québec, SE Canada 45.58N 74.10W
13 N11 Ste-Agathe-des-Monts Québec, SE Canada 46.03N 74.19W
180 I16 Sainte Anne island Inner Islands, NE Seychelles
9 Y16 Ste.Anne Manitoba, S Canada 49.40N 96.40W
47 R12 Ste-Anne Grande Terre, E Guadeloupe 16.13N 61.22W
47 Y6 Ste-Anne SE Martinique 14.25N 60.53W
13 Q10 Ste-Anne ∽ Québec, SE Canada
13 W6 Ste-Anne-des-Monts Québec, SE Canada 49.07N 66.28W
12 M10 Ste-Anne-du-Lac Québec, SE Canada 46.51N 75.20W
13 U4 Ste-Anne, Lac ◎ Québec, SE Canada
13 S10 Ste-Apolline Québec, SE Canada 46.47N 70.15W
13 U7 Ste-Blandine Québec, SE Canada 48.22N 68.27W
13 R10 Ste-Claire Québec, SE Canada 46.30N 70.40W
13 Q10 Ste-Croix Québec, SE Canada 46.36N 71.42W
110 B8 Ste.Croix Vaud, SW Switzerland 46.49N 6.31E
105 P14 Ste-Énimie Lozère, S France 44.21N 3.26E
29 Y6 Sainte Genevieve Missouri, C USA 37.57N 90.01W
105 S12 St-Egrève Isère, E France 45.15N 5.40E
41 T12 Saint Elias, Cape headland Kayak Island, Alaska, USA 59.48N 144.36W
41 U11 Saint Elias, Mount ▲ Alaska, USA 60.18N 140.57W
8 G8 Saint Elias Mountains ▲ Canada/USA
57 Y10 St-Élie N French Guiana 4.49N 53.21W
105 O10 St-Eloy-les-Mines Puy-de-Dôme, C France 46.07N 2.50E
13 R7 Ste-Marguerite ∽ Québec, SE Canada
13 S7 Ste-Marguerite-Nord-Est ∽ Québec, SE Canada
13 V4 Ste-Marguerite, Pointe headland Québec, SE Canada 50.01N 66.43W
13 R10 Ste-Marie Québec, SE Canada 46.28N 71.00W
47 Q11 Ste-Marie NE Martinique 14.48N 61.01W
181 P16 Ste-Marie NE Réunion
105 U6 Ste-Marie-aux-Mines Haut-Rhin, NE France 48.16N 7.12E
10 J14 Ste-Marie, Lac ▣ Québec, S Canada
180 K4 Sainte Marie, Nosy island E Madagascar
104 L8 Ste-Maure-de-Touraine Indre-et-Loire, C France 47.06N 0.38E
105 R4 Ste-Menehould Marne, NE France 49.06N 4.54E
Ste-Perpétue see Ste-Perpétue-de-l'Islet
13 S9 Ste-Perpétue-de-l'Islet var. Ste-Perpétue. Québec, SE Canada 47.02N 69.54W
47 X11 Ste-Rose Basse Terre, N Guadeloupe 16.20N 61.41W
181 P16 Ste-Rose E Réunion
9 W15 Ste.Rose du Lac Manitoba, S Canada 51.04N 99.31W
104 J11 Saintes anc. Mediolanum. Charente-Maritime, W France 45.45N 0.37W
47 X7 Saintes, Canal des channel SW Guadeloupe
Saintes, Îles des see les Saintes
181 P16 Ste-Suzanne N Réunion
13 P10 Ste-Thècle Québec, SE Canada 46.48N 72.31W
105 Q12 St-Étienne Loire, E France 45.25N 4.22E
104 M4 St-Étienne-du-Rouvray Seine-Maritime, N France 49.22N 1.07E
Saint Eustatius see Sint Eustatius
12 M11 Ste-Véronique Québec, SE Canada 46.30N 74.58W
13 T7 St-Fabien Québec, SE Canada 48.19N 68.51W
13 P7 St-Félicien Québec, SE Canada 48.38N 72.29W
13 O11 St-Félix-de-Valois Québec, SE Canada 46.10N 73.25W
105 Y14 St-Florent Corse, France, C Mediterranean Sea 42.41N 9.19E
105 Y14 St-Florent, Golfe de gulf Corse, France, C Mediterranean Sea
105 P6 St-Florentin Yonne, C France 48.00N 3.46E
105 N9 St-Florent-sur-Cher Cher, C France 47.00N 2.13E
105 P12 St-Flour Cantal, C France 45.01N 3.04E
28 H2 Saint Francis Kansas, C USA 39.45N 101.31W
85 H26 St.Francis, Cape headland S South Africa 34.11S 24.45E
29 X10 Saint Francis River ∽ Arkansas/Missouri, C USA
24 J8 Saint Francisville Louisiana, S USA 30.46N 91.22W
13 Q12 St-François ∽ Québec, SE Canada
47 Y6 St-François Grande Terre, E Guadeloupe 16.15N 61.16W
13 R11 St-François, Lac ◎ Québec, SE Canada
29 X7 Saint Francois Mountains ▲ Missouri, C USA
St-Gall/Saint Gall/St.Gallen see Sankt Gallen
104 L16 St-Gaudens Haute-Garonne, S France 43.07N 0.43E
13 R12 St-Gédéon Québec, SE Canada 45.51N 70.36W
189 X10 Saint George Queensland, E Australia 28.04S 148.39E
66 B12 St George N Bermuda 32.24N 64.42W
40 K15 Saint George Saint George Island, Alaska, USA 56.34N 169.30W
23 S14 Saint George South Carolina, SE USA 33.10N 80.34W
38 J8 Saint George Utah, W USA 37.06N 113.35W
11 R12 St.George, Cape headland Newfoundland and Labrador, E Canada 48.26N 59.17W
195 P11 St.George, Cape headland New Ireland, NE PNG 4.49S 152.52E
40 J15 Saint George Island island Pribilof Islands, Alaska, USA
25 S10 Saint George Island island Florida, SE USA
101 J19 Saint-Georges Liège, E Belgium 50.36N 5.20E
13 R11 St-Georges Québec, SE Canada 46.07N 70.40W
57 Z11 St-Georges E French Guiana 3.55N 51.49W
47 R14 St.George's ● (Grenada) SW Grenada 12.03N 61.45W
11 R12 St.George's Bay inlet Newfoundland and Labrador, E Canada
99 G21 Saint George's Channel channel Ireland/Wales, UK
195 P10 St.George's Channel channel NE PNG
66 B11 St George's Island island E Bermuda
101 I21 Saint-Gérard Namur, S Belgium 50.20N 4.47E
St-Germain see St-Germain-en-Laye
13 P12 St-Germain-de-Grantham Québec, SE Canada 45.49N 72.32W
105 N5 St-Germain-en-Laye var. St-Germain. Yvelines, N France 48.52N 2.04E
104 H8 St-Gildas, Pointe du headland NW France 47.09N 2.25W
105 R15 St-Gilles Gard, S France 43.41N 4.24E
104 I9 St-Gilles-Croix-de-Vie Vendée, NW France 46.41N 1.55W
181 O16 St-Gilles-les-Bains W Réunion 21.01S 55.13E
104 M16 St-Girons Ariège, S France 42.58N 1.07E
Saint Gotthard see Szentgotthárd
110 G9 St.Gotthard Tunnel tunnel Ticino, S Switzerland
99 H22 St Govan's Head headland SW Wales, UK 51.35N 4.55W
36 M7 Saint Helena California, W USA 38.29N 122.30W
67 F24 Saint Helena ◇ UK dependent territory C Atlantic Ocean
69 O12 Saint Helena island C Atlantic Ocean
85 E25 St.Helena Bay bay SW South Africa
67 M16 Saint Helena Fracture Zone tectonic feature C Atlantic Ocean
36 M7 Saint Helena, Mount ▲ California, W USA 38.40N 122.39W
23 S15 Saint Helena Sound inlet South Carolina, SE USA
33 Q7 Saint Helen, Lake ◎ Michigan, N USA
191 Q16 Saint Helens Tasmania, SE Australia 41.21S 148.15E
99 K18 St Helens NW England, UK 53.28N 2.43W
34 G10 Saint Helens Oregon, NW USA 45.55N 122.51W
34 H10 Saint Helens, Mount ☒ Washington, NW USA 46.24N 121.49W
99 L26 St Helier ○ (Jersey) S Jersey, Channel Islands 49.12N 2.07W
13 S9 St-Hilarion Québec, SE Canada 47.34N 70.24W

◆ Country ● Country Capital ◇ Dependent Territory ○ Dependent Territory Capital ◆ Administrative Region ✕ International Airport ▲ Mountain ▲ Mountain Range ☒ Volcano ∽ River ◎ Lake ▣ Reservoir

◆ COUNTRY
◆ COUNTRY CAPITAL
◇ DEPENDENT TERRITORY
◇ DEPENDENT TERRITORY CAPITAL
◆ ADMINISTRATIVE REGION
✕ INTERNATIONAL AIRPORT
▲ MOUNTAIN
▲ MOUNTAIN RANGE
▲ VOLCANO
≈ RIVER
⊗ LAKE
⊠ RESERVOIR

Samakov – San Juan de Limay

Samakov see Samokov
44 B6 Samalá, Río ≈ SW Guatemala
42 J3 Samalayuca Chihuahua, N Mexico 31.14N 106.28W
179 Q17 Samales Group island group Sulu Archipelago, SW Philippines
161 L16 Sāmalkot Andhra Pradesh, E India 17.03N 82.15E
47 P8 Samaná var. Santa Bárbara de Samaná. E Dominican Republic 19.11N 69.19W
47 P8 Samaná, Bahía de bay E Dominican Republic
46 K4 Samana Cay island SE Bahamas
142 K17 Samandağı Hatay, S Turkey 36.06N 35.56E
155 P3 Samangān ◈ province N Afghanistan
Samangān see Āybak
172 P8 Samani Hokkaidō, NE Japan 42.07N 142.57E
56 C13 Samaniego Nariño, SW Colombia 1.22N 77.34W
179 R12 Samar island C Philippines
131 S6 Samara prev. Kuybyshev. Samarskaya Oblast', W Russian Federation 53.14N 50.15E
131 S6 Samara ✕ Samarskaya Oblast', W Russian Federation 53.11N 50.27E
131 T7 Samara ≈ W Russian Federation
119 V7 Samara ≈ E Ukraine
195 N17 Samarai Milne Bay, SE PNG 10.37S 150.39E
Samarang see Semarang
144 G9 Samarian Hills hill range N Israel
56 L9 Samariapo Amazonas, C Venezuela 5.13N 67.47W
175 O8 Samarinda Borneo, C Indonesia 0.30S 117.09E
Samarkand see Samarqand
Samarkandskaya Oblast' see Samarqand Viloyati
Samarkandski/Samarkandskoye see Temirtau
Samarobriva see Amiens
153 N11 Samarqand Rus. Samarkand. Samarqand Viloyati, C Uzbekistan 39.39N 66.55E
152 M11 Samarqand Viloyati Rus. Samarkandskaya Oblast'. ◈ province C Uzbekistan
145 S6 Sāmarrā' C Iraq 34.13N 43.52E
131 R7 Samarskaya Oblast' prev. Kuybyshevskaya Oblast'. ◈ province W Russian Federation
159 Q13 Samastīpur Bihār, N India 25.52N 85.46E
78 L14 Samatiguila NW Ivory Coast 9.51N 7.36W
Samawa see As Samāwah
143 Y11 Şamaxı Rus. Shemakha. E Azerbaijan 40.38N 48.34E
158 H6 Samba Jammu and Kashmir, NW India 32.31N 75.07E
81 K18 Samba Equateur, NW Dem. Rep. Congo (Zaire) 0.13N 21.16E
81 N21 Samba Maniema, E Dem. Rep. Congo (Zaire) 4.40S 26.22E
175 Oo6 Sambaliung, Pegunungan ▲▲ Borneo, N Indonesia
160 M11 Sambalpur Orissa, E India 21.28N 83.04E
69 X12 Sambao ≈ W Madagascar
174 Kk7 Sambas, Sungai ≈ Borneo, N Indonesia
180 K2 Sambava Antsiranana, NE Madagascar 14.16S 50.10E
176 Ww9 Samberi Papua, E Indonesia 1.07S 135.54E
158 J10 Sambhal Uttar Pradesh, N India 28.34N 78.34E
158 H12 Sāmbhar Salt Lake ◎ N India
109 N21 Sambiase Calabria, SW Italy 38.58N 16.16E
118 H5 Sambir Rus. Sambor. L'vivs'ka Oblast', NW Ukraine 49.29N 23.09E
84 C13 Sambo Huambo, C Angola 13.07S 16.06E
Sambor see Sambir
63 E21 Samborombón, Bahía bay NE Argentina
101 H20 Sambre ≈ Belgium/France
45 V16 Sambú, Río ≈ SE Panama
169 Z14 Samch'ŏk Jap. Sanchoku. NE South Korea 37.21N 129.12E
Samch'ŏnpŏ see Sach'ŏn
83 I21 Same Kilimanjaro, NE Tanzania 4.02S 37.46E
110 J10 Samedan Ger. Samaden. Graubünden, S Switzerland 46.31N 9.51E
84 K12 Samfya Luapula, N Zambia 11.25S 29.30E
147 W13 Samḩān, Jabal ▲ SW Oman
117 C18 Sámi Kefallonía, Iónia Nisiá, Greece, C Mediterranean Sea 38.15N 20.39E
58 F10 Samiria, Río ≈ N Peru
Samirum see Semirom
143 V11 Şämkir Rus. Shamkhor. NW Azerbaijan 40.51N 46.03E
178 J7 Sam, Nam Vtn. Sông Chu. ≈ Laos/Vietnam
Samnān see Semnān
Sam Neua see Xam Nua
77 P10 Samnū C Libya 27.19N 15.01E
198 Bb7 Samoa off. Independent State of Samoa, var. Sāmoa; prev. Western Samoa. ◆ monarchy W Polynesia
198 C8 Sāmoa island group American Samoa
183 T9 Samoa Basin undersea feature W Pacific Ocean
Sāmoa-i-Sisifo see Samoa
114 D8 Samobor Zagreb, N Croatia 45.48N 15.38E
116 H10 Samokov var. Samakov. Sofiya, W Bulgaria 42.19N 23.34E
113 H21 Šamorín Ger. Sommerein, Hung. Somorja. Trnavský Kraj, W Slovakia 48.01N 17.18E
117 M19 Sámos prev. Limín Vathéos. Sámos, Dodekánisa, Greece, Aegean Sea 37.46N 26.58E
117 M20 Sámos island Dodekánisa, Greece, Aegean Sea
Samosch see Szamos
173 Ff5 Samosir, Pulau island W Indonesia
Samothrace see Samothráki
117 K14 Samothráki Samothráki, NE Greece 40.28N 25.31E
117 J14 Samothráki anc. Samothrace. island NE Greece
117 A15 Samothráki island Iónia Nisiá, Greece, C Mediterranean Sea
Samotschin see Szamocin
Sampê see Xiangcheng
174 M10 Sampit Borneo, C Indonesia 2.30S 112.30E
174 M10 Sampit, Sungai ≈ Borneo, N Indonesia
Sampoku see Sanpoku
195 P11 Sampun New Britain, E PNG 5.19S 152.06E
81 N24 Sampwe Katanga, SE Dem. Rep. Congo (Zaire) 9.17S 27.22E
27 X8 Sam Rayburn Reservoir ⊞ Texas, SW USA
178 Ii6 Sam Sao, Phou ▲▲ Laos/Thailand
97 H22 Samsø island E Denmark
97 H23 Samsø Bælt channel E Denmark
178 Jj7 Sâm Sơn Thanh Hoa, N Vietnam 19.43N 105.52E
142 L11 Samsun anc. Amisus. Samsun, N Turkey 41.16N 36.22E
142 K11 Samsun ◈ province N Turkey
143 R9 Samtredia W Georgia 42.09N 42.20E
61 E15 Samuel, Represa de ⊞ W Brazil
178 H15 Samui, Ko island SW Thailand
Samundari see Samundri
155 U9 Samundri var. Samundari. Punjab, E Pakistan 31.04N 72.58E
143 X10 Samur ≈ Azerbaijan/Russian Federation
143 Y11 Samur-Abşeron Kanalı Rus. Samur-Apsheronskiy Kanal. canal E Azerbaijan
Samur-Apsheronskiy Kanal see Samur-Abşeron Kanalı
178 Hh11 Samut Prakan var. Muang Samut Prakan, Paknam. Samut Prakan, C Thailand 13.33N 100.13E
178 H11 Samut Sakhon var. Maha Chai, Samut Sakorn, Tha Chin. Samut Sakhon, C Thailand 13.31N 100.15E
Samut Sakorn see Samut Sakhon
178 H11 Samut Songhram prev. Meklong. Samut Songkhram, SW Thailand 13.25N 100.01E
79 N12 San Ségou, C Mali 13.18N 4.51W
113 O15 San ≈ SE Poland
147 O15 Şan'ā' Eng. Sana. ● (Yemen) W Yemen 15.24N 44.13E
114 F11 Sana ≈ NW Bosnia and Herzegovina
82 O12 Sanaag off. Gobolka Sanaag. ◈ region N Somalia
116 J8 Sanadinovo Pleven, N Bulgaria 43.33N 25.00E
205 P11 Sanae South African research station Antarctica 70.19S 1.31W
145 Y10 Sanāf, Hawr as ◎ S Iraq
81 E15 Sanaga ≈ C Cameroon
56 D12 San Agustín Huila, SW Colombia 1.52N 76.13W
179 S16 San Agustin, Cape headland Mindanao, S Philippines 6.17N 126.12E
39 Q13 San Agustin, Plains of plain New Mexico, SW USA
40 M16 Sanak Islands island group Aleutian Islands, Alaska, USA
200 P11 San Ambrosio, Isla Eng. San Ambrosio Island. island W Chile
San Ambrosio Island see San Ambrosio, Isla
175 S10 Sanana Pulau Sanana, E Indonesia 2.04S 125.58E
175 S10 Sanana, Pulau island Maluku, E Indonesia
148 K5 Sanandaj prev. Sinneh. Kordestān, W Iran 35.18N 47.01E
37 P8 San Andreas California, W USA 38.10N 120.40W
2 C13 San Andreas Fault fault W USA
56 G8 San Andrés Santander, C Colombia 6.52N 72.52W
63 C20 San Andrés de Giles Buenos Aires, E Argentina 34.27S 59.27W
39 R14 San Andres Mountains ▲▲ New Mexico, SW USA
43 S15 San Andrés Tuxtla var. Tuxtla. Veracruz-Llave, E Mexico 18.27N 95.18W
27 P8 San Angelo Texas, SW USA 31.27N 100.26W
109 A20 San Antioco, Isola di island W Italy
44 F4 San Antonio Toledo, S Belize 16.13N 89.02W
64 G11 San Antonio Valparaíso, C Chile 33.35S 71.34W
196 H6 San Antonio Saipan, S Northern Mariana Islands
39 R13 San Antonio New Mexico, SW USA 33.53N 106.52W
27 R12 San Antonio Texas, SW USA 29.25N 98.29W
56 M11 San Antonio Amazonas, S Venezuela 3.31N 66.46W
56 I7 San Antonio Barinas, C Venezuela 7.24N 71.28W
57 O5 San Antonio Monagas, NE Venezuela 10.03N 63.45W
27 S12 San Antonio ✕ Texas, SW USA 29.31N 98.11W
San Antonio see San Antonio del Táchira
San Antonio Abad see Sant Antoni de Portmany
27 U13 San Antonio Bay inlet Texas, SW USA
63 E22 San Antonio, Cabo headland E Argentina 36.45S 56.40W
46 A5 San Antonio, Cabo de headland W Cuba 21.51N 84.58W
107 T11 San Antonio, Cabo de headland E Spain 38.50N 0.09E
56 H7 San Antonio de Caparo Táchira, W Venezuela 7.34N 71.28W
64 J5 San Antonio de los Cobres Salta, NE Argentina 24.10S 66.17W
56 H7 San Antonio del Táchira var. San Antonio. Táchira, W Venezuela 7.49N 72.27W
37 T15 San Antonio, Mount ▲ California, W USA 34.18N 117.37W
65 K16 San Antonio Oeste Río Negro, E Argentina 40.45S 64.58W
27 T13 San Antonio River ≈ Texas, SW USA
56 J5 Sanare Lara, N Venezuela 9.45N 69.39W
105 T16 Sanary-sur-Mer Var, SE France 43.07N 5.48E
27 X8 San Augustine Texas, SW USA 31.31N 94.06W
147 T13 Sanāw var. Sanaw. NE Yemen 18.00N 51.00E
43 O11 San Bartolo San Luis Potosí, C Mexico 22.19N 100.04W
109 L16 San Bartolomeo in Galdo Campania, S Italy 41.24N 15.01E
108 K13 San Benedetto del Tronto Marche, C Italy 42.57N 13.52E
44 E3 San Benito Petén, N Guatemala 16.55N 89.58W
27 T17 San Benito Texas, SW USA 26.07N 97.37W
56 E6 San Benito Abad Sucre, N Colombia 8.55N 75.01W
37 P11 San Benito Mountain ▲ California, W USA 36.21N 120.37W
37 O10 San Benito River ≈ California, W USA
110 H10 San Bernardino Graubünden, S Switzerland 46.21N 9.13E
37 U15 San Bernardino California, W USA 34.06N 117.15W
37 U15 San Bernardino Mountains ▲▲ California, W USA
64 H11 San Bernardo Santiago, C Chile 33.36S 70.40W
42 J8 San Bernardo Durango, C Mexico 25.58N 105.27W
170 F12 Sanbe-san ▲ Kyūshū, SW Japan 35.09N 132.36E
San Bizenti-Barakaldo see San Vicente de Barakaldo
42 J12 San Blas Nayarit, C Mexico 21.33N 105.17W
42 H8 San Blas Sinaloa, C Mexico 26.05N 108.44W
45 V14 San Blas off. Comarca de San Blas. ◈ special territory NE Panama
45 U14 San Blas, Archipiélago de island group NE Panama
25 Q10 San Blas, Cape headland Florida, SE USA 29.39N 85.21W
45 V14 San Blas, Cordillera de ▲▲ NE Panama
64 J8 San Blas de los Sauces Catamarca, NW Argentina 28.18S 67.12W
108 G8 San Bonifacio Veneto, NE Italy 45.22N 11.14E
31 S12 Sanborn Iowa, C USA 43.10N 95.39W
42 M7 San Buenaventura Coahuila de Zaragoza, NE Mexico 27.03N 101.33W
107 S5 San Caprasio ▲ N Spain 41.45N 0.26W
64 G13 San Carlos Bío Bío, C Chile 36.25S 71.58W
42 E9 San Carlos Baja California Sur, W Mexico 24.52N 112.15W
43 N5 San Carlos Coahuila de Zaragoza, NE Mexico 29.00N 100.51W
San Carlos, Estrecho de see Falkland Sound
43 P9 San Carlos Tamaulipas, C Mexico 24.36N 98.42W
44 L12 San Carlos Río San Juan, S Nicaragua 11.06N 84.46W
45 T16 San Carlos Panamá, C Panama 8.28N 79.58W
179 P9 San Carlos off. San Carlos City. Luzon, N Philippines 15.57N 120.18E
38 M14 San Carlos Arizona, SW USA 33.21N 110.27W
63 G20 San Carlos Maldonado, S Uruguay 34.46S 54.58W
56 K5 San Carlos Cojedes, N Venezuela 9.39N 68.34W
San Carlos see Quesada, Costa Rica
San Carlos see Luba, Equatorial Guinea
63 B17 San Carlos Centro Santa Fe, C Argentina 31.45S 61.04W
179 Q13 San Carlos City Negros, C Philippines 10.34N 123.24E
San Carlos de Ancud see Ancud
65 H16 San Carlos de Bariloche Río Negro, SW Argentina 41.07S 71.15W
63 B21 San Carlos de Bolívar Buenos Aires, E Argentina 36.15S 61.06W
56 H6 San Carlos del Zulia Zulia, W Venezuela 9.01N 71.58W
56 L12 San Carlos de Río Negro Amazonas, S Venezuela 1.54N 67.54W
San Carlos, Estrecho de see Falkland Sound
38 M14 San Carlos Reservoir ⊞ Arizona, SW USA
44 M12 San Carlos, Río ≈ N Costa Rica
67 D24 San Carlos Settlement East Falkland, Falkland Islands
63 C23 San Cayetano Buenos Aires, E Argentina 38.19S 59.37W
105 O8 Sancerre Cher, C France 47.19N 2.53E
164 G7 Sanchakou Xinjiang Uygur Zizhiqu, NW China 39.58N 78.26E
Sanchoku see Samch'ŏk
43 O12 San Ciro San Luis Potosí, C Mexico 21.40N 99.49W
107 P10 San Clemente Castilla-La Mancha, C Spain 39.24N 2.25W
37 T16 San Clemente California, W USA 33.25N 117.36W
63 E21 San Clemente del Tuyú Buenos Aires, E Argentina 36.25S 56.45W
37 S17 San Clemente Island island Channel Islands, California, W USA
105 O9 Sancoins Cher, C France 46.49N 3.00E
195 Z17 San Cristobal var. Makira. island SE Solomon Islands
63 B16 San Cristóbal Santa Fe, C Argentina 30.19S 61.13W
46 B4 San Cristóbal Pinar del Río, W Cuba 22.43N 83.03W
47 O9 San Cristóbal var. Benemérita de San Cristóbal. S Dominican Republic 18.26N 70.07W
56 H7 San Cristóbal Táchira, W Venezuela 7.46N 72.15W
San Cristóbal see San Cristóbal de Las Casas
43 U16 San Cristóbal de Las Casas var. San Cristóbal. Chiapas, SE Mexico 16.43N 92.40W
200 Oo8 San Cristóbal, Isla var. Chatham Island. island Galapagos Islands, Ecuador, E Pacific Ocean
44 D5 San Cristóbal Verapaz Alta Verapaz, C Guatemala 15.22N 90.25W
46 F6 Sancti Spíritus Sancti Spíritus, C Cuba 21.54N 79.27W
105 O11 Sancy, Puy de ▲ C France 45.33N 2.48E
97 D15 Sand Rogaland, S Norway 59.28N 6.16E
175 Oo2 Sandakan Sabah, East Malaysia 5.52N 118.04E
190 K9 Sandalwood South Australia 34.51S 140.13E
Sandalwood Island see Sumba, Pulau
96 D11 Sandane Sogn og Fjordane, S Norway 61.46N 6.13E
116 G12 Sandanski prev. Sveti Vrach. Blagoevgrad, SW Bulgaria 41.36N 23.18E
78 J11 Sandaré Kayes, W Mali 14.36N 10.22W
97 J19 Sandared Västra Götaland, S Sweden 57.43N 12.46E
96 N12 Sandarne Gävleborg, C Sweden 61.15N 17.15E
194 E10 Sandaun prev. West Sepik. ◈ province NW PNG
98 K4 Sanday island NE Scotland, UK
179 N14 Sand Cay island W Spratly Islands
33 P15 Sand Creek ≈ Indiana, N USA
97 H15 Sande Vestfold, S Norway 59.34N 10.13E
97 H16 Sandefjord Vestfold, S Norway 59.07N 10.13E
79 O15 Sandégué E Ivory Coast 7.58N 3.33W
79 P14 Sandema N Ghana 10.42N 1.17W
39 O11 Sanders Arizona, SW USA 35.13N 109.21W
26 M11 Sanderson Texas, SW USA 30.08N 102.23W
25 U4 Sandersville Georgia, SE USA 32.58N 82.48W
94 H4 Sandgerdhi Sudhurland, SW Iceland 64.01N 22.42W
30 K14 Sand Hills ▲▲ Nebraska, C USA
27 S14 Sandia Texas, SW USA 27.59N 97.52W
37 T17 San Diego California, W USA 32.43N 117.09W
27 S14 San Diego Texas, SW USA 27.45N 98.14W
142 F14 Sandıklı Afyon, W Turkey 38.28N 30.16E
158 L12 Sandila Uttar Pradesh, N India 27.05N 80.37E
123 J15 San Dimitri, Ras var. San Dmitri Point. headland Gozo, NW Malta 36.04N 14.12E
174 Gg11 Sanding, Selat strait W Indonesia
32 J3 Sand Island island Apostle Islands, Wisconsin, N USA
97 C16 Sandnes Rogaland, S Norway 58.51N 5.45E
94 F13 Sandnessjøen Nordland, C Norway 66.00N 12.37E
81 L24 Sandoa Katanga, S Dem. Rep. Congo (Zaire) 9.39S 22.58E
113 N15 Sandomierz Rus. Sandomir. Świętokrzyskie, C Poland 50.42N 21.44E
Sandomir see Sandomierz
56 C13 Sandoná Nariño, SW Colombia 1.13N 77.29W
108 I7 San Donà di Piave Veneto, NE Italy 45.37N 12.34E
128 K14 Sandovo Tverskaya Oblast', W Russian Federation 58.26N 36.30E
177 Ff7 Sandoway Arakan State, W Burma 18.28N 94.19E
99 M24 Sandown S England, UK 50.39N 1.11W
97 B19 Sandoy Dan. Sandø Island Faeroe Islands 61.52N 6.51W
41 N16 Sand Point Popof Island, Alaska, USA 55.20N 160.30W
67 N24 Sand Point headland E Tristan da Cunha
33 R7 Sand Point headland Michigan, N USA 43.54N 83.24W
34 M7 Sandpoint Idaho, NW USA 48.16N 116.33W
95 H14 Sandsele Västerbotten, N Sweden 65.16N 17.40E
8 I14 Sandspit Moresby Island, British Columbia, SW Canada 53.13N 131.49W
29 P9 Sand Springs Oklahoma, C USA 36.08N 96.06W
31 W7 Sandstone Minnesota, N USA 46.07N 92.51W
38 K15 Sand Tank Mountains ▲▲ Arizona, SW USA
33 S8 Sandusky Michigan, N USA 43.24N 82.47W
33 S11 Sandusky Ohio, N USA 41.27N 82.42W
33 S12 Sandusky River ≈ Ohio, N USA
85 D22 Sandverhaar Karas, S Namibia 26.49S 17.25E
97 L24 Sandvig Bornholm, E Denmark 55.15N 14.45E
97 H15 Sandvika Akershus, S Norway 59.54N 10.28E
96 N13 Sandviken Gävleborg, C Sweden 60.37N 16.49E
32 M11 Sandwich Illinois, N USA 41.39N 88.37W
Sandwich Island see Éfaté
Sandwich Islands see Hawaiian Islands
159 V16 Sandwip Island island SE Bangladesh
9 U12 Sandy Bay Saskatchewan, C Canada 55.31N 102.14W
191 N16 Sandy Cape headland Tasmania, SE Australia 41.27S 144.43E
178 Mm14 Sandy Cay island NW Spratly Islands
38 L3 Sandy City Utah, W USA 40.36N 111.53W
33 U12 Sandy Creek ≈ Ohio, N USA
23 O5 Sandy Hook Kentucky, S USA 38.09N 83.05W
20 K15 Sandy Hook headland New Jersey, NE USA 40.27N 73.59W
Sandykachi/Sandykgachy see Sandykgaçy
152 J15 Sandykgaçy var. Sandykgachy, Rus. Sandykachi. Mary Welaýaty, S Turkmenistan 36.34N 62.28E
152 L13 Sandykly Gumy Rus. Peski Sandykly. desert E Turkmenistan
Sandykly, Peski see Sandykly Gumy
9 Q13 Sandy Lake Alberta, W Canada 55.50N 113.30W
10 B8 Sandy Lake Ontario, C Canada 53.00N 93.25W
10 B8 Sandy Lake ◎ Ontario, C Canada
25 S3 Sandy Springs Georgia, SE USA 33.57N 84.23W
26 H8 San Elizario Texas, SW USA 31.35N 106.16W
101 L25 Sanem Luxembourg, SW Luxembourg 49.33N 5.55E
44 K5 San Esteban Olancho, C Honduras 15.18N 85.45W
107 O6 San Esteban de Gormaz Castilla-León, N Spain 41.34N 3.13W
42 E5 San Esteban, Isla island NW Mexico
San Eugenio/San Eugenio del Cuareim see Artigas
64 H11 San Felipe var. San Felipe de Aconcagua. Valparaíso, C Chile 32.45S 70.42W
42 D3 San Felipe Baja California, NW Mexico 31.02N 114.55W
42 N12 San Felipe Guanajuato, C Mexico 21.27N 101.12W
56 K5 San Felipe Yaracuy, NW Venezuela 10.25N 68.40W
46 B5 San Felipe, Cayos de island group W Cuba
San Felipe de Aconcagua see San Felipe
San Felipe de Puerto Plata see Puerto Plata
39 R11 San Felipe Pueblo New Mexico, SW USA 35.25N 106.27W
San Feliú de Guixols see Sant Feliu de Guíxols
200 Oo11 San Félix, Isla Eng. San Felix Island. island W Chile
San Felix Island see San Félix, Isla
56 L11 San Fernando de Atabapo Amazonas, S Venezuela 4.00N 67.42W
42 C4 San Fernando var. Misión San Fernando. Baja California, NW Mexico 29.58N 115.14W
43 P9 San Fernando Tamaulipas, C Mexico 24.51N 98.09W
179 P9 San Fernando Luzon, N Philippines 16.45N 120.21E
179 P10 San Fernando Luzon, N Philippines 15.01N 120.41E
106 J16 San Fernando prev. Isla de León. Andalucía, S Spain 36.28N 6.12W
47 U14 San Fernando Trinidad, Trinidad and Tobago 10.16N 61.27W
37 S15 San Fernando California, W USA 34.16N 118.26W
56 L7 San Fernando var. San Fernando de Apure. Apure, C Venezuela 7.54N 67.28W
San Fernando de Apure see San Fernando
64 L8 San Fernando del Valle de Catamarca var. Catamarca. Catamarca, NW Argentina 28.28S 65.46W
San Fernando de Monte Cristi see Monte Cristi
43 P9 San Fernando, Río ≈ C Mexico
25 X11 Sanford Florida, SE USA 28.48N 81.16W
21 P9 Sanford Maine, NE USA 43.26N 70.46W
23 T10 Sanford North Carolina, SE USA 35.28N 79.10W
27 N2 Sanford Texas, SW USA 35.42N 101.31W
41 T10 Sanford, Mount ▲ Alaska, USA 62.21N 144.12W
44 G8 San Francisco var. Gotera, San Francisco Gotera. Morazán, E El Salvador 13.40N 88.06W
45 R16 San Francisco Veraguas, C Panama 8.14N 80.58W
179 Pp11 San Francisco var. Aurora. Luzon, N Philippines 13.22N 122.31E
37 L8 San Francisco California, W USA 37.46N 122.25W
56 H5 San Francisco Zulia, NW Venezuela 10.36N 71.39W
36 M8 San Francisco ✕ California, W USA 37.37N 122.23W
37 N9 San Francisco Bay bay California, W USA
63 C24 San Francisco de Bellocq Buenos Aires, E Argentina 38.42S 60.01W
42 I6 San Francisco de Borja Chihuahua, N Mexico 27.57N 106.42W
44 J6 San Francisco de la Paz Olancho, C Honduras 14.55N 86.13W
42 J7 San Francisco del Oro Chihuahua, N Mexico 26.52N 105.49W
42 M12 San Francisco del Rincón Jalisco, SW Mexico 20.57N 101.54W
47 O8 San Francisco de Macorís C Dominican Republic 19.15N 70.15W
San Francisco de Satipo see Satipo
San Francisco Gotera see San Francisco
San Francisco Telixtlahuaca see Telixtlahuaca
109 K23 San Fratello Sicilia, Italy, C Mediterranean Sea 38.00N 14.35E
San Fructuoso see Tacuarembó
84 C12 Sanga Cuanza Sul, NW Angola 11.10S 15.27E
58 C5 San Gabriel Carchi, N Ecuador 0.37N 77.49W
165 S15 Sa'ngain Xizang Zizhiqu, W China 30.46N 98.45E
160 E13 Sangamner Mahārāshtra, W India 19.37N 74.18E
158 H12 Sāngāner Rājasthān, N India 26.48N 75.48E
Sangan, Koh-i- see Sangān, Kūh-e
155 N6 Sangān, Kūh-e Pash. Koh-i-Sangan. ▲ C Afghanistan
126 Ll10 Sangar Respublika Sakha (Yakutiya), NE Russian Federation 63.48N 127.37E
175 O8 Sangasanga Borneo, C Indonesia 0.36S 117.12E
105 N1 Sangatte Pas-de-Calais, N France 50.56N 1.41E
109 B19 San Gavino Monreale Sardegna, Italy, C Mediterranean Sea 39.33N 8.47E
59 D16 Sangayan, Isla island W Peru
32 L14 Sangchris Lake ⊞ Illinois, N USA
175 P15 Sangeang, Pulau island S Indonesia
118 I10 Sângeorgiu de Pădure prev. Erdăt-Sângeorz, Sîngeorgiu de Pădure, Hung. Erdőszentgyörgy. Mureș, C Romania 46.27N 24.49E
118 I9 Sângeorz-Băi var. Singeroz Băi, Ger. Rumänisch-Sankt-Georgen, Hung. Oláhszentgyörgy; prev. Sîngeorz-Băi. Bistrița-Năsăud, N Romania 47.24N 24.40E
37 R10 Sanger California, W USA 36.42N 119.33W
27 T5 Sanger Texas, SW USA 33.21N 97.10W
Sângerei see Sîngerei
103 L15 Sangerhausen Sachsen-Anhalt, C Germany 51.28N 11.18E
47 S6 San Germán W Puerto Rico 18.05N 67.02W
San Germano see Cassino
167 N2 Sanggan He ≈ E China
175 Oo16 Sanggar, Teluk bay Nusa Tenggara, S Indonesia
174 L8 Sanggau Borneo, C Indonesia 0.07N 110.34E
81 H16 Sangha ≈ Central African Republic/Congo
81 G16 Sangha-Mbaéré ◈ prefecture SW Central African Republic
155 Q15 Sānghar Sind, SE Pakistan 26.10N 68.58E
117 F22 Sangiás ▲ S Greece 36.39N 22.24E
Sangihe, Kepulauan see Sangir, Kepulauan
175 S4 Sangihe, Pulau var. Sangir. island N Indonesia
56 G8 San Gil Santander, C Colombia 6.34N 73.07W
108 F12 San Gimignano Toscana, C Italy 43.30N 11.00E
154 M8 Sangin var. Sangin. Helmand, S Afghanistan 32.03N 64.49E
109 O21 San Giovanni in Fiore Calabria, SW Italy 39.16N 16.42E
109 M16 San Giovanni Rotondo Puglia, SE Italy 41.43N 15.43E
108 G12 San Giovanni Valdarno Toscana, C Italy 43.34N 11.31E
Sangir see Sangihe, Pulau
175 Rr6 Sangir, Kepulauan var. Kepulauan Sangihe. island group N Indonesia
Sangiyn Dalay see Erdene, Govĭ-Altay, Mongolia
Sangiyn Dalay see Erdenedalay, Dundgovĭ, Mongolia
Sangiyn Dalay see Nomgon, Ömnögovĭ, Mongolia
Sangiyn Dalay see Öldziyt, Övörhangay, Mongolia
169 Y15 Sangju Jap. Shōshū. C South Korea 36.26N 128.09E
178 Ii11 Sangkha Surin, E Thailand 14.36N 103.43E
175 Oo7 Sangkulirang Borneo, N Indonesia 1.00N 117.56E
175 Oo7 Sangkulirang, Teluk bay Borneo, N Indonesia
161 E16 Sāngli Mahārāshtra, W India 16.55N 74.37E
81 E16 Sangmélima Sud, S Cameroon 2.57N 11.55E
37 V15 San Gorgonio Mountain ▲ California, W USA 34.06N 116.50W
39 T8 Sangre de Cristo Mountains ▲▲ Colorado/New Mexico, C USA
63 A20 San Gregorio Santa Fe, C Argentina 34.18S 62.01W
63 F18 San Gregorio de Polanco Tacuarembó, C Uruguay 32.37S 55.49W
47 V14 Sangre Grande Trinidad, Trinidad and Tobago 10.35N 61.07W
165 N16 Sangri Xizang Zizhiqu, W China 29.17N 92.01E
158 H9 Sangrūr Punjab, NW India 30.16N 75.52E
46 I11 Sangster off. Sir Donald Sangster International Airport, var. Montego Bay. ✕ (Montego Bay) W Jamaica 18.30N 77.54W
61 G17 Sangue, Rio do ≈ W Brazil
107 R4 Sangüesa Navarra, N Spain 42.34N 1.16W
63 C16 San Gustavo Entre Ríos, E Argentina 30.40S 59.22W
Sangyuan see Wuqiao
42 C6 San Hipólito, Punta headland W Mexico 26.57N 114.00W
25 W15 Sanibel Sanibel Island, Florida, SE USA 26.27N 82.01W
25 V15 Sanibel Island island Florida, SE USA
62 F13 San Ignacio Misiones, NE Argentina 27.13S 55.29W
44 F2 San Ignacio prev. Cayo, El Cayo. Cayo, W Belize 17.09N 89.02W
59 L16 San Ignacio Beni, N Bolivia 14.54S 65.34W
59 O18 San Ignacio Santa Cruz, E Bolivia 16.27S 60.57W
44 M14 San Ignacio var. San Ignacio de Acosta. San José, W Costa Rica 9.46N 84.10W
42 E6 San Ignacio Baja California Sur, W Mexico 27.18N 112.51W
42 J10 San Ignacio Sinaloa, W Mexico 23.55N 106.25W
58 B9 San Ignacio Cajamarca, N Peru 5.03S 79.03W
San Ignacio de Acosta see San Ignacio
42 D7 San Ignacio, Laguna lagoon W Mexico
10 I6 Sanikiluaq Belcher Islands, Nunavut, C Canada 55.16N 77.44W
179 Pp9 San Ildefonso Peninsula peninsula Luzon, N Philippines
Saniquillie see Sanniquellie
63 D20 San Isidro Buenos Aires, E Argentina 34.28S 58.31W
45 N14 San Isidro var. San Isidro de El General. San José, SE Costa Rica 9.21N 83.42W
San Isidro de El General see San Isidro
56 E5 San Jacinto Bolívar, N Colombia 9.52N 75.10W
37 U16 San Jacinto California, W USA 33.47N 116.58W
37 V15 San Jacinto Peak ▲ California, W USA 33.48N 116.40W
63 F14 San Javier Misiones, NE Argentina 27.49S 55.06W
63 C16 San Javier Santa Fe, C Argentina 30.34S 59.58W
107 S13 San Javier Murcia, SE Spain 37.49N 0.49W
63 D18 San Javier Río Negro, W Uruguay 32.40S 58.07W
63 C16 San Javier, Río ≈ C Argentina
Sanjiang see Jinping, Guizhou
166 L12 Sanjiang var. Guyi, Sanjiang Dongzu Zizhixian. Guangxi Zhuangzu Zizhiqu, S China 25.49N 109.31E
Sanjiang Dongzu Zizhixian see Sanjiang
Sanjiaocheng see Haiyan
171 Kk13 Sanjō var. Sanzyô. Niigata, Honshū, C Japan 37.39N 139.00E
59 M15 San Joaquín Beni, N Bolivia 13.03S 64.47W
57 O6 San Joaquín Anzoátegui, NE Venezuela 9.21N 64.30W
37 O9 San Joaquin River ≈ California, W USA
37 P10 San Joaquin Valley valley California, W USA
63 A18 San Jorge Santa Fe, C Argentina 31.49S 61.49W
195 W15 San Jorge island N Solomon Islands
42 D3 San Jorge, Bahía de bay NW Mexico
San Jorge, Isla de see Weddell Island
65 J19 San Jorge, Golfo var. Gulf of San Jorge. gulf S Argentina
San Jorge, Gulf of see San Jorge, Golfo
196 K8 San Jose Tinian, S Northern Mariana Islands 15.00S 145.38E
179 Pp12 San Jose Mindoro, N Philippines 12.20N 121.07E
37 N9 San Jose California, W USA 37.18N 121.53W
63 F14 San José Misiones, NE Argentina 27.46S 55.46W
59 P19 San José var. San José de Chiquitos. Santa Cruz, E Bolivia 14.13S 68.04W
44 M14 San José ● (Costa Rica) San José, C Costa Rica 9.55N 84.05W
44 C7 San José var. Puerto San José. Escuintla, S Guatemala 13.55N 90.48W
42 G6 San José Sonora, NW Mexico 27.31N 110.09W
107 U11 San José Eivissa, Spain, W Mediterranean Sea 38.55N 1.18E
56 H5 San José Zulia, NW Venezuela 9.58N 72.22W
44 M14 San José off. Provincia de San José. ◈ province W Costa Rica
63 E19 San José ◈ department S Uruguay
44 M13 San José ✕ Alajuela, C Costa Rica 10.03N 84.12W
San José see San José del Guaviare, Colombia
San José see San José de Mayo, S Uruguay
San José see Sant Josep de sa Talaia, Ibiza, Spain
179 P9 San Jose City Luzon, N Philippines 15.49N 120.57E
179 Pp13 San Jose de Buenavista Panay Island, C Philippines 10.44N 122.00E
San José de Cúcuta see Cúcuta
63 D16 San José de Feliciano Entre Ríos, E Argentina 30.21S 58.47W
57 O6 San José de Guanipa var. El Tigrito. Anzoátegui, NE Venezuela 8.54N 64.10W
64 I9 San José de Jáchal San Juan, W Argentina 30.15S 68.46W
42 G10 San José del Cabo Baja California Sur, W Mexico 23.01N 109.40W
56 G12 San José del Guaviare var. San José. Guaviare, S Colombia 2.34N 72.37W
63 E20 San José de Mayo var. San José. San José, S Uruguay 34.19S 56.42W
56 I10 San José de Ocuné Vichada, E Colombia 4.10N 70.21W
43 O9 San José de Raíces Nuevo León, NE Mexico 24.32N 100.15W
65 K17 San José, Golfo gulf E Argentina
42 F9 San José, Isla island W Mexico
45 U16 San José, Isla island SE Panama
27 U14 San Jose Island island Texas, SW USA
64 I10 San Juan San Juan, W Argentina 31.36S 68.26W
47 N9 San Juan var. San Juan de la Maguana. C Dominican Republic 18.46N 71.13W
59 E17 San Juan Ica, S Peru 15.22S 75.08W
47 U5 San Juan ○ (Puerto Rico) NE Puerto Rico 18.28N 66.06W
64 H10 San Juan off. Provincia de San Juan. ◈ province W Argentina
47 U5 San Juan var. Luis Muñoz Marin. ✕ NE Puerto Rico 18.27N 66.05W
San Juan see San Juan de los Morros
64 O7 San Juan Bautista Misiones, S Paraguay 26.39S 57.08W
37 O10 San Juan Bautista California, W USA 36.50N 121.34W
San Juan Bautista see Villahermosa
San Juan Bautista Cuicatlán see Cuicatlán
San Juan Bautista Tuxtepec see Tuxtepec
81 C17 San Juan, Cabo headland S Equatorial Guinea 1.09N 9.25E
107 S12 San Juan de Alicante País Valenciano, E Spain 38.25N 0.27W
56 H7 San Juan de Colón Táchira, NW Venezuela 8.01N 72.16W
42 L9 San Juan de Guadalupe Durango, C Mexico 25.12N 100.50W
San Juan de la Maguana see San Juan
56 G4 San Juan del Cesar La Guajira, N Colombia 10.45N 73.00W
42 L15 San Juan de Lima, Punta headland SW Mexico 18.34N 103.40W
44 I8 San Juan de Limay Estelí, NW Nicaragua 13.10N 86.36W

◆ Country ● Country Capital ◇ Dependent Territory ○ Dependent Territory Capital ◈ Administrative Region ✕ International Airport ▲ Mountain ▲▲ Mountain Range Volcano ≈ River ◎ Lake ⊞ Reservoir

San Juan del Norte – Santiago de Cuba

45 N12 **San Juan del Norte** *var.* Greytown. Río San Juan, SE Nicaragua *10.54N 83.42W*
56 K4 **San Juan de los Cayos** Falcón, N Venezuela *11.06N 68.25W*
42 M12 **San Juan de los Lagos** Jalisco, C Mexico *21.15N 102.15W*
56 L5 **San Juan de los Morros** *var.* San Juan. Guárico, N Venezuela *9.52N 67.22W*
42 K9 **San Juan del Río** Durango, C Mexico *25.12N 100.50W*
43 O13 **San Juan del Río** Querétaro de Arteaga, C Mexico *20.21N 100.01W*
44 J11 **San Juan del Sur** Rivas, SW Nicaragua *11.14N 85.52W*
56 M9 **San Juan de Manapiare** Amazonas, S Venezuela *5.15N 66.04W*
42 E7 **San Juanico** Baja California Sur, W Mexico
42 D7 **San Juanico, Punta** *headland* W Mexico *26.01N 112.17W*
34 G6 **San Juan Islands** *island group* Washington, NW USA
42 I6 **San Juanito** Chihuahua, N Mexico
42 I12 **San Juanito, Isla** *island* C Mexico
39 R8 **San Juan Mountains** ▲ Colorado, C USA
56 E5 **San Juan Nepomuceno** Bolívar, NW Colombia *9.57N 75.06W*
46 E5 **San Juan, Pico** ▲ C Cuba *21.58N 80.10W*
203 W15 **San Juan, Punta** *headland* Easter Island, Chile, E Pacific Ocean *27.03S 109.22W*
44 M12 **San Juan, Río** ~ Costa Rica/Nicaragua
43 S15 **San Juan, Río** ~ SE Mexico
39 O8 **San Juan River** ~ Colorado/Utah, W USA
San Julián *see* Puerto San Julián
63 B17 **San Justo** Santa Fe, C Argentina *30.46S 60.31W*
111 W5 **Sankt Aegyd-am-Neuwalde** Niederösterreich, E Austria *47.51N 15.34E*
111 U9 **Sankt Andrä** *Slvn.* Šent Andraž. Kärnten, S Austria *46.46N 14.49E*
Sankt Andrä *see* Szentendre
Sankt Anna *see* Sântana
110 K8 **Sankt Anton-am-Arlberg** Vorarlberg, W Austria *47.08N 10.11E*
103 E16 **Sankt Augustin** Nordrhein-Westfalen, W Germany *50.46N 7.10E*
Sankt-Bartholomäi *see* Palamuse
103 F24 **Sankt Blasien** Baden-Württemberg, SW Germany *47.43N 8.09E*
111 R3 **Sankt Florian am Inn** Oberösterreich, N Austria *48.24N 13.27E*
110 I7 **Sankt Gallen** *var.* St.Gallen, *Eng.* Saint Gall, *Fr.* St-Gall. Sankt Gallen, NE Switzerland *47.25N 9.22E*
110 H8 **Sankt Gallen** *var.* St.Gallen, Eng. Saint Gall, Fr. St-Gall. ◆ *canton* NE Switzerland
110 J8 **Sankt Gallenkirch** Vorarlberg, W Austria *47.00N 10.59E*
111 Q5 **Sankt Georgen** Salzburg, N Austria *47.59N 12.57E*
Sankt Georgen *see* Đurđevac, Croatia
Sankt-Georgen *see* Sfântu Gheorghe, Romania
111 R6 **Sankt Gilgen** Salzburg, NW Austria *47.46N 13.21E*
Sankt Gotthard *see* Szentgotthárd
103 E20 **Sankt Ingbert** Saarland, SW Germany *49.16N 7.07E*
Sankt-Jakobi *see* Viru-Jaagupi, Lääne-Virumaa, Estonia
Sankt-Jakobi *see* Pärnu-Jaagupi, Pärnumaa, Estonia
Sankt Johann *see* Sankt Johann in Tirol
111 T7 **Sankt Johann am Tauern** Steiermark, E Austria *47.20N 14.27E*
111 Q7 **Sankt Johann im Pongau** Salzburg, NW Austria *47.22N 13.13E*
111 P6 **Sankt Johann in Tirol** *var.* Sankt Johann. Tirol, W Austria *47.31N 12.25E*
Sankt-Johannis *see* Järva-Jaani
110 L8 **Sankt Leonhard** Tirol, W Austria *47.05N 10.53E*
Sankt Margarethen *see* Sankt Margarethen im Burgenland
111 Y5 **Sankt Margarethen im Burgenland** *var.* Sankt Margarethen. Burgenland, E Austria *47.49N 16.37E*
Sankt Martin *see* Martin
111 X8 **Sankt Martin an der Raab** Burgenland, SE Austria *46.59N 16.12E*
111 U7 **Sankt Michael in Obersteiermark** Steiermark, SE Austria *47.21N 14.59E*
Sankt Michel *see* Mikkeli
Sankt Moritz *see* St.Moritz
110 E11 **Sankt Niklaus** Valais, S Switzerland *46.09N 7.48E*
111 S7 **Sankt Nikolai** *var.* Sankt Nikolai im Sölktal. Steiermark, SE Austria *47.18N 14.04E*
Sankt Nikolai im Sölktal *see* Sankt Nikolai
111 U9 **Sankt Paul** *var.* Sankt Paul im Lavanttal. Kärnten, S Austria *46.42N 14.53E*
Sankt Paul im Lavanttal *see* Sankt Paul
Sankt Peter *see* Pivka
111 W9 **Sankt Peter am Ottersbach** Steiermark, SE Austria *46.49N 15.48E*
128 J13 **Sankt-Peterburg** *prev.* Leningrad, Petrograd, *Eng.* Saint Petersburg, *Fin.* Pietari. Leningradskaya Oblast', NW Russian Federation *59.55N 30.25E*
102 H8 **Sankt Peter-Ording** Schleswig-Holstein, N Germany *54.18N 8.37E*
111 V4 **Sankt Pölten** Niederösterreich, N Austria *48.14N 15.37E*
111 W7 **Sankt Ruprecht** *var.* Sankt Ruprecht an der Raab. Steiermark, SE Austria *47.10N 15.41E*
Sankt Ruprecht an der Raab *see* Sankt Ruprecht
Sankt-Ulrich *see* Ortisei
111 T4 **Sankt Valentin** Niederösterreich, C Austria *48.09N 14.30E*
Sankt Veit am Flaum *see* Rijeka
111 T9 **Sankt Veit an der Glan** *Slvn.* Šent Vid. Kärnten, S Austria *46.46N 14.22E*
101 M21 **Sankt-Vith** *var.* Saint-Vith. Liège, E Belgium *50.16N 6.07E*
103 E20 **Sankt Wendel** Saarland, SW Germany *49.28N 7.10E*
111 R6 **Sankt Wolfgang** Salzburg, NW Austria *47.43N 13.30E*
81 K21 **Sankuru** ~ C Dem. Rep. Congo
42 D8 **San Lázaro, Cabo** *headland* W Mexico *24.46N 112.15W*
143 O16 **Şanlıurfa** *prev.* Sanli Urfa, Urfa, *anc.* Edessa. Şanlıurfa, S Turkey *37.07N 38.45E*
143 O16 **Şanlıurfa** *prev.* Urfa. ◆ *province* SE Turkey
143 O16 **Şanlıurfa Yaylası** *plateau* SE Turkey
63 B18 **San Lorenzo** Santa Fe, C Argentina *32.37S 60.48W*
59 M21 **San Lorenzo** Tarija, S Bolivia *21.27S 64.47W*
58 C5 **San Lorenzo** Esmeraldas, N Ecuador *1.15N 78.51W*
44 H8 **San Lorenzo** Valle, S Honduras *13.25N 87.27W*
58 A6 **San Lorenzo, Cabo** *headland* W Ecuador *0.57S 80.49W*
107 N8 **San Lorenzo de El Escorial** *var.* El Escorial. Madrid, C Spain *40.36N 4.07W*
42 E5 **San Lorenzo, Isla** *island* NW Mexico
59 C14 **San Lorenzo, Isla** *island* W Peru
65 G20 **San Lorenzo, Monte** ▲ S Argentina *47.40S 72.12W*
42 I9 **San Lorenzo, Río** ~ C Mexico
106 J15 **Sanlúcar de Barrameda** Andalucía, S Spain *36.46N 6.21W*
106 J14 **Sanlúcar la Mayor** Andalucía, S Spain *37.24N 6.13W*
42 F11 **San Lucas** Baja California Sur, NW Mexico *22.49N 109.52W*
42 E6 **San Lucas** *var.* Cabo San Lucas. Baja California Sur, W Mexico *27.13N 112.15W*
42 G11 **San Lucas, Cabo** *var.* San Lucas Cape. *headland* W Mexico *22.52N 109.55W*
San Lucas Cape *see* San Lucas, Cabo
64 J11 **San Luis** San Luis, C Argentina *33.18S 66.18W*
44 E4 **San Luis** Petén, NE Guatemala *16.16N 89.27W*
42 D2 **San Luis** *var.* San Luis Río Colorado. Sonora, NW Mexico *32.25N 114.48W*
44 M7 **San Luis** Región Autónoma Atlántico Norte, NE Nicaragua *13.58N 84.10W*
38 H15 **San Luis** Arizona, SW USA *32.27N 114.45W*
39 T8 **San Luis** Colorado, C USA *37.09N 105.24W*
56 J4 **San Luis** Falcón, N Venezuela *11.08N 69.36W*
64 J11 **San Luis** *off.* Provincia de San Luis. ◆ *province* C Argentina
43 N12 **San Luis de la Paz** Guanajuato, C Mexico *21.15N 100.33W*
42 K8 **San Luis del Cordero** Durango, C Mexico *25.25N 104.09W*
42 D4 **San Luis, Isla** *island* NW Mexico
44 E6 **San Luis Jilotepeque** Jalapa, SE Guatemala *14.36N 89.40W*
59 M16 **San Luis, Laguna de** ◎ NW Bolivia
37 P13 **San Luis Obispo** California, W USA *35.16N 120.39W*
39 R7 **San Luis Peak** ▲ Colorado, C USA *37.59N 106.55W*
43 N11 **San Luis Potosí** San Luis Potosí, C Mexico *22.09N 100.57W*
43 N11 **San Luis Potosí** ◆ *state* C Mexico
37 O10 **San Luis Reservoir** ⊡ California, W USA
San Luis Río Colorado *see* San Luis
39 S8 **San Luis Valley** *basin* Colorado, C USA
109 C19 **Sanluri** Sardegna, Italy, C Mediterranean Sea *39.34N 8.54E*
63 D23 **San Manuel** Buenos Aires, E Argentina *37.46S 58.49W*
38 M15 **San Manuel** Arizona, SW USA *32.36N 110.37W*
108 F11 **San Marcello Pistoiese** Toscana, C Italy *44.03N 10.46E*
109 N20 **San Marco Argentano** Calabria, SW Italy *39.31N 16.07E*
56 E6 **San Marcos** Sucre, N Colombia *8.37N 75.12W*
44 M14 **San Marcos** San José, C Costa Rica *9.39N 84.00W*
44 B5 **San Marcos** San Marcos, W Guatemala *14.57N 91.46W*
44 F6 **San Marcos** Ocotepeque, SW Honduras *14.23N 88.57W*
43 O16 **San Marcos** Guerrero, S Mexico *16.47N 99.29W*
27 S11 **San Marcos** Texas, SW USA *29.52N 97.56W*
44 A5 **San Marcos** *off.* Departamento de San Marcos. ◆ *department* W Guatemala
San Marcos de Arica *see* Arica
42 E6 **San Marcos, Isla** *island* W Mexico
108 H11 **San Marino** ● (San Marino) C San Marino *43.53N 12.27E*
108 I11 **San Marino** *off.* Republic of San Marino. ◆ *republic* S Europe
64 I11 **San Martín** Mendoza, C Argentina *33.04S 68.28W*
56 F11 **San Martín** Meta, C Colombia *3.43N 73.42W*
58 D11 **San Martín** *off.* Departamento de San Martín. ◆ *department* C Peru
204 I5 **San Martín** *Argentinian research station* Antarctica *68.18S 67.03W*
65 H16 **San Martín de los Andes** Neuquén, W Argentina *40.10S 71.22W*
106 M8 **San Martín de Valdeiglesias** Madrid, C Spain *40.21N 4.24W*
65 G21 **San Martín, Lago** *var.* Lago O'Higgins. ◎ S Argentina
108 H6 **San Martino di Castrozza** Trentino-Alto Adige, N Italy *46.16N 11.50E*
59 N16 **San Martín, Río** ~ N Bolivia
San Martín Texmelucan *see* Texmelucan
37 N9 **San Mateo** California, W USA *37.33N 122.19W*
57 O6 **San Mateo** Anzoátegui, NE Venezuela *9.34N 64.30W*
44 B4 **San Mateo Ixtatán** Huehuetenango, W Guatemala *15.48N 91.30W*
59 Q18 **San Matías** Santa Cruz, E Bolivia *16.19S 58.23W*
65 K16 **San Matías, Golfo** *var.* Gulf of San Matías. *gulf* E Argentina
San Matías, Gulf of *see* San Matías, Golfo
13 O8 **Sanmaur** Québec, SE Canada *47.52N 73.47W*
167 T10 **Sanmen Wan** *bay* E China
166 M6 **Sanmenxia** *var.* Shan Xian. Henan, C China *34.46N 111.16E*
Sânmiclăuş Mare *see* Sânnicolau Mare
63 D14 **San Miguel** Corrientes, NE Argentina *28.02S 57.38W*
59 L16 **San Miguel** Beni, N Bolivia *16.43S 61.06W*
44 G8 **San Miguel** San Miguel, SE El Salvador *13.27N 88.10W*
42 L6 **San Miguel** Coahuila de Zaragoza, N Mexico *29.10N 101.28W*
42 J9 **San Miguel** *var.* San Miguel de Cruces. Durango, C Mexico *24.25N 105.55W*
45 U16 **San Miguel** Panamá, SE Panama *8.26N 78.57W*
37 P12 **San Miguel** California, W USA *35.45N 120.42W*
44 B9 **San Miguel** ◆ *department* E El Salvador
43 N13 **San Miguel de Allende** Guanajuato, C Mexico *20.54N 100.46W*
San Miguel de Cruces *see* San Miguel
San Miguel de Ibarra *see* Ibarra
63 D21 **San Miguel del Monte** Buenos Aires, E Argentina *35.25S 58.49W*
64 J7 **San Miguel de Tucumán** *var.* Tucumán. Tucumán, N Argentina *26.46S 65.15W*
45 V16 **San Miguel, Golfo de** *gulf* S Panama
37 P15 **San Miguel Island** *island* California, W USA
44 L11 **San Miguelito** Río San Juan, S Nicaragua *11.22N 84.52W*
45 T15 **San Miguelito** Panamá, C Panama *8.58N 79.31W*
59 N18 **San Miguel, Río** ~ E Bolivia
58 D6 **San Miguel, Río** ~ Colombia/Ecuador
42 I7 **San Miguel, Río** ~ N Mexico
44 G8 **San Miguel, Volcán de** ⛰ SE El Salvador *13.27N 88.18W*
167 Q12 **Sanming** Fujian, SE China *26.10N 117.37E*
108 F11 **San Miniato** Toscana, C Italy *43.40N 10.53E*
San Murezzan *see* St.Moritz
Sannär *see* Sennar
109 M15 **Sannicandro Garganico** Puglia, SE Italy *41.49N 15.31E*
42 H6 **San Nicolás** Sonora, NW Mexico *28.31N 109.24W*
63 C19 **San Nicolás de los Arroyos** Buenos Aires, E Argentina *33.17S 60.12W*
37 R16 **San Nicolas Island** *island* Channel Islands, California, W USA
Sânnicolaul-Mare *see* Sânnicolau Mare
118 E11 **Sânnicolau Mare** *var.* Sânnicolaul-Mare, *Hung.* Nagyszentmiklós; *prev.* Sânmiclăuş Mare, Sînnicolau Mare. Timiş, W Romania *46.05N 20.38E*
126 L15 **Sannikova, Proliv** *strait* NE Russian Federation
78 K16 **Sanniquellie** *var.* Saniquillie. NE Liberia *7.24N 8.45W*
172 N9 **Sannohe** Aomori, Honshū, C Japan *40.23N 141.16E*
Santtaler Alpen *see* Kamniško-Savinjske Alpe
171 K15 **Sano** Tochigi, Honshū, S Japan *36.19N 139.36E*
113 O17 **Sanok** Podkarpackie, SE Poland *49.31N 22.14E*
56 E5 **San Onofre** Sucre, NW Colombia *9.45N 75.33W*
59 K21 **San Pablo** Potosí, S Bolivia *21.43S 66.37W*
179 P11 **San Pablo** *off.* San Pablo City. Luzon, N Philippines *14.04N 121.16E*
San Pablo Balleza *see* Balleza
37 N8 **San Pablo Bay** *bay* California, W USA
42 C6 **San Pablo, Punta** *headland* W Mexico *27.12N 114.30W*
45 R16 **San Pablo, Río** ~ C Panama
179 Q11 **San Pascual** Burias Island, C Philippines *13.06N 122.59E*
123 J16 **San Pawl il-Bahar** *Eng.* Saint Paul's Bay. E Malta *35.57N 14.24E*
63 C19 **San Pedro** Buenos Aires, E Argentina *33.37S 59.42W*
64 K5 **San Pedro** Jujuy, N Argentina *24.13S 64.51W*
62 G13 **San Pedro** Misiones, NE Argentina *26.37S 54.12W*
44 H1 **San Pedro** Corozal, NE Belize *17.58N 87.55W*
42 L8 **San Pedro** *var.* San Pedro de las Colonias. Coahuila de Zaragoza, NE Mexico *25.47N 102.57W*
64 O5 **San Pedro** San Pedro, SE Paraguay *24.04S 57.03W*
64 O6 **San Pedro** *off.* Departamento de San Pedro. ◆ *department* C Paraguay
79 N16 **San Pedro** ✕ (Yamoussoukro) C Ivory Coast *6.49N 5.14W*
46 G6 **San Pedro** ~ C Cuba
San Pedro *see* San Pedro del Pinatar
78 M17 **San-Pédro** S Ivory Coast *4.45N 6.37W*
44 D5 **San Pedro Carchá** Alta Verapaz, C Guatemala *15.30N 90.12W*
37 S16 **San Pedro Channel** *channel* California, W USA
64 I5 **San Pedro de Atacama** Antofagasta, N Chile *22.52S 68.10W*
San Pedro de Durazno *see* Durazno
42 G5 **San Pedro de la Cueva** Sonora, NW Mexico *29.16N 109.46W*
San Pedro de las Colonias *see* San Pedro
58 B11 **San Pedro de Lloc** La Libertad, NW Peru *7.27S 79.34W*
107 S13 **San Pedro del Pinatar** *var.* San Pedro. Murcia, SE Spain *37.49N 0.46W*
47 P9 **San Pedro de Macorís** SE Dominican Republic *18.28N 69.19W*
42 C3 **San Pedro Mártir, Sierra** ▲ NW Mexico
San Pedro Pochutla *see* Pochutla
44 D2 **San Pedro, Río** ~ Guatemala/Mexico
42 K10 **San Pedro, Río** ~ C Mexico
106 J10 **San Pedro, Sierra de** ▲ W Spain
44 G5 **San Pedro Sula** Cortés, NW Honduras *15.26N 88.01W*
San Pedro Tapanatepec *see* Tapanatepec
64 I4 **San Pedro, Volcán** ▲ N Chile *21.46S 68.13W*
108 E7 **San Pellegrino Terme** Lombardia, N Italy *45.53N 9.42E*
27 T16 **San Perlita** Texas, SW USA *26.30N 97.38W*
San Pietro *see* Supetar
San Pietro del Carso *see* Pivka
109 A20 **San Pietro, Isola di** *island* W Italy
34 K7 **Sanpoil River** ~ Washington, NW USA
171 L12 **Sanpoku** *var.* Sampoku. Niigata, Honshū, C Japan *38.32N 139.33E*
42 C3 **San Quintín** Baja California, NW Mexico *30.21N 115.58W*
42 B3 **San Quintín, Bahía de** *bay* NW Mexico
42 B3 **San Quintín, Cabo** *headland* NW Mexico *30.22N 116.01W*
64 I12 **San Rafael** Mendoza, W Argentina *34.43S 68.15W*
43 N9 **San Rafael** Nuevo León, NE Mexico *25.01N 100.33W*
36 M8 **San Rafael** California, W USA *37.58N 122.31W*
39 Q11 **San Rafael** New Mexico, SW USA *35.03N 107.52W*
56 H4 **San Rafael** *var.* El Moján. Zulia, NW Venezuela *10.58N 71.45W*
44 J8 **San Rafael del Norte** Jinotega, NW Nicaragua *13.10N 86.10W*
44 J10 **San Rafael del Sur** Managua, SW Nicaragua *11.51N 86.24W*
38 M5 **San Rafael Knob** ▲ Utah, W USA *38.46N 110.45W*
37 Q14 **San Rafael Mountains** ▲ California, W USA
44 M13 **San Ramón** Alajuela, C Costa Rica *10.04N 84.27W*
59 E14 **San Ramón** Junín, C Peru *11.08S 75.19W*
63 F19 **San Ramón** Canelones, S Uruguay *34.18S 55.55W*
64 K5 **San Ramón de la Nueva Orán** Salta, N Argentina *23.07S 64.19W*
59 O16 **San Ramón, Río** ~ E Bolivia
108 B11 **San Remo** Liguria, NW Italy *43.48N 7.46E*
56 J3 **San Román, Cabo** *headland* NW Venezuela *12.10N 70.01W*
63 C15 **San Roque** Corrientes, NE Argentina *28.34S 58.45W*
196 I4 **San Roque** Saipan, S Northern Mariana Islands *15.15S 85.46E*
106 K16 **San Roque** Andalucía, S Spain *36.13N 5.22W*
27 R9 **San Saba** Texas, SW USA *31.12N 98.43W*
27 Q9 **San Saba River** ~ Texas, SW USA
63 D17 **San Salvador** Entre Ríos, E Argentina *31.37S 58.30W*
44 F7 **San Salvador** ● (El Salvador) San Salvador, SW El Salvador *13.42N 89.12W*
44 A10 **San Salvador** ◆ *department* C El Salvador
44 F8 **San Salvador** ✕ La Paz, S El Salvador *13.27N 89.04W*
46 K4 **San Salvador** *prev.* Watlings Island. *island* E Bahamas
64 J5 **San Salvador de Jujuy** *var.* Jujuy. Jujuy, N Argentina *24.10S 65.19W*
44 F7 **San Salvador, Volcán de** ⛰ C El Salvador *13.58N 89.14W*
79 Q14 **Sansanné-Mango** *var.* Mango. N Togo *10.21N 0.28E*
47 S5 **San Sebastián** W Puerto Rico *18.21N 67.00W*
65 J24 **San Sebastián, Bahía** *bay* S Argentina
Sansenhō *see* Sach'ŏn
108 H12 **Sansepolcro** Toscana, C Italy *43.34N 12.12E*
109 M16 **San Severo** Puglia, SE Italy *41.40N 15.22E*
114 F11 **Sanski Most** Federacija Bosna I Hercegovina, NW Bosnia & Herzegovina *44.43N 16.40E*
176 Ww9 **Sansundi** Papua, E Indonesia *0.42S 135.48E*
168 K9 **Sant** *var.* Mayhan. Övörhangay, C Mongolia *46.02N 104.00E*
106 K11 **Santa Amalia** Extremadura, W Spain *39.00N 6.01W*
62 F13 **Santa Ana** Misiones, NE Argentina *27.22S 55.34W*
59 L16 **Santa Ana** Beni, N Bolivia *13.43S 65.37W*
44 E7 **Santa Ana** Santa Ana, NW El Salvador *13.58N 89.34W*
42 F4 **Santa Ana** Sonora, NW Mexico *30.33N 111.07W*
37 T16 **Santa Ana** California, W USA *33.45N 117.52W*
57 N6 **Santa Ana** Nueva Esparta, NE Venezuela *9.15N 64.39W*
44 A9 **Santa Ana** ◆ *department* NW El Salvador
Santa Ana de Coro *see* Coro
37 U16 **Santa Ana Mountains** ▲ California, W USA
44 E7 **Santa Ana, Volcán de** *var.* La Matepec. ⛰ W El Salvador *13.49N 89.36W*
42 J7 **Santa Barbara** Chihuahua, N Mexico *26.46N 105.46W*
37 Q14 **Santa Barbara** California, W USA *34.24N 119.40W*
44 G6 **Santa Bárbara** Santa Bárbara, W Honduras *14.57N 88.15W*
56 L11 **Santa Bárbara** Amazonas, S Venezuela *3.55N 67.06W*
56 I7 **Santa Bárbara** Barinas, W Venezuela *7.48N 71.10W*
44 F5 **Santa Bárbara** ◆ *department* NW Honduras
Santa Bárbara *see* Iscuandé
37 Q15 **Santa Barbara Channel** *channel* California, W USA
Santa Bárbara de Samaná *see* Samaná
37 R16 **Santa Barbara Island** *island* Channel Islands, California, W USA
56 E5 **Santa Catalina** Bolívar, N Colombia *10.34N 75.22W*
45 R15 **Santa Catalina** Bocas del Toro, W Panama *8.46N 81.18W*
37 T17 **Santa Catalina, Gulf of** *gulf* California, W USA
42 F8 **Santa Catalina, Isla** *island* W Mexico
37 S16 **Santa Catalina Island** *island* Channel Islands, California, W USA
43 N8 **Santa Catarina** Nuevo León, NE Mexico *25.39N 100.30W*
62 H13 **Santa Catarina** *off.* Estado de Santa Catarina. ◆ *state* S Brazil
Santa Catarina de Tepehuanes *see* Tepehuanes
62 L13 **Santa Catarina, Ilha de** *island* S Brazil
47 Q16 **Santa Catherina** Curaçao, C Netherlands Antilles *12.07N 68.46W*
46 E5 **Santa Clara** Villa Clara, C Cuba *22.25N 78.00W*
37 N9 **Santa Clara** California, W USA *37.20N 121.57W*
38 J8 **Santa Clara** Utah, W USA *37.07N 113.39W*
Santa Clara *see* Santa Clara de Olimar
63 F18 **Santa Clara de Olimar** *var.* Santa Clara. Cerro Largo, NE Uruguay *32.54S 54.55W*
63 A17 **Santa Clara de Saguier** Santa Fe, C Argentina *31.21S 61.49W*
Santa Coloma *see* Santa Coloma de Gramanet
107 X5 **Santa Coloma de Farners** *var.* Santa Coloma de Farnés. Cataluña, NE Spain *41.52N 2.39E*
Santa Coloma de Farnés *see* Santa Coloma de Farners
107 W6 **Santa Coloma de Gramanet** *var.* Santa Coloma. Cataluña, NE Spain *41.28N 2.13E*
106 G2 **Santa Comba** Galicia, NW Spain *43.01N 8.49W*
Santa Comba *see* Uaco Cungo
106 H8 **Santa Comba Dão** Viseu, N Portugal *40.22N 8.07W*
84 C10 **Santa Cruz** Uíge, NW Angola *6.56S 16.25E*
59 N19 **Santa Cruz** *var.* Santa Cruz de la Sierra. Santa Cruz, C Bolivia *17.49S 63.10W*
64 G12 **Santa Cruz** Libertador, C Chile *34.39S 71.16W*
44 K13 **Santa Cruz** Guanacaste, W Costa Rica *10.15N 85.34W*
46 I12 **Santa Cruz** W Jamaica *18.03N 77.41W*
66 P6 **Santa Cruz** Madeira, Portugal, NE Atlantic Ocean *32.43N 16.46W*
37 N10 **Santa Cruz** California, W USA *36.58N 122.01W*
65 H20 **Santa Cruz** *off.* Provincia de Santa Cruz. ◆ *province* S Argentina
59 O18 **Santa Cruz** ◆ *department* E Bolivia
Santa Cruz *see* Viru-Viru
Santa Cruz *see* Puerto Santa Cruz
Santa Cruz Barillas *see* Barillas
61 O18 **Santa Cruz Cabrália** Bahia, E Brazil *16.16S 39.03W*
Santa Cruz de El Seibo *see* El Seibo
66 N11 **Santa Cruz de la Palma** La Palma, Islas Canarias, Spain, NE Atlantic Ocean *28.40N 17.46W*
Santa Cruz de la Sierra *see* Santa Cruz
107 O9 **Santa Cruz de la Zarza** Castilla-La Mancha, C Spain *39.59N 3.10W*
44 C5 **Santa Cruz del Quiché** Quiché, W Guatemala *15.01N 91.08W*
107 N8 **Santa Cruz del Retamar** Castilla-La Mancha, C Spain *40.07N 4.13W*
Santa Cruz del Seibo *see* El Seibo
46 G7 **Santa Cruz del Sur** Camagüey, C Cuba *20.44N 78.00W*
107 O11 **Santa Cruz de Mudela** Castilla-La Mancha, C Spain *38.37N 3.27W*
66 Q11 **Santa Cruz de Tenerife** Tenerife, Islas Canarias, Spain, NE Atlantic Ocean *28.28N 16.15W*
66 P11 **Santa Cruz de Tenerife** ◆ *province* Islas Canarias, Spain, NE Atlantic Ocean
62 K9 **Santa Cruz do Rio Pardo** São Paulo, S Brazil *22.52S 49.37W*
63 H15 **Santa Cruz do Sul** Rio Grande do Sul, S Brazil *29.42S 52.25W*
59 C17 **Santa Cruz, Isla** *var.* Indefatigable Island, Isla Chávez. *island* Galapagos Islands, Ecuador, E Pacific Ocean
42 F8 **Santa Cruz, Isla** *island* W Mexico
37 Q15 **Santa Cruz Island** *island* California, W USA
195 X8 **Santa Cruz Islands** *island group* E Solomon Islands
65 I22 **Santa Cruz, Río** ~ S Argentina
38 L15 **Santa Cruz River** ~ Arizona, SW USA
63 C17 **Santa Elena** Entre Ríos, E Argentina *30.58S 59.46W*
44 F2 **Santa Elena** Cayo, W Belize *17.08N 89.04W*
27 R16 **Santa Elena** Texas, SW USA *26.43N 98.30W*
58 A7 **Santa Elena, Bahía de** *bay* W Ecuador
57 R10 **Santa Elena de Uairén** Bolívar, E Venezuela *4.40N 61.03W*
44 K12 **Santa Elena, Península** *peninsula* NW Costa Rica
58 A7 **Santa Elena, Punta** *headland* W Ecuador *2.11S 81.00W*
106 L11 **Santa Eufemia** Andalucía, S Spain *38.36N 4.54W*
109 N21 **Santa Eufemia, Golfo di** *gulf* S Italy
107 S4 **Santa Eulalia de Gállego** Aragón, NE Spain *42.16N 0.46W*
107 V11 **Santa Eulalia del Río** Ibiza, Spain, W Mediterranean Sea *39.00N 1.33E*
63 B17 **Santa Fe** Santa Fe, C Argentina *31.36S 60.46W*
107 N14 **Santa Fe** Andalucía, S Spain *37.10N 3.43W*
39 S10 **Santa Fe** *state capital* New Mexico, SW USA *35.41N 105.56W*
63 B15 **Santa Fe** *off.* Provincia de Santa Fe. ◆ *province* C Argentina
Santa Fe *see* Bogotá
46 C6 **Santa Fé** *var.* La Fe. Isla de la Juventud, W Cuba *21.39N 82.45W*
45 R16 **Santa Fé** Veraguas, C Panama *8.28N 81.03W*
Santa Fe de Bogotá *see* Bogotá
62 J7 **Santa Fé do Sul** São Paulo, S Brazil *20.13S 50.55W*
59 B18 **Santa Fe, Isla** *var.* Barrington Island. *island* Galapagos Islands, Ecuador, E Pacific Ocean
25 V9 **Santa Fe River** ~ Florida, SE USA
61 M15 **Santa Filomena** Piauí, E Brazil *9.06S 45.52W*
42 G10 **Santa Genoveva** ▲ W Mexico *23.07N 109.56W*
159 S14 **Santahar** Rajshahi, NW Bangladesh *24.45N 89.03E*
62 G11 **Santa Helena** Paraná, S Brazil *24.53S 54.19W*
56 J5 **Santa Inés** Lara, N Venezuela *10.37N 69.18W*
65 G24 **Santa Inés, Isla** *island* S Chile
64 J13 **Santa Isabel** La Pampa, C Argentina *36.11S 66.59W*
45 U14 **Santa Isabel** Colón, N Panama *9.31N 79.12W*
195 W14 **Santa Isabel** *var.* Bughotu. *island* N Solomon Islands
Santa Isabel *see* Malabo
60 D11 **Santa Isabel do Rio Negro** Amazonas, NW Brazil *0.40S 64.55W*
63 C15 **Santa Lucia** Corrientes, NE Argentina *28.58S 59.05W*
59 I17 **Santa Lucía** Puno, S Peru *15.45S 70.34W*
63 F20 **Santa Lucía** *var.* Santa Lucia. Canelones, S Uruguay *34.25S 56.25W*
44 B6 **Santa Lucía Cotzumalguapa** Escuintla, SW Guatemala *14.20N 91.00W*
109 L23 **Santa Lucia del Mela** Sicilia, Italy, C Mediterranean Sea *38.07N 15.16E*
37 O11 **Santa Lucia Range** ▲ California, W USA
42 D9 **Santa Margarita, Isla** *island* W Mexico
63 G15 **Santa Maria** Rio Grande do Sul, S Brazil *29.40S 53.48W*
37 P13 **Santa Maria** California, W USA *34.56N 120.25W*
66 Q4 **Santa Maria** ✕ Santa Maria, Azores, Portugal, NE Atlantic Ocean
66 P3 **Santa Maria** *island* Azores, Portugal, NE Atlantic Ocean
Santa Maria *see* Gaua.
64 J7 **Santa María** Catamarca, N Argentina *26.38S 66.01W*
Santa María Asunción Tlaxiaco *see* Tlaxiaco
42 G9 **Santa María, Bahía** *bay* W Mexico
85 L21 **Santa Maria, Cabo de** *headland* S Mozambique *26.05S 32.58E*
106 G15 **Santa Maria, Cabo de** *headland* S Portugal *36.57N 7.55W*
46 J4 **Santa Maria, Cape** *headland* Long Island, C Bahamas *23.40N 75.20W*
109 J17 **Santa Maria Capua Vetere** Campania, S Italy *41.04N 14.15E*
61 M17 **Santa Maria da Vitória** Bahia, E Brazil *13.25S 44.09W*
57 N9 **Santa María de Erebato** Bolívar, SE Venezuela *5.09N 64.49W*
106 G7 **Santa Maria da Feira** Aveiro, N Portugal *40.55N 8.31W*
57 N6 **Santa María de Ipire** Guárico, C Venezuela *8.51N 65.21W*
Santa Maria del Buen Aire *see* Buenos Aires
42 J8 **Santa María del Oro** Durango, C Mexico *25.57N 105.22W*
43 N12 **Santa María del Río** San Luis Potosí, C Mexico *21.48N 100.42W*
Santa Maria di Castellabate *see* Castellabate
109 Q20 **Santa Maria di Leuca, Capo** *headland* SE Italy *39.48N 18.21E*
110 K10 **Santa Maria-im-Münstertal** Graubünden, SE Switzerland *46.36N 10.25E*
59 B18 **Santa María, Isla** *var.* Isla Floreana, Charles Island. *island* Galapagos Islands, Ecuador, E Pacific Ocean
42 J3 **Santa María, Laguna de** ◎ N Mexico
63 G16 **Santa Maria, Rio** ~ S Brazil
45 R16 **Santa María, Río** ~ C Panama
38 J12 **Santa Maria River** ~ Arizona, SW USA
109 G15 **Santa Marinella** Lazio, C Italy *42.01N 11.51E*
56 F4 **Santa Marta** Magdalena, N Colombia *11.13N 74.13W*
106 J11 **Santa Marta** Extremadura, W Spain *38.37N 6.39W*
Santa Maura *see* Lefkáda
37 S15 **Santa Monica** California, W USA *34.01N 118.29W*
118 F10 **Sântana** *Ger.* Sankt Anna, *Hung.* Újszentanna; *prev.* Sîntana. Arad, W Romania *46.19N 21.30E*
63 F16 **Santana, Coxilha de** *hill range* S Brazil
63 H16 **Santana da Boa Vista** Rio Grande do Sul, S Brazil *30.52S 53.03W*
63 F16 **Santana do Livramento** *prev.* Livramento. Rio Grande do Sul, S Brazil *30.52S 55.30W*
107 N2 **Santander** Cantabria, N Spain *43.28N 3.48W*
56 F8 **Santander** *off.* Departamento de Santander. ◆ *province* C Colombia
Santander Jiménez *see* Jiménez
Sant'Andrea *see* Svetac
109 B20 **Sant'Antioco** Sardegna, Italy, C Mediterranean Sea *39.03N 8.28E*
107 V11 **Sant Antoni de Portmany** *Cas.* San Antonio Abad. Ibiza, Spain, W Mediterranean Sea *38.58N 1.18E*
107 Y10 **Santanyí** Mallorca, Spain, W Mediterranean Sea *39.24N 3.07E*
106 J13 **Santa Olalla del Cala** Andalucía, S Spain *37.54N 6.13W*
37 R15 **Santa Paula** California, W USA *34.21N 119.03W*
38 L4 **Santaquin** Utah, W USA *39.58N 111.46W*
60 I12 **Santarém** Pará, N Brazil *2.25S 54.40W*
106 G10 **Santarém** *anc.* Scalabis. Santarém, W Portugal *39.13N 8.40W*
106 G10 **Santarém** ◆ *district* C Portugal
46 F4 **Santaren Channel** *channel* W Bahamas
56 K10 **Santa Rita** Vichada, E Colombia *4.51N 68.27W*
196 B16 **Santa Rita** SW Guam
44 H5 **Santa Rita** Cortés, NW Honduras *15.10N 87.54W*
42 E9 **Santa Rita** Baja California Sur, W Mexico *27.28N 100.33W*
56 H5 **Santa Rita** Zulia, NW Venezuela *10.33N 71.31W*
61 I19 **Santa Rita de Araguaia** Goiás, S Brazil *17.17S 53.13W*
Santa Rita de Cassia *see* Cássia
63 D14 **Santa Rosa** Corrientes, NE Argentina *28.18S 58.04W*
64 K13 **Santa Rosa** La Pampa, C Argentina *36.37S 64.15W*
63 G14 **Santa Rosa** Rio Grande do Sul, S Brazil *27.49S 54.28W*
60 E10 **Santa Rosa** Roraima, N Brazil *3.41N 62.29W*
58 B8 **Santa Rosa** El Oro, SW Ecuador *3.27S 79.57W*
59 I16 **Santa Rosa** Puno, S Peru *14.38S 70.48W*
36 M7 **Santa Rosa** California, W USA *38.26N 122.42W*
39 U11 **Santa Rosa** New Mexico, SW USA *34.54N 104.43W*
57 O6 **Santa Rosa** Anzoátegui, NE Venezuela *9.36N 64.16W*
44 A3 **Santa Rosa** *off.* Departamento de Santa Rosa. ◆ *department* SE Guatemala
Santa Rosa *see* Santa Rosa de Copán
65 J15 **Santa Rosa, Bajo de** *basin* E Argentina
44 F6 **Santa Rosa de Copán** *var.* Santa Rosa. Copán, W Honduras *14.46N 88.48W*
56 E8 **Santa Rosa de Osos** Antioquia, C Colombia *6.40N 75.27W*
37 Q15 **Santa Rosa Island** *island* California, W USA
25 O9 **Santa Rosa Island** *island* Florida, SE USA
42 E6 **Santa Rosalía** Baja California Sur, W Mexico *27.19N 112.16W*
56 K6 **Santa Rosalía** Portuguesa, NW Venezuela *9.01N 69.02W*
196 C15 **Santa Rosa, Mount** ▲ NE Guam
37 V16 **Santa Rosa Mountains** ▲ California, W USA
37 T2 **Santa Rosa Range** ▲ Nevada, W USA
64 M8 **Santa Sylvina** Chaco, N Argentina *27.49S 61.07W*
Santa Tecla *see* Nueva San Salvador
63 B19 **Santa Teresa** Santa Fe, C Argentina *33.30S 60.45W*
61 O20 **Santa Teresa** Espírito Santo, SE Brazil *19.51S 40.49W*
109 M23 **Santa Teresa di Riva** Sicilia, Italy, C Mediterranean Sea *38.00N 15.25E*
63 E21 **Santa Teresita** Buenos Aires, E Argentina *36.34S 56.43W*
63 H19 **Santa Vitória do Palmar** Rio Grande do Sul, S Brazil *33.31S 53.25W*
37 Q14 **Santa Ynez River** ~ California, W USA
Sant Carles de la Rápida *see* Sant Carles de la Ràpita
107 U7 **Sant Carles de la Ràpita** *var.* Sant Carles de la Rápida. Cataluña, NE Spain *40.37N 0.36E*
107 W5 **Sant Celoni** Cataluña, NE Spain *41.39N 2.25E*
37 U17 **Santee** California, W USA *32.50N 116.58W*
23 T13 **Santee River** ~ South Carolina, SE USA
42 K15 **San Telmo, Punta** *headland* SW Mexico *18.19N 103.30W*
109 O17 **Santeramo in Colle** Puglia, SE Italy *40.46N 16.45E*
107 X5 **Sant Feliu de Guíxols** *var.* San Feliú de Guixols. Cataluña, NE Spain *41.46N 3.01E*
107 W6 **Sant Feliu de Llobregat** Cataluña, NE Spain *41.22N 2.00E*
108 C7 **Santhià** Piemonte, NE Italy *45.21N 8.11E*
63 F15 **Santiago** Rio Grande do Sul, S Brazil *29.10S 54.52W*
64 H11 **Santiago** *var.* Gran Santiago. ● (Chile) Santiago, C Chile *33.30S 70.40W*
47 N8 **Santiago** *var.* Santiago de los Caballeros. N Dominican Republic *19.27N 70.42W*
42 G10 **Santiago** Baja California Sur, W Mexico *23.32N 109.45W*
43 O8 **Santiago** Nuevo León, NE Mexico *25.22N 100.09W*
45 R16 **Santiago** Veraguas, S Panama *8.06N 80.58W*
59 E16 **Santiago** Ica, SW Peru *14.13S 75.43W*
106 G3 **Santiago** *var.* Santiago de Compostela, *Eng.* Compostella; *anc.* Campus Stellae. Galicia, NW Spain *42.52N 8.33W*
64 H11 **Santiago** *off.* Región Metropolitana de Santiago, *var.* Metropolitan. ◆ *region* C Chile
64 H11 **Santiago** ✕ Santiago, C Chile *33.27S 70.40W*
106 G3 **Santiago** ✕ Galicia, NW Spain
78 D10 **Santiago** *var.* São Tiago. *island* Ilhas de Sotavento, S Cape Verde
Santiago *see* Santiago de Cuba, Cuba
Santiago *see* Grande de Santiago, Río, Mexico
44 B6 **Santiago Atitlán** Sololá, SW Guatemala *14.36N 91.13W*
45 Q16 **Santiago, Cerro** ▲ W Panama *8.27N 81.42W*
Santiago de Compostela *see* Santiago
46 I8 **Santiago de Cuba** *var.* Santiago. Santiago de Cuba, E Cuba *20.01N 75.50W*

◆ Country
● Country Capital
◇ Dependent Territory
○ Dependent Territory Capital
◆ Administrative Region
✕ International Airport
▲ Mountain
▲ Mountain Range
⛰ Volcano
~ River
◎ Lake
⊡ Reservoir

Santiago de Guayaquil *see* Guayaquil

64 K8 **Santiago del Estero** Santiago del Estero, C Argentina 27.51S 64.15W

63 A15 **Santiago del Estero** *off.* Provincia de Santiago del Estero. ◆ *province* N Argentina

42 I8 **Santiago de los Caballeros** Sinaloa, W Mexico 25.33N 107.22W
Santiago de los Caballeros *see* Santiago, Dominican Republic
Santiago de los Caballeros *see* Guatemala, Guatemala

44 F8 **Santiago de María** Usulután, SE El Salvador 13.28N 88.28W

106 F12 **Santiago do Cacém** Setúbal, S Portugal 38.01N 8.42W

42 J12 **Santiago Ixcuintla** Nayarit, C Mexico 21.49N 105.07W
Santiago Jamiltepec *see* Jamiltepec

26 L11 **Santiago Mountains** ▲ Texas, SW USA

42 J9 **Santiago Papasquiaro** Durango, C Mexico 25.03N 105.25W
Santiago Pinotepa Nacional *see* Pinotepa Nacional

58 C8 **Santiago, Río** ≈ N Peru

42 M10 **San Tiburcio** Zacatecas, C Mexico 24.07N 101.28W

107 N2 **Santillana** Cantabria, N Spain 43.24N 4.06W

56 I5 **San Timoteo** Zulia, NW Venezuela 9.49N 71.04W
Santi Quaranta *see* Sarandë
Santissima Trinidad *see* Chilung

107 O12 **Santisteban del Puerto** Andalucía, S Spain 38.15N 3.10W

107 U7 **Sant Jordi, Golf de** *gulf* NE Spain

107 U11 **Sant Josep de sa Talaia** *var.* San José, Ibiza, Spain, W Mediterranean Sea 38.55N 1.18E

168 G6 **Santmargats** *var.* Holboo. Dzavhan, W Mongolia 48.35N 95.25E

107 T8 **Sant Mateu** País Valenciano, E Spain 40.28N 0.10E

27 S7 **Santo** Texas, SW USA 32.35N 98.06W
Santo *see* Espiritu Santo

62 M10 **Santo Amaro, Ilha de** *island* SE Brazil

63 G14 **Santo Ângelo** Rio Grande do Sul, S Brazil 28.16S 54.15W

78 C9 **Santo Antão** *island* Ilhas de Barlavento, N Cape Verde

62 J10 **Santo Antônio da Platina** Paraná, S Brazil 23.20S 50.05W

60 C13 **Santo Antônio do Içá** Amazonas, N Brazil 3.04S 67.55W

59 Q18 **Santo Corazón, Río** ≈ E Bolivia

46 E5 **Santo Domingo** Villa Clara, C Cuba 22.34N 80.15W

47 O9 **Santo Domingo** *prev.* Ciudad Trujillo. ● (Dominican Republic) SE Dominican Republic 18.30N 69.57W

42 E8 **Santo Domingo** Baja California Sur, W Mexico 25.31N 111.54W

42 M10 **Santo Domingo** San Luis Potosí, C Mexico 23.18N 101.42W

44 L10 **Santo Domingo** Chontales, S Nicaragua 12.15N 85.06W

107 P4 **Santo Domingo de la Calzada** La Rioja, N Spain 42.25N 2.57W

58 B6 **Santo Domingo de los Colorados** Pichincha, NW Ecuador 0.16S 79.11W
Santo Domingo Tehuantepec *see* Tehuantepec

57 O6 **San Tomé** Anzoátegui, NE Venezuela 8.54N 64.14W
San Tomé de Guayana *see* Ciudad Guayana

107 R13 **Santomera** Murcia, SE Spain 38.03N 1.05W

107 O2 **Santoña** Cantabria, N Spain 43.27N 3.28W
Santorín *see* Santoríni

117 K22 **Santoríni** *var.* Santorin; *prev.* Thíra *anc.* Thera. *island* Kykládes, Greece, Aegean Sea

62 M10 **Santos** São Paulo, S Brazil 23.55S 46.22W

67 J17 **Santos Plateau** *undersea feature* SW Atlantic Ocean

106 G6 **Santo Tirso** Porto, N Portugal 41.20N 8.25W

42 C2 **Santo Tomás** Baja California, NW Mexico 31.31N 116.25W

44 L10 **Santo Tomás** Chontales, S Nicaragua 12.04N 85.01W

44 G5 **Santo Tomás de Castilla** Izabal, E Guatemala 15.40N 88.36W

42 B2 **Santo Tomás, Punta** *headland* NW Mexico 31.30N 116.40W

59 H16 **Santo Tomás, Río** ≈ C Peru

59 J18 **Santo Tomás, Volcán** ⚡ Galapagos Islands, Ecuador, E Pacific Ocean 0.46S 91.01W

63 F14 **Santo Tomé** Corrientes, NE Argentina 28.31S 56.03W
Santo Tomé de Guayana *see* Ciudad Guayana

100 H10 **Santpoort** Noord-Holland, W Netherlands 52.25N 4.37E
Santurce *see* Santurtzi

107 O2 **Santurtzi** *var.* Santurce, Santurzi. País Vasco, N Spain 43.19N 3.03W
Santurzi *see* Santurtzi

65 G20 **San Valentín, Cerro** ▲ S Chile 46.36S 73.17W

44 F8 **San Vicente** San Vicente, C El Salvador 13.37N 88.44W

42 C2 **San Vicente** Baja California, NW Mexico 31.18N 116.12W

196 H6 **San Vicente** Saipan, S Northern Mariana Islands

44 B9 **San Vicente** ◆ *department* E El Salvador

106 I10 **San Vicente de Alcántara** Extremadura, W Spain 39.21N 7.07W

107 N2 **San Vicente de Barakaldo** *var.* Baracaldo, *Basq.* San Bizenti-Barakaldo. País Vasco, N Spain 43.16N 2.58W

59 E15 **San Vicente de Cañete** *var.* Cañete. Lima, W Peru 13.04S 76.25W

106 M2 **San Vicente de la Barquera** Cantabria, N Spain 43.23N 4.24W

56 E12 **San Vicente del Caguán** Caquetá, S Colombia 2.07N 74.46W

44 F8 **San Vicente, Volcán de** ⚡ C El Salvador 13.34N 88.50W

45 O15 **San Vito** Puntarenas, SE Costa Rica 8.49N 82.58W

108 I7 **San Vito al Tagliamento** Friuli-Venezia Giulia, NE Italy 45.54N 12.55E

109 H23 **San Vito, Capo** *headland* Sicilia, Italy, C Mediterranean Sea 38.11N 12.41E

109 P18 **San Vito dei Normanni** Puglia, SE Italy 40.40N 17.42E

166 L17 **Sanya** *var.* Ya Xian. Hainan, S China 18.17N 109.32E

85 J16 **Sanyati** ≈ N Zimbabwe

27 Q16 **San Ygnacio** Texas, SW USA 27.04N 99.25W

186 L6 **Sanyuan** Shaanxi, C China 34.40N 108.55E

126 LJ12 **Sanyyakhtakh** Respublika Sakha (Yakutiya), NE Russian Federation 60.34N 124.09E

152 J15 **S.A.Nyýazow Adyndaky** *Rus.* Imeni S.A.Niyazova. Mary Welaýaty, S Turkmenistan 36.44N 62.23E

84 C10 **Sanza Pombo** Uíge, NW Angola 07.20S 16.00E
Sanzyô *see* Sanjô

106 G14 **São Bartolomeu de Messines** Faro, S Portugal 37.12N 8.16W

62 M10 **São Bernardo do Campo** São Paulo, S Brazil 23.41S 46.29W

63 F15 **São Borja** Rio Grande do Sul, S Brazil 28.34S 56.01W

106 H14 **São Brás de Alportel** Faro, S Portugal 37.09N 7.55W

62 M10 **São Caetano do Sul** São Paulo, S Brazil 23.37S 46.34W

62 L9 **São Carlos** São Paulo, S Brazil 22.01S 47.52W

62 P16 **São Cristóvão** Sergipe, E Brazil 10.58S 37.10W

62 F15 **São Francisco de Assis** Rio Grande do Sul, S Brazil 27.15S 54.55W

60 K13 **São Félix** Pará, NE Brazil 6.43S 51.55W
São Félix *see* São Félix do Araguaia

61 J14 **São Félix do Xingu** Pará, NE Brazil 6.37S 51.58W

62 Q9 **São Fidélis** Rio de Janeiro, SE Brazil 21.37S 41.40W

78 D10 **São Filipe** Fogo, S Cape Verde 14.52N 24.28W

62 K12 **São Francisco** São Paulo, S Brazil 26.16S 48.39W

46 G13 **São Francisco, Ilha de** *island* S Brazil

62 P16 **São Francisco, Rio** ≈ E Brazil

62 G16 **São Gabriel** Rio Grande do Sul, S Brazil 30.20S 54.17W

62 P10 **São Gonçalo** Rio de Janeiro, SE Brazil 22.48S 43.02W

83 H23 **Sao Hill** Iringa, S Tanzania 8.19S 35.10E

62 R9 **São João da Barra** Rio de Janeiro, SE Brazil 21.37S 41.04W

106 G7 **São João da Madeira** Aveiro, N Portugal 40.52N 8.28W

60 M12 **São João de Cortes** Maranhão, E Brazil 2.30S 44.27W

81 M21 **São João del Rei** Minas Gerais, NE Brazil 21.07S 44.15W

61 N15 **São João do Piauí** Piauí, E Brazil 8.21S 42.13W

60 M13 **São João dos Patos** Maranhão, E Brazil 6.28S 43.43W

60 C11 **São Joaquim** Amazonas, NW Brazil 0.08S 67.10W

63 J14 **São Joaquim** Santa Catarina, S Brazil 28.20S 49.55W

62 L7 **São João da Barra** São Paulo, S Brazil 20.36S 47.50W

96 N6 **São Jorge** *island* Azores, Portugal, NE Atlantic Ocean

63 K14 **São José** Santa Catarina, S Brazil 27.34S 48.39W

62 M8 **São José do Rio Pardo** São Paulo, S Brazil 21.37S 46.52W

62 K8 **São José do Rio Preto** São Paulo, S Brazil 20.50S 49.20W

62 N10 **São José dos Campos** São Paulo, S Brazil 23.07S 45.52W

63 H15 **São Lourenço do Sul** Rio Grande do Sul, S Brazil 31.25S 52.00W

60 F11 **São Luís** Roraima, N Brazil 1.11N 60.15W

60 M13 **São Luís** *state capital* Maranhão, NE Brazil 2.34S 44.16W

60 M12 **São Luís, Ilha de** *island* NE Brazil 2.34S 44.16W

63 F14 **São Luiz Gonzaga** Rio Grande do Sul, S Brazil 28.24S 54.58W

106 I10 **São Mamede** ▲ C Portugal 39.18N 7.19W

49 U8 **São Manuel** *see* São Manuel, Rio

61 H15 **São Manuel, Rio** *var.* São Mandol, Teles Pirés. ≈ C Brazil

62 C11 **São Marcelino** Amazonas, NW Brazil 0.53N 67.16W

60 N13 **São Marcos, Baía de** *bay* N Brazil

62 Q9 **São Mateus** Espírito Santo, SE Brazil 18.43S 39.52W

62 J12 **São Mateus do Sul** Paraná, S Brazil 25.51S 50.24W

96 P3 **São Miguel** *island* Azores, Portugal, NE Atlantic Ocean

62 G13 **São Miguel d'Oeste** Santa Catarina, S Brazil 26.45S 53.34W

47 P9 **Saona, Isla** *island* SE Dominican Republic

180 H12 **Saondzou** ▲ Grande Comore, NW Comoros

105 R14 **Saône** ≈ E France

105 Q9 **Saône-et-Loire** ◆ *department* C France

78 D9 **São Nicolau** *Eng.* Saint Nicholas. *island* Ilhas de Barlavento, N Cape Verde

32 L15 **Sara, Lake** ⊚ Illinois, N USA

25 N8 **Saraland** Alabama, S USA 30.49N 88.04W

62 M10 **São Paulo** *state capital* São Paulo, S Brazil 23.33S 46.39W

62 K9 **São Paulo** *off.* Estado de São Paulo. ◆ *state* S Brazil
São Paulo de Loanda *see* Luanda

62 I7 **São Pedro do Rio Grande do Sul** *see* Rio Grande

106 H7 **São Pedro do Sul** Viseu, N Portugal 40.46N 7.58W

62 K7 **São Pedro e São Paulo** *undersea feature* C Atlantic Ocean 1.25N 28.54W

61 M14 **São Raimundo das Mangabeiras** Maranhão, E Brazil 07.00S 45.30W

61 Q14 **São Roque, Cabo de** *headland* E Brazil 5.28S 35.16W
São Salvador/São Salvador do Congo *see* M'Banza Congo, Angola
São Salvador *see* Salvador, Brazil

62 N10 **São Sebastião, Ilha de** *island* S Brazil

85 N19 **São Sebastião, Ponta** *headland* C Mozambique 22.09S 35.33E

106 F13 **São Teotónio** Beja, S Portugal 37.30N 8.41W
São Tiago *see* Santiago

62 B18 **São Tomé** ● (Sao Tome and Principe) São Tomé, S Sao Tome and Principe 0.25N 6.39E

62 B18 **São Tomé** × São Tomé, S Sao Tome and Principe 0.23N 6.43E

62 B18 **São Tomé** *Eng.* Saint Thomas. *island* S Sao Tome and Principe

62 B17 **Sao Tome and Principe** *off.* Democratic Republic of Sao Tome and Principe. ◆ *republic* E Atlantic Ocean

76 H9 **Saoura, Oued** ≈ NW Algeria

62 M10 **São Vicente** S Brazil. São Paulo, S Brazil 23.55S 46.25W

106 O5 **São Vicente** Madeira, Portugal, NE Atlantic Ocean 32.48N 17.03W

78 C9 **São Vicente** *Eng.* Saint Vincent. *island* Ilhas de Barlavento, N Cape Verde
São Vicente, Cabo de *see* São Vicente, Cabo de

106 F14 **São Vicente, Cabo de** *Eng.* Cape Saint Vincent, *Port.* Cabo de São Vicente. *headland* S Portugal 37.01N 9.01W
Sápai *see* Sápes
Sapaleri, Cerro *see* Zapaleri, Cerro

175 T11 **Saparua, Pulau** *island* E Indonesia
Saparoea *see* Saparua

175 T11 **Saparua** *prev.* Saparoea. Pulau Saparua, C Indonesia 3.34S 128.37E

174 Hh8 **Sapat** Sumatera, W Indonesia 0.18S 103.18E

59 U17 **Sapele** Delta, S Nigeria 5.54N 5.43E

25 X7 **Sapelo Island** *island* Georgia, SE USA

25 X7 **Sapelo Sound** *sound* Georgia, SE USA

116 K13 **Sápes** *var.* Sápai. Anatolikí Makedonía kai Thráki, NE Greece 41.01N 25.42E

175 P16 **Sape, Selat** *strait* Nusa Tenggara, S Indonesia

117 D22 **Sapiénza** *var.* Sapiéntza. *island* S Greece
Sapiénza *see* Sapiénza
Sapir *see* Sappir

52 I15 **Sapiranga** Rio Grande do Sul, S Brazil 29.39S 50.58W

158 L11 **Sárda** *Nep.* Kali. ≈ India/Nepal

158 G10 **Sardárshahr** Rājasthān, NW India 28.24N 74.32E

109 C18 **Sardegna** *Eng.* Sardinia. ◆ *region* Italy, C Mediterranean Sea

109 A18 **Sardegna** *Eng.* Sardinia. *island* Italy, C Mediterranean Sea
Sardinal Guanacaste, NW Costa Rica 10.30N 85.38W
Sardinia *see* Sardegna

123 K8 **Sardinia-Corsica Trough** *undersea feature* Tyrrhenian Sea, C Mediterranean Sea

24 L2 **Sardis** Mississippi, S USA 34.25N 89.55W

24 L2 **Sardis Lake** ⊚ Mississippi, S USA

107 S8 **Sarrión** Aragón, NE Spain 40.09N 0.49W

94 H11 **Sarek** ▲ N Sweden

94 H11 **Sarektjåhkkå** ▲ N Sweden 67.28N 17.56E

155 N3 **Sar-e Pol** *var.* Sar-i-Pul, Sar-e Pol, N Afghanistan 36.16N 65.55E

155 O3 **Sar-e Pol** *var.* Sar-e Pol. ◆ *province* N Afghanistan

148 J6 **Sar-e Pol-e Ẕahāb** *var.* Sar-e Pol, Sar-i Pul, Kermānshāh, W Iran 34.28N 45.52E

155 U8 **Sārābādi** E Iraq 33.00N 44.52E
Sāqqiz *see* Saqqez

62 N10 **São dos Campos** São Paulo, S Brazil 23.07S 45.52W

45 W12 **Sarstoon** ≈ Belize/Guatemala
Sarstún, Río *see* Sarstoon

25 M9 **Sartang** ≈ NE Russian Federation

105 X16 **Sartène** Corse, France, C Mediterranean Sea 41.37N 8.58E

104 K7 **Sarthe** ◆ *department* NW France

104 K7 **Sarthe** ≈ N France

117 H15 **Sárti** Kentrikí Makedonía, N Greece 40.04N 23.59E

127 V5 **Sartoba** Samarskaya Oblast', W Russian Federation 53.05N 51.09E

172 Pp2 **Sarufutsu** Hokkaidō, NE Japan 45.17N 142.24E

172 Oo7 **Saru-gawa** ≈ Hokkaidō, NE Japan

27 X10 **Saratoga** Texas, SW USA 30.15N 94.31W

20 K10 **Saratoga Springs** New York, NE USA 43.04N 73.47W

131 P8 **Saratov** Saratovskaya Oblast', W Russian Federation 51.33N 45.57E

131 P8 **Saratovskaya Oblast'** ◆ *province* W Russian Federation

131 Q7 **Saratovskoye Vodokhranilishche** ⊞ W Russian Federation

172 Q5 **Saroma** Hokkaidō, NE Japan 44.01N 143.43E

172 Q5 **Saroma-ko** ⊚ Hokkaidō, NE Japan

117 H20 **Saronikós Kólpos** *Eng.* Saronic Gulf. *gulf* S Greece
Saronic Gulf *see* Saronikós Kólpos

108 D7 **Saronno** Lombardia, N Italy 45.37N 9.01E

142 B11 **Saros Körfezi** *gulf* NW Turkey

111 N20 **Sárospatak** Borsod-Abaúj-Zemplén, NE Hungary 48.18N 21.36E

131 O4 **Sarova** Respublika Mordoviya, W Russian Federation 54.39N 43.09E
Sarova *see* Sarov

131 P12 **Sarpa, Ozero** ⊚ SW Russian Federation

131 P12 **Sarpa** Respublika Kalmykiya, SW Russian Federation 47.00N 45.42E

131 P12 **Sarpa, Ozero** ⊚ SW Russian Federation

95 J16 **Sarpsborg** Østfold, S Norway 59.16N 11.09E

105 U4 **Sarralbe** Moselle, NE France 48.59N 7.01E
Sarre *see* Saar, France/Germany
Sarre *see* Saarland, Germany

105 U5 **Sarrebourg** *Ger.* Saarburg. Moselle, NE France 48.44N 7.03E
Sarrebruck *see* Saarbrücken

105 U4 **Sarreguemines** *prev.* Saargemund. Moselle, NE France 49.06N 7.04E

106 I3 **Sarria** Galicia, NW Spain 42.46N 7.25W

107 S8 **Sarrión** Aragón, NE Spain 40.09N 0.49W

44 F4 **Sarstoon** ≈ Belize/Guatemala

196 M16 **Satawal** *island* Caroline Islands, C Micronesia

201 R17 **Satawan Atoll** *atoll* Mortlock Islands, C Micronesia

25 Y12 **Satellite Beach** Florida, SE USA 28.10N 80.35W

104 K13 **Sauveterre-de-Guyenne** Gironde, SW France 44.43N 0.02W

121 O14 **Sava** *Rus.* Sava. Mahilyowskaya Voblasts', E Belarus 53.57N 30.47E

86 H11 **Sava** *Eng.* Save, *Ger.* Sau, *Hung.* Száva. ≈ SE Europe

44 J5 **Savá** Colón, N Honduras 15.30N 86.12W

35 Y8 **Savage** Montana, NW USA 47.28N 104.17W

191 N16 **Savage River** Tasmania, SE Australia 41.34S 145.15E

198 Aa7 **Savaiʻi** *island* NW Samoa

176 V8 **Savalou** S Benin 7.58N 1.58E

32 K10 **Savanna** Illinois, N USA 42.05N 90.09W

25 X6 **Savannah** Georgia, SE USA 32.01N 81.00W

29 R2 **Savannah** Missouri, C USA 39.56N 94.49W

22 H10 **Savannah** Tennessee, S USA 35.13N 88.15W

23 O12 **Savannah River** ≈ Georgia/ South Carolina, SE USA
Savannakhét *see* Khanthabouli

46 H12 **Savanna-La-Mar** W Jamaica 18.13N 78.07W

161 F17 **Savanūr** Karnātaka, W India 14.58N 75.05E

95 J16 **Sävar** Västerbotten, N Sweden 63.52N 20.33E
Savaria *see* Szombathely

160 C11 **Sāvarkundla** *var.* Kundla. Gujarāt, W India 21.21N 71.20E

118 F11 **Săveni** Botoşani, N Romania 47.57N 26.49E
Săvîrşin, Hung. Soborsin; *prev.* Săvîrşin. Arad, W Romania 46.00N 22.15E

142 L5 **Savaştepe** Balıkesir, W Turkey 39.19N 27.37E
Savat *see* Savot
Sávdijárś *see* Skaulo

85 N18 **Save** Inhambane, E Mozambique 21.07S 34.35E

85 L17 **Save** *var.* Sabi. ≈ Mozambique/ Zimbabwe *see also* Sabi
Save *see* Sava

79 R15 **Savè** SE Benin 8.04N 2.28E

148 M6 **Saveh** Markazī, W Iran 35.03N 50.21E

63 C16 **Sauce Corrientes** NE Argentina 30.07S 58.50W
Sauce *see* Juan L.Lacaze

105 N16 **Sauveterre Ariège, S France** 43.15N 1.34E

105 U5 **Saverne** *var.* Zabern; *anc.* Tres Tabernae. Bas-Rhin, NE France 48.45N 7.22E

NORTH AMERICA

CANADA
PAGES 8–16

UNITED STATES OF AMERICA
PAGES 17–41

MEXICO
PAGES 42–43

BELIZE
PAGES 44–45

COSTA RICA
PAGES 44–45

EL SALVADOR
PAGES 44–45

GUATEMALA
PAGES 44–45

HONDURAS
PAGES 44–45

SOUTH AMERICA

GRENADA
PAGES 46–47

HAITI
PAGES 46–47

JAMAICA
PAGES 46–47

ST KITTS & NEVIS
PAGES 46–47

ST LUCIA
PAGES 46–47

ST VINCENT & THE GRENADINES
PAGES 46–47

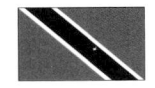
TRINIDAD & TOBAGO
PAGES 46–47

COLOMBIA
PAGES 56–57

AFRICA

URUGUAY
PAGES 62–63

CHILE
PAGES 64–65

PARAGUAY
PAGES 64–65

ALGERIA
PAGES 76–77

EGYPT
PAGES 76–77

LIBYA
PAGES 76–77

MOROCCO
PAGES 76–77

TUNISIA
PAGES 76–77

LIBERIA
PAGES 78–79

MALI
PAGES 78–79

MAURITANIA
PAGES 78–79

NIGER
PAGES 78–79

NIGERIA
PAGES 78–79

SENEGAL
PAGES 78–79

SIERRA LEONE
PAGES 78–79

TOGO
PAGES 78–79

BURUNDI
PAGES 82–83

DJIBOUTI
PAGES 82–83

ERITREA
PAGES 82–83

ETHIOPIA
PAGES 82–83

KENYA
PAGES 82–83

RWANDA
PAGES 82–83

SOMALIA
PAGES 82–83

SUDAN
PAGES 82–83

EUROPE

SOUTH AFRICA
PAGES 84–85

SWAZILAND
PAGES 84–85

ZAMBIA
PAGES 84–85

ZIMBABWE
PAGES 84–85

DENMARK
PAGES 94–97

FINLAND
PAGES 94–95

ICELAND
PAGES 94–95

NORWAY
PAGES 94–97

MONACO
PAGES 104–105

ANDORRA
PAGES 106–107

PORTUGAL
PAGES 106–107

SPAIN
PAGES 106–107

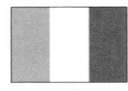
ITALY
PAGES 108–109

SAN MARINO
PAGES 108–109

VATICAN CITY
PAGES 108–109

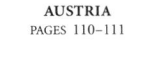
AUSTRIA
PAGES 110–111

BOSNIA & HERZEGOVINA
PAGES 114–115

CROATIA
PAGES 114–115

MACEDONIA
PAGES 114–115

MONTENEGRO
PAGES 114–115

SERBIA
PAGES 114–115

BULGARIA
PAGES 116–117

GREECE
PAGES 116–117

MOLDOVA
PAGES 118–119

ASIA

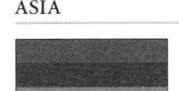
ARMENIA
PAGES 142–143

AZERBAIJAN
PAGES 142–143

GEORGIA
PAGES 142–143

TURKEY
PAGES 142–143/116–117

IRAQ
PAGES 144–145

ISRAEL
PAGES 144–145

JORDAN
PAGES 144–145

LEBANON
PAGES 144–145

IRAN
PAGES 148–149

KAZAKHSTAN
PAGES 150–151

KYRGYZSTAN
PAGES 152–153

TAJIKISTAN
PAGES 152–153

TURKMENISTAN
PAGES 152–153

UZBEKISTAN
PAGES 152–153

AFGHANISTAN
PAGES 154–155

PAKISTAN
PAGES 154–157

TAIWAN
PAGES 166–167

JAPAN
PAGES 170–172

BURMA
PAGES 173–176

CAMBODIA
PAGES 173–176

LAOS
PAGES 173–176

PHILIPPINES
PAGES 173–176

THAILAND
PAGES 177–179

VIETNAM
PAGES 177–179

AUSTRALASIA & OCEANIA

MAURITIUS
PAGES 180–181

SEYCHELLES
PAGES 180–181

AUSTRALIA
PAGES 188–191

NEW ZEALAND
PAGES 192–193

PAPUA NEW GUINEA
PAGES 194–195

FIJI
PAGES 194–195

SOLOMON ISLANDS
PAGES 196/201

VANUATU
PAGES 196/201

Selected glossary

Abyssal plain A broad plain found in the depths of the ocean, more than 10,000 ft (3000 m) below sea level.

Air mass A huge, homogeneous mass of air, within which horizontal patterns of temperature and humidity are consistent. Air masses are separated by fronts.

Alluvial fan Large fan-shaped deposit of fine *sediments* deposited by a river as it emerges from a narrow, mountain valley onto a broad, open plain.

Alluvium Material deposited by rivers. Nowadays usually only applied to finer particles of silt and clay.

Anticline A geological fold which forms an arch shape, curving upwards in the rock strata.

Aquifer A body of rock which can absorb water.

Arête A thin, jagged mountain ridge which divides two adjacent cirques, found in regions where *glaciation* has occurred.

Artesian well A naturally occurring source of underground water, stored in an *aquifer*.

Atoll A ring-shaped island or coral reef often enclosing a lagoon of sea water.

Badlands A landscape that has been heavily *eroded* and dissected by rainwater, and which has little or no vegetation.

Back slope The gentler windward slope of a sand dune or gentler slope of a *cuesta*.

Bajos An *alluvial fan* deposited by a river at the base of mountains and hills that encircle desert areas.

Bar, coastal An offshore strip of sand or shingle, either above or below the water. Usually parallel to the shore but sometimes crescent-shaped or at an oblique angle.

Barchan A crescent-shaped sand dune, formed where wind direction is very consistent. The horns of the crescent point downwind and where there is enough sand the barchan is mobile.

Base level The level below which flowing water cannot erode the land.

Basement rock A mass of ancient rock often of *Pre-Cambrian* age, covered by a layer of more recent *sedimentary rocks*. Commonly associated with *shield* areas.

Bedrock Solid, consolidated and relatively unweathered rock, found on the surface of the land or just below a layer of soil or weathered rock.

Bluff The steep bank of a meander, formed by the erosive action of a river.

Breccia A type of rock composed of sharp fragments, cemented by a fine-grained material such as clay.

Butte An isolated, flat-topped hill with steep or vertical sides, buttes are the eroded remnants of a former land surface.

Calcite Hexagonal crystals of calcium carbonate.

Caldera A huge volcanic vent, often containing a number of smaller vents, and sometimes a crater lake.

Carbonation Process whereby rocks are broken down by carbonic acid. Carbon dioxide in the air dissolves in rainwater, forming carbonic acid.

Castle kopje Hill or rock outcrop, especially in southern Africa, where steep sides, and a summit composed of blocks, give a castle-like appearance.

Cataracts A series of stepped waterfalls created as a river flows over a band of hard, resistant rock.

Chernozem A fertile soil, also known as 'black earth' consisting of a layer of dark topsoil, rich in decaying vegetation, overlying a lighter chalky layer.

Confluence The point at which two rivers meet.

Continental drift The theory that the continents of today are fragments of one or more prehistoric *supercontinents* which have moved across the Earth's surface, creating ocean basins.

Continental shelf An area of the continental *crust*, below sea level, which slopes gently.

Continental slope A steep slope running from the edge of the continental shelf to the ocean floor.

Core The centre of the Earth, consisting of a dense mass of iron and nickel.

Coulées A US / Canadian term for a ravine formed by river *erosion*.

Craton A large block of the Earth's *crust* which has remained stable for a long period of geological time. It is made up of ancient *shield* rocks.

Cretaceous A period of geological time beginning about 145 million years ago and lasting until c. 65 million years ago.

Crevasse A deep crack in a *glacier*.

Crust The hard, thin outer shell of the Earth. It floats on the *mantle*, which is softer and more dense.

Crystalline rock Rocks formed when molten *magma* crystallizes (*igneous rocks*) or when heat or pressure cause re-crystallization (*metamorphic rocks*).

Cuesta A hill which rises into a steep slope on one side but has a gentler gradient on its other slope.

Delta Low-lying, fan-shaped area at a river mouth, formed by the *deposition* of successive layers of *sediment*.

Denudation The combined effect of *weathering*, *erosion*, and mass movement, which, over long periods, exposes underlying rocks.

Deposition The laying down of material that has accumulated: after being eroded and then transported by wind, ice, or water; as organic remains, such as coal and coral; as the result of evaporation and chemical *precipitation*.

Depression 1 In climatic terms it is a large low pressure system; 2 a complex fold, producing a large valley, which incorporates both a *syncline* and an *anticline*.

Detritus Piles of rock deposited by an erosive agent such as a river or *glacier*.

Distributary A minor branch of a river, which does not rejoin the main stream, common at *deltas*.

Divide A US term describing the area of high ground separating two *drainage basins*.

Donga A steep-sided gully, resulting from *erosion* by a river or by floods.

Drainage basin The area drained by a single river system, its boundary is marked by a *watershed* or *divide*.

Drumlin A long, streamlined hillock composed of material deposited by a *glacier*. They often occur in groups known as swarms.

Earthflow The rapid movement of soil and other loose surface material down a slope, when saturated by water.

Ephemeral A non-permanent feature, often used in connection with seasonal rivers or lakes in dry areas.

Epicentre The point on the Earth's surface directly above the underground origin or focus of an earthquake.

Erg An extensive area of sand dunes, particularly in the Sahara.

Erosion The processes which wear away the surface of the land. *Glaciers*, wind, rivers, waves and currents all carry debris that causes erosion.

Escarpment A steep slope at the margin of a level, upland surface. In a landscape created by folding, escarpments (or scarps) frequently lie behind a more gentle backward slope.

Esker A narrow, winding ridge of sand and gravel deposited by streams of water flowing beneath or at the edge of a *glacier*.

Erratic A rock transported by a *glacier* and deposited some distance from its place of origin.

Eustacy A world-wide fall or rise in ocean levels.

Exfoliation A kind of *weathering* whereby scale-like flakes of rock are peeled or broken off by the development of salt crystals in water within the rocks.

Extrusive rock *Igneous rock* formed when molten material (*magma*) pours forth at the Earth's surface and cools rapidly. It usually has a glassy texture.

Fault A fracture or crack in rock, where strains (*tectonic* movement) have caused blocks to move, vertically or laterally, relative to each other.

Ferrel cell A component in the global pattern of air circulation, which rises in the colder *latitudes* (60° N and S) and descends in warmer latitudes (30° N and S).

Fissure A deep crack in a rock or a *glacier*.

Fjord A deep, narrow inlet, created when the sea inundates the *U-shaped valley* created by a *glacier*.

Flash flood A sudden, short-lived rise in the water level of a river or stream, or surge of water down a dry river channel, or wadi, caused by heavy rainfall.

Flood plain The broad, flat part of a river valley, adjacent to the river itself, formed by *sediment* deposited during flooding.

Fold A bend in the rock strata of the Earth's *crust*, resulting from compression.

Frost shattering A form of *weathering* where water freezes in cracks, causing expansion. As temperatures fluctuate and the ice melts and refreezes, it eventually causes the rocks to shatter.

Geosyncline A concave fold (*syncline*) or large depression in the Earth's *crust*, extending hundreds of kilometres.

Geothermal energy Heat derived from hot rocks within the Earth's *crust* and resulting in hot springs, steam, or hot rocks at the surface.

Geyser A jet of steam and hot water that intermittently erupts from vents in the ground in areas that are, or were, volcanic.

Glaciation The growth of *glaciers* and *ice sheets*, and their impact on the landscape.

Glacier A body of ice moving down-slope under the influence of gravity and consisting of compacted and frozen snow.

Glacio-eustacy A worldwide change in the level of the oceans, caused when the formation of *ice sheets* takes up water or when their melting returns water to the ocean.

Glaciofluvial To do with glacial *meltwater*, the landforms it creates and its processes; *erosion*, transportation and *deposition*.

Glacis A gentle slope or pediment.

Gondwanaland The *supercontinent* thought to have existed over 200 million years ago in the southern hemisphere.

Graben A block of rock let down between two parallel faults. Where the graben occurs within a valley, the structure is known as a *rift valley*.

Grease ice Slicks of ice that form in Antarctic seas, when ice crystals are bonded together by wind and wave action.

Groundwater Water that has seeped into the pores, cavities, and cracks of rocks or into soil and water held in an *aquifer*.

Gully A deep, narrow channel eroded in the landscape by ephemeral streams.

Guyot A small, flat-topped submarine mountain, formed as a result of subsidence which occurs during *sea-floor spreading*.

Hadley cell A large-scale component in the global pattern of air circulation. Warm air rises over the Equator and blows at high altitude toward the poles, sinking in subtropical regions (30° N and 30° S) and creating high pressure. The air then flows at the surface towards the Equator in the form of trade winds.

Hamada An Arabic word for a plateau of bare rock in a desert.

Hanging valley A tributary valley that ends suddenly, high above the bed of the main valley.

Headwards The action of a river eroding back upstream, as opposed to the normal process of downstream *erosion*. Headwards erosion is often associated with gullying.

Hoodos Pinnacles of rock which have been worn away by *weathering* in semi-arid regions.

Horst A block of the Earth's crust that has been left upstanding by the sinking of adjoining blocks along fault lines.

Hot spot A region of the Earth's *crust* where high thermal activity occurs, often leading to volcanic eruptions.

Hydrolysis The chemical breakdown of rocks in reaction with water, forming new compounds.

Ice Age A period in the Earth's history when surface temperatures in the temperate *latitudes* were much lower and ice sheets expanded considerably. There have been ice ages from *Pre-Cambrian* times onwards.

Ice cap A permanent dome of ice in highland areas.

Ice floe A large, flat mass of ice floating free on the ocean surface. It is usually formed after the break-up of winter ice by heavy storms.

Ice sheet A continuous, very thick layer of ice and snow. The term is usually used of ice masses which are continental in extent.

Ice shelf A floating mass of ice attached to the edge of a coast. The seaward edge is usually a sheer cliff up to 100 ft (30 m) high.

Ice wedge Massive blocks of ice up to 6.5 ft (2 m) wide at the top and extending 32 ft (10 m) deep.

Iceberg A large mass of ice in a lake or a sea, which has broken off from a floating ice sheet (an *ice shelf*) or from a *glacier*.

Igneous rock Rock formed when molten material, *magma*, from the hot, lower layers of the Earth's crust, cools, solidifies, and crystallizes, either within the Earth's *crust* (intrusive) or on the surface (extrusive).

Inselberg An isolated, steep-sided hill, rising from a low plain in semi-arid and savannah landscapes.

Interglacial A period of global climate, between two *ice ages*, when temperatures rise and *ice sheets* and *glaciers* retreat.

Intraplate volcano A volcano that lies in the centre of one of the Earth's *tectonic plates*, rather than, as is more common, at its edge.

Intrusion (intrusive *igneous rock*) Rock formed when molten material, *magma*, penetrates existing rocks below the Earth's surface before cooling and solidifying.

Isostasy The state of equilibrium that the Earth's *crust* maintains as its lighter and heavier parts float on the denser underlying *mantle*.

Isthmus A narrow strip of land connecting two larger landmasses or islands.

Joint A crack in a rock, formed where blocks of rock have not shifted relative to each other, as is the case with a *fault*. Joints are created by folding; by shrinkage in *igneous rock* as it cools or *sedimentary rock* as it dries out; and by the release of pressure in a rock mass when overlying materials are removed by *erosion*.

Kame A mound of stratified sand and gravel with steep sides, deposited in a *crevasse* by *meltwater* running over a *glacier*. When the ice retreats, this forms an undulating terrain of hummocks.

Karst A barren limestone landscape created by carbonic acid in streams and rainwater, in areas where limestone is close to the surface.

Kettle hole A round hollow formed in a glacial deposit by a detached block of glacial ice, which later melted. They can fill with water to form kettle-lakes.

Lagoon A shallow stretch of coastal salt-water behind a partial barrier such as a sandbank or coral reef. Also used to describe the water encircled by an *atoll*.

Laterite A hard red deposit left by chemical *weathering* in tropical conditions, and consisting mainly of oxides of iron and aluminium.

Latitude The angular distance from the Equator, to a given point on the Earth's surface. Imaginary lines of latitude running parallel to the Equator encircle the Earth, and are measured in degrees north or south of the Equator. The Equator is 0°, the poles 90° South and North respectively. Also called parallels.

Laurasia In the theory of *continental drift*, the northern part of the great *supercontinent* of Pangaea. Laurasia is said to consist of North America, Greenland and all of Eurasia north of the Indian subcontinent.

Lava The molten rock, *magma*, which erupts onto the Earth's surface through a volcano, or through a *fault* or crack in the Earth's *crust*.

Leaching The process whereby water dissolves minerals and moves them down through layers of soil or rock.

Levée A raised bank alongside the channel of a river. Levées are either man-made or formed in times of flood when the river overflows its channel, slows and *deposits* much of its *sediment* load.

Lithosphere The rigid, upper layer of the Earth, comprising the *crust* and the upper part of the *mantle*.

Loess Fertile, fine-grained, yellow deposits of unstratified silts and sands.

Longitude A division of the Earth which pinpoints how far east or west a given place is from the Prime Meridian (0°) which runs through the Royal Observatory at Greenwich, England (UK). Imaginary lines of longitude are drawn around the world from pole to pole. The world is divided into 360 degrees.

Longshore drift The movement of sand and silt along the coast, carried by waves hitting the beach at an angle.

Magma Underground, molten rock, which is very hot and highly charged with gas. It is generated at great pressure, at depths 10 miles (16 km) or more below the Earth's surface.

Mantle The layer of the Earth between the *crust* and the *core*. It is about 1800 miles (2900 km) thick.

Massif A single very large mountain or an area of mountains with uniform characteristics and clearly defined boundaries.

Meltwater Water resulting from the melting of a *glacier* or *ice sheet*.

Mesa A broad, flat-topped hill, characteristic of arid regions.

Metamorphic rocks Rocks which have been altered from their original form, in terms of texture, composition and structure by intense heat, pressure or by the introduction of new chemical substances – or a combination of more than one of these.

Milankovitch hypothesis A theory suggesting that there are a series of cycles that slightly alter the Earth's position when rotating about the Sun.

Mistral A strong, dry, cold northerly or north-westerly wind, which blows from the Massif Central of France to the Mediterranean Sea.

Mohorovicic discontinuity (Moho) The structural divide at the margin between the Earth's *crust* and the *mantle*. On average it is 20 miles (35 km) below the continents and 6 miles (10 km) below the oceans.

Monsoon A wind which changes direction bi-annually. The change is caused by the reversal of pressure over landmasses and the adjacent oceans. Because the inflowing moist winds bring rain, the term monsoon is also used to refer to the rains themselves.

Moraine Debris, transported and deposited by a *glacier or ice sheet* in unstratified, mixed, piles of rock, boulders, pebbles and clay.

Mountain-building The formation of fold mountains by tectonic activity. Also known as orogeny, mountain-building often occurs on the margin where two *tectonic plates* collide.

Nappe A mass of rocks which has been overfolded by repeated thrust faulting.

Oasis A fertile area in the midst of a desert, usually watered by an underground *aquifer*.

Oceanic ridge A mid-ocean ridge formed, according to the theory of plate tectonics, when plates drift apart and hot *magma* pours through to form new oceanic crust.

Onion-skin weathering The weathering away or exfoliation of a rock or outcrop by the peeling off of surface layers.

Outwash plain Glaciofluvial material (typically clay, sand and gravel) carried beyond an *ice sheet* by *meltwater* streams, forming a broad, flat deposit.

Oxbow lake A crescent-shaped lake formed on a river *flood plain* when a river erodes the outside bend of a meander, making the neck of the meander narrower until the river cuts across the neck. The meander is cut off and is dammed off with *sediment*, creating an oxbow lake.

Oxidation A form of chemical *weathering* where oxygen dissolved in water reacts with minerals in rocks – particularly iron to form oxides.

Pack ice Ice masses more than 10 ft (3 m) thick that form on the sea surface and are not attached to a landmass.

Pancake ice Thin discs of ice, up to 8 ft (2.4 m) wide which form when slicks of *grease ice* are tossed together by winds and stormy seas.

Pangaea In the theory of *continental drift*, Pangaea is the original great land mass which, about 190 million years ago, began to split into Gondwanaland in the south and Laurasia in the north, separated by the Tethys Sea.

Pediment A gently sloping ramp of bedrock below a steeper slope, often found at mountain edges in desert areas, but also in other climatic zones. Pediments may include depositional elements such as *alluvial fans*.

Periglacial Regions on the edges of *ice sheets* or *glaciers* or, more commonly, cold regions experiencing intense frost action, permafrost or both.

Permafrost Permanently frozen ground, typical of Arctic regions.

Permeable rocks Rocks through which water can seep, because they are either porous or cracked.

Phreatic eruption A volcanic eruption which occurs when lava combines with groundwater, superheating the water and causing a sudden emission of steam at the surface.

Pingo A dome of earth with a core of ice, found in tundra regions. Pingos are formed either when groundwater freezes and expands, pushing up the land surface, or when trapped, freezing water in a lake expands and pushes up lake sediments to form the pingo dome.

Placer A belt of mineral-bearing rock strata lying at or close to the Earth's surface, from which minerals can be easily extracted.

Plate, plate tectonics The study of tectonic plates, that helps to explain *continental drift*, mountain formation and volcanic activity. The movement of tectonic plates may be explained by the currents of rock rising and falling from within the Earth's *mantle*, as it heats up and then cools. The boundaries of the plates are known as plate margins and most mountains, earthquakes and volcanoes occur at these margins. Constructive margins are moving apart; destructive margins are crunching together and conservative margins are sliding past one another.

Pleistocene A period of geological time spanning from about 5.2 million years ago to 1.6 million years ago.

Plutonic rock Igneous rocks found deep below the surface. They are coarse-grained because they cooled and solidified slowly.

Polje A long, broad depression found in karst (limestone) regions.

Polygonal patterning Typical ground patterning, found in areas where the soil is subject to severe frost action, often in *periglacial* regions.

Porosity A measure of how much water can be held within a rock or a soil.

Pre-Cambrian The earliest period of geological time dating from over 570 million years ago.

Precipitation The fall of moisture from the atmosphere onto the surface of the Earth, whether as dew, hail, rain, sleet or snow.

Pyramidal peak A steep, isolated mountain summit, formed when the back walls of three or more cirques are cut back and move towards each other. The cliffs around such a horned peak, or horn, are divided by sharp *arêtes*.

Pyroclasts Fragments of rock ejected during volcanic eruptions.

Quaternary The current period of geological time, which started about 1.6 million years ago.

Reg A large area of stony desert, where tightly-packed gravel lies on top of clayey sand. A reg is formed where the wind blows away the finer sand.

Resistance The capacity of a rock to resist denudation, by processes such as *weathering* and *erosion*.

Ria A flooded *V-shaped river valley* or estuary, flooded by a rise in sea level (eustacy) or sinking land. It is shorter than a fjord and gets deeper as it meets the sea.

Rift valley A long, narrow depression in the Earth's crust, formed by the sinking of rocks between two faults.

Roche moutonée A rock found in a glaciated valley. The side facing the flow of the glacier has been smoothed and rounded, while the other side has been left more rugged because the *glacier*, as it flows over it, has plucked out frozen fragments and carried them away.

Runoff Water draining from a land surface by flowing across it.

Sabkha The floor of an isolated depression that occurs in an arid environment – usually covered by salt deposits and devoid of vegetation.

Salt plug A rounded hill produced by the upward doming of rock strata caused by the movement of salt or other evaporite deposits under intense pressure.

Sastrugi Ice ridges formed by wind action. They lie parallel to the direction of the wind.

Scree Piles of rock fragments beneath a cliff or rock face, caused by mechanical *weathering*, especially *frost shattering*, where the expansion and contraction of freezing and thawing water within the rock, gradually breaks it up.

Sea-floor spreading The process whereby *tectonic plates* move apart, allowing hot magma to erupt and solidify.

Seamount An isolated, submarine mountain or hill, probably of volcanic origin.

Sediment Grains of rock transported and deposited by rivers, sea, ice or wind.

Sedimentary rocks Rocks formed from the debris of pre-existing rocks or of organic material. They are found in many environments on the ocean floor, on beaches, rivers and deserts.

Seif A sand dune which lies parallel to the direction of the prevailing wind. Seifs form steep-sided ridges, sometimes extending for miles.

Selva A region of wet forest found in the Amazon Basin.

Shale (marine shale) A compacted *sedimentary rock*, with fine-grained particles. Marine shale is formed on the seabed. Fuel such as oil may be extracted from it.

Sheetwash Water that runs downhill in thin sheets without forming channels. It can cause *sheet erosion*.

Sheet erosion The washing away of soil by a thin film or sheet of water, known as *sheetwash*.

Shield A vast stable block of the Earth's *crust*, which has experienced little or no mountain-building.

Sinkhole A circular depression in a limestone region. They are formed by the collapse of an underground cave system or the chemical *weathering* of the limestone.

Slip face The steep leeward side of a sand dune or slope. Opposite side to a back slope.

Soil creep The very gradual downslope movement of rock debris and soil, under the influence of gravity. This is a type of mass movement.

Solifluction A kind of soil creep, where water in the surface layer has saturated the soil and rock debris which slips slowly downhill. It often happens where frozen top-layer deposits thaw, leaving frozen layers below them.

Spit A thin linear deposit of sand or shingle extending from the sea shore.

Stack A tall, isolated pillar of rock near a coastline, created as wave action erodes away the adjacent rock.

Strike-slip fault Occurs where plates move sideways past each other and blocks of rocks move horizontally in relation to each other, not up or down as in normal faults.

Subduction zone A region where two *tectonic plates* collide, forcing one beneath the other.

Submarine fan Deposits of silt and alluvium, carried by large rivers forming great fan-shaped deposits on the ocean floor.

Supercontinent A large continent that breaks up to form smaller continents or that forms when smaller continents merge.

Syncline A basin-shaped downfold in rock strata, created when the strata are compressed, for example where *tectonic plates* collide.

Tableland A highland area with a flat or gently undulating surface.

Tectonic plates Plates, or tectonic plates, are the rigid slabs which form the Earth's outer shell, the *lithosphere*. Eight big plates and several smaller ones have been identified.

Thermokarst Subsidence created by the thawing of ground ice in *periglacial* areas, creating depressions.

Till Unstratified glacial deposits or drift left by a *glacier or ice sheet*. Includes mixtures of clay, sand, gravel and boulders.

Topography The typical shape and features of a given area such as land height and terrain.

Tombolo A large sand spit which attaches part of the mainland to an island.

Transform fault In *plate tectonics*, a fault of continental scale, occurring where two plates slide past each other, staying close together for example, the San Andreas Fault. The jerky, uneven movement creates earthquakes but does not destroy or add to the Earth's *crust*

Trench (oceanic trench) A long, deep trough in the ocean floor, formed, according to the theory of *plate tectonics*, when two plates collide and one dives under the other, creating a *subduction zone*.

Tropic of Cancer A line of *latitude* or imaginary circle round the Earth, lying at 23° 28′ N.

Tropic of Capricorn A line of *latitude* or imaginary circle round the Earth, lying at 23° 28′ S.

U-shaped valley A river valley that has been deepened and widened by a *glacier*. They are characteristically flat-bottomed and steep-sided and generally much deeper than river valleys.

V-shaped valley A typical valley eroded by a river in its upper course.

Wadi The dry bed left by a torrent of water. Also classified as a ephemeral stream, found in arid and semi-arid regions, which are subject to sudden and often severe *flash flooding*.

Watershed The dividing line between one *drainage basin* an area where all streams flow into a single river system – and another. In the US, watershed also means the whole drainage basin of a single river system – its catchment area.

Waterspout A rotating column of water in the form of cloud, mist and spray which form on open water. Often has the appearance of a small tornado.

Weathering The decay and break-up of rocks at or near the Earth's surface, caused by water, wind, heat, or ice, organic material or the atmosphere. Physical weathering includes the effects of frost and temperature changes. Biological weathering includes the efects of plant roots, burrowing animals and the acids produced by animals, especially as they decay after death. Carbonation and hydrolysis are among many kinds of chemical weathering.

Picture Credits

DORLING KINDERSLEY *would like to express their thanks to the following individuals, companies and institutions for their help in preparing this Atlas.*

Earth Resources Mapping Ltd., *Egham, Surrey*
Brian Groombridge, World Conservation Monitoring Centre, *Cambridge*
The British Library, *London*
British Library of Political and Economic Science, *London*
The British Museum, *London*
The City Business Library, *London*
King's College, *London*
National Meteorological Library and Archive, *Bracknell, Berkshire*
The Printed Word, *London*
The Royal Geographical Society, *London*
University of London Library
Paul Beardmore
Philip Boyes
Hayley Crockford
Alistair Dougal
Nick Drake
Reg Grant
Louise Keane
Zoe Livesley
Laura Porter
Jeff Eidenshink
Chris Hornby
Rachelle Smith
Ray Pinchard
Robert Meisner
Fiona Strawbridge
Wim Jenkins

T = top, B = bottom, A=above, L = left, R = right, C = centre

Every effort has been made to trace the copyright holders and we apologize in advance for any unintentional omissions. We would be pleased to insert the appropriate acknowledgement in any subsequent edition of this publication.

Adams Picture Library: 88CLA; **G Andrews:** 194CR; **Ardea London Ltd:** K Ghana 156C; M Iljima 140TC; R Waller 154TR; **Aspect Picture Library:** P Carmichael 137CRB, 166TR; G Tompkinson 202TRB; **Axiom:** C Bradley 154CA, 165CA; J Holmes xivCRA, xxivBCR, xxviiCRB, 156TCR, 172BC, 172TL, J Morris 77TL, 77CRB, J Spaull 134BL; **Bridgeman Art Library, London / New York:** Collection of the Earl of Pembroke, Wilton House xxBC; **The J. Allan Cash Photolibrary:** xlBR, xliiCLA, xlivCL, 8BC, 62CL, 71CLB, 72CL, 74CLB, 77BR, 78BC, 89BL, 111BR, 144BCL, 147TL, 160CR, 186BR, 189TR; **Bruce Coleman Ltd:** 88BC, 100CL, 102TC; S Alden 198BR; Atlantide xxviTCR, 144BR; E Bjurstrom 147BR; S Bond 98CRB; T Buchholz xvCL, 96TR, 130TCL; J Burton xxiiiC; J Cancalosi 189TRB; B J Coates xxvBL, 198BC; B Coleman 65TL; B & C Colhoun 2TR, 38CB; A Compost xxiiiCBR; Dr S Coyne 47TL; G Cubitt xviTCL, 173BCL, 186TR, 192TR; P Davey xxviiCLB, 123BL; N Devore 201CBL; S J Doylee xxiiCRR; H Flygare xviiCRA; M P L Fogden 17CB; Jeff Foott Productions xxiiiCRB, 9CRA; M Freeman 93BRA; P van Gaalen 88TR; G Gualco 146C; B Henderson 200CR; Dr C Henneghien 71C; HPH Photography, H Van den Berg 71CR; C Hughes 71BCL; C James xxxixTC; J Johnson 41CR, 207TR; J Jurka 93CA; S C Kaufman 30C; S J Krasemann 35TR; H Lange 8TRB, 70CA; C Lockwood 34BC; L C Marigo xxiiBC, xxviiCLA, 51CRA, 61BR; M McCoy 195TR; D Meredith 3CR; J Murray xvCR, 187BR; Orion Press 172TR; Orion Services & Trading Co. Inc. 171TR; C Ott 18BL; Dr E Pott 14C, 42CL, 89C, 95TL, 204CLB; F Prenzel 197C, 200CB; M Read 44BR, 45CRB; H Reinhard xxiiCR, xxviiTR, 204BR; L Lee Rue III 157BCL; J Shaw xixTL; K N Swenson 204BC; P Terry 117CR; N Tomalin 56BCL; P Ward 80TC; S Widstrand 59TR; K Wothe 93C, 181TCL; J T Wright 131BR; **Colorific:** Black Star / L Mulvehil 162CL; Black Star / R Rogers 59BR; Black Star / J Rupp 167BCR; Camera Tres / C. Meyer 61BRA; R Caputo / Matrix 80CL; J. Hill 119CLB; M Koene 57TR; G Satterley xliiCLAR; M Yamashita 162BL, 179CA; **Comstock:** 110CRB; **D Cousens:** 153 CRA; **Sue Cunningham Photographic:** 53CR; **James Davis Travel Photography:** xxxviTCB, xxxviTR, xxxviCL, xxxiii CRA; 11CA, 21BC, 51TLB, 58BCR, 59CLA, 63BCL, 95BC, 96TC, 104TR, 122CB, 164BC, 187CRA, 203BR; **G Dunnet:** 128CA; **Environmental Picture Library:** Chris Westwood 130C; **Eye Ubiquitous:** xCA; Marcus Stone xxxiii tr; L. Fordyce 10CLA; L Johnstone 6CRA, 30BLA, 32CB; S. Miller xxiCA; M Southern 75BLA; **Chris Fairclough Colour Library:** xliBR; **Ffotograff:** C Aithie 137CL, N. Tapsell 164CL; **Geoscience Features:** xviBCR, xviBR, 104CL, 110BC, 127BR; Solar Film 66TC; **Robert Harding Picture Library:** xviiTC, xxivCR, xxxC, xxxvTC, Gavin Heller xxxiii cl; 2TLB, 3CA, 13CRB, 13CR, 39BC, 40CRA, 52BL, 97BR, 101CR, 116CR, 126BL, 138CLA, 148CB, 149TL, 153TR, 162TR, 173CA, 177BR; P G. Adam 11TCB; D Atchison-Jones 72BLA; J Bayne 74BCL; B Schuster 82CR; C Bowman 52BR, 55CA, 64CL, 72CRL; C Campbell xxiBC; G Corrigan 165CRB, 167CRB; P Craven xxxvBL; R Cundy 71BR; Delu 81BC; A Durand 113BR; Financial Times 148BR; R Frerck 53BL; T Gervis 3BCL, 7CR; I Griffiths xxxCL, 79TL; T Hall 177CRA; D Harney 148CA; S Harris xliiiBCL; G Hellier xvCRB, 135BL; F Jackson 143BCR; Jacobs xxxviiTL; P Koch 145TR; F Joseph Land 125TR; Y Marcoux 16BR; S Massif xvBC; A Mills 90CLB; L Murray 116TR; R Rainford xlivBL; G Renner 76CB, 204C; C Rennie 50CL, 118BR; R Richardson 120CL; P Van Riel 50BR; E Rooney 128TR; Sassoon xxivCL, 154CLB; P Scholey 184TR; M Short 143TL; E Simanor xxviiCR; V Southwell 145CR; J Strachan 44TR, 113BL, 136BCR; C Tokeley 140CLA; A C Waltham 167C; T Waltham xviiBL, xxiiCLLL, 144CRB; Westlight 39CR; N Wheeler 145BL; A Williams xxxviiiBR, xlTR; A Woolfitt 97BRA; **Paul Harris:** 126TR, 174TC; **Hutchison Library:** 6BL, 140BCL; P. Collomb 143CR; C. Dodwell 139TR; S Errington 72BCL; P. Hellyer 148BC; J. Horner xxxiTC; R. Ian Lloyd 134CRA; N. Durrell McKenna xxviBCR; J.Nowell 135CLB, 149TC; A Zvoznikov xxiiCL; **Image Bank:** 89BR; J Banagan 202BCA; A Becker xxivBCL; P Hendrie 174BC; M Isy-Schwart 200C, 203CL; M Khansa 124BR; K Forest 169TR; Lomeo xxivTCR; T Madison 177CR; C Molyneux xxiiCRRR; K Mori 200TC; C Navajas xviiiTR; Ocean Images Inc. 198CLB; J van Os xviiTCR; S Proehl 6CL; T Rakke xixTC, 66CL; M Reitz 206CA; M Romanelli 177BL; G A Rossi 157BCR, 184BLA; B Roussel 111TL; S Satushek xviiBCR; Stock Photos / J M Spielman xxivTRL; **Images Colour Library:** xxiiCLL, xxxixTR, xliCR, xliiiBL, 3BR, 21BR, 39TL, 46TL, 64TC, 93BR, 104CLB, 105CR, 156CL, 171CL, 172TRB, 188CA; **Impact Photos:** J & G Andrews 194BL; C. Bluntzer 162BR; Cosmos / G. Buthaud 67BC; S Franklin 130BL; A. le Garsmeur 137CRA; A Indge xxviiTC; C Jones xxxiCB, 72BL; V. Nemirousky 143BR; J Nicholl 78TCR; C. Penn 197BR; G Sweeney xviiBR, 206CB, 206TR; **JVZ Picture Library:** T Nilson 135TC; **Frank Lane Picture Agency:** xxiTCR, xxiiiBL, 95TR; A Christiansen 60CRA; J Holmes xivBL; S. McCutcheon 3C; Silvestris 181TCR; D Smith xxiiBCL; W Wisniewsli 126TL, 205BR; **Leeds Castle Foundation:** xxxviiBC; **Magnum:** Abbas 85CR, 142CA; S Franklin 134CRB; D Hurn 4BCL; P. Jones-Griffiths 203BL; H Kubota xviBCL, 162CLB; F Maver xviBL; S McCurry 75CL, 141BCR; G. Rodger 76TR; C Steele Perkins 74BL; **Mountain Camera / John Cleare:** 159TR; C Monteath 159CR; **Nature Photographers:** E.A. Janes 114CL; **Natural Science Photos:** M Andera 112C; **Network Photographers Ltd.:** C Sappa / Rapho 121BL; **N.H.P.A.:** N. J. Dennis xxiiiCL; D Heuchlin xxiiiCLA; Jane Gifford xxxiii bl; S Krasemann 13BL, 27BR, 40TC; K Schafer 51CB; R Tidman 166CLB; D Tomlinson 151CR; M Wendler 50TR; **Nottingham Trent University:** T Waltham xivCL, xvBR; **Novosti:** 150BLA; **Oxford Scientific Films:** D Allan xxiiTR; H R Bardarson xviiiBC; D Bown xxiiiCBLL; M Brown 146BL; M Colbeck 153CAR; W Faidley 3TL; L Gould xxiiiTRB; D Guravich xxiiiTR; P Hammerschmidy / Okapia 89CLA; M Hill 59TL, 205TR; C Menteath 140TR; J Netherton 2CRB; S Osolinski 84CA; R Packwood 74CA; M Pitts 187TC; N Rosing xxiiiCBL, 9TR, 207BR; D Simonson 59C; Survival Anglia / C Catton 143TR; R Toms xxiiiBR; K Wothe xxiBL, xviiCLA; **Panos Pictures:** B Aris 141C; P Barker xxivBR; T Bolstao 159BR; N Cooper 84CB, 159TC; J-L Dugast 177CB, 178BC; J Hartley 75CA, 92CL; J Holmes 155BC; J Morris 78CLB; M Rose 152TR; D Sansoni 161CL; C Stowers 169TL; **Edward Parker:** 51TL, 51CLB; **Pictor International:** xivBR, xvBRA, xixTCL, xxCL, 3CLA, 19BR, 22TR, 22CRB, 25BCA, 25CL, 28CB, 29BC, 32CA, 35TRB, 36BC, 36BR, 36CR, 40CB, 40CL, 45CL, 65BR, 67TC, 84CL, 85CLB, 101BR, 109CLA, 177TCR, 178BR, 179CR, 188CLB, 193TL; **Pictures Colour Library:** xxiBCL, xxiiBR, xxviBCL, 6BR, 13TR, 14TC, 17TR, 21TL, 22BL, 26C, 26CLA, 29TR, 34TRB, 38BC, 43CA, 45CRA, 70BL, 92TCB, 96BL, 101BL, 108CA, 109CLB, 109CR, 109BR, 119BL, 170BC, 171BR, 198CL; **Planet Earth Pictures:** 200BL; D Barrett 154CB, 192CA; R Coomber 17BL; G Douwma 180BR; E Edmonds 181BR; HC Heap 124TR; J Lythgoe 206BL; A Mounter 137BCR, 180CR; M Potts 6CA; P Scoones xxTR; J Walencik 112TR; J Waters 55BCL; **Popperfoto:** Reuters / J Drake xxxiiCLA; **Rex Features:** 170CR; Antelope xxxiiCLB; M Friedel xxiCR; I McIlgorm xxxCBR; J Shelley xxxCR; Sipa Press xxxCR; Sipa Press / Alix xxxCBL; Sipa Press / Chamussy 184BL; **Russia & Republics Photolibrary:** M Wadlow 120CR, 121CL, 128BC, 128CL, 129TL, 129BR, 130TCR; **Science Photo Library:** CNES, 1990 Distribution Spot Image 137BL; Earth Satellite Corporation xixTRB, xxxiCR, 51BCL; F Gohier xiCR; J Heseltine xviTCB; K Kent xvBLA; P Menzell xvBL; N.A.S.A. xBC; D Parker xivBC; University of Cambridge Collection Air Pictures 89CLB; RJ Wainscoat / P Arnold, Inc. xiBC; D Weintraub xiBL; **South American Pictures:** 59BL, 64TR; R Francis 54BL; Guyana Space Centre 52TR; T Morrison 51CRB, 51BL, 52CR, 54TR, 56TR, 62BL, 63C; **Southampton Oceanography:** xviiiBL; **Sovofoto / Eastfoto:** xxxiiCBR; **Spectrum Colour Library:** 52BC, 166BC; J King 151BR; **Frank Spooner Pictures / Gamma:** 28CRB; E. Baitel xxxiiBC; Bernstein xxxiCL; Contrast 114CR; Diard / Photo News 115CL; Liaison / C. Hires xxxiiTCB; Liaison / Nickelsberg xxxiiTR; Liaison / Vogel 140BL; Marleen 115TL; Novosti 118CA; P. Piel xxxCA; N Quidu 135CL; H Stucke 196CLB, 202CA; Torrengo / Figaro 80BR; A Zamur 115BL; **Still Pictures:** C Caldicott 79TC; A Crump 201CL; M & C Denis-Huot xxiiBL, 80CR, 83BL; M Edwards xxiCRL, 55BL, 66CR, 71BLA, 161BR; J Frebet 55CLB; H Giradet 55TC; M Gunther 123BC; E Parker 54CL; R Seitre 137CA, 138BL, 138TL; **Tony Stone Images:** xxviTR, 4CA, 7BL, 7CL, 11CRB, 41BR, 60C, 99BC, 103BR, 108TR, 111CL, 111CRB, 141BR, 170CLB, 171C,188CB, 189BR, 196BC, 198TR; G Allison 20TR, 33CRB, 195CRB; D Armand 12TCB; D Austen 188TR, 194CL, 195CL; J Beatty 76CL; O Benn xxviBR; K Biggs xxiTL; R Bradbury 46BR; R A Butcher xxviTL; J Callahan xxviiCRA; P Chesley 193BCL, 196C; W Clay 32BL, 33CRA; J Cornish 98BL, 109TL; C Condina 43CB; T Craddock xxivTR; P Degginger 38CLB; Demetrio 5BR; N DeVore xxivBC; A Diesendruck 62BR; S Egan 89CRA, 98BR; R Elliot xxiiBCR; S Elmore 21C; R Frerck 122TR; J Garrett 75CR; S Grandadam 12BR; R Grosskopf 30BL; D Hanson 106BC; C Harvey 71TL; G Hellier 112BL, 172CR; S Huber 105CRB; D Hughs xxxiBR; A Husmo 93TR; G Irvine 33BC; J Jangoux 60CL; G Johnson 138CLB; D Johnston xviiTR; A Kehr 115C; R Koskas xviTR; J Lamb 98CRA; J Lawrence 77CRA; L Lefkowitz 7CA; M Lewis 47CLA; S Mayman 57BR; Murray & Associates 47CR; G Norways 106CA; N Parfitt xxviiCL, 70TCR, 83TL; R Passmore 123TR; N Press xviBCA; E Pritchard 90CA, 92CLR; T Raymond 23BL, 31TR; L Resnick 76BR; M Rogers 82BR; A Sacks 30TCB; C Saule 92CR; S Schulhof xxivTC; P Seaward 36CL; M Segal 34BL; V Shenai 158CL; R Sherman 28CL; H Sitton 142CR; R Smith xxvBLA, 58C; S Studd 110CLA; H Strand 51BR, 65TR; P Tweedie 185CR; L Ulrich 19BL; M Vines 19TC; A B Wadham 62CR; J Warden 65CLB; R Wells 25CRA, 199BL; G Yeowell 36BL; **Telegraph Colour Library:** 63CRB, 63TCR, 163TL; R Antrobus xxxixBR; J Sims 28BR; **Topham Picturepoint:** xxxiCBL, 137BCL, 139CR, 168BR, 174TR, 176BC; 184BL; **Travel Ink:** A Cowin 90TR; **Trip:** 146BR, 150CA, 161CRA; B Ashe 165TR; D Cole 202BCL, 202CR; D Davis 91BL; I Deineko xxxiTR; J Dennis 24BL; Dinodia 160CL, Eye Ubiquitous / L Fordyce 2CLB; A Gasson 155CR; W Jacobs 45TL, 56BL, 185BC, 186CLA, 193BCR, 197BL; P Kingsbury 114C; K Knight 185BR; V Kolpakov 153BL; T Noorits 89TL, 121BR, 152CL; R Power 43TR; N Ray 176CA; C Rennie 118CLB; V Sidoropolev 151TR; E Smith 191BC, 191TL; **Woodfin Camp & Associates:** 94BLR; **World Pictures:** xvCRA, xviiCRA, 16CRB, 24CL, 25BC, 26BL, 37BL, 42TR, 53TR, 73BR, 82TCR, 84TR, 85BL, 88BCR, 98TC, 100BL, 102CR, 103CR, 105BC, 107TC, 123CB, 124BL, 163BL, 167BCL, 168CLB, 180CLB, 180BC, 187BL, 190CB, 191C, 192CL, 193CR; **Zefa Picture Library:** xviBLR, xviiBCL, xviiiCL, 3CL, 11BC, 12TC, 17CA, 23TL, 24CRB, 27BL, 34TCR, 38BCR, 61BCL, 67TCL, 71CLA, 81TL, 83BR, 89CRB, 94C, 100C, 101TL, 102BL, 109TR, 120CRB, 122BL, 126CB, 128CLA, 170CA, 191TR; Anatol 115BR; Barone 116BL; Brandenburg 5C; A J Brown 46TR; H J Clauss 57CLB; Damm 73BC; Evert 94BL; W Felger 3BL; J Fields 201CRA; R Frerck 4BL; G Heil 58BR; K Heibig 117BR; Heilman 30BC; Hunter 8C; Kitchen 8TR, 14CL, 14BL, 16TR; Dr H Kramarz 7BLA, 127CRA; Mehlio 161BL; J F Raga 26TR; Rossenbach 107BR, 122CA; Streichan 91TL; T Stewart 11TR, 21CR; Sunak 56BR, 168TR; D H Teuffen 97TL; B Zaunders 42BC. **Additional Photography:** Geoff Dann; Rob Reichenfeld; H Taylor; Jerry Young.

◆ COUNTRY ● COUNTRY CAPITAL ◇ DEPENDENT TERRITORY ○ DEPENDENT TERRITORY CAPITAL ◆ ADMINISTRATIVE REGION ✈ INTERNATIONAL AIRPORT ▲ MOUNTAIN ▲▲ MOUNTAIN RANGE VOLCANO 𝄐 RIVER ⊛ LAKE ⊠ RESERVOIR

353

◆ Country
● Country Capital
◇ Dependent Territory
○ Dependent Territory Capital
⬖ Administrative Region
✕ International Airport
▲ Mountain
▲▲ Mountain Range
Volcano
≈ River
⊚ Lake
▣ Reservoir

W

◆ Country ● Country Capital ◇ Dependent Territory ○ Dependent Territory Capital ◆ Administrative Region ✕ International Airport ▲ Mountain ▲ Mountain Range Volcano ∼ River ⊚ Lake ⊠ Reservoir

● COUNTRY   ● COUNTRY CAPITAL   ○ DEPENDENT TERRITORY   ○ DEPENDENT TERRITORY CAPITAL   ◆ ADMINISTRATIVE DIVISION   ✕ INTERNATIONAL AIRPORT   ▲ MOUNTAIN   ▲ VOLCANO   ✦ MOUNTAIN RANGE   ～ RIVER   ▨ LAKE   ▤ RESERVOIR

◆ Country
● Country Capital
◇ Dependent Territory
○ Dependent Territory Capital
⬖ Administrative Region
✕ International Airport
▲ Mountain
▲▲ Mountain Range
Volcano
~ River
◎ Lake
⊠ Reservoir

X

◆ Country
● Country Capital
◇ Dependent Territory
○ Dependent Territory Capital
◆ Administrative Region
✖ International Airport
▲ Mountain
▲▲ Mountain Range
Volcano
∽ River
◎ Lake
⊞ Reservoir

Y

◆ Country
● Country Capital
◇ Dependent Territory
○ Dependent Territory Capital
◈ Administrative Region
✈ International Airport
▲ Mountain
▲▲ Mountain Range
Volcano
≈ River
◎ Lake
▣ Reservoir

Z

◆ Country
● Country Capital
◇ Dependent Territory
○ Dependent Territory Capital
◈ Administrative Region
✕ International Airport
▲ Mountain
⛰ Mountain Range
🌋 Volcano
≈ River
◎ Lake
▣ Reservoir

◆ Country
● Country Capital
◇ Dependent Territory
○ Dependent Territory Capital
◐ Administrative Region
✕ International Airport
▲ Mountain
▲▲ Mountain Range
Volcano
≈ River
◎ Lake
⊠ Reservoir

TROIS SAUTS – TÜRKMENGALA

57 Y12 **Trois Sauts** S French Guiana 2.15N 52.52W
101 M22 **Troisvierges** Diekirch, N Luxembourg 50.07N 6.00E
125 Ee12 **Troitsk** Chelyabinskaya Oblast', S Russian Federation 54.04N 61.31E
129 T9 **Troitsko-Pechorsk** Respublika Komi, NW Russian Federation 62.39N 56.06E
131 V7 **Troitskoye** Orenburgskaya Oblast', W Russian Federation 52.23N 56.24E
Troki *see* Trakai
96 F9 **Trolla** ▲ S Norway 62.41N 9.47E
97 J18 **Trollhättan** Västra Götaland, S Sweden 58.16N 12.19E
96 G9 **Trollheimen** ▲▲ S Norway
96 E9 **Trolltindan** ▲ S Norway 62.30N 7.43E
60 H11 **Trombetas, Rio** ~ NE Brazil
132 L16 **Tromelin, Île** *island* N Réunion
94 I9 **Troms** ◈ *county* N Norway
94 I9 **Tromsø** *Fin.* Tromssa. Troms, N Norway 69.42N 19.00E
86 F5 **Tromsøflaket** *undersea feature* W Barents Sea
Tromssa *see* Tromsø
96 H10 **Tron** ▲ S Norway 62.12N 10.46E
37 U12 **Trona** California, W USA 35.46N 117.21W
65 G16 **Tronador, Cerro** ▲ S Chile 41.12S 71.51W
96 H8 **Trondheim** *Ger.* Drontheim; *prev.* Nidaros, Trondhjem. Sør-Trøndelag, S Norway 63.25N 10.24E
96 H7 **Trondheimsfjorden** *fjord* S Norway
Trondhjem *see* Trondheim
109 J14 **Tronto** ~ C Italy
Troodos *see* Ólympos
124 N3 **Troódos** *var.* Troodos Mountains. ▲▲ C Cyprus
Troodos Mountains *see* Troódos
98 I13 **Troon** W Scotland, UK 55.32N 4.41W
109 M22 **Tropea** Calabria, SW Italy 38.40N 15.52E
38 L7 **Tropic** Utah, W USA 37.37N 112.04W
66 L10 **Tropic Seamount** *var.* Banc du Tropique. *undersea feature* E Atlantic Ocean 23.49N 20.40W
Tropique, Banc du *see* Tropic Seamount
Tropoja *see* Tropojë
115 L17 **Tropojë** *var.* Tropoja. Kukës, N Albania 42.25N 20.09E
Troppau *see* Opava
97 O16 **Trosa** Södermanland, C Sweden 58.54N 17.34E
120 H12 **Troškūnai** Utena, E Lithuania 55.36N 24.55E
103 G23 **Trossingen** Baden-Württemberg, SW Germany 48.04N 8.37E
119 T4 **Trostyanets'** *Rus.* Trostyanets. Sums'ka Oblast', NE Ukraine 50.29N 34.58E
119 N7 **Trostyanets'** *Rus.* Trostyanets. Vinnyts'ka Oblast', C Ukraine 48.35N 29.10E
118 L11 **Trotuş** ~ E Romania
46 M8 **Trou-du-Nord** N Haiti 19.34N 71.57W
27 W7 **Troup** Texas, SW USA 32.08N 95.07W
15 H8 **Trout** ~ Northwest Territories, NW Canada
35 N8 **Trout Creek** Montana, NW USA 47.51N 115.40W
34 H10 **Trout Lake** Washington, NW USA 45.59N 121.33W
10 B9 **Trout Lake** ◎ Ontario, S Canada
35 T12 **Trout Peak** ▲ Wyoming, C USA 44.36N 109.33W
104 L4 **Trouville** Calvados, N France 49.21N 0.07E
99 L22 **Trowbridge** S England, UK 51.19N 2.13W
25 Q6 **Troy** Alabama, S USA 31.48N 85.58W
29 Q3 **Troy** Kansas, C USA 39.46N 95.05W
29 W4 **Troy** Missouri, C USA 38.58N 90.58W
20 L10 **Troy** New York, NE USA 42.43N 73.37W
23 S10 **Troy** North Carolina, SE USA 35.21N 79.53W
33 R13 **Troy** Ohio, N USA 40.02N 84.12W
27 T9 **Troy** Texas, SW USA 31.12N 97.18W
116 I9 **Troyan** Lovech, N Bulgaria 42.53N 24.43E
116 I9 **Troyanski Prokhod** *pass* N Bulgaria 42.48N 24.38E
151 N6 **Troyebratskiy** Severnyy Kazakhstan, N Kazakhstan 54.21N 66.07E
105 Q6 **Troyes** *anc.* Augustobona Tricassium. Aube, N France 48.18N 4.04E
119 X5 **Troyits'ke** Luhans'ka Oblast', E Ukraine 49.55N 38.18E
37 W7 **Troy Peak** ▲ Nevada, W USA 38.18N 115.27W
115 G15 **Trpanj** Dubrovnik-Neretva, S Croatia 43.00N 17.18E
Tršćanski Zaljev *see* Trieste, Gulf of
Trst *see* Trieste
115 N14 **Trstenik** Serbia, C Serbia 43.38N 21.01E
130 I6 **Trubchevsk** Bryanskaya Oblast', W Russian Federation 52.33N 33.45E
Trubchular *see* Orlyak
39 S10 **Truchas Peak** ▲ New Mexico, SW USA 35.57N 105.38W
149 P16 **Trucial Coast** *physical region* C UAE
Trucial States *see* United Arab Emirates
37 Q6 **Truckee** California, W USA 39.18N 120.10W
37 R5 **Truckee River** ~ Nevada, W USA
131 Q13 **Trudfront** Astrakhanskaya Oblast', SW Russian Federation 45.56N 47.42E
12 I9 **Truite, Lac à la** ◎ Québec, SE Canada
44 K4 **Trujillo** Colón, NE Honduras 15.59N 85.54W
58 C12 **Trujillo** La Libertad, NW Peru 8.04S 79.02W
106 K10 **Trujillo** Extremadura, W Spain 39.28N 5.52W
56 I6 **Trujillo** Trujillo, NW Venezuela 9.19N 70.37W
56 I6 **Trujillo** *off.* Estado Trujillo. ◈ *state* W Venezuela
Truk *see* Chuuk
Truk Islands *see* Chuuk Islands
31 U10 **Truman** Minnesota, N USA 43.49N 94.26W
29 X10 **Trumann** Arkansas, C USA 35.40N 90.30W
38 J9 **Trumbull, Mount** ▲ Arizona, SW USA 36.22N 113.09W
116 F9 **Trŭn** Pernik, W Bulgaria 42.51N 22.37E
191 Q8 **Trundle** New South Wales, SE Australia 32.55S 147.43E
133 U13 **Trung Phân** *physical region* S Vietnam
Trupcilar *see* Orlyak
11 Q15 **Truro** Nova Scotia, SE Canada 45.20N 63.14W
99 H25 **Truro** SW England, UK 50.16N 5.03W
27 P5 **Truscott** Texas, SW USA 33.43N 99.48W
118 K9 **Truşeşti** Botoşani, NE Romania 47.45N 27.01E
118 H6 **Truskavets'** L'vivs'ka Oblast', W Ukraine 49.15N 23.30E
97 H22 **Trustrup** Århus, C Denmark 56.20N 10.46E
8 M11 **Trutch** British Columbia, W Canada 57.42N 123.00W
39 Q14 **Truth Or Consequences** New Mexico, SW USA 33.07N 107.15W
113 F15 **Trutnov** *Ger.* Trautenau. Královéhradecký Kraj, NE Czech Republic 50.34N 15.52E
105 P13 **Truyère** ~ C France
116 K9 **Tryavna** Lovech, N Bulgaria 42.52N 25.30E
30 M14 **Tryon** Nebraska, C USA 41.31N 100.56W
117 J16 **Trypití, Akrotírio** *var.* Ákra Tripití. *headland* Ágios Efstrátios, E Greece 39.28N 24.58E
96 I11 **Trysilelva** ~ S Norway
114 D10 **Tržac** Federacija Bosna I Hercegovina, NW Bosnia and Herzegovina 44.58N 15.48E
Tržaški Zaliv *see* Trieste, Gulf of
112 G10 **Trzcianka** *Ger.* Schönlanke. Piła, Wielkopolskie, C Poland 53.01N 16.24E
112 E7 **Trzebiatów** *Ger.* Treptow an der Rega. Zachodnio-pomorskie, NW Poland 54.04N 15.14E
113 G14 **Trzebnica** *Ger.* Trebnitz. Dolnośląskie, SW Poland 51.18N 17.03E
111 T10 **Tržič** *Ger.* Neumarktl. NW Slovenia 46.22N 14.17E
Trzynietz *see* Třinec
Tsabong *see* Tshabong
168 G7 **Tsagaanchuluut** Dzavhan, C Mongolia 47.06N 96.40E
168 M8 **Tsagaandelger** *var.* Haraat. Dundgovĭ, C Mongolia 46.30N 107.39E
Tsagaanders *see* Bayantümen
168 G7 **Tsagaanhayrhan** *var.* Shiree. Dzavhan, W Mongolia 47.30N 96.48E
Tsagaannuur *see* Halhgol
Tsagaan-Olom *see* Tayshir
Tsagaan-Ovoo *see* Nariynteel
Tsagaantüngi *see* Altantsögts
168 H6 **Tsagaan-Uul** *var.* Sharga. Hövsgöl, N Mongolia 49.33N 98.36E
168 J5 **Tsagaan-Üür** *var.* Bulgan. Hövsgöl, N Mongolia 50.30N 101.28E
131 P12 **Tsagan Aman** Respublika Kalmykiya, SW Russian Federation 47.37N 46.43E
25 V11 **Tsala Apopka Lake** ◎ Florida, SE USA
Tsamkong *see* Zhanjiang
Tsangpo *see* Brahmaputra
Tsant *see* Deren
85 G17 **Tsao** North-West, NW Botswana 20.08S 22.29E
180 I4 **Tsaratanana** Mahajanga, C Madagascar 16.46S 47.40E
116 N10 **Tsarevo** *prev.* Michurin. Burgas, E Bulgaria 42.10N 27.51E
Tsarigrad *see* İstanbul
Tsaritsyn *see* Volgograd
128 G13 **Tsarskoye Selo** *prev.* Pushkin. Leningradskaya Oblast', NW Russian Federation 59.42N 30.24E
119 T7 **Tsarychanka** Dnipropetrovs'ka Oblast', E Ukraine 48.56N 34.29E
85 H21 **Tsatsu** Southern, S Botswana 25.21S 24.45E
83 J20 **Tsavo** Coast, S Kenya 2.58S 38.28E
85 E21 **Tsawisis** Karas, S Namibia 26.18S 18.07E
Tschakathurn *see* Čakovec
Tschaslau *see* Čáslav
Tschenstochau *see* Częstochowa
Tschernembl *see* Črnomelj
30 K6 **Tschida, Lake** ⊠ North Dakota, N USA
Tschorna *see* Mustvee
85 I17 **Tsebanana** Central, NE Botswana 19.50S 26.29E
Tsefat *see* Zefat
168 G8 **Tseel** Govĭ-Altay, SW Mongolia 45.45N 95.54E
130 M13 **Tselina** Rostovskaya Oblast', SW Russian Federation 46.31N 41.01E
Tselinograd *see* Astana
Tselinogradskaya Oblast' *see* Akmola
Tsengel *see* Tosontsengel
168 J8 **Tsenher** *var.* Altan-Ovoo. Arhangay, C Mongolia 47.24N 101.51E
Tsenher *see* Mönhhayrhan
169 N8 **Tsenhermandal** *var.* Modot. Hentiy, C Mongolia 47.45N 109.03E
Tsentral'nyye Nizmennyye Garagumy *see* Merkezi Garagumy
85 E21 **Tses** Karas, S Namibia 25.54S 18.09E
Tseshevlya *see* Tsyeshawlya
168 E7 **Tsetseg** *var.* Tsetsegnuur. Hovd, W Mongolia 46.30N 93.16E
Tsetsegnuur *see* Tsetseg
Tsetsen Khan *see* Öndörhaan
168 J7 **Tsetserleg** Arhangay, C Mongolia 47.28N 101.19E
168 H6 **Tsetserleg** *var.* Halban. Hövsgöl, N Mongolia 49.30N 97.33E
168 J8 **Tsetserleg** *var.* Hujirt. Övörhangay, C Mongolia 46.50N 102.38E
79 R16 **Tsévié** S Togo 6.25N 1.13E
85 G21 **Tshabong** *var.* Tsabong. Kgalagadi, SW Botswana 26.01S 22.24E
85 G20 **Tshane** Kgalagadi, SW Botswana 24.02S 21.54E
Tshangalele, Lac *see* Lufira, Lac de Retenue de la
85 H17 **Tshauxaba** Central, C Botswana 19.56S 25.09E
81 F21 **Tshela** Bas-Congo, W Dem. Rep. Congo 4.55S 13.01E
81 K22 **Tshibala** Kasai Occidental, S Dem. Rep. Congo 6.53S 22.01E
81 J22 **Tshikapa** Kasai Occidental, SW Dem. Rep. Congo 6.23S 20.47E
81 L22 **Tshilenge** Kasai Oriental, S Dem. Rep. Congo 6.16S 23.48E
81 L24 **Tshimbalanga** Katanga, S Dem. Rep. Congo 9.42S 23.04E
81 L22 **Tshimbulu** Kasai Occidental, S Dem. Rep. Congo 6.27S 22.54E
Tshiumbe *see* Chiumbe
81 M21 **Tshofa** Kasai Oriental, C Dem. Rep. Congo 5.13S 25.13E
81 K18 **Tshuapa** ~ C Dem. Rep. Congo
85 J21 **Tshwane** *var.* Epitoli, *prev.* Pretoria. ● (South Africa-administrative capital) Gauteng, NE South Africa 25.40S 28.11E
116 G7 **Tsibritsa** ~ NW Bulgaria
Tsien Tang *see* Puyang Jiang
116 I12 **Tsigansko Gradishte** ▲ Bulgaria/Greece 41.24N 24.41E
14 G3 **Tsiigehtchic** *prev.* Arctic Red River. Northwest Territories, NW Canada 67.24N 133.40W
129 Q7 **Tsil'ma** ~ NW Russian Federation
121 J17 **Tsimkavichy** *Rus.* Timkovichi. Minskaya Voblasts', C Belarus 53.04N 26.58E
130 M11 **Tsimlyansk** Rostovskaya Oblast', SW Russian Federation 47.39N 42.05E
131 N11 **Tsimlyanskoye Vodokhranilishche** *var.* Tsimlyansk Vodoskhovshche, *Eng.* Tsimlyansk Reservoir ⊠ SW Russian Federation
Tsimlyansk Reservoir *see* Tsimlyanskoye Vodokhranilishche
Tsimlyansk Vodoskhovshche *see* Tsimlyanskoye Vodokhranilishche
Tsinan *see* Jinan
Tsing Hai *see* Qinghai Hu, China
Tsinghai *see* Qinghai, China
Tsingtao/Tsingtau *see* Qingdao
Tsingyuan *see* Baoding
Tsinkiang *see* Quanzhou
Tsintao *see* Qingdao
85 D17 **Tsintsabis** Otjikoto, N Namibia 18.44S 17.57E
180 H8 **Tsiombe** *var.* Tsihombe. Toliara, S Madagascar
126 Kk14 **Tsipa** ~ S Russian Federation
180 H5 **Tsiribihina** ~ W Madagascar
180 I5 **Tsiroanomandidy** Antananarivo, C Madagascar 18.43S 46.01E
201 U13 **Tsis** *island* Chuuk, C Micronesia
Tsitsihar *see* Qiqihar
131 Q3 **Tsivil'sk** Chavash Respubliki, W Russian Federation 55.51N 47.30E
143 T9 **Ts'khinvali** *prev.* Staliniri. C Georgia 42.12N 43.58E
121 J19 **Tsna** ~ SW Belarus
128 I15 **Tsna** *var.* Zna. ~ W Russian Federation
168 G9 **Tsogt** *var.* Tahilt. Govĭ-Altay, W Mongolia 45.20N 96.42E
168 K10 **Tsogt-Ovoo** *var.* Doloon. Ömnögovĭ, S Mongolia 44.28N 105.22E
168 L10 **Tsogttsetsiy** *var.* Baruunsuu. Ömnögovĭ, S Mongolia 43.46N 105.28E
Tsoohor *see* Hürmen
171 H16 **Tsu** *var.* Tu. Mie, Honshū, SW Japan 34.40N 136.30E
171 K13 **Tsubame** *var.* Tubame. Niigata, Honshū, C Japan 37.39N 138.55E
171 Ii13 **Tsubata** Ishikawa, Honshū, SW Japan 36.33N 136.42E
172 Q6 **Tsubetsu** Hokkaidō, NE Japan 43.43N 144.01E
171 Kk16 **Tsuchiura** *var.* Tutiura. Ibaraki, Honshū, S Japan 36.03N 140.09E
172 N7 **Tsugaru-kaikyō** *strait* N Japan
171 Kk13 **Tsugawa** Niigata, Honshū, C Japan 37.40N 139.26E
172 Oo5 **Tsukigata** Hokkaidō, NE Japan 43.18N 141.37E
170 Dd15 **Tsukumi** *var.* Tukumi. Ōita, Kyūshū, SW Japan 33.02N 131.51E
Tsul-Ulaan *see* Bayanuur
85 D17 **Tsumeb** Otjikoto, N Namibia 19.13S 17.42E
85 F17 **Tsumkwe** Otjozondjupa, NE Namibia 19.35S 20.26E
170 Cc16 **Tsuno** Miyazaki, Kyūshū, SW Japan 32.43N 131.32E
170 D11 **Tsuno-shima** *island* SW Japan
171 H14 **Tsuruga** *var.* Turuga. Fukui, Honshū, SW Japan 35.38N 136.01E
170 F15 **Tsurugi-san** ▲ Shikoku, SW Japan 33.50N 134.04E
170 Dd15 **Tsurumi-zaki** *headland* Kyūshū, SW Japan 32.55N 132.03E
171 L11 **Tsuruoka** *var.* Turuoka. Yamagata, Honshū, C Japan 38.43N 139.48E
171 Hh15 **Tsushima** *var.* Tusima. Aichi, Honshū, SW Japan 35.10N 136.45E
170 C10 **Tsushima** *var.* Tsushima-tō, Tusima. *island group* SW Japan
Tsushima-tō *see* Tsushima
170 E12 **Tsuwano** Shimane, Honshū, SW Japan 34.28N 131.43E
170 Ff13 **Tsuyama** *var.* Tuyama. Okayama, Honshū, SW Japan 35.03N 133.57E
85 G19 **Tswaane** Ghanzi, W Botswana 22.21S 21.52E
121 N16 **Tsyakhtsin** *Rus.* Tekhtin. Mahilyowskaya Voblasts', E Belarus 53.52N 29.43E
121 P19 **Tsyerakhowka** *Rus.* Terekhovka. Homyel'skaya Voblasts', SE Belarus 52.13N 31.24E
121 I17 **Tsyeshawlya** *Rus.* Cheshevlya, Tseshevlya. Brestskaya Voblasts', SW Belarus 53.13N 25.49E
Tsyurupinsk *see* Tsyurupyns'k
119 R10 **Tsyurupyns'k** *Rus.* Tsyurupinsk. Khersons'ka Oblast', S Ukraine 46.34N 32.42E
Tu *see* Tsu
194 H13 **Tua** ~ C PNG
Tuaim *see* Tuam
192 L6 **Tuakau** Waikato, North Island, NZ 37.16S 174.56E
99 C17 **Tuam** *Ir.* Tuaim. W Ireland 53.31N 8.49W
193 K14 **Tuamarina** Marlborough, South Island, NZ 41.27S 174.00E
Tuamotu, Archipel des *see* Tuamotu, Îles
199 M10 **Tuamotu Fracture Zone** *tectonic feature* E Pacific Ocean
203 W9 **Tuamotu, Îles** *var.* Archipel des Tuamotu, Dangerous Archipelago, Tuamotu Islands. *island group* N French Polynesia
Tuamotu Islands *see* Tuamotu, Îles
183 X10 **Tuamotu Ridge** *undersea feature* C Pacific Ocean
178 Ii5 **Tuân Giao** Lai Châu, N Vietnam 21.34N 103.24E
179 P8 **Tuao** Luzon, N Philippines 17.42N 121.25E
202 B15 **Tuapa** NW Niue 18.57S 169.58W
45 N7 **Tuapi** Región Autónoma Atlántico Norte, NE Nicaragua 14.10N 83.18W
130 K15 **Tuapse** Krasnodarskiy Kray, SW Russian Federation 44.07N 39.07E
175 Nn2 **Tuaran** Sabah, East Malaysia 6.12N 116.12E
106 I6 **Tua, Rio** ~ N Portugal
198 B7 **Tuasivi** Savai'i, C Samoa 13.37S 172.07W
193 B24 **Tuatapere** Southland, South Island, NZ 46.09S 167.43E
38 M9 **Tuba City** Arizona, SW USA 36.08N 111.14W
144 H11 **Ţūbah, Qaşr aţ** *castle* 'Ammān, C Jordan 31.22N 36.39E
Tubame *see* Tsubame
174 Ll14 **Tuban** *prev.* Toeban. Jawa, C Indonesia 6.55S 112.01E
147 O16 **Tuban, Wādī** *dry watercourse* SW Yemen
63 K14 **Tubarão** Santa Catarina, S Brazil 28.29S 49.00W
100 O10 **Tubbergen** Overijssel, E Netherlands 52.25N 6.46E
Tubeke *see* Tubize
103 H22 **Tübingen** *var.* Tuebingen. Baden-Württemberg, SW Germany 48.31N 9.04E
131 W6 **Tubinskiy** Respublika Bashkortostan, W Russian Federation 52.48N 58.18E
101 G19 **Tubize** *Dut.* Tubeke. Wallon Brabant, C Belgium 50.43N 4.14E
78 J16 **Tubmanburg** NW Liberia 6.50N 10.53W
179 Qq15 **Tubod** Mindanao, S Philippines 7.58N 123.46E
77 T7 **Ţubruq** *Eng.* Tobruk, *It.* Tobruch. NE Libya 32.04N 23.58E
203 T13 **Tubuai** *island* Îles Australes, SW French Polynesia
Tubuai, Îles/Tubuai Islands *see* Australes, Îles
42 F3 **Tubutama** Sonora, NW Mexico 30.51N 111.31W
56 K4 **Tucacas** Falcón, N Venezuela 10.46N 68.19W
61 P16 **Tucano** Bahia, E Brazil 10.52S 38.48W
59 P19 **Tucavaca, Río** ~ E Bolivia
112 H8 **Tuchola** Kujawsko-pomorskie, C Poland 53.36N 17.49E
113 M17 **Tuchów** Małopolskie, SE Poland 49.53N 21.04E
25 S3 **Tucker** Georgia, SE USA 33.53N 84.10W
29 W10 **Tuckerman** Arkansas, C USA 35.43N 91.12W
66 B12 **Tucker's Town** E Bermuda 32.19N 64.42W
Tuckum *see* Tukums
38 M15 **Tucson** Arizona, SW USA 32.13N 111.00W
64 J7 **Tucumán** *off.* Provincia de Tucumán. ◈ *province* N Argentina
Tucumán *see* San Miguel de Tucumán
39 V11 **Tucumcari** New Mexico, SW USA 35.10N 103.43W
60 H13 **Tucunaré** Pará, N Brazil 5.15S 55.49W
57 Q6 **Tucupita** Delta Amacuro, NE Venezuela 9.01N 62.04W
60 K13 **Tucuruí, Represa de** ⊠ NE Brazil
112 F9 **Tuczno** Zachodnio-pomorskie, NW Poland 53.12N 16.08E
Tuddo *see* Tudu
107 Q5 **Tudela** *Basq.* Tutera; *anc.* Tutela. Navarra, N Spain 42.04N 1.37W
106 M6 **Tudela de Duero** Castilla-León, N Spain 41.35N 4.34W
168 G6 **Tüdevtey** *var.* Oygon. Dzavhan, N Mongolia 48.57N 96.33E
144 K6 **Tudmur** *var.* Tadmur, Tamar, *Gk.* Palmyra; *Bibl.* Tadmor. Ḩimş, C Syria 34.36N 38.15E
120 J4 **Tudu** *Ger.* Tuddo. Lääne-Virumaa, NE Estonia 59.12N 26.52E
Tuebingen *see* Tübingen
126 H16 **Tuekta** Respublika Altay, S Russian Federation 50.51N 85.52E
106 I5 **Tuela, Rio** ~ N Portugal
159 X12 **Tuensang** Nāgāland, NE India 26.16N 94.45E
142 L15 **Tufanbeyli** Adana, C Turkey 38.15N 36.13E
Tüffer *see* Laško
194 M15 **Tufi** Northern, S PNG 9.04S 149.15E
199 L3 **Tufts Plain** *undersea feature* N Pacific Ocean
Tugalan *see* Kolkhozobod
69 V14 **Tugela** ~ SE South Africa
23 P6 **Tug Fork** ~ S USA
41 P15 **Tugidak Island** *island* Trinity Islands, Alaska, USA
179 P8 **Tuguegarao** Luzon, N Philippines 17.36N 121.47E
127 N13 **Tugur** Khabarovskiy Kray, SE Russian Federation 53.43N 137.00E
167 P4 **Tuhai He** ~ E China
106 G4 **Tui** Galicia, NW Spain 42.02N 8.37W
79 O13 **Tui** *var.* Grand Balé. ~ W Burkina
59 J16 **Tuichi, Río** ~ W Bolivia
66 Q11 **Tuineje** Fuerteventura, Islas Canarias, Spain, NE Atlantic Ocean 28.18N 14.03W
45 X16 **Tuira, Río** ~ SE Panama
Tuisarkan *see* Tūysarkān
Tujiabu *see* Yongxiu
131 W5 **Tukan** Respublika Bashkortostan, W Russian Federation 53.58N 57.29E
175 R13 **Tukangbesi, Kepulauan** *Dut.* Toekang Besi Eilanden. *island group* C Indonesia
153 V13 **Tŭkhtamish** *Rus.* Toktomush, *prev.* Tokhtamyshbek. SE Tajikistan 37.51N 74.41E
192 O12 **Tukituki** ~ North Island, NZ
Tu-k'ou *see* Panzhihua
124 N15 **Tūkrah** NE Libya 32.28N 20.36E
14 G2 **Tuktoyaktuk** Northwest Territories, NW Canada 69.27N 133.00W
173 Ff6 **Tuktuk** Pulau Samosir, W Indonesia 2.32N 98.43E
Tukumi *see* Tsukumi
120 E9 **Tukums** *Ger.* Tuckum. Tukums, W Latvia 56.58N 23.12E
83 G24 **Tukuyu** *prev.* Neu-Langenburg. Mbeya, S Tanzania 9.13S 33.39E
Tukzār *see* Tokzār
43 O13 **Tula** *var.* Tula de Allende. Hidalgo, C Mexico 20.01N 99.17W
43 O11 **Tula** Tamaulipas, C Mexico 22.59N 99.43W
130 K5 **Tula** Tul'skaya Oblast', W Russian Federation 54.10N 37.39E
Tulach Mhór *see* Tullamore
Tula de Allende *see* Tula
165 N10 **Tulage Ar Gol** ~ W China
195 X15 **Tulaghi** *var.* Tulagi. Florida Islands, C Solomon Islands 9.04S 160.09E
Tulagi *see* Tulaghi
43 P13 **Tulancingo** Hidalgo, C Mexico 20.34N 98.24W
37 R11 **Tulare** California, W USA 36.12N 119.21W
31 P9 **Tulare** South Dakota, N USA 44.43N 98.29W
37 Q12 **Tulare Lake Bed** *salt flat* California, W USA
39 S14 **Tularosa** New Mexico, SW USA 33.04N 106.01W
39 P13 **Tularosa Mountains** ▲▲ New Mexico, SW USA
39 S15 **Tularosa Valley** *basin* New Mexico, SW USA
85 E25 **Tulbagh** Western Cape, SW South Africa 33.16S 19.09E
58 C5 **Tulcán** Carchi, N Ecuador 0.44N 77.43W
119 N13 **Tulcea** Tulcea, E Romania 45.11N 28.48E
119 N13 **Tulcea** ◈ *county* SE Romania
Tul'chin *see* Tul'chyn
119 N7 **Tul'chyn** *Rus.* Tul'chin. Vinnyts'ka Oblast', C Ukraine 48.40N 28.48E
Tuléar *see* Toliara
37 O1 **Tulelake** California, W USA 41.57N 121.30W
118 J10 **Tulgheş** *Hung.* Gyergyótölgyes. Harghita, C Romania 46.57N 25.46E
Tuli *see* Thuli
27 N4 **Tulia** Texas, SW USA 34.32N 101.45W
15 Gg6 **Tulita** *prev.* Fort Norman, Norman. Northwest Territories, NW Canada 64.55N 125.25W
22 J10 **Tullahoma** Tennessee, S USA 35.21N 86.12W
191 N12 **Tullamarine** ✕ (Melbourne) Victoria, SE Australia 37.40S 144.46E
191 Q7 **Tullamore** New South Wales, SE Australia 32.39S 147.35E
99 E18 **Tullamore** *Ir.* Tulach Mhór. C Ireland 53.16N 7.30W
105 N12 **Tulle** *anc.* Tutela. Corrèze, C France 45.16N 1.46E
111 X3 **Tulln** *var.* Oberhollabrunn. Niederösterreich, NE Austria 48.19N 16.01E
111 W4 **Tulln** ~ NE Austria
24 H6 **Tullos** Louisiana, S USA 31.48N 92.19W
99 F19 **Tullow** *Ir.* An Tullach. SE Ireland 52.48N 6.43W
189 W5 **Tully** Queensland, NE Australia 18.03S 145.55E
128 J3 **Tuloma** ~ NW Russian Federation
116 K10 **Tulovo** Stara Zagora, C Bulgaria 42.34N 25.34E
29 P9 **Tulsa** Oklahoma, C USA 36.09N 95.59W
159 N11 **Tulsipur** Mid Western, W Nepal 28.01N 82.22E
130 K6 **Tul'skaya Oblast'** ◈ *province* W Russian Federation
130 L14 **Tul'skiy** Respublika Adygeya, SW Russian Federation 44.26N 40.12E
194 K8 **Tulu** Manus Island, N PNG 1.58S 146.50E
56 D10 **Tuluá** Valle del Cauca, W Colombia 4.01N 76.16W
118 M12 **Tuluceşti** Galaţi, E Romania 45.35N 28.01E
41 N12 **Tuluksak** Alaska, USA 61.06N 160.57W
43 Z12 **Tulum, Ruinas de** *ruins* Quintana Roo, SE Mexico 20.13N 87.24W
126 Ii15 **Tulun** Irkutskaya Oblast', S Russian Federation 54.28N 100.18E
174 Ll15 **Tulungagung** *prev.* Toeloengagoeng. Jawa, C Indonesia 8.03S 111.54E
195 S11 **Tulun Islands** *var.* Kilinailau Islands; *prev.* Carteret Islands. *island group* NE PNG
130 M4 **Tuma** Ryazanskaya Oblast', W Russian Federation 55.09N 40.27E
56 B12 **Tumaco** Nariño, SW Colombia 1.51N 78.46W
56 B12 **Tumaco, Bahía de** *bay* SW Colombia
Tuman-gang *see* Tumen
44 L8 **Tuma, Río** ~ N Nicaragua
97 O16 **Tumba** Stockholm, C Sweden 59.12N 17.49E
Tumba, Lac *see* Ntomba, Lac
174 M9 **Tumbangsenamang** Borneo, C Indonesia 1.16S 112.21E
191 Q10 **Tumbarumba** New South Wales, SE Australia 35.47S 148.03E
58 A8 **Tumbes** Tumbes, NW Peru 3.33S 80.27W
58 A9 **Tumbes** *off.* Departamento de Tumbes. ◈ *department* NW Peru
21 P5 **Tumbledown Mountain** ▲ Maine, NE USA 45.27N 70.28W
9 N13 **Tumbler Ridge** British Columbia, W Canada 55.06N 120.51W
178 I12 **Tumbŏt, Phnum** ▲ W Cambodia 12.23N 102.57E
190 G9 **Tumby Bay** South Australia 34.22S 136.05E
169 Y10 **Tumen** Jilin, NE China 42.58N 129.52E
169 Y11 **Tumen** *Chin.* Tumen Jiang, *Kor.* Tuman-gang, *Rus.* Tumyn'tszyan. ~ E Asia
Tumen Jiang *see* Tumen
57 Q8 **Tumeremo** Bolívar, E Venezuela 7.19N 61.28W
161 G19 **Tumkūr** Karnātaka, W India 13.19N 77.06E
98 I10 **Tummel** ~ C Scotland, UK
196 B15 **Tumon Bay** *bay* W Guam
79 P14 **Tumu** NW Ghana 10.51N 1.58W
60 I10 **Tumuc Humac Mountains** *var.* Serra Tumucumaque. ▲▲ N South America
Tumucumaque, Serra *see* Tumuc Humac Mountains
191 Q10 **Tumut** New South Wales, SE Australia 35.19S 148.12E
Tumyn'tszyan *see* Tumen
Tūn *see* Ferdows
47 U14 **Tunapuna** Trinidad, Trinidad and Tobago 10.38N 61.23W
62 K11 **Tunas** Paraná, S Brazil 24.57S 49.05W
Tunbridge Wells *see* Royal Tunbridge Wells
116 L11 **Tunca Nehri** *Bul.* Tundzha. ~ Bulgaria/Turkey *see also* Tundzha
143 O14 **Tunceli** *var.* Kalan. Tunceli, E Turkey 39.07N 39.34E
143 O14 **Tunceli** ◈ *province* C Turkey
158 J12 **Tūndla** Uttar Pradesh, N India 27.13N 78.13E
83 I25 **Tunduru** Ruvuma, S Tanzania 11.07S 37.21E
116 L10 **Tundzha** *Turk.* Tunca Nehri. ~ Bulgaria/Turkey *see also* Tunca Nehri
168 I6 **Tünel** *var.* Bulag. Hövsgöl, N Mongolia 49.51N 100.41E
161 H17 **Tungabhadra** ~ S India
161 F17 **Tungabhadra Reservoir** ◎ S India
203 P2 **Tungaru** *prev.* Gilbert Islands. *island group* W Kiribati
179 Q16 **Tungawan** Mindanao, S Philippines 7.33N 122.22E
Tungdor *see* Mainling
174 Hh9 **Tungkal** ~ Sumatera, W Indonesia
T'ung-shan *see* Xuzhou
167 Q16 **Tungsha Tao** *Chin.* Dongsha Qundao, *Eng.* Pratas Island. *island* S Taiwan
167 S13 **Tungshih** *Jap.* Tōsei. N Taiwan 24.13N 120.54E
14 G7 **Tungsten** Northwest Territories, W Canada 62.00N 128.09W
Tung-t'ing Hu *see* Dongting Hu
58 A13 **Tungurahua** ◈ *province* C Ecuador
97 F14 **Tunhovdfjorden** ◎ S Norway
24 K2 **Tunica** Mississippi, S USA 34.40N 90.22W
77 N5 **Tunis** *var.* Tūnis. ● (Tunisia) NE Tunisia 36.52N 10.10E
77 N5 **Tunis, Golfe de** *Ar.* Khalīj Tūnis. *gulf* NE Tunisia
77 N6 **Tunisia** *off.* Republic of Tunisia, *Ar.* Al Jumhūrīyah at Tūnisīyah, *Fr.* République Tunisienne. ◆ *republic* N Africa
Tūnisīyah, Al Jumhūrīyah at *see* Tunisia
Tūnis, Khalīj *see* Tunis, Golfe de
56 G9 **Tunja** Boyacá, C Colombia 5.33N 73.22W
95 F14 **Tunnsjøen** *Lapp.* Dåtnejaevrie. ◎ C Norway
41 N12 **Tuntutuliak** Alaska, USA 60.21N 162.40W
153 U8 **Tunuk** Chuyskaya Oblast', C Kyrgyzstan 42.11N 73.55E
11 Q6 **Tunungayualok Island** *island* Newfoundland and Labrador, E Canada
64 H11 **Tunuyán** Mendoza, W Argentina 33.28S 69.01W
207 P14 **Tunu** ◈ *province* E Greenland
64 I11 **Tunuyán, Río** ~ W Argentina
Tunxi *see* Huangshan
Tuodian *see* Shuangbai
Tuoji *see* Zhongba
37 P9 **Tuolumne River** ~ California, W USA
Tuong Buong *see* Tương Đương
178 J7 **Tương Đương** *var.* Tuong Buong. Nghê An, N Vietnam 19.14N 104.30E
166 I13 **Tuoniang Jiang** ~ S China
Tuotuo He *see* Togton He
Tuotuoheyan *see* Tanggulashan
Tüp *see* Tyup
62 J9 **Tupã** São Paulo, S Brazil 21.57S 50.28W
203 S10 **Tupai** *var.* Motu Iti. *atoll* Îles Sous le Vent, W French Polynesia
63 G15 **Tupanciretã** Rio Grande do Sul, S Brazil 29.06S 53.48W
24 M2 **Tupelo** Mississippi, S USA 34.15N 88.42W
126 L14 **Tupik** Chitinskaya Oblast', S Russian Federation 54.21N 119.56E
61 K18 **Tupiraçaba** Goiás, S Brazil 14.33S 48.40W
59 L21 **Tupiza** Potosí, S Bolivia 21.27S 65.45W
9 N13 **Tupper** British Columbia, W Canada 55.30N 119.59W
20 J8 **Tupper Lake** ◎ New York, NE USA
152 J10 **Tuproqqal'a** *Rus.* Turpakkla. Xorazm Viloyati, W Uzbekistan 40.52N 62.00E
64 H11 **Tupungato, Volcán** ▲ W Argentina 33.27S 69.42W
169 T9 **Tuquan** Nei Mongol Zizhiqu, N China 45.21N 121.36E
56 C13 **Túquerres** Nariño, SW Colombia 1.06N 77.37W
159 U13 **Tura** Meghālaya, NE India 25.33N 90.14E
126 J10 **Tura** Evenkiyskiy Avtonomnyy Okrug, N Russian Federation 64.19N 100.16E
125 F11 **Tura** ~ C Russian Federation
146 M10 **Turabah** Makkah, W Saudi Arabia 21.27N 41.40E
57 O8 **Turagua, Cerro** ▲ C Venezuela 6.59N 64.34W
192 L12 **Turakina** Manawatu-Wanganui, North Island, NZ 40.03S 175.13E
193 K15 **Turakirae Head** *headland* North Island, NZ 41.26S 174.54E
194 G13 **Turama** ~ S PNG
126 I15 **Turan** Respublika Tyva, S Russian Federation 52.11N 93.40E
192 M10 **Turangi** Waikato, North Island, NZ 39.01S 175.46E
152 F11 **Turan Lowland** *var.* Turan Plain, *Kaz.* Turan Oypaty, *Rus.* Turanskaya Nizmennost', *Turk.* Turan Pesligi, *Uzb.* Turon Pasttekisligi. *plain* C Asia
Turan Oypaty/Turan Pesligi/Turan Plain/Turanskaya Nizmennost' *see* Turan Lowland
144 K7 **Ţurāq al 'Ilab** *hill range* S Syria
121 K20 **Turaw** *Rus.* Turov. Homyel'skaya Voblasts', SE Belarus 52.04N 27.41E
146 L2 **Ţurayf** Al Ḩudūd ash Shamālīyah, NW Saudi Arabia 31.43N 38.39E
Turba *see* Teruel
56 E5 **Turbaco** Bolívar, N Colombia 10.19N 75.25W
154 K15 **Turbat** Baluchistān, SW Pakistan 26.02N 62.56E
Turbat-i-Haidari *see* Torbat-e Ḩeydarīyeh
Turbat-i-Jam *see* Torbat-e Jām
56 D7 **Turbo** Antioquia, NW Colombia 8.06N 76.43W
Turčianský Svätý Martin *see* Martin
118 H10 **Turda** *Ger.* Thorenburg, *Hung.* Torda. Cluj, NW Romania 46.34N 23.49E
148 M7 **Ţūreh** Markazī, W Iran
203 X12 **Tureia** *atoll* Îles Tuamotu, SE French Polynesia
112 I12 **Turek** Wielkopolskie, C Poland 52.01N 18.30E
95 L19 **Turenki** Etelä-Suomi, S Finland 60.55N 24.37E
Turfan *see* Turpan
151 R8 **Turgay** *Kaz.* Torghay. Akmola, W Kazakhstan 51.43N 72.46E
151 N10 **Turgay** *Kaz.* Torgay. ~ C Kazakhstan
150 M8 **Turgayskaya Stolovaya Strana** *Kaz.* Torgay Üstirti. *plateau* Kazakhstan/Russian Federation
Turgel *see* Türi
116 L8 **Tŭrgovishte** *prev.* Eski Dzhumaya. Tŭrgovishte, N Bulgaria 43.15N 26.33E
116 L8 **Tŭrgovishte** ◈ *province* N Bulgaria
142 C14 **Turgutlu** Manisa, W Turkey 38.30N 27.43E
142 L12 **Turhal** Tokat, N Turkey 40.22N 36.04E
120 H4 **Türi** *Ger.* Turgel. Järvamaa, N Estonia 58.49N 25.25E
107 S9 **Turia** ~ E Spain
60 M12 **Turiaçu** Maranhão, E Brazil 1.40S 45.22W
Turin *see* Torino
118 I3 **Turiys'k** Volyns'ka Oblast', NW Ukraine 51.05N 24.31E
Turja *see* Tur"ya
126 K15 **Turka** Respublika Buryatiya, S Russian Federation 53.02N 108.19E
118 H6 **Turka** L'vivs'ka Oblast', W Ukraine 49.07N 23.01E
83 H16 **Turkana, Lake** *var.* Lake Rudolf. ◎ N Kenya
151 P16 **Turkestan** *Kaz.* Türkistan. Yuzhnyy Kazakhstan, S Kazakhstan 43.18N 68.18E
153 Q12 **Turkestan Range** *Rus.* Turkestanskiy Khrebet. ▲▲ C Asia
Turkestanskiy Khrebet *see* Turkestan Range
113 M23 **Túrkeve** Jász-Nagykun-Szolnok, E Hungary 47.07N 20.48E
27 O4 **Turkey** Texas, SW USA 34.23N 100.54W
142 H14 **Turkey** *off.* Republic of Turkey, *Turk.* Türkiye Cumhuriyeti. ◆ *republic* SW Asia
189 N4 **Turkey Creek** Western Australia 16.54S 128.12E
28 M9 **Turkey Creek** ~ Oklahoma, C USA
39 T9 **Turkey Mountains** ▲▲ New Mexico, SW USA
31 X11 **Turkey River** ~ Iowa, C USA
131 N7 **Turki** Saratovskaya Oblast', W Russian Federation 52.00N 43.16E
124 Nn2 **Turkish Republic of Northern Cyprus** ◇ *disputed territory* Cyprus
Türkistan *see* Turkestan
Turkistan, Bandi-i *see* Torkestān, Selseleh-ye Band-e
Türkiye Cumhuriyeti *see* Turkey
152 K12 **Türkmenabat** *prev. Rus.* Chardzhev, Chardzhou, Chardzhui, Lenin-Turkmenski, *Turkm.* Chärjew. Lebap Welaýaty, E Turkmenistan 39.07N 63.30E
152 A11 **Türkmen Aylagy** *Rus.* Turkmenskiy Zaliv. *lake gulf* W Turkmenistan
Turkmenbashi *see* Türkmenbaşy
152 A10 **Türkmenbaşy** *Rus.* Turkmenbashi; *prev.* Krasnovodsk. Balkan Welaýaty, W Turkmenistan 40.00N 53.04E
152 A10 **Türkmenbaşy Aylagy** *prev. Rus.* Krasnovodskiy Zaliv, *Turkm.* Krasnowodsk Aylagy. *lake gulf* W Turkmenistan
152 J14 **Türkmengala** *Rus.* Turkmen-kala; *prev.* Turkmen-Kala. Mary Welaýaty, S Turkmenistan 37.25N 62.19E

◆ Country
● Country Capital
◇ Dependent Territory
○ Dependent Territory Capital
◈ Administrative Region
✕ International Airport
▲ Mountain
▲▲ Mountain Range
Volcano
~ River
◎ Lake
⊠ Reservoir

Toppenish – Trois-Rivières

34 J10 Toppenish Washington, NW USA 46.22N 120.18W
189 P4 Top Springs Roadhouse Northern Territory, N Australia 16.37S 131.49E
201 U11 Tora island Chuuk, C Micronesia
Toraigh see Tory Island
201 U11 Tora Island Pass passage Chuuk Islands, C Micronesia
149 U5 Torbat-e Ḩeydarīyeh var. Turbat-i-Haidari. Khorāsān-Razavī, NE Iran 35.18N 59.12E
149 V5 Torbat-e Jām var. Turbat-i-Jam. Khorāsān-Razavī, NE Iran 35.16N 60.36E
41 Q11 Torbert, Mount ▲ Alaska, USA 61.30N 152.15W
33 P6 Torch Lake ◎ Michigan, N USA
Törcsvár see Bran
Torda see Turda
106 L6 Tordesillas Castilla-León, N Spain 41.30N 5.00W
94 K13 Töre Norrbotten, N Sweden 65.55N 22.40E
97 L17 Töreboda Västra Götaland, S Sweden 58.40N 14.07E
97 J21 Torekov Skåne, S Sweden 56.25N 12.39E
94 O3 Torell Land physical region SW Svalbard
119 Y8 Torez Donets'ka Oblast', SE Ukraine 48.02N 38.45E
103 N14 Torgau Sachsen, E Germany 51.34N 13.01E
Torgay Üstirti see Turgayskaya Stolovaya Strana
Torghay see Turgay
97 N22 Torhamn Blekinge, S Sweden 56.04N 15.49E
101 C17 Torhout West-Vlaanderen, W Belgium 51.04N 3.06E
108 B8 Torino Eng. Turin. Piemonte, NW Italy 45.03N 7.39E
172 Q13 Tori-shima island Izu-shotō, SE Japan
83 F16 Torit Eastern Equatoria, S Sudan 4.27N 32.31E
195 O11 Toriu New Britain, E PNG 4.39S 151.42E
154 M4 Torkestān, Selseleh-ye Band-e var. Bandi-i Turkistan. ▲ NW Afghanistan
106 L7 Tormes ↝ W Spain
Tornacum see Tournai
Torneå see Tornio
94 K12 Torneälven var. Torniojoki, Fin. Tornionjoki. ↝ Finland/Sweden
94 I11 Torneträsk ◎ N Sweden
11 O4 Torngat Mountains ▲ Newfoundland and Labrador, NE Canada
26 H8 Tornillo Texas, SW USA 31.26N 106.06W
94 K13 Tornio Swe. Torneå. Lappi, NW Finland 65.50N 24.17E
Torniojoki/Tornionjoki see Torneälven
63 B23 Tornquist Buenos Aires, E Argentina 38.05S 62.13W
106 L6 Toro Castilla-León, N Spain 41.31N 5.24W
64 H9 Toro, Cerro del ▲ N Chile 29.10S 69.43W
79 R12 Torodi Tillabéri, SW Niger 13.05N 1.46E
Törökbecse see Novi Bečej
195 S12 Torokina Bougainville Island, NE PNG 6.12S 155.04E
113 L23 Törökszentmiklós Jász-Nagykun-Szolnok, E Hungary 47.10N 20.25E
44 G7 Torola, Río ↝ El Salvador/Honduras
Toronaíos, Kólpos see Kassándras, Kólpos
12 H15 Toronto Ontario, S Canada 43.42N 79.25W
33 V12 Toronto Ohio, N USA 40.27N 80.36W
Toronto see Lester B.Pearson
29 P6 Toronto Lake ▣ Kansas, C USA
37 V16 Toro Peak ▲ California, W USA 33.31N 116.25W
128 H16 Toropets Tverskaya Oblast', W Russian Federation 56.29N 31.37E
83 G18 Tororo E Uganda 0.46N 34.12E
142 H16 Toros Dağları Eng. Taurus Mountains. ▲ S Turkey
191 N13 Torquay Victoria, SE Australia 38.21S 144.18E
99 J24 Torquay SW England, UK 50.28N 3.30W
106 M5 Torquemada Castilla-León, N Spain 42.02N 4.17W
37 S16 Torrance California, W USA 33.49N 118.19W
106 G12 Torrão Setúbal, S Portugal 38.18N 8.13W
106 H8 Torre, Alto da ▲ C Portugal 40.21N 7.31W
109 K18 Torre Annunziata Campania, S Italy 40.45N 14.27E
107 T8 Torreblanca País Valenciano, E Spain 40.13N 0.12E
106 L15 Torrecilla ▲ S Spain 36.38N 4.54W
107 P4 Torrecilla en Cameros La Rioja, N Spain 42.18N 2.33W
107 N13 Torredelcampo Andalucía, S Spain 37.45N 3.52W
109 K17 Torre del Greco Campania, S Italy 40.46N 14.22E
106 I6 Torre de Moncorvo var. Moncorvo, Tôrre de Moncorvo. Bragança, N Portugal 41.10N 7.03W
106 J9 Torrejoncillo Extremadura, W Spain 39.54N 6.28W
107 O8 Torrejón de Ardoz Madrid, C Spain 40.27N 3.28W
107 N7 Torrelaguna Madrid, C Spain 40.49N 3.33W
107 N2 Torrelavega Cantabria, N Spain 43.21N 4.03W
109 M16 Torremaggiore Puglia, SE Italy 41.42N 15.17E
106 M15 Torremolinos Andalucía, S Spain 36.37N 4.30W
190 I6 Torrens, Lake salt lake South Australia
107 S10 Torrent Cas. Torrente var. Torrent de l'Horta. País Valenciano, E Spain 39.27N 0.28W
Torrent de l'Horta/Torrente see Torrent
42 L8 Torreón Coahuila de Zaragoza, NE Mexico 25.47N 103.21W
107 R13 Torre Pacheco Murcia, SE Spain 37.43N 0.57W
108 A8 Torre Pellice Piemonte, NE Italy 44.49N 7.12E
107 O13 Torreperogil Andalucía, S Spain 38.01N 3.16W
63 J15 Torres Rio Grande do Sul, S Brazil 29.19S 49.46W
Torrès, Îles see Torres Islands
197 B10 Torres Islands Fr. Îles Torrès. island group N Vanuatu
106 G9 Torres Novas Santarém, C Portugal 39.28N 8.31W
189 V1 Torres Strait strait Australia/PNG
106 F10 Torres Vedras Lisboa, C Portugal 39.04N 9.15W
107 S13 Torrevieja País Valenciano, E Spain 37.58N 0.40W
194 F9 Torricelli Mountains ▲ NW PNG
98 G8 Torridon, Loch inlet NW Scotland, UK
108 D9 Torriglia Liguria, NW Italy 44.31N 9.08E
106 M9 Torrijos Castilla-La Mancha, C Spain 39.58N 4.18W
20 L12 Torrington Connecticut, NE USA 41.48N 73.07W
35 Z15 Torrington Wyoming, C USA 42.04N 104.10W
Torröjen see Torrön
96 F16 Torrön prev. Torröjen. ◎ C Sweden
107 N15 Torrox Andalucía, S Spain 36.45N 3.58W
96 N13 Torsåker Gävleborg, C Sweden 60.31N 16.30E
97 N21 Torsås Kalmar, S Sweden 56.24N 16.00E
97 J14 Torsby Värmland, C Sweden 60.07N 13.00E
97 N16 Torshälla Södermanland, C Sweden 59.25N 16.28E
97 B19 Tórshavn Dan. Thorshavn Dependent territory capital Faeroe Islands 62.02N 6.47W
Torshiz see Kāshmar
152 I9 To'rtko'l var. Türtkül, Rus. Turtkul'; prev. Petroaleksandrovsk. Qoraqalpog'iston Respublikasi, W Uzbekistan 41.34N 61.00E
47 T9 Tortola island C British Virgin Islands
108 D9 Tortona anc. Dertona. Piemonte, NW Italy 44.54N 8.52E
109 L23 Tortorici Sicilia, Italy, C Mediterranean Sea 38.01N 14.49E
107 U7 Tortosa anc. Dertosa. Cataluña, E Spain 40.49N 0.31E
Tortosa see Ţarţūs
107 U7 Tortosa, Cap headland E Spain 40.43N 0.55E
46 L8 Tortue, Île de la var. Tortuga Island. island N Haiti
57 Y10 Tortue, Montagne ▲ C French Guiana
Tortuga, Isla see La Tortuga, Isla
Tortuga Island see Tortue, Île de la
56 C11 Tortugas, Golfo gulf W Colombia
47 T5 Tortuguero, Laguna lagoon N Puerto Rico
143 Q12 Tortum Erzurum, NE Turkey 40.15N 41.30E
Torugart, Pereval see Turugart Shankou
143 O12 Torul Gümüşhane, NE Turkey 40.34N 39.18E
112 J10 Toruń Ger. Thorn. Toruń, Kujawsko-pomorskie, C Poland 53.01N 18.36E
97 K20 Torup Halland, S Sweden 56.57N 13.04E
120 I6 Tõrva Ger. Törwa. Valgamaa, S Estonia 58.00N 25.54E
Törwa see Tõrva
98 D13 Tory Island Ir. Toraigh. island NW Ireland
113 N19 Torysa Hung. Tarca. ↝ NE Slovakia
Törzburg see Bran
128 J16 Torzhok Tverskaya Oblast', W Russian Federation 57.04N 34.55E
170 Ee15 Tosa Kōchi, Shikoku, SW Japan 33.28N 133.25E
170 E16 Tosa-Shimizu var. Tosasimizu. Kōchi, Shikoku, SW Japan 32.46N 132.55E
Tosasimizu see Tosa-Shimizu
170 Ee16 Tosa-wan bay SW Japan
85 H21 Tosca North-West, N South Africa 25.51S 23.56E
108 F12 Toscana Eng. Tuscany. ◆ region C Italy
109 E14 Toscano, Archipelago Eng. Tuscan Archipelago. island group C Italy
108 G10 Tosco-Emiliano, Appennino Eng. Tuscan-Emilian Mountains. ▲ C Italy
Tōsei see Tungshih
171 J18 To-shima island Izu-shotō, SE Japan
153 Q9 Toshkent Eng./Rus. Tashkent. ● (Uzbekistan) Toshkent Viloyati, E Uzbekistan 41.19N 69.17E
153 Q9 Toshkent ✕ Toshkent Viloyati, E Uzbekistan 41.13N 69.15E
153 P9 Toshkent Viloyati Rus. Tashkentskaya Oblast'. ◆ province E Uzbekistan
128 H13 Tosno Leningradskaya Oblast', NW Russian Federation 59.34N 30.48E
165 Q10 Toson Hu ◎ C China
168 H6 Tosontsengel Dzavhan, NW Mongolia 48.42N 98.14E
168 J6 Tosontsengel var. Tsengel. Hövsgöl, N Mongolia 49.29N 101.09E
152 I8 Tosquduq Qumlari prev. Goshquduq Qum, Rus. Peski Taskuduk. desert W Uzbekistan
107 U4 Tossal de l'Orri var. Llorri. ▲ NE Spain 42.24N 1.15E
63 A15 Tostado Santa Fe, C Argentina 29.14S 61.43W
120 F6 Tõstamaa Ger. Testama. Pärnumaa, SW Estonia 58.19N 23.58E
102 I10 Tostedt Niedersachsen, NW Germany 53.16N 9.42E
142 J11 Tosya Kastamonu, N Turkey 41.01N 34.01E
97 F15 Totak ◎ S Norway
107 R13 Totana Murcia, SE Spain 37.45N 1.30W
96 H13 Toten physical region S Norway
85 G18 Toteng North-West, C Botswana 20.19S 22.57E
104 M3 Tôtes Seine-Maritime, N France 49.40N 1.02E
Totigi see Tochigi
Totio see Tochio
Totis see Tata
201 U13 Totiw island Chuuk, C Micronesia
129 N13 Tot'ma var. Totma. Vologodskaya Oblast', NW Russian Federation 59.58N 42.42E
Tot'ma see Sukhona
57 V9 Totness Coronie, N Surinam 5.51N 56.19W
44 C5 Totonicapán Totonicapán, W Guatemala 14.54N 91.18W
44 A2 Totonicapán off. Departamento de Totonicapán. ◆ department W Guatemala
63 B18 Totoras Santa Fe, C Argentina 32.34S 61.10W
197 K15 Totoya island S Fiji
191 Q7 Tottenham New South Wales, SE Australia 32.16S 147.23E
171 Gg13 Tottori Tottori, Honshū, SW Japan 35.28N 134.14E
170 Ff13 Tottori off. Tottori-ken. ◆ prefecture Honshū, SW Japan
78 I6 Touâjîl Tiris Zemmour, N Mauritania 22.03N 12.39W
78 L15 Touba W Ivory Coast 8.16N 7.40W
78 G11 Touba W Senegal 14.55N 15.53W
76 E7 Toubkal, Jbel ▲ W Morocco 31.00N 7.50W
34 K10 Touchet Washington, NW USA 46.03N 118.40W
105 P7 Toucy Yonne, C France 47.45N 3.18E
79 O12 Tougan W Burkina 13.06N 3.03W
76 L7 Touggourt NE Algeria 33.07N 6.04E
79 Q12 Tougouri N Burkina 13.22N 0.25W
78 J13 Tougué NW Guinea 11.28N 11.48W
78 K12 Toukoto Kayes, W Mali 13.24N 9.52W
105 S5 Toul Meurthe-et-Moselle, NE France 48.40N 5.54E
78 L16 Toulépleu var. Toulobli. W Ivory Coast 6.37N 8.27W
167 S14 Touliu C Taiwan 23.44N 120.27E
13 U3 Toulnustouc ↝ Québec, SE Canada
Toulobli see Toulépleu
105 T16 Toulon anc. Telo Martius, Tilio Martius. Var, SE France 43.07N 5.55E
32 K12 Toulon Illinois, N USA 41.04N 89.54W
104 M15 Toulouse anc. Tolosa. Haute-Garonne, S France 43.36N 1.24E
104 M15 Toulouse ✕ Haute-Garonne, S France 43.38N 1.19E
79 N16 Toumodi C Ivory Coast 6.34N 5.01W
76 G9 Tounassine, Hamada hill range W Algeria
177 G7 Toungoo Pegu, C Burma 18.57N 96.25E
104 L8 Touraine cultural region C France
Tourane see Đa Nâng
105 P1 Tourcoing Nord, N France 50.43N 3.10E
106 F2 Touriñán, Cabo headland NW Spain 43.02N 9.20W
78 J6 Tourine Tiris Zemmour, N Mauritania 22.22N 11.49W
104 J3 Tourlaville Manche, N France 49.39N 1.34W
101 D19 Tournai var. Tournay, Dut. Doornik; anc. Tornacum. Hainaut, SW Belgium 50.36N 3.24E
104 L16 Tournay Hautes-Pyrénées, S France 43.10N 0.16E
Tournay see Tournai
105 R12 Tournon Ardèche, E France 45.04N 4.49E
105 R9 Tournus Saône-et-Loire, C France 46.33N 4.53E
61 Q14 Touros Rio Grande do Norte, E Brazil 5.10S 35.28W
104 L8 Tours anc. Caesarodunum, Turoni. Indre-et-Loire, C France 47.22N 0.40E
191 Q17 Tourville, Cape headland Tasmania, SE Australia 42.09S 148.20E
168 L8 Töv ◆ province C Mongolia
56 H7 Tovar Mérida, NW Venezuela 8.21N 71.45W
130 L5 Tovarkovskiy Tul'skaya Oblast', W Russian Federation 53.41N 38.18E
Tovil'-Dora see Tavildara
Tövis see Teiuş
143 V11 Tovuz Rus. Tauz. W Azerbaijan 40.58N 45.41E
172 N9 Towada Aomori, Honshū, C Japan 40.36N 141.11E
172 N9 Towada-ko var. Towada Ko. ◎ Honshū, C Japan
192 K3 Towai Northland, North Island, NZ 35.29S 174.06E
20 H12 Towanda Pennsylvania, NE USA 41.45N 76.25W
31 W4 Tower Minnesota, N USA 47.48N 92.16W
175 Pp8 Towera Sulawesi, N Indonesia 0.29S 120.01E
Tower Island see Genovesa, Isla
188 M13 Tower Peak ▲ Western Australia 33.23S 123.27E
37 U11 Towne Pass pass California, W USA
31 N3 Towner North Dakota, N USA 48.20N 100.27W
35 R10 Townsend Montana, NW USA 46.19N 111.31W
189 X6 Townsville Queensland, NE Australia 19.24S 146.52E
Towoeti Meer see Towuti, Danau
175 Q10 Towori, Teluk bay Sulawesi, C Indonesia
154 K4 Towraghoudī Herāt, NW Afghanistan 35.12N 62.19E
23 X3 Towson Maryland, NE USA 39.22N 76.33W
175 Q11 Towuti, Danau Dut. Towoeti Meer. ◎ Sulawesi, C Indonesia
Toxkan He see Ak-say
26 K9 Toyah Texas, SW USA 31.18N 103.47W
172 Nn6 Tōya-ko ◎ Hokkaidō, NE Japan
171 Ii13 Toyama Toyama, Honshū, SW Japan 36.41N 137.12E
171 Ii13 Toyama off. Toyama-ken. ◆ prefecture Honshū, SW Japan
171 J13 Toyama-wan bay W Japan
170 F16 Tōyo Ehime, Shikoku, SW Japan 33.57N 133.02E
170 Ee14 Tōyo Kōchi, Shikoku, SW Japan 33.28N 134.13E
Toyohara see Yuzhno-Sakhalinsk
171 Hh16 Toyohashi var. Toyohasi. Aichi, Honshū, SW Japan 34.45N 137.22E
Toyohasi see Toyohashi
171 I16 Toyokawa Aichi, Honshū, SW Japan 34.49N 137.22E
171 Gg13 Toyooka Hyōgo, Honshū, SW Japan 35.33N 134.48E
171 Kk12 Toyosaka Niigata, Honshū, C Japan 37.54N 139.12E
171 I16 Toyota Aichi, Honshū, SW Japan 35.04N 137.09E
172 Pp2 Toyotomi Hokkaidō, NE Japan 45.07N 141.45E
170 Dd12 Toyoura Yamaguchi, Honshū, SW Japan 34.09N 130.55E
Toytepa see To'ytepa
153 Q10 To'ytepa Rus. Toytepa. Toshkent Viloyati, E Uzbekistan 41.04N 69.22E
76 M6 Tozeur var. Tawzar. W Tunisia 34.00N 8.09E
41 Q8 Tozi, Mount ▲ Alaska, USA 65.45N 151.01W
143 Q9 Tqvarch'eli Rus. Tkvarcheli. NW Georgia 42.51N 41.42E
Trâblous see Tripoli
143 O11 Trabzon Eng. Trebizond; anc. Trapezus. Trabzon, NE Turkey 41.00N 39.43E
143 O11 Trabzon Eng. Trebizond. ◆ province NE Turkey
11 P13 Tracadie New Brunswick, SE Canada 47.31N 64.57W
Trachenberg see Żmigród
13 O11 Tracy Québec, SE Canada 45.59N 73.07W
37 O8 Tracy California, W USA 37.43N 121.27W
31 S10 Tracy Minnesota, N USA 44.14N 95.37W
22 K10 Tracy City Tennessee, S USA 35.15N 85.44W
108 D7 Tradate Lombardia, N Italy 45.43N 8.57E
86 F6 Traena Bank undersea feature E Norwegian Sea
31 W13 Traer Iowa, C USA 42.11N 92.28W
106 J16 Trafalgar, Cabo de headland SW Spain 36.10N 6.03W
Traiectum ad Mosam/Traiectum Tungorum see Maastricht
Tráigh Mhór see Tramore
9 O17 Trail British Columbia, SW Canada 49.04N 117.46W
60 B11 Traíra, Serra do ▲ NW Brazil
111 V5 Traisen Niederösterreich, NE Austria 48.03N 15.37E
111 W4 Traisen ↝ NE Austria
111 X4 Traiskirchen Niederösterreich, NE Austria 48.01N 16.18E
Trajani Portus see Civitavecchia
Trajectum ad Rhenum see Utrecht
121 H14 Trakai Ger. Traken, Pol. Troki. Vilnius, SE Lithuania 54.39N 24.58E
Traken see Trakai
99 B20 Tralee Ir. Trá Lí. SW Ireland 52.16N 9.42W
99 A20 Tralee Bay Ir. Bá Thrá Lí. bay SW Ireland
Trá Lí see Tralee
Trälleborg see Trelleborg
Tralles see Aydın
63 J16 Tramandaí Rio Grande do Sul, S Brazil 30.01S 50.11W
110 C7 Tramelan Bern, W Switzerland 47.13N 7.07E
Trá Mhór see Tramore
99 E20 Tramore Ir. Tráigh Mhór, Trá Mhór. S Ireland 52.10N 7.10W
97 L18 Tranås Jönköping, S Sweden 58.03N 15.00E
64 J7 Trancas Tucumán, N Argentina 26.10S 65.19W
106 I7 Trancoso Guarda, N Portugal 40.46N 7.21W
97 H22 Tranebjerg Århus, C Denmark 55.51N 10.36E
97 K19 Tranemo Västra Götaland, S Sweden 57.30N 13.19E
178 Gg16 Trang Trang, S Thailand 7.33N 99.36E
176 W14 Trangan, Pulau island Kepulauan Aru, E Indonesia
Trâng Dinh see Thât Khê
191 Q7 Trangie New South Wales, SE Australia 32.01S 147.58E
96 K12 Trängslet Dalarna, C Sweden 61.22N 13.43E
109 N16 Trani Puglia, SE Italy 41.16N 16.24E
63 F17 Tranqueras Rivera, NE Uruguay 31.13S 55.45W
65 G17 Tranqui, Isla island S Chile
41 V6 Trans-Alaska pipeline oil pipeline Alaska, USA
205 Q10 Transantarctic Mountains ▲ Antarctica
Transcarpathian Oblast see Zakarpats'ka Oblast'
Transilvania see Transylvania
Transilvaniei, Alpi see Carpaţii Meridionali
Transjordan see Jordan
180 L11 Transkei Basin undersea feature SW Indian Ocean
119 O10 Transnistria cultural region E Moldova
127 N17 Trans-Siberian Railway Railroad Russian Federation
Transsylvanische Alpen/Transylvanian Alps see Carpaţii Meridionali
96 K12 Transtrand Dalarna, C Sweden 61.06N 13.19E
118 G10 Transylvania Eng. Ardeal, Transilvania, Ger. Siebenbürgen, Hung. Erdély. cultural region NW Romania
178 Jj15 Tra Ôn Vinh Long, S Vietnam 9.58N 105.58E
109 H23 Trapani anc. Drepanum. Sicilia, Italy, C Mediterranean Sea 38.02N 12.31E
178 J12 Trâpeăng Vêng Kâmpóng Thum, C Cambodia 12.37N 104.58E
116 L9 Trapoklovo Sliven, C Bulgaria 42.40N 26.36E
191 P13 Traralgon Victoria, SE Australia 38.15S 146.35E
78 H9 Trarza ◆ region SW Mauritania
Trasimenischersee see Trasimeno, Lago
108 H12 Trasimeno, Lago Eng. Lake of Perugia, Ger. Trasimenischersee. ◎ C Italy
97 J20 Träslövsläge Halland, S Sweden 57.02N 12.18E
Trás-os-Montes see Cucumbi
106 I6 Trás-os-Montes e Alto Douro former province N Portugal
178 I13 Trat var. Bang Phra. Trat, S Thailand 12.16N 102.30E
Trá Tholl, Inis see Inishtrahull
Traù see Trogir
111 T4 Traun Oberösterreich, N Austria 48.14N 14.13E
111 S5 Traun ↝ N Austria
Traun, Lake see Traunsee
103 N23 Traunreut Bayern, SE Germany 47.58N 12.36E
111 S5 Traunsee var. Gmundner See, Eng. Lake Traun. ◎ N Austria
Trautenau see Trutnov
23 P11 Travelers Rest South Carolina, SE USA 34.58N 82.26W
190 L8 Travellers Lake seasonal lake New South Wales, SE Australia
33 P6 Traverse City Michigan, N USA 44.45N 85.37W
31 R7 Traverse, Lake ◎ Minnesota/South Dakota, N USA
193 I16 Travers, Mount ▲ South Island, NZ 42.01S 172.46E
9 P17 Travers Reservoir ▣ Alberta, SW Canada
178 Jj15 Tra Vinh var. Phu Vinh. Tra Vinh, S Vietnam 9.57N 106.19E
27 S10 Travis, Lake ▣ Texas, SW USA
114 H12 Travnik Federacija Bosna I Hercegovina, C Bosnia and Herzegovina 44.14N 17.40E
111 V11 Trbovlje Ger. Trifail. C Slovenia 46.09N 15.03E
25 V13 Treasure Island Florida, SE USA 27.46N 82.46W
Treasure State see Montana
195 S14 Treasury Islands island group NW Solomon Islands
108 D9 Trebbia anc. Trebia. ↝ NW Italy
102 N8 Trebel ↝ NE Germany
105 O16 Trèbes Aude, S France 43.12N 2.25E
Trebia see Trebbia
113 F18 Třebíč Ger. Trebitsch. Vysočina, S Czech Republic 49.13N 15.52E
115 I16 Trebinje Republika Srpska, S Bosnia and Herzegovina 42.42N 18.19E
Trebišnica see Trebišnjica
115 H16 Trebišnjica var. Trebišnica. ↝ S Bosnia and Herzegovina
113 N20 Trebišov Hung. Tőketerebes. Košický Kraj, E Slovakia 48.36N 21.44E
Trebitsch see Třebíč
Trebizond see Trabzon
Trebnitz see Trzebnica
111 V12 Trebnje SE Slovenia 45.54N 15.01E
113 D19 Třeboň Ger. Wittingau. Jihočeský Kraj, S Czech Republic 49.00N 14.46E
106 J15 Trebujena Andalucía, S Spain 36.52N 6.10W
102 I7 Treene ↝ N Germany
Tree Planters State see Nebraska
111 S9 Treffen Kärnten, S Austria 46.40N 13.51E
Trefynwy see Monmouth
104 G5 Tréguier Côtes d'Armor, NW France 48.50N 3.12W
63 G18 Treinta y Tres Treinta y Tres, E Uruguay 33.12S 54.19W
63 F18 Treinta y Tres ◆ department E Uruguay
125 E11 Trëkhgornyy Chelyabinskaya Oblast', C Russian Federation 54.42N 58.25E
116 F9 Treklyanska Reka ↝ W Bulgaria
175 R10 Treko, Kepulauan island group N Indonesia
104 K8 Trélazé Maine-et-Loire, NW France 47.27N 0.28W
65 K17 Trelew Chubut, SE Argentina 43.13S 65.15W
97 K23 Trelleborg var. Trälleborg. Skåne, S Sweden 55.22N 13.10E
115 P15 Trem ▲ SE Serbia 43.10N 22.12E
13 N11 Tremblant, Mont ▲ Québec, SE Canada 46.13N 74.34W
101 H17 Tremelo Vlaams Brabant, C Belgium 50.59N 4.34E
109 M15 Tremiti, Isole island group SE Italy
32 K12 Tremont Illinois, N USA 40.30N 89.31W
38 L1 Tremonton Utah, W USA 41.42N 112.09W
107 U4 Tremp Cataluña, NE Spain 42.09N 0.53E
32 J7 Trempealeau Wisconsin, N USA 44.00N 91.25W
13 P8 Trenche ↝ Québec, SE Canada
13 O7 Trenche, Lac ◎ Québec, SE Canada
113 I20 Trenčiansky Kraj ◆ region W Slovakia
113 I19 Trenčín Ger. Trentschin, Hung. Trencsén. Trenčiansky Kraj, W Slovakia 48.54N 18.03E
Trencsén see Trenčín
Trengganu see Terengganu
63 A21 Trenque Lauquen Buenos Aires, E Argentina 36.00S 62.46W
12 J14 Trent ↝ Ontario, SE Canada
99 N18 Trent ↝ C England, UK
Trent see Trento
108 F5 Trentino-Alto Adige prev. Venezia Tridentina. ◆ region N Italy
108 G6 Trento Eng. Trent, Ger. Trient; anc. Tridentum. Trentino-Alto Adige, N Italy 46.04N 11.07E
12 J15 Trenton Ontario, SE Canada 44.06N 77.36W
25 V10 Trenton Florida, SE USA 29.36N 82.49W
25 R1 Trenton Georgia, SE USA 34.52N 85.27W
33 S10 Trenton Michigan, N USA 42.08N 83.10W
29 S2 Trenton Missouri, C USA 40.04N 93.37W
30 M17 Trenton Nebraska, C USA 40.10N 101.00W
20 J15 Trenton state capital New Jersey, NE USA 40.13N 74.44W
23 W10 Trenton North Carolina, SE USA 35.03N 77.20W
22 G9 Trenton Tennessee, S USA 35.58N 88.56W
38 L1 Trenton Utah, W USA 41.53N 111.57W
Trentschin see Trenčín
Treptow an der Rega see Trzebiatów
63 C23 Tres Arroyos Buenos Aires, E Argentina 38.21S 60.16W
63 J15 Três Cachoeiras Rio Grande do Sul, S Brazil 29.21S 49.48W
108 E7 Trescore Balneario Lombardia, N Italy 45.43N 9.52E
43 V17 Tres Cruces, Cerro ▲ SE Mexico 15.28N 92.27W
59 K18 Tres Cruces, Cordillera ▲ W Bolivia
115 N18 Treska ↝ NW FYR Macedonia
115 I14 Treskavica ▲ SE Bosnia and Herzegovina
61 J20 Três Lagoas Mato Grosso do Sul, SW Brazil 20.46S 51.43W
42 H12 Tres Marías, Islas island group C Mexico
61 M19 Três Marias, Represa ▣ SE Brazil
65 F20 Tres Montes, Península headland S Chile 46.49S 75.29W
107 O3 Trespaderne Castilla-León, N Spain 42.46N 3.24W
62 G13 Três Passos Rio Grande do Sul, S Brazil 27.28S 53.55W
63 A23 Tres Picos, Cerro ▲ E Argentina 38.10S 61.54W
65 G17 Tres Picos, Cerro ▲ SW Argentina 42.22S 71.51W
62 I12 Três Pinheiros Paraná, S Brazil 25.25S 51.57W
61 M21 Três Pontas Minas Gerais, SE Brazil 21.33S 45.18W
Tres Puntas, Cabo see Manabique, Punta
62 P9 Três Rios Rio de Janeiro, SE Brazil 22.06S 43.15W
Tres Tabernae see Saverne
Trestenberg/Trestendorf see Tăşnad
43 R15 Tres Valles Veracruz-Llave, SE Mexico 18.14N 96.03W
96 H12 Tretten Oppland, S Norway 61.19N 10.19E
Treuburg see Olecko
103 K21 Treuchtlingen Bayern, S Germany 48.57N 10.55E
102 N13 Treuenbrietzen Brandenburg, E Germany 52.06N 12.52E
97 F16 Treungen Telemark, S Norway 59.00N 8.34E
65 H17 Trevelín Chubut, SW Argentina 43.02S 71.27W
Treves/Trèves see Trier
108 I13 Trevi Umbria, C Italy 42.52N 12.46E
108 E7 Treviglio Lombardia, N Italy 45.31N 9.34E
106 J4 Trevinca, Peña ▲ NW Spain 42.10N 6.49W
107 P3 Treviño Castilla-León, N Spain 42.45N 2.41W
108 I7 Treviso anc. Tarvisium. Veneto, NE Italy 45.40N 12.15E
99 G24 Trevose Head headland SW England, UK 50.33N 5.03W
Trg see Feldkirchen in Kärnten
191 P17 Triabunna Tasmania, SE Australia 42.33S 147.55E
23 W4 Triangle Virginia, NE USA 38.30N 77.17W
85 L18 Triangle Masvingo, SE Zimbabwe 20.58S 31.28E
117 L23 Tría Nisía island Kykládes, Greece, Aegean Sea
Triberg see Triberg im Schwarzwald
103 G23 Triberg im Schwarzwald var. Triberg. Baden-Württemberg, SW Germany 48.07N 8.13E
159 P11 Tribhuvan ✕ (Kathmandu) Central, C Nepal
56 C9 Tribugá, Golfo de gulf W Colombia
189 W4 Tribulation, Cape headland Queensland, NE Australia 16.14S 145.48E
110 M8 Tribulaun ▲ SW Austria 46.59N 11.18E
9 U17 Tribune Saskatchewan, S Canada 49.16N 103.50W
28 H5 Tribune Kansas, C USA 38.28N 101.45W
109 N18 Tricarico Basilicata, S Italy 40.37N 16.09E
109 Q19 Tricase Puglia, SE Italy 39.56N 18.21E
Trichinopoly see Tiruchchirāppalli
117 D18 Trichonída, Límni ◎ C Greece
161 G22 Trichūr var. Thrissur. Kerala, SW India 10.31N 76.13E
Tricorno see Triglav
191 O8 Trida New South Wales, SE Australia 33.02S 145.03E
37 S1 Trident Peak ▲ Nevada, W USA 41.52N 118.22W
Tridentum/Trient see Trento
111 T6 Trieben Steiermark, SE Austria 47.29N 14.27E
103 D19 Trier Eng. Treves, Fr. Trèves; anc. Augusta Treverorum. Rheinland-Pfalz, SW Germany 49.45N 6.39E
108 K7 Trieste Slvn. Trst. Friuli-Venezia Giulia, NE Italy 45.39N 13.45E
Trieste, Golfo di/Triest, Golf von see Trieste, Gulf of
108 J8 Trieste, Gulf of Cro. Tršćanski Zaljev, Ger. Golf von Triest, It. Golfo di Trieste, Slvn. Tržaški Zaliv. gulf S Europe
111 W4 Triesting ↝ W Austria
Triêu Hai see Quang Tri
Trifail see Trbovlje
118 L9 Trifeşti Iaşi, NE Romania 47.30N 27.31E
111 S10 Triglav It. Tricorno. ▲ NW Slovenia 46.22N 13.40E
106 I14 Trigueros Andalucía, S Spain 37.24N 6.49W
117 E16 Tríkala prev. Trikkala. Thessalía, C Greece 39.33N 21.46E
117 E17 Trikeriótis ↝ C Greece
Trikkala see Tríkala
Trikomo/Tríkomon see Iskele
99 F17 Trim Ir. Baile Átha Troim. E Ireland 53.34N 6.46W
110 E7 Trimbach Solothurn, NW Switzerland 47.21N 7.49E
111 Q5 Trimmelkam Oberösterreich, N Austria 48.02N 12.55E
31 U11 Trimont Minnesota, N USA 43.45N 94.42W
Trimontium see Plovdiv
Trinacria see Sicilia
161 K24 Trincomalee var. Trinkomali. Eastern Province, NE Sri Lanka 8.34N 81.13E
67 K16 Trindade, Ilha da island Brazil, W Atlantic Ocean
49 Y9 Trindade Spur undersea feature SW Atlantic Ocean
113 J17 Třinec Ger. Trzynietz. Moravskoslezský Kraj, E Czech Republic 49.42N 18.37E
59 M16 Trinidad Beni, N Bolivia 14.52S 64.54W
56 H9 Trinidad Casanare, E Colombia 5.25N 71.39W
46 E6 Trinidad Sancti Spíritus, C Cuba 21.48N 80.00W
39 U8 Trinidad Colorado, C USA 37.10N 104.31W
63 E19 Trinidad Flores, S Uruguay 33.34S 56.54W
47 Y17 Trinidad island C Trinidad and Tobago
Trinidad see Jose Abad Santos
47 Y16 Trinidad and Tobago off. Republic of Trinidad and Tobago. ◆ republic SE West Indies
65 F22 Trinidad, Golfo gulf S Chile
63 B24 Trinidad, Isla island E Argentina
109 N16 Trinitapoli Puglia, SE Italy 41.22N 16.06E
57 X10 Trinité, Montagnes de la ▲ C French Guiana
27 W9 Trinity Texas, SW USA 30.57N 95.22W
11 U12 Trinity Bay inlet Newfoundland and Labrador, E Canada
41 P15 Trinity Islands island group Alaska, USA
37 N2 Trinity Mountains ▲ California, W USA
37 S4 Trinity Peak ▲ Nevada, W USA 40.13N 118.43W
37 S5 Trinity Range ▲ Nevada, W USA
37 N2 Trinity River ↝ California, W USA
27 V8 Trinity River ↝ Texas, SW USA
Trinkomali see Trincomalee
181 Y15 Triolet NW Mauritius 20.04S 57.31E
109 O20 Trionto, Capo headland S Italy 39.37N 16.46E
173 Ee4 Tripa, Krueng ↝ Sumatera, NW Indonesia
Tripiti, Ákra see Trypití, Akrotírio
144 G6 Tripoli var. Tarābulus, Ţarābulus ash Shām, Trâblous; anc. Tripolis. N Lebanon 34.30N 35.42E
31 X12 Tripoli Iowa, C USA 42.48N 92.15W
Tripoli see Ţarābulus
117 F20 Trípoli prev. Trípolis. Pelopónnisos, S Greece 37.31N 22.22E
Tripolis see Tripoli, Lebanon
Trípolis see Trípoli, Greece
31 Q12 Tripp South Dakota, N USA 43.12N 97.57W
159 V15 Tripura var. Hill Tippera. ◆ state N India
110 K8 Trisanna ↝ W Austria
102 H8 Trischen island NW Germany
67 M24 Tristan da Cunha ◇ dependency of Saint Helena SE Atlantic Ocean
69 P15 Tristan da Cunha island SE Atlantic Ocean
67 L18 Tristan da Cunha Fracture Zone tectonic feature S Atlantic Ocean
178 J14 Tri Tôn An Giang, S Vietnam 10.25N 105.01E
178 Ll11 Triton Island island S Paracel Islands
161 G24 Trivandrum var. Thiruvanathapuram. Kerala, SW India 8.30N 76.57E
113 H20 Trnava Ger. Tyrnau, Hung. Nagyszombat. Trnavský Kraj, W Slovakia 48.22N 17.36E
113 H20 Trnavský Kraj ◆ region W Slovakia
Trnovo see Veliko Tŭrnovo
Trobriand Island see Kiriwina Island
Trobriand Islands see Kiriwina Islands
9 Q16 Trochu Alberta, SW Canada 51.48N 113.12W
111 U7 Trofaiach Steiermark, SE Austria 47.24N 14.56E
95 F14 Trofors Troms, N Norway 65.31N 13.19E
115 E14 Trogir It. Traù. Split-Dalmacija, S Croatia 43.32N 16.13E
114 F13 Troglav ▲ Bosnia and Herzegovina/Croatia 44.00N 16.36E
109 M16 Troia Puglia, SE Italy 41.21N 15.19E
109 K24 Troina Sicilia, Italy, C Mediterranean Sea 37.48N 14.33E
181 O16 Trois-Bassins W Réunion 21.04S 55.18E
103 E17 Troisdorf Nordrhein-Westfalen, W Germany 50.49N 7.09E
76 H5 Trois Fourches, Cap des headland NE Morocco 35.27N 2.58W
13 T8 Trois-Pistoles Québec, SE Canada 48.07N 69.10W
101 L21 Trois-Ponts Liège, E Belgium 50.22N 5.52E
13 P11 Trois-Rivières Québec, SE Canada 46.21N 72.34W

◆ Country ● Country Capital ◇ Dependent Territory ○ Dependent Territory Capital ◆ Administrative Region ✕ International Airport ▲ Mountain ▲ Mountain Range ⛰ Volcano ↝ River ◎ Lake ▣ Reservoir
339

TIMUR, BANJARAN – TOPOZERO, OZERO

174 H3 **Timur, Banjaran** ⛰ Peninsular Malaysia
179 R17 **Tinaca Point** headland Mindanao, S Philippines 5.35N 125.18E
56 K5 **Tinaco** Cojedes, N Venezuela 9.42N 68.27W
66 Q11 **Tinajo** Lanzarote, Islas Canarias, Spain, NE Atlantic Ocean 29.03N 13.40W
195 W8 **Tinakula** island Santa Cruz Islands, E Solomon Islands
56 K5 **Tinaquillo** Cojedes, N Venezuela 9.52N 68.19W
118 F10 **Tinca** Hung. Tenke. Bihor, W Romania 46.46N 21.58E
161 J20 **Tindivanam** Tamil Nādu, SE India 12.15N 79.40E
76 E9 **Tindouf** W Algeria 27.43N 8.09W
76 E9 **Tindouf, Sebkha de** salt lake W Algeria
106 J2 **Tineo** Asturias, N Spain 43.19N 6.25W
79 R9 **Ti-n-Essako** Kidal, E Mali 18.30N 2.27E
191 T5 **Tingha** New South Wales, SE Australia 29.56S 151.13E
Tingis see Tanger
Tinglett see Tinglev
97 F24 **Tinglev** Ger. Tinglett. Sønderjylland, SW Denmark 54.57N 9.15E
58 E12 **Tingo María** Huánuco, C Peru 9.19S 75.56W
Tingréla see Tengréla
164 K16 **Tingri** var. Xêgar. Xizang Zizhiqu, W China 28.40N 87.04E
97 M21 **Tingsryd** Kronoberg, S Sweden 56.30N 15.00E
97 P19 **Tingstäde** Gotland, SE Sweden 57.45N 18.36E
64 H12 **Tinguiririca, Volcán** ▲ C Chile 34.52S 70.24W
96 F9 **Tingvoll** Møre og Romsdal, S Norway 62.55N 8.13E
194 M9 **Tingwon Island** island N PNG
196 K8 **Tinian** island S Northern Mariana Islands
Ti-n-Kâr see Timétrine
Tinnevelly see Tirunelveli
97 G15 **Tinnoset** Telemark, S Norway 59.43N 9.03E
97 F15 **Tinnsjø** ◎ S Norway
Tino see Chino
117 J20 **Tínos** Tínos, Kykládes, Greece, Aegean Sea 37.32N 25.10E
117 J20 **Tínos** anc. Tenos. island Kykládes, Greece, Aegean Sea
159 R14 **Tinpahar** Jhārkhand, NE India 25.00N 87.43E
124 O14 **Tin, Ra's al** headland N Libya 32.36N 23.10E
159 X11 **Tinsukia** Assam, NE India 27.28N 95.19E
78 K10 **Tintâne** Hodh el Gharbi, S Mauritania 16.25N 10.08W
64 L7 **Tintina** Santiago del Estero, N Argentina 27.03S 62.42W
190 K10 **Tintinara** South Australia 35.54S 140.04E
106 I14 **Tinto** ∽ SW Spain
79 S8 **Ti-n-Zaouâtene** Kidal, NE Mali 19.56N 2.45E
Tiobraid Árann see Tipperary
30 K3 **Tioga** North Dakota, N USA 48.24N 102.56W
20 G12 **Tioga** Pennsylvania, NE USA 41.54N 77.07W
27 T5 **Tioga** Texas, SW USA 33.28N 96.55W
37 Q8 **Tioga Pass** pass California, W USA 37.53N 119.15W
20 G12 **Tioga River** ∽ New York/Pennsylvania, NE USA
176 Y11 **Tiom** Papua, E Indonesia 3.49S 138.22E
Tioman Island see Tioman, Pulau
174 I5 **Tioman, Pulau** var. Tioman Island. island Peninsular Malaysia
20 C12 **Tionesta** Pennsylvania, NE USA 41.31N 79.30W
20 D12 **Tionesta Creek** ∽ Pennsylvania, NE USA
173 G11 **Tiop** Pulau Pagai Selatan, W Indonesia 3.12S 100.21E
175 Qq12 **Tioro, Selat** var. Tiworo. strait Sulawesi, C Indonesia
79 O12 **Tiou** NW Burkina 13.42N 2.34W
20 H11 **Tioughnioga River** ∽ New York, NE USA
176 U10 **Tip** Papua, E Indonesia 1.50S 130.04E
76 J5 **Tipasa** var. Tipaza. N Algeria 36.34N 2.27E
Tipaza see Tipasa
44 J10 **Tipitapa** Managua, W Nicaragua 12.10N 86.04W
33 R13 **Tipp City** Ohio, N USA 39.57N 84.10W
33 O12 **Tippecanoe River** ∽ Indiana, N USA
99 D20 **Tipperary** Ir. Tiobraid Árann. S Ireland 52.28N 8.10W
99 D19 **Tipperary** Ir. Tiobraid Árann. cultural region S Ireland
37 R12 **Tipton** California, W USA 36.02N 119.19W
33 P13 **Tipton** Indiana, N USA 40.19N 86.00W
31 Y14 **Tipton** Iowa, C USA 41.46N 91.07W
29 U5 **Tipton** Missouri, C USA 38.39N 92.46W
38 I10 **Tipton, Mount** ▲ Arizona, SW USA 35.32N 114.11W
22 F8 **Tiptonville** Tennessee, S USA 36.22N 89.28W
10 E12 **Tip Top Mountain** ▲ Ontario, S Canada 48.18N 86.06W
161 G19 **Tiptūr** Karnātaka, W India 13.17N 76.31E
Tiquisate see Pueblo Nuevo Tiquisate
60 L13 **Tiracambu, Serra do** ⛰ E Brazil
Tirana see Tiranë
115 K19 **Tirana Rinas** ✕ Durrës, W Albania 41.25N 19.41E
115 L20 **Tiranë** var. Tirana. ● (Albania) Tiranë, C Albania 41.19N 19.49E
115 K20 **Tiranë** ◐ district W Albania
146 I5 **Tīrān, Jazīrat** island Egypt/Saudi Arabia
108 F6 **Tirano** Lombardia, N Italy 46.13N 10.10E
190 I2 **Tirari Desert** desert South Australia
119 O10 **Tiraspol** Rus. Tiraspol'. E Moldova 46.50N 29.34E
192 M8 **Tirau** Waikato, North Island, NZ 37.59S 175.44E
142 C14 **Tire** İzmir, SW Turkey 38.04N 27.45E
143 O11 **Tirebolu** Giresun, N Turkey 41.01N 38.49E
98 F11 **Tiree** island W Scotland, UK
Tîrgovişte see Târgovişte
Tîrgu see Târgu Cărbuneşti
Tîrgu Bujor see Târgu Bujor
Tîrgu Frumos see Târgu Frumos
Tîrgu Jiu see Târgu Jiu
Tîrgu Lăpuş see Târgu Lăpuş
Tîrgu Mures see Târgu Mureş
Tîrgu-Neamţ see Târgu-Neamţ
Tîrgu Ocna see Târgu Ocna
Tîrgu Secuiesc see Târgu Secuiesc
155 T3 **Tirich Mīr** ▲ NW Pakistan 36.12N 71.51E
78 J5 **Tiris Zemmour** ◐ region N Mauritania
Tirlemont see Tienen
131 W5 **Tirlyanskiy** Respublika Bashkortostan, W Russian Federation 54.09N 58.32E
Tîrnava Mare see Târnava Mare
Tîrnava Mică see Târnava Mică
Tîrnăveni see Târnăveni
Tírnavos see Týrnavos
Tirnovo see Veliko Tŭrnovo
160 J11 **Tirodi** Madhya Pradesh, C India 21.40N 79.43E
110 K8 **Tirol** off. Land Tirol, var. Tyrol, It. Tirolo. ◐ state W Austria
Tirolo see Tirol
Tirreno, Mare see Tyrrhenian Sea
109 B19 **Tirso** ∽ Sardegna, Italy, C Mediterranean Sea
97 H22 **Tirstrup** ✕ (Århus) Århus, C Denmark 56.17N 10.36E
161 I21 **Tiruchchirāppalli** prev. Trichinopoly. Tamil Nādu, SE India 10.49N 78.43E
161 H23 **Tirunelveli** var. Tinnevelly. Tamil Nādu, SE India 8.45N 77.43E
161 J19 **Tirupati** Andhra Pradesh, E India 13.39N 79.25E
161 I20 **Tiruppattūr** Tamil Nādu, SE India 12.28N 78.31E
161 H21 **Tiruppūr** Tamil Nādu, SW India 11.04N 77.19E
161 I20 **Tiruvannāmalai** Tamil Nādu, SE India 12.13N 79.07E
114 L10 **Tisa** Ger. Theiss, Hung. Tisza, Rus. Tissa, Ukr. Tysa. ∽ SE Europe see also Tisza
Tischnowitz see Tišnov
9 U14 **Tisdale** Saskatchewan, S Canada 52.51N 104.01W
29 O13 **Tishomingo** Oklahoma, C USA 34.14N 96.40W
97 M17 **Tisnaren** ◎ S Sweden
113 F18 **Tišnov** Ger. Tischnowitz. Jihomoravský Kraj, SE Czech Republic 49.21N 16.24E
Tissa see Tisa/Tisza
76 J6 **Tissemsilt** N Algeria 35.37N 1.48E
159 S12 **Tista** ∽ NE India
114 L8 **Tisza** Ger. Theiss, Rom./Slvn./SCr. Tisa, Rus. Tissa, Ukr. Tysa. ∽ SE Europe see also Tisa
113 L23 **Tiszaföldvár** Jász-Nagykun-Szolnok, E Hungary 47.00N 20.16E
113 M22 **Tiszafüred** Jász-Nagykun-Szolnok, E Hungary 47.34N 20.45E
113 L23 **Tiszakécske** Bács-Kiskun, C Hungary 46.55N 20.04E
113 M21 **Tiszaújváros** prev. Leninváros. Borsod-Abaúj-Zemplén, NE Hungary 47.55N 21.03E
113 N21 **Tiszavasvári** Szabolcs-Szatmár-Bereg, NE Hungary 47.57N 21.24E
Titibu see Chichibu
59 I17 **Titicaca, Lake** ◎ Bolivia/Peru
202 H17 **Titikaveka** Rarotonga, S Cook Islands 21.16S 159.45W
160 M13 **Titilāgarh** Orissa, E India 20.18N 83.09E
174 Gg4 **Titiwangsa, Banjaran** ⛰ Peninsular Malaysia
Titograd see Podgorica
Titose see Chitose
Titova Mitrovica see Kosovska Mitrovica
Titovo Užice see Užice
115 M18 **Titov Vrv** ▲ NW FYR Macedonia 41.58N 20.49E
96 F7 **Titran** Sør-Trøndelag, S Norway 63.40N 8.20E
33 Q8 **Tittabawassee River** ∽ Michigan, N USA
118 J13 **Titu** Dâmboviţa, S Romania 44.40N 25.31E
81 M16 **Titule** Orientale, N Dem. Rep. Congo 3.19N 25.23E
25 X11 **Titusville** Florida, SE USA 28.34N 80.48W
20 C12 **Titusville** Pennsylvania, NE USA 41.36N 79.39W
78 G11 **Tivaouane** W Senegal 14.59N 16.50W
115 I17 **Tivat** SW Montenegro 42.25N 18.43E
12 E14 **Tiverton** Ontario, S Canada 44.15N 81.31W
99 J23 **Tiverton** SW England, UK 50.54N 3.30W
21 O12 **Tiverton** Rhode Island, NE USA 41.38N 71.10W
109 I15 **Tivoli** anc. Tiber. Lazio, C Italy 41.58N 12.45E
27 U13 **Tivoli** Texas, SW USA 28.26N 96.54W
176 W11 **Tiwarra** Papua, E Indonesia 2.54S 133.52E
147 Z8 **Ţīwī** NE Oman 22.43N 59.20E
Tiworo see Tioro, Selat
176 Ww12 **Tiyo, Pegunungan** ⛰ Papua, E Indonesia
43 Y11 **Tizimín** Yucatán, SE Mexico 21.10N 88.09W
76 K5 **Tizi Ouzou** var. Tizi-Ouzou. N Algeria 36.44N 4.06E
76 D8 **Tiznit** SW Morocco 29.43N 9.39W
115 I14 **Tjentište** Republika Srpska, SE Bosnia and Herzegovina 43.23N 18.42E
Tjepoe/Tjepu see Cepu
100 L7 **Tjeukemeer** ◎ N Netherlands
Tjiamis see Ciamis
Tjiandjoer see Cianjur
Tjilatjap see Cilacap
Tjiledoeg see Ciledug
97 F23 **Tjæreborg** Ribe, W Denmark 55.28N 8.34E
97 I18 **Tjörn** island S Sweden
94 O3 **Tjuvfjorden** fjord S Svalbard
Tkvarcheli see Tqvarch'eli
42 L8 **Tlahualilo** Durango, N Mexico 26.06N 103.25W
43 P14 **Tlalnepantla** México, C Mexico 19.37N 99.09W
43 Q13 **Tlapacoyán** Veracruz-Llave, E Mexico 19.57N 97.18W
43 P16 **Tlapa de Comonfort** Guerrero, S Mexico 17.33N 98.33W
42 L13 **Tlaquepaque** Jalisco, C Mexico 20.36N 103.19W
Tlascala see Tlaxcala
43 P14 **Tlaxcala** var. Tlascala, Tlaxcala de Xicohténcatl. Tlaxcala, C Mexico 19.17N 98.15W
43 P14 **Tlaxcala** ◐ state S Mexico
Tlaxcala de Xicohténcatl see Tlaxcala
43 P14 **Tlaxco** var. Tlaxco de Morelos. Tlaxcala, S Mexico 19.37N 98.07W
Tlaxco de Morelos see Tlaxco
43 Q16 **Tlaxiaco** var. Santa María Asunción Tlaxiaco. Oaxaca, S Mexico 17.18N 97.42W
76 I6 **Tlemcen** var. Tilimsen, Tlemsen. NW Algeria 34.52N 1.21W
Tlemsen see Tlemcen
144 L4 **Tlété Ouâte Rharbi, Jebel** ▲ N Syria
118 J7 **Tlumach** Ivano-Frankivs'ka Oblast', W Ukraine 48.53N 25.00E
131 P17 **Tlyarata** Respublika Dagestan, SW Russian Federation 42.10N 46.30E
118 K10 **Toaca, Vârful** prev. Vîrful Toaca. ▲ NE Romania 46.58N 25.55E
Toaca, Vîrful see Toaca, Vârful
197 C13 **Toak** Ambrym, C Vanuatu 16.21S 168.16E
180 J4 **Toamasina** var. Tamatave. Toamasina, E Madagascar 18.10S 49.22E
180 J4 **Toamasina** ◐ province E Madagascar
180 J4 **Toamasina** ✕ Toamasina, E Madagascar 18.10S 49.22E
23 X6 **Toano** Virginia, NE USA 37.22N 76.46W
203 U10 **Toau** atoll Îles Tuamotu, C French Polynesia
47 T6 **Toa Vaca, Embalse** ⊡ C Puerto Rico
64 K13 **Toay** La Pampa, C Argentina 36.43S 64.22W
165 R14 **Toba** Xizang Zizhiqu, W China 31.16N 97.37E
171 Hh16 **Toba** Mie, Honshū, SW Japan 34.28N 136.49E
173 Ff5 **Toba, Danau** ◎ Sumatera, W Indonesia
47 Y16 **Tobago** island NE Trinidad and Tobago
155 Q9 **Toba Kākar Range** ⛰ NW Pakistan
175 T10 **Tobalai, Selat** strait Maluku, E Indonesia
175 Q9 **Tobamawu** Sulawesi, N Indonesia 1.16S 121.42E
107 Q12 **Tobarra** Castilla-La Mancha, C Spain 38.36N 1.40W
155 U9 **Toba Tek Singh** Punjab, E Pakistan 30.54N 72.30E
175 T6 **Tobelo** Pulau Halmahera, E Indonesia 1.45N 127.58E
12 E12 **Tobermory** Ontario, S Canada 45.13N 81.39W
98 G10 **Tobermory** W Scotland, UK 56.37N 6.12W
172 Oo5 **Tōbetsu** Hokkaidō, NE Japan 43.12N 141.28E
188 M6 **Tobin Lake** ◎ Western Australia
9 U14 **Tobin Lake** ◎ Saskatchewan, C Canada
37 T4 **Tobin, Mount** ▲ Nevada, W USA 40.25N 117.28W
171 L10 **Tobi-shima** island C Japan
174 J11 **Toboali** Pulau Bangka, W Indonesia 2.57S 106.25E
150 M8 **Tobol** Kaz. Tobyl. Kostanay, N Kazakhstan 52.42N 62.36E
150 L8 **Tobol** Kaz. Tobyl. ∽ Kazakhstan/Russian Federation
125 F11 **Tobol'sk** Tyumenskaya Oblast', C Russian Federation 58.15N 68.12E
Tobruch/Tobruk see Ţubruq
129 R3 **Tobseda** Nenetskiy Avtonomnyy Okrug, NW Russian Federation 68.37N 52.24E
Tobyl see Tobol
129 Q6 **Tobysh** ∽ NW Russian Federation
56 F10 **Tocaima** Cundinamarca, C Colombia 4.30N 74.37W
61 K16 **Tocantins** off. Estado do Tocantins. ◐ state C Brazil
61 K15 **Tocantins, Rio** ∽ N Brazil
25 T2 **Toccoa** Georgia, SE USA 34.34N 83.19W
171 K15 **Tochigi** var. Totigi. Tochigi, Honshū, S Japan 36.24N 139.42E
171 Kk15 **Tochigi** off. Tochigi-ken, var. Totigi. ◐ prefecture Honshū, S Japan
171 K13 **Tochio** var. Totio. Niigata, Honshū, C Japan 37.27N 139.00E
97 J15 **Töcksfors** Värmland, C Sweden 59.30N 11.49E
44 J5 **Tocoa** Colón, N Honduras 15.36N 86.01W
64 H4 **Tocopilla** Antofagasta, N Chile 22.06S 70.08W
64 I4 **Tocorpuri, Cerro de** ▲ Bolivia/Chile 22.25S 67.52W
191 O10 **Tocumwal** New South Wales, SE Australia 35.53S 145.35E
56 K4 **Tocuyo de La Costa** Falcón, NW Venezuela 11.02N 68.27W
158 H13 **Toda Rāisingh** Rājasthān, N India 26.01N 75.34E
108 H13 **Todi** Umbria, C Italy 42.46N 12.25E
110 G9 **Tödi** ▲ NE Switzerland 46.52N 8.53E
176 Uu9 **Todlo** Papua, E Indonesia 0.46S 130.50E
172 N12 **Todoga-saki** headland Honshū, C Japan 39.33N 142.02E
61 P17 **Todos os Santos, Baía de** bay E Brazil
42 F10 **Todos Santos** Baja California Sur, W Mexico 23.26N 110.14W
42 B2 **Todos Santos, Bahía de** bay NW Mexico
Toeban see Tuban
Toekang Besi Eilanden see Tukangbesi, Kepulauan
Tōen see T'aoyüan
193 D25 **Toetoes Bay** bay South Island, NZ
9 Q14 **Tofield** Alberta, SW Canada 53.22N 112.39W
8 K17 **Tofino** Vancouver Island, British Columbia, SW Canada 49.05N 125.51W
201 X17 **Tofol** Kosrae, E Micronesia
97 J20 **Tofta** Halland, S Sweden 57.10N 12.19E
97 H15 **Tofte** Buskerud, S Norway 59.31N 10.33E
97 F24 **Toftlund** Sønderjylland, SW Denmark 55.12N 9.04E
200 S13 **Tofua** island Ha'apai Group, C Tonga
197 B10 **Toga** island Torres Islands, N Vanuatu
171 Kk17 **Tōgane** Chiba, Honshū, S Japan 35.32N 140.22E
82 N13 **Togdheer** off. Gobolka Togdheer. ◐ region NW Somalia
Toghyzaq see Toguzak
171 Ii12 **Togi** Ishikawa, Honshū, SW Japan 37.06N 136.43E
41 N13 **Togiak** Alaska, USA 59.03N 160.31W
175 Qq8 **Togian, Kepulauan** island group C Indonesia
79 Q15 **Togo** off. Togolese Republic; prev. French Togoland. ◆ republic W Africa
168 F8 **Tögrög** Govĭ-Altay, SW Mongolia 45.51N 95.04E
168 J9 **Tögrög** var. Hoolt. Övörhangay, C Mongolia 45.31N 103.06E
Tögrög see Manhan
165 N12 **Togton He** var. Tuotuo He. ∽ C China
Togton Heyan see Tanggulashan
150 L7 **Toguzak** Kaz. Toghyzaq. ∽ Kazakhstan/Russian Federation
39 P10 **Tohatchi** New Mexico, SW USA 35.51N 108.45W
203 O7 **Tohiea, Mont** ▲ Moorea, W French Polynesia 17.33S 149.48W
95 O17 **Tohmajärvi** Itä-Suomi, E Finland 62.12N 30.19E
143 N14 **Tohma Çayı** ∽ C Turkey
95 L16 **Toholampi** Länsi-Suomi, W Finland 63.46N 24.15E
Töhöm see Mandah
25 X12 **Tohopekaliga, Lake** ◎ Florida, SE USA
171 J17 **Toi** Shizuoka, Honshū, S Japan 34.55N 138.45E
202 B15 **Toi** N Niue 18.57S 169.51W
95 L19 **Toijala** Länsi-Suomi, W Finland 61.09N 23.51E
175 Qq9 **Toima** Sulawesi, N Indonesia 0.48S 122.21E
170 C17 **Toi-misaki** headland Kyūshū, SW Japan 31.21N 131.18E
175 Rr17 **Toineke** Timor, S Indonesia 10.06S 124.22E
Toirc, Inis see Inishturk
37 U6 **Toiyabe Range** ⛰ Nevada, W USA
Tojikiston, Jumhurii see Tajikistan
153 R12 **Tojikobod** Rus. Tadzhikabad. C Tajikistan 39.08N 70.54E
170 F13 **Tōjō** Hiroshima, Honshū, SW Japan 34.54N 133.15E
41 T10 **Tok** Alaska, USA 63.20N 142.59W
172 P5 **Tokachi-dake** ▲ Hokkaidō, NE Japan 43.24N 142.41E
172 Pp7 **Tokachi-gawa** var. Tokati Gawa. ∽ Hokkaidō, NE Japan
171 Hh16 **Tōkai** Aichi, Honshū, SW Japan 35.01N 136.51E
113 N21 **Tokaj** Borsod-Abaúj-Zemplén, NE Hungary 48.07N 21.25E
171 Jj13 **Tōkamachi** Niigata, Honshū, C Japan 37.08N 138.46E
193 D25 **Tokanui** Southland, South Island, NZ 46.33S 169.01E
82 I7 **Tokar** var. Ţawkar. Red Sea, NE Sudan 18.27N 37.40E
142 L12 **Tokat** Tokat, N Turkey 40.19N 36.34E
142 L12 **Tokat** ◐ province N Turkey
Tokati Gawa see Tokachi-gawa
169 X15 **Tŏkchŏk-gundo** island group NW South Korea
Tŏke see Taka Atoll
202 J9 **Tokelau** ◇ NZ overseas territory W Polynesia
Tőketerebes see Trebišov
Tokhtamyshbek see Tŭkhtamish
26 M6 **Tokio** Texas, SW USA 33.09N 102.31W
Tokio see Tōkyō
201 W11 **Toki Point** point NW Wake Island 19.19N 166.36E
Tokkuztara see Gongliu
153 V7 **Tokmak** Kir. Tokmok. Chuyskaya Oblast', N Kyrgyzstan 42.49N 75.18E
119 V9 **Tokmak** var. Velykyy Tokmak. Zaporiz'ka Oblast', SE Ukraine 47.13N 35.42E
Tokmok see Tokmak
192 Q8 **Tokomaru Bay** Gisborne, North Island, NZ 38.10S 178.18E
171 Hh16 **Tokoname** Aichi, Honshū, SW Japan 34.54N 136.49E
172 Qq5 **Tokoro** Hokkaidō, NE Japan 44.06N 144.03E
192 M8 **Tokoroa** Waikato, North Island, NZ 38.14S 175.52E
172 Q6 **Tokoro-gawa** ∽ Hokkaidō, NE Japan
78 K14 **Tokounou** C Guinea 9.43N 9.46W
40 M12 **Toksook Bay** Alaska, USA 60.33N 165.01W
Toksu see Xinhe
Toksum see Toksun
164 L6 **Toksun** var. Toksum. Xinjiang Uygur Zizhiqu, NW China 42.46N 88.37E
153 T8 **Toktogul** Talasskaya Oblast', NW Kyrgyzstan 41.51N 72.56E
153 T9 **Toktogul'skoye Vodokhranilishche** ⊡ W Kyrgyzstan
Toktomush see Tŭkhtamish
200 Ss12 **Toku** island Vava'u Group, N Tonga
172 Qq14 **Tokunoshima** Kagoshima, Tokuno-shima, SW Japan
172 Q14 **Tokuno-shima** island Nansei-shotō, SW Japan
170 Ff15 **Tokushima** var. Tokusima. Tokushima, Shikoku, SW Japan 34.04N 134.28E
170 F15 **Tokushima** off. Tokushima-ken, var. Tokusima. ◐ prefecture Shikoku, SW Japan
Tokusima see Tokushima
170 E13 **Tokuyama** Yamaguchi, Honshū, SW Japan 34.04N 131.48E
171 Jj16 **Tōkyō** var. Tokio. ● (Japan) Tōkyō, Honshū, S Japan 35.40N 139.45E
171 J15 **Tōkyō** off. Tōkyō-to. ◐ capital district Honshū, S Japan
171 K17 **Tōkyō-wan** bay S Japan
151 T12 **Tokyrau** ∽ C Kazakhstan
155 O3 **Tokzār** Pash. Tukzār. Sar-e Pol, N Afghanistan 35.47N 66.28E
151 W13 **Tokzhaylau** prev. Dzerzhinskoye. Almaty, SE Kazakhstan 45.49N 81.04E
201 U12 **Tol** atoll Chuuk Islands, C Micronesia
192 Q9 **Tolaga Bay** Gisborne, North Island, NZ 38.22S 178.17E
180 I7 **Tôlañaro** prev. Faradofay, Fort-Dauphin. Toliara, SE Madagascar
168 D6 **Tolbo** Bayan-Ölgiy, W Mongolia 48.22N 90.22E
Tolbukhin see Dobrich
62 G11 **Toledo** Paraná, S Brazil 24.45S 53.41W
56 G8 **Toledo** Norte de Santander, N Colombia 7.16N 72.28W
179 Qq13 **Toledo** off. Toledo City. Cebu, C Philippines 10.23N 123.39E
107 N9 **Toledo** anc. Toletum. Castilla-La Mancha, C Spain 39.52N 4.01W
32 M14 **Toledo** Illinois, N USA 39.16N 88.15W
31 W13 **Toledo** Iowa, C USA 42.00N 92.34W
33 R11 **Toledo** Ohio, N USA 41.39N 83.33W
34 F12 **Toledo** Oregon, NW USA 44.37N 123.56W
34 G9 **Toledo** Washington, NW USA 46.27N 122.49W
44 F3 **Toledo** ◐ district S Belize
106 M9 **Toledo** ◐ province Castilla-La Mancha, C Spain
27 Y7 **Toledo Bend Reservoir** ⊡ Louisiana/Texas, SW USA
106 M10 **Toledo, Montes de** ⛰ C Spain
108 J12 **Tolentino** Marche, C Italy 43.08N 13.17E
Toletum see Toledo
96 H10 **Tolga** Hedmark, S Norway 62.25N 11.00E
164 J3 **Toli** Xinjiang Uygur Zizhiqu, NW China 45.55N 83.33E
180 H7 **Toliara** var. Toliary; prev. Tuléar. Toliara, SW Madagascar 23.19S 43.40E
180 H7 **Toliara** ◐ province SW Madagascar
Toliary see Toliara
56 D11 **Tolima** off. Departamento del Tolima. ◐ province C Colombia
175 Pp7 **Tolitoli** Sulawesi, C Indonesia 1.04N 120.49E
97 K22 **Tollarp** Skåne, S Sweden 55.55N 14.00E
102 N9 **Tollense** ∽ NE Germany
102 N10 **Tollensesee** ◎ NE Germany
38 K13 **Tolleson** Arizona, SW USA 33.25N 112.15W
152 M13 **Tollimarjon** Rus. Talimardzhan. Qashqadaryo Viloyati, S Uzbekistan 38.22N 65.31E
Tolmein see Tolmin
108 J6 **Tolmezzo** Friuli-Venezia Giulia, NE Italy 46.27N 13.01E
111 S11 **Tolmin** Ger. Tolmein, It. Tolmino. W Slovenia 46.12N 13.39E
Tolmino see Tolmin
113 J25 **Tolna** Ger. Tolnau. Tolna, S Hungary 46.25N 18.46E
113 I24 **Tolna** off. Tolna Megye. ◐ county SW Hungary
Tolnau see Tolna
81 I20 **Tolo** Bandundu, W Dem. Rep. Congo 2.57S 18.35E
Tolochin see Talachyn
202 D12 **Toloke** Île Futuna, W Wallis and Futuna
32 M13 **Tolono** Illinois, N USA 39.59N 88.16W
107 Q3 **Tolosa** País Vasco, N Spain 43.09N 2.04W
Tolosa see Toulouse
175 Qq10 **Tolo, Teluk** bay Sulawesi, C Indonesia
41 R9 **Tolovana River** ∽ Alaska, USA
127 Oo10 **Tolstoy, Mys** headland E Russian Federation 59.12N 155.04E
65 G15 **Toltén** Araucanía, C Chile 39.13S 73.10W
65 G15 **Toltén, Río** ∽ S Chile
56 E6 **Tolú** Sucre, NW Colombia 9.31N 75.34W
43 O14 **Toluca** var. Toluca de Lerdo. México, S Mexico 19.19N 99.40W
Toluca de Lerdo see Toluca
43 O14 **Toluca, Nevado de** ▲ C Mexico 19.05N 99.45W
131 R6 **Tol'yatti** prev. Stavropol'. Samarskaya Oblast', W Russian Federation 53.31N 49.27E
126 H14 **Tom'** ∽ S Russian Federation
79 O12 **Toma** NW Burkina 12.46N 2.51W
32 K7 **Tomah** Wisconsin, N USA 43.59N 90.31W
32 L5 **Tomahawk** Wisconsin, N USA 45.27N 89.40W
119 T8 **Tomakivka** Dnipropetrovs'ka Oblast', E Ukraine 47.47N 34.45E
172 O6 **Tomakomai** Hokkaidō, NE Japan 42.38N 141.32E
172 P3 **Tomamae** Hokkaidō, NE Japan 44.18N 141.38E
106 G9 **Tomar** Santarém, W Portugal 39.36N 8.25W
127 O15 **Tomari** Ostrov Sakhalin, Sakhalinskaya Oblast', SE Russian Federation 47.47N 142.09E
117 C16 **Tómaros** ▲ W Greece 39.31N 20.45E
Tomaschow see Tomaszów Lubelski, Poland
Tomaschow see Tomaszów Mazowiecki, Poland
63 E16 **Tomás Gomensoro** Artigas, N Uruguay 30.28S 57.28W
119 N7 **Tomashpil'** Vinnyts'ka Oblast', C Ukraine 48.32N 28.31E
Tomaszów see Tomaszów Mazowiecki
113 P15 **Tomaszów Lubelski** Ger. Tomaschow. Lubelskie, E Poland 50.28N 23.22E
Tomaszów Mazowiecka see Tomaszów Mazowiecki
112 L13 **Tomaszów Mazowiecki** var. Tomaszów Mazowiecka; prev. Tomaszów, Ger. Tomaschow. Łodzkie, C Poland 51.33N 20.00E
42 J13 **Tomatlán** Jalisco, C Mexico 19.53N 105.18W
170 F12 **Tombara** Shimane, Honshū, SW Japan 35.04N 132.46E
83 F15 **Tombe** Jonglei, S Sudan 5.52N 31.40E
25 N4 **Tombigbee River** ∽ Alabama/Mississippi, S USA
84 A10 **Tomboco** Zaire, NW Angola 6.47S 13.18E
79 O10 **Tombouctou** Eng. Timbuktu. Tombouctou, N Mali 16.47N 3.03W
79 N9 **Tombouctou** ◐ region W Mali
39 N16 **Tombstone** Arizona, SW USA 31.42N 110.04W
85 A15 **Tombua** Port. Porto Alexandre. Namibe, SW Angola 15.49S 11.52E
85 J19 **Tom Burke** Limpopo, NE South Africa 23.07S 28.01E
152 L9 **Tomdibuloq** Rus. Tamdybulak. Navoiy Viloyati, N Uzbekistan 41.48N 64.33E
152 L9 **Tomditov-Togʻlari** ⛰ N Uzbekistan
64 G13 **Tomé** Bío Bío, C Chile 36.39S 72.53W
60 L12 **Tomé-Açu** Pará, NE Brazil 2.25S 48.09W
97 L23 **Tomelilla** Skåne, S Sweden 55.33N 14.00E
107 O10 **Tomelloso** Castilla-La Mancha, C Spain 39.09N 3.01W
12 H10 **Tomiko Lake** ◎ Ontario, S Canada
79 N12 **Tominian** Ségou, C Mali 13.18N 4.39W
175 Pp8 **Tomini, Gulf of** var. Teluk Tomini; prev. Teluk Gorontalo. bay Sulawesi, C Indonesia
Tomini, Teluk see Tomini, Gulf of
172 Ii15 **Tomioka** Fukushima, Honshū, C Japan 37.19N 140.57E
172 Jj15 **Tomioka** Gunma, Honshū, S Japan 36.15N 138.51E
115 G14 **Tomislavgrad** Federacija Bosna I Hercegovina, SW Bosnia and Herzegovina 43.43N 17.15E
189 O9 **Tomkinson Ranges** ⛰ South Australia/Western Australia
126 Ll12 **Tommot** Respublika Sakha (Yakutiya), NE Russian Federation 58.56N 126.24E
175 Rr7 **Tomohon** Sulawesi, N Indonesia 1.19N 124.49E
56 K9 **Tomo, Río** ∽ E Colombia
115 L21 **Tomorrit, Mali i** ▲ S Albania 40.43N 20.12E
9 S17 **Tompkins** Saskatchewan, S Canada 50.03N 108.49W
22 K8 **Tompkinsville** Kentucky, S USA 36.42N 85.41W
175 Pp7 **Tompo** Sulawesi, N Indonesia 0.56N 120.16E
188 I8 **Tom Price** Western Australia 22.48S 117.49E
126 H13 **Tomsk** Tomskaya Oblast', C Russian Federation 56.30N 85.04E
12[illegible] G[illegible]12 **Tomskaya Oblast'** ◐ province [illegible] Russian Federation
20 K16 **Tom[illegible]** New Jersey, NE USA 39.56N 7[illegible]
Tom Steed [illegible] Steed Reservoir
28 L12 **Tom Steed Reservoi[illegible]** [illegible] Steed Lake. ⊡ Oklahoma, C USA
176 Vv10 **Tomu** Papua, E Indonesia 2.07S 133.01E
194 F13 **Tomu** ∽ W PNG
164 H6 **Tomür Feng** var. Pobeda Peak, Rus. Pik Pobedy. ▲ China/Kyrgyzstan 42.02N 80.07E see also Pobedy, Pik
201 N13 **Tomworoahlang** Pohnpei, E Micronesia
43 U17 **Tonalá** Chiapas, SE Mexico 16.03N 93.43W
108 F6 **Tonale, Passo del** pass N Italy 46.16N 10.37E
171 Ii13 **Tonami** Toyama, Honshū, SW Japan 36.39N 136.57E
60 C12 **Tonantins** Amazonas, W Brazil 2.58S 67.30W
34 K6 **Tonasket** Washington, NW USA 48.41N 119.27W
57 Y9 **Tonate** var. Macouria. N French Guiana 05.00N 52.28W
20 D10 **Tonawanda** New York, NE USA 43.00N 78.51W
175 Rr7 **Tondano** Sulawesi, C Indonesia 1.19N 124.55E
175 Rr7 **Tondano, Danau** ◎ Sulawesi, N Indonesia
106 H7 **Tondela** Viseu, N Portugal 40.31N 8.04W
97 F24 **Tønder** Ger. Tondern. Sønderjylland, SW Denmark 54.57N 8.52E
Tondern see Tønder
171 K16 **Tone-gawa** ∽ Honshū, S Japan
149 N4 **Tonekābon** var. Shahsawar, Tonkābon; prev. Shahsavār. Māzandarān, N Iran 36.49N 51.51E
Tonezh see Tonyezh
200 S15 **Tonga** off. Kingdom of Tonga, var. Friendly Islands. ◆ monarchy SW Pacific Ocean
183 R9 **Tonga** island group SW Pacific Ocean
85 K23 **Tongaat** KwaZulu/Natal, E South Africa 29.31S 31.09E
167 Q13 **Tong'an** var. Datong, Tong an. Fujian, SE China 24.43N 118.07E
29 Q4 **Tonganoxie** Kansas, C USA 39.06N 95.05W
41 Y13 **Tongass National Forest** reserve Alaska, USA
200 Qq16 **Tongatapu** ✕ Tongatapu, S Tonga 21.10S 175.10W
200 R15 **Tongatapu** island Tongatapu Group, S Tonga
200 S14 **Tongatapu Group** island group S Tonga
183 S9 **Tonga Trench** undersea feature S Pacific Ocean
167 N8 **Tongbai Shan** ⛰ C China
167 P8 **Tongcheng** Anhui, E China 31.16N 117.00E
166 L6 **Tongchuan** Shaanxi, C China 35.10N 109.03E
166 L12 **Tongdao** var. Tongdao Dongzu Zizhixian; prev. Shuangjiang. Hunan, S China 26.06N 109.46E
165 T11 **Tongde** var. Gabasumdo. Qinghai, C China 35.13N 100.39E
101 K19 **Tongeren** Fr. Tongres. Limburg, NE Belgium 50.46N 5.28E
169 Y14 **Tonghae** NE South Korea 37.25N 129.08E
166 G13 **Tonghai** var. Xiushan. Yunnan, SW China 24.06N 102.45E
169 X8 **Tonghe** Heilongjiang, NE China 46.00N 128.45E
169 W11 **Tonghua** Jilin, NE China 41.43N 125.56E
194 L8 **Tong Island** island N PNG
169 Z6 **Tongjiang** Heilongjiang, NE China 47.39N 132.29E
169 Y13 **Tongjosŏn-man** prev. Broughton Bay. bay E North Korea
169 V7 **Tongken He** ∽ NE China
178 K7 **Tongking, Gulf of** Chin. Beibu Wan, Vtn. Vinh Bắc Bộ. gulf China/Vietnam
169 U10 **Tongliao** Nei Mongol Zizhiqu, N China 43.37N 122.15E
167 Q9 **Tongling** Anhui, E China 30.54N 117.51E
167 R9 **Tonglu** Zhejiang, SE China 29.49N 119.37E
197 D14 **Tongoa** island Shepherd Islands, S Vanuatu
64 G9 **Tongoy** Coquimbo, C Chile 30.20S 71.28W
166 L11 **Tongren** Guizhou, S China 27.43N 109.10E
165 T11 **Tongren** var. Rongwo. Qinghai, C China 35.31N 101.58E
Tongres see Tongeren
159 U11 **Tongsa** var. Tongsa Dzong. C Bhutan 27.33N 90.30E
Tongsa Dzong see Tongsa
Tongshan see Fuding, Fujian, China
Tongshan see Xuzhou, Jiansu, China
Tongshi see Wuzhishan
165 P12 **Tongtian He** ∽ C China
98 I6 **Tongue** N Scotland, UK 58.29N 4.24W
46 H3 **Tongue of the Ocean** strait C Bahamas
35 X10 **Tongue River** ∽ Montana, NW USA
35 W11 **Tongue River Reservoir** ⊡ Montana, NW USA
165 V11 **Tongwei** Gansu, C China 35.09N 105.15E
165 W9 **Tongxin** Ningxia, N China 37.00N 105.41E
169 U9 **Tongyu** var. Kaitong. Jilin, NE China 44.49N 123.08E
166 J11 **Tongzi** Guizhou, S China 28.07N 106.49E
168 F8 **Tonhil** var. Dzüyl. Govĭ-Altay, SW Mongolia 46.09N 93.55E
42 G5 **Tónichi** Sonora, NW Mexico 28.34N 109.33W
83 D14 **Tonj** Warab, SW Sudan 7.18N 28.40E
158 H13 **Tonk** Rājasthān, N India 26.10N 75.49E
Tonkābon see Tonekābon
29 N8 **Tonkawa** Oklahoma, C USA 36.40N 97.18W
178 Ii12 **Tônlé Sap** Eng. Great Lake. ◎ W Cambodia
104 L14 **Tonneins** Lot-et-Garonne, SW France 44.21N 0.21E
105 Q7 **Tonnerre** Yonne, C France 47.50N 4.00E
Tonoas see Dublon
37 U8 **Tonopah** Nevada, W USA 38.04N 117.13W
1[illegible] **Tonoshō** Okayama, Shōdo-shima, SW Japan 34.29N 134.10E
45 S17 **[illegible]nosí** Los Santos, S Panama 7.2[illegible] [illegible].25W
97 H16 **Tønsb[illegible]** Vestfold, S Norway 59.16N 10.2[illegible]
41 T11 **Tonsina** Alaska, USA 61.39N 145.10W
97 D17 **Tonstad** Vest-Agder, S Norway 58.40N 6.42E
200 S14 **Tonumea** island Nomuka Grou[illegible] W Tonga
143 O11 **Tonya** Trabzon, NE Turkey 40.52N 39.16E
121 K20 **Tonyezh** Rus. Tonezh. Homyel'skaya Voblasts', SE Belarus 51.49N 27.48E
38 L3 **Tooele** Utah, W USA 40.31N 112.18W
126 Ii15 **Toora-Khem** Respublika Tyva, S Russian Federation 52.25N 96.01E
191 O5 **Toorale East** New South Wales, SE Australia 30.29S 145.25E
85 H25 **Toorberg** ▲ S South Africa 32.02S 24.02E
120 G5 **Tootsi** Pärnumaa, SW Estonia 58.35N 24.46E
191 U3 **Toowoomba** Queensland, E Australia 27.34S 151.54E
29 Q4 **Topeka** state capital Kansas, C USA 39.03N 95.40W
113 M18 **Topľa** Hung. Toplya. ∽ NE Slovakia
126 H14 **Topki** Kemerovskaya Oblast', S Russian Federation 55.12N 85.40E
Toplicza see Toplița
118 J10 **Toplița** Ger. Töplitz, Hung. Maroshévíz; prev. Toplița Română, Hung. Oláh-Toplicza, Toplicza. Harghita, C Romania 46.57N 25.22E
Toplița Română/Töplitz see Toplița
Toplya see Topla
113 I20 **Topoľčany** Hung. Nagytapolcsány. Nitriansky Kraj, SW Slovakia 48.33N 18.10E
42 G8 **Topolobampo** Sinaloa, C Mexico 25.37N 109.02W
118 I13 **Topoloveni** Argeş, S Romania 44.49N 25.01E
116 L11 **Topolovgrad** prev. Kavakli. Khaskovo, S Bulgaria 42.06N 26.20E
Topolya see Bačka Topola
128 I6 **Topozero, Ozero** ◎ NW Russian Federation

◆ Country
● Country Capital
◇ Dependent Territory
○ Dependent Territory Capital
◐ Administrative Region
✕ International Airport
▲ Mountain
⛰ Mountain Range
▲ Volcano
∽ River
◎ Lake
⊡ Reservoir

85 M15 **Tete** Tete, NW Mozambique
16.14S 33.34E

85 M15 **Tete off.** Província de Tete. ◆
province NW Mozambique

9 N15 **Tête Jaune Cache** British
Columbia, SW Canada
52.52N 119.22W

192 O8 **Te Teko** Bay of Plenty, North
Island, NZ 38.03S 176.48E

195 U15 **Tetepare** *island* New Georgia
Islands, NW Solomon Islands

118 M5 **Teteriv** *Rus.* Teteriv. ☌ N Ukraine

102 M9 **Teterow** Mecklenburg-
Vorpommern, NE Germany
53.46N 12.34E

116 I9 **Teteven** Lovech, N Bulgaria
42.54N 24.19E

203 T10 **Tetiaroa** *atoll* Îles du Vent,
W French Polynesia

107 P14 **Tetica de Bacares** ▲ S Spain
37.15N 2.31W

119 O6 **Tetiyiv** *Rus.* Tetiyev

41 T10 **Tetlin** Alaska, USA
63.08N 142.31W

35 R8 **Teton River** ☌ Montana,
NW USA

76 G5 **Tétouan** *var.* Tetouan, Tetuán.
N Morocco 35.33N 5.22W

Tetova/Tetovë *see* Tetovo

116 L7 **Tetovo** Razgrad, N Bulgaria
43.49N 26.21E

115 N18 **Tetovo Alb.** Tetova, Tetovë, *Turk.*
Kalkandelen. NW FYR Macedonia
42.01N 20.58E

117 E20 **Tetrázio** ▲ S Greece

Tetschen *see* Děčín

Tetuán *see* Tétouan

203 Q8 **Tetufera, Mont** ▲ Tahiti,
W French Polynesia
17.40S 149.25W

131 R4 **Tetyushi** Respublika Tatarstan,
W Russian Federation
54.55N 48.46E

110 I7 **Teufen** Sankt Gallen,
NE Switzerland 47.24N 9.24E

42 L12 **Teul** *var.* Teul de Gonzáles
Ortega. Zacatecas, C Mexico
21.30N 103.28W

109 B21 **Teulada** Sardegna, Italy,
C Mediterranean Sea 38.58N 8.46E

Teul de Gonzáles Ortega *see*
Teul

9 X16 **Teulon** Manitoba, S Canada
50.20N 97.14W

44 I7 **Teupasenti** El Paraíso, S Honduras
14.14N 86.43W

172 Oo3 **Teuri-tō** *island* NE Japan

102 G13 **Teutoburger Wald** *Eng.*
Teutoburg Forest. *hill range*
NW Germany

Teutoburg Forest *see*
Teutoburger Wald

95 K17 **Teuva** *Swe.* Östermark. Länsi-
Suomi, W Finland 62.28N 21.45E

109 H15 **Tevere** *Eng.* Tiber. ☌ C Italy

144 G9 **Teverya** *var.* Tiberias, Tverya,
Northern, N Israel 32.48N 35.31E

98 K13 **Teviot** ☌ SE Scotland, UK

Tevli *see* Tewli

125 FJ12 **Tevriz** Omskaya Oblast', C Russian
Federation 57.30N 72.13E

193 B24 **Te Waewae Bay** *bay* South Island,
NZ

99 L21 **Tewkesbury** C England, UK
51.58N 2.09W

121 F19 **Tewli** *Rus.* Tevli. Brestskaya
Voblasts', SW Belarus
52.20N 24.13E

165 U12 **Têwo** *var.* Dêngdagoin. Gansu,
C China 34.05N 103.15E

27 U12 **Texana, Lake** ☉ Texas, SW USA

29 S14 **Texarkana** Arkansas, C USA
33.26N 94.02W

27 X5 **Texarkana** Texas, SW USA
33.25N 94.03W

27 N9 **Texas off.** State of Texas; also
known as The Lone Star State. ◆
state S USA

27 W12 **Texas City** Texas, SW USA
29.22N 94.54W

43 P14 **Texcoco** México, C Mexico
19.31N 98.52W

100 I6 **Texel** *island* Waddeneilanden,
NW Netherlands

...à M14 **Texhoma** Oklahoma, C USA
36.30N 101.46W

27 S...ehoma Texas, SW USA
36.30N 101.46W

W12 **Texico** New Mexico, SW USA
34.23N 103.03W

26 L1 **Texline** Texas, SW USA
36.22N 103.01W

43 P14 **Texmelucan** *var.* San Martín
Texmelucan. Puebla, S Mexico
19.13N 98.25W

29 S12 **Texoma, Lake** ☉ Oklahoma/
Texas, C USA

27 N9 **Texon** Texas, SW USA
31.13N 101.42W

126 J12 **Teya** Krasnoyarskiy Kray,
C Russian Federation 60.27N 92.46E

85 J23 **Teyateyaneng** NW Lesotho
29.04S 27.51E

128 M16 **Teykovo** Ivanovskaya
Oblast', W Russian Federation
56.49N 40.31E

128 M16 **Teza** ☌ W Russian Federation

43 S12 **Teziutlán** Puebla, S Mexico
19.49N 97.22W

159 W12 **Tezpur** Assam, NE India
26.39N 92.47E

15 L6 **Tha-Anne** ☌ Nunavut,
NE Canada

85 K23 **Thabana Ntlenyana** *var.*
Thabantshonyana, Mount
Ntlenyan. ▲ E Lesotho
29.26S 29.16E

Thabantshonyana *see*
Thabana Ntlenyana

85 J23 **Thaba Putsoa** ▲ C Lesotho
29.48S 27.46E

178 I8 **Tha Bo** Nong Khai, E Thailand
17.52N 102.34E

105 S12 **Thabor, Pic du** ▲ E France
45.07N 6.34E

Tha Chin *see* Samut Sakhon

177 G2 **Thagaya** Pegu, C Burma
19.19N 96.16E

178 J10 **Thai, Ao** *see* Thailand, Gulf of

178 J7 **Thai Binh** Thai Binh, N Vietnam
20.27N 106.19E

178 J10 **Thai Hoa** *var.* Nghia Đan. Nghê
An, N Vietnam 19.21N 105.26E

---

178 Hh10 **Thailand off.** Kingdom of
Thailand, *Th.* Prathet Thai;
prev. Siam. ◆ *monarchy*
SE Asia

178 Hh13 **Thailand, Gulf of var.** Gulf of
Siam, *Th.* Ao Thai, *Vtn.* Vinh Thai
Lan. *gulf* SE Asia

Thai Lan, Vinh *see*
Thailand, Gulf of

178 J9 **Thai Nguyên** Bắc Thai,
N Vietnam 21.36N 105.49E

178 J9 **Thakhek** *prev.* Muang
Khammouan. Khammouan, C Laos
17.24N 104.50E

159 S13 **Thakurgaon** Rajshahi,
NW Bangladesh 26.04N 88.34E

155 S6 **Thal** North-West Frontier
Province, NW Pakistan
33.24N 70.31E

177 G16 **Thalang** Phuket, SW Thailand
08.00N 98.21E

Thalassery *see* Tellicherry

178 I10 **Thalat Khae** Nakhon Ratchasima,
C Thailand 15.15N 102.24E

111 Q5 **Thalgau** Salzburg, NW Austria
47.49N 13.19E

110 G7 **Thalwil** Zürich, NW Switzerland
47.16N 8.34E

85 I20 **Thamaga** Kweneng, SE Botswana
24.40S 25.31E

Thamarīd *see* Thamarit

147 V13 **Thamarīt** *var.* Thamarīd,
Thumrayt. SW Oman
17.39N 54.01E

147 P16 **Thamar, Jabal** ▲ SW Yemen
13.46N 45.32E

192 M6 **Thames** Waikato, North Island,
NZ 37.10S 175.33E

12 D17 **Thames** ☌ Ontario, S Canada

99 O22 **Thames** ☌ S England, UK

192 M6 **Thames, Firth of** *gulf* North
Island, NZ

12 D17 **Thamesville** Ontario, S Canada
42.33N 81.58W

147 S13 **Thamūd** N Yemen 17.17N 49.57E

178 Gg9 **Thanbyuzayat** Mon State,
S Burma 15.58N 97.43E

158 I9 **Thānesar** Haryāna, N India
29.58N 76.51E

178 Jj7 **Thanh Hoa** Thanh Hoa,
N Vietnam 19.49N 105.48E

Thanintari Taungdan *see*
Bilauktaung Range

161 I21 **Thanjāvūr** *prev.* Tanjore. Tamil
Nādu, SE India 10.46N 79.09E

Thanlwin *see* Salween

105 U7 **Thann** Haut-Rhin, NE France
47.51N 7.04E

178 H16 **Tha Nong Phrom** Phatthalung,
SW Thailand 7.24N 100.04E

178 H13 **Thap Sakae** *var.* Thap Sakau.
Prachuap Khiri Khan, SW Thailand
11.30N 99.34E

178 H13 **Thap Sakau** *see* Thap Sakae

100 L10 **'t Harde** Gelderland,
E Netherlands 52.25N 5.52E

158 D11 **Thar Desert** *var.* Great Indian
Desert, Indian Desert. *desert* India/
Pakistan

189 V10 **Thargomindah** Queensland,
C Australia 28.00S 143.47E

145 S7 **Tharthār, Buhayrat ath** ☉ C Iraq

145 R7 **Tharthār, Wādī ath** *dry
watercourse* N Iraq

178d Jj7a **Tha Sae** Chumphon, SW Thailand

178 H15 **Tha Sala** Nakhon Si Thammarat,
SW Thailand 8.43N 99.54E

116 I13 **Thásos** Thásos, E Greece
40.46N 24.43E

117 I14 **Thásos** *island* E Greece

59 N14 **Thatcher** Ari... W USA
32.47...

178 Jj5 ...lam Trâng Dinh. Lang...
...etnam 16.55N 97.19E

178 J9 **That Phanom** Nakhon Phanom,
E Thailand 16.52N 104.41E

178 I10 **Tha Tum** Surin, E Thailand
15.18N 103.39E

105 P16 **Thau, Bassin de var.** Étang de
Thau. ☉ S France

Thau, Étang de *see* Thau,
Bassin de

177 G3 **Thaungdut** Sagaing, N Burma
24.25N 94.45E

178 Gg8 **Thaungyin Th.** Mae Nam Moei.
☌ Burma/Thailand

178 J9 **Tha Uthen** Nakhon Phanom,
E Thailand 17.31N 104.34E

111 W2 **Thaya** *var.* Dyje. ☌ Austria/Czech
Republic *see also* Dyje

29 V8 **Thayer** Missouri, C USA
36.31N 91.34W

177 F7 **Thayetmyo** Magwe, C Burma
19.19N 95.10E

177 F6 **Thazi** Mandalay, C Burma
20.49N 96.04E

Thebes *see* Thíva

46 L5 **The Carlton** *var.* Abraham
Bay. Mayaguana, SE Bahamas
22.21N 72.56W

58 H9 **The Crane** *var.* Crane. S Barbados
13.06N 59.26W

34 I11 **The Dalles** Oregon, NW USA
45.36N 121.10W

30 M14 **Thedford** Nebraska, C USA
41.58N 100.34W

The Hague *see* 's-Gravenhage

Theiss *see* Tisa/Tisza

15 I6 **Thelon** ☌ Northwest Territories/
Nunavut, N Canada

9 V15 **Theodore** Saskatchewan,
S Canada 51.25N 103.01W

23 N8 **Theodore** Alabama, S USA
30.33N 88.10W

38 L13 **Theodore Roosevelt Lake**
☉ Arizona, SW USA

Theodosia *see* Feodosiya

Theophilo Ottoni *see*
Teófilo Otoni

15 K13 **The Pas** Manitoba, C Canada
53.49N 101.09W

31 T14 **The Plains** Ohio, N USA
39.22N 82.07W

Thera *see* Santorini

117 J23 **Thérèse, Île** *island* Inner Islands,
NE Seychelles

Therezina *see* Teresina

117 L22 **Thérma** Ikaría, Dodekánisa,
Greece, Aegean Sea 37.38N 26.18E

Thermae Himerenses *see*
Termini Imerese

Thermae Pannonicae *see* Baden

**Thermaic Gulf/Thermaïkós
Sinus** *see* Thermaïkós Kólpos

123 Gg10 **Thermaïkós Kólpos** *Eng.*
Thermaic Gulf; *anc.* Thermaicus
Sinus. *gulf* N Greece

Thermiá *see* Kýthnos

117 L17 **Thérmo** Dytikí Ellás, C Greece
39.08N 26.32E

117 E18 **Thérmo** *var.* Thérmo. Dytikí Ellás,
C Greece 38.32N 21.42E

25 V14 **Thermopolis** Wyoming, C USA
43.39N 108.12W

191 P10 **The Rock** New South Wales,
SE Australia 35.18S 147.07E

205 O5 **Theron Mountains** ▲ Antarctica

117 G18 **Thespés** Stereá Ellás, C Greece
38.18N 23.08E

117 E16 **Thessalía** *Eng.* Thessaly. ◆ *region*
C Greece

12 C10 **Thessalon** Ontario, S Canada
46.15N 83.32W

117 G14 **Thessaloníki** *Eng.* Salonica,
Salonika, *SCr.* Solun, *Turk.* Selānik.
Kentrikí Makedonía, N Greece
40.37N 22.58E

117 G14 **Thessaloníki** ✈ Kentrikí
Makedonía, N Greece
40.30N 22.58E

Thessaly *see* Thessalía

86 B12 **Theta Gap** *undersea feature*
E Atlantic Ocean

99 P20 **Thetford** E England, UK
52.25N 0.45E

13 R11 **Thetford-Mines** Québec,
SE Canada 46.07N 71.16W

115 K17 **Theth** *var.* Thethi. Shkodër,
N Albania 42.25N 19.45E

Thethi *see* Theth

101 L20 **Theux** Liège, E Belgium
50.33N 5.48E

47 V9 **The Valley** ○ (Anguilla) ○
E Anguilla 18.12N 63.00W

29 N10 **The Village** Oklahoma, C USA
35.33N 97.33W

27 W10 **The Woodlands** Texas, SW USA
30.09N 95.27E

24 J9 **Thibodaux** Louisiana, S USA
29.48N 90.49W

31 S1 **Thief Lake** ☉ Minnesota, N USA

31 S1 **Thief River** ☌ Minnesota, C USA

31 S1 **Thief River Falls** Minnesota,
N USA 48.07N 96.10W

34 G14 **Thielsen, Mount** ▲ Oregon,
NW USA 43.09N 122.04W

Thielt *see* Tielt

108 G7 **Thiene** Veneto, NE Italy
45.43N 11.28E

Thienen *see* Tienen

105 P11 **Thiers** Puy-de-Dôme, C France
45.51N 3.33E

78 F11 **Thiès** W Senegal 14.51N 16.51W

83 I19 **Thika** Central, S Kenya
1.03S 37.04E

157 K18 **Thiladhunmathi Atoll** *var.*
Tiladummati Atoll. *atoll*
N Maldives

Thimbu *see* Thimphu

159 T11 **Thimphu** *var.* Thimbu; *prev.* Tashi
Chho Dzong. ● (Bhutan) ● W Bhutan
27.29N 89.37E

94 H2 **Thingeyri** Vestfirðir, NW Iceland
65.52N 23.28W

192 H1 **Three Kings Islands** *island group*
N NZ

183 P10 **Three Kings Rise** *undersea
feature* W Pacific Ocean

79 O18 **Three Points, Cape** *headland*
S Ghana 4.43N 2.03W

31 P10 **Three Rivers** Michigan, N USA
41.56N 85.37W

27 S13 **Three Rivers** Texas, SW USA
28.27N 98.10W

85 G24 **Three Sisters** Northern Cape,
South Africa 31.51S 23.04E

34 H13 **Three Sisters** ▲ Oregon,
NW USA 44.08N 121.46W

195 Z16 **Three Sisters Islands** *island group*
SE Solomon Islands

21 Q6 **Throckmorton** Texas, SW USA
33.10N 99.10W

188 M10 **Throssell, Lake** *salt lake* Western
Australia

117 K25 **Thrýptis** *var.* Thrýptis. ▲ Kríti,
Greece, E Mediterranean Sea
35.06N 25.51E

178 Jj14 **Thu Dâu Môt** *var.* Phu
Cương. Sông Bé, S Vietnam
10.58N 106.40E

178 Jj6 **Thu Đô** ✈ (Ha Nôi) Ha Nôi,
N Vietnam 21.13N 105.46E

101 G21 **Thuin** Hainaut, S Belgium
50.21N 4.18E

34 H3 **Thul** Sind, SE Pakistan
28.16N 68.49E

Thule *see* Qaanaaq

85 J18 **Thuli var.** Tuli. ☌ S Zimbabwe

110 D9 **Thun Fr.** Thoune. Bern,
W Switzerland 46.46N 7.37E

12 H11 **Thunder Bay** S Canada
48.27N 89.12W

32 M1 **Thunder Bay** *lake* S Canada

33 R6 **Thunder Bay** *lake bay* Michigan,
N USA

32 N11 **Thunderbird, Lake**
☉ Oklahoma, C USA

30 L8 **Thunder Butte Creek** ☌ South
Dakota, N USA

110 E9 **Thuner See** ☉ C Switzerland

178 H16 **Thung Song** *var.* Cha Mai.
Nakhon Si Thammarat,
SW Thailand 8.10N 99.40E

79 N16 **Tiébissou** *var.* Tiebissou. C Ivory
Coast 7.10N 5.10W

110 H7 **Thur** ☌ NE Switzerland

110 G6 **Thurgau Fr.** Thurgovie. ◆ *canton*
NE Switzerland

110 I9 **Tiefencastel** Graubünden,
S Switzerland 46.40N 9.33E

110 I7 **Tiegenhof** *see* Nowy Dwór Gdański

T'ieh-ling *see* Tieling

100 K13 **Tiel Gelderland, C Netherlands
51.54N 5.04E

169 W7 **Tieli** Heilongjiang, NE China
46.55N 128.01E

169 V11 **Tieling var.** T'ieh-ling. Liaoning,
NE China 42.19N 123.52E

158 L4 **Tielongtan** China/India
35.03N 79.31E

99 D19 **Thurles** Ir. Durlas. S Ireland
52.40N 7.49W

---

(0) F8 **Thompson** ☌ Alberta/British
Columbia, SW Canada

35 O8 **Thompson Falls** Montana,
NW USA 47.36N 115.20W

31 Q10 **Thompson, Lake** ☉ South
Dakota, N USA

36 M3 **Thompson Peak** ▲ California,
W USA 41.00N 123.01W

29 S2 **Thompson River** ☌ Missouri,
C USA

193 A22 **Thompson Sound** *sound* South
Island, NZ

15 Hh1 **Thomsen** ☌ Banks Island,
Northwest Territories, N Canada

25 V4 **Thomson** Georgia, SE USA
33.28N 82.30W

105 S10 **Thonon-les-Bains** Haute-Savoie,
E France 46.22N 6.30E

105 O15 **Thoré** ☌ S France

29 P11 **Thoreau** New Mexico, SW USA
35.24N 108.10W

Thorenburg *see* Turda

94 J3 **Thórisvatn** ☉ C Iceland

94 P4 **Thor, Kapp** *headland* S Svalbard
76.25N 25.01E

94 I4 **Thorlákshöfn** Suðurland,
SW Iceland 63.51N 21.24W

Thorn *see* Toruń

27 T10 **Thorndale** Texas, SW USA
30.36N 97.12W

12 H10 **Thorne** Ontario, S Canada

99 J14 **Thornhill** S Scotland, UK
55.13N 3.46W

27 U8 **Thornton** Texas, SW USA
31.24N 96.34W

Thornton Island *see*
Millennium Island

12 H16 **Thorold** Ontario, S Canada
47.09N 79.15W

34 J9 **Thorp** Washington, NW USA
47.03N 120.40W

205 S3 **Thorshavnheiane** *physical region*
Antarctica

94 L1 **Thórshöfn** Norðhurland Eystra,
NE Iceland 66.09N 15.18W

178 J14 **Thôt Nôt** Cân Thơ, S Vietnam
10.16N 105.31E

104 K8 **Thouars** Deux-Sèvres, W France
46.59N 0.13W

104 K9 **Thouet** ☌ W France

Thoune *see* Thun

20 H7 **Thousand Islands** *island* Canada/
USA

37 S15 **Thousand Oaks** California,
W USA 34.10N 118.50W

116 L12 **Thrace** *cultural region* SE Europe

116 J13 **Thracian Sea Gk.** Thrakikó
Pélagos; *anc.* Thracium Mare. *sea*
Greece/Turkey

**Thracium Mare/Thrakikó
Pélagos** *see* Thracian Sea

Thrá Lí, Bá *see* Tralee Bay

35 R11 **Three Forks** Montana, NW USA
45.53N 111.34W

166 M8 **Three Gorges Dam** *dam* Hubei,
C China 30.55N 111.00E

166 L9 **Three Gorges Reservoir** ☉
C China

9 Q16 **Three Hills** Alberta, SW Canada
51.43N 113.15W

191 N15 **Three Hummock Island** *island*
Tasmania, SE Australia

---

23 W2 **Thurmont** Maryland, NE USA
39.36N 77.22W

Thure *see* Thurø By

97 H24 **Thurø By** *var.* Thurø. Fyn,
C Denmark 55.03N 10.43E

12 M12 **Thurso** Scotland, SE Canada
45.36N 75.13W

98 J6 **Thurso** N Scotland, UK
58.34N 3.31W

204 I10 **Thurston Island** *island* Antarctica

110 I9 **Thusis** Graubünden, S Switzerland
46.40N 9.27E

178 K6 **Tiên Yên** Quang Ninh, N Vietnam
21.19N 107.24E

97 E21 **Thyborøn** *var.* Tyborøn.
Ringkøbing, W Denmark
56.40N 8.12E

205 U3 **Thyer Glacier** *glacier* Antarctica

117 L20 **Thýmaina** *island* Dodekánisa,
Greece, Aegean Sea

85 N15 **Thyolo** *var.* Cholo. Southern,
S Malawi 16.03S 35.11E

191 U6 **Tia** New South Wales, SE Australia
31.14S 151.51E

H5 **Tía Juana** Zulia, NW Venezuela
10.18N 71.22W

166 J14 **Tiancheng** *see* Chongyang

166 I4 **Tiandong** *var.* Pingma. Guangxi
Zhuangzu Zizhiqu, S China
23.37N 107.06E

167 O3 **Tianjin** *var.* Tientsin. Tianjin Shi,
E China 39.12N 117.06E

167 P3 **Tianjin Shi** *var.* Jin, Tianjin,
T'ien-ching, Tientsin. ◆
municipality E China

165 S10 **Tianjun** *var.* Xinyuan. Qinghai,
C China 37.16N 99.03E

166 J13 **Tianlin** *var.* Leli. Guangxi
Zhuangzu Zizhiqu, S China
24.27N 106.03E

165 W11 **Tianshui** Gansu, C China
34.33N 105.51E

156 I7 **Tianshuihai** Xinjiang Uygur
Zizhiqu, W China 35.16N 79.30E

167 S10 **Tiantai** Zhejiang, SE China
29.11N 121.01E

166 J14 **Tianyang** *var.* Tianzhou. Guangxi
Zhuangzu Zizhiqu, S China
23.45N 106.54E

Tianzhou *see* Tianyang

165 U9 **Tianzhu** *var.* Huazangsi, Tianzhu
Zangzu Zizhixian. Gansu, C China
37.01N 103.04E

Tianzhu Zangzu Zizhixian *see*
Tianzhu

203 Q7 **Tiarei** Tahiti, W French Polynesia
17.31S 149.19W

76 J6 **Tiaret** *var.* Tihert. NW Algeria
35.23N 1.18E

79 N17 **Tiassalé** S Ivory Coast

198 Bb8 **Ti'avea** Upolu, SE Samoa
13.58S 171.30W

Tiba *see* Chiba

62 J11 **Tibagi** *var.* Tibají. Paraná, S Brazil
24.28S 50.28W

62 J10 **Tibagi, Rio** *var.* Rio Tibají.
☌ S Brazil

Tibají *see* Tibagi

Tibají, Rio *see* Tibagi, Rio

145 Q9 **Tibal, Wādī** *dry watercourse*
S Iraq

54 G9 **Tibaná** Boyacá, C Colombia
5.19N 73.25W

76 J6 **Tibati** Adamaoua, N Cameroon
6.28N 12.37E

78 K15 **Tibé, Pic de** ▲ SE Guinea
8.39N 8.58W

115 I9 **Tiber** *see* Tivoli, Italy

Tiber *see* Tevere, Italy

Tiberias *see* Teverya

144 G9 **Tiberias, Lake** *var.* Chinnereth,
Sea of Bahr Tabariya, Sea of Galilee,
Ar. Bahrat Tabariya, *Heb.* Yam
Kinneret. ☉ N Israel

69 Q5 **Tibesti** *var.* Tibesti Massif, *Ar.*
Tibisti. ▲ N Africa

Tibesti Massif *see* Tibesti

Tibetan Autonomous Region
see Xizang Zizhiqu

Tibet, Plateau of *see*
Qingzang Gaoyuan

Tibisti *see* Tibesti

188 M10 **Tibooburra** New South Wales,
SE Australia 29.24S 142.01E

97 L18 **Tibro** Västra Götaland, S Sweden
58.25N 14.10E

42 B1 **Tiburón, Isla** *var.* Isla del
Tiburón. *island* NW Mexico

Tiburón, Isla del *see* Tiburón, Isla

25 W14 **Tice** Florida, SE USA
26.40N 81.49W

75 Yazov **Tichau** *see* Tychy

155 Q12 **Thul** Sind, SE Pakistan

78 K9 **Tichit** *var.* Tichitt. Tagant,
C Mauritania 18.25N 9.31W

81 J18 **Tichitt** *see* Tichit

110 G11 **Ticino** *var.* Tessin. ◆ *canton*
S Switzerland

108 D8 **Ticino** *Ger.* Tessin. ☌
Italy/Switzerland

110 H11 **Ticino** *Ger.* Tessin. ◆
W Switzerland

Ticinum *see* Pavia

43 X12 **Ticul** Yucatán, SE Mexico
20.21N 89.29W

97 K18 **Tidaholm** Västra Götaland,
S Sweden 58.12N 13.55E

Tidjikdja *see* Tidjikja

78 J8 **Tidjikja** *var.* Tidikdja; *prev.* Fort-
Cappolani. Tagant, C Mauritania
18.30N 11.24W

175 S7 **Tidore, Pulau** *island* E Indonesia

175 S7 **Tidore, Pulau** *island* E Indonesia

175 S7 **Tidra, Île** *see* Et Tidra

---

127 Pp8 **Tilichiki** Koryakskiy Avtonomnyy
Okrug, E Russian Federation
60.25N 165.55E

158 I7 **Tienen** *var.* Thienen, *Fr.*
Tirlemont. Vlaams Brabant,
C Belgium 50.48N 4.56E

Tiêu Giang, Sông *see*
Tien Giang, Sông

153 X9 **Tien Shan** *Chin.* Thian Shan, Tian
Shan, T'ien Shan, *Rus.* Tyan'-Shan'.
▲ C Asia

Tientsin *see* Tianjin

Tientsin *see* Tianjin Shi

97 O14 **Tierp** Uppsala, C Sweden
60.19N 17.30E

64 H7 **Tierra Amarilla** Atacama,
N Chile 27.28S 70.16W

39 R9 **Tierra Amarilla** New Mexico,
SW USA 36.42N 106.31W

43 R15 **Tierra Blanca** Veracruz-Llave,
E Mexico 18.28N 96.21W

43 O16 **Tierra Colorada** Guerrero,
S Mexico 17.10N 99.36W

65 I17 **Tierra Colorada, Bajo de la**
basin E Argentina

65 I25 **Tierra del Fuego off.** Provincia
de la Tierra del Fuego. ◆ *province*
S Argentina

65 J20 **Tierra del Fuego** *island*
Argentina/Chile

56 D7 **Tierralta** Córdoba, NW Colombia
8.10N 76.04W

106 L10 **Tiétar** ☌ W Spain

62 L10 **Tietê, Rio** ☌ S Brazil

34 I9 **Tieton** Washington, NW USA
46.41N 120.43W

33 S12 **Tiffin** Ohio, N USA 41.06N 83.10W

33 Q11 **Tiffin River** ☌ Ohio, N USA

25 U7 **Tifton** Georgia, SE USA
31.27N 83.31W

Tiflis *see* T'bilisi

175 Ss11 **Tifu** Pulau Buru, E Indonesia
3.46S 126.36E

197 K6 **Tiga, Île** *island* Îles Loyauté,
W New Caledonia

40 L17 **Tigalda Island** *island* Aleutian
Islands, Alaska, USA

117 I15 **Tigáni, Akrotírio** *headland*
Límnos, E Greece 39.50N 25.03E

175 O1 **Tiga Tarok** Sabah, East Malaysia
6.57N 117.07E

119 O10 **Tighina** *Rus.* Bendery; *prev.*
Bender. E Moldova 46.51N 29.27E

127 P10 **Tigil'** Koryakskiy Avtonomnyy
Okrug, E Russian Federation
57.43N 158.39E

151 X9 **Tigiretskiy Khrebet**
▲ E Kazakhstan

81 F14 **Tignère** Adamaoua, N Cameroon
7.25N 12.49E

13 Q15 **Tignish** Prince Edward Island,
SE Canada 46.58N 64.03W

145 X10 **Tigris** *Ar.* Dijlah, *Turk.* Dicle.
☌ Iraq/Turkey

78 G9 **Tiguent** Trarza, SW Mauritania
17.15N 16.00W

76 M10 **Tiguentourine** E Algeria
27.59N 9.16E

79 V10 **Tiguidit, Falaise de** *ridge*
C Niger

147 N13 **Tihāmah** *var.* Tehama. *plain* Saudi
Arabia/Yemen

Tihert *see* Tiaret

153 O7 **Ti-hua/Tihwa** *see* Ürümqi

43 Q13 **Tijuana** Baja California,
NW Mexico 32.31N 117.01W

42 E2 **Tikal** Petén, N Guatemala
17.16N 89.37W

160 I9 **Tikamgarh** *prev.* Tehri. Madhya
Pradesh, C India 24.43N 78.49E

164 L7 **Tiklamlik** Xinjiang Uygur Zizhiqu,
NW China 40.43N 81.59E

79 P12 **Tikaré** N Burkina 13.16N 1.39W

203 T9 **Tikehau** *atoll* Îles Tuamotu,
C French Polynesia

203 V9 **Tikei** *island* Îles Tuamotu, C French
Polynesia

125 R7 **Tikhoretsk** Krasnodarskiy
Kray, SW Russian Federation
45.50N 40.07E

128 I13 **Tikhvin** Leningradskaya
Oblast', NW Russian Federation
59.37N 33.29E

199 L10 **Tiki Basin** *undersea feature*
S Pacific Ocean

192 Q8 **Tikitiki** Gisborne, North Island,
NZ 37.49S 178.23E

81 J18 **Tiko** Sud-Ouest, SW Cameroon
4.04N 9.21E

145 S6 **Tikrit var.** Tekrit. N Iraq
34.36N 43.42E

128 I8 **Tiksha** Respublika Kareliya,
NW Russian Federation
64.07N 32.31E

122 L7 **Tikshozero, Ozero**
☉ NW Russian Federation

123 O8 **Tiksi** Respublika Sakha
(Yakutiya), NE Russian Federation
71.40N 128.46E

173 O8 **Tiku** Sumatera, W Indonesia
0.24S 99.55E

44 L13 **Tilapa** San Marcos, SW Guatemala
14.32N 92.12W

44 L13 **Tilarán** Guanacaste, NW Costa
Rica 10.28N 84.57W

101 I18 **Tilburg** Noord-Brabant,
S Netherlands 51.34N 5.04E

12 D17 **Tilbury** Ontario, S Canada
42.15N 82.25W

55 I9 **Tilcara** Jujuy, NE Argentina
23.35S 65.23W

190 K6 **Tilcha** South Australia
29.35S 140.52E

Tilcha Creek *see* Callabonna
Creek

31 Q14 **Tilden** Nebraska, C USA
42.03N 97.49W

27 R13 **Tilden** Texas, SW USA
28.28N 98.34W

12 H10 **Tilden Lake** Ontario, S Canada
46.35N 79.36W

99 J19 **Tilford** Texas, S USA

97 O8 **Tilemsi, Vallée de** ▲ C Mali

---

119 P9 **Tiliilihul** *Rus.* Tiligul.

119 P10 **Tilihul's'kyy Lyman** *Rus.*
Tiligul'skiy Liman. ◆ S Ukraine

Tilimsen *see* Tlemcen

79 R11 **Tillabéri** *var.* Tillabéry. Tillabéri,
W Niger 14.12N 1.25E

79 R11 **Tillabéri** ◆ *department* SW Niger

Tillabéry *see* Tillabéri

34 I12 **Tillamook** Oregon, NW USA
45.27N 123.50W

34 H2 **Tillamook Bay** *inlet* Oregon,
NW USA

157 Q22 **Tillanchāng Dwip** *island* Nicobar
Islands, E Indian Ocean

97 N15 **Tillberga** Västmanland, C Sweden
59.52N 16.39E

23 S10 **Tillery, Lake** ☉ North Carolina,
SE USA

79 T10 **Tillia** Tahoua, W Niger
16.13N 4.51E

25 N8 **Tillmans Corner** Alabama,
S USA 30.35N 88.10W

12 F17 **Tillsonburg** Ontario, S Canada
42.51N 80.41W

117 N22 **Tílos** *island* Dodekánisa, Greece,
Aegean Sea

191 N5 **Tilpa** New South Wales,
SE Australia 30.56S 144.24E

Tilsit *see* Sovetsk

33 N13 **Tilton** Illinois, N USA
40.06N 87.39W

130 K7 **Tim** Kurskaya Oblast', W Russian
Federation 51.39N 37.11E

56 C12 **Timaná** Huila, S Colombia
1.56N 75.57W

Timan Ridge *see* Timanskiy
Kryazh

129 Q8 **Timanskiy Kryazh** *Eng.* Timan
Ridge. *ridge* NW Russian Federation

193 G20 **Timaru** Canterbury, South Island,
NZ 44.23S 171.15E

131 N6 **Timashevo** Samarskaya
Oblast', W Russian Federation
53.22N 51.13E

130 K13 **Timashevsk** Krasnodarskiy
Kray, SW Russian Federation
45.37N 38.57E

130 K13 **Timbaki/Timbákion** *see*
Tympáki

24 J4 **Timbalier Bay** *bay* Louisiana,
S USA

24 J4 **Timbalier Island** *island*
Louisiana, S USA

194 K5 **Timbe** ☌ C Papau New Guinea

78 L10 **Timbedgha** *var.* Timbédra.
Hodh ech Chargui, SE Mauritania
16.16N 8.13W

Timbédra *see* Timbedgha

34 G10 **Timber** Oregon, NW USA
45.42N 123.19W

189 O3 **Timber Creek** Northern Territory,
N Australia 15.35S 130.21E

30 M8 **Timber Lake** South Dakota,
N USA 45.25N 101.01W

70 D12 **Timbio** Cauca, SW Colombia
2.22N 76.41W

56 C12 **Timbiquí** Cauca, SW Colombia
2.41N 77.41W

85 O17 **Timbue, Ponta** *headland*
C Mozambique 18.49S 36.22E

Timbuktu *see* Tombouctou

176 Vv10 **Timbuni, Sungai** ☌ Papua,
E Indonesia

175 Oo4 **Timbun Mata, Pulau** *island*
E Malaysia

79 P8 **Timétrine** *var.* Ti-n-Kâr. *oasis*
C Mali 19.18N 0.09W

79 V9 **Timfi** *see* Týmfi

Timfristos *see* Tymfristós

176 X12 **Timía** Agadez, C Niger
18.07N 8.49E

176 X12 **Timika** Papua, E Indonesia
4.39S 137.15E

77 O7 **Timimoun** C Algeria
29.18N 0.21E

78 F8 **Timiris, Cap** *see* Timirist, Râs

78 F8 **Timirist, Râs** *var.* Cap Timiris.
headland NW Mauritania
19.18N 16.28W

151 S17 **Timiryazevo** Severnyy
Kazakhstan, N Kazakhstan

118 E3 **Timiş** ◆ *county* SW Romania

118 H7 **Timişoara, Lake** *Fr.* Lac.

118 I11 **Timiskaming, Lake** *see*
Témiscamingue. ☉ Ontario/
Québec, SE Canada

118 J12 **Timişoara** *Ger.* Temeschwar,
Temeswar, *Hung.* Temesvár; *prev.*
Temeschburg. Timiş, W Romania
45.46N 21.16E

118 I12 **Timişoara** ✈ Timiş, W Romania
45.50N 21.21E

Timkovichi *see* Tsimkavichy

79 V9 **Ti-m-Meghsoi** ☌ NW Niger

102 K8 **Timmendorfer Strand**
Schleswig-Holstein, N Germany
53.59N 10.50E

12 F15 **Timmins** Ontario, S Canada
48.09N 80.00W

23 R12 **Timmonsville** South Carolina,
SE USA 34.07N 79.56W

32 N5 **Timms Hill** ▲ Wisconsin, N USA
45.27N 90.12W

176 Vv9 **Timóforo** ☌ Papua, E Indonesia

114 F14 **Timok** ☌ E Serbia

60 N10 **Timon** Maranhão, E Brazil
5.07S 42.52W

175 S17 **Timor** *island* East Timor/Indonesia

175 S17 **Timor Sea** *sea* E Indian Ocean

Timor Coast *see* East Timor

Timor Timur *see* East Timor

Timor Trench *see* Timor Trough

198 P9 **Timor Trough** *var.* Timor Trench.
undersea feature NE Timor Sea.

63 A21 **Timote** Buenos Aires, E Argentina
35.22S 62.13W

56 I9 **Timotes** Mérida, NW Venezuela
8.57N 70.46W

27 O8 **Timpson** Texas, SW USA
31.54N 94.24W

126 L13 **Timptón** ☌ NE Russian
Federation

95 H17 **Timrå** Västernorrland, S Sweden
62.28N 17.19E

22 J10 **Tims Ford Lake** ☉ Tennessee,
S USA

174 Hh7 **Timun Pulau Kundur, C Indonesia
0.49N 103.23E

◆ Country ● Country Capital ◇ Dependent Territory ○ Dependent Territory Capital ◈ Administrative Region ✕ International Airport ▲ Mountain ▲▲ Mountain Range ⩚ Volcano ≈ River ◎ Lake ▣ Reservoir

◆ Country ● Country Capital ◇ Dependent Territory ○ Dependent Territory Capital ◈ Administrative Region ✕ International Airport ▲ Mountain ▲▲ Mountain Range ⋏ Volcano ≈ River ◎ Lake ⊠ Reservoir

◆ Country
● Country Capital
◇ Dependent Territory
○ Dependent Territory Capital
◐ Administrative Region
✕ International Airport
▲ Mountain
▲▲ Mountain Range
Volcano
~ River
◎ Lake
⊠ Reservoir

◆ Country
● Country Capital
◇ Dependent Territory
○ Dependent Territory Capital
◈ Administrative Region
✈ International Airport
▲ Mountain
▲▲ Mountain Range
⛰ Volcano
≈ River
◎ Lake
⊠ Reservoir

T

◆ Country
● Country Capital
◇ Dependent Territory
○ Dependent Territory Capital
◈ Administrative Region
✈ International Airport
▲ Mountain
▲▲ Mountain Range
⩘ Volcano
≈ River
⊛ Lake
⊠ Reservoir

◆ Country
● Country Capital
◇ Dependent Territory
○ Dependent Territory Capital
⬖ Administrative Region
✕ International Airport
▲ Mountain
▲▲ Mountain Range
⛰ Volcano
≈ River
◎ Lake
▣ Reservoir